1947

Larousse Gastronomique

SHELL-FISH. Mussels à la marinière (*Robert Carrier*)

LAROUSSE GASTRONOMIQUE

THE ENCYCLOPEDIA
OF FOOD, WINE & COOKERY

by Prosper Montagné

INTRODUCTIONS BY A. ESCOFFIER AND PH. GILBERT

EDITED BY CHARLOTTE TURGEON AND NINA FROUD

1000 Illustrations Including
Many in Full Color

CROWN PUBLISHERS, INC. · NEW YORK

Larousse Gastronomique

was first published in France by
Augé, Gillon, Hollier-Larousse, Moreau et Cie
(Librairie Larousse), Paris

Text translated from the French by
Nina Froud, Patience Gray, Maud Murdoch
and Barbara Macrae Taylor

Edited by Charlotte Turgeon and Nina Froud

Seventh Printing, September, 1966

Library of Congress Catalogue
Card Number: 61-15788

Printed in the U.S.A.

Prefaces

by Auguste Escoffier and Philéas Gilbert to the original edition of Larousse Gastronomique

Publishers' note

Escoffier died before the first edition of Larousse Gastronomique *was published in 1938; the great 'king of cooks and the cook of kings' wrote his preface after reading the first draft of the manuscript. Philéas Gilbert later saw the complete work and added a supplementary preface.*

The history of the table of a nation is a reflection of the civilization of that nation. To show the changes in the order and serving of meals from century to century, to describe and comment on the progress of the French cuisine, is to paint a picture of the many stages through which a nation has evolved since the distant times when, as a weak tribe, men lived in dark caves, eating wild roots, raw fish and the still pulsating flesh of animals killed with the spear.

It is this history that is the subject of *Larousse Gastronomique*, in which Prosper Montagné has outlined in some thousand pages all the improvements brought to the culinary art from prehistoric times to the present day. Presented in the form of a dictionary, it sums up all that has been achieved by the science of alimentation, and everything in it has been minutely studied and described.

Those who make a profession of gastronomy will find in this book matter for comparison between what used to be the art of good eating and what it is today. Housewives will be particularly interested in the evolution of the table through the ages, its refinements modified in each epoch—to a certain extent by the exigencies of reigning fashions. Professional cooks, both men and women, will be able to draw inspiration from the principles of a culinary technique founded on the universally recognized knowledge and authority of the author. The text of the book and the recipes are enlivened by attractive anecdotes and legendary tales.

While waiting to read them in print, I went through the innumerable manuscript pages of this encyclopedia and I am still under the spell cast by this work. How could it have been completed so rapidly? For the author had only one collaborator, albeit an eminent one, who was entrusted with all scientific and medical subjects, and the material was prepared in less than three years.

Larousse Gastronomique is a model of exactitude and precision in all that concerns the etymology of certain words, the definition of culinary terms, the origin of foods in everyday use and the many recipes for each given dish.

Numerous descriptive photographs illustrate certain subjects, and there are some very attractive reproductions of antique engravings. Magnificent colour plates show finished dishes with their appropriate garnishes.

Such a work would have been incomplete, and the authors were well aware of this, had not considerable space been reserved for the riches of our famous French vineyards. The greatest of these, classified, are shown together in explicit tables.

Finally, the biographies of certain *maîtres de cuisine* and some gastronomes of great renown are for ever immortalized in these pages, and a culinary and gastronomical bibliography mentions a great number of works, some of which are perhaps unknown to the bibliophiles.

All those who make a cult of good eating and good drinking will find that Prosper Montagné's *Larousse Gastronomique* is indeed a work that they will consult with interest and one that will have a prominent place in their library. And this will be the author's merited and just reward, which I heartily applaud.

Auguste Escoffier

In his preface, Escoffier outlined the opinion he formed after having read the first draft of the *Larousse Gastronomique*. This manuscript was later considerably revised and completed. Being in a more favourable position than he, it was on the study of these final pages that my judgment was based; it conforms with that of Escoffier and is all the better founded because I have been able to see for myself what he predicted.

Escoffier and I, old friends of Prosper Montagné, realized that he had undertaken a formidable task, one of which only the authors of culinary works can understand the importance, but knowing his capacity for work and his inflexible willpower, his extensive erudition and his professional knowledge, which puts him in the first place among great cooks of our time, we were certain that he would bring it to a successful conclusion.

As Escoffier wrote, it is to all those who have anything to do with food or who are interested in the history of the cuisine and the table, that this book is addressed. It is—dare I say it—the apotheosis of the professional work of Prosper Montagné.

Larousse Gastronomique must become—and it already is—a *vade-mecum* for everyone, a reliable counsellor ready to be consulted at any moment and on no matter what subject connected with the alimentary sciences and the arts of the table.

Like Escoffier, I wish heartily that such a magnificent and persevering effort may find its reward in the welcome of those for whom it was conceived, a welcome which it deserves from any point of view.

Philéas Gilbert

Contents

List of Colour Plates

Introduction

to the English Language Edition

It is nearly a quarter of a century since Prosper Montagné compiled his monumental work to the glory of the French kitchen. *Larousse Gastronomique* has been printed no less than ten times in France but has never before been translated. Small wonder, for it contains well over a million words and must be the longest single volume cookery book ever written.

This English language edition is an Anglo-American venture and has been more than three years in preparation. As editors our chief aim has been to present as faithful a version as possible of the original work. Prosper Montagné was one of the greatest masters in the history of French cooking, and as a guide to the theory and practice of the culinary art his book has never been rivalled. It ranges from the aristocratic recipes of Carême (many of them so extravagant as to be of purely historical interest today, but they set the standards for more than a century of great cooking) to the simplest traditional recipes of the French countryside. To attempt to 'modernize' or rewrite a classic encyclopedia of this kind would have been, we feel, a great mistake. We have therefore revised or amended the text only when it was necessary or useful to do so. Chemical analyses and all medical and dietary information which is obsolete or inaccurate for us today have been omitted, as have some of the very curious articles on foreign cooking. There still remained over 13,000 pages of manuscript of the essential *Larousse Gastronomique*!

The original French measurements in gram weights have been retained, together with conversions to cup, tablespoon and teaspoon measurements. The cup referred to in the text is an 8-ounce American standard measuring cup. Comprehensive conversion tables for French, English and American systems of measuring foodstuffs are given at the beginning of the book. Occasional liberties have been taken in proportionately increasing or decreasing by small amounts all ingredients in a recipe to make the measurements less awkward, but only when the end results would be in no way altered.

The text has been arranged in alphabetical order, and when the French title of a recipe or article has been translated, the original French is given as well. There is a complete French index at the end of the book, so that it is an easy matter to look up a recipe or article under either its French or English title. The system of cross-referencing recipes operates as follows: where a recipe is listed with an asterisk it can be found in its alphabetical order in the encyclopedia; otherwise a bracketed cross-reference indicates the main section in which it appears.

In translating culinary terms we have tried to use those which will be understood by both British and American readers, and have cross-referenced or given alternatives in brackets when using names which are not common to both countries. French *abats*, for example, are offal in England and variety meats in America, so we have cross-referenced both terms. Some vegetables have a variety of names: for example what the French and Americans call chicory the English call endive, and what the French and Americans call endive the English call chicory. In America aubergines are egg-plants; *courgettes* remain *courgettes* or may be described as zucchini, baby marrows or Italian marrows depending on where you buy them.

Meat is cut up in different ways in France, England and U.S.A. Charts showing the principal cuts used in all three countries are included in the text, and the English and American cuts most closely approximating to the French cuts are indicated in the recipes where necessary.

Salt water fish found off European shores are in many cases not to be found off the American coast, so we have on occasion suggested a similar species which could if necessary be substituted for the fish prescribed in the French recipe.

Flour differs in weight and quality in every country in the world. Unless otherwise specified, the flour used in the transferred measurements is an all-purpose variety, untouched by bleaching agents. Cake flour is specified in certain recipes.

Sugar is refined in many ways. Unless otherwise specified, ordinary granulated sugar is to be used. Castor sugar corresponds to American 'fine granulated' and is termed 'fine'.

Many of the recipes in this encyclopedia cater for large numbers of people, and it would be merely pedantic to try to standardize quantities. The intelligent cook will be able to adapt them to the particular need of the moment. However, it is a fact that French cooks, while laying down very clear and precise rules, tend to be vague about *exact* measurements. Montagné will specify a 'spoonful' of this and that and he takes it for granted that the reader will discover his or her specific requirements by practical experiment. Here we have tried to help by indicating tablespoon or teaspoon measures where applicable. But *you* will be the final arbiter of taste. Remember that to the French the preparation of a meal is a work of art; they believe that without creative endeavour and a loving imagination on the part of the cook very little can be achieved. *Larousse Gastronomique* was not designed to help the lazy cook, but everyone who regards cooking and the preparation of food as something more than a necessity should find this great book a never-ending source of inspiration in the kitchen.

Table of Comparative Measures

Note

Published for use throughout the world, this edition of LAROUSSE GASTRONOMIQUE contains American and British equivalents as well as original French measurements in all recipes. Occasionally what appears to be a discrepancy in conversion may occur. In fact this results from proportionate alteration of quantities throughout that recipe in order to avoid awkward fractions in measurements.

The cups and tablespoons quoted, together with the French measures, in this book are American Standard, which are slightly smaller in capacity than British Standard cups and spoons. The American and Canadian Standard ½ pint measuring cup has a capacity of 8 fluid ounces; the British Standard Imperial ½ pint measuring cup has a capacity of 10 fluid ounces. The American and Canadian Standard measuring tablespoon measures ¾ fluid ounce; the British Standard tablespoon measures 1 fluid ounce. 3 teaspoons are equal to 1 tablespoon. All measurements refer to LEVEL spoons and cups.

LIQUID MEASURES

French	British	American
1 litre	1¾ pints	4¼ cups or 1 quart 2 ounces
1 demilitre (½ litre)	¾ pint (generous)	2 cups (generous) or 1 pint (generous)
1 decilitre (1/10 litre)	3–4 ounces	½ cup (scant) or ¼ pint (scant)

WEIGHT

French	British and American
1 gram	.035 ounce
28·35 grams	1 ounce
100 grams	3½ ounces
114 grams	4 ounces (approx.)
226·78 grams	8 ounces
500 grams	1 pound 1½ ounces (approx.)
1 kilogram	2·21 pounds

APPROXIMATE EQUIVALENTS FOR BASIC FOODS

	French	British	American
Almonds, blanched, whole	150 grams	5½ ounces	1 cup
Baking powder	4·3 grams	1 teaspoon (approx.)	1 teaspoon (approx.)
	30 grams	1 ounce	2½ tablespoons
Breadcrumbs, dry	90 grams	3¼ ounces	1 cup
,, fresh	45 grams	1½ ounces	1 cup
Butter	15 grams	½ ounce	1 tablespoon
	125 grams	4 ounces	½ cup
	500 grams	1 pound (generous)	2 cups
Cheese	500 grams	1 pound (generous)	1 pound (generous)
,, (grated Parmesan)	100 grams	4 ounces (scant)	1 cup (scant)
Coffee, medium ground	85 grams	3 ounces	1 cup
Cornstarch (cornflour)	10 grams	⅓ ounce	1 tablespoon
Cream of tartar	3–4 grams	⅛ ounce	1 teaspoon
Fish	500 grams	1 pound (generous)	1 pound (generous)
Flour (unsifted, all purpose)	35 grams	1$\frac{3}{16}$ ounces	¼ cup
	70 grams	2⅜ ounces	½ cup
	142 grams	4¾ ounces	1 cup
	500 grams	1 pound (generous)	3½ cups
,, (sifted, all purpose)	32 grams	1 ounce (generous)	¼ cup
	60 grams	2⅛ ounces	½ cup
	128 grams	4¼ ounces	1 cup
,, (sifted cake and pastry flour)	30 grams	1 ounce	¼ cup
	60 grams	2 ounces	½ cup
	120 grams	4 ounces	1 cup
Fruit (fresh)	500 grams	1 pound (generous)	1 pound (generous)
,, (dried)	500 grams	1 pound (generous)	2 cups
Gelatine (leaf sheets)	6 medium size leaves	1 ounce	2 tablespoons
,, (granulated)	150 grams	5⅓ ounces	1 cup
Meats	500 grams	1 pound (generous)	1 pound (generous)
,, (diced)	226 grams	8 ounces	1 cup
Mustard (dry)	15 grams	½ ounce	2 tablespoons

	French	British	American
Pepper (whole white)	30 grams	1 ounce (generous)	3⅚ tablespoons
,, (whole black)	30 grams	1 ounce (generous)	4½ tablespoons
,, (powdered)	30 grams	1 ounce (generous)	4 tablespoons
Raisins (seeded)	12 grams 200 grams	⅖ ounce 6⅔ ounces	1 tablespoon 1 cup
,, (seedless)	10 grams 160 grams 500 grams	⅓ ounce 5⅓ ounces 1 pound	1 tablespoon 1 cup 3 cups
Rice	240 grams	8 ounces	1 cup
Salt	15 grams	½ ounce	1 tablespoon
Spices (ground)	2½ grams 15 grams	1/12 ounce ½ ounce	1 teaspoon 2 tablespoons
Sugar (fine granulated)	5 grams 15 grams 60 grams 240 grams	⅙ ounce ½ ounce 2 ounces 8 ounces	1 teaspoon 1 tablespoon ¼ cup 1 cup
,, (powdered)	34 grams 68 grams 140 grams	1 ounce (generous) 2 2/7 ounces 4 4/7 ounces	¼ cup ½ cup 1 cup
,, (confectioner's or icing)	35 grams 70 grams 140 grams	1 ounce (generous) 2 2/7 ounces 4 4/7 ounces	¼ cup ½ cup 1 cup
,, (brown)	10 grams 80 grams 160 grams	⅓ ounce 2⅔ ounces 5⅓ ounces	1 tablespoon ½ cup 1 cup
Vegetables (fresh)	500 grams	1 pound (generous)	1 pound (generous)
,, (dried: lentils or split peas)	500 grams	1 pound (generous)	2 cups

Larousse Gastronomique

(*Robert Carrier*)

Artichokes à la hollandaise

ABAISSE—A term in pastry-making, for which there is no English equivalent, used generally to describe a piece (or sheet) of pastry, rolled out to a certain thickness, depending on the use for which it is intended. This word is also used to describe a layer of sponge cake or biscuit.

ABAT-FAIM ('Hunger-killer')—A substantial dish which is served first or early in the meal.

ABATTE—A popular corruption of the French word *battre* ('to beat'). An *abatte* is a kind of rather thick, double-edged flat knife used for flattening meat.

ABEL-MUSK. AMBRETTE—An aromatic plant originating in Martinique, the seeds of which give off a very strong flavour of musk. In India these seeds are mixed with coffee to flavour it and to heighten its stimulating properties.

Ambrette is also the name of a variety of pears which have a slight scent of ambergris.

ABLUTIONS, TABLE—The custom of passing bowls to guests at table, to enable them to rinse their fingers at the end of a meal, or after eating certain dishes, goes back to the times of great antiquity. This was common practice with the ancient Egyptians, the Greeks and the Romans.

The ancients not only washed their hands before a meal, but also between each course of the dinner. 'This practice is found among all the peoples of antiquity and is explained by necessity, since in those days food was taken with the fingers. A servant poured over the fingers of the guest the contents of a vessel which usually contained scented water. In other circumstances, hands were simply washed in a basin.' (*Vie Privée des Anciens* by Louis Nicolas Menard.)

ABOMASUM. CAILLETTE—Fourth stomach of the ruminants. Dried reed (solid rennet) or the extract obtained by infusion (liquid rennet) are used in the cheese-making industry for coagulating milk.

ABONDANCE—Wine diluted with water.

This word ironically describes the drink which in days gone by used to be served in schools or colleges, where wine was scarce and water abundant. The term is used, deprecatingly, of a wine excessively watered down.

ABRASTOL—A compound of sulpho-naphthol. An antiseptic (the use of which is forbidden) sometimes used to preserve wines and other alcoholic drinks. It causes a red coloration by ammoniacal ferrous sulphate.

ABROTONITE—Wine in which, in ancient times, people used to infuse a sort of artemisia, so-called *Southernwood abrotanum*, to flavour it.

ABSINTH. ABSINTHE—Liqueur made by maceration and distillation of leaves of wormwood (*artemisia absinthium*) with the addition of other bitter or aromatic plants (fennel, anise, Chinese anise, star anise, hyssop, etc.).

Absinth wine. VIN D'ABSINTHE—Wine spiced by infusion of wormwood leaves.

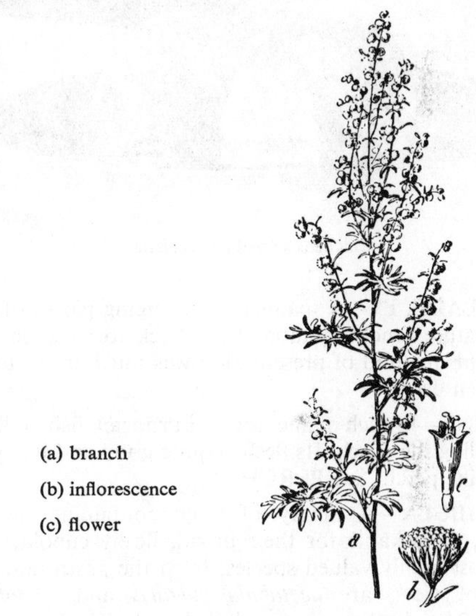

Wormwood

ABSORPTION (whimsical gastronomy)—A meal offered to the senior group of the French Military Academy of Artillery and Engineering by the junior group. 'There one absorbs enough things to justify the name of solemnity.' (Lorédan Larchey.)

'*Absorption* is the annual reunion at which old boys and freshmen fraternise in the glimmer of punch flames and to the glug-glug of champagne bottles. It takes place on the first day of the senior group's return.' (G. Maillard, 1866.)

ABSTINENCE—The days of abstinence are those on which one should abstain trom meat, without being obliged to fast.

ABUTILON—A plant, more than sixty varieties of which are known throughout the various parts of the world.

In Brazil the species known in botany under the name of *abutilon esculentum* is edible. The Brazilians call it *benças de deos*. They eat its flowers cooked with meat.

In Europe *abutilon* is generally cultivated as a flower-bed plant for the beauty of its flowers, but very rarely for the purpose of using it as food.

In some countries, particularly in Asia and in the West Indies, its leaves are eaten cooked in the manner of sorrel or spinach. In India the natives are very fond of the species known as *abutilon indicum*.

ACACIA—Acacia blossoms are used for making fritters and also for a home-made liqueur.

Acacia blossom fritters. See FRITTERS, *Blossom and flower fritters*.

Acacia blossom ratafia. See LIQUEURS, *Acacia liqueur or ratafia*.

ACANTHUS (Brank-ursine). ACANTHE—This plant, with decorative, elegantly cut-out leaves, is commonly found in Southern France. Its leaves, when young, are eaten as a salad.

ACARNE—Name given to European fish commonly known as *sea-bream*.

ACAVUS. ACAVE—A variety of snail common in French vineyards and gardens.

Chickens served *en accolade*

ACCOLADE, IN—A manner of arranging pieces of the same nature—meat, poultry, fish—back to back on one dish. This method of presentation was much in vogue in the olden days.

ACELINE—French name for a European fish a little resembling the perch. Its flesh is quite good and it is prepared like perch. See PERCH.

ACETABULA—A family of fungi containing several species, remarkable for their broad, fleshy cupola. The two most highly valued species, from the gastronomical point of view, are *acetabula vulgaris* and *acetabula sulcata*. They both grow in secluded spots. The first looks different in the spring and in the autumn. The acetabula differ in colour, from bright red to orange-yellow and dark brown.

All the methods of preparation given in the recipes for other fungi, field mushrooms, cantharellus, etc., can be applied to these species. See Mushroom.

ACETABULUM—Ancient Romans used the word *acetabulum* to describe a vessel intended to contain vinegar.

ACETIC ACID. ACÉTIQUE—The acid which forms the basis of vinegar. It is used in confectionery, in the cooking of sugar.

ACETIFICATION—Reaction which transforms wine alcohol (or any other alcoholic liquid) into acetic acid. This reaction, fostered by different industrial processes (see VINEGAR), is due to the action of yeast, the *mycoderma aceti*.

ACETIMETER. ACÉTIMÈTRE—Instrument by means of which the degree of concentration of vinegar is assessed.

ACETO-DOLCE ('Sour-sweet')—Italian commercial product which is consumed as hors d'oeuvre. It is a mixture of various vegetables and fruit which, after having been pickled in vinegar, are preserved in jars in a syrup of muscat grape, must and honey with mustard added.

ACETOMEL—Sour-sweet syrup made of honey and vinegar. It is used in preserving fruit: quinces, pears or grapes thus preserved take the name of *aceto-dolce*, i.e. sour-sweet fruit.

ACETONE—Colourless, inflammable liquid, of pungent and burning taste; its smell resembles that of quinces. Acetone is produced in the organism in the course of partial decomposition of fatty matter, particularly when the diet does not allow a sufficient quantity of carbohydrates. This arises in the case of starvation and above all in severe cases of diabetes.

ACHAR. ACHARD—This word, which has come down to us from the Persian *atchar*, through India, describes various kinds of fruit, vegetables, very young and tender buds of palm cabbage (palmetto), or bamboo shoots, pickled in various ways and strongly spiced. It is generally coloured with saffron. This condiment is greatly valued in the whole of the Indian Archipelago, in Mauritius and in the Bourbon Island (Réunion Island).

Lemon achar (Creole recipe). ACHARDS DE CITRONS—Choose thin-skinned lemons and quarter them. Squeeze out the juice and remove the pips of these pieces of lemon. Leave them to steep in layers of kitchen salt.

To prepare, take off the salt and put the lemons into plenty of cold water for 24 hours, changing the water several times.

Boil in fresh water until the lemons become quite soft. Strain off the water. Dry the lemons and put to marinate in the following sauce:

Pound a large onion, a large piece of ginger (this, along with pimento, allspice, Bourbon saffron and Indian curry powder, can be bought in specialty or delicatessen shops) and pimento in a mortar into a fine paste. Add vinegar and a teaspoon of Bourbon saffron. Blend all with best quality olive oil, in sufficient quantity to make sure that the lemons, packed into jars, will be covered completely.

Palmetto achar (Creole recipe). ACHARDS DE PALMISTE—Palmettos (palm-cabbage) can be bought in delicatessen or specialty shops. Take them out of the tin carefully, put into a glass jar, pour in enough good quality oil to cover, having first got rid of the oil in which the palmetto was packed.

Vegetable achar (Creole recipe). ACHARDS DE LÉGUMES—Cut into thin straws 1½ inches in length, carrots, cucumbers—from which the seeds and the pulp have been removed—large fresh pimentos, with the interior thrown away, young French beans, cauliflower in little flowerets and cabbage leaves in pieces. Spread coarse salt over these vegetables and impregnate them well with it. After 36 hours they will have given out water. Drain them well, dry and season with the same sauce as described in the recipe for *Lemon achar* above. To preserve the achar, cover completely with good quality oil and seal the jars hermetically.

ACHILLEA (milfoil). ACHILLÉE—Plant, of which one species, *achillea patarnica*, which grows in woods, is edible. Its tender young leaves are added to salads.

ACID. ACIDE—A chemical hydrogen compound recognizable by its property of causing litmus solution to turn red.

ACIDIFIERS. ACIDIFIANTS—Foods which supply the organism with an excess of acid and which tend to acidify the tissue fluids. The acid quality of the foods must not be confused with their acid taste; certain foods, whilst having an acid taste, such as lemons, for example, are not acidifiers.

In a general manner, meat (and this includes the flesh of fish) and all food of animal origin (with the exception of milk and blood) are acidifiers. Among the vegetables, grains and cereals and foods derived from them (pasta products, flour, bread), the blossoms and the buds are acidifiers.

Meat, game, sea fish, offal, cereals, flour, pasta, pastry and bread are powerful acidifiers. Ham, fresh-water fish, eggs, butter, fats, chocolate, asparagus, hop shoots, Brussels sprouts, artichokes, onions, chestnuts, peanuts, walnuts, hazelnuts and almonds are less seriously acidifying.

ACIDIFY. ACIDIFIER—To add acid (lemon juice, vinegar or verjuice) to a culinary preparation.

ACIDIMETER. PÈSE-ACIDE—A calibrated hydrometer for determining the density of acids.

ACIDITY. ACIDITÉ—Acid taste. It exists naturally in certain vegetables and fruit and disappears or diminishes as a result of a 'blanching' operation. See BLANCHING.

ACIDULATE. ACIDULER—To render a dish slightly acid, sour or piquant by the addition of lemon, vinegar, etc.

ACIDULATED. ACIDULÉ—Term which is only used to describe mineral waters charged with carbonic acid.

ACON—Name given to an implement used by the mussel farmers who gather mussels bred in mussel beds in the cove of Aiguillon, near La Rochelle.

The use of this tool goes back to ancient times. It is mentioned in Charlemagne's *Capitularies*.

ACORN. GLAND—Fruit of the oak tree. Some types are edible, and were eaten by certain Asian peoples before they discovered cereals. In some countries, such as Spain, acorns are eaten raw or roasted. Acorn flour, which unlike chicory has costive properties, is used as a substitute for coffee. For this purpose, the roasted acorns of the ballota oak are most commonly used.

Acorn barnacles stuck to a piece of shell

ACORN BARNACLE. BALANE—A small shell-fish with a conical irregular shell which is found in all seas, attached to rocks. It is also commonly called *acorn-shell* and *turban-shell*. Its flesh is quite delicate. This crustacean is prepared like crab.

ACQUETTE—An old spirituous and very aromatic liqueur, much prized in Italy and throughout the south of France. Its appearance resembles that of *Danziger Goldwasser* (Danzig eau-de-vie). There are two ways of making it and it is sold under two different names: *Silver-Acquette*, in Italian *Aqua bianca*, and *Gold-Acquette*, or *Aqua d'oro*.

Silver acquette is made as follows:

Ceylon cinnamon	½ pound (250 grams)
Cloves	1 ounce (30 grams)
Nutmeg	1 ounce (30 grams)
85° alcohol	22 quarts (20 litres)

Steep these various ingredients in alcohol for 24 hours, then distil without rectifying; you will obtain 22 quarts (20 litres) of liqueur. Then, dissolve 53 pounds (25 kilograms) of sugar in 12 quarts (11 litres) of water and add the syrup obtained to the result of the distillation; leave to rest for the time required, filter and put into each bottle a crushed silver leaf.

To prepare gold acquette take:

Ceylon cinnamon ..	½ pound (250 grams)
Cloves	½ ounce (15 grams)
Angelica roots	3 ounces (75 grams)
Daucus of Crete ..	3 ounces (75 grams)
Fresh lemon (peel of) ..	1½ ounces (40 grams)
85° alcohol	22 quarts (20 litres)

Proceed as for preparing silver acquette, with just one difference, that you put into each bottle a crushed gold leaf.

ACRIDOPHAGE—One who feeds on locusts. This food may seem extraordinary to the epicures of Europe, but it is quite acceptable to African gastronomes.

It appears that the taste of locusts resembles, if somewhat remotely, that of raw shrimps.

ACROAMA—Greek word, adopted by the Romans. It means 'that to which one listens', further extended to mean 'that to which one pays attention'.

For greater enjoyment of their guests, the patricians made a habit of summoning musicians, poets, actors of comic and other, at times very licentious, scenes, men and women dancers, jugglers, acrobats, tumblers, dwarfs, and even gladiators and savage beasts to perform at meal times.

To the Romans this word *acroama* meant not only these various types of entertainment, but also the actors of spectacles of this sort.

The custom of the *acroama* continued through the centuries that followed but took on the name of *entremets* ('between courses'). These *entremets* had nothing in common with what, under the same name, figures on the menu today as a course of vegetables succeeding the roast, or with the sweet courses which are served at the end of a meal. *Acroama*, and the 'spectacular entremets' which succeeded it, were enacted all through the meal.

There are dinner hosts today who, in order to imitate the fashions which have spread from America, offer their guests dancing between courses. Guests who take part in these dances allow delicacies which have been served to them to congeal on their plates. This fashion is hardly compatible with true gastronomy!

ACTINIA (Sea anemone). ACTINIE—Although the actinia (sea anemones) are urticating (stinging) animals, they are used as food in certain localities. The inhabitants of southern coasts of France relish a species of actinia which they call *rastègne* and maintain that their taste resembles that of crabs.

In the winter, *actinia coriacea*, vulgarly known as 'mule's backside', can be found in the marshes of Rochefort, and the *actinia edulis* (*actigne*) can also be found along the coast of Provence.

ADOC—Name sometimes given to sour milk.

ADULTERATION. FALSIFICATION—A deliberate lowering of the quality of foodstuffs for the purpose of illicit gain.

AEGINETIA. AEGINETIE—Plant, of which the species known as *aeginetia indica* comes from India. It is the *tsiem-cumulu* of the people of the coast of Malabar. The natives were the first to have had the ingenious idea of preparing it with nutmeg and sugar; it thus constitutes an excellent masticatory (chewing gum), strengthens the teeth and counteracts unpleasant breath. As such, it is widely used in England and America.

AFRIANDER—French culinary term which means to tempt, make an appeal by the pleasant appearance of a dish.

AFTER-TASTE. ARRIÈRE-GOÛT—Taste which returns to the mouth after ingestion of certain foods and beverages.

Agami

AGAMI (Trumpeter)—A bird of the wader family of which the *Guiana agami* is a prototype. Its flesh has appreciable merit. The agami is used in cookery mainly in South America, boiled in consommé or braised with rice.

Agami à la chilienne—Choose as tender an agami as possible. Pluck, draw, singe and clean it. Prepare a garnish of rice cooked in fat stock with pimentos. Bard it and put to braise in a braising pan with the usual accompaniments of vegetables and spices and some dry white wine.

Separately, braise in veal jelly stock 12 medium-size onions stuffed with a *salpicon** of sweet pimentos blended with a few tablespoons of reduced *Velouté**. Prepare also 1 pound of *Okra in tomato sauce**.

As soon as the agami is cooked, remove from the braising pan. Glaze it in the oven.

Strain the pan juices, remove excess fat and reduce to the desired consistency.

Put the agami on a large dish, arrange the garnishes around and pour the sauce over it.

AGAPE (Love feast)—This was the name of the meals which the early Christians held together in church, in memory of the Last Supper which Jesus had with the Apostles. The Council of Carthage abolished the agapes in 397 A.D. in order to put an end to the calumnies of which they were the object.

The meals held by the early Christians in the catacombs in memory of the martyrs were also called agapes.

This word nowadays is used to define an important family meal.

AGAR-AGAR (Bengal isinglass)—A product obtained from various seaweeds, known also under the name of *Japanese moss, Ceylon moss.*

Agar-agar is found in the form of thin, crinkly, whitish, transparent strips. It gets slightly swollen in cold water and considerably so in boiling water, in which it finally dissolves. A fairly stiff jelly can be obtained from it, which is used in bacteriology.

Its neutral taste permits it to be used in cooking and in confectionery for making jellies.

It is by regurgitating sea-weed of this type that the salangane (Chinese swallow) builds its nest, so much prized by the Chinese under the name of *bird's nests*, for which factory-made agar-agar is often passed off in France.

Agar-agar always contains the carapaces of diatoms (microscopic unicellular algae) easily identifiable under the microscope, which helps to discover any fraudulent use of this product.

AGARIC—A genus of fungi; the cap is compact and the gills radiating.

These fungi grow profusely in damp and shaded places. They are also found in fields, on tree trunks, in caves and on decayed wood. There are about 2,000 known species of agarics and quite a large number of them are edible. The poisonous species are chiefly found among the genus called *Amanita*.

Among the edible agarics are the following:

Edible agaric or *cultivated mushrooms*, grown around Paris—the classic type of mushroom. This is often described under the generic name of 'champignon' without any other qualification.

Agaric oronge, *agaric* (*odorain*) or *St George's agaric* and the *cultivated agaric*, which is commonly found in the Paris region.

Among the poisonous species are the *amanita phalloides* (death cap), *amanita verna* (fool's mushroom) and *amanita virosus* (destroying angel).

To prepare edible agarics, sauté in a shallow pan in oil or butter; dress with fine herbs, *à la provençale*, *à la bordelaise* (see GARNISHES), *à la crème* (see SAUCE). They can also be used as a garnish for an infinite number of dishes.

AGATHON—Poet, born in Athens, and not in Samos, as certain authors maintain.

Agathon was magnificently generous in spending money for the table which, no doubt, gave rise to a great deal of jesting on the part of Aristophanes and other dramatists.

Some people claim that Plato's *Banquet* was composed at his table.

AGAVE—A genus of South American plants belonging to the family *Agavacea*—a native of Mexico. In Cuba and Mexico its pulp is fermented to make an alcoholic beverage which is called *pulque*.

AGI or AJI. AGY—Guinea or red Indian dwarf pepper, a species of capsicum. It is a kind of pimento grown in Peru. See PEPPER.

AGNOLOTTI. Agnolotti à la Piémontaise (Italian cookery)—Prepare a noodle paste in the following manner: put 1 pound (500 grams) of flour in a circle or a 'fountain' on a table. In the middle of this circle put 4 yolks of eggs, a generous tablespoon (20 grams) of butter, a pinch of salt and a scant $\frac{1}{4}$ cup (1 decilitre) water.

Knead for 10 minutes but avoid giving too much body to the paste.

Roll out the paste with a rolling-pin as thin as possible. On this piece of rolled-out paste put in a horizontal line little heaps of forcemeat each the size of a walnut (see FORCEMEAT, *Beef forcemeat*), spacing them at a distance of 2 inches from each other and 2 inches from the edge of the paste.

Fold the overlapping edge of the paste over this row of agnolotti. Press down around each heap of forcemeat, to make the paste stick well.

Cut out the agnolotti with a crescent-shaped fluted-edge pastry cutter, thus obtaining little turnovers.

Poach them in boiling salted water, allowing $1\frac{1}{2}$ teaspoons of salt per quart of water (10 grams per 1 litre), for 10 minutes. Drain and put in a dish, serve with a sauce made from the braised beef left over from the forcemeat and grated Parmesan cheese.

AGONE D'ISTRIA (Smaris graerlis). AGON—This fish abounds in the Italian lakes of Como and Garda. In Italy it is known under the name of *sardina*, and it has the same taste and is similar in size.

All the recipes given for sardine (see SARDINE) can be applied to it. It can also be salted in the same manner as sardines.

AGORANOME—Inspector of markets in ancient Greece. He controlled the price of goods and was responsible for the implementation of the laws relating to these markets. The *agoranome* of the Greeks corresponded to the *aedile* of the Romans.

AGOU—The *Agou* or *Negroes' Sagou* resembles small-grain millet. This grain is of brownish-grey colour with a yellow spot where it joins the stem. It is cooked like rice. Flour made from it serves to make cakes and porridge.

AGOUTI—Genus of rodents of Cavy or Guinea-pig family. Animal the size of a hare which is found in Brazil where it is called *cotia*, in Guiana, in the Dominican Republic and, generally, in all the West Indies. The agouti can live in Europe if they are protected from the cold.

The flesh is good to eat, even though the flavour is rather strong. It is prepared like sucking-pig. See PORK, *Piglet*.

AGRAS (Granulated almond milk)—The agras is a sort of iced beverage, or, to be exact, a *granité* which is made in Algeria. It is made from almonds and verjuice.

Ingredients. 1 cup (5 ounces) (150 grams) of sweet almonds, 1 quart (1 litre) of verjuice, 1 pint ($\frac{1}{2}$ litre) of water, 1 cup (150 grams) of sugar or brown sugar.

Method of preparation. Blanch the almonds after having scalded them with boiling water. Pound them in a mortar as finely as possible, moistening them with a little of the water. When they form a paste, dilute with the rest of the water and verjuice and strain through a napkin, then put under a press to extract all the liquid. 1 cup (150 grams) of white wine vinegar combined with 1 quart (1 litre) of water could be substituted for the verjuice and water.

Sweeten the liquid thus obtained with brown sugar, or, if this is not available, with granulated sugar, and strain through a napkin once again, but without pressing this time.

Stand this mixture in an ice-pail, surround by a mixture of crushed ice and sea-salt (coarse salt), allowing 10 per cent of salt, and leave to chill. Loosen the parts which get stuck to the walls of the ice-pail about every quarter of an hour. When the whole mixture acquires a granulated texture, serve it in sherbet glasses and put half a coffee spoonful of kirsch into each glass.

AGUAXIMA—A species of Brazilian pepper possessing the same properties as ordinary pepper.

AGUNCATE—A fruit grown in Peru, known in Lima under the name of *palta*. It is shaped like a calabash (gourd), is green in colour and has a varnished appearance. Its skin comes away from the flesh easily when the fruit is ripe. This flesh, somewhat insipid, is eaten with salt. It has something in common with the flesh of avocado pear (Alligator pear). See AVOCADO PEAR.

AIGRE DE CÈDRE (French name for Citrus Medica)—Fruit of a citron tree cultivated in Provence, around Grasse and Nice and in Italy at San Remo and near Genoa.

It makes a very refreshing summer drink.

AIGUILLETTE—An *aiguillette* means a thin slice or slices cut lengthways on the breast of poultry and winged game.

Strictly speaking, the word should only be used to describe thin slices of fowl, but it is often used to describe thin slices of meat too, e.g. 'cut a fillet of beef into *aiguillettes*'. *Aiguillette* is also used to describe the top of rump. See BEEF.

AILLADE—Definition used in the south of France, which applies, according to the district, Languedoc or Provence, to preparations which, although they differ somewhat, are all made of garlic.

Firstly, *aillade* sauce, a sort of *vinaigrette** with garlic and sometimes including shallots, chives and other garnishes. *Aillade* sauce is served with cold meat and fish, with potatoes and, generally, with all dishes served *à la vinaigrette*.

Secondly, bread *à l'aillade*, a slice of toasted bread, thoroughly rubbed with garlic and sprinkled with olive oil. This aillade in Provence is the equivalent of the 'garlic capon' in Languedoc.

Certain authors also mention other regional preparations known under the name of aillade. Among these are:

Aillade albigeoise which is nothing more than an *aioli.**

Aillade à la toulousaine, which is also *aioli* but incorporates a certain quantity of blanched and pounded walnuts.

All these preparations are very appetizing but something of an acquired taste, garlic being their outstanding characteristic. They are excellent for seasoning salads.

AIOLI or AILLOLI—Take 4 large cloves of garlic, remove the sprout and with 1 yolk of egg pound into a fine paste in a mortar. Season with a pinch of salt, and continue to pound adding 1 cup ($2\frac{1}{2}$ decilitres) of oil, little by little, as for mayonnaise. Stir this mixture vigorously. When finished, it should have the appearance of a thick smooth mayonnaise.

Aioli is served mainly with boiled fish, hot or cold, but can also be served with cold meat, or could be used for seasoning salads and cooked vegetables.

Garnished aioli. AIOLI GARNI—This dish, very popular in Provence, is composed of various ingredients, such as boiled cod, snails cooked in salt water, with fennel and onions stuck with a clove, boiled carrots, French beans, artichokes cooked in salt water, potatoes in jackets, hard-boiled eggs, etc., to which small octopi, boiled in salted water with herbs, are sometimes added. All these are arranged on a large dish and served with aioli.

The preparation of this dish, says J. B. Reboul, one of the *maîtres de cuisine* in Provence, demands a great deal of artistic arrangement. Not all the ingredients which we have enumerated, however, are absolutely essential. There is no set rule on this point. One should proceed according to one's tastes and the means at one's disposal.

Aioli à la grecque—A sort of vinaigrette sauce which is prepared as follows: combine pounded walnuts, almonds and hazelnuts, fresh breadcrumbs, sieved and soaked in milk, and pounded garlic. Blend with oil, vinegar and lemon juice. For fried and boiled fish.

ALARIA—A genus of sea-weed of which five species are known and which are found in all the seas of northern Europe.

One variety (*alaria esculenta*) known under the name of *badderlocks* in Scotland and of *murlins* in Ireland, is abundant in England and all the Atlantic costs. It is eaten in Scotland, in Ireland and in the Faroe Islands; but only the central vein of it is consumed. The taste of this cartilaginous vein is slightly sweet.

ALBACORE—A species of tunny (tuna) fish.

ALBARELLE—A genus of edible fungi which grows on chestnut trees and white poplars.

ALBATROSS. ALBATROS—Sea-fowl with very tough flesh. That of the young birds is eaten, nevertheless, and is prepared like wild duck. See DUCK, *Wild duck*.

ALBIGEOISE—Garnish for large and small cuts of meat. It consists of stuffed tomatoes and potato croquettes.

ALBUFÉRA, D'—Definition applying to various kinds of dishes chiefly characterized by the sauce which goes with them.

The name of d'Albuféra was first used by Carême, or more certainly by his successor, Plumery. We thus believe that we have an authentic recipe for *Duckling à la d'albuféra* which differs a little from the present-day method. It is known that Marshal Suchet was made Duke of d'Albuféra in 1812 after the victories of Oropeza, Murviedro and Valencia in Spain. The lake of d'Albuféra is near Valencia. See DUCK, CHICKEN.

ALBUMEN—A constituent of seeds containing food reserves for the plant in germination. Albumen is sometimes farinaceous, as in cereals, such as maize, barley, corn and rye; sometimes oily or fleshy, as in coconut palm and in black poppy. In certain palms it reaches the hardness of ivory. The albumen contained in coconuts is in the form of a periferic layer; in the centre is the cavity, of greater or lesser size, filled with liquid commonly called coconut milk.

A great variety of grain is used in domestic economy, in medicine and in arts for its albumen. Thus the cereals furnish us with flour, the coffee shrub with an alkaloid known as caffein. The black poppy produces poppy-seed oil, used as food almost universally. The seeds of certain species of nymphaea, very pleasant to the taste, are greatly used in China and Annam as food. The kernels of a pine growing in Provence and in Italy contain an albumen of an oily consistency and of a very delicate flavour, which makes them much valued articles in confectionery, particularly in the making of sugared pine-nuts. A good number of palm trees furnish edible oil and oil for lighting. Linseed oil comes from the seeds of flax.

A species of dwarf palm, native of Peru, produces a voluminous fruit known among the natives as *cana* or *cabeza de negro*. The albumen of its seeds is, when the fruit is green, liquid, of a pleasant taste and capable, by fermentation, of producing a wine which is thought quite highly of in the country. When ripe the fruit, on the contrary, acquires great hardness. It can then be put to the same uses as ivory. In the trade, for this is an article of export, it is known under the name of *raw ivory* (morfil) or *vegetable ivory*. When burned, it furnishes a product which compares favourably with ivory black, which is obtained from elephants' teeth and tusks.

ALBUMIN. ALBUMINE—Viscous whitish matter of a slightly salty taste, of which the white of egg is an example, containing albumin up to 59 per cent of its total weight. (See EGGS.) It is also found in blood serum, in milk and plants, particularly in the seeds of dried vegetables. That is why the water in which peas, beans and lentils are cooked becomes viscous when cooled. Albumin is soluble in water in its raw state but coagulates at a temperature of 158°—176°F. and then becomes insoluble.

By evaporating the white of egg at a temperature of about 120°F., albumin in the form of thin yellowish transparent sediment resembling paste, can be obtained.

Albumin is used in confectionery instead of white of egg for certain kinds of whisked-up paste, marshmallow, liquorice, Montelimar nougat and various meringue products.

It is also used in the biscuit and cake-making industry where it replaces eggs in the manufacture of cheap biscuits and white of egg in almond paste. To use it, it must be dissolved in about seven times its weight of cold water.

ALBUMINOIDS. ALBUMINOIDES—Substances possessing properties akin to those of albumin (coagulable by heat), also called nitrogenous, quarternary or proteinic substances. They exist in all the living organisms, whether animal or vegetable.

ALBUNDIGAS (Mexican cuisine)—The origin of *albundigas* appears to be Spanish or Mexican. In Mexico it is almost a national dish.

Combine 1 pound (500 grams) of finely chopped fillet of beef and ¼ pound (125 grams) of fairly coarsely chopped fat bacon. Season with salt and pepper. Add a little crushed garlic and a teaspoon of chopped parsley and bind with an egg. Shape into slightly thickish cakes. Fry in clarified butter. Put into an ovenproof dish. Cover with tomato sauce. Cook in the oven for 20 minutes. Serve with *Rice à la créole*.*

The albundigas can also be made from a mixture of veal and pork.

The Mexicans make a soup which is called by the same name; here is the recipe for it:

Ingredients. For 3 quarts (3 litres) of light stock or water, take ½ pound (250 grams) of fillet of pork, veal or beef, 5 new, medium-sized onions, one clove of garlic, 4 green pimentos, 3 peeled tomatoes with the seeds taken out, 3 tablespoons (50 grams) of butter, 1 heaped tablespoon (20 grams) of wheat flour and the same amount of sieved breadcrumbs, ½ teaspoon (5 grams) of coriander, thyme or, better still, marjoram, which has a more delicate flavour, a whole egg and 1 tablespoon (15—20 grams) of salt.

Method of preparation. Slice the onions and pimentos and brown in butter; at the last moment, add slightly crushed garlic. When the onions are done, sprinkle with flour, stir, allow to brown lightly, then add meat, bread and other condiments, previously passed through a mincer. Add egg and blend well. Moisten with stock or boiling water and leave to simmer for a quarter of an hour.

Put all this forcemeat, while still hot, into a pastry (forcing) bag with a ring at the end. Hold the bag over a saucepan of boiling stock. With a small knife cut into little slices the sausage which you squeeze out of the bag.

Poach these quenelles, simmering lightly, with the saucepan uncovered. At the last moment, add peeled, chopped tomatoes, softened in butter, to the soup.

Alcarraza

ALCARRAZA (Water-cooler). ALCARAZAS—The French have borrowed this word from the Spanish, which in turn was borrowed from the Arabic *alkourraz* (pitcher). In Egypt, the alcarraza is called *bardak*, which in French has become *bardague* and *balasse*. This is a Turkish word, which appears to derive from the Arabic root *bara*, meaning to cool, from which *barrada*, like alcarraza, meaning a vessel intended for cooling liquids, is certainly derived and which has brought into being the Spanish word *albarrada*.

These porous, unglazed jugs of various shapes are filled with water and hung in the shade in a draught. The water oozes through the pores of the jug and evaporates. The hotter the outside temperature and the drier the air, the quicker the evaporation. The heat necessary for evaporation is extracted from the liquid inside the jug which is thus cooled.

ALCAZAR (Pastry)—Line a sponge tin with *Lining paste* (see DOUGH). Prick the bottom and spread with 2 tablespoons of apricot jam. Fill three-quarters of the tin with the following mixture:

Ingredients. 1 cup (125 grams) of icing sugar, 4 whites of egg, 4 tablespoons (60 grams) of powdered almonds, 4 tablespoons (60 grams) of flour, 2 tablespoons (25 grams) of melted butter, kirsch.

Method of preparation. Beat the sugar and the whites of egg on the fire to obtain a firm meringue, then add powdered almonds, flour and, finally, melted butter mixed with half a wine-glass of kirsch. Spread on a buttered and floured baking sheet. Bake in the oven (350 °F.) for 50-60 minutes and turn out on to a wire tray.

Garnish with uncooked almond paste, pound for pound (see ALMOND) piped through in criss-cross lines making lozenge shapes. Make a border of almond paste around and put in a hot oven to colour the almond paste. Cover with thick apricot jam and put half a pistachio nut in the middle of each lozenge.

You can also cover the whole with a layer of apricot jam and sprinkle with chopped roasted almonds.

ALCOHOL. ALCOOL—Liquid obtained by distilling fermented liquors.

In chemistry, all organic substances composed of carbon, hydrogen and oxygen, capable of being combined into an acid to form an ether are defined as alcohol. Among these alcohols, we shall deal only with *ethyl alcohol* or wine alcohol, also called wine spirit. It is the principal product of the fermentation of sweet liquids formed by the double decomposition of glucose under the action of a yeast, a microscopic vegetable cell which, for its proliferation, decomposes glucose into carbonic acid and alcohol, and results also in by-products of some fragrant and sapid substances. See BEER, WINE.

Alcohol is produced by fermenting natural sweet juices (grapes, apples, sugar cane, beetroot, etc.) or the amyloide musts, subjected to a preliminary fermentation, which transforms starch into glucose: wort of cereals (beer), potatoes, etc.

The distillation of these musts and worts produces spirits (see SPIRITS); the concentration and rectification of these spirits produces industrial alcohols.

Absolute 100 per cent alcohol is a laboratory product; it is a caustic liquid, which boils at 78·3°C. and, having a great attraction for water, can be kept only with the greatest precautions.

Officinal (medicinal) 95° alcohol is a colourless mobile liquid, volatile, without residue, of a pleasant odour and a burning taste, which boils at 79·9°C. It can be mixed with water in all proportions, with contraction, that is to say that the total volume of the mixture is lower than that of the components and with emission of heat.

85° alcohol is commonly called 'three-six' (*trois-six*) because three parts of this alcohol, mixed with an equal quantity of pure water, produces six parts of ordinary eau-de-vie.

Alcohol possesses antiseptic properties; it is a diffusible stimulant which has numerous uses in therapeutics.

In its chemical composition alcohol approaches sugars (one molecule of glucose is split, by fermentation, into two molecules of alcohol). It possesses tangible but mediocre alimentary properties, because it decomposes too quickly in the organism and the energy released can only be used to a small degree, mainly because it becomes a toxic substance when taken in large doses. See ALCOHOLISM.

ALCOHOLISM. ALCOOLISME—Intoxication produced by the abuse of liquids containing alcohol. There are three distinct forms:

(1) **Inebriety**—Occurring when alcohol reaches a certain degree, variable with individuals, manifesting itself in the following manner: *First degree:* Sensation of well-being, stimulation of the intellectual faculties and the imagination; slight swelling of the face; *Second degree:* Mental incoherence, diminution of muscular strength, titubation, lack of movement co-ordination, congestion of the face, overpowering drowsiness; *Third degree:* Loss of mobility, sensitiveness and will.

(2) **Acute intoxication**—Early symptoms the same as in inebriety, but the period of excitation is very short, resulting quickly in somnolence, which can develop into a coma and even death through cerebral or pulmonary congestion.

(3) **Chronic alcoholism**—Repeated abuse of alcoholic liquids produces lesions of the stomach (gastritis), of the liver (cirrhosis), of the kidneys (nephritis), and of the nervous system (delirium, neuritis).

ALE—English beer, lightly hopped and slightly bitter. It is used in cooking for making various cheese dishes, notably for Welsh rarebit. See WELSH RAREBIT.

Ale is obtained by rapid fermentation and acquires strength on maturing. *Stout* and *porter* are brewed from roasted grain: ale is made from grain in its natural state.

It used to be a tradition in wealthy English families at the birth of a son to fill one of several barrels of ale specially brewed for the occasion. The barrels, hermetically sealed, were not opened until the son and heir reached his majority. On this memorable day, which was called 'the coming of age', and was celebrated with great pomp, all the tenants, friends and servants were invited to a great repast and, after the banquet, the famous beer, which had attained the age of twenty-one years, was passed round.

Ale posset—Heat a quart (litre) of ale, seasoned with a little sugar, a pinch of powdered ginger and grated nutmeg. Boil a quart (litre) of unskimmed milk and mix it, while still boiling, with the ale.

Toast and ale—An English beverage which used to be served in the winter, after dinner, at the same time as the cheese.

Method. Bring 1 litre of old ale, to which a coffee spoonful of ginger has been added, to the boil, pour it, whilst almost boiling, into an English jug with a metal lid, into which a thick slice of bread toasted on both sides has been put. Leave the ale to stand for a little while before serving.

ALECTRYON—A big tree of which the best-known species is found in New Zealand.

Its red-coloured fruit is much prized for its pleasant acid taste. Very refreshing beverages are made from it. An excellent oil is extracted from its seeds, and is exported.

ALEMBIC. ALAMBIC—Apparatus used for distilling. It is composed of a boiler in tinned copper, either equipped with a water bath, or not, as the case may be, surmounted by a cap with a *serpentine*, i.e. a tin or tinned copper spiral coil leading from it. The liquid to be distilled is put direct into the boiler, in the case of a naked flame still, or into the water bath contained in it, and the container is then put on a fire. Under the action of the heat, alcoholic vapours are first given off, pass into the serpentine, which is cooled by flowing water, and condense. The old method in Charente used to be to use naked flame stills heated by wood; the first produce obtained (*le brouillis*—'murky') had to be distilled and passed through once again.

A series of improvements have been introduced in the old-fashioned still to obtain alcohol at the first attempt, and to ensure continuous feeding of the apparatus. The traditionalists insist however that all these improvements have increased the taste of the boiler and result in inferior products.

In industry, more complicated apparatus, distilling towers, with rectifiers, etc., are used.

ALGAE. ALGUE—Plants which live in water. The nutritive value of the algae is indubitable and has generally been more conclusively proved than that of fungi. During the 1914-18 war, these plants were used as fodder for horses.

As far as feeding humans is concerned, it would appear that for certain small tribes of the extreme north the algae constitute an exceptional nourishment in cases of food shortage. In Scotland, certain species are eaten regularly.

In the Far East, certain types of algae are much valued. They serve as a basis for numerous manufactured foodstuffs, the consumption of which is considerable. A great number of algae are consumed in Japan. It is from certain laminaria species that the Japanese prepare the *Kombu*, or rather *Kombus*, as there are several dishes prepared from algae which are thus called.

The algae are soaked in vinegar for a long time. When they are thoroughly steeped in vinegar, they are dried in the open air. The leaves are then scraped with a knife to remove the skin, which comes away in scraps. After this the white, subjacent pulp is scraped. This pulp is dried and crushed into powder, or, according to circumstances, cut into little geometrical shapes. It is then used for preparing soups and stews. With the fragments of the same pulp, boiled in soya sauce, a condiment is prepared which is much prized in Japan and which is to some extent similar to anchovy essence.

The central part of these algae is put to cook with fish, vegetables and soups, to heighten the flavour of these dishes. A beverage is made from pulverized *Kombu* moistened with boiling water, which is drunk as tea. The *Kombu* is also added to stews and it is widely used for spicing rice. Cut into pieces and dried by a fire, the *Kombu* can be eaten as it is, dry, or softened by dipping into boiling water for a few moments.

The Japanese also eat another variety of artificially cultivated algae. After a thorough washing, it is dried in the sun, then lightly toasted and after being broken into small pieces it is thrown into soups and sauces to flavour them.

Another algae product which is often used in Japan is the *kantus*, a sort of glue or gelatine, which is found in the form of white, shiny, half-transparent shavings or flakes. The *kantus* is used like tapioca for preparing jellies, soups and sauces.

ALGERIA. ALGÉRIE—Algeria is an essentially agricultural country, especially in the Tell region where cereal cultivation predominates. Pasture lands extend to the high plains, while the mountains and land unsuitable for agriculture are covered with forest. This country, therefore, possesses important resources. In times of antiquity it was one of Rome's granaries.

Algerian cereals are found in every form: cereals, wheat, barley, oats, maize, millet, etc. We know that wheat especially is valued for the manufacture of pasta and semolina products, as it produces paste which, while swelling in the process of cooking, retains its form.

The Algerian vineyards are extensive. The wines, processed by improved methods, are appreciated in all the countries of the world. They are generally strong in alcohol content and lend themselves to blending and travel in all climates.

Not only do the Algerian vineyards produce interesting wines but they also provide dessert grapes, which make their appearance on the French market from the month of June.

Among other equally early fruit are plums and greengages and almonds, but specifically Algerian are oranges, tangerines, dates and figs. The two latter are exported in considerable quantities dried. A great part of the production of oranges and tangerines is used locally for the manufacture of liqueurs.

Vegetable farming produces excellent quality potatoes, beans, artichokes, tomatoes, peas, carrots, melons, watermelons and aubergines (eggplants). Olives are cultivated in the littoral regions and in a few higher regions—up to 900 metres (almost 3,000 feet) in altitude. Refineries situated on the spot produce a very good quality oil, easy-flowing, fruity, golden.

The coasts furnish all the fish and crustaceans of the Mediterranean, as well as *fruits de mer*, very similar to those found on the coast of Provence.

The pasture lands of the interior provide nourishment for considerable herds of livestock, about ten times as rich in sheep as in bovines. This explains why in Arab cookery, examples of which are given below, many more recipes for mutton are given than for beef, etc. Specifically

Algerian animals, such as camels or gazelles, come on the menu more in the nature of a gastronomical curiosity and are treated in rather an exceptional manner.

Arab cuisine or 'tent cookery'. CUISINE ARABE—This type of food is simple and healthy; milk, oil, semolina, rice, dates, vegetables, pasta products, condiments and meats which go into its composition, are all excellent and, simply treated, produce easily digestible dishes.

The method of slaughter used by the Arabs, which consists of severing the neck, the windpipe and the two jugular veins, without lifting the knife off until the severance is complete, is to be particularly recommended.

The Arabs eat only the flesh of animals; the blood is forbidden. The Koran authorizes a choice of foods which the Arabs are permitted to eat. This includes aquatic animals, all the poultry and all birds, except birds of prey—day or nocturnal, all livestock animals, camels, oxen, sheep, etc. with the exception of pig and wild boar.

The lawmaker advises his faithful: 'Do not eat in a crouching or huddled position, as this position disposes to too much eating, but sit around the table in such a manner as to appear always ready to get up'.

Arabs generally drink only once, after a meal, when a communal vessel (*guerba*), containing spring water or milk makes the round of those participating in the meal.

The person drinking should not breathe into the bowl containing the liquid; he must remove it from his lips before beginning to breathe again. Then he can resume drinking. A cup of coffee and a pipe of tobacco always concludes the meal of the true Arab.

The coffee, a Moslem beverage, the inseparable companion of tobacco (these two constitute the two great pleasures of the Arab) is very rich in tonic substances and, therefore, very healthy in a country where the summer temperature varies between 77°F. and 122°F.

Arabs drink no wine; the Koran forbids it.

One of the authors of the commentaries to the Koran, Sidi Dylaleddine, thinks, however, that the Prophet simply wanted to forbid an excess of wine drinking, and that wine is permitted provided one does not get drunk.

Another, going one better, said: 'Eat and drink but without excess, for God loves not him who commits excess'.

Arab gastronomical customs—'When the food is served,' says El Syauté, 'help yourself from around the edge of the dish, leaving the middle, as the blessing of heaven will descend upon it'.

The laws of hospitality are rigorously observed by the Moslems. If a stranger, be he well or poorly dressed, appears at the entrance to a tent, or at the door of a house, and asks for hospitality, the master of the household immediately answers: 'Be welcome', and bids him enter, indicating a place on the carpet or mat which covers the floor. Immediately the visit is treated as a festive occasion and the guest is offered a cup of coffee or tea and whatever there is ready to eat.

Hospitality is a duty of every good Moslem.

When a native family offers you some *messelmen*, some *sebaas-el-aarroussa*, a kind of biscuit in the shape of a tapering finger or little hands in sponge cake, this is a manifestation of welcome.

The pattern of the hand which is seen on the cakes, on the tents, on the walls of native houses, as well as on doors or windows is a symbol of power arising from an historical episode.

Moses, having changed his rod into a serpent, showed his dazzling hand to the Pharaoh, as if to bear witness to his power. The faithful have adopted the symbol of the hand of Moses, as protection from the evil eye.

A very rigid period of fasting, the *Ramadan*, is prescribed for all Moslems during all daylight hours of the entire month of Ramadan, which is the ninth month of the Mohammedan year.

The word '*Ramadan*' comes from a verb which means to rain, because it washes away the sins of the flesh and cleanses the impurities of the heart.

The period of fasting was laid down by Mohamed, during the second year of the Hegira, to consecrate, for religious practice, the memory of what happened to the first man when he ate the forbidden fruit. Adam, banished from the Garden of Eden, cried bitterly, but his repentance was not accepted by God until thirty days after his fall, when his body had been cleansed of the impurities with which his disobedience had tainted him, and posterity was thus condemned to a consecutive fast of thirty days a year.

During the month of Ramadan the Moslems must abstain from food, drink and smoke from sunrise to sunset.

In North Africa, where Islam is the predominating religion, an artillery salvo proclaims to the faithful the beginning of Ramadan. During the whole month a cannon fired once at sunset announces each evening the cessation of fasting.

The Ramadan ends with pantagruelian feasts, called Aid-el-Kébir, which have several features in common with the Christian Christmas dinner. The Moslems, who cannot celebrate this feast at home, gather in native cafés.

Culinary specialities of North Africa:

Aâssida—Flour boiled in water, mixed with butter.

Bascoutou—Spanish loaf made of yolks of egg, flour and orange blossoms.

Bissar—Dried beans cooked in water and oil until they form a sort of jelly; eaten hot or cold.

Bouzellouf—Sheep's head, singed on a brisk fire to remove all hairs, then boiled and seasoned with oil, vinegar, salt, pepper and garlic.

Breyes beylicales—Little squares of semolina mixed with pistachio nuts, walnuts and almonds.

Brik—Eggs in puff pastry, fried in oil.

Cacao—This preparation, which is formed in the shape of little reddish-brown lozenges, is made from sugar, pistachio nuts, almonds and lemon essence.

Chekchuka. TCHEKCHOUKA—A dish made of sweet or strong peppers, tomatoes, little marrows (zucchinis) or aubergines (eggplants), cut in pieces and fried in olive oil with garlic and onion, the whole either mixed with beaten eggs or not, as the case may be, and cooked for a few minutes on a slow fire.

Cherba-bel-frik—Green corn soup.

Djendjelem—Bought ready-made. It is a sort of whitish, soft paste, made of sugar, ginger, starch and a pinch of pepper.

Dolma—Mixture of rice, chopped meat and onions, the whole strongly seasoned and wrapped in cabbage leaves, cooked in a casserole, covered with water, with fire below and above. Similar to Turkish dolma.

Douara—Boiled pluck and tripe, seasoned with cummin and spices.

Guizada—A sort of scalloped little cookies made from semolina and eggs, baked in the oven.

Homse—Little balls of paste dried and coated with honey.

Kabab—Mutton cut into squares, braised in butter, seasoned with salt and pepper and served with a strong garnish of sliced onions and parsley.

Kefta—Chopped and spiced mutton, shaped into rissoles and grilled on a wood fire.

Khali—Dried mutton, cooked in oil and fat and thus preserved.

Liani—Lamb stew with chick-peas, seasoned with wild parsley.

Makrouda—A variety of lozenges made of pastry stuffed with dates.

M'darbel—Mixture of fried marrows (zucchinis) and little pieces of beef fried in oil, highly seasoned with pimento and slightly dressed with vinegar.

Mekechter—Chicken fricassée with chick-peas.

Merga—Stock made of mutton or chicken, or both, strongly aromatized and spiced, which the Arabs drink only when it is very cold or in cases of illness.

M'habia—Cake made from milk, semolina, pistachio nuts, walnuts and pine-nuts.

M'hamsa—Soup with pasta products and tomatoes.

Mokh—Sheep's brains and tongue, strongly spiced with garlic, cayenne pepper and wild parsley.

Osbane—Forcemeat made from sheep's pluck and meat, chopped, mixed with rice, seasoned with red pepper and spices, for stuffing sheep's intestines.

Rim-bel-terfass—A stew made of gazelle meat, with Saharan truffles (Sahara dish).

Sferia—Mixture of chopped mutton and onions, seasoned with salt, pepper and cummin, shaped into little balls, dipped in eggs and fried in butter.

Tadjin helou—Very delicate stew, made of mutton or beef, vegetables in season and dried fruit, prunes or raisins, and a few quinces, covered with pie pastry and cooked in the oven.

Terbia-bel-hebar—Macedoine of vegetables served with a roast bustard (little bustard or field-duck).

Tleiti—Macaroni garnished with chopped meat and eggs cooked in the oven.

Tomina—Coarse semolina cooked in an earthenware casserole and plunged into butter and boiling honey.

Yubbo—Cake made from honey, olive oil, rose petals, flour and dandelion.

Other specialities include *lagni*, much-valued palm-milk, *leban*, which is nothing but whey, and *kefir* made from cow's, goat's or sheep's milk; *chreyba*, *rahat-loucoum*, *sahleb*, *rogagues*, *messemen*, *makroutes*, *stuffed dates*, etc.

Also added to this list must be all the *tadjins*, the *mechoui*, the *couscous* (see COUSCOUS), with its various accompaniments (for which recipes will be found under COUSCOUS), the delicacies of Tunisian and Israeli cuisine, which will enable us to realize that regional African cookery need not fear comparison with the metropolitan.

ALGÉRIENNE (A L')—This is the name of a garnish, applicable principally to meat, consisting of small tomatoes braised in oil and sweet potato croquettes, or sweet potatoes cooked in butter.

ALICA—The Romans called by this name a food product of which they were very fond. It was composed of paste made from a cereal called *zea*, to which a sort of clay, *creta*, which is found between Naples and Pouzzoles, was added. It is recorded that Augustus annually paid the sum of twenty thousand sesterces to the Neapolitans for exclusive supplies of this clay.

ALICANTE WINE—A very famous dessert wine which is cultivated in Spain, in the province of Alicante. This wine, which has considerable alcoholic content, is very similar to the *Muscat de Frontignan*.

ALICUIT (Languedoc cuisine)—Ragoût of giblets (principally turkey gizzards and pinions) prepared as described in the recipe for *Turkey giblets bonne-femme*. See GIBLETS.

This ragoût is also called *alicot*. In all its forms the etymological root is retained: *ali*, *ailes* (*wings*); *cuit*, *cuites* (*cooked*).

ALKALESCENTS. ALCALINASANTS—Foods, the total mineralization of which includes an excess of basic elements (lime, soda, potassium, magnesia).

Milk and blood are the only alkalescents of animal origin; with the exception of cereals and products derived from them, and some vegetables of which we consume the flowers (artichoke) or buds (asparagus, Brussels sprouts), all the foods of vegetable origin are alkalescents, including all acid-tasting fruit such as lemons, red currants, etc.

Celery, Jerusalem artichokes, turnips, carrots, beetroot, cucumbers, cabbage, dandelion, endives, lettuce, tomatoes, spinach, oranges, tangerines and lemons are very strong alkalescents.

Less powerful alkalescents are: milk, potatoes, cauliflower, fruit.

ALKALI VOLATILE. ALCALI VOLATIL—Commonly known as liquid ammonia. It is a colourless liquid, having an extremely strong pungent smell, the fumes of which can even prove to be poisonous. Alkali is lighter than water and has a very pronounced smell of urine.

It is used in confectionery as a dissolvent for cochineal carmines.

ALKALOIDS—Nitrogenous basic substance of vegetable origin, having a powerful action on the organism, even when absorbed in very small quantities. (The stimulants contained in coffee, tea and chocolate are alkaloids.)

ALKERMES—An old cordial which used to be very fashionable in days gone by. This liqueur, which is red, the coloration being produced by kermes, hence the name, is flavoured with nutmeg, cinnamon, bay leaf and cloves. The infusion of these aromatics is distilled and mixed with sugar.

ALLEMANDE SAUCE (Carême's recipe)—This name is given to a classic white sauce, made with *Velouté** blended with yolks of egg and cream. The recipe for this sauce, which is one of the best in the French culinary repertoire, as it is made nowadays, is given in the section devoted to sauces.

In spite of its name, this sauce in no way originates in Germany. It is so called, according to Carême, because it is light in colour, to differentiate it from *Espagnole sauce*, which is dark.

Moreover, this latter sauce does not appear to have originated in Spain either.

There is, in the French culinary repertoire, a very great number of terms which, although borrowed from other countries, serve to describe dishes of entirely French origin. Modern authors also refer to the *Allemande* as *Parisienne sauce*. See SAUCE.

Carême's recipe—Carême first of all gives the recipe for preparing *Velouté sauce*, then goes on to describe how, with this *Velouté* (see SAUCE), to prepare *Allemande sauce*.

'Pour into a saucepan half the velouté and the same quantity of good chicken consommé, in which you will have put a few mushrooms (stalks and peel), and as much salt as can be held on the point of a knife.

'After having placed on a brisk fire, stir the sauce with a wooden spoon until it comes to the boil; then, put it on the edge of the stove, cover and leave to simmer for about an hour; then skim off fat and put back on a high flame stirring with a wooden spoon to prevent it sticking to the bottom of the pan. When this sauce is perfectly cooked, it should coat the surface of a spoon quite thickly. When poured, it should be the same consistency as red-currant jelly, if it has reached the ideal point in its cooking.

'Then, you remove the saucepan from the fire, prepare a liaison using 4 yolks of egg, mix with 2 tablespoons of cream and, having passed it through a sieve, add best butter the size of a small egg, in small pieces; then pour it little by little into the *velouté*, stirring carefully with a wooden spoon to make sure that the liaison is blended in smoothly. When it is all perfectly incorporated, replace the *allemande* on a moderate fire and keep on stirring. As soon as a few bubbles start to rise, remove from heat; add as much grated nutmeg as can be held on the point of a knife. When well blended, pass through a sieve.'

ALLIARIA (Jack-by-the-hedge). ALLIARE—This plant has a very pronounced taste of garlic. Its leaves are chiefly used as a pharmaceutical plaster, but it can be used as a condiment in seasoning salads. It is common in the north temperate regions of Europe.

ALLIGATOR—A species of American crocodile, commonly called *cayman*. While we are still waiting for Fulbert-Dumonteil's dream to come true—he wanted the whole of natural history and its subjects to go through our saucepans—the alligator has already become part of the gastronomical world. Not only do the natives who capture it eat its slightly musky flesh, but a slice of alligator is sometimes served in London and Paris.

This, however, is rather unusual, and the sauces and garnishes which accompany it are the only excuse. The most valued parts of the reptile are the paws or flappers, since the alligator, although less aquatic than most crocodiles, also lives in water. These flappers are prepared *à l'américaine*, *à l'indienne* or in any other slightly spiced manner. See TURTLE.

ALLSPICE. TOUTE-ÉPICE—Name for the seed of Jamaica pepper and for that of cultivated nigella.

ALLUMETTES—A kind of hors-d'oeuvre, or small entrée. They are strips of puff pastry accompanied by different garnishes cooked in the oven.

Little cakes also made of puff pastry and filled or garnished with various mixtures are likewise called *allumettes*.

Allumettes (hot hors-d'oeuvre)—Roll out a strip of puff pastry to a thickness of $\frac{1}{8}$-$\frac{1}{4}$ inch, about 3 inches wide and of indeterminate length. Cover the surface of this strip with *Fish forcemeat* or any other indicated mixture (see FORCEMEAT), cut into rectangles, put on a baking tray and bake in the oven (400°F.) for about 15 minutes.

Allumettes à la périgourdine—Coat the puff pastry with a *purée of chicken livers** mixed with finely chopped truffles. Bake in the oven.

Allumettes à la reine—Coat the puff pastry with a very finely minced mixture of breast of chicken, truffles and mushrooms blended with thick *Velouté sauce* (see SAUCE). Bake in the oven.

Allumettes à la toscane—Sprinkle the sheet of puff pastry, while rolling it out, with grated Parmesan. Cut into strips as usual and bake in the oven.

Ox palate allumettes. ALLUMETTES DE PALAIS DE BOEUF—'Take two ox palates cooked in water; after removing the skin, cut into strips the size of matchsticks and marinate in lemon juice or vinegar, a little salt, parsley in sprigs and whole spring onions; when they have taken on a flavour, drain and dip into batter made in the following manner: put into a saucepan two good handfuls of flour, a spoonful of fine oil, a little finely ground salt and dilute it, little by little, with beer, until the batter has a consistency of thick cream; dip your palate strips into it and fry until they are a nice colour. Serve as hot as possible.' (*La Cuisine Bourgeoise*, 1769, Paris.)

Allumettes (cakes)

ALLUMETTES (cakes)—These little cakes were created, it is said, by a pastry-cook of Swiss origin who, towards the end of the last century, was established at Dinard (Ille-et-Vilaine). M. Lacam, who wrote a history of pastry-making, describes the invention as follows: 'Planta, that's the name of the above-mentioned pastry-cook, one day had some icing left over and did not know what to do with it. Having softened this icing he added a pinch of flour to it, to prevent the sugar from running in the heat of the oven, then he spread it on a sheet of puff pastry, which he cut into little sticks, and baked them in the oven'.

And this is how the *allumettes*, a sort of dry *petits fours* which are so popular these days, were invented.

Method. Roll out some puff pastry to a thickness of $\frac{1}{8}$ inch. Cut this pastry into strips 3 inches wide. Spread a thin layer of royal icing (see ICING) on these strips. Cut the strips into pieces about 1 inch wide and put them on a baking tray. Bake in the oven (400°F.) for 12 minutes.

ALMOND. AMANDE—In general, any seed enclosed in a kernel of a nut or stone fruit. In particular, fruit of the almond tree. There are two varieties: *sweet almond* and *bitter almond*. They come mostly from North Africa, Provence, Italy and Languedoc and from California, U.S.A. More than half their weight is oil, which is extracted and of which there are two varieties: oil which is used principally in perfumery, and that used in pharmaceutics for the manufacture of soothing emulsions.

The almond tree is mentioned in Genesis, and almonds figure among the fruit offered to Joseph.

COUNTRY ALMOND (Indian Almond Tree). BADAMIER—This tree, which is also called *catappa*, grows generally in Asia. The fruit is an almond, of a pleasant taste, from which an oil somewhat similar to olive oil is extracted.

Another species of country almond produces resinous and aromatic matter, a kind of gum benzoin, which is used in confectionery.

Aboukir almonds (confectionery). AMANDES D'ABOUKIR —*Petit four*, made of kirsch-flavoured, green-coloured almond paste, shaped in the form of a green almond, stuffed with a blanched almond. The aboukirs are coated with gum or iced with sugar cooked to the condition of large crack. See SUGAR.

Almond

Almond and puff pastry gâteau. GÂTEAU FEUILLETÉ AUX AMANDES—This gâteau is known under the name of *Pithiviers.**

Almond butter. BEURRE D'AMANDES—Pound 1 cup (150 grams) of freshly-blanched almonds finely in a mortar until they are reduced to paste, adding a few drops of cold water to prevent them from turning into oil. Continue to pound and add ½ pound (250 grams) of fresh butter. Pass through a very fine sieve.

This butter is used for flavouring certain sauces or cream soups and also as an element in cold *hors d'oeuvre*.

Almond cake—This is made like plum cake using 1 pound (500 grams) of butter, ½ pound (250 grams) of almonds pounded with 2 eggs, 10 whole eggs (put in one by one), 4⅔ cup (600 grams) of sieved flour mixed with 1 teaspoon (5 grams) of baking powder and grated rind of 2 lemons. Decorate the top of the cake with halves of blanched almonds.

Almond cookies. PAINS ANGLAIS—Small dry cookies prepared in the following manner.

Ingredients. 2 cups (250 grams) of sieved cake flour, ½ pound (250 grams) of ground almonds, 1¾ cups (250 grams) of castor (fine) sugar, ¼ pound (125 grams) of butter, 4 eggs, half a liqueur glass of rum.

Method. Put the flour on the table in a circle, make a well in the middle and put into it the almonds, the sugar and the butter, the latter well softened. Break the eggs into these ingredients, pour on the rum and mix the paste without kneading it, to prevent burning (if the paste is too firm, add a yolk of egg).

Roll the paste into sausages, cut into pieces and roll into little balls on a lightly-floured table.

Put the pieces of pastry on a buttered tray, spacing them out a little. Brush with two coats of egg. Slit each little ball slightly with the blade of a wet knife.

Bake for 20 minutes in a slow oven (using two baking trays).

Almond cookies (lemon flavoured). PAINS ANGLAIS AU CITRON—Pound ½ pound (250 grams) of blanched almonds finely with 1¾ cups (250 grams) of fine sugar and 2 whole eggs.

Sieve 2 cups (250 grams) of sieved cake flour, spread in a circle on the table and put the almond and sugar paste in the middle. Add ⅘ cup (200 grams) of butter and the grated rind of 1 lemon (or orange). Knead well together.

Divide the paste into pieces about the size of a walnut. Sprinkle the table lightly with flour and roll these pieces of paste into little cigars, pointed at the ends. Put them on a buttered baking sheet, slit in the middle with a knife, brush with beaten egg and bake in a hot oven from 8 to 10 minutes.

Almond cream. CRÈME D'AMANDES—Prepare 2 cups (½ litre) of *crème pâtisserie* in the usual manner, cool it and add to it ½ pound (250 grams) of fieshly-blanched almonds pounded into a smooth paste with 1 cup (250 grams) of sugar and ½ pound (250 grams) of butter.

This cream is used for filling sweet dishes. For *crème pâtisserie* see CREAM, *French pastry cream.*

Almond loaf. PAIN COMPLET—A cake made of almond paste in the shape of a wholemeal loaf.

Almond milk. LAIT D'AMANDES—The codex gives the following recipe for almond milk:

Ingredients. ⅓ cup (50 grams) sweet blanched almonds, 2 tablespoons (50 grams) white sugar, 5 tablespoons (100 grams) distilled water.

Method. Pound the almonds and the sugar with a small quantity of water in a marble mortar to obtain a very smooth paste. Force through a fine sieve.

Almond nougat. NOUGAT AUX AMANDES—Dry in the oven 1 pound (500 grams) of almonds, blanched and chopped. Put these almonds in a copper bowl in which 1½ cups plus 2 tablespoons (400 grams) of sugar, flavoured with a squeeze of lemon juice, has been boiled to a pale caramel. Stir this mixture with a spatula.

While the mixture is still hot, put it into greased moulds of different shapes.

The nougat can also be spread on an oiled marble slab, so that it forms a thin layer which can then be cut into different shapes.

Nougat prepared in this way can be shaped into bowls, baskets, clogs and other objects.

Almond paste I. PÂTÉ D'AMANDES—Crush 1 pound (500 grams) of blanched almonds. Put them in a mortar, add the flavouring chosen (vanilla, scented sugar or liqueur). Add, little by little, 2 pounds (a kilogram) of sugar cooked to the condition of large crack (see SUGAR). Mix the sugar and the almond paste well, stirring vigorously with the pestle.

Almond paste II. PÂTÉ D'AMANDES—*Ingredients.* 3 cups (475 grams) sweet almonds, 2 tablespoons (25 grams) bitter almonds, 5 grams gum tragacanth, ¾ cup (100 grams) of icing sugar, one white of egg, juice of one lemon.

Method. Pound the almonds with the juice of the lemon and pass through a fine strainer. Put into a copper pan. Add icing sugar and white of egg. Stir this mixture, drying it gently over the fire. Incorporate in it the gum tragacanth dissolved in a little water.

To be perfect this paste must not stick to the fingers. It is used in layers in various sweet dishes and *petits fours.*

Almond praline. PRALIN AUX AMANDES—Melt 2 cups (500 grams) of castor (fine) sugar slowly in a copper pan. Cook it until it reaches the degree of light caramel (180°F.). Add to this sugar 3 cups (500 grams) of raw (shelled but unskinned) well-dried almonds.

Tip all this mixture on to an oiled marble slab. Allow to cool. Pound the mixture in a mortar. Pass it through a fine sieve. Keep this dry almond powder in tins with well-fitting lids.

Almond tartlets. TARTELETTES AMANDINES—For these very delicate little tartlets, Edmond Rostand, in *Cyrano de Bergerac*, gives a recipe in verse which is attributed to Ragueneau, the famous pastry-cook who lived in the seventeenth century. Here is this poetical recipe:

Comment on fait les tartelettes amandines

Battez pour qu'ils soient mousseux,
Quelques oeufs;
Incorporez à leur mousse
Un jus de cédrat choisi;
Versez-y
Un bon lait d'amande douce;
Mettez de la pâté à flan
Dans le flanc
De moules à tartelette;
D'un doigt preste abricotez
Les côtés;
Versez goutte à gouttelette
Votre mousse en ces puits, puis
Que ces puits
Passent au four, et, blondines,
Sortant en gais troupelets,
Ce sont les
Tartelettes amandines!

Beat your eggs, the yolk and white
Very light;
Mingle with their creamy fluff
Drops of lime juice, cool and green;
Then pour in
Milk of almonds, just enough.
Dainty patty pans, embraced
In puff-paste—
Have these ready within reach;
With your thumb and finger, pinch
Half an inch
Up around the edge of each—
Into these, a score or more,
Slowly pour
All your store of custard; so
Take them, bake them golden-brown—
Now sit down! . . . .
Almond tartlets!*

Bitter almonds. AMANDES AMÈRES—Bitter almonds owe their bitterness to the relatively considerable quantity of prussic acid contained in them. They should, therefore, be used only in moderation.

They are used in pastry-making for flavouring icings and cream fillings, and in confectionery in the form of essence for flavouring sweets, liquors, etc.

These almonds are not used as dessert fruit and their oil is poisonous.

Blanched almonds. AMANDES MONDÉES—Dried almonds from which the skin has been removed. Proceed in the following manner: put the almonds into a sieve; plunge into a saucepan of boiling water. Draw the saucepan to the side of the stove.

Drain the almonds little by little, as soon as you can see that the skin comes off when pressed with the fingers. Skin them quickly and cool in cold water. Drain, dry and, if they are meant for keeping, put to dry in a very slow oven on a sieve or fine grill. Put into a tin or a jar with a well-fitting lid. Keep in a dry place.

Chopped almonds. AMANDES HACHÉES—Chop blanched almonds into small pieces of desired size, according to the use for which they are ultimately intended.

Coloured almonds. AMANDES COLORÉES—In pastry-making and confectionery shredded or ground almonds in all colours are used either for making coloured nougat, for coating sweets, or for making decorations for *petits fours*, little fancy cakes and biscuits (U.S. cookies), large cakes and sweet dishes coated with a fondant icing.

The preparation of these almonds is the same whatever their colour.

The best process is to dissolve the colouring matter (which may be liquid, paste or powder) in a sufficient quantity of alcohol to moisten all the almonds. Put these into a round basin or bowl and pour over them a part of the colouring matter dissolved in alcohol; stir briskly to mix well and continue adding colouring matter until the desired tint is obtained. When the almonds are coloured lay them out on a piece of paper and expose them to a gentle heat. Sieve them when they are dry and decant into hermetically sealed containers.

Flavouring appropriate to the colour may be added: thus pink may be scented with raspberry essence; mauve with violet, etc.

Diced almonds. AMANDES EN DÉS—Blanched, halved almonds, cut into dice of desired size according to the use for which they are ultimately intended. These are used for sweet dishes and in pastry-making.

Raw almonds. AMANDES BRUTES—This is the name given in pastry-making and confectionery to almonds which have simply been taken out of their hard shells but are still covered with the brown skin.

Almonds for which there is the greatest demand in pastry-making are those with hard shells from Provence.

Medium-sized almonds grown in the plains are greatly valued; they sometimes contain quite a high percentage of bitter almonds. These are used for preference in making almond paste.

The *béraude* almonds, broad and fleshy, contain a smaller percentage of bitter almonds and are chiefly shredded or ground and used for sprinkling on small cakes and fancy biscuits or for covering sweets.

The *Tournefort* almonds are irregular in shape and very small, but because of their excellent flavour they are in great demand for making almond paste.

Roasted almonds. AMANDES GRILLÉES—Shred the almonds and dry in the oven until they turn pale golden.

Salted almonds. AMANDES SALÉES—Put sweet blanched almonds in the oven to make them a pale yellow colour, turning once. Then fry them until golden in butter with a pinch of saffron, red pepper and ginger. Drain on a cloth and, after cooling, coat the almonds with a clear solution of gum arabic and sprinkle with fine salt.

* *From Brian Hooker's translation of* Cyrano de Bergerac *by Edmond Rostand. Published by Heinemann in association with Allen & Unwin.*

Shredded almonds. AMANDES EFFILÉES — Shredded almonds are used a great deal in pastry-making and in confectionery; shredded and roasted, they are used for coating the sides and sometimes the whole of sweet dishes. Shredded unroasted (white), they are used for coating almond *petits fours* (fancy cakes and biscuits—U.S. cookies), for cooked nougat and for Montelimar nougat. They also enter into the composition of *petits fours*, *meringues*, *tuiles aux amandes*, etc.

There are several very practical instruments for shredding almonds, but this operation can be done equally well by hand. The almonds should be cut lengthways and each almond can be shredded into 12 to 15 pieces. The almonds are shredded as soon as they are blanched, before they are dried; after shredding, they are put on a metal sheet, placed to dry in a very slow oven and turned three times a day. Keep in hermetically sealed tins.

Sugared almond. DRAGÉE—An almond coated with hard sugar.

Sugared almonds, made from almonds encased in sugar or rather honey, have been known from the earliest times.

It is said that the Romans made them and also that in the year 177 B.C. a patrician Roman family, the illustrious Fabian family, used, as a token of rejoicing, to distribute sugared almonds to the populace on the occasion of a birth or marriage in the family. It is thus plain that the habit of serving sugared almonds at the celebration of a birth goes back a long way.

It is difficult to make sugared almonds in household kitchens. However, nowadays excellent sugared almonds are manufactured commercially. Some are made with windfall almonds, others with hazelnuts or pistachios. Others are filled with a few drops of liqueur, chocolate, almond or filbert paste, etc.

Sweet almonds. AMANDES DOUCES—Sweet almonds are in great demand in pastry-making and in confectionery; all Spanish and Italian almonds are sweet.

Green sweet almonds are greatly esteemed as dessert fruit and are consumed in great quantities. They are less oily and for that reason easier to digest than dry almonds.

Whole almonds. AMANDES ENTIÈRES—When a recipe in pastry-making and confectionery calls for a certain amount of whole almonds, this means blanched almonds and not raw almonds, which are always referred to as raw, meaning with the thin brown skin left on.

ALMONDS, EARTH. AMANDES DE TERRE—This is the name of the *cyperus* tubers, a plant which grows in marshy places in countries with hot and temperate climates.

These tubers are in the shape of little almonds, brown on the outside. The flesh inside is very white. They are very starchy in substance. They are eaten raw, like nuts, or they can be cooked as chestnuts. They are also made into a kind of flour.

ALOCASIA—Plant originating in the Indies. Nowadays about fifteen species of it are known. The most important one is a native of Ceylon but has spread throughout the greater part of the Indian subcontinent, where its voluminous rhizomes, after a prolonged period of cooking, serve as a food.

ALOE. ALOÈS—A genus of shrubby plants belonging to the family *Liliaceae*. From the leaves of this plant a purgative gum resin is extracted. Certain species found in Cochin-China (Vietnam) produce an edible starch.

ALOUMÈRE—A type of agaric of a sweetish taste. It is chiefly found under elder trees. Prepare as cultivated mushrooms. See MUSHROOMS.

ALPHEUS. ALPHÉE—A kind of crustacean, the body of which, a little compressed, resembles that of crayfish. Some of them are common to all the coasts of France, on the Atlantic side, as well as on the Mediterranean. Other species are peculiar to the Mediterranean. Yet others live in the seas of Asia, Australia and America.

Although it lacks the fine quality of the spiny lobster, this crustacean is the object of regular fishing and is generally esteemed.

All the methods of preparation given for lobster or the crayfish are applicable to it.

Gastronomic map of Alsace

ALSACE—The Alsatian larder is well stocked with numerous and excellent foods.

Butcher's meat in this region is of good quality. Pork is particularly full-flavoured. The *seigneur cochon* (the 'noble pig') is held in great honour in Alsace.

'The Benedictine monks who were the first to maintain ponds for keeping fish and to make the first steps in pisciculture, were also the first to realize the advantages which could be derived from breeding pigs', says Paul Bouillard, in an essay on Alsatian cookery. With this pig breeding gradually improving, they have succeeded in producing admirable pork, with firm flesh and delicate flavour. The Strasbourg pork butchers, who are masters of their art, transform it into various preparations, which are enjoyed not only by the gourmands of Alsace, but also of Paris, for the Alsatian pork produce is found in all good Paris houses.

Alsatian charcuterie (pork butchery produce): (1) Little Strasbourg sausages (*knackwurst*); (2) Saveloys; (3) Thann sausage; (4) *Metwurst*; (5) Black pudding with tongue; (6) Ham sausage (*Schinkenwurst*); (7) Schwartenmagen; (8) Bierwurst; (9) Veal roll; (10) Schwartwurst; (11) Strasbourg sausage; (12) Mulhouse sausage; (13) Lyon type sausage made in Strasbourg; (14) Leberwurst; (15) Tongue roll with truffles; (16) Veal roll with *foie gras*

Alsatian geese are famous for the delicacy of their flesh. It is from these geese, by the way, specially fattened up for the purpose, that the magnificent liver is obtained, which the Alsatian master-cooks know so well how to transform into those celebrated *pâtés* and *terrines*.

The vegetables of the Alsatian kitchen-garden are beautiful and good. Alsatian orchards produce delectable fruit of which some, such as *quetsches* (Alsatian plums) and mirabelle plums, are not only good to eat fresh but are also used for the preparation of exquisite *eaux-de-vie* (see SPIRITS). And the list would not be complete without a mention of the cherries and the raspberries, which are distilled into very famous liqueurs.

The freshwater fish of Alsace are renowned, too. Who does not know the succulence of the Rhine salmon, the river trout, the crayfish from the streams in the Vosges, the eels, the tench and the bream, from which delicious *matelotes au vin d'Alsace* are prepared?

With such food supplies—and we have by no means mentioned all of them—the Alsatian master-cooks and *cordon-bleu* chefs cannot help but cook well. The Alsatian meal is a perfect epicurean symphony.

The following are the principal dishes, dishes truly of the country, although we have not, of course, listed the magnificent *Choucroute de Strasbourg*, nor the sublime *Pâté de foie gras* with truffles.

Culinary specialities of Alsace—*Alsatian potée*; *matelote of fish de l'Ill*; *crayfish 'cardinalised' in Alsatian wine*; *stuffed carp à l'alsacienne*; *crayfish flan*; *stuffed breast of veal*; *hot meat pâté*; *onion flan* or *zewelewaï*; *civet of hare with noodles*; *saddle of hare à la crème*; *beckenoffe*, a kind of *estouffade* made with mutton, pork and potatoes, which—to justify its name—must be cooked in a baker's oven; *fat geese à l'alsacienne*; the *schifela*, i.e. shoulder of pork with pickled turnips; *ham cooked in pastry*; *fricassée of chicken à l'alsacienne*; *salmis of goose*; *turkey with chestnuts*; *calf's liver fritters*; *chartreuse of partridges*; the *kalereii*, a kind of pork brawn; *Strasbourg black puddings*; *saveloys and sausages*; *stuffed sucking pig 'à la peau de goret'*; *red cabbage with chestnuts*; *potatoes à l'alsacienne*; *kohl-rabi à la crème*; *noodles à l'alsacienne*; *knepfle*, a kind of fritters; *milchstriwle*; *bretzel*; *schenkele*; *beignets de carnaval* (carnival fritters); different sorts of Alsatian tarts; *kougloff* or *kugelhopf*; *kouguel juif*; *bilberry flan*; *kaffeekrantz*, etc.

Alsatian *kugelhopf*

Alsatian wines—To accompany all these good things, Alsace produces, in addition to a delicious beer, rare and precious wines.

The wines of Alsace are in a special category among the great wines of France. By the richness of their bouquet, their fruity taste and their freshness, they are very close to those of Moselle and the German Rhine, which is quite natural as they are the products of the same variety of vine.

In lower Alsace there are some thirty vineyards, including the *rieslings* of Wolxheim and Molsheim, the *klevner* of Heiligenstein, the *traminer* of Gertwiller (white grapes); the white wines of Andlau, Barr, Dambach, Kintzheim, and the red wines of Marlenheim and Ottrot.

In upper Alsace there are the *riesling* of Guebwiller and of Ribeauville, the *gentil* and the *sporen* of Riquewihr, the *geisburger* of Kaysersberg, the *klevner* of Colmar, the *gries* of Ammerschwihr. Then there are the white wines of Beblenheim, Katzenthal, Ingersheim, and Mittelwihr.

Vines, Alsace (*French Government Tourist Office*)

The following are some of the characteristics of the wines of Alsace:

Riesling is a fresh wine the very fine aroma of which recalls a little the mixed perfumes of cinnamon, orange peel and cloves.

Traminer is a very round, velvety wine, aromatic and with a sweet taste.

Gentil, an issue of the white grapes of the *Pinot* family, has an exquisite delicacy. It only seems to need a red cloak to be mistaken for one of the great Burgundy wines.

Muscat has a very pronounced musky taste.

Sylvaner is one of the pleasantest wines to drink, but its bouquet is less pronounced.

Famous *eaux-de-vie* are distilled in Alsace. Among the most appreciated are: *Kirsch* (cherry); *Quetsche* (plum); *Framboise* (raspberry); *Mirabelle* (golden plum); and *Prunelle* (sloe).

ALSACIENNE (A L')—Definition applying to a very great number of preparations. The predominating ingredients featured in dishes thus prepared are sauerkraut, ham and Strasbourg sausage. See SAUERKRAUT.

Certain preparations based on *foie gras* are also described by this name.

ALSTROEMERIA. ALSTROEMÈRE—A genus of root tubers. Some fifty species of this plant are known, all originating in the hot or temperate regions of South America. One of them, cultivated in Chile, is known under the name of *linct*. It produces the *chûno*, a kind of arrowroot, which is extracted from the tubers in the same way that starch is extracted from potatoes. See ARROWROOT.

In the West Indies the roots of *Maranta arundinacea* are sold regularly in the market under the name of *white topinambour* (Jerusalem artichoke, i.e. *Helianthus tuberosa*); its roots are edible and lend themselves to the same methods of preparation as potatoes. They are exported to all the markets of Europe.

ALUM. ALUN—Double sulphate of aluminium and potassium, or of ammonia; salt of astringent taste.

This was once used in confectionery, to set the colour of crystallized fruit, and in pastry-making to prevent the white of egg from curdling whilst being whisked. Such use is now forbidden by law.

ALUMINITE—A sort of fire-proof earthenware with an alumina basis. All earthenware is composed of silicates of alumina, to which other substances are added. Aluminite possesses in alumina (oxide of aluminium) a source of strength much superior to that of other earthenware and acquires, as a result of this, a great resistance to fire.

ALUMINIUM—Ductile resistant metal, possessing the appearance of silver, the principal characteristic of which is its extreme lightness.

Aluminium is ideal for the manufacture of kitchen utensils, but care must be taken when cleaning aluminium receptacles and the use of soap and, above all, of washing soda crystals must be taboo. Soda, as well as its components, voraciously eats into aluminium.

AMANITA. AMANITE—A genus of fungi of the agaric group of which there are numerous species. Some of these are edible, others dangerous and even deadly. It is, therefore, very important to learn to recognize them. See MUSHROOMS.

AMARANTH. AMARANTE—This plant is cultivated in France mainly for the beauty of its flowers. In Italy, however, tender leaves of one variety of amaranth are eaten, prepared rather like spinach.

AMBERGRIS. AMBRE GRIS—An intestinal concretion of the sperm-whale. It is found floating on the surface of the seas in the Far East, in the form of wax-like substances, dotted with yellow and black spots, and possessing a strong and pleasant smell. Used in ancient pharmacopoeia as an antispasmodic, it was also credited with aphrodisiac and restorative properties. Brillat-Savarin, in a positively ecstatic outpouring, sings praises of the restorative powers of ambergris chocolate.

This product, which was formerly used in confectionery and in cookery, is today used in perfumery as a fixative.

In *Méditation VI* Brillat-Savarin refers to ambergris chocolate as the 'chocolate of the afflicted': 'I knew that Marshal Richelieu, of glorious memory, constantly chewed ambergris lozenges; as for myself, when I get one of those days when the weight of age makes itself felt—a painful thought—or when one feels oppressed by an unknown force, I add a knob of ambergris the size of a bean, pounded with sugar, to a strong cup of chocolate, and I always find my condition improving marvellously. The burden of life becomes lighter, thought flows with ease and I do not suffer from insomnia, which would have been the invariable result of a cup of coffee taken for the same purpose'.

Brillat-Savarin also highly praises the powers of ambergris in his *Magistères Restaurants*.

AMBIGU (Cold collation)—*Trévoux Dictionary* gives the following definition: 'A mixed collation at which meat and fruit are served together in such a manner as to make one wonder whether it is a simple collation or a supper'

In other dictionaries the same definition, or nearly the same, is given with the proviso that the dishes served at this kind of a meal must be cold.

In his *Dictionnaire Universel de Cuisine* Joseph Favre says that the word *ambigu* is applicable to a meal which is taken between luncheon and dinner, or between dinner and luncheon, and at which all the dishes, the sweet courses and the dessert are served at the same time.

We think that this definition should apply specifically to a night meal, a supper, served in the course of a *soirée* (an evening party), between midnight and two o'clock in the morning.

AMBROSIA. AMBROISIE—Food of the gods of Olympus. A metaphor descriptive of a particularly delectable food or drink.

AMÉLÉON—A French word used in Normandy for a particular kind of cider.

AMÉRICAINE (A L')—Name given to various methods of preparation of meat, fish, eggs, vegetables. Among these preparations the best known is *Lobster à l'américaine*. See LOBSTER.

The foundation of this preparation is *Tomato fondue** cooked with oil and butter and spiced with chopped onion, shallots, garlic, parsley, chervil and tarragon. The moistening consists of white wine or brandy and the final thickening is effected with the coral of these crustaceans, kneaded with butter.

AMERICAN COOKERY. CUISINE AMÉRICAINE—The history of American cooking, and in this instance we speak of cooking in the United States, is closely related to the history of the country. When the early settlers arrived, they found the Indians who had been living off the land for centuries, eating the animals and birds of plain and forest, the fish and shellfish from ocean, lake, river, and stream, wild fruits and nuts, a large variety of greens, and corn (maize). Most of the settlers, beginning with the Spanish explorers in the 1500s, followed by the British in the 1600s, and not long after, the Dutch, the French, the Germans, and the Scandinavians, arrived in the New World with domestic animals and native plants to start a new life near to the one they had left behind. Many of them incorporated into their traditional eating habits certain Indian foods, especially corn. By the nineteenth century, people from every corner of the globe had come to this country, settling in different areas. Thus regional cooking in the United States can be attributed in part to the resources of an area, but also to the people who settled there and adapted their native cooking habits to what nature had to offer.

Many factors enter into the American gastronomical picture. Most important are the natural resources of the whole country, modern food handling and rapid transportation, food technology, nutritional emphasis, and communication.

The climatic and geographical conditions of the country are so varied that from the fertile valleys, vast forests and plains, lakes, rivers and streams, and extensive coastal regions, almost every food known to man can be produced within its borders. With modern techniques of food handling and rapid transportation, the produce of any one section of the country can be enjoyed in any other. For example, oranges and grapefruit grown in Florida or California are sold in every State in the Union. Maine lobsters are served in Texas, and oysters and crabs from Maryland are served fresh in Chicago. This means that very few foods are unique to any one area, but there are still special dishes that certain localities claim as their own. To mention a few, *Baked beans and brown bread* belong to Boston and *Lobster stew* to Maine. *Fried chicken*, *Hominy grits* and *Pecan pie* are at home south of the Mason-Dixon line; *Roast pork* tastes best in Iowa; and New Orleans is where one finds the best of Creole cooking.

Food technology, which concerns itself in part with the processing and packaging of food, takes much of the hard work of food preparation out of the home or restaurant kitchen and does it in a factory. This, plus country-wide distribution, tends to standardize American food. The whole country is highly nutrition-conscious. Great emphasis is placed on the importance of eating foods with high vitamin and mineral content; food is advertised and sold quite as much for its food value as for its enjoyment. Food-fads extolling the health-giving properties of one food or another come and go, but the basic requirements for nutritional health remain constantly in the minds of most Americans, professional and domestic, who plan meals.

The food business, with its main contributing subdivisions, represents a major part of American industry. One sub-division is communication, with cookbooks, magazine articles, newspaper columns, radio and television programmes all dealing with the production and preparation of food. The United States can boast its share of gourmets who strive constantly, through the various media of communications, to raise the gastronomical standards of the country and their efforts are not without result.

Hotels and restaurants in the United States, as in most countries, range from the simplest to the most luxurious. In large cities such as New York, Chicago and San Francisco, there are many restaurants which specialize in food from other countries. In large cities generally, the better restaurants combine American cooking with international cooking, the French variety having the predominant influence. Outside the cities and across the width and breadth of the country there are thousands of small inns, restaurants, and hotels. Some of the establishments specializing in regional cookery have attained national reputations. Peculiarly American are the eating-places dedicated to eating as quickly as possible for as little money as possible. These include lunch counters where quick order meals are served, cafeterias where patrons serve themselves from a wide variety of foods, the ubiquitous hot-dog and hamburger stands, and drive-ins where meals are served to guests in their cars.

Certain American gastronomical habits that impress visitors to the country are the speed with which most people eat, the number of foods that are served simultaneously on a plate, the sweet jellies and conserves served with meat and vegetables, and the great quantities of dairy produce used. These are admittedly American characteristics, but the nature of the country, plus the international quality of its population, make it impossible to summarily define American cookery, other than to say that America is capable of producing and cooking the finest food in the world. Favourite American foods are *Beef Steak*, *Lamb chops*, *Ham*, *Chicken* and *Lobster*, *Corn on the Cob*, *Apple pie* and *Ice cream*.

AMERICAN PARTRIDGE. COLIN—Bird of the partridge family, a little larger than quail, very common in America. See QUAIL.

The *colin loui*, also called *American quail* (Bob-white, Virginian colin) is highly esteemed in the United States and is today acclimatized in England.

For its culinary preparation, see QUAIL and PARTRIDGE.

AMIENS—This town in Picardy is famous, gastronomically speaking, for its *Duck pâté* (see PÂTÉ), for its *andouillettes** and its macaroons.

AMIRAL (A L')—A name given to fish dishes, mostly. The characteristic feature of these dishes is their garnish, composed of fried mussels and oysters, crayfish tails and truffles, to which peeled mushrooms (see MUSHROOMS) are added. The sauce is a *Normandy sauce* flavoured with crayfish butter. See SAUCE.

AMMOCOETE. AMMOCÈTE—A fish having a certain similarity with the eel and even more so with the lamprey. They are found in the mouth of the Seine.

The methods of preparation given for eel and lamprey are applicable to this fish. See EEL and LAMPREY.

AMMONIA. AMMONIAC—Gas resulting from the combination of nitrogen and hydrogen. Possessing strong alkaline and caustic properties, this gas is irrespirable, causes sneezing, watering of the eyes and coughing; it is easily soluble in water and so diluted constitutes liquid ammonia or volatile alkali, an aqueous solution of ammonia (ammonium hydrate).

AMMONIA, CARBONATE OF. AMMONIAQUE, CARBONATE D'—These salts decompose under the action of heat, into ammonia and carbonic acid (carbon dioxide) both gaseous, without leaving any residue. It is used in certain preparations under the name of *baking powder* or *Alsatian yeast*, to render non-fermented dough spongey and porous. The gases, in escaping, occupy a greater volume than the grains of flour and form vacuoles in the dough; they then disappear completely if the heat of the oven is sufficiently strong.

AMMOPERDRIX. AMMAPERDRIX—A type of partridge which is found in Algeria, Egypt, Israel, India and Persia. It is a variety of the European partridge.

The Ammoperdrix does not differ from the red-legged partridge except by its smaller size, and the absence of the tarsal spur. These birds like hiding in rocky places and feed, like the French partridges, on plants more or less analogous to thyme and wild thyme. They are sometimes found on the Mediterranean coast of France, wandering about in the fields. All the methods of preparation given for partridge are applicable to this bird. See PARTRIDGE.

AMOMUM. AMOME—Plant (perennial herb of the ginger family) native of Asia and Africa. The species known under the scientific name of *amomum cardamomum* produces globular pods often called *cardamon*, and used as a substitute for true *cardamom*.

It is exported in considerable quantity from Siam, from Singapore and from Saigon. In France this seed is known under the name of grains of paradise, Malaguetta pepper, Guinea grains. It is also used as a condiment as a substitute for pepper.

AMOURETTES—Culinary name for the spinal marrow of oxen and calves. Calf's *amourettes*, very delicate in flavour, are used as garnish for patties, hot pâtés, pies, vol-au-vent, etc.

Amourettes can also be prepared as an independent dish, in the form of fritters, croquettes or fried in batter, etc.

In addition to recipes given specially for the preparation of amourettes, the majority of the recipes given for calf's and lamb's brains—with which the spinal marrow has a certain similarity—can be applied to them.

Before being treated in one way or another, the amourettes should be boiled in *court-bouillon*,* as described in the case of calf's and lamb's brains. See OFFAL OR VARIETY MEATS.

AMPHICLES—Celebrated cook of ancient Greece.

More than any of his colleagues of that distant epoch, Amphicles deserves to be rescued from oblivion. He could discern all that was barbarous and ostentatiously foolish in the culinary methods of his time and, in his teachings, as in practice, he applied himself to the task of bringing to them a saner logic. 'Amphicles loved to leave the fruits of nature in their simplicity. He liked to have a hare cooked on a spit and served underdone, discreetly seasoned with coriander and fennel. He maintained that a sucking pig should be boiled and put simply on a bed of sage. He wrapped larks in vine leaves and red mullet in fig leaves and had them cooked in the cinders. No-one knew better than he how to harmonize a piece of flesh with an aromatic. No-one disapproved more than he did of the practice of disguising the flavour of meat or vegetable. Even in the sauces, this friend of Theotime used spices sparingly. Where his predecessors indiscriminately mixed the most ill-matched condiments, where his emulators, whimsical to excess, would be lavish with twenty kinds of ingredients, Amphicles confined himself to the choice of two or three'.

If we spoke of this cook of the past at such length, it was to give an example to many modern practitioners, who are convinced that the virtue of the culinary arts lies principally in extravagance of preparations.

AMPHITRYON (host)—Most of the dictionaries and the authors of gastronomical books, such as Brillat-Savarin, Grimod de la Reynière, Berchoux, Monselet and Chavette, define this word as 'one who entertains one to dinner'.

All the gastronomical writers have laid down precepts on the relationships of hosts and guests. The most famous of these works is the *Manuel des Amphitryons* by Grimod de la Reynière.

Nearer to our time, a practitioner of great spirit and of not lesser munificence, Auguste Michel, dedicated to 'the man who receives at his table' a book full of useful hints concerning the role of the host. Its title was *Le Manuel des Amphitryons au debut de XXe siècle*.

To the original meaning of the word amphitryon an ironical nuance has been added, at times even a pejorative connotation. The same applies, in gastronomical spheres, to the word 'gourmand' which used to mean nothing more than 'one who is appreciative of good things to eat and drink' and which today is used in a definitely derogatory sense and for many people is synonymous with glutton and 'greedy-guts'.

Strictly speaking, the word amphitryon only means host and does not, and should not, apply except to a person who entertains someone at his table.

We find it difficult to imagine what a host was like in ancient times. Among the most celebrated amphitryons, whether historical or legendary, was Lucullus. He can be taken as a model of amphitryons, who offered his guests really magnificent feasts.

The historians have given us accounts of the lavishness of Maecenas' table, who is also described as a great master of the art of entertaining; Heliogabalus, famous for the extraordinary luxury of his table; Apicius—there were three men of this name in ancient Rome. See APICIUS.

Another great host was Ashurbanipal, one of the most sumptuous kings of Assyria. Belshazzar, too, must have been an amphitryon on a grand scale, because even today, speaking of a truly magnificent banquet, we still say that it was 'a veritable Belshazzar's feast'.

'For a rich man', writes Grimod de la Reynière, 'the best role in the world is that of host'.

Berchoux, for his part, says:

'S'il est un rôle noble et bien digne d'envie,
C'est celui d'un mortel qui fait en sa maison,
Les honneurs de sa table en digne amphitryon.'

'If there is a noble role, a truly enviable one,
It is that of a mortal who in his house makes
The honours of his table worthy of an amphitryon.'

Greek amphora

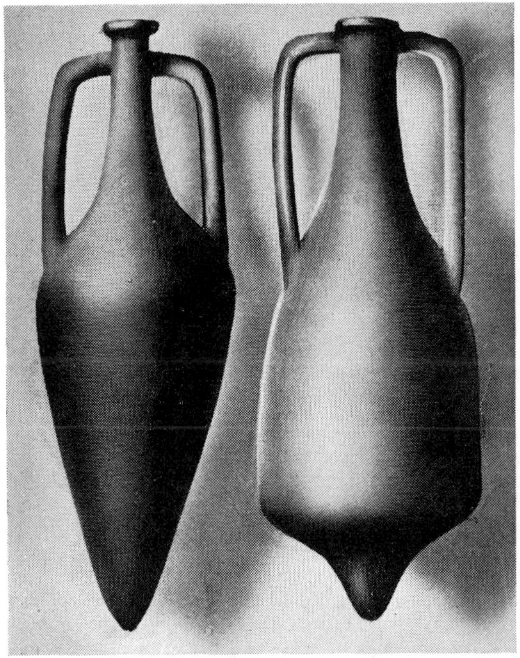

Terra-cotta amphorae for storing oil or wine

AMPHORA. AMPHORE—A two-handled terra-cotta vessel of elongated form. It is of Greek origin, the Romans having taken it from Greece. This vessel, frequently ornamented with a design, even with remarkable sculptures, served as a container for wine, and was also used for storing oil. It was often surmounted by a lid of the same material as the vessel, ending in a point.

AMYGDALINE. AMYGDALIN—Term applied to all substances, cakes or sweets, which contain almonds.

ANADONTA. ANODONTE—A genus of mollusc which lives exclusively in fresh water. The anadonta have a large thin shell, and lack hinge teeth. In Europe, chiefly in Italy and in the south of France, the species called *anadonta cygnea* are eaten like mussels.

The *anadonta cygnea* are found mainly in ponds; they can be up to 8 inches in length. As to the species commonly known as *bernacle* (barnacle), it is of much more modest dimensions and lives in rivers and streams.

The valves of the shell of another species of anadonta sometimes reach very large dimensions and are used, mainly in northern Europe, for skimming cream off the milk. In northern France the shells of the mollusc intended for this use are called *écalottes.*

ANAGNOSTE—A name given in Rome to the slave whose job it was to read during meals.

This custom was widespread from the time of the Emperor Claudius. In our days the custom hardly exists, except in some nunneries and monasteries; not so long ago it was still in force in France in educational establishments run by church authorities.

The anagnost of these latter establishments could be considered a privileged person. He took his meals after his comrades and was, more often than not, favoured by being given more choice and more copious portions. This post was much sought after by the pupils.

ANALECT. ANALECTE—Name given to the slave whose job it was to collect the remains of a meal.

What happened to left-overs in Rome? History does not tell us. One must presume that these remains of food were tidied up, arranged artistically and sold in special markets, as in the case of 'arlequins' of modern kitchens. See ARLEQUINS.

ANALEPTIC. ANALEPTIQUE—A building-up diet which restores exhausted forces. It applies to light foods which are easy to digest and which rapidly produce a sensation of well-being; full-bodied wines, beef-tea, meat jellies, tapioca and chocolate are all analeptics.

ANALYSIS. ANALYSE—In chemistry this term means resolution of a body into simple constituent elements.

ANAPHYLAXIS. ANAPHYLAXIE—Word created by Professor C. Richet to define a curious phenomenon discovered by him—the property of certain poisons of increasing, instead of diminishing, the sensitiveness of an organism to their action.

Food anaphylaxis. ANAPHYLAXIE ALIMENTAIRE—Some people, following the ingestion of certain foods such as bread, eggs, milk, honey, chocolate, etc. are subject either to skin eruptions, more often of the nettle-rash kind, or a respiratory disorder akin to asthma, or severe headaches.

The desensitization treatment is a delicate one and belongs entirely to the realm of medicine.

ANCHOVY. ANCHOIS—Small sea fish, 6 inches long. When it is fresh its back is of a beautiful green colour which later turns a dark greenish blue, then almost black, all of which helps to determine its freshness. It can be distinguished from the sardine by its projecting snout, and its large mouth, which stretches almost to the gills.

Anchovy is very delicate when fresh but can only be eaten in this state in the countries where it is caught. The best ones come from the Mediterranean region, from Nice and Catalonia, where they are very big.

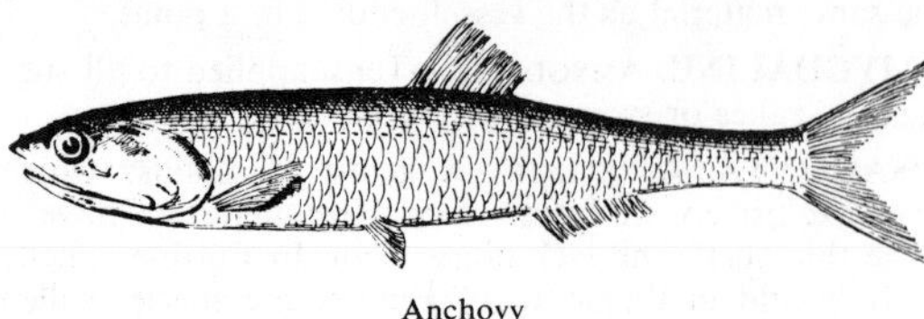

Anchovy

Method of preparation. Cut the head off and clean out the inside. Wipe the fish without pressing too hard so as not to damage them as their flesh is very fragile.

The most popular and the best method of cooking fresh anchovy is frying in olive oil.

When fresh anchovy are large, all the recipes given for fresh sardines in this book can be applied to them.

Anchovy is mostly prepared in brine. It is in this form that it is found on all the markets of Europe. It is either preserved in oil or pickled.

Anchovies à la silésienne. ANCHOIS À LA SILÉSIENNE—Prepare 6 fresh anchovies in fillets and leave them to soak for half an hour in white wine.

Rub soft roes of 2 salted herrings (having previously soaked them in water if necessary) through a fine sieve and add to this one spoonful of finely chopped shallot and parsley. Thin down this purée with white wine in which the anchovies were soaked. Spread this mixture on the bottom of an *hors-d'oeuvre* dish. Put the anchovy fillets on it in a criss-cross pattern. Surround with a border of a mixed salad—half of boiled potatoes and half of good, sharp apples, both cut in small dice and well seasoned. Garnish with small sprigs of parsley, sliced lemon and beetroot, and just before serving sprinkle with olive oil.

Put these fillet strips into an *hors-d'oeuvre* dish, arranging them suitably. Decorate with yolks and whites of hard boiled eggs, chopped separately, and chopped parsley and capers. Sprinkle the fillets with a few spoonfuls of olive oil.

The arrangement of anchovy fillets in porcelain, cut-glass or silver *hors-d'oeuvre* dishes lends itself to an infinite variety of artistic expression. Slices of lemon, quartered lettuce hearts, small gherkins cut in various shapes, beetroot cut in rounds or crescents, etc., can also be added to the ingredients mentioned above.

Anchovy fillets à la suédoise. FILETS D'ANCHOIS À LA SUÉDOISE—Arrange the anchovy fillets, prepared in the usual manner, on a foundation of salad composed of tart red apples and cooked beetroot, cut in small dice, seasoned with oil, vinegar, salt and pepper.

Surround this salad with a garnish of little bunches of parsley, yolks and white of hard boiled eggs, and cooked truffles, all chopped separately and arranged in individual groups.

Sprinkle with a few tablespoons of oil.

Portuguese anchovy fillets. FILETS D'ANCHOIS PORTUGAISE—Prepare de-salted anchovies in fillets. Cut them into thin strips or use canned fillets.

Separately prepare a *fondue* of tomatoes (see TOMATO), cooked lightly in oil.

Line the bottom of an *hors-d'oeuvre* dish with this *fondue*. Put the anchovy fillets on top of it, arranging them in a criss-cross pattern. Decorate with capers, chopped parsley, slices of peeled lemon and sprinkle with a few tablespoons of olive oil.

Anchovy toast. TOASTS AUX ANCHOIS—Garnish lightly toasted rectangular pieces of bread with fillets of anchovies. Sprinkle with breadcrumbs fried in butter and put in the oven for a moment to brown the top.

Medallions of anchovy à la niçoise. MÉDAILLONS D'ANCHOIS À LA NIÇOISE—Roll up anchovy fillets or purchase the canned or bottled variety. Spread round slices of bread, without crusts, with butter mixed with very thick *tomato purée** and put a slice of hard boiled egg on top. Put a rolled fillet of anchovy on the egg. Garnish these medallions with stoned black olives and sprinkle them with a little chopped tarragon. Arrange on a paper doyley and garnish with curly parsley.

Medallions of anchovy à la niçoise; Anchovy canapés

Anchovy canapés. CANAPÉS AUX ANCHOIS—Arrange the anchovy fillets, cut in small pieces, on long slices of bread with the crusts off, spread with a light coating of *Maître d'hôtel butter*. (See BUTTER.) Put between the pieces of anchovies yolks and whites of hard boiled eggs, chopped separately, and some chopped parsley. Arrange on a paper doyley and garnish with curly parsley.

Anchovy fillets. FILETS D'ANCHOIS—De-salt the anchovies, trim them, that is remove bones and skin. Wipe these fillets with a cloth and cut into two or three strips lengthways (canned fillets may be used).

Preserved anchovies. CONSERVE D'ANCHOIS—As soon as the anchovies are caught, remove the heads, the gall bladder and the intestines (by pressing with the thumb).

Put them in layers, in a small barrel, with salt mixed with red ochre (or powdered brick) in the proportions of

12 pounds (6 kilos) of salt to 1 pound (500 grams) of powdered brick.

Lay the anchovies in layers of 2½ inches, separated from each other by a layer of salt and brick ¾ inch thick.

When the barrel is full, put on the lid (this must have a hole pierced in the middle). Through this hole pour a concentrated solution of sea salt on the anchovies.

Leave the barrels in the sun, covered with a brick. The heat of the sun produces a kind of fermentation which preserves the fish and ensures their keeping quality, whilst the brick prevents the brine from evaporating.

When the degree of fermentation is considered sufficient, put a cork in the hole in the lid.

Anchovies preserved in brine can then be used as *hors-d'oeuvre* and for other preparations.

Rolled anchovies à la Talleyrand. PAUPIETTES D'ANCHOIS À LA TALLEYRAND—Trim and flatten the fillets. Roll them around a bit of purée of pickled tunny (tuna fish) with finely chopped truffles added to it and bound with a tablespoon of mayonnaise.

Arrange these rolled stuffed anchovies on fairly thick slices of hard boiled egg; put in an *hors-d'oeuvre* dish and surround with a *chiffonnade** of finely shredded lettuce.

Decorate with rounds of lemon and beetroot and sprinkle with oil.

Rolled anchovies à la tartare. PAUPIETTES D'ANCHOIS À LA TARTARE—Trim, flatten and roll the anchovy fillets around a core of purée of horse-radish and fresh butter (grate the horse-radish finely and knead it with butter).

Put the rolled anchovies on round, rather thick slices of cooked beetroot (cut with fluted cutters) and arrange them in an *hors-d'oeuvre* dish. Decorate with chopped hard boiled eggs, parsley and capers. Sprinkle with oil.

Rolled anchovies with hard boiled eggs. PAUPIETTES D'ANCHOIS AUX OEUFS DURS—Having trimmed and flattened the anchovy fillets, roll them into little rolls. Canned or bottled anchovies may be used.

Arrange these rolled anchovies in an *hors-d'oeuvre* dish, decorate with chopped hard boiled eggs, parsley and capers, and sprinkle with oil.

Soused anchovies. ANCHOIS MARINÉS—Clean 1 pound (500 grams) of fresh anchovies (in principle, all the preparation can only be done where the fish is actually caught). Lay them out on a plate, sprinkle with salt and leave to saturate in this seasoning for 2 hours.

Fry them quickly in smoking hot oil just to stiffen them; drain, put into an earthenware dish and cover with a marinade prepared in the following manner.

Heat the oil in which the anchovies were cooked (adding 5 or 6 tablespoons of fresh oil). Fry in it a finely sliced medium-sized onion and a sliced carrot. Add 3 unpeeled cloves of garlic.

Moisten with ⅓ cup (1 decilitre) of vinegar and ⅓ cup (1 decilitre) of water. Season with fine salt, add a sprig of thyme, half a bay leaf, 3 sprigs of parsley and ½ teaspoon of crushed peppercorns.

Boil for 10 minutes; pour while boiling on the anchovies. Leave to souse for 24 hours. Serve in an *hors-d'oeuvre* dish with slices of lemon.

ANCHOYADE (Provençal cookery)—A preparation based on anchovy paste. Pound the anchovies in a mortar, add olive oil and a few drops of vinegar. Spread this paste on slices of home-made bread, sprinkle with chopped onion and hard boiled egg. Sprinkle with oil and brown in the oven.

Anchoyade à la niçoise—Add chopped shallots and parsley to anchovy paste, moisten with olive oil and spread this mixture on slices of toast or bread fried in oil until golden.

Sprinkle with breadcrumbs mixed with chopped parsley and garlic, and olive oil. Brown in the oven.

ANCIENNE (A L')—Name given to preparations treated according to the precepts of the old school and almost always composed of mixed garnishes.

These dishes are mostly represented by braised pieces such as stew, simmered slowly for a long time. The most characteristic type is *Rump of beef à l'ancienne*. See BEEF.

This term also applies to dishes served with ragoûts in pastry shells baked blind (empty), cocks' combs and kidneys, quenelles of truffles and mushrooms. For *Chicken sauté à l'ancienne mode*, see CHICKEN, and for *Escalopes of calf's sweetbreads à l'ancienne*, see OFFAL OR VARIETY MEATS.

Finally, the term *à l'ancienne* applies to *blanquettes** and *fricassées** of veal and chicken treated in a special way. See VEAL.

ANDALOUSE (A L')—Name given to different preparations characterised mainly by tomatoes, sweet pimentos and sometimes chipolata sausages; aubergines (eggplants) and rice pilaf. See EGGS, *Eggs à l'andalouse*, CHICKEN, *Chicken à l'andalouse*.

ANDOUILLE—A very popular large sausage, composed of a large pig intestine filled with strips of chitterlings and stomach of the same animal. It is generally served cold, as an *hors-d'oeuvre*, cut in thin slices in the case of large andouille of Vire or other origin. These sausages are sold cooked.

Uncooked andouilles should be, in the first place, poached in slightly salted water, allowed to cool and then grilled as chitterlings and black (U.S.A., blood) puddings. They can be accompanied by various garnishes, but the most usual garnish is mashed potato. See PORK.

ANDOUILLETTES (Chitterlings)—Andouillettes are prepared as andouilles using smaller intestines. The most famous come from Cambrai, Caen and Troyes. Andouillettes, like andouilles, are sold ready to cook, i.e. poached and cooled.

All that remains to do is to make a few surface slits and grill them on a low fire. They are served with various garnishes but mainly, as in the case of andouilles, with mashed potatoes.

Andouillettes à la lyonnaise—Slit the andouillettes and cook them in a frying pan in lard (or butter); when two-thirds done, add a finely chopped onion previously lightly cooked in lard or butter. Finish cooking together. At the last moment, add a spoonful of vinegar and spoonful of chopped parsley.

Andouillettes à la lyonnaise can be served with mashed potatoes or sautéed potatoes.

Andouillettes à la strasbourgeoise—Grill 4 slit andouillettes on a low fire. Arrange them on braised sauerkraut and serve with boiled or steamed potatoes.

For various other preparations of andouilles and andouillettes see PORK.

ANDROPOGON (Blue grass)—A genus of plant of the *Graminacaea* family. Numerous species of it are known; one of them is the sugar cane.

Several of the plants are used for infusion, like tea.

ANETHOLE. ANÉTHOL—A compound of hydrocarbide, similar to essence of terebenthene, and of a special element, capable of crystallization, possessing a strong smell of anise. It constitutes the major part of the essences of anise, fennel, star anise and tarragon. It is used for flavouring sweets and certain dishes and liqueurs.

ANETHUM—See FENNEL.

ANGEL CAKE—See CAKE.

ANGEL-FISH (Squatina squatina). ANGE DE MER—A kind of dog-fish with a large, depressed body, with pectoral and ventral fins seeming to continue the lateral line of the body in all its thickness. The tail is big and rounded. The back is covered with a hard skin of brownish-green colour, with small whitish and green spots. The belly is whitish. This fish is the intermediary type between the family of *squali* (sharks) and that of ray and skates.

The fishermen of the French coasts call this fish *angelot* or *angel.*

It is also known as Monk-fish. On the east coast of America a very similar fish is caught. It is called angler-fish or monkfish.

The catch is very abundant. The flesh of the angel-fish is quite delicate and recalls that of the ray.

All the methods of preparation given for the latter are applicable to angel-fish. See RAY.

Angelica

ANGELICA. ANGÉLIQUE—A genus of plants of the family *Umbelliferae*, the prototype of which is generally known under the common name of *angelica, angelic herb.* It is a large biennial herb rendered hardy by scientific cultivation. It looks exactly like wild angelica.

Angelica officinalis grows wild in the Alps, in the Pyrenees and in northern Europe. It has always been valued as a stimulant, stomachic, carminative and anti-spasmodic.

Today, it is cultivated mostly for the sake of its roots and stalks.

The fresh stalks, candied in sugar, make a pleasant preserve, used by confectioners and wine and spirit merchants under the name of Niort angelica, Nevers angelica, Châteaubriand angelica.

The roots, which come principally from Bohemia, are rugose, grey outside and white inside. They are aromatic, musky, have a sweet taste to begin with, which later becomes acrid and bitter.

They contain a volatile oil, angelicine, angelic acid, tannin, malic acid, pectic acid, the malates, etc. These roots possess very strong digestive and antidyspeptic properties, owing to which they enter into the composition of melissa cordial and several other liqueurs such as chartreuse, vespetro, gin and English bitters.

Angelica liqueur. LIQUEUR D'ANGÉLIQUE—Put 2 pounds (1 kilo) of angelica stalks, cut into small pieces, to macerate for a month in 1 quart (1 litre) of brandy, in a bottling jar. See that the jar is hermetically sealed and expose it to the sun whenever possible.

Add from 1 to 1½ pounds (600 to 800 grams) of lump sugar dissolved in very little water.

Pass the whole through a silk sieve or fine muslin, pressing it. Leave to stand for a few hours, then filter the liqueur through paper.

Decant into bottles, cork and seal.

Candied angelica. ANGÉLIQUE CONFITE—Cut the angelica stalks into pieces of 6 to 8 inches; soak them in cold water.

Plunge them into a pan of boiling water until the pulp begins to give slightly when pressed with the fingers. Cool under a cold tap, drain and peel, taking care to remove all stringy parts.

Put into a syrup of 1 cup of sugar to 1 cup of water for 24 hours.

Drain; cook the syrup to 225°F. and pour it over the pieces of angelica.

Repeat this operation for 3 days. On the fourth day cook the syrup to small pearl, i.e. 245°F. Put angelica into this syrup and bring it to the boil several times.

Remove the pan from the fire and let it stand.

Drain the pieces of angelica on a sieve. When they become dry, lay them out on a marble slab, sprinkle with fine sugar and put them to dry in a very slow oven. Put into tins.

ANGELS ON HORSEBACK (English cookery). ANGES À CHEVAL—This hot *hors-d'oeuvre* is prepared in the following manner; take nice fat oysters out of their shells, drain their liquor and remove their beards, wrap each one in a very thin rasher of bacon, thread on little metal skewers, season with salt and pepper and grill. Arrange on fingers of toast.

Just before serving sprinkle with breadcrumbs fried in butter.

ANGLAISE—In cookery the term *anglaise* is applied to a mixture composed of eggs, oil (half a tablespoon per egg), salt and pepper. Various ingredients which have to be dipped in breadcrumbs are first coated with this mixture. Ingredients coated with this are said to be '*à l'anglaise*' and are then fried in butter, oil or other fat or deep-fried.

ANGLAISE (A L')—Name given to various preparations most frequently cooked in water (see MUTTON, *Leg of mutton*) or in white stock (see CHICKEN, *English boiled chicken.*)

This term also applies to the following: fish simply poached in *court-bouillon*;* fish grilled or fried in bread-crumbs; vegetables, mainly potatoes, boiled in water or steamed. See POTATOES, *Potatoes à l'anglaise.*

Grilled fish à l'anglaise. POISSONS GRILLÉS À L'ANGLAISE—This method of cooking applies to all fish. The large fish are cut into slices or steaks, the small ones are cooked whole, after having a few slits cut in them. Fish, whole or sliced, is coated with oil or melted butter and seasoned with salt and pepper before being put under a grill. It must be cooked on a low flame.

When fish with a delicate flesh is being grilled, such as whiting, fresh sliced cod, etc., it should be dusted with flour and immediately sprinkled with melted butter or oil before putting it under the grill.

Grilled fish à l'anglaise is served simply with melted butter or *Maître d'hôtel butter* (see BUTTER) and (optionally) with potatoes steamed or cooked in salted water and drained.

ANGLAISE (Custard) — Variously - flavoured custard made of yolks of egg, sugar and milk. See CREAM, *Custard cream.*

ANGLER (U.S.A. ANGLERFISH). LOTTE DE MER, BAUDROIE—This fish, also called *Lophius angle-fish* and *frog-fish,* is extremely ugly. Its foreparts are very broad while its hindquarters are exceedingly narrow. Its head, which is enormous, is very flat and spiky. Along its back, one behind the other, it has three very mobile filaments. The first, which is the largest, ends in a sort of flail shaped like a spear-head which can lash out in all directions. It is believed that the angler uses this as bait to attract its prey.

The skin of the angler is olive-brown along the back and grey on the belly. It is flabby and sticky and entirely without scales. Instead it is covered with bony filaments similar to the spikes on its head.

The angler is used mainly as an ingredient of *bouillabaisses** and other fish soups, but it can be cooked in the same way as cod and other large sea fish.

However it is prepared, angler fish should be rather highly-seasoned, since it is a somewhat tasteless fish. In U.S.A. the anglerfish while plentiful is not widely marketed. White fish fillets or steaks can be used in the following recipes.

Angler à l'anglaise. LOTTE DE MER À L'ANGLAISE—Fillet a medium-sized raw angler. Trim the fillets. Flatten and season with salt and pepper. Dip them in egg and breadcrumbs. Fry them in butter, browning on both sides. Serve on a long dish, covered with *maître d'hôtel* butter. See BUTTER.

Boiled angler with various sauces. LOTTE DE MER BOUILLIE—Skin the angler completely. Cut it into thick steaks. Cook in a *court-bouillon** as for *boiled cod* (see COD). Serve with any sauce suitable for boiled fish.

Cold angler pâté. PÂTÉ FROID DE LOTTE DE MER—Proceed as for *Cold eel pâté.* See EEL.

Fillets of angler braised in white wine. FILETS DE LOTTE DE MER BRAISÉS AU VIN BLANC—Trim and flatten the fillets. Season with salt and pepper. Lay them in a buttered baking-tin. Moisten with white wine fish essence (*fumet**). Cook in a moderate oven.

Drain the fillets. Serve on a long dish with a white wine sauce made from the cooking stock. See SAUCE, *White sauces.*

Fried angler. LOTTE DE MER FRITE—Cut the fillets of angler into strips. Dip them in milk. Flour lightly. Deep-fry in boiling fat.

Drain and season. Serve on a napkin, garnished with fried parsley and lemon.

Hot angler pâté. PÂTÉ CHAUD DE LOTTE DE MER—Made from fillets of angler and pike or whiting stuffing in the same way as *Hot eel pâté.* See EEL.

Matelot of angler. MATELOTE DE LOTTE DE MER—Cut the fillets of angler into squares. Cook them *en matelote* in white or red wine as for *Eel en matelote.* See EEL.

ANGLET—Town situated 2-3 miles from Bayonne, near the sea. A very famous white wine is produced there, dry and heady, which is called *vin de sable.* Rock salt also comes from Anglet.

ANGOULÊME—A town in the Charente where famous brandies are distilled. A famous partridge pâté is also made at Angoulême.

ANGOUMOIS—Angoumois is situated between the Poitou and the Périgord, the Limousin and the Saintonge. Such a neighbourhood could not help but turn the inhabitants of this province into gastronomes—all the more so, since the food products are excellent.

Ground and feathered game abound in Angoumois. Fresh-water fish of all kinds are to be found there. The river Touvre, which flows by the gates of Angoulême, is still, as Clement Marot said, 'paved with trout, edged with eels and crayfish', and these delicious fish and crustaceans are made into mouth-watering *matelotes.*

Various species of mushroom are gathered in Angoumois. In the quarries round about Angoulême very good quality cultivated mushrooms are grown, which in delicacy of flavour rival the famous mushrooms cultivated in the quarries around Paris.

Cattle bred for food in this region is of good quality and the meat is excellent.

Excellent poultry is also raised there; the Barbezieux chickens are particularly held in high repute.

Culinary specialities—*Friture charentaise* composed of various small-sized fish; *cagouilles* stuffed or in ragoût. (By *cagouilles* we mean snails and the inhabitants of the Charente are so fond of them that they are nicknamed *cagouillards.*)

The *tourtière* (raised pie made of chicken and salsify); jugged hare, to which in Angoumois red currant jelly is added; *preserved duck,* which is eaten with sautéed potatoes done in goose fat, or with *ceps* sautéed *à la bordelaise*; the *gigorit* or lamb's pluck; the stuffed cabbage, which is called *farée*; a range of various *pâtés* which are made in this region, such as *pâté de foie gras truffée of Barbezieux and Angoulême,* the *partridge pâté of Ruffec,* the *lark pâtés of Exideuil.* Sausages, saveloys, black puddings, chitterlings and other pork butchery produce are all excellent.

Among the sweet dishes and cakes there are the *marvels,* a sort of fritters; cheese cake, made of Ruffec cheese; chocolate tartlets flavoured with brandy.

Wine—The wines of the Angoumois region are of average quality and are drunk only locally.

Among the wines most highly thought of by the inhabitants are the white wines of *Saint-Brice* and the wines of *Saint-Radegonde,* near Barbezieux.

As table wines, these are rather mediocre but they are excellent for distilling purposes. Charente brandy is made from this wine.

The vines cultivated in the chalky soil of the Cognac, Châteauneuf, Archiac and Barbezieux, produce wine which is made into brandies (cognac des bois), which are divided into *fins bois, bons bois ordinaires, bois communs.*

An intermediate quality between the champagne brandy and the cognac des bois is obtained with the *borderies,* which are cultivated in a narrow strip of country, both chalky and sandy, situated north of Cognac. (*See map of Angoumois on next page.*)

ANGREC—A genus of plants, some of the best known of which grow in Bourbon (Réunion) Island and Madagascar, others on the Cape of Good Hope and on the west coast of Africa. The most important species is the *angraecum fragrans*; its leaves furnish the *faham*, or tea of the Island of Bourbon, which is widely used in the same way as China tea.

ANIMELLES—This is a culinary term for the testicles of male animals, in particular those of rams. In the past *animelles* were very much in vogue in France, Spain and Italy. For recipes see OFFAL OR VARIETY MEATS, *Animelles*.

ANISEED (SWEET CUMIN). ANIS VERT—Plant with ovoid seeds, slightly contracted at the top, with a ribbed surface and a short hard pubescence of a greyish-green colour.

The seeds sold in the shops must be cleaned of the earth which often sticks to them. Parsley seed, with the pubescence removed, is sometimes fraudulently sold as aniseed. Aniseed is used in confectionery, in pastry-making and distilling.

Aniseed cookies (Alsatian pastry). PAINS À L'ANIS—Mix 3½ cups (500 grams) of fine castor (powdered) sugar and 12 eggs in a copper basin. Beat the mixture with a whisk as for an ordinary sponge cake.

When the mixture is well whisked, add 4 cups (500 grams) of sieved cake flour, 1¼ cups (200 grams) of cornstarch and ⅓ cup (50 grams) of aniseed (in grains). Mix well.

Take up the mixture with a tablespoon, about the size of a macaroon, and drop on to a moistened baking sheet.

Put the little cookies into a warm place to dry. When they begin to rise slightly, bake in a low oven.

Aniseed-flavoured sugar. SUCRE ANISÉ—Aniseed-flavoured sugar is used for various preparations. The proportion of aniseed may vary, to render the sugar more or less scented.

When it is intended for the preparation of aniseed cake, 3 tablespoons (25 grams) of aniseed are added to 1 pound (500 grams) of castor sugar. If, on the other hand, it is wanted to flavour a sponge cake, a biscuit, a custard or cream, where a considerable quantity of it is incorporated, much more will be required and the proportion of aniseed can go up to ⅔ cup (100 grams) per pound of sugar.

Method. Pick over the aniseed carefully and rub on a fine sieve to remove stalks. Put to dry for 12 hours in a slow oven. Pound with lump sugar. Sift through a fine sieve, to obtain a very fine powder and pound whatever remains in the silk sieve again until the whole has been sifted.

ANISETTE—Liqueur based on aniseed.

The best anisette liqueur in France is made at Bordeaux.

Dutch anisette is also held in very high repute.

For the method of preparation of this liqueur see LIQUEURS, *Anise or anisette liqueur*.

ANJOU—Land of sweetness and harmony where the cuisine and wines match the nature.

'Its cuisine is as mellow as its skies, harmonious as its horizons. Did not one of Anjou's wittiest sons, and a

Gastronomic map of Angoumois, Aunis and Saintonge

great gourmet, the humourist Curnonsky, say that Anjou is to gastronomy what Racine is to literature?'

Thus another native of Anjou, and a great gastronome, Henry Coutant, defines its cuisine and adds: 'As to its wines, they are like the humour of its inhabitants: light and sparkling, of incomparable taste, but at times also malicious and treacherous towards those who have no idea how to face up to their caprices with adequate preparation. Admirable wines, however, which merit one of the first places among the great wines of France.'

Anjou cattle, bred for food, gives meat of excellent quality. The Maine region cattle is famous for the quality of its meat, and so is the Cholet cattle.

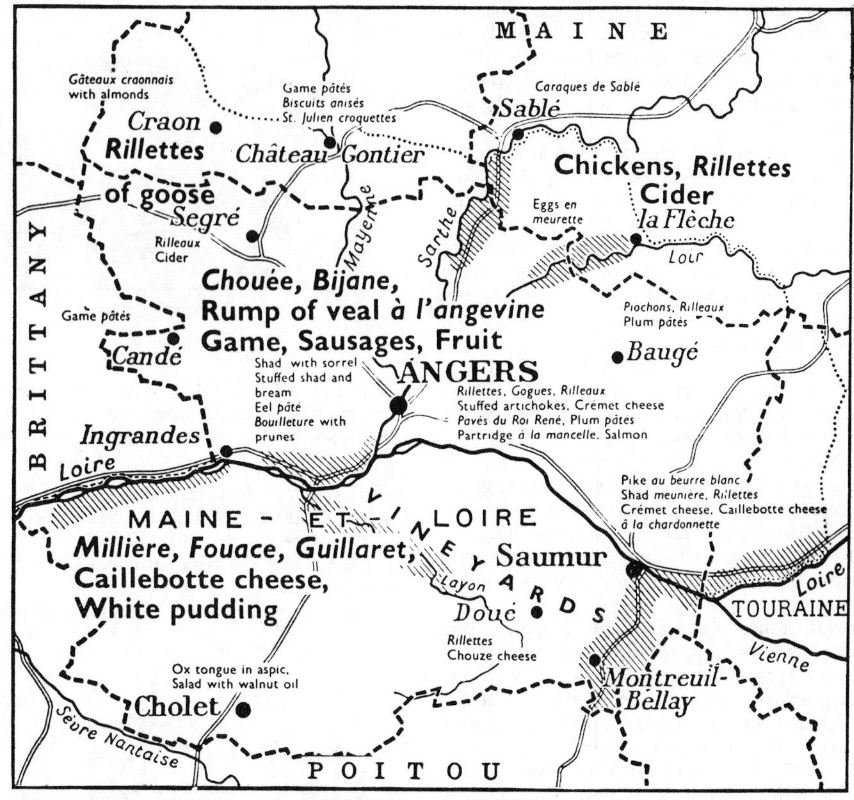

Gastronomic map of Anjou

The Loire near Saumur (*French Government Tourist Office*)

Anjou pork is of the greatest delicacy and various locally made pork butchery produce—*rillettes*, potted pork mince, sausages, andouilles, black (U.S.A. blood) puddings—are admirable 'bacchic spurs', as Rabelais called them, just the thing to make one appreciate the fragrant wines of the Anjou vineyards.

Anjou chickens are tender and plump. They are made into exquisite fricassées.

'The fish which the Loire so generously offers us between Saumur and Champtoceaux is more delicate than anywhere else,' declares an Anjou gourmand. Its pike are among the finest; its shad, its tench and its bream know no rivals. For the first two fish the cooks of Anjou have transmitted from generation to generation the recipe for a succulent sauce, *beurre blanc* (white butter) the creamy taste of which is a fragrant delight. Tench and bream, particularly bream, are done chiefly with a sorrel stuffing which makes a savoury foundation for their flesh.

The Loire salmon are famous; they are considered the best of all French river salmon.

Poultry is excellent in Anjou. The whole world knows the glory of *Capon de la Flèche* and *Chicken du Mans.*

First-class ground and feathered game are also found here.

Anjou vegetable gardening produce is superb. The green cabbages of this region, the *piochous*, as they are called, are well known and are made into those excellent fricassées which delight the lovers of country dishes.

The Anjou orchards produce superb fruit, pears,

dessert and cider apples, plums and strawberries. 'We must pay homage to the fruit of Anjou,' said gastronome Henry Coutant, 'which forms a vegetable aristocracy of this province of France.'

Anjou cheeses are excellent. The famous Angers *crémets* (soft fresh cream cheeses) should really be classed more among the sweet courses than among the cheeses. These *crémets*, which are generally eaten with sugar, can also, however, be sprinkled with salt and flavoured with chives.

With food produce of such quality the master cooks and *cordons bleus* of Anjou, who have always been fine cooks, cannot help their cuisine being excellent—and excellent it is.

Anjou culinary specialities are numerous. Here are some of them, chosen from the most typical dishes: *Saumur rillettes*, *rillons* (greaves), *potted pork mince*, *white puddings* and other *charcuterie*, made from the excellent pork of the region.

Bouilleture, a sort of *matelote* of various types of fish, principally eels; *stuffed shad*; *bream in butter*; *pike or shad au beurre blanc* (white butter); *matelotes* of fresh-water fish; *perch with prunes*; *fish stews*; *eel pâté*.

Rump of veal à l'angevine; *pig's fry*; *gogue*; *fricassée of chicken*; *partridge à la mancelle*; *chouée* (boiled green cabbage sprinkled with butter); *fricassée of green cabbage*; *fricassée of cauliflower*; *green salads with walnut oil*.

Notable cheeses include the Saumur *chouzé*, *caillebotte à la chardonette* and the Saumur and Angers *crémets* (cream cheeses).

Other famous dishes are *bijane*, or 'magpie' soup (similar to the Saintonge broth); bread crumbled into sweetened red wine; roast with hot wine; *millière* (maize meal and rice porridge); *fouée* (a sort of very flat girdle-cake made of bread dough, spread with butter); *fouace* (flat cakes baked in the hearth). Rabelais speaks of '*fouaciers* of Lerné (or Lernay), of Maine and Loire', which shows how long these cakes have been known. *Guillaret* or *échaudé*; Angers aniseed biscuits; prune paste. The *fouace* and the *guillaret* are not delicate pastries; in the past they used to be sold in the markets and at fairs in western France. Their main quality was their power to provoke thirst.

Wines—All the white wines of Anjou are very well known.

Wines of the Layon valley. Beaulieu, Faye, Rablé, Thouard.

Wines of the Loire coteaux. Monjeau, Murs, Roche-aux-Moines, Soulaines and and, above all, Coulée de Serrant, very fine wines, with a strong bouquet and an agreeable earthy tang.

White wines of Saumur. These are very fine light wines, notable among them being: Brèze, Montsoreau, Parnay, Souzay. A good many of these wines are made into sparkling wines (Saumur sparkling wines).

Red wines of the Saumur region. Among these wines, all with a strong bouquet, *Champigny* is worthy of mention.

In the south-east of this department, neighbouring on the Nantes region, *Muscadet*—a very pleasant white wine—is produced. Finally, there are *Rougets*, the pale-red and rosé wines obtained from red grapes pressed before fermentation.

Good *marc* brandies (distilled from the husks of grapes after the wine has been made) and some widely renowned liqueurs, such as *Guignolet d'Angers*, are also produced in this region.

Among the beverages of the region, *Segré cider*, which is excellent, should not be overlooked.

ANNA POTATOES. POMMES DE TERRE ANNA—A method of preparing potatoes cut in thin round slices, cooked in butter, in a special utensil or a covered terrine. See POTATOES.

Casserole for Anna potatoes

ANNETTE POTATOES. POMMES DE TERRE ANNETTE—Prepared like *Anna potatoes*, but the potatoes should be shredded into fine *julienne*.* See POTATOES.

ANON—Fish of the genus *Gadus*. This fish, one of the varieties of haddock, abounds in vast numbers in the English Channel. Its flesh is very white and laminated. The fishing season for it is mainly January and February. In U.S.A. hake and cusk (usually sold in fillets), are very similar to this fish.

For cookery purposes it is treated as *Whiting*.*

Anona: (1) Custard apple; (2) Bullock's heart; (3) Purple apple

ANONA. ANONE—The *anona* or *small purple apple* is the fruit of a tree which grows in tropical regions and in southern California (U.S.A.). This fruit, both in colour and shape, resembles an artichoke, the difference being that its skin is shiny.

The flesh of the anona, which can be found in France in shops specializing in exotic produce, is cream coloured, a little less white than that of the large *purple apple*, sweet and strongly scented. It is only eaten raw.

ANTHRACITE—Coal remarkable for its great purity; one of the fuels which is used, in preference, for heating and cooking.

ANTIDOTE. CONTRE-POISON—Substance capable of neutralizing the toxic properties of another element, by forming with it an insoluble non-toxic combination.

ANTISEPSIS. ANTISEPSIE—Method which aims at the prevention of putrefaction or infection by use of chemical substances. The salting and smoking of meat actually constitutes an application of the antiseptic treatment, as also the use of vinegar in marinades, and of salt or alcohol for preserving fruit. With exceptions, the use of antiseptics as preservatives for food substances is usually to be condemned.

ANTISEPTICS. ANTISEPTIQUES — Substances which counteract putrefaction, fermentation and infection. See PRESERVATION.

ANVERSOISE (A L')—Method of preparing large and small pieces of meat, calf's sweetbreads and eggs. These are garnished with hop stalks in butter or cream and potatoes fried in butter.

AOUDZÉ—Name given in Ethiopia to a strongly-spiced sauce which is made of pimento, ginger, cloves and an aromatic plant somewhat similar to thyme, known as *zégakelie*.

The Ethiopians serve this sauce with a dish which they call *brondo* of which they are very fond.

APÉRITIF—The old pharmacopoeia recognized *major bitters* (roots of parsley, fennel, asparagus and butcher's broom) and *minor bitters* (roots of maidenhair fern, couch-grass, thistle, rest-harrow and strawberry-plant). The term as used today only applies to stimulants of appetite.

Apéritifs served in cafés are drinks of a greater or lesser degree of bitterness, variously flavoured, which are drunk neat or diluted with water. They generally have a strong alcoholic content, because the essences of which they are composed are not soluble except in strong alcohol (which is why they go cloudy when mixed with water) and this alcohol content to a great extent nullifies the beneficent action of the bitters.

But, through sheer force of habit (or perhaps through imagination), some people think that they have no appetite unless they have their daily apéritif (or apéritifs). It is this fact which has led to the coining of the phrase that if an apéritif can open the appetite, it does so with a skeleton key. Be this as it may, the apéritif was, and still is, a traditional rite in certain circles.

For many people, the apéritif hour is the moment of relaxation after a day's work, before the family meal. It is important to others as a social occasion.

La Partie de Plaisir, an engraving by de Moitte after a painting by Lancret

APHORISMS AND AXIOMS. APHORISMES ET AXIOMES —Short pithy maxims, expressing rules and precepts of gastronomy, hygiene and everything generally pertaining to the table, the most celebrated of which are those of Brillat-Savarin, given by this master of gastronomical sciences as a preface to *Physiologie du goût*. Here they are:

(1) The universe is nothing except for life and everything that lives has to feed itself.

(2) Animals feed; man eats; only a man of wit knows how to eat.

(3) The destiny of nations depends on their manner of eating.

(4) Tell me what you eat, and I shall tell you what you are.

(5) The Creator, by making man eat to live, invites him to do so with appetite and rewards him with pleasure.

(6) Gourmandism is an act of judgment, by which we prefer things which have a pleasant taste to those which lack this quality.

(7) The pleasures of the table belong to all ages, to all conditions, to all countries and to every day; they can be associated with all the other pleasures and remain the last to console us for the loss of the rest.

(8) The table is the only place where one is never bored during the first hour.

(9) The discovery of a new dish does more for the happiness of mankind than the discovery of a star.

(10) Those who give themselves indigestion or get drunk, do not know how to eat or drink.

(11) The correct order of foods is starting with the heaviest and ending with the lightest.

(12) The correct order of beverages is starting with the most temperate and ending with the most heady.

(13) To claim that wines should not be changed is a heresy; the palate becomes saturated and after the third glass the best of wines arouses nothing but an obscure sensation.

(14) A dessert without cheese is like a beautiful woman with one eye.

(15) One can learn to cook, but a restaurateur is born.

(16) The most indispensible quality of a cook is punctuality; it should also be that of a guest.

(17) To wait too long for a late-comer is to show a lack of consideration for all those present.

(18) He who receives his friends and gives no personal attention to the meal which is being prepared for them, is not worthy of having friends.

(19) The mistress of the house must always make sure that her coffee is excellent, and the master of the house that his wines are choice.

(20) To invite someone is to take charge of his happiness during the time he spends under your roof.

Some of Brillat-Savarin's aphorisms, notably the one which claims that 'One can learn to cook, but a good restaurateur is born' are rather disputable!

There are many other gastronomic aphorisms. We quote some which are attributed to the actor Des Essarts, who, according to a contemporary author, had an appetite proportionate to his corpulence (Des Essarts was very fat) and was as much a gastronome as a man of wit —qualities which often go together.

Some people claim that he was the precursor of Brillat-Savarin. A good dinner would put him into good spirits. He would eloquently analyse the qualities of each dish and create amusingly bizarre combinations of words:

'Good cookery is the food of a pure conscience.'

'Let the leg of mutton be awaited as the first lovers' meeting, mortified as a liar caught in the act, golden as a young German girl and bloody as a Carib.'

'Take advantage of the gracious condescension of the elegant calf's kidney, multiply its metamorphoses: you can, without giving it any offence, call it the chameleon of cuisine.'

'Make an amiable intermediary of an egg, which comes

between the various parts (of food) to bring about difficult reconciliations.'

'Mutton is to lamb what a millionaire uncle is to his poverty-stricken nephew.'

'The benevolence of wrapping the partridge in a vine leaf brings out its quality, just as the barrel of Diogenes brought forth the qualities of the great thinker.'

'Never forget that the pheasant must be awaited like the pension of a man of letters who has never indulged in epistles to the ministers nor written madrigals for their mistresses.'

Des Essarts, born at Langres in 1740, was one of the best actors of the Comédie-Française. He died suddenly in 1793, on hearing of the arrest of one of his best friends.

The poets and prose writers of the past have also formulated gastronomical aphorisms and axioms.

Horace, who set great store by the cleanliness of the table and above all insisted that one should be able to see one's reflection mirrored in the plates and glasses, formulates his desires as follows:

'The stomach heaves when one receives from a valet a goblet bearing the greasy imprint of his sauce-stained fingers, and when one sees at the bottom the filthy dregs collected there.'

Plutarch makes this statement—which he attributes to Aemilius Paulus, the conqueror of Persia: 'The same intelligence is required to marshal an army in battle and to order a good dinner. The first must be as formidable as possible, the second as pleasant as possible, to the participants'.

In these words Plutarch gives a valuable lesson to all would-be gastronomes, to those who—at any rate, at the present time—frequently compose menus which would give no pleasure to a true gastronome.

Rabelais categorically declares that only 'candle-lit' dinners and suppers are pleasing. He goes on to say: 'There is no good cheer except at night, when the lanterns are in place with their gentle flickering lights'.

Nearer to our own time, other writers and gastronomes have formulated many aphorisms which may be taken as sound gastronomical rules.

Thus Carême gives the following advice to ministers and diplomats: 'The culinary art follows diplomacy and every prime minister is its tributary'.

Talleyrand knew this only too well. He used to advise French ambassadors at the courts of foreign sovereigns to rely more on their casseroles for the success of their missions, than on their secretaries.

Carême also says: 'To preside over a political chamber or to hold a post in an embassy, is to take a course in gastronomy'.

Another of Carême's aphorisms stresses how very important is the part played by cookery: 'When there is no more cookery in the world, there will be no more letters, no quick and lofty intelligence, no pleasant easy relationships; no more social unity'. (*Pâtissier pittoresque.*)

Sainte-Beuve is responsible for this aphorism: 'Intellectual men who quickly wolf down whatever nourishment is necessary for their bodies with a kind of disdain, may be very rational and have a noble intelligence, but they are not men of taste'.

Monselet, who was a gastronome and extremely witty, formulated numerous aphorisms in his writings. Here is one to show the social importance of dinners when they are good.

'Tout se fait en dînant dans le siècle où sommes,
Et c'est par les dîners qu'on gouverne les hommes.'

'Everything is done at dinner in the century in which we live, and it is by these dinners that men are governed.'

And now for some which we have culled from various books which Monselet wrote to the glory of gastronomy:

'Gastronomy is the joy of all conditions and all ages. It adds wit to beauty.'

'A gourmet is a being pleasing to the heavens.'

'All passions, rationalized and controlled, become an art: gastronomy, more than any other passion, is sensitive to rationalism and direction.'

'Ponder well on this point: the pleasant hours of our life are all connected by a more or less tangible link, with some memory of the table.'

'How many flowers there are which only serve to produce essences, which could have been made into savoury dishes.'

And finally, he gives in his *Letters to Emily* the following advice to all women: 'Enchant, stay beautiful and graceful, but to do this, eat well. Bring the same consideration to the preparation of your food as you devote to your appearance. Let your dinner be a poem, like your dress'.

The feast of the fat (J.-J. de Lusse, late 18th century)

The feast of the lean (J.-J. de Lusse, late 18th century)

Lucien Tendret, whose great-uncle was Brillat-Savarin, in his book *La Table au pays de Brillat-Savarin*, also created a few gastronomical aphorisms. They are no doubt less famous than those of the author of *Physiologie du goût*, but a few of them, nevertheless, deserve to be quoted here:

'Cuisine is both an art and a science; it is an art when it strives to bring about the realization of the true and the beautiful, called *le bon* (the good) in the order of culinary ideas. As a science, it respects chemistry, physics and natural history. Its axioms are called aphorisms, its theorems recipes, and its philosophy gastronomy.'

'The beautiful and the good are identical but the fleeting impressions created by the work of a cook or a musician disperse even as they are being experienced. Raphael's painting *The Transfiguration* is immortal, but Carême's *Ragoût de truffes à la parisienne* lasts while it is being eaten, just as roses last as long as their fragrance can be enjoyed.'

'The cook is no less than an artist, and even if he may not be on the level of Polygnotus and Phidias, he has his part and his place in civilization as a whole.'

'Skilful and refined cookery has always made its appearance during the most glorious epochs in history.'

'Vatel is not less famous than his master, the conqueror of Rocroi, and if glory is nothing but smoke, then Antonin Carême has made as much of it as Napoleon.'

'To give life to beauty, the painter uses a whole range of colours, musicians of sounds, the cook of tastes—and it is indeed remarkable that there are seven colours, seven musical notes and seven tastes.'

Lucien Tendret also made the following remarks illustrating the importance of good cuisine in diplomatic affairs:

'Political issues are decided at table. Talleyrand has often been indebted for his successes to the skilful creations of Antonin Carême.'

'At the time of the Congress of Vienna, the ambassador (Talleyrand), taking leave of Louis XVIII, said to him: "Please believe me, Your Majesty, I need saucepans more than written questions".'

'Monsieur Guizot assures us that while he was ambassador in London, his cook was more useful to him politically than his secretaries.'

Also from his pen, drafted in the form of axioms, came the following advice to hosts and guests:

'To order and conduct a dinner is given only to fine gastronomes, of delicate and cultivated tastes; an able host is as rare as a good cook.'

'One only dines well at the homes of true gastronomes who feel all the nuances; the least puffiness spoils the loveliest of faces and attention to detail creates perfection.'

'With money anyone can offer succulent dishes and famous wines, but courtesy and kindness cannot be bought.'

'To make people who have no appetite eat, to make the wit of those who have it sparkle, to enable those who want these qualities to find them—this is the supreme science of a gastronome-host.'

And to emphasize what he says, Lucien Tendret adds:

'French conversation was born in the salons of the eighteenth century; from the dining-rooms of the Regent, from those of President Hénault, Baron Holbach and Madame Geoffrin, emerged a society, sceptical of truth and impious, but permeated with suave urbanity and that ingenious and enlightened courtesy, which has since spread throughout Europe and has become one of the salient characteristics of modern civilization.'

Another word of advice to hosts:

'The gourmets, if they are not seated comfortably and have no elbow room, count both the wines and the food for nothing.'

And here is yet another which Jean Richepin gives in his poem *At Table*:

Est-on dix, y compris la famille, on se serre!
Mais pas trop cependant, et sans être à l'étroit
Il faut qu'on ait de l'air aux coudes, et le droit
De faire en bavardant, si l'on veut, de grandes gestes;
Grignotés de profil, les mets sont indigestes.

'We are ten, with the family, sit closer together!
But not too closely, we don't want to be cramped
We must have elbow room, and be able
To talk and make gestures, if we feel so inclined;
Sitting sideways and picking at food is courting indigestion.'

And finally, a remark which will reassure people who think they are doing something wrong in giving themselves up to the pleasures of the table. Lucien Tendret says:

'The casuists have classed gluttony as one of the seven deadly sins, but if it is not tainted by the vice of drinking to inebriation or eating to excess, it deserves to be on a par with the theological virtues.'

'Those who have a profound indifference to the pleasures of the table are generally gloomy, charmless and unamiable.'

Apophthegms. APOPHTEGMES GOURMANDS—The aphorisms of Brillat-Savarin, quoted above, are known throughout the world. Much less known are the gastronomical apophthegms which the author of *Physiologie du goût* has set forth in various meditations on the code of the table. Here are some which have a special bearing on cookery:

Cookery. 'Cooking is one of the oldest arts and one which has rendered us the most important service in civic life.'

'The science which feeds men is worth at least as much as the one which teaches how to kill them.'

'Once fire was discovered, the instinct for improvement made men bring food to it, first to dry it, then to put it on the coals to cook.'

'Cookery made great progress when fire-resisting vessels in bronze or clay appeared.'

'Meals, in the sense in which we understand this word, began with the second age of the human species.'

'In the state of society in which we now find ourselves, it is difficult to imagine a nation which lived solely on bread and vegetables.'

Gourmandism and Gourmands. 'Gourmandism is an ardent, rational and habitual preference for things which flatter the taste.'

'From whatever point of view you look at gourmandism, it deserves nothing but praise and encouragement.'

'Gourmandism is one of the main links uniting society.'

'If there are gastronomes by predestination, then there are also some by circumstance.'

Taste. 'Taste is simple in its action, that is to say, it cannot react to two flavours at once.'

'Man's palate, by the delicacy of its texture and of the various membranes which surround it, gives sufficient proof of the sublimity of functions for which it is intended.'

The five senses. Painting by Ténier

Appetite and digestion. 'Appetite proclaims itself by a slight sensation of languor in the stomach and a feeling of tiredness.'

'Digestion is an absolutely mechanical function, and the digestive organs can be thought of as a mill equipped with bolters.'

'To understand digestion as a whole, it must be linked with its antecedents and its consequences.'

'Digestion, of all the bodily functions, is the one which exercises the greatest influence on the mental state of an individual.'

'Some people are in a bad temper while digestion is in progress; it is therefore not the time either to suggest projects or to ask favours of them.'

'Theory and experience both prove that the quality and quantity of food have a powerful influence on work.'

'A badly-nourished man cannot adequately cope with the effort of continuous work for any length of time.'

Obesity and Thinness. 'Obesity is never found among the savages or among the classes of society where the people have to work to eat, and where they only eat to live.'

'Thinness is not a great drawback for men, but it is a dreadful misfortune for women.'

Foods. 'By foods one means substances which, introduced into the stomach, can be assimilated by digestion and restore the energy lost by the human body.'

'We were not satisfied with the qualities which nature gave to poultry; art stepped in and, under the pretext of improving fowls, has made martyrs of them.'

'Poultry is for cookery what canvas is for painting, and the cap of Fortunatus for the charlatans. It is served to us boiled, roast, hot or cold, whole or in portions, with or without sauce, and always with equal success.'

'Three lands of ancient France contest the honour of producing the best poultry: the Caux, Le Mans and Bresse.'

'Turkey is undoubtedly one of the best gifts that the New World has made to the Old.'

'Game provides the delights of our table; it is healthy, rich, savoury food, excellent in taste and easy to digest, especially when young.'

'Under the direction of an erudite chef game goes through many skilful modifications and transformations, and provides most of the full-flavoured dishes which constitute superlative cuisine.'

'The taste of a Périgord partridge is not the same as that of a Sologne partridge.'

'If the garden warbler were the size of a pheasant, it would most certainly cost as much as an acre of land.'

'The quail is the sweetest and the nicest of game birds. It is an act of ignorance to serve it in any other way but roasted.'

'A woodcock is in its full glory only when roasted actually before the very eyes of the hunter, above all the hunter who shot it.'

'In the hands of an able cook, fish can become an inexhaustible source of perpetual delight.'

'The smelt is the garden warbler of the water; the same smallness, the same high flavour, the same superiority.'

APICIUS—There were three Romans by the name of Apicius. All three were famous, not for their genius, their virtues or their great qualities, but for their gluttony and achievements in the gastronomical art.

The first lived under Sulla, the second under Augustus and Tiberius, and the third under Trajan. It is the second

Apicius who is the most famous and it is of him that Seneca, Pliny, Juvenal and Martialis have spoken so much. Athenaeus says that he spent immense sums to satisfy his gluttony and that he invented several kinds of cakes which bear his name. Seneca, who was his contemporary, tells us that he ran a sort of school of 'good fare'. He adds that Apicius, having got into heavy debt, was at last forced to examine that state of his affairs and that, seeing that he had only 250,000 Roman pounds left (some authors say forty million sesterces, in other words, an income of £80,000), he killed himself, fearing that such a sum would not be enough for him to live on.

Pliny often speaks of the ragoûts which Apicius invented, and calls him *nepotum omnium altissimus gurges*.

The third Apicius lived under Trajan. Having invented a secret method of preserving oysters, he managed to deliver some very fresh ones to the Emperor, who was at the time busy fighting the Parthians.

The name of Apicius was not only given to cakes but spread to several kinds of sauces.

There exists, under the name of Coelius Apicius, a treatise *De re culinaria* printed for the first time in Milan (1498); the critics do not think, however, that it was written by one of the three men named Apicius. Martin Lister produced a magnificent edition of this book entitled *De obsonis et condimentis, sive de arte coquinaria* (London, 1705), of which 125 copies were printed.

Did Imperial Rome have her gastronomes in the strictest sense of this word, and were the illustrious personages, whose prowess at table has been described in history or legend, real connoisseurs of culinary matters?

On this point, Carême, who made a profound study of the history of ancient Rome, says that Roman cookery was 'fundamentally barbaric'.

What the historians tell us of the three men named Apicius leads us to agree with Carême. The Roman table certainly was sumptuous and magnificent, in the spectacular sense, but it was not at all refined.

Rome, at the time of Apicius, governed the whole world, at any rate the world as it was then known. She dictated her laws to distant provinces. From these subjugated provinces she received great quantities of various food products. Gallia Narbonensis sent her her pork. Africa and Asia sent her, as tributes from the vanquished to the conqueror, a thousand and one exquisite things, which her cooks, who had been trained in their art by experts from Greece, prepared in a manner, if not perfect, at least lavish and, above all, ostentatious.

It was during this epoch of Apicius that, to dazzle his guests, an amphitryon offered them a ragoût composed entirely of song-birds' tongues, and showered rose petals upon them. It was then, too, that the guests, indolently reclining on the triclinium couches, did themselves proud on sows, stuffed to bursting-point with all sorts of little dainties, half of the sow being boiled and half roast—a reminder, no doubt, of the legendary *Porc à la troyenne*.

APONOGETONACEAE. Aponogetons — Flowering rush family, represented by one genus *Aponogeton*. Their leaves float on the surface of the water, rather like those of water-lilies.

The *Aponogeton dystachyon* is widely cultivated in the temperate parts of Europe. For some years now it has become completely naturalized at Montpellier, where its young shoots are eaten and called *Cape asparagus*. In U.S.A. the common names for this plant are *Cape pond weed* or *water hawthorn*.

APOPHORETA—Name given by the ancient Romans to the gifts which the host made to his guests for members of their families. These gifts were often of great value. They were mostly precious dishes or vases which had been used at the feast. Sometimes the slaves who served at table were also presented to the guests.

APOTHECA—Roman name for a room, situated under the roof of a house, so arranged that the smoke of various fireplaces passed through it, with the sole purpose of boiling down the famous Caecubum wine to the desired syrupy consistency.

APPAREIL—In French culinary terminology this word is used to describe all simple or mixed preparations that go into the making of dishes. It is synonymous with the word mixture.

For example, the following terms are used: *appareil à soufflé* (soufflé mixture); *appareil à biscuit* (sponge mixture); *appareil à crème renversée* (custard mixture), etc.

François Appert

APPERT—François Appert was the inventor of a method of preserving various foods in tinplate canisters and wide-mouthed bottles.

Biographies of the inventor of canned foods are somewhat contradictory. In some we are told that Appert was a cook, that he learned to cook at the court of King Christian IV, established himself as a confectioner in Paris in 1805, and that it was in his confectionery laboratory that he began to put his invention into practice.

In other biographies we are told that Appert was a chemist, born at Massy (Seine et Oise) in 1750, and that he died in 1841.

Appert based his work on the principle, popularized later by the works of Pouchet, Pasteur and other scientists, that fermentation and consequently decomposition of organic substances, could not take place if air was excluded.

It was Chevalier-Appert who perfected the work of Appert in 1852. He thought of using the sterilizer, which until then had entirely different uses, and of putting the food containers into it and raising the temperature.

As it was essential to know the internal degree during this operation, in order not to impair the quality of the substances being preserved, frequently very delicate, Chevalier-Appert also invented a manometer.

The only manometers then in existence were manometers for steam boilers, which only measured heat to an approximation of a few degrees, whereas for preserving food, heat had to be measured to a degree or sometimes even to half a degree, to ensure preservation and at the same time to keep the taste of the product preserved.

In 1852 Chevalier-Appert took out a patent, establishing the date of his invention, and so became the founder of a great industry, which today sends out its innumerable products all over the world. And it was thanks to the original invention of François Appert that enormous canning factories have been created and put into operation, both in the old world and the new.

APPETENCE—A feeling which brings desire for food; this is the first stage of appetite.

APPÉTIT—Common name for chives in French. See CHIVES.

APPETITE. APPÉTIT—Psychologists define under the term natural appetite the tendencies which instinctively cause us to satisfy the needs of the body.

In physiology appetite is defined as something rather different from hunger. Hunger in reality is nothing more than the need to eat, whereas appetite is the lure of pleasure which one experiences whilst eating, brought about by a particular condition of the organism.

Brillat-Savarin, however, in his definition, appears to give the word appetite the meaning of hunger. 'Movement and life cause a continual loss of substance in the human body; and the human body, this extremely complicated machinery, would soon be out of service, had Providence not equipped it with a device which gives warning the moment its forces are out of balance with its needs.

'This device is appetite. This word means the first sensation of the need to eat.'

The sensation of hunger, at regular meal-times with civilized people, disappears if it is not satisfied at the usual hour. The appetite is stimulated by the sight and smell of food; bitter substances frequently awaken lost appetite by releasing digestive secretions.

In certain psychic and mental cases, appetite can degenerate into a craving for offensive and non-edible substances.

The opposite of appetite is *anorexia*, which means distaste for food.

APPIGRET—An old French word which Rabelais used to define gravy, juice, seasoning.

APPLE. POMME—Apples are the fruit of a tree belonging to the family *Rosaceae*.

The numerous varieties of apples are divided into cooking and eating apples.

The following varieties are considered the best French eating apples: *Reinette grise*, quite big, with a firm, crisp flesh, fragrant and a good keeping apple; *Reine des reinettes*, big, round, yellow streaked with russet, keeps until the summer; *Reinette franche*, medium size, cylindrical in shape, yellowish-green with brown spots, fragrant and keeps well; *Reinette de Canada*, large, flattened, yellow skin with thin russet and slight flush.

Calvilles, characterized by ribbed sides at neck; *Calville blanche*, big, conical, irregular, pale yellow in colour, sometimes with a slight red flush on one side, very aromatic with a pronounced taste of pineapple; *Calville rouge*, of the same form as the preceding apple, greenish-yellow with dark crimson flush, often having a light raspberry flavour.

Apple is an excellent dessert fruit, easily digestible if well chewed. It is used in cookery in innumerable sweet dessert dishes, for jellies, etc. In confectionery it is used for making apple butter and apple sugar. Apple juice also provides cider, and calvados (or apple-jack) is distilled from it.

Baked apples in pastry or douillon normand. RABOTTES DE POMMES, DOUILLON NORMAND—Choose big sound baking apples and core them with a corer. Make a circular incision around the middle, to prevent their bursting. Fill the middle, hollowed out by the corer with butter kneaded with sugar (and with a pinch of cinnamon, if liked).

Baked apples in pastry (*Douillon normand*)

Enclose each apple in a piece of *lining paste* (see DOUGH), rolled out not too thick. Put a little circlet of lining paste (cut out with a fluted-edged cutter) on top of each apple. Brush with beaten egg and rib the outside of the apples lightly with a knife.

Bake in a moderate oven from 25 to 30 minutes. Serve piping hot.

Note. The apples can be peeled before being put into pastry. They can also be cooked first (as for *Apples bonne femme*). In that case the baking will only take 15 minutes. Lining paste can be replaced by left-over pieces of puff pastry.

Apples bonne femme. POMMES BONNE FEMME—Make a slight circular incision around the middle of some baking apples, core them with a corer, to remove the central part containing the pips.

Put them into a buttered fireproof dish. Fill the middle with a little butter mixed with fine castor sugar. Pour a few tablespoonfuls of water in the pan, bake gently in the oven and serve in the same dish.

Apples Bourdaloue. POMMES BOURDALOUE—Prepare, using apples poached in syrup (whole, halved or quartered) as described in the recipe for *Apricots Bourdaloue*. See APRICOT.

Apple butter, marmalade—See JAM, *Apple jelly*; MARMALADE, *Apple marmalade*.

Buttered apples. POMMES AU BEURRE—Peel some baking apples, core them with a corer and parboil for 2 minutes in boiling water with a dash of lemon juice added to it. Drain the apples, put them into a buttered fireproof dish, sprinkle with fine sugar, moisten with a few tablespoonfuls of water (or light syrup) and cook gently in the oven.

Serve each apple on a round croûton of bread fried in butter. Dilute the pan juices with a few tablespoonfuls of water, add a little butter and pour over the apples.

Apple cake (English cookery)—Peel, core, quarter and slice 6 medium-sized cooking apples. Cook in a pan with 6 tablespoons (100 grams) of butter or melted beef bone-marrow and season with a pinch of powdered cinnamon. As soon as the apples are cooked, rub them through a sieve.

Put the pulp back into the pan, add 2 tablespoons of arrowroot or cornstarch and 1 cup (250 grams) of fine sugar, and cook, stirring with a wooden spoon, until the mixture reaches a firm consistency.

Put the pulp into a bowl; allow to cool, then add 2 whole eggs and 6 yolks, whisked as for omelette; blend well and pour this mixture into a simple straight mould, smeared with butter and sprinkled with flour.

Cook in a pan of hot water or *bain-marie** in a slow oven (325°F.) for 1 hour. Turn out on to a round dish; serve with *zabaglione*.*

This sweet can also be served cold. It is really a soufflé, not a cake.

Apples au chambertin. POMMES AU CHAMBERTIN—Peel some apples and core them with a corer. Poach them in sweetened Chambertin wine, allowing $1\frac{1}{3}$ cups (300 grams) of sugar per quart (litre) of wine. Leave the apples to cool in this syrup. Arrange in a fruit dish or a timbale. Boil down the syrup by half, leave until cold, then pour over the apples.

Apple charlotte—See CHARLOTTE.

Apple compote—See COMPOTE.

Apples Condé. POMMES CONDÉ—Prepare as described in the recipe for *Apricots Condé*. See APRICOT.

Apples à la crème au kirsch. POMMES À LA CRÈME AU KIRSCH—Peel, core and cook the apples in a vanilla-flavoured syrup. Leave to cool in the syrup. Drain, dry and arrange them in a glass goblet (or a fruit dish). At the last moment top with half-whipped fresh cream, sweetened with sugar and flavoured with kirsch.

Note. Apples, prepared as described above, can be topped with cream flavoured with various liqueurs, such as anisette, benédictine, cassis, chartreuse, raspberry liqueur, rum, etc.

Crêpes stuffed with apples (Apple pancakes). CRÊPES FOURRÉES AUX POMMES—Prepare the *crêpes** in the usual manner and coat with greatly concentrated *Apple marmelade* (*Apple sauce*).*

Roll the pancakes or fold them in four. Put them on a baking sheet, sprinkle with icing sugar and glaze quickly in the oven. Serve on a folded napkin.

Note. Stuffed crêpes are usually called *pannequets* in French.

Apple croûte. CROÛTE AUX POMMES—Using apples poached in vanilla-flavoured syrup (in halves or quarters), prepare as described in the recipe for *Apricot croûte*. See APRICOT.

Apples Figaro. POMMES FIGARO—'Scald about a pound and a quarter of chestnuts, remove the shells and the inner grey skin, put them into a narrow pan with a vanilla bean and enough milk (previously boiled) to cover them completely and simmer gently for 45 to 50 minutes.

'Using an apple corer, core some medium-sized apples and peel them. Cook them in a light syrup, strongly flavoured with vanilla, keeping them a little firm (it is enough for the pulp just to be softened).

'Shred fifteen almonds, roast them lightly (letting them go slightly *yellow*, not *brown*). Add to these almonds 3 tablespoons (50 grams) of coarsely crumbled *marrons glacés*.

'Make a cream, using $\frac{2}{3}$ cup (150 grams) of castor (fine) sugar, 4 yolks of egg, $1\frac{1}{2}$ tablespoonfuls of flour and 2 cups (4 decilitres) of vanilla-flavoured, boiled milk. After boiling this cream for one minute, remove from heat and incorporate 2 tablespoonfuls of butter. Do not allow to boil again after this. Rub the chestnuts through a sieve quickly, put this purée into a sauté pan and add $\frac{1}{2}$ cup (125 grams) of castor sugar and $\frac{3}{4}$ cup ($1\frac{1}{2}$ decilitres) of cream. Stir on the fire for 2 minutes, then spread on a dish.

'Place the well-drained apples on this chestnut purée, pour over the cream and sprinkle with almond and chestnut mixture.' (Philéas Gilbert.)

Apple flambé au kirsch (or other liqueurs). POMMES FLAMBÉES AU KIRSCH—There are two ways of preparing this dish:

(1) Core the cooking apples with a corer, peel them and poach in a light, vanilla-flavoured syrup. Drain them, put into a low-shaped silver timbale or a fireproof china or glass dish. Sprinkle with kirsch, heat and set alight just before serving.

(2) Put the peeled and cored apples into a buttered dish. Sprinkle with sugar and melted butter and bake slowly in the oven.

Put into a low-shaped silver, fire-proof china, or glass dish, sprinkle with kirsch and, just before serving, set alight.

Note. Apple flambé can also be set alight with brandy, raspberry eau-de-vie, calvados, quetsche, rum, or any other liqueur with high-degree alcohol content.

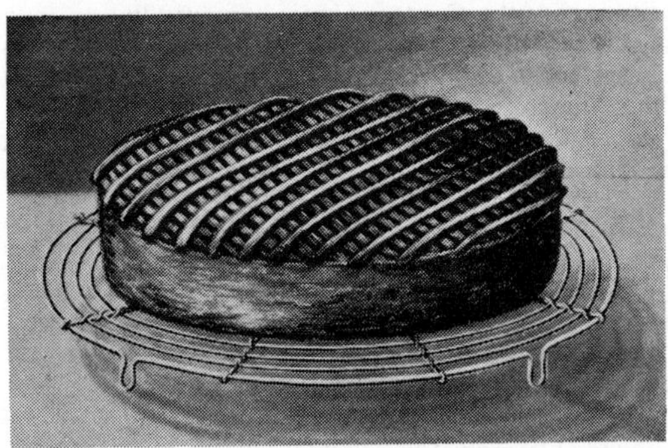

Apple flan

Apple flan—See TARTS AND FLANS.

Apple fritters—See FRITTERS, *Dessert* (*sweet*) *fritters*.

Apple glacé à l'impératrice. POMMES GLACÉES À L'IMPÉRATRICE—Using dessert apples, poached in syrup and well drained, prepare as described in the recipe for *Peaches à l'impératrice*. See PEACHES.

Apple gratiné. POMMES GRATINÉES—Peel tart apples, cut into quarters and cook in vanilla-flavoured syrup, keeping them a little firm. Drain and dry.

Arrange in an oven-proof dish on a layer of apple sauce (see below) prepared as for a *charlotte*. Scatter some crushed macaroons on top, sprinkle with a little melted butter and brown the top in a slow oven.

Note. For this dish apples can also be cut into quarters and cooked in butter, instead of being poached in syrup.

Apple jelly—See JAM, jellies.

Apple mousse à la Chantilly. MOUSSE AUX POMMES À LA CHANTILLY—Prepare a very fine, thick, vanilla-flavoured apple *marmelade* (apple sauce).* Cool the *marmelade* and whisk it on ice, adding to it a few tablespoonfuls of fresh thick cream, making sure that the mixture does not lose its consistency. Pour into a glass goblet or a fruit dish, piling it up in a dome.

Top with vanilla-flavoured whipped cream, whisked stiff.

Apple omelette à la normande. OMELETTE FOURRÉE AUX POMMES DITE À LA NORMANDE—Make the omelette in the usual manner using eggs seasoned with sugar. Just before folding, fill the omelette with concentrated apple *marmelade* (apple sauce)* or with tart apples, peeled, diced, cooked in butter and mixed with a little apple *marmelade* or with thick fresh cream.

Arrange the omelette on a long dish. Sprinkle with sugar and glaze with a glazing iron or with a salamander.

Apple pectin. JUS DE POMMES—This juice, very mucilaginous in consistency, is used for preparing apple jelly, described elsewhere in this book. See JAMS AND JELLIES.

It is also used for preparing a great many other jellies made of fruit with too high a water content, which without such addition would not have the desired consistency and stand a risk of fermenting.

Used in the right proportions, apple juice does not alter the flavour of the fruit to which it is added.

To obtain about 4½ (U.S.A. 5½) pints (2½ litres) of apple juice, cut 36 sound apples in quarters, without peeling or coring them, as both the peel and the pips provide a great deal of mucilaginous matter.

Put them in a copper basin with 3½ (U.S.A. 4⅜) pints (2 litres) of water. Cover the basin hermetically and cook on not too brisk but sustained heat until the apple quarters become soft enough to give easily when pressed with a finger.

Pour into a tammy cloth placed over the bowl and let the juice drip through without pressing the apple quarters. Use this juice as indicated in the recipe.

Note. The residue, i.e., the apple pulp which remains in the tammy, can be used for preparing apple *marmelade* (apple sauce)* or paste. It can also be used for various sweet flans, loaves, soufflés.

Apple pie—See PIE.

Apple pudding—See PUDDING.

Apples with rice. POMMES GRATINÉES AU RIZ—Prepare ¼ pound (125 grams) of sweetened rice (see RICE). Put into an ovenproof dish in layers alternating with ½ pound (250 grams) of apples, sliced and cooked in butter.

Smooth the surface of the top rice layer and cover with 10 apple quarters, cooked in butter.

Sprinkle with crushed macaroons and a tablespoonful of melted butter and brown the top. Serve in the same dish, handing kirsch-flavoured *Apricot sauce* separately.

Apples with rice and meringue. POMMES MERINGUÉES AU RIZ—Using quarters of apples, poached in vanilla-flavoured syrup or cooked in butter, proceed as described in the recipe for *Apricots and rice with meringue*. See APRICOT.

Apple ring à la normande. BORDURE DE POMMES À LA NORMANDE—Peel, halve and core the apples and cook them in vanilla-flavoured syrup. Allow to cool in the syrup. Drain and dry.

Prepare a mixture from *crème moulée* (see CUSTARD, *Vanilla custard*) and cook it in a *bain-marie** in a plain border mould. Leave the border until cold.

Turn out the border on to a round dish. Fill the inside with well-dried apple halves, piling them up into a dome.

Decorate by piping very firm whipped cream through a forcer with a fluted nozzle. Serve with calvados-flavoured *Apricot sauce* (see SAUCE).

Apple ring Brillat-Savarin. BORDURE DE POMMES BRILLAT-SAVARIN—Fill a *savarin*,* steeped in syrup and flavoured with rum, with stewed apples bound with rum-flavoured confectioner's custard (French pastry cream). See CREAM.

On top of the savarin put apple halves, poached in vanilla-flavoured syrup, well drained and coated with reduced apricot pulp. Decorate with halves of fresh walnuts, crystallized cherries and lozenges of angelica. Serve with rum-flavoured custard.

Apple rissoles. RISSOLES DE POMMES—Roll out a piece of puff paste (see PASTRY) and cut into little circlets 3 to 4 inches in diameter.

Put a good tablespoonful of greatly concentrated apple *marmelade* (apple sauce),* flavoured with kirsch or any other liqueur in the middle of each circlet. Fold the pastry to enclose the filling completely and seal the edges, moistening them with water.

Just before serving, fry in smoking hot deep fat.

Drain the rissoles and arrange on folded napkins. Serve kirsch-flavoured *Apricot sauce* separately.

Note. Apple (or other fruit) rissoles can also be prepared using lining paste or common brioche dough. These rissoles can be made in different shapes. See RISSOLE.

Apple sauce. MARMELADE DE POMMES—Prepare by cooking quartered apples in very little water until soft. Force through a strainer. Add a pinch of salt and enough sugar to sweeten. Boil down until thick. Lemon juice is sometimes added.

Apple soufflé. SOUFFLÉ AUX POMMES—Using apple pulp and a special cream, prepare as described in the recipe for fruit soufflés. See SOUFFLÉ.

APPLE-CORER. VIDE-POMMES—Tube-shaped implement for taking the cores out of apples.

APPRÊT—In French cookery this word means a finished culinary preparation.

APRICOT (Prunus Armeniaca). ABRICOT—Fruit of the apricot tree, brought from Armenia into Italy at the beginning of our era, but not widely known in Europe until the fifteenth century.

The musk-apricot, so justly famous for its succulent flesh, is found in the south of France, in Algeria and in Spain.

In Auvergne, another much-prized variety of apricot is cultivated with success, for the high quality of jam which is produced from it.

Among the best varieties of apricots is clingstone, a species of apricot with white flesh which adheres strongly to the stone. It has a somewhat tart flavour. Peach-apricot, a choice fruit, is much sought after for the delicacy of its flesh; it is very fragrant, juicy and sweet.

Apricot is one of the fruits most used in pastry-making and confectionery. It is used in a number of preparations, such as sweet courses and confectionery. It is one of the best comfits. It also makes excellent tarts, delicious compotes and a mouth-watering jelly.

Compotes can also be made from green preserved apricots, which should be peeled before being bottled. They can also be preserved in brandy.

Apricots à l'ancienne. ABRICOTS À L'ANCIENNE—Divide large apricots into halves and poach in vanilla-flavoured syrup.

Remove, arrange on a layer of sponge cake soaked in rum and coated with a layer of apple sauce.

Sprinkle with chopped almonds, sugar and a little melted butter. Put in the oven to set.

Serve with apricot jam, diluted with a little water, heated, strained and laced with rum.

Apricot barquettes. BARQUETTES AUX ABRICOTS—See BARQUETTE.

Apricot bombe. BOMBE ABRICOTINE—Line the mould with chocolate ice cream. Fill with *mousse (bombe) mixture* (see ICE CREAMS AND ICES), flavoured with apricot brandy or apricot purée.

Apricot bouchées. BOUCHÉES À L'ABRICOT—These cakes can be made either with *Genoese* or *Sponge* batter and are filled and coated with apricot jam.

Ingredients. 1¼ cups (250 grams) of fine sugar, 8 whole eggs, 1¾ cups (200 grams) of sieved cake flour, ¾ cup (200 grams) of best butter, a small glass of kirsch or rum.

Method. Beat the sugar and the eggs in a red copper basin on a low fire (or over hot water). When the mixture becomes light, frothy and whitish, blend in carefully the sieved flour and the melted butter (to which the flavouring chosen has been added).

Pour the mixture into shallow round moulds (cake or muffin tins) filling up to three-quarters. Cook for about 20 minutes in a slow oven. Turn out and allow to cool. When quite cold, cut each bouchée in half with a very thin sharp knife, to avoid crumbling the sponge. Spread with kirsch-flavoured apricot jam, then sandwich the bouchées together again. Brush with concentrated apricot jam and coat the sides all round with chopped roasted almonds. Decorate the top with half a glacé cherry.

Apricots Bourdaloue (I). ABRICOTS BOURDALOUE—Cook 16 halves of apricots in a light vanilla-flavoured syrup. Remove, drain, arrange in a shallow china fireproof dish filled up to two-thirds with semolina cooked with milk and bound with two yolks of egg (see SEMOLINA, *English semolina pudding*).

Cover the apricots with a light layer of semolina, sprinkle with the crumbs of 2 crushed macaroons and a teaspoon of fine powdered or castor sugar; put in a very hot oven for a few moments to glaze the top.

Serve with an apricot and kirsch sauce (apricot jam, thinned down with the syrup in which the apricots were cooked, strained and laced with a tablespoon of kirsch).

Apricots Bourdaloue (II). ABRICOTS BOURDALOUE—Apricots Bourdaloue are also prepared by placing apricots halved, and cooked lightly in syrup, on a layer of *Frangipane cream** in an ovenproof dish or on a flan shell.

Sprinkle with crushed macaroons and melted butter and glaze in the oven.

Serve with *Apricot and kirsch sauce.*

Candied apricots or apricot comfits in brandy. ABRICOTS CONFITS À L'EAU-DE-VIE—For this method of preserving, choose very small, firm apricots of uniform size.

Proceed to whiten as described in the recipe for candied apricots. Put them into syrup having first soaked them in water. 'Dress' them up to 25° (average syrup density) and leave them in syrup at this degree for 4 days. Drain them, put into glass jars which should be filled with the following mixture:

Syrup in which the fruit was candied: 1 quart (1 litre).

Neutral alcohol, tasteless, of 90°: 1 quart (1 litre).

Mix these two liquids and pour over the fruit, so that it is well submerged.

Put a piece of vanilla bean, or 1 teaspoon of vanilla extract or 1 wine-glass (1 decilitre) of rum or kirsch, according to taste, into the jars, per 2 quarts (2 litres) of liquid. Seal the bottles with cork lids or jar tops. Keep in a cool place, protected from both heat and humidity. At the end of one month the fruit will be ready for use.

Candied or crystallized apricots (Apricot comfits). ABRICOTS CONFITS—Choose very firm white apricots of uniform size. Make a light incision at the opposite end to the stalk.

Put them, a few at a time, into a copper basin full of cold water, so that they are submerged completely.

Put the basin on a low flame. As soon as the apricots rise to the surface, take them out of the water with a perforated spoon. Feel them to see if they have become much softer; this operation constitutes the 'whitening'.

Soak the apricots for 12 hours in cold water, changing the water every 2 hours.

Prepare a syrup (1 cup sugar to $1\frac{3}{4}$ cups water boiled to 215°-220°F. or 18°—syrup gauge). Pour this boiling syrup on the drained apricots, and put into a copper basin.

Bring to the boil on a high flame; decant the syrup and the apricots into an earthenware bowl and allow to rest until the following day.

On the following day, drain the apricots, put the syrup to boil (measured by the syrup gauge, it should not be above 12° (very light)). Add $\frac{1}{4}$ cup sugar and bring this syrup to 18° in syrup gauge (light). When it is boiling, throw the apricots in and bring to the boil, then decant into an earthenware bowl (this operation is called 'to give a dressing'). Continue to give a dressing in this manner every other day and, each time, bring the syrup up 6° or make it a little heavier by adding sugar, and by boiling it down when there is too much of it.

The syrup must always cover the fruit completely. When the syrup comes up to 30° (average syrup density) that is after the third dressing, do not bring up the syrup by more than 4° and give the dressings only every 3 days. Proceed in this manner until the syrup reaches 36° (moderately thick). Now proceed to stone the apricots. To do this, introduce a copper needle at the stalk end and push the stone towards the incision made in the beginning of the operation. Then take several damaged apricots, cut them into pieces the size of the stones removed. Stuff the apricots with these pieces to keep them round and lay them neatly in an earthenware bowl. Bring the syrup to the boil, check the degree and pour it, boiling, on the apricots. Allow the whole to cool. Keep the jars in a cool, dry place. Cover them with greaseproof paper, as you would jam.

Caramel apricots in brandy (Petits fours). ABRICOTS (À L'EAU-DE-VIE) AU CARAMEL—Drain the preserved apricots as described in the recipe for *Crystallized apricots.* Roll them in powdered gum arabic.

Dip them, one by one, into sugar cooked to *crack condition.* See SUGAR.

Put them, spacing them out carefully, on a slightly oiled marble slab.

When they are completely dry, put into fluted paper cases.

Apricot charlotte. See CHARLOTTE, *Fruit charlottes.*

Colbert apricots. ABRICOTS COLBERT—Divide the apricots in halves, remove the stones, poach the apricots in a light syrup (flavoured with vanilla, if liked).

Simmer gently for 8 to 10 minutes, depending on the ripeness of the fruit. Allow to cool in the syrup.

To serve, arrange the halved apricots in a fruit dish; add a few drops of kirsch to the syrup and pour it over the fruit.

For this compote the halved apricots can be peeled. To make this operation easier, plunge the apricot halves for a second into boiling water or syrup.

This compote can be flavoured by adding to it a few of the almonds extracted from the apricot kernels and blanched.

Apricot compote. See COMPOTE.

Condé apricots (old recipe). ABRICOTS CONDÉ—Cook the halved apricots as usual, in syrup. Drain, arrange on a *savarin,** prepared in the usual manner. Top with apricot syrup flavoured with kirsch. See SAVARIN (this is a round cake with a hollow centre, moistened with rum).

Garnish the middle with a mixture of $\frac{1}{4}$ cup of corn meal or maize flour, cooked in double boiler with 4 cups scalded sweetened, vanilla-flavoured milk until thick and diluted with cream. Around the *savarin* put little cork-shaped croquettes also made of corn meal or maize flour mixture.

Condé apricots (I). ABRICOTS CONDÉ—Fill three-quarters of a shallow china fireproof dish with *dessert rice* (see RICE). Arrange on this rice 16 apricot halves, cooked in syrup and drained.

Decorate with glacé cherries and lozenges of angelica. Heat thoroughly in the oven and serve with *Apricot and kirsch sauce*, or serve this sauce separately.

Condé apricots (II). ABRICOTS CONDÉ—Arrange the apricot halves on a border of *dessert rice*. See RICE.

Decorate with glacé cherries and angelica diamonds. Stud the apricots with a row of halved, blanched almonds.

Put in the oven to heat and serve *Apricot and kirsch sauce* separately.

Apricot coupe. See ICE CREAMS AND ICES.

Apricot croûte. CROÛTE AUX ABRICOTS—Arrange a dozen slices of stale *savarin** in a circle, as described in the recipe for *Fruit croûte*, replacing the pineapple slices by a layer of apricot jam spread evenly on the savarin slices. See CROÛTES, *Fruit croûtes*.

Lay 16 apricot halves, cooked in syrup and drained, on this circle of savarin slices.

Decorate with crystallized fruit; heat in the oven and serve with apricot and kirsch sauce, madeira sauce, or other sauce.

Crystallized apricots in brandy (petits fours). ABRICOTS (À L'EAU-DE-VIE) CRISTALLISÉS—Using apricots which have been preserved in brandy (see *Candied apricots in brandy*), put on a flat sieve and drain for two hours. Melt a little gum arabic in water to obtain a fairly liquid glue.

Put these well-drained apricots into a small bowl, pour a little of the melted gum arabic over them, shake gently to make sure that all the apricots are properly coated. Remove and roll them, one at a time, in crystallized sugar.

Put them in a flat sieve or grille. Then, when they are quite dry, put them into fluted paper cases.

Apricots à la diable. ABRICOTS À LA DIABLE—Spread the flat side of 8 large macaroons with a layer of apricot jam flavoured with kirsch.

Arrange these macaroons, curved side up, in a circle, in a flat fireproof dish; put on each macaroon two apricot halves, cooked in syrup and drained; spread the whole with a few tablespoons of *Praline custard cream*. See CREAM.

Sprinkle the apricots with icing sugar or castor sugar and glaze in a very hot oven.

When ready to serve, add to the dish a few tablespoons of apricot sauce laced with kirsch.

Apricots flambé in kirsch. ABRICOTS FLAMBÉS AU KIRSCH—Put the apricot halves, cooked in syrup, into little individual metal or fireproof porcelain dishes (2 or 3 halves of fruit per dish).

Add to each dish 2 tablespoons of the syrup in which the apricots were cooked, blended with some corn starch or arrowroot.

Heat to boiling point. When ready to serve, put into each dish a teaspoon of kirsch and set it ablaze.

Apricot flan. See TART.

Apricot fritters. See FRITTERS.

Apricot ice cream. See ICE CREAMS AND ICES.

Apricots à l'impératrice (I). ABRICOTS À L'IMPÉRATRICE—Fill three quarters of a glass or cut-glass dessert dish of about 8 inches in diameter, with *Rice à l'impératrice*. See RICE.

Put to set in a cold place, on ice if possible.

Arrange 20 apricot halves, cooked in vanilla-flavoured syrup and well drained, on the rice in a circle. Decorate apricot halves with glacé cherries and angelica lozenges.

Top the apricots with a light coating of red-currant jelly. See JAM, *Currant jelly*.

Keep on ice until ready to serve.

To serve, put the dish on a larger one covered with a napkin and surround with crushed ice.

Apricots à l'impératrice (II)
(*National Milk Publicity Council*)

Apricots à l'impératrice (II). ABRICOTS À L'IMPÉRATRICE—Prepare *Rice à l'impératrice* in a charlotte mould. See RICE.

Turn it out into a shallow glass or crystal fruit bowl.

Arrange around it a circle of choice halved apricots, cooked and drained. Decorate with glacé cherries and angelica lozenges.

This method of presentation may be applied to all fruit desserts *à l'impératrice*.

The rice can also be served in a savarin mould, turned out on to a round dish and filled with apricot halves in the middle.

Apricot jam. See JAM.

Apricot omelette. See EGG, *Omelette: jam and fruit omelette*.

Apricot omelette
(*British Egg Information Service*)

Apricot oreillons. OREILLONS D'ABRICOTS—halved apricots are called *Apricot oreillons*. They are bottled plain, or with syrup like whole stoned apricots.

Apricot pudding. See PUDDING, *Fruit pudding*.

Apricot sauce. See SAUCE, *Dessert sauces*.

Apricot soufflé. See SOUFFLÉ, *Sweet soufflé*.

Apricots preserved in syrup. CONSERVE D'ABRICOTS AU SIROP—The procedure is exactly the same as for compote of apricots in syrup. See COMPOTE, *Preserved fruit in compote*.

Apricots with rice. ABRICOTS AU RIZ—Cook 1 cup of rice in 2 cups milk flavoured with ½ cup sugar and ½ teaspoon of vanilla, or any other flavouring.

Put the rice into a fruit dish and arrange halved apricots, cooked in syrup and strained, on top of it.

Sprinkle with a few tablespoons of apricot sauce, laced with kirsch, or serve as they are.

This sweet can be served hot or cold. The surface of the rice can be glazed before the halved apricots are put on.

The rice can also be bound with yolks of egg. See RICE, *Dessert rice*.

Apricots and rice with meringue. ABRICOTS MERINGUÉS AU RIZ—Put into a fireproof dish a layer of dessert rice 1 inch thick and a little smaller in diameter than the bottom of the dish.

Arrange on this bed of rice 24 halves of apricots, cooked in vanilla-flavoured syrup and well drained.

Place these apricot halves in such a manner as to form a round layer equal to that of rice.

Cover with ordinary *meringue*.* Smooth the surface and the edges carefully; pipe some meringue for decoration; sprinkle with icing sugar and bake in a moderate oven. At the last moment, place in a very hot oven to make the meringue golden.

When removed from oven, pipe apricot and red-currant jam into the hollows in meringue decoration, alternating the colours.

This dessert is mostly served hot, but it can also be served cold.

Pineapple, bananas, cherries, peaches, pears and apples can be prepared in the same manner. The fruit should previously be poached in vanilla-flavoured syrup, or stewed in butter, and used whole, halved, in slices or in dice.

Apricot tarts and tartlets. See TART AND TARTLET.

APRICOTING. ABRICOTER—This is a term used in pastry-making to define the operation which consists of covering a cake or a sweet with a thin layer of apricot jam, boiled down to thicken, flavoured with a liqueur and passed through a fine strainer.

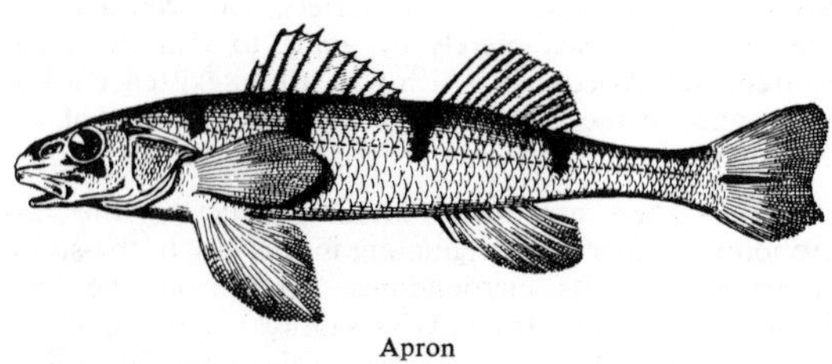

Apron

APRON—A small European fish with a rounded elongated body covered with very rough scales; its head is flattened, the snout protrudes above its mouth; its dorsal fins are placed at a distance from each other; its gill slits are very big. Only two species of apron are known; one which is found in the Danube and the *common apron* which abounds in the Rhone and all its tributaries.

The apron rarely exceeds 7 inches in length. The upper part of its body is yellowish-brown streaked with darkish bands or stripes which come down its sides. Its belly is a greyish white; its fins are yellow spotted with grey. Its flesh is very succulent and resembles that of perch; it is much appreciated by all the gastronomes. For culinary preparation see PERCH.

ARAB COOKERY. See ALGERIA.

ARAPÈDE—French name for a univalve shell-fish commonly found in Provence. It is prepared as cockles.

ARBOIS—A small town in the Jura. Its vineyards produce a white wine called Arbois, which is classed in the second category. This wine is very spirituous and has a great keeping quality. The wines of Arbois, like those of Château-Chalon and Pupillin, also of the Jura Department, are made dry or sparkling. These wines are known as *vins de l'Étoile*.

ARBUTUS BERRY. ARBOUSE—Fruit of the cane apple, a shrub which is found in profusion in the southern parts of North America, Mexico, southern Europe and the Canary Islands.

This shrub, which is grown in some parts of southern France, mainly in the Languedoc, is also known as *strawberry-tree*. It owes this name to the shape and colour of its fruit, which resembles the strawberry but has neither its scent nor its melting flesh.

Italy, Spain and Algeria are the main suppliers of wine and spirits distilled from the arbutus berry.

The fruit of the arbutus berry yields wine, spirits and a liqueur called *crème d'arbouse*, which has the reputation of being helpful to digestion.

The berries are very fleshy when ripe, sweet, and have a faint acid after-taste. They are reputed to be astringent and diuretic.

ARCA—A bivalve mollusc commonly known as *arch*. Its shells, which are of rather a dark colour, are found on all the coasts of France.

This mollusc is eaten raw or is prepared in the same way as mussels.

ARCACHON—This town, situated on the southern shores of the Bassin d'Arcachon (an inlet of the Bay of Biscay) is dear to the hearts of gastronomes and lovers of oysters. Arcachon is famous for its magnificent oyster beds.

ARCANETTE—Name given in Lorraine to a species of small local teal. It differs from an ordinary teal and from garganey in that it does not migrate and is found in its native land all the year round. Its flight is short but swift. Arcanette shooting is like duck shooting, the two species being of similar behaviour.

The flesh of this species of teal is excellent and much appreciated by all gastronomes. In taste it can be compared to that of wild duck.

For culinary preparation, see DUCK.

ARCH. See ARCA.

ARCHANGELICA. ARCHANGÉLIQUE—A genus of plants (of the family *Umbelliferae*) generally known under its common names of *angelica*, *angelica officinalis*, *garden angelica*, etc. In appearance it does not differ from *wild angelica*. See ANGELICA.

ARCHESTRATUS—Greek poet of about 350 B.C., who, it is said, was a very great gastronome. He was the author of a work in verse of which only a few very short fragments have survived to our day. It is called *Gastronomy*.

Archestratus was born, it is believed, in Athens, although some say in Gela, the ancient town in southern Sicily, and he lived in Syracuse for a long time. He was chiefly renowned for the numerous voyages he made to collect notes on methods relative to food and eating habits of the nations.

Archestratus is sometimes referred to as a cook. It is apparent, however, from the writings of authors of the time that he was much more of a gastronome, plus a very able writer, and not at all a cookery technician. It can be said that he was the Brillat-Savarin of the time of Pericles. Archestratus was not a cook at all, he was the prototype of the gastronomical globe-trotter.

The most reliable data we have concerning this poet-gastronome comes from *Deipnosophistai* or *Specialists in Dining* by Athenaeus, a work translated into French from the Latin text by Michel de Marolles in 1680. There we find all that appertains to gastronomy, to food production, to cookery and to solemn ceremonies.

Here is what Barthélemy, inspired by Athenaeus, says: 'This author was a friend of one of Pericles' sons. He crossed many lands and seas to find out for himself what was the best they had to offer. In his voyages he studied not the manners and customs of peoples, which it is useless to study, since it is impossible to change them, but he went into the laboratories where the delights of the table were manufactured and had no dealings except with people who catered for these pleasures. His poem is a shining treasure and does not contain a single verse which is not a plea for gastronomy.

'Chrysippus considers the lessons of Archestratus to be the fundamental point of the Epicurean doctrine and the true theogony of philosopher-gourmands. His principle was that when the number of guests exceeds three or four, then it becomes nothing more than a gathering of labourers or soldiers devouring their plunder. It would appear that these lessons did not help him to get rich, as Plutarch reports this exclamation of a partisan of the poet and his doctrine: "Oh, Archestratus, why did you not live under Alexander! Each of your verses would have earned you Cyprus or Phoenicia as reward".'

ARCHIDUC (A L')—A term applying to a great number of preparations. All the dishes *à l'archiduc* are usually seasoned with paprika, or Hungarian red pepper, and blended with cream. See EGGS and CHICKEN, *Chicken sauté*.

ARCHIL (ORCHIL, DYER'S MOSS). ORSEILLE—Bluish red paste made out of lichen, used as colouring matter. It is mainly used for tinting pickled tongue—*langue à l'écarlate*.

ARDENNAISE (A L')—A term applying mostly to dishes of small birds cooked in a *cocotte* with juniper berries. See THRUSH.

The same name also applies to a method of preparing crayfish.

ARDOISE (Slate)—In gastronomical terminology the name of *ardoise* is somewhat whimsically bestowed on the bills presented for meals taken in cheap restaurants, because in the past these bills were written on a slate.

ARENGA PALM—Palm tree. Its trunk is covered with a very thick layer of pith which produces a large quantity of amyloide substance, obtained by making an incision on the trunk; from the clusters, which develop all the year round between the lower leaves, there is a flow of sweet sap which, by a simple evaporation, furnishes a kind of sugar of a brownish colour and, by a process of fermentation, a palm wine.

In England and in some parts of France where imported sago is to be had, fruit of the sugar palm, gathered green, is candied and much valued as a stomachic. See SAGO.

ARGENTEUIL (Asparagus)—Asparagus cultivated in the Argenteuil region, in Seine-et-Oise, enjoys world-wide reputation. It has no rivals. See ASPARAGUS.

ARGUS PHEASANT—Bird of the family *Phasianidae*. It is thus called because of the great number of 'eyes' on its magnificent plumage. It bears some resemblance to peacock and is found in Java and Sumatra.

The flesh of argus pheasant is very delicate. All the methods of preparation given for pheasant are also applicable to argus pheasant. See PHEASANT.

ARIÈGE—The Ariège department of France, situated on the Spanish frontier, between Haute-Garonne in the west and Pyrénées-Orientales in the east, is chiefly famous for the mineral waters of its thermal springs at the spas Ax and Aulus.

Among Ariège culinary specialities there are many excellent dishes, lavish and rich in good fat meat.

Excellent *confits d'oie** are made in this region. The Ariège geese have a very fine flesh. Ariège pork is also excellent, and is made into very fine pork butchery products. Ariège hams and sausages are famous. See LANGUEDOC.

ARIÉGEOISE (A L')—Name given to various dishes almost all of which include the following ingredients as garnish: green cabbage and pickled pork, and sometimes kidney beans. See CHICKEN, *Stuffed chicken à l'ariégeoise*. MUTTON, *Stuffed breast of mutton à l'ariégeoise*.

ARLEQUIN (Harlequin)—The *arlequin* is, or rather was, for it is almost a thing of the past, an assortment of scraps and odds and ends of food, bought from bottle-washers or washers-up of restaurants. These were tidied up and sold to people of small means, who could, for the price of a few sous, thus procure for themselves the illusion of having a good meal. These bits and pieces are also called '*bijoux*' (jewels). Privat d'Anglemont says: 'Arlequin is so called because these dishes are composed of bits and pieces, thrown together in a haphazard fashion, just like the parti-coloured tights of the citizen of Bergamo. These pieces of meat are very copious and yet they are sold indiscriminately for a sou a piece. The bucket costs 3 francs. There you can find everything, from truffled chicken and game to beef and cabbage'.

It must be said that these pieces of meat and other food were by no means thrown together indiscriminately, but arranged with method and propriety. One could easily see this for oneself merely by going to visit the great Marché aux Arlequins, which was still in existence a few years ago, in the middle of Paris, by the market of the Madeleine.

ARLES—There are many famous products in the gastronomical repertoire originating in this city in the south of France and its surroundings. Apart from the celebrated *saucisson d'Arles* (Arles sausage), this region, so well sung by Mistral, produces excellent oil. See PROVENCE.

ARLÉSIENNE (A L')—Name which applies to different preparations characterized some by a garnish composed of aubergines (egg-plants) fried in oil, sautéed tomatoes and onion rings dredged in flour and fried; others by a garnish of whole little tomatoes, peeled and stewed in butter, and very tender pickled chicory hearts fried in oil. See CHICORY.

The third garnish bearing the same name is composed of small tomatoes stuffed with rice pilaf and browned on top, and large olives stuffed with chicken forcemeat with anchovy butter and new potatoes.

ARMADILLO. Tatou—Small toothless mammal covered with scales found in South America. It is about the size of a guinea-pig, but more highly esteemed as meat.

Cave at Condom, Gers, a leading centre of Armagnac distillation (*French Government Tourist Office*)

ARMAGNAC—Region in the old province of Gascony, now almost entirely included in the department of Gers. The Armagnac brandies are famous, second only to those of Charente. The best are distilled from the Bas-Armagnac wines, at Nogaro, Cazambon and Gabaret. See SPIRITS.

ARMORICAINE—Armorica (older Aremorica) was the ancient name for a region in north-west France comprising the coast of Gaul, between the Seine and Loire rivers.

Armoricaine nowadays is the name given to a very choice variety of oysters. See OYSTERS.

ARMORICAINE (A L')—Corruption by certain authors of the name of dishes called *à l'américaine*, particularly lobster. As a result of this corruption, this dish, so typically Provençal, has been placed under the patronage of legendary Armorica.

AROMA. Arome—Gastronomically speaking, this word describes the characteristic fragrance of various dishes. The word aroma has a greater force of expression than either *odour* or *smell*. The word perfume, on the other hand, is more specifically reserved for essences and other non-edible substances. It is right and proper that gastronomical literature should have a terminology of its own. We say, the aroma of this consommé, the aroma of this *fumet*,* the aroma of this coffee.

AROMATIC PLANTS. Plantes aromatiques—A great number of aromatic plants, either with a bland or pungent aroma, are used as flavourings in cookery.

The following are among the herbs and aromatic plants most commonly used in the kitchen: *parsley*, *chervil*, *tarragon*, *rosemary*, *thyme*, *bay leaf*, *wild thyme*, *sage*, *savoury* (see CONDIMENTS) and the following aromatics: *garlic*, *shallots*, *spring onions*, *chives* and *onions*.

AROMATICS. Aromates—Taken in its general sense, this word describes all substances which give out an odour of varying degrees of sweetness. The greatest number of aromatics is provided by plants of hot countries, notably Arabia. We are only concerned here with aromatics used in cookery, pastry-making and confectionery. Without indulging in the excesses of the ancient practice, when such scents as rose-water and benzoin were used on every possible occasion, present-day cookery has at its disposal a great number of aromatics. The following are among those most widely used as condiments: *dill*, *betel pepper*, *cinnamon*, *cloves*, *coriander*, *bay leaf*, *mace*, *mustard*, *nutmeg*, *pepper* and *thyme*. Next come the aromatics used mostly for flavouring culinary preparations: *ambergris*, *anise*, *star anise*, *basil*, *cummin*, *fennel*, *juniper*, *ginger*, *horse-radish*, *rosemary*, *sage*, etc.

Some aromatic plants are frequently used fresh, for instance, *chervil*, *tarragon*, *parsley*, etc. The essence extracted from the peel of *oranges*, *lemons* and *tangerines* is also used. Pastry-making and confectionery, in addition to the aromatics mentioned above, also use *vanilla*, *tea*, *chocolate* and *coffee*.

Garlic, *spring onions*, *shallots* and *onions* are dealt with at length under separate entries in their alphabetical order, as well as the aromatic roots of carrot, celery and parsnip, which are really more vegetables than aromatics.

Medieval directions concerning the use of aromatics in cookery are numerous and varied. Some denounce it, others tolerate it and yet others demand it. In old cookery practice, which is so often praised nowadays, the use of aromatics and strong seasoning was abused. Modern cookery has, in part, done away with these excesses. See SEASONING; CONDIMENTS.

AROMATIZE. Aromatiser—To impart some aroma to a culinary preparation or a pastry. Pastry is also aromatized with liqueurs.

ARPENTEUR—Common French name for plover.

ARQUEBUSE—An old liqueur made of various aromatic plants.

Eau d'arquebuse—Also known under the name of *eau d'arquebusade*. This beverage is obtained by infusion or maceration of vulnerary plants (kidney vetch, lady's finger, wound-wort).

ARRACACHA or ARRACACIA—Plant, native of Columbia, which grows in the Andes and in North America.

Its roots, which are very farinaceous, produce a flour which is eaten in its country of origin. The roots can also be cooked like *yams* and *sweet potatoes*.

The starch which is extracted from the roots of the arracacha is similar to arrowroot.

ARRACK. Arack—Name given to a spirit distilled from fermented rice. Arrack is also distilled either from sugar and coconut milk left to ferment, or from the juice which seeps through incisions made on the coconut palm. In Réunion Island, in Madagascar and in most parts of the South African sub-continent, where sugar cane is cultivated, the name of arrack is also given to a spirit distilled from fermented *cane-juice* (sugar cane juice squeezed out under a press).

Arrack is imported into Europe and is esteemed as a liqueur by many people.

ARROWROOT—Name given to starch food materials obtained from the roots and rhizomes of various unrelated plants of the tropical regions.

There is a legend that this name originated because the Indians considered the sap obtained from the rhizomes capable of healing wounds caused by arrows. Hence the name in English, *arrow-root*. The fact is, however, that arrowroot takes its name from the American Indian word for flour-root, *araruta*.

The chief of these plants is the *West Indian arrowroot*, thus called because the flour produced from it originated in the West Indies. The English introduced it into India and it is also called *West Indian salep*.

This plant also grows in Madagascar.

Arrowroot is eminently edible and is imported into Europe in vast quantities.

This very delicate starch is used in thickening soups and gravies, as well as in the preparation of blancmanges, milk puddings and numerous sweet dishes.

Easily digestible arrowroot is especially valued as a food for young children, invalids and the aged.

Arrowroot liaison. Liaison à l'arrowroot—Pour into a quart (litre) of boiling veal (or other) stock, 1 tablespoon (7 to 8 grams) of arrowroot, well blended with a little cold stock or water. Mix, bring to the boil and strain.

Arrowroot porridge. Bouillie à l'arrowroot—Pour into 2 cups of boiling milk, sweetened (⅓ cup sugar) or salted (1 teaspoon salt), 2 or 3 large tablespoons of arrowroot diluted with ¼ cup cold milk. Mix well. Cook gently from 8 to 10 minutes stirring from time to time.

Stock can be used instead of milk.

Arrowroot pudding. See PUDDING, *Semolina pudding*.

ARSENIC—An element which is normally present in minute doses in the tissues of the human body (thyroid gland, thymus gland, mammary gland, head and body hair). Certain vegetables (kohl-rabi, turnips, certain cereals), sea-fish, sea-salt, milk and yolk of egg contain small quantities of it, sufficient for the requirements of the organism.

ARTAGNAN (A L')—Name of a garnish composed of cèpes prepared *à la béarnaise* (see SAUCE), little stuffed tomatoes and cork-shaped potato croquettes.

This garnish is served with large or small pieces of meat and with poultry.

ARTICHOKE. Artichaut—Vegetable derived from the cardoon vastly improved by scientific methods.

This plant has been cultivated in France since the beginning of the sixteenth century and is mentioned by Rabelais.

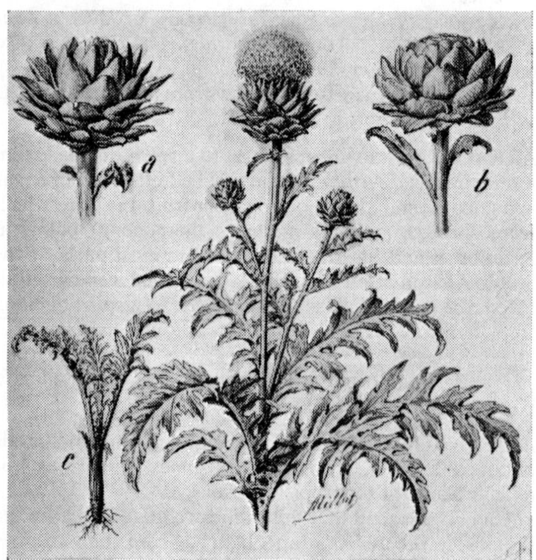

Artichoke showing inflorescence
a) Large green of Laon; (b) Camus of Brittany; (c) Artichoke bud

Among the great number of species which are cultivated all over France, but particularly in Roussillon, in Provence and in Brittany, the following varieties are much valued in cookery: *large green of Laon*, *large camus of Brittany*, and *green of Provence*.

It lends itself to numerous delicious culinary compositions. When it is young, and therefore very tender, it is eaten raw, *à la croque au sel*, which means with 'nought but a grain of salt', *à la poivrade*,* and *à la vinaigrette*.*

Artichoke hearts, cooked and chilled, make one of the best garnishes for cold dishes. They can be stuffed with various ingredients. They are also used in the preparation of *hors-d'oeuvre*.

See also JERUSALEM ARTICHOKE.

WHOLE ARTICHOKES.

Artichokes barigoule. Artichauts barigoule—Prepare the artichokes as described in *whole boiled artichokes*.

Fill the inside with a *duxelles** mixture, adding to it a quarter of its volume in finely shredded fat bacon, the same amount of chopped lean ham and some chopped parsley.

Surround the artichokes with rashers or strips of fat bacon and braise them as described in the recipe for *large braised artichokes stuffed au gras*.

Finish as described in that recipe.

Note. A variant of this recipe consists of cooking the stuffed artichokes in oil with a little white wine.

In home cookery, in the absence of *demi-glace* (see SAUCE), the braising liquor can be thickened with *kneaded butter* (see BUTTER).

Whole boiled artichokes. Artichauts entiers bouillis—Cut off the stalks, pull off hard outer leaves and trim off the leaves with scissors. Shorten them neatly and evenly, cutting off tops to two-thirds of their height. Wash, tie with string around the largest circumference, and put bases downwards into a saucepan of boiling salted water.

Cook, keeping the water boiling, until done—the cooking time depending on size and age of the artichokes.

Drain, dry on a cloth, remove string and serve as indicated in the recipe chosen.

The artichokes must not be overcooked. To ensure this, test the bottom of the vegetable which, when cooked, should 'give' under very light pressure.

If the artichokes are to be served cold, cool them in cold water as soon as they are cooked.

Boiled artichokes with various cold sauces. Artichauts bouillis—Boil, cool and serve with one of the following sauces: *mayonnaise*, *mustard*, *tartare*, *vinaigrette*. See SAUCE.

To serve artichoke cold, scoop out the choke and remove the leaves from around the choke. Turn them upside down to form a cup, and replace them in the cavity left by the removal of the choke. Put a pinch of chopped chervil and parsley on these leaves.

Boiled artichokes with various hot sauces. Artichauts bouillis—Boil as described in the recipe for *whole boiled artichokes*; serve with one of the following sauces: *butter*, *white*, *cream*, *hollandaise*, *mousseline*. See SAUCE.

Large braised artichokes stuffed au gras (with meat). Gros artichauts braisés farcis au gras—Pare and trim the artichokes. Blanch for 5 minutes in boiling, salted water. Plunge into cold water or leave under a running tap to cool, drain and remove the choke.

Season, stuff as desired, wrap them in a thin rasher or slice of fat bacon and tie with a string. Melt some butter in a sauté pan, put in finely shredded bacon, onions and carrots and place the artichokes on this foundation. Season and add a *bouquet garni*.*

Simmer under a lid in butter and a small quantity of white wine until the liquor is almost completely boiled down; then add a few tablespoons of veal stock and cook in the oven (350°F.) with lid on, 55 minutes to an hour. Baste frequently during cooking.

Drain the artichokes, remove string, take off the bacon and put the artichokes on a round dish.

Strain the liquor in which the artichokes were cooked, skim off surplus fat, strain, add *demi-glace*,* veal stock or any other sauce, according to the recipe, boil down and pour over the artichokes.

Preparation of artichokes

Large braised artichokes stuffed au maigre (without meat). GROS ARTICHAUTS BRAISÉS FARCIS AU MAIGRE—Proceed as described above, leaving out the bacon and replacing veal stock by vegetable stock.

Small braised artichokes. PETITS ARTICHAUTS BRAISÉS—These are served as garnish and as vegetable. Choose very young small artichokes; pare them, trim off the stalks evenly and rub the bottoms with lemon; blanch in boiling water with salt and vinegar added to it, dip in cold water to cool, drain and put (bases downwards) into a buttered sauté or heavy frying-pan on a foundation of vegetables, as described in the recipe for *large braised artichokes*. Cook over a low heat with the lid on for about 10 minutes and finish cooking as described above.

Drain the artichokes. Use them as indicated. Strain the braising liquor, reduce, skim off surplus fat and pour the sauce over the artichokes.

Note. Small braised artichokes can also be prepared *au maigre* (without meat) by following the instructions given for large braised artichokes *au maigre*.

One can, provided one works sufficiently quickly to prevent the artichokes from going black, put them into a buttered sauté pan without blanching.

Artichokes Clamart. ARTICHAUTS CLAMART—Choose 12 very small young artichokes; trim them and put in a sauté or heavy frying-pan with plenty of butter.

Add 2 cups ($\frac{1}{2}$ litre) of fresh garden peas and 2 shredded lettuce hearts.

Season with salt and sugar. Moisten with 3 tablespoons of water. Cook with lid on, simmering gently.

At the last moment add a tablespoon of fresh butter. Serve in a vegetable dish.

This vegetable, being delicate and fragile, can be prepared in a bi-metal or an aluminium sauté pan, or in an earthenware or enamelware *cocotte*, and served in the same dish (to avoid damaging in transferring).

Artichokes Crécy. ARTICHAUTS CRÉCY—Proceed as described in the preceding recipe replacing peas and lettuce by an equal quantity of very small young carrots, correctly peeled.

Artichokes à la diable or Carciofo à l'inferno (Italian cookery). ARTICHAUTS À LA DIABLE—Trim lightly the tips of very tender medium-sized artichokes. Remove the choke, blanch, drain and fill the artichokes with a mixture of breadcrumbs, chopped garlic, capers and parsley, salt and pepper.

Put into a sauté pan with oil, packing them in rather tightly. Sprinkle generously with olive oil and season. Cook in the oven, uncovered, basting frequently.

When cooked, the artichokes should be crisp at the tips.

Arrange on a round dish and sprinkle with the oil in which they were cooked.

Dried artichokes. CONSERVE D'ARTICHAUTS SÉCHÉS—Trim the artichokes, then blanch them for 5 minutes in water with 1 per cent of sulphurous acid added to it.

Drain them and put to dry on trays in the sun or in a slow oven. (They can also be threaded on a string and dried in the open air.)

For this method of preserving artichokes, blanching water must not be salted, otherwise saline particles would impregnate the artichokes, thus drawing humidity and thereby preventing dessication.

Fried artichokes. See *Artichoke hearts fried in batter*.

Artichoke fritters. BEIGNETS D'ARTICHAUTS—These can be served as *hors-d'oeuvre* or as a vegetable. See HORS-D'OEUVRE, *Fritters*.

Artichokes à la lyonnaise. ARTICHAUTS À LA LYONNAISE—Proceed as described in the recipe for *Artichokes barigoule*, replacing the *duxelles** mixture by sausage-meat with a quarter of its weight of chopped lightly fried onion and chopped parsley added to it.

Artichokes à la ménagère. ARTICHAUTS À LA MÉNAGÈRE—Proceed as described in the recipe for *Artichokes barigoule*, replacing the *duxelles** mixture by chopped boiled beef, mixed with finely shredded fresh bacon and chopped parsley.

Artichokes mirepoix. ARTICHAUTS MIREPOIX—Put 12 small artichokes prepared as described in the recipe for *Artichokes Clamart* into a sauté pan on a foundation of $\frac{2}{3}$ cup (2 decilitres) *Vegetable mirepoix*,* mixed with 2 tablespoons of lean ham cut into tiny dice. See MIREPOIX.

Simmer for 5 minutes over a low flame, keeping the pan uncovered. Moisten with 4 tablespoons of white wine. Simmer 5 minutes, add $\frac{1}{3}$ cup (1 decilitre) of veal stock, cover with a lid and simmer for 35 minutes.

Serve in a vegetable dish. Pour the *mirepoix* over the artichokes and sprinkle with chopped parsley.

Pickled artichokes. CONSERVE D'ARTICHAUTS—Trim freshly-gathered artichokes. Put them, whole or in quarters, in water with 1 per cent of sulphurous acid added to it.

Blanch them, allowing 10 minutes for whole artichokes and 5 minutes for quarters, in salted water, (allowing 10 per cent of salt), drain and dip in cold water.

Drain them again, put into cans and pour in the following pickling brine:

For 20 quarts (litres) of water: 2 pounds (1 kilo) of well-refined salt and 20 grams of sulphurous acid.

Weight of cans	Cooking time with 230°F. pressure sterilizer	Cooking time in a bain-marie or canning kettle
1 pound (500 grams)	30 minutes	1 hour
2 pounds (1 kilogram)	40 minutes	1½ hours
4 pounds (2 kilograms)	60 minutes	2 hours

Pickled artichokes à la grecque. CONSERVE D'ARTICHAUTS À LA GRECQUE—This is a pickle for which only small artichokes are used. Large artichokes have to be cut in quarters, which changes the aspect of this *hors-d'oeuvre*.

Method. Pare and trim uniformly 100 small artichokes of the same size.

Plunge them, as they are trimmed, into the following previously-prepared mixture:

5 quarts (5 litres) water; 1 pint (½ litre) olive oil; 1½ tablespoons (10 grams) coriander; 1 teaspoon (5 grams) peppercorns; 1½ tablespoons (25 grams) salt; a large *bouquet garni* composed of thyme, bay leaf, fennel and a stalk of celery; and the juice of 10 lemons strained through a muslin bag. Bring the artichokes to the boil and continue boiling for 8 to 10 minutes at the most.

For a smaller quantity (20 artichoke hearts or quarters), see *aubergines* (*egg-plant*) *à la grecque*. Cook 8 to 10 minutes at the most.

Transfer them, with their liquor, into a large earthenware crock and allow to cool.

Put into 4-quart or 8-pint cans. Fill with the liquor to within the width of a finger from the top. Seal hermetically and put to boil 20 minutes for pint (½ litre), and 30 minutes for quart (litre) cans.

Artichokes à la poivrade. See HORS-D'OEUVRE.

Purée of artichokes for garnish. PURÉE D'ARTICHAUTS—Half cook artichoke hearts in a white vegetable court-bouillon and simmer in butter. Rub through a fine sieve. Heat the purée and add butter or cream, as directed in the recipe.

Depending on the final use for which this purée is intended, thicken its consistency by adding an equal amount of potato purée.

Purée of artichokes soubisée for garnishes. PURÉE D'ARTICHAUTS SOUBISÉE—Proceed as described in the preceding recipe. Add to the artichoke purée one third of its volume of onion purée *Soubise*. See PURÉES.

Artichoke salad. See SALAD, *Mixed salads*.

Artichoke soufflé. See SOUFFLÉS, *Soufflé of various vegetables*.

Artichoke stalks. MOELLE D'ARTICHAUT—Peel the stalks of large artichokes, taking care to remove all the woody casing. Cut these stalks into sticks 2 inches long. Blanch in salt water flavoured with lemon.

When they are blanched, artichoke stalks can be prepared in various ways: simmered in butter or cream in a covered pan; in *fritots**; *à la grecque**; curried; with gravy; sautéed in butter, etc.

ARTICHOKE HEARTS. FONDS D'ARTICHAUTS—Artichoke hearts prepared as described below can be served as a vegetable or as a garnish. When sliced and blended with a sauce, white or brown, they should be served in a vegetable dish, in a *gratin* dish, or in a *croustade*,* timbale or vol-au-vent cases. For preparation of the hearts, see *Artichoke hearts in court-bouillon*.

Artichoke hearts à l'allemande. FONDS D'ARTICHAUTS À L'ALLEMANDE—Blanch the artichokes lightly and stew in butter. Transfer into a vegetable dish and cover with *Allemande sauce*. See SAUCE.

If the artichoke hearts are too big, cut them into slices.

Artichoke hearts à la béchamel. FONDS D'ARTICHAUTS À LA BÉCHAMEL—Proceed as above, using *béchamel sauce*. See SAUCE.

Artichoke hearts cooked in butter. FONDS D'ARTICHAUTS ÉTUVÉS AU BEURRE—Pare and trim the artichoke as described in next recipe. Rub them with lemon and blanch for 10 minutes in boiling salt water acidulated with a few drops of lemon juice.

Drain, put in a well-buttered sauté pan, season, sprinkle with melted butter, cook with a lid on from 18 to 25 minutes, depending on their size.

Use as indicated in the recipe chosen.

Artichoke hearts in court-bouillon. FONDS D'ARTICHAUTS AU BLANC—Strip off the outside leaves of medium-sized artichokes. Trim them as evenly as possible, leaving only the fleshy middle part. Remove the choke, trim the hearts and rub them with lemon. Put into acidulated cold water as each one is trimmed.

Put the artichoke hearts to cook into a boiling *white vegetable court-bouillon*. See COURT-BOUILLON.

Cook until done or blanch, as required, depending on the final use for which they are intended.

Drain the artichoke hearts and use as recommended in the recipe.

Artichoke hearts à la crème. FONDS D'ARTICHAUTS À LA CRÈME—Proceed as above. As soon as the artichoke hearts are cooked, pour boiling cream over them. Simmer down by half. Transfer the artichoke hearts into a vegetable dish. Add some butter to the sauce, strain it and pour over the artichokes. Cream sauce can also be used for pouring over artichoke hearts. See SAUCE.

Artichoke hearts fines herbes. FONDS D'ARTICHAUTS FINES HERBES—Blanch lightly, slice, fry in butter in a shallow pan. Transfer into a vegetable dish, sprinkle with chopped chervil and parsley.

When the artichokes are very tender slice them raw and then fry in butter.

Artichoke hearts fried in batter. FONDS D'ARTICHAUTS EN FRITOT—Blanch the artichoke hearts, slice them and marinade in oil, lemon juice, salt, pepper and *fines herbes*.* When required, dip them into batter and deep-fry.

Drain, dry, season with fine salt, arrange them in a heap on a folded napkin and garnish with fried parsley.

Garnished artichoke hearts. FONDS D'ARTICHAUTS GARNIS—Artichoke hearts used principally as a garnish for hot and cold dishes can be filled with various mixtures. Here are the main ingredients which can be added to them: for hot dishes, the artichoke hearts, cooked in *white vegetable court-bouillon* (see COURT-BOUILLON) and simmered in butter, are filled at the last moment with vegetables or other ingredients, but are not put in the oven to brown the tops, as recommended for stuffed artichoke hearts.

Artichoke hearts intended as a garnish for cold dishes are cooked in this *court-bouillon*, drained, dried, filled with various vegetables set with a jelly, or seasoned with vinaigrette or mayonnaise, or other *salpicons*.* Artichoke hearts are used plain, or covered with aspic jelly, or *chaud-froid sauce*, and decorated as desired.

Filled artichoke hearts as garnish for cold dishes—Fill hearts with various compound butters; caviar; shrimps; crayfish; lobster and other shell-fish; various vegetables; hard boiled eggs; meat, fish and shell-fish purées; various salpicons, etc.

Filled artichoke hearts as garnish for hot dishes—*Anversoise*: hop shoots in cream; *argenteuil*: purée of white asparagus; *bretonne*: purée of kidney beans; *Compoint*: purée of green asparagus; *Conti*: lentil purée: *écossaise: brunoise** of carrots, celery, French beans and onions; *macédoine* of vegetables in butter; *princess*: asparagus tips and diced truffles; *Saint-Germain*: purée of fresh garden peas; *various thick sauces* such as *béarnaise, Choron, Henri IV, paloise*; *Vichy*: carrots à la Vichy.

Artichoke hearts can, in fact, be filled with all the *salpicons* given in this dictionary.

Artichoke hearts à la hollandaise. FONDS D'ARTICHAUTS À LA HOLLANDAISE—Cook in a *court-bouillon (IV)*,* drain, put in a vegetable dish and cover with *Hollandaise sauce*. See SAUCE.

Artichoke hearts Mornay. FONDS D'ARTICHAUTS MORNAY—Simmer in butter in a covered pan. Put into a fireproof dish coated with *Mornay sauce* (see SAUCE). Cover with the same sauce, sprinkle with grated Parmesan cheese and melted butter and brown the top.

Pickled artichoke hearts. CONSERVE DE FONDS D'ARTICHAUTS—Choose small, very tender artichokes. Trim them correctly with a special turning peeler or by hand, and put them, as they are trimmed, into water with 1 per cent sulphurous acid added to it. Blanch for 5 minutes in salted water (8 per cent salt), drain and cool in cold water.

Drain again, put into cans and pour in the same pickling brine as above.

Weight of cans	Cooking time with 230°F. pressure sterilizer	Cooking time in a bain-marie or canning kettle
1 pound (500 grams)	20 minutes	40 minutes
2 pounds (1 kilogram)	30 minutes	60 minutes

Artichoke hearts stuffed à la cévenole. FONDS D'ARTICHAUTS FARCIS À LA CÉVENOLE—Blanch the artichoke hearts thoroughly. Simmer in butter. Garnish with a *chestnut purée* flavoured with *Soubise purée* (see PURÉES). Sprinkle with grated Parmesan cheese and melted butter and brown the top.

Artichoke hearts stuffed à la chalonnaise. FONDS D'ARTICHAUTS FARCIS À LA CHALONNAISE—As above with a *salpicon à la chalonnaise*. See SALPICON.

Artichoke hearts stuffed à la duxelles. FONDS D'ARTICHAUTS FARCIS À LA DUXELLES—As above with very thick *duxelles*.*

Artichoke hearts stuffed à la florentine. FONDS D'ARTICHAUTS FARCIS À LA FLORENTINE—Fill the artichoke hearts, simmered in butter, with spinach also simmered in butter. Pour over *Mornay sauce* (see SAUCE), sprinkle with grated cheese and brown the top.

Artichoke hearts stuffed à la lyonnaise. FONDS D'ARTICHAUTS FARCIS À LA LYONNAISE—As above, with sausagemeat mixed with chopped onion lightly fried in butter.

Artichoke hearts stuffed à la niçoise. FONDS D'ARTICHAUTS FARCIS À LA NIÇOISE—Blanch the artichoke hearts, fry them in oil, fill with *tomato fondue*,* sprinkle with breadcrumbs and melted butter and brown the top.

Artichoke hearts stuffed Piémontaise. FONDS D'ARTICHAUTS PIÉMONTAISE—Simmer them in butter in a covered pan. Fill with *Risotto à la Piémontaise* (see RICE), sprinkle with grated Parmesan cheese and brown the top.

Artichoke hearts stuffed Soubise. FONDS D'ARTICHAUTS FARCIS SOUBISE—As above with a thick *Soubise purée*. See PURÉES.

ARTICHOKE QUARTERS. QUARTIERS D'ARTICHAUTS—Pare and trim medium sized artichokes. Cut them into quarters. Trim these quarters carefully, rub with lemon, blanch for 6 minutes in salted and acidulated boiling water. Put under a cold tap to cool and drain.

Dry, finish off and use as directed in recipe.

In addition to the specific recipes given in this section, most of those given for small whole artichokes and some of those given for artichoke hearts can be applied to artichoke quarters.

Artichoke quarters in butter. QUARTIERS D'ARTICHAUTS AU BEURRE—Thoroughly blanch quarters of 6 artichokes; put them into a well-buttered sauté or heavy frying pan. Season, moisten with 3 tablespoons of water, sprinkle with a tablespoon of melted butter, bring to the boil, cover with a lid and simmer gently for 30-35 minutes. Serve in a vegetable dish with the pan juices poured over.

Artichoke quarters aux fines herbes. QUARTIERS D'ARTICHAUTS AUX FINES HERBES—Prepare as in recipe for *Artichoke quarters in butter*. Put in a vegetable dish. Dilute the pan juices with $\frac{1}{3}$ cup (1 decilitre) of white wine, boil down, add 3 tablespoons ($\frac{1}{2}$ decilitre) of thickened veal stock and boil for a few moments. Strain this sauce, add to it one tablespoon of butter, a few drops of lemon juice and one tablespoon of chopped *fines herbes*.* Pour over the artichoke quarters.

Note. These quarters can also be prepared *au maigre* (without stock). Proceed as described in the recipe for artichoke quarters in butter, but finish off with lemon juice and chopped *fines herbes*.

Artichoke quarters fried in batter. QUARTIERS D'ARTICHAUTS EN FRITOT—Using well-trimmed, blanched and marinaded artichoke quarters, proceed as described in the recipe for *Artichoke hearts fried in batter*.

Artichoke quarters à la grecque. QUARTIERS D'ARTICHAUTS À LA GRECQUE—Using well-trimmed artichoke quarters, proceed as described in the recipe for *Pickled artichokes à la grecque*. These are served as cold *hors-d'oeuvre*.

Artichoke quarters à l'italienne. QUARTIERS D'ARTICHAUTS À L'ITALIENNE—Proceed as described in the recipe for *Artichoke quarters aux fines herbes*. Finish off with *Italian sauce*. See SAUCE.

Artichoke quarters au jus. QUARTIERS D'ARTICHAUTS AU JUS—Proceed as described in the recipe for *Artichoke quarters aux fines herbes*, but omit the herbs.

Artichoke quarters à la lyonnaise. QUARTIERS D'ARTICHAUTS À LA LYONNAISE—Proceed as described for *Artichoke quarters aux fines herbes*. Finish off with *Lyonnaise sauce*. See SAUCE.

Artichoke quarters à la moelle. QUARTIERS D'ARTICHAUTS À LA MOELLE—Cook the artichoke quarters as described for those *au jus*. Finish off with *Marrow sauce* (see SAUCE), and garnish with thin slices of bonemarrow, poached and drained.

Artichoke quarters à la portugaise. QUARTIERS D'ARTICHAUTS À LA PORTUGAISE—Simmer the quarters in 4 tablespoons oil with 3 tablespoons chopped onions. Add

2 peeled, pressed-out and pounded tomatoes and a little grated garlic and chopped parsley. Cook uncovered, simmering gently.

Serve in a vegetable dish sprinkled with chopped parsley.

WINTER ARTICHOKE. ARTICHAUT D'HIVER—Another name for *Jerusalem artichoke*.

ARTOCARPUS. ARTOCARPE — See BREAD-FRUIT TREE.

ARTOIS AND BOULONNAIS—The principal food resources of this ancient province of France come from the sea.

Boulogne is certainly the most important fishing port in France, with the best supplies of herrings and mackerel. Whole convoys of lorries carrying mackerel, herrings, gurnet (gurnard) and other fish leave this seaport every day with supplies of fish for all parts of France.

The climate of this region, rather variable, is damp and not suitable for fruit-growing. Not much fruit is found there, except cider apples. Cider, along with beer, is the main beverage of the region.

Artois market-gardening produces very good vegetables. Those from around Saint-Omar are particularly fine.

Good quality beef and mutton is produced in Artois.

Poultry and game of this region are of average quality.

Rivers and ponds abound in fish of all kinds; magnificent salmon in the estuary of the small coastal rivers and, in the Canche, trout with flesh of great delicacy.

Culinary specialities. These are not very numerous. Almost all of them are based on sea food: fish, crustacea and shell-fish.

The principal specialities of the region are: *andouilles** d'Arras and various other pork butchery products, such as *saucisses de campagne* (country sausages), black (blood) puddings, Valencienne tongue.

Beer soup and *leek soup*, the latter very popular in Artois and in Flanders.

The *hotch-potch*, a dish of Flemish origin, *woodcock pâté* of Montreuil-sur-Mer, excellent dishes which are hardly ever made nowadays; *Wild rabbit with prunes or raisins*, a speciality of Valenciennes; *Goose à la flamande*.

Jellied eel, the *caudière de Berck*, a kind of *matelote* similar to the *chaudrée* of Aunis and, finally, a whole range of fish dishes, from *mackerel à la boulonnaise* to more complicated dishes made of various kinds of sea-fish: burbot, turbot, striped mullet, smelt, coalfish (green pollack), bass, sole, red mullet, skate.

Boulogne is above all the town of herrings and mackerel. According to an ancient document, herring and mackerel fishing can be traced back to the year 809. Since that distant epoch fishing methods have developed more and more, and the trade in herrings—dried, smoked, pickled or ready for serving—has assumed enormous proportions. Nor must we forget all the various preparations of canned herring which are sent from Boulogne all over France.

Herrings are prepared in different ways. There are *bloaters*, slightly salted and smoked herrings; *salted herrings* proper; *smoked herrings* called gendarmes; *kippers*, cured and split; *herrings pickled in white wine*; *cured herring fillets in oil*; and various other preparations of this excellent fish which are eaten as *hors-d'oeuvre*.

Excellent canned mackerel comes from Boulogne too, which is also eaten as *hors-d'oeuvre*.

Among the pastries and confectionery products are the Arras '*hearts*' and *caramels*, the Lille *délices*, the Cambrai *bêtises* and the Berck *chiques*.

ARUM MACULATUM—This plant is also known under the names of *lords and ladies*, *cuckoo-pint*, *calf's foot* and *wake-robin*. In French it is also called pepper-cabbage (*chou-poivre*) because of the acridity of its leaves and rhizomes. In U.S.A. it is sometimes called *wild-ginger* for the same reason.

These rhizomes, or roots, are much valued by the Arabs, who eat them cooked in the cinders.

ASAFOETIDA—Resinous gum extract of some oriental palms. In spite of its offensive smell, some people in the East and Far East use it as a condiment. The Romans were very fond of it and used to add it to a great number of dishes, under the name of *sylphium* or *silphion*.

ASBESTOS. AMIANTE—Fibrous mineral substance which is found in eruptive rocks. Asbestos fibres are sufficiently flexible to be plaited and woven. The principal characteristic of asbestos is its incombustibility. A piece of asbestos fabric put in the middle of a blazing fire-place can remain there a long time without suffering any damage. The ancients, who used asbestos napkins and tablecoths, used to clean them by this process. In the present day, asbestos is still used for table-mats. The properties of asbestos are also exploited for interior lining of kitchen stoves on all sides. Asbestos, being a very bad conductor, does not absorb heat, as metal would, but reflects it by radiation.

Owing to this radiating property the maximum of heat is obtained with the minimum of fuel, which results in a considerable saving of expense.

ASCALAPHUS—Ascalaphus, the legend tells us, was Pluto's cook and Proserpine's guardian. This position of confidence brought him misfortune. Ceres turned him into an owl because he revealed that Proserpine—whom Jupiter wanted to return to her mother, Ceres, on condition that she had eaten nothing in the infernal regions—had eaten six grains of pomegranate.

Minerva, wishing to console him in his misfortune, took him under her protection.

This is a wonderful myth for the cooks, who can glory in the fact that one of their ancestors was thus adopted by the goddess of wisdom, although they must regret the fact that Ascalaphus' indiscretion resulted in such trying consequences for Proserpine.

ASH. FRÊNE—The young shoots of this tree can be eaten in a salad. The seeds are sometimes preserved.

ASHDRINK. FRÉNETTE—A very economical drink which is said to be healthy. Its basis is ash leaves. The recipe is as follows:

Boil 2½ ounces (75 grams) of ashleaves and 1¾ ounces (55 grams) of roasted chicory in 3 quarts (3 litres) of water; dissolve in another pot 5 pounds (2 kg. 500 grams) of sugar and 1¼ ounces (40 grams) of citric acid in 2 quarts (2 litres) of water. Mix the two liquids; let cool, add ¾ ounce (25 grams) of yeast dissolved in water and pour the whole into a barrel. Add enough water to make 50 quarts (50 litres) and leave to ferment for 12 days. Keep in tightly closed bottles.

This makes a kind of lemonade with a certain amount of alcohol content at a very low price.

ASHES. CENDRES—Residue after combustion. Various foods are cooked in the ashes of a wood fire, notably chestnuts, potatoes and truffles.

ASIALIA. ASIALIE—A deficiency, absence of saliva. It occurs in certain diseases and in certain nervous conditions.

ASITIA. ASITIE—Forced abstinence. Loss of desire for food.

ASPARAGUS. Asperge—A genus of *Liliaceae*, containing more than 100 species found in temperate and warm regions of Europe and America.

Asparagus grows wild in meadows and bushy places, especially in sandy soil, over a great part of France, as well as on sandy coasts on the Atlantic and the Mediterranean side.

Officinal asparagus (or common asparagus) has been widely cultivated since time immemorial as a garden vegetable. Its young sprouts, or shoots, are eaten either whole or just the tips, i.e. the terminal buds.

In Spain, young shoots of a certain species armed with long and sharp-pointed thorns, which cover the stem and the branches, are also eaten.

A great number of asparagus varieties exist, but from the culinary point of view these varieties can be reduced to several main types, which are: *French asparagus*, of which the best known and the most delicious is *Argenteuil asparagus*; *Italian asparagus* or *purple Genoa asparagus*; *white Belgian asparagus*; *white German asparagus* and, finally, *green asparagus*, which is subdivided in two types, small, used for garnishes and known as *asparagus tips*, and large, which is prepared like *Argenteuil asparagus*.

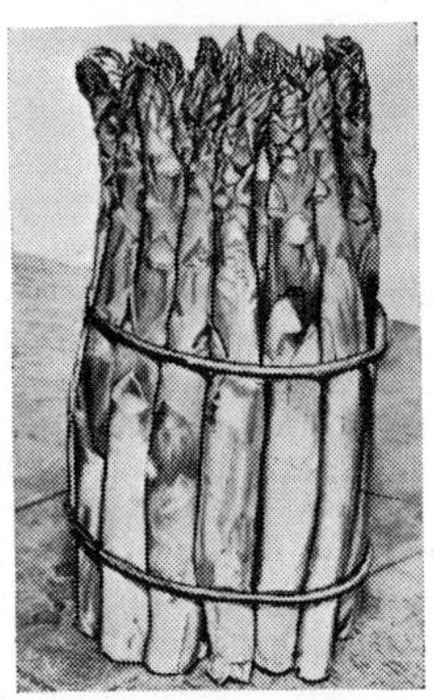

Lauris asparagus

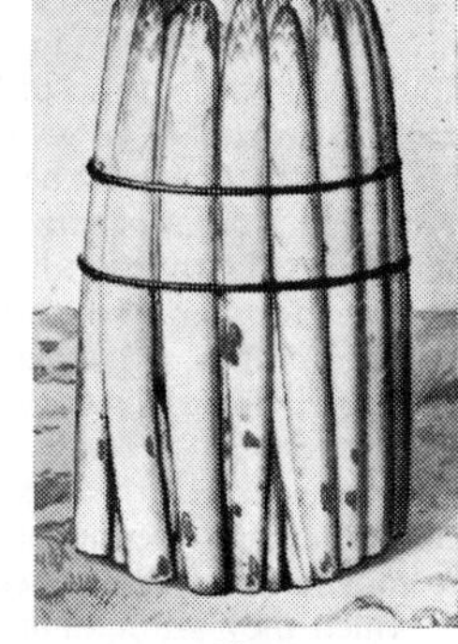

Argenteuil asparagus

From the month of February early asparagus can be found in France, and it is usually sold at very high prices.

The ancients knew and cultivated asparagus but seem to have had a predilection for wild asparagus.

In France, asparagus came into vogue during the reign of Louis XIV, thanks to Quintinie, who was the first to use asparagus beds to cater for the tastes of *Le Roi Soleil*. He was thus able to supply the royal kitchen with asparagus all the year round.

Method of preparation. The preparation of large asparagus is very simple. After scraping, or better still, peeling them, they are washed and tied into not-too-big bundles and put to cook in plenty of salted boiling water, allowing 1½ teaspoons (10 grams) of salt per quart (litre) of water. As soon as they are cooked, asparagus should be drained thoroughly and arranged on a napkin-covered dish, or on a special asparagus dish equipped with a strainer. Hot or cold asparagus is served with various sauces.

The duration of the cooking period, which varies between 18 and 22 minutes, depends on the nature of asparagus and also on the taste of the people for whom it is cooked. In principle, asparagus should not be overcooked, as this renders it watery and tasteless.

Note. At the end of the season asparagus becomes a little bitter and it is wise to put it into fresh water after it is cooked.

When asparagus is to be served cold, it should be dipped into cold water or left under a running tap to cool it. Generally speaking, for 4 persons from 4 to 5¼ pounds (2 kg. to 2 kg. 500 grams) of asparagus is allowed. For this quantity 1 to 1½ cups (3 to 4 decilitres) of sauce will be required.

Canned asparagus. Conserve d'asperges—This should not be attempted except with freshly gathered asparagus.

Scrape off the skin, dry carefully, *without washing*. Cut off the ends very evenly to have them all the same length. Arrange them in bundles choosing stalks of the same thickness to ensure even cooking.

Put the asparagus, matching them in thickness, into an asparagus boiling basket, the bundles put in standing and not too tightly packed. Boil in 8 per cent salted water in an asparagus boiler equipped with special devices controlling the movement of the basket.

Lower the basket so that the asparagus tips are immersed up to one-third of their length and allow to boil for 3 minutes.

Disengage the basket and drop it down lower into the boiler, so that two-thirds of the asparagus tips are immersed and boil for another 3 minutes.

Remove the basket and plunge into a tub of cold running water (the tub should be supplied with water from underneath in such a way that the jets of water cannot damage the asparagus tips). Leave the asparagus in this water for about an hour. Drain with great care.

Put them into cans or into glass jars, placing some heads up, others down. Cover with salted water, allowing ½ pound (300 grams) of refined salt to 10 quarts (10 litres).

Weight of cans	Cooking time in a 238°F. sterilizer	Cooking time in a bain-marie
1 pound (500 grams)	10 minutes	20 minutes
2 pounds (1 kilogram)	15 minutes	30 minutes
4 pounds (2 kilograms)	20 minutes	40 minutes

Canned green asparagus tips. Conserve de pointes d'asperges vertes—Divide the asparagus stalks into three parts: the base, the middle and the tips.

First put the bases (the hardest parts) into a saucepan of salted boiling water and boil them for 2 minutes. Then add the middle sections and boil for another 2 minutes. Finally, add the tips and boil for 2 minutes. Drain very carefully.

Put them into cans, cover with brine, in a proportion of ½ pound (300 grams) of purified salt to 10 quarts (10 litres) of water.

Weight of cans	Cooking time in a 230°F. sterilizer	Cooking time in a bain-marie
1 pound (500 grams)	10 minutes	20 minutes
2 pounds (1 kilogram)	15 minutes	30 minutes
4 pounds (2 kilograms)	—	40 minutes

Cream of asparagus soup. See SOUP, *Cream soups*.

Asparagus heaped in a croustade à la Carême. BUISSON D'ASPERGES EN CROUSTADE À LA CARÊME—Cook the tips of very thick white asparagus in salted water, keeping them a little underdone. Drain and dry on a napkin. Coat each one with a layer of aspic mayonnaise. Chill thoroughly in a refrigerator or in an ice-box.

Asparagus heaped in a croustade à la Carême

Arrange in a heap in a low flan shell, made of pie pastry and baked blind, and filled half-way with a salad of green asparagus tips and truffles, seasoned with oil and lemon juice.

Asparagus à la flamande. ASPERGES À LA FLAMANDE—Serve hot with melted butter and halves of hot hard boiled eggs served separately.

The guests mash the eggs and add them to the melted butter.

Asparagus fried in batter. FRITOT D'ASPERGES—Cook the tips of large white or green asparagus in salted boiling water for 5 minutes. Drain, dry and marinate for 30 minutes, in oil, lemon juice or vinegar, salt and pepper. At the last moment, dip the asparagus tips into a light batter and fry in deep fat, smoking hot. Drain, dry, season with fine salt and arrange in a heap on a napkin.

Asparagus à la Fontenelle. ASPERGES À LA FONTENELLE—Boil the asparagus in salted water and drain. Serve with melted butter.

After dipping the asparagus in melted butter, the guests dip them into a soft boiled egg.

Asparagus au gratin (*H. J. Heinz*)

Asparagus au gratin. ASPERGES AU GRATIN—Cook in salted water and drain thoroughly. Put in a fireproof dish, arranging them symmetrically in tiers.

Pour *Mornay sauce* (see SAUCE) over the tips. Cover the parts untouched by sauce with a piece of greaseproof paper. Sprinkle the sauce with grated Parmesan cheese and melted butter and brown the top. Remove the paper before serving.

Asparagus à la milanaise. ASPERGES À LA MILANAISE—Proceed as described in the recipe for *Asparagus au gratin*, but omitting Mornay sauce.

Asparagus à la Mornay. ASPERGES À LA MORNAY—Another name for *Asparagus au gratin*.

Asparagus with noisette butter. ASPERGES AU BEURRE NOISETTE—Cook the asparagus according to the usual method. Serve *Noisette butter* (see BUTTER) separately. Or else arrange cooked and well-drained asparagus on a dish (without a napkin). Keep warm in the oven. Just before serving sprinkle with sizzling *noisette butter*.

Asparagus à la polonaise. ASPERGES À LA POLONAISE—Proceed as described in the recipe for *Asparagus au gratin*, covering the tips with chopped yolks of hard boiled eggs and parsley.

When ready to serve, pour some sizzling *noisette butter* in which white freshly grated breadcrumbs have been fried until light golden.

Or else arrange the asparagus on an asparagus serving-dish. Serve butter *à la polonaise* separately.

Asparagus soufflé. See SOUFFLÉ, *Soufflé of various vegetables*.

Asparagus tips for garnishes. POINTES D'ASPERGES—Scrape, if necessary. Cut the tips into 1½-2 inch lengths and tie into bundles. Cook as described in the recipe for *Green asparagus tips*.

If this garnish is used for hot dishes, the asparagus tips should be added to the dishes at the very last moment, having been cooked in water and dressed with butter, or cream, as the case may be.

Asparagus makes an excellent garnish for eggs: scrambled, lightly boiled, *au plat*, poached or in an omelette; for some fish dishes; for meat served in small portions: cutlets, escalopes, noisettes, small fillets, tournedos, etc.; for calf's sweetbreads and, finally, for fowls and chickens.

When asparagus tips are intended for garnishes or cold salads, they must be dipped in cold water as soon as they are cooked and well drained. Depending on the final use for which they are intended, they can be seasoned with vinaigrette, or mayonnaise, or bound with meat jelly.

Asparagus tips in butter. POINTES D'ASPERGES AU BEURRE—Cook the diced part of the asparagus, drain well and put into a pan and dry them for a few moments on the fire. Add to them for ½ pound (250 grams) asparagus 5 tablespoons (75 grams) of butter divided into very small pieces. Stir gently so as not to damage the asparagus. Heap in a *timbale*, shallow platter or a vegetable dish. Put on top the tips, heated in salted water and untied.

Green asparagus tips. POINTES D'ASPERGES VERTES—Break off the hard stalks, keeping the tender parts of green asparagus. Tie into bundles of 8 to 10 shoots. Cut into dice the lower part of these bundles, keeping the actual tips tied together.

Put the diced asparagus to cook in salted boiling water. After 4 minutes of boiling, add the bundles of tips. Cook, boiling briskly, with the saucepan uncovered, from 6 to 8 minutes. Drain the diced asparagus and the bundles. Dip in cold water to cool. Proceed as indicated in the recipe.

Purée of green asparagus. PURÉE D'ASPERGES VERTES—Rub through a fine sieve asparagus tips cooked in fast-boiling salted water and drained. Heat the purée, add butter and cream, according to individual recipes. This purée is used as a garnish.

White asparagus with fried bread. CROÛTE GRATINÉE AUX ASPERGES BLANCHES—Blanch 1 pound (500 grams) of white asparagus tips in salted water for 8 minutes, drain and simmer in butter until done. Cut some stale de-crusted bread into slices 4 inches long and 2½ inches wide and fry in butter. Put 6 to 8 asparagus tips on each slice of fried bread, sprinkle with grated Parmesan cheese, pour on the butter in which the asparagus was cooked and brown the top lightly.

White asparagus with melted butter. ASPERGES BLANCHES AU BEURRE FONDU—Cook the asparagus in salted water, drain and serve, piping hot, with warm melted butter. The butter should be melted on a gentle heat and seasoned with salt, pepper and a dash of lemon juice.

Purée of white asparagus. PURÉE D'ASPERGES BLANCHES —Blanch 1 pound (500 grams) of white asparagus tips for 8 minutes and simmer lightly in butter. Season with salt and pepper. Moisten with 1-1½ cups (2½ decilitres) of thick *Béchamel* (see SAUCE). Boil for 15 minutes. Rub through a fine sieve. Heat the purée and add butter.

This purée is used as a garnish for poached or lightly boiled eggs, for small pieces of meat, for chicken, for filling patties, tartlets and other preparations of a similar nature.

White asparagus salad. SALADE D'ASPERGES BLANCHES— Cook the asparagus tips in salted water. Drain, dip in cold water, drain again and dry. Arrange in a salad bowl or an *hors-d'oeuvre* dish. Pour over well-whisked vinaigrette, or a mixture of oil, lemon juice, salt and pepper, all well whisked, so that the sauce covers the asparagus in a layer. Serve very cold.

White asparagus with cold sauces. ASPERGES BLANCHES AVEC SAUCES FROIDES—Cool the asparagus. Arrange on an asparagus serving dish. Serve with one of the following sauces: *mayonnaise*, *mustard*, *tartare*, *vinaigrette*. See SAUCE.

White asparagus with hot sauces. ASPERGES BLANCHES AVEC SAUCES CHAUDES—Boil the asparagus in salted water and drain. Serve separately one of the sauces recommended, such as *butter*, *bâtarde*, *Chantilly*, *cream*, *hollandaise*, *maltaise*, *mousseuse*, *noisette*. See SAUCE, *White sauces*.

ASPERULA. ASPÉRULE—Plant both useful and pleasant. It is also called *sweet woodruff*, *mugwort*, *sweet grass* and *quinsy wort*. Its white flowers are taken as an infusion and are also used for distilling liqueurs.

In some northern countries it is also used for flavouring sausages.

ASPIC—Term which applies to a way of arranging cold dishes. It consists of putting slices or fillets of chicken, game, various meats, fish, vegetables, fruit, etc., into moulded jelly.

Many authors believe that this name comes from the serpent called asp, 'whose icy coldness recalls that of the jelly'. This explanation seems to be a trifle far-fetched. It makes more sense to presume that it is derived from the Greek word *aspis*, which means buckler or shield. It was, in fact, in this form that the first moulds were made; others were made in the shape of a coiled snake, probably to justify the name aspic.

Whatever its origin may be, the word aspic is applied to very different preparations. We speak, for instance, of *foie gras in aspic*, or *chicken in aspic*, or *partridge in aspic*, or *lobster in aspic*, or *fillets of sole in aspic*.

For methods of aspic preparations of meat, chicken, game, shell-fish, fish, see the following entries in their alphabetical order: CHICKEN, LOBSTER, PHEASANT, SHRIMP, SOLE.

Sweet dishes made of fruit and set in jelly moulds are also called *aspics*. The word aspic is used, too, for the actual jelly. See JELLY.

In his book devoted to cold entrées, Antonin Carême describes the method of preparing aspic jelly as follows: 'After having cleaned and singed two chickens, wash them thoroughly, then truss, tucking the legs under, and place into a small *marmite*,* with a round of veal, some other veal trimmings and a little ham. Add six boned and blanched calf's feet, fill the *marmite* with water and leave to cook on the edge of the stove. By this process a much lighter aspic is obtained, which is, consequently, easier to clarify. After having skimmed it thoroughly, add half a bay leaf, a little thyme and basil, a good bunch of parsley and spring onions, two carrots and two onions. Keep the jelly simmering gently for four hours.

'When the aspic is ready, strain it through a napkin. Boil down (reduce) by half a ragoût spoonful of good tarragon vinegar, with a pinch of mignonette, four cloves, a little mace and a little salt. Pour the jelly over this and remove from the stove. (This step may be omitted.)

'Whisk 4 whites of egg with a glass of good white wine or Madeira and the same amount of veal stock if you wish to give it some colour. If not, omit the veal stock. When this mixture is well whisked, add it to the jelly, which you have replaced on a high flame, and stir constantly with an egg-whisk until boiling is established, then draw back to the edge of the stove or turn heat down to very low.

'Cover, to make the white of egg rise to the surface of the jelly, and leave to simmer for 2 minutes, after which it should be clear.

'As soon as the jelly begins to boil and the whites are well mixed, it should be tasted and a little salt added, if necessary.

'After having strained the aspic through a napkin (a thin napkin, rinsed out in water and wrung out well) tied to the four legs of a wooden stool, or an upturned chair, use it as indicated for each speciality.'

This recipe of Carême's is perfectly explicit. It describes the various phases of the preparation of aspic jelly: the method of cooking and the method of clarifying. In another article, Carême tells us how aspic jellies should be coloured:

'One of the principal presentations of cold dishes consists of these good, clarified, transparent jellies of two colours only—one should be white and the other of a good strong colour.' And, always precise in his instructions, the master tells us, in a marginal note, how the great Laguipière achieved perfect colourings for his jellies: 'He melted some good sieved sugar and, without moistening it, let it colour little by little on red-hot cinders, which takes a quarter of an hour. When it is a good amber-red caramel, moisten with half a glass of water and put it on a livelier fire. After several minutes of boiling, you will have a very clear, beautiful amber-red caramel, totally unlike the bitter caramel which is allowed to get black on a high flame and which is commonly called "monkey's blood".'

Modern day practice can but draw inspiration from these lessons. And, in any case, modern methods differ very little from those of the past.

The stock for jellies, meat and meatless (see JELLIES), is made practically as it was then. The clarifying process differs a little. This can be judged from the recipe given under the entry entitled JELLIES and the one given below.

Clarification of aspic jelly. To clarify 5 quarts (5 litres) of jelly stock add 1 pound (500 grams) of lean minced beef and 3 whites of egg and put into a pan with a fairly flat bottom. Add a tablespoon of tarragon and a tablespoon of chervil, roughly chopped.

Stir with a whisk. Pour on the jelly stock which should be slightly tepid, with *all* the fat skimmed off. Bring to the boil whisking constantly.

As soon as boiling is established, remove to the edge of the stove. Simmer gently for 35 minutes.

Strain through a napkin (which should be rinsed out in water and thoroughly wrung out).

Jelly cut in this way must be sufficiently solid and very clear.

When a great number of croûtons have to be made, the jelly is poured out into a large shallow baking dish to set.

The strips of jelly to be cut up are placed flat on a damp cloth (moistened and wrung out), stretched out on the table, and are cut up with a knife if the croûtons are a rectilinear shape, or with a pastry-cutter if they are variously shaped.

Arrangements of aspic, after Carême

Aspic jelly can be flavoured with various dessert wines: Frontignan, Port, Sherry, Marsala, Madeira, Malvasia (Malvoisie).

These wines, which are only added to the jelly when it is tepid, are used in the proportion of $\frac{1}{3}$ cup (1 decilitre) per quart (litre) of jelly in the case of dessert wines, and $\frac{2}{3}$ cup (2 decilitres) in the case of Champagne, Sauternes, Alsatian, or other white wines.

All the instructions for making various aspic jellies will be found under entries entitled JELLIES, *Meat jellies*.

Aspics in moulds. Aspics are set in plain moulds, charlotte type moulds, or moulds with a hole in the middle, plain or patterned.

The bottom and the inner walls are coated with a thin layer of jelly, as indicated in each recipe. On the walls thus coated are put various decorative elements. These elements, which differ according to the type of aspics, are most frequently composed, for meat, chicken or game aspics, of truffles, white of hard boiled eggs, little pieces of cooked lean ham or salt beef tongue and for fish or crustacean aspics, of truffles, whites of hard boiled eggs, the coral or eggs of the crustaceans, or little pieces of smoked salmon.

All these decorations should be simple. A garnish of neat, round slivers of truffles, alternating with thin circles of whites of hard boiled eggs, makes a perfect pattern when seen through a transparent jelly.

Aspic croûtons. CROÛTONS DE GELÉE—Pieces of aspic cut as a rule into triangles, but sometimes in different shapes such as crescents, rectangles, medallions, etc.

The technical term *croûtonner de gelée* means to surround some cold article with croûtons of jelly correctly cut up.

Aspic of freshwater crayfish tails. ASPIC DE QUEUES D'ÉCREVISSES—Cook the crayfish *à la mirepoix*.* Shell the tails and arrange them in a plain round mould lined with jelly. Fill the mould either with a *crayfish mousse** or a *Russian salad* (see SALAD). Chill on ice.

Aspic of fish. ASPIC DE POISSONS—Aspic of fish can be made with fish of various kinds, cut in fillets, slices or medallions. Fill the middle of the aspic dishes either with a fish mousse composition appropriate for the particular dish, with Russian salad, or with any other mixture normally used for cold dishes.

Aspic of foie gras (I). ASPIC DE FOIE GRAS—Put into a plain round mould, lined with jelly, uniform slices of foie gras, garnished with large slivers of truffles.

Fill the mould with half-set jelly. Leave on ice to set. Serve on a round plate or in a glass dish.

Aspic of foie gras (II). ASPIC DE FOIE GRAS—Line the walls of a plain mould with truffles cut into neat round slices, round pieces of ham or pickled tongue and, if desired, rings of white of hard boiled eggs. Coat the mould with port-flavoured jelly (or jelly flavoured with any other heavy wine).

Fill the mould with jelly. Chill on ice or in the refrigerator.

Turn out the aspic straight on to a serving dish or on to a slice of buttered bread (cut to the shape of the aspic).

Chicken in aspic (*Robert Carrier*)

Surround with chopped jelly. Decorate the dish with a border of jelly triangles.

This aspic can also be made by filling the mould with slices of foie gras or shell-shaped pieces of foie gras cut out with a shell-shaped scoop.

A fluted mould can equally well be used for this aspic.

Aspic of frogs' legs à l'ancienne. ASPIC DE GRENOUILLES À L'ANCIENNE—Poach trimmed frogs' legs in white wine flavoured with a sprig of thyme and a little bay leaf. Leave to cool in their liquor.

Drain, dry and coat half of them completely with a *White chaud-froid sauce* (based on meatless stock), and the other half with a chaud-froid sauce coloured with crayfish butter. See SAUCE, *Compound sauces*.

Put the frogs' legs on a wire tray, one by one, and leave them to get quite cold. Decorate with truffles cut in thin round slices, or in any other shape. Coat with aspic jelly.

Arrange frogs' legs around the walls of a plain mould, coated with jelly, following the directions for the general method of arranging aspic dishes, and alternating with peeled crayfish tails.

Fill the middle of the mould with a *Parisian salad* (see SALAD), dressed with mayonnaise strengthened with gelatine.

Finish by pouring a thin layer of aspic jelly over the whole and chill on ice.

To serve: turn out on to a round dish. Decorate with a border of aspic jelly *croûtons*.*

Little chicken aspics (*Brown and Polson*)

Aspic of poultry and feathered game. ASPIC DE VOLAILLES —These aspics are prepared using slices of chicken or game, coated with white or brown chaud-froid sauces, according to the nature of the dish, and filling the mould either with a chicken or game mousse, or with some other mixture normally used for cold dishes. See CHICKEN, PHEASANT, PARTRIDGE.

Aspic of shrimps or other crustaceans. ASPIC DE CREVETTES—Coat the bottom and the walls of an aspic mould with very clear fish jelly. Decorate the walls of the mould with trimmed, pink, peeled shrimp tails and little pieces of truffles. Fill the middle of the mould with a cold shrimp mousse, mixed with shrimp tails and truffles in large dice. Fill the mould with jelly and leave on ice to set.

Crayfish aspics can be prepared in the same way, using trimmed crayfish tails and crayfish mousse. *Spiny lobster* or *lobster aspics* are made using slices of one or the other of these crustacea and the appropriate mousse.

ASSIETTE—See PLATE.

Assiette anglaise—An assortment of cold meats arranged on a plate or a dish.

In principle, this assortment consists of York ham, salt beef tongue, rib of beef or roast beef. Mortadella, galantine, etc., are sometimes added to it.

This meat is garnished with chopped jelly, cress and gherkins. The *assiette anglaise* is served chiefly at lunch.

The term *assiettes assorties* describes various preparations served as *hors-d'oeuvre*. This term, however, really belongs to the old cuisine. *Hors-d'oeuvre* are nowadays usually served in special *hors-d'oeuvre* dishes.

These *assiettes assorties* in the past also used to be called *assiettes volantes*.

Assiettes volantes—This term describes a selection of several articles on one plate in the manner of an *hors-d'oeuvre*, particularly various kinds of salty things cut in thin slices.

In the old days there used to be a course known as *assiettes volantes*, which consisted of a great number of preparations of very different kinds.

Assiettes garnies—At the beginning of the nineteenth century this term also applied to a dish. 'Lunch', says Carême, 'consisted of six *assiettes* (dishes), on which veal cutlets, fish, chicken, game, a side-dish of vegetables and soft boiled eggs were served'.

ASTI—Italian town situated about 25 miles from Turin. This town, which is the ancient *Asta Colonia* or *Asta Pompeia* of the Romans, is famous for its sparkling wine, made from moscato grapes, called *Asti Spumante*. See WINE.

Astragal
(a) Astragalus of Crete; (b) Liquorice vetch; (c) Fruit

ASTRAGAL (Milk vetch). ASTRAGALE—Many varieties of astragal grow in Asia; it is also found in the temperate regions of the Lebanon. One variety of milk vetch produces gum tragacanth, which is used in confectionery and pastry-making.

Another variety produces fruit in the form of pods which, before the seeds contained in them are formed, resemble worms. In the past these pods used to be added to salads, just to mystify the guests. These astragalus pods are also pickled in vinegar like capers.

There is yet another variety of astralagus, the seeds of which, when ripe, are used in cookery.

ASTRINGENT—Binding, contracting. The vegetable astringents owe their property to tannin. Among them are cutch, bark of oak, quinquina, leaves of walnut tree, of arbutus tree, of bramble, lemon juice, quinces, etc.

ASTRODERME—Sea-fish of an unusual appearance, yellowish-pink on the back and sides with black round spots, alternating with silvery spots on the belly. Young astrodermes have purplish-blue bodies and silvery bellies. This fish, called *feï d'Aermica* by Nice fishermen, is well known along the whole of the Mediterranean coast of France (Côte d'Azur).

It is chiefly used as an ingredient for bouillabaisse.

ATHENAEUS—Greek writer, born in Naucratis, in Egypt, under the reign of Marcus Aurelius. He was still living in the reign of Alexander Severus, towards the year 228 A.D.

Only one of his works has survived, entitled *Deipnosophistai* or *Specialists in Dining*, which is a gem of erudition, giving much information which we should otherwise lack in ancient history.

In the *Specialists in Dining* there are several passages relating to flowers and fruit and their various uses, both practical and pleasurable.

ATHÉNIENNE (A L')—Name applying to various dishes, all of which are usually flavoured with lightly-fried onion and are garnished with aubergines (egg-plants), tomatoes and sweet pimentos.

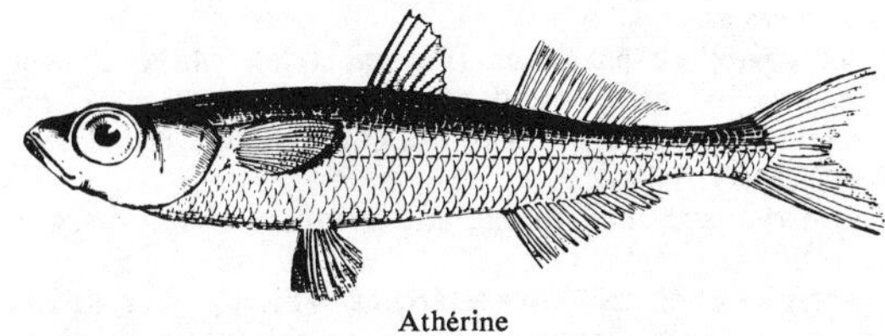

Athérine

ATHÉRINE—Little fish, with a long spindle-shaped body, covered with rounded scales at posterior end. Their sides have a silvery stripe. The head is flattened on the top, the upper jaw is shorter than the lower and the teeth are very small.

Two species of this fish are known on the coasts of France where they are called *prêtre* and *faux éperlan*. Common names in English are *silverside* and *sand-smelt*, and the fishermen take enormous catches. Other species are found in the estuaries and Mediterranean coast lakes. In the U.S.A., smelts correspond to this fish. Its flesh is quite delicate in flavour and athérines are usually fried in deep fat, but all recipes suitable for small bass can be applied to this fish.

ÂTRE (HEARTH-STONE)—This word is no longer used today except to describe the central part of the baker's or pastry-cook's oven.

In the past, when a great number of dishes were cooked in the fireplace, the part of the fireplace where the fire was actually made was called the *âtre* (hearth).

It was in the hearth that stews and other preparations which take a long time were slowly cooked, surrounded by hot coals.

All these dishes are today made in ovens heated by coal, gas, electricity or oil.

Quite a few gastronomes protest against these methods of cooking, maintaining that, prepared in this way, dishes cannot taste as good as when cooked by the old methods. Experience shows that there is nothing to this claim. When well-made utensils are used (and kitchen utensils have today reached a high point of perfection) food can be cooked successfully, whatever the product and whatever the method.

ATRIPLEX—Herbaceous plant of the same family as spinach, orach, and the goosefoot genus *Chenopodium*.

The atriplex is commonly known as garden orach; it is cultivated and grows all over France. This plant is prepared like spinach. See ORACH.

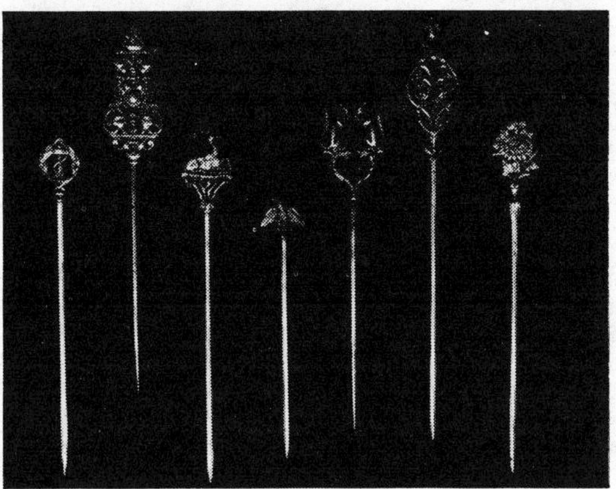

Antique attelets
(Collection of Dr. Gottschalk. *Photograph Larousse*)

ATTELET—This word comes from the Latin *hasta*, meaning staff, rod, and in the past was spelled *hatelet*. It is often used, quite incorrectly, to describe little metal skewers on which various small pieces of meat, sheeps' kidneys, lambs' sweetbreads, larks, etc. are threaded.

To be more precise, an *attelet* is a little utensil in the shape of a pin (or skewer), but with an ornamented top. These, with truffles, cocks' combs, crayfish and other articles threaded on them, are used solely for decorating hot or cold dishes served in a grand style.

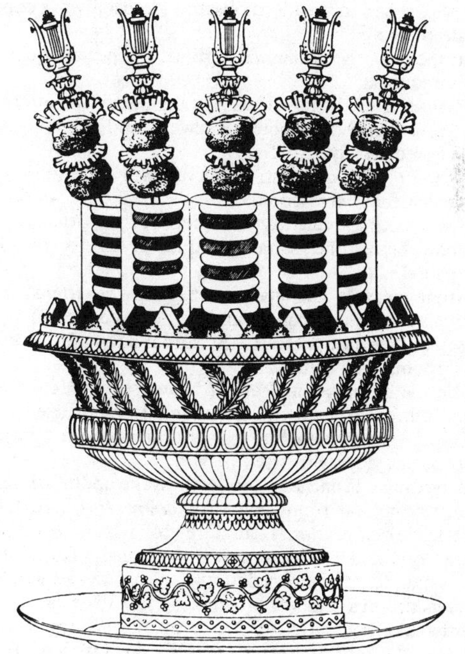

The use of attelets, after Carême

For arranging these grand *entrées*, Carême advocated the use of a great number of attelets. In modern culinary technique this means of decoration has been practically abandoned. Modern cooks disdain the use of anything which is not actually edible.

We hasten to add that, no doubt, the attelets accompanying Carême's *entrées* and *removes* were edible and we are only too ready to admit that these arrangements certainly were beautiful. But requirements of modern service, as well as a new orientation of taste, have forced the modern cook to look for other methods of dressing dishes.

ATTENDU—French culinary term applied to a dish or beverage the consumption of which is intentionally postponed to improve it. Thus a pheasant should be *attendu* (kept hung) before being eaten.

ATTEREAU (Skewer)—In his *Dictionnaire de cuisine et d'économie* (Paris, 1836), Burnet, one-time steward of the Royal Household, gives the following definition of *attereau*: 'Name which keepers of eating houses attribute to a kind of ragoût made of fillet of veal, cut in very thin slices: they are studded with lardoons and are cooked in a pie-dish with a little stock poured over them'.

This definition seems rather erroneous, all the more astonishing because Carême, in his works published before Burnet's dictionary, gives a recipe for attereau, in particular for ox palate *en attereau*, and the method of preparation he describes shows that this dish is in no way a ragoût. And even before Carême, *attereaux* were prepared in a way which differs little from the present-day practice.

At the present time, *attereau*, which describes first of all a metal skewer on which various articles were threaded, is also used to described the dish itself. This dish is mostly served as *hors-d'oeuvre*, but can, supplemented by a garnish, be served as a small *entrée*.

The attereaux differ distinctly from *brochettes* by the fact that they are dipped in a sauce, to give them a firm coating, rolled in breadcrumbs and almost always cooked by deep frying.

In the past the *attereaux* were set in special square or plain moulds.

Various ingredients which go to make up the attereaux can be cooked on wooden skewers and after cooking transferred to silver attelets.

The attereaux can also be served without the skewers on which they were cooked.

Sweet courses can also be prepared *en attereau*, the method being the same as that given for savoury *attereaux*.

Attereaux à la chalonaise. Make up the *attereaux* by threading on cocks' combs and kidneys, cooked in *White court-bouillon* (see COURT-BOUILLON), and drained, mushrooms and truffles.

Dip the *attereaux* in *Villeroi sauce* (see SAUCE). Roll them in breadcrumbs and fry in smoking hot deep fat.

Drain, season with fine salt and arrange on a napkin or paper doyley, with fried parsley.

Attereaux à la duchesse (dessert). Make up the *attereaux* by threading on round slices of *crème frite* (see CUSTARD, *Fried custard*) mixture to which 2 crushed macaroons and 1 tablespoon of crystallised fruit, cut in very small dice and steeped in rum, have been added. Roll in breadcrumbs and fry in smoking hot deep fat.

Attereaux à l'écossaise. Make up the *attereaux* using pieces of *Pickled ox tongue* (see OFFAL OR VARIETY MEATS), mushrooms and rather thick slices of truffles. Finish as described in the recipe for *Attereaux à la chalonaise*.

Attereaux à la maraîchère. Make up the *attereaux*, using pieces of turnip-rooted celery (celeriac), previously simmered in butter, mushrooms and pieces of cooked ham. Finish as described in the recipe for *Attereaux à la chalonaise*.

Attereaux à la niçoise. Make up the *attereaux*, using large stoned olives, stuffed with a purée of anchovies, mushrooms and pieces of pickled tunny. Dip them into *Villeroi sauce* with a tablespoon of concentrated tomato purée and chopped tarragon added to it. Finish as described in the recipe for *Attereaux à la chalonaise*.

Attereaux à la normande. Make up the *attereaux* by threading on plump mussels cooked *à la marinière*, drained and stuffed with a finely pounded fish forcemeat, and mushrooms cut in round slices. Finish as described in the recipe for *Attereaux à la chalonaise*.

Attereaux à la piémontaise. Make up the *attereaux*, using round slices or square pieces of polenta cooked with butter and rather thick slices of truffles. See POLENTA.

Dip them in egg and breadcrumbs and deep fry in sizzling fat.

Attereaux à la Saint-Hubert. Make up the *attereaux* by threading on slices of pheasant, grouse, or any other winged game, sliced mushrooms and pieces of cooked lean ham. Dip the *attereaux* into *Villeroi sauce* (see SAUCE) with concentrated game stock reduced to a *fumet** added to it, and finish as described in the recipe for *Attereaux à la chalonaise*.

Attereaux au parmesan (Parma style). Make up the *attereaux* by using round or square pieces of semolina, cooked with butter, and round slices of Gruyère cheese. See SEMOLINA.

Dip the *attereaux* in egg and breadcrumbs and fry in deep fat.

Attereaux of calf's sweetbreads Villeroi. ATTEREAUX DE RIS DE VEAU VILLEROI—Make up the *attereaux* using uniform pieces of calf's sweetbreads, previously braised in a *White court-bouillon* (see COURT-BOUILLON). Finish as described in the recipe for *Attereaux à la chalonaise*.

Attereaux of chicken livers à la mirepoix. ATTEREAUX DE FOIES DE VOLAILLE À LA MIREPOIX—Make up the *attereaux* by threading on chicken livers, fried in butter, drained and cooled, pieces of cooked lean ham, and mushrooms cut in round slices. Coat the *attereaux* with a *fondue** of root vegetables cut into very small cubes called *mirepoix*,* roll in breadcrumbs and finish as described in the recipe for *Attereaux à la chalonaise*.

Attereaux of lambs' brains Villeroi. ATTEREAUX DE CERVELLE D'AGNEAU VILLEROI—Make up the *attereaux* by threading on pieces of lambs' brains, previously cooked in *White court-bouillon* (see COURT-BOUILLON), allowed to cool and drained. Before threading them on, season the pieces of brains with salt, pepper, a spoonful of oil, a few drops of lemon juice and a little chopped parsley. Finish as described in the recipe for *Attereaux à la chalonaise*.

Attereaux of calves' brains are prepared in the same manner.

Attereaux of lambs' sweetbreads Villeroi. ATTEREAUX DE RIS D'AGNEAU VILLEROI—Make up the *attereaux* by threading on lambs' sweetbreads, previously braised in *White court-bouillon* (see COURT-BOUILLON). Finish off as described in the recipe for *Attereaux à la chalonaise*.

Attereaux à la Villeroi can, in addition to the basic element, also contain mushrooms cooked in *White mushroom court-bouillon* and cut in round slices.

Attereaux of ox palate. ATTEREAUX DE PALAIS DE BOEUF—Cut the ox palate, cooked as described under *Ox palate*, into little round slices. Put them on skewers, in alternate rows with fried mushroom heads and slivers of truffles.

Coat the skewers (with the ingredients threaded on them) in *Villeroi sauce* (see SAUCE). Allow to cool. Dip them in egg and breadcrumbs and roll into cylindrical shape.

When ready, deep fry in sizzling fat. Arrange on a napkin, garnish with fried parsley. Serve *Périgueux sauce* (see SAUCE) separately.

Attereaux of lambs' sweetbreads Villeroi

Attereaux of oysters Monselet. ATTEREAUX D'HUÎTRES MONSELET—Make up the *attereaux* by threading on oysters, previously poached and drained, mushrooms, cooked and cut in round slices, and slices of truffles cut rather thick. Finish as described in the recipe for *Attereaux of brains*, using *Villeroi sauce* (see SAUCE) based on fish stock boiled down to a *fumet*.*

Attereaux of pineapple (dessert). ATTEREAUX D'ANANAS —Make up the *attereaux* by threading on pieces of pineapple. Dip them into a *crème frite* (see CUSTARD, *Fried custard*) mixture and breadcrumbs. Fry in smoking hot deep fat. Drain and sprinkle with sugar. Serve *Apricot sauce* (see SAUCE, DESSERT SAUCES) laced with kirsch at the same time.

Attereaux of salmon. See SALMON.

Attereaux Pompadour (dessert)—Make up the *attereaux* by threading on round slices of stale brioche alternating with apricot halves, cooked in syrup and well drained. Dip them in a *crème frite* (see CUSTARD, *Fried custard*) mixture flavoured with kirsch. Roll in breadcrumbs and fry in smoking hot deep fat. Drain and dredge with sugar.

Attereaux Victoria (dessert)—Make up the *attereaux* by threading on round slices of plum pudding, alternating with round slices of cooking apples steeped in rum. Dip in egg and breadcrumbs and fry in smoking hot deep fat. Drain and dredge with sugar.

AUBENAS—Small town in the Ardèche department where truffles are found which, although not rivalling the flavour of the Périgord product, are excellent.

Marrons glacés and other greatly prized chestnut preserves are also made at Aubenas.

AUBERGINE OR EGG-PLANT—Fruit of a plant originating in India known also in France under the name of *melongena* and *morelle*. It has been cultivated in France since the beginning of the seventeeth century. In U.S.A. it is almost always called egg-plant.

There is a great number of varieties of this plant.

The best known, or at least the most used in cookery, is the *long purple*, which is used as a vegetable and as a garnish. Among other edible varieties are: the *Barbentane aubergine*, the *round purple aubergine*, the *giant New York aubergine* and the *round Chinese aubergine*.

Methods of preparation. There are many recipes for cooking aubergines (egg-plant). The initial preparation varies greatly.

When this vegetable is to be stewed, baked in the oven or fried, it must be steeped in salt for 30 minutes to make its excess water ooze out.

After this the aubergine is thoroughly dried and cooked as indicated in the recipes.

Various uses. Aubergines, cut in dice and fried in butter or oil, can be used as a garnish for the following: eggs (*sur le plat*, scrambled, poached, in omelette or fried), fish *meunière*, lamb or mutton chops or cutlets or noisettes, tournedos and chicken, fried or *en cocotte* (see CHICKEN). Sliced in halves lengthways, fried or grilled, they can be used for arranging poached eggs and fillets of fish. Peeled, cut in thick round slices and fried or grilled, they can be used as a foundation for escalopes, noisettes, tournedos and other small pieces of meat.

Varieties of aubergines

(1) Long purple (2) Very early Barbentane
(3) Very large round purple (4) Very early dwarf purple

Aubergines or egg-plant à la crème—Peel 2 good firm aubergines. Cut them in round slices $\frac{1}{4}$ inch thick and steep in salt for 30 minutes. Dry and simmer (stew) in butter in a sauté or heavy frying-pan.

At the last moment add ½ cup (1½ decilitres) of cream sauce. Stir, taking care not to damage the aubergines. Arrange in a vegetable dish. Dilute the pan juices with 1 cup (3 decilitres) of cream. Boil down by half, take off the fire and add 3 tablespoons (50 grams) of fresh butter. Strain and pour over the aubergines.

Fried aubergines or egg-plant. AUBERGINES FRITES—Cut the aubergines into thin round slices, dredge with flour and plunge them into a deep pan of sizzling oil.

Drain, season with fine salt and arrange on a napkin.

Aubergines intended for deep frying can also be cut into thick square pieces, or can be cut fan-wise.

Aubergines or egg-plant au gratin—Cut the aubergines in half lengthways. Make a few shallow incisions and leave in a dish with salt.

Fry in sizzling oil. Drain and with a spoon carefully scoop out the pulp without damaging the outside skin. Chop the pulp and add to it an equal quantity of *duxelles** mixture and a tablespoon of chopped parsley.

Fill the aubergine skins with this mixture and put into a buttered or oiled fireproof dish. Sprinkle with finely-grated breadcrumbs, fresh or toasted, and melted butter or oil and brown the top.

When cooked, pipe a border of *demi-glacé** around the aubergines.

Aubergines or egg-plant au gratin à la catalane—Fill aubergine halves with their chopped pulp with one chopped hard boiled egg, a tablespoon of chopped onion lightly fried in oil, and a tablespoon of finely grated breadcrumbs, mixed with chopped parsley and garlic, added to it. Finish cooking as above.

Aubergines or egg-plant au gratin à l'italienne—Fill the aubergine halves with their chopped pulp mixed with an equal quantity of risotto and a little chopped parsley and garlic. Finish cooking as above.

Aubergines or egg-plant au gratin à la languedocienne—Fill the aubergine halves with their chopped pulp mixed with sausage meat and chopped parsley and garlic. Finish cooking as above.

Aubergines or egg-plant au gratin à la portugaise—Fill the aubergine halves with their chopped pulp mixed with an equal quantity of chopped tomatoes lightly fried in butter with chopped onion, parsley and garlic. Finish cooking as above.

Aubergines or egg-plant au gratin à la reine—Fill the aubergine halves with their chopped pulp mixed with an equal quantity of *salpicon** of chicken bound with 2 tablespoons of thick *Velouté sauce* (see SAUCE). Finish cooking as above.

Aubergines or egg-plant au gratin à la toulousaine—Peel the aubergines, cut into thick slices, across or lengthways; leave in a dish sprinkled with salt. Dry, toss in a pan of hot oil.

Arrange in layers in a fireproof dish, in rows, alternating with an equal amount of tomatoes cut in half and also tossed in oil.

Sprinkle generously with freshly grated breadcrumbs mixed with chopped garlic and parsley. Pour on a little oil and brown in the oven. This dish is sometimes also called *Aubergines à la languedocienne*.

Aubergines or egg-plant au gratin à la turque—Fill aubergine halves with their chopped pulp mixed with an equal quantity of braised chopped mutton and rice cooked in water (taking these ingredients in equal proportions). Add chopped garlic and parsley and a small pinch of cayenne. Brown the top. When cooked, pipe a border of tomato sauce around the aubergines.

Aubergines or egg-plant in gravy. AUBERGINES AU JUS—Proceed as described in the recipe given for *Aubergines à la crème* but substitute thickened veal gravy.

Aubergines or egg-plant à la grecque (hors-d'oeuvre)—Peel 2 large aubergines, cut in dice or thick square pieces. Throw them, a few at a time, into a *court-bouillon** prepared as described in the recipe for *Artichokes à la grecque*.* Bring to a full boil. Then cook for 12 to 15 minutes. Transfer into a *terrine* with the liquor. Serve in an *hors-d'oeuvre* dish.

Grilled aubergines or egg-plant. AUBERGINES GRILLÉES—Peel the aubergines, cut them into thick slices, across or lengthways, leave to stand in a dish with salt. Dry, brush with oil and grill on a gentle heat.

If these aubergines are intended to be served as a vegetable, arrange them in a crown on a round dish and dab with a few tablespoons of *Maître d'hôtel butter*. See BUTTER.

Aubergines or egg-plant Imam Baaldi (Turkish cookery)—'Take good sound aubergines, slit them along their entire length, *without peeling them*, and scoop out some of the pulp.

'Prepare a stuffing composed of aubergine pulp, tomatoes, onions and currants, fry this mixture in oil and fill the aubergines with it.

'As soon as the aubergines are filled with the stuffing, put them into an earthenware dish and pour on enough oil to cover them completely. Add a little thyme and bay leaf to the oil. Cook for three hours on a low fire until the aubergines are quite soft. Allow to cool. This dish should be served very cold. If possible, prepare it the day before it is wanted, to allow the aubergines to saturate in the oil.'

Imam Baaldi in Turkish means 'the priest has fainted'. According to an anecdote connected with oriental cookery, when aubergines prepared in this manner were offered to a certain imam, he was so moved by the fragrance of the dish that he fainted from sheer gastronomical joy.

Aubergines or egg-plant à l'ornaise—Cut the aubergines into chunks about 2 inches long, make a few slits in them and leave to stand in a dish with salt.

Dry, cook in oil and drain. Scoop out the pulp, chop it and mix it with an equal quantity of rice cooked in oil or butter, with diced sweet peppers, tomato sauce and chopped parsley and garlic added to it.

Fill the chunks with this mixture. Arrange them in an oiled fireproof dish, scatter breadcrumbs on top, sprinkle with oil and brown the top.

Aubergine or egg-plant purée (garnish). PURÉE D'AUBERGINES—Peel the aubergines, cut them in slices across and leave to stand in a dish with salt. Dry and put to cook in a covered casserole with a little butter and salt.

Rub through a fine sieve. Heat the purée, add 2 tablespoons of butter and transfer into a vegetable dish.

A few tablespoons of thick *Béchamel* (see SAUCE) can be added to the aubergines before rubbing them through a sieve. The purée will thus have a more substantial consistency and be whiter.

Aubergine or egg-plant salad. SALADE D'AUBERGINES—Peel the aubergines, cut into thin slices and leave to stand in a dish with salt. Dry, season *à la vinaigrette*,* and add chopped chervil and tarragon.

Note. This salad can also be prepared of aubergines cooked in salted water, drained and dried.

Sautéed aubergines or egg-plant. AUBERGINES SAUTÉES—Peel the aubergines and cut them into pieces ¾-inch square. Leave to stand in a dish with salt. Dry, dredge with flour and sauté them on a brisk fire, in oil, butter or other fat, according to taste.

Serve in a vegetable dish sprinkled with chopped parsley.

Aubergines (egg-plant) Imam Baaldi (*Robert Carrier*)

Aubergines or egg-plant soufflées—Prepare the aubergines as described in the recipe for *Aubergines au gratin*. Rub the scooped-out pulp through a sieve. Add an equal quantity of thick *Béchamel*. See SAUCE.

Bind with yolks of egg and season with salt, pepper and a little grated nutmeg. At the last moment, incorporate whites of egg whisked into a stiff froth.

Fill the aubergine skins with this mixture and put them into a fireproof dish.

Cook in a moderate oven from 8 to 10 minutes. Serve at once.

Aubergines or egg-plant soufflées à la hongroise—Proceed as above, adding 2 tablespoons of chopped onion lightly fried in butter and seasoned with paprika to the filling.

Aubergines or egg-plant soufflées au parmesan—As above adding 2 tablespoons of grated Parmesan cheese to the filling.

AUBLET—A name given in some parts of France to *bleak*, a small river fish of the carp family.

AUDE—This department is formed of the lower part of Languedoc, a region where, from time immemorial, good cookery has been held in great esteem.

Among the excellent specialities of Aude (which will be found in their alphabetical order) there is a world-famous dish called the *cassoulet*. There are two kinds of cassoulet in Aude—the cassoulet of Castelnaudary and cassoulet of Carcassonne—and in addition there is yet another, in Languedoc, the cassoulet of Toulouse. Their origin goes back much further than is generally believed, because, according to reliable historians, white beans, introduced by the Arabs, were cultivated in Gallia Narbonensis long before beans were brought from America. The Arabs taught the inhabitants of that country to prepare a *mutton ragoût with white beans*, which can be considered the ancestor of the present-day cassoulet.

See CASSOULET for further details of this culinary glory of the Provence region.

AUK. ALQUE—Name of birds of the great order *Charadriiformes*, of which several species have become extinct. The *little auk* measures only 15 inches when fully grown. Its wings are equipped for flying which enables the bird to escape from the relentless pursuit of fishermen hunting it.

Although originating in arctic regions, it is frequently to be seen, in autumn and winter, on the coasts of England, Scotland, Belgium and France. It migrates even as far as Spain, Portugal, Italy and Algeria. Not infrequently it breeds on the French ocean coasts. The Icelanders call it *Alka* (*aalga*) or *klumba*. The flesh and fat of these birds are greatly valued by fishermen, who snare them among the rocks where they choose to nest.

AUNIS AND SAINTONGE—The region of Aunis has fertile well-cultivated lands where crops of cereals, vegetables and fruit of the first quality are gathered.

Animals raised for food in this region produce meat of excellent quality, including some very good lamb.

From the neighbouring sea and lakes come fish and shellfish famous for their succulence.

Among the specialities of this district are the oysters of Marennes, La Tremblade and of Château d'Oléron, white or stained with fine green weed from the fattening ponds, which are considered the best in the world; the *Portuguese oysters* which are bred here have a delicious flavour.

A great number of other shellfish is also found at Aunis, including mussels and clams of Cléron and La Rochelle, cockles which are found in the green weed of the fattening ponds at Marennes, all excellent shellfish. There are also prawns (*salicoques*) which are locally called *chevrettes* and shrimps which are called *boucs*. Among the many fish found in this region (La Rochelle, after Boulogne, is the greatest fishing port in France) are hake coalfish (U.S.A. pollock), soles which, sold immediately after being caught and not having been trawled, are excellent, fresh sardines known as Royan sardines which enjoy a universal reputation, grey mullet, called *meuils* locally, which have very white and delicate flesh, and brill (U.S.A. sea-perch).

In the Charente and Sèvre Niortaise and their tributaries, there are eels, which have a delicate flesh. These are cooked here in the best manner possible, stewed or *en matelote*.

Fruit and vegetables are particularly good. Garden peas of Aunis have the reputation of being tender and sweet and it is this variety of peas which is canned at Bordeaux and La Roche-sur-Yon. Broad beans from Marennes and the island of Oléron are considered the best in the world. Kidney beans and red beans (*mogettes*) are excellent.

The orchard and vegetable garden produce includes the *brugnons* (nectarines) of Saintonge, the apples of Saint-Porchaire (*reinettes grises* and *clochard*, which are exported to England), white *chasselas* grapes, cultivated mushrooms and other mushrooms such as *cèpes*, Saintonge oranges, *milk agarics*, *brunettes* (*psalliota*), *pleurote du panicot* (argouane), oyster mushroom, etc.

Ground and winged game of this region is of excellent quality.

First quality butter is made in Aunis, which can be compared to the best Normandy butter.

Culinary specialities. The *mouclade* (mussels *à la crème*), *mussel soup*, *roast mussels* (cooked on cinders), *oysters with sausages*, *razor-fish soup* (solen), *razor-fish* stuffed with breadcrumbs mixed with chopped garlic and parsley and browned on the top, *scallops aux fines herbes*, *ragoûts of lavagnons*, *small cuttle-fish fried in deep fat*, *deep fried crameou* (crabs which have shed their shells), *hake soup* (made with the fish-head), the *chaudrée* (*matelote* resembling the Boulogne codière), *roast eel*, *fried eels du Mignon*.

Special meat and poultry dishes include chicken fricassée with onions and potatoes, the *civet* of Aunis which is made of pig's fry, a *salmi* of sea-birds, various pork butchery produce; *rillettes* (potted pork), head cheese, *pâtés* and *terrines*, and white and black pudding.

Other special dishes of this region include *roast garlic*, cooked on the cinders, which is eaten with butter, *curds à la chardonnette*, *jonchée*, a kind of cream cheese made of ewe's or goat's milk, various *fouaces* (scones) and *coireaux* (made of maize flour), *la fouée* (oil seed cake), *gâteau d'Assemblée*, Easter gâteau, *Taillebourg brioches*, grape jelly, Pons rusks, Frangipane tart.

Wines. Saintonge produces table wines of average quality, almost all of which are used for distilling purposes. In a coastal stretch, about 12 miles wide, from the Vendée to nearly Royan, grapes are grown from which brandies of the *bois communs* category are distilled. In another stretch of land of about the same size, slightly further away from the sea, grapes are gathered which go into the making of brandies of the *bois ordinaires* category, whilst in a third stretch which includes Saint-Jean-d'Angély, and all the south and east of Saintogne touching Angoumois, grapes are cultivated which produce brandies of the *bons bois*, *fins bois*, and even fine champagne categories.

In this region, the proprietors of vineyards make a

liqueur wine for themselves and their friends, white or sometimes red, which is locally called *pineau*. It is made by pouring local brandy on the must during fermentation.

Not to be overlooked, too, is the angelica liqueur which is a speciality of Matha.

AURILLAC—Town in the Auvergne region, which is the centre of the production of *Cantal* cheese.

AURIOL—Name for mackerel in Marseilles.

AUROCHS—Wild ox, ox of the plains. This animal, which in the past used to be found in the forests of temperate Europe, is now only found, and in very small numbers, in Lithuania, in the Carpathians and in the Caucasus.

The meat of aurochs is prepared as ordinary beef.

AURORE (A L')—Name applied principally to a sauce, the recipe for which is given in the section on sauces, and consequently also to all the dishes cooked with this sauce.

This name is also given to a dish of stuffed hard boiled eggs. See EGGS, *Aurora eggs*.

This name further applies to an all-the-year-round cheese made in Normandy.

AUTOCLAVE (Pressure cooker) — High-pressure steam vessel. A sort of boiler, with very strong walls, which can be closed hermetically, provided with a safety valve and capable of raising the temperature of the water above boiling point.

No living bacteria can survive the temperature of 248°F. in a liquid medium over a certain period of time. Thus the autoclave is used in the canning industry to sterilize food products contained in hermetically sealed cans. See PRESERVATION OF FOOD.

This instrument was invented by Denis Papin and the original Papin marmite (the ancestor of the steam engine) has become popular once again in the form of pressure cookers, which, by bringing food to a temperature often reaching 284°F., make it possible to cook in a very short time dishes which would take much longer cooked by the ordinary method.

The results, although acceptable in a good many cases, are, however, far from being as good as those obtained by the traditional methods. The decomposition of certain foods, meat in particular, is taken much further than in ordinary cooking. Furthermore, vitamins can be entirely destroyed.

If pressure cookers were to be used exclusively this could lead to certain maladies (e.g. scurvy), which also occur in the case of people who live only on sterilized food. Several such cases have been reported.

AUTO-INTOXICATION, DIGESTIVE—This form of intoxication, due to healthy foods (particularly albuminoids) ingested in excessive quantity and subjected to bacterial putrefaction in the intestines, should not be confused with alimentary intoxication due to ingestion of toxic foods or foods which have gone bad.

AUTRICHIENNE (A L')—This expression is applied to various preparations characterized, as in the case of those called *à la hongroise*, by being seasoned with paprika, or Hungarian pepper, and sometimes by the addition of onion, lightly fried, of fennel or sour cream.

AUVERGNE—There are many people who believe that the cookery of this region consists entirely of lavish cabbage soup or *potée*, made of fresh and salt pork. It is true that this is typical of all the meals, grand or simple, served in this region and one which particularly suits the taste of the local inhabitants—but it is by no means the one and only local dish. Nor is it unique to Auvergne.

Each region of France, including the Île de France, has its *potée*. There is the Bourguignonne *potée*, a wonderful dish, the Alsatian *potée* which, too, is succulent, as is that of Cantal, the Languedoc *potée*, which is very savoury and, finally, the Parisian *potée* which figures daily on the bills of fare of the capital's restaurants. There are besides many other *potées* in France, recipes for which will be found in their alphabetical order, under SOUP, all of which are made of fresh or salt pork as a basic element, with cabbage, carrots, onions, leeks and potatoes completing the dish.

Auvergne
(*French Government Tourist Office*)

Auvergne, the ancient province of France which includes the departments of Puy-de-Dôme and Cantal, and a part of the Haute-Loire, is a fertile land of copious and rich cookery.

Excellent vegetables are grown in Auvergne. The orchards of Limagne produce choice dessert fruit (apricots, peaches, apples, pears, cherries) and also supply the important crystallized fruit industry of Clermont-Ferrand. The succulence of Auvergne walnuts and chestnuts is also well known.

Cattle raised for food provides excellent meat. In the mountainous pasture lands very good quality oxen are raised which give meat of exquisite flavour. Mutton, particularly that from sheep raised in Vassivières and Chaudesaigues, is greatly valued.

The pork of Auvergne is known for the delicacy of its flesh. This is made into many kinds of exquisite local products which can be found not only in the shops of Paris but also in other big cities.

The poultry of this region, no doubt, has not the quality of that raised at Bresse, but nevertheless the quality of its flesh is delicate.

The game of Auvergne, both ground and winged, cannot be compared with that of Sologne either, but it is of good quality.

The freshwater fish there is exquisite. Carp, perch, tench, pike and eels abound in the rivers and lakes and provide the ingredients for succulent matelotes. It is said, and rightly, that the trout found in the rivers of Massiac, Aurillac, Murols and Marsenac, are most delicate and are exquisite prepared *au bleu* or *à la meunière*. The flesh of the *salmon* of Brioude, in delicacy, is comparable to that of the Loire salmon.

In the spring, exquisite mushrooms, particularly succulent *morels*, are gathered in the woods and forests of Auvergne.

The vineyards of this region do not produce any great red or white wines. They produce only some very good table wines. The inhabitants of this region declare, however, and no doubt they are right, that the Chanturgne red wine is a nectar which should be drunk with the various culinary specialities of the region.

Gastronomic map of Auvergne

Culinary specialities of Auvergne. The culinary specialities of this region are not very numerous. In the first place there is the succulent *potée*, which is made of salt pork as a basic ingredient, with cabbage, carrots, turnips, onions, leeks and potatoes, as accompaniments, and with garlic as a local touch (we are below the Loire here). The *Soupe au farci* is a sort of rustic *pot-au-feu* in which a cabbage stuffed with sausage-meat flavoured with chopped garlic and parsley is cooked.

The pork butchery products are numerous and delicious: the *hams*, large and small *country sausages*, black puddings (blood sausage), *greaves* (cracklings) and *fricandeau** which are not, as their name might suggest, made of slices of veal, but of a sort of pork pâté cooked in caul or in a sheet of salt pork.

Among the strictly local specialities are the following: *tourte à la viande*, a pie made in a shallow pie-dish, lined with puff pastry and filled with pork and veal forcemeat; *omelette brayaude*, an omelette which is made of diced potatoes and lean bacon, and which, before being turned in the frying-pan, is filled with thick cream and grated cheese; *friands de Saint-Flour*, which have a great deal in common with those which are found in the Parisian shops selling pork butchery produce; *leg of lamb brayaude*, which is, of course, studded with garlic, and is braised with the usual vegetables and aromatics in white wine and is normally served with red beans, with little onions, and sometimes with braised cabbage; the *truffade*, which is potatoes cooked in a shallow pan with lean rashers of bacon, flavoured with garlic, with fresh Tomme cheese cut in small dice added at the last moment; *potatoes with bacon*, prepared in much the same way as everywhere else; the Murat *pickled pork*; *coq au vin*, a grand dish which is made in one of the inns at the top of Puy-de-Dôme and the *tripoux* of Saint-Flour.

Among the fish dishes, Ussel *jellied eel* is worthy of note, and among game dishes the Brioude *thrush cutlets*.

The pasta products of Clermont-Ferrand, too, are very well known.

Finally, among sweet dishes and confectionery products, are the *flagnarde*, *milliards de cerise*, Clermont-Ferrand *angelica*, the Thiers *crunchies*, the Riom *échaudé*, the Murat *cornets*, the Saint-Flour *bêtises* and *farces*, the Aurillac *chestnut tart* and *buckwheat pancakes*.

Cheeses of Auvergne include the famous *Cantal* cheese, which is known throughout the world, the *bleu d'Auvergne*, the small *riommois* cheeses and *goat milk cheese*.

AUVERNAT—Variety of vine, native of Auvergne and cultivated around Orleans. It is best known because of Boileau and does indeed produce wine which, as that poet says, is heady and of a strong colour. As far back as the days of Louis XIV, inn-keepers were in the habit of mixing it with lighter and less coloured wines, such as the *lignage*, to obtain pale or rosé wines, which were sold under the name of Ermitage, and which are now known under different names.

AVICE—French pastry-cook, contemporary of Antonin Carême. In his books, Carême speaks of him with great respect and gives him first place among the pastry-cooks of that brilliant epoch.

AVINER—French word meaning to season, or impregnate a new wine cask to make it lose the taste of wood.

To season a vat also means to press the grapes as the vat is being filled.

AVOCADO PEAR. Avocat—The fruit of the avocado tree, native of tropical and sub-tropical America.

The fruit, usually pear-shaped, is of greenish or purplish colour.

The kernel, in the middle of the pulp, is about the size of a walnut. The flesh of the avocado is much prized by the Americans. It is thick, buttery, spreads like butter, and is nutty in taste.

Avocado pear is not sweet but slightly acid, and contains 2 per cent of proteins and a strong proportion of oil (20 per cent), which makes it very nourishing.

It is eaten plain or seasoned with *Vinaigrette sauce* (see SAUCE). In the United States it is often served as a salad. (See illustration opposite.)

AVOCET. Avocette—A genus of wading birds. It is found in countries with cold or temperate climates, particularly along the coasts of Europe and America.

The flesh of the avocet, although quite delicate, savours of the food it lives on, which consists almost entirely of fresh fish, worms and aquatic insects. The

Avocet

European avocet is about the size of a pigeon. It is recognizable by its pied plumage. Avocet shooting is practised in the Poitou.

All the culinary methods given for *teal* can be applied to avocet.

AYAPANA—Plant originating in South America. Its leaves, exuding a pleasant aroma, are used as infusions, aperients and soporifics.

The infusion is made in the same way as tea, but as the smell of the ayapana is very strong, 12 or 13 leaves are enough for a six-cup teapot.

Ayapana blends perfectly with yolks of egg and cream.

AZAROLE—Fruit of the Neapolitan medlar, common name of a shrub known as *crataegus azarolus*, which is of the same species as hawthorn. It is also called *épine d'Espagne* in France. This shrub is similar to a service-tree.

The Neapolitan medlar is indigenous to the whole of the Mediterranean area and it is also cultivated in the Paris region. The medlar berry is oval, reddish or yellowish in colour, acid and slightly sweet in taste. It is used for compotes, confectionery and a greatly-prized liqueur.

Azarole: Fruit and branches

In Provence, in Italy and in Spain, as well as throughout the whole of Algeria, it is used for making a jam which is very popular.

AZI OR AZY—French term for rennet which is made from whey to which a certain amount of vinegar is added.

AZYMOUS (Bread). Azyme—Etymologically, the word azymous means *unleavened.*

The Jews had two ways of making their unleavened bread, either by previously grilling the flour, or by using ordinary flour. This flour was kneaded with warm water and salted, allowing 1½ teaspoons (10 grams) of salt per pound of flour. The paste was rolled out to a thickness of ⅓ inch and put on a metal sheet; the rolled-out piece of pastry was then pricked and baked in a slow oven.

Unleavened bread made out of grilled oatmeal flour is prepared in the same manner.

Avocado pear

BABA—Cake made of leavened dough, mixed with raisins, and steeped in kirsch or rum after cooking.

It is generally acknowledged that the invention of this cake belongs to King Stanislas Leczinski. Some authors however state that this royal gastronome did not invent the baba we know, nothing like it in fact, but that he simply invented a new way of eating a kugelhopf, which has been made in Lemberg (Lvov) since 1609, by sprinkling this cake with rum and setting it alight as one does a plum-pudding.

The kugelhopf done in this way had an enormous success at the court of Lorraine, where it was always served accompanied by a sauce-boat containing sweetened and spiced Malaga wine.

King Stanislas was a fervent reader of the *Thousand and One Nights* (in Galand's translation) and named his favourite sweet after one of the heroes of his favourite book, Ali Baba.

This cake was introduced to Paris at the beginning of the nineteenth century by a pastry-cook called Sthorer, who had seen it made in Lunéville, where the court of Poland was transferred. Keeping the same name, he made this cake a great speciality of his establishment in Rue Montorgueil. Later the cake was simply called baba.

Baba was in great vogue. Sthorer made the babas in advance, then moistened them with a brush just before selling them. Later, the process was to immerse them in rum-flavoured syrup.

Towards 1840 a cake of a similar nature was made in Bordeaux which was called *fribourg*.

Baba

At the same time a Parîsian Maître Pâtissier, Julien, by omitting raisins from the dough, giving the cake another shape and changing the syrup in which it was steeped (this syrup remained the secret of his establishment for a long time), created the *brillat-savarin*, which later became simply savarin.

'He gave', says Lacam, 'to his friend Bourbonneux, with whom he worked at Chiboust's, the idea of creating —using the same dough, but this time baked in a hexagonal mould—a cake which was christened *gorenflot*, after one of the heroes of *La Dame de Monsoreau*, which the two friends had just heard together. Alexandre Dumas himself later took this name for the commune of Gorenflos, near Amiens'.

Here is the recipe used by the pastry-cooks for babas:

Ingredients. 3¾ cups (500 grams) of sifted bread flour, 1¼ cups (300 grams) of butter, 1 heaping tablespoon (20 grams) of sugar, ⅔ ounce (20 grams) of yeast, 7 whole eggs, ½ cup (1 decilitre) of warm milk, 6 tablespoons (50 grams) currants, 4 tablespoons (50 grams) golden sultanas, 1½ teaspoons (10 grams) salt.

Method. Put the sieved flour into a large wooden bowl, make a well in the middle, put salt and yeast into this well, having diluted the yeast with warm milk.

Add eggs and work the paste with the hands to mix well.

Detach those portions of it which stick to the walls of the bowl and add to the paste. Distribute softened butter in small quantities over the paste. Cover and keep the paste in a warm place until it has doubled its original bulk.

Then add sugar and knead the paste so that it may absorb the butter. Add raisins and currants and mix well.

Put the paste into large, well-buttered moulds or into special moulds, as directed in the recipe, filling the moulds only up to one-third of their height. Bake in a hot oven and allow to cool before turning out of the mould. Pour syrup over the cake and sprinkle with the liqueur recommended: rum, kirsch, or other.

Syrup for babas. SIROP À BABA—In principle this syrup is prepared by adding 1 cup (2½ decilitres) of rum to 3 cups (1½ litres) of syrup (2 cups sugar and 1½ cups water) cooked to 220°F.

Various establishments use different flavourings to aromatize the syrup, mainly a small quantity of coriander.

BABIROUSSA—This mammal, allied to the wild boar, differs from the latter by the number and curious development of the canines.

Its general appearance and its squat shape give it a

certain similarity to the rhinoceros. Like the latter, it lives in the swampy forests of the Malay Archipelago. It is fairly easily tamed. Its flesh, which is prepared in the same way as that of wild boar, is much prized. See WILD BOAR.

BACCHANALIA—Festivals celebrated in honour of Bacchus. These festivals, it is said, began in Egypt, then passed to Phoenicia, Greece and Italy.

BACCHANTE—Priestess, votary of Bacchus.

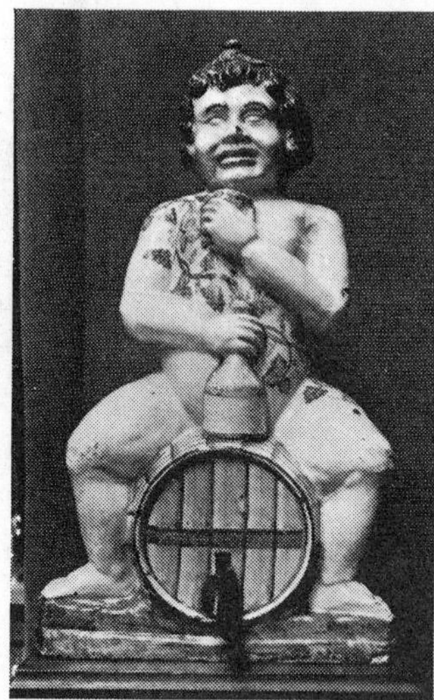

Bacchus on a barrel of wine.
Faience (Larousse)

BACCHUS—Roman god of wine, the Dionysus of the Greeks. He was born, according to legend, in Thebes, in Boeotia.

The nymph Leucothea and the infant Bacchus. Bas-relief Musée de Latran (*Photograph Anderson*)

Jupiter (Zeus) was his father. Semele, his mother, was one of the daughters of Cadmus and Hermione.

Semele wanted to see her lover in all his majesty and Jupiter (Zeus) came accordingly attended by lightning and thunderbolts, by which Semele was instantly consumed. Bacchus would also have perished, if Jupiter (Zeus) had not had him saved by Vulcan who pulled the young fruit of Love out of the dead body lying at his feet. Macris, the daughter of Aristaeus, received the child into her arms and Sabazius put him in the god's thigh. He remained in Jupiter's thigh all the time necessary to complete the nine months of his gestation.

The nymphs of Nysa nursed him and brought him up with all the care of a mother. From the hands of the Nymphs, Bacchus passed into those of the Muses and Silenus. The Muses initiated him into knowledge of harmony and dance, Silenus taught him viniculture and the making of wine.

Enthusiasm, comfortable life, abundance, civilization, all these the ancients attributed to the myth of Bacchus.

The god of wine was considered as the friend of Ceres, goddess of corn-bearing and agriculture; Ceres and Bacchus were a sacred couple par excellence. The one without the other, thought the ancients, 'taught incomplete agriculture and gave only insufficient food'. The solid and the liquid, that which sustains and that which animates, good sense and enthusiasm, that is what complete life is.

BACON—In the past this word used to mean in France pork in general, and more particularly salt pork and pig's back-fat.

This old French word, as so many others, has passed into the English language and has returned to us to serve as a definition for *lard maigre fumé* (bacon).

'A big hog (bacon) had been killed', we read in Segretain Moine's medieval tale. And in the fable of Cockayne we read:

Si païs si a non Coquaigne
Qui plus i dort, plus i gaigne.
De bars, de saumons et d'aloses
Sont toutes les maisons encloses;
Si chevron i sont d'esturgeon;
Les couvertures de bacons
Et les lates sont de saucisses.

In this land, the land of Cockayne
The more one sleeps, the more one would gain by it;
With bass, salmon and shad
All the houses are enclosed:
Their rafters are made of sturgeon,
The roof of bacon,
And the slates are sausages.

BACONIQUE—This adjective used to be applied in France to meals which consisted exclusively of pork, fresh or salt, and prepared in various ways.

The name used to describe these meals, which was used in France until the sixteenth century, proves that the word bacon is indeed a word of French origin.

BADIAN ANISE. Badiane—Fruit of a tree of the same name having a taste of anise. It is better known under the name of *star anise* and is also called Chinese anise. It is used as a carminative, in the form of an infusion ($1\frac{3}{4}$ to 2 ounces per quart; 50 to 60 grams per litre) and in the preparation of certain liqueurs. Its taste is more pungent than that of green anise, and the essence to which this fruit owes its aroma is toxic if taken in heavy doses.

Cases of poisoning, as a result of taking too strong an infusion, have in fact been known.

In India, China and Japan this plant is burned to scent the houses; it is eaten after a meal to freshen the mouth and it is also mixed with tea and liqueurs.

Badian anise, which was brought into Europe by an English sailor at the end of the sixteenth century, is used in the manufacture of the Bordeaux *anisette*.

The seeds of badian anise are used in confectionery and pastry-making. In some northern countries it is used for flavouring bread.

BAGRATION—The name of a Russian general who fought against Napoleon, which is given to various dishes: Bagration soup, Bagration salad. See SOUP and SALAD.

BAIN-DE-PIED (FOOTBATH)—In colloquial French this term is used to describe an excess of liquid of any kind (principally coffee) when it overflows from the cup into which it is poured and spills into a saucer.

Formerly, coffee cups had rather deep saucers in which our forefathers used to cool coffee before drinking it, which was quite wrong, as coffee should be drunk very hot.

This word is still used sometimes to describe too full a glass of brandy, but only in establishments where liqueurs are not served in appropriate glasses.

BAIN-MARIE—In cookery and confectionery, this term generally applies to a utensil—a vessel containing hot water in which sauces and dishes can be kept hot in small pans, until required. The vessel is usually half-filled with water, which is kept hot either by placing it on the corner of the stove, over a low heat, in the oven or heating it by steam, gas or electricity. In this bain-marie white sauces bound with yolks or cream, such as *béarnaise*, *hollandaise*, *allemande*, white wine, etc. or garnish ragoûts, simple or mixed, in white or brown gravy, and various purées and salpicons can be kept hot.

Cooking in a bain-marie—This method consists of cooking in a receptacle, in a casserole or a pan, filled with water kept near boiling-point, certain delicate dishes, such as scrambled eggs, butter sauces, emollients and other preparations which otherwise may disintegrate or turn 'oily' if they are cooked on a direct heat. In U.S.A. a utensil called the *double boiler* is used for this purpose.

Custard creams, various puddings, meat and fish loaves, compound mousses, etc., are also cooked in a bain-marie.

In French the name *bain-marie* is also applied to a utensil which is used for sterilizing babies' bottles.

BAISER—In some regions of France this is the name given to two very small meringues joined together with some fairly thick cream or other mixture.

BAJET—A species of oyster commonly found on the coast of West Africa. The shell of this oyster is very flat, round and thicker than that of ordinary oysters. The flesh is edible but not very delicate.

BAKERY. BOULANGERIE—Place where bread baked by the baker is sold.

The first bakers to have come to Italy were those whom the Romans brought from Greece following their campaign against Philip, Hannibal's foolhardy ally. Later, together with the freed slaves, they formed an organization which enjoyed considerable privileges.

Like all the corporations in France, the bakers' corporation was formed as a kind of a confraternity, or religious society, under the name of *talemeliers*, by which they were then known. Their statutes can be traced back to the time of Saint Louis, but the oldest set of regulations in existence is that preserved for us by Estienne Boileau at the beginning of the *Registres des métiers* (Register of Trades), collected about 1260.

A Roman baker, after a fresco in Pompeii

The first clause decrees: 'No-one may become a *talemelier* in the suburbs of Paris who does not buy the right to the trade from the King'.

One of their privileges was the buying and reselling of pigs without paying for this right, because they needed pigs to eat the bran which was not yet in those days separated from the flour.

To become a master baker and to have the right to practise his profession, a baker had to serve a four-years' apprenticeship, to buy the master's certificate from the King or from the King's Pantler and, in order to receive it, submit to a series of rather bizarre formalities, the mystical significance of which today escapes us completely. Thus, the new master baker had to present himself before the head of the community, where the collector of taxes and all the master bakers of the town and their first assistants were gathered and 'the new baker had to deliver his pot and his walnuts to the head of the community and say: "Master, I have completed my four years' training . . . ." And the master must ask the tax collector if this were true. The master must then give the new baker his pot and his walnuts and order him to throw them at the wall. While he is throwing them, the master and all the rest of those present go outside. Then they go back into the house where the chief must hand them fire and wine and each of the bakers, the new baker and the master valets must all give the master a *denier* (penny) for the fire and the wine served to them.'

From that time, the right of inspection was established. Bread of insufficient weight was confiscated and distributed to the poor, the violation of the law being left to the discretion of the head of the community. The appeals were brought before the Grand Pantler, whose judgment was final. The penalty was simple: the punishment was a fine of 6 *deniers* (pennies). Philip the Fair who introduced reforms into this legislation, decreed that the fines should be discretionary and proportionate to the offence. He appointed the Provost of Paris to be the bakers' judge and considerably reduced their privileges. He left the trade of bakery free; he forbade the buying of grain on the markets for resale and permitted private persons to do the buying as wholesale merchants.

In 1366, in a decree of March 12th, Charles V ordered that the bakers, both in Paris and outside, should bring their bread to the market on market days and that they should all make bread of the same weight, the same flour, the same content and at the same price, and that they should make two kinds of bread: one which cost 4 *deniers* and the other which cost 2 *deniers*, the price being determined by weight.

In July and December 1372, the King again revised the bakery question. He decided that the price of bread should be fixed in Paris in accordance with the varying prices of grain. When grain cost 8 sous, white bread or *pain de chailli* costing 2 *deniers* a loaf should weigh 30 ounces in dough, and 25½ ounces when baked. The *bourgeois* loaf of the same price should weigh 45 ounces in dough and 37½ ounces when baked. And, finally, inferior quality *pain de brode*, costing 1 *denier*, should weigh 42 ounces in dough and 36 ounces baked.

At the beginning of the fourteenth century Charles VI decreed:

'That the bakers may not buy or cause to be bought either grain or flour on the Paris markets if the market has not been open at least one hour.

'That no baker can at the same time be a miller or a measurer of grain.

'That the bakers may not buy grain except through the intermediary of a sworn-in measurer'.

The rigours of an interminable war, the scarcity and high prices of cereals, the sale of bread against uncertain payment and other causes forced many of the disheartened bakers to give up their trade under the reign of Charles VI and to destroy their ovens. A written decree was issued in February 1415 ordering them to rebuild the ovens without delay on pain of banishment.

A few months later numerous regulations were issued to the effect that 'white bread shall be sold at 3 Paris minted *deniers* (pennies), wholemeal bread at 2 Paris *deniers*, bread with barley admixture 2 Tours minted *deniers* for 13 ounces'. In addition, the bakers had to make these prices known to their customers and could not get more than 6 dozen 13-ounce white loaves out of a setier (an old measure of weight, about 8 pints).

Charles VII, by an order of September 19th, 1439, introduced a few new regulations: 'The weights for weighing grain and flour in Paris shall be kept in a place chosen by the municipal magistrates. White bread, *when it is permitted to be baked*, shall be sold by measures of six ounces at the price of eight ounces of wholemeal bread. The measurers shall each Saturday make a survey of the price of grain, wheat, rye, and barley, sold in the three markets at Les Halles, Grève and Martroi. The price of bread shall be published and posted up in the said markets. The bakers shall not buy grain before noon'.

This last regulation shows the extent to which the custom of making their own bread had spread among the bourgeois classes and secured for them the facilities for buying grain. It aimed at preventing the bakers from bulk buying and maintaining their monopoly.

Under Louis XI a decree of June 1467 concerning trades ordered that 'all the guilds of the city of Paris should have their coat of arms and their own banner; each is to have a different insignia and all must have a white cross in the middle'.

During the sixteenth century the relation of the price of grain to the price of bread, and of the quantity of flour to the quantity of grain and the regulations governing trading hours at the markets went on without great modifications.

Having settled the question of the trade itself, legislation turned to the bakers. A somewhat peculiar decree of May 13th, 1569, announced that all members of the bakers' guild had to be constantly dressed in a shirt, drawers, without trunk hose, and wear a cap. In short, dressed in such a costume they had to be working all the time and never go out, except on Sundays and such closing days as were laid down in the regulations: 'And they are forbidden to gather together, to set up monopolies, to wear a sword, dagger or any other weapon, or to wear coats, hats and trunk hose, except on Sundays and other holidays, on which days only are they permitted to wear hats, hose and coats of grey or white woollen cloth and not of any other colour, on pain of imprisonment and corporal punishment and confiscation of the said coats, hose and hats'.

The seventeenth century marks a milestone in the history of Parisian bakery trade in the improvements in manufacture, the introduction of the custom of selling flour without bran to Paris bakers, the celebrated *pain mollet* (bread roll) process, the regulation forbidding the use of brewers' yeast and, finally, the greatly increased number of markets.

At the beginning of that century the vogue for the bread baked by the Chapter of the Cathedral of Notre Dame, which was called *pain de chapitre* (Chapter loaf), passed in preference for the favourite bread of Queen Marie de Medici. The *Queen's bread* was salted and prepared with brewers' yeast. Then came bread known as the *pains à la Montauron*, which was kneaded with milk as *pains à la Ségovie*. The *Gentilly* bread was made with butter. There were also the *pain mollet* (rolls), *horn-shaped loaves*, *pain Blême* (pale bread) and *pain à la citrouille* (pumpkin loaves) which were the monopoly of bakers specializing in small loaves.

Richelieu did away with many out-of-date measures and introduced bold reforms into legislation, which are in force to this day. In his general order to the Paris police, issued on March 30th, 1635, he introduced the following regulation: 'Grain merchants shall not make their purchases except outside the ten leagues (40 kilometres) limit around Paris. Small loaf bakers and pastry-cooks shall not buy grain before 11 o'clock in the summer and noon in the winter; big loaf bakers shall not buy grain before 2 o'clock, to enable the needs of the bourgeois to be supplied first. The bakers shall put their distinctive trade mark on their loaves. They shall keep scales and weights in their shops on pain of being deprived of licence or even more severe punishment'.

This regulation laid down that 'all large loaf bakers both of this city and outside, bringing their bread to the markets, should sell it themselves, or by the efforts of their wives, children or servants without going through *regrattiers* (hucksters) and middlemen.

'The bakers shall not keep nor store away in nearby houses, nor take away, what is left of the unsold bread; they have to sell it within three days of baking. Otherwise the left-over bread will have to be sold at a reduced price and the bakers shall not raise the price for the freshly-baked bread, but rather have to reduce it'.

During the Fronde (the rising of the aristocracy and the Parliament against Mazarin, 1648-53), the high price of flour, caused by the difficulties of transporting it to Paris, and then the high price of bread, led to measures which we have already mentioned: in 1650 sifted or bolted flour began to make its appearance, which enabled a greater quantity to be transported at one time and the transport of bran no longer had to be paid for as part of the flour. From that time the bakers were no longer allowed to raise pigs and they had to sell those they had to villagers.

In 1666, under the reign of Louis XIV, a curious case was argued, the funny side of which was recorded by Ed. Fournier, *Molière et le procès du pain mollet* (Molière and the bread roll) in the *Revue Française*. (A man called Poquelin, a relative of Molière, was involved in the case.) After this there was a verdict which declared that the use of brewers' yeast was detrimental to health and, therefore, forbidden.

Precautions for the wholesomeness of food went so far as to protect even the grain under ground against influences known to be harmful. For instance, an order forbade the farmers to dung their land with faeces unless faecal matter 'has been left for a considerable time in a public pit and freed from its bad properties'.

Towards 1710 bakers, says Delamare, 'could sell their bread during the morning and until noon at whatever price they wished. In the afternoon they were not allowed to raise the morning price, and from 4 o'clock, if they had any bread left over, they had to sell it at a reduced price to be able to dispose of the whole lot'.

At this time, and even from the time of Sauval, the number of bread markets had been raised to fifteen, to which 500 to 600 bakers came from the city and the outlying suburbs and from 934 to 1,034 from Gonesse, Corbeil and Saint-Germain-en-Laye. They were distributed in the following manner: Grandes Halles, 342; Halles de la Tonnellerie, 104; Place Maubert, 159; Saint-Jean cemetery, 158; Marché-Neuf de la Cité, 89; rue Saint-Antoine, in front of the Jesuits' church, 148; Quai des Augustins, 92; Petit Marché du Faubourg Saint-Germain 147; in front of Quinze-Vingts church in the rue Saint-Honoré, 95; Place du Palais Royale, 40; in front of the Hotel des Bâtiments royaux, in rue Saint Honoré, 30; Marché des Marais du Temple, 46; in front of the Temple, 22; at the place where the Porte Saint-Michel was, 36; at the Halle du Faubourg Saint-Antoine, 16.

There the bread of the privileged master bakers was sold, and, much to their despair, also bread baked by bakers who plied their trade without holding master bakers' certificates. These unauthorized bakers lived around the Temple, Saint-Jean-de-Latran, Saint-Denis, La Châtre and Quinze-Vingts. They enjoyed the same rights in the city as the people from outside, except for the master bakers, who enjoyed all the privileges conferred by the licence.

The time had come for the community to receive its most important privilege: Louis XIV abolished the jurisdiction of the Royal Pantler.

A law passed in 1678 had put the artisans and merchants of the suburbs on the same footing as those of the town. The edict of Louis XIV invited members of the bakers' profession to participate in this doubtful blessing, and newly-qualified masters of the trade henceforth were enabled to practice on the same conditions by paying the same dues.

The payment of dues! That, no doubt, was the principal aim of the order. Two years had passed: 1709 and 1710—years of appalling poverty and shortages. The following year was not much better. The State was in dire straits, the Treasury depleted, the people pressed to the limit. What was desired, it appears, was to increase taxation even further by imposing it on the suburban bakers, as well as on those of the city, and by extracting from both sums which the authorities deemed to be the just remuneration for this so-called privilege.

Then followed the addition to the law forbidding the bakers to withdraw from the market before they had sold all their bread, of a clause making it compulsory for each baker to bring a certain quantity of bread to the market (Abbé Jaubert, *Dictionnaire Universel des Arts et Métiers, 1773*) and never to hand over anything that was left to a man who was a stranger to the city bakers. That was a great hardship for, after a certain hour, the bakers had to get rid of their bread at all costs. They could not recoup by cheating on the weight, as they were obliged to 'mark each loaf clearly showing its weight and the weight thus shown should correspond to the actual weight on pain of confiscation and fine'. (Hurtault, *Dictionnaire Historique de Paris, 1779*.)

At this period, the apprenticeship, which lasted five years, had to be followed by four years of working for the guild. After these nine years, the worker, unless he were the master baker's son, had to present his *chef-d'oeuvre* and, on paying for a 40-pound and a 900-pound certificate, might finally practise as a master baker.

Boulanger-cabaretier (miniature from the Bibliothèque de L'Arsenal)

Thus matters continued until the French Revolution, but, even after 1789, the breadmaking industry remained under strict control. It was only in 1863 that it became free.

Baker's assistant. MITRON—This French term, it is said by some authorities, comes from the paper head-dress or *mitre* which, formerly, bakers wore at work.

Bakery equipment—The original equipment used in the bakery has changed very little since the time of ancient Greece and Rome. Kneading by hand was done for many centuries in a huge wooden trough, rather longer than it was wide, which stood on four legs. This kneading-trough had a flat cover which was called the *tour*. The modern kneading-troughs are made of metal. As to the ovens, until the nineteenth century they remained as they were in the days of the Romans and as they are shown in Diderot's *Encyclopaedia*: a block of masonry, with the actual baking oven inside, square in shape with all the inside edges rounded off, and surmounted by a dome called the *chapelle*. The walls were at least 20 inches thick and the oven was heated with wood.

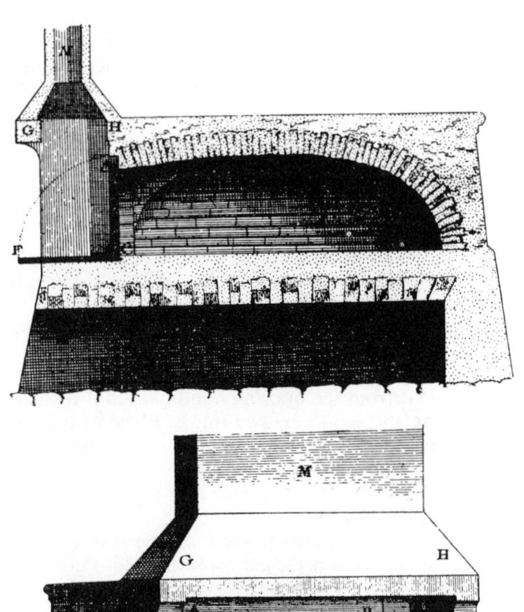

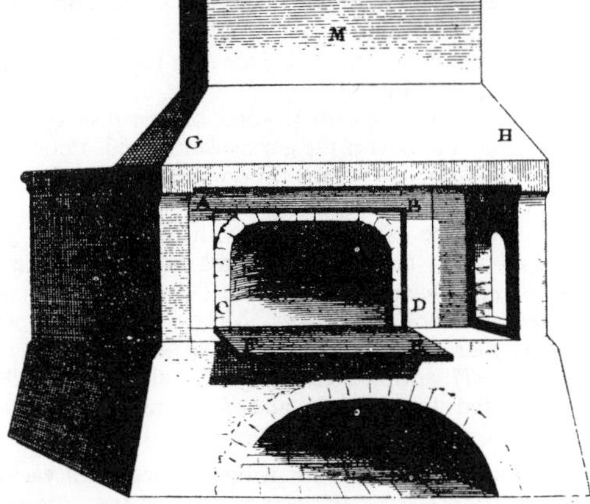

Bakers' ovens, reproduced from Diderot's *Encyclopaedia*

Modern bakeries are equipped with mechanical kneading machines.

The first step towards progress in oven heating was the replacement of wood by coal, which was burnt in a special fireplace below the opening of the oven. Then came gas, oil heating and electricity. The heating technique underwent further improvement with the introduction of pipes containing a liquid, which is first heated in a coal-fired chamber and circulates round the oven: this heating system has the advantage of being continuous, very even, clean and economical.

In France bread making is still carried on to a great extent in small-scale establishments, with a few workers under one master-baker, which produce a few hundred-weight of bread per day. However, the trend is towards mass production and large factories are in existence where highly-developed mechanization and technical organization result in very large production capacity.

The work involved in transforming flour into bread is described under the entry entitled BREAD.

BALACHAN—Seasoning much used in Siam. In Tonkin it is known under the name of *nukemum*. It is equivalent to the *poppadom* of South China.

It is made of small shrimps which are pounded with salt into a sort of thick brine which is dried in the sun.

Balachan, it is said, stimulates the appetite and fortifies the stomach.

BALAINE OR BALEINE—The name of a restaurant-keeper who ran '*Le Rocher de Cancale*', in rue Montorgueil. Grimod de la Reynière, who gave parties at his restaurant, spoke very highly of him. Carême considered him to be a second-rate caterer.

BALAOU—French name for a small fish which is very similar to the sardine. It abounds in Martinique. Its flesh is very delicate and easily digestible.

All the methods of cooking sardines can be applied to balaou.

BALLOTTINE—This term describes a kind of galantine which is normally served as a hot entrée, but can also be served cold.

The ballottine is made of a piece of meat, fowl, game, or fish, which is boned, stuffed and rolled into the shape of a bundle.

To be precise, the term *ballottine* should apply only to a piece of butcher's meat, boned, stuffed and rolled, but it is in fact also applied to various dishes which are actually galantines.

Ballottine of lamb à la boulangère. BALLOTTINE D'AGNEAU À LA BOULANGÈRE—Prepare as *Shoulder of lamb à la boulangère*. See LAMB.

Ballottine of lamb à la bourgeoise. BALLOTTINE D'AGNEAU À LA BOURGEOISE—Prepare like *Ballottine of lamb braised à la bonne femme*, replacing the garnish indicated in that recipe by garnish *à la bourgeoise*, which should be cooked with the meat. See GARNISHES.

Ballottine of lamb à la bourguignonne. BALLOTTINE D'AGNEAU À LA BOURGUIGNONNE—Braise the ballottine in red wine. When it is nearly cooked, drain it and strain the liquor. Put it back into the earthenware cooking dish with garnish *à la bourguignonne* (mushrooms, bacon cut in large dice, blanched and lightly fried, and small glazed onions). Pour the sauce over the ballottine and finish cooking together.

Ballottine of lamb braised à la bonne femme. BALLOTTINE D'AGNEAU BRAISÉE À LA BONNE FEMME—Stuff a boned shoulder of lamb with sausage meat mixed with chopped onion, lightly fried in butter or lard, and chopped parsley.

Roll the shoulder into a ballottine and secure with string. Brown it in the oven. Put into an oval earthenware *cocotte* (deep dish) with 12 medium-sized onions lightly fried in butter and 6 medium-sized rashers (100 grams) of lean bacon cut in dice and blanched. Add a *bouquet garni*. Moisten with $\frac{2}{3}$ cup (2 decilitres) of dry white wine. Boil down the wine. Add enough thickened meat stock just to cover the ballottine. Bring to the boil. Cover the *cocotte* with a lid and put it in the oven for 45 minutes. Add 2 cups (500 grams) of potato balls. Cook together in the oven from 30 to 35 minutes. Drain the ballottine, remove string, put it back in the *cocotte* and serve.

Ballottine of lamb, braised, with various garnishes. BALLOTTINE D'AGNEAU BRAISÉE—Prepare the ballottine and braise it in a deep oval earthenware dish, as described in the preceding recipe, without adding bacon, potatoes and onions. When the ballottine is cooked, drain it and remove string. Arrange on a serving dish, surround with the garnish recommended or, according to circumstances, serve this garnish separately. Boil down the braising liquor, remove surplus fat, strain and pour over the ballottine.

Garnishes which are most suitable for this dish, the recipes for which will be found under GARNISHES, are as follows: *bouquetière*, *Bretonne*, *Bruxelloise*, *chipolata*, *Flamande*, *jardinière*, *Macédoine*, *Milanaise*, *Nivernaise*, or this dish may be served with *noodles*, *rice pilaf*, or *risotto*.

Ballottine can also be served with various fresh vegetables, dressed with butter or cream, braised or glazed vegetables, and potatoes prepared in various ways.

Ballottine of lamb, cold, with various garnishes. BALLOTTINE D'AGNEAU FROIDE—When the ballottine is quite cold, pour a little cold liquid aspic jelly and leave until set. Arrange on a serving dish, straight on the dish or, according to the nature of the garnish, on a de-crusted buttered croûton, and put the garnish around. Decorate with chopped jelly.

All the garnishes recommended for cold meat and poultry are suitable for cold ballottine.

Ballottine of lamb in jelly

Ballottine of lamb in jelly. BALLOTTINE D'AGNEAU À LA GELÉE—Stuff a boned and flattened shoulder with galantine forcemeat (see FORCEMEATS), mixed with a *salpicon** composed of tongue *à l'écarlate*, ham and truffles. Roll, wrap in a piece of muslin and tie with string.

Cook in jelly stock as described in the recipe for *galantine*.

Drain the ballottine, unwrap and wrap up again tightly in a cloth, securing with string at each end and in the middle. Cool under a press.

Unwrap the ballottine and glaze it with cold but liquid aspic jelly (made from the stock in which it was cooked, clarified and reinforced with gelatine, if necessary).

Arrange on a serving dish, surrounded with chopped jelly.

You can also, instead of serving the ballottine on a platter, put it into an oval earthenware or porcelain terrine, or in a glass dish, and cover it with half-set jelly.

Ballottine of mutton. BALLOTTINE DE MOUTON—Proceed as described for *Ballottine of lamb*.

Ballottine of pork braised with various garnishes. BALLOTTINE DE PORC BRAISÉE AVEC GARNITURES DIVERSES —Bone a shoulder of pork and prepare as *Ballottine of lamb*.

When the ballottine is braised, drain it, remove string, glaze with jelly and serve with one of the garnishes normally used for meat (see GARNISHES). Boil down (reduce) the braising liquor, remove fat, strain and pour over the ballottine.

Ballottine of pork in jelly. BALLOTTINE DE PORC À LA GELÉE—Bone a shoulder of pork and prepare as *Ballottine of lamb in jelly*.

Garnish and serve as described in the recipe for *Ballottine of lamb*.

Ballottine of veal. BALLOTTINE DE VEAU—Take a boned shoulder or a thin slice of chump end of loin (U.S.A. sirloin steak or cutlet) and proceed as described in the recipe for *Ballottine of lamb*.

Ballottine of veal can be prepared either hot or cold and can be served with one of the garnishes usually recommended for meat.

Ballottine of chicken with a dark sauce with various garnishes. BALLOTTINE DE POULARDE (À BRUN)—Bone a medium-sized fowl in the usual manner. See GALANTINE.

Stuff it with a quenelle or finely-pounded pork forcemeat. See FORCEMEATS.

Boil the ballottine in a napkin (previously soaked in hot water and wrung out) and secure with string giving the ballottine the right shape.

Put the ballottine to cook in a braising pan with just enough chicken stock to cover the fowl. Bring to the boil, cover and then simmer gently for 50 minutes.

Drain the ballottine, keep it hot for 10 minutes in the oven. (This resting is necessary to ensure that the forcemeat settles properly.)

Remove fat from the braising liquor, strain it through a muslin bag and reduce by two-thirds. Blend with a cup (2 decilitres) of thickened rich veal stock and strain through a fine strainer.

Unwrap the ballottine and glaze it in the oven, basting with the thickened gravy.

Arrange on a long dish straight on the dish or on a croûton. Surround with the garnish indicated. Pour over a few tablespoons of the gravy and serve the rest separately in a sauceboat.

This ballottine can be served with the following garnishes: noodles, celery, mushrooms or chipolata, *à la bouquetière*, *Demidoff* (see *Chicken Demidoff*), *espagnole*, *financière*, *Godard*, *Milanaise*, *Niçoise*, *orientale*, *périgourdine*, *piémontaise*, *portugaise*, *Rossini* (see *Chicken à la Rossini*) and, in general, with all the garnishes recommended for chicken and fowl served in small pieces prepared with a dark sauce.

Ballottine of chicken (with a light sauce) with various garnishes. BALLOTTINE DE POULARDS À BLANC—Prepare and cook the ballottine as described above and glaze it lightly.

Arrange on a fried croûton, or on a foundation of rice or semolina (this is optional and is only intended to improve the appearance of the dish).

Surround by the garnish recommended and serve with a *Velouté* or *Suprême sauce* (see SAUCE) incorporating in it the liquor in which the ballottine was cooked.

This ballottine can be served with the following garnishes: with celery, mushrooms, noodles, rice, *Albuféra*, *à l'Anversoise*, *banquière*, *Chivry* (see *Chicken Chivry*), *demi-deuil*, *ivoire* (see *Chicken à l'ivoire*), *princesse*, *régence*, *Toulouse*, and, generally, with all the garnishes recommended for poultry prepared with a light sauce.

Small ballottines of chicken. PETITES BALLOTTINES DE VOLAILLES—Tiny ballottines made of chicken's legs, when the wings and breast are used for some other dish.

The legs are boned and stuffed as described in the first recipe for *Ballottines of chicken*. They are braised *à brun* or *à blanc* and garnished and served as described in the directions for *Ballottines of chicken*.

Sometimes this dish is given the shape of a ham knuckle, in which case it is served under the name of *Jambonneaux de volailles.*

Ballottine of chicken in jelly (chaud-froid) (I). BALLOTTINE DE POULARDE À LA GELÉE (EN CHAUD-FROID)—Prepare and cook as described in the preceding recipes.

According to the type of recipe, finish cooking as indicated in the recipes for *Chicken in jelly, mayonnaise, Néva, parisienne.* See CHICKEN, *Cold chicken.*

Ballottine of chicken in jelly (II). BALLOTTINE DE POULET À LA GELÉE—Prepare and cook the ballottine as described in the preceding recipes.

Unwrap and allow to cool in its liquor, strained and with the fat removed.

Arrange the chicken on a serving dish, glaze and decorate with jelly made from the stock in which it was cooked, as described in the recipe for *Chicken in jelly.* See CHICKEN, *Cold chicken.*

Ballottine of glazed chicken (chaud-froid). BALLOTTINE DE POULET GLACÉE EN CHAUD-FROID—Proceed with a cooked ballottine as described above and chilled and prepared as in the recipe for *Chaud-froid of chicken.* See CHICKEN.

Ballottines of various poultry. BALLOTTINE DE VOLAILLES—Proceed with various types of poultry: ducks, turkeys, pigeons or guinea-fowl, as described in the recipe for *Ballottine of chicken.*

Forcemeat for stuffing ducks and guinea-fowls can be mixed with one-third of its volume of *foie gras.*

According to the method chosen, chopped truffles can also be added to the stuffing.

Ballottines of duck, turkey, pigeons and guinea-fowl are served cold or hot and accompanied by all the garnishes recommended for chicken in general.

BALM. BAUME—Name commonly applied to various aromatic plants of the mint type.

Garden balm (Costmary) was known in ancient cookery. Sweet trefoil or blue melilot or Swiss melilot are used in some regions of Switzerland for flavouring certain cheeses.

BALSAM. BALSAMINE DES BOIS—Plant of the family *Balsaminaceae* which is erroneously presumed to be poisonous. Its tender leaves can be prepared like those of sorrel.

BAMBELLE—French name for a small fish of the carp family. It abounds in some of the Swiss lakes.

All the recipes given for carp are applicable to it. See CARP.

BAMBOO. BAMBOU—Arborescent reeds (a genus of woody-stemmed grasses) grown in tropical countries. Its young shoots are edible and when pickled in vinegar are called *achard* or *bamboo shoots* and are sold, canned, as a luxury product.

The shoots, which are spiky, are eaten fresh in China, Indo-China, India, Japan, etc. like asparagus, or stewed with meat like cabbage.

The Japanese pickle tender bamboo shoots in saké vinegar (saké is a spirit distilled from rice). In the Sunda Isles bamboo stems are pickled in palm vinegar.

The pith of various species of bamboo is very sweet and a sort of syrup oozes from it which is greatly prized. The fruit of the bamboo which succeeds the flower, in some cases seen only once in 25 years, is the size of a pear and is formed of a great number of edible seeds resembling ripe ears of maize or Indian corn. This fruit is greatly valued in Japan.

As young bamboo shoots are covered with very fine but sharp hairs, it is advisable before cooking them to have these removed in one way or another, to prevent serious accidents which may lead to an intestinal perforation.

BANANA. BANANE—Fruit of the banana tree which grows in tropical regions. About 30 species of it are known. This fruit has a taste which appeals to many people. The taste varies according to species.

In the Hindu religion there is a legend according to which the banana was the fruit which was forbidden to Adam and Eve in the terrestrial paradise which, says the legend, was situated on the island of Ceylon. According to the same legend, it was banana leaves that the parents of the human race used to cover their nakedness. This belief explains the names of *Adam's fig-tree* and *Paradise banana,* which the Indians have given to two species of banana trees.

Very rich in nutritive substances, the banana is considered a particularly recommendable food. This statement, however, requires certain reservations.

Bananas intended for export are harvested while still green and unripe, put into stores or warehouses to ripen and, depending on distribution, sold in varying degrees of ripeness.

Canary bananas and *American bananas* are to be found in great abundance. The first is sweeter, more fragrant and arch-shaped; the second is bigger and longer. When choosing bananas from a bunch, pick those of a uniform golden yellow colour, without any black spots, which are signs of decay.

A bunch can contain up to 200 bananas and can weigh 70 to 80 pounds.

When bananas are cut unripe their flesh is white and almost tasteless. It often happens that people who have never eaten bananas before try them for the first time in their unripe state and, naturally, form a very unfavourable opinion of the fruit. As bananas mature, they become sweet, like chestnuts, and even sweeter, and acquire a very pleasant smell. They even retain it when dried in the oven for keeping purposes. When perfectly ripe, bananas are eaten either raw or cooked, but when they are green it is absolutely essential to cook them.

As to dried bananas, their calorific value goes up to about twice that of meat. Is it surprising, therefore, that this fruit plays such an important part in the diet of certain vegetarian peoples and is almost sufficient alone to ensure them their existence? That is why Stanley exclaimed, with more truth than meets the eye, 'When there is no more wheat, barley, rice, sorghum or millet, we'll eat bananas'.

Baked bananas. BANANES AU FOUR—Bake the bananas in the oven without peeling them. Serve with melted butter and fine granulated sugar.

These bananas can also be served with a red fruit jelly.

Bananas Beauharnais. BANANES BEAUHARNAIS—Scrape 6 peeled bananas and put them into a buttered fireproof dish. Dust with sugar, sprinkle with 4 tablespoons of white rum and heat on the stove, then cook in the oven for 5 minutes. Pour over thick cream, sprinkle with crushed macaroons and a little melted butter and glaze in a very hot oven. Serve in the same dish.

Bananas Bourdaloue. BANANES BOURDALOUE—Peel and poach the bananas in syrup and proceed as described in the recipe for *Apricots Bourdaloue.* See APRICOTS.

Bananas in butter. BANANES AU BEURRE—Peel and scrape bananas and put them into a buttered fireproof dish. Sprinkle with sugar. Cook gently in the oven (350°F.) for 20-30 minutes.

Banana compote. See COMPOTE.

Bananas Condé. BANANES CONDÉ—Peel and poach the bananas and proceed as described in the recipe for *Apricots Condé*. See APRICOTS.

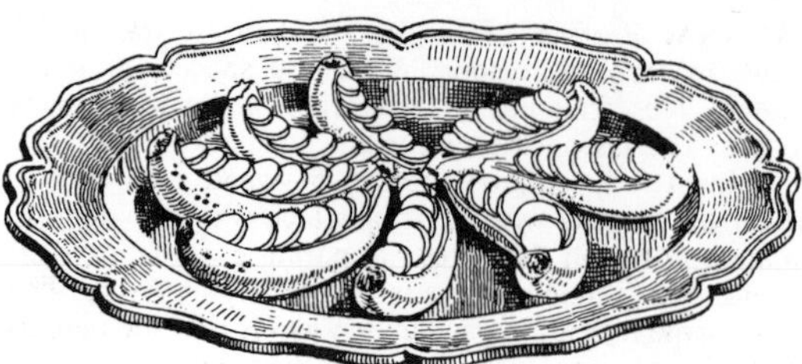

Bananas *à la créole*

Bananas à la créole. BANANES GRATINÉES À LA CRÉOLE—Choose good firm bananas and cut lengthwise. Remove the fruit without breaking the skin. Soak the skins for 2 minutes in boiling water, drain and dip them in cold water to cool. Cut each banana half into 6 slices and put these to steep for 30 minutes with sugar and rum.

Fill the banana skins up to two-thirds with dessert rice (see RICE) mixed with a *salpicon** of crystallized fruit (cherries, apricots, candied peel, etc.) and flavoured with rum.

On this rice arrange the banana slices in a neat row. Put the fruit on a baking tray, sprinkle with finely ground macaroons and melted butter and put in a very hot oven for a few moments to brown the top.

Put the bananas on a round dish covered with a paper doyley. Serve rum-flavoured *Apricot sauce* (see SAUCE) separately.

Banana croûtes à la Bauvilliers. CROÛTES AUX BANANES À LA BAUVILLIERS—Cut a stale brioche into a dozen rectangular slices 2½ inches long and a little wider than a banana.

Put these slices on a baking tray, sprinkle with fine sugar and glaze in the oven.

Meanwhile, peel 6 bananas and divide in halves lengthways. Put these halves on a buttered baking tray, sprinkle with fine sugar and cook in the oven for 5 minutes.

Arrange the bananas alternating with slices of brioche in a circle, on a round fire-proof dish.

Fill the middle with a composition of semolina cooked with milk, sugar and vanilla, bound with yolks of eggs (see SEMOLINA, *English semolina pudding*) and mixed with a *salpicon** of preserved fruit steeped in maraschino.

Sprinkle the whole dish with finely-crushed macaroons and melted butter and brown the top in the oven.

Just before serving, surround with a ring of *Apricot sauce* (see SAUCE), flavoured with maraschino.

Banana croûtes à la maltaise. CROÛTES AUX BANANES À LA MALTAISE—Prepare as described in the recipe for *Banana croûte à la Bauvilliers*, replacing semolina by very thick *French pastry cream* (see CREAM), flavoured with grated orange peel.

Decorate the circle of bananas with candied orange-peel and halved almonds.

Bananas flambé. BANANES FLAMBÉES—Peel and scrape the bananas and cook them in vanilla-flavoured syrup (see *Banana fritters (III)*). Drain and put into a timbale or a shallow ovenproof dish. Sprinkle with brandy, kirsch, calvados, rum or any other liqueur. Set alight when serving.

Instead of poaching, the bananas can also be cooked in butter.

Banana flan or tart à la crème. FLAN DE BANANES À LA CRÈME—Peel the bananas and divide in halves lengthways. Put them in a buttered dish, sprinkle with fine sugar and cook in the oven.

Arrange the banana halves in a short pastry flan filled with *French pastry cream* (see CREAM). Sprinkle with crushed macaroons and brown the top in the oven.

Fried bananas (garnish for meat). BANANES FRITES—Divide the bananas in two lengthways and marinate for ½ hour in oil, lemon juice, salt and pepper.

Dip into a light batter. Fry at the last moment.

As a dessert or sweet course, these are the same as *Banana fritters*.

Fried bananas with cream

Banana fritters (I). BEIGNETS DE BANANES—Divide the bananas in half lengthways and steep them for an hour in rum or kirsch and sugar.

When required, dip them into a batter and deep-fry in sizzling fat.

Drain, dry, sprinkle with fine sugar and serve on a napkin.

After frying, the fritters can also be glazed in the oven.

Banana fritters (II) (à l'ancienne). BANANES EN BEIGNETS À L'ANCIENNE—Halve the bananas, steep them in some liqueur, and sandwich together with *French pastry cream* (see CREAM), flavoured with grated orange-peel. Dip in batter. Finish as described above.

Banana fritters (III) (Creole cookery). BANANES EN BEIGNETS—*Batter*. Make a smooth, rather thick paste, using 3 large tablespoons of flour and warm water. Add a large tablespoon of good olive oil. Leave to stand for 2 to 3 hours, stirring from time to time. Just before using, whisk 2 whites of egg into a very stiff froth and fold into the batter gently. Dip each piece of banana in this batter and fry in very hot fat.

Preparation of bananas. Cut in two lengthways and poach in thick vanilla-flavoured sugar syrup (1 cup sugar and ¾ cup water boiled to 220°F.). Allow to cool and use each piece of banana as described above. Sprinkle the fritters with fine sugar.

Grilled bananas. BANANES GRILLÉES—Peel the bananas, scrape, coat them with melted butter and grill on a gentle heat.

Arrange on a round dish and sprinkle with fine sugar.

Prepared in this way, bananas may have thick cream poured over them.

When arranged on a dish, these bananas can also be sprinkled with brandy, kirsch or rum, and set alight.

Bananas with meringue. BANANES MERINGUÉES—Peel and poach the bananas in syrup and proceed as described in the recipe for *Apricots with meringue*. See APRICOTS.

Banana mousse glacée. See ICE CREAMS AND ICES, *Fruit mousses*.

Bananas à la norvégienne. BANANES À LA NORVÉGIENNE —Cut a slit lengthwise around 6 large bananas. Remove the top skin and scoop out the pulp without damaging the bottom skin.

Fill the bananas up to three-quarters with *Banana ice cream* (see ICE CREAMS AND ICES). Pipe *Italian meringue* (see MERINGUE), flavoured with vanilla through a pastry or forcing-bag.

Put the bananas on a dish and place the dish in the oven in a pan of crushed ice. Leave in the oven, which should be very hot (475°F.), just as long as is necessary to make the meringue golden. Serve immediately.

Banana salad (Cold hors-d'oeuvre). SALADE DE BANANES —Peel the bananas, cut into thin slices and dress *à la vinaigrette* or with mayonnaise.

Banana is often used in mixed salads.

Banana soufflé. SOUFFLÉ AUX BANANES—Put a tablespoon of flour and a very small pinch of salt into a saucepan. Blend into a smooth paste, avoiding formation of lumps, with $\frac{1}{3}$ cup (1 decilitre) of cold milk, previously boiled with 2 tablespoons (35 grams) of sugar and half a vanilla bean or $\frac{1}{2}$ teaspoon of vanilla extract added after the cooking.

Cook for 2 minutes stirring all the time. Remove from heat. Rub the pulp of 4 bananas through a fine sieve, mix with 2 yolks of eggs and a heaped tablespoon of best butter, and add this to the cream in the saucepan. At the last moment, add 3 very stiffly beaten whites of eggs.

Butter a soufflé dish, sprinkle it with fine sugar and pour in the mixture. Bake in a slow oven (325°F.) from 12 to 15 minutes, or longer, depending on the size of the soufflé.

Banana soufflé may be flavoured with rum or kirsch. It can be put into banana skins (see preceding recipe) or into little fire-proof metal or china cassolettes.

BANGI—A small tree which grows in the Philippines. It is lactescent and produces a rather pleasant green-coloured fruit, the size of an orange.

BANILLES—A French name given to small pods, long and tapering, which have some similarity with vanilla bean. These pods contain a very fragrant, sugary juice which is often used in the manufacture of ordinary chocolate, instead of real vanilla.

BANQUET—The word banquet seems to come from the word *banc* (bench) and, to explain how a derivative, meaning a meal taken in company, was formed from the name of a seat, it has been suggested that it was on benches that the first Christians sat as they celebrated their agapes in the catacombs.

Whatever the origin of the word banquet, it signifies a rather solemn and sumptuous meal given to a large number of guests. A banquet is given on festal or ceremonial occasions, or it is given to bring together people with the same religious or political ideas, the same literary or artistic (or sometimes just gastronomical!) tastes, people of the same social status or profession, people of the same geographical or ethnic origin and so on.

People therefore gather round the same table, either owing to the necessities imposed by family life, or else to mark an important occasion and to affirm mutual ideas —intellectual or sentimental.

The origins of these two reasons for gathering round a table go back to the earliest times.

On the other hand, primitive men quite naturally took their meals with their families, as it has been established that the very first men did not live by themselves, but in groups, just like many animals do, such as monkeys or elephants. These family meals consisted of rough foods that had not yet been improved by planned cooking. As soon as fire was discovered men brought meats near to it, first to dry them, then to grill and cook them.

This discovery of fire rendered the habit of gathering round the hearth to have a meal even more natural.

Archaeologists have supplied us with invaluable information about our ancestors' meals: prehistoric strata plainly show traces of fire, heaps of ashes, in which were found bones of animals that had been used for food, and by which different prehistoric eras can be identified.

The mystic character of a banquet is also to be found in prehistory. In the origins of all the manifestations of human activity there was magic, namely the need of man to make the mysterious forces of nature favourable to him. On the walls of the *Trois Frères* caves in Ariège, a primitive artist has painted the figure of a sorcerer in ceremonial robes, who seems to be performing a sacred dance in the middle of an immense herd. It was a sort of incantation to make hunting successful; and when the vanquished animal lay on the ground, it was naturally divided into two parts. The first for the benevolent divinities, the other for the tribe, clan or family. So men grew used to meeting to divide amongst themselves the chosen bits of the animal, and they continued to do this on the occasion of the two great events in their lives: birth and death. These were the first banquets.

Enormous progress was made in cooking when clay or bronze vessels were invented, vessels that could withstand fire and in which meats, vegetables and fish, seasoned and spiced, could be cooked.

Ever since then, large gatherings at table became possible. The era of banquets began, and the most magnificent were those that took place in the fertile lands of the orient, especially rich in spices and flavourings.

The banquets of the Egyptians. According to Herodotus, the Egyptians believed that the manner in which nourishment was taken was at the root of most illnesses. They were very careful in their cooking, therefore, and very discerning in their choice of foods.

Descriptions have been preserved of Egyptian feasts, at which, contrary to the custom of most Eastern countries, the woman took charge of the organization of meals, directed the service and presided at the table.

The guests, arriving in palanquins, were ushered into the first room, where they washed their feet and hands. They then disported themselves in various games, before the feast. At the entrance to the banqueting hall servants crowned the guests with wreaths of flowers, the first drinks were served and, after the usual prayers, the meal began.

The Egyptians were not in the habit of reclining on couches at mealtimes; often there was not even a table, the various dishes being served in baskets, placed near the guests. Boy and girl musicians provided music on the harp, lyre and tambourine, blending the harmony of their instruments with the fragrance of the dishes and the measured movements of the dancing girls. Sometimes even acrobats and pantomimists performed their comic or daring turns during or after the meal.

Herodotus, Athenaeus and Plutarch have recorded the fact that in order to inspire the guest to enjoy all the terrestrial pleasures to the full, a coffin was sometimes brought in at the end of the meal, with an imitation skeleton in it, so that in front of the image of death, more value was set on the joys of life in general and the joys of the table in particular.

The banquets of the Assyrians and the Chaldeans. Strabo tells us that the epitaph inscribed on the tomb of Sardanapalus reads as follows: 'Sardanapalus, the son of Anacyndara, had the towns of Anchiale and Tarsus built in a day. Passer-by, drink, eat and be merry, for nothing else matters!'.

This legendary king, the last descendant of Semiramis, was, as is known, surprised by his enemies while he was giving a magnificent banquet in gratitude to his victorious soldiers.†

The Assyrians, essentially a military people, always celebrated the victories of their armies. In this land of the Euphrates and the Tigris, manners were more barbaric than on the banks of the Nile; but if the people lived poorly on a land often devastated by wars, the rich relished delicate, carefully prepared dishes. In an Assyrian bas-relief, we can see the king reclining languidly on a sumptuous couch, the queen sitting at his feet, the table richly decked, slaves charming the guests with the music of their string instruments. The vessels which are on the table have no feet, they were designed to be quaffed in one copious draught. Maspéro, in his *Lectures Historiques* gives the following description of one of these banquets, given by Ashur-bani-pal, the king under whom Nineveh reached the height of its power:

'The doors of the palace remained open to all comers for seven days. Multi-coloured draperies were hung on the walls, transforming the courtyards into immense banqueting halls. People crowded into them from morning till night, stretching out on state couches or sitting on seats, ordering whatever they liked. The slaves had been ordered to refuse them nothing, but to bring to everyone whatever they desired. Women and children, as well as men, were admitted to this largesse. Nor were soldiers, whose duty prevented them leaving the barracks, forgotten: the king sent food and drink to those who could not come, and in such a profusion that they had nothing to regret.

'In the palace halls Ashur-bani-pal received the heads of the palace and the Ministers of State. They sat on double seats, two on one side of a small table and two on the other facing them. The chairs were high and had no backs or footrests, or anything else for the guests to lean on. The honour of dining with the king must be bought at the price of some discomfort. The tables were covered with fringed tablecloths on which the slaves placed the dishes.'

In Babylon, the inner precincts of which could enclose Paris four times, there were orchards and gardens capable of supplying the town with food during a long siege. The sumptuousness of their banquets equalled that of the Assyrians.

According to the biblical story told in the Book of Daniel, the King of Babylon, Belshazzar (Bel-shar-utsur), was surprised by Cyrus during the great feast when the sacred vessels (which Nebuchadnezzar had carried off from the Temple of Jerusalem) were served at the orgies of his courtesans and concubines.

†Lemprière tells a somewhat different story. According to him, Sardanapalus never was much of a soldier. In fact, he was celebrated for his luxury and voluptuousness. The greater part of his time he spent in the company of his eunuchs and he was given to 'disguising himself in the habit of a female and spinning wool for his amusement'. This effeminacy made him unpopular with his officers and they rose against him. On rare occasions only did he bestir himself to appear at the head of his army. Sardanapalus was beaten and besieged in the city of Ninus for two years. When he despaired of success, he burned himself in his palace, with his eunuchs, concubines and all his treasures. None of which prevented his being made a god after death.—*Editor.*

Ashur-bani-pal (669-626 B.C.) feasting with his queen
(*Assyrian palace relief from the British Museum*)

The Banquets of the Hebrews. The Hebrews were nomads for a long time, having come out of Chaldea to occupy the land of Canaan. When they decided to stay on the banks of the Jordan, a period of prosperity and peaceful life enabled them to partake of the pleasures of the table. At first they were simple pleasures, if the Holy Scripture is to be believed: 'and Judah and Israel dwelt safely, every man under his vine and fig tree, from Dan even to Beer-sheba, all the days of Solomon'.

Later luxury and refinement were introduced and their banquets became very elaborate. At the time of the Kings, the Hebrews sat down to take their meals. Later they adopted the habit of reclining on couches to eat. Then they perfumed their wine and added fragrant essences to it, and the prophet, condemning all this luxury, said to the people of Sion: 'Therefore now shall they go captive with the first that go captive, and the banquet of them that stretched themselves shall be removed'.

As soon as the guest arrived at the house prepared for the banquet, holy water and perfumes were poured on him, he was crowned with flowers and took his place according to his rank. Glass vessels with relief designs on them were placed in front of him and utensils of bronze, gold and silver were set on the table. When one wanted to do special honours to a guest, one served him a double helping. Ecclesiasticus says: 'A seal of emerald in a rich setting of gold is the melody of music with good wine'.

And the Hebrews, according to the prophet Isaiah, had in their feasts 'the harp, and the tabret and pipe, and wine'.

For a long time women were not admitted to the feasts, but then came a time when they were accepted. Ezekiel says: 'and thou satest upon a stately bed, and a table prepared before it, whereupon thou hast set mine incense and mine oil'. They brought in Sabeans from the desert, who put bracelets on the women's wrists and magnificent crowns on their heads.

The banquets of the Persians. The splendour of Susa and Ecbatana, where the Persian kings spent the winter, is well known through the testimony of historians and the discoveries of archaeology. The magnificence of their tables was in no way inferior to that of the other oriental courts.

The Persian kings' tables were lavish, if we are to go by what Athenaeus says: 'One thousand animals are slaughtered daily for the King's table; these comprise horses, camels, oxen, asses, deer and most of the smaller animals. Many birds are also consumed, such as Arabian ostriches—and the creature is large—geese, and cocks'. They sometimes used to roast animals whole. The Book of Esther describes a banquet given by Ahasuerus, at which Queen Vashti's fall from favour was proclaimed after she had refused to appear at the King's orders. This magnificent banquet, served in the palace gardens, lasted seven days. White, green and hyacinth coloured tapestries were attached with cords of fine scarlet linen with silver rings to marble columns. The couches were silver and gold on floors of porphyry, alabaster and streaked marble. Drinks were poured into gold cups of different shapes and there was an abundance of wine. The manner of drinking was as ordered.

The banquets of the Greeks. Ancient Greeks organized banquets or City Feasts for social or religious ends.

In addition to these banquets, where all the citizens were assembled, and which could take place only on solemn festivals, religion prescribed that every day there should be a sacred meal. For this purpose, men chosen by the city were required to eat together, in its name, within the enclosure of the prytaneum, in the presence of the sacred fire and the protecting gods. The Greeks were convinced that, if this repast was interrupted but for a single day, the State was menaced with the loss of the favour of its gods.

At Athens, the men who took part in the common meal were selected by lot, and the law severely punished those who refused to perform this duty. The citizens who sat at the sacred table were clothed for the time in sacerdotal character; they were called *Parasites.* This word which, at a later period, became a term of contempt, was in the beginning a sacred title. In the time of Demosthenes the parasites had disappeared; but the prytanes were still required to eat together in the prytaneum. In all cities there were halls destined for community meals.

At this meal, every guest had a crown upon his head; it was a custom of the ancients to wear a crown of leaves or flowers when one performed a religious act: 'the more one is adorned with flowers', they said, 'the surer one is of pleasing the gods'. For the same reason the banqueters were clothed in robes of white; among the ancients white was the sacred colour which pleased the gods.

In the Odyssey, Homer describes the banquet given by Telemachus to Athene who has assumed the appearance of Mentor, a Taphian chieftain: 'She found the Suitors sitting on hides of oxen they had slaughtered and playing draughts, while their squires and pages were busy round them, squires blending wine and water in mixing-bowls, and the pages carving meat in lavish proportions or washing the tables with sponges before setting them ready. . . . Presently a maid came with water in a handsome golden jug and poured it out over a silver basin so that they could rinse their hands. She then drew a polished table to their side and a staid housekeeper brought some bread and set it by them, with a choice of dainties, helping them liberally to all she could offer. Meanwhile, a carver dished up for them on platters slices of various meats and put gold cups beside them, which a steward filled up with wine. . . .'

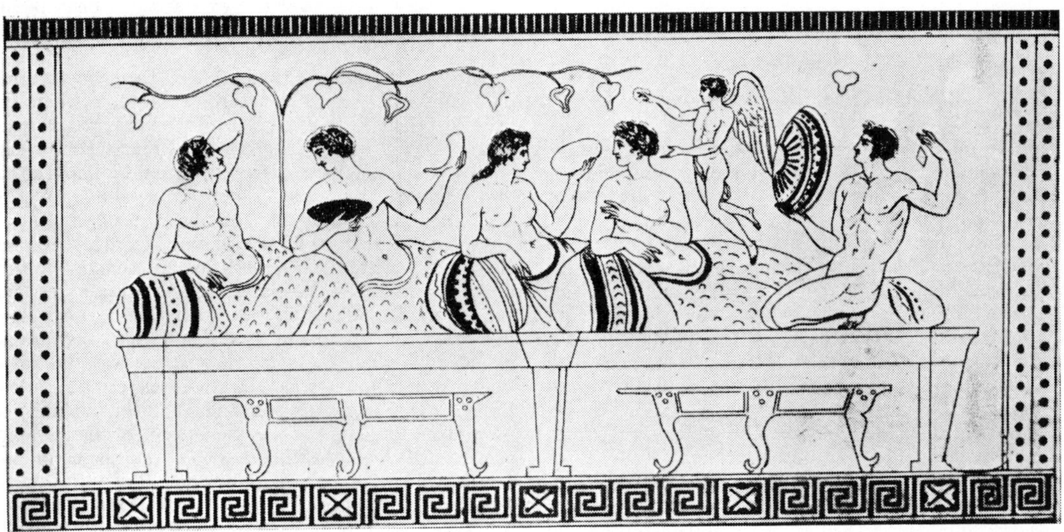

Fresco showing a meal in Greek times

We have few descriptions of the great Greek banquets, but we know, nevertheless, that women were never invited, that the guests' shoes were taken off before they entered the place of the banquet, that after they lay down on couches they washed, and that the banquet only began after the gods of the home and country had been invoked. The napkin was unknown for a long time and they ate with their hands. The guests wore crowns of flowers; they said that the perfume they exuded soothed the headaches caused by the wine. They sang, young girls entertained the guests by playing the harp and the lute and there were famous dancing girls. Plutarch suggested that these pleasures prevented quarrels and disagreements among the guests who became very excited at the end of the meals.

Dancing and music at a Greek banquet

But, notwithstanding the abundance of dishes at Greek banquets, it is claimed that they were always inferior in quality to those of the Romans in the time of the empire.

We know that some of the ancient Greek peoples took all their meals together, thus making them into something like banquets. Community meals were also part of the social order in Sparta, where under the laws of Lycurgus all the townspeople ate together the famous broth which some authors claim to have been only a hash of various meats, with a high fat content, and spiced with vinegar.

'This broth', says Plutarch, 'was appreciated by the Lacedaemonians above all other dishes'.

The Banquets of the Romans. The gastronomical splendours of Imperial Rome are famous to this day. From Apicius, who spent vast sums of money on the satisfaction of his stomach, to Lucullus who sent explorers to new countries in search of new foods, history has kept for us the magnificence of an era dedicated to physical pleasures, and particularly to the delectations of the table.

The Romans often sacrified the dishes themselves to presentation, setting and ostentation. At one meal Heliogabalus served his guests 600 ostrich brains, peas with grains of gold, lentils with precious stones, and other dishes with pearls and amber. In his golden palace, Nero had ceilings that opened to shower flowers on the guests. Cleopatra, Queen of Egypt, who introduced Roman luxury to her court, having come to Antony in Gilicia, gave him a truly regal meal: 'All the dishes were of gold, set with precious stones of the finest craftsmanship. The walls were covered with purple and gold cloth. Having arranged twelve couches each of three places, she invited Antony and the people he wished to bring with him. When Antony expressed astonishment at all this luxury, Cleopatra presented it all to him'. The next day, the preparations were even more sumptuous. Thus protocol, richness, and abundance were the rule in the Roman banquets.

The dining-room where the Romans took their meals was called the *triclinium*. This was so called because it was the custom to put only three couches around one table. The fourth side remained free so as to make serving easier and to leave room for the entertainment which the dancers, mimes, 'palestrites' and sometimes gladiators provided for the guests. This figure three could, say some historians, have another meaning. As on each of the couches there was room only for three persons—the number of the Graces—the total number of guests sitting around the table was symbolically that of the Muses.

However, this rule could not always be complied with, especially when the feast was a special one or when there were more numerous guests. But in the placing of guests the figure three was always taken as a basis. So, in important gatherings, nine, fifteen or thirty places were reserved on each couch. On these couches the guests were placed, in accordance with protocol, in the following order: (1) the place of the host; (2) his wife or a relative; (3) that of an intimate friend or a privileged guest, or (4) the consular place, or place of honour, and (5), (6), (7), (8), (9), the other guests.

On these couches the guests usually half-reclined, with the left arm supported by a cushion.

Each guest brought his own napkin. Some poetic satirists of the time tell us that sometimes the guests stole their neighbours' napkins.

On arrival, the guests changed from their town clothes into white robes. They had to enter the room where the feast was held with the right foot. They reclined on couches which were arranged around the table in different ways, taking their places in order of importance. Slaves removed the guests' shoes to put sandals on their feet. They performed their ablutions after each course. They tied a fine napkin around their neck and had another beside them, because for a long time the Romans ate with their fingers. After invoking the Penates, Lares and Jupiter, the feast began. It was usually in three parts. The first course, during which a light wine was drunk, included the *hors-d'oeuvre*. The second was the *coena* (meal) proper, after which sacrifices were made to the Lares amid silence. The pieces reserved for this purpose were taken to the fire as was the ancient custom. A slave entered the room bearing a goblet in his hand and offered a libation to propitious gods. The third course was the dessert, which was usually composed of fresh or dried fruit, or fruit in pastries. But in a menu found in Pompeii, this part of the meal had amongst other things sow's udders, wild boar's head, fricassée of wild duck, a cream made of flour and Vicence cakes.

Sometimes the guests used to pick off rose petals from their crowns and drop them into the wine served to them by young servants, and then drink the liquid and the petals together. Musicians, singers, reciters and dancers appeared at important feasts. Sometimes there were gladiator fights, acrobats and clowns.

The combination of these rich surroundings, the sumptuousness of the cooking and the abundance of the festivities, created in the Roman banquets a magnificence never equalled before or since.

Trimalchio's feast. Trimalchio's feast, which is described for us by Petronius, can be taken as the prototype of the great banquets of ancient Rome. It would appear that Petronius' story is a little tendentious and that in this narration he wanted mainly to record, perhaps with a satirical intention, the exaggerated luxury of the grandiose and barbaric feasts given by Nero. We can, nevertheless, find in this account of Petronius a relatively faithful description of what a great feast in imperial Rome was like.

'. . . The first course is brought in, which could not be more splendid. On a tray of relishes stood a small figure of an ass in Corinthian bronze, carrying twin baskets, one of which contained green and the other black olives. On the back of the animal were two silver dishes—their rims engraved with the name of Trimalchio and the weight of the metal. Salvers, moulded like bridges, contained dormice, seasoned with honey and poppy seeds. There were also sizzling sausages on a silver gridiron with Syrian plums and pomegranate seeds placed beneath it. . . . A tray was placed before us containing a basket in which there was a hen, carved out of wood, wings spread out as if she were sitting. Up stepped two slaves and, after rummaging in the straw, took out pea-fowls' eggs, distributing them among the guests. I am afraid they might have been already hatched, but let us see if they are still edible. For the purpose of eating these eggs, spoons weighing at least half a pound each were handed to us and we broke the eggs, which were made of light pastry looking exactly like the shell.

'I was just about to throw away the one which was served to me, as I thought it was addled and had become a chicken already, when one of the guests, who was an old hand at these tricks, stopped me: "There is something in it," said he, "I don't know what it is, but it is excellent." I then looked in the shell and found a fine, plump beccafico (garden-warbler) in it, deliciously spiced, hidden inside the yolk. . . .

'Crystal flagons, carefully sealed, were brought in. Around the neck of each bottle hung a label worded thus: "*Falernian opimian wine 100 years old*". (Falernian wine was made in the Campanian vineyards round Falerno, under the shadow of Vesuvius, and was praised by many Latin poets. Opimian wine was vintaged when Opimius was Consul, in the year 633 of Rome (121 B.C.)—*Editor*.) While tippling, we admired the sumptuousness of the feast and a slave put on the table a silver skeleton so perfectly made that the joints and backbone could be articulated in all directions. After the slave had made the springs of this automaton work several times and made it go through various contortions, Trimalchio began to recite:

"Man has so little, alas! and of his years
the thread is so short and fragile!
The grave is following in our footsteps,
but in their rapid flight
let us grace our moments with pleasure".

'This elegy was interrupted by the arrival of the second course, the appearance of which did not come up to our expectations. However, a new marvel soon attracted everyone's attention. This was a globe-shaped tray with the twelve signs of the zodiac reproduced on it in a circle. Above each one the chef had placed dishes which in their shape or nature had some analogy with the particular constellation: over Aries (the Ram) were chick peas, over Taurus (the Bull) a piece of beef, over Gemini (the Twins) kidneys and testicles, over Cancer (the Crab) a simple crown, over Leo (the Lion) African figs, over Virgo (the Virgin) the uterus of a sow, over Libra (the Scales) a pair of scales with a pie on one side and a cake on the other, over Scorpio (the Scorpion) a small sea-fish, over Sagittarius (the Archer) a hare, over Capricorn (the Goat) a lobster, over Aquarius (the Waterbearer) a goose and over Pisces (the Fish) two surmullets. In the middle of this contraption on a tuft of artistically-cut turf reposed a honeycomb. An Egyptian slave served hot bread all round from a silver dish, and, whilst doing his round, he screeched a raucous song from the pantomime Silphium. We were glumly preparing to attack this rather coarse fare, when Trimalchio said to us: "Let us eat; believe me, you have the most succulent of meals before you".

'As he said this four slaves hurried towards the table and, dancing in time to music, removed the top part of the globe-shaped tray. And lo, a new course was before our eyes; plump chickens, sows' udders, a hare with wings fastened to its back, symbolizing Pegasus. We also noticed at the corners of the tray four figures of Marsyas, with highly-seasoned fish sauce dripping from their bellies over the fish, which were floating about, as if they were in a regular canal. At this sight, the slaves began to applaud and we followed their example. Then it was with a smile of satisfaction that we set to to attack these exquisite dishes. . . .

'The slaves spread coverings on our couches which had hunters with their hunting spears, in fact the whole hunting scene, embroidered on them. We did not as yet know what this meant, when, suddenly, a great noise was heard outside and Laconian hounds rushed into the room and began running around the table. They were followed by a platter on which lay the most enormous wild boar. On its head was perched a cap of a freed slave; on his tusks hung down two baskets lined with palm leaves, one was filled with Syrian dates, the other with Theban dates. Little sucking-pigs, made of pastry and baked in the oven, surrounded the animal as if they were pressing on the teats, thus giving the guests enough indication to see that it was a breeding sow that was served to them. The guests to whom these were offered had permission to take them away. . . .

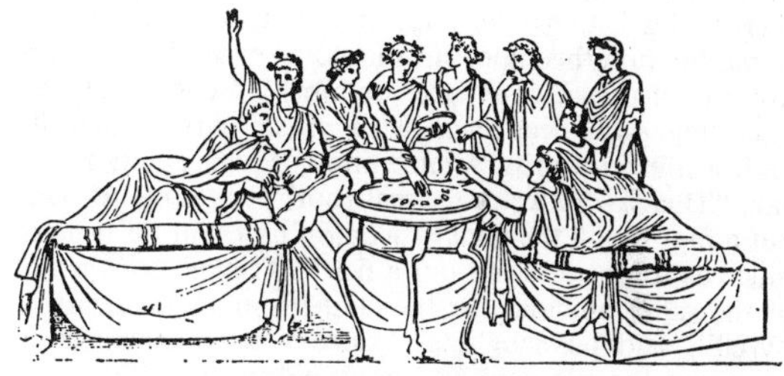

A Roman banquet

'Drawing his hunting knife, a slave gave the wild boar a great stab in the belly and suddenly, from the opening in the animal's side, flew out thrushes. Vainly the birds tried to escape, flying round and round the room: birdcatchers provided with fowlers' rods instantly caught them and by order of their master offered one to each guest. Then Trimalchio said: "Just look if this glutton hasn't swallowed all the acorns in the forest". Immediately, the slaves ran to the baskets hanging from the animal's tusks and distributed to us equal portions of Syrian and Theban dates.

'When the table had been cleared in time to music, we saw three white pigs, muzzled and adorned with little bells, enter the room. The slave who was driving them told us that one of them was two years old, the other three, and the third was six years old. I for one thought that these pigs which were brought in were those acrobatic pigs that have been seen in the circuses and that we were about to be shown some extraordinary trick. But

Trimalchio dispelled our speculations: "Which of the three", asked he, "would you like to eat? It will be prepared for you at once. Country cooks cook a chicken, a pheasant or some other suchlike kickshaws but mine will boil a whole calf all at once. Call the cook!" And without giving us the embarrassment of having to make a choice, he ordered the oldest pig to be slaughtered.

'Trimalchio, turning to us with a gracious expression, said: "If this wine is not to your taste, I shall have it replaced by another. Prove to me that you find it good by doing it justice. Thanks to the favour of the gods I do not have to buy it, for all that flatters your taste is grown on my estate, which I have not visited yet. I am told it is somewhere around Tarracina and Tarentum. Now I feel like joining Sicily to some of my property so that if I ever fancy going to Africa, I shall be able to do so without leaving my estate. . . .".

'Trimalchio was still rambling on, when an enormous pig was served to us on a tray which took up a great part of the table. The guests expressed their wonder at the rapidity with which the cook worked; each swore that any other cook would take longer just to prepare a fowl, and what increased our astonishment even further was the fact that the pig seemed to us even bigger than the wild boar which had been served to us earlier. In the meantime Trimalchio, examining the animal very closely, said: "What do I see here? This pig has not been cleaned. No, to be sure, it has not been gutted. Bring the cook here at once". The poor devil approached the table, trembling, and owned that he had forgotten. "What! Forgotten!" cried Trimalchio in a great fury. "Wouldn't one think, from the way he speaks, that he has merely neglected to season it with pepper and cummin? Off with your clothes, knave!" Immediately the culprit's clothes were stripped off, and he stood between two torturers. His downcast and pitiful look softened the hearts of all those present and each one of us hastened to plead for mercy. "Such things do happen", said we, "we beg you to pardon him this time, but should he ever do this again, not one of us will intercede for him!" I could not help regarding such negligence with much harsher severity and, leaning towards Agamemnon, I whispered in his ear: "This slave must be a real fool! Forgetting to clean out a pig! By all the gods! I wouldn't let him off if he so much as forgot to clean out a fish!" Trimalchio was not of the same opinion, for he suddenly made a decision. "Well", said he, laughing, "since your memory is so poor, gut the pig here and now, before us". The cook put on his tunic again, seized a knife, and with a trembling hand slashed the animal's paunch in several places, and out of these slits, which kept widening owing to the pressure of the weight inside, black puddings and sausages began to pour forth. At the sight of this unexpected feat all the guests began to applaud and shout, "Vivat Gaius!".

'The cook was given the privilege of drinking in our presence and he received a silver crown.'

Banquet at the court of Domitian. Dion Cassius, who wrote a *Roman History* in 80 volumes, based on an annalistic scheme from the mythical beginnings to the reign of Severus Alexander, describes a banquet given by Domitian in these words:

'This is how Domitian treated the chief senators and other knights whom he had invited to dinner. He had a room prepared, the ceiling, the walls and the floor of which were all covered with black. The chairs were of the same colour. The guests were brought in one by one, at midnight, alone, without any of their servants.

'To begin with each guest had a pillar placed before him, like those that are put on tombs, on which the name of everyone was engraved and on top of which stood a lamp of the sort that are usually hung up in sepulchres. Naked young slaves, with blackened bodies, as terrible to behold as ghosts, came into the room. They executed a mournful dance around the guests, then stopped and stood still. They then served the guests in dishes all the instruments and ornaments that are used at funerals. Stricken with fear and trembling they expected to have their throats cut at any moment. What added to their agonies of fear was the silence which reigned among them, as if they were already dead, and Domitian, just to cheer them up, discoursed on nothing but murders and massacres.

'At last, he dismissed them. Having first sent away their servants who were waiting for them in the lobby, he then ordered unknown men to escort his guests home, some in litters, others in chariots, which made the guests more apprehensive than ever.

'On arrival at home, scarcely had they begun to breathe, when they were told that someone was asking for them in the name of the Emperor. They gave themselves up for lost, but the visitors were Domitian's messengers, carrying, in procession, one the silver pillar of which I spoke earlier, the second the vessels that were used at table, the third some other precious object artistically decorated and, lastly, they received the slaves who played the parts of phantoms and who served them, but well washed and clothed. They thus passed the whole night in fear, receiving these various presents in turn one after another.'

The banquets of the Gauls (100 B.C.). The food of the early Gauls mainly consisted of fresh or salt pork, the animals they raised or killed in the forests, and milk.

Their meals were long, plentiful and bore the stamp of a vulgar sort of luxury.

Diodorus Siculus tells us that at their meals the Gauls were served by their children or by young people of both sexes.

They had their tables placed near a brazier, with spits and cauldrons, in which their food was cooked.

Posidonious, the Greek stoic philosopher, has left us a rather curious description of such a meal:

'Around a very low table, there were bundles of straw or hay, on which the guests sat. A little bread and great quantities of meat, boiled, roasted on the spit, or grilled (all the present-day methods of cooking meat were, as can be seen, known to our ancestors), constituted the meal.

'The food is served in a clean way, on silver or copper dishes (the plating of copper and tin was already known at that time) in rich houses and in earthenware or wooden ones in the homes of the poor.

'Each man takes a whole joint and bites it; it is a lion's meal. Should the piece be too tough or too big, they use for cutting it a small knife the sheath of which is attached to the scabbard of the sword. A single drinking vessel, either earthenware or metal, is handed by the slaves and makes its rounds as often as possible, but one drinks little at a time.'

From these vessels the Gauls used to drink various wines, and also from the horns of wild oxen, ornamented with gold and silver rings, and sometimes from the skulls of their enemies killed in battle or of their own dead parents, whose memory they thus wanted to honour, out of respect and filial piety. In particular they drank the wine of Bézier or Vienna, wines which the Romans esteemed greatly, because they had a taste of pitch.

Italian and Greek wines were also to be seen on the tables of the rich. These were taken in small quantities, diluted with a little water. The poor gorged themselves on beer and hydromel (honey diluted with water, with herbs and spices added).

'Fish is in great demand in the areas near the sea, rivers and streams. The Gauls eat it mainly grilled, seasoned with salt and cummin and sprinkled with vinegar.

'On special days a round table is set up and the guests sit around it in a circle. The middle place is given to the most distinguished or the most valiant; he is like the *Coryphaeus*—leader of the chorus. Next to him sits the master of the house, then all the other guests in order of importance. Behind is the circle of *clients*, who accompany their masters in battle, some carrying shields, others lances. They eat as other guests.

'After a feast the Gauls would start a fight, at first just for amusement, but they would soon get excited and the fighting would become so fierce that they would have to be separated.

'There was an ancient custom which decreed that the legs of the animals served should be allotted to the bravest, that is to those who were declared to be such. This was a source of quarrels and, often, fights to the death.'

The banquets of the Gallo-Romans. The Gallo-Romans, at any rate those who belonged to the rich classes, had adopted Latin customs and had their meals in dining-rooms in all respects resembling those of Rome and Pompeii. Their banquets were, in fact, modelled on the Roman. It appears, however, that the custom of reclining on a couch at mealtimes was discarded by the Gallo-Romans early on.

De la Bédolière, in his *Histoire des Moeurs et de la Vie Privée des Français*, thus describes the banquets of the Gallo-Romans:

'Great State banquets are generally given in the evening. The table, ornamented with incrustations, is round, covered with a fine tablecloth. The couches, which follow the contours of the table, are in the shape of an arch, or the Greek letter *Sigma*. Some Gauls, disdaining the indolence of the Romans, use benches, stools, and other wooden seats covered with a carpet instead of couches.

'The architricline announces that dinner is served. The guests wash their hands, which they will do again after the first course. They put on special robes and sandals, which they will leave at the lower end of the *sigma*. They unfold their napkins, if they have brought them, for the host does not provide these. Then they take their places around the table.

'The slaves bring in a great quantity of meat, roast or boiled, which is carved with great skill and dexterity by servants in charge of this job. The meal always starts with a tasting of *mulsum* or *medum*, mulled wine, mixed with honey. . . . A salver (*repositorium*) is placed in the centre of the table, and various dishes are put on it one after the other; fresh eggs, quarters of beef, mutton, pork, goat, all seasoned with yolks of egg, black pepper, brine, cummin, salt from the salt mines or residue from boiled sea-water. . . . As a dessert, after having consumed an endless number of various dishes, the guests are served hot or cold tarts, honey cakes, soft cheese, grilled escargots, medlars, chestnuts, figs, Gaul peaches and fresh and dried grapes. At the end of the meal hot mulsum is brought in once again and the slaves distribute toothpicks made of feathers, wood and silver.

'To satisfy all the senses, the dining-room and the *sigma* are strewed with leaves of laurel, ivy, verdant vine-branches; both the guests and the servants are crowned with flowers. Garlands of roses hang from the handles of *canthares*. Large baskets, placed on the table as well as on the *abacus* or sideboard, are full of bunches of cytisus (laburnum), saffron (crocus), privet, marigolds and rosemary, and their fragrance mingles with that of Arabian aromatics smouldering in the three-legged brazier.'

The banquets of the Franks. Gallo-Roman manners were adopted by the Franks to such an extent that Caius Sollius Apollinaris Sidonius states that one could find in their meals 'the elegance of Greece, the abundance of Gaul, the dispatch of Italy, the pomp of a public ceremony allied to the fastidiousness of a private table, of the order befitting a king's palace'. Floral decoration played a great part in the banquets of that epoch. At times meals were served on tables covered with a thick carpet of roses instead of tablecloths. But it was with the coming of Charlemagne that the Franks began to invest their feasts with the greatest splendour. That great Emperor was the first to introduce the ceremonial which was later adopted by the kings of France.

We find the following description of a banqueting hall in *La France* of Le Bas:

'The walls, instead of being whitewashed stone, were carpeted with ivy. The floor was strewn with flowers so that it was like walking on an enamelled field. Silver lilies contrasted in it with crimson poppies and the room was scented with delightful perfumes.

'As for the table itself, it had more roses on it than a whole field. It was not an ordinary tablecloth that was covering it, it was roses; they chose something that flatters the sense of smell and covers the table at the same time, in preference to linen.'

And here is another description of a feast of the Franks in *L'Art Culinaire* by the Marquis de Cussy:

'The Franks, as well as the Gallo-Romans, also adopted the custom of Thermae between dinner and supper and washed their hands before meals. . . . Authors of the time mention silver tables, all sorts of utensils in gold and silver, enormous basins—one weighing 170 pounds belonged to a patrician called Mummol; another, weighing 72 pounds, belonged to Arnould, the bishop of Metz and plushy and downy tablecloths and napkins.'

The Franks kept open table and had a very thorough code of table manners. We know that they had the custom of drinking in turn, passing the wine round in the same cup. They considered that any lamp desecrated the feast table. So the rooms where their meals were held were not lit except for torches held by slaves.

Meal served to Grandgousier, Gargantua's father, from an old edition of the works of Rabelais

French banquets from the Middle Ages to the fifteenth century—During the Middle Ages, in the great houses, the beginning of a feast was announced by the sound of a horn. That was a privilege reserved for the highest personages in the kingdom. Others had to be content with bells, as in monasteries. The first act of the guests before sitting down was to wash their hands with perfumed water. Then damsels and young pages handed napkins to them. The presentation of a napkin to the sovereign was considered as a very great honour to be performed by the chamberlain or some other gentleman of high standing. And, as all food was eaten with the hands, since forks had not yet come into use, the ablutions were often repeated in the course of the meal, as well as at the end of it.

The guests were seated in order of precedence, the master of the house at the head of the table, the ladies taking their places with the family. The king ate alone. His table was covered with a tablecloth and the servants brought him knives, spoons and bowls.

Most of the time, goblets and tankards did not figure on the table. These vessels were put on a sideboard or a buffet (credence-tables), and the pages and valets filled and brought them to the guests. This manner of serving beverages during meals survived until the end of the eighteenth century.

Then came bread. Grace was said and after that the first dishes were carried in by the servants with great pomp, sometimes even announced by a flourish of trumpets. The dishes were tasted or touched with a talisman to make sure they were not poisoned.

In royal courts these tests were carried out with great solemnity. Luxury, pomp and abundance were at this time at their height. First soups were served, then fish, but it was among the side-dishes that roast peacocks, with gilded bills and claws, dressed in their rich plumage, swans and pheasants, presented in a similar manner, together with calves and pigs, made their appearance. The *dessert*, fruit and creams, preceded the end of the meal, which was concluded with dried fruit preserves, pastry and hippocras (spiced wine). As soon as the tables were cleared and the washing of hands completed, the guests stood up and said grace. After which the valets brought in aromatized wines and various beverages and sweetmeats, which constituted the *boute-hors*, or 'issuing from the table' and were consumed standing up. Then came the minstrels and troubadours, trouvères (epic poets), buffoons, jugglers and jesters. Before the fourteenth century, entertainments provided during a meal were real spectacles.

The chronicles of the time have recorded for us a description of these great feasts, with their unparalleled luxury. They mention certain princes who had dishes served by armed valets on horseback. Others had horns to herald the arrival of each course, blown by minstrels astride oxen, dressed in scarlet. Accounts of the feasts given by Louis IX at Saumur, at which three thousand knights were present, or of the table of Queen Blanche, the mother of the king, entertaining twenty archbishops or bishops, or of the king's table, where the King of Navarre was served by Joinville (the famous French historian, 1224-1319) whilst the Count d'Artois carved before his brother the king, give some semblance of an idea of the spendour of the banquets of this royal epoch.

French banquets with entertainments given by Charles V to the Emperor of Germany. In 1378, the Emperor Charles IV, accompanied by his son, went to Paris to see the King of France, who was his nephew and godson. This visit was the occasion of magnificent feasts, lengthy accounts of which are given in the official chronicles of Charles V. The banquet took place on January 6th in the great hall of the Palace. More than eight hundred persons were invited to it. The high table was set at the top end of the room, under a gold cloth canopy, with three valances of blue velvet, adorned with fleurs-de-lys, to mark the places of the three sovereigns. The Archbishop of Rheims, the Emperor, the King of France, the King of the Romans, the Bishop of Brunswick, the Bishop of Paris and the Bishop of Beauvais sat at the high table.

Kings at table (*Woodcut, Lyon, 1508*)

The banquet was to have had four courses, each course consisting of ten pairs of dishes. But the Emperor, who was old and suffering from gout, began to look tired and so the King ordered one of the courses to be omitted to reach the time for entertainment sooner. In those days the word 'entremets' meant entertainment provided between two courses. The entertainment was described at length in the chronicles and represented the capture of Jerusalem by the crusaders.

French banquets of the sixteenth century. The great banquets of the sixteenth century show a predilection for fine table linen, rich table-service and decorations not only for the table, but also for dressers, sideboards and credence-tables, which formed part of the furniture of banqueting halls.

Massive silver and gold pieces, richly wrought and engraved, magnificent Faïence and Nevers porcelain, priceless Venetian glassware, were set out on fine linen tablecloths. Henri III liked to have the tablecloths finely pleated and goffered, exactly like the ruffs or frills which were then worn round the neck.

This was the time when the fork and the long-handled spoon came into use.

The order of dishes served at banquets was the same as before, but cooking had become much more refined. Belon, in his book *Histoire de la nature des oiseaux*, gives us a description of one of these feasts: 'For entrées we had a thousand little disguises of flesh, as soups, fricassées, hashes, salads. The second course consisted of a roast joint, a boiled joint, various meats, both butcher's and game. To end with there were cold things, such as fruit, milk products, sweetmeats, cakes, hot buns, mouth-watering little cakes, portions of cheese, chestnuts, short-shank Capendy apples, a salad of lemons or pomegranates'.

Under François I, the luxury of the table was worthy of the Renaissance, of which the king was the moving spirit. The châteaux of Amboise and Montmorency saw magnificent banquets. Catherine de Medici was sumptuously received by the city of Paris in 1549. 30 peacocks, 33 pheasants, 21 swans, 9 cranes, 33 ducks, 33 ibises, 33 egrets, 33 young herons, 30 young goats, 99 young pigeons, 99 turtle doves, 13 partridges, 33 goslings, 3 young bustards, 13 young capons, 90 quails, 66 boiling chickens, 66 Indian chickens, 30 capons, 90 spring chickens in vinegar, 66 chickens 'cooked as grouse', were served at this banquet. There were a great number of other dishes from which, in principle, butcher's meat was excluded, being considered too ordinary, which, however, did not prevent the organizer of this monster banquet from serving to his guests many young piglets, rabbits, and a vast quantity of vegetables, such as asparagus, broad beans, peas and artichokes.

In 1571, the city of Paris again put itself to extraordinary trouble and expense in honour of Elizabeth, Queen of Austria, the wife of Charles IX, on the occasion of his triumphal entry into the capital. The banquet, which was given in his honour, consisted entirely of fish dishes, the day being Friday. Among other things, 1,000 frogs, 200 white herrings and 200 pickled herrings, 18 big turbots, 18 brill, 18 mullets, 50 pounds of whale meat, 18 trout, 50 carps, 18 lampreys, and 200 big larval lamprey figured in the menu.

A curious document, preserved in the Archives of the Nord department, gives us the list of dishes served on the occasion of the marriage of Maître Baude Cuvillon (Conseiller et Maître ordinaire de la Chambre des comptes) in 1571. It is entitled *Devise pour le souper des nopces de Maistre Baulde Cuvillon*. If we are to believe this document, the nuptial agapes consisted of two meals: first—banquet number one, in the afternoon, then about midnight, a sort of supper called *disner de chauldéau*. On the menu for this dinner, the first and second courses are called *first* and *second* plates, and the dessert is called *issue*.

Under Henri IV, with whose reign the sixteenth century ended and the seventeenth began, there is a not a single important banquet to report.

French banquets of the seventeenth century. Under the reign of Louis XIII the luxury of the banquets underwent great changes: there was less display of sumptuousness and more evidence of striving after harmony and simplicity. The arrangement of the menus, too, was better.

Two documents, pertaining to the reign of Louis XIV, will enable the reader to assess the complications of a big banquet and give an idea of the really enormous number of dishes which could be presented on one table.

Here is how Nicolas de Bonnefons, in a work entitled *Délices de la Campagne*, published about 1652, describes a dinner:

'The great fashion is to place four fine soups at the four corners with four dish stands between each two, with four salt-cellars placed near the soup tureen. On the dish-stands are placed four entrées, in low pie-dishes *à l'italienne*. Guests' plates should be deep, so that they can use them for soup, or for helping themselves to whatever they wish to eat, without having to take it spoonful by spoonful out of the serving dish, as they might otherwise be disgusted at the sight of a spoon, which had been in the mouth of a person, being dipped into the serving-dish without being wiped.'

This recommendation is rather extraordinary and proves that even in the great houses, in the middle of the seventeenth century, when a meal was eaten in a family circle or among friends, all those present at table dipped into the same soup-tureen.

'The second course,' continues Nicolas de Bonnefons, 'will consist of four substantial dishes set in the corners, a *court-bouillon*, a piece of beef, a good big roast and salads on plates. The third course will consist of roast poultry and game, small roasts on plates and all the rest. The middle of the table remains free as otherwise the head steward will have difficulty in reaching it, because of the size of the table. Should it be desirable to fill the centre space, melons, various salads in a bowl, or on little plates to make serving them easier, oranges and lemons and preserves in syrup on marzipan biscuits, also on plates, could be put there.'

Directions for ceremonial dinners and feasts give a good idea of the profusion and variety of dishes served on these occasions.

'I am of the opinion that for a company of thirty persons of high standing, whom one would wish to treat sumptuously, one should lay the table for that number, allowing the space of a chair between each seat (excellent advice which should be noted), putting fourteen covers on each side, one at the top of the table and one at the bottom. The table should be wide, the tablecloth should reach to the floor on all sides, there should be several salt-cellars and dish-stands in the middle for putting various dishes on.

'*First course*. Thirty bowls will be served which will contain only broths, hashes and panadas; there should be fifteen with whatever flesh is in it in whole pieces and the other fifteen of hash on bread boiled to pulp; serve alternatively, putting a good *potage de santé* at the top end and on the other side a *potage de la Reine*, made of minced partridge or pheasant. Then below the *potage de santé* another hash on mushrooms, artichokes, and other disguises, and opposite that, a bisque. Below the other hash, a *potage garni*, below the bisque, a pigeon or another bird; continue like this until the end, always alternating a strong broth with a clear.

studded with tooth-picks, musk pastilles or Verdun (sugared) almonds in small pieces of sugar paste flavoured with musk and amber.

'The head steward will give orders that the napkins be changed at least after every two courses. To clear the table, he will begin to remove plates at the lower end, whilst his assistant will remove the plates, salt-cellars and everything else on the table except the tablecloth, finishing up at the high end, where he will attend to the ablutions whilst his second in command will dispose of the plates.

Feast given by Louis XIII to the Chevaliers du Saint-Esprit on March 14th, 1635
(*Engraving by A. Bosse*)

'*Second course*. This will be composed of all sorts of ragoûts, such as fricassées, *court-bouillons*, venison haunches roast and baked in pastry, pâtés in puff pastry, entrée pies, hams, tongues, andouilles, large and small sausages and melons and entrée fruit. . . . The head steward should never set a dish full of big pieces of meat before important personages, as this may obstruct the serving and cause this personage to be forced to divide the piece to give to others.

'*Third course*. This will consist of all the big roasts such as partridges, pheasants, woodcock, wood-pigeons, young turkeys, chickens, young hares, rabbits, whole lambs, and other such like, with oranges, lemons, olives and sauceboats in the middle.

'*Fourth course*. This will be the small roasts such as snipe, thrushes, larks and all sorts of small fried things.

'*Fifth course*. Whole salmon, trout, carp, pike and various fish pies, interspersed with fricassées of turtle served with the shell on top, and crayfish.

Sixth course. This should consist of all sorts of side dishes made with butter or lard, all sorts of eggs, both in lamb gravy and fried, and others with sugar, cold and hot, with jellies of all colours and blancmanges, and artichokes, cardoons and celery dressed with pepper, on plates placed in the middle of the table.

'*Seventh course*. This will consist only of fruit, with creams and a few biscuits. Almonds and green walnuts should be served on dish-stands.

'*Eighth course*. The last course (the issue) should consist of all sorts of preserves, in syrup and dried, marzipans, bunches of fennel, sprinkled with sugar in all colours,

'I have written this for reasonable men,' concludes the author, 'as must be those who take upon themselves to conduct banquets, which is perhaps one of the most difficult tasks to accomplish, all the more so because one is dependent on so many different kinds of people, different in spirit and humour whom it is necessary to assemble at a given place and precise time. Also one is subject to censure from people in high quarters, whose lack of appetite or bad temper will cause them to criticize something that is very pleasing to others.' A difficult art indeed! But what painter, what author would not say the same of his?

The second document about provisioning a banquet in the time of Louis XIV appears in *La Vie Privée des Français* by Le Grand d'Aussy who describes an eight-course meal as follows:

'For the *first course*: various kinds of soups, meats cut into slices, sausages and other similar things.'

The *second course* was composed of fritures, *daubes*, *courts-bouillons*, game, ham, smoked pig's or ox tongue, forcemeats, hot pâtés, salads, melons.

For the *third course* there were capons, partridges, pheasants, woodcocks, wood-pigeons, young turkeys, young hares, rabbits, lambs, all roasted on a spit and served, as was then the custom, with oranges and lemons and garnished with olives.

The *fourth course* consisted of small birds: larks, ortolans, thrushes and snipe. During this course, calves' sweetbreads and various other *béatilles* were served.

The *fifth course*, the main object of which was to 'remove the taste of meat' consisted of various freshwater fish: salmon, trout, pike, carp, all of which were cooked in pastry. Crayfish and even turtle were also served with this course.

A royal banquet
during the reign of Louis XIV

During the *sixth course* the dishes of the previous course were removed and replaced by fruit, in syrups or sprinkled with sugar, and various sweets were served, such as cooked creams, blancmanges, etc. This course also included variously prepared vegetables, which were served before the sweet dishes.

The *seventh course*, which constituted what we now know as *dessert*, included pastries of all kinds and fresh fruit.

Finally, during the *eighth course*, which was also called the '*issue de la table*', the guests were served with preserves, in syrups and dried, crystallized fruit, fennel in sugar, pastilles and sugared almonds.

We have quite a lot of information on the manner in which the service at the king's table was organized.

The daily meals of King Louis XIV were as scrupulously regulated as State banquets. They were governed by a strict protocol and all the acts of this gastronomical ceremony were carried out in accordance with the rules laid down by etiquette.

'The king lunched at one o'clock. As soon as the signal for the meal was given by one of his officers, who had no other duty to perform, a procession would start on the ground floor of the building, which had for a long time been a military hospital. The ground floor of it then was occupied by the cousins, and the various other storeys by officers and servants of the royal household, more than 1,500 persons in all, taking orders from the Lord Chief Steward, a post which was always held by a prince of the blood.

'Immediately after him came the Head Steward, also a gentleman of high rank, who was more specifically entrusted with the running of the domestic side which, however, did not prevent the best names of France from being included in the ranks of this service, at least on the higher level. The Marquis de Livry, Mestre de camp (colonel) of an infantry regiment, held this office for a long time. He and his successors had charge of seven of the services. The first two, the *bread-store* and *wine-supplies*, were particularly earmarked for the royal family. The other five constituted the management of general supplies (*le grand commun*) and dealt with all the food requirements of the Palace.' (This word *commun* has remained in the vocabulary of cuisine and the term is applied in all the big hotels to everything concerned with the feeding of the personnel. Thus, the word *communard*, the origins of which go back a long way, is a cook who has to prepare the meals for his comrades-in-arms.)

'The bakery and wine department alone employed about fifty persons, masters of the kitchen, equerries, roast cooks, soup cooks, down to kitchen errand-boys, familiarly called *galopins*.

'And so, at a signal barked out by the officer, a procession was formed. At the head of it marched two archers—constables of the watch or bodyguards; then, behind the gentleman-usher, came the Lord Steward of the Royal Household, carrying his scarlet staff—his badge of office. Then followed a gentleman-in-waiting, the general controller of the household, and other gentlemen of less exalted rank, preceding the clerks of the kitchen carrying plates, the *nef*, or a basket in which knives, spoons, forks, toothpicks, salt, ginger, pepper, saffron and all the oriental spices were kept.

Spoon, knife and fork belonging to Louis XIV

'Two archers—constables of the watch—completed the procession. Thus escorted, the king's food crossed the courts, ascended stairs. People bowed to the dishes which were to have the honour of being tasted by Louis XIV, but when they arrived in the royal chamber of His Very Christian Majesty, they were half-cold. . . .

'The ceremonial continued to run its course and the dishes became totally cold. While one of the ushers went to announce to the king the arrival of his meal, the Lord Steward bowed to the *nef* (the cutlery basket) which had been placed on the table, then took the napkins out of it which a gentleman-in-waiting received between two gold plates. Meanwhile, another gentleman-in-waiting was "tasting" the first dish. Had this contained any quick-killing poison, the sovereign would have been saved; if the poison were slow in action the gentleman-in-waiting would die at the same time as the king and be a witness of such an exalted event!

'Then the king sat down and, at long last, began to eat. Should he wish to drink, the official cup-bearer would call out in a loud voice: "Drink for the King". After which he would salute His Majesty, go to the sideboard and take from it a tray with a covered glass, a decanter of wine and a carafe of water. He would then walk back to the table, salute a second time, pour wine and water out of the two carafes into a silver-gilt cup, then present himself before the *chef de gobelet* who would proceed to "taste" the contents of the little cup. The gentleman-in-waiting then carried out another "test" and would finally present the uncovered glass to the king, who helped himself, drank and gave the glass to the prostrate cup-bearer.

'In spite of this protocol, the meals sometimes lacked dignity. The Duke of Luynes testifies to this:

' "During the suppers which Louis XIV was wont to have with the princesses and the ladies at Marly, it sometimes happened that the king, who was very dexterous, amused himself by throwing little rolls of bread at the ladies and allowed all of them to throw them at him. Monsieur de Lassoy, who was very young and who had never before been present at one of these suppers, told me that he was extremely surprised to see bread rolls being thrown at the king, and not only rolls, but also apples and oranges. It is said that Mademoiselle de Vautois, lady-in-waiting to the Princess de Conti, the king's daughter, who was hurt when the king threw a roll at her, threw a salad at him, fully seasoned."

'These manners, which strike us as somewhat barbarous, were nevertheless a sign of great progress at the court, where the civilizing influence of the Italian queens had only just begun to be felt. For instance, to quote but one example, it was Louis XIV who introduced the fork into general use. Before him, the spoon and the knife—the same sort of knife which in remote villages is used to this day to spike pieces of food on a plate—were hardly used. The fork is certainly mentioned in the inventory of Charles VI. On the other hand we know that Henri III and his favourites tried to bring it into fashion. But their patronage did it more harm than good and the moralists of the time ridiculed these affected ignoramuses who, instead of taking food delicately between three fingers, as decreed by the rules of the social code, resorted to such a ridiculous instrument.'

French banquets of the eighteenth century. The reign of Louis XV also knew the splendours of the table. A document of the time gives us details of the pomp which accompanied the royal banquet given on October 25th, 1722, at Reims, on the occasion of the anointing of the king:

'In one of the halls of the archiepiscopal palace, five tables were laid. The king's table was placed on a rostrum, with four steps leading to it, under a purple velvet canopy with golden fleur-de-lys. To the right and left were four other tables, which were to be occupied by peers, ecclesiastical and lay, ambassadors, chamberlains and other gentlemen. On the left of the royal table a tribune had been erected, from which the Duchess of Lorraine watched the ceremony with several foreign princes who were present incognito.

'The tables were ready. The Duke of Brissac, the Grand Pantler of France, had the king's cover laid and brought His Majesty's cadenas. He was accompanied by the chief cup-bearer who was carrying the saucer, the glasses and the carafe, and by the Esquire Trenchant, carrying the big spoon, the fork and the knife. All these personages were richly dressed in mantles of black velvet and gold cloth.

'The Grand Master of ceremonies then informed the Lord Chief Steward of the royal household that the food was ready, and the latter announced this to the king who ordered the meal to be served.

'At the head came the oboes, the trumpets and the flutes, sounding fanfares. Then came the heralds, the Grand Master of Ceremonies, twelve stewards of the royal household, carrying their staffs, the Lord Head Steward, the Prince de Rohan, his Grand-Maître staff in his hand; the Duke de Brissac, carrying the first dish, and then the gentlemen-in-waiting to his Majesty, carrying the other dishes. The Marquis de la Chenaye, the Esquire Trenchant in Chief, then arranged the dishes on the king's table and tasted them as a precaution. Then the Prince de Rohan, preceded by a similar procession, went to fetch the monarch, who came into the banqueting hall with his suite in the following order:

'Oboes, trumpets, flutes, heralds, masters of ceremony and their aides, stewards of the household, Marshal de Talard, the Count de Matignon, the Count de Médair, the Marquis de Guébriant, who carried the offerings, Marshal d'Estrées carrying the crown of Charlemagne and walking in the middle of a group consisting of Marshal d'Uxelles and Marshal de Tessé, the Prince de Rohan, the Prince de Turenne, the Grand Chamberlain of France, the Duke de Villequier, first gentleman-in-waiting (gentleman of the chamber), Marshal de Villars, representing the Commander-in-Chief, holding his sword unsheathed, with his officer-ushers on each side of him carrying their maces. The ecclesiastic and lay peers came next, walking on either side of the king, who had the Dukes de Villeroi and d'Harcourt, his captains and guards and the Duke de Charrost, his commanding-officer, walking beside him. The Scottish guards walked through the aisles. The king had a diamond crown on his head and the sceptre and the ivory hand of Justice in his hands.

'The Archbishop of Reims supported him by the right arm. The Prince of Lorraine carried the train of the royal robe and the Guard of the Great closed the procession. The king having arrived at his table, the Archbishop said grace, then the crown of Charlemagne, the sceptre and the hand of Justice were placed on purple velvet cushions on the corners of the table, and those who carried them stood beside them throughout the whole dinner.

'Marshal de Villars, holding his sword unsheathed, with his ushers carrying their maces at his side, then took his place in front of the king's table, facing His Majesty; the Prince of Lorraine had taken his place behind the king's armchair and the Duke de Villeroi and the Duke d'Harcourt sat down on either side of him. The Prince de Rohan remained standing on the right of the king and handed him his napkin before and after the dinner. The Great Pantler, the Great Wine-steward and the Master of the Horse took up their positions in front of the table to be available to perform their duties: the first to change the king's plates, napkins and cutlery; the second to serve beverages whenever the king wished to drink, tasting the wine and water destined for the king before giving it to him; the third passing and clearing

BEEF. *Above:* Tournedos Helder, Fillets Clamart.
Centre: Beef salad à la parisienne.
Below: Rib of beef with spring vegetables (*Écu de France*)

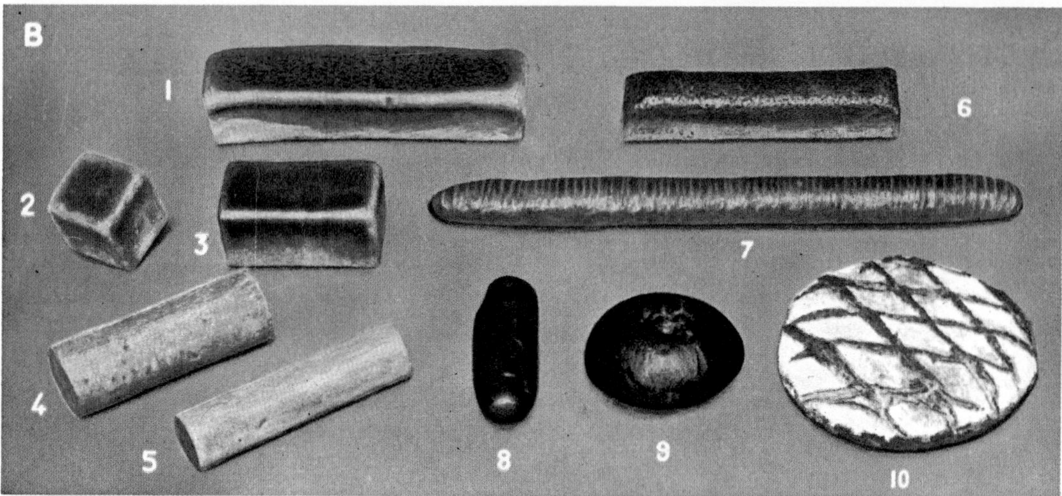

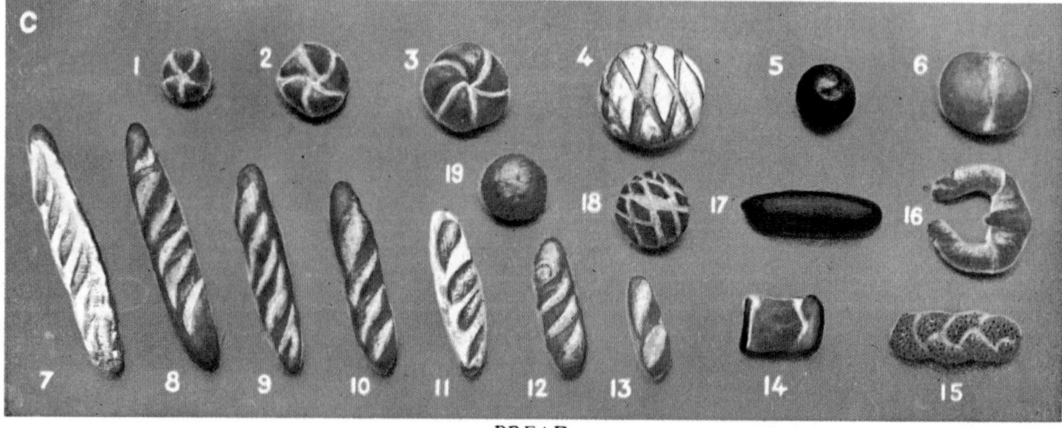

BREAD

A:
1. Pain marchand de vin;
2. Baguette anglaise;
3. Baguette gruau;
4. Joko court;
5. Joko long;
6. Baguette ficelle;
7. Couronne

B:
1. Pain de mie;
2-3. Mie royale;
4-5. Royal sandwich;
6. Pain de seigle à huîtres;
7. Pain gibier;
8. Seigle russe;
9. Boule de seigle;
10. Miche de seigle

C:
1-3. Empereur;
4. Galette;
5. Benoiston;
6. Pistolet;
7, 9. Grand opéra;
8-12. Opéra;
13. Lunch;
14. Brillat-Savarin;
15. Pain Buda;
16. Croissant;
17. Pain sandwich;
18. Boule de fromage;
19. Galette

(*From the original French edition of* Larousse Gastronomique)

away dishes and bringing nearer those which the king wished to have. The *nef* was placed in the corner of the room and Abbé Milon, the King's Almoner, was entrusted with opening it each time that it pleased His Majesty to change his napkin. The other courses were served by His Majesty's household officers with the same processions and the same ceremony as the first. The last course, which consisted of fruit, was served by the Duke de Brissac, the Grand Pantler of France.

'Then two tables were set at the Town Hall. Marshal Villars, the Prince de Rohan, the Marshals of France who carried the royal insignia, the captains of the guard, the captain of the Cent-Suisses, the Great Pantler, the Great Cup-bearer, the Equerry Trenchant and the Chief Lord Steward sat at the first table. At the second sat the four barons who escorted the Holy Ampulla and several other courtiers. These tables were also served by the notables and officers of the town of Reims.'

Banquet given by the Duke of Alba to celebrate the birth of the Prince of Asturias in 1707

'During this sumptuous banquet the Duchess of Lorraine who, from her tribune, could see all these succulent dishes filing past without being able to touch them, quietly nibbled biscuits, with which she was fortunately provided, and offered them to the *incognito* princes, who by this time were also beginning to reach the end of their tether.

'Soon after the king took his place at table, the ecclesiastical and lay peers, the nuncio, the ambassadors, the Guard of the Great Seal, the Grand Chamberlain, the first Gentleman of the Chamber, the Knights of Saint-Esprit, who carried the offerings, and the introducers of the ambassadors took their places at the four tables laid for them and were served by the notables of Reims, at whose expense the banquet was given. After the dinner, the Archbishop of Reims said grace—the Duchess of Lorraine by this time had reached her reserves of dried prunes—and the king was re-conducted to his apartments in the same order and with the same ceremony with which he was ushered in.

French banquets at the end of the eighteenth century. The great banquets of the eighteenth century were, in their composition and service, no less sumptuous than the grandiose affairs of the preceding century. It was also the era of the birth of little dinners and suppers, which were so favourable to progress in cookery. Already French cuisine, without lowering its principles, or impoverishing them in any way, had become modified and simplified to a great extent. The predecessors of Carême were formulating the new culinary laws and Laguipière, Lasne, Boucher, Riquette and Avice established a sort of *charte gourmande*, 'gastronomical charter'.

Under Louis XVI, we are told by Madam de Genlis, the princes, the ministers 'and all the people who occupied important posts had to live in grand style. All kept an open table in Paris at least three times a week, and in Versailles and Fontainebleau every day'.

It was still the custom for the king to take his meals in public which, in fact, amounted to a sort of 'banquet'—somewhat on the spectacular side.

Water jug
(early seventeenth century)

Wine jug
(early seventeenth century)

Sugar caster
(late seventeenth century)

Ewer
(early eighteenth century)

Sugar basin
(Picasso, 1740)

Sauceboat
(Depris, 1723)

Teapot
(Germain, 1750)

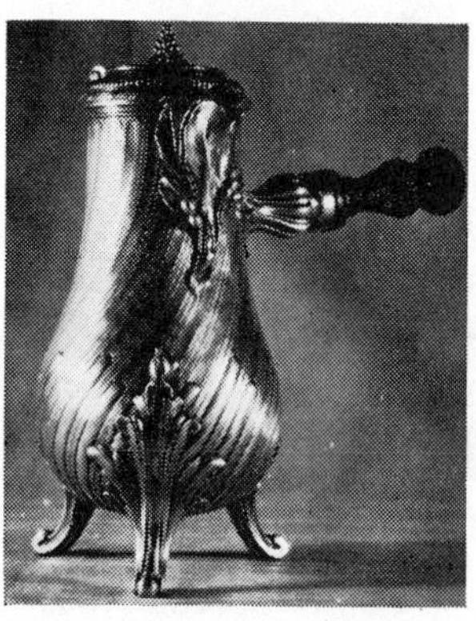

Coffee pot
(Germain, 1750)

Tray
(Germain, 1756)

Teapot
(Germain, late eighteenth century)

Tureen
(Joubert, 1761)

Cooler for glasses
(1790)

TABLE SILVER

Dufort de Cheverny says in his *Memoirs*, speaking of Choiseul: 'At that time (1759) he dined at two o'clock precisely, and all the foreigners, who had been presented, and all the courtiers were received. The big table was laid for thirty-five persons and there was another one all ready out of sight. A valet counted the guests as they entered and as soon as the number exceeded thirty-five, the other table was laid. The silver tableware, in vast quantity, was magnificent and lent a brilliant lustre to the table.'

Banquet given in honour of Louis XVI and Queen Marie Antoinette on the occasion of the birth of the Dauphin in 1785 (*Louvre*, engraving on metal)

Louis XVI and his family often took their meals in public. Madame Campan tells us in her *Memoirs* that on one occasion 'the ushers allowed all people who were decently dressed to enter. As dinner-hour came, one met these good people on the stairs. Having seen the Dauphine eat her soup, they were dashing to see the princes eat their boiled beef, and then rushed, out of breath, to watch the Ladies eat their dessert. This spectacle gave happiness to the provincials.'

Let's face it, the spectacle must have been a little ridiculous too!

Louis XVI always dined in public on Sundays, with the queen. This dinner took place in the ante-chamber of the queen's apartments, as in those days the dining-room, in the sense in which we now understand the word, did not exist. But, according to d'Hézecques, who was a page to Louis XVI, the queen did not eat during this 'spectacular' meal, as she dined later in her apartments. The king, who was blessed with a good healthy stomach, really did eat and, it would appear, with a good appetite.

Louis XVI, although he was what we commonly call 'a good trencherman', plying a good knife and fork (a big eater running a good second to Louis XIV in this respect) was not a gastronome as we understand this word today. Even at the most critical time of his life when he was a prisoner at the Temple, Louis XVI kept his good appetite. It was true that it was no longer a question of banquets in the gastronomical sense of the word, but, if we are to believe Franklin's testimony, the ordinary bill of fare of the imprisoned king and his family was comfortable: 'The dinner consisted of three soups, four entrées, three roast dishes, each of three pieces, four sweet courses, a plate of fancy cakes, three compotes, three dishes of fruit, three loaves of bread with butter, one bottle of Champagne, one small carafe of Bordeaux wine, one of Malvoisie, one of Madeira and four cups of coffee.'

Supper was similar to dinner in the composition of its menu. The National Convention was not so hard on its prisoner as is generally believed.

Madame Vigée-Lebrun's Greek supper. Among the famous meals given at the end of the eighteenth century there was one—a supper given by Madame Vigée-Lebrun—which had enormous repercussions. So many absurd stories circulated about this supper which, it is said, was extravagant to the extreme, that Madame Lebrun felt it was her duty to put things straight and, in her *Memoirs*, she described this much-discussed supper.

'Here, my dear, is the exact account of the most brilliant supper I ever gave, in the days when people never stopped talking about my luxurious and magnificent mode of living.

'One afternoon, when I had invited twelve or fifteen people to hear a reading to be given by the poet Lebrun, my brother read me—while I was resting—a few pages of the *Travels of Anacharsis*. When he came to the passage describing a Greek dinner and the manner of preparing several sauces, he said: "We should try them this evening". I immediately had my cook come up, gave her the necessary instructions and it was decided that she would make a certain sauce for a chicken and another for the eel. As I was expecting some very beautiful women, I decided we should all dress up in Grecian costumes and give Monsieur de Vaudreuil and Monsieur Boutin, who I knew were not coming until ten o'clock, a surprise. I had in my workroom the draperies which I used to drape my models and this was enough to provide all the dresses, while the Count de Parois, who occupied my house at rue de Cléry, had a superb collection of foreign vases. He came to my house that very day at about four o'clock. I told him about my plan and got him to bring me some of his urns and vases, from which I made my choice. I cleaned them all myself and I put them on a bare mahogany table.

Having done this I put an immense folding screen behind the chairs, which I had taken the care to disguise, covering it with drapery caught here and there, as you see in Poussin's paintings. A hanging lamp shed a strong light on the table. Everything was ready, including my costumes, when Joseph Vernet's charming daughter Madame Chalgrin, arrived. She was the first. At once I dressed her and arranged her hair. Then came Madame de Bonneuil, so famous for her beauty, Madame Vigée, my sister-in-law, who, without being pretty, had the loveliest eyes in the world—and there they were, the three of them, transformed into Athenians. Lebrun (Pindar) came in. We removed the powder from his hair, undid his side-curls and I fixed a crown of laurel leaves on his head, which I had just used for painting the young Prince Henri Lubomirski in *Amour de la Gloire*. The Count de Parois happened to have a purple cloak, which served me for draping my poet and with it, in a twinkling of an eye, I transformed Pindar into Anacreon. Then came the Marquis de Cubières. Whilst they went to fetch his guitar for him, which he turned into a golden lyre, I dressed him up. I also provided a costume for M. de Rivière (my sister-in-law's brother), Cinguené and for Chaudet (the famous sculptor).

'Time was getting on, I had not much time to think about myself. I was as usual wearing a white tunic-shaped dress (which nowadays is called a blouse) so all I had to do was to put on a veil and fix a chaplet of flowers on my hair. I only had time to see to my daughter, a sweet child, and Mademoiselle de Bonneuil, who was as lovely as an angel. Both of them were ravishing to look at, carrying a very light antique vase, preparing to serve us with a drink.

'At half-past nine the preparations were complete and as soon as we took our places the effect was so novel, so picturesque, that each of us got up in turn to look at those seated at table.

'At ten o'clock we heard the carriage of the Count de Vaudreuil and Boutin and when these two gentlemen arrived at the dining-room door—I had both the swing-doors wide open—they found us singing Gluck's chorus from *Le Dieu de Paphos et de Cnide* with M. de Cubières accompanying us on the lyre.

'In all my life I have never seen two faces more astonished and more bemused than those of M. de Vaudreuil and his companion. They were astounded and charmed to such a degree that they remained standing for some time before they could bring themselves to take the places which we had kept for them.

'In addition to the two dishes of which I have already told you, we had for supper a sweet made of honey and currants and two dishes of vegetables. It is true we did drink a bottle of old Cyprus wine which had been given to me as a present; that was all the excess. Nevertheless we remained seated at table for a long time; Lebrun recited several odes of Anacreon which he had translated, and I don't think that I have ever spent a more amusing evening.'

Rumour ran in Versailles that this supper cost 20,000 francs. In Rome the figure was raised to 40,000 francs, in Vienna to 60,000, in Petersburg to 80,000. In fact it cost Madame Lebrun 15 francs.

Imperial State dinners. Gala dinners at the Imperial Court were magnificent. Some historians say that although this Court was a long way away from being a gourmand court, in the sense in which the Court of the Bourbons was, generally speaking it enjoyed excellent cuisine.

But in the Tuileries as well as in the palaces of the great dignitaries of the Empire, the cooks succeeded each other in too great numbers and too rapidly.

The State dinner under the Empire never lasted longer than a quarter of an hour. At least, this is what the historians tell us, but we find it extremely difficult to believe. If the laws of gastronomy were so little known at Court, however, it was not the same in the case of the great dignitaries of the Empire.

French banquets of the nineteenth century. The beginning of the nineteenth century was marked by the publication of *La Physiologie du Goût*—a work in which Brillat-Savarin established the art of arranging banquets harmoniously.

To ensure that a meal is perfect, said Brillat-Savarin, one should see to it:

'That the number of guests does not exceed a dozen, so that conversation can constantly be general.

'That they should be most carefully chosen, that their professions be different but their tastes similar and with such points of contact that one will not have to resort to the odious formality of presentations.'

In prescribing that the number of guests seated at the same table should not exceed a dozen, Brillat-Savarin no doubt was thinking only of an intimate dinner. It is obvious that the number of guests at a great gala dinner can greatly exceed this figure without any detrimental effect either on the quality of the food or on the efficiency of the service.

'That the dining-room be luxuriously lit, the cloth be of the utmost cleanliness and the temperature from 13 to 16 degrees by the Réaumur thermometer (61-66°F.).

'That the men be witty without pretensions and the women charming without being too coquettish.

'That the choice of dishes should be exquisite but restrained in number and the wines of the first quality, each the best of its kind.

'That the order, for the former, should be from the most substantial to the lightest and, for the latter, from the lightest to those with the greatest bouquet.

'That the speed of eating should be moderate, dinner being the last affair of the day and that the guests behave like travellers who aim to arrive at the same destination together.

'That the coffee be scalding hot (and made with skill, the master ought to add, for how rare are the homes where this beverage is as it should be!) and the liqueurs specially chosen by the master of the house.'

Now for the 'rules' for after dinner: 'That the salon be sufficiently spacious to organize a game of cards, for those who cannot do without, and to leave enough room to enable the rest to enjoy conversation.

'That the guests be held by the pleasure of the company and stirred by the hope that the evening will not pass without some further entertainment.'

At the same epoch, another gastronome, Grimod de la

Reynière, also established a *Charte de bon manger* which enjoys authority to this day.

In his *Manuel des Amphitryons* Grimod de la Reynière decreed the laws governing the banquets.

He himself gave grand dinners. But Grimod de la Reynière was a somewhat eccentric gastronome. The *mortuary dinner* which he once gave to some of his friends bears witness to this eccentricity.

Grimod de la Reynière one day gave a dinner for which he sent out invitations in the form of obituary notices, which ran as follows:

'You are requested to attend the funeral and obsequies of a big feed which will be given by M. Balthazar Grimod de la Reynière, Esquire, Advocate to Parliament, drama correspondent of the *Journal de Neufchâtel*, at his home in Champs-Elysées on the first day of February, 1783.

'The arrival is fixed for 9 o'clock and supper will take place at 10 o'clock.

'You are requested not to bring any lackeys as there will be enough servants.

'Neither pig nor oil will be missing from the supper.

'You are requested to bring this invitation, without which admittance will be refused.'

The guests, arriving at the appointed hour, were first confronted by a Premier Suisse, especially posted, who asked them whether they were going to Monsieur de la Reynière, the *oppressor of the people*, or Monsieur de la Reynière, the *defender of the people*. After they replied that they were going to the defender of the people, the Swiss made a tick on the invitation and the guests passed through into a place which looked like a guardroom full of men, dressed and armed after the fashion of heralds of long ago. These conducted the guests into the first room where there was a kind of *frère terrible*; he had a helmet on his head, with the vizor lowered, and was clad in a coat of mail with a dagger at his side. He made the second tick on the invitation and ushered the guests into a second room. There they were faced with a man in a robe and square cap who asked them all sorts of questions about their address and their status. He drew up a report, and, after having taken their card, announced them in the assembly room where two actors, dressed up as choir-boys, burned incense before the guests.

The guests, numbering twenty-two in all, two of them being women dressed up as men, passed through a dark room and immediately a curtain went up and revealed the banqueting hall. In the middle of the table, instead of a centre-piece, stood a catafalque and each guest had a coffin standing upright behind him. Old-fashioned lamps and about 300 candles provided lighting for the room.

Around the room ran a gallery intended for spectators, enabling them to catch a glimpse of the banquet. With this in view, M. de la Reynière sent out 300 invitations.

The fashionable restaurants. The nineteenth century saw the start of the great vogue for certain restaurant-keepers. In their restaurants magnificent dinners were given almost every day, the menu of which was, no doubt, less overloaded with various dishes than those of the gala dinners of the preceding century, but which was more logically composed and certainly more elegant.

Dinner given on March 7th, 1806, by the Paris print dealers to their fellow dealer Le Clerc. The legend on the print bears the following inscription: 'They beg him to accept this light sketch as a token of their esteem and friendship. May he remember them sometimes in his retirement and for a long time enjoy the happiness he deserves for his kindness of heart and probity'.

Such was the case of the '*dîner médité*' which took place at the celebrated *Rocher de Cancale*. Here is a description of it which was left to us by a gastronomical chronicler of the time:

'This dinner took place at the end of the winter of 1834 at *Rocher de Cancale*. It was given by Lord W. and was presided over by an English general. Monsieur de Cussy wrote the menu as dictated to him by some whimsical mind.

'Dinner was served at six o'clock sharp. We were, said one of the diners, at the time at a quarter past six in a state of grace, that is, full of appetite.

'Six Marenne oysters were served to each guest, followed by six spoonfuls of soup. There was a choice of two soups. The majority preferred a cream of crab soup, which was excellent. The second soup was *printanier*, based on clear stock. It was mainly this soup which revealed the first sensations. I remember the chairman, I can see him now, hear him saying to us in his most solemn voice: "I advise discretion, gentlemen. No distractions. Remember, I know the menu. We shall be at table for three hours." A "bravo" was heard, which was almost immediately checked.

'It was then that the dinner unrolled in all its freshness and delicacy, in the Russian style, each dish being announced in a loud voice, then cut and served on burning hot plates. The way it was done was perfect—it had everything; disposition, sequence. The quality was of the highest, the seasoning accurately computed, the whole, or rather the sequence, for that's what matters most at an ambigu, was harmonious, when suddenly a dreadful calamity occurred. A head waiter, a young man recently arrived from Bergerac, tried to serve punch *à la romaine* instead of a rum sherbet between two courses. Nobody had any warning. You can imagine the effect of this innovation! All the bright faces darkened. The host, a man of great tact, was disconcerted for a moment, then he exclaimed: "This is a misfortune. It's a lost outpost!" Punch *à la romaine* was taken away. It passed like a cloud. A glass of unique Madeira and a glass of vermouth brought back some of the joy to the faces.

'I have forgotten the details of the dinner. I noted, at the second course, a ham roasted on a spit, proudly lying on a bed of spinach; it was eaten piping hot, and washed down by a few glasses of Clos-Vougeot; God's goodness has seldom ripened such another one; it came from Monsieur Ouvrard. I remember the grouse which had come from Scotland that morning. I also remember exquisite salads and sweet dishes, made of sugar, which Carême had first made for the Prince de Talleyrand. The dessert was all it should have been in such knowledgeable company. It was pleasant, fresh and limited; it consisted of several kinds of cheese. Berthe, who is today an officer at the Russian Court, an author of an excellent little book on the subject, defined some dispositions. The table was covered with flowers—these were the contribution of greenhouses. Spring was then not far off, it would soon be giving us ordinary flowers and all these atoms of life which are dispersed in the air in May, June, and July. We did not part before three o'clock in the morning, after some splendid tea and in the glow of charming anecdotes.' (*Almanac des Chasseurs et des Gourmands.*)

Under the Second Empire, there were a great number of magnificent gastronomical galas. Dinners at court were, in general, quite sumptuous.

In the sections headed COOKING and MENUS examples are given of what these State dinners were like at the time.

The great banquets of today. Most banquets of the past were remarkable for the prodigious number of guests who attended them and for the even more prodigious quantity of food which was served.

But at these banquets not all the dishes included in the different courses of the menu were served to all the guests. Whilst some ate turbot or salmon, others had to make do with whiting or even cod. This also applied in the case of *removes*, *entrées*, roast meat courses and sweets.

At the great modern dinners, at which up to several hundred guests may be present (and in the twentieth century there have been banquets for 30,000 and even 50,000 persons), all the guests, if the service is correctly executed, eat the same dishes at the same time.

No doubt the number of the dishes of which a great modern dinner consists has been considerably reduced (quite rightly so) and, although the number of courses remains the same, each of these courses nowadays consists only of one, or rarely, of two dishes.

It is a rule that a great banquet, apart from the time devoted to speeches (for there are speeches at all the big dinners) does not last more than an hour and a quarter, so far as the actual serving of dishes is concerned. It would be difficult, therefore, to serve the multitude of dishes, which were an essential part in all the banquets of the past, in such a short space of time.

For some idea of the courses which it is more or less customary to include in the menu of a modern banquet, and the general organization, see MENUS and SERVICE.

BANQUIÈRE (A LA)—Garnish used for chicken, calf's sweetbreads, vol-au-vent. It is composed of quenelles, mushrooms, thin slivers of truffles and *banquière* sauce. See GARNISHES.

BANTAM—The name of a variety of Java chickens, after the town from which they originated. These birds have a very delicate flesh and are prepared as ordinary chickens.

BANVIN—French word for the feudal right which allowed the seigneur to sell his wine on his estate for a certain time, to the exclusion of all other persons. The proclamation announcing the day from which private persons could sell new wine, in some parts of the country, is also called *banvin*.

BANYULS—A commune in the Eastern Pyrenees producing a very famous dessert wine: Grenache or Rancio. Only wines made from grapes gathered in a part of the commune of Cerbère, Port-Vendres and Banyuls-sur-Mer are called *Banyuls*.

BAOBAB—The baobab, a tropical African tree, is the largest known.

The fruit of the baobab is called *monkey-bread*, because monkeys eat it.

Its pulp, which is very sweet with a slight acid flavour, is made into a refreshing drink much prized by the local inhabitants of the regions where this magnificent tree grows. A great deal of this beverage is consumed in Morocco and in Egypt.

The Africans dry the leaves of the baobab in the shade, then reduce them to powder, which they call *lalo*, and mix it with their food.

BARAQUILLES—A hot *hors-d'oeuvre* of former days. The *baraquilles* were triangular little patties, filled with a *salpicon** of winged game fillets, calf's sweetbreads, foie gras, truffles and mushrooms, bound with Madeira-flavoured *allemande* sauce. *Baraquilles* were also prepared as rissoles.

BARASHEK IZ MASLA (BUTTER LAMB) (Russian cookery)—Using butter, which has been rendered very firm by being left in iced water, make a model of a lamb on a board.

Cover this with butter pressing down with a coarse-weave cloth or canvas to give the appearance of fleece.

Mark the eyes with two little circles of truffle, or two little raisins.

Put a small green branch in the lamb's mouth.

This symbolic lamb, in Russia, is a feature of the traditional table laid for the ritual Easter meal.

BARBADOS CREAM. CRÈME DES BARBADES—Liqueur which used to be very fashionable in the past. It was made of lemon, orange and citron peel, mace, cinnamon, cloves, sugar and eau-de-vie.

BARBANTANE—A dessert wine made from grapes grown in the Barbantane region, a little commune in the Bouches-du-Rhône.

BARBAREA. BARBARÉE—This plant is also called *Herb of St Barbara, winter cress, treacle mustard wormseed, treacle wormseed* and *yellow rocket*. It is similar to cress in taste and has the same antiscorbutic properties.

This plant grows wild in sandy and damp places.

A variety of barbarea, called *land cress* or *American cress* (U.S.A. common *winter-cress*) is cultivated and eaten in salads.

Barbarea can be prepared in all the ways recommended for cress.

In certain regions this plant is mixed with spinach.

BARBARIN—French name for a fish of the mullet family.

BARBARINE—A variety of marrow (U.S.A., squash), of various shapes and sizes. Most frequently the barbarine is of elongated form rather like a cucumber, and usually plain yellow or parti-coloured, sometimes striped with green.

The best barbarines are pale yellow. All the recipes given for marrows and cucumbers are applicable to barbarines.

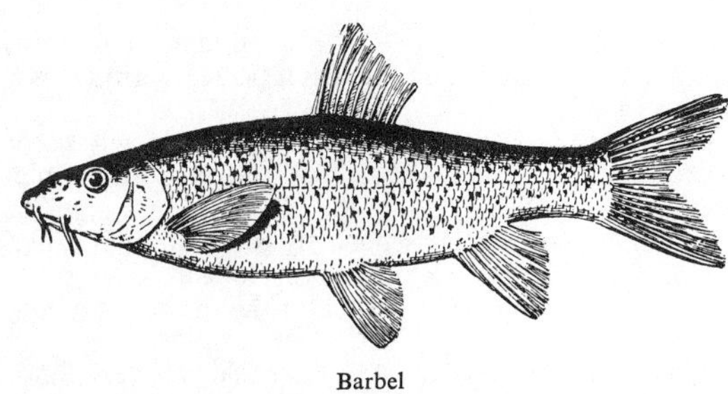

Barbel

BARBEL. BARBEAU, BARBILLON—This river fish is recognizable by the barbels situated some at the end of the snout, others at the corner of the jaws.

In France, only the *common barbel* is known, which is found in all the rivers, and the *southern barbel*, which is found in the south of France, in the Alpes-Maritimes, and in the Pyrenées-Orientales.

The flesh of the barbel is rather insipid and it has too many bones to be pleasant.

The large barbel, those found in the Loire, which are considered the best, may be poached, braised, baked or roast. The small ones, usually called *barbillons*, are served grilled or fried. Recipes for barbel can be applied to the *catfish* of U.S.A.

The soft roes of barbel are quite delicate. The hard roes are supposed to be poisonous.

Boiled barbel with various sauces. BARBEAU BOUILLI—Poach the barbel in a *court-bouillon with vinegar (IV)*. See COURT-BOUILLON.

Drain it thoroughly and arrange on a napkin. Garnish with boiled potatoes and fresh parsley. Serve it, as recommended in individual recipes, with a *White sauce, Butter sauce, Hollandaise sauce, Caper sauce*, or melted butter. See SAUCE.

Barbel à la bourguignonne. BARBEAU À LA BOURGUIGNONNE—Proceed as described in the recipe for *Brill à la bourguignonne*. See BRILL or FLOUNDER.

Fried barbel. BARBILLON FRIT—Proceed as described in the recipe for *Fried bass*. See BASS.

Grilled barbel. BARBILLON GRILLÉ—Proceed as described in the recipe for *Grilled bass*. See BASS.

Barbel à la meunière. BARBILLON À LA MEUNIÈRE—Proceed as described in the recipe for *Bass à la meunière*. See BASS.

Barbel à la mode des mariniers. BARBEAU À LA MODE DES MARINIERS—Clean and scale a 2-pound barbel and cut off wattles and fins. Put the soft roe, if any, back into the fish, seasoned with salt and pepper.

Fry 2 chopped onions and 4 shallots lightly in butter without allowing them to colour and strew these on the bottom of a shallow earthenware dish with 7 or 8 chopped dried walnuts and ¼ pound (125 grams) of chopped mushrooms. It is preferable to use field mushrooms, morels or St George's agarics, but, if these are not available, cultivated mushrooms will do. Make a few slits in the fish, season it with salt and pepper and put on the above ingredients. Add 2 glasses of red wine and 7 tablespoons (100 grams) of butter, divided into tiny pieces. Bring to boil on the top of the stove, then cook in a hot oven basting frequently, for 35 minutes. 10 minutes before the end of cooking, sprinkle with breadcrumbs and melted butter and brown the top. By the end of cooking the wine should be almost completely reduced (boiled away). When the fish is taken out of the oven, sprinkle it with chopped parsley.

Barbel en matelote. See MATELOTE.

Roast barbel. BARBEAU RÔTI—Insert fillets of anchovy into the flesh of a medium-sized barbel, sprinkle with oil (or butter), season and roast, either in the oven or on a spit, basting frequently during cooking.

Arrange on a long dish. Dilute the pan juices with white wine, reduce, add a spoonful of butter and a dash of lemon juice and serve with the fish.

Anchovy butter or *Maître d'hôtel butter* can be served at the same time.

BARBERON—Name used in some parts of the south of France for salsify.

BARBERRY. ÉPINE-VINETTE—A very common prickly shrub. Its green berry can be pickled in vinegar, like capers. This fruit ripens in November. When ripe, the berries are red and contain a great deal of malic and citric acid. They are used to make syrup, jam, and even a kind of wine.

Dry candied barberries. ÉPINE-VINETTE CONFITE AU SEC—'Take some large barberries very ripe and of a fine red colour. Leave them in clusters. For 2 pounds of berries, cook 2½ pounds of sugar to the *large feather* (232°F.—see SUGAR). Put in the barberries and boil very hastily to produce 10 to 12 bubbles.

'Take off the stove. When the fruit is beginning to cool, put it in a hot cupboard leaving it to drain on a cloth until next day. Put it on sheets of paper to drain further.

'Dust the clusters of berries with fine sugar rubbed through a drum sieve (a very fine sieve). Put them to dry in a hot cupboard.' (Old recipe.)

BARBOTEUR ('PADDLER')—Common French name for the domestic duck. See DUCK.

BARBOTTE or BARBOTE—French common name for river burbot or eelpout.

BARD. BARDER—To bard means to cover a piece of meat, poultry, game or, more rarely, a large fish before braising it, with thin slices of bacon or salt or fresh pork kept in place with the aid of string.

After cooking the barding fat is usually removed. Its main purpose is to protect delicate parts of the meat, or breast of poultry.

It is, however, customary to serve roast game—woodcock, quail, pheasant, partridge, etc.—with the fat or bacon which was used for barding.

BARDING FAT. BARDE—Slices of fat bacon or pork fat (fresh or salted) for enveloping poultry and game as well as various cuts of butcher's meat before they are braised, poached or roasted.

Barding fat should be cut in very thin slices and of a suitable length and width for enveloping the pieces of meat.

Barding fat or bacon is also used for lining pâtés cooked in pie-crust and terrines.

BARIGOULE—French name for a mushroom which in the south of France is also called *brigoule* and *bourigoule*. It is very good to eat.

BARIGOULE (A LA)—Some authors of culinary books say that the term *à la barigoule*, given to stuffed artichokes, is derived from the name of the mushroom which is used in the south of France for filling these artichokes.

BAR-LE-DUC—Town in Lorraine which is famous for its red-currant jams.

Grapes cultivated in the Bar-le-Duc region produce quite well-known white wines and red table wines of the *vin ordinaire* category.

BARLEY. ORGE—One of the most ancient cultivated cereals, which still exists in its original form on the shores of the Red and Caspian seas.

Barley grain is poorer in gluten than wheat and its flour does not form an elastic paste when mixed with water. It is therefore not suitable as a bread-stuff. Barley bread (generally mixed with wheat) used to be made in the past; it is very rarely made nowadays. It was heavy and difficult to digest but produced a sensation of repletion, sought by agricultural workers. The advantage of this bread was that it could be kept for a long time.

A barley decoction and infusion (barley water) was one of the most popular medicines used by Hippocrates, who, depending on the case, prescribed it to be taken with or without grains. Barley water is refreshing, viscous and emollient. It is made by boiling 2 teaspoons (20 grams) of pearl barley, washed in cold water, until completely cooked, in enough water to leave one quart (litre) of liquid after boiling. Allow to stand for a moment and strain, pressing well.

Barley is used in cookery in the form of *hulled barley* and *pearl barley*. It is mainly used for soups, creams, meal (*bouillie*). Hulled or pearl barley is also used as garnish for *ragoûts*. See MUTTON, *Ragoût of mutton with barley*.

Barley sugar (Confection). SUCRE D'ORGE—Cook 1 cup (250 grams) of hulled barley with 5 quarts (litres) of water for 5 hours.

Strain the liquid (which resembles a light white-coloured jelly) and decant.

Add some sugar, previously cooked to soufflé degree (228°F.), to this liquid and cook until sugar reaches crack degree (310°F.). Pour the sugar on to an oiled marble slab (or on to an oiled metal sheet). When it begins to cool off, cut into long strips and twist.

This is the original method of making barley-sugar sticks. The modern method is to make them out of drawn sugar.

Consommé with pearl barley. CONSOMMÉ À L'ORGE PERLÉ—Put 3½ tablespoons (100 grams) of pearl barley (previously washed in warm water) into 2½ quarts (litres) of consommé (meat stock). Add a stalk of celery. Simmer gently for 2 hours.

Cream of barley soup. See SOUPS AND BROTHS.

Hulled barley broth. DÉCOCTION D'ORGE MONDÉ—Into a large stock pot put 3½ tablespoons (100 grams) of hulled barley (washed and soaked in warm water for an hour). Add 3½ quarts (litres) of water, 4 teaspoons (25 grams) of salt, 2 carrots, 1 onion studded with a clove, 4 leeks and 2 stalks of celery.

Simmer very gently for 3 hours and strain. This barley broth is most refreshing.

Mutton broth with barley. See SOUPS AND BROTHS, *Mutton broth*.

Sprouted barley. See BEER.

BARNACLE. BERNACLE—Common name for the ordinary *patella* (limpet), mollusc with a conical-shaped shell, which attaches itself to rocks by the sea. It is called by various names in various regions in France: *flie*, *bassin*, *jamble* or *arapède*. Its flesh is rather hard. It is eaten raw, plain or with *vinaigrette* dressing. Small-sized limpets (barnacles) can be cooked like mussels, big ones can also be grilled with butter.

BARNACLE-GOOSE. BARNACHE, BERNACLE—A bird of passage having a certain similarity to the greyleg goose. It is also called *oie-marine* (sea-goose) in French.

Barnacle-goose comes to the French coast in winter.

Its flesh is edible but indigestible. It is prepared as greyleg goose.

BARON—This is the name of a large joint of mutton comprising the saddle and the two legs. This term is also applied to lamb.

In England where this term originated, it is only used for a large piece of beef—a baron of beef: roast of double sirloin.

In U.S.A. the term is used mostly for lamb, indicating the hindquarters (both legs and both loins).

The following anecdote is told on the subject of *baron* or sirloin of beef.

King Henry VIII, who was a big eater, was very fond of roast beef. One day, enraptured by the sight of a magnificent double sirloin set before him, he conferred knighthood upon it. The noble title bestowed on this piece of beef by word of royal mouth has been sanctioned by custom and the cut is known to this day as *sirloin* and a *baron of beef*.

The baron, or sirloin of beef, is generally prepared as a roast and mostly cooked on a spit. In England, where this dish is much esteemed, it is served with Yorkshire pudding, which is made out of a kind of batter, cooked in the dripping-pan under the roasting joint.

Barons of mutton or lamb are also served roasted. These joints are garnished with various vegetables, or they can be served with their own gravy, garnished with watercress. See LAMB and MUTTON.

BARQUETTES—This term describes oval-shaped tartlet shells.

These shells, as those for ordinary tartlets, are filled whilst uncooked with various compositions, or they can be cooked blind, that is to say, empty, and then filled, as in the case of strawberry or raspberry tartlets.

Barquettes are also used for *hors-d'oeuvre* or a small *entrée*, and recipes for these will be found in the section on HORS-D'OEUVRE.

For more sweet barquettes, see TARTLETS.

Savoury barquettes

Apricot barquettes (I). BARQUETTES AUX ABRICOTS—Make flaky pastry (see DOUGH), using 2 cups (250 grams) sieved flour, 1 teaspoon (5 grams) salt, 2 teaspoons (10 grams) sugar, 1 yolk of egg, 10 tablespoons (150 grams) butter and $\frac{1}{3}$-$\frac{1}{2}$ cup (1 decilitre) water.

Line the boat-shaped tartlet tins with this pastry, rolled out to a thickness of $\frac{1}{8}$ inch and cut out with a fluted oval-shaped cutter.

Prick the bottom to prevent the pastry rising during cooking and sprinkle with a small pinch of fine sugar. Stone the apricots, if fresh fruit is used, and cut each apricot into four pieces.

Arrange these quarters in the tartlets, skin side down. Cook in a moderate oven (350°F.) for about 20 minutes. Take out of tins and allow to cool on a wire cake tray. Spoon some very fine apricot jam into the tartlets. Break the apricot stones, blanch the kernels contained in them, and put two halves of these almonds in each tartlet.

Apricot barquettes (II). BARQUETTES AUX ABRICOTS—In classical pastry-making boat-shaped tartlet tins are usually lined with puff pastry.

The method of lining the tins and of filling, baking and finishing the apricot tartlets is the same as in the preceding recipe.

Apricot barquettes à l'ancienne. BARQUETTES AUX ABRICOTS À L'ANCIENNE—Line the barquette tins with flaky pastry and bake the tartlets blind (empty).

Put in them a layer of vanilla-flavoured *Butter cream*. See CREAM.

Place in each tartlet half an apricot, cooked in vanilla-flavoured syrup.

Decorate with halves of blanched almonds and crystallized cherries.

BARREL. BARIL—A small cask of variable capacity (usually 72 litres, or 78·12 quarts) which is used as container for brandy, vinegar, oil, anchovies, herrings or other fish, olives, etc.

BARRIQUE—A large cask or barrel, usually a wine barrel, used for transporting liquids in France. Its capacity varies in different regions. In Bordeaux and in the south of France, it is about 225 litres, in Cognac about 205 litres, in Mâcon about 213 litres, and in Nantes, about 210 litres.

BARROT—This is a French word for the small barrel containing anchovies. The term applies only to anchovy barrels.

BARSAC—A commune in the Gironde where one of the great white Bordeaux wines is produced.

Barsac is a wine which is greatly prized by gastronomes. It has a great vigour and a very pronounced bouquet. It is a little less soft than the Sauternes wines and there is a local saying that 'the barsac is the male and the sauternes the female'.

According to the classification established in 1855 for the great white wines of the Gironde, *Château-Climens* and *Château-Coutet* are the two finest growths, and *Château-Broustet-Nérac*, *Château-Caillou*, *Château-Doisy* (Doisy-Daene), *Château-Doisy* (Doisy-Dubroca), *Château-Myrat* and *Château-Suau* are in the second category.

BASELLA (Indian spinach). BASELLE—Edible plant, native of tropical countries. It is cultivated in certain parts of France.

It is prepared as *spinach.**

Basil

BASIL. BASILIC—Plant (mainly tropical genus of annual or perennial herbs or shrubs) cultivated in our gardens for the sake of its characteristic fragrance.

There are several varieties of basil: *Sweet basil*, the leaves of which are dried and used as a condiment in cookery, *Monk's basil* which can also be similarly preserved and *Bush basil*. The latter is often grown as a pot herb, which makes it available at a moment's notice. It is used in Provence together with garlic for flavouring the *pistou*—a very popular soup in this region.

In the past basil used to be considered a royal plant; only the sovereign (*basileus*) could cut it and even then—we are told—only with a golden sickle. Things are different nowadays. The plant has come into common use. There was a time when it was almost compulsory in the decoration of cobblers' workshops.

BASIN. BASSIN—Kitchen utensil, most frequently made of copper, but can also be made of other metals (aluminium, nickel, etc.).

Semi-spherical non-tinplated copper basins are used for cooking syrups, jellies, jams and marmalades.

There are also iron basins for deep frying and tinned iron basins for washing-up.

BASQUAISE (A LA)—Garnish for large cuts of meat, composed of fried cèpes, Anna potatoes (in dariole moulds) sprinkled with chopped Bayonne (raw cured) ham.

BAS-ROND—Term incorrectly used by some writers of culinary works, instead of *baron* due no doubt to their ignorance of etymology. See BARON.

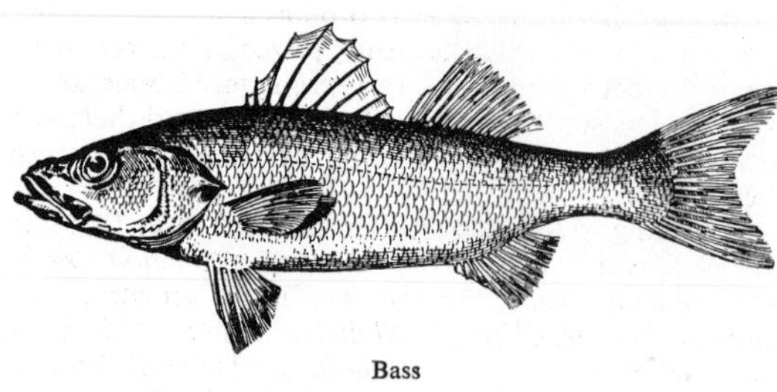

Bass

BASS. BAR—This fish, which is also called *sea-dace*, *sea-wolf* or *sea-perch* (the latter because of its resemblance to the fresh-water perch) abounds in the Mediterranean.

It is also found, but in smaller numbers, in the Atlantic Ocean. It does not normally cross the English Channel and very rarely penetrates into the Baltic.

Two species of bass are known: the *common bass*, often called *sea-wolf*, on the Mediterranean coast, and *striped bass*. The first is seen a great deal in French markets; it is recognizable by its silvery grey-blue back and by its white belly. The bass of the U.S.A., while not identically the same, can be prepared in the same way.

The flesh of the bass is very delicate. It lends itself to an infinite number of preparations.

To clean the fish. Clean out the fish through the gills and a light incision made on the belly. Do not scale the bass, if it is to be poached. Scale it, without breaking the skin, if it is to be braised, fried or grilled. Wash and dry.

According to the recipe chosen, make a few light incisions on the fleshy part of the back, slit it along the backbone, or cut into uniform-sized pieces.

Boiled or poached bass with various sauces. BAR BOUILLI (POCHÉ)—Put the bass into a *court-bouillon of salted water (III)*.*

As soon as boiling is established, draw the pan away to the edge of the burner and poach, simmering lightly.

Drain the bass, put it on a dish covered with a napkin, (or on a strainer—a perforated dish which allows drainage) and garnish with fresh parsley.

Serve *Hollandaise sauce*, or any other sauce recommended for boiled fish, or melted butter, separately. See SAUCE.

Note. Boiled bass, as all poached fish, is served with steamed or boiled potatoes.

Braised bass with various sauces and garnishes. BAR BRAISÉ—Having cleaned the bass in the usual manner, spread the inside with a large piece of butter kneaded with chopped parsley and seasoned with salt and pepper. Season on the outside. Put it on a grid of a fish-kettle, on a foundation of shredded carrots and onions lightly fried in butter. Add a *bouquet garni.** Moisten, for a bass weighing 2 pounds (1 kilogram), with 1¼ cups (3 decilitres) of dry white wine and sprinkle with 2 tablespoons of melted butter.

Bring to the boil, then cook in the oven, uncovered, basting frequently and allowing 25 to 30 minutes for a bass weighing 2 pounds (1 kilo).

Drain the bass, and arrange on a serving dish. Surround with the garnish indicated and pour over it the braising liquor, reduced and with butter added, or, depending on the nature of the dish, serve it with *Espagnole sauce* (made with fish stock) or with *Velouté* (see SAUCE).

Braised bass can be accompanied by all the garnishes recommended elsewhere for all large braised fish. See BRILL, TURBOT, SALMON.

Cold bass with various sauces. BAR FROID—Cook the fish, whole or in large pieces, in a *court-bouillon of salted water (III)*.*

Allow to cool in the liquor. Drain, arrange on a napkin and garnish with fresh parsley.

Serve it with one of the cold sauces usually served with cold fish (mayonnaise, or related sauces).

Cold bass can also be prepared by following one of the recipes given for salmon and salmon trout. Cold bass cooked in *court-bouillon* can also be served with all the garnishes normally used for large cold fish, such as hard-boiled eggs, stuffed artichoke hearts, lettuce hearts, little *macédoines of vegetables** in dariole moulds, etc.

Curried bass à l'indienne. BAR AU CURRIE, À L'INDIENNE—Cut the bass into uniform pieces. Cook as described in the recipe for *Curried fillets of brill*. See BRILL or FLOUNDER.

Bass Dugléré. BAR DUGLÉRÉ—Scale bass weighing 1½ pounds (750 grams), cut it across into 6 or 8 pieces of equal size. Melt some butter in a sauté pan, put in a tablespoon of chopped onion, 4 peeled, pipped and chopped tomatoes, 1 tablespoon of coarsely chopped parsley, a sprig of thyme, a quarter of a bay leaf and as much grated garlic as can be held on the point of a knife. Put the bass on this foundation, season, moisten with ½ cup (1 decilitre) of dry white wine, bring to the boil, cover, and cook in the oven from 12 to 15 minutes. Drain the pieces of bass, arrange on a long dish in the shape of the fish.

Remove thyme and bay leaf from the pan, add 2 tablespoons of *Velouté sauce* (see SAUCE) made of fish stock; cook down and incorporate 4-5 tablespoons (60-80 grams) of butter. Pour this sauce over the fish and sprinkle with chopped parsley.

One can, instead of using *Velouté sauce*, thicken the sauce with a tablespoon of kneaded butter, or with a tablespoon of flour mixed with 2 tablespoons of water (this last type of liaison is called *à la meunière*).

Fillets of bass. FILETS DE BAR—Bass is rarely prepared in fillets. When this method is adopted, the fillets should be skinned and well trimmed. All the recipes given for whole bass, as well as those given for *bream* (U.S.A., porgy or scup), *mullets* or river *trout*, can be applied to fillets of bass.

All the recipes given for *fresh cod*, *whiting*, *mackerel* and generally, for all sea-fish, can also be applied to fillets of bass.

Fried bass. BAR FRIT—This method is suitable for small-size bass.

Scale the bass, make a few slits and soak it in cold, boiled, salted milk. Dredge with flour and fry in sizzling deep fat (oil for preference).

Drain, dry, sprinkle with fine very dry salt, arrange on a napkin and garnish with fried parsley and slices of lemon.

One can, when no small bass are available, prepare large fish in this way, cut into slices or steaks.

Bass au gratin. BAR AU GRATIN—This method is mostly applied to fillets of bass. Proceed as described in the recipe for *Sole au gratin*. See SOLE.

Grilled bass with various sauces. BAR GRILLÉ—This method is applied to bass of medium size. Scale the fish, make a few shallow incisions, season, dredge in flour, brush with oil or melted butter and put to cook on a grill on a moderate heat.

Turn the bass once during cooking and baste with oil or butter from time to time.

Arrange it on a long dish (either straight on the dish or on a strainer or on special crinkly paper). Garnish with fresh parsley and surround with slices of decoratively cut lemon.

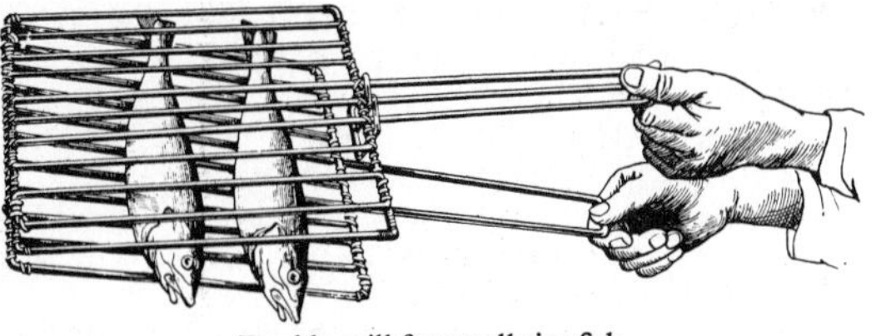

Double grill for small size fish

Serve with *Maître d'hôtel butter*, *Anchovy butter*, *Ravigote butter*, or one of the special sauces recommended for grilled fish.

Bass à la livornaise. BAR À LA LIVORNAISE—This method is suitable for small-size bass. Scale 4 bass, season and put them in a well-buttered or oiled fireproof dish on a foundation consisting of 1 cup (2 decilitres) of tomato *fondue*,* mixed with plenty of chopped onion and flavoured with as much pounded garlic as can be held on the point of a knife.

Scatter breadcrumbs on top, sprinkle with oil and cook in the oven for about 15 minutes.

When taken out of the oven, sprinkle with chopped parsley.

Bass à la meunière. BAR À LA MEUNIÈRE—This method is suitable for small-size bass. Scale them, make a few incisions, season, sprinkle with flour and cook in a frying-pan in previously heated butter. For this method it is preferable to use an oval-shaped pan. See FRYING-PAN.

When the fish is cooked and nicely golden on both sides, arrange in a long dish, sprinkle with chopped parsley and a few drops of lemon juice as well as with the butter left over from frying, heated until it browns, adding, if necessary a little fresh butter.

Serve at once, as the butter should look frothy.

Bass prepared *à la meunière* may be served with various garnishes. Information will be found in the recipe for *Sole meunière*.

Bass à la portugaise (I). BAR À LA PORTUGAISE—This method is suitable for bass of medium size or cut in pieces.

Scale a bass weighing about ¾ pound (300 to 400 grams). Slit lightly along the back, season, put in a buttered pan, moisten with a liquid consisting of equal proportions of white wine and concentrated fish stock boiled down to the consistency of *fumet*,* cover and cook for 15 minutes.

Drain the bass, put in a fireproof dish and surround with a border of very thick *Tomato fondue à la portugaise* (see FONDUE). Boil down the pan juices, add 3 tablespoons of *Velouté sauce* (see SAUCE) based on fish stock and some butter, and pour it over the bass.

Glaze in a very hot oven, sprinkle with chopped parsley and serve in the same dish.

Bass à la portugaise (II). BAR À LA PORTUGAISE—Proceed as described in the recipe for *Bass Dugléré* (but leaving the fish whole). Arrange in a long fireproof dish, pour over the reduced (boiled down) pan juices to which some butter has been added, sprinkle with breadcrumbs and glaze in a very hot oven.

Bass à la provençale. BAR À LA PROVENÇALE—Scale the bass, make a few shallow slits, season, dredge with flour and fry it briskly in oil in a pan.

When it is cooked and nicely golden on both sides, put it in a long fireproof dish.

Cover with *Provençale sauce*, sprinkle with breadcrumbs and oil and put in a very hot oven for a few moments to set the top.

When taken out of the oven, sprinkle with chopped parsley.

Stuffed braised bass with various garnishes. BAR BRAISÉ FARCI—Stuff the bass with one of the special forcemeats recommended for large fish. Braise it as described above.

Arrange on a serving-dish, surround with the prescribed garnish and pour over the sauce recommended.

BASTE. JUTER—To pour roasting or braising stock over a joint to keep it moist during cooking.

BASTION—Method of arranging cold dishes in aspic which used to be very popular in the past. This style of serving was applied principally to fish, particularly to *eel*.

BAT—French culinary term for tail of fish. The length of fish is measured from eye to tail.

BAT. CHAUVE-SOURIS—Little mammal provided with membranous wings which enable it to fly, whose meat is esteemed in certain oriental countries, notably in China.

BA-TA-CLAN—Pastry dessert invented, it is said, by Lacam, the celebrated Parisian pastry-cook, which is still made in good Paris cake-shops.

Ingredients. 1½ cups (250 grams) freshly blanched almonds, 1⅔ cups (375 grams) vanilla flavoured sugar (or add 1½ teaspoons vanilla extract to rum), 1 cup (125 grams) sieved flour, 9 eggs and ⅓ cup (1 decilitre) of rum.

Method. Pound the almonds in a mortar, adding to them the eggs, one by one. When the mixture is well pounded, add sugar and rum.

Put the mixture into a bowl, add flour and stir until quite smooth.

Put the mixture into a flat tin with fluted edges. Bake in a moderate oven. When cooked, take out of the oven and ice with vanilla icing.

BÂTARDE—Name given to *Butter sauce* (*I*), (see SAUCE).

BATEAUX—French name for small china, glass or metal containers used for serving cold *hors-d'oeuvre*. These containers are boat-shaped, hence their name.

BÂTONNETS or BÂTONS—Various preparations shaped in the form of little sticks.

Almond bâtonnets. BÂTONNETS AUX AMANDES—These little fancy biscuits (cookies) come in the category of *petits fours*.

Ingredients. 1½ cups (250 grams) blanched almonds, 1 cup (250 grams) of sugar, 3 whites of egg and ⅓ cup (1 decilitre) of rum.

For icing the bâtonnets. Beaten whites of egg and crystallized sugar.

Method. Pound the almonds and the sugar together in a mortar, moistening them with whites of egg. Add the rum.

Blend into a smooth paste and roll out ⅛ inch thick on a marble slab lightly dusted with flour.

Cut this paste into strips 3 inches in width, then into sticks ¾ inch in width. Dip the little sticks into lightly beaten whites of egg, then into crystallized sugar. Brush baking trays with butter, sprinkle with flour, put the sticks on them and bake in a moderate oven (350°F.).

Bâtons with vanilla icing. BÂTONS GLACÉS À LA VANILLE —Pound 1½ cups (250 grams) of blanched almonds with 1 cup (250 grams) of sugar. Add 3 whites of egg and ½ a teaspoon of vanilla extract to this mixture.

Spread this mixture on a marble slab and roll out until the paste is ⅓ inch thick and 6 inches wide. Coat this rolled-out piece of paste with a layer of vanilla-flavoured *Royal icing* (see ICING).

Cut into sticks ¾ inch wide. Brush a baking tray with butter, sprinkle with flour, put the sticks on it and bake in a moderate oven (350°F.).

Chocolate bâtonnets. BÂTONNETS AU CHOCOLAT—Dry *petits fours* made of almonds and cocoa.

Ingredients. 1½ cups (250 grams) of almonds, 1 cup (250 grams) of sugar, 1¾ cups (200 grams) of cocoa, 2 tablespoons (30 grams) vanilla-flavoured sugar, 3 whites of egg (½ teaspoon vanilla extract may be added to replace dry vanilla).

Method. Proceed as described in the recipe for *Almond bâtonnets*.

Cummin bâtonnets. BÂTONNETS AU CUMIN—Dry *petits fours* which are prepared in the following manner:

Add cummin to *Short pastry dough (II)*, (see DOUGH) when rolling it out. Cut it into little sticks, roll the sticks, put them on a buttered baking tray, brush with egg and cook in a hot oven (400°F.).

Hazel-nut bâtonnets. BÂTONNETS AUX AVELINES—These little dry *petits fours* are made in the same way as *Almond bâtonnets*, but replace almonds with hazel-nuts, blanched and dried in the oven, and flavour the mixture with kirsch.

Iced puff pastry bâtons. BÂTONS FEUILLETÉS GLACÉS—Roll out *Puff pastry* (see DOUGH), very thin. Cut it into strips 3 inches wide. Ice these strips with *Royal icing* (see ICING), and cut them across into pieces 1½ inches wide. Put on a baking tray and bake in a hot oven (400°F.).

Jacob's bâtons. BÂTONS DE JACOB—Little cakes made of *Chou pastry** in the shape of little sticks, filled with French pastry cream and coated on top with sugar cooked to crack degree (320°F.). See ÉCLAIR.

Royal bâtons. BÂTONS ROYAUX—This old-fashioned hot *hors-d'oeuvre* is prepared in the following manner:

Roll out a piece of short pastry, cut into small rect-angles, slit and fill the middle of each with a chicken and partridge forcemeat. Roll into little sticks, sealing the pastry well. Deep fry in smoking hot fat.

Serve in a heap on a napkin garnished with fried parsley.

BATTERS FOR FRYING. PÂTE À FRIRE.

Frying batter (I) (Carême's recipe)—'Put 12 ounces (3 cups) of sifted flour into a small bowl, dilute it with slightly warmed water in which you have melted 2 ounces (4 tablespoons) of best butter. Tip the pan and blow on the water, to make butter pour out first. Pour on enough water to make rather a soft paste, free from lumps. Add a pinch of fine salt, 2 tablespoons of brandy, fold in 2 stiffly beaten whites and use at once'.

Frying batter (II)—Mix 2⅛ cups (250 grams) of sifted flour, a good tablespoon of oil, a pinch of fine salt, ¾ cup (1½ decilitres) of beer, 1 cup (2 decilitres) of warm water and a tablespoon of brandy into a smooth batter. At the last moment, fold in two stiffly beaten whites of egg.

Frying batter (III) (for unglazed fruit and flower fritters)—

Ingredients. 2⅛ cups (250 grams) of sifted flour, 2 table-spoons of melted butter, 1 teaspoon (5 grams) of salt, ¾ cup (1½ decilitres) of beer, 1¼ cups (2½ decilitres) of water, one tablespoon of brandy, 2 whites of egg whisked into a stiff froth.

Method. Put the flour, salt and melted butter into a big bowl, so as to be able to mix all the ingredients properly. Dilute with beer and warm water, without stirring too much.

Just before using, fold in the stiffly beaten whites.

Frying batter (IV) (for fruit fritters glazed in the oven)—*Ingredients.* 2⅛ cups (250 grams) of sifted flour, 2 table-spoons of melted butter, a good pinch of sugar, a pinch of salt, ¾ cup (1½ decilitres) of beer, 1 cup (2 decilitres) of water, one whole egg, one tablespoon of brandy.

Method. Mix the batter as described in the preceding recipe. Keep in a warm place to make it ferment. Just before using, whisk the batter.

Note. Fruit fritters which are to be glazed, are drained after frying, placed on a metal sheet, sprinkled with icing sugar and set in a hot oven to glaze.

Frying batter (V) (for vegetable fritters)—Mix 2⅛ cups (250 grams) of sifted flour in a bowl with 4 tablespoons of melted butter, 2 whole eggs, a good pinch of salt and the necessary quantity of water to make not too thick a batter.

This batter must be prepared at least an hour before use.

Frying batter (VI) (for meat and fish fritters)—Put 2⅛ cups (250 grams) of sifted flour into a bowl, make a well in the middle and put into it a good pinch of salt, 4 table-spoons of oil (or melted butter) and 2 cups (4 decilitres) of slightly warm water.

Mix these ingredients well with a wooden spoon, with-out too much stirring if the batter is to be used at once. If, on the other hand, the batter is made in advance, it can be stirred a lot.

Just before using, add 4 whites of egg whisked into a very stiff froth.

Frying batter (VII) (à la provençale)—'Into a bowl put 3 cups (12 ounces) of flour, 2 yolks of egg, 4 tablespoons of Aix oil, and enough cold water to mix the flour into a soft paste. Add a grain of salt, two stiffly-beaten whites and use.' (Carême's recipe.)

Batters (sweet)—See DOUGH.

BAVARIAN CREAM. BAVAROIS—In the past this cold sweet used to be called *fromage bavarois*. This is the name Carême gives it in his *Traité des entremets de douceur*.

Did this preparation, which is composed of an English custard, whisked with gelatine and with fresh whipped cream added to it, originate in Bavaria, as its name would seem to imply? We do not really know the answer, but we are inclined to think that the name *bavarois* was given to the sweet by a French chef who practised his art in some stately home in Bavaria.

In any case, this dish, of solid consistency, should not be confused with the liquid preparation known as the *bavaroise*,* which used to be called *crème bavaroise* (*Bavarian cream*), and according to culinary historians, was invented in Bavaria towards the end of the seven-teenth century.

The *bavarois* in the olden days were prepared quite differently from the present-day method. The mixture was not bound with yolks of egg, but only with clarified isinglass. We quote several of Carême's recipes for this type of *bavarois*.

Bavarian cream à la cévenole. BAVAROIS À LA CÉVENOLE —Coat a simple round mould with a hole in the middle, with a layer of *Vanilla Bavarian cream.** Fill the mould with a composition of *Vanilla Bavarian cream** mixed with a purée of marrons glacés, and flavoured with kirsch. Chill in the refrigerator.

Unmould on to a round dish. Decorate with *Chantilly cream* (see *CREAM*). Surround with marrons glacés.

Fruit Bavarois (*Robert Carrier*)

Bavarian cream à la créole. BAVAROIS À LA CRÉOLE—Coat a mould with sweet almond oil and fill it with alternate layers of equal thickness of rum-flavoured Bavarian cream and a pineapple-flavoured Bavarian cream, mixed with a *salpicon** of bananas steeped in rum.

Turn out on to a round round dish, decorate with *Chantilly cream* (see CREAM) piped through a pastry bag and sprinkle with shredded blanched pistachio nuts.

Bavarian cream à la normande. BAVAROIS À LA NORMANDE—Line the mould with a layer of calvados-flavoured Bavarian cream. Fill the mould with thick *apple-sauce*,* whisked with gelatine dissolved in water, and finished off with whipped cream.

Turn out on to a glass dish. Surround with quarters of apples cooked in syrup and well drained.

Bavarian cream au parfait amour. FROMAGE BAVAROIS AU PARFAIT AMOUR (CARÊME)—'Shred half the peel of a small citron as finely as possible. Drop it into 2 glasses of boiling milk, add 6 crushed cloves, 8 ounces (240 grams) of sugar, leave to infuse for an hour and strain through a tammy-cloth.

'Add 1 ounce (30 grams) of isinglass and enough cochineal essence to give the mixture a pretty pink colour.

'Put into a bowl of ice. As soon as the mixture begins to set fold in whipped cream, after which complete the operation in the usual manner.'

Bavarian cream with pistachio nuts. FROMAGE BAVAROIS AUX NOIX VERTES (Carême)—'Shell about 100 choice pistachio nuts, pound them in a mortar, moistening with a little water from time to time, to prevent them from turning oily. Then put them into a small bowl and little by little add 2 glasses of very cold cream in which you have dissolved 8 ounces (240 grams) of sugar. Leave to infuse for one hour after which strain through a fine sieve.

'Add 1 ounce (30 grams) of slightly warm clarified isinglass; pour the mixture into a tin-plated mould 10 inches in diameter and 4 inches in depth, or pour it into a large pipe-clay bowl, or into a medium-sized terrine, which you will set in 15 pounds of crushed ice. After 15 minutes, begin to stir the mixture with a large silver spoon and continue to do so from time to time. As soon as it begins to set stir all the time, to achieve a smooth flowing mixture.

'Then, little by little, add well-drained whipped cream the same volume as the mould which you are going to use. Blend the mixture thoroughly to fold in the whipped cream, which will thus give you a perfectly mellow and velvety *fromage bavarois*. Pour it into a mould and place the mould on ice. After leaving it on ice for a good hour and a half you can turn it out.'

Bavarian cream aux roses. FROMAGE BAVAROIS AUX ROSES (Carême)—'Take about 30 choice freshly-picked roses and after stripping off the petals put them with a pinch of cochineal grains into 8 ounces (240 grams) of clarified boiling sugar syrup. Cover the infusion and, when it is just warm, add 1 ounce (30 grams) of isinglass, then strain the mixture through a napkin and set on ice. When the mixture begins to set fold in whipped cream. Complete as usual.'

Fruit Bavarian cream. BAVAROIS AUX FRUITS—This is prepared in the following manner:

Composition. Put into a bowl 2½ cups (5 decilitres) of whatever fruit purée is chosen mixed with 2½ cups (5 decilitres) of heavy (30°) syrup. Add the juice of 3 lemons and 4 tablespoons (30 grams) of gelatine, dissolved and strained through a muslin bag. Blend well.

Incorporate in the mixture a pint of cream, stiffly whipped. Stir.

Moulding and serving. Proceed as described in the recipe for *Vanilla Bavarian cream.*

Mocha coffee Bavarian creams. FROMAGE BAVAROIS AU CAFÉ MOKA (Carême)—'Take 6 ounces (180 grams) of mocha coffee beans, put into a small saucepan and place on a moderate fire, stirring constantly until they acquire a fine reddish-yellow colour. As soon as the coffee-beans become oily the roasting is complete. Drop the coffee grains into 3 glasses of boiling milk, cover and leave to infuse. When the infusion is just warm, strain it through a napkin. Mix with 8 ounces (240 grams) of sieved sugar and 1 ounce (28-30 grams) of isinglass. Blend until perfectly smooth and strain through a napkin once again. Put the mixture on ice and when it begins to set, add to it a plateful of whipped cream. Complete the procedure as usual.'

Strawberry Bavarian cream. BAVAROIS AUX FRAISES—Prepare the Bavarian cream using 1¼ cups of strawberry pulp rubbed through a fine sieve, 1¼ cups (2½ decilitres) of heavy (30°) syrup, 2 tablespoons (15 grams) of gelatine, dissolved and strained through a muslin bag, the juice of 1 lemon and 1¼ cups (2½ decilitres) of cream, whipped.

Put into a mould and chill on ice or in a refrigerator. Turn out on to a round dish. Surround with big hulled strawberries, sprinkled with fine sugar.

Apricot, pineapple, peach, pear, raspberry and other fruit bavarois can be prepared in the same way.

Striped bavarois

Striped chocolate and vanilla Bavarian cream. BAVAROIS RUBANÉ AU CHOCOLAT ET À LA VANILLE—Striped Bavarian creams are made of Bavarian creams of various colours and flavours, which are put into the mould in alternate layers.

Instead of putting the *bavarois* into a mould to set, it can be put into glass and cut-glass dishes. In this way, the work is done much more quickly and, besides, a lighter composition is obtained, as the amount of gelatine can be considerably reduced.

Ingredients. 8 yolks of egg, 1 cup (250 grams) of fine sugar, 2½ cups (5 decilitres) of milk, 1 vanilla bean, 1¾ ounces (50 grams) of chocolate, 1½ to 2 tablespoons (10 to 14 grams) of powdered gelatine, 1 pint (½ litre) of cream, whipped, some sweet almond oil, salt.

Method. Put the sifted sugar, a pinch of salt and the yolks into a saucepan. Stir until the mixture is perfectly homogenous. Moisten with milk previously boiled with vanilla (or add 1½ teaspoons vanilla extract when custard is removed from the heat). Soak the gelatine in cold water and add to the mixture. Mix.

Keep the custard on a low heat stirring constantly.

When it thickens sufficiently to coat a spoon, remove from heat.

Strain the custard and divide in two parts. Add to one part chocolate softened on a gentle heat and blend.

Finish each of the mixtures separately, incorporating whipped cream in them when they begin to set.

Brush a mould with a hole in the middle with sweet almond oil or rinse in ice water. Fill with alternate layers of the above mixtures, taking care not to add a new layer until the preceding one has set properly.

Place the mould into a bowl of crushed ice or in the refrigerator and leave to set from 1½ to 2 hours.

To serve, dip the mould quickly into warm water, wipe it and turn the *bavarois* on to a napkin-covered dish or into a cut-glass bowl.

Striped Bavarian cream (various flavours). BAVAROIS RUBANÉS AUX PARFUMS DIVERS—Proceed as described in the previous recipe to make striped Bavarian cream using variously flavoured mixtures. Variegated Bavarian cream can thus be made by using alternate layers of vanilla and strawberry mixture (or any other red-coloured fruit), vanilla and coffee, vanilla and apricot, vanilla and pistachio nuts, etc.

Vanilla Bavarian cream. BAVAROIS À LA CRÈME—Here is the modern method of preparing *bavarois*.

Composition. Blend together in a saucepan 2 cups (500 grams) of fine sugar, 16 yolks of egg, and a very small pinch of salt.

When the mixture becomes quite smooth, moisten with a quart (litre) of milk, which has previously been boiled and flavoured with a vanilla bean, or add 2 teaspoons vanilla extract after removing from the heat. Add 3 tablespoons (25 grams) of gelatine, soaked in cold water.

Keep this mixture on the burner, stirring all the time, until it coats the wooden spoon, but *do not allow it to boil.*

Transfer this custard into a bowl and allow to cool, fanning it frequently.

As soon as the composition begins to set fold into it 1 quart (1 litre) cream stiffly whipped and ½ cup (100 grams) of powdered sugar.

Moulding of bavarois. Take a mould with a hole in the middle, coat it with sweet almond oil (or rinse with iced water), and put into it the above composition, filling the mould to the brim. Cover with a circle of white paper.

Put the mould into a container of crushed ice or in the refrigerator and chill for about two hours.

Serving of bavarois. Dip the mould quickly into a bowl of warm water, dry it and turn out the *bavarois* on to a dish, which may be covered with a folded napkin or a paper doyley, or into a low glass dish.

Note. The mould in which the *bavarois* is set can be coated with sugar cooked to a light caramel instead of being greased with sweet almond oil.

It can also, instead of being set in a mould, be served in a glass dessert dish or in a low-shaped silver timbale. *Bavarois* composition which is served in the latter manner needs less gelatine and will, therefore, be more delicate.

The composition described above may be flavoured with different flavouring agents. The same recipe may be used for preparing *bavarois* flavoured with coffee, chocolate, tea, brandies and various liqueurs (anisette, armagnac, calvados, curaçao, fine champagne brandy, kirsch, kummel, rum, etc.), lemon, tangerine, orange and praline of burnt almond, hazel nuts, etc.

Vanilla Bavarian cream. FROMAGE BAVAROIS À LA VANILLE (Carême)—'Put a good vanilla bean into 3 glasses of boiling cream. Put the infusion on the edge of the stove and reduce by one-third. Add 8 ounces (240 grams) of sieved sugar and 1 ounce (30 grams) of isinglass.

'Blend the whole perfectly, and when the mixture is just warm, strain through a napkin. Put on ice and when the mixture begins to set fold in whipped cream.'

BAVAROISE—Hot beverage which used to be served in the past at evening parties and which deserves to be revived, as it is both delicious and relieves congestion of the chest.

Bavaroise (I)—Add 1 cup (2 decilitres) of very strong tea to a yolk of egg which you have put in a glass (or some other receptacle) with a tablespoon of fine sugar and a tablespoon of sugar syrup (220°F.) and whisk vigorously until the mixture becomes frothy. Add some boiled milk and 5 teaspoons of kirsch.

The *bavaroise* can be flavoured with rum, maraschino, or any other liqueur. It can also be made with chocolate.

Bavaroise (II)—Put into a saucepan ½ cup (125 grams) fine sugar and 4 yolks of egg. Beat this mixture with a whisk until thick.

Add one by one the following ingredients: ¼ cup (½ decilitre) of 220°F. syrup, 1¼ cups (2½ decilitres) of freshly-made scalding hot tea and the same amount of boiling milk. Whisk until the mixture is very frothy. Then add ⅓ to ½ cup (1 decilitre) of whatever liqueur is preferred, such as rum, kirsch, calvados, etc.

The *bavaroise* can also be flavoured with orange, lemon or vanilla. For these various preparations, infuse the flavouring chosen in boiling milk.

BAVAROISE AUX CHOUX—A French slang expression meaning a mixture of absinth and orgeat.

BAY. LAURIER-SAUCE—Bay leaves are a traditional ingredient of the *bouquet garni.** The berries of the bay tree are used in a distillation of the spirit of aromatic herbs called Fioravanti.

BAYONNE—This town in the Basses-Pyrénées where, according to some authors of culinary works, the cold egg and oil sauce, called mayonnaise, was invented, which, therefore, should really be called *bayonnaise*, is famous throughout the whole world for its salt hams, known as *Bayonne hams*.

This kind of ham is not actually made at Bayonne but at Orthez, a little neighbouring town.

It is mostly eaten raw. It is also used to improve the flavour of ragoûts and sauces and cooked as a garnish for variously prepared eggs.

The gastronomical repertoire of Bayonne and its region also includes many excellent local dishes. There are magnificent *garbures** (a hotch-potch of cabbage, bacon, goose-fat and rye bread popular in the Pyrenees district) and not only preserved goose, but also preserved pork (*confit de porc*) which is locally called *méthode*.

All the pork butchery produce of the Bayonne region is exquisite, above all the black (blood) puddings.

As for sweet dainties, Bayonne has the *pâté de cédrat* (a citron preserve) and its famous *chocolates*.

Among local wines is the white wine made from grapes grown in Anglet, quite a fine wine called *vin de sable*, as the vine which produces it grows in a very sandy soil very close to the sea shore.

BEAN. HARICOT—A pulse of which there are many varieties, some edible and others ornamental.

Among the edible varieties are the climbing beans which grow to a height of 6 to 9 feet. These are trained on to bean-poles. There are also dwarf varieties, which are short and need no support. In most varieties the pod is tender and edible when young. Edible bean pods fall under the general heading of green beans. In some varieties the pod remains tender and good to eat even when fully grown, but in the case of shelling or parchment skinned beans, it becomes tough and leathery.

BEAN, BROAD (U.S.A. Shell Bean). FÈVE—An annual plant of the *Leguminosae* family, cultivated for its seeds, which serve as food for man and for animals. The broad bean, of which the *Windsor* is best known, is the common bean of Europe. Other well-known broad beans are the *Lima bean*, a species originating in South America and cultivated extensively in California; the *Soy bean* of China, Japan and India, now very widely cultivated. Some beans such as the Scotch *Horse bean* and the *Cowpea* of Southern U.S.A. are used chiefly for forage.

To cook fresh broad beans. Shell the beans. Remove the rather tough outer skin and put them to cook in boiling salt water with a bunch of savory.

Drain and proceed according to the recipe selected.

Fresh broad beans à l'anglaise. FÈVES FRAÎCHES À L'ANGLAISE—Cook the beans as indicated above, but leaving them in their skins. Drain and serve in a vegetable dish. Serve fresh butter separately.

Fresh broad beans in butter. FÈVES FRAÎCHES AU BEURRE —Proceed as for *peas in butter*, with chopped savory added.

Broad beans in cream. FÈVES À LA CRÈME—Proceed as for *Peas in butter*.* Moisten with thick fresh cream. Simmer for a few seconds. Serve in a vegetable dish.

Broad beans à la croque-au-sel. FÈVES À LA CROQUE-AU-SEL—This is the name given to fresh broad beans served raw as an *hors-d'oeuvre*. The guests shell the beans themselves and season them with coarse salt. This *hors-d'oeuvre* is very popular all over the south of France.

Fresh broad beans à la française. FÈVES FRAÎCHES À LA FRANÇAISE—Shell and skin the beans and stew as for *peas à la française* with a bunch of savory.

Purée of fresh broad beans for garnishing. PURÉE DE FÈVES FRAÎCHES—Proceed as for *Purée of fresh garden peas*. See PEAS.

Purée of bean soup. POTAGE PURÉE DE FÈVES—See SOUPS AND BROTHS.

Fresh broad beans with savory. FÈVES FRAÎCHES À LA SARRIETTE—Shell and skin the beans. Cook them in boiling salt water, with a bunch of savory. Drain the beans and put them in a pan. Toss them for a few seconds on the fire to evaporate as much moisture as possible. Add fresh butter cut into tiny pieces. Mix carefully so as not to damage the beans.

BEAN (FIELD). FÉVEROLE—A kind of European broad bean, smaller than the common broad bean. The beans usually remain white. These beans are used in the same way as broad beans.

Field-bean flour is sometimes added to wheaten flour for the manufacture of bread.

BEANS (FLAGEOLET). HARICOTS FLAGEOLETS—These beans, whether fresh or dried, are used mainly as a garnish for meat dishes. They are excellent with large and small cuts of mutton or lamb. They make very delicately flavoured purées.

Flageolets are not common in U.S.A.

Fresh flageolets. HARICOTS FLAGEOLETS FRAIS—These beans, which are greenish in colour and very small, are cooked in the same way as *Fresh white haricot beans*. All recipes for haricot beans are suitable for *flageolets*.

Dried flageolets. HARICOTS FLAGEOLETS SECS—Proceed as for *Dried white haricot beans*.

BEANS, FRENCH (STRING). HARICOTS VERTS—This vegetable, which is very easy to prepare, is most delicately flavoured.

It is wise to ensure that the beans are absolutely fresh, that is to say, very recently picked.

To cook French beans. If the beans are picked as soon as the pods are formed they will not be stringy and therefore need only be topped and tailed. With older beans, it is necessary to cut away the stringy edges. Wash the beans in cold water.

Put them in a large saucepan full of boiling salt water, $1\frac{1}{2}$ teaspoons (9-10 grams) of salt to every quart (litre) of water. Leave the saucepan uncovered and cook over a very hasty flame. Taste from time to time. When the beans are tender but still firm in texture, they are ready. They must not be overcooked.

Drain them thoroughly and proceed according to the recipe.

Note. If the beans are to be kept for use later or are to be dressed with oil and vinegar as a salad, they should be put in a colander under running cold water.

If they are to be served immediately in butter, cream, or in some other way, they should not be cooled after having been boiled in salt water.

The boiling of beans is sometimes called *blanching* in France. This is a misnomer since, in fact, they are fully cooked.

French (or string) beans à l'anglaise. HARICOTS VERTS À L'ANGLAISE—Boil the beans in salt water. Drain and dry in a cloth. Serve them in a vegetable dish. Serve fresh butter separately.

French (or string) beans à la bonne femme. HARICOTS VERTS À LA BONNE FEMME—Boil the beans in salt water until they are three parts cooked. Drain thoroughly and dry in a cloth. Fry in a saucepan allowing for 1 pound (500 grams) of beans, 7 ounces (200 grams) of diced lean bacon, previously well blanched. Add the beans. Moisten with a few tablespoons of thickened brown veal stock. Cover the pan and simmer slowly until the beans are cooked. Just before serving, add butter. Sprinkle with chopped parsley and serve in a vegetable dish.

French (or string) beans in browned butter. HARICOTS VERTS AU BEURRE NOISETTE—Boil the beans in salt water as indicated above. Drain and dry them in a cloth. Brown some butter in a pan. Add the beans. Season and toss them in the butter until they have absorbed it well. Serve sprinkled with chopped parsley, in a vegetable dish.

French (or string) beans in butter, à la maître d'hôtel. HARICOTS VERTS AU BEURRE, DITS À LA MAÎTRE D'HÔTEL—Boil the beans as indicated above. Drain them thoroughly. Toss them in a pan on the stove for a few moments until all the moisture left in them has evaporated.

Season and blend with butter cut into tiny fragments, 6 to 7 tablespoons of butter to a pound (500 grams) of beans. Toss the beans in the butter so that they are all evenly coated. Serve, sprinkled with chopped parsley, in a vegetable dish.

French (or string) beans in cream (I). HARICOTS VERTS À LA CRÈME—Boil the beans in salt water until they are three-parts cooked. Drain and dry in a cloth. Toss in butter for a few seconds. Cover with thick fresh cream. Simmer them until the sauce has been reduced to half its original volume. Season. Serve in a vegetable dish.

French (or string) beans in cream (II). HARICOTS VERTS À LA CRÈME—Boil the beans in salt water until they are three-parts cooked. Drain and dry in a cloth. Simmer them until they are cooked in a rather thin *Béchamel sauce* (see SAUCE). Just before serving, add butter. Serve in a vegetable dish.

Note. French (or string) beans prepared in this way and sprinkled with chopped parsley are called *Haricots verts à la tourangelle*.

Dried French (or string) beans. HARICOTS VERTS SECS—Dried French beans soaked for a long time in cold water can be cooked like fresh French beans.

French (or string) beans à la française. HARICOTS VERTS À LA FRANÇAISE—Slice the beans, raw, into pieces about 1 inch long. Proceed as for *Peas à la française*.

French (or string) beans au gratin. HARICOTS VERTS AU GRATIN—Proceed as for *French beans in cream*. Put the beans in a buttered ovenware dish with grated cheese in it. Pour melted butter over the beans and sprinkle grated cheese over the dish. Brown slowly.

French (or string) beans in gravy. HARICOTS VERTS AU JUS—Boil the beans in salt water until they are three-parts cooked only. Stew them slowly in butter. When they are cooked, moisten with a few tablespoons of thickened brown gravy. Serve in a vegetable dish.

French (or string) beans à la lyonnaise. HARICOTS VERTS À LA LYONNAISE—Boil 1 pound (500 grams) of French (or string) beans in salt water. Drain and dry in a cloth. Brown lightly in a pan ¾ cup (150 grams) of finely-sliced onions. Add the beans. Season with salt and pepper. Sauté these ingredients together until the beans are very slightly browned. Sprinkle with chopped parsley. Add a little vinegar. Serve in a vegetable dish.

French (or string) beans à la maître d'hôtel. HARICOTS VERTS À LA MAÎTRE D'HÔTEL—See *French beans in butter*.

Mixed beans (Panachés). HARICOTS VERTS PANACHÉS—Boil separately in salt water, equal quantities of French (or string) beans and small fresh kidney beans (*flageolets*). Drain thoroughly. Blend the two kinds of beans in butter or cream.

French (or string) beans à la normande. HARICOTS VERTS À LA NORMANDE—Proceed as for *French beans in cream*. After the beans are cooked, blend in yolks of eggs. Just before serving, add butter.

French bean salad

French (or string) bean salad. SALADE DE HARICOTS VERTS—Boil the beans in salt water. Drain and dry in a cloth. Serve in a salad bowl with a French dressing.

This salad can also be seasoned while the beans are still hot. In this case, it is flavoured with finely chopped mixed herbs and often also with finely sliced onion rings.

French (or string) beans sautéed in butter. HARICOTS VERTS SAUTÉS AU BEURRE—Boil the beans in salt water. Drain and dry in a cloth. Sauté in a heavy iron pan with butter, browning them slightly. Sprinkle with chopped parsley.

French (or string) beans sautéed à la provençale. HARICOTS VERTS SAUTÉS À LA PROVENÇALE—Proceed as for *French beans sautéed in butter*, substituting oil for the butter. Just before serving, add garlic and chopped parsley.

Preserved French (or string) beans—Beans may be preserved for future use by bottling, tinning (canning), drying, or freezing. See PRESERVATION OF FOODS.

Purée of French (or string) beans. PURÉE DE HARICOTS VERTS—Boil the beans in salt water. Drain and dry in a cloth. Stew them for a few minutes in butter. Rub through a fine sieve. Add to this purée half the volume of purée of dried kidney beans (*flageolets*) or the same quantity of mashed potato. Heat up the mixture and, just before serving, add butter.

French (or string) beans in tomato sauce. HARICOTS VERTS À LA TOMATE—Boil the beans in salt water until they are three parts cooked. Drain thoroughly and dry in a cloth. Stew for a few moments in butter. Add a few tablespoons of tomato sauce. Simmer. Sprinkle with chopped parsley, and serve in a vegetable dish.

BEANS, LIMA. HARICOTS DE LIMA—Lima beans or *Cape peas* are immensely popular in America. They are green like *flageolets* and about the size of broad beans.

All recipes for *Fresh white haricot beans* or *flageolets* are suitable for lima beans.

BEANS, RED. HARICOTS ROUGES—

Fresh red beans (U.S.A. kidney beans). HARICOTS ROUGES FRAIS—These beans should be cooked in the same way as *Fresh white haricot beans*. All recipes for white beans are suitable for red beans.

Dried red beans. HARICOTS ROUGES SECS—These beans should be cooked in the same way as *Dried white haricot beans*. All recipes for dried white beans are suitable for dried red beans.

Red beans in red wine à la bourguignonne. HARICOTS ROUGES AU VIN ROUGE, DITS À LA BOURGUIGNONNE—Cook the beans in equal parts of water and red wine with the usual herbs and a piece of blanched lean bacon or lean smoked bacon.

When the beans are cooked, drain them. Put them in a frying-pan with butter and the bacon, coarsely chopped. Fry them and then add kneaded (creamed) butter. Serve in a vegetable dish.

BEAN, TONKA—The seed of a pulse rich in coumarin (a fragrant crystalline substance, analogous to volatile oils and camphor). It is used in the manufacture of some liqueurs.

BEANS, FRESH WHITE HARICOT. HARICOTS BLANCS FRAIS—

To cook fresh white haricot beans. Usually these beans are put into boiling salt water, 1½ teaspoons (10 grams) of salt to 1 quart (litre) of water with aromatic vegetables and a *bouquet garni*.* (Dry white haricot beans, on the other hand, must be put into cold water.)

The fresh beans can also be cooked as follows:

Brown very lightly in butter a medium-sized carrot and onion cut in quarters. Add enough water to cover the beans completely when they are put in, with a little to spare. Add a *bouquet garni* and ¾ pound (300 grams) of blanched lean bacon to every 3 quarts (litres) of water. Bring to the boil, skin and season with salt. After the stock has boiled for 25 minutes, add the beans and simmer gently.

This method of cooking greatly improves the flavour of the beans. White beans prepared in this way can be dressed in a number of different ways.

Fresh white beans à la bretonne. HARICOTS BLANCS FRAIS À LA BRETONNE—Cook the beans as indicated above. Drain and put them in a pan. Blend in *Bretonne sauce* (see SAUCE). 1¼ cups (2½ decilitres) of sauce should be used to a quart (litre) of cooked beans. Simmer the beans in the sauce for a few minutes. Sprinkle with chopped parsley. Serve in a vegetable dish.

Fresh white beans in butter. HARICOTS BLANCS FRAIS AU BEURRE—Cook the beans as indicated above. Drain them. Put them in a saucepan and toss them over a flame for a few seconds to dry them. Blend in 5 tablespoons (80 grams) of butter to every quart (litre) of cooked beans. Serve in a vegetable dish.

Fresh white beans en cassoulet. HARICOTS BLANCS FRAIS EN CASSOULET—The *cassoulet* of Languedoc is usually made from dried white haricot beans, but it may also be made from fresh beans. For the recipe, see CASSOULET.

Fresh white beans in cream. HARICOTS BLANCS FRAIS À LA CRÈME—Dry the beans for a few seconds on the stove after they have been cooked as described above and well drained. Cover the beans with thick fresh cream. Simmer until the cream has been reduced to half its volume. Add several spoonfuls of fresh cream. Mix and serve in a vegetable dish.

Estouffat* of fresh white beans à l'occitane. ESTOUFFAT DE HARICOTS BLANCS FRAIS À L'OCCITANE—Brown in butter or goose fat ½ pound (250 grams) of belly of pork or salt pork, diced and blanched. When the pork begins to fry, add 1 medium to large chopped onion (150 grams), 2 peeled, squeezed and coarsely chopped tomatoes and a little crushed garlic. Cook for 10 minutes. Add to this stock 1½ quarts (litres) white haricot beans cooked as indicated above. The beans should, however, be only three parts cooked. They must be drained before they are added to the stock. Cover and cook. Serve in a vegetable dish.

Seven ounces (200 grams) of pork-skin or bacon-rind, rolled and tied, may be added when cooking the beans. Later, when the whole dish is ready the skin should be coarsely diced and added to the *estouffat*.*

Fresh white beans à la lyonnaise. HARICOTS BLANCS FRAIS À LA LYONNAISE—Cook the beans as described above and drain well. To each quart (litre) of cooked beans add 2 medium-sized onions (200 grams) finely sliced and cooked slowly in butter until tender. Simmer together for a few minutes in a casserole. Add 2 tablespoons of chopped parsley.

Fresh white beans with parsley. HARICOTS BLANCS FRAIS AUX FINES HERBES—Proceed as for *Fresh white beans in butter*, with chopped parsley added.

Purée of fresh white beans. PURÉE DE HARICOTS BLANCS FRAIS—Cook the beans as indicated above. Rub them through a fine sieve and drain thoroughly.

Warm this purée, stirring vigorously with a wooden spoon until it is very smooth. Just before serving add fresh butter, 6 tablespoons (90-100 grams) of butter to 2 cups (500 grams) of purée.

If required, before adding the butter, mix a few tablespoons of boiled milk, cream or stock, in which the beans were cooked, with the purée.

If the beans are to be served as a vegetable or garnish, however, the purée should be left fairly thick.

Fresh white bean salad. SALADE DE HARICOTS BLANCS FRAIS—Cook the beans as described above. Drain them thoroughly. Put them in a salad bowl. Dress them with oil and vinegar and season with salt, pepper and chopped mixed herbs (parsley, chervil and chives). Mix well.

This salad needs a lot of seasoning. Onion rings or chopped onion may be added to it.

BEANS, DRIED WHITE HARICOT (U.S.A. Horticultural). HARICOTS BLANCS SECS—Before cooking in water, meat or vegetable stock, dried white haricot beans are usually soaked for a long time in water. This traditional practice is a bad one. If dried beans or other dried vegetables have to be soaked they should be left for a short time only. Some recipes recommend 12 or even 24 hours of soaking, whereas in fact soaking, even for a few hours, may cause slight fermentation which noticeably spoils the flavour of the beans and can also make them slightly poisonous. To swell the beans, 1½ to 2 hours of soaking in cold water is sufficient.

If the beans are of good quality and have been dried within the year, they can be cooked without soaking.

To cook dried white beans. Pick through the beans and wash them. Put them in a deep saucepan with plenty of cold water. Bring the water slowly to the boil. Skim. Season. Flavour with aromatic vegetables (onions stuck with cloves, quartered carrots, a *bouquet garni** with a small clove of garlic). Cover and simmer very slowly.

In some cases, especially for *cassoulet** and *estouffat** it is advisable to cook the dried beans with fat. This is done by adding to the stock salted bacon, chine of salt pork or knuckle of pork and fresh pork skin. This adds to the flavour of the beans.

Once cooked, dried white beans can be used in the same ways as fresh white beans: in butter, *à la bretonne*, *en cassoulet*, in cream, *en estouffat*, with herbs, *à la lyonnaise*, as a purée, in salad, etc.

Dried white beans à l'américaine. HARICOTS BLANCS SECS À L'AMÉRICAINE—Cook the beans in the usual way, with the addition of a pound (500 grams) of lean bacon to a quart (litre) of dried haricot beans. After cooking, drain, trim and dice the bacon. Drain the beans and mix with tomato sauce. Add the bacon to this mixture and simmer. Serve in a vegetable dish.

Dried white beans à l'anglaise. HARICOTS BLANCS SECS À L'ANGLAISE—Boil the beans in water with seasoning and the usual herbs. Drain them. Serve them in a vegetable dish. Serve fresh butter separately.

Dried white beans à la berrichonne. HARICOTS BLANCS SECS À LA BERRICHONNE—Proceed as for *Dried white beans au gratin*. Put alternate layers of beans and thick mutton hash in an ovenware dish. Sprinkle with breadcrumbs. Pour melted butter over it and brown.

Dried white beans à la charcutière. HARICOTS BLANCS SECS À LA CHARCUTIÈRE—Cook the beans with a piece of de-salted lean raw ham and the usual herbs.

When the ham is cooked, drain it and dice coarsely. Drain the beans thoroughly. For 2 quarts (litres) of cooked beans use ¾ cup (150 grams) of chopped onions and brown these in butter in a saucepan. Add the beans and simmer. Add the diced ham to this mixture.

Put the beans in a buttered ovenware dish. Press down into the beans 6 little flat pork sausages (*crépinettes**) cooked in butter. Sprinkle with breadcrumbs. Pour over the dish the butter in which the sausages have been cooked. Brown slowly.

Dried white beans au gratin. HARICOTS BLANCS SECS AU GRATIN—Cook the beans in the usual way. Drain them thoroughly. Mix some concentrated veal stock with the beans. Put them in a buttered ovenware dish. Sprinkle them with toasted breadcrumbs. Pour melted butter over them. Brown them slowly.

Dried white beans in tomato sauce. HARICOTS BLANCS SECS AUX TOMATES—Cook the beans in the usual way. Drain them well. To each quart (litre) of cooked beans add 1½ cups (3 decilitres) of *tomato fondue** flavoured with a touch of garlic and a tablespoon of chopped parsley. Simmer all together in a pan for a few minutes. Serve in a vegetable dish.

BEAR. OURS—A perfectly edible animal but rarely used in the kitchen. Bear meat can only be used after it has been marinated for a long time.

This meat, which is not particularly tasty and is often tough, can be prepared in any way suitable for wild boar or venison. Some gastronomes consider bear's paws to be a great delicacy.

Bear ham. JAMBON D'OURS—This ham, which is common in Russia and some European countries, is cured in exactly the same way as pork ham. It is eaten cooked or raw. All recipes for pork ham are suitable for bear ham.

Bear's paw. PATTE DE L'OURS—Bear's paw is the earliest delicacy known to the Chinese, for even Mencius, the great philosopher of the pre-Christian era, who lived about a hundred years after Confucius, said: 'Fish is what I like, so are bear's paws; but if I cannot have both, I will forego the fish and choose the bear's paw. Similarly, I love life and I also love righteousness; but if I cannot have both, I will forego life and choose righteousness'. (Mencius, Book VI, Part I, Chapter 10.)

Unfortunately, bear's paw is fast becoming a delicacy of historical interest only, for its supply is very limited. There was a restaurant in Canton which claimed to be able to produce buffalo feet as a substitute and challenged guests to tell the difference. Skilfully prepared buffalo's feet can taste rather like bear's paw and can fool those who have not tasted bear's paw before, or who may have tasted it but are no connoisseurs.

Bear's paw chiefly is a delicacy of North China and is considered the domain of the cooks of the Shantung or Honan schools. The taste of bear's paw, like caviar, cannot really be compared to anything—it is unique. Mr F. T. Cheng, the one-time Chinese Ambassador to the Court of St James's, who certainly knew all about it, said: 'The nearest comparison is that it is like the fat part of the best ham, or rather much better, for it has not the greasiness of the latter. It is so smooth and delicious that it simply melts in one's mouth'.

Method. Wrap the paw in *clean* mud and bake in the oven. When the mud becomes firm like clay, take the paw out of the oven. Leave until cold and tear off the mud. This will automatically bring the hairy skin off the paw.

Then, simmer in water to get the paw softened, changing the water frequently, to get rid of its gamey smell and taste.

When it has become soft and 'tasteless', a condition that is essential, cook it until tender over a simmering fire with shredded chicken meat, lean ham, sherry and just enough water to enable the ingredients to yield a rich and thick gravy.

To serve. Cut in slices, like ham.

BEARBERRY. RAISIN D'OURS—See ARBUTUS.

BÉARN, THE BASQUE COUNTRY, BIGORRE—In these three picturesque provinces of the Pyrenées the art of cookery has never ceased to be honoured and practised.

'In the Béarn,' says Curnonsky, 'we have eaten as many local dishes and drunk as much local wine as our capacity would permit. . . . Almost everywhere, in the big hotels as well as in the little country inns, we found not only a cordial welcome (which is natural in France) but absolute cleanliness, attentive service and plentiful healthy food, prepared with care and taste.

'We met some great chefs, cooks and cordons-bleus who truly deserve the title of rare artists and we have had an opportunity of appreciating the talents of several admirable *cuisiniers* worthy of beatification.

'The number of Basque or Béarnais gastronomes appears to us to equal that of the Bresse and Lyon regions, which means that they ought to represent about five-sixths of the population.'

This type of praise should not come as a surprise. In fact, 'no matter what part of Hautes or Basses-Pyrénées you visit, never hesitate to stop at a modest inn or to enter the dining-room of an unpretentious hostelry. Express your desire to try the local dishes and a few moments later you will be enjoying them, and, what is probably more wonderful still, your digestion will not be

Map of Béarn

Sauveterre de Béarn, Béarn (*French Government Tourist Office*)

in the least taxed, a "digestion without remorse", as an old Pau doctor used to say'.

Let us now enumerate the gastronomical riches of the three Pyrenean provinces.

First of all, there is an unsurpassable soup, at once a soup and a substantial dish, the *garbure*, and its friend and companion, *lou trebuc*, a portion of preserved goose or pork; the *toulia* in Bigorre and the *ouliat* in Béarn, onion soup to which a dash of vinegar is sometimes added and which is also made of cheese, tomatoes, leeks and garlic, when it takes the name of *soupe du berger*.

In the chapter on meat the historic dish, *poule au pot d'Henri IV*, will be found, and also the lamb of the Ossau valley, in Béarn, as tender as a strawberry and of a flavour which never fails to arouse the admiration of the guest; *mutton cutlets* (chops) of Barèges, the *daube à la béarnaise*, or *estouffat*; *preserved goose*, *pork*, *turkey* and *duck*.

As an accompaniment to all these delicious dishes, the Béarn produces excellent local wines, like all the wines made from grapes gathered in the Adour region.

Gastronomes know the wines of *Madiran*, *Portet* and *Jurançon*. The last one is a historic name; it is known that Henri IV was very fond of the Jurançon wine.

The Madiran is a tonic wine, and easily digestible. It is drawn from the wood and bottled after five or six years. Once bottled, it does not reach its full splendour and maturity for another ten years.

The vine-growers of Béarn have a distinct taste for 'maderization' (a polite description of the bottle stink of a wine which has been kept too long) and treat the *Portet* and the *Jurançon* to have this taste. To them 'maderization', which is a deficiency, is considered a good quality.

Paul de Cassagnac, a great gourmet and gourmand, who very carefully studied the wines of the Adour basin, quotes among the most remarkable vintage years of the Madiran those of 1870 (unobtainable, alas!), 1886, 1898, 1904 and 1916. And this learned gastronome says that he has had an occasion to drink a Madiran of 1848 which was still 'at the height of its form'.

'The *Portet* is a white wine. It is gathered late. In the olden days people waited for the "noble rot" (*passerillage*) to do its work and generally did not harvest it until about Christmas time. Nowadays the grapes are gathered at the end of the vintage season, towards the end of November.

'The *Portet* is sweet and soft, or dry, depending on the year.

'The characteristic feature of the *Jurançon* is first of all its great sweetness, with which nothing in France can compare. And what is remarkable, is that its sweetness does not destroy its bouquet nor turn it into a syrup.

'The vintage years are mostly irregular, often the good qualities of *Jurançon* are swamped in the excess of sugar. 1886, 1905 and 1916 produced splendid results.'

A red *Jurançon* (*Bouchy*) is also made in Béarn; it is certainly esteemed as a table wine but cannot compare with white *Jurançon*.

BÉARNAISE SAUCE—According to some authors of culinary works, this sauce, one of the best in French classical cookery, originated in Béarn.

They say, in order to justify this claim, that originally the sauce was made of oil, not butter.

Other authors (and it would appear that these are nearer the truth) say that this sauce was made for the first time in the Henry IV pavilion, at Saint-Germain-en-Laye; that it was made with butter from the beginning and that it was thus named in honour of King Henry IV, the *Great Béarnais*, whose name, in fact, figures gloriously on the signboard of the old restaurant at Saint-

Germain-en-Laye. The recipe for *Béarnaise sauce* will be found in the section on SAUCES.

BEAST. BÊTE—In culinary language this stands for any quadruped which can be used as food for man.

Animals intended for slaughter, which come under the general term of *live-stock*, are enumerated under that heading.

In addition, some beasts of burden, such as horse, mule, donkey and camel, are perfectly edible.

Among the barnyard animals, specifically raised for food, are pigs, rabbits and goats.

Among the wild animals, i.e., ground game, all of which are edible (and some very good to eat indeed), are deer, chamois, fallow-deer, red deer, wild boar, as well as the female and the young of these species.

The so-called wild beasts, such as lions, tigers, panthers, etc., are used as food in certain countries.

Normally, in cattle-farm and barnyard language, oxen, cows, bulls, goats and rams are referred to as horned cattle.

BEATER (kitchen utensil). ABATTE—The word *abatte* is a popular corruption of the word *battre* (to beat). An *abatte* is a kind of rather thick, double-edged flat knife used for flattening meat.

BÉATILLES (Titbits)—This name was used in the past to describe a collection of small articles, such as cocks' combs and kidneys, lambs' sweetbreads, mushrooms, which are used as a garnish for *vol-au-vent*, *patties* and *tourtes*.

These ingredients were usually bound with a *Velouté sauce* or *Suprême sauce* (see SAUCE). See TOURTE, *Tourte d'entrée à l'ancienne*.

Ragoût of béatilles (titbits)—Here is an old recipe for preparing *béatilles*.

'Gently cook in butter ½ pound (250 grams) of lambs' sweetbreads (which have previously been soaked in cold water and blanched). Cook ¼ pound (125 grams) of cocks' combs scalded, skinned and soaked thoroughly in cold water, in a *court-bouillon*,* and 1 ounce (25 grams) of cocks' kidneys, cooked simply in ½ cup (a decilitre) of Madeira and a spoonful of butter. Sauté briskly in butter ½ pound (250 grams) of chicken livers, trimmed, sliced and seasoned with salt and pepper. Cook ½ pound (250 grams) of cultivated trimmed and washed mushrooms in butter. Put the lambs' sweetbreads, livers, cocks' combs and kidneys and the mushrooms into a saucepan. Add ¼ pound (125 grams) of truffles cut in thick slices. Moisten with ¾ cup (1½ decilitres) of Madeira. Simmer with a lid on.

'Meanwhile, prepare a white sauce, called *Velouté* (see SAUCE), using good concentrated chicken stock. Add to it half of its volume of fresh cream. Cook down by half. Lace with a little Madeira, add some butter, strain and pour this sauce over the ragoût.'

BEAUGENCY—A small town in the Loiret, producing wine which resembles slightly the Basse-Bourgogne (Lower Burgundy) wines.

BEAUHARNAIS (A LA)—Method of preparing small cuts of meat, mainly tournedos.

The garnish consists of small artichoke hearts with *Béarnaise sauce* (see SAUCE), with a purée of tarragon added to it, and little potato balls.

BEAUJOLAIS—The wine of this region, which administratively belongs partly to the Department of Rhône, is attached to the vineyards of the Bourgogne province. It is an excellent red wine, most pleasant to drink (especially in large glasses). This wine is very fruity; its colour is a rich brilliant ruby. *Beaujolais* does not improve with age.

BEAUNE—Small town in the Côte-d'Or, famous throughout the world for the excellence of its wines, made from grapes gathered in the surrounding region.

Côte de Beaune produces both red and white wines.

Among the red are those of Corton, Santenot, Pommard, Volnay, Beaune, Hospice de Beaune and Monthéle.

Among the white wines are those of Meursault, Mont-

A Beaujolais wine-cellar (*French Government Tourist Office*)

rachet, Puligny, Chevalier-Montrachet, Bâtard-Montrachet, and the white Corton known under the name of Charlemagne.

BEAUVILLIERS—Beauvilliers was a great *cuisinier*. He served as Steward of the Household to the Count of Provence and Attaché Extraordinary of the royal households.

The restaurant which he founded (in 1782, according to Brillat-Savarin; in 1786 according to others) was situated at 26 Rue de Richelieu and was called *La Grande Taverne de Londres*. It can be considered the first real restaurant to be opened in Paris.

During the turmoil of the revolution it had to close its doors. Towards the end of the Directory, Beauvilliers reopened his restaurant. In 1824 he wrote his book *L'Art du Cuisinier*, which for a long time remained an authoritative standard work.

'Beauvilliers had a prodigious memory. He recognized and welcomed people whom he had not seen for twenty years, people who may only have eaten at his restaurant once or twice.

'He would advise which dish not to take, which to snap up and would then order a third one that no one else would have thought of; he would have wine brought up from the vaults, to which only he had the key. . . . But this role of a host lasted but a moment and having accomplished it, he would vanish. And a little while later the amount of the dinner bill (check) and the bitterness of paying it showed clearly that one had dined with a great restaurateur.

'Beauvilliers made his fortune, lost it and made it again several times.

'We do not know in what state he was financially when death surprised him, but it is unlikely that his estate amounted to *spolia opima*.' (Brillat-Savarin.)

BEAUVILLIERS—Garnish for braised meat served in a large cut. It consists of spinach kromeskies, tomatoes stuffed with a purée of brains and salsify sautéed in butter.

BEAUVILLIERS and BONVALET—These two cakes, the recipes for which are almost identical, were created towards the middle of the nineteenth century.

The first does not owe its name to the Duke of Beauvilliers, the preceptor of the Duke of Bourgogne, nor to the Abbess of Montmartre of the same name, but to one of Beauvilliers' old pupils, Monnier, who had set up a cake shop in Rue Monsieur-le-Prince and, as homage to his teacher, named his creation after him. This was the first cake intended for travel, wrapped in tinfoil. It was rather indigestible, containing a little over a pound (525 grams) of flour for 1 pound of sugar, whereas, according to Lacam, a cake should never contain more than ¾ pound (375 grams) of flour per pound (500 grams) of sugar.

The *Bonvalet* cake was not created in the pastry-making establishment bearing that name. The credit for it goes to a man called Jules Leroy, head pastry-cook at Machin's, 99 Rue de Turenne, and he dedicated it to a Monsieur Bonvalet in 1869.

Here is the recipe for these cakes, as given by Philéas Gilbert:

Pound 1½ cups (200 grams) of almonds with an equal amount of sugar, add five whites of egg, little by little. Rub this mixture through a sieve and keep by.

Meanwhile in a bowl blend 2 cups (500 grams) of sugar with ⅔ cup (350 grams) of butter and 4 whole eggs, added one at a time. When the mixture is quite smooth, add the almonds, 1½ cups (175 grams) of fine cake flour, the same amount of rice flour, and potato flour. Then add 7 whites of egg whisked into a stiff froth. Cook in a slow oven (325°F.) in a special cake-baking tin (with a hole in the middle) called *à trois frères*, sprinkled with potato flour.

When this sponge cake, for it is a sponge cake, is cold, ice it with kirsch icing and fill the centre of the cake with *Chantilly cream* (see CREAM) or *Plombière ice cream*. See ICE CREAMS and ICES.

BEAVER. CASTOR—A mammal rather rare in Europe but common in U.S.A. whose meat is sometimes eaten, but which has a rather disagreeable musky flavour.

BEC (BEAK)—Word often used in French colloquial expressions, such as *rincer le bec* (to wet one's whistle), which means to drink; *tortiller du bec* (to wolf down, make short work of food), which means to eat; *fin bec*, which means a gourmet.

BEC-PLAT ('Flat-beak', i.e. Shoveller)—Common French name for spoon-bill duck, thus called because of its flat beak. It can be prepared in all the ways suitable for *Wild duck*. See DUCK.

BEC-POINTU—French name for White Skate. They call it 'sharp beak' because its head is more elongated and the body more oval. It can be prepared as ordinary *skate*.

BÉCARD (Hooked nose)—French term for old male salmon. Its snout begins to protrude like a hooked beak, hence the name. See SALMON.

Bécasseau

BÉCASSEAU—French name for the young of woodcock, until its seventh month.

All the methods of preparation given for woodcock are applicable to them, but they are mostly cooked on a spit.

BÉCHAMEIL (Louis de)—Marquis de Nointel, a financier who made his fortune during the Fronde (the rising of the aristocracy and the Parliament against Mazarin in 1648-53) and got himself the post of Lord Steward of the Royal Household to Louis XIV, a job for which only very high-ranking gentlemen were eligible, and which was in no way like the post which is nowadays fulfilled by a *maître d'hôtel* of a big restaurant. The invention of béchamel sauce is attributed to him but it had, no doubt, been known for a long time under some other name. It is more likely, however, to be the invention of a court chef who must have dedicated it to Béchameil as a compliment.

The old Duke d'Escars said: 'That fellow Béchameil has all the luck. I was serving breast of chicken *à la crème* twenty years before he was born, yet, as you can see, I have never yet had the chance of giving my name to the most insignificant of sauces!'

BÉCHAMEL (Sauce)—Was *béchamel sauce* (which some people would spell *béchamelle*) really invented by Marquis Louis de Béchameil? Was this financier a gastronome and a gourmet and was he in any way competent in the culinary art?

We do not know this for certain but everything seems

to indicate that the *béchamel sauce*, being a major sauce, must have been, if not invented, at least perfected by one of the *queux de semestre*—cooks in the six-months' service of the royal kitchen.

Some dictionaries give quite erroneous definitions of this major sauce.

Originally, the *béchamel* was made by adding a liberal amount of fresh cream to a thick *velouté* sauce. Nowadays *béchamel* is made by pouring boiling milk on white *roux* (blend of butter and flour). When a meat *béchamel* is wanted, a certain amount of lean veal, diced and simmered in butter with a minced onion is added. See SAUCE.

Béchamel sauce (Carême's recipe)—'When the *velouté* is thick and just at the moment when you are going to bind it with a liaison of yolks and cream, pour into the *velouté*, little by little, thick cream and then you reduce (cook down) this *béchamel*, taking care to stir with a wooden spoon to make sure the sauce does not stick to the bottom of the pan. When it is simmered down to the desired consistency, it should just coat lightly the garnish for which it is intended; then you remove it from the fire, add to it a piece of butter the size of a walnut and a few tablespoons of very thick double cream to make it whiter. Then add a pinch of grated nutmeg, pass it through a white tammy and keep hot in a *bain-marie*.'

Note. In a marginal note Carême says: 'Boil down 2 pints (about 1 litre) of hot milk by two-thirds and use instead of cream, if the latter cannot be obtained except the day before it is required, which renders it extremely liable to have a sourish taste, whereas by using hot milk no such risk can be incurred. When it is possible to obtain good double cream, it should be used cold, and blended with the *velouté* a little at a time.'

BECQUETER—French slang word, which means 'to peck at food'.

BEDSTRAW. GAILLET—A plant of the *Rubiaceae* family. The flowering tops of the yellow bedstraw or *cheese-rennet* contain a substance which is used in the curdling of milk. It is used in the cheese-press in the preparation of Cheshire cheese.

BEE. ABEILLE—Insect which produces honey, greatly valued since the dawn of history.

BEECH. HÊTRE—The beech is a handsome tree found in upland groves. The fruit of the beech or beech-nut is good to eat. Beech oil is extracted from these nuts, and is second only to olive oil in quality.

Beech-nut. FAINE—The fruit of the beech tree. Its flavour is midway between that of the hazel-nut and the chestnut, with a slightly astringent taste which is dispelled by roasting, as in the case of chestnuts.

Oil is extracted from it which has a distinctive, not unpleasant flavour.

BEEF. BOEUF—Beef is the best, the most fortifying and most nourishing of all butcher's meat.

In France, there are three qualities of meat, graded according to breed, age, state of fattening, work done and even sex of the animal (for beef includes the meat of ox, heifer, cow and bull).

The best meat, especially for roasts, comes from five- to six-year old grass-fattened oxen. Younger oxen, belonging to an early maturing breed, give, at least in France, more tender but less palatable meat.

The English began to specialize in rearing and feeding cattle for beef long before the French did. County Durham shorthorns were imported into France to improve the strain of bovine stock reared for beef production. The Durham-Manceau cross-breeds, Charolais, Limousin, Garonne, Normandy and Salers oxen also show a natural predisposition for fattening.

Prime beef is of a brilliant red colour, firm and elastic to the touch. It has a very fresh light smell; the fat intermingles with the lean, peppering it with white, or slightly yellowish grains of fat. A sheet of blotting-paper applied to the surface should never be covered with greasy spots, as in the case of horse-meat.

Cattle market at Bordeaux (*French Government Tourist Office*)

Beef is classified in three categories according to its market value, which depends on how firm and fine-grained is the texture, as well as on the proportion of sinews, fascia and fat:

First category. Fillet, porter-house steak, sirloin, top of rump, rump steak, silverside and inner parts of the flank and round.

Second category. Top of sirloin, plate, top ribs, fore-rib and three-rib, shoulder of beef, chuck end of clod, and clod.

Third category. Flank, brisket, leg of beef, neck, ox-cheek, shin, ox-knees, or shin of beef, and knuckle.

Yield of carcase.

Sirloin (with fillet, porter-house steak, rump steak, aitch-bone and top of rump)	15·0%
The ribs (including top of sirloin, plate and rib)	7·5%
Hindquarter (silverside, flank and leg)	20·0%
Shoulder (rib, meat taken off the bone, shoulder of beef)	15·0%
Lower sections	32·5%
Fat	10·0%

Cows' meat is inferior to that of ox, generally speaking, except in the case of young heifers and sterile cows, whose flesh can often be superior to that of oxen. Bull's meat is tough; it swells a great deal in cooking, but is not suitable for anything except the stockpot, and the meat of a young bullock is preferable to that of a fully-grown bull.

Aiguillette de boeuf—French culinary term, for the part which is also called *pointe de culotte* and *pièce de boeuf*. This is the top part of the rump and is usually braised or poached.

Baron of beef. BARON DE BOEUF—Joint served in

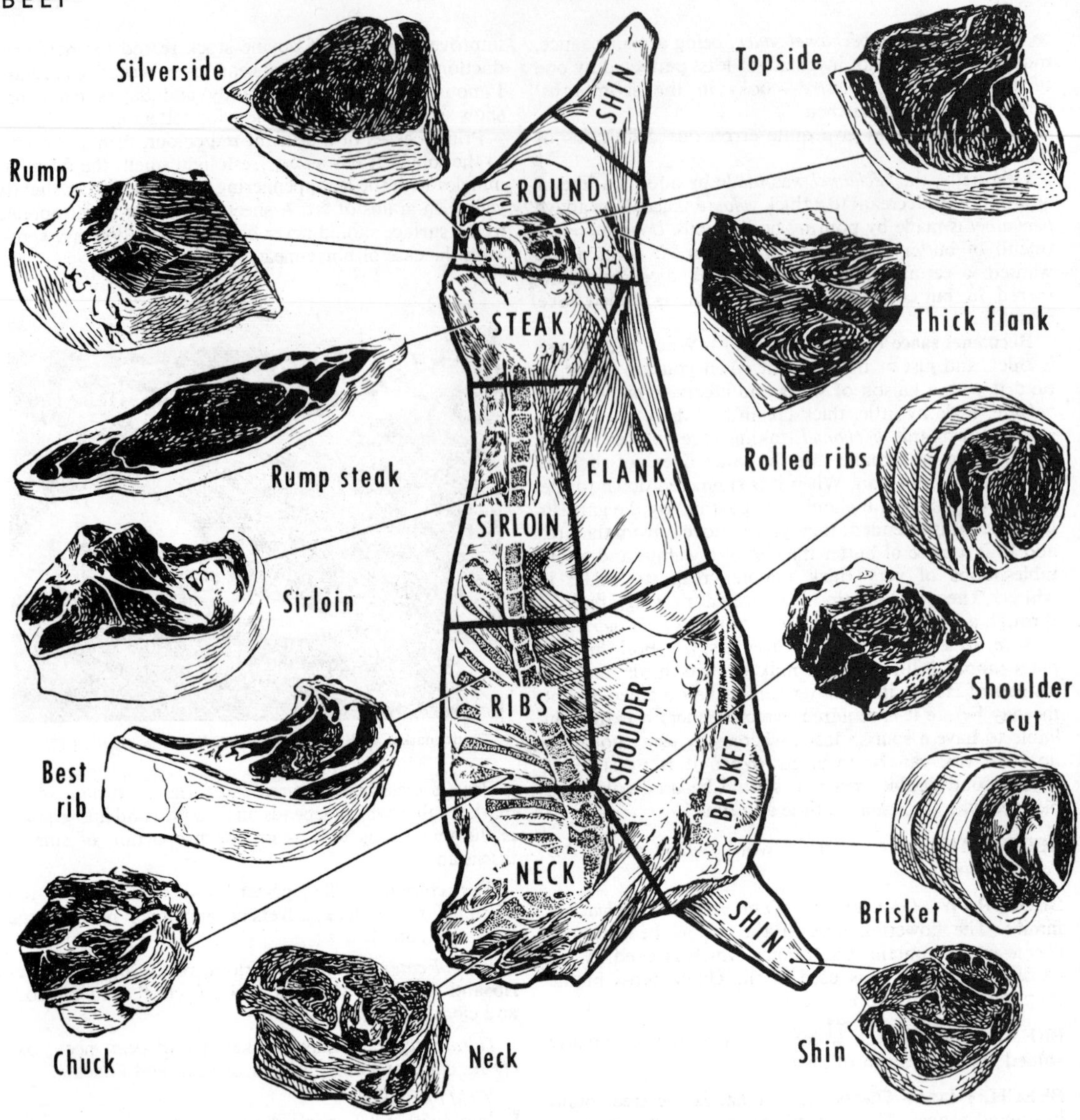

Chart of cuts of beef, English style

England at Christmas time, which comprises the two sirloins and a part of the ribs.

This huge joint is treated as *Roast sirloin à l'anglaise*.

Beefsteak. BIFTECK—This word, of English origin, defines a slice of beef taken from the fillet and grilled. This name is also given to a slice of beef taken from the sirloin, or *contre-filet*.

Instead of grilling beefsteak, it may also be fried in butter or lard. For recipes see *Entrecôte*, *Chateaubriand*, *Contre-filet*, etc.

In France, minced beef, served raw or cooked, for which various recipes are given is also called *bifteck*.

Beefsteak à l'américaine. BIFTECK À L'AMÉRICAINE—Trim ¾ pound (400 grams) of fillet of beef, cut off fat, chop the meat finely and shape into 4 round flat little cakes.

Put them on a serving-dish.

Make a little nest in the centre of each 'steak' and slip a raw yolk of egg into it.

Serve separately chopped onion and parsley and capers pickled in vinegar.

This dish is often prescribed in a building-up diet.

Beefsteak à l'andalouse. BIFTECK À L'ANDALOUSE—Chop ¾ pound (400 grams) of beef finely, add to it 4 tablespoons (50 grams) of chopped onion, lightly fried in butter with as much pounded garlic as can be held on the point of a knife. Season and shape into 4 flat round cakes. Dredge with flour and fry these briskly in oil.

Arrange them on a round dish, each placed on half a tomato sautéed in oil.

Fill the centre of the dish with rice pilaf. Dilute the pan juices left over from frying the meat with a ½ cup (a decilitre) of sherry; boil down, add butter and pour over the fillets.

Beefsteak à cheval. BIFTECK À CHEVAL—Season the steak with salt and pepper, sauté quickly in hot butter. Arrange on a plate with one or two eggs, fried in butter, on top. Pour over butter and juices from cooking.

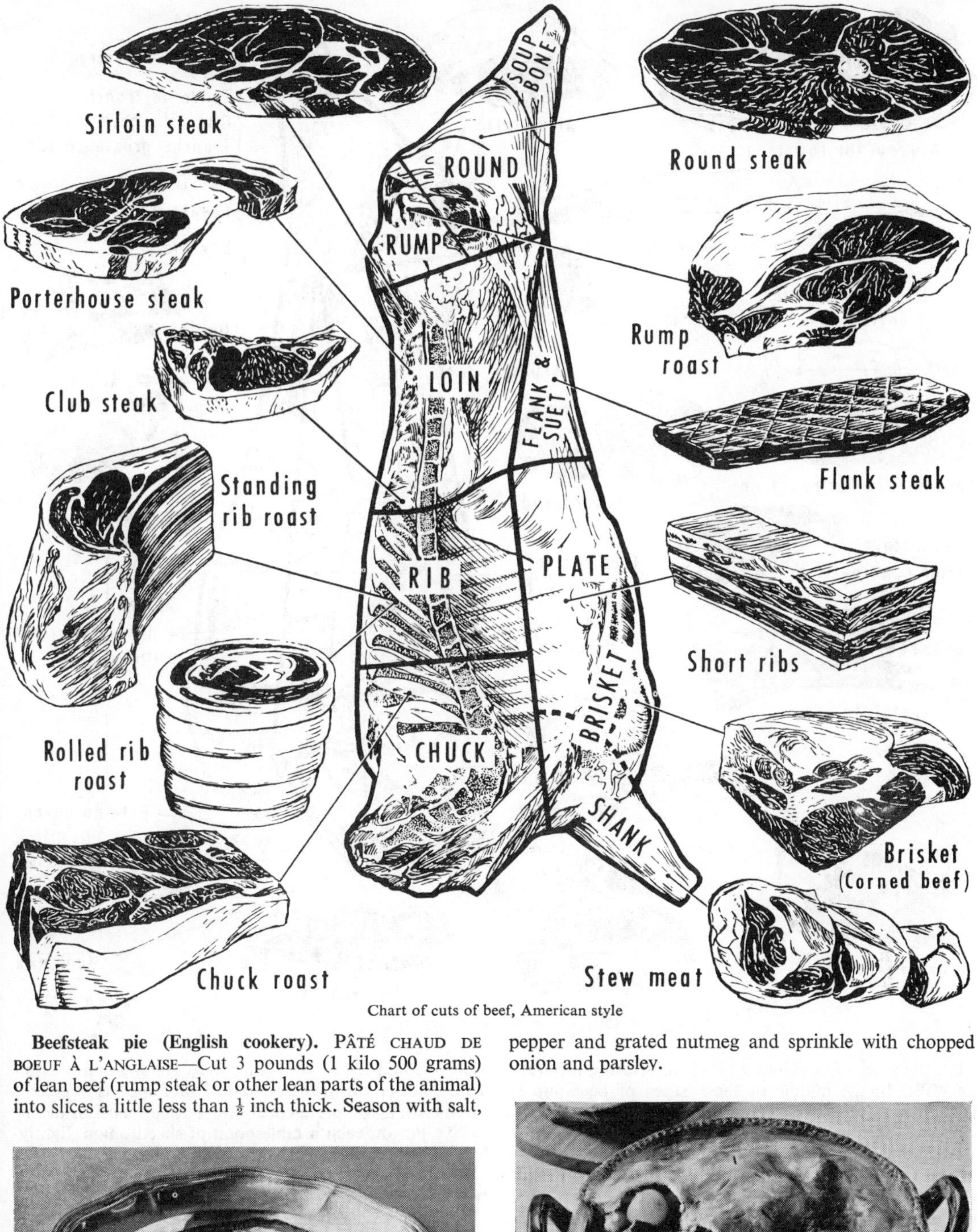

Chart of cuts of beef, American style

Beefsteak pie (English cookery). PÂTÉ CHAUD DE BOEUF À L'ANGLAISE—Cut 3 pounds (1 kilo 500 grams) of lean beef (rump steak or other lean parts of the animal) into slices a little less than ½ inch thick. Season with salt, pepper and grated nutmeg and sprinkle with chopped onion and parsley.

Bifteck à cheval

Beefsteak pie

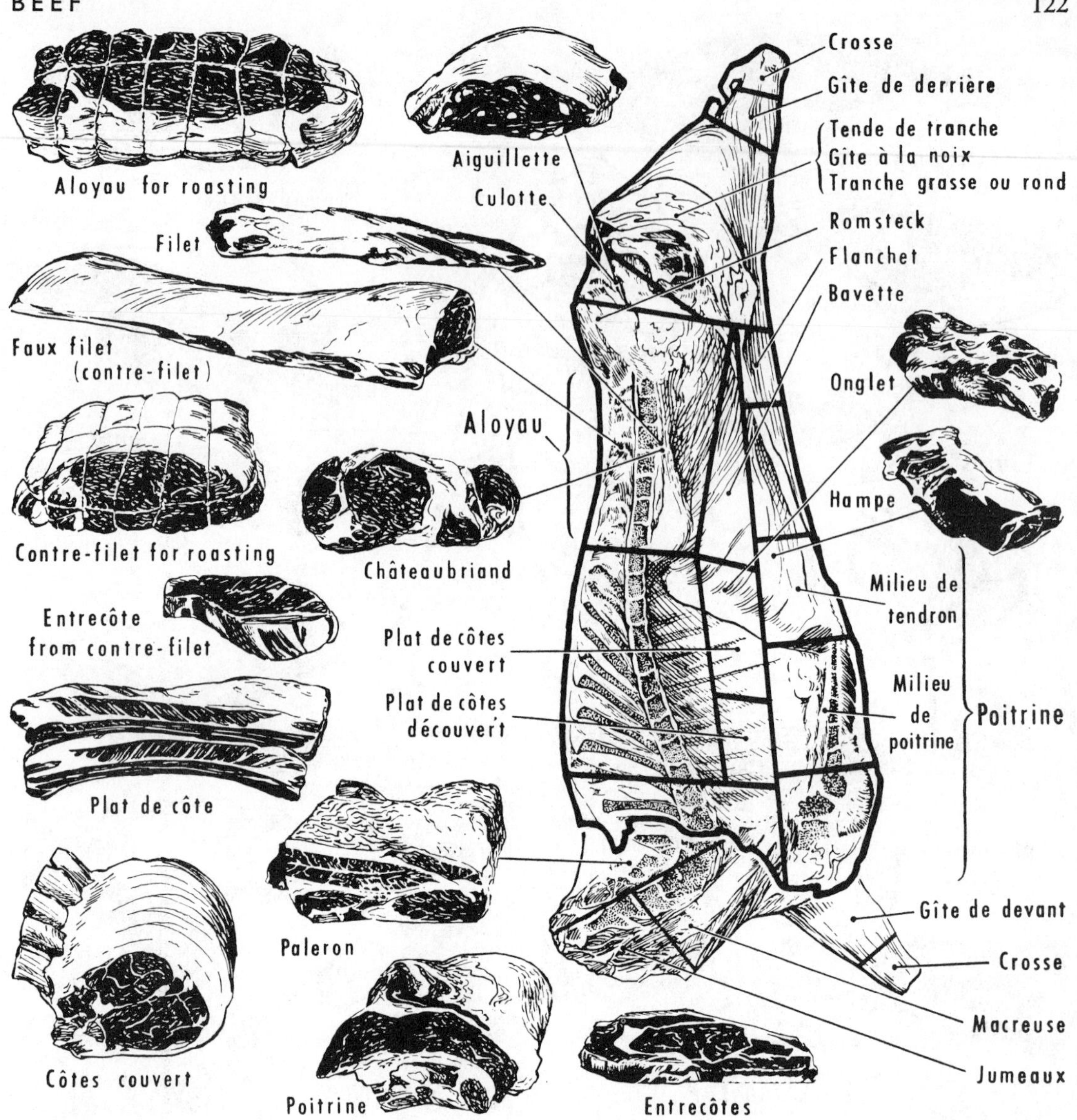

Chart of cuts of beef, French style

Put the slices of beef into a pie-dish, pressing towards the walls. In the middle of these slices of beef put 2 medium-sized potatoes cut into small pieces (optional). Moisten with stock (or water).

Wet the edge of the pie-dish, put a border of pastry around it, moisten it with a little water and put on a lid of pie or puff pastry. Seal the edges, ornament the top with pieces of pastry cut in fancy shapes, brush over with beaten egg yolk and make a hole in the centre to allow steam to escape.

Bake in a moderate oven from 1½ to 2 hours.

English beefsteak pie should be served hot. Cooking time should be adjusted according to the nature of the meat used.

Beefsteak à la russe (bitok). BIFTECK À LA RUSSE—For each serving, trim ¼ pound (125 grams) of lean beef; cut away all fat and remove sinews. Chop finely and add 2 tablespoons (30 grams) of butter. Season with salt, pepper and nutmeg. Shape into flat round cakes, flour each one and fry in clarified butter. Arrange on a dish. To the butter left in the pan add 2 tablespoons of cream (sour cream, for preference) and 1 tablespoon of *demi-glace*.* Put on each a tablespoon of sliced onion, lightly fried in butter. Garnish with sautéed potatoes.

Another way is to dip the bitok into egg and bread-crumbs and then fry in butter.

A dish is served sometimes under the name of *Bifteck à la russe* in which the chopped onion, which is normally put on the bitok, is replaced by a fried egg.

Beefsteak tartare. BIFTECK À LA TARTARE—Proceed as described in the recipe for *Beefsteak à l'américaine* but omit the raw yolk. Serve *Tartare sauce* separately. See SAUCE.

Cold boiled beef. BOEUF BOUILLI DE DESSERTE—Left-over pieces of boiled beef, cut in rather thick slices, served with various sauces.

Cold boiled beef à la parisienne. BOEUF BOUILLI FROID À LA PARISIENNE—Cut the beef into thin slices. Arrange on a long dish in one very straight row. Around it, dispose in separate, alternating groups, boiled potatoes (peeled and cut in round slices), sliced tomatoes, French (string) beans, quarters of hard boiled eggs, watercress and any other vegetables in season. Decorate the meat with thin onion rings. Sprinkle with *Vinaigrette sauce* (see SAUCE) and chopped parsley, chervil and tarragon. Serve very cold.

Left-over pieces of boiled beef can also be prepared in various other ways, including the following: *boulettes, croquettes, kromeskies, en fritot* (i.e. fried in deep fat), *en miroton.*

Boiled beef à la diable. BOEUF BOUILLI À LA DIABLE—Cut boiled beef into rather thick slices. Spread these slices with mustard, sprinkle with melted butter or oil and cover on both sides with white breadcrumbs. Grill on a low heat, making both sides golden. Serve *Diable sauce* separately. See SAUCE.

Boiled beef à la hongroise. BOEUF BOUILLI À LA HONGROISE—Cut the beef into large dice, brown in a sauté pan, in which ½ cup (100 grams) of chopped onion for 1 pound (500 grams) of beef have been fried lightly. Season with paprika. At the last moment, add *Cream sauce*. See SAUCE.

Boiled beef with horseradish sauce. BOEUF BOUILLI SAUCE RAIFORT—Beef from the stockpot with *Horseradish sauce* served separately. See SAUCE.

Boiled beef à l'indienne. BOEUF BOUILLI À L'INDIENNE—Like *Boiled beef à la hongroise*, substituting curry powder for paprika. Serve *Rice à l'indienne* separately. See RICE.

Boiled beef au pauvre homme (old recipe). BOEUF BOUILLI AU PAUVRE HOMME—'When you have any boiled beef left over, cut it into slices, arrange on a dish, sprinkle with salt, pepper, chopped spring onions and parsley, add a little dripping or fat skimmed off the stockpot, a pinch of garlic, a glass of stock or water, a little breadcrumbs and leave to simmer for a quarter of an hour on hot ashes.' (This dish, it is said, was considered a great treat by King Louis XV.)

Boiled beef with piquante sauce. BOEUF BOUILLI SAUCE PIQUANTE—Beef from the stockpot, with *Piquante sauce* served separately. See SAUCE.

Boiled beef à la provençale. BOEUF BOUILLI À LA PROVENÇALE—Prepare as *Boiled beef à la hongroise*, substituting for the cream sauce an equal quantity of a not-too-thick *Tomato fondue** flavoured with garlic. Heap on a platter and sprinkle with chopped parsley.

Boiled beef with root vegetables. BOEUF BOUILLI AUX RACINES—Boiled beef served with various stockpot vegetables, such as carrots, turnips, leeks.

Sea salt, gherkins, pickles, etc., are served at the same time.

Boiled beef sauté à la lyonnaise. BOEUF BOUILLI SAUTÉ À LA LYONNAISE—Cut 1 pound (500 grams) of boiled beef into small slices and fry in cooking fat or butter. Add 1¼ cups (250 grams) of sliced onions, previously fried in butter or other fat. Cook together, season with salt and pepper. Heap on a serving platter; sprinkle with chopped parsley and 2 tablespoons of vinegar heated in the pan in which the beef was cooked.

Boiled beef sauté Parmentier. BOEUF BOUILLI SAUTÉ PARMENTIER—Cut 2 medium-sized potatoes (300 grams) into large dice and cook in butter in a frying-pan. When nearly done, remove from the pan. In the same butter brown 2 cups (500 grams) of left-over pieces of beef cut into 1¼ square inch pieces. Add the potatoes and fry everything together. Heap on a serving platter and sprinkle with chopped parsley.

Boiled beef with tomato sauce. BOEUF BOUILLI SAUCE TOMATE—Beef from the stockpot with *Tomato sauce* served separately. See SAUCE.

Beef bouillon. BOUILLON DE BOEUF—This stock, which constitutes the basis of clear soups, is also used for moistening sauces.

'Beef', said Carême, 'is the soul of cookery.' Beef stock is obtained by cooking lean beef with aromatic vegetables such as carrots, onions, leeks, celery and parsnips, in water for about 4 hours. When the stock is to be served as soup, a certain quantity of turnips is added to the above vegetables.

For the method of preparation of beef stock, see SOUP, *Clear soup*.

Braised beef. ESTOUFFADE DE BOEUF—Fry lightly ½ pound (300 grams) of lean diced blanched bacon in butter in a sauté pan. Drain it and in the same butter fry 3 pounds (1½ kilos) of beef, taken half from the shoulder and half from the rib, cut into square pieces, each weighing about 3½ ounces (100 grams), until quite brown. Add 3 medium-sized onions cut into quarters. Season with salt and pepper, add pounded thyme and bay leaf and a crushed clove of garlic.

When all these ingredients are nicely browned, sprinkle in 2 tablespoons of flour. Let this flour colour slightly, stirring all the time. Moisten with ½ cup (1 decilitre) of red wine and the same amount of stock. Blend well, add a *bouquet garni** and bring to the boil. Cover the pan and cook in a slow oven from 2½ to 3 hours.

Drain on a sieve placed over a bowl. Put the pieces of beef and bacon into a sauté pan, add to them ½ pound (300 grams) of mushrooms, sliced or cut in quarters and sautéed in butter. Skim surplus fat off the sauce; boil it down to the desired consistency, strain and pour over the meat. Simmer gently for 25 minutes. Heap on a serving platter.

Brisket. POITRINE DE BOEUF—This part of beef is used for the stockpot. It can also be cooked as forequarter flank.

Carbonades of beef à la flamande. CARBONADES DE BOEUF À LA FLAMANDE—Cut 1½ pounds (750 grams) of lean beef (thick skirt, or chuck) into thin slices.

Season the slices with salt and pepper, brown quickly on both sides in sizzling fat (lard or clarified stock fat).

Remove the carbonades from the sauté pan and in the same fat fry 1¼ cups (250 grams) of sliced onions until golden, then remove from pan.

Put the carbonades and the onions into a casserole in alternate layers and add a *bouquet-garni.**

Moisten with liquor obtained in the following way: Dilute the pan juices with 3 cups (6 decilitres) of beer and a few tablespoons of stock. Thicken with 3 tablespoons (60 grams) of *Brown roux,** add a good tablespoon of brown sugar, stir, cook for a few moments and strain through a fine strainer.

Bring to the boil, cover with a lid and cook in the oven for 2½ hours. Heap on a serving platter.

Carbonades of beef with Lambic (Belgian cookery). CARBONADES DE BOEUF AU LAMBIC—Cut the carbonades and fry as described above in the recipe for *Carbonades of beef à la flamande.*

Remove from the pan and in the same fat fry the onions (chopped instead of sliced). Brown lightly, sprinkle in a good tablespoon of flour and cook for a few moments.

Put the carbonades into a casserole, season, add a *bouquet garni,** moisten with Lambic (strong Belgian beer), and bring to the boil. Cover the casserole with a lid and cook in a hot oven for 2½ hours.

Chateaubriand (Porterhouse steak)—A thick slice of beef fillet taken from the middle, weighing between $\frac{3}{4}$ to $1\frac{3}{4}$ pounds (400 to 800 grams).

The *Chateaubriand* is mostly grilled, garnished with *Château potatoes* (see POTATOES) and served with *Colbert sauce* or *Maître d'hôtel butter*. The *Chateaubriand* can also be cooked in any way suitable for T-bone steak, fillets and rump steaks.

The *Chateaubriand* can be either grilled or fried.

Grilled. Brush the *Chateaubriand* with butter or other fat and season. Put first under a high grill to seal the meat juices. Then lower the heat and cook as desired, keeping it a little underdone. Serve and garnish as indicated in the recipe.

Fried. Season the *Chateaubriand*, heat some butter in a sauté pan and put in the *Chateaubriand.*

Fry briskly but avoid leaving the pan on a high flame as this may cause the meat to get dry. Keep underdone.

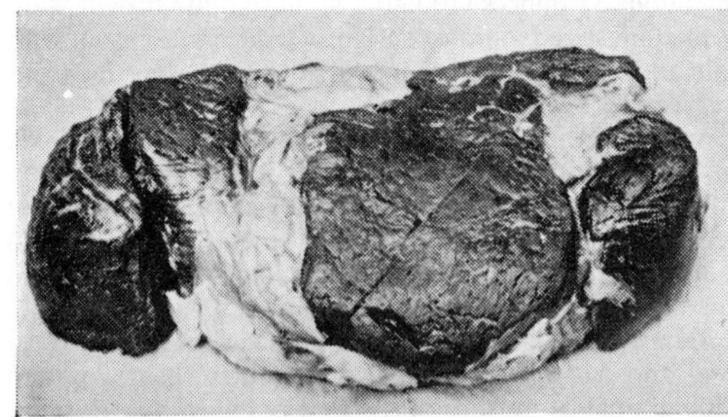

Chateaubriand

Arrange, garnish and serve with a sauce made from suitably diluted pan juices, as indicated in the recipe.

All the garnishes recommended for T-bone and rump steaks and the majority of those recommended for tournedos and small fillet steaks are applicable to *Chateaubriands.*

Contre-filet (U.S.A. Sirloin)—Cut situated partly above the loins and partly above the chine. It is classed in the first category of beef. This cut can be either roasted or braised, having first been boned, trimmed and dressed. Cut into thickish slices it is served grilled, as T-bone or rump steaks.

Contre-filet

Roast. The *contre-filet* (*U.S.A. sirloin*) is treated like all brown meat; it should be rosy on the inside. This is achieved by allowing 15 minutes' cooking time per pound if cooked in the oven, and 15 to 18 minutes, if cooked on a spit. When roasting the *contre-filet* with the bones, as is customary in England, allow 4 or 5 minutes extra time per pound.

Braised. Proceed as described in the recipe for *Braised beef.* Allow from 3 to 4 pounds (1 kilo 500 grams to 2 kilos) of untrimmed *contre-filet* for 10 persons. The weight may be increased as this meat is very good cold.

Served as a remove, the *contre-filet*, braised or roasted, is generally accompanied by vegetables.

If it is to be served grilled, cut into thickish slices and cook as described in the recipes for *Beefsteak*, *Sirloin steak*, *Rumpsteak.*

If the *contre-filet* is to be served roasted, bard it with bacon rashers, cover the rashers with barding fat (U.S.A. pounded suet), tie with string and roast either in the oven or on a spit.

Arrange on a big long dish, previously heated. Surrounded with the garnish recommended and serve either with its own gravy or the sauce indicated in the recipe.

Contre-filet (U.S.A. Sirloin), braised à l'ancienne. CONTRE-FILET BRAISÉ À L'ANCIENNE—Proceed as described in the recipe for *Top of rump braised à l'ancienne.*

Contre-filet (U.S.A. Sirloin) braised à la bourgeoise. CONTRE-FILET BRAISÉ À LA BOURGEOISE—Proceed as described in the recipe for *Top of rump à la bourgeoise.*

Contre-filet (U.S.A. Sirloin roast), cold, with various salads. CONTRE-FILET FROID GARNI—Arrange as described in the recipe for *Contre-filet, jellied.* Serve with whatever salad you like, either plain or mixed.

Note. For serving in grand scale buffets, cold *contre-filet* can be garnished with small timbales of vegetable salad, stuffed artichoke hearts, hard boiled eggs, lettuce hearts, etc. To make serving easier, however, it is preferable to decorate the *contre-filet* only with jelly and cress and serve the other garnish separately.

Contre-filet (U.S.A. Sirloin roast), jellied. CONTRE-FILET À LA GELÉE—This method is also used for serving left-over pieces of roast *contre-filet.*

Trim the piece, coat with slightly-coloured strong aspic jelly, arrange on a large dish, garnish with chopped jelly and watercress and put jelly croûtons around the border of the dish.

Contre-filet (U.S.A. Sirloin) with garnishes. CONTRE-FILET GARNI—Below we give the garnishes which are suitable for this cut of meat. For their method of preparation, see entry headed GARNISHES. (Garnishes followed by the letter (b) are suitable for *Braised contre-filet.*)

Algérienne, *Alsacienne* (b), *Anversoise*, *Béatrix*, *Bouquetière*, *Bourguignonne* (b), *Brillat-Savarin*, *Bruxelloise*, *Châtelaine*, *Chipolata sausages* (b), *Clamart*, *Dauphine*, *Duchesse*, *Favorite*, *Flamande* (b), *Française*, *Hongroise*, *Jardinière*, *Languedocienne*, *Lorraine* (b), *Lyonnaise* (b), *Macédoine*, *Maraîchère*, *Mentonnaise*, *Milanaise*, *Modderne*, *Niçoise*, *Nivernaise*, *Orientale*, *Piémontaise*, *Portugaise*, *Printanière*, *Provençale*, *Richelieu*, *Romaine*, *Sarde.*

In addition to the garnishes listed above, the *contre-filet* (sirloin) roasted or braised, can also be served with buttered or braised green vegetables, potatoes prepared in various ways, macaroni or other pasta products, rice pilaf or risotto, and, finally, purées of dried vegetables. These various garnishes are generally served in a separate dish.

Coquilles (scallop shells) au gratin (I). COQUILLES DE BOEUF AU GRATIN—Fill scallop shells with well-seasoned mixed cold beef, bordered with a purée of *Duchess potatoes* (see POTATOES). Sprinkle with grated cheese and breadcrumbs. Pour over some melted butter and brown in the oven.

Coquilles (scallop shells) au gratin (II). COQUILLES DE BOEUF AU GRATIN—Fill the shells, edged with half-slices of boiled potatoes, coated with a tablespoon of *Italian sauce* (see SAUCE), with thin slices of cold boiled beef. Put a mushroom on each shell. Cover with the sauce. Finish in the way described above.

Under HORS-D'OEUVRE a number of recipes will be found for preparing coquilles, hot and cold. See HORS-D'OEUVRE, *Scallop shells.*

Beef à la créole (Créole cookery). BOEUF À LA CRÉOLE—Put some fat and a tablespoon of olive oil into a casserole. Place two big sliced onions on the bottom and on top of this the beef, cut in large square pieces as for *Beef ragoûts.* Add a tablespoonful of tomato sauce, a clove of garlic, a sprig of thyme and parsley and a few pinches of saffron. Cook gently for 3 hours with a lid on. The beef and the onions give out enough juice, but if at the end of cooking the juice becomes too concentrated, add a few drops of water or stock. If, on the other hand, there is too much sauce, boil it down.

Daube of beef. DAUBE DE BOEUF—This old dish is prepared in different ways in different regions. In principle, it consists of a piece of butcher's meat or a large fowl, cooked in a *daubière** in braising liquor, with white or red wine added to it. But whereas in some provinces the meat (usually taken from the rump) is cooked whole, in others it is cut into square pieces or thick escalopes.

Prepared in this way, the *daubes* are very similar to *Braised beef.*

Daube of beef à l'ancienne. DAUBE DE BOEUF À L'ANCIENNE—Lard a piece of rump with thick lardoons (strips of salt pork) and marinate for a few hours in white wine and brandy, with sliced carrots and onions, parsley, thyme, bay leaf and pounded garlic, and proceed as described in the recipe for *Braised top of rump.*

Daube of beef à la béarnaise. DAUBE DE BOEUF À LA BÉARNAISE—Cut 4 pounds (2 kilos) of beef, taken from rump or shoulder of beef, into 2-inch square pieces. Lard each of these pieces of beef transversely with a thick lardoon (strip of salt pork), rolled in chopped parsley and garlic, seasoned with powdered thyme and bay leaf and sprinkled with brandy. Leave these pieces of meat to marinate for 2 hours in red wine and brandy, with sliced carrots and onions, a sprig of parsley and thyme and a bay leaf. Dry the pieces of beef in a cloth, dredge with flour and put in layers into a *daubière** lined with slices of Bayonne ham, alternating with layers of carrots and onions cut in round slices, lightly fried in lard or goose fat. Put a *bouquet garni** in the middle. Bring the wine in which the meat was marinated, with all its vegetables, to the boil, add to it 2 or 3 crushed cloves of garlic and a few tablespoons of stock, and simmer for 25 minutes. Strain and pour over the meat. There should be enough liquor to cover the meat completely.

Cover the *daubière* with a lid, sealing it with a strip of flour and water paste. Bring to the boil on top of the stove, then cook in the oven, maintaining even heat, for 4 hours. Serve in the *daubière*, having first removed the *bouquet garni** and skimmed off surplus fat.

In Béarn, this *daube* is served with *broyo* instead of bread.

Daube of beef à la provençale. DAUBE DE BOEUF À LA PROVENÇALE—Cut the beef into square pieces, lard them and marinate for 2 hours as described above, but using white wine instead of red and adding 3 spoonfuls of oil to it. Drain the pieces of beef and put them into a *daubière* which should be large enough to take all the ingredients. Spread the pieces of meat in layers alternating with fresh bacon rinds cut into small dice, bacon, blanched and cut into large dice, sliced carrots, chopped onions, raw chopped mushrooms, peeled, seeded and chopped tomatoes, some pounded cloves of garlic and stoned black olives. Put a good *bouquet garni** in the middle of all these ingredients and, besides the usual aromatic herbs, add a small piece of bitter orange peel.

Daube à la provençale (*Brown & Polson*)

Pour the marinating liquor over the whole, add some veal stock to complete the moistening, put on the lid, seal it with a strip of flour and water paste and cook in a moderate oven for 5 or 6 hours.

Serve in the *daubière*, having first removed the *bouquet garni* and skimmed off surplus fat.

Entrecôte or Steak—Entrecôte, by definition, is the part of the meat between the bones of the ribs of beef. A slice taken from the *contre-filet* or from the rump is often served under this name.

For culinary purposes they are often treated in the same way. The real *entrecôte* is mostly grilled, whereas a slice of *contre-filet* (U.S.A. sirloin), often called *rumpsteak* in France, is occasionally fried in butter.

These steaks are more generally boned before being grilled. When the pieces are thick, however, rib bones are sometimes left on.

Grilled. Trim and flatten the steak, brush with butter or oil, season and cook under a grill, first on a brisk then on a lowered heat. Arrange and serve as indicated in the recipe.

Sautéed. Trim and flatten the steak, season it and sauté briskly in butter. Arrange and garnish as indicated in the recipe. Pour over the pan juices left over from frying, having diluted them and finished off as described in the recipe.

In France, a steak taken from ribs of beef, or *contre-filet* (sirloin), of a pound (400 to 500 grams) or a little less is considered sufficient for 4 persons.

Entrecôte or Steak à la béarnaise—Grill the steak; arrange on a dish and garnish with *Château potatoes* (see POTATOES) and watercress. Serve *Béarnaise sauce* (see SAUCE) separately.

Entrecôte or Steak à la Bercy—Grill the steak. Arrange on a dish and cover with *Bercy butter.* See BUTTER, *Compound butters.*

Entrecôte or Steak à la bonne femme, or 'Grand-mère'—Sauté the steak quickly in butter, browning on both sides. Surround it in the sauté pan with 12 small glazed onions, 2 blanched potatoes cut to look like small olives and 2 ounces (50 grams) of salt pork or of bacon, diced and blanched. Finish cooking together. Arrange in an oval-shaped earthenware dish, with the garnish surrounding it. Dilute the butter left in the sauté pan with ¼ cup (½ decilitre) of stock or water and pour over the dish. Sprinkle with chopped parsley.

Entrecôte or Steak à la bordelaise—Grill the steak. Arrange on a dish, put on top 10 slices of poached and drained bone marrow. Serve *Bordelaise sauce* separately.

Note. The steak can also be served sautéed with the pan juices added to the sauce.

Entrecôte or Steak à la bourguignonne—Sauté the *entrecôte* in butter. Arrange in a dish, surround with and garnish *à la bourguignonne* (see GARNISHES). Dilute the pan juices with ½ cup (1 decilitre) of red wine, add ½ cup (1 decilitre) of *demi-glace*,* boil down, strain and pour over the dish.

Entrecôte or Steak à la fermière—Prepare *Steak à la bonne femme*, replacing the garnish indicated for that recipe by ¾ cup (1½ decilitres) of *Vegetable fondue* (see FONDUE). Arrange on a dish, pour over the pan juices, diluted with white wine and thickened veal gravy.

Entrecôte or Steak à la forestière—Prepare *Steak with mushrooms* (*I*) or (*II*), replacing the mushrooms by the garnish called *à la forestière*. See GARNISHES.

Entrecôte or Steak à la hongroise—Season the steak with paprika and sauté it in butter. When three-quarters done, add a tablespoon of chopped onion, lightly fried in butter and seasoned with salt and paprika. Arrange the steak on a dish. Dilute the pan juices with ½ cup (1 decilitre) of white wine, add ½ cup (1 decilitre) of thin *Velouté sauce* (see SAUCE). Cook for a few moments and pour over the steak. Serve with boiled potatoes.

Entrecôte or Steak à la lyonnaise (I)—Sauté the steak in butter. When three-quarters done, add 2 tablespoons of chopped onion, lightly fried in butter. Arrange the steak on a dish. Dilute the pan juices with one tablespoon of vinegar and 2 tablespoons of white wine, add ½ cup (1 decilitre) of *demi-glace*;* boil down, add a tablespoon of chopped parsley and pour over the steak.

Note. The sauce can be strained.

Entrecôte or Steak à la lyonnaise (II)—Proceed to cook as above. Dilute the pan juices with vinegar and white wine. Add stock and thicken the sauce with kneaded butter. See BUTTER, *Compound butters*.

Entrecôte or Steak maître d'hôtel—Grill the steak. Serve *maître d'hôtel butter* on top or separately. See BUTTER, *Compound butters*.

Entrecôte or Steak marchand de vin—Grill the steak. Serve with *Marchand de vin butter* on top or separately. See BUTTER, *Compound butters*.

Entrecôte or Steak à la ménagère—Prepare as *Entrecôte à la bonne femme*. Replace the garnish recommended in that recipe by an equal quantity of small glazed onion, carrots correctly cut down to uniform size and shape and three-quarters cooked, and mushrooms. Arrange on a dish, pour over the pan juices diluted with white wine and thickened veal gravy.

Entrecôte or Steak à la minute—Flatten the steak to make it as thin as possible. Season and sauté in butter. Arrange on a dish, and pour over it the butter in which it was cooked, piping hot and with a few drops of lemon juice and half a tablespoon of chopped parsley added to it.

Entrecôte or Steak Mirabeau—Grill the steak. Arrange on a dish, decorate with anchovy fillets and tarragon leaves, garnish with stoned, blanched olives and serve with anchovy butter, either putting a little on top, or handing it separately. See BUTTER, *Compound butters*.

Entrecôte or Steak with mushrooms (I). ENTRECÔTE AUX CHAMPIGNONS—Sauté the steak in butter. When three-quarters done, add 8 mushroom caps to the sauté pan. Arrange the steak on a long dish, finish cooking the mushrooms and put them around the meat.

Dilute the butter left in the sauté pan with ½ cup (1 decilitre) of white wine, add ½ cup (1 decilitre) of *demi-glace*,* boil down, strain, add a teaspoon of fresh butter and pour over the meat.

Entrecôte or Steak with mushrooms (II). ENTRECÔTE AUX CHAMPIGNONS—Proceed as above. Dilute the pan juices with white wine, add stock and thicken with *kneaded butter*. See BUTTER, *Compound butters*.

Entrecôte or Steak à la niçoise—Sauté the steak in butter or oil. Arrange on a dish, garnish with *Tomato fondue à la niçoise*,* new potatoes cooked in butter and black olives. Pour over the pan juices, diluted with white wine and tomato-flavoured veal stock.

Entrecôte or Steak à la tyrolienne—Grill the steak, arrange on a dish, top with onion rings fried in butter, surround with a border of *Tomato fondue** and sprinkle with chopped parsley.

Entrecôte or Steak au vert-pré—Grill the steak, arrange on a dish, garnish with straw potatoes alternating with little bunches of watercress and serve topped with *Maître d'hôtel butter*. See BUTTER, *Compound butters*.

Entrecôte or Steak à la viennoise (Austrian cookery)—Beat the steak to flatten thoroughly, season with salt and paprika, dredge with flour and sauté briskly in lard. Arrange on a dish, cover with onion rings, fried in lard, drained and dressed with butter and vinegar.

Serve boiled potatoes separately.

Beef essence. ESSENCE DE BOEUF—Concentrated meat juice prepared as described under *Beef-tea*.

Filets mignons—These cuts are taken from the centre fillet. The *filet mignon* is trimmed into the shape of a triangle; its weight varies according to the size of the fillet. If it is too big, it can be divided in two and thus provide two *filets mignons*.

This part of the fillet of beef can also be used for the preparation of *Steak on skewers*, *bitki*, *pilafs* and quick *sautés*.

Grilled. Flatten the *filet mignon* slightly, season it, dip into melted butter and cover with breadcrumbs, pressing with the flat part of the knife to make the breadcrumbs adhere properly.

Sprinkle with melted butter and cook under a low grill. Arrange on a dish and serve with the garnish and sauce recommended in the recipe.

Since the fillet is cooked in breadcrumbs, the sauce accompanying it should be served separately.

Sautéed. Flatten the *filet mignon*, season it and sauté briskly in butter.

Arrange on a dish, serve with a garnish and sauce recommended in the recipe.

We consider it unnecessary to give special formulae for sautéed *filet mignon*. It can be prepared in any way suitable for *entrecôtes*, *rumpsteaks* and other cuts. In addition, all the recipes given for *escalopes* of veal, *noisettes* and *tournedos* can be applied to *filet mignon*.

Filets mignons en chevreuil—These cuts are taken from the centre fillet.

Trim, flatten lightly, and lard the fillets with strips of bacon, inserting them in a rosette pattern. Leave to marinate from 24 to 28 hours in the summer, from 3 to 4 days in the winter. See MARINADES.

Take the fillets out of the marinade and dry them in a cloth. Sauté as quickly as possible in clarified butter or oil.

Arrange on a dish and serve with the garnish and sauce recommended in the recipe.

The following are the most appropriate garnishes for

Entrecôte Mirabeau (*Robert Carrier*)

Ragoût of beef (*Robert Carrier*)

filet en chevreuil: *celeriac*, *lentils*, *chestnuts*, *onions à la Soubise*. They can also be served with fresh or dried *noodles*, *rice pilaf*, *risotto*, etc.

Filets en chevreuil can also be prepared *au chasseur*, *à la hongroise*, *à la poivrade*, *à la romaine*, *en venison*, etc.

Fillet of beef (U.S.A. Tenderloin). FILET DE BOEUF—The fillet is the undercut of sirloin, a muscular mass of pyramidal form situated in the lumbar region near the kidneys. The centre fillet is used for making tournedos and *filets mignons*. The middle of the fillet, after the fat and sinews have been removed, makes tender and delicate roasts, or, cut into slices of desired thickness, delicious grills. The top of the fillet, less delicate in taste, more sinewy than the middle, is used for the same purposes.

Whatever the method of preparation, allow 12 to 15 minutes' cooking time per pound (kilogram) of meat cooked in the oven (450°F.) and 15 to 18 minutes, cooked on a spit.

Method of preparation. Trim the fillet, that is remove all skins and sinews.

Cut into rather thick slices if it is to be served as a *chateaubriand*, as grilled fillet, *tournedo* or *filet mignon* and prepare all these various dishes as described in the appropriate recipes.

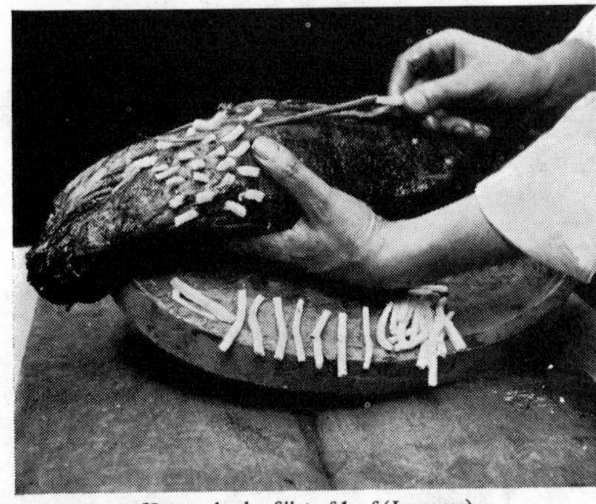

How to lard a fillet of beef (*Larousse*)

Trim the fillet, if it is to be served whole. Lard it with thin strips of bacon or bard it with rashers and secure with string, or, depending on the instructions given in the recipe chosen, stud it with little pieces of tongue *à l'écarlate* (salt beef tongue), ham, or truffle cut into little studs.

Tie the fillet with string, roast it in the oven or on a spit, fry or braise it, according to the recipe chosen. Follow the special instructions for braising, frying, roasting, under CULINARY METHODS.

When the fillet is cooked, untie the string and remove barding.

Arrange on a large, long, heated dish, surround with the garnish indicated and serve with its own juice or the sauce recommended.

In the olden days the fillet of beef used to be left to marinate from 12 to 24 hours before cooking.

Fillet of beef (U.S.A. Tenderloin) with garnish. FILET DE BOEUF GARNI—This is served as a remove. For various garnishes suitable for fillet of beef (U.S.A. Tenderloin), fried or roast, see GARNISHES. In the list of recommended garnishes, which is given below, garnish followed by the letter (f) is intended only for fried fillets; all the others are suitable both for fried and roast fillets.

Anversoise, *Béatrix*, *Bouquetière*, *Brillat-Savarin*, *Bruxelloise*, *Châtelaine* (f), *Clamart*, *Dauphine*, *Duchesse*, *Favorite*, *Financière* (f), *Forestière*, *Française* (f), *Frascati* (f), *Godard* (f), *Hongroise*, *Jardinière*, *Italienne* (f), *Languedocienne*, *Macédoine*, *Massenet* (f), *Mentonnaise* (f), *Milanaise* (f), *Moderne* (f), *Niçoise*, (f), *Nivernaise* (f), *Orientale*, *Parisienne*, *Piémontaise* (f), *Portugaise*, *Printanière*, *Provençale* (f), *Renaissance* (f), *Richelieu*, *Romaine* (f), *Romanov* (f), *Sarde* (f), *Saint-Germain*, *Viennoise* (f).

In addition to the garnishes indicated above, fried or roast fillet of beef can also be accompanied by buttered or braised vegetables, potatoes and purées of various vegetables. These purées should be served separately in timbales or vegetable dishes.

Fillet of beef (U.S.A. Tenderloin), London House. FILET DE BOEUF LONDON HOUSE—This is the same as *Fillet Prince Albert*.

Fillet of beef (U.S.A. Tenderloin) Matignon. FILET DE BOEUF MATIGNON—Lard a fillet with pieces of *tongue à l'écarlate* (salt beef tongue) (see OFFAL OR VARIETY MEATS) and truffles cut into little strips. Cover with a layer of *matignon*, wrap in wide, thin rashers of bacon and secure with string. See MATIGNON.

Put into a long narrow braising pan as indicated under CULINARY METHODS.

Moisten with Madeira and cook with a lid on for 1 hour. Drain the fillet, remove the bacon rashers and the *matignon*.

Glaze the fillet in the oven, arrange on a big, long dish, either straight on the dish or placing it on a croûton of fried bread.

Surround with garnish *à la matignon*. Strain the braising liquor, skim off surplus fat, pour a little of the sauce around the fillet and serve the rest separately.

Fillet of beef (U.S.A. Tenderloin) à la périgourdine. FILET DE BOEUF À LA PÉRIGOURDINE—Insert slivers of truffle into the fillet, bard it, tie with string and braise in Madeira-flavoured braising stock. Drain, remove barding bacon and glaze. Arrange on a serving dish. Surround with little slices of *foie gras* tossed in butter and little tartlets filled with a *salpicon** of truffles. Reduce (boil down) the braising liquor, strain and pour over the fillet.

Fillet of beef (U.S.A. Tenderloin) Prince Albert. FILET DE BOEUF PRINCE ALBERT—Take a good trimmed fillet of beef. Lard it with very fine strips of larding bacon. Slit it open, by cutting it longitudinally, but without separating the two halves completely.

Fill the inside with pieces of uncooked *foie gras* seasoned and studded with pieces of truffles.

Close the fillet, tie with string and brown quickly in the oven on all sides.

Put into a braising pan with the ingredients indicated in the recipe for *Fillet of beef Matignon*.

Moisten with port, cook in the oven and complete as described in the above-mentioned recipe.

Surround with *Prince Albert garnish* which consists of large truffles cooked in Madeira and mushroom caps cooked in butter.

This fillet of beef is also known as *Prince of Wales* and *London House*.

Another way of doing it is to stuff it with slices of *foie gras* and truffles incorporated in a forcemeat consisting of one-third minced fillet of beef and two-thirds *foie gras*, rubbed through a sieve and with chopped truffles added.

Instead of larding it with strips of bacon it is sometimes studded with truffles.

Fillet of Beef (U.S.A. Tenderloin) Stroganoff. Slice 2 pounds of fillet into thin strips. Sprinkle with salt and black pepper and keep 2 hours in a cool place.

Make a light *roux* by blending 2 tablespoons of hot butter with 1½ tablespoons of flour and adding 2 cups hot beef stock. When well blended add ¼ cup sour cream. Either a teaspoon of prepared mustard or tomato paste may be added.

Saute 1 medium-size onion, minced fine, and the beef strips in 2 tablespoons of butter over high heat. When brown, combine with the sauce and simmer 15 minutes.

Fillet of beef (U.S.A. Tenderloin) on skewers. BROCHETTES DE FILET DE BOEUF—This is prepared of square pieces of fillet of beef, taken from the fillet (U.S.A. tenderloin), pieces of lean bacon, blanched and fried, and mushrooms, in the same way as *Fillets of mutton on skewers*. See MUTTON.

Cold fillet of beef (U.S.A. Tenderloin). FILET DE BOEUF FROID—There are innumerable ways of presenting cold beef fillets. By changing the method of serving and the garnish, they can be varied *ad infinitum*.

They can be garnished with various vegetables, boiled, drained, allowed to cool and mixed with half-set aspic jelly. These vegetables are disposed around the fillet in separate groups, or they can be used mixed or individually for filling artichoke hearts, tartlets baked blind (tartlet shells), in little hollowed-out unsweetened brioches, etc.

Cold fillets can also be garnished with various *mousses* set in dariole moulds, lined with aspic jelly and decorated.

There are no hard and fast rules about the manner of serving these cold dishes. It can be simplified or complicated as desired, according to circumstances.

Full instructions for these preparations, as well as a list of appropriate garnishes will be found under the entry entitled COLD FOODSTUFFS.

Jellied cold fillet of beef (U.S.A. Tenderloin). FILET DE BOEUF FROID À LA GELÉE—This method is mostly applied to left-over pot-roasted or roasted fillet. If the piece is big enough to be served whole, cover it with aspic jelly, arrange on a long dish and decorate with chopped jelly and watercress.

If the opposite is the case, cut the fillet into thin slices, arrange on a long or round dish and garnish with chopped jelly and watercress.

The fillet can also be trimmed and placed whole in a long glass dish, a terrine or a shallow serving dish and covered completely with meat aspic jelly flavoured with Madeira, port, or sherry.

Whatever method of serving is adopted, it is advisable always to serve a green or a vegetable salad with the fillet. It is also desirable to accompany this dish with some cold sauce: *mayonnaise*, *rémoulade*, *tartare*, etc. See SAUCE.

Cold fillet of beef (U.S.A. Tenderloin) à la niçoise. FILET DE BOEUF FROID À LA NIÇOISE—Roast or pot-roast the fillet, keeping a little underdone on the inside. Leave to get quite cold. Trim and put into a rectangular rather narrow mould, with a flat or rounded bottom, lined with tarragon-flavoured jelly and decorated with pieces of white of hard boiled eggs, truffles and tarragon leaves, blanched, dipped into cold water and drained.

Fill the mould with jelly and leave to set, on ice or in the refrigerator.

Turn out on to a long dish, on a foundation of a thin layer of tarragon-flavoured jelly.

Surround with 12 small tomatoes, emptied without being damaged, marinated in oil, vinegar, salt and pepper and stuffed with a *salpicon** of truffles at the last moment and 12 small artichoke hearts filled with a salad of green asparagus tips. Put a heap of big, stoned olives, stuffed with anchovy butter and glazed with aspic jelly at each end of the dish.

Put a little chopped jelly between each group of garnish and decorate the border of the dish with jelly croûtons.

Cold fillet of beef (U.S.A. Tenderloin) à la parisienne. FILET DE BOEUF FROID À LA PARISIENNE—Pot-roast or roast the fillet and leave to cool.

Trim it on the sides and underneath, dry and coat with jelly.

Arrange on a big, long dish, either straight on the dish, or on a buttered croûton of bread, or on a foundation of cooked rice.

Surround with 24 small timbales of *Macédoine of vegetables*,* mixed with aspic jelly (set in dariole moulds). Decorate the edges of the dish with jelly croûtons. Serve *Mayonnaise sauce* (see SAUCE) separately.

Although *attelets* are merely decorative elements, the arrangement of cold fillets may be completed by the addition of these articles. The *attelets* should carry ingredients appropriate to the garnish used.

Cold fillet of beef (U.S.A. Tenderloin), à la russe. FILET DE BOEUF À LA RUSSE—Cook the fillet as described in the recipe for *Cold fillet of beef à la parisienne* and leave to get quite cold. Cut out the central part, leaving only a 'frame', with a narrow strip of about 2 inches at each end.

Cut the scooped-out meat into thin slices. Put these slices back into the hollowed-out meat case, pressing them in tightly.

Cover the fillet with good strong aspic jelly flavoured with Madeira and with chopped truffles added to it.

Arrange the fillet on a bread croûton or a foundation of cooked rice.

Surround with 12 halves of hard boiled eggs, stuffed, decorated and covered with jelly, 12 artichoke hearts filled with a salad of vegetables dressed with gelatine-strengthened mayonnaise, and 2 lettuce hearts cut in quarters.

Cold fillet of beef (U.S.A. Tenderloin) à la strasbourgeoise. FILET DE BOEUF FROID À LA STRASBOURGEOISE—Prepare and cook the fillet as described in the recipe for *Fillet of beef à la Prince Albert*, studding it with truffles instead of strips of larding bacon. Leave to get completely cold.

Trim on the sides and underneath and cover with jelly flavoured with port.

Arrange the fillet on a buttered croûton of bread or on a foundation of cooked rice.

Put at each end of the dish a heap of truffles cooked in port, cooled and dipped in jelly; garnish the sides of the dish with chopped jelly and small bunches of fresh parsley. Decorate the border of the dish with jelly croûtons. The fillet, trimmed and cut short, can also be served in an oval-shaped terrine and covered completely in port-flavoured jelly.

Fillets of beef steaks (U.S.A. Tenderloin steaks). FILETS DE BOEUF DE DÉTAIL—Slices cut off the fillet of beef weighing from 5 to 6½ ounces (150 to 200 grams). They can be prepared in any way suitable for steaks, rump steak and tournedos.

Grilled. Trim and slightly flatten the fillet, brush with butter or other fat, season and grill on a brisk fire.

Arrange it on a dish and garnish as indicated in the recipe.

Sautéed. Season the fillet and put to cook in a sauté pan in which some butter has been heated. Keep slightly underdone.

Arrange on a dish and serve with the garnish and sauce

Grilled petits filets (*Swift & Co*)

recommended in the recipe.

Small fillets of beef. PETITS FILETS DE BOEUF—Name given to small slices of fillets (taken from the narrow part of the cut) cut a little bigger than tournedos. All the methods of preparation given for tournedos are applicable to small fillets but grilling is the most popular method of cooking them.

Small fillets of beef à la niçoise. PETITS FILETS DE BOEUF À LA NIÇOISE—Sauté the little fillets in butter, drain them and arrange on a round dish, each placed on a croûton of bread fried in butter. Fill the middle of the dish with cooked French beans dressed with butter and put between each fillet a little heap of small potatoes (or potato balls) cooked in butter.

Dilute the pan juices with white wine, add some *Tomato fondue** flavoured with a little bit of garlic and chopped tarragon, and pour the sauce over the fillets. Top each with a rolled anchovy fillet and sprinkle with chopped parsley.

Petits filets a la nicoise (*Larousse*)

Beef forcemeat for agnolotti—See FORCEMEAT.

Forequarter flank (U.S.A. Shank). PLAT-DE-CÔTE—This is the name of the top part of the rib. It is mostly used for the stockpot.

It can also, after having been pickled in brine for several days, be poached in water with vegetables and aromatics and served hot with some appropriate garnish. The following are among the garnishes usually served with this cut: braised red cabbage, braised green cabbage, butter beans, or some other similar vegetable, and purées of fresh or dried vegetables.

This cut can also be used for making stews and can be prepared as *Pressed beef*.

Fricadelles, made of cooked beef. FRICADELLES DE BOEUF AVEC VIANDE CUITE—Mince 1½ pounds (750 grams) of cooked beef (remains of a piece of boiled or braised beef) and mix it with 2 cups (350 grams) of very thick potato purée. Add ¾ cup (150 grams) of chopped onion; bind with 2 whole eggs, season with salt, pepper and grated nutmeg and mix well.

Divide this mixture into pieces of about 3½ ounces (100 grams) each. Roll them on a board sprinkled with flour and shape into rather thick, flat cakes.

Brown them on both sides in butter or other fat. Finish cooking in the oven.

Arrange on a serving dish and serve with some well-spiced sauce, such as *Piquante*, or *Robert*, or with a vegetable purée.

Fricadelles, made of raw beef. FRICADELLES DE BOEUF AVEC VIANDE CRUE—Chop together 1½ pounds (750 grams) of lean beef, ½ pound (250 grams) de-crusted bread, soaked and squeezed out, and 1½ cups (350 grams) of butter. Add to this mixture ⅔ cup (125 grams) of onion chopped and lightly fried in butter and a spoonful of chopped parsley.

Bind this forcemeat with 3 whole eggs, season with salt, pepper and a pinch of grated nutmeg and mix well.

Using this mixture, prepare the *fricadelles* as described in the preceding recipe. Cook and serve them in the same manner.

Beef glaze. GLACE DE BOEUF—This is obtained by reducing (boiling down) very concentrated beef stock to a syrupy consistency.

This glaze is used for flavouring sauces, gravies and stews. See EXTRACTS, *Meat extract*.

Goulash (Hungarian cookery). GULYAS DE BOEUF—The goulash, or rather, the goulashes, as there are a great number of stews under this generic name in Hungary, are a way of stewing beef (or other meat), spiced with paprika, or Hungarian red pepper.

These stews, in Hungary as in France, are prepared in different ways. Two of the most popular methods of preparing beef goulash are given below.

Hungarian goulash (I). GULYAS DE BOEUF À LA HONGROISE—Fry together in ¼ pound (125 grams) of lard 3 pounds (1 kilo 500 grams) of lean beef, taken from the shoulder or rib, cut into square pieces of about 3½ ounces (100 grams), and ½ pound (250 grams) of onions cut into rather large dice. Season with salt and a teaspoon of paprika.

When all the ingredients are nicely browned, add 1 pound (500 grams) of tomatoes, peeled, seeded and cut in dice. Moisten with 1 cup (2 decilitres) of water, bring to the boil, cover with a lid and simmer for 1½ hours. Then add 1 cup (2 decilitres) of water to the stew, put in 3 medium-sized potatoes cut into quarters and continue to cook for about another hour. Serve in a timbale or a deep dish.

Hungarian goulash (II). GULYAS DE BOEUF À LA HONGROISE—Brown together in lard beef cut in pieces and onion chopped in large pieces. Season with salt and paprika.

When all the ingredients get brown, sprinkle in 2 tablespoons of flour. Allow the flour to cook for a few moments. Add enough clear brown stock to cover the meat. Add 1 cup (2 decilitres) of tomato purée and a *bouquet garni.** Stir, bring to the boil, then cover and cook in the oven for an hour and a half. Serve in a deep dish. Serve boiled potatoes separately.

Beef gravy. JUS DE BOEUF—This gravy is usually called in French *jus de viande* (meat juice). It is used in building-up diets and is obtained by pressing grilled lean slices of beef lightly in a special apparatus.

Beef au gros sel. BOEUF AU GROS SEL—Stockpot boiled meat, served hot, garnished with the vegetables with which it was cooked and sea salt. See *Bouillon, beef*; SOUP, *Clear soup*.

Hamburger steak (also called steak à l'allemande). BIFTECK À LA HAMBOURGEOISE—Chop finely ¾ pound (400 grams) of beef, taken from top of contre-filet or fillet (U.S.A. tenderloin or sirloin). Add 4 tablespoons (50 grams) of chopped, lightly fried onion and 2 raw eggs. Season well with salt, pepper and grated nutmeg and shape into 4 flat round cakes.

Dredge with flour and fry in clarified butter keeping them a little underdone on the inside (it is said that they are just right when little beads of blood form on the surface). Arrange on a round dish. Put on each steak a tablespoon of thinly sliced onion fried in butter.

Beef hash. HACHIS DE BOEUF—This type of dish really belongs only in home cookery. It is made out of left-over meat, mainly boiled or braised.

A great number of recipes for the preparation of beef hashes will be found under the section entitled HASHES. They can be made in scallop shells, as *kromeskies, croquettes, aux fines herbes, à la hongroise, à l'italienne, à la lyonnaise, Parmentier, à la polonaise, à la portugaise.*

Keftedes of beef (German cookery). KEFTEDES DE BOEUF—Prepare *Hamburger steaks* (see above) omitting the onion garnish.

This method of preparation can also be applied to other meat. It is very similar to *bitki* or *cutlets à la Pozharsky*, which can be made of veal, chicken or game and even fish.

Ox (beef) liver. FOIE DE BOEUF—This is less delicate than calf's liver. Nevertheless, all recipes for calf's liver are suitable for ox (beef) liver. See OFFAL OR VARIETY MEATS.

Beef marrow on toast. CROÛTES À LA MOELLE—Fry some rectangular slices of bread in butter. Put on them chopped beef marrow combined with some concentrated veal stock, flavoured with chopped shallot which has been simmered in a little white wine. Put four slices of marrow, which have been poached without boiling in salt water beforehand, and thoroughly drained, on top of this mixture.

Cover the marrow with breadcrumbs fried in butter (or with fine fresh breadcrumbs). Season with fresh ground pepper. Brown in a hot oven. Serve at once.

Medallions of beef fillet. MÉDAILLONS DE FILET DE BOEUF—Little round slices of fillet, a bit smaller than tournedos. Their weight varies between 3 to 3½ ounces (80 and 100 grams) and they can be prepared in any way suitable for *tournedos* or *noisettes*. They are sometimes called *coeur de filet de boeuf.*

Miroton of beef. MIROTON DE BOEUF—Arrange thin slices of left-over boiled beef, putting them quite flat overlapping slightly in a long earthenware or metal fire-proof dish, on a very thick foundation of *Lyonnaise sauce* (see SAUCE) and sliced onions lightly fried in butter. Pour some *Lyonnaise sauce* over the meat, sprinkle with melted butter or dripping and gently brown the top in the oven. Sprinkle with chopped parsley and serve in the same dish.

Miroton Parmentier. MIROTON DE BOEUF PARMENTIER—This is prepared as described in the preceding recipe, in a fireproof dish, the beef surrounded with a border of rather thick potato purée.

Paupiettes of beef. PAUPIETTES DE BOEUF—*Paupiettes* are little *ballottines** made of thin slices of various meats, stuffed with whatever mixture desired, and rolled.

Method. Flatten thoroughly thin slices of beef taken from top of contre-filet, silverside or shoulder of beef (U.S.A. sirloin, top of round or chuck). Season with salt and pepper. Cover with a layer of pork sausage or any other well-spiced forcemeat. Roll into the shape of large corks, wrap in thin rashers of bacon and secure with string.

Braise the *paupiettes* in the usual manner, moisten with white wine or Madeira, depending on the nature of the dish. See CULINARY METHODS, *Braising*.

Remove barding bacon, arrange the *paupiettes* on a serving dish, add whatever garnish is recommended, and pour over the braising liquor, boiled down and strained.

Note. All the garnishes indicated for braised beef can be served with *paupiettes*. Certain types of garnish, such as *bourgeoise, chipolata sausages*, small onions, or other similar accompaniment should be cooked with the *paupiettes*, added when the latter are half cooked, finishing cooking together, covered with strained braising liquor.

Paupiettes of beef can be prepared *à la bourguignonne*, that is to say, braised in red wine. In this case, the special garnish—small onions, lardoons (strips of salt pork) and mushrooms—must be cooked with the *paupiettes.*

Paupiettes of beef are often called *oiseaux sans tête* (birds without heads). This is quite wrong, as the latter dish, which originates in Belgium and is called *loose-vinken*, is made by stuffing slices of beef not with a force-meat, but simply with a big lardoon, seasoned with spiced salt. Like ordinary *paupiettes, oiseaux sans tête* are rolled into the shape of large corks, barded, and cooked like *Carbonnades à la flamande*, i.e., braised with finely-sliced onion lightly fried in butter and moistened with beer (Lambic).

Paupiettes of beef à la hongroise. PAUPIETTES DE BOEUF À LA HONGROISE—Prepare the *paupiettes* in the usual manner, but stuff them with a veal forcemeat mixed with chopped onion lightly fried in butter. Put them into a sauté pan on a foundation of thinly sliced onion lightly fried in butter. Season with salt and paprika. Simmer for 10 minutes under a lid. Moisten with dry white wine, allowing 1 cup (2 decilitres) for 10 *paupiettes*. Boil down, then add 2 to 2½ cups (4 or 5 decilitres) of light *velouté sauce* (see SAUCE). Put a *bouquet garni** in the middle of the dish. Bring to the boil, cover the sauté pan and set to cook in the oven, basting frequently. When the *paupiettes* are nearly done, drain them, remove barding, put back into the sauté dish and add 20 small mushrooms lightly tossed in butter. Add a little cream to the sauce, reduce (cook down), strain and pour over the *paupiettes*. Finish cooking together. Arrange the *paupiettes* on a round dish, each placed on an oval-shaped croûton fried in butter. Cover with the sauce and mushrooms.

Paupiettes of beef with risotto. PAUPIETTES DE BOEUF AU RISOTTO—Cook the *paupiettes* as described above. Glaze them, arrange on a round dish and serve with *risotto* (see RICE). Reduce (simmer down) the liquor in which the *paupiettes* were braised, strain it and pour over them.

Paupiettes of beef Sainte-Menehould. PAUPIETTES DE BOEUF SAINTE-MENEHOULD—Prepare the *paupiettes* as described above and braise until three-quarters done.

Allow to cool in their strained braising liquor. Drain, dry, spread with mustard flavoured with a pinch of cayenne pepper. Sprinkle with melted butter, roll in fresh breadcrumbs and cook under a moderate grill.

Arrange on a round dish. Garnish with watercress and serve with the braising liquor reduced (boiled down) and strained.

Paupiettes of beef with various vegetables. PAUPIETTES DE BOEUF AUX LÉGUMES—Having braised the *paupiettes* as described above, serve them garnished with various vegetables, disposed around them or served separately. They can be accompanied by buttered vegetables (French or string beans, broad beans, green peas, etc.), braised vegetables (celery, endive, lettuce); glazed vegetables (carrots, turnips, small onions, etc.), potatoes prepared in various ways and purées of dried or fresh vegetables.

Porterhouse steak—See CHATEAUBRIAND.

Pressed beef. BOEUF PRESSÉ—Pressed beef, which is served as an *hors-d'oeuvre*, can be found ready-cooked in the shops and it is very rarely done in the home.

Method of preparation. Take 6 pounds (3 kilos) of brisket, lean and fat mixed, prick it with a thick trussing needle and pickle in brine for 8 to 10 days, depending on season, the pickling process being completed quicker in summer than in winter.

The pickling brine is the same as that used for *Pickled scarlet beef or ox tongue* (see OFFAL) and care must be taken to see that the beef is completely submerged in the liquid, which can be ensured by covering it with a wooden board and putting a weight on top.

Just before putting the meat to cook, wash it in cold water and cut into pieces to fit the sizes of the moulds in which they will later be placed. Cook in water with a carrot cut in quarters and a bunch of leeks making sure that the meat is cooked thoroughly. After cooking, drain the pieces of meat, put into square moulds, cover with a wooden board and put a weight on top.

When the meat is quite cold, take out of the moulds and coat on all sides with a gelatine mixture, diluted and coloured reddish-brown by the addition of burnt sugar and carmine, putting on several layers. The meat will thus be enclosed in a protective covering which will guarantee it against contact with air and will keep for some time.

To serve, cut into the thinnest possible slices, arrange on a dish and decorate with fresh parsley.

Beef ragoûts. RAGOÛTS DE BOEUF—Pieces of rump, shoulder or rib are used for these ragoûts.

Bone the meat and cut into pieces of about 3½ ounces (100 grams).

Brown in dripping or butter, with onions and carrots cut into quarters. Season with salt and pepper.

When the meat and the vegetables acquire a nice colour, sprinkle in some flour, moisten with clear brown stock and mix. Add a *bouquet garni** and a crushed clove of garlic. Cook with a lid on, simmering gently, for an hour and a half. Drain on a sieve, put the pieces of meat, packing them in flat, into an earthenware casserole big enough to take the meat and the garnish. On top of the meat put the garnish indicated (which varies depending on the nature of the dish). Boil down (reduce) the sauce, skim off fat, strain and pour over the ragoût. Finish cooking in the oven, keeping the casserole uncovered, for an hour and a half.

Garnishes suitable for beef ragoûts. Bourgeoise, Bourguignonne, chipolata sausages, mushrooms, chestnuts, salsify.

Note. These beef ragoûts can be moistened with red wine. When thus cooked they are called *Beef à la bourguignonne*, a very popular dish not only in Burgundy, where it seems to originate, but also in Paris, where it figures almost daily on the menus of small restaurants, especially those kept by wine merchants and dealers. On these menus this dish is elliptically described as *Bourguignon*.

The garnish for *Beef à la bourguignonne* consists of lean rashers of bacon, scalded and browned, small glazed onions and mushrooms, whole if they are small, sliced if large.

Rib of beef. CÔTES DE BOEUF—This cut, also called *train de côtes*, consists of the muscles which cover the top part of the ribs and the vertebrae. It is divided into *train de côtes découvert*, from the fourth to the seventh vertebra, and *train de côtes couvert*, from the eighth to the last dorsal vertebra. The rib is classed by some in the first and by others in the second category of beef.

When boned, the rib is cut in transversal slices or *entrecôtes*, which are then generally grilled. See *Entrecôte*.

Roast or braised whole, ribs of beef are excellent. In big restaurants roast rib of beef is served on a trolley, i.e. a mobile hotplate, and is carved before the guests. The garnish for the joint and its gravy or sauce that goes with it, are also kept on the same trolley in *bains-marie* (double boilers).

Roast rib of beef is treated like all red meats and must be under-done on the inside. This is achieved by allowing 15 to 18 minutes per pound cooking time, when cooked in the oven, and 20 to 22 minutes cooked on a spit, for whole rib well hung and trimmed.

Braised rib of beef is prepared in the same way as *Pièce de boeuf* (U.S.A. Rump). See *Rump*.

It is advisable, for either roasting or braising, to choose rather big joints, to avoid the meat becoming dried up. For 10 persons allow an untrimmed rib of beef weighing from 3 to 4 pounds (1 kilo 500 grams to 2 kilos). This weight may be exceeded as cold roast rib of beef provides a very good dish.

Rib of beef (roast or braised) is served with all the garnishes recommended for *contre-filet* and *fillet*.

When *roasted*, it is usually served with its own gravy, clear and strong; when *braised*, with the braising liquor boiled down.

The left-overs of rib of beef can be made into various dishes, recipes for which are given under ÉMINCE, HASH, SALPICON.

Method of preparation. Roast in the oven: Trim and cut short the ribs. Cover with pieces of fat beaten flat and secure with string.

Brush with dripping, sprinkle with salt, put in a roasting pan and cook in the oven (400°F.), uncovered, allowing 15 to 18 minutes per pound.

Take the rib of beef out of the oven, remove string, trim and keep hot until ready to serve. Garnish and serve as indicated in the recipe.

Another method (as done in Parisian restaurants): Put the rib of beef, trimmed and tied, into a braising pan and coat with a layer of sea salt moistened with water, about 1 inch thick.

Cook as described in the preceding recipe.

Protected by this crust of salt, which solidifies when heated, the ribs cook through gradually. For serving, remove the salt crust.

Roasting on a spit. Trim the rib. Tie with string as described above. Put on an English spit.

Brush with dripping, season with salt and cook before a lively fire to begin with, to seal the juices.Then reduce to a more moderate heat, to ensure that the meat cooks through. Take off the spit and proceed as described above.

Rib of beef roasted on a spit should be taken off the

spit and kept in a slow oven for a certain time, from 30 minutes to one hour, depending on size (this applies to *whole roast rib*). The cooking is thus completed and the meat settles in the gentle heat and becomes more tender.

Ribs of beef à la bouquetière. CÔTE DE BOEUF À LA BOUQUETIÈRE—Cut a thick slice (containing two bones) off a trimmed rib of beef. Season this slice of rib and cook in a sauté pan in clarified butter.

Drain, arrange on a long dish, garnish with vegetables disposed in separate groups: little carrots and turnips cut down to a uniform size, or scooped out with a special round spoon, French (string) beans, artichoke hearts stuffed with garden peas, new potatoes cooked in butter, flowerets of cauliflower.

Dilute the pan juices with Madeira, add a little *demi-glace** and pour over the rib of beef.

Braised rib of beef. CÔTE DE BOEUF BRAISÉE—Proceed as described in the recipe for *Braised beef*.

Note. To braise, use pieces of rib, cut in thick transversal slices, weighing from 4 to 6 pounds (2 to 3 kilos).

Rib of beef with garnish. CÔTE DE BOEUF GARNIE—For various garnishes suitable for roast or braised ribs of beef, see GARNISHES. The following are the principal garnishes; letter (b) following the name of the garnish indicates that it is intended for braised rib of beef:

Bourgeoise (b), *Bourguignonne* (b), *Bruxelloise*, *Chipolata sausages* (b), *Dauphine*, *Duchesse*, *Flamande*, *Hongroise*, *Jardinière*, *Lorraine*, *Lyonnaise*, *Macédoine*, *Maraîchère*, *Milanaise*, *Moderne*, *Nivernaise*, *Parisienne*, *Piémontaise*, potatoes cooked in various ways, *Portugaise*, *Richelieu*.

In addition to these garnishes, roast ribs of beef can be served with buttered or braised vegetables and purées of vegetables and pulse foods.

Jellied ribs of beef. CÔTE DE BOEUF À LA GELÉE—The following method is used for serving left-over roast rib of beef:

Trim the joint, cover with strong slightly coloured aspic jelly, arrange on a big dish, garnish with chopped jelly and watercress and decorate the border of the dish with jelly croûtons.

Jellied rib of beef can be accompanied by various plain or mixed salads.

Roast ribs of beef, à l'anglaise. CÔTE DE BOEUF RÔTI À L'ANGLAISE—Roast the rib as described in the preceding recipes but allow a little more cooking time.

Serve with Yorkshire pudding, baked in the dripping-pan if the joint is cooked on a spit, or in an ordinary pan, using beef drippings for fat, if the joint is cooked in the oven. See YORKSHIRE PUDDING.

Roast rib of beef (boned and rolled)

Decorating a roast (*French Government Tourist Office*)

Roast beef. ROSBIF—Rib roasts, either standing or boned and rolled, fillets (U.S.A. Tenderloin), sirloin and rump make excellent roasts. The meat should be covered with dripping or other fat and roasted in a moderately hot oven (400°F.). To have the meat cooked medium-rare one should allow 15 minutes per pound. Some authorities advise longer, slower cooking.

Rump of beef. CULOTTE DE BOEUF—This cut represents all that is left of the hindquarter after the sirloin has been cut off. This is a first category cut and is braised and used for stocks.

The *top of rump* is usually braised or poached. This cut is commonly known as *pièce de boeuf*.

Braised or poached top of rump is served as a remove. All the recipes applicable to it will be found under *Top of rump*.

Rumpsteak. ROMSTECK—Rumpsteak is a slice of beef, varying in thickness, taken from the top of sirloin (U.S.A., face of the rump), or the lower part of the sirloin, also called *culotte* in French, formed by the thick, fleshy parts which cover the pelvic girdle. This cut is used for roasts and is also excellent when braised, but is chiefly preferred grilled.

In France, erroneously, a slice of *contre-filet* is sometimes called rumpsteak.

Rumpsteak can be cooked in any way suitable for beefsteaks, and fillets.

Grilled. Proceed as described for *Entrecôte, grilled*.

Sautéed. Proceed as described for *Entrecôte sautéed*.

Salt (U.S.A., Corned) and smoked beef. BOEUF SALÉ ET FUMÉ—The method is suitable principally for brisket, but top of rump and shoulder of beef (chuck) can also be prepared in this manner.

After having been kept in brine (as ox tongue) for a period of time according to season, these cuts are de-salted and put to cook in water, allowing 15 minutes per pound.

Salt beef is served hot, accompanied by various vegetables (braised red or green cabbage, sauerkraut) and, in general, with all vegetables normally served with poached beef.

Salt beef is also used as an element for the *potée*. It can be served cold. For this it is cooled under a press, as described in the previous recipe for *Pressed beef*.

Smoked beef, which must be pickled in brine before being smoked, is prepared in the same way as salt beef. It is served hot or cold.

Sautés of beef. SAUTÉS DE BOEUF—These are prepared from parts of rump and centre fillet cut into pieces weighing on the average 1½ ounces (50 grams).

Method of preparation. Season the pieces of fillet with salt and pepper. Sauté briskly in butter in a sauté pan, keeping underdone on the inside. Remove from the sauté pan as soon as the meat is nicely browned and keep hot. Dilute the pan juices with white wine, or any other wine, depending on the method of preparation. Add some thickened brown veal gravy or *demi-glace*,* boil down and strain this sauce. Put the pieces of beef back into the sauté pan. Pour the sauce over them, re-heat without boiling and heap on a serving dish.

Note. The sautés of fillet of beef can be cooked with various garnishes, such as mushrooms, which should be cooked in the same butter in which the beef has been cooked; truffles, cut in thick slices, lightly tossed in the same butter; potatoes, generally cut in dice and fried in butter, added to the beef after it has been transferred into a timbale; fresh buttered or glazed vegetables.

The following methods are also suitable for preparing sautés of beef: *à la crème*, the pan juices being diluted with Madeira and moistened with fresh cream; *à la bourguignonne*, pan juices diluted with red wine, with a garnish of lean rashers of bacon, blanched and fried lightly, small glazed onions and mushrooms sautéed in butter; *à la provençale*, pan juices diluted with white wine and moistened with *tomato fondue*.*

Sauté of beef can also be served surrounded with a border of rice pilaf or risotto.

Shank (U.S.A.)—See *Forequarter flank*.

Shoulder of beef (U.S.A. Chuck). PALERON DE BOEUF—The name of the fleshy part of the ox-shoulder. This cut is mainly used for making stock, but it can also be braised, as top of rump, and made into stews.

Sirloin (U.S.A. Loin). ALOYAU DE BOEUF—This cut, which is classed in the first category of beef, constitutes the part of the animal from the hook to the first ribs. It includes the *contre-filet* or *faux-filet* (U.S.A., Sirloin) and the *beef fillet* (U.S.A., Tenderloin). It is only called *aloyau* (sirloin) when it includes these two cuts, which should be cooked together, without boning. This cut is not found in retail markets in U.S.A., but a *Sirloin roast* can substitute in the following recipes.

When the sirloin is cooked whole, the top has to be trimmed off slightly and the ligament all along the chine has to be severed in several places. The fillet, which is just inside this cut, should have quite a lot of fat left on it, only some of the fat surrounding it should be cut off. After having been thus trimmed, the joint is seasoned inside with salt and pepper and tied with a string to help it keep its correct shape during cooking.

The sirloin, served as a meat remove, is generally roasted. It is cooked either on a spit or in the oven and kept a little underdone inside. The sirloin can also be braised. In this case, instead of cooking it whole, it is cut across into pieces of 4 to 6 pounds (2 to 3 kilos), which are then braised in the usual manner. See CULINARY METHODS, *Braising*.

Sirloin (U.S.A.)—See *Contre-filet*.

Sirloin à la d'Albuféra (Carême's recipe). ALOYAU À LA D'ALBUFÉRA—'After having prepared, braised and glazed your sirloin in the usual way, pour around it a ragoût made in the following manner: Put some of the pan juices and a little fresh butter into a sauce called *à la Tortue* (see SAUCE), add to it a plateful each of lightly fried calf's sweetbreads, salt beef tongue and mushrooms, bring the ragoût to the boil once and serve. Dispose around the meat a garnish of sliced fillets of young rabbit *à la Orly*: decorate the joint with 10 *attelets**: put on the attelet first a plump double cock's comb, then a slice of rabbit *à la Orly*, then another cock's comb and a glazed black truffle. Serve the ragoût in two sauceboats.'

Braised sirloin. ALOYAU BRAISÉ—Trim a piece of sirloin weighing from 4 to 6 pounds (2 to 3 kilos). Cut across the joint, with the grain of the meat. Lard it with thick lardoons, seasoned with salt, pepper and spices, sprinkled with chopped parsley and steeped for an hour in a sprinkling of brandy with carrots and onions. Secure with string.

Braise it in the usual manner.

Reduce the pan juices, skim off fat, strain and pour over the sirloin before serving.

Braised sirloin with various garnishes. ALOYAU BRAISÉ AVEC GARNITURES DIVERSES—Braise the sirloin as described above. Serve it with one of the following garnishes, disposed around the meat or served separately, according to the ingredients of which it is composed: *Bourgeoise*, *Bruxelloise*, Celery, Chipolata Sausages, Sauerkraut, Kohlrabi, *Dubarry*, *Duchesse*, *Flamande*, *Jardinière*, *Milanaise*, *Napolitaine*, Noodles, *Piémontaise*, Various Potatoes, *Provençale*, *Richelieu*, *Risotto*. See GARNISHES.

Sirloin, left-over pieces braised or roast. DESSERTE DE L'ALOYAU—All the recipes given for the preparation of *rib of beef* or *contre-filet* are applicable to sirloin.

Bones which remain after the meat has been completely used up can be used for making beef stock. See STOCKS.

Roast sirloin. ALOYAU RÔTI—This can be cooked whole or in pieces. Cut off the top and trim the sirloin.

Trim the joint, leaving a light layer of fat on the fillet, to prevent it from drying during cooking, and tie with string.

Roast it, on a spit or in the oven, by following the instructions given for the cooking of red meats (see CULINARY METHODS). Allow 12-15 minutes per pound at 450°F. Garnish with watercress and serve its own gravy separately.

Roast sirloin à l'anglaise. ALOYAU RÔTI À L'ANGLAISE—Trim and tie the joint, enclose in paste made of flour and hot water with one quarter of its weight of chopped and salted beef fat added to it.

When the sirloin is nearly cooked, remove the crust and brown the joint before a lively fire.

Serve with *Yorkshire pudding** cooked in the roasting pan, and the joint's own gravy.

Roast sirloin with various garnishes. ALOYAU RÔTI—Roast the joint as described above. Serve it with one of the garnishes recommended for *Braised sirloin*.

In addition to these garnishes, the sirloin, braised or roasted, can be accompanied by all the garnishes recommended for *Contre-filet* (U.S.A. Sirloin), *Rib* and *Fillet of beef* (U.S.A. Tenderloin).

Sliced beef with various sauces. ÉMINCÉS DE BOEUF—Left-over poached, braised or roast meat is usually used for preparing this dish.

Cut the piece of meat, *contre-filet* or fillet, into thin slices. Arrange them on a serving dish. Pour over them whatever sauce is recommended, *which should be absolutely boiling* so that the meat will be heated through.

On no account must the slices of roast beef be allowed to boil. The following sauces are particularly suitable for this dish: *Bordelaise*, *Bourguignonne*, *Charcutière*, *Chasseur*, *Duxelles*, *fines herbes*, *Italian*, *Lyonnaise*, *Madeira*, *Piquante*, *Poivrade*.

This dish can be served with various garnishes, depending on their nature. The garnish can either be disposed around the meat, or served separately, in a timbale.

Steak—See *Entrecôte, Beefsteak, Chateaubriand, Contre-filet*, etc., in this section.

Ox tail—See OFFAL OR VARIETY MEATS.

Beef-tea—This is a sort of concentrated consommé or meat juice, obtained by cutting lean beef into small dice and putting, without adding to it, into a wide-necked bottle which can be sealed hermetically, or into a special screw-top small pewter receptacle (American marmite) which is put into a pan of boiling water for 40 or 50 minutes.

Thus 1 pound (500 grams) of meat will give about 5 ounces (150 grams) of liquid, of a pleasant taste.

Beef-tea has a greater nutritive value than ordinary meat-stock (see SOUP, *Clear soup*), but it is chiefly a stimulant, useful, in small doses, for convalescents for stimulating the secretion of digestive glands and awakening the appetite.

Tenderloin (U.S.A.)—See *Fillet of beef.*

Tip of sirloin (thin hind-quarter flank). BAVETTE D'ALOYAU—This cut is formed by the lateral abdominal wall. With careful trimming, it can be used for steaks, a little firm but very juicy.

This cut can also be used for *pot-au-feu*.

Tongue—See OFFAL OR VARIETY MEATS, *Beef or Ox tongue*.

Top of rump. PIÈCE DE BOEUF (POINTE DE CULOTTE)—See *Rump of beef.* In French culinary language, top of rump can be called *Pointe de culotte*, but it is more frequently described on the menus as *Pièce de boeuf.*

Method of preparation: Braised. Lard a 6-pound (3 kilo) piece of top of rump with large lardoons (strips of salt pork), well seasoned and sprinkled with brandy. Season the meat with fine salt, pepper and spices and tie with string.

Marinate for 5 hours in advance, if the recipe calls for such treatment, in white or red wine with thyme, bay leaf, parsley and a crushed clove of garlic.

Drain and dry the meat with a cloth. Brown in butter or other fat and put into a braising pan on a foundation of 2 large onions and 2 carrots cut into round slices and lightly fried in butter, 3 pounds (1½ kilos) of fleshy bones and a calf's knuckle chopped into small pieces and browned in the oven. Add a strong *bouquet garni** and two calf's feet, boned, scalded, dipped in cold water and tied with string. Also add the bones taken out of the feet, cut in half lengthways and browned in the oven.

Moisten with the marinating liquor, cover the braising pan and cook on the edge of the stove until the liquor is almost completely reduced.

Add enough slightly thickened veal stock mixed with 3 tablespoons of tomato sauce to just cover the meat.

Bring to the boil. Cover the braising pan and put in a slow oven for about 4 hours.

To serve. Drain the meat, untie and glaze it in the oven, basting with its own gravy.

Arrange on a large dish, surround with the garnish recommended, disposed in separate groups, and pour over it the braising liquor, boiled down, strained and with the fat skimmed off.

Poached. Lard with large lardoons or leave the meat as it is, as indicated in the recipe.

Tie with string and put to cook, with the usual garnish, in a large stockpot as indicated for *pot-au-feu*. Bring to the boil, remove scum, season and leave to simmer gently, the pan three-quarters covered, for 4 to 5 hours.

To serve. Drain the meat, remove string, arrange on a large dish, and surround with the garnish indicated. Serve its own strained liquor, grated horseradish and sea-salt separately.

Cooked in this way the top of rump makes a soup and a meat course at the same time. To give the soup more body and flavour, all the basic elements and a certain quantity of fleshy bones, chopped into small pieces, should be added to it.

Top of rump à la bourgeoise. PIÈCE DE BOEUF À LA BOURGEOISE—Take a 6-pound (3-kilo) piece of rump and insert into it large lardoons, previously left to steep in brandy and spices.

Season it and put to marinate in 2½ cups (5 decilitres) of white wine for 6 hours.

Cook in a braising pan with vegetables and other garnish as indicated for *Braising of meats*, and following all the instructions given in that recipe. See CULINARY METHODS.

When three-quarters cooked, drain the meat, put it into a casserole with 4 medium to large carrots cut into small uniform pieces, two-thirds cooked in stock, and 12 small glazed onions. Add calf's feet, braised with the meat, boned and cut into pieces. Strain the braising liquor, skim off fat and pour over the meat. Cook with a lid on for one and a quarter hours.

To serve. Drain the meat, put it on a large dish, surround with the garnish disposed in separate groups and pour over the concentrated liquor.

Top of rump à la bourguignonne. PIÈCE DE BOEUF À LA BOURGUIGNONNE—Insert large lardoons (strips of salt pork) into a 6-pound (3-kilo) piece of rump and marinate in brandy for 6 hours.

Braise it in red wine following the instructions given in the recipe for *Braising of meats*, with the usual vegetables and garnish. See CULINARY METHODS.

When three-quarters cooked, drain the meat and put it into a *daubière** with garnish *à la bourguignonne* and its braising liquor, strained with the fat skimmed off. (See GARNISHES.) Simmer gently.

Braised top of rump à l'ancienne. PIÈCE DE BOEUF BRAISÉE À L'ANCIENNE—Trim top of rump in the usual manner, tie it and braise. When the meat is still a little on the firm side, drain, put under a press, in a pan or a deep dish which can, by pressing on the sides, help to keep the shape of the meat. Leave like that to get cold.

Trim all round, cut out the central part, leaving a meat case about ¾ inch thick.

Brush this case with beaten egg and cover with white breadcrumbs mixed with grated Parmesan cheese. Press well to make the breadcrumbs adhere, put the meat case in a pan, sprinkle with melted butter and put in the oven to colour on all sides.

Meanwhile, cut the meat taken out of the central part into very thin slices. Put them into a sauté pan, add thin slices of tongue *à l'écarlate* (salt beef tongue) and some sliced mushrooms, lightly fried in butter. Moisten with a few tablespoons of concentrated braising liquor, strained and with the fat skimmed off. Add ¼ cup (½ decilitre) of Madeira and leave to stew without boiling.

To serve. At the last moment, put these slices into the hollowed-out piece of meat, placed on a large round dish. Serve the remainder of the sauce separately.

Top of rump à la mode. PIÈCE DE BOEUF À LA MODE—Proceed as described in the recipe for *Top of rump à la bourgeoise*, replacing white wine by red.

Top of skirt (U.S.A. short ribs). ONGLET DE BOEUF—This cut, although a little firm is very flavoursome and, above all, very juicy.

It can be prepared in any way suitable for *Beef steaks.*

It is also used for carbonades, for extracting meat juice and for beef sautées.

Method of cooking. Grill or sauté.

Tournedos—Small slices of fillet of beef, cut round and rather thick, weighing about $3\frac{1}{2}$ to 4 ounces (100 to 125 grams). These are also called *Medallions of fillet of beef.*

Method. Tournedos are mainly fried in butter, in a mixture of butter and oil, and sometimes simply in oil.

Their preparation is similar to that given for *Noisettes of mutton*. Like the latter, the tournedos must be cooked very quickly, to make sure that they remain rosy on the inside.

The tournedos can also be grilled. For this method of cooking, see instructions given for *Filets mignons, grilled.*

Tournedos, either grilled or fried, are arranged, garnished and served with the appropriate sauce as indicated in individual recipes. Depending on the nature of the garnish chosen, and in order not to smother the tournedos underneath all this garnish, they are sometimes raised on grilled or fried croûtons, or, better still, on little potato cakes, artichoke hearts, small mounds of rice, etc.

The recipes which follow indicate garnishes and sauces, instructions for which will be found under entries entitled GARNISHES and SAUCE, in their alphabetical order.

In addition to these recipes, all those given for *Escalopes of veal* (see VEAL) and *Noisettes of lamb and mutton* (see LAMB, MUTTON) can be applied to tournedos and medallions of beef fillet.

Tournedos Abrantès—Season the tournedos with salt and paprika and sauté them in oil. Arrange on grilled round slices of aubergines (egg-plant) and fill the middle of the dish with potatoes cut down to look like cob nuts or olives, cooked in butter. Add one tablespoon of chopped onion lightly fried in oil and a *salpicon** of peeled pimentos to the pan juices; blend in a few tablespoons of tomato sauce and pour over the tournedos.

Tournedos à l'algérienne—Season the tournedos with salt and paprika and sauté them in butter.

Arrange on fried croûtons and surround with *Garnish à l'algérienne* (see GARNISHES). Dilute the pan juices with white wine and tomato-flavoured veal stock and pour over the tournedos.

Tournedos archiduc—Sauté the tournedos in butter and arrange on little duchess potato cakes. Garnish with very small croquettes of calf's brains. Put on each tournedo 2 slivers of truffle, tossed in butter. Dilute the pan juices with sherry; add fresh cream and veal stock in equal proportions, season with paprika, cook down, strain and pour over the tournedos.

Tournedos à la béarnaise—Arrange grilled tournedos on a round dish. Garnish with small *Château potatoes* (see POTATOES). Serve *Béarnaise sauce* (see SAUCE) separately.

Tournedos à la bordelaise—Grill the tournedos, arrange on a dish, put on top of each one a thin slice of poached and drained marrow and decorate the middle of this slice of marrow with a pinch of chopped parsley. Serve *Bordelaise sauce* (see SAUCE) separately.

Tournedos chasseur—Sauté the tournedos in butter. Arrange in a crown on a round dish (putting them either straight on the dish, or on croûtons fried in butter). Slice raw mushrooms and put them into the sauté pan in which the tournedos were cooked. Add a small spoonful of chopped shallot. Season, brown for a few moments, moisten with dry white wine, add a few tablespoons of *demi-glace** or thickened veal gravy and boil for 2 minutes. Add 2 teaspoons of chopped parsley, chervil and tarragon. Add a little butter to the sauce and pour it over the tournedos.

Tournedos Choron—Sauté the tournedos in butter. Arrange on fried croûtons. Garnish with artichoke hearts stewed in butter and filled with garden peas (or asparagus tips) dressed with butter.

Pour on each tournedo a ring of thick *Choron sauce* (see SAUCE). Dilute the pan juices with white wine and thickened veal gravy and pour a few tablespoons of this sauce over the tournedos.

Tournedos à la Clamart—Sauté the tournedos in butter. Arrange on a dish, garnish with artichoke hearts (simmered) in butter and filled either with fresh garden peas dressed with butter, or with a purée of fresh peas, and little new potatoes cooked in butter, or potatoes cut down to look like cob nuts or olives. Dilute the pan juices with white wine and thickened veal gravy and pour over the tournedos.

Alternatively, grill the tournedos, arrange on a dish and garnish with garden peas *à la française*.

Tournedos Helder—Sauté the tournedos in butter. Arrange on fried croûtons. Put on each of the tournedos a ring of *Béarnaise sauce* (see SAUCE) and, in the middle of this *béarnaise* a teaspoon of thick *Tomato fondue*. Garnish with potatoes cut to look like cob nuts fried in butter. Dilute the pan juices with white wine and thickened veal gravy and pour over the tournedos.

Tournedos Henri IV—Sauté the tournedos in butter. Arrange on fried croûtons. Put on each of the tournedos a small artichoke heart filled with thick *Béarnaise sauce* (see SAUCE). Put a sliver of truffle on each artichoke heart. Garnish with potatoes cut to look like cob nuts or olives. Dilute the pan juices with Madeira and *demi-glace** and pour over the tournedos.

Tournedos Marguery

Tournedos Marguery—Sauté the tournedos in butter. Arrange each on an artichoke heart filled with a *salpicon** of truffles *à la crème*. Fill the middle of the dish with morels fried in butter and put a few cock's combs and kidneys between each of the tournedos. Dilute the pan juices with port, add fresh cream, reduce (cook down) and pour over the tournedos.

Tournedos Masséna—Grill the tournedos and arrange on artichoke hearts simmered in butter. Put on each of the tournedos a slice of poached bone marrow. Cover with *Marrow sauce (I)* (see SAUCE), and put a pinch of chopped parsley in the middle of each slice of marrow.

Tournedos with mushrooms—Sauté the tournedos in butter. When half cooked, put into the same sauté pan some small mushrooms, previously lightly fried in butter, and finish cooking together. Arrange the tournedos in a crown on a round dish, putting them either straight on the dish or placing each on a croûton fried in butter. Put the mushrooms around the tournedos. Dilute the pan juices with Madeira, moisten with *demi-glace** or thickened veal gravy and pour over the tournedos.

Tournedos à la périgourdine—Sauté the tournedos, arrange on fried croûtons, put on each 4 thin slices of truffles, tossed in the same butter in which the tournedos were cooked. Dilute the pan juices with Madeira and *demi-glace** and pour over the tournedos.

Tournedos à la portugaise—Sauté the tournedos in butter and oil. Arrange on a dish. Garnish with very small stuffed tomatoes and *Château potatoes* (see POTATOES). Dilute the pan juices with white wine and tomato-flavoured veal stock and pour over the tournedos.

Tournedos Rossini—Sauté the tournedos in butter and arrange on croûtons. Put on each a slice of *foie gras* tossed in butter, and on top of this, three good slices of truffles, heated in the same butter in which the tournedos were cooked.

Dilute the pan juices with Madeira and *demi-glace** (see SAUCE) and pour over the tournedos.

Tournedos Saint-Germain—Sauté the tournedos in butter, arrange on fried croûtons and garnish with a rather thick purée of fresh peas.

Dilute the pan juices with thickened veal gravy and pour over the tournedos.

Alternatively, sauté the tournedos in butter and arrange in little tartlet shells, filled with a purée of fresh peas.

Garnish with little new potatoes cooked in butter and young glazed carrots, disposed in alternating groups. Dilute the pan juices as described above and pour over the tournedos. Serve *Béarnaise sauce* (see SAUCE), separately.

Note. In addition to the recipes given above, tournedos can be treated in any way suitable for small cuts of meat, especially as described in recipes for *Noisettes of mutton.* See MUTTON.

Sautéed or grilled tournedos can also be garnished with all sorts of vegetables, dressed with butter or fresh cream, such as French (string) beans, kidney beans, peas, asparagus tips.

They can also be garnished with fresh vegetables cooked in butter or braised, such as cucumbers, endive, lettuce, small marrows, aubergines (egg-plant), celeriac, celery, spinach, etc., as well as with potatoes cooked in various ways, purées of fresh or dried vegetables, rice pilaf, risotto, and various pasta products and cereals.

Beef à la vinaigrette. BOEUF À LA VINAIGRETTE—Boiled beef cut in thin slices or dice, seasoned with oil, vinegar, salt, pepper, onion and chopped parsley. Often sliced boiled potatoes are added.

BEEF-EATERS—This is the nickname by which some of the Yeomen of the Guard on duty at the Tower of London are known. There would appear to be a great deal of uncertainty about the origin of the word. It has been suggested that it was derived from the French *Beaufaitier*—one who attends the buffet, but this has been rejected. Some authorities maintain that it means 'an eater of beef', a servant, rather like the old English *hlafaeta*, or loaf-eater. There are also references to this word being attributed to Cosimo, Grand Duke of Tuscany, who in 1669 described these yeomen as receiving a large daily ration of beef, which might justify their being called 'beef-eaters'.

The guard made its first official appearance, according to the official Tower of London information book, as a body fifty strong at Henry VII's coronation at Westminster Abbey on October 30th, 1485.

BEER. BIÈRE—Beer is a generic term used for all fermented malt beverages, including porter, ale and stout. It is a beverage obtained through the action of yeast on an infusion of cereals, previously malted. It is a refreshing and slightly stimulating drink that has food value. The word 'beer' may come from the Hebrew. The Hebrew word for grain (i.e. the most important element used in the preparation of beer) retains the root *bre*. On the other hand, the Saxon word for barley is *bere* and it seems quite natural that from *bere* the Germans should have made *bier*, the French *bière* and the English *beer*.

It should also be pointed out that the Latin word *cerevisia*, from which we have *cervoise* (in the old days given in France to a kind of beer) comes from a word which is found again in most Indo-Germanic languages and which means 'a grain of corn'. The name of Ceres, goddess who presided over the harvest, has also the same origin.

The invention of fermented beverages from grain is attributed to the Egyptians. The manufacture of alcoholic liquor from grain was practised by the Egyptians at least 5,000 years ago, and papyri of the period around 1300 B.C. referred to the regulation of beer-shops to prevent people over-indulging in beer. They knew several kinds of beer and they made a kind of wine out of barley which they called *xithum*.

From the earliest times beer has been used by many different races.

The Pannonians who lived along the Danube used to make a potent drink out of barley and millet. According to Ammianus, a similar beverage existed in Illyria. Tacitus said that ancient Teutons gladly indulged in drinking and made a kind of wine out of fermented barley and wheat. 'The people of the west', said Pliny, 'get drunk on *mouldy grain*.'

All this proves conclusively that beer was known among the most ancient peoples. But the beer which was made by these people was not made to be kept.

Hops were not introduced in the brewing of beer until very much later in the Netherlands and in England in the fifteenth century.

In all regions and at all latitudes, beer is brewed from various cereals: wheat, oats, rice (the Japanese saké), millet, maize (U.S.A. corn), sorghum, etc., and even out of starchy roots (sweet potatoes, cassava), when cereals are not available.

In Europe, beer is mostly brewed from barley, usually flavoured with hops.

Starch contained in cereals cannot be directly fermented. It has, therefore, to be treated, in order to be transformed into a soluble sugar called maltose. (In U.S.A. corn or rice is added to the malt barley to modify the protein content and for flavour.)

To achieve this transformation the biological process of germination is resorted to in the industry, during which ferments or enzymes intervene and render soluble the nutrient matter originally meant for the embryo.

Malting, the name given in brewing to this operation, consists of spreading the grain, slightly moistened, in a thin layer in warm moist chambers where it is often stirred; under these conditions the barley soon germinates and then takes the name of malt. As soon as the acrospire, as it is known in brewing, reaches a certain length, germination is stopped by a drying process at a relatively high temperature which depends on the degree of roasting desired to obtain a coloured wort. During the germination process, enzymes are produced which transform the starch into maltose and soluble dextrines. Next is the *mashing* operation, which consists of mixing the malt with water. When all the soluble substance has been removed, the wort so produced is sterilized by boiling with hops. The hops also lend it a distinctive flavour and aroma.

This 'bitter' wort is then cooled and made to ferment by the addition of yeast. Two main kinds of yeast can be distinguished: a top fermentation yeast, which releases a large quantity of carbon dioxide and collects on the surface of the liquid thus forming a head. This is used to make ale, porter and stout whereas the other type, bottom fermentation yeast, is produced at a comparatively cool temperature and collects at the bottom of the container; this is used in the making of lager beer.

A type of yeastless beer, known under the names of *lambic* and *faro*, is manufactured on a very small scale mainly in Belgium. Its very slow fermentation is achieved by 'wild' yeasts of the atmosphere, without avoiding a parallel development of lactic or acetic ferment, which lends this beer a relatively high acidity.

When the fermentation is complete, some beers are still a long way from being ready for drinking: they must undergo an additional fermentation, like wine, which takes place in tuns, in very cool cellars. The beer becomes slowly clarified, although sometimes clearing or filtration has to be done, which demands very great precautions to avoid too great loss of carbon dioxide.

In bottom fermentation beers, there may be several months of this 'lagering' before the beer is released for consumption. Handling of the product, which can so easily be spoilt, requires the greatest care; it is drawn off into sterilized barrels, always of small capacity, or into bottles which are usually pasteurized if they are destined to be exported or stored for some time.

Beer may be sold straight from the 'wood', the cask being in the bar, but more often the beer is pumped from the casks by means of 'beer engines', the handles of which are fixed to the bar. When beer has to remain on draught a certain length of time, an additional source of pressure is provided by means of compressed carbon dioxide. Bottled beer is preferable for domestic use where only an occasional consumption is expected.

Pale ale is manufactured from malt which has simply been dried. Dark beer is obtained from a highly-roasted malt wort often coloured by adding burnt sugar.

There are several times as many brands of beer as there are breweries, each wishing its beers to have their special characters. Brewers attach great importance to the water they use. It must be chemically and bacteriologically pure and beer character is related to the type and composition of waters used.

In general beer contains from 3% to 6% alcohol (3½% in U.S.A.) by weight, sometimes more, particularly in English beers. Some of the unfermented carbohydrates help to give that feeling of 'body' which connoisseurs call palatefulness. Carbon dioxide forms the substantial froth or 'head' which indicates skilful brewing and careful drawing.

In beers of low quality other bitter substances were at one time substituted for hops. The use of pine buds, bark of willow, box-wood, gentian, or even *quassia amara* (bitter ash), might have been acceptable from the point of view of health, but their use has long since been discontinued, certainly in the United Kingdom and in the United States, where official figures show beer to be brewed wholly from cereals, hops and sugar.

Ale, stout and porter are consumed in much greater quantities in Europe than in U.S.A. Some ale is manufactured in the United States but all but a few American breweries limit themselves to producing a lager beer which, in general, is lighter-bodied than the European varieties. There is both importing and exporting ofbeer between Europe and the United States.

Barley beer. CERVOISE—Drink of the ancient Gauls, made of a decoction of barley, fermented with a kind of yeast, perhaps derived from fermenting grapes, which produced a kind of barley wine rather than a beer in the ordinary sense of the word.

Ginger beer. BIÈRE DE GINGEMBRE—Boil 5 pounds loaf sugar, 3 ounces of ground ginger and 3 gallons of water for 1 hour. When cold, add the juice and thinly peeled rind of 5 lemons. Put ¼ cup of brewer's yeast on a slice of toast and add. Put all into a tub and cover with a thick cloth for two or three days, then strain through a cloth, bottle, cork securely and tie the corks down. This will be ready to drink in four or five days. If stronger ginger beer is desired, add more ginger.

Home-made beer (I). BIÈRE DE MÉNAGE—To make 33 quarts (30 litres) of beer, allow ¼ pound (125 grams) of hops, 9 cups (2 litres) of ordinary barley, 2¼ pounds (1 kilo 125 grams) of sugar, 1¾ ounces (50 grams) of brewer's yeast and ⅓ ounce (10 grams) of chicory as colouring agent.

Put the barley into a stockpot with 22 quarts (20 litres) of water and cook for 2 hours.

As soon as the barley is cooked, add the hops and the chicory and leave to infuse. Strain and pour into a 30-litre tun.

Add sugar dissolved in 11 quarts (10 litres) of water and mix. Leave the tun uncovered. On the following day add the yeast, previously dissolved in a little hot water.

Stir with a stick. Leave the tun open for 6 days. Add more liquid every morning and evening to replace liquid lost through fermentation.

On the seventh day, bung the barrel and on the eighth, bottle the beer. Cork the bottles, having first boiled the corks in water for 5 minutes.

Home-made beer (II). BIÈRE DE MÉNAGE—Put a good handful of hops, 3½ ounces (100 grams) of hulled barley and 1 pound (500 grams) of sugar into 4 quarts plus 1 cup (4 litres) of water. Boil for ½ hour.

Remove from heat, add ⅓ ounce (10 grams) of baker's yeast and dilute with 11 quarts (10 litres) of water. Leave to ferment for 4 days. Bottle and tie down the corks.

A little bit of burnt sugar may be added to this beer to give it some colour.

Home-made beer (III). BIÈRE DE MÉNAGE—2 pounds (1 kilo) of roasted and ground barley, 4 pounds (2 kilos) of barley ground on the previous day, 28 pounds (14 kilos) of glucose, 5 ounces (150 grams) of gentian, 6⅔ ounces (200 grams) of hops, 2⅓ ounces (70 grams) of orange zest, ½ ounce (15 grams) of cinnamon (in sticks) and 28 quarts (25 litres) of water.

Cook all the ingredients together for 2 hours. Leave to stand then filter the wort into a barrel at a temperature of 68°F. (20°C.).

Madder beer. BIÈRE DE GARANCE—Chop the roots of madder, put into a vat with water, brewer's yeast and sugar. Leave to ferment 5 to 6 days.

Bottle and cork well.

Malt beer. BIÈRE DE MALT—This beer is obtained by adding concentrated malt extract to the wort and letting it ferment slightly. It has much greater nutritive properties than ordinary beer and is used as a tonic, or for nursing mothers.

Beer soup (German cookery). SOUPE À LA BIÈRE—Dilute ½ cup (150 grams) of light *roux** made of butter and flour with 1½ quarts (litres) of light beer. Mix well. Season with salt and pepper. Add 2 teaspoons (12 grams) of fine sugar and a very small pinch of powdered cinnamon, bring to the boil, then simmer for 25 minutes.

Just before serving, thicken with 1 cup (2 decilitres) of double cream. Pour boiling into a soup tureen, over thin slices of toast.

BEESTINGS. AMOUILLE—The name commonly given to the first milk of a cow after parturition. Special properties are attributed to it.

BEESWAX. Cire—A product transformed from the honey absorbed by the working bee which it uses to construct the cells in honey-combs and in the interior of the hive.

By analogy the name *cires végétales* is given to substances extracted from certain vegetables, in particular from certain palms.

BEET—See BEETROOT.

BEETROOT (U.S.A. Beets). Betterave—There are many varieties of this plant, some cultivated solely for distillery purposes, some as animal foodstuff and some, as in the case of *garden beet*, as vegetable.

Among the best varieties of garden beetroot are the following: red stump-rooted, dark red Massy, large red, early red globe, dark red turnip-rooted Egyptian, red globe summer beet, dark red globe early beet.

The Romans cultivated beetroot and used its leaves as a vegetable.

In Russian cookery both the roots and the leaves of beets are used a great deal, notably for various soups. See SOUPS AND BROTHS, *Beetroot soup à la Russe*.

For information on sugar beet, see SUGAR.

Beetroot leaves are perfectly edible. They are used a great deal in many recipes, but in France it is mostly the roots, boiled or baked, that are used as garnish for salads, *hors-d'oeuvre* and various game entrées.

Method of preparation. Wash and scrub the beets with a brush. Dry them and bake in the oven (baker's or pastry-cook's oven, if possible).

They are ready when they begin to give a little, if pressed with a finger. Remove from oven and keep in a cool place.

Beetroot à l'anglaise. Betteraves à l'anglaise—Choose tender beets, peel them, cut into thick slices and boil in salted water. Drain, dry and serve. Hand fresh butter separately.

Beetroot barquettes. Barquettes de betteraves—Prepare the barquettes as for *hors-d'oeuvre*. Fill with cooked beetroot, cut in small dice and dressed with *Vinaigrette* or *Mayonnaise*. See SAUCE.

Beetroot à la béchamel. Betteraves à la béchamel—Bake 2 beets in the oven, peel and cut into fairly thick slices. Simmer gently in a sauté pan with 2 tablespoons of butter and a pinch of salt.

Transfer into a vegetable dish, cover with not too thick *Béchamel sauce* (see SAUCE), with butter added to it.

Beetroot in cream. Betteraves à la crème—Cut beets into round slices and stew in butter. Put into a vegetable dish.

Dilute the pan juices with 2 cups (4 decilitres) of previously boiled cream.

Cook down by half, season, remove from heat, blend in 4 tablespoons (60 grams) of butter and pour this cream over the beets.

Beetroot for garnishes and other purposes. Betteraves pour garnitures—Bake the beets in the oven, allow to cool thoroughly and peel. Cut into round slices, either plain or fluted-edged, into crescent shapes, large or small dice or shred into a *julienne*.* Prepared in this way beetroot can be served as a garnish for hot dishes, for *hors-d'oeuvre* and for salads.

Beetroot in gravy. Batteraves au jus—Proceed as described in the recipe for *Beetroot in cream*, replacing the latter by 1 cup (2 decilitres) of thickened brown veal gravy. Allow the beets to boil in the gravy for a few moments. Heap on a shallow dish.

Beetroot à la lyonnaise. Betteraves à la lyonnaise—Melt 3 tablespoons (50 grams) of butter in a pan, add 4 tablespoons of finely chopped onion, cook gently without allowing it to colour, add beetroot cut in round slices and simmer together for a few moments.

A few minutes before serving, moisten with 1 cup (2 decilitres) of thickened brown veal gravy.

Beetroot à la poitevine. Betteraves à la poitevine—Put round slices of beetroot to stew for a few moments in 1 cup (2 decilitres) of *Lyonnaise sauce* (see SAUCE). At the last moment, add a tablespoon of vinegar.

Stuffed beetroot cassolettes. Cassolettes de betteraves garnies—These are served as *hors-d'oeuvre*. Choose large beets, bake them in the oven and cut into thick slices. Scoop out these slices and trim them to look like little *cassolettes*. Fill them with any cold *hors-d'oeuvre* composition: *salpicons** of hard boiled eggs, fish, or vegetables, dressed with mayonnaise; various purées, etc.

BEGONIA—Some varieties of this plant are edible. The leaves of these can be prepared in the same way as sorrel.

BÉGUINETTE—Name used in some parts of France for the garden warbler.

BEIGNETS—See FRITTERS.

Beignets (petits fours) (I)—Pound 3 cups (500 grams) of blanched almonds with 2 cups (500 grams) of sugar and 5 whites of egg.

Soften this paste by adding two whole eggs to it. Flavour it, according to taste, with vanilla, orange or lemon peel or shredded crystallized pineapple. Colour it either with carmine or green vegetable colouring agent. Fold in 16 stiffly beaten whites of egg. Put into buttered and floured petits fours moulds of various shapes. Decorate with pieces of candied orange or pineapple. Sprinkle with icing sugar. Bake in a slow oven.

Beignets (II)—Pound together in mortar 1½ pounds (250 grams) of blanched almonds and 1 cup (250 grams) of sugar. Add one white of egg to the mixture and soften it further by blending in one whole egg. Flavour with vanilla or any other flavouring.

Whisk 8 whites of egg into a very stiff froth and fold them into the mixture.

Put the mixture into small fancy biscuit moulds, sprinkle with icing sugar and bake in a slow oven.

BELLE-ALLIANCE—A variety of winter pear (December and January). The skin of this pear is yellowish on one side and red on the other. It is an excellent dessert fruit.

BELLE-ANGEVINE—A variety of winter pear which reaches considerable dimensions. Its skin is green at first, then becomes a bright yellow, flushed with red and pitted with brown.

This pear, which is in season in February and March, is really a show-piece. It is better to look at than to eat and is used mostly for filling large decorative baskets of fruit.

BELLE-CHEVREUSE—A variety of peach. The skin of this fruit is a beautiful bright red. It should be eaten when it is just ripe; when it is too ripe, its flesh becomes 'sleepy'.

BELLE-DE-BERRY—Another name for a variety of pear called *Poire de curé*.

BELLE-ET-BONNE—Variety of pear. Its flesh is rather mediocre and it is usually cooked in syrup or red wine.

BELLE-GARDE—Peach which ripens in September and October. Its flesh is slightly on the firm side. This fruit is mostly used for compotes and in pastry-making.

BELLONE—A variety of very large figs, which grow in Provence. They are used for preserves.

BELSHAZZAR. BALTHAZARD—In colloquial usage this word stands for copious meals—an allusion to the famous feasts mentioned in the Bible.

BELUGA (Huso Huso)—Russian name for white sturgeon of the Black Sea, Caspian Sea and other waters. It is the largest of the sturgeon family, producing the best caviar.

BÉNARI—Local French name for a variety of ortolans found in the Languedoc district.

They are fattened in the same way as the Landes district ortolans.

For methods of culinary preparation, see ORTOLAN.

BÉNÉDICTIN (Cake)—*Ingredients.* 1½ cups (250 grams) of ground almonds, 1 cup (250 grams) of fine sugar, 4 whole eggs, 12 yolks of eggs, 1 cup (100 grams) minus 2 tablespoons of sieved flour, ⅔ cup (100 grams) of potato flour, Benedictine.

Method. Put the almonds, sugar, 2 whole eggs and 12 yolks into a bowl.

Cream this mixture, working in a cool place, and blending as for a sponge. When it is very smooth, add the rest of the eggs, one by one.

Incorporate in the mixture, first a tablespoon of Benedictine liqueur, then the flour and the potato flour, sieved together on to a piece of paper.

Butter square baking tins, sprinkle them with flour and fill two-thirds full with the cake mixture. Bake in a 350°F. oven.

Take out of the tins as soon as they are baked and leave to cool on a wire cake cooler, laying them wide side up. While they are cooling, about 10 minutes after taking them out of the oven, sprinkle each cake with about a liqueur glassful of Benedictine and as soon as they have absorbed this, cover the top and the sides with a light layer of thick apricot jam.

Decorate all around the sides with chopped roasted almonds at about ⅓ inch from the top. Leave the cake to get cold.

When it is quite cold, prepare a fondant icing of a pale yellow colour, flavoured with Benedictine, and a pale mauve fondant icing. (See ICING.) Ice the top of the cake with yellow-coloured fondant icing, and with a forcing bag pipe the mauve fondant mixture, laying threads in a diagonal pattern. Trace a second row of diagonal threads at right-angles, to form squares.

Decorate the middle of each square with half a pistachio nut.

Note. The same mixture can be used for preparing little iced *petits fours*. The cake is baked, then steeped in liqueur and coated with apricot jam as above. The cake is then cut into uniform squares, which are iced with pale yellow fondant icing flavoured with Benedictine. On each *petit four* a pale mauve fondant spiral is traced, starting in the centre and stopping at the edge.

BENEDICTINE—Old French liqueur of wide renown. It was invented and has for many years been made by the Benedictine monks at the Abbey at Fécamp.

BÉNÉDICTINE (A LA)—Garnish suitable for poached fish or eggs. It is composed of a *brandade** of cod and truffles.

BERCHOUX (Joseph)—This French poet, who was born at Saint-Symphorien-de-Lay (Loire) in 1765 and died at Marcigray (Saône-et-Loire) in 1839, made a great name for himself in gastronomical literature, due to a poem entitled *Gastronomie* which appeared in 1800.

Joseph Berchoux (1765–1839)

Berchoux was certainly not a gastronome, and even less of a gourmet-connoisseur, and in this poem you will not find enlightenment on the art of cookery, let alone gastronomy.

However, it deserves to be read for its zest, for its light-hearted and witty tone, for its harmonious, albeit at times somewhat solemn style. To this day the poem can be read with pleasure and Berchoux is rightly considered to be one of the most famous among the '*pères de la table*', along with Grimod de la Reynière, Brillat-Savarin and de Cussy.

The works of these writers, assembled in one volume, were published by Charpentier in 1829, under the title of *Les Classiques de la Table*.

Bergamot

BERGAMOT ORANGE. BERGAMOTE—Fruit of the

bergamot tree. It is a kind of lemon, having a very acid but very pleasant taste.

Highly-scented essential oil extracted from its rind is used in perfumery, pharmaceutics and in confectionery. Candied bergamot peel is used in pastry-making and cookery for flavouring cakes and sweet dishes.

BERGAMOT PEAR. BERGAMOTE—This name is applied to several varieties of pears. The *bergamote d'automne* (*autumn bergamot*) is the best.

BERLINGOT—A hard sweet candy flavoured with various flavourings, most frequently with peppermint.

Several regions of France each have their own speciality of *Berlingots*.

BERNARD (Émile)—Famous chef of the nineteenth century who practised his art at the court of Wilhelm I, King of Prussia.

In collaboration with Urbain Dubois he wrote one of the best culinary works of the nineteenth century: *Cuisine classique*.

BERRY—The Berry is the best sheep-producing country of France. Sheep raised in that region are famous and connoisseurs of good meat praise them highly.

But lamb and mutton are by no means the only form of gastronomical riches of Berry. The fame of the wines of Cher dates a long way back. 'The neighbourhood of Sancerre', wrote a historian, Jean Chaumeau, the Seigneur de Lassay, 'is surrounded by little hillocks, almost entirely under vineyards which produce a great quantity of very good and excellent wines every year'.

'The most famous of all these wines', says Hugues Lapaire, a native of Berry, in *Cuisine berrichonne*, 'is the one which comes from the grapes harvested at Chavignol, on the slopes of the Bouffants, the Countess's vineyard which is locally called *Sauvignon*'.

In the Boischaux, at La Châtre, on the gentle slopes of the Berry countryside, at Quincy, Reuilly, Marmagne, to the south-west, at Mornay-sur-Allier, Sagonne, around Saint-Amand, at Châteaumeillant, Menneton, Azay, grapes are cultivated which produce fine wines, and all over Upper and Lower Berry a pale-red wine is produced, which is sometimes a little rough and, as the peasants say, has the taste of *terre noir* (i.e., soil).

The Chavignol, which the experts call by the pretty name of *Moustille*, was greatly esteemed by Balzac. The good lady of Nohant, so the story goes, was a first-rate cook and also thought highly of this wine.

Chavignol, a really capital wine, goes extremely well with all the local dishes of this region.

To tell the truth, Berry does not have any sumptuous dishes in its gastronomical repertoire which could be compared with those of certain other provinces, but the cuisine of the Berry region is distinguished by its agreeable simplicity, its almost rustic quality.

The larder here is nevertheless well stocked. Here you will find the fine poultry of Bourges and a great variety of fresh-water fish, among which we must particularly mention the Vierzon *lamprey*. Excellent vegetables and fine fruit are cultivated in Berry. Game, both ground and winged, is plentiful and of exquisite quality.

Culinary specialities of this region include:

Rich soups with *truches* or *tartouffes*, i.e. potatoes; with *reuves* and salt pork. 'We are great soup-eaters in

Gastronomic map of Berry

this country', says Hugues Lapaire, 'and in some places, they eat soup in the morning, at midday and at night'.

The *Sanguine*, a sort of pancake made of chicken's blood called *sanquette* in the south-west of France; various *Matelotes*; the *Citrouillat* or pumpkin-pie; the *Sauciaux*, a kind of peasant pancake; the *Truffiat*, a home-made potato scone; the *Grignaudes*, country flat-cakes made of pork greaves or cracklings; *Poulet en barbouille*, which is chicken cooked with its own blood; the old-fashioned *Matafan* (pancake); and the potato *Gouère* or *Gouèron*.

Argenton-sur-Creuse (*French Government Tourist Office*)

BESAIGRE—French technical term used to indicate that a wine is beginning to turn sour.

BESI—Word used in Franche-Comté and in the Jura region for salted and dried cow's meat. Also a generic term for several varieties of pears.

Besi de Caissoy—A variety of winter pear which is also called *Rousette d'Anjou*.

Besi d'Héry—Winter pear which takes its name from a forest in Brittany where it originated.

Besi de la Motte—Autumn pear with very white and succulent flesh.

BÊTE A CORNE ('HORNED BEAST')—Slang term which used to mean a fork, because in the olden days the forks had only two prongs.

BÊTE DE COMPAGNIE—This term is used in France to describe a wild boar between one and two years old. See WILD BOAR.

BÊTE ROUSSE—This term is used in France to describe a wild boar between six months and one year old.

BEURRÉ—A sort of juicy pear including many varieties, among which are the *beurré gris* and the *beurré d'hiver nouveau* which reach maturity in January and February, the *beurré Capiannont* (October and November), the *beurré Giffard* which is ripe at the end of July, and the *beurré Diel*. These pears are all dessert fruits.

BEVERAGE. Boisson—Liquid taken by the mouth to maintain or re-establish normal proportion of water in the organism.

Our bodies contain approximately 70% water, eliminating daily an average of 4 pints. When the water content is lowered to some considerable degree, the sensation of thirst appears. We therefore have to replace the water eliminated, partly by solid foods which always contain a considerable proportion of water, partly by liquids. In addition to water contained in food the body needs 3-4 pints of water each day.

Water is in fact the only liquid which is indispensable.

However, at all times and in all countries man has always striven either after sapidity or stimulation, which water alone could not give him, and has invented an innumerable quantity of beverages.

Apart from milk (see MILK), which the specialists consider not a drink but a liquid food, we can classify beverages into five categories:

(1) *Pure water* and mineral waters (see WATER).

(2) Aromatic and stimulating *infusions* (see INFUSIONS, HERBAL TEAS, COFFEE, CHOCOLATE, MATÉ, TEA) as well as various preparations based on these: *Bavarian creams*, *iced coffee*, *bishop*, etc., which are dealt with in their alphabetical order.

(3) *Fruit juices*, freshly extracted and not modified by fermentation, which are drunk either in their pure state (grape juice), or mixed with water and sugar (lemonade, orangeade, etc.) which are dealt with in their alphabetical order.

(4) *Fermented beverages*, the principal of which, in France, is *wine*, then *beer*, *cider*, *perry*, *hydromel*, and various *fruit liqueurs*. These are all dealt with separately in alphabetical order, but there is another large group of fermented or compound beverages, referred to as economical or medicinal, which will be found in this section.

(5) *Fermented and distilled beverages* or mixtures and preparations based on alcoholic drinks, dealt with in alphabetical order.

Quantity and temperature of beverages. The normal intake of beverages varies according to their nature, the requirements of the organism, outside temperature and state of health.

Generally speaking, excessive intake of liquids diminishes appetite and impedes digestion. In some cases it is advisable to increase the intake of liquids in order to improve elimination and cleanse the organism. In others, as we shall see when we examine certain types of diets, it is advisable to reduce the intake of liquids.

Should beverages be taken during meals or between them? Man alone drinks while eating; all other animals separate their solid feeding from absorption of liquid.

A pint of water drunk on an empty stomach leaves it in less than half an hour. The water would remain in the stomach much longer if accompanied by other food.

A meal eaten without drinking is digested quicker and better. It is advisable, therefore, in diets for people suffering from dyspepsia and enteritis, to separate the intake of solids and liquids, let them drink *before* the meal (from an hour to three-quarters of an hour) so as to ensure that the stomach is empty in time for the meal. The result will not be the same if the liquid is taken after the meal: the stomach will be full and the conditions will be the same as when drinking during a meal.

There is no justification for this dissociation of liquids and solids in the case of perfectly healthy people, provided the amount of drink taken is not so excessive as to impede digestion.

The amount of drink, and, of course, no hard and fast rules can really be laid down for it, should not exceed two ordinary glasses at one meal.

The need to drink, thirst itself, also depends on the composition of the meal. Too much meat, highly-spiced dishes, and, above all, excessive use of salt, considerably increase the sensation of thirst. Diet consisting mainly of vegetables, containing little salt, does not provoke thirst nearly so much.

The temperature of beverages must also be taken into account. Moderately warm they dilate the blood vessels of the stomach, are better absorbed and quench the thirst more efficiently. If too cold, they will, on the contrary, cause the contraction of the abdominal capillary system and may lead to disorders, at times of a serious nature, colic, precordial anxiety and even syncopes (loss of consciousness from fall of blood pressure). These disorders are more likely to occur if one drinks a certain quantity of *cold* liquid quickly. To prevent such occurrences, sportsmen are always advised to drink hot beverages after violent exercise. Such accidents occur much less frequently with *iced* drinks, because these can only be swallowed in small sips.

The reaction to various temperatures of beverages varies according to their nature. Below 42°F. or 46°F. water gives the impression of being ice cold, it is pleasantly cool at 54°F., it becomes warm and unpleasant at 62°F. and at 78°F. it is absolutely nauseating. At the same temperature, aerated water seems colder, owing to the release of carbon dioxide. At 42°F. it seems ice cold and can only be taken in small sips, it remains cold up to 50°F. and pleasantly cool up to 62°F. and 64°F.

Immediately after milking the temperature of milk varies between 92-94°F.; at 132-134°F. it seems very hot indeed and causes perspiration.

The best temperature for an average white wine is about 50°F. Some wines, such as Sauternes, can be chilled (*frappés*) with a cooling solution which lowers the temperature considerably.

Sparkling wines should be cooled only by ice, without adding any salt (which is an expedient for clients who are in a hurry). These wines lose a great deal of their quality at a temperature below 42°F.

Red wines, at any rate the great wines of Bordeaux, are served *chambrés* (with the chill taken off and brought to room temperature), that is to say, slowly, without application of direct heat, brought up to 60-65°F. Burgundy wines are drunk at a cooler temperature and the light white wines only stand to gain by being served cold.

FERMENTED BEVERAGES. BOISSONS FERMENTÉES—We give below a few old recipes for home-made and medicinal beverages; it is interesting to consider also the origins of this kind of drink.

Water is the only liquid drunk by the animals, whereas man demands more from a drink than a simple quenching of thirst, just as in his food he is looking for more than just an appeasement of hunger.

We are concerned here with a purely psychic phenomenon, found among all people, even among the least developed intellectually, which has manifested itself from the earliest times.

It was not, therefore, a mere flash of wit on the part of the physiologist, Professor Schiff, when he said that the first two mental functions which distinguish man from other species are his taste for fermented beverages and games of chance! He continued: 'To think that these two factors, against which all the moralists cry out, were responsible for the development of the human mind!'

The manufacture of fermented drinks, in effect, demands a whole series of operations, often very complicated, and it is extremely difficult to believe that their sequence was discovered by a mere chance.

Spontaneous fermentation of grapes, apples, oranges, pineapples, may have produced a pleasant drink by chance; this is true in the case of coconut milk, the sap of palm trees, maple trees, birch trees, sycamores, etc., but it becomes more difficult to make mere chance account for the alcoholic fermentation of cows', mares' and she-camels' milk, which does not take place of its own accord. Still more complicated, owing to the absence of these basic materials, is the transformation of cereal crops, as their alcoholic fermentation necessitates a prior diastatic fermentation. See BEER.

Cabaretier selling drinks in the seventeenth century
(*Guérard*)

The most curious case is that of small tribes, which, having neither fruit nor cereals nor milk at their disposal, have, nevertheless, managed to produce an intoxicating beverage from the tubers of cassava or sweet potatoes. As it is not possible to render starch fermentable by germination, the problem had to be solved by the use of digestive ferments, by salivary ptyalin. The raw roots (for this method of manufacture has been found among savages who did not even know the art of making fire) are chewed and insalivated by the women of the tribe, who then spit it out into a tub, leaving the atmosphere to take care of transforming starch, saccharified by this process which to us appears repugnant, into alcohol.

So, if the abuse of fermented beverages is blameworthy, their use does seem to be an instinctive need peculiar to mankind, which strict legislation may restrain, but has never yet managed to eliminate for any length of time. We have no data on the duration of prohibition in Sparta; it is very probable that it did not survive Lycurgus, to whom the responsibility for it is attributed.

In times much nearer to our own the total prohibition introduced in the United States proved in practice impossible to enforce, in spite of all the efforts of the authorities.

Barley cordial (shrub). BOISSON D'ORGE—Into 22 quarts (20 litres) of water put 1 pound (500 grams) of ordinary barley and 7 ounces (200 grams) of couch-grass.

Boil and add 3½ ounces (100 grams) of liquorice cut into small pieces.

Leave to get cold, strain and bottle.

Barley water. EAU D'ORGE—Put a handful of barley into a kettle. Pour on boiling water and put the kettle on the fire. As soon as the liquid boils, throw the water away and replace by fresh water. Allow to boil for 15 to 20 minutes.

If pearl or hulled barley is used (1 tablespoon per quart (litre) of water), there is no need to boil it in two waters. Cook the barley until the grains split.

Cider type drink. BOISSON FACON CIDRE—Put into a large receptacle 11 quarts (10 litres) of water, 1 quart (litre) of double beer, ⅓ ounce (10 grams) of citric acid and a large glass of brandy.

Stir to blend well. Decant into bottles and tie down the corks. This drink will be ready for use in 5-6 days' time.

Clairet—Boil 13 pounds (6 kilos 500 grams) of carrots and 4 ounces (120 grams) of liquorice roots in 11 quarts (10 litres) of water. Strain the liquid under a press.

Add ½ pound (250 grams) of tartaric acid, ½ pound (250 grams) of ground ginger, 4 pounds (2 kilos) of brown sugar and 2 quarts (2 litres) of brandy to the strained liquid.

Pour the whole into a barrel of 100 quarts (litres) capacity. Fill with water.

Leave to stand for 8 days, then bottle, cork, and tie down the corks.

Economical drink (I). BOISSON ÉCONOMIQUE—To make 60 quarts (litres), put 4 quarts (litres) of red or white wine into a tun, add 56 quarts (litres) of water, 4 pounds (2 kilos) of sugar (having dissolved it before putting into the tun), a small lemon cut into pieces and tied in a muslin bag. Leave for 5-6 days, stirring once a day, then at the end of 8 days, decant into bottles. Leave the bottles upright.

Economical drink (II). BOISSON ÉCONOMIQUE—Put into a receptacle 20 quarts (litres) of water, 1 quart (litre) of wine, 2 pounds (1 kilo) of sugar and 1 lemon cut into slices. Leave to macerate for 4 days, stirring once a day. Bottle and tie down the corks. This drink will be ready for use in 4 to 6 days' time.

Elderblossom cordial (shrub). BOISSON DE SUREAU—Take a barrel of about 70 quarts (60 litres) capacity, enlarge the bung hole and fill the barrel with water. Put the following ingredients into a bag: 4 pounds (2 kilos) of refined sugar (for preference) or, if that is not available, ordinary granulated, 3½ ounces (100 grams) of dried elderblossom, 1¾ ounces (50 grams) of hops, 1 lemon cut into pieces and the juice squeezed into the water and 1 cup (25 centilitres) of vinegar. Leave to infuse for 5 days stirring with a stick once a day. Leave to rest on the sixth day and bottle on the seventh (decanting into champagne bottles, if possible). Tie down the corks. This beverage will be ready for use in five days' time. Keep the bottles upright in the cellar.

Elder and lime cordial (shrub). BOISSON DE SUREAU ET TILLEUL—Mix a handful each of elder and lime-tree leaves with 7⅔ quarts (7 litres) of water.

Add ½ pound (250 grams) of sugar, 2 lemons and 1 glass of vinegar. Leave to macerate for 3 days, stirring once a day. Strain, bottle and tie down corks. This beverage will be ready for use in five days' time.

Hippocras. HYPOCRAS — Spiced wine, tonic and stomachic, which used to be very popular. There have been various kinds of hippocras (the beverage takes its name from the fact that it used to be strained through a filter called *Hippocrates' sleeve*) such as: beer hippocras, cider hippocras, red wine hippocras, white wine hippocras, etc.

Hippocras can be based on infusing flavour of any stone fruit, oranges, vanilla, wormwood, violets, etc.

Here are some recipes taken from old works:

Angelica hippocras. HYPOCRAS À L'ANGÉLIQUE—Leave ¼ ounce (8 grams) of fresh angelica and a pinch of ground nutmeg to infuse in a quart (litre) of cold wine (white or red) for 2 days.

Add sugar and a little brandy to taste. Filter.

Juniper hippocras. HYPOCRAS AU GENIÈVRE—Leave 1 ounce (30 grams) of crushed juniper berries to infuse in 1 quart (litre) of cold wine, mixed with 1½ ounces (45 grams) of alcohol, for 24 hours. Then add a little vanilla and 9 tablespoons (75 grams) of powdered sugar and filter.

Raspberry hippocras. HYPOCRAS À LA FRAMBOISE—Put 1 pound (500 grams) of freshly gathered sound raspberries into a straining funnel. Place the straining funnel over a bowl, pour in 1 quart (litre) of red wine, sweeten with sugar, add 2 ounces (60 grams) of wine alcohol and filter.

Hippocras with spices. HYPOCRAS AUX ÉPICES—Infuse ⅛ ounce (4 grams) of cinnamon, ½ ounce (15 grams) of nutmeg, a pinch of mace and 3 cloves, all ground into powder, in 1½ ounces (45 grams) of alcohol.

At the end of 2 days add 1 quart (litre) of white or red wine, 3 drops of amber essence and 9 tablespoons (75 grams) of powdered sugar and stir.

Leave to stand for 24 hours, then filter.

Honey water. EAU MIELLÉE—Dissolve some pure honey in hot water, add a little rum or brandy to the mixture, according to taste. This beverage can also be acidulated with a dash of vinegar. It is a refreshing drink but does not keep.

Hop drink. BOISSON AU HOUBLON—Put into a 20-quart (litre) crock 2 pounds (1 kilo) of sugar, 2 handfuls of hop flowers, 8 to 10 orange leaves and a glass of vinegar.

Fill with water. Leave to macerate for 2 days, stirring frequently. Strain through a cloth, decant into bottles, cork and tie down cork.

Hydromel (I) (Codex recipe)—Dilute 3½ ounces (100 grams) of very pure white honey in 1 quart (litre) of warm water and strain.

Vinous hydromel is made out of one part honey and three parts water.

Hydromel (II)—Dissolve the honey in water, allowing 2 pounds (1 kilo) per quart (litre), add animal charcoal and filter the liquid to purify it. Then add brandy, amounting to a quarter of the water used, having previously left the brandy to stand for a few days with elder blossom, Florentine iris (Iris root) and a few bitter almonds.

Leave the mixture in the sun for 15 days, filter and it will be ready for bottling.

Kefir—This beverage, made from fermented cows' milk, has for a long time been used in the countries bordering on the Caucasus.

The fermented kefir is dried, preserved and transported in the form of grains.

These grains, called *pousse toujours* in French, possess a valuable property: they can multiply indefinitely by fermentation. This being so, a minute quantity of this product is enough to produce any amount of kefir.

Allow 1⅓ ounces (40 grams) of kefir for 1 quart (litre) of water. Put the kefir into a stone jug, dilute with water, sweeten slightly, stir and allow to stand for 24 hours. Stir again, allow to stand and at the end of 4 days put into bottles.

Ready for use in 6 or 7 days' time after bottling.

Lemonade—See section on LEMONADE.

Fizzy lemonade. LIMONADE GAZEUSE—Ordinary lemonade aerated with carbon dioxide by means of aerating apparatus.

Lemonade with pomegranate juice. LIMONADE AU SUC DE GRENADE—Take the seeds out of 6 ripe red pomegranates and extract the juice from them either by pressing in a fruit squeezer or by rubbing through a sieve.

To this pomegranate juice add the juice of 2 lemons and 2 oranges as well as the zest of one lemon and one orange. Add twice as much water as there is juice, sugar to taste, then strain through a silk sieve and chill the lemonade.

Liquorice and orange water. EAU DE RÉGLISSE À L'ORANGE—Put 2¾ to 3½ ounces (80 to 100 grams) of well washed liquorice roots, cut into very small pieces, into a pan. Add ⅓ ounce (10 grams) of orange zest.

Cover with 4 quarts (litres) of water, boil for 5 minutes, strain through a cloth and the drink will be ready for use at once.

Oatmeal water. EAU DE GRUAU—Using oatmeal proceed as described in the recipe for *Barley water* (see above).

Orangette or Frénette cordial (shrub). BOISSON ORANGETTE OU FRÉNETTE—Take 1¾ ounces (50 grams) of ash-tree leaves, peel of 10 oranges, 6 pounds (3 kilos) of granulated sugar, 1¾ ounces (50 grams) of citric acid, 1 ounce (30 grams) of brewers' yeast, burnt sugar.

Boil the ash-tree leaves with the orange peel for 25 or 30 minutes in 2 quarts (litres) of water. Strain through a cloth.

Dissolve 6 pounds (3 kilos) of granulated sugar in the above liquid. Add 1¾ ounces (50 grams) of citric acid. Put into a barrel of about 50 quarts (litres) capacity.

Dilute 1 ounce (30 grams) of yeast with cold water, mix with 2 tablespoons of burnt sugar and add to the barrel. Fill with water, leave to ferment for 8 days, then bottle and cork.

Beverage made out of pea-pods. BOISSON DE COSSES DE POIS VERTS—Put pods of green peas into a stockpot and add plenty of water to them. Boil for 3 hours.

Leave to get cold, add a good handful of sage for 10 quarts (litres) of liquid.

Leave to ferment in a barrel.

Draw off, bottle and tie down corks.

Golden rhubarb cordial (shrub). EAU DORÉE DE RHUBARBE—Tonic and apéritif obtained by macerating a piece of rhubarb in a jug of water.

Rice water. EAU DE RIZ—Proceed as described in the recipe for *Barley water*.

Three flowers cordial (shrub). BOISSON DE TROIS FLEURS—Put 2 ounces (60 grams) of hop flowers, 2 ounces (60 grams) of violet flowers and 1⅓ ounces (40 grams) of elder blossom into 22 quarts (20 litres) of boiling water Boil for 5 minutes then strain through a fine cloth.

Pour this liquid into a barrel with 9 pounds (4 kilos 500 grams) of brown sugar; mix, add a pint (½ litre) of vinegar and ⅜ ounce (12 grams) of brewer's yeast, broken up into pieces.

Fill the barrel with 87 quarts (80 litres) of water, stir vigorously to mix well, bung the barrel and leave to ferment.

Wine-flavoured water. EAU VINEUSE—A beverage for convalescents, made by adding a small quantity of Bordeaux or Burgundy wine to water or soda water. A little sugar and lemon essence is sometimes also added.

Bitter wines. VINS AMERS—Apart from medicinal wines, the most popular bitter wines which are to be found in the shops are *Quinquina*, *Absinthe*, *Gentian*.

Blackcurrant wine. VIN DE CASSIS—Put ripe blackcurrants into a tub, squash them and leave for 24 hours.

Rub through a sieve or a coarse cloth and keep the juice separately. Cover the remaining *marc* with water, equalling in volume the amount of juice extracted, and leave to macerate for 12 hours, then press through again. Mix the two juices, measure and add ¼ cup (50 grams) of sugar per quart (litre) of liquid.

Pour the liquid into a barrel or some other receptacle and leave to ferment.

When the fermentation begins to be established, bung the barrel, leaving an opening the size of a vent-peg.

After a few days, remove bung, to allow carbon dioxide to escape.

Repeat this operation from time to time until there is no longer any risk of too great an expansion of gas, then bung for good. Draw off at the end of six months.

Cherry wine. VIN DE CERISES—Proceed as described in the recipe for *Blackcurrant wine*.

Fig wine or figuette. VIN DE FIGURES FIGUETTE—Put 2 pounds (1 kilo) of dried figs and 10 juniper berries into a small barrel.

Add 10 quarts (litres) of water and leave to macerate from 6 to 8 days. Strain the liquid, bottle it and leave to rest 4 or 5 days before using.

Ginger wine. VIN DE GINGEMBRE—Put 16 pounds (8 kilos) of sugar into 40 quarts (litres) of boiling water. When the sugar dissolves, add ¾ pound (350 grams) of pounded ginger roots.

Boil for a quarter of an hour, then remove from heat.

When the liquid is nearly cold, add ½ pound (250 grams) of brewer's yeast. Leave to ferment in a barrel. Draw off after fermentation, and when the wine is quite clear, decant into bottles.

Juniper wine. VIN DE GENIÈVRE—Mix 10 pounds (5 kilos) of honey (or brown sugar) with 4 pounds (2 kilos) of brewer's yeast and 100 pounds (50 kilos) of crushed juniper berries. Add 100 quarts (litres) of hot water. Add a little crushed coriander. Pour this mixture into a cask and stir vigorously for 5 minutes. Cover with boards, hermetically if possible.

Leave to ferment in a place with a temperature of 77°F.

When the fermentation is complete and the wine has become clear, draw off into a keg and put into a place with a temperature not exceeding 59°F. At the end of one month, draw off again and keep in a cellar in a very full, well-bunged keg. After one year, decant into bottles.

Juniper wine, called genevrette. VIN DE GENIÈVRE, DIT GENEVRETTE—Put 50 quarts (litres) of juniper berries into 100 quarts (litres) of water, add 2 handfuls of wormwood and leave to ferment in a cool place for one month, then filter and bottle.

The supply of this beverage may be prolonged by leaving the berries in the receptacle and adding water to replace liquid drawn off.

This is a bitter, aromatic, stimulating beverage and at one time was very popular in the Gâtinais.

Raisin wine. VIN DE RAISINS SECS—Put 1 quart (litre) of raisins, 1¼ cups (300 grams) of granulated sugar and ¼ cup (½ decilitre) of wine vinegar into a small 15-quarts (litres) barrel. Add water. Leave to macerate for 8 days, then bottle. The wine will be ready for use 8 days after bottling in the winter, and 4 days in the summer.

BÉZIERS—This town of the Hérault department may be considered the capital of French red table wines. The Hérault department is one of the four departments of France which produce the greatest proportion of the wine harvested in the country.

The culinary specialities of Béziers and its surroundings are the same as those found in all towns of the Languedoc.

They include *escargots à la lodévoise*, *cabassols*, *manouls* and small *Béziers pâtés*, known as *pâtés de Pézenas; flaunes* or *flauzonnes de Lodève*, *fouaces aux frittons* and *oreillettes*.

BEZIEU SOEP OR RED-CURRANT SOUP (Belgian cuisine). SOUPE AUX GROSEILLES—Cook some vermicelli in water. When the vermicelli is ready, add salt, bind with a liaison of potato flour diluted in a little cold water and add some red-currant juice with a little sugar.

BICARBONATE OF SODA. BICARBONATE DE SOUDE—In medicine, this is used as an alkali and antacid.

In cooking it is used to soften the water used for certain vegetables. It is sometimes added to the water used for carrots prepared *à la Vichy*.

BICHIQUES—Tiny fish. See CURRY, *Bichique curry*.

BIGARADE SAUCE—See SAUCE.

BIGARREAU—A variety of hard-fleshed cherry. There are red and white varieties. See CHERRY.

BIGNON (Louis)—One of the greatest restaurateurs of the nineteenth century.

Having completed his training in the kitchen of the Café d'Orsay (which today no longer exists), he took charge of the Café Foy, which he re-organized completely and made one of the best restaurants in Paris.

In 1847 he handed over this establishment (which has now also disappeared) to his brother, who had just married Mademoiselle Callot, a daughter of a director of one of the most celebrated restaurants of the time 'Les Frères Provençaux'.

Bignon then took over the management of Café Riche. A remarkably intelligent man, he did not limit his activities only to cookery, but also took a lively interest in vine-growing and agriculture. With a few friends he founded the *Société des Agriculteurs de France*. He was later elected a member of the *Société Nationale d'Agriculture* and of the *Conseil supérieur de l'agriculture, du commerce et de l'industrie*.

In the world exhibitions which were held in Paris and London from 1862 to 1880, he received the highest awards for agricultural produce, wines and selected products which he exhibited.

All the famous people of that epoch, all the great artists, all the great writers used to be frequent visitors to Bignon's restaurant. Café Riche was the most famous restaurant in Paris and its renown was world-wide.

Many magnificent dishes, which to this day figure on the menus of the best restaurants of the world, were invented at the Café Riche. *Sole à la Riche* and *Woodcock à la Riche* both originated there.

In 1867, Louis Bignon was awarded the Legion of Honour. He was the first French restaurant-keeper to have attained this distinction; it was in fact bestowed upon him not in his capacity of a great restaurateur, but that of a famous agriculturist.

In 1878, still in the same capacity, he was made Officer of the Legion of Honour and at the same time awarded the *palmes académiques*.

Louis Bignon, who was held in high esteem by all his colleagues, was elected president of the restaurant and bar-keepers' union of the Seine department.

In his guide to the *Pleasures of Paris*, Alfred Delvau, one of the wittiest historiographers of Parisian life, speaking of Café Riche (for some time it had been the fashion among reporters to refer to it as Café Iche) wrote: 'Many men of letters lunch there, many men of letters dine there, as well as a great number of stockbrokers. . . . Bignon's cellar is respectably stocked with good vintage wines, to which gastronomes do due justice. For in the Café Riche, people drink even more than they eat. . . . The favourite dish of the people who go to have supper at Bignon senior's is *Sole aux crevettes* (sole with shrimps) which they wash down with red Bouzy. And very good it is, *sole aux crevettes* at the Café Riche. The red Bouzy is very good, too!

'Nor let us forget the sauce, the famous sauce of this restaurant, which is neither *sauce au fumet*, nor *sauce au blanc*, neither *sauce Robert*, nor *sauce au velouté*, neither *sauce à la béchamel*, nor *sauce perlée*, neither *sauce au pauvre homme* nor *sauce bonne femme*, nor yet *sauce salmis*, it is not this and it is not that, but quite simply *sauce du Café Riche* and the secret of the head cuisinier.'

BIGOS (Polish cookery)—This dish is served in Poland at lunch or dinner as a main course. It is made of sauerkraut, prepared in a somewhat different way to that of Alsace.

Wash 8 pounds (4 kilos) sauerkraut in several waters. Put it into a saucepan, pour on enough cold water to cover, bring to the boil, drain on a sieve, add 2 pounded onions and 4 cooking apples, peeled and cut in small dice, and mix well.

Prepare cooked meats in advance, such as venison, chicken, mutton, duck, ham, sausages and pickled pork.

Put the sauerkraut and the meat into a casserole, arranging it in layers and putting a little butter on each layer. Moisten with stock, cover and cook in the oven for 2 hours.

Twenty-five minutes before serving add sauce to the sauerkraut, prepared by diluting a butter and flour *roux** with the liquor in which the sauerkraut was cooked.

BIJANE—A sort of cold soup very popular in the Anjou region. It is prepared by putting crumbled bread into sweetened red wine.

BILBERRY. MYRTILLE—A small plant common in upland woods (naturalized in U.S.A.). The purplish, rather tart berries can be stewed and are used in jam (see WHORTLEBERRY), syrups and liqueurs.

Bilberry

BILE—Thick, ropy, greenish-yellow, bitter fluid secreted by liver. In cookery and industry bile is called gall.

BINDENFLEISCH—A Swiss gastronomical delicacy. Made from best quality beef, it goes through a pickling process and is then air dried at altitudes of from 3000 to 5000 feet during the cold winter months. When the meat reaches a certain point of ripeness it is pressed into proper shape. Occasionally stag meat is treated in the same way. Cut in paper thin slices, it is served as an hors d'oeuvre with brown bread and a glass of red wine.

BIRD. OISEAU—A great number of wild and domestic birds are edible. But this word does not figure on the menu, except in the expression *petits oiseaux*. In classic French cookery the term *oiseau* covers various small birds of the sparrow type, which are generally roasted or cooked on skewers like larks.

BIRD'S-FOOT TREFOIL (U.S.A. Lotus). LOTIER—This leguminous plant grows abundantly in meadows, along the highways and in fields of cereal crops.

The leaves, stems and flowers of the bird's-foot trefoil have a pleasant fragrance, especially when dried.

They can be used to flavour marinades.

In some districts the leaves and flowers of this plant are used to impart the flavour of wild rabbit to hutch rabbits. The rabbit is drawn and then stuffed with a handful of bird's-foot trefoil leaves and flowers.

BISCOTTE—See RUSK.

BISCUIT—This French term, in principle applied to a floury confection which undergoes double baking, has acquired a great many meanings and covers cakes, home-made biscuits (U.S.A. cookies), factory-made biscuits, army biscuits and even medicinal biscuits.

The word biscuit is also used in French to describe an iced sweet, made of ice cream mixture, simply because the portions are cut to look like biscuits. See ICE CREAMS AND ICES, *Neapolitan ice cream*.

Army biscuits. BISCUITS DE GUERRE—These used to be made of a fairly substantial paste (1 part water for 6 parts flour), baked from 20 to 25 minutes and cooled off until completely dry. Sometimes a little leaven was added to the paste and invariably some seasoning (see BREAD) to give this dough a little taste, as it had no salt in it. The biscuits were difficult to chew and were not much good in soups as they did not absorb enough liquid when soaked.

After 1894, as a result of the work carried out by the army chemist Balland, to whom we owe innumerable analyses of food products, biscuit was replaced by *army bread*. This had practically the same water content as the biscuit. It was made of flour, bolted up to 75% and fermented by yeast. It was dried and delivered in the shape of 50-gram flat loaves pricked all over. This bread was porous and absorbent. Nevertheless it was not popular with the soldiers. The ration was 550 grams in peace-time and 600 grams in action.

Sweet biscuits (U.S.A. Cookies). BISCUITS DE PÂTISSERIE—**Apricot biscuits (cookies) (Petits fours).** BISCUITS À L'ABRICOT—*Ingredients.* 2 cups (500 grams) of sugar, 16 eggs, 5 cups (625 grams) of sieved flour, ¼ cup (50 grams) of vanilla-flavoured sugar. Vanilla extract may be substituted.

Method. Cream the yolks and the sugar in a bowl, blend in flour and whites of egg whisked into a stiff froth, folding in gently and lightly to prevent breaking up the paste, which should be very firm.

Grease tins with butter, sprinkle with flour and half fill with the biscuit mixture, piping it through a forcing-bag. Put a spot of apricot jam in the middle, and cover with biscuit mixture.

Sift sugar over and bake in a moderate oven (375°F.) for 20 minutes. Take out of baking tins, allow to cool and store in biscuit tins.

Chocolate soufflé biscuits (cookies). BISCUITS SOUFFLÉS AU CHOCOLAT—Warm 2 cups (500 grams) of fine sugar and 10 whites of egg on a gentle heat, whisking all the time. When the mixture acquires sufficient consistency, add 10½ ounces (300 grams) of softened chocolate, well blended with 2 whites of egg.

Pipe through a forcing-bag on to a baking sheet, buttered and dusted out with flour.

Bake in a moderate oven (350°F.).

Note. Instead of piping this mixture on to a baking sheet, it can be poured into little frilly paper cases for baking.

Genevese biscuits (cookies). BISCUITS GENEVOIS—Put ½ cup (125 grams) of fine sugar into a bowl with 3 yolks of egg, one whole egg, a little grated lemon rind and a pinch of salt. Stir the mixture with a wooden spoon for 2 minutes.

Add 3 tablespoons (45 grams) of melted butter, 4 tablespoons (35 grams) of ground almonds, 1 cup (125 grams) of sieved flour and, at the last moment, 3 whites of egg whisked into a stiff froth.

Pour the mixture into finger-shaped moulds, which have been buttered and dusted out with a mixture of fine sugar and cornflour (cornstarch). Bake in a very slow oven. Take out of the moulds and dry off on a sieve before storing in biscuit tins.

Ginger biscuits (cookies). BISCUITS AU GINGEMBRE—Put ½ cup (125 grams) of fine sugar into a bowl with 4 yolks of egg, and 2 teaspoons (5 grams) of ground ginger.

Stir this mixture with a wooden spoon until it is quite smooth.

Add 6 tablespoons (60 grams) of rice flour and 3 tablespoons (30 grams) of potato starch and fold in 4 whites of egg whisked into a stiff froth.

Pipe this mixture through a forcing-bag with a plain nozzle on to greased paper in the shape of little sticks 2 inches long.

Sprinkle with sugar, put on a baking sheet and bake in a 350°F. oven for 8 to 10 minutes.

Detach the biscuits and leave to dry on a sieve before storing in biscuit tins.

Lemon biscuits (cookies). BISCUITS AU CITRON—Put ¼ cup (60 grams) of fine sugar and 2 yolks of egg into a bowl and cream together until the mixture becomes firm.

Add grated rind of 1 lemon, mix with a wooden spoon, and add ¼ cup (30 grams) of sifted flour, 2 tablespoons (20 grams) of potato starch, a teaspoon of ground almonds and 2 whites of egg whisked into a stiff froth.

Pipe this mixture through a forcing-bag on wafer paper in the shape of macaroons 1¼ inches in diameter.

Sprinkle with powdered sugar, put on a baking sheet and bake in a slow oven (325°F.).

Detach the biscuits and store in a biscuit tin.

Biscuits mousseline à l'orange—*Ingredients.* 1 cup (125 grams) of sifted flour, ¾ cup (125 grams) of potato flour, 3½ cups (500 grams) of fine castor sugar, 1 teaspoon (25 grams) of orange-flavoured sugar, 10 eggs (whites and yolks separated), a small pinch of salt.

Method. Cream the yolks and the sugar in a bowl until the mixture is perfectly smooth.

Whisk the whites into a very stiff froth and fold into the yolks. Blend.

Add the flour and the potato flour and mix well.

Butter biscuit tins (using very hot melted butter), sprinkle the entire surface with icing sugar and fill the tins with the biscuit mixture.

Sprinkle with icing sugar and bake in a hot oven.

Take the biscuits out of their baking tins, ice with curaçao-flavoured icing and decorate the tops with candied orange peel.

Small unleavened biscuits. PETITS PAINS AZYME—*Ingredients.* 3¾ cups (500 grams) of sieved flour, 2 cups (500 grams) of fine castor sugar, 8 eggs, a pinch of salt, water.

Method. Mix the flour and the sugar, spread on the table making a well in the centre, put the salt into it and dissolve it with a few drops of water. Add the eggs, breaking them into the middle of the flour, and mix, keeping the dough rather firm. If necessary, add a little water.

Leave the dough to rest in a cool place. Roll it out with a pin and cut out with a plain round pastry cutter.

Place these circlets of dough on a lightly buttered baking sheet. Prick them all over, brush with milk and bake in a slow oven.

BISHOP (mulled wine). BISCHOF—A hot beverage very popular in northern European countries.

The *bischof* (the word can also be spelt *bishop*) is heated wine, spiced with orange and lemon peel, cinnamon, cloves, and sometimes, star anise. It is served mostly at dances and evening parties. In England *bishop* was the name once given to hot, sweetened and spiced port by Oxford and Cambridge undergraduates.

Iced bishop. BISCHOF GLACÉ—Pour a bottle of champagne, 2½ cups (5 decilitres) of lime-blossom tea into a bowl, and add an orange and half a lemon cut into thin slices.

Add a sufficient quantity of heavy (32°) sugar syrup to bring the mixture to a light syrup consistency (18°). Leave to steep in a cool place for one hour. Strain through a fine strainer.

Ice as a granité. At the last moment, add 4 small glasses of fine champagne brandy; serve in punch glasses.

Rhine wine bishop. BISCHOF AU VIN DU RHIN—Melt on the stove ½ pound of sugar mixed with grated rind of 1 orange and 1 lemon, 2 cloves, and a small stick of cinnamon in 1½ cups of water. Cook for 5 minutes.

Add one bottle of Rhine wine. Heat on the fire until a light white foam is formed on the surface.

Strain through a fine strainer. Serve in a jug or in a large silver punch bowl.

The bishop can also be prepared with Bordeaux or Burgundy wine, white or red, with champagne or any other wine.

To make it more stimulating, a little Madeira, sherry or marsala is sometimes added to this drink.

BISON—A genus of wild cattle, closely allied to the ox and yak. It differs from the ox by its shorter, wider skull, the way in which the line of the back falls away from the rounded humped shoulders, and by the thick woolly coat covering head and fore-quarters and by its beard.

The American species of this quadruped is different from the European bison, which is found, or at any rate, used to be found (as the animal is becoming more and more rare), in some parts of Russia.

Its flesh can be prepared in any way suitable for beef.

BISQUE—Nowadays this is the French name of a culinary preparation in the form of a purée, more particularly a purée of crayfish, or other shellfish, served as a thick soup.

In the olden days it was something quite different. In the beginning of the nineteenth century the word *bisque* was not applied exclusively to shellfish preparations and such things as *pigeon bisque*, *quail bisque*, etc., can be found in the recipes of that period. E. Darenne, writing on the subject of bisque in *La Cuisine Française*, says: 'A number of dictionaries give this simple definition to the word bisque: "Soup made out of the flesh of crayfish".

'Opinions are widely divided on the origin of the word bisque. Old cookery books and the most authoritative sources lead us to believe that at the beginning the word bisque did not have the same meaning. The book by Vincent La Chapelle published in 1752 gives a recipe for crayfish soup, served with pieces of crusty bread boiled to pulp, covered with crayfish flesh; this soup was not called bisque.

'Bisque soups in the eighteenth century were made of all sorts of poultry and game (without any shellfish at all), and were not, therefore, purées, but a simple presentation of *boiled* poultry or game, sometimes served with a garnish of cocks' combs and kidneys.

'For the first time, in 1758, in the last edition of *Dons de Comus*, we come across a recipe for a quail soup with crayfish, which really was a bisque soup, made of quails, topped with crayfish purée. We also find a recipe for a bisque soup made of pigeons with crayfish, which contains the following note: "All that is bisque must settle on the bottom of the plate and form a little *gratin*".

'We therefore come to the conclusion that originally *bisque* meant a soup, with some sort of meat, as was already the fashion, and breadcrumbs.

'What could have given the crayfish purée (bound in some kind of liaison) the name of *bisque soup*, was the addition, as described above, of crayfish meat to various soups, which were then called bisques.'

The bisques, whether they were made of shellfish, poultry or game, have always been considered high style preparations and have always been rather excessively spiced.

These dishes have never been considered suitable for invalids. Such was the opinion of Mellin de Saint-Gelais, chaplain to François I, expressed in verse:

Quand on est fébricitant,
Ma Dame, on se trouve en risque,
Et pour une assez longtemps,

De ne point manger de bisque:
Si rude et si fâcheux risque
Que je bisque en y songeant!

When one is feverish,
Ma Dame, one runs the risk
And for quite a long time,

Not to eat any bisque:
Such an unkind and troublesome risk,
That I feel vexed to think of it!

For recipes for *Crab bisque*, *Crayfish bisque*, *Lobster bisque* and *Spiny lobster bisque*, see SOUP.

BISTORT. BISTORTE—A plant, the roots of which are twisted in an S-shape.

These are farinaceous and are eaten by the Samoyeds instead of bread. They bake them on hot coals.

A variety of this plant is found in some high Alpine regions. Its tender leaves are eaten like spinach.

BITOK (Russian cookery). BITOKE—The *bitok* can be made of any kind of meat (beef, mutton, pork, veal, chicken, rabbit, etc.). For the simplest everyday kind the meat is minced, has milk-soaked bread and finely chopped onion (either raw or lightly fried) added, is seasoned and put through a mincer again once or twice to ensure perfect smoothness. It is then shaped into round little cakes (as distinct from the lozenge-shaped *kotlety*), about 1½ inches in diameter dredged in flour, fried in butter in a deep pan, covered with sour cream and simmered for 5 to 7 minutes.

BITTER. AMER—Having an unpleasant, wormwood taste. Among the bitter plants which are used for making infusions or decoctions are the following: *wormwood, camomile, chicory, fumitory, gentian, germander, hops, lichen, wild pansy, lesser centaury, quassia amara* (bitter ash), *cinchona, rhubarb.*

According to Foussagrives, infusions or liqueurs made of the bitter plants may be divided into five classes: (i) *purgative bitters,* based on rhubarb, aloes, etc.; (ii) *nauseous bitters,* based on camomile; (iii) *astringent bitters,* which, with the bitter substance content of tannin, include cinchona, knapweed, bark of chestnut tree, etc.; (iv) *stimulating bitters* (apéritifs) based on wormwood, peel of bitter oranges, gentian, germander, hops, etc.; (v) *convulsing* or *toxic bitters* which include the *nux vomica* and other products which belong in the province of medicine and not of distillery.

BITTER ASH. BOIS-AMER—Another name for *quassia amara** which is used in the preparation of apéritifs.

BLACK CUMIN. NIGELLE—The name given to a plant of the *Renunculus* family, whose seeds are used as a spice in India and the Mediterranean region. The pungent seeds can be used instead of pepper.

BLACKBIRD. MERLE—A bird of the thrush family, with black plumage and yellow beak. Its flesh is aromatic in flavour and slightly bitter. It is most fragrant in autumn. Corsican blackbirds enjoy a great reputation. For methods of cooking blackbirds, see THRUSH.

BLACKCURRANT. CASSIS—Fruit of the blackcurrant bush which is used to make a well esteemed liqueur (see RATAFIA) and preserves.

BLADDER. VESSIE—Membraneous bag in animals, used after butchering in charcuterie (pork butchery) and cookery to prepare certain dishes, for example *Rouen duckling en chemise.* See DUCK.

BLAISOIS or BLÉSOIS—Small regions of France (Touraine), which was already known under this name at the time of the Carolingian empire.

As in the case of all riparian lands bordering on the Loire, Blaisois is a land where, from time immemorial, the inhabitants have enjoyed the cult of good food.

The culinary specialities of Blaisois are rather similar to those of nearby Orléanais.

The Blois *rillettes* and *greaves* (cracklings) are well-known for their quality. All the pork butchery produce of this region is excellent and connoisseurs particularly appreciate the big sausages, *andouillettes* and *black (blood) puddings* (see PORK).

Notable too are the game pâtés, mostly winged game, above all the lark pâtés which are made in the same shape as the famous Pithiviers pâtés, and the celebrated *Chartres pâté,* which is made of partridges.

Also excellent are the pikes, carps and other fresh-water fish of this region, where it is prepared *en matelote,** stewed, or *au beurre blanc* (see PIKE).

Butchers' meat in Blaisois is of good quality.

Finally, there are the following specialities, greatly esteemed by all true gastronomes: *Lapereau à la solognote* (young rabbit cooked in the Sologne style), *Gâteau Pithiviers* (see PITHIVIERS), *Tarte des demoiselles Tatin* (see TART), *Lamotte-Beuvron* (tart) and Orléans *Cotignacs** (quince paste).

Wines of Blaisois and Orléanais are among the category normally known as *Demoiselles d'honneur.* Of the Orléans wines, Saint-Jean-de-Braye, Meung and Beaugency and of the Blois wines Côte-des-Grouets enjoy the greatest popularity among the gastronomes.

These wines very often suffer from a lack of sun and tend to set one's teeth on edge, but they go perfectly with the local dishes of the region.

BLANC—French culinary term used mainly to describe a *court-bouillon,* a mixture of water and flour in which various substances, such as white offal (variety meats) and certain vegetables are cooked. A *court-bouillon* in which cultivated mushrooms are cooked is also called *blanc.* See COURT-BOUILLON.

This name is also applied to white stock, based either on veal or chicken. See STOCKS, *White stocks.*

The term *blanc* is also used to define breast of chicken or other poultry and these are described on the menus as *Blanc de volaille,* etc.

BLANC DE BLANC—Name given to Champagne made from Pinot-Chardonnay white grapes.

BLANCHING. BLANCHIR—An operation consisting of boiling, for varying lengths of time, various ingredients in salted water either to harden them, or, as in the case of some green vegetables, to cook them.

Some ingredients, previously soaked in cold water, are blanched in water (gradually brought to the boil), as in the case of calf's head and trotters, calf's and lamb's sweetbreads, etc., both to cleanse them and to harden the skin.

Bacon (pork) fat, generally cut in large dice, is blanched to extract surplus salt, before frying it.

Certain green vegetables, such as green cabbages, onions, etc., are blanched to reduce their pungency.

Other vegetables and fruit, such as tomatoes, peaches, etc., are scalded (blanched) to render them easier to peel.

One author of a culinary work suggested the use of a word *blanchi gumage* to describe the operation which consists of cooking some green vegetables (brussels sprouts, fresh kidney beans, French beans, garden peas) *wholly* in salted water, but this word has not caught on in culinary terminology.

BLANCHING (Nuts). MONDER—To clean by removing skin, husk, etc. It is used especially of skinning almonds, walnuts, pistachios and hazelnuts.

Boiling water is poured over the shelled nuts to soften the skin.

BLANCMANGE. BLANC-MANGER—In early culinary history this was a much prized jelly.

If we are to take Grimod de la Reynière's word for it, the blancmange originated in Languedoc. And, said he, 'the simplest cooks in Montpelier make it excellently, but the sort made in Paris is seldom edible.'

According to Grimod de la Reynière, this dish was very difficult to make. 'Only two or three cooks of the old school were reputed to know how to make it and we are very much afraid that the secret may have been lost since the Revolution.'

In spite of this pessimistic remark, we think that it is possible to make this dish perfectly in our time. And for making it well, we give a few recipes below.

'These delicious sweets,' said Carême in his *Traité des*

entremets de douceur, 'are greatly esteemed by gastronomes, but, to be enjoyed, they must be extremely smooth and very white. Given these two qualities (so rarely found together), they will always be preferred to other creams, even to transparent jellies. This is because almond is very nourishing and contains creamy, balsamic properties which are just right for sweetening the bitterness of humours.'

Blancmange (Carême's recipe). BLANC-MANGER—'Throw into boiling water a pound of sweet almonds and about twenty bitter almonds; after having blanched them, leave them to soak in a bowl of cold water, which renders them singularly white. Drain them on a sieve and then rub in a napkin.

'Pound them in a mortar, moistening them, little by little, with half a spoonful of water at a time, to prevent them turning into oil. When they are pounded into a fine paste, take them out of the mortar and put into a bowl. Dilute these almonds with 5 glasses of filtered water, adding it a little at a time. Then, spread a clean napkin over an oval dish, pour the blancmange into it and, with two people twisting the napkin, press out all the almond milk, then put in 12 ounces of granulated sugar and rub through a silk sieve. The sugar being on the bottom, strain the blancmange through a napkin once again, then add to the almond milk 1 ounce 4 grains of isinglass, clarified and a little warmer than tepid, so that it can be blended perfectly with the blancmange, which you will then pour into a mould.

'The mould, before this operation, should be placed into a container with 15 pounds of crushed ice; and 3 hours later, when it is ready to serve, turn out the sweet in the usual manner.'

To make rum blancmange, add ½ glass of good rum to the mixture described above. To make a maraschino blancmange, add ½ glass of maraschino.

'To serve this sweet in little pots (the sort of little pots used for creams), prepare two-thirds of the quantity given in the preceding recipe; you will, however, need a little less isinglass, as blancmange served in little pots has to be more delicate than when it is to be turned out.'

Proceeding on all points as described in the above recipe, one can, according to Carême, make blancmanges flavoured with citron, vanilla, coffee, chocolate, pistachio nuts, hazelnuts and strawberries, as well as whipped cream.

Blancmange (modern method). BLANC-MANGER—*Ingredients for 5 persons.* 1½ cups (240 grams) of sweet almonds, 1 tablespoon (10 grams) of bitter almonds, 1 pint (½ litre) of cold water, 1 cup (200 grams) of lump sugar, ½ ounce (15 grams) of gelatine, ½ cup (1 decilitre) of rum or kirsch.

Method. Scald the almonds with boiling water, skin them, wash in plenty of water and put into a perfectly clean mortar. Pound as finely as possible, sprinkling them with a few drops of cold water, taken from the pint allowed. When the almonds have been reduced to a very fine paste, dilute it with the rest of the water.

Put a coarse linen cloth over a bowl and pour the contents of the mortar into this cloth. Press vigorously, twisting the cloth and squeezing the pocket holding the almonds, to extract all the milk. Put the almonds back into the mortar and pound once again, adding enough fresh water to extract 1 pint (½ litre) of almond milk.

Put the gelatine, properly softened, into a saucepan with the almond milk and lump sugar. Place the saucepan on a fire and stir with a wooden spoon until boiling is established. Then strain the mixture through a fine strainer or a napkin into a clean bowl and leave to cool. When it is just tepid, add the liqueur or the flavouring chosen and mix.

Grease a *bavarois* mould with sweet almond oil, shake out any surplus, fix it in crushed ice, without salt, and when the mixture is cold, pour it into the mould before it sets (if it sets, it has to be warmed gently to render it liquid once again).

After an hour the blancmange can be served. Take the mould off the ice, dip into water for a moment, wipe the mould and turn out the blancmange on to a napkin-covered dish.

BLANQUET—A variety of French pear which ripens in July or August. There are two kinds: the *large* and the *small blanquet*. These pears are mediocre in flavour and are used mostly for compotes.

BLANQUETTE—A white ragoût, based on lamb, veal or chicken meat, bound with a liaison of yolks of egg and cream and accompanied by a garnish consisting, in principle, of small onions cooked in *court-bouillon** and mushrooms, but other ingredients are sometimes added to the garnish.

Method of preparation of all the meats. Cut the meat into square pieces, of about 2 inches. Put them into a saucepan and cover with white stock or water. Season, bring to the boil and remove scum.

Add an onion studded with a clove, a carrot and a *bouquet garni.** Simmer gently for 45 minutes for lamb or chicken and 1¼ hours for veal.

Drain the pieces, trim them, put them into a sauté pan with small onions and mushrooms cooked in a *white court-bouillon.**

At the last moment, pour over the meat a *velouté** prepared by thickening the liquor with white *roux** and binding with a liaison of yolks and cream.

Acidulate by adding a little lemon juice. Serve in a timbale, sprinkle with chopped parsley and garnish with heart-shaped croûtons fried in butter.

Blanquette à la ménagère, also called Fricassée—Fry pieces of meat, as described above, in butter, without allowing them to brown.

Sprinkle with flour, stir and do not allow it to turn yellow, moisten with white stock or water, bring to the boil, season and add an onion stuck with a clove, a carrot and a *bouquet garni.**

Finish cooking and complete the garnishing as indicated in the recipe; bind with a liaison of yolks and cream as described above in the recipe for *Blanquette*. For further recipes for various blanquettes, see LAMB, VEAL, CHICKEN.

BLANQUETTE DE LIMOUX—Sparkling white wine (more often aerated) which is made at Limoux, in the Aude. This wine is slightly sweet. Like all sparkling or sweet wines, it should be served very cold, even iced.

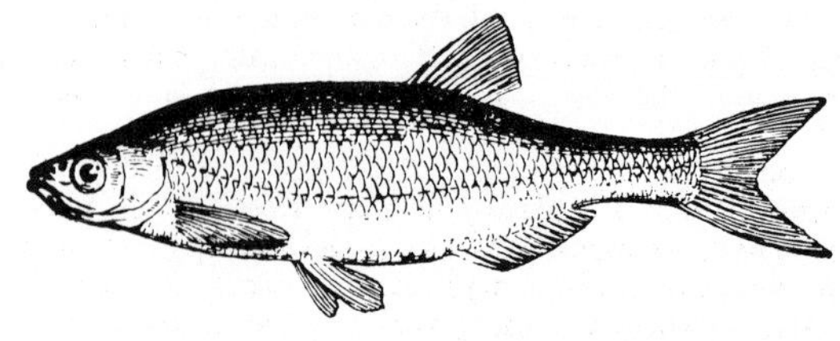

Bleak

BLEAK (ABLET). ABLETTE—A small European fresh-water fish. Its length hardly exceeds 4 inches. Its flesh is white and rather insipid. It is used mostly for frying.

BLENNY. Blennie cagnette—A genus of European freshwater fish. All the other members of the Blenny family are sea fish (forming a sub-order of percomorph fishes).

A characteristic which is common to all blennies is the absence of scales, the body being covered with a layer of viscous mucus of exceptional thickness.

This fish varies in size from 4 to 6 inches and is fawn-coloured, speckled with brown, with brown transversal strips along the back.

The blenny abounds in the waterways of the Hérault department. It is particularly plentiful in Agde, where it is called *lièvre* (hare), because the shape of its head resembles that of the hare's a little.

It is also found in the lake of Bourget and the fishermen of this region call it *chasseur* (hunter).

In other regions it is known as *bavecca.*

The blenny's flesh is white and quite good in flavour. It is mainly fried but can also be used as an ingredient for *matelotes.**

BLETTE—Name given in some parts of France to white beet or chard.

BLEU (to cook au bleu)—Method applied to freshwater fish, mainly to trout. This method consists of plunging the fish, *absolutely fresh, if not actually alive*, into a boiling *court-bouillon,** generally a mixture of water and vinegar, seasoned with salt and sometimes spiced with thyme and bay leaf.

Cooked in this way, the skin of the fish, especially that of trout, takes on a slightly bluish colour. To accentuate this blueing, the fish can be sprinkled with pure vinegar, before immersing it in *court-bouillon.*

All fish cooked *au bleu* is generally served with melted butter, handed separately. It can also be served with *Hollandaise sauce* (see SAUCE), or any other white sauce specially recommended for poached fish.

BLIND, BAKE. Cuire a blanc—This describes an operation which consists of baking a flan (pie shell) or other crust 'blind', i.e. empty. Thus certain kinds of tart and flan cases are baked in the oven filled with some dried vegetables, which are removed once the case is cooked. The cases are then filled with the ingredients indicated in the recipe.

Cuire au blanc also describes the operation which consists of cooking certain substances (mostly white offal or variety meats) in a special *court-bouillon.**

Frying-pan for blini

BLINI (Russian cookery)—Blini are pancakes which have been made in Russia from time immemorial and especially during Shrovetide. Recipes for *blini* and various fillings are given under HORS-D'OEUVRE.

A. Petit, in his interesting work *Traité de la cuisine russe*, says that during Shrovetide, 'from the humblest cottage to the richest palace, they all have their blini, twice a day, the whole of that week; it is a treat for everybody and the masters attach all the more importance to it, because it is often very difficult to find cooks who can make them well.'

Batter for blini. Pâté à blinis—Prepare a light batter, using $\frac{2}{3}$ ounce (20 grams) of yeast diluted in a pint ($\frac{1}{2}$ litre) of warm milk and 6 tablespoons (50 grams) of sieved flour. Put this batter in a bowl in a warm place and leave it to ferment for 2 hours.

Then add to it 2 cups (250 grams) of sieved flour, 4 yolks of egg, $1\frac{1}{2}$ cups (3 decilitres) of warm milk and a pinch of salt.

Mix all these ingredients thoroughly, but without allowing the mixture to get heavy. At the last moment add 4 whites of egg whisked into a stiff froth and $\frac{1}{2}$ cup (1 decilitre) of cream, whipped. Leave the batter to rise for about 35 minutes. Out of this batter make little pancakes, frying them in butter as ordinary pancakes but using special small frying-pans.

BLOATER. Craquelot—A variety of slightly salted and smoked herring which is served mainly in England, in the morning, for breakfast and also for high tea.

The bloater is grilled on a low fire and served with melted butter or *Maître d'hôtel butter* (see BUTTER, *Compound butters*) served separately.

BLOCK. Billot—Thick, short piece of tree-trunk, usually placed on three legs, which serves for chopping up meat.

A butcher's block is usually an upright table made of wood, enclosed in a wooden frame.

BLOND DE VEAU—A French culinary term which describes (or used to in the past, for this term is hardly used in the present day) white veal stock.

Carême, in his *Traité de sauces*, uses this term.

White veal stock is used in the preparation of some brown sauces (see SAUCE) or for glazing certain substances.

BLOND DE VOLAILLE—A synonym of *fond blond*, clear or thickened chicken stock. See SAUCE, *brown sauces.*

Rich veal or chicken stocks are used as liquor for braising certain vegetables, such as cardoons, celery, artichoke hearts, lettuces, etc.

BLONDINER—A word used or perhaps even invented by Alexandre Dumas, describing the action of making sliced onion, fried in butter, turn a pale yellow colour, not quite browning it.

BLONDIR—This French culinary term describes the operation which consists of browning very lightly any substance fried in butter, oil, or some other fat.

The term *faire blondir* also describes the cooking of flour and butter mixture, which constitutes a light *roux.* See ROUX.

BLOOD. Sang—The blood of butchered animals has no part in nutrition but it has a number of industrial uses (the treatment of wines, clarification of sugar, the manufacture of coal products, fertilizers, etc.).

The blood of the pig (often mixed with other blood) is used to make *boudin* (black pudding), and the blood of rabbit, hare and chicken is used to thicken the dishes called *civets*, which—after the blood has been added—must not be heated above 158°F., the temperature above which blood coagulates and the mixture curdles.

BLOOD PUDDING—See PORK.

BLUE GAZELLE. GAZELLE BLEUE—A type of edible goat found mainly at the Cape. Its meat, which is very delicate, is cooked like roebuck.

BOAR—See WILD BOAR.

BOCAL—Wide-mouthed, short-necked glass bottle or jar for bottling or pickling vegetables and fruit (gherkins, capers, small onions, mixed vegetables, cherries, small melons, etc.) or for preserving fruit in brandy.

BODY (to have). CORPS (AVOIR DU)—One says that a wine has body when it produces a sensation in the mouth of plenitude, of *solidité*, resulting from a harmonious combination of strength and flavour, and the content of essence and tannin.

BOILING. ÉBULLITION—The movement of a liquid in the process of vaporization. Boiling takes place when, as a result of heating, the steam pressure is at least equal to that of the liquid.

While a liquid is boiling its temperature remains constant. The boiling point of water has been taken as the norm for comparative purposes, and stands at 100°C. (212°F.). This temperature decreases by about a third of a degree per 100 metres of altitude.

BOIS DE SAINTE-LUCIE—Name of a variety of cherry-tree, distinguishable by the fragrance of its wood.

BOLÉE—Term applied to a receptacle, usually brown earthenware, which is used for drinking cider in Normandy and Brittany.

This term also applies to the cider contained in the receptacle. Thus it is said: 'Boire une bolée de cidre'—'To drink a bowlful of cider'.

BOLETUS (Cèpe). BOLET—A genus of fungi of which about 70 species are known in France. Unless one is an expert, the only boletus mushroom which can safely be gathered is the *boletus edulis*, known in France as *cèpe de Bordeaux* and *tête de nègre* when it is young. It has then a bronze-coloured cap, white underneath, on a white and swollen stem. As it grows, the cap becomes a lighter brown, begins to overlap the stem, the underneath becomes yellow, later the tubes turn green and can be removed like the choke of a cooked artichoke.

This mushroom is found in woods, under oak, chestnut and beech trees and sometimes under pines. In the Paris region it appears in April and is sometimes very plentiful in the autumn.

The underneath may be white, yellow or greenish but never red. The stem is white, yellow or brown; it should never have any red spots. The flesh which is exposed to the air remains white and never becomes green; its taste is very pleasant, never bitter.

Very old cèpes, with green tubes and damaged by slugs, should be avoided.

The cèpe is a highly-prized mushroom; it is, however, a little indigestible. According to some authorities, its nutritive value, like that of other fungi, is insignificant, in spite of misleading analyses, as nitrogenous substances contained in fungi escape the chemical processes of digestion. See MUSHROOMS.

BOMBE (Ice cream). BOMBE GLACÉE—Ice cream which used to be made in a spherical shaped mould, hence its name. In modern culinary practice it is made in a simple, conical mould.

In the past the bombes were made of ordinary ice cream mixture disposed in concentric layers in the mould.

In the present day, they are made of a very light mixture, enclosed in an ordinary ice cream or water ice mixture. See ICE CREAMS, *Bombes*.

BONBON (Sweet, candy)—According to some authorities, the word bonbon was invented by children, whose first words are generally repetitions of two syllables.

Have the bonbons of our time anything in common with the *dulcia* of the Romans? We do not know the answer, but we think at any rate that the word *dulcia* at the time of the Romans must have meant not only a sweetmeat, but covered the whole range of sweet dishes which we now call *entremets de sucre* (sweet courses or desserts).

One thing is certain, that sweets could not have been made in Europe until sugar was brought from the Orient by the returning crusaders in the thirteenth century. It is known that the first experiments with sugar-cane juices were carried out by the Jews in Sicily towards A.D. 1230.

Before that time, the bonbons, which were not yet thus called, used to be made in France with fruit juice and honey, flavoured with amber or cinnamon.

The art of making sweets spread very rapidly. To make them appeal to the ladies at court, as well as to the great gentlemen who also had a liking for sweetmeats, confectionery methods were improved and the variety of sweets increased.

During the brilliant epoch of the Renaissance this art was carried even further. All the great gentlemen used to carry bonbonnières full of sweets, which they offered to the ladies. These bonbonnières were often veritable works of art, some of them set with precious stones.

It is said that Henry IV always had his pockets full of sweets, so as to be able to offer them to the ladies.

As time went on, the art of confectionery continued to make strides forward. The variety of sweets which are made nowadays is infinite.

All these sweets can be classified in four principal groups as follows: *dragées* (sugar-coated almonds) and *pralines*; *bonbons fondants*; *boiled sweets* and *pastilles*.

Various other confectionery preparations which are now factory-made, are also classed in the category of bonbons, such as *caramels*, *butterscotch*, *toffee*, *fruit paste*, a certain number of marzipan preparations, *crystallized fruit* and, finally, *walnuts*, *almonds* and *hazelnuts* dipped into sugar cooked to crack degree.

BON-CHRÉTIEN—A pear of which two varieties are known: one ripens in summer, the other in winter.

The flesh of this pear is quite sweet but a little gritty. It is mostly eaten cooked.

BONE. OS—Any of the separate parts of a vertebrate skeleton, forming its framework. Bones are composed of a cartilaginous substance impregnated with calcareous salts.

By boiling in water, especially under pressure, they produce gelatine. The bones, 'make-weight' in butchery terminology, added to stock give it a gelatinous consistency without improving its taste or increasing its nutritive value.

Uses of bones and meat parings. After a prolonged cooking, the bones still retain a considerable quantity of extractive juices and gelatine. As a result of a second and, of course, prolonged cooking these juices and the gelatine can be extracted and a palatable stock obtained, which, flavoured with vegetables and suitably seasoned, may provide a soup.

Reduce (boil down) this stock until it becomes syrupy and is transformed into *meat jelly*. This jelly, which is used for strengthening soups and sauces, can be kept indefinitely.

To extract all the juices, the bones should be broken up as small as possible. This second stock, naturally, is not really an economical proposition, unless it can be done without using any further fuel.

It is, therefore, to be undertaken only if one has a permanent fire at one's disposal.

BONE-MARROW. MOELLE—A soft, fatty substance contained in long bones commonly called marrow-bones.

Spinal marrow is that part of the central nervous system contained in the spinal cord. The spinal marrow of butcher's meat sold in sections is called in French *amourette*. See OFFAL OR VARIETY MEATS.

Beef bone-marrow. MOELLE DE BOEUF—This, extracted raw from the large bones of the thigh or shoulder of beef, has many uses in the kitchen.

The marrow, cut into fairly thick slices (using a knife dipped in boiling water), poached without boiling in salt water and drained, is used to garnish steaks.

Beef bone-marrow, diced, poached and drained, is also used in various brown sauces.

Bone-marrow canapés. CANAPÉS À LA MOELLE—Made from the marrow of the large marrow-bone cooked in the pot-au-feu or *petite marmite* (see SOUPS AND BROTHS).

These canapés can be served in two ways:

(1) Spread the marrow on neat slices of toast. Season these canapés with salt and freshly-ground pepper.

(2) Spread a *salpicon** of marrow (poached and well drained) on rectangular slices of toast. Decorate the top of the *salpicon* with strips of marrow, poached in salt water and drained, or seasoned with peppercorns ground in a mill. Sprinkle with fresh breadcrumbs tossed in butter and drained. Put the canapés in the oven for a few seconds.

Bone-marrow on fried bread. CROÛTES À LA MOELLE—Made with hollowed-out crusts of sandwich loaf fried in butter like canapés.

Bone-marrow fritots. FRITOTS À LA MOELLE—Cut the beef marrow into slices $\frac{1}{8}$-inch ($\frac{1}{2}$ centimetre) thick. Stick these slices together in pairs with some kind of forcemeat (preferably *à gratin*). Steep them for 20 minutes in oil, lemon juice, salt, pepper and chopped parsley.

Just before serving, dip these slices of marrow in a light batter. Deep-fry in very hot fat. Drain and dry in a cloth. Serve in a clump on a napkin. Garnish with fried parsley.

Salpicon of bone-marrow. SALPICON DE MOELLE—Dice the marrow more or less finely as required. Poach without bringing to the boil. Blend with *Demi-glace sauce* (see SAUCE), flavoured if desired with shallot cooked in white wine until all the liquid has evaporated.

This is used as a filling or garnish for flaky pastry vol-au-vents, canapés, fried bread (in fancy shapes), coddled or poached eggs, artichoke hearts, large mushrooms, etc.

Bone-marrow sauce. SAUCE À LA MOELLE—A sauce served with meat, grilled or sautéed fish and poached or coddled eggs. See SAUCE.

Small vol-au-vents with bone-marrow. BOUCHÉES À LA MOELLE—Small flaky pastry vol-au-vents filled while hot with a *salpicon** of beef bone-marrow blended with *Demi-glace sauce* (see SAUCE) (or very concentrated veal stock), flavoured if desired with a little shallot cooked in white wine until all the liquid has evaporated.

BONING. DÉSOSSER—The process of removing the bones from a joint of meat, poultry or any other food, whether cooked or raw, which contains bones.

The boning of raw meat or poultry requires skill, since if possible the bones must be taken out without damage to the meat.

BONITO. BONITE—A small species of tunny, commonly found in the Mediterranean and on the Atlantic coast where French fishermen also call it *germon*. It is an important fish of the North American Pacific coast. It is prepared in the same way as tunny (tuna).

BONNE-DAME—Common name for orach in France. See ORACH.

BONNES-MARES—Red wine of the Côte-d'Or. See WINE.

BONNET-TURC—French name for a variety of pumpkin.

BONVALET (cake)—This cake, which is almost identical to a cake called Beauvilliers, was created in 1869 by a pastry-cook called Jules Leroy, who was in charge of the *Maison Machin*. See BEAUVILLIERS.

BOOPS. BOGUE—A Mediterranean fish of which two species are known: the *common boops* which reaches 14 inches in length, and the *bogue saupe*.

This fish, which can be served fried, *à la meunière*, and poached and which is also used in bouillabaisse, is remarkable for the brightness of its colour—olive-yellow on the back and silver on the belly.

BORAGE. BOURRACHE—Herbaceous perennial plant. Its flowers are cooked in some regions of France as fritters. The young leaves are used for flavouring salads, iced drinks, herbal tea and vegetables. They are also used for flavouring claret cup.

BORAX OR SODIUM PERBORATE. BORATE DE SOUDE—This was sometimes fraudulently used, under various fancy names such as preservative powder, anti-ferment, etc., for preserving meat, fish, butter, wine, etc.

Its use was forbidden in France by an order of July 14th, 1891.

It is easily discoverable by chemical analysis and can be recognized by the intensification of green colour which it gives to a Bunsen burner flame, in common with all boron salts.

BORD-DE-PLAT—A small utensil used in the kitchen to protect the border of a dish on which food in sauce is being served.

Border protectors are made of tin-plated iron or any other metal. They are round or oval and vary in diameter.

BORDEAUX—The town of Bordeaux can be considered one of the capitals of French gastronomy. Its culinary glory equals that of Lyon, where, according to connoisseurs, the art of good food has reached the level of the sublime. *Gourmands*, who are connoisseurs of good things to eat, and *gourmets*, who are experts in the subtle art of wine tasting, hold this town of the ancient province of Guyenne in particular regard.

The natives of Bordeaux like good food. To compose their menus they have choice products at their disposal. From the sea they get excellent fish, crustacea and shellfish (among which the Marenne oysters must be mentioned).

The cooks of this region have always been great masters of their art.

Bordeaux, whose wines and food were being sung long ago by the poet Decimus Magnus Ausonius, born in A.D. 310, is the birthplace of one of the greatest men in French classical cookery: Dugléré. He had for a long time been in charge of the kitchens at the *Café Anglais* in Paris, which at the time was frequented by kings, princes and all the most illustrious gastronomes of Europe.

The principal culinary specialities of the Bordeaux region are: *Crayfish à la bordelaise*, *Lamprey with leeks*, *Mussels à la bordelaise*, *Escargots à la Caudéran*, *Fried whitebait*, *Sausages with oysters*, *Entrecôte à la bordelaise*, *Leg of lamb à la ficelle* (a close relative of Alexandre Dumas' *Chicken à la ficelle*), *Chicken sauté à la bordelaise*, *Pauillac lamb à la persillade*, *Foie gras with grapes*. *Terrine de Nérac*, *Pâté de foie gras aux truffes*, *Cèpes à la bordelaise*, *Aubergines sauté with garlic*, *the Millas*, *Pancakes à la bordelaise*, and finally, all those famous varieties of cakes made by the pastry-cooks of Bordeaux.

With such *harnois de gueule* ('grub'), one can appreciate the good wines of Guyenne. And to make one taste these wines all the better, excellent cheeses are produced throughout the Bordeaux region.

Wines of Bordeaux. This generic term describes all the wines, red and white, made from the grapes gathered in the department of Gironde, and, mainly, in the parts of this department lying along the course of the rivers Garonne, Dordogne and Gironde. A map will be found in the section on WINE.

The great divisions of this vineyard region are: *Médoc*, *Graves*, *Sauternes*, *Entre-deux-Mers*, *Libourne*, *Bourg*, and *Blaye*.

These great divisions are themselves sub-divided into regions which take the names of the communes and their wines are specially classified for trade.

A Bordeaux vineyard (*French Government Tourist Office*)

Médoc wines. VIN DE MÉDOC—The name Médoc defines a strip of land about fifty miles long and six miles wide along the left bank of the Gironde, between Bordeaux-Bacalan and Pointe de Grave.

Classification of the great Médoc wines

First growth

	Commune
Château-Lafite	Pauillac
Château-Margaux	Margaux
Château-Latour	Pauillac
Château-Haut-Brion	Pessac (Graves)

Château-Haut-Brion, commune of Pessac, is not actually part of the Médoc region, but of Graves, and is the only one to figure in the *first growth* category.

Second growth

	Commune
Mouton-Rothschild	Pauillac
Rauzan-Ségla	Margaux
Rauzan-Gassies	Margaux
Léoville-Lascases	Saint-Julien
Léoville-Poyferré	Saint-Julien
*Léoville-Barton	Saint-Julien
Durfort-Vivens	Margaux
Lascombes	Margaux
Gruaud-Larose-Sarget	Saint-Julien
Gruaud-Larose	Saint-Julien
Brane-Cantenac	Cantenac
Pichon-Longueville	Pauillac
Pichon-Longueville-Lalande	Pauillac
Ducru-Beaucaillou	Saint-Julien
Cos d'Estournel	Saint-Estèphe
Montrose	Saint-Estèphe

Third growth

	Commune
Kirwan	Cantenac
Issan	Cantenac
Lagrange	Saint-Julien
*Langoa	Saint-Julien
*Giscours	Labarde
Malescot Saint-Exupéry	Margaux
Cantenac-Brown	Cantenac
Palmer	Cantenac
La Lagune	Ludon
Desmirail	Margaux
Calon-Ségur	Saint-Estèphe
*Ferrière	Margaux
Marquis d'Alesme-Becker	Margaux

Fourth growth

	Commune
Saint-Pierre-Sevestre	Saint-Julien
Saint-Pierre-Bontemps	Saint Julien
Duluc-Branaire-Ducru	Saint-Julien
*Talbot d'Aux	Saint-Julien
Duhart-Milon	Pauillac
Poujet	Cantenac
La Tour Carnet	Saint-Laurent
Lafon Rochet	Saint-Estèphe
*Beychevelle	Saint-Julien
Le Prieuré	Cantenac
Marquis de Terme	Margaux

Fifth growth

	Commune
*Pontet-Canet	Pauillac
Batailley	Pauillac
Grand-Puy Lacoste	Pauillac
Grand-Puy Ducasse	Pauillac
Lynch Bages	Pauillac
Lynch Moussas	Pauillac
Dauzac	Labarde
Mouton d'Armailhacq	Pauillac
Le Tertre	Arsac
Haut-Bages	Pauillac
Pédesclaux	Pauillac
Belgrave	Saint-Laurent
Camensac	Saint-Laurent
Cos-Labory	Saint-Estèphe
Clerc Milon	Pauillac
*Croizet Bages	Pauillac
*Cantemerle	Macau

Note. Categories marked with * are those which have never been granted the right to be château bottled.

It should be pointed out that, in addition to the wines of the classed growths given above, there are also a great number of other wine-producing estates called *crus bourgeois.* These produce wines which are greatly prized by the consumers and, quite rightly, often fetch the same price as certain wines classed in fourth and fifth growths. Among the most famous of these are the following:

	Commune
Château-Sénejac	Le Pian
Château-Lahourringue	Macau
Château-d'Arsac	Arsac
Château-Martinens	Cantenac
Château-Labégorce	Margaux
Château-Laurent	Margaux
Château-Citran	Avensac
Château-Belais	Soussac
Château-Chasse-Spleen	Moulis
Château-Gastebois	Moulis
Château-Brillette	Moulis
Château-Mauvezin	Moulis
Château-Poujeaux	Moulis
Château-Maucaillou	Moulis
Château-Fourcas	Listrac
Château-Fonréaud	Listrac
Château-Clarke	Listrac
Château-Larose-Trintaudon	Saint-Laurent
Château-Larose-Perganson	Saint-Laurent
Château-La-Couronne	Pauillac
Château-Constant Bages	Pauillac
Château-Haut-Pauillac	Pauillac
Château-Bellegrave	Pauillac
Château-Haut-Bages	Pauillac
Château-Fontbadet	Pauillac
Château-Liversan	Saint-Sauveur
Château-Leroc	Saint-Estèphe
Château-Le-Crock	Saint-Estèphe
Château-Phélan-Ségur	Saint-Estèphe
Château-Pomys	Saint-Estèphe
Château-Canteloup	Saint-Estèphe

Geographically Médoc is divided into *Petite Flandre de Médoc*, *Bas-Médoc*, *Haut-Médoc* and *Palud*, but all the wines produced in these different divisions are known as Médoc wines.

'The wines of Médoc have a particular personality; they can be distinguished by a very slight harshness peculiar to them, their lingering fragrance, their aromatic savour, their mellowness and bouquet which survives even after being kept for a great many years. They are generous without being heady, and their colour, a beautiful garnet-red when young, turns a tawny ruby with age.

'They are more soft and flowing and ready for consumption sooner in the communes of Blanquefort and Castelnau cantons than in the cantons of Saint-Laurent, Pauillac and Lesparre, whose wines are less stable and therefore take longer to become mellow.' (Ernest Verdier: *An abridged monograph and classification of the great French* wines.)

Graves—*Graves* or *Graves de Bordeaux*, which comes after Médoc, going down towards the south of France, also occupies a strip of territory averaging about 9 miles in width, parallel to the course of the Gironde, between Bordeaux and Langon.

The name *Graves* comes from the nature of the soil which is gravelly. The northern part of this strip of land produces mainly red wines, the southern, white wines.

'Red Graves wines possess a great softness and a very distinctive fine bouquet, and their pleasant taste makes them sought after everywhere by those who prefer easy-flowing, easy-to-drink wines.

'There are two kinds of white wines: dry and vigorous, which are used like white Burgundy wines, and sweet and fragrant, like the wines of Sauternes.

'The principal growths of red Graves wines, which—with the exception of Haut-Brion—have not been officially classified, can, by reason of their quality and prices reached, be classified as follows:

	Commune
Château-Haut-Bailly	Léognan
Château-Pape Clément	Pessac
La Mission Haut-Brion	Pessac
Smith Haut-Lafite	Martillac
Haut-Brion Larrivet	Léognan
Haut-Brion Verthanon	Pessac
Château-Camponac	Pessac
Château-Olivier	Léognan
Château-Charbonnieux	Léognan
Domaine de Chevalier	Léognan
Latour Haut-Brion	Talence
Labuthe Haut-Brion	Gradignan
Château-Brown-Léognan	Léognan
Château du Bouscaut	Cadaujac

'The other growths are classified in the categories of *Bourgeois supérieurs* and *Bons artisans.*

'There are two types of white Graves wines. The northern part of Graves produces very little white wine, whereas the southern part, including the part below the

Pressing grapes at Saint-Émilion
(*French Government Tourist Office*)

stream of Gamort in the canton of Labrède and the whole of the canton of Podensac, produces mainly white wines and, whilst there is no official classification for them, it can be said that the wines of Portets, Podensac, Virelade, Illat and Cérons have many admirers.' (Ernest Verdier.)

The Sauternes region—This region comprises the communes of Bommes, Fargues, Barsac, Preignac and Sauternes.

'The wines of this region are generally of a pale golden colour, warm to look at; they have a distinctive bouquet and, depending on the growth and the year, vary in stillness, softness and aromatic savour.'

The great wines of Sauternes were given the following classification in 1855 by the Bordeaux *Chambre Syndicale des Courtiers*:

First great growth

	Commune
Château-Yquem	Sauternes

First growths

	Commune
Château-La Tour Blanche	Bommes
Château-Peraguey	Bommes
Château-Vigneau	Bommes
Château-Suduiraut	Preignac
Château-Coutet	Barsac
Château-Climens	Barsac
Château-Guiraud	Sauternes
Château-Rieussec	Fargues
Château-Rabaud	Bommes

Second growths

	Commune
Château-Myrat	Barsac
Château-Dorsy	Barsac
Château-Peixotto	Bommes
Château-d'Arche	Sauternes
Château-Filhot	Sauternes
Château-Broustet-Nérac	Barsac
Château-Caillou	Barsac
Château-Suau	Barsac
Château-de Malle	Preignac
Château-Romer	Preignac
Château-Lamothe	Sauternes

'In addition to the officially classified wines, other growths enjoying the same popularity as wines classified in the second growth category and reaching the same price, must be mentioned. They are: Château-Roumieux, Château-Cantegril, Château-Piada, Château-Pernaud, and Château-du-Cloziot from the commune of Barsac, and Château-La Montagne from the commune of Preignac.

'Apart from the officially classified wines, the Sauternes region also produces wines in the *Bourgeois supérieurs* and *Bons Artisans* grades, which are usually sold under the name of the commune from which they come.

'On the slopes of the right bank of the Garonne, from Saint-Macaire to Baurech, there are communes which produce greatly esteemed white wines, somewhere in between the wines of Graves and those of Sauternes. These are: Sainte-Croix-du-Mont, Loupiac, Baurech, Tabanac, Langoiran, Le Tourne, Haux, Capian, Lestiac, Paillet, Rions, Laroque, Beguey, Cadillac, Cabarnac, Montprinblanc, Omet, Donzac, Verdelais, etc.' (Ernest Verdier.)

Saint-Émilionnais—Saint-Émilion, say C. Coks and E. Feret, in their book *Bordeaux et ses vins*, is not limited to the boundaries of the commune.

Saint-Émilionnais comprises on the one hand the slopes of Saint-Émilion, Saint-Christophe-de-Barde, Saint-Laurent-des-Combes, Saint-Hippolyte, Saint-Étienne-de-Lisse, which make up the great Saint-Émilion, and on the other hand the surrounding district of the commune, also the commune of Pomerol and finally the vineyards of Libourne and of the surrounding communes on the left bank of the Isle, tributary of the Dordogne.

The wines of Saint-Émilion have all the characteristics of wines from slopes with stony subsoil like that of Bourgogne. They have a beautiful dark colour, a distinctive, very marked bouquet, a strong aromatic savour, and much warmth, they are full-bodied but easy-flowing, keep well, and improve in quality with age.

There has never been an official classification of the Saint-Émilion wines. In Saint-Émilion itself, the first great growth, are the following: *Château-Ausone, Château-Belair-Marignan, Château-Magdelaine, Château-Beauséjour, Château-Canon Saint-Émilion, Château-Fonplegade, le clos Fourtet, Château-Pavie et le domaine de Pavie, cru le Cadet, Cadet Pineau-Bon, Château-Coutet, Château-Bellevue, Le Prieuré.*

Among the Saint-Émilion Graves: *Château-Cheval Blanc, Château-Figeac.*

Saint-Christophe-des-Bardes: *Château-Haut-Sarpe, Château-Laroque.*

Saint-Laurent-des-Combes: *Château-Larcis-Ducasse.*

The wines of Pomerol have all the characteristics of Saint-Émilion wine, but they are more supple and ready for consumption more quickly.

The first growths are: *Château-Petrus, Château-Vieux Certan, l'Evangile, Château-La-Conseillante, Château-Certan, Château-Trotanoy, Château-Lapointe,* etc.

In all other communes of Saint-Émilionnais, good ordinary wines are produced.

Fronsadais, which takes its name from the town of Fronsac, occupies the slopes which overlook the corner formed by the right banks of the Isle and the Dordogne at their junction. This region produces wines much valued as table wines.

BORDELAISE (A LA)—Culinary term which applies to a great number of different dishes which belong to four categories. The first is characterized by the *Sauce bordelaise*, with white or red wine and marrowbone fat; the second by the addition of *cèpes*; the third by the *Mirepoix* and the fourth by a garnish consisting of *artichokes* and *potatoes*. These basic principles can be varied by the incorporation of different other ingredients.

This term also applies to various sweet courses (desserts), cakes, etc. See MUSHROOMS, *Cèpes à la bordelaise*, CRAYFISH, MIREPOIX, SAUCE.

BORDER (Ring). BORDURE—Culinary term which defines certain dishes, whose main characteristic is that they are served either in or on a substance shaped or moulded in the form of a ring or crown.

The substances which are used for these borders vary greatly. Thus, borders can be made of *quenelle* or other forcemeat, *rice*, *semolina* and *duchess potatoes* for hot dishes; *jelly*, *custards and creams*, *rice à l'impératrice*, etc., for cold and sweet dishes.

This term also applies to a method of decoration, very popular at one time but hardly ever seen nowadays, which used to be made either of noodle paste or short pastry, cut out in fancy shapes and stuck on to the edges of previously heated dishes with a mixture of flour and white of egg.

In the same way, borders are made of small croûtons of bread, cut into various shapes and fried in butter, which are also stuck on to the inside edge of the serving dish with a mixture of flour and white of egg.

Fancy jelly shapes arranged in a border round a dish (*Larousse*)

The edges of cold dishes can have a similar border around them made of jelly cut into the shape of croûtons.

Vegetable borders, for hot entrées, are prepared in a similar manner.

Finally, the term *bordure* (border) is also applied to the round or oval-shaped metal utensils, plain or patterned, which are put in the dish to keep various elements of the garnish in place.

Ring (border) of béatilles à l'ancienne. BORDURE DE BÉATILLES À L'ANCIENNE—Fill a round, plain, buttered border mould with a veal or chicken *Mousseline forcemeat à la crème* (see FORCEMEAT). Poach gently in the oven in a *bain-marie** (pan of hot water).

When cooked, remove from the oven and allow to stand for a few moments for the forcemeat to settle. Turn the border out on to a round dish.

At the last moment, fill the middle with a ragoût composed of lambs' sweetbreads, cocks' combs and kidneys, truffles and mushrooms, in a *Velouté sauce* (see SAUCE) flavoured with Madeira-laced *Truffle fumet* (see FUMET). Garnish with slivers of truffles heated in a little concentrated meat stock.

Ring (border) for brains à la piémontaise. BORDURE DE CERVELLE À LA PIÉMONTAISE—Butter a plain round ring (border) mould and fill it with rather compact *Risotto* (see RICE). Press the rice in well. Put the mould in the oven for a few minutes to heat it thoroughly.

At the last moment, turn out on to a round dish. Fill the middle with little escalopes of *Calf's brains à la poulette* (see OFFAL OR VARIETY MEATS) mixed with sliced mushrooms. Decorate the brains with a circle of thin slices of truffles, heated in a little concentrated meat stock.

Egg ring (border) Brillat-Savarin. BORDURE D'OEUFS BRILLAT-SAVARIN—Fill a plain border mould with *Veal forcemeat à la crème* (see FORCEMEAT) and poach in the oven in a *bain-marie** (pan of hot water). Turn out on to a round dish. At the last moment fill the middle of the dish with eggs scrambled with Parmesan and diced truffles. Sprinkle with grated Parmesan, pour over a little melted butter and brown the top quickly in a very hot oven.

Egg ring (border) à la princesse. BORDURE D'OEUFS PRINCESSE—Prepare as *Egg ring (border) Brillat-Savarin*, using scrambled eggs with asparagus tips and truffles. In the same manner variously prepared eggs can be served, such as scrambled eggs with crayfish, shrimps, *fruits de mer*, mushrooms, truffles, tomatoes, etc.

When these ingredients are served as Lenten entrées, the borders should be made of *Cream fish forcemeat*. See FORCEMEAT.

Fish forcemeat ring (border) with various garnishes. BORDURE DE FARCE DE POISSONS—These rings, which are served as Lenten fare, are made of *Cream fish forcemeat* (see FORCEMEAT) of pike, whiting or other fish, moulded and baked as described above.

They are filled with a ragoût of fish or shellfish, the following being particularly suitable for the purpose: *Ragoût of fruit de mers* in *Shrimp*, *Nantua* or *Normande sauce*; oysters and mushrooms in *Velouté sauce*; *Mussels à la poulette*; Shrimp tails; slices of lobster or spiny lobster *à la crème* or *à l'américaine*; *Purées* or *salpicons* of various fish with truffles and mushrooms.

Ring (border) of frogs' legs vert-pré. BORDURE DE GRENOUILLES VERT-PRÉ—Prepare the frogs' legs as described in the recipe for *Frogs' legs in aspic à l'ancienne* (see ASPIC), coating them only with *White chaud-froid sauce* (see SAUCE), then cover with jelly.

Prepare a jelly ring decorated with little circlets of truffles.

Season cooked and well-drained green asparagus tips with oil, vinegar, salt and pepper.

To serve. Turn the ring out on to a round dish, put the frogs' legs on it, overlapping them slightly, fill the middle with a salad of asparagus tips, blended with some concentrated aspic jelly to impart to them a more solid consistency and complete the decoration with a nice round truffle dipped in jelly.

Game forcemeat ring (border) with various garnishes. BORDURE DE FARCE DE GIBIERS—These are made of *Game forcemeat à la crème*. See FORCEMEAT.

These rings are usually filled with purées or *salpicons** of game in *White* or *Brown sauce*. See SAUCE.

Piping a border of duchess potatoes through a forcing-bag

Potato ring (border). BORDURE DE POMMES DE TERRE—This is usually made out of *Duchess potato mixture* (see POTATOES), which is piped through a forcing-bag on to a buttered dish, or moulded by hand into a ring, the height depending on the nature of the garnish.

The middle of the dish is filled with the ingredients prescribed, such as little slices of cooked fish, covered with *Mornay sauce*; slices of various shellfish; hashes of various kinds of meat; vegetables cooked in butter, etc.

Generally speaking, this potato ring (border) is sprinkled with grated Parmesan and the top browned in the oven or under a grill. Before being browned the ring should be brushed with beaten egg.

Ring (border) of sole à la normande

Rice ring (border) with various garnishes. BORDURES DE RIZ—These rings (borders) are usually prepared out of *rice pilaf*, *risotto*, or rice cooked in consommé and bound with egg, put into buttered ring moulds.

Press the rice well into the mould. Set the mould in the oven for a few minutes and, at the last moment, turn the rice out of the mould on to a serving dish.

Fill the middle of the dish with various ingredients, such as: mixed ragoûts in *White* or *Brown sauce*; various *salpicons*,* etc.

Semolina ring (border) with various garnishes. BORDURES DE SEMOULE—Prepare like *Rice ring*, using semolina cooked in consommé and bound with egg.

Ring (border) of sole à la normande. BORDURE DE SOLES À LA NORMANDE—Prepare a *Cream fish forcemeat* (see FORCEMEAT), bake and turn it out on a round dish. Fill the centre with a *ragoût* of mussels, shrimp tails and mushrooms, bound with *Normande sauce*. See SAUCE.

Arrange on the ring little sole fillets which have been rolled up and cooked in white wine. Put on each fillet an oyster, poached and debearded. Cover with *Normande sauce* and decorate with thin strips of truffles. Put round the border crayfish cooked in *court-bouillon** and on the ragoût, arranged in a dome, smelts or gudgeon fried in breadcrumbs.

Veal or chicken forcemeat ring (border) with various garnishes. BORDURES DE FARCE DE VEAU, DE VOLAILLE—Prepare the ring of the forcemeat indicated as described in the recipe for *Ring of béatilles à l'ancienne*.

Turn the ring out on to a round dish. Fill the centre with a simple or mixed garnish, as indicated in the recipe.

The following are particularly suitable for such a garnish: *Veal amourettes à la poulette*, *Cocks' combs and kidneys à la crème*, slices of chicken in *Velouté sauce*, *Lamb's or calf's brains à la poulette*, *Veal or chicken hash à la crème*, simple or mixed *salpicons*,* in *White* or *Brown sauce*, or *Purée of chicken in Velouté sauce*, eggs scrambled with various ingredients, fresh vegetables dressed with butter or cream, *Macédoine of vegetables*, blended with butter or cream, various mushrooms *à la crème*.

Cold rings (borders) for entrées or sweet dishes. BORDURES FROIDES D'ENTRÉES, D'ENTREMETS—These borders are usually made of aspic or fruit jelly. Cold entrée borders can also be made out of *foie gras*, ham, game, chicken or fish mousses.

Rings (borders) for sweets (desserts). BORDURES D'ENTREMETS—These are made from various compositions and can be prepared hot or cold.

For the latter, they are usually made from a *custard* (see CREAMS and CUSTARD) cooked in a *bain-marie** (pan of hot water) and the mould is generally caramelized.

When quite cold, the rings (borders) are turned out on to a serving dish and the middle is filled with various mixtures, such as macédoines of fruit, whipped cream flavoured with vanilla or other flavouring, purée of various fruit, etc.

Dessert rings can also be made from *Dessert rice* (see RICE) and *semolina*.* Whether cold or hot, they are filled with macédoines of fruit or any other mixture suitable for a hot sweet.

Custard ring (border) with mirabelles à la vosgienne. BORDURE DE MIRABELLES À LA VOSGIENNE—Prepare a kirsch-flavoured *Custard cream*. See CREAMS.

Fill a plain ring mould with straight sides, previously coated with caramel, with this composition and cook in a *bain-marie** (pan of hot water). Allow to cool completely before turning out.

Cook the mirabelles in syrup. Prepare whipped cream or *Crème Chantilly*. See CREAMS.

Turn out the kirsch cream ring on to a dish. Wipe off any liquid around the ring. Fill the middle with well-drained mirabelles. Before serving, top fruit with whipped cream. Serve with mirabelle sauce laced with kirsch.

Rice ring (border) with cherries. BORDURE DE RIZ AUX CERISES—Fill a buttered ring mould with *Dessert rice* (see RICE). Heat the mould for a few minutes in the oven. Turn it out on to a round dish. Fill the centre with stoned cherries simmered in syrup, and combined with a little gooseberry jelly.

Rice ring (border) à la créole. BORDURE DE RIZ À LA CRÉOLE—Butter a Savarin ring mould and fill with sweetened dessert rice.

Fluted and plain ring moulds (*Larousse*)

Turn out this border on to a round dish and fill the middle with about 20 half slices of pineapple, poached in vanilla-flavoured syrup.

Decorate with preserved cherries and lozenges of angelica. Heat in the oven and serve with rum-flavoured *Apricot sauce*. See SAUCE.

Rice ring (border) Montmorency. BORDURE DE RIZ MONTMORENCY—Fill a buttered ring mould with sweetened dessert rice, pressing it in well to ensure that there are no holes. Cover and cook in the oven for a few minutes. Then remove and turn out on to a round dish.

Fill the middle of the dish with stoned cherries, cooked in syrup and well drained, laying them out in layers and putting a layer of hot *French pastry cream* (see CREAMS) between each layer of cherries. Finish with a layer of cherries, piling them slightly into a dome shape. Sprinkle the top with crushed macaroons, pour over some melted butter and glaze quickly in a scorching-hot oven. Serve kirsch-laced *Cherry sauce* separately. See SAUCE.

Semolina ring (border) filled with various fruit. BORDURE DE SEMOULE GARNIE DE FRUITS—Fill a buttered ring mould with sweetened dessert semolina, pressing it well into the mould. Heat for a few minutes in a low oven.

Turn the border out on to a round dish. When ready to serve, fill with various fruit, cooked in vanilla-flavoured syrup and well drained, such as: halved apricots, sliced pineapple, cherries, pears and apples in quarters, etc.

Heat in the oven for a few minutes. Pour over a few tablespoons of liqueur-flavoured apricot or other fruit sauce which goes with the filling.

BORIC (Acid). BORIQUE—Sometimes used as a preservative agent. See BORAX.

BORSCH—See SOUPS.

BOTER MELK OR BUTTER MILK (Belgian cookery) —Boil 2 quarts (litres) of butter milk with a relative quantity of pearl barley and a little brown sugar. Cook together for $1\frac{1}{2}$ or 2 hours and, just before serving, blend in a little corn-flour (cornstarch) diluted with cold water.

Another popular way of dealing with butter milk is to cook it with pearl barley and then add some treacle (molasses) to it.

Butter milk is also cooked (and this not only in Belgium but also in Northern France) with vermicelli, rice, semolina and tapioca. Currants, sultanas and cooking apples are sometimes added.

BOTTLE. BOUTEILLE—Oenology, the science which deals with wine, gives the following definition to the word bottle: 'A glass phial of various shapes and colours according to the nature of the wine it is intended to contain'. This means that Bordeaux wines should not be bottled in Burgundy wine bottles and vice versa. No doubt this law can be transgressed when it is a question of ordinary simple table wines, in fact, most of these wines are sold in so-called Saint-Galmier bottles. As far as bottles of very old wines and wines of great growths are concerned, their contents must be decanted into carafes for serving, for the custom of serving bottles of very old wines out of wicker cradles is not approved by the gastronomes.

(1) Double litre; (2) Litre; (3) Half-litre; (4) Bordeaux bottle; (5) Anjou fillette; (6) Demi-Anjou; (7) Anjou; (8) Maconnaise; (9) Champagne; (10) Burgundy; (11) Saint-Galmier; (12) Chianti bottle; (13) Alsatian so-called 'flute' wine bottle

Contents of bottles in France—Here is the text of a decree concerning the application of the law of January 1st, 1930:

Article 1. Under the conditions of paragraph 3 of article 2 given below, it is forbidden to put on sale or to sell wines other than sparkling wines, wines imported in bottles and wines intended for export, in bottles other than:

(1) Bottles known as *bordelaise*, *bourguignonne* and *mâconnaise*, the type and capacity of which are indicated in the table appended to the Bill passed on June 13th, 1866, concerning trade usages;

(2) Bottles which correspond to the following characteristics:

Type	*Capacity*
Double litre	200 centilitres
Litre	100 ,,
Half-litre	50 ,,
Saint-Galmier	90 ,,
Anjou..	75 ,,
Demi-Anjou	37·5 ,,
Fillette d'Anjou or (Fillette) de Touraine	35 ,,
Rhine wine	72 ,,

The capacity indicated in paragraphs (1) and (2) above is that of a receptacle measured at neck rim at a temperature of 15°C. This capacity has a tolerance of 2%.

Article 2. It will not be permitted to use bottles the appearance of which answers the description given in Article 1 which have not the legal minimum capacity, unless these bottles bear a label indicating their capacity.

In the case where, in accordance with the preceding paragraph, a label is used, this should bear, in addition to the indication of the minimum capacity, the indication of the degree of alcohol contained in the wine, where such indication is compulsory.

Article 3. The conditions laid down in this decree are not applicable to:

(1) Bottles containing wines made before the publication of this decree and put into the above-mentioned bottles before the said publication;

(2) Receptacles other than bottles, such as carafes, cellar jugs, pitchers, etc., in which wines are served for consumption on the premises.

BOTULISM. BOTULISME—Serious infection caused by anaerobic bacteria (the organism involved is *Clostridium botulinum*) which develop in canned meat, fish or vegetables, both home- and factory-made. It differs from ptomaine poisoning in that the substances affected by the botulism baccilus (ham, pork produce and other canned goods) show no sign of putrefaction although at times they do have a peculiar sour smell.

The disease manifests itself by gastric pains, occasionally accompanied by attacks of vomiting, and by constipation which resists all medicines. Later, marked disturbances of vision, such as double vision and loss of power to accommodate the eyes, symptoms of soft palate, etc., appear. It is often very serious and can cause death. It must be treated only by a doctor.

To avoid the occurrence of botulism only properly-sterilized canned goods must be used. Vacuum, even a perfect one, is not a sufficient guarantee, because anaerobes develop even in the absence of oxygen. So far as food pickled in brine is concerned, it should contain at least 10% of sodium chloride. If vinegar is used for pickling, its acetic acid content should be more than 2%. Finally, all suspect canned foods and those having a rancid smell, however slight, should be avoided, as should foods showing signs of fermentation (bubbles of gas, bulging lids).

Members of the *Bouche du roi* carrying in the collation

BOUCHE DU ROI—Under the old régime this term was used to describe the service which dealt with the kitchens of the Royal household.

These services, under certain kings, at times employed over 500 people (most of whom only worked for six months each year), were exclusively concerned with the King's table and were absolutely distinct from the so-called common service, which was in charge of kitchen and supply arrangements for the officers and certain members of the royal household.

Bouche du roi included the following: the actual service dealing with food supplies, the Pantler's office and the Royal Butler's office.

The Pantler's office had charge of everything concerned with the King's tableware, bread and all accessories of the table. The personnel consisted of thirteen heads of service, four *assistants*, one *keeper of table service*, one *sommier*, one *washer-up* and several boys whose job it was to assist the high-ranking officials in charge of these various posts.

The Butler's office was mainly concerned (as its name implies) with the beverages to be served to the King. This service consisted of thirteen *heads of service*, five *assistants*, four *sommiers* (officers in charge of directing convoys of pack animals carrying baggage whenever the King travelled or was at war).

It was the head of the Butler's office who had to take to the King's closet (*cabinet*) a loaf of bread, two bottles of wine, two bottles of water, two napkins and some ice for His Majesty's canteen every day, before His Majesty was up.

This canteen, which really constituted the King's emergency stock (and which he—no doubt—shared with Molière one evening) remained in the King's closet (*cabinet*) so that his needs could be satisfied promptly should he require a drink. The tasting of these emergency stock beverages were carried out by the officers of the Royal Butler's office before the first valet of the King.

The personnel of the Royal Butler's office also included four wine bearers, two palfrey drivers and several boys.

When the King went hunting the first wine runner used to carry a chest, covered with a red cloth bearing the arms of France, containing two silver flagons, one with wine, the other with water, biscuits, bread, fruit, jams and table linen. The palfrey driver 'drove a horse carrying baskets in which were various cold viands and other dishes, sufficient for two meals'.

The most important service, naturally, was for the

BARQUETTES AND TARTLETS

(*From the original French edition of* Larousse Gastronomique)

CAKE. Quatre-quarts

actual Royal kitchens. This consisted of the following: two *ordinary equerries*, eight *serving equerries*, four *master-cooks*, four *cooks in charge of roasting*, four *soup cooks*, four *pastry-cooks*, three *galopins* or kitchen errand boys, who were the *commis* of the kitchens of those days.

In addition, there were four *water carriers*, four *fuel carriers*, four *keepers of the table service*, two *ushers*, five *sommiers*, two *heralds*, four *armchair-carriers*, valets of *sert-d'eau* and four *washers-up*.

The Royal household food supply service, which, as we have said, also included a separate department of the *common kitchen*, as distinct from the Royal kitchen, was obviously an important one. To these services were also added those of the other members of the Royal family; the Queen's, the Dauphin's, the Dauphine's, bringing up the total of servants and officials to a great number.

Until the end of Louis XIV's reign, all the officials of the Royal household were members of the aristocracy; some of them even belonged to the most illustrious families in the kingdom.

All the supplies for this service were bought by these gentlemen. But towards the end of the reign of Louis XIV, owing to severe fiscal laws at the time, these supplies became prohibitively expensive and the high-ranking noblemen no longer sought this excessively onerous position and the duties had to be passed on to rich burghers, who paid a very high price to obtain them.

BOUCHÉES—This is the name of little puff pastry patties, baked blind (empty) and filled with various compositions.

There are also various kinds of *petits fours* called *bouchées*. These *bouchées* are chocolate sweets with various centres: praliné, nougat, toffee, liqueur-flavoured creams, etc. They are manufactured in factories.

A great number of recipes for the preparation of puff pastry *bouchées* will be found in the section entitled *Hot hors-d'oeuvre*. See also *Puff pastry cases* (patty shells). See DOUGH.

BOUDY—Apples of a very beautiful appearance but rather mediocre in taste. Because of their beauty they are used mainly for decorating fruit baskets. They can also be cooked.

BOUFFOIR—French word for the bellows which the butchers use to force air under the skin and into the cellular tissues of the carcases.

BOUGRAS (Périgord cookery)—Soup prepared from cabbage, leeks, onions and potatoes, using water in which black puddings were cooked for stock.

This soup, much appreciated in Périgord, is cooked mainly at Shrovetide when pigs are slaughtered and the delicious Périgord black puddings are made. Here is the recipe:

Bring the water in which the black puddings were cooked to the boil, put in it for 5½ pints (2½ litres) of water, the heart of a curly green cabbage, cut into slices and blanched, carrots, turnips, leeks, celery and onions in quarters. Simmer gently for 40 minutes. Add 2 large potatoes (400 grams) cut into thick round slices and cook together for 35 minutes.

Fifteen minutes before serving drain some of the vegetable garnish, cut into slices and fry to colour slightly. Sprinkle with flour, moistened with a few tablespoons of stock and add to the soup (this is called *fricassée* in Périgord, and is added to most soups). Pour the boiling soup into a soup tureen over very thin slices of home-made bread.

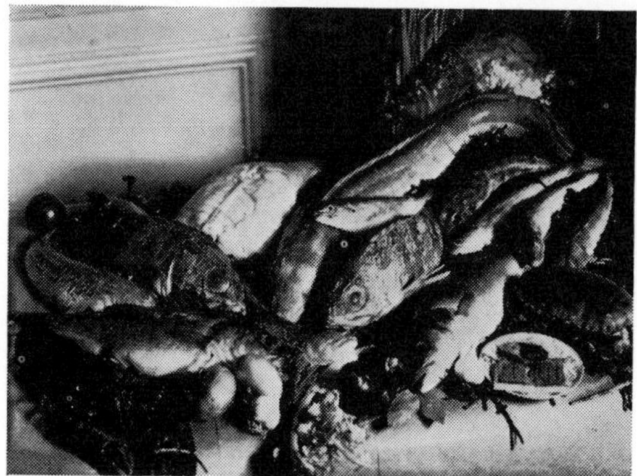

Ingredients for a Marseilles bouillabaisse (*Larousse*)

BOUILLABAISSE—Most dictionaries define *bouillabaisse* as a Provence dish made out of fish cooked in water or white wine, flavoured with garlic, parsley, saffron, pepper, bay leaf, etc. This 'etc.' no doubt means all the other essential ingredients of bouillabaisse, such as oil and tomatoes, without which there would be no bouillabaisse.

All along the Mediterranean coast, from Cap Cerbère to Menton, a great variety of bouillabaisses is prepared, all slightly different from each other, but, to the purists, there is only one real and authentic bouillabaisse and that is the one made in the Mediterranean region from Marseilles to Toulon. All the other bouillabaisses, however succulent they may be (and those made at Nice, Menton and many other places are exquisite), do not exist for the true connoisseurs of this saffron-flavoured soup.

These lovers of bouillabaisse invest this preparation with divine origins, attributing its invention to Venus. They say that the goddess of love took the fancy one day to prepare this soup as a treat for her handsome husband Vulcan, mainly with the purpose of inducing sound sleep in him, sleep which Venus planned to exploit for her own ends. In the time of antiquity it was considered that saffron-flavoured fish soup acted as a soporific, but this opinion is disproved today.

Numerous writers have sung the praises of bouillabaisse, in prose and in verse. Méry has dedicated to it a poem, in which, among other things, he tells us what fish to use for it. True, in his list of the *fruits de mer*, indispensable for this soup, he forgets to mention the spiny lobster, whiting and various other sea foods which are a must for the bouillabaisse.

Méry tells us that the credit for the invention of this fish soup goes not to Venus, but to a certain abbess of a Marseilles convent. He says:

'*Pour le vendredi maigre, un jour, certaine abbesse*
D'un couvent marseillais créa la bouillabaisse.'

'For a Friday abstinence meal, one day, a certain abbess
Of a Marseilles nunnery created the bouillabaisse.'

This does not seem acceptable, for we find mention of various fish soups of the ancient Greeks, which could very well be considered as a kind of bouillabaisse.

But Méry, who is not bothered by such trifles, goes on to tell us what is a real bouillabaisse and what fish should go into the making of it:

Ecoutez bien ceci, vieux cuisiniers novices,
Qui faites des homards avec des écrevisses,
Et qui croyez qu'on peut, chez Potel ou Chabot,
Traduire mon plat grec en tranches de turbot.
L'heure est enfin venue où notre capitale
Peut joindre à ses banquets la table orientale,
Et donner aux gourmands, chez le restaurateur,
Un ragoût marseillais et non un plat menteur.

A ce plat phocéen, accompli sans défaut,
Indispensablement, même avant tout, il faut
La rascasse, poisson, certes, des plus vulgaires.
Isolé sur un gril, on ne l'estime guère,
Mais dans la bouillabaisse aussitôt il répand
De merveilleux parfums d'où le succès dépend.
La rascasse, nourrie aux crevasses des syrtes,
Dans les golfes couverts de lauriers et de myrtes,
Ou devant un rocher garni de fleurs de thym.

Puis les poissons nourris assez loin de la rade,
Dans le creux des récifs: le beau rouget, l'orade,
Le pagel délicat, le saint-pierre odorant,
Gibier de mer suivi par le loup dévorant,
Enfin, la galinette, avec ses yeux des bogues,
Et d'autres, oubliés par les ichthyologues
Fins poissons que Neptune, aux feux d'un ciel ardent,
Choisit à la fourchette et jamais au trident.

Hearken to me, old cooks and new,
All those who make lobsters out of prawns
And think that one can, Chez Potel or Chabot,
Translate my dish into slices of turbot.
The hour has come at last, when our capital
Can add oriental dishes to her banquets
And give the gourmands in a restaurant
A real Marseilles ragoût, and not a lying dish.

For this Phocaean dish, accomplished without fault,
Above all, is indispensible the rascasse,
'Tis true, a very common fish.
Served on a grill alone, it does not find favour,
But in a bouillabaisse it does exude
A marvellous aroma on which success depends,
The rascasse feeds in crevasses, in quicksands,
In bays shaded with laurel and myrtle bushes
Or around rocks covered with flowering thyme.

Then the fish which feed away from the roads,
Among the reefs: the beautiful red mullet and orades,
The delicate sea-bream, the sweet-smelling Saint-Pierre,
Sea-game escaping from the devouring sea-perch,
And finally, the galinette, with its boops' eyes,
And others, forgotten by the ichthyologists,
Fine fish, that Neptune, in the fire of a blazing sky,
Spikes on a fork, and never on a trident.

In some regions, notably in Perpignan, potatoes are added to the bouillabaisse and often the saffron is omitted, which brings this soup nearer to the *chaudrée** or the *cotriade*.* At Sète a garlic-flavoured fish soup is made which is somewhat similar to the Flemish *water zootje*.* And finally various places specialize in *bourrides*,* which are, in fact, a kind of bouillabaisse, or, perhaps, more like the *cotriades**, similar to those cooked by the Breton fishermen.

Ingredients for bouillabaisse—The Provence bouillabaisse, or, more correctly, the Marseilles bouillabaisse, for this is how it is chiefly referred to, must be made of the following fish: rascasse, chapon, saint-pierre, conger-eel, lophius (angler-fish), red mullet, rouquier, whiting, sea-perch, spiny lobster, crabs and other shell-fish. (Many of the fish used for the bouillabaisse, such as the traditional *rascasse*, are not found except in the Mediterranean, they are virtually unknown in England and America, and no English name for them exists. To make up for these non-existent varieties of fish, many others obtainable both in England and the U.S.A. can be recommended as suitable for the bouillabaisse, such as gurnet, mackerel, small turbot, fresh tunny, perch, pike, grayling, trout, eel-pout and various rock fish.)

All these fish, both those with a firm flesh and those with tender flesh, should be cut into uniform-sized pieces. To these ingredients, which are essentially Mediterranean fish, no mussels or other such molluscs should be added, as is the wont of many Paris restaurants.

To make enough bouillabaisse for 8-10 persons you will need about 6½ pounds (3 kilos) net, of fish and crustacea.

Method of preparation. Put into a high-walled big casserole 1 cup (200 grams) of chopped onions, 3 large seeded and chopped tomatoes, 8 small cloves (40 grams) of pounded garlic, a sprig of fennel and 3 sprigs of bruised parsley, a sprig of thyme, a bay leaf and a piece of dry orange peel. On top of all these vegetables and aromatics first put the crustacea, then on top of these the firm-fleshed fish. Sprinkle with 1 cup (2 decilitres) of olive oil and season with salt and freshly-ground pepper. Add a good pinch of powdered saffron with enough water to cover the fish completely.

Boil briskly, with a lid on, for 7 to 8 minutes. Then add the fish with delicate flesh, such as whiting and red mullets, and cook together, still allowing to boil briskly. Total cooking time of a bouillabaisse does not exceed 14 to 15 minutes.

Arrange the pieces of fish and crustaceans on a large, deep round dish standing on another deep dish containing slices of home-made bread. Strain the soup over these, sprinkle the soup and the fish with roughly chopped parsley and serve everything together at the same time.

Note. Some authorities prescribe two-thirds chopped onions and one-third chopped leeks for bouillabaisse.

Instead of moistening the bouillabaisse with water, fish stock (prepared in advance out of fish heads and trimmings), can be used.

The bread used for the bouillabaisse should be neither toasted nor fried. In Marseilles special bread, called *marette*, is used for this purpose.

To make good bouillabaisse, one of the essential points to observe is to cook it as quickly as possible—which results in the soup having the right consistency.

To obtain this consistency, some authorities suggest the addition of a spoonful or two of butter at the last moment. To us, the use of butter in a Provençal dish seems to be quite wrong and we feel that it is possible to give the bouillabaisse the desired smoothness without resorting to the addition of butter as a liaison. Some Paris restaurants, where the bouillabaisse is supposed to be a great speciality, serve it in too thick a soup, which is a pity.

Bouillabaisse Borgne (Provençal cookery)—This kind of bouillabaisse, which has nothing in common with the real Marsellaise bouillabaisse, is called *l'aigo-sau-d'iou* in Provence. This is how it is made:

Cook some potatoes cut into circles ⅛ inch (½ centimetre) thick slowly in fish stock prepared as described in the recipe for *Bouillabaisse à la parisienne*.

When the potatoes are done, slip into the stock very

fresh eggs, one by one, taking care not to break them. Poach these eggs.

Pour the soup into a tureen over slices of bread, and arrange the potatoes and the poached eggs on another dish. Sprinkle with parsley and serve the two dishes at the same time.

Cod bouillabaisse. BOUILLABAISSE DE MORUE—This dish, which is prepared as *Bouillabaisse à la parisienne*, is a kind of stew rather than a soup. For method of preparation, see COD.

Ocean bouillabaisse. BOUILLABAISSE DE L'OCÉAN—Although the bouillabaisse is essentially a Mediterranean, if not a Provençal, dish, a kind of bouillabaisse is made on the Atlantic coast, for which we give the recipe below:

Heat 6 tablespoons of olive oil and 2 tablespoons of butter in a big saucepan and fry in it 5 big chopped onions, a pound of potatoes cut into slices, and 4 chopped leeks. Add a little thyme, savoury and fennel, a bay leaf, 4 cloves, 4 cloves of garlic, 2 stalks of celery, 4 peeled and chopped tomatoes and a pinch of saffron.

Cut into slices 4 whitings, 1 conger-eel, 3 red mullets, 3 mackerels, a few sardines (fresh), 2 small lobsters or 2 crabs and some Dublin Bay prawns, cut into chunks.

Season with salt, pepper and a little cayenne pepper and add enough dry white wine and water to cover the fish.

Separately, cook 1 quart (litre) of mussels and, when done, discard the shells and add the mussels and the liquor they were cooked in, to the fish.

Bring to the boil then simmer gently on the edge of the burner for 30 minutes.

Fry some slices of bread until golden and pour over them the strained fish stock. Arrange the fish on a separate dish and serve at the same time as the soup.

Bouillabaisse à la parisienne—Fry briskly $\frac{3}{4}$ cup (150 grams) of chopped onion and 6 tablespoons (75 grams) of chopped leeks (using only the white parts) in $\frac{3}{4}$ cup ($1\frac{1}{2}$ decilitres) of oil, without allowing them to colour. Moisten with 3 cups (6 decilitres) of white wine, then add 1 quart (litre) of water. Add to this stock 4 peeled, seeded and chopped tomatoes, 4 crushed cloves of garlic, a sprig of thyme and a bay leaf. Season with salt, pepper and a good pinch of powdered saffron. Add to this stock heads and trimmings of fish intended for another dish. Cook briskly for 20 minutes and strain through a fine strainer.

Pour this stock over the fish for the bouillabaisse: gurnet, red mullet, whiting, conger-eel, weever, spiny lobster and mussels. All these fish and crustaceans should be cut into regular chunks and laid flat in a deep pan, the mussels, well washed, should be placed on top and the whole seasoned with salt and pepper and sprinkled with chopped parsley and oil.

Cook briskly for 15 minutes. At the last moment effect a liaison by adding 3 tablespoons of kneaded butter.

Arrange the fish in a *timbale*.* Pour the soup into another *timbale* over slices of bread (cut from the long thin kind of loaf), grilled and rubbed with garlic.

Sardine bouillabaisse. BOUILLABAISSE DE SARDINES—Heat some oil in a shallow frying-pan and fry 1 chopped onion and 2 leeks. Add a big tomato, peeled, seeded and chopped, 2 pounded cloves of garlic, 1 bay leaf, 1 sprig of fennel and a small piece of orange peel.

Moisten with 3 cups ($\frac{3}{4}$ litre) of water. Season with salt, pepper and a pinch of saffron.

Add 6 sliced potatoes, not too thinly cut (waxy potatoes are best for this dish as they are less likely to disintegrate). Cook with a lid on.

When the potatoes are nearly done, arrange on top of them 2 pounds (1 kilo) of fresh sardines, cleaned out, scaled and washed. Cook for 7 or 8 minutes.

Strain the soup over the slices of home-made bread laid in a deep dish. Arrange the potatoes and the sardines on another dish. Sprinkle with chopped parsley.

Spinach bouillabaisse (Provençal cookery). BOUILLABAISSE D'ÉPINARDS—This dish, called locally the *bouiabaisso d'espinarc*, in no way resembles the *bouillabaisse provençale*. It is essentially a home dish, which is very popular in Marseilles. Here is a recipe contributed by the great master of Provençal cuisine, J. B. Reboul:

'Pick over and wash 2 pounds (1 kilo) of spinach, cook for 5 minutes in boiling water, then dip into cold water and drain, press with the hands to extract all water and chop.

'Put $\frac{1}{4}$ cup ($\frac{1}{2}$ decilitre) of oil into an earthenware casserole, add a chopped onion, previously fried lightly without browning, and the spinach. Cook on a low fire for 5 minutes, stirring all the time.

'When the spinach is nicely seared, add five sliced waxy potatoes. Season with salt, pepper and a little saffron. Moisten with a quart (1 litre) of boiling water, add 2 chopped cloves of garlic and a sprig of fennel, and leave to cook, covered with a lid, on a low flame.

'When the potatoes are cooked, break into the pan 4 eggs and cook gently. Serve the dish as it is.'

BOUILLANT—In the olden days this name was given to a small puff pastry patty, generally filled with a *salpicon** of chicken, which had to be served 'boiling hot'.

These small puff pastry pies were usually served as a hot *hors-d'oeuvre*. See HORS-D'OEUVRE, *Hot hors-d'oeuvre, Small patties and rissoles*.

BOUILLANTE—This name was given in the past to a soup, which, by definition, had to be served 'boiling hot'.

In barrack-room slang this soup was also known by the name of *mouillante*.

BOUILLE—French name for a vessel used for transporting milk.

BOUILLETURE OR BOUILLITURE (Anjou cookery)—A kind of *matelote*,* made mainly of eel, moistened with red wine, thickened with kneaded butter, garnished with mushrooms, little onions and—a local touch—with prunes.

This *matelote** is served garnished with slices of toast. Hard boiled eggs cut into quarters can also be added, but this is very rarely done.

BOUILLI—Abbreviation of *boeuf bouilli*, i.e., boiled beef.

In the history of mankind the method of cooking meat by boiling it in water, which necessitates the use of earthenware or metal utensils, obviously came later than cooking direct on the naked fire, such as grilling or roasting. The discovery of the method of boiling meat has certainly had the greatest influence on the subsequent development of the culinary art.

Brillat-Savarin dedicated paragraph II of *Méditation VI* to the subject of boiled beef together with a lively criticism of those who like it.

'Boiled beef is a wholesome food which appeases hunger promptly and is quite easily digestible but by itself has no great restorative powers, as in the process of boiling the meat loses a part of the juices which can be converted into animal matter.'

This assertion is rather debatable, since modern experts tell us that the only nutritive part of the *pot-au-feu** is not the stock but the piece of meat used for preparing it.

The master also adds that boiled beef loses half its weight.

He then goes on to enumerate, rather sarcastically, various classes of people who eat boiled beef:

'First—the stick-in-the-muds who eat it because their parents eat it and who, following this practice with blind submissiveness, even expect to be imitated by their children.

'Secondly—the impatient, who abhor inactivity at table and have formed the habit of pouncing upon the first thing that is served (*materiam subjectam*).

'Thirdly—the couldn't-care-less brigade, who, not being blessed with the sacred spark, consider meals as forced labour, putting all that can nourish them on the same level and behaving at table "like an oyster in its bed".

'Fourthly—the devourers, having an appetite of which they try to conceal the full extent, who hasten to cram down into their stomachs the first victim which presents itself, to appease the gastric fires consuming them, to serve as a foundation for all the other consignments which they propose to dispatch to the same destination.'

Brillat-Savarin, who most certainly did not like boiled beef, adds sententiously that 'Professors never eat boiled beef, out of respect for their principles and because they know the incontestable truth that *boiled beef is flesh without its juice*'.

Brillat-Savarin's somewhat contestable pronouncements on the subject of boiled beef can perhaps be justified by the fact that in his day boiled beef out of the stockpot was served even at great banquets as a remove (separate course), which he emphasizes in a marginal note in which he says that 'boiled beef has disappeared from the really carefully planned dinners' and that it has been replaced by 'a roast fillet, turbot or a matelote'.

For recipes for *Boiled beef*, see BEEF.

BOUILLON—French term for stock or broth. Normally in cookery this describes the liquid of the stockpot. In classical cookery terminology this liquid is usually called *consommé blanc*, to distinguish it from *clarified consommé*, also referred to as *double* or *rich consommé*.

Plain white stock serves as a basis for all soups, clear and thickened. It is also used instead of special basic preparations (highly seasoned beef broth, veal broth, veal broth doubled with chicken stock, etc.) for making white or brown sauces.

For the method of preparation of *Stock* or *Consommé*, see SOUP.

Stock is a basic liquid obtained by prolonged boiling of meat and vegetables in slightly salted water.

The *bouillon* was and remains one of the basic elements of French cookery, both in modest home kitchens and in the most sumptuous establishments.

Clear soup is a food of mediocre nutritive value (which can, however, be increased by the addition of pasta products, bread and various substances) but an excellent 'quickener' of digestion and a stimulant which tones up the heart and slightly raises the blood pressure. It has an action, so far still shrouded in mystery, similar to that of coffee and chocolate which, from the moment it is ingested, creates the sensation of well-being, even before a small part of it can be absorbed, and this makes it a 'nervine' food, similar to these beverages.

Clarification of bouillon. CONSOMMÉ BLANC SIMPLE—The object of clarifying *bouillon*, as the name indicates, is to make ordinary *bouillon* from the soup kettle more limpid. The process also improves the taste because the operation is accomplished not only with white of egg but with a given quantity of lean beef and vegetables cut into very small dice.

The *bouillon* clarified in this way is then called *consommé*.

In domestic cookery, stock is served without clarification. This *bouillon* or stock (which is served as a soup after adding various garnishes, principally some form of pasta) is made with a number of elements, some nutritive (beef and fowl), others aromatic (carrots, turnips, leeks, parsnips, onion, celery, garlic, cloves).

This is called white *consommé*. It is used not only for making soups, but also to add to stews and braises.

The *bouillon*, also called simple *consommé* to distinguish it from clarified *consommé* (often called double *consommé* in *grande cuisine*), must have a delicious flavour.

If the cooking has been done correctly, the *bouillon* or stock will be clear. That is why in domestic cookery it should not really be necessary to clarify *bouillon*.

Method of clarifying bouillon. Put 1½ pounds (750 grams) of lean meat and 2 leeks cut up into small dice into a deep pan with a thick flat bottom. Add a fresh white of egg.

Mix these ingredients with a whip. Add 2½ quarts (litres) of lukewarm *bouillon* from the marmite. Continue to whip the contents of the pan until boiling is established.

Draw the pan to the corner of the fire and *simmer* (not boil) for 1½ hours.

Pass the *consommé* through a cloth.

Bouillon de noce (wedding soup) (Périgord cookery)—This Périgord clear soup is really a version of *olla-podrida*.* Four different kinds of meat are used as a nutritive basis for it, namely: beef, a veal knuckle, a stuffed chicken and a turkey.

All these are cooked in stock flavoured with the usual vegetables with the addition of Swiss chard. This stock is coloured by adding to it onion, fried in lard until golden.

Vermicelli is added to the soup and it is served in Périgord at important gala dinners.

Cereal bouillons (stocks). BOUILLONS DE CÉRÉALES—These decoctions have a rather thick consistency and are in no way unpleasant to the taste. They can easily be adapted for a particular purpose by adding fruit juices or other substances to them. They are rich in assimilable mineral substances and soluble nutritive matter which, being responsible for giving vegetable embryo the nutriment necessary for growth, have a particularly beneficial effect on growing children. According to Dr. Springer's formula, a soup spoonful each of wheat, oats, barley, rye, maize and bran have to be boiled for a long time in about 3 quarts (litres) of water, until the liquid is reduced to 1 quart (litre). After cooking, strain and add either salt or sugar. This formula can be modified by adding buckwheat or leguminous plants, as in Dr. Comby's formula, which uses, for the same process, 1 ounce (30 grams) of each of the following substances: wheat, barley, crushed maize, white dried beans, lentils and dried peas.

Herb bouillon (stock). BOUILLON AUX HERBES—The following is the formula given in the 1884 Codex for the old-fashioned herb stock:

Fresh sorrel leaves	40 grams
Fresh lettuce leaves	20 grams
Fresh chervil leaves	10 grams
Sea salt	2 grams
Fresh butter	5 grams
Water	1 litre

Wash the leaves, cook until done and add salt and butter. Strain.

Here is a formula for a vegetable stock for children, given by Dr. Méry and modified by Dr. Leclerc:

Carrots	45 grams
Potatoes	60 grams
Turnips	15 grams
Dried peas	6 grams
Dried beans	6 grams

Boil for 4 hours in 3 litres of water in a covered stock-pot. Allow to reduce to 1 litre and add 5 grams of salt.

Rice flour or other cereals are then added to this stock, or it can be used as a basis for various soups.

Quick meat bouillon (stock). BOUILLON DE VIANDE EXTEMPORANÉ—In a brochure which appeared about 1800, in an article entitled *Quick-made stock*, Cadet de Vaux describes how to prepare an excellent clear soup in half an hour.

The utensil recommended for this by Cadet de Vaux is a *fourneau-déjeuner*, which was heated either by burning paper or alcohol under it. To this day utensils similar to the one advocated by Cadet de Vaux can be found in shops specializing in camping equipment. Here is the actual recipe:

'Take 2 glasses, i.e. 10 ounces, of water, 4 ounces of meat, some carrot, parsnip, onion, celery (in all about 1 ounce) and if you wish to add an aromatic, a third of a clove and a piece of garlic the size of a lentil.

'Chop the meat, as the greatest division of substances yields the maximum of their nutritive elements. Soften the vegetables on red-hot ashes: softened in this way and cooked in their own juice, they have more taste and yield their sweet juices more easily. Cut them into thin round slices. To divide the clove, it is put between two sheets of paper and crushed with a blunt instrument. Treated in this way, it rapidly communicates its fragrance to the stock. If garlic is added, it should be scraped with a knife. Put everything into a saucepan, add water and salt, stir with a spoon and cover with a lid.

'Your stockpot thus prepared, heat it by burning paper under it. Six minutes is enough to bring it to the boil. It will be difficult to remove scum, so leave it. Paper, which burns too quickly, can be substituted by an alcohol burner. To do so, remove the saucepan, place it on a grid, put under it a spirit lamp with a thin, short wick. Once the stockpot has been heated, the smallest flame will be enough to keep it simmering.

'The stock requires no attention at all and you can forget it completely for about half an hour. It would even do no harm to leave it a little longer. After half an hour, however, it can be considered ready. The stock should be strained through a silk strainer.'

Note. According to Cadet de Vaux, the ordinary proportions for stock are 1 pound of meat per pint (a French pint equals nearly an English quart, i.e. 93 centilitres), 40 ounces in weight, and 4 ounces of vegetables per pound of meat.

Vegetable bouillon (stock). BOUILLON DE LÉGUMES—Good flavoursome clear soups can be made using only vegetable stock as a basis and vegetarian cookery books give many and varied recipes for these.

Clear vegetable soups can be used in children's diets to replace milk partially and in diets for invalids as lightly remineralizing diuretic beverages. With tapioca or vermicelli added, these soups acquire slightly more nutritive value.

BOUILLON—This used to be, and still is, the French name either for little restaurants serving meals mostly at a fixed price or for restaurants with a limited selection *à la carte*.

Before Duval, who, in 1860, created this type of restaurant, or rather improved it, so-called Dutch 'Bouillons' existed in Paris, but they had no success at all and disappeared very quickly.

BOUILLON AVEUGLE—A colloquial French expression which is applied to mediocre clear soup on the surface of which it is not possible to see any of those limpid little round spots of fat, which are called *eyes*.

It must be said, however, that a clear soup can be perfectly delicious even though *blind*, i.e. with all the fat carefully skimmed off.

BOULE DE NEIGE—Name given in certain regions of France to edible agaric.

BOULE DE NEIGE (pastry)—Cakes made in the shape of balls and covered with whipped cream all over.

These cakes are most frequently made of layers of fine sponge coated with butter cream.

The term is also applied to an iced sweet, made of bombe ice cream mixture set in a round mould and, at the last moment, covered with whipped cream. See SNOWBALL.

BOULE DE SON ('Bran Ball')—Slang term used to describe ration bread. It was thus called because of the relatively high proportion of bran which went into its preparation.

BOULETTE—This name is given to a dish prepared out of some mixture (forcemeat, hash or purée) which is given a spherical form. *Boulettes* are often made from pieces of left-over meat or fish.

Boulettes are dipped in egg and breadcrumbs and fried in deep fat. They are also cooked in the oven, after having been brushed with lard or butter.

BOUQUET. BOUQUET DE VIN—The wine bouquet is due to ethers and essences (or essential oils) which are extremely volatile. In the process of evaporation these essences release the multiple aromas pertaining to each wine.

The four elements which determine the quality of a wine are the colour, the bouquet, fruitiness and vinosity (the flavour and strength of wine). The quality of a wine lies in the right proportion of all these elements.

BOUQUET GARNI—Aromatic herbs or plants tied together into a little faggot. The proportion of these plants—parsley, thyme and bay leaf—is adjusted depending on the nature of the dish. *Bouquets garnis* can be *small*, *medium* and *large*. In the composition of the bouquet the strength of thyme and bay leaf must be taken into account and these aromatics should be used sparingly.

Simple bouquets are also used, prepared only of sprigs of parsley.

And, finally, for certain kinds of dishes, aromatic bouquets are made containing highly-scented plants and herbs such as *basil*, *celery*, *chervil*, *tarragon*, *burnet*, *rosemary*, *savory*, etc.

The bouquets are removed from stews and sauces before serving.

BOUQUETIÈRE (A LA)—Name of a garnish used for meat dishes. It is composed of various vegetables disposed in bouquets. See GARNISHES.

BOURBONNAIS—The Bourbonnais, ancient province of France, forms the whole of the department of Allier and a small part of Puy-de-Dôme, Creuse and Cher.

The 'Bourbonnichons' (i.e. natives of the district) are generally hearty eaters and enjoy good and copious country dishes.

The larder of this district is well stocked with various food products. Highest quality beef, mutton and pork are produced here. The rivers and ponds abound in succulent fish: carp, pike, eel, which are cooked *en matelote** or *au bleu.** The streams abound in trout and crayfish.

Very good game, both ground and winged, is also found in this district. Poultry raised here perhaps cannot be compared to that of Bresse, but is, nevertheless, excellent, particularly geese.

The vegetable gardens and the orchards of Bourbonnais produce choice vegetables and fruit.

Among the culinary specialities of this region are the following, the recipes for which will be found in alphabetical order in the book: *freshwater matelotes and stews*, *pike à la crème*, Montluçon and Moulin *meat pies*, *sheep's tongues with turnips*, *goose stew*, called *oyonnade* locally, *pompe aux grattons*, *potato pâté*, *mihior* or *millias*, rather similar to the one made in Languedoc, *cherry tarts*, *pancakes*, which are called *sauciaux* locally, *pear gâteaux*, the *gounerre*, which is a kind of potato pie, the *Gannat brioche*, *tarte bourbonnaise*, a healthy and pleasant country cheesecake for which the recipe is as follows: Take some sweet, fresh cream cheese without any trace of sourness. Pound it in a bowl with fine salt, 4 eggs, 4 tablespoons (60 grams) of very fresh butter and 4 tablespoons of flour. When the paste is very smooth and completely free from lumps, spread it in a buttered low pie-dish, indent 7 or 8 holes with a finger and put a piece of fresh butter the size of a cob nut in each. Bake in a slow oven for ½ hour. Sprinkle with sugar before serving.

Finally, in Allier and the neighbouring departments a great number of confectionery and pastry specialities are made, some of which are produced in factories and are very famous.

Beverages. The wines of Bourbonnais have an interesting bouquet. Among the most famous are those of Chemilly, Huriel, Couraud, Chareilles, Billy, Souvigny, Saint-Pourcin—these are little wines which are drunk locally and which are much appreciated by those who like light wines.

The mineral waters of Bourbonnais are very famous, especially those of Vichy.

From time immemorial Vichy has been a famous watering-place. Its hot mineral waters, which later, in bottles bearing white and black labels, were to take its name into all the corners of the world, were well known to the Romans. Numerous objects of antiquity discovered in the substratum of the present-day town bear witness to that, as do the remains of a Roman road from Feurs to Clermont-Ferrand, which passed near the springs.

In the middle ages, Vichy—a peaceful little village—was the seat of a castellany, which was acquired in 1344 by Pierre I of the House of Bourbon. His son, Louis II, in 1411 founded a Celestine monastery and it is to these monks, who propagated the virtue of its waters, that Vichy partly owes its fame.

The religious wars, from which this town suffered a great deal, arrested its progress to an extent. Under the reign of Henri IV its fame began to spread and in 1605 a general administration of mineral and medicinal waters was created in France. Vichy became its headquarters in 1648.

The popularity of Vichy water grew during the seventeenth and eighteenth centuries. Louis XIV protected its early fortune. The letters of Madame de Sevigné, who went there for a cure in 1676 and 1677, completed its rise to success. In 1716 Louis XV endowed the Vichy hospital. Louis XVI's aunts, Adélaide and Victoire, having undergone a successful treatment, decided to build a new establishment to replace the modest 'Maison du Roi' built in the reign of Louis XIII. The Vieux Parc was laid out during the First Empire. Later, in 1821, the Duchess of Angoulême laid the foundation stone of the establishment. Finally, in 1853, the mineral waters concession was granted to a company.

The many seasons which the Emperor Napoléon III held at Vichy, where he even had a villa built, added further lustre to the fame of this spa.

BOURGEOISE (A LA)—Name which is applied to various dishes, mainly to large pieces of braised meat, prepared *à la mode bourgeoise*. These dishes always include a garnish composed of carrots cut down to a uniform size, small onions and large dice of lean bacon. See GARNISHES and BEEF, *Top of rump à la bourgeoise*.

BOURGUEIL—Very famous wine made from the grapes gathered in Indre-et-Loire, in the commune of the same name.

BOURGUIGNONNE (A LA)—See the beginning of the article on BURGUNDY.

BOURRIDE (Provençal cookery)—For 2 pounds (1 kilo) of various small fish put the following ingredients into a small casserole: 2 quarts (litres) of water, 2 onions, 2 tomatoes, 2 cloves of garlic—all finely chopped—and a *bouquet garni.*

Add a little bitter orange peel, season, then add 2 good tablespoons of olive oil and a little saffron. Put in the fish and allow to boil fast for ¼ hour.

Strain the stock through a sieve, pressing the vegetables. Bind the stock with a liaison of 2 yolks of egg mixed with some *ailloli.** Simmer lightly and pour into a soup tureen on slices of bread. Serve the fish separately.

BOURRU (wine)—Term which in the past was used to describe spiced wine. Today, new wine is often called *Vin bourru.*

BOUTEILLER (Charge de)—This title in the olden days was given to the man in charge of the wine cellar of the king, of a prince, or of some other great aristocrat. At the court of the kings of France this post was always held by some of the highest ranking gentlemen in the kingdom. Today the word *bouteiller*—which in fact is hardly ever used—is synonymous with *sommelier* (wine waiter).

BOUT-SAIGNEUX—French butchery expression meaning the neck of a calf or a sheep.

BOUVILLON—The word *bouvillon* in French is applied to a young steer until it loses its first milk tooth.

BOUZY—White wine of the Champagne district which is classed among the best wines of this region.

BOWL. Bol—Little basin of varying capacity, generally made of porcelain, but can also be in earthenware, glass or metal.

This receptacle is sometimes used in France for hot drinks, coffee, chocolate or tea with milk served at breakfast.

The term *punch bowl* is applied to a bigger receptacle, usually made of silver, in which punch and mulled wine are prepared.

In French the word *bol* also applies to little china,

glass or metal finger-bowls put before guests at the end of a meal, before serving sweets and after serving fish, shellfish, etc.

In the past, porcelain, pottery, silver and even gold basins were used for this purpose. These were circulated around the table and the servant poured scented water on the fingers of the guests.

In the more distant past, special dining-room wash-stands were used.

The only vestiges left of these articles of furniture, which were widely used from the Middle Ages until the eighteenth century, are the little china or copper fountains that can still be found in antique shops or in old lodging-houses in the provinces.

In times gone by these could be seen in monastery refectories, in dining-halls of châteaux, palaces, stately houses, etc. Some were big, made of lead, stone, marble or bronze set in little niches in walls or placed on iron stands.

To realize how indispensable these articles were, it must be remembered that until the middle of the sixteenth century, forks were not used at table and that for a long time it was customary for two people to eat out of one bowl. It was only in the seventeenth century that the fork was introduced into more general use.

It was, therefore, essential to have washing arrangements handy for the guests actually in the room where the meals took place.

The finger-bowls which are in use nowadays are much less ostentatious. They should be used, too, in the most discreet fashion.

Fruit bowls. BOL AUX FRUITS—In the past this term figured on menus and described the item which we now call fresh fruit salad. See FRUIT, *Fruit salad.*

BOWELS. BOYAUX—Intestines of slaughtered animals. Pigs' intestines are mainly used in pork butchery for making *andouilles** and *andouillettes.**

These belong to the domain of pork butchery and are made of all the intestines except the smallest ones, which are used as casings for sausages, and *fat* intestines which are used in the preparation of certain sausages, notably Lyon sausages. For method of preparation see recipes for *andouilles* (see PORK).

Pigs' intestines are divided into two categories: the *big* and the *small*. The first include the *rectum* and the *caecum*; the latter are referred to as the *smallest*.

Before being used pigs' intestines should be prepared and cleaned with minute care.

BRABANÇONNE (A LA)—Garnish for large pieces of meat composed of endives and potato croquettes. This garnish is often supplemented by hop shoots cooked with butter or cream.

BRAINS. CERVELLE—Culinary name for the brain substance of edible animals. Because of their soft consistency they are considered as an easily digestible substance, often given to invalids and children; this digestibility is not reliably proved, as a great many people cannot tolerate them.

Before being put to use, brains must first be freed of any blood attaching to them, by soaking, and cooked in a *court-bouillon.** For their various uses, see OFFAL OR VARIETY MEATS.

BRAISE. BRAISER—To cook various food products by braising in a special utensil called a *daubière** or a braising pan.

BRAISING. BRAISAGE—Method of cooking which can be applied to most food substances. This is usually done in an air-tight pan adding very little liquid.

All the instructions relevant to braising will be found in the section entitled CULINARY METHODS.

Braising pan (braisière)

BRAISING PAN. BRAISIÈRE—Utensil which is made in all kinds of metal, tinned copper, nickel, aluminium, enamelled cast-iron, as well as in earthenware and fireproof porcelain.

This utensil, which is also called a *daubière*, is generally rectangular in shape and has a well-fitting deep cover on which live charcoals are placed, or rather used to be placed, as braised dishes are now done in the oven and the method of cooking by action of heat above as well as below is not used any more.

In restaurant (we might as well say bad restaurant) terminology, the word *braisière* is applied to any kind of a stock, made out of various meat trimmings and bones, which is used for the preparation of basic sauces.

This stock is used instead of *estouffade** and clear beef or veal stock, which along with white *consommé* should be used for the moistening of *roux.**

BRAMBLE (Blackberry). RONCE—Very common prickly bush whose berries can be used to make syrup and jam. The young shoots can be eaten like asparagus.

BRAN. SON—Envelope of the grain which is separated from the flour by milling.

BRANDADE—A method of preparing pounded salt cod which is very popular in Languedoc and Provence. This dish, like many of the specialities of this region, is flavoured with garlic and is prepared by stirring vigorously and constantly with a wooden spoon, maintaining the same moderate heat throughout the operation and adding oil little by little. See COD, *Brandade of salt cod.*

BRANDEVIN—Spirit distilled from wine. See SPIRITS.

BRANDEVINIER—Name used in France to describe a man who in some regions goes about the countryside with his still, for distilling spirit from wine, marc or fruit.

BRASSERIE—An establishment where beer and cider are made or sold. Breweries, of which there are a great many in Germany and in the eastern regions, were not established in Paris and other parts of France until the middle of the nineteenth century. Brasseries in modern times are cafés or restaurants where food and drink are served.

Certain types of brasseries used to serve as a meeting-place for politicians, artists, men of letters and bohemians. Among the brasseries which have either become converted into something else or have disappeared altogether, are the brasseries in Rue des Martyrs, where Nadar, Pelloquet and Privat d'Anglemont used to hold forth, where Villiers de l'Isle-Adam mused and brooded, where Baudelaire dreamt up ways of astounding people and where Courbet held long discussions with Carjat.

Brasserie Pousset, which at one time was the centre

where literary men and journalists went to seek refreshment and a pick-me-up after the theatre, in the end became the meeting-place of government and colonial officials. Other famous brasseries were the Brasserie du Petit-Poucet, where one could meet Ponchon and Grenet-Dancourt, where Séverine amused himself preparing beef salads for his friends, and Brasserie Steinbach in the Quartier Latin where Jean Moréas used to call for a chat with Maurice Maindron or Paul Mounet.

BRAZIL NUT. Noix du Brésil—Fruit of the bertholettia, a tree which can grow to 114 feet (35 metres) in height. It grows in Latin America, especially in Paraguay and Brazil. In France, this nut is also known as American chestnut. In South America it is called *juvia*; the Portuguese call it *castenas de maranon*.

Its shell, which has three sharp edges, is brown and hard. Its white kernel is similar in flavour to coconut and hazelnut.

BREAD. Pain—Dough made of flour and water, fermented and baked.

The cereals were first used in the form of a meal, then as a kind of cake made out of a mixture of meal or flour and honey, oil, sweet wine, various grains, fruit and meat.

The Hebrews, the Egyptians and the Chinese introduced flat cakes made out of flour and water dough baked without leaven. The discovery of fermented bread, no doubt an accidental one, which observation enabled people to repeat, is attributed to the Egyptians, who used the leaven of sour dough, left over from the previous bread-making, and the must of grapes, kneaded with flour and dried in the sun.

The use of fermented bread spread very quickly but did not supersede the old method of making unleavened flat cakes, which were the only bread known to the Roman soldiers. In the Middle Ages, under the name of *trenchers* they were used instead of plates and as dishes for cutting up meat; they were then eaten or thrown to the poor.

The making of bread—The flour, which must be kept for at least 15 days after milling, first of all goes through a kneading operation, which consists of moistening it with water after mixing it with yeast.

The leaven, which gives the dough the ferments (alcohol barm and associated fungus) necessary for transforming sugar into alcohol and carbon dioxide, is taken either from a previous kneading or can be a mixture of yeasts (brewer's yeast or special baker's yeast) when kneading is done with yeast, which is the usual method.

The flour is put in a bowl, a well is made in the centre, yeast and warm water are added and the mixture is left to ferment for 4 to 5 hours, to form the 'main leaven'. It is then 'refreshed' by adding an equal weight of flour to obtain the 'first leaven', then, after some time, more flour is added in lesser or greater quantity, depending on the time of the year, to obtain the 'second leaven' or *tout point*, which represents either half or a third of an ovenful or batch of loaves.

During the final kneading the required quantity of flour is added to it and the dough is moistened with warm salted water allowing on the average 1½ pounds (750 grams) of salt per 230 pounds (100 kilograms) of flour; this operation is called *frase* (kneading) and it is followed by *contre-frase* (second kneading) which is very hard work when it has to be done by hand and consists of moulding the dough into one lump, leaving it to rise, then allowing it to subside, dividing, stretching and kneading it into one lot again—and all these operations have to be done very quickly. In modern establishments they are done by easier and more hygienic methods in mechanical kneaders.

When the kneading is completed, a certain quantity of dough is removed, if necessary, for subsequent use, and the rest is left to stand, in a kneading-trough or in a similar receptacle, covered with a cloth.

Bread kneaded with leaven is whiter and has more taste than bread kneaded only with diluted yeast.

Through the action of leaven, the released carbon dioxide puffs up the dough and when it reaches double its original volume, it is divided into loaves, the underside is sprinkled with wholemeal flour, rice flour or finely ground maize (corn meal) and put in the oven.

The oven is heated to between 225-300°C. (437-581°F.), in such a way as to sear the whole surface of the loaf immediately, while the interior continues to ferment briskly. Carbon dioxide swells the dough, forms holes in the bread and causes the surface to bulge. When the inside temperature reaches 60°C. (140°F.), the starch is transformed into starch-paste and fermentation ceases when the temperature goes up to 80°C. (176°F.). When the inside temperature reaches 100°C. (212°F.), the crust loses a great proportion of water by evaporation (the crust of a loaf made of dough containing 45-48% of water will not contain more than 24%, while the crumb (soft part) will contain the same proportion as the dough).

When the temperature of the oven (which will have gone down while the bread was being put into it) reaches 200°C. (392°F.) the starch is roasted; water steam is then injected (or in more primitive bakeries the oven is simply sprayed with water) to prevent the formation of too thick a crust. The baking time varies according to the size of the loaves.

The total loss of water is proportional to the size of the loaf; to obtain 1,000 grams (2 pounds 3 ounces) of bread, 1,140 grams (2 pounds 5 ounces) of dough will be needed for loaves of 4 kilograms (8 pounds 3 ounces) and 1,670 grams (3 pounds 6 ounces) for loaves of 1 kilogram (2 pounds 3 ounces).

If the fermentation of the dough is excessive, carbon dioxide is released before the loaves are placed in the oven and the bread will be heavy and compact with a cavity between the crumb and the crust.

The alcohol, which forms during fermentation, evaporates during baking as well as carbon dioxide, which continues to be released during cooling. A condensation of steam takes place during this cooling-off period in newly-baked bread, which then begins to look greasy and shiny.

Qualities of bread—A good quality loaf should have a pale yellow or a light brown bottom crust and a golden yellow or light brown top crust, which should be thick, domed and resonant when tapped. Both the crusts should adhere to the crumb and together equal one-fifth of the weight of the loaf (the thicker the crust, the less water there is in a loaf). If the crusts of a slice of bread are pressed together the slice should quickly regain its original shape.

The crumb should be homogenous, without any white or yellowish lumps, without grey, red or black spots; it should not stick to the fingers; the holes in it should be uneven, not too big (which is a sign of badly-kneaded dough), nor too small (which is a sign of insufficient fermentation); the smell should be sweet, the taste clean and pleasant.

Too white a crumb is a sign of rice flour having been added; greyish-brown crumb shows that rye or buckwheat flour has been added.

Along with the traditional methods of bread-making, efforts have always been made and are still being made to render bread more nutritious, and to give it a better appearance.

Slightly brownish bread, made out of less bolted (lower extraction) flour, which used to be made in the country in days gone by, kept fresh for a long time, especially if barley or potato flour were added to the dough; its taste was very pleasant but this bread has almost disappeared from use in France owing to preference for white bread.

If kept for a long time, bread becomes stale, the crumb dries up and the crust grows soft. This phenomenon is not due solely to the loss of water (stale bread contains only about 1% less water than fresh bread), but to a partial transformation of starch into dextrine. By heating stale bread (which causes it to lose 3% of its water content), a sort of distillation process is achieved, moisture from the crust penetrates the crumb, giving it, for a short space of time, the appearance of fresh bread.

Varieties of bread—There are many varieties of bread, distinguishable by their composition, shape or weight. In France ordinary or household bread weighing from 2 to 4 kilograms (4 to 8 pounds), long and cylindrical in shape, is flattened on the top, and slashed with slanting or parallel markings. The *boulot* or *bouleau* loaf is the same shape, but floured on the top. The *polka loaf* is long or round, with a hard crust, slashed with lozenge-shaped decorations. A *split loaf* is made by joining two long loaves together; it is thicker and has less crust. The *round loaf* is of the traditional round shape, the upper crust having a domed top; the *crown loaf*, as its name implies, is circular in form.

Fancy loaves, sold by the piece and not by weight, are made out of highest quality flour and shaped either into batons, with a golden brown or floured surface, or into flat loaves or small rolls of various shapes.

The *Vienna loaf* is kneaded with a certain quantity of milk. The *tin* or *pan loaf*, square-shaped with a very thin crust, is used in France mainly for toast, canapés, garnish croûtons and sandwiches. Lastly, on the borderline between the domains of bakery and pastry-making we have brioche dough loaves and puff pastry croissants.

Bread containing some or all of the bran and germ of the grain and endosperm has always been advocated; these loaves, always darker in colour, theoretically are more nutritive but being less easily assimilated by the intestines, the advantages are rather problematical.

Wholemeal bread is made from a meal milled from and containing the entire wheat grain. In some parts of Germany very dark bread (pumpernickel) is made of coarse unbolted rye.

Flour for fine bread is usually wheaten, but in many countries rye is the principal bread grain. Barley bread, or rather bread made out of a mixture of barley and wheat, used to be made and kept fresh for a long time, but it was very coarse, as can be judged from the saying 'as coarse as barley bread', because it is very difficult to hull barley.

Rye bread, made of 15% bolted whole rye, has a heavy compact texture; bread made out of a mixture of rye and wheat (one part rye to three parts wheat) keeps well and is sold as quality bread.

'Gluten' bread, manufactured for diabetics, has gluten added to the dough; it contains up to 40% starch.

Unleavened bread is much less used than ordinary bread; it is still used in some countries, Sweden for example, where it is served with *hors-d'oeuvre*.

Adulteration of bread—The most prevalent method is to retain as great a proportion of water in bread as possible, but there are other fraudulent practices, involving the use of grain poor in gluten content and adding various 'improving agents' to the flour, thus rendering bread-making easier. These 'improving agents' are various chemical products. This process, condemned by all nutritionists, has contributed not a little to the disfavour in which bread is held by dieticians.

Digestibility of bread—Bread is a food which is used, and abused, more than any other, especially in France. For many it is the staple food, which children are taught —and forced—to eat with all other food; in many circles the quantity of bread consumed exceeds in volume that of all other foods put together.

Bread (good bread, that is) taken in moderate quantities is an excellent food, but it should not be consumed in excessive quantities.

The crust is more digestible than the crumb, both because being hard it has to be chewed with greater care and because one eats less of it. For the same reason, toasted bread is better for dyspeptics, who will thus be forced to chew it more thoroughly and will be less tempted to over-eat.

The difference in the composition of the crust and the crumb lies mainly in the latter's greater water content.

There are various prejudices concerning bread, the worst being the preference for white bread. This, having been reserved for the richer classes in times gone by, was always coveted by the less favoured classes. To satisfy them, the use of higher extracted flour was resorted to for the manufacture of 'rich' bread and artificially-bleached flour for the other kinds.

The principal drawback of excessively white bread, so popular at present, is that it does not maintain its fresh goodness for more than a day.

Methods for making good bread—Below we give, quoting from Carême, three Edlin recipes.

'Cooks', he writes, 'who travel with their gastronomically-minded masters can, from now on, by following this method, procure fresh bread every day.'

Ordinary method—'Put 5 pounds of flour in the mixing trough. Make a well in the middle and put in 3 ounces of yeast.

'Moisten with warm water and mix until the consistency of brioche dough is reached, kneading well and adding 2 ounces (¼ cup) of fine salt, diluted in a little warm water.

'Cover and put in a warm place to ferment and rise.

'After having left the dough in this condition for an hour or two, depending on the time of year, knead it again, then cover and leave for another 2 hours.

'Meanwhile heat the oven.

'Divide the dough into 8 equal parts and shape into loaves or whatever form you choose.

'Put them in the oven as quickly as possible. When baked, rub the crust with a little butter, for this gives it a fine golden colour.'

French rolled loaf. PAIN FRANÇAIS EN ROULEAU—'Put 5 pounds of sieved flour into a kneading trough. Knead it with 2 pints (4 cups) of milk, ½ pound of warm butter, 4 ounces of yeast and 2 ounces of salt.

'When all the ingredients have been mixed, knead with a sufficient quantity of hot water. Mix well, cover and leave for 2 hours. Then shape into rolls and put them on baking trays or tin-plated metal sheets and leave on the oven, or some other warm place, to rise for an hour. Bake in a very hot oven for 20 minutes.'

Loaf à la terrine or à la grecque. PAIN À LA TERRINE, À LA GRECQUE—'Put 5 pounds of fine flour into a big wooden mixing bowl, or into an ordinary bowl. See that both the vessel and the flour are slightly warm (put them on the oven or some other warm place an hour before beginning to make bread), add 3 ounces of yeast and a sufficient quantity of water or milk to make the dough rather soft (add 2 ounces of salt).

'After kneading thoroughly, cover and keep on the oven or in some other warm place for 3 hours. Divide into 8 loaves and put these into buttered terrines.

'Place in a very hot oven. When the bread is nearly baked, remove from the terrines and put on baking trays or metal sheets for a few minutes to let them brown a little.'

Consecrated bread. PAIN BÉNIT—Consecrated bread, which is distributed in churches of big towns, is most frequently made of fine brioche dough.

In the country the dough for consecrated bread is made like brioche dough using the following ingredients: 2 pounds (1 kilo) of sieved flour, 1 pound (500 grams) of butter, $\frac{2}{3}$ ounce (20 grams) of brewers' yeast, 1 pint ($\frac{1}{2}$ litre) of boiled milk and a pinch of salt.

Diet breads.—PAINS DE RÉGIME—Various diet breads for dyspeptics, diabetics, etc., are found in French shops under various trade names, depending on their composition and shape: slices of toasted bread, biscottes, gressins, longuets, etc., made with or without salt. All these types of bread are manufactured by the bakery industry.

English or tin loaf. PAIN ANGLAIS, DIT AUSSI PAIN DE MIE—This bread is baked in France specially for various culinary uses (croûtons, white breadcrumbs, etc.) or for making sandwiches, canapés served as *hors-d'oeuvre* or for toast served with tea.

English loaves can be of different shapes and weight. They are most frequently baked in rectangular tins, which makes it very easy to cut off the crust (used for making white breadcrumbs). Stale bread is often used.

This type of loaf is also used for making hollowed-out *croustades** in which various ragoûts, purées, etc., are served.

Finger rolls (I). PETITS PAINS AU BEURRE—*Ingredients.* 1 pound (500 grams) of sieved flour, 5 ounces (150 grams) of butter, 1 ounce (30 grams) of brewers' yeast, $1\frac{1}{3}$ cups (4 decilitres) of boiled milk, $\frac{2}{3}$ cup (2 decilitres) of fresh cream, a small pinch of salt.

Method. Using one-third of the flour, the yeast and the milk, prepare the leaven (in a hot bowl). When the leaven rises nicely, add it to the rest of the flour, which should be spread on the table in a circle with a well in the middle into which the butter, the cream and the salt have been put. Knead as brioche dough.

Put this dough into an earthenware bowl, sprinkled with flour, and cover with a cloth.

Leave to rise in a slightly warm place. Divide the dough into small parts, pat them into little boat-shaped rolls and bake in a hot oven.

Finger rolls (II), with milk. PETITS PAINS AU LAIT—*Ingredients.* 2 pounds (1 kilo) of sieved flour, $1\frac{1}{3}$ ounce (40 grams) of bakers' yeast, $\frac{1}{2}$ pound (250 grams) of butter, $1\frac{2}{3}$ cups (5 decilitres) of boiled milk, $\frac{1}{3}$ cup (30 grams) of fine castor sugar, a pinch of salt and a little warm water.

Method. Spread the flour on the table in a circle, into the well in the middle put the sugar, salt and butter; moisten with the milk and add a little warm water. Knead with the leaven and leave until the next morning.

Divide the dough into small (60- or 80-gram) pieces and shape into slightly oval rolls. Split the rolls slightly in the centre, brush with beaten egg and bake in a hot oven.

Finger rolls (III), with eggs. PETITS PAINS AUX OEUFS—These are made like *Finger rolls (I)*, replacing fresh cream by 4 yolks of egg.

Plaited bread. NATTE—Bread baked in the form of a plait.

Bread for soups. PAIN POUR POTAGES—This bread, which is made in the shape of a long thin roll and is sold only in big Paris bakeries, is prepared of dough very rich in gluten. These rolls are cut into very thin round slices and then dried in the oven, or they can be cut and hollowed out in various shapes. See CROÛTES.

Unleavened bread. PAIN AZYME—The Book of Exodus tells us that in their haste to leave Egypt the Jews forgot to bring yeast with them, and that for a long time after that they had to eat unleavened bread.

The Israelites perpetuated the memory of this privation by eating only unleavened bread during Pesach. This is how this bread is made:

Knead some sieved wheaten flour with water and salt into a slightly softish paste.

Put this paste, rolled out into round or square pieces one centimetre thick on metal sheets. Prick them all over and bake in a low oven.

Unleavened or offering bread. PAIN AZYME À HOSTIE—Sieve the flour through a silk sieve. Dilute this flour with enough slightly salted water to obtain a softish paste, as for wafers called *oublies*.

Pour this paste into special moderately-hot irons in such a way as to dry the paste without allowing it to colour. Leave to dry in the oven laid out on wicker trays. Store in a dry place in wooden boxes with well-fitting lids.

BREADCRUMBS—The French word *chapelure* comes from *chapeler* which used to mean to crush bread which had been dried very slowly in the oven.

There are white breadcrumbs, obtained by sieving stale white bread through a metal sieve with a fairly large mesh, used for crumbing objects destined for frying. Loaf bread, called 'English bread' in France, is generally used for this purpose. When French bread is used, the operation is easier if, after the removal of the crust, the bread is rolled in a lightly floured cloth. Then this bread passes much more easily through the meshes of the sieve, or through the holes in a strainer.

White breadcrumbs can be kept for two or three days. If one takes the precaution of drying the breadcrumbs gently above the stove, without allowing them to brown, they keep much longer.

Golden breadcrumbs are prepared by drying bread crusts in a very slow oven. Once dry and slightly coloured these crusts are pounded in a mortar (or crushed with a rolling-pin) and then passed through a wire-mesh sieve. This type of breadcrumb will keep indefinitely in a lidded glass jar in a dry atmosphere.

Golden breadcrumbs (if white breadcrumbs are not available) can be used for coating meat and fish with egg and breadcrumbs before frying, but they are mainly used for sprinkling over preparations which are cooked *au gratin*.

BREADCRUMB (TO). PANER—To coat an object with breadcrumbs before frying it in clarified butter.

Coat with butter and breadcrumbs. PANER AU BEURRE—To brush various meats, before grilling them, with plenty of melted butter, then roll in freshly grated breadcrumbs.

Coat with breadcrumbs à la milanaise. PANER À LA MILANAISE—As *à l'anglaise* but adding to the breadcrumbs one-third of their volume of grated Parmesan cheese.

Coat with egg and breadcrumbs. PANER À L'ANGLAISE—To cover various objects (fillets of fish, escalopes, cutlets, etc.) previously seasoned and dipped in egg beaten as for an omelette with a little oil, salt and pepper, with freshly grated white breadcrumbs (or failing that, with white toasted breadcrumbs), before frying them in clarified butter.

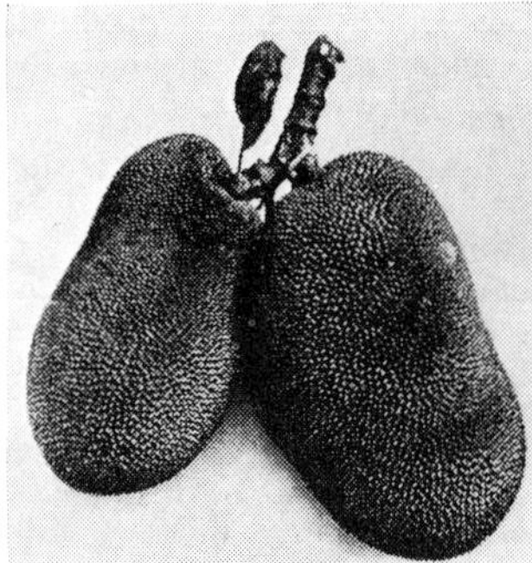

Bread-fruit

BREAD-FRUIT TREE. ARBRE À PAIN—A genus of plants which includes the sago palm and raffia palm.

It is a beautiful tree, its timber is soft and its leaves are deeply divided. It is a native of the tropical regions of Asia and the South Sea Islands. They are cultivated throughout the islands of the Asiatic archipelago and in the Pacific islands close to the equatorial region.

The tree attains a height of 50 to 65 feet. It contains a milky juice, thick and viscous, which is made into a kind of glue used for various purposes. The juice, which hardens on exposure to air, is used by the natives of the South Seas to waterproof canoes, etc. The timber, although not very hard, is used in the building of huts and canoes. The fibrous inner bark is beaten out and made into a kind of cloth. The leaves, which reach enormous dimensions, serve as roofing for dwellings and as wrapping for food. The dried spikes of the male flowers are used as tinderwood. The fruit itself is large and spherical and of a greenish-yellow colour; it provides an important article of food for a great many islanders. When fully ripe it has a sweetish taste, goes bad very quickly, is laxative and indigestible. But before reaching full ripeness (which is the moment chosen for gathering it) the flesh is firm and white, mealy and rich in starch, and has almost all the nutritive qualities of wheaten bread. It is cut in slices and baked or toasted on hot coals; or it can be baked whole in the oven until the outside skin acquires a darkish colour. Prepared in this way it is a valuable food, healthy and very nutritious; its taste recalls that of freshly-baked bread with a slight hint of artichoke and Jerusalem artichoke.

It is claimed that two or three of these trees produce a sufficient quantity of fruit to provide food for one man for a whole year. The seeds are also edible; they are roasted in the cinders or cooked in water, like chestnuts, which they resemble a little in taste and size.

A small quantity of fruit and the green ocrea of the bread-fruit tree are exported.

Another species of the bread-fruit tree, called the *jack tree*, has fruit structurally resembling the bread-fruit, which is eaten on a vast scale, but which is greatly inferior to the bread-fruit proper in taste. Its ocrea is eaten like chestnuts.

BREAD SAUCE (English cookery)—Sauce made of milk and breadcrumbs. It is served with roast game. (See SAUCE.) In England fried breadcrumbs are usually served at the same time as this sauce.

Bream

BREAM. BRÈME—A European freshwater fish. In appearance it resembles the carp. All the recipes given for carp can be applied to bream. (See CARP.) It is mostly used for *matelotes** and fish stews.

BRÈDES (Creole cookery)—This was the name given in some of the old French colonies to a dish made out of leaves of different plants, such as watercress, tips of pumpkin shoots, cabbage, spinach, lettuce. This dish is a speciality of Réunion Island; it is very refreshing and is served with *rice à la créole*.*

Cabbage brèdes. BRÈDES DE CHOU—Take a white cabbage. Trim each leaf removing the tough centre vein. Taking a few leaves at a time, shape into bundles and shred finely as for sauerkraut.

Cut some bacon into strips and fry it in a cast-iron casserole until it is light golden. Add a pinch of finely pounded ginger and a chopped tomato. Moisten with a little water. Allow to simmer for 20 minutes. Put the shredded cabbage into this sauce. Cook for about 1½ hours and turn into a vegetable dish, serving *rice à la créole** separately.

Lettuce brèdes. BRÈDES DE LAITUES—For 6 persons allow 3 to 4 heads of cabbage-lettuce. Wash the leaves. Cut them lengthways. Soak in cold water. Prepare in the same manner as *Watercress brèdes* but use less sauce and allow shorter cooking time.

Pumpkin brèdes. BRÈDES DE CITROUILLE—Take some tips of pumpkin shoots, about 8 inches in length, with their leaves and stalks. Detach the leaves one by one. Leave a piece of stalk ⅓ inch long on each leaf and peel off all skin and stringy parts. Scrape off all green knots. Wash carefully and leave to soak in cold water. Drain. Put some good fat into a casserole, add some diced bacon and brown a chopped onion in this mixture. Add a large, skinned, seeded and quartered tomato and some salt, garlic and ginger, pounded in a mortar. Simmer for a few moments. Add the prepared pumpkin shoots to the casserole and simmer gently without adding any water.

Spinach brèdes. BRÈDES D'ÉPINARDS—Prepare as above, blanching the spinach before putting it into the sauce.

Watercress brèdes. BRÈDES DE CRESSON—Wash and pick over the cress as for a salad. Put enough good fat into a *coquelle* (a cast-iron casserole) and add 5 ounces (150 grams) of thickly sliced bacon and a chopped onion. Fry until golden. Pound 2 cloves of garlic, a pinch of ginger and salt in a mortar and add to the casserole; add a peeled, seeded and sliced tomato. Allow to brown for a few moments, then add 1½ large glasses of water. Reduce the sauce slightly, and put in the cress to simmer until it is done. Serve with plenty of sauce and hand *Rice à la créole* separately.

Chicken giblets, previously cooked, can be used instead of bacon, and stock can be used instead of water for cooking the cress.

BRESOLLES—According to some culinary authorities, this dish was invented by the chef in charge of Marquis de Bresolles' kitchen who, naturally, called it after his master. Here is how it is made:

'Chop finely ½ pound (250 grams) of lean ham with onions, a few spring onions (scallions), some mushrooms and a clove of garlic. Season this forcemeat with salt, pepper and a little grated nutmeg. Then add a little olive oil.

'Put a layer of this forcemeat into a buttered earthenware casserole. On the top of the forcemeat lay thin slices of veal, beef or mutton and continue in alternating layers of forcemeat and slices of meat until the casserole is filled up to ⅛ inch from the top. Cover with a lid and cook in the oven.

'Turn out on to a round dish. Garnish with braised chestnuts and pour over some *Demi-glace sauce* (see SAUCE) flavoured with Madeira.'

Specialities of Bresse (*French Government Tourist Office*)

BRESSE—The name of this ancient part of France is known throughout the world for the excellence of the poultry raised there, which is rightly considered the best in France.

Bresse chickens and capons have been eulogized by all the 'Peers of the table' and numerous poets have sung their praises in verse.

BRESTOIS—Cake which used to be made in Brest. Here is the recipe:

Put 12 eggs and 3½ cups (500 grams) of fine sugar into a copper basin and whisk this mixture over a low heat as for Genoese pastry.

Add 5 ounces (1 scant cup) (150 grams) of sweet blanched almonds, pounded in a mortar with 3 whole eggs. Flavour this composition with a few drops of lemon essence, a little bitter almond essence and a small glass of curaçao. Whisk the mixture thoroughly to make it frothy and, at the last moment, add 1½ cups (375 grams) of melted butter and 3 cups (375 grams) of sieved (cake) flour. Blend well.

Put this mixture into buttered brioche moulds. Bake in a slow oven. This type of cake, if wrapped in foil, will keep in a perfect condition for a long time. It is a kind of 'travelling cake' (*gâteau de voyage*).

BRETON (Gâteau)—Although this gâteau is presented under the Breton banner it does not, in fact, originate in Brittany. It was created at about 1850 by a Monsieur Dubusc, chief of the Seugnot laboratories in Rue du Bac.

The *Breton* is usually made, or rather, used to be made, as a great number of these large cakes are no longer made nowadays, in the shape of a *gâteau monté*, a cake with *mille-feuilles*, or some other big piece of pastry superimposed on it. It was made out of almond biscuit paste.

The *Breton* was assembled by placing different cakes on top of one another, icing each with a different colour fondant icing and then decorating it.

BRETON FAR. FAR BRETON—A kind of cream flan (tart). This Breton speciality is made commercially.

BRETONNE (A LA)—Most dishes prepared *à la bretonne* include a garnish of beans cooked *à la bretonne*. (See BEAN, *White beans*). Thus *Leg* or *Shoulder of mutton à la bretonne* is roasted or pot-roasted (more rarely braised), and served with beans. See MUTTON.

There is also the *Purée bretonne* which is made of beans cooked *à la bretonne* and served, clarified, as a soup, or if a thicker consistency is retained, as a vegetable or a garnish for meat.

Finally, there is the *Sauce bretonne*, which is poured over poached or soft boiled eggs and braised fillets of fish. This does not contain any beans but is made by adding finely-shredded carrots, celery and leeks, lightly tossed in butter, to thick *velouté sauce* with cream, or to white wine sauce. See SAUCE and SOLE, *Sole à la bretonne*.

BRETONNEAU—An old name for turbot, used in Normandy.

BRIE—Name of an ancient province of France, situated to the east of Paris, with the town of Meaux as capital. This province in the past was divided into three regions: Brie champenoise (Meaux), Brie française (Brie-Comte-Robert) and Brie pouilleuse (Château-Thierry). These regions were part of the Government of Champagne.

The name of Brie is known throughout the world for the excellent cheeses which are produced there.

This region has no other gastronomical specialities. Its cuisine is the same as that of the Île-de-France and, therefore, similar to the one which constitutes the basis of Parisian cookery.

BRIE CHEESES—See CHEESE.

BRIGNOLE—A kind of dried plum which gets its name from the town of Brignolles (in the department of Var). It is used in compotes in the same way as dried apricots and prunes.

BRILL. BARBUE—Flat sea-fish, possessing a certain similarity to turbot, from which it differs by its smaller size, by its slightly more elongated shape and by the tiny scales which cover its skin. Its flesh is very delicate and very light.

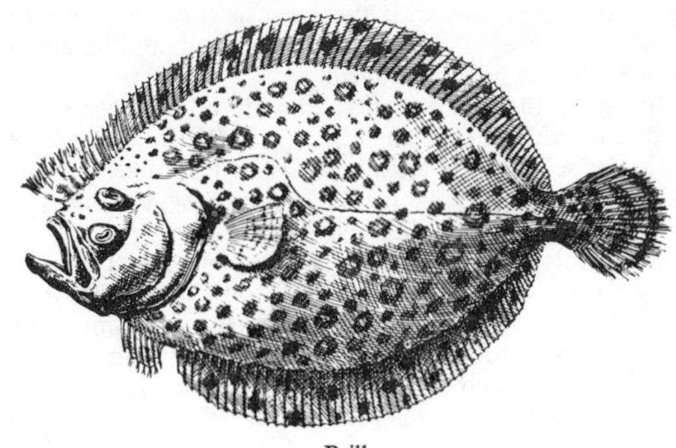

Brill

This fish abounds in all the seas of Europe, but the brill caught in the Atlantic ocean is of the greatest gastronomical value. While not the identical fish, *grey sole*, a species of flounder, seems to resemble *brill* the closest. Other species, the *dab*, the *winter flounder* and *lemon sole*, can all be prepared in the same way.

To clean the fish. Clean the brill by making a transversal incision under the head on the dark side. Scale on both sides and trim all round. Trim the tail to shorten it slightly and wash the fish. Depending on the final use for which it is intended, cut in half, in slices or in fillets.

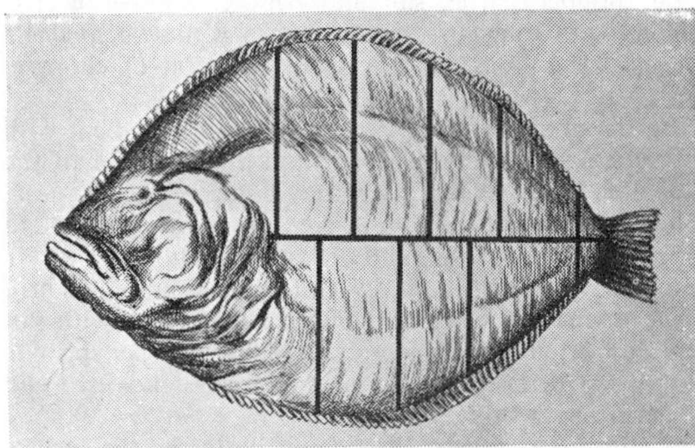

How to divide a brill

Brill à l'américaine. Barbue à l'américaine—Cook a medium-sized brill as described in the recipe for *Brill in white wine*.

Drain, arrange on a long dish and garnish with slices of a small lobster or crayfish *à l'américaine*. See LOBSTER.

Pour over *Américaine sauce* (see SAUCE) with the reduced (boiled down) liquor in which the fish was braised added to it.

Brill à l'amiral. Barbue à l'amiral—Put a 2-pound brill, scaled and slit lengthways on the dark side, on the buttered grid of a turbot-kettle or shallow pan. Season, pour in enough white wine fish stock (boiled down to the consistency of a *fumet**) to reach the level of the fish.

Bring to the boil. As soon as boiling is established, cover the turbot-kettle and put to cook in the oven from 25 to 30 minutes.

During cooking baste the fish with its own liquor, but only when the flesh is partly cooked. If basted earlier there is a risk of the brill splitting.

Drain the brill. Turn it out whole on to a large flat dish, dark side up. Remove all the dark skin. Turn the brill again, this time turning it on to a serving-dish. Trim off all the side bones without damaging the brill.

Serving. Wipe off carefully the liquid which may have come out of the fish on the serving-dish, dry the borders of the dish.

Heat for a moment in the oven. Cover the brill with *Normande sauce* made from the liquor left over from cooking the fish, strained, boiled down (reduced) and finished off with a little *Crayfish butter*. See BUTTER, *Compound butters*, and SAUCE, *White sauces*.

Dispose the following garnish around the brill: 24 oysters, fried in egg and breadcrumbs, 24 mussels *à la Villeroi*; 8 small scallop shells filled with crayfish tails *à la Nantua*, with the top slightly browned under the grill. Decorate the brill with 24 very thin slices of truffle, heated in butter and seasoned with salt and pepper.

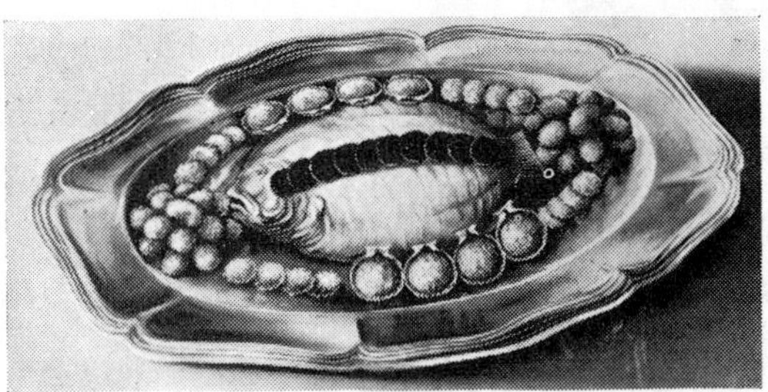

Brill à l'amiral

Note. The method of cooking *Brill à l'amiral* has been explained at some length as the method is rather similar for all large flat braised fish, except in so far as removing the dark skin and side bones is concerned, which, of course, could only apply to such flat fish as brill, turbot, large soles (U.S.A. flounders).

The braising of large fish should be done in very little *court-bouillon** and the stock or *fumet** used must be very well flavoured.

The sauce which accompanies braised fish can be prepared in advance, but it is an absolute must that the liquor in which the fish is cooked should be added to it, after it has been boiled down (reduced) to the desired degree.

There are variations on the theme of *Brill à l'amiral*: sometimes the fish is glazed by dotting it with crayfish butter and heating it in the oven; it is then surrounded with the garnish described above and the sauce served separately.

The garnish itself is sometimes modified. The shells containing crayfish tails are replaced by little boat-shaped tartlets or patties *à la Nantua*.

The garnish is completed by the addition of whole mushrooms cooked in *court-bouillon*.*

Brill à la Bercy. Barbue à la Bercy—Make a few longitudinal incisions on the back, on the dark side of a brill weighing 1½ pounds (750 grams), lifting the fillets lightly. Season inside and outside. Butter a long fireproof dish, sprinkle it with a tablespoon of chopped shallots and parsley and put the fish into it.

Moisten with ½ cup (1 decilitre) of white wine and ½ cup (1 decilitre) of concentrated fish stock boiled down to the consistency of *fumet*.* Scatter the surface of the brill with 3 tablespoons (50 grams) of butter divided into tiny pieces. Bring to the boil and put in the oven to cook for 12 to 15 minutes, basting frequently.

Three minutes before the end of cooking, put the dish in the hottest part of the oven to glaze the fish. The liquor should by this time be boiled down to the desired consistency.

Boiled or poached brill with various sauces. BARBUE BOUILLIE POCHÉE—Put the brill on a grid of a turbot-kettle or on a wire grill in a shallow pan, completely immersed in a cold *court-bouillon** composed of water and salted boiled milk in equal proportions.

Put on a moderate heat. As soon as boiling is established, skim off the impurities which rise to the surface of the liquid, draw the turbot-kettle to the edge of the burner, cover the brill with a napkin and leave it to simmer, so that the water just *shivers* imperceptibly, allowing 12 minutes cooking time per pound.

Remove the napkin, and lift the grid to drain the brill thoroughly.

Slide it on to a napkin-covered dish or on a special perforated dish. Garnish with boiled potatoes and fresh parsley.

Serve with one of the sauces recommended for boiled fish.

Depending on size, the brill can be cut in half or in portions before cooking.

To give the fish a more shiny look, it is usually brushed over with melted butter just before serving.

Brill à la bonne femme. BARBUE À LA BONNE FEMME—This is prepared as *Brill à la Bercy*, adding ¼ pound (125 grams) of raw, thinly sliced cultivated mushrooms and moistening with white wine and a few tablespoons of *Velouté sauce* (see SAUCE) based on fish stock.

Bring to the boil on the stove, then finish cooking in the oven. Glaze.

Brill à la Bourguignonne. BARBUE À LA BOURGUIGNONNE—Put a brill, seasoned with salt and pepper, into a buttered pan. Surround with 24 small glazed onions and 12 small mushrooms. Moisten with 2 cups (4 decilitres) of red (Burgundy) wine. Add a *bouquet garni.** Cook in the oven with a lid on.

Arrange the brill on a serving-dish. Dispose the garnish around and cover with the sauce prepared as follows:

Boil down the liquor in which the fish was cooked until it reaches the concentrated consistency of a *fumet*,* blend in 2 tablespoons of *Kneaded butter* (see BUTTER), boil for a few moments, add 5 tablespoons (80 grams) of butter, blend well and strain.

The brill can also be moistened with red wine fish stock boiled down to the consistency of a *fumet.**

After the fish is cooked, the stock is boiled down and mixed with a few tablespoons of *Espagnole sauce* based on fish stock (see SAUCE). After the sauce has been cooking for a few minutes, add butter to it.

Braised brill with various garnishes. BARBUE BRAISÉE—Put the brill, cleaned out as usual, seasoned with salt and either stuffed or not, as the case may be, on the buttered grid of a turbot-kettle, or wire grill in a shallow pan.

Put the grid with the fish into the turbot-kettle, on a foundation of sliced carrots and onions lightly fried in butter, little sprigs of parsley, thyme and a bay leaf.

Add enough cold concentrated fish stock until it reaches the level of the fish. Bring to the boil, then cook in a slow oven, basting frequently.

Drain the brill, trim it and, if it is not stuffed, remove the centre bone, to make serving much easier. To remove this bone proceed as follows: Put a large oval dish, generously spread with butter, over the fish, still on the grid. Turn the dish over so that the brill is on top, dark side up. Carefully separate the fillets, remove the central bone and close the fillets again.

Now again place a well-buttered serving-dish on the boned brill, turn the dish over and you will have the fish on the serving-dish white side up.

Garnish as indicated in the recipe. Cover with a sauce made to harmonize with the garnish used, a sauce to which, whatever its nature, concentrated and strained braising liquor must be added.

Braised brill may be moistened with red wine fish stock (reduced to the consistency of a *fumet**), in which case it can be served with all the garnishes recommended for fish prepared in this manner: *Bourguignonne*, *Chambertin*, *Mâconnaise*, etc. See GARNISHES.

Brill braised in white wine can be served with one of the garnishes normally used for fish cooked in white wine, especially those recommended for soles. It must be served with a sauce which goes with the garnish.

Brill Brancas. BARBUE BRANCAS—Scale and trim a brill weighing 1½ pounds (750 grams). Cut into uniform pieces.

Shred an onion, leek and half a heart of celery into a fine *julienne.** Put these vegetables into a small sauté pan with 2 tablespoons (25 grams) of butter and a pinch of salt. The cooking must be done on a very gentle heat and the garnish should, therefore, be prepared a little in advance. Do not allow to colour. When the vegetables are three-quarters done, add ¼ pound (125 grams) of equally finely shredded mushrooms. This *julienne** is called *bretonne*.

Peel 4 medium-sized tomatoes and remove seeds. Chop the tomatoes coarsely and put to cook in a little sauté pan in which a tablespoon of chopped onion has previously been sautéed in butter without browning. Add a little chopped garlic, salt and pepper. Simmer gently, stirring from time to time to obtain a *tomato fondue.** At the last moment add a small spoonful of chopped parsley.

Butter an earthenware ovenproof dish, sprinkle it with salt and freshly ground pepper and line it with half the vegetable *julienne** described above. Put a *bouquet garni** into one corner of the dish in such a way as to be able to take it out easily at the end of the cooking.

Spread the *julienne* evenly and put the pieces of brill on it, giving the fish its original shape. Season with salt and pepper, cover with the rest of the *julienne*, sprinkle with a few drops of lemon juice and moisten with 1 cup (2 decilitres) of white wine.

Scatter a few very small dabs of butter on the surface of the fish. Put on the stove. As soon as boiling is established, put to cook in a slow oven from 15 to 18 minutes, basting frequently.

Five minutes before taking out of the oven, put an even border of *Tomato fondue à la portugaise** around the brill. Wipe the edges of the dish carefully, glaze in a very hot oven and sprinkle with chopped parsley at the last moment.

This method of cooking, evolved from the Dugléré method of preparation, is applicable to a great number of fish, such as *young turbot*, *sole*, *whiting*, *fresh cod*, *plaice* (U.S.A. flounder).

The principle of cutting into pieces is generally adopted, but the fish may also be cooked whole.

Brill à la cancalaise. BARBUE À LA CANCALAISE—Cook the brill in white wine as described in the recipe for *Brill à l'amiral*. Drain thoroughly. Arrange on a serving-dish. Garnish with oysters poached in their own liquor, drained and with the beards removed. (The oysters can be laid out on the fish or disposed around it.) Cover with *Normande sauce* (see SAUCE) in which the reduced (boiled down) liquor left over from cooking the fish and the oysters has been incorporated.

Brill cardinal. BARBUE CARDINAL—Slit the fish on the dark side. Remove the central bone, taking care not to tear the white skin. Season the inside. Stuff the brill with a finely pounded *Pike forcemeat* (see FORCEMEAT) finished off with lobster butter (or crayfish butter, as this dish can be made with either of these crustacea).

Poach the brill in a little white wine. Drain, arrange on a serving-dish and garnish on top with slices of lobster or crayfish. Cover with *Cardinal sauce* (*I*) (see SAUCE, *White sauces*). Sprinkle with chopped coral.

Brill au chambertin. BARBUE AU CHAMBERTIN—Cook in concentrated fish stock made with Chambertin wine, as described in the recipe for *Brill à la bourguignonne*, making the sauce with Chambertin instead of Burgundy.

Usually, *Brill au chambertin* is garnished only with mushrooms cooked with the fish, whereas brill prepared *à la bourguignonne* is garnished with mushrooms and little glazed onions.

Sometimes the garnish is completed by the addition of *Fillets of sole en goujons*, i.e. cut up in strips, floured and fried in butter (see SOLE). This garnish is added to the dish after the sauce has been poured over the fish.

Brill in champagne, called à la champenoise. BARBUE AU CHAMPAGNE, DIT À LA CHAMPENOISE—Bone and stuff the brill with a *Cream pike forcemeat* (see FORCEMEAT) season with salt and pepper and put into a fireproof dish on a foundation of *julienne** of cultivated mushrooms lightly tossed in butter.

Moisten with dry champagne. Scatter very small pieces of butter on top. Bring to the boil and put in the oven to cook, basting frequently.

Drain. Add 3 tablespoons of *Velouté sauce* (see SAUCE) based on fish stock and 5 tablespoons of cream to the liquor in which the brill was cooked. Add butter to this sauce, pass through a strainer and pour over the brill. Glaze quickly in a very hot oven.

The brill may be served plain or garnished with *Fillets of sole en goujon* (see SOLE) fried in butter, which are arranged in bouquets at both ends of the dish.

Brill Chérubin. BARBUE CHÉRUBIN—Season the brill with paprika, put into a buttered pan on a foundation of a fine *salpicon** of carrots, leeks and celery, moisten with very concentrated fish stock and cook in the oven, basting frequently.

Drain the brill, arrange it on a long dish, surround with bouquets of very thick *tomato fondue*,* alternating with bouquets of truffles cut in large dice.

Reduce (boil down) the liquor in which the fish was cooked to the concentrated consistency of a *fumet*,* strain, add a *julienne** of sweet (red) pimentos lightly fried in butter; incorporate all this in *Hollandaise sauce* (see SAUCE) and pour over the brill. Glaze quickly in a very hot oven.

Cold brill with various sauces. BARBUE FROIDE—Cook the fish as described in the recipe for *Boiled brill*. Allow to cool in the liquor in which it was cooked, drain and arrange on a napkin-covered dish or on a dish with a perforated top which allows for draining. Garnish with fresh parsley or lettuce hearts. Serve with mayonnaise or any other sauce specially recommended for cold fish.

Cold brill can be garnished with hard boiled eggs, *macédoine* of vegetables, cucumbers, and, generally, with all garnishes ordinarily used for cold fish.

Brill with crayfish, called à la Nantua. BARBUE AUX ÉCREVISSES, DITE À LA NANTUA—Prepare (whole or in fillets) as *Brill with shrimps*, replacing shrimp tails by crayfish tails, and covering with *Nantua sauce*, with the reduced (boiled down) liquor in which the fish was cooked added to it. See SAUCE, *Compound sauces*.

Brill in cream au gratin. BARBUE À LA CRÈME AU GRATIN—Prepare as *Creamed cod au gratin*, using brill cut into pieces. See COD.

Brill à la dieppoise. BARBUE À LA DIEPPOISE—The brill may be left whole or filleted. Cook in a little white wine. Drain and arrange on a serving-dish. Surround with garnish *à la dieppoise* (mussels cooked in white wine and peeled shrimp tails). Pour over *White wine sauce* (*I*) (see SAUCE, *White sauces*) to which the concentrated pan juices have been added. Serve as it is or glaze in a very hot oven.

Brill Dugléré. BARBUE DUGLÉRÉ—Cut into pieces. Prepare as described in the recipe for *Bass Dugléré*. See BASS.

Brill à la fermière. BARBUE À LA FERMIÈRE—There are two ways of preparing fish (generally flat fish) *à la fermière*. We give both the methods below:

First method. Put the brill seasoned with salt and pepper, in a buttered oval fireproof dish, on a foundation composed of 4 tablespoons of *fondue** of the following vegetables: carrots, onions, leeks and celery, shredded and lightly cooked in butter. Cover the fish with similarly prepared vegetables.

Moisten with a few tablespoons of dry white wine or concentrated fish stock based on white wine reduced (boiled down) to the condition of a *fumet** (see STOCK, *Fish stock*). Scatter over some very small dabs of butter. Cook in a slow oven, basting frequently. When the fish is done, add 3 tablespoons of cream. Glaze in the oven.

Second method. Put the fish in a buttered dish, on a foundation of chopped onion lightly fried in butter. Cover it with sliced mushrooms. Moisten with red wine. Scatter some very small dabs of butter. Cook in the oven. Strain the pan juices, bring to the boil, thicken with kneaded butter. Add a little fresh butter, pour the sauce over the fish and glaze quickly in the oven.

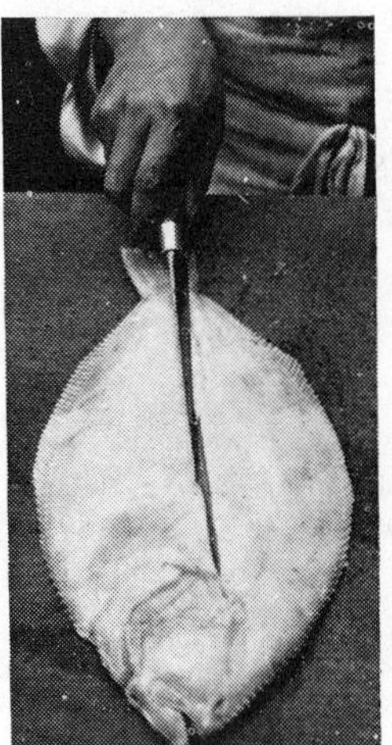
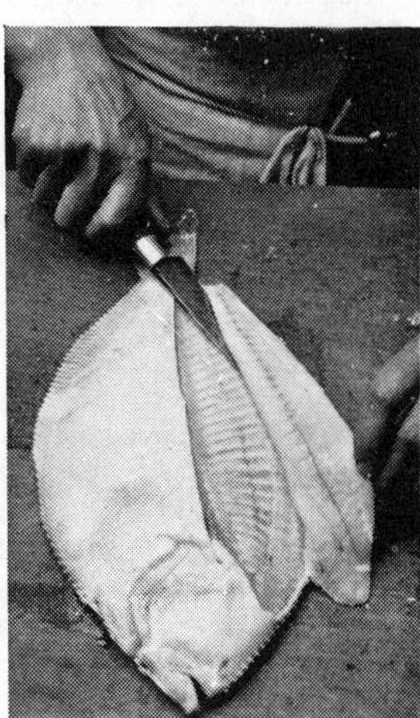

How to fillet brill (*Larousse*)

Fillets of brill. FILETS DE BARBUE—Brill, like other fish, is filleted in the following manner:

After dressing the fish, i.e. after it has been cleaned out, scaled and washed in the usual way, put it on the table dark side down. Slit it in the middle, right down from head to tail. Through this incision slide the knife under the fillets to lift them, pressing towards the edges to sever them completely from the body of the fish.

Proceed in the same way to remove the fillets on the dark side.

Put the fillets flat on the table, skin side down. Slide the blade of a thin sharp knife between the flesh and the skin, holding the fillets at one end so as to remove the skin in one motion.

All the methods of preparation given above for whole brill can be applied to fillets of brill. Recipes which follow can also be applied to them, as well as to whole brill or to fillets of other fish.

Fillets of brill à l'anglaise. FILETS DE BARBUE À L'ANGLAISE—Flatten the fillets slightly, and dip in egg and breadcrumbs.

Fry them in clarified butter until both sides are golden.

Arrange on a long dish and put some softened *Maître d'hôtel butter* (see BUTTER, *Compound butters*) on each fillet. Put decoratively cut half-slices of lemon round the border of the dish.

Note. Fillets of fish simply grilled and accompanied by melted butter and boiled potatoes are often served under the name of fillets of brill, or other fish, *à l'anglaise*.

Fillets of brill à la créole. FILETS DE BARBUE À LA CRÉOLE—Season the fillets with salt and paprika, dredge with flour, fry in a pan in butter or oil.

Arrange on a serving-dish. Surround with halved tomatoes cooked in oil, each filled with a spoonful of *Rice pilaf*, and sweet pimentos, peeled, cut in square pieces and cooked in oil. Add a tablespoon of chopped garlic and parsley to the sizzling hot oil left over from the frying. Sprinkle the fillets with lemon juice, then pour over the oil and serve.

Curried fillets of brill. FILETS DE BARBUE À L'INDIENNE—Season the fillets with salt and pepper and put into a fireproof dish on a foundation composed of ½ cup (100 grams) of chopped onions, lightly fried in butter, seasoned with curry powder and spiced with as much pounded garlic as can be held on the point of a knife.

Put on the fish 4 peeled, seeded and chopped tomatoes. Moisten with ¾ cup (1½ decilitres) white wine. Scatter tiny dabs of butter, cook in the oven for 10 minutes, basting frequently. Add 1 cup (2 decilitres) of thick cream. Finish cooking in the oven, basting frequently. Serve *Rice à l'indienne* separately. See RICE.

Fillets of brill à la Duxelles. FILETS DE BARBUE À LA DUXELLES—Season the fillets with salt and pepper, dredge with flour and fry in a pan in a mixture of oil and butter. Arrange on a serving-dish, on a foundation composed of a *duxelles** mixture, bound with *Tomato sauce* (see SAUCE). Garnish with slices of peeled lemon, sprinkle with chopped parsley and pour over it the butter left over from the frying, sizzling hot.

Fillets of brill Richelieu. FILETS DE BARBUE RICHELIEU—Dip in egg and breadcrumbs and cook in butter until both sides are golden. Arrange on a serving dish. Garnish with thin slices of truffles heated in butter. Put dabs of *Maître d'hôtel butter* on top. See BUTTER, *Compound butters.*

Fillets of brill à la toulonnaise. FILETS DE BARBUE À LA TOULONNAISE—Season the fillets with salt and pepper and dip them in egg and breadcrumbs. Fry in oil until both sides are golden.

Arrange on an oval dish on a bed of rather thick *Tomato fondue** (cooked in oil with chopped onion and a pinch of pounded garlic).

Surround with aubergines (egg-plant) cut in large dice, fried in oil. Put on the fillets a row of thin slices of lemon. Sprinkle with a few tablespoons of sizzling hot oil.

Fillets of brill à la tyrolienne. FILETS DE BARBUE À LA TYROLIENNE—Season the fillets with salt and paprika, brush with oil and grill on low heat. Arrange on a serving-dish on a bed of *Tomato fondue,** not too thick. Cover with onion rings fried in oil.

Fillets of brill Véron. FILETS DE BARBUE VÉRON—Cut the fillets of brill in half lengthways, season with salt and pepper, dip in melted butter and then in breadcrumbs, sprinkle with melted butter and cook under a low grill. Arrange on a serving-dish on a layer of *Véron sauce*. See SAUCE.

Brill à la florentine. BARBUE À LA FLORENTINE—Cook in very little concentrated white wine fish stock. Drain, arrange on a serving-dish on a foundation of leaf spinach cooked in butter. Cover with *Mornay sauce* (see SAUCE), sprinkle with grated cheese and melted butter and glaze quickly. (This method is mostly used for fillets cooked in white wine and always in very little liquid.)

When cooking whole fish, it is advisable to remove the central bone once it is cooked, and to trim it all round before arranging it on spinach.

Fried brill. BARBUE FRITE—This method is only suitable for brill of small size. After cleaning in the usual manner, soak in milk, lightly dredge in flour and deep fry in sizzling fat, preferably oil.

Drain the fish, dry with a cloth, season with very fine dry salt, serve on a napkin garnished with fried parsley and lemon.

Brill au gratin. BARBUE AU GRATIN—Using small-sized brill proceed as described in the recipe for *Sole au gratin*. See SOLE.

Grilled brill. BARBUE GRILLÉE—Put a medium-sized brill on a grill and make a few shallow incisions, season with salt and pepper, brush with oil or butter and grill on a low heat.

Arrange on a hot dish and garnish with slices of lemon and fresh parsley.

Serve separately *Maître d'hôtel butter* (see BUTTER, *Compound butters*) or any other sauce specially recommended for grilled fish.

Brill can also be grilled cut in slices or in fillets.

Jellied brill with various garnishes. BARBUE GLACÉE À LA GELÉE—Cook the brill, either stuffed or not, as the case may be, in very little concentrated stock, based either on white or red wine depending on the nature of the dish.

Allow it to cool in its own strained liquor. Take it out of the stock when it is quite cold. Trim and dry the brill and arrange on a serving-dish. Coat it with jelly, clarified in the usual manner. See JELLY.

Jellied brill can be served with various garnishes. All the garnishes recommended elsewhere in the book for *Cold salmon* can be applied to brill. See SALMON.

Brill à la mâconnaise. BARBUE À LA MÂCONNAISE—Bone a medium-sized brill, taking care not to tear the white skin. Season inside and stuff with fish forcemeat mixed with dry *duxelles** and chopped parsley.

Cook in a pan in concentrated fish stock based on red (Mâcon) wine, as described in the recipe for *Brill à la bourguignonne*.

Drain the brill thoroughly and arrange on a serving-dish. Surround with very small white cèpes, briskly fried in butter and spiced with chopped shallots. Cover with a sauce prepared as described in the recipe for *Brill à la bourguignonne*. Simmer (stew) small artichoke hearts in butter, fill with a *salpicon** of truffles *à la crème*, brown the top and use to put round the fish.

Brill à la marinière. BARBUE À LA MARINIÈRE—As *Brill in white wine*. Surround with *Marinière garnish* (see GARNISHES), cover with *Marinière sauce*. See SAUCE.

Brill à la ménagère. BARBUE À LA MÉNAGÈRE—Put the fish, seasoned with salt and pepper, into a fireproof dish, on a foundation of chopped onions, lightly fried in butter and spiced with pounded thyme and bay leaf. Moisten with red wine. Cook with a lid on.

Arrange the brill on a serving-dish. Thicken the pan juices with kneaded butter, bring to the boil, add fresh butter and pour over the fish.

Brill Mornay. BARBUE MORNAY—This method is chiefly used for fillets of brill.

Cook the brill in concentrated fish stock using very little liquid, arrange on a serving-dish lined with a layer of *Mornay sauce* (see SAUCE). Cover with *Mornay sauce*. Sprinkle with grated cheese (Gruyère and Parmesan mixed) and melted butter and brown the top quickly.

Brill with mushrooms. BARBUE AUX CHAMPIGNONS—Cook the fish whole, in fillets or cut in pieces, with mushrooms, in a concentrated white wine fish stock. Allow 20 carefully peeled mushroom caps for a brill weighing $1\frac{1}{2}$ pounds (750 grams). As soon as the brill is cooked, drain thoroughly, arrange on a serving-dish and surround with the mushrooms. Prepare a *White wine sauce I* as usual, incorporating the liquor in which the fish was cooked (see SAUCE). Serve as it is or glaze the fish quickly in a very hot oven.

Brill with mussels and other shellfish. BARBUE AUX MOULES—Cook the brill in very little concentrated fish stock. Drain it, arrange on a serving-dish, surround with mussels, cooked in white wine and taken out of their shells. Cover with white wine sauce or *Normande sauce* (see SAUCE) with the concentrated liquor in which the fish and the mussels were cooked added to it.

Brill cooked in this manner can also be garnished with other shellfish.

Brill à la normande. BARBUE À LA NORMANDE—Cook the brill in very little concentrated fish stock. Drain it well, arrange on a serving-dish and surround with the various elements of garnish *à la normande* (see GARNISHES). Cover with *Normande sauce* (see SAUCE) with the liquor in which the fish was cooked boiled down and added to it.

The method of preparation known as *à la normande* is mostly applied to sole, but may also be applied to all flat fish, such as turbot, brill, plaice, etc. See SOLE, *Sole à la normande*.

Brill with oysters. BARBUE AUX HUÎTRES—Cook the brill, whole or cut in pieces, in very little concentrated white wine stock. Drain it and arrange on a serving-dish.

Poach the oysters, remove beards and garnish the fish. Pour over white wine sauce to which the liquor in which the fish and the oysters were cooked have been added.

Brill sur le plat. BARBUE SUR LE PLAT—This method is chiefly used for brill of small size.

Proceed as described in the recipe for *Sole sur le plat*. See SOLE.

Brill à la portugaise. BARBUE À LA PORTUGAISE—Using brill, whole or cut in pieces, proceed as described in the recipe for *Bass à la portugaise*. See BASS.

Brill à la provençale. BARBUE À LA PROVENÇALE—As *Bass à la provençale*.

Brill in red wine. BARBUE AU VIN ROUGE—Cook the brill in very little concentrated fish stock based on red wine. Drain and arrange on a serving-dish. Prepare red wine sauce incorporating in it the liquor in which the fish was cooked, thicken with kneaded flour and butter or blend with *Espagnole sauce* based on fish stock (see SAUCE). Add a little butter, strain and pour over the brill.

Brill à la russe. BARBUE À LA RUSSE—Using medium-sized brill proceed as described in the recipe for *Sole à la russe*. See SOLE.

Brill in scallop shells. COQUILLES DE BARBUE—Pipe a good border of *Duchess potato mixture* (see POTATOES) around the edges of scallop shells, or metal or ovenproof china shells. Cover the centre of the shells with *Mornay sauce* (see SAUCE). Arrange little slices of hot brill on this sauce. Pour on *Mornay sauce*, scatter grated cheese on top, sprinkle with melted butter and brown the top quickly.

Brill with shrimps. BARBUE AUX CREVETTES—Cook the brill in very little white wine fish *fumet*.*

Drain the fish. Garnish on the sides with peeled shrimp tails. Pour over shrimp sauce to which boiled down liquor left over from cooking the fish has been added.

Brill stuffed with salmon (saumonée) with various sauces and garnishes. BARBUE SAUMONÉE—Take a brill weighing about 4 pounds (2 kilos) and clean in the usual manner. Slit lengthways in the middle on the dark side. Bone the fish through this opening, that is remove the central bone (taking care not to tear the white skin).

Season on the inside and stuff the brill with a cream *forcemeat* made of salmon (see FORCEMEAT) either with or without truffles, according to the nature of the dish.

Put the fish, laying it very flat, in a well-buttered ovenproof dish. Season, moisten with 2 cups (4 decilitres) white wine fish *fumet** and poach gently in the oven with a lid on. Drain the brill, dry and arrange on a serving-dish. Cover with *Normande sauce* (see SAUCE) with the pan juices boiled down and added to it.

Note. When the fish is garnished, cover it with a sauce which goes with the garnish.

Prepared in this manner, brill stuffed with salmon (*saumonée*) may be served with various garnishes and sauces. All the methods of preparation given elsewhere in this book for brill and sole poached in white wine, can be applied to this dish. The following garnishes are most suitable for it: *à l'amiral, cancalaise, cardinal, champenoise, diplomate, Nantua, Normande, Polignac, Victoria.*

Stuffed brill with various garnishes. BARBUE FARCIE—Bone the brill as described in the recipe for *Brill stuffed with salmon*. Stuff with a *fish forcemeat* (see FORCEMEAT). Poach in a little concentrated fish stock.

Drain the fish, arrange on a serving-dish, surround with the garnish recommended and pour over some sauce which goes well with this garnish.

All the methods of preparation given for *Braised brill in white or red wine* can be applied to stuffed brill.

Brill à la venitienne. BARBUE À LA VENITIENNE—As *Sole à la venitienne*.

Brill à la Victoria. BARBUE À LA VICTORIA—Cook the brill as described in the recipe for *Brill in white wine*. Drain it, arrange on a long dish and garnish with a *salpicon** of the flesh of spiny lobster (U.S.A. crayfish) and truffles. Cover with *Victoria sauce** (see SAUCE). Glaze quickly in the oven.

Brill in white wine. BARBUE AU VIN BLANC—Season the brill inside and outside and put in a buttered dish with a finely sliced medium-sized onion and a *bouquet garni*.* Moisten with a few tablespoons of white wine or concentrated fish stock based on white wine and boiled down to the consistency of a *fumet*.* Cook on a low heat with a lid on.

Drain the brill. Arrange it on a serving-dish and wipe off any liquid which it may have given out.

Cover with *White wine sauce* (see SAUCE) using the liquor in which the fish was cooked as basis.

The brill can be served as it is, plain, or it can be glazed quickly in a very hot oven or under the grill.

Brillat-Savarin

BRILLAT-SAVARIN (Jean Anthelme)—French magistrate, politician and gastronome, born at Belley in 1755, died in Paris in 1826.

He started his career as a lawyer at the Court of Belley, became deputy of the National Assembly in 1789, was made mayor and commander of the National Guard of Belley in 1793, was banished under the Reign of Terror, fled to Switzerland, then spent three years as a refugee in America.

He returned to France in September 1797 and, having had his name removed from the list of emigrés, became first a commissioner to the army in Germany under Augereau, then the commissioner with executive powers at the court of the department of Seine-et-Oise, and, finally, member of the Supreme Court of Appeal (Germinal year VIII). *Germinal* is the seventh month of the French Republican calendar—March/April.

He published various pamphlets: *Vues et projets d'économie politique* (1801); a fragment of a work entitled *Théorie judiciaire* (1808); *De la Cour suprême* (1814); *Essai historique et critique sur le duel* (1819).

But these works would not have saved his name from oblivion had he not published shortly before his death *La Physiologie du goût*, a gastronomical work on which he had been engaged for a long time and which is one of the best in existence.

BRILLAT-SAVARIN—Method of preparing meat served in small pieces, mainly lamb and mutton *noisettes*. The garnish which accompanies these dishes consists of small duchess potato *cassolettes**, filled with a *salpicon** of foie gras and truffles, and green asparagus tips in butter.

BRINDE—Old French word for a two-handled cup for wine.

BRINE. SAUMURE—Solution of sea-salt, to which is often added sugar, saltpetre and aromatics, in which foodstuffs are immersed in order to preserve them.

Liquid brine. SAUMURE LIQUIDE—For scarlet (pickled) tongues and pressed beef. *Method.* Put into a large receptacle 5 quarts (litres) of water; 5 pounds ($2\frac{1}{2}$ kilograms) of grey (rock) salt; 2 cups (300 grams) of brown sugar; 5 ounces (150 grams) of saltpetre; 15 peppercorns; 15 juniper berries; a branch of thyme and a bay leaf.

Boil for 25 minutes. Allow to cool.

Pour this brine over the tongues or other pieces of meat which have been pricked, rubbed with salt and saltpetre and put into a receptacle.

Cover with a piece of wood pressing well down. Keep in a cool place.

Note. Six days of soaking in brine are necessary in summer and eight in winter.

Full brine pickle (for various meats). GRANDE SAUMURE —*Method.* Put into a large copper vessel 25 quarts (litres) of water, 25 pounds ($12\frac{1}{2}$ kilograms) of grey (rock) salt, $2\frac{3}{4}$ pounds (1 kilo 350 grams) of saltpetre and $5\frac{1}{2}$ cups (800 grams) of brown sugar.

Bring to the boil over a strong heat.

Test the density of the brine by putting into it a peeled potato. If this floats on top, the proportion of salt is too high and more water should be added; if on the contrary the potato sinks to the bottom, the liquid should be reduced until the potato will float more or less in the middle.

Remove the brine from the fire and allow it to cool.

Pour it, perfectly cold, over the meat in the special tub, after the latter has been trimmed, deeply pricked with a large needle and rubbed with salt mixed with saltpetre.

Note. The brine tub is usually made of cement, glazed brick, stone or slate.

It must be provided with a grille in the bottom on which the meat to be salted is placed.

Pickling, for a piece of meat weighing 8 to 10 pounds (4 to 5 kilograms), must continue for at least 8 days.

If larger sized cuts are being used it is better to inject brine into the interior of the meat with a special pump.

BRIOCHE—Cake made out of yeast dough, often made in the shape of a circle or a ball surmounted by a head.

The name of this cake, according to some etymologists, is derived from two old words *bris* (break) and *hocher* (stir) which put together have resulted in the word *brioche*. This etymological explanation, which appears to be a little whimsical, is today generally accepted. Some authors maintain, however, that the word comes from Brie, the name of a district of France famous for its manufacture of an excellent cheese, where, it is said, this cake was invented. According to these authors, the brioche pastry was originally made out of Brie cheese.

Until the middle of the eighteenth century brioches were made in Paris with baker's yeast. Brewer's yeast, which had been in use for a long time in Poland and Austria, was introduced into Alsace and Lorraine when the court of King Stanislas was transferred to Lunéville. In the olden days the brioches of Gisors and Gournay, great butter marketing centres, used to be famous.

Here is a recipe given by Monsieur Sansvoisin:

'On market or feast days they sell up to 250 to 300 kilograms of brioches in Gisors. The dough is made the night before (1 kilogram of flour, of which about a quarter is used for mixing with the yeast, 10 grams of yeast, 7 or 8 eggs); the dough is then mixed with the yeast and 800 grams of butter "breaking" the dough which "uses the butter". The dough is kept in a bowl and is shaped into brioches only just before putting them in the oven. Prepared in this way the brioches remain light, keep well and retain the flavour of butter without having any taste of yeast.'

Using the various brioche doughs, for which recipes are given in this section and under DOUGH, a great number of sweet dishes (desserts) can also be prepared. Brioche dough can be used for cases for sweet or savoury dishes, for rissoles, for sweet and savoury flans and a great many other dishes and pastries.

For the preparation of various *hors-d'oeuvre* and certain small hot *entrée* dishes a so-called 'common' brioche dough is made, the recipe for which will be found in this section. It is this dough which is normally used for the preparation of *coulibiac*, Russian hot pies (see COULIBIAC), rissoles and other dishes.

Simple brioche dough. PÂTE À BRIOCHE ORDINAIRE—A detailed recipe is given for ordinary brioche dough under DOUGH. In this section will be found various methods of preparing cakes made out of this dough.

Ingredients. $3\frac{3}{4}$ cups (500 grams) of sieved flour, $\frac{1}{2}$ pound (250 grams) butter, 6 eggs, $\frac{1}{2}$ ounce (15 grams) of yeast, $2\frac{1}{2}$ teaspoons (15 grams) of salt, 5 teaspoons (25 grams) of sugar and $\frac{1}{3}$ cup (1 decilitre) of warm water.

Method. Proceed as described in the recipe for *Brioche dough*. See DOUGH.

Common brioche dough. PÂTE À BRIOCHE COMMUNE—

Ingredients. $3\frac{3}{4}$ cups (500 grams) of sieved flour, $\frac{7}{8}$ cup (200 grams) of butter, 4 eggs, $\frac{1}{2}$ ounce (15 grams) yeast, $2\frac{1}{2}$ teaspoons (15 grams) salt, a pinch of sugar and 10 tablespoons ($1\frac{1}{2}$ decilitres) of warm milk.

Method. Proceed as described in the recipe for *Brioche dough*. See DOUGH.

This dough is used for *hors-d'oeuvre* and small hot *entrée* dishes.

Dough for brioche mousseline. PÂTE À BRIOCHE MOUSSELINE — Make a brioche dough as described under DOUGH, using $1\frac{2}{3}$ cups (400 grams) of butter for $3\frac{3}{4}$ cups (500 grams) of flour. Add 4 tablespoons (60 grams) of softened butter per pound of dough.

Brioche en couronne

Brioche en couronne (crown-shaped brioche)—Roll the brioche dough into a round loaf, put it on a baking sheet, shape into a crown and make a few light incisions on the surface. Brush with beaten egg and bake in a moderate oven.

Brioche Goubaud

Brioche Goubaud—Line a buttered straight-sided round cake tin (*moule à manqué*) with brioche dough. Take similar dough, roll it out, cut into pieces, stuff each piece with a *salpicon** of preserved fruit, steeped in rum or some liqueur, and fill the mould with these little fruit pies. Leave to rise in a warm place. Brush with beaten egg and bake in the oven. When ready, take out of the oven and brush the top with diluted apricot jam.

Brioche mousseline

Brioche mousseline—This is baked in a plain, tall round mould, the height of which is further extended by wrapping a piece of buttered greaseproof paper around the top and tying it with a piece of string.

Butter this mould well and fill it up to two-thirds with fine brioche dough. Leave the dough in the mould to rise, then bake in a moderate oven.

Note. The dough for this brioche has quite a lot of yeast which renders it extremely light.

Cheese brioche. BRIOCHE AU FROMAGE—This is either baked in a fluted mould or shaped like a crown, using ordinary brioche dough with some Gruyère cheese, cut into very little dice or grated, added to it. Allow $\frac{1}{2}$ pound (250 grams) of cheese for 4 pounds (2 kilograms) of dough.

Filled brioches à la bohémienne or bouchées glacées. BRIOCHES GARNIES À LA BOHÉMIENNE—Tiny brioches, three-quarters scooped out and filled with various mixtures: *mousses*, *purées*, *salpicons*, etc.

Fruit briochin. BRIOCHIN AUX FRUITS—Using a fairly tall flan (tart) ring, put it on a buttered baking sheet and line with rather firm brioche dough. Line the bottom of the flan with *frangipane.** On this frangipane put whatever fruit is chosen, sliced or diced and steeped in kirsch, maraschino or some other liqueur. Cover with a lid of brioche dough. Leave to rise for an hour. Brush with beaten eggs and bake in a good oven. Sprinkle the cake with icing sugar.

This cake can be filled with all sorts of fruit: stoned cherries, halved apricots, cooking apples prepared as for a *charlotte*, cooked and stoned prunes, etc.

Large brioches à tête. GROSSES BRIOCHES À TÊTE—This is the most popular type of this excellent cake. Here is the recipe:

Butter a big fluted mould and put a piece of brioche dough, rolled into a ball, into the mould so that it fills it to within the width of one finger from the top. Make a hole in the middle of this dough by inserting three fingers into it. Into this hollow put a smaller ball of brioche dough, which has been tapered down to a point at its lower end. Make a few light incisions in the surface of the

Brioche à la tête made from simple brioche dough

dough in the mould. Brush with beaten egg and bake in a good oven.

Brioche à tête can be made without a mould by putting the ball of dough on a buttered baking sheet and proceeding as described above.

Small brioches. PETITES BRIOCHES—These are baked in small fluted moulds called 'brioche moulds' in the same way as large *brioches à tête*.

BRIOCHE (TO MAKE A)—'*Faire une brioche*' means make a blunder or bloomer, 'to drop a brick'.

This is how the expression originated:

After the foundation of the Paris Opéra (which goes almost as far back as the invention of the brioche) the musicians of the orchestra had the idea of punishing any member of the orchestra who was guilty of playing out of tune by making him pay a fine. The total sum of the fines collected was spent on brioches which were eaten by all the members at a gathering for which a date was fixed. The musicians who were thus fined had to wear a badge representing a brioche in their buttonholes.

These facts soon became known to the general public and thus the expression 'to make a brioche' passed into general speech when one wanted to say that someone had acted foolishly or made a silly mistake.

BRIOLET—Slang word synonymous with '*piquette*' (i.e. wine of poor quality). An allusion to a Brie wine which is rather mediocre: 'This is Brie wine, it makes goats dance'.

BRIOLI (Corsican cookery)—Chestnut meal, prepared as polenta, with the addition of milk or cream.

BRIONNE—Another French name for chayote, a vegetable of the *Cucurbutaceae* family. See CHAYOTE.

BRISSE (Baron)—Master of the wolf-hunt and author of culinary works.

Baron Brisse adopted a picturesque style in his culinary works. His recipes were romanticized. They were not at all precise and at times even inexecutable. In this respect, Baron Brisse greatly resembled good old Alexandre Dumas who in his *Grand Dictionnaire de Cuisine* gave some very odd recipes. . .

Thus, Baron Brisse speaks of turkeys 'in blossom' and refers to tomato as 'red mustard'. He also said: 'There is as much difference between a mackerel and a red mullet as there is between a miller and a bishop'.

He made another curious remark to the effect that 'the disappearance of hot *hors-d'oeuvre* was the result of the excessive development of women's skirts'. He wrote this in 1866 in *La Liberté* at a time when enormous crinolines were the rage. 'In a properly administered house the over-expenditure on one side has to be balanced by economy on the other.'

His main works are: *La Cuisine à l'usage des ménages bourgeois et des petits ménages* (P. Marpon & Flammarion, undated publication); *Baron Brisse's 365 menus* (*La Liberté*, 1867); *La Petite cuisine du Baron Brisse* (*Le Petit Journal*, 1870); *366 Menus* (P. Donnaud, 1872); *La Cuisine en Carême* (P. Dentu, 1882).

Gastronomic map of Brittany

A Breton farm-house (*French Government Tourist Office*)

Sampling the culinary specialities of Brittany (*French Government Tourist Office*)

BROCCIO—See CHEESE.

BRITTANY. BRETAGNE—Many, no doubt misguided, gastronomes say (and write) that Breton cuisine is generally mediocre and that there are no culinary specialities in this region worthy of the attention of a true gastronome.

This judgment is quite wrong. Cooking could not be mediocre in a province which has for centuries produced butter rivalling that of Normandy in quality, and where exquisite cream can be obtained at all times. In Brittany choice food products are found in abundance, whether they originate in the sea or on land. Excellent sheep (notably 'salt-meadow' sheep) and cattle are raised.

And, surely, one would confer the title of *haute gastronomie* on the land where simple fishermen have created that excellent sea-food soup called the *cotriade*, where the magnificent *beurre blanc*, which in delicacy rivals that of Anjou, is served with pike and Loire shad and has always proved a delight to any gastronome who had the joy of tasting it.

Among the sea-foods are Cancale and Morbihan oysters, as well as oysters found in the rivers Auray and Belon; clams, cockles, scallops, winkles, ormers, haliotes, spiny lobsters, crabs, shrimps, Lorient sardines, conger eels (which are made into *cotriade*, so popular with the Breton fishermen), soles, brill, turbot, plaice, mackerel, herrings, tunny.

The rivers produce pike, carp, trout, eels, shad; the Odet and Aulne salmon is famous.

Butchers' meat is of good quality; mutton is choice and pork is excellent.

Among the poultry a particular mention should be made of the excellent Nantes ducklings and succulent young turkeys.

The ground and winged game of this region is famous.

Notable too are the Roscoff cauliflowers and artichokes; they are sent to the markets of London and Paris. Breton potatoes must be mentioned, and Plougastel strawberries and apples.

Beverages. Cider is the usual drink of the Bretons. Among the famous growths, those of Pleudihen, Fouesnant, Clohars and Saint-Féréou must be mentioned.

The muscatel wines of Saint-Herblon, Ancenis, Bouzille and Vallet are excellent and Brittany supplies finest quality *eaux-de-vie* distilled from cider and marcs.

Culinary specialities. The best known Breton culinary specialities are *Cornouailles buckwheat and bacon soup*, the *cotriade*—the soup of the Breton fishermen similar to the *chaudrée** of the Aunis sailors, *Morlaix hams*, *Ancenis andouilles* and *sausages*, large *Andouilles de Bretagne*, excellent *black puddings*, *Quimperlé andouillettes*, *Pike au beurre blanc*, *Shad à la crème*, *Nantes bacon*, *Roast leg of salt-meadow lamb with beans* called '*a la bretonne*', *Buckwheat girdlecakes* and *pancakes*, *Quimperlé oat loaf à la crème*, *Quimper pancakes*, *Morlaix brioches*, *Lorient and Quimper cakes*, *Rennes mingaux* (a kind of cream cheese similar to the Saumur *crémets*), *Nantes flat cakes and guillarets*, *biscuits*.

Two chefs from Quimper (*French Government Tourist Office*)

BROCCOLI. CHOUX BROCOLIS—The flower heads which develop in the leaf axils are eaten before they are fully grown. They are also called broccoli tips.

Culinary preparation of broccoli. All the methods of preparation given for cauliflower apply to broccoli.

The flower in this type of cabbage is generally very small. In some varieties it is hardly bigger than a nut. Broccoli is also eaten for its leaves as well as its flowers.

BROCKET. DAGUET—The name given to a young stag,

between one year and eighteen months old. The French name *daguet* comes from *dague*, dagger, and refers to the shape of the young stag's horns.

In cookery, all recipes for roebuck are suitable for brocket. See ROEBUCK.

BROOKLIME. BECCABUNGA—This plant is also called *Water pimpernel.* It is a kind of European cress which grows wild on the banks of streams and ponds.

It is eaten in salads like watercress and can be prepared in all the ways suitable for the latter. See CRESS.

It is ordinarily used as a condiment for salad.

BROUET, BRODIUM, BRODO—In the past all these words were synonymous with *soup*. The word may come from the German *brot*, which means bread. *Brodo* means soup in Italian.

Brouet was the national dish of the Spartans. It consisted of a mixture of chopped meat, pork fat, vinegar and salt.

Plutarch says that the Spartans much appreciated this dish, although it must have been rather mediocre in taste. We borrow the following story from him:

'It is said that to have black *brouet* (broth) Dionysius —the tyrant of Sicily—bought a Spartan cook and ordered him to prepare a dish without economizing on anything that ought to go into it. But hardly had he touched the dish when he was overcome with disgust and threw down the portion he had taken, declaring that he found it very bad indeed. Then, the man who prepared it answered that he was not surprised at all, as the seasoning was missing. "Which?" asked Dionysius. "Weariness after a hunt or foot-race on the banks of the Eurotas, hunger and thirst," replied the cook, "these are the things that make the Spartan dish taste good." '

Athenaeus tells us that the Spartans soon gave up their *brouet*: 'They abandoned their austerity, gave up their temperance and gave themselves up to pleasures', certainly including those of the table.

BROUILLY—Very famous red Beaujolais wine.

BROUTES or BROUTONS (Béarn cookery)—In Béarn this name is given to old cabbage shoots. This dish is served mainly during Lent.

Trim and wash the cabbage and cook in salted water. Drain and dry. Season with oil and vinegar.

In some villages in the Basses-Pyrénées a mixture of leeks and white cabbage, cooked together, drained, pressed and cut into pieces, is also called *broutes*.

BROYE (Béarn cookery)—Meal prepared out of white or roasted maize (corn) flour.

'If white, that is to say unroasted, flour is used, make the *broye* as an ordinary *bouilli.** Bring some vegetable stock or simply salted water to the boil and little by little add the flour until a paste of a fairly firm consistency is obtained.

'When the *bouilli* is cooked, and it should be stirred all the time during cooking, it is served with a ladle, which should be dipped in fat to prevent the *bouilli* sticking to it.

'If roasted flour is used (*troustado* or *tourrado*, as they say in Béarn), you make a well out of it, moisten with the liquid indicated, blend well and proceed to cook.

'Cold broye can be cut into slices and fried in sizzling fat until golden'. (From *La Cuisine en Béarn*, by Simin Palay.)

BRUGNON—A French name for nectarine or smooth-skinned peach. For methods of preparation, see PEACH.

BRÛLOT ('FIRE-BRAND')—Colloquialism meaning a piece of sugar put into a spoon, soaked in brandy, rum or kirsch and set alight over a cup of coffee.

As soon as the flame dies out, this mixture is poured into the coffee.

True lovers of coffee and gastronomes do not like brûlot much; they prefer to drink the liqueur separately.

BRUNOISE—This word has the following meanings:

(1) A method of shredding vegetable very finely. (Thus, people speak of *shredding carrots, leeks, celery, into a brunoise.*) All these ingredients are then cooked in butter or some other fat.

(2) A mixture of vegetables, such as carrots, onions, leeks, celery and sometimes turnips slowly cooked in butter. This sort of *brunoise* is used for making soups or as a supplementary element for certain forcemeats, sauces and *salpicons.**

(3) A mixture of vegetables cut into small dice which is used as an aromatic element for crayfish and other dishes. See CRAYFISH, TRUFFLES.

Brunoise—The ingredients of a *brunoise* vary according to the nature of the basic soup. A plain *brunoise* may be nothing more than a single vegetable, such as carrot, turnip, celery, artichoke. Generally, two or three spoonfuls of this preparation are added to every quart (litre) of soup, according to whether or not the soup contains any other garnish.

Dice the vegetables into pieces about $\frac{1}{8}$ inch across; simmer them in butter in a covered pan, adding a little clear soup.

This *brunoise* may be served by itself or added to other soups, such as soups made from white meat of poultry, pickled tongue, game of all kinds, fillets of fish, etc.

Vegetable brunoise for soups. BRUNOISE DE LÉGUMES POUR POTAGES—Cut the following into dice $\frac{1}{2}$ inch square: 3 small carrots (150 grams), $\frac{1}{2}$ small turnip (100 grams), 2 leeks (75 grams), 1 very small onion (25 grams) and 2 stalks of white celery (50 grams). Season these vegetables with salt and a pinch of castor (fine) sugar and simmer them in a covered pan on a low heat with 3 tablespoons (50 grams) of butter. When they are nicely softened add 1 cup of stock and leave to cook for 15 minutes. At the last moment, add a tablespoon of garden peas and a tablespoon of diced French string beans, cooked in water.

BRUSH. PINCEAU—Utensil consisting of hair or bristle attached to a handle used in the kitchen for brushing various articles intended for grilling with melted butter or oil.

The brush is also used in pastry-making for buttering baking-tins and other utensils and for brushing the tops of pastries with beaten egg.

BRUSSELS SPROUTS. CHOUX DE BRUXELLES—The buds which develop in the leaf axils are eaten between October and the end of March.

Boiled Brussels sprouts. CHOUX DE BRUXELLES À L'ANGLAISE—Trim the sprouts, which means removing outer leaves which are either too hard or too withered and cutting the base of each sprout. Wash them well.

Cook the sprouts in boiling salted water, drain and arrange them in a vegetable dish. Serve fresh butter separately.

Brussels sprouts with butter. CHOUX DE BRUXELLES AU BEURRE—Having partially cooked the sprouts in boiling salted water, drain them well and put them in a sauté pan with some heated butter. Season. Simmer gently in the butter. Serve in a vegetable dish.

Brussels sprouts with cream. CHOUX DE BRUXELLES À LA CRÈME—Half-cook the sprouts in salted boiling water, drain them well and simmer in butter. Cover them with boiling fresh cream. Add butter. Arrange in a dish.

They can also be moistened with a *Cream sauce*, instead of cream. See SAUCE.

Brussels sprouts à l'indienne. CHOUX DE BRUXELLES À L'INDIENNE—Simmer the sprouts in butter. Moisten with a curry sauce. Arrange them inside a border of rice cooked in the Indian way. See RICE.

Brussels sprouts au jus. CHOUX DE BRUXELLES AU JUS—Simmer the sprouts in butter. At the end of the cooking, moisten with a few tablespoons of rich veal stock. Cook a little more, and turn into a vegetable dish.

Brussels sprouts à la milanaise. CHOUX DE BRUXELLES À LA MILANAISE—Boil the sprouts. Drain them well. Arrange them in a dome on a buttered dish, which has been sprinkled with grated cheese. Sprinkle abundantly with more grated cheese, and pour over some melted butter. Brown in the oven. At the last moment pour on some *Noisette butter*. See BUTTER, *Compound butters*.

Brussels sprouts Mornay. CHOUX DE BRUXELLES MORNAY—This is prepared in the same way as *Cauliflower Mornay** with the sprouts arranged in a dome on a gratin dish.

Brussels sprouts with noisette butter. CHOUX DE BRUXELLES AU BEURRE NOISETTE—Boil the sprouts in salt water, drain them and arrange in a dish. At the moment of serving sprinkle them with a little lemon juice and pour over some tablespoons of butter which has been heated in a pan until it has turned golden brown.

Brussels sprouts à la polonaise. CHOUX DE BRUXELLES À LA POLONAISE—Prepared in a vegetable dish like *Cauliflower à la polonaise.**

Brussels sprouts purée. PURÉE DE CHOUX DE BRUXELLES—Prepared with blanched Brussels sprouts simmered in butter, in the same way as *Cauliflower purée.**

Brussels sprouts salad. SALADE DE CHOUX DE BRUXELLES—Boil the sprouts; drain them well. Arrange them in a salad bowl; season with oil, vinegar, salt and pepper. Sprinkle with chopped chervil or with salad herbs.

Brussels sprouts sautéed in butter. CHOUX DE BRUXELLES SAUTÉS AU BEURRE—Boil the sprouts; drain them. Put them in a dish with some heated butter and sauté lightly so that they brown. Arrange in a dish, sprinkled with chopped parsley.

BUCCAN. BOUCAN—The place where the Indians used to cure their meat. The word also applies to the actual grid on which the smoking was done.

BUCKWHEAT. BLÉ NOIR—A variety of Saracen corn.

Buckwheat (Russian soup garnish). GRUAU DE SARRASIN, BLÉ NOIR—Moisten 2 pounds (1 kilo) of buckwheat with 3 cups (7 to 8 decilitres) of salted warm water. Work it to a smooth paste. Put this paste in a deep saucepan. Press it down well. Bake in a hot oven for 2 hours.

Take the mixture out of the oven. Remove the crust which has formed on the surface. Turn out the buckwheat mixture into a saucepan without touching the crust which has formed at the bottom and on the sides of the pan.

Work the dough with 7 tablespoons (100 grams) of butter. Spread it out on a slab so that it is $\frac{1}{3}$ inch thick. Leave it to cool under a weight.

Using a round pastry-cutter $\frac{3}{4}$-inch in diameter, cut it into biscuit shapes. Brown these in butter. Arrange them on a napkin. Serve with broth.

Buckwheat kasha—See KASHA.

BUFFALO. BUFFLE—Member of the ox tribe which is found in hot swampy countries of the old world. Buffaloes are domesticated in Italy and Asia. The American buffalo, more properly called bison, is much larger than the Asiatic buffalo. Formerly very abundant, this animal, which is the only member of the ox family indigenous to America, is fast becoming extinct. The flesh of Asiatic, African and Italian buffaloes can be prepared in any manner suitable for beef. See BEEF.

BUFFET (RESTAURANT)—In culinary terminology, the word *buffet* means a fairly large tiered table, often set at the entrance to one of the rooms of a restaurant, on which various dishes of meats, poultry, fish, cold sweets as well as pastries, are arranged in a decorative manner.

Fruit in boxes or elegant baskets is also placed on these tables. Buffets of large restaurants, always artistically presented, also often have a display of choice vegetables, such as garden peas, French (string) beans, asparagus, as well as the best of cultivated mushrooms and, when in season, cèpes, morels and truffles.

Tempting poultry, game, both ground and winged, fresh caviar and a great selection of other choice products are also displayed on the buffet, as well as fish, crustacea and shellfish arranged on boards covered with seaweed.

The buffet of a large restaurant is, in fact, a show of choice edibles.

Large tables, generally tiered, with a display of foods of all kinds, set in a ballroom (or near a ballroom) are also called buffets. At these the food is dispensed by a butler and the guests come to be served either with refreshments: sandwiches, or cold meats, or pastries, and various drinks: champagne, port, orangeade, lemonade, chocolate, bavaroise, etc., or to have *consommé* served in cups.

Buffets of this type are also arranged for wedding lunches.

At large receptions of the days gone by the buffets used to be magnificent. Those arranged by Carême remain to this day models of this method of serving food.

BUFFETER—Old French word (used by Rabelais in this sense) which described the action of drawing-off wine from a barrel and replacing it by water.

'*Servir à buffet*' used to mean to serve guests with wine liberally watered down.

BUGEY—Bugey includes the part of Savoy annexed by Henri IV which is the department of Ain of today.

In the olden days the chief town of the department of Bugey was Belley, a town famous in the annals of gastronomy, firstly because Brillat-Savarin was born there and, secondly and mainly, because its cuisine is one of the best in France.

The crayfish which is caught in the streams of Bugey is renowned. Nantua, in particular, is celebrated for its crayfish.

All the famous cheeses of Burgundy are to be found there and gastronomes can wash down these cheeses with excellent local wines.

Meat is also excellent in that fortunate land. The lamb there equals in quality that of the best salt-meadow lamb. Choice plump capons, chickens, ducks, can be (or at any rate used to be) found in the markets of Bugey. Trout and pike abound in the rivers and the Bourget lake supplies lavaret, perch and char. The country hams here are superb. The hillsides and the plains provide succulent game. This fertile region also produces truffles, morels, and an infinite variety of other mushrooms.

Culinary specialities. Lucien Tendret, the grand-nephew of the author of *La Physiologie du goût*, wrote an extremely appetizing description of the dishes of this region. He devoted a book, entitled *La Table au pays de Brillat-Savarin*, to these specialities. According to him, the following are the principal specialities of Bugey:

As *hors-d'oeuvre*, or rather as 'thirst raisers', first come various pork butchery products, notably *salt ham* and Belley *sausage*; then the Belley *fondue*, for which Brillat-Savarin, in his treatise on *haute gastronomie* gives such a mouth-watering recipe, the Bugey *rissoles*, *'cardinalized' crayfish*, *crayfish croquettes*, *timbale of crayfish tails à la Nantua*, *char prepared à la façon du lac du Bourget*, *Lavaret quenelles* and *gâteaux*, *crayfish tails au gratin*, *pike à la crème*, *fillet of beef studded with black truffles as prepared in Monsieur Brillat-Savarin's house at Vieu* (a long title, but the dish is excellent), *braised leg of mutton with onions*, *round of veal with Valromey black morels*, *calves' sweetbreads with black truffles*, *stuffed calves' ears*, the majestic *truffled turkey*, *turkey giblets with chestnuts*, *Bresse plump truffled chicken*—'steamed' (which resembles the celebrated chicken of Madame Filloux at Lyon in more ways than one), *chicken fricassée*, *chicken Célestine*, *gâteau de foies blondes* (light liver gâteau) 'swimming in crayfish tail sauce', *jugged hare de Diane de Châteaumorand*, Bernardini *salmis of woodcock*.

To quote further from Lucien Tendret's book, and these are splendid things, there are the three pâtés of Belley: the *Chapeau de Monseigneur Gabriel Cortois de Quensey*, the *Toque de Président Adolphe Clerc*, and, last, but not least, the most glorious *Oreiller de la belle Aurore*, a grandiose pâté, made of different kinds of game, which was prepared in Paris in all the restaurants to mark the Brillat-Savarin centenary.

Finally, we must mention *prickly cardoon with black truffles*, with '*turkey juice*' sauce, *glazed turnips*, *potatoes à la savoyarde*, *rape* (turnip) *à la crème*, *farcettes*, *timbale of macaroni*, *white truffles à la crème*, *sauté of black truffles*, the *salé* of Bugey, the national dish of this region, which 'used to be eaten as a four o'clock snack, washed down with glassfuls of new wine from the hillsides of Belley—a little "proud" but wholesome and of slightly sour taste'; the Belley *anguries*, a sort of water-melon salad, served as an *hors-d'oeuvre*.

Local wines perform miracles, as accompaniments to all these good things. First of all, there are the great wines of Mâcon, then among the vintage wines, those of Virien, Manicle, Poulet, Culoz and Seyssel must be mentioned, particularly the latter, a white wine of which Brillat-Savarin was particularly fond and which, quite wrongly, we think, is now made into a sparkling wine.

Here is a recipe for a very famous dish—the Bugey *Rissoles*:

'The Bugey rissole is a hot *hors-d'oeuvre*. It is in no way inferior to the *bouchée à la reine* (see HORS-D'OEUVRE, *Hot hors-d'oeuvre*, *patties à la reine*). At Belley rissoles are eaten at Christmas and the housewife would not dream of preparing them at any other time. Pastry-cooks and bakers used to make excellent little pies on Christmas Eve which, after the midnight mass, they served piping hot to warm the stomachs of the faithful.

'The following proportions will make a dozen rissoles:

'Cut ½ pound (250 grams) of roast turkey and 5 ounces (150 grams) of tripe (thoroughly cleaned and cooked for 3 hours in a *court-bouillon** of white wine and beef stock, seasoned with salt, pepper, onions and a bouquet of thyme and chervil) into small dice, about ⅓ inch square.

'Put a piece of fresh butter and a chopped onion into a saucepan and cook it without allowing it to brown. Put in the meats, season with salt and pepper: sauté for 5 or 6 minutes and moisten with ½ glass of gravy from a roast turkey.

'Simmer until the liquor is reduced by half, then add 2 tablespoons (40 grams) of beautiful, black, shiny currants. Take the saucepan off the fire, turn the mixture into a dish and allow to cool.

'Meanwhile prepare puff pastry. Cut into rectangular pieces ⅛ inch thick, 4 inches long and 2¼ inches wide.

'Put some filling on these pieces of pastry, fold them over, brush with beaten egg and bake in the oven.' (Lucien Tendret.)

BUGLOSS. Buglosse—Common name for Anchusa, a plant which is also known as alkanet. Its flowers are eaten as a salad. It is said that this salad (which used to be considered a tonic) was a great favourite of Louis XIII.

In some regions the leaves of bugloss are eaten prepared in the same way as spinach.

BUGNES—A kind of fritter, made out of rolled dough and fried in oil.

BULBOUS CHERVIL. Cerfeuil bulbeux—Biennial plant cultivated for its tuberous roots, rich in fecula and with a very aromatic flavour.

The bulbous roots of this chervil are prepared like Chinese artichokes.

BULBOUS CICUTA. Cicutaire bulbeuse—A type of hemlock, the roots of which, cut into slices, are eaten in salad, particularly in Austria and in Prussia.

BULL. Taureau—The flesh of young bulls, always a little tougher than that of beef, is nevertheless of good quality; that of old stud animals is very tough and often musky in taste.

BULLRUSH. Massette—An aquatic plant which grows along the edges of ponds and swamps and the banks of rivers. The leaves and young shoots are eaten in salad. The roots, which are fleshy and full of starch, are also edible.

BULLY-BEEF. Endaubage—A slang term for tinned meat supplied to the armed forces.

BUNDENFLEISCH—German word which in translation means Grisons salt beef.

Pickle a lean piece of beef for 6 days, then take out of the brine and hang for 5 or 6 months.

This pickling is done in the Swiss canton of Grisons in November, and the meat thus salted is sold to the public only the following April.

In the Oberland Grisons beef taken out of the brine is put into a smoke-curing house for one day.

In the canton of Engadine, where this sort of pickling is done commercially on a great scale, beef is not smoke-cured.

BUNG. Bonde—Wooden stopper for barrel bung-holes.

BUNTING. Bruant—A genus of aquatic web-footed birds, found in the marshes of Bresse and Dauphiné.

It is prepared in the same way as wild duck.

BURBOT. Lotte de rivière—A species of fish whose characteristic features are long dorsal fins, an equally long tail fin and drooping barbels on the chin. It is a fresh-water fish.

Burbot liver. Foie de lotte de rivière—Burbot liver is usually prepared in the same way as the soft roes of various fish. However, it requires longer poaching than soft roes.

This liver is highly prized by connoisseurs. It is used in various Lenten garnishes, after being poached in white wine. Pâtés are also made from burbot liver. See PÂTÉ.

Spring in Burgundy (*French Government Tourist Office*)

BURDOCK (Butter-bur, Beggar's buttons). BARDANE—A hardy perennial plant which grows along paths on the roadside and in the hedgerows. It is also called *herbe aux teigneux* (scurvy grass) because in the past its leaves were used as poultices for certain kinds of sores.

In Scotland young shoots and peeled roots of burdock are used in cooking; they are prepared as salsify.

BURGUNDY. BOURGOGNE—Burgundy is undoubtedly the region of France where the best food and the best wines are to be had. It was in its capital Dijon—a city of *haute gourmandise*—that the first, and most magnificent, gastronomical fair in France was organized.

Nature has been particularly lavish with Burgundy in so far as the riches of the table are concerned. It enjoys the esteem of the gastronomes of the entire world for the quality and variety of its wines, made from the grapes gathered in its vineyards, which, along with those of the Aquitaine, are the most perfect wines that could possibly be found.

The cuisine of Burgundy is of the same level of excellence as its wines: it is all at once powerful and delicate, created for healthy appetites and strong stomachs. 'This cuisine is not concerned with dishes made out of nothing, which are worth nothing except for the charm of an ingenious seasoning, exquisite but misleading works of art. What it needs first and foremost is a substantial and strong foundation, which demands rich accompaniments and vigorous sauces.' (Report in *Touring Club*.)

We are, moreover, beholden to this excellent cuisine for a method of preparation called *à la bourguignonne*.

It is used mainly for large cuts of braised meat (also for eggs, fish and poultry). Its main features are a red wine sauce and a garnish composed of mushrooms, little onions and lardoons (the latter are omitted when preparing fish).

Burgundy, as we said, is particularly favoured by the gods presiding over the delights of the table, delights considered vulgar by some but which, according to Brillat-Savarin, can be revealed only to men of intellectual capacity.

All the departments of this old province are lands where gastronomy flourishes.

The Ain is the district where the best poultry in the world is raised, and where the town of Belley is situated, where everything speaks of Brillat-Savarin, and Nantua—the name that evokes in every true gastronome visions of crayfish *à la crème*; the Saône-and-Loire has the town of Mâcon, which has given its name to one of our best wines; the Côte-d'Or, with Dijon, may be said to be one of the capitals of gastronomy, and, finally, the Yonne produces the delightful Chablis wines, so esteemed by gourmets.

The Burgundy larder is abundantly rich. In the pasture lands of Charolais cattle are raised which give succulent beef. The poultry of Bresse is considered among the best in France. In the Morvan various ground and winged game abounds. The experts maintain—and it would appear that they are right—that the woodcock of the Dombes marshes is unequalled.

In the ponds, rivers and streams of Burgundy, delicate fish are found, such as pike, char, trout, salmon trout, crayfish, etc.

The escargots of Burgundy are known throughout the whole world as being the most succulent.

Among other excellent products of this region are the Courtivron and Oyonnax morels, St. George's agaric, cèpes and other mushrooms which are found in great abundance in the woods and fields, and the choice vegetables cultivated in Auxonne and around Dijon.

The fruit of the Burgundy orchards is varied and mouth-watering. Some, such as Saint-Bris cherries, for example, are famous. The blackcurrants too are worthy of mention, being used not only to prepare the famous

Cassis liqueur made in Dijon, but also for a vast number of sweetmeats. The famous Dijon mustard has, quite rightly, for centuries been considered the best; condiments seasoned with vinegar, such as pickled gherkins, are also made in Dijon.

Burgundy truffles although, perhaps, inferior in aroma to those of Périgord or Lot are, nevertheless, invaluable for lending fragrance to local dishes. Brillat-Savarin spoke of them very harshly, saying that 'they are tough and lack oats', a judgment which is somewhat difficult to explain.

The region which, with Bordeaux and Champagne, produces the most magnificent wines in France produces excellent cheeses to accompany them. Among the cheeses most highly esteemed by gastronomes are *Gex blue-veined cheese* which has a certain similarity to *Roquefort*; the *Soumaintrin*, the *Cîteaux*, *Beugnon*, *Butteaux*, *Germigny*, *Pougny*, the famous *Époisses* cheeses (which are made in the Yonne), *Saint-Florentin*, *Passin* which, according to some experts, is as good as the best *Gruyère*, various *Morvan goat* cheeses and the *Saône-et-Loire cream* cheeses.

For centuries Burgundy has been the land of great gastronomical feasts. Brillat-Savarin, who was a Burgundy man, a native of Bugey, has eulogized the table of this region and has left us his accounts of its glories.

The most characteristic Burgundy feasts were given at the time of grape-harvesting. Philéas Gilbert wrote a lovely description of these magnificent feasts: 'From the moment the village crier had sounded the call (the roll of the drum before the proclamation), when only the "*père de la vigne*" and the masters of wine layering had the word, until the evening, when the last cask of grapes crushed by the wine-press was poured into the vats, all was joy and song.

'And as a compensation for the midday meal, the supper menu promised a veritable feast, with the traditional *potée*—its robust fragrance teasing the men and women wine harvesters long before it was ready. *La tisane de choux sucrée avec le lard*, as Henri II used to say. Then there was *goose à la taribaude*, and a sheep, sacrificed for the occasion and transformed into strange yet exquisite ragoûts. The flesh of this sheep, the grandam of the flock, at times tasted of wool grease (to say nothing of its toughness!) but, to make it go down, the pot-bellied jugs poured forth cool wine; it was "plenty of grub" and carousing to one's heart's content. . .

'Ah! Those admirable Burgundian meals, when a great

Gastronomic map of Burgundy

profusion of delectable dishes is served, such as escargots —*à la bourguignonne*, naturally!—*meurette** of various fish; *andouillettes** with beans; a succulent *daube** of beef; the traditional *ferchuse à la ménagère*, *flammiche aux poireaux*, *fouée au lard*, and the Burgundy *rigodon*!'

To Philéas Gilbert, the escargot, prepared in accordance with the Burgundian rites, eaten scalding hot as it is taken out of its garlic-scented butter bath, symbolizes the gastronomy of Burgundy. But there is an infinite variety of other dishes to delight the heart and palate. The following are the most typical culinary specialities, the recipes for which will be found elsewhere in this book in alphabetical order:

Potée bourguignonne, which is rather similar to various French *potées*, for each region of France has its *potée*, the *meurette*,* the *pochouse*,* and various freshwater fish *matelotes*,* *beef à la bourguignonne*, a dish which by a felicitous shortening is simply called *bourguignon* in Paris, which, naturally, must be made with red wine, *round of veal à la crème*, *andouille with white beans*, the *ferchuse* (a corruption of the word *fressure*, i.e. pluck); *daube bourguignonne*, *flammiche** *with leeks*, *fouée*, which is a sort of a cream flan filled with slices of bacon and sprinkled with walnut oil, *poulet au sang* (this dish is found in almost all the regions of France, but in Burgundy it is prepared in a special manner), *young pigeons à la gobinette*; *canard au laurier*, *jugged hare à la bourguignonne*, *saddle of hare à la Piron*, a creation of Maître Racouchot, who also created the celebrated pâté which bears his name, *omelette au sang*.

Then there are *pike à la crème*, Arnay-le-Duc *andouille*, Sens *andouillette*, the celebrated Dijon *ham with parsley*, the *sausages* of Belley (Brillat-Savarin's native place), *crayfish tails à la Nantua*, *pike quenelles with crayfish*, Pernollet *chicken à la crème*, *coq au chambertin*, *sucking-pig à la bourguignonne*, *ham rigodon* and a whole range of excellent pork butchery produce, large and small sausages, black pudding and pork pies, which are made in the Côte-d'Or, Ain, Saône-et-Loire and in Yonne, all of which are excellent 'thirst promoters', as Rabelais described them.

Burgundian specialities (*French Government Tourist Office*)

Among the cakes, sweets and pastries of the Burgundy region are the *rigodon** (which can also be made as a dessert or sweet course), *Lower Burgundy girdle cakes*, *Upper Burgundy girdle cakes*, known as *pognon*; *pancakes*, called *matefaims* in Upper Burgundy; *bugnes* or *couques*, Sens and Auxerre *gougère*, Louhans *corgniottes*, the *Chamoure*—a kind of marrow flan which is mainly made in Lower Mâconnais, fruit *tartouillat*, *tarte aux boulettes*, *flamusse bressane* and *gaudes*.

Among local pastry and confectionery specialities are the Dijon *nonnettes* and *pain d'épice*, Avallon and Chablis *biscuits*, Sens *macaroons*, Chablis *meringues*, Arnay-le-Duc *marzipans*, *nougatines*, *black currant fondants*, *sugar-coated cherries* (cherries in petticoats), excellent jams, among which the most famous are the Chanceaux *raisiné* and *confiture d'épine-vinette*, and Flavigny aniseed sweets.

To conclude the list of local produce are the greatly esteemed *cassis* liqueurs, made at Dijon, and *prunelle*, made at Flavigny.

Wines of Burgundy—The vineyards which produce the grapes for the great Burgundy wines are situated on the east side of the Côte-d'Or, between Dijon and Santenay.

This part of the Côte-d'Or department, about 31 miles long, is divided into *Côte de Nuits*, stretching from Dijon to Cargolin, and *Côte de Beaune*, from Ladoix-Serrigny to Santenay.

The wines of Côte de Nuits are full-bodied and preserve their qualities well. These are great wines but they need a certain time for developing. Those of Côte de Beaune are fine with an excellent bouquet; when young they are more supple than those of Côte de Nuits.

About 75,000 acres of vineyards are cultivated in Burgundy, which produce over 26 million gallons of wine of world renown.

To describe the wines of Burgundy we cannot do better than quote Dr. Lavalle: 'They have an exquisite finesse of the bouquet and a flavour at once hot and delicate which lasts a few moments and leaves a sweet and fragrant after-taste, ruby colour of perfect limpidity and beneficient action on the digestive organs—such are the high qualities of the wines of Côte-d'Or, the first wines in the world.

'The wine, to merit the approbation of a gourmet, must be of pure and not too dark a colour. Its translucence must be completely unclouded and if a little of it is poured on to some metal surface and disperses in little droplets, these should resemble nothing so much as the purest of rubies.

'The palate and the sense of smell should be at once struck by the flavour and the aroma released and the reaction of all the other organs should be so similar to those of the sense of taste and smell that it should be impossible to tell which of the organs is affected most.'

Below we give the classification of the Burgundy wines, carried out more than eighty years ago by Dr. Lavalle which is still valid today. A map will be found in the section on WINE.

Classification of the great wine growths of Burgundy.

Côte de Nuits.

GEVREY-CHAMBERTIN

Grand first growths. Chambertin, Chambertin Clos de Bèze.

First growths. Clos Saint-Jacques, Fouchères, Grande Chapelle, Mazy-Haut, Upper Ruchottes, Charmes, Grillottes, Véroilles, Etrournelles, Castiers.

MOREY

Grand first growth. Clos de Tart.

First growths. Bonnes Mares (a part), Lambray, Clos de la Roche.

CHAMBOLLE-MUSIGNY

Grand first growths. Grands-Musigny, Petits-Musigny.

First growths. Bonnes Mares (a part), Varoilles, Fuées, Cras, Amoureuses.

VOUGEOT

Grand first growth. Clos Vougeot.
First growths. Upper part.
Second growths. Central part.
Third growths. Lower part.

FLAGEY-ECHÉZEAUX

Grand first growth. Grands Echézeaux.
First growths. Orveau, Poulaillères, Murs du Clos, Upper Echézeaux, Achausses, Cruots, Champs-Traversins, Lower Rouges, Beaux Monts Bas.

VOSNE-ROMANÉE

Grand first growths. Romanée-Conti, Richebourgs, Tâche, Romanée.
First growths. Romanée Saint-Vivant, Gaudichots, Malconsorts, Grande rue, Varvilles-sous-Richebourg.

NUITS-SAINT-GEORGES

First growths. Saint-Georges, Vaucrains, Cailles Forets, Pruliers, Boudots, Cras, Murgers, Thorey, Argillats, Chabiots, Rousselot, Chaignots, Chaînes-quarte, Champs-Perdrix, Charmottes, Crots, Ferrières, Procès, Richemonnes, Roncières, Vignes-Rondes, Poulettes.

Côte de Beaune.

ALOXE-CORTON

First growths. Corton Clos du Roy, Renardes, Chaumes, Bressandes, Perrières, Fiètres, Grèves, Languettes, Pougets, Meix, Vigne-au-Saint.

PERNAND

First growth. Vergelesses.

SAVIGNY

First growths. Vergelesses, Jarrons, Marconnets Hauts et Bas, Jarrons-Guettes, Gravains, Carrières.

BEAUNE

Grand first growths. Fèves, Grèves, Cras, Champs-Pimonts.
First growths. Aigrots, Avots, Clos de la Mousse, Mignotte, Coucheriats, Clos de Mouches, Vignes-Franches, Clos du Roi, Blanches-Fleurs, Boucherottes.

POMMARD

First growths. Arvelets, Rugiens, Reufène, Clos de la Commaraine, Fremiets et Jarolières, Epenots, Charmots, l'Argillière and Pezerolles, Boucherottes, Poutures, Croix Noires, Chaponnières, Rugiens-Haut, Clos Blanc and Clos de Cîteaux.

VOLNAY

Grand first growths. Cailleret, Cailleret-Dessus, Caillerets, Champans, Chevret, Fremiets, Pousse d'Or, Angles and Pointes d'Angles, Barre, Carelle, Sous-Chapelle and Rougirots, l'Ormeau, Mitans.

MONTHÉLIE (above Volnay)

First growths. Champs Fullots and Clou des Chênes.

MEURSAULT

Grand first growths. Santenots du Milieu, Santenots.
First growths. Cras, Clos des Mouches, Pelures.

CHASSAGNE-MONTRACHET

First growths. Clos Saint-Jean, Clos Pitois, Torgeots, Boudriotte, Maltroie, Brussanes, Caillerets, Changains.

SANTENAY

First growths (supérieures). Clos Tavanne, Gravières, Bussanes.
First growths. Boichot, Beauregard, Beaurepaire, Maladière, Grand Clos Rousseau, Comme, Passe-Temps.

White Burgundy wines—The great Burgundy growths also produce very famous white wines, some in very minute quantity, such as Corton and Charlemagne at Pernand; others in very appreciable quantities. All these vineyards are situated on the Côte de Beaune and here is their classification by commune:

MEURSAULT

Grand first growths. Perrières (Upper and Lower).
First growths. Santenots blancs, Upper Genevrières, Upper Charmes, Bouchères, Tessons, Goutte d'Or.

PULIGNY-MONTRACHET

Grand first growth (outstanding). Montrachet (Puligny and Chassagne).
First growths. Chevaliers-Montrachet, Bâtard-Montrachet, Caillerets, Combettes, Platières, Référés and Charmes.

It will be observed that different communes often use the same name to define the climates, as for example: Cras, Charmes, Perrières, Combes, etc.

BUSH (IN A). BUISSON (EN)—Method of arranging various ingredients, particularly crustacea: *Crayfish en buisson, Lobsters en buisson, Spiny lobster en buisson.*

Various small fried articles, such as smelts, croquettes, etc. are also arranged in a 'bush'.

BUSTARD. OUTARDE—Genus of bird of the family *Otidae* found both in hot and temperate regions of the Old World.

The *Great Bustard* (*Otis tarda*) (the largest land bird in Europe, where it comes in December and stays until March) is known both for the delicacy of its flesh and its size.

The *Little Bustard* (*Otis tetrax*), the smaller of the species, is still more highly prized. It comes to Beauce and Berry in April. It is non-migrant in Spain, Italy, Greece and Sardinia. It can be distinguished from the Great Bustard by its smaller size and even more by the fact that the special feather structures on the head so peculiar to the male of the Great Bustard species is absent in the case of the Little Bustard.

The principal method of cooking bustard is roasting. All the methods indicated for the preparation of the domestic goose and the Nantes duckling can be applied to it.

BUTCHER'S BROOM. PETIT-HOUX—Shrub with bitter roots, which is one of the five roots used for aperitifs. Its young shoots are edible and are prepared like asparagus.

BUTCHER'S SHOP. BOUCHERIE—Shop for the retail sale of meat for human consumption.

The meat trade, which includes all the operations from the slaughter of the animals to cutting the meat into pieces for sale, has a very long history. Although in the most ancient times no special individuals were recognized as being entirely responsible for this work, it is known that the Jewish High Priest—performing the sacrificial offering—was the real precursor of the butcher. We see in the Greek bas-reliefs the high priest represented killing the bull before slitting its throat. The same method was to be adopted for centuries by professional butchers.

Human sacrifices and holocausts have led to people

killing their own animals in Egypt, in Greece and elsewhere. In Egypt, before the altar where a sacrifice was to take place, a fire used to be lit, wine was offered and a god was invoked. Then the throat of the victim was slit, the head severed and the carcase skinned. After imprecating curses upon the head, it was taken to the market and if a Greek merchant could be found operating in the locality it was sold to him; if a Greek merchant could not be found it was thrown in the river. In sacrifices to Isis, after the bull was skinned, the intestines were removed but the viscera and the fat were left in the carcase. The legs, the end of the tail, the shoulders and the neck were cut off; when this was done, the rest of the carcase was filled with bread, honey, raisins, figs, rosemary, myrtle and other aromatic substances and thus prepared it was roasted on the altar, sprinkled with great quantities of oil.

With the Romans, sacrifices took place in much the same way; but the Romans were too civilized to indulge in the gross practice of butchery and they created a kind of monopoly for the men whom they entrusted with this task, giving them special privileges to compensate them for the fact that their occupation was held in contempt by the higher classes.

They operated in one part of the town and were subject to very severe police regulations, as already in those days the future power of this corporation was feared. Under Nero, the Roman butcher's shop was an establishment just as imposing and elegant and as well situated as the Baths, the Aqueduct and the other monuments of Rome, which was then at her height. The development of the town made it necessary later to establish two other butcher's shops also subjected to the same regulations. Butchers specializing in buying and selling pigs were called *suarii*.

In the wake of the Roman armies engaged in the conquest of Gaul came the purveyors, some of whom were entrusted with the task of buying and looking after cattle, in order to supply not only the army but also the conquered territories. It is very likely that this was the ancient origin of the guild of master butchers into which no ordinary person was allowed to enter. It was, in a way, a duty handed from father to son or to other male relatives, no right being passed on to daughters, wives or illegitimate children. When the family died out because of the lack of a male heir, the inheritance reverted to the Guild.

In France, according to F. Dornier, 'it is only by Royal Decree of 730 that it became permissible for a man who had served a three-year apprenticeship and had bought, dressed, cut and sold meat for three further years, to aspire to Mastership provided, however, that he bought the companion's Diploma, the cost of which was 202 pounds and the Mastership which cost 900 pounds'.

This Guild was directed by a chief, elected by a majority vote, who took the title of *Master of Master Butchers*. Unless found guilty of maladministration, his appointment was for life. He settled all disputes among his members and administered the common property. The prosecution was presented to him by a *Procureur d'office* (procurator) and the judgment pronounced by a registrar. These two appointments were also made by election. Appeals were made before the Provost of Paris whose decision was final.

The Butchers' Guild had its phases of prosperity and its phases of financial straits. At the beginning, free to sell not only beef, veal, mutton, lamb, pork and sucking-pig, but also sea and river fish, a privilege which was won with great difficulty from Philippe le Hardi, they only needed to acquire the right to sell poultry and game, to assemble in their hands all the animal products required by man. It is not even certain that butchers did not sometimes do this. So, under Charles VI, butchers were as much to be feared in France as they were, for a much longer time, in England. They even indulged in the pretentious fantasy of building a special chapel and forming themselves into a religious corporation. They wore chasubles at certain ceremonies and formed processions chanting hymns.

When people reach such an apogee of glory and arrogance, their decline is near, and that is precisely what happened. Charles VI, alarmed by the abuse of administrative authority by this Corporation, seized the opportunity (which had arisen as a result of a political uprising within the Corporation) to ruin the organization. After revoking their privileges and completely destroying their property, he forbade the butchers to gather as a community. Two years had hardly gone by when they regained their original power. They regained favour as a result of intrigues but lost some of their rights. The authority to sell pigs was taken away from them and given to the pork butchers. The sale of lambs and sucking-pigs was also forbidden to them, as was the sale of fish.

In spite of this semi-disgrace, they quickly regained their power and soon became so rich and so proud that they abandoned their work and left their meat stalls to their assistants. But a law of April 2nd, 1465, compelled them to work at their stalls themselves, or at least to employ paid servants for this purpose, failing which they were subject to a penalty or to the loss of their meat stalls. It was only by a new law of March 4th, 1557, that they were released from this obligation and it became possible for them to employ qualified men on their premises, subject to the annual approval of the Provost of Paris or his lieutenant.

In 1587 these new butchers, tired of their allegiance to master butchers, asked to be raised to the status of tradesmen. The master butchers immediately opposed this motion; this did not prevent Parliament from granting, on December 22nd, 1589, Letters of Patent creating this community, provided they joined the old guild and that the Statutes, registered on the same day, should be compulsory for all of them.

According to these Statutes every butcher was expected always and throughout the year to have meat on his stall. They were forbidden to:

(1) Sell outside their stall.
(2) Open new stalls, move their stalls without authority or reduce the number of stalls they possessed.
(3) Keep open after 6 p.m. except on holidays and Saturdays when they could remain open until 10 p.m.
(4) Open on holidays and Sundays except from Trinity Sunday to September 8th because of hot weather, but never on Ascension Day.
(5) Exhibit meat on Abstinence Days or during Lent in more than one stall out of ten, and this only for the sick.
(6) Solicit custom or abuse the customers.
(7) Slaughter animals without informing the police and without paying for this right.
(8) Cook meat, or sell cooked meat.
(9) Run an inn, a fruit shop, a public-house, or pursue any trade other than that of butcher.

They were expected to sell meat from healthy animals, which had been properly slaughtered and not died from disease or suffocation, to prepare it in a clean way and to sell it at the right time, neither too fresh nor kept for too long, i.e., more than 2 days in the winter and 1½ days in summer, this meat becoming, after this period, unfit for human consumption.

The law of May 4th, 1540, which fixed the maximum rent for stalls in the town at 16 *livres parisis* (francs, minted in Paris, of 25 sous), was maintained and, to prevent the landlords from avoiding this and thereby forcing the butchers to increase the price of their meat, the rent was governed by a legal authority.

The sale of meat measured out by hand, on which police officers and butchers' representatives did not see eye to eye, was forbidden. In their own interest, the butchers had substituted this custom for the use of weights, which were already in common use under Charlemagne, as can be seen from his *Capitulary* (a collection of ordinances). This method of approximate estimation, which caused continual arguments, was for ever banished, at least in the capital, and was replaced by the system of scales as the one which offered the greatest fairness and best guarantee for the buyer. Fines, distraints by seizure, confiscations and even corporal punishment and penalties involving loss of civil rights were inflicted on the law-breakers. It was the duty of the Provost of Paris to see to it that these Statutes were carried out. Then this became the responsibility of the Lieutenant of Police in 1667, when this post was created.

The Royal regulations were maintained until the end of absolute monarchy. It was Napoleon who succeeded in doing away with privately owned slaughter-houses. He created the public slaughter-house. As soon as butchers were forced to take their animals there, two distinct branches of the industry developed: the wholesale trade and the retail trade. The first covered the purchase of livestock, transport to the slaughter-house, and the work of the scalding-room. The second merely consisted of retailing the carcases of meat to the consumer.

To facilitate the wholesale trade, cattle markets were created in the nineteenth century, such as at Sceaux, Pontoise, and Passy for the Paris area. A fund was also set up from which the butchers obtained the necessary money for purchases with a charge of 5% and with a proviso that the loan be repaid within a fortnight. Thus the butchers kept one of their most ancient privileges. Their creditors could not press their claims on the eve of or on market day, nor seize the meat in the shop. These conditions were essential to safeguard the town's meat supplies.

'The number of shops in Paris under Napoleon was fixed at 400 and anyone who gave the necessary guarantees was eligible. Their price rose up to 200,000 or 300,000 francs and parents used to ponder whether to buy a notary's practice or a butcher's shop for their sons. That was the time when butchers were held in high regard. On Thursdays they disported themselves, splitting the pavement of the Poissy road and competing in feats of strength as in the Roman Circus.

'Hardly deigning to count the receipts in their shops, which they left in the lily-white hands of some *dame de compagnie*, they spent the evening dressed in their brown suits and wearing kid gloves in the most comfortable salons. That was the time when the Boeuf-Gras (fatted ox) festivals were celebrated with much pomp, magnificence and éclat. The Government, dazzled by this display of opulence, thought it opportune to raise the number of shops to 600. The result was so unfortunate and so many bankruptcies followed that the number was quickly reduced to 500.'

During the nineteenth century the meat trade became free but there was a transition period during which, in order to set up business, it was necessary to pay a fee of 3,000 francs, to prove that an apprenticeship had been served and that one possessed the necessary knowledge to retail meat, present a certificate of good conduct and character and undertake not to leave the business without giving the Prefecture three months' notice. Towards the middle of the last century there were only 500 retail butcher shops left. Police regulations laid down the details relating to the running of the shops. They had to be tiled, well positioned, well ventilated. No butcher could set up business before the Police Commissioner of his area had visited the premises and given his approval; any shop owner who displayed meat outside his shop was fined. Finally, any shop which did not display any meat for three consecutive days was closed for six months.

Since 1863 the meat trade has been free and the number of shops has increased considerably. They are still controlled by police regulations, but the Butchers' Guild no longer has the prerogatives it had under the old régime.

Nowadays, the work of retail butchers hardly ever includes the killing of animals, which is carried out in slaughter-houses, except in a very few localities where the butcher does the slaughtering himself. The bulk of the work is the preparation of cuts of meat for cooking purposes and the butcher often takes it upon himself to string, stuff and dress the joints (cuts).

This carving and preparatory work is carried out on chopping-blocks and slabs. The chopping-block is a section of a tree-trunk, usually elm, with a cross-grained surface, mounted on three legs. The slab, a kind of large bench, has a cross-grained wooden working surface, and an upright section with fittings for tools and large drawers. The tools include choppers, saws and knives of various sizes; the latter are sometimes placed in a wooden case, which in French is called *boutique*. These tools are often seen in the kitchens of large catering establishments which buy complete carcases or large cuts wholesale or direct from the slaughter-house for their cooks to carve and prepare.

Butchers' shops are also provided with scales (which must be kept very clean), marble tables and faience plates to display the meat. Modern rules of hygiene being to protect all food products from dust, many butchers' shops are provided with display counters enclosed in glass and with means of refrigeration. Uncut carcases are hung from rails, provided with hooks and enclosed in a refrigerated chamber, or in a large refrigerator.

The walls and floor are tiled and kept scrupulously clean.

Employees are dressed in light-coloured clothes and wear white aprons. These include butchers' boys and shopmen, but there are men who fulfil both functions. Sales are generally supervised by the owner or manager, who should mainly be a specialist in the art of carving, preparing and displaying the cuts.

BUTTER. BEURRE—Fatty substances extracted from the milk of mammals, known and used as food by man from the most ancient time.

The origin of butter, in fact, goes back to the early nomadic people who, to prepare it, used the milk of cows, ewes, goats, mares, she-asses and even she-camels, which they raised for their domestic needs and which followed them in all their peregrinations.

The Aryans brought butter to the inhabitants of India, who, very soon, began to consider it a sacred food.

This precious food figures in their mythological geography as Salmala, a river of butter which meandered its sinuous way around one of the seven concentric zones symbolizing the earth, situated around Meron, which was considered to be the axis of the world.

The Hebrews knew butter and used it not only as food but also as medicine.

Genesis tells us that Abraham offered butter, a symbolic food, to three men who came to his tent in the plains of Mamre. In his proverbs, Solomon says: 'Surely, the churning of milk bringeth forth butter . . .' which shows that churning was known to the Hebrews.

History tells us that the Scythians also had butter and brought it to the Greeks. From them butter entered into the realm of pure gastronomy, its use spread very quickly throughout the civilized world, concurrently with that of oil and other fatty substances.

People living in some southern countries however, like the Romans, used oil much more than butter in their cooking. This preference still persists in certain parts of the south of France, mainly in Provence, where oil plays the principal part in all the dishes.

Clarification of butter—See CLARIFICATION.

Preparation of butter—Milk fat globules are found in a relatively stable state of emulsion. They separate, however, when the liquid is left to stand and rise to the surface in the form of cream. If milk is subjected to a series of repeated shocks, which constitutes the *churning* operation, these globules are agglutinated into a compact mass which is butter.

Qualities of butter—Good butter must have semi-soft consistency at ordinary temperature; it must not ooze little droplets, which indicates too strong a proportion of water and insufficient drying; it should have a very pleasant gentle aroma, the taste should be fresh and wholesome and when taken in the mouth it should melt on the tongue without leaving any curds.

To work butter. DÉLAITER—The process of washing butter to remove the residual buttermilk.

Butter shells or pats. COQUILLES DE BEURRE—Prepared in this way, butter is served as part of the *hors-d'oeuvre*. The shells are made by scraping butter (which should be very firm) with a special tool.

The round pats are stamped out with special moulds, generally made of box-tree wood.

When served with *hors-d'oeuvre*, butter can also be presented in a loaf of any size, simply put in an *hors-d'oeuvre* dish or some other receptacle.

Cocoa butter. BEURRE DE CACAO—Fatty substance expressed from roasted cocoa beans. This is found in shops in the form of rectangular shiny blocks, yellowish-white in colour. Its taste is sweet and pleasant, recalling that of chocolate.

It melts at a temperature between 30°C. and 33°C. and stays liquid by supercooling at a lower temperature, solidifying only at 23°C.

This product, of which there are several brands, is sterilized and, therefore, keeps very well. It contains absolutely no water and is easily digestible, perhaps more so even than ordinary butter. Its taste is absolutely neutral and can in no way be compared to that of butter.

Coconut butter. BEURRE DE COCO—A vegetable butter frequently used in France is *coconut butter*. The *copra* (albuminous lining of the interior of the coconut), dried and put under a great pressure, yields an oil, used in soap-making. This oil, after bleaching and various other processes, is transformed into an edible product, of fairly firm consistency, which has the appearance of butter.

Fried butter. BEURRE FRIT—Prepare ½ pound (250 grams) of butter as described in the recipe for *Butter cooked on a spit*. Divide this butter into portions of 3 tablespoons (50 grams) each. Shape them into little balls, roll in breadcrumbs to give them three coatings and, when required, deep fry in smoking hot fat. Drain and arrange on a napkin.

Butter prepared in this way is served as an accompaniment to poached fish.

Nutmeg butter. BEURRE DE MUSCADE—Fatty substance expressed from nutmegs. It is found in shops in the form of rectangular leaves covered with palm leaves. It is of brownish-yellow colour, veined with red, very unctuous to the touch and has a smell of nutmeg.

It is used mainly in pharmaceutics.

Butter cooked on a spit. BEURRE À LA BROCHE—A preparation which used to be in vogue in years gone by but which is not done nowadays.

It was made in the following manner: Soften 1 pound (500 grams) of butter to a malleable paste, add to it some chopped chervil, tarragon and chives and some lemon juice. Season and shape into a ballottine.

Put on a wooden spit and chill thoroughly in an ice-box.

When the block of butter is quite hard, coat it with three layers of breadcrumbs in such a way as to enclose it entirely in a thick coating of breadcrumbs.

Put the butter before a very lively fire. Sprinkle it with melted butter. Cook from 8 to 10 minutes until the outside crust acquires a good colour. Serve at once.

Butter on a spit is not really a dish. It is simply an original way of serving melted butter with poached fish or a boiled vegetable.

Walnut butter, hazelnut butter, peanut butter. BEURRE DE NOIX, NOISETTES, ARACHIDES—These are factory-made products high in nutritive value.

COMPOUND BUTTERS. BEURRES COMPOSÉS—This term applies to the following:

(1) Butters mixed with one or more substances, generally reduced to a purée or chopped.

(2) Butters cooked to various degrees, or simply melted and seasoned, spiced and used as accompaniment to various fish, meat and vegetable dishes.

Compound butters of the first category are used either as a supplementary element in sauces and various dishes, or as an auxiliary element in dressing certain cold dishes, or as garnish for cold *hors-d'oeuvre*.

Almond butter. BEURRE D'AMANDES—Pound 2½ ounces (75 grams) of sweet blanched and washed almonds into a fine paste, adding a few drops of cold water to prevent their turning into oil. Add 10 tablespoons (150 grams) of butter. Rub through a fine sieve.

Uses. Garnish for cold *hors-d'oeuvre*, and also used as final liaison for soups and some white sauces.

Anchovy butter. BEURRE D'ANCHOIS—De-salt and dry 2½ ounces (75 grams) of anchovy fillets and pound them in a mortar with ¾ cup (200 grams) of butter. Rub through a fine sieve.

Uses. The same as those indicated for *Garlic butter*. Anchovy butter is also used as an accompaniment for grilled fish and meat.

Bercy butter. BEURRE BERCY—Add 1½ tablespoons of finely chopped shallots to 1 cup (2 decilitres) of white wine and reduce (boil down) by half. When the liquor is almost cold, add to it ¾ cup (200 grams) of fresh softened butter, 1 pound (500 grams) of beef bone marrow, cut in dice, poached in salted water and drained, a tablespoon of chopped parsley and the juice of half a lemon. Season with 1¼ teaspoons (8 grams) of fine salt and a pinch of freshly ground pepper.

Uses. Accompaniment to grilled meat and fish. It is served either on or under the grilled meat or fish, or, if preferred, separately, in a sauceboat.

Brown butter. BEURRE NOIR—A quotation from Rabelais proves the great age of this culinary preparation: 'He remained stunned and battered, one eye "*au beurre noir*" '. In this sense, '*avoir un oeil au beurre noir*' means to have a black eye!

Brown butter is served with eggs, various fish (see SKATE), vegetables boiled in salted water, brains and a large number of other dishes.

Cook 10 tablespoons (150 grams) of butter in a pan to a dark brown tone, *not black*. When it reaches this point, add to it 2 tablespoons of fresh, picked-over, washed and well-dried leaves of parsley and a tablespoon of capers. Pour the butter into a sauceboat or over the dish with which it is served, adding to it a tablespoon of vinegar heated in the same pan.

For *Eggs with browned butter*, omit the parsley and the capers.

Caviar butter. BEURRE DE CAVIAR—Pound 2½ ounces (75 grams) of pressed caviar in a mortar. Add 10 tablespoons (150 grams) of butter. Blend well. Rub through a fine sieve.

Uses. As a garnish element for *Canapés à la russe* and for various cold *hors-d'oeuvre*. It is also used as a supplementary element for certain fish forcemeats.

Chive butter. BEURRE DE CIBOULETTE—Prepare as *shallot butter*, using green chives.

Uses. The same as those for shallot butter.

Chivry butter. BEURRE CHIVRY—Blanch 2 teaspoons each (150 grams) of parsley, tarragon and chervil leaves, fresh burnet and chives for 3 minutes in salted water. Drain these herbs, dip in cold water, and dry. Pound them in a mortar with 1½ tablespoons (20 grams) of chopped, blanched shallots. Add 10 tablespoons (150 grams) of butter. Rub through a fine sieve.

Uses. Supplementary element for white sauces and garnish for cold *hors-d'oeuvre*.

This compound butter is also called *butter ravigote*.

Colbert butter. BEURRE COLBERT—Prepare *Maître d'hôtel butter*. Add, for 6 tablespoons (100 grams) of butter, 1 teaspoon of chopped tarragon and 1 tablespoon of dissolved meat jelly.

Uses. Accompaniment for fried fish *à la Colbert* and for grilled meat and fish.

Crab butter. BEURRE DE CRABES—Prepared as *Shrimp butter*, using small crabs, cooked in *court-bouillon** and drained.

Uses. The same as those for shrimp butter.

Crayfish butter (cold). BEURRE D'ÉCREVISSES (À FROID)—Prepared as *Shrimp butter* (cold), using shells and trimmings of crayfish cooked *à la mirepoix.**

Uses. The same as for shrimp butter.

Crayfish butter (hot). BEURRE D'ÉCREVISSES (À CHAUD)—Pound finely in a mortar the shells and trimmings of crayfish cooked *à la mirepoix* (the tails being used for some other dish). Add the same amount of fresh butter and blend well.

Put this mixture into a small saucepan. Stand the saucepan in a larger pan of hot water (which will amount to a *bain-marie*). Let the crayfish butter melt slowly. When it is completely melted, pour it through a cloth, placed over a bowl of iced water. Twist the cloth over the water to squeeze out all the butter.

Allow the butter which has then been strained on to ice to set. When it is completely solidified, take it out of the bowl. Dry on a cloth.

Uses. Supplementary element for sauces, gravies, thick shellfish soups, fish forcemeats and shellfish ragoûts.

Garlic butter. BEURRE D'AIL—Peel, blanch, drain and dry 8 cloves (100 grams) of garlic and pound finely in a mortar with 8 tablespoons (200 grams) of fresh butter. Rub through a fine sieve.

Uses. Supplementary element for certain sauces, garnish for cold *hors-d'oeuvre.*

Gascogne butter. BEURRE DE GASCOGNE—This should not be confused with *aioli*, which in the south of France is called *beurre de Provence.*

Gascogne butter is also prepared with garlic, but the garlic is first cooked for a few minutes in salted water, then drained and pounded with a little good fat and seasoned with salt and pepper.

This garlic butter is used for seasoning kidney beans and for sprinkling grilled mushrooms.

Green butter. BEURRE VERT—Ordinary butter, softened to a paste and mixed with green spinach, prepared in the following manner: pick over, wash and dry the spinach leaves and pound them in a mortar, uncooked. Put the spinach into a very strong cloth, twist the cloth to extract all the juice from the spinach, which should be collected into a little saucepan, set this juice to coagulate in a *bain-marie** (double boiler) and turn out on to a fine cloth stretched over a receptacle.

Scrape off the green residue which remains on the cloth with a spoon. This substance is called *vert d'épinard* (spinach green).

To this spinach green add double its weight in butter. Rub this butter through a fine sieve or a tammy.

Uses. The same as for *Chivry butter*. It is also used like *Montpellier butter.*

Hazelnut butter. BEURRE DE NOISETTE—Prepared like *Almond butter*, using lightly-roasted hazelnuts or filbert nuts.

Uses. The same as for *Almond butter*.

Herring butter. BEURRE DE HARENG—Made of fillets of pickled herrings, as *Anchovy butter*.

Uses. The same as for *Anchovy butter*.

Horseradish butter. BEURRE DE RAIFORT—Pound in a mortar ⅓ cup (75 grams) of grated horseradish. Add 1 scant cup (200 grams) of butter. Rub through a sieve.

Uses. The same as for *Garlic butter*.

Kneaded butter. BEURRE MANIE—Blend 5 tablespoons (75 grams) of butter and ¾ cup (100 grams) of flour into a smooth paste.

Kneaded butter is used as a quick liaison to bind certain sauces, notably those called *à la matelote*.

Lemon butter. BEURRE DE CITRON—Add finely grated rind of 1 lemon to ¾ cup (200 grams) of butter. Season with salt and white pepper. Blend well.

Uses. Garnish for cold *hors-d'oeuvre*.

Lobster butter (cold). BEURRE DE HOMARD (À FROID)—Using the creamy parts, the coral and the eggs of the lobster (cooked in *court-bouillon**), proceed as described in recipe for *Shrimp butter* (*cold*).

Uses. The same as for *Shrimp butter* (*cold*).

Lobster butter (hot). BEURRE DE HOMARD (À CHAUD)—Using shells and trimmings of lobster, cooked in *court-bouillon** or *à la mirepoix** prepare as *Crayfish butter* (*hot*).

Uses. The same as for hot crayfish butter.

This butter is often called red colouring butter. In principle, the latter is prepared by pounding together in a mortar the coral, or eggs of the various crustaceans, cooked in *court-bouillon* with an equal quantity of butter.

COQUILLES SAINT-JACQUES AND ESCARGOTS MAISON (*Nézard-Debillot*)

(*From Curnonsky:* Cuisine et Vins de France)

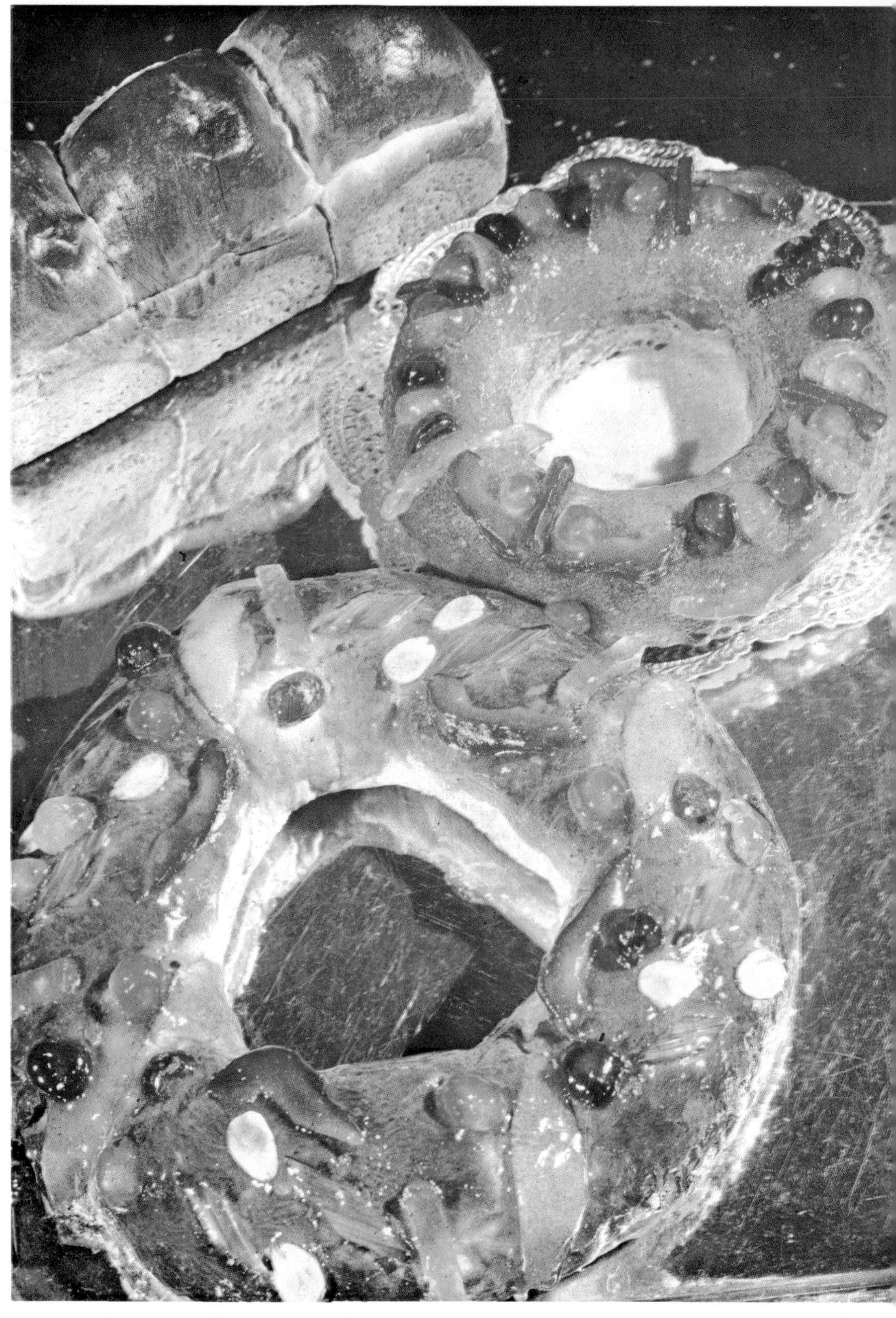

BRIOCHE. Pain brioché, Savarin, Brioche décorée (*Duchesse A*

(*From the original French edition of* Larousse Gastronomique)

Maître d'hôtel butter. BEURRE À LA MAÎTRE D'HÔTEL—Mix $\frac{3}{4}$ cup (200 grams) of fresh butter with $1\frac{1}{2}$ tablespoons of chopped parsley, 1 teaspoon (6 grams) of fine salt, a small pinch of freshly ground pepper and a dash of lemon juice and stir with a spoon until it forms a smooth paste.

Uses. Accompaniment for grilled meat and fish, fish fried in egg and breadcrumbs and various boiled vegetables.

Melted *Maître d'hôtel butter* may be served separately or put on or under the ingredients which it accompanies, depending on the nature of the dishes.

Marchand de vins butter. BEURRE MARCHAND DE VINS—Add 2 tablespoons (30 grams) of finely chopped shallots to $1\frac{1}{2}$ cups (3 decilitres) of red wine and simmer down by half. To this liquor add a large tablespoon of dissolved meat jelly (or 2 tablespoons of rich brown veal stock). Add 10 tablespoons (150 grams) of butter softened into a paste, a tablespoon of chopped parsley and the juice of a quarter of a lemon. Season with salt and pepper and blend well.

Uses. This butter is specially used as an accompaniment for *Grilled rump steak à la marchand de vin.*

Marseilles butter. BEURRE DE MARSEILLES—Name ironically used for oil, in the same way as garlic is referred to as Marseilles vanilla.

Melted butter. BEURRE FONDU—This is made by gently melting finest butter, seasoned with salt and a pinch of white pepper and acidulated with a few drops of lemon juice, on a low heat.

Uses. Accompaniment for poached fish and boiled vegetables.

Meunière butter. BEURRE À LA MEUNIÈRE—In principle this butter is used for cooking the ingredients (mostly fish) with which it is to be served. It can however, be prepared separately in the following manner:

Heat the butter in a pan until it acquires a light brown colour. At the last moment add a dash of lemon juice and some salt and pepper.

Uses. Accompaniment for fish prepared *à la meunière* (see BASS, *Bass à la meunière*) and certain vegetables, poached or simmered in butter.

Montpellier butter. BEURRE DE MONTPELLIER—This is mainly used for dressing cold dishes, particularly fish. It can be considered more a decorative element than an accompaniment.

However, this butter, prepared as described below (and not obtained by colouring ordinary butter with green vegetable colouring matter) is delicious and makes a perfect accompaniment to cold fish.

Method of preparation. (1) In a copper basin quickly blanch in salted water the following herbs, picked over and washed: 4 tablespoons each (20 grams) of parsley, chervil, cress, tarragon, chives and a small handful (25 grams) of spinach leaves.

Also blanch in salted water 3 tablespoons (40 grams) of chopped shallot.

Drain these herbs and condiments, dip them in cold water and press well to extract all the water.

(2) Pound all these ingredients in a mortar, adding the following: 3 medium-sized gherkins, 1 tablespoon of well-pressed capers, 4 de-salted anchovy fillets, and 1 small clove of garlic.

When all the ingredients have been reduced to a smooth paste, add to them 5 tablespoons (75 grams) of butter, 3 yolks of hard boiled eggs and 2 raw yolks of eggs.

Finally, still pounding with a pestle, little by little, add 1 cup (2 decilitres) of olive oil. Season with salt and a pinch of cayenne pepper. Rub through a fine sieve or tammy. Put the butter into a bowl and stir with a whisk until quite smooth.

When *Montpellier butter* is prepared specially for decorating cold dishes and for spreading on croûtons, raw yolks of egg and oil are omitted. This decorative butter is spread in a uniform layer on a sheet and left to cool.

Mushroom butter. BEURRE DE CHAMPIGNONS—Slice 1 cup (150 grams) of cultivated mushrooms; toss briskly in butter, season with salt and pepper and pound finely in a mortar. Add 10 tablespoons (150 grams) of fresh butter, blend and rub through a fine sieve.

Uses. Supplementary element for white sauce and garnish for cold *hors-d'oeuvre.*

Mustard butter. BEURRE DE MOUTARDE—Add 2 tablespoons of mustard to 1 cup (scant) (200 grams) of butter softened to a paste. Blend well.

Uses. The same as those for *Anchovy butter.*

Noisette butter. BEURRE NOISETTE—Heat and cook butter in a pan to a light hazelnut colour. This butter is poured over the dishes with which it is served, piping hot, or, if the butter is to be served separately, poured, equally sizzling hot, into a sauceboat, into which the juice of one lemon has previously been squeezed. *Noisette butter* is served with eggs, lambs' or calves' brains, skate (cooked in *court-bouillon**), soft roes, and various vegetables, cooked in water and well drained.

Paprika butter. BEURRE DE PAPRIKA—Blend into a smooth paste 1 scant cup (200 grams) of butter, seasoned with 1 tablespoon (5 grams) of paprika.

Uses. Garnish for *canapés* and other cold *hors-d'oeuvre.*

Pistachio butter. BEURRE DE PISTACHES—This is prepared like *Almond butter*, using blanched pistachio nuts.

Uses. The same as almond butter.

Printanier butter. BEURRE PRINTANIER—This is prepared by pounding in a mortar an equal quantity of butter and green vegetables (green peas, asparagus tips, French beans, etc.) cooked in water, drained and dried. Blend and rub through a fine sieve.

Uses. Garnish for cold *hors-d'oeuvre,* liaison for thickened soups and for some white sauces.

Ravigote butter. BEURRE RAVIGOTE—Name for *Chivry butter.*

Red butter. BEURRE ROUGE—Name given to *Lobster butter* and butter mixed with other shellfish.

Salmon butter. BEURRE DE SAUMON—This can be prepared using either fresh or smoked salmon. Using one or the other, proceed as described in the recipe for *Herring butter.*

Sardine butter. BEURRE DE SARDINES—This is prepared like *Herring butter*, using fillets of sardines in oil.

Uses. The same as those for *Herring butter.*

Shallot butter. BEURRE D'ÉCHALOTE—Shred, blanch, drain and dry 8 shallots (125 grams) and pound them finely in a mortar. Add 8 tablespoons of butter and rub through a fine sieve.

Uses. Mainly as an accompaniment to grilled meat and fish.

Shrimp butter (cold) BEURRE DE CREVETTES (À FROID)—Pound 5 ounces (150 grams) of cooked shrimps finely in a mortar with an equal amount of butter. Rub through a fine sieve.

Uses. Supplementary element for fish sauces and garnish for cold *hors-d'oeuvre* and cold fish.

Shrimp butter (hot). BEURRE DE CREVETTES (À CHAUD)—Using cooked shrimps prepare in the same way as *Crayfish butter* (*hot*).

Uses. The same as those for hot *Crayfish butter.*

Shrimp butter, as in the case of other crustaceans, may

be made using only the shells if the flesh is needed for some other dish.

Butter for snails à la bourguignonne. BEURRE POUR ESCARGOTS, À LA BOURGUIGNONNE—The following proportions have been established for 100 good-sized escargots:

Add the following ingredients to 1½ pounds (700 grams) of best (unsalted) butter: 6 tablespoons (70 grams) of finely chopped shallots, 2 cloves of garlic pounded into paste, 2 good tablespoons of chopped parsley. Season with 3 teaspoons (24 grams) of salt and ¼ teaspoon (4 grams) of pepper. Blend well.

Uses. For filling escargot shells cooked *à la bourguignonne*.

Soft roe butter. BEURRE DE LAITANCES—This butter, which is mainly used as a garnish for cold *hors-d'oeuvre*, is prepared by pounding together in a mortar equal quantities of soft roes of pickled herrings and butter. This butter is then rubbed through a sieve.

This butter can also be prepared by pounding in a mortar ¼ pound (125 grams) of soft roes of various fish (especially those of carp), poached, cooled and well dried, with ¾ cup (200 grams) of butter.

This is used as a supplementary element for some fish sauces.

Spiny lobster butter. BEURRE DE LANGOUSTE—Prepare, using shells and trimmings of the spiny lobster (U.S.A. crayfish) as *Lobster butter*.

Sweet pimento butter. BEURRE DE POIVRONS DOUX—Pound finely in a mortar 6 tablespoons (150 grams) of sweet pimentos (red or green) previously stewed in butter. Add a scant cup (200 grams) of butter and rub through a fine sieve.

Uses. The same as for *Garlic butter*.

Tarragon butter. BEURRE D'ESTRAGON—Blanch 4 tablespoons (125 grams) of fresh tarragon leaves for 2 minutes in salted boiling water. Drain, dip in cold water, dry and pound in a mortar with ¾ cup (200 grams) of fresh butter. Rub through a fine sieve.

Uses. Supplementary element for various sauces and garnish for cold *hors-d'oeuvre*, especially *Canapés à la russe*. See HORS-D'OEUVRE, *Cold hors-d'oeuvre*.

Tomato butter. BEURRE DE TOMATES—Soften ¾ cup (200 grams) of butter into a paste, add 1 cup (2 decilitres) of concentrated tomato juice and blend well.

Uses. The same as those for *Anchovy butter*. It is also used as a liaison for thickened soups and white sauces.

Truffle butter. BEURRE DE TRUFFES—Pound in a mortar 4 small (100 grams) fresh truffles with 10 tablespoons (150 grams) of butter. Rub through a fine sieve.

Uses. Garnish for *canapés* and other cold *hors-d'oeuvre*.

Tunny (tuna fish) butter. BEURRE DE THON—Prepare as *Anchovy butter* using tunny in oil.

Uses. The same as for *Anchovy butter*.

Walnut butter. BEURRE DE NOIX—This is prepared like *Almond butter*, using dried, blanched walnuts.

Uses. The same as for *Almond butter*.

BUTTER CREAMS—See CREAM.

BUTTER-DISH. BEURRIER—Small dish used for serving butter on the table. Some butter dishes are made in such a way that the butter is always kept under salted water. Thus enclosed, the butter can be kept fresh for a longer period. There are more modern types consisting of a double-wall bell-shaped cover in porous earthenware filled with water which is replaced every day. The bell-shaped cover is placed over the butter contained in a glass dish.

BUTTERMILK. BABEURRE—Buttermilk is the milk which is left after churning the butter. This product differs, depending on whether fresh or sour milk is being churned, and on whether or not the cream is taken off by centrifugal machinery or not. In principle, buttermilk differs from ordinary skimmed milk in that skimming is taken much further and that it has been subjected to the beginning of lactic fermentation.

It has the same composition as milk, excluding cream, of which it nevertheless retains a small proportion as no churning, however complete, can remove it entirely. It contains all the casein, which differentiates it from whey, and this casein, following acidification, undergoes changes which render it more soluble and more digestible. It contains all the mineral salts found in milk and a proportion of lactose which has not yet been transformed into lactic acid.

Buttermilk soup. SOUPE DE BABEURRE—Mix a little flour (wheat, barley, rice, etc.) allowing one tablespoon per quart (litre), in a small quantity of cold buttermilk, blending to avoid lumps. Add this mixture to heated buttermilk, which is gently brought to the boil in a porcelain or enamel casserole. Allow to boil down by about one quarter and sweeten with sugar, allowing ⅓ cup (70-90 grams) of sugar (sometimes less) per quart (litre).

The object of adding flour is to break up the globules of casein and thus make it more digestible. Prepared in this way, buttermilk soup has a nutritive value to a considerable extent approaching that of human milk.

BUTYRIC ACID. BUTYRIQUE—Acid which develops in butter by oxidation and which causes it to become rancid.

BUTYROMETER. BUTYROMÈTRE—Instrument consisting of a calibrated glass tube for measuring the butter content of milk.

The milk is mixed with a certain volume of ether which dissolves the butter. Then an equal volume of alcohol is added. The butter floats on the surface in the form of an oily layer and its thickness, measured by the graduation of the tube, clearly shows the proportion of butter.

CABARET—In a general sense, this word today defines a tavern where drinks can be bought or, more often, are consumed on the premises, and where food is sometimes served.

In French the word 'cabaret' is often taken to have a derogatory connotation, although in the last few years it has been rehabilitated somewhat, for it is now used in France to describe quite elegant establishments, frequented by high society, where entertainment is provided, and where prices are always rather high.

A great deal has been written on the origin of this word. Each of its syllables has been well and truly twisted in an effort to wrench its etymology from it. Some authorities go back as far as ancient Hebrew language—it is said that the word *cabaret* comes from *cabar* (to assemble). Others, delving into old Celtic, claim that it has been derived from two words *cab* (head) and *aret* (*aries*—i.e. ram), citing cases of this animal being consecrated to Bacchus as proof. We feel that it is not necessary to look any further than medieval Latin, the common source of so many French words, and investigate the verb *cabare* (to dig, to make a cave), which strikes us as being the most natural source of the word.

History. The *cabarets* owe more than their name to the Romans. The inn-sign, this picturesque distinguishing mark, the symbolic appeal to the customer; the cork, the clump of ivy or yew, whose shade invites the drinker and which Olivier Basselin knew so well—all these have been taken over from ancient Rome. In the words of the poet, the witty inventor of the Norman *Vaudevires*:

'*Il vaut bien mieux cacher son nez dans un grand verre.*
Il est mieux assuré qu'en un casque de guerre;
Pour cornette ou guidon suivre plutôt on doit
Les branches d'hierre ou d'if qui montrent où l'on boit.'

'It is better to bury one's nose in a big glass.
It's more protected thus than in a soldier's helmet;
And for a standard or a pennant, it is best to follow
The branch of ivy or of yew, which shows one where to drink.'

The inn-keepers of ancient Rome used to cut Bacchus' thyrsus to hang it over their inns, to advertise, with barefaced effrontery, the dreadful mixture which they were pleased to call *cecubae* and *falernian opimian* wine.

The fir-cone, another ornament of Bacchus' sceptre, was also adopted into the heraldic arms of the French *cabarets*. It became a sign of the most famous tavern in Paris, perhaps the same that Villon praised and Boileau reviled.

Well over a hundred years ago Edouard Fournier and Arthur de Beauplan described the old taverns as follows:

'In the twelfth century, the dark and grimy Paris, which Philippe Auguste was beginning to dream of cleaning up, was surrounded with gardens where people could go for a drink.

'Outside these miserable walls, there was a green oasis, which became alive on holidays with a joyous throng of people who flocked here to find in pleasure a revenge against boredom.

'These rustic gatherings, so regularly frequented by the little people and the bourgeoisie were even then called *courtilz* or *courtilles*. And even in those days the enclosed space of their clumps of trees and kegs was protected by lattice-work, as can be seen from the *Rusticon* miniature in the Bibliothèque de l'Arsenal.

'The role of the rustic tavern has been to cling closely to the walls of the town and to enliven the approaches to it. Paris was in those days of such a size that a pig fair outside the city walls took place just where the rue Montesquieu and the Porte St. Honoré are today, exactly at the spot where the *Café de la Régence* is now, so that one is not surprised to learn that the *courtilles* used to flourish where today the most popular districts and some of the most elegant streets are situated.

'Often, traces of some of these *courtilles*, encroaching on large vineyards, still bounded by these districts, can be found in the names of the streets.

'Thus, the *Clos Georgeot* which spread its vineyards on the southern slopes of the Butte Saint-Roch has given its name to a little street close to the Palais Royal.

'The *Clos de Posteries*, traversed by the *Rue des Postes*, is also represented by the *Impasse des Vignes*.

'Further, there are some which have left nothing but their names, such as *Clos Vignerai*, *Clos des Champeaux*, *Clos Gauthier*, the first of which used to be situated on a part of the Jardin du Luxembourg, the second between rue Saint-Denis and les Halles and the last in Montmartre.

'These *clos*, the approaches to which were enlivened by the popular *courtilles*, were sometimes a part of a nobleman's domain, and then the vineyards were well guarded—it was the forbidden fruit. But the people—gluttons and as vain as the fox in the fable—and, like the fox, always disparaging what they could not have, consoled themselves by the proverb: "*Courtilles* vines—they look fine, but there's nothing in them". They thus scoffed at the *courtille Barbette*, country seat of the Provost of merchants, and burned down both the house and the

A *cabaret* during the reign of François I (*Flemish School*)

vineyard during a riot. And when they got to the *Clos de la Ville-l'Evêque*, a famous episcopal courtille, it was not just caustic jibes that they aimed at the fat canons, hiding under heavily-laden climbing vines, who had gathered for a "theological banquet".

'On the other hand, the people reserved their most cheerful greetings for the little Tournelles garden, where Jehan de Meung, their beloved patron, had established his poetical *courtille*. Later, passing through rue des Jardines-Saint-Paul, they would lovingly point out, in the middle of this shady retreat, the verdant nook where Rabelais found pantagruellic inspiration, in the wine that maketh glad the heart of man.

'But when the holidays came, when the people felt they were free for a few days, and were not afraid to forget themselves beside a jug of wine, when the hot sun rays invited them to leave their damp and smoky dwelling-places, they would venture into the country, in groups, as far as the most distant *courtilles*.

'But, as we know, not every day is a holiday. Whilst fully conscious of the truth of this old axiom, the people did not feel the need to satisfy their daily thirst during the week any the less. On Sundays they could regard it as a duty.

'They needed therefore, in the absence of the *courtilles* reserved for carousing on good feast days, some place not far from where they lived where they could minister to the caprices of this daily thirst. These places were the first *cabarets*.

'In the thirteenth century there were 90 publicans in Paris, and we could give you their names and addresses, as well as those of 3 goose merchants, 21 *cuisiniers*, 24 inn-keepers, 23 cooks, in all 161 caterers who in those days represented the food industry of the good city of Paris. But what use would it be to you to know that Péronelle, the beer-seller, used to live in rue Thibault-aux-Dez, or that Robert-the-Breton kept a pub at Deux-Portes with Master Yves, his companion?

'You would sooner prefer to learn something about the appearance of these public places and the customs and habits of the people who frequented them.

'And first of all, you must understand, that in those days a drinker worthy of the name never mistook a *cabaret* for a tavern. He knew well that only in a tavern did he have the right to install himself for the purpose of eating and drinking without hindrance. For he was strictly forbidden to enter a *cabaret* and still more so to sit down or have the table laid.

'A stout wooden trellis work—the survival of which can still be seen in the iron railing, to this day used by the wine merchants—guarded the entry to the houses of *cabaret* keepers. Through an opening cut in the trellis-work the publican handed the wine to the customer (the wine which he brought in *longues bottes de verre*). The transaction completed, he had to hold the jug, which he used as a measure, upside down, to show that there was no possible way of drinking on his premises the wine which had been bought. Such were the official orders of the provost and the inn-keeper had to abide by this method of selling "by means of a cut door and an over-turned jug"!'

In the centuries which followed, little by little, the cabarets started to be identified with taverns until the two words became synonymous.

Some cabarets, frequented by writers, especially in the seventeenth century, acquired lasting fame, among them *Le Mouton blanc* (in rue du Vieux-Colombier), where Racine, La Fontaine and Boileau used to meet; *Le Sabot* (rue du Pot-de-Fer) where Ronsard used to come in for a drink and which Chapelain also visited;

L'Écu d'Argent, which, in a way, was the home of Ménage; *La Pomme de Pin* (rue de la Licorne), the *scholars'* meeting-place, mentioned by Rabelais. Notable among eighteenth century inns were *Le Caveau* (on the Buci crossroads) where Collé, Piron and many other epicureans used to gather to sing their bawdy songs and where in 1737 the Caveau society was formed; the *Chat blanc* (rue de la Vieille-Lanterne), on the railing of which the hanging body of Gérard de Nerval was found.

CABARET (LIQUEUR STAND)—A liqueur set, including glasses and decanters, presented either on a tray or in a special cabinet.

CABBAGE. CHOU—The species type seems to be of European origin, and prior to the Aryan invasion. Highly esteemed by the Greeks and particularly by the Romans, the cabbage seems to have been unknown to the Hebrews. It is not mentioned in the Bible.

Apart from sea-kale, no species of cabbage survives in a wild state.

Innumerable varieties have been developed by cultivation. These include: green cabbages, cabbage with full heart (*choux pommés*), cauliflowers, broccoli, Brussels sprouts, red cabbages, kohlrabi and *choux-navets*.

The various kinds of white cabbage are used chiefly for the preparation of sauerkraut. One can, however, apply to all white cabbages all the methods of cooking indicated for cabbage hearts and greens.

Green cabbage hearts and greens are braised. They are also used as an element in peasant soups.

Red cabbage is braised, but as a rule is not blanched before braising. This type of cabbage is also served raw, cut into narrow strips, and marinated with vinegar and aromatics.

GREEN CABBAGE. CHOUX VERTS.

Boiled cabbage. CHOU VERT À L'ANGLAISE—Cut a cabbage into quarters. Remove the fibrous part of the stem and the coarse outer leaves. Cook in salt water until just tender. Drain, press between two plates to extract the moisture. Slice this pressed cabbage into rectangles.

Green cabbage prepared in this way is used as a vegetable served with melted butter, or as a garnish.

Braised cabbage. CHOU VERT BRAISÉ—Divide a cabbage of moderate size into quarters, blanch, put under the cold tap, and drain. Break up the cabbage, and remove the thick portions of the stem. Season with salt, pepper, grated nutmeg. Put the cabbage into a deep casserole which has been lined with strips of larding bacon. Add an onion stuck with a clove, a large carrot cut into quarters and a *bouquet garni*.* Moisten with stock which has not been skimmed of its fat (if there is no fat, add 3 tablespoons of clarified fat to it). Cover with strips of fat bacon. Start cooking on top of the stove. Cover the pan and put it in a moderate oven for about 1½ hours.

A piece of lean pork can be added which has been properly blanched beforehand.

Braised cabbage can be used as a vegetable but, more often, it appears as one element in a garnish.

Cabbage in marinade. CHOU VERT MARINÉ—This is prepared like *Red cabbage in marinade*.*

Cabbage salad. SALADE DE CHOU VERT—Slice the cabbage finely. Blanch for 15 minutes in salted water. Put under the cold tap, drain and dry. Season with oil. vinegar, salt and pepper like an ordinary green salad.

Little stuffed cabbage balls. PETITS CHOUX POUR GARNITURE—Divide a large cabbage into quarters, wash, blanch for 8 to 10 minutes in salt water, rinse and drain.

Remove all the leaves, trim them by paring the ribbed stalks. Make a stuffing with the tender inner leaves, and an equal quantity of forcemeat. Put a little round of stuffing on each leaf, and roll into tight balls. Braise in the usual way.

Stuffed cabbage balls are used to garnish large joints which are either braised or boiled. The cabbage leaves can be stuffed with all kinds of hashes or purées.

Stuffed cabbage. CHOU VERT FARCI—Blanch a whole cabbage in salted water. Put it under the cold tap, drain it, and remove the stem.

Put the cabbage on a damp cloth, spread out on the table, and large enough to enclose the cabbage. Open out the cabbage beginning with the outer leaves. Stuff the heart first with a ball of forcemeat (fine pork stuffing). Close the leaves round this, and then fill the outer leaves closing them in to reform the shape of the cabbage. Wrap the cabbage up in thin strips of bacon fat. Tie it up in the cloth and make fast with string. Put it in a braising-pan lined with bacon skins and slices of onion and carrot.

Cover the cabbage with a fat stock. Braise for about 1½ hours.

Drain the cabbage, untie it, and remove the bards. Set it on a round dish and pour over it the liquor in which it has cooked, boiled down (reduced) with or without the addition of a little rich brown sauce, and serve the rest of the concentrated liquor separately.

This type of stuffed cabbage is served as a garnish for large joints, being first cut into thick slices.

The cabbage can be prepared in another way. When it has been opened, remove the heart. Chop the tender leaves and mix them with the stuffing. Stuff the cabbage with this mixture and braise it.

Stuffed cabbage à la provençale (Niçoise cooking). CHOU FARCI—Blanch a large cabbage for 8 minutes in salted water, rinse in cold water, drain it, and remove the large outer leaves.

Remove the ribbed stems and spread the leaves out flat on a thin damp cloth, or piece of muslin, stretched out on the table.

Chop the inside leaves of the cabbage. Stuff the outer leaves with the chopped-up leaves and the following ingredients, arranged in layers: ½ pound (250 grams) of blanched beet leaves; 7 ounces (200 grams) of lean pork cut into dice and browned; 1 medium-sized onion (100 grams), chopped, lightly fried in butter; 2 large tomatoes, peeled, seeded and chopped; ⅓ cup (100 grams) of blanched rice; 1 cup (125 grams) of fresh green peas; 1½ pounds (750 grams) of sausage meat seasoned with a crushed garlic clove.

Fold the cabbage leaves round the stuffing in the form of a ball. Tie up the cloth or muslin.

Put the cabbage into the *pot-au-feu* prepared in the usual way, but using mutton instead of beef. Cook for about 3½ hours very gently.

Drain the cabbage; set it on a round dish. Pour over it a few tablespoons of the cooking liquor.

Note. This dish, which is fundamental to the *cuisine niçoise* can be served with the soup from the *pot-au-feu* in which it has cooked.

Stuffed cabbage rolls. CHOU VERT FARCI EN BALLOTTINE—Lay out some slices of larding bacon on a damp cloth and arrange some cabbage leaves which have been blanched, rinsed and dried, on top, the leaves overlapping to form a rectangle. Put some stuffing in the form of a roll in the centre of the leaves. Wrap the leaves round the stuffing,

Stuffed cabbage à la provençale (*Robert Carrier*)

Stuffed cabbage rolls

enclose them in the cloth and tie it up with string. Braise in the manner indicated above.

This type of stuffed cabbage is served as a garnish for large joints, being first cut into thick slices.

RED CABBAGE. CHOUX ROUGES.

Red cabbage à la flamande. CHOU ROUGE À LA FLAMANDE—Shred the cabbage after cutting it into quarters, washing it, and removing the hard core and stem.

Season the cabbage with salt and pepper and sprinkle with a few drops of vinegar. Put into an earthenware casserole with butter. Put on the lid, cook on a gentle heat. When the cabbage is three-quarters cooked, add 3 tart apples, peeled, and cut into quarters. Season with a tablespoon of brown sugar. Finish the cooking on a low heat; cooking time is approximately 2 hours.

Red cabbage à la limousine. CHOU ROUGE À LA LIMOUSINE—Shred the cabbage and put it into an earthenware casserole. Moisten with bouillon; add 4 tablespoons of pork fat, peeled raw chestnuts chopped up (20 chestnuts for a cabbage of average size). Season with salt and pepper. Cook with the lid on for about 2 hours.

Red cabbage in marinade. CHOU ROUGE MARINÉ—Shred the cabbage after removing the hard core and ribs; put it in a terrine; sprinkle with fine salt. Leave for 48 hours, stirring from time to time.

Drain the cabbage. Put it in an earthenware bowl with peppercorns, fragments of bay leaf and a clove of garlic. Cover with vinegar which has been boiled and allowed to cool. Marinate for 24 to 48 hours.

Red cabbage in marinade is used as an *hors-d'oeuvre*. It is also served with boiled beef.

Stalks and stumps of red and green cabbage. MOELLE DE CHOU ROUGE ET CHOU VERT—The core of the stalks and stumps of these vegetables is usually discarded, but it can be very tasty and can, if well cooked, provide very good dishes.

Trim the stalks or stumps, that is to say, remove all the woody outer casing. Blanch whole if they are to be served with the vegetable. If they are to be cooked separately, cut into rounds or some other shape. After blanching, these stalks and stumps can be prepared in the same way as artichoke stalks or endive stumps.

CABBAGE PALM. PALMISTE—Name given to the terminal bud of several species of palms.

Cabbage palm en daube (Creole cookery). PALMISTE EN DAUBE—Put some good fat into a copper sauté pan. Put in pieces of cabbage palm shoots, cut lengthways into strips of about 2 inches, tied in bundles to keep them together. First parboil in water and drain well on a napkin.

Brown on a low fire for about ½ hour, add a tablespoon of flour and blend it in, frying it lightly. Add ½ teaspoon of tomato purée.

Moisten with very concentrated chicken stock, prepared in advance from chicken giblets.

Cook for several minutes, put in the oven for a while without allowing the top to brown and serve in very little sauce.

CABERNET—A variety of wine-making grapes grown extensively in the Bordeaux vineyards. There are two species: *cabernet-franc* and *cabernet-sauvignon*.

CACHALOT (SPERM-WHALE)—Sea mammal, the flesh of which is sometimes used as food.

CACHAT CHEESE—See CHEESE.

CACHOU. CACHUNDÉ—Aromatic tablets used in the Far East, to which stomachic properties are attributed. They are mainly used to freshen and sweeten breath and are made of amber, musc, sandalwood, sweet calamus, galingale, cinnamon, bole, etc.

CADENAS—A kind of container, with grooves, which closed like a drawer. This was used in the Royal households for the same purpose as the *Nef*, a basket containing Royal cutlery, napkins, etc. It contained the fork, the knife and the spoon, the bread being placed on the dish. The *cadenas* were still in use in the sixteenth century. Under Louis XIV it became a hexagonal tray on which the napkin, the fork, the knife and the spoon were placed. The Grand Pantler had the *nef* and the *cadenas* conjoined on his coat-of-arms—as insignia of his office.

CAFÉS—Establishments where, in principle, only liquid refreshments are served. In the beginning they served only coffee.

Three years after the departure of Suleiman Aga, who, in 1669, brought coffee in large quantities to France, an Armenian called Pascal opened a coffee-shop at the Saint-Germain fair. The Armenian's shop was always full and he did a roaring trade. After the fair, he went to Quai de l'École and opened a new shop but did not have the same success as at the Saint-Germain fair. Pascal then went to London, where coffee had been known since 1652. After Pascal, another Armenian, called Maliban, opened a new café, but a little while later went to Holland, leaving his house to a man called Grégoire, who moved his establishment to rue Mazarine to be near the Comédie, which was then in that street, opposite rue Guénégaud.

At the same period in Paris a little lame man called Candiol went about carrying a hawker's tray with all sorts of domestic utensils. He also sold coffee which could be drunk at home. His price was two *sous* a cup, including sugar. His associate, Joseph, opened a café at the bottom of the Notre-Dame bridge, and a Levantine from Aleppo, called Etienne, opened another one in rue Saint-André-des-Arts, facing the Saint-Michel bridge. But these miserable cafés were really no more than dirty little smoking-saloons, frequented only by confirmed smokers, travellers from the Lebanon and several Knights of Malta. The coffee sold in these shops was extremely mediocre and badly served. In 1754 there were already 56 cafés in Paris; by the end of the eighteenth century their number rose to 600.

The cafés very soon replaced the cabarets as meeting-places for men of letters. Among such literary cafés the first, chronologically, was the *Café du Parnasse* at the bottom of the Pont-Neuf, near the Samaritaine; then

Café Frascati in the early nineteenth century

the *Veuve Laurent*, in rue Dauphine, and the *Café Procope* whose fame goes back to the eighteenth century when it counted among its regulars Buffon, Gilbert, Marmontel, Voltaire, d'Holbach, Diderot, d'Alembert and others.

The widow Fournier, whose café in rue Saint-Antoine was founded by a man called Baptiste in 1690, was the first to have conceived the idea of providing her regular customers with newspapers to read. She subscribed to *Gazette de France*, *Mercure* and *Journal des Savants*. The *Café des Grâces*, in rue l'Arbre-Sec, was the first establishment in Paris to have public billiards. The *Café de la Régence* became the meeting-place of chess-players and Jean Jacques Rousseau tried his skill there against the celebrated Philidor. During the Revolution the cafés played an important role as meeting-places of secret committees of Members of the National Convention and as tribunes for orators.

The *Palais-Royal cafés*, too, have had their hour of fame: *Café de Foy*, *Café de la Rotonde*, *Café Corazza* and *Café Lamblin* were the meeting-places of Bonapartist officers on 'half-pay'.

Under the Second Empire the Boulevard cafés, the *Café Riche* and, above all, *Café Frascati*, were the meeting places of writers, dramatists and journalists. When *Frascati's* disappeared, it was replaced in this function by *Café Napolitain* until the deaths of Catulle Mendès, Ernest La Jeunesse and Gomez-Carrillo.

In the Latin Quarter, Jean Moréas held court at *Café Vachette*.

Today the cafés, although more numerous and more luxurious than ever, have not the same political and literary influence, with the exception perhaps of a few Left Bank establishments, which still serve as a coterie for young literary and artistic movements.

CAFFEINE. Caféine—Alkaloid substance contained in coffee, which acts on the nervous system. Coffee soothes, eliminates the feeling of tiredness and exhaustion, makes mental work easier, dispels drowsiness. A bigger dose can bring on nervous excitation, trembling, insomnia.

CAILLEBOTTE (CURDS)—Name given in certain regions of France to curdled milk, drained in a muslin bag and eaten fresh.

CAILLETOT—Name commonly used in Normandy for young turbot.

CAILLIER—French name for a wooden vessel which was used in the Middle Ages and until the end of the sixteenth century as a drinking cup. They were made in the shape of a bowl of average size supported by a leg, the whole carved out of one piece of wood. There were also such bowls made in a very much larger size which served as containers for wine, the bowl-shaped lids being used as drinking vessels.

CAKE. Gâteau—The word *gâteau*, some authorities say, comes from the word *gasteau*, which itself derives from the term *gastel*, which, in old French, meant a delicate food that quickly deteriorates, (*gâter*—to spoil).

This etymology seems to us somewhat dubious but, for want of a better one, we are compelled to accept it.

But what we can say is that the generic term '*gâteau*' or cake designates all types of pastry and cakes in the strict sense of the term, while the word '*entremets*' ('sweet', U.S.A. 'dessert') applies more especially to sweet preparations such as creams, fritters, charlottes, tarts, flans and pies, puddings, soufflés and all kinds of ices, which belong to the domain of the cook rather than that of the confectioner.

For the most part, moreover, cakes are made from a somewhat limited number of basic doughs. In fact, there are only eight such doughs in French confectionery: flaky pastry (*feuilletage*), short pastry (*pâte brisée*), sweet pastry (*pâte sucrée*), brioche, savarin cake, baba, Génoise cake, choux pastry.

To these doughs may be added, for the preparation of various cakes, a large number of mixtures of additional ingredients such as almond paste, various kinds of sugar icing, fondant, French pastry cream (*crème pâtissière*), frangipane cream and other creams, *praline*,* etc.

In France, as well as in many other countries, there are symbolic cakes. These cakes, which in some cases have been made for centuries, are eaten, as it were, ritually, on certain feast days. Such, for example, is the Twelfth-Night cake, which symbolizes, gastronomically, the great feast of the Epiphany.

In France, from the very earliest times, a large number

Ancient gâteaux or centre-pieces, after Carême: Turkish pavilion; Ruins of a rotunda; Large fountain

of provinces have produced pastries peculiar to themselves.

Thus in Artois were made the *gâteaux razis*, and in Bourbonnais the ancient '*tartes de fromage broyé, de crème et de moyeux d'oeulz*'. Flat-cakes were made in Normandy, Picardy and Poitou and in some provinces of the south of France. Many of these cakes are still made. They are called variously *fouaces, fouaches, fouées* or *fouyasses*, according to the district. See HEARTH-CAKE.

It was usual in Paris, at Whitsuntide, to throw down upon the heads of the worshippers gathered under the vaulted roofs of the Cathedral of Notre-Dame, *nieules* and *oublies* (wafers), local Parisian confections. At the same time blazing wicks were showered on the congregation. This custom was not abandoned until the seventeenth century.

Among the many pastries which, in Paris and other great cities of the realm, were in high favour from the twelfth to the fifteenth centuries, we single out the following: the *échaudés* of which two variants, the *flageols* and the *gobets* were especially prized by the people of Paris; the *darioles*,* which were then a kind of little tartlet covered with narrow strips of pastry. Two kinds of *darioles* were made, one filled with cream cheese, the other with a kind of frangipane cream. The *talemouses*, known today as *talmouses* (cheese turnovers), of which those called '*St. Denis*' were held in the highest repute, were also much appreciated at that time. (See HORS-D'OEUVRE, *Hot hors-d'oeuvre*.)

Also highly-prized were the *casse-museaux** a dry hard pastry still made today, the *ratons* and the *petits choux*, and finally the *gâteaux feuilletés* which are mentioned in a Charter by Robert, Bishop of Amiens in 1311, and which proves that flaky pastry was known in France long before the seventeenth century, when, some writers claim, the process of making flaky pastry was invented by Claude Gelée, the painter.

In the centuries following, the number and variety of cakes was ever growing. In Paris, and in a good many other towns of the realm, pastry-cooks who, of course, were organized into guilds, produced not only the pastries listed above, but also *gâteaux bavueuls, gâteaux joyeux, brioches, bridaneaux, pains d'épices*, waffles of various kinds, marzipan biscuits, tarts and flans garnished in various ways; *pâtes royales* which were a kind of meringue; almond cakes, dough-cakes, Beauce cakes, Milanese cakes, cracknels and *flamiches*.

CAKES AND SMALL CAKES—To describe even briefly all the gâteaux, large and small, which are made in France is an impossibility because of their great number. We list below the French names of the principal ones and recipes for many of them will be found in this section or in alphabetical order throughout the book.

Alcazar, Allumettes, Almond cake, *Amandines*, Angel cake, Apple cake.

Baba, Bâton de Jacob, Biscuits de Bruxelles, Biscuits à la cuiller, Biscuits de Savoie, Bouchées à l'abricot, Boule de neige, Brestois, Breton, Brioche, Brioche Goubaud, Briochin.

Chausson aux pommes, Cornets à la crème, Conversation, Croquembouche.

Dampfnudeln, Darioles, Dartois, Dijon, Duchesse, Dumpling.

Échaudés, Éclairs.

Feuilleté aux amandes, Flan aux abricots, Flan aux abricots à l'alsacienne, Flan aux cerises, Flan aux fruits, Flan meringué, Flan aux mirabelles, Flan aux pêches, Flan aux poires, Flan aux pommes, Flan aux pommes grillé, Flan aux prunes.

Galette feuilletée, Galette à l'orange, Gâteau de cit-

Large cakes: Dijon, Madasgar; St James (*Larousse*

rouille, *Gâteau de voyage*, *Génoise à l'abricot*, *Génoise au chocolat*, *Génoise au moka*, *Génoise à la normande*, *Gimblette*, *Gorenflot*, *Gougère*.

Jalousie.

Kiche, *Kouglof*, *Kulich*, *Langues de chat*.

Macaroons, Madeira cake, *Madeleines*, *Malgache*, *Manchons*, *Mandarine*, *Manqué*, *Marignan*, *Mascotte*, *Massepain*, *Massillon*, *Mazarin*, Meringues, *Merveilles*, *Milanais*, *Millefeuilles*, *Millasous*, *Mirliton de Rouen*, *Moka*, *Mokatine*, *Moques*, *Monte-Cristo*, *Montmorency*, *Mousseline*.

Nantais, *Napolitain*, *Nemours*, *Néroli*, *Norvégien*, *Nougat*, *Nougatine*.

Oublies.

Pain anglais, *Pain à l'anis*, *Pain azyme*, *Pain complet*, *Pain de maïs*, *Pain de la Mecque*, *Palets de dames*, *Palmiers*, *Paneton*, *Parisien*, *Pastis du Béarn*, *Pavé au chocolat*, *Pavé aux fruits*, *Pavé au moka*, *Pavé aux noisettes*, *Pithiviers*, Plum cake, *Pogne de Romans*, *Pont-neuf*, *Poupelin*, *Profiteroles*, Punch cake, *Puits d'amour*.

Quatre-quarts, *Quiche*, *Quillet*.

Rabotte, *Ramequin*, *Religieuse*, *Richelieu*, *Rigodon*.

Gâteau Saint-Honoré (*Larousse*

Sablés, *Sacristains*, *Saint-Honoré*, *Saint-James*, *Saint-Michel*, *Savarin*, *Savarin à la crème*, *Savarin aux cerises*, *Schaleth à la juive*, Shortbread, *Solilème*, *Souvarov*, *Spéculos*, *Strizel*, *Strudel*, *Sultane*.

Tarte alsacienne, *Tarte aux fruits à l'allemande*, *Tarte aux fruits à l'anglaise*, *Tarte aux fruits*, *Tarte des demoiselles Tatin*, *Tarte au riz*, *Tarte à la rhubarbe*, *Tartelettes*, *Tôt-fait*, *Tantes*, *Trois-frères*.

Vacherin, *Victoria cake*.

Almond cake—See ALMOND.

Angel cake (American pastry)—Whisk 8 whites of egg until very stiff, adding 1 teaspoon cream of tartar at foamy stage. Add 1¼ cups of fine granulated sugar.

Fold in 1 cup of sifted flour, 1 teaspoon vanilla extract or 1½ teaspoons of vanilla-flavoured sugar. Avoid whisking too much.

Put this mixture into a large unbuttered angel cake pan, with a centre tube.

Bake in a slow oven (325°F.) for about 1 hour. Invert the pan on a cake rack and cool before taking the cake out of the mould.

Apple cake—See APPLE.

Christmas yule log. BÛCHE DE NOËL—Symbolic cake sold by all French confectioners at Christmas time. This log, generally made of a sheet of *Génoise cake pastry*,* spread with various creams (usually a butter cream) and rolled into the shape of a log, is decorated by using a forcing (pastry) bag with a fluted nozzle, filled with a chocolate or coffee butter cream and icing the cake in lengthwise strips to represent the bark of the log.

Note. At Christmas another symbolic cake is also made in France. It is shaped like a wooden shoe. This cake, generally made of nougat, is decorated with *petits fours*.*

German Easter cake (Ostertorte)

Easter cake, German (Ostertorte)—Make a sponge cake dough of 1 cup (125 grams) of sifted flour, 7 tablespoons (100 grams) of sugar, 5 eggs (yolks and whites separated) and 7 tablespoons (100 grams) of butter.

Place this dough in a cake tin with sloping sides. Bake in a hot oven (375°F.) 40 to 45 minutes.

Turn the cake out of the mould. Allow it to cool. Cut it across into two equal halves. Spread one half with coffee-flavoured butter-cream. Stick the two halves together. Ice the cake with *fondant* icing. See ICING. Decorate it with a border of butter-cream put through a forcing (pastry) bag and with little chocolate eggs each sitting on a little nest of the same cream. In the centre of the cake place a little chick made of sugar surrounded by 4 little chocolate eggs, each in its nest of butter-cream.

Fruit loaf or Bireweck (Alsatian pastry). PAIN DE FRUITS (PÂTISSERIE ALSACIENNE)—*Ingredients*: *Paste*. 7½ cups (1 kilo) of sieved bread flour, 1 ounce (30 grams) of yeast. (This paste is moistened with the liquid in which the fruit is cooked.)

Fruit. 1 pound (500 grams) of fresh or dried pears, ½ pound (250 grams) of fresh or dried apples, ½ pound (250 grams) of prunes, ½ pound (250 grams) of dried figs, ½ pound (250 grams) of peaches, ¼ pound (125 grams) of stoned dates, ½ pound (250 grams) of seedless Malaga raisins, ⅔ cup (100 grams) of citron candied peel, 1⅔ ounces (50 grams) of angelica, ¼ pound (125 grams) of whole almonds, ¼ pound (125 grams) of hazelnuts, 1 cup plus 2 tablepoons (125 grams) of shelled walnuts, ⅓ cup (50 grams) each lemon and orange rind cut into *julienne** strips, ⅔ cup (50 grams) of star anise, a pinch of spices and 2 quarts, 6 ounces (2 litres) of kirsch.

Method. Cook the pears, apples, prunes, peaches and dates in water, keeping them rather firm.

Make the dough, using flour and yeast and the water in which the fruit was cooked as liquid for moistening it. Leave the dough to rise for 2 hours.

Put the dough into a large bowl, add the well-drained fruit to it and mix well.

Add the raisins, almonds, hazelnuts, walnuts, dates, citron candied peel and angelica, cut in small dice, the orange and lemon peel, as well as the anise and the spices. Moisten with kirsch and blend well to incorporate all the fruit.

Divide the paste into 6-7-ounce (200-gram) pieces, shape them into small loaves, brush with water and bake in a low oven for 1¾ hours.

flour and ¼ pound (125 grams) of melted butter. Blend well.

Butter the cake tins, put a piece of buttered paper on the bottom, pour in the cake mixture and bake in a moderate oven.

Kulich (Russian Easter cake)—Place in a bowl (which has been warmed in advance) 11 cups (1 kilo 500 grams) of flour. Make a well in the centre. Place in this well 1 ounce of yeast which has been dissolved in ¼ cup of warm milk with ¼ cup of flour added to make a leaven. Work the yeast mixture into the flour. Cover the bowl and stand in a warm place for 1¼ hours to allow the dough to rise.

Add 1 pound (500 grams) of butter, half-melted, 10 whole eggs, 1 cup (250 grams) of fine sugar and a pinch of salt.

Beat the mixture until it is no longer sticky to the touch and comes away cleanly from the bowl.

Now take another 7½ cups (1 kilo) of flour, and work it in little by little, beating the dough lightly until it is thoroughly mixed. Add ½ pound (250 grams) each of sultanas, currants and raisins, cleaned and with the stalks removed. Leave the dough to rise once more in a warm place.

When the dough is well risen, turn it out on a floured table. Keep a small piece for the decoration of the cake and make the rest of the dough into a large ball. Place this in a very large, well-buttered baking-tin.

Roll out the remaining dough and cut it into fairly long, wide strips. Twist them. Decorate the cake with these twisted strips. Allow the cake to rise again for ½ hour.

Brush the cake with a mixture of egg yolks and sugar, sprinkle chopped almonds on top and bake in a hot oven.

It is customary in Russia to ice and decorate the top of the cake, after it has been turned out of the baking-tin and set on a large dish.

Small cakes (*Larousse*)

Genoa cake (I). PAIN DE GÊNES (I)—*Ingredients.* 1⅓ cups (325 grams) of granulated sugar, 1 pound (500 grams) of blanched almonds, 10 tablespoons (150 grams) of butter, ⅔ cup (100 grams) of cornflour, corn or potato starch, 5 eggs, powdered vanilla and rum or curaçao.

Method. Pound the almonds with the sugar to reduce them to powder. Put this mixture into a bowl and stir with a wooden spoon, adding the eggs one by one. Continue to stir the mixture for 10 minutes, then add the cornflour, vanilla and the liqueur. Incorporate melted butter and mix, lifting the batter.

Put this mixture into buttered cake tins (there are special ones for this cake) with a piece of buttered paper on the bottom. Bake in a moderate oven.

Genoa cake will keep well for 5 or 6 days.

Genoa cake (II). PAIN DE GÊNES (II)—Pound 2¾ cups (375 grams) of fine castor sugar in a mortar with 6 eggs and 2 drops of bitter almond essence. When the mixture is very frothy, pour in ½ cup (65 grams) of sieved cake

Maids of honour. DEMOISELLES D'HONNEUR—The recipe for these little cakes which, in England, used to enjoy a great reputation, was for a long time, so it is said, kept a secret. History goes so far as to relate that it was Anne Boleyn, then a maid of honour at the English Court, who was the first to make these cakes, in the hope of pleasing King Henry VIII, who was very fond of his food. And it was King Henry who, finding them excellent, called them *maids of honour*, which has been their name ever since.

It is said that the secret recipe for this cake was bought for a thousand pounds. *Maids of honour* were once the speciality of Richmond (Surrey). A confectioner there claimed to have the secret recipe and he alone, it was said, could make the true maids of honour, which he sent out daily in large numbers all over the country.

The cakes are like little tarts of light puff pastry, with a filling made of egg, ground almonds and lemon.

Mecca cakes. PAINS DE LA MECQUE—The paste for these is the same as *Chou paste*. See CHOUX.

Force the paste through a pastry bag on to a metal baking-sheet, squeezing it out in the shape of little eggs. Brush with beaten egg, sprinkle with granulated sugar and bake in a hot oven.

Plum cake—English cake which is prepared as follows:

Put 1 pound (500 grams) of butter into a bowl, soften it until it becomes creamy, then whisk until it turns white. Add 3½ cups (500 grams) of fine sugar. Whisk again for a few minutes, then incorporate in the mixture 8 to 9 eggs, putting them in one by one and whisking all the time. Add ½ pound (250 grams) of chopped candied peel (lemon, orange and citron), 1 cup (200 grams) of stoned Malaga raisins, 1 cup (150 grams) of best sultanas and 1¼ cups (150 grams) of currants.

Add 4 cups (500 grams) of sifted cake flour, mixed with 1½ teaspoons (6 grams) of baking powder, and, finally, put in the grated rind of 2 lemons and 3 tablespoons (4 centilitres) of rum.

Line a rectangular baking-tin with greased paper so that it extends above the rim of the tin by 1½ inches.

Pour the cake mixture into the tin, taking care not to fill it over two-thirds, to allow the cake to rise.

Bake in a moderate oven for 2 hours, 45 minutes.

Note. The plum cake can also be baked in round or square tins.

Punch-cake—Fill a charlotte mould with Savoy sponge-cake mixture. Cook this cake in the oven. Turn it out and leave it to stale for two days.

Cut the cake horizontally in three slices of equal thickness, each of these slices constituting a cake which is soaked in rum and covered with apricot jam. Decorate with meringue. Finish in the oven.

Meringue for the punch-cake. Put into a saucepan 4 tablespoons (100 grams) of apricot jam which has been put through a fine sieve: add ¼ cup (½ decilitre) of rum, a spoonful of curaçao and ½ cup (100 grams) of fine sugar. Mix into this jam 6 stiffly beaten egg whites.

Spice cake—In principle rye flour should be used for the spiced loaf, but if it is not available, ordinary wheaten flour can be used. It is not necessary to use best quality honey for this cake.

There are two methods of preparing it:

First method. Heat 1 pound (500 grams) of honey nearly to boiling-point and remove scum which rises to the surface. Put 3¾ cups (500 grams) of sieved bread flour into a bowl, make a well in the centre, pour in the honey and stir with a wooden spoon. As some flours are more absorbent than others, it may be necessary to add a little more to obtain a firm paste. Roll this paste into a ball, wrap in a cloth and leave to prove for an hour. At the end of this time, add ⅜ ounce (12 grams) of powdered yeast (dried chemical yeast which is used without moistening) and knead vigorously to give it body.

Second method. Mix 3¾ cups (500 grams) of sieved bread flour and 1 pound (500 grams) of honey, leave to stand and knead as described above, adding ¾ cup (100 grams) of fine sugar, ⅜ ounce (12 grams) of dried yeast, used as indicated previously, 1½ teaspoons (5 grams) of baking powder, ⅓ cup (50 grams) of blanched, dried and chopped almonds, 1½ tablespoons (30 grams) of candied and chopped orange and lemon peel.

To this dough, which is obviously superior to the first, the following ingredients can also be added, if liked: ⅓ ounce (10 grams) of aniseed, a good pinch of cinnamon, the same amount of finely pounded cloves, and ½ tablespoon of grated or chopped orange or lemon peel.

Baking. Whatever dough you choose, roll it out to the desired thickness and put it on a baking-sheet, with slightly buttered edges. The paste can also be put into square or other baking tins. Bake in a moderate oven. As soon as the spiced loaf is baked, brush the surface quickly with milk sweetened with a lot of sugar (it should be like a thick syrup) and leave for a few seconds in the oven. Sweetened milk can be replaced by sugar syrup cooked to thread degree. See SUGAR.

Wheaten flour can be replaced by rye flour.

Twelfth-Night cakes. GÂTEAUX DES ROIS—Even though the celebration of the religious rites associated with such festivals as Christmas, New Year and Twelfth Night is tending to decline, the gastronomic custom of baking Twelfth-Night cake is still observed.

To be sure, the mystical significance of these festivals is virtually unknown today, and no one now chants when the 'king' drinks, the old couplet of our forefathers:

Laus au roy! Nous la lui devons.
Il a beu dru! . . . A nous! beuvons.

Laud the king, we owe it to him.
He has drunk lustily. It is our turn now.
Come, let us drink.

But things were very different in past ages. The kind of celebration which takes place in most French homes when the Twelfth-Night cake is eaten is a relic of the pagan feast called the *Basilinda.* It is believed that the word *phoebe* (which is the name given to the bean or other symbolic favour which is baked in the cake) is a corruption of the word *éphèbe* which to the Romans meant 'a son of the house'.

It was once customary to say '*Éphèbe*' (young man) to a child who was hidden under the table and who, from there, pointed out the guests who were to receive the pieces of ritual cake. He would reply '*Domine*'. Then would follow questions regarding the persons who were to receive the piece which held the *phoebe*.

In the seventeenth century, the priests of Saint-Germain launched a very vigorous attack on the Twelfth-Night cake ceremonial. But, long before that, attention had been drawn to the excesses to which this custom could give rise.

There was in Cambridge a manuscript by Thomas Neagorgus from which Pasquier quotes a passage referring to this festival:

'At last comes the blessed day of the Magi who, led by a star, came to offer gifts to the new-born Christ. There is much talk everywhere of these kings, who were only three in number.

'Many come together to dine then and elect a king by lot or vote. This king chooses ministers for himself. Next, he opens the feast which lasts for several days, the celebrations continuing until there are only empty purses left, and the creditors come to be paid.

'Their sons then make haste to follow their example; they too elect a king and hold sumptuous banquets either with stolen money, or at their parents' expense, thereby learning luxury and larceny at one and the same time.

'Finally, on the same day, the head of the family, the good master, causes to be brought forth, according to his means and the number of his guests, a cake in which has been hidden a silver coin which must serve as a token. He cuts the cake into as many pieces as there are members of his family present and gives each one his piece. At the same time, he keeps back one for "the infant Jesus", for "the Virgin" and for the "Magi". He then gives these to the poor in their names. Whosoever receives the piece containing the silver coin is recognized as king, and all the guests shout for joy.'

Nowadays, the ceremonial attending the distribution among the guests of pieces of the Twelfth-Night cake is no doubt somewhat different and certainly does not last as long as it used to. Nevertheless, custom demands that the person or persons on whom the lot has fallen as king or queen of the feast should, in their turn, give dinner-parties at their homes, parties during which the symbolic cake is served.

The nature of this cake varies in different regions of France. In Paris, and in all the neighbouring provinces of Île-de-France, Twelfth-Night cake is a flaky pastry *galette*.* In all the districts of the south-east and south-west, this cake is made from yeast-dough, more or less the same as *brioche** dough, and is in the form of a crown.

Bordeaux Twelfth-Night cake (I). GÂTEAU DES ROIS DE BORDEAUX—3¾ cups (500 grams) sieved flour, 1 cup (200 grams) butter, 1 cup (200 grams) fine sugar, ¾ ounce (20 grams) of yeast, 8 whole eggs, 2 tablespoons (10 grams) salt, 1 grated lemon-rind.

Method. Make a ring of the flour on the table. Place in the middle the yeast and salt. Mix. Knead the dough, adding the eggs one by one, the lemon-rind, the sugar, mixed in a little at a time, and finally the butter softened to a creamy texture. Mix all these ingredients thoroughly.

Place this dough, which should be fairly limp, in a bowl, and let it stand in a warm place through the night, during which it will rise.

Next day, break down the dough, as for *brioche*,* and divide it into equal parts, each of which should be made into the shape of a crown, and then placed on buttered paper. Leave it to rise in a hot cupboard. Allow the crowns to cool. Brush them with beaten egg. Arrange round the top thin slices of citron and crystallized sugar. Bake in a medium oven.

Bordeaux Twelfth-Night cake (II). GÂTEAU DES ROIS BORDELAIS—Make a yeast dough of 2 cups (250 grams) of sieved flour and ¾ ounce (20 grams) of yeast. (The dough should be fairly limp. To obtain the required consistency add water as necessary.) Leave the dough to rise in a warm place.

Take 8 cups (1 kilo) of sieved flour. Make a well in it.

Place in the centre of the well 8 whole eggs and a very small pinch of salt.

Make a lukewarm syrup of 1 cup (250 grams) of sugar, the grated rinds of 2 lemons and of 2 oranges, a ½-pint combination of orange-flower water, water and rum; stir gently together. Add to the ingredients in the well and mix gradually with the flour. When these ingredients are well blended, add the yeast dough and mix thoroughly.

Place the dough in a floured bowl. Leave it to rise in a warm place. Break down the dough.

On the floured table, shape the dough into a crown. Place it on a strong sheet of buttered paper on a baking-sheet. Press pieces of citron into the top of the crown. Leave it to rise. Brush with yolk of egg. Bake in a slow oven (300°F.) for 1¼ hours or until cake shrinks from cake pan.

Limoux Twelfth-Night cake. GÂTEAU DES ROIS DE LIMOUX—This cake, which is also in the shape of a crown, is made with a yeast dough similar to that used for the *Bordeaux Twelfth-Night cake*. The Limoux cake is richly decorated with candied citron.

Wedding cake. GÂTEAU DE NOCE—In England, in the homes of rich and poor alike, the centre-piece of the wedding reception is the wedding cake. But this cake is a symbol rather than a delicacy, a tradition handed down from one century to the next, whose origins are lost in the mists of antiquity. The wedding cake is, above all, a monumental cake and it is obviously impossible to make a very large cake with a mixture which is too crumbling, too fine or too light.

Massive a wedding cake must always be, since, after the wedding, it must be cut up into ten, twenty, a hundred or a thousand slices, according to the extent of the family's circle of acquaintances. Each piece of cake is placed in a box, especially made for the purpose, a box lavishly decorated and gilded, to be sent to the four corners of the earth so that relations and friends in the most distant parts of the world may receive a souvenir from the mother country. This cake may cost anything from one to a hundred pounds.

Here are the ingredients from which the wedding cake mixture is made. It is the same as that used for ordinary plum cake: 2 pounds (1 kilo) butter, 2 pounds (1 kilo) sugar, 1 pound (500 grams) ground almonds or pounded almonds mixed with some of the eggs, 1 pound (500 grams) chopped candied peel, 1 pound (500 grams) each stoned raisins, sultanas and currants, 9½ cups (1 kilo 250 grams) flour mixed with 2 teaspoons (8 grams) of baking powder and sieved, 16-18 whole eggs, according to size, 1 tablespoon (15 grams) allspice, ½ cup (1 decilitre) rum. See *Plum cake*.

Line the bottom and sides of the required number of graduated baking-tins with paper. Fill the tins with this mixture. Bake 2½-3 hours at 375°F.

The tiers of the cake must be made several days in advance to give the mixture time to settle.

To decorate the cake. Trim each tier so that it is perfectly flat and perfectly round. Spread each tier with apricot jam. Cover them completely with a layer of almond paste ½ centimetre thick. Level the tops of the tiers with a rolling-pin. Leave them to dry for 24 hours. Ice the sides of each tier, covering all parts which will still be visible when the tiers are set one on top of the other.

Arrange the tiers on top of one another on a low stand of the same diameter as the base of the cake.

Decorate the cake with sugar motifs of different shapes with *Royal icing* (see ICING), using an icing-horn (pastry tube).

Place on the top tier an allegorical motif or a vase of flowers with the sprays trailing over the cake.

CAKE RACK OR TRAY. GRILLE—A flat wire tray on which cakes are set to cool when they are taken out of the oven.

CALABASH GOURD OR BOTTLE GOURD. CALEBASSE—The fruit of the calabash tree (*Crescentia cujete* of the family *Bignoniaceae*) of which several species are known. One species has long leaves, green hard shell with acid white pulp inside, which in tropical America and the West Indies is made into a highly esteemed syrup. Calabash pipes (imported from South Africa), drinking vessels and other articles are made from these gourds.

CALAMARY (SQUID). CALMAR—Common name for certain varieties of cephalopoda, which have elongated bodies and arms or tentacles with suckers on tips.

They are found mainly in mid-ocean depths or way out to sea, but come to spawn near the coasts.

Like cuttle-fish, calamary have, situated near the heart, a bag containing a dark liquid, a kind of ink which is used in painting under the name of *sepia*.

The fleshy body of the calamary or the visceral sac is enclosed in a muscular mantle, tapering towards the base and ending with wing-shaped appendages. Inside the body there is a transparent shell.

This mollusc is considered a great delicacy in the Mediterranean region. In Provence it is known under the name of *Tantonnet*.

Stuffed calamary (squid) à la marseillaise. CALMAR FARCI À LA MARSEILLAISE—'Take 4 calamaries (squid), remove the black ink bag and the cranial cartilage. Remove the tentacles and wash the calamaries.

'Put the body sacs flat on a cloth. Chop an onion finely, fry it in a few tablespoons of oil, add the finely chopped tentacles, 2 or 3 equally finely chopped tomatoes, season and fry together. Soak a piece of French bread the size of a fist in milk, squeeze it out and add to the frying-pan, together with 2 cloves of garlic chopped with parsley. Blend well, moisten with 2 tablespoons of hot water, add 2 or 3 yolks of egg and remove from heat. You should now have a forcemeat fairly thick in consistency and of good flavour.

'Fill the calamaries up to three-quarters, sew them up to enclose the forcemeat and put them one by one into a sauté pan with some oil.

'Separately, fry a finely chopped onion in oil. Add a bay leaf, a crushed clove of garlic and blend in a tablespoon of flour. Moisten with a glass of white wine and an equal quantity of hot water. Season with salt and pepper and leave to simmer for ¼ hour. Strain this sauce over the calamaries, sprinkle with breadcrumbs and oil and brown the top in a slow oven. Serve at once with the sauce poured over.

'The calamaries can also be stuffed with chopped tentacles and spinach.' (Reboul's recipe from *La Cuisine provençale*.)

CALAPPA (BOX-CRAB). CALAPPE (COQ DE MER)—A crustacean which has a certain similarity to the crab.

CALF—See also VEAL.

Calf's brains—See OFFAL (VARIETY MEATS).

Calf's crow. FRAISE DE VEAU—The crow is the membrane which covers the intestines of the calf or lamb. This may be cooked in various ways. See OFFAL (VARIETY MEATS), *Calf's mesentery*.

In whatever fashion the crow is to be prepared it must first be cooked in a flour-and-water stock, as for *Calf's head*.

Calf's ears. OREILLES DE VEAU—Calf's ears, whatever method of preparation it is desired to apply to them, must first be carefully cleaned and strongly blanched. See OFFAL (VARIETY MEATS).

Calf's feet. PIEDS DE VEAU—Having been blanched and cooked in a flour-and-water stock, like *Calf's head*, the feet may be finished off in various ways. For their preparation see OFFAL (VARIETY MEATS).

Calf's head. TÊTE DE VEAU—Calf's head is prepared in numerous ways. It is most often served *à la vinaigrette* after having been blanched and cooked in a flour-and-water stock.

For the different methods of preparation see OFFAL (VARIETY MEATS).

Calf's heart. COEUR DE VEAU—This can be prepared in different ways. All the recipes given for veal kidneys are applicable. Calf's heart may also be cooked whole, braised, pot roasted, or roasted. See OFFAL (VARIETY MEATS).

Calf's kidneys. ROGNONS DE VEAU—See OFFAL (VARIETY MEATS).

Calf's liver. FOIE DE VEAU—See OFFAL (VARIETY MEATS).

Calf's sweetbreads. RIS DE VEAU—Calf's sweetbreads are considered the most delicate of the white offal or variety meats. They can be cooked whole, sliced in *médaillons* or in various ways. Under OFFAL (VARIETY MEATS) will be found numerous recipes for preparing them.

Calf's tongue. LANGUE DE VEAU—This can be braised, or may be poached in a flour-and-water stock in the same way as *Calf's head*. See OFFAL (VARIETY MEATS).

Calf's udder. TÉTINE DE VEAU—This is mostly used in Jewish cookery, taking the place of bacon fat.

After having been soaked in cold water and blanched, the udder can be braised. It is served like the *noix* and the *fricandeau*.

CALORIE—Unit of heat. *Large or great calorie* is the amount of heat required to raise 1 kilogram of water 1°C.; the *petite calorie* is the amount of heat necessary to raise 1 gram of water from 14·5°C. to 15·5°C. The calorie is used as a unit in expressing the heat and energy-producing qualities of food.

Food substances, in the final analysis, are the combination of results produced by the energy borrowed from solar radiations—the source of all energy on earth.

On their decomposition, which is effected first by digestion and then by a transformation which they undergo in our organism, these substances restore this energy, which can be measured by the heat released.

Numerous experiments which have been carried out have enabled scientists to establish the co-efficients of calories released by albuminoids, fats and carbohydrates. Knowing the composition of a food product, it is possible to calculate its value in energy, measured in calories.

It should, however, always be borne in mind that, in practice, these figures can only be *approximate and average* and one should not draw too rigid conclusions from them.

CAMBACÉRÈS (Jean-Jacques, Régis de)—Cambacérès was the Second Consul appointed by Bonaparte after the *coup d'état* of 18 Brumaire, then High Chancellor of the Empire, later made Duke of Parma. He was born in Montpellier in 1753 and died in Paris in 1824.

It is said that Cambacérès was a great gastronome, but it would appear, from what contemporary gossip-writers tell us, that he was rather an eccentric type of a gastronome and something of a snob, even before this word was invented. Duchardon (in *Avant de quitter la table*) writes: 'His quarrels with his table-companion, d'Aigrefeuille (another gastronome of the time), on the subject of turbot's tongue, about which they both raved, and which d'Aigrefeuille managed to purloin before the fish appeared on the table, are legendary.' Legendary indeed and, as is the case with most legends, not very reliable. Turbot's tongue, as that of most fish, does not, in fact, constitute a choice morsel over which true gastronomes would quarrel. This anecdote, even if it is true, only goes to prove that Cambacérès was not a very knowledgeable gastronome. Here is what Jean Lhomer, advocate at the Court of Appeal, says in his essay about the celebrated diplomat:

'Cambacérès had, after Talleyrand, the best table in Paris. It used to be said: "At the Emperor's table one dines very quickly, at the High Chancellor's very well and at the Chief Treasurer's—not at all." Marco de

Cambacérès (1753–1824)

Saint-Hilaire wrote in his diary, "Yesterday I had the honour of being admitted to the table of Consul Cambacérès and I must confess that out of the four courses—each of which consisted of at least 16 or 18 dishes, and about a quarter of which I had no chance of tasting—there was not one single one which would not have been approved by Lucullus or Apicius, of gastronomical memory. It is beyond doubt that under the Republic, cuisine in France has made enormous steps forward, and I proclaim it here and now to be the best in the world".'

Cambacérès prepared his dinners (himself compiling the menus) with meticulous care and amazing taste. In his *Memoirs*, Bourienne tells us: 'During the Congress of Lunéville, the First Consul, on being informed that mail-coaches were carrying a lot of goods, in particular delicacies for the table of prominent persons, gave an order that henceforward postal services were to carry nothing but despatches. That very evening, Cambacérès came into the salon, where I was alone with the First Consul, who was already laughing at the embarrassment he caused to his colleague. "Well, what can you want at this hour, Cambacérès?" "I have come to ask you to make one exception in the order you have given the Director of Post. How do you expect us to make friends with people if we can't give them elegant dishes? You know yourself that, to a great extent, it is at one's table that one governs." The First Consul laughed a great deal, called him a glutton and finished by slapping him on the shoulder and saying, "Console yourself, my poor Cambacérès, and don't be angry. The mail-coaches will continue to carry your truffled turkeys, your Strasbourg pâtés, your Mayence hams and your partridges." '

CAMEL—CHAMEAU—Family of mammals which include large animals with one or two humps. The latter are known as dromedaries. Moses forbade the Israelites to eat camels' meat. The Arabs are not bound by this edict, but only eat camels when they are young and the meat tender.

From the time of Gallien, camels' meat was regarded with favour. Aristophanes maintains that it was served to royalty, and Aristotle praises it.

The hump, the feet and the stomach are the parts most appreciated by connoisseurs.

Camel couscous (Arab cooking). COUSCOUS AU CHAMEAU—Prepare the couscous in the usual way, but substituting young camel's meat for the mutton. See COUSCOUS.

Camel escalopes with pimentos and aubergines (eggplant). TRANCHES DE CHAMEAU AUX POIVRONS ET AUBERGINES—Sauté in butter slices or escalopes of camel meat taken from the sirloin, which have been marinated with oil, lemon juice, salt, pepper and spices.

Drain the slices, and set them on a round dish. Put on each slice two rounds of aubergines sautéed in oil. Pour over the juices of the meat to which have been added (for 4 escalopes) 2 sweet pimentos, peeled, cut into strips and simmered in oil, a $\frac{1}{2}$ cup ($1\frac{1}{2}$ decilitres) of white wine, $1\frac{1}{4}$ cups (3 decilitres) of tomato purée, and a little garlic. Sprinkle with chopped parsley.

Camel's feet à la vinaigrette. PIEDS DE CHAMEAU À LA VINAIGRETTE—Soak the feet of a young camel. Cook them in a *White court-bouillon* in the same way as for *Calf's feet*. See OFFAL (VARIETY MEATS). Drain them. Serve with *Vinaigrette sauce*. (See SAUCE, *Cold sauces*.)

Roast camel's fillet. FILET DE CHAMEAU RÔTI—This is how the fillet of a young camel or camel colt is prepared.

Marinate the fillet with oil, lemon juice, salt, pepper and spices. Roast it on a spit in the same way as for a beef fillet.

The fillet can be larded with strips of larding bacon.

Roast camel's hump. BOSSE DE CHAMEAU RÔTIE—Only the hump of a very young camel is prepared in this way.

Marinate the meat with oil, lemon juice, salt, pepper, spices. Roast it in the same way as for roast sirloin of beef. (See BEEF.) Serve with its own gravy and watercress.

Camel's paunch à la marocaine. VENTRE DE CHAMEAU À LA MAROCAINE—Marinate a piece of camel's paunch weighing 4 pounds (2 kilos) trimmed and tied with string, with oil, lemon juice, spices and the usual vegetables. Brown in oil in an earthenware casserole. Remove it when it is properly browned all over. Then put 2 sliced medium onions into the casserole. Simmer gently and when they are soft add 4 tomatoes, peeled, seeded and chopped, 4 large sweet pimentos, peeled, seeded and cut into dice, a root of fennel, its outer parts removed and the inner core cut into four, and 4 sliced cloves of garlic. Season with salt and pepper. Cook for 15 minutes.

Return the camel's paunch to the casserole. Pour over it 2 cups (4 decilitres) of good stock. Add the liquor from the marinade. Add a *bouquet garni* consisting of parsley, thyme, bay and zest of orange. Simmer for $2\frac{1}{2}$ hours. Add $\frac{1}{2}$ pound (250 grams) of rice after removing the *bouquet garni*. Cook for a further 25 minutes.

Take out the meat, and set it on a large round dish with the rice on each side.

Camel pilaf. PILAF DE CHAMEAU—This is prepared with lean camel's meat taken from the fillet or sirloin in the same way as *Mutton pilaf*. See PILAF.

Ragoût of camel with tomato sauce. RAGOÛT DE CHAMEAU À LA TOMATE—This is prepared with camel meat cut into square pieces, marinated in oil, lemon juice, salt, pepper, spices, in the same way as *Ragoût of mutton* with tomato sauce. See MUTTON.

Camel ribs with rice. CÔTES DE CHAMEAU AU RIZ—Trim the camel ribs. Marinate them with oil, lemon juice, salt, pepper, spices.

Sauté them in butter, lard or oil. Drain them of fat,

and set them on a round dish. Garnish with a *Rice pilaf*. (See PILAF.) Dress with a sauce made with the juices remaining in the pan to which a few tablespoons of stock have been added, and a little tomato sauce seasoned with garlic.

All the methods of preparation applying to ribs of veal or of pork can be applied to camel's ribs.

CAMEMBERT CHEESE—See CHEESE.

CAMOMILE (or CHAMOMILE)—Common name of a genus of herbs of the composite family. The best known is *Anthemis nobilis* which is used for medicinal purposes. Its dried flower-heads are used as infusion and the usual dose is 5 grams per litre of boiling water. This infusion, known as 'camomile tea' is bitter and astringent.

CAMPANULA. CAMPANULE—This common field plant, which has a purplish-violet flower, is edible and can be eaten in salad (both leaves and roots), if picked before the plant develops its stalk.

CAMPEACHY WOOD (LOGWOOD). BOIS DE CAMPÊCHE—Tree which grows profusely in Mexico chiefly around Campeachy Bay, hence its name. Its wood, by a process of boiling, produces colouring matter—red on contact with acids, turning violet on contact with alkali. Deprived of its toxic properties, it is used in the manufacture of liqueurs and for improving the colour of wine.

CAN, DRUM. BIDON—Originally wooden jug of 5 litres capacity; nowadays metal container for liquids.

As a slang expression in French this word has taken the same meaning as *bedon* (belly).

CANAPÉS—The primary meaning of this word is a slice of crustless bread, cut in rectangular shapes, the size and thickness of which varies depending on the nature of ingredients to be put on them.

Canapés which are also called *croûtons* are made of toasted or fried bread and can either be spread with various mixtures or left plain, depending on the nature of the dishes for which they are to serve as an accompaniment.

Canapés are mostly used as an accompaniment to winged game, and, in this case, they are spread with *à gratin forcemeat* or some other forcemeat and when actually at table the trail intestines of birds, whcih are not drawn for cooking, are also spread on the *canapés*. Recipes for preparing these will be found under the entries entitled RÔTIES (i.e. TRAIL and WOODCOCK).

Canapés (hors-d'oeuvre)—These *canapés*, which are made from crustless bread, home-made bread, common brioche or pastry, are garnished with various compositions.

Recipes for this type of *canapé*, some of which are referred to as *Canapés à la russe*, will be found in the section entitled HORS-D'OEUVRE. See *Cold hors-d'oeuvre*.

Canapés for various dishes—These *canapés* are cut and browned in the same way as those described above. They are mostly described as croûtons and are used as foundations for fried or grilled escalopes, noisettes, tournedos, kidneys, etc.

CANARY-GRASS. ALPISTE—A genus of plants of the graminacae family, one species of which is cultivated in the Canary Islands for its seed, rich in edible starch, which the local inhabitants use as food. It was first introduced into Spain; from there it was brought to the south of France, where it became quickly naturalized. In some parts of France it is called canary grain, bird grain or spike grain.

The other species of this plant are suitable only for forage.

CANCALAISE, A LA—Lenten garnish composed of oysters and shrimps' tails in *Normande sauce*. See SAUCE.

CANCALE—Small fishing port situated near the English Channel and famous for its 'blonde' plump oysters.

CANE. CANNE—Name commonly given to different species of reeds. *Sweet calamus* was used in the past as an infusion. The roots of *Giant* or *Bamboo* reed are still used in popular medicine as an infusion against lacteal disorders. *Sugar cane* produces sugar.

Cane juice. VESOU—The liquid juice which comes out of sugar cane crushed by the mill. It is also called *vin de canne* (cane wine).

CANNELONI. CANNELONS GARNIS—A pasta dish which is served as an *hors-d'oeuvre* or as a small *entrée*. See HORS-D'OEUVRE, *Hot hors-d'oeuvre*.

CANNING—See PRESERVATION OF FOOD.

CANON—Old French wine measure of one-sixteenth of a litre. Slang term for a unit of liquid measure used by the wine merchants. The word comes from *canon*, which means a *glass* in masonic terminology.

CANTAL CHEESE—See CHEESE.

CANTALOUP—The name of a melon which is thus called because originally it was mainly grown at Cantalupo, near Rome. See MELON.

CANTEEN. CANTINE—Camp or barrack shop for liquor and provisions, refreshment room at work, etc.

The name also applies to a small box containing cooking equipment for officers, and to a vessel for carrying liquids.

CAPELIN OR CAPLIN. CAPELAN, CAPEL—Small Mediterranean fish which is prepared as *Whiting*.*

CAPENDU—French name of a variety of red apples with a very short stalk.

CAPER. CÂPRE—The floral bud of the caper-bush, which grows wild in the south of France, in Algeria, Turkey, in Asia Minor, etc. Capers are pickled in vinegar and used as seasoning and condiment. The best are the round (*nonesuch*) capers from the departments of Var and Bouches-du-Rhône. They are firmer and smaller than the English capers, and should not be confused with pickled nasturtium seeds.

CAPITAINE—French name for sea-fish which resembles carp and is cooked in the same manner. See CARP.

CAPON. CHAPON—Young cock which has been castrated and fattened to improve its flavour. Capons are prepared in the same way as chickens. See CHICKEN.

Capon in a pastry crust 'belle aurore'. CHAPON EN PÂTÉ BELLE AURORE—Bone a capon. Spread out the boned capon on a table, season with salt and spices. Prepare two stuffings separately. The first is made with the meat of a fowl, with lean pork, pork fat and ham, seasoned and combined with egg. The second stuffing is made with *à gratin forcemeat** (prepared with chicken livers, partridge livers, beef marrow, truffles and chopped mushrooms), the whole well-seasoned and combined with egg. Stuff the capon with these two stuffings in alternate layers, and dispose between the layers thin strips of veal fillet, lean pork, breast of chicken, wings of red partridge, saddle of hare, and veal sweetbreads (blanched and cooled under pressure), all these ingredients being marinated for a considerable time in oil, cognac, lemon juice and spices beforehand. Complete the composition of the galantine with quartered truffles. Make the stuffed capon into the form of a substantial roll, tie it up in a cloth, secure with string and cook in a *daubière** for 45 minutes on a foundation of aromatic vegetables (onion, carrots, celery) moistened with a very little stock and flavoured with Madeira wine. Drain the capon and cool it as quickly as possible. Remove the string and cloth in which it is wrapped, and lay it on a sheet of fine pastry, set on an iron baking-sheet. Cover with a second sheet of the same pastry, and join the edges of the two sheets of pastry to form a rather long oval. Decorate the top of the crust with cut-out pastry decorations. Make a hole in the top so that the steam can escape. Gild with egg yolk and bake in a moderate oven. As soon as the pâté is cooked pour in a few tablespoons of strong chicken stock improved with Madeira, and very much concentrated. Serve separately a ragoût of mushrooms and truffles sautéed in butter, and *Suprême sauce* (see SAUCE) with a little Madeira added.

CAPONATA (Sicilian cookery)—Peel 4 aubergines (eggplant) and cut them into large dice. Sprinkle with salt and when they have yielded their juice, fry them in oil.

Prepare 3 tablespoons (50 grams) of capers, ½ cup (100 grams) of black olives, 1 head or heart of blanched celery, 4 de-salted anchovies, the whole shredded into *julienne** strips.

Meanwhile, slice a white onion thinly and fry it lightly in oil. Add 3 tablespoons (50 grams) of sugar and 1 cup (2 decilitres) of *tomato purée*. Cook down well until it takes on a dark colour, after which add ¼ cup of vinegar. Leave to simmer for a few minutes, season generously, add some chopped parsley and mix this sauce with the aubergines and the other ingredients mentioned above. Put this mixture into a vegetable-dish, piling it up into a dome shape. Decorate the top with slices of spiny lobster, tunny (tuna) fish in oil and *poutargue* (salted and dried grey mullet roes).

This dish is served both in the summer and in the winter. It is advisable to prepare it well in advance to allow all the ingredients to be permeated by the sweet-sour taste of the tomato sauce.

CAPUCIN—Name by which the French hunters call the hare. See HARE.

CARAFE—A large-based glass or crystal bottle or flagon used for water or wine. A *carafon* is a small carafe.

CARAMEL (BURNT SUGAR)—Caramel is used in cookery for colouring clear soups, stews, gravies, and sauces, brown stocks, jellies, etc. It is also used in pastry-making. Although this adjuvant appears useless in home cookery where every effort should be made to preserve the natural colour of the dishes, we deem it necessary to give the method for its preparation.

'Melt some good sugar without moistening it and allow it to colour slightly on the red coals, which takes a quarter of an hour. When it acquires an amber-red colour, moisten it with a glass of water and put on a high flame. After boiling for a few minutes you will have caramel of a beautiful amber-red, that has nothing in common with the bitter caramel, which is allowed to go black on a high flame and which is commonly called "*monkey's blood*".' (From Carême.)

Keep in small bottles with longitudinally-incised corks which allow the caramel to be poured drop by drop.

Caramels (confectionery). CARAMELS MOUS—*Ingredients.* 2¾ cups (375 grams) of fine sugar, 3 cups (75 centilitres) of double cream, 7 tablespoons (100 grams) of finest butter, 3½ ounces (100 grams) of glucose (or 5 tablespoons of dark corn syrup), 1 vanilla bean.

Method. Put the sugar, cream, glucose (or corn syrup) and vanilla into an untinned copper basin. Put to boil on a high flame stirring all the time with a wooden spoon. Place a bowl of very cold water nearby and as soon as the sugar begins to boil, dip your hand into water and wipe the sides of the basin to detach the sugar which is beginning to crystallize. Perform this operation as quickly as possible, and dip your hand immediately into cold water. When the sugar has reached the degree of cooking known as *thread*, add the butter in small pieces stirring with a wooden spoon all the time. Cook until the ball degree is reached. Remove the basin from heat. Pour the sugar on a slightly oiled marble slab, keeping it in check with oiled iron or wooden rulers, which should be put in such a way as to form a sort of frame, the sugar layer having a thickness of ¼ inch. Remove the vanilla bean, leave until completely cold, then cut into small squares of desired dimensions.

Note. When the sugar is poured on the marble slab, the bottom of the basin should on no account be scraped, as this would cause the mixture to go gritty.

Coffee caramels. CARAMELS MOUS AU CAFÉ—The same method as above. Flavour with ⅓ cup (1 decilitre) of triple strength coffee essence.

Caramels with hazelnuts. CARAMELS MOUS AUX AVELINES—Pound finely 2½ ounces (75 grams) of blanched hazelnuts in a mortar or by machine. Put into a bowl, moisten with a pint of boiling milk and strain through a cloth, pressing out thoroughly. Add sugar and cream and proceed as described above.

Pistachio-nut caramels. CARAMELS MOUS AUX PISTACHES—The same method as above. At the last moment add 5 ounces (150 grams) of blanched and finely chopped pistachio nuts. Vanilla flavouring may be added to all these different preparations.

CARAMELIZE. CARAMÉLISER—To caramelize a mould, in which a cream or some other mixture is put for cooking in a *bain-marie** (pan of hot water), means to coat it with sugar cooked to caramel degree. To do that, heat in this mould one or several pieces of sugar moistened with a little water, until the sugar acquires a brown colour. (See SUGAR, *Cooking of sugar.*) The mould should then be rotated in such a way as to coat the interior with the caramel completely and evenly. The mould can also be caramelized by brushing on sugar cooked to caramel degree. Creams, custards, and other mixtures are caramelized by adding to them some sugar cooked to caramel degree.

Caraway

CARAWAY. CARVI—Umbelliferous plant producing black seeds, whose odour, and taste is halfway between that of aniseed and fennel. Caraway seeds are used to flavour certain cheeses and cakes. The seeds which have a carminative effect were included in the carminative compounds of the old pharmacopoeia.

The leaves and the white shoots in its first season gathered before the flower stalks have begun to shoot have a sharp and aromatic taste. They can be eaten in salads, as a vegetable or in soup. They are also used for flavouring a marinade.

CARBON DIOXIDE. CARBONIQUE—Gaseous body formed by the union of one atom of carbon and two atoms of oxygen. This gas is found in the atmosphere from which it is absorbed by plants and these, under the influence of solar radiation, combine it with hydrogen thus obtaining complex hydro-carbon and fat syntheses. Soluble in cold water, it forms carbonic acid which is found in many mineral waters (acidulated waters). When introduced under pressure into ordinary water, it forms artificial soda-water.

Carbon dioxide is released in large quantities during alcoholic fermentation; it is this gas which forms froth on sparkling wines, beer, cider, etc.

Carbon dioxide, compressed highly, is used in many industrial processes; in particular, it is used for drawing beer, served as 'draught' beer.

This gas has no liquid state. When it is heavily cooled or when it is decompressed and projected on to a cold surface, it solidifies in the form of snow which, in turn, vaporizes without becoming a liquid and absorbing a large quantity of heat in the process.

This property has been successfully exploited in the refrigerating industry where blocks of solid carbon dioxide (U.S.A. dry ice) are used instead of ice for the cold storage of perishable goods, for air conditioning, etc. The substitution of ice by solid carbon dioxide results in a great saving of space and completely avoids humidity.

Carbon dioxide is not suitable for breathing and it may cause asphyxia when it is found in large concentration in confined spaces, in vats for harvested grapes, etc. In small doses, however, it is a stimulant.

CARCASE. CARCASSE—Bone structure of an animal, term used in French particularly of a fowl. Sheep's carcase, in butcher's parlance: the body of the slaughtered animal, drawn and trimmed.

CARDAMINE OR LADY'S SMOCK. CRESSON DES PRÉS—Common plant, of American origin: with lilac flower-spikes, edible. It is eaten as salad; it has the same taste as watercress, but less strong. It contains vitamins and is recommended for scorbutic complaints.

CARDAMON. CARDAMOME—Common name for *Elettaria Cardomum*, a species belonging to the Ginger family, whose aromatic seeds are used as a spice.

CARDINAL (A LA)—One should say '*au Cardinal*' but the form '*à la Cardinal*' is normally used. It applies to a fish garnish composed of little *coquilles cardinal*, mushrooms, slices of truffle.

CARDINAL FISH. APOGON—Name of one of the varieties of red mullet, which is found in the Mediterranean. It is said that this is the king of mullets. For culinary preparation, see MULLET. In U.S.A. *Redfish* found from New Jersey to Texas is very similar.

CARDINALISER—This is a term used in French kitchen parlance for crustaceans which are made to turn red by plunging them into a boiling *court-bouillon*. Rabelais used this expression: 'Exceptez les escrevisses que l'on cardinalise à la cuicte.' (With the exception of crayfish which are cardinalized in cooking.)

CARDOON—Plant of the same genus as the artichoke, of which the stems are eaten. The principal varieties are the *cardon de Tours*, *plein inerme*, *improved white*, etc. The *cardon de Tours* is the best, but the stems are rather spiny.

However the cardoons are to be prepared, they have first to be cooked in white vegetable *court-bouillon.** They are then simmered in the required sauce.

Cardoons, to cook—Remove the hard stems and those that are wilted. Then remove the tender stalks one by one and divide them into 3-inch long slices. Remove all the stringy parts from the pieces and rub each one with half a lemon to prevent them from turning black.

Put them in a special white vegetable *court-bouillon** which has already been prepared and kept on the boil.

Add the heart of the cardoon, carefully trimmed.

Set to boil, stirring to prevent the vegetable sticking to the bottom of the pan.

Cover the pan; cook at a simmer for about 2 hours.

Cardoons in béchamel sauce. CARDONS À LA BÉCHAMEL—Drain and dry the cardoons after cooking them in a white *court-bouillon.** Simmer them in butter with the lid on for 15 minutes.

Add 1 cup (2 decilitres) of *Béchamel sauce*. (See SAUCE.) Simmer for 5 minutes.

Arrange in a dish.

Cardoons in butter. CARDONS AU BEURRE—Cook in a white *court-bouillon.** Drain them and stew them in butter with the lid on for 20 minutes. Arrange in a dish.

Cardoons with cream (I). CARDONS À LA CRÈME—Cook the cardoons, drain them and simmer them in butter; moisten with 1 cup (2 decilitres) of *Cream sauce* (see SAUCE). Simmer for 5 minutes. Arrange in a dish.

Cardoons with cream (II). CARDONS À LA CRÈME—Cook, drain and simmer the cardoons in butter. Take them out of the butter. Put them in a dish. Pour 1½ cups (3 decilitres) of fresh cream into the sauté pan. Boil down by half. Take the pan off the fire, add 3 tablespoons (50 grams) of butter; strain through a sieve on to the cardoons.

Cardoons aux fines herbes (I). CARDONS AUX FINES HERBES—Stew the cardoons in butter; drain them. Moisten with a few tablespoons of *fines herbes sauce* (see SAUCE). Simmer for 10 minutes and turn out into a dish.

Cardoons aux fines herbes (II). CARDONS AUX FINES HERBES—Proceed in the same way as for cardoons with butter. Add chopped parsley and chervil.

Fried cardoons. CARDONS FRITS—Cook the cardoons in the usual way and drain. Dry them, marinate for 30 minutes with oil, lemon juice and chopped parsley, dip in a light frying batter and fry in boiling oil at the last moment.

Drain again, season with fine salt; arrange cardoons in a pile on a napkin.

Cardoons à la grecque. CARDONS À LA GRECQUE—Divide the cardoons into little slices; trim them, rub them with lemon juice and throw them into a *court-bouillon* made in the same way as for *Artichokes à la grecque*. (See ARTICHOKE.) Finish as described in this recipe.

They are served as an *hors-d'oeuvre*.

Cardoons à l'italienne. CARDONS À L'ITALIENNE—Proceed in the same way as for *Cardoons aux fines herbes*. Moisten with *Italian sauce*. See SAUCE.

Cardoons à l'italienne gratinés. CARDONS À L'ITALIENNE GRATINÉS—Prepare the cardoons as described in the preceding recipe. Put the cardoons in a gratin dish. Cover them with sauce, sprinkle with fine breadcrumbs, pour over some melted butter and brown quickly in the oven.

Cardoons au jus. CARDONS AU JUS. Drain the cardoons after cooking them in a *court-bouillon.** Put them in a vegetable dish. Arrange the heart of the cardoon cut into slices on top.

Pour over a few tablespoons of thick brown veal sauce to which some butter has been added.

Cardoons à la lyonnaise. CARDONS À LA LYONNAISE—Proceed in the same way as for *Cardoons à l'italienne*. Moisten with *Lyonnaise sauce*. See SAUCE.

Cardoons with marrow (I). CARDONS À LA MOELLE—Drain the cardoons after cooking them in *court-bouillon.** Put them in a dish. Put the hearts of the cardoons cut into slices on top, alternating with slices of marrow poached in salt water and well drained.

Cover the dish with a few tablespoons of *Marrow sauce*. (See SAUCE.) Sprinkle with chopped parsley.

Cardoons with marrow (II). CARDONS À LA MOELLE—Arrange the cardoons in a pyramid on a round dish. Cover them with the rounded slices of cardoon heart and pour over some *Marrow sauce* (see SAUCE), and sprinkle with chopped parsley.

Arrange round the edge of the dish some little hollowed-out *croûtes* made of bread, gilded with butter and filled with poached marrow cut into dice.

The hollowed-out *croûtes* can be replaced by little *bouchées* made of puff pastry.

The marrow hash can have chopped shallot and chopped parsley added to it, combined with a concentrated veal sauce or with dissolved meat glaze.

Cardoons à la milanaise. CARDONS À LA MILANAISE—Cook the cardoons in *court-bouillon,** drain and dry them. Arrange on a fireproof dish, in regular layers, sprinkling each layer with grated Parmesan. Sprinkle with melted butter and brown in the oven. When removed from the oven, sprinkle with brown butter.

Cardoons Mornay. CARDONS MORNAY—Arrange the cooked and drained cardoons in a buttered gratin dish.

Cover them with *Mornay sauce* (see SAUCE). Sprinkle with grated Parmesan. Pour over a little melted butter and brown in a very hot oven.

Cardoons with Parmesan (à blanc). CARDONS AU PARMESAN (À BLANC)—Proceed in the same way as for *Cardoons Mornay*.

Cardoons with Parmesan (à brun). CARDONS AU PARMESAN (À BRUN)—Arrange the cardoons, cooked and drained, in a buttered gratin dish; cover them with a *Demi-glace sauce** (see SAUCE). Sprinkle them with Parmesan and brown them in the oven.

Raw cardoons à la Piémontaise. Cardialla Piemontese (Italian cooking). CARDONS CRUS À LA PIÉMONTAISE—Clean some fine white cardoons. Remove the fibres and the thin skin on the inside of the stalks. Plunge them into fresh water, lightly acidulated with lemon juice. Divide the stalks into pieces about 2 inches (4 to 5 centimetres) long.

Serve them as they are, arranged in an *hors-d'oeuvre* dish, with the following sauce:

Put $\frac{3}{4}$ cup (200 grams) of butter in a casserole with $\frac{2}{3}$ cup (150 grams) of olive oil, 4 shredded cloves of garlic and 6 de-salted anchovy fillets, cut into dice. Five minutes before serving this sauce heat it up, but take care not to allow the garlic to brown. It must remain white.

Add to this sauce one or two white truffles, peeled and sliced (with a special slicer) into very thin strips. Mix. Serve hot.

This sauce is usually prepared at table in front of the guests.

Cardoon purée. PURÉE DE CARDONS—Prepare the cardoons as for *Cardoons with butter*, cooking them well. Pass through a fine sieve. Heat the purée and add butter.

One-third of its volume of potato purée can be added to the cardoon purée. A few tablespoons of thick *Béchamel sauce* can also be added.

Cardoon salad. SALADE DE CARDON—Cut up the cardoons which have already been cooked in a *court-bouillon,** drained and dried.

Arrange in a dish. Season with oil, vinegar, salt and pepper. Sprinkle with chopped parsley and chervil.

Cardoons with various sauces. CARDONS AVEC SAUCES DIVERSES—Drain the cardoons; arrange them on a napkin or on a grid; serve with the following sauces handed separately; *butter*, *cream*, *hollandaise*, *Hungarian* or *mousseline*. See SAUCE.

Antonin Carême (1784–1833)

CARÊME—The actual Christian names of this illustrious cook were Marie-Antoine, although he signed his works Antonin Carême. He was born in Paris on June 8th, 1784, and died there on January 12th, 1833.

His father was a poor working man weighed down with progeny, who had so much difficulty in feeding his family that he found it simplest to abandon little Antoine after a farewell meal in a tavern at the city gate, leaving him provided with this one and only viaticum: 'Go, little one. In this world there are excellent callings. Leave us to languish; misery is our lot and we must die of misery. This is the time of fine fortunes, it only needs wit to make one, and wit you have. Go, little one, and perhaps this evening or tomorrow some fine house will open its doors to you. Go with what God has given you'.

The boy, thus abandoned, could have knocked on the door of a carpenter or of a locksmith or of a clothes merchant. Destiny led him to a humble cookshop, the owner of which gave him his first lesson in cooking. The man who has been called the *Cuisinier des rois et le Roi des cuisiniers* (the Cook of kings and the King of cooks) made his début in the meanest of cookshops. A precarious beginning! But, by some providential accident, Carême was set to work in a type of activity for which he had been endowed with magnificent gifts. The speed with which he rose—starting from such a modest beginning—revealed him as something of a prodigy. 'Although born into one of the poorest families of France,' he says in his recollections, 'of a family of twenty-five children, although my father literally threw me into the street to save me, fortune smiled very soon upon me and a good fairy has often taken me by the hand to lead me to the goal. In the eyes of my enemies, and I have many, I have more than once appeared as a child spoiled by fortune. I have accepted and refused on several occasions, the finest posts. I have left the first houses of Europe in order to record my own experiences, and those of a few great contemporaries who scarcely existed any more when I wrote except in my memory'.

Carême very soon began work in a restaurant in the capacity of kitchen help. He was then fifteen years old. His passionate application to work, his frenzy for learning, his wise intuition for the secrets and resources of his art, his serene authority, his progress from such a sudden and easy beginning, all these qualities designated him as a person of exceptional quality. Very soon he moved to the celebrated *pâtissier* Bailly, rue Vivienne, who had M. de Talleyrand as a client, who was, under the First Empire, the most splendid amphitryon and for whom Carême later worked.

M. de Talleyrand, who did not always have stable convictions and who rallied with enthusiasm to the regime which had just triumphed, was none the less an extremely clever diplomat and made gastronomy subserve his political combinations.

On leaving for the Congress of Vienna where he was able to obtain important advantages for France he declared proudly to Louis XVIII, the gourmet king, who was well able to understand the words: 'Sire, I have more need of casseroles than of written instructions'.

Carême has left us an account of the time he spent with the famous Bailly: 'At 17,' he writes, 'I was with M. Bailly, as his first *tourtier*. This good master showed a lively interest in me. He allowed me to leave work in order to draw in the print room. When I had shown him that I had a particular vocation for his art he confided to me the task of executing *pièces montées* for the Consul's (Napoleon's) table. The Peace of Amiens had just been signed (1802). The Consul had dictated it! I used my drawings and my nights in the service of M. Bailly. His kindness, it is true, rewarded my trouble. It was with him that I became an inventor. At that time, the illustrious Avice flourished in the realm of *pâtisserie*; his work served as my instruction. The knowledge of his procedures gave me courage, and I did all I could to follow him, but not to imitate him.'

In brief, he executed extraordinary decorative pieces which provoked general admiration. 'But,' he confesses, addressing himself to the younger generation, 'how many sleepless nights I spent before I reached that point. I could not give my attention to my drawings and calculations until after nine or ten at night, with the result that I toiled for the greater part of the night'. This young pastry-cook who based his set pieces on the engravings in great (French) collections which were his study even in his tenderest years, reveals preoccupations which, at first sight, may seem peculiar. Said Carême, 'A gastronomic painter (of whom there are many) was explaining to us one day that there was an undesirable relationship between the culinary art and the fine arts. To support this paradoxical thesis, this painter invoked the very terms used by the critics who speak of *cuisine*, *colours*, *pâte savoureuse*, *jus*, *crude colours*, even *rissolés*, and compared the manner in which the artist sets out his colours on the palette with that in which a chef enriches a sauce and measures his seasoning. He further recalled that Claude Gellée, called le Lorrain, the Raphael of landscape, was in his youth apprenticed to a pastrycook at Toul.'

Carême himself associated confectionery with architecture and he wrote the following sentence, quoted by Anatole France: 'The fine arts are five in number, to wit: *painting*, *sculpture*, *poetry*, *music*, *architecture—whose main branch is confectionery*'.

Carême entered the service of M. de Lavalette, who kept a famous table and who entertained the most distinguished men of his day in politics, the army, the arts and sciences. Here Carême worked, as he puts it, to further the union of delicacy, order and economy! He stayed twelve years with Prince Talleyrand whose table, he declared, was furnished at once with grandeur and wisdom.

Next, Carême was summoned to the office of chief cook to the Prince Regent in England. Here he stayed for two years. During his service with the Prince, Carême pursued a course of rational and healthy gastronomy. Every morning he explained the properties of each individual dish to the Prince. 'Carême,' said his royal master one day, 'You will kill me with a surfeit of food. I have a fancy for everything you put before me. The temptation is really too great.' 'Your Highness,' replied Carême (who relates this conversation in the preamble to his *Cuisinier parisien*, 'my great concern is to stimulate your appetite by the variety of my dishes. It is no concern of mine to curb it.'

The English fogs depressed him. He returned to France. When the Prince Regent, later King George IV, asked him to return, he offered munificent terms which would assure Carême's present and future prosperity. But Carême refused. Nothing could be more noble than the reasons he gave for his decision. He did not like London where 'all was sombre', where he was cut off from his friends and deprived of 'that most, most alluring French conversation'. Further, he wanted to 'take advantage of the time still left to him by divine providence to finish his books'. 'They have been my whole life's preoccupation. What anxieties do they not represent, and how I have tortured myself in body and spirit by wakeful nights!' This chef, who loved glory above all else and who looked upon his profession as a sacred trust, was much in demand by kings and other great personages.

We find him at St Petersburg with the Czar Alexander, at the Court of Vienna, at the British Embassy (in Paris), at the Congress of Aix-la-Chapelle, in the households of the Princess Bagration and Lord Stewart, and finally with the Baron de Rothschild, where he remained for seven years. While he was with this prince of finance, the Rothschild table was considered the best in Europe. M. de Rothschild, having just bought the Ferrières estate, offered him the opportunity of directing the kitchens of the Château, and added that he could, if he wished, retire there. Carême declined this offer. His strength was exhausted by the unremitting labours of thirty years.

'My prayer', he added, 'is not to end my days in a château but in humble lodgings in Paris.' 'And', he declared, 'to publish a comprehensive survey of the state of my profession at the present time.' He fell gravely ill and was forced to take to his bed. His great anxiety, on his bed of pain, was his fear of leaving unfinished works which he regarded as essential to the future of his art. He died, still under the age of fifty years, on January 12th, 1833, burnt out, according to Laurent Tailhade, by the flame of his genius and the fuel of his ovens. His last moments of life were spent in dictating admirable notes to his daughter.

Carême's life is a model of probity and nobility. Money meant nothing to him. His art alone was important. He prized nothing but the glory of his profession. His very conception of culinary art is in tune with the grandeur of his character. It was always Carême's ideal to present sumptuously the culinary marvels with which he enriched the tables of kings. It has already been said that he looked upon confectionery as a branch of architecture. Nothing could be more meticulous than the drawings he made for set pieces, aspics, galantines, baskets of fruit, etc., or even simple borders. He had a thorough grounding in the study of classical architecture. He was so much in love with architecture that he prepared a vast plan for the embellishment of St Petersburg. He offered the dedication to the Czar Alexander who, in accepting it, presented him with a diamond ring. Carême designed for the table of Louis XVIII an opulent centre-piece composed of seven trophies. It never got beyond the model stage: 'The Restoration,' he remarked, 'was not always magnanimous and gracious'.

Nowadays, we no longer approve of this ostentatious manner of setting out cooked dishes. We have banished display from our tables, as much for the sake of hygiene as for reasons of expediency. But it must be remembered that Carême worked for the great ones of the earth and wanted his art to 'serve as a foil to European diplomacy'. Nevertheless, while he considered cooking must be decorative, he was equally emphatic that it must be hygienic. He himself was extremely sober and considered that 'good cooking should strengthen the life of old societies'.

He wrote in a majestic style in the manner of Buffon, pompous as his architectural creations in pastry. He died poor, leaving only his works, listed below:

Le Maître d'hôtel français, or comparisons of ancient and modern cookery considered from the point of view of the plan and the arrangement of menus according to the four seasons, in Paris, St Petersburg, London and Vienna, by Carême, 2 volumes.

Le Pâtissier royal parisien, elementary and practical treatise by Carême, etc. 2 volumes. New edition, ornamented with 41 plates by the author, 2 volumes.

Le Cuisinier parisien, by the same. New edition, 1 volume.

L'Art de la cuisine au dix-neuvième siècle, by Carême, 5 volumes.

Le Pâtissier pittoresque, by the same; ornamented with 128 plates by the author.

In the first of these works Carême set out the arrangement of the menus in the manner in which he himself composed them, successively for King George IV, for the Austrian court, for the Emperor Alexander, during his stay in Paris, and for the Congress of Aix-la-Chapelle.

It might be advantageous for those interested in the minutiae of historical detail to examine the dinner menus of the King of England or of Monsieur de Metternich, on a particular day of the year. Could not one here obtain the key to more than one transaction, and was not the meekness of the Russian autocrat during the Conventions of 1814 perhaps to be explained by the excellence of Carême's blancmange?

One of these historic glimpses is particularly mouth-watering. It is a Lenten menu, seventy covers worthy of a conclave: a cucumber soup *à la hollandaise*, truffled sturgeon croquettes, fish pudding *à la Richelieu*, a galantine of eels with crayfish butter, roast teal with orange sauce.

On reading these works one gets an impression of the exalted view Carême takes of his art:

'If my age does not give me the advantage of citing myself as a pupil of the most elect establishment of the ancient nobility,' he says in his preface, 'I can say without vanity that I was brought up among men of reputation in those times. It was under M. Richaut, the famous sauce cook of the house of Condé that I learned the preparation

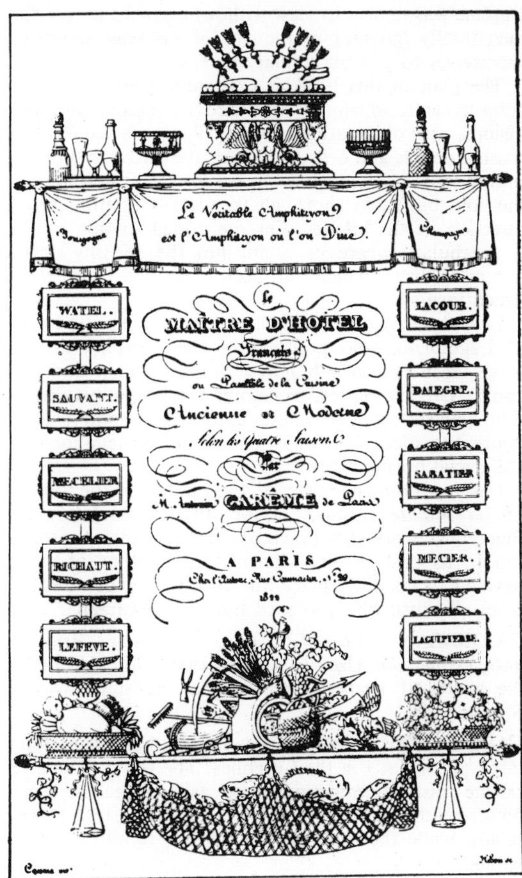
Le Véritable Amphitryon
est l'Amphitryon où l'on Dîne.
Le
MAÎTRE D'HÔTEL
Français
ou Parallèle de la Cuisine
Ancienne et Moderne
selon les Quatre Saisons,
Par
M. Antonin CARÊME de Paris
A PARIS
WATEL.
SAUVANT.
MECELIER.
RICHAUT.
LAFEVE.
LACOUR.
DALEGRE.
SABATIER.
MECIER.

Title page of one of Carême's works

of sauces, during the splendid festivities held at the Hôtel de Ville in Paris under the orders of M. Lasne that I learned the best part of cold buffet cookery, at the Elysée Napoléon under the auspices of Messrs. Robert and Laguipière that I learned the elegance of modern cookery and the working of a large establishment. Since the renaissance of the art, I have been constantly employed at dinners and festivities. I have seen a great deal, made valuable observations, and have profited from them.'

There is an unusual erudition in Carême's works. He prefaced his own formulation of modern menus with a treatise on ancient cookery which required a great deal of research and which bears witness to a devoted passion for his profession. There is nothing stranger than the menu of a dinner unearthed by Carême which was served in 1745 to Louis XV by Héliot, the Dauphine's '*écuyer ordinaire de la bouche*'. This dinner consisted entirely of beef! From the ungarnished soup made with shin of beef to the brain fritters served with lemon juice, nothing but this common-or-garden animal featured on the monarch's table. Carême recalls that one of Marshal Davoust's cooks prepared a dinner consisting entirely of horse-meat during the long siege of Hamburg, of which Davoust was the Governor. But he adds that necessity forced him to this pass, for which he deserved praise, whereas the Dauphine's chef, author of a deplorable menu, was merely an ignorant and mediocre person.

Le Pâtissier royal parisien is filled with the sentiment which earned Juvenal his immortality: indignation.

Carême was unable to view without disgust the fact that men totally ignorant of the art of cooking permitted themselves to publish culinary works.

The plan of this book is extremely methodical. The subjects with which he deals are marketing and provisions, with observations on their freshness, quality and season, details and organization of the larder, major and minor sauces, *consommés*, *hors-d'oeuvre*, frying, sweets, the cold buffet, in short, all the details relating to the direction of the kitchen. Carême added to this treatise a vocabulary where he establishes the spelling of the names of dishes which had been travestied by so many practitioners.

Le Cuisinier parisien is dedicated to the departed spirit of Laguipière, who perished in the Moscow disaster which cost France a hundred thousand men and fifty cooks. 'Oh, my master,' exclaimed Carême in his dedication, 'you suffered persecution in life, and to add insult to injury, you died in the midst of the most cruel agonies in the glacial northern cold'.

Carême should be regarded, even today, as the founder of '*la grande cuisine*,' classic French cookery. His theoretical work, his practical work as an inventor of sauces, as pastrymaker, designer and author of works devoted to cooking, place him at an immense distance from all those who preceded him in his career.

CARIBBEAN CABBAGE. CHOU CARAIBE—Root of *arum esculentum*. Used in Asia, Africa, and cultivated in the south of France. Prepared in the same way as *Swedes*.*

CARLINE THISTLE—Plant which grows in the mountains, particularly in the Cévennes. The root of the great carline thistle is sometimes used as a drug. The young flower-heads are edible and have a nutty taste, eaten in salads, while the roots have a flavour recalling that of fennel.

CARMINATIVE. CARMINATIF—A medicament which prevents the formation or provokes the expulsion of gases contained in the intestines. The kind of carminative which featured in the old pharmacopoeia consisted in grains of aniseed, coriander, fennel and caraway in equal parts.

CARMINE. CARMIN—Substance derived from cochineal, of a vivid scarlet red colour, non-toxic, used to colour a variety of food substances.

CARNATION. OEILLET—The petals of the carnation flower are used to make a syrup and a ratafia.

CARNIVAL. CARNAVAL—The period between Epiphany and Ash Wednesday, given up to all kinds of rejoicing, and in particular to the pleasures of the table.

CAROLINA—Commercial name for a type of rice. See RICE.

CAROLINE—Name given in pastry-making to small *éclairs* served as an *hors-d'oeuvre*.

CAROTENE—Yellow colouring matter, widespread in the vegetable world, which is not exclusively found in carrots, but also in spinach, lettuce, peas, pumpkins, cabbage, oranges, etc. It is also found in butter and yolks of egg. This substance seems to play an important role in the growth of animals and is transformed in the animal organism into vitamins. Its properties emphasize once again the importance of fresh vegetables in diet.

CARP. CARPE—A freshwater fish which is not mentioned in ancient history. It probably originated in China and was imported into England in 1614 and into Holland and Scandinavia about 1660. In 1876, it was brought to the U.S.A., put in fish ponds in Washington, D.C., and in 1879 distributed to twenty-five states and territories. It is very abundant in the Middle West and sold in the principal eastern cities of U.S.A.

Mirror carp

The carp has a small mouth, provided with four fleshy appendages called barbules, and no teeth. The river carp has brownish scales on the back, golden yellow scales on its flanks, greenish-white scales on the stomach. The carp which inhabits lakes and ponds often has a muddy smell, and is darker in colour. The few fish with which one might confuse the carp have no barbules. Carp can grow to an enormous size. The best season for eating them is between November and the end of March.

In French rivers, carps are found weighing from 12 to 16 pounds (6-8 kilos), fish which are not more than eight or ten years old, which to some extent invalidates the claims of longevity made for the Fontainebleau carp, said to be contemporaries of François I, and those of Chantilly which are said to have been hand-fed by the great Condé. It is also known that the lakes of the royal or princely domains cannot possibly be inhabited by centenarian carps owing to the fact that they are emptied from time to time and re-stocked with fish.

There are several species of carp of which the chief ones are the mirror carp, leather carp, the Kollar carp, and the Bohemian carp.

The mirror carp was called the queen of carp in the old days, on account of the great delicacy of its flesh. It is more hardy than the common carp, grows more rapidly, and attains a larger size.

The leather carp resembles the mirror carp; it is entirely without scales, the skin is rather thick and has the appearance of brownish leather, from which it derives its name.

The Kollar carp is seldom found in France but is very abundant in Belgium, in Germany and in Hungary.

At one time this carp was found in the Enghien lake near Paris, but it has almost disappeared.

In U.S.A., the average market carp weighs from 2-7 pounds. Also known as Winter Carp or Golden Carp, Buffalo fish is very similar to carp and can be prepared in the same way.

All these species of carp can be prepared in the same way as the common carp.

Carp à l'alsacienne. CARPE À L'ALSACIENNE—Fill a carp of medium size with a *Fish cream stuffing* (see FORCEMEAT, *Fish forcemeat*). Poach it in a little white wine.

Put it on a serving-dish. Garnish with *Sauerkraut garnish* (see GARNISHES) and boiled potatoes.

At the same time serve the liquor in which it has cooked after boiling it down, thickening it with *Kneaded butter* (see BUTTER) and at the last moment adding a little fresh butter.

Carp cooked in beer (German cookery). CARPE À LA BIÈRE—Season a carp of moderate size, which can be stuffed or not, as the case may be. Put it in a fish kettle on a foundation of 1 large (150 grams) onion, lightly fried in a little butter, without browning, plus a small piece (30 grams) of gingerbread cut into little squares, and 2 stalks (50 grams) of celery, finely sliced. Add a *bouquet garni.** Pour over the fish some light beer, sufficient to almost cover the fish. Poach in a slow oven. When it is cooked remove the fish on to a long platter. Garnish it with the carp's roes, poached and sliced. Serve the fish with a sauce made by boiling down by one-third the liquor in which it has cooked, passing it through a fine sieve, and adding some fresh butter before serving.

Carp au bleu. CARPE AU BLEU—Small carp are used for this preparation. Proceed in the same way as for *Blue trout*. See TROUT.

Carp cooked *au bleu* are served hot, accompanied by melted butter or *hollandaise sauce*, cold, with *ravigote sauce*. See SAUCE.

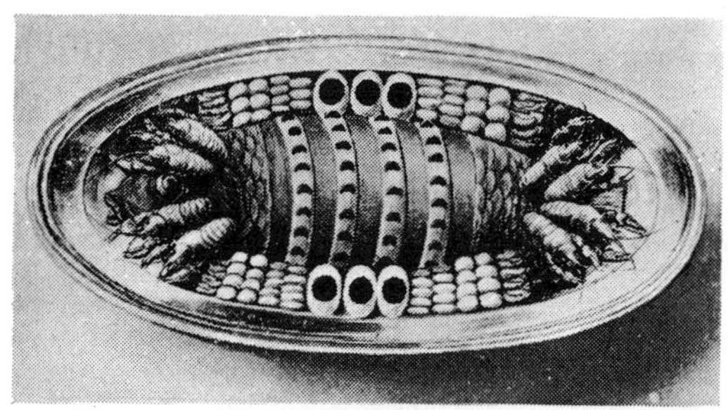

Carp Chambord

Carp Chambord. CARPE CHAMBORD—Stuff a carp weighing 4-6 pounds (2-3 kilos) with a delicate *Fish cream stuffing* (see FORCEMEAT, *Fish forcemeat*). Sew it up. Neatly remove a strip of skin from both sides of the fish, leaving the skin towards the stomach untouched to hold in the stuffing. Lard the skinned portion with little strips of fat bacon, or stud it with truffle slices. (Alternatively this part can be spread with a thin layer of fish stuffing garnished with little slices of truffle cut in crescent shapes.)

Put the carp on the drainer of the fish kettle and settle this in the utensil on a base of herbs and vegetables which with some mushroom peelings have been lightly fried in butter. Add a *bouquet garni.**

Pour on some fish stock (see STOCK) which has been prepared with red wine to reach two-thirds up the sides of the fish. Braise in a slow oven (325°F.).

Drain the fish. Lay it on a platter. Glaze it. Surround it with a *Chambord garnish* (see GARNISHES) in which each element is separately disposed in groups. Put a little *Genevoise sauce* (see SAUCE) in the bottom of the dish which has been prepared with the liquor from the braised carp, and serve the rest of the sauce separately.

Cold carp. CARPE FROID —All the methods of preparation given for *Cold salmon* (see SALMON) and *Salmon trout* (see TROUT) apply to carp.

Carp au court-bouillon. CARPE AU COURT-BOUILLON—Poach the fish in a *court-bouillon* (prepared with red or white wine) containing aromatic vegetables and seasoning. See COURT-BOUILLON.

Drain the carp. Lay it on a napkin. Garnish it with fresh parsley.

Serve with melted butter or with any other sauce normally used with poached fish.

Fillets of carp. FILETS DE CARPE—Lift the fillets from an uncooked moderate-sized carp. Trim the fillets. Season them. Poach them in a shallow-lidded pan in a little concentrated fish stock.

Drain the fillets, and set them on a serving-dish. Cover them with one of the following sauces: *cream*, *fines herbes*, *hollandaise*, *marinière*, *normande*, *white ine*, or any sauce suitable for poached fish. See SAUCE.

Fillets of carp can be accompanied by any of the garnishes appropriate to poached fish, and particularly those given for sole, or fillets of sole. See SOLE.

Fried carp. CARPE FRITE—This method applies particularly to very small carp. Deep fry the fish in boiling oil. Drain them and wipe them with a cloth. Season with fine salt. Arrange them on a napkin in a dish, and garnish with fried parsley and quarters of lemon.

Grilled carp à la maître d'hôtel. CARPE GRILLÉE À LA MAÎTRE D'HÔTEL—Small carp are prepared in this way. Follow the instructions for *grilled bass*. See BASS.

Carp à la juive. CARPE À LA JUIVE—Cut a carp of moderate size into even slices. Put the slices into a pan with 1 medium (100 grams) onion chopped and 3 (50 grams) chopped shallots which have already been lightly cooked in ⅔ cup (2 decilitres) of oil without browning. Sprinkle the contents of the pan with 2½ tablespoons (35 grams) of flour. Almost cover the fish with white wine and fish stock (or water). Season with salt and a touch of cayenne. Add 2 crushed garlic cloves and a *bouquet garni.** Sprinkle with a few tablespoons of oil. Bring to the boil, and then simmer gently with the lid on for 20 minutes.

Drain the carp slices. Set them on a long dish, disposing them in such a way as to reform the shape of the carp.

Boil down the liquor in which the fish has cooked by two-thirds, and beat in ⅔ cup (2 decilitres) of oil off the fire before pouring it over the carp. Leave to cool. At the moment of serving sprinkle with chopped parsley.

Carp à la juive à l'orientale. CARPE À LA JUIVE À L'ORIENTALE—This is prepared in the same way as *Carp à la juive*, but after the sauce has been reduced and the oil incorporated, add a pinch of saffron and 2 tablespoons (30 grams) of chopped almonds, previously blanched and peeled.

Carp à la juive with parsley. CARPE À LA JUIVE AU PERSIL—Prepared in the same way as *Carp à la juive* with the addition of several sprigs (50 grams) of fresh parsley to the cooking liquor, the fish slices being sprinkled abundantly with chopped parsley at the moment of serving.

Carp à la juive with raisins. CARPE À LA JUIVE AUX RAISINS—This is prepared in the same way as *Carp à la juive*. Add to the boiled-down liquor in which it has cooked, and in which the oil has already been incorporated, 2 teaspoons (15 grams) of powdered sugar, 2 tablespoons of wine vinegar, 4 tablespoons (40 grams) of seeded Malaga raisins, and 4 tablespoons (50 grams) of Smyrna and Corinth (seedless) raisins. The raisins must first be allowed to swell in lukewarm water, then drained.

Matelote of carp. CARPE EN MATELOTE—This is prepared with the carp cut into slices in the same way as *Matelote of eels*. See EELS, see MATELOTE.

Carp à la polonaise. CARPE À LA POLONAISE—Stuff a carp of moderate size with a fish stuffing. Put it in a fish kettle on a foundation of 2 tablespoons (50 grams) of chopped onion and 1½ tablespoons (25 grams) of chopped shallot. Add a *bouquet garni.** Season. Almost cover the carp with liquor consisting of half red wine and half fish stock. Add 3 large pieces (100 grams) of gingerbread cut into large squares. Braise gently on top of the stove or in the oven.

Drain the carp. Set it on a serving-dish and cover it with the following sauce:

Prepare a pale caramel syrup with 4 tablespoons (50 grams) of sugar and ½ cup (1 decilitre) of vinegar. Add the liquor in which the fish has cooked, passed through a fine sieve. Boil this concoction, and complete the sauce with 4 tablespoons (100 grams) of butter and 2½ tablespoons (50 grams) of flaked almonds which have been lightly grilled.

Carp quenelles. QUENELLES DE CARPE—These are prepared with carp meat in the same way as *Pike quenelles*. See PIKE.

As soon as large carp quenelles have been poached they are served on *croustades feuilletée** or on croûtons, fried in butter. They are accompanied by various garnishes, and are covered with a sauce suitable for the kind of garnish used. See QUENELLE, *Fish quenelles*.

Carp quenelles are also used as an element in the garnish of large braised fish, and as a garnish for fish pies.

Roast carp. CARPE RÔTIE—This is prepared, with or without stuffing, in the same way as *Roast pike*. See PIKE.

Carps' roes. LAITANCES DE CARPES—Carps' roes are often used as one element of the garnish for large braised fish. They can also be served alone as a hot *hors-d'oeuvre* or as a little *entrée*.

In general, before being put to these uses, carps' roes (and those of other fish) should be poached in a *court-bouillon*,* very little liquid being used, or cooked in butter seasoned with a little lemon juice in a covered pan.

They can then be prepared according to the instructions given under the different recipes for SOFT ROES.

Stuffed carp à l'ancienne. CARPE FARCIE À L'ANCIENNE—Take a large soft-roed carp. Scale it. Remove the flesh of a small eel and 8 brined anchovies which have been properly de-salted. Make a *quenelle forcemeat* (see FORCEMEAT), but without adding any sauce. Keep it rather firm.

'Be careful when removing the flesh of the carp from the bones to leave the backbone intact, complete with head and tail.

'Blanch the roes. Cut them into several pieces. Sauté them in butter with a little lemon juice, then add some truffles and mushrooms, and combine this with a few tablespoons of thick *Allemande sauce*.' See SAUCE.

'Take a tin tray of the same length as the carp, and butter it thickly. Lay on this a layer of forcemeat about 2 inches deep in the form of the carp, set the backbone, to which head and tail are still adhering, in place. Cover the bone with a little more forcemeat and then apply the ragoût of truffles, mushrooms and carps' roes. On top of this lay about an inch of stuffing keeping carefully to the shape of the carp. Smooth the surface with the blade of a knife dipped in hot water.

'Butter a baking-sheet large enough to hold the carp, and sprinkle breadcrumbs on the butter. Put the tin tray on which the carp has been prepared over the heat for a few minutes so that the butter melts and it is then possible to slide the fish on to the baking-sheet.

'Then with the aid of a pastry brush cover the fish with beaten egg. Sprinkle with fine dry breadcrumbs, pressing them on with a knife, and pour on melted butter. Then, with the tip of a little silver spoon press in a pattern of scales beginning at the head.

'Three-quarters of an hour before serving put the carp in the oven.

'Take care to baste it often with clarified butter so that it acquires a fine golden colour. At the end of the prescribed time, when you are certain that it is ready, slide a long slice between the baking-sheet and the card and slide it on to the serving-dish. Put in the dish a little *Sauce financière* (see SAUCE), based on fish essence and serve some more sauce in a sauceboat.' (*L'Art de la cuisine française, de Carême*, by Plumerey.)

CARPILLON OR CARPEAU—French names for very small carp, given also to a species of little mullet which does not spawn. This fish, which is found in the Rhône, the Saône and other European rivers, is treated in the same way as carp. Its flesh is tender and delicate.

CARPION—A variety of trout which is principally found in alpine streams.

All the methods of preparation indicated for river trout can be applied to it. See TROUT.

CARRIER-PIGEON. BISET—Wild pigeon which is also called *rock-pigeon*. It is smaller than ring-dove (or wood-pigeon). Its plumage is slate-grey.

It can be prepared in any way suitable for the domestic pigeon. See PIGEON.

This name is also given in France to a marsh bird, rather similar to the wild duck, which is cooked in the same way. See DUCK, *Wild duck*.

CARROTS. CAROTTES—Root vegetables which occur in a great many culinary preparations, either used as an aromatic base or as a garnish. Prepared alone, they provide very refreshing vegetable dishes.

The carrot contains a notable amount of sugar which adds to its nutritive properties.

There is a variety of types. Carrots old or new are in supply all the year round.

The following recipes are intended for new carrots. If old specimens are used the orange part should be blanched before treating according to the various methods indicated below.

Carrots in béchamel sauce. CAROTTES À LA BÉCHAMEL—Cook the carrots in boiling water or prepare them in the same way as *Glazed carrots*. Add at the last moment, a few tablespoons of *Béchamel sauce*. See SAUCE.

Boiled carrots. CAROTTES À L'ANGLAISE—Cook some tender carrots in boiling water. Drain them, put them in a vegetable dish. Serve fresh butter separately.

Buttered carrots. CAROTTES AU BEURRE—Boil the carrots. As soon as they are cooked, drain them, return them to the pan, add a little butter and shake it so that each carrot receives a coating of butter.

Carrots en cheveux d'ange (angel's hair). CAROTTES EN CHEVEUX D'ANGE—A kind of carrot jam which used to be prepared in the south-west of France. See CHEVEUX D'ANGE.

Carrots à la crème (I). CAROTTES À LA CRÈME—Boil the carrots. As soon as they are cooked cover them with boiling cream. Cook down by two-thirds. Serve in a vegetable dish.

Carrots à la crème (II). CAROTTES À LA CRÈME—Choose a pound (500 grams) of carrots of the same size, turn them neatly, put them in a pan, just as they are if they are young, and blanched, rinsed in cold water, and strained if they are old. Cover the carrots with cold water. Season with a pinch of salt, castor (fine) sugar, and add 2 tablespoons (50 grams) of butter. Bring to boiling-point, then reduce the heat and leave them to cook until the liquid is syrupy. Test the carrots to make sure they are cooked. If they are still hard, add a few tablespoons of hot water and boil down again until the liquid again becomes syrupy.

Pour boiling fresh cream over the carrots, to cover them.

Bring this preparation to the boil, lower the heat, and simmer until the cream has boiled down a little, then add a spoonful of butter, mixing it in gently. Place in a vegetable dish or use as a garnish according to the recipe's instructions.

Carrots aux fines herbes (I). CAROTTES AUX FINES HERBES—Proceed in the same way as for *Glazed carrots*. Sprinkle with chopped parsley and chervil.

Carrots aux fines herbes (II). CAROTTES AUX FINES HERBES—Pare some tender carrots. Slice them neatly. Blanch for 5 minutes. Drain them and cook in a little butter in a pan. Season with salt and a pinch of sugar. At the last moment sprinkle with chopped parsley and chervil.

Carrot flan or tart. FLAN DE CAROTTES—Partly fill the bottom of a baked pastry shell with a purée of carrots, lightly sugared.

Cover the purée with finely sliced carrots which have already been cooked according to instructions for *Glazed carrots*.

Cover with the liquor in which the carrots have been cooked, properly reduced to a syrupy consistency.

Set in a hot oven for a few minutes.

This flan can be prepared with a greater quantity of sugar as a sweet.

Glazed carrots (I). CAROTTES GLACÉES—Pare or turn as perfectly as possible some young carrots. Leave whole ones of moderate size, halve the larger ones.

Put them in a pan, cover with cold water. Add for each pint (½ litre) of water 1 teaspoon (6 grams) of salt, 1 tablespoon (30 grams) of sugar, and 4 tablespoons (60 grams) of butter.

Set to boil on a lively heat and as soon as boiling is established lower the heat, cover the pan, and simmer until the liquid is practically evaporated.

At this point the carrots should be cooked. Shake the pan so that the carrots are properly covered with the syrupy liquid, and use them according to instructions.

If old carrots are used cut them in quarters. Use only the orange part, which should be sliced into neat strips, and blanched in boiling salted water first of all.

Glazed young carrots (II). CAROTTES NOUVELLES GLACÉES—Neatly pare some little new carrots chosen all of the same size.

Put them in a pan. Cover with stock. Add for 1 pound (500 grams) of carrots 2½ tablespoons (40 grams) of butter, a pinch of salt and a teaspoon of sugar.

Cook gently with the lid on until the liquid is entirely boiled down. When the carrots are cooked and the reduction of the liquid produces a kind of syrup, roll the carrots in this syrup so that each one is coated with it.

Carrots au jus. CAROTTES AU JUS—Proceed in the same way as for *Glazed carrots*,* but at the last moment add a few tablespoons of rich brown veal stock. Simmer for a few minutes and serve in a vegetable dish.

Carrot purée (I). PURÉE DE CAROTTES—Cook in salted water, with the addition of a teaspoon of sugar and a tablespoon of butter, 1 pound (500 grams) of sliced new carrots. Drain the carrots as soon as they are cooked and put them through a fine sieve.

Heat the purée. Add a little of the cooking liquor if the purée is too thick, and incorporate at the last moment 3 tablespoons (50 grams) of fresh butter. Mix well and serve. For an ordinary occasion one can use the carrots from *pot-au-feu** in this way.

Carrot purée (II). PURÉE DE CAROTTES—Proceed in the same way as for *Carrot purée (I)*, but 10 minutes after setting the carrots on the stove add a quarter of their volume of sliced potatoes.

Carrot purée with cream. PURÉE DE CAROTTES À LA CRÈME—Proceed in the same way as for *Carrot purée (I)*. Finish the purée with 4 tablespoons of boiled cream and a tablespoon of fresh butter.

Carrot purée with rice. PURÉE DE CAROTTES AU RIZ—The same method as *Carrot purée (I)*, but with the addition of a quarter of the carrots' weight in rice added when setting the carrots to cook. Finish in the same way.

The addition of potatoes or rice in carrot purées helps to improve their consistency. They are prepared in this way when used for garnishes.

Carrot soufflé. SOUFFLÉ DE CAROTTES—Put ½ pound (250 grams) of carrots prepared as for a purée, through a fine sieve. Remove the moisture from the purée by allowing it to boil for a few moments over a lively heat.

Take the pan off the fire, add 3 egg yolks. At the last moment mix and incorporate 3 beaten egg whites which should be really stiff.

Put this preparation in a buttered soufflé dish. Cook in the oven (400°F.) for about 15 minutes, and serve at once.

Little carrot soufflés. PETITS SOUFFLÉS AUX CAROTTES—Proceed in the same way as for *Carrot soufflé*. Put the soufflé mixture in little fireproof dishes, and cook for 6 to 8 minutes.

Carrot timbale. PAIN DE CAROTTES—Sieve ½ pound (250 grams) of carrots cooked as for a purée. Put the purée in a pan on the fire to dry out for a few minutes, add 3 whole eggs, stir them into the purée, and turn out into a buttered charlotte mould.

Cook in a pan of hot water or *bain-marie* in a moderate oven (350°F.) for 30 minutes. Take out of the oven, and allow to stand a few minutes before turning it out.

Serve with *béchamel sauce*, with cream, or with a *hollandaise* sauce. See SAUCE.

The buttered mould can be decorated with rounds of cooked carrots before putting in the purée.

Carrots à la Vichy. CAROTTES À LA VICHY—Pare and slice evenly a bunch of new carrots.

Put into a pan, and cover with water. Add for each pint (½ litre) of water 1 teaspoon (6 grams) of salt, 1 tablespoon (30 grams) of sugar and 4 tablespoons (60 grams) of butter, and cook in the same manner as for *Glazed carrots*.

When the liquid is very concentrated and the carrots are really glazed, arrange them in a vegetable dish, and sprinkle them with chopped parsley.

Old carrots can also be used for this preparation. Only use the orange parts, cut into strips, and blanch them in salted boiling water, before setting them to cook with the other ingredients.

Sometimes Vichy water is used as the cooking liquor, or, failing this, a light pinch of bicarbonate of soda.

CARVING. DÉCOUPAGE—The action of cutting up meat, poultry, game, etc. to serve it at table. In former times, the carving of meat was considered a noble art, one exercised solely by high officials of royal or princely households and known as *esquires tranchants*.

In royal households, the *esquire tranchant* was usually a nobleman and he always carried out his duties with his sword at his side.

The art of skilful carving was looked upon as so essential by our forefathers that it was taught to well-born men as an indispensable part of good education. Moreover, the last tutor provided for young noblemen was a master of carving.

For a long time in France in the best society, the carving and serving of food was carried out by the head of the household, who regarded it as a matter of honour to carve skilfully, and was far from believing that he was demeaning himself by carrying out a task which today in large establishments is undertaken at table by a *maître d'hôtel* or in the pantry, by the chef or *cuisinière*.

Moreover, the introduction in France of the *service à la Russe*, which, as is well-known, consists in presenting the diners with the food already carved, has caused the decline at the French table of this gracious custom. Since then, private households in which, before the marvelling guests, the host proceeds to carve the meat himself, often with consummate skill, have become rare.

But this modification in the customs attending service at table has in no way diminished the science of carving though it is true that one no longer sees a great personage, perhaps even a king, at some great banquet, skilfully carving a bird and handing it to his delighted guests, as King Louis-Philippe of France is said to have done.

In modern times, the *esquire tranchant* has disappeared. The carving of meat is done, at least in large restaurants, by a specialist known as the carver. This craftsman, though he may not have the glamour of his predecessor, the *esquire tranchant*, has often professional qualifications of the highest order, more numerous and varied, no doubt, than those of the old official of the royal household.

The modern carver, who, almost always, has the status of *maître d'hôtel*, must know his job inside out. In addition to a complete knowledge of cooking, a true carver must have some knowledge of anatomy. He must have great manual skill and a reserve of physical strength, so as to be able to sever the joints of the animals he has to carve. He must also have an intimate knowledge of the grain and texture of every piece of meat which he has to carve, and he must work with elegance and delicacy.

Quite a number of restaurant carvers have won a world-wide reputation. Such a one, among those who are no more, was the famous Joseph Dugnol, who founded the Taverne Joseph, and who was a master in the art of carving. One of his contemporaries thus describes one of the feats accomplished by this most able man:

'It was at a dinner held by M. Paillard for a few important members of the Paris press. In front of the spellbound guests, Joseph Dugnol, who was in charge of the dining-room of this famous establishment, carved a Rouen duckling while holding it up impaled on the prongs of a fork, so that there was nothing to support it. He carved this duck into very thin fillets all of which fell, in perfect order, on to the dish underneath. And that,' adds the narrator, 'with admirable despatch and in less time than it takes to tell.'

Such another was the celebrated Frédéric Delair, the great Frédéric of the Tour d'Argent who was also a past master in the complex art of jointing and carving poultry, especially Rouen duckling which, as is generally known, was the great speciality of his restaurant.

Other great *maîtres d'hôtel* of the first restaurants in Paris were true masters in the art of jointing and carving. Among these master-craftsmen were Louis Barraya who was in charge of the Café de Paris, Armenonville, the Pré-Catalan and Fouquet's, and Léopold Mourier, also formerly in charge of the above-named restaurants.

Principles in carving. As a general principle, all meat should be carved vertically, across the grain of the meat. The slices must be as large and as level as possible.

The leg of lamb or mutton only is an exception to this rule. It can be carved in two ways, either parallel to or at right angles to the bone.

Ham, whether boned or not, is always carved vertically towards the bone.

To carve a chicken, begin with the leg. Stick the fork into the thigh keeping it upright and pressing down on it, in fact using it as a lever to raise the leg as the knife slides along the carcase to sever the sinews. Sever the cartilage of the joint.

Next, remove the wing. For this purpose, secure the fork under the wing. Feel for the joint with the knife.

Thirdly and finally, the carcase is cut up. Lay the chicken on its back. Hold it firm by wedging the fork high up in the breast. With the knife, divide the carcase lengthwise along the breastbone.

Nantes duck is jointed (cut up) in exactly the same way as chicken. To joint a Rouen duck, begin by detaching the two legs, as for chicken, but instead of proceeding to remove the breast, it is first carved into thin slices. For this operation, lay the duck on its back and shave off the two halves of the breast on either side of the breastbone.

Next, pressing firmly down with the fork, cut the breast horizontally into very thin slices.

The wings are removed last of all.

CASEIN. Caseine—Albumenoid substance in milk which is coagulated by rennet, the fermentation of which is the origin of all cheeses.

CASHEW. Acajou—A name given to different varieties of trees. The type commonly known as 'pear-cashew' is cultivated in the tropical regions. Its fruit, the so-called *cashew-nut*, is kidney-shaped and contains an edible white nut of sweet and agreeable taste.

The fleshy part around this nut is called the 'cashew-pear', which is eaten throughout the whole of South America and some European countries. It is eaten without any preparation. It has a very pleasant taste, though slightly tart. Mixed with sugar, it can be made into excellent preserves, which are imported into Europe, as well as an extremely refreshing beverage.

Fermented, the cashew-nut fruit produces a kind of wine, which is quite famous in Brazil, and a vinegar—known as *anacard* or *cashew-nut vinegar*.

CASKING. Entonner—Pouring liquid into a cask.

CASSATA. Cassates—A kind of Neapolitan ice cream, made with mousse mixture coated with ices. It is sold in slices.

CASSAVA. Manioc—A plant native to the West Indies and Equatorial America, and Florida in U.S.A. The root, which is a fleshy tuber, contains edible starch. The sap, which contains hydrocyanic acid, is poisonous. This is eliminated by fermentation and cooking. Some varieties are sweet, containing no poison. These can be eaten plain (roasted on embers).

In South America, cassava is used in the manufacture of tapioca. The roots are grated and left to ferment. They are then pressed. The residue, baked into a flat cake and powdered, forms a *farinha* (Portuguese for meal). The starch of cassava dried quickly by heat when in a moist condition agglomerates into small masses known as tapioca.

In Florida, cassava is used as food for man and for beasts, and is used to make starch and glucose.

CASSE-MUSEAU (Jawbreaker)—A very hard cake, very much in vogue in former times, but which is hardly ever made today. Here is a recipe for this cake, which dates from 1730:

'Take some cream cheese, 4 eggs, ¼ pound (125 grams)

of butter, the juice of ½ lemon, 2¼ cups (300 grams) of flour and a pinch of salt.

'Combine all these ingredients into a soft paste and let it rest.

'Make the *casse-museaux* in the form of very little buns. Put them in the oven at a low temperature.

'After 15 minutes in the oven, take them out. Split them open with scissors, and put them back in the oven to finish cooking.'

Casse-Museau landais (Landes jawbreaker)—Work together in a terrine 2 pounds (1 kilo) of flour, 6 eggs, and 6 little local cheeses (about 1 pound of soft dark yellow cheese)—the little cheeses made in the Landes resemble Bondon—a pinch of salt, a tablespoon of olive oil, and a little glass of brandy. Mix well in order to produce a paste which is soft and without lumps. Leave this to rest for 3 hours. Then divide it into portions the size of an egg, with the help of a tablespoon. Put these on greased paper on a metal sheet, and cook in a slow oven (325°F.) for about 30 minutes.

CASSEROLE—Cooking utensil made in copper, aluminium, stainless steel, nickel, or other metals, and also in terracotta, in fireproof porcelain, in tempered glass, and in enamelled cast-iron. Many are decorative enough to use as serving dishes.

Casseroles are usually made in a rounded form and are furnished with a handle or handles. When deep-sided, the form most common in U.S.A., they are often used in the oven; when shallow-sided, they are normally called *sautoirs*, *sauteuses*, *plats à sauter* (sauté-pan or U.S.A. frying-pan).

CASSEROLE—In French cooking the term casserole also denotes a preparation generally made with rice, which, after cooking, is fashioned in the shape of a casserole, or more properly in that of a timbale. Casseroles are also made with a preparation of duchess potatoes, in this case being known as a *Casserole of potatoes*. This type of case has various fillings.

In U.S.A. a *casserole* defines a dish made of two or more elements, the basis of which can be rice, any paste (macaroni, spaghetti, etc.) in combinations with meat or fish plus a sauce or gravy, and often a variety of vegetables. This one-dish-meal can be prepared in advance and cooked and served in a decorative *casserole*. Such a dish is very popular in homes where there are no servants to help prepare or serve meals.

Fillings for rice casseroles—All the fillings indicated elsewhere for timbales, small patty shells, *vol-au-vent*, can be used for this *entrée*. These casseroles can also be filled with various minced meats (poultry, game, etc.), with fricassées of fowl with truffles, with various preparations of lambs' sweetbreads, truffled *foie gras* escalopes, and with all kinds of ragoûts and salpicons (compound of various products, cut into dice, and held together with sauce or forcemeat), prepared with or without meat and meat stock.

Rice casserole à l'ancienne. CASSEROLE AU RIZ À L'ANCIENNE—This hot entrée was often featured in old culinary practice. It is made less today which is a pity because this method of presenting a dish is excellent and has a delightful appearance. Here is Carême's recipe:

'The rice casserole is as elegant as it is rich; its shape and appetizing appearance give it a distinct character; it is certainly the most arresting entrée cooked in the oven.

'For a dinner which includes eight entrées, one prefers to serve a handsome casserole of rice rather than a hot *pâté* or *vol-au-vent*, and such a preference is right for the casserole is the most attractive of the coloured entrées.

'*Method of preparation.* After having washed 2 pounds of Carolina rice in lukewarm water several times, put the rice in a large casserole 10 inches in diameter in order the better to handle it in due course. Put it on the fire, with cold water, and after it has boiled for a few seconds drain it.

'Then cover the rice with good beef stock to about double its volume, and add for good measure some fat-skimmings from a chicken broth. Which means that if the rice measures an inch deep in the pan you can cover it with 2 inches above its surface with stock (without counting the chicken fat, 2 tablespoons in all).

'Put the casserole on a good fire. As soon as the rice begins to boil draw it to one side of the fire, the more easily to remove the small amount of scum that will appear. That done, put the casserole on hot cinders. Cover it without putting coals on the lid.

'Care must be taken that the rice is simmering the whole time. After simmering for about an hour stir it with a spatula so that the grains burst evenly. Let it simmer for another 20 to 25 minutes, then stir it again. If you find that it is soft and easy to crush between the fingers take it off the fire.

'But in the contrary case add a little more stock, and leave it to cook until it is perfectly done. Then stir it for a few minutes with the spatula.

'When the rice is no longer hot, work it well for a time with a spatula or wooden spoon so that every grain is crushed. If you judge it necessary to add a little stock do so, a little at a time, but the rice must be firm although malleable.

'When this is done, mould the rice casserole on a metal sheet or baking-tin. To this end pour out the rice in a mass and form it into a shape 4 to 5 inches high, 7 inches in diameter, working it smooth with the fingers.

'To embellish it, use the point of a knife and slices of carrot which you cut up to make them suitable for such work (the carrots are used to emphasize the form of the casserole).

'But take care that this form of decoration projects and does not get confused with the mass of rice.

'Cover the surface of the rice casserole with clarified butter, which helps to produce a more vivid colour, then set it on an andiron (iron tripod) and put it in a hot oven. The time it takes to cook is about 1½ hours. The colour should be a vivid yellow.

'When it is cooked, remove the cover which you have outlined on the top in forming the casserole, by incising with a sharp pointed knife the rounded top, taking care to remove all the rice inside which does not adhere to the gilded outer crust, so that the crust itself is quite thin.

'Then mix a large spoonful of rice from the interior of the casserole in a little pan with a little *béchamel sauce* (if the filling is to employ this sauce), or a little *Spanish sauce* (if the casserole is to be filled with a ragoût prepared with Spanish sauce), or any other sauce (see SAUCE) and, at the moment of serving, garnish the interior of the casserole crust which is then filled with whatever preparation is indicated. Before serving, lightly glaze the projections of the *casserole*.

'When a *consommé de bouillon* (beef stock doubled with veal and fowl) and clear chicken fat is lacking, it can be replaced by adding water, butter and salt to the rice. The casserole is not appreciably different, the result the same, and the rice is much whiter.' (Caréme, *Le Pâtissier royal.*)

Little casseroles of rice. CASSEROLETTES DE RIZ—'These little casseroles are made in exactly the same way as casserole of rice. They are made to measure 2¼ inches high and 3 inches in diameter. Place them on a metal sheet 3 inches apart to enable each to acquire the proper colour. Put them in a hot oven, and take them out when they are all a good golden colour.

'At the moment of serving fill them with the appropriate ragoût.' (Carême's recipe.)

CASSIA. CASSE—The pod of a leguminous plant divided into compartments, each enclosing a fairly large seed, surrounded by a brownish pulp, which is sweet, slightly acid, with a flavour resembling that of the prune.

This pulp has laxative properties; when sieved it forms the *casse mondée* of old times.

Manufacture of cassis, Dijou
(*French Government Tourist Office*)

CASSIS—District in the Bouches-du-Rhône area where an excellent wine is produced. The limits of the Cassis territory were fixed by ministerial decree (May, 1936). Beyond these limits no wine is authorized to bear the name of Cassis.

CASSOLETTE—Little dishes in fireproof porcelain, metal or tempered glass, of different shapes and capacity, used for presenting *hors-d'oeuvre*, hot or cold, little *entrées* and also some desserts. In U.S.A., these are called individual casseroles.

Cassolettes are also made with a preparation of duchess potatoes. These are produced by deep-fat frying, emptied after frying, and filled with various fillings.

Cassolettes served as an *hors-d'oeuvre* or as a little *entrée* are filled with *salpicons* or with various *ragoûts*, combined by means of a brown or white sauce. (See HORS-D'OEUVRE, *Hot hors-d'oeuvre*.)

Cassolettes served as sweets are filled with creams, with various sweetened pastes, with fruits poached in syrup.

CASSOULET—Haricot (shell) bean stew which is made more especially in Languedoc where it originates. The *cassoulet* is prepared with pork and mutton, with goose or duck, in an earthenware utensil which used to be known as the *cassole d'Issel* from whence derives its name.

Franc-Nohain, humorous poet, sang the praises of Languedoc Cassoulet in his *Nouvelle cuisinière bourgeoise* (a book in which many pungent poems are to be found). He even gives a recipe in verse for *cassoulet*, the substance of which is here extracted from the poem:

'On a moderate fire I see two casseroles. In one, a leg of *confit d'oie* or *confit de canard* (preserved goose or duck) as well as little sausages, ribs of pork and loin of mutton, are browning. Do not forget the flavouring, 2 tomatoes and 2 onions cut in four. Meanwhile the white Soissons haricots are cooking gently in the other utensil. Let the cooking proceed for 2 hours, and then dispose the beans and meat in the same earthenware vessel, in such a way that the goose or duck, mutton and pork are distributed between layers of haricot beans, all ready to melt in the mouth. After which put the cassoulet in the oven. Then on the surface of the dish a golden crust forms, thick and fat. Break it because this element must be incorporated

Cassoulet (*Robert Carrier*)

with the rest of the ingredients. Put it back in the oven, wait until another crust forms, which must be broken, and this must be done six times. Serve after breaking the crust seven times. Unctuous and perfect, in Languedoc a royal feast, this is called a haricot cream or *cassoulet*.'

Anatole France loved the cassoulet. He especially prized the one made by a certain Madame Clémence, rue Vavin.

In *Histoire comique* he wrote the following:

'I am going to lead you to a little tavern in the rue Vavin, chez Clémence, who only makes one dish, but a stupendous one: *le cassoulet de Castelnaudary*.

'*Le cassoulet de Castelnaudary* contains legs of *confits d'oie* (preserved goose), haricot beans previously blanched, pork fat, and little sausages. To be good it must have cooked very slowly for a long time. Clémence's cassoulet has been cooking for twenty years. She replenishes the pot sometimes with goose, sometimes with pork fat, sometimes she puts in a sausage or some haricots, but it is always the same cassoulet. The basis remains, and this ancient and precious substance gives it a taste, which one finds in the paintings of the old Venetian masters, in the amber flesh tints of their women. Come, I wish you to taste Clémence's cassoulet.'

There are three kinds of cassoulets; that of Castelnaudary, that of Carcassonne, and that of Toulouse.

Certain gastronomes deny this and maintain that there is only one cassoulet, that of Castelnaudary.

Serious culinary writers recognize this trinity. Joseph Favre says in his *Dictionnaire universel de la cuisine*, that 'Toulouse, Castelnaudary and Carcassonne make a speciality of this dish'.

Urbain Dubois says that the cassoulet is a very popular dish in the various districts of Languedoc, and chiefly in the Aude, the Haute-Garonne, and as far as the borders of the Hautes-Pyrénées. He adds that the Carcassonne method is characterized by 'leg of mutton, partridge and *confit d'oie* (preserved goose)'.

The three types of cassoulet should have the following differences: that of Castelnaudary (the forebear, the leader), is prepared with fresh pork, ham, knuckle of pork, and fresh bacon rinds; that of Carcassonne with the addition to the above of a shortened leg of mutton, and partridges in season; that of Toulouse, always in addition to the ingredients already mentioned for the *cassoulet de Castelnaudary*: breast of pork, Toulouse sausage, mutton (neck or boned breast) and *confit d'oie* (preserved goose) or *confit de canard* (preserved duck).

So much for principles. In current practice, in the Parisian restaurant just as in those of Languedoc, the rules relating to the different constituents are not always observed, and more or less universally the cassoulet, which is after all nothing but a succulent *estouffade* of pork and mutton, with haricot (shell) beans, is prepared with pork meat, fresh or salted (in various forms), with mutton and preserved goose or duck. In the homes of Languedoc it is customary (or at least it was in the old days) to complete the cooking of the cassoulet in a large earthenware terrine made of Issel clay in the baker's oven, heated with brushwood of mountain furze.

In Languedoc the way in which the cassoulet is made varies according to whoever is preparing it. Some cook the haricots, pork, mutton, bacon skins and sausages together, and then arrange these in alternate layers in the special terrine, covering the surface with a thick sprinkling of breadcrumbs, and then consign it to the baker's oven to cook gently for some hours.

Cassoulet de Castelnaudary (I)—Here is a 'simple' recipe confided to us by a gourmand of Castelnaudary:

Simmer some white haricot (shell) beans in a glazed earthenware pot known as a *toupin* (Pamiers or Cazères haricots are the best) with the usual seasoning, meats, and aromatic vegetables (without forgetting the garlic, the soul of Languedoc cooking!).

Drain them when they are properly cooked but whole and unbroken, put them in their special earthenware pot (in Issel clay) which has been lined with fresh bacon skins cooked with the haricots, knuckle of pork, breast of pork, sausage, a leg of *confit d'oie* (preserved goose).

Sprinkle with a layer of coarse breadcrumbs and add goose fat. Put into the baker's oven (heated with mountain furze), and cook gently for several hours.

When a good golden crust has formed on the surface of the cassoulet stir it in with the aid of a spoon and repeat this operation at least two or three times.

'And so', says our gourmand, 'you will obtain a cassoulet which you can serve with either a fine red Aquitaine wine, or with an old Minervois wine.'

Cassoulet de Castelnaudary (II)—After giving this recipe, which we have experimented with ourselves and found to be excellent, it behoves us to give the one which we ourselves execute.

For eight people. Put a quart (litre) of dried white haricot (shell) beans (previously soaked in cold water for several hours, but not for too long or they may begin to ferment) with ½ pound (300 grams) of salt breast of pork, approximately ⅓ pound (200 grams) of de-salted bacon skins (rolled up and held fast with thread), a carrot, an onion stuck with cloves, and a *bouquet garni** containing 3 cloves of garlic into an earthenware pot. Season with salt, but not too much (on account of the salt pork), and add sufficient water to just cover the beans. Simmer gently on a very low heat which will result in the haricots being perfectly cooked and unbroken.

In another pan, brown 1½ pounds (750 grams) of loin of pork and 1 pound (500 grams) of boned loin of mutton, well seasoned with salt and pepper in lard or goose fat. When the meat is well browned put into the pan in which they have been cooked 2 medium-sized onions (200 grams) chopped fine, a *bouquet garni* and 2 crushed cloves of garlic. Continue cooking with the lid on and moisten from time to time with good gravy or beef stock (one can add at will a few teaspoons of tomato purée to the sauce, or 3 fresh chopped tomatoes peeled, with the seeds removed, and chopped).

When the haricots are nearly cooked, remove the carrot, onion, *bouquet garni*, and put in the pork, the mutton, a garlic sausage, a leg of *confit d'oie* or *confit de canard* (preserved goose or duck), and perhaps a home-made sausage.

Simmer gently for an hour.

Remove the pieces of meat from the haricot beans. Cut the pork, mutton and goose up into slices of equal size. Cut the bacon skins into rectangular pieces, the garlic sausage into slices (with the skin removed), and the sausage into little slices.

Put into a large deep-set earthenware pot lined with bacon skins a layer of haricot beans; on top of this a layer of the various meats, with some of their sauce. Put more haricots on top, and continue to fill the pot with alternate layers, seasoning each one with a little freshly ground pepper. On the last layer of haricots lay slices of salt pork, and bacon skins, with some slices of garlic sausage.

Sprinkle with white breadcrumbs, and pour over them a little goose fat. Cook gently in the oven (if possible in a baker's oven) for about 1½ hours. Serve the cassoulet in the pot in which it has cooked.

CASTAGNACI (Corsican cookery)—Thick fritters or waffles made with chestnut flour.

CASTIGLIONE (A LA)—Preparation of small pieces of butcher's meat. The Castiglione garnish consists of large mushrooms stuffed with rice and browned in the oven, of aubergines (egg-plants) sautéed in butter, and slices of poached beef marrow. See GARNISHES.

CASTRATE. CHÂTRER—The castration of animals destined for the butcher, to hasten their fattening.

The word *châtrer* is also applied to the removal of the intestines of crayfish (U.S.A. crawfish) before cooking. In order to do this the central part of the tail is pinched and the intestines emerge.

CAT. CHAT—Domestic cat whose edible meat has a flavour halfway between that of rabbit and that of hare. Cat's meat has often been eaten in periods of famine or of siege. Legend has it that in the cook-shops the cat is often used in the making of rabbit fricassées. Examination of the bones would easily enable one, in case of doubt, to distinguish between the one animal and the other.

CATALANE (A LA)—Garnish for large pieces of butcher's meat composed of aubergines (egg-plants) sautéed in oil and pilaf of rice. See GARNISHES.

CATECHU. CACHOU—Thick sap which comes from a variety of Indian acacia (catechu), *Areca catechu* betel nut. The catechu is found in compact, heavy, friable, irregular masses, brownish on the outside and reddish-brown on the inside. It should neither stick to the tongue nor tint the saliva red.

Its taste, at first bitter and astringent, becomes sweet and clean—without any smell. The most highly prized are the *Ceylon catechu* and that of Pegu (Burma), which has medicinal properties.

The catechu contains a strong proportion of tannin, which gives it its astringent properties.

Catechu tablets are made out of 50 grams of powdered Pegu catechu, 400 grams of icing sugar and 50 grams of gum tragacanth mucilage. (Extract from the Codex formula.)

CATFISH. POISSON-CHAT—American river fish found principally in the Mississippi basin. It has six barbels or feelers about the mouth reaching from 12 to 24 inches in length; the flesh is delicate and there are not too many bones.

CATSUP OR KETCHUP—Condiment of English origin, widely used both in England and U.S.A. It has a tomato base and is highly spiced.

CAUF. BANNETON—A receptacle with holes which permits fish to be kept alive in water. This word is also used to describe a baker's bread-basket.

CAUL. CRÉPINE—Membrane enclosing the paunch of animals, used for butcher's meat, and more especially that of pork and mutton. In French, this is also called *toilette*.

CAULIFLOWER. CHOU-FLEUR—These vegetables are oriental in origin and have been known in Italy since the sixteenth century. A delicate food which must always be bought with its green leaves (which are in fact edible), an indication of freshness.

Boiled cauliflower. CHOU-FLEUR À L'ANGLAISE—This means cooking a cauliflower in boiling salted water, draining it, and arranging it on a napkin, or on a grid, and serving with melted butter.

According to the English method a cauliflower served in this way must be cooked whole with two rows of tender leaves enveloping the flower-head. It is also customary in England to serve the cauliflower on a thick slice of toast, the object being to absorb the excess moisture.

Note. In domestic cookery where one should attempt to make the best of the raw material at hand it often happens that considerable portions, which are perfectly edible, are removed during preparation. This is particularly the case with the cauliflower, the flower-heads only being used. The leaves, ribs, and stems are, however, excellent. They should be trimmed and cooked with the white part.

These latter portions can also be used for soup, *hors-d'oeuvre*, etc. Using these various parts of the vegetable also diminishes the cost.

Boiled cauliflower with various sauces (cold). CHOU-FLEUR BOUILLI—Cook the cauliflower in the same way as above. Drain it, put it under the cold tap. Arrange the florets in their original form. Serve with *Vinaigrette sauce*, *Mayonnaise* or some other cold sauce. See SAUCE, *Cold sauces*.

Boiled cauliflower with various sauces (hot). CHOU-FLEUR BOUILLI—Divide the raw cauliflower into little florets, trim them, and boil them in salted water. Drain them. Arrange them on a napkin, or on a grid, giving them their original form. Garnish with fresh parsley.

Serve with one or other of the usual sauces for boiled vegetables: melted butter, *cream*, *hollandaise*, *white sauce*, etc. See SAUCE.

Cauliflower with brown butter or noisette butter. CHOU-FLEUR AU BEURRE NOIR—Arrange the cauliflower florets, which have been boiled in salted water, in the form of a dome, on a dish. Sprinkle with chopped parsley, and a thread of lemon juice. At the moment of serving cover the cauliflower with brown butter, or with noisette butter. See BUTTER, *Compound butters*.

Cauliflower with cream. CHOU-FLEUR À LA CRÈME—Cook the cauliflower in the way described above. Then simmer it slightly in butter. Rearrange the florets in their original form. Cover it with a *Cream sauce*. See SAUCE.

Cauliflower fritters. CHOU-FLEUR EN FRITOTS—Cook the cauliflower florets in salted water, keeping them rather firm. Drain them. Soak them for 30 minutes in oil, lemon juice, chopped parsley, salt and pepper.

At the right moment dip the florets in a *light batter* (see BATTER). Fry in deep fat. Arrange on a napkin; sprinkle with fried parsley. Serve with tomato sauce, handed separately.

Cauliflower au gratin. CHOU-FLEUR AU GRATIN—Blanch the cauliflower florets in boiling salted water, drain them, and then simmer them in butter. Arrange them on a buttered gratin dish, covered with *Mornay sauce* (see SAUCE). Sprinkle with grated cheese and melted butter. Brown in the oven.

Cauliflower à la milanaise. CHOU-FLEUR À LA MILANAISE—Blanch the cauliflower florets in boiling salted water, drain them, and then cook them gently in butter. Sprinkle with grated Parmesan cheese and melted butter. Brown in the oven. At the moment of serving pour on a little *noisette butter*. See BUTTER, *Compound butters*.

Cauliflower Mornay. CHOU-FLEUR MORNAY—Prepared in the same way as *Cauliflower au gratin*.

Cauliflower mould. PAIN DE CHOU-FLEUR—This is made in the same way as *pain de chicorée*, with a purée of cauliflower. See CHICORY/ENDIVE.

Cauliflower à la polonaise. CHOU-FLEUR À LA POLONAISE—Arrange the cooked cauliflower on a round buttered dish. Sprinkle it with hard yolks of egg mixed with chopped parsley. At the moment of serving pour over the cauliflower some *noisette butter** (see BUTTER, *Compound butters*) in which some fine breadcrumbs have been fried (about ⅔ cup (30 grams) of breadcrumbs per 6 tablespoons (100 grams) of butter). Serve at once; the butter should be frothy.

Cauliflower purée. PURÉE DE CHOU-FLEUR—Put some cooked cauliflower through a fine sieve, having first drained it thoroughly and dried it for a moment in the oven. Heat the purée and add one-quarter of its weight of potato purée. Finish with fresh cream and butter. Season, and mix well.

Cauliflower salad

Cauliflower salad. SALADE DE CHOU-FLEUR—Arrange a cauliflower which has been boiled in salted water, and properly drained, in a dish. Season with oil, vinegar, salt and pepper. Sprinkle with chopped chervil. Lemon juice can replace the vinegar.

Cauliflower sautéed in butter. CHOU-FLEUR SAUTÉ AU BEURRE—Divide a cauliflower into little florets and blanch them. Drain well and put them in a pan in which some butter is heating. Cook at a good heat so that the cauliflower florets are lightly browned. Arrange in a dish (as usual arranging them in their original form). Pour the butter in which the cauliflower has cooked over the dish.

Cauliflower soufflé. SOUFFLÉ DE CHOU-FLEUR—Prepared with cauliflower boiled in salt water and passed through a fine sieve, in the same way as for *Chicory soufflé*. See CHICORY/ENDIVE.

Cauliflower au gratin

Stalks and stumps of cauliflower. MOELLE DE CHOU-FLEUR—The core of the stalks and stumps of this vegetable is usually discarded, but it can be very tasty and can, if well cooked, provide very good dishes.

Trim the stalks or stumps, that is to say, remove all the woody outer casing. Blanch whole if they are to be served with the vegetable. If they are to be cooked separately, cut into rounds or some other shape. After blanching, these stalks and stumps can be prepared in the same way as artichoke stalks or endive stumps.

CAVAILLON—Little town in the Vaucluse district which has given its name to a kind of melon. See MELON.

CAVEAU—Little cellar sometimes reserved for fine wines.

CAVEAU (LE)—Literary society, bacchic and gastronomic, founded in 1729 by Piron, Collé, Gallet and Crébillon *fils*.

CAVIARE—The roe of the various members of the sturgeon family, lightly salted or marinated. There are different qualities of caviare. Caviare is also made from the roes of beluga, sevruga, sterlet, keta, or dog-salmon, etc.

Caviare was known by our forbears. Rabelais mentions it in *Pantagruel*, under the name of *caviat*. He also speaks of *la bourtargue*, which is a kind of caviare prepared with red mullets' roes.

In Savary's *Dictionnaire du Commerce* (1741) one reads on the subject of caviare, which was then called *kavia*, 'It is beginning to be known in France where it is not despised at the best tables'.

The mention in Rabelais proves that caviare was known in France some four hundred years ago. Caviare is served as an *hors-d'oeuvre*.

CAVOUR (A LA)—Method of preparing small pieces of butcher's meat, especially veal escalopes and calves' sweetbreads. These are dressed on little circles of polenta, garnished with grilled mushrooms filled with a purée of chicken livers and slices of truffle.

CAYENNE PEPPER. POIVRE DE CAYENNE—See PEPPER, *Red pepper or Pimento*.

CELERY. CÉLERI—A cultivated form of wild celery. Used a great deal by the Romans, celery did not come into cultivation until the sixteenth century. In some cases growers have tried to develop the leaves, in others the root.

This plant contains an essential oil, which is highly aromatic. According to the different varieties, either the stems are eaten, elongated by trussing or culture in the dark, or the roots (celeriac). Both are eaten raw, in salad, or cooked.

Branch (forced) celery. CÉLERI EN BRANCHES—*Method of preparation*—Trim off the upper branches of the celery in order to conserve only the tender parts, measuring between 7-8 inches.

Remove the green outer stems, and trim the root.

Wash the base of the celery taking meticulous care, allowing water to run between the stems, so that all earth or other foreign matter is washed away.

Pare the outer stems to remove the fibres.

Blanch the celery sticks in boiling salted water for 10 minutes.

Plunge them in cold water, drain and wipe dry.

Spread them out on a cloth, open them slightly and season inside. Then tie them together, two or three at a time, and put them in a deep casserole which is already buttered and lined with bacon rinds, hashed onions and sliced carrots. Just cover the onions and carrots with a white stock from which not all the fat has been skimmed, or with beef stock.

Set on the stove, to start cooking. Then put the casserole in the oven at a low temperature for about 1½ hours.

Celery can be prepared '*au maigre*' by omitting the bacon rinds, and replacing the stock with water.

Celery with béchamel sauce. CÉLERIS À LA BÉCHAMEL—Braise the celery, drain it, divide it lengthways in two. Fold each portion in half.

Set in a buttered pan. Simmer for 10 minutes. Cover with a *béchamel sauce*, not too thick. (See SAUCE.) Simmer again for a few minutes.

Celery in butter. CÉLERIS AU BEURRE—Trim, wash and blanch the celery sticks for 10 minutes in salted water. Divide them in two lengthways and bend each portion in half, and put them in a very well-buttered pan. Season. Moisten with a few tablespoons of white stock or water and cook covered for 45 minutes or 1 hour.

Celery with cream. CÉLERIS À LA CRÈME—Pare and shorten the sticks of celery. Wash them and remove the fibres from the outside stems.

Blanch in salted boiling water. Plunge them in cold water, drain, and dry.

Divide the sticks in halves lengthways. Arrange them in a well-buttered casserole. Season. Cover with a light bouillon (or with water if you want to serve them '*au maigre*').

Bring to the boil on top of the stove. Cover the pan and put it in the oven for about an hour.

Drain the celery. Bend the pieces in half. Put them on a vegetable dish.

Strain their liquor, skim it, and boil it down. Add to it 6-8 tablespoons (½ decilitre) of *béchamel sauce*. See SAUCE.

Moisten with ⅔ cup (2 decilitres) of rather thick fresh cream. Boil down by half, incorporate a tablespoon of butter, mix, and strain through a sieve. Pour this sauce over the celery.

Celery à la grecque (cold hors-d'oeuvre). CÉLERIS À LA GRECQUE—Trim the celery sticks, wash well, divide into quarters and prepare them in the manner described for *Artichokes à la grecque*. See ARTICHOKE.

Celery à l'italienne. CÉLERIS À L'ITALIENNE—The same as for *Cardoons à l'italienne*.*

Celery au jus. CÉLERIS AU JUS—The same as for *Cardoons au jus*.*

Celery with marrow. CÉLERIS À LA MOELLÈ—The same as for *Cardoons with marrow*.*

Celery Mornay. CÉLERIS MORNAY—The same as for *Cardoons à la Mornay*. See CARDOON.

Celery with Parmesan. CÉLERIS AU PARMESAN—The same as for *Cardoons with Parmesan*.*

Celery purée. PURÉE DE CÉLERIS—Using braised celery, cooked with beef bouillon or water, prepare the purée in the same way as for *Cardoon purée*.* The purée can be prepared with the addition of potatoes used in the proportion of a third of the volume of the celery, which improves the consistency.

Celery with various sauces. CÉLERIS AUX SAUCES DIVERSES—Pare, wash and blanch celery and cook completely in salted water. Drain and serve like asparagus, with sauces handed separately. See SAUCE.

Celery vinaigrette. CÉLERIS À LA VINAIGRETTE—Scrape and wash the celery, which should be white and tender. Arrange the sticks in a crystal glass. Serve with a *Vinaigrette sauce* (see SAUCE) handed separately.

CELERY ROOTS OR CELERIAC. CÉLERI-RAVE—Celeriac is a variety of celery having a large edible root. Wash and pare the celeriac. Divide into quarters and cut into chunks, or large slices. Blanch them for 5 minutes in boiling salted water, plunge into cold water, drain and wipe dry. Then stew them in butter adding a little white stock or water. All the recipes for branch celery are applicable to celeriac.

After having divided the celeriac into quarters, and cutting them into chunks or thick slices, they are first of all cooked in stock or water.

The following recipes can also be applied to this vegetable.

Celeriac julienne. JULIENNE DE CÉLERI-RAVE—Used as a garnish. Pare a root of celeriac. Wash it and cut it into matchstick strips, very fine or less so according to the result required. Put the *julienne** into a sauté-pan in which a tablespoon of butter has been heated. Season with salt and a little powdered sugar. Simmer gently.

Use the preparation according to the requirements of the recipe.

Celeriac purée. PURÉE DE CÉLERI-RAVE—Garnish for large or small pieces of butcher's meat. The purée is prepared in the same way as for *Cardoon purée*. See CARDOON.

Salpicon of celeriac. SALPICON DE CÉLERI-RAVE—Cut the celeriac into squares of a suitable size. Blanch in salted water, drain, and stew in butter. Use the *salpicon** according to the requirements of the recipe.

Stuffed celeriac à la paysanne. CÉLERI-RAVE À LA PAYSANNE—This is used as a garnish. Pare 2 celeriac roots. Divide them into slices 1 inch thick. Trim the slices into rounds.

Blanch for 5 minutes in salted water, plunge into cold water, drain, and dry the slices in a cloth. Scoop a hollow in each slice to half its depth.

Cut the pulp which has been hollowed out into squares, and add double the quantity of carrot and onion *brunoise** sautéed in butter and seasoned with salt and pepper.

Stuff the celeriac rounds with this mixture. Put them in a butter dish, dust them with grated cheese. Sprinkle with melted butter and brown in a moderate oven.

Note. All the stuffings used for tomatoes and artichoke hearts can be applied equally well to celeriac.

CELLAR. CAVE—Underground room, with or without an arched ceiling, in which wine is kept. A good cellar must be cool (50-54°F.), slightly damp, and the air must circulate a little.

Liqueur cellar. CAVE À LIQUEURS—Chest, the work of a cabinet-maker or goldsmith, which is used to lock up precious flagons and sometimes liqueur glasses.

CELLULOSE—A more or less hard substance constituting the tissue of vegetable matter.

CENDRÉ DE LA BRIE—An Ile-de-France cheese which is eaten between September and May.

CÈNE—Long ago this word was synonymous in France with the word meal (*repas*) but it is now used solely to designate the Last Supper taken by Christ with the apostles, before the Passion.

CÉPAGE—Plant, variety of vine. French vines, restocked with American vines, have been grafted on to the ancient vine stocks, which are recognized as the best in each region.

The number of vine varieties is considerable. Among the principal vine stocks there are:

In Bordeaux: the *Cabernet franc*, the *Cabernet Sauvignon*, the *Merlot*, the *Malbec*, the *Verdot*, for red wines;

the *Sauvignon*, the *Semillon*, and the *Muscadelle* for white wines.

In Burgundy: the *Pinots* and the *Gamay*, red and white; in Champagne, the *Pinot noir* and the *Pinot chardonny*; along the Loire, the *Gamay blanc*, the *Breton* (which is the same as the *Bordeaux Cabernet*) and the *Pinot de la Loire* are shared among the vineyards, and one can also name the *Syrah* (Hermitage wine), the *Picquepoul du Gers*, from which the Armagnac brandies are distilled, while the same plant under the name of *Folle blanche* serves in Charentes as the chief element of cognac.

The Jura wines come principally from the *Pinot blanc* and the *Poulsart*; the muscat wines of Roussillon derive from the *Alicante*; the *Grenache*, the *Aramon* and the *Carigane* are the vine-stocks with a high yield, cultivated in the departments of Aude, Herault and Gard.

Among the notable vine-stocks producing grapes for the table are the various *chasselas*, the *muscats*, white and red, the *oeillade*, etc.

CÈPE—French name for boletus or edible mushroom. Recipes will be found under MUSHROOM.

CEREALS. CÉRÉALES—Designations of farinaceous foodstuffs, which may or may not be suitable for bread, which are the basis of human diet.

Oats, wheat, maize, millet, barley, rice, rye, and Indian millet are the graminaceous crops; only buckwheat belongs to the polygonaceous group.

All cereals are capable of being made into bread, if need be, but wheat and rye are more especially reserved for this purpose.

CERVELAS—Large short sausage, made of pork meat interlarded with pork fat, seasoned usually with garlic.

This type of *charcuterie* (cooked pork meats) is so-called because formerly brains, particularly pigs' brains, formed part of its composition. For the preparation of *cervelas*, also called *saucisson de Paris*, see SAUCISSON, *Parisian saucisson*.

CHABLIS—Little town in the district of Yonne famous for its white wines. See WINE.

CHABOISSEAU—Mediterranean fish of the Cottus family. The *chaboisseau* is called 'scorpion', 'sea-devil', 'toad' locally on account of its strange appearance. It is also known as 'tadpole' (on account of its large head), 'grumbler', and 'sea-cock', on account of the rumbling sound it produces when held in the hand. The flesh of this fish is fairly delicate, and is used especially in *bouillabaisse* and fish soups. It should not be eaten during the spawning season from November to May.

CHABOT—Freshwater fish of the cottus family, which has fairly delicate flesh. The chabot should not be confused with the *chevaine* (chub) although chub in France are sometimes called *chabot*.

CHALK. CHAUX—Calcium oxide, found in various combinations and in different forms in organic tissue.

Very often drinking-water contains too high a proportion of calcium salt and is termed *hard water*. This hard water prevents the perfectly satisfactory cooking of vegetables, and is not good for lathering; one can, at least in part, remove the calcium salts from drinking water by decanting it after prolonged boiling and subsquent cooling, but it must then be aerated by beating.

CHAMBERTIN—Vineyard on the Côte d'Or in the commune of Gevrey-Chambertin. See WINE.

CHAMBRER—A term referring to wines removed from the cellar a few hours before they are required, in order to bring them slowly up to the same temperature as the room. All the red Bordeaux wines must be *chambrés*.

CHAMOIS—Wild mammal, bearing some resemblance to the goat. It is found in the high alps and in the Pyrenees, where it is known as *Izard* (Isard).

Chamois meat is considered excellent venison, enjoyed particularly when the animal is young. It is tougher when the chamois is older, and needs to be properly marinated before cooking.

It is prepared in the same ways as *Roebuck*.*

CHAMPAGNE—This province, which comprises approximately the four departments of Marne, Ardennes, Haute-Marne and Aube, has a world-wide reputation on account of its great sparkling white wines.

The cooking in the Champagne province is excellent, but its repertoire is rather limited.

The local *charcuterie* is in the first rank of gastronomic specialities, particularly the delicious *andouillettes* of Bar-sur-Aube and Bar-sur-Seine: the *andouillettes de mouton* of Troyes, and the *langues fourrées* of the same town; the famous pigs' trotters '*à la Sainte-Menehould*'; the Reims hams and knuckles, and many other *charcuterie* specialities which are famous.

The butchers' meat in this region, particularly the mutton, is excellent. Poultry-raising produces fairly good birds; the vegetable plot and the orchard also provide products of excellent quality.

Freshwater fish have a certain delicacy, notably the carp, pike, trout and salmon, the latter fish being of migratory habit.

In this region excellent game, both furred and feathered, is found, and the thrushes of the Ardennes in particular are greatly prized by connoisseurs.

Among the dishes of Champagne are the *matelotes** prepared in the Champagne manner, that is to say employing champagne; *la Potée champenoise*: the *Quartier de mouton à la champagne*; the *Boudin de lapin à la Sainte-Menehould*; Thrushes *à l'ardennaise*; the *Poulet à la peau de goret*; the *Gougère de l'Aube* (which resembles the one prepared in Burgundy); the *salade de pissenlit au lard*; and, as a sweet, the *Beignets au fromage blanc*.

Old champagne bottles

Wines. The cellars of Champagne are famous. One single wine embellishes them, a truly precious wine, a wine for kings, champagne.

One could well devote a whole volume to describing the history of champagne, a complete history of this magnificent wine. We must be content here with only a brief note.

This wine, '*aimable, fin et élégant*', which has conquered the whole world and which no longer needs its well-earned praise, is the outcome of a series of operations and meticulous manipulations.

The vineyards which produce the grapes used in the production of the great Champagne wines occupy the surrounding slopes of the *montagne de Reims* (Hills of Reims) from Damery as far as Villedommange on the one hand, and, on the other, the hillsides of Epernay and Avize from Boursault to Vertus.

On the slopes of the *montagne de Reims* which face east between Ambonnay and Verzenay, one sees in successive terraces facing south first of all, and dominating the

On the slopes of Epernay facing north-east, running parallel with the Marne, are the vines of Boursault, Vauciennes and Epernay. Facing east one sees those of Chouilly, Pierry, Saint-Martin-d'Ablois, Moussy, Vinay and Monthelon.

On the hillsides of Avize and then on those of Epernay are the vineyards of Cramant, Avize, Oger, le Mesnil-sur-Oger, all famous for their fine wines made from white grapes, and finally the vines of Vertus.

Gastronomic map of Champagne

Marne, the vines of Damery, Cumières, Dizy, Hautvillers (where sparkling wine originated), Champillon, Ay—a vineyard which produces the most perfect wine where body and delicacy are united—Mareuil-sur-Ay, Avenay, Tours-de-Marne, Tauxières and Bouzy. Facing east one sees the vines of Ambonnay, Trépail and Villers-Marmery, facing north-east there are the vines of Verzy, Verzenay, Mailly, Ludes, Chigny, Rilly-en-Montagne, Villers-Allerand, Chamery, Ecueil, Sacy and Villedommange.

Here is the order in which the Champagne wine trade classes the vineyards:

Premiers grands crus. Black grapes: Ay, Bouzy, Ambonnay, Verzenay, Verzy (black), Mailly. *White* grapes: Cramant, Avize, Oger.

Deuxièmes grands crus. Black grapes: Mareuil-sur-Ay, Dizy, Hautvillers, Champillon, Avenay, Trépail, Villers-Marmery, Cuis, Grauves, Ludes, Chigny, Cumières, Rilly-la-Montagne, Chouilly, Pierry, Vertus. *White* grapes: Verzy, Trépail, Villers-Marmery, Cuis, Grauves,

Chouilly (these communes produce both black and white grapes).

Troisèmes crus. Epernay, Villers-Allerand, Chamery, Ecueil, Villedommange, Saint-Martin-d'Ablois, Mancy, Vinay and Monthelon, and finally Boursault and Vauciennes.

CHAMPAGNE (Fine) — Name designating certain brandies made in the Charentes area. The famous name given to the locality which produces these brandies is due it is said to a resemblance between the soil and the chalky sub-soil with that of the Champagne of north-west France. See CHARENTE, *Eau-de-vie.*

CHAMPAGNISER—To produce the sparkling quality, or to treat wines according to the Champagne method.

CHAMPIGNY (pastry cookery)—Use some puff pastry (*pâté feuilletée*) which has been rolled out six times (see DOUGH), and roll it out to a thickness not more than $\frac{1}{8}$ inch in a square shape of the size in which the pastry is required. Fill the centre of the pastry with a good layer of apricot jam without sieving it, so that the whole fruits are retained (the jam should be flavoured with a little kirsch and contain some apricot kernels). Moisten the edges of the pastry and cover this layer with a second sheet of pastry, $\frac{1}{8}$ inch thick, made in the same way. Press the edges well together all round to join the two layers, and prevent the apricot jam from seeping through during the cooking. Pattern the edges by indenting with a fork, and brush the surface with beaten egg. Cook in a moderate oven for 25 to 30 minutes. Sprinkle with icing sugar and glaze.

Note. To prevent the jam from seeping out during the cooking, a ribbon of pastry is often imposed round the edges.

CHAMPOREAU—This used to denote a combination of weak *café au lait* and some kind of liqueur.

Today it signifies black coffee with the addition of a certain quantity of eau-de-vie, cognac, armagnac, rum or kirsch.

One says in slang language '*faire champoreau*'.

CHANFAINA (Spanish cookery)—Cook a lamb's liver in salt water (or a pig's liver; this dish is prepared with one or the other). Separately cook two large chopped onions in oil. When the onion is almost cooked add pimentos cut into small pieces, chopped parsley and chopped fresh mint. Season with salt, pepper, cinnamon and cumin. Cook for a few minutes. Then put in the liver cut up into large dice. Cook on a fairly strong heat for a few minutes. Moisten with a few tablespoons of the liquor in which the liver has been cooked. Boil for 5 minutes. Add a small quantity of breadcrumbs cooked in water in the manner of a bread *panada** to bind the sauce. Season highly.

CHANTERELLE (Cantharellus cibarius)—Edible mushroom also known in France under the name of *girolle*. See MUSHROOMS.

CHANTILLY—Name given to a variety of preparations. Denotes, in the first place, fresh cream beaten to the consistency of a mousse, sweetened and flavoured with vanilla or other flavours. It also means a hollandaise sauce to which whipped cream has been added; also a cold sauce, composed of mayonnaise and whipped cream. These last two sauces are also known under the name of *mousseline*. Finally the name is given to various culinary preparations and pastry confections. See *Chicken à la Chantilly*, *Charlotte à la Chantilly*.

CHAP. Bajoue—The lower jaw, or half of cheek (especially of pig).

CHAPELER—The French verb denotes in culinary terms the preparation of breadcrumbs by crushing with a bottle or rolling-pin bread which has been dried in the oven (or *chapelé*), and passing it through a metal sieve. In the old days grilled bread was called in France '*pain cappelé*'. The term '*chapeler un plat*' meant to brown the dish in the oven after dusting it with breadcrumbs (*chapelure*). See BREADCRUMBS.

CHAPON (Mediterranean cooking)—A slice of French bread rubbed with garlic and seasoned with oil and vinegar. In the south of France, and especially in Languedoc, bread treated in this way is added to salads, particularly to chicory salad.

CHAR OR CHARR. Omble chevalier—Fish of the salmon genus, found in the deep lakes and rivers of Switzerland and Savoy, resembling the trout, with finer scales and teeth and black spots on the sides. The flesh of the char is very delicate. It is prepared like *Salmon trout*. See TROUT.

CHARCOAL. Charbon—Result of the incomplete combustion of organic matter. Granulated or reduced to a powder charcoal is capable of absorbing a high proportion of gas, and of absorbing colouring matter or odours.

For these purposes vegetable charcoal is used, made from a non-resinous wood (poplar), or from animal charcoal. There are today specially 'activated' charcoals capable of considerable powers of absorption.

Charcoal is used to take the colour out of wine and liqueurs, to remove the smell of putrefaction, and to purify water.

CHARCUTERIE (Pork butchery)—The art of preparing various meats, in particular pork, in order to present them in the most diverse ways.

The pig, whose meat prepared by modern pork butchers in such a variety of ways is the delight of gourmets, was despised by the Egyptians, and Moses included it among the impure meats which he forbade the Hebrews to eat. The most ancient peoples of the East did not know sausages in any form, pâtés or hams, etc.

The Greeks rehabilitated the animal so far as to make it the favourite victim in the sacrifices offered to the gods. They also used pork fat in cooking. The Romans probably learned from them the elementary preparations of pork. They elaborated the art and since then Italy has remained in the forefront in the manufacture of the most delectable forms of *charcuterie*.

One law, the *porcella* law, determined the manner of raising, feeding, killing and preparing pigs in Rome. This same law controlled the profession of pork butchery. Pork meat was treated in several ways in the time of the Roman Empire and was preserved by mixing it with salt, spices and aromatics. *Mortadellas*, *salamis*, and all the Italian specialities were very probably made under other names at that time, more or less in the same way as today. Particularly appreciated were the uterus and the udder before the animal had begun to breed. As for the various preparations which appeared on Roman tables in the form of small or large sausages, they had their names: *farcimina*, *tobelli*, *tomacula* and *tomacina*, etc. It was therefore among the Romans that the art of pork butchery was developed.

This art was more or less preserved during the Middle Ages in France, but the métier of pork butchery was for a long time confused with that of *cuisinier-oyer* which, in the fourteenth century comprised only two categories: that of the *chaircutiers* and that of the *rostisseurs* (roasting chefs). It was in 1476 that the charcutiers obtained the monopoly of selling pork meat, cooked or

Charcuterie, Bayonne (*French Government Tourist Office*)

raw (fat pork only in the latter case), but they were not allowed to kill the pigs themselves and had to buy the pork meat from the butchers.

Until the fifteenth century the *chaircutiers* sold cooked meats almost exclusively. Fresh pork meat, like other meat, was part of the butchers' trade. The statutes of January 17th, 1475, recognized the sole rights of the *chaircutiers-saucissiers boudiniers* to sell pork meat either cooked or prepared in the form of *cervelas*, sausages, black puddings (U.S.A. blood sausages) etc. (Franklin).

In the sixteenth century they finally obtained the right to kill the pigs themselves. An order of March 26th, 1664, forced them to buy their pigs at a distance of 21 leagues from Paris, a decree which is no longer in force since the creation of stockyards in the city itself.

All Parisians know the famous *foire aux jambons* (Ham Fair) which is held on the boulevard Richard-Lenoir before Holy Week. The little stalls are laden for several days with all the *charcuterie* specialities from the French provinces, and even from abroad. Auvergne and Lorraine seem to dominate with their concentration of sausages, small and large, their hams, puddings, pâtés, etc. This fair dates from the remote past and is said to have begun in front of Notre Dame.

CHARD. Carde—Name given in olden days to white beet. See BEETROOT.

CHARENTE—This name is famous throughout the world for its magnificent brandies known under the name of *Cognac*.

These are made from the wines produced in the department of Charente-Maritime.

Eaux-de-vie of Charente—The general classification of the vineyards of the Charente region is arranged in the following order:

Grande champagne, *petite champagne*, *borderies*, *fins-bois*, *bons-bois*, *bois ordinaires*, and *bois du terroir*.

Grande champagne includes the whole of the canton of Segonzac, and part of the Cognac canton south of the Charente river.

'The brandy of this region is the prototype of the brandies of Charente; it is characterized by a very delicate aroma, recalling the gentle perfume of the vine in flower, and by a vigorous and full savour which is translated in the tasting into prolonged and pleasurable sensations. This brandy is warm without burning the palate, and its colour, if it has aged in an ideal situation, is a very pale gold.

'*Petite champagne* encloses the *Grande champagne* in a half-circle. It is limited on the north by the course of the Charente, between Mosnac and Merpins, then, to the east, by a line running from Mosnac to Barbezieux, on the south by the road running from Barbezieux to Jonzac, and finally on the west by the course of the river Seugne, from Jonzac to Beillant.

'The brandies of this region, without having the great finesse of those of *Grande champagne*, approach them to a certain degree, particularly in the bordering vineyards, and are excellent.

'The *borderies*, as the name implies, form a series of little hills along the banks of the Charente, from Cognac to Chérac, and stretch northwards as far as the heights of Saint-Sulpice and Menac. This borders on the vast plain of the Pays-Bas.

'The *borderies* produce good brandies with aroma, a certain finesse and a full body. They are less mellow than the *champagne* brandies, but have more body.

'The *fins-bois* and *bons-bois* surround the three preceding areas in the form of a pentagon whose upper angle touches Saint-Jean-d'Angély, and whose limits are successively the road from Saint-Jean-d'Angély to Angou-

Some charcuterie products: (1) Paris ham; (2) Rolled shoulder; (3) Galantine of boar's head; (4) Pain de rillettes; (5) Rillons de Tours; (6) Black pudding; (7) Foie gras sausage; (8) *Filet de Saxe*; (9) Liver pâté; (10) Rabbit galantine; (11) Poultry galantine; (12) Brawn; (13) Truffled poultry galantine; (14) Truffled foie gras galantine (*Larousse*)

lême, the line of the railroad from Angoulême to Chalais, a line drawn from Chalais to Montendre, the road from Montendre to Saujon, and finally a line running from Saujon to Saint-Jean-d'Angély.

'The *bois* brandies have a smooth quality, but, compared with those of *champagne* they are soft, with less finesse and offer briefer pleasures to the palate.

'All the other vineyards of Charente and the islands produce ordinary brandies, but worthy of imbibing.' (From *Les Dissertations gastronomiques* by Ernest Verdier.)

Not only must the brandies of the Charente area come from the areas defined in the accompanying chart in order to have the right to a Cognac label, but the wines on which they are based must derive solely from the following vine-stocks: *Sémillon*, *Folle-blanche*, *Colombac*, *Blanc rainé*, *Jurançon blanc*, *Montils* and *Sauvigon*.

CHARLOTTE—Two kinds of rather different desserts are known by the name of Charlotte. One, *Charlotte russe*, is prepared with *Bavarian cream** which is set in a plain round mould lined round the sides and at the bottom with sponge fingers, and served cold; while the other, the *Fruit Charlotte* (and more especially *Apple Charlotte* which seems to have been the first of this kind), is made with a confection of fruit in a mould lined with thin slices of buttered bread, usually served hot. The only thing in common between these two charlottes is their exterior form.

The second charlotte was certainly invented a long time before the *Charlotte russe*, which was created by Carême, and to which he had given the name *Charlotte parisienne*, having had this idea, he says, while starting up his own establishment, because the first *Charlottes russes* to make their appearance were at the tables of ministers of security, and foreign ministers. I sent them, adds Carême, 'all ready to serve along with the orders for pastry sweets which were placed with me by the great houses. (Carême, *Pâtissier royale*.)

Carême, then, invented the *Charlotte russe*, and from the preceding remarks it appears—although denied by the majority of the great chef's biographers—that Carême certainly was established in Paris, for a short time no doubt, but it is not known exactly in what locality.

Fruit charlottes. CHARLOTTES DE FRUITS:

Apple charlotte. CHARLOTTE DE POMMES—Line the bottom and the sides of a charlotte mould with slices of bread cut in the form of hearts, and dipped in melted butter for the bottom, and for the sides sliced in the form of rectangles exactly the same height as the mould and also dipped in melted butter.

Fill the mould lined with bread with a preparation of apple made in the following way:

Slice 12 apples which have been cut in quarters. Put the apples in a sauté-pan (heavy frying-pan) in which 3 tablespoons (50 grams) of butter have been heated. Add 2 large tablespoons of powdered sugar, a pinch of cinnamon and a little lemon rind (or flavour with vanilla). Cook the apples on a hot flame, stirring continuously with a spatula. When the preparation is considerably thickened add 3 or 4 tablespoons of apricot jam.

Fill the mould with this, being careful to fill the top and a little more. Place a slice of bread trimmed into a round and dipped in butter on top of the apple.

Cook in the oven at a good heat (350°F.) for 35 to 40 minutes. Let the charlotte rest for a few minutes before turning it out, so that the apple settles. Turn out on to a round dish. Serve with an apricot sauce passed separately.

Note. Charlottes can be prepared in the same way with various fruits, such as pears, quinces, apricots, peaches, plums. The consistency of the fruit must be kept very stiff, because if too liquid, it would soften the bread lining the mould and the dessert would disintegrate when turned out of the mould.

Charlottes can also be filled with a fruit filling and with *French pastry cream* or with *frangipane pastry cream.* See CREAM.

Schaleth à la juive is also a kind of charlotte, but for this confection the utensil in which it is cooked is a cast-iron cocotte, which is lined with a noodle paste, and the apple filling is garnished with Malaga raisins, Corinth raisins, Smyrna raisins, moistened with Malaga wine and combined with eggs. See SCHALETH.

Apple charlotte with rice. CHARLOTTE DE POMMES AU RIZ—Line a thickly-buttered charlotte mould sprinkled with dried breadcrumbs, with a layer of *dessert rice* (see RICE), $\frac{1}{3}$ inch thick. Fill the mould to within $\frac{1}{3}$ inch from the top with very stiff apple filling. Cover with dessert rice and put in a gentle oven (325°F.) for 30 minutes. Let it rest for a few minutes and turn it out on to a round dish. Serve a fruit sauce or a *Zabaglione** at the same time.

Cold charlottes. CHARLOTTES FROIDES:

Charlotte à la Chantilly—Use a straight-sided mould; lining a mould with slanting sides is more difficult.

For an ordinary mould, 18 to 20 sponge fingers are needed. Some are cut into triangles and are used to line the bottom of the mould. Arrange these triangles in the mould, the round sides downwards and press them well together (this will form a rosette). At the centre of the rosette put a sponge finger cut into a circle.

Trim the ends and sides of the other sponge fingers. Set them in the mould, upright, the rounded side touching the lining of the mould, well pressed together one against the other. Beat 2 cups (5 to 6 decilitres) of thick, fresh cream (kept on ice or in a cold place until the moment of beating). The cream must be so firm that it sticks to the whisk, which is to say it must have almost the consistency of beaten egg whites.

Mix $\frac{3}{4}$ cup (125 grams) of powdered sugar with the cream and a heaping tablespoon of vanilla sugar or 1 teaspoon vanilla extract. Put the cream in the lined mould, and turn out at once on to a dish in which a napkin has been placed.

Charlotte à la parisienne (Carême's recipe)—'Take 6 ounces of sponge fingers which are frosted on one side and a little packet of green pistachio biscuits (dry cakes). Cut the latter into thin slices and then into diamond shapes, $\frac{1}{2}$ inch long. Make a double star with them in the bottom of a plain mould in the form of an octagon. Then, using the sponge fingers cut into suitable shape, fill the bottom of the mould. With the rest of the sponge fingers line the sides of the mould, setting them upright and close together. Take care to place the glazed side against the mould.

'Then you fill the charlotte with the preparation known as *Bavarian cream à la vanille,** but you put it in only when it is due to be served. Once the mould is filled you cover the *Bavarian cream* with sponge fingers. The mould is then surrounded with broken ice, and 40 minutes later you turn it out on to a silver dish.'

Charlotte plombières—Prepared in the same way as *Vanilla ice cream charlotte,** with a filling of *Plombières ice cream.** See ICE CREAMS AND ICES.

Charlotte russe—Line a round mould with sponge fingers cut into the form of hearts for the bottom of the mould, and for the sides with sponge fingers which have been trimmed at the end and down the sides. Place these upright round the inside of the mould, pressed well together, and projecting about an inch above the top of the mould.

Fill the charlotte with a preparation of *Bavarian cream.** Freeze in the refrigerator. Turn out on to a round dish, covered with a napkin.

Charlottes russes can be filled with *Bavarian cream* of different flavours.

Vanilla ice cream charlotte. CHARLOTTE GLACÉE À LA VANILLE—Line the charlotte mould with sponge fingers as described in the preceding recipe.

At the moment of serving fill the mould with vanilla ice or with a vanilla filling for a *bombe.** See ICE CREAM AND ICES.

Note. In the same way one can prepare iced charlottes filled with ice cream of various flavourings, or with various fillings for iced *bombes.*

CHARQUICAN-CHILENO (Chilean cookery)—This dish is the national dish of Chile. Sauté the *charqui* (lean beef), cut into large blocks in oil with garlic and coarsely chopped onion and moistened with brown stock. Add carrots, turnips, tomatoes, little peas in their pods, pumpkin, celery, green haricots and pimentos cut into large pieces. Braise and serve in deep soup plates. Fried potatoes can be added.

CHARTREUSE—Liqueur made by the monks of Chartreux. The approximate composition of this liqueur is as follows:

Balm, 1 pound 7 ounces (640 grams); hyssop, 1 pound 7 ounces (640 grams); angelica leaves, 11 ounces (320 grams); cinnamon bark, $3\frac{1}{2}$ ounces (100 grams); mace, $1\frac{1}{2}$ ounces (40 grams); saffron, $1\frac{1}{2}$ ounces (40 grams).

Infuse for 10 days in 11 quarts (10 litres) of distilled alcohol, add 2 pounds 10 ounces (1,200 grams) of white sugar.

CHARTREUSE—This name is hardly used nowadays, except to denote a preparation composed of partridges and cabbage, but in the old days the word applied to a variety of preparations which included neither feathered game, nor cabbage, but which were all characterized by an arrangement of the principal element in a mould, round or oval, and without decoration, lined either with vegetables arranged in orderly rows or with other substances similarly arranged.

'The Chartreuse is undoubtedly the queen of entrées which one can serve; it is composed of roots and vegetables, but is only perfect in May, June, July and August, that smiling and propitious season, when everything is renewed in nature, and seems to invite us to take fresh trouble in our preparations on account of the delicacy of these excellent products.' (Carême: *Traité des entrées chaudes.*)

But this remark on the necessity of employing only fresh vegetables for the creation of chartreuses does not prevent Carême from giving a variety of recipes in which no vegetables feature at all; excellent recipes, all the same.

Chartreuse à la parisienne, en surprise (Carême's recipe)—'You cook 8 fine round truffles in the ashes or in champagne; when they are cold, you pare them and cut them in the direction of the greatest length with a cutter 9 millimetres ($\frac{1}{4}$ inch) in diameter. Then you peel 100 crayfish tails (these can be replaced by carrots prepared in the same way as for *Chartreuse of partridge*, see PARTRIDGE), and you begin to form a crown on the bottom of the mould which you have already buttered. You trim your (columns of) truffles and place them on the crayfish tails, but you place them in such a way as to make a Greek border. You add chicken fillets which you have already stiffened with butter, and then suitably trimmed. Then you set on top of this border a crown of crayfish tails to form a parallel with the crayfish border underneath, so that the Greek border is framed with crayfish tails.

'Then you chop very finely the trimmings of the truffles, and scatter them on the bottom of the mould, which you then carefully cover with an inch-thick layer of *chicken quenelle forcemeat*. Then you cover the Greek border. Then, the mould being filled on the bottom and round the sides with forcemeat, you fill the middle with a *Blanquette of chicken* (see BLANQUETTE.) (Carême does not say so, but the pieces of chicken have to be boned), with sweetbreads, of veal or lamb, or with some slices of game fillets, or with a ragoût "*à la financière*"* or "*à la Toulouse*",* but the mould must not be filled above a line 1·3 centimetres (½ inch) below the rim, and the ragoût should be put in cold.

'Then you make a cover of forcemeat on a round of buttered paper 5 inches in diameter and 1·3 centimetres (½ inch) thick. You place this cover on top of the filling (stuffing side down) which is then by this means contained on all sides by forcemeat. To remove the paper you put on it, for a second only, a hot lid which melts the butter and immediately the paper can be removed. The forcemeat lid is joined to the forcemeat surround with the point of a knife.

'The chartreuse being completed in this way you cover the top with a circle of buttered paper, you then put it in a *bain-marie** for a good hour and a half. When it is cooked you set it on its dish, removing the mould.

'Decorate the top in the following manner: place on the top of the chartreuse round the edge a crown of little white mushrooms, and in the middle a pretty rosette, which you have prepared in advance, of 8 *Filets mignons à la Conti* of fowl or game according to the nature of the basic ragoût, in the form of a crescent.

'Set a mushroom in the middle of this rosette.

'Serve at once, and glaze the dish if you like, but I prefer it without that, bearing in mind that the strips of white chicken combined with the Greek border of truffles make the best possible effect.'

'This kind of entrée', says Carême, 'has the elegance and the quality desired, and can certainly take its place with the old *grenades* and the forcemeat *turbans*.*

'It seems to me that one could serve in the same manner "*loaves*" *of chicken, of foie gras, or of fish as a cold entrée*.'

Chartreuse of partridge, or pheasant. CHARTREUSE DE PERDRIX, DE FAISAN—See PARTRIDGE, PHEASANT.

Little chartreuses of larks à la francaise. PETITES CHARTREUSES DE MAUVIETTES À LA FRANÇAISE—Prepared in dariole moulds (individual custard moulds), which must not be too small, in the same way as *Chartreuse of partridge*. See PARTRIDGE.

The larks, boned and stuffed with a *gratin forcemeat* (see FORCEMEAT), with *foie gras* and truffles, are rolled into a neat shape and set to cook in cabbage.

The dariole moulds are lined with glazed carrots and glazed turnips turned in the form of small balls, with peas and diced green haricot beans cooked in salted water, all these vegetables disposed in alternate layers and kept in place by a layer of quenelle forcemeat. The larks, individually wrapped in braised cabbage, are placed one in each mould. Cover them with a quenelle forcemeat. Cook in a pan of hot water or *bain-marie* in the oven for 30 minutes.

Turn the little chartreuses out on to a round dish. Pour over them a game sauce, made with rich game stock.

CHASSE ROYALE—A roast composed of various game arranged in a pyramid on a great dish.

CHASSELAS—A species of vine-stock considered with good reason to provide the best dessert grapes. These grapes are known throughout the world. The grapes themselves take their name from the vine-stock.

The fame of the Fontainebleau *chasselas* is established everywhere. It is believed that the origin of its cultivation at Thoméry and in the neighbourhood is by Swiss importation in the sixteenth century. The principal variety of Swiss vine-stock is the *fendants* which are none other than *chasselas*. The importation of *chasselas* into Switzerland itself goes back to the time when the Roman legions settled in Helvetia after its conquest by Julius Caesar, and it is believed that this Roman importation took place by means of cuttings made in Turkey. In fact the *chasselas* vines have always been widely grown in the gardens of the Mussulmans, who had a very wide choice of all kinds of fruit for cultivation. The Turkish origin of the *chasselas* was affirmed by a former ambassador to Constantinople, who thought he had discovered documents in the Turkish archives leaving no doubt on the matter.

The black variety of *chasselas* has never been seen, only the white variety, or the rose or violet varieties, obtained by authentic selection and budding.

However, it is well known that in the wild state all vines have black grapes. The white variety is an accidental degeneration, brought about by cultivation. This fact has been very clearly demonstrated in the last few years by the creation, by means of selection, of white varieties of most of our black grapes (*Aramon*, *Pinot*, *Gamay*).

Chicken sauté chasseur (*Mac Fisheries*)

CHASSEUR (A LA)—*Chasseur* denotes a method of preparation applying to small pieces of butcher's meat, fowl, eggs, characterized by a garnish of cultivated mushrooms, sliced, sautéed, flavoured with shallots and moistened with white wine. See *Tournedos chasseur*, under BEEF.

CHÂTEAU (STEAK, POTATOES, SAUCE)—This term applies to a slice of porterhouse steak (sirloin uppercut), but rather thick, 1½-2 pounds (800 grams to 1 kilo) or a slice cut from a rib of beef.

This piece of meat which in restaurants is called *entrecôte château* (porterhouse steak) is generally grilled.

The name also applies to potatoes cut into long strips and cooked in butter. See POTATOES.

In restaurants, it is also given as an abbreviation of Châteaubriand sauce.

CHATEAUBRIAND—A method of preparing a beef fillet invented by Montmireil, chef to Chateaubriand. It is wrong, we think, to spell the word *Châteaubriant*.

The *chateaubriand* is a thick slice taken from the middle of the fillet which is grilled and served garnished with *château* potatoes (potatoes trimmed into thick strips and cooked in butter) and accompanied by *château* sauce or *Béarnaise* sauce.

More rarely the *chateaubriand* is sautéed in butter. See *Chateaubriand** under BEEF.

CHÂTEAUNEUF-DU-PAPE (wine)—The red wines vintaged at Châteauneuf-du-Pape, the little commune of Vaucluse, have a great reputation. When they are matured, which means to say ten years old, they are heady, with a good bouquet and a fine perfume.

The region, outside which the labelling of wine as Châteauneuf-du-Pape is forbidden, was fixed by ministerial decree in May 1936.

These wines have been famous for a long time. When Pope Urban X wished to transfer the papal chair from Avignon to Rome he met with a great deal of opposition from a number of Cardinals who did not wish to leave a part of the country producing such exquisite wines.

It is said that Petrarch wrote in answer to a letter from Urban X expressing his astonishment at the Cardinals' attitude: 'Très Saint Père, the princes of the church value the wine of Provence and know that French wines are rarer at the Vatican than Holy Water.'

One can see that the letters patent of nobility of Châteauneuf-du-Pape are not only ancient but magnificent.

CHATOUILLARD (POTATOES)—Name given to potatoes which are cut with a special instrument into long ribbons and deep fried. See POTATOES.

Chatouillard was also the nickname given to an expert chef, an excellent *rôtissier* or *friturier*.

CHAUD-FROID—Preparation of fowl or game which is cooked as a hot dish, but served cold.

The paternity of this cold dish, one of the most refined in the French culinary repertoire, is, it seems, wrongly attributed to one named Chaufroix, *entremetteur* in the royal kitchens of Louis XV. (For an appreciation of the role of an *entremetteur*, see the entry ENTREMETS.*)

Philéas Gilbert says in this connection that both history and fact show without doubt that the *chaud-froid* was born at the Château Montmorency in 1759, and that it was given its name by the Maréchal de Luxembourg himself. The name of this dish should be spelt *chaud-froid* and not *chaufroix*.

This is how the *chaud-froid* was invented:

'The Maréchal de Luxembourg had invited that evening a large and brilliant assembly to his castle at Montmorency.

'His table was moreover famous as one of the best in the French kingdom.

'While waiting for grace to be said the guests were already discussing and praising the splendours of the menu, when silence fell in the salons, up till then, noisy with talk; a valet announced the arrival of a royal courier, bearer of a message to the Maréchal requiring his immediate presence at the King's Council.

'There was instant dismay; disappointment showed itself on every face, there were whispered protests, the spell was broken.

'But briefly the Maréchal gave his orders, commanded that his absence should in no way delay the serving of the banquet, and left.

'The guests took their places at the table in an atmosphere of constraint, uneasy in the absence of their host, and only paying distracted attention to the dishes served with unaccustomed despatch.

'The Maréchal returned, very late, and imperiously demanded to be served, but he only wanted a single dish, and this dish was a fricassée of chicken embalmed in its ivory-coloured sauce which the famished Maréchal tasted with pleasure. Nothing remains so firmly in the mind as a dish which has been enjoyed, and some days afterwards, conferring with the director of his kitchens, the Maréchal expressed the wish for the succulent cold fricassée to be served again.

'The dish was presented under the name refroidi, but this name displeased the Maréchal who insisted that it should appear on the menu under the name of *chaud-froid*.' (Philéas Gilbert.)

Some authors maintain that the origin of the *chaud-froid* is much earlier than the eighteenth century, and set it back as far as Roman times.

In order to justify this hypothesis, they base it on the fact that when the excavations at Pompeii were in progress in 1885, a vase was found containing fragments of meat in jelly, bearing the inscription ***calidus-frigidus***, which must needs be translated as *chaud* and *froid*.

But such a discovery does not necessarily prove that the ancient Romans knew the preparation of fowl or game which is the actual *chaud-froid* as presented for the first time by the Maréchal de Luxembourg's master cook!

Chauds-froids—(*Chaufroids* is also written but it is incorrect) are in fact no other than chicken fricassées or salmis of game served cold, covered with their gravy and glazed with aspic. But these dishes, simple to make, are delicious if prepared in a proper manner.

According to ancient practice, the *chauds-froids* were

Chaud-foid of poultry presented on a dish; behind, the three-tiered plinth made of breadcrumb on which it is mounted decorated in an elaborate way. They were arranged as a rule on a decorated base (this arrangement was used still more recently); the pieces of chicken or game were arranged in a pyramid, covered with the prescribed sauce, decorated with truffle, hard boiled egg whites, tongue or other items, glazed with aspic jelly, and set on *gradins* (see TIERED PLINTH), ornamental stands sculpted out of bread disposed in tiers.

This rather complicated arrangement has been replaced with a much simpler one which consists of placing the pieces of chicken or game in a crystal bowl or silver timbale covered with the appropriate *chaud-froid* sauce and glazed with a clear aspic jelly. This method which is both simple and elegant permits the use of aspics containing scarcely any gelatine and therefore having more delicacy.

The bowls or timbales are set on a dish covered with a folded napkin and surrounded with crushed ice.

Recipes for *chauds-froids* of *chicken*, *pheasant*, *partridge*, *quails*, *thrushes*, will be found under these headings.

We give here Carême's recipe for the *Chaud-froid of chicken in aspic*, to show how this important cold entrée was made in the old days.

Chaud-froid of chicken in aspic (Carême's recipe). CHAUD-FROID DE POULET À LA GELÉE—'After having lightly singed 5 fine farmyard chickens (6 months old), you cut them up in the approved manner; soak them for not more than 2 hours in lukewarm water; drain them; then plunge them into cold water and put them in a pan with enough stock to cover them completely. Put the pan on a hot fire and boil for a few minutes; then drain the pieces and put them in cold water. When they are cold, trim the pieces of chicken and set them in a pan in which some good butter is melting. When all the pieces are suitably trimmed, set the pan containing them on a moderate fire and sauté; then sprinkle with a little handful of flour; continue to sauté over the fire; then pour in the stock in which the chicken has blanched after straining it; stir the contents of the pan, set it on the fire, season the fricassée with salt, a little nutmeg, a bouquet composed of parsley, spring onions, thyme, bay, basil, and 2 onions stuck with 2 cloves, and 12 peeled mushrooms. When the contents of the casserole have reached the boil, draw it to the side of the fire, and ½ hour later you skim the fricassée carefully, which should by now be cooked; then you remove the pieces of chicken with a perforated spoon, draining them carefully, and place them one by one in a casserole, which you cover.

'Reduce the sauce to a proper consistency, remove it from the fire, and 2 minutes later incorporate 5 egg yolks; return the pan to the fire, stirring all the time, until the sauce almost reaches the boil. Then pass the sauce through a fine sieve. As soon as it is cold pour one-third into the fricassée which you shake once or twice and set for ½ hour on crushed ice; then arrange the fricassée in the following manner:

'Begin by placing the legs of the chicken in the form of a crown on the entrée dish; in the middle you place the wings; above the legs you put the parsons' noses and the breasts. On top of these you put the fillets, as close together as possible.

'As much height as possible should be given to this entrée, which should be crowned with a fine truffle cooked in Champagne, and topped with a very white double coxcomb.

'Having completed this arrangement, work the sauce with the addition of 4 spoonfuls of lukewarm aspic jelly (see ASPIC) which should make it very smooth and thick; then you cover the surface of the fricassée (removing the truffle which is later replaced). Surround the piece with chopped aspic and a fine border of aspic in two colours cut in decorative shapes. Then serve the dish.' (Carême, *Le Pâtissier parisien.*)

CHAUDRÉE DE FOURAS—Fish soup which is prepared in the following way: Prepare a *court-bouillon* with herbs, white wine, a piece of butter and seasoning.

Cut various fish into pieces: conger eel, whiting, sole, plaice, *raiteau*, etc.

First put into the *court-bouillon* the firm fish such as conger eel, a few minutes later add the less firm fish.

Boil for ¼ hour. Add butter. Serve the soup and the fish separately.

CHAUDRON (cauldron)—A little cauldron usually in copper, used for culinary purposes.

Confit d'oie, *Confit de porc* (preserved goose and pork), are cooked in this utensil. Untinned copper cauldrons may also be used for home-made jams and preserves.

Chayotes

CHAYOTE—A name given to *Sechium edile*, a vine of the gourd family (*Cucurbitaceae*). It is widely cultivated in tropical America for its edible tubers and fruit, known variously as *custard marrow*, *vegetable pear*, *pepinella*. The fruit is in the form of a large green pear with deep ribbing. The *Chayote* is grown in Algeria and is exported to Europe. See also CUSTARD MARROW.

CHEESES. FROMAGES—Cheese is a product of curds, drained and, more often than not, fermented. From the earliest times, cheese has been made in stock-rearing countries to use up surplus milk. Nowadays, there are so many different kinds of cheese that no list, however long, could possibly claim to be complete. Every country, every district has its own special cheese. Many local cheeses have a deservedly high reputation. Switzerland produces its Gruyère and Emmenthal; England, its Cheshire, Cheddar and Stilton; Italy, Parmesan and Gorgonzola; Holland, its Gouda and Edam, and so on. It may justly be claimed, however, that no country has so great a variety and range of cheeses as France, where almost every rural district has its own local cheese.

Fresh cheeses are distinct from other cheeses in not being fermented. They are produced by spontaneous coagulation (*fromage à la pie*,* white cheese) or coagulation under pressure (*petit-suisse*, double-cream).

Fermented cheeses made from raw curds are of two kinds: the *soft* cheeses (Brie, Coulommiers, Camembert, Livarot, Pont-L'Evêque, etc.), and the *hard* cheeses

(Dutch, Cantal, Cheshire, Roquefort, Gorgonzola, etc.). There are also *cheeses made from scalded curds* (Gruyère, Emmenthal, Parmesan, Port-Salut, etc.).

Making cheese at Beaufortin
(*French Government Tourist Office*)

A very brief glance at the many and complex operations which go to the making of cheeses, especially soft cheeses, may help towards an appreciation of the infinite diversity of the end products. The milk of cows, goats and ewes, and sometimes other mammals, can be used skimmed, partly skimmed or whole, or even enriched with added cream.

Coagulation can take place spontaneously, that is to say by the natural fermentation of the milk, or it can be induced by the addition of certain vegetable juices. Most often, it is brought about by the action of rennet, a curdling agent extracted from the stomachs of young mammals. Rennet may be used in solid form, dried or fresh. It may be used in liquid form, plain or seasoned with herbs.

Curdling with rennet may be carried out in different ways. The milk may be left to curdle in cold surroundings. In this case very little rennet is used. It may be curdled at a higher temperature (100-104°F.) in which case a strong dose of rennet is required.

For soft cheeses, the curds are carefully cut up into fairly large pieces; for hard cheeses the curds are broken up into tiny crumbs, several times over, even after fermentation has begun.

The moulding of the cheese, which is the last stage in the drainage of the curds, is carried out in osier baskets, earthenware, pottery, wooden or tinplate moulds. These are usually covered with a cloth. For soft cheeses, the curds are carefully broken up before being put in the moulds. For hard cheeses, all moisture is expelled by putting the curds through a press or by draining them between two boards with weights on top.

At this stage, the process of fermentation begins. Theoretically this process is divided into three stages which, in practice, tend more or less to overlap:

(1) *The action of the ferments in the milk* which attack the lactose (sugar of milk) and turn it into lactic acid.

(2) *The culture of fungi* which appear on the surface of the curds and quickly form a thick and furry fungoid skin (known in the cheese trade as the 'white'). These fungi feed on the lactic acid, as soon as it is formed, up to the time when all the lactose has been used up. They also play a part in the maturing of the curds. In particular, it is these fungi which give to certain cheeses their characteristic and much-prized bitter flavour; but their action must not be allowed to proceed unchecked.

(3) *The culture of secondary microbes.* These are organisms of various kinds, microbes, fungi, mildew, mainly red or orange in colour (known in the cheese trade as the 'red'). Their function is to inhibit, by co-existence, the too-rapid breeding of the fungi of the second phase. Once the 'red' has been formed, the cheeses settle down and mature more or less quickly according to their nature.

Among gastronomes, opinion is sharply, though unequally, divided on the subject of cheese, which has its passionate enemies and passionate devotees. These last are in the majority and it is generally admitted that cheese is an indispensable concomitant of all meals, enhancing the flavour of wines to such an extent that it is sometimes called the 'drunkard's biscuit'.

Brillat-Savarin used to say that 'a dessert without cheese is a beautiful woman with only one eye', and Briffault enunciated this aphorism: 'Cheese complements a good meal and supplements a bad one'.

The serving of cheese. In France, cheeses, of whatever kind, are always served before the sweet (dessert). Thus they would normally follow the main course, or the salad, if this should be served separately after the meat and vegetables.

Each cheese is usually served on a separate plate alone and unadorned. But cheeses may also be served on a cheese-board.

The practice followed in certain restaurants of grating the cheeses in advance and even covering them with rind after they have been grated, is not recommended. True connoisseurs of cheese are absolutely opposed to it.

It is, on the other hand, considered highly desirable to serve fresh butter at the same time as the cheese. In this way, the diners may take butter or not, as they please. Generally, connoisseurs prefer not to take butter with their cheese.

Savoury biscuits (U.S.A., crackers) of various kinds and slices of black bread may also be served with cheese.

With certain cheeses, notably Munster, it is usual to serve cumin, with which the diners may season their cheese. Fresh heads of celery or bulb fennel also provide a suitable garnish for cheese.

With cheeses, especially fermented and strong cheeses, red wine, Burgundy or Claret, should be served. Rhône wines, especially those with a good deal of body and a powerful aroma, may also be served with cheese.

It is the custom in France to offer the cheese first to the master of the house. He examines it and then drives the knife into it before it is handed round to the guests. This applies, of course, to whole cheeses, for there are always shy guests who are reluctant to broach, say, an uncut Camembert.

Various laws, decrees and judicial precedents regulate the legal use of the names given to various French cheeses. The name Roquefort, for instance, is strictly reserved for cheeses coming from an area whose boundaries are clearly laid down. In the case of other cheeses, such as Camembert, Brie, Port-Salut, the name must be followed by a clear indication of the department or district in which the cheese has been made.

(A) Principal French Cheeses: (1) Brie de Meaux; (2) Saint-Nectaire; (3) Bleu d'Auvergne; (4) Camembert; (5) Pont-l'Evêque; (6) Livarot; (7) Tomme; (8) Reblochon; (9) Munster; (10) Port-Salut; (11) Fourme d'Ambert; (12) Maroilles; (13) Roquefort; (14) Excelsior. (C) Principal local cheeses: (1) Brie de Melun; (2) Vic-en-Bigorre; (3) Fromage au foin de Pithiviers; (4) Rollot; (5) Guerbigny; (6) Saint-Marcellin; (7) Montréal; (8) Langres; (9) Boulette d'Avesnes; (10) Gex; (11) Dauphin; (12) Olivet Bleu; (13) Puant macéré; (14) Pouligny; (15) Cantal; (16) Cendré d'Auvergne; (17) Sainte-Maure; (18) Brillat-Savarin; (19) Fromage de Curé; (20) Chatillon-sur-Cher. (B) Some foreign cheeses: (1) Caccio Cavale; (2) Gouda; (3) Cheshire; (4) Gorgonzola; (5) Fat Dutch cheese; (6) Boule de Lille (Oude Kaas, hollandais); (7) Gjetöst; (8) Gammelöst; (9) Etuvé; (10) Fribourg; (11) Kaunas; (12) Emmenthal; (13) Cheshire cream; (14) Little Gouda. (*Fromages de la maison Androuët. Photograph, Larousse*)

To our knowledge, there are some 400 different cheeses being made in France alone. To describe all these, it would be necessary to write a separate book some hundreds of pages long. This section, however, lists the most appreciated French cheeses as well as many foreign cheeses which are obtainable in France and elsewhere.

Aettekees—Belgian cheese which can be eaten from November to May.

Amou—Cheese made in Béarn, which can be eaten from October to May.

Arrigny—A winter cheese made from November to May in the Champagne region.

Asco—Corsican cheese which can be eaten from October to May.

Autun—This cheese is called 'cow cheese' and can be eaten all the year round.

(Les) Aydes—This cheese from the Orléanais district is good to eat between October and June.

Banon—Cheese made in Provence, in the foothills of the Alps, which may be eaten from May to November.

Beaufort—Savoy cheese which can be eaten all the year round.

Beaumont—Savoy cheese which can be eaten from October to June.

Beaupré de Roybon—Cheese made in the Dauphine which can be eaten from November to April.

Bleu d'Auvergne—A blue mould cheese which is also known under the name of *Bleu de Salers* and can be eaten from November to May. It is usually made of a mixture of goats', ewes' and cows' milk.

Bleu de Basillac—Cheese made in the Limousin department which can be eaten from November to May. It resembles Roquefort.

Blue mould French cheeses. BLEUS FRANÇAIS—In France there are a number of these cheeses, which have something in common with *Roquefort* but are less delicate in flavour. Among the best of these are: *Bleu d'Auvergne** which is made chiefly in the Mont-Dore district; *Fourme d'Ambert**; *Grand bornant* and *Thônes* of the Haute-Savoie; the Blue cheese of *Gex*,* which is made from cows' milk in the Ain Department; *Champoléon* from the Queyras (in the High Alps); *Saint-Marcellin** and *Sassenage*,* made in the Isère district; *Septmoncel*,* made in the Jura mountains. These cheeses are described in alphabetical order in this section.

Blue cheeses from other lands—A great many blue mould cheeses are made outside France. They include Tyrolean blue from Rastadt; *cabrales* from the Asturias; Portuguese *Castello-branco*; *Sarrazin* from Sarraz in Switzerland; *Stilton* from England; the Italian *Stracchino* which has something in common with *Gorgonzola*. (See *Gorgonzola* and *Stilton*.)

Bondon—A variety of cheese which is made in Normandy, mostly around Rouen. It is a whole-milk, small, loaf-shaped cheese, rather like Gournay in texture, but with 2% sugar added. It is about 3 inches high and from 1½ to 2 inches in diameter.

Bosson macéré—A French winter cheese made in Provence which can be eaten from December to March.

(La) Bouille—A cheese made in Normandy which can be eaten between October and May.

Boule de Lille—A Dutch cheese, known in Holland under the name of *Oude Kaas*, which can be eaten all the year round.

Boulette d'Avesnes, also Boulette de Cambrai—The name of an all-the-year-round cheese made in Flanders from November to May.

Brie—This cheese certainly has a claim to nobility. As long ago as the fifteenth century, Charles d'Orléans, father of Louis XII, used to order Bries by the dozen to give as New Year presents to his friends. Two centuries later, St Amant, that great poet of good living, devoted a much-quoted ode to 'this gentle jam of Bacchus':

Sus! qu'à plein gosier on s'écrie:
Bény soit le territoire de Brie.
Pont-l'Evêque, arrière de nous!
Auvergne et Milan, cachez-vous.
C'est luy seulement qui mérite
Qu'en or sa gloire soit escrite;
Je dis en or avec raison,
Puisqu'il feroit comparaison
De ce fromage que j'honore
A ce métal que l'homme adore:
Il est aussi jaune que luy;
Toutefois ce n'est pas d'ennuy,
Car, si tost que le doigt le p esse,
Il rit et se crève de gresse. . . .
Hé! pourquoy n'est-il infiny
Tout aussi bien en sa matièrè
Qu'il l'estoit en sa forme entière?
Pourquoy tousjours s'apetissant,
De lune devient-il croissant? . . .

Now then, let us shout with all our might:
Blessed be the land of Brie.
Pont-l'Evêque, get thee behind us!
Auvergne and Milan, out of our sight.
Brie alone deserves that we
Should record her praises in letters of gold.
Gold, I say, and with good reason,
Since it is with gold that one must compare
This cheese to which I now pay homage.
It is as yellow as the gold worshipped by man,
But without its anxiety
For one has only to press it with one's fingers
For it to split its sides with laughter
And run over with fat.
Why then, is it not endless
As indeed its circular form is endless?
Why must its full moon, eternally appetizing,
Wane to a crescent? . . .

The cheese of Brie has not deteriorated since that time. On the contrary, it has actually improved in quality and is now more uniformly good, since the local farmers, abandoning the old methods, use the ferments tested and recommended by the Ferté-sous-Jouarre Laboratory.

Experiments carried out in that laboratory made it possible to isolate the particular micro-organism which is active in the last phase in the maturing of Brie, and which gives to the crust of the cheese its peculiar reddish colouring, known in the cheese trade as the 'red'.

Brie is fully ripe when the cheese is all of the same texture. When pressure is exerted on the surface of a section the cheese should bulge but not run.

Brie is made in various sizes. A large Brie may be up to 22 inches (54 centimetres) in diameter, a medium Brie up to 16 inches (42 centimetres), a small one not more than 13 inches (33 centimetres). There are different kinds of Brie known as Bries *fermiers*, *laitiers* and '*façon Coulommiers*'.*

It takes from 13 to 20 litres (14 to 22 quarts) of milk to make a cheese, according to size. Although whole milk is always used, some experts advise a little skimming —bringing the percentage of cream down to 25 to 27% —because, they maintain, a higher cream content makes the cheese bitter.

A good Brie must have a reddish crust with a few

traces of white, but no blackish streaks. It must be creamy but not runny, and should be pale yellow in colour.

Brie de Coulommiers—This differs from the usual *Brie de Meaux* in that a little cream is often added to it. A considerable quantity is added if the cheese is to be eaten fresh ('double-cream'), a smaller amount if it is to be left to mature.

Brie de Melun—This is made in thicker and smaller rounds than the Brie de Meaux. It is a special cheese with a much more pronounced aroma, being saltier and more piquant. It is sometimes called *Brie d'amateur*.

Brie de Provins—This is made in the same way as the Brie de Meaux, but is a little different in shape, being thicker and smaller in circumference.

Brie is a winter cheese (November to May).

Brillat-Savarin—Cheese made in Normandy which can be eaten all the year round.

Brinzen—Hungarian cheese made out of fresh ewes' milk, mixed with rennet. It is dried for 10 or 12 days, kneaded with 3 % of salt, then put into drums and pressed.

Broccio—A Corsican cheese, made from goats' milk or sour ewes' milk, very delicate, and similar in appearance to '*petit-suisse*'. A large proportion of this cheese is exported.

It is eaten plain, in fritters or in ravioli. It is also used as a stuffing for vegetables. A special cake called *Fiadene* is made with it.

Caccio-cavallo—An Italian cheese made in the region of Naples from skimmed cows' milk, moulded in the shape of gourds and left to dry straddled on sticks —hence the name.

Misled by the name, the astronomer Lalande claimed that it was made from mares' milk. This mistake proved a vast source of amusement to the Italian gastronomes of the time. Some Caccio-cavallo addicts are not satisfied with merely having the cheese dried, but insist on its being smoke-cured as well, as was done far back in the time of the Romans.

The monument to Mme Harel, the creator of Camembert cheese

Cheddar cheese

Cachat—A cheese very popular in Provence. It is made from ewes' milk, ripened with vinegar, then pressed. It is eaten in an onion skin, and usually served with Châteauneuf wine.

Cachat can be eaten from May to November.

Camembert—A soft cheese, invented, or rather perfected, in about the year 1790, by a local farmer's wife, Mme Harel, to whom, in grateful memory, a statue has been erected in the little village of Camembert, near Vimoutiers (Orne).

Good quality Camembert is made from whole unskimmed milk.

Camembert is made mainly in the winter by a process very similar to that used in the manufacture of Brie, but the micro-organisms are different and give to the cheese a slight characteristic bitterness which the makers attribute to the oat-straw of the wicker trays.

Camembert, which is chiefly made in the regions of Vimoutiers and Livarot, is disc-shaped, thicker and much smaller than Brie. Like Brie, its crust must be a yellowish-orange without any black streaks. The cheese must be pale yellow, smooth and without holes. It must not be runny.

Camembert is made today all over France and even in other countries, but it is laid down by law that its place of origin must be indicated.

The Camembert 'season' lasts from October to June.

Cancoillotte—A special very strong cheese mixture made in Franche-Comté, which has to be melted before serving. It can be eaten from September to June.

Cantal—A hard, strong cheese made in Auvergne, which is also known as 'Fourme de Salers'. It can be eaten the whole year round but is particularly recommendable from November to May.

Carré de Bonneville—Normandy cheese, eaten between September and June.

Caseum—Coagulated casein or fresh cheese.

Chabichou—Poitou cheese, which is eaten from April to December. It is made from goats' milk and is soft and sweet.

Chabissous or Cabecous—Little cheeses made with goats' or ewes' milk.

Chaingy—A cheese made in Orléans which can be eaten from September to June.

Champenois—Cheese still called Riceys-Cendré which can be eaten between September and June.

Chaource— This cheese, which is made in the Champagne district, is somewhat similar to *Soumaintrain*, a cheese made in the Yonne region. It may be eaten from November to May.

Chaumont—Cheese made in the Champagne region which can be eaten from November to May.

Cheddar—English cheese eaten all the year round.

English Cheshire cheese

Cheshire—A hard, cows' milk English cheese made in two colours: red and white. It can be eaten all the year round.

Chester—Name by which Cheshire cheese is known in France.

Chevret—A Bresse cheese made from goats' milk which can be eaten from December to April.

Chevrotins—Name given to a cheese produced in Savoy. It is made of dried goats' milk and is eaten from March to December. The *chevrotins de Moulins* are little cheeses made in Bourbonnais.

Chevrotton de Mâcon—A cheese also called Mâconnais that can be eaten from May to September.

Cierp de Luchon—A cheese made in the Comté de Foix which is eaten from November to May.

Comté—Jura cheese which can be eaten all the year round.

Coulommiers—This comes into the category of soft cream cheeses. It is made in the Brie district in the neighbourhood of Coulommiers (Seine-et-Marne).

Coulommiers cheeses are usually eaten fresh, after salting. They may also be processed like Brie, that is to say, kept until they are covered with white mould.

A good Coulommiers must have a white crust, with a slight greyish tinge. It must be creamy to the touch, and slightly yellowish inside.

Cream cheese. FROMAGE À LA CRÈME—There are several ways of making this cheese. It may simply be a matter, as with double-cream, of adding some cream to the milk before introducing the rennet, or the so-called 'cream cheese' may be made from milk which has been completely skimmed. This cheese is worked with fresh cream after draining, and then put into moulds to complete the drainage.

Crème des Vosges—Alsatian soft cream cheese eaten between October and April.

Crottin de Chavignol—Semi-hard goats' milk cheese made in Berry, which can be eaten from May to December.

Curé—See *Nantais cheese.*

Dauphin—A cheese made in Northern France, good to eat between November and May.

Decize—A Nivernais cheese which can be eaten all the year round. It resembles Brie.

Demi-sel—A small whole-milk soft cheese somewhat similar to double-cream. The curd, after being drained, sieved and put in moulds, has 1 to 1·5% of salt added to it.

Double-cream. DOUBLE-CRÈME—French soft cream cheese in which the milk is enriched with added cream, increasing the weight by one-sixth. A small quantity of rennet is mixed with it so that the slow process of coagulation lasts about 24 hours. The curd, wrapped in a cloth, is put under weights to drain. Next, cream is worked into it. The curds are moulded and wrapped in waxed paper.

Dunlop—A Scottish cheese somewhat similar to Cheshire and Double-Gloucester, but which, in the opinion of English gastronomes, is much superior to both. Sir Walter Scott was enthusiastic about this cheese.

Dutch cheeses—There are a great many of these. The best known, Edam, is made in a number of European countries and in America. It is made from partly skimmed milk, curdled in 15 to 20 minutes with a strong dose of rennet. Fermentation is very slow, and allowed to continue until a hard non-porous rind is formed. As soon as the cheese is fully fermented, the cheese is painted over with a coating of linseed oil. Sometimes it is given a further coating of paraffin. The cheese is coloured with annatto (dye).

Edam cheese is yellow-red when stove-dried, softish and free of holes.

Emmenthal—A Swiss hard cheese named after the high Emme valley (in the Berne Canton), but made all over Switzerland where there is highland pasture. As the transport of butter from these mountain districts would be uneconomic, Emmenthal cheese is usually made from whole milk. However, in some parts these difficulties have been overcome, so that, nowadays, a semi-fat Emmenthal is made.

In almost all respects, Emmenthal cheese is manufactured in the same way as Gruyère. The round Emmenthal cheeses are larger than Gruyères, weighing from 120 to 200 pounds; their rind is straw-coloured.

The cheese is creamier than Gruyère, less pungent and, usually, less salty. It has a good many holes, called 'eyes', usually three to every bore-hole made. These eyes are fairly large, but should not exceed a two-franc piece in diameter.

Epoisses—A whole-milk, mould inoculated, soft French cheese made in almost every part of Burgundy and in central France. Its name comes from a village on the Côte d'Or.

The milk is curdled with a special rennet, flavoured with black pepper, clove and fennel, salt and brandy. It is eaten either fresh or ripened.

The cheese is left in cellars to ripen for a longer or shorter time according to whether it is to be eaten '*passé*' (over-ripe) or '*coulant*' (runny).

The fresh cheese is eaten in summer; the ripe cheese in winter or spring (November to June).

Ercé—A cheese made in the Ariège district. It is good to eat between November and May.

Étuvé—A semi-hard Dutch cheese which is good to eat all the year round.

Excelsior—A Normandy cheese which is good to eat all the year round.

Feuille de Dreux—A cheese made in the Île-de-France. It is good to eat between November and May.

Fin de Siècle—A Normandy cheese which is good to eat all the year round.

Fleur de Decauville—A cheese made in the Ile-de-France. It is good to eat between December and May.

Fontine—A cheese made in Franche-Comté all the year round.

Foutina—An Italian soft, creamy cheese used in making a kind of fondue made in the Val d'Aosta.

Fourme—Cheese from the Limagne. There are the cheeses of *Ambert*, of *Montbrisson*, of *Salers*, etc., known as *Fourme d'Ambert*, *Fourme de Montbrisson*, *Fourme de Salers*. The latter is sometimes sold under the name of *Cantal*. These cheeses are generally best from November to May.

Friesche Kaas—A soft Dutch cheese which can be eaten between November and May.

Frinot—Cheese made in the region of Orléans which can be eaten between November and June.

Fromage à la pie (fresh unfermented cheese)—Usually made on farms, for immediate consumption, from skimmed milk. It may also be made in the home from whole milk.

The milk is left to stand in a cool place (60 to 75°F). Curdling takes place at the end of 24 to 36 hours, through the action of the lactic ferment.

This cheese can also be made with rennet.

Fromage à la pie is eaten fresh, with fresh cream added. It may be seasoned with sugar or salt and pepper according to taste, and a little chopped chives for added flavour.

Géromé—A cheese made in the Vosges, round and about Gérardmer. Its name is a corruption of Gérardmer.

It is made from whole milk and rennet.

It is ripened in cellars for 4 months, until the crust has taken on a tawny colour. Sometimes aniseed, fennel or caraway seeds are added. Géromé is a winter cheese, eaten between November and April.

Gervais—Well-known make of *Petit-suisse*. See *Petit-suisse*, in this section.

Gex—This French blue-veined cheese is manufactured at Gex, principal town of the Ain department, between November and May, from unskimmed whole milk, coagulated in 2 hours at 85 to 92°F.

Before it is offered for sale, it is stored for a fortnight in ripening cellars where its special qualities develop.

The 'blue' which is due to the *penicillum glaucum* is self-generating and appears during processing without the aid of any foreign body.

The chief characteristic of Gex cheese, which distinguishes it from all others, is that (except for the blue streaks) it remains pure white.

It takes from 2 to 4 months to ripen completely.

Gjetöst—A brown-coloured Norwegian cheese which can be eaten all the year round. It is made of goats' milk.

Gloucester—There are two English cheeses of this name: the famous *Double Gloucester* and *Single Gloucester*.

Double Gloucester—the shape and size of a large grindstone, crumbly in texture, has a strong but mellow and delicate flavour. It ripens slowly (this process takes about 6 months) and keeps well.

Single Gloucester, made during spring and summer, ripens in a couple of months. It is flat and round, in fact similar to *Double Gloucester* in shape, and has a soft and open texture. It is excellent for toasting.

Glux—A Nivernais cheese which can be eaten all the year round.

Goats' milk cheeses. FROMAGE DE CHÈVRE—In different parts of France, a great many cheeses are made from goats' milk. Among these, which are usually eaten fresh, but may also be eaten very ripe, are *Chabichous*, made in the Poitou district; *Pamproux*; *La Mothe-Sainte-Hérave*; *Rougerets* or *Rougernis*, made in the Lyonnais and Bourbonais districts; *Rigottes* from Condrieu; *Cabrious* from the *Cévennes*; the cheeses of *Châteauroux* and *Sainte-Maure*; *Vendômes* and *Loches*.

Gorgonzola—This semi-hard cheese takes its name from a little village near Milan. It is made by a rather complex process.

Good Gorgonzola, which is a spring and summer cheese, has a thin rind. The cheese should be streaked with blue, but not excessively, and should be yellowish white in colour.

Gouda—A Dutch cheese made from whole milk, very similar to *Cantal* but made without preliminary fermentation.

Gournay—A French whole-milk, soft cheese made at Gournay, in Normandy, and in neighbouring districts.

Gruyère—The Gruyère valley is situated in the Fribourg Canton, dominated by the Moléson. It has given its name to a cheese which is also made in the Cantons of Vaud and Neuchâtel. The true Gruyère is only made in French Switzerland.

Formerly, only semi-fat cheeses or cheeses made from skim milk were manufactured, the cream being used for butter which could be economically exported. Nowadays whole milk Gruyères are also made, especially for export.

This cheese is not well-known in France. It is often confused with Emmenthal (see *Emmenthal*). Sometimes cheesemongers advertise '*a genuine Gruyère from Emmenthal*' which is like saying '*genuine Brie from Camembert*'! This cheese is made in rounds of 100 to 120 pounds. The rind is golden-brown. The cheese is waxy, more or less dry according to age. It is scored with cracks underneath through which drops of serum ooze out. To satisfy the demands of the French market which expects 'eyes' in the cheese, it is processed in such a way for export that little holes appear. These are always smaller than the holes in Emmenthal. The export cheeses are also less salty than those made for local consumption. To enhance the pungent flavour of this excellent cheese, it is usual in Switzerland to preserve the pieces in a cloth soaked in salted water or white wine.

Gruyère is manufactured in cheese factories in the mountains, close to the pastures.

Gruyère keeps for a very long time uncut. Some connoisseurs demand a very ripe cheese, others prefer it fairly fresh. For '*fondue*'* a mixture of the two kinds is normally required.

Gruyère (Crème de)—For some years now, little triangles of processed cheese have been sold, carefully wrapped in silver paper. This cheese is made from Comté and sometimes even from Gruyère.

At first, this cheese was produced mainly as a means of using up defective cheeses, but it has gained so much in popularity that it is now manufactured from cheese made especially for the purpose. Indeed, there are now a great number of processed and packaged cheeses (called creams) made from a variety of basic cheeses.

Their indeterminate flavour does not always appeal to the connoisseur, but their success is easily explained. They are processed and packaged in a very convenient and hygienic form, having no rind and leaving no waste.

Gruyère de 'Comté'—A number of 'Gruyère type' cheeses are made today in countries all over Europe and even in America. For a long time a type of Gruyère has been manufactured in the Jura. Although this cheese is really more like Emmenthal than Gruyère, it is sold as Gruyère. Some makes are of excellent quality and, if they were sold under the name of their locality, they could only gain in reputation.

Guerbigny—A cheese from Picardy, which can be eaten between October and May.

Guéret—A cheese made in Guéret, a city of the department of Creuse. It is sometimes also called *Creusois*.

Hervé—A soft, fermented cheese made in Belgium, from cows' milk, curdled with rennet, and drained under great pressure in square moulds.

Hervé is made from November to May, in three qualities: extra cream, cream, and partly skimmed milk. It is turned out in cubes, ripened in dark cellars, wrapped in cloths steeped in beer.

Huppemeau—A cheese made at Huppemeau in the Loire-et-Cher region. It is somewhat similar to Brie.

Incheville—A Normandy cheese which may be eaten from November to May.

Jonchée—Cheese made from ewes' or goats' milk. Half the milk is boiled with a few bay leaves. This is mixed with the remainder of the milk which is raw. It is curdled with rennet and decanted into little pots.

Kauna—A Lithuanian cheese which can be eaten all the year round.

Kummel—Dutch cheese with caraway seeds, which can be eaten all the year round. It is also called *Leidsche Kaas*.

(Les) Laumes—This cheese from Burgundy is good to eat between November and July.

Levroux—This goat cheese made in and around Berry is good to eat between May and December.

Leyden—Leyden cheese is made in the same way as Edam. It is often flavoured with cumin, cloves or even cinnamon. Some connoisseurs prefer Dutch cheese stove-dried. This makes it less creamy but improves its flavour. Leyden is also known as *Leidische Kaas* and *Kummel*.

Limbourger—A semi-hard, fermented cheese made in Belgium, Alsace and Germany. The whole-milk curds are kneaded with chives, parsley and tarragon, then put in moulds and dried in the sun. The surface is made non-porous by salting and brushing.

Livarot—A small town in the Calvados region has given its name to a soft paste cheese (usually coloured annatto-brown or deep red). This cheese is only good to eat between February and June, and is best in January, February and March.

Malakoff—This cheese is similar to Neufchâtel. It is made in the shape of discs, 2 inches in diameter and from $\frac{1}{3}$ to $\frac{1}{2}$ inch thick.

Manicamp—A Picardy cheese which can be eaten between October and July.

Maroilles—This semi-hard, full-flavoured cheese, square in shape, takes its name from a village in the Avesnes district, but it is manufactured in Thiérache and all over Picardy.

The whole-milk curds are salted, dried very quickly and then stored in a cellar where, at frequent intervals, the cheese is turned over brushed and washed with beer. It is good to eat between November and June and is also called *Marolles* or *Marole*.

Metton—A cheese from the Jura mountains which can be eaten from October to June.

Monsieur—A cheese made in Normandy. It is good to eat between November and June.

Mont-Cenis—A large, round, semi-hard, blue-veined whole-milk cheese somewhere between a Roquefort and a Gorgonzola. It ripens in cellars where it acquires its characteristic blue streaks.

Mont d'Or—This cheese, which once had a great reputation, was made along the banks of the Saône, round about Lyons. Only the milk of stable-fed goats was used. The cheese was ripened in cellars for 5 to 6 weeks.

This excellent cheese now exists only in memory. The cheese which now bears its name is made almost all over France, is manufactured from cows' milk and bears very little resemblance to the original cheese. The best is made at Mont d'Or, according to some authorities. It can be eaten from December to April.

Morbier—A cheese from Bresse which is good to eat between November and July.

(La) Mothe-Sainte-Héraye—A goat cheese from Poitou which is good to eat between May and November. Also called *Lamothe-Bougon*.

Munster Cheese—This semi-hard, fermented, whole-milk cheese, which is made in Alsace, in the Munster valley (Upper Rhine), is much prized by lovers of cheese. It is usually flavoured with caraway or anise seed. It is good to eat between November and April.

Murols—A Limagne cheese, good to eat between November and June.

Mysöst—A Norwegian cheese which can be eaten all the year round.

Nantais—This Breton cheese, sometimes called *fromage de curé*, is good to eat all the year round.

Neufchâtel or Bondon—Small French, loaf-shaped cheese made from skimmed milk, whole milk or with added cream, according to the type of cheese required. It is ripened in a drying room, on straw bundles, until a skin, white at first and later bluish, forms on the surface (first skin). The ripening is then completed in cool, well-aired store rooms until a second skin forms, this time red in colour. The cheese is a rather dark yellow.

Niolo—A Corsican cheese, which is good to eat between October and May.

Noekkelöst—A Norwegian cheese which can be eaten all the year round.

Olivet—Name of a whole-milk, mould-inoculated cheese, made in the small town of Olivet, in the Loiret.

This cheese is made of ewes' milk, in round discs about $1\frac{1}{4}$ inches thick and 6 inches in diameter.

The curd is white and rather salty. This cheese can be eaten from October to June. There is another type of Olivet cheese, called *Olivet Cendré*, which is good to eat from October to June. Fresh creamy Olivet cheese is sold in the summer months.

Oloron—Cheese from Béarn which is also called *fromage de la Vallée d'Ossau*, which should be eaten from October to May.

Paladru—Cheese made in Savoy, which can be eaten from November to May.

Parmesan—This famous cheese, which keeps for a very long time, is made in Lombardy and in the Romagna under various names. The name 'Parmesan' is used abroad for export cheeses of this type. Parmesan is made with skimmed milk.

During the ripening process, which is very slow, it sometimes happens that harmful microbes cause liquid patches in the cheese. These patches, which may be compared to abscesses in animal tissues, are dealt with surgically by Italian cheese-makers. They test the cheese by tapping it with a hammer. When they detect a soft patch, they open up the cheese, cut out the diseased section and cauterize the 'wound' with a red-hot iron. The ripening period lasts for nearly four years. At the end of this process the cheese may be kept for a very long time, twenty years or even longer.

Parmesan is a hard cheese which can be eaten all the

year round. It is golden yellow in colour and should sweat very slightly.

Pavé de Moyaux—Normandy cheese to be eaten from November to June.

Pelardon de Ruoms—A goat cheese made in Ardèche which can be eaten from May to November.

Petit-carré—This cheese has the same flavour and texture as Malakoff. It is square in shape, 2 inches across and approximately ½ inch thick.

Petit-suisse—A very creamy unsalted French cheese of the double-cream type, small and cylindrical in shape. It is made from whole milk, with 20% proportion of fresh cream added. In spite of its name, it was first made, not in Switzerland, but in Gournay in Normandy (Seine-Inférieure). The Gervais *Petit-suisse* is the best known make. Manufacturing this cheese is a delicate process, to which the most up-to-date scientific methods of production and supervision must be applied.

Picodon de Dieulefit—Cheese made in the Dauphiné which can be eaten from May to December.

Pithiviers au foin—Cheese made in the Orléans region and ripened on hay, which can be eaten from October to May.

Pontgibaud cheese (Puy-de-Dôme)—Made in exactly the same way as *Roquefort*,* but from cows' milk.

This cheese is eaten all the year round, except in midsummer.

Pont-l'Evêque—A French semi-hard, fermented cheese. It is made from whole or skimmed milk. It is shaped in square moulds, salted and processed like the Bondon of Neufchâtel. It is ripened in cellars. This takes from 3 to 4 months or less if the cheese is very rich in cream. Pont-l'Evêque is a summer and autumn cheese. (It can be eaten the whole year round except for August.) It should have a wrinkled crust, greyish yellow in colour. The cheese is softish and pale yellow in colour.

Port-Salut—A superb creamy, yellow, whole-milk cheese.

It was first made at the Trappist Monastery of Port du Salut, near Laval. The name of Port-Salut was given to it by a company establisqed at Entrammes (Mayenne Department) where it is still made. It is made in Trappist monasteries all over the world according to a secret formula.

Pouligny-Saint-Pierre—A famous cheese made from May to December in Berry.

Puant Macéré—Cheese from the region of Nord, eaten from November till June.

Pultöst—Norwegian mountain farm cheese which can be eaten all the year round.

Reblochon—A soft cheese made in Savoy. It is made of ewes' milk, and is eaten from October to June.

Récollet de Gérardmer—Cheese from the Vosges, which is eaten from October to April.

Remondou—Belgian cheese called '*Fromage piquant*' which is eaten from November to June.

Riceys cendré—Cheese sometimes called *Champenois*, which can be eaten from September to June.

Rigotte de Condrieu—A semi-hard, small creamy goats' cheese of the Lyon district which can be eaten from May to November.

Rocamadour—This community in the Lot, celebrated for its picturesque setting and its places of pilgrimage, has given its name to a cheese which can be eaten from November to May. It is a very small ewes' milk cheese weighing 2 ounces.

Rollot—Cheese in the form of a disc resembling Brie and Camembert, although smaller, which comes from Picardy and which can be eaten from October to May. It is also called *Bigolot*.

Romalour—A cheese from the Loire district which can be eaten all the year round.

Roquefort—The true Roquefort cheese, made in the little town of that name in the Saint-Affrique district (Aveyron), is manufactured exclusively from ewes' milk, sheep being the only animals which can subsist on the arid pastures of the Causses.

The unique feature of this cheese is that the curds are mixed with a special type of breadcrumb. The bread is dried and then ground to a fine dust, in which a special greenish mould has been allowed to develop. To ensure the right conditions for ripening, the cheeses are stored in damp, very cool caves (40° to 48°F.), such as the natural caves which are to be found in the Causses region.

After 30 or 40 days, the cheese is ready for sale to the consumer, but before it takes on the pungent flavour which makes it so sought-after by the connoisseur, it must be left to ripen for a much longer period. In fact, in the view of the experts, it should be kept for a year.

A good Roquefort has a grey rind. The cheese is yellowish, very fatty and evenly veined with blue. If it is too white in appearance and chalky in texture, it is not completely fermented.

The season for Roquefort lasts from May to September. A number of different districts in France produce a 'Roquefort-type' cheese; but these may not be sold under the name of Roquefort.

On the subject of Roquefort, there is a story which, though it has not the merit of novelty, gave much pleasure to our ancestors towards the middle of the seventeenth century.

A certain Gascon, very fond of his food, having been entertained to a sumptuous dinner, had a whole Roquefort cheese set before him. Simulating embarrassment, he asked: 'Where shall I broach it?'

'Wherever you please,' was the reply.

'In that case,' retorted the sponger, 'I will broach it at home.' And he ordered his valet to carry off the cheese.

Rouennais—Normandy cheese which can be eaten from October to May.

Rougeret—Small goat cheese which is made near Mâcon. Is also known under the name of *Maconnet*.

Saint-Agathon—Breton cheese that can be eaten from October to July.

Saint-Florentin—This Burgundian cheese is good to eat from November to July. It is soft and salty.

Saint-Marcellin—This cheese, manufactured chiefly at Saint-Marcellin, principal town of the Isère district, was formerly made exclusively from goats' milk. Today, both cows' milk and ewes' milk are added or are used as a substitute for the goats' milk.

Saint-Rémi—A square cheese made in Franche-Comté and Haute-Savoie. It is soft and resembles Pont l'Evêque.

Sainte-Maure—Touraine cheese, good to eat from May to November. It is a soft creamy goat-milk cheese.

Sassenage—A semi-hard, blue-veined cheese made in the Isère, good to eat from November to May.

Septmoncel—A small village in the Jura Department, which has given its name to a 'Roquefort-type' cheese made round about Saint-Claude which is judged excellent by connoisseurs. It is made in the same way as Gex cheese. Curds from two milkings are sometimes put together without mixing to produce a cheese known as 'bastard Septmoncel'.

Serré or Seray—The whey, which is the residue in the manufacture of cheese, sometimes still contains a certain proportion of butter, and a considerable quantity of casein and soluble albumen. This is particularly the case where curdling takes place quickly (by scalding). The butter can be extracted from this whey, after which, if it is first allowed to become acid, it can be curdled a second time with rennet. By this means it is possible to precipitate the serum containing the soluble albumen and separate it from the lactose and mineral salts.

This preparation is called *serré* and is used both as human and animal food.

In some regions, notably in the Glaris district, the *serré* (called *ligger* in German) is pounded with herbs, wild celery in particular. This mixture is dried and made into slabs which are called *schabzigger*. Grated and mixed with butter, this cheese, which has a strongly aromatic flavour, is held in high esteem by some connoisseurs. For some years, under the name of *crème de Glaris*, this cheese, mixed with butter, has been sold wrapped in silver paper.

Soumaintrin, also called Saint-Florentin—This Burgundian cheese is regarded as the *prime vintage* among all those made in the Armance valley in Burgundy.

It is round in shape and weighs approximately a pound. It is yellow in colour, with a yellowish orange rind, and is eaten from November to July.

Soya—This cheese has been made in China from time immemorial and is the result of fermentation in the juices extracted from soya-beans.

The soya-beans, softened and swollen by soaking, are put through a press. The liquid thus extracted is mixed with a little sulphate of lime or magnesium. It coagulates into a grey mass which is left to ferment like curds in the cheese industry.

Stilton cheese

Stilton cheese—An English cheese made from whole milk with cream added. It takes a very long time to ripen. The cheese is marked with grey and green streaks. The cheese should not be cut but scooped out of the centre. A little sherry or port should be poured on to it and left to soak into the cheese.

Stracchino—Italian soft goat cheese.

Strong cheese. FROMAGE FORT—This preparation, exceedingly savoury and strong-smelling, is especially well liked in the Morvan and Lyons districts.

Successive layers of milk cheese, grated or thinly sliced, salt and mixed herbs (leek juice is sometimes used), and sometimes a little cream are put in glazed stoneware jars. The jars are filled to the top with white wine laced with brandy. They are hermetically sealed and left in a warm place for two or three weeks to ferment.

Tête de Mort—Name sometimes given in France to the Dutch *Edam* cheese.

Tomme—Cheese of the Savoy, of which several varieties exist. *Tomme de Beauges* and *Tomme au fenouil* are good to eat from September to June; *Tomme de Boudave* is eaten from October to July.

Trappistes—Cheeses of which the most popular variety is known as Port-Salut, because it is made by the Trappist monks of Port-du-Salut in the Mayenne, but of which there are several other types in various regions of France. They include Trappiste of Cîteaux (Burgundy), Trappiste of Bricquebec (Normandy), Trappiste of Mont-des-Cats (Picardy), Trappiste of Sainte-Anne-d'Auray (Brittany) and Trappiste of Tamie (Savoy). These cheeses may be eaten all the year round.

Troô—This Touraine cheese can be eaten from May to January.

Troyes—This creamy cheese can be eaten from November to May. It is a soft cheese, resembling Camembert. It is also known as *Barberey*.

Vacherin—A soft cheese made in the Jura, in Switzerland and in Franche-Comté. It is good to eat from November to May.

Valençay—This soft goat-milk cheese from the Berry district is good to eat from May to December.

Vestgötaöst—Swedish cheese which can be eaten all the year round.

Vendôme—There is a soft Vendôme cheese, made in Orléans, which is good from October to June. There is also a hard ewes' milk cheese ripened under ashes which is good in the same months, and is also called Vendôme.

Vic-en-Bigorre—Béarnaise winter cheese which can be eaten from October to May.

Villedieu—Normandy cheese which may be eaten all the year round.

White cheese. FROMAGE BLANC—Made from whole milk, treated with rennet, and eaten fresh in summer. (See *Fromage à la pie.*)

CHEESE-RENNET. CAILLE-LAIT — Name given to various plants, the flowers and leaves of which have the property of curdling milk. Yellow bedstraw (*Galium verum*, family *Rubiaceae*) is most commonly used for this purpose.

CHEF DE CUISINE—Director responsible for a kitchen team. See COOKING.

The role of the present-day *chef de cuisine* corresponds to that of *officier de bouche* in great houses in the old days, and in earlier times to that of *maître des garnisons des cuisines royales* or *grand-queux*.

CHEMISIER—To coat with a thin layer of aspic jelly the lining of a mould, or to coat some substance with aspic jelly.

CHEMIST'S JAR. CHEVRETTE—Faience vase, oblong in form, with a large mouth, and projecting spout, and a handle on the opposite side. In the old days only chemists (U.S.A., druggists) had the right to possess and exhibit this kind of vase in the windows of their shops. These jars have been replaced by glass jars filled with red or green coloured water which chemists stand in their windows, ornaments which are now tending to disappear.

The word *chevrette* also denotes a kind of iron tripod on which casseroles and *marmites* are put.

CHENU—Colloquial term, a synonym for excellent when applied to very old wine. Chenu, which means 'the white hair of old age', is applied to a wine mellowed by old age.

CHERRY. CERISE—Fruit of a tree of the *Rosaceae* family of which the numerous varieties stem from two primitive species:

The *Wild Cherry*, or *Bird Cherry*, originating in Persia

and Armenia, from which derive the sweet cherries which divide into the *Heart Cherry* with soft flesh and coloured juice, and the *White-heart Cherry*, with hard flesh and colourless juice.

The *Morella Cherry* (*Prunus cerasus*) whose origin is uncertain, stems perhaps from the above species; it grows in Greece and in Italy, and its introduction has been falsely attributed to Lucullus in the latter country. The morella cherries, greatly improved by cultivation, still have a slightly acidulated taste.

There are innumerable varieties, some early-fruiting, ripening in May; others, late-fruiting, which ripen in August or September.

Cherries are one of the most refreshing fruits, and the most highly thought of. They can be preserved by drying in the sun or over heat, by preserving in sugar or in brandy. Jams, jellies, syrups are made from them (see JAM, SYRUPS). They are used for distilling (see KIRSCH), and liqueurs are made with them (see MARASCHINO).

Their stalks used in infusions are a popular diuretic.

Cherries à l'allemande (I). CERISES À L'ALLEMANDE—This cold *hors-d'oeuvre* is made commercially, but it can be prepared in the following way:

Trim the stalks of some morella cherries which are only just ripe, and put the cherries in a jar in the same way as for *gherkins.**

Cover them with aromatic vinegar prepared in the following way: put into a quart (litre) of vinegar, 1⅓ cups (200 grams) of light brown sugar, a fragment of stick cinnamon, a little grated nutmeg and 3 cloves. Boil, and allow to cool before pouring over the cherries. Leave the cherries in this concoction for 15 days.

Cherries à l'allemande (II). CERISES À L'ALLEMANDE—Put the cherries with their stalks removed in a dish and cover them with brown sugar. Put the dish in a very slow oven and leave it there until the cherries are slightly softened.

When the cherries have cooled put them in a glass jar and cover them with aromatic vinegar, prepared as above, but using less brown sugar. Leave for 15 days before use.

Note. With either method, one can add thyme, bay and tarragon to taste.

Cherries prepared *à l'allemande*, served also under the name of sweet-sour cherries, are used to accompany boiled meats, cold meat, in the same way as gherkins.

Cherries in brandy. CERISES À L'EAU-DE-VIE—*Formula A*: Choose well-grown cherries not yet quite ripe. Cut half the stalk and arrange the cherries in a glass jar. Cover with good brandy in which some sugar has been dissolved in the proportion of ½ pound (250 grams) of sugar to 1 quart (litre) of brandy. Hermetically seal the jar.

Using this method whole cherries are obtained, of a good colour and firm, but very strong in alcohol, which more easily penetrates the interior of the fruit than water. To obtain cherries less penetrated with alcohol, one should proceed with the following formula:

Formula B: Shorten the cherry stalks, and pierce each cherry with the point of a needle at the opposite end from the stalk. Throw them in cold water. Drain them and put them in a terrine, covering them with a syrup made with sugar and water in the proportion of 4 pounds (2 kilos) of sugar for one quart (litre) of water. Cover the terrine and leave the cherries to absorb the syrup for 24 hours. Drain them, arrange them in a glass jar, and cover with the syrup, which has been reduced and to which, after cooling, 2 parts of brandy have been added for one part of syrup. Close the jar hermetically.

Cherries with claret. CERISES AU CLARET—Put 1 pound (500 grams) of fine cherries in a silver timbale or in an enamelled casserole or pan, having removed the ends of the stalks. Pour over these cherries, in a sufficient quantity just to cover them, some red Bordeaux wine with sugar added and flavoured with a little cinnamon. Cook covered for 10 to 12 minutes on a gentle heat. Leave the cherries to cool in their syrup. Pour off the wine and boil it down by a third. Add 3 tablespoons of gooseberry jelly. Mix well. Pour this syrup over the cherries. Serve cold with sponge fingers.

This dish is also called *Cherry soup à l'anglaise*.

Cherry compote. COMPOTE DE CERISES—Prepared with stoned cherries in the same way as *Apricot compote*. See COMPOTE.

Cherry condé. CERISES CONDÉ—Prepared with stoned cherries cooked in a vanilla syrup, like *Condé apricots*. See APRICOT.

Cherry coupe—See ICE CREAMS AND ICES.

Cherry croûtes. CROÛTES AUX CERISES—Prepared with stoned cherries cooked in syrup, like *Apricot croûte*. See APRICOT.

Cherry flan. FLAN DE CERISES—Pastry sweet composed of a pastry shell or flan case made with sweetened pastry, filled with raw stoned cherries, baked in the oven. Cherry tarts or flans are also prepared with cream *à l'alsacienne* or *à la flamande*. See TARTS.

Cherry fritters. BEIGNETS AUX CERISES—The cherries are stoned, soaked with kirsch and sugar, or some other liqueur, dipped in light frying batter and fried. See FRITTERS.

Cherry ice. GLACE AUX CERISES—Pound a quart of stoned cherries or crush in a mortar or blender. Add the pounded cherry kernels to this pulp. Soak the mixture for an hour in a quart (litre) of syrup (2 cups sugar to 4 cups of water) flavoured with kirsch. Pass through a fine sieve and add the juice of a lemon. This preparation should measure 21° on the syrup gauge.

Freeze the mixture in the usual way. See ICE CREAMS AND ICES.

Cherry jam. CONFITURE DE CERISES—This jam is prepared as a rule with 1½ pounds (750 grams) of lump sugar for each 2 pounds (kilo) of fruit. If the fruit is not very sweet the jam is made with an equal weight of sugar and fruit. See JAM.

Cherries jubilee. CERISES JUBILÉ—Simmer some fine, stoned cherries in syrup. Drain them, put them into little silver, fireproof porcelain or glass ovenproof dishes. Pour the syrup in which they have cooked over them, after boiling it down and adding to it a little cornstarch or arrowroot diluted with cold water.

Then pour into each dish a tablespoon of warmed kirsch, and set flame to it at the moment of serving.

Cherry meringue tart or flan with rice. FLAN DE CERISES MERINGUÉES AU RIZ—Put a layer of dessert rice (see RICE) in a round gratin dish. Put a thick layer of stoned cherries which have been cooked in the oven with a little sugar on top of the rice. Cover with ordinary meringue. Decorate the top with arabesques in meringue and proceed in the same way as for *Apricots and rice with meringue*. See APRICOT.

Cherry mousse—See ICE CREAMS AND ICES.

Cherry sauce—See SAUCE, *Dessert sauces*.

Cherry soufflé Montmorency. SOUFFLÉ AUX CERISES DIT MONTMORENCY—Add 2 cups (400 grams) of cherry purée to 1 pound (500 grams) of sugar boiled in 1 quart of water to the crack stage (310°F.). Fold in 10 whites of egg beaten stiff.

Make the soufflé in the usual way. See SOUFFLÉ.

The soufflé can also be prepared with cream. See SOUFFLÉ, *Cream soufflés*.

Cold cherry soufflé. Soufflé glacé aux cerises—Use the preparation for *Iced cherry mousse* (see ICE CREAMS AND ICES). Fill a soufflé dish with this mixture, first attaching a shield of white paper round the top of the soufflé dish to reach a good inch above it, fixed with butter or tied with string.

Once the soufflé has set in the refrigerator the paper border is removed.

Little iced cherry soufflés (or those in which other fruits are used) are prepared in the same way.

Danish cherry tart or flan. Flan de cerises à la danoise—Fill a flaky pastry shell or flan case with stoned cherries soaked in sugar and sprinkled with a pinch of cinnamon.

Cover the cherries with a prepared mixture of 6 tablespoons (120 grams) of softened butter, 6 tablespoons (120 grams) of sugar, ½ cup (120 grams) of powdered almonds and 2 eggs.

Cook the tart or flan in the oven at a moderate temperature (375°F.). Leave it to cool, and then cover it with gooseberry jelly and glaze with rum.

Cherries in vinegar. Cerises au vinaigre—Remove the stalks from some fine cherries which are ripe and free from imperfections. Put them in a glass jar, alternating layers of cherries with powdered sugar, with a few cloves and some fragments of cinnamon. Continue the layers of cherries and sugar until the jar is full, then pour over some white wine vinegar, which has been boiled with lemon rinds, and allowed to cool.

Close the jars hermetically with corks covered with linen, or with sulphurized paper. Instead of alternating the layers of cherries with layers of sugar, one can also boil the sugar with the vinegar. The white sugar can be replaced by light brown sugar, about 2 pounds (1 kilo) of brown sugar to every quart (litre) of vinegar.

CHERRY-BAY (U.S.A. CHERRY LAUREL). Laurier-cerise—The leaves of this shrub emit a smell of bitter almonds when they are rubbed between the fingers. They are used to flavour creams of various kinds. They must be used circumspectly, however, as they contain an appreciable amount of poisonous hydrocyanic acid.

CHERVIL. Cerfeuil—Pot-herb with stiff stems and curly leaves, originating in Russia and western Asia; cultivated from the beginning of the Christian era. It is used chopped for seasoning.

Wild chervil, sweet Cecily, which has darker leaves, less denticulated, has a more bitter flavour.

CHERVIS—Plant originating in China. The very sweet and aromatic root was greatly sought after in the old days, but it is no longer much esteemed.

CHESTNUTS. Châtaignes—Chestnuts grow two or three together in a prickly shell. A number of chestnut varieties exist, improved by cultivation. The species whose fruit contains only a single large nut are called '*marrons*'.

This fruit has a very high food value and is a basic element in certain regions: *Creuse*, *Limousin*, *Haute-Vienne* and especially *Corsica*. The chestnuts are eaten raw, boiled, steamed and grilled. They are used for various preparations of a culinary nature and in the confection of sweets and pastries.

Chestnuts are preserved by drying and flour is made of them, as a rule by very primitive means. This flour, which is white with here and there red particles (debris of the outer skin) in inferior types, has a sweet flavour, an agreeable smell and makes a non-elastic paste when combined with water.

Chestnut flour is used to make a kind of porridge, and various dishes. In Corsica it is eaten in various forms of which the most important are:

Polenta. Chestnut flour, sieved, thrown into boiling water, lightly salted, mixed with a spatula until the paste is sufficiently dried out, and no longer adheres to the sides of the casserole; then poured on to a floured cloth and cut into slices with a thread. These slices are either eaten as they are, with *broccio* (Corsican cheese) or grilled or fried. See POLENTA.

Brilloli. A kind of porridge made with chestnut flour to which milk or cream is added.

Ferinana. This is *brilloli* with oil added.

Tourte. Porridge to which aniseed with pine kernels and dried raisins have been added, poured into a baking-dish and cooked in the oven.

Pislicine. A cake prepared with a chestnut porridge fermented with yeast, and flavoured with aniseed.

Castagnacci. Thick fritters using a chestnut flour base.

Peeling chestnuts. Slot the surface of the chestnuts on the domed face. Put them in a baking-tin with a little water. Roast them in the oven for 8 minutes. Peel them while they are still hot.

Another method. Slot the chestnuts as indicated above. Put them, a few at a time, into boiling fat. Deep-fry for 2 minutes. Drain. Peel them while they are still hot.

Chestnut barquettes. Barquettes aux marrons—Line barquette tins with *Fine pastry dough* (*I*) (see DOUGH). Bake blind (empty). When they are ready, fill them with a purée of *marrons glacés* (or purée of chestnuts cooked in milk), flavoured with kirsch. Ice the barquettes with kirsch-flavoured *Fondant icing*. See ICING.

Boiled chestnuts. Marrons bouillis—Put the chestnuts in a saucepan. Cover them with cold water. Season with a tiny pinch of salt and flavour with a little celery, star anise, Chinese anise or any other spice.

Bring to the boil. Cover and simmer gently for 45 minutes to 1 hour.

Drain the chestnuts and serve them wrapped in a folded napkin, or in a wooden bowl, covered with a napkin.

Braised chestnuts. Marrons braisés—Peel the chestnuts as indicated above. Lay them flat in a buttered dish. Put into the middle of the dish a *bouquet garni* with plenty of celery. Season. Barely cover the chestnuts with very thick concentrated veal stock. Cover the pan and cook in the oven without stirring, so as not to break the chestnuts.

Chestnuts prepared in this way are used as a garnish for various main dishes.

Chestnut compote. Compote de marrons—Cook the chestnuts in a light syrup flavoured with vanilla. Serve in a glass bowl. Pour the cooking syrup (boiled down if necessary) over the chestnuts.

Chestnuts prepared in this way can be served either hot or cold, and may be flavoured with kirsch or any other liqueur.

Chestnut confection. Pâté de marrons—'Shell the chestnuts, put into water to blanch, peel off the skin, pound in a stone mortar and weigh. Separately, clarify the same amount of sugar, cooked to ball degree (250°F.) take off the fire and mix with half its weight of apricot jam or apple jelly. Stir, combine all the ingredients together, spread on a slate slab or a metal sheet to a thickness of two or three lines (see WEIGHTS AND MEASURES) and put into a drying oven. On the following day, cut into squares, lay out on a sieve, turning them from time to time, and when they are quite dry store in boxes.' (*Le Confiseur moderne.*)

Chestnut croquettes. CROQUETTES DE MARRONS—Chop *marrons glacés* very finely. Chestnuts boiled in milk sweetened with vanilla sugar may also be used. Blend with thick *French pastry cream* (see CREAM). Spread the mixture on a baking sheet. Leave to cool.

Divide the mixture into small portions. Flour each piece and dip in egg and freshly made breadcrumbs. The pieces may be shaped as corks or into any other shape desired. Deep-fry in clarified butter. Serve on a napkin. Serve *Apricot sauce* (see SAUCE) flavoured with kirsch separately.

Marrons glacés—*Marrons glacés* are first preserved and then glazed. This is a long and extremely intricate process and is therefore seldom undertaken in the home.

Chestnut jam. CONFITURE DE MARRONS—Make a chestnut purée with milk or water. Put it in a bowl with an equal weight of sugar, a vanilla pod and ½ cup (1 decilitre) of water to every 2 pounds (1 kilo) of the mixture. Warm gently, stirring constantly. The jam is ready if it comes away from the bottom of the pan when stirred with the skimmer.

To ensure longer preservation, put the jam in special jars and sterilize as for bottled fruit.

Chestnut Mont-Blanc (sweet dessert). MONT-BLANC AUX MARRONS—Shell the chestnuts, leaving the inner skin. Put in a saucepan. Cover with water and bring to the boil. Then remove the inner skin, taking care not to let the chestnuts get cold.

Simmer the chestnuts very gently in milk with sugar and vanilla. When they are ready, drain them (unless all the moisture has been evaporated in cooking) and rub them through a wire sieve as follows:

Place the sieve over a large plain ring baking-tin. Rub the chestnuts through with a mortar or wooden mushroom, so that the sieved chestnuts look like vermicelli and thus line the walls of the baking-tin.

If any chestnut purée has fallen outside the tin, add it to the rest. Do not put any pressure on the purée so that when it is turned out on the serving-dish, it retains the appearance of vermicelli.

Turn this border out on to a large round dish. When it is quite cold, fill the centre with *Chantilly cream* flavoured with vanilla. Shape the cream into a dome.

Chestnut purée. PURÉE DE MARRONS—Remove the shell of the chestnuts, leaving the inner skin intact. Plunge them in boiling water. Drain and skin. Cook the chestnuts in white stock seasoned with a little celery. (If a meatless purée is required, cook in water.) Drain and rub through a fine sieve. Put the purée in a saucepan and warm, stirring constantly. Just before serving, add fresh butter and a few tablespoons of fresh cream.

Chestnut purée soup or cream. POTAGE PURÉE (OU CRÈME) DE MARRONS—See SOUPS AND BROTHS, *Purée soups*.

Chestnuts and rice. BORDURE DE MARRONS AU RIZ—Peel the chestnuts and cook in a light syrup flavoured with vanilla.

Drain and arrange them in a pyramid surrounded by a border of rice prepared as for *Condé apricots*. (See APRICOT.) Decorate the top of the border with crystallized fruit and halved almonds. Serve with *Apricot sauce* flavoured with kirsch. See SAUCE, *Dessert sauces*.

Roast chestnuts. MARRONS GRILLÉS—Cut a ring round the chestnuts making sure not to damage the kernels. Put them in a special chestnut pan. Roast them on hot embers or on the stove, tossing them frequently so that all are thoroughly cooked.

Chestnut soufflé. SOUFFLÉ DE MARRONS—Make a chestnut purée with stock or milk as desired, and use this to make a soufflé, proceeding as for *Potato soufflé*. See SOUFFLÉ.

Sweet chestnut soufflé. POUDING SOUFFLÉ AUX MARRONS—Peel 2 pounds (1 kilo) of chestnuts and make a purée by cooking them in a light syrup, flavoured with vanilla. Add to this purée, while stirring it on the stove to evaporate the moisture, ⅔ cup (150 grams) of fine sugar and 6½ tablespoons (100 grams) of butter.

Remove the pan from the stove and blend in 8 yolks of egg. Whisk 6 whites of egg until they are very stiff. Blend them in at the last minute.

Pour the mixture into a plain round buttered mould. Put the mould in a pan of water and bake in the oven. Serve *custard** or *zabaglione** separately.

Stewed chestnuts as a garnish. MARRONS ÉTUVÉS POUR GARNITURE—Peel the chestnuts as indicated above. Put them in a buttered pan. Cover with clear white stock (or, for fish or vegetable dishes, with water). Add a pinch of salt, a small spoonful of fine sugar and a stick of celery.

Bring rapidly to the boil. Cover and leave to simmer very slowly for 45 minutes.

Serve as indicated in the recipe for the main dish.

CHEVALER—This is a technical French culinary term indicating the symmetrical arrangement of the various elements of a dish placed one upon the other.

CHEVALET—A slice of bread trimmed '*en chevalet*' and covered with wafer thin slices of fat pork or butter, on which chicken *filets mignons* (breasts) are placed to give them a correct form while cooking.

CHEVEUX D'ANGE—This preparation with a carrot base is hardly ever used today. It was popular about 80 years ago in the south-west of France. It is prepared in the following way: Cut 1 pound (500 grams) of the orange part of carrots into thin slices or a fine *julienne*.*

Put the carrots into a copper pan or failing that into an ordinary pan in which 2 cups (500 grams) of sugar have been set to boil in water. There must be sufficient water to cover the carrots. Cook, keeping the pan on the boil until two-thirds of the liquid has evaporated. Add the rind of a lemon finely chopped and a few drops of lemon juice.

Turn out the marmelade into a dish or pour into a carrot mould. Leave to cool and then turn out. These carrots can also be flavoured with vanilla.

The sweet Chantilly ring *au cheveux d'ange* and tarts and tartlets *aux cheveux d'ange* can be made with carrots prepared '*en cheveux d'ange*'.

The name *Cheveux d'ange* is also given to a very fine type of vermicelli.

CHEVRIER—A type of haricot *flageolet* (bean) which stays green; cultivated especially in the neighbourhood of Arpajon, it bears the name of the originator of this variety. See BEAN.

CHIANTI—Well-known Italian red wine, produced chiefly in the district of Chianti Ferrese in the Province of Siena in Tuscany.

CHICK-PEA (Cicer arietinum). POIS CHICHE—Plant (of the family *Leguminosae*) originating in the Mediterranean area, one species of which is cultivated in France.

In south-western France chick-peas are cooked *en*

*estouffade**. They are used in Spain a great deal, being an essential ingredient of many soups. Chick-peas are also very popular in North Africa. They are essential as part of the garnish for the classic *Couscous*.

Chick-peas (Catalan style). POIS CHICHES À LA CATALANE —Soak the chick-peas until they become quite soft. Boil them in water with the usual vegetable garnish (like white dried beans), *bouquet garni** and piece of bacon. Season with salt and pepper. Add a few tablespoons of oil to form a layer of fat on the surface. Add some Spanish sausages called *chorizos**. Simmer very gently for about 4 hours.

Drain the chick-peas, remove the vegetable garnish and the *bouquet garni** and put the chick-peas into a saucepan. Add a few tablespoons of tomato purée. Add the chorizos and the bacon, cut in uniform pieces. Add a pinch of garlic and a few tablespoons of the liquid left over from boiling the chick-peas. Simmer for an hour and serve in a timbale.

CHICKEN. POULETS, POULARDES, VOLAILLE—Chicken is the generic term used to describe the barnyard fowl and includes in modern parlance everything from the very young chicken (*poussin*) to the large hen suitable only for the stock pot. The spring chicken (*poulet de grain* and *poulet de reine*) weigh from 1½ pounds to 3½ pounds. Fat hens or roasting chicken weigh from 3½ to 5½ pounds and are called *poulardes* in French. The larger birds and capons are also called chicken in most French markets and on most menus. All recipes for the different kinds of chicken are grouped together in alphabetical order in this section after the general cooking instructions which follow.

A good *poulet* has tender flesh, elastic, not flabby; the breastbone gives when it is pressed from side to side; the feet can be black or white according to the breed but never yellow. The comb should be small and unformed, the skin loose and white and the 'parson's nose' white or pinkish with a knob of fat above reaching the backbone.

The principal types of French hens are those of Bresse, Houdan, La Flèche, Crèvecoeur, Barbezieux, Faverolles and Le Mans.

General cooking instructions for chicken. The quantity of meats used as flavouring in slow cooking and the aromatic bases used in braising depend on the size of the bird. The same is true of the cooking liquor added. There should be as little as possible of this, so as not to dissipate the delicate flavour.

Sauces accompanying braised fowl are made with the liquor in which it was cooked, strained, and with all grease skimmed off, and finished according to the recipe.

Boiled or poached chicken is cooked in white stock (chicken or veal) or in a pale beef stock.

Failing a previously prepared stock, a savoury base can be made with the neck, the head and the crop and the feet cooked in water with aromatic vegetables and the usual seasonings.

Boiled chicken is accompanied by white or pale sauce, made, as a general principle, with the liquor in which it was cooked. To this end a white *roux* should be made in advance with butter and flour cooked gently together without colouring, and moistened with some of the chicken broth when this is about three-quarters cooked. Nevertheless, whenever possible, these white sauces should be prepared with their own special white bases and only reinforced with a little chicken broth. Such a sauce would have the stalks and caps of mushrooms added should the recipe so demand.

Different ways of finishing these sauces are given in the list of white sauces. See SAUCE.

Chicken baked in butter (i.e. cooked in the oven in a covered dish) is accompanied by the cooking juices skimmed of fat, diluted as necessary, and thickened or not according to taste. Cream is sometimes used.

Chicken baked *à la Matignon* is accompanied by the cooking juices diluted with wine, blended with veal or chicken stock and bound with rich brown sauce.

The garnish for a chicken dish is either cooked with the chicken or prepared separately, according to the recipe.

In none of the recipes that follow should all the sauce be used to coat the bird. A very little sauce only should be poured over it and the rest should be handed separately in a sauceboat.

Some instructions for cooking large fowls call for stuffings and prepared mixtures. See FORCEMEAT.

Serving and arrangment. In garnished chicken dishes, particularly those served at large dinners, the bird is often left whole. This calls for a fairly decorative presentation. It is important however that the garnish should not cancel out the flavour of the dish.

Garnishes should be arranged so that the food can still be quickly served. It is a good idea not to set all the accompaniments on the main dish, but to use only a small part as a garnish and serve the rest separately when handing the sauce, all piping hot.

In making an ornamental arrangement set the fowl on a base of fried bread, so as to keep it separate from the garnish. In the past these garnishes consisted of the most complicated borders of bread cut in fancy shapes, designs made of *pasta*, of rice etc. Modern practice has done away with these excesses, but although decorative presentations of uncut chicken have been considerably simplified, their elegance is undiminished.

Methods of preparation.

Braised fat hens and capons—Draw, singe and clean the chicken; truss it as illustrated. Lard the breast with bacon fat, truffles or tongue, having previously dipped the chicken for a moment into boiling stock to solidify the flesh.

Cover the breast with a bard of bacon fat big enough to protect this delicate part of the bird during cooking, so that it does not become too dry.

Brown the chicken in a hot oven, then put it into a heavy braising pan with the ingredients used for braising white meat. (See CULINARY METHODS, *Braising*.)

Pour in the liquid indicated, bring to the boil, cover the pot and cook in the oven, basting frequently.

Drain the chicken; remove the bard and trussing string and glaze in the oven, basting it with the cooking liquor.

Set it on a slice of fried bread (or directly on to the

Braised chicken (*Mac Fisheries*)

(1) Pierce with threaded trussing needle the left thigh, the breast and the right thigh

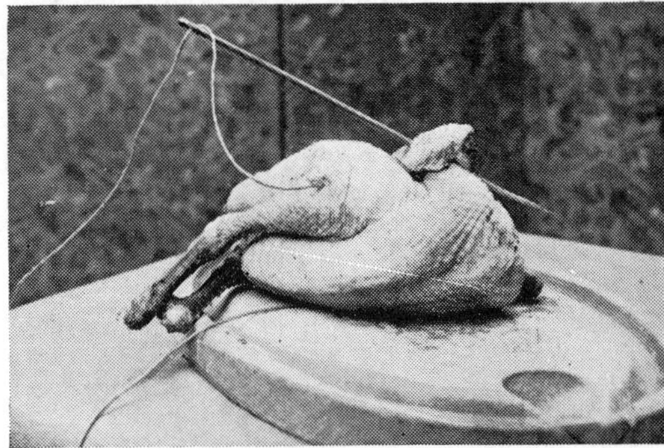

(2) Lay the chicken on its left side and sew through the right wing

(3) The chicken is on its right side; cross the back and pierce the right wing

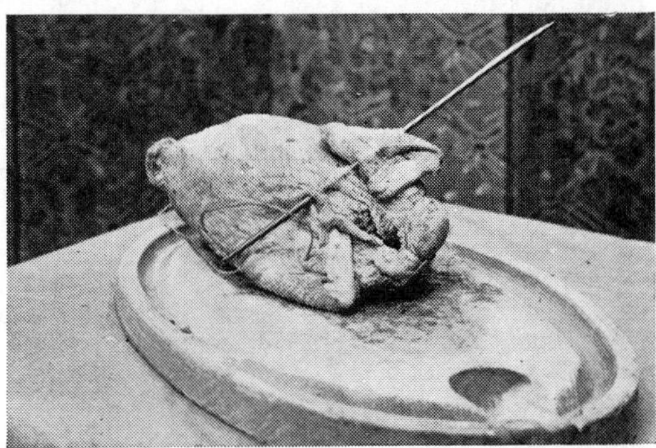

(4) Bring the two ends of string together and tie them

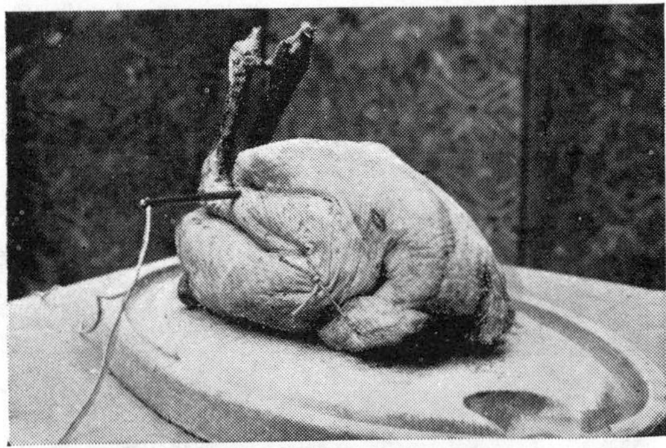

(5) Pass the needle through the lower part of the drumsticks and under the breast from left to right

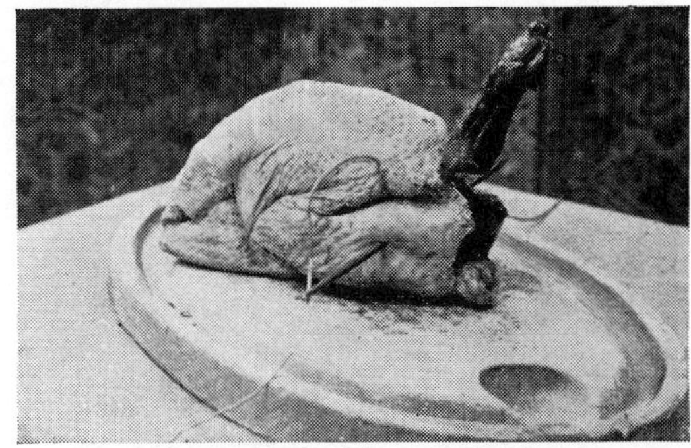

(6) Next pierce the lower part of the body from right to left

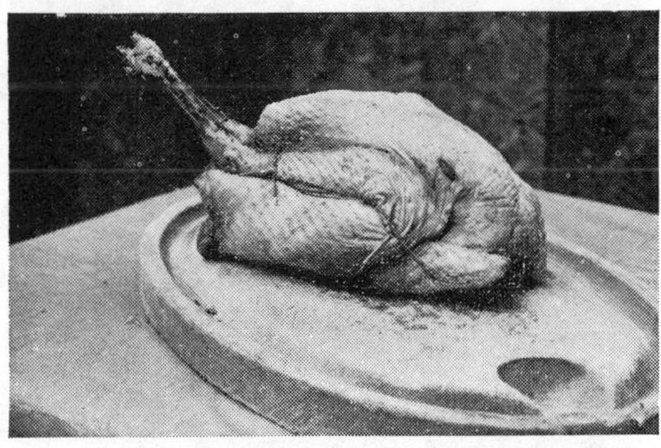

(7) Pull the two ends of the string and tie them

(8) Chicken barded and trussed, ready to braise or roast

HOW TO TRUSS A CHICKEN

plate), garnish it according to the recipe, and serve it with the liquid in which it was cooked, finished off according to the instructions, or with whatever sauce is indicated.

Poached or boiled fat hens and capons—Clean and truss the chicken as for braised chicken. Rub the breast and legs with a slice of lemon to keep them white.

According to the recipe lard or stud the breast with fat or seasoning. Cover with a bard of bacon fat.

Put in a deep saucepan; cover with white stock.

Bring to the boil and cook quickly for a few moments; skim; cover the saucepan and simmer very slowly.

To test whether the chicken is cooked, prick a fleshy part with the point of a knife. If a clear, pinkish juice escapes it is done.

Drain the chicken; remove the bard and the trussing string. Set on its dish and garnish according to the instructions. Serve with a white sauce to which must always be added some of the liquor in which the chicken was cooked.

Fat hens and capons baked in butter—Clean, truss and bard the chicken as for braised chicken.

Put in a heavy-bottomed pot, pour over melted butter, season and cook quickly for a few moments over a good heat; then cook in the oven, covered, basting frequently with its butter.

Take out the chicken, remove the bard and the trussing string, set on a dish and garnish according to the recipe. Serve with its cooking juices diluted and finished off according to the formula for the particular preparation.

Fat hens and capons baked à la Matignon—Clean, draw, truss and bard the chicken as for braised chicken. Put it in a deep saucepan or braising pan whose base is lined with *Matignon** half-cooked in butter.

Pour over melted butter, season and cook in the oven, covered, basting frequently with its butter.

When the chicken is cooked and golden brown, moisten with concentrated veal or chicken stock or with such other liquid as the recipe prescribes; baste the bird with this juice. Take out the chicken, remove the bard and trussing string.

Set on the dish and garnish according to the recipe and serve with its own cooking juice, diluted and finished off according to the instructions.

Fat hens and capons baked à la Matignon (old style)—Crisp in butter the flesh of a fowl prepared as for braised chicken. Cover it in a thick layer of *Matignon*; bard it and wrap it in a sheet of buttered paper; cook in the oven or on the spit. As soon as the bird is cooked unwrap it, take off the bard and remove the *Matignon*. Put the chicken in a saucepan, pour over Madeira; reduce the liquid and finish with veal stock that has been reduced and thickened. Remove all fat and strain.

Set the chicken on a dish and garnish it according to the recipe; serve with its cooking liquid finished off according to the instructions.

Note. The many recipes given below can be augmented by serving braised, boiled and baked chicken with different vegetables, with *pasta* and with other garnishes described in the course of this dictionary.

Recipes.

Chicken à l'allemande. POULARDE À L'ALLEMANDE—Poach the chicken in a white stock. Set on a dish; coat with *Allemande sauce* (see SAUCE) to which part of the reduced cooking liquor has been added.

Chicken Ambassadrice. POULARDE AMBASSADRICE—Stuff the chicken with a mixture of lamb's sweetbreads, truffles and mushrooms bound with a *Velouté sauce* (see SAUCE); cook it covered, in the oven *à la Matignon*.

Surround with 8 pastry cases filled with sautéed chicken livers, cock's combs and kidneys. Put on each tartlet a slice of truffle heated in butter.

Coat the chicken with the cooking juices diluted with Madeira and rich thickened brown veal stock.

Chicken à l'andalouse. POULARDE À L'ANDALOUSE—Stuff the chicken with rice mixed with small pieces of lean ham and seasoned with paprika.

Cook the chicken in butter in a heavy stew pan or hermetically sealed braising pan, adding (*for flavouring only*) one large onion and a *bouquet garni**. Prepare separately a garnish *à l'andalouse*. See ANDALOUSE.

Set the chicken on a long dish; surround it with this garnish and sprinkle it with its cooking juices diluted with white wine, to which thickened rich brown veal gravy with tomato purée have been added.

Chicken à l'anversoise. POULARDE À L'ANVERSOISE—Stuff the chicken with hop shoots in cream (see HOPS). Bake it with butter in a covered dish until it is three-quarters cooked.

Put in a casserole with $1\frac{3}{4}$ cups (400 grams) of potatoes, cut to look like olives and fried lightly in butter. Finish cooking in the oven.

Pour over a small quantity of the pan juices, diluted with white wine and thickened rich brown veal gravy. Serve in the casserole.

Chicken in aspic. POULARDE EN ASPIC—Cut the breast and wings of a cold, boiled chicken into thin slices, coat with *White chaud-froid sauce* (see SAUCE). Decorate with truffles and glaze with chicken jelly.

Set these prepared pieces in an aspic mould that has been lined with a layer of jelly.

Fill the middle of the mould with a chicken mousse made of the flesh of the chicken legs with addition of *foie gras* (see MOUSSES). Fill the mould with the jelly; allow to cool and chill on ice.

Turn out the aspic on to a round dish, straight on to the dish or raised on a croûton of bread. Garnish with chopped jelly.

Roasting chickens, Angers (*French Government Tourist Office*)

Chicken à l'Aurora. POULARDE À L'AURORE—Poach the chicken in white stock. Set it on a dish; coat with *Aurora sauce* (see SAUCE) to which has been added a small quantity of the reduced cooking liquor.

This chicken may be stuffed with cream *Quenelle forcemeat* (see FORCEMEAT) flavoured with strong tomato purée.

Chicken ballottines. BALLOTINES DE VOLAILLE—Prepared using either a whole chicken, boned, filled with a stuffing of some kind, rolled in a ballottine and braised or poached (see BALLOTTINE), or with legs of large chickens prepared in the same manner. The latter are usually called *Jambonneaux de volaille.*

Chicken à la banquière. POULARDE À LA BANQUIÈRE—Stuff the chicken with rice half-cooked in white stock mixed with 2 tablespoons of truffles cut in dice. Poach in white stock. Set on a round plate.

Surround with 10 *quenelles** of chicken forcemeat, 10 mushrooms and 10 rather thick slices of truffles.

Coat with *Banquière sauce*. See SAUCE.

Chicken blanquette. BLANQUETTE DE VOLAILLE—The same as a ragoût of poultry prepared *à blanc*. See BLANQUETTE.

Chicken with blood. POULET AU SANG—This can only be prepared using a chicken bled on the premises, the blood being essential to bind the sauce.

The chicken is cut in pieces and fried in butter as for a fricassée. Once the pieces of chicken are quite firm, they are taken out of the pan and in the same butter are lightly cooked 12 small onions and 12 small pieces of bacon. Add 12 mushrooms, and when these are all just cooked remove them from the pan.

Put in the pan a tablespoon of flour, colour it lightly. Stir in 2 cups (half a litre) of red wine and a few tablespoons of *pot-au-feu* broth. Mix the sauce well, season and strain.

Put back in the pan the pieces of chicken and its garnish. Put in the middle a *bouquet garni**. Pour over the strained sauce. Cook with the pan covered for about 45 minutes. At the last moment bind the sauce with the chicken's blood to which 2 or 3 tablespoons of red wine have been added to prevent it from coagulating. Add a good tablespoon of brandy and set it alight. Serve in a deep dish garnished with heart-shaped croûtons of bread fried in butter.

Boiled chicken à l'anglaise I. POULARDE POCHÉE À L'ANGLAISE—Poach in a white stock. Surround with 8 small slices of tongue and alternate small mounds of celery, peas, carrots and turnips cooked in water.

Boiled chicken à l'anglaise II. POULARDE POCHÉE À L'ANGLAISE II—Poach in water with a carrot cut in quarters, an onion stuck with a clove, a bunch of herbs and a piece of lean bacon weighing slightly less than a pound, well blanched.

Set on a dish. Surround with the bacon cut in squares.

Serve at the same time a sauceboat of *Parsley sauce* (see SAUCE) and a sauceboat of the chicken broth.

Boiled chicken à l'anglaise III. POULARDE POCHÉE À L'ANGLAISE—Poach the chicken in a white stock with 20 small carrots, as many pieces of turnip, cut into balls, and two celery hearts.

Set on a dish. Surround with these vegetables, arranged alternately, with the addition of French (string) beans and cauliflower cooked in water.

Serve with *Butter sauce* (see SAUCE) with capers and a sauceboat of the chicken broth.

Chicken à la bonne femme. POULARDE À LA BONNE FEMME—Cook the chicken, covered, in the oven with butter. When it is half-cooked add 5 rashers (strips) (100 grams) of lean bacon cut in dice and blanched, and 20 small onions. Cook in the oven for 15 minutes.

Add 2 cups (500 grams) of potatoes cut to look like olives (or an equivalent quantity of new potatoes). Finish cooking together, basting frequently.

Put the chicken and its garnish in a casserole or on a dish. Pour over the butter it was cooked in, having added to it 4 tablespoons of thickened rich brown veal gravy. This chicken can be cooked in an earthenware casserole and brought in it to the table.

Chicken bouchées, canapés, croûtes and tartelettes— All these are filled with a *salpicon** of poultry finished off with truffles, mushrooms or other ingredient and bound with a white or brown sauce.

Chicken boudins à la Richelieu. BOUDINS DE VOLAILLE À LA RICHELIEU—Line small, oval or rectangular well buttered moulds, with fine *Chicken forcemeat à la crème* (see FORCEMEAT). Fill these moulds with a *salpicon** of breast of chicken, truffles and mushrooms, blended with very thick *Allemande sauce* (see SAUCE). Cover with another layer of chicken forcemeat, which should be well smoothed over with the blade of a knife dipped in cold water.

Poach these quenelles (for these *boudins* are no more than stuffed quenelles) in the oven, placing the moulds in a pan of hot water. Turn out of the moulds, dry, dip in egg and breadcrumbs and fry until light golden in clarified butter.

Arrange the little puddings in a turban on a round napkin-covered dish, packing them in fairly tightly. Garnish the middle of the dish with fried parsley. Serve *Périgueux sauce* or *Suprême sauce* with diced truffles added to it, separately. See SAUCE.

Chicken *boudins* can also be prepared in the following manner:

Roll the chicken forcement, which should be of a fairly firm consistency, into little cylinders. Poach them. Slit open these large quenelles on one side, stuff with the *salpicon** indicated and close the opening. Dip in egg and breadcrumbs and fry in clarified butter.

Chicken à la bourgeoise. POULARDE À LA BOURGEOISE—Cook the chicken, covered, in the oven with butter. When it is half-cooked add 5 rashers (strips) (100 grams) of lean bacon cut in dice, 20 small onions and 20 small carrots. Finish cooking together, basting frequently.

Put the chicken and its garnish in an earthenware dish; pour over its cooking juices diluted with white wine and thickened rich veal gravy.

Chicken à la bourguignonne. POULARDE À LA BOURGUIGNONNE—Brown in 2 tablespoons (25 grams) of butter 5 rashers (strips) (100 grams) of lean bacon, cut in dice and blanched. Add 20 small onions and 20 sliced mushrooms.

Take out all these ingredients and brown the chicken in the same butter.

Take out the chicken. Dilute the juices in the pan with 2 cups (4 decilitres) of red wine. Boil down to half the volume. Add 2 cups (4 decilitres) of rich brown gravy, cook at boiling point for 5 minutes and add a *bouquet garni**.

Put the chicken back in the saucepan. Cook quickly over a good heat for a few moments. Then cook on a very low heat for 45 minutes to one hour.

Put the chicken and its accompaniments on an earthenware dish or a plate; pour the sauce over, having first removed the herbs.

Note. As with all chickens cooked *à la bourgeoise, Chicken à la bourguignonne* can also be cooked in an earthenware casserole and served in the same dish.

Chicken brochettes. BROCHETTES DE VOLAILLE—Made with slices of chicken (raw or cooked), threaded on metal skewers alternately with pieces of lean bacon and mushrooms. These skewers are coated in egg and breadcrumbs and grilled.

Chicken broth (English and American cooking)—For this chicken soup see SOUPS AND BROTHS.

Chicken capilotade. POULET EN CAPILOTADE—Use for this dish any left-overs of boiled, braised or roasted chicken.

The chicken is taken off the bones, cut in thin slices, and put to simmer in a previously prepared sauce such as *Chasseur*, *Italian*, *Portuguese*, *Provençal*, etc. See SAUCE.

The *capilotade* is served in a deep dish.

Chicken casserole. POULARDE EN CASSEROLE—Put the chicken, trussed for boiling, into a pot or casserole in which some butter has been heated. Season with salt and pepper. Cook in the oven at a good heat for 45 to 55 minutes for a chicken weighing 3 to 3½ pounds (1 kg. 500 grams to 1 kg. 800 grams).

At the last moment pour over 4 or 5 tablespoons of thickened rich brown veal stock.

Chicken casserole à la bonne femme. POULARDE EN CASSEROLE À LA BONNE FEMME—As above, adding to the chicken, when it has been well browned in butter, small pieces of lean bacon, blanched, small onions that have been tossed in butter and potatoes cut into olive-shaped pieces.

Chicken with celery. POULARDE AUX CÉLERIS—*Brown.* Cook the chicken with butter, in a covered casserole, in the oven.

Set on a dish. Surround with braised quartered celery hearts. Pour over the cooking juices, diluted with white wine and with rich thickened brown veal gravy.

Alternatively, the chicken may be braised with celery, previously blanched.

White. As for *Chicken à l'allemande**. Surround the chicken with braised celery. Pour over *Allemande sauce.* See SAUCE.

Chicken à la Chantilly. POULARDE À LA CHANTILLY—Stuff the chicken with cooked rice mixed with truffles or *foie gras* cut in dice. Cook, covered, in the oven with butter, but do not allow to brown.

Set on a dish. Surround with 8 large whole truffles cooked in port wine and 8 slices of *foie gras* that have been lightly fried in butter.

Dilute the pan juices with white stock, add some thick chicken *Velouté sauce* (see SAUCE), simmer down by half, at the last moment add a few tablespoons of whipped cream and pour over the chicken.

Chaud-froid of chicken in jelly

Chaud-froid of chicken. CHAUD-FROID DE VOLAILLE—A cold entrée. Prepared with chicken poached in a flour-and-water stock and jointed. The pieces are coated with *Chaud-froid sauce* (white or brown) (see SAUCE), decorated with truffles or similar garnish, glazed with jelly, set on a dish or in a bowl and again covered with jelly.

Chicken à la Chevalière. POULARDE À LA CHEVALIÈRE—Take off the wings of two chickens, leaving the pinions on them. Trim them, insert small pieces of bacon fat under the skin and braise them in Madeira-flavoured braising stock.

Detach the four breasts; trim and flatten them a little, stud with pieces of tongue and truffles and put them in a buttered dish. (These breasts are cooked last.)

Cook the four leg joints, the ends of the wings and the carcases (these last cut in two pieces each) as a fricassée in the usual way.

Drain and wipe the cooked leg joints, coat them with egg and breadcrumbs and fry in clarified butter.

Arrange in a pastry case about 2½ inches deep the pieces of carcase and wingtips. Pour over them the strained fricassée sauce.

On top of the carcases arrange the leg joints and between each leg and the next set a wing. On top of everything put the quickly poached breasts.

Serve the rest of the fricassée sauce, to which mushrooms and truffles have been added separately.

Chicken chipolata. POULARDE CHIPOLATA—Braise the chicken in brown gravy. Surround with a garnish of chipolata sausages (see GARNISHES). Pour over the pan juices diluted with Madeira and mixed with rich *Brown sauce*. See SAUCE.

Chicken à la Chivry. POULARDE À LA CHIVRY—Poach the chicken in white stock.

Surround with 10 artichoke bottoms garnished with asparagus tips or little fresh peas. Pour over *Chivry sauce I.* See SAUCE.

A variation is to serve the chicken with *Chivry sauce* poured over and a garnish of mixed vegetables.

Chicken à la Clamart. POULARDE À LA CLAMART—Half-cook in butter a chicken trussed as for boiling. Put in an earthenware casserole. Add a quart (litre) of fresh *peas à la française*, three-quarters cooked. Cover with a lid and finish cooking together in the oven. Serve in the same casserole.

Note. Small chicken prepared in the same way are called *Poulets à la Clamart.*

Chicken in cocotte. POULARDE EN COCOTTE—This title describes a chicken cooked in a pot or casserole and served in the same receptacle.

Chicken compote. POULET EN COMPOTE—Truss the chicken as for boiling. Prepare as for *Pigeon compote.**

Chaud-froid of chicken (Reine Pédauque)

Chicken consommé—See SOUPS AND BROTHS.

Chicken à la crapaudine. POULET À LA CRAPAUDINE—Prepare, using a small roasting chicken, as *Pigeon à la crapaudine*.*

Chicken côtelettes. CÔTELETTES DE VOLAILLE—Under this name are known the following:

(1) The breasts of poultry removed when raw and cooked separately to be served as a small entrée.

(2) A kind of *croquettes* made with a chicken cutlet mixture, formed into the shape of cutlets, coated in egg and breadcrumbs and fried in butter.

(3) A variety of *quenelles* made with a poultry forcemeat and poached in a special mould.

To prepare chicken breasts—Remove the breasts of a small roasting chicken or a fat hen (*poularde*) after having taken off the skin.

Allow the wingtips to remain on the joint. Flatten lightly after having fixed the *filet mignon* underneath. (The *filet mignon* is the small piece of breast lying against the bone after the main part of the breast has been sliced away.)

To cook in butter 'à brun'—Season the côtelettes, sprinkle with flour and sauté them in clarified butter as quickly as possible. Cook very lightly as these pieces are extremely delicate and are liable to become tough if they are over-cooked.

Dish, garnish and add sauce according to the recipe. Put paper frills on the ends.

According to the recipe the côtelettes are served on croûtons, on bases of various kinds, on vegetables, etc.

To cook in butter 'à l'anglaise'—Season the côtelettes, sprinkle them with flour and coat with egg and breadcrumbs. Cook in clarified butter.

Dish, garnish and add sauce according to the recipe.

Chicken côtelettes may be coated with breadcrumbs to which chopped truffles or other ingredients have been added.

To cook 'à blanc', or poach—Season the côtelettes, brush with melted butter and lay them flat in a buttered sauté pan. Add a few drops of lemon juice; cover the sauté pan and cook for 6 to 8 minutes in a very hot oven.

Dish, garnish and add sauce according to the recipe.

The cooking of *chicken côtelettes 'à blanc'* must be extremely rapid and done without boiling. The liquid must be limited to the few drops of lemon juice indicated above.

Chicken côtelettes à l'anglaise. CÔTELETTES DE VOLAILLE À L'ANGLAISE—Season and coat the côtelettes in egg and breadcrumbs. Sauté in butter. Dish; garnish with a green vegetable tossed in butter. For sauce, serve thickened brown veal gravy.

Chicken côtelettes Heider. CÔTELETTES DE VOLAILLE HEIDER—Cook the côtelettes in white stock. Dish and garnish with a *salpicon** of carrots, artichoke bottoms, truffles and mushrooms cooked slowly in butter.

Coat with rich chicken *Velouté sauce* (see SAUCE) diluted with a tablespoon of tomato juice, with butter added and strained.

Chicken côtelettes maréchale. CÔTELETTES DE VOLAILLE MARÉCHALE—Coat the côtelettes with egg and breadcrumbs adding to the breadcrumbs a third of their volume of chopped truffles. Sauté in butter.

Arrange on a platter; put on top of each côtelette 2 slices of truffles; sprinkle with *Noisette butter*. See BUTTER, *Compound butters*.

Chicken crépinettes. CRÉPINETTES DE VOLAILLE—Prepared like *Pork crépinettes* with a *salpicon** or purée of chicken. See CRÉPINETTES.

Chicken croquettes. CROQUETTES DE VOLAILLE—Combine 1 cup of finely chopped chicken with $\frac{1}{3}$ cup of thick *Velouté sauce* (see SAUCE). Bind with an egg yolk and season well with salt, pepper and lemon juice. Cool thoroughly. Make into small oval croquettes. Coat with beaten egg and fine breadcrumbs and fry in deep fat.

Chicken with cucumber. POULARDE AUX CONCOMBRES—Follow recipe for *Chicken à l'allemande*. Set on a dish. Surround with cucumber cut in chunks and simmered in butter. Pour over *Allemande sauce*. See SAUCE.

Chicken curry I. CARI DE POULET—For this dish of Eastern origin, Plumerey, the successor of Carême (*L'Art de la Cuisine au XIXe siècle*) gives the following recipe:

'Toss in butter two chickens cut in pieces with one pound of uncooked ham cleaned of salt and cut in dice; add a good tablespoon of flour and moisten with light veal stock; put in a *bouquet garni** and two teaspoonfuls of curry powder.

'After it is cooked, boil down (reduce) the sauce without thickening it too much. It should look to the eye like a pale Espagnole sauce, lightly coloured with saffron.'

For accompaniment to this curry, Plumerey says that there should be served rice lightly fried in butter and cooked in stock like a rice pudding in a charlotte mould, which is certainly wrong, because with all curry dishes only Indian-style rice should be served.

Chicken curry II. CARI DE POULET—After having drawn, plucked and jointed a medium-sized chicken, divide each joint into three or four pieces (when cutting up chicken joints be careful not to splinter the bones into tiny fragments).

Put these pieces of chicken to cook in a saucepan in which you have previously cooked in lard or butter 2 chopped-up medium-sized onions, 3 to 4 ounces (100 grams) of ham cut in small pieces, and 2 medium-sized eating apples peeled and chopped up, the whole seasoned with crushed garlic, thyme, bay leaf, cinnamon, cardamom and powdered mace.

When the pieces of chicken are quite firm, shake them about without letting them colour too much and sprinkle them with two teaspoons of curry powder. Add 2 peeled, seeded and crushed tomatoes and mix well.

Put in $1\frac{1}{2}$ cups ($2\frac{1}{2}$ decilitres) of coconut milk (or almond milk). Cook very gently in a covered saucepan for about 35 minutes.

Ten minutes before serving, add $\frac{3}{4}$ cup ($1\frac{1}{2}$ decilitres) of thick fresh cream and the juice of a lemon. This sauce must be thickened to the desired consistency by boiling down.

Set the chicken in a bowl and serve with rice which you will have prepared, not in the form of a 'pudding' as Plumerey advises, but in the following fashion:

Cook $\frac{1}{2}$ pound (250 grams) of rice for 15 minutes in salt water, stirring often, drain it and wash several times in cold water; put it on a flat dish wrapped in a napkin. Let it dry, either in a special drying oven or in the ordinary oven at a very low heat for 15 minutes. (Mont-Bry's recipe.)

Chicken curry (Creole cookery). CARI DE POULET—Joint a medium-sized chicken. Brown the pieces very lightly in good fat, taking care not to let them become dry. Leave in the same container to simmer on a very low flame, with $\frac{1}{4}$ cup of finely chopped onion. *This must not be allowed to turn yellow.* Add next 2 small tomatoes, peeled, seeded and chopped. Stir the mixture. Leave to simmer for a quarter of an hour. Add 2 teaspoons of saffron, previously pounded in a mortar with the following ingredients: a sprig of thyme and a sprig of parsley, a clove of garlic, a piece of stem ginger. Leave these spices to soak into the chicken before moistening the curry with a glass of luke warm water, poured into the pan a little at a time. This is not a very liquid sauce. Simmer for two hours and serve with *Creole rice*. See RICE.

Chicken à la Cussy. POULARDE À LA CUSSY—Braise the chicken in brown butter. Surround with a *Cussy garnish*. See GARNISHES.

Pour over the cooking juices diluted with port wine and rich *Brown sauce*. See SAUCE, *Basic sauces*.

Chicken à la d'Albuféra. POULARDE À LA D'ALBUFÉRA—Stuff the chicken with rice half-cooked in white stock, mixed with small pieces of truffles and foie gras. Poach in white stock.

Set on its dish; surround with 8 small pastry cases filled with small chicken quenelles, cock's kidneys, round slices of truffles and button mushrooms bound with *d'Albuféra Sauce* (see SAUCE). Coat the chicken with d'Albuféra sauce.

Chicken demi-deuil. POULARDE DEMI-DEUIL—Poach the chicken in a white stock.

Surround with 8 pastry cases filled with a mixture of lamb's sweetbreads and mushrooms bound in a thick chicken *Velouté sauce* (see SAUCE). Put on top of each tartlet a small round truffle cooked in Madeira. Pour over *Suprême sauce*. See SAUCE.

Chicken demi-deuil is also called *Poached chicken Lyonnaise*.

Chicken Demidoff I. POULARDE DEMIDOFF—Cook the chicken, covered, in the oven *à la Matignon**.

Surround with 8 artichoke bottoms garnished with some vegetables cooked to a purée. Put on each artichoke bottom an onion ring dipped in batter and fried. Put in the middle of each onion ring a slice of truffle.

Pour over the cooking juices diluted with Madeira and rich *Brown sauce*. See SAUCE.

Chicken Demidoff II. POULARDE DEMIDOFF—Cook the chicken, covered, in the oven with butter.

When it is three-quarters cooked, put it in a casserole with 1½ cups (3 decilitres) of mixed vegetables cooked to a purée, with mushrooms and truffles.

At the last moment add 2 medium-sized truffles cut in slices.

Pour over the cooking juices diluted with port wine and thickened rich brown veal stock.

Chicken à la Derby. POULARDE À LA DERBY—Stuff the chicken with rice cooked in butter mixed with truffles cut in large dice. Cook, covered, in the oven.

Surround with 8 large truffles, cooked in port wine, and 8 slices of foie gras sautéed in butter.

Pour over the cooking juices diluted with the port wine and thickened rich brown veal gravy.

Chicken à la Doria. POULARDE À LA DORIA—Poach the chicken in white stock. Take it out of the liquid, remove the barding and trussing string. Cut off the breast fillets. Take out the small bones from the interior of the carcase.

Fill the chicken with the following mixture prepared in advance:

Bind a mixture of 3½ ounces (100 grams) of cock's combs and kidneys, ⅜ cup (100 grams) of button mushrooms and 3 medium-sized (100 grams) truffles cut to look like olives with 1½ cups (3 decilitres) of very thick chicken *velouté sauce* (see SAUCE, *Basic sauces*). Chill.

Fill the chicken with this mixture, giving the bird its original shape. Arrange on top the breast fillets, cut into very fine strips.

Pour over some very thick *Allemande sauce* (see SAUCE). Sprinkle with grated Parmesan and brown lightly in the oven.

Put the chicken on a dish and surround it with 8 large chicken *quenelles** decorated with truffles, 8 medium-sized truffles cooked in champagne, 8 fried cock's combs, and 8 large mushrooms.

Pour into the bottom of the dish a few tablespoons of *Suprême sauce*. See SAUCE.

Émincés of Chicken. ÉMINCÉS DE VOLAILLE—Left-over chicken (poached, braised or roasted), boned, and cut into thin slices. Set on a serving dish; coat with any sauce; heat without boiling.

Chicken filets. FILETS DE VOLAILLE—Under this name are known the *côtelettes* or *suprêmes* of chicken (and other poultry), i.e. the breasts removed when raw and cooked in various ways. See the recipes given under *Côtelettes* and *Suprêmes*.

Chicken filets mignons. FILETS MIGNONS DE VOLAILLE—Long thin strips cut from the suprêmes of poultry. These *filets*, after having been encrusted with thin slices of truffles or pickled tongue, are formed into rings or arcs and are placed on top of the *suprêmes* which are cooked separately. They can also be prepared by themselves when there are a sufficient number to make a light side dish.

Chicken à la financière. POULARDE À LA FINANCIÈRE—Braise the chicken. Surround with a *Financière garnish*. See GARNISHES.

Pour over *Financière sauce* (see SAUCE) to which have been added some of the juices in which the chicken was cooked.

Chicken forcemeat—See FORCEMEAT.

Chicken fricassée—See also FRICASSÉE.

Chicken fricassée à la minute. FRICASSÉE DE POULET À LA MINUTE—'After having cut up two chickens in the ordinary way, put them in a saucepan with 3 tablespoons (6 ounces) of fine butter, melted.

'Toss them about so that they become firm without colouring, add two rather small tablespoons of flour, season with salt, pepper and grated nutmeg and add as much water as will make a slightly thickened sauce; add half a dozen little onions, previously blanched, and a *bouquet garni** and cook on a good heat, taking care that the chicken does not stick and that the sauce is boiled down (reduced) little by little. At the end of 25 minutes test one of the legs (it should be cooked); throw in ½ pound (250 grams) of mushrooms, remove grease, bind the sauce with four egg yolks, beaten together, and finish with some lemon juice.' (Plumerey's recipe.)

Chicken fritot. FRITOT DE VOLAILLE—Small entrée prepared with slices of cooked chicken, marinated with oil, lemon juice and herbs, dipped in batter and fried in deep fat or oil. See also FRITTERS.

Chicken galantine—See GALANTINE.

Chicken giblets. ABATIS DE VOLAILLE—Poultry giblets in the proper sense are composed of wingtips, neck, gizzard, liver and heart. For cooking, see GIBLETS.

Chicken à la Godard. POULARDE À LA GODARD—Braise the chicken. Surround with a *Godard garnish*. See GARNISH.

Pour over *Godard sauce* (see SAUCE) to which some of the cooking juices have been added.

Grilled chicken. POULARDE GRILLÉE—Cut the chicken open down the back, push the ends of the legs into the flesh, flatten lightly, and season with salt and pepper. Brown it on both sides in butter, then cover on both sides with freshly grated breadcrumbs and grill under a gentle heat. The chicken can also be divided into joints as for *Chicken sauté*.

Grilled chicken (*Mac Fisheries*)

Grilled chicken is served with a rather highly seasoned sauce such as *Diable*, *Mustard*, *Béarnaise*, etc. See SAUCE.

Grilled chicken diable. POULET GRILLÉ DIABLE—Truss the chicken as for boiling and split it through the back. Flatten it slightly, season with salt and pepper, spread it with butter, and half-cook it in the oven.

Smear the chicken with a little mustard to which some cayenne has been added; coat with freshly sieved bread-crumbs; sprinkle with melted butter. Finish cooking the chicken under the grill, at a gentle heat, letting it colour well.

Set the chicken on a round dish bordered with gherkins and half-slices of lemon and serve with *Diable sauce*. See SAUCE.

Hungarian chicken. POULARDE À LA HONGROISE—Stuff the chicken with rice three-quarters cooked and seasoned with paprika.

Cook covered with butter in the oven; set on a dish and pour over the pan juices diluted with white wine and *Hungarian sauce*. See SAUCE.

Chicken Grimod-de-la-Reynière—See *Chicken à la Nantua III.*

Chicken ham. JAMBON DE POULET—A name given in France to the thigh of a large chicken, which is boned, stuffed, trussed in the shape of a little ham and braised in Madeira.

Chicken hash. HACHIS DE VOLAILLE—Made with left-over poultry (poached or braised), boned and chopped or cut in very small dice. See HASH.

Chicken à l'imperiale. POULARDE À L'IMPÉRIALE—Stuff the chicken with a mixture composed of 5 ounces (150 grams) of lamb's sweetbreads, $\frac{3}{4}$ cup (100 grams) of button mushrooms, 3 medium-size truffles (100 grams) shaped to look like olives, and bound with 1 cup (2 decilitres) of mushroom purée and 1 cup (2 decilitres) of thick chicken *Velouté sauce* (see SAUCE). Cook, covered, in the oven without allowing it to colour.

Put on a dish. Surround with 8 pastry cases filled with small pieces of *foie gras*, 8 large mushrooms cooked in butter and garnished with asparagus tips and 8 small artichoke bottoms simmered gently in butter and filled with chopped truffles.

Coat lightly with a sauce prepared using the cooking juices as for *Chicken à la Chantilly**.

Chicken à l'indienne. POULARDE À L'INDIENNE—Poach the chicken in a white stock or cook it covered in the oven with butter.

Set on a dish; pour over *Curry sauce* (see SAUCE) and serve with *Rice à l'indienne.**

Chicken à l'ivoire. POULARDE À L'IVOIRE—Poach the chicken in a white stock.

Set on a dish and surround with 20 mushroom heads and 20 chicken quenelles; pour over *Suprême sauce*. See SAUCE.

Cold chicken Isabelle. CHAUD-FROID DE POULARDE ISABELLE—Cut the chicken in pieces, soak in cold water, drain and put in a shallow pan. Pour over it 1 cup ($\frac{1}{2}$ pint) concentrated veal stock, flavoured with mushroom essence.

The chicken being cooked, drain it. Strain the cooking juices into a basin and use them to moisten a *roux** made with 5 tablespoons (75 grams) of butter and the same quantity of flour cooked together. Add a teaspoonful of paprika. Allow to cook, and skim. Bind the sauce with 2 yolks of egg beaten up in a little cream; cook it gently to the right consistency and strain it over the pieces of chicken, which will have had their skin and any scraps of garnish removed and been placed in a shallow pan. Add at this point a *julienne* of sweet pimentos cut in very thin strips. Simmer for a few minutes.

Put the pieces of chicken in a glass dish, arranging them symmetrically; cover them completely with their sauce, and when quite cold decorate with small pieces of truffles and sweet pimentos.

Coat completely with a thin layer of jelly, which should be almost colourless and very clear. (M. Apollon Callat's recipe.)

Chicken jambalaya (Indian cookery). JAMBALAIA DE POULET—A kind of pilaf made from rice cooked *à l'indienne*. See RICE.

Dice coarsely $\frac{1}{3}$ cup (150 grams) of raw, lean ham. Sauté in butter in a heavy pan.

When the ham is almost cooked, mix with it 1 cup (250 grams) cooked diced chicken without bones or skin.

Sauté these ingredients together for a few seconds. Season with red pepper and add 1 cup (200 grams) of *Rice à l'indienne*, cooked separately.

Mix and serve in a deep dish.

Jellied chicken in casserole. POULARDE EN TERRINE À LA GELÉE—Bone a plump fowl, with the exception of the legs. Stuff with a forcemeat made of equal parts of veal, fresh pork fat and *forcemeat à gratin*, the whole well seasoned, bound with two eggs and flavoured with brandy and essence of truffles.

Put in the middle of the forcemeat half a raw *foie gras* studded with four quarters of truffles. Reform the shape of the chicken. Truss it as for boiling, bard with a slice of fat bacon and cook, covered, in the oven with Madeira. Remove from dish and cool. Dilute the pan juices. Remove the trussing string and the barding, wipe the chicken and put it in an oval earthenware dish on a base of well-set jelly. Cover completely with jelly to which the diluted cooking juices have been added. Leave to chill for at least 12 hours.

Jellied chicken with champagne. POULARDE AU CHAMPAGNE EN GELÉE—Put into a plump chicken a whole *foie gras*, trimmed and studded with truffles, soaked in brandy and spices and cooked in butter for a few minutes (the chicken should be opened on top and the breastbone taken out).

Cook, covered, in the oven in butter. When the chicken is cooked, dilute its cooking juices with $2\frac{1}{2}$ cups (5 decilitres) of dry champagne. Reduce (boil down). Add $2\frac{1}{2}$ cups (5 decilitres) of chicken jelly. (See JELLY.) Boil for a few moments. Strain through a muslin.

Put the chicken in a large oval earthenware dish. Cover with the jelly.

Cool completely; when the jelly is quite set take off with the help of a spoon any fat that is sticking to the surface, and so as to remove every bit, wipe over two or three times with a cloth wrung out in very hot water.

Note. This chicken dish must be prepared at least 12 hours in advance.

Jellied chicken may be flavoured with different wines.

Jellied chicken with foie gras (canned). POULARDE AU FOIE GRAS À LA GELÉE—Prepare as for *Jellied chicken in casserole*. Drain, remove the trussing strings and wings. Put, breast downwards, into a large tin just big enough to hold the chicken. Cover with its cooking liquor, clarified. Solder the tin, make a mark on the top with solder. Put the tin into a pot and cover completely with water. Bring to the boil and continue to boil, *without interruption*, for an hour.

Drain the tin and leave to cool, keeping it upside down so that the breast of chicken is in jelly and the fat goes to the bottom of the tin.

Chicken with tarragon in jelly

Chicken with tarragon in jelly. POULARDE À L'ESTRAGON DANS SA GELÉE—Truss the chicken as for boiling, put in a saucepan and cover with white stock prepared in the usual way. Add a generous quantity of tarragon.

Cook very gently for an hour. Leave to cool in its own liquid.

Drain the chicken, take off the trussing string and wipe carefully.

Reheat the cooking liquor, from which all grease has previously been removed, and strain it through muslin. Add to it the required quantity of gelatine, soaked in cold water.

Pour this, when just lukewarm, into a saucepan in which ½ cup (100 grams) of chopped lean beef, the white of an egg and a handful of tarragon leaves roughly chopped have been mixed together with a whisk. Cook over a good heat for a moment, whisking lightly.

As soon as it comes to the boil, remove the saucepan to a very low heat and cook very slowly for 25 minutes.

Strain the jelly through a cloth, adding, when it has cooled a little, ½ cup (1 decilitre) of Madeira.

When it is nearly cold, half fill an oval glass dish or an earthenware pot with some of this jelly.

When the jelly has set, put the chicken on top.

Decorate it with broad leaves of tarragon, blanched, trimmed, drained and dipped one by one in half-set jelly. Arrange these leaves in garlands, in fans or any other way according to fancy, on the breast of the chicken. Three-quarters cover the chicken with the rest of the jelly, which must be used when it is half set.

Place the dish on ice or in the refrigerator until the moment of serving. (*Chicken with tarragon* can also be arranged on a round platter.)

Chicken Katoff. POULET KATOFF—Grill a chicken (split down the back and lightly flattened) as for *Chicken à la diable*.

Set it on a round dish on a cake made of *Duchess potato* (see POTATOES), brushed with egg and browned in the oven. Surround with thickened rich brown veal stock with butter added.

Chicken kromeskies—CROMESQUIS DE VOLAILLE—Prepared with a *croquette mixture**, wrapped in pig's caul (or pork fat), dipped in batter and fried. See CROQUETTES.

Chicken Lambertye. POULARDE LAMBERTYE—Poach a fat hen, trussed for boiling, in white chicken stock. Allow it to cool completely in its own liquid.

Make a circular incision round the breast and remove it. Fill the inside with a *foie gras mousse**, rounding the top nicely to reform the shape of the chicken. Coat the chicken legs with *White chaud-froid sauce*. See SAUCE.

Place over the mousse the chicken breasts cut in slices, coated with the sauce and decorated with truffles and rounds of tongue, glazed with jelly.

Set the chicken on a long dish, placed on a croûton of bread or a bed of rice (or set it in an oval glass dish on a jelly base). Garnish with jelly shapes or chopped jelly.

Chicken à la languedocienne. POULARDE À LA LANGUEDOCIENNE—Cook the chicken, covered, in the oven with butter.

Set on a dish; surround with 8 *tomatoes à la languedocienne* and 4 aubergines (egg-plant) cut in rounds and lightly fried in oil.

Pour over the cooking juices diluted with white wine, seasoned with a crushed clove of garlic and with the addition of thickened rich brown veal gravy. Sprinkle with chopped parsley.

Chicken livers. FOIES DE POULETS—Chicken livers are used mostly as a garnish. They are also used for forcemeat.

They may, however, be served grilled on skewers, sautéed, with mushrooms, in pilafs and risottos, and used in *terrines* and *pâtés*.

Cold chicken loaf. PAIN DE VOLAILLES FROID—Prepare cold *Chicken mousse* mixture and decorate as for all other cold loaves; *game*, *foie gras*, *fish*, *crustaceans*, setting it in a plain round mould, coated with jelly and decorated with pieces of truffles, white of hard-boiled egg, pickled tongue, etc.

Chicken loaf (hot). PAIN DE VOLAILLE—Prepare a *Mousseline forcemeat*. See FORCEMEAT.

Butter a plain round mould with a hole in the middle and fill with the above forcemeat to within ¼ inch from the top.

Poach the loaf in the oven in a *bain-marie** (pan of hot water) from 45 minutes to an hour, depending on the size of the mould.

When the loaf is cooked, leave it to settle for a few moments before turning out. Turn out on to a round dish, either straight on the dish or on a round croûton fried in butter.

Surround the loaf with the garnish indicated and pour over the sauce appropriate to the garnish.

The following garnishes and sauces are suitable for hot chicken loaves: *Clamart* (peas) and *Cream sauce;* mushrooms and *Allemande sauce*; *Hongroise* (*salpicon** of mushrooms and onions disposed in separate groups) and *Hungarian sauce; Monselet* (coarsely diced artichoke hearts and truffles disposed in separate groups) and *Suprême sauce*; *Montpensier* (asparagus tips in butter, slivers of truffles) and *Allemande sauce; Nantua* (crayfish tails, slivers of truffles) and *Nantua sauce;* asparagus tips and *Velouté sauce* cooked with cream. See GARNISHES, SAUCE.

Chicken à la lyonnaise or demi-deuil. POULARDE À LA LYONNAISE, DITE DEMI-DEUIL—Poach in a white chicken stock the chicken, stuffed with a fine truffled forcemeat and with little pieces of truffle inserted under the skin without breaking it.

Surround the chicken with vegetables cooked in the chicken broth and accompanied by the poaching liquor strained through a fine strainer.

Note. This way of cooking chicken is the great culinary speciality of the city of Lyons and is known all over the world as *Poularde de Madame Filoux.*

Chicken Maeterlinck. POULARDE MAETERLINCK—Stuff a chicken with a chopped-up mixture of cock's combs and kidneys, lamb's sweetbread's, truffles and mushrooms bound with very thick chicken *Velouté sauce* (see SAUCE) and fresh cream (this mixture must be quite cold before it is put in the chicken). Truss the chicken and bard it with a piece of bacon fat held in place with two pieces of string. Put the bird in a deep and heavy pot with butter, strips of fresh bacon rind, carrots and onions cut in rounds. Season with salt. Cook in the oven, covered, for 45 minutes.

Drain the chicken; remove the trussing string. Put in an oval earthenware casserole. Surround it with 6 medium-sized truffles, peeled, seasoned with salt, pepper and nutmeg, and 6 small slices of *foie gras* heated in butter. For the sauce dilute the cooking juices with 1¼ cups (2½ decilitres) of sherry and 2 cups (4 decilitres) of thickened strained brown meat gravy. Add 4 tablespoons of brandy and set alight. Seal the lid of the casserole with flour-and-water paste. Cook in the oven, in a good heat for 35 minutes. Serve in the casserole. (M. Mouy's recipe.)

Marinade of chicken. MARINADE DE VOLAILLE—Prepared in the same way as *Chicken fritot*, using uncooked chicken.

Chicken à la Matignon. POULARDE À LA MATIGNON—Stuff the chicken with *forcemeat à gratin** mixed with one-third of its volume of *Quenelle stuffing*. See FORCEMEAT.

Brown in the oven. Take out and allow to cool.

Cover it entirely with a thick coating of *Matignon** (vegetable mixture).

Wrap the chicken in a pork caul or sheet of salt pork, and tie firmly. Braise.

Set on a dish; surround with 8 braised lettuces, and pour over the cooking juices diluted with Madeira and rich *Brown sauce*. See SAUCE.

Chicken mayonnaise. MAYONNAISE DE VOLAILLE—Slices of cooked chicken (or other poultry) seasoned with oil, vinegar, salt and pepper, set on shredded lettuce in a salad dish, coated with mayonnaise and garnished with lettuce hearts and quartered hard-boiled eggs, capers and anchovy fillets. See MAYONNAISE.

Chicken médaillons. MÉDAILLONS DE VOLAILLE—There are several kinds. Some are prepared with a *croquette** mixture shaped into discs, coated in egg and breadcrumbs and sautéed in butter; others are made from *quenelle forcemeat* (see FORCEMEAT) or *chicken mousse**, moulded into little cakes. These *médaillons* are poached and belong to the category of *chicken quenelles*. See QUENELLES. A third kind is made with the flesh of a boned fowl, chiefly the white meat, and some *médaillons* are cut from the breasts or *suprêmes* of raw chicken, lightly flattened and cut into round or oval pieces.

Methods of preparing these last two types are given below.

Chicken médaillons à l'algérienne. MÉDAILLONS DE VOLAILLE À L'ALGÉRIENNE—Coat in egg and breadcrumbs *médaillons* made with chopped chicken meat sautéed in butter.

Set each *médaillon* on top of a half tomato grilled and stuffed with rice pilaf mixed with sweet peppers cut into dice. Surround with light *Tomato sauce*. See SAUCE.

Chicken médaillons Beauharnais. MÉDAILLONS DE VOLAILLE BEAUHARNAIS—Season the *médaillons*, cut when raw from the breasts, and sauté them in butter.

Set on croûtons of bread fried in butter. Put each *médaillon* on top of a small artichoke bottom cooked in butter and garnished with a tablespoon of *Beauharnais sauce* (see SAUCE). Place a slice of truffle on each artichoke bottom. Surround with thickened brown veal gravy mixed with butter.

Chicken médaillons cut from the breast. MÉDAILLONS DÉTAILLÉS SUR FILETS DE VOLAILLE—Remove the breast from a roasting chicken or fat hen.

Cut each, according to size, into 2 or 3 slices, as regular in shape as possible. Flatten these lightly and trim them into rounds or ovals.

Cook according to the recipe, following the instructions given under *Chicken Côtelettes* and *Suprêmes*.

Note. The *filets mignons* may be left with the *médaillons*. They may also be cooked separately, as for *Suprêmes of chicken* and served on top of the *médaillons*.

The legs, wings and carcases of the chickens used for the *médaillons* can be used up by following the instructions given under *Chicken ballottines*.

Chopped chicken médaillons. MÉDAILLONS EN CHAIR DE VOLAILLE HACHÉE—Bone the breasts of a roasting chicken or fat hen. Chop them, adding 1¼ cups (60 grams) of breadcrumbs soaked in milk and squeezed out, and 4 tablespoons (60 grams) of butter. Add to the mixture 2 tablespoons of fresh cream; season with salt, pepper and nutmeg.

Form out of this mixture 4 nicely shaped *médaillons*. Coat them with egg and breadcrumbs or dredge with flour and sauté in clarified butter.

These *médaillons* may be prepared more economically using the whole of the bird. The carcase, neck, head and feet can be used separately either to prepare chicken stock or soup, or a sauce to accompany the *médaillons*.

Chicken médaillons Dunan. MÉDAILLONS DE VOLAILLE DUNAN—Coat with egg and breadcrumbs *médaillons* made of chopped chicken meat mixed with a *salpicon** of lean ham and mushrooms. Sauté in butter.

Set in tartlets baked blind (cooked empty) and filled with a *salpicon** of truffles *à la crème*.

Serve Madeira sauce (see SAUCE) separately.

Chicken médaillons à l'écarlate—MÉDAILLONS DE VOLAILLE À L'ÉCARLATE—Season *médaillons* and poach them in white stock.

Set in a dish in the form of a turban, alternating them with round slices of pickled tongue heated in white stock.

Pour into the bottom of the dish a few tablespoons of *Allemande sauce*. See SAUCE.

Chicken médaillons à l'égyptienne. MÉDAILLONS DE VOLAILLE À L'ÉGYPTIENNE. Season médaillons with paprika; sauté them in butter.

Arrange in the form of a turban alternating them with rounds of aubergines (egg-plant) sautéed in butter. Garnish the middle of the dish with pilaf rice. Surround with *Tomato sauce* (see SAUCE) to which has been added the cooking juices diluted with white wine.

Chicken médaillons Fédora. MÉDAILLONS DE VOLAILLE FÉDORA. Season the *médaillons* and poach them in white stock.

Set on croûtons of bread fried in butter; garnish with cucumbers cut into uniform pieces and stewed in butter; coat with the cooking juices diluted with cream and chicken *Velouté sauce*. See SAUCE.

Chicken médaillons Grignan. MÉDAILLONS DE VOLAILLE GRIGNAN—Make *médaillons* using chopped chicken meat, keeping them not too thick; sprinkle with flour, dip in beaten egg and cover with finely chopped truffles. Cook in butter.

Arrange on artichoke bottoms cooked in butter. Garnish with a ragoût of *chicken quenelles* (see QUENELLES), and cocks' combs and kidneys, bound with *Allemande sauce*. See SAUCE.

Chicken médaillons à la mantouane. MÉDAILLONS DE VOLAILLE À LA MANTOUANE—Season médaillons and coat them *à la milanaise* (with egg and breadcrumbs mixed with grated Parmesan). Sauté in butter.

Set in tartelettes (baked empty), each filled with a spoonful of macaroni bound with Parmesan to which a *julienne* (thin strips) of lean ham and pickled tongue has been added. Put a slice of truffle on top of each *médaillon*.

Chicken médaillons à la turque. MÉDAILLONS DE VOLAILLE À LA TURQUE—Season with paprika *médaillons* cut from the breasts and sauté in butter.

Set on top of *Rice pilaf* (see PILAF). Coat with the cooking juices diluted with white wine and veal gravy flavoured with tomato.

Chicken à la milanaise I. POULARDE À LA MILANAISE—Stuff the chicken with *macaroni à la Milanaise**. Cook it, covered, in the oven in butter.

Set in an earthenware dish and pour over the cooking juices diluted with white wine and thickened rich brown veal gravy, with tomato purée added.

Chicken à la milanaise

Chicken à la milanaise II. POULARDE À LA MILANAISE—Stuff the chicken with a mixture composed of sliced lamb's sweetbreads, tongue, lean ham, mushrooms and truffles, bound with rich brown sauce flavoured with tomato. Braise the chicken.

Set on a dish and surround with 8 timbales of *Macaroni à la milanaise* (made in dariole moulds).

Pour over the cooking juices diluted with Madeira and *rich brown sauce* (see SAUCE) flavoured with tomato.

Chicken mousse and mousselines. MOUSSE ET MOUSSELINES DE VOLAILLES—An entrée, cold or hot, prepared with *Chicken mousseline forcemeat*. See FORCEMEAT.

Chicken with mousseline forcemeat—Poach the chicken in a white stock. Drain it, take off the breast fillets as for *Chicken à la Doria**.

Fill the inside of the bird with *Mousseline forcemeat* (see FORCEMEAT), with the addition of one-third of purée of *foie gras*. Arrange this stuffing in layers, alternating it with the pieces of breast fillets.

Round off the top of the forcemeat and smooth it over, giving it the shape of the bird.

Put the chicken in a dish and cook in a low oven, setting the dish in a tray containing hot water.

Place on a serving dish, surround with one of the garnishes recommended for chicken poached in a white stock. See GARNISHES.

Chicken with mushrooms. POULARDE AUX CHAMPIGNONS—*Brown.* Cook the chicken, covered, in the oven with butter; 10 minutes before taking it out add 20 large mushrooms. Surround with the mushrooms. Pour over the pan juices, diluted with white wine and mixed with rich *Brown sauce*. See SAUCE.

White. As for *Chicken à l'allemande*. Surround with 20 large mushrooms cooked without allowing them to colour. Pour over *Allemande sauce*. See SAUCE.

Chicken à la Nantua I. POULARDE À LA NANTUA—Poach the chicken in a white stock.

Set it on a dish, surround with 20 quenelles made of *chicken forcemeat* (see FORCEMEAT) with *Shrimp butter* (see BUTTER) added, and 8 boat-shaped pastry shells filled with shrimps in a *Nantua sauce*. See SAUCE.

Place on each little boat a fine slice of truffle; pour over the chicken *Suprême sauce* (see SAUCE) finished with shrimp butter.

Chicken à la Nantua II. POULARDE À LA NANTUA—Stuff the chicken with a purée of shrimps mixed with a very thick chicken *Velouté sauce* (see SAUCE). Poach in a white stock.

Set on a dish and pour over *Suprême sauce* (see SAUCE) finished with *Shrimp butter*. See BUTTER.

A few pieces of truffle may be added to the shrimp purée.

Chicken à la Nantua III. POULARDE À LA NANTUA—Poach the chicken, drain it, cut off the breast fillets and stuff it in the same way as *Chicken à la Doria*, replacing the mixture used in that recipe with purée of shrimps mixed with very thick chicken *Velouté sauce*. See SAUCE.

Reform the chicken, put back on top the pieces of breast fillets, cut in thin strips. Pour over *Allemande sauce* (see SAUCE). Sprinkle with Parmesan and brown the top.

Set the chicken on a dish, surround it with little tit-bits in the Nantua style and serve with *Suprême sauce* (see SAUCE), finished with *Shrimp butter* (see BUTTER), passed separately.

Prepared in this way the chicken is also known under the name of *Chicken Grimod-de-la-Reynière*.

Chicken à la Néva. POULARDE À LA NÉVA—Stuff the chicken, which has been opened from the back and the breastbone removed, with a fine chicken *forcemeat** to which has been added some raw *foie gras* and truffles cut in dice. Truss as for boiling, and poach in chicken stock. Allow to cool.

When the chicken is quite cold, wipe it and coat with white *Chaud-froid sauce* (see SAUCE) prepared with some of the chicken broth.

Glaze the chicken with jelly and allow to set firmly.

Set the chicken either on a bed of rice, on a slice of bread spread with butter or directly on to the plate. Put at each end of the plate on silver or glass scallop shells vegetable salad in mayonnaise (the salad rounded into a dome and decorated with truffles). Garnish the edges with jelly shapes.

Note. Chicken à la Néva can also be served in the same way as *Chicken Lambertye*, that is to say, having been cooked and cooled, the breast can be removed and its

CHEESES OF EUROPE

(*From the original French edition of* Larousse Gastronomique)

DUCK. Braised duck

(*Robert Carrier*)

meat sliced and arranged on the rest of the chicken, coated with white *Chaud-froid sauce*, decorated with truffles and glazed with jelly. Chicken prepared in this way may, instead of being placed on a bed of rice, be set in an oval bowl and coated with jelly.

Chicken à la niçoise I. POULARDE À LA NIÇOISE—Cook the chicken, covered, in the oven in butter.

Set it on a dish, surround with 8 quartered artichokes simmered in butter, 8 braised courgettes (zucchinis), 8 to 10 (200 grams) small new potatoes, cooked in butter, and some black olives.

Pour over the cooking juices diluted with white wine, seasoned with a crushed clove of garlic and thickened rich brown veal gravy, flavoured with tomato purée. Sprinkle with chopped tarragon.

Chicken à la niçoise II. POULARDE À LA NIÇOISE—Cook the chicken covered, in the oven with butter.

Set in an earthenware dish with tomatoes cooked gently in butter, courgettes (zucchini) cut in large dice and tossed in oil, new potatoes cooked in butter and black olives.

Pour over the cooking juices prepared as above. Sprinkle with chopped tarragon.

Chicken with noodles I. POULARDE AUX NOUILLES—Stuff the chicken with noodles half-cooked in salt water, drained and dressed with butter and grated cheese. Cook it, covered, in the oven with butter.

Set it on a dish; pour over the pan juices, diluted with white wine and thickened rich brown veal gravy flavoured with tomato purée.

Chicken with noodles II. POULARDE AUX NOUILLES—Cook the chicken, covered, in the oven with butter.

Set in an earthenware dish on a layer of noodles cooked in salt water and dressed with butter and grated cheese. Pour over the cooking juices diluted as above.

Chicken with oysters. POULARDE AUX HUÎTRES—Poach the chicken in white stock. Set it on a dish, surround it with 24 oysters poached in their own liquor, bearded and drained. Pour over *Suprême sauce* (see SAUCE) to which some of the boiled-down oyster liquor has been added.

The oysters may be served on little pieces of fried bread or toast, or may be put in the sauce.

Chicken Panurge. ETUVÉE DE POULET PANURGE—Cut the chicken up as for a fricassée. Season with salt and pepper and put it in a shallow pan in two spoonfuls of butter. Sauté the chicken in this butter over a hot flame until the flesh is quite firm. Take it out of the pan.

In the butter put 1½ cups (3 decilitres) of mixed vegetables, carrots, onion and celery previously cut in thin pieces, and lightly tossed in butter.

Put the pieces of chicken on the layer of vegetables, laying them as flat as possible. Pour in dry white wine. Boil down the liquid. Pour over a little fresh cream. Cook gently, covered, for 25 minutes. Add 24 stoned olives. Simmer for a few minutes.

Set the chicken in a bowl or a deep dish. Pour over the sauce, to which has been added a good tablespoon of butter. Put on top of the chicken thin slices of the gizzard which has been peeled, trimmed, cooked in consommé and fried in butter, and thin slices of the liver also fried in butter. Garnish with heart-shaped bread croûtons fried in butter.

Chicken à la parisienne. POULARDE À LA PARISIENNE—Remove the breastbone and stuff the chicken with a *Fine panada forcemeat* (see FORCEMEAT). Truss the bird and poach in a white stock.

Drain the chicken when it is cold; take off the pieces of breast. Take out the stuffing, cut it in large dice and add it to a cold chicken mousseline forcemeat. With this mixture refill the interior of the chicken, rounding it out to remake the shape of the chicken. Coat with white *chaud-froid sauce*. See SAUCE.

On the stuffing, place the breasts cut into thin slices, coated with the sauce, decorated with truffles and tongue and glazed with jelly.

Set the chicken on a long dish on a slice of bread spread with butter. Surround with vegetable salad moulded in darioles lined with jelly and decorated with truffles.

Ornament the edges of the dish with jelly shapes and garnish the bottom of the plate with chopped jelly.

Chicken pâté (Hot)—See PÂTÉ, *Hot chicken pâté.*

Chicken pâté (Cold)—See PÂTÉ, *Cold pâtés.*

Chicken à la périgourdine. POULARDE À LA PÉRIGOURDINE—Stuff the chicken with foie gras and truffles cut in large dice, seasoned with salt and spice and moistened with brandy. Cook it, covered, in the oven with butter, or braise it.

Set it on a dish. Surround with truffles, whole or in quarters, that have been put to cook with the chicken 8 or 10 minutes before cooking was completed. Pour over the chicken the cooking juices diluted with Madeira and rich *Brown sauce*. See SAUCE.

This chicken can be cooked in an oval earthenware casserole and served in the same dish.

Chicken pie—See PIE.

Chicken pie à la créole. PÂTÉ DE POULET À LA CRÉOLE—Make some *brioche** pastry very slightly sweetened and salted, tinted pale yellow with saffron. Prepare separately a *Chicken curry*, boiling down (reducing) the sauce as much as possible. Make a forcemeat with a blend of fat and lean pork, salted and very well peppered, and cook it for a moment in some fat. Take the brioche pastry, spread it out and give it the shape of a tart, hollow in the middle. Put a layer of forcemeat in the bottom, place on top the pieces of curried chicken, cover with another layer of forcemeat, and bring brioche pastry over the top, rounding it off as the tart is closed.

Put it to bake gently in the oven so that it rises slowly. The middle should rise more than the sides. Serve hot or cold according to taste.

Chicken à la piémontaise I. POULARDE À LA PIÉMONTAISE—Stuff the chicken with risotto mixed with 3½ ounces (100 grams) of white truffles cut in dice. Cook, covered, in the oven with butter.

Set on a dish; pour over the cooking juices diluted with white wine and mixed with thickened rich brown veal gravy.

Chicken à la piémontaise II. POULARDE À LA PIÉMONTAISE—Cook the chicken, covered, in the oven with butter. Set in an earthenware dish garnished with a cheese risotto.

Cover the chicken with 3½ ounces (100 grams) of white truffles cut in thin slices.

Pour over the cooking butter mixed with 4 tablespoons of thickened rich brown veal gravy.

Chicken pilaf. PILAF DE VOLAILLE—In restaurants this pilaf is generally prepared of chicken cooked in advance, cut in small square pieces and sautéed in butter. The chicken is then added to the rice, which is placed in a ring (border) mould, as described in the recipe for *Chicken liver pilaf* (see PILAF). A few tablespoons of concentrated brown veal gravy or *Demi-glace sauce* (see SAUCE) is poured on the pilaf.

A better result is obtained by proceeding as follows:

Prepare the rice in the usual manner. Arrange the rice in a border on a round dish. Fill the middle with chicken prepared in the following manner:

Cut the chicken into small uniform pieces. Season with salt and pepper and sauté in butter and drain.

Dilute the pan juices with ½ cup (one decilitre) of white wine. Add 1½ cups (3 decilitres) of brown veal stock and a tablespoon of tomato purée. Boil for a few moments. Strain the sauce. Replace the chicken in the sauté pan and simmer for a few moments.

Chicken à la polonaise. POULET À LA POLONAISE—Stuff a chicken with a *gratin forcemeat* mixed with a little bread that has been soaked and squeezed out, and chopped parsley (see FORCEMEAT). Truss it as for boiling. Brown quickly in very hot butter. Put it in an earthenware casserole and finish cooking in the oven.

Take off the trussing strings, squeeze over a few drops of lemon juice, then, at the last moment, sprinkle with browned butter in which some fine breadcrumbs have been fried, allowing ⅓ cup (30 grams) of breadcrumbs to 10 tablespoons (150 grams) of butter.

Chicken à la portugaise I. POULARDE À LA PORTUGAISE—Cook the chicken, covered, in the oven with butter. Set it on a dish; surround with 8 medium-sized tomatoes stuffed and topped with browned crumbs.

Pour over the cooking juices diluted with white wine and thickened with brown veal gravy flavoured with tomato and a clove of garlic.

Chicken à la portugaise II. POULARDE À LA PORTUGAISE—Cook the chicken, covered, in the oven with butter. When it is three-quarters cooked, put in the pot 8 medium-sized tomatoes, peeled, cut in large dice and lightly cooked in butter with a tablespoon of chopped onion.

Set the chicken in an earthenware dish with the cooked tomato and moisten with the diluted cooking juices. Sprinkle with chopped parsley.

Chicken princess. POULARDE PRINCESSE—Poach the chicken in a minimum quantity of white chicken stock.

Set on a round dish. Surround with a garnish composed of 8 pastry cases filled with buttered asparagus tips and truffles simmered in butter. Pour over the chicken some *Allemande sauce*. See SAUCE.

Chicken purée. PURÉE DE VOLAILLE—Purée made of chicken poached in a white stock. This purée is served by itself or used as garnish or filling.

It is sometimes called *Purée à la reine*, and used as garnish for large and small entrées made with pastry, such as *bouchées*, rissoles and vol-au-vent.

Chicken purée, finished off with cream, is also used for the soup called *Coulis* à la reine*.

Chicken quenelles. QUENELLES DE VOLAILLE—Prepared with various forcemeats and in different sizes. See FORCEMEAT.

Chicken à la régence. POULARDE À LA RÉGENCE—Insert pieces of bacon fat into the chicken and braise it in brown butter.

Set it on a plate and surround with 8 slices of calf's sweetbreads sautéed in butter, 8 truffles cooked in Madeira, 12 chicken quenelles, 8 cock's combs and 8 large prawns (shrimps) cooked in bouillon.

Pour over *Régence sauce* (see SAUCE) with some of the cooking liquor added to it.

Instead of being sliced, whole braised sweetbreads can be used.

Chicken à la reine. POULARDE À LA REINE—Stuff the chicken with the same mixture as for making *chicken croquettes**; poach in a white stock, with the minimum of liquid.

Set on a round dish; surround with small pastry cases filled with *chicken purée**.

Put on each pastry case, in the form of a lid, a thin slice of truffle. Pour over *Allemande sauce*. See SAUCE.

Chicken à la Renaissance. POULARDE À LA RENAISSANCE—Poach in a white stock with the minimum of liquid. Set the chicken on a round dish. Surround it with *Renaissance garnish* (see GARNISHES). Pour over *Suprême sauce* (see SAUCE), made with mushroom essence.

Chicken with rice à la Bourbon (Creole cooking). POULARDE AU RIZ À LA BOURBON—Put a chicken in a saucepan with some fat and lightly brown it. Add an onion that has been finely chopped and cooked without allowing it to colour, 2 whole carrots, a bunch of herbs, salt, pepper and a spoonful of tomato purée. Add enough stock to ensure that the chicken will be tender. Cook on a very gentle heat for about 1½ hours and boil down the liquid.

The evening before or very early in the morning you will have made a light stock, using the giblets, scraps of meat, and a strip of the skin of fresh pork (or bacon rinds). You will use this stock to finish cooking your rice, which will have been first scalded and drained. The rice must be soft and supple. When it is cooked put it on a dish or shape it with a mould into the form of a crown.

Cut up your chicken and arrange the pieces in the middle. Strain the juice, and pour over the dish. Decorate your turban of rice with rounds of carrot.

Chicken and rice with suprême sauce. POULARDE AU RIZ SAUCE SUPRÊME—Cook a chicken trussed as for boiling and covered with a bard of bacon fat in a white stock. When half-cooked, drain the chicken. Put the stock through a fine strainer and replace the chicken in the pot. Add ½ pound (250 grams) of rice, blanched and drained. Add the stock to a point two fingers above the rice. Add 2 tablespoons of butter. Finish cooking all together, over a gentle heat.

Using part of the cooking liquor prepare a *Suprême sauce*. See SAUCE.

Set the chicken on a large round dish. Flank in on each side with rice.

Serve with *Suprême sauce* and a sauceboat of the chicken broth, handed separately.

Roast chicken. POULARDE RÔTIE—Truss the chicken and season inside and outside. Cover the breast with a thin slice of bacon fat.

Cook in the oven, allowing 45 minutes for a bird of 3 pounds (1 kilo 500 grams) and 50 to 55 minutes on the spit for a bird of the same weight.

Set the chicken on a long dish. Serve with the cooking juices and watercress.

Roast chicken à l'anglaise. POULARDE RÔTIE À L'ANGLAISE—Roast the chicken in the usual way. Put on a long dish, surround with slices of bacon or grilled sausages and serve with *Bread sauce*. See SAUCE.

Note. Roast chicken à l'anglaise may also be prepared in the same way as *Roast turkey à l'anglaise* (see TURKEY), that is to say, stuffed with a sage stuffing.

Chicken with rock (coarse) salt. POULARDE AU GROS SEL—Poach the chicken in white stock.

Set it on a dish and serve it with its cooking liquor strained separately, and some rock (coarse) salt.

This chicken can be served surrounded with carrots and onions cooked in the chicken broth.

Chicken Rosière. POULARDE ROSIÈRE—Stuff a chicken which has been drawn and carefully cleaned, with a pound of *chicken forcemeat with cream* (see FORCEMEAT). Truss it, laying the feet flat against the sides, rub it all over with lemon juice and wrap it entirely in bards of bacon fat. Line the bottom of an oval-shaped casserole with fresh bacon rinds, cut in strips, rounds of carrot and onion and a bunch of herbs. Place the chicken on top and add white veal stock in sufficient quantity to cover the chicken. Cook (with the lid on), ensuring that the simmering is slow and steady, for about 50 minutes.

In addition, blanch, trim and press under a weight for half an hour 3 nice calfs' sweetbreads, having removed all membranes. About 35 minutes before serving, cut the sweetbreads in slices a bare $\frac{1}{3}$ inch thick, arrange them in a pan and just cover with white veal stock. Add a piece of butter and cook, keeping the liquid just simmering.

Prepare $1\frac{1}{2}$ pints ($\frac{3}{4}$ of a litre) of *Fresh mushroom purée* (see MUSHROOMS). To this purée add 1 cup (2 decilitres) of fresh cream to bring it to the consistency of an ordinary sauce, and mix into it 1 cup (150 grams) of mushrooms cooked and chopped.

Drain the chicken, remove the barding and trussing strings; set it on a round dish and surround with the slices of sweetbread. Coat the chicken and the garnish with some of the sauce and serve the rest separately.

Chicken à la Rossini. POULARDE À LA ROSSINI—Cook the chicken, covered, in the oven in butter. Set on a dish and surround it with 8 slices of *foie gras* tossed in butter.

Place on each slice of *foie gras* 2 slices of truffle heated in butter.

Pour over the chicken its cooking juices diluted with Madeira and truffle-flavoured rich *Brown sauce* (see SAUCE). The slices of *foie gras* may be placed in pastry cases or on round slices of bread fried in butter.

Chicken salad. SALADE DE VOLAILLE—Prepare using sliced cooked chicken, set on a foundation of shredded lettuce, season with *Vinaigrette sauce* (see SAUCE) and garnish with lettuce hearts and quartered hard-boiled eggs.

Chicken sauté. POULETS SAUTÉS—Small tender fowls, such as pullets weighing from $1\frac{3}{4}$ to $3\frac{1}{2}$ pounds (900 to 1,800 grams), are better for this dish than fat fowls and capons, which are seldom prepared in this way.

Only exceptionally, too, are spring chickens cooked in this manner.

The cooking of chicken sauté is done in butter, in oil or in fat. It must be done rapidly. Once cooked and crisp, the pieces *must not be allowed to boil in their juices.*

Nevertheless, one way to cook chicken sauté (known as the 'white' style) is when the pieces are slowly simmered in butter without having been previously fried. This method of preparation applies to chickens finished in cream or *Velouté sauce*. See SAUCE.

Cutting the chickens. Divide up the chicken into joints. Cut away the leg at its thickest part, having cut through the joint.

Remove the lungs which will be found in the carcase.

When the feet must be cooked with the other pieces, it is a good idea to heat them to make skinning easier.

Spring chickens are simply divided in two. These halves are lightly flattened.

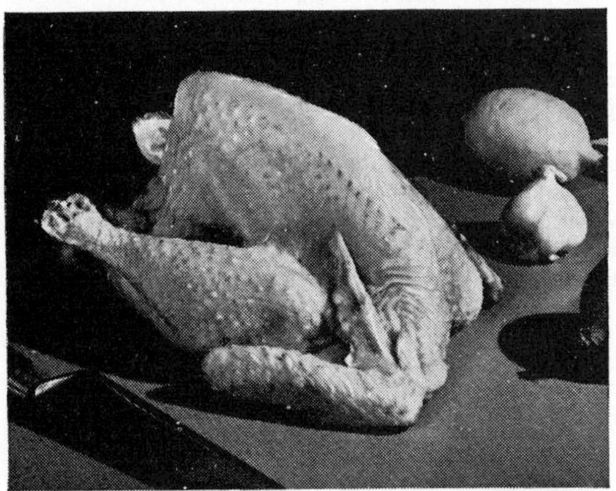

How to joint a chicken (*Mac Fisheries*)

Method of cooking. Brown. A BRUN—Season the pieces of chicken with salt and pepper. Arrange them, as flat as possible, fleshy parts downwards, in a sauté dish in which 2 to 3 tablespoons (30 to 40 grams) of butter have previously been heated (oil or fat may be used).

Brown the pieces of chicken well on both sides.

Cover and cook over a low heat, or in a 375°F. oven.

After 6 or 8 minutes, take out the wings and the pieces of breast. Keep them warm (these parts being the most delicate are cooked the soonest).

Let the legs and carcases cook for 8 to 12 minutes, according to size.

Take out the pieces of chicken, remove the cooking fat (all or part according to the recipe); dilute the juices in the sauté dish with the liquid indicated: white or other wine, stock, meat juices, etc.

Boil down (reduce) the resultant liquor by half and finish by adding the prescribed sauce.

Put back the pieces of chicken (wings and breasts above) in the sauté dish and keep covered in a warm place, *but avoid boiling.*

Set on a dish and garnish according to the recipe.

Chicken sauté garnished with mushrooms

Brown, 'à la ménagère'. A BRUN À LA MÉNAGÈRE—Brown and cook the pieces of chicken as above.

Take them out of the sauté dish; put in the cooking butter a tablespoon of flour. Let it colour lightly.

Dilute with wine or other liquid, following the recipe. Boil down; add 1 cup (2 decilitres) of white stock, consommé or water.

Cook for 12 to 15 minutes, stirring with a wooden spoon. Strain the sauce.

Put back the pieces of chicken in the sauté dish. Pour the sauce over and keep warm in a covered pot *but avoid boiling.*

White. A BLANC—Arrange the pieces of chicken, seasoned, in a sauté dish where 2 to 3 tablespoons (30 to 50 grams) of butter have been heated.

Make the pieces of chicken firm by sautéing lightly on all sides *without letting them brown.*

Cover the sauté dish; cook at moderate heat (taking out the wings and breasts first as described above).

Take out the other pieces; pour off the butter; dilute the pan juices with white stock, mushroom juice or cream and add the prescribed sauce.

Serve and garnish according to the particular recipe.

Note. Over and above the very numerous formulae which follow for chicken sauté, further variations may be made by serving with different garnishes, such as: sautéed aubergines (egg-plant), glazed carrots, thin chips of celeriac, brussels sprouts in butter, cucumbers, baby marrows (zucchinis), gombos (gumbos), sweet corn in butter or cream, small glazed onions, noodles, macaroni, rice, etc.

In the recipes which follow it is indicated that the diluted pan juices of the chicken sautées should have sauces, such as reduced and thickened brown veal stock or rich *Brown sauce* (*demi-glace*) (see SAUCE), completed, if necessary, with tomato sauce, added to them.

In home cooking these ingredients are not always available. The cooking method described above as *à la ménagère*, i.e. housewife style, should then be applied.

When the sauté preparations are diluted with wine and white stock or broth, the sauce may be thickened by the addition of a little butter and flour worked together. The same applies to 'white' chicken sautés.

Chicken sauté Alexandra. POULET SAUTÉ ALEXANDRA—Sauté the chicken in butter in the 'white' style.

Dilute the cooking juices with ½ cup (1 decilitre) of white stock; reduce. Stir in ½ cup (1 decilitre) of chicken *Velouté sauce* (see SAUCE), add two tablespoons of *Soubise purée* (see PURÉE). Finish with two tablespoons of cream and 2½ tablespoons (40 grams) of butter. Strain the sauce.

Chicken sauté à l'algérienne. POULET SAUTÉ À L'ALGÉRIENNE—Sauté the chicken in oil, browning it; when half-cooked add a tablespoon of chopped onion.

Take out the chicken; put in the sauté dish a crushed garlic clove and two tomatoes, peeled, drained and crushed; cook 8 minutes, stirring.

Put back the chicken in the sauté dish; let it simmer 8 to 10 minutes without boiling.

Set the chicken on a dish, garnish with 2 aubergines (egg-plant) cut in dice; sauté in oil. Pour over the sauce, sprinkle with chopped parsley.

Chicken sauté ambassadrice. POULET SAUTÉ AMBASSADRICE—Sauté the chicken in butter, browning it.

Dilute the juices in the pan with ¼ cup (½ decilitre) of Madeira; boil down the liquid; pour in ¾ cup (1½ decilitres) of thickened rich brown veal gravy. Cook at boiling point for a few moments.

Set the chicken on a dish, garnish with 8 cock's combs and 8 cock's kidneys cooked in light stock, 4 chicken livers sautéed in butter, 8 mushrooms which have been sautéed with the chicken and 8 slices of truffle; coat with the sauce.

Chicken sauté à l'ancienne mode. POULET SAUTÉ À L'ANCIENNE MODE—Sauté the chicken in butter, without browning it.

Dilute the juices in the pan with ½ cup (a decilitre) of white stock or mushroom stock, boil down to two-thirds of its volume, stir in ¾ cup (1½ decilitres) of chicken *Velouté sauce* (see SAUCE), cook for 5 minutes at boiling point, incorporate 3 tablespoons (50 grams) of butter and strain. Add 2 tablespoons of chopped truffles and ½ cup (a decilitre) of port.

Set the chicken on a dish; coat with the sauce and garnish with rosettes of puff pastry.

Chicken sauté Annette. POULET SAUTÉ ANNETTE—Sauté the chicken in butter, browning it.

Dilute the juices in the pan with some white wine; add a chopped shallot; boil down the liquid, then add ¾ cup (1½ decilitres) of thickened rich brown gravy. Cook for a few moments at boiling point. Finish with a spoonful of chopped parsley, chervil and tarragon, a squeeze of lemon juice and a tablespoon of fresh butter.

Set the chicken in a crust of *Annette potatoes* (see POTATOES). Coat with the sauce.

Note. The crust of Annette potatoes is made with straw potatoes cooked in butter in a sauté pan like Anna potatoes, but with a sort of iron pie dish put in the middle of the potatoes, so that they form a hollow cake.

Chicken sauté Archduke. POULET SAUTÉ ARCHIDUC—Sauté the chicken in butter but without colouring it. When it is half-cooked add 2 tablespoons of chopped onion lightly cooked in butter and a good pinch of paprika.

Dilute the cooking juices with ½ cup (a decilitre) of white wine, boil down, pour in ¾ cup (1½ decilitres) of cream and cook at boiling point for a few moments. Incorporate in the sauce 3 tablespoons (50 grams) of butter and a squeeze of lemon juice and strain.

Set the chicken on a dish, garnish with cucumbers cut in chunks and simmered in butter. Coat with the sauce.

Chicken sauté Archduke Salvator. POULET SAUTÉ ARCHIDUC SALVATOR—Prepare the chicken as for *Chicken sauté Archduke.*

Set it on a *Potato galette* (see GALETTE) garnish with cucumbers simmered in butter, sautéed mushrooms and slices of truffle.

Note. There are numerous ways of cooking *Chicken Archduke.* Only the basic recipe is more or less invariable. The chicken must be sautéed without allowing it to colour, onion and cream must be added, but the method of diluting the juices can be varied by using brandy or Madeira. The sauce can be finished off with whisky or port; the garnish can be of cucumbers, mushrooms, quartered artichokes or truffles.

Chicken sauté with artichokes. POULET SAUTÉ AUX ARTICHAUTS—Sauté the chicken in butter, browning it. When it is half-cooked, add 12 quarters of artichokes, well blanched. Finish cooking all together.

Take out the chicken and artichokes. Dilute the juices in the pan with ½ cup (a decilitre) of white wine, boil down, pour in ¾ cup (1½ decilitres) of thickened rich brown veal gravy.

Set the chicken on a dish, and garnish with the quarters of artichokes; coat with the sauce. Sprinkle with chopped parsley.

The chicken may also be garnished with artichoke bottoms, cooked in a flour-and-water *court-bouillon**, sliced and sautéed with the chicken.

Chicken sauté with basil. POULET SAUTÉ AU BASILIC—Sauté the chicken in butter, browning it.

Dilute the juices in the pan with 1 cup (2 decilitres) of white wine and add a tablespoon of chopped basil.

Boil down the liquid by half. Incorporate 3 tablespoons (50 grams) of butter; mix together.

Set the chicken on a dish and coat with its juice.

Chicken sauté à la biarrotte. POULET SAUTÉ À LA BIARROTTE—Sauté the chicken in oil, browning it.

Dilute the juices in the pan with white wine, boil down and pour in ½ cup (a decilitre) of *Tomato sauce* (see SAUCE); add a crushed clove of garlic.

Set the chicken on a dish; garnish with ¼ pound (125 grams) of cèpes sautéed in oil, 1 cup (125 grams) of potatoes, dice and sautéed in oil, an aubergine (egg-plant) peeled, cut in dice and sautéed in oil and a medium-sized onion cut in rings and fried, all disposed in separate groups round the chicken.

Chicken sauté à la bohémienne. POULET SAUTÉ À LA BOHÉMIENNE—Sauté the chicken (seasoned with paprika) in oil, browning it. When it is half-cooked, add 4 sweet pimentos peeled and cut in large strips, 2 tomatoes peeled and cut in thick slices, a medium-sized onion cut in small dice and blanched, a crushed clove of garlic and a teaspoon of chopped fennel.

Dilute the juices in the pan with white wine; add ¼ cup (half a decilitre) of thickened rich brown veal gravy and finish with a squeeze of lemon juice.

Set the chicken on a dish; coat with the sauce and serve *rice à l'Indienne** at the same time.

Chicken sauté Boivin. POULET SAUTÉ BOIVIN—Cook lightly in butter, browning a little on both sides, a chicken cut up as for fricassée. When the pieces are lightly browned put in the pan 24 small onions that have been tossed in butter, 12 quarters of small artichokes, blanched, and 24 small new potatoes all the same size and shape. Season all the garnishes set round the chicken. Cook, covered, on a gentle heat.

Drain the pieces of chicken. Set them on a round dish and dispose the garnish of little onions, artichokes and potatoes around them. Pour over the chicken the cooking juices diluted with *pot-au-feu* broth, with the addition of 2 tablespoons of dissolved meat glaze, sharpened with a squeeze of lemon juice, and with butter added. (*Mont-Bry's recipe.*)

Chicken sauté à la bordelaise

Chicken sauté à la bordelaise. POULET SAUTÉ À LA BORDELAISE—Sauté the chicken in a mixture of oil and butter.

Finish as in the recipe for *Chicken sauté with white wine.* Add to the sauce a tablespoon of *Tomato sauce* (see SAUCE) and a crushed clove of garlic.

Set the chicken on a dish and garnish it with 1 cup (125 grams) of potatoes, sliced and sautéed in butter, 2 medium-sized artichokes cut in quarters, blanched and cooked in butter, several sprigs (25 grams) of fried parsley, and 2 medium-sized onions cut in rounds and fried. Coat with the sauce.

Chicken sauté à la bourguignonne. POULET SAUTÉ À LA BOURGUIGNONNE—Sauté the chicken in butter, browning it. When it is three-quarters cooked add 12 small glazed onions, 12 mushrooms lightly cooked in butter and 4 slices (50 grams) of lean bacon cut in large dice, blanched and lightly fried.

Take out the chicken and its accompaniments. Dilute the juices in the pan with 1 cup (2 decilitres) of red wine, add a crushed clove of garlic, boil down to two-thirds, add ¾ cup (1½ decilitres) of rich *Brown sauce* (see SAUCE), cook at boiling point for a few moments and strain.

Set the chicken on a dish; surround it with the garnish, coat with the sauce.

Note. Some heart-shaped croûtons of bread fried in butter may be added.

Chicken sauté à la bourguignonne or matelote. POULET SAUTÉ À LA BOURGUIGNONNE, EN MATELOTE—Fry in butter 4 slices (50 grams) of lean bacon cut in big dice and blanched. Add 12 small onions, blanched; cook till golden and add 12 small raw mushrooms.

Drain this mixture and brown quickly in the same fat a chicken cut into pieces in the ordinary way. When the chicken is half-cooked, put the garnish back in the pan, cover and cook for 15 minutes.

Take out chicken and garnish. Dilute the juices in the pan with 1 cup (2 decilitres) of red wine, boil down to half and thicken with a tablespoon of butter worked together with flour. Strain.

Set the chicken on a dish, surrounded with its garnish and pour the sauce over it.

Chicken sauté in butter or à la minute. POULET SAUTÉ AU BEURRE (À LA MINUTE)—Sauté the chicken in butter, browning it.

Set it on a dish, squeeze some lemon juice over the top, pour over the cooking butter, very hot, and sprinkle with chopped parsley.

Chicken sauté with cèpes I. POULET SAUTÉ AUX CÈPES—Sauté the chicken in oil or butter and oil mixed. When it is three-quarters cooked, add $\frac{5}{8}$ pound (300 grams) of firm white cèpes, cut up into rather thick slices and sauteéd in oil. Finally sprinkle over a chopped onion.

Drain the chicken and cèpes. Dilute the juices in the pan with $\frac{1}{2}$ cup (a decilitre) of white wine, reduce and finish with 3 tablespoons (500 grams) of butter.

Set the chicken on a dish, garnish with the cèpes, coat with the juice and sprinkle with chopped parsley.

Note. Preserved cèpes may also be used. If liked, a crushed clove of garlic may be added.

Chicken sauté with cèpes II. POULET SAUTÉ AUX CÈPES—Prepare the chicken as for *Chicken sauté with white wine.* Set it on a dish, garnish with *Cèpes à la bordelaise* (see MUSHROOMS). Coat with the sauce. Sprinkle with chopped parsley.

Chicken sauté chasseur (*Batchelors*)

Chicken sauté chasseur. POULET SAUTÉ CHASSEUR—Sauté the chicken in a mixture of oil and butter. When it is three-quarters cooked, add $\frac{1}{4}$ pound (125 grams) of raw, sliced mushrooms.

Dilute the juices in the pan with $\frac{1}{2}$ cup (a decilitre) of white wine. Add a chopped shallot, reduce, add $\frac{3}{4}$ cup ($1\frac{1}{2}$ decilitres) of thickened rich veal gravy and $\frac{1}{4}$ cup ($\frac{1}{2}$ decilitre) of *Tomato sauce* (see SAUCE). Cook at boiling point for a few moments, add a tablespoon of brandy and a tablespoon of parsley, chervil and tarragon finely chopped.

Set the chicken on a dish, coat with the sauce and sprinkle with chopped parsley.

Chicken sauté with chayotes. POULET SAUTÉ AUX CHAYOTTES—Proceed as for *Chicken sauté with artichokes.*

Set the chicken on a dish; garnish with quarters of chayotes or custard marrows stewed in butter, and coat with the sauce. See CUSTARD MARROW.

Chicken sauté with cream. POULET SAUTÉ À LA CRÈME—Sauté the chicken in butter, but without browning it. Dilute the juices in the pan with $1\frac{1}{4}$ cups ($2\frac{1}{2}$ decilitres) of cream. Boil down to half. Add, at the last moment, $2\frac{1}{2}$ tablespoons (40 grams) of butter.

Set the chicken on a dish and coat it with the sauce. The diluted cooking juices may be thickened with one or two spoonfuls of chicken *Velouté sauce*. See SAUCE.

Curried chicken sauté. POULET SAUTÉ AU CURRIE—See *Chicken sauté à l'indienne.*

Chicken sauté Demidoff. POULET SAUTÉ DEMIDOFF—Sauté the chicken in butter, browning it. When it is half-cooked add $\frac{3}{4}$ cup ($1\frac{1}{2}$ decilitres) of purée of cooked chopped vegetables *à la Demidoff.*

At the end of cooking add 2 medium-sized truffles cut in slices and a tablespoon of curly parsley leaves, blanched.

Take out the chicken and its garnish, dilute the juices in the pan with $\frac{1}{4}$ cup ($\frac{1}{2}$ decilitre) of Madeira; boil down and add $\frac{3}{4}$ cup ($1\frac{1}{2}$ decilitres) of rich *Brown sauce.* See SAUCE.

Set the chicken on a dish, cover with the vegetables, coat with the sauce and garnish with a dozen round slices of onion dipped in batter and fried.

Chicken sauté Duroc. POULET SAUTÉ DUROC—Proceed as for *Chicken sauté chasseur.*

Garnish the chicken with 8 very small tomatoes peeled and simmered in butter and with $1\frac{1}{2}$ cups (150 grams) of small new potatoes cooked in butter. Coat with the sauce, sprinkle with chopped parsley.

Chicken sauté à l'écossaise. POULET SAUTÉ À L'ÉCOSSAISE—Sauté the chicken in butter, browning it.

Dilute the juices in the pan with $\frac{1}{4}$ cup ($\frac{1}{2}$ decilitre) of sherry, reduce and add $\frac{3}{4}$ cup ($1\frac{1}{2}$ decilitres) of thickened rich brown veal gravy. Cook at boiling point for a few moments; finish with $2\frac{1}{2}$ tablespoons (40 grams) of butter.

Set the chicken on a dish, garnish with buttered French (string) beans and tongue and truffles, cut in thick strips and heated in sherry. Coat with the sauce.

Chicken sauté fermière (or à la paysanne). POULET SAUTÉ FERMIÈRE (DIT AUSSI À LA PAYSANNE)—Sauté the chicken as above. Add $\frac{3}{4}$ cup ($1\frac{1}{2}$ decilitres) of *Vegetable fondue* (see FONDUE). Finish cooking together.

Set the chicken and vegetables in an earthenware dish or casserole, add a tablespoon of lean ham cut in dice. Simmer covered in the oven.

At the last moment sprinkle over the cooking juices diluted with $\frac{3}{4}$ cup ($1\frac{1}{2}$ decilitres) of thickened rich veal gravy.

Chicken sauté aux fines herbes I. POULET SAUTÉ AUX FINES HERBES—Sauté the chicken in butter, browning it.

Dilute the juices in the pan with $\frac{3}{4}$ cup ($1\frac{1}{2}$ decilitres) of white wine, add a chopped shallot, boil down, and add $\frac{3}{4}$ cup ($1\frac{1}{2}$ decilitres) of thickened rich brown veal gravy. Cook at boiling point for a few moments. Finish with half a tablespoon of parsley, chervil and tarragon, finely chopped, a squeeze of lemon juice and a tablespoon of fresh butter.

Set the chicken on a dish and pour the sauce over it.

Chicken sauté aux fines herbes II. POULET SAUTÉ AUX FINES HERBES—Sauté the chicken as above. Set it on a dish and sprinkle over its cooking juices diluted with ¼ cup (½ decilitre) of white wine, mixed with a chopped shallot and half a tablespoonful of parsley, chervil and tarragon finely chopped. Draw away from the fire and add 3 tablespoons (50 grams) of butter and a squeeze of lemon.

Chicken sauté à la florentine. POULET SAUTÉ À LA FLORENTINE—Proceed as for *Chicken sauté with Madeira* (see *Chicken sauté with various wines*). Set the chicken in a border of *risotto* (see RICE) mixed with 2 tablespoons of chopped truffles. Coat with the sauce well cooked down.

Chicken sauté à la forestière. POULET SAUTÉ À LA FORESTIÈRE—Proceed as for *Chicken sauté with mushrooms*.

Replace the latter by 1 cup (150 grams) of morels sautéed in butter, 1½ cups (150 grams) of diced potatoes sautéed in butter and ¾ cup (100 grams) of small, blanched cardoons.

Chicken sauté with hop shoots. POULET SAUTÉ AUX JETS DE HOUBLON—Sauté the chicken in butter, browning it.

Dilute the juices in the pan with white wine, boil down, then add thickened rich brown veal gravy.

Set the chicken on a dish, garnish with a generous ½ pound (300 grams) of hop shoots in cream. Coat with the sauce.

Chicken sauté with hop shoots in cream I. POULET SAUTÉ AUX JETS DE HOUBLON À LA CRÈME—Prepare the chicken as for *Chicken sauté with cream*.

Set it on a dish and garnish with hop shoots in cream. Coat with the sauce.

Chicken sauté with hop shoots in cream II. POULET SAUTÉ AUX JETS DE HOUBLON À LA CRÈME—When the chicken is cooked, take it out of the sauté pan. Put in some butter and a tablespoon of flour. Cook without colouring. Stir in ½ cup (1 decilitre) of white stock or consommé. Boil down (reduce) to one-third. Finish with 3 tablespoons of cream.

Set on a dish and garnish as above.

Chicken sauté à l'indienne I. POULET SAUTÉ À L'INDIENNE—Sauté the chicken in butter or oil but without browning it. Put in the pan at the same time a large onion, finely chopped, and a tablespoon of curry powder.

As soon as the pieces of chicken are firm, sprinkle over a tablespoon of flour; cook for a moment, stirring; pour in 1 cup (2 decilitres) of white stock. Add a *bouquet garni** and cook, covered, like a fricassée.

Set the chicken in a timbale, coat with the sauce which has been somewhat cooked down, either strained or not, and with a squeeze of lemon juice added.

Serve at the same time *Rice à l'indienne*.*

Note. The liquid used may be one-half coconut or almond milk and one-half white stock.

The tablespoon of flour may be left out and the sauce completed with some chicken *Velouté sauce* (see SAUCE).

Chicken sauté à l'indienne II. POULET SAUTÉ À L'INDIENNE—Cut up the chicken into 15 or 20 small pieces, that is to say, divide each of the joints into two or three pieces according to size.

Put the chicken into a saucepan in which there have previously been heated some butter (with oil or with lard), a large chopped onion, 3½ ounces (100 grams) of ham, cut in very small dice, and a large grated eating apple.

Add a sprig of thyme, a bay leaf, a pinch of cardamom, a pinch of cinnamon, a pinch of mace (the outer case of the nutmeg) and 2 crushed cloves of garlic.

Sprinkle over 4 teaspoons of curry powder. Mix.

Add 2 tomatoes peeled and seeded; pour in 2 cups (4 decilitres) of coconut milk and cook for 40 minutes.

At the last moment add a cup (decilitre) of double cream and the juice of a lemon.

Set in a bowl and serve with *Rice à l'indienne**.

Note. Methods of preparing various Indian ragoûts (curries of mutton, lamb, chicken, fish, etc.) are numerous. Each Indian cook has his own, and if the basic principle, whose characteristic is the curry seasoning, does not vary, the recipes differ greatly from each other in requiring different ingredients. We have often seen curries finished off with a great variety of accompaniments which formed a sort of garnish to the main dish. Among these are—in addition to the traditional Indian-style rice—yellow rice (rice cooked with saffron), boiled cabbage mixed with mashed potatoes and sprinkled with curry, Indian pancakes, extra-thin flat cakes made of fine wheaten flour, etc.

Very often in France *Chicken sauté à l'indienne* is prepared by adding a quantity of curry powder to a chicken sauté, cooked without browning, its sauce bound with a chicken *Velouté sauce*. See SAUCE.

Chicken sauté à l'italienne I. POULET SAUTÉ À L'ITALIENNE—Sauté the chicken in a mixture of oil and butter, browning it.

Dilute the juices in the pan with ¾ cup (1½ decilitres) of *Italian sauce*. See SAUCE.

Set the chicken on a dish and coat it with the sauce. Sprinkle with chopped parsley.

Chicken sauté à l'italienne II. POULET SAUTÉ À L'ITALIENNE—Sauté the chicken in oil and butter. When it is half-cooked add a spoonful of chopped onion half-cooked in butter, then, lastly, a chopped shallot and 4 good tablespoons of mushrooms either chopped or cut into little dice.

Dilute the juices in the pan with ½ cup (one decilitre) of white wine, boil down, add ½ cup (1 decilitre) of rich, thickened brown veal stock and ¼ cup (½ decilitre) of *Tomato sauce* (see SAUCE). Cook for a few moments at boiling point, then add a tablespoon of lean ham chopped finely and a spoonful of parsley, chervil and tarragon, chopped together.

Set the chicken on a dish; coat it with the sauce.

Chicken sauté à la japonaise (Japanese style). POULET SAUTÉ À LA JAPONAISE—Sauté the chicken in butter, browning it. When it is half-cooked add a generous ½ pound (300 grams) of Japanese artichokes, lightly blanched and drained. Finish cooking together.

Finish off as for *Chicken sauté with artichokes*.

Chicken sauté à la livonienne. POULET SAUTÉ À LA LIVONIENNE—Sauté the chicken in butter, without browning. When it is three-quarters cooked add ½ pound (250 grams) of morels sautéed in butter.

Dilute the juices in the pan and finish as for *Chicken sauté with cream*.

Set the chicken on a dish, and garnish with the morels. Coat with the sauce, to which a tablespoon of chives, chopped and blanched, has been added.

Scatter on top of the morels 2 tablespoons of bread-crumbs fried in butter.

Chicken sauté à la lyonnaise. POULET SAUTÉ À LA LYONNAISE—Sauté the chicken in butter, browning it. When it is half-cooked, add 2 large onions finely chopped and sautéed in butter. Finish cooking together.

Dilute the juices in the pan with 2 tablespoons of vinegar. Boil down, then mix in 1 cup (2 decilitres) of thickened rich brown veal gravy or rich *Brown sauce* (see SAUCE). Set the chicken on a dish, coat with the sauce and sprinkle with chopped parsley.

Chicken saute à la marengo (*Robert Carrier*)

Chicken sauté à la Marengo. POULET SAUTÉ À LA MARENGO—Sauté the chicken in oil, browning it. Dilute the juices in the pan with ½ cup (a decilitre) of white wine, cook down, pour in ¾ cup (1½ decilitres) of thickened rich brown veal gravy. Add a crushed clove of garlic, cook at boiling point for a few minutes; strain.

Set the chicken on a dish; garnish with 8 mushrooms (sautéed with the chicken) 4 very small fried eggs (or just the yolks), 4 large crayfish trussed and cooked in *court-bouillon* and 4 heart-shaped croûtons fried in butter.

Place on the chicken 8 slices of truffles sautéed in butter, coat with the sauce and sprinkle with chopped parsley.

Chicken sauté en matelote—See *Chicken sauté à la bourguignonne*.

Chicken sauté à la meunière. POULET SAUTÉ À LA MEUNIÈRE—Proceed as for *Chicken sauté in butter*, adding chopped parsley, lemon juice and 3 or 4 tablespoons of rich veal gravy or rich *Brown sauce*. See SAUCE.

Chicken sauté Mireille. POULET SAUTÉ MIREILLE—Sauté the chicken in butter, browning it. Dilute the juices in the pan with ½ cup (a decilitre) of white wine; cook down, then stir in ¾ cup (1½ decilitres) of thickened rich brown veal gravy and ¼ cup (½ decilitre) of *Tomato sauce* (see SAUCE). Cook at boiling point for a few moments.

Set the chicken on a dish; garnish with 8 endive hearts (gourilos) in cream and 8 very small tomatoes peeled, drained and simmered in butter. Coat the chicken with the sauce.

Chicken sauté Monselet. POULET SAUTÉ MONSELET—Sauté the chicken in butter, browning it; when it is three-quarters cooked add 2 artichoke bottoms, blanched and cut in slices, and, when the cooking is finished, two medium-sized truffles cut in slices.

Take out the chicken and its accompaniments, dilute the juices in the pan with ½ cup (1 decilitre) of white wine, cook down, then add ¾ cup (1½ decilitres) of thickened rich brown veal gravy, and cook at boiling point for a few moments.

Set the chicken on a dish, garnish with the artichokes and truffles; coat with the sauce.

Chicken sauté with morels and other mushrooms. POULET SAUTÉ AUX MORILLES—Proceed as for *Chicken sauté with mushrooms* replacing the latter with a generous ½ pound (300 grams) of morels (or an equivalent quantity of other mushrooms).

Chicken sauté with mushrooms. POULET SAUTÉ AUX CHAMPIGNONS—Sauté the chicken in butter, browning it; when it is three-quarters cooked add ½ pound (250 grams) of sliced mushrooms.

Dilute the juices in the pan with ¼ cup (½ decilitre) of Madeira, boil down, add ¾ cup (1½ decilitres) of thickened rich brown veal gravy. Cook for a few moments at boiling point. Set the chicken on a dish; garnish with the mushrooms and coat with the sauce.

Note. It is useless, and indeed a bad thing, to cook the mushrooms in a flour-and-water stock before adding them to the chicken. Preserved mushrooms may be used, cooked lightly in the same way.

Chicken sauté Niçoise. POULET SAUTÉ NIÇOISE—Sauté the chicken in oil, browning it. Dilute the juices in the pan with ½ cup (1 decilitre) of white wine, add a crushed clove of garlic, cook down and add ¾ cup (1½ decilitres) of *Tomato sauce*. See SAUCE.

Set the chicken on a dish, garnish with 8 quarters of artichokes stewed in butter, 4 baby marrows (zucchini), braised, 1 cup (125 grams) of small new potatoes cooked in butter and 12 stoned black olives; coat with the sauce and sprinkle with chopped tarragon.

Chicken sauté with oysters I. POULET SAUTÉ AUX HUÎTRES—Sauté the chicken in butter, without colouring it.

Dilute the juices in the pan with ½ cup (a decilitre) of white wine and the liquor from 12 oysters previously poached in their own juice. Boil down, add ½ cup (1 decilitre) of chicken *Velouté sauce* (see SAUCE). Cook at boiling point for a few moments. Add 2½ tablespoons (40 grams) of butter and a squeeze of lemon juice; strain.

Set the chicken on a dish, garnish with the drained oysters and coat with the sauce.

Chicken sauté with oysters II. POULET SAUTÉ AUX HUÎTRES—Sauté the chicken in butter, without browning it; when it is half-cooked add a tablespoon of blanched chopped onion.

Take out the chicken; sprinkle with a tablespoon of flour and add the liquor of the poached oysters and ½ cup (1 decilitre) of mushroom or white stock. Cook for 10 minutes. Add 2 tablespoons of cream and 2 tablespoons (30 grams) of butter. Strain. Finish as above.

Chicken sauté panetière. POULET SAUTÉ PANETIÈRE—Prepare as for *Chicken sauté with cream.*

Set on a round of bread, trimmed, dried in the oven and spread with a layer of purée of *foie gras.*

Garnish with morels (or other mushrooms) in cream. Coat with the sauce.

Chicken sauté with paprika. POULET SAUTÉ AU PAPRIKA—Season the chicken with paprika. Sauté it in butter, without colouring it and finish off as for *Chicken sauté with cream.*

Chicken sauté parisienne. POULET SAUTÉ PARISIENNE—Proceed as for *Chicken sauté in white wine.* Set the chicken on a thick layer of *Duchess potato mixture* (see POTATOES) brushed with egg and browned in the oven. Garnish with buttered asparagus tips. Coat with the sauce.

Chicken sauté Parmentier. POULET SAUTÉ PARMENTIER—Sauté the chicken in butter. When it is two-thirds cooked, add 4 potatoes cut in large dice, blanched and half-cooked in butter.

Finish off as for *Chicken sauté with white wine.*

Set the chicken on a dish, garnish with the potatoes, coat with its sauce and sprinkle with chopped parsley.

Chicken sauté à la périgord. POULET SAUTÉ À LA PÉRIGORD—See *Chicken sauté with truffles.*

The truffles, instead of being cut in thick slices, may be cut to look like small olives.

Chicken sauté petit-duc. POULET SAUTÉ PETIT-DUC—Sauté the chicken in butter, browning it. Dilute the juices in the pan with ¼ cup (½ decilitre) of Madeira, cook down, add ¾ cup (1½ decilitres) of rich *Brown sauce* (see SAUCE). Cook at boiling point for a few moments.

Set the chicken on a dish, garnish with morels and truffle slices sautéed in butter. Coat with the sauce.

Chicken sauté à la piémontaise. POULET SAUTÉ À LA PIÉMONTAISE—Proceed as for *Chicken sauté with white wine.*

Set in a border of risotto mixed with white truffles cut in little dice. Put on the chicken round slices of white truffle lightly heated in butter and pour the sauce over it.

Chicken sauté à la portugaise. POULET SAUTÉ À LA PORTUGAISE—Sauté the chicken in oil. When it is two-thirds cooked, add a tablespoon of chopped onion.

Take out the chicken; put in the sauté pan 4 tomatoes peeled, drained and pressed and a clove of crushed garlic. Season, pour in ½ cup (a decilitre) of white wine, boil down the liquid by half. Add 3 tablespoons of thickened rich brown veal gravy.

Set the chicken on a dish; coat with the sauce; sprinkle with chopped parsley.

Chicken sauté à la provençale. POULET SAUTÉ À LA PROVENÇALE—Proceed as for *Chicken sauté à la portugaise.*

Set the chicken on a dish, garnish with 20 stoned and blanched olives and 8 small mushrooms sautéed in oil. Coat with the sauce and decorate with 8 anchovy fillets. Sprinkle with chopped parsley.

Chicken sauté Rivoli. POULET SAUTÉ RIVOLI—Sauté the chicken in butter, browning it. When it is three-quarters cooked add 4 potatoes sliced and sauté in butter. When cooking is complete add 2 chopped-up truffles of medium size.

Take out the chicken and garnish and put in an earthenware dish.

Dilute the juices in the pan with ¼ cup (½ decilitre) of sherry, cook down, add ¾ cup (1½ decilitres) of thickened rich brown veal gravy and pour over the chicken.

Chicken sauté à la romaine. POULET SAUTÉ À LA ROMAINE—Sauté the chicken in oil, browning it. Dilute the juices in the pan with ½ cup (a decilitre) of Asti wine, cook down, then pour in ¾ cup (1½ decilitres) of thickened rich veal gravy and ½ cup (1 decilitre) of tomato sauce.

Set the chicken on a layer of leaf spinach, simmered in butter and mixed with 2 diced anchovy fillets. Coat with the sauce.

Chicken sauté Stanley. POULET SAUTÉ STANLEY—Sauté the chicken in butter, but without colouring it. When it is half-cooked add 2 large onions chopped up finely.

Set the chicken in a casserole or earthenware dish and garnish with mushrooms cooked in butter.

Dilute the onions and cooking juices with 1 cup (2 decilitres) of cream, cook for 10 minutes and put through a sieve.

Reduce the onion purée by a quarter; season with a pinch of curry and a *soupçon* of cayenne, and add, at the last moment, 2½ tablespoons (40 grams) of butter. Coat the chicken with this sauce and put 8 slices of truffle on top.

Chicken sauté with tarragon. POULET SAUTÉ À L'ESTRAGON—Like *Chicken sauté aux fine herbes,* replacing shallot, parsley and chervil with an equivalent quantity of chopped tarragon.

Set the chicken on a dish and decorate with blanched tarragon leaves.

Chicken sauté with truffles. POULET SAUTÉ AUX TRUFFES—Sauté the chicken in butter, browning it. When it is cooked, put on the chicken 12 nice, rather thick, slices of raw truffle. Leave to cook, covered, for 5 minutes.

Take out the chicken and truffles. Dilute the pan juices and finish off as for *Chicken sauté with mushrooms.*

Fresh or preserved truffles may be used. In the case of the latter, their reduced juices are added to the sauce.

Chicken sauté à la viennoise. POULET SAUTÉ À LA VIENNOISE—As for *Chicken sauté Archduke,* but without the onion. Garnish with cooked buttered cucumbers.

Chicken sauté with various wines. POULET SAUTÉ AU VIN—Sauté the chicken in butter, browning it.

Dilute with the wine desired, add thickened rich brown veal gravy and finish in the ordinary way.

Note. These preparations are designated by the name of the wine used: Chablis, Graves, Pouilly, Frontignan, Sauternes, Madeira, Port, Sherry, Champagne, etc.

Chicken sauté with red wine is always called *à la bourguignonne*. See COQ AU VIN.

Chicken sauté with white wine. POULET SAUTÉ AU VIN BLANC—Sauté the chicken in butter, browning it.

Dilute the juices with ½ cup (a decilitre) of white wine, cook down, pour in ¾ cup (1½ decilitres) of thickened rich brown veal gravy, cook at boiling point for a few moments and finish off with 3 tablespoons (50 grams) of butter.

Set the chicken on a dish and coat with the sauce.

Chicken sauté à la zingara. POULET SAUTÉ À LA ZINGARA—Season the chicken with paprika, sauté it in oil, browning it. When it is cooked, put in the sauté pan 4 spoonfuls of *Zingara garnish**.

Take out the chicken and its garnish. Dilute the cooking juices with ¼ cup (½ decilitre) of Madeira; cook down and add ¾ cup (1½ decilitres) of rich *Brown sauce* (see SAUCE) flavoured with tomato.

Set the chicken on a dish; dress with the Zingara garnish, arranged in two heaps, and add four small slices of toast with a thin slice of ham tossed in butter on each. Coat with the sauce and sprinkle with chopped parsley.

The slices of ham may also be served in little tartlet shells of thin pastry.

Chicken in scallop shells. COQUILLES DE VOLAILLE—See HORS-D'OEUVRE, HOT, *Scallop shells of poultry*.

Chicken soufflé. SOUFFLÉ DE VOLAILLE—Prepared in this way:

Using raw chicken: Add to 2 pounds (a kilo) of *Chicken mousseline forcemeat* (see FORCEMEAT) 5 stiffly beaten egg whites. Put this mixture in a buttered soufflé dish. Cook gently in the oven for 35 to 40 minutes.

Using cooked chicken: Pound finely in a mortar some cooked chicken meat, adding for every 2 cups (500 grams) of the meat 6 tablespoons of thick cold *Béchamel sauce* (see SAUCE). Season and rub through a sieve.

Heat this purée, *without allowing it to boil*, add 3 tablespoons (50 grams) of butter, 5 egg yolks and, at the last moment, 6 stiffly beaten egg whites.

Put the mixture in a buttered soufflé dish; cook in the oven at a gentle heat.

Cream of chicken soup. CRÈME DE VOLAILLE—Soup made with chicken cooked in a veal or chicken stock, pounded to a purée and finished off with *Velouté sauce* and cream. See SOUPS AND BROTHS.

Chicken Souvarov. POULARDE SOUVAROV—Stuff the chicken with a mixture of chopped *foie gras* and truffles, seasoned with salt and spices and sprinkled with a few drops of liqueur brandy.

Cover and cook in the oven with butter till three-quarters done. Put into a casserole with 8 medium-sized truffles, seasoned and simmered in butter for 5 minutes.

Moisten the chicken with the cooking juices diluted with Madeira, boiled down, and mixed with some rich *Brown sauce* (see SAUCE) made with the truffle juices. Cover, sealing the lid opening with flour-and-water paste.

Finish cooking in the oven for 20 to 25 minutes.

Spring chicken (baby chicks), POUSSIN—This name generally describes a chicken newly hatched whose flesh, not yet formed, is scarcely edible, by reason of its softness and insipidity. This flesh, it is said, is even difficult to digest.

In culinary terminology the word means young pullets, well formed, whose flesh has all the necessary firmness and savour (in U.S.A. these are called *broilers*).

The name is also given to a very small chicken, of which the best type is Hamburg chicken. These chickens have delicate flesh and can be prepared in any of the ways given for small roasting chickens.

Spring chicken (cold). POUSSIN FROID—Prepared in any of the ways given for cold chicken or pigeon dishes.

Usually before being prepared for a cold dish of one kind or another, the chicken is stuffed with forcemeat or with *foie gras* and truffles cut in dice. For certain dishes the spring chickens are boned.

Spring chicken en compote. POUSSIN EN COMPOTE—Stuffed with a fine forcemeat (made with the chicken liver).

Prepared as for *Compote of pigeon*. See PIGEON.

Spring chicken (fried). POUSSIN FRIT—Cut up the chicken into pieces of equal size. Season with salt and pepper. Roll the pieces in flour, coat with egg and breadcrumbs.

At the last moment fry them in deep fat. Arrange on a napkin and garnish with fried parsley and quarters of lemon.

The pieces of chicken may and should be marinated in oil, lemon juice, salt and pepper before being floured.

Spring chicken grilled à la diable. POUSSIN GRILLÉ À LA DIABLE—Prepared as for *Grilled chicken à la diable*.

Spring chicken in marinade (fried). POUSSIN EN MARINADE (FRIT)—Cut the chicken in quarters and take out the greater part of the small bones. Marinate the pieces with oil, lemon juice, salt, pepper, chopped herbs.

Just before serving dip these pieces in a light batter and fry in deep fat.

Drain the pieces, and arrange on a napkin. Garnish with fried parsley. Serve *Tomato sauce* (see SAUCE) separately.

This dish is often served under the name of 'fritot' of chicken. This is wrong, because, in principle, 'fritot' is made of previously cooked substances.

Spring chicken with peas. POUSSIN AUX PETITS POIS—Prepared like *Pigeon with Peas**.

Spring chicken à la piémontaise. POUSSIN À LA PIÉMONTAISE—Fill the chicken with a mixture made of fine *forcemeat*, the liver chopped up and some onion lightly cooked in butter. Truss as for boiling. Cook in butter, browning it all over. Drain, and take off the trussing strings; set in the middle of a risotto arranged as a border on a round dish. Sprinkle the chicken with its juices, diluted with white wine, thickened rich brown veal gravy, with a little tomato purée added, all cooked down together.

Spring chicken à la polonaise. POUSSIN À LA POLONAISE—Stuffed chicken with a *gratin forcemeat* (see FORCEMEAT) mixed with soaked and pressed bread, with butter and chopped parsley added.

Cook in a casserole. Finish off as for *Chicken à la polonaise*.

Roasted spring chicken. POUSSIN RÔTI—Put inside the chicken a *bouquet garni* and a spoonful of butter, to which the chicken liver, chopped, and well seasoned with salt, pepper and a little grated nutmeg has been added. Truss the chicken, bard it with bacon fat and put it on the spit. Cook on a good heat, basting frequently.

When it is three-quarters cooked, sprinkle with fresh breadcrumbs. Let it take a good colour and serve with its own juices, handed separately. (Prosper Salles' recipe.)

Spring chicken à la sicilienne. POUSSIN À LA SICILIENNE—Cook some *lasagne** in salt water; drain and reheat for a few moments in very hot butter, and bind with a purée of pistachio nuts. Season well. Allow to cool. Stuff the chicken with this mixture and truss it as for spit roasting. Cook at a good heat, basting frequently. When it is three-quarters cooked sprinkle with freshly grated bread-crumbs, let it colour and serve with its own juices, handed separately.

Spring chicken à la tartare. POUSSIN À LA TARTARE—Split the chicken down the back, season, brush over with melted butter, sprinkle with breadcrumbs and grill on a gentle heat.

Serve *Tartare sauce* (see SAUCE) separately.

Spring chicken à la viennoise. POUSSIN À LA VIENNOISE—Divide the chicken into quarters. Season them, sprinkle with flour, coat with egg and breadcrumbs and cook in clarified butter (or in lard), browning them well on both sides (or cook them in deep fat).

Arrange on a napkin and garnish with fried parsley and quarters of lemon.

Chicken Stanley. POULARDE STANLEY—Poach the chicken in a white stock to which have been added 4 large onions, chopped.

Set the chicken on a dish; surround it with 20 large mushrooms and 8 tartlets filled with chopped up truffles.

Coat the chicken with *Stanley sauce* (see *Chicken sauté Stanley*) and finish off with the onions cooked in the stock, strained through a cloth.

Stuffed chicken à l'ariégeoise. POULET FARCI À L'ARIÉGEOISE—Stuff a chicken with a forcemeat made in this way: soak in milk 4 cups (250 grams) of crustless bread. Squeeze this bread, put in a basin, add to it 3 to 4 ounces (100 grams) of chopped raw ham, the liver of the chicken, also chopped up, the chicken gizzard chopped very finely, 2 cloves of garlic, finely chopped, 2 tablespoons of chopped onion cooked lightly in fat. Bind this forcemeat with a whole egg and the blood of the hen. Season with salt, pepper and grated nutmeg and add a large tablespoon of chopped parsley.

Truss the chicken as for boiling. Put it to cook in a *pot-au-feu* with a piece of beef and a piece of chined salt pork (pork back).

The chicken being cooked, take off the trussing strings and set it on a long dish. Surround with a garnish composed of stuffed cabbage fashioned into balls, potatoes cut into large round slices and cooked in the *pot-au-feu* broth, and the chined pork, boned and cut into nice little slices.

Serve separately *Tomato sauce* (see SAUCE) seasoned with garlic.

When this chicken dish is prepared, the *pot-au-feu* broth is served as soup, generally with rice or vermicelli.

Stuffed chicken à la mode de Sorges (Périgord cookery). POULET FARCI À LA MODE DE SORGES—Stuff the chicken with a forcemeat made of chopped chicken liver, stale breadcrumbs, chopped bacon and parsley, spring onions, shallot and garlic, all finely chopped, the whole well seasoned with salt, pepper and grated nutmeg, and bound with the blood of the chicken and egg yolks.

Brown the chicken all over in goose fat. Put it in a deep earthenware dish. Cover with boiling water. Season with salt and pepper. Bring to the boil, skim, add 3 carrots, 2 turnips, the white parts of 3 leeks tied in a bunch, a celery heart, a large onion stuck with a clove and some beet stalks tied in a bunch. Cook like a *pot-au-feu*, very slowly, for about an hour.

Drain the chicken. Take off the trussing strings, put the chicken on a dish, surround with its garnish, the carrots and turnips cut in pieces.

Serve separately *Sorges sauce*, which is a highly seasoned vinaigrette sauce, with chopped parsley, spring onions and shallots added to it, bound with the yolks of 2 eggs cooked for 3 minutes in boiling water. Finish with the whites of these eggs recooked in the chicken broth and cut in dice.

In Périgord the broth is served first, poured over slices of toasted bread or garnished with macaroni.

Suprêmes of chicken. SUPRÊMES DE VOLAILLE—Under this name are known the wings (but more normally in English the breast and wings) of poultry, removed when raw.

These suprêmes, which are also called *côtelettes* or *filets*, are separated and served as small entrées.

Note. When *suprêmes* of *poularde* or fat hen are used, they should each be divided into two or three slices. These slices, lightly flattened, and trimmed into oval shapes, are afterwards cooked like *Chicken côtelettes.*

Suprêmes of chicken ambassadrice. SUPRÊMES DE VOLAILLE AMBASSADRICE—Sauté in butter. Place on a dish, garnish with chicken livers sautéed in butter, with cocks' combs and kidneys and truffles cut into the shape of olives. Dilute the pan juices with Madeira and thickened brown veal gravy and pour over the dish.

Place on top of these suprêmes the *filets mignons* (the pieces that lie against the breastbone) studded with truffles.

Suprêmes of chicken Camerani. SUPRÊMES DE VOLAILLE CAMERANI—Coat the *suprêmes* with egg and bread-crumbs, adding to the crumbs one-third of their volume of chopped truffles, and sauté in butter.

Set on a foundation of noodles. For sauce use the cooking juices, diluted with Madeira and thickened brown veal gravy, to which has been added a spoonful of *julienne** of celery and truffles, cooked in butter until tender.

Suprêmes of chicken Carême. SUPRÊMES DE VOLAILLE CARÊME—Slit open the *suprêmes* into 'purses' and fill them with a thick mushroom purée, to which a fine *julienne** of cocks' combs and truffles has been added. Sauté in butter.

Set on croûtons of bread fried in butter and garnish with *Chicken quenelles* (see QUENELLES), truffles cut into the shapes of olives and mushrooms. For sauce use thickened brown veal gravy with tomato and butter.

Place on top of the suprêmes the *filets mignons* (chicken breast) studded with pickled tongue.

Suprêmes of chicken à la florentine. SUPRÊMES DE VOLAILLE À LA FLORENTINE—Poach in a veal or chicken stock till three-quarters cooked. Coat with *Mornay sauce* (see SAUCE) to which some *chicken essence* has been added. Sprinkle with grated Parmesan and brown quickly.

Suprêmes of chicken Gabrielle. SUPRÊMES DE VOLAILLE GABRIELLE—Remove the *suprêmes*, without detaching the *filets mignon*, which lie against the breastbone. Cover them with a thin layer of *mirepoix** cooked in butter until tender. Coat with egg and breadcrumbs. Sauté in butter.

Set on a serving dish and garnish with shredded lettuce dressed with very thick cream. Sprinkle with *Noisette butter*. See BUTTER, *Compound butters.*

Suprêmes of chicken à l'impériale. SUPRÊMES DE VOLAILLE À L'IMPÉRIALE—Stud the *suprêmes* with semi-circles of truffles and pickled tongue. Cook in a white stock.

Set into *barquettes* cooked empty, filled with a *Purée of truffles à la crème**. Coat lightly with *Suprême sauce*. See SAUCE.

Place the *filets mignons* (chicken breast), studded with truffles, on top of the *suprêmes.*

Suprêmes of chicken marquise. SUPRÊMES DE VOLAILLE MARQUISE—Sauté in butter. Set on a serving dish and garnish with small *bouchées** of puff pastry filled with a *salpicon** of cocks' combs and kidneys and truffles bound with cream.

Coat with the pan juices diluted with cream, to which 2 tablespoons of truffles and butter have been added. Place the *filets mignons*, poached in a white stock, on top of the *suprêmes*.

Suprêmes of chicken Montpensier. SUPRÊMES DE VOLAILLE MONTPENSIER—Coat the *suprêmes* with egg and breadcrumbs and sauté them in butter.

Set on a serving dish; garnish with asparagus tips in butter and put two slices of truffles on top of each *suprême*.

Sprinkle with *Noisette butter* (see BUTTER, *Compound butters*), and for sauce use concentrated thickened brown veal gravy.

Suprêmes of chicken à la Périgueux. SUPRÊMES DE VOLAILLE À LA PÉRIGUEUX—Sauté in butter. Set on croûtons of bread fried in butter, garnish with slices of truffles and coat with *Demi-glace sauce* (see SAUCE) flavoured with Madeira.

Suprêmes of chicken Pojarski. SUPRÊMES DE VOLAILLE POJARKSI—Chop the flesh of the *suprêmes*, adding $1\frac{1}{4}$ cups (60 grams) of breadcrumbs, soaked in milk and squeezed, 4 tablespoons (60 grams) of butter and 1 or 2 tablespoons of fresh cream; season with salt, pepper and nutmeg.

Reform the *suprêmes* into their original shape, flour them lightly and sauté in butter.

Set on a serving dish, garnish with a green vegetable in butter and sprinkle with *Noisette butter*. See BUTTER, *compound butters*.

Suprêmes of chicken princesse. SUPRÊMES DE VOLAILLE PRINCESSE—Cook in a veal or chicken stock. Set on croûtons of bread fried in butter, coat with *Allemande sauce* (see SAUCE) and place on each *suprême* two slices of truffles. Set on top the *filets mignons* (chicken breast) studded with truffles.

Suprêmes of chicken Richelieu. SUPRÊMES DE VOLAILLE RICHELIEU—Coat the *suprêmes* with egg and breadcrumbs. Sauté in butter.

Set on a serving dish; coat with *Maître d'hôtel butter* (see BUTTER, *compound butters*), place 4 slices of truffles on top of each *suprême*.

Suprêmes of chicken Rossini. SUPRÊMES DE VOLAILLE ROSSINI—Sauté in butter. Set on croûtons of bread fried in butter and garnish with slices of *foie gras* sautéed in butter and slices of truffles. Serve with *Madeira sauce*. See SAUCE.

Suprêmes of chicken, with various vegetables. SUPRÊMES DE VOLAILLE AUX LÉGUMES DIVERS—Season the *suprêmes* and sauté them in butter.

Set on a serving dish and garnish with one or the other of the following vegetables: aubergines (egg-plant) cut in dice and fried in butter; peeled mushrooms; braised endives; cucumber cut in chunks and simmered in butter; French (string) beans in butter; braised lettuces; macédoine of vegetables in butter; pease in butter or *à la française;* asparagus tips in butter or cream; various vegetable purées, etc.

For sauce use the cooking juices diluted with white wine and thickened brown veal gravy.

Suprêmes of chicken Verdi. SUPRÊMES DE VOLAILLE VERDI—Sauté in butter. Set on a serving dish in a pastry shell filled with diced macaroni drained and bound with *Purée of foie gras**. Put two slices of truffles on top of each suprême and coat lightly with *Demi-glace sauce* (see SAUCE) finished off with Marsala.

Add the *filets mignons* each cut in 3 slices, coated in egg and breadcrumbs and sautéed in butter.

Chicken with tarragon

Chicken with tarragon I. POULARDE À L'ESTRAGON—Poach a chicken in white stock with a good bunch of tarragon.

Set on a dish and decorate with previously blanched tarragon leaves.

Pour into the bottom of the dish several tablespoons of the cooking liquor, strained, thickened with arrowroot, and with some chopped tarragon added.

Serve the rest of the cooking liquor in a sauceboat.

Chicken with tarragon II. POULARDE À L'ESTRAGON—Cook the chicken, covered, in the oven with butter. Put it in an earthenware dish, pour over its cooking juices, diluted with white wine, to which a handful of crushed tarragon and some thickened rich veal gravy have been added.

Chicken timbale. See TIMBALE and CROÛTES.

Chicken Toscane. POULARDE TOSCANE—Stuff the chicken with a scant $\frac{1}{4}$ pound (100 grams) of spaghetti cooked in water, mixed with $3\frac{1}{2}$ ounces (100 grams) of *Purée of foie gras*, 2 large truffles (75 grams) cut into dice and $\frac{1}{2}$ cup (50 grams) of grated Parmesan, season and bind the mixture with 4 tablespoons of thickened rich brown veal gravy.

Cook as *Chicken à la Derby*, and prepare the sauce as indicated in that recipe.

Set on a dish; surround with 8 little cases filled with ham, tongue and truffles, the mixture bound with rich *Brown sauce* (see SAUCE), flavoured with tomato, and eight slices of *foie gras*, previously tossed in butter.

Pour the pan juices over the chicken.

Chicken Toulouse. POULARDE TOULOUSE—Poach the chicken in a white stock. Set on a dish; surround with *Toulouse garnish* (see GARNISH) and pour over *Allemande sauce*. See SAUCE.

Chicken with truffles. POULARDE AUX TRUFFES—Cook the chicken covered with butter in the oven.

Put it in an earthenware casserole with $\frac{1}{2}$ pound (250 grams) of raw truffles cut in thick slices. Moisten with the cooking butter, cover the dish and keep it for a few moments in a low heat.

At the last moment sprinkle over the cooking juices diluted with Madeira and mixed with rich *Brown sauce*. See SAUCE.

Chicken with truffles à la périgourdine. POULARDE TRUFFÉE À LA PÉRIGOURDINE—'Having drawn and singed a fine fat hen without damaging the skin, have two pounds of good truffles washed and peeled, and cut them into the shape and size of pigeon's eggs. Keep the scraps and chop them up; take half a pound of chicken fat and an equal quantity of fresh fat bacon, melt them over a gentle heat, press the liquid fat through a strainer and put it in a saucepan with the truffles, salt, pepper, spices, half a bay leaf, a very small sprig of thyme, a little grated nutmeg, and the chopped truffles and let them simmer, covered, for a quarter of an hour. Take out and allow to cool. Fill the chicken with this mixture, taking care to close the opening. Put the chicken in an earthenware pot and cover it with the outside skin of the truffles, which you will have kept; leave the chicken like this for three or four days.

'The day that you serve it, take off the truffle skins, which you will toss in butter with an onion, a carrot, and a sprig of parsley; set the chicken on a skewer, cover with bards of fresh pork fat and over them the vegetables and truffles, wrap up in double sheets of oiled paper; set on a spit and give an hour-and-a-half's cooking, sprinkling often with water. Five minutes before serving, unwrap the chicken, leave it to brown nicely, take off the spit, remove the bards and serve with *Perigueux Sauce*' (see SAUCE). (Plumerey's recipe.)

Chicken turban (ring). TURBAN DE VOLAILLE—Using thin slices of raw chicken line a buttered savarin (ring) mould, overlapping the edges a little. Cover with a thin layer of *Chicken mousseline forcemeat* (see FORCEMEAT). Fill the mould with a *salpicon** of cooked chicken, truffles and mushrooms, bound with *Allemande sauce* (see SAUCE). Cover with another thin layer of the forcemeat folding overlapping edges of the sliced chicken over it. Poach the 'turban' in the oven in a *bain-marie* for about 40 minutes.

Allow to rest for a few moments after cooking before turning out of the mould. Fill the middle of the 'turban' with some kind of garnish and serve with *Suprême* or *Allemande sauce*. See SAUCE.

Chicken à la viennoise. POULET À LA VIENNOISE—This method applies mainly to small spring chickens, but can perhaps be applied to small tender roasting chickens (*poulets de grain*).

Cut the chicken into joints. Season the pieces with salt and pepper, flour them, dip in egg beaten up with a little oil, salt and pepper, and cover with freshly made breadcrumbs. Cook in clarified butter or lard. Serve on a napkin, garnished with fried parsley and quarters of lemon.

This chicken may also be fried in deep fat.

Chicken vol-au-vent—See VOL-AU-VENT.

Chicken wings—See PINIONS.

CHICORY (U.S. Endive). ENDIVE—This variety of Magdebourg chicory is known in France and U.S.A. as *endive* and in Belgium, where it is grown in large quantities, as *chicorée de Bruxelles*. It is also called *witloof* and *barbe-de-bouc* (goat's beard) in Belgium.

The roots of the chicory plant, obtained by etiolation, are very white and delicate. This vegetable comes into season in about October and is available all through the winter. Chicory (endive) is eaten raw, in salad or cooked in various ways.

Method of cooking. Trim and wash the chicory, leaving it in water for as short a time as possible. Put it in a saucepan with, for 1 pound (500 grams) of the vegetable, 2 tablespoons (30 grams) of butter, a pinch of salt, the juice of a quarter of a lemon and ½ cup (1 decilitre) of water.

Cover the saucepan and bring to the boil. Simmer slowly but steadily for 45 minutes.

Another method. Trim and wash the chicory (U.S. endive) and put it in a saucepan with 3 tablespoons (50 grams) of butter, a pinch of salt and a few drops of lemon juice. Cover and stew for 45 minutes. Chicory cooked in this way can be prepared according to the recipes given below. It must be noted that chicory must never be parboiled before stewing.

Chicory (U.S. Endive) à la béchamel. ENDIVES À LA BÉCHAMEL—Cook the chicory as indicated above. Put the shoots in a vegetable dish. Cover with *Béchamel sauce* (see SAUCE), with the cooking stock of the chicory, boiled down and buttered, added.

Chicory (U.S. Endive) with butter. ENDIVES AU BEURRE—Cook as indicated in first recipe. Put the chicory in a vegetable dish. Mix a piece of fresh butter with the cooking stock and pour over the vegetable.

Chicory (U.S. Endive) with brown or noisette butter. ENDIVES AU BEURRE NOIR—Cook the chicory as indicated in the first recipe. Drain. Arrange very flat on a long dish Pour on lemon juice. Just before serving, cover with piping hot *Brown* or *Noisette butter*. See BUTTER, *Compound butters*.

Chicory (U.S. Endive) chiffonnade. CHIFFONNADE D'ENDIVES—Remove the outer leaves of the shoots. Wash them quickly and dry them. Shred them finely. Cook the shredded chicory in butter in a covered pan with a pinch of salt and sugar.

Chicory (U.S. Endive) chiffonnade with cream. CHIFFONNADE D'ENDIVES À LA CRÈME—Proceed as ndicated in the first recipe. Just before serving, moisten with a few tablespoons of fresh cream.

Chicory (U.S. Endive) with cream. ENDIVES À LA CRÈME—Proceed as indicated in the first recipe. Five minutes before serving, moisten with 1 cup (2 decilitres) of boiling cream. Boil fast for a few seconds. Put the chicory in a vegetable dish. Pour on the cooking stock with a little fresh butter added.

Chicory (U.S. Endive) à la flamande. ENDIVES À LA FLAMANDE—Another name for *Chicory with butter*.

Chicory (U.S. Endive) fritots. ENDIVES EN FRITOT—Cook the chicory as indicated in the first recipe. Drain and dry thoroughly in a cloth. Quarter the shoots. Steep them in a marinade of oil, lemon juice, salt and pepper. Just before serving dip them in light batter and deep-fry. Serve on a napkin, garnished.

Chicory (U.S. Endive) au gratin. ENDIVES AU GRATIN—Cook the chicory in butter. Arrange in a buttered ovenware dish dusted with grated cheese. Sprinkle the chicory with grated cheese. Pour on melted butter. Brown in oven.

Chicory (U.S. Endive) in gravy. ENDIVES AU JUS—Cook as indicated in the first recipe. Arrange the chicory in a vegetable dish. Pour on a few tablespoons of very concentrated brown veal stock with the cooking stock of the chicory added to it.

Chicory (U.S. Endive) à la grecque (hors-d'oeuvre). ENDIVES À LA GRECQUE—Trim some very small chicory shoots. Wash them quickly and dry in a cloth. Plunge them at once into a stock prepared as indicated for *Artichoke à la grecque**. Complete cooking as indicated in that recipe.

Chicory (U.S. Endive) à la meunière. ENDIVES À LA MEUNIÈRE—A name commonly applied to *Chicory with brown butter*.

Chicory (U.S. Endive) à la milanaise. ENDIVES À LA MILANAISE—Cook the chicory as indicated in first recipe. Arrange in an ovenproof dish.

Proceed as indicated for *Asparagus à la milanaise.*

Chicory (U.S. Endive) à la Mornay. ENDIVES À LA MORNAY—Cook the chicory as indicated in first recipe. Arrange in an ovenproof dish and cover with *Mornay sauce* (see SAUCE) (with the concentrated stock of the chicory). Sprinkle with grated cheese. Pour on melted butter and brown in a very hot oven.

Chicory (U.S. Endive) à la polonaise. ENDIVES À LA POLONAISE—Cook the chicory as indicated in first recipe. Arrange in a vegetable dish or on a long serving dish.

Proceed as indicated for *Asparagus à la polonaise.*

Purée of chicory (U.S. Endive). PURÉE D'ENDIVES—Cook the chicory as indicated in the first recipe. Rub through a sieve. Heat the purée and add to it, according to the directions in the selected recipe, a little butter or some cream.

This purée can be thickened with a few tablespoons of *Béchamel sauce* or thick *Velouté sauce* (see SAUCE), or a third of its weight of mashed potatoes. It can also be completed with a little concentrated brown veal stock.

Chicory (U.S. Endive) salad I. SALADE D'ENDIVES—Wash and dry the chicory. Remove faded leaves. Separate the remaining leaves. Halve each one. Serve in a salad bowl, seasoned with oil, lemon juice or vinegar, salt and pepper.

Chicory (U.S. Endive) salad II. SALADE D'ENDIVES—Trim the chicory. Wash and dry it in a cloth. Shred the shoots across. Serve in a salad bowl dressed as indicated in the previous recipe.

Chicory, with the leaves whole or shredded, can also be dressed with *mayonnaise* (see SAUCE, *cold sauces*).

Cooked chicory can also be made into a salad.

Chicory (U.S. Endive) soufflé. SOUFFLÉ D'ENDIVE—Using cooked chicory rubbed through a fine sieve, proceed as indicated for *Endive soufflé.* See ENDIVE.

CHICORY GOURILOS (endive stumps)—*Gourilos* is the name given to the stumps of endive and chicory. These stumps, when they are fully grown and tender, make a delicately flavoured vegetable.

They can be prepared in different ways: as an hors-d'oeuvre, *à la greque* or otherwise; as a vegetable, in butter or cream, in gravy, fried, grilled, etc.

Method. Trim the stumps and wash them. Boil them in salt water until just tender.

Drain and leave to cool. Dry them and cook according to the following recipes.

Chicory or endive gourilos in butter. GOURILOS AU BEURRE—Blanch 12 *gourilos.* Put them in a frying pan with 3 tablespoons (50 grams) of butter and 2 tablespoons of water. Cover and cook for 40 minutes. Arrange in a vegetable dish. Pour on them the butter in which they have been cooked, with a tablespoon of water or white stock added.

Chicory or endive gourilos in cream. GOURILOS À LA CRÈME—Cook as for *Gourilos in butter.* When they are ready, add $\frac{3}{4}$ cup ($1\frac{1}{2}$ decilitres) of boiling hot fresh cream. Simmer for 8 minutes. Arrange the *gourilos* in a vegetable dish and pour on the cream.

Chicory or endive gourilos à la grecque. GOURILOS À LA GRECQUE—Blanch the gourilos and prepare them as for *Artichoke à la grecque**.

Fried chicory or endive gourilos. GOURILOS FRITS—Blanch the gourilos; drain, leave to cool, chill and dry them. Steep them in oil, lemon juice, salt and pepper for 25 minutes. Coat them with a thin frying batter and fry in boiling deep fat. Drain. Sprinkle with salt. Arrange them in a clump on a napkin, or use as a garnish as desired.

Chicory or endive gourilos in gravy, bone-marrow sauce, velouté sauce or other sauces. GOURILOS AU JUS, À LA MOELLE, AU VELOUTÉ—Proceed as in recipes for *cardoons** or *celery**, using these various sauces.

Grilled chicory or endive gourilos. GOURILOS GRILLÉS—Blanch and soak the gourilos in oil and lemon juice as for *fried gourilos.* Grill them under a low flame, moistening them with a little oil from time to time.

Chicory or endive gourilos sauté with chopped herbs, à l'italienne, à la lyonnaise, à la provençale, etc. GOURILOS SAUTÉS AUX FINES HERBES, À L'ITALIENNE, À LA LYONNAISE, À LA PROVENÇALE—Proceed as for *Artichoke hearts,* using these various methods.

Chicory (in coffee). CHICORÉE À CAFÉ—The use of the wild chicory root as a substitute for or adulterant in coffee dates back to 1769, shortly after this beverage came into fashion. Used first in Sicily, then in Germany, the preparation of this plant has given rise to an important industry. The roots, cut up into *cosettes,* are dried and reduced to a more or less fine grain or powder. Commercially the different types are known as *gros-grains,* from selected *cosettes* (roots); *demi-grains,* from small *cosettes*; chicory *courantes,* and chicory in powder form.

Chicory has a much greater food value than coffee, which is of little importance in view of the small amount consumed; it produces an infusion of a dark colour and has laxative properties. It prevents caffeine poisoning which would frequently occur if a person drank an excess of coffee, correctly made.

But coffee addicts do not admit of the slightest addition of chicory in coffee, and they are justified.

CHIFFONNADE—In cooking, all plants, herbal or otherwise, which are cut into fine strips or ribbons are denoted by this term. It is more especially used to denote a mixture of sorrel and lettuce cut into julienne strips and cooked in butter.

Most of the *chiffonnades* are used as a garnish for clear or thick soups.

Lettuce chiffonnade cooked in butter. CHIFFONNADE DE LAITUE AU BEURRE—Slice the leaves of a lettuce into fine strips, leaving aside the coarser leaves. Put the sliced lettuce in a pan in which some butter is melting, 2 tablespoons of butter for every $\frac{1}{2}$ pound (250 grams) of lettuce. Season. Cook gently until the vegetable liquor has completely evaporated.

Lettuce chiffonnade with cream. CHIFFONNADE DE LAITUE À LA CRÈME—Prepared in the same way as *Lettuce chiffonnade cooked in butter.* When the lettuce has softened, moisten with a few tablespoons of fresh cream and boil down (reduce) until vegetable liquor has evaporated.

This chiffonnade can also be moistened with cream sauce.

Mixed chiffonnade (garnish for soups). CHIFFONNADE MÉLANGÉE—Prepared in the same way as *Lettuce chiffonnade,* with a mixture in equal parts of sorrel leaves and lettuce leaves.

Sorrel chiffonnade. CHIFFONNADE D'OSEILLE—Prepared with sorrel leaves in the same way as *Lettuce chiffonnade.* Sorrel chiffonnade is used especially for making *Potage santé.* See SOUPS AND BROTHS.

CHIMNEY HOOK. CRÉMAILLÈRE—A toothed pot-hook

used for suspending cauldrons and cooking pots in the chimney.

The symbolic expression *pendre la crémaillère* (to hang up the chimney hook) designates the first meal given to inaugurate a new home.

CHINCHARD. See SAUREL.

CHINE. CHAINE—In culinary parlance the chine represents the bony part adhering to the fillet of a loin of veal, mutton, lamb or pork, and equally to the bony part of a rib or sirloin of beef.

CHINESE ARTICHOKE. CROSNE DE JAPON—Plant originating in China and Japan, cultivated for the first time in France at Crosnes (Seine-et-Oise) for its tubers, which are edible. It is also called *knot-root*, *chorogi* and *Japanese artichoke*.

This vegetable, which is delicious when fresh, is extremely white. Those tubers which have dried out and have been revived by soaking, and are sometimes sold as fresh, can be recognized by a brownish discolouration.

Method of preparation. Put the tubers in a strong linen cloth with a handful of sea salt, and shake them well. Wash them and remove any skin that is left.

Blanch them in salted water. Simmer in butter without allowing them to brown.

After being prepared in this way, the tubers can be either served as they are as a vegetable, or used to garnish some kind of roast.

They can also be prepared *à la crème*, with *fines herbes*, *au jus*, and in general in all the ways given for *Jerusalem artichokes*.*

CHINESE CABBAGE or PE-TSAI. CHOU DE CHINE—This type of cabbage, in which the heart is oval in shape with very tightly closed leaves, is fairly common.

All the methods of preparation given for green cabbage can be applied to it. It can also be used raw in salad or in a marinade, like red cabbage.

CHINOIS (fruit)—Name given in France to little Chinese oranges, green or yellow, which are crystallized or preserved in brandy.

CHINOIS (utensil)—Conical strainer with a fine mesh.

CHIPOLATA—Garnish consisting of braised chestnuts, little glazed onions, diced breast of pork, chipolata sausages, and sometimes glazed carrots. See GARNISHES.

Applies to cuts of butcher's meat and to chicken.

Chipolata was originally an Italian ragoût with an onion foundation. The word is also applied to little sausages enclosed in sheep's intestines.

CHIQUETER—To indent with a little knife the margins of a vol-au-vent case, the rim of a tart, or various gâteaux.

CHIVES. CIBOULETTE, CIVETTE—Chives are used as a culinary seasoning, chiefly in green salads.

CHOCOLATE. CHOCOLAT—The dried, roasted and polished 'nibs' or almonds of the cacao bean are crushed and the resulting thick liquor is, if of good quality, about fifty per cent cocoa fat. When the liquor is partially defatted it is cooled and solidifies into a hard block, known as *bitter chocolate*. This is the type that is used for baking in U.S.A. The cooking chocolate most generally used in England and France is a mixture of the chocolate liquor with some of the fat removed and sugar added. In England this is known as *pure chocolate* and in the U.S.A. as *bitter-sweet chocolate*. *Milk chocolate* has powdered or condensed milk added to the sweetened chocolate and is variously flavoured with vanilla, almond, cinnamon, etc. Chocolate used in confectionery for coating bon-bons has added amounts of cocoa fat. When most of the cocoa fat is extracted from the chocolate liquor, the chocolate block that results is powdered into cocoa which contains only 18% fat.

Chocolate was brought to Europe by the Spaniards who had discovered it in Mexico in 1519. Its use spread through Europe soon after.

'Chocolate', says Brillat-Savarin, 'is one of the most effective restoratives. All those who have to work when they might be sleeping, men of wit who feel temporarily deprived of their intellectual powers, those who find the weather oppressive, time dragging, the atmosphere depressing; those who are tormented by some preoccupation which deprives them of the liberty of thought; let all such men imbibe a half-litre of *chocolat ambré* (see AMBER), using 60 to 72 grains of amber per half-kilo, and they will be amazed.' The grain, an old-fashioned measure, equals about the twentieth part of a gram, and we might add, *ambre gris* is meant, a greyish substance which exhales a smell analagous to musk, and not yellow amber which is an entirely different thing. Such chocolate no longer exists.

To increase the flavour of the chocolate Brillat-Savarin divulges the secret which Mme. d'Arestrel, Mother Superior of the Convent of the Visitation at Belley, revealed to him: 'When you want to taste good chocolate' said that religious gourmande, 'make it the night before, in a faïence coffee pot, and leave it. The chocolate becomes concentrated during the night and this gives it a much better consistency.'

Preparation of chocolate (Beverage). CHOCOLAT—A generous ounce (40 grams) of good sweet chocolate is needed for a breakfast cup. Put the chocolate broken up into pieces with a small quantity of water or hot milk in a casserole on a gentle heat. Cover the pan, let the chocolate soften, remove from the fire and whip into a smooth paste with a whip or wooden spoon; add first of all two or three tablespoons of boiling liquid (water or milk) to dilute the paste, then the rest of the liquid, still boiling, continuing to stir all the time. To retain the full aroma of the chocolate (the same applies to cocoa) it must never be allowed to boil.

CHOESELS (Belgian cookery)—A ragoût composed of tripe and pancreas.

Cleaned, with the fat removed, pancreas resembles meat and is of the same colour, but it is flat and elongated. Beef pancreas, which is usually used for *choesels*, weighs about 1 pound (500 grams).

Considering with what abundance the portions are served (particularly in Brussels) one may well ask oneself how many horned beasts would have to be slaughtered every day to supply the innumerable restaurants which serve this favourite dish from seven until midnight (and which is eaten in Brussels in a quite particular way in December).

It might be concluded, therefore, that one is likely to meet *choesels* of doubtful authenticity, but this is not so: the dish is cooked according to the correct recipe, but the pancreas is reinforced, most agreeably, by other equally delicate parts of the animal's anatomy, which, bulk apart, impart their respective qualities to the flavour of the dish. In this way ox-tail, kidneys, *quenelles* of calves' sweetbreads, and breast and feet of lamb feature with honour in *choesels*.

But even though the basic ingredients of this preparation remain fixed, the manner of combining them varies with the interpreter.

As a rule, the seasoning consists of onions, thyme, bay, cloves, nutmeg, pepper and salt; the sauce is combined with a good glass of Madeira, or for passionate connoisseurs, with strong Belgian beer (*Lambic*).

Choesels à la Bruxelloise—Put ½ cup (100 grams) of clarified beef fat (from the roast) into a pan, heat it smoking hot, and then brown an ox-tail cut into pieces, and two calf's (U.S. veal) sweetbreads. Reduce the temperature and cook gently for 45 minutes. Then add 2 pounds (1 kilo) of breast of veal to the stew, cut into regular pieces, and 1 large sliced onion. Continue to cook for a further 30 minutes, stirring the while. Then add a beef kidney cut into large pieces. When the kidney has stiffened, moisten the stew with 1½ cups (3 decilitres) of *lambic* (Belgian beer). Put in a strong *bouquet garni**. Season with salt and a little cayenne.

Cook gently for 30 minutes. Add the *choesels* (beef pancreas), and to increase the liquor, a bottle of *lambic* and 2½ cups (5 decilitres) of the liquor in which some mushrooms have been cooked (see *Court-bouillon XVIII, white, for mushrooms**). (Paul Bouillard's recipe.)

CHOPE—Goblet of glass or earthenware containing about one-third of a litre (12 ounces or 1½ cups) in which beer is drunk.

CHOPINE—Old measure for wine corresponding to half a litre.

CHOPPING. HACHAGE—The chopping of food in French is called *hachage* or *hachement*.

Hachage can also mean the food which has been chopped. Thus, it is possible to speak of an onion *hachage*, though the more common expression is *hachis*.

The chopping of meat with an ordinary chopper is done on a special cylindrical chopping block, usually made of cross-grained planks. These planks are set upright in a wooden frame, pressed very tightly one against the other.

The chopping blocks or tables must not be washed with water but merely scraped with a special scraper, thoroughly dried with sawdust, and then rubbed clean.

'CHOPS'. BABINES—Slang name for lips of some animals, such as dogs or monkeys. The popular expression 'to lick one's chops' indicates satisfaction experienced by savouring a tasty dish.

CHORIZOS D'ESTRAMADURE—Highly-spiced sausages, used a great deal in Spain.

'Trim a fresh fillet of pork, add the same quantity of pork fat, and a pig's liver. Chop all this together and pound it in a mortar. Season with salt, spices, sweet red peppers, a pinch of cayenne pepper, a few juniper berries, sieved and pounded. When the whole is properly mixed, add a few tablespoons of tomato purée, and stuff the preparation in sausage skins (well-soaked intestines). String up into sausages of the same size as a *Cervelas**; rub each sausage with good oil; and hang in the chimney for 6 or 7 days.

'Each evening when damping down the fire, throw on a few handfuls of juniper berries. These little sausages, which are cooked with *garbanzos* (chick-peas) in Spain, are excellent.' (Plumerey's recipe.)

CHOU (Pastry)—This little bun is made with *chou* pastry, which is pushed through a forcing (pastry) bag on to a metal baking tray. The *chou*, which must always be made in a round form, is either served as it is, or stuffed with cream or some other preparation.

Chou pastry or cream puff pastry. PÂTÉ À CHOU—Ordinary *chou* pastry (with which a great number of cakes, large and small, are made) is made in the following way:

Ingredients. 4¼ cups water (1 litre); 1½ cups (375 grams) butter, 3¾ cups (500 grams) sifted flour; 1 tablespoon (16 grams) salt; 1½ tablespoons (25 grams) sugar; 16 eggs; 1 good tablespoon orange blossom water or 1 teaspoon orange extract.

Method. Boil the water, butter, salt and sugar together in a deep pan with a flat bottom. When the mixture boils, take the pan off the fire and pour in the sifted flour; mix well. Dry out the mixture over a low heat, working it with a wooden spoon until the mixture comes away from the sides of the pan and oils a little. Then add the eggs, off the fire, two by two, working vigorously all the time, and finally the flavouring. Other flavouring may be used.

Note. Various cakes such as *Éclairs, Jacob's ladders, Saint-Honoré, Profiteroles,* etc. are made with this pastry. *Soufflé fritters* are also made with it.

Cooking the choux or cream puffs—Put the mixture through a forcing (pastry) bag with a simple round nozzle in little collops on to a buttered baking tray, allowing a little distance between each. Make them about the size of a walnut, or smaller if they are used as *Profiteroles.* Gild them with beaten egg. Cook them in the oven at a good moderate heat (400°F.) for 15 minutes.

These little buns are filled with confectioner's custard or *French pastry cream* (see CREAM) or with any other composition according to the recipe, once they are cold.

Choux or cream puffs à la cévenole—These are made like *Choux or cream puffs à la crème**. Fill with a purée of chestnuts mixed with whipped cream, flavoured with kirsch, once they are cold.

Choux or cream puffs à la Chantilly—Prepare and cook the puffs in the same way as *Choux or cream puffs à la crème**. Leave them to cool, split them and fill with *Chantilly cream* (see CREAM) flavoured with vanilla.

Chocolate choux or cream puffs. CHOUX AU CHOCOLAT—Prepared in the same way as *Coffee choux or cream puffs*, below.

Coffee choux or cream puffs. CHOUX AU CAFÉ—Fill the puffs once cooked with *French pastry cream* (see CREAM) flavoured with coffee essence.

They can be glazed with sugar flavoured with coffee.

Choux or cream puffs à la crème—Make the puffs in the usual way. When they are cold, slit them on one side, and fill the interior with a *French pastry cream* (see CREAM). Close the puffs and sprinkle with icing sugar.

Choux or cream puffs à la frangipane—The same as *Choux or cream puffs à la crème**, with *Frangipane cream.* See CREAM.

Glazed choux or cream puffs. CHOUX GLACÉS—Ordinary puffs filled with cream or any other preparation and glazed with sugar which is cooked to the 'crack' degree. See SUGAR, *Sugar boiling*.

Choux or cream puffs Montmorency—Made like *Choux or cream puffs à la crème.* Fill the puffs when cold with a mixture of cherries and *French pastry cream* (see CREAM) flavoured with cherry brandy.

Choux or cream puffs à la normande—*Choux* filled with a stiff apple purée mixed with a third of its weight of *French pastry cream* (see CREAM) flavoured with calvados.

CHRISTMAS. Noël—It was in the fourth century that Pope Julius I fixed December 25th as the date on which the birth of Christ was to be celebrated.

In France, the main Christmas meal is served on the night of 24th to 25th December after the celebration of Midnight Mass. This meal is called the *réveillon*.

The menu of the *réveillon* and of Christmas Day itself—essentially a family celebration—must include dishes which have, so to speak, a ritual significance. However rich the dishes in the *réveillon* menu, even if they include expensive delicacies such as *foie gras*, truffles, game of various kinds, rare fish and shellfish, they must also include, in deference to tradition, a black or white pudding, sometimes both, and a goose or turkey with chestnuts, which, naturally, are often enriched with truffles.

In Britain Christmas Day is celebrated gastronomically with even more splendour than in France.

'For many of the islanders,' wrote Alfred Suzanne in his book *La Cuisine anglaise et américaine* (English and American cookery) 'this anniversary is memorable (apart from all religious significance) because it evokes a great slaughter of turkeys, geese and all kinds of game, a wholesale massacre of fat oxen, pigs and sheep; they envisage garlands of black puddings, sausages and saveloys . . . mountains of plum-puddings and oven-fulls of mince-pies . . . .

'On that day no one in England may go hungry . . . . This is a family gathering, and on every table the same menu is prepared. A joint of beef, a turkey or goose, which is usually the *pièce de résistance*, accompanied by a ham, sausages and game; then follow the inevitable plum-pudding and the famous mince pies.'

Chub

CHUB. Chevaine, chevesne—Freshwater fish with a long spindly body, the dorsal fin set below the ventral opening.

The *common chub* called, in English, *Coheven, Nab, Botling*, is called in French *Meunier, Cabot, Chabot, Chavanne, Testard, Rotisson, Caboda*, etc. and sometimes reaches a size of 20 inches.

In U.S.A. chubs, known as the longjaw, blackfin and the bloater, are found in the Great Lakes. Lake Superior is the source of most of the blackfin, which is the only chub used extensively as fresh fish.

All the recipes given for the *Fera** (a fish belonging to the salmon family) are applicable to chub. This fish is also used as one element in the *matelote**.

CHUTNEY—A condiment of Indian origin which is found ready-made commercially.

This product is a kind of purée made with seeded Malaga raisins, which are pounded in a mortar with garlic, shallots, pimentos, apple, mustard, brown sugar and vinegar.

Preparation. Put in a quart (litre) of white vinegar which has been brought to the boil; 3 pounds (1,500 grams) of cooking apples, peeled and sliced. Cook them. Add 1 pound (500 grams) of brown sugar; 1 ounce (30 grams) of chilis, cut up fine; 1 cup (200 grams) of seeded Malaga raisins, cut up and washed; 1 pound (500 grams) of preserved lemon peel cut up fine; 1 pound (500 grams) of preserved ginger, cut into large dice; 2 crushed cloves of garlic. Season with 2 tablespoons (30 grams) of salt; 4 ounces (125 grams) of mustard grains and 2 tablespoons (15 grams) of powdered ginger. Add, if possible, 1 pound (500 grams) of preserved mangoes. Cook all this for about 8 minutes. Put the preparation, while hot, into glass jars which have been heated with boiling water, and cork them with fitting corks, which have been boiled for 8 minutes.

It is preferable to use ordinary bottling jars with rubber rings and screw caps. The screw caps are removed when the preserve has cooled.

CIDER. Cidre—Fermented drink with an apple base. This drink was already being made in Normandy in the thirteenth century and is mentioned in the Chronicles of Charlemagne. Special apples are used to make it, sweet, acid and tart, the varieties of which, differentiated by cultivation, have given a reputation to certain localities in which cider is produced. There are early and late species. In general, a good cider is made with ⅓ sweet apples and ⅔ sour and acid apples. The early-ripening apples are usually put in the press as soon as they are ready; the rest have to be stored in attics, and not in heaps at the foot of trees, contrary to some ideas.

The apples are crushed and then put in a press; the *marc* (what is left of the fruit after the juice has been pressed out) is submitted to a second pressing after it has been sprinkled with water.

The fermentation is established in the same way as with wine. Cider is subject to the same diseases as wine, and the same remedies can be applied to it.

There are different commercial brands of cider: *sweet cider*, and *bottled cider*, sparkling or not, according to whether it has been bottled before or after complete fermentation in cask.

It is a very refreshing beverage, generally less alcoholic than wine.

CIGAR, CIGARETTE—Considered solely from the gastronomic point of view, tobacco rounds off a meal in a pleasant way for those who like it. Smoking before or even during the meal is a heresy and destroys the sense of taste.

Professional tasters are obliged to renounce smoking altogether.

CINNAMON. Cannelle—Bark of the cinnamon tree. The name is also given to other kinds of bark which resemble cinnamon in smell or flavour. The highly esteemed and the only medicinal species is the *Ceylon cinnamon* which is found in the shops in the form of thin little sticks (about ⅓ inch in diameter) and up to a yard in length at times, consisting of rolled pieces of bark, each piece about a quarter of a millimetre thick.

It is yellowish in colour, easily breakable, with a spicy aroma and a very fine, sweet, hot taste.

The Chinese cinnamon (*cassia lignea*) is found in shorter, thicker sticks, formed of one layer of rolled bark, yellowish-brown in colour, with a few brown or blackish spots, easily breakable but with a less pleasant aroma and taste.

Cinnamon contains an essential volatile oil.

Powdered cinnamon is often made from inferior quality bark and is subject to a great many adulterations. Cinnamon in sticks is sometimes dried up (with the essential oils extracted) before being sold, but this sort of fraudulent practice is rare.

CINNAMONE—Name given in the old days to a spice which is probably cinnamon (*cannelle*).

CISELER—French term for making superficial incisions on the back of a fish to hasten its cooking under the grill or in any other manner.

Also applied to the slicing of any kind of leafy herb which is to be cut up into *Julienne** strips or into a *chiffonnade**.

CITRIC ACID. CITRIQUE—Organic acid found not only in lemons but in a great number of fruits (oranges, gooseberries, raspberries, etc.) and in some other plants. It is extracted from lemon juice, or it is prepared commercially by a special fermentation of glucose. It appears in fairly large fragile crystals, with an agreeable but acid flavour, highly soluble in water. It is easily kept in a dry state, but solutions of citric acid are rapidly invaded by moulds.

Citric acid is used for making lemonade. It also enters into the composition of orange and lemon syrups, etc.

Citric acid syrup. SIROP D'ACIDE CITRIQUE—See SYRUP.

CITRON. CÉDRAT—A species of lemon with a very thick coruscated skin, which is cultivated on the coast of the Mediterranean.

This fruit, which is very perfumed, is seldom eaten in a natural state, like the ordinary type of orange or lemon. Because of the thickness of its skin it is chiefly preserved, and in this form is used a great deal in cake-making and confectionery.

In Corsica, where the culture of this lemon species is extensive, a liqueur called *cédratine* is made with the fruit of this tree.

CITRONELLA. CITRONELLE—Common name for *Collinsonia canadensis*, a coarse plant of the mint family.

Citronella exudes a strong penetrating scent, rather like lemon. The leaves are used for seasoning. Digestive liqueurs are made from its flowers.

CITRUS AURANTIUM. BIGARADIER—The green leaves of this tree, called orange leaves, are principally used as tea. See TISANE.

The flowers, called *orange blossoms*, are used in confectionery, pharmaceutics and perfumery (distilled orange blossom water, essence of neroli).

CITRUS BALOTINUM. BALLOTIN—A variety of orange tree. Its leaves, larger than those of ordinary orange trees, are serrated around the edges. The fruit of this tree is somewhat similar to the lemon and has the same properties.

CITRUS BIGARDIA (Seville orange). BIGARDE—A species of bitter orange which is used in confectionery and in distilling certain liqueurs and beverages.

This orange is also used in cookery for spicing various sauces intended for game, in particular for waterfowl. See SAUCE.

It is also used for making bitter orange marmalade.

CITRUS MEDICA—See AIGRE DE CÈDRE.

CIVET—The word *civet* particularly applies to ragoûts of furred game, which are moistened with red wine, garnished with little onions, lardoons and mushrooms, and combined, when cooked, with the blood of the animal in question. This liaison with blood is essential to the dish.

The name of this preparation comes from the word *cive* (green onion) because in the past the dish was flavoured with these onions.

Although an old dictum maintains that 'to make a *civet*, first take a hare', one can, in fact, make the dish with any kind of furred game, and also with feathered game or fowl. There are even *civets de viandes* in some districts, and spiny lobster *civets* in Languedoc.

Civet of hare. CIVET DE LIÈVRE—See HARE.

Civet of spiny lobster. CIVET DE LANGOUSTE—See SPINY LOBSTER, *Spiny lobster stew*.

CLAFOUTI—A homely preparation in Limousin, this is a kind of fruit pastry or thick fruit pancake, made usually with black cherries.

Ingredients. 1 cup (125 grams) of flour, 2 eggs, ¾ cup (100 grams) of powdered sugar, half of which is reserved to sprinkle over the fruit, 1 cup (2 decilitres) of boiled milk, a pinch of salt, and 2 cups (400 grams) of cherries. Put the pastry and then the stoned cherries in a buttered flan case and cook in the oven.

CLAIRE—The name of the marine enclosures in the Marennes region where the oysters are left to go green. See *Green Marennes oysters* under OYSTER.

CLAIRET—Formerly *clairet* was a spiced and flavoured wine.

This wine was well known at the time of Charlemagne. It was then called *vin piment*, or simply *piment*. In this form it was a wine drunk as an apéritif, made in the same way that vermouth and other mixed wines are made now.

This made-up wine was not the same thing as *vin clairet*, which formerly was a natural, raw wine, neither red nor white, a sort of 'grey wine' as it would be called nowadays. It was of this *vin clairet* that the poets sang in the eighteenth century. The other *clairet* of the fourteenth and fifteenth centuries was also praised by poets who 'regarded it as the masterpiece of human industry to have united at one time in one drink the strength and aroma of wine, the sweetness and savour of honey and the perfume of far away spices, so rich and costly.'

Le Grand d'Aussy says that at this period: 'One would say that something had been lacking at a feast if "piment" had not been served', this being the name given to the wine in the thirteenth century. Like many other good things eaten and drunk, *clairet* or *piment* was made in the religious houses.

The *Pouillis* (statements of ecclesiastical profits in a province), said le Grand d'Aussy, prove that in the twelfth and fourteenth centuries the priors of the deanery of Châteaufort were required to provide on the Feast of the Assumption, each in turn, *piment* for the chauvines (nuns or postulants).

Le Grand d'Aussy also says that this apéritif was made only with *vin clairet*, that is to say with wine that was neither white nor red. It had several different shades: grey, straw coloured, 'partridge-eye', etc.

CLAIRETTE—Name given to a sparkling white wine made in Drôme.

CLARET—Name given in England to red Bordeaux wines.

CLAM. PALOURDE—A name applied to many edible bivalve molluscs which live in slimy sand and are found at low tide.

Some of these molluscs are cultivated in special beds along the beaches of Auray, Croisic and in the Bay of Bourgneuf.

Auray and Roscoff are the principal French centres of the clam trade.

In many of the places along the Atlantic coast the name *palourde* (clam) is also applied to various other molluscs: *tapé à stries croisées, tapé virginal, tapé à stries fines*, which are called *palourdou* in La Rochelle.

In Provence these molluscs are called *clovisses*.

Palourde is the common name given to many varieties of clams in most parts of France.

These molluscs are mainly eaten raw but they can be cooked in the same manner as mussels.

There are two sorts of clams: *soft shelled clams* and *hard shelled clams*.

The North American peoples are very fond of this shellfish. In the United States it is prepared in innumerable ways.

Fresh clams are eaten in the same way as oysters.

All the recipes given for *clovisses*, oysters, mussels and other shellfish can be applied to them.

Clams à l'américaine—Prepared in the same way as *Oysters à l'américaine.**

Clam chowder. CLAMS EN SOUPE—See SOUP.

Clams with cream. CLAMS À LA CRÈME—The same as *Oysters à la crème*.

Clams with cream are served in silver dishes, or in fire-proof porcelain, in *croustades*,* in little puff-paste tarts, and in vol-au-vents.

Clams à la diable—Like *Devilled oysters*. See OYSTER.

Fried clams. CLAMS FRITS—Like *Fried oysters*. See OYSTER.

Clam fritters. CLAMS EN BEIGNETS—Made in the same way as *Oyster fritters*.

Clams as garnish—Cook them in their own liquor, without allowing it to boil, in the same way as *Oysters for garnishing*.

Clams au gratin—The same as *Oysters au gratin.**

Grilled clams with various sauces. CLAMS EN BROCHETTES—Prepare like *Grilled oysters*. See OYSTER.

Served with *Diable, Indian, Niçoise, Provençale* sauce etc. See SAUCE.

Clams Mornay—The same as *Oysters à la Mornay.**

Clams à la polonaise—Like *Oysters à la polonaise.**

Clams on the half shell (Cold hors-d'oeuvre). CLAMS AU NATUREL—Fresh clams are served each in their bottom shell on ice, in the same way as fresh oysters.

Fresh clams are accompanied by various sauces: *Shallot, Horseradish, Vinaigrette*, etc. They are served with lemon, crackers, toast, with or without butter. Little Necks and Cherrystones are the names given to these small hard shelled clams.

Clams à la Villeroi—Like *Oysters à la Villeroi.**

CLARIFICATION—Operation which consists in clarifying certain food substances, usually a liquid.

The process of clarification varies according to the nature of the substance.

Clarification of bouillon—See BOUILLON.

Clarification of butter—This is done by fusion and decanting. Heat the butter on a *very gentle heat:* the butter melts and appears as clear as olive oil while a whitish deposit forms on the bottom of the pan. Strain the clear butter off into another receptacle.

Clarification of liquids and fruit juices. Nearly all liquids can be clarified by filtering; fruit juices are clarified by light fermentation.

Clarification of sugar—See SUGAR.

CLARY. ORVALE—Common name of the *Salvia sclarea* (herb of the sage family) formerly used in England for flavouring certain kinds of pastries. When infused in wine, it communicates to it a muscat taste. It is one of the herbs used in making Italian vermouth.

CLAVARIA OR CLUB-TOP MUSHROOM. BARBE-DE-CHÈVRE, CLAVAIRE—A capless, spindle-shaped mushroom which grows like a little bush, divided into branches, of various colours: white, pink or purple. It is edible but tough, indigestible and rather insipid. The best is yellow clavaria.

It can be prepared like other mushrooms, that is, sautéed in oil, or butter, *à la provençale, à la crème*, etc.

CLAYÈRE—An oyster bed where oysters are fattened.

CLAYON—French word for a little mat of rush or straw on which certain foods are put. The same name is given to small wire trays used by pastry-cooks.

CLIMAT—Certain vineyards, especially in the *Côte de Nuits* district, are called *climats*, because each one has a specific climatic condition.

CLISSE—Little tray or mat made in wicker or rush used to drain cheeses. Also a wicker covering round a bottle.

CLOCHE—This can mean a silver or plated cover to keep dishes warm. It also means a glass cover under which cheese is kept.

A *cloche* is also the name of a glass utensil which is used to cover certain things while cooking. See MUSHROOMS, *Mushrooms sous cloche*.

CLOS DE VOUGEOT (Wine)—The name of Vougeot is famous throughout the world. This charming village produces an excellent wine which is classed among the outstanding Burgundies as *Tête de Cuvée no*. 1.

Vougeot lies about 3 miles (5 kilometres) from Nuits, 12½ miles (20 kilometres) from Beaune, which is its district centre, and 11 miles (13 kilometres) from Dijon.

The vines which are grown are: for the fine wines of *Clos de Vougeot*, the *Pinots;* for the ordinary wines in other parts of the commune, the *Gamays*.

Clos de Vougeot wines have been declared 'perfect' by the specialists who have analysed them. These wines have a *grande finesse* and a great delicacy.

CLOSE (Jean-Joseph)—Famous pastry-cook born in Normandy. It is said that Close invented the *Pâté de foie gras aux truffes* about 1782, when he was in service with the Maréchal de Contade, governor of the province of Alsace at that time.

Culinary history relates that Close (his name is also spelt Clause), having realised what a *foie gras* could become in the hands of a clever chef, 'had elevated it to a sovereign dish by strengthening and concentrating the prime ingredient.... .in surrounding it with a forcemeat of veal and chopped pork fat,' and finally 'by adding to it the truffle, that culinary jewel.'

It does seem, however, that well before this time, and well before Close, the *pâté* and the *terrine de foie gras* were known in the south-west of France. See FOIE GRAS.

Some historians say that Close was only a populariser in Alsace of a dish already known in the south of France. Perhaps he also perfected this dish a little.

CLOTH FILTER. Blanchet—White woollen cloth filter for straining syrup and thick liquids.

CLOUD. Louchir—To become cloudy. This term is used of a liquid which is no longer clear.

CLOUTER (To stud)—An operation consisting of the insertion of small pieces of some substance or other in the shape of little studs into the surface of butcher's meat, fowl, game or fish.

To this end, truffles, cooked ham, and scarlet tongue are used for the *cloutage* (studding) of meat, fowl, game.

Fish are studded with truffles, with fillets of anchovy and with gherkins.

CLOVE. Girofle (Clou de)—Flowers of the clover-tree picked in bud and dried in the sun. The clove-tree probably comes originally from China. It was first cultivated in the Moluccas by the Dutch, who had the monopoly. It was introduced into Réunion and Mauritius by Governor Poivre, and later into the West Indies, Cayenne and Zanzibar.

Cloves have a four-sided stem and a calyx with four sepals. They have an aromatic scent and a hot spicy flavour. They are used for seasoning in cookery. They are sometimes sold mixed with cloves which have already been used in the manufacture of dyes or liqueurs. Sometimes the clove matrix or fruit of the clove tree are sold as cloves.

CLOVISSE—Bi-valve mollusc which is identical to *palourde* (a variety of clam); it is eaten fresh like oysters or cooked like mussels.

Clovisse is the Provençal name for *Vénus treillissée.* The genus *Vénus* comprises more than 150 species.

In Paris certain inferior bi-valves called *clovisses,* which bear absolutely no resemblance to the Mediterranean *clovisses,* are sold by the litre. This type of shell-fish has a similar outward form; but the shell is soft whereas the *Vénus provençale* is thick and strong in mother-of-pearl. These pseudo-clovisses, which come from the sands of the oceanic coast have, moreover, a wavy edge to the shell.

The Marseilles *clovisse* is not only remarkable for its beautiful mother-of-pearl; it is distinguished from the *Vénus de l'océan* by its marvellous cleanliness, just like the rock mussel.

It only lives in fine sand, never in mud, and keeps away from all forms of putrefaction.

This is an exquisite shell-fish, eaten fresh, with or without lemon.

Clovisses are prepared in the same way as mussels; see MUSSEL.

CLUPEIDAE. Clupes—Under this name a very important family of sea-water and fresh-water fishes are included, among which are the shad, herring, sardine and anchovy.

CNICAUT—A kind of edible wild cardoon, with a taste of cabbage.

COAGULATE. Figer—To thicken or congeal, when applied to fats.

COAL FISH. Charbonnier—A kind of cod fished in the North Sea. Prepared like cod. See COD.

COASTER. Galerie (bordure) de plat—A ring of silver or silver-plate made to fit the inner diameter of round dishes. This circle, more or less ornamental, is set in the well of the dish to hold in position the garnishes arranged round the main course.

COAT. Enrober—To coat food with a protective covering.

In cookery this term is mainly used of dipping food either in batter or in a sauce which masks it entirely, such as a *chaud-froid* sauce.

COCA—Peruvian shrub, the leaves of which are chewed by the Indians. Considered an economical food its properties are due to the effect produced by its alkaloid, cocaine, which is as stimulating as tea or coffee.

It is used as an infusion, as a wine, as an elixir. It is also used as an ingredient of certain cakes.

COCHINEAL. Cochenille—An insect used to prepare a magnificent red dye, called carmine.

The best known *cochineal* is that of nopal (cochineal cactus).

The female insect is used, collected after being fertilised and before the complete development of the eggs; gray cochineals are the most sought after, but there are also red and black varieties.

They are dried after being put in the oven on metal sheets for a few moments, or plunged into boiling water.

Carmine is used for colouring in cooking and cake-mixing.

COCHLEARIA—Type of cruciferous plant, of which one species, the wild horse-radish (*Cochlearia de Bretagne*) grows on the sea coast, particularly in Brittany, in England and in Ireland. It is known in the United States as 'Scurvy-grass'.

Its new leaves, having a taste of mustard, are edible and are eaten in salads or as a vegetable in certain countries, particularly Ireland.

COCIDO (Spanish cookery)—The name of a popular Spanish soup. This soup is also known under the name of *Olla podrida.**

COCK. Coq—Culinary synonym for chicken in certain dishes: *Coq au vin,* coq en pâté,** etc.

COCK-A-LEEKIE (or Cocky-Leeky, Scottish cookery) —Soup made of cock and leeks. See SOUP.

COCK'S COMB. Crête de coq—Fleshy excrescence, often voluminous, found on the heads of cocks and other gallinaceans. It is used chiefly as a garnish for entrées.

Method of cleaning and cooking cock's combs: Prick the combs lightly with a needle and put them under the cold tap, pressing them often with the fingers to dispel the blood.

Put them in a pan and cover with cold water. Put the pan on a lively heat and leave it there until the water reaches a temperature of 104°F. to 113°F. At this temperature the skin of the combs begins to detach itself.

Drain the combs and rub them one by one in a cloth sprinkled with fine salt.

Remove the outer skin completely; put the combs to soak once again and when they are white, plunge them in a boiling *White court-bouillon* (see COURT-BOUILLON) and let them cook for 35 minutes.

Turn them out into a basin and use according to instructions.

Attelets of cocks' combs. ATTELETS DE CRÊTES DE COQ—These decorative skewers, which were very much in use in the old days, are hardly ever seen today (see ATTELET). Almost always, when they were used to decorate removes or entrées, the principal elements of the decoration were cocks' combs.

Skewers which were garnished entirely with cocks' combs were made in the following way:

Attelets de crêtes chaudes—Cook the cocks' combs keeping them as white as possible and rather firm. Drain and wipe them. Piece the combs with decorative skewers, the frilled edge uppermost.

Attelets de crêtes froides—These are prepared in the same way as above, with fine cold cocks' combs, which are cased in jelly, once mounted on the skewers.

They are also made with cocks' combs covered in a *chaud-froid sauce* (see SAUCE), white or brown, and then covered with a coating of aspic jelly.

But these recipes are only given for the record, since these decorative accessories are hardly ever used today.

Cocks' comb barquettes and tartlets. BARQUETTES ET TARTELETTES DE CRÊTES DE COQ—These are made in the same way as barquettes and tartlets filled with various salpicon preparations. See HORS-D'OEUVRE, Hot hors-d'oeuvre.

Cocks' combs en atteraux—CRÊTES DE COQ EN ATTERAUX—Cook the cock's combs in the manner described above. Let them cool. Drain and wipe them. Marinate them in oil, lemon juice, and chopped parsley.

Drain them; impale them three at a time on silver skewers; dip in egg and breadcrumbs; at the last moment fry in clarified butter.

Cocks' combs en atteraux à la Villeroi. CRÊTES DE COQ EN ATTERAUX À LA VILLEROI—Cover the cocks' combs, which have been cooked in a *White Court-Bouillon* (see COURT-BOUILLON), drained and dried, with *Villeroi* sauce (see SAUCE). Allow to cool on a grid. Paint the combs with egg and sprinkle with breadcrumbs.

At the last moment, fry them in clarified butter.

Salpicon of cocks' combs à blanc. SALPICON DE CRÊTES DE COQ À BLANC—Cut up the cocks' combs into dice of a suitable size according to the nature of the preparation, after having cooked them in the manner described above. Heat them for a few moments in Madeira (or in any other wine or liqueur). Combine them with a few tablespoons of *Velouté sauce*, or with *Allemande sauce*. See SAUCE.

This salpicon is used as a filling for *bouchées*,* *barquettes*,* *tartlets*,* or other similar preparations.

Salpicon of cocks' combs à brun. SALPICON DE CRÊTES DE COQ À BRUN—Prepared in the same way as *Salpicon of cocks' combs à blanc*,* but replacing the white sauce with a very concentrated and thickened brown stock, to which Madeira has been added before boiling down.

Stuffed cocks' combs. CRÊTES DE COQ FARCIES—Choose very large combs and cook them in *White Court-Bouillon* (see COURT-BOUILLON) keeping them rather firm. Let them cool; drain them; wipe them. Slit them down the centre of the fattest part. Stuff each with a small ball of fowl stuffing (or with any other forcemeat). Cover the combs in *Villeroi sauce* (see SAUCE). Paint them with egg and sprinkle with crumbs. Fry at the last moment in clarified butter.

COCKLE. BUCARDE—A European marine bivalve mollusc of the genus *Cardium* found mainly at the mouth of rivers. The type found on the Atlantic coast of France, called *Bucarde sourdon*, is edible. It is also known in France under the names of *Coque*, *Sourdon* and *Poor man's oyster*.

Cockles are eaten raw and can also be prepared like *mussels*.*

COCKTAIL—A cocktail is a drink of spiritous liquor mixed with other liquid and aromatic ingredients, stirred or shaken with ice and served ice cold in special cocktail glasses. The origin of the word *cocktail* is uncertain. Probably Anglo-American, it might refer to the titillation resulting from the mixture of coloured liqueurs, or, according to certain etymologists, because the primitive cocktail of the Manhattan pioneers consisted in cocks' tails, dipped in a concoction of pimentos with which they tickled their throats to incite them to drink. The French origin of the word *coquetel* is, however, admitted by a number of authors, who maintain that it was in Bordeaux, towards the end of the eighteenth century, that this sort of drink was invented.

The cocktail party is a phenomenon of the mid-twentieth century. It is a method of entertaining small or large gatherings. On such an occasion one or more kinds of cocktails are served as well as 'straight' liquor, usually Scotch, Irish, Bourbon or Rye whisky, served poured over ice cubes ('on the rocks') or with crushed ice ('in a mist'), and served in short glasses or mixed with water or carbonated water and served in long 'highball' glasses. Accompanying these drinks are so called finger foods, which are hors-d'oeuvre that can be eaten while holding the glass. These hors-d'oeuvre can range from the very simple to the very elaborate.

There are a great many cocktails which have been in vogue from time to time, either for their exotic nature, or for their fantastic name, but certain mixtures have stood the test of time and continue to win the approval of connoisseurs. These include the following:

Martinis (Gin and Vermouth)—Dry Martini is 3 parts gin, 1 part dry French vermouth, with a garnish of an olive, a twist of lemon peel or a pearl onion, in which case the drink is called a Gibson. Proportions may vary; some people prefer a straight Martini which means less gin and more vermouth. A sweet Martini would contain 5 parts gin and 1 part sweet Italian vermouth, and is garnished with a twist of orange peel.

Pink Gin—A Pink Gin is made by putting some Angostura bitters in a glass and agitating the glass so that the bitters coat the sides and bottom; the bitters are then poured from the glass and gin is added until the drink is pale pink.

Gin and Dubonnet (Dubonnet Cocktail)—2 parts Dubonnet and 1 part gin, combined with cracked ice and shaken hard in a cocktail shaker and strained into stemmed cocktail glasses.

Manhattans—3 parts whisky (Rye, Bourbon or Scotch), 1 part sweet Italian vermouth and a dash of Angostura bitters. Garnish (optional): a maraschino cherry.

Dry Manhattan (Bronx)—3 parts whisky (Rye, Bourbon or Scotch), 1 part dry French vermouth. Garnish: a twist of lemon peel.

Whisky sour—4 parts whisky (Rye, Bourbon or Scotch), 1 part orange juice, 1 part lemon juice, sweetening to taste. Garnish (optional): maraschino cherry, orange peel or lemon peel.

Old-fashioned—Whisky (Rye, Bourbon or Scotch), Angostura bitters or cherry juice, sugar. Garnish (optional): cherries, orange slices, lemon slices or pineapple wedges. A small lump of sugar moistened with the Angostura bitters or cherry juice is placed in an 'old fashioned' glass. Ice cubes are added and 2-3 ounces of whisky are poured over them. One or more of the garnishes are added or, if preferred, a piece of lemon peel is twisted over the drink. A muddler (stirring stick) is placed in each glass.

Rum Daiquiri—1 part lime juice, 1 part sugar syrup, 4 parts Bacardi rum. Blend syrup and lime juice. Add rum and finely crushed ice. Shake hard and strain into chilled stemmed glasses.

Cocoa pods

COCOA (Beans). CACAO—Seeds contained in a sort of pod, which is the fruit of the Cacao tree.

This pod is gathered when ripe and split, after having been piled up for a few days. The beans, covered with fleshy pulp, are put to ferment which destroys the germ and permits the beans to be shelled. They are then dried either in silos or in the open air, the first method being considered the best. There is a great number of varieties and the highest quality cocoa comes from Venezuela and Guatemala. It can be recognised by the thickness of the shell, covered with an earthy ochre-coloured pulp. The bean is of a purplish-blue colour. Ecuador cocoa beans are bigger, covered with a brown shell and the inside is brown, almost black. Brazil varieties of cocoa, including the Maragnan, are flatter in shape. They are not silo dried, the inside is purple, bluish or purplish-blue. Guiana cocoa beans are small, with a grey shell and a brown inside. Cocoa from the West Indies is not silo dried. Different characteristics make it possible to distinguish the cocoa of Jamaica, Martinique, Guadeloupe, etc. The beans should have a clean smell, without any suggestion of mustiness or any foreign odour. They should not have any worm holes and must not contain any grit or other foreign matter.

Columbus was, according to legend, the first European to see cocoa in use, but the specimens he took back to Spain were not considered of any value. Cortés found it widely grown and used in Mexico in 1519. The Aztecs grew it for many generations and their Emperor Montezuma and his court are reputed to have consumed 50 large jars a day! There was, of course, no sugar and the drink was flavoured with vanilla and drunk cold.

In Europe, the Spaniards more or less imitated the Aztec method of preparing 'chocolate', flavouring it with chillies and other hot spices and making it into a souplike concoction.

Chocolate became a fashionable drink in France and the first record of its use in England was at Oxford in 1650. Seven years later a Frenchman opened a 'cocoahouse' in Bishopsgate Street, London. The price of chocolate was then from 10 to 15 shillings a pound. Under Charles II the duty payable on chocolate in its finished state was 8 shillings a gallon.

Later someone (it has never been quite established who the genius was) thought of adding sugar to chocolate and Pepys in his diary, after his first taste of '*jucalette*', described it as 'very good'.

During the eighteenth century, cocoa houses were fashionable resorts, each having a particular literary, political or gambling clientèle. Thus, White's, once notorious as a gaming house, later became White's Club in St. James's Street, one of the oldest clubs in England.

Chocolate was, of course, prepared by hand and Dr. Joseph Fry of Bristol was the first (having bought the patent rights from Walter Churchman, who had been making chocolate since 1728) to manufacture it on a big scale, introducing a steam-engine for grinding the cocoa beans in 1795. Dr. James Baker founded the first chocolate factory in America in 1780. Both businesses still exist.

All this, of course, was still cocoa, or drinking chocolate. It is not definitely known exactly when chocolate was first sold for eating, probably not until Victoria's reign. Cadbury's price list, as late as 1842, shows only one brand of eating chocolate.

Roasted cocoa. CACAO TORRÉFIÉ—The cocoa beans have only a very light smell and a bitter taste. Roasting, as in the case of coffee, is necessary to release the aroma.

After roasting the beans are pulverised and presented in various forms.

Cocoa powder. POUDRE DE CACAO SOLUBLE—Cocoa with reduced fat content treated with potassium (of which it must not contain more than 3.5 grams per 100). It is soluble.

Cocoa, among its principal aromatics, contains various alkaloids, the most important of which are theobromine and caffeine.

Cocoa, which contains about 17% of nitrogenous matter, 25.5% fats and 38% carbohydrates, has an important food value and, above all, a stimulating action which produces an immediate result, even before it has had time to be assimilated. It is mainly taken in the form of chocolate.

Preparation of cocoa—To prepare an excellent breakfast beverage, cocoa can be used instead of slab chocolate. The boiling liquid (water or milk) is poured on cocoa powder, mixed with fine sugar according to taste, and stirred with a wooden spoon until perfectly blended.

A smooth paste can be made by mixing cocoa powder with sweetened condensed milk and then adding boiling water.

Cocoa powder can also be sprinkled into a saucepan of milk or water on the fire and stirred until boiling is established.

Cocoa shells. Coques de cacao—The membranous shells of husked cocoa beans can be used to prepare a very pleasant beverage, resembling chocolate, which possesses fortifying properties, owing to the vitamin content. Allow a tablespoonful of cocoa shells per cup of this infusion.

Coconuts

COCONUT. Noix de coco—Fruit of the coconut tree, belonging to the palmtree family. The sap is used to make fermented drinks called generically Palm Tree wines.

Gathered before the fruit is ripe, the coconut contains a kind of milk or cream. When ripe the nut has a hollow centre and adheres to the shell, is of a hard consistency and has a flavour recalling that of nuts.

Coconut is used for many culinary preparations, for cake-making and for confectionery.

Dried and with the fibrous outer skin removed, the coconut is called copra and is used for making an industrial oil, used in soap manufacture.

Purified and deodorized, this fat (coconut oil has a firm consistency at ordinary temperatures) is called cocoa butter. There are a number of commercial products under this name. It is fatty, pure, almost without water content, odourless and tasteless, and very digestible. It is also used in certain diets when butter cannot be assimilated (which is rare) and especially in vegetarian cookery.

Coconut milk. Lait de coco—Used to moisten curry sauces.

Method. Mix with 1½ cups (3 decilitres) warm milk 14 ounces (400 grams) of fresh finely grated coconut. Strain through a muslin bag.

COCO-PLUM. Icaque—The coco-plum is the fruit of the tropical coco-plum tree. The coco-plum may be eaten fresh or preserved like prunes.

COCOSE—Butter made from coconut.

COCOTTE—This name is applied to utensils which are either round or oval in shape, in which certain foods are cooked, particularly meat, fowl and game.

Cocottes (B.E.D.A.)

Cocottes are made in earthenware or in fire-proof porcelain, in metal (tinned copper, nickel, aluminium, stainless steel, cast iron, silver or bi-metal) and in tempered glass.

The dishes cooked in these utensils, in which they are generally served, are described as *en cocotte* or *en casserole*.

Cod

COD. Cabillaud, Cabliaud—Large fish of the genus *Gadus*, to be found in Northern Atlantic waters. It has an elongated body with little soft grey scales. It is olive-brown in colour with yellow and brown spots on its back and flanks, which are white like its belly. A cod can weigh as much as 80 pounds. In France fresh cod is called *Cabillaud* and salt cod is called *Morue*. The flesh is white and flaky.

Cod was introduced into general use in France in the fifteenth century by Basque fishermen.

The Basque mariners, occupied from time immemorial with whaling, pressed on in pursuit of these enormous cetaceans into the depths of the Northern seas and, in the fourteenth century, reached the shores of Newfoundland. In the reign of François I, France had taken possession of this territory, to which the abundance of fish which visit its shores attracted French fishermen. In the seventeenth century it was considered that this fish was one of the best that could be found.

Fresh cod can be prepared in many different ways. In addition to the recipes given below for cod, this fish, whole or in pieces, steaks or fillets, can be prepared in any way suitable for *brill*,* *turbot*,* *haddock*,* and, generally, any other large fish.

The following recipes are particularly suitable for cod: *Bercy*, *Bonne femme*, *Normande*, *Portugaise*, *Provençale*.

Cod à l'américaine. CABILLAUD À L'AMÉRICAINE—This is prepared in slices or fillets as described in the recipe for *Brill à l'américaine*.*

Cod à l'anglaise. CABILLAUD À L'ANGLAISE—Cut the fish into slices $1\frac{1}{4}$ inches thick (taken from the middle part of the fish for preference). Season with salt and pepper and dredge in flour. Dip into beaten egg mixed with some oil and seasoned with salt and pepper, then cover with white breadcrumbs.

Cook in clarified butter until both sides are golden.

Arrange on a serving dish. Top with half-melted *Maître d'hôtel butter*. See BUTTER, *Compound butters*.

Boiled cod (hot) with various sauces. CABILLAUD BOUILLI (CHAUD)—Poach the cod whole or in pieces or steaks (the latter not too thin) in *Court-bouillon III*.*

Do not put the fish into the *court-bouillon* until it is cold. Bring the liquid to the boil, then remove the saucepan to the edge of the stove and leave to poach without allowing it to boil.

Drain the fish. Arrange it on a napkin-covered dish, garnish with fresh parsley and boiled potatoes, which can also be served separately.

Serve with one of the special sauces recommended for boiled fish, such as *Anchovy*, *Butter*, *Caper*, *Shrimp*, *Fines herbes*, *Hollandaise*, *Lobster*, *Ravigote*, etc. See SAUCE, *White and brown sauces*.

Boiled cod (cold) with various sauces. CABILLAUD BOUILLI (FROID)—Cook the fish as described in the preceding recipe; cook only until the fish is two thirds done, so that the cooking process can be completed while it is left to cool in the *court-bouillon*.*

Drain the fish when it is cold, dry on a cloth and arrange on a napkin-covered dish.

Garnish with fresh parsley, or, depending on the method of serving, with lettuce hearts and quartered hard boiled eggs.

Serve separately one of the cold sauces recommended for cold fish, such as *Gribiche*, *Mayonnaise*, *Ravigote*, *Rémoulade*, *Tartare*, *Green*, *Vincent*. See SAUCE, *Cold sauces*.

Cod à la boulangère. CABILLAUD À LA BOULANGÈRE—Season a chunk of cod with salt and pepper. Put it into an oven-proof dish. Sprinkle with melted butter and brown lightly in the oven.

Surround with potatoes cut in thin round slices and similarly sliced onions. Season the potatoes with salt and pepper and powdered thyme and bay leaf. Sprinkle with a little melted butter.

Bake in the oven basting frequently during cooking.

Sprinkle with chopped parsley and serve in the same dish in which it was cooked.

Cod braised in white wine. CABILLAUD BRAISÉ AU VIN BLANC—This dish can be made out of cod slices, steaks, chunks or skinned fillets.

Proceed as described in the recipe for *Brill in white wine*. See BRILL.

Cod braised in white wine, with various garnishes. CABILLAUD BRAISÉ AU VIN BLANC—All the methods of preparation given for brill, sole, whiting and other braised and garnished fish can be applied to cod (cooked in chunks, slices or fillets).

Cod with melted butter. CABILLAUD AU BEURRE FONDU—Cook the cod whole or in chunks in the salted water *Court-bouillon III*.*

Drain. Separately serve melted butter and boiled potatoes, as is usually done with poached fish.

Cold cod with various sauces. CABILLAUD FROID—Poach the fish in salted water, whether whole or in pieces. Leave to cool in the liquor in which it was cooked. Drain, arrange on a napkin-covered dish and garnish with parsley. Separately serve *Mayonnaise*, *Tartare sauce*, *Vinaigrette* or any other sauce recommended as an accompaniment for cold fish. See SAUCE, *Cold sauces*.

All the garnishes indicated for cold bass are suitable for cod. See GARNISHES.

Cod à la crème. CABILLAUD À LA CRÈME—Season slices of cod with salt and pepper. Fry in butter. When the slices of fish are half cooked, moisten with thick fresh cream, covering them to about halfway. Finish cooking under a lid. Put the cod on a serving dish. Boil down (reduce) the cream, add 2 or 3 tablespoons of fresh butter to it and pour over the fish.

Cod cooked in cream. CABILLAUD ÉTUVÉ À LA CRÈME—Bone a medium-sized cod. Skin the fillets and cut into pieces 2 inches square. Season them with salt and pepper. Fry $\frac{3}{4}$ cup (150 grams) of chopped onion lightly in butter in a sauté pan without allowing it to colour and add the fish. Fry the pieces of cod on all sides. Moisten with 1 cup (2 decilitres) of dry white wine. Simmer several minutes. Add 2 cups (4 decilitres) of not too thick *Cream sauce*. (See SAUCE). Finish cooking under a lid, simmering gently.

Creamed Cod au gratin. CABILLAUD CRÈME GRATIN—Butter a round or oval-shaped dish and pipe a fairly high border of *Duchess potatoes* (see POTATOES) round the edges.

Put a few tablespoonfuls of *Mornay sauce* (see SAUCE) on the bottom of the dish. Fill up to two-thirds of the height of the border with slices of cod, heated in butter. Cover with Mornay sauce, sprinkle with grated cheese, brush the border with beaten egg, sprinkle with melted butter and brown in a moderate oven.

Cod or Chrysophrys Curry (Créole Cookery). CARI DE COLIN—Take the tail of a codfish and fry it in fat. Take it out of the fat and keep warm. Put in this fat $\frac{1}{3}$ cup of finely chopped onions, add about a tablespoon of fresh tomato or tomato purée, some saffron (about a dessert-spoonful), thyme, parsley, two cloves of garlic, ginger. All these ingredients must be mixed in a mortar before they are put in the fat. Moisten with a large glass of luke-warm water. Simmer for a few minutes. Put the codfish tail in this sauce. Add 3 tablespoons of best olive oil. Simmer for about 40 minutes. Put in the oven for a few minutes and serve with *Créole rice*. See RICE.

Cod à la dieppoise. TRONÇONS DE CABILLAUD À LA DIEPPOISE—*Sauce and garnish:* Prepare in advance $2\frac{1}{2}$ cups (5 decilitres) of concentrated fish stock known as *fumet* (see FUMET). Clean and open a pint (half a litre) of mussels in the usual manner. Have ready 2 ounces (60 grams) of shrimps' tails (to obtain this volume of shelled shrimps' tails, that is to say only the flesh, allow 5 ounces or 150 grams of shrimps gross).

Using 2 tablespoons (25 grams) of butter and 2 table-spoons (25 grams) of flour, prepare a white *roux*.* Dilute it with fish *fumet** and $\frac{1}{2}$ cup (one decilitre) of well strained liquor left from cooking the mussels. Season with a pinch of pepper and a little grated nutmeg. Bring to the boil stirring all the time, add a small *bouquet garni** and, if possible, a tablespoon of onion peel. Allow to simmer gently for 20 minutes.

To cook the fish: Make a few small incisions on both sides of the fillets (this is to facilitate even heat penetration into the flesh).

Season the piece with fine salt and put into a dish with a glass of white wine and 2 tablespoons (30 grams) of butter in tiny pieces. Bring to the boil then continue to cook in a moderate oven from 15 to 18 minutes basting the fish frequently.

Last-minute operations: Strain the sauce through a strainer into another saucepan. Add the liquor in which the fish was cooked and 2 yolks of egg diluted with a few tablespoons of mushroom stock. Keeping on the fire, stir for a few minutes, then remove from heat and finish off with 4 tablespoons (60 grams) of butter.

To this sauce add the mussels (taken out of their shells and kept hot) and the shrimps' tails and do not allow to boil again. Arrange the fish on a long dish and surround with the sauce and the garnish. (Philéas Gilbert.)

Cod Dugléré. CABILLAUD DUGLÉRÉ. Cut the fish into steaks. Proceed as described in the recipe for *Bass Dugléré.* See BASS.

Cod fillets. FILETS DE CABILLAUD—Carefully skin the cod fillets and cut into rather big pieces (or leave the fish whole, if it is small).

Prepare by following one of the recipes given for whole or sliced cod, or bass, whiting or sole.

Cod à la flamande. CABILLAUD À LA FLAMANDE—From the middle of the cod cut 4 uniform pieces, each weighing from 3½–4 ounces (100–125 grams). Season with salt and freshly ground pepper.

Put these slices into a baking pan, well buttered and sprinkled with a good tablespoon of chopped shallots and a tablespoon of chopped parsley.

Cover with dry white wine. On each piece of cod put a slice of peeled lemon, without seeds, and bring to the boil on the top of the stove.

Finish cooking in the oven, allowing about 12 minutes.

Drain the fish and arrange on a long dish.

Bring the pan juices to the boil, add a tablespoon of butter, pour over the fish and sprinkle with chopped parsley.

Fried cod (*Mac Fisheries*)

Fried cod. CABILLAUD FRIT—Cut the fish into slices about 1 inch thick. Dip in cold boiled milk. Dredge with flour and deep fry in sizzling fat, preferably oil.

Drain the fish, dry with a cloth and sprinkle with very fine salt. Arrange on a napkin-covered dish and garnish with fried parsley and quarters of lemon.

Fried cod in breadcrumbs. CABILLAUD FRIT PANÉ—Dip the slices of cod in egg and breadcrumbs and fry as above.

Drain, season, arrange on a napkin, garnish with fried parsley and lemon and serve with *Maître d'hôtel butter* (see BUTTER, *Compound butters*).

Fried cod Orly. CABILLAUD FRIT ORLY—Prepare, in fillets, like *Whiting Orly.* See WHITING.

Cod au gratin. CABILLAUD AU GRATIN—Using cod steaks or fillets, prepare like *Brill au gratin.**

Grilled cod. CABILLAUD GRILLÉ—Cut the fish into steaks, approximately 1½ inches thick. Season with salt and pepper, sprinkle with melted butter or oil and cook under a moderate grill.

Arrange on a serving dish. Put a slice of carefully peeled lemon on each cod steak and garnish with fresh parsley.

Serve with *Maître d'hôtel butter* or one of the sauces recommended for grilled fish. See BUTTER, *Compound butters*, and SAUCE.

Cod à la hollandaise. CABILLAUD À LA HOLLANDAISE—In salt water *Court-bouillon III,** cook a piece of cod, taken from the middle, and some floury (mealy) potatoes, whole if they are small, cut in quarters if they are big.

Drain the fish and arrange on a serving dish. Surround with potatoes (*these should be cooked with the fish*) which have been dried off a bit in the saucepan, and turned, to break them up a little.

Serve melted butter separately.

This dish must not be confused with *Cod with hollandaise sauce,** In the latter dish, the cod, whole or in slices or steaks, is cooked in a *court-bouillon** and Hollandaise sauce is served separately.

Cod à l'indienne. DARNES DE CABILLAUD À L'INDIENNE—Season 4 cod steaks or slices with salt and pepper. Put them into a pan on a foundation of 4 tablespoons (50 grams) of chopped onions lightly fried in butter, 2 medium-sized tomatoes, peeled, seeded and chopped, as much grated garlic as can be held on the point of a knife and a tablespoon of chopped parsley. Sprinkle with 2 tablespoons (25 grams) of butter, in very small pieces. Moisten with ¾ cup (1½ decilitres) of dry white wine. Bring to the boil on the stove then bake in the oven for 10 minutes. Baste with thick fresh cream. Finish cooking, basting frequently. Serve *Rice à l'indienne** separately.

Cod steaks can also be prepared in the following manner: season with salt and pepper. Cook in a concentrated fish stock boiled down to the consistency of a *fumet.** Drain, arrange on a long dish, cover with *Curry sauce* (see SAUCE) to which the concentrated pan juices have been added. Serve *Rice à l'indienne** separately.

Cod à la meunière. CABILLAUD À LA MEUNIÈRE—Cut the cod into slices and proceed as described in the recipe for *Bass à la meunière.**

Cod Mornay. CABILLAUD MORNAY—Cut the fish into thin slices or fillets. Cook in very little white wine. Put in an oven-proof dish. Cover with *Mornay sauce* (see SAUCE), sprinkle with grated cheese and melted butter. Brown the top in the oven or under a grill.

Cod Mornay in shells I. COQUILLES DE CABILLAUD MORNAY—This is for using up left-overs. Put some *Mornay sauce* to cover the bottom of the shells (either metal, oven-proof china or scallop shells may be used). Fill with little slices of hot cod. Cover with *Mornay sauce* (see SAUCE). Sprinkle with grated cheese and melted butter and brown the top quickly.

Cod Mornay in shells II. COQUILLES DE CABILLAUD MORNAY—Prepare as above, putting the pieces of cod into shells around the edges of which a border of *Duchess potato* mixture (see POTATOES) has previously been piped through a forcing (pastry) bag with a fluted nozzle.

Roast cod. CABILLAUD RÔTI—This is prepared using cod whole or cut in large chunks. Season the fish with salt and pepper. Sprinkle with oil and a dash of lemon juice and leave to steep in this seasoning for an hour.

Drain the fish, put on a spit and secure with string. Brush with melted butter and roast before a brisk fire, basting with butter frequently.

Remove the fish from the spit. Arrange on a serving dish. Dilute the dripping pan juices with white wine and serve with the fish.

The cod may also be roasted in the oven. In this case, it should be placed on a grid to prevent its lying in the pan juices.

Cod in shells à la florentine. CABILLAUD EN COQUILLES À LA FLORENTINE—Proceed as described in the recipe for *Cod in shells au gratin*, lining the bottom of the shells with a tablespoon of leaf spinach, blanched and simmered in butter.

Cod in shells au gratin. CABILLAUD EN COQUILLES AU GRATIN—Put a border of sliced mushrooms around the edges of the shells. Cover the bottom with *Mornay sauce* (see SAUCE). Fill with small pieces of cod, put a cooked mushroom in the middle, cover with *Mornay sauce*, sprinkle with grated breadcrumbs and melted butter and brown the top.

When ready to serve, sprinkle with chopped parsley. To keep the fish from spilling out of the shells, a border of *Duchess potatoes* (see POTATOES) can be piped round the edges.

Cod in shells à la Nantua. CABILLAUD EN COQUILLES À LA NANTUA—Proceed as described in the recipes for *Cod Mornay in shells* replacing *Mornay sauce* by *Nantua sauce* (see SAUCE). At the last moment, put a large slice of truffle, heated in butter, into each shell.

Cod in white wine. CABILLAUD AU VIN BLANC—Using cod slices or fillets proceed as for *Brill in white wine*.*

SALT COD. MORUE—In France cod is mainly eaten salted (*morue verte*) and dried. As a general rule, salt cod should be treated as follows before it is prepared for the table:

Wash thoroughly, under a running tap if possible, otherwise in several waters. Poach in water without salt.

In certain cases salt cod, always washed first to remove salt, is used raw, that is without being poached in water.

To cook salt cod: Wash under the cold tap. Cut into pieces larger or smaller according to the recipe chosen. Soak for 24 to 36 hours in cold water. Drain the cod and put it in a pan, covered with cold water. Heat and at the first signs of bubbling, skim the water and lower the heat. Cover and poach (*the water must not boil*) for 15 to 18 minutes according to the size of the pieces. Drain the cod and proceed as indicated in the recipe selected.

Note. There is a practice (general in former times, and still followed by a good many people today) of cooking salt cod in rainwater and always in an earthenware casserole.

Salt cod à l'anglaise I. MORUE À L'ANGLAISE—Poach the cod in water. Drain. Lay it on a napkin. Garnish with fresh parsley. Serve separately parsnips boiled in salt water and drained, and Scotch hard boiled egg sauce, melted butter flavoured with lemon, with diced hot hard boiled eggs and parsley chopped and blanched.

Salt cod à l'anglaise II. MORUE À L'ANGLAISE—Wash and soak fillets of salt cod to remove all salt. Cut the raw fillets into thin slices. Flatten gently. Dip in egg and breadcrumbs. Fry in butter. Arrange on a long dish. Cover with partly melted *Maître d'hôtel butter* (see BUTTER, *Compound butters*). Serve with boiled potatoes.

Salt cod à la bamboche. MORUE À LA BAMBOCHE—Cut raw fillets of cod (washed and soaked to remove all salt) into thin slices, about the size of a fillet of sole. Dip in milk and flour. Twist into spirals. Deep-fry in boiling fat (preferably oil).

Drain, dry in a cloth. Fill a bowl with a *macédoine** of vegetables blended with butter or cream, and arrange the fillets on top.

Salt cod à la béchamel. MORUE À LA BÉCHAMEL—Poach the cod in water. Skin, trim and flake, keeping it very hot. Spread it in layers in a deep round dish, pouring over each layer a few tablespoons of *Béchamel sauce* (see SAUCE) with butter and fresh cream added.

Salt cod à la bénédictine. MORUE À LA BÉNÉDICTINE—Wash and soak 2 pounds (a kilo) of cod to remove all salt. Boil. Drain, skin and bone. Flake the cod. Dry in the oven for a few minutes.

Mix in a mortar with 3 cups (500 grams) of boiled potatoes which have been drained and dried in the oven.

Work this mixture with a pestle so that it absorbs 1 cup (2 decilitres) of oil and 1½ cups (3 decilitres) of boiled milk, taking care to add those ingredients alternately, a little at a time.

When the mixture is smooth and moist, put it in a buttered baking dish. Smooth the surface. Pour on melted butter and brown in the oven.

Note. Brandade of salt cod with truffles is often served under the name of *salt cod à la bénédictine*. This dish is, of course, a kind of *brandade* with potatoes, browned in the oven.

Salt cod à la Benoiton. MORUE À LA BENOITON—Brown very lightly in oil and butter ¾ cup (150 grams) of finely sliced onions. Sprinkle with 2 tablespoons (30 grams) of flour. Let this flour cook for a few seconds. Moisten with 3 cups (6 decilitres) of red wine and ¾ cup (1½ decilitres) of fish *fumet*.* Season with salt and pepper. Add a crushed clove of garlic, and mix. Cook for 15 minutes. Add five potatoes which have been peeled, boiled in salt water and sliced round. On top of these potatoes, put 2 pounds (a kilo) of boiled cod, flaked.

Tip the whole contents of the saucepan in one movement into a buttered baking dish. Smooth the surface carefully. Sprinkle with breadcrumbs. Pour on melted butter. Brown in the oven.

Boiled salt cod with various sauces. MORUE BOUILLIE—Wash and soak fillets of cod to remove all salt. Cut into pieces of equal size. Roll these pieces into scrolls and tie them. Poach in water as indicated in the introduction to this section.

Drain the cod scrolls. Untie them. Serve on a napkin, garnished with fresh parsley. Serve boiled potatoes separately, and one or other of the sauces usually served with fish fried in a *court-bouillon*,* such as *Bâtarde*, *Caper*, *Cream*, *Curry*, *Parsley*, *Hollandaise*, *Mustard*, *Ravigote*, *Saint-Malo*, etc. See SAUCE.

Bouillabaisse of salt cod I. BOUILLABAISSE DE MORUE—Cook in oil without browning ½ cup (100 grams) of onion and ¼ cup (50 grams) of leek, chopped. When these vegetables are very tender, add two tomatoes, skinned, with the seeds removed and coarsely chopped, and a crushed clove of garlic. Cook very quickly for 5 minutes. Moisten with ½ cup (a decilitre) of white wine and 2½ cups (5 decilitres) of water (or fish *fumet**) and add a generous pinch of saffron. Boil. Put in this stock 1½ pounds (750 grams) of fillet of salt cod cut into square pieces and well washed to remove salt. Pour in 3 tablespoons of oil. Season with a pinch of freshly ground pepper. Cover the saucepan and boil hastily for about 25 minutes. At the last minute add a tablespoon of chopped parsley.

Brandade of salt cod *(Robert Carrier)*

Serve the *bouillabaisse* in a deep round bowl, with slices of bread toasted in the oven.

Note. As with *Bouillabaisse à la Marseillaise*, the soup of the *bouillabaisse* can be served in a tureen with slices of French bread in it, and the fish served separately in a deep dish.

Bouillabaisse of salt cod II (à la ménagère). BOUILLABAISSE DE MORUE À LA MÉNAGÈRE—Cook very slowly in ½ cup (a decilitre) of oil, ½ cup (100 grams) of finely sliced onions and ¼ cup (50 grams) of leek, also finely sliced. The vegetables must not brown. When they are cooked add two crushed cloves of garlic.

Moisten with a quart (litre) of water. Season with salt and pepper. Add a pinch of saffron and a *bouquet garni.** Boil. Put in the saucepan 2 cups (300 grams) of thickly sliced potatoes and boil hastily for 12 minutes.

Put in 1½ pounds (750 grams) of salt cod, treated as indicated above, and cut into square pieces. Pour 3 tablespoons of oil into the saucepan. Cover and boil fast until it is ready. Just before serving, add a tablespoon of chopped parsley. Remove the *bouquet garni.*

Serve the *bouillabaisse* in a deep round bowl or a deep dish. Serve with slices of ordinary toasted bread, rubbed with garlic and soaked in a few tablespoons of the cooking stock.

Brandade of salt cod. BRANDADE DE MORUE—Wash and soak 2 pounds (1 kilo) of salt cod to remove salt. Cut it into square pieces. Poach in water for not more than 8 minutes. Drain the cod. Skin and bone it. Flake.

Take a heavy, flat-bottomed saucepan. Heat 1 cup (2 decilitres) of olive oil in it until it begins to smoke. Put in the cod, and add a small crushed clove of garlic. Work the mixture on the stove with a spoon made of very hard wood until it is reduced to a smooth paste. Turn the heat very low and keep on working the *brandade* with the wooden spoon, adding, a little at a time, 2–2½ cups (4 to 5 decilitres) of oil. Still stirring constantly, add at the same time as the oil about 1¼ cups (2½ decilitres) of boiled milk (or fresh cream), poured in a little at a time. Season with salt and white pepper.

Note. When the *brandade* (which must be prepared on the stove over a gentle heat) is ready, it should have the appearance of a white paste. very smooth, with the consistency of mashed potatoes.

Serve the *brandade* in a round bowl or deep dish, moulding it into the shape of a dome. Garnish with triangles of sandwich bread fried in oil or butter (or with croûtes of ordinary French bread, also fried in oil).

Brandade of salt cod à la Nantua. BRANDADE DE MORUE À LA NANTUA—Prepare the *brandade* as indicated above, moistening it with fresh cream. Serve it in a bowl in layers. Alternate each layer with 3 tablespoons of *ragoût** of fresh-water crayfish tails. Surround with strips of truffle tossed in butter and garnish with slices of bread fried in butter.

Brandade of salt cod with truffles. BRANDADE DE MORUE AUX TRUFFES—Make the *brandade* as indicated above. Add, at the end, coarsely diced truffles tossed in butter. Serve in a bowl. Cover with strips of truffle tossed in butter. Surround with slices of bread fried in butter.

Salt cod with brown butter. MORUE AU BEURRE NOIR—Put the cod, poached, drained and trimmed, on a serving dish.

Dry for a few seconds in the oven. Pour on a few drops of vinegar or lemon juice. Sprinkle with chopped parsley, and capers if desired. At the last minute pour sizzling brown butter over the cod, allowing 7 tablespoons of butter per pound of fish.

Note. The cod can also be prepared as follows:

Brandade of salt cod with truffles

Put the cod on a serving dish. Pour vinegar over it. Sprinkle capers on top. At the last minute, pour on brown butter in which 3 tablespoons of small sprigs of parsley taken off the stalk have been fried.

Salt cod with noisette butter. MORUE AU BEURRE NOISETTE—Poach and trim the cod. Put it on a serving dish. Squeeze lemon over it. Sprinkle with chopped parsley. At the last moment pour on a few tablespoons of noisette butter (butter heated in a frying pan until it is as brown as a hazel nut).

Salt cod à la crème. MORUE À LA CRÈME—Proceed as for *Salt cod with béchamel*, using *béchamel* sauce enriched with fresh cream. Serve in a deep round dish.

Salt cod à la crème au gratin. MORUE À LA CRÈME AU GRATIN—Poach, trim and flake the salt cod, and proceed as for *Creamed cod au gratin.*

Salt cod à la créole. MORUE À LA CRÉOLE—Poach, drain, trim and flake the cod. Make a dome of it in a buttered baking dish on a bed of a tomato fondue prepared as follows:

Cook ¾ cup (150 grams) of finely sliced onions in a mixture of oil and butter until they are very tender. Skin 4 tomatoes, remove seeds and crush. Add them to the onions. Also add 4 skinned, coarsely diced sweet peppers. Season with salt and pepper, and flavour with a little chopped garlic.

On top of the cod put a few slices of tomato sautéed in oil, and halved sweet peppers, skinned and also sautéed in oil. Pour on a little oil. Bake in the oven for a few minutes. Just before serving squeeze a little lemon juice over the fish, and sprinkle with chopped parsley.

Croquettes of salt cod. CROQUETTES DE MORUE—Made in the same way as other croquettes, with boiled salt cod, left to cool and diced.

Cooked mushrooms and diced truffles may be added to the croquettes, as with most other croquettes. See CROQUETTE.

Curried salt cod, called à l'indienne. MORUE AU CURRIE, DITE À L'INDIENNE—Boil the cod. Trim and flake it. Put it in 2½ cups (5 decilitres) of *Curry sauce* (see SAUCE). Mix gently. Serve in a deep round dish. Serve *Rice à l'indienne** separately.

Salt cod en escabèche. MORUE EN ESCABÈCHE—Wash and soak fillets of cod to remove salt. Cut into thin slices. Proceed as for *Anchovies à la grecque.* See HORS-D'OEUVRE, *Cold hors-d'oeuvre.*

Fillets of salt cod Orly. FILETS DE MORUE ORLY—Cut the cod, raw, into thin slices. Steep for an hour in a marinade of oil, lemon-juice and chopped parsley. Just before serving, dip in a light batter and deep-fry. Garnish with fried parsley and serve with *Tomato sauce.* See SAUCE.

Fish balls of salt cod à l'américaine. CROQUETTES DE MORUE À L'AMÉRICAINE—Take equal parts of *Duchess potato mixture* (see POTATOES) and flaked boiled cod with bones and skin carefully removed. Bind the mixture with a few tablespoons of *Béchamel sauce*. See SAUCE. Season well and mix. Leave to cool.

Divide this mixture into small parts. Roll into balls on a floured table. Dip in egg and breadcrumbs. Deep-fry. Serve on a napkin, garnished with fried parsley. Serve with *Tomato sauce*. See SAUCE.

Fried salt cod. MORUE FRITE—Wash and soak a fillet of cod to remove salt. Cut into thin slices. Dip the slices into boiled milk. Drain and flour lightly. Deep-fry in boiling fat (preferably oil). Drain, dry in a cloth, season with very dry table salt (though only if the cod is completely free from salt). Serve on a napkin, garnished with fried parsley and lemon.

Fritot of salt cod. MORUE EN FRITOT—Poach and flake the cod. Steep in a marinade of oil, lemonjuice, pepper and chopped parsley. Just before serving, dip in a light batter and deep-fry. Thin slices of raw salt cod, similarly steeped and coated with batter, may also be used. Serve on a napkin garnished with fried parsley. Serve *Tomato sauce* separately. See SAUCE.

Salt cod à la hongroise. MORUE À LA HONGROISE—Line a frying pan with chopped onions seasoned with paprika. Cook slowly in butter until very tender. Cut into square pieces 2 pounds (1 kilo) of cod and remove salt as indicated above. Lay the cod on top of the onions. Cover with a layer of onions, cooked in the same way. Moisten with ¾ cup (1½ decilitres) of dry white wine. Add 1 cup (150 grams) of coarsely diced cultivated mushrooms. Cover and cook for 6 minutes. Moisten with a few tablespoons of thick fresh cream. Cover and simmer for 10 minutes. Serve in a deep round dish.

Salt cod à la languedocienne. MORUE À LA LANGUEDOCIENNE—Remove salt from 2 pounds (a kilo) of cod as indicated above. Cut into square pieces and boil in water. It should be taken out while the flesh is still rather firm. Drain the cod and put it in a *ragoût* of potatoes prepared as follows: Cut 2 pounds (a kilo) of potatoes to look like big olives or into quarters. Brown lightly in oil.

Sprinkle with 2 tablespoons of flour. Fry for a few seconds, shaking the pan constantly. Add a crushed clove of garlic. Moisten with a few spoonfuls of the cod cooking stock. Add a *bouquet garni.** Season with a little salt and pepper if necessary, bearing in mind that the cooking stock is already salty.

Cover and bake in the oven for 25 minutes. Remove the *bouquet* and sprinkle with chopped parsley.

The pieces of cod having been put on top of the *ragoût*, pour oil over it and finish cooking in the oven for 5 to 6 minutes.

Salt cod à la lyonnaise (Carême's recipe). MORUE À LA LYONNAISE—'After having prepared and boiled the cod in water, drain it so that it can be flaked. Put the flaked cod in a saucepan and set this on hot embers. Cover and put glowing coals on top to dry off any water that may be left in the cod (or dry in the oven).

'Dice three large white onions. Throw them into a frying pan in which half a pound of butter has been melted. Cook the onions over a gentle heat until they are a fine golden colour. As soon as they are ready, brown the cod in the pan. Season with pepper, grated nutmeg and the juice of a lemon, and serve.'

Salt cod à la maître d'hôtel. MORUE À LA MAÎTRE D'HÔTEL—Poach in water and flake the cod. Put in a deep, round dish with alternate layers of peeled, boiled potatoes, sliced round. Cover with partly melted *Maître d'hôtel butter*. See BUTTER, *Compound butters*.

Salt cod mayonnaise. MAYONNAISE DE MORUE—Made with cod poached in water, trimmed and flaked, in the same way as *Cold salmon mayonnaise*. See SALMON.

Salt cod à la meunière. MORUE À LA MEUNIÈRE—Slice raw fillets of cod. Flour and fry in butter. Put on a long dish. Squeeze a few drops of lemon over it. Sprinkle with chopped parsley. Pour the sizzling butter over the fish.

Salt cod Mireille. MORUE MIREILLE—Take some raw cod fillets. Thoroughly remove salt as indicated above. Cut into neat pieces of equal size. Flour. Brown quickly in smoking oil. Prepare a fondue of tomatoes as follows: Cook in oil, without browning, 4 tablespoons (50 grams) of chopped onion. Skin 4 tomatoes, remove seeds and chop coarsely. Add these to the onions, with half a clove of chopped garlic. Season with salt and pepper and a teaspoon of saffron. Cook until almost all the water of the tomatoes has evaporated. Moisten with 1½ cups (3 decilitres) of white wine. Cook for 10 minutes.

Serve on a round dish with a border of *Rice pilaf* (see PILAF). Cover with the sauce.

Arrange whole black olives on top. Sprinkle with chopped parsley.

Salt cod Mornay. MORUE MORNAY—Boil, drain and trim pieces of cod. Put in an ovenware dish on a layer of *Mornay sauce* (see SAUCE). Cover the fish with the same sauce. Sprinkle with grated cheese. Pour on salted butter, and brown in the oven.

Salt cod à l'occitane. MORUE À L'OCCITANE—In a deep round ovenware dish, heat 5 tablespoons of oil with a clove of garlic. Add the ingredients in layers: 1½ pounds (750 grams) of salt cod, poached, trimmed and flaked; 3 hard boiled eggs cut into thick slices; 4 peeled, boiled potatoes, cut into round slices; a large tomato, peeled, coarsely diced and cooked in oil; 24 black olives; 1 tablespoon of capers. Decorate the top of the dish with slices of hard boiled eggs, black olives and slices of lemon with all rind and skin removed. Pour on a few tablespoons of oil. Season with freshly ground pepper. Warm gently. Sprinkle with chopped parsley.

Salt cod à la parisienne. MORUE À LA PARISIENNE—Boil, drain and trim slices of cod. Put on a serving dish. Cover with finely diced hard boiled eggs, capers and chopped parsley. Squeeze lemon juice over it. Just before serving, pour on a few tablespoons of browned butter in which 4 tablespoons of fresh breadcrumbs have been fried.

Salt cod Parmentier. MORUE PARMENTIER—Boil, drain and flake the cod. Put in a buttered ovenware dish. Cover with a light purée of potatoes. Sprinkle with grated cheese. Pour on melted butter. Brown in the oven.

Salt cod à la Provençale. MORUE À LA PROVENÇALE—Make 2½ cups (5 decilitres) of *Tomato fondue** with oil, flavoured with garlic. Add to it 2 pounds (1 kilo) of cod poached in butter, trimmed and flaked. Add salt and pepper. Sprinkle with crushed parsley. Cover and simmer for a few minutes. Serve in a deep, round dish.

Salt cod en rayte. MORUE EN RAYTE—Brown in oil in a saucepan ½ cup (100 grams) of chopped onion. Add 2 tablespoons of flour. Cook for a few seconds on the stove, stirring. Moisten with 2 cups (half a litre) of red wine and the same quantity of boiling water. Mix. Season with pepper and a very little salt (the cod being salted). Add 2 cloves of garlic and a *bouquet garni.** Add a tablespoon of tomato purée. Boil.

To this sauce, add 1½ pounds (750 grams) of fillets of cod with the salt removed, floured and deep-fried in oil. Add 2 teaspoons of capers. Cover and simmer for a few minutes.

Rougail of salt cod and tomatoes—See ROUGAIL.

Salt cod salad. SALADE DE MORUE—Mix in a salad bowl round slices of peeled, boiled potatoes and cod, boiled, drained, trimmed and flaked. If desired, add chopped onion. Season with oil and vinegar. Sprinkle with chopped parsley, chervil and tarragon.

Salt cod with spinach au gratin. MORUE AUX ÉPINARDS GRATINÉE—Wash and soak the cod to remove salt. Cut into slices of equal size. Poach in water. Drain the cod. Skin and bone it. Flake. Heat 1 cup (2 decilitres) of oil in a pan until it begins to smoke. Take enough spinach to produce a pound (500 grams) when cleaned. Remove stalks. Wash, parboil for 5 minutes in boiling salt water, drain and chop coarsely. Put it in the smoking oil. Season with salt, pepper and a touch of nutmeg. Add a little crushed garlic. Add to this spinach the flaked cod. Add a few spoonfuls of *Béchamel sauce** (see SAUCE). Mix and arrange in a round buttered fireproof dish. Shape into a dome and smooth. Sprinkle with breadcrumbs. Pour oil over it. Brown gently in the oven.

Salt cod with tomatoes à la marseillaise. MORUE AUX TOMATES À LA MARSEILLAISE—Cut the raw cod into square pieces. Flour and deep-fry in oil. Simmer for 10 minutes in *Tomato fondue** strongly flavoured with garlic.

Vol-au-vent of salt cod. VOL-AU-VENT DE MORUE—This type of vol-au-vent is usually made by filling the flaky pastry cases with *Brandade of salt cod* (see above) with or without truffles.

Vol-au-vents can also be filled with flaked cod mixed with colloped (sliced) truffles and mushrooms, and blended with either a meatless *Velouté sauce* or a *Cream sauce*. See SAUCE.

COD-BURBOT—Fresh water fish of the codfish type. The cod-burbot is also known as burbot, eel-pout and coney fish. The method of cooking is the same as for river burbot. See BURBOT. In U.S.A., the burbot, also called *fresh water cusk*, is found in the Great Lakes and in smaller lakes and rivers across the northern latitude of the country.

COFFEE, COFFEE-SHRUB. CAFÉ—The coffee bean from which the beverage is brewed is a species of the madder family called *Coffea Arabica.*

History, or perhaps legend, tells us that the first man to drink coffee, at least according to Scheha Beddin, an Arab author of the fifteenth century, was the Mufti of Aden, who lived in the beginning of the ninth century. According to another tradition, we owe the discovery of coffee to a certain Mullah (a Mahometan priest) called Chadely or Scyadly, whose name, it is said, is still venerated in the Middle East. This holy man, upon finding himself often overcome by sleep in the middle of his prayers, attributed his drowsiness to the half-heartedness of his devotions, and his over-scrupulous conscience tormented him. Chance, or, according to the legend, the Prophet, touched by his sorrow, led him to encounter a herdsman, who told him that each time his goats ate the berries of a certain shrub, they would remain awake, jumping and gambolling the whole night. The Mullah expressed the wish to see this extraordinary plant and the herdsman showed him a pretty little shrub with a greyish bark and brilliant foliage, the slender branches of which, at the axils of their leaves, had bunches of small white flowers mingled with clusters of small berries, some green, others, riper ones, of a clear yellow colour and yet others, which had reached complete maturity, of the size, shape and colour of a cherry. It was the coffee-shrub. The Mullah wished to test the unusual virtues of these berries. He made himself a very potent brew and spent the whole night in a state of delicious intoxication which, however, in no way affected his intellectual capacities. He told his dervishes about his discovery and soon coffee became much in demand with devout Moslems, as a divine gift brought by an angel from heaven to the faithful. The use of coffee then spread from Aden to Medina, Mecca and throughout the rest of the Middle East. Coffee was taken during prayers, in the mosques, even at the Holy Temple at Mecca and before the tomb of the Prophet.

Coffee, in the Middle East, is one of the first necessities of life. One of the commitments which a Turk takes on, it is said (or, at any rate, used to take on in the past), towards the woman he marries, is the promise that she shall never go short of coffee.

Coffee was hardly known in Europe before the seventeenth century. Travellers, who had acquired the habit of drinking this beverage in the East, imported it at first for their personal use. Pietro della Valle brought it to Italy in 1615, La Royne to Marseilles in 1644, Thévenot to Paris in 1647, but even before Thévenot a certain Levantine in 1645 established a shop in Petit-Châtelet where for some time, but without great success, he sold a coffee decoction which he then called *cahove* or *cahouet* (a name probably derived from the Arabic *quhwah*, in Turkey pronounced *kahvah* or possibly from Kaffa in the Ethiopian highlands where the plant is native). It was Suleiman Aga, the ambassador of the Sublime Porte to the Court of Louis XIV in 1669 who popularized coffee in France. As laid down by Turkish custom, he offered it to all who came to visit him. The vogue for coffee then spread throughout high society and created a furore. Coffee was as rare as it was in keen demand and the price was high.

The Dutch founded the East India coffee trade when they introduced coffee into Java about 1690, but it was thanks to a Frenchman, Desclieux, that coffee was introduced into the Western Hemisphere. He, under the patronage of Louis XIV, defied great hardships in order to bring one tiny coffee plant seedling to Martinique. Once there, the plant flourished and from there seedlings were taken to French Guiana and thence to Brazil, and from there it spread to Central America. Brazil is the greatest producer of coffee.

The best varieties of coffee had for a long time been those which came from Arabia, known as *moka* or *Yemen* coffee, as well as coffee from the Bourbon (or Réunion) Island and Martinique. The names have been preserved in the trade to distinguish three types of coffee, although the designation in no way implies its origin.

The three types are:

Moka—small irregular grains, yellowing in colour and convex on both sides.

Bourbon—medium-sized grains, yellowing, oblong.

Martinique—the biggest grains, rounded at the ends, greenish in colour.

Like wine, coffee gives the greatest production in the plains but the best qualities come from the higher parts of the torrid zone, particularly from Central America (Guatemala, Salvador, Honduras, Nicaragua and Costa Rica), as well as from the northern part of South America (Venezuela and Colombia) whose products are always rated among the first. Arabian coffee is very rarely to be found on the market. The same applies to Martinique coffee, which figures in commercial statistics only as a memory.

The coffee plant is a large evergreen shrub with dark shiny leaves. The cherry-like fruit is soaked, de-pulped, dried and the seed is then polished to remove the parchment-like husk and outer filament. The seeds are then classified as to size and ripeness.

Coffees of various origins are usually blended in the trade in different proportions.

When green, coffee keeps for a long time, provided it is protected from damp; keeping it, in fact, improves it. It is entirely devoid of smell.

To release the aroma, coffee has to be roasted, an operation which many coffee lovers insist on performing themselves.

Well-roasted coffee should be brown, of varying degrees of darkness, but never black. If not sufficiently roasted, it produces a colourless infusion, and is rough and astringent. If over-roasted, it produces a black infusion, bitter and unpleasant.

During industrial roasting process a small quantity of sugar molasses or various other products is sometimes added, to 'coat' the berries. This coating, which is permissible by law, gives the berries a better colour and more shiny appearance, prevents the loss of aroma and has a further advantage for the merchant of increasing the weight and, frequently, allows him to use inferior quality or damaged grains.

After roasting, coffee does not keep its aroma for long; it is, therefore, better not to roast or not to buy it all roasted in quantities exceeding one's needs, and it is advisable to keep it in jars and tins with well-fitting lids.

Grinding is the last operation through which coffee has to go before being actually made. Ideally, coffee should be ground immediately before being made, as ground coffee quickly loses its aroma. The operation itself is too well known to require description.

Soluble coffee, more commonly known as instant coffee, was the invention of a Mr. G. Washington, an Englishman living in Guatemala. While waiting for his wife one day to join him in the garden for coffee, he noticed on the spout of the silver coffee pot, the fine powder, which seemed to be the condensation of the coffee vapours. This intrigued him and led to his discovery of soluble coffee. In 1906 he started experiments and put his product on the market in 1909. Since that time many varieties of instant coffee have appeared on the market with great commercial success.

There are four basic methods of brewing coffee: *boiling*, *steeping*, *percolating* and *filtering*. Coffee experts consider filtering the best method of extracting the soluble essences of ground coffee. The coffee is contained in a paper or cloth filter. Boiling water is poured over the grounds and allowed to flow into a container where it will not come into contact again with the grounds. For perfect coffee, earthenware or glass receptacles should be used, since contact with metal lowers the quality of the drink.

Bourbon créole coffee. CAFÉ CRÉOLE BOURBON—Créole coffee must be strong and fragrant. 15 grams, or one heaped tablespoonful of ground coffee should be allowed per cup. Put into the filter as many spoonfuls of coffee as you want cups, press down well and proceed in the following manner:

Put your filter into a *bain-marie** (which must not be boiling) just to keep the coffee hot. Keep some boiling water in a separate receptacle especially for this purpose. First steep the coffee thoroughly, then, little by little, add a tablespoonful of water. Let it drip through until you have obtained the required amount of coffee. Serve very hot in a coffee pot which has previously been scalded. The preparation of créole coffee takes over an hour.

Coffee with milk, with cream. CAFÉ AU LAIT, À LA CRÈME—The addition of a quantity of milk or cream to black coffee reduces its stimulating properties and turns it into a real food. Coffee can also be actually made with milk, according to an old process revived by M. Louis Forest. Milky coffee, which has a mildly laxative effect on most people, has been blamed for all sorts of harmful effects, but these allegations have never been proved.

Iced coffee. CAFÉ GLACÉ—Prepare the coffee in the usual manner, using 3 cups (300 grams) of freshly ground coffee and 3 cups (¾ litre) of boiling water. Pour this infusion into a bowl with 2½ cups (600 grams) of lump (or granulated) sugar. Dissolve the sugar and chill the infusion.

Then add to the coffee a quart (litre) of vanilla-flavoured boiled milk, which should be completely cold, and a pint (½ litre) of fresh cream. Freeze in an ice-pail keeping the composition a little on the liquid side. Serve in cups. If served with whipped cream, it is called *Café liégeois*.

Uses of coffee—Coffee is used for flavouring a great number of cold and hot sweets. In all these dishes coffee is used in the form of an essence, which is prepared by putting plenty of coffee powder with very strong coffee into the upper part of the coffee-pot.

To flavour creams (English custards, etc.) roast the coffee grains in the oven (on a metal sheet), grind and put them into boiling milk. Cover this milk with a cloth and leave to infuse for a few minutes (see CREAMS, ICE CREAMS AND ICES, PARFAIT). Industrially produced coffee essence and 'instant' coffee can also be used for flavouring creams.

Coffee with caffeine extracted. CAFÉ DECAFÉINÉ—In order to render coffee less harmful and to extract the caffeine, attempts have been made to rob coffee of its alkaloid substance (see CAFFEINE). This operation, which is nowadays done on a great scale (and done very efficiently) consists, after having broken up the beans by steam, of subjecting them to the action of either chloroform or some other solvent, then of eliminating this liquid by heating and roasting.

After having been roasted, the coffee, from which the solvent has removed the caffeine and a sort of gum, retains the same taste as coffee which has not been treated, without having any of the stimulating properties.

Coffee substitutes—The number of products which aim at replacing coffee is considerable. Various grains and roots have been used to this effect, or for adulterating purposes. Apart from chicory, the most important adulterants are the following: *fig*, *date*, *acorn* (mildly astringent), *malt*, *barley* and other roasted *cereals*, often flavoured with steam passed through coffee, *chick-pea* and *lupins*, used a great deal in Brittany. This is by no means a complete list.

The majority of these products, even though their flavour may only have a very remote resemblance to that of real coffee, are at least harmless.

COGNAC—Little town in the district of Charente which has given its name to famous brandies. See CHARENTE and SPIRITS.

The distillation of wines which provide the various cognacs is done in a special way, by the method of *brouillis* and *repasses*. The special qualities of the *champagnes*, the *borderies*, the *fins-bois*, and the *bons-bois*, etc., are not apparent until the brandy has been allowed to age from 15 to 25 years in barrels of the white oak of the district, or in Limousin oak. Several brandies are blended together to obtain a perfect bouquet, a complete and harmonious ensemble; then the blend is allowed to

Cognac country (*French Government Tourist Office*)

age, in order that the constituent Charente brandies may unite and justify the poet's definition:

'Liquid gold which sleeps in cask, and seems to be made of the distilled rays of the sunrise.'

For the boundaries of the Cognac region and its various subdivisions, see map below.

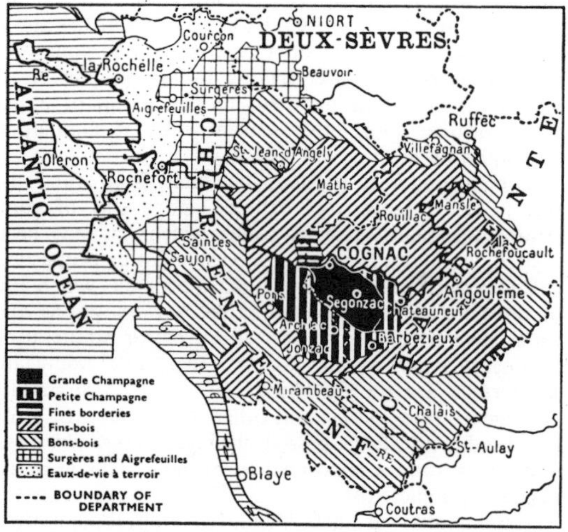

Map of the Cognac-producing areas

COLA. KOLA—An African tree. Its seeds, which are a flattened oblong in shape, have a bitter and astringent flavour. These seeds, incorrectly called nuts, are chewed by the natives. They contain a high proportion of caffeine, theobromine, and a glucoside, kola red. It is a tonic and stimulant, an 'ersatz' or economy food like coffee, without any real nutritive value. It is used as a colouring matter, a liquid flavouring extract, in wines, etc.

Cola cream. CRÈME À LA KOLA—This cream is made by adding a variable amount of essence of cola nut to some kind of sweetened substance. This is a most refreshing dish. The cream used can be either rather thick for *French pastry cream* (crème patissière) or *frangipane* cream, or a butter cream (see CREAM). Cola cream which can be flavoured with orange essence, is used to fill or decorate cakes and pastries such as *Genoese cake, choux,* éclairs, tartlets*, etc.

It is possible to buy cola cakes, which can be served with afternoon tea.

COLBERT (A LA)—Name given particularly to a preparation of fried fish. These fish are egg-and-crumbed before being fried. See SOLE COLBERT.

This name is also applied to a specially prepared butter, which is in fact served with the fish prepared *à la Colbert*. See BUTTER, *Compound butters*.

Cold table

COLD FOODSTUFFS, PRESENTATION OF COLD DISHES. PLATS FROIDS—'The basis of a cold buffet,' wrote Carême, 'is attractive presentation. Judicious cooking and careful seasoning are also supremely important. Good jellies are essential. These must be clarified, perfectly transparent, and of two colours only. One of these must be white, the other some bold, attractive shade (emerald green is by far the best).'

Carême's reference to 'emerald green' must certainly be a slip of the pen, because, in a marginal note, he gives detailed instructions for the preparation of this 'bold, attractive shade':

'I have never seen a more beautiful jelly of this colour than M. Laguipière's. This is how he made it. He melted some good, fine, dry sugar, and then left it for a quarter of an hour on red embers to colour slowly.

'When it turned to a beautiful caramel, reddish-amber in colour, it was moistened with half a glass of water and brought to the boil over a higher flame. After it had boiled for a few minutes, he had a very transparent caramel, of a beautiful reddish-amber colour, which bore no resemblance to that caramel of sugar blackened over a strong flame and referred to in French slang as *jus de singe* (monkey's blood).'

If Carême coloured aspic jelly with a caramel prepared in this fashion, he could scarcely have turned out an aspic of emerald green!

For the presentation and decoration of cold dishes,

FISH. *Above:* Eel en brochette, Cod à la hollandaise. *Below:* Sole à l'amiral (*Prunier*)

(*From Curnonsky:* Cuisine et Vins de France)

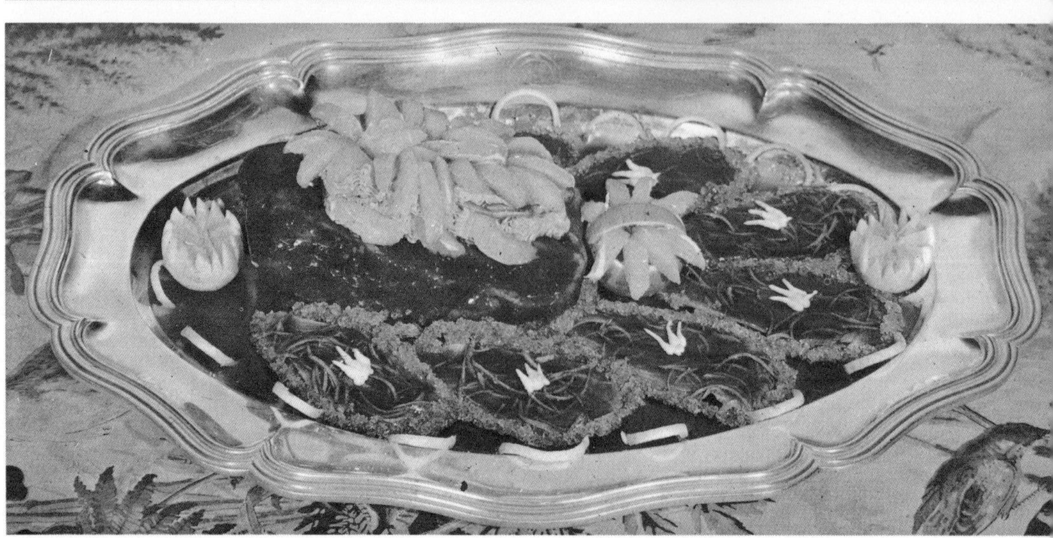

DUCK. *Above:* Duckling à l'alsacienne, Duck au chambertin, Roast duckling garnished with olives and tomatoes *Below:* Duck à l'orange

(Reine Péda

(*From the original French edition of* Larousse Gastronomique)

Carême also recommends the use of 'beautiful magnonnaise sauces'—(this was his name for mayonnaise)—'one white and the other a fine pistachio-green, ravigote sauce and Montpellier butter, coloured a very delicate green and very highly seasoned.

'Entrées,' Carême goes on to say, 'must be dressed with care, glazed with an attractive light jelly, the whole presented artistically, decorated *as simply as possible* with truffles, meat from the breasts of chicken and pickled ox-tongue, and garnished with fine rounds of jelly, arranged tastefully to form rich and elegant borders . . . these are the essentials in the presentation of handsome, cold dishes.'

We are of the same opinion. The presentation of cold dishes must never be either over-elaborate or finicky. A dish of food, whether hot or cold, should not be a work of architecture. Concluding his lesson on the presentation of cold dishes, Careme says that 'they must be set on handsome plinths, very white, smooth and elegant in shape,' (he also taught the art of making these plinths). He was, no doubt, giving voice to the taste of his own day, a taste which, very fortunately, no longer prevails today, when even at state banquets, all superfluous decoration is avoided in the presentation of cold dishes.

The simpler the presentation of a cold dish, the handsomer it is. But there are still artists in this field who remain obstinately faithful to the old customs. It is for these that we quote Carême's rules for the presentation of cold dishes:

'*Ribs of beef:* Dressed in their natural shape, garnished with their own bones, which must be carefully scraped to make them very white. The dish to be surrounded by a border of jelly.

'*Fillets of beef:* Dressed in a long rectangle; glazed and decorated with jelly; border as above.

'*Noix de veau* (see VEAL)*: Well presented and decorated with *tétine*, trimmed into an attractive shape, and presented in its natural whiteness. Glaze the remainder of the *noix* and decorate with jelly only.' (By *tétine*, Carême means the layer of fat which covers part of the noix de veau.)

'*Chauds-froids* of chicken:* Arrange in a pyramid and cover with a very transparent sauce. Crown the pyramid with a fine black truffle and a very white double cock's comb.

'Scatter here and there on the high points of the pile little clumps of lightly chopped jelly. These touches of decoration have great distinction and are most effective. Complete the effect with a pretty border of very clear jelly, tastefully arranged.

'This is an *entrée* in the best of taste and having great distinction.

'*Galantines of poultry:* These must be garnished with a good forcemeat (stuffing) using plenty of truffles, whole and diced, with pickled ox-tongue or calves' tongue and calves' udder. Lightly glaze the whole.

'*Salmis:** Presented and decorated in the same way.

'*Chicken salads:* These must be presented like fricassées *en chaud-froid.** Instead of crowning them with a truffle, place on the top half a hard boiled egg with the heart of some salad vegetable upon it (lettuce for preference).

'This salad should be served with a good mayonnaise, either white or green. Make a border of hard boiled eggs or coloured butter, decorated with fillets of anchovy.

'*Eel galantines:* These should be presented in the shape of a bastion. It should be set upon a bed of Montpellier butter and decorated with jelly. Make a border of jelly or coloured butter garnished with little sprigs of tarragon.

'*Salmon steaks:* These should be shown in their natural colour or masked with Montpellier butter. Decorate the top with jelly, truffle, breast of chicken or pickled tongue, so that the decoration is all the same colour. Make a border of coloured butter or jelly.

'*Salads of fillets of sole or other fish:* Arrange in a circle inside a border of moulded jelly. The same arrangement is suitable for fillets of turbot, trout, salmon, brill, pike and perch. But, for whole perch, cover the fish with white mayonnaise, decorated with truffles only. Make a border of jelly in two colours.'

After giving the details of these different methods of presentation, Carême remarks that dilettantes admire and artists practise them. 'Cold dishes are everything in themselves, or they are nothing. The man of talent brings out all their inherent beauty; the man without taste detracts from it and makes them insipid.'

While having lost none of its elegance, the cold dish, in modern practice, is presented in a much simpler way. The old methods, which were inspired by architecture rather than by the arts of the kitchen, have been completely abandoned and it is now established that all the garnishes of any cold dish whatsoever must be grouped in the simplest and most rational manner possible round the main dish, without any seeking after architectural effects.

Today dishes are made in shapes perfectly adapted to their purpose. On these the food, presented in the simplest possible way and discreetly decorated, is much more elegant than that which, in former times, was presented on wooden supports covered with butter or plinths (*mandrins*, see WOODEN PLINTH) ornamented with so-called artistic figures.

In this kind of presentation, the first object is to make the most of the intrinsic shape and colour of the main dish, and to surround it only with those garnishes which would normally be eaten with it. Thus, the plinth, so fashionable in former times, is now quite out of favour.

The radical reform in the presentation of cold dishes has been well received by discerning diners and persons of good taste everywhere. Food presented in this way seems to them less pretentious and fussy. It no longer evokes for them that chain of laborious processes involved in the preparation of certain large cold cuts, set on very elaborate plinths, and more often than not, garnished with ingredients which offended against the laws of the palate.

Some time ago there was an attempt to bring back into fashion this elaborate ornamentation of cold dishes. The odd thing is that those most in favour of this revival of the so-called *decorative* presentation of cold dishes were the disciples of that great Italian 'futurist' master, Marinetti. Fortunately, this attempt met with no success whatever.

COLIFICHET—A dry cake, without butter or salt, made for birds.

In the repertoire of *pâtisserie* (even *grande pâtisserie*) this word does not only denote bird cake. In the old days *pièces montées* (set pieces) which decorated the table and buffets were called *colifichets*, in order to differentiate between them and the serious dishes.

Colifichets, although almost entirely composed of edible substances, were laden with ornamental details.

Carême, in speaking of the decorative pieces, wrote: 'This brilliant sideline does not suffer from mediocrity, and in this connection I compare a good maker of *colifichets* to a distinguished *modiste*, gifted with perfect taste and an inventive imagination, whose industrious fingers, with a minimum of material, make charming things which seduce and captivate. Again, we have to make with fragments of *pâtisserie*, which means with practically nothing, things which are graceful and pretty and which at the same time excite the appetite. Such are the secrets of this profession which demands a great deal of skill, of patience, taste and precise arrangement. It is the details of the *pièces montées* which are difficult; it is here that the great talent of the exponents of the art of *colifichet*, shines.

'It is not enough to make flower-shaped ornaments and pretty little cakes; one must also know that such and such an article will go well with such and such a thing; and that the whole, grouped with taste, will make a pleasing ensemble.'

This remark of Carême's on the *colifichet* shows that in *pâtisserie* the word denotes what is still called a *pièce montée*.

In current practice this is rarely, if ever, made. One can, however, occasionally see some specimens in culinary exhibitions, where they feature only as essays in retrospection.

COLIN—This name is given in Paris markets to hake. This fish, whose flaky flesh is fairly delicate, is also called *saumon blanc* (white salmon).

The head and back of the *colin* are grey in colour, the stomach is white and lightly silvered.

In former times, before the opening up of north Atlantic fishing, the *colin* was salted and replaced salt cod in all the European markets.

All the methods of preparation given for cod are applicable to *colin* (hake). See COD.

COLLAGE—Operation which has as its aim the clarification of alcoholic beverages by precipitating the solid matter which they contain, and which is capable of spoiling their keeping qualities. See WINE.

COLLE—Synonym for gelatine in culinary terms. Also used in popular language for butter sauce: *sauce colle*.

COLLER—The operation consisting in adding dissolved gelatine to a preparation to give it body.

COLLOP. ESCALOPER—To cut meat or vegetables into thick or thin slices.

COLOCASIA. CARAIBE (CHOU)—*Colocasia esculenta* (family *Araceae*), tuberous herb native of the Moluccas (Spice Islands).

In the West Indies not only its tubers but also its leaves are eaten, as cabbage, hence the French name, *caraibe* (*chou*).

COLOCYNTH—Member of the gourd family, the fruit of which is very rich and many coloured, used as a table ornament. The pulp is extremely bitter and a violent purgative.

COLOMBINES—Kind of croquettes with an outer layer of semolina with Parmesan. See HORS-D'OEUVRE, *Hot hors-d'oeuvre*.

COLONNE—Utensil used to core certain fruits (apples), to cut certain vegetables into the shape of a column. This utensil is also called *moule à colonne*.

COLOURING. COLORANTS—The colourings used in cookery, in cake-making, and in confectionery, are for the most part of vegetable origin, and in consequence harmless; others are of insect origin, like the carmine of cochineal, or of mineral origin, and there are some derived from coal.

COLZA—Colza or rapeseed is an oleaginous plant sometimes used to adulterate mustard seed.

COMFITS. CONFIT—Fruits or vegetables preserved in sugar, brandy, or vinegar. See GHERKINS, CAPERS, FRUIT.

COMFREY. CONSOUDE—Name of various plants, some of which are edible and are used in salad, or cooked, like corn-salad.

COMINÉE DE GELINES (ancient recipe)—The ancestor of the *Chicken fricassée* seems to be the *Cominée de Gelines*, for which one of the most ancient culinary treatises (1290), the *Traité où l'on enseigne à faire appareiller et assaisonner toutes viandes*, gives the following recipe:

'If you wish to make *cominée de gelines*, take the chickens and cook them in wine and water, and boil them, and skim off the fat, and take out the chickens, and after that take egg yolks.

'Beat them well, and dilute them with chicken stock, and put in some cumin, and put all together. There is your cominée.'

Fruit compote

COMPOTE—This word denotes a preparation of fresh or dried fruit cooked either whole or cut into quarters according to the nature of the fruit, in a thick or thin syrup and flavoured or not with various aromatics, such as vanilla, lemon or orange zest, cinnamon, clove, etc.

Dried fruits, prunes, apricots, apples, pears, etc., must be soaked for some length of time in cold water before being cooked in the syrup.

Compotes are usually served cold. They can be sprinkled with kirsch or some other liqueur after being put in a dish.

Simple Compotes consist of one type of fruit cooked in syrup.

Compotes Composées consist of a macedoine of various fruits. These are served in the same way as simple *compotes*, that is to say, the fruits are arranged in a dish and the syrup in which they have been cooked is poured over them, or they can be covered with a fruit jelly (quince, gooseberry, apple, etc.).

The word *compote* is also used for certain dishes (of pigeon, partridge) which have been cooked for a considerable time.

COMPOTES OF FRESH AND DRIED FRUITS. COMPOTE DE FRUITS FRAIS ET SECS:

Apple compote. COMPOTE DE POMMES—Made with whole fruit, in which case core them first with an apple-corer and peel them, or with fruit cut into halves or quarters, peeled and with the pips removed. Put the fruit in a syrup of $\frac{3}{4}$ cup sugar to $1\frac{1}{3}$ cups water with or without a vanilla flavouring.

Watch the cooking, and remove at once those apples or segments of apple which are cooked.

Arrange in a fruit dish and pour the cooking syrup over the fruit.

Apricot compote I. COMPOTE D'ABRICOTS—Cut the apricots in half; pound the kernels of these apricots; cook the halved apricots in a syrup ($1\frac{1}{2}$ cups of sugar to $2\frac{1}{2}$ cups of water). Arrange the fruit in a dish. Put a halved almond on each fruit. Pour the cooking syrup over them.

Apricot compote II. COMPOTE D'ABRICOTS ÉTUVÉE—Arrange the apricot halves in a fireproof dish. Sprinkle with sugar and put to cook in a slow heat (250°F.). Serve in a fruit dish.

Banana compote. COMPOTE DE BANANES—Peel the bananas and remove the strips of fibre. Cook them for five minutes in a heavy sugar syrup. Flavour with kirsch.

Cherry compote I. COMPOTE DE CERISES—Put the stoned cherries in a sugar syrup which has been cooked to the large ball stage (see SUGAR). Use $\frac{3}{4}$ cup (300 grams) of sugar for each pound of cherries (net weight). Cook with the lid on for 8 minutes over low heat; stir from time to time. Arrange the fruit in a dish; pour over the cooking syrup; flavour with kirsch or cherry brandy.

Cherry compote II. COMPOTE DE CERISES—Put the stoned cherries in a deep dish; put a little bag containing 12 crushed kernels in the middle of the fruit; sprinkle copiously with powdered sugar. When the cherries are swimming in juice rendered by the sugar, cook them in the oven in a covered dish.

Fig compote (dried figs). COMPOTE DE FIGUES SÈCHES—Prepared in the same way as *Prune compote.**

Fig compote (fresh figs). COMPOTE DE FIGUES FRAÎCHES—Peel the figs, which should be selected for ripeness and of equal size; put them in a boiling syrup ($1\frac{1}{2}$ cups sugar to $2\frac{1}{2}$ cups water), flavoured with vanilla. Poach for a few minutes.

Arrange the fruit in a dish. Pour over them the cooking syrup.

Peach compote. COMPOTE DE PÊCHES—Peel the peaches, cook them whole or cut in half in a syrup ($\frac{3}{4}$ cup sugar to $1\frac{1}{3}$ cups water) flavoured with vanilla.

Pear compote. COMPOTE DE POIRES—If the pears are small leave them whole, and peel them carefully; if they are large, cut into quarters or halves. Trim them.

Poach fruit in boiling vanilla syrup ($\frac{3}{4}$ cup sugar to $1\frac{1}{3}$ cups water), cooking them only very slightly if the fruit are soft.

If this *compote* is made with firm pears (cooking pears) rub the fruit with lemon and blanch them for a few minutes before putting them in the cooking syrup flavoured with vanilla.

Pineapple compote. COMPOTE D'ANANAS—Cut a fresh pineapple into slices after having removed the outside and the hard core. Cook the slices in vanilla flavoured syrup. Arrange the fruit in a dish in the form of a circle. Pour over the cooking syrup. Flavour according to taste with kirsch or with any other liqueur.

This compote can be made with canned pineapples.

Plum compote. COMPOTE DE PRUNES—Prepared especially with mirabelle plums or with greengages, but can be made with any variety of plum.

Stone the fruit; poach them in a syrup of $\frac{3}{4}$ cup sugar to $1\frac{1}{3}$ cups water for 10 to 12 minutes.

Prune compote. COMPOTE DE PRUNEAUX—Soak the prunes in cold water long enough for them to swell. Put them to cook in a syrup, $\frac{3}{4}$ cup sugar to $1\frac{1}{3}$ cups of liquid, consisting of half red wine and half water and flavoured with cinnamon or with lemon zest. Cook very slowly.

This compote can also be prepared in a syrup made without red wine.

All dried fruit compotes are prepared in the same way, cooking the fruit in a thin syrup.

Raspberry compote. COMPOTE DE FRAMBOISES—Arrange the fruit in a fairly deep dish. Pour over a few tablespoons of boiling syrup.

Strawberry compote. COMPOTE DE FRAISES—Prepared in the same way as *Raspberry compote.*

COMPOTES OF PRESERVED FRUITS. COMPOTE DE FRUITS EN CONSERVE:

Apricot compote. COMPOTE D'ABRICOTS—Choose fruits of the same ripeness, preferably not quite ripe rather than overripe. Prick them with the point of a knife and put them in a basin. Cover with a cold syrup (4 cups sugar to $1\frac{1}{2}$ cups water) weighing 32 degrees or 225°F. on the saccharometer. Leave them to soak in the syrup for 3 hours.

While the fruit is soaking prepare a syrup of 26 degrees or 220°F. with lump sugar.

Clarify the syrup with white of egg—one white of egg for 2 quarts (litres) of syrup. Strain the syrup through a straining bag or cloth. Leave to cool.

Drain the apricots. Put them into wide-mouthed jars. Cover the apricots with the boiling clarified syrup so that it reaches at least 1 inch (3 centimetres) above the level of the fruit. Cover the jars with caps, several types of which are made commercially.

Lay some straw, hay or sacking on the bottom of a large preserving pan or use a wire rack made for this purpose; arrange the bottles in such a way that they do not touch. Fill the pan with cold water: the water must entirely cover the bottles. Put the pan on the fire. When the water is boiling rapidly, allow a full ten minutes before removing the bottles. Wipe them and seal them.

Keep the bottles in a cool place away from the light.

Note. Halved apricots can also be used for the compote. To do this, they are halved, put in a basin and soaked in a heavy syrup. Half the number of stones are cracked, the kernels peeled, and put into the preserving jars with the halved apricots.

The process for capping and boiling is the same as specified above.

Compote of cherries, peaches, plums and other fruits for preserving—All these fruits are prepared for preserving in the same way as apricots. According to their special nature the boiling period is increased or diminished.

COMPOTIER—A deep dish on a raised base in which fruits, compotes, jams and various other cold sweets are served. China or crystal fruit dishes are also used for fresh fruits.

CONCASSER—This is the French term for rough chopping of some substance with a knife, or for breaking it up by pounding in a mortar.

CONDÉ (Pâtisserie)—Roll out a piece of left-over *flaky pastry* (see DOUGH) in strips about 10 inches long, 4 inches wide and ¼ inch thick.

Cover this strip with a layer of *royal almond icing* called Condé (see below). Divide the strip into rectangles 1½ inches wide. Lift the rectangles with the blade of a large knife and put them on a baking tray. Powder them with icing sugar. Cook in a gentle oven.

Preparation of the Condé—Work ¾ cup (100 grams) of icing sugar and 2 egg whites in a basin. When the mixture has acquired a certain consistency add peeled almonds which have been finely chopped, in sufficient quantity to form a fairly thick paste.

CONDIMENT SET. HUILIER—A piece of table ware often consisting of two glass bottles in a metal, wooden or pottery frame. In former times, the condiment set was a magnificent piece of silverware, placed on the table for decoration rather than use.

CONDIMENTS—Aromatic substances which are added to food to improve its flavour.

Although the term 'seasoning' is reserved more especially for substances which are added during the cooking, while condiments apply to those which are added at table to the food already prepared, the two words are often used interchangeably in current speech.

All substances used as condiments, with the exception of salt and saltpetre, are of vegetable origin and it is vegetarian people, particularly those who inhabit the hot regions of the globe, who use strong condiments the most.

According to their dominant flavour one can class condiments into salt, acid, bitter, aromatic, sweet, etc.

Salt condiments—Sodium chloride or sea salt is the only table condiment of mineral origin. It is, besides, the condiment *par excellence*, a fact underlined by numerous metaphors.

In fact, salt is at one and the same time an element which is an integral part of our tissues and of our body fluids, and an actual condiment. All our foods contain a more or less strong proportion of salt; in spite of this there are very few culinary preparations which do not require its use.

Saltpetre (azotate or potassium nitrate) is hardly used in cooking, but is employed in the salting industry to accentuate the red colouring of meats.

Acid condiments—Vinegar, verjuice, the juice of lemon or tamarind, etc. exert a strong influence on the gustatory papillae and encourage salivary secretion. In the same category can be included all vegetables preserved in vinegar; salted cucumbers, which become acid through fermentation; capers, nasturtium flowers, Indian pickles, purslane, sweet-sour cherries, sea-fennel or samphire, little onions in vinegar, little melons in vinegar.

Bitter condiments—Garlic, shallot, Welsh onion, spring onion, onion, rocamble (Spanish garlic), leeks, are vegetable seasonings rather than condiments, but are sometimes used in a raw state as condiments; mustard, horse-radish, sometimes the radish, are proper condiments, arousing the appetite.

Bitter aromatic condiments—Pepper is the chief example of this group; its aromatic qualities are largely lost in the process of cooking, and to preserve all its flavour it should be added after cooking.

Paprika, the various types of pimento and ginger produce a scale of flavours which, when necessary, reinforce the flavour of pepper.

Among the principal aromatic condiments are dill, anise, basil, cocoa, coffee, cinnamon, chervil, coriander, cumin, tumeric, tarragon, fennel, juniper, clove, bay, mace, mint, nutmeg, parsley, saffron, sage, savory, thyme, vanilla, orange and lemon zest, and the various aromatic vegetables.

Sweet condiments—Sugar and its derivatives (syrups, etc.), as well as honeys, are proper foods at the same time as being condiments. In certain countries some *compotes* (whortleberries, gooseberries) are used as condiments. With a flavour which is at the same time sweet and acidulated, they are often served with roast or boiled meats, especially with game.

Sweet condiments also include the *aceto-dolce* of the Italians, a preserve of fruit and vegetables in vinegar sweetened with concentrated grape must or with honey, and preserved fruits with mustard.

Fat condiments—Sometimes the fatty elements (oils, butter, fats) are classed as condiments, because they are used for seasoning; they are in reality foods, not condiments.

Ready-made condiments—There are a number of condiments prepared industrially, which acquire a distinct individuality according to the proportions in which the specific ingredients are used, such as the English sauces (Worcestershire, Harvey, etc.), ketchups, curry powders, prepared mustards, soya sauce, etc.

CONFECTIONER'S CUSTARD. CRÈME PÂTISSIÈRE—See CREAMS, *French pastry cream.*

CONFECTIONERY. CONFISERIE—A branch of cookery occupied with the transformation of sugar into sweets.

Confectionery nowadays tends more and more to become an industry of which the products are sold in special shops; one of the branches of confectionery is concerned with the making of chocolates. Long ago in antiquity the Egyptians, the Arabs and the Chinese prepared sweetmeats based on various fruit juices and honey. In Europe the use of sugar was not widespread until after the time of the Crusades, and even then remained for a long time in the hands of apothecaries. However, in the fifteenth century the crystallized fruits of Auvergne enjoyed a well-deserved reputation, as well as the sugared almonds flavoured with *amber* or musk, and the '*gigembrats de Montpellier*'. In 1660, the regulations promulgated by Colbert underlined the importance of the manufacture of the sugared almonds of Verdun. In *Diderot's Encyclopedia* several plates show the work of the confectioner. In the nineteenth century the discovery of sugar beet juice and the advance of mechanical appliances assured the rapid development of sweet-making.

CONFIT—Meat of pork, goose, duck, turkey, etc., cooked in its own fat, and preserved in a receptacle, completely immersed and covered in the same fat, which prevents it from coming in contact with the air.

Confit d'oie (Preserved goose)—Portions of goose cooked in goose fat and preserved in stoneware pots. See GOOSE.

Confit de porc (Preserved pork) (Gascon cookery)—Portions of pork meat which after having been marinated in salt with spices are cooked in melted pork fat.

Confit de porc, which is used a great deal in Gascon cookery, is preserved in stoneware pots in the same way as *confit d'oie* (preserved goose).

CONGER EEL. CONGRE—Large fish, also called *anguille de mer* (sea eel), found in the seas of the temperate zone, particularly in those of northern Europe.

Confectioners at work, from Diderot's *Encylopédie*

The best known type is the common conger.

The flesh of the conger eel has a certain resemblance to that of eels, but is less delicate.

The conger eel is chiefly used for making fish soups, notably the *bouillabaisse*, but can be cooked in all the ways given for eel. See EEL.

CONSOLANTE—In common French restaurant-kitchen parlance, the glass of wine, beer or cider, served to the team of cooks in the course of their work is called a *consolante*.

CONSOMMÉ—Meat stock which has been enriched, concentrated and clarified. See BOUILLON, *Clarification of bouillon*.

For the preparation of various consommés (simple consommés chicken, game, fish consommés) see SOUP, *Clear soups*. Under this heading the necessary instructions for preparing garnishes for the various consommés will be found.

CONTISER—A French term for encrusting chicken fillets, or those of game or fish (chiefly sole), with truffles or other elements, cut in the shape of little cocks' combs. These various objects, previously soaked in white of egg (in order to make them adhere properly), are set at regular intervals into superficial cuts made in the fillets.

CONVERSATION (Pâtisserie)—Roll out a piece of puff pastry (*pâte feuilletée*) which has already been rolled out five times (see DOUGH). Set out some tartlet moulds close together on a table, moisten each one slightly, then lay the sheet of pastry on top of the moulds. Take a lump of pastry, flour it lightly, and press it gently into each mould so that the pastry adheres to the bottom and sides of the moulds. Half fill the bottom of each tartlet with a preparation of almonds made according to the directions given for *Dartois cakes*,* or with *French pastry cream* (see CREAM) to which some powdered almonds have been added.

Moisten the edges of the tartlets lightly and place on them a second sheet of pastry, made slightly thinner than the first.

Roll the pastry roller over the sheet of pastry, which will result in cutting it on the brim of the moulds, at the same time sealing the edges of the pastry lining of the tartlets.

On the top of the tarts put a layer of firm *Royal icing* (see ICING), made with $1\frac{3}{4}$ cups (250 grams) of icing sugar and one white of egg worked well together, and with the addition of a light pinch of flour in order to prevent its running.

Put thin bands of pastry made from the trimmings crosswise on top of the tarts, pressing the ends against the sides of the moulds. Cook the cakes in the oven at a moderate temperature.

COOK. Cuisinière—A woman responsible for the preparation and cooking of food is called a *cuisinière* in French.

The word *cuisinière* is also used in France to describe a small household cooker (stove).

COOKIES—See BISCUIT.

COOKING. Cuisine—In French the word *cuisine* denotes both the art of preparing dishes (cooking) and the place (kitchen) in which they are prepared.

The art of cooking is extremely ancient. The first cook was a primitive man who, having put a hunk of meat close to the fire, which he had lit to warm himself, discovered that the meat heated in this way was not only more tasty but easier to masticate.

From this moment cooking was born, and progressed thanks to further discoveries.

An ingenious man found a means of heating water in a stone hollowed out into the form of a basin. Then the clay vase succeeded this primitive pot.

The spit and the pot, however rudimentary these utensils proved in the beginning, allowed man to undertake all kinds of culinary operations.

Prehistoric discoveries provide much data on the

origin of cooking—fragments of pottery, flint or bronze instruments, animals' bones, the traces of hearths, lake dwellings, and much more.

Cooking among the Egyptians and Assyrians is described under BANQUET.

Greek cooking—In Greece for a long time no other cook was known than the *mageiros*, who was not in fact a real cook, but a mixer of dough, a baker. The name *mageiros* derives from *magis, madza,* meaning a kind of barley bread or kneaded cake, or from *masso, matto,* meaning to knead.

In the time of Homer it appears that the *mageiros* did not exist. Female slaves ground the corn and prepared the food. If Homer's accounts in the Iliad and the Odyssey are to be believed, it was the host himself, however exalted he might be, who, with the help of friends, themselves men of rank, prepared and cooked the meals, when he received distinguished guests.

Later, the *mageiros*, at the same time as making bread, was given the task of cooking for his masters.

This servant became in course of time *chef de cuisine* (head cook) in the absolute sense of the word, and especially on those days when, in the preparation of a great feast, he was given assistants. Then he became an *archimageiros* or, as one would say today, a *gros bonnet*.

In the kitchens of great houses of this time, placed under the direction of a steward, called the *eleatros*, there was a whole hierarchy of slaves, each one having clearly defined duties; thus, one of the slaves called the *opsonomos* or *agorastes* (the part of the city where the market was held was called the *agora*) had the task of buying the food. Another slave, called the *opsartytes*, was charged with lighting and maintaining the fires; he also did certain rough jobs, and prepared the food for the household slaves.

A woman, the *demiourga*, made nothing but the sweetmeats and other delicacies. In Greece women had free access to and performed various tasks in the kitchen.

Other slaves were occupied in the preparation of meals or in serving at table: the *trapezopoios*, who laid the table and, once the meal was over, washed the dishes; the *oinophoros*, who was charged with the wine; the *oinochoikos*, a young slave whose task was to fill the wine cups of the guests.

In the fourth century B.C., Athenian cooks, as depicted in the Greek theatre, were often nothing but slaves.

In spite of their low estate they seem to have played quite an important role in the life of the city, judging by the taunts the poets levelled at their pretensions.

'They were artists in their way; their apprenticeship lasted two years, under the direction of a cook of reputation, and during this time they wore the apron of the apprentice.

'In order to acquire this difficult *métier* the apprentice cook did not learn from his masters alone. He was given books which set down the rules of his art, and if he was zealous, he passed the night in studying them.

'It was only after long study that he could aspire to become one of those illustrious artists whose names were quoted, and who became famous through the creation of a single dish.' (C. Darenberg and E. Saglio, *Dictionnaire des antiquités grecques et romaines.*)

In Greece, cooks had become persons of importance. In Athens they ruled as masters over all the other slaves in the household. A special law permitted the cook who invented a new dish the sole privilege of making it and selling it to the public, and a proverb of that time, which proves the importance that cooks then enjoyed, said, 'When the cook makes a mistake, it is the flute player who receives the blows.'

A Greek cook introduced on the scene by Athenaeus says with some pride:

'I have earned in my profession as much as any comedian has ever earned in his own: my art is a smoke-blackened empire . . . It was I who prepared the *abyrtake* for Seleucus. I introduced the use of the royal lentil to Agathocles of Sicily; but I still haven't said the main thing. True that Lachares feeding his friends during a famine feasted Minerva without her companions, but it is I who feed Jupiter and all his train.' (Deipnosophistai.)

A great number of Greek cooks left an illustrious name behind them. Cadmos was cook to the King of Sidon in Phoenicia, and, according to legend, introduced writing into Greece.

There was indeed a whole literature of gastronomy and cooking of extreme brilliance in Greece, a literature of which, apart from some fragments which remain to us after the burning of the library in Alexandria, we now possess only the authors' names.

The best known of them is Archestratus of Syracuse who travelled the world not only to describe its customs, but also and in particular, to record its eating habits. A great number of other writers wrote on good living at this epoch, and in this way challenged the practitioners of the time to improve their art.

The culinary equipment of the Greeks was rather rudimentary, at least in the first centuries of their history. However, the manufacture of kitchen utensils was gradually perfected. Marmites, casseroles, cauldrons, gridirons, besides being made in a more practical way, were sometimes made in precious metal, silver or gold, and magnificently decorated. The various objects from the Bosco-Reale Treasure, preserved in the Louvre in Paris, bear testimony to the splendour of these culinary utensils.

Greek cauldrons were usually in bronze or iron, but sometimes in silver. In general, these utensils were of ovoid form or in the shape of a truncated cone. Their base was always rounded. They were furnished with chains, fixed or mobile, and most of them had a cover, which permitted meats to be cooked or stewed in the minimum of liquor.

Among these vessels were the following: the *chytra* and the *chutros*, which were quite common earthenware pots made without ornament; the *kakkabe* (or *kakkabos*), which was a kind of metal pot.

There were also in the Greek kitchen the *lebes*, a large basin of metal with an almost spherical form; the *olla*, ancestor of the present-day marmite and made in earthenware.

The casseroles or pans used by the Greeks were generally of bronze, fairly similar in shape to those we use nowadays. Their frying pans (the Greeks particularly enjoyed fried food) more or less resembled the utensil we use today.

There were also in the Greek kitchens special dishes for cooking eggs. The cavities made in these dishes were of different size; Athenaeus says: 'The first row belongs to peacocks' eggs, the second to gooses' eggs, the third to chickens' eggs.' (Deipnosophistai.) These utensils were usually placed on a metal support which was called the *eugytheke*.

To heat beverages the Greeks had kettles made of bronze, of graceful form and bearing a great resemblance to those used today.

For the same purpose, they used amphorae with a double bottom, made in such a way that the liquids put in them could be heated without upsetting. These amphorae were in fact made on the principle of the *bain-marie* (double boiler) and were very similar to those used today.

For serving food, the Greeks had a number of utensils, some in earthenware, others in metal. These included the *kane*, a very concave dish provided with two horizontal handles; the *pazopsis*, equally deep, made in fine pottery, in bronze, in silver, sometimes even in gold, and always richly decorated.

Other receptacles in the form of bowls were used for gruel, sauces, and certain rather liquid stews.

For serving certain dishes there were plates called *ichthuai*, dishes which were nearly always decorated with representations of fishes, because, as is known, for a long period fish constituted the principal food of the Greeks.

Greek drinking vessels, which were as a rule richly decorated, were called *patarion* or *poterion*.

Roman cooking—In early Rome, as in the early Greek period, there were no cooks in their own right. The bakers existed in their stead, and carried on their *métier*.

Cooking in the first centuries of the Roman era was very rudimentary, and in order to make the simple dishes with which the Romans nourished themselves, there was no need of talented practitioners.

It was not until after the war against Antiochus the Great (year 568 according to the Roman calendar) that the Romans came to know the luxury of banquets, and in consequence, had clever cooks to prepare them. Titus Livy expressly says: 'The army from Asia introduced a foreign luxury to Rome; it was then the meals began to require more dishes and more expenditure . . . the cook, who had up to that time been employed as a slave of low price, become dear: what had been nothing but a *métier* was elevated to an art.'

An event which led to a total reform of the table among the Romans, and which contributed towards the increasingly important role of the cook in society, was the deputation sent to Athens to bring back the laws of Solon, and to study Greek Art and Letters. Not only *littérateurs* and *savants*, but also cooks and gastronomes were brought back to Rome.

The high society of Rome treated these cooks not as servants or as slaves, but as important persons worthy of admiration. The Roman cooks, in fact, formed themselves into a kind of society, almost a hierarchy. One among them gave himself the title, rather vainglorious perhaps, of *vicarius supra coenas*, another called himself, in imitation of his Greek *confrères*, an *archimagirus*.

Under the Emperor Hadrian, cooks went so far as to form an Academy: *Collegium coquorum* whose centre was on the Palatine Hill.

Some authors say that, drunk with their success, the Roman cooks became vain, arrogant, and conceited, and even, according to C. Dezobry, 'made of their masters their very slaves.' But these vain practitioners were often treated in the most severe manner: 'If the skill of the artist had failed, if he had served some ill-prepared dish, the cook was put in irons on the spot, or else was led to the *triclinium* (dining-room) by two henchmen and severely flogged in the presence of the guests.' (C. Dezobry, *Rome au siècle d'Auguste*.)

The cooks of ancient Rome were very highly paid. The triumvir Antony gave the house of a citizen of Magnesia to Queen Cleopatra's cook to reward him for having served an admirable meal.

As with the Greeks, the kitchen staff of the large Roman households was made up of slaves, each one having his specific tasks. The division of work which is today the rule of the kitchen was already in existence. In these households there was the actual *coquus*, who was in some respects the *gros bonnet* ('big noise'), then there was the *focarius*, the man charged with keeping the fires going, the *coctor*, whose duty it was to superintend the cooking of certain dishes, such as the braises, the *pistor* or *pinsitor*, who was a kitchen help, his duty being to prepare the stuffings, to pound various foods (the Romans had a great taste for purées), and also to grind corn to make bread and cakes.

There was also a whole crowd of slaves attached to the kitchen and the dining room; the *condus*, who conducted the household management and ordered and stored the food; the *doliarius*, who managed the cellar; the *structor*, whose role consisted in arranging the food on the serving platters; the *captor*, who carved the meat; the *proegustator*, a reliable man who tasted the dishes; the *aquarius*, who was responsible for the supply of water.

As regards the service of the triclinium (dining room) there was the *tricliniarcha*, whose duties comprised a similar function to that of the butler in a large household today; the *pocillator*, who poured wine into the drinking vessels; there was also a servant of high rank, the *nomenclator*, a kind of chief of protocol, who, in large households where a great deal of entertaining took place, arranged the order of the guests.

For a long time in ancient Rome and under the Republic the chief food, the national dish almost, consisted of a kind of gruel made of cereals which was called *puls* or *pulmentus*, and which was prepared with barley or with spelt (German wheat), was roasted, pounded up, and cooked with water, to make a kind of porridge having a great similarity to the *polenta* which is still eaten today in Italy. This kind of porridge was made in a bronze cauldron.

The Romans called a great variety of liquid foods similar to what we today call bouillon (broth) by the name of *potus*, which comes from the verb *potare*, to drink.

From this word *potus* all the terms denoting preparations which are more or less liquid such as *potées*, *potages*, *pot-au-feu*, derive. But under the Empire an increasing decadence, gluttony and extravagant luxury at table became the characteristic of Roman cooking. The stories of writers and historians are very illuminating (see under BANQUET, *Trimalchio's feast*). But if luxury at table was excessive, it is no less certain that taste and moderation were entirely absent from these gastronomic displays.

Carême, who made a thorough study of Roman cuisine, declared that it was fundamentally heavy and without refinement.

The Roman taste for meat was carried to an extreme. The consumption of meat became so exaggerated that more than once restrictive measures had to be taken. Under Alexander Severus meat had risen to such a high price that it was expressly forbidden by law to kill sows which had recently littered, sucking pigs, cows and heifers.

The consumption of meat was not restricted to ordinary domestic animals. Heliogabalus, following the culinary precepts of Apicius, sometimes had camel served at his table.

The Romans even tried eating elephant. Pliny tells us that only the trunk found favour with amateurs. But the explanation he gives of the Roman gastronomes' particular taste for this part of the animal is somewhat specious. 'Of the cartilage of this trunk,' he says, 'is made a dish which is singularly prized for the sole reason, I think, that one imagines one is eating ivory itself.'

Maecenas, says Pliny, was the first to serve at his table the meat of an ass's foal. In his time it was much preferred to that of the wild ass; after him, this taste passed out of fashion.

Cato the Censor, says Pliny again, reproached his contemporaries with their taste for the loin of the roe-buck, which divides into three parts and of which only the middle part, called the saddle, was served at table.

'The first Roman to have a roe-buck served whole was Servilius Rullus, a luxury common today, because nowadays, two or three roe-buck are set on the table at the same time, and these do not represent the entire meal, but only the first course.'

Eulius Lupinus was the first, according to Pliny, who thought of the idea of parks in which the roe-buck and other wild animals could be raised. He set up herds of wild animals in the neighbourhood of Tarquinia. Without delay Lucullus and Hortensius followed this example.

But the Romans did not wish to confine themselves only to wild animals. The most various animals were introduced into their diet. 'Our fathers,' says Pliny, 'regarded puppies still at suck as a food of such purity that they used them as victims for expiatory sacrifices. Young dogs were sacrificed and still today (Pliny's day) the meat of puppies is served at meals in honour of the gods. This meat was used solemnly in the inaugural meals for sovereigns, as is shown in the comedies of Plautus.'

Dormice were also very much appreciated by the Romans, who called them *glires*. Varron says that they were fattened by shutting them up in casks where, deprived of light, they were fed on chestnuts, acorns, and nuts.

Fulvius Hirpinius invented a special cage for fattening guinea pigs. This cage, called the *gliriarium*, replaced the cask.

In the serving of their meals the Romans certainly valued above all both the eccentric and the colossal.

The kitchen itself was one of the most spacious rooms in the whole house. This was in fact essential, as the household slaves ate in this room, and they were always very numerous.

In town houses this room, which was used only for preparing the food, was, in contrast, extremely restricted.

C. Garnier and A. Ammann give a fairly precise picture of the kitchen in Roman dwellings:

'The cooking range was the chief ornament of the kitchen. It occupied a corner of the room and consisted of a block of masonry enclosed by brickwork and divided into little compartments, each of which was a separate oven.

'The kitchen furniture was completed by a number of accessories. A large table in hard stone on which the meats were cut up was also provided with a little cavity in which various culinary ingredients were pounded; various utensils were suspended from the walls; there was a little well which supplied the water for household requirements and a stone sink in one corner of the room furnished with a drain to draw off the dirty water.'

Mazois, in the *Palais de Scaurus*, described how the kitchen was arranged and equipped in the house of a great Roman personage:

'Scaurus's kitchen is arched, its dimensions are of enormous size; it is 148 feet long; and it will not astonish you when you think of the banquets he gives and the great number of guests, freed men, and slaves, he has to feed. Here the fireplace is, as in my own home, elbow-high, but vast and made in such a way as to easily draw off the smoke; because, in winter, a house filled with smoke, however beautiful it may otherwise be, is uninhabitable, particularly if green wood or new brushwood are burnt. As for the decoration of the kitchen, this has, as mine has, a painting representing one of those ridiculous sacrifices made to the goddess *Fortunax*. This painting is surrounded with paintings of all those victuals necessary for a great feast: fish ready for cooking; hams; venison ready for the spit; birds, hares and an infinity of other objects. I have gone one further than the researches undertaken by all those amateurs of cooking, who try to make their kitchens clean and agreeable, by making the kitchen floor of a composition used particularly in Greece. The method of doing this may be of use to you if you ever return to your own country. After having dug out about two feet and beaten the earth well, I have laid a layer of broken brick inclined in such a way as to drain the water away into a specially made drain. On this layer I have spread a bed of well beaten charcoal, and on the top of this a third layer, half a foot deep, of cement made of lime, sand and pounded charcoal, or hot cinders. I then polished this rendering with pumice stone. This produces a paving of fine black colour which has the special property of absorbing any water that falls on it; with the result that the floor of this kitchen is always dry and the persons who work there never get cold feet even when they go barefoot.

'Near the kitchen there are subsidiary rooms, such as the *olearium* where oil is kept in great *dolia* (earthenware pots four feet in diameter); the *horreum* where a great many things are kept, such as winter provisions, honey, fruits, dried raisins, salt meats, and in general all the provisions necessary for a great household. These various store-rooms are under the surveillance of a store-keeper called *promuscondus*, who keeps a check on all the food-stuffs and supplies and delivers them to the servants when required. The steward sees to the maintaining of the supplies in these store-rooms and cellars; their extent and the amount of provisions they contain make them resemble actual shops.'

The kitchen utensils used by the Romans were similar to those used by the Greeks, both as to material and shape.

For cooking meat, the Romans used a grill which they called *craticula*.

They also had a great number of pastry moulds, sieves, skimmers, ladles, all of these utensils more or less resembling those we use today.

Cooking and eating habits of the Gauls—The cooking of the Gauls was not very choice, and we can only get a slight idea of it from Latin writers.

Strabo wrote: 'The Celts eat bread in very small quantity with a great deal of meat either boiled, roast or grilled. Their rivers and the two seas which surround them provide fish which they season with cumin and vinegar, as they use very little oil, it being scarce in their country. As for cumin, they add it to all their beverages.

'The drink of the rich is wine, which they bring from Italy and the neighbourhood of Marseilles, and which is served to them in the following way: the servant charged with this task brings in each hand a bowl of earthenware or silver, similar to a marmite and filled with wine. Each one draws from the bowl. Little is drunk at a time, but they drink often, and wine is almost always unadulterated.'

The Gauls loved spiced dishes. The few recipes which we give below show the taste that these people had for strong condiments:

Oleogarum—This is made with lovage, coriander, rue, and broth, honey and a little oil; or with thyme, savory, pepper, honey, broth and oil.

Oxygarum—Made with half an ounce of pepper, with three scruples of masterwort or gallic benzoin, six scruples of cardamon grains, six scruples of cumin, one scruple of mint leaves, six scruples of dried mint flowers.

Mix these with honey and when you wish to serve the dish, add some broth and vinegar.

Note. A scruple is $\frac{1}{24}$ ounce.

Method of preparing cranes and ducks—Wash and trim the crane (or the duck) and put it in an earthenware marmite. Add water, salt and dill. Let it reduce by half and then put the whole into a cauldron with oil and broth, a bouquet of marjoram and coriander. When the crane is on the point of being cooked, add a little heated wine. Pour over a mixture of honey, lovage, cumin, coriander, roots of benzoin, rue and pounded caraway, with vinegar. Put some starch in the pan and make the liquid boil. Put your crane on a dish and pour the sauce over it.

Stuffing for dormice—Make this with the meat of the dormouse with powdered pepper, nuts, benzoin and broth. Put the dormice on a tile after sewing them up, and put them in the oven. They can also be cooked in a copper boiler.

Sauce for all kinds of game, boiled or roast—Take eight scruples of pepper, rue, garden lovage, parsley seeds, juniper, thyme, dried mint and three scruples of penny-royal. Grind the lot to powder and make it into a single mass by adding honey to it. Use this for *oxygarum*.

Sauce for langoustes and shrimps—Made with pepper, mint, rue, nuts, honey, vinegar, broth and wine.

Seasoning for haricots verts—Made of salt, cumin, oil and a little wine.

Method of preparing snails—Take snails which have been fattened with milk, sponge and wipe them; remove the shells, leave them for a day in salt water, fry them in oil, and serve them with *oleogarum*.

Sauce for melons—This is a mixture of pepper, mint, pennyroyal, honey or wine made from raisins dried in the sun, with broth and vinegar. Benzoin (benjamin) is sometimes added.

Rose or violet shrub—Soak some roses or violets for seven days in wine. Take them out, put fresh flowers in their place, and leave to soak again for seven days. Strain the wine in which the flowers have infused, and when you wish to drink it, add some honey to it.

Cooking and eating habits of the Franks and Merovingians—'Once established in Gaul, the Franks imitated the luxurious example set by the Romanized Gauls. They ate reclining on couches in dining-rooms round tables decorated with flowers.

'Coarser and more barbarous than the Gauls who were already initiated into the resources of culinary science, the Franks borrowed from them their various dishes and their cooking remained very much the same as that of the Romanized Gauls, entirely Roman.

'The manuscripts which dealt with this subject were for a long time only repetitions of the rules set down by *Apicius*.

'One can see that pepper, honey, wine, vinegar, meat broth and certain aromatic plants formed the basis of all seasonings.' (From *L'Art culinaire* of the Marquis de Cussy.)

It was at the end of the Merovingian period that the convents, which had preserved all the traditions of the gourmands, increased in number in France, and from then on great progress was made in culinary matters.

French cooking and eating habits in the Middle Ages—Viollet-le-Duc, in the course of his studies of architecture in the Middle Ages, gives a picture of what kitchens were like at the time:

'In the houses of the Middle Ages chimneys were large and high; generally, a man could get inside the chimney without bending, and ten or twelve people could sit easily round the hearth. Inside these chimneys strong andirons were needed, called *landiers*, to hold the enormous logs which were put on the fire, and to prevent them from rolling into the room. There were kitchen andirons and those for other apartments; the former were rather complicated in form because they were put to various uses. Their uprights were furnished with supports or hooks to take the spits; they were surmounted by an extension in the form of a small brazier on which certain dishes could be prepared, or kept warm.

'In the kitchens, the division of the stoves into several compartments as is frequently the case in our day, was seldom seen; the dishes were cooked on the fire itself, and one can easily understand that these fierce fires did not allow dishes which required constant stirring to be prepared, or dishes which needed to be made in small frying pans.

'The andiron-braziers, filled with charcoal, were at a convenient level and set at some distance from the actual fire and thus facilitated the preparation of these dishes. Sometimes the andiron-braziers were divided into two compartments, in which case it was possible to prepare and cook four dishes outside the hearth; over the hearth were suspended one or many pots, by means of chimney hooks or tripods; in front of the fire there were one or two spits turning, with several pieces of meat. Only in this way was it possible to prepare a copious meal. As a rule a huge chain was fitted to the head of the andirons so that they could be drawn closer together or further apart.

'Before the twelfth century only roast meats and boiled vegetables were eaten, the art of making stews being almost unknown. What was needed in the kitchen were good clear fires, large hearths on which numerous and long spits could be set, and space for suspending vast cauldrons.

'The architects of the twelfth century began to install ovens in kitchens, and tables on which to arrange the food before serving it. From the fourteenth century the use of sauces was a much appreciated part of the culinary art; it was no longer sufficient to serve roast and boiled

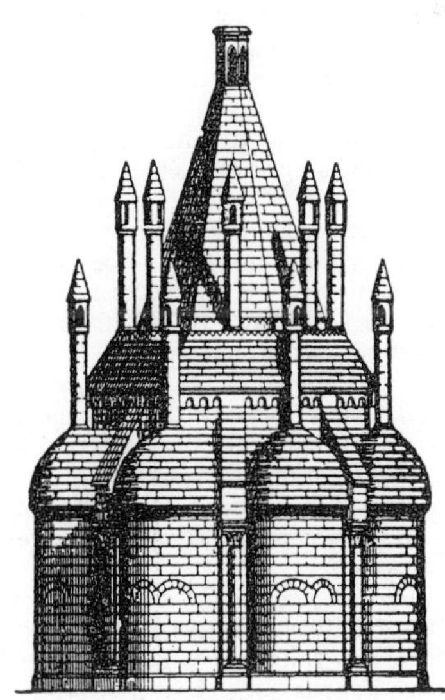

Fontevrault Abbey; the kitchen

meats at table. Now ovens were needed to make the more diverse dishes which were served at the big feasts held at this time. Also from this time on the fixed equipment of the kitchens was more and more improved.

'In the castles and convents of the Middle Ages the chimney was not always built against the wall in the chamber reserved for cooking, but it was sometimes disposed in the middle of the vaulted roof, the hearth being set in the centre of the room. A kitchen of this kind resembled a tower open at the top without any joists separating the intervening space into floors, with a diameter decreasing continuously towards the top. A kitchen of this kind can still be seen in the Palace of the Popes at Avignon.'

French cooking in the fourteenth and fifteenth centuries—It is in *Le Viandier*, the work of Taillevent, that we find all the information on the culinary practices and table habits of these times.

Soups were a kind of gruel, made with milk and very often flavoured with honey, saffron and sweet wine. These gruels were thickened with *moyeux* (egg yolks) and with butter.

Rice soups were also made, various purées, which were a kind of *garbures**, and in which slices of bread were put. At that time they were called *soupes* (sops), a generic name which for this reason has been given to soups themselves.

Among the dishes of the time were *chaudumer* or *chaudemer*, which was a kind of *matelote**, but which was made with freshwater fish cooked first on the grill.

Brouet was made of calves' meat, with fowl or with conies (rabbits) cut up into pieces. The meat was put to brown in *sein de lard* (lard) with onions and crushed almonds and moistened with wine and stock. These were kinds of ragoût or more properly *sautés*, more or less like those made today.

The *hochepot* (hotchpotch) was a preparation which at that time was similar to that called *brouet*, but to which grilled bread or grated breadcrumbs were added to effect the thickening. This dish, obviously, bears no resemblance to the dish known by that name today.

The *galimafrée* was a dish very much appreciated at the time. The word *galimafrée* had not the unhappy connotation it has today, when according to the dictionaries it is synonymous with a rotten stew (*mauvais ragoût*). Then, the dish was made with mutton or with fowl cooked, chopped, simmered with hashed onion and moistened with *Cameline* sauce, one of the chief sauces of the time.

The *morterel* was also a kind of hash made with pheasant's meat, kid's leg and mesentery, bound with eggs.

In the same book, *Le Viandier*, Taillevent gives recipes for seventeen sauces, including *cameline*, a kind of brown meat sauce; *jauce; dodine* (made in three different ways); *saulce Robert*, so wholesome and necessary, according to Rabelais, for duck, rabbits, roasts, fresh pork, eggs, salt cod, and other meats.

Philéas Gilbert notes in *La Technique culinaire à travers les âges*, that at this time the thickening of sauces with flour was completely unknown. The thickening was done with grilled or ordinary bread.

The three *dodines* mentioned by Taillevent were, in fact, sauces which accompanied various dishes and not dishes in themselves.

In order to give a picture of what cooking was like in the fourteenth and fifteenth centuries we give the menu of a banquet served by Taillevent to King Charles VI.

First course: Capons with cinnamon broth; chickens with herbs; new cabbage, and then venison.

Second course: a fine roast, peacocks or *sebererau*, capon pies, leverets in vinegar, and capons in unfermented wine.

Third course: Partridges *à la trimolette*, stewed pigeons, venison *pâtés*, jellies and *leschées* (probably slices of buttered bread.)

Fourth course: as sweets (desserts) pear pies, almonds, sugared tarts.

No document mentions cooking under Louix XI, and it is to be surmised that in his castle of Plessis-les-Tours his conversations with his crony Tristan were on subjects far removed from that of the art of good eating.

It does seem, however, that Louix XI did not despise the pleasures of the table. In his castle in Touraine, a district which has always maintained the cult of good living, and where gay and light-hearted wines have always been made, the King and his good companions must have feasted often and without any doubt magnificently.

French cooking in the sixteenth century—Under François I the days of heavy feasting and tremendous drinking bouts recounted by Rabelais were revived.

It is from this time that the books on cookery which are really worthy of the name actually date.

In 1543, *La Fleur de toute cuisine* appeared, by Pierre Pidoux, and in 1570, the *Viandier de Taboureau*, which in many respects was inspired by Taillevent's book.

The conclusion of this book is rather curious. '*Dist Taboureau que mon livre est parfait . . . loué soit celui qui m'a fait et la douce mère Marie.*' ('Taboureau says that my book is perfect . . . Let Him who made me be praised and the sweet Mother Mary'.)

Cooking flourished in the reign of François I. Already the refinements of the Italian Renaissance had penetrated into France, and both art and letters had received the happy impetus of a new culture. The table in France became more magnificent than it had ever been.

Menus included fish, fowl, feathered game and venison; butcher's meat and vegetables featured very little.

Kitchen implements of this time were much the same as those of the Middle Ages, although these were augmented by larger pieces, and notably by enormous copper *daubières**.

Under the following reigns, as a result of the disturbances caused by the imperial and religious wars, expenses had to be cut down and the pleasures of the table restricted. 'Then,' says Brantôme, 'it was by fits and starts that good living was maintained.'

But in the time of King Henry II, prosperity returned and the culinary art made rapid progress. The magnificence of the feasts was tremendous. Dishes were served in great style, such as those which featured in the menu served on the 5th March, 1558 to King Henry II, a meal which included a profusion of lampreys in a Hippocras sauce, lavish hot-pots, ducklings *à la Malvoisie*, slices of muraena (an eel-like fish) served with a sauce of egg yolks and herbs, ducks *à la didone*, sturgeon fillets *à la lombarde*, quarters of roe-buck, partridges *à la tonelette*, and a whole series of sweets such as *darioles, oriflans* and *échaudés*.

At the end of the sixteenth century and until the reign of Henry IV, Italian cooks and pastry cooks were introduced into France under the influence of Catherine and Marie de Médici. At that time the Italian *maîtres queux* (head chefs) were considered the best in the world.

These Italian cooks, against whose instruction the French practitioners had the good sense not to revolt, taught them a great many recipes which have since remained in the French repertoire.

This was due to the fact that French cooks were

A sixteenth century kitchen.
After Christiano di Messiburgo, Ferrare 1549

already aware of their rôle and their social importance. They knew very well what consideration was due to them, and for this were, in fact, rather ridiculed by their contemporaries, notably by Montaigne who reports, not without mockery, a conversation with one of them:

'He discoursed on this science of cookery with a gravity and a magisterial air as if he was discussing with me a great point in theology.

'He interpreted for me the differences in appetite, that which one has on an empty stomach, that which one has following on the second and third course, the means to arouse it and to stimulate it; the order of his sauces, first of all in general and then particularising the quality of their ingredients and their effects. And all this in rich and magnificent phrases such as one would use to discuss the government of an empire.'

French cooking in the seventeenth century—The reign of Henry IV is symbolised by the famous 'hen' which the good King wished all his subjects to be able to put in the pot on Sundays. But this is by no means the only feature of this period. There were many notable cooks, one of whom, La Varenne, the chef of the Marquis d'Uxelles' kitchens, was also at the end of his life a kind of statesman.

The reign of Louis XIII was relatively insignificant from the point of view of cooking, but the dawn of the *Grand Siècle* was about to begin, and cooking was to receive a serious impetus founded on the instruction of the *Cuisinier Français* by La Varenne, which appeared in 1651, the first book to fix the rules and the principles of working, and to establish some order in cooking.

In 1691 another book appeared, *Le Cuisinier Royal et Bourgeois* by Massialot, who, like La Varenne, gave precise and clear culinary instructions. It is apparent from this book that culinary preparations were growing more varied, and that dishes were beginning to be embellished with names of famous people or of royal favourites. It was also at this time that menus mention the *olla*—the Spanish *olla podrida*—introduced into French cooking at the request of Maria Theresa, wife of the great king; the multiple hors-d'oeuvre, the monumental removes, *entremets** in the real meaning of the word, because in the preceding centuries not a culinary preparation but a spectacle was offered to the guests under this name. Now, too, the different courses in a gala dinner were arranged in a logical way.

The *Grand Siècle* was also great gastronomically speaking, but under the Great King cooking was spectacular and ostentatious rather than fine and delicate.

It was in the reign of Louis XIV that the culinary weapons of the Middle Ages were replaced by a *batterie de cuisine** (see KITCHEN EQUIPMENT) which included a great number of new utensils, and utensils in tinplate and wrought iron began to appear. A little later utensils made in silver were seen.

The festivities of the Superintendent Fouquet in his Château de Vaux, and those of the Prince of Condé at Chantilly were particularly sumptuous. The famous Vatel was *maître d'hôtel* of the Grand Condé, which was an extremely important position.

There were numerous and magnificent gastronomic manifestations in the seventeenth century. All the *grands seigneurs* took a great interest in matters relating to food. And the master cooks, in gratitude for the interest they took in cooking, made a point of giving their names to the new dishes they composed. For this reason many people believe today that such a dish in the French repertoire was conceived, created, even prepared by the men of high standing or the noble ladies whose name they bear. For instance, it is frequently believed that *Béchamel* sauce was invented by the Marquis de Béchamel, which some call *Béchameil*, that the Richelieu garnish was invented by the Maréchal Duc de Richelieu, that the invention of *Carré de mouton à la purée de lentilles* (loin of mutton with lentil purée) is due to the Princesse de Conti and that the *Côtelettes d'agneau Maintenon* (lamb cutlets Maintenon)* were invented by the widow of the poet Scarron. The honour should be bestowed where it is legitimately due, on those artists who actually invented these dishes, and who are sometimes very little known.

At this time table manners were less extravagant than those fashionable in the preceding century. If Louis XIV was a great eater, a much too great eater to be a true

Seventeenth century cook (*Mariette*)

gourmand, he did at least have the merit of establishing a new protocol of the table at court, which consisted in serving the different dishes separately. Before his time everything was thrown together, pell-mell, making a monstrous pyramid which is amusingly described by Boileau in his *Festin ridicule:*

Sur un lièvre flanqué de six poulets étiques,
S'élevaient trois lapins, animaux domestiques,
Qui, dès leur tendre enfance élevés dans Paris,
Sentaient encor le chou dont ils furent nourris.
Autour de cet amas de viandes entassées,
Régnait un long cordon d'alouettes pressées,
Et sur les bords du plat, six pigeons étalés
Présentaient pour renforts leurs squelettes brulés.

On top of a hare surrounded by six emaciated pullets,
Lay three rabbits, domestic animals,
Who, raised since their tender infancy in Paris,
Smelt still of the cabbage on which they had been fed.
Round this mass of piled up meats
Reigned a long border of pressed larks,
And on the edges of the dish, six pigeons spread out
Exposed their burnt skeletons as a reinforcement.

In the seventeenth century a great quantity of dishes were served at each meal. As proof we have the enumeration that Molière's Maître Jacques makes to Harpagon, and the description that a number of documents give of the meals served at the royal table of Louis XIV.

The Palatine Princess wrote: 'I have seen the King eat, and that very often, four plates of different soups, an entire pheasant, a partridge, a large plateful of salad, mutton cut up in its juice with garlic, two good pieces of ham, a plateful of cakes, and fruit and jams.'

In 1708, Fagon, His Majesty's last doctor, noted: 'The King, tired out and in low spirits, was constrained to eat meat on a Friday, and wished to be served only with crusts, a pigeon soup, and three roast chickens. The following day he was served with a soup with a fowl, three roast chickens of which he took as on Friday, four wings, the white meat and a leg. The day after that he hardly ate any entrée, and contented himself with four wings, the white meat and some of the legs of the chickens.'

We know what Saint-Simon wrote on the royal appetite. The great biographer says, 'All his life he had eaten very little bread, and for some time past only the soft part as he had no teeth. Soup in very large quantities, fine hashes and eggs were used as a supplement. As he became in the last year of his life more and more subject to constipation, Fagon gave him a great deal of iced fruits to begin his meal, such as melons, figs, over-ripe to the point of rottenness, and for his dessert a great many other fruits, followed by a quantity of sweet things which always delighted him. All the year round he ate a great deal of salad at supper. His soups, of which he had several morning and evening, and each one in quantity without prejudice to the rest, were full of juice and full of nourishment, and everything he ate was very highly spiced, at least twice as spiced as is ordinarily the case, and very strong indeed.' It was, incidentally, due to Louis XIV that the custom of serving sweets, formerly reserved for fête days, was introduced; his taste for sweet things brought them into daily use.

In general, the menus were equally copious in the great houses and among the rich bourgeois of the time, and it seems that the master chefs or the *cordons bleus* who had to prepare these meals had a great deal to do. A fairly clear idea of this can be had from reading the description of a meal for eight or ten people given in the *Délices de la campagne*, by Nicolas de Bonnefons, valet to the King about 1652, which is reproduced in the section entitled BANQUET.

French cooking under the Regency—History has judged the eight years of the Regency rather severely. But, if under Philippe d'Orléans, these years were disastrous from a political, economic and national point of view, they did at least have some distinction as regards gastronomy, and it is from this time that the true French cuisine dates.

While the Regency lasted, the ovens of the great houses in the kingdom were hardly ever idle, and the gifted cooks who directed the kitchens of the Palais Royal, of the Trianon and the other princely houses had to accomplish feats of prowess to give full and entire satisfaction to the refined table companions who were the guests of the Regent.

The Regent himself took a hand with the pastry, according to the anecdotes of this amiable time. In *La vie privée d'autrefois*, Franklin wrote: 'For the little suppers given by the Regent, the dishes were prepared in special rooms on the same floor, where all the utensils were made of silver; the *roués* often worked with the cooks.'

The menu of one of these suppers to which the Regent invited his *roués*, a menu for twelve which was half *gras* and half *maigre*, gives a better picture of the state of the cuisine of that time when it was particularly brilliant than does a long dissertation. This meal is, in fact, a key to the nomenclature of principal dishes in fashion at the time, and also a kind of specification, as some of the elements of the dishes are mentioned:

First course: Joint of salt beef, garnished with carrots and potatoes.

Two soups: one made of a pike cullis, one of turnips with a duck thereon.

Two fish dishes: a carp *à l'anglaise*; freshwater fish consisting of twenty-four little perch and four little pikes.

Ten entrées: Mutton fillets larded and glazed with gherkins on top; two chickens stuck with parsley, espagnole sauce; pike *à la polonaise;* perch *à la genevoise* (six perch and one bottle of white wine); sauerkraut with one pike; twenty-five oysters cooked with a pint of cream; *noix de veau à la néapolitaine;* three partridges *en levrault* (leveret); two fine eels *à la bavaroise* and half a hundred fine crayfish; roe-buck kidneys in marinade.

Two dishes of pâtisseries: a cake filled with an apricot *marmelade;* an iced tart (six peaches iced and a pint of cream).

Four roasts: Fried smelts (crumbed); two *poulardes;* two fried soles; two wild ducks.

Four different salads, with sauces.

Four little hot entremets: six veal sweetbreads larded and glazed; pig's trotters *Sainte-Menehould;* dried peas *à la crème;* dessert apples *à la chinoise.*

At this period kitchen arrangements became more sensible and kitchen utensils more practical. Until the beginning of the eighteenth century, cooking was done on the fire and on charcoal braziers: then all kitchens were provided with a stove called a *potager* supplied with twelve or twenty grates (foyers) according to the size of the household. This arrangement persisted until the time when the cast-iron stove heated with coal came into use.

French cooking under Louis XV—Cooking in the reign of Louis XV was more or less the same as under the Regency. The nobility of that time were extremely interested in the culinary art. They were 'gastronomic snobs' and wished to have dishes named after them, whether these had been invented in their own house or not. It is to this period that we owe the *Bouchées de la Reine*, named in honour of Marie Leczinska, wife of Louis XV; the *Cailles à la Mirepoix* (Quails), the *Timbale Pompadour*, and all those other dishes which the chefs of these illustrious personages baptised with the names of their masters.

The menus served at the court of Louis XV by Heliot, *écuyer de la bouche* of Madame Dauphine de France, were really grandiose. A part of these menus drawn from the original source was published by Carême in his *Maitre d'hôtel français*. From these it is possible to detect a certain progress in cooking, but Philéas Gilbert notes that the menus were presented in the form of placards or inscriptions on a card '*whose dimensions are those of electoral notices and in which figure:* 4 *ollas and* 8 *lesser soups;* 12 *fish entrées;* 32 *entrées and* 44 *lesser entrées;* 12 *removes;* 4 *hors-d'oeuvre before the King;* 2 *grands entremets;* 32 *roasts;* 2 *lesser roasts at the ends of the table;* 2 *little dishes before the King;* 40 *cold entremets and* 48 *hot entremets*.'

It is obvious that to execute a menu of this importance it was necessary to have a very considerable number of master cooks.

In the time of Louis XV a number of culinary books appeared. The principal and most interesting ones were the *Cuisinier moderne* by Vincent de la Chapelle, published first in English in 1733, and then translated into French in 1735, and the *Dons de Comus*, a work which appeared without the author's name but which was written by Marin, *maître d'hôtel* of the Maréchal de Soubise. This work was preceded by a *Discours préliminaire* remarkable both for its style and documentation, and attributed to the Jesuit fathers, Pierre Brunoy and Hyacinthe Bourgeant.

Carême considered the work of Vincent de la Chapelle as the best of the books which had appeared in the seventeenth and eighteenth centuries. He valued less the work of Marin, whom he regarded as the compiler of Chapelle.

As far as the *Cuisinier moderne* is concerned, he criticises the author for having given certain dishes inadmissible names, such as *Filet de boeuf en talon de botte*, *Semelles de faisan à la Conti*, *Veau roulé en crotte d'âne*, and above all that of *Potage à la jambe de bois*, which he found altogether grotesque.

Among the simple bourgeois at this time, meals were also more regulated as far as their composition was concerned, and with more order than in the previous century.

Here, according to Brillat-Savarin, is the usual composition of a meal served among the middle classes of society. In 1740 a dinner for ten people would consist of:

First course: Le bouilli (boiled meat); an entrée of veal cooked in its juice; an hors d'oeuvre.

Second course: a turkey; a dish of vegetables; a salad; a cream.

Third course: cheese; fruit; a pot of jam.

It is understood, although Brillat-Savarin does not exactly stipulate it, that by the word *bouilli* not only the piece of boiled beef was meant, but also the soup in which it was cooked, which was served before it.

'The plates were only changed three times; after the soup, for the second course, and for dessert.

'Coffee was seldom served, but quite often a ratafia of cherries or carnations, which was a fairly new introduction.'

French cooking at the time of Louis XVI—During the first years of the reign of Louis XVI there was a continued tendency to refine culinary methods and to establish more order and more logic, as well as a greater elegance in the composition of the menus for grand galas. There were at this time, says Brillat-Savarin in his *Histoire de la cuisine* (*Physiologie du goût*, *Meditation XXVII*), great improvements in all branches of catering.

'All the professions in which the aim is to prepare or to sell food, such as cooks, caterers, *pâtissiers*, confectioners, grocers, have multiplied on an ever increasing scale . . . Physics and chemistry have been called to the aid of cooking. The most distinguished intellects have not thought it an unworthy task to occupy themselves with our basic needs and have introduced improvements ranging from the workman's simple *pot-au-feu* to the transparent extracts (Brillat-Savarin means here the aspic jellies) which are served only in gold or crystal.

'New professions have arisen, for example the confectioners of *petits fours*, who lie half way between the *pâtissiers* proper and the confectioners . . . The art of preserving food has also become a distinct profession . . . Horticulture has made enormous progress, (horticulture had already been carried to a high degree of perfection by La Quintinie, in the reign of Louis XIV), the hot-houses have put tropical fruits before us, various types of vegetable have been introduced by cultivation or importation. Wines of all countries have been cultivated, imported and presented in a regular order, Madeira which paves the way for the meal, the wines of France, which are divided among the courses, and those of Spain, which crown the meal.

'The French cuisine has appropriated foreign dishes, such as caviare and beefsteak; seasoning such as curry and soya; drinks like punch, and others . . . Coffee has become popular, in the morning as nourishment, and after dinner as an exhilarating and tonic drink.

'Finally,' added Brillat-Savarin, 'the word gastronomy had been resuscitated from the Greek; it had a gentle sound to French ears, and although hardly understood, it was enough to pronounce it to bring a smile of hilarity to every face.'

It was under the reign of Louis XVI, in 1765 according to some and in 1770 according to others, that the first restaurant came into being. See RESTAURANT.

A glance at the menus of restaurateurs at the end of the eighteenth century provides information on the general state of cooking at that time. These menus included 12 soups; 24 hors d'oeuvre; 15 or 20 entrées of beef; 20 entrées of mutton; 30 entrées of fowl or game; 12 or 20 entrées of veal; 12 dishes of pâtisserie; 24 dishes of fish; 15 roasts; 50 entremets; 50 desserts.

French cooking during the period of the Revolution and the Empire—The author of *Avant de quitter la table* described the state of French cuisine at the time of the Revolution as follows:

'There were other preoccupations than the confection of cullises, roasts, and the arrangement of menus . . . the poor chefs were forgotten; a new austerity prevailed over the extravagances of yesterday, and the supreme *bon ton* was to assume a spartan simplicity.

'But the pleasures of the table never lose their rights, and the new masters of France soon tired of so much virtue, and once again in Paris and in the provinces, there was a return to good living. Besides, the chefs of the great houses of the nobility, finding themselves unemployed on the emigration of their masters, put themselves at the service of the sovereign people (or at least of those who governed them), and soon the ovens were heated once again throughout the country, and particularly in Paris, in the Palais ex-Royal, Rue Montorgueil, and the Boulevard du Temple.

'Men of talent, such as Brillat-Savarin and Grimod de la Reynière, began to assemble their observations, and to experiment in order to write their works. In 1798, when he was sixteen years old, Carême, the man who was going to write the new 'culinary charter', after a period of six years in a modest cabaret on the outskirts of Paris where he learned the rudiments of his art, had started as a pastrycook with Bailly. The *maison Bailly*, which was one of the leading Paris pâtisseries, supplied the Prince de Talleyrand, who, as is well known, kept a sumptuous table, and two years later in this famous house, Carême was first pastry-maker (Tourier).'

In the relatively calmer period of the Directory, the great bourgeois households reorganised themselves, new restaurants opened, and cooking became once again as grandiose as it had been in the time of Louis XV.

Under the Directory, an attempt was made to reconstitute official dinners and suppers. Ostentation was re-established in serving food; magnificent buffets were prepared for balls, buffets which were overladen with enormous cold *pièces* decorated to excess.

Even if the emphasis was on luxury rather than on a well-chosen ensemble in these great festivities, nevertheless both in Paris and in the provinces, more rational menus were introduced, less overcharged with a multiplicity of dishes than in former reigns.

The following menu bears testimony to this—countersigned by General Barras, one of the five members of the Directory.

Potage (Soup):

Aux petits oignons, à la ci-devant minime (with little onions)

Relevé (Remove):

Tronçons d'esturgeon à la broche (Sturgeon roast on the spit)

Six Entrées:

Un sauté de turbot à l'homme de confiance, ci-devant maître d'hôtel (Turbot *sautéed maître d'hôtel*)

Anguilles à la tartare (Eels, tartare sauce)

Concombres farcis à la moelle (Cucumbers stuffed with marrowfat)

Un ci-devant saint-pierre, sauce aux câpres (John Dory, caper sauce)

Vol-au-vent de blancs de volaille à la béchamel (Vol-au-vent of breast of chicken with béchamel sauce)

Filets de perdrix, en anneaux pour ne pas dire en couronnes (Fillets of partridge in rings, so as not to say 'crowns')

Two plats de rôt:

Goujons du département (Gudgeon)

Une carpe au court-bouillon (Carp in court-bouillon)

Six Entremets:

Lentilles à la ci-devant Reine (lentils *à la Reine*)

Betteraves blanchies, sautées au beurre (Beetroots blanched and sautéed in butter)

Culs d'artichauts à la ravigote (Purée of artichokes *à la ravigote*)

Oeufs à la neige (Eggs *à la neige*)

Gelée au vin de Madère (Madeira wine jelly)

Beignets de crème à la fleur d'oranger (Cream fritters)

Salade:

Céleri en remoulade (Celery in remoulade sauce)

Vingt-quarte assiettes de dessert (Twenty-four dishes of dessert)

This menu is annotated by Varras, who was a connoisseur of *cuisine*. Very justly, he remarks that it contains too much fish. 'Remove the gudgeon,' he says. And he recommends that 'the placing of cushions on the chairs of the citizens Tallien, Talma, Beauharnais, Hingerelot and Osbirande should not again be forgotten . . .

'The first Empire passed in the clash of arms and in triumphal trumpetings marked by splendid fêtes and immense banquets.'

But, if we are to believe F. Masson, the position of chef in the Imperial Court was no sinecure.

The chefs came and went very frequently. 'Was it,' he writes, 'due to the bad ventilation in the kitchens, or to the severe economy established in the household which reduced them strictly to their 2,400 francs wages? After Gaillon, who accompanied the General (Napoleon) into Egypt and who was retired with the position of *garde des bouches* at Fontainebleau; after Danger, who also went on the Egyptian expedition and who even ran the risk of death when, on the return, the silver was stolen at six *lieues* from Aix-en-Provence, there was a succession of chefs (at the court) after 1802; Vénard de la Borde, Coulon, Farcy, Laguipière, (the great *maître queux* of whom Carême speaks with so much enthusiasm), the artist whom Murat attached to his person and who died on the retreat from Russia; Debray, Lecomte, Heurtin, Lacombe, Lemoigne. Ferdinand was the cook at Elba, and Dousseau the chef de cuisine during the Hundred Days . . . ' (F. Masson, *Napoléon chez lui.*)

Too frequent changes in the kitchen team were the cause of the service at table lacking the necessary correctness. One single practitioner, says F. Masson, remained in the Imperial kitchens from the beginning of the reign until the end, the chief pastrycook, Lebeau, 'who was, it is said, the restorer of French pâtisserie, and who, from the moment he entered the household of the First Consul, made a sensation with his inventions of charming *pièces montées*.'

Among the many practitioners who exercised their art in the service of the Imperial Court, and contributed to the extravagance of the great gastronomic galas which took place at that time, was the man who was certainly the most devoted of Napoleon's servants, since he followed him to St. Helena and who, in spite of countless difficulties, applied himself to the task of encouraging the appetite of the fallen Emperor, just as he did at the Tuileries in the time of his greatness. This great chef, whom Carême venerated as a god, was Chandelier.

It was at this time that Carême himself, the great master of culinary art, collected the material with which he wrote his work on the art of French *cuisine* in the nineteenth century.

In this ten year period of great official dinners (called *extraordinaires*) Carême, while still continuing his innovations in pâtisserie, perfected his knowledge of culinary matters. He was seen at the Tuileries, at the great dinners of the Galeries given by Talleyrand, at the fêtes of the Hôtel de Ville, where the new marshals of France, the new nobility, ministers and ambassadors jostled one another; he was seen at the Elysée-Napoléon with the great Laguipière.

As a *pâtissier* he had taken the place of famous executants who had come to the end of their careers, such as Avice, Tiroloy, the one time chef of the Soubise household, Feuillet of the house of Condé, Lecoq, who had worked in the royal household under Louis XVI.

Studying under the celebrated chefs of the moment, he gained rapid promotion, and in his works he expresses his gratitude, notably to Richaud, the most famous *saucier* of his time, to Lasnes, who taught him the secrets of the cold table, to Riquette, former first chef to

A kitchen in the early nineteenth century

the Czar, to Bouchet, the supervisor of the house of Talleyrand, and above all, to Laguipière.

French cooking at the beginning of the nineteenth century—Kitchens of this time, even the best equipped kitchens, had very mediocre implements and the various cooking stoves were very rudimentary. Carême has left us a forceful picture of these kitchens at the hour of work, of the *coup de feu* as the French say today.

'Imagine yourself in a large kitchen such as that of the Foreign Ministry at the moment of a great dinner (Talleyrand was Foreign Minister at the time). There one sees twenty chefs at their urgent occupations, coming, going, moving with speed in this cauldron of heat. Look at the great mass of live charcoal, a cubic metre, for the cooking of the entrées, and another mass on the ovens for the cooking of the soups, the sauces, the ragoûts, the frying and the bains-marie.

'Add to that a heap of burning wood in front of which four spits are turning, one of which bears a sirloin weighing from 45 to 60 lb., another a piece of veal weighing 35 to 45 lb., the other two for fowl and game.

'In this furnace everyone moves with tremendous speed; not a sound is heard; only the chef has the right to make himself heard, and at the sound of his voice, everyone obeys. Finally, to put the lid on our sufferings, for about half an hour the doors and windows are closed so that the air does not cool the dishes as they are being dished up. And in this way we pass the best days of our lives.

'But,' adds Carême, 'honour commands. We must obey even though physical strength fails. But it is the burning charcoal which kills us!'

Victor Hugo gives another description of a kitchen, which dates from about the middle of the same century.

'At Sainte-Menehould I have seen a fine sight, the kitchen of the Hôtel de Metz.

'This is a real kitchen. An immense room. One wall occupied by copper pans, the other by faïence; in the middle facing the windows, the chimney, an enormous cavern filled with a splendid fire. On the ceiling, a black network of smoke-encrusted beams from which hang all kinds of delectable things, baskets, lamps, a meat safe, and in the centre a large openwork net in which vast pieces of bacon are suspended. Inside the chimney, beside the turnspit, the chimney hook and the cauldron, glitter a dazzling array of a dozen scoops and tongs of all shapes and sizes. The glowing hearth shoots beams of light into all the corners, cuts out great shadows on the ceiling, casts a fresh rose tint on the blue faïence, and makes the fantastic edifice of pans glow like a wall of fire. If I were Homer or Rabelais I would say, "This kitchen is a world, and this chimney is the sun."

'It is a world indeed in which a whole republic of men, women and animals move, of boys, servants, scullions, carters seated at table, of pans and braziers, of simmering pots, sizzling frying-pans, of cards, pipes, children at play and cats and dogs and the master who keeps an eye on it all. *Mens agitat molem.*

'In one corner, a huge clock with weights and chain soberly tells the time to all these busy people. Among the innumerable things which hang from the ceiling, I particularly admired one on the evening I arrived; it was a little cage in which a little bird was sleeping. This bird seemed to me to be the most admirable emblem of confidence. This cavern, this forge of indigestion, this terrifying kitchen is day and night full of noise, but the bird sleeps. The men swear, the women quarrel, the children cry, the dogs bark, the cats miauw, the clock chimes, the chopper falls, the dripping pan squeaks, the turnspit creaks, the fountain drips, the bottles weep, the windowpanes shiver, the diligences pass under the arch like thunder, but the little ball of feathers does not move.'

This romantic kitchen may have been in the poet's eyes a fine thing, but to ours it seems extremely unpractical.

During the Restoration, Brillat-Savarin's *La Physiologie du Goût* appeared, and this fact alone is a revelation of the importance that gastronomy and progress in cuisine had at that time.

In the restaurants of the Palais Royal small and great dinners were on the increase.

Véry made his fortune; Achard began to make his; Beauvilliers made a third; and Madame Sallot, whose shop at the Palais Royal hardly measured two yards square, sold as many as 12 thousand little pâtés a day (*Physiologie du Goût*).

Perhaps one should regard this figure given by Brillat-Savarin as a little exaggerated. But it must be admitted that, thanks to the efforts made by all the restaurateurs and master cooks of that day to satisfy the tastes of their innumerable clientele, the progress made in cookery was important.

Under the reign of Louis-Philippe the culinary art was rather less in favour. Everyone in the entourage of the King, who was essentially economical, applied himself to simple living to the point of stinginess. The dinners at the Tuileries were extremely bourgeois in their presentation.

Louis-Philippe lived as a bourgeois; he was all order and economy. He pushed this last virtue so far as to assign to the caterers of the second zone the supply of dinners at fixed prices to the château. The price of these dinners was between 5 and 10 francs per head according to the importance of the guests.

As can be imagined, under such a régime the culinary art could hardly make progress, as no encouragement came from the court.

However, it was in this reign of the 'bourgeois' King that the most famous clubs and gastronomic coteries were founded.

These societies held their sessions in the best restaurants of the time, and can be considered as the forerunners of the *Académie des gastronomes* founded by Curnonsky. Brillat-Savarin had already predicted the creation of a gastronomic academy, but the programme that the author of *La Physiologie du Goût* established for this *Académie des gastronomes* is rather nebulous.

The brief Republic of 1848 had its patriotic banquets where according to the historians of that period the menus consisted only of veal and salad.

French cooking during the period of the Second Empire—It may be true that the Second Empire was 'the reign of electro-plated ware and tinsel, the time of crinolines and prefects' but it was also a period particularly favourable to *cuisine*.

In the reign of Napoleon III there were at the Tuileries, and in the various châteaux in which the court stayed, some magnificent festivities always accompanied by splendid banquets. And, given the professional merit of the *maîtres queux* who at that time directed the kitchens of the great houses in France, one can be certain that the great dinners of the time achieved the highest perfection.

It was at this time too that the first edition of the *Cuisine classique by* Urbain Dubois and Auguste Bernard appeared, a magnificent work which still speaks with authority today, and which has done more for professional instruction than the work of Carême himself, which sometimes makes difficult reading. Very great masters exercised their art at the time in France. Among them were Armand Gouffé and Joseph Gastilleur.

'On ordinary occasions,' says Madame de Carette, 'the table at the Tuileries was rich and elegant, and the food exquisite and delicate.' (*Souvenirs intimes de la cour des Tuileries.*)

'One ate at almost all seasons strawberries, peaches, little new peas, from the greenhouses of the châteaux of Versailles . . . . There were four double courses, which means today, two soups, two removes, four entrées, two roasts, etc.

'The kitchens in the Tuileries were in the basement and the dishes arrived by lifts installed behind the Gallery of Diana.'

Even for ordinary dinners the menus at the Tuileries contained a fairly large number of dishes.

Although the cuisine of the Second Empire was in high social circles quite as brilliant and quite as delicate as that of the time of the Restoration, many chroniclers criticised the culinary practices of the time and complained that the cooking was thoroughly mediocre.

In the *Courrier de Paris* of 27th March, 1858, we find a severe critic of the cooking and of the chefs of the time:

'A good dinner is a rare thing today. Gastronomy is like poetry: it has fallen into a complete decadence . . .

'The causes of this decadence are well known: thoughtlessness, fatuity, overweening ambition are only small and ordinary sins; the most complete self-abandonment, the absence of convictions, greed, these are what have troubled the limpid sources from which gastronomic delights should flow with an enchanted murmur.

'The present generation eats and knows not how to eat . . . It is the enemy of that *grande cuisine* which was France's glory. The chefs are the cause of this indifference which is blamed on us. They have muddled everything, spoilt everything, exhausted everything.'

And the Baron Brisse wrote in the *Liberté* of 1st January, 1866, on the eve of the Great Universal Exhibition which was visited by William I, King of Prussia, the Czar of all the Russias, and many other monarchs and princes of Europe: 'Is the *cuisine* in decline in France? Incontestably yes. Our chefs are aware of this, even more than their predecessors: science comes to their aid, but also the material conditions of the culinary art are completely changed.'

On the 7th June, 1867, during the Universal Exhibition, the dinner of the three Emperors took place in the Café Anglais in the famous salon of the *Grand Seize*. The guests at this quasi-historic dinner were all illustrious personages. There were the Czar, the Czarevitch, the King of Prussia, William I and several Grand Dukes. Under the heading *MENU* the composition of this meal will be found. It cost 400 francs per cover, a considerable sum at that time.

Old kitchen, Hospice de Beaune (*French Government Tourist Office*)

A French cook surveys his handiwork
(*French Government Tourist Office*)

Guides to French cooking of the late nineteenth and early twentieth century—Since the end of the nineteenth century French culinary art has perhaps reached the highest point of perfection. The end of that century and the early part of this were notable for the many excellent books on cookery, starting with those written by Urbain Dubois and Bernard, by Gouffé, by Joseph Favre and other practitioners of the culinary art. From 1900 were published such books as Escoffier's *Guide Culinaire* (in collaboration with Philéas Gilbert), *Plaisirs de la Table* by Nignon, *Le Grand Livre de la Cuisine* by Prosper Salles, works of far-reaching importance, which are known throughout the world. Many other books, less important in the history of cooking but equally interesting, came from the pen of master cooks such as Alfred Suzanne, Dietrich, Garlin, Ferdinand Werner and Bouzy.

It is true that these books treat only of theoretical instruction and often there is a large gap between theory and practice. Still, the fact that they came to be written proves that culinary practice, the rules of which they establish, was highly developed. From all points of view the present-day chef must have the same qualities as those at the beginning of the last century, of whom the poet Désaugiers wrote:

Un cuisinier, quand je dine,
Me semble un être divin
Qui, du fond de sa cuisine,
Gouverne le genre humain.
Qu'ici bas, on le contemple
Comme un ministre du ciel,
Car sa cuisine est un temple
Dont les fourneaux sont l'autel.

'A cook, when I dine, seems to me a divine being, who from the depths of his kitchen rules the human race. One considers him as a minister of heaven, because his kitchen is a temple, in which his ovens are the altar.'

COOT. Foulque—This bird is in some ways similar to a moor-hen. Like the latter it has dark flesh which is dry and not strongly flavoured.

There are several varieties of coots in France: *foulque morelle*, *foulque macroule*, also known as *foulque judelle*, *foulque à crête du Cap*, (African or crested coot) and *foulque bleue du Portugal*. It is found in England but is not so popular as it formerly was. There are several species in the U.S.A. but they are never marketed.

Coot

The coot is classified by the church as Lenten fare. All ways of cooking a wild duck apply to a coot. It is very good when eaten fresh, if skinned immediately after shooting (the skin is in fact oily and smelly) and cooked in a casserole with a piece of larding bacon.

COPEAUX (TWISTS) (Petits fours)—These little confections are made of a similar preparation to that given for *langues de chat*.

This preparation is squeezed out of a forcing bag on to a baking tray and cooked in a hot oven. When cooked, and while the little *gâteaux* are still malleable, they should be rolled on a moderate-sized stick into twists.

COPPER. Cuivre—A metal extensively used in the manufacture of a number of different cooking utensils. Copper being a very good conductor of heat, copper cooking pans have the advantage of spreading the heat out evenly and thus cooking the food right through.

Copper salts were long regarded as virulent poisons. Careful experiments have proved this false: these salts, like sulphates and acetates (verdigris), mainly tend to cause nausea and vomiting.

In fact, in minute but measureable doses, copper is one of the mineral elements in the human organism and some foodstuffs.

COQ—Name of the chef aboard ship. Also the French word for COCK. *Coq* is usually used on menus.

Coq en pâte—This dish is so-called, but as a rule it is prepared with a fine chicken and not a cock, not even a capon. And the result is much better if one proceeds in the following way, as it used to be done long ago:

The chicken being dressed, that is to say emptied (from the front), singed and cleaned, remove the breast bone. Stuff the bird copiously with *foie gras* and truffles cut into large pieces, seasoned with salt, spices and moistened with a little cognac, and with a small amount of delicate forcemeat. Truss the chicken *en entrée* (i.e. the legs inserted into the sides of the chicken).

Brown on all sides in butter. Cover the chicken with a *matignon*, made of 1 medium sized carrot, 1 medium small onion, 2 tablespoons (25 grams) of celery, all sliced, and cooked gently in butter until soft, seasoned with salt, pepper, thyme and powdered bay, with the addition at the end of the cooking of 2½ ounces (75 grams) of lean raw ham sliced very finely. Wrap up the chicken in a pig's caul soaked in cold water or in a sheet of salt pork. Put it on a sheet of *Lining pastry* (see DOUGH)—using 3¾ cups (500 grams) of flour, 10 oz. (300 grams) of butter, one egg, ⅔ cup (1½ decilitres) of water, 1½ teaspoons (10 grams) of salt. Cover the chicken with another sheet of the same pastry. Join the edges well and pinch them

Coq au vin (*Robert Carrier*)

together. Gild the surface of the pastry. Make an opening to allow for the escape of steam. Cook in the oven at a good heat for about an hour.

Nowadays a fat chicken or cock cooked in pastry is more often prepared like this: Stuff the chicken and brown it in butter in the same way as described above. Put it in an oval terrine which exactly contains it. Cover the terrine with *pâte à foncer* (ingredients for this are specified above). Gild the pastry. Cook in the oven.

The cock or chicken in pastry must be accompanied by a *Périgueux sauce* (see SAUCE) served separately.

Coq au vin (from an old recipe)—Cut up a young chicken into six pieces. Heat in 3 tablespoons (45 grams) of butter in an earthenware pot, 3 ounces (90 grams) of lean breast of pork, cut into dice, and some little onions. When these are browned, put in the pieces of chicken, a garlic clove chopped fine, a *bouquet garni**, *morels** or other mushrooms. Sauté till golden on a lively heat, with the lid on; take off the lid and skim off the fat. Pour over a little good brandy, set light to it, and then pour on a pint (demi-litre) of old Auvergne wine. After cooking on a good fire for 15 to 20 minutes take out the chicken, and pour over it the sauce, thickened with the blood of the chicken mixed with the pounded liver and some brandy. Do not cook the sauce after this liaison, because the sauce will curdle. Lacking the blood, the sauce may be thickened with *Kneaded butter*. See BUTTER.

COQUE DU LOT—This cake is made in the region of Lot for the Easter celebrations.

Ingredients. 2 pounds (1 kilo) flour; 6 whole eggs; $\frac{1}{4}$ pound (125 grams) butter; $3\frac{1}{2}$ ounces of citron (100 grams), cut in thin, long slices; $\frac{5}{6}$ ounce (25 grams) of yeast, or 1 large yeast cake; flavouring composed in thirds of lemon essence, orange flower water and rum.

Method. With the above ingredients prepare a dough like *Brioche dough* (see DOUGH). When the dough has risen, make it into the shape of an oval loaf; put it on a board; leave it to rise again; cook in a hot oven.

COQUERET—Popular name for the strawberry-tomato. Common plant in the south of Europe, of which the fruit is edible.

COQUES A PETITS FOURS—These *coques*, put two together joined with a very stiff fruit *marmelade* or with some other composition, are subsequently glazed with *fondant*. See ICING.

The mixture: Pound together 1 pound (500 grams) of dry peeled almonds and 1 pound (500 grams) of sugar. Add to this mixture when it is well worked, one white of egg beaten stiff. Mix well.

Pass the mixture through a forcing bag (pastry bag) on to a sheet of greaseproof paper in a series of balls. Sprinkle with icing sugar. Cook in a slow oven.

The mixture can also be made in the following way:

Grind 1 pound (500 grams) of peeled almonds and mix with 1 pound (500 grams) of fine sugar, and 5 egg whites.

Put this mixture in a basin, add 5 tablespoons (50 grams) of fecula (potato flour), a teaspoon of powdered vanilla or 2 teaspoons vanilla extract, and finally, 5 egg whites beaten stiff.

COQUETIER—An egg cup used for keeping eggs upright when served boiled in their shells. The French word *coquetier* is also applied to tradespeople dealing in eggs and poultry.

COQUILLE—Kitchen utensil which is filled with charcoal. Used for roasting various joints cooked on the spit.

The name is also given to little dishes made in the form of a shell. They are made in fireproof porcelain, in tempered glass, in metal. The deep shell of the scallop is also used to the same effect.

Various preparations are put in these shells, such as *salpicons*, purées, ragoûts, simple or complex, chicken fillets, or portions of fish or shellfish.

All these articles are enveloped in various sauces, and having been sprinkled with grated breadcrumbs and grated cheese, they are browned in the oven or under the grill.

CORDER—In French a pastry is said to be *cordée* when too much water has been used in the mixing. This fault must be avoided as sweets made with such pastry are hard as leather.

CORIANDER—The rounded fruits of this umbelliferous plant are about ⅛ to ¼ inch in diameter, light yellow brown in colour, with a particularly aromatic smell, and with a taste at the same time sweet and bitter.

Coriander is used in the flavouring of spirits, and in the seasoning of a large variety of foods, including meats, cheeses, pickles, salads, soups, puddings and pastries.

CORKSCREW. TIRE-BOUCHON—Instrument in the form of a spiral, the stem of which can be flat or rounded, used to extract the cork from a bottle. With a rounded stem there is less risk of cutting or breaking the cork.

CORN (Maize). MAÏS—A graminaceous plant, also known as Indian corn and corn-on-the-cob.

This plant is of South American origin. It was cultivated by the Peruvians before the arrival of the Spanish settlers.

Corn (maize) was introduced into France in the sixteenth century and a great many varieties are now grown there.

In France corn (maize) flourishes especially in the wine-growing districts.

The grain is enclosed in a strong fibrous casing with tasselled tops. Its flour makes a special kind of bread which is very popular in America. It contains a high proportion of oil and does not keep.

Fresh corn-on-the-cob is not much used in French cooking. In America on the other hand, it is eaten in considerable quantity.

Boiled fresh corn-on-the-cob I. MAÏS FRAIS AU NATUREL —Choose very fresh corn-cobs. The corn should be tender and milky. Boil them in plenty of salt water leaving them wrapped in their leaves, or strip the leaves before boiling.

Boil quickly for about 15 minutes.

Drain the cobs. Fold back the leaves, if not already stripped, so as to expose the cob. Serve on a napkin or wire tray. Serve fresh butter separately.

Fresh corn-on-the-cob can also be steamed.

Boiled fresh corn-on-the-cob II. MAÏS FRAIS AU NATUREL —Sever the stem of the corn at the base. Remove the green leaves and the silky threads underneath.

Plunge into *unsalted* boiling water with milk (1 pint of milk to every 5 quarts of water). Boil quickly for 10 minutes.

Fresh corn à la béchamel. MAÏS FRAIS À LA BÉCHAMEL—Boil the cobs as indicated for *Boiled fresh corn-on-the-cob*. Strip the cobs and mix the corn with *Béchamel sauce*. (See SAUCE).

Corn bread (American). PAIN DE MAÏS—Mix 3 cups (500 grams) of corn meal (maize flour), 1¾ cups (250 grams) of sieved wheat flour, 4 teaspoons (20 grams) of sugar, 1⅝ tablespoons (20 grams) of baking powder, 1½ teaspoons (10 grams) of salt and 6 tablespoons (100 grams) of butter in a bowl.

Blend in 4 yolks of egg beaten with a pint (½ litre) of milk and ½ cup (a decilitre) of double cream, stirring as little as possible. Fold in 4 whites of egg, whisked into a stiff froth and pour immediately into well-buttered muffin pans, filling them up to three-quarters of their height.

Bake at once in a hot oven for 25 or 30 minutes.

Note. This bread is served hot, straight from the oven, at breakfast.

Fresh corn in butter. MAÏS FRAIS AU BEURRE—Strip the cobs and proceed as for *Peas in butter**.

Fresh corn in cream. MAÏS À LA CRÈME—Strip the cobs and proceed as for *Peas à la crème**.

Grilled fresh corn. MAÏS FRAIS GRILLÉ—Put the cobs on a gridiron. Cook in a hot oven. When the grains have swollen and are a good colour, take the cobs out of the oven.

Strip the cobs. Serve the corn on a napkin. Grilled corn can also be served on the cob.

Corn en suso with chicken giblets (Créole cookery). MAÏS EN SUSO AUX ABATIS DE POULET—Suso is a kind of porridge made from maize flour (corn meal). It must not be too thick and should be simmered very slowly for a long time.

Cut the giblets into pieces of equal size. Brown them in fat. Moisten with a little water. Add 2 tablespoons of tomato purée and season. When the mixture is completely cooked, drain off the stock and keep it to moisten the flour.

When the giblets are ready, drain them. Wash some maize flour (which is about the same consistency as coarse semolina). Put it in the pan in which the giblets have been browned (with chopped onion). Put the giblets back in the pan. Add the stock little by little and cook slowly.

CORN OIL. HUILE DE MAÏS—Corn (maize) oil is a non-hydrogenated oil which is used extensively in the U.S.A. for salad dressings, for frying and as a shortening in baking.

CORN SALAD. MÂCHE—A variety of *valeriana* also known as *lamb's lettuce*. This plant, which grows wild in Europe, North Africa and Asia Minor, has been greatly improved by cultivation. In Europe it is on the market between the end of the summer and the beginning of winter. It is mainly eaten in salad. Corn salad was brought to America in the early part of the nineteenth century and is cultivated commercially and in home gardens.

Corn salad can also be cooked like spinach. See SPINACH.

CORNELIAN CHERRY. CORNOUILLE—Reddish fruit, the size of an olive, with a tart taste, which is preserved in honey or sugar. It is preserved in pickle, like olives, and a jelly is made with it. It is also called a Cornel.

CORNET—This word can have the following meanings:

(1) A twist of paper used to wrap up certain goods.
(2) A pastry in the form of a horn.
(3) A thin slice of ham, of tongue, or of other meat, rolled in the shape of a horn.
(4) In terms of butchery in France the larynx of butcher's carcases is called a *cornet*.

Cornet for ornamenting. CORNET À DÉCORER—The paper cornet which used to be used for ornamenting cold dishes and in pâtisserie is today replaced, more or less everywhere, by the forcing bag (pastry bag).

Carême, in the *Discours préliminaire du Pâtissier royal* (the foreword to his book *Le Pâtissier royal*), says, 'I must give an honourable mention to the man who invented the procedure of the paper cornet, used now to decorate and to embellish with meringue our modern sweets.

'I have been told that this ingenious idea belonged to a fashionable pastrycook in Bordeaux; others have said that it was a decorative pastrycook in Bordeaux. Whoever he was, I am grateful to the inventor for this delightful innovation; I very much regret not being able to associate his name with that of men of reputation.'

From this remark made by Carême, it would appear that the paper cornet was not used in pâtisserie until the beginning of the nineteenth century.

This seems improbable, particularly if one thinks that in preceding centuries, and especially in the eighteenth century, the decoration of cold dishes and of sweets had been carried to the heights of perfection.

However, speaking of this cornet, new to him, Carême says that it enables one 'to make things to perfection and with a scarcely perceptible lapse of time, while before it came into use we took three times as long to make the same things.'

And Carême adds (indicating in doing so the future uses to which the forcing bag would be put) that one can use the cornet 'to form sponge fingers, *croquettes à la reine*, and *biscottes à la parisienne*'.

CORNFLOWER. BLUET—This flower of a lovely blue colour (called Bachelor's Button in the U.S.A.) was once used, pounded with sugar, in pastry-making. However, blue colour is seldom used in cookery and nowadays it is only very rarely used for creams, custards and certain other preparations.

CORNSTARCH OR CORNFLOUR. FÉCULE DE MAÏS—A white flour used for thickening and in puddings which is milled from corn (Indian corn or maize).

COROZO—White substance taken from the seeds of the fruit of a palm tree, used in industry. Corozo flour has been used as bran flour for bread, but today this usage is forbidden.

CORSICA. CORSE—Island in the Mediterranean which forms a French department. Corsican cookery is very simple. The Corsican is frugal as a rule; and if he does not, as he used to in the old days, content himself with lunching *dans le tiroir* ('out of a drawer'), which means to say that the main part of his meal consists of chestnuts kept in the drawer of a cupboard, he eats certain dishes based on fish, crustaceans, and other *fruits de mer* which abound on all the shores of the island.

The Corsican larder is, however, quite well supplied. The sea produces fish in abundance, shellfish, langoustes of exquisite delicacy and other crustaceans.

In the lakes and streams of the island, lampreys and trout are found—admirable delicacies. The vegetable plot produces good vegetables, and succulent fruits grow in the orchards: plums, peaches, cherries, almonds abound, as well as the same fruits as in Italy, oranges and citrons. Corsican figs are renowned. Olives and chestnuts are harvested everywhere on the island. Vines prosper and give wines of good quality.

Sartine, Corsica

In the Maquis, Arbutus trees are found which produce red acid fruits reminiscent of strawberries.

Sheep are reared which produce good meat; goats are eaten usually when they are young, and there are pigs of very good quality, with which several excellent types of charcuterie are made.

Game is abundant in Corsica. One still finds, though rather rarely, the *mouflon*, or wild sheep. Woodcock abound in the forests and the blackbirds, fed on myrtle and arbutus, have a very succulent taste. The old French proverb which says *Faute de grives, on mange les merles* (Failing thrushes, one eats blackbirds) could hardly apply to Corsica, where the hunter who has killed a few of these delicate birds deplores the fact that one or two thrushes are found among them.

The most notable Corsican cheese is *broccio*, with which various sweets are made, such as *fritelle* and *figadone*.

Corsican wines are varied, and some, without being able to rival those of Guyenne, Burgundy, or the Côtes du Rhône, are nevertheless excellent. Among them are those of *Cap Corse*, *Porto-Vecchio*, *Cervione*, *Olmeto*, *Corte*, and the heady *Malvoisies*, made in the neighbourhood of Cap Corse.

Culinary specialities of Corsica—Among the fish and crustacean dishes are the various fish soups, some of them similar to the Marseilles *bouillabaisse*, and, of course, flavoured with garlic, pimento, capsicum, and saffron; the *anchoïade*, similar to the one made in Nice, and various foods which come into the category of hors-d'oeuvre, all kinds of shellfish, little crustaceans and other *fruits de mer* which are eaten raw or cooked in a *court-bouillon*. Stockfish deserves a special mention. It is prepared in the same way as in Nice, as is the langouste which is cooked in a *court-bouillon* or braised, and various local fish which are fried in olive oil, braised, baked in the oven, or cooked in various other ways similar to those employed on the mainland.

Among other specialities there are: the *Lonzo*, a fillet

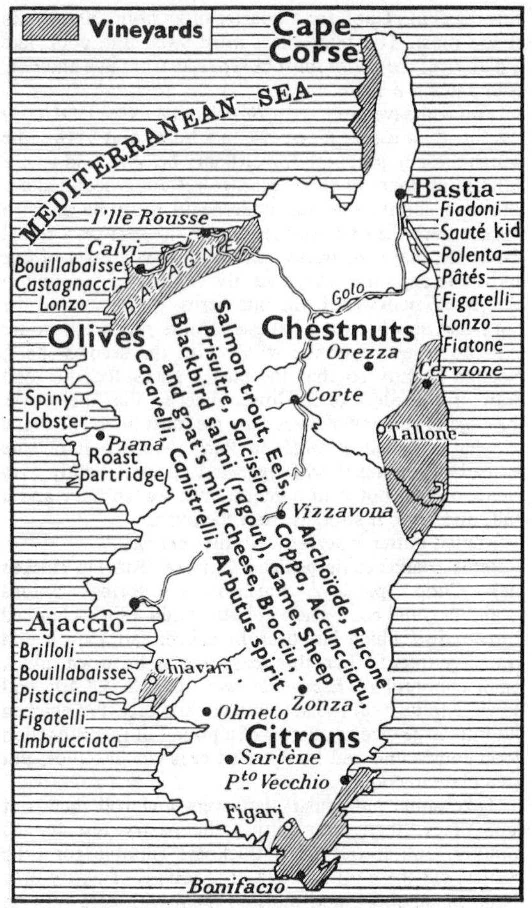

Gastronomic map of Corsica

of pork prepared in a special way, and which is the typical dish of the country (see LONZO); *Coppa*, a kind of highly flavoured sausage; *Prisuttu*, raw ham; *Omelette au broccio* (*broccio* is a Corsican cheese); *Figatelli*, a kind of sausage made of pig's liver; *Ragoût of pork*, with beans; *Stuffatu* of mutton; *Assaignes; Pebronata* of beef, braised beef flavoured with juniper; *Strisciule* made with goat's meat cured in the sun; *Cabris* and *cabiros* (kid), roasted or stewed; *Micisca*, fillet of pork slashed, marinated, smoked and cooked on a grill; *Tripa*, sheep's belly or intestines stuffed with a mixture of spinach, beet, *fines herbes*, combined with sheep's blood, tied up like a *boudin* (black pudding), and cooked in salted water.

Corsican *Polenta* is made in the same way as in Italy—in Italy polenta is made with maize (corn) flour, in Corsica with chestnut flour; *Accunciatu*, a stew with goat meat or with lamb or mutton, with potatoes, and finally *Tripette*, which are made with sheep's small intestines cut into squares, fried, sautéed in lard with tomatoes and various condiments. The *Ragoût de mouflon* is now rarely made on the island, since the wild sheep have almost disappeared.

More sumptuous dishes include *Blackbirds* (those famous blackbirds) which are roasted, usually wrapped in sage leaves, or made into salmis or pâtés; *Woodcock alla cacciatore; Salmis of partridges; Wild boar with Pebronata sauce.*

Among sweet dishes are *Brioli*, made with chestnut flour; *Fritelle*, a kind of fritter with *broccio* cheese; *Fladene*, a kind of tart made with broccio and flavoured with vanilla; *fijadone*, another flan, *Panette dolce*, a kind of bread made with eggs and sugar, decorated with raisins (these are eaten especially at Easter); *Torta*, a cake decorated with pine-kernels or almonds and flavoured with aniseed; *Migliassis*, cakes baked in the oven on chestnut leaves; preserves made with citron and other island fruits; chestnuts cooked in various ways and with which various pastries are made.

COSAQUE—A sweet which is wrapped in paper and which explodes when both ends are pulled.

The paper also contains a motto.

COTEAUX (ORDRE DES)—In the seventeenth century the name *coteaux* was given to people of refined taste, who not only were able to distinguish the best wines and from which hillside or from which vineyard they came, but who had the same exquisite taste for everything which concerned good living. Many writers of the time speak of these *coteaux*.

'The dinner given by Monsieur Valavoir', wrote the Marquise de Sévigné, 'completely surpassed our own, not on account of the quality of the dishes, but by reason of their extreme delicacy, which surpassed that of the *coteaux*.' The poet de Villiers wrote:

Ces hommes admirables,
Ces petits délicats, ces vrais amis de tables,
Eux qu'on en peut nommer les dignes souverains,
Savent tous les coteaux où croissent les bons vins.
Et leur goût leur ayant acquis cette science,
Du grand nom de Coteaux *on les appelle en France.*

These admirable men,
These fastidious people, these true friends of good living,
One can name them worthy sovereigns,
They who know all the slopes on which the good wine grows.
Their science having been acquired through taste
They are called in France by the great name of *Coteaux*.

The connoisseurs of good living were jokingly called '*profès dans l'ordre des coteaux.*'

The origin of this title given to gourmands is explained by an author of the time. One day a M. de Lavardin, Bishop of Mans, was chaffing Saint-Evremond, who was dining with him, on his refinement. 'These gentlemen', said he, speaking of him, of Count d'Olonne and of the Marquis du Bois-Dauphin, 'exaggerate everything from the need to refine everything. They are not able to drink unless the wine comes from one of the hillsides of Aï, of Haut-Villiers, or Avenau.'

Saint-Evremond did not fail to retail this criticism to his friends, and they repeated the words of the prelate so often that in the end they were called '*les trois coteaux*' (the three hillsides), after which the *Ordre des coteaux* very soon came into being.

COTIGNAC—Quince paste. The most famous of these pastes is the one made industrially at Orléans.

CÔTOYER—A French culinary term which means to turn a joint in the oven in such a way as to expose in turn every side to the maximum heat.

COTRIADE OR BRETON BOUILLABAISSE—As in the *bouillabaisse*, the more fish there are in the *cotriade*, the better it is.

These fish should be chosen among the following: sardine, mackerel, John Dory, *daurade* (chrysophrys), *baudroie* (sea devil), hake, conger eel, gurnet, red mullet, etc. One or two large fish heads can be included to excellent effect.

Heat some butter or lard in a cauldron (on a wood fire) and cook some quartered onions in it. When the onions begin to turn a pale gold, moisten with water, allowing a pint (half a litre) per person. Add potatoes, cut in quarters. Put in some thyme, bay and other aromatic herbs. Bring to the boil. Then put in the fish on top of the potatoes, cut into slices. Cook rapidly.

Pour the liquor on to slices of bread (in a tureen) and serve the fish separately on a large dish, with the potatoes.

COUCH GRASS. CHIENDENT—Very common plant of which the rhizomes are used in the form of infusion as a diuretic.

COUCHER—French term meaning to turn out a preparation (stuffing, pâté or purée) either in a round or long shape, on a baking sheet with the help of a forcing (pastry) bag (or cornet) with a round or fluted nozzle.

COUCOUZELLE—French name given to the fruits of a variety of gourd which is picked before it is fully grown; also called *courgettes* in France, and *zuchetti* or *zucchini* in Italy. They are called *zucchini* in the United States and in England. See ITALIAN MARROWS.

COULAGE—Disease of grapes. Also, waste resulting from inadequate supervision in kitchen work.

COULIBIAC (Russian cookery)—The coulibiac is a hot fish pie.

Here is the recipe given by Plumerey in *L'Art de la cuisine française au XIX*[e] *siècle:*

'In St. Petersburg, this pie is made with salmon and sometimes with *soudac* (pike-perch), but on state occasions the *soudac* is replaced with *sterlet* (the most prized fish in Russia).

'In Paris, where we have neither the one nor the other of these fish, we replace it to advantage with turbot. The description that I give here of this pie is one which will serve 12 to 14 persons. It will be easy for whoever makes it to increase or diminish it according to the number of guests.

'Take a slice of salmon 4 inches high, and a piece of turbot of the same size; remove the flesh and cut it up into a dozen square pieces; chop a great deal of parsley, spring onion (scallion), and a little chives and two punnets (small baskets) of mushrooms; set these aromatics with half a pound of butter in a large sauté pan, with salt, pepper, allspice, clove, nutmeg and cinnamon; when they are softened, add half a glass of Madeira wine; put in the pieces of both fish, and simmer gently, with heat above and below, until perfectly cooked.'

Note. In those days they used to put live charcoal on the lids of copper pans to provide heat 'above' as well as below.

'Take out the pieces of fish from the pan and let them cool; put a good spoonful of *Espagnole sauce* (see SAUCE) into the *fines herbes;* reduce, and put in a basin to cool for use later on.

'Hard boil 6 eggs and chop the whites and the yolks. Now take half a pound of *kache* (buckwheat); put it in a pan with the same volume of water, a little butter and salt; as soon as it begins to boil take it off the fire, add two ounces of fine butter which you mix in well, put the pan on the grate with the heat above and below, and surrounded with hot cinders. (In the old days, dishes were cooked on a *paillasse*, a kind of grate filled with ashes and burning coal.) Cook for a quarter of an hour, 20 minutes at the most. The buckwheat must swell and cook like Indian rice; the grains must be separate from one another; pour out on a plate.

'You will have prepared a *Brioche dough* (see DOUGH) less fine than usual; if you are in a hurry and have some dough already prepared for ordinary *brioche*, add to it a handful of flour; in either case, roll it out twice; make it into two sheets; the one underneath must be an inch thicker than the one above; put the thickest on a metal sheet; set a layer of buckwheat on it, then a layer of fine herbs and eggs, then the sauce, then a layer of fish, on top of this the buckwheat, the fine herbs, the sauce and the eggs, and so on until all these various preparations are used up; then cover the whole with the second sheet; moisten slightly so that the pastry sticks together and draw up the edges of the lower sheet so that they cover the edge of the upper sheet. The pie must be in the shape of what is called a *pantin* in Paris. Moisten it outside instead of gilding it with egg, and cover it lightly with breadcrumbs; put it in a gentle oven for an hour and a half, and serve it straight from the oven.

'Melted butter is served with the *coulibiac.*'

Petits coulibiacs de poulet à la russe (Russian chicken pie)—'Chop parsley, mushrooms, spring onions (scallions), and cook them in butter; add a little chopped horse-radish which has been blanched, salt, pepper and grated nutmeg; when this seasoning is browned add a small spoonful of *Espagnole sauce* (see SAUCE); boil down, and take off the fire; add cooked breast of chicken cut into large dice, a quarter of a pound of rice cooked in good consommé and hard boiled eggs cut into dice; put on a plate to cool.

'Take some puff pastry left-overs and roll them out four times; then after letting the pastry rest for 10 minutes, roll it out to a thickness suitable for little patties; cut them out; put 24 little rounds of pastry on a damp metal sheet, and moisten them with care; put on each a little lump of the mixture; cover and press together to close the little patties; moisten them and sprinkle with fresh grated breadcrumbs.

'Cook in a medium oven (375°F.) for 25 to 30 minutes; give them a good colour and serve.' (Plumerey's recipe.)

These little patties are served as a hot entrée.

COULIS (CULLIS)—In the old days sauces in general were called *coulis* (cullis). To be more precise, coulis are various meat juices obtained in a natural way, which means to say, juices which run out of the meat during the cooking.

Some authors say that rather liquid purées should be designated *coulis*, and that this should not be used except for chicken purées, game purées, fish purées, and those of crustaceans and vegetables.

Some of these *coulis* can, according to the same authors, be served as soup. The principal type, they say, is *Potage à la reine*.

As well as juice, *coulis* (or cullis) is none other than what we call today veal stock (*fonds de veau*) and which Carême called *blond de veau.*

In modern practice the word *coulis* is often used to denote certain thick soups which are made with a purée of some crustacean: *coulis d'écrevisses* (crayfish cullis), *coulis de crabes* (crab), *de homard* (lobster), *de crevettes* (prawns), is often used instead of *bisque d'ecrevisses*, etc.

COULOMMIERS CHEESE—See CHEESE.

COUP D'AVANT—This expression applies to the glass of wine, of liqueur or even of alcohol, which is taken immediately before the meal. In fact, this picturesque term is hardly ever used any more.

More often the term *coup d'après* is used for the generous glass of wine which is often drunk after the soup.

This custom has been transmitted from generation to generation, and is still found in different countries, particularly among rural communities.

The picturesque language of the Middle Ages gave names to the different drinks which were imbibed in particular circumstances. At court, and among the great, there was the *Vin du coucher* (night-cap); in the middle of a meal, the *Coup du milieu* was drunk (this custom still exists in Champagne) and it is probably in the same manner that wine taken on leaving, at a time when hardly anyone travelled except on horseback, was given the name of *Coup de l'étrier* (stirrup cup).

COUP DE FEU—The alteration to a joint (charring) when it has been subjected to a too lively heat.

This expression is also used in professional cookery for the hours devoted to serving up.

Serving up, which takes place morning and evening at the meal time, is preceded by work which is called *mise en place.*

COUP DE VIN—The amount of wine that can be drunk at a single gulp.

COUPAGE—Mixing of various wines to obtain a commercial blend of colour, strength, and uniform taste.

COUPE JACQUES—Fruit soaked in liqueurs and covered with various ices. See ICE CREAMS AND ICES.

COURGETTES—See ITALIAN MARROWS.

COURT-BOUILLON—An aromatic liquor (liquid) in which meat, fish and various vegetables are cooked.

COURTS-BOUILLONS FOR HORS-D'OEUVRE:

Court-bouillon I, à la grecque, for marinating vegetables. COURT-BOUILLON À LA GRECQUE, POUR LÉGUMES MARINÉS—Put ½ cup (1 decilitre) of olive oil in a pan; 3½ cups (7 decilitres) of water and the strained juice of 2 lemons. Add a strong *bouquet garni* composed of parsley roots, celery, fennel, thyme and bay; 12 to 15 coriander seeds and the same number of peppercorns. Boil for 20 minutes. Use according to instructions. This amount of liquor will cook 25 to 30 little artichokes trimmed, or an equal quantity of any other vegetable prepared *à la grecque.*

Court-bouillon II, à la grecque, for marinating fish. COURT-BOUILLON À LA GRECQUE, POUR POISSONS MARINÉS—Simmer gently ½ cup (100 grams) of finely chopped onion in ¾ cup (1½ decilitres) of olive oil. Cook the onion without allowing it to brown.

Moisten with ¾ cup (1½ decilitres) of white wine, ¾ cup (1½ decilitres) of water and the strained juice of one lemon.

Add an unpeeled, crushed, clove of garlic, a *bouquet garni* composed of 2 parsley roots, a branch of thyme, a bay leaf, and a good branch of fresh fennel, 10 or 12 coriander seeds and 2 sweet pimentos skinned and cut into strips. Season with ¾ teaspoon (4 grams) of salt and a pinch of freshly ground pepper.

Boil for 15 minutes. Use according to the recipe.

This amount of *court-bouillon* is sufficient for 1 pound (500 grams) of fish (net weight).

COURTS-BOUILLONS FOR FISH AND CRUSTACEANS:

Court-bouillon III, salt water court-bouillon. COURT-BOUILLON À L'EAU SALÉE—This is simply composed of salt water in the proportion of 1½ teaspoons (9-10 grams) of salt to a quart (litre) of water. It is used to poach various fish such as sea-perch, sea-dace, coalfish, cod, whitefish, haddock, etc.

Court-bouillon IV, for salmon and salmon trout. COURT-BOUILLON POUR SAUMONS ET TRUITES SAUMONÉES—This is made with water, lemon juice or vinegar, sliced onions and carrots, parsley, thyme, bay leaf, salt, peppercorns. These fish can also be cooked in a white wine *court-bouillon.*

Court-bouillon V, for lobster and other crustaceans. COURT-BOUILLON POUR LANGOUSTES ET AUTRES CRUSTACÉS—This is made with water, thinly sliced carrots and onions, parsley, thyme, bay leaf, salt and peppercorns.

Court-bouillon VI, for lobster and other crustaceans. COURT-BOUILLON POUR LANGOUSTES ET AUTRES CRUSTACÉS—A *court-bouillon* more often used for cooking crustaceans is made simply with salt water, flavoured only with thyme and bay.

Court-bouillon VII au bleu for river trout, carp, pike—This is made of salt water, with the addition of vinegar, flavoured with carrots and sliced onions, parsley, thyme, bay leaf, salt and pepper. See TROUT, *Blue trout.*

Court-bouillon VIII, white wine, à la hongroise. COURT-BOUILLON AU VIN BLANC, À LA HONGROISE—Melt 2 large tablespoons of minced onion in a tablespoon of butter until it is completely soft. Season with salt and paprika pepper and add a *bouquet garni* of thyme and bay leaf.

Moisten with 2½-3 cups (6 decilitres) of dry white wine. Boil for 8 minutes.

This *court-bouillon* is used for fish prepared as hors-d'oeuvre. It can be made with olive oil instead of butter.

Court-bouillon IX, vegetable. COURT-BOUILLON AUX LÉGUMES—Melt 2 tablespoons (25 grams) of onions and 2 tablespoons (25 grams) of carrots, chopped very fine, in a spoonful of butter, until they are completely cooked. Season with salt and pepper. Add 2 crushed garlic cloves and a *bouquet garni.*

Moisten with 2½-3 cups (6 decilitres) of dry white wine. Boil for 10 minutes. This is used for fish and other articles served as an hors-d'oeuvre.

It can be made with oil instead of butter.

Court-bouillon X, au vert—Melt in 3 tablespoons of butter, 2 handfuls (100 grams) of sorrel leaves, a few very young nettle leaves (25 grams), and several sprigs of parsley leaves (10 grams), 1 tablespoon (5 grams) each of savory, of burnet, of green sage, 1 teaspoon (2 grams) of tarragon and a branch of thyme. Season with salt and pepper; moisten with 2½-3 cups (6 decilitres) of white wine. Cook for 8 minutes.

Used for little fish cooked 'au vert' (set to stiffen in herbs before the white wine is added).

After cooking the fish, the *court-bouillon* is slightly thickened with egg yolks, and acidulated with a few drops of lemon juice.

See EEL, *Eels au vert.*

Court-bouillon XI, white wine, for fish in marinade. COURT-BOUILLON AU VIN BLANC POUR POISSONS MARINÉS—Put 2 very tender small carrots (50 grams) cut in thin scalloped rounds, 1 small onion (50 grams) cut in thin slices, 2 sticks of celery sliced finely, 2 sliced shallots, a little handful of parsley stalks, 2 sprigs of thyme and a bay leaf in a sauté-pan.

Moisten with 1 cup (2 decilitres) of white wine and ½ cup (a decilitre) of vinegar; season with a pinch of salt and a little freshly ground pepper.

Boil for 15 minutes. Pour this with the vegetables over the fish prepared *à la marinade* (see MARINADE); cook these according to instructions given in the recipe.

The vegetables in this *court-bouillon* should be correctly sliced, and scalloped if possible, because they are served as a rule with the marinated fish.

Court-bouillon XII, white wine à la mirepoix (for braised or poached fish). COURT-BOUILLON AU VIN BLANC À LA MIREPOIX—Moisten with one cup (2 decilitres) of dry white wine, one cup (2 decilitres) of vegetable *mirepoix** (carrot, leek, onion, celery, thyme and a bay leaf ground to powder) which has been gently simmered in butter.

Boil down by two thirds. Finish the *court-bouillon* with the addition of 1½ cups (3 decilitres) of fish *fumet**. Boil for 10 minutes. Use according to instructions.

Court-bouillon XIII, champagne à la mirepoix. COURT-BOUILLON AU VIN DE CHAMPAGNE À LA MIREPOIX—Proceed in the same way as for *Court-bouillon XII*, using champagne instead of white wine.

Court-bouillon XIV, red wine à la mirepoix. COURT-BOUILLON AU VIN ROUGE À LA MIREPOIX—Proceed in the same way as for *Court-bouillon XII*, replacing the white wine with burgundy or claret. For all the *courts-bouillons à la mirepoix* mushroom peelings can be used.

COURTS-BOUILLONS OR BLANCS FOR MEAT. BLANCS POUR VIANDES:

Simple court-bouillon XV, for meats and offal (variety meats)—Use salted water (to cover) 2 tablespoons each shredded carrots and onions, 1 *bouquet garni*, 10 peppercorns, 1 clove garlic. Boil the *court-bouillon* for 10-15 minutes before adding the meat.

Court-bouillon XVI, white, for meat. BLANC POUR VIANDES—This is used for cooking certain parts of offal (variety meats), such as sheep's tongue and feet, calf's head etc., as well as for cock's combs and kidneys.

Proceed as described in the recipe for *Court-bouillon XIX, for vegetables*, adding one medium sized carrot, cut in quarters, one onion studded with a clove and a *bouquet garni**.

Put the meat to be cooked into boiling *court-bouillon.*

White court-bouillon XVII, for cooking calf's head. BLANC POUR CUIRE LA TÊTE DE VEAU—Mix flour with cold water (using a heaped tablespoon per quart (litre) of water) until smooth. Pass this mixture through a fine strainer. Pour into a saucepan, big enough to take the head, either whole or divided in halves, or cut into pieces. Season with 1 teaspoon (6 grams) of salt and add one tablespoon of vinegar per quart (litre) of water. Bring to the boil, add a large onion studded with two cloves and a good *bouquet garni* consisting of a sprig of parsley, thyme and bay leaf. When this stock is boiling, put in the calf's head wrapped in a fine muslin cloth. Add ½ pound (250 grams) of beef (or veal) fat chopped and soaked in cold water. This fat, upon melting, will form a protective layer over the calf's head and will prevent it from going black.

White court-bouillon XVIII, for mushrooms. BLANC POUR CHAMPIGNONS—This is also used for other vegetables. Bring 3 tablespoons (45 grams) of butter, the juice of half a lemon and 1 teaspoon (6 grams) of salt to the boil in ½ cup (1 decilitre) of water.

Mushrooms, or other vegetables, should be put to cook in this liquor when it is boiling.

White court-bouillon XIX, for vegetables. BLANC POUR LÉGUMES—This is used for cooking certain vegetables which are liable to turn dark, such as chards, cardoons, artichoke hearts, salsify, etc.

Mix 2 tablespoons (25 grams) of flour with 4 tablespoons of water into a smooth paste. Add one quart (litre) of water, mix and strain through a fine strainer. Season with 1 teaspoon (6 grams) of salt, add the juice of half a lemon and 2 or 3 tablespoons of raw, chopped suet.

Boil for a few moments, then add whatever vegetable is being cooked.

This *court-bouillon* can be spiced with an onion studded with a clove and a *bouquet garni**, but this addition is not necessary if the ingredients cooked in a *court-bouillon* have to be seasoned at the final stage of cooking.

The *court-bouillon* only serves to cook the vegetables and keep them very white. It is with this aim in view that a certain quantity of suet is added (and may be replaced by butter), as it forms an isolation layer, protecting the vegetables from contact with air.

A couscous bowl

COUSCOUS OR COUSCOUSSOU—North African culinary speciality, the origin of which dates from earliest times. Couscous is made with millet flour or with crushed rice, and with meat (mutton, chicken, etc.).

According to some authors, the word couscous means *becquetée* (pecked at), or food which a bird takes in its beak and which it rolls into minute morsels in order to feed its young. Léon Isnard, who wrote a very interesting book on African cooking, adds:

'It seems that the word couscous is a Gallic version of *rac keskes*, which means *crushed small.*

'By a phonetic deviation of the names *koskos*, *keuscass*, *koskosou*, *kouskous*, used currently in different parts of North Africa to denote an earthenware receptacle or one made of alfa grass pierced with holes, and which is set on top of another utensil containing boiling water or stock, a receptacle in which the semolina is put to steam, the name couscous has been given to the preparation made in this receptacle.

'The inhabitants of North Africa included as a rule under this name all kinds of dishes made with flour, white or brown (buckwheat flour), and steamed in the *keskass*, a vase similar to a basin.

'But we think that the word *couscous* or *kouskoussou* is onomatopoeic, the letters and syllables having no other role than to evoke the sound made by the steam as it passes through the holes of the utensil in the process of cooking.

'In Kabylia one says *sekjou;* in the Mozabite dialect the expression *ouchéou* is used, still with the imitative sound. However, by some inexplicable deviation the people of Oued-Rigt have adopted the word *gouni*, borrowed from the Berbers.'

There are a great many ways of preparing couscous. We cite those in practice in Algeria and Tunisia.

Cooking the crushed grain by steaming—Put the crushed grain, already moistened with water and swollen, in the cooking vessel (a colander or strainer can be used, fitted in the marmite) without pressing it.

Put some water or stock to boil in the marmite, in the proportion of one quart (litre) to 1 pound (500 grams) of couscous (i.e. crushed grain).

When the liquid begins to boil, put the vessel containing the crushed grain (couscous) on top of the marmite, without covering it. (The vessel in which the grain is steamed must never come into contact with the boiling water.)

A damp cloth should be placed between the two vessels at the point of contact to prevent the escape of steam round the edge. When the steam begins to rise, allow 40 minutes cooking. Remove from the fire. Turn out the grain on to a large plate in order to work out any lumps that may have formed. Fork it over, and moisten with two glasses of water and a spoonful of oil. Add salt and pepper.

Leave for 15 minutes. Return the marmite to the heat, and when it boils put the couscous back in the steaming vessel, and steam for a further 20 minutes.

Turn out on to a serving dish. Mix in 6 tablespoons (100 grams) of butter.

Cooking the crushed grain in boiling water—For this method of cooking, the steaming vessel is dispensed with. Soak the couscous in the same way as above, then throw it into the boiling water or stock, stirring the while. Use a quart (1 litre) of strained stock, or milk or water. Add butter and draw off the fire after about 15 minutes cooking. Leave it for a little and serve very hot accompanied by various meats or vegetables, either disposed on top of the couscous or served separately.

Armenian couscous. Couscous arménien—This couscous is prepared like the Arab couscous with crushed grain, chick peas, slices of carrots and new turnips, fragments of white cabbage; with hashed mutton browned in oil. Hot pimento sauce is served separately.

Moroccan couscous. Couscous marocain—Pass a pound (500 grams) of finely ground hard wheat through a fine sieve into a deep earthenware dish. Incorporate water, drop by drop, working it well with the hands until it is all reduced to a fine-grained consistency. This requires a lot of patience, and if it is not forthcoming a lumpy mass will result. When this is done, put the grain in a strainer and steam it over a *bain-marie* or pan of hot water for 15 minutes. Then put the couscous in a sauté-pan and separate the grains with the hands, adding a little lukewarm water. Put it back to cook for another ten minutes, then separate it out again, and mix in butter and salt. (Some people add raisins, but this is a matter of taste.)

'Here now is the recipe for *tagine*, which always accompanies the couscous.

'For 12 people: 2 fairly large chickens, a shoulder and a neck of mutton, cut up, the chicken in quarters, the mutton cut in the usual way for sautéing. Brown the meat in chicken fat with 4 large carrots and 4 onions cut up in large dice. Sprinkle with a spoonful of ground red pepper and moisten generously with mutton and chicken stock. Add some crushed tomatoes, a strong bouquet garni with celery, and a sachet containing pepper corns, cloves, saffron, cinnamon and cumin.

In the course of the cooking, add some quartered artichokes, *garbanzos* (chick-peas), turnips, beans, marrow and courgettes cut in large dice, all these vegetables in equal quantities.

Allow one hour for the cooking, as the meat must be well cooked. The whole ragoût should be immersed in the stock, and served in earthenware pots without removing the fat.' (R. Pénet.)

Mutton couscous 'chtitra'. Couscous au mouton 'chtitra'—For 6 or 8 persons, prepare and steam a pound (500 grams) of couscous.

Separately prepare the following ingredients: a leg of mutton cut into square pieces, 3 chopped cloves of garlic, 3 little Cayenne red peppers chopped up, 2 soup-spoonfuls of sweet red pepper powder, a spoonful of oil, salt, pepper, parsley and chopped chervil, and put these ingredients in a cocotte.

Moisten the whole with water (about one quart or litre).

Simmer this concoction for at least 3 hours; when cooked and ready to serve, pour some of the liquor from the meats to which 6 tablespoons (100 grams) of butter have been added, over the couscous.

Arrange the couscous on a huge dish, place the various meats neatly on top of it, and serve the rest of the sauce separately.

COUSINETTE (Béarnaise cooking)—A soup made with spinach, sorrel, lettuce, and other green herbs, all of which are cut up finely.

COVER. Couvert—The word *couvert* (cover) denotes a number of things, slightly differing from one another.

Couvert is used to denote the collection of utensils set out on a table which has been laid. The expression *lever* or *enlever le couvert* (to clear the table) denotes the operation of clearing the table once the meal is over.

The same word applies as well to the number of guests present at a meal: *un diner de* 20, *de* 100 *couverts* (a dinner of 20, of 100 covers).

Couvert also denotes a fixed charge written on the menu and on the bill in French restaurants, which is added to the amount charged for the dishes consumed. The price of the *couvert* varies according to the restaurant.

More generally the word *couvert de table* (table-setting) denotes the three individual utensils used by the diner: the knife, the fork and the spoon.

Assembled, they form such a rational ensemble, the knife for cutting, the fork for piercing the solid food, and the spoon for liquid foods, that one is tempted to believe they were created on the same day. However, this is far from the case. Several centuries separate the invention of these three objects.

The most ancient of the three is certainly the knife, because one of man's very first needs, even in primitive times, was to make a tool with which the meat obtained by hunting could be cut up. The making of bronze and iron instruments was still unknown, he had recourse to flints and a volcanic substance known as obsidian. Fractured into thin fragments, black obsidian has the double property of being extremely hard and as sharp as glass. A piece of obsidian fitted between two little bands of wood or bone, bound with plaited fibres, made one of the first knives, and placed at the end of an arrow or a spear became a weapon. Later, human industry replaced the obsidian knives by those of bronze, then iron and steel. According to Ammien Marcellin, bronze knives made all in one piece were used by the Gauls 'who used them to divide the largest pieces of meat', and from the tenth century the town of Beauvais had the exclusive monopoly for their manufacture.

The fork, which originally had only two prongs, is a more recent invention than the knife.

As for the spoon, it was probably contemporary with the knife for the good reason that if our ancestors were willing to eat solid foods with their hands, it must still have been essential to them to make spoons for liquids, even if these were merely simple shells with a wooden handle attachment. The making of spoons in metal goes back at least as far as the making of metal knives. From the excavations which have supplied so many everyday articles in bronze, now to be seen in the different museums, one finds a great many spoons of different shape and size, the form of the spoon being in some cases rounded, in others more elongated, very similar in fact to the different spoons used today, and among all these objects only one or two forks are seen, which do not seem to have been used for eating.

In the fourteenth century, the richest houses, even the palaces of princes, numbered far more spoons than forks among their splendid silverware. Piers Gaveston, Edward II's favourite, possessed 69 silver spoons and 3 forks. These, according to the inventory, were designed for eating pears. Queen Clémence of Hungary (1328) left at her death 30 spoons and a single fork. M. le comte de Laborde, the source of this information, adds: 'From the thirteenth century forks existed for certain exceptional dishes, but were not used in the common run of things'.

The general use of the fork in the seventeenth century dates from the influence of a famous beau, M. de Montausier.

Not only has the *couvert* (place setting) composed of these three classic pieces become in our day a matter of general use, but by ingenious modifications the table setting has been adapted to various types of dishes and food, and a whole series of utensils have been developed to satisfy particular requirements. Thus we have a luncheon table setting, one for sweets, or cakes, for dessert, for fruit, for strawberries, for fish, for crayfish. Sometimes only one of the utensils is modified in its shape or size in order to suit a special use. There have been spoons for absinthe, for porridge, for jam, for coffee, for ices, spoons for infusions, for liqueurs, for moka, for eggs, syrup, soda, tea, glasses of water.

Among the special forks there is one for winkles, for snails, for oysters, for vegetables, for fish and for melons.

These three individual implements which make up the couvert or table-setting are augmented by certain special instruments for eating lobster, artichokes, asparagus, snails, etc.

COW. Vache—In butchery sterile cows or heifers are more often sought after as meat than bullocks.

The flesh of old cows, worn out by calving and lactation, is tough and of inferior quality. For culinary preparation see BEEF.

COW-PARSNIP. Berce—Common weed in meadows and hedges, also called *Meadow-parsnip* and *Hog-weed.* This is a plant of the family *Umbelliferae* which grows in damp and marshy places. In Siberia its young shoots are eaten like asparagus. In Lithuania and Poland its leaves and seeds are made into a kind of rather potent beer.

CRAB. Crabe—A crustacean of the *Decapoda* order. There are many species which are edible.

Crabs and crustaceans in broth (Creole cookery). Crabes en bouillon—Melt in fat some hashed onion, some tomato, pounded ginger, thyme, 2 cloves of garlic, and those parts of the crab not usually eaten (or the shells of the prawns or other crustaceans which are being cooked). Keep aside the edible portions. Moisten the preparation in the pan with broth. Leave this concoction to simmer gently, for about 2 hours. Pass it through a fine sieve, or tammy, pressing to obtain a thick sauce. Take a casserole, put in a little fat, a teaspoon of saffron, some pimento. Lightly brown the pieces of crab or other shell fish and pour over them the sauce which has been obtained. Let it cook for some minutes and serve hot in a tureen with *Rice à la créole**.

Cold Crab. Crabe froid—Cook the crab in a court-bouillon (the court-bouillon prepared in the same way as that used for cooking all shellfish, composed of water, salt, thyme and bay leaf). Leave to cool. Arrange on a napkin; garnish with fresh parsley. Serve with *Mayonnaise sauce*, *Tartare sauce*, *Gribiche sauce*, *Green sauce*, or some other cold sauce. See SAUCE.

In England, fishmongers sell cold crab already prepared (dressed crab).

The meat, mashed up with the help of two forks, is seasoned with a sauce made with the crab's liver, English

HOW TO PREPARE CRAB (*photographs Mac Fisheries*)

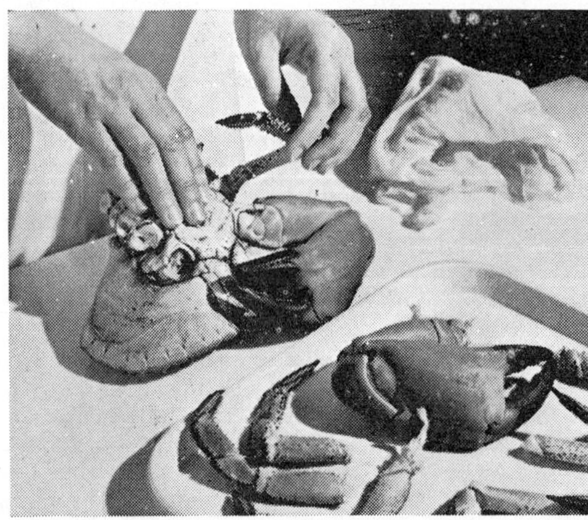

To twist off the legs and claws, wipe crab with damp cloth. Place on back with tail flap facing. Remove claws and legs by twisting inwards and towards you

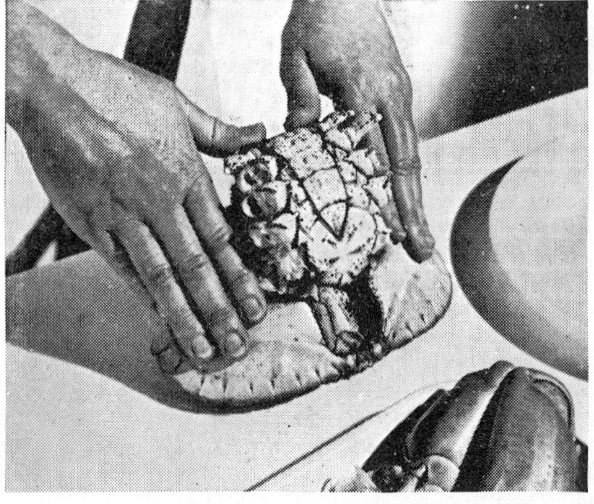

To separate body from shell, place thumbs under tail flap and push upwards until the body breaks away from the shell

HOW TO PREPARE CRAB (continued)

To remove mouth and stomach bag, place shell with mouth facing you. Press thumbs down and forward on mouth until this, and stomach bag attached breaks away with a click

To remove the stomach, take hold of the mouth and stomach bag and carefully remove them; they should come away in one piece. Discard them

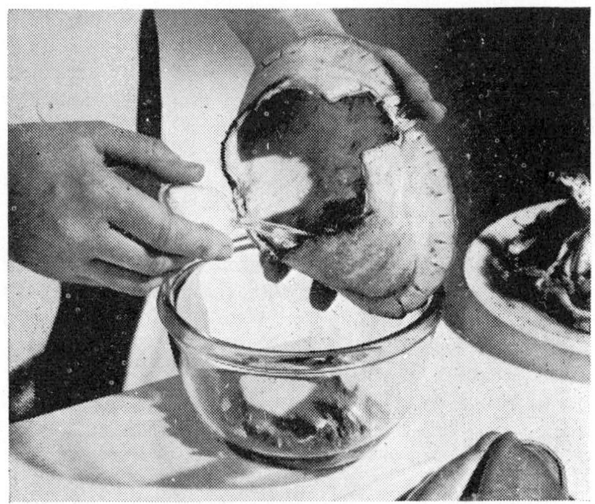

To remove meat, ease round inside shell with handle of a spoon, loosening soft brown meat. Turn all the meat into a basin, leaving the shell clean

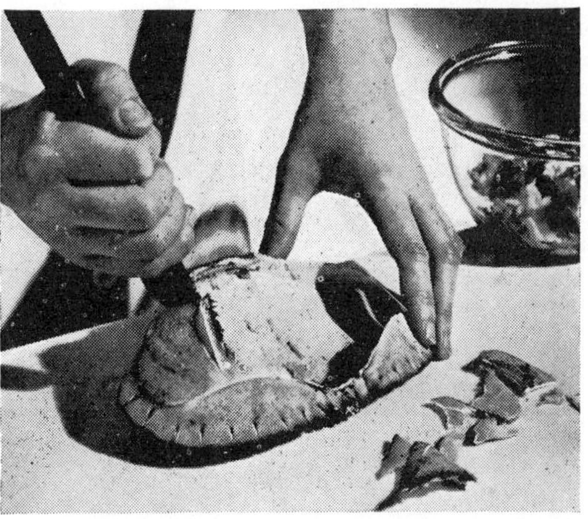

To trim shell, tap 'false line' round shell cavity with knife handle, press with thumbs till edges of shell wall break away neatly. Scrub and dry the shell and oil lightly

Taking body of crab, discard 'dead men's fingers'. Remove brown meat, adding to basin. Scoop white meat from leg sockets, keeping free from bone; put in second basin

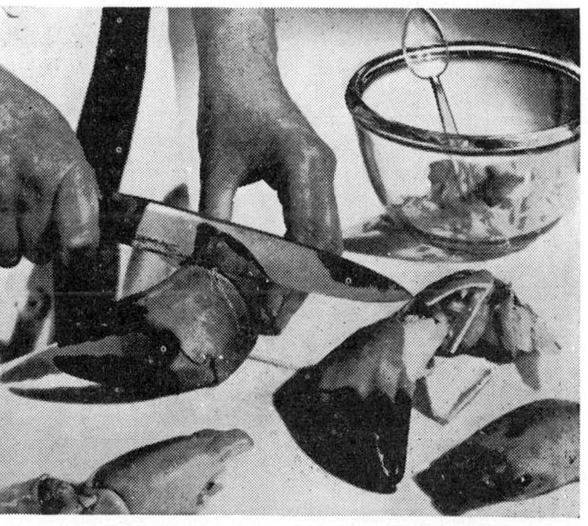

Twist first joint off claws to remove meat. With back of heavy knife tap sharply round centre of claws broadest part till shell cracks apart; empty both into white meat basin

Dressed crab (*Mac Fisheries*)

mustard, oil and vinegar, and is then put back in the shell. The preparation is smoothed with a knife and the surface decorated with yolks of egg and chopped parsley. The crab is served with a *Mayonnaise sauce*.

Crab au gratin—Cook a large crab in a *court-bouillon**. Let it cool. When cold remove the claws and legs. Then, using the point of a knife, make an incision underneath the crab's shell in such a way as to detach the upper part.

Remove the meat from claws and legs, and from the shell. Cut the meat into large dice or mash it up with the help of two forks. Put the meat back in the hollow shell, which should be cleaned with hot water and covered on the bottom with a few tablespoons of *Mornay sauce* (see SAUCE) to which the crab's liver and the creamy parts are added finely pounded. Cover with the same sauce. Sprinkle with grated cheese; pour over some melted butter. Brown in a moderate oven.

CRACK (Small or large). CASSE (PETIT, GROS)—A degree of cooking sugar. See SUGAR.

CRACKNEL (Biscuit) (Dry petit four). CRAQUELIN—Knead 2 cups (250 grams) of sifted cake flour with 10 tablespoons (150 grams) of butter, 2 egg yolks, ½ cup of cold milk, 2 tablespoons (30 grams) of sugar and a pinch of salt.

Leave the pastry to rest for 2 hours. Roll it out to ⅛ inch thickness.

Cut this pastry sheet into 2 inch square pieces. Arrange them on a baking sheet. Gild with egg. Cook in a very hot oven. Sprinkle with vanilla-flavoured sugar.

CRAMIQUE (Belgian pâtisserie)—A kind of brioche bread which has Corinth raisins in it.

CRANBERRY OR MOSSBERRY—Fruit of a small shrubby plant which grows in the boggy regions of North America and Europe and which is edible. Cranberries, which look rather like small cherries, and are of the same size, the colour of which varies from a clear pink to a deep red, have an acid flavour, astringent, slightly bitter, and are unpleasant in a raw state. Cooked, they produce a compote and a jelly with a delicate taste, very much appreciated in Anglo-Saxon countries. Cranberry jelly is traditionally used as a condiment with game and fowl such as duck and goose.

Here is the formula for cranberry jelly, according to Dr. Leclerc: 'Cook the berries, which have been covered fairly liberally with water, until they are soft, for about 15 minutes, then add 1⅓ cups (325 grams) of sugar for each pound (½ kilo) of fruit and cook again until the consistency of a thick syrup is achieved, which will form into a jelly when cool.'

CRANE. GRUE—A bird of the wader group, seldom used for food nowadays. The Romans greatly prized this bird, which they fattened specially to give it a richer flavour. In the Middle Ages, the crane was among the game-birds eaten in the best society. Only very young birds can be eaten. Crane is cooked in the same way as bustard (see BUSTARD).

CRAPAUDINE (A LA).—This is the name for a preparation of fowl, particularly of pigeon; see PIGEON.

Some authors say that this name comes from the word *crapaud*, toad, and that the name was given to the dish because the birds, trussed in this way, have the form of a toad.

Others maintain that the word comes from the ordeal called *crapaudine* which was inflicted long ago on men belonging to disciplinary orders, and that the name was given to pigeons prepared in this way because once trussed they recalled the attitude of men subjected to this ordeal.

CRAQUELIN—A kind of cake given this name because, being very dry, it crunches between the teeth. This kind of pâtisserie is made in different ways. Sometimes it is made in the same way as Reims biscuits, sometimes with dough (*pâté à échaudée*).

CRAYFISH, FRESHWATER. ÉCREVISSE—A freshwater crustacean of which there are many known breeds. The flesh of the freshwater crayfish is somewhat firm, as with all shell-fish, but it is subtly and delicately flavoured.

In the U.S.A., crayfish (also called crawfish) are rare in the Eastern part of the country but easily obtainable in the West and parts of the Mid-West.

Crayfish bisque or coulis. BISQUE (COULIS) D'ÉCREVISSES—This thick soup is made with crayfish cooked *à la mirepoix*. While pounding the crayfish in a mortar, add some cooked rice. See SOUPS AND BROTHS, *Purée of crayfish soup*.

Crayfish à la bordelaise. ÉCREVISSES À LA BORDELAISE—'Make a very fine *mirepoix* of vegetables. Toss the crayfish in butter separately. Season with salt, pepper and spices.

'Pour brandy over the crayfish and set alight. Moisten with white wine. Add the *mirepoix* and cook all together for about 20 minutes.

'Drain the crayfish and put them in a deep round silver dish.

'Bind the cooking stock with 3 or 4 yolks of eggs. Mix in a generous piece of best butter. Season very well.

'Mask the crayfish with this sauce and serve at once, piping hot.' (Recipe of M. Sicard, proprietor of the *Chapon Fin* at Bordeaux.)

Bush of crayfish. BUISSON D'ÉCREVISSES—A *buisson* in French is a small bush or clump. Cook the crayfish in *court-bouillon* as indicated for *Crayfish à la nage*. Leave them to cool.

Arrange them on a special graduated stand fixing them by the tail to the teeth. Garnish with bunches of fresh parsley.

The crayfish can also be piled into a pyramid on a folded napkin.

Crayfish croûtes. CROÛTES AUX ÉCREVISSES—Using a *Ragout of crayfish tails à la Nantua*, proceed as for *Mushroom croûte**.

Crayfish flan with cheese. FLAN AUX ÉCREVISSES GRATINÉ—Fill a flan crust baked blind (baked pie shell) with a *ragoût of Crayfish tails à la Nantua**. Sprinkle with grated cheese. Pour on melted butter. Brown in the oven.

Crayfish as a garnish. ÉCREVISSES POUR GARNITURE—Wash and gut the crayfish. As indicated in the recipe, either truss them (that is to say fasten the claws to the tail) or leave them as they are. Put them in a boiling *court-bouillon* of water, salt, thyme and bay leaf. Boil until cooked. Use them hot or cold, according to the recipe.

Crayfish à la liégeoise. ÉCREVISSES À LA LIÉGEOISE—Cook the crayfish in a *court-bouillon* as indicated for *Crayfish à la Nage*. Drain the crayfish and arrange them in a deep round dish. Strain the cooking stock. Boil down (reduce) to a quarter of its volume. Mix in, for ½ cup (1 decilitre) of stock, 7 tablespoons (100 grams) of butter. Whisk thoroughly. Pour this sauce over the crayfish. Sprinkle with chopped parsley.

Crayfish à la marinière. ÉCREVISSES À LA MARINIÈRE—Sauté the crayfish in boiling butter over a very hot flame. When they are all well browned, season with salt, pepper, a little powdered thyme and bay leaf and moisten with enough dry white wine to cover the crayfish.

Cover the saucepan and boil hastily for 12 minutes. Put the crayfish in a bowl. Boil down the stock and add a little meatless *velouté* to it. Take it off the stove and mix in 2 or 3 tablespoons of butter. Pour this sauce over the crayfish and sprinkle with chopped parsley.

Crayfish mousse I à l'ancienne (cold). MOUSSE FROIDE D'ÉCREVISSES À L'ANCIENNE—Cook 36 medium-sized crayfish *à la mirepoix*. Drain them and shell the tails. Pound the shells in a mortar with the *mirepoix*, adding 3 tablespoons (50 grams) of butter, ¾ cup (1½ decilitres) of cold meatless *Velouté* and ½ cup (1 decilitre) of melted aspic jelly.

Rub this mixture through a sieve. Put it in a saucepan. Work on ice for a few minutes, adding 2 cups (4 decilitres) of fresh partly-whipped cream, and the crayfish tails, shelled and diced.

Line a charlotte mould with white paper and fill the mould with this mixture. Leave to chill thoroughly on ice or in a refrigerator, until just before serving.

Turn out the mousse on a serving dish. Decorate the top with slices of truffle which have been dipped in half-set jelly. Surround the mousse with chopped aspic jelly.

Crayfish mousse II (cold). MOUSSE FROIDE D'ÉCREVISSES—Prepare the mousse as indicated in previous recipe. Line a charlotte mould with aspic jelly and decorate the bottom and sides with shelled crayfish tails and strips of truffles.

Crayfish mousse can also be served in a glass or silver bowl, completely covered with aspic jelly.

Crayfish mousselines à la Nantua (hot). MOUSSELINES D'ÉCREVISSES À LA NANTUA—Use *Fine cream forcemeat* (see FORCEMEAT) made with fillet of pike or whiting mixed with purée of crayfish tails. When the forcemeat is ready, add chopped crayfish tails. Fill small buttered cylindrical moulds with this mixture. Stand in water and poach in the oven.

Turn out the *mousselines* on a round dish, each one set on a round of sandwich bread fried in butter, or if preferred, arrange them straight on the dish.

Cover with *Nantua sauce* (see SAUCE). Decorate the top of each *mousseline* with a large, thick strip of truffle.

Note. Crayfish *mousseline* can be served with various garnishes and masked with a sauce chosen to blend with these garnishes: *cancalaise**, *normande*, *cardinal*, *Victoria**, etc.

These *mousselines* are also often used to garnish large braised fish.

They can be served also in tartlets baked blind (empty) or with artichoke hearts cooked in butter instead of on fried bread *croûtons*. The same mixture can be used to make large hot mousses which are poached in charlotte moulds stood in water.

Crayfish mousselines (cold). MOUSSELINES FROIDES D'ÉCREVISSES—These are made with a mousse mixture prepared as in the recipe for *Crayfish mousselines à la Nantua* (*hot*). Line small cylindrical or other moulds with jelly, decorate with crayfish tails and truffles. Fill these moulds with the mousse mixture and chill on ice.

Crayfish à la nage. ÉCREVISSES À LA NAGE—Gut 48 crayfish, that is to say, remove the intestinal matter in the centre of the tail. Wash them and plunge them immediately into a stock prepared as follows:—

Slice 3 small carrots (100 grams) into thin rounds, either fluted or plain. Put them in a saucepan with ½ cup (100 grams) of small finely chopped onions, 4 sliced shallots, a small crushed clove of garlic, a sprig of thyme, half a bay leaf, a handful of parsley heads. Moisten with 2 cups (4 decilitres) of white wine and 1 cup (2 decilitres) of water. Season with salt and freshly ground pepper. Cook for 15 minutes.

Cook the crayfish in this *court-bouillon* for 10 minutes, tossing from time to time. Season with a touch of cayenne pepper and leave to cool in a bowl in the cooking stock.

Serve in a crystal bowl or salad bowl in the stock.

Crayfish puffs. FRIANDS AUX ÉCREVISSES—Proceed as for *Crayfish roll*, using flaky pastry cut into triangles.

Crayfish rolls. CHAUSSONS AUX ÉCREVISSES—Cut small round pieces out of a rolled-out layer of flaky pastry (see DOUGH). Fill with a heaped tablespoon of *Crayfish tail ragoût à la Nantua**. This must be placed in the centre of each round when completely cold. Roll the dough and seal the edges. Brush the top of the rolls with egg. Lightly score the top. Bake in a slow oven. Serve piping hot.

Crayfish rolls des Dames de Bous. CHAUSSONS DE QUEUES D'ÉCREVISSES DES DAMES DE BOUS—'Cook 100 crayfish *à la mirepoix* with white wine not forgetting to season the *court-bouillon* rather highly.' According to Mme. de Loiseau, residuary legatee of the recipes of Mme. de Marron, this seasoning must be a mixture of 'all the main types of pepper.'

'With the shelled tails of the crayfish, make a *Ragoût à la Nantua** finishing it as indicated in the recipe for this *ragoût*.

'Leave the *ragoût* to cool. At the same time, poach some carp soft roes in white wine and leave to cool.

'Roll out a round layer of *flaky pastry* (see DOUGH) and put it on a baking sheet. Spread it on one side only with the ragoût and the soft roes enriched with a liberal quantity of thick slices of truffles seasoned with salt, pepper and spices and sprinkled with liqueur brandy.

'Roll the pastry into a scroll, carefully sealing the edges. Score light diagonal lines on the scroll. Brush with egg and bake in a hot oven.

'When it is ready, pour into the scroll through the opening known as "the chimney", a little very hot *crayfish butter*. See BUTTER, *Compound butters*.

Fried crayfish rolls. RISSOLES AUX ÉCREVISSES—Proceed as for *Crayfish rolls*. Having made the rolls as indicated in the recipe, deep-fry them instead of baking them in the oven. When they are a good colour, drain them. Season with table salt. Arrange on a napkin, garnished with fried parsley.

Crayfish tails au gratin. GRATIN DE QUEUES D'ÉCREVISSES—Prepare the crayfish tails as indicated for *Crayfish tail ragoût à la Nantua*. Put the ragoût in a buttered ovenware dish. Sprinkle with grated cheese, preferably Parmesan. Pour on melted butter. Brown slowly in the oven.

Crayfish tail gratin à la façon de Maître La Planche. GRATIN DE QUEUES D'ÉCREVISSES À LA FAÇON DE MAÎTRE LA PLANCHE—'Using crayfish cooked *à la mirepoix*, prepare a *ragoût* of crayfish tails thickened with rather thick, highly seasoned crayfish purée.

'Put this *ragoût* in a buttered ovenware dish with alternate layers of fresh truffles cut into thick slices, seasoned and tossed in very hot butter.

'Sprinkle with finely grated cheese. Brown in a moderate oven, taking care to stand the dish in warm water to prevent the sauce from curdling.'

Crayfish tail ragoût à la Nantua. QUEUES D'ÉCREVISSES À LA NANTUA—Make $\frac{3}{4}$ cup ($1\frac{1}{2}$ decilitres) of *mirepoix* by cooking slowly in butter until very tender, a mixture of finely diced carrots, onions and celery with powdered thyme and bay leaf. Toss 48 crayfish tails in this mixture. Season with salt and pepper. Moisten with 1 cup (2 decilitres) of white wine. Cover the saucepan and cook for 10 minutes.

Drain the crayfish. Shell the tails. Pound the shells and the *mirepoix* in a mortar and add *Béchamel sauce* to this purée as indicated in the recipe for Nantua sauce. See SAUCE.

Put the crayfish tails in a small pan with a tablespoon of butter. Heat without browning. Sprinkle with a tablespoon of flour. Mix thoroughly. Moisten with 2 tablespoons of brandy and $\frac{1}{2}$ cup (1 decilitre) of rather thick cream. Mix.

Leave to simmer on a very low heat for 8 minutes. Add the *Nantua sauce* prepared separately. Take the sauce off the stove and mix in 4 tablespoons (60 grams) of butter.

Note. According to the purpose for which this ragoût is to be used, the whole or only part of the *Nantua sauce*, made with the pounded shells, is added to it. If the *ragoût* is to be used as the sole filling of a vol-au-vent or pie, and if the tails of the crayfish are small, more tails will be required. However, this *ragoût* is mainly used as a garnish. It can be served with a host of other garnishes such as mushrooms, truffles, oysters, etc.

Crayfish tails in shells. COQUILLES DE QUEUES D'ÉCREVISSES—Line some little silver, fireproof, china or glass shells with *Mornay sauce* (see SAUCE) flavoured with crayfish butter (see BUTTER, *compound butters*). Pipe a narrow border of Duchess potato mixture (see POTATOES) round the shell.

On top of the sauce, arrange 6 to 8 shelled crayfish tails. Cover with *Mornay sauce*. Sprinkle with grated cheese. Pour on melted butter and brown quickly in the oven.

In the same way, using different sauces and garnishes, crayfish tails can be prepared in shells *à la normande*, *à la cardinal*, with mushrooms, etc.

Crayfish timbale à l'ancienne. TIMBALE DE QUEUES D'ÉCREVISSES À L'ANCIENNE—Prepare *Crayfish tail ragoût à la Nantua**. Line a shallow pie dish with *Fine lining pastry* (see DOUGH) lined in its turn with a thin layer of *Fine pike forcemeat* (see FORCEMEAT). Mix some coarsely diced truffles tossed in butter and left to cool, with the *ragoût* and fill the piecrust with the mixture.

Cover the *ragoût* with a layer of pike forcemeat. Cover the pie with a layer of pastry and seal. Decorate the top with flaky pastry motifs.

Make a small hole in the middle of the cover for the escape of steam. Brush with egg. Bake in a slow oven for 45 minutes to an hour.

When the pie is ready, pour into it a few tablespoons of rather thin *Nantua sauce* (see SAUCE). Serve on a napkin.

Crayfish timbale à la mode de Chavillieu. TIMBALE DE QUEUES D'ÉCREVISSES À LA MODE DE CHAVILLIEU—Cook 100 crayfish *à la mirepoix* with white wine. Drain them. Shell the tails and put them straight into a pan with melted butter. Pound the shells finely in a mortar. Divide the resulting purée into two halves. With one half of the purée make crayfish butter. See BUTTER, *Compound butters*.

Mix the rest of the crayfish purée with an equal quantity of *Béchamel* (see SAUCE), which has been diluted with fresh cream. Put this purée through a sieve, working it with a spatula.

When these ingredients are ready, heat the crayfish tails in the butter, *without browning*. Pour on a little fresh cream and blend in the crayfish purée.

Mix on the stove; moisten with thick fresh cream. At the last moment when the ragoût has thickened to the required consistency, mix in some of the crayfish butter mentioned above. Spice the dish with a little cayenne pepper and flavour with a few drops of liqueur brandy.

Keep hot in a double saucepan.

Separately, prepare 24 forcemeat balls made with a lavaret stuffing. (This is a cream stuffing made with filleted fish, whites of egg and thick fresh cream.) Poach these forcemeat balls slowly and keep them hot. Fill a piecrust of fine pastry baked blind (empty) with alternate layers of crayfish tail ragoût and forcemeat balls. The crust must be piping hot when filled. Cover the top of the pie with a few tablespoons of *Nantua sauce* (made with the rest of the purée and the crayfish butter), and decorate with large, thick slices of truffle, seasoned with salt and pepper, tossed in butter and flavoured with a little liqueur brandy. Cover with the top of the pie and serve piping hot.

Crayfish vol-au-vent. VOL-AU-VENT AUX ÉCREVISSES—Make a vol-au-vent case in the usual way. See VOL-AU-VENT. Fill with a *Crayfish tail ragoût à la Nantua**.

Little crayfish vol-au-vents, barquettes or tartlets—See HORS-D'OEUVRE, *Hot hors-d'oeuvre*.

CREAM (from milk). CRÈME DU LAIT—As well as the fat globules which make butter, cream contains a proportion of water, which varies according to the method of extracting it, some casein, lactose, and mineral salts. See MILK.

There is a distinction between single cream obtained by skimming milk which has been allowed to settle in shallow bowls, which contains 10 to 20 per cent of butter, and double cream obtained by a separating machine which must contain at least 30 per cent of butter. Possible adulterants are the addition of starch, fecula (potato flour), gelatine, but these are easy to detect as the cream in such a case has a mealy or gluey flavour.

Good cream is as a rule easy to digest, but a number of people find it harder to digest than butter.

CREAM CHEESES—See CHEESE.

CREAM SAUCE—See SAUCE.

CREAM SOUPS—These thickened soups have a basis of cereal, vegetables, fowl, fish or crustaceans. For their preparation, see SOUPS AND BROTHS.

CREAMS. CRÈMES—The French word *Crème* applies to whipped cream, butter and custard creams used to garnish pastries and cakes, custard cream sauces and soups.

Almond cream. CRÈME D'AMANDES—*Ingredients.* 3 cups (500 grams) almonds; 2 cups (500 grams) sugar; 1 pound (500 grams) butter; 8 eggs.

Method. Pound the peeled almonds with the sugar, moistening them with two of the eggs.

When the almonds have acquired the consistency of a paste, add the butter (softened into a paste). Continue to work the mixture, adding one by one the rest of the eggs.

Butter creams. CRÈMES AU BEURRE—There are two ways of making butter creams, which are used for garnishing cakes and pastries. One combines butter with *Custard cream** and the other is made with sugar syrup, beaten egg yolks and butter. Both types of butter creams are flavoured variously with mocha, praline, chocolate, vanilla or any liqueur.

Butter cream (with custard) I. CRÈME AU BEURRE—Prepare a *Custard cream** as described below. Beat it until it is lukewarm. Then incorporate 2 cups (450 grams) of butter in little dollops for every 3 cups (6 decilitres) of custard, beating all the time. Flavour the custard with vanilla sugar, or with some other flavouring according to the recipe.

Butter cream (with custard) II. CRÈME AU BEURRE—*Ingredients.* 12 egg yolks; 1 pound (500 grams) fine sugar; 1 cup (2 decilitres) fresh cream; 2 cups (450 grams) of butter; one pod vanilla or 2 teaspoons vanilla extract.

Method. Work together in a basin the sugar, the egg yolks, the vanilla, and the cream, until the preparation has a good consistency.

Put the basin over a low heat, or over a sauté-pan or a casserole half full of hot water, and whip the mixture on a gentle heat until it becomes frothy, light and whitish. Take it off the fire and continue to whip until it cools. Incorporate this custard with the butter which has been worked to a cream. Mix well.

These custard creams can be flavoured in various ways, with vanilla, lemon, orange or mandarin zest; with coffee, chocolate, tea or with liqueurs.

Butter cream with syrup. CRÈME AU BEURRE AU SIROP—Boil 2 cups sugar and 1½ cups water to 220°F. (making 5 decilitres of syrup). Infuse the prescribed flavouring in the resulting syrup (vanilla, zest, etc.). Pour the boiling syrup very gradually over 12 egg yolks, beating constantly. Pass this preparation through a cloth (optional) and add 2 cups (450 grams) of butter, mixing it in well.

Chantilly cream. CRÈME CHANTILLY—For one quart (litre), put a pint (½ litre) of thick fresh cream in a basin. The cream should have been kept in a cool place or on ice for 24 hours if possible. Beat the cream until it doubles its volume. Drain the cream on a tammy (fine sieve). At the last moment add 4 tablespoons (60 grams) of sugar and a teaspoon of vanilla sugar or 1 teaspoon vanilla extract.

Chantilly cream with fruit. CRÈME CHANTILLY AUX FRUITS—This can be made with all kinds of fruit pulp, but strawberry or raspberry pulp is the most suitable. Add to the cream which has been whipped till stiff a third of its volume of fruit pulp passed through a silk tammy. Arrange in a fruit bowl or a crystal dish.

Coffee custard cream. CRÈME AU CAFÉ—Prepared in the same way as vanilla flavoured *Custard cream**, with milk in which some roasted coffee beans have been infused.

Custard cream. CRÈME À L'ANGLAISE (CRÈME FRANÇAISE)—Work 8 egg yolks, 1 cup (250 grams) of fine sugar, and a minute pinch of salt in a pan with the aid of a spatula until the mixture has a homogeneous consistency and forms into ribbons when the spatula is raised above the pan. Moisten gradually with 2½ cups (5 decilitres) of boiled milk which has been flavoured, according to taste, with vanilla, lemon or orange zest.

Mix well. Keep the pan on the fire stirring all the time until the contents almost reach the boil. At this point, the egg yolks being sufficiently cooked, the custard should cling to the spatula.

Pass the custard through a fine sieve, or through a silk tammy, and keep it warm in a bain-marie (double boiler) if required to accompany a hot pudding, or turn it out into a basin and keep in a cool place if the custard is to be served cold. In the latter case it should be stirred while cooling to prevent a skin forming.

This custard cream can be made more cheaply by diminishing the number of egg yolks (6 instead of 8) and by adding to the egg yolk and sugar mixture a small teaspoon of arrowroot or fecula (potato or corn starch). This addition gives more consistency to the custard and prevents it from clotting if it has been allowed to overheat.

This custard, which is used to accompany a great many sweets (desserts), has a delicate taste.

It is also used, after incorporating a specific quantity of gelatine, for cold sweets such as *Bavarois**, *Charlottes**, *Rice à l'impératrice**, etc.

Custard Cream au miroir. CRÈME AU MIROIR—Custard cream presented in a bowl or dish, which is glazed with the aid of a salamander or hot poker.

Custard cream filling for waffles I. CRÈME POUR FOURRER LES GAUFRES—Chill a basin and work in it with a whip, 1 cup (250 grams) of butter, ¾ cup (250 grams) of icing sugar, 7 ounces (200 grams) of praline.

When this mixture has acquired a homogeneous consistency, use it as a filling for waffles.

Custard cream filling for waffles II. CRÈME POUR FOURRER LES GAUFRES—Put ½ pound (250 grams) of lump sugar and a ½ cup (1 decilitre) of water in a pan. Cook till it reaches the 'ball' stage (see SUGAR). Skim and strain the syrup. Put 15 egg yolks in a basin; pour the sugar syrup over them, letting it fall in a thin thread. Mix. Add 1 cup (250 grams) of butter which has been worked into a cream, then, beating all the time, add 7 ounces (200 grams) of praline.

Although praline is the flavouring indicated for these creams, it is equally possible to use coffee, chocolate, vanilla or orange flavouring.

Custard cream with gelatine. CRÈME ANGLAISE COLLÉE—Used for cold sweets (desserts). Prepare the custard as described above. As soon as it is cooked, add 1–1½ tablespoons (20–25 grams) of granulated gelatine which has been soaked in cold water or 8 to 10 leaves of gelatine, and let it dissolve in the preparation while stirring.

Strain the custard, and stir it until it cools.

Custard cream with liqueurs. CRÈME À L'ANGLAISE AUX LIQUEURS—Prepare the custard cream in the same way as *Custard cream with gelatine** and when it is completely cool, add a good tablespoon of liqueur: curaçao, kirsch, maraschino, rum, etc.

Custard cream flavoured with tea. CRÈME ANGLAISE AU THÉ—This is prepared like *Moka custard cream**, replacing the coffee with a strong infusion of tea.

The custard can also be made by moistening the mixture of egg yolks and sugar with milk in which tea leaves have been infused (without boiling).

Frangipane pastry cream. CRÈME PÂTISSIÈRE, DITE FRANGIPANE—*Ingredients.* 1⅝ cups (200 grams) sifted flour; 4 whole eggs; 6 egg yolks; 4 cups (a litre) of milk; 4 tablespoons (60 grams) of butter; 7 tablespoons (100 grams) fine sugar, ⅝ cup (60 grams) crushed macaroons; a small pinch of salt.

Method. Work together in a pan the whole eggs and the egg yolks, the flour and the sugar. When the preparation is smooth and forms a ribbon (when the spatula is lifted out of the pan), add the milk and the butter. Cook on the fire, working continuously with the spatula. Add in the last place the crushed macaroons.

Let the cream cook, stirring from time to time, to prevent a skin forming.

French pastry cream or Confectioner's custard. CRÈME PÂTISSIÈRE—This preparation, which is very much used in pâtisserie as a filling for large and small *gâteaux*, is equally used in the preparation of puddings, both hot and cold. We give two methods of making it, the first being more economical than the second.

First method. Put the following ingredients in a thick-bottomed pan: ½ cup (60 grams) of sifted flour, ¾ cup (175 grams) of sugar, a very small pinch of salt, 1 tablespoon (15 grams) of good quality butter and 4 whole eggs. Work this mixture with a spatula or a wooden spoon.

Add 2 cups (half a litre) of boiling milk in which a vanilla pod has been infused or add 1 teaspoon vanilla extract. After mixing, put the pan on the fire and let it boil for a few minutes, taking care to stir constantly to prevent the cream from catching on the bottom of the pan.

Turn it out into a basin. Stir the cream from time to time as it cools.

Second method. Follow the same procedure, but modify the proportions of the ingredients used thus: ½ cup (65 grams) of flour, 1 cup (250 grams) of sugar, 6 egg yolks, a pint (half a litre) of milk flavoured with vanilla, a pinch of salt.

Moka custard cream. CRÈME ANGLAISE AU MOKA—This is prepared in the same way as a simple *custard cream**, but the mixture of egg yolks and sugar is moistened with milk in which some freshly roasted coffee beans have been infused. (The infusion is made by heating the milk and coffee beans without allowing it to boil.)

Plombières cream. CRÈME PLOMBIÈRES—'Put 8 egg yolks in a casserole and a tablespoon of rice flour. Add 3 glasses (cups) of good milk, almost boiling; put the pan on a moderate heat and stir continuously with a wooden spoon. When the mixture begins to thicken, remove it from the fire and continue to stir until it acquires a perfectly smooth consistency; after this, cook it for a further few minutes. This cream must be of the same consistency as an ordinary *French pastry cream**. Then, mix in ¾ cup of fine sugar and a minute pinch of salt. Pour the mixture into another pan and set it on ice, stirring from time to time. In cooling it thickens a little. When the cream is cold, and at the moment of serving, mix in a good half glass of liqueur and then a saucerful of good, whipped cream which has been properly drained on a cloth. The whole, well amalgamated, should produce a light velvety cream of a perfect consistency. Then dress the cream in a silver dish, or in small pots or in a pastry case, in a specially made biscuit case, or in a dish-shaped vehicle of almond paste.' (From *Le cuisinier royal*, by Viard and Fouret, 1828.)

Praline custard cream. CRÈME PRALINÉ—Add *Praline** to *Custard cream**.

St. Honoré cream. CRÈME SAINT-HONORÉ—This is the same as *French pastry cream** (or confectioner's custard) to which beaten whites of egg are added, very stiff, when the cream is still boiling. Use 16 egg whites for a cream made with 1 quart, 3 ounces (litre) of milk, 2 cups (500 grams) of sugar and 16 egg yolks.

CREAM HORNS A LA CHIBOUST. CORNETS FEUILLETÉS À LA CRÈME, DITS À LA CHIBOUST—*Ingredients for 12 cornets.* 1 pound (500 grams) puff pastry (see DOUGH); 1¼ cups (150 grams) fine sugar; 5 egg yolks; 4 whites of egg; 5 tablespoons (50 grams) flour; 2 cups (½ litre) milk; half a pod vanilla or 1 teaspoon vanilla extract; and a pinch of salt.

Method. Prepare the pastry as directed under the heading *Puff pastry* (see DOUGH). As soon as it is ready, and rested, roll it out with the rolling pin to a thickness of ⅛ inch.

Cut the sheet into 12 strips about 1 inch wide and 10 inches long. Roll these strips round cornet-shaped moulds.

Arrange the cornets on a wet iron baking sheet; let them rest for 10 minutes; gild them with egg and set to cook in a hot oven for 12 to 15 minutes. When they are nearly cooked, sprinkle them with icing sugar and glaze them. As soon as they glisten, take them out of the oven.

The Cream. The foundation of this preparation is the *Crème pâtissière* (French pastry cream). Put the sieved flour, the fine sugar and the pinch of salt in a pan. Add the egg yolks and whip until the mixture is smooth.

Moisten with the milk, which has first been boiled with half a vanilla pod; mix carefully and cook on a good heat, beating all the time until the cream has acquired the desired consistency. The cooking must be rapid and should not require more than 5 minutes. This operation constitutes the *crème pâtissière*. To obtain the *crème Chiboust*, it only needs the addition, when still hot, of 4 egg whites which have been beaten until very firm.

Fill the cornets, completely cold, with the cream, using a forcing bag (pastry bag) with a round nozzle, or, failing this, a cornet of greaseproof paper.

CRÉCY (A LA)—A name given to various preparations, and notably to a soup called *Purée Crécy*. All the preparations named in this way include an obligatory garnish of carrots, and some are exclusively composed of carrots. See SOUPS AND BROTHS.

This name has been given to various preparations on account of the excellent quality of the carrots harvested at Crécy, a little town in the Seine-et-Marne.

However, some authors insist that the name of this soup comes not from that of the chief town of the Seine-et-Marne district, but from that of a little town in the Somme, near which the Battle of Crécy took place in 1346. Monselet seems to lean towards this view, as can be seen from his sonnet called *La Purée Crécy*:

Au jour de dîme et de taille
Crécy fut une bataille,
Dont le pays maltraité
Garde la plaie au côté.
Combat d'estoc et de taille!
De cette cruelle entaille,
O contraste! Il n'est resté
Qu'un potage réputé.
Le temps a, pour nos détresses,
D'irrésistibles caresses
Dont chaque âge est adouci.
Légumes taillés en pièces
Disent seuls, en ce temps-ci
Les grands combats de Crécy!

This sonnet is a play on the word '*taille*', and does not really bear translating. The sense of it is this: In the days of tithes and taxes there was a battle at Crécy from which the district suffered considerably. But of this cut-and-thrust fighting, this cruel slashing, nothing remains but a famous soup. Time has a way of alleviating distress, and vegetables cut into pieces are the only record nowadays of the great fights at Crécy.

CRÉMANT—This word is used to denote Champagne wines which have a creamy froth and not much of it.

CRÈME (A LA)—This name is given to meat and vegetable preparations the pan juices of which are mixed with fresh cream (e.g. *Mushrooms à la crème*).

CRÈME RENVERSÉE—This is made like *Caramel custard* (see CUSTARD), a custard cream poured into a mould, cooked in the oven in a bain-marie (pan of hot water), and turned out when cold.

CRÉMETS D'ANGERS, DE SAUMUR—Cream cheeses to which whites of egg are added. These are prepared by adding little by little fresh cream whipped very stiff, whites of egg equally well whipped, whipping all the time so that the various elements are properly amalgamated. Little perforated moulds are filled with this preparation, covered with fine muslin, and left to drain in a cool place. At the moment of serving, the *crémets* are turned out of their moulds on to a fruit dish or a deepset dish and covered with fresh cream.

CRÉOLE (A LA)—This is a term applying to various culinary preparations which contain as a rule a rice garnish prepared as a pilaf, or *à la Créole*, a garnish which is completed by sweet peppers simmered in a little oil, and also with tomatoes.

À la Créole can also apply to sweet dishes. All these, or at least the greater number, are prepared with rice, and as a rule are flavoured with orange.

Crêpes (*French Government Tourist Office*)

CRÊPES. PANCAKES—A preparation composed of a batter made with eggs and flour, which is poured sparingly into a frying-pan, and fried on both sides.

Crêpe batter I—Put 3¾ cups (500 grams) of sifted flour, 1 cup minus 2 tablespoons (200 grams) of fine sugar, a light pinch of salt, and the inside of a vanilla pod (or 1 teaspoon vanilla extract added after the eggs), into a basin.

Add 8 whole eggs and 4 yolks one by one, working the batter with a wooden spoon.

When this preparation is properly amalgamated, add 3 cups (¾ litre) of milk, and 2–3 tablespoons of fresh thick cream. Add 2–3 tablespoons of Cognac to the batter (or some other liqueur), and 2 tablespoons (25 grams) of butter which has been heated until it has acquired a slight nutty colour.

Note. This batter should be made a little in advance and allowed to stand for a time before use.

Crêpe batter II—Put 3¾ cups (500 grams) of flour, 10 tablespoons (150 grams) of fine sugar, and a pinch of fine salt in a basin. Add 10 eggs. Work the mixture until it is thoroughly smooth, then add 1½ cups (3 decilitres) of

Crêpes filled with strawberries

fresh cream, ¼ cup (½ decilitre) of cognac, 5 tablespoons (80 grams) of melted butter and 4 cups (1 litre) of milk. Strain through a fine sieve. Add ¼ cup (½ decilitre) of orgeat syrup, and 1 heaped cup (100 grams) of macaroons which have been crushed fine. Flavour to taste.

Crêpe batter III—3¾ cups (500 grams) of flour; 10 tablespoons (150 grams) of sugar; a pinch of salt; 10 eggs. Work the mixture and add 2 cups (4 decilitres) of cream and 2 cups (half a litre) of milk. Flavour to taste.

Crêpe batter IV—3¾ cups (500 grams) of sifted flour, 10 tablespoons (150 grams) of sugar; a pinch of salt; 4 whole eggs and 5 yolks. Work the mixture; add 4 cups (1 litre) of milk and finish with 6 egg whites beaten very stiff. Flavour to taste.

Savoury crêpe batter V. PÂTE À CRÊPES SALÉES—This is used for soup garnishes and hot hors d'oeuvre. Work 2 cups minus 2 tablespoons (250 grams) of sifted flour and 4 eggs together in a basin; season with 1½ teaspoons (10 grams) of fine salt. Moisten with 3 cups (¾ litre) of boiled milk, which has been boiled down by one third.

Note. The milk can be replaced by stock or broth.

Alsatian crêpes. CRÊPES ALSACIENNES—Pancakes made from a *crêpe batter**. These are filled with redcurrant or raspberry jelly, sprinkled with sugar and glazed in a very hot oven.

Apple crêpes—See APPLE, *Crêpes stuffed with apple.*

Buckwheat crêpes, called galetous. CRÊPES AU BLÉ NOIR, DITES GALETOUS—Put 2 tablespoons of olive oil in a basin with 2 small glasses of brandy, 2 pinches of salt, 2 cups of curdled (sour) milk, 3¾ cups (500 grams) of buckwheat flour. Mix together.

Add 8 whole eggs, put in one by one, and work the mixture well to avoid its becoming lumpy.

Cook the pancakes on a griddle which has been rubbed with butter or fat.

This is a Breton speciality.

Crêpes à la cévenole—Make the crêpes with a sweetened batter in the usual way. When they are cooked, spread them out on the table, and cover each one with a thin layer of a purée of *marrons glacés* (see CHESTNUTS) flavoured with rum.

Roll the pancakes up and arrange them on a fireproof dish. Glaze them in a fierce oven.

Crêpes as a soup garnish, and for other purposes—Prepared in the ordinary way, with the unsweetened pancake batter, or with *Savoury crêpe batter**. See GARNISHES.

Raspberry crêpes. CRÊPES AUX FRAMBOISES—Cover very thin pancakes with raspberry purée which has been thickened with *French pastry cream* (see CREAM). Remove stems of raspberries and soak the fruit in sugar and liqueur. Roll the pancakes up. Trim them on a slant at both ends. Arrange them on a dish. Sprinkle with icing sugar. Glaze pancakes in very hot oven.

Crêpes with Roquefort. CRÊPES AU ROQUEFORT—Make some very small pancakes with an unsweetened batter. Put these pancakes on the table and spread them with the following preparation:

Add to 4–6 tablespoons of *Béchamel** (see SAUCE), 2–3 tablespoons of Roquefort cheese which has been worked into a paste. Season with pepper and a little nutmeg and mix well.

Roll up the pancakes. Arrange them on a fireproof dish. Sprinkle them with grated cheese. Glaze them rapidly in the oven.

Note. Crêpes with Gruyère, Parmesan, Cantal, Brie, Edam cheeses, can be made in the same way.

Crêpes Suzette—Make the pancakes very thin, with a batter flavoured with curaçao and mandarin orange juice.

Spread the pancakes with the following mixture: work 3 tablespoons (50 grams) of butter into a cream with 5 tablespoons (50 grams) of fine sugar. Add, working the mixture with a spatula, the juice of a mandarin orange, its zest grated fine, and 2 tablespoons of curaçao.

When the pancakes are lined with this preparation, fold them over into four, and serve very hot.

CRÉPINETTES—Little flat sausages, encased in caul. All the preparations made in this form are, as a rule, enclosed in a layer of forcemeat. Paper-thin slices of salt pork can be substituted for the caul.

Crépinettes, whatever their composition (all kinds are made), are, as a rule, grilled. Before setting them on the grill, they are bathed in melted butter, or fat, and they are covered entirely with fresh breadcrumbs. *Crépinettes* can also be sautéed or cooked in the oven.

Very small *crépinettes* are also made under the name of *Pieds cendrillon* which in the old days were wrapped in sheets of paper, and put to cook in hot cinders. Nowadays these are cooked in the same way as crépinettes, or they can be enclosed in a thin sheet of fine pastry and cooked in the oven.

Crépinettes are usually accompanied by a purée of potatoes when they are grilled, or cooked in the oven. They can also be served with a fairly strongly seasoned sauce handed separately, and if they are truffled, with a *Périgueux sauce* (see SAUCE).

When the *crépinettes* are truffled, whatever the basic ingredient is, truffles cut into dice are incorporated in the stuffing and a large slice of truffle placed on top of the stuffing before enclosing it in the caul.

Crépinettes Cendrillon—See PORK, *Cinderella pork crépinettes.*

Chicken crépinettes. CRÉPINETTES DE VOLAILLE—Made with a hash of fowl to which truffles and mushrooms are added, incorporated in a very concentrated *Velouté sauce* (see SAUCE) in the same manner as *Lamb crépinettes.*

Lamb crépinettes. CRÉPINETTES D'AGNEAU—Prepared with hashed lamb, mushrooms, and truffles, with a white or brown sauce, enclosed in a delicate forcemeat and wrapped in caul.

Pork crépinettes. CRÉPINETTES DE PORC—These are simply flat sausages.

Crépinettes Sainte-Ménehould—Made with a hash of pig's trotters, bound with a very concentrated thick brown veal gravy (with or without the addition of truffles cut in dice), enclosed in a fine pork forcemeat (with or without truffles), and enveloped in caul.

Truffled crépinettes. CRÉPINETTES TRUFFÉES—Made with sausage meat, or with a fine pork forcemeat with the addition of truffles cut into dice. Divide this into portions weighing $3\frac{1}{2}$ ounces (100 grams). Put each portion on to a piece of caul. Wrap it in the caul.

Cover the *crépinettes* with melted butter. Grill them on a gentle heat. Accompany with a purée of potatoes, and *Périgueux sauce* (see SAUCE) served separately.

Veal crépinettes. CRÉPINETTES DE VEAU—Made with a veal hash incorporated in a white or brown sauce, in the same way as *Lamb crépinettes**.

CRESS. CRESSON—This name is given to two plants of rather different aspect, although both have the same properties.

One is *watercress*, the other *garden cress.*

To these two species should be added *lady's smock* the leaves of which are sweeter than those of watercress and are eaten in salad in the spring; the *rock cress* which is eaten in salad in the Vosges, and which has a more bitter taste than watercress; and *wild cress* which has the same uses as the other cresses.

Cress has a special taste, slightly bitter and piquant, recalling that of mustard.

The cress most used in cooking is watercress. It is used raw, to garnish grilled and roast meats, or in salad. Less often is it cooked, although it provides excellent dishes.

Cress when eaten in a raw state should be carefully picked over, the thicker stems removed as well as the yellowing or faded leaves, carefully washed and properly drained.

The washing of the cress should be done quickly, and it should not be left to soak in water. For recipes, see WATERCRESS.

CRESTED LARK. COCHEVIS—See LARK.

CRETAN DITTANY. DICTAME DE CRÈTE—An aromatic labinate formerly used in treacle. It is sometimes used in the manufacture of liqueurs.

CREUX (Wine)—A French term applied to wine which lacks body.

CREVER (To burst)—This is a French term applied to rice which is brought to a certain point or condition by boiling. Many people have an erroneous idea of what this condition should be, because the word *crever* gives a false idea that rice should be cooked to the point of bursting, which in fact transforms it into a glutinous mass, both displeasing and insipid. See RICE.

CRICKET. CRIQUET—Insect of the same family as the grasshopper. It is eaten in some countries.

CROCODILE—A kind of reptile with very strong smelling flesh which is, however, edible and appreciated in certain countries, on account of the restorative properties which it is said to possess. See ALLIGATOR.

CROISSANT—A crescent-shaped roll generally made with *pâte feuilletée* (puff pastry), or with a leavened dough for which we give the recipe below.

The origin of this delicious pastry—because the croissant is more of a pastry than a bread—is extremely ancient; it dates from the year 1686 and it was first created in Budapest.

In that year, the Turks were besieging the city. To reach the centre of the town they had dug underground passages. Bakers who worked during the night heard the noise made by the Turks and gave the alarm. The assailants were repulsed.

Croissants and breakfast rolls

In order to reward the bakers who had saved the city in this way, they were granted the privilege of making a special pastry which, in memory of the emblem which decorates the Ottoman flag, had to take the form of a crescent.

Put 3¾ cups (500 grams) of sifted flour on the table in the form of a crown. Put ⅝ ounce (20 grams) of dry yeast in the middle of the flour. Moisten the yeast with a little lukewarm milk and incorporate one quarter of the flour. Let the dough rise.

Then add a pinch of salt, ¾ cup (200 grams) of butter and ¾-1 cup (2 decilitres) of milk. Mix these elements well incorporating the remaining flour and work the dough moistening it if necessary with a little milk. The dough should be firm, rather than soft. Roll it into a ball, cover it with a cloth and leave it to rise.

When the dough has risen divide it into pieces the size of an egg. Roll out the pieces of dough with a rolling pin, giving them an oval shape. Roll up each piece and shape it into a crescent. Put them on a baking sheet. Leave them to rise.

Moisten them with a paintbrush dipped in milk and cook in a hot oven.

As soon as they are cooked, baste them with a mixture of 3 tablespoons of potato flour and 2 cups (half a litre) of boiled water.

Almond croissants (dry petits fours). Croissants aux amandes—Pound 2 cups (300 grams) of peeled almonds and 1⅓ cups (300 grams) of vanilla-flavoured sugar in mortar, moistening little by little with white of egg in sufficient quantity to obtain a paste which can be rolled out by hand. Add 2 tablespoons of flour to this paste.

Jam croissants

Divide it into pieces the size of a nut. Roll these with floured hands into a rather pointed cigar shape.

Dip them in beaten egg and roll them in chopped almonds. Arrange them on sheets of paper laid on baking sheets, giving them the shape of small crescents. Gild with egg. Cook for 8 to 10 minutes in the oven at a medium heat. As soon as they are cooked paint them with very sweetened milk.

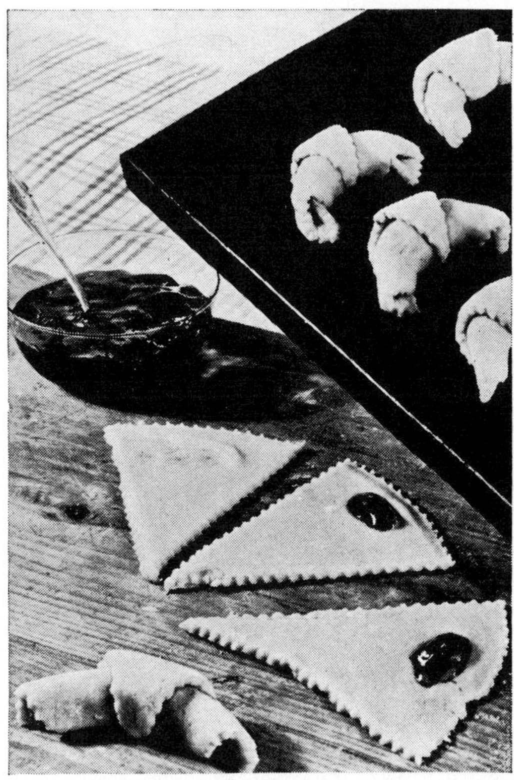

Shaping jam croissants (Austrian pâtisserie)

Jam croissants (Austrian pâtisserie). Croissants aux confitures—Cut some *Puff pastry* (see DOUGH) into triangular pieces (with a fluted pastry cutter). Put a teaspoon of gooseberry (or any other) jam on each of these paste triangles on one side. Roll these up in the manner indicated for ordinary croissants. Put them on a baking sheet. Gild them with egg. Cook them in the oven at a good heat. When you take them out, sprinkle with fine sugar.

CROMESQUI (KROMESKY)—Little preparations made with some kind of *salpicon** enclosed in a pig's caul (or slices of salt pork), dipped in frying batter and deep-fat fried.

Served as a hot hors d'oeuvre, or as a small entrée. See HORS D'OEUVRE, *Hot hors d'oeuvre*.

CROP. Jabot—A dilation of the gullet forming a pouch in birds, especially grain-eating birds. In the drawing of poultry and winged game, the crop is removed.

CROQUANT (Pâtisserie)—A kind of *petit-four* which, as its name indicates, crunches when bitten.

Pound fine in a mortar 1½ cups (250 grams) of almonds to which 4 egg whites are added little by little; add 2 cups

(500 grams) of fine sugar, 2 tablespoons of vanilla sugar or 1 teaspoon vanilla extract and strain through a fine sieve.

Make little boat-shapes with the paste; roll them in brown sugar; put them on a buttered baking sheet. Cook in a very moderate oven.

CROQUANTE (Pâtisserie)—This large piece of pâtisserie, which used to be made a great deal in the old days to decorate large buffets, or to serve as a tailpiece to a dinner, is hardly ever made today.

It was prepared by surrounding a large mould (which was tinned on the exterior) with bands of almond paste. These bands were arranged in a kind of trellis on the mould (sticking those parts which crossed over each other with beaten egg), and it was cooked in the oven to give it colour. When the paste was cooked, it was left to cool and was then turned out.

This was glazed with strained apricot marmalade, the croquante was then set on a pastry base, covered with sugar, green or pink, and the top of the cake was filled with rounds of puff paste, the centres of which were emptied and filled with preserved cherries.

Under the same name, sweets were prepared in the old days with almond paste arranged as a basket, which was filled at the last moment with vanilla ice or an ice with any other flavour.

Croquantes were also made with little jumbles of almond paste glazed, some with pink icing, others with white icing. These little *bonnes bouchées* were arranged one on top of the other, topped with an aigrette in spun sugar.

CROQUE AU SEL (A LA)—This is said of food which is eaten raw as a rule with no other seasoning than salt: *Artichokes à la croque au sel*, for instance.

CROQUEMBOUCHE—This word is also written croque-en-bouche, and dictionaries on this account say that the word means all kinds of pâtisserie which crunches and crumbles in the mouth.

Croquembouches can be made of various compositions and are, in fact, made with ingredients which crunch between the teeth because they are all glazed with sugar which is cooked *au cassé* (to the crack stage).

The typical *croquembouche* is that made of little *choux profiteroles** filled with some kind of cream, glazed with sugar, and arranged one on top of the other.

Croquembouches can also be made of jumbles, of Genoese pastries, of meringues, almond paste, and with various fruits. Among these last, the one most frequently made today is the *croquembouche* of oranges.

Croquembouche of marrons glacés—'Grill 60 fine Spanish chestnuts, and after having peeled them and removed any traces of burning, glaze them by dipping them in sugar cooked to the *crack stage* (see SUGAR) and put them, as soon as glazed, into a simple round mould 7 inches across and 5 inches high.

'The *croquembouche* has to be piled up at the last minute before serving, because the moisture contained in the chestnuts tends to soften the sugar and make it lose both its consistency and its brilliance.' (Carême.)

Croquembouche of oranges—Dip some segments of orange to which the thin skin is still adhering in some sugar cooked to the crack stage.

Arrange these segments one on top of the other (in a *croquembouche* mould) beginning at the bottom. When the sugar is cold, lightly heat the periphery of the mould and then remove it. Set the *croquembouche* on a pastry base. Finish the decoration of the *croquembouche* by

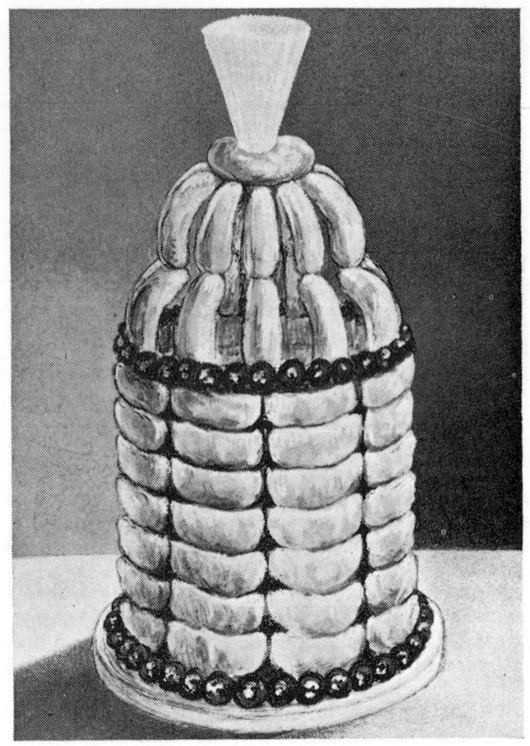

Croquembouche of oranges

adding more orange segments dipped in glazing sugar to round off the top, and complete with an aigrette of spun sugar. Decorate the top and bottom of the croquembouche with preserved cherries glazed with sugar cooked to the crack stage.

CROQUE-MONSIEUR—A rather fantastic name for a kind of hot sandwich which is served as an hors d'oeuvre or as a small entrée. It can also feature in the list of small dishes for lunch, tea, etc.

Cut some slices $3\frac{1}{2}$ inches long and $2\frac{1}{4}$ inches wide and $\frac{1}{8}$ inch thick, from a fresh loaf, or failing that use some stale bread. Spread with butter on one side only and lay a thin slice of Gruyere cheese on top. Put a slice of lean ham on top of the cheese, and close the sandwich. Fry till golden in a frying pan in clarified butter.

CROQUETS—Dry *petits fours* of which the most famous are those of the Bordeaux area.

Bar almond croquets. CROQUETS DE BAR AUX AMANDES—*Ingredients.* $3\frac{1}{2}$ cups (500 grams) of castor (powdered) sugar; $\frac{1}{2}$ pound (250 grams) of powdered almonds; $2\frac{1}{4}$ cups (275 grams) of sifted flour; 8 egg whites; 2 teaspoons (10 grams) of vanilla sugar or 1 teaspoon vanilla extract.

Method. Moisten the sugar and powdered almonds in a basin with the egg whites, worked in one at a time. Mix in lightly the flour and vanilla sugar, which have been sifted together through a sieve.

Arrange on a baking sheet in the shape of thin leaves (using a thin piece of card bent into leaf shape, or with a special metal cutter).

Cook in a gentle oven; remove from the baking sheet while still hot and leave to cool on a marble slab. Store in a jar or tin, and keep in a dry place.

Bordelais croquets. CROQUETS BORDELAIS—Finely pound 2 cups (300 grams) of peeled almonds in a mortar with 1½ cups (150 grams) of unpeeled almonds, 2/3 cups (300 grams) of sugar, ½ cup (120 grams) of butter, 2 whole eggs, the grated zest of lemon (or orange), a packet of powdered yeast and a pinch of salt.

Once pounded, coarsely chop up this preparation and roll it into the form of a large *boudin* (black pudding), slightly flattened at the edges. Put it on a baking sheet. Gild with egg; score it; cook for 15 minutes in a moderate oven. Cut into even slices.

CROQUETTES—Small preparations made in various forms with a mixture which as a rule is a *salpicon** combined with a white or brown sauce, and which contains as well as the basic element, mushrooms, truffles, and sometimes lean ham, all these ingredients being chopped up fine.

Croquettes are also made with potatoes or other vegetables, fresh or dried; with rice cooked in broth or simply boiled, with various forms of pasta combined with cheese and a *Béchamel sauce.* See SAUCE.

Croquettes are also made with a hash or a forcemeat of various meats or fish.

Finally there are sweet croquettes made with rice cooked in milk, with semolina, or with a salpicon of fruit combined with a very stiff *French pastry cream.* See CREAM.

Croquets is the name given to a number of croquettes made with a basic element of pasta.

Preparation of croquettes—Put in a sauté-pan a salpicon made up of 2 cups (500 grams) of the principal element (fowl, game, veal, lamb, offal, or variety meat, cut up into very small dice). Add for 2 cups (500 grams) of meat, ½ pound (250 grams) of cultivated mushrooms (cooked) cut into dice, and 3 ounces (85 grams) of diced truffles. Moisten this hash with ½ cup (1 decilitre) of Madeira, and heat in the oven, covering the pan.

Then add 2 cups (4 decilitres) of *Velouté sauce* (see SAUCE) which has been boiled down, and to which 3 egg yolks have been added after the desired thickness is reached.

Mix on the fire, stirring the mixture with a spatula.

Put this preparation into a buttered baking dish, spreading it out into an even layer. Dab the surface with butter to prevent a crust forming. Allow it to cool completely before making the croquettes.

Note. Quite often croquettes made with various meats, with fowl or game, have a hash of lean cooked ham or tongue added to them.

Croquettes made with fish or crustaceans have only mushrooms and truffles added to them as a complementary element.

The croquettes can be combined with a *Brown sauce* (see SAUCE) instead of a *Velouté*, that is to say, with a good veal stock which has been greatly concentrated and combined with yolks of egg.

Forming the croquettes—Divide the mixture into portions of about 2 ounces (50 to 10 grams). Roll these portions on a floured table.

Dip them in a mixture of egg and olive oil beaten together, cover them entirely with fine breadcrumbs and shape them into corks, balls, eggs, rectangles, etc.

Cooking the croquettes—Arrange the croquettes on a grill or in the frying basket, and plunge them all together in boiling oil. Cook them until they are crisp and golden.

Drain them, sponge them with a cloth, sprinkle with fine salt.

Serving croquettes—Arrange them in the form of a pyramid or turban on a dish covered with a napkin or with a paper doyley. Garnish with curled parsley.

They can also be arranged in a mound in a nest of straw potatoes.

Sauces and garnishes for croquettes—The sauces which accompany croquettes vary with their composition.

Note. When croquettes are served as a little entrée, they are sometimes accompanied by a garnish of fresh vegetables to which butter has been added, or with a purée of vegetables, fresh or dry. In this case, the croquettes should be made in rectangular form in order that they can be arranged in the form of a turban.

Croquettes can be used as a garnish for large roasts, for fowl, game or fish. In this case they should be made very small.

Croquettes, with the exception of sweet croquettes, are served as hors d'oeuvre or as little entrées.

The composition of the following croquettes will be found under HORS D'OEUVRE, *Hot hors d'oeuvre: Beef, Brains, Cress, Foie gras, Game, Lobster, Oyster, Vegetables, Macaroni, Montrouge, Cod, Fish, Potatoes, Printanière, Various meats, Viennoise, Poultry,* etc.

Apricot croquettes I. CROQUETTES AUX ABRICOTS—Cook 1 pound (500 grams) of apricots in syrup, drain them, dry them and cut them up into large dice. Bind the apricots with 2 cups (4 decilitres) of *Fried custard cream* (see CUSTARD CREAMS). Flavour this preparation with kirsch. Let it cool.

Divide it up into 2 ounce (60 gram) portions. Roll the portions in flour, then in egg and breadcrumbs. Deep fry at the last moment.

Arrange the croquettes on a napkin; serve with *Apricot sauce* (see SAUCE) flavoured with kirsch.

Apricot croquettes II. CROQUETS AUX ABRICOTS—Cook some halved apricots in a vanilla syrup. Drain them well, and then fill each half with a tablespoon of *Frangipane pastry cream* (see CREAM), flavoured with kirsch. Put two apricot halves together and envelop each reconstructed apricot in a coating of cooked semolina (see SEMOLINA). Dip in egg and in breadcrumbs and fry at the last moment. Serve with an *Apricot sauce* flavoured with kirsch. See SAUCE.

Brie cheese croquettes. CROQUETTES DE FROMAGE DE BRIE—Put 3 tablespoons (30 grams) of sifted flour in a casserole with 3 tablespoons of rice flour. Moisten with ½ cup (a decilitre) of milk. Add ½ pound (250 grams) of Brie cut into little pieces and 5 tablespoons (75 grams) of butter divided into little pieces. Season with a pinch of salt, a pinch of cayenne, and a little grated nutmeg. Cook on a good heat, stirring uninterruptedly until the cream has a sufficient consistency. Spread it out on a buttered baking sheet; leave to cool. Cut it into rectangular pieces. Dip in egg and in breadcrumbs. Fry the croquettes.

This cream is used as soon as cooked to fill tartlets or *barquettes* served as a hot hors-d'oeuvre.

Chestnut croquettes I. CROQUETTES DE MARRONS—Prepare a chestnut purée in the usual way by peeling the chestnuts, cooking them in a light syrup flavoured with vanilla, and passing them through a fine sieve. Let their moisture evaporate over heat, add 5 egg yolks and 3 tablespoons (50 grams) of butter for 2 cups (500 grams) of purée. Make the croquettes using 1 heaped tablespoon (60 grams) of the purée for each. Dip them in egg and breadcrumbs, and deep fry in boiling oil.

Arrange the croquettes on a napkin, serve with apricot sauce flavoured with kirsch, or with any other sauce suitable for sweets.

Chestnut croquettes II. CROQUETTES DE MARRONS—Crumble some *marrons glacés* (see CHESTNUTS). Add for every pound (500 grams), 2 cups (4 decilitres) of *French pastry cream* (see CREAM) flavoured with kirsch, or with any other liqueur. Let this mixture cool. Make it into croquettes. Finish in the same way as for *Apricot croquettes**.

Gruyère cheese croquettes. CROQUETTES DE FROMAGE DE GRUYÈRE—Put ¾ cup (100 grams) of sifted flour in a pan with 5 tablespoons (50 grams) rice flour, 3 eggs and 2 egg yolks. Mix with a spoon. Moisten with 2½ cups (5 decilitres) of boiled milk; season with a pinch of salt, a small pinch of cayenne, and a little grated nutmeg. Bring to the boil. Let the mixture cook on a good heat for 5 minutes, stirring constantly to prevent it from sticking to the bottom of the pan. Remove the pan from the heat. Add ¼ pound (125 grams) of grated Gruyère. Spread out the mixture on a baking sheet; leave to cool; cut into rectangles. Dip in egg and breadcrumbs; fry in boiling oil.

This cream can also be used to garnish canapés, *barquettes*, fried bread, or tartlets, which are then browned in the oven, and served as a hot hors d'oeuvre.

Mussel croquettes. CROQUETTES DE MOULES—Cook 2 quarts (litres) of mussels in white wine with sliced onion, parsley, thyme and bay leaf.

Drain the mussels, and take them out of their shells. Dry them on a cloth, put them in a sauté-pan, with an equal quantity of mushrooms cut into dice, and simmered in butter.

Combine with a *Béchamel sauce* (see SAUCE) to which the liquor in wihch the mussels have been cooked has been added, and the sauce suitably cooked down (reduced). Leave to cool.

Make the croquettes, dip them in egg and breadcrumbs, and fry in the usual way.

Potato croquettes. CROQUETTES DE POMMES DE TERRE—Prepared with a *Duchess potato* mixture. See POTATOES.

In order to vary this kind of dish, when served as a hot hors-d'oeuvre or used as a garnish, it is possible to add various ingredients to the basic *duchess* preparation, such as finely hashed ham, mushrooms, truffles, or a fairly thick tomato sauce, chopped onion lightly cooked in butter, *Mirepoix**, *Duxelles**, etc.

Rice croquettes (savoury). CROQUETTES DE RIZ—Croquettes are prepared either with rice cooked with butter and bound with egg at the end of cooking, or with cheese risotto.

Make the croquettes in the usual way and fry in deep fat, smoking hot. Arrange in a heap on a napkin, garnish with fried parsley. Serve with tomato sauce.

Rice croquettes (sweet). CROQUETTES DE RIZ—Rice croquettes can be used as a sweet course or pudding. Prepare ½ cup (125 grams) of sweetened rice (see RICE). As soon as it is cold, divide it into portions of 1 heaped tablespoon (60 grams). Dip in egg and breadcrumbs, and make the croquettes in the shape of apricots, apples or little pears. They can also be made in the form of large corks, in flattened rounds, or in rectangles.

Fry, and arrange in the form of a pyramid. Serve an apricot or some other fruit sauce with the croquettes.

Rice croquettes, stuffed. CROQUETTES DE RIZ FOURRÉES—Divide some cooked sweetened rice into balls of 1 heaped tablespoon each (60 grams). Put the balls on a floured table. Slit them slightly and fill with a small spoonful of *fruit marmelade* (see JAM) or with a very thick *French pastry cream* (see CREAM). Close up the slit; dip in egg and breadcrumbs, and fry in the usual way.

Rice croquettes in the old sytle. CROQUETTES DE RIZ À LA MANIÈRE ANCIENNE—'Cook ¾ cup (six ounces) of Carolina rice in good stock; then work it with 1–2 tablespoons of thick *Velouté sauce* (see SAUCE), 2–3 tablespoons of grated Parmesan cheese, and a little nutmeg.

'When this is well amalgamated, divide it into ten equal portions. With one of these portions, make a kind of cup in the hollow of the left hand with the thumb and the forefinger, in which you put a small spoonful of a fine salpicon (fowl, game, combined with reduced *velouté*), close in the edges of the little cup in such a way as to completely enclose the filling in the rice; after that, proceed in the same way for the rest of the rice. Roll in grated Parmesan (very fine), and then in the palm of the hand (to make the croquettes completely round).' (Carême's recipe).

Having made the croquettes in this way, dip them in egg and breadcrumbs mixed with very finely grated Parmesan cheese, and deep fat fry them. Arrange them on a napkin, and garnish with fried parsley.

La Varenne croquettes—Make some very large very thin crêpes with an unsweetened *crêpe batter**. Cover the crêpes with a layer of finely chopped mushrooms which have been cooked in butter and combined with a thick tomato sauce. Roll up the pancakes, cut each one into three or four slices, according to their length. Dip the slices in egg and breadcrumbs, and fry them at the last moment. Arrange them piled up on a napkin and garnish with fried parsley.

CROQUIGNOLLES PARISIENNES (Pâtisserie)—*Ingredients.* 4 cups (500 grams) flour; 4½ cups (600 grams) icing sugar; 10 whites of egg; flavouring to taste, vanilla, zest, various liqueurs.

Method. Mix half the egg whites with the icing sugar. Add the sifted flour then, mixing well, the rest of the egg whites.

Press the mixture through a forcing (pastry) bag on to a buttered baking sheet in various shapes; leave to dry out for a few hours. Cook in a moderate oven.

Note. In various regions of France, *croquignolles* are made in a way which differs slightly from those made in Paris. The best known ones are those of Navarre in the Basses-Pyrenées. These are made very much in the same way as those above, with the following ingredients: 1 pound (500 grams) sifted cake flour, 1 pound (500 grams) icing sugar, 7 whites of egg, 4 drops lemon essence (or powdered vanilla), 2 tablespoons brandy.

Follow the same method of combining the ingredients and the same way of cooking them as for *Croquignolles parisiennes.*

CROUSTADE (PIE, PASTY)—The word *croustade* denotes various dishes made, as a rule, with pastry (flaky pastry, or puff pastry) which are filled with ragoûts, with salpicons, or with other preparations.

Croustades are also made with bread which is hollowed out in order to receive some kind of filling. These are filled with the same types of filling as those mentioned above, after having been gilded in the oven or fried in deep fat.

Croustades are made both big and small. The small type are used as a hot hors d'oeuvre, or as a little entrée.

Both kinds of croustades can be filled with all the usual ragoûts and salpicons normally used for filling *tourtes* and vol-au-vent cases. They can also be filled with various vegetables, mixed with butter or combined with cream, and with various purées (meat, fowl, fish, crustaceans).

Bread croustade. CROUSTADE DE PAIN DE MIE—This is made with stale bread. Cut a thick slice 2–4 inches thick from a loaf. Trim this slice to give it the required shape (round, oval, square). Decorate the outside with knife-cuts. On the top cut it round with the point of the knife (to mark the lid).

Sandwich bread hollowed out to make a croustade

Croustade made from a hollowed-out bread roll

Fry the croustade in deep fat. Drain when it is golden. Remove the cover. Through this opening remove the crumb from the inside. Line the croustade with a thin layer of some kind of forcemeat. Dry this forcemeat by leaving the croustade for a moment at the opening of the oven.

Then fill the croustade with the required ragoût. Arrange on a napkin.

Fillings for bread croustades—All the fillings given elsewhere for *timbales** and *vol-au-vent** can be used to fill bread croustades.

Bread croustade filled with a sauté of poultry *en Bellevue* after Carême

Little butter croustades. PETITES CROUSTADES DE BEURRE—Shape a slab of butter into a square 1½ inches thick. Chill the butter on ice. When it is firm, cut it up with a pastry cutter dipped in hot water in rounds 1 inch in diameter.

Dip these rounds in egg and breadcrumbs twice over. Make a circular incision in the top of the croustade with a plain pastry cutting wheel. Fry in boiling oil.

Drain the croustades. Remove the lid; pour off the butter inside; fill the croustades with some kind of filling.

Little croustades (hot). PETITES CROUSTADES CHAUDES—Nowadays these croustades are made by lining round or oval tartlet moulds with *Sweet pastry dough* (see DOUGH; this is a short crust reinforced with an egg and a small quantity of sugar). These are then cooked blind (unfilled) and filled afterwards with the indicated filling. See HORS-D'OEUVRE, *Hot hors-d'oeuvre*.

The little croustades are used as a hot hors d'oeuvre or as a little entrée.

In the old days, these were made in dariole moulds. These croustades are also made with various compositions, for instance, rice, semolina, a preparation of *Duchess potato mixture* (see POTATOES), macaroni, noodles, etc.

Little duchess potato croustades. PETITES CROUSTADES EN POMMES DE TERRE DUCHESSE—Spread out the *Duchess potato mixture* (see POTATOES) on a baking sheet in an even layer 1½ inches thick. Leave to cool.

Cut it into *croustades* with a simple round pastry cutter. Dip them in egg and breadcrumbs and finish in the same way as described for *Little noodle croustades**. Fry them. Fill them in the same way.

Little noodle croustades. PETITES CROUSTADES DE NOUILLES—'Prepare a *noodle paste* with 12 egg yolks (see NOODLE). Having rolled out the paste and cut it into narrow strips in the usual way, put it into a pan of salted boiling water, a little at a time. After a few minutes' boiling, drain the noodles in a large colander and sauté them in a pan with ¼ pound (4 ounces) of butter and a little salt. Pour them out into a large sauté-pan and spread out the noodles to a depth of 2½ inches. These croustades may be made with commercially prepared noodles.

'When they are cold, turn them out onto a marble slab and cut your croustades with a simple round pastry cutter ¼ inch in diameter.

'The croustades, once cut, are dipped in egg and breadcrumbs. Mark the lid with a round pastry cutter, smaller than the size of the croustade, fry them in deep fat.

'Drain them; remove the lids; take out the centre leaving only a thin casing. Fill them with the indicated filling.' (Carême's recipe.)

These croustades can be filled with all the salpicons and other indicated preparations for *tartlets**, *croûtes**, *bouchées**, and other similar preparations.

Little rice croustades. PETITES CROUSTADES DE RIZ—These are made with rice cooked in bouillon, or simply boiled, allowed to cool, and cut into shape with a round pastry cutter, in the same way as *Little noodle croustades**.

Little semolina croustades. PETITES CROUSTADES DE SEMOULE—The same as *Little noodle croustades** with semolina cooked in stock, or plain boiled.

Note. Once the semolina has been cooked, it can be combined with egg yolks.

Little vermicelli croustades. PETITES CROUSTADES DE VERMICELLE—The same as *Little noodle croustades** with vermicelli cooked in stock, or plain boiled.

CROÛTES—Under this name various rather different preparations are designated, some made of bread, some of brioche dough, or other types of bread dough, and which are used either with soups or as an hors-d'oeuvre.

Croûtes made of bread are also used to garnish certain preparations. *Croûtes* made of bread and used as a garnish are more commonly called *croûtons*.

CROÛTES FOR SOUP:

Croûtes for croûte au pot—Divide a French load (*flûte*) into 2 inch slices. Cut each slice in half lengthwise. Remove the soft part. Dry the crusts in a slow oven, or, alternatively, arrange them on a dish, sprinkle them with the fat skimmed from the *pot-au-feu*, and gild them in the oven.

Diablotins. CROÛTES DITES DIABLOTINS—Divide a French loaf into slices 2½ to 3 inches thick. Cover the slices with a thick *Béchamel sauce* (see SAUCE) to which some grated cheese has been added, seasoned with a little cayenne. Arrange on a gratin dish, sprinkle with cheese. Brown in the oven. Serve separately.

Sliced croûtes en dentelle. CROÛTES ÉMINCÉES DITES EN DENTELLE—Cut a French loaf into thin slices. Dry the slices. Serve separately.

When French bread is not available, these can be made with ordinary bread, or with Viennese *baguettes*.

Stuffed croûtes for croûtes au pot or for garbure. CROÛTES FARCIES—Cut a loaf of French bread into slices 1½ inches thick. Take out three-quarters of the soft part. Dry the crusts in the oven. Stuff them with the vegetables from the *marmite*, either chopped or put through a sieve. Arrange them on a dish, sprinkle with grated cheese; pour over them some melted butter; brown in the oven. Serve as an accompaniment to the soup.

Note. The croûtes can also be made with very small round rolls which are emptied of crumb, dried, stuffed, sprinkled with cheese and butter, and browned in the oven.

CROÛTES FOR HORS-D'OEUVRE OR SMALL ENTRÉES—These are a kind of small *croustade** made with stale bread. With the help of a simple round cutter the croûtes are cut out of slices of bread about 1 inch thick. The cover of the croute is marked out by pressing a smaller circular cutter into the bread and cutting only half-way into it.

The croûtes are then fried; they are drained; the incised portion is removed, then they are filled with various fillings.

Croûtes with grated cheese. CROÛTES AU FROMAGE GRATINÉES—Cut some thick slices about ¾ inch thick from a stale loaf. Trim them into an oval shape. Fry these slices lightly in butter until they are golden. Cover them with a layer of *Béchamel sauce* (see SAUCE) to which some thick cream has been added and some grated cheese, the sauce being cooked down (reduced) to a thick consistency and passed through a sieve. Put on top of each a thin slice of Gruyère. Sprinkle with a few fine, dry breadcrumbs; pour over some melted butter. Brown in a hot oven. Serve at once.

Croûtes with mushrooms. CROÛTES AUX CHAMPIGNONS —Mushrooms prepared *à la crème* are used as a stuffing for brioche croutes in the form of a galette, large or small, which is hollowed out, buttered and gilded in the oven. (A galette is a kind of round open tart, made with puff pastry and various fillings, see GALETTE.)

For the preparation of *Mushrooms à la crème*, see MUSHROOMS.

As a rule these croûtes are made with cultivated mushrooms, but they can be made with all kinds of mushrooms such as cèpes, morels, chanterelles, etc. They are served hot.

Croûtes à la Nantua—Combine some *Béchamel sauce* (see SAUCE) with a little crayfish butter, and with this preparation cover some small slices of bread cut into rectangles and fried in butter. On this layer of sauce, put some peeled crayfish tails. Cover with a cream sauce to which some crayfish butter has been added. Sprinkle with fine breadcrumbs. Pour over some melted butter. Brown quickly in a very hot oven. Shrimps can be substituted for the crayfish.

Croûtes à la reine—Cover some slices of fried bread with a purée of fowl cooked *à la crème**. Sprinkle with white breadcrumbs. Pour over some melted butter. Brown in a hot oven.

Croûtes Saint-Hubert—The same as *Croûtes à la reine*, but replacing the purée of fowl with a game purée, which has been combined with a very concentrated game stock.

Croûtes with truffles I. CROÛTES GRATINÉES AUX TRUFFES—Cut in thick slices some cleaned and peeled truffles. Season with salt and pepper and dip for a few moments in melted butter.

Set these slices, overlapping one over the other, on square slices of bread that have been lightly cooked in butter. Sprinkle with grated Parmesan and pour over a few drops of melted butter. Put for a few moments under the salamander or in a very hot oven. Serve on a napkin or goffered paper.

Croûtes with truffles II. CROÛTES AUX TRUFFES—Made like *Croutes with mushrooms* with truffles prepared *à la crème*.

CROÛTES FOR DESSERTS.

Croûte dorée—This sweet was very popular in the old days, but is hardly ever made today, a matter for regret as it is excellent. It is made with stale brioche cut into slices ⅓ inch thick. These are soaked in cold sweetened milk flavoured with vanilla, which are then gilded in clarified butter, after soaking them in a mixture of slightly sweetened beaten egg.

The brioche slices cooked in this manner are arranged on a napkin and sprinkled with vanilla sugar. See also GOLDEN CROÛTES.

Fruit croûtes. CROÛTES AUX FRUITS—Cut a stale *savarin** into ⅛ inch slices. (The savarin should not have been soaked in syrup.) Put these slices on a baking sheet and sprinkle them with fine sugar. Glaze them in the oven.

Cut a piece of white loaf into a conical shape, fry it, and put it in the centre of a round dish. Arrange the savarin slices round the centre cone, alternating them with slices of pineapple cooked in syrup, and cut in the same shape as the savarin slices, in the form of a crown.

Arrange some quartered pear and apple slices, which have been cooked in syrup and well drained, alternately on top of the crown. Fill the inside of this border with a mixture of fruits which have been cooked in syrup and drained. Decorate the border with preserved cherries and lozenges of angelica, quartered preserved apricots, with oranges preserved in brandy (*chinois*), and almond halves. Stick a decorative skewer (*hâtelet*) decorated with various preserved fruits into the central cone.

Heat this confection in a very moderate oven, and at the moment of serving cover it with an *Apricot sauce* (see SAUCE) flavoured with kirsch, and serve some more of this sauce separately.

Croûtes garnished with other fruits are made in the same way. The principal element can be any fruit such as apricots, peaches, pears, nectarines, plums, etc., cooked in syrup.

Golden croûtes. PAINS À LA ROMAINE DITS AUSSI CROÛTES DORÉES—*Ingredients.* ½ pound (250 grams) of stale brioche, 1 pint (half a litre) of milk, 6 tablespoons (100 grams) of butter, ½ cup (125 grams) of fine sugar, half a vanilla bean, 2 eggs.

Method. Cut the brioche into somewhat thick uniform slices.

Put them to soak in milk, previously boiled with the sugar and vanilla and allowed to cool.

Dip the brioche slices one at a time in eggs beaten with a little fine sugar and fry in a pan in which some butter has been heated.

When both sides are nicely golden, drain the slices, arrange them on a dish and sprinkle with fine sugar.

Croûtes au madère—This is made of slices of savarin and pineapple, like the *Fruit croûte**. Fill the centre of the crown with a mixture of fruits cooked *en compote** and cut into rather large pieces, to which some Corinth, Smyrna and Malaga raisins have been added. These must be washed, their stalks removed, and allowed to swell in luke-warm water. Cover the croûte with an *Apricot sauce* (see SAUCE) flavoured with Madeira. Serve a little more of this sauce separately.

Croûte Montmorency—Cut a stale brioche into slices ½ inch thick in the shape of a half moon. Put the slices on a baking sheet, sprinkle them with sugar, and glaze them in the oven.

Cover each slice with a thin layer of *Frangipane pastry cream* (see CREAMS) flavoured with cherry brandy, and arrange them in the form of a crown, set very close together on a round dish.

Fill the centre of the crown with stoned cherries which have been cooked in a vanilla syrup and then drained. Arrange the cherries in the form of a dome. Decorate the top of the border with preserved cherries, angelica lozenges, and halved almonds. Cover with red currant jelly laced with cherry brandy, and serve a little of this sauce separately.

Croûtes à la normande—Arrange some slices of stale brioche, glazed with sugar, and covered with a thick purée of apple, prepared as for a *Charlotte** and finished with thick cream, in the form of a crown on a round dish.

Fill the centre of the crown with quartered apples cooked in a syrup flavoured with vanilla. Cover with apple sauce flavoured with Calvados. Serve a little of this sauce separately.

CROÛTES FOR MIXED ENTRÉES—These croûtes are made of pastry (see DOUGH) either fine or ordinary or with puff pastry leftovers, in the same way as for a *pastry case* (shell).

According to the nature of the dish, the cases are cooked blind (unfilled) or filled with whatever preparation is indicated in the recipe.

CROÛTON—End of a long loaf. Synonym for *quignon*.

Also bread cut into dice and fried in butter, served as an accompaniment to soup.

Bread Croûtons—These slices of bread used as a base for certain preparations are made in various forms. They are cut from a stale white loaf.

According to the nature of the objects which they are to accompany, croûtons are either fried in butter, grilled or simply dried in the oven.

Besides the little croûtons, hardly more than ¼ inch in thickness, supports are made in various forms and in different sizes, on which large *pièces* are arranged.

Except for the large croûtons used as a mount for game, and which, after having been gilded with butter or with fat from the joint, are stuffed, the greater part of these croûtons-supports are not considered edible. Their only rôle is to support large hot or cold joints in order to be able to display the various garnishes round them without concealment. All excessive trimmings should be avoided in these arrangements, which must be simple in order to be effective.

Croûtons for garnishes—These croûtons are made of white bread cut in different ways, as a rule in the form of hearts. They are cooked in oil or butter.

They are used to garnish various dishes which are presented in their sauce, such as *Blanquette de veau*, *Civet*, *Chicken fricasee*, *Chicken Marengo*, *Salmis*. The garnish of croutons in this last dish is usually covered with a *gratin forcemeat* (see FORCEMEAT).

Croûtons cut in the form of *dents de loup* (wolves' teeth) are used to garnish spinach and other vegetable purées; those cut into lozenge shapes are used for fish prepared *à la normande**.

Finally, those croûtons cut in the form of crests, which are also made of white bread fried in butter, are used to separate the groups of different articles in a complex garnish.

Croûtons for scrambled eggs or omelettes—These are made of white bread cut up into dice. They are fried in butter and added to scrambled eggs, once these are ready; they are also put into the omelette preparation when it is being beaten.

Besides the croûtons put into the scrambled eggs, this egg dish is also served with croûtons cut in *dent de loup* shapes (wolf's teeth) fried in butter.

CROW. CORBEAU—The meat of this bird, except when young, is too tough and fibrous to be considered as a food. Nevertheless, in many forest regions where crows abound, they are often eaten or at least, to be more correct, they are used to make a soup which is as a rule far from succulent. This soup can, however, be tasty if one takes care to follow the humorous advice of Cuniset-Carnot, in his interesting *Vie aux champs*. The recipe is simple. One has only to make, according to the sacred rites, an ordinary, good *pot-au-feu**. On the lid of the pot (the lid is reversed for the purpose) one puts a plucked crow. Then after 5 or 6 hours of gentle cooking one '..... throws the crow in the fire and enjoys the pot-au-feu .....'

We advise our readers, if the occasion occurs when they have to prepare crows—we must emphasise *very young crows*—to prepare them as the English do, that is to say in a pie.

CROWN. COURONNE—This word applies to a method of dressing a dish in the form of a crown. The word is, in culinary terms, synonymous with *turban** or ring. In French, *Brioche en couronne* denotes a type of dough cake made in this shape. See BRIOCHE.

CROWN-PIGEON (Squab). GOURA—Crown pigeon, known as *goura* or *pigeon couronné* is cooked in the same way as the common pigeon or squab.

CRU—The soil in which a plant or a fruit has grown. This is applied particularly to wine.

CRUCHADE—A kind of 'porridge' which is made with milk or water and with maize flour (corn meal).

This porridge has a great similarity to *miliasse* or *millat*, which is made in the south-west of France, and also to *polenta* which is made in the south-east, and in Italy. It is made particularly in the Bordeaux region. See MILIASSE.

CRUET STAND (U.S. Castor set). MÉNAGÈRE—A table set made up of glass bottles and jars sunk into a wooden or metal base with a central stem and handle.

CRUSH. ÉCRASER—To flatten and break aromatic seeds. or bread baked hard in the oven, into breadcrumbs, etc.

CRUSTACEANS. CRUSTACÉS—Animals with a hard, shelly crust and jointed extremities, generally aquatic, some species of which are used in cooking: crabs, crayfish, lobsters, langoustes, etc.

For the various dishes made with these different crustaceans, see the recipes given under their names.

Crustaceans have a very firm close-grained flesh, and an agreeable taste, but are not easy to digest; they enjoy a reputation as aphrodisiacs, due probably to the very strong condiments with which they are often flavoured.

Main types of edible shellfish: (1) Common oyster (huître); (2) Portuguese oyster; (3) and (4) Mussels (moules); (5) Clam; (6) and (7) Clovisse; (8) *Praire*; (9) and (10) Cockles (coques); (11) *Lavignon*; (12) *Vernis*; (13) *Fléon*; (14) Razor shell; (15) and (16) Scallops (Coquille Saint-Jacques); (17) *Amande-de-mer*; (18) *Dosinie exolète*; (19) *Ormer*; (20) Winkle; (21) Whelk; (22) Limpet

As far as their freshness is concerned, the same considerations apply as to fish.

The various crustaceans are described under their individual names.

Mussels à la marinière (*Mac Fisheries*)

CUCKOO. COUCOU—Bird which can be eaten. Prepared like thrushes.

CUCUMBER. CONCOMBRE—Genus of plants belonging to the gourd family, with large elongated fruits.

Cucumbers originated in the north-west of India where they grow in a wild state. They have been cultivated in Hindustan for three thousand years.

There are a large number of species, white or green, with smooth or rough skin, early or late fruiting, of various forms. This vegetable is very watery and contains very little nutritive value.

It is eaten cooked and, more often raw in salads; it contains a rather bitter juice which should be removed by salting and then pressing, before seasoning.

Cucumbers are preserved in brine, or they are allowed to ferment for a certain time.

Cucumbers in butter I. CONCOMBRES AU BEURRE—Peel the cucumbers; divide them in quarters; trim the quarters into chunks. Blanch and drain them.

Put them in a buttered sauté-pan; season, and cook gently, covered.

Cucumbers in butter II. CONCOMBRES ÉTUVÉS AU BEURRE—Divide a large cucumber into transverse slices. Cut each slice into 4 or 5 pieces according to their size, and trim them into a regular shape.

Put 3 tablespoons (50 grams) of butter, a pinch of salt and 3 tablespoons of water into a sauté-pan. Start cooking on a good heat, and then reduce the heat. Cover the pan and cook at a simmer for 45 minutes.

At the last moment add 2 tablespoons of butter and put the vegetable into a dish.

Cucumbers à la crème. CONCOMBRES À LA CRÈME—Prepare the cucumbers in the same way as for *Cucumbers with butter*. When they are three-quarters cooked, cover them with boiling cream. Finish cooking in the cream.

Cucumbers à la crème can also be prepared by moistening them when almost cooked with a *Cream sauce* (see SAUCE).

Cucumbers à la dijonnaise (Hors d'oeuvre). CONCOMBRES À LA DIJONNAISE—Cut two green cucumbers into regular slices, divide the slices into quarters, and trim them into a regular shape. Put them in boiling water which has been salted with a few drops of wine vinegar added, and boil for 2 minutes.

Drain them and put them in a colander under a cold tap. Then simmer them for 12 minutes in a small casserole with 2 tablespoons of olive oil, a tablespoon of vinegar, a pinch of salt and a pinch of paprika; at the last moment add 2 spoonfuls of *Dijon mustard;* mix well and turn out into a dish; keep in a cool place.

Cucumbers au gratin. CONCOMBRES GRATINÉS AU PARMESAN—Trim the cucumbers into even slices. Blanch them lightly, and stew them in butter.

Arrange them in a buttered gratin dish sprinkled with grated Parmesan. Sprinkle with more grated Parmesan; pour over some melted butter. Brown in the oven.

Cucumbers à la grecque (Hors d'oeuvre). CONCOMBRES À LA GRECQUE—Divide a large cucumber in quarters and trim each quarter into a regular shape. Put them into a court-bouillon made with $1\frac{1}{2}$ cups (3 decilitres) of water, $\frac{1}{2}$ cup (1 decilitre) of oil, the juice of a lemon, a *bouquet* of celery, fennel, thyme, bay, a strong pinch of coriander, salt and pepper.

Boil for 8 minutes. Drain the cucumbers, put them in a little dish. Pour the liquor in which they have been cooked, boiled down (reduced) by half and cooled, over them. Keep in a cool place, and serve very cold.

Cucumbers au jus. CONCOMBRES AU JUS—Prepared in the same way as *Cucumbers with butter*, with the addition at the end of the cooking time of a few tablespoons of very concentrated veal gravy.

Cucumbers Mornay. CONCOMBRES MORNAY—Prepare the cucumbers in the same way as *Cucumbers with butter**. Put them in a gratin dish covered with *Mornay sauce* (see

SAUCE). Pour some more sauce over them. Sprinkle with grated cheese; pour over some melted butter. Brown in the oven.

Cucumber purée. PURÉE DE CONCOMBRES—Peel two large cucumbers; split them lengthways and remove the seeds; cut into slices; simmer the slices in butter; add half their quantity of potatoes cut in quarters. Moisten with consommé or water, season, boil till soft, and drain. Sieve cucumbers and potatoes; put the purée in a pan over heat; add a few teaspoons of butter and thick fresh cream and work the mixture till smooth.

Cucumber salad. SALADE DE CONCOMBRES—Peel the cucumbers; split them in half lengthwise; remove the seeds; slice them finely.

Spread the cucumber slices on a cloth; sprinkle them with fine salt; leave them for 30 minutes; drain them; season with oil, vinegar, salt and pepper and chopped chervil. Arrange in a salad bowl or in an hors-d'oeuvre dish.

Green cucumbers are normally prepared in this way. These can be seasoned with a vinaigrette sauce without first being salted.

Stuffed cucumbers. CONCOMBRES FARCIS—Cut twelve slices $1\frac{3}{4}$ inches thick from cucumbers of medium size; peel them, put them in a casserole containing boiling salted water and boil for 5 minutes. After this, drain the pieces, and scoop out a hollow in each to hold the stuffing.

Mix two good tablespoons of *Duxelles** with $\frac{1}{2}$ pound (250 grams) of veal forcemeat (see FORCEMEAT) or failing this, pork forcemeat and add a tablespoon of chopped parsley, 4 tablespoons (60 grams) of chopped onion which has been cooked in butter and cooled. With the aid of a spoon or a forcing (pastry) bag fill the cucumbers with the stuffing.

Line the bottom of a sauté-pan with pork skins or bacon rinds, slices of carrot and onion and a *bouquet garni**. Set the cucumbers side by side on this foundation. Add enough stock (only slightly salted) to reach two thirds up the sides of the cucumbers; bring to the boil. Put a sheet of buttered paper over the cucumbers, cover the pan and cook gently in the oven for 35 minutes.

Put the cucumbers on a dish; strain the cooking liquor and boil down rapidly to 1 cup (2 decilitres); thicken slightly with a brown sauce or with *Kneaded butter* (see BUTTER) and pour over the cucumbers.

CUIRE VERT—This is a colourful expression indicating the point to which certain pieces of butchers' meat must be cooked in order that they are very underdone (*très saignantes*).

The expression *cuire bleu* is also used.

CUISSON—This term has several meanings in French. They are: (1) The cooking of any kind of food; (2) Cooking-time; (3) Liquid used in the cooking of certain foodstuffs; *cuisson* of mushrooms, *cuisson* of calves' head. In such cases, *cuisson* really means stock or clear soup.

CUISSOT—See HAUNCH.

CULINARY ART. ART CULINAIRE—'Cookery is an old art', said the Marquis de Cussy, 'as it goes back to Adam'.

All authors agree that the culinary art came to us from the Orient, the cradle of civilisation.

The culinary art is closely bound with the general history of man. 'Does not this art,' asks Brillat-Savarin, 'in fact embrace all the branches of human activity; is not the art of feeding oneself one of the primordial needs of man?'

The same author, with a view to demonstrating the usefulness for those who practise cookery, of knowing all the resources of their art, tells the following story.

'The Prince de Soubise planned to give a party one day which was to have ended with a supper, and he demanded a menu for it.

'His major-domo presented himself at the levée with a beautiful card, decorated with vignettes and the first entry on which the prince's eye fell was: "Fifty hams".

' "Really, Bertrand!" said he, "I think you exaggerate: fifty hams! Are you proposing to regale the whole of my regiment?"

' "No, my Prince, only one ham will appear on the table, but I need all the rest for my *sauce espagnole*, for my stocks, for my garnishes . . . "

' "Bertrand, you are robbing me, and this is not to be allowed."

' "Ah! Monseigneur," replied the artist, hardly able to control his feelings, "you do not know my resourcefulness! Order them, and I shall reduce these fifty hams, which obscure your judgment, until they can go into a crystal flagon not bigger than my thumb."

'What can one answer to such an assertion? The Prince smiled, bowed his head and the order was approved.'

Of course, the imagination of a real artist of *cuisine* is infinite, and he can, when he knows his job through and through, do magnificent things, but the example quoted by Brillat-Savarin does not perhaps really show how great are the resources of cookery.

For a short history of cookery, see the entry on COOKING.

CULINARY METHODS—All culinary operations, from the simplest to the most complicated, must be carried out according to precise rules. These rules together constitute what are nowadays called the principles of cookery. It is advisable to adhere scrupulously to these principles in order to achieve success in the preparation of simple as well as complex dishes.

The culinary rules governing the different methods of cooking foodstuffs are listed below in alphabetical order.

Braising of meat. BRAISAGE DE VIANDES—This method of cooking meat is chiefly used for red meats, such as beef and mutton, but can also be used for white meats, such as lamb and veal.

It can also be used, by slightly modifying the procedure, for pork and venison.

Large poultry is also braised, and the method may be used with large fish, though in this case the fish is really stewed with a very little liquid rather than braised in the strict sense of the word.

Red meat, before being braised, should first be interlarded, that is to say it must have thick lardoons seasoned with spices, moistened with brandy and often sprinkled with chopped parsley, inserted into it, using a larding needle.

Generally speaking, large cuts of butchers' meat (and also large cuts of venison) are steeped in a marinade for a time before braising. See MARINADE.

Large cuts of meat for braising are moistened with a braising stock prepared in advance. It goes without saying that in household kitchens, a different procedure may be adopted. The meat can be moistened either from the stockpot or even with water, though it must be admitted that braising cuts moistened with water are less tasty. In any case, it is always advisable to add to the stock (of whatever kind) white or red wine, the marinade and the aromatic vegetables of the marinade.

Instructions for braising large cuts of butcher's meat are given under BEEF.

Garnishes for braised butcher's meat—More often than not, the meat is braised *à la bourgeoise*, and consequently has such vegetables as carrots and onions added to it towards the end of the cooking. Braised cuts can also be served with various additional garnishes, such as vegetables braised in gravy, stuffed vegetables, macaroni prepared in different ways, risotto, etc.

Braising of white meat—Strictly speaking, cuts of white meat, veal in particular, should be *pot-roasted* rather than *braised*. Nevertheless, cuts of white meat can be braised in the same way as red meat, but using very little stock. See POT-ROASTING below.

Braising of large poultry—As in the case of white meat, large poultry is usually pot-roasted rather than braised. In any case, if it is braised it is advisable to use very little stock in the cooking.

Clarifying and enriching soups, stocks and jellies. CLARIFICATION DES BOUILLONS, FONDS ET GELÉES—The purpose of this operation is to make soups, stocks and jellies at once more limpid and tastier. This applies to sweet jellies as well as to fish and meat stocks.

After clarification and subsequent enriching with a given quantity of chopped lean beef and white of egg, the soup is known as *consommé*. $\frac{1}{2}$ to $\frac{3}{4}$ pound (250 to 350 grams) of chopped lean beef are required for every quart (litre) of soup (also known as plain *consommé*) to ensure adequate clarification. For jelly stocks, which are very concentrated in themselves, about $\frac{1}{4}$ pound (100 to 150 grams) per quart (litre) is required. See JELLY.

Where appropriate, chopped poultry may be used instead of chopped beef. A small quantity of white of egg and aromatic ingredients in the form of finely diced vegetables must always be used.

In clarifying sweet jellies (made with fruit, wine or liqueur) white of egg only is used. See JELLY, *Fruit jelly*.

Clarified *consommé* and jellies of various kinds must be strained after boiling (the time varies with the type of jelly). The old method in France is as follows:

Wet a cloth of some closely woven material and wring it out. Fix it to the four legs of an upturned wooden stool. Under this cloth, place a bowl or pan large enough to take the whole of the stock. Skim all fat off the stock and pour it into the well of this improvised strainer. This method is especially suitable for straining large quantities of liquid. For smaller amounts, wet and wring out the cloth, lay it on top of a pan or bowl, and lift up the corners.

Deep-frying. FRITURE—A detailed study of the theory and practice of deep-frying is to be found in the section devoted to this subject. See DEEP-FRYING. This method of cooking foodstuffs is used a great deal in the kitchen, and fried foods, well prepared, are always much prized by gastronomes.

Gratins—This is the name given to dishes which, after having been subjected to intense heat in the oven or under the grill, acquire a crisp golden-brown crust.

To assist in the formation of this crust, sprinkle the food either with fresh or lightly toasted breadcrumbs or with grated cheese, Parmesan in particular, and pour on melted butter.

Food to be served *au gratin* may or may not be blended with white or brown, meat or meatless, sauces.

Gratins can be made with either *raw* or *cooked* food. The most common raw gratins are made of fish covered with *Duxelles sauce*. (See SAUCE). Instructions for this method of cooking are to be found under *Sole au gratin*.

A recipe for cooking raw vegetables *au gratin* is given under *Potatoes à la dauphinoise*. See POTATOES.

Fish prepared with a white gratin sauce are usually poached in concentrated fish stock, drained, covered with a meatless white sauce, sprinkled with cheese (or breadcrumbs) and browned very quickly.

When browning a *gratin*, the dish should always be set on a wire tray separating it from the oven shelf, or in a dish half full of hot water. This prevents the sauce from spoiling and the fats from separating out.

Grilling (U.S. Broiling). GRILLADE—Grilling, like roasting, is a method of cooking by intense heat. By this method, all the nourishing juices are sealed into the meat by the crust formed on the surface.

The importance of this browned crust depends on the size and nature of the cut. The sealing of the exposed parts necessary for the successful grilling of red meat must not, however, be carried to excess so that the outside is actually charred.

The source of heat must be carefully regulated so as to obtain a more or less intense heat according to requirements.

The fuel traditionally used for grilling in France is small charcoal (known as *braise*).

The charcoal, when it is thoroughly alight, must be spread out to form a 'bed' in a grill-pan with a well-regulated draught. This bed of charcoal must vary in depth according to the size and nature of the meat to be grilled.

Both gas and electric grills are extremely practical. Whatever grill is used, it must be scrupulously clean, and must be heated before the meat is laid upon it or under it for cooking.

The desired heat having been attained, the food to be grilled must be basted with clarified or purified butter, oil or fat, and seasoned. Meat, whether red or white, must always be gently flattened and trimmed before cooking. Fish, whether large or small, must be scored with a knife, well coated with oil or butter, and seasoned.

Fish which is rather dry has a tendency to stick to the bars of the grill and should therefore be floured before being coated with butter or oil. This will form a covering inside which the fish will cook without becoming too dry.

Grilling food should be turned over with a palate knife once or twice during cooking, and frequently basted with butter, oil or fat. A fork or other sharp implement should never be used for turning. The easiest way of basting during cooking is to use a brush.

The grilled food is ready when, if lightly touched with the fingertip, it resists pressure. Tiny pinkish droplets appearing on the browned surface are another indication that it is fully cooked.

As a general rule, grilled white meat should be less browned than red meat. A less intense heat should be used and, as in the case of roast white meat, the browning and cooking should take place simultaneously.

The grilling of fish should be carried out at moderate heat, and the fish should be basted frequently.

Often, tiny pieces of meat or fish for grilling are dipped in fresh breadcrumbs before being placed on the grill. These must first be coated with oil or melted butter and then rolled in the breadcrumbs. To ensure that the pieces of meat or fish are well coated with breadcrumbs, they should be pressed down with the flat of a knife.

With poultry or other larger pieces to be grilled in breadcrumbs, the pieces should first be grilled or roasted plain and then, when three parts cooked, covered with breadcrumbs as indicated for *Chicken à la diable* (devilled). See CHICKEN.

Interlarding meat. PIQUAGE DES VIANDES—Certain cuts of meat, such as fillet of beef, leg of veal, etc., are interlarded with best pork fat cut into small neat lardoons. In the same way poultry, veal sweetbreads, veal chops and, less commonly, large fish such as carp, sturgeon, etc., are interlarded with very small lardoons.

To interlard a fillet of beef: First trim the meat, that is to say, skin it and remove all tendons. Next, using a larding needle threaded with a lardoon, thread it into the fillet, following the grain of the meat. The depth of the stitch is determined by the length of the lardoon. Each lardoon must project ¾ inch on either side.

Having thus made a first transverse row with the lardoons, thread the second row of lardoons through the meat, alternating them with the first, also at a distance of ¾ inch from each other. Make sure that the lardoons always project over the meat by the same length. Keeping the spacing even, thread as many double rows of lardoons into the meat as its length requires. It should be noted that, where the meat is narrower, fewer lardoons are required.

Finally, the fillet being completely interlarded, trim the lardoons so that the ends are of equal length. Tie the fillet crosswise to keep it round in shape. Put it on a spit or, if it is to be roasted in the oven, in a roasting tin fitted with a grid.

To interlard a fricandeau or leg of veal: Trim the joint as indicated in the appropriate section under VEAL. Next, interlard as indicated for fillet of beef.

To interlard saddles of mutton, roebuck, baron of hare, haunch of venison, etc.: Proceed as indicated above, adapting the thickness of the lardoons to the size of the meat, and leaving more or less space between the rows according to the size of the cut.

Interlarding of small cuts of meat, veal sweetbreads, etc.: Interlard with best lardoons, chops, escalopes, *grenadins* and medallions of veal for braising. These lardoons must be cut very fine and the needle used must be proportionately small.

Small round portions of meat may be interlarded by threading the lardoons into them in the form of a rosette. This method can also be used with beef and mutton *filets mignons*. Veal sweetbreads can be interlarded so that the lardoons form a rosette, or with alternate rows of lardoons as for fillet of beef. Veal sweetbreads, before interlarding, must be soaked in water, blanched, cooled under running water, and left to get quite cold under a weight.

Interlarding of poultry and game: Only large poultry for braising is interlarded. To make this operation easier, singe with a rather hot flame the part of the breast to be interlarded, or dip it in boiling water to make the flesh more firm.

Only old game for braising, such as partridge, pheasant or hazel-grouse, is interlarded. Proceed as for poultry, using very small lardoons.

Poaching. POCHAGE—This method of cooking can be used with an infinite variety of foodstuffs. Red and white meat, poultry and fish can all be poached, as well as eggs, fish and meat balls, *mousses* and *mousselines*. The latter are poached in a double saucepan. Sweetbreads are poached in a very little stock.

Poaching is a very gentle simmering in liquid. The amount of water or stock used depends on the food to be poached. Red meat is poached in a white stock with vegetables or, as is customary with *Leg of lamb à l'anglaise*, (see LAMB), in boiling salt water.

White butcher's meat is seldom poached. On the other hand, the term 'poaching' may fairly be applied to the method of cooking used in preparing lamb and veal *en blanquette**.

Large poultry to be poached is put into cold white stock. The liquid is brought to the boil, skimmed, seasoned as with *pot-au-feu**. Thereafter the poultry must simmer very gently in the stock.

According to the recipe chosen, poultry for poaching can be either stuffed or plain, trussed as for an entrée. Depending on the manner in which it is finally to be served, it can be larded with best lardoons or studded with pieces of ham, tongue or truffles cut into the shape of little pegs.

To protect the breast during cooking, poultry should be barded. To test whether or not the poultry is ready, prick the thigh. When the juice exuded is white or barely tinged with pink, the bird is cooked.

After cooking, poultry is drained and untrussed. The barding is removed at the same time. It should be served on a large dish on fried bread, or some other foundation, depending on the type of bird, and surrounded with an appropriate garnish.

The stock, strained and skimmed of fat, is finished as indicated in the recipe used, or boiled down and added to the sauce to be served with the dish.

Large fish poached whole or in slices is cooked in much the same way as braised fish, The only difference is that poached fish is now browned after cooking; it is moistened with very concentrated fish stock (*fumet*)*.

Thick slices of fish are prepared in the same way. Poached fillets of fish (brill, whiting, sole, turbot, etc.) must be put in a buttered baking dish, seasoned, moistened with a few tablespoons of very concentrated fish stock (*fumet**) and cooked in the oven.

Poached eggs must be cooked in boiling salt water to which a few drops of vinegar have been added.

Fish or meat balls, shaped with a spoon or piped, must be put into a buttered pan, covered with boiling salt water and simmered very slowly.

Food poached on the double-saucepan principle, such as *mousses*, *mousselines*, moulds, puddings, etc., must be stood in baking tins or pans half full of hot water and cooked in a very slow oven.

Pot-roasting. POÊLAGE—This is a method of slow-cooking by steam. A casserole with a tightly fitting lid is used. The food is cooked in butter or fat and flavoured with vegetables which have been cooked slowly in butter until very tender.

Pot-roasted meat, poultry or fish must be basted frequently during cooking. When it is ready, take it out of the casserole. Serve on a dish or, where appropriate, in a *cocotte** dish. Remove most of the cooking fat.

Swill the casserole with wine or stock as indicated in the recipe. Boil for a few seconds. Strain and pour the stock over the dish.

Pot-roasting à la Matignon: Brown lightly in butter the meat or fish to be pot-roasted. Cover with a thick layer of *matignon* or *fondue** of root vegetables. (See MATIGNON.) Wrap in buttered (grease-proof) paper and cook in the oven in a braising pan, or on the spit. After cooking, unwrap, place on a dish, surround with appropriate garnishes and pour on the stock to which the *matignon* has been added before straining.

Braising à la matignon can also be carried out by lining the braising pan with the *fondue* of root vegetables and placing the meat, fish or poultry (which should be liberally basted with butter) on top.

Ragoûts—Although food *en ragoût* is always *stewed*, a *ragoût* is somewhat different from a stew. The French equivalent of our stew is a *ragoût à blanc* or *à l'anglaise*.

All details and recipes for the preparation of *ragoût* dishes are to be found under RAGOÛT.

Roasting. RÔTISSAGE—The process described as roasting can be used in the cooking of meat, poultry, game, as well as large fish and shell-fish.

The distinctive feature of this form of cooking by concentration is that the internal juices are preserved. This preservation is assured by carefully controlled cooking, which consists of adapting the intensity of the cooking heat to the nature and size of the food.

In his *Principes et lois culinaires* Reculet thus defines the roasting process:

'Cooking by concentration works by means of transmission and not, as is the case with boiling, by means of insinuation. The concentrating agent, whether ponderable or imponderable, attacks and envelopes the substance subjected to its action. The first coating is heated, the juices are driven inwards towards the centre, and the crust forms on the surface. The heat of the first coating is transmitted to the second and so on. The juices sealed in by the outer coating, being unable to escape from the tissues generate heat themselves and contribute powerfully to the cooking of the whole.'

There are two ways of roasting: (1) by the action of a naked flame, that is to say on the spit; (2) by radiant heat, that is to say in the oven.

There is no question but that spit roasts are superior to oven roasts. This is due to the free evaporation of substances placed before an open fire, as opposed to those cooked in an enclosed oven which are enveloped and radically altered by the vapour produced.

But modern equipment, at least in kitchens of average size, seldom includes an open wood or even coal fire. Almost everywhere, roasts are cooked in coal, gas or electric ovens. These, however, being extremely well designed, produce the very best results in the preparation of dishes of all kinds, and they do sometimes incorporate an automatic spit.

Roasting in the oven. RÔTIS AU FOUR—The intensity of the cooking heat must be regulated to suit the roast, as for spit-roasting.

Roasts which are to be underdone must be put in a very hot oven to seal them thoroughly. When the crust is formed the heat must be lowered. With a solid fuel cooker, the roast should be moved to a cooler part of the oven and the roasting pan stood in another pan if necessary. It is absolutely essential for oven roasts to be raised above the bottom of the roasting pan on a grid. In France roasting pans are almost always fitted with such grids.

Basting of oven roasts should be carried out as for spit roasts.

The exact moment when the roast is ready can be recognised simply by touch and, in this regard, only practice makes perfect.

It does not take long to acquire the knack of knowing when the roast is ready. If in doubt, however, follow the instructions in the section on *cooking-time for roasts*, and look for the following indications.

When red butcher's meat (beef and mutton) is perfectly cooked, a small prick will make it exude drops of pale pink blood.

In the case of white meat (veal, lamb, pork) the juice exuded must be colourless.

Poultry is perfectly cooked when, if tilted on a plate, pure white juice pours out of the body. As long as there are any reddish traces, the poultry is not fully cooked.

Winged and ground game should, as a rule, always exude a pinkish juice. It should be tested in the same way as red meat.

Poultry and game should be trussed, barded or, if required by the recipe, interlarded with best lardoons.

The purpose of barding with pork fat (or fat bacon) is to protect the delicate parts of the breast from the intensity of the heat and also to impregnate the flesh with fat to make it more tender.

Barding is done by tying the fat to the bird with two or three lengths of string.

After cooking, the fat is removed, though, in the case of some winged game, it is served on the bird.

Large cuts of meat are also sometimes barded. More often, however, the delicate parts of these cuts are protected with well-flattened pieces of beef or veal fat.

Strictly, roasts should be served as soon as they are removed from the spit or the oven. For red meat, however, it is advisable to take it out of the oven or off the spit a few moments before it is quite ready and to keep it hot in front of an open oven until it is to be served. While it is standing the meat seems to settle in some way so that it becomes easier to carve.

Spit roasting. RÔTIS À LA BROCHE—Whatever fuel is used, wood, coal, coke, etc., the intensity of heat must always depend upon the nature of the food to be cooked. Thus, red meat, very rich in juices, must first be browned and then subjected to an even heat to ensure that the meat is cooked right through.

Anthracite, which gives an intense heat without producing flames, is very suitable for the cooking of red meat.

For white meat, the heat must be adjusted so that the external browning and internal cooking (which must be complete) take place simultaneously.

The same principles apply to the roasting of poultry.

Spit-roasted food must be basted frequently. Contrary to a practice which is all too common, this basting should be done with the fat floating on the top of the liquid in the dripping pan and not with the gravy itself. Basting with pure fat produces a tender, well-browned roast, whereas basting with gravy, even hot gravy, prevents the roast from browning.

Gravy of the roast. JUS DE RÔTIS—In household cookery it is absolutely essential to extract all the goodness in the roasting or dripping pan by immediate dilution and boiling.

So that the gravy should retain the full flavour of the roast, water or very clear stock should be used.

In this way, the gravy obtained is pure in flavour and pleasanter than gravies made from stocks.

The gravy of a roast should not be completely skimmed of fat. Sauceboats can be obtained made in such a way as to enable the guests to take their gravy with or without fat according to taste.

By the above method only a small amount of gravy is obtained, but this is sufficient to go with the roast. One large tablespoon for each guest is ample.

The serving of roasts—This is not at all complicated. The roast, if it is a joint or a bird, is simply laid on a very hot dish and garnished, if desired, with very fresh watercress which must first be picked over, washed and thoroughly drained.

The gravy must always be served separately, but just before serving the cooking fat may be poured over the roast. In some parts of northern and eastern France, a thick purée of apples and stewed fruit is often served with roasts. These *compotes** and purées should be only very slightly sweetened.

Winged game (other than wild duck, pintail and teal), must be served on canapés (or slices of bread) of various sizes, fried in butter and spread with *à gratin* forcemeat. See FORCEMEAT.

Game birds are generally garnished with watercress and lemons, halved or quartered. In the case of wild duck, teal, pintail and other wildfowl, orange is sometimes served instead of lemon.

In England, roast winged game is often garnished with potato crisps. (See POTATOES.) Bread sauce and fried breadcrumbs are also served in addition to the gravy. See SAUCE.

With roast venison and small ground game, redcurrant jelly and chestnut purée are often served.

Winged game is no longer served *en volière*, that is to say dressed in its own feathers which have been specially treated for the purpose. This practice was in favour in former times.

Average cooking time for roasts (home cooking)—

Beef.

Sirloin: 10 to 12 minutes per pound.

Sirloin roast à l'anglaise: 15 to 18 minutes per pound.

Contre-filet or faux filet: Boned, from 10 to 12 minutes per pound. On the bone, from 14 to 16 minutes per pound.

Rib: in the oven: 15 to 18 minutes per pound; *on the spit:* 18 minutes, but as soon as the meat is taken off the spit it must be put in a warm oven for 30 minutes or longer, according to size. Under this very moderate heat, the cooking is completed without sizzling and the rib retains all its internal juices.

Faux filet: See *Contre-filet*.

Fillet: in the oven: 12 to 15 minutes per pound *on the spit:* 15 to 18 minutes.

Mutton.

Baron: 15 to 18 minutes per pound (preferably in the oven).

Breast: 18 to 25 minutes per pound.

Shoulder: 18 to 20 minutes per pound.

Leg: 20 to 25 minutes per pound.

Saddle: 15 to 18 minutes per pound.

Veal.

Breast: 30 minutes per pound.

Top loin or fillet: 35 minutes per pound.

Lengthwise cut of chump end (*U.S. Tenderloin*) 35 minutes per pound.

Lamb.

For cooking roasts of lamb proceed as indicated for cuts of mutton.

Pork.

Breast: 25 to 30 minutes per pound.

Fillet: 30 to 35 minutes per pound.

Roast Nantes duckling

Poultry.

Nantes Duckling: A bird of average size, about 2 pounds in weight: roast quickly, 35 to 40 minutes *on the spit;* 30 to 35 minutes *in the oven.*

Rouen Duckling: A bird of average size, roast very quickly, 18 to 25 minutes.

Large Turkey: (9–15 pounds); 25 minutes per pound.

Very Large Turkey: (15–30 pounds); 15 to 20 minutes per pound.

Small Turkey: (3 pounds); 45 to 50 minutes per pound.

Goose: 25 to 35 minutes per pound *on the spit;* 25 to 30 minutes per pound *in the oven.*

Pigeon: 20 to 25 minutes *on the spit;* 18 to 20 minutes *in the oven.*

Guinea-fowl: 20 to 25 minutes per pound *on the spit;* 18 to 20 minutes per pound *in the oven.*

Chicken: (3–4 pounds); 60 minutes *on the spit;* 45 to 60 minutes *in the oven.*

Cockerel: (2–2½ pounds) 30 to 35 minutes *on the spit;* 25 to 30 minutes *in the oven.*

Spring Chicken: 15 to 20 minutes per pound *on the spit;* 12 to 15 minutes per pound *in the oven.*

Winged Game.

Woodcock: 18 to 20 minutes *on the spit;* 15 to 18 minutes per pound *in the oven.*

Snipe: 9 to 12 minutes *on the spit;* 9 to 10 minutes per pound *in the oven.*

Pipit, also called *garden warbler:* 8 to 10 minutes.

Quail: 12 to 15 minutes *on the spit;* 10 to 12 minutes per pound *in the oven.*

Wild Duck; 18 to 20 minutes *on the spit;* 20 to 30 minutes *in the oven.*

Woodgrouse; 25 to 30 minutes *on the spit;* 20 to 25 minutes *in the oven.*

Pheasant: 30 to 35 minutes *on the spit;* 25 to 30 minutes *in the oven.*

Hazel-grouse; 20 to 25 minutes *on the spit;* 15 to 18 minutes *in the oven.*

Thrush; 12 to 15 minutes *on the spit:* 10 to 12 minutes *in the oven.*

Grouse: Proceed as for *hazel-grouse.*

Lark: Proceed as for *pipit.*

Blackbird: Proceed as for *thrush.*

Bunting: 6 to 8 minutes.

Partridge: 20 to 22 minutes *on the spit;* 18 to 20 minutes *in the oven.*

Pintail: 18 to 20 minutes *on the spit;* 15 to 18 minutes *in the oven.*

Plover: 15 to 18 minutes *on the spit;* 12 to 15 minutes *in the oven.*

Teal: 15 to 18 minutes *on the spit;* 12 to 15 minutes *in the oven.*

Lapwing: Proceed as for *plover.*

Ground game and venison.

Haunch of roebuck: 15 to 20 minutes per pound *on the spit;* 12 to 15 minutes per pound *in the oven.*

Saddle of roebuck: 15 to 20 minutes per pound *on the spit;* 12 to 15 minutes per pound *in the oven.*

Young rabbit: 25 to 30 minutes *on the spit;* 18 to 20 minutes *in the oven.*

Baron of hare: 20 to 22 minutes per pound *on the spit;* 18 to 20 minutes per pound *in the oven.*

Young wild boar (*breast or saddle*)*:* 20 to 25 minutes per pound *on the spit;* 18 to 20 minutes per pound *in the oven.*

Sauté—This method of cooking is generally used for small pieces of food only. A wide, shallow frying pan is used so that the food may cook fairly quickly. In France these frying pans are called *sautoirs*, *plats à sauter* or *sauteuses.*

The cooking is done in fat, butter or oil, which is first heated in the pan. The food is seasoned and, when the butter or fat is *thoroughly heated* and not before, laid flat in the pan so that it is thoroughly sealed.

Small cuts of meat treated in this way are:

Red meat: Rump and fillet steaks, medallions and *tournedos* (beef), cutlets and *noisettes* (mutton).

White meat: Veal chops and escalopes or veal Sweetbreads; cutlets or *noisettes* of lamb.

Red meat must be sautéed as quickly as possible in clarified butter.

White meat can be sautéed in fresh butter and, after sealing, may cook more slowly. But in all cases these cuts must be sautéed on the stove with the pan uncovered.

Sautéed poultry (cockerels, chickens of medium size, pigeons, etc.) are always jointed. The same principles apply as in the case of white meat.

On the other hand, when dealing with rather large poultry, the pieces may, when they are well browned on both sides, be left to cook further with the pan covered and left to cook on the stove.

Serving. Sauté dishes, butcher's meat or poultry, must be taken out of the pan and served as indicated in the selected recipe. According to the meat or poultry used, the dishes are arranged with pieces of fried bread cut into suitable shapes. After garnishing, the cooking stock, diluted with red or white wine or white or brown stock (thickened or clear), or with cream or some other suitable liquid, is poured over the dish.

Mixed sautés—This name is given to various *ragoûts** whose gravy is not thickened with flour. Generally these *ragoûts*, made up mostly of small pieces of boned lamb, beef, mutton or veal, are fried in butter, fat or oil.

Thereafter they are cooked in their own stock, diluted with various liquids, as in the case of ordinary *ragoûts*.

Various garnishes are served with these 'sautés'. They are presented in deep round dishes.

CUMIN—A plant whose seeds, long and spindle-shaped, dull yellow or light brown in colour, are five-sided, smooth or covered with tiny hairs, which makes it possible to distinguish them from other seeds with which they are sometimes adulterated.

They are acrid and spicy in taste.

Cumin is used for seasoning and in the preparation of liqueurs. Bread is also made with cumin seeds.

Wild cumin is sometimes used, especially in certain cheeses, such as Münster cheese.

CUP. Tasse—Receptacle made of china or metal in various shapes, provided with a handle of one kind or another. Ranging from the smallest to the largest, we have the coffee cup, the tea cup and the breakfast cup.

CUP-BEARER. Échanson—An official charged with the duty of pouring wine for a king or other great personage.

The title of *Senior Cup-Bearer* or *Butler of France* was a purely honorific one under Louis XIV. This officer had no duties though there were 24 gentlemen under his command, serving *par quartiers*, at a salary of 700 livres.

The armorial bearing of this office showed 2 silver-gilt bottles engraved with the arms of the king, supporting the arms of the holder of the office.

The functions of this Grand-Officer fell gradually into disuse, until finally they were exercised only at coronations, ceremonial feasts, at Communion Supper on Maundy Thursday, etc. The office itself was sometimes left vacant. The last Butler of France under the old monarchy was the Marquis de Lamermary, appointed to this post in 1702.

CURAÇAO—A liqueur made from the rind of Seville oranges and brandy or gin.

CURCUMA—An Indian plant whose yellowish rhizome has an acrid and bitter flavour and smells of saffron and ginger. Powdered, the rhizome is used in curry powder and English mustard.

CURD. Caillé—Precipitate or coagulum which is formed in milk subjected to the action of rennet or acidified by lactic ferments.

It is a result of the precipitation of casein and contains varying proportions of butter, depending on whether or not the milk has previously been skimmed.

When curd is obtained by the action of rennet, the serum still contains a considerable proportion of casein, which can be precipitated by a second coagulation; the serum of milk curdled by acidification contains very little casein.

Curd can be eaten as it is or with cream. See CHEESE, *cream cheese*.

Curdling is the first operation in the manufacture of *cheese**.

CURING—See PRESERVATION OF FOOD.

CURLEW. Courlis—Wader, a marsh bird which is not highly esteemed from the culinary point of view. Cooked in the same way as *plover**.

CURRANT. Groseille—There are various types of currant, the best-known being red, white and black currants.

Red and white currants are cultivated in several regions of France, notably on the outskirts of Paris, and in the Meuse and Puy-de-Dôme districts.

Black currants are grown mainly on the Côte d'Or.

In Dijon black currants are used to make the *Cassis de Dijon*, a liqueur which is internationally famous. See CASSIS.

Red and white currants can be eaten raw, as a dessert, but they are more commonly used in jellies, syrups and in various sweets.

Red and white currants are used at Bar-le-Duc to make a jelly which enjoys a great reputation.

Currant compote. Compote de groseilles—Wash and clean the currants. Put them in a bowl. Pour over them a boiling syrup (2 cups sugar plus 1½ cups water) at 35° or boiled to 250° F. Serve in a glass bowl.

Currant jam. Confiture de groseilles—See JAM, *Jellies*.

Currant juice for ices—Proceed as for strawberry ice mixture. See STRAWBERRY.

CURRY. Cari—A curry is a combination of spices, thoroughly dried and ground to a powder and cooked slowly in clarified butter, vegetable oil or soured milk before adding the fish, meat, eggs or vegetables that are to be 'curried'. Curry powders may consist of a combination of as few as five spices or as many as fifty. The curry powders bottled and sold in grocery shops are usually a combination of fifteen or twenty herbs, seeds and spices but those who really appreciate curry have special combinations of spices to go with various dishes, which sometimes call for mild subtle seasonings and other times for hotter ones. The strength of a curry depends on how much chili is used. The following are the principal ingredients of curry powder:

Allspice, anise, bay leaves, cinnamon, caraway, celery seed, cloves, coriander, cumin, curry leaves, dill, fennel, fenugreek (seeds and leaves), garlic, ginger, mace, mustard, nutmeg, pepper (white and black), paprika, poppy seeds, saffron, turmeric, mint, cubeb berries, sumach seeds, juniper berries, zedoary root, salt.

For the preparation of different curries see MUTTON, CHICKEN.

Bichique curry (Creole cookery). CARI DE BICHIQUE—The *bichique* is a minute fish found near the island of Réunion. This fish is exported in tins. It is prepared as follows:

Put some good quality fat or oil in a saucepan. Heat a finely chopped onion in this fat until golden. For a small tin of *bichique* add a large tomato, peeled and seeded and cut into tiny pieces, and a coffee spoonful of Réunion saffron. Cover and stew for a few seconds. Pound together in a mortar, some ginger, a clove of garlic, a sprig of parsley and salt. Mix this thoroughly with the ingredients already in the saucepan. Mix in the fish by shaking the pan. Do not stir or they may break, as they are very fragile. Leave to soak for 20 minutes. Cover the pan and put it in a moderate oven. Leave it in the oven for 20 to 25 minutes. Serve with *Rice à la créole* (see RICE).

Bringelle curry (Créole cookery). CARI DE BRINGELLES—Cut some lean and fat pork into large cubes as for a stew. Brown these pieces lightly in fat with some finely chopped onion. Add 2 teaspoons saffron, some parsley, thyme, garlic, a piece of stem ginger well crushed, and chopped tomatoes. Slice some aubergines (egg-plant) into rounds and dip them in water slightly seasoned with salt and vinegar. Drain them thoroughly and put them in a saucepan with the pork. Moisten with a little olive oil. Cover. Stir from time to time, crushing the aubergines with the spoon. Allow 2½ hours for cooking on a low flame. Serve when the sauce is thick.

CUSTARD. CRÈME—Custard is a mixture of beaten eggs and milk variously sweetened and flavoured and cooked either over hot water or baked in an oven.

Caramel custard

Caramel custard. CRÈME MOULÉE AU CARAMEL—Fill a plain round mould with a preparation of *Vanilla custard*, first lining the interior of the mould with caramel. Cook the custard in the oven at a gentle heat, setting the mould in a pan half filled with hot water. Take it out, and let it cool. Turn the caramel custard out on to a serving dish.

Fried custard. CRÈME FRITE—Put 1¾ cups (250 grams) of sifted flour in a pan with ½ cup (125 grams) of fine sugar, 12 egg yolks and 4 whole eggs and a small pinch of salt. Moisten with a quart (litre) of milk which has been boiled with a vanilla pod (or any other desired flavour). Add 3½ tablespoons (50 grams) of butter. Mix until there is no trace of lumps. Cook on the stove in the same way as *French pastry cream* (see CREAM) stirring all the time. Spread out this cream, which must have a proper consistency, on a buttered baking sheet in an even layer, about ¼ inch thick. Allow to cool. Cut in rectangular pieces, or squares or rounds. Cover the pieces with beaten egg and breadcrumbs.

At the last moment, fry them in deep boiling fat. Drain the pieces; dry them on a cloth. Arrange them on a napkin or on a doyley. Sprinkle them with powdered sugar. Serve with an *Apricot sauce* (see SAUCE) flavoured with kirsch or with some other liqueur.

Vanilla custard. CRÈME MOULÉE À LA VANILLE—Dissolve 7 tablespoons (100 grams) of sugar in a pint (½ litre) of boiled milk. Add half a vanilla pod or 1 teaspoon vanilla extract. Let it infuse for 20 minutes. Pour this little by little over 2 whole eggs and 4 egg yolks beaten together in a basin. Mix well. Strain through a silk tammy or fine sieve. Remove the froth which forms on the surface of the cream.

Fill a simple mould (charlotte mould) with this preparation. Cook the custard cream in the oven in a bain-marie. Let it cool thoroughly before attempting to turn it out.

CUSTARD APPLE OR BULLOCK'S HEART. COROSSOL—This is the vulgar name for a species of anona and its fruit.

This fruit is one of the most sizable known. It sometimes attains a weight of 8 to 10 pounds (4 kilos). In contrast the tree that produces it is stunted and bare.

The fruit, which resembles a large pimento in shape, has a skin tender green in colour, smooth, with here and there little hairy protuberances.

The pulp of this fruit is white, compact, and full of black seeds of the size of an apricot kernel.

This pulp, when the fruit is ripe, gives off a very agreeable odour; the taste is lightly acid. When crushed and mixed with four or five times its volume of water, it produces a liquid similar to milk, which after being sweetened and chilled makes a very pleasant drink.

CUSTARD MARROW. CHAYOTE—This vegetable, which is also known in France under the name of *brionne*, is the fruit of a climbing plant belonging to the same family as marrows.

The custard marrow is a native of Mexico and the Antilles. Its cultivation has spread to other hot countries, notably Algeria.

The fruit of the custard marrow is in the form of a large green pear with deep ribbing. Its surface is somewhat spiny; the flesh is white, firm, homogenous, not very watery, without smell or too pronounced a taste.

This vegetable is prepared in a great many ways. Before cooking it must be blanched or cooked *au blanc*, like *Cardoons**, being first cut up into quarters and then trimmed into lozenge-shaped pieces.

Custard marrows in béchamel sauce. CHAYOTES AU BLANC—Prepared in the same way as *Custard marrows à la crème*, but moistening them with a not too thick *Béchamel sauce* (see SAUCE) in place of fresh cream.

Braised custard marrows au jus. CHAYOTES BRAISÉES AU JUS—Divide the custard marrows into quarters. Trim these quarters into lozenge-shaped pieces; blanch in boiling salted water. Drain.

Put them in a buttered pan, lined with strips of bacon rind, carrots and onions cut into rounds. Season. Moisten with a consommé, from which not all the fat has been skimmed, sufficient to cover the vegetables. Cook with the lid on. When the liquor is reduced to a glaze add a few tablespoons of rich brown veal stock. Simmer. Drain the custard marrows and arrange them in a dish. Pour over them a sauce made by reducing (boiling down) the liquor remaining in the pan, adding butter and straining through a sieve.

Custard marrows with butter. CHAYOTES AU BEURRE—Divide the custard marrows into quarters, trim each quarter into large lozenge-shaped pieces. Cook them in a *White court-bouillon for vegetables* (see COURT-BOUILLON) in the same way as *cardoons* or *salsify*, but keeping them firm.

Drain and dry them, put into a sauté-pan or heavy frying pan in which three tablespoons of butter have been heated. Moisten with three tablespoons of veal or chicken consommé or water. Cook gently under cover.

When they are cooked, arrange them in a dish. Pour over them the liquor in which they have cooked with a little butter added.

They can also be cooked in the following way: Blanch the quartered custard marrows in salted water. Drain and put them in a buttered pan. Moisten with consommé or water. Cook gently with the lid on. Finish in the same way as above.

Custard marrows à la crème. CHAYOTES À LA CRÈME—Cook the custard marrows in the same way as for *Custard marrows with butter**. When they are nearly cooked cover them with fresh boiled cream; finish cooking with the lid on.

Arrange the custard marrows in a dish. Pour over them the cream in which they have cooked.

Custard marrows à la créole. CHAYOTES À LA CRÉOLE—Divide the custard marrows into quarters. Blanch them well in salted water. Put them in a sauté-pan or heavy frying pan in which ½ cup (100 grams) of chopped onions have been cooked in butter and oil (half and half). Add 3 tomatoes, peeled, seeded and coarsely chopped, a *bouquet garni** and a minced clove of garlic. Cook with the lid on.

Arrange the custard marrows on a round dish in the middle of a border of rice, cooked in bouillon. Sprinkle the custard marrows with chopped parsley.

Custard marrow fritters. CHAYOTES EN FRITOT—Divide the custard marrows into quarters. Cook them in a *White court-bouillon for vegetables* (see COURT-BOUILLON). Drain and dry them. Put them in a marinade of olive oil, lemon juice, salt and pepper. Dip each piece in a light batter. Deep fry in boiling oil. Arrange on a napkin and garnish with fried parsley.

Custard marrows used as a garnish. CHAYOTES POUR GARNITURES—Quartered custard marrows, cooked in butter or braised, can be used as an element in the garnish of eggs, fish, small pieces of butcher's meat, fowl, etc.

When used to garnish eggs or fish, the custard marrows are usually cut up into large dice, blanched and cooked in butter.

To garnish pieces of butcher's meat or fowl, the custard marrows are trimmed into large lozenge shapes, cooked in butter or braised, and when they are nearly cooked, the juices of the meat or fowl which they are to accompany are added to them.

Custard marrows au gratin. CHAYOTES AU GRATIN—Cut the custard marrows into quarters, cook them in a *White court-bouillon for vegetables* (see COURT-BOUILLON), simmer them in butter, arrange in a buttered gratin dish and sprinkle with grated cheese; pour some melted butter over them. Cook in a moderate oven.

Custard marrows à la grecque. CHAYOTES À LA GRECQUE—Divide the custard marrows into segments. Blanch in salted water. Cook them in a court-bouillon in the same way as *Aubergines (egg-plant) à la grecque**. Let them cool in their liquor before serving. Used as an hors-d'oeuvre.

Custard marrows à la martiniquaise. CHAYOTES À LA MARTINIQUAISE—Press boiled custard marrow in a cloth to extract the maximum of water, then pound the pulp with bread dipped in milk. Cook some very finely chopped onion in a casserole in butter; add the custard marrows and bread with a little salt and pepper and milk. Turn out into a vegetable dish, smooth the surface and pour over it a spoonful of olive oil, sprinkle with grated breadcrumbs and set in a moderately hot oven. (Recipe taken from the *Bulletin de la société d'horticulture d'Algérie*.)

Custard marrows Mornay. CHAYOTES MORNAY—Prepared in the same way as *Custard marrows au gratin**. The custard marrows are arranged on a dish on a layer of *Mornay sauce* (see SAUCE), covered with the same sauce, sprinkled with grated cheese and browned in the oven.

Custard marrow salad. SALADE DE CHAYOTES—Divide the custard marrows in quarters. Cook them in a *White court-bouillon for vegetables* (see COURT-BOUILLON). Drain and slice them. Arrange in a salad bowl. Season with oil, vinegar, pepper and chopped herbs.

Stuffed custard marrows. CHAYOTES FARCIES—Divide the custard marrows in half crossways. Trim the halves and hollow them out slightly. Blanch them in salted water, drain and dry them.

Simmer them gently in butter. When the vegetables are nearly cooked fill them with a mixture of pork forcemeat and dry *duxelles**.

Arrange the forcemeat in the form of a dome; put the custard marrows on a buttered gratin dish; sprinkle with dried breadcrumbs and melted butter, and brown gently in the oven.

Custard marrows prepared in this way can be served as a vegetable or used as an element in the garnish of a particular dish.

Instead of stuffing them with a pork forcemeat, they can be filled with one or other of the preparations indicated for various stuffed vegetables. See TOMATO, AUBERGINE, etc.

CUTTING BOARD. PLANCHE À DÉCOUPER—Beechwood board used for cutting up meat, provided with a groove and a hole to catch the juices.

CUTTLE-FISH. SEICHE, SÈCHE—Cephalopod mollusc with an internal shell (cuttle-bone), secreting an inky liquid (sepia). The tough flesh becomes eatable if it is vigorously beaten; it was popular with the Romans and is still liked in certain regions, notably in Spain. Powdered cuttle-bone was formerly used as an absorbent.

Cuttle-fish is prepared like octopus.

CUVE—A large tun made of wood, cement or even metal, in which the grapes are pressed for wine and in which red wine is fermented.

CUVEAU—French name for a small vat.

CUVÉE—The product of a particular wine press. A *cuvée* is always a mixture of grapes, either taken from different parts of a large vineyard, as in the Bordeaux district, or bought from different growers under similar climatic conditions, as in Burgundy, or the product of different harvests in the same region, as in Champagne and on the slopes of the Rhône. The final result depends upon the quality of the vintage and the skilful balance of the mixture.

Dab

DAB. Limande—A flat fish of the *Pleuronect* family, with scales almost as rough as a file. It is oval and less elongated than the sole. Its right side, where the eyes are placed, is coloured, with a semi-circular lateral line running from head to tail. Its blind side is white. It is between 8 and 12 inches long. The flesh is white, rather soft, but easily digested. The American dab is only slightly different.

All recipes for *plaice* are suitable for dab.

DACE. Dard—A fresh-water fish of the *Chevaine* family. In France it is also known as *Aubourg*, *Gravelet* or *Vandoise*.

It is caught in most of the rivers of Central France. It is rather leathery to eat and is usually prepared *en matelote*.

DAGH KEBAB (Turkish cookery)—Pieces of shin veal skewered with slices of white onions and tomatoes between, grilled and sprinkled with thyme. This dish is served with pilaf of rice and ladies' fingers (okra) or some other garnish.

DAHLIA—An ornamental plant, originally found in Mexico, which owes its name to the botanist Dahl of Antwerp. Dahlia tubers are edible and are similar to the Jerusalem artichoke in flavour. They are cooked in the same way as *Jerusalem artichokes**.

DAIKON—A large Japanese radish which can be eaten raw, like the common radish, or cooked like turnips after being parboiled.

DAISY. Paquetette—One of the commonest field flowers. Its young leaves and buds are eaten in salads.

DAME-BLANCHE (Cold sweet or dessert)—A kind of Plombières ice cream. For a recipe for this ice cream, see ICE CREAMS AND ICES.

DAMPFNUDELN (German pastry)—*Ingredients.* 3¾ cups (500 grams) of sieved flour; 3 cups (100 grams) of sugar; 5 yolks of egg; 6½ tablespoons (100 grams) of melted butter; 1 cup (2 decilitres) of milk, ⅓ ounce (10 grams) yeast; a small pinch of salt; the rind of a lemon.

Method. Make a leaven with a quarter of the flour, the yeast and the milk, which should be slightly warmed. Keep the leaven in a moderate temperature.

When the leaven has doubled in volume, mix in the melted butter, a little at a time, the salt, the lemon rind, the yolks of egg, the sugar and the rest of the flour.

Put this dough on a floured table and dredge with flour. Roll it out with a rolling pin. Leave to stand for 5 minutes. Cut it into rounds (with a pastry-cutter). Put these rounds on a floured cloth. Leave to rise in a mild temperature for an hour. Baste with butter. Sprinkle with fine sugar. Bake in a slow oven.

Dampfnudeln are usually served with stewed fruit or jam. The rounds can also be filled with a small spoonful of very

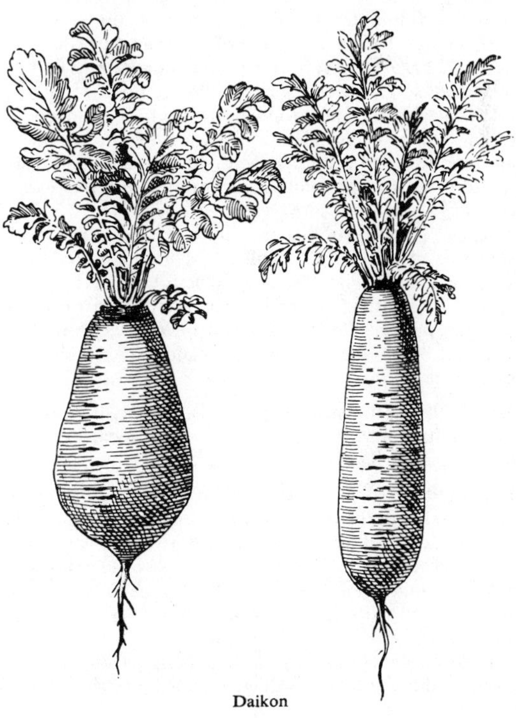

Daikon

thick apricot purée flavoured with rum. In this case, lift up the edges of each round, fold inwards and seal. Put the pastries on a buttered baking sheet with the join downward.

DANDELION. PISSENLIT—A weed with toothed or pinnated leaves and yellow flowers.

This is most frequently merely gathered in the fields, from November to March, but there are improved varieties such as *plein coeur amélioré* and *très hâtif*, which are cultivated.

Tender young dandelion leaves are eaten raw, in salads. They can also be cooked like *spinach**.

DARIOLE—Nowadays this name is applied to a small cylindrical mould. In former times there was a small pastry known as *dariole* for which these moulds were used. Here is a recipe for *darioles:*

Line *dariole* moulds with *Puff pastry* (see DOUGH) folded and rolled out 6 times. Fill these moulds with *Frangipane cream* (see CREAM) mixed with plenty of almonds and flavoured with kirsch or some other liqueur. Bake in a hot oven. When the *darioles* are ready, sprinkle with sugar.

DARNE—This is the name given in France to a thick slice of a large raw fish. This cut used to be called, more logically, a *dalle* (slab).

Darnes of fish can be prepared in different ways: poached, braised, grilled or sautéed in butter (see SALMON and other large fish). We give below a typical recipe.

Darne of salmon à l'ancienne. DARNE DE SAUMON À L'ANCIENNE—Season with salt and pepper a *darne* of salmon weighing about a pound (between 500 and 600 grams). Put it in an oval buttered dish. Moisten with ½ cup (a decilitre) of white wine and the same quantity of very concentrated fish stock. Add a small sliced onion, a *bouquet garni* and the trimmings and peelings of mushrooms, the mushrooms to be used later for the garnish.

Bring to the boil on the stove. Put it in the oven and cook for 20 minutes, basting from time to time.

10 minutes before taking out of the oven, put round the salmon 12 raw mushrooms, peeled, trimmed and without their stalks. Drain the salmon. Put it on a long dish. Garnish with the mushrooms, arranged at each end of the dish. Top each mushroom with an oyster, poached and drained, and decorate each one with a strip of truffle tossed in butter. Surround the salmon with 6 fresh-water crayfish, tossed and cooked in a *court-bouillon**.

Sauce. Reduce (boil down) the cooking stock of the salmon and thicken with yolks of egg and butter in the same way as a *white wine sauce* (see SAUCE). Finish the sauce with a tablespoon of liqueur brandy and a touch of cayenne pepper. Pour this sauce in a circle round the salmon. Serve the rest of the sauce separately in a sauceboat.

DARTOIS—Tiny snacks served as an hors-d'oeuvre or light main course. Recipes for these are given under *hot hors-d'oeuvre*. See HORS-D'OEUVRE.

DARTOIS (Pastry)—Make two layers of *Puff pastry* (see DOUGH). Fill the middle with almond cream and cover with the second layer. Brush the top with egg, leaving the edges untouched or the pastry will not rise during baking.

With a small knife, lightly mark dividing lines at evenly spaced intervals to indicate where the pastry is to be cut after baking.

Bake in a moderate oven. When the pastry is ready, sprinkle the top lightly with icing sugar. Put the pastry back in the oven, until the sugar forms a glaze on top. Cut into sections at once, following the lines marked out before baking. The lower half of this cake can be made with flaky pastry trimmings. This is quite a common practice. In some cases, the bottom layer of pastry need be only ⅛ inch thick. The upper layer should be about ¼ inch thick.

Dartois (*Larousse*)

When the puff pastry is rolled out 6 times as indicated above, however, both layers should be of the same thickness, a little less than ¼ inch.

Cream for filling dartois—Pound finely in a mortar ½ cup (125 grams) of sugar with ¼ pound (125 grams) blanched almonds, adding 2 eggs to prevent the mixture from becoming oily. Soften ¼ pound (125 grams) of butter to a paste. Add it to the mixture. Add a small glass of rum and, if desired, 2 tablespoons of *French pastry cream* (see CREAM).

A good cream can also be made by simply mixing ground almonds with *French pastry cream* and flavouring the mixture with vanilla or rum. In this case, the greatest care must be taken to seal the layers of pastry together as the cream boils during cooking, thus becoming runny and tending to ooze out, which not only spoils the appearance of the pastry but also its delicate flavour, since not enough cream is left between the layers.

Dates and date-palm

DATE. DATTE—The fruit of the date-palm was known to the Chaldeans in antiquity. It grows wild in the area bounded by the Euphrates and the Nile, and is cultivated in the desert oases of Southern Algeria and Tunisia. The male and female principles grow on separate trees and artificial pollination is therefore necessary.

There are hard and soft dates, the latter being more highly prized. The best dates come from Tunisia, Algeria and Western Asia. They are about the size of a thumb, with yellowish-red skin, and have a sweet winy flavour. Excellent dates are now grown in South Carolina and Arizona (U.S.A.).

Dates are highly nourishing. They provide food for wandering desert tribes. An intoxicating wine and a spirit are made from them. A drink made from dates steeped in water or milk is sometimes used as a palliative for coughs. Dates were one of the four fruits used for chest and throat ailments in early medicine. The others were the fig, the jujube and the raisin.

Date Fritters—See FRITTER, *Sweet (dessert) fritters.*

Stuffed dates (*Claire*)

Stuffed dates (petits fours). DATTES FOURRÉES—Slit the dates down one side and stone them. Stuff each date with a knob of almond paste (about the size of a hazel-nut) flavoured with kirsch or rum, or with pistachio nut paste. Sprinkle the dates with crystallized sugar.

DAUBE—A method of cooking meat. Although this method can be used not only for beef but also for other meat, as well as poultry and game, the term *daube* without qualification often means a cut of beef cooked *en daube*, that is to say braised in stock, generally red wine stock enriched with various nourishing ingredients and well seasoned with herbs.

The name *Daube à l'avignonnaise* designates a dish made with mutton cooked in red wine. See MUTTON.

For different kinds of *daube* see BEEF, MUTTON, TURKEY, PHEASANT.

In ancient cookery the term *daube* was reserved almost exclusively for braised meat to be eaten cold.

This is far from being the case today, for now a *daube* is almost always served hot.

DAUBIÈRE—A type of casserole used in France, as its name indicates, for the cooking of *daubes*. It can be made of stoneware, earthenware or tinned copper.

In former times *daubières* had very deep lids so that they could be covered with live charcoal and ashes.

DAUCUS—An umbrella plant whose aromatic seeds, used medicinally in former times, are now used in the preparation of some liqueurs.

Old daubière (*Larousse*)

DAUMONT (A LA)—A method of preparing large fish. The *Daumont* garnish comprises *quenelles**, soft roe, mushrooms and fresh-water crayfish tails all served with *Nantua sauce*. See GARNISHES.

Dauphiné (*French Government Tourist Office*)

DAUPHINÉ—The Dauphiné region stretches from the Alps to the Rhône Valley. In the north it borders on the Lyonnais district and the Bresse area from which it is separated by the Rhône. In the south it is neighboured by Provence without any clear-cut geographical line of demarcation. Its north-eastern border is Savoy on the edge of the high, mountainous Isère valley. This region, therefore, has a great diversity of geographical and climatic conditions, which explains the variety of its produce. The Rhône Valley, which brings the Dauphiné close to Provence, has a climate favourable to the cultivation of spring vegetables and orchards (especially peaches and apricots), and its sunlit slopes bear the famous Rhône vineyards, often terraced. In the extreme south, even olive trees are to be found. In contrast, the valleys of the Alps provide rich pasture for rearing great numbers of cows which yield excellent milk. Here too are fine chestnut groves from which the chestnuts known as Lyon chestnuts are gathered. There are also hazel-nut trees which yield an abundant crop of the finest nuts. The honey of these upland pastures is highly prized. The lakes, torrents and rivers provide delicate fish such as their renowned trout and crayfish. In some places truffles are found, and morels and cèpes are common in the woods.

and in autumn with pumpkin. In the Drôme area, a *pogne* is a kind of *brioche*. The *pogne* of Romans enjoys an especially high reputation. Among the sweet specialities are Valence *pognes* and *meringues*, the honey *tourons* of Gap, the sweetmeats of Voiron and the famous nougat of Montélimar.

Wine is the normal drink in the region. The wines of the Rhône slopes have some very highly reputed vintages,

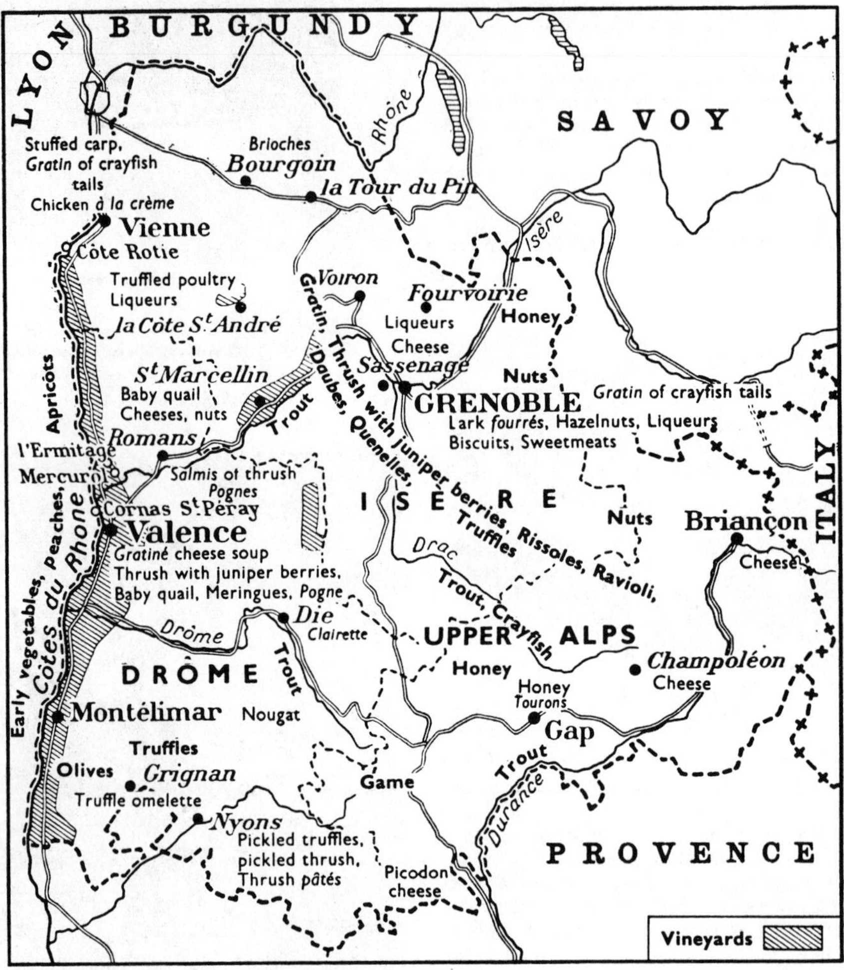

Gastronomic map of Dauphiné

Regional cookery shows a marked predeliction for *gratin* dishes. These are made not only with *macaroni* and *potatoes* but also with *chopped porridge*, *white beet*, *swedes*, *cèpes* and even *crayfish tails*.

Daubes are favourite dishes and those of Vienne enjoy a considerable reputation. Among the specialities of this region the following must be mentioned: *Grills à la marinière; Défarde; Baby quails; Thrush with juniper berries; Thrush pâtés des Alpes; Salmis of thrush; Pickled thrush* and the *pickled truffles* of Nyons which are excellent.

The dairy farms in these magnificent alpine pastures provide milk which is used to manufacture cheeses such as Sassenage, Saint-Marcellin, Champoléon, Pelvoux, Briançon and white cheese *tomme* (a cheese made from fermented butter milk). The characteristic regional pastry is the *pogne*, an immense tart filled in summer with fruit

such as those of *l'Ermitage*, *Crozes*, *Mercurol* and the *Côte rôtie* made in the neighbourhood of Vienne.

DAUPHINE (A LA)—A name given to several different dishes. Most commonly it is used for a potato preparation made from *Duchess potato mixture* and *Chou paste*. This mixture is shaped into balls and deep-fried. See POTATOES.

DAUPHINOISE (A LA)—This designation usually indicates a method of preparing potatoes. See POTATOES.

DECANT. DÉCANTER—To pour any liquid from one container into another. Wine is decanted into a carafe to get rid of the deposit formed at the bottom of the wine bottle.

This operation must be carried out with great care,

training a light on to the carafe to make sure that it is clear, and allowing as little as possible of the residue to get into the carafe.

Butter is also said to be decanted when it is melted and purified by being transferred from one container to another.

DECOCTION—The process of boiling a solid for a period in water. *Clear soup* is a decoction of meat. The decoction of vegetable matter has the disadvantage of sapping many of its nutritive properties and evaporating its volatile elements.

DECOMPOSITION—The destruction of a body by the disintegration of its elements.

DEEP-FRYING. FRITURE—Deep-frying is carried out by immersing certain foods in a large, deep pan of boiling fat. The French term for deep-frying is *friture*, a word also applied to the fat used in deep-frying.

In the great kitchens of a hotel or restaurant, deep-frying is almost always carried out successfully, but this cannot be said of home cooking, where more often than not the methods and ingredients used are quite unsuitable.

In great kitchens a large number of different fats are available. These are chosen with care and used lavishly. In private households, the fats used are all too often impure, and, for reasons of economy, the housewife uses her fats too sparingly.

This is a false economy. Deep-frying can only be successful if a great deal of fat is used. The more fat the less waste, since, where too little fat is used, it is absorbed into the food and the pieces stick to one another and become soggy. Food fried in abundant fat is crisp, firm and cooked all through. The food is properly sealed at the outset and therefore does not absorb the fat.

It follows naturally from this principle that there must be ample room in the cooking utensil. This should be a large, deep pan, round or oval in shape. It should be made in a single piece, of sheet-iron or hammered copper.

As it is often necessary to fry a number of things at the same time, it is desirable to have at least two such pans in every kitchen. One of these should be kept exclusively for fish.

Other necessary equipment for deep-frying are grids, baskets and skimmers.

The deep-frying pan must be carefully cleaned each time it is used. The fat must be strained through muslin. The pan must then be thoroughly cleaned inside and out. When this is done, the fat may be poured back into the pan for storage.

Deep-frying fats—Although, theoretically, any fats, butters or oils may be used for deep-frying, it would be well to note that they are not all equally suitable for the purpose.

The best fat to use in all deep-frying is ox (beef) kidney fat (suet), clarified and purified with scrupulous care.

After it is clarified, this fat is quite odourless, and can be heated up to 375°F. without burning. It should be noted that ox kidney fat is the cheapest available. If it is carefully looked after, it can be used over and over again.

A little veal fat can be added if desired, but veal fat must not be used alone, since it deteriorates very quickly.

An alternative household fat can be prepared by mixing in equal parts ox-kidney fat with lard or oil. However, these mixtures, apart from being more expensive, cannot be heated to the same high degree without burning, nor can they be used again as much.

Mutton fat should *never* be used in deep frying, since it impregnates the food with a detestable taste of tallow.

Among the fats which are suitable for frying certain special foods are olive oil, which can be heated to 500°F.–550°F. without burning, and is very suitable for fish, fritters, rice and cream croquettes, etc., and—though it is a somewhat expensive luxury—clarified butter, which may be used in the preparation of delicately flavoured sweets. Ground-nut (peanut) oil and cereal oils are also very good for deep-frying.

The cheaper vegetable oils include various types of coconut butter. They are quite suitable in certain cases, but are still a poor substitute for ox-kidney fat.

The fat of duck, goose and other fat poultry, as well as lard, may be used with butter for browning or in the preparation of *roux**, but again, ox-kidney is more efficient.

In his book, *Le Cuisinier Practicien*, Reculet made the following wise pronouncements:

'The amount of fat used in frying must always depend upon the size of the object to be fried, because, the greater the quantity of liquid, the more it can hold the heat. Hence, it is able to counteract the cooling caused by the immersion of the object and the moisture given off during cooking.

'In a busy kitchen it is desirable to have two lots of cooking fat, one white, one brown. The white fat is fresh or at least little used: it should be used for all deep-frying except for fish. The brown fat, darkened by long service in "white frying", should be used for fish.

'This use of brown fat in frying fish is purely a matter of economy, since obviously good white fat is preferable in all cases.

'There are several indications to be seen when frying oil becomes hot:

(1) A slight tremor on the surface.
(2) Quite a strong characteristic smell.
(3) A dry whitish vapour given off by the fat.

'It is possible to test the heat of the fat by adding a drop of water to it or by dipping any substance into it other than purified fat. If the sound of sizzling is deep and low, the fat is boiling, if it is sharp and high, the fat is frying or crying out that it is hot enough. This is the moment at which to put into it whatever is to be fried.'

According to their nature and greater or lesser liquid content, foods are immersed in the frying fat at different degrees of heat.

Vegetables and fruit, which always have a high proportion of water in them, are fried in moderately hot fat. This applies particularly to potatoes.

Fish and other large foodstuffs are also deep-fried in moderately hot fat; they would not be cooked right through if they were sealed at once by contact with too intense a heat.

Very hot fat is used for foodstuffs which must be sealed instantly, for instance anything dipped in egg and breadcrumbs or batter. This also applies to pre-cooked foods such as croquettes and other similar dishes.

Finally, very hot fat is used for very small foodstuffs which must be sealed immediately. *Soufflé* potatoes too must be dropped into very hot fat after having first been cooked in moderately hot fat.

This was Brillat-Savarin's theory of deep-frying:

'Not all liquids exposed to the action of fire can absorb the same amount of heat; nature has not endowed them all equally. This phenomenon, which is one of nature's secrets, is called *calorific capacity*.

'Thus, one may with impunity dip one's finger into boiling spirits of wine, where one would withdraw it hastily from brandy, and still more hastily from water, while any contact with boiling oil would cause an intensely painful blister, since oil can hold at least three times as much heat as water.

'It is as a result of these differences that hot liquids act in different ways upon the foodstuffs which are immersed in them.

'Those cooked in *water* are softened and reduced by boiling. Soups and extracts are their by-products. Foods cooked in *fat*, on the other hand, are compressed; they take on a dark colouring, and in the end become charred.

'In the first case, water dissolves and absorbs into itself the inherent juices of the foods cooked in it; in the second, the juices are preserved intact because they are insoluble in oil. If, in the long run, fried foods become desiccated, it is because over-exposure to heat has evaporated all the moisture in them.

'These two methods of cooking are known by different names. The process of boiling foodstuffs in oil or fat is known as *frying*.

'I believe I have already stated that, in terms of officinal ratio, oil and fat are more or less synonymous, fat being none other than solidified oil and oil none other than liquid fat . . .

'The whole virture of good frying lies in the element of *surprise*. The boiling liquid, with its capacity to brown or char, carries out a surprise attack on the surface of foodstuffs plunged into it, at the very moment of immersion.

'By means of this surprise attack, a kind of shell is formed round the food, which prevents the fat from penetrating it and seals the juices within it. These juices are thus cooked within the shell so that the full flavour of the food is preserved.

'In order that the surprise attack may take place, the boiling liquid must have attained a sufficient degree of heat for its action to be sudden and instantaneous; but to reach this point, it must be heated for quite a long time over a very hot flame.

'You will doubtless have observed that when foodstuffs are well fried, neither salt nor sugar will dissolve on their surface, though it will be necessary to add one or other of these seasonings according to the nature of the food. To overcome this difficulty, pound the salt and sugar very finely, so that they will stick to the surface of the food. Thus, when they are sprinkled on the food, they will season it by juxtaposition.

'Experience has taught that olive oil should be used only for very quick frying or for processes which do not require great heat. This is because olive oil, if heated for a long time, develops an unpleasant taste which it is difficult to eradicate.' (*Physiologie du Goût*.)

DEEP-FRYING BASKET. GRILLE—A small wire utensil in which food is contained for deep-frying. Fried foods can be lifted out of the fat all at once in this utensil.

DEER. CERF—Wild mammal which up to six months old is called fawn, in both sexes, up to one year old a *young stag*, then *brocket*, or *young hind*, from one to two years old, then *three year old*. Between five and six years old it becomes a *five-pronger*, *old stag* or *grand old stag* if it lives longer.

Deer's flesh is tender up to one year, and from then on becomes more and more tough. It is particularly indigestible and even poisonous when the deer has been brought down after a long chase.

Hartshorn, rich in mucilage, used to be used in the old days to make jellies. All methods of preparation given for the buck are applicable to the doe.

DEFRUTUM—A Latin term frequently used by Apicius (a celebrated gastronome of the time of the Emperors Augustus and Tiberius), and found in very ancient recipes, to designate grape juice reduced by evaporation to a third of its volume. This juice was widely used in Roman cookery.

DÉGLAÇAGE—A technical term in French cookery for the operation of pouring any liquid into the pan in which food has been cooked in butter or some other fat.

Most commonly wine is used for this purpose. It is heated and stirred in the pan so that all the concentrated juices are incorporated into it. White or brown stocks, cream or vinegar can also be used.

DÉGLACER—A technical term in French cookery for the dilution of the concentrated juices in a pan in which meat, poultry, game or fish has been roasted, braised or fried. For this purpose, white or red wine, Madeira or some other heavy wine, clear soup, stock and sometimes cream are used.

DÉGORGER—A term used in French cookery meaning to soak food for a variable length of time in cold water to free it from any impurities it may contain.

Thus, calves' heads and veal sweetbreads are soaked in water to make them very white.

The term is also used of the operation of clearing champagne bottles of the impurities contained in the wine.

DÉGRAISSER—A term in French cookery meaning to skim off excess fat which forms on the surface of a liquid (clear soup, sauce, etc.).

The term is also used to describe the operation of cutting away some of the fat which forms a coating on a joint of meat.

All fat thus removed, whether from liquids or meat (except that of mutton or lamb) must be clarified. It can then be used for deep-frying.

DÉGRAISSIS—A term used in French cookery for the fat skimmed off a clear soup stock or sauce. This fat, which must be clarified, is known in France as *economy fat*. It is used either to fry certain vegetables or as deep-frying fat.

DEHYDRATING. DÉSHYDRATER—A synonym for drying. See DRYING.

DÉJEUNER—The French *déjeuner* (luncheon) means breaking fast or taking the first meal of the day after a night of fasting.

Nowadays, in France, the first meal of the day (breakfast) is called the *petit déjeuner* or *premier déjeuner* (i.e. little or first *déjeuner*) to distinguish it from *déjeuner* which is taken in the middle of the day.

The institution of this midday meal in France dates back to the French Revolution. In the eighteenth century, the main meal of the day, dinner, was taken first at midday and later at one o'clock. The *déjeuner*, taken upon waking, consisted of a soup or coffee with milk.

The Constituent Assembly began its deliberations at about midday, to rise at about six o'clock. It was, therefore, necessary to change the dinner hour to six o'clock and since the Members could not sit fasting, they were obliged to take a second breakfast at about eleven o'clock in the morning. This second *déjeuner* was more substantial than the first, since it included eggs and cold meat. If the Goncourt brothers, Edmond (1822–1896) and Jules (1830–1870), are to be believed, it was Mme. Handy who invented fork luncheons, by setting out cutlets, kidneys and sausages on a buffet in her café on the boulevards opposite the Comédie-Italienne, and pressing her clients to take these savouries with their meal.

Le petit déjeuner (Boucher)

Nowadays, in France, luncheon has largely usurped the place of dinner. It is made up of the same dishes and is eaten later and later in the day.

One could discourse at great length on the advantages and disadvantages of this state of affairs, if such discussion were likely to have any influence on accepted manners and customs. It is certain that a heavy dinner, especially when eaten very late at night, as is becoming more and more common in France, tends to be followed by an uncomfortable and restless night. On the other hand it can be argued that too elaborate a luncheon, too liberally washed down with wines and spirits, as many business luncheons' are, makes work almost impossible for the rest of the afternoon.

DÉLICE—This word, which in French strictly means a certain type of pastry, is nowadays misused by some pretentious *maîtres d'hôtel* in the drawing up of their menus.

Having no precise culinary meaning, the word (which implies delectability), is exploited for its very vagueness, implying in advance that the dish offered is delectable, though, in fact, all it does is to put the wary patron on his guard.

DEMI—In English the term 'half' is used of a glass of beer holding approximately half a pint.

In France, a *demi* is a glass of beer holding about 30 centilitres, so that patrons get approximately three *demis* to a litre. See TANKARD OR BEER-GLASS.

DEMI-DEUIL (A LA)—This term (which, literally translated, means 'in half-mourning') is applied mainly to poached poultry and veal sweetbreads braised in a white sauce.

The food cooked in this way is masked with *Suprême sauce* and garnished with truffles, which explains why these dishes are so called. See GARNISHES.

DEMIDOFF—The name of a princely Russian family. Prince Anatole Demidoff, married to Princess Mathilde, daughter of King Jérôme Bonaparte, but soon divorced, was one of the most celebrated gastronomes of the Second Empire. For this reason, an elaborate method of preparing large poultry in particular was called after him. See CHICKEN, *Chicken Demidoff*.

DEMI-ESPAGNOLE—By *demi-espagnole*, Carême means what today is called *demi-glace*. See SAUCE.

'Pour half the *grande espagnole* into a saucepan with the same volume of good clear chicken soup to which have been added the trimmings of mushrooms and truffles.' And Carême adds instructions for the preparation of this soup in a marginal note.

'This *consommé* is made with the carcases and giblets of two chickens, moistened with good stock (too much salt must be particularly avoided). Next, add a carrot, a couple of onions, and, after having skimmed it carefully, let it simmer. About two hours later, strain it through muslin or sieve without pressure. Leave it to stand, and then strain it thoroughly before using.

'Put the saucepan on a hot fire and stir with a special *espagnole* wooden spoon until it is bubbling all over. Then move it to the corner of the stove; skim carefully and remove every trace of fat. In this state, leave it for a full three-quarters of an hour. After this, skim off the fat, and put the stock on a hot fire.

'Stir the *espagnole* with a wooden spoon, to prevent it from boiling over, which will otherwise happen because of the very rapid boiling necessary to preserve as far as possible the essence which is really the palpable spirit of the sauce.

'While working the sauce, you will see it gradually taking on that brilliant glaze which delights the eye when it first appears. Finally, when it is suitably reduced, strain through a tammy cloth.'

DEMI-GLACE—A brown sauce made by boiling and skimming *Espagnole sauce* and mixing in white stock, *estouffade* or clear soup.

This sauce is usually flavoured with Madeira or sherry. See SAUCE.

DEMI-JOHN. DAME-JEANNE—A large earthenware or glass bottle.

DEMI-SEL CHEESE—See CHEESE.

DEMI-TASSE—In France a *demi-tasse* can mean either a very small cup or a cup of black coffee.

DÉNERVER—A term in French cookery denoting the removal of tendons, membranes, gristle, etc. from meat (poultry, game, etc.).

DENIER (EN)—Potato crisps are sometimes called *en denier* in France because they are cut in the shape of a coin. (The *denarius* from which the word denier derives, was a Roman coin.) See POTATOES.

DENSIMETER. DENSIMÈTRE—An instrument designed to measure the density of liquids. Anometers and alcoholometers are densimeters constant in weight but variable in volume, made in the form of a hollow glass rod weighted with lead or mercury. The rod sinks into the liquid to a greater or lesser depth and the density is recorded by means of a scale marked on the side.

There are a great many different types of densimeter for different types of liquid. These are usually sold with conversion tables indicating the allowances to be made for temperature, and enabling the readings to be converted to the centesimal or some other scale.

DENSITY. DENSITÉ—The degree of consistence of a body or substance, measured by the ratio of the mass to the volume, or by the quantity of matter in a unit of bulk. In practice, this is the ratio of the volume of a body to the same volume of distilled water at a temperature of 4°C. (39.2°F.). The measuring of density with special instruments makes it possible readily to assess the alcohol content of a liquid, the sugar content of a syrup, etc.

DENT-DE-LOUP (Wolves' fang)—This name is given in France to several kinds of decorative motif used in the presentation of dishes:

(1) Slices of sandwich bread cut into triangles and fried in butter or oil These triangles are used to garnish a number of different dishes.

(2) Triangles cut out of strips of jelly. These are used to garnish cold dishes.

DERBY—A name mainly applied to a method of preparing large poultry. See CHICKEN.

This method of preparing poultry was devised by M. Jean Giroix when he was in charge of the kitchens of the Hôtel de Paris at Monte-Carlo.

DÉROBER—A French term used in cookery for the removal of the skins of shelled broad beans.

It can also mean the peeling of potatoes and other vegetables.

M. A. Désaugiers (1772–1827)

DÉSAUGIERS—Marc-Antoine Désaugiers, a talented writer of satirical songs, was born at Fréjus (Var) in 1772 and died in Paris in 1827.

Désaugiers, immortal author of M. et Mme. Denis, can be numbered among the gastronomic poets, for he wrote a great many songs extolling the joys of the table. Some of these songs are still sung today, when as in our forefathers' time, each guest at the table takes his turn at singing a song over the dessert.

Désaugiers, who was secretary of the *Caveau Moderne*, a French literary, gastronomic and also somewhat bacchanalian society, wrote his will, in a manner of speaking, in the last couplet of his *Chanson à manger* (Eating Song).

Here are the last wishes of this amiable epicurean:–

Je veux que la mort me frappe
Au milieu d'un grand repas
Qu'on m'enterre sous la nappe
Entre quatre larges plats,
Et que sur ma tombe on mette
Cette courte inscription:
Ci-gît le premier poète
Mort d'une indigestion.

I pray that death may strike me
In the middle of a large meal.
I wish to be buried under the tablecloth
Between four large dishes.
And I desire that this short inscription
Should be engraved on my tombstone
Here lies the first poet
Ever to die of indigestion.

And in another song, *Ma tactique*, he tells us how he was able to brave, unharmed, 'the murderous hand of that black trio, the Fates':

Si, jusqu'ici du noir trio
La main meurtrière
N'a pas mis, d'une coup de ciseau,
Fin à ma carrière,
C'est que, jusqu'ici, le bravant,
J'ai toujours dit, en bon vivant,
Parques en arrière
Momus, en avant!

If, up to now
The murderous hand
Of the black trio
Has not, with a single snap of the scissors,
Put an end to my career,
It is because, up to this moment,
I have always faced them boldly
And cried as a man of good cheer should:
Back Fates, forward Momus.

(Momus was the Greek God of revelry.)

DESESSARTS—One of the greatest actors of the Comédie-Française in his day. He was born at Langres in 1740 and died at Barèges in 1793. He was also a celebrated gastronome.

'Desessarts,' says Emile Deschanel in *l'Histoire des comédiens*, 'had an appetite worthy of his size, but he was also a connoisseur. He was very witty. A good dinner sent his spirits soaring. He would analyse elegantly the qualities of each dish, and, in order to describe them more vividly, would coin amusingly bizarre words.

'If his fellow-diners were amiable and good trenchermen, the sybarite gaiety of Desessarts would express itself lyrically in poetic phrases such as "the boar, prince of the forests, whose ferocious pride is humbled when he is baked in a pâté".'

Desessarts was, like all gourmets, a splendid fellow. His talent was as straightforward as his character. Infectious gaiety and bluntness mixed with bonhomie were distinctive traits both of his art and his disposition.

DESSERT—The last course of a meal. Nowadays, in France, dessert comprises cheese, sweets (which were formerly served before the dessert) and fruit.

In former times at great banquets, dessert, which was the fifth course of the meal, was often presented in magnificent style. Large set pieces fashioned in pastry, described often and in great detail by Carême, whose accounts are accompanied by splendid illustrations, were placed on the table at the beginning of the meal. These handsome set pieces, which owed more to architecture than to the art of cooking, had a purely decorative function. Just before the sweet course, a multitude of sweets were elegantly arranged, in a pre-determined order, on the table with the set pieces, for every ceremonial table was laid in accordance with a detailed plan, and the dishes had to harmonize with gold plate, crystal, magnificent baskets of fruit (with the fruit piled into pyramids) and the tall candelabra whose candles lit the table.

Dessert arranged in this way presented a magnificent spectacle, and, before starting on the meal, the guests were able to admire the superb artistry of the arrangements.

Dessert (after Carême, *Le Confiturier Royal*)

Though the presentation of dessert in our own day is somewhat less ostentatious than it was in our father's time, it is no less pleasing to behold. Now, more than in other times, flowers are used for table decoration. Fruit too, is often placed on the table before the beginning of the meal and this too contributes, in the most appropriate way, to its embellishment. The giant candelabra and tall fruit baskets have disappeared, but other accessories, no less magnificent, have taken their place.

Modern dessert in France
(*Orfèvrerie Christofle*)

The 'table-ends', those large gâteaux mounted on sugar plinths, which were once very fashionable, have now also disappeared.

Sweets, hot or cold, are served as dessert—after the cheese, as a matter of course in France. Although less ostentatious than in former times, modern desserts are no less sumptuous or succulent.

DESICCATION—The process of drying or dehydrating foodstuffs. A number of foodstuffs are commonly preserved by desiccation. See PRESERVATION OF FOOD.

DÉTREMPE—A technical term in confectionery meaning a mixture of flour and water to be used in the preparation of pastries.

For example, the French use the expression *faire la détrempe du feuilletage* for making the flour and water mixture used in the preparation of flaky pastry.

DEVIL-FISH. Diable de mer—This is another name for the Anglerfish found on the North American and European sides of the Atlantic. It is also sometimes known as *Sea-Frog*, *Miller's Thumb*, and *Bull-Head*.

This fish has acquired these nicknames because of its odd shape. 'It seems,' says an old French writer, 'to be nothing but head and tail.'

In the U.S.A. this fish is also known as *Goose Fish*, *All-Mouth Monkfish*, and *Fishing Frog*.

DEVILLED (A LA DIABLE)—This is the name given to a method of preparation, especially suitable for poultry. The bird is slit open along the back, spread out flat, seasoned, grilled and then, after cooking, sprinkled with fresh breadcrumbs and browned under the grill.

Poultry cooked in this way must always be served with *Diable sauce*. See SAUCE.

DEXTRIN (British gum). Dextrine—A product obtained by splitting starch. Dextrin is a powdery substance, white or slightly yellowish. When mixed with water it forms a thick, viscous paste.

DEXTROSE—The scientific name for glucose, so called because, in polarization, it causes deviation to the right.

DIABLE—A cookery utensil made in the form of two porous earthenware pans, one of which fits on to the other as lid. Some vegetables and fruit (potatoes, chestnuts) can be cooked in this type of pan without liquid.

In France a sheet-metal draught device for solid fuel cookers is also known as a *diable.*

DIABLE (A LA)—See DEVILLED.

DIABLOTINS—Round slices of French bread about $\frac{1}{3}$ inch thick, covered with a mixture of thick *Béchamel* flavoured with grated cheese and cayenne pepper. These slices are sprinkled with grated Parmesan cheese and browned. They are served with soup.

In earlier times the name *Diablotins* was given in France to a variety of confectioner's cream fritters.

Chocolates sold in paper cases and accompanied by a motto are also called *diablotins.*

DIAPHRAGM. Coffre—Part of the body of man or beast which contains the ribs. The French word *coffre* is applied to the carapace of certain crustaceans.

For instance, '*Remplissez de chiffonade de laitue le coffre de la langouste*' (i.e. 'Stuff the carapace of the langouste with a lettuce chiffonade').

DIASTASIS. Diastase—A ferment which develops in grain and tubers at the moment of germination. This ferment liquefies the starch and then turns it into sugar.

DICING. Couper en dés—Cutting various foodstuffs into large or small cubes or squares. Thus ham, artichoke hearts, truffles, mushrooms, etc. when cut in this way are said to be diced.

DIEPPOISE (A LA)—A method of preparation special to sea-water fish. Fish *à la Dieppoise* is cooked in white wine, garnished with mussels and shelled fresh-water crayfish tails, and masked with a white wine sauce made with the cooking stock of the fish and mussels. See *Brill à la Dieppoise*.

DIET. Régime alimentaire—Methodical and reasoned use of food in health as in sickness.

DIETETICS. Hygiène alimentaire—Dietetics are concerned with certain special aspects of food: the analysis of its components, the study of its effect upon digestion, of the way in which it is assimilated into the body, of its energy-potential, and the working out of balanced invalid diets.

DIGESTER. Digesteur—A piece of apparatus on the pressure cooker principle. It can be hermetically sealed and is fitted with a safety-valve, thus enabling food to be subjected to higher temperatures than that of boiling water. See PRESSURE-COOKER.

DIGESTIBILITY—The assimilability of foodstuffs into the digestive system. The layman recognises food as digestible if it produces no unpleasant sensation in the course of digestion. To the expert, digestibility is determined by the proportion of elements in food which can be thoroughly assimilated into the human organism.

This portion is variable in different foods and depends also upon the state in which they are eaten, upon the manner in which they are cooked, upon the amount eaten and upon the other foods eaten at the same time, and is assessed only on the basis of a perfectly healthy digestion.

Some foods, such as sugar which leaves no residue, are completely digestible; with most other foods there is a larger or smaller proportion of waste.

In a normal mixed diet the proportion of digestible matter is 97% in meat and eggs; 94% in milk; 79% in bread; 80 to 85% in pulses and potatoes. In fats, the proportion of digestible matter is 95% in meat, eggs and milk; 100% of the carbohydrates in milk are digestible, in cereals in the form of flour or bread, 99%; in pulses and potatoes 96%. About 10% of wastage is a fair average, especially as most people eat more than is strictly necessary.

DIGESTIVE. DIGESTIF—That which promotes digestion.

The *digestive juices* are elements in the secretions of the digestive glands which cause foodstuffs to undergo changes which render them assimilable. The principle digestive juices are: *ptyalin* in saliva, *pepsin* and *rennet* in the stomach, *amylase*, *trypsin* and *lipase* in the pancrease; *erepsin* and *invertin* in the intestine.

Several of these juices are taken in the form of medicine to supplement deficiencies in the natural secretions. Apart from these juices there are, strictly speaking, no medicines helpful to the digestion. Bitter medicines increase the appetite; alkalines and acids neutralize excess acids or alkalis in the stomach, but are not, in the exact sense of the word, *digestives*. As for liqueurs taken after meals with coffee, from the medical point of view, they do not deserve the name *digestive* which is sometimes bestowed upon them.

DIJON—The capital of the ancient province of Burgundy is a town of high gastronomic repute and has many specialities. Among these the most famous are *Dijon mustard*, *Gingerbread*, *Cassis*, *Jambon persillé* (ham sprinkled with parsley); *Gras-doubles à la dijonnaise* (tripe *à la dijonnaise*); *Beef à la bourguignonne; Ferchuse; Snails à la bourguignonne; Meurette*. There are many other special dishes which are described in detail under Burgundy. See BURGUNDY.

DILUTING. DÉLAYER—Adding liquid to another liquid or semi-solid substance.

DINNER. DÎNER—This word is derived from the low Latin *di-coenare*, *disnare*.

Dinner is the main meal of the day.

The ancient Greeks usually dined towards evening. In ancient Rome dinner or supper was taken at the ninth or tenth hour, that is to say between 3 and 4 in the afternoon.

The Roman dinner menu was made up as follows:

First course (*gustatus*): eggs, various vegetables (these were probably seasoned with vinegar.)

Second course (*mensa prima*): various stews and, so say some translators of Latin texts, roast veal.

Third course (*mensa secunda*): pastries and various jams, fruit and sweetmeats.

At great Roman banquets, five or even six courses were served.

The banquet menus of ancient Greece were similar in character, but in Greece it was customary to serve boiled fowl as a first course, as a kind of soup.

In France, the dinner hour has shifted about a good deal. Under King Charles V (1337–1380), the main meal of the day was taken at nine o'clock in the morning. This meal, it is believed, was somewhat similar to the English breakfast.

Under Louis XIII (1610–1643) dinner was served at midday. In the seventeenth century, it became customary to serve this meal after mass, that is to say between eleven in the morning and midday.

Under Louis XV (1715–1774), the dinner hour was put forward again so that, from this time forth, dinner became the main meal of the day as it is now. It was then served at about two o'clock in the afternoon. Nowadays the normal dinner hour is between 7 and 8 in the evening, though in France it is commonly served much later than this and is often in the nature of supper.

DIPLOMAT. DIPLOMATE—This name is given to several quite different dishes. See PUDDING, *Diplomat pudding*, SAUCE, *Diplomat sauce*.

DISH STAND. PORTE-PLAT—Basket or support used for carrying dishes. A sort of metal or porcelain tray or mat on which dishes are placed.

DISINFECTING. DÉSINFECTION—This term, which once meant to deodorize, today means to purify or render aseptic by destroying harmful germs.

Disinfecting is obligatory in contaminated areas, especially those where provisions are kept.

In the case of foodstuffs which are in the least degree contaminated chemical disinfectants are usually ineffectual and their use in such cases must be condemned.

DISPENSAIRE—The name given in former times to a book of recipes.

DISSECTING. DISSECTION—This term is sometimes used instead of jointing, e.g. *dissecting a chicken*.

DISTILLATION—The process of separating the more volatile from the less volatile components in a liquid by vaporization (through heating) followed by condensation (through chilling).

In industry, very large apparatus is used to distil fermented fruit juices or cereal decoctions in the production of commercial alcohol or spirits. See SPIRITS.

DIURETIC. DIURÉTIQUE—Having the property of increasing the volume of urine. In the old *Codex Pharmacopoeiae*, the diuretic plants mentioned are the dried roots of smallage, asparagus, fennel, parsley and knee-holly.

DIVE—An old French word, short for divine, now only used in the expression *la dive bouteille* (the divine bottle), a quotation from Rabelais' *Gargantua*.

DIVER OR LOON. PLONGEON—Web-footed birds of the *Gaviiformes* order, very similar to duck. The flesh is tough, oily and fishy, yet there are people who eat it.

DOBULE—Common French name for the European chub, which is found in lakes, ponds and rivers. This fish tastes a little like the *féra*. It is cooked in the same way as *féra*. See FÉRA.

DOE. BICHE—The doe is the female of deer. The meat of this animal, when it is killed outside the mating season, is similar to that of the roe-buck.

Before preparing this meat in any way (all methods indicated for venison are applicable to it) it should be marinated. See MARINADE.

DOE OR ROE DEER. CHEVRETTE—See preceding entry.

DOG. CHIEN—Carnivorous domestic mammal whose meat is edible and is eaten in certain countries. In China there is a breed of dogs (Chow dogs) specially fattened for the table.

Dogfish

DOGFISH. AIGUILLAT—Common name for the fish of the *squalus acanthias* species, also called the *Piked dogfish* or *Spur dogfish.* This fish has a strong spike of horny substance in front which reaches up to a yard in length. It is a bluish-grey on the back and dirty white on the belly. It feeds on fish, crustaceans, and molluscs. Its flesh is white and not very delicate. Its liver oil is used in the treatment of skins; its own skin is used by turners for polishing wood and ivory.

For cooking purposes, dogfish can be prepared by following the recipes given for cod and other large fish (see COD); its flesh can be made into soup, thin but quite nutritive, especially if pasta products, cereals, or bread are added to them.

The name dogfish is given to other species of fish on both sides of the North Atlantic.

DOLIC. DOLIQUE—A group of pulses, several of which are edible. Among these, the most important is the soya or Chinese bean. See SOYA BEAN.

DOLMAS OR DOLMADES (Turkish cookery)—*Dolmas* are prepared by stuffing vine-leaves, first blanched and thoroughly drained, with a stuffing of minced lamb and cooked rice. These leaves are rolled into balls and braised in very little stock with oil and lemon juice added.

Dolmas can also be made with cabbage leaves, fig leaves or the leaves of the hazel-nut tree.

In Turkey, *dolmas* are often cooked in sheep-tail fat.

Dolma is also the term used in the Middle East for a dish of mixed stuffed vegetables, aubergines (egg-plants), tomatoes, artichoke hearts and *courgettes* (zucchini).

DOM PÉRIGNON—A celebrated monk of the Abbey of Hartvilliers near Epernay, who achieved fame by discovering the process of making sparkling champagne.

DONKEY, ASS'S FOAL. ÂNE, ÂNON—Little used for food, the donkey's meat is nevertheless tasty, much superior in flavour to that of horse; it is used mainly in the manufacture of certain types of sausage. Wild donkey used to be considered choice venison in the Orient.

Donkey meat, and certainly that of ass's foals, has been used in cookery for a long time. It was highly valued by the Romans. Maecenas, it is said, treated his guests to a stew of marinated donkey meat.

In France, in the sixteenth century, Chancellor Duprat had donkeys bred and fattened for his table. During the blockade of Malta by the English and the Neapolitans, the inhabitants of Malta, reduced to eating all sorts of domestic animals, dogs, cats, rats and donkeys, became so fond of the flesh of the latter that they even preferred it to beef and veal. During the seige of Paris, donkey meat, along with the flesh of many other less edible animals, helped to appease the pangs of hunger of the beseiged.

Culinary preparation of donkey meat is the same as for horsemeat or beef. The meat of an ass's foal under two years old is very delicate and is used in making pâtés, which in quality rival those made of veal.

Among the dishes made of donkey meat, there is one which evokes a painful hour of French history; the cook to Wilhelm, the king of Prussia, at a luncheon given to Napoleon III at Sedan, served, it is said, *donkey's brains à la diplomate*. We find it difficult to believe in the veracity of this story.

DORADE—See SEA BREAM.

DORMANT—A large silver or gold centrepiece which used, in former times to stand on the dining table. It was similar to an *épergne.*

DORMOUSE. LOIR—A small rodent found in Southern Europe. It is about the size of a rat. It was highly esteemed by the gastronomes of Rome, where the dormouse was fattened in cages and cooked with honey and poppy seed. It was eaten at the beginning of a feast.

DORURE (Gilding)—This is a term used in French cookery for beaten whole eggs or egg yolks, thinned with a little water, brushed on to pastry and some other mixtures such as *Duchess potato mixture* (see POTATOES).

The egg is brushed on to the pastry with a pastry-brush made of silk or feathers.

DOTTEREL. GUIGNARD—A European bird of passage of the wader group. Its flesh is rather tasteless. All recipes for *Plover** are suitable for dotterel.

DOUBLE-CREAM (Cheese). DOUBLE-CRÈME—See CHEESE.

DOUBLE SAUCEPAN (U.S. Double boiler). DOUBLE-FOND—Two saucepans fitting together. Food which must not come in contact directly with the heat of the cooker is placed in the upper saucepan. The lower saucepan contains water which is brought to the boil, so heating the contents of the upper saucepan.

DOUBLER—A term in French cookery, meaning to fold in two a layer of pastry, a cut of meat or a fillet of fish. It also means to cover pastries on a baking sheet with another baking sheet to protect them from the heat of the oven.

DOUGHS, PASTRY, BATTERS:

Brioche dough I. PÂTE À BRIOCHE—*Ingredients.* $3\frac{3}{4}$ cups (500 grams) of sieved flour, $1\frac{1}{2}$ cups (400 grams) of butter, $\frac{1}{3}$ ounce (10 grams) of dried yeast, 6 eggs, 3 tablespoons (25 grams) of fine sugar, $1\frac{1}{2}$ teaspoons (10 grams) of salt and $\frac{1}{2}$ cup (1 decilitre) of warm water.

Method. The leaven: Put a quarter of the flour in a circle on the table, put the yeast in the middle, dilute with a little water, moisten and mix as usual keeping the dough rather soft. Roll into a ball, make a crossways incision on the top, put into a small bowl, cover it and leave in a warm place for the paste to ferment and double its volume.

The dough: Put the rest of the flour in a circle on the table, put 4 eggs and 2 tablespoons of warm water in the middle, moisten the dough, and knead it.

Add sugar and salt dissolved in a few drops of water, then incorporate the previously softened butter.

Add the remaining 2 eggs, one by one, while continuing to mix the dough.

Mix everything together well.

Spread the dough on the table, pour the leaven into the centre and blend it in as described for the butter above.

Put the dough into a bowl, cover with a cloth and put in a warm place to rise.

Five or six hours later beat the dough and from then on keep in a cool place until needed.

Brioche dough II. PÂTE À BRIOCHE COMMUNE—*Ingredients.* 3¾ cups (500 grams) of sieved flour, ¾ cup (200 grams) of butter, ⅓ ounce (10 grams) of yeast, 4 eggs, 1 teaspoon (5 grams) of fine sugar, 1½ teaspoons (10 grams) of salt, ½ cup (1 decilitre) of warm water (or milk).

Method. Proceed as described in the recipe for ordinary *brioche dough.*

Note. As this dough has to be rolled with a rolling pin, it should be kept rather firm.

When it is intended for pies to be served as entrée, or for coulibiacs, the sugar can be omitted, although the small amount of sugar indicated above is only meant to give a little colour to the dough.

Mousseline brioche dough. PÂTE À BRIOCHE MOUSSELINE —*Method.* Prepare the dough as described in the recipe for ordinary brioche.

Add 4 tablespoons (60 grams) of softened butter per pound of dough.

Shape the dough into a ball, put it into a well buttered mould, taking care not to fill it above two thirds.

Put in a warm place and leave until the dough rises to the top of the mould (to let the dough rise in the mould, put a band of buttered greaseproof paper around it, tied with string).

Bake in a slow oven.

Chou paste I (d'office) (Cream puff pastry). PÂTE À CHOU D'OFFICE—Pour 4 cups (a litre) of water, with ¾ cup (200 grams) of butter and 1½ teaspoons (10 grams) of salt into a pan. Bring to the boil. Remove from fire and add 4¾ cups (625 grams) of sieved flour, pouring it all in at once. Mix well.

Cook this composition on the fire, stirring with a wooden spoon until it dries and comes away from the walls of the pan.

Remove from fire and, stirring vigorously with a wooden spoon, add from 12 to 14 eggs (depending on size) putting them in two at a time.

This paste has many applications in cookery. It is used for making gnocci *à la viennoise*, for preparing dauphine potato mixture, etc.

Chou paste II (Cream puff pastry). PÂTE À CHOU ORDINAIRE—Chou paste can be moistened with milk instead of water. The eggs can be added one by one, stirring the mixture with a wooden spoon all the time.

Dumpling dough. PÂTE À DUMPLING—*Ingredients.* 3¾ cups (500 grams) of sieved flour, 10 ounces (300 grams) of suet (net weight), 3 tablespoons (50 grams) of sugar, 1½ teaspoons (10 grams) of salt and 1 cup (2 decilitres) of water.

Method. Remove all skin and fibre from the suet (choose very dry suet), shred and chop it up very finely with a knife dipped in flour.

Put the flour in a circle on the board, place the suet in the middle, adding sugar, salt and water.

Mix to a fairly stiff paste, shape into a ball and keep in a cool place until needed.

Flaky pastry. FEUILLETAGE—Flaky pastry, the most delicate of all pastries, is said by some historians to have been invented by Claude Gelée, called le Lorrain, the famous seventeenth century painter, or, others say, by a chef called Feuillet who was chief pastrycook to the house of Condé.

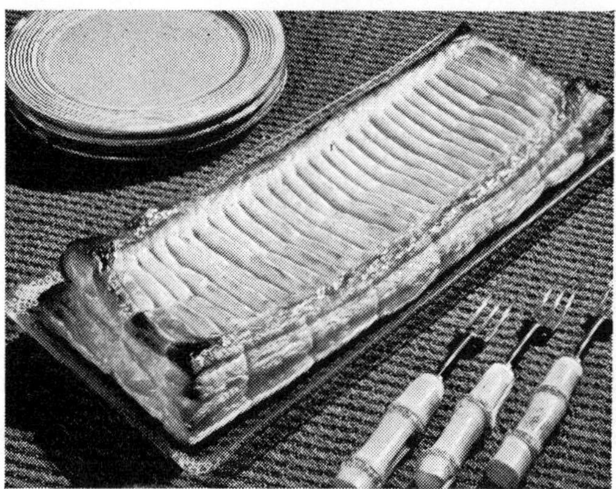

Flaky pastry

It would be hard to decide which theory is correct. It certainly seems more logical to attribute this invention to a pastrycook than to a painter, but there is no reliable documentary evidence to support this view, and moreover, it would seem rather childish to suppose that the word *feuilletage* (flaky or leaved pastry) derives from Feuillet.

Carême eulogises Feuillet who was undoubtedly a great pastrycook. In his *Pâtissier Royal*, Carême says: 'Richaud spurred me on to work twice as hard by speaking to me often of the great Feuillet: from the 1st of January to the 31st December, his pastries were delicious.' But Carême stops there, and nowhere in his learned treatises on pastry does he say that Feuillet was the inventor of flaky pastry. In contrast, Joseph Favre is very definite on this subject. In his *Dictionnaire Universel de Cuisine* he says outright that Feuillet was 'the inventor of flaky pastry.'

It appears, however, from the study of documents of a much earlier date than the lifetime of either the painter Claude Gelée or the pastrycook Feuillet, that flaky pastry was known not only in the Middle Ages but also in ancient Greece. In a charter drawn up by Robert, Bishop of Amiens (1311), flaky pastry cakes are mentioned.

Claude Gelée who, it is said, served a pastrycook's apprenticeship, was, therefore, not the inventor of this delicious pastry. He merely brought it back into fashion in his own time, since, no doubt, he had a special liking for it.

Some authorities attributed the invention of this pastry to a man called Saupiquet, who was master-chef to the Baron de la Vieuville, under Henry IV of France. However, it has been proved that long before this time *fleurons* (decorative motifs in flaky pastry) were served at the court of the Dukes of Tuscany. They were used as a garnish for macaroni and spinach.

Finally, some historians hold that flaky pastry made with oil, which for a long time was the monopoly of the town of Cahors, was created in the reign of Charles V (of France), that is to say in the fourteenth century, long before the painter Claude Gelée was born.

Flaky pastry or puff paste (Modern recipe). PÂTE FEUILLETÉE, FEUILLETAGE—First prepare a flour and water paste in the following manner:

Put 3¾ cups (500 grams) of sieved flour on a board in a circle, making a well in the middle. Since flours differ, the proportion of water to flour is variable. Into the centre of this circle put in 1½ teaspoons (10 grams) of salt and from

1. Water is poured on the salt in the middle of the well

2. Mixing flour and water

3. Method of putting butter on the paste

4. How butter is enclosed in the paste

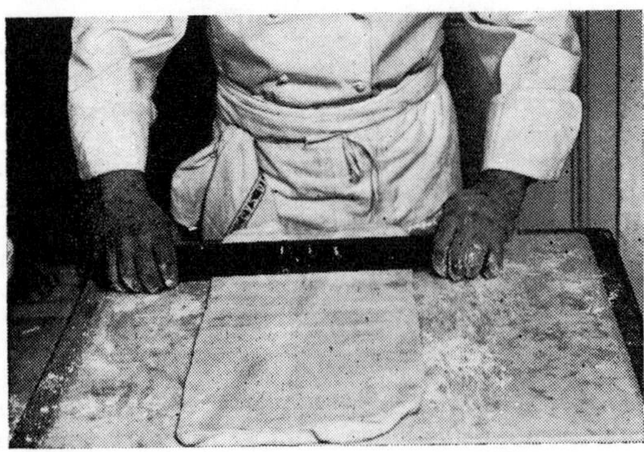

5. Rolling out for the first time: the paste is rolled out in a rectanglar sheet

6. Rolling out for the second time: the rectangle of paste is folded in three

7. Second turn: turn the paste before rolling it out

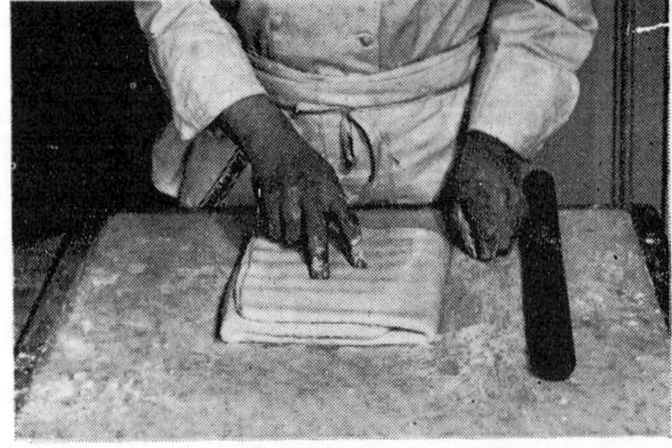

8. Making a mark on the paste to indicate that it has been given two turns

MAKING FLAKY PASTRY (Cookery classes, Gaz de Paris, *Photograph Larousse*)

FRUIT

(*From the original French edition of* Larousse Gastronomique)

GAME. Hare pâté *(Robert Car*

1¼ to 1½ cups (2½ to 3 decilitres) of water. Mix and knead until the dough is smooth and elastic. Roll into a ball and let it stand for 25 minutes.

Roll out the paste into a sheet, about 8 inches (20 centimetres) square and of even thickness throughout. Put 1 pound (500 grams) of kneaded butter in the middle of this paste. Fold the ends of the paste over the butter in such a way as to enclose it completely. Leave to stand for 10 minutes in a cold place.

Give two turns to this paste. This operation is called *tourage* in French and it is done in two parts;

(1) Roll the paste with a rolling pin (on a *lightly floured* board) in such a way as to obtain a rectangle 24 inches (60 centimetres) long, 8 inches (20 centimetres) wide and ½ inch (1½ centimetres) thick.

(2) Re-fold this strip in three. This operation is known as *giving* a turn, i.e. the second turn is done by rolling out the folded paste in the opposite direction, and so forth.

Give four more turns to the paste, leaving it to stand for 10 minutes between each operation.

After having been given the six prescribed turns, the puff paste is ready for use.

Note. The purpose of turning and rolling is to spread the butter evenly in the paste and to ensure the regularity of its development during cooking.

Before being added to the flour and water paste, the butter should be kneaded on a lightly floured marble slab, so as to give the two elements (the flour and water paste and the butter) a similar consistency. It can be kneaded in a floured cloth.

During preparation, flaky pastry (puff paste) should be kept in a cold place. But it should never be put directly on ice; this may cause the butter to harden and it will then not be easy to incorporate in the paste.

The rolling out of paste and manipulating it on the table requires the table or board to be floured, but only a very small quantity of flour should be used for dusting the board.

Flaky pastry or puff paste (Carême's recipe). PÂTE FEUILLETÉE, FEUILLETAGE—In the old culinary practice puff paste was prepared in a manner very different from the present day practice. Eggs used to be added to it, which is never done nowadays.

Here is a recipe given by Carême:

Method. 'Having put a litron (about 800 grams) of sieved flour on the board, place the tips of your fingers in the middle and spread it in a circle with the inside diameter of four inches; this operation is known in the profession as "*making a well*", as the flour, disposed in this manner will, as shall be seen later, have water in the middle required for moistening it.

'In the centre of this well, put 2 *gros* (see WEIGHTS AND MEASURES) of fine salt, 2 yolks of egg, a piece of butter the size of a walnut and nearly a glass of water. Stir this mixture with the tips of your fingers (using the right hand only and keeping the fingers spread out) and, little by little, mix in the flour, adding a little water if necessary, so that the paste is moistened, has the right consistency and is slightly firm. Then stir it a little, pressing with the hand on the board in such a way as to achieve, after a few minutes' work, a paste which is soft to the touch and as smooth as satin.

'It is important to note that this paste should neither be too firm nor too soft—it should be just in between. It is, however, better for it to be a little on the soft side rather than too hard.

'This procedure will apply equally in the winter and summer, although many people claim that in the winter the paste should be firmer than in the summer, because of the difference of these two seasons.

'As far as hardness of butter is concerned, this reasoning has an element of truth in it, for the winter is propitious to our work whilst the summer makes our operations difficult and laborious, sometimes leading to unsatisfactory results, especially in the case of puff paste, which cannot be well done in the summer without cooling it on ice, which then renders the butter as firm as in the month of January.

'When the paste is made as described above, take out three quarters (three *quarterons*) of the butter which you had put (twenty minutes before beginning to make the paste), in pieces, into a bucket of well water with several pounds of washed and broken ice. Dry and knead this butter in a napkin, to extract water and, at the same time, to make it supple and smooth.

'Roll the paste out in a rectangular sheet; put the butter in the middle and cover it by folding the edges of the paste over it. Make sure that it is entirely enclosed with an even thickness of paste all round. This part of the operation, as well as turning, should be done as quickly as possible; with this in view you should roll it out with a rolling pin on a marble slab or other surface. When the rolled out sheet of paste is about three feet long and eleven or twelve inches wide, fold one foot of one end of the sheet, then the same with the other end, thus the sheet of paste should be folded in three layers of equal length. Roll out the paste again to the same dimensions as above, turning it before rolling so that its former width becomes its length; fold it again in the same way, roll out so that it is two inches longer than it is wide, put it quickly into a pan lightly sprinkled with flour and stand on six pounds of crushed ice spread out to cover the same length and width as the pan. Cover the paste with a piece of paper on top of which you stand a pan filled with a pound of crushed ice.

'After three or four minutes, remove the top pan, turn the paste upside down and cover again. Then you begin the same operation all over again, after which you give the paste two turns as described. Put the puff paste on ice again, turning it as carefully as before; then you give another turn and a half or two turns, depending on the use for which it is intended.'

Among the notes made by Carême on the making of puff paste, there are two important points, which we feel we should quote in their entirety:

'Generally, care should be taken to sprinkle the top and bottom of the puff paste with flour very sparingly when turning it, otherwise it goes grey in the baking.

'Then, when the puff paste has been given the last turn, it should be used at once, that is to say it should be placed in the oven in the space of four, six or, at the most, eight minutes after the last rolling out. If it is thoughtlessly made ready 20 or 25 minutes before it can be put in the oven, then instead of being clear and light, it will be dull and tough. This is due, I presume, to the fact that during this period of waiting the consistency of the paste goes slack; this causes it to lose some of its elasticity, which is so evident in its first strength, and for this reason it is essential, as far as possible, to complete the preparation of puff paste just a few minutes before it can be put in the oven.' (*Le pâtissier royal.*)

Flaky pastry or puff pastry made with oil. PÂTE FEUILLETÉE À L'HUILE—'Proceed as described in the recipe for *Pudding pastry or Suet flaky pastry*, the only difference being that instead of using lard use oil, adding 1½ cups (12 ounces) of oil during the rolling and turning. Then cut as usual.' (Carême's recipe.)

'I give these various methods of making puff paste.' says Carême, 'for the benefit of cooks in distant countries, to which they are inclined to travel, where butter may be in short supply or even altogether unknown, as in the case told to me by the famous Laguipière of the voyage to America which he made with the Comte d'Estaing, during his conquest of the island of Grenada in 1779, where all pastry was made out of suet, there being absolutely no butter.'

This sort of puff paste, which one might be forced to make in foreign lands, is suitable only for pastry served hot.

Semi-flaky pastry or rough puff paste. PÂTE DEMI-FEUILLETÉE, DEMI-FEUILLETAGE—Having finished cutting out your puff paste into patties, vol-au-vent, etc., collect the left over pieces together into a ball.

This paste, rolled out to the desired dimensions, can be used for making boat-shaped tartlets, croustades, tartlets, etc. This paste is also called *rognures* ('scraps').

Three-minute flaky pastry or puff paste. PÂTE FEUILLETÉE EN TROIS MINUTES—*Ingredients.* 3 cups (400 grams) of sifted flour, 1 pound (500 grams) of butter, $1\frac{1}{2}$ teaspoons (10 grams) of salt and 1 cup ($\frac{1}{4}$ litre) of water.

Combine all the ingredients, give the paste four turns. After these four turns the paste can be used.

Viennese flaky pastry or puff paste. PÂTE FEUILLETÉE À LA VIENNOISE—*Ingredients.* $3\frac{3}{4}$ cups (500 grams) of sifted flour, 1 pound (500 grams) of butter, 2 yolks, 1 cup ($2\frac{1}{2}$ decilitres) of water and $1\frac{1}{2}$ teaspoons (10 grams) of salt.

Method. Mix half the flour with the yolks, water and salt.

Separately, mix the rest of the flour with one third of the butter, blending them with a knife.

Roll out the flour, yolk and water paste into a thin square sheet. Shape the butter and flour mixture into a square of a smaller size and put it on the paste square.

Enclose this butter in the paste, folding the edges as usual.

Roll out the paste as described in puff paste recipe.

Flour and water dough. PÂTE À L'EAU—This paste is used for luting, or hermetically sealing, earthenware casserole and cocotte lids.

It is made by mixing flour with enough warm water to obtain a soft paste. Use as indicated.

Leavened dough for tarts. PÂTE LEVÉE POUR TARTES—The best recipe for leavened paste for tarts is the same as for brioche dough.

A more ordinary dough can be made using $3\frac{3}{4}$ cups (500 grams) of sifted flour, 4 eggs, $1\frac{1}{2}$ teaspoons (10 grams) of salt, $1\frac{1}{2}$ tablespoons (20 grams) of sugar, $\frac{1}{3}$ ounce (10 grams) of yeast, a cup (a quarter of a litre) of milk and $\frac{7}{8}$ cup (200 grams) of butter.

Proceed as described in the recipe for *Brioche dough.*

Fine lining paste or pastry dough I. PÂTE À FONCER FINE—*Ingredients.* $3\frac{3}{4}$ cups (500 grams) of sifted flour, $1\frac{1}{4}$ cups (300 grams) of butter, one egg, $\frac{1}{2}$–$\frac{3}{4}$ cup ($1\frac{1}{2}$ decilitres) of water, 5 tablespoons (50 grams) of fine sugar, $1\frac{1}{2}$ teaspoons (10 grams) of salt.

Method. Spread the flour in a circle on the board, make a well in the middle and put in egg, butter, water, sugar and salt. First mix all these ingredients together, then, little by little, incorporate the flour.

Knead twice, roll the paste in a ball and wrap in a cloth.

Keep in a cold place until ready for use. Lining paste should always be made several hours before it is needed, and the less this paste is handled the better, as it quickly becomes tough.

Lining paste (ordinary) or pastry dough II (Tart pastry). PÂTE À FONCER ORDINAIRE—*Ingredients.* $3\frac{3}{4}$ cups (500 grams) of sifted flour; $\frac{1}{2}$ pound (250 grams) of butter; $\frac{3}{4}$ to 1 cup (2 decilitres) of water; $1\frac{1}{2}$ teaspoons (10 grams) of salt.

Method. Proceed as described in the recipe for *Fine lining paste.*

Pastry dough for hot or cold pâtés (pies)—See PASTRY.

Pudding Pastry—see DUMPLING DOUGH.

Pudding pastry or suet flaky pastry (Carême's recipe). PÂTE FEUILLETÉE À LA GRAISSE DE BOEUF—'Having removed skin and fibre from a pound of suet, chop it up very finely and put in a mortar with a tablespoon of good olive oil. Then, as you pound it, little by little, add several more tablespoons of oil, to give it body and to soften it at the same time, in such a way that, as a result of this operation, the suet becomes as soft and easy to work as butter.

'Then proceed to use it as butter, in the same proportions. Mix it with the flour and water paste as described above.

'You can use lard instead of oil. By using suet and lard in equal proportions, very good puff paste is obtained, very agreeable to the palate, but it must be eaten hot.'

Note. This type of puff paste is very suitable for entrée pies. See TOURTES (PIES).

Puff pastry—See FLAKY PASTRY.

Savarin dough I. PÂTE À SAVARIN—*Ingredients.* 4 cups (500 grams) of sifted cake flour, $\frac{1}{2}$ pound (250 grams) of butter, $\frac{1}{4}$ cup (50 grams) of sugar, $1\frac{1}{2}$ teaspoons (10 grams) of salt, $\frac{1}{3}$ ounce (10 grams) of yeast, 6 to 8 eggs, 1 cup (2 decilitres) of milk.

Method. Take a third of the flour and prepare the leaven, incorporating in it the yeast dissolved in 1 to $1\frac{1}{2}$ cups (2 or 3 decilitres) of warm water. Blend perfectly and leave to rise, until the leaven more than doubles its volume.

Spread the rest of the flour in a circle on the board, make a well in the middle, and add salt and two thirds of the eggs. Work the mixture by hand to give it more body, then add the rest of the eggs and the milk. Knead until the paste no longer sticks to the hands.

Then add the butter quickly and pour in the leaven. Blend the mixture to make it smooth and, *last of all,* add the sugar.

Put the dough into a bowl, stand in a cool place, covering the bowl with a cloth to prevent the formation of a crust, and leave until the following day.

The baking of savarin. A mould with a special border, called a *savarin mould,* is used for baking this cake.

Butter the mould and fill it half-way with the above dough.

Stand the mould in a warm place and leave the dough to rise until it fills the mould completely.

Bake in a hot oven from 20 to 35 minutes, according to the size of the mould.

Savarin dough II. PÂTE À SAVARIN—This is a shorter formula. The ingredients are identical.

Put the sifted flour into a bowl. Mix the leaven and the dough in the order described above. Add the butter, melted and still warm. Then add the leaven and the sugar and use at once.

Savarin dough III. PÂTE À SAVARIN—*Ingredients.* $3\frac{3}{4}$ cups (500 grams) of sifted flour, $1\frac{1}{3}$ cups (375 grams) of butter, 2 tablespoons (20 grams) of fine sugar, $\frac{2}{3}$ ounce (20 grams) of yeast, 8 eggs, $\frac{1}{2}$ cup (one decilitre) of milk, $1\frac{1}{2}$ teaspoons (10 grams) of fine salt.

Method. Put the sifted flour into a bowl, make a well in the middle and put in the yeast.

Moisten the yeast with warm milk and stir it to dilute.

Add the eggs one by one, mixing the paste with the hands to blend well.

Put the butter, previously softened and divided into small pieces, on the paste.

Cover the bowl and stand in a warm place to ferment, until the dough doubles its volume.

Add salt. Knead the dough with the hands to incorporate the butter properly and continue to do so until the dough acquires sufficient body to be lifted in one block.

Then add the sugar and knead a few minutes longer to blend well.

Savarin dough IV. PÂTE À SAVARIN—*Ingredients.* 3¾ cups (500 grams) of sifted flour, 1⅓ cups (350 grams) of butter, 2 teaspoons (10 grams) of sugar, ⅓ ounce (10 grams) of yeast, 7 eggs, ½ cup (one decilitre) of milk, 1½ teaspoons (10 grams) of fine salt.

Method. Prepare a leaven, using a quarter of the flour, the yeast and the warm milk. Put this leaven into a small bowl, cover and stand in a warm place to ferment.

Separately, mix the rest of the flour with half the butter, the eggs and the salt. Blend well, kneading the paste by hand.

Add the leaven, the rest of the softened butter and the sugar. Continue to knead the dough for a few moments.

Short pastry I. PÂTE SÈCHE SUCRÉE—*Ingredients.* 3¾ cups (500 grams) of sifted flour, ⅞ cup (200 grams) of butter, 3 eggs, 1 heaping cup (150 grams) of fine castor sugar, half a spoonful of orange blossom water or ½ teaspoon orange extract.

Method. Proceed as described in the recipe for *Lining paste or Pastry dough.*

Short Pastry II. PÂTE SUCRÉE—*Ingredients.* 1⅝ cups (250 grams) of sifted flour, 5 tablespoons (75 grams) of sugar, ⅞ cup (200 grams) of butter, 1 egg, a small pinch of salt and lemon peel, or vanilla-flavoured sugar.

Method. Spread the flour in a circle, make a well in the middle and put in the sugar (without mixing it), the butter, well softened, the salt and the egg.

Mix all these ingredients, with the exception of flour, into a soft paste, then crumble them with flour, kneading the paste as little as possible, just enough to make it hold together.

Leave it to harden for two hours, then roll out and cut.

BATTERS AND DOUGHS FOR BISCUITS ETC.:

Baba batter. PÂTE À BABA—*Ingredients.* 3¾ cups (500 grams) of sieved flour, 1¼ cups (300 grams) of butter, 7 eggs, ⅔ ounce (20 grams) of yeast, 4 teaspoons (20 grams) of sugar, ½ cup (100 grams) of raisins and sultanas (half and half), ½ cup (1 decilitre) of warm milk, 2½ teaspoons (15 grams) of salt.

Method. Proceed as for making a *Savarin**. When the batter is ready, add the raisins, sultanas and sugar.

Pour into buttered baba moulds, filling only one third of the moulds.

Bake in a hot even oven, like *savarins.**

When cooked, pour over them sugar syrup, flavoured with rum or any other liqueur.

Batter for small tea biscuits. PÂTE À PETITS GÂTEAUX—*Ingredients.* 4 cups (500 grams) of sifted cake flour, 1¼ cups (300 grams) of sugar, 1 whole egg, 4 yolks of egg, one tablespoon of orange blossom water or 1 teaspoon of orange extract.

Method. Mix the paste in the usual manner, knead it twice, roll into a ball and leave to stand in a cold place for an hour or two.

Preparation of biscuits. Roll out the paste to a thickness of ⅓ inch. Cut it out with pastry cutters of different shapes. Put the biscuits on a baking tray, brush them with beaten egg, decorate, as desired, with halved almonds, cherries, candied peel, etc., and bake in a hot oven. When ready, remove from oven, brush over with a solution of gum arabic or boiling milk, mixed with sugar and reduced to a syrupy consistency. Treated in this manner, the biscuits look more shiny and keep better.

Crêpe batter.—See CRÊPES.

Crêpe batter (sweet). PÂTE À PANNEQUETS—Put 1⅝ cups (250 grams) of sifted flour, ½ cup (100 grams) of fine sugar and a pinch of salt into a bowl.

Add 6 whole eggs. Stir the mixture with a wooden spoon until smooth.

Dilute with 3¼ cups (7½ decilitres) of boiled milk (flavoured with vanilla, orange, or lemon, depending on the nature of the pancakes).

Add a tablespoon of butter heated to *noisette* colour (see BUTTER) and a spoonful of brandy or rum. Blend well.

Cussy batter. PÂTE À CUSSY—*Ingredients.* 1¾ cups (250 grams) of fine sugar, 1 cup (150 grams) of rice flour, 7 whole eggs, 4 tablespoons (65 grams) of butter, 1 tablespoon (15 grams) of vanilla-flavoured sugar, a pinch of salt.

Method. Put the eggs, sugar, vanilla-flavoured sugar and the salt into a basin.

Whisk the eggs on a low heat. When the mixture is well whisked, add the rice flour and the melted butter.

Batter for Vienna fritters. PÂTE À BEIGNETS VIENNOIS—Proceed as described in the recipe for *Brioche dough* using the following ingredients: 3¾ cups (500 grams) of sieved flour, ⅚ cup (200 grams) of butter, 6 eggs, ⅔ ounce (20 grams) of yeast, 2½ teaspoons (15 grams) of salt, 1 tablespoon (15 grams) of sugar and ½ cup (one decilitre) of milk.

Batter for soufflé fritters (or Pets de nonne). PÂTE À BEIGNETS SOUFFLÉS—Prepare in exactly the same way as *Chou paste*, adding 4 teaspoons (20 grams) of sugar for the proportions indicated in that recipe.

Galette batter. PÂTE À LA GALETTE—*Ingredients.* 4 cups (500 grams) of sifted cake flour, 1½ cups (375 grams) of butter, ¾ cup (1½ decilitres) of water, 1½ tablespoons (15 grams) of fine sugar and 1½ teaspoons (10 grams) of salt.

Method. Mix as described in the recipe for *Lining paste.* Roll the paste into a ball without kneading. Leave to stand in a cool place for two hours.

Give the paste 3 turns, leaving it to stand for 10 minutes between each turn.

Leave to stand for a few minutes before use.

Batter for little salted galettes (biscuits). PÂTE À PETITES GALETTES SALÉES—*Ingredients.* 2 cups (250 grams) of sifted cake flour, ½ cup (120 grams) of butter, ½ cup (1 decilitre) of milk, 2 tablespoons (20 grams) of fine sugar and 1½ teaspoons (10 grams) of salt.

Method. Put the flour on a board in a heap, make a well in the middle and put the sugar and salt into it. Add slightly warmed milk and butter, knead all together, roll into a ball and leave to stand for half an hour.

To make the galettes. Roll the paste out until it is no more than ⅛ inch (half a centimetre) in thickness.

Prick it over the whole surface with a metal fork. Cut out with a 6-inch round pastry cutter.

Put the galettes on a metal tray and bake them in a hot oven for about 10 minutes.

Genoese batter. PÂTE À GENOISE—*Ingredients.* 3⅛ cups (375 grams) of sifted cake flour, 3½ cups (500 grams) of fine sugar, ⅞ cup (200 grams) of melted butter, 16 eggs flavouring.

Method. Put the sugar and the eggs into a copper basin. Blend them. Put on a low heat on the stove or over a pan of hot water and beat with a whisk until the mixture makes a ribbon.

Remove from heat and, stirring gently with a wooden spoon, add the flavouring chosen, the flour and the melted butter, pouring it in a small thread.

Put into buttered and floured tins or pan, according to recipe. Bake in a hot oven.

Note. Genoese paste may be flavoured with vanilla sugar, vanilla extract, lemon or orange peel, or some liqueur.

Gougère batter. PÂTE À GOUGÈRE—Proceed as described in the recipe for ordinary *Chou paste*, replacing water by milk and omitting the sugar and the flavouring.

Having added eggs to the paste, finish it off with ½ pound (250 grams) of Gruyère cheese cut in very small dice.

Manqué batter. PÂTE À MANQUÉ—*Ingredients.* 3½ cups (500 grams) of fine sugar, 3¼ cups (400 grams) of sifted cake flour, 1¼ cups (300 grams) of butter, 18 yolks, 16 stiffly beaten whites, 3 tablespoons of rum.

Method. Cream the yolks and the sugar in a bowl until the mixture becomes white and light.

Add rum and flour, mix, then fold in stiffly beaten whites, and last of all, pour in melted butter.

Butter moulds *à manqué*, dust with flour, pour in the mixture and bake in a medium oven.

Mazarin batter. PÂTE À MAZARIN—Mixture of baba and brioche dough in equal proportions.

This paste is usually baked in plain genoese cake tins.

Fine sponge cake or biscuit batter. PÂTE À BISCUITS FINS—*Ingredients.* 3½ cups (500 grams) of fine sugar; 10 eggs (yolks and whites separated); 1 cup (125 grams) of sieved cake flour; ¾ cup (125 grams) of potato flour; 3 tablespoons (25 grams) of vanilla-flavoured sugar; a small pinch of salt.

Method. Blend the yolks with the sugar, vanilla-flavoured sugar and salt in a bowl with a wooden spoon. When the mixture is quite smooth, add the whites, whisked into a stiff froth, then add the flour and the potato flour.

Italian sponge cake or biscuit batter. PATE Â BISCUITS ITALIENS—*Ingredients.* ½ pound (250 grams) of sugar, 4 eggs (yolks and whites separated), 1 cup (125 grams) of sieved cake flour, salt.

Method. Put the sugar into a pan, moisten with ¼ cup (½ decilitre) of water, cook to hard ball degree (see SUGAR) and allow the sugar to cool to half its temperature.

Add the yolks to the sugar, then the flour and finally fold in the stiffly beaten whites.

Ordinary sponge cake or biscuit batter. PÂTE À BISCUITS ORDINAIRE—*Ingredients.* 1¾ cups (250 grams) of fine sugar; 8 eggs (yolks and whites separated); 1¼ cups (150 grams) of sifted cake flour; salt.

Method. Proceed as described in the recipe for *Fine sponge cake or biscuit batter*.

Reims sponge cake or biscuit batter. PÂTE À BISCUITS DE REIMS—*Ingredients.* 12 eggs, 1¼ cups (300 grams) of castor sugar, 1½ cups (180 grams) of sieved cake flour, one spoonful of vanilla-flavoured sugar, a small pinch of salt or 1 teaspoon vanilla extract.

Method. Put the sugar, 12 whites of egg and 10 yolks into a bowl and whisk this on a low heat until the mixture becomes firm and smooth. Add flour and vanilla-flavoured sugar. Mix with a wooden spoon.

Swiss sponge cake or biscuit batter. PÂTE À BISCUIT DE SAVOIE—*Ingredients.* 3½ cups (500 grams) of fine sugar, 1½ cups (185 grams) of sieved cake flour, 1¼ cups plus 1 tablespoon (185 grams) of cornstarch (cornflour), 14 yolks, 14 stiffly beaten whites of egg, one spoonful of vanilla-flavoured sugar or 1 teaspoon vanilla extract.

Method. Blend the sugar and the yolks together in a bowl until the mixture forms a ribbon. Add the flour, cornstarch, vanilla-flavoured sugar and the stiffly beaten whites. Mix quickly.

Butter a special baking tin, sprinkle with cornstarch carefully and pour in the mixture, filling only two thirds of the tin.

Bake in a slow but continuous oven.

Sponge cake or biscuit batter, whisked on the fire. PÂTE À BISCUITS SUR LE FEU—Put 12 eggs into a copper pan. Add 3½ cups (500 grams) of fine sugar and a small pinch of salt. Keeping the pan on the edge of the burner, whisk the mixture until it becomes very firm and smooth.

Still whisking, add 1⅓ cups (225 grams) of potato flour.

Sponge fingers batter. PÂTE À BISCUIT À LA CUILLER—*Ingredients.* 3½ cups (500 grams) of castor sugar, 3 cups plus 2 tablespoons (375 grams) of sieved flour, 16 eggs, one tablespoon of orange blossom water or ½ teaspoon orange or lemon extract.

Method. Mix the yolks and the sugar in a bowl. Keep on creaming the mixture until it forms a ribbon.

Add the flavouring, pour in the flour, then fold in 16 whites of egg whisked into a stiff froth. Lift the mixture with a wooden spoon to incorporate the whites evenly.

To make the biscuits. Put into a savoy (large pastry) bag with a plain ¾ inch nozzle. Pipe the biscuits on to strong paper in little sticks of uniform size. Sprinkle with plenty of fine sugar. Shake off the surplus sugar, lifting the two ends of the paper.

Moisten the biscuits with a few drops of cold water (which will ensure beading) and bake in a very slow oven.

DOUILLET (Pig au père). COCHON AU PÈRE—A very popular dish in the repertoire of an earlier age. Pierre de Lune, esquire of the household of the Prince de Rohan (1734–1803) gives the following recipe:

'Cut the pig into pieces. Blanch the pieces, interlard with pork fat cut partly from the outer layer and partly from the belly. Put them in a cloth, seasoned with salt, pepper, whole cloves, nutmeg, bayleaves, green lemons, spring onions. Cook in a pot with clear soup and a little white wine. Make sure that the dish is highly seasoned. Leave to stand until lukewarm. Serve on a napkin with slices of lemon.'

DOVE. COLOMBE—See PIGEON.

DOYENNE—A variety of pear which melts in the mouth and is very sweet. See PEAR.

DRAFF. DRÈCHE—A by-product of barley used in brewing. It is also used for fodder.

DRAGONET. DOUCETTE—Another name for corn salad. See CORN SALAD.

DRAINING. ÉGOUTER—Draining off drop by drop all excess liquid from foodstuffs which have been washed, or boiled and cooled under running water.

DRESSING (Poultry, game and fish). HABILLAGE—The dressing of poultry or winged game consists in plucking, drawing, singeing, trimming and trussing. The dressing of fish consists in scaling, gutting and trimming.

All these operations must be carried out before the birds and the fish are ready for cooking.

DRINKING STRAW. CHALUMEAU—Hollow stem of straw, glass or metal, paper or plastic used for imbibing iced drinks.

DRIPPING PAN. Lèchefrite—A rectangular pan, usually of metal, which is placed underneath food roasted or grilled on a spit.

The gravy of the roast drips into the pan.

DROMEDARY. Dromadaire—A camel with only one hump. Its flesh is cooked in the same way as that of camel. See CAMEL.

DRUM. Estagnon—A container in which liquids, especially oil, are transported.

DRUPE—A general French term for a fruit with a single stone.

DRYING. Dessécher—Dehydrating a solid of any kind by putting it on the stove for a few seconds. Thus green vegetables boiled in salt water are *dried* or more accurately *dehydrated* when they are stood for a very short time over a very hot flame. The purpose of this operation is to evaporate excess moisture absorbed by the vegetables during cooking. Once they have been dried, the vegetables are tossed in butter or prepared for the table in some other way.

In France, the term *dessécher* (drying) is also used of cooking *panadas* and dough on the stove. See PANADA and DOUGH, *Chou paste*.

The term drying is not synonymous with *reducing*. This last term refers only to the process of boiling certain liquids so that they are reduced in volume.

DUBARRY (garnish)—Small flowerets of cauliflower covered with *Mornay sauce* (see SAUCE) sprinkled with grated cheese and breadcrumbs and browned.

Sauce. A *Demi-glace sauce* (see SAUCE) blended with the diluted meat juices of the main dish.

Use for large cuts of meat.

DUBLIN BAY PRAWNS (French LANGOUSTINE; Italian SCAMPI)—The common names for the *nephrops norvegicus*. This shell-fish is about the size of a prawn. I is orange in colour with white-tipped claws and legs. I does not change colour in cooking.

They are prepared in the same way as shrimps and are served as hors-d'oeuvre.

They can also be prepared *à l'américaine** or *à la bodelaise**. All recipes for fresh-water *crayfish* and shell-fish generally are suitable for Dublin Bay Prawns.

Duchesse d'Angoulême pears (*Wide World*)

DUCHESSE—A winter pear which makes an excellent table fruit.

DUCHESSE (A LA)—A name given to various preparations, especially a method of preparing potatoes. See POTATOES, *Duchess potatoes*.

DUCHESSE MIXTURE—A purée of potatoes blended with yolks of egg. It is made into *Duchess potatoes* (see POTATOES) and into borders, savoury cases, etc.

DUCHESSES (Petites)—*Petits fours* which are made as follows:

Pound in a mortar 2 ounces (60 grams) of sweet almonds and the same quantity of hazel-nuts blended with the white of an egg. Add $1\frac{3}{4}$ cups (300 grams) of fine sugar, $\frac{1}{3}$ cup (50 grams) of vanilla-flavoured sugar and $1\frac{2}{3}$ ounces (50 grams) of bitter-sweet chocolate. Now add to this mixture 3 whites of egg and mix thoroughly. Pipe this mixture into little balls on a baking sheet. Bake in a moderate oven.

DUCK. Canard—Web-footed water bird of which many species are known.

Varieties of domestic ducks are bred, some for food, others for pleasure, because of the beauty of their plumage.

Their ancestor is the Mallard duck (*le canard sauvage*), which is found in Europe, Asia, North America and North Africa.

In French classical cookery Rouen and Nantes ducks enjoy the highest esteem for their gustatory qualities.

The different types of ducks raised in France for food include *Duclair* which is a variety of *Rouen duck; Barbary duck*, which, when mated with *Rouen*, produces the *Mulard duck*, which is bred specially for the production of foie gras.

The *Barbary duck* (which in French is also called *Canard d'Inde*) is raised mainly in the southern and south-eastern regions of France. Its flesh is rather mediocre and sometimes is so musky as to be even uneatable, which, according to some authorities, has led to this palmiped being called *musk-duck*. There is another school which believes that 'musk-duck' is a corruption of 'Muscovy duck' and, furthermore, this bird, in spite of the unpleasant association of its name, has no odour of musk.

The young birds are fairly good to eat, the old are tough and have a strong odour, which, it is said, they develop after they have acquired their red wattles. Hill, in 1864, as an explanation of their name, writes that they originally came from the Mosquito coast, Nicaragua, the land of the Muysca Indians, whence the name Musco duck, later corrupted to Muscovy.

The *Nantes duck* is a magnificent bird, with fine, delicately flavoured flesh. It is smaller in size than the *Rouen duck*. When fully developed, that is at four months, it hardly ever exceeds 4 pounds (2 kilos) in weight, whilst the *Rouen duck* weighs easily 5 to 6 pounds. It is bled before cooking.

The *Rouen duckling* owes its reputation, as well as the fine quality of its flesh and the particular taste of the flesh to the method by which it is killed: it is smothered, so that it is not bled as are all other fowl (except guinea-fowl, which in the south-western part of France is often shot, like game). The fact that it loses none of its blood before being cooked makes the flesh of the *Rouen duck* stay red and gives it a special flavour much prized by the connoisseurs.

Note. Ducks which are killed without bleeding are rarely marketed in the U.S.A. Ducks killed in this manner should be cooked the same day to avoid the development of dangerous toxins.

Other breeds of ducks raised for food are *Aylesbury duck*, a bird which has a certain similarity to the *Rouen duck* and which the English greatly appreciate; the black *Cayuga*, which is also called *Great American duck*, a very big-sized bird with delicate flesh; the *Pekin duck*, a small-sized bird with yellow plumage and bright yellow feet and bill, excellent in flesh quality. In the U.S.A. domestic ducks are sold at 5–6 pounds, ducklings at 3½–4 pounds. Wild ducks are shot in large numbers during the hunting season. The most prized is the *Canvasback*.

The age and tenderness of ducks can be determined by the flexibility of their pinions and under-bill—these should be soft enough to be bent back easily.

Rich Romans, according to Martial, were very fond of duck, but—and this is a curious thing—they only ate the breast, which is natural enough, and the brains, which is rather strange.

In the fifteenth and sixteenth centuries, according to the historians of the time, in particular Scaliger and Munster, it was generally believed that the duck evolved from plants or was the result of the decomposition and transformation of leaves.

This popular belief was perhaps due to the fact that, at that time, the only wild ducks known were those which inhabited the vicinity of ponds and marshes and fed on worms and insects and hatched their eggs among decomposing plants.

Duck breeding—It is generally thought that the duck, being an aquatic animal, can only be raised in places situated near water or on river-banks. This opinion is erroneous as many poultry-breeders have proved.

In Normandy a great quantity of ducks are raised in localities without any source of water.

The famous *Rouen duckling* is raised mainly around Yvetot, where you will not find a river or even a spring within a radius of 25 miles.

The celebrated duck pâtés, made in Amiens and justly enjoying a great reputation, are made from the flesh of ducks raised a long way away from running water.

In Normandy a two-month old duck of large-sized breed, raised a long way away from any source of water, is considered the best and commands the highest prices of the market.

In Languedoc and various other parts of south-western France, where big ducks are bred for the manufacture of foie gras, the flesh of these ducks is preserved in fat, like that of geese, and this preserved duck is esteemed by the gastronomes even more than the *confit d'oie* (preserved goose). *Mallard ducks* are also preserved in brine.

The famous truffled *terrines* and *pâtés* of world renown are also made from the livers of these ducks.

In French culinary parlance, duck is always described as *caneton* (i.e. *duckling*) and as nowadays young birds are always used (or should be), this description is perfectly justified.

Duckling d'Albuféra. CANETON D'ALBUFÉRA—'Clean and truss two very young ducklings as for an entrée. Cut 12 pieces of uncooked Bayonne ham into heart-shaped slices. Melt ¾ cup (6 ounces) of the best butter into a casserole, put in first the ham, then the 2 ducklings and add a *bouquet garni**, an onion studded with 2 cloves and half a wine glass of Madeira.

'Cover with a piece of buttered paper, bring to the boil, and put on a *paillasse** (a brick oven with glowing charcoal), with hot coals above and below the casserole, without the heat being too lively, so that the ducklings are cooked without being fried. After 20 minutes, turn the ducklings, remove the onion and the *bouquet garni**. Leave for another 20 minutes, then drain the ducklings, remove trussing string and arrange on a serving dish. The birds should be a lovely colour. Garnish with the slices of ham. Skim off surplus fat from the pan juices, add 2 tablespoonsful of *Financière sauce* (see SAUCE) and 2 small baskets (¼ pound) of very small correctly peeled mushrooms. Pour this sauce over the ducklings.' (From *L'Art de la cuisine française au XIX siècle.*)

Duckling à l'alsacienne. CANETON À L'ALSACIENNE—Braise a Nantes duckling in the usual manner.

Arrange it on a serving dish. Surround with sauerkraut which has been braised separately with streaky bacon and the usual garnishings. Garnish the border of the dish with this bacon, cut into rectangular pieces, and 6 smoked Strasbourg sausages poached in water.

Strain the braising liquor, spoon some over the duckling and serve the rest separately.

Ballottine of duckling (hot). BALLOTTINE DE CANETON—Bone a Nantes duckling and carefully remove all the flesh, leaving only the skin. Remove all sinews from flesh. Dice the fillets and chop the rest of the meat finely with an equal weight of fresh fat bacon, half of its weight of lean veal and 4 tablespoons (75 grams) of *Panada**.

Pound the whole mixture in a mortar adding 4 yolks of egg. Season with salt, pepper and spices. Rub this forcemeat through a sieve. Add 5 ounces (150 grams) of uncooked *foie gras* (duck's liver) cut in large dice and briskly tossed in butter, 5 ounces (150 grams) of truffles cut in large dice and the diced duck breast fillets. Add 2 tablespoons of brandy and blend well.

Spread the duck's skin on the table, on a piece of muslin cloth which has been soaked in cold water and wrung out. Stuff the skin with the forcemeat and roll into a *ballottine**. Secure with string at both ends and in the middle.

Poach the ballottine in stock prepared using a veal knuckle and the bones and trimmings of the duckling. Drain the duckling when it is done (allow about 1¼ hours), unwrap and glaze in the oven.

Arrange on a serving dish. Surround with the garnish indicated in the recipe. Spoon over a little of the braising liquor, boiled down and strained, and serve the rest separately in a sauceboat.

Hot ballottine of duckling may be served with most of the garnishes indicated for braised or broiled poultry. See GARNISHES. The following are the most suitable: *Chatelaine*, *Chipolata*, *Forestière*, *Godard*, braised chestnuts, braised lettuce, other vegetables braised or cooked in butter (and, depending on the nature of these vegetables, they are either disposed around the ballottine or served separately in a vegetable dish).

Ballottine of duckling (cold). BALLOTTINE DE CANETON—This ballottine, so far as preparation and cooking is concerned, is made in the same way as *Hot ballottine*, but a greater quantity of duck's liver and truffles are added to the forcemeat.

After cooking, unwrap the ballottine, then wrap once again in the same cloth very tightly and put to cool under a press.

To serve, unwrap, glaze with liquid aspic jelly, arrange on a dish and surround with chopped jelly.

Cold ballottine of duckling can also be served in a glass dish or in a *terrine*.

Duckling à la bordelaise. CANETON À LA BORDELAISE—Stuff a duckling with a finely pounded forcemeat, mixed with the duck's chopped liver, a little shallot, garlic, a tablespoon of chopped parsley, chopped stoned and blanched olives, seasoned with salt, pepper and spices and bound with an egg.

Truss the duckling as for an entrée and fry in butter in an earthenware cocotte until it is golden on all sides, then add 500 grams of choice, white, firm cèpes, which have been trimmed, washed, lightly tossed in oil and seasoned with salt and pepper. Cook in a hot oven. When the duckling is done, remove trussing string and put back into the cocotte. Pour over 4 or 5 tablespoons of thickened brown veal gravy, sprinkle with chopped parsley and serve in the cocotte in which it was cooked.

Braised Nantes duckling

Braised duckling with various garnishes. CANETON BRAISÉ—Truss a large Nantes duckling as for an entrée. Put it into a braising pan on a foundation of fresh bacon rinds, one carrot and a medium-sized onion sliced and tossed in butter. Add a *bouquet garni** composed of parsley, thyme and bay leaf. Season. Cook with a lid on for about 15 minutes. When the duckling is nicely browned on all sides, moisten with $\frac{3}{4}$ cup ($1\frac{1}{2}$ decilitres) of white wine.

Cook down, then add $1\frac{3}{4}$ cups ($3\frac{1}{2}$ decilitres) of slightly thickened brown veal or chicken stock.

Bring to the boil on the stove, then cook in a hot oven with the braising pan covered, for about an hour.

Drain the duckling, remove trussing string, arrange on a serving dish and surround with the garnish indicated. Boil down and strain the braising liquor, spoon over a little of it on the duck and serve the rest separately in a sauce-boat.

Nantes braised duckling may be served with all the garnishes recommended for braised and broiled poultry. The garnishes which are most suitable for this dish, some of which should be cooked with the duckling, are as follows:

Fermière, *Languedocienne*, *Macédoine*, *Toulousaine*. See GARNISHES.

Braised duckling can also be accompanied by one particular article, generally a vegetable sautéed in butter or braised, such as carrots, turnips, celeriac, cucumbers, small glazed onions, peas, tomatoes, etc.

Casserole of duckling with various garnishes. CANETON EN CASSEROLE—Prepare, either broiled or in casserole, like *Casserole of chicken* (see CHICKEN).

Duckling prepared in this manner is served with *Bonne-femme* (see GARNISHES), *Paysanne** or some other garnish which should be, in principle, cooked with the bird in an earthenware casserole.

Duckling à la chipolata. CANETON À LA CHIPOLATA—Braise the duckling in the usual manner. When it is nearly done, drain and remove trussing string. Put the duckling back in the casserole with a chipolata garnish composed of 10 braised chestnuts, 10 small glazed onions, 10 lean rashers (slices) of bacon—blanched and fried lightly—and 18 carrots cut down to the size of olives and glazed. Boil down the braising liquor, strain and pour over the duckling. Finish cooking together. At the last moment add 10 small chipolata sausages cooked in butter.

Arrange the duckling on a round dish, surround with the garnish disposed in separate groups. Pour over the sauce.

Cold duckling. CANETON FROID—Duckling can be prepared in any manner suitable for cold chicken. See CHICKEN.

Fillets of duck à la bigarade—FILETS DE CANARD À LA BIGARADE—'Remove the breast fillets and the legs of two wild ducks. Put them into an earthenware dish with salt, coarse-ground pepper, parsley, thyme, bay leaf, chopped shallots, lemon juice and a quarter of a glass of good oil. Keep them in this seasoning for three quarters of an hour before they are required, turning frequently.

'Thread them on a skewer, then put them on a spit, without packing too tightly, sprinkling with the seasoning in which they were steeped.

'As soon as you feel them becoming firm to the touch, take them off the skewer. Wash the fillets and put them one by one into a sauté pan in which a piece of game jelly the size of a walnut has been melted, with an equal amount of butter and the juice of half a lemon. Arrange and serve with *Bigarade sauce* (see SAUCE).' (Plumerey's recipe.)

Duckling with olives. CANETON AUX OLIVES—Braise the duckling in the usual manner, cooking it until three quarters done. Strain the braising liquor, put the duckling back in it and add $\frac{1}{2}$ pound (250 grams) of stoned and blanched olives. Finish cooking together on a slow heat.

Duckling can also be cooked with stuffed olives.

Duckling à l'orange (braised), or à la bigarade. CANETON À L'ORANGE, À LA BIGARADE—Braise a Nantes duckling in the usual manner.

Drain, remove trussing string and arrange on a serving dish. Pour over *Bigarade sauce* prepared in the following manner: strain the braising liquor into a small saucepan, in which 2 lumps of sugar, moistened with 2 tablespoons of vinegar, have previously been cooked to caramel degree, and boil down. Add the juice of one orange and half a lemon. Boil down again and strain. At the last moment add the blanched and drained rind of one orange and half a lemon shredded into a fine *julienne**.

Duckling à l'orange or à la bigarade (broiled). CANETON À L'ORANGE, À LA BIGARADE—Pan fry the duckling in butter keeping it a little underdone. Drain, remove trussing string and arrange on a serving dish.

Dilute the pan juices with $\frac{1}{2}$ cup (1 decilitre) of white wine. Add $1\frac{1}{2}$ cups (3 decilitres) of clear veal stock or *Demi-glace sauce* (see SAUCE). Add sugar and vinegar cooked to caramel degree as described above and allow to boil for a few moments. Add the juice of one orange and half a lemon and finish off as described above.

This duckling can be garnished with carefully peeled slices of orange.

In principle, sauce for *Duckling à l'orange* should be made of the rind of bitter, not sweet, oranges or Seville oranges.

It was the latter kind of orange that was always used in the olden days.

Duck pâté, cold. PÂTÉ FROID DE CANETON—Prepare in the same manner as *Cold chicken pâté*. See PÂTÉ, *Cold pâtés*.

Duck pâté, hot. PÂTÉ CHAUD DE CANETON—Using boned, stuffed and truffled duck, proceed as described in the recipe for *Hot chicken pâté*, See PÂTÉ, *Hot pâtés*.

Duckling with peas I. CANETON AUX PETITS POIS—In the same pan brown together in butter 12 small uniform-sized onions and 6–7 ounces (200 grams) of blanched bacon cut in large dice. Remove these from the pan and

How to carve a roast duck (*Photograph Larousse*)
1. First cut off the legs

2. Place the bird on its back and cut vertically along the length of the breastbone

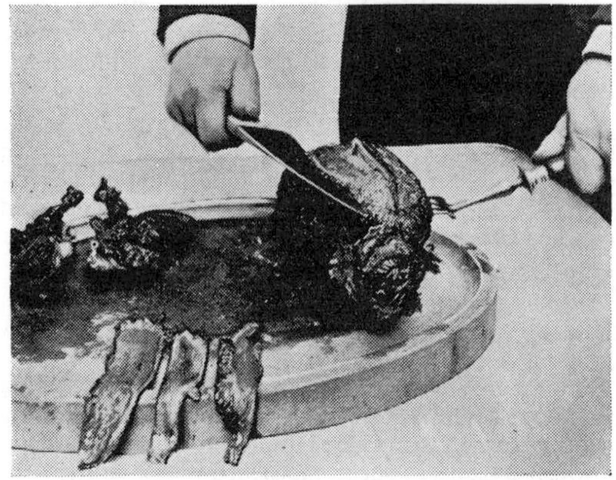

3. Cut off the breast meat in long thin slices

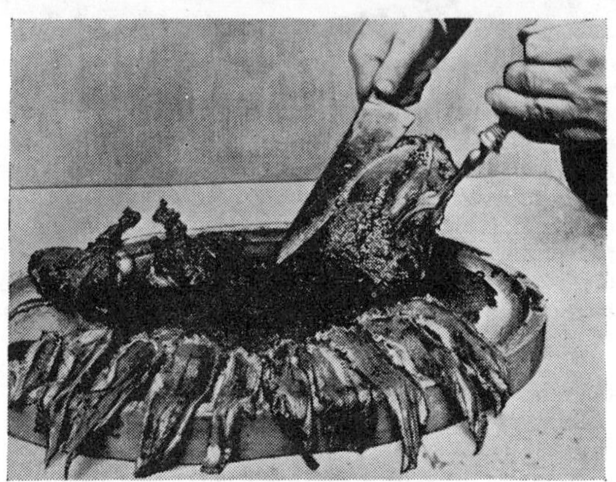

4. Repeat the operation on the other side

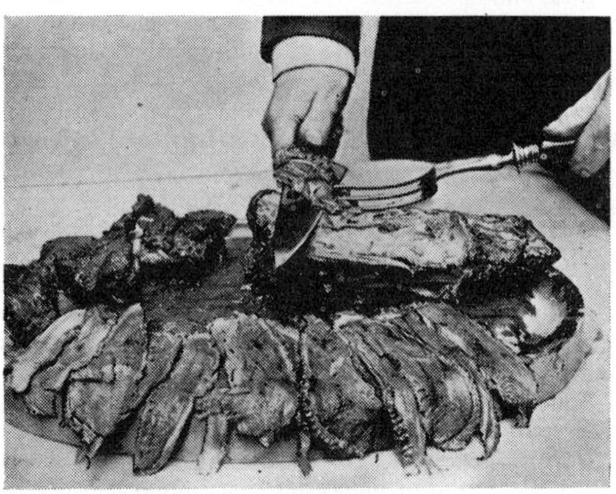

5. Finally cut off the two wings

in the same butter sear a Nantes duckling, trussed as for an entrée. Brown it well on all sides and drain.

Dilute the pan juices with ½ cup (1 decilitre) of white stock. Add 1¼ cups (2½ decilitres) of veal and chicken stock and put the duckling into this liquor. Add a quart (litre) of fresh garden peas, the small onions and pieces of bacon and a *bouquet garni**. Season and add a teaspoon of sugar. Simmer gently with a lid on. Drain the duckling. Arrange it on a serving dish. Put the peas around. Boil down the pan juices and pour over the bird.

A lettuce shredded into a *chiffonnade**, or left whole and tied with string, can be added to the peas. If left whole, it should be cut into quarters when serving, and arranged on the peas.

Duckling with peas II. CANETON AUX PETITS POIS—Cook the duckling in an earthenware casserole, keeping it a little underdone.

When cooked, add a quart of fresh garden peas, cooked *à la française*. See PEAS. Leave to infuse for a few moments without allowing it to boil.

Roast duckling. CANETON RÔTI—Truss the duckling and roast it in the oven or on a spit, allowing 35 minutes cooking time in the oven and from 40 to 45 minutes on the spit, for a bird weighing 2½ pounds (1 kg. 200 grams).

Duckling with sauerkraut. CANETON À LA CHOUCROUTE—This is prepared in the same way as *Duckling à l'alsacienne**. Surround with sauerkraut braised in the usual manner. Garnish with pieces of streaky bacon (cooked with the sauerkraut) and saveloys, Strasbourg or Frankfurt sausages. Pour over the liquor in which the duckling was braised.

Duckling with turnips (braised). CANETON AUX NAVETS—Brown a Nantes duckling, trussed as for an entrée. When it is nicely brown on all sides, take it out of the pan and drain. Remove butter from the pan and put into the pan ¾ cup (1½ decilitres) of dry white wine and 2 cups (4 decilitres) of *Espagnole sauce* (see SAUCE) or veal stock. Add a *bouquet garni**. Replace the duckling into the sauce and simmer gently.

Separately, in the butter left over from browning the

duckling, cook 3–4 small turnips, cut down to a uniform size. Season and sprinkle with a spoonful of sugar, which will enable them to be glazed more quickly. Sauté the turnip on a brisk fire.

Have ready 24 small onions, half cooked in butter.

When the duckling is half cooked drain it and strain the liquor. Put the duckling back into the pan and add the turnips and the onions. Pour in the sauce. Finish cooking together in a slow oven.

Arrange the duckling on a serving dish, dispose the garnish around it, pour the sauce over and serve piping hot.

ROUEN DUCKS. CANARDS ROUENNAIS—See note under DUCK.

Ballottine of Rouen duckling. BALLOTTINE DE CANETON DE ROUEN—Prepare like *Ballottine of duckling*.

Rouen duckling à la bigarade. CANETON ROUENNAIS À LA BIGARADE—Prepare, braised or broiled, like *Duckling à l'orange*.

The Rouen duckling is rarely braised, but it can be cooked in this manner and is excellent.

Rouen duckling au chambertin. CANETON ROUENNAIS AU CHAMBERTIN—Braise the duckling, trussed as for an entrée, in braising liquor based on red wine (Chambertin). When it is nearly cooked, put into another pan. Add ¼ pound (125 grams) of pork or bacon cut in large dice, blanched and fried lightly, and 24 mushroom caps (heads), peeled and lightly tossed in butter.

Boil down the braising liquor, strain, pour over the duckling and finish cooking in the oven with a lid on.

Rouen duckling in champagne. CANETON ROUENNAIS AU CHAMPAGNE—Broil the duckling in butter. When it is nearly cooked, put it into an oval-shaped, earthenware cocotte.

Dilute the pan juices with 1½ cups (3 decilitres) of dry champagne, add a few tablespoons of thickened brown veal stock and pour over the duckling. Finish cooking in the oven with a lid on. Serve in the cocotte in which it was cooked.

Chaud-froid of Rouen duckling. CHAUD-FROID DE CANETON DE ROUEN—Cook the duckling in the oven keeping it a little underdone. Remove the legs. Cut the breast fillets into not too thin strips. Using the carcase and the trimmings, roughly chopped, prepare a *Brown chaud-froid sauce* and mix it with aspic jelly, flavoured with Madeira or some other liqueur wine. See SAUCE, *Compound sauces*.

Coat the pieces of duckling fillets with this half-set sauce. Put on a grid to cool. Decorate with pieces of truffles, white of hard boiled egg and pickled tongue and glaze with jelly.

Arrange in a dish in pyramid shapes. Garnish with chopped jelly and surround the border of the dish with jelly croûtons.

Chaud-froid of Rouen duckling (Nantes duckling cannot be prepared in this way) may also be arranged in a glass dish with the jelly poured over the sliced duckling.

Rouen duckling en chemise I. CANETON ROUENNAIS EN CHEMISE—Remove the breastbone of a Rouen duckling, stuff it *à la rouennaise** and truss as for an entrée. Roast as quickly as possible from 8 to 12 minutes. Leave to get cold then enclose the bird in a large pork bladder, previously soaked in cold water, placing the bird with the rump towards the opening of the bladder. Tie the opening with string. Poach in a clear braising stock for 45 minutes.

Arrange the duckling on a serving dish as it is, bladder and all. To serve, take the duckling out of the bladder and proceed as described in the recipe for *Duckling à la rouennaise*.

Rouen duckling en chemise II. CANETON ROUENNAIS EN CHEMISE—Remove the breastbone, stuff the duck and truss as for an entrée.

Wrap in a napkin which has been soaked in water and wrung out. Tie like a *galantine**. Poach in double veal broth from 40 to 50 minutes.

Drain, unwrap and wrap in a fresh fringed napkin. Arrange on a serving dish. Surround with carefully peeled orange quarters. Serve *Rouennaise sauce* separately (see SAUCE).

Rouen duckling with cherries. CANETON ROUENNAIS AUX CERISES—Truss the duckling as for an entrée. Broil it in a pan with butter. When it is nearly cooked, put it into an oval-shaped earthenware cocotte with ½ pound (250 grams) of stoned Morello cherries. Dilute the pan juices with Madeira, add 1 or 2 tablespoons of brown veal stock and put over the duckling.

Simmer in the oven for a few minutes. Serve in the same cocotte.

Rouen duckling, cold. CANETON ROUENNAIS FROID—As in the case of Nantes duckling, the Rouen duckling, roast or broiled, may be served cold garnished with watercress. To be served in this way it should be cooked longer than required for serving it hot.

Galantine of Rouen duckling. GALANTINE DE CANETON DE ROUEN—Prepare like *Galantine of chicken*, adding to the forcemeat a certain quantity of *à gratin forcemeat*. See GALANTINE.

Jellied Rouen duckling en daube. CANETON ROUENNAIS EN DAUBE À LA GELÉE—Prepare like *Daube of pheasant in jelly*. See PHEASANT.

Jellied strips of Rouen duckling à l'orange

Jellied strips of Rouen duckling à l'orange. AIGUILLETTES DE CANETON DE ROUEN GLACÉES À L'ORANGE—Prepare the duckling as described in the recipe for *Chaud-froid of duckling*. Cut the breast fillets into thin strips. Coat these strips with *Chaud-froid sauce à l'andalouse* (see SAUCE), decorate with truffles and orange peel cut into little strips and glaze with jelly. Keep cold in a refrigerator. Using the flesh of the legs, make a mousse as described in the recipe for *Poultry mousses* (see MOUSSE) adding some diced truffles. Line a dome shaped (or a parfait) mould with this mousse and put on ice to set.

When the mousse is well chilled, turn it out on to a round dish, placing it on a croûton of crustless bread, spread with butter.

Cover this mousse shape with chaud-froid covered duckling strips, putting them close to each other. Spoon a little half-set jelly on the bottom of the dish. Cut oranges into basket-shapes, scoop out the pulp, half fill with port jelly, decorate with carefully peeled orange sections and put these orange baskets around the mousse shape.

Decorate the top by spiking on with a decorative skewer half an orange with a big truffle in it.

Chill in the refrigerator.

Rouen duckling Lambertye. CANETON DE ROUEN LAMBERTYE—Proceed as described in the recipe for *Chicken Lambertye*, replacing the chicken mousse indicated in that recipe by duck mousse.

Set in *Chaud-froid sauce, brown* (see SAUCE).

Rouen duckling mousse I. MOUSSE DE CANETON DE ROUEN—Prepare like *Chicken mousse, cold*, replacing the chicken by duck.

Rouen duckling mousse II and mousselines. MOUSSE ET MOUSSELINES DE CANETON ROUENNAIS—These are prepared as described in the recipe for *Soufflé Rouen duckling*, the *mousse* in a charlotte form or in a mould with a hole in the middle, poached in the oven in a *bain-marie** (pan of hot water), the *mousselines* in similar small moulds, also poached in the oven in a *bain-marie**. See MOUSSE.

Rouen duckling pâté. PÂTÉ DE CANETON DE ROUEN—See PÂTÉS.

Rouen duckling in port. CANETON ROUENNAIS AU PORTO—Truss a Rouen duckling as for an entrée and cook in butter, keeping it slightly underdone.

Drain and arrange on a long dish. Pour over a few tablespoons of port sauce prepared in the following manner: Dilute the pan juices, in which the duckling was cooked, with 1¼ cups (2½ decilitres) of port, add 1¼ cups (2½ decilitres) of thickened brown veal gravy, bring to the boil, simmer for a few moments, add some butter and strain.

Serve the rest of the sauce separately in a sauceboat.

Rouen duckling can be prepared in the same way with Madeira, Frontignan, sherry or any other liqueur wine, by replacing port with one of these wines.

Duck press

Pressed Rouen duckling. CANETON ROUENNAIS À LA PRESSE—Cook the duckling from 18 to 20 minutes. Send it to the table where it will be treated as follows: Remove the legs, which, considering the cooking time allowed, will still be raw. Ordinarily these legs are not served. They can, however, be served if they are grilled first on a brisk fire. (Before putting them under the grill make a few shallow incisions on the underside, season with salt, pepper and a little pounded clove and brush with butter.)

Carve the breast into very thin slivers. Arrange these on a dish, standing on a hotplate (for, we repeat, this dish is actually prepared at table before the guests), in which ½ cup (1 decilitre) of good red wine has been boiled down to almost nothing. Season with freshly ground pepper.

Cut up the carcase, sprinkle with very good red wine and press it. Add 2 tablespoons of brandy to the juice obtained and pour over the sliced duckling. Scatter a few small pieces of butter. Heat on the hotplate without allowing the sauce to boil. Put the grilled duckling's legs at each end of the dish and serve.

Duckling à la rouennaise. CANETON À LA ROUENNAISE—Stuff the duckling with a forcemeat prepared in the following manner: Fry a good tablespoon of chopped onion in ¼ pound (125 grams) of chopped bacon fat, without allowing it to colour. Add the duckling's liver, supplemented by one or two chicken livers (or ducks' livers, if available), cut into thin slices. Season with salt and pepper, sprinkle with spices and chopped parsley and fry as quickly as possible. Leave until cold, then pound in a mortar and rub through a sieve.

After the duckling has been stuffed truss it as for an entrée. Cook in a very hot oven from 20 to 30 minutes, depending on the size of the bird.

Serve with *Rouennaise sauce* (see SAUCE).

To serve *Duckling à la rouennaise*, proceed as follows: Remove the legs, make a few shallow incisions in them, season and grill.

Cut the breast into thin slivers. Put these slivers on the borders of a buttered, oval-shaped dish, placed on a hotplate. Fill the middle of the dish with the stuffing contained in the carcase. Put the grilled legs at each end of the dish.

Chop the carcase into big pieces, put it under a duck press, sprinkling it with 2 or 3 tablespoons of brandy and a dash of lemon juice. Add the juice thus obtained to some Rouennaise sauce, blend and pour some over the sliced duckling. Serve the rest of the sauce separately in a sauceboat.

Salmis of duckling à la rouennaise. CANETON EN SALMI À LA ROUENNAISE—Remove the breastbone and truss the duckling as for an entrée. Put it into a red-hot oven to stiffen and sear it. Leave until just warm, then wipe on a cloth.

Remove the legs, make a few shallow incisions on the underside, season and grill them.

Carve the breast into thin slivers and put them in rows on a big, long, buttered dish. Sprinkle with a small spoonful of finely chopped shallot and season with crushed sea salt, freshly ground pepper and spices.

Chop up the carcase, sprinkle it with half a glass of full-bodied red wine and press. Pour the juice obtained over the sliced duckling.

Scatter a few small pieces of butter, heat the dish for a moment on the stove and put under the grill for a few moments to glaze the meat. Place the grilled legs, one at each end of the dish and serve at once.

Different restaurants have different ways of preparing *Salmis of duckling à la rouennaise*. Quite often it is no more than *Stuffed duckling à la rouennaise*, the recipe for which is given above (see *Duckling à la rouennaise*).

In some restaurants in Rouen, whence this dish originated, the sliced duckling (cooked from 10 to 12 minutes) is covered with *Red wine sauce* (see SAUCE), spiced with shallots, flavoured with a tablespoon of brandy, and thickened with raw chopped duck liver.

In other Rouen restaurants the following method is adopted: Roast the duckling before a lively fire from 12 to 14 minutes (with the liver put inside the duckling, having removed the gall bladder), cut the breast into sliver-thin slices, put them on a long dish, buttered and sprinkled with a tablespoon of chopped shallot, season with freshly ground salt, pepper and spices and sprinkle with a few drops of fine champagne brandy.

Chop up the carcase and the liver. Moisten with half a glass of red wine and press. Mix the juice obtained with a good spoonful of melted butter and pour over the duck slices.

Glaze as described above.

In Duclair, the home of the famous ducklings, a slightly different method is used: Bone the duckling to the wing joints, put the liver inside the bird, trim it, truss and roast on the spit from 20 to 22 minutes, depending on size.

Carve the breast into sliver-thin slices and arrange them on a dish around the carcase filled with the following purée: Fry a large chopped onion in butter without allowing it to colour, sprinkle with port and Burgundy wine, reduce, add the duckling's liver, pounded in a mortar, and the blood of the pressed out carcase. Heat well.

As can be seen, there are numerous ways of preparing duckling *à la rouennaise*, which should be called *Salmis of duckling à la rouennaise*. It is a very famous dish.

Soufflé Rouen duckling. CANETON ROUENNAISE SOUFFLÉ—This is very much a grand style dish: it is excellent but rather expensive as, in principle, two ducklings should be used, one—the larger of the two—to be used for serving and a smaller one for making a forcemeat to stuff the larger one.

This is how *Duckling soufflé à la rouennaise* is made, which is also called *Soufflé of duck rouennaise:*

Truss the duck as for an entrée and roast in the oven, keeping in rather underdone.

Remove the breast fillets and keep hot, for tartlets or for stuffing the duck when it is cooked.

Remove the breastbone in such a way as to make the carcase into a sort of case. Season the duck inside with salt, pepper and spices and sprinkle with a tablespoon of brandy. Stuff the carcase with a forcemeat prepared separately, using the flesh of the second duck (choose a small-sized bird for this), boned and treated as described in the recipe for *Mousseline forcemeat* (see FORCEMEAT), 5 ounces (150 grams) of uncooked *foie gras* and the livers of the ducks which are being cooked. Spread this forcemeat in the carcase, piling it up to give the duck its original shape. Cover with a piece of buttered paper. Tie this paper on with a piece of string to keep the forcemeat well enclosed during cooking. Put the stuffed duck in a roasting pan, sprinkle with melted butter and poach in a slow oven from 20 to 25 minutes.

Remove the paper covering the duck and arrange it on a long dish. Surround with little tartlets, baked blind (empty), filled with a *salpicon** of truffles and mushrooms, blended with greatly concentrated *Madeira sauce* (see SAUCE), place a slice of duck on each tartlet and top with a good sliver of truffle, heated in butter. Serve *Rouennaise sauce* or *Périgueux sauce* separately (see SAUCE).

Note. The fillets, instead of being sliced and arranged in tartlets disposed around the duck, can be cut into very thin slices and encrusted in the mousseline forcemeat used for the stuffing.

The same forcemeat can be used for making Rouen duck *mousses* and *mousselines*, which are prepared, the former in charlotte forms or moulds with a hole in the middle; the latter in small individual moulds. They are poached in the oven in a *bain-marie** (pan of hot water).

The same composition can also be used for preparing *Duck soufflé en timbale*. Put the mixture into big or small buttered soufflé moulds and bake in the oven as an ordinary soufflé. See SOUFFLÉS, *Savoury soufflés*.

Suprême of Rouen duckling. SUPRÊMES DE CANETON ROUENNAIS—Remove the breast fillets of a Rouen duckling. Cut each fillet into two or three pieces lengthways depending on their size. Beat them to flatten slightly, season with salt and pepper, put in a buttered dish and poach with a lid on, keeping them a bit underdone.

Duck fillets prepared in this manner can be served with various garnishes and sauces. Thus, they can be prepared *à la bigarade*, with shredded orange and lemon rind and *Bigarade sauce;* with Morello cherries, stoned and cooked in Madeira with concentrated Madeira-flavoured veal gravy, blended with a little butter; garnished with mushrooms sautéed in butter; *au chambertin*, arranged on croûtons fried in butter, garnished with sliced mushrooms fried in butter and slices of truffles in *Chambertin sauce; au porto*, arranged on croûtons fried in butter with *Port sauce* poured over them; *à la périgourdine*, arranged on fried croûtons, spread with foie gras, garnished with slivers of truffles and served with *Madeira*, *Port* or *Sherry sauce;* with *truffles*, arranged on croûtons fried in butter, garnished with thick slices of truffles sautéed in butter and served with Madeira sauce *à l'orange*, arranged on croûtons fried in butter, garnished with orange rind shredded into *julienne** strips, surrounded with carefully peeled sections of orange and served with *Orange sauce*.

Terrine of Rouen duckling. TERRINE DE CANETON DE ROUEN—Using duck flesh, fine forcemeat and truffles, prepare like *Terrine of duckling*. See TERRINE.

Timbale of Rouen duckling Voisin. TIMBALE DE CANETON ROUENNAIS VOISIN—This dish was one of the specialities of the famous Voisin restaurant, which is no longer in existence. The recipe was as follows:

Roast a Rouen duckling, keeping it a little underdone. When it is quite cold, remove the breast fillets.

Chop up the carcase and the trimmings and use them for making a *Salmis sauce* (see SAUCE, *Brown sauces*). Strain the sauce, remove surplus fat, add to it an equal quantity of meat jelly, reduce (cook down) and strain through a muslin cloth.

Coat a *timbale* with this sauce. When it sets put in a layer of sliced fillets of duckling, previously coated with the same sauce and left to set, alternating with slivers of truffles. Continue in this manner until the *timbale* is filled in alternating rows of sliced duck and truffles, spooning some half-set jelly on each row.

Finish off with a slightly thicker layer of jelly. Put the *timbale* on ice or in a refrigerator and chill well.

Rouen duckling with truffles. CANETON ROUENNAIS AUX TRUFFES—This method of preparation is suitable only for fillets or suprêmes (breasts) of Rouen ducklings.

Cook the duckling in the oven, keeping it a little underdone. Cut the breast fillets into thick slices. Arrange these slices in a silver dish with good thick slices of truffles, tossed in butter. Keep hot without allowing to boil.

Chop the carcase and the parings into biggish pieces, moisten with Madeira, port or sherry and reduce. Add a few spoonfuls of concentrated *Demi-glace* (see SAUCE). Allow to boil for a few moments, then strain through a fine strainer. Bring this sauce to the boil, add a tablespoon of brandy, which has previously been set alight, and 2 tablespoons of butter. Pour the sauce over the duckling fillets.

WILD DUCKS. CANARDS SAUVAGES—Among the wild ducks used in cookery, the most popular, and the biggest, is the green-head or Mallard, known in France as *Canard sauvage* or just *Un sauvage*.

This duck, with exquisitely flavoured flesh, is found in the vicinity of fresh water ponds and lakes from October to March. Its plumage varies depending on sex, age and season. The plumage of the male is green and red, with touches of brown and grey. The female is brown.

The flesh of other species of wild ducks, most of which are also used in the kitchen, and which are found in France, is less delicate than that of the Mallard. These other species include the *Pintail*, the *Sheld-duck* and the *Gadwell*.

Other water game of the same family, which is defined by the generic term of *waterfowl*, includes the *Spoonbill* or *Shoveller-duck*, the flesh of which is succulent, and the *Teal*, a small but excellent bird.

Some members of the waterfowl family are canonically considered as lenten fare, such as the *Pintail*, the *Teal* and *Gargney*, whereas the mallard is considered as meat.

All the methods of preparation suitable for mallard are also applicable to pintail, sheld-duck, teal and gargney.

Wild duck à la bigarade. CANARD SAUVAGE À LA BIGARADE—Roast or broil the wild duck and prepare as *Nantes duckling à l'orange*.

Wild duck au chambertin. CANARD SAUVAGE AU CHAMBERTIN—Roast or broil the duck, keeping it a little underdone (from 18 to 20 minutes). Arrange on a serving dish. Prepare *Chambertin sauce* (see SAUCE), add to it some of the diluted pan juices left over from cooking the duck and pour over the dish. *Wild duck au chambertin* is usually garnished with truffles and mushrooms.

Salmis of wild duck. SALMIS DE CANARD SAUVAGE—Cover a wild duck with a *Mirepoix**, wrap in a piece of paper and put to cook on a spit. After cooking for half an hour unwrap, test to see if the duck is done, and cut up as for a salmis in the usual manner.

'Put the joints into a casserole, together with the blood which comes out of them, to keep hot, making sure that it neither boils nor dries up.

'Have some concentrated, rather thick, *Financière sauce* (see SAUCE) ready in a *bain-marie** (double boiler). Put the bones and parings into a saucepan with half a glass of good red Bordeaux wine, a quarter of a shallot, one clove and a pinch of coarsely ground pepper. Boil to reduce by half then add the Financière sauce and cook until it reaches the consistency of a salmis sauce. Strain, add a tablespoonful of olive oil and the juice of a quarter of a lemon. Arrange the pieces of duck on heart-shaped croûtons, garnish with sliced truffles and mushrooms and pour over the sauce.' (Plumerey's recipe.)

Salmis of wild duck à la minute. SALMIS DE CANARD SAUVAGE À LA MINUTE—'Prepare the duck as described in the preceding recipe. While it is cooking, chop some parsley, mushrooms and shallots very finely, toss them lightly in butter in a sauté pan with salt, pepper and a little grated nutmeg. Moisten with three quarters of a glass of good white Chablis wine, boil down (reduce) by half, add a good tablespoon of *Espagnole sauce* (see SAUCE), remove from heat and add half a tablespoon of the best mustard.

'Take the duck off the spit, joint it and put the pieces into a sauté pan, turning them gently on the fire without allowing to boil. Put in a little game jelly to melt and a piece of butter the size of a small walnut. Serve with the sauce poured over.' (Plumerey's recipe.)

Wild duck à l'orange. CANARD SAUVAGE À L'ORANGE—Broil or pan-roast the duck. Proceed as described in the recipe for *Nantes duckling à l'orange, à la bigarade*.

Wild duck in port. CANARD SAUVAGE AU PORTO—Broil or pan-roast the duck and proceed as described in the recipe for *Rouen duckling in port*.

Wild duck à la presse. CANARD SAUVAGE À LA PRESSE—Roast the duck from 18 to 20 minutes. Proceed as described in the recipe for *Rouen duckling à la presse*.

Roast wild duck. CANARD SAUVAGE RÔTI—Roast the duck on a brisk fire, either on a spit or in the oven, from 18 to 20 minutes.

Arrange on a serving dish. Garnish with lemon and orange slices. Dilute the pan juices and serve separately.

Wild duck à la tyrolienne. CANARD SAUVAGE À LA TYROLIENNE—'Stew some cooking apples and add a little cinnamon and mace just to infuse the hot apples with these aromatics.

'Stuff the duck, trussed as for an entrée, with the stewed apples and sew up both the neck and the rump, to make sure the apples are kept in.

'At the moment of putting on a spit to roast, bring a third of a glass of vinegar to the boil with a piece of butter the size of a small walnut, half a coffee spoonful of castor (fine) sugar and a little coarsely ground pepper. Baste the duck with this preparation constantly during cooking, having placed a dripping pan or a sauté dish beneath it to catch the juices. As soon as the cooking is completed (it should not take more than 30 or 35 minutes) take the duck off the spit, remove trussing strings and arrange on a dish. Strain the pan juices into a saucepan, heat, add half a tablespoonful of red-currant jelly and pour this sauce over the duck.' (Plumerey's recipe.)

DUCK PRESS. PRESSE À CANARD—Kitchen utensil, different from a meat press, in that it serves the sole purpose of extracting the juices from the carcase of duck.

DUNAND—There were two master chefs of this name, the father and the son, who were equally famous. The elder Dunand was of Swiss origin. He joined the French army and became chef to the Prince de Condé.

His son succeeded him and became comptroller of this great household. When, in 1793, the Prince emigrated, the younger Dunand followed him and, for 12 years, was in charge of his kitchens.

Then, being a sick man and above all with a nostalgic longing to see Paris once more, he returned to France and, having re-established himself, entered the service of Napoleon I as chef. He remained in the service of the Emperor until he left for Saint Helena. Sick man as he was, Dunand, to his great sorrow, was unable to go into exile with his master.

He retired to Switzerland. He left to the Lausanne Museum the Emperor's personal table-service which had been presented to him by his master.

According to anecdote, it is to Dunand the younger that we owe the invention of the dish known as *Chicken sauté Marengo*.

DUXELLES—A kind of mushroom hash. According to some experts, the name *duxelles* derives from *Uxel*, a small town of the Côtes-du-Nord. Others believe, with better reason, that this dish was so-called because it was created by La Varenne, an official of the household of the Marquis d'Uxelles.

Method. Thoroughly clean and trim $\frac{1}{4}$ pound (125 grams) of mushrooms (or peelings and stalks) and chop them finely. Put them in a cloth and twist tightly to extract all liquid as thoroughly as possible. Lightly brown in butter half an onion, chopped. Add 2 chopped shallots, salt, pepper, nutmeg and the mushrooms, chopped and squeezed. Stir over a lively flame so that any surplus moisture left in the mushrooms is evaporated while at the same time the mushrooms are thoroughly cooked. Leave to get quite cold and keep in a cold place, covered with buttered paper.

EARTH-NUTS. TERRE-NOIX—Tuberous root about the size of a nut, black outside and white inside, of a plant whose scientific name is *Carum bulbocastanum*. It tastes like chestnut and is prepared in the same ways. The seeds of the plant are sometimes used in place of caraway.

ÉCHAUDÉ—Pastry made with dough which is first poached in water, then dried in the oven.

The invention of this pastry is attributed to Charles-Paul Favart, father of the French dramatist, who in 1710 was established as a pastrycook in the Rue de la Verrerie in Paris.

It is probable that Favart's 'invention' consisted merely in improving and altering the shape of this pastry and thereby bringing it into fashion.

This pastry was known in France long before Favart's time. It is mentioned, in fact, in a charter of 1202 where it is described as 'buns called *eschaudati*'. This name was given to the pastry because hot water was poured on to the dough to make it rise.

Échaudés (Carême)—*Ingredients.* $3\frac{3}{4}$ cups (500 grams) of flour, $\frac{1}{2}$ cup (125 grams) of oil, $1\frac{1}{2}$ teaspoons (10 grams) of salt, $\frac{2}{3}$ cup (2 decilitres) of water.

Method. Mix and knead the dough in the usual way. Leave to stand for 2 hours, wrapped in a cloth. Divide into small pieces (each weighing from 25 to 30 grams). Shape these pieces into balls. Flatten them slightly and press three fingers into them to make them hollow. Poach the *échaudés* in water. Drain and dry them in a cloth. Leave to dry for 2 hours.

Put them on a baking sheet. Bake in a hot oven for 25 to 30 minutes.

ÉCLAIR—A small pastry made with *Chou paste* (see DOUGH) filled with *French pastry cream* (see CREAM) flavoured with vanilla, coffee or chocolate and iced with fondant icing.

Method. Pipe the éclairs on to a baking sheet (using a plain round nozzle) in the shape of fingers. Brush with egg. Bake in a hot oven.

As soon as the éclairs are cold, slit them along one side and fill them, using a forcing bag, with confectioner's cream (French pastry cream) (see CREAM) flavoured with vanilla, coffee or chocolate. Ice the top of the éclairs with hot fondant icing flavoured to blend with the filling. See ICING.

Éclairs can also be filled with different mixtures such as: *Crème Chiboust* (see CREAM), *Chantilly*, *Purée of marrons glacés* or *salpicons* of various kinds of fruit blended in confectioner's cream.

Éclairs filled with various creams and iced with caramel sugar instead of fondant icing are known in France as *Bâtons de Jacob.*

Small éclairs à la hollandaise. PETITS ÉCLAIRS À LA HOLLANDAISE—These éclairs are served as hors-d'oeuvre.

Method. Pipe the éclairs, made of unsweetened chou paste, on to a baking sheet, making them smaller than ordinary éclairs. They should be about $1\frac{1}{2}$ inches long.

Brush with egg and bake in a slow oven. Leave them until they are quite cold.

The filling. Pound in a mortar a large filleted herring, trimmed, soaked to remove all salt, and dried in a cloth. While pounding, add 2 yolks of hard boiled egg and 5 tablespoons (80 grams) of butter. Rub through a fine sieve.

Put this filling in a bowl. Work with a spatula, after adding half a tablespoon of chopped chives and half a tablespoon of chopped parsley.

Make a small slit in the side of the éclair. Fill them through this slit, using a forcing (pastry) bag.

Brush the top of the éclairs with melted butter and, while the butter is still runny, sprinkle the surface with a little chopped yolk of hard boiled egg and chopped parsley. Serve the éclairs on a doyley on a round dish.

ÉCUELLE—A deep dish used for serving vegetables.

EEL. ANGUILLE—A snake-like fish with viscous and very slippery skin. When caught in fast flowing water, its flesh is very delicate. Eel from running water of a river is therefore always preferable to that from a pool. It can be recognised by its light brown skin, with shades of green on the back and silver on the belly. The flesh of eels from a pool or pond of stagnant water is slimy. Its skin is dark brown on the back and dirty yellow on the belly.

But whatever the source of eels, they must always be kept alive until the moment of preparation. They should be kept in a fish-pond or in a large bucket of water, which should be changed frequently.

Eel's flesh is extremely nourishing, but a little heavy. It becomes more easily digestible if, before cooking, the layer of fat between the skin and the flesh is removed.

There are several varieties of sea eels, the best of which is *Moray* (*Muarena*). This fish was much valued by the ancient Romans; they used to breed it in fish-ponds, expensive establishments situated near the banks of a river or sea-shore. Among the sea eels we must also mention the *Conger eel*, chiefly used for *bouillabaisse**, but which can also serve to make excellent *matelotes**. And, finally, there is yet another sea fish which has something in common with the eel, both in shape and in taste, the *Lamprey*, which goes up the rivers in the spring. The

Eels from Angers (*French Government Tourist Office*)

lamprey's flesh is delicate in flavour and it can be prepared in the same way as eel.

Method of preparation. Cleaning: We repeat, eel must be kept alive until the last moment.

Before skinning it, stun it by banging the head hard against a stone.

As soon as the eel is dead, hang it up on a hook by a string tied at the neck. Make a circular incision below the string. Turn the skin back all round the neck in such a way as to be able to hold it with a cloth. Tear it off in one go.

Trim the eel and clean it out by making a very light incision along the belly. Cut off the head, which should be thrown away, and cut it into slices or leave whole as directed in the recipe.

Bring to the boil, cover with a lid and simmer on the edge of the stove 20 to 25 minutes.

Drain the pieces of eel and put them into an earthenware dish. Pass the liquid in which the eel was cooked through a fine strainer and pour it into the dish.

Eel cooked in this way in *court-bouillon** can then be prepared *à la bourguignonne*, fried, grilled *à la tartare*, *en matelote**, in a white or brown sauce, etc.

Note. Small sized eels intended for frying are not cooked in *court-bouillon** prior to frying.

The same applies to large eels cut in fillets or slices, or left whole for boning and stuffing.

You can also, instead of skinning the eel whole, cut it into chunks; put them under a grill for a few moments under a brisk flame, turning them to catch the skin on all sides. Under the action of the fire the skin blisters and can then be taken off very easily.

This method of skinning also has the advantage of removing the excess fat and thus rendering the fish more easily digestible.

Court-bouillon cooking—This method is given for an eel weighing about 1½ pounds (700 to 800 grams). Depending on the final use for which it is intended, the eel is first cooked in a *wine court-bouillon** (white or red wine) with vegetables. Proceed as follows:

Cut the eel into pieces of about 2½ inches, or leave whole, as directed in the recipe. Put into a well-buttered sauté or heavy frying pan on a foundation of shredded onions and carrots, allowing 3 tablespoons (50 grams) each of chopped onions and carrots per quart (litre) of liquid, pressing down well to make the fish lie flat. Add a crushed clove of garlic and a good *bouquet garni**. Season with salt and freshly ground pepper; pour in enough wine to cover the fish, red or white, according to the individual recipe.

Eel à l'anglaise. ANGUILLES À L'ANGLAISE—Cut fillets of boned eel into collops or 2-inch pieces. Flatten these collops and marinate them for half an hour in oil, lemon juice or vinegar, salt and pepper.

Coat them with a *panne à l'anglaise** (see BREADCRUMB) (dip in lightly beaten egg and roll in breadcrumbs) and fry them at the last moment. Serve with a *Butter sauce* to which a little anchovy butter has been added. See SAUCE.

Ballottine of eel, or stuffed eel. BALLOTTINE D'ANGUILLE (ANGUILLE FARCIE)—This dish is served hot or cold. When hot, ballottine of eel can be served with all the garnishes and sauces recommended for large size braised fish. When cold, all the recipes given for cold fish can be applied to it.

Cold ballottine of eel is also called galantine of eel. *Bastion of eel*, a cold dish which was very popular in old cookery, and which is almost never done nowadays, used to be made from ballottine of eel.

Cold ballottine of eel should be made from eel slightly smaller in diameter and can be served as an hors-d'oeuvre called *Eel sausage*.

Cold ballottine of eel, also called Galantine of eel or Eel sausage or Stuffed jellied eel. BALLOTTINE D'ANGUILLE FROIDE; GALANTINE, SAUCISSON D'ANGUILLE; ANGUILLE FARCIE À LA GELÉE—Bone the eel and fill with the stuffing desired, as described above.

Poach gently in red or white wine *court-bouillon** according to the recipe chosen.

Drain the ballottine, unwrap and then wrap again in a muslin cloth once it has been carefully rinsed and wrung out. Tie with string, tightening it a little and put under a press on a board.

Leave for 12 hours to get cold. Unwrap the ballottine of eel, dry, trim and coat with jelly or *chaud-froid* (see SAUCE) as required by recipe.

Serve and garnish as described in the recipe.

Note. The fish stock for cold ballottine of eel is made with red or white wine. This stock should have plenty of taste and a generous allowance of gelatinous substances.

After the ballottine is cooked, the stock is clarified as described in the recipe for preparing fish jelly (see JELLY) and used for coating the eel and for garnishing it.

All relative information on stuffing for ballottine of eel will be found in the article entitled *Forcemeats for fish*. See FORCEMEAT.

For the arrangements and the garnish of ballottine of eel (cold), follow the directions given for cold preparations of large size fish.

When the ballottine of eel is prepared simply in jelly, and has therefore no garnish to go with it, it is preferable to serve it completely covered in its jelly, in a deep oval terrine, in a glass dish, or in a silver *timbale*. The receptacle containing it is placed on a long dish and surrounded by crushed ice.

Hot ballottine of eel. BALLOTTINE D'ANGUILLE CHAUDE—Bone a large eel, skinned and trimmed, with the head and tail piece cut off.

Flatten it slightly, season with salt, pepper and spices.

Fill with the required stuffing. Distribute this stuffing evenly in such a manner as to make the eel look normal when you put it back into shape.

Wrap the ballottine in a muslin cloth and tie it at both ends, as well as in three or four places in the middle.

Put into a buttered fish kettle with a grill. Cover with the liquid required according to recipe (either white or red wine).

Bring to the boil. As soon as boiling is established, cover and leave to poach gently.

Drain and unwrap the eel. Put in a fireproof dish, glaze in the oven, basting frequently with its thickened pan juices.

Arrange and garnish the ballottine as described in the recipe chosen and serve with the sauce recommended.

The liquid for boiling ballottine of eel is made of white or red wine. It should be well reinforced with other taste-giving elements. Strengthen it, therefore, by putting into it the bones and trimming from various fish in addition to the eel being cooked.

The aromatic elements of this fish stock, vegetables—shredded or diced—previously sautéed in butter, and the *bouquet garni**, should be strong and abundant.

After cooking the ballottine of eel, this liquor should be used for the preparation of the sauce to accompany it. All relative information on this stuffing for ballottine of eel will be found in the article entitled *Forcemeats for fish.* See FORCEMEATS.

Note. In addition to the recipes given below for ballottine of eel, all those given for large size braised fish can be applied to it. Among these, the following are very suitable for ballottine of eel: *bretonne, Chambord, chinonaise, Daumont, Joinville, matelote, Nantua, normande.* Ballottine of eel, poached in white or red wine, can also be accompanied by a simple garnish, arranged around the dish or served separately, such as mushrooms, various croquettes, *macédoine** of vegetables with butter or cream potatoes prepared in various ways, rice pilaf or risotto.

Ballottine of eel à l'ancienne. BALLOTTINE D'ANGUILLE À L'ANCIENNE—Stuff the eel with whiting forcemeat with diced truffles added to it. Poach it in a *court-bouillon** with white wine (see above).

Drain, glaze, arrange on a foundation of fish forcemeat, or on a rectangluar croûton of bread, without crusts, fried in butter.

Surround with *Garnish à l'ancienne**.

Cover with *Normande sauce* (see SAUCE) diluted with the liquor left over from cooking the eel, boiled down (reduced) and with a finely shredded *Mirepoix** of vegetables and Madeira added to it.

Ballottine of eel à la bourguignonne. BALLOTTINE D'ANGUILLE À LA BOURGUIGNONNE—Stuff the eel with a pike or whiting forcemeat mixed with chopped parsley. Poach it in a red wine *court-bouillon**. Drain, glaze, arrange on a croûton of crustless bread fried in butter.

Surround with *Garnish à la bourguignonne.* Cover with *Bourguignonne sauce* made with the liquor left over from cooking the fish (see SAUCE).

Ballottine of eel à la gauloise. BALLOTTINE D'ANGUILLE À LA GAULOISE—Stuff the eel with pike or whiting forcemeat, mixed with a *salpicon** of truffles and mushrooms. Poach in a white wine *court-bouillon** (see above).

Drain, arrange on a croûton of crustless bread fried in butter. Surround with little artichoke hearts filled with carp's soft roes cooked in butter and little pie pastry boats filled with *Crayfish tails à la Nantua**.

Reduce the liquor in which the eel was cooked, thicken with several tablespoons of thin *Espagnole sauce* (see SAUCE), add butter, strain and pour over the dish.

Bastion of eel. BASTION D'ANGUILLE—Method of serving cold eel which was very popular in times gone by but which is very seldom executed nowadays.

Bone 2 large eels, fill them with a fish stuffing (pike or whiting) with diced truffles added to it. Wrap the eels in a fine cloth or a piece of muslin and secure with string to help keep the shape. Cook in white wine with a well flavoured fish stock.

Drain, unwrap and cool under a press.

Cut the eels into chunks of about 4 inches in length. Coat the chunks with a *Chaud-froid sauce* prepared with the liquor in which the fish was cooked (see SAUCE) and decorate with truffles and white of egg. Glaze with liquid jelly.

Arrange the chunks of eel on a bed of cooked rice or on a buttered croûton of bread, placing them upright, next to each other, thus building up a bastion. Garnish the border of the dish with halved hard boiled eggs and jelly croûtons.

Note. Poached fillets of sole, cooled under a press and cut to look like crenellation loopholes or in some other pattern, with detail filled in in truffles, jelly croûtons and, finally, *Montpellier butter* or some other compound butter (see BUTTER, *Compound butters*) can be used as decorative elements for bastions of eel.

These dishes can only be prepared for very grand buffets.

Eel à la bonne femme. ANGUILLE À LA BONNE FEMME—Put an eel of average weight, either cut in pieces or left whole and rolled into a ring, into a sauté or heavy frying pan on a foundation composed of four good tablespoons of chopped onion lightly fried in butter. Season with salt and pepper; add a *bouquet garni** and moisten with 1 cup (3 decilitres) of white wine. Poach gently, with a lid on, for 25 minutes.

Drain the eel, arrange on a round dish on croûtons of bread fried in butter (or, if left whole, on a large round croûton fried in butter); garnish with potatoes cut in large dice, fried in butter.

Cover the eel with the pan juices in which it was cooked, boiled down by half, blended with a tablespoon of kneaded butter and either passed through a strainer or not, as required. Sprinkle with chopped parsley.

Collared eel, cold. ROULADE D'ANGUILLE FROIDE—Using a boned eel, stuffed with whatever stuffing is preferred, and twisted into a ring, proceed as described in the recipe for *Ballottine of eel, cold.*

Arrange and garnish the collared eel, following the directions given for cold ballottine of eel or those for all jellied stuffed fish.

Collared eel à l'angevine. ROULADE D'ANGUILLE À L'ANGEVINE—After skinning the eel in the usual manner, bone it completely. Lay it flat on a table. Season with salt and pepper; spread the inside with pike forcemeat bound with an egg and with a *salpicon** of mushrooms and truffles added to it.

Reshape the eel. (Roll it up from the head, or broad end, to the tail end.) Wrap in rashers of fat bacon. Twist into a ring and tie with string.

Meanwhile, in a sauté or heavy frying pan (for an eel weighing 3 pounds or $1\frac{1}{2}$ kilos) fry lightly in butter a large onion and a carrot cut into round slices. On these vegetables, evenly spread out in the pan, put the eel. Place a large *bouquet garni** including—in addition to the usual herbs—a leek and a branch of savory.

Moisten the eel with white Anjou wine, not too sweet, in sufficient quantity just to cover it. Bring to the boil and remove scum.

Simmer gently without a lid for 35 minutes.

Drain the eel. Unwrap, put into another pan with 24 peeled mushrooms tossed in butter.

Pour over it a sauce made in the following manner: Prepare a white *roux** made of 3 tablespoons (50 grams) of butter and 4 tablespoons (60 grams) of flour. Dilute with the liquor in which the fish was cooked, passed through a fine strainer. Blend well. Add the parings of the mushrooms used for garnish. Boil down on full heat, adding, when boiled down, about 1⅓ cups (3½ decilitres) of fresh cream. Simmer.

When the sauce reaches the desired consistency add to it (off the boil) 6 tablespoons (100 grams) of *Crayfish butter* (see BUTTER, *Compound butters*).

Collared eel à la bordelaise. ROULADE D'ANGUILLE À LA BORDELAISE—Stuff the eel with *Fish forcemeat* (see FORCEMEAT) flavoured with anchovy butter with chopped parsley added to it. Twist into a ring. Poach in *Court-bouillon** made of red Bordeaux wine (see above).

Drain, arrange on a round dish. Put into the middle of the dish some cooked mushrooms, cèpes for preference, arranged in a pyramid.

Pour over the liquor in which the fish was cooked, thickened with kneaded butter and strained, as indicated for thin *Bordelaise sauce* (see SAUCE). Garnish with heart shaped croûtons fried in butter.

Note. Chunks of stuffed eel *à la bordelaise* are prepared in the same manner.

Collared eel à la royale. ROULADE D'ANGUILLE À LA ROYALE—Roll a medium sized eel into a ring. Poach in a white wine *court-bouillon** (see above) with a *mirepoix** of vegetables. Leave to get cold in its liquor. Drain, dry and coat in *Villeroi sauce* (see SAUCE).

Put the eel thus coated in a round frying basket and fry in deep fat at the last moment.

Drain and arrange on a round napkin covered dish.

Fill the middle with a mound of soft roes *à la Villeroi*. Surround with dressed crayfish, cooked in *court-bouillon**, alternating with little bunches of fried parsley.

Serve separately *Normande sauce* with chopped truffles added to it. See SAUCE.

Eel coulibiac (Russian cookery). COULIBIAC D'ANGUILLE Follow the directions given for *Salmon coulibiac**. Replace the salmon by boned eel cut in collops or 2-inch slices.

Little eel coulibiacs. PETITS COULIBIACS D'ANGUILLE—See SALMON, *Small salmon coulibiacs*.

Eel in cream with paprika, or à la hongroise. ANGUILLE À LA CRÈME, AU PAPRIKA, DITE À LA HONGROISE—Cut an eel weighing about 1½ pounds (700 to 800 grams) into pieces. Put the pieces into a sauté or heavy frying pan on a foundation of a medium sized onion, shredded, and, lightly fried in butter; sprinkle in paprika; add a *bouquet garni**; season.

Moisten with white wine in sufficient quantity to cover the fish. Bring to the boil, cover with a lid and cook for 20 minutes. 8 minutes before the end of cooking, put 12 peeled mushroom heads into the pan.

Drain the pieces of eel and the mushrooms. Arrange each piece of eel on a rectangular croûton fried in butter, garnish with the mushrooms and keep hot.

Boil down (reduce) the pan juices by half and pass through a fine sieve. Add 2 tablespoons of thin *Velouté sauce* (see SAUCE) and ⅔ cup (2 decilitres) of cream. Cook until the sauce coats the surface of a spoon. Add 5 tablespoons (75 grams) of butter, strain the sauce and pour it over the eel.

Eel à la diable. ANGUILLE À LA DIABLE—Roll a medium sized eel into a ring. Poach it in a white wine *court-bouillon**. Leave to cool in this liquor.

Drain, dry, coat with mustard, sprinkle with melted butter and dip in breadcrumbs mixed with a pinch of cayenne pepper. Sprinkle with melted butter again and grill gently.

Arrange on a round dish, surround with a border of gherkins and half slices of decoratively cut lemon. Serve *Diable sauce* separately (see SAUCE).

Eel à la fermière. ANGUILLE À LA FERMIÈRE—Cut an eel weighing about 1½ pounds (700 to 800 grams) into pieces and put them in a sauté or heavy frying pan on a foundation composed of ⅔ cup (2 decilitres) of a *fondue** of vegetables. Season with salt and pepper.

Moisten with ¾ cup (2½ decilitres) of white wine; add a *bouquet garni**. Bring to the boil, cover with a lid and cook for 25 to 30 minutes.

Drain the pieces of eel, arrange on golden croûtons of bread fried in butter.

Reduce the pan juices, thicken with heavy cream and pour the sauce over the eel.

Fricassée of eel. ANGUILLE EN FRICASSÉE—Cut an eel weighing about 1½ pounds (700–800 grams) into 2½ inch pieces and put into a buttered sauté or heavy frying pan. Season with salt and pepper.

Add 12 well blanched onions (raw if they are young) and a *bouquet garni**. Moisten with water and white wine in equal proportions. Bring to the boil, cover with a lid and simmer for 25 to 30 minutes. 5 minutes before the end of cooking, add 10 sliced mushrooms.

Drain the eel, heap in a shallow platter and garnish with well drained little onions and mushrooms.

Strain the pan juices, add 3 tablespoons of thin *Velouté* (see SAUCE) and boil down (reduce) by half.

Make a *liaison* by blending in 2 yolks of egg diluted with ⅓ cup (1 decilitre) of cream. Add 3 tablespoons (50 grams) of butter, pass through a strainer and pour over the fish. Garnish with heart shaped croûtons fried in butter.

Fried eel. ANGUILLE FRITE—Choose small sized eel; skin, make light incisions on the back, twist into rings or into figure-of-eight shapes, secure with skewers.

Soak in milk, dredge with flour and fry in deep fat. Arrange on a napkin; garnish with fried parsley and quarters of lemon.

Fried eel Orly. ANGUILLE FRITE ORLY—Cut eel fillets into slices.

Flatten these slices, season and dip into a light batter.

Deep fry at the last moment. Arrange on a napkin, garnish with fried parsley and serve with *Tomato sauce* (see SAUCE).

Instead of dipping the eel slices into batter, they can be done in lightly beaten egg and breadcrumbs.

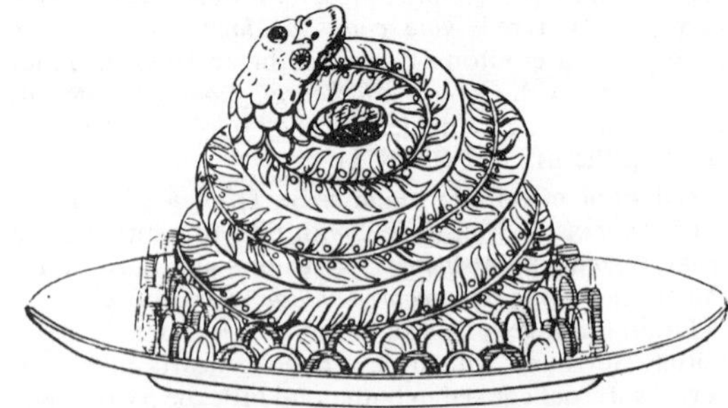

Galantine of eel arranged in a coil, after Carême

Galantine of eel arranged in a coil. GALANTINE D'ANGUILLE EN VOLUTE—Bone a large size eel. Stuff it with *Pike forcemeat à la crème* (see FORCEMEAT) with a

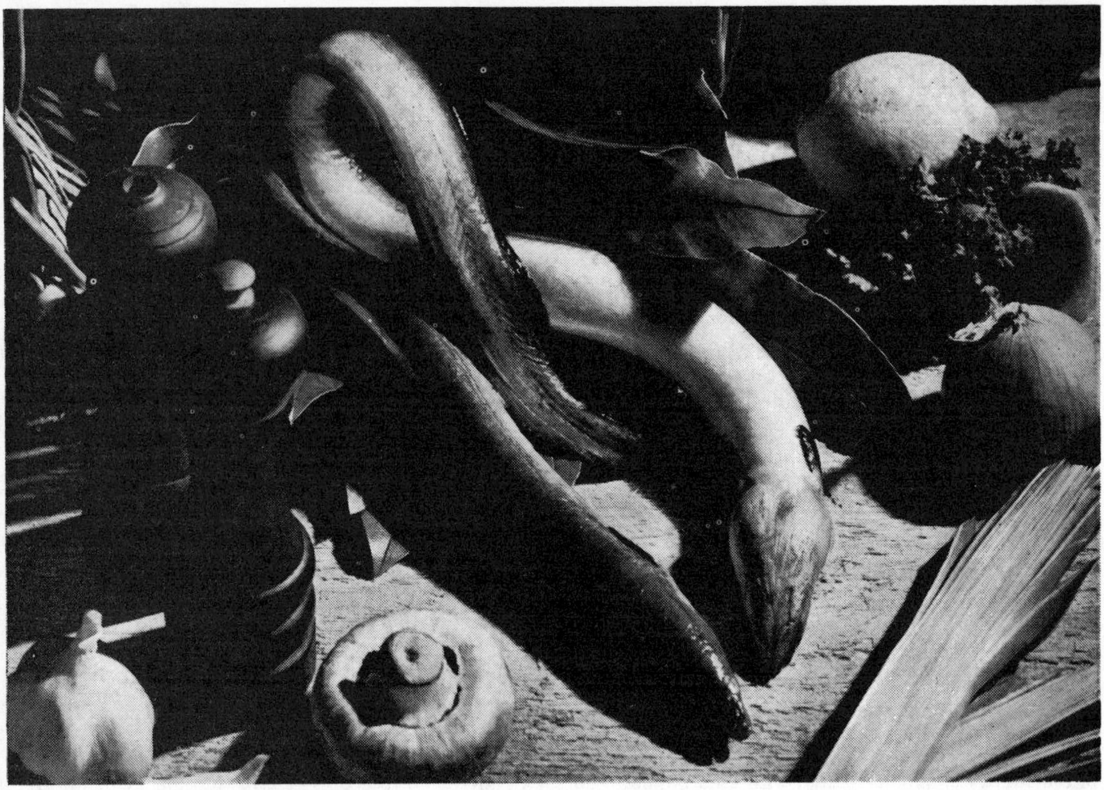

Eel en matelote (*Robert Carrier*)

*salpicon** of fillets of sole and truffles added to it. Twist the eel, coiling it upwards into a dome shape, securing with string to help it keep this shape. Cook in a well flavoured white wine fish stock.

Drain the eel. Allow to cool. Cover with *Chaud-froid sauce* prepared with the liquor in which the fish was cooked (see SAUCE). Decorate the eel with truffles and white of hard boiled egg. Glaze with fish jelly.

Arrange the eel on a round dish, on a bed of cooked rice on a croûton of bread spread with butter, or on another foundation.

Galantine of jellied eel. GALANTINE D'ANGUILLE À LA GELÉE—This is another name for *Cold ballottine of eel.*

Grilled eel maître d'hôtel. ANGUILLE GRILLÉE MAÎTRE D'HÔTEL—Prepare the eel as described for *Eel à la diable*, but without coating it with mustard. Arrange on a round dish. Cover with softened *Maître d'hôtel butter* (see BUTTER, *Compound butters*), or, if preferred, serve this butter separately.

Grilled eel can be served with all the sauces specially recommended for grilled fish.

Eel à l'italienne. ANGUILLE À L'ITALIENNE—Take a medium sized eel, cut in uniform pieces and seasoned, and fry briskly in a sauté or heavy frying pan in oil, just to stiffen it.

Remove from the pan and in the same oil brown 2 tablespoons of chopped onion. When the onion is nearly done, add a small spoonful of chopped shallots and $\frac{1}{4}$ pound (125 grams) of mushrooms cut in very small dice (or mushroom stalks). Put the eel back into the pan; add $\frac{1}{3}$ cup (1 decilitre) of white wine and $\frac{3}{4}$ cup ($2\frac{1}{2}$ decilitres) of tomato sauce. Simmer gently, with a lid on, 25 to 30 minutes. Heap in a shallow platter, sprinkle with chopped parsley, chervil and tarragon.

Eel en matelote. ANGUILLE EN MATELOTE—Cut a skinned eel into pieces; prepare as described in the recipe for *Matelote à la marinière* or *à la meunière*, according to the method chosen. See MATELOTE.

Eel en matelote à la normande. ANGUILLE EN MATELOTE À LA NORMANDE—Cut the eel into pieces and proceed as described in the recipe for *Matelote à la normande**.

Eel à la meunière. ANGUILLE À LA MEUNIÈRE—Divide small size eels into pieces of $3\frac{1}{2}$–4 inches. Season, dredge with flour and fry in butter.

Arrange on a long dish, scatter chopped parsley on top, sprinkle with lemon juice and, at the last moment, cover with *Noisette butter* (see BUTTER, *Compound butters*).

Hot eel pâté or eel pie (English cookery). PÂTÉ CHAUD D'ANGUILLE À L'ANGLAISE—Cut trimmed fillets of eel into collops or slices of about $2\frac{1}{2}$ inches. Blanch them in salted water.

Drain in a sieve, allow to cool, season with salt, pepper and grated nutmeg and sprinkle with chopped parsley.

Arrange these eel collops in an English pie dish or deep terrine, oval in shape for preference, alternating them with layers of sliced hard boiled eggs, seasoned as the eel.

Moisten with white wine in sufficient quantity almost to cover the fish. Scatter over a few small dabs of butter.

Cover with a piece of rolled out *Puff pastry* (see DOUGH). Brush with beaten egg, crimp the edges and make an opening in the middle of the pie crust to allow steam to escape. Bake in a moderate oven for an hour and a half. At the moment of serving, through the opening in the top pour into the pie a few tablespoons of thin *Demi-glace* (see SAUCE).

Hot eel pâté aux fines herbes, called à la ménagère. PÂTÉ CHAUD D'ANGUILLE AUX FINES HERBES DITE À LA MÉNAGÈRE—Cut eel fillets into uniform collops or 2-inch slices. Flatten lightly, season with salt, pepper and spices, arrange in a pie dish and sprinkle with a few tablespoons of white wine, a little brandy and a dash of olive oil. Leave to marinate in a cool place for 2 hours.

Drain and dry the collops, fry them briskly in butter just to stiffen them and sprinkle liberally with chopped shallots and parsley. Remove the pan from heat, pour over the liquor in which the eel was marinated and leave to stand until quite cold.

Line an oval shaped pie dish with pie pastry, put on it a layer of pike forcemeat with chopped parsley added to it, spreading it evenly over the bottom and walls of the pie dish. Put the eel collops on top.

Lay out the collops very flat, alternating with layers of pike forcemeat. Sprinkle each layer with the marinating liquor.

Finish with a layer of forcemeat $\frac{3}{4}$ inch thick. Sprinkle this last layer with melted butter.

Cover with a rolled out piece of pastry, proceeding with this operation as described in the recipe for *hot pâtés* (see PÂTÉ). Decorate the top with pastry rolled out very thin and cut in fancy shapes. Make a chimney or an opening in the top to allow steam to escape. Brush the pie crust with egg.

Bake in a moderate oven for 2 hours.

Take out of the pie dish, arrange on a long serving dish. Through the opening in the top pour in a few tablespoons of thin *Demi-glace* (see SAUCE).

The eel collops can be studded with anchovy fillets, if liked. Anchovy butter or dry *Duxelles** mixture can also be added to the pike forcemeat.

Hot eel pâté à la Nantua. PÂTÉ CHAUD D'ANGUILLE À LA NANTUA—Proceed as described in the recipe for *Hot eel pâté aux fines herbes*, using eel collops studded with truffles, pike forcemeat flavoured with *Crayfish butter* (see BUTTER, *Compound butters*) with some crayfish tails added to it.

At the last moment, pour into the pâté a few spoonfuls of thin *Velouté sauce* (see SAUCE), flavoured with crayfish butter.

Hot eel pâté with truffles. PÂTÉ CHAUD D'ANGUILLE AUX TRUFFES—Proceed as described in the recipe for *Hot eel pâté aux fines herbes*, using collops of eel studded with truffles and pike forcemeat with diced truffles added to it.

Put into the pâté, alternating with rows of large slices of truffles, cut rather thick.

At the last moment, pour into the pâté a few tablespoons of thin *Demi-glace* (see SAUCE) with chopped truffles added to it.

Eel pâté, cold, or eel pie. PÂTÉ FROID D'ANGUILLE À L'ANGLAISE—Proceed as described in the recipe for *Hot eel pâté or eel pie.* Allow to cool for several hours before serving.

Cold eel pâté à la ménagère. PÂTÉ FROID D'ANGUILLE À LA MÉNAGÈRE—Proceed as described in the recipe for *Hot eel pâté aux fines herbes.*

When the pâté is quite cold, through the opening in the top pour in enough liquid fish aspic jelly (made from eel bones) to fill the space created as a result of evaporation during cooking.

Leave to get cold for 12 hours.

Cold eel pâté à la Nantua. PÂTÉ FROID D'ANGUILLE À LA NANTUA—As *Hot eel pâté à la Nantua.*

Finish with fish aspic jelly. Leave to get cold for 12 hours.

Cold eel pâté with truffles. PÂTÉ FROID D'ANGUILLE AUX TRUFFES—As *Hot eel pâté with truffles.*

Finish with fish aspic jelly based on truffle essence. Leave to get cold for 12 hours.

Note. Cold eel pâté (eel pie) can also be prepared by filling it with a completely boned eel, stuffed with whatever stuffing is indicated in the recipe, and reshaped into a *ballottine**, or twisted into a ring.

All the directions relating to this mode of preparation will be found in the recipe for *Cold eel tourte Rabelais.*

Eel pie—See *Eel pâté, Eel tourte.*

Eel à la piémontaise. ANGUILLE À LA PIÉMONTAISE—Prepare a medium sized eel as described in the recipe for *Grilled eel maître d'hôtel.* Arrange in a shallow dish on a foundation of *Risotto à la piémontaise* (see RICE). Surround with a border of *Tomato sauce* (see SAUCE). The eel can also be prepared cut in pieces.

Eel à la poulette. ANGUILLE À LA POULETTE—Fry gently in butter, in a heavy frying or sauté pan, 2 tablespoons of chopped onion, without allowing it to colour.

Toss in this onion a medium size eel, cut into uniform pieces, just to stiffen it.

Season with salt and pepper; sprinkle in a good spoonful of flour; moisten with white wine, pouring in enough to cover the fish. Add a *bouquet garni**. Simmer gently with a lid on for 25 to 30 minutes.

10 minutes before serving add 12 peeled and sliced mushrooms.

Put the eel into a *timbale* and garnish with the mushrooms.

Cover with the sauce, thickened with yolks of egg, as described in the recipe for *Poulette sauce*, and strained. See SAUCE. Sprinkle with chopped parsley.

Eel à la provençale. ANGUILLE À LA PROVENÇALE—Fry gently in oil 2 tablespoons of chopped onion. Toss briskly in this onion a medium size eel, cut in uniform slices, just to stiffen it.

Season with salt and pepper; add 4 tomatoes peeled, seeds pressed out and chopped, a *bouquet garni** and a little crushed garlic. Moisten with ½ cup (1 decilitre) of white wine. Simmer gently, with a lid on, for 25 to 30 minutes. 10 minutes before serving, add 20 black olives. Simmer slowly. Heap on a shallow platter and sprinkle with chopped parsley.

Eel with risotto—See *Eel à la piémontaise.*

Eel à la romaine. ANGUILLE À LA ROMAINE—Cut a medium size eel into pieces of about 2 inches.

Season these pieces with salt and pepper and fry them briskly in a sauté or heavy frying pan, in butter, just to stiffen them.

Add to the pan 2 cups (½ litre) of freshly shelled small garden peas, a small lettuce shredded into a *chiffonnade**, 3 tablespoons (50 grams) of butter and 2 tablespoons of white wine. Cook slowly, uncovered.

At the last moment, blend in half a tablespoon of kneaded butter. Heap on a shallow platter.

Eel on skewers à l'anglaise. ANGUILLE EN BROCHETTE À L'ANGLAISE—Bone the eel and cut into uniform pieces.

Marinate for an hour in oil, lemon juice, pepper, salt and chopped parsley.

Drain them, dredge in flour, then dip in egg and roll in breadcrumbs.

Thread on metal skewers, putting a slice of fairly fat bacon between each piece. Grill on a low flame.

Arrange on a long dish; garnish with fresh parsley, surround with half slices of decoratively cut lemon. Serve with *Tartare sauce* (see SAUCE).

Eel à la tartare I. ANGUILLE À LA TARTARE—Cut the eel into uniform pieces and cook in a white wine *court-bouillon**. Allow to cool in this liquor.

Drain, dry, dip in egg and breadcrumbs and fry at the last moment. Arrange on a napkin, garnish with fried parsley and serve *Tartare sauce* separately. See SAUCE.

Eel à la tartare II. ANGUILLE À LA TARTARE—Cook the eel as described above. Drain, dry, coat with melted butter and roll in finely grated breadcrumbs.

Sprinkle with melted butter and grill on a gentle heat. Arrange on a long dish, surround with a border of gherkins and half slices of decoratively cut lemon. Serve *Tartare sauce* separately (see SAUCE). Fried or grilled *eel à la tartare* can also be cooked whole, twisted into a ring.

Hot eel tourte. TOURTE CHAUDE D'ANGUILLE—Proceed as described in the recipe for *Hot eel pâté aux fines herbes,* using a round pie dish, with very slightly raised edges.

Cold eel tourte. TOURTE FROIDE D'ANGUILLE—Proceed as described in the recipe for *Cold eel pâté à la ménagère,* using a round pie dish, with very slightly raised edges.

Cold eel tourte Rabelais. TOURTE FROIDE D'ANGUILLE RABELAIS—Bone an eel, flatten it, put into a shallow dish, season with salt, pepper and spices, sprinkle with a few spoonfuls of white wine, a little brandy and olive oil. Leave to marinate in a cool place for one hour.

Put the eel flat on a table, stuff with *Whiting forcemeat* (see FORCEMEAT), studding it—in alternate layers—with shelled crayfish tails, olives stuffed with anchovy fillets, and truffles cut in square pieces.

Line a round pie dish with very slightly raised edges with pie pastry and put a layer of whiting forcemeat mixed with chopped parsley. Reshape the eel and put it into the pie dish.

Fill the middle of the pie with very small rolled fillets of sole, half of them stuffed with whiting forcemeat mixed with *Crayfish butter* (see BUTTER, *Compound butters*), the other half with *Whiting forcemeat* mixed with a purée of truffles.

Cover the whole with an even layer of *Whiting forcemeat aux fines herbes* (see FORCEMEAT, *Fish forcemeat II*).

Cover the pie with a rolled out piece of pastry. Seal the edges and decorate the top with pastry cut in fancy shapes.

Brush with beaten egg. Make an opening in the middle to allow steam to escape.

Bake in a moderate oven for about an hour.

Leave until quite cold. Pour into the tourte a few spoonfuls of fish aspic jelly. Serve on a napkin.

Eel à la tyrolienne. ANGUILLE À LA TYROLIENNE—Cook the eel as described in the recipe for *Grilled eel maître d'hôtel.*

Arrange in a circle on a round dish on a *fondue** of tomatoes. See TOMATO. Garnish the middle of the dish with onion rings fried in butter. Sprinkle with chopped parsley.

Eels au vert. ANGUILLES AU VERT—Skin two eels of about ¾ pound (300 to 400 grams) each. Divide each into 8 chunks of about 2 inches.

Toss them, just to stiffen them, in a sauté or heavy frying pan in which the following ingredients have already been fried lightly in 50 grams of butter: 2 handfuls of spinach leaves, prepared in the same manner (or, if available, an equal quantity of tender nettle leaves), a pinch of tarragon leaves, 2 tablespoons of pounded parsley leaves, a pinch of burnet and a few leaves of sage.

Season the chunks of eel with salt, freshly ground pepper and a very small pinch of powdered thyme and bay leaf.

Add 1⅔ cups (5 decilitres) of white wine. Bring to the boil. Cover with a lid and draw the pan away to the side of the burner. Simmer for 10 minutes.

Bind the liquor with 3 yolks of egg, add a dash of lemon juice. Transfer into an earthenware dish and keep in a very cold place.

To serve, arrange the chunks of eel in an hors-d'oeuvre dish and pour over the liquor they were cooked in, or, if they have been transferred to a dish which can be put on the table, serve them as they are.

Eel Villeroi. ANGUILLE VILLEROI—Cut the eel into pieces about 2 inches long. Poach in a white wine *court-bouillon** (see above). Allow to cool in this liquor.

Drain the pieces of eel, dry them and coat with *Panne à la Villeroi.*

Fry the eel at the last moment. Drain, arrange on a napkin, garnish with fried parsley and quarters of lemons. Serve *Tomato sauce* (see SAUCE) separately.

Whole eel can also be prepared *à la Villeroi.*

EFFERVESCENCE—The release of gas in a liquid.

EGG-HOLDER, WIRE. OEUFRIER—Utensil used for soft boiling eggs.

EGGNOG. LAIT DE POULE—A nourishing drink made from yolks of egg mixed with a pint of sweetened water or milk, flavoured with orange-flower water, vanilla or grated nutmeg, and laced with rum or brandy.

The Germans make a beer eggnog which they call *biersuppe.* This is prepared as follows:

Boil 2¼ quarts (2 litres) of beer with 1 pound (500 grams) of sugar, a pinch of salt, a little grated lemon rind and cinnamon. Add 8 yolks of egg mixed with a tablespoon of cold milk. Strain and chill. Just before serving, add a cup (¼ litre) of fried black bread *croûtons*, ¾ cup (120 grams) of raisins and 1 cup (120 grams) of currants, cooked in a pint (½ litre) of water and well drained.

EGG-PLANT—See AUBERGINE.

Eggs (*Sougez*)

EGGS. OEUFS—The eggs of birds, fish and even of reptiles can all be used as food. Hens' eggs, however, play much the most prominent part in the kitchen and it is with them that the following article mainly deals.

Eggs are very nutritious, and are particularly important during growth. They are often eaten raw, particularly in country districts. The raw egg is very easily assimilated by the stomach. In practice it appears that it is as easily digested as a soft boiled egg.

Boiled eggs and *eggs en cocotte* are easily digestible, except if the latter are served with a heavy garnish such as foie gras, truffles, mushrooms etc.

Poached and *soft boiled eggs* are equally digestible as long as they are not accompanied by rich garnishes.

The same applies to *omelette* and *scrambled eggs* though these two dishes—even without any garnish, are not as easily digestible as those mentioned above.

Fried eggs are also fairly easily digestible if they are not too much browned in the butter or fat in which they are cooked. But they are never digested quite as quickly as eggs boiled *à la coque*, *en cocotte*, *poached* or *soft boiled.*

Hard boiled eggs where the *albumin* is always very congealed, take longer to digest than any of the others. A hard boiled egg cut into very small fragments is more easily digested.

It has been proved that in general, no matter in what form eggs are taken, they produce a quicker feeling of satisfaction than the equivalent amount of meat.

Choice of eggs—A fresh egg is heavy. When a fresh egg is shaken it should feel well-filled. As the shell of the egg is porous, the water which encloses the inner part of the egg evaporates. An egg loses a tiny fraction in weight every day.

It is easy to find out the state of freshness of any egg by plunging it into a solution of 12% salted water (kitchen salt). If the egg is very fresh, it falls at once to the bottom of the liquid. If it is a few days old it floats in the liquid. If it is bad it floats on top of the liquid. This method does not apply to eggs which have been preserved in water and limestone or any other liquid.

Composition of the egg—The average weight of a hen's egg is 2 ounces. The shell weighs on an average 12% of the total weight of the egg and is made of a calcareous, porous substance, pervious to air, water and smells. It is lined with a delicate membrane, the pellucid membrane, which separates itself from the shell at the larger end of the egg to form the air chamber. The size of this air chamber is in inverse proportion to the freshness of the egg—the fresher the egg, the smaller the chamber.

The albumen, or white of the egg, is a thick, viscous, transparent liquid, with a high percentage of water. It can be considered as an albuminous solution with some mineral substances. This albumen is soluble in cold water, congeals at 70°C. (158°F.) and remains from then on insoluble. It forms about 58% of the total weight of the egg.

The vitellus, or yolk of the egg (30% of the total weight), is an opaque, soft substance which congeals in the heat. The yolk is composed of albumin, fats containing vitamins, lecithines, nucleines, cholesterines and mineral substances including a ferruginous pigment, *hematogene*, which gives it its colour.

The composition of the egg varies with the breed of the hen and its diet (diet also influences the flavour of the eggs). The best eggs come from poultry kept in the open, allowed to forage for worms, and receiving the right proportion of grains and greenery. A diet too rich in insects, or one composed of substances causing constipation (thereby favouring the laying of eggs) such as powdered meat, fish, blood, etc., gives a bad taste to the eggs and make them unfit for children to eat.

Ostrich, turkey, goose, peacock and duck eggs are bigger than hens' eggs; pigeon, guinea-fowl, pheasant, partridge, lapwing, plover and gulls' eggs are smaller. All these are of a very similar composition except for duck and goose eggs which are more oily.

Preservation of eggs—Eggs are preserved by the exclusion of air. They can either be dipped into a proprietary solution and then stored, or they can be kept submerged in a solution of waterglass. It is not advisable to use preserved eggs for boiling.

Eggs can also be preserved by dessication into powder.

Methods of cooking eggs—Although eggs can be prepared in an infinite number of ways, the basic methods of cooking them are few.

In cooking and baking only absolutely fresh eggs should be used. Certain methods of cooking eggs, namely *à la coque**, soft boiled* and poached* should only be used when the eggs are not more than a day or two old. Ideally only eggs laid on the day itself should be used, but that is often difficult to arrange.

Boiled eggs and garnished eggs en cocotte (*Robert Carrier*)

EGGS, BASIC RECIPES:

Boiled eggs (hard boiled). OEUFS DURS—Plunge the eggs into a pan of boiling water, keep on the boil for 8 to 10 minutes according to the size of the eggs.

Drain and put the eggs into cold water or under a cold water tap. Peel them and use them hot or cold according to the recipe chosen.

Boiled eggs (soft boiled). OEUFS MOLLETS—Plunge the eggs into a pan of boiling water. Cook for 3–4 minutes. Put the eggs under cold water and shell them. Keep the eggs warm in a pan of very hot salted water until the moment of serving.

Serving: Drain the eggs. Arrange and garnish them or serve them with a sauce according to the recipe chosen.

Soft boiled eggs are served and garnished in the same way as poached eggs.

Eggs en cocotte, cassolettes ou caissettes. OEUFS EN COCOTTE—This way of preparing eggs derives from a combination of *eggs à la coque** and *poached eggs**.

Method. Warm the cocottes, cassolettes or caissettes (made of china, clay, metal or fireproof glass—round or oval shaped). Butter the inside of the dishes lightly or coat them according to the recipe with a purée or a similar preparation.

Break the eggs and put them into the moulds. Use one or two eggs for each mould according to the recipe.

Put the moulds into a dish half filled with warm water. Cook them in the oven for 6 to 8 minutes depending on how many eggs are in each dish.

Salt the eggs when taking them out of the oven.

Serving. Clean the exterior of the moulds well, put them on a flat dish covered with a napkin or a paper doyley. Serve *au naturel* or garnish according to the recipes given in another place.

Eggs à la coque. OEUFS À LA COQUE—

First method. Plunge the egg into a pot of boiling water. An egg of average weight should be left for 3 minutes. A larger egg should be left for half a minute longer in the boiling water.

Second method. Plunge the eggs into boiling water; boil for one minute. Draw the pot away from the fire and leave the eggs in the hot water for 3 minutes.

Third method. Put the eggs in a saucepan. Cover them completely with cold water. Let them come to the boil and remove the eggs from the saucepan as soon as the water is really boiling.

Fourth method. Cook the eggs by steam in special pans for 3 minutes.

Note. The times given above are those necessary for normal cooking methods. According to the taste of the diners, cooking time can be increased or reduced.

Fried eggs. OEUFS FRITS—There are two ways of preparing these eggs.

Fried. Put one egg at a time into plenty of fat, oil or butter. The white should cover the yolk.

Sautéed. In a frying pan, with fat, oil or butter done on one side only or on both sides, turned over on to a dish or plate.

Method. Heat oil well in a small frying pan. Use sufficient oil to enable the egg to swim. Break the egg into a cup and season with salt. Put it into the hot oil and with a wooden spoon gather the white around the yolk, as it gets sealed by the boiling oil.

Serving. Drain the eggs on a cloth, arrange and garnish them as indicated for each recipe.

Eggs in a mould. OEUFS MOULÉS—This dish belongs to the *grand cuisine*, but it can easily be prepared in a home kitchen.

Fried egg and bacon

Method. Cover the inside of castle pudding moulds with a good coating of butter and sprinkle them according to the recipe with parsley, ham, truffles, or any other suitable article chopped or cut into different shapes. Break the eggs into the lined moulds.

Cook in a bain-marie (pan of hot water) for 8 to 12 minutes. Leave in the moulds for a few minutes before taking out.

Serving. Put the eggs on rounds of bread or square pieces of sandwich loaf which have been toasted or fried. Moulded eggs can also be served on tartlets or round *croustades**, on artichoke hearts or in a different way according to the recipe chosen. Garnish and serve with a suitable sauce.

Note. For certain dishes these eggs are cooked in differently shaped moulds, simple or fluted. Their preparation is the same.

Omelette—The difficulty of preparing an omelette is more apparent than real. Success is assured if the following points are observed.

The flame must be very high.

Use only a frying pan which is absolutely clean and in which nothing else is ever cooked.

Beat the eggs moderately and only at the last moment.

Do not put too much butter or other fat into the frying pan.

Finally, have confidence in yourself.

Omelette (*Brown and Polson*)

Method. The following quantities are sufficient for four people.

Beat 8 eggs in moderation. Season with fine salt and if desired with freshly ground pepper.

Heat 2 to 2½ tablespoons (30 to 40 grams) of butter in the frying pan and add the eggs. Put on a high flame. Mix with a fork. Shake the eggs in the pan to ensure that the omelette is evenly cooked all over. Fold it over once and turn it upside down with one quick movement on to a warmed dish.

Serving. Garnish the omelette and choose a sauce as described in the various omelette recipes in this section.

Rub a piece of butter over the top of the omelette to make it look shiny.

Poached eggs. OEUFS POCHÉS—*Method.* Choose a suitable pan. Fill with salted water—1½ teaspoons (10 grams) of salt to 1 quart (1 litre) of water. Add 1 tablespoon of vinegar to each quart (litre). Bring to the boil. Break the eggs and put them in the liquid exactly on the spot where it is bubbling. Simmer very gently for 3 minutes.

Drain the eggs one after the other with the help of a skimmer. Put each one separately into fresh water. Trim the eggs, i.e. remove the blisters (with fresh eggs trimming should hardly be necessary). Put in a dish with very hot salted water and leave them there until they are served.

Serving. Drain the eggs and dry them. Put the eggs according to the recipe on fried or grilled crusts of bread which can be hollowed out if desired. Poached eggs can also be served on *croustades* made from very fine lining dough or puff pastry (see DOUGH) in tartlets or on a foundation of rice, semolina, potatoes, artichoke hearts, etc.

Garnish and cover with a sauce according to the recipe chosen.

Scrambled eggs. OEUFS BROUILLÉS—Well prepared scrambled eggs are a very delicious dish, but it is vital that they should be cooked with care—they must be smooth and creamy.

Like omelette, scrambled eggs can be garnished in various ways.

First method. The following quantities are enough for four people. Choose a small frying pan with a thick bottom or a small saucepan. Melt 3 tablespoons (50 grams) of butter. Break 8 eggs and beat *lightly* as for an omelette. Season and put in the pan.

Cook over a low heat, i.e. on the corner of the stove and stir constantly with a wooden spoon.

Gather into the middle the parts of the eggs which have been cooked on the sides of the pan. When the eggs are cooked, remove them from the stove and add 4 tablespoons (60 grams) of butter cut into small pieces. Mix well and keep hot in a *bain-marie* (pan of hot water) until the moment of serving.

Serving. Garnish according to the recipe chosen and serve in a pie dish or in a vegetable dish.

Second method. Use a double saucepan. Fill the larger pan half way up with warm water. Put the butter and the beaten eggs in the smaller pan. Cook over a low heat, stirring with a wooden spoon.

When the eggs are cooked, add butter, cut into small pieces as described above.

Note. According to the recipe chosen, two or three tablespoons of fresh cream can be added to scrambled eggs after they are cooked.

Scrambled eggs can be served in small or large *croustades** made from puff pastry, in *timbales** made from best plain pastry, in *cassolettes**, in hollowed out vegetables or in metal or china pie dishes.

Eggs sur le plat or shirred eggs. OEUFS SUR LE PLAT—For this extremely simple way of cooking eggs use special individual pans or large pans. Individual pans, holding one or two eggs, are the only means of cooking eggs to the taste of each diner.

For two eggs. Coat the pan with 1 teaspoon (6 to 8 grams) of butter. Heat on the stove. Break the eggs into the pan. Pour some drops of melted butter on the yolks.

Cook in the oven. Cooking time depends on the texture desired. Season with salt on taking out of the oven. In France eggs cooked in this way are sometimes called *oeufs miroir* ('looking-glass eggs'), because, after cooking, the albumin forms a kind of varnish on the yolks.

Serving. Garnish or cover with a sauce according to instructions given further on in alphabetical order.

EGG DISHES:

Eggs à l'africaine (soft boiled or poached). OEUFS À L'AFRICAINE—Arrange the eggs in a turban (ring) on a layer of *Couscous**.

Peel some aubergines (egg-plants), cut into large dice, sauté them in oil and put into the middle of the turban.

Peel some sweet peppers, cut into dice and cook in a *consommé* (see SOUPS AND BROTHS). Make a *Tomato sauce* (see SAUCE), add the peppers and pour it over the eggs.

Eggs à l'agenaise (sur le plat). OEUFS À L'AGENAISE—Sauté chopped onions in some goose fat and when cooked add a little garlic and chopped parsley. Put a tablespoon of the onion mixture in individual fireproof dishes and break an egg in each dish.

Garnish with some aubergines (egg-plant), peeled, cut into large dice, and sautéed in goose fat.

Aladdin eggs (baked). OEUFS ALADDIN—Bake the eggs on a foundation of onions sautéed in butter until they are very soft.

Garnish with bouquets of *Sweet peppers à l'orientale* (see PEPPERS) and saffron-flavoured *Risotto* (see RICE). Surround with a border of *Tomato sauce* (see SAUCE).

Aladdin eggs (soft boiled or poached). OEUFS ALADDIN—Arrange the eggs like a turban (ring) on a layer of saffron-flavoured *Risotto* (see RICE).

Peel some sweet peppers, cut them into large dice and cook *à l'orientale* (see PEPPERS). Garnish the middle of the dish with these peppers.

Mask the eggs with *Tomato sauce* (see SAUCE) spiced with a pinch of cayenne.

Eggs à l'alsacienne I (deep fried). OEUFS À L'ALSACIENNE—Arrange the fried eggs on a layer of braised sauerkraut alternating them with slices of ham. Surround with a border of *Demi-glace sauce* (see SAUCE).

Eggs à l'alsacienne II (soft boiled or poached). OEUFS À L'ALSACIENNE—Arrange the eggs in a dish on a layer of braised sauerkraut. Garnish with thin slices of cooked ham. Cover with *Demi-glace sauce* (see SAUCE).

Eggs à l'alsacienne III (sur le plat). OEUFS À L'ALSACIENNE—Fry the eggs in goose fat. Garnish with a tablespoon of braised sauerkraut and a slice of ham. Surround with a border of *Demi-glace sauce* (see SAUCE).

Ambassadrice eggs I (soft boiled or poached). OEUFS AMBASSADRICE MOLLETS, POCHÉS—Make some *croustades** with puff pastry, garnish with a *salpicon** of truffles and foie gras, blend with a very concentrated *Demi-glace sauce* (see SAUCE) flavoured with Madeira. Put the eggs on the garnished *croustades* and mask them with a *Suprême sauce* (see SAUCE). Garnish the middle of the dish with asparagus tips blended with butter.

Ambassadrice eggs II (en cocotte). OEUFS AMBASSADRICE EN COCOTTE—Line the cocotte dishes with *Purée of foie gras** and sprinkle them with chopped truffles. Break the eggs into the lined dishes and cook them in a *bain-marie* (pan of hot water). When the eggs are cooked, take them out and garnish with asparagus tips and surround the yolk with *Suprême sauce* to which sherry has been added (see SAUCE).

Ambassadrice eggs III (sur le plat). OEUFS AMBASSADRICE SUR LE PLAT—Cook the eggs according to the usual method. When taking them out of the oven, garnish the eggs with a *salpicon** of foie gras, truffles and asparagus tips. Surround with a border of *Suprême sauce* to which sherry has been added (see SAUCE).

Amélie eggs I (soft boiled or poached). OEUFS AMÉLIE MOLLETS, POCHÉS—Arrange the eggs on *croustades** made from puff pastry garnished with a fine *mirepoix** of vegetables (cooked in butter until they are very soft) and with a little Madeira wine, poured into the pan after the vegetables have been taken out.

Mask the eggs with a *Cream sauce* (see SAUCE). Garnish with morels cooked in cream.

Amélie eggs II (sur le plat). OEUFS AMÉLIE SUR LE PLAT—Make a *mirepoix** of vegetables with Madeira and cook the eggs on this. Garnish with morels cooked in cream.

Eggs à l'américaine I (deep fried). OEUFS À L'AMÉRICAINE FRITS—Cook the eggs with butter in a frying pan. Arrange them on a dish. Garnish with two slices of grilled bacon (the bacon can also be sautéed in a frying pan) and half a grilled tomato.

Eggs à l'américaine II (soft boiled or poached). OEUFS À L'AMÉRICAINE—Arrange the eggs on fried bread or on *croustades**. Garnish with pieces of *lobster or spiny lobster à l'américaine**. Pour *Américaine sauce* over the eggs. See SAUCE.

Note. These eggs can also be served with left-overs of *lobster or spiny lobster à l'américaine**. Instead of using pieces use the meat of the claws and the trunk cut into dice.

Eggs à l'américaine III (sur le plat). OEUFS À L'AMÉRICAINE SUR LE PLAT—Put in a buttered frying pan 2 pieces of *lobster or spiny lobster à l'américaine.* Break two eggs on to the collops. Bake in the oven; surround with *Américaine sauce* (see SAUCE).

Anchovy eggs I (soft boiled or poached). OEUFS AUX ANCHOIS MOLLETS, POCHÉS—Arrange the eggs on bread fried in butter on both sides or on *croustades** made from puff pastry.

Mask the eggs with *Anchovy Sauce* (see SAUCE). De-salt anchovy fillets, shape them into rings and put one on each egg.

Anchovy eggs II (sur le plat). OEUFS AUX ANCHOIS SUR LE PLAT—De-salt the anchovies and cut into dice. Sprinkle these dice into a buttered pan; break the eggs on to them. Surround the yolks with thin anchovy fillets rolled into rings.

Anchovy eggs III (deep fried). OEUFS AUX ANCHOIS FRITS—Deep-fry the eggs in oil. Arrange each egg on an oval piece of bread, fried in butter on both sides and garnished with thin fillets of anchovy arranged criss-cross. Sprinkle with *Noisette butter* (see BUTTER, *Compound butters*).

Eggs à l'ancienne I (soft boiled or poached). OEUFS À L'ANCIENNE—Arrange the eggs on a mound of rice which has been cooked in meat stock.

Cover the eggs with a *Velouté sauce* (see SAUCE). Put a small teaspoon of *julienne** of truffles blended with a thick *Madeira sauce* (see SAUCE) between the eggs.

Eggs à l'ancienne II (cold). OEUFS À L'ANCIENNE—Use soft boiled eggs or poached eggs. Mask them with a *White chaud-froid sauce* (see SAUCE) to which Madeira has been added. Decorate with truffles and glaze with jelly. Serve them in a crystal dish or on a metal dish lined with a layer of chicken jelly.

Separate the eggs with slices of pickled tongue cut into fluted half-circles. Cover with a thin jelly. Put chopped jelly into the middle of the dish. Keep in a cold place until the moment of serving.

Eggs à l'andalouse I (sur le plat). OEUFS À L'ANDALOUSE—Before cooking the eggs in oil, rub the dish with garlic. Peel sweet peppers, cut them into dice and cook them gently in oil; add *Tomato fondue** and garnish the eggs with the mixture.

Eggs à l'andalouse II (deep fried). OEUFS À L'ANDALOUSE—Deep-fry the eggs in oil. Arrange them in the shape of a crown, alternating them with grilled halved tomatoes.

Garnish the middle of the dish with sweet peppers cooked in oil and roundels of onions fried in oil.

Eggs à l'anglaise I (sur le plat). OEUFS À L'ANGLAISE—Put a grilled slice of bacon into a buttered dish. Break two eggs over the bacon; cook in the oven.

Eggs à l'anglaise II. OEUFS À L'ANGLAISE—Cook the eggs in butter in a frying pan. Cut them with a round plain biscuit cutter in such a way as to keep only a thin white rim round the yolk.

Arrange on round pieces of sandwich loaf which have been either toasted or fried in butter.

Surround with veal stock or serve veal stock separately.

Eggs à l'antiboise. OEUFS À L'ANTIBOISE—Roll in flour four tablespoons of *nonats** and sauté in butter in a frying pan. When the *nonats* are brown, add a tablespoon of Gruyère cheese cut into very small dice and a little crushed garlic.

Break four eggs into the same pan; cook in the oven. Turn upside down on to a hot dish. Sprinkle with chopped parsley.

Eggs à l'anversoise (soft boiled or poached). OEUFS À L'ANVERSOISE—Serve the eggs on bread fried in butter on both sides. Garnish with hop shoots cooked in butter. Mask with *Cream sauce* or *Suprême sauce* (see SAUCE), depending on whether the dish is to be served as a Lenten dish or not.

Eggs à l'anversoise (sur le plat). OEUFS À L'ANVERSOISE—Garnish the eggs after they have been baked with a tablespoon of hop shoots cooked in butter or cream. Surround with a border of boiling cream.

Apicius eggs (soft boiled or poached). OEUFS APICIUS—Serve the eggs on large grilled mushrooms. Garnish the middle of the dish with a ragoût of *Crayfish tails à la Nantua**. Mask the eggs with *Normande sauce* (see SAUCE). Put between each of the eggs a tablespoon of a *salpicon** made from truffles cooked in butter.

Archiduc eggs I (soft boiled or poached). OEUFS ARCHIDUC MOLLETS, POCHÉS—Arrange the eggs on pieces of bread fried in butter on both sides or on *croustades** made from puff pastry.

Mask with *Suprême sauce* (see SAUCE), add chopped onions cooked gently in butter until they are very soft; season with paprika. Garnish with truffles cut into dice and lightly fried in butter.

Archiduc eggs II (sur le plat). OEUFS ARCHIDUC SUR LE PLAT—Break the eggs into a baking dish lined with chopped onions lightly fried in butter until very soft and seasoned with paprika.

Garnish with diced truffles cooked in butter. Surround with *Suprême sauce* (see SAUCE), to which paprika has been added.

Eggs argenteuil I (soft boiled or poached) OUEFS ARGENTEUIL MOLLETS, POCHÉS—Arrange the eggs on pieces of bread fried in butter on both sides or on puff pastry *croustades**.

Mask with *White asparagus purée* (see PURÉE) to which *Velouté sauce* (see SAUCE) has been added in the proportion of three to one.

Garnish with white asparagus tips cooked in butter.

Eggs Argenteuil II (sur le plat). OEUFS ARGENTEUIL SUR LE PLAT—Put one tablespoon of fresh cream into a buttered dish. Break the eggs into this. Cook in the oven.

Garnish with white asparagus tips cooked in butter.

Eggs Argenteuil III. OEUFS ARGENTEUIL—Line a dish with *White asparagus purée* (see PURÉE). Break the eggs into it. Cook in the oven.

Garnish with green asparagus tips cooked in butter. Surround with *Velouté sauce* or *Cream sauce* (see SAUCE).

Eggs Argenteuil IV (cold). OEUFS ARGENTEUIL FROIDS—Mask the eggs with a *Chaud-froid sauce* (see SAUCE). Decorate with green asparagus tips and glaze with jelly, by spooning some aspic jelly over them.

Use a round plate or a crystal dish with a shallow rim. Make a salad of white asparagus tips seasoned with *Jellied mayonnaise* (see SAUCE). Arrange this salad on the dish very neatly and put the eggs on it with chopped jelly in the middle.

Armenonville eggs (soft boiled or poached). OEUFS ARMENONVILLE—Arrange the eggs on small oval pieces of toast made from ordinary unsweetened brioche dough, grilled. Mask with a *Velouté sauce* (see SAUCE) to which sherry has been added. Garnish with bouquets of very small carrots cooked in cream and asparagus tips sautéed with butter.

Auber eggs I (soft boiled or poached). OEUFS AUBER MOLLETS, POCHÉS—Stuff halved tomatoes with a *Chicken forcemeat* (see FORCEMEAT) mixed with chopped truffles. Put one egg on each.

Make a *Velouté sauce* (see SAUCE) flavoured with tomato paste. At the last minute, add a *julienne** of truffles cooked in sherry. Mask the eggs with this sauce.

Auber eggs II (cold). OEUFS AUBER—Mask the eggs with a *White chaud-froid sauce* (see SAUCE) to which *Tomato essence* has been added (see ESSENCE). Decorate them with truffles and glaze with jelly.

Hollow out some tomatoes, marinate them and fill them with diced breast of chicken and truffles, seasoned with a gelatine-strengthened mayonnaise. Put one decorated egg on each stuffed tomato. Arrange on a dish in the shape of a crown and garnish with chopped jelly.

Eggs with aubergines I (baked). OEUFS AUX AUBERGINES SUR LE PLAT—Line the pan with diced aubergines (egg-plant) sautéed in butter. Break the eggs on to the aubergines, cook in the usual way.

Eggs with aubergines II (deep fried). OEUFS AUX AUBERGINES FRITS—Deep fry the eggs in oil. Arrange them in a ring alternating with slices of aubergines (egg-plant) cut lengthwise and deep fried in oil or grilled. Garnish with fried parsley.

Eggs with aubergines (egg-plant) à la sicilienne (soft boiled or poached). OEUFS AUX AUBERGINES À LA SICILIENNE—Cut the aubergines (egg-plant) lengthwise in half. Score the pulp. Salt them and leave to render their liquid for an hour. Cook in oil in a frying pan.

Remove the pulp of the aubergines without tearing the skins. Let the pulp dry a little on the stove. Add twice its volume of *Mornay sauce* (see SAUCE).

Mask the bottom of the aubergines with a tablespoon of this purée. Put one egg in each halved aubergine. Arrange them in a buttered fireproof dish. Cover the eggs with the remaining purée to which fresh cream has been added. Sprinkle with grated cheese. Brown in a hot oven.

Augier eggs (sur le plat). OEUFS AUGIER—Line a buttered dish with a purée made of sweetbreads and chopped chervil. Break the eggs on to the purée. Surround the yolks with a ring of fresh cream. Bake in the oven.

Aurora eggs I (soft boiled or poached). OEUFS À L'AURORE MOLLETS, POCHÉS—Arrange the eggs on pieces of bread fried in butter on both sides or on puff pastry *croustades**. Mask them with *Aurora sauce* (see SAUCE).

Sprinkle with chopped yolks of hard boiled eggs. Surround with a rim of tomato sauce.

Aurora eggs II (stuffed hard boiled). OEUFS À L'AURORE DURS FARCIS—Cut the eggs lengthwise. Take the yolks out. Mix two thirds of the yolks with an equal weight of very thick *Béchamel sauce* (see SAUCE) and butter. Season and add a pinch of chopped herbs.

Stuff the eggs with this mixture heaping it into a dome.

Mask a baking dish with *Mornay sauce* (see SAUCE) and arrange the eggs on it.

Sprinkle them with grated cheese and pour on a little melted butter. Brown in a very hot oven.

When taking the dish out of the oven, sprinkle with the remaining chopped hard boiled yolks and surround with a rim of *Tomato sauce* (see SAUCE).

Eggs à l'auvergnate (soft boiled or poached). OEUFS À L'AUVERGNATE—Cook some cabbage in meat stock and drain. Sauté in butter or lard in a frying pan. Arrange the eggs on the cabbage alternating them with roundels of sausage, deep fried in butter.

Cover with a concentrated veal stock to which butter has been added.

Babinski eggs (sur le plat). OEUFS BABINSKI—After the eggs are cooked, garnish them with very small cork-shaped chicken croquettes and with a tablespoon of morels in cream. Surround with very concentrated veal stock to which butter has been added.

Bachaumont eggs (en cocotte). OEUFS BACHAUMONT—Butter the cocottes and line them with a celeriac purée. Break the eggs on to the purée. Cook in the oven in a *bain-marie**.

When taking out of the oven, season, and surround with a ring of *Cream sauce* (see SAUCE) mixed with chopped chervil.

Eggs and bacon I (baked). OEUFS AU BACON SUR LE PLAT—Put in a dish some thin slices of bacon lightly browned in butter. Break the eggs into the dish and pour the fat rendered by the bacon over them. Bake in the oven.

Eggs and bacon II (fried). OEUFS AU BACON POÊLÉS—Grill some bacon. Cook the eggs in a frying pan with butter over a hot flame and garnish with the bacon. Season. Slide on to a plate.

Eggs and bacon III (deep fried). OEUFS AU BACON FRITS—Deep fry the eggs in oil. Arrange in a turban (ring), alternating with bacon which has been either grilled or deep fried in oil. Garnish with fried parsley.

Bagration eggs I (soft boiled or poached). OEUFS BAGRATION, MOLLETS, POCHÉS—Serve the eggs in a flan crust baked blind (baked pie shell). Garnish with macaroni cooked in water, cut into dice, blended with cream and mixed with truffles cut into dice. Mask with *Cream sauce* (see SAUCE).

Bagration eggs II (in a mould). OEUFS BAGRATION, MOULÉS—Take a buttered mould and line it with macaroni cooked in water. The macaroni must mount the walls of the mould in spiral fashion. Spread *Quenelle forcemeat* (see FORCEMEAT) on the macaroni and break the eggs into this. Cook in a *bain-marie* (pan of hot water).

Empty the moulds and stand them on small round *croustades**. Mask with *Cream sauce* (see SAUCE). Put on each egg a round slice of truffle cooked in butter.

Bagration eggs

Balmoral eggs (en cocotte). OEUFS BALMORAL—Line cocotte dishes with a layer of vegetable *mirepoix**. Break the eggs on the *mirepoix*. Bake in the oven in a *bain-marie* (pan of hot water).

Season when taking out of the oven and garnish with a tablespoon of mushrooms cut into dice, fried in butter, blended with a little concentrated veal stock.

Bamboche eggs (deep fried). OEUFS BAMBOCHE—Deep fry the eggs in oil. Arrange them in a circle on a *macédoine** of vegetables blended with cream.

Garnish the centre of the dish with thin strips of fried cod as described for *Salt cod à la bamboche* (see COD).

Banville eggs (soft boiled or poached). OEUFS BANVILLE —Boil some artichoke hearts in *court-bouillon** and sauté them lightly in butter. Arrange the eggs on the artichoke hearts and mask them with *Chivry sauce* (see SAUCE). Garnish the centre of the dish with slightly thickened *Chicken forcemeat à la crème* (see FORCEMEAT).

Eggs à la bayonnaise (deep fried). OEUFS À LA BAYONNAISE—Deep fry some slices of bread and the eggs in oil. Cut small round slices of Bayonne ham and deep fry them in oil. Arrange the eggs on the fried bread, alternating them with the fried ham. Garnish with sautéed cèpes. Raw Italian ham (*prosciutto*) may be used in place of Bayonne ham.

Eggs à la béarnaise (soft boiled or poached). OEUFS À LA BÉARNAISE—Make small oval flat cakes using *Duchess potato mixture* (see POTATOES). Bake in the oven until golden brown. Spread each of these with concentrated veal gravy to which butter has been added. Serve *Béarnaise sauce* separately (see SAUCE).

Eggs à la Beauharnais (soft boiled or poached). OEUFS À LA BEAUHARNAIS—Cook some artichoke hearts in butter. Arrange one egg on each heart. Garnish with *Beauharnais sauce* (see SAUCE). Cover with a concentrated *Demi-glace sauce* (see SAUCE), to which butter has been added.

Eggs à la Beaumont. OEUFS À LA BEAUMONT—'Using ten eggs make the following preparations: 10 oval *croustades** made from left-over puff pastry, a pint (½ litre) of thin *Béchamel sauce* (see SAUCE).

'Cook three large artichoke hearts, trim them well and cut them into small squares; stew them very gently in butter. Take a third of the stewed artichoke hearts and pass them through a fine sieve. Mix the purée with the *Béchamel sauce*. To complete the sauce add at the last minute about 3 tablespoons (40 to 50 grams) of butter.

'Cook the tips of a pound (400 grams) of green asparagus in salt water. Drain the asparagus but do not rinse in cold water. At the last minute, season the asparagus tips with salt, pepper, and a pinch of grated nutmeg and dress with butter. Mix in the remainder of the cut-up artichoke hearts.

'Poach the eggs, bearing in mind that eggs cooked in this way should be absolutely fresh. Drain them and plunge into lukewarm water. Then drain and dry on a cloth. Trim the eggs and arrange them in a circle, each egg resting on a *croustade**. Cover them with the sauce; put some chervil on each egg and arrange in the centre of the circle, the garnish consisting of artichokes and asparagus tips'. (Philéas Gilbert.)

Eggs à la béchamel. OEUFS À LA BÉCHAMEL—See *Eggs with cream.*

Belle-Hélène eggs (soft boiled or poached). OEUFS BELLE-HÉLÈNE—Make some oval-shaped *croquettes** from left-over poultry meat, dip them in egg and breadcrumbs and fry them in butter. Put one soft boiled or poached egg on each croquette. Mask the eggs with *Colbert butter* (see BUTTER, *Compound butters*). Garnish with asparagus tips. Surround with a ring of *Velouté sauce* (see SAUCE).

Eggs à la bellevilloise (sur le plat). OEUFS À LA BELLEVILLOISE—Line a dish with chopped onion cooked in butter until very soft. Put the eggs on the onions and garnish with two slices of grilled *andouillettes**. Bake in the oven.

Take the dish out of the oven and surround the eggs with a ribbon of *Lyonnaise sauce* (see SAUCE).

Eggs à la bénédictine (soft boiled or poached). OEUFS À LA BÉNÉDICTINE—Pound some cod with garlic, oil and cream and add some chopped truffles. Arrange the eggs on the mixture and mask with a *Cream sauce* (see SAUCE).

Bérangère eggs (soft boiled or poached). OEUFS BÉRANGÈRE—Garnish a flan crust baked blind (a baked pie shell) with a layer of thick *Soubise purée* (see PURÉE). Put the eggs on this layer and mask them with *Mornay sauce* (see SAUCE). Sprinkle grated cheese over the pie and pour melted butter over the cheese. Brown quickly in the oven.

Bérangère eggs (en cocotte). OEUFS BÉRANGÈRE—Butter some cocottes. Line them with a thin layer of forcemeat stuffing made from poultry and truffles. Break the eggs into the cocottes. Cook in the usual way. When the eggs are cooked, garnish them with a tablespoon of ragoût made from cocks' combs and kidneys blended with a *Suprême sauce* (see SAUCE).

Bercy eggs (sur le plat). OEUFS BERCY—Bake the eggs in the usual way. When cooked, garnish them with a small grilled or fried sausage. Surround with a ring of *Tomato sauce* (see SAUCE).

Berlioz eggs (soft boiled or poached). OEUFS BERLIOZ—Make some oval *croustades** from *Duchess potato mixture* (see POTATOES). Brown them in the oven. Fill the *croustades* with a *salpicon** of truffles and mushrooms blended with a thick *Madeira sauce* (see SAUCE). Put the eggs on the garnished *croustades.*

Mask the eggs very lightly with a *Suprême sauce* (see SAUCE). Fill the middle of the dish with fried *Cock's combs à la Villeroi**.

Bernis eggs (soft boiled or poached). OEUFS BERNIS—Make some round *croustades** with a little rim from puff pastry. Garnish them with a layer of chicken purée. Arrange the eggs in the *croustades.*

Mask the eggs with a *Suprême sauce* (see SAUCE). Garnish the centre of the dish with green asparagus tips blended with butter.

Eggs Bernis (cold). OEUFS BERNIS—Use poached eggs. Wrap them in white *Chaud-froid sauce* (see SAUCE). Decorate the eggs with truffles and glaze with jelly.

Take a crystal dish. Line with a layer of *chicken mousse**. Arrange the eggs on the mousse leaving space between each egg for a bouquet of green asparagus tips. Spoon over the whole dish some half-set jelly. Keep very cold until the moment of serving.

Note. It is more convenient to serve the eggs in individual dishes. Small cassolettes made from metal, crystal or china, or shell dishes made from the same materials could be used.

Bizet eggs (in a mould). OEUFS BIZET—Butter some individual moulds and line them with finely chopped pickled tongue and truffles. Break the eggs into the moulds. Poach them in a *bain-marie* (pan of hot water).

Cook some artichoke hearts in butter. Take the eggs out of the moulds and put one egg on each artichoke heart. Mask with *Périgueux sauce* (see SAUCE). Put a slice of truffle on each egg.

Eggs à la bohémienne (soft boiled or poached). OEUFS À LA BOHÉMIENNE—Make some *croustades** from puff pastry and garnish them with purée of *foie gras*. Put the eggs on the purée. Cover them with *Velouté sauce* (see SAUCE). Cut some lean ham into short matchsticks and heat these up in Madeira. Put the ham on the eggs. Surround with a ring of light veal jelly.

Bonvalet eggs (soft boiled or poached). OEUFS BONVALET —Make some *croûtons**. Hollow them out slightly. Brown them in butter and put the eggs into the hollows.

Mask with a *Velouté sauce* (see SAUCE). Surround them with a ribbon of thick tomato-flavoured *Béarnaise sauce* (see SAUCE) piped through a paper forcing (pastry) bag. Put on each egg a slice of truffle heated in butter.

Eggs à la bordelaise I (sur le plat). OEUFS À LA BORDELAISE—Chop some cèpes and sauté them *à la bordelaise*. Break the eggs on the mushrooms and cook in the usual way.

Eggs à la bordelaise II (deep fried). OEUFS À LA BORDELAISE—Deep fry the eggs in oil. Deep fry some oval croûtons in oil. Arrange the eggs on the croûtons and garnish with cèpes cooked *à la bordelaise*.

Eggs as a border to spinach

Eggs as a border I (with various garnishes). OEUFS EN BORDURE—Hard boil the eggs. Cut them into quarters or thick roundels, or halve the eggs.

Use a plain ring mould. Butter it well. Arrange the eggs with the yolks facing outward. Fill the mould, using a forcing (pastry) bag, with forcemeat made of meat, fish or vegetables (see FORCEMEAT). Press the forcemeat down to avoid empty spaces. Cover with a lid and cook in a *bain-marie* (pan of hot water), in the oven on a low heat.

Turn the mould out onto a round dish, taking care not to remove it too soon, so that the ingredients all come out well pressed together.

Fill the middle with some garnish. Use either creamed mushrooms or sautéed mushrooms, a macédoine of vegetables, asparagus tips or other green vegetables in butter or with cream, spinach leaves or spinach purée, sautéed aubergines (egg-plant), etc.

Spoon some *Cream sauce* (see SAUCE) or any other suitable sauce over the border.

Eggs as a border II. OEUFS EN BORDURE—Use hard boiled eggs. Cut them into thick round slices. Bake a flan crust (pie shell). Arrange the eggs in a circle round the edges of the flan, alternating them with round slices of ham, pickled tongue, calf's brain sautéed in butter, aubergines (egg-plant) or courgettes (zucchini) sautéed in butter, or with any other garnish that goes well with hard boiled eggs.

Fill the middle of the flan with one of the garnishes described in the previous recipe (*Eggs as a border with various garnishes*). Cover the eggs with *Cream sauce* (see SAUCE) or any other sauce suitable to the chosen garnish.

Eggs as a border III (cold). OEUFS EN BORDURE—Hard boil some eggs. Cut them into halves, quarters or thick roundels. Line some ring moulds with very white jelly. Put the eggs on to the jelly and decorate them with small pieces of truffle, pickled tongue, lean ham, or any other suitable garnishes. Fill up with half set jelly. Leave to set on ice.

Turn the eggs out of the mould on to a round dish. Garnish the middle of the dish with a vegetable salad seasoned with gelatine-strengthened *mayonnaise* or with any other similar garnish. Surround with *Jelly triangles**.

Eggs as a border IV. OEUFS EN BORDURE—Take a plain ring mould. Line it with jelly. Decorate with the white of hard boiled eggs, truffles, etc.

Using a forcing (pastry) bag fill the ring with stuffing prepared from the yolks of the hard boiled eggs rubbed through a sieve with purée of *foie gras* in the proportion of three to one. Fill the mould with half-set jelly. Leave to set in the refrigerator.

Turn the mould out on to a round dish. Put in the centre of the mould a round *croûton** made from a sandwich loaf, spread with yellow butter. Remove the yolks from halved hard boiled eggs; add some *foie gras* and rub them together through a sieve. Stuff the whites, heap these eggs in a pyramid on the *croûton*, decorate them with truffles and spoon some jelly over them.

Garnish the edge of the border with *jelly triangles*.

Note. In France these eggs are also called *Jellied eggs à la française*.

Eggs à la bourguignonne (poached). OEUFS À LA BOURGUIGNONNE—Boil for a few minutes 3 cups (6 decilitres) of red wine to which the following have been added: a pinch of salt, pepper, a small handful of parsley, a twig of thyme, a fragment of a bay leaf, a crushed clove of garlic.

Strain the wine and poach 6 very fresh eggs in it.

Drain the eggs and arrange them on *croûtons** made from home made bread, deep fried in butter. Cover the eggs with *Bourguignonne sauce* (see SAUCE) made by blending butter mixed with flour into the red wine in which the eggs were cooked.

Or: Arrange the eggs on *croûtons* made from round slices of bread deep fried in butter.

Garnish with sautéed mushrooms and small glazed onions. Cover with *Bourguignonne sauce* (see SAUCE).

Eggs à la bretonne I (soft boiled or poached). OEUFS À LA BRETONNE—Arrange the eggs on *croûtons** deep fried in butter. Cover them with *Bretonne sauce* (see SAUCE).

Or: Arrange the eggs in hollowed out *croûtons* deep fried in butter (or in *croustades* or tartlets) filled with white bean purée. Cover with concentrated veal gravy to which butter has been added.

Eggs à la bretonne II (sur le plat). OEUFS À LA BRETONNE —Bake the eggs in the usual way. When they are cooked, surround them with a ribbon of *Bretonne sauce* (see SAUCE).

Or: Make a thick purée of white beans. Put them through a forcing bag along the edge of a buttered pan.

Break the eggs into the pan and fry them in the usual way.

Brillat-Savarin eggs I (soft boiled or poached). OEUFS BRILLAT-SAVARIN—Bake a flan crust (pie shell) blind. Garnish with morels sautéed in butter. Put the eggs on the mushrooms. Mask them with a concentrated *Velouté sauce* (see SAUCE) to which a little sherry and butter has been added. Put green asparagus tips dressed with butter into the centre of the dish.

Brillat-Savarin eggs II (baked). OEUFS BRILLAT-SAVARIN SUR LE PLAT—Bake the eggs in the usual way. Garnish them with morels sautéed in butter and asparagus tips. Surround them with sherry-flavoured *Velouté sauce* (see SAUCE).

Brillat-Savarin eggs III (en caissettes), OEUFS BRILLAT-SAVARIN—Butter some small caissettes made of china. Garnish them with a spoonful of sautéed morels. Put the eggs on these and bake in the oven in a *bain-marie* (pan of hot water).

When ready, garnish them with asparagus tips and surround with a ribbon of *Velouté sauce* (see SAUCE) flavoured with sherry.

Brimont eggs (soft boiled or poached). OEUFS BRIMONT—Make a large puff pastry *croustade** with a rim. Fill it with mushrooms cooked in cream. Put the eggs on the mushrooms. Mask them with a thick *Velouté sauce* (see SAUCE) made from chicken stock with Madeira and cream added. Garnish the centre of the dish with small round chicken *croquettes**. Put a slice of truffle on each egg.

Eggs à la bruxelloise I (soft boiled or poached). OEUFS À LA BRUXELLOISE—Hollow out some *croûtes* from a sandwich loaf. Bake them a golden colour in the oven (or use tartlets baked blind). Garnish them with minced chicory simmered in butter and blended with a *Béchamel sauce* (see SAUCE). Put the eggs in the *croûtes* on the sauce and spoon over them some *Cream sauce* (see SAUCE).

Eggs à la bruxelloise II (sur le plat). OEUFS À LA BRUXELLOISE—Put halved braised chicory in a buttered dish. Break the eggs on the chicory and cook them in the usual way. When the eggs are cooked, surround them with a ribbon of *Cream sauce* (see SAUCE).

Cardinal eggs I (soft boiled or poached). OEUFS CARDINAL—Bake some tartlets blind (empty). Garnish them with spiny lobster blended with a *Béchamel sauce* (see SAUCE). Put the eggs on the lobster and mask with *Cardinal sauce* (see SAUCE). Garnish each egg with a slice of truffle.

Cardinal eggs II (in a mould). OEUFS CARDINAL—Butter some individual moulds and sprinkle them with lobster coral. Break the eggs into the moulds and cook them in a *bain-marie* (pan of hot water). Garnish some tartlets with lobster blended with a *Béchamel sauce* (see SAUCE). Turn the moulds out into the tartlets. Mask them with *Cardinal sauce* (see SAUCE). Heat some sliced truffles in butter. Put one on each egg.

Carême eggs I (soft boiled or poached). OEUFS CARÊME—Cook some artichoke hearts in butter. Arrange the eggs on them. Garnish the dish with a ragoût made of sweetbreads, truffles and mushrooms.

Mask with a thick *Velouté sauce** (see SAUCE), one third of which should be veal stock. Add cream and Madeira to the velouté.

Cut slices of pickled tongue with a fluted biscuit-cutter and put one slice of these on each egg.

Carême eggs II (in a mould). OEUFS CARÊME—Use small hexagonal individual moulds. Line them with pickled tongue and truffle cut into very small pieces. Break the eggs into the lined moulds and steam them.

Garnish and mask with sauce as described in the above recipe.

Carême eggs III (cold). OEUFS CARÊME—Poach the eggs and trim them so that only very little of the white remains. Line some small hexagonal moulds with jelly and decorate them with truffles and pickled tongue cut into small pieces. Put the eggs into the moulds. Fill them with Madeira-flavoured jelly. Chill on ice.

Take the eggs out of the moulds. Have some artichoke hearts ready, cooked in *court-bouillon** and masked with jelly. Put one egg on each heart.

Make an aspic of sweetbread and truffles; put it in a conical mould. Arrange the eggs on a dish around the aspic.

Cook small mushrooms in *court-bouillon**; mask them with a *White chaud-froid sauce* (see SAUCE), and decorate them with a piece of truffle shaped like a lozenge. Put a decorated mushroom on each egg.

Eggs à la carmélite (soft boiled or poached). OEUFS À LA CARMÉLITE—Bake a flan crust blind (bake a pie shell). Garnish it with *Mussels in cream**. Arrange the eggs on the mussels and garnish them with a *White wine sauce* (see SAUCE).

Carmen eggs (shirred). OEUFS CARMEN SUR LE PLAT—Bake the eggs. Then cut them with a round biscuit-cutter in such a way that only a narrow ribbon of white is left round the yolk. Cut round *croûtons** and deep fry them in oil. Cover each *croûton* with a round slice of ham tossed in a frying pan. Put one egg on each slice of ham. Mask the eggs with *Tomato sauce* (see SAUCE) seasoned with paprika and with butter added.

Carnavalet eggs (soft boiled or poached). OEUFS CARNAVALET—Arrange the eggs on *spinach subrics**. Arrange them in a circle on a dish. Garnish the middle of the dish with a *macédoine* *of vegetables blended with a *Béchamel sauce* (see SAUCE). Mask the eggs with a *Cream sauce* (see SAUCE).

Eggs à la catalane (fried). OEUFS À LA CATALANE—Fry halved tomatoes and thinly sliced aubergines (eggplant) in oil. Use a separate frying pan for each vegetable. When they are cooked mix the vegetables together and season with salt and pepper. Add garlic and chopped parsley and arrange on a dish.

Cook the eggs in a frying pan and slide them on to the vegetables.

Eggs à la charcutière I (deep fried). OEUFS À LA CHARCUTIÈRE—Deep fry the eggs. Arrange them on a dish in the shape of a crown, alternating them with flat grilled sausages wrapped in caul (pork fat) *crépinettes.* Garnish with fried parsley. Serve separately *Charcutière sauce* (see SAUCE).

Eggs à la charcutière II (soft boiled or poached). OEUFS À LA CHARCUTIÈRE—Fry or grill small flat pork sausages wrapped in caul (pork fat) *crépinettes.* Arrange the eggs on the sausages. Cover with very concentrated *Charcutière sauce* (see SAUCE).

Chartreuse eggs (in a mould). OEUFS EN CHARTREUSE—Cut carrots and turnips with a round spoon-shaped cutter into tiny balls, cut French (string) beans into dice. Cook each of these vegetables, as well as green peas, separately in salt water. Drain the vegetables and toss them in melted butter. Line buttered moulds with the vegetables.

Break the eggs into the lined moulds and cook in a *bain-marie**.

Make some round *croûtes* and hollow them out slightly. Bake them in the oven until they are a golden colour. Fill them with braised well drained cabbage.

Take the eggs out of the moulds and put them on the cabbage in the hollowed *croûtes*, separating each moulded egg from the next with a slice of cooked sausage. Mask the eggs with concentrated veal stock to which butter has been added.

Eggs au chasseur I (sur le plat). Oeufs au chasseur—When the eggs are cooked garnish them with sautéed chicken livers. Surround with a ribbon of *Chasseur sauce* (see SAUCE). Sprinkle with chopped parsley.

Finely sliced mushrooms can be added to the chicken livers.

Eggs au chasseur II (soft boiled or poached). Oeufs au chasseur—Bake some tartlets blind. Fill them with sautéed chicken livers. Arrange the eggs on the liver. Cover with *Chausseur sauce* (see SAUCE). Sprinkle with chopped parsley.

Chateaubriand eggs (soft boiled or poached). Oeufs Chateaubriand—Cook some artichoke hearts in butter. Fill with a thick *Béarnaise sauce* (see SAUCE). Arrange the eggs on the hearts. Mask them with very concentrated veal stock to which butter has been added. Garnish the centre of the dish with asparagus tips cooked in butter (or with any other green vegetable prepared in butter).

Eggs à la châtelaine I (soft boiled or poached). Oeufs à la châtelaine—Bake some tartlets blind (empty). Garnish them with a *Chestnut purée* to which a purée of *Soubise* (see PURÉE) weighing a quarter of the chestnut purée has been added. Arrange the eggs on the purée mixture, cover with a poultry *Velouté sauce* (see SAUCE).

Eggs à la châtelaine II (cold). Oeufs à la châtelaine—Mask the eggs with *Chaud-froid sauce* (see SAUCE). Decorate them with pickled tongue and truffles and glaze with jelly.

Line a glass dish with a jellied chestnut mousse. Arrange the eggs on the mousse. Cover them with a thin layer of half set jelly.

Eggs à la Chaville (sur le plat). Oeufs à la Chaville—Line the dish with a tablespoon of *salpicon** of mushrooms cooked in butter. When the eggs are cooked, garnish with a tablespoon of *Tomato fondue** to which chopped tarragon has been added.

Chénier eggs (soft boiled or poached). Oeufs Chénier—Make some *Rice pilaf* (see PILAF). Add a little saffron. Arrange in little moulds. Put one egg on each mould. Garnish with aubergines (egg-plant) cut into rounds and fried in oil. Mask with *Tomato sauce* (see SAUCE).

Eggs à la chevalière (soft boiled or poached). Oeufs à la chevalière—Bake a flan crust blind (bake a pie shell). Arrange the eggs along the edge. Garnish the centre of the crust with a ragoût made of cock's combs and kidneys and mushrooms blended with a *Velouté sauce* (see SAUCE). Spoon over the eggs some *Suprême sauce* (see SAUCE). Dip some cock's combs in egg and breadcrumbs and fry them. Put one comb between each egg and arrange one slice of truffle on each egg.

Eggs à la Chevreuse (sur le plat). Oeufs à la Chevreuse—Make a thick purée of French (string) beans. Pipe a layer of this purée around the edge of a buttered dish. Break the eggs into the middle of the dish. Sprinkle with grated cheese and bake.

Eggs à la Chimay (stuffed). Oeufs à la Chimay—Cut hard boiled eggs lengthwise. Remove the yolk and pound it; add an equal quantity of dry *Duxelles**. Stuff the halved whites of egg with this mixture.

Arrange the stuffed eggs in a buttered dish. Cover with *Mornay sauce* (see SAUCE). Sprinkle with grated cheese. Pour melted butter over them. Brown the top in the oven or under a grill.

Eggs with chipolatas (baked). Oeufs aux chipolatas—Line a dish with chopped onions cooked in butter until they are very soft. Break the eggs on to the onions. Put a grilled chipolata sausage on each side of the yolk. Pour melted butter over the dish. Cook in the oven. Surround with concentrated veal stock.

Eggs à la Chivry (soft boiled or poached). Oeufs à la Chivry—Arrange the eggs on fried *croûtons**. Garnish with green asparagus tips cooked in butter. Cover with *Chivry sauce* (see SAUCE).

Choron eggs (soft boiled or poached). Oeufs Choron—Make some oval *croûtons** with a fairly deep groove around the edge. Deep fry them in butter. Put the eggs on the *croûtons*. Mask them with a *Cream sauce* to which *Tomato sauce* has been added (see SAUCE).

Pipe a ribbon of thick *Béarnaise sauce* (see SAUCE) into the groove surrounding the croûtons. Garnish with small green peas cooked in butter.

Eggs à la Clamart (soft boiled or poached). Oeufs à la Clamart—Bake tartlets. Fill them with green *peas à la française*. Arrange the eggs on the peas. Cover with *Cream sauce* (see SAUCE) to which *Green pea butter* has been added (see BUTTER) *Compound butters*.

Eggs à la Clarence (soft boiled or poached). Oeufs à la Clarence—Bake tartlets. Fill them with a *julienne** of pickled tongue, truffles and mushrooms. Arrange the eggs in the tartlets. Cover with *Réforme sauce* to which butter has been added (see SAUCE).

Garnished eggs en cocotte

Eggs en cocotte with cream. Oeufs en cocotte à la crème—Put a tablespoon of boiling cream in the *cocottes*. Break the eggs on to the cream. Put a piece of butter the size of a hazelnut on the yolk. Bake in the oven in a *bain-marie* (pan of hot water).

Eggs en cocotte à la duxelles. Oeufs en cocotte à la duxelles—Line buttered cocotte dishes with a dry *duxelles mixture**. Break the eggs into the cocotte. Bake in the oven in a *bain-marie*. Remove from the oven, surround the yolks with a ring of concentrated veal gravy to which butter has been added.

Eggs en cocotte in gravy. Oeufs en cocotte au jus—Cook in the same way as *Eggs en cocotte with tarragon*, leaving out the tarragon and using very concentrated veal gravy.

Eggs en cocotte, au naturel—See EGGS, BASIC RECIPES.

Eggs en cocotte with Parmesan cheese. OEUFS EN COCOTTE AU PARMESAN—Cook in the same way as *Eggs en cocotte with cream.* Sprinkle grated Parmesan cheese on the eggs and pour melted butter over them. Bake in the oven in a *bain-marie* (pan of hot water).

Eggs en cocotte à la périgourdine. OEUFS EN COCOTTE À LA PÉRIGOURDINE—Line the cocotte dish with a purée of *foie gras*. Break the eggs on to the purée; put a piece of butter, the size of a hazelnut, on the yolks. Cook as described above. Bake in the oven in a *bain-marie* (pan of hot water). When cooked, surround the yolks with a ring of *Périgueux sauce* (see SAUCE).

Eggs en cocotte à la rouennaise. OEUFS EN COCOTTE À LA ROUENNAISE—Prepare in the same way as *Eggs en cocotte à la périgourdine*, using *Gratin stuffing* (see FORCEMEAT) instead of purée of *foie gras*. Surround with a ring of *Red wine sauce* (see SAUCE) to which butter has been added.

Eggs en cocotte à la strasbourgeoise. OEUFS EN COCOTTE À LA STRASBOURGEOISE—Line the cocotte dishes with chopped truffles. Cook the eggs in the oven in a *bain-marie* (pan of hot water). Garnish each cocotte dish with a collop of foie gras sautéed in butter. Surround with a ring of concentrated *Demi-glace sauce* (see SAUCE) to which Madeira and butter have been added.

Eggs en cocotte with tarragon. OEUFS EN COCOTTE À L'ESTRAGON NATUREL—See EGGS, BASIC RECIPES. When the eggs are cooked, pour a ring of concentrated veal gravy flavoured with tarragon around the yolks. Blanch and drain some tarragon leaves. Surround the yolk with these in the shape of a star.

If desired buttered cocotte dishes can be lined with chopped tarragon.

Eggs en cocotte à la tartare. OEUFS EN COCOTTE À LA TARTARE—Mince finely some raw beef, add chopped chives and season with salt and pepper. Line cocotte dishes with this mixture and break the eggs into them. Pour a ring of fresh cream around the yolks. Bake in the oven in a *bain-marie* (pan of hot water).

Colbert eggs (soft boiled or poached). OEUFS COLBERT—Arrange the eggs in *croustades** garnished with a *macédoine** of vegetables blended with a *Béchamel sauce* (see SAUCE). Mask the eggs with *Colbert butter*. See BUTTER, *Compound butters*.

Comtesse eggs (soft boiled or poached) OEUFS COMTESSE—Bake some tartlets. Garnish them with a *salpicon** of truffle and mushrooms. Mask with *Suprême sauce* (see SAUCE) flavoured with sherry. Put one slice of truffle on each egg.

Condé eggs I (sur le plat). OEUFS CONDÉ SUR LE PLAT—Make a purée of red beans. Pipe a border of this on to a buttered dish. Grill or deep fry two slices of lean bacon. Break the eggs on to the dish and cook in the usual way.

Condé eggs II. OEUFS CONDÉ—Bake the eggs as described in the recipe above. When taking them out of the oven garnish them with two very small chicken croquettes. Surround with a ring of *Suprême sauce* (see SAUCE).

Eggs Conti I (sur le plat). OEUFS CONTI—Line a buttered dish with a tablespoon of lentil purée. Break the eggs into the dish. Bake in the usual way.

This dish can be enriched by the addition of two thin slices of lean bacon sautéed in butter or grilled.

Eggs Conti II (soft boiled or poached). OEUFS CONTI—Line a pie-dish with a purée of lentils. The purée should not be too thick. Arrange the eggs on the purée.

Eggs à la coque. OEUFS À LA COQUE—For the method of cooking eggs à la coque see under general instructions for cooking eggs.

Egg côtelettes (hard boiled). OEUFS EN CÔTELETTES—Cut the white and the yolk of the hard boiled eggs into dice. Mix and blend this salpicon with a thick *Béchamel sauce* (see SAUCE) to which raw yolks of egg have been added. Chill.

Divide this mixture into portions weighing 2 ounces (60 grams). Shape into the form of cutlets (chops). Dip into egg and breadcrumbs.

Just before serving deep fry. Arrange on a circle on a round dish. Put a frill on each cutlet and garnish with fried parsley. Serve *Tomato sauce* or any other suitable sauce separately. (See SAUCE.)

Note. Egg cutlets can also be served with a variety of garnishes, such as: green vegetables with butter or with cream; *macédoine**; *Tomato fondue**; *Risotto* (see RICE) different kinds of pasta; various kinds of purée, etc.

The mixture for egg cutlets may be varied. Diced mushrooms and truffles may be added or, if a meat mixture is preferred, diced ham or diced pickled tongue can be used.

Egg cutlets can be cooked in clarified butter instead of being deep fried.

Eggs with cream. OEUFS À LA CRÈME—Break the eggs into individual buttered fireproof dishes. Surround with a ribbon of fresh cream. Cook.

Or: Cook the eggs in the usual way. Once cooked, surround them with a ribbon of *Cream sauce* (see SAUCE).

Eggs with cream sauce (soft boiled or poached). OEUFS À LA CRÈME—Deep fry croûtons in butter. Put the cooked eggs on the croûtons and cover them with *Cream sauce* (see SAUCE).

Eggs à la Crécy I (soft boiled or poached). OEUFS À LA CRÉCY—Arrange the eggs in a pyramid on a pie dish on a foundation of *Carrot purée*. Cover the eggs with *Cream sauce* (see SAUCE).

Eggs à la Crécy II (baked). OEUFS À LA CRÉCY—Spread a tablespoon of *Carrot purée* on the bottom of small buttered baking dishes. Break the eggs into the dishes. Cook in the usual way. Surround with a ribbon of *Cream sauce* (see SAUCE.)

Eggs à la créole (deep fried). OEUFS À LA CRÉOLE—Deep fry the eggs in oil. Grill some halved courgettes (zucchinis). Arrange the eggs on a dish on the halved courgettes, leaving the centre of the dish free. Fill the centre of the dish with *Rice à la créole**. Pour *Noisette butter* over the eggs (see BUTTER, *Compound butters*).

Eggs à la cressonière I (soft boiled or poached). OEUFS À LA CRESSONIÈRE—Cover a pie dish with with *Watercress purée**. Arrange the eggs on it. Cover them with *Cream sauce* (see SAUCE) or with concentrated veal stock to which butter has been added.

Eggs à la cressonière II (baked). OEUFS À LA CRESSONIÈRE—Pipe a border of very thick *Watercress purée** on to a buttered dish. Break the eggs into the dish. Surround the yolks with a ribbon of *Cream sauce* (see SAUCE). Bake in the oven.

Egg croquettes (hard boiled). OEUFS EN CROQUETTES—Prepare the croquette mixture as described in the recipe for *Egg côtelettes* (bound with *White sauce* or *Béchamel sauce*).

Shape the mixture, when it is cold, in the form of eggs or any other shape, dip in egg and breadcrumbs, fry at the last moment.

Arrange in a heap on a napkin, with fried parsley.

Serve *Tomato* or *Cream sauce* separately. (See SAUCE.)

Daudet eggs (soft boiled or poached). OEUFS DAUDET—Arrange the eggs on puff pastry *croustades** covered with chopped breast of chicken. Cover with a purée of truffles bound with a rich *White sauce* (see SAUCE).

Daumont eggs (soft boiled or poached). OEUFS DAUMONT—Arrange the eggs on large cultivated mushrooms cooked in butter, garnished with a salpicon of *Crayfish tails à la Nantua**. Cover with *Nantua sauce* (see SAUCE); put a sliver of truffle on each egg.

Delmonico eggs (soft boiled or poached). OEUFS DELMONICO—Cover the eggs with *Mornay sauce* (see SAUCE) mixed with chopped truffles. Put them on a low *croustade** of noodles filled with a mixture of lamb's sweetbreads, mushrooms and truffles, blended with very concentrated *Madeira sauce*. Glaze in the oven.

Demi-deuil eggs (soft boiled or poached). OEUFS DEMI-DEUIL—Arrange the eggs in a low puff pastry shell filled with mushrooms in cream. Cover with *Suprême sauce* (see SAUCE). Garnish the middle of the dish with diced truffles blended with very concentrated *Madeira sauce* (see SAUCE).

Eggs à la diable (fried). OEUFS À LA DIABLE—Fry the eggs in sizzling (nearly brown) butter. Turn them without breaking the yolks. Arrange on a very hot dish. Sprinkle with brown butter and a dash of vinegar heated in the pan.

Eggs à la Diane (soft boiled or poached). OEUFS À LA DIANE—Arrange the eggs on hollowed out slices of bread, fried in butter, garnished with a purée of game. Cover with *Salmis sauce* (see SAUCE) to which diced truffles and butter have been added.

Dino eggs (soft boiled or poached). OEUFS DINO—Arrange the eggs in tartlets lined with finely shredded breast of chicken and cèpes (or small cultivated mushrooms) mixed with cream.

Top with *Curry sauce* (see SAUCE).

Duchess eggs (soft boiled or poached). OEUFS À LA DUCHESSE—Arrange the eggs on little oval potato cakes baked golden in the oven. Boil down (reduce) veal stock, add butter to it and pour it over the eggs.

Duxelles eggs (soft boiled or poached). OEUFS À LA DUXELLES—Arrange the eggs on oval-shaped *croûtons*, cooked in butter and garnished with thin slices of ham tossed in butter. Cover with buttered *Duxelles sauce* (see SAUCE). Sprinkle with chopped parsley.

Easter eggs. OEUFS DE PÂQUES—Hard boiled eggs with dyed or painted shells, or confections made of sugar, chocolate etc., moulded in the shape of eggs, which it is customary to offer at Easter.

It is perhaps to the Phoenicians that we owe our Easter eggs. According to their belief, night—the beginning of all things—begot an egg, from which came love and the human race. Towards Easter the sun reaches the Equator, the long nights pass, the primeval egg breaks and mankind is born.

In the past people used to be quite content to exchange eggs at Easter, which were merely hen's eggs, dyed or decorated with artistic designs.

The most popular colour for Easter eggs is bright red. In Germany and some parts of France these eggs used to be hidden in the garden and the children would come searching for them, rejoicing when they found them in a green nest.

This is how hard boiled eggs used to be dyed in various colours:

Coral red. Put very fresh eggs into a saucepan in which water, seasoned with salt and acidulated with a dash of lemon juice has been boiled for 45 minutes with a sachet containing 5 ounces (150 grams) of cochineal (for 2 quarts (litres) of water) and $1\frac{5}{8}$ ounces (50 grams) of alum. Cook the eggs, keeping up sustained boiling for 12 minutes. Drain, dip in cold water and dry.

Dark maroon. Cook the eggs as described above in water mixed with $\frac{1}{2}$ pound (250 grams) of campeche wood, $\frac{1}{6}$ ounce (5 grams) each of alum and salt.

Green. Cook the eggs as described above in water mixed with spinach, scalded, drained and pounded in a mortar.

Yellow. Cook the eggs in salted water mixed with yellow onion peel, a pinch of saffron and a dash of lemon juice.

Modern vegetable dyes make colouring eggs a very simple process.

Eggs à l'écarlate I (cold). OEUFS À L'ÉCARLATE—Cover soft boiled or poached eggs with half-set jelly, to which some chopped pickled tongue has been added. Arrange the eggs in a shallow dish (or a glass or crystal dish), on slices of pickled or smoked tongue. Cover with jelly.

Eggs à l'écarlate II (soft boiled or poached). OEUFS À L'ÉCARLATE—Arrange the eggs on croûtons fried in butter. Cover them with buttered *Tomato sauce* (see SAUCE). Sprinkle with diced, smoked or pickled tongue.

Eggs à l'écarlate III (sur le plat). OEUFS À L'ÉCARLATE—Put a spoonful of concentrated *Tomato sauce* (see SAUCE) into a buttered heat-proof dish. Break the eggs into the dish, sprinkle with pickled or smoked tongue, cut into tiny dice. Bake until the white is set.

Edward VII eggs (soft boiled or poached). OEUFS EDOUARD VII—Place the eggs on a *Risotto* (see RICE) mixed with diced truffles, separating each egg with a sliver of pickled or smoked tongue, cut in the shape of a cock's comb, and heated in sherry. Cover the eggs with concentrated veal gravy with some butter added to it and garnish each with a slice of truffle.

Elizabeth eggs (stuffed). OEUFS ELISABETH—Cut off the ends of hard boiled eggs so as to make them look like little barrels. Take out the yolks, taking care not to break the whites.

Rub the yolks through a fine sieve. Mix with an equal quantity of rather thick *Artichoke purée*, add some chopped truffles and season. Fill the eggs with this mixture piling it up on the top.

Place each egg on an artichoke heart previously stewed in butter. Cover with *Mornay sauce* (see SAUCE). Sprinkle with grated cheese and melted butter. Brown the top.

Arrange the eggs in a crown on a round dish. Fill the centre with a *Ragoût of truffles** cooked in Madeira.

Esau eggs (soft boiled or poached). OEUFS ESAU—Arrange the eggs in a pyramid on a lentil purée. Garnish with heart-shaped croûtons fried in butter. Pour concentrated veal gravy with some butter added to it over the eggs.

Or: Arrange the eggs on a *croustade** of de-crusted bread, fried, hollowed out and filled with a lentil purée. Cover with a buttered concentrated veal gravy.

Eggs à l'espagnole I (cold). OEUFS À L'ESPAGNOLE—Cover the eggs with meat jelly to which a little *Tomato jelly* has been added. Decorate each one with a ring of thoroughly blanched onion, garnish with a pinch of chopped parsley in the middle, and spoon over some half-set jelly. Arrange the eggs on round, buttered pieces of toast. Surround with very small tomatoes with the seeds taken out, dressed with oil, vinegar, salt and pepper, and filled with diced sweet green pimentos, seasoned *à la vinaigrette*.

Eggs à l'espagnole II (fried). OEUFS À L'ESPAGNOLE—Fry the eggs in oil. Arrange them in a crown alternating with halved tomatoes fried in oil. Fill the centre of the dish with onion rings fried in oil. Pour a ring of *Tomato sauce* (see SAUCE) mixed with a *salpicon** of sweet pimentos around the eggs.

Eggs à l'espagnole III (soft boiled or poached). OEUFS À L'ESPAGNOLE—Arrange the eggs on tomatoes cooked in oil, filled with a *salpicon** of sweet pimentos. Fill the centre of the dish with onion rings fried in oil. Cover the eggs with *Tomato sauce* (see SAUCE), flavoured with red Spanish pepper.

Eggs à l'espagnole IV (sur le plat). OEUFS À L'ESPAGNOLE—Line a fire-proof dish with a spoonful of thinly sliced onion, lightly fried in butter, and seasoned with red Spanish pepper. Break the eggs into the dish. Cook as usual. Garnish with a good spoonful of *Tomato fondue** mixed with diced sweet pimentos cooked in butter.

Favart eggs (soft boiled or poached). OEUFS FAVART—Arrange the eggs in little tartlet cases, filled with a *salpicon** of calf's sweetbreads, truffles and mushrooms blended with *Velouté sauce* (see SAUCE). Fill the middle of the dish with large truffled quenelles. Cover with *Suprême sauce* (see SAUCE).

Eggs à la flamande I (soft boiled or poached). OEUFS À LA FLAMANDE—Arrange the eggs on a layer of chicory (Belgian endive), cooked in butter.

Cover with *Allemande sauce* or *Cream sauce* (see SAUCE), depending on whether the dish is intended for a meat or Lenten meal.

Or: Arrange the poached eggs on croûtons fried in butter. In between each egg put a head of chicory (Belgian endive) cooked *à la flamande* and folded over. Boil down the liquor left over from braising the endives, add cream, bring to the boil, add a little fresh butter and pour over the eggs.

Eggs à la flamande II (sur le plat). OEUFS À LA FLAMANDE—This usually means *Eggs à la bruxelloise*, that is to say garnished with a *chiffonnade* of chicory (U.S. Belgian endive) cooked in butter. Poached, soft boiled or fried eggs can also be garnished with hop shoots cooked in butter or cream. Prepared in this way they are also called *Eggs à la flamande*.

Florentine eggs (soft boiled or poached). OEUFS À LA FLORENTINE—Arrange the eggs in a fireproof dish, on a layer of spinach cooked in butter. Cover with *Mornay sauce* (see SAUCE). Sprinkle with grated cheese and melted butter and brown the top quickly in a very hot oven.

Florentine eggs (sur le plat). OEUFS À LA FLORENTINE—Fill the buttered dishes with a layer of spinach simmered in butter. Cover with a light *Mornay sauce* (see SAUCE). Sprinkle with grated cheese and melted butter. Brown in a very hot oven.

Eggs à la forestière (poached). OEUFS À LA FORESTIÈRE—Arrange the eggs on *croustades** filled with morels fried in butter, mixed with bacon, cut in small dice, blanched and fried lightly in butter. Cover the eggs with *Chateaubriand sauce* (see SAUCE). Sprinkle with chopped parsley.

Florentine eggs (*Robert Carrier*)

THE LARDER. Franz Snyders (*Musée de Bruxelles*)

(*From the original French edition of* Larousse Gastronomique)

PÂTISSERIE. Petits-fours, Croquembouche, small fancy cakes (*Rey*)

(*From the original French edition of* Larousse Gastronomique)

Eggs à la forestière (sur le plat). OEUFS À LA FORESTIÈRE—Fill the dishes with diced blanched bacon lightly fried in butter. Break the eggs into the dishes. Put on each side a spoonful of morels fried in butter. Cook in the oven. Season after cooking. Pipe a ring of *Chateaubriand sauce* (see SAUCE) around the edges.

Georgette eggs (poached). OEUFS GEORGETTE—Put a small poached egg into a potato that has been baked in the oven, partly hollowed out and filled with a spoonful of ragoût of *Crayfish tails à la Nantua*. Cover with *Nantua sauce* (see SAUCE). Sprinkle with grated Parmesan and melted butter. Brown the top in a very hot oven.

Grand Duke eggs I (soft boiled or poached). OEUFS GRAND-DUC—Arrange the eggs on oval-shaped croûtons fried in butter (or on low puff pastry shells). Put a sliver of truffle on each egg. Cover with *Mornay sauce* (see SAUCE). Sprinkle with grated cheese and melted butter. Brown the tops in a very hot oven. Garnish with buttered asparagus tips.

Grand Duke eggs II (sur le plat). OEUFS GRAND-DUC—Cover the eggs with a light *Mornay sauce* (see SAUCE). Sprinkle with grated cheese and melted butter. Cook in a very hot oven. Garnish with diced truffles and asparagus tips.

Eggs au gratin (soft boiled or poached). OEUFS AU GRATIN—Prepare like *Mornay eggs*.

Halévy eggs (soft boiled or poached). OEUFS HALÉVY—Arrange the eggs in tartlets baked blind (unfilled); garnish with a *salpicon** of chicken blended with *Velouté sauce* (see SAUCE). Cover half with *Allemande sauce*, half with *Tomato sauce* to which butter has been added. (See SAUCE.)

Hard boiled eggs with chicory (U.S. Belgian endive). OEUFS DURS SUR CHICORÉE—Arrange the eggs in a vegetable dish on braised chicory (cooked in stock or cream). Cover with concentrated veal gravy or a light *Cream sauce* (see SAUCE).

Hard boiled eggs with various garnishes. OEUFS DURS AVEC GARNITURES DIVERSES—Shell the eggs (boiled as described under EGGS, BASIC RECIPES). Heat them in salted boiling water; drain and dry them.

Arrange and garnish them as indicated in the various recipes.

Hard boiled eggs on a macédoine of vegetables. OEUFS DURS SUR MACÉDOINE DE LÉGUMES—Arrange the eggs in a pie dish on a *macédoine* of vegetables, blended with butter or cream.

Hard boiled eggs on various purées. OEUFS DURS SUR PURÉES—Hard boiled eggs can be served with a purée of asparagus, carrots, celery, mushrooms, chicory, lettuce, chestnuts, sorrel, sweet potato or Jerusalem artichokes.

Hard boiled eggs with watercress. OEUFS DURS À LA CRESSONIÈRE—Arrange the eggs on a bed of *Watercress purée**. Cover with *Cream sauce* (see SAUCE).

Eggs (in cups) à la hollandaise. OEUFS EN TASSE À LA HOLLANDAISE—Butter three tea cups and coat with grated cheese on the inside. Put a layer of diced ham in each cup and pour in an egg whisked as for an omelette. Cover with a layer of ham and finish off with a thick layer of cheese. Cook for 12 minutes in a *bain-marie* (pan of hot water). Serve with *Tomato sauce* (see SAUCE).

Eggs à l'italienne I (fried). OEUFS À L'ITALIENNE—Fry the eggs in oil. Arrange them in a crown on a round dish, alternating with thin slices of ham sautéed in butter. Pour a few tablespoons of *Italian sauce* (see SAUCE) over the eggs.

Eggs à l'italienne II (soft boiled or poached). OEUFS À L'ITALIENNE—Cut crusts off slices of bread, fry in butter, spread with a *salpicon** of chopped ham blended with Madeira-flavoured *Demi-glace sauce* (see SAUCE) and arrange the eggs on top. Add some butter to *Italian sauce* (see SAUCE) and pour over the eggs. Sprinkle with chopped parsley.

Eggs à l'italienne III (sur le plat or cooked in a cocotte) OEUFS À L'ITALIENNE—Butter a fire-proof dish or a cocotte, and break the eggs over a foundation of lean chopped ham. Cook in the usual manner. When ready, pour a ring of *Italian sauce* (see SAUCE) around the eggs.

Jeanette eggs (en cocotte). OEUFS JEANETTE EN COCOTTE—Put a layer of *Chicken quenelle mixture* in a cocotte as a foundation. Break the eggs into the cocotte. Cook as usual. Garnish with asparagus tips. Pour a ring of *Velouté sauce* around the dish. See SAUCE.

Jellied eggs à la française. OEUFS GLACÉS À LA FRANÇAISE—See *Eggs as a border IV*.

Jellied tarragon eggs, also called à la Chartres. OEUFS À L'ESTRAGON À LA GELÉE (À LA CHARTRES)—Arrange the eggs (poached or soft boiled) in moulds the shape of half an egg, or dariole moulds coated with white tarragon-flavoured meat jelly and decorated with blanched tarragon leaves. Fill the moulds with jelly and set on ice.

Turn the eggs out at the last moment. Arrange them in a crown. Fill the centre with chopped jelly. Decorate the dish with jelly croûtons cut in the shape of wolves' teeth.

Or: Arrange the poached eggs decorated with tarragon leaves and glazed with jelly on a deep glass or metal dish on a layer of thin slices of cooked ham.

Preparing eggs à la hollandaise (*Claire*)

Cover with half-set jelly. Chill thoroughly on ice before serving.

This last method is the one most frequently used in restaurants. (Poached or soft boiled eggs can also be arranged in individual little china *cassolettes* lined with a thin slice of ham and filled with jelly.)

Jockey club eggs. OEUFS JOCKEY-CLUB—Fry the eggs individually. Cut them with a cutter in such a way as to leave only a thin band of white around the yolk. Put each egg on a grilled croûton of bread spread with a purée of foie gras. Arrange the eggs in a crown on a round dish. Fill the middle of the dish with sliced calf's kidney sautéed in Madeira. Put a sliver of truffle on each egg.

Egg kromeskies (hard boiled). OEUFS EN CROMESQUIS—Prepare an egg croquette mixture (see recipe for *Egg côtelettes*); add truffles and mushrooms; bind with *Allemande sauce* (see SAUCE), allowing 1½ cups (3½ decilitres) for 2 cups (500 grams) of *salpicon**. Leave the mixture to cool.

Divide into small portions. Make into oval or cork-shaped cakes.

At the last moment dip into a light batter and fry in deep fat.

Drain on a cloth, season with very fine dry salt. Arrange on a napkin and garnish with fried parsley. Serve *Tomato sauce* separately. See SAUCE.

If this dish is intended for Lenten fare, replace the *Allemande* sauce by *Béchamel*.

Egg kromeskies à la polonaise. OEUFS EN CROMESQUIS À LA POLONAISE—Prepare the mixture as described above and, when cold, divide into small portions. Shape into little rectangles and wrap each one in a very thin *crêpe* (pancake). At the last moment, dip into a light batter and deep fry. Serve *Tomato sauce* or *Piquante sauce* separately (see SAUCE).

Eggs à la languedocienne (fried). OEUFS À LA LANGUEDOCIENNE—Fry the eggs in oil. Arrange each on a round slice of aubergine (egg-plant) fried in oil. Fill the middle of the dish with garlic-flavoured *Tomato fondue**. Sprinkle with *Noisette butter* (see BUTTER, *Compound butters*).

Eggs à la Lorraine (sur le plat). OEUFS À LA LORRAINE—Butter a dish, line with thin rashers of grilled bacon and slivers of Gruyère cheese. Break the eggs into dish. Pour a ring of fresh cream around the yolks. Bake in the oven in the usual manner.

Lucullus Eggs (soft boiled or poached). OEUFS LUCULLUS—Arrange each egg on an artichoke heart cooked in butter and filled with a *salpicon** of lambs' sweetbreads, truffles and mushrooms bound with concentrated *Velouté sauce* (see SAUCE).

Cover the eggs with *Suprême sauce* (see SAUCE) to which some diced truffles have been added. Put some foie gras cut in large dice in the middle, season with salt and pepper and toss briskly in butter. Put a *Cock's comb à la Villeroi* between each egg.

Eggs à la maraîchère (sur le plat). OEUFS À LA MARAÎCHÈRE—Line the bottom of a dish with a tablespoon of lettuce, sorrel and chervil, shredded into a *chiffonnade** and tossed in butter. Break the eggs into the dish. Add a thin rasher of bacon sautéed in butter. Bake in the oven in the usual manner.

Marianne eggs (soft boiled or poached). OEUFS MARIANNE—Put each egg on half a tomato, seeded, cooked in butter and filled with a very thick *Tomato fondue**. Put on each egg a round slice of black Madagascar potato cooked in butter. Top with *Maître d'hôtel butter* (see BUTTER, *Compound butters*) mixed with dissolved meat jelly.

Marivaux eggs (soft boiled or poached). OEUFS MARIVAUX—Arrange the eggs in a flan (pie) case baked blind (unfilled), garnished with a *salpicon** of mushrooms and truffles. Have ready some very concentrated Madeira-flavoured *Demi-glace sauce* (see SAUCE), add a little butter to it and pour over the eggs.

Masséna eggs (soft boiled or poached). OEUFS MASSÉNA—Place each egg on an artichoke heart cooked in butter and filled with very thick *Béarnaise sauce* (see SAUCE). Put a slice of poached marrowbone fat on each egg. Surround with ring of *Marrow sauce I* (see SAUCE) and sprinkle the marrow with a pinch of chopped parsley.

Massenet eggs (soft boiled or poached). OEUFS MASSENET—Put the eggs into *croustades** made of *Duchess potato mixture* (see POTATOES), filled with a *salpicon** of French (string) beans dressed with butter. Cover with *Marrow sauce I* (see SAUCE). Sprinkle with chopped parsley.

Eggs à la ménagère. OEUFS À LA MÉNAGÈRE—Fry the eggs in butter. Put them in a dish on a bed of stock-pot vegetables, sliced and sautéed in butter. Surround with a ring of *Tomato sauce* (see SAUCE).

Meyerbeer eggs (sur le plat). OEUFS MEYERBEER—Garnish the cooked eggs with grilled lamb kidney (without breadcrumbs). Surround with a ring of *Périgueux sauce* (see SAUCE).

Eggs à la milanaise (fried). OEUFS À LA MILANAISE—Fry the eggs in oil. Arrange in a pyramid on a bed of *Macaroni à la milanaise** and surround with a ring of *Tomato sauce*. (see SAUCE).

Mirette eggs (poached). OEUFS MIRETTE—Poach the yolks only. Arrange, placing each in a tartlet case, bake blind (unfilled) and garnish with a *salpicon** of chicken breast and truffles, blended with Madeira-flavoured, thick *Velouté sauce*. Pour *Suprême sauce* over the eggs. (See SAUCE).

Miroir eggs. OEUFS MIROIR—See EGGS, BASIC RECIPES, *Shirred eggs*.

Monselet eggs (soft boiled or poached). OEUFS MONSELET—Arrange the eggs on artichoke hearts cooked in butter. Cover with *Velouté chicken sauce* (see SAUCE) mixed with a third of its volume of veal stock and the same quantity of cream, flavoured with sherry and cooked down. Garnish with diced truffles cooked in butter and minute potato croquettes.

Montrouge eggs I (soft boiled or poached). OEUFS MONTROUGE—Arrange the eggs in tartlet cases baked blind (unfilled) and garnish with a *Purée of mushrooms*. Cover with *Suprême sauce* (see SAUCE).

Montrouge eggs II (sur le plat or en cocotte). OEUFS MONTROUGE—Butter the dishes and pipe a border of *Mushroom purée** through a forcing bag. Break the eggs into the dishes. Surround the yolks with a ring of fresh cream. Bake in the oven in the usual manner.

To prepare eggs *en cocotte*, break the eggs into a cocotte lined with *Mushroom purée**. Surround the yolks with a ring of fresh cream. Cook in the oven in a *bain-marie* (pan of hot water).

Mornay eggs I (soft boiled or poached). OEUFS MORNAY—Put the eggs into a fire-proof dish on a layer of *Mornay sauce* (see SAUCE) (or on croûtons fried in butter). Cover with *Mornay sauce*, sprinkle with grated cheese and melted butter and brown the top in the oven.

Mornay eggs II (sur le plat). OEUFS MORNAY—Break the eggs into a dish lined with *Mornay sauce* (see SAUCE). Cover with *Mornay sauce*. Sprinkle with grated cheese and melted butter and brown the top in the oven.

Eggs à la Nantua I (soft boiled or poached). OEUFS À LA NANTUA—Arrange the eggs in tartlets filled with *Crayfish*

Mornay eggs sur le plat

*tails à la Nantua**. Cover with *Nantua sauce* (see SAUCE). Put a sliver of truffle on each egg.

Eggs à la Nantua II (sur le plat). OEUFS À LA NANTUA—Butter a dish, fill with crayfish tails, break in the eggs and cook in the oven. Put a sliver of truffle on each yolk. Cover with *Nantua sauce* (see SAUCE).

Eggs with noisette butter (baked). OEUFS AU BEURRE NOISETTE—Heat the butter in the pan until it becomes light brown or 'noisette'. Break the eggs into the heated butter. Bake in the usual way.

Eggs à la normande (soft boiled or poached). OEUFS À LA NORMANDE—Arrange the eggs on puff pastry *croustades**, filled with a *salpicon* of mussels, mushrooms and shrimps' tails, bound with *Normande sauce* (see SAUCE). Put a poached and de-bearded oyster on each egg. Cover with *Normande sauce.* Put a sliver of truffle on each egg.

Omelette—See under separate heading at the end of this section.

Eggs opera (sur le plat). OEUFS OPÉRA—Garnish the cooked eggs on one side with sliced chicken livers sautéed in Madeira and on the other with asparagus tips. Surround with a ring of veal gravy, cooked down and with butter added to it.

Eggs à la parisienne (sur le plat). OEUFS À LA PARISIENNE—Line egg dishes with a layer of chicken forcemeat mixed with pickled smoked tongue, truffles and chopped mushrooms, and put in the eggs. Cook as usual and surround with a ring of *Demi-glace sauce* (see SAUCE).

Parmentier eggs I. OEUFS PARMENTIER—Bake four large potatoes in the oven. Halve them and scoop out the pulp taking care not to break the skin. Blend the scooped out pulp with butter and cream and season. Line the potato skins with this pulp and break an egg into each shell. Sprinkle with cream and bake in the oven.

Or: Prepare the potatoes as described above. Put a small poached egg into each potato. Cover with *Mornay sauce* (see SAUCE). Sprinkle with grated cheese and melted butter and brown the top in the oven.

Parmentier eggs II. OEUFS PARMENTIER—Butter the egg dish and line with diced potatoes fried in butter. Break the eggs into the dish, surround with a ring of cream and cook in the oven.

Eggs à la Polignac (cooked in moulds). OEUFS À LA POLIGNAC—Butter individual plain round moulds, put a sliver of truffle in each and break in the eggs. Cook in a *bain-marie* (pan of hot water). Turn out the eggs on to croûtons fried in butter. Top with *Maître d'hôtel butter* (see BUTTER, *Compound butters*) mixed with dissolved meat jelly.

Eggs à la portugaise I (soft boiled or poached). OEUFS À LA PORTUGAISE—Arrange each egg on half a tomato cooked in oil. Cover with *Portugaise sauce* (see SAUCE).

Eggs à la portugaise II (sur le plat). OEUFS À LA PORTUGAISE—Butter a dish, put in a spoonful of *Tomato fondue**, break the eggs into the dish and cook in the oven.

Princess eggs (soft boiled or poached). OEUFS PRINCESSE—Arrange the eggs on fried croûtons (or in puff pastry *croustades**), cover with *Suprême sauce* (see SAUCE), garnish with asparagus tips and chicken breast shredded into *julienne** strips and put a sliver of truffle on each egg.

Eggs à la printanière I (soft boiled or poached). OEUFS À LA PRINTANIÈRE—Arrange the eggs on a puff pastry foundation, covered with a *printanière** of vegetables dressed with cream. Prepare *Suprême sauce* (see SAUCE), add *Printanier butter* to it and pour over the eggs. (See BUTTER, *Compound butters.*) Garnish with asparagus tips in butter.

Eggs à la printanière II (cold). OEUFS À LA PRINTANIÈRE—Arrange the eggs (soft boiled or poached) in a low glass dish on a bed of *macédoine** of vegetables dressed with mayonnaise strengthened with gelatine. Garnish the middle of the dish with green asparagus tips. Decorate the eggs with tarragon leaves. Cover with half-set jelly.

Eggs à la provençale I (soft boiled or poached). OEUFS À LA PROVENÇALE—Arrange each egg on a halved tomato cooked in oil. Cover with a clear, garlic-flavoured *Tomato fondue**. Garnish the middle of the dish with aubergines (egg-plant) cut in large dice and fried in oil. Sprinkle with chopped parsley.

Eggs à la provençale II (sur le plat). OEUFS À LA PROVENÇALE—Rub the bottoms of the egg dishes with garlic and line with round slices of aubergines fried in oil. Break the eggs into the dishes. Bake in the oven. Pour a ring of *Provençale sauce* (see SAUCE) around the yolks.

Eggs à la provençale III (fried). OEUFS À LA PROVENÇALE—Fry the eggs in oil and arrange each on a halved tomato, also fried in oil. Put a slice of aubergine (egg-plant) fried in oil, on each egg. Garnish with fried parsley.

Eggs à la provençale IV (fried). OEUFS À LA PROVENÇALE—Cook thinly sliced aubergines (egg-plant) in oil. Spread these slices on a round dish, alternating with halved tomatoes, pressed, seeded and fried in oil. On this foundation put the fried eggs (either turned or not, as desired) and sprinkle with sizzling butter to which a spoonful of chopped parsley mixed with chopped garlic has been added.

Eggs à la provençale V (glazed in jelly). OEUFS À LA PROVENÇALE—Coat the eggs (soft boiled or poached) with tomato-flavoured, gelatine-strengthened *mayonnaise.* Decorate with tarragon leaves, spoon over a little liquid jelly to glaze. Arrange each egg on a halved tomato, seeded and steeped in oil, vinegar, salt and pepper and stuffed with a salad consisting of diced potatoes and aubergines (egg-plants), dressed with garlic-flavoured *mayonnaise.* Arrange the eggs in a crown on a round dish and garnish with chopped parsley.

Rachel eggs. OEUFS RACHEL—Cook the eggs in butter in a pan. Trim with a round pastry-cutter so as to leave only a thin band of white around the yolk.

Arrange each egg on a round slice of bread fried in butter. Cover with *Marrow sauce* (see SAUCE) and put a thin slice of poached marrow on each egg.

Eggs à la reine I (soft boiled or poached). OEUFS À LA REINE—Arrange the eggs in tartlets filled with *Chicken purée** and cover with *Suprême sauce* (see SAUCE).

Eggs à la reine II (sur le plat or en cocotte). OEUFS À LA REINE—Butter the egg dishes and pipe a border of *Chicken purée** through a forcing (pastry) bag. Break the eggs into these dishes. Surround the yolks with a ring of thick chicken *Velouté sauce* (see SAUCE) with cream. Cook in the oven in the usual manner.

Eggs en cocotte à la reine are prepared in the same way in individual cocottes lined with *Chicken purée*.

Eggs à la romaine (fried). OEUFS À LA ROMAINE—Fry the eggs in oil. Chop some spinach roughly, toss in *Noisette butter* and mix with diced anchovies. Put the eggs on this foundation and sprinkle with *Noisette butter* (see BUTTER, *Compound butters*).

Rossini eggs I (soft boiled or poached). OEUFS ROSSINI—Arrange each egg on a slice of *foie gras* sautéed in butter. Put 2 slices of truffle, tossed in butter, on each egg. Cover with Madeira-flavoured *Demi-glace sauce* (see SAUCE).

Or: Arrange the eggs in puff pastry tartlets filled with *foie gras* cut in large dice. Garnish with slivers of truffles. Prepare a Madeira-flavoured *Demi-glace sauce*, cook down (reduce), add some butter and pour over the eggs.

Rossini eggs II (sur le plat or en cocotte). OEUFS ROSSINI—Butter the dishes, line with a *salpicon** of foie gras and truffles, break in the eggs and bake in the oven. Surround with a ring of concentrated and buttered Madeira-flavoured *Demi-glace sauce* (see SAUCE).

Rossini eggs en cocotte are prepared in the same way, using cocottes instead of individual egg dishes.

Rothomago eggs. OEUFS ROTHOMAGO—Line the egg dishes with slices of ham, tossed in butter. Break the eggs into the dishes. Cook in the usual manner. When cooked, garnish with grilled chipolata sausages. Surround with a ring of *Tomato sauce* (see SAUCE).

Eggs à la royale. OEUFS À LA ROYALE—Arrange the eggs on puff pastry cases filled with a *salpicon** of truffles blended with very concentrated Madeira-flavoured *Demi-glace sauce* (see SAUCE). Cover with *Velouté chicken sauce* (see SAUCE), mixed with a purée of truffles, diluted with cream and flavoured with Madeira.

Eggs à la Saint-Hubert (soft boiled or poached). OEUFS À LA SAINT-HUBERT—Arrange in a pie dish on a foundation of hashed venison (or any other ground game). Cover with game *Poivrade sauce* (see SAUCE). Garnish with puff pastry crescents or heart-shaped *croûtons* fried in butter.

Scotch eggs I (soft boiled or poached). OEUFS À L'ÉCOSSAISE—Arrange the eggs on puff pastry croûtes covered with *Salmon purée* (see PURÉE). Cover with *Shrimp sauce* (see SAUCE). Decorate each egg with a sliver of truffle.

Scotch eggs II. OEUFS À L'ÉCOSSAISE—Make a forcemeat using finely minced cooked ham, 2–3 pounded anchovy fillets and enough fresh breadcrumbs to give the forcemeat 'body'. Season with salt, pepper and mixed spices, bind with raw egg and blend well. Shell some hard boiled eggs and coat each one with the forcemeat. Dip in egg and breadcrumbs and deep fry in hot fat.

Scrambled eggs. OEUFS BROUILLÉS—For method of preparation see EGGS, *Basic recipes*.

Scrambled eggs à l'américaine. OEUFS BROUILLÉS À L'AMÉRICAINE—Add diced bacon, fried in butter, to the scrambled eggs. Heap the eggs on a warm platter and garnish with rashers of grilled bacon and halved grilled tomatoes.

Note. The same name also applies to scrambled eggs with sliced lobster (or spiny lobster *à l'américaine*). Recipes for these dishes will be found under entry entitled *Scrambled eggs à l'armoricaine*.

Scrambled eggs à l'ancienne. OEUFS BROUILLÉS À L'ANCIENNE—Add mushrooms and truffles, cut in dice and tossed in butter, to the scrambled eggs. Arrange in a flan case, baked blind (tart shell). Garnish with cocks' kidneys in sherry-flavoured *Velouté sauce* (see SAUCE) diluted with cream. Surround with *Cocks' combs Villeroi*. Surround with a ring of sherry-flavoured *Suprême sauce* (see SAUCE).

Scrambled eggs à l'antiboise. OEUFS BROUILLÉS À L'ANTIBOISE—Prepare the eggs in the usual manner. Arrange in a deep oven-proof dish, putting them in layers alternating with small, sliced vegetable marrows (zucchini, or summer squash) sautéed in oil and *Tomato fondue**. Finish with a layer of eggs. Sprinkle with grated Parmesan and melted butter. Brown the top quickly in a hot oven.

Scrambled eggs Argenteuil. OEUFS BROUILLÉS ARGENTEUIL—Prepare the eggs in the usual manner. Garnish with white asparagus tips, half cooked in salted water and simmered in butter. Surround with a ring of *Cream sauce* (see SAUCE). Decorate with *croûtons* cut in the shape of wolves' teeth, fried in butter.

Scrambled eggs à l'arlesienne. OEUFS BROUILLÉS À L'ARLÉSIENNE—Scramble the eggs with some garlic-flavoured *Tomato fondue**. Cook long small vegetable marrows (zucchini) in butter, halve them, remove the pulp. Chop this pulp and mix with the scrambled eggs. Fill the halved marrows with the scrambled eggs and put them on a buttered fire-proof dish. Sprinkle with grated Parmesan and melted butter. Brown the top quickly and surround with a ring of *Tomato sauce* (see SAUCE).

Scrambled eggs à l'armoricaine. OEUFS BROUILLÉS À L'ARMORICAINE—Prepare the eggs in the usual manner. Arrange in a deep dish, in layers, alternating with a *salpicon** of *Lobster* or *Spiny lobster à l'américaine* (see LOBSTER). Put slices of lobster or spiny lobster on the eggs and surround with a ring of *Sauce à l'américaine* (see SAUCE).

Scrambled eggs with artichokes. OEUFS BROUILLÉS AUX ARTICHAUTS—Mix the eggs with artichoke hearts (previously cooked), sliced or cut in dice and sautéed in butter.

Garnish the top with sliced artichoke hearts sautéed in butter and bread croûtons, cut in the shape of wolves' teeth, fried in butter. Surround with a ring of concentrated veal gravy.

Scrambled eggs à la Bercy. OEUFS BROUILLÉS À LA BERCY—Arrange the eggs in a deep dish and garnish with chipolata sausages, grilled or cooked in butter. Surround with a ring of *Tomato sauce* (see SAUCE).

Scrambled eggs with cèpes. OUEFS BROUILLÉS AUX CÈPES—Slice the cèpes, sauté in butter or oil and add to the eggs. Arrange in a deep dish, placing the cèpes in the middle; garnish with bread croûtons, cut in the shape of wolves' teeth and fried in butter. Surround with a ring of concentrated veal gravy.

Scrambled eggs with chicken livers. OEUFS BROUILLÉS AUX FOIES DE VOLAILLES—Heap the scrambled eggs on a heated platter, garnish with chicken livers, sliced, sautéed in butter and bound with *Demi-glace sauce* (see SAUCE). Sprinkle with chopped parsley.

Scrambled eggs Clamart. OEUFS BROUILLÉS CLAMART—Mix the eggs with *Green peas cooked à la française*. Garnish with a little heap of peas on top.

Scrambled eggs with crayfish. OEUFS BROUILLÉS AUX ÉCREVISSES—Prepare as *Scrambled eggs with shrimps*, using crayfish tails and *Nantua sauce* (see SAUCE).

Scrambled eggs 'l'échelle'. OEUFS BROUILLÉS 'L'ÉCHELLE'—Prepare scrambled eggs with cheese. Butter an earthenware dish and line it with *croûtons* of crustless bread, lightly fried in butter, covered with thick slices of truffles heated in butter and seasoned with salt and pepper. Put the eggs into the dish.

Smooth the surface of the eggs, sprinkle with grated cheese and melted butter and brown the top briskly.

Scrambled eggs à l'espagnole I. OEUFS BROUILLÉS À L'ESPAGNOLE—Garnish the scrambled eggs with diced tomatoes cooked in oil mixed with a *salpicon** of sweet pimentos. Decorate the top with onion rings fried in oil.

Scrambled eggs à l'espagnole II. OEUFS BROUILLÉS À L'ESPAGNOLE—Prepare the eggs in the usual manner, add a *salpicon** of sweet pimentos and put into halved, seeded tomatoes, cooked in oil. Garnish with onion rings fried in oil.

Scrambled eggs à la forestière. OEUFS BROUILLÉS À LA FORESTIÈRE—Garnish the scrambled eggs with morels, fried in butter with chopped shallot and diced lean bacon. Arrange a little mound of morels on top. Surround with a ring of *Demi-glace sauce* (see SAUCE) and sprinkle with chopped parsley.

Scrambled eggs Georgette. OEUFS BROUILLÉS GEORGETTE —Bake large long potatoes in the oven, and scoop out three quarters of the pulp. Scramble the eggs in the usual manner and put into the potatoes.

Put a spoonful of *Crayfish tails à la Nantua** on each potato. Serve on a napkin-covered dish.

Scrambled eggs with ham or bacon. OEUFS BROUILLÉS AU JAMBON, AU LARD MAIGRE (OU BACON)—Add to the eggs, when they are cooked, some diced ham or bacon, blanched and fried lightly.

Heap the eggs on a warm platter and put little slices of lightly fried ham or rashers (slices) of bacon on top.

Scrambled eggs Massenet. OEUFS BROUILLÉS MASSENET —Garnish the eggs with artichoke hearts, diced and sautéed in butter. Arrange in a timbale and garnish with small slices of *foie gras*, slivers of truffles and asparagus tips. Surround with a ring of concentrated (reduced) veal gravy.

Scrambled eggs with mushrooms (various). OEUFS BROUILLÉS AUX CHAMPIGNONS—Add to the eggs some cultivated (or other) mushrooms sliced or cut into dice, sautéed in butter and seasoned with salt and pepper.

Garnish with sliced mushrooms and bread croûtons cut in the shape of wolves' teeth. Surround with a ring of concentrated veal gravy.

Scrambled eggs à la Nantua. OEUFS BROUILLÉS À LA NANTUA—Scrambled eggs garnished with diced crayfish tails and truffles, decorated with *Crayfish tails à la Nantua** and some sliced truffles heated in butter.

Scrambled eggs à la normande. OEUFS BROUILLÉS À LA NORMANDE—Cook the eggs in the usual manner and arrange in a flan case, baked blind (unfilled) and garnished with mussels, taken out of their shells and bound with *Velouté sauce* (see SAUCE), based on fish stock and diluted with cream. Garnish the top with oysters, poached in their own liquid and de-bearded, slivers of truffles tossed in oil and shrimps' tails in *Shrimp sauce* (see SAUCE). Surround with croûtons shaped to look like wolves' teeth, fried in butter and surround with a ring of *Normande sauce* (see SAUCE).

Scrambled eggs panetière. OEUFS BROUILLÉS PANETIÈRE —Scramble the eggs and add mushrooms and ham, diced and fried in butter. Hollow out a round loaf, cut as a *croustade*, butter on the inside and brown very lightly in the oven. Fill this *croustade* with the scrambled eggs, sprinkle with grated cheese and melted butter and brown the top briskly.

Scrambled eggs Parmentier. OEUFS BROUILLÉS PARMENTIER—Heap the scrambled eggs on a heated platter and garnish with diced potatoes, sautéed in butter and rolled in meat jelly. Sprinkle with chopped parsley.

Scrambled eggs à la périgourdine. OEUFS BROUILLÉS À LA PÉRIGOURDINE—Prepare as *Scrambled eggs Rossini.*

This dish can also be made by adding a *salpicon** of foie gras and truffles to the scrambled eggs.

Scrambled eggs with potatoes. OEUFS BROUILLÉS AUX POMMES DE TERRE—Like *Scrambled eggs Parmentier.* Can also be made with potatoes boiled with their skins, then peeled, sliced and sautéed in butter.

Scrambled eggs princesse. OEUFS BROUILLÉS PRINCESSE—Garnish the eggs with asparagus tips simmered in butter. Arrange in a timbale, or in a flan case, baked blind (tart shell). Put on top some chicken breast cut into *julienne** strips, bound with *Suprême sauce* (see SAUCE) and slivers of truffles tossed in butter. Surround with a ring of *Suprême sauce.*

Scrambled eggs à la reine. OEUFS BROUILLÉS À LA REINE —Arrange the eggs in vol-au-vent cases, in rows alternating with thick *Chicken purée.* Serve with a ring of *Suprême sauce* (see SAUCE).

Scrambled eggs à la romaine. OEUFS BROUILLÉS À LA ROMAINE—Scramble the eggs in the usual manner with some grated Parmesan cheese; arrange in an earthenware dish, or a low timbale, on a bed of leaf spinach, cooked in butter and mixed with diced anchovy fillets. Sprinkle with grated Parmesan cheese and melted butter and brown the top.

Scrambled eggs Rossini. OEUFS BROUILLÉS ROSSINI—Arrange the eggs in a timbale, or a flan case baked blind (unfilled tart shell), garnish with slices of *foie gras* sautéed in butter and slivers of truffles heated in butter. Surround with a ring of very concentrated Madeira-flavoured *Demi-glace sauce* (see SAUCE).

Scrambled eggs Sagan. OEUFS BROUILLÉS SAGAN—Scrambled eggs with cheese, arranged in a timbale or a flan case baked blind (tart shell), garnished with little escalopes of brains, dredged in flour and sautéed in butter, and slivers of truffles heated in butter, served with a ring of concentrated veal gravy.

Scrambled eggs Saint-Hubert. OEUFS BROUILLÉS SAINT-HUBERT—Heap the scrambled eggs on a warm platter; garnish with game purée bound with *Demi-glace sauce* based on concentrated game stock (see SAUCE).

Scrambled eggs with salpicon of lobster, spiny lobster or other shell-fish. OEUFS BROUILLÉS AU SALPICON DE HOMARD (DE LANGOUSTE ETC.)—As *Scrambled eggs with shrimps*, using a *salpicon** of the shell-fish indicated, served with *Cream sauce with white wine* (see SAUCE), finished off with the compound butter relevant to the particular shell-fish.

Scrambled eggs with shrimps. OEUFS BROUILLÉS AUX CREVETTES—Add to the eggs some peeled shrimps' tails heated in butter. Heap on a warm platter. Garnish the top with a little mound of shrimps' tails heated in butter or in *Shrimp sauce* (see SAUCE). Surround with croûtons cut in the shape of wolves' teeth fried in butter. Pour a ring of *Shrimp sauce* round the eggs.

Scrambled eggs with truffles. OEUFS BROUILLÉS AUX TRUFFES—Prepare the scrambled eggs in the usual manner. When cooked, add the truffles, diced and tossed in butter. (Either fresh or canned truffles can be used.) Heap on a warm platter and garnish with slices of truffles and croûtons cut to look like wolves' teeth.

Sévigné eggs (soft boiled or poached). OEUFS SÉVIGNÉ—Arrange the eggs on a round dish, placing each on half a braised lettuce. Cover with *Suprême sauce* (see SAUCE). Put a sliver of truffle on each egg.

Eggs with shrimps (baked). OEUFS AUX CREVETTES—Put a spoonful of shrimp tails into a buttered pan. Break the eggs into the dish. Bake in the ordinary way. Surround with a ribbon of *Shrimp sauce* (see SAUCE).

Eggs with shrimps (soft boiled or poached). OEUFS AUX CREVETTES—Fill some tartlets (baked blind) with shrimps blended with *Shrimp sauce* (see SAUCE). Arrange the eggs on this mixture. Cover with the sauce.

Eggs with shrimps (cold). OEUFS AUX CREVETTES—Coat dariole moulds with *Fish aspic jelly* (see ASPIC). Line the walls of these moulds with shrimps' tails, spooning over a little liquid jelly to set them.

Put a very small soft boiled egg into each mould. Fill with jelly and chill on ice.

Turn out the eggs. Put each on a small round grilled croûton, spread with shrimp butter (see BUTTER, *Compound butters*). Arrange in a crown.

Garnish the middle of the dish with a salad composed of diced potatoes and shrimps' tails dressed with mayonnaise strengthened with gelatine.

Decorate the top of each egg with three shrimps' tails arranged to look like a plume. Surround the croûtons with fish aspic jelly.

Snow eggs

Snow eggs. OEUFS À LA NEIGE—A sweet made of whites of egg and sugar, coated with vanilla-flavoured English custard.

Whisk the eggs and add sugar to them, as for a meringue. With a tablespoon take as much of the meringue mixture as the spoon will hold comfortably (which will give them egg shape) and drop, spoonful by spoonful, into a saucepan of boiling milk, sweetened with sugar and flavoured with vanilla. Poach these eggs in milk, turning them to ensure even cooking.

As soon as they become firm, drain them on a hair sieve.

Using the milk left from poaching these eggs, make an English custard as described in the appropriate recipe (see CREAMS).

Arrange the eggs in a fruit dish and when the custard is cold, pour it over them.

Eggs à la soubise (hard boiled). OEUFS DURS À LA SOUBISE—Arrange hard boiled eggs in a pie dish, on *Onion purée* (see PURÉE). Cover with *Cream sauce* (see SAUCE).

Spanish eggs—See *Eggs à l'espagnole.*

Stanley eggs (soft boiled or poached). OEUFS STANLEY—Arrange the eggs in tartlet cases, baked blind (unfilled) and filled with a *Soubise purée* (see PURÉE). Cover with *Curry sauce* (see SAUCE).

Tarragon eggs (sur le plat). OEUFS À L'ESTRAGON—Put a spoonful of tarragon-flavoured veal gravy into a buttered dish. Break the eggs into the dish. Cook until the whites are set. Pour a ring of the gravy around the eggs. Decorate with blanched tarragon.

Tarragon eggs, also called eggs à la Chartres (soft boiled or poached). OEUFS À L'ESTRAGON, DITS AUSSI À LA CHARTRES—Arrange the eggs on round or oval-shaped *croûtons* fried in butter. Cover them with tarragon-flavoured veal gravy. Decorate with tarragon leaves, blanched and well-drained.

Eggs à la tripe, also called eggs à la béchamel soubisée (hard boiled). OEUFS À LA TRIPE (OEUFS À LA BÉCHAMEL SOUBISÉE)—Cut the hard boiled eggs into quarters or thick round slices. Arrange in a pie dish. Cover with *Soubise sauce* (see SAUCE).

Verdier eggs (stuffed). OEUFS VERDIER—Stuff halved hard boiled eggs with a mixture of the hard boiled yolks rubbed through a sieve and cooked *foie gras* (the latter added in the proportion of one third).

Arrange the eggs in a gratin dish on a layer of sliced onions, lightly cooked in butter, blended with a spoonful of *Béchamel sauce* (see SAUCE) and seasoned with curry.

Cover with *Béchamel sauce* mixed with a *julienne** of truffles. Sprinkle with Parmesan. Brown the top in a very hot oven.

Victoria eggs (soft boiled or poached). OEUFS VICTORIA—Arrange the eggs in puff pastry cases filled with a *salpicon** of spiny lobster (or lobster) and truffles, bound with *Victoria sauce* (see SAUCES). Put a slice of spiny lobster (or lobster) and a sliver of truffle on each egg.

Eggs à la Villeroi (soft boiled or poached). OEUFS À LA VILLEROI—Small-sized eggs are used for this dish. Dry the eggs in a cloth, coat with *Villeroi sauce* (see SAUCE) and leave to get thoroughly cold.

Dip in egg and breadcrumbs. Fry at the last moment. Arrange in a crown on a napkin. Garnish with fried parsley. Serve *Tomato sauce* (see SAUCE) separately.

Eggs à la Zingara (soft boiled or poached). OEUFS À LA ZINGARA—Arrange the eggs on oval-shaped croûtons fried in butter, covered with a thin slice of lean ham. Cover with *Zingara sauce*. See SAUCE.

OMELETTE—The etymology of this word is uncertain, bnt it may have been derived from *amelette*, which is a corruption of *alemette*, derived from *alemelle* or *alumette*, or slice—as this dish is often flat in shape.

Ancient Romans used the name *ova mellita* to define eggs beaten with honey and cooked in an earthenware dish. It, therefore, seems more logical to presume that the word omelette has been derived from *ova mellita.*

The following story is also told on the subject of the origin of the word omelette:

The King of Spain was taking a walk in the country one day. Feeling very hungry and being a long way from any inn, he went into a peasant's hut and asked the peasant to prepare some food quickly for him and his suite.

The man set to work, and with a speed which delighted the hungry King, proceeded to cook some beaten eggs in oil in a pan.

'Quel homme leste (What an agile man)!' exclaimed the King on savouring the dish, which it appears he had never tasted before . . .

And from that day, say some authors, beaten eggs cooked in a pan have been called *omelette*, in memory of the *homme leste*, who had the honour of serving this dish to the King of Spain.

What weakens this story somewhat is the fact that in Spain an omelette is called *tortilla* . . .

In this section recipes for sweet (dessert) omelettes will be found at the end. The recipe for basic omelettes appears under EGGS, BASIC RECIPES.

Filled omelettes. OMELETTE FOURRÉES—The omelettes, before being folded, can be filled with various mixtures (*forcemeat**, *purée**, *salpicon**), as indicated in individual recipes.

This garnish should be hot when put into the omelette and folded in carefully, to make sure that once the omelette is dished the filling will not drop out.

A large omelette can also be filled with a separately cooked smaller omelette in which case the colour and the flavour of the two omelettes should be completely different.

Flat omelettes. OMELETTES PLATES—These are cooked in a pan, in butter, oil or other fat, and made flat, that is to say, resembling rather a thick pancake.

Tomato omelette and bacon (*Bacon Information Council*)

Omelettes garnies—The garnish, as indicated in individual recipes, can either be added when the eggs are beaten, or put in the omelette when folding it.

In addition to the interior garnish or filling, a small quantity of the same ingredients is put on top of the omelette. If this garnish includes a liaison sauce, or is bound with butter, a shallow cut is made lengthwise in the surface when the omelette is done, to accommodate it.

Most filled and garnished omelettes are served with a ring of sauce suitable for the garnish.

Cheese mousseline omelette (*The Cheese Bureau*)

Omelette mousseline—Mix 6 yolks of eggs with 2 tablespoons of cream. Season with salt and pepper.

Add the whites, whisked into a very stiff froth. Fold in quickly. Using this composition, make an omelette like a thick pancake.

This omelette can also be made fluffy.

Omelette Agnès Sorel—Before folding, fill the omelette with sliced mushrooms, sautéed in butter and bound with a *Chicken purée**.

Decorate the top with round slices of pickled or smoked tongue. Reduce (boil down) some veal gravy, add butter to it and pour it around the omelette.

Omelette Albina—Add some truffles, cut in small dice, to the eggs while beating them. Cook the omelette in the usual manner. Before folding, put in a filling of rather thick *Chicken purée.* Pour a ring of *Velouté sauce* (see SAUCE) mixed with cream around the omelette.

Omelette à l'alsacienne (Alsatian omelette)—Fry the omelette in goose fat. Fill it with braised, well-drained sauerkraut.

Put thin slices of ham on the omelette and surround with a ring of *Demi-glace sauce* (see SAUCE).

Anchovy omelette. OMELETTE AUX ANCHOIS—Beat the eggs with the fillets of one de-salted anchovy, rubbed through a sieve. Cook the omelette as usual.

Cut de-salted anchovy fillets into thin strips and place these on the omelette.

Omelette André-Theuriet—Fill the omelette, before folding it, with *Morels à la crème*. Transfer to a dish and garnish with bunches of asparagus tips in butter. Put some slivers of truffles tossed in butter on top and surround with a ring of *Suprême sauce* (see SAUCE).

Omelette Archiduc—Season the eggs with salt and pepper. Add 1 or 2 tablespoons of chopped onion, melted in butter and seasoned with paprika. Beat the eggs and prepare the omelette in the usual manner.

Garnish with slivers of truffles heated in butter and surround with a ring of paprika sauce.

Omelette Argenteuil—Cook the omelette in the usual manner. Before folding it, fill it with 3 tablespoons of white or green asparagus tips in butter.

Put a tablespoon of asparagus tips on top. Surround with a ring of *Allemande sauce*, or *Cream sauce* (see SAUCE), if the dish is meatless.

Artichoke omelette. OMELETTE AUX ARTICHAUTS—Add artichoke hearts, half cooked, sliced and sautéed in butter to the eggs when beating them. Prepare the omelette in the usual manner. Garnish with a row of sliced artichoke hearts, sautéed in butter. Serve with a ring of reduced (concentrated) veal gravy, with butter added to it.

Omelette with asparagus tips. OMELETTE AUX POINTES D'ASPERGES—Add to the eggs, while beating them, some green asparagus tips, diced and tossed in butter. Make the omelette in the usual manner. Put a little bunch of asparagus tips on the omelette and sprinkle with melted butter.

Aubergine omelette I. OMELETTE AUX AUBERGINES—Add 2 tablespoons of aubergines (egg-plant), diced and sautéed in butter or oil, to the eggs when beating them.

Cook the omelette as described.

Aubergine omelette II. OMELETTE AUX AUBERGINES—Prepare the omelette as usual. Put a row of round slices of aubergine (egg-plant) fried in butter or oil, on top.

Sprinkle with chopped parsley and surround with a ring of *Demi-glace sauce* or *Tomato sauce* (see SAUCE).

Bacon omelette. OMELETTE AU BACON—Add 4 tablespoons of bacon, diced and lightly fried in butter, to the eggs while beating them.

Prepare the omelette in the usual manner. Garnish the top with 6 thin rashers of bacon fried in butter.

Omelette à la Bércy—Add some chopped *fines herbes* to the eggs when beating them and prepare the omelette as usual. Garnish with small chipolata sausages, grilled or sautéed. Surround with a ring of *Tomato sauce* (see SAUCE).

Omelette à la bigourdine—Fill the omelette with truffles and foie gras cut in large dice. Serve with a ring of *Madeira sauce* (see SAUCE).

Omelette à la bouchère—Fill the omelette before folding it with bone marrow fat cut in dice, poached and bound with liquid meat jelly.

Put a row of poached marrow slices on top and spoon over some liquid meat jelly.

Brillat-Savarin's tunny omelette (or Omelette du curé). OMELETTE AU THON—From the short series of recipes by the illustrious gastronome we consider it interesting to reproduce that for *Tunny* (*tuna*) *omelette*, as given to him, but in the version invented for Monseigneur de la T., by his chef, Frédéric. (See also Omelette de Savarin.)

'*Preparation of tunny omelette:* For 6 persons, take two well washed soft carp roes, which you will blanch by plunging them into slightly salted, boiling water for five minutes.

'Have a piece of tunny, the size of a chicken's egg ready for use. Add to it a small shallot chopped into minute particles.

'Chop together the soft roes and the tunny in such a way as to blend them thoroughly. Put the mixture into a saucepan with a sufficient amount of the best butter, to sauté until the butter is melted. This constitutes the speciality of the omelette.

'Take a second piece of butter (the size being left to your discretion) blend it with parsley and spring onions, put into a pisciform dish intended for the omelette. Sprinkle with a dash of lemon juice and put on hot coals.

'Proceed to beat a dozen eggs (the fresher the better), add the tunny and roe mixture to them and stir to blend well.

'Fry the omelette in the usual manner; try to make it longish, thick and fluffy. Transfer it adroitly to a dish which you have ready to receive it, and serve at once.

'These dishes should be reserved specially for elegant luncheons, for connoisseurs, where people know what's what and where they eat in a leisurely manner; above all, these dishes should be washed down with some good wine and you will see wonders.

'*Theoretical notes on the preparation:* The soft roes and the tunny should be sautéed without allowing them to boil, to stop them going hard, which would prevent their blending with the eggs smoothly.

'The dish should be deep enough to collect the sauce which should be served with a spoon.

'The dish itself should be warmed slightly, for, if it is cold the porcelain will extract all the heat from the omelette and there will not be enough heat left to melt the maître d'hôtel butter on which it is laid.'

Omelette à la bruxelloise—Choose very small Brussels sprouts, cook them in salted water until three quarters done, then drain, dry and fry in a pan in butter.

Put the seasoned beaten eggs into the pan and cook the omelette in the usual manner. Serve with a ring of concentrated veal gravy.

Carrot omelette—See *Omelette à la Crécy.*

Omelette with cèpes. OMELETTE AUX CÈPES—Add some cèpes, sliced and fried in butter (or oil) and some chopped parsley to the eggs when beating them. Cook the omelette in the usual manner. Put on the omelette a row of sliced cèpes, fried in butter.

Omelette chasseur—Fill the omelette with sautéed chicken livers mixed with sliced mushrooms. A bouquet of the same ingredients should be reserved for garnishing the omelette on top. Serve with a ring of *Chasseur sauce* (Hunter sauce). See SAUCE. Sprinkle with chopped parsley.

Omelette à la châtelaine—Fill the omelette with chestnuts, braised, mashed and bound with greatly reduced (concentrated) veal gravy. Serve with a ring of *Cream sauce* (see SAUCE).

Omelette with chervil. OMELETTE AU CERFEUIL BULBEUX—Add some turnip-rooted chervil chopped and cooked in butter and some chopped chervil to the eggs while beating them.

Make the omelette in the usual manner.

Chicken liver omelette. OMELETTE AUX FOIES DE VOLAILLES—Fill the omelette with chicken livers, sliced, sautéed briskly in butter and bound with concentrated *Demi-glace sauce* (see SAUCE).

Decorate the top with a little mound of chicken livers prepared as above and serve with a ring of Madeira-flavoured *Demi-glace sauce* (see SAUCE).

Omelette Choisy—Fill the omelette with *Chiffonnade of lettuce with cream* (see LETTUCE). Serve with a ring of *Cream sauce* (see SAUCE).

Omelette Clamart—Fill the omelette with *Peas à la française* (keeping the liaison rather thick). Make a slight cut in the top of the omelette lengthways and put a tablespoon of peas on top.

Omelette à la Crécy I—Add 2 tablespoons of *Carrots à la Vichy** to the eggs while beating them. Make the omelette in the usual manner.

Omelette à la Crécy II—Fill the omelette with 2 good tablespoons of rather thick *Carrot purée.*

Decorate the top with a row of sliced carrots cooked in butter. Serve with a ring of *Cream sauce* (see SAUCE).

Omelette with croûtons. OMELETTE AUX CROÛTONS—This can be made flat or fluffy.

Flat. Cut some bread into large dice and fry in butter in a pan. Beat the eggs with some chopped parsley, and pour over the croûtons. Make the omelette as a pancake.

Fluffy. Fry the diced bread in butter and add to the eggs while beating them together with some chopped parsley. Fry the omelette in the usual manner.

Omelette Diane—Make an omelette using beaten eggs and mushrooms, sliced, fried in butter and seasoned with salt and pepper.

When folding, fill it with a *salpicon** of partridge, or any other winged game, and truffles, bound with concentrated *Velouté sauce* (see SAUCE) based on game *fumet**. Garnish the top of the omelette with a row of truffle slices, tossed in butter. Serve with a ring of *Demi-glace sauce* (see SAUCE) based on game stock. The *salpicon** is prepared out of left-over pieces of game.

Omelette diplomate—Using 3 eggs make a flat omelette. Put the omelette on a round dish and cover the top with a layer of lobster and truffle *salpicon** bound with *Béchamel sauce* (see SAUCE) flavoured with lobster butter and brandy.

On top of this put a second 3-egg omelette keeping it rather creamy. Cover with *Mornay sauce* (see SAUCE), flavoured with lobster butter. Sprinkle with grated Parmesan and melted butter and brown the top briskly in a very hot oven.

Omelette Du Barry—Boil a cauliflower divided into flowerets in salted water; drain and fry quickly in clarified butter. When done pour in the eggs, beaten with chopped chervil and seasoned with salt and pepper.

Cook the omelette as a pancake and serve with a ring of *Cream sauce* (see SAUCE).

Omelette à la duxelles—Fill the omelette with *Duxelles** mixture mixed with diced ham. Serve with a ring of tomato-flavoured *Demi-glace sauce* (see SAUCE).

Omelette à la fermière—Add to the eggs while beating them 3 tablespoons of a *paysanne** of vegetables, composed of carrots, onions and celery, sliced, lightly fried in butter and seasoned with salt, pepper and half a tablespoon of chopped parsley.

Fry 2 tablespoons of diced lean ham lightly in butter. Pour the eggs over the ham and fry the omelette as a pancake.

Omelette à la flamande—Fill the omelette with shredded chicory (U.S. Belgian endive) cooked in butter and bound with cream. Serve with a ring of *Cream sauce* (see SAUCE).

Omelette Feydeau

Omelette Feydeau—Prepare a very creamy omelette (i.e. keeping it rather liquid). Transfer it to a hot dish. Open it completely and fill with a *Mushroom purée**.

On this omelette place a row of very small soft poached eggs (one per guest). Cover with *Mornay sauce* (see SAUCE) mixed with a *julienne** of truffles. Sprinkle with grated Parmesan and brown the top quickly.

Omelettes aux fines herbes—Usually, and quite wrongly, this omelette is prepared by adding only chopped parsley to the eggs. Actually, omelette *aux fines herbes* should contain chopped parsley, chervil, tarragon and even spring onions or chives and there must be enough of all these aromatic herbs to make the omelette green.

In the olden days the words '*fines herbes*' meant a mixture, not only of various aromatic herbs, but also of mushrooms and, sometimes, chopped truffles.

Omelette à la florentine I—Fill the omelette with leaf spinach cooked in butter. Serve with a ring of *Béchamel sauce* (see SAUCE).

Omelette à la florentine II—Fill the omelette with spinach cooked in butter. Cover with a light *Mornay sauce* (see SAUCE) sprinkle with grated Parmesan and melted butter and brown the top quickly.

Omelette à la forestière—Add to the eggs while beating them 2 tablespoons of lean bacon, diced and fried in butter. Fill the omelette with morels, sautéed in butter, bound with concentrated veal gravy and sprinkled with chopped parsley. Serve with a ring of concentrated veal gravy with some butter added to it.

Omelette à la gasconne—Add to the eggs while beating them some diced, unsmoked ham, and thinly sliced onions, fried lightly in butter (or goose fat), as well as some chopped garlic and parsley. Fry the omelette like a pancake in butter or goose fat.

Omelette à la grecque—Beat the eggs, add chopped onion lightly fried in butter and diced sweet pimentos and make two flat omelettes. Put one of these omelettes on a round dish, spread with a layer of mutton hash and cover with the second omelette.

Surround with a ring of garlic-flavoured *Tomato sauce* (see SAUCE) and sprinkle with chopped parsley and *Noisette butter* (see BUTTER, *Compound butters*).

Ham omelette. OMELETTE AU JAMBON—As *Bacon omelette*, using diced lean ham.

Omelette à la hongroise (Hungarian omelette)—Dice some lean ham (not smoked) and fry lightly in butter. Add an equal quantity of onions cut in very small dice and also fried in butter. Season with paprika.

Pour the eggs into the pan. Make a pancake omelette and serve with a ring of *Hungarian sauce* (see SAUCE).

Omelette with hop shoots. OMELETTE AUX JETS DE HOUBLON—Fill the omelette with *Hop shoots à la crème*. Serve with a ring of *Cream sauce* (see SAUCE).

Japanese omelette. OMELETTE À LA JAPONAISE—Fill the omelette with *Chinese artichokes**, cooked in butter and sprinkled with chopped parsley. Serve with a ring of *Cream sauce* (see SAUCE) .

Omelette à la jardinière—Cook some vegetables, such as carrots, turnips, French string beans, peas, potatoes, etc., in water or stock, according to the nature of the vegetable, and fry lightly in butter.

Into the same pan pour the beaten eggs and make a flat omelette.

Garnish the top of the omelette with asparagus tips and little flowerets of cauliflower. Serve with a ring of *Cream sauce* (see SAUCE).

Omelette à la jurassienne I—Add some lean bacon, diced, scalded and lightly fried in butter and some chopped spring onions to the eggs while beating them.

Fill the omelette when folding with sorrel cooked in butter.

Omelette à la jurassienne II—Beat the eggs with chopped sorrel, cooked in butter, and some spring onions. Fry some diced lean bacon in butter and pour the eggs into the same pan. Make a flat omelette.

Kidney omelette. OMELETTE AUX ROGNONS—Prepared with calf's or lamb's kidneys, cut in small dice, sautéed in butter and bound with Madeira-flavoured, concentrated *Demi-glace sauce* (see SAUCE).

Fill the omelette with the kidneys prepared as described. Garnish on top with a spoonful of sautéed kidneys. Serve with a ring of Madeira-flavoured *Demi-glace sauce*.

This omelette can also be made using sliced, instead of diced, kidneys.

Lobster omelette. OMELETTE AU HOMARD—Prepare as *Shrimp omelette*, using a *salpicon** of lobster bound with *Lobster sauce* (see SAUCE).

Omelette à la lorraine—Add to the eggs while beating them some diced lean bacon sautéed in butter (or grilled), some shredded Gruyère cheese and chopped spring onions. Make a flat omelette or a fluffy omelette.

Omelette à la lyonnaise—Add to the eggs, while beating them, some finely sliced onions, lightly fried in butter, and chopped parsley. Make the omelette in the usual manner.

This omelette can also be made flat. When ready, arrange on a dish, sprinkle with a few drops of vinegar, heated in the same pan, and pour over it some *Noisette butter* (see BUTTER, *Compound butters*).

Omelette Louis Forest—Beat the eggs with truffles, cut in dice and cooked in butter, and make two flat omelettes. Put one of these omelettes on a round dish. Spread with little slices of fresh foie gras sautéed in butter and cover with the second omelette. Spoon over some concentrated, Madeira-flavoured veal gravy and sprinkle with *Noisette butter* (see BUTTER, *Compound butters*).

Omelette Maintenon—Fill the omelette with a *salpicon** of chicken, truffles and mushrooms, bound with *Velouté sauce* (see SAUCE) diluted with cream. Make the omelette in the usual manner, keeping it very creamy. Cover with *Béchamel sauce with onion* (see SAUCE); sprinkle with grated Parmesan and melted butter and brown the top quickly in oven or under a grill.

Marrow omelette. OMELETTE À LA MOELLE—This can be made flat or fluffy.

Flat. Garnish the omelette, having put it on a dish, with slices of bone marrow fat, poached in salt water and drained. Spoon over a little liquid meat jelly on each slice of marrow and serve with a ring of *Marrow sauce* (see SAUCE).

Fluffy. Fill the omelette with a *salpicon** of bone marrow fat, bound with *Marrow sauce*. Garnish the omelette on top with slices of marrow, poached in salted water and drained. Serve with a ring of *Marrow sauce*.

Omelette with morels. OMELETTE AUX MORILLES—Add to the eggs, while beating them, some morels sautéed in butter and some chopped parsley. Fry the omelette in the usual manner.

Omelette with morels à la crème. OMELETTE AUX MORILLES À LA CRÈME—Fill the omelette with *Morels à la crème* and serve with a ring of *Cream sauce* (see SAUCE).

Omelette à la ménagère—Cut some left-over pieces of boiled beef into little dice, fry lightly in butter and add an equal quantity of diced onion, also cooked in butter.

Beat the eggs with chopped parsley, season with salt and pepper, pour into the pan and make a pancake omelette.

Omelette Mistral—Fry some diced aubergines (egg-plant) in oil. Into the same pan pour the eggs, mixed with tomatoes, diced and lightly fried in butter, chopped parsley and a pinch of garlic. Make the omelette like a pancake.

Omelette Monselet—Fill the omelette with a *salpicon** of artichoke hearts and *Truffles à la crème*. Garnish the omelette on top with slivers of truffles heated in butter. Serve with a ring of Madeira-flavoured *Demi-glace sauce* (see SAUCE).

Omelette Montbry—Beat the eggs together with some grated horse-radish, chopped spring onions, parsley and the usual seasoning. Make two flat omelettes. Put one of them on a buttered round dish. Spread with a *salpicon** of celeriac (i.e. turnip-rooted celery) bound with *Cream sauce* (see SAUCE) and seasoned with paprika. Cover with the second omelette. Spoon over some light *Mornay sauce* (see SAUCE), sprinkle with grated Parmesan and melted butter and brown the top quickly.

Mushroom omelette. OMELETTE AUX CHAMPIGNONS—Add 2 good tablespoons of mushrooms, sliced and sautéed in butter, to the eggs while beating them.

Keep a dozen of the best slices of mushrooms to decorate the omelette.

Omelette à la nancéienne

Omelette à la nancéienne—This can be made flat or fluffy.

Flat. Make two flat omelettes, using eggs beaten together with chopped onion, lightly fried in butter, and chopped parsley. Put one of the omelettes on a round dish. Put on it round slices of black pudding, lightly fried in butter. Cover with the second omelette and sprinkle with chopped parsley. Pour round the omelette some concentrated veal gravy and sprinkle with *Noisette butter* (see BUTTER, *Compound butters*).

Fluffy. Fill the omelette (made of eggs beaten with lightly fried chopped onion and chopped parsley) with chunks of fried black pudding. Reduce (concentrate) some veal gravy, add butter to it and pour a ring of this sauce around the omelette.

Omelette à la Nantua—Fill the omelettes with crayfish tails bound with *Nantua sauce* (see SAUCE). Garnish the omelette on top with crayfish tails and slivers of truffles. Serve with a ring of the sauce.

Omelette à la niçoise—Make a flat omelette using eggs mixed with *Tomato fondue** and chopped parsley and garlic.

Garnish the omelette with anchovies laid in a criss-cross pattern. Sprinkle with *Noisette butter* (see BUTTER, *Compound butters*).

Omelette à la normande—Fill the omelette with a *ragoût* of shrimps' tails and mushrooms, bound with *Normande sauce* (see SAUCE). Put on the omelette some oysters, poached in their own liquid and de-bearded, and some slivers of truffles. Serve with a ring of *Normande sauce*.

Okra (gombos) omelette à la créole. OMELETTE AUX GOMBOS À LA CRÉOLE—Add to the eggs while beating them some diced onions and peeled and diced sweet pimentos, both cooked in butter, and some chopped parsley.

Fill the omelette with okra (gombos) cooked in butter, mixed with *Tomato fondue** and flavoured with a pinch of garlic. Serve with a ring of *Tomato sauce* (see SAUCE).

Or: Make a flat omelette and serve the okra *ragoût* on top.

Omelette à la parisienne—Add to the eggs while beating them some chopped onion lightly fried in butter and some chopped mushrooms sautéed in butter. Make the omelette in the usual manner. Cover with chipolata sausages, cooked in butter or grilled. Serve with a ring of concentrated veal gravy with butter added to it.

Omelette Parmentier—This can be made flat or fluffy.

Flat. Add to the eggs, just before frying the omelette, some potatoes cut in small dice, fried in butter and chopped parsley. Make a pancake omelette.

Fluffy. Fry the omelette in the usual manner, using eggs to which diced fried potatoes and chopped parsley have been added at the last moment.

Note. Omelette Parmentier can also be made with potatoes sautéed in butter (boiled with their skins, peeled, then sliced and sauteéd in butter), or with raw potatoes, sliced and sautéed in butter.

To prepare an omelette using raw potatoes proceed as follows:

Sauté the potatoes in a pan. When they are lightly fried, add to them the beaten eggs, seasoned and mixed with some chopped parsley. Fry a pancake omelette.

Omelette pascale—Make an omelette, using eggs mixed with lean bacon, diced, scalded and lightly fried in butter, and chopped parsley.

Omelette à la paysanne—Add to the eggs, while beating them, some chopped sorrel, lightly fried in butter, potatoes, cooked in their skins, peeled, cut in round slices and fried in butter, and some pounded parsley and chervil.

Fry a flat pancake omelette.

Omelette à la polonaise (Polish omelette)—Fill the omelette with mutton hash bound with *Demi-glace sauce* (see SAUCE). Garnish on top with a dollop of *Tomato fondue**. Sprinkle with chopped parsley and serve with a ring of *Tomato sauce* (see SAUCE).

Potato omelette—OMELETTE AUX POMMES DE TERRE—See *Omelette Parmentier.*

Omelette à la portugaise—Fill the omelette with *Tomato fondue** and serve with a ring of *Tomato sauce* (see SAUCE).

Princess omelette I. OMELETTE PRINCESSE—Add to the eggs, while beating them, some green asparagus tips in butter. Make the omelette in the usual manner. Put a row of truffle slices, heated in butter, on top of the omelette. Serve with a ring of *Suprême sauce* (see SAUCE).

Princess omelette II. OMELETTE PRINCESSE—Make an omelette using eggs mixed with diced truffles. Fill it with asparagus tips bound with cream. Garnish on top with a little bunch of green asparagus tips. Serve with a ring of *Suprême sauce* (see SAUCE).

Omelette à la provençale—Cook some peeled, seeded and diced tomatoes in butter or oil. Season with salt and pepper and add a pinch of garlic.

Beat the eggs with some pounded parsley, pour into the pan and fry the omelette in the usual manner.

Omelette à la romaine—Fry two flat omelettes, using eggs beaten together with chopped onion, sweated in butter, and some chopped parsley. Spread one of these omelettes with leaf spinach, cooked in *Noisette butter* (see BUTTER) and mixed with diced anchovy fillets. Cover with the second omelette.

Spoon over some *Mornay sauce* (see SAUCE), not too thick. Sprinkle with grated Parmesan and melted butter. Brown the top quickly.

Omelette Rossini—Add to the eggs, while beating them, a *salpicon** of *foie gras* and truffles. Make the omelette in the usual manner. Garnish with small slices of *foie gras* and slivers of truffles. Serve with a ring of Madeira-flavoured *Demi-glace sauce* (see SAUCE).

Omelette à la rouennaise—Fill the omelette with a duck liver purée. Serve with a ring of red wine, boiled down (reduced) and blended with some meat jelly and butter.

Omelette à la royale—Using eggs mixed with a purée of truffles, make a small omelette. Fill it with a *ragoût* of cocks' combs and kidneys, mushrooms and truffles, bound with *Velouté sauce* (see SAUCE) diluted with cream.

Beat some eggs mixed with fresh cream, season with salt and pepper and make a big omelette. When folding, fill this with the smaller truffled omelette.

Put this omelette on a big, long dish. Garnish the top with small slices of foie gras, alternating with slivers of truffles. Serve with a ring of port-flavoured *Suprême sauce* (see SAUCE).

Omelette à la Saint-Flour—Add to the eggs, while beating them, some sliced onions lightly fried in lard and some bacon, diced, scalded and fried lightly. Using half this egg mixture, make a flat omelette. Spread this omelette with a layer of braised, mashed cabbage. Cover with the second omelette, made out of the rest of the eggs. Serve with a ring of *Tomato sauce* (see SAUCE).

Omelette à la Saint-Hubert—Fold into the omelette some purée of game meat, bound with thick *Demi-glace sauce* (see SAUCE), based on concentrated game stock.

Put on the omelette a row of sliced mushrooms, lightly fried in butter. Serve with a ring of *Demi-glace sauce.*

Omelette with salsify and Brussels sprouts, called à la maraîchère. OMELETTE AUX SALSIFIS ET AUX CHOUX DE BRUXELLES, DITE À LA MARAÎCHÈRE—Fold into the omelette some salsify (previously cooked in a *court-bouillon**), cut in dice, tossed in butter and bound with thick *Velouté sauce* (see SAUCE). Put around the omelette a garnish consisting of potatoes cut to look like cob-nuts and Brussels sprouts sautéed in butter. Serve with a ring of concentrated *Demi-glace sauce* (see SAUCE) with butter added to it.

Omelette de Savarin (according to Frédéric)—'The original recipe was the source of memorable discussions between the *Directeur de la table* of the Archbishop (a Canon and master of gastronomy) and the *Chef de cuisine*, at which Frédéric declared himself totally against the massacre of the soft roes and emphatically repudiated the use of shallot. The Monseigneur, who acted as arbiter, declared his wish to preserve neutrality, on condition that Frédéric's omelette, a Lenten mortification dish, left nothing to be desired. At any rate, the principle had to be respected.

'Frédéric absolutely refused to use more than eight eggs in an omelette, and those who have to hold the handle of the frying pan cannot but approve of this. His method of procedure was as follows: The roes, instead of being chopped, were cut into thin slices and done "*à la meunière*". The tunny (he used tunny in oil more often than not) was dried on a cloth, cut into a fairly coarse *salpicon*, seasoned and simmered in butter. The eggs, beaten simply to assure the blending of the whites and the yolks, were mixed with two spoonfuls of very thick fresh cream. At a precise moment, when the butter was singing in the omelette pan, the sliced roes and the diced tunny were married in a shrimp sauce, discreetly seasoned and amply enriched with cream. And the centre of the omelette, cooked to just the right consistency and folded twice, received this "cardinalized" *ragoût.*

'Arranged on its serving dish, the omelette or omelettes, depending on the number of guests present, was frugally covered with the same sauce, decorated with some large slices of truffles, to provide a sober note of mourning, and served at once, as Frédéric, whose tyranny was dreaded by the servants, always insisted that the house steward be present during the preparation so that the omelette would not be kept waiting even for a second.

'Sometimes, for a change, the omelette, prepared as described, was girdled with *fried frogs' legs.*

'It is also to this chef, a man of rare talent, that the creation of the transcendent *Prelate's omelette* is attributed.' (Philéas Gilbert.)

Omelette à la savoyarde—Fry sliced potatoes in a pan. Into the same pan pour the eggs, mixed with shredded Gruyère. Fry like a pancake omelette.

Sea food omelette. OMELETTE AUX FRUITS DE MER—Beat the eggs with chopped parsley and chervil, season with salt and pepper and make two pancake omelettes.

Put one of the omelettes on a round oven-proof dish and cover it with a *ragoût* composed of mussels, shrimps, tails, cockles and other shell-fish, bound with *Shrimp sauce* (see SAUCE). Cover with the second omelette, pour over some cream sauce flavoured with shrimp butter and glaze quickly in the oven.

Shrimp omelette. OMELETTE AUX CREVETTES—Fill the omelette with peeled shrimps' tails bound with *Shrimp sauce* (see SAUCE). Serve with a ring of Shrimp sauce.

Sorrel omelette I. OMELETTE À L'OSEILLE—Add to the eggs, while beating them, 4 tablespoons of sorrel, shredded into a *chiffonnade** and lightly fried in butter. Make the omelette in the usual manner.

Sorrel omelette II. OMELETTE À L'OSEILLE—Fill the omelette with a *chiffonnade** of sorrel bound with cream. Serve with a ring of *Cream sauce* (see SAUCE).

Spanish omelette I. OMELETTE À L'ESPAGNOLE—Add to the eggs, while beating them, some sweet pimentos, diced or shredded into *julienne** strips and cooked in butter, diced tomatoes cooked in butter and a pinch of chopped garlic and parsley. Fry the omelette like a pancake.

Spanish omelette II. OMELETTE À L'ESPAGNOLE—Slice some sweet pimentos and fry in oil. Beat the eggs with chopped parsley, garlic, salt and pepper and pour over the pimentos. Fry the omelette like a pancake. Serve with a ring of *Tomato sauce* (see SAUCE).

Spinach omelette. OMELETTE AUX ÉPINARDS—Sweat the leaf spinach in butter and mix with the eggs while beating them. Cook the omelette like a pancake.

Spiny lobster omelette (Crawfish omelette). OMELETTE À LA LANGOUSTE—Prepare a *Shrimp omelette** using a *salpicon** of spiny lobster, bound with a sauce flavoured with Spiny lobster butter.

Spring onion omelette. OMELETTE À LA CIBOULETTE—Add some chopped spring onions to the eggs while beating them. Make the omelette in the usual manner.

Sweet corn omelette. OMELETTE AU MAIS À LA CRÈME—Fill the omelette with *Fresh corn in cream* (see CORN) and serve with a ring of *Cream sauce* (see SAUCE).

Sweet pimento omelette. OMELETTE AUX PIMENTS DOUX—Add to the eggs, while beating them, some sweet pimentos (green, yellow or red), peeled, coarsely shredded and cooked in oil. Fry a pancake omelette.

This omelette, which is usually fried in oil, may be spiced with a pinch of pounded garlic.

Sweet potato omelette. OMELETTE AUX PATATES—Prepare as *Omelette Parmentier*, using sweet potatoes fried in butter.

Swiss omelette. OMELETTE À LA SUISSE—Beat the eggs, add some grated Emmenthal cheese and cream and make a flat omelette.

Omelette à la Talleyrand—Add to the eggs, while beating them, some diced onions, lightly fried in butter seasoned with a pinch of curry powder. Cook a flat omelette. Garnish it with slices of calf's sweetbreads, dipped in egg and breadcrumbs and sautéed in butter. Serve with a ring of *Cream sauce* (see SAUCE).

Tomato omelette. OMELETTE AUX TOMATES—Prepare like *Omelette à la provençale*. The garlic seasoning may be omitted.

Truffle omelette. OMELETTE AUX TRUFFES—Add to the eggs, while beating them, some truffles cut in dice and lightly tossed in butter. Make the omelette in the usual manner.

Garnish with slivers of truffles tossed in butter. Serve with a ring of *Demi-glace sauce* (see SAUCE) flavoured with Madeira and truffle essence.

Two-coloured omelette. OMELETTE PANACHÉE—Make a 3-egg creamy omelette (i.e. keeping the interior semi-liquid), using beaten eggs mixed with a rather thick spinach purée, or equally thick tomato pulp, or any other ingredient which can lend colour to the eggs.

Make another omelette, using 6 eggs. When folding this omelette, put the smaller one inside it. Arrange the omelette on a long dish. Surround with a ring of *White*, *Brown* or *Tomato sauce* (see SAUCE).

Vegetable marrow (zucchini) omelette. OMELETTE AUX COURGETTES—This can be made flat or fluffy.

Flat. Cut the marrows into thin slices and sauté in butter. Beat the eggs with chopped parsley, season with salt and pepper and pour over the marrows. Cook the omelette as a pancake.

Fluffy. Add the marrows, diced and sautéed in butter (or oil) and chopped parsley to the eggs. Make the omelette in the usual manner.

Omelette à la verdurière—Add to the eggs, while beating them, a *chiffonnade** of sorrel and lettuce, melted in butter, and some chopped parsley, chervil and tarragon. Make a flat omelette. Sprinkle with *Noisette butter* (see BUTTER, *Compound butters*).

Omelette viveur—Fry 2 diced artichoke hearts (previously cooked in a *court-bouillon**) briskly in clarified butter. Remove from the pan and in the same butter quickly fry 2 tablespoons of celeriac (turnip-rooted celery), cut in large dice and blanched in salted water. Drain the celeriac. In the same butter quickly fry 3 ounces of fillet of beef, well trimmed, cut into dice and seasoned with salt and paprika.

Put the artichokes and the celeriac back into the pan and mix. Beat the eggs with chopped parsley and chervil and pour into the same pan. Make a flat omelette.

SWEET (DESSERT) OMELETTES.
OMELETTES D'ENTREMETS:—

Omelette à la Célestine—This omelette, which used to be very popular in the past, is really a group of three small omelettes, filled with apricot jam, arranged in a row on a long dish, sprinkled with castor (fine) sugar and glazed in a hot oven.

Omelette à la dijonnaise—Beat the eggs with sugar, finely crushed macaroons and fresh, double (heavy) cream. Make two flat omelettes. Put one on a round, ovenproof dish, spread with a layer of very thick *French pastry cream* (see CREAM), mixed with ground almonds and flavoured with black currant jam, and cover with the second omelette. Cover the top and the sides with meringue. Sprinkle with icing sugar, glaze quickly in a very hot oven and serve with a ring of blackcurrant jam.

Frangipane omelette. OMELETTE À LA FRANGIPANE—Beat 10 eggs with 3 tablespoons of sugar, 2 tablespoons of melted butter, ½ cup (1 decilitre) of cream and a small pinch of salt.

Using these eggs, make 10 small flat omelettes. When cooked, put them on a baking sheet. Spread each one with a layer of *Frangipane* (see CREAM), fold, cut off the ends, sprinkle with fine sugar, glaze quickly in a very hot oven and serve heaped on a dish.

Jam omelette. OMELETTE AUX CONFITURES—Prepare like *Jam and fruit omelette*, replacing the fruit by rather thick jam.

Jam and fruit omelette. OMELETTE À LA CONFITURE ET AUX FRUITS—Beat the eggs, seasoned with fine sugar and a small pinch of salt. Fry the omelette in butter in the usual manner. When folding, put in the fruit indicated in the individual recipes—usually fruit cooked *en compote* (in vanilla-flavoured syrup), drained, bound with a jam suitable for the fruit and flavoured with some liqueur. Arrange the omelette on a long dish, sprinkle with fine sugar, and make a criss-cross pattern by applying a red hot glazing iron or pass quickly under the grill.

Liqueur omelette flambée. OMELETTE AUX LIQUEURS FLAMBÉE—*Rum omelette* is the prototype of these omelettes.

Beat the eggs, seasoned with sugar and a small pinch of salt and cook the omelette in butter, as usual, keeping it very creamy (i.e. semi-liquid inside). Sprinkle with fine sugar, pour over sufficient warmed rum and set it alight at the moment of serving.

Note. In the same way omelettes can be made with armagnac, calvados, cognac, whisky, kirsch and other spirits distilled from various fruit, such as plums, raspberries, mirabelles, and all sorts of other fruit liqueurs.

Normandy apple omelette. OMELETTE À LA NORMANDE—Beat the eggs with sugar and fresh cream. When ready fold in the following composition:

Norwegian omelette or Baked Alaska (*Robert Carrier*)

For a 10-egg omelette: Cut 3 cooking apples into quarters, peel, slice into fairly big slices and cook in butter with vanilla-flavoured sugar. As soon as the apples are cooked, add 4 tablespoons of fresh double cream; cook to the desired consistency and flavour with 2 tablespoons of calvados.

Glaze the omelette with a red hot glazing iron (or under the grill) and surround with a ring of fresh double (heavy) cream.

Norwegian omelette (U.S. Baked Alaska). OMELETTE À LA NORVÉGIENNE—It is said that the invention of the surprise omelette, called '*à la norvégienne*', is attributed to an American-born physicist called Benjamin Thompson whose work in England earned him the title of Count Benjamin Thompson Rumford. This omelette was launched into popularity about 1895, at the Hotel de Paris in Monte Carlo, by Jean Giroix, who was then in charge of the kitchens there.

If, however, we are to believe the culinary column of the *Liberté*, in which Baron Brisse wrote on 6th June 1866, it was the master-cook of the Chinese Mission, visiting Paris at the time who, if not invented, at least popularised this paradoxical omelette, which combines the cold and the hot. Here is what Baron Brisse wrote on the subject:

'During the stay of the Chinese Mission in Paris, the master-cooks of the Celestial Empire have exchanged civilities and information with the chefs of the Grand-Hotel. (The Grand-Hotel was opened in 1862 and its first chef was called Balzac.)

'The French chef in charge of sweet courses is particularly delighted with this circumstance. He has learnt from his Chinese colleague *the method of baking vanilla and ginger ices in the oven.*

'Here is how to proceed with this delicate operation:

'Chill the ice until hard, wrap each in a very light pastry crust and put in the oven.

'The pastry is baked before the ice protected by the pastry shell can melt. This phenomenon is explained by poor conductibility of certain substances.

'The gourmets can thus give themselves the double pleasure of biting through piping hot crust and cooling the palate on contact with fragrant ices.'

Preparation. Put an oval-shaped piece of Genoese cake $\frac{3}{4}$ inch (2 centimetres) thick on a long dish, sprinkle with liqueur (kirsch, maraschino or any other), and place the ice, appropriately flavoured, a cream ice or a fruit ice, on the cake.

Cover the ice completely with a layer of ordinary *meringue** (or *Italian meringue*). Smooth over the meringue, decorate the omelette by piping some of the meringue mixture through a forcing (pastry) bag and sprinkle with icing sugar. Bake in a very hot oven so that the meringue becomes golden very quickly without allowing the heat to penetrate through the ice.

Note. The piece of cake is often spread with a *salpicon** of fruit.

Norwegian omelette with pineapple. OMELETTE À LA NORVEGIENNE À L'ANANAS—Proceed as described in the recipe for *Norwegian omelette* using pineapple ice cream and pineapple cooked in syrup, cut in dice and steeped in kirsch, as a filling.

Omelette Reine Pédauque—Beat the eggs with powdered sugar, fresh cream and some ground almonds and make two flat omelettes. Put one of these in an oven-proof dish. Spread it with a thick layer of apple purée, mixed with fresh cream and flavoured with kirsch. Cover with the second omelette and then cover the whole with a layer of meringue. Sprinkle with icing sugar and put in a very hot oven until the meringue sets and is golden.

Soufflé omelette. OMELETTE SOUFFLÉE—In the olden days soufflé omelette mixture used to be cooked in a frying pan like an ordinary omelette. In present day culinary practice, a soufflé omelette is much more of a soufflé than an omelette. Instead of being cooked in a special timbale, it is baked in a long dish. The mixture is prepared as follows:

Blend $1\frac{1}{4}$ cups (250 grams) of powdered sugar and 6 yolks of eggs (with the flavouring indicated: vanilla, or grated lemon or orange rind) in a bowl, until the mixture turns white and forms a ribbon.

Beat 8 whites of egg into a very stiff froth and fold in gently into the above mixture.

Preparation. Butter a long, oven-proof dish, sprinkle it with fine sugar, pour in the omelette mixture, piling it into a dome shape. Smooth the surface with the blade of a knife. Decorate the omelette by piping some of the mixture, kept specially for this purpose, through a forcing bag with a plain nozzle. Sprinkle with fine sugar and bake in a very hot oven. The cooking time depends on the size of the omelette. Sprinkle with icing sugar and, at the last moment, glaze in a very hot oven.

This omelette may be flavoured with coffee, chocolate or various liqueurs.

Strawberry omelette. OMELETTE AUX FRAISES—Make an omelette, beating the eggs with sugar, a small pinch of salt and a little cream. Fold in the strawberries, previously steeped in rum or kirsch and sugar.

Sprinkle the omelette with fine sugar and glaze under the grill (broiler). Surround with crushed strawberries, sprinkled with sugar and flavoured with liqueur.

Omelette with sugar. OMELETTE AU SUCRE—Beat the eggs together with the sugar and a very small pinch of salt and cook as an ordinary omelette. Sprinkle it with fine sugar and either make a criss-cross pattern with a special glazing iron or glaze under a grill. Flavour, as desired, with grated orange, lemon or tangerine rind.

FISHES' EGGS. OEUFS DE POISSONS—Eggs of certain kinds of fish are used as food. The most highly esteemed are those of the sturgeon and sterlet, which are used for preparing *Caviare;* and those of salmon, which are used for preparing *Red caviare;* and those of mullet, from which the *Poutargue* is made. Other edible fishes' eggs include those of the shad (Shad Roe), of which the Americans are very fond, and those of fresh or pickled herring (Herring Roe), which are quite delicate in taste. The eggs of various crustaceans are also frequently eaten.

LAPWING AND PLOVER EGGS. OEUFS DE VANNEAU ET DE PLUVIER—These eggs are a little bigger than pigeons' eggs. The shell is pale green with small black spots.

They are greatly prized by some gastronomes, not for their gustative qualities, which are in no way superior to those of hen's eggs, but because of their rarity.

When they appear on the market in France, at the beginning of spring, lapwing and plover eggs are sold at very high prices.

Lapwing and plover eggs can be prepared in any way suitable for ordinary eggs, but it is more usual to serve them hard boiled and cold, as an hors-d'oeuvre.

The sale of both these is forbidden in England and unknown in U.S.A.

Lapwing eggs in aspic. OEUFS DE VANNEAU EN ASPIC—Hard boil and shell the eggs. Put them point downwards into an aspic mould, coated with jelly and decorated with pieces of truffles, pickled tongue, tarragon leaves, etc. Put the mould on ice and fill with aspic jelly. Leave to set. Turn out on to a napkin-covered dish.

Lapwing eggs Brillat-Savarin. OEUFS DE VANNEAU BRILLAT-SAVARIN—Decorate the eggs (hard boiled, shelled and well dried), with pieces of truffles and coat with half-set jelly.

Arrange in baked barquettes filled with *Crayfish mousse**. Arrange on a napkin.

Lapwing eggs Cambacérès. OEUFS DE VANNEAU CAMBACÉRÈS—Put the eggs, points downwards, into individual dariole moulds, coated with jelly and decorated, on bottom and walls, with crayfish tails and truffle. Fill the moulds with jelly and leave on ice to set.

Turn out the eggs, placing each on an artichoke heart (cooked in *court-bouillon**), filled with green asparagus tips and seasoned with oil and vinegar. Arrange on a round dish and garnish with chopped jelly.

Lapwing eggs Grimod-de-la-Reynière. OEUFS DE VANNEAU GRIMOD-DE-LA-REYNIÈRE—Hard boil the eggs, shell, dry on a cloth and coat with *White chaud-froid sauce* (see SAUCE). Decorate with truffles and spoon over some white jelly to glaze the decorations.

Arrange each in a baked barquette, and fill with diced truffles, dressed with gelatine-strengthened mayonnaise. Surround the eggs with peeled pink shrimp tails. Serve on a napkin-covered dish.

Hard boiled lapwing eggs. OEUFS DE VANNEAU DURS—Put the eggs into boiling water and allow 8 minutes' cooking time from the moment boiling is re-established.

Drain the eggs, dip in cold water and shell.

Note. After having been cooked in this manner, the albumen of these eggs takes on a milky colour and always remains a little soft.

When served as hors-d'oeuvre, these eggs should be half shelled and arranged in a watercress nest.

Lapwing eggs in nests. OEUFS DE VANNEAU AU NID—Arrange the eggs, hard boiled and shelled, in a nest made of *Montpellier butter* (see BUTTER, *Compound butters*), piped through a forcing (pastry) bag with a small round nozzle. Garnish with chopped jelly.

Princess lapwing eggs. OEUFS DE VANNEAU PRINCESSE—Hard boil the eggs, shell, dry on a cloth and coat with white, sherry-flavoured *Chaud-froid sauce* (see SAUCE). Decorate with pieces of truffles and glaze with jelly. Arrange each in a baked barquette, filled with asparagus tips seasoned with oil and vinegar.

Surround the eggs with a ring of chopped jelly.

Note. All the recipes given above for lapwing eggs are applicable to plover eggs.

Pigeon, ring-dove and other birds' eggs are prepared in the same way.

Lapwing eggs are rarely served hot. An omelette made of lapwing eggs would be too heavy a dish.

REPTILES' EGGS, TURTLE EGGS. OEUFS DE REPTILES, OEUFS DE TORTUE—Reptiles' eggs are very little used in European cookery. They are, however, much prized by the Arabs and the Indians, who are particularly fond of the cayman's eggs.

EGG-PLANT—See AUBERGINE.

EGG-TIMER. SABLIER—A small glass utensil made of two bulbous containers narrowing in the middle where they communicate by means of a very small opening.

One of the containers contains a fixed quantity of sand, which, when the utensil is turned upside down, passes into the other container, taking 3 minutes to do so—the ordinary time taken to boil an egg.

EGLANTINE, DOG-ROSE. ÉGLANTIER—A wild rose bush. The hips of this plant are red, ovoid and elongated and contain a dozen small hairy ossicles.

The pulp of these hips has astringent properties and is used to make jam.

Dog-rose hip preserve is still sometimes used for chronic diarrhoea. It is prepared by steeping the hips, with the seeds and hair scraped out, in white wine and cooking the pulp in 1½ times its weight in sugar.

EGYPTIAN LOTUS. NELUMBO—An aquatic plant also known as *Nile lily*. This magnificent plant, which was the sacred lotus of Ancient Egypt, is now no longer found on the Nile, but it still grows in India and China. Its leaves and roots are edible. Its fruit contains up to 30 kernels which are very delicate in flavour.

ELDERBERRY GOURILOS. MOELLE DE SUREAU—Green elderberry stalks, after paring away all the woody outer casing, can be cooked in the same way as artichoke stalks or endive stumps. (See CHICORY.)

ELEPHANT—Elephant meat is edible but leathery. The trunk and feet of elephant are regarded as great delicacies.

ELIXIR—A liquid manufactured by dissolving various elements in alcohol or wine containing a high proportion of alcohol. The Old Codex Pharmacopoeia included a large number of formulae for elixirs. Some of these have come down to us. The present Codex includes only 6, among which are elixir of cola, elixir of *garus* and the elixir of the *Grande Chartreuse*.

Elixir of cola. ÉLIXIR DE COLA—*Ingredients*. 1⅝ ounces (50 grams) of fluid extract of cola; 3⅛ ounces (100 grams) of alcohol 60° proof; 3⅛ ounces (100 grams) of plain syrup and 25 ounces (750 grams) of Lunel wine.

Elixir of Garus. ÉLIXIR DE GARUS—Steep for 2 days in 32 ounces (1 kilo) of spirits of *Garus* 1 gram of vanilla and 50 centigrams of saffron.

Infuse for half an hour in 16 ounces (500 grams) of boiling water, ⅝ ounce (20 grams) of Canadian maidenhair fern. Add 6⅝ ounces (200 grams) of distilled orange flower water and 2 pounds (1 kilo) of white sugar. Mix this syrup. Add the spirits to it. Leave to cool and filter.

Elixir of the Grande Chartreuse. ÉLIXIR DE LA GRANDE CHARTREUSE—Steep the following for 8 days in 11 quarts (10 litres) of alcohol: fresh melissa and hyssop leaves, 21 ounces (620 grams) of each; 10⅝ ounces (320 grams) of angelica leaves; 5⅓ ounces (160 grams) of cinnamon pod; mace and saffron, 1⅓ ounces (40 grams) of each. Distil. Add 5¼ cups (1,260 grams) of white sugar.

ELK. ÉLAN—A wild ruminant found in northern Europe. The elk is the largest stag now in existence.

It is edible. All recipes for stag and fallow deer are suitable for elk. (See DEER and FALLOW DEER.)

EMBONPOINT—Etymologically, this word indicates a degree of corpulence in which fat is in proportion to size, but it is now commonly used as a euphemism for slight obesity. Connoisseurs of good food are proud of their '*embonpoint*', but, whatever their weight may be, they will never admit to being fat.

ÉMINCÉ—A dish made with left-over roast or braised meat. The meat, thinly sliced, is put in an ovenware dish and covered with some sauce or other, such as *Bordelaise*, *Mushroom*, *Chasseur*, *Italian*, *Piquante*, *Poivrade*, *Robert*, *Tomato*, etc. (See SAUCE.)

These slices of meat must be heated only in the sauce poured over them, and the dish *must not boil*, especially if roast meat is used.

Beef, roebuck, mutton or lamb are most commonly used for this dish. It is sometimes made with poultry.

Émincés of beef with bordelaise sauce. ÉMINCÉS DE BOEUF SAUCE BORDELAISE—Arrange the slices of beef on a dish. Garnish with strips of poached beef bone-marrow. Cover with *Bordelaise sauce* (see SAUCE).

Émincés of beef chasseur. ÉMINCÉS DE BOEUF CHASSEUR—Arrange the slices of beef on a long dish. Cover with boiling *Chasseur sauce* (see SAUCE).

Émincés of beef à l'italienne. ÉMINCÉS DE BOEUF À L'ITALIENNE—Proceed as for *Émincés of beef chasseur*, covering the meat with *Italian sauce* (see SAUCE).

Émincés of beef à la lyonnaise. ÉMINCÉS DE BOEUF À LA LYONNAISE—Proceed as for *Émincés of beef chasseur*, covering the meat with *Lyonnaise sauce* (see SAUCE).

Émincés of beef with mushrooms. ÉMINCÉS DE BOEUF AUX CHAMPIGNONS—Arrange the slices of beef on a long dish. Put whole or sliced mushrooms, tossed in butter, on top of the slices. Cover with boiling *Madeira sauce* (see SAUCE).

Émincés of beef with piquante sauce. ÉMINCÉS DE BOEUF SAUCE PIQUANTE—Proceed as for *Émincés of beef chasseur*, covering the meat with *Piquante sauce* (see SAUCE).

Émincés of beef with Poivrade sauce. ÉMINCÉS DE BOEUF SAUCE POIVRADE—Proceed as for *Émincés of beef chasseur*, covering the meat with *Poivrade sauce* (see SAUCE).

Émincés of beef with Robert sauce. ÉMINCÉS DE BOEUF SAUCE ROBERT—Proceed as for *Émincés of beef chasseur*, covering the meat with *Robert sauce* (see SAUCE).

Émincés of beef with tomato sauce. ÉMINCÉS DE BOEUF SAUCE TOMATE—Proceed as for *Émincés of beef chasseur*, covering the meat with *Tomato sauce* (see SAUCE).

After being covered with the sauce indicated, émincés can be garnished in various ways. The garnishes most suited to these dishes are: sauté potatoes, green vegetables tossed in butter or cream; braised vegetables; purées of pulses and chestnuts; *pasta* of various kinds, pilaf of rice and risotto.

Émincés of mutton or lamb. ÉMINCÉS DE MOUTON, D'AGNEAU—Proceed as for *Émincés of beef*, using left-over roast or braised mutton or lamb.

These *émincés* can be prepared *à la bordelaise;* with mushrooms; *au chausseur; à l'italienne; à la lyonnaise;* with *Piquante sauce; Poivrade sauce; Robert sauce; Tomato sauce.* (See SAUCE.)

Émincés of pork. ÉMINCÉS DE PORC—Proceed, using slices of left-over pork, as for *Émincés of beef.*

Émincés of poultry. ÉMINCÉS DE VOLAILLE—Make with thin slices of left-over poultry, roast or poached. All methods of serving *Émincés of beef* are suitable for *Émincés of poultry*. They can also be covered with white sauces, such as *Cream sauce; Curry* (in this case, served with *Rice à l'indienne**); *Suprême; Ravigote; Hongroise.* (See SAUCE.)

Émincés of roebuck. ÉMINCÉS DE CHEVREUIL—Proceed, using slices of left-over roast roebuck, as for *Émincés of mutton.*

Émincés of roebuck and other ground game can be covered with all sauces especially suitable for ground game, e.g. *Grand veneur*, *Romaine.* (See SAUCE.)

Émincés of veal. Émincés de veau—Prepared, à *brun*, like *Émincés of beef*, *à blanc*, like *Émincés of poultry*.

ÉMINCER—A term in French cookery meaning to slice meat, vegetables or fruit very finely. Carrots and turnips are finely sliced for a *paysanne* preparation. Mushrooms are finely sliced to be sautéed in butter. Finely sliced potatoes, apples, etc. are also said to be *émincé*.

EMPOTAGE—A term in French cookery designating all the ingredients put in a braising pan. The French talk of the meat and vegetables of the *empotage*.

EMPOTER—French term meaning to put various ingredients in a stockpot or braising pan.

EMULSION—A liquid of milky appearance containing minute drops of oil or fat in more or less stable suspension.

Emulsions have greater stability when the liquid is slightly alkaloid and proteid, with a somewhat viscous consistency. Milk, for instance, is an emulsion of cream globules.

The name emulsion is also given in cookery to a mixture of oil or butter with yolks of egg, such as mayonnaise or hollandaise sauce.

Plain almond emulsion or milk of almonds. EMULSION SIMPLE D'AMANDES, LAIT D'AMANDES—$1\frac{2}{3}$ ounces (50 grams) blanched sweet almonds, 3 tablespoons (50 grams) white sugar, 1 quart (litre) distilled water, (codex formula).

Pound the almonds with the sugar and a little water in a marble mortar to the consistency of a very smooth paste. Dilute this paste with the rest of the water. Rub through a cloth.

ENDAUBAGE—A term used in French cookery designating the supplementary ingredients used in the braising of meat.

ENDIVE AND CHICORY
1. Louviers endive (U.S. chicory) **2.** Barbe-de-Capucin (wild chicory) **3.** Chicory (U.S. Belgian endive) **4.** Endive (U.S. chicory, escarole)

ENDIVE (U.S. CHICORY). CHICORÉE—A genus of plants cultivated for its leaves, and of which the two principal species, *Wild chicory* and *Garden chicory*, provide a very large number of varieties in cultivation.

Wild chicory, which grows of its own accord in meadows and in hedgerows, is hardly ever eaten except in salad. Even then it is better to cut it into narrow strips to make it easier to eat. This salad, very bitter, is quite appreciated. It is eaten in the spring.

Wild chicory improved by cultivation produces fleshy and tender leaves. These are eaten in salads but can be braised or stewed in butter, in the same way as indicated in the following recipes for *endive*.

There is great confusion about the names *Endive* and *Chicory*. In England *endive* usually means the curly-leaved salad plant, which is generally called *chicory* in the U.S.A. What the French and Americans call *endive* or *Belgian endive* is called chicory in England. To add to the confusion, the two words are sometimes used interchangeably in both England and in America. For the sake of clarity we are giving preference to the English usage.

Endive (U.S. chicory) with béchamel sauce. CHICORÉE À LA BÉCHAMEL—Braise in beef stock or cook in salted boiling water. Add to the cooked endive at the last moment some tablespoons of *Béchamel sauce* (see SAUCE) and some fresh butter. Arrange in a vegetable dish.

Braised endive (U.S. chicory). CHICORÉE BRAISÉE AU GRAS—Remove the leaves which are too hard or too green. Cut the rest from the stump. Wash the leaves in several waters. Drain them and blanch for 10 minutes in rapidly boiling salted water.

Drain, put under the cold tap, press the endive, and chop it up very fine.

Put it in a casserole in which a white *roux** has been made. For 1 pound (500 grams) of endive use 3 tablespoons (40 grams) of butter and 3 tablespoons (50 grams) of flour; season with salt, pepper, sugar and grated nutmeg. Moisten with 2 cups (6 decilitres) of consommé, or white stock; mix; bring to the boil on top of the stove and then put the casserole in the oven and cook covered for an hour and a half.

Finish in the manner indicated in the recipe.

Buttered endive (U.S. chicory). CHICORÉE AU BEURRE—Braise in beef stock or cook in salted boiling water. Add to the cooked endive at the last moment 3–5 tablespoons (50 to 80 grams) of butter for every pound (500 grams) of vegetable. Arrange in a vegetable dish.

Endive (U.S. chicory) with cream. CHICORÉE À LA CRÈME—Cooked in the same way as *Chicory in butter**. Finish with ½ cup (1½ decilitres) fresh cream.

Cream of endive (U.S. chicory) soup. POTAGE CRÈME DE CHICORÉE—See SOUPS AND BROTHS.

Endive (U.S. chicory) à la flamande. CHICORÉE À LA FLAMANDE—Trim and wash the endive, blanch it, drain it and simmer it in butter without chopping it up. Finish in the same way as for *Endive with cream.**

Endive (U.S. chicory) au gratin. CHICORÉE AU GRATIN—Put the braised endive in a fireproof oven dish covered with some *Béchamel sauce* (see SAUCE). Sprinkle with grated cheese and pour over some melted butter. Brown gently in the oven.

Endive (U.S. chicory) au jus. CHICORÉE AU JUS—Braise the endive in good beef stock on a foundation of sliced root vegetables (carrots, onions etc.). Strain the reduced liquor in which the endive has been cooked and add to it at the last moment some spoonfuls of very rich veal stock.

Endive (U.S. chicory) loaf. PAIN DE CHICORÉE—Combine 1 pound (500 grams) of *Braised endive* with 3 beaten eggs. Season with salt, pepper and nutmeg. Mix well.

Put this preparation in a buttered mould. Cook in a pan of hot water or bain-marie in the oven for 25 minutes.

Allow it to rest for a few moments before turning it out on to a round dish.

Cover with *Allemande sauce** or with *Cream sauce* (see SAUCE).

Endive (U.S. chicory) au maigre. CHICORÉE ÉTUVÉE AU MAIGRE—Blanch the endive; put it in a colander under the cold tap; drain and dry it.

Put it in a pan with 3 tablespoons (50 grams) of butter for every pound (500 grams) of endive. Season. Moisten with about 2 cups (5 or 6 decilitres) of water, and cook in the oven covered for an hour and a half.

Finish according to instructions in the recipe.

A white *roux** of flour and butter can be added.

Endive (U.S. chicory) purée. PURÉE DE CHICORÉE—Rub braised or stewed endive through a sieve. Add *Béchamel sauce*, thick *Velouté sauce* (see SAUCE), or very rich veal gravy, or fresh butter, according to the recipe. Arrange in a vegetable dish.

In order to improve the consistency of this purée one can add a third or a quarter of its weight of potato purée.

Endive (U.S. chicory) salad. SALADE DE CHICORÉE—See SALAD.

Endive (U.S. chicory) soufflé. SOUFFLÉ DE CHICORÉE—Put ½ pound (250 grams) of braised endive, which has been cooked in beef stock or *au maigre* (in butter and water) through a sieve. Combine with 3 egg yolks; season with salt, pepper and nutmeg, and at the last moment incorporate 3 well beaten egg whites.

Pour into a buttered soufflé dish; smooth the surface and cook in the oven (400°F.) for 15 to 18 minutes. Serve at once.

Endive (U.S. chicory) soufflé with Parmesan. SOUFFLÉ DE CHICORÉE AU PARMESAN—Made in the same way as *Endive soufflé*. Add ½ cup (50 grams) of grated Parmesan to the soufflé.

Little endive (U.S. chicory) soufflés (hot hors d'oeuvre). PETITS SOUFFLÉS DE CHICORÉE—The same as above. Put the preparation into little individual soufflé dishes of porcelain, metal or paper. Cook in the oven (400°F.) for 8 to 10 minutes.

Endive (U.S. chicory) subrics. SUBRICS DE CHICORÉE—Prepared with *Braised endive* in the same way as *Spinach subrics**.

Gourilos

ENDIVE (U.S. CHICORY) GOURILOS. MOELLE DE CHICORÉE—The stumps of curly endive are often called *moelles* in France, but they are also known as *gourilos*.

Blanch in salt water containing lemon or vinegar and drain well. After blanching, endive stumps can be prepared in various ways: cooked in butter or cream in a covered pan; fried; in *fritots**; grilled; *à la grecque**; curried; sautéed, etc. For recipes see CHICORY GOURILOS.

ENGLISH COOKERY. CUISINE ANGLAISE—The essence of English cookery lies in choosing ingredients of the finest quality and cooking them so that their flavour and texture are fully developed. This is done with the minimum addition of ingredients to mask the fine natural taste of the original food.

England has long been a producer of beef, mutton, lamb, pork, pheasant, grouse, partridge, duck, salmon, sole, plaice, turbot, halibut, butter and cheese, etc. of a quality unsurpassed anywhere else in the world. Dishes from these prime materials cooked by roasting, grilling, frying or baking can be relied on to give food which is not only good to eat but is also easily digested. These foods are more suitable for service in the home than the restaurant because deterioration takes place rapidly if kept even for a short time after cooking. A first-class English cuisine is therefore, only possible in a restaurant with good *à la carte* service.

Puddings, pies and tarts are another important aspect of English cooking. A great number of different recipes for baked, boiled and steamed puddings made mainly from flour, fat, eggs and fruit are given in any English basic cookery book—in fact the variety of puddings available is probably greater than in any other country in the world. The main meal of the day usually includes a cooked second course, which may be one of these puddings or one with milk as the main ingredient, such as rice pudding, or it may be a pie or tart having pastry as one of its main ingredients.

Cakes, scones and biscuits constitute a basic part of English cookery, eaten usually at the tea meal in the late afternoon. There are many varieties, a number of which are fairly plain, having a smaller proportion of fat, sugar and eggs than those of other countries. Another basic constituent of the tea meal is thinly sliced brown or white bread and butter.

Vegetable cookery is not a highly developed art in England. As long ago as the eighteenth century foreigners said that English cooks seemed incapable of turning out a good vegetable dish. A German named Moritz in 1872 wrote of his landlady's meal that 'An English dinner for such lodgers as I am, generally consists of a piece of half-boiled or half-roasted meat, and a few cabbage leaves boiled in plain water, on which they pour a sauce made of flour and butter.' It is very usual for a main meal to include potatoes as one of the two vegetables served, both of which are cooked by boiling in plenty of water.

Popular dishes for which England is justly famous include pork pies, the best ones being made in the Midlands; bacon and egg—thin smoked back rashers lightly fried and served with slices of bread crisply fried and a lightly fried egg—a delicious dish whether served for breakfast, lunch or supper; Lancashire hotpot—a stew of meat, potatoes and onions cooked slowly for a long period in the oven; Cornish pasties—diced lamb, potato and shredded onion cooked in individual cases of short pastry and served either hot as part of the main meal or cold as a snack or picnic dish. Other delicious specialities are Christmas pudding, mince pies, stew with dumplings, Welsh rarebit, Yorkshire pudding, steak and kidney pudding, and kippers, particularly those cured in wood smoke for which the Isle of Man is famous.

ENTRECÔTE—This term in French means literally 'between the ribs', and is used of a steak taken between two ribs of beef.

The term is also used for a slice taken from the *contre-filet* or faux filet of beef, but a true *entrecôte* is that cut between the ribs.

This cut is usually grilled or fried. For various recipes, see BEEF.

ENTRECUISSE—A term in French cookery for the fleshy thigh of poultry or winged game. This is to distinguish it from the lower half of the leg or 'drumstick'.

ENTRE-DEUX-MERS—The name given in France (it means 'between two seas') to the area of Bordeaux situated between the Garonne and the Dordogne, and which stretches to the south-eastern boundary of the Gironde department and overlaps with the Lot-et-Garonne department.

White and red wines are made from the grapes grown in this region. Some of these enjoy a high reputation. Others are of poor quality but are used for the distillation of high-grade spirits.

ENTRÉE—Although in French the word *entrée* literally means 'beginning', it does not in the culinary sense mean *first course* as some people seem to believe. The *entrée* is the course which, in a full French menu, follows the *relevé* (remove) or intermediate course which, in its turn, follows the fish (or whatever dish may be served in place of it). In other words, the *entrée* is the third course.

This course is usually a dish served with a white or brown sauce. It can also be a cold dish. At a large formal dinner, it is usual to serve several *entrées*, which must be distinctly different from one another in character.

Finally, though this is unusual, the *entrée* may be made up of fish dishes with various garnishes and white or brown sauces.

Mixed *entrées*, that is to say composite dishes, can also be served.

Mixed entrées—Under this heading there is an infinite variety of dishes, the chief of these being casseroles of rice with various garnishes, hot pâtés made with poultry, game, meat and offal (variety meats), fish and shell-fish, pies, savoury tartlets and vol-au-vents. These entrées are served after the principal *entrées*.

ENTRELARDER—A French culinary term for cooking slices of meat with alternate layers of pork fat.

The term is especially used in the past participle to designate a joint of meat with plenty of intra-muscular fat. In this case, it is a synonym of streaky. See MEAT.

ENTREMETS—Literally *entremets* means 'between dishes'. In old French the term covered the *ensemble* of dishes which followed the roast, and included not only sweets but also vegetables.

In the fourteenth, fifteenth, sixteenth and seventeenth centuries, *entremets* meant not only food but also any kind of entertainment in the middle of the meal, provided by buffoons, minstrels, troubadours, acrobats, dancers and other performers. A special décor, often very elegant, was provided for this entertainment. This was made, not by cooks, but by special craftsmen and sometimes consisted of a papier mâché fortress or some other edifice.

Nowadays, the word *entremets* means sweets (desserts) and these are served in France after the cheese. Recipes for the main sweets in the modern repertoire are given under their names in alphabetical order.

Most sweets served nowadays fall into one of the following categories:

1. Batter sweets (crêpes, fritters, etc.).
2. Cooked creams and custards.
3. Egg sweets (sweet omelettes, etc.).
4. Fruit sweets (cooked or raw).
5. Ices and ice creams.
6. Meringue sweets.
7. Pastry sweets (tarts, pies, flans, etc.).
8. Puddings.
9. Rice and semolina sweets.
10. Whipped cream sweets.

EPERGNE. MÉNAGÈRE—A table-centre of 3, 4 or 8 glass, porcelain or metal bowls attached to an ornamental metal stem. In France, *epergnes* are still used as hors d'oeuvre sets for serving pickles such as gherkins, salted cucumbers, small pickled melons, capers and other similar delicacies. They can also be used for serving stewed fruit or iced *petits fours*.

ÉPIGRAMME—A common definition of *épigramme* is 'a white lamb stew in which some of the internal parts of the lamb are used'. *Épigramme* of lamb, however, is in no sense a stew, and the expression 'internal' parts might suggest that such organs as sweetbreads and kidneys are used. This is not so, however, since an *épigramme* is made with breast of lamb and cutlets (chops).

An *épigramme of lamb*, therefore, consists of two cuts, both cooked 'dry'. These two pieces are a slice of breast and a cutlet (chop). They are dipped in egg and breadcrumbs and grilled or fried. Instructions for the preparation of *épigrammes* are given under LAMB.

Philéas Gilbert explains the origins of the term *épigramme* as follows:

'It was towards the middle of the eighteenth century. One day when she was entertaining a large and elegant assembly at her table, a young and pretty marquise overheard one of her guests remark that when he was dining the previous evening with the Comte de Vaudreuil, he was charmingly received and, furthermore, had had a feast of excellent epigrams. The marquise, though pretty and elegant, was somewhat ignorant of the meaning of words.

'At once she summoned her master chef who, according to the story, was called Michelet.

' "Michelet", she said to him, "To-morrow, I shall require a dish of *épigrammes*!"

'The chef did not bat an eyelid. He withdrew pondering the problem deeply. He consulted his colleagues. He looked up old recipes, but found no reference to anything of the kind. None of his colleagues had ever heard of the said dish.

'But no French master-chef is ever at a loss. Since he could discover nothing about the dish he had been asked to prepare he set about to invent one. Next day, inspiration came and he created a most delicate dish.

'At dinner, the guests, who were the same as those present the night before, fell into ecstasies over the exquisite dish put before them and, after complimenting the lady of the house, desired to know its name. With perfect sang-froid the master chef replied "Épigrammes of lamb à la Michelet."

'Everyone laughed. The marquise was triumphant, though she could not understand the amusement of her guests. And, from that moment, the culinary repertoire of France was enriched by a name still used to this day.

'But whereas this name was originally used for slices of breast of lamb dipped in breadcrumbs, fried in butter and arranged in a circle (according to Tavenet) round a *blanquette* of lamb, by the end of the eighteenth century it had been completely transformed into what it is today, that is to say cutlets and slices of breast, dipped in egg and breadcrumbs and fried in butter or grilled.'

ÉPINE D'HIVER—The name of a winter pear. It is tender and fragrant to eat. (See PEAR).

ÉPINÉE—A French dialect name for chine of pork. (See PORK).

EPIPHANY. Épiphanie—Epiphany or Twelfth Night (known in France as the Feast of the Kings) is celebrated on January 6th. In France it is an occasion for great feasting.

Twelfth cake, the symbolic cake containing the traditional bean (or favour) is always eaten on Twelfth Night. It is made of risen dough either in the shape of a ring or a flaky pastry in the shape of a *galette*, according to the region.

ÉPONGER—A term in French cookery for the process of drying parboiled or boiled vegetables by putting them on a cloth after draining to get rid of all surplus moisture.

Some deep fried foods are drained in a cloth. This process is also known as *éponger*.

ERDBEERKUCHEN (German pastry)—A German strawberry tart. See TART, *Fruit tart à l'allemande*.

ERMITAGE WINE—This name is sometimes written with an 'H' (Hermitage). The wine, which is made in the Drôme department, enjoys a great reputation. There are both red and white Ermitage wines, made from grapes grown on the slopes of l'Ermitage in the commune of Tain on the left bank of the Rhône.

There are different types of soil in this area, and the vineyard is divided into 3 sections or *mas*, each very different in geological structure from the others. One, the *mas de Bossard*, is a granite slope, another, the *mas de Méal*, is alluvial soil, and the third, the *mas de Greffieux*, is clay.

Ermitage wine is perfect only when made from grapes from all three sections of the vineyard.

White Ermitage wine is a fine golden yellow. It has a fairly strong bouquet. The red wine, when it is young, is of a faded purple colour. It should be left to mature for a while, otherwise it tastes slightly bitter.

ERMITE—The name given in France to a very old wild boar which is also known as *solitaire*. The meat of old wild boar is leathery. Only young boar is eaten. In France, a young boar is known as a *marcassin* or *bête rousse*. (See WILD BOAR).

ERVY—A soft cheese made in the Champagne district. It is good to eat between November and May. It resembles Camembert.

ÉRYTHRIN—The generic name for several varieties of fish, rather thick and rounded in body with large heads and rounded jaws.

Three or four varieties are to be found in the lakes and rivers of hot countries.

This fish is excellent to eat. It is cooked in the same way as sea-perch.

ESCABÈCHE—See HORS-D'OEUVRE, *Cold hors-d'oeuvre*.

ESCALOPE, COLLOP—Slices of meat or fish of any kind flattened slightly and fried in butter or some other fat.

In former times the term was used of a dish of sliced meat, for instance, sliced mutton would be called *une escalope de mouton*.

ESCAROLE. Scarole—A variety of salad green with wide dark green leaves which are curled to a greater or lesser degree, sometimes blanched by being surrounded by earth or by being cultivated in cellars in the dark.

Escarole is chiefly eaten raw in salad, but can also be cooked in a great many ways.

All the methods of preparation given for *endive* and *chicory* are applicable to this variety.

Auguste Escoffier in front of a sugar model of Grosvenor House, London

ESCOFFIER, AUGUSTE—It was in 1847 at Villeneuve-Loubet, a charming little town in the Alpes-Maritimes, that Auguste Escoffier was born.

He was a very great cook and well deserved his title of 'the king of chefs and the chef of kings'. He was certainly greater than Carême. It was mainly in England that this master pursued his culinary art.

In 1890, in association with Ritz and Echenard, two great masters of the hotel business, he opened the Savoy Hotel in London. He remained in this illustrious establishment until 1898 when, for personal reasons, he gave up the direction of the Savoy kitchens to take charge of those of the Carlton Hotel, then one of the most famous in Europe.

It was while he was in charge of the Carlton kitchens that, as a reward for all he had done to enhance the prestige of French cooking throughout the world, Escoffier was made a Chevalier of the Legion of Honour in 1920. President Poincaré, then visiting London, handed him the Cross personally.

In 1928, Escoffier received the rosette of an Officer of the Legion. This was presented to him by President Herriot at a magnificent banquet held in his honour at the Palais d'Orsay in Paris.

Escoffier's culinary career was supremely brilliant. He was regarded as the emperor of the world's kitchens. This honorific title was conferred upon him by the Emperor William II, when this monarch spent some time on the steamer 'Imperator' of the Hamburg-America Line which Escoffier had joined to take charge of the imperial kitchens.

In the course of a conversation with Escoffier the Emperor, congratulating him, said: 'I am the Emperor of Germany, but you are the Emperor of chefs.'

Having started his career at the age of 12 (in 1859), Escoffier retired from active duties at the Carlton in London in 1921. He was then 74 years of age and had practised his art for 62 years. In all the history of cookery, there is no other example of such a long professional career.

Escoffier died in February, 1935. He was nearly 89 years old.

The culinary writings of Escoffier are works of authority. The best known are *Le Guide Culinaire*, written in collaboration with Philéas Gilbert and Émile Fetu; *Le Livre des Menus; Les Fleurs en cire; Ma Cuisine; Le Riz; Le Carnet d'Épicure.*

ESPAGNOLE—This is the name given in cooking to one of the basic brown sauces. It is also called *sauce-mère* (parent-sauce) which indicates that it can be used as a basis for a vast number of derivative brown sauces. Some gastronomes regard it as a somewhat inferior sauce, but this point of view seems quite unjustified when *Espagnole sauce* is made as it should be, and succulent in consequence.

Admittedly, it would be rather extravagant today to make a '*petite*' or '*demi-espagnole*' according to the recipe given by Carême. This is his recipe for what he called '*petite-espagnole*'.

'Take a deep saucepan, 7 inches across. Put in two slices of Bayonne ham three or four *lignes* thick. Place on top a *noix* of veal and two partridges. Add enough stock just to cover the veal only. Cover and put on a hot fire. When the liquid is reduced, cover the fire with red embers (or on a modern cooker, move it to the coolest part), to sweat the veal, so as to extract all the juice.

'This is necessary so as to increase the volume of the concentrated stock, which will result in a finer *espagnole*.

'Towards the end of the reduction of the stock, take great care not to leave it unattended, in case the resulting essence is scorched by the heat.

'Finally, when the stock is reduced to a coating on the bottom of the pan, that is to say, when there is practically none left, or rather when the little that is left begins to be almost imperceptibly tinged with gold, remove the pan from the stove, then prick the *noix* of veal with the point of a knife so that its juice mingles with the essence. Put the saucepan back on the stove on a low heat and leave it for about an hour. Then watch the essence as it gradually turns to a clear red colour.

'To simplify this operation, scrape off a little of the essence with the point of a knife. Roll it between the fingers. If it rolls into a ball, the essence is perfectly reduced. If it is not, it will stick the fingers together.

'Now, remove the saucepan from the stove and put it aside for a quarter of an hour for the essence to cool. It will then dissolve more readily. Next fill the saucepan with clear soup or stock and put it on the corner of the stove. As soon as it comes to the boil, and after having skimmed it, pour two ladles of it into the *roux*.'

Here, we must interpolate Carême's instructions for the preparation of this *roux*.

'Melt four ounces of butter and add to it sieved flour to make a rather liquid *roux*. Then put it on red-hot embers (or with a modern cooker, on a low heat or in the oven). Take care to stir it from time to time so that little by little the whole of the mixture turns a beautiful golden colour. When adding the liquid, do not forget that the *roux* must not be on the fire while you are mixing in the first spoonfuls of *espagnole* (or stock); but it should be put on the stove later, so that it may be added boiling hot to the rest of the stock.

'When the two ladles of stock are poured into the roux, stir it so as to turn this mixture into a perfectly smooth *espagnole*. Now pour it into the saucepan with the veal *noix*. Add a bouquet of parsley and spring onions, seasoned with half a bay leaf, a little thyme, two chives, and especially mushroom trimmings. Leave the *espagnole* to simmer on the corner of the stove. Stir it. After boiling for a full hour, skim off the fat. Half an hour later skim off the fat again.

'Rub through a tammy cloth into a bowl, stirring from time to time with a wooden spoon so that no skim forms on the surface, as easily happens when the sauce is exposed to the air'. (Extract from *Le pâtissier royal; Traité des entrées chaudes.*)

It must be admitted that nowadays this parent-sauce is made by a somewhat different method. But in good restaurants where this sauce is still used (though it is usually replaced by brown stock or veal concentrate), it is made with the same care as Carême prescribes.

Only the meat used in the preparation of the moistening stock is a little different from that indicated by Carême. Thus, a shoulder of veal is used instead of a *noix* and partridge is not used in the stock. See SAUCE, *Espagnole sauce*. See also DEMI-ESPAGNOLE.

ESQUIRE TRENCHANT—A servant or high dignitary officiating at ceremonial banquets.

In former times, in great households, the esquire trenchant was second to the major-domo in rank. In lesser households, the two offices were combined.

At Court, the arms of the Grand Carver, whose functions latterly were purely honorific, were supported by a crossed knife and fork with crowns at the end of each handle and fleurs-de-lys in saltire above.

The Queens of France also had their master-carvers but the title of Grand Carver was exclusive to the King's household.

ESSAI or ESSAY—The *Essai* at the French Royal Courts

was the ceremony of tasting the King's food and drink. The cups which were used for tasting wines etc. were also called *essais*.

The fear of poison, which, in the Middle Ages, was far from fantastic, gave rise to a complicated ceremonial attending the sovereign's meals. In France, this was minutely regulated by court etiquette, which continued with slight modifications up to the Revolution, to be revived under the Empire.

The knife, fork, spoon, toothpick, salt-cellar, spices and napkin were locked in the *cadenas* or *nef*, in those days part of the ceremonial silver.

In later times the *cadenas* (which had once been a worked casket) was merely a tray on which the sovereign's cutlery was laid. The *nef*, which was a piece of goldsmith's work, originally in the form of a ship, changed in appearance, but its use remained the same as long as the monarchy lasted. It held the Royal Napkin between two scented cushions, the salt-cellar, the spices and the cutlery.

The *nef* was carried in procession, escorted by two armed bodyguards and constantly watched by them, under the supervision of the *maître d'hôtel* (in those days a prince or high-ranking nobleman). All those present, whatever their rank, made way for the procession and knelt as it passed. The *nef* was laid either on the dining table itself or on the '*table du prêt*', where the tasting was done.

The cover could be lifted only by the almoner, and the napkin was always presented to the King by a prince.

The *maître d'hôtel* rubbed all the cutlery and the viands with balls of bread crumbs and caused them to be eaten before his eyes by the squires of the pantry, who, previously, had subjected to the same ordeal the servants who had handed them the dishes.

In earlier times, instead of bread, certain objects were used which, it was believed, had the property of changing colour or disintegrating when in contact with a poison. Among these objects, very expensive because of their rarity, are mentioned the tongue of a serpent (which was really nothing but a shark's tooth), certain precious stones and, above all, the horn of the fabulous unicorn, for which a narwhal's spike was used.

For drinks, the ceremonial was equally complicated. When the king called for a drink, the cup-bearer (who was not allowed to leave the table) made a sign to the wine-butler and his assistant. The first of these brought the wine in a flagon, and the king's glass, covered; the second, a silver jug full of water. Both these functionaries were escorted by guards. The cup-bearer took the glass and uncovered it; the wine-butler poured in the wine, then the water. The cup-bearer poured some of this watered wine into two little silver-gilt cups. He drank from one; the wine-butler drank from the other. Only then did the cup-bearer proffer the cup, now covered once more, across the table to the king. He did not uncover it until the very moment that the king was about to drink.

The same ceremonial took place for the queen, who also had a right to the *nef*. By special favour, Louis XIV bestowed the same prerogative upon the dauphine (the wife of the heir to the throne).

In some royal households, the cup or glass was fitted with a smaller vessel which was at the same time cover and taster.

When the king was entertained by one of his subjects, it was incumbent upon the host to comply with all the formalities of the *essai*, and it was a great mark of confidence (on the part of the sovereign) to dispense with them, as King Henry IV did for Mme. de Montpensier.

On the death of the sovereign, the *table de prêt*, with all the objects of the *essai*, were set next to the bed in which he lay.

ESSENCE—A liquid, usually oily and volatile, extracted by the distillation of vegetable substances in water: essence of anise, cinnamon, lemon, oranges, roses, etc.

Anchovy essence. ESSENCE D'ANCHOIS—A commercial product which is used in the preparation of *Anchovy butter* (see BUTTER, *Compound butters*) and to flavour certain sauces, stuffings, salads, etc.

Essence of bitter almonds. ESSENCE D'AMANDES AMÈRES—A product which is made and sold commercially.

Essence of chervil. ESSENCE DE CERFEUIL—Proceed as for *Essence of tarragon*, using chervil in place of tarragon.

Essence of fish. ESSENCE DE POISSON—For $2\frac{1}{2}$ cups (5 decilitres) put in a saucepan: 2 pounds (1 kilo) of bones and trimmings of sole, whiting, brill or other white fish; 1 small onion sliced (50 grams); $\frac{1}{2}$ cup (100 grams) of mushroom trimmings; a sprig of parsley and a few drops of lemon juice. Moisten with a quart (litre) of strained fish stock or essence and 1 cup (2 decilitres) of white wine.

Bring to the boil. Skim. Boil steadily for 30 to 35 minutes. Strain through muslin. Boil down (reduce) to half its volume.

This essence, which is fairly rich, is used for poaching fish or can be used, after concentrating, in the preparation of *Normande* and *White wine* sauces or other special sauces served with fish. See SAUCE.

Essence of game. ESSENCE DE GIBIER—Game stock reduced (cooked down) to the consistency of thick meat jelly.

Essence of garlic. ESSENCE D'AIL—Used to flavour certain dishes. It is made by pouring boiling white wine or vinegar on to crushed cloves of garlic. The liquid is strained and reduced.

Essence of mushrooms. ESSENCE DE CHAMPIGNONS—This is merely the liquid, greatly concentrated, in which mushrooms have been cooked. It is used to flavour sauces.

Essence of onion and shallot. ESSENCE D'OIGNON, D'ÉCHALOTE—These essences are made by infusing finely sliced onions or shallots in white wine or vinegar.

Essence of parsley. ESSENCE DE PERSIL—Proceed as for *Essence of tarragon*.

Essence of tarragon. ESSENCE D'ESTRAGON—An infusion of fresh tarragon in white wine or vinegar, strained and reduced.

Essence of tomato. ESSENCE DE TOMATES—Rub 1 pound (500 grams) of very ripe raw tomatoes through a fine sieve. Boil the pulp until it is reduced to half its volume. Rub through a sieve, pressing hard with a spoon. Boil this pulp again until it thickens to a syrupy consistency. Rub through muslin.

Cooked in this way, tomato pulp makes a kind of jelly which can be kept for several days.

It is used as an additional ingredient for sauces, stuffing and other mixtures.

Essence of truffles. ESSENCE DE TRUFFES—Made from truffle peelings infused in Madeira or any other heavy wine.

ESTAMINET—A name given in former times in France to cafés where patrons were permitted to smoke.

Nowadays, an *estaminet* is the frontage of a restaurant or café entirely open to the street; but in this sense the word is seldom used. It is more often used of a basement tavern.

ESTOUFFADE—(1) A dish whose ingredients are slowly stewed. (2) Clear brown stock used to dilute sauces and moisten braised meat and *ragoûts*. See STOCK.

ESTOUFFAT—A Languedoc dialect form of *étuvée* (dish stewed very slowly). In that region, it is mainly used to designate a stew of haricot (dry) beans and pork.

ÉTOUFFÉE—A method of cooking food in a tightly closed vessel with very little liquid or even without liquid, often called *à l'étuvée*.

ÉTOURDEAU—A name given in some parts of France to a young capon.

ÉTUVÉE (A L')—A method of cooking food. See ÉTOUFFÉE.

ÉTUVER—To cook food in covered pan, without moistening. This method of cooking is suitable for all kinds of meat, poultry, vegetables and fruit.

A suitable quantity of butter, fat or oil is added.

ÉVENT—The French name for the deterioration which is caused, especially in wine, by too long exposure to the air. The '*taste of évent*' is the washy flavour in wine which has lost its aroma through oxidation.

EVERLASTING PEA. JAROSSE, JAROUSSE—Popular name for the cultivated vetch. In France, it is also sometimes called *Auvergne lentil.*

EWE. BREBIS—In culinary practice, the flesh of a ewe, when young, is used as ordinary mutton. See MUTTON.

In some regions of south-western France, ewe's meat is pickled in the same way as pork.

EWER. AIGUIÈRE—A vessel intended to contain water for service at table. The word *Aiguière* comes from Old French *aigue*, i.e. water.

The existence of the ewer goes back to times of antiquity and although its shape, decoration, and the material from which it was made, varied with time, country and purpose for which it was intended, its essential forms have never changed much. In general, it is a vessel of elongated form, with a foot, a handle and a spout. To get an idea of the riches which the gold and silver smiths lavished on ewers destined for the tables of the French nobility from the twelfth to seventeenth century, one cannot do better than to read through the accounts and inventories of these noblemen, many of which were collected by Gay in his *Archeological Glossary*. Gold, precious stones and the finest enamels were destined for their manufacture. One of the most beautiful examples is in chased silver and was part of the treasure discovered in 1830 at Berthonville, near Bernay, in the Eure. It is kept in the museum of medals in the French *Bibliothèque Nationale*.

EXOCOETUS. EXOCET—This fish, commonly known as *flying-fish*, is edible. It is prepared in the same way as mackerel.

EXTRACT. EXTRAIT—A product obtained by evaporating animal or vegetable juice. According to the degree of evaporation a moist or dry extract can be obtained. The cooking stock of meat, reduced to a coating in the pan, is an extract.

The extracts most commonly used in great kitchens, other than extract of mixed meat, (*glace de viande*) are those of *beef, veal, poultry* and *game*.

Extracts of fish can also be made, but these are termed *essences* or *fumets*.

The term can be extended to cover concentrated vegetable essences. These play the same part in vegetarian cooking as meat extracts play in the cooking of meat. These concentrates are made from various root vegetables, and from mushrooms, tomatoes and truffles.

Among the vegetable extracts much used in the kitchen is soya sauce, which, if added to *coulis**, *ragoûts**, and other meat or vegetarian dishes, enhances their flavour without destroying their own particular taste. See SOYA.

Chicken extract. GLACE DE VOLAILLE—Reduce clear chicken stock in the same way as indicated in the recipe for *Meat extract II.*

Fish extract. GLACE DE POISSON—See ESSENCE, *Fish essence.*

Game extract. GLACE DE GIBIER—Reduce clear game stock in the same way as for *Meat extract II.*

Meat extract I (old recipe). GLACE DE VIANDE—Our forefathers knew how to make meat extracts. They compressed them into cubes and used them when required in the preparation of soups and sauces.

These meat extracts were, on the whole, much the same as those sold nowadays, but were made from various ingredients which might seem somewhat extravagant today. Here is a recipe for cubes of meat extract, 'easy to carry, and which will keep for a year or more.' It is taken from *Les Secrets de la nature et de l'art concernant les aliments* (1769).

'Take a quarter of a large beef carcase, a whole calf (or part of it only according to size), two sheep, two dozen old hens and cocks, or a dozen old turkeys, plucked and drawn. After all the fat has been removed from these animals, and the feet of the calves and sheep have been separately cleaned and scalded, put all the ingredients in a large boiler. Prepare a decoction of 12 to 14 pounds of ground hartshorn boiled in water and put through a press while it is still very hot. Add this to the boiling meat and poultry. Next, add 4 pails of well-water. Cover the boiler with a tight-fitting lid and seal the edges with flour and water paste. Place on top a 50 to 60 pound weight; let the ingredients simmer gently without skimming, for 6 hours or even longer if necessary, that is to say until they are sufficiently cooked for the meat to fall easily away from the bones. Now remove the largest carcases from the boiler, leaving the pot on the boil so that all the meat is kept as hot as possible. Chop up the meat as soon as it is taken out of the pot and put it in a large press fitted with hot iron plates, to extract all the juices. These operations must be carried out with the utmost possible speed. When all the meat has been through the press, add the extract to the hot stock in the boiler. Then, as quickly as possible, pour all the liquid through a large hair-sieve.'

Meat extract II (modern recipe). GLACE DE VIANDE—Reduce to half its volume 10 quarts (litres) of *brown stock*. Remove all fat and see that the stock is as clear as possible.

Strain this stock through muslin, and boil it down further; strain once more. Repeat this procedure until the stock is reduced to the required consistency, that is to say until it coats the back of a spoon. Skim it constantly at each successive stage of boiling. Each time it is strained, transfer the stock to a smaller saucepan and reduce the heat as the stock thickens.

Pour the extract into little jars and keep it in a cool place.

Meat extracts (commercially prepared). EXTRAITS DE VIANDE DU COMMERCE—These extracts, which are manufactured commercially, are mainly used in household kitchens. They are not intended for restaurant kitchens where, ideally, sauces are made with special stocks prepared by cooking beef, veal or poultry in a lot of water, and flavouring them with pot vegetables.

FAGOUE—A name given in the French tripe-trade to the pancreas and sometimes to calf's sweetbreads.

Antique faience of Nevers, Strasbourg and Rouen

FAIENCE—An opaque type of pottery, whitish in colour or tinted to a greater or lesser degree. The earthenware is covered with tin-glaze (lead glaze made opaque by the addition of tin ashes) so that the colour of the earthenware is completely masked. This pottery takes its name from the Italian town of Faenza.

Very little is known about the origins of faience pottery. Nevertheless, from the very earliest times, a brilliant, vitreous lead glaze coloured by means of metallic oxides was known to potters. It is to be seen in the hypogeum of Ancient Egypt, on its vases, funeral images, and also on the glazed bricks which decorated the walls of Nineveh and Babylon.

The ancient mosques of Asia Minor have preserved to us the magnificent craftsmanship of the Persians who passed on their skill to the Arabs.

From the thirteenth century, there were important centres for the manufacture of faience in Spain, at Malaga and Majorca, which gave its name to the Italian *majolica*. Up to the seventeenth century, the most famous factories were in Valencia.

But it was mainly through the discovery of tin-glaze by Luca della Robbia, towards the middle of the fifteenth century, that the ceramic industry was able to develop, first at Faenza and then in various other Italian towns, whose names have become famous, notably Urbino, Gubbio, Deruta, Durante, Venice, Milan, and Turin.

In France, in the sixteenth century, faience pottery called Henry II faience was made, the most important being the very individual pieces made by Bernard Palissy. At the same period, Italian potters tried to introduce the faience industry into France. The Conradi, coming from Savona, settled at Nevers. Early abortive attempts were made in the sixteenth century to make faience in Rouen, but it was only in the seventeenth century that this town produced the beautiful specimens which remain one of the glories of the French faience industry. These were very fashionable in the eighteenth century and were copied everywhere, both in France and other countries. Moustiers, from the end of the seventeenth century, made famous faience pieces in the style of Tempesta, or copied from Bérain and Bernard Toro. At Strasbourg, the Hannong family in the eighteenth century created a style quickly adopted by the factories of Lunéville and Niederwiller. In Paris, at Saint-Cloud, Meudon, Lille and Marseilles, there were also a large number of less important factories.

Outside France, some of the finest work was produced at Delft in Holland, which was, for a long time, the most active centre of the faience industry in Europe.

Fine pottery, called clay pottery, made its appearance towards the middle of the eighteenth century, and this industry was most fully developed in England, in the towns of Leeds and Burslem. In France, this type of pottery was made especially at Pont-aux-Choux, in Paris, at Lunéville and Orléans.

With the advent of porcelain, faience became less sought-after and less highly-prized. But modern faience manufacturers have given a new lease of life to this type of pottery.

FAISANDAGE—The French term for red meat which is in the condition which, in England, is known as 'high'. It is derived from *faisan* (pheasant).

When it is fresh, pheasant is tough and without much flavour. It grows tender and its aroma develops after it has been hung for a longer or shorter time, depending upon the temperature. Nowadays, pheasant is no longer hung, as advocated by Montaigne, 'until it develops a marked smell'.

In Brillat-Savarin's time, pheasant was not considered fit for the gastronome's table, except in a state of complete putrefaction. This authority recommends, in effect, that it should be kept, unplucked, until its *breast turns green*, so that it has to be held together for roasting on the spit by a slice of bread tied on with ribbon.

Grimod de La Reynière declared that it was ready when, being hung up by the tail, it fell down of its own accord. '*Pheasant*,' he says in a weighty phrase, 'wishes to be waited for as a government pension is waited for by a man of letters who never learnt how to flatter anyone!' To make his meaning perfectly clear, he continues: 'a pheasant killed on Shrove Tuesday will make perfect eating on Easter Day!'

Apart from a few sportsmen in love with tradition, most people have today abandoned these excesses.

Winged game and ground game, when hung for a certain length of time, acquire a flavour similar to that of pheasant.

This habit of hanging meat until it is high, though approved of by a few connoisseurs, usually motivated by snobbery, is properly reprehended by those concerned with hygiene and also by the true gastronome.

FAISELLE. FAISSELLE—An osier or pottery basket used for draining cheeses. Also the table on which the apple residue is drained after the brewing of cider.

FALCON. FAUCON—A bird of prey, trained to hunt on the wing. According to Tournefort, the French botanist and traveller, (1656–1708), it is delicate to eat and need not be hung.

FALERNIAN WINE. FALERNE—A Campagna wine celebrated in verse by the poet Horace.

FALLOW-DEER. DAIM—A wild ruminant, somewhat rare in France. In the language of venery, it is known as a *fawn* up to 8 months. It loses its horns twice before it is fully grown. A full-grown fallow-deer can be recognised by the palms between the branches of its antlers. The female of the fallow-deer is called a *doe*.

The meat of young fallow-deer is very delicate. That of the full-grown animal is leathery and must be steeped in a marinade. See MARINADE FOR VENISON.

All recipes for roebuck (venison) are suitable for fallow-deer. See ROEBUCK.

Roast haunch of fallow-deer (venison) à l'anglaise. HANCHE DE DAIM RÔTIE À L'ANGLAISE—The haunch of venison is highly prized in England and is hung for quite a long time until it is high.

It keeps very well for several days if care is taken to hang it in a room well-aired by a draught. Before hanging, the venison should be rubbed all over with a mixture of flour and pepper. The purpose of the flour is to keep out the damp and that of the pepper to keep away the flies.

Before impaling the venison on the spit, trim it and coat it with ordinary flour and water paste.

Wrap it, coated with this mixture, in thick paper secured with several lengths of string.

Roast for 4 hours, basting frequently.

(Care must be taken not to cut the fat off the venison. The fatter it is the better.)

Ten minutes before removing the roast from the spit, unwrap it and scrape off the flour and water paste. Pour melted butter over it and sprinkle with salt and flour. Put it closer to the fire so that it is nicely browned.

With roast haunch of venison, it is usual to serve boiled French beans or chestnut purée, and red currant jelly in a sauceboat. Haunch of stag is cooked in the same way, but is less highly prized than that of fallow-deer.

FALSE OATS. FROMENTAL—A variety of oats.

FANCHETTE OR FANCHONETTE (Confectionery)—This gâteau, which was very popular in the past, is scarcely ever made today. This is a pity because it is excellent. It is made in a deep round baking tin similar to that used for hot *pâtés*.

Line this baking tin with flaky pastry dough which has been rolled out and folded into 3 upon itself six times (*Twelfth Night galette* mixture; see GALETTE). Fill this crust with a cream made like French pastry cream, with the following ingredients: 12 yolks of eggs, ¾ cup (100 grams) of powdered sugar, ¾ cup (100 grams) of unsifted flour, 2½ cups (5 decilitres) of fresh thick cream, a tablespoon of vanilla-flavoured sugar, or 1 teaspoon of vanilla extract, a pinch of salt.

Bake the gâteau in a slow oven. When it is cold, cover with meringue. Decorate the top with meringue, piping it through a forcing bag. Sprinkle with sugar. Brown in the oven. Serve warm.

FANES—A name given in France to the stalks, green or dry, of plants not cultivated for fodder.

The *fanes* of some pot vegetables are edible. Turnip stalks (turnip-tops) can be cooked like spinach, but only if they are tender.

FANTAISIE—In France, the word '*Fantaisie*' must appear on the label of synthetic products ('*fantaisie*' liqueurs, jams etc.). '*Fantaisie*' bread in France is bread sold by the piece and not by weight.

FAR—A porridge made from hard wheat flour. More commonly, the term designates a kind of flan (tart) made in Brittany.

FAR POITEVIN—A kind of *farci** made in Poitou. It is made from all kinds of green vegetables and herbs (sorrel, green cabbage, white beet tops, lettuce). These are shredded raw, mixed with chopped pork fat and blended with cream and eggs, and flavoured with chopped chive and parsley, highly seasoned, and wrapped in green cabbage leaves and lettuce leaves (put in a net), and cooked in a hot-pot made with fresh and salt pork and flavoured with the usual vegetables.

FARCI—This is a dish made most commonly in the south of France. It is cooked in stock and prepared in different ways.

In its most usual form, the *farci* is a cabbage stuffed with sausage-meat or some other forcemeat, wrapped in muslin (U.S. cheese cloth) and cooked in stock.

Farci can also be prepared *à la niçoise*. See SOU FASSUM.

This dish can also be made by stuffing a piece of breast of veal with any kind of forcemeat. This too is cooked in stock. See SOUP.

FARINACEOUS. FARINEUX—Containing flour or with a high starch content. Cereals, pulses and potatoes are usually referred to as *farinaceous foods*.

FARINIÈRE (Flour bin)—A receptacle for flour. In Provençal kitchens flour for dredging fish is kept in a flat box with a sliding cover which is attached to the salt-bin.

FARO—Belgian beer, only slightly fermented. It is relatively sour and often has sugar added to it.

FASÉOLE—A species of haricot (U.S. shell) bean, cultivated in southern regions. These beans are prepared in the same way as white haricot beans. See BEANS.

FAT. GRAISSE—A greasy substance which melts at a low temperature. It is found in animal tissue and in some vegetable substances.

There are fats in almost all muscular animal tissue. Fat also surrounds many animal organs. It forms deposits equal to at least a thirtieth of the weight of the whole body.

There are three principal constituents in fat: *Stearin*, *Olein* and *Margarine*. *Stearin* is solid at normal temperatures, *olein* liquid. *Margarine* has an intermediate consistency.

Industrially prepared cooking fats. GRAISSES ALIMENTAIRES INDUSTRIELLES—Various cooking fat mixtures, besides cocoa-butter (see BUTTER), margarine and vegetable cooking fat, are manufactured commercially.

Economy fats. GRAISSE D'ÉCONOMIE—It goes without saying that all fats produced in the preparation of *pot-au-feu* and dripping of various kinds, should be carefully collected and preserved.

Once they are clarified, they can be used in the cooking of a variety of dishes.

Clarification of economy fat. Carefully skim off all the fat on the surface of the stock pot. Put it in an earthenware bowl, straining it through a fine sieve. Leave it to get cold overnight. Next day, prick the layer of fat in two places and pour off through the holes all the liquid (stock) which is underneath the congealed fat.

Thus separated from its liquid, the fat can be used in the cooking of vegetables (it is especially recommended for braised cabbage) but, not having been clarified, in other words completely dehydrated, it cannot be used for frying.

When the fat is to be used for frying, it must be processed as follows:

Put the fat in a saucepan; melt it, first over a low heat, then over a higher flame. Keep the fat on the boil until it stops giving off the steam produced by the liquid contained in it.

As soon as this steam stops rising, remove the pan from the stove, otherwise the fat will burn and become bitter in taste.

Strain through a fine sieve or muslin.

Pour it into an earthenware bowl and store in a cool, dry place.

Note. This fat can be further improved by the addition of a third of its weight of lard.

Dripping may also be added to the stock pot and clarified with it, but care should be taken never to use mutton dripping in this way.

Frying fat. GRAISSE À FRITURE—This is generally made from clarified beef-kidney fat (suet). See CULINARY METHODS, FRYING.

Fat for plinths. GRAISSE À COULER POUR SOCLES—A mixture of the fat of sheep's kidneys and lard which is used, or rather was formerly used, to make plinths and mould decorative motifs to adorn them.

This special fat is prepared as follows:

Trim the mutton fat carefully and chop it into tiny pieces.

Soak it in cold water until it is very white.

Put it in a saucepan with a little water. Melt it on a low heat, with the saucepan covered. Stir frequently. When it is thoroughly melted and clarified, squeeze it through muslin. Let it stand for a few minutes.

Next, mix in three quarters of its volume of very white lard, obtained by melting the fat of fresh pork.

Stir the mixture with a spoon until it begins to congeal, then add a few drops of citric acid.

Before pouring into the plinth moulds, this fat must be gently heated.

Nowadays, only pork butchers make these plinths in France, and then only at Christmas time.

Modelling fat or wax. GRAISSE À MODELER, STÉATOPLASTIQUE—For the sake of the record, we recall that kind of fat which, in former times, was used in France to model decorative motifs and to make so-called 'artistic' plinths.

This wax is prepared in exactly the same way as fat for plinths (see previous recipe), except that equal parts of lard and mutton fat are used.

It is put in an earthenware bowl and left to get completely cold. It is then turned out and grated into fine shavings. These shavings are put on a damp cloth spread out on the table. Just before using, the fat is kneaded into a ball. After kneading, it should be smooth and very malleable.

FAUBONNE—A thick soup made with purée of white haricot (shell) beans with a plain *julienne* of vegetables added. See SOUPS AND BROTHS.

FAUVES (Wild animals)—This is a French hunting term used especially of animals of the deer family, such as stag, fallow-deer, chamois and roebuck, as opposed to *black game*, such as boar, and *red game*, such as fox.

FAUX-FILET OR CONTRE-FILET—Part of the sirloin of beef taken from either side of the chine in the lumbar region. In U.S.A. this is called the *tenderloin.* For the cooking of this cut, see BEEF.

FAVEROLLES—Name used in the south of France for all kinds of haricot (U.S. shell) beans. These are also called *faverottes* and *favioles* in this region.

FAVRE (JOSEPH)—Joseph Favre was not only one of the greatest nineteenth-century chefs, but also one of the finest writers on culinary matters.

He was the author of the *Dictionnaire universel de cuisine et d'hygiène alimentaire*, a work in four volumes which contains not only a large number of recipes, but a very interesting history of cookery.

Joseph Favre was also the founder of the first Academy of Cookery, which no longer exists today.

FAWN. FAON—The young of a roe-doe, hind or fallow-doe. For the preparation of fawn, see ROEBUCK.

FEDELINI—An Italian *pasta* in the form of narrow ribbons. All recipes for *macaroni* are suitable for *fedelini.*

FENDANT WINE—The name of a Valais vine, cultivated in the Vaud Canton in Switzerland. It is said that this vine is merely a variety of Chasselas. Wine made from Fendant grapes has a strong aroma and is very heady. It is invariably served with the famous cheese *Fondue valaisienne.* See FONDUE, *Cheese fondue I.*

Fennel

FENNEL. FENOUIL—An aromatic flowering umbelliferous plant of Italian origin which is now widely cultivated. It has a slight flavour of aniseed.

The edible part of this plant is the very fleshy bulbous stem at the base of the leaf-stalk. This stem, which in French cookery is called *fenouil tubereux*, and which the Italians, who are very fond of it, call *finocchio*, is cooked like celery. It can be eaten raw or cooked. In England it is called *Florence fennel.*

Both the bulbous stem and the leaves of the fennel plant are used in cookery to flavour a large number of dishes. Fennel is an excellent condiment.

Fennel with bone-marrow. FENOUIL À LA MOELLE—Braise in fat. Complete cooking as for *Cardoons with marrow.* See CARDOON.

Fennel in butter. FENOUIL ÉTUVÉ AU BEURRE—Fennel can be cooked without meat-stock or fat. Proceed as follows:

Put the fennel stems, parboiled (whole or quartered), in a well buttered pan. Moisten with a few tablespoons of water. Season. Cover and simmer gently. Serve the fennel bulbs in a bowl. Pour on the cooking stock with butter added.

Fennel in cream. FENOUIL À LA CRÈME—Fennel stems, simmered in butter or braised in fat as indicated above, can be put into a cream sauce and simmered for a few minutes before serving.

Fennel au gratin. FENOUIL AU GRATIN—Stew the fennel stems in butter or braise in fat. Put them in a buttered ovenware dish. Sprinkle with grated cheese. Pour on melted butter. Brown in the oven.

Fennel in gravy. FENOUIL AU JUS—Braise in fat. Simmer for a few minutes in concentrated brown veal stock.

Fennel à la grecque. FENOUIL À LA GRECQUE—Proceed as indicated for *Artichokes à la grecque.* (See ARTICHOKE, *Pickled artichokes.*) Fennel prepared in this way is served as an hors-d'oeuvre.

Fennel cooked in meat stock. FENOUIL AU GRAS—Trim the fennel stems. Parboil for 5 minutes in boiling salt water. Cool under running water. Drain and dry in a cloth. Quarter them or, if they are small leave whole. Put them in a pan lined with pork-skin, onions and carrots cut into rounds. Moisten with a few tablespoons of rather fat stock. Boil. Cover the pan. Cook slowly in the oven.

FENNEL-PEAR (FENOWLET). FENOUILLET—A variety of pear which (like fennel) tastes slightly of aniseed. Three varieties are grown in France: the *fenouillet gris*, the *fenouillet gros*, and the *fenouillet rouge*.

FENNEL-WATER. FENOUILLETTE—A liqueur made from fennel seeds. This liqueur is made commercially.

FENUGREEK. FENUGREC—An unusual Asiatic herb with slightly bitter aromatic seeds sometimes used in making curry.

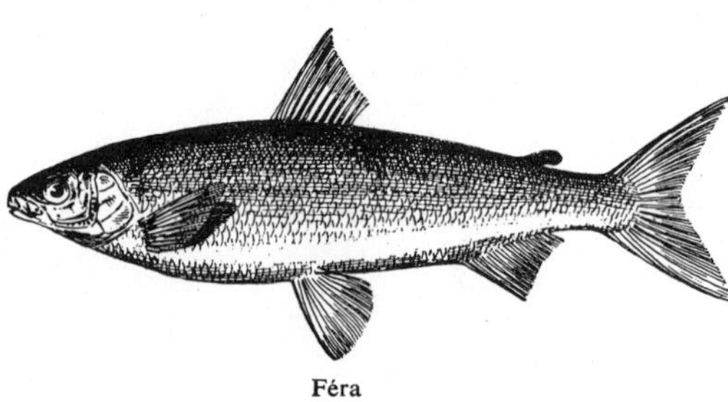

Féra

FÉRA—A breed of salmon found in Lake Geneva and several other lakes in Switzerland, Bavaria and Austria.

This fish, which is exceedingly delicate, is very similar to the lavaret, but the two fish differ in shape. The *féra's* body is more compact, its scales are larger and its jaws, sloping obliquely back, are somewhat truncated.

The colouring of the *féra* varies with the season, the age of the fish and its habitat.

The *white féra* is found particularly in very deep waters, the *black féra* in waters of average depth: the *blue féra*, which is really the young *féra*, has a bluish rather than greenish shimmer on the upper part of its body.

The Lake Geneva *féra* is the most highly prized. It is generally thought that the best Lake Geneva *féra* are those caught on the sandbank called the *Travers* where the water is very shallow, the sandbank forming a barrier across the lake near the port of Geneva. This fish, which fills out very rapidly by feeding on a winged insect called the caddis-fly which is plentiful in this area about May, is very fat, white and extremely delicate. The fishermen of Geneva sell this fish under the name of *Féra de Travers.*

North American *land-locked salmon*, fished in Eastern Canadian and New England lakes, may be prepared like *féra.*

Féra à la meunière—Scale, gut and wash the féra. Dry thoroughly and season with salt and pepper. Dip in flour and, after shaking off excess flour, cook in fresh butter in an iron frying pan.

Baste frequently with the cooking butter, over a moderate heat. Drain the fish. Put on a dish. Sprinkle with chopped parsley. Pour on a few drops of lemon juice and the cooking butter, piping hot. If there is not enough of this, add one or two tablespoons of fresh butter to it.

Serve at once.

FERCHUSE—This dish is a culinary speciality of Burgundy. In former times it was traditionally made on the day when the pig was killed. Its name *ferchuse* is a corruption of *fressure* (pluck). See PLUCK.

Method. Take a large saucepan with a heavy base. Melt in it 1 pound (500 grams) of fresh chopped pork fat. When it is melted bring to the boil, put in all the pork pluck (heart, liver and lungs), cut into square pieces and season with salt, pepper and spices.

Brown the pluck very quickly. When browned, sprinkle with 3 heaped tablespoons of flour. Mix well, stirring with a wooden spoon and cook until the flour is golden in colour.

Moisten with 2 parts of red wine and 1 part of water or, to give more flavour to the dish, with stock. Altogether there should be enough liquid to cover all the pluck completely.

Bring to the boil. As soon as the liquid is boiling steadily, add 8 chopped shallots, 6 crushed cloves of garlic and a large *bouquet garni.* Simmer slowly for another 45 minutes.

FERMENTATION—The chemical change induced by the action of bacteria.

Alcoholic Fermentation: See ALCOHOL, WINE, BEER, etc.

Fermentation of milk: See MILK, CHEESE.

Putrid fermentation: See PUTREFACTION.

FERMIÈRE (A LA)—A special method of preparing braised or pot-roasted meat, with a garnish of carrots, turnips, celery and onions cooked slowly in butter until very tender. See FONDUE, *Vegetable fondues.*

FERN. FOUGÈRE—The young shoots of certain ferns (such as the male fern and bracken) are edible and can be served like male *hop-flower stalks.*

The underground stems or rhizomes of bracken have also been eaten in the form of flour in times of famine.

FEUILLANTINE—This name is given in France to puff-pastries made with flaky pastry dough rolled out and folded into three upon itself 6 times. These pastries are cut out of the dough in strips $1\frac{1}{2}$ to 2 inches long and $\frac{2}{3}$ inch wide. They are brushed with white of egg, sprinkled with granulated sugar and baked in a moderate oven.

Feuillantines are served with afternoon tea and also, instead of wafers, with ice cream.

FEUILLETON—This is the name given in France to a preparation made from thin slices of veal or pork, beaten very flat, which are spread with layers of stuffing and laid one on top of the other. When it is built up, the *feuilleton* is wrapped in thin slices of pork fat or pork caul, and braised in the usual way.

Feuilleton of veal à l'ancienne. FEUILLETON DE VEAU À L'ANCIENNE—For a *feuilleton* weighing 4 pounds (2 kilos), cut 10 thin slices from the *noix* or *sous-noix* (U.S. loin) of veal. Flatten these slices with a beater to make them rectangular in shape. Season with salt, pepper and a pinch of spices.

Cut a very thin slice of pork fat rather larger than the slices of veal. Spread a slice of veal with the fine pork stuffing, a third of its weight of a gratin stuffing (see FORCEMEAT) and a third of its weight of dry *Duxelles** added, and bound with eggs. Lay the slices of veal one on top of the other, spreading each one with stuffing and ending with a layer of stuffing. Cover with a thin slice of pork fat. Fold the edges of the lower slice of pork fat so that they cover the sides of the *feuilleton.* Fold the edges of the upper slice over those of the lower slice. Tie the *feuilleton* neatly into shape. Put it in a buttered stewpan lined with bacon rinds, onions and carrots sliced into rounds. Add a *bouquet garni.* Cover and simmer for 20 minutes. Moisten with 1¼ cups (2½ decilitres) of white wine. Reduce. Add 1¼ cups (2½ decilitres) of brown veal stock. Boil down to a concentrated jelly. Moisten with 2½ cups (5 decilitres) of good stock. Cover and cook in the oven for 1 hour, 45 minutes, basting frequently.

Drain the *feuilleton.* Untie it and put it on a serving dish. Pour on a few tablespoons of the fat of the braising stock. Glaze in the oven, basting frequently during this final operation. Surround the *feuilleton* with a *Bourgeoise* garnish (see GARNISHES) or any other garnish of braised vegetables such as celery, chicory, lettuce, cucumbers, etc.

Remove the fat from the braising stock. Strain and, if necessary, boil down (reduce). Pour a few tablespoons of this stock over the meat, and serve the rest separately.

Note. To ensure that the *feuilleton* is perfectly rectangular in shape it can be boxed in with thin rectangular pieces of white wood laid on the top, bottom and sides, and kept in position with string.

This dish can also be made with different mixtures, stuffings and *salpicons.*

It can be braised in Madeira instead of white wine.

Another method is to moisten it with red wine and prepare it *à la bourguignonne.* When prepared in this way the garnish of strips of pork belly (pork fat), blanched and fried, half-cooked small onions and mushrooms must be put to simmer with the meat.

Feuilleton of cold veal in jelly. FEUILLETON DE VEAU FROID À LA GELÉE—Prepare and cook the *feuilleton* as for *Feuilleton of veal à l'ancienne* or *à la périgourdine.* Cool under a weight. Trim the *feuilleton* and put it in an oval bowl on a bed of well-set jelly. Pour over it enough half-set jelly to cover it (the jelly having been enriched with the braising stock diluted with unthickened meat juice). Chill on ice.

Using the same method, *feuilletons* of pork or large poultry can be made and served hot or cold. Poultry *feuilletons* can be braised in white stock (see CULINARY METHODS), and served with a sauce and garnish especially suitable for poultry entrées.

Feuilleton of veal à la périgourdine. FEUILLETON DE VEAU À LA PÉRIGOURDINE—Prepare the *feuilleton* as indicated for *Feuilleton of veal à l'ancienne*, spreading the slices of meat with a stuffing made of two-thirds foie gras and one-third fine stuffing, with diced truffles added. Braise in Madeira. Garnish with strips of truffle and slices of foie gras sautéed in butter.

FEUILLETTE—A cask roughly equivalent to the English quarter-cask, with a capacity of 114 to 140 litres. The *ordinary feuillette* holds 133 to 135 litres and the *large feuillette* up to 140 litres. The *Burgundy feuillette* only holds 112 to 114 litres.

FIASQUE—A wine flask (*fiasco* in Italian) with a wide base and long neck. It is usually wrapped in straw.

The Florentine flask has a capacity of 2 quarts, 14 ounces for oil and 3 quarts, 1 ounce for wine.

FIATOLE—Common French name for a Mediterranean fish. It is striking in appearance with golden yellow bars and spots on its leaden grey skin. It is flat and as broad as it is long. It is fairly delicate to eat. All recipes for turbot are suitable for this fish. See TURBOT.

FIÉLAS—This is the name given in Provence to the conger-eel, which is one of the ingredients of *bouillabaisse.* It can also be stewed, cooked *en matelote*, etc. in the same way as eel. See CONGER-EEL.

FIELD-POPPY OIL. HUILE D'OEILLETTE—Edible oil obtained by pressing the seeds of the white poppy.

This oil is also known in France as white oil and *olivette.* It has the same culinary uses as olive oil.

FIELDFARE. LITORNE—A large type of thrush with greyish head-feathers. It is less delicate than the true thrush. All recipes for thrush are suitable for fieldfare.

FIG. FIGUE—The fruit of the *fig-tree*, a tree or bush which seems to have come originally from the East. It was certainly known in the very earliest times.

There are three types of fig, the *white fig*, the *purple fig* and the *red fig.* These three types are sub-divided into a large number of varieties.

In France, the most highly prized of these varieties is the *Marseillaise fig.* It is a fruit of medium size with a yellowish white skin slightly tinged with gold. Its pulp is white and succulent. This fig is in season from August to October. The *Bellona fig*, a rather large purple-skinned fig with red pulp, is quite sweet. It is in season from July to October. The black *Banissotte fig*, a large fruit with a rather thick skin, is purple with rather sweet red pulp. It is in season from August to the coming of the first frosts.

Among the varieties cultivated in central and western France are:

(1) *the white fig of Argenteuil*, known also as *blanquette* and *madeleine*, a fruit of medium size, elongated in shape, greenish-yellow in colour with very sweet, white pulp. It is in season in mid-July and again at the end of September.

(2) *the red fig of Argenteuil*, also known as *dauphine*, a large fattish fruit, with purplish skin and pale red pulp. It is fairly sweet and is in season in August.

(3) *the barbillone fig*, a medium-sized fruit with purplish skin and rather firm white pulp. It is fairly sweet and is in season in mid-July and again in September.

There are a great many other varieties of fig which are mostly similar in colour and flavour to those mentioned above. Among these varieties are : *the large yellow Smyrna fig, the Bordeaux fig, the russet pear fig, the Moissonne fig*, etc.

Generally speaking, fresh figs are eaten raw. They are served as hors-d'oeuvre, like melon, in some parts of France and Italy. In Paris, figs are generally eaten as dessert.

Figs can also be cooked in various ways. All recipes for apricots are suitable for figs.

A fermented drink is made from figs and also a spirit which is highly prized by the Arabs.

In Central Europe roast figs are used, as chicory is in France, to flavour coffee.

Dried figs. Figues sèches—In the South of France, figs are preserved by drying in the sun. Very ripe autumn fruit is used. The figs, spread out on hurdles, are exposed to the sun. They are taken indoors at night. They have to be turned over several times during the drying and, before they are completely dried, they are slightly flattened. Treated in this way, figs will keep a very long time.

More commonly, and especially in countries where figs are intensively cultivated, the drying is done industrially in hot rooms.

Dried figs are eaten as they are. They can also be stewed, like all other dried fruits, and are used in various sweets and pastries.

Fig fritters. Beignets de figues—Peel the figs and quarter them. Steep them for 30 minutes in brandy or some other liqueur and sugar.

At the last moment, dip them in light batter and deep-fry. See FRITTERS.

Fig jam.—See JAM, *marmelade.*

Stewed figs—See COMPOTE.

Fig tart—See TART.

Fig wine or figuette. Vin de Figue, Figuette—A medicinal drink made from dried figs.

FILBERT (Corylus avellana). Aveline—Another name for hazelnut.

The filbert-tree, which produces these nuts, is a variety of common hazel tree. They are thus called because they are ripe about St. Philbert's day—August 22nd.

Recipes for filbert nuts will be found under HAZEL-NUT.

FILLET. Filet—The undercut of the sirloin of beef. A cut taken from the fleshy part of the buttocks of other butcher's meat.

For methods of preparation see BEEF, MUTTON, VEAL, PORK.

Filet mignon—In France this term designates a small cut of meat taken from the end of the beef fillet. *Filets mignons* are grilled or sautéed. See BEEF.

More loosely this term is applied to the fillet proper of some meat such as lamb, mutton, veal and pork. See LAMB, MUTTON, VEAL, PORK.

Fillets of fish. Filets de poisson—Fish cut lengthwise off the central bone before cooking, e.g. fillets of sole, whiting, etc.

Fillets of poultry and winged game. Filets de volaille, de gibiers de plume—In France a *filet* as applied to game or poultry is, in the strict sense,

(1) the under part of the breast of poultry and winged game.

(2) the breasts themselves of poultry or game, cut off before cooking and prepared in various ways, whole or, when they are too fat as in the case of turkeys, cut into fillets, that is to say into thin slices.

Usually, the breasts of poultry and game are known in cookery as *suprêmes.* They are also called, though in our opinion improperly, *cutlets.*

FILLETTE—The French name for a small wine-bottle used mainly for Anjou wines. Its capacity is about a third of a litre.

FINANCIÈRE (A LA)—A method of preparing meat and poultry. *Financière* garnish (which is also used to fill pies and vol-au-vents) consists of cocks' combs and cocks' kidneys, *quenelles,* lambs' sweetbreads, mushrooms, olives and strips of truffles.

FINES HERBES—Generally speaking, this term is used not of mixed herbs but simply of chopped parsley. Thus an *Omelette aux fines herbes* is an omelette containing only chopped parsley in addition to the usual seasoning.

Actually, *fines herbes* should be a mixture of herbs, such as parsley, chervil, tarragon and even chives.

Indeed this was the original meaning of the term. In earlier times chopped mushroom and even truffles were added to the herbs listed above.

FINTE—A fish somewhat similar to the shad. Like the shad, it returns to the rivers to spawn, but about a month later.

It differs from the shad in shape, being rather more elongated. Unlike the shad it has very sharp teeth in both jaws. The *finte* is prepared in the same way as the common shad. See SHAD.

FIREDOG. Landier—Large kitchen andiron.

In his *Dictionnaire raisonné du mobilier français, de l'époque carolingienne à la Renaissance,* Viollet Le Duc thus defines antique firedogs and describes their uses in the kitchens of our ancestors:

'Stoves divided into several compartments were much less frequently used in kitchens than they are today. The food was cooked over the open fire. It will be readily understood that, in view of the great heat of the fire, it was impossible to use it for certain dishes which had to be stirred during cooking or which were prepared in small cooking pots.

'Stoves filled with live charcoal were propped on fire-dogs away from the hearth and at a convenient height for working. They made cooking very much easier. The kitchen staff even ate their food off these little stoves and kept themselves warm at the same time.

'Kitchen firedogs,' Viollet Le Duc adds, 'were simple in design, though they were forged with great care, but those designed for living apartments were often very richly ornamented with scroll-work. Few firedogs made before the fifteenth century have much artistic merit.'

FIRECREST, FIRE-CRESTED WREN. Roitelet—Small singing bird, which in France unfortunately enters sometimes into the confection of *brochettes* of small birds. Prepared like LARK.

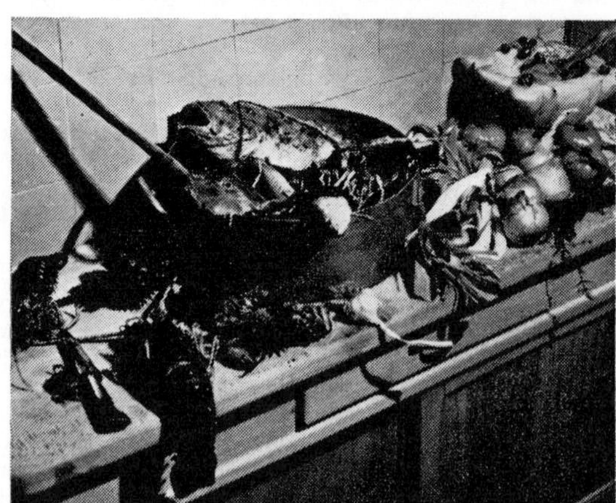

Fish for bouillabaisse (*French Government Tourist Office*)

FISH. Poissons—Most fish are edible and the fish world presents an enormous source of food. The most nourishing fish are river eels and lampreys, then come salmon,

salmon trout, mackerel, turbot, fresh herring and the conger eel. Among the least nourishing, although they are by no means to be despised, are bream, sole and lemon sole.

The water content of all fish is much the same—75%. The albuminoids also vary very little from species to species—they constitute about 18%. The fats are found in more variable quantities. There are fish very rich in fat content, such as eel (26%), fish fairly rich in fats such as lamprey (12.5%), shad (8.42%), mackerel (8.31%), sturgeon (7.91%), herring (6%) and lean fish such as pike, ray and bream.

The flesh of fish, therefore, in content does not differ greatly from the flesh of land animals; it may perhaps contain slightly less nitrogenous substances, but the fat content and the proportion of mineral is substantially the same, in particular that of phosphorated compounds. Owing to the fact that fish (particularly lean fish) is easily digestible, it is an excellent food for sedentary workers.

From the practical point of view, it is interesting to note the quantity of waste of a whole fish. Thus carp, fresh cod and sole carry 50%, bass 47%, perch, trout 44%, small frying fish, such as gudgeon and smelts, from 40% to 30% and the fresh sardine only 20% of wastages.

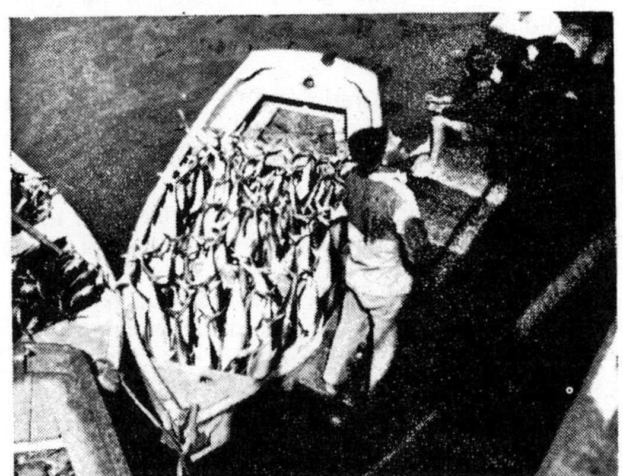

Landing the catch, Britanny (*French Government Tourist Office*)

The freshness of fish—Fish is subject to speedy decay by bacterial action and often causes food poisoning if it is not absolutely fresh.

At the market the freshness of fish can be recognised by the firmness of the flesh; clean fresh smell, without any suggestion of anything musty, unpleasant, sweetish or pungent; bright eyes, which should stand out and not be embedded in the orbits; brightness of scales and the colour of the gills, which must be bright red.

The ray is perhaps the only fish which can stand a slight degree of mortification; it can be eaten when not entirely fresh.

Flat fish—There are two kinds of flat fish: *fish flattened vertically*, such as ray or skate, the upper, exposed side being dark and the underside white, and the *fish flattened laterally*, which are the real flat fish, the white and dark sides representing the flanks, the back and the belly being represented by the flattened sides; the two eyes are both on the same side (the coloured side) and, depending on the position of the eyes, flat fish are classified into *dextral species*, if the eyes lie on the right side of the head, and *sinistral species*, if they are on the left. The anus is always visible on the underside. Plaice, flounder, sole and lemon sole are right-sided, while sardine, turbot and brill are left-sided.

Poisonous fish—The flesh of certain varieties of fish, generally those inhabiting tropical seas, is permanently poisonous; other species, such as grey gurnard, carp-bream, garfish, etc. become poisonous at certain times.

Venomous fish—These fish, the flesh of which is often excellent, must not be confused with fish mentioned in the preceding paragraph. Venomous fish have dorsal fins armed with spines which are grooved and provided with poison glands. These can cause very painful and even dangerous wounds if they are handled without due precaution, as, for instance, in the case of the weever or sting-fish.

Recipes—For recipes for different fish, see BRILL, COD, PLAICE, SOLE etc.

Fish mousse. MOUSSE DE POISSON—*Ingredients.* 2 pounds (1 kilo) of fish (net weight); 4 to 5 whites of egg; 5 cups (1¼ litres) of fresh thick cream; 1½ teaspoons (10 grams) of salt; ¼ teaspoon (3 grams) of white pepper; pinch of spices.

Method. Pound the fish, seasoned with salt, pepper and spices, in a mortar as finely as possible. While pounding add the whites of egg a little at a time. Rub the mixture through a fine sieve.

Put it in a pan and leave it to stand on ice (or in a cool place) for 2 hours.

Next, add the cream, a little at a time, stirring with a wooden spoon.

Cooking. Fill a plain deep, round mould (or a mould with a hole in the middle) three quarters full with this mixture. Stand in water and poach in a moderate oven. Allow 30 to 35 minutes for a quart (litre) capacity mould. Leave to stand for a few seconds before turning out.

Fish mousses, garnishes and sauces—Appropriate garnishes are:

Cancalaise; various species of mushrooms and fungi, sautéed in butter; *Shrimps; Dieppoise; Fresh-water cray-fish; Joinville; Nantua; Marinière; Mussels; Normande; Green peas in butter; Asparagus tips in butter; Princesse; Trouvillaise; Victoria.*

Recipes for all the garnishes are given under GARNISHES. Fish mousses are covered with one or other of the following sauces (to blend with the garnish selected):

Aurore, Cardinal, Cream, Shrimp, Curry, Diplomate, Parsley, Lobster, Joinville, Marinière, Nantua, Normande, Ravigote, Riche, Vénitienne, Victoria, White wine. See SAUCE.

Fish roes on toast. CROÛTES AUX LAITANCES—Put some roes (carp roes, herring roes, etc.) on slices of bread which have been cut into rectangles and fried in butter. The roes should be poached first of all in a little butter and lemon juice. Sprinkle with breadcrumbs which have been fried in butter. Squeeze over some lemon juice and put in a hot oven. Sprinkle with chopped parsley.

FISH KETTLE (FISH BOILER). POISSONNIÈRE—A kitchen utensil intended for cooking fish. It usually contains a removable grid which makes it possible to take out the fish without breaking it.

FISSURELLE—A species of gasteropod mollusc in a conical shell similar to that of the limpet or barnacle. It has radiating ribs and is perforated at the tip. *Fissurelles* live in temperate and tropical waters and there are about a hundred different types. The Greek *fissurelle*, called *St. Peter's ear*, is very common in the Mediterranean.

All recipes for octopus are suitable for this mollusc. See OCTOPUS.

FISTULANE—The common French name for a kind of headless mollusc, also known as *gastrochère*. Its shell is tubular. *Fistulanes* are cooked in the same way as cockles.

Fistulina Hepatica

FISTULINA HEPATICA. FISTULINE HÉPATIQUE—A somewhat tasteless edible fungus which grows on the trunks of oak trees. It is commonly known in France as *langue-de-boeuf* (ox-tongue) or *foie-de-boeuf* (ox-liver). In U.S.A. it is known as *Liver fungus*.

FLAGEOLET (small kidney bean)—A dwarf bean which is shelled for eating. See BEANS.

FLAKES. FLOCON—The name given to certain cereals, flattened in a rolling-mill and used (in France) as a garnish in soups or as an ingredient of porridges, e.g. *corn flakes*.

FLAMANDE (A LA)—The name of a kind of hot-pot (see SOUPS). This name is also given to a garnish, especially for large cuts of meat served as an intermediate course. It consists of braised cabbage, carrots, diced belly of pork and potatoes. See GARNISHES.

The name *à la flamande* is also applied to a method of preparing asparagus. See ASPARAGUS.

FLAMBART—This is the name given in French pork butchery to the residual fat collected in the preparation of various pork products.

FLAMICHE—Legrand d'Aussy, (a French scholar, 1737–1800) thus described the *flamiche* as it was made in his day: 'It is a kind of *galette* made with baker's dough. It is rolled out with a rolling pin and put in the oven while the wood is burning. As soon as it has been thoroughly heated, it is taken out of the oven and spread with butter. It is eaten as soon as it comes out of the oven.'

Nowadays the name *flamiche* is given to a kind of leek tart made in Burgundy and Picardy.

To make this tart proceed as follows: Line a buttered tart tin with pastry, fill with sliced white leeks, cooked slowly in butter until very tender, blended with yolks of egg and well seasoned. Cover with a thin layer of lining pastry. Press the edges together and crimp them. Brush with egg. Bake in a very hot oven. Serve at once. In some parts of France, this tart is made with a mixture of flour, yolks of egg, yeast, sugar and rum or brandy. The result is more in the nature of a sweet.

In former times, in some parts of northern France, the *flamiche* was made with a pound (500 grams) of brie or camembert cheese, a pound (500 grams) of butter, 1½ pounds (750 grams) of flour, 8 whole eggs and a pinch of salt.

The butter and cheese were kneaded together. With the flour, eggs, salt and a little water, a dough was made which was left to stand before rolling out. When it was rolled out the mixture of butter and cheese were laid on it and it was folded into three and rolled out three times. The dough was then rolled out again and cut into little sticks which were put on a buttered baking sheet and baked in a hot oven.

FLAMINGO—A wader with webbed feet. The Romans considered it a delicacy though it is less highly prized nowadays. This bird is cooked in the same way as *Bustard**.

FLAMIQUE—A form of *flamiche* made in some parts of Northern France.

FLAMRI—*Flamri* is a kind of semolina pudding, usually served cold, covered with a purée of raw red fruit. It is made as follows: Boil 2 cups (½ litre) of white wine with the same quantity of water. Gradually pour into it ½ pound (250 grams) of fine semolina. Mix. Simmer gently for 25 minutes. To this 'porridge' add 1¼ cups (300 grams) of fine sugar, 2 whole eggs, a pinch of salt and, at the last moment, 6 stiffly beaten whites of egg. Pour this mixture into a plain buttered mould. Put in a pan of hot water and bake. Leave to cool.

Turn out the pudding on to a serving dish. Pour over it a purée of sweetened raw red fruit (strawberries, red currants, raspberries).

FLAMUSSE (Burgundian pastry)—A kind of flan made of lining (pie) pastry with a cheese-flavoured cream blended with eggs.

FLAN—A pastry preparation whose name comes from the metallurgical term flan, a metal disc. The flan has been in existence for many centuries. The Latin poet Fortunatus (530–609 A.D.) mentions it. He says that Saint Radegonde, as an exercise in mortification, made flans but ate only the coarse outer crust, made of rye or oatmeal dough.

In cookery, or rather in the language of confectionery, the term flan is used of various pastry preparations filled or plain, and usually round in shape.

In some parts of France, however, the term is used to designate a set cream preparation (caramel pudding, for instance).

In essence, a flan is no more than a kind of open tart filled with fruit, cream, stuffing or some other filling.

Flans are served as hors-d'oeuvre or as a light main course, and as such have a savoury filling. They are also served as a sweet. Recipes for savoury flans and some sweet flans are given below. A large number of recipes for sweet flans is given under TART. (In U.S.A. a *flan* is known as a *tart* or *pie*.)

Flan cases—Made in the same way as tart cases, and are either baked blind (unfilled) or with the indicated filling.

These flan cases are made according to the particular preparation with various types of pastry, such as short pastry, fine lining or ordinary pastry, sweet pastry, semi-flaky pastry, or with left-overs of puff pastry. See TART. (Illustrated at top of next page.)

Apple flan Grimaldi. FLAN AUX POMMES GRIMALDI—Cut four big cooking apples into quarters and cook them in vanilla-flavoured syrup. Drain and arrange in a flan case (U.S. pie shell) filled with rice, prepared in the following manner:

Bake the flan case blind (that is to say without any filling), in a flan ring. When ready, fill this flan case with sweetened rice, cooked as described in the appropriate recipe (see RICE), mixed with a *salpicon** of candied orange peel, shredded very finely, flavoured with curaçao and with a good tablespoonful of butter added to it.

How to prepare flan cases

Put the well-drained apple quarters on this rice, sprinkle with crushed macaroons and castor (fine) sugar and glaze in the oven.

Note. This flan is served hot, accompanied by curaçao-flavoured English custard (see CREAM).

Flan à la bordelaise—Bake a flan crust blind (empty). Fill with a coarse *salpicon** of beef bone-marrow mixed with diced, lean, cooked ham and blended with very thick *Bordelaise sauce* (see SAUCE). Decorate the top, alternating them with strips of bone-marrow cut rather thick, poached and drained, and fresh flap mushrooms (cèpes), sliced and sautéed in oil. Sprinkle with toasted breadcrumbs. Pour on melted butter. Brown quickly in a very hot oven. Sprinkle with chopped parsley.

Flan à la bourguignonne—Bake a flan crust blind (empty). Fill with a mixture prepared as follows: Simmer in butter, without browning, 10 sliced white leeks. When these leeks are very tender, add 1½ to 2 cups (3 to 4 decilitres) of *Béchamel sauce* (see SAUCE) enriched with ½ cup (1 decilitre) of fresh cream, boiled and strained. Sprinkle with grated cheese. Pour on melted butter. Brown in the oven.

Brillat-Savarin flan. FLAN BRILLAT-SAVARIN—Bake blind (empty) a flan crust made of *Fine lining pastry* (see DOUGH). On taking it out of the oven, fill this crust with very creamy scrambled eggs with truffles. Decorate the top with strips of raw seasoned truffle dipped in melted butter. Sprinkle with grated Parmesan. Pour on melted butter. Brown in a very hot oven.

Carrot flan à la flamande. FLAN DE CAROTTES À LA FLAMANDE—Fill an unbaked flan (tart) crust with carrots, finely chopped and boiled in a little water, butter, sugar and flavouring to taste. Moisten with a few tablespoons of custard, slightly thickened with potato-flour or arrowroot.

Bake in a moderate oven. Just before taking out of the oven, sprinkle with icing sugar and leave in the oven until it is evenly glazed. This flan can be served hot or cold.

Cheese flan. FLAN AU FROMAGE—Line a flan (pastry) ring, standing on a buttered baking sheet, with *Fine lining pastry* (see DOUGH). Fill with a mixture prepared as follows: Boil 2 cups (half a litre) of thick fresh cream with 3 tablespoons (50 grams) of butter. Season with salt, pepper and nutmeg. Add ¾ cup (100 grams) of sieved flour and mix on the stove to obtain a rather thick cream.

Take the pan off the stove and add to the cream 4 yolks of egg and 1½ cups (150 grams) of grated Gruyère cheese. Blend into the mixture the whites of the eggs, beaten to a very stiff foam.

Bake the flan in a hot oven.

Other types of cheese, such as Cantal, Dutch cheese, Parmesan, etc., can be used for this flan.

Cheese flan Juliette Récamier. FLAN DU FROMAGE JULIETTE RÉCAMIER—Stand a flan (pastry) ring on a buttered metal baking sheet. Line with *Fine lining pastry* (see DOUGH). Fill the bottom of the flan with beef bone-marrow dipped in concentrated veal stock, flavoured with chopped parsley, shallot cooked in white wine until all the moisture has evaporated, and seasoned with salt, pepper and grated nutmeg.

Fill the flan half-full of cream made like *French pastry cream* (see CREAM) but unsweetened, with grated cheese and a little fresh cream added. Bake in a moderate oven.

As soon as the flan is ready, turn it out. Put it on a round ovenware dish. Decorate the top with a few table-spoons of very soft scrambled eggs flavoured with cheese. Sprinkle with grated cheese and brown as rapidly as possible.

Chicken liver flan Chavette. FLAN DE FOIES DE VOLAILLE CHAVETTE—Make a flan crust of *Fine lining pastry* (see DOUGH) and bake blind (before filling).

Prepare a ragoût of chicken livers made as follows: Trim 1 pound (500 grams) of chicken livers and cut into rather thick pieces. Season these livers with salt and pepper and sauté quickly in sizzling butter. Drain the livers and keep hot. In the same butter, sauté quickly ½ cup (100 grams) of sliced mushrooms. Season the mush-rooms. Drain and keep warm with the chicken livers.

Pour 1 cup (2 decilitres) of Madeira into the pan in which the livers and mushrooms have been cooked. Reduce (boil down). Add 1¾ cups (3½ decilitres) of rather thin *Béchamel sauce* (see SAUCE) and 1 cup (2 decilitres) of fresh cream. Add to this sauce the pieces of livers and mushrooms and cook until it is fairly thick. Strain the sauce through a sieve and add the livers and mushrooms to it. Keep hot without bringing to the boil.

Scramble some eggs in the usual way (they should be rather soft). When they are ready, add 2 tablespoons of grated Parmesan and 2 tablespoons of butter.

Put the chicken livers and mushrooms at the bottom of the flan. Cover with the eggs scrambled with Parmesan. Sprinkle with grated cheese. Pour on melted butter. Brown in a very hot oven. (This flan can be made with livers of other poultry.)

Fresh-water crayfish flan à la Nantua. FLAN D'ÉCREVISSES À LA NANTUA—Bake a flan (tart) crust blind. Fill with a *ragoût* of *Crayfish tails à la Nantua** mixed with truffles. Brown quickly in a very hot oven.

All shell-fish flans, with shrimps, crabs, lobsters and spiny lobster, are prepared in this way.

The truffles can be omitted.

Flan à la financière—Bake a flan crust blind (empty). Garnish with a *Ragoût à la financière** thickened with very concentrated *Demi-glace* (see SAUCE) flavoured with Madeira. Sprinkle with breadcrumbs. Brown in the oven.

Flan à la florentine—Bake a flan crust blind (empty). Fill with a layer of spinach (cooked whole, drained, squeezed, coarsely chopped and simmered in butter). Cover with *Mornay sauce* (see SAUCE). Sprinkle with grated cheese. Pour on melted butter. Brown in a hot oven.

Leek flan with cheese. FLAN DE POIREAUX AU FROMAGE—Stand a large flan (pastry) ring on a buttered baking sheet. Line with *Fine lining pastry* (see DOUGH) and bake blind (empty).

When it is ready, turn out the crust and put it on a large round ovenware dish. Line the flan with a few tablespoons of *Mornay sauce* (see SAUCE). Arrange on top a few large white leeks, parboiled for a very short time and simmered in butter.

Cover with *Mornay sauce* enriched with butter. Sprinkle with grated Parmesan. Pour on melted butter. Brown in the oven.

This flan can also be made with small onions instead of leeks. In this case the onions must be well glazed before they are arranged on the bed of *Mornay sauce.*

Raspberry cream flan. FLAN AUX FRAMBOISES À LA CRÈME—Remove stems from raspberries. Cover with sugar. Arrange on a baked flan or tart shell a *French pastry cream* (see CREAM) flavoured with vanilla. Cover with raspberries and a small amount of raspberry jelly.

Flan à la reine—Bake a flan crust blind (empty). Fill with a chicken *Salpicon à la reine**.

Sprinkle with toasted breadcrumbs. Brown in a very hot oven. Decorate the top of the flan with a border of strips of truffle.

Rice flan—See RICE.

Flan à la Sagan—Bake a flan crust blind (empty). Line the bottom with a *salpicon** of mushrooms and truffles blended in cream and seasoned with curry-powder. On top of the *salpicon* arrange slices of calves' brains sautéed in butter. Put a strip of truffle on top of each slice. Cover with *Mornay sauce* (see SAUCE) flavoured with curry. Sprinkle with grated cheese. Pour on melted butter. Brown quickly in a very hot oven.

Seafood flan. FLAN AU FRUIT DE MER—Bake blind (empty) a flan crust of *Fine lining pastry* or *Flaky pastry* (see DOUGH). When the flan is ready, fill with a seafood *ragoût* (oysters, mussels, fresh-water crayfish tails, cockles and other shell-fish). Blend in rather thick *Normande sauce* (see SAUCE). Sprinkle with toasted breadcrumbs. Pour on melted butter. Brown rapidly in a very hot oven.

Shell-fish flan. FLANS DE CRUSTACÉS—Using cooked lobster, crayfish or some other shell-fish, and a sauce appropriate to the fish chosen, proceed as indicated in the recipe for *Fresh-water crayfish flan à la Nantua* in this section.

Sole flan à la normande. FLAN DE SOLES À LA NORMANDE—This dish is merely fillets of sole prepared *à la normande* (see SOLE) arranged as a border in a flan crust baked blind (empty). Cover with *Normande sauce* (see SAUCE) and garnish as indicated for *Fillets of sole à la normande*.

Fish flans of all kinds can be made in the same way. Collops or fillets of the selected fish are first poached in white wine (or, simply, in butter) and arranged as a border in the flan. Any meatless garnish can be put in the flan, covered with a sauce appropriate to the garnish used.

FLANCS DE TABLE—It was customary in former times to flank the main dish, set in the centre of the dining table, with other dishes. These dishes, which were often large set-pieces of pastry, were placed on the table at the beginning of the meal and left there until the end. In France these dishes were known as *flancs de table*.

FLANDERS. FLANDRES—The cookery of this northern province has much in common with that of Artois and Picardy.

More or less the same stock and produce are to be found there as in Artois.

Among the characteristic dishes of French Flanders are: the *Baby chitterlings of Cambrai and Armentières;* the *Smoked tongues of Valenciennes;* the *Craquelots of Dunkirk*, which are herrings smoked with the leaves of the hazelnut tree; *Soupe verte* (green soup); *Flemish hot-pot; Poule au blanc* (chicken in white sauce); *Rabbit with prunes; Tartine de beurre.*

Among the best known sweets and pastries are: the *Apple pâté of Avesnes;* the *Craquelins of Roubaix;* the *Carrés* of Lannoy; the *Koke-boterom of Dunkirk*, small buns made with eggs and butter, sweetened and decorated with raisins; *Red plum tarts; Couques;* the *Bêtises de Cambrai.*

Good cheeses are made in French Flanders. Those of Bergues, Mont-des-Cats and Marolles (a very pungent cheese) are the best known.

Beer is the local drink, and good quality spirits are distilled from juniper and beetroot.

FLANGNARDE—This flan, which is also sometimes called *flognarde*, is made in Auvergne and Limousin.

Proceed as follows:

Put 3 spoonfuls of flour in a bowl. Break three eggs into it. Add a very little salt. Sweeten. Mix to a smooth paste, adding $1\frac{1}{2}$ pints (three quarters of a litre) of milk, boiled and cooled. Flavour with vanilla or grated lemon rind.

Pour this mixture through a strainer into a deep buttered ovenware dish. Dot neatly with small pieces of butter.

Bake in a very hot oven. Serve hot or cold in the baking dish.

FLANK. FLANCHET—A cut of beef between the fat slice and the breast. See BEEF.

FLATTEN. APLATIR—A culinary term indicating an action which renders a piece of meat (entrecôte, rump steak, escalope, cutlet, *noisette**, etc.) thinner by beating it with a beater or mallet. Flattening meat in this manner makes it easier to cook and renders it relatively more tender.

FLAVOURING. PARFUM—In old culinary practice (before the eighteenth century) flavourings very different from those in use today were resorted to, often excessively, in various culinary preparations.

Not only simple aromatic plants, such as thyme, bay leaf, savoury, coriander, aniseed, marjoram, sage, etc., were used to this end, but even more exotic aromatics: the essence of roses or other flowers, origanum, benzoin, amber, etc.

These aromatics are only used nowadays (and even then in very small doses) in the preparation of sweet courses, in pastry-making and in confectionery.

Liqueur wines such as Madeira, Frontignan, port, sherry, etc. are widely used nowadays for flavouring numerous culinary preparations.

Various brandies (cognac, armagnac, calvados, etc.) are used for flavouring sauces and gravies and for bringing out the taste of preparations, such as game stews, salmis, shell-fish *à l'américaine* or *à la bordelaise*, woodcock flambé, pressed wild ducks, etc.

The seasoning of culinary preparations (the purpose of which is to give relish to food) is achieved with the aid of spices and aromatics. All the information relative to these aromatic plants and their uses in the kitchen will be found in the entry entitled CONDIMENTS.

FLEURON—A small flaky pastry motif used to decorate certain dishes and the top of pâtés in pastry crust.

FLEURS DE VIN—Little whitish or bluish flakes, due to the development of *mycoderma vini*, in wines on the turn. The appearance of these flakes generally precedes acid fermentation.

FLOATING ISLAND. Île flottante—In former times, this sweet was much in favour. It is rather less commonly seen today. This is a pity because it is excellent.

Method. Cut into thin even layers a stale *Savoie* (sponge) cake which has been baked in a round cake tin. Steep the slices in kirsch and maraschino. Spread each one with a layer of apricot jam and sprinkle with chopped blanched almonds and cleaned dried currants. (These must be washed and thoroughly drained.)

Build up the cake into its original shape by laying the slices one on top of the other.

Ice the cake with *Chantilly cream* (see CREAMS) flavoured with vanilla.

Put the cake in a glass bowl. Decorate it with almonds, chopped pistachio nuts and currants.

At the last moment pour chilled vanilla-flavoured custard into the bowl.

The pulp of strawberries, raspberries or red currants, sieved and sweetened, may be used instead of custard.

FLORENTINE (A LA)—A method of preparation used mainly for fish and eggs. The fish, eggs, etc. are set on a bed of spinach stewed in butter, covered with *Mornay sauce* (see SAUCE) sprinkled with grated cheese and browned.

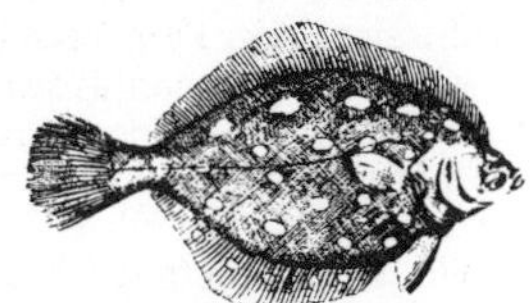

Flounder, plaice

FLOUNDER. Flet, flétan—The common name for a fish of the same family as the brill, dab, lemon-sole, sole and turbot.

While these others never leave the sea, the flounder, though also a salt-water fish, is often found in fresh water. Flounders are even caught in the river Seine between Pont-de-l'Arche and Les Andelys.

The flounder is oval in shape and is covered with tiny scales. Flounders vary in colour from greenish brown to blackish yellow, with yellow, orange or reddish markings.

In France it is sometimes known as *flendre* (or *flondre*) *de rivière* or *picard*. In former times it was called *flétan*, which is the French name for halibut, a quite different fish, more elongated in shape, which is found in northern waters.

In Northern countries of Europe, especially Norway, flounders are preserved by drying and smoking.

Flounders can also be eaten fresh. They are quite delicate but less so than brill and turbot. All recipes for brill and turbot are suitable for flounders.

The flounder plays an important part in American cookery, often taking the place of sole and turbot, which are not found in American waters and, having to be imported, are always rather expensive.

FLOUR. Farine—Flour is the finely ground and bolted meal of wheat and other cereals, including rye, buckwheat, rice oatmeal and maize (corn), but since wheat with its content of gluten is best for breadmaking, the word flour generally connotes wheat flour. The milling of grain for flour dates back to prehistoric times. What, for centuries, was the hard domestic job of producing flour that could be made into bread has developed through the ages into a large industry. There is evidence that wheat or corn was crushed and used as food at least 6,000 years ago; the pounding stones used for this purpose have been discovered in archeological diggings in the British Isles, Switzerland and elsewhere.

The Romans invented slightly conical millstones (querns) which were turned by hand or by slave and beast according to size. Once the grain was crushed the flour was bolted through horsehair sieves to produce different grades of flour. The invention of the water-propelled mill dates from about the time of the birth of Christ and it was also at this time that flat millstones were proved preferable to the conical shaped.

Windmills first appeared in Europe in about 1300 and were widely used until the invention of the steam engine in 1760. From then on rapid advances were made, culminating in the invention of the roller mills, invented and perfected in Switzerland (1834–1836). The roller system with many modern mechanical improvements is still in use in all large commercial mills.

The wheat kernel is composed of three parts; the *Endosperm*, the *Germ* or *Embryo* and the *Bran*. The object of milling is to separate the endosperm from the bran and germ, because the white flour is derived from the endosperm which generally comprises 84% of the kernel as opposed to the 2% content of germ and 14% content of bran. Modern commercial milling of wheat first cleans the wheat by means of air blasts and disk separators. After this dry cleaning or scouring, the wheat is moistened by one method or another and allowed to 'temper'. This hardens the bran and makes the separation more complete.

The separation is accomplished by alternated reductions (rollings at varying tensions) and purifications (classifications by mechanized winnowing and sifting of the endosperm particles, the bran chips and the germ). The results of these successive reductions and purifications are blended into various standard and commercial blends (Patents and Clear Grades) depending on the amount of germ and bran left in the endosperm flour. Freshly milled white flour is pale yellow but becomes white with ageing. To hurry this process most mills use a chemical agent which is rigorously controlled by the government. Vitamin content lost in this process is usually replaced.

Graham flour is unbolted wheat meal ground from the whole kernel. *Whole wheat*, *Whole meal* or *Entire wheat* flour contains all of the kernel except a portion of the bran.

FLOURING. Fariner—To sprinkle lightly with flour fish or some other food to be deep fried.

To dip in flour, before dipping in egg and breadcrumbs, small pieces of meat, usually escalopes and cutlets of veal and lamb cutlets, before frying in butter.

FLOUTES (Alsatian cookery)—Quenelles made with mashed potatoes. See POTATOES.

FLUKE. CARRELET—See PLAICE.

FLÛTE—This is the long French roll very popular in the Paris region. The *Flûte à potage* is a long French roll used for making croûtes served with broths and hot-pots.

FLUTE. CANNELER—Culinary term describing the operation of cutting vegetables, fruit and the edges of some sweet courses, in a decorative manner. Thus vegetables, mushrooms and lemons can be decoratively cut with kitchen knives or with special tools. Circles of pastry cut with a fluted-edged pastry cutter are said to be *cannelé*. The same term is used in the operation of marking the sides of a cake with a small knife, although the last-named operation is more often called *chiquetage* (i.e. *pinking*).

FOGOSCH—This fish, which is very delicate in flavour, is scarcely ever found anywhere else than in Lake Platen in Austria. It grows to a fair size and often weighs between 16–20 pounds (8–10 kilos).

When sliced raw the flesh of the *fogosch* is almost transparent. When it is cooked, it is white.

All recipes for sea-perch and chrysophrys are suitable for this fish.

A pâté de foie gras shaped and decorated by hand, from an 18th century document

FOIE GRAS: Goose and duck foie gras—Preparations made from the livers of fattened geese and ducks were known to the Ancients.

The goose was regarded by the Romans not only as a sacred animal, from the time when a goose saved the Capitol, but also as a succulent one, for its meat and liver were highly prized by the gourmets of this period.

The Romans used various methods of fattening ducks and thereby causing a considerable swelling of the liver.

History tells us that in order to fatten goose livers Scipio Metellus, a Roman gastronome, had the idea of plunging the livers, warm from the still panting bird, in a bath of milk and honey, where they were left for several hours. When taken out of the milk, the livers were considerably swollen and it is said (though we can scarcely believe it) endowed with a richer flavour.

One thing is certain, the fat goose livers upon which the Romans feasted were very large indeed.

In cookery the name *foie gras* is used only of goose or duck liver fattened in a special way.

These livers, especially those of geese, sometime grow to a considerable size. The livers of Toulouse and Strasbourg geese sometimes weigh as much as 4 pounds (2 kilos).

Foie gras is regarded as one of the greatest delicacies available. 'The goose,' says C. Gerard, author of *L'Ancienne Alsace à table*, 'is nothing, but man has made of it an instrument for the output of a marvellous product, a kind of living hothouse in which grows the supreme fruit of gastronomy.'

This 'fruit' is foie gras, from which are made the succulent potted products and marvellous *pâtés* made in some French towns such as Strasbourg, Toulouse, Périgueux, Nancy, etc.

The finest foies gras come from geese reared in Alsace and south-western France. Toulouse foies gras are greatly sought after. Duck foie gras is also very delicate, but having a tendency to disintegrate in cooking, lends itself less satisfactorily to the many ways, hot or cold, in which foie gras can be prepared. Other European countries (besides France) produce very good goose foie gras, notably Austria, Czechoslovakia and the Duchy of Luxemburg.

The quality of foie gras can be judged primarily by its colour and also by texture. It should be creamy-white, tinged with pink and very firm.

Foie gras aspic—See ASPIC.

Foie gras en Bellevue—Line a plain mould with jelly. Decorate with strips of truffle and the whites of hard boiled egg. Cover these with a second layer of jelly. Leave on ice until thoroughly set. Put in slices of poached foie gras or neat slices of potted foie gras with truffles. Fill the mould with half-set jelly. Chill on ice.

Turn out on a dish covered with a napkin.

Foie gras en brioche (hot)—Season some truffles and pour brandy over them. Take a large, very firm foie gras which will not disintegrate in cooking. Stud it with the truffles. Season with spiced salt. Pour brandy over it and leave it to steep for several hours in this seasoning.

Wrap the foie gras in a piece of pork caul (or in very thin slices of pork fat) and cook in a slow oven for 18 to 20 minutes. Leave to cool.

Put it in a plain, round, buttered baking tin lined fairly thickly with ordinary unsweetened *Brioche dough**. Cover with a layer of dough. Tie a strip of buttered paper round the tin, to prevent the dough from overflowing during baking. Leave the dough to rise in a warm place.

Bake in a hot oven for 50 minutes to an hour. To test whether the foie gras is cooked, drive a long skewer into it. If the skewer comes out quite clean, the foie gras is ready. Turn out the brioche and serve as it is. A fluted mould can also be used for *foie gras en brioche*. In this case the dough should be shaped as for a *Brioche à tête**.

Foie gras en brioche (cold)—Proceed exactly as for *Foie gras en brioche* (*hot*). Leave to cool before serving.

Foie gras en chausson—Proceed as for *Foie gras en brioche*.

Stud the foie gras with truffles and cook for 18 to 20 minutes. Put it on a rather stiff layer of *Brioche dough**. Roll the dough in a scroll shape. Bake in the oven. Serve hot or cold.

Foie gras en cocotte or en casserole—Trim a large, very firm foie gras and stud with truffles seasoned with spiced salt and sprinkled with brandy. Season the foie gras with spiced salt (see SALT), pour on brandy and leave to steep in the seasoning for 12 hours.

Brown the foie gras in very hot butter. Put it in an oval ovenware dish. Moisten with the cooking stock, moistened with Madeira (or any other heavy wine) and very concentrated thickened brown veal stock. Cover the dish. Seal with a strip of dough. Cook in a slow oven for 45 minutes to an hour, according to the size of the foie gras. Serve as it is, in the cooking dish.

Foie gras crêpes (pancakes) à la Périgourdine. PANNEQUETTES DE FOIE GRAS À LA PÉRIGOURDINE—Make some thin unsweetened pancakes in the usual way. Fill them with foie gras mixed with chopped truffles and flavoured with a little armagnac. Roll the pancakes into scrolls. Trim at each end and halve them. Put them on a buttered dish. Sprinkle lightly with fried breadcrumbs. Warm for a few minutes in the oven.

Foie gras crépinettes à la Périgueux. CRÉPINETTES DE FOIE GRAS À LA PÉRIGUEUX—Proceed as for *Crépinettes of chicken.* In the middle of the stuffing of each *crépinette* (flat sausage made with stuffing wrapped in pork caul or thin slices of pork fat), put a slice of foie gras well browned in butter.

Foie gras cutlets, croquettes and kromeskies. CÔTELETTES, CROQUETTES, CROMESQUIS DE FOIE GRAS—These different preparations, which are served as hot hors d'ouevre or a light main course, are made from *salpicon* of liver, usually with diced truffles added, in the same way as chicken cutlets, croquettes and kromeskies. See HORS-D'OEUVRE.

Foie gras 'eggs' (cold). OEUFS DE FOIE GRAS FROIDS—Made with foie gras mousse shaped in little egg-shaped moulds. A truffle is placed in the middle of the mousse which, when it is quite cold is coated with jelly and covered with brown or white *Chaud-froid sauce* (see SAUCE).

The 'eggs' are then built up into a pyramid on a napkin or put in a nest of butter piped through a forcing bag.

Escalopes of foie gras Cambacérès—Sauté slices of foie gras in butter. Put each one on an artichoke heart stewed in butter, filled with a *salpicon* of mushrooms in cream.

On top of each escalope arrange 2 thick strips of truffle. Pour on the dish the cooking stock diluted with Madeira, and thickened with *Demi-glace* (see SAUCE) flavoured with *Essence of truffles**.

Escalopes of foie gras en chaud-froid—Slices of foie gras (plain or truffled) covered with *White chaud-froid sauce* (see SAUCE), moistened either with clear brown veal stock or chicken essence, decorated with truffles, whites of hard boiled egg, pickled tongue, and high-lighted with jelly.

The escalopes can be served in little individual paper cases, silver, porcelain or glass shells, each one on a bed of chopped jelly.

The escalopes can also be arranged in a circle in a glass bowl on a bed of jelly set hard. They are then covered with jelly. Or they can be heaped into a dome on a platform of sandwich bread, cut round.

Escalopes of foie gras with grapes. ESCALOPES DE FOIE GRAS AUX RAISINS—Sauté slices of foie gras in butter. Drain them. Put each one on an oval slice of bread fried in butter. Decorate with large, peeled grapes. Dilute the cooking juices with Frontignan or any other heavy wine. Boil down the mixture. Add a few tablespoons of thickened brown veal stock. Boil again. Cover the escalopes with this sauce.

Escalopes of foie gras with grapes and truffles (cold). ESCALOPES DE FOIE GRAS AUX RAISINS ET AUX TRUFFES—Cook the foie gras in its own fat. Cut into neat slices. On top of each escalope place a wide strip of truffle, dipped in jelly so that it will stick to the escalope. Glaze with jelly.

Arrange the escalopes in a circle in a shallow glass bowl or a shallow silver dish. In the middle, heap a dome of large fresh peeled grapes which have been steeped in a little liqueur brandy. Cover the whole dish with very clear jelly flavoured with port or any other heavy wine. Chill thoroughly on ice or in the refrigerator.

Escalopes of foie gras Montrouge—Sauté slices of foie gras in butter. Arrange them in a circle, each on a round slice of bread fried in butter. Pile rather thick *Mushroom purée** in the middle of the dish. Cover the escalopes with their cooking juices diluted with Madeira and veal stock.

Escalopes of foie gras Richelieu—Dip the slices of foie gras in egg and breadcrumbs. Sauté in clarified butter. Arrange them in a circle on a serving dish. Pour over them diced truffles in melted butter, flavoured with a little Madeira or some other heavy wine.

Escalopes of foie gras à la romaine—Sauté slices of foie gras in butter. Arrange on rounds of bread fried in butter. Cover with *Romaine sauce* (see SAUCE). Fill the middle of the plate with rice cooked in butter.

Escalopes of foie gras with truffles. ESCALOPES DE FOIE GRAS AUX TRUFFES—Sauté slices of foie gras in butter. Arrange on rounds of bread fried in butter. Cover with slices of truffle heated in the butter in which the escalopes have been cooked. Dilute the cooking juices with Madeira or some other heavy wine and *Demi-glace* (see SAUCE) and pour this sauce over the dish.

Foie gras à la financière—Stud a foie gras with truffles. Season with spiced salt. Pour on brandy. Leave to steep for a few hours in this seasoning. Wrap the foie gras in pork caul or thin slices of pork fat. Cook it in a braising stock moistened with Madeira for 40 to 45 minutes.

Drain the liver. Put it on a slice of bread fried in butter or straight on to a serving dish. Surround with a *Financière garnish* (see GARNISHES) to which the braising stock of the liver, concentrated and strained, has been added.

Foie gras loaf (hot). PAIN DE FOIE GRAS—This dish is more a soufflé than a loaf and is usually described as such on restaurant menus. See MOUSSE, *Foie gras mousse.*

Foie gras loaf in jelly. PAIN DE FOIE GRAS À LA GELÉE—Poach a large fat liver in Madeira-flavoured liquid jelly. Allow to cool, drain the liver and cut one lobe into 8 uniform-sized slices.

Remove fat from the liquor in which the liver was poached and add to it an equal quantity of aspic jelly based on concentrated truffle stock simmered down to the consistency of a *fumet**. Add a small glass of fine champagne brandy, reduce (boil down) the liquor by half and bind with a liaison of 4 yolks of egg. Heat, incorporate $\frac{7}{8}$ cup (200 grams) of butter and proceed as described in the recipe for *Hollandaise sauce* (see SAUCE, *Cold sauces*).

When this emulsion is just warm, add to it 2 leaves (1 teaspoon) of gelatine soaked in warm water and the rest of the liver rubbed through a fine sieve. Blend without stirring too much.

Coat a big round mould with very clear jelly. Decorate the walls of the mould with slivers of truffles. Fill with the liver composition putting it in layers and alternating with layers of sliced liver and slivers of truffles. Cover with a layer of jelly. Leave to set in a cooler or on ice.

Turn out on to a round dish, placing the loaf either straight on the dish, or on a buttered crustless croûton, or any other foundation. Garnish the dish with jelly croûtons.

Foie gras medallions. MÉDAILLONS DE FOIE GRAS—Slices of foie gras are sometimes called medallions. Medallions of foie gras can be served hot or cold. See above, *Escalopes of foie gras*.

Foie gras mousse (cold). MOUSSE DE FOIE GRAS—Prepare the mousse mixture as follows:

Rub cooked foie gras through a fine sieve. Put this purée in a bowl with 1¼ cups (2½ decilitres) of melted jelly and 2 cups (4 decilitres) of *Chicken velouté* (see SAUCE) to every quart (litre) of purée. Work this mixture gently on ice. Season. At the last moment add about 2 cups (4 decilitres) of partly whisked fresh cream.

Put this mixture in a plain round mould lined with jelly and decorated with truffles, the whites of hard boiled eggs or some other suitable ingredient. Fill the bowl only to within ½ inch of the top. Cover the mousse with a layer of jelly. Chill in the refrigerator.

Turn the mousse out on to a buttered slice of bread or straight on to a serving dish. Surround with chopped jelly and make a border of rounds of jelly (cut out with a pastry-cutter).

Foie gras mousse can be made in a fancy mould. It is also possible, and it is now usual, to serve foie gras mousse in a round silver dish on a layer of set jelly. Smooth the top of the mousse, which should be slightly domed in the middle. Decorate the top with handsome strips of truffle and glaze with jelly.

Foie gras mousse can also be served in a glass bowl, on a bed of jelly set hard and covered with jelly.

Foie gras mousse (hot). MOUSSE DE FOIE GRAS (CHAUDE)—See MOUSSE, *Foie gras mousse*.

Foie gras mousselines (cold). MOUSSELINES DE FOIE GRAS—Use the same mixture as for *Foie gras mousse (cold)*. Put this mixture into little cups. Decorate with truffles. Glaze with jelly.

This mixture can also be shaped in egg-shaped or other moulds. In this case, they are covered with jelly.

Diced truffles may be added to the mousse or mousseline mixture.

Foie gras with paprika (cold). FOIE GRAS AU PAPRIKA—Stud the foie gras with truffles. Season with salt and paprika. Pour brandy over it. Wrap it in a piece of pork caul and poach in Madeira. When the liver is cooked, drain it and leave to cool. Unwrap it. Press it into shape in a fine cloth. Cover with *Chaud-froid sauce* flavoured with paprika (see SAUCE). Decorate with strips of truffle and sweet peppers, green and red, cut into rings and poached for a few seconds in jelly.

Glaze the foie gras with jelly. Put it in an oval glass dish or a silver bowl. Cover with very clear jelly, flavoured with port or any other heavy wine.

Parfait of foie gras (cold)—This name is given to several preparations which differ quite considerably from one another.

In former times a *Parfait of foie gras* was a mousse of foie gras in jelly. Nowadays, it is a whole foie gras, studded with truffles, poached in a Madeira-flavoured aspic stock, cooled and served in jelly.

Some writers on cookery describe as a *parfait* a pâté of foie gras in pastry crust, which is the same as an ordinary *Pâté de foie gras*, except that instead of the empty pockets on the surface (which appear when the pâté is cold) being filled with butter or goose fat, they are filled with jelly.

It would seem that the term *parfait*, which implies a dish of exceptional gastronomic merit, should be reserved for truffled foie gras, poached in Madeira and jelly stock, cooled and served in very clear jelly.

Pâté de foie gras de Périgueux (old recipe)—'To 2 pounds of truffles add 12 foies gras' (in those days fat white chicken livers were mainly used), '3 pounds of pork fat, parsley, spring onions and mushrooms. Chop the lot. Make the pâté high enough to use up all the mixture. Make it of chopped pork fat covered with a layer of sliced truffles seasoned with fine salt and fine spices mixed, and *fines herbes;* next, another layer of pork fat and on top of that a layer of foie gras seasoned as indicated above, and mushrooms, parsley and spring onions. Continue building up the pâté in the same order until all the ingredients are used up. Cover the whole with slices of pork fat. Finish as usual. Cook and leave to cool for a final course.' (*Dictionnaire portatif de cuisine*, Paris, 1767).

Truffled pâté de foie gras (*Presse Moderne*)

Truffled pâté de foie gras. PÂTÉ DE FOIE GRAS TRUFFÉ—*Ingredients.* 2 very firm foies gras; 2 pounds (1 kilo) pork and foie gras forcemeat; ¾ pound (400 grams) truffles; 2 pounds (1 kilo) pastry dough; salt, pepper, spices, brandy, Madeira.

Method. Stud the foie gras with truffles, peeled and quartered or, if small, left whole. These should be seasoned with *spiced salt* (see SALT) and sprinkled with brandy. Season the livers with spiced salt and leave to steep in brandy and Madeira for 2 hours.

Line a pâté mould (a hinged round or oval mould) with the pastry dough (made with butter or lard). This must be made in advance and left to stand for a long time (see PASTRY DOUGH FOR PÂTÉS).

Line the bottom and sides of the pastry with part of the stuffing. Put in foie gras, pressed close together. Cover with a domed layer of stuffing. On top of this, lay a slice of pork fat and half a bay leaf and a small sprig of thyme. Cover the pâté with a layer of dough and seal the edges. Decorate the top of the pâté with decorative pastry motifs shaped with pastry cutters (lozenges, leaves, crescents, etc.) or strips of plaited dough forming a dome and pressed down at the edges. In the middle put 3 or 4 round pieces of dough shaped with a fluted pastry-cutter. Make a hole in the middle of these for the escape of steam during baking. Brush with egg. Bake in a fairly hot oven, allowing 15 to 20 minutes per pound (30 to 35 minutes per kilo).

Cool the pâté in the mould. When it is luke-warm pour into it either half-melted lard, if it is to be kept for some time, or, if it is to be used at once, Madeira-flavoured jelly.

Pâté de foie gras must be made at least 12 hours before using. The mould can be lined with a stuffing made entirely of foie gras instead of with pork stuffing.

Small truffled pâtés de foie gras (old recipe). PETITS PÂTÉS DE FOIE GRAS AUX TRUFFES—'Take foies gras and stud with truffles. Make a foie gras stuffing especially for the purpose. Prepare little individual pâtés. Put the stuffing at the bottom, a piece of foie gras on top and a truffle at each side. Cover with stuffing. Finish, brush with egg and put them in the oven. When they are ready, uncover them, pour a little essence into them and serve.' (*Le Cuisinier Gascon*, Amsterdam, 1747).

Potted foie gras with truffles. TERRINE DE FOIE GRAS AUX TRUFFES—Cut a large foie gras in half. Trim the halves (the trimmings are used to make the forcemeat), and stud them with large pieces of truffle. Season the foie gras with *Spiced salt* (see SALT). Pour brandy over it and steep for an hour or two in this seasoning.

Line an oval ovenware dish with thin slices of pork fat. Put in it a fairly thin layer of a forcemeat made with $\frac{3}{4}$ pound (375 grams) of lean pork, 1 pound (475 grams) of fresh pork fat, the trimmings of the foie gras (about 7 ounces or 200 grams), 5 ounces (150 grams) of diced or chopped truffles, flavoured with $\frac{1}{4}$ cup ($\frac{1}{2}$ decilitre) of Madeira or brandy and seasoned with 2 tablespoons (25 grams) of spiced salt. Put half a foie gras on top of this forcemeat. Cover with a layer of truffled forcemeat. Put the other half of foie gras on top. Cover with the remainder of the forcemeat. Press down well to flatten all the ingredients. Cover with a thin slice of pork fat. On top of this put half a bay leaf and a small sprig of thyme. Cover the dish and seal with flour and water paste. Cook in the oven, standing in a pan half-full of hot water, for 45 minutes to an hour, according to the size of the dish.

Leave to cool under a light weight until the following day. Next day, turn it out (this can be more easily done if the dish is first stood for a few seconds in hot water). Remove the slices of lard covering the potted foie gras. Dry the foie gras with a cloth, pressing a little so as to make the forcemeat quite firm. Before replacing it in the container, line the bottom of the container with a layer of lard mixed with goose fat (which was exuded in cooking). Pour a similar mixture of fat, almost cold, over the foie gras. Leave to chill in the refrigerator for at least 10 hours. Serve as it is in the cooking dish.

Note. It is advisable to prepare potted foie gras (and other potted preparations containing foie gras) at least 24 hours before using.

To make it easier to serve in individual portions, potted foie gras is made in restaurant kitchens in rectangular earthenware, porcelain or metal dishes.

Potted foie gras with truffles à la façon périgourdine. TERRINE DE FOIE GRAS À LA FAÇON PÉRIGOURDINE—Take a large very firm foie gras and soak all night in cold water. Drain and dry in a cloth.

Make several incisions in the lobes of the foie gras, and put into each one a piece of truffle. Season the foie gras with salt and spices.

Completely line a *terrine* with thin slices of fresh pork fat. Put the foie gras into it. Press it well down into the container. Cover with a thin layer of lean and fat pork, chopped and seasoned together. Pour on a few tablespoons of good spirits, and on top of the whole mixture put a little luke-warm melted goose fat.

Cover the *terrine* and seal the edges with flour and water paste. Stand it in a pan half-full of hot water. Cook evenly in a hot oven for about an hour. Leave under a light weight until quite cold. When the foie gras is very cold, pour on a few tablespoons of goose fat and when this is quite set, add a little melted lard. Cover the *terrine*. Seal with a strip of gummed silver paper. Keep in a cool, dry place.

Preserved potted foie gras in goose fat. CONSERVE DE FOIE GRAS AU NATUREL EN TERRINE—Season the foie gras with *Spiced salt* (see SALT). Steep in brandy for a few hours. Dry it. Cook it gently, that is to say poach it in clarified goose fat. Drain the foie gras. Put it in a round *terrine* just large enough to contain it. Cover with goose fat. Leave until quite cold. Now, pour over it a thin layer of melted lard. Leave to cool. Cover the terrine. Seal the edges with a strip of gummed silver paper.

Prepared in this way and kept in a dry, cool place, foie gras will keep for a very long time.

Quenelles of foie gras—See QUENELLES.

Foie gras rissoles. RISSOLES DE FOIE GRAS—Cut a layer of *Flaky pastry dough* (see DOUGH) into small shapes with a round fluted pastry cutter. In the middle of each one put a heaped spoonful of *salpicon** of foie gras with diced truffles added, seasoned and flavoured with a little brandy.

Roll the pastry into scrolls, sealing the edges carefully. Deep fry at the last moment. Arrange in a clump on a napkin. Garnish with fried parsley. Serve *Périgueux sauce* (see SAUCE) separately.

Foie gras shells in jelly. COQUILLES DE FOIE GRAS À LA GELÉE—A method of presenting potted foie gras or foie gras cooked in its own fat. These shells, which must be very carefully shaped, are cut out with a shell-shaped scoop with sharp edges. They can also be made with an ordinary tablespoon. To prevent the foie gras from sticking to the spoon or scoop, dip in hot water before cutting the foie gras.

The foie gras shells are served in individual metal, porcelain or glass shells, or arranged in a pyramid on a napkin. In either case, they are decorated with chopped jelly.

Foie gras soufflé. SOUFFLÉ DE FOIE GRAS—Rub through a fine sieve 10 ounces (300 grams) of carefully trimmed raw foie gras, which has been pounded in a mortar with 3 whites of egg. Put the mixture in a bowl and work on ice, incorporating about $1\frac{1}{2}$ cups (3 decilitres) of thick fresh cream, added to the mixture little by little. Finally, add 3 to 4 whites of egg beaten to a stiff foam. Fill a buttered soufflé dish with this mixture. Stand it in a pan of water and cook for 30 to 35 minutes.

Serve separately *Périgueux sauce* or *Madeira sauce* (see SAUCE) with *truffle essence* (see ESSENCE).

Foie gras soufflé can also be made with purée of cooked foie gras.

Foie gras Souvarov—Brown a firm foie gras in very hot butter, after seasoning it and leaving it to steep in brandy. Put it in an oval earthenware heatproof dish with large quartered truffles. Pour on a little *Demi-glace sauce* (see SAUCE) diluted with *Truffle essence* (see ESSENCE). Cover the dish and seal with a strip of dough. Cook in a moderate oven for 40 to 50 minutes according to the size of the foie gras. Serve as it is in the cooking dish.

Foie gras tart à l'ancienne. TOURTE DE FOIE GRAS À L'ANCIENNE—Roll out a layer of *Fine lining pastry* (see DOUGH) and cut it round. Fill the middle with a layer of *Mousseline forcemeat* (see FORCEMEAT) mixed with a little foie gras purée and chopped truffles, leaving a border of $1\frac{1}{2}$ inches.

Lay on this stuffing 10 slices of foie gras, seasoned and steeped in brandy, and the same number of rather thick strips of raw truffle. Put these strips of truffle on top of the slices and cover the whole with a thin layer of stuffing. Cover with a round piece of rolled-out pastry and seal the edges carefully. Pink the edge of the tart. Make a hole in the middle. Decorate the top with little flaky pastry motifs or score with shallow criss-cross lines. Brush with egg and bake in the oven for 45 to 50 minutes. When the tart is ready, pour in, through the hole in the middle, a few spoonfuls of very concentrated *Demi-glace sauce* (see SAUCE) flavoured with *Essence of truffles**. This tart can equally well be made with *Flaky pastry* (see DOUGH).

Foie gras tart with truffles (cold). TOURTE DE FOIE GRAS AUX TRUFFES—Using *Fine lining pastry* (see DOUGH) make the tart as indicated for *Foie gras tart à l'ancienne*. When it is ready leave it to cool. When it is cold, pour into it through the hole in the centre a few tablespoons of Madeira-flavoured jelly.

Tinned foie gras in goose fat. CONSERVE DE FOIE GRAS AU NATUREL—Oval tins are used for this purpose. Put into them very firm foies gras, seasoned and steeped for 2 hours in brandy. Put a little goose fat in the tins. Seal them. Stand them in water and *boil steadily* for 1½ hours for tins weighing 2 pounds (1 kilo) and 1 hour for tins weighing 1 pound (500 grams).

Drain the tins. Leave to cool. Dry thoroughly and keep in a cool, dry place.

Truffled foie gras in Madeira (hot). FOIE GRAS TRUFFÉ AU MADÈRE—This dish is made with foie gras studded with truffles and cooked in its own fat. It is then put in a silver dish or glass bowl and drowned in jelly flavoured with Madeira, port, sherry, or any other heavy wine.

Stud a foie gras with truffles and pour brandy over it. Leave to steep in this seasoning. Wrap the foie gras in a piece of pork caul or thin slices of pork fat. Put it in a small braising dish lined with fresh pork skin and sliced onions and carrots, tossed in butter. Cover and simmer for 7 to 8 minutes on the stove. Moisten with 1¼ cups (2½ decilitres) of Madeira. Simmer several minutes. Add 1½ cups (3 decilitres) of concentrated brown veal stock. Cook in the oven for 45 minutes.

Drain and unwrap the foie gras. Put it on a serving dish; strain and skim all fat off the stock. Cover the foie gras with the stock.

Truffled foie gras in Madeira (cold). FOIE GRAS TRUFFÉ AU MADÈRE—Proceed exactly as for *Truffled foie gras in Madeira (hot)*. When the liver is cooked, drain and unwrap it. Put it in a terrine just large enough to hold it. Strain the cooking stock and pour it over the foie gras. Leave it to cool for 12 hours. Next day, skim the layer of fat which will have formed on the sauce. Serve it as it is, in the terrine.

Note. When *Foie gras in Madeira* is to be served cold, the veal stock must be of a kind that will readily set into a jelly.

Truffled foie gras in port (cold). FOIE GRAS TRUFFÉ AU PORTO—Proceed as for *Truffled foie gras in Madeira (cold)*, using jelly flavoured with port. Even when ruby port is used, the jelly should be amber-coloured.

FOLLE-BLANCHE—The name of a vine bearing white grapes, which grows in the Charentes region. The wine made from these grapes is of rather poor quality, but it is used in the distillation of brandy.

FONDANT—See ICING.

FONDANTS (croquettes)—See HORS-D'OEUVRE, *Hot hors-d'oeuvre*.

FONDUE—This name applies to a number of different dishes. For instance, it is the name for a kind of cheese sauce which originally came from Switzerland. The recipe for this follows under *Cheese fondue I*.

Under the same name—though quite unjustifiably—goes a dish of scrambled eggs with cheese of which an original recipe can be found in Brillat-Savarin's *Physiologie du Goût*. See *Cheese fondue II*.

Certain vegetable preparations are also called *fondue*. The vegetables in question are cooked for a very long time in butter or lard or oil until they are reduced to pulp, i.e. become *fondues*. Different vegetable *fondues* can be used as constituent elements in a great many dishes.

Carrot fondue. FONDUE DE CAROTTES—Gently cook very finely sliced or shredded carrots in butter, in a covered pan. Season with salt and a pinch of sugar.

To avoid the carrots being fried in the butter add from time to time a few drops of water or *bouillon*.

Cook the carrots until they are reduced to a pulp, i.e. become *fondues*.

Celery fondue. FONDUE DE CÉLERI—This dish can be done with celery or celeriac. Gently cook in butter adding a few drops of water or bouillon, 1 pound (500 grams) of celery finely sliced, cut like matchsticks or diced. Season. Cook until the moisture has completely evaporated.

Cheese fondue

Cheese fondue I. FONDUE DE FROMAGE—This dish originates in the French-speaking part of Switzerland. It consists of grated cheese melted in white wine, seasoned with pepper and flavoured at the last minute with a little kirsch.

The *Valais fondue* contains no butter, no eggs, no flour or starch of any kind and no chemical products in its original form. It is prepared in a small casserole and served on a hot plate (or trivet). Each person round the table dips a piece of bread spiked on the end of his fork into the dish.

The *Fribourg* (*Freiburg*) *fondue* is prepared with Vacherin cheese. Vacherin is made in Savoy from cows' milk and is a soft cheese.

The *Neuchâtel fondue* has Gruyère cheese as a basis. For this dish stale and fresh cheese are mixed.

This dish has undergone various modifications and most gastronomic writers who have described it have given different recipes which are as complicated as they are inexact.

Cheese fondue II according to Brillat-Savarin. FONDUE AU FROMAGE BRILLAT-SAVARIN—This is the name the author gives to a dish of scrambled eggs with cheese in his book *Physiologie du goût*. The following is a translation of the original recipe.

'Recipe of *fondue* as found in M. Trollet's papers. He was bailiff of Mondon in the Canton of Berne.

'Weigh the number of eggs which you want to use. This

number depends on how many people are going to eat with you.

'Take a piece of good Gruyère weighing a third and butter weighing a sixth of the weight of the eggs.

'Break the eggs and beat them well in a casserole. Add the butter and the cheese, grated or minced.

'Put the casserole on a hot stove and stir with a wooden spoon until the mixture has suitably thickened and is smooth. Add a very little or hardly any salt, depending on the age of the cheese. Add a good portion of pepper, which is one of the distinguishing characteristics of this ancient dish. Serve on a lightly heated dish.'

Chervil tuber fondue. FONDUE DE CERFEUIL TUBÉREUX—Prepared in the same way as *Celery fondue**.

Chicory fondue. FONDUE D'ENDIVES—Mince finely 1 pound (500 grams) of raw chicory. Cook gently in butter in a covered pan. Season.

This *fondue* is served as a garnish for egg and fish dishes as well as cuts of meat, and poultry or vegetable dishes.

Fennel tuber fondue. FONDUE DE FENOUIL TUBÉREUX—Prepared and used in the same way as *Celery fondue**.

Leek fondue. FONDUE DE POIREAUX—Shred or cut into fine slices the white part of leeks and cook gently in butter until very soft. Season.

Used in sauces, stuffings, stews; as garnish for eggs, fish, meat, poultry and vegetables.

Lettuce fondue. FONDUE DE LAITUES—This is prepared in the same way as *Lettuce chiffonnade**.

It is used as constituent element in thick or thin soups; it is also used as a garnish for eggs and dishes of small cuts of meat or poultry.

Mushroom fondue. FONDUE AUX CHAMPIGNONS—Mince the mushrooms, thicken with cream, and brown in the oven.

Onion fondue. FONDUE D'OIGNONS—1 pound (500 grams) shredded or finely chopped onions are gently cooked in butter in a covered pan without allowing them to colour. To avoid the onions getting fried, moisten them from time to time with water or stock. Season.

Sorrel fondue. FONDUE D'OSEILLE—This is prepared in the same way as *Sorrel chiffonnade**.

It is used as a constituent element in thick and thin soups and as an egg garnish with small cuts of meat and with poultry.

Sweet pepper fondue. FONDUE DE PIMENTS DOUX—Cut 1 pound (500 grams) of sweet peppers (pimentos) very finely like matchsticks; peel and remove seeds and stalk. Cook gently until soft in butter or oil. Season.

Use in hot and cold sauces, in different kinds of stuffings, with soft eggs, in omelettes, with hot or cold fish, with crustaceans, with meat, poultry and vegetables.

Tomato fondue. FONDUE DE TOMATES—Gently cook 1 medium sized onion (100 grams) chopped in butter or a butter and oil mixture. For some dishes you can also cook them in oil only. When the onions begin to colour, add six tomatoes. The latter must be peeled, seeded, cut into pieces or chopped. Season with salt and pepper. Add one grated clove of garlic. Cook gently until the liquid of the tomatoes has almost disappeared. Add half a tablespoon of chopped parsley at the last minute.

Note. Tomato fondue is used for an infinite number of dishes, mainly for those called *à la provençale*, *à la portugaise*, or *à la madrilène*. It is a garnish for eggs and for vegetables such as mushrooms, small vegetable marrows (zucchinis), aubergines (egg-plant), artichoke hearts, etc. When made with oil, and chilled, tomato fondue is often used in the preparation of cold hors-d'oeuvre.

Tomato fondue à la niçoise. FONDUE DE TOMATES, DITE À LA NIÇOISE—This is prepared in the same way as *Tomato fondue** with the addition of tarragon and chopped chervil. It is used in the same dishes.

Tomato fondue à l'orientale. FONDUE DE TOMATES À L'ORIENTALE—This dish is prepared in the same way as *Tomato fondue**, with the addition of a pinch of saffron. Its uses are the same.

Vegetable fondue. FONDUE DE LÉGUMES—Cut into small slices two carrots, a tender turnip, the white part of a leek, and a medium-sized onion. Add a quarter of a celery root also cut into thin slices.

Mix all these ingredients, season with salt and a teaspoon of castor or powdered sugar. Add a large tablespoon of butter and cook in a covered heavy pan.

When the vegetables are quite soft and of a good mahogany colour add $\frac{1}{3}$ to $\frac{1}{2}$ cup (1 decilitre) of thin veal stock or, failing that, water to which a little veal jelly has been added.

Cook very slowly until all the liquid has disappeared.

This fondue is used as a garnish for meat sautés, eggs or fish.

FONTAINEBLEAU—This town is well known in the gastronomic world because of its famous grapes, which are found in and near Thomery (see GRAPES) and also because of its succulent cream-cheese, which is eaten as a sweet (dessert).

FOOL—Fruit purée. Fruit of almost any variety is cooked with very little water and passed through a fine sieve. The pulp is sugared and kept cool—on ice if possible. At the last minute whipped cream is added to the pulp in the proportion of two to one, mixed gently and served in sherbet glasses.

FORCEMEATS OR STUFFINGS. FARCES—Forcemeats or stuffings, which are a mixture of ingredients minced or chopped and spiced, are among the preparations most widely used in cooking.

They figure in most dishes made from pork products, in pâtés, potted preparations, galantines and *ballottines**.

They are used to stuff or garnish eggs, fish, poultry, game, meat, vegetables, etc.

Forcemeats are also used, especially that known as *godiveau*, which is one of the oldest preparations in French cookery, in the making of forcemeat balls, borders, mousses, moulds, etc.

There are, moreover, an infinite number of forcemeats or stuffings which can be made with or without meat, though all of them derive from 5 basic forcemeats. These are:

(1) *Pork forcemeat;*

(2) *Veal and fat forcemeat, known as godiveau;*

(3) *Fine forcemeat, with cream;*

(4) *Forcemeat made of special ingredients*, with or without meat;

(5) *Gratin forcemeat*.

Usually, forcemeats used in cookery, whether or not they contain meat, are given substance by the addition of various *panadas* (see below).

Most forcemeats made of butchers' meat, poultry or game are bound with eggs.

Panada for stuffings or forcemeats. PANADE—A *panada* is a preparation made with various flours or bread, usually boiled in water or milk or stock and used to bind stuffings or forcemeats.

Generally, *panadas* are added to stuffings in the proportion: 2 parts basic ingredients to 1 part *panada*.

The *panada* should not be added to the forcemeat or

stuffing until it is completely cold. To speed up the cooling process, spread out the force on a buttered dish. Cover with buttered paper to prevent a crust from forming through exposure to the air. For the preparation of various *panadas* see PANADA.

Seasoning and binding of forcemeats or stuffing for galantines, pâtés and potted preparations—For every pound (500 grams) of forcemeat, 2 tablespoons (½ ounce) (12–15 grams) of spiced salt (salt, pepper and spices) and ⅓ cup (¾ decilitre) of brandy or cognac are used as seasoning. To bind, use 1 egg for every pound (500 grams) of forcemeat stuffing.

FORCEMEATS OR STUFFINGS MADE WITH BEEF, VEAL, PORK, GAME AND POULTRY. FARCES DE CHAIR DE VEAU, DE PORC, DE GIBIER, DE VOLAILLE:

Beef forcemeat for agnolotti. FARCE DE BOEUF POUR LES AGNOLOTTI—This forcemeat is made of 1 pound (500 grams) of beef braised in red wine.

When completely cooked, remove the beef, chop and add to it ½ pound (250 grams) of chopped braised cabbage.

Add to the forcemeat ½ cup (50 grams) of grated Parmesan cheese and season with salt, pepper and spices.

Pass the sauce in which the beef was braised through a fine sieve, and use it as was already described above, for serving with agnolotti.

Chicken (or other poultry) forcemeat. FARCE DE VOLAILLE—Prepare like *Veal and pork forcemeat* using the following ingredients: ½ pound (250 grams) of chicken (or other poultry meat, such as turkey, pigeon, duck, guinea-fowl), 3½ ounces (100 grams) of lean veal, 3½ ounces (100 grams) of pork, 15 ounces (450 grams) of fresh bacon, 2 eggs, ¾ cup (1½ decilitres) of brandy and 5 to 6 teaspoons (25 to 30 grams) of *Spiced salt* (see SALT).

Note. This forcemeat can also be prepared using only the meat of fowl indicated and fresh bacon.

Forcemeat or stuffing for galantines, pâtés and potted preparations. FARCE POUR GALANTINES, PÂTÉS, TERRINES—*Ingredients.* ½ pound (250 grams) of lean veal (net weight); 1 pound (500 grams) of lean pork (net weight); 1 pound (500 grams) of fresh pork fat; 2 eggs; 6 tablespoons (45 grams) of *spiced salt* (see SALT); ¾ cup (1½ decilitres) of brandy.

Method. Dice the veal, pork and pork fat. Pound these ingredients in a mortar with the seasoning and brandy. Add the eggs and mix well. Rub through a fine sieve. Stir until the stuffing is very smooth.

Game forcemeats, various. FARCE DE GIBIERS—Prepare like *Chicken (or other poultry) forcemeat*, replacing chicken by the game meat.

Game stuffing for pâtés and potted preparations. FARCE DE GIBIER POUR PÂTÉS ET TERRINES—Using whatever game is indicated in the recipe, proceed as for *Chicken (or other poultry) forcemeat.*

To render this stuffing more delicate, the trimmings of fresh foie gras are added to it.

It can also be enriched by the addition of *à gratin game stuffing* and some very concentrated game essence.

A gratin calves' liver forcemeat or stuffing for borders and hot pâtés. FARCE À GRATIN DE FOIE DE VEAU—*Ingredients.* 10 ounces (300 grams) trimmed calves' liver; ½ pound (250 grams) fat belly of pork (pork fat); ½ cup (75 grams) cultivated mushroom peelings; 3 tablespoons (40 grams) chopped shallots; 1¼ cups (150 grams) butter; 4 teaspoons (20 grams) salt; 1½ teaspoons (4 grams) pepper; ½ teaspoon (2 grams) of cloves; a small sprig of thyme; half a bay leaf; ¾ cup (1½ decilitres) white wine; 3 egg yolks.

Method. Brown the diced belly of pork in 3 tablespoons (50 grams) of butter in a pan. Remove the pork from the pan, and, in the same butter, brown very quickly the calves' liver diced. Put the diced pork back in the pan. Add the mushroom peelings and shallots. Season and spice. Sauté the mixture on a very hot flame for 2 minutes. Take the calves' liver out of the pan. Dilute the stock with the white wine. Cook down and add this reduced stock to the liver. Pound in a mortar, adding the rest of the butter and the yolks of egg. Mix well. Rub through a sieve. Put the mixture in a bowl. Whip with a wooden spoon until it is very smooth.

The mixture is added to forcemeats for pâtés and potted products. It is also used in the preparation of borders and poultry or game moulds.

If appropriate to the purpose for which it is to be used, truffle peelings may be added to this forcemeat and pounded with the calves' liver. A little concentrated *Espagnole sauce* can also be added (see SAUCE).

A gratin game stuffing. FARCE À GRATIN DE GIBIER—Proceed as for *à gratin calves' liver forcemeat*, using the following ingredients:

½ pound (250 grams) of livers of various types of game, ¼ pound (125 grams) belly of pork (pork fat); ½ pound (250 grams) young rabbit meat (net weight after trimming); 1⅔ ounces (50 grams) of foie gras; 2 tablespoons (25 grams) of butter; 3 yolks of egg; *Espagnole sauce* (see SAUCE) made with game essence. Seasoning and spices as for *à gratin calves' liver forcemeat;* ½ cup (7 decilitres) of Madeira.

This stuffing is used for the same purpose as *à gratin calves' liver stuffing*. It is especially used for hot pâtés and game pies.

A gratin poultry liver forcemeat or stuffing. FARCE À GRATIN DE FOIES DE VOLAILLE—Proceed as for *à gratin calves' liver stuffing*, substituting an equal quantity of carefully trimmed poultry livers for the calves' liver. This is used for pâtés and potted preparations.

Mousseline forcemeat. FARCE À LA CRÈME, DITE MOUSSELINE—*Ingredients.* 2 pounds (1 kilo) of boned veal, poultry or game, trimmed, with all gristle, tendons, etc., removed; 4 whites of egg; 6 cups (1½ litres) of thick fresh cream; 3 teaspoons (18 grams) of salt; ½ teaspoon (3 grams) of white pepper.

Method. Pound the meat finely in a mortar. Season. Add the whites of egg a little at a time, pounding well with the pestle. Rub through a fine sieve.

Put the forcemeat in a pan. Make it smooth by stirring vigorously with a wooden spoon. Keep it cool, on ice if possible, for 2 hours.

When it is quite cold, add the cream a little at a time, stirring vigorously with a wooden spoon. (The mixture should be stirred on ice.)

Use for fine forcemeat balls, mousses and mousselines.

Panada forcemeat I, fine. FARCE À LA PANADE—*Ingredients.* 2 pounds (1 kilo) veal or poultry, boned and trimmed, with all gristle and tendons removed; 1½ cups (500 grams) *panada;* 1 pound (500 grams) butter; 4 whole eggs; 8 yolks; 2 teaspoons (12 grams) salt; ½ teaspoon (2 grams) white pepper; pinch (1 gram) grated nutmeg.

Method. Dice the veal or poultry. Pound in a mortar with seasoning. Take the pounded meat out of the mortar and put in the *panada*. Add butter. Put back the pounded meat and pound vigorously with the pestle. See PANADA.

Now add the eggs and the yolks, one or two at a time. Rub the forcemeat through a fine sieve. Put it in a bowl. Work well with a wooden spoon until very smooth. This forcemeat may be made in an electric blender.

It is used for plain forcemeat balls, borders, moulds, and to stuff poultry, meat, etc.

Panada forcemeat II, fine (game). FARCE À LA PANADE—Proceed as for *Panada forcemeat I*, using boned and trimmed game.

This stuffing is used for plain forcemeat balls, borders, moulds, and to stuff game birds.

Panada forcemeat III, fine (with cream). FARCE À LA PANADE ET À LA CRÈME—*Ingredients.* 2 pounds (1 kilo) veal or poultry, boned and trimmed, with all gristle and tendons removed; 1¼ cups (400 grams) *Panada C**; 4 whites of egg; 6 cups (1½ litres) double cream; 1 teaspoon (5 grams) salt; ½ teaspoon (2 grams) white pepper; pinch (1 gram) grated nutmeg.

Method. Pound the meat or poultry with the seasoning and the whites of egg, adding a little at a time. Still pounding, add the *Panada C*. Pound vigorously with the pestle until the ingredients are thoroughly mixed.

Rub the forcemeat through a fine sieve. Put it in a pan. Keep it on ice for an hour.

After this, stirring vigorously with a wooden spoon, add, a little at a time, a third of the cream indicated. At the very last, stirring constantly, add the rest of the cream, partly whipped.

This forcemeat may be prepared in an electric blender and is used for fine forcemeat balls.

Forcemeat or stuffing for pâté de foie gras or potted foie gras. FARCE POUR PÂTÉ DE FOIE GRAS—*Ingredients.* ¾ pound (375 grams) lean pork (net weight); 15 ounces (450 grams) fresh pork fat; ½ pound (250 grams) fresh foie gras (the trimmings of the livers used to make the *pâté* or potted foie gras); 4 teaspoons (25 grams) *Spiced salt* (see SALT); ½ cup (1 decilitre) brandy.

Method. Pound finely in a mortar the meat indicated above. Add the seasoning and the brandy. Rub through a sieve.

Périgourdine forcemeat. FARCE PÉRIGOURDINE—This forcemeat, which is wrapped in white cabbage leaves, is made with breadcrumbs steeped in clear soup or milk, and chopped fresh pork, or, as appropriate, chopped ham or pork fat. Chopped parsley and garlic are added to it and it is bound with yolks of egg and seasoned with salt, pepper and spices.

The stuffed cabbage, rolled into a large ball, is wrapped in muslin (U.S. cheese cloth) and braised.

This forcemeat is also used to stuff pot-roasted chicken. In this case, the liver and blood of the chicken are added to it.

Pork forcemeat or stuffing, fine. FARCE FINE DE PORC—Made with lean pork and pork fat, in the same way as ordinary pork forcemeat. The mixture is then rubbed through a sieve. It is used for the same purposes as ordinary pork forcemeat.

Pork forcemeat or stuffing, ordinary. FARCE DITE CHAIR À SAUCISSES—Mix equal quantities of finely minced lean pork and pork fat. Season with 2 tablespoons (15 grams) of *Spiced salt* (see SALT) per pound (500 grams).

Used for *crépinettes*, sausages, stuffed vegetables, etc.

Poultry forcemeat or stuffing for pâtés and potted preparations. FARCE DE VOLAILLE—*Ingredients.* 1¼ pounds (600 grams) poultry (net weight); 7 ounces (200 grams) veal (net weight); 30 ounces (900 grams) fresh pork fat; 4 eggs; 3 tablespoons (50 grams) *Spiced salt* (see SALT); 1¼ cups (2½ decilitres) brandy.

Method. Dice the poultry, veal and fat. Pound finely in a mortar with the seasoning. Add the eggs and the brandy. Mix well. Rub through a sieve.

Poultry forcemeat or stuffing for poached, braised or roast poultry. FARCE POUR VOLAILLES POCHÉES, BRAISÉES, RÔTIES—This stuffing is usually made with sausage meat, with chopped parsley added. Sometimes chopped onion, cooked slowly in butter until very soft, and breadcrumbs are also added.

Poultry forcemeat for truffled poultry. FARCE TRUFFÉ—Coarsely dice 2 pounds (1 kilo) of fresh pork fat and ½ pound (250 grams) of raw foie gras. Pound these ingredients in a mortar. Add the truffle peelings (thoroughly cleaned). Season with salt, pepper and a pinch of spices. When the mixture is very smooth, take it out of the mortar. Cook gently over a very low flame and rub through a fine sieve.

Slowly melt 1 pound (500 grams) of this truffled fat. Add to it (for young turkey of about medium weight, 8 pounds or 4 kilos), 1⅔ to 2 pounds (800 grams to 1 kilo) of peeled truffles (the peelings having been used, as indicated above, to flavour the pork fat), quartered if large or whole if small. Season with salt, pepper, powdered thyme and bay leaf. Poach on a low heat for 8 to 10 minutes. Leave the truffles to cool, covered. When they are quite cold, add them to the pork fat. Add a little brandy and mix thoroughly.

Quenelle forcemeat I. FARCE À GODIVEAU À LA GRAISSE, À LA GLACE—*Ingredients.* 2 pounds (1 kilo) of lean veal trimmed, with gristle and tendons removed (mainly *noix* of veal), 1 pound (500 grams) well-dried beef suet (net weight after trimming); 8 whole eggs; 5 teaspoons (25 grams) salt; 2 teaspoons (5 grams) white pepper; pinch (1 gram) of grated nutmeg; 1½ pounds (700–800 grams) chopped ice, or failing this, 3½ to 4 cups (7–8 decilitres) of iced water.

Method. Mince separately the veal, diced, and the suet, finely minced. Add the seasoning indicated.

Still keeping them separate, pound the veal and the suet. Put the veal and the suet together and pound them to a fine paste. Add the eggs one by one, still pounding. Rub through a fine sieve. Spread the mixture out on a plate, and leave it on ice till the next day.

Next day, pound the stuffing once more in the mortar, adding the ice, broken into small pieces and put in gradually. Mix well with the pestle.

Test the forcemeat by poaching a small piece. Add a little iced water, if it is too firm, or a little white of egg, if it is too soft.

This stuffing is made into forcemeat balls which are served in vol-au-vents, pies or pastry, or used to garnish large cuts of meat or poultry.

Quenelle forcemeat II. FARCE À GODIVEAU À LA CRÈME—*Ingredients.* 2 pounds (1 kilo) trimmed *noix* or loin of veal; 2 pounds (1 kilo) beef suet (net weight after skinning and trimming); 4 whole eggs; 3 yolks; 3½ cups (7 decilitres) fresh cream; 5 teaspoons (25 grams) salt; 2 teaspoons (5 grams) pepper; pinch (1 gram) nutmeg.

Method. Chop the veal and pound it in a mortar. Pound the suet separately. Mix the veal and the suet. Add the seasoning, the eggs and yolks, put in one by one, mixing vigorously with the pestle.

Rub the stuffing through a fine sieve. Spread it out well on a board. Leave it on ice until the next day.

Next day, pound the stuffing once more in the mortar, which should be chilled in advance with ice. Still pounding, add the cream a little at a time.

Test the forcemeat as indicated in the preceding recipe, adjusting the consistency if necessary. This forcemeat is used in the same way as *Quenelle forcemeat I*.

Quenelle forcemeat balls. FARCE À GODIVEAU—These balls can be piped through a forcing (pastry) bag, like any other forcemeat balls, but they are usually rolled by hand and poached in salt water.

They can also be poached dry, as follows:

Pipe through a forcing bag with a plain nozzle on to buttered paper laid on a buttered baking sheet. Put the balls fairly close together when piping them on to the paper.

Cook in a moderate oven for 7 to 8 minutes. When, at the end of this time, little pinkish beads of fat begin to appear on the surface, this indicates that the balls are ready.

Take them out of the oven. Overturn the paper on a board or marble slab. Peel off the sheet of paper, holding it at one corner, when the forcemeat balls are almost cold. Put them on a dish and use as required.

Veal forcemeat for borders, large stuffed forcemeat balls, linings (for the presentation of hot entrées). FARCE DE VEAU POUR BORDURES, GROSSES QUENELLES FOURRÉES, FONDS DE PLAT—*Ingredients.* 2 pounds (1 kilo) lean veal (net weight after trimming); 1 cup (300 grams) *Panada A**; 5 whole eggs; 8 yolks; ¼ cup (½ decilitre) very thick *Béchamel sauce* (cold) (see SAUCE); 3 teaspoons (20 grams) salt; ¾ teaspoon (3 grams) white pepper; pinch (1 gram) of grated nutmeg.

Method. Dice the veal and pound it finely in a mortar with seasoning. Take it out of the mortar and put the *panada* in its place. Pound this until it is very creamy. Add the veal and the butter, and pound until all the ingredients are thoroughly mixed. Still pounding, add the eggs and yolks one at a time, then the *Béchamel sauce.* Rub the stuffing through a sieve. Put it in a bowl. Work with a spatula until it is very smooth.

Veal and pork forcemeat. FARCE DE VEAU ET DE PORC—Chop separately 10 ounces (300 grams) of round of veal, ½ pound (250 grams) of lean pork and ½ pound (250 grams) of fresh fat bacon.

Pound these ingredients together in a mortar, add to them 2 whole eggs and ½ cup (one decilitre) of brandy, season with *Spiced salt* (see SALT) and rub through a sieve.

FORCEMEATS OR STUFFINGS MADE WITH FISH. FARCES DE POISSONS, CRUSTACES:

Anchovy forcemeat or stuffing I. FARCE AUX ANCHOIS—Make a white *roux* of 1 tablespoon of butter and 2 of flour. Moisten with ½ cup (a decilitre) of boiling milk.

Cook for a few minutes over a very hot flame, stirring with a wooden spoon. When this mixture is very thick, remove it from the stove.

Add a whole egg, 2 yolks and the fillets of 4 anchovies, which have been soaked in cold water to remove the salt. Rub through a fine sieve.

Cook the mixture for a few seconds, stirring constantly. Rub through muslin.

This stuffing is used as a filling for savoury tarts, *dartois*, small pâtés, pies, etc.

Anchovy forcemeat or stuffing II. FARCE D'ANCHOIS—'After soaking some large anchovies to remove the salt, clean them perfectly and bone them. Take 10 ounces of these anchovy fillets (about 325 grams) and toss for not more than 2 minutes in 8 tablespoons (4 ounces) of butter, seasoned with 2 tablespoons of *fines herbes*, a touch of nutmeg and a very little *Spiced salt* (see SALT).

'When the mixture is cold, pound the fillets of anchovy without their seasoning with ½ cup (6 ounces) of milk *panada**. Next add the cooking butter with the *fines herbes*. After having pounded this mixture for 5 minutes, add 8 tablespoons (4 ounces) of butter (crayfish butter or some other kind) and 3 yolks of egg. When all the ingredients are pounded to a smooth paste, take out the stuffing and use it.' (Carême's recipe.)

This mixture is used mostly for stuffing large fish. It can also be used to stuff vegetables, artichoke hearts, mushrooms, tomatoes, etc. to provide a Lenten dish.

Fresh-water crayfish forcemeat. FARCE D'ÉCREVISSES—Proceed as for *Prawn or shrimp forcemeat.*

Cream forcemeat or stuffing (Lenten). FARCE À LA CRÈME (MAIGRE)—Proceed in all particulars as indicated for *Veal or poultry forcemeat*, using fish instead of meat. Pike, whiting or some other suitable fish may be used.

Fish forcemeat. FARCE DE POISSON—*Ingredients.* 2 pounds (1 kilo) (net weight) of pike (or other white-fleshed fish); 1¼ cups (400 grams) of frangipane or rice panada; 4 whites of egg; 2 teaspoons (30 grams) of salt; 2 teaspoons (5 grams) of pepper and a small pinch of grated nutmeg.

Method. Prepare as *Quenelle forcemeat.* See FORCEMEATS MADE WITH BEEF, VEAL ETC.

Fish forcemeat II. FARCE POUR POISSON—Chop finely 10 ounces (300 grams) (net weight) of whiting or any other white fish. Add to this 3¾ cups (200 grams) of breadcrumbs, soaked in milk and squeezed; 3 tablespoons (50 grams) of butter; a tablespoon of chopped blanched chives; a tablespoon of chopped chervil and parsley. Season with salt, pepper and nutmeg. Bind with 2 whole eggs or 1 whole egg and 3 yolks. Mix thoroughly.

Mousseline forcemeat for fish mousses and mousselines. FARCE MOUSSELINE—*Ingredients.* 2 pounds (1 kilo) fish, skinned and boned (pike, whiting, sole, salmon, trout, etc.); 4 or 5 whites of egg; 5 cups (1¼ litres) fresh cream; 1½ teaspoons (10 grams) salt; ½ teaspoon (2 grams) white pepper; pinch (1 gram) of grated nutmeg.

Method. Pound the fish in a mortar with the seasoning. Add the whites of egg, a little at a time. Rub the mixture through a fine sieve. Put it in a bowl. Stir on ice with a spatula until it is very smooth. Leave it on ice for 2 hours. Now add the cream, a little at a time, stirring it in gently with the spatula.

This mixture is used for light fish quenelles, mousses and mousselines, and also for stuffing large braised fish.

Panada forcemeat with butter (Lenten). FARCE À LA PANADE ET AU BEURRE (MAIGRE)—Proceed as for *Veal or Chicken forcemeat*, using fish (pike, whiting or some other suitable fish).

This is used for plain fish quenelles, borders, moulds, and for stuffing large fish.

Panada forcemeat for fish and shell-fish mousses. FARCE POUR MOUSSES DE POISSONS ET DE CRUSTACÉS (À LA PANADE)—Proceed as for *Mousseline forcemeat for fish mousses*, using the following ingredients: 2 pounds (1 kilo) boned and skinned fish (net weight); 1½ cups (450 grams) frangipane *panada**; 4 whites of egg; 6 cups (1½ litres) cream; salt, pepper, grated nutmeg.

The addition of the *panada* to this forcemeat gives it body, but makes it less delicate in flavour.

It is used for the same purposes as *Mousseline forcemeat for fish mousses.*

Pickled herring or sardine forcemeat. FARCE DE HARENGS SAURS, DE SARDINES—Proceed, using fillets of pickled herring or sardines, as for *Anchovy forcemeat I.*

This is used for the same purpose as *Prawn forcemeat.*

Pike forcemeat, fine, à la lyonnaise or Godiveau lyonnaise. FARCE DE BROCHET À LA LYONNAISE, DITE GODIVEAU LYONNAISE—*Ingredients.* 1 pound (500 grams) pike (skinned and boned, net weight); 1 pound (500 grams) beef suet (trimmed and minced, net weight); 1 pound (500 grams) *Panada B**; 4 whites of egg; 2¼ teaspoons (15 grams) salt; 1 teaspoon (3 grams) pepper; pinch (1 gram) nutmeg.

Method. Pound the fat, the *panada*, and the whites of egg in a mortar. Add the pike and the seasoning. Work the stuffing vigorously with the pestle. Rub through a fine sieve. Put it in a bowl and work with a spatula until the mixture is very smooth. All this may be accomplished with an electric blender.

This forcemeat is used for large fish balls known as *Quenelles lyonnaises.*

Note. The distinctive feature of pike balls (*Quenelles à la lyonnaise*), which as a general rule should be shaped in a spoon and poached in salt water, is that they swell up appreciably in cooking. To cause the *quenelles* to swell, simmer them for 10 minutes in the sauce served with them. This is usually a meatless *Espagnole sauce* (see SAUCE) containing mushrooms, stoned olives, truffles and other small delicacies.

When pike *quenelles* are served with a thick sauce, such as *Nantua*, lobster, shrimp, white wine or other white sauce suitable for fish and shell-fish, they should simply be poached in salt water. After draining and drying them in a cloth, serve them on bread fried in butter, artichoke hearts or flaky pastry. Garnish, and cover with the sauce indicated in the selected recipe.

Prawn or shrimp forcemeat. FARCE DE CREVETTES—Pound in a mortar ¼ pound (125 grams) of prawns or shrimps with 7 tablespoons (100 grams) of butter. Rub through a fine sieve. Add to this mixture half its volume of yolks of hard boiled eggs, rubbed through a fine sieve. Mix well.

This mixture is used for cold hors-d'oeuvre.

Shellfish cream forcemeat, fine. FARCE FINE DE CRUSTACÉS À LA CRÈME—Proceed, using shellfish, as indicated for *Mousseline forcemeat.*

This is used for the same purpose as *Pike forcemeat.*

MISCELLANEOUS FORCEMEATS OR STUFFINGS. FARCES DIVERSES:

Brain forcemeat or stuffing. FARCE DE CERVELLE—See OFFAL OR VARIETY MEATS.

Fish forcemeat. FARCE POUR POISSON—Soak 4½ cups (250 grams) of breadcrumbs in milk and squeeze them. Beat it in a bowl. Add 6 tablespoons (75 grams) of finely chopped onion cooked slowly in butter until very soft; 1½ tablespoons (20 grams) of chopped shallot, cooked in white wine until all the moisture has evaporated; ½ cup (100 grams) of raw mushrooms, chopped and squeezed (or 3 tablespoons of dry *Duxelles**); and a tablespoon of chopped parsley. Bind with 2 whole eggs. Season with salt, pepper and grated nutmeg.

According to the nature of the dish for which the forcemeat is to be used, a touch of garlic may be added.

Fish forcemeat à la provençale. FARCE POUR POISSON À LA PROVENÇALE—Cook slowly ½ cup (100 grams) of finely chopped onions in 4 tablespoons of oil until very tender. Add a finely chopped clove of garlic and 1 cup (150 grams) of chopped raw mushrooms. Brown for a few seconds on the stove.

Remove the pan from the stove and add 4½ cups (250 grams) of freshly grated breadcrumbs, a heaped tablespoon of chopped chives, a heaped tablespoon of chopped parsley and chervil and three chopped hard boiled eggs.

Season with salt, pepper and grated nutmeg and mix.

Forcemeats for various fungi and mushrooms: cèpes, cultivated mushrooms, morels, St. George's mushrooms, etc. FARCE DE CHAMPIGNONS DIVERS—Proceed, using one or other of these fungi, first tossed in butter, as for *Truffle forcemeat*. These forcemeats are used in the same way as truffle forcemeat.

Garlic forcemeat—See GARLIC.

A gratin forcemeat for canapés and croûtons. FARCE À GRATIN—Heat in a pan 5 ounces (150 grams) of grated fresh pork fat. When it is very hot, put in it 10 ounces (300 grams) of trimmed chicken livers, 1½ tablespoons (15 grams) of sliced shallots, 2 tablespoons (20 grams) of mushroom peelings, a sprig of thyme, half a bay leaf. Season with salt, pepper and a little spice. Brown the livers quickly over a very hot flame to seal them.

Leave to cool. Pound in a mortar. Rub through a sieve or reduce to a purée in an electric blender. Keep in an earthenware container in a cool place. Cover with buttered paper. Prepared in this way, the forcemeat will keep for several days.

It is used to spread croûtons of fried bread used as a base for small roast game birds, and to spread the pieces of fried bread served with salmis and civets.

Ravioli forcemeat—See RAVIOLI.

Sage and onion stuffing (English cookery). FARCE À LA SAUGE—This is used to stuff poultry, especially duck and goose.

Bake in the oven 2 large onions in their skins. Leave to cool. Skin and chop them.

Mix with 3 cups (150 grams) of breadcrumbs, first dipped in milk and squeezed, and an equal quantity of beef suet, cooked and chopped. Season with 2 tablespoons of chopped sage, salt and pepper, and mix thoroughly.

Truffle stuffing. FARCE AUX TRUFFES—'Chop 5 ounces of very black truffles; then toss them for a few minutes in 8 tablespoons (4 ounces) of butter seasoned with 2 tablespoons of *Spiced salt* and a touch of nutneg. Drain the truffles on a plate, then pound 3 ounces of *Panada C.**

'When the truffles are cold, put them in the mortar and pound them with the *panada* for a few minutes. After this, add the butter in which the truffles were cooked, and pound together until the mixture is perfectly smooth. Finally, mix in three yolks of egg.' (Carême's recipe.)

This forcemeat is used for stuffing poultry and winged game and for meat or fish *paupiettes**. It is also used in various hot pâtés.

Truffled stuffing. FARCE TRUFFÉE—This is used for stuffing turkeys, capons, chickens and winged game. See TURKEY, *Truffled turkey* and *Chicken with truffles.*

Vegetable stuffings (various). FARCE POUR LÉGUMES—This mixture which is used to stuff certain vegetables, such as mushrooms, egg-plant (*aubergines*), very small vegetable marrows (*courgettes* or *zucchini*), tomatoes, artichoke hearts, etc., is really a thickened *Duxelles sauce* (see SAUCE) to which is added, in some cases, the pulp of the vegetables, scooped out after they have been cooked in oil.

Yolk of egg stuffing. FARCE DE JAUNES D'OEUFS—*Cold:* Rub through a fine sieve the yolks of 10 hard boiled eggs. Put these yolks in a bowl. Add 7 tablespoons (100 grams) of butter softened to a paste. Season with salt and white pepper. Mix.

This is used as a spread in cold hors-d'oeuvre, especially for *canapés à la russe*. It is also used as filling for halved hard boiled eggs, artichoke hearts, and small barquettes or tartlets served as garnishes with cold dishes.

Hot: Rub the yolks of hard boiled eggs through a sieve. Season. Mix with half their weight of thick *Béchamel sauce* (see SAUCE) passed through muslin or a fine sieve.

This stuffing is used mainly to fill hard boiled eggs prepared *au gratin* (see EGGS, *Eggs à la Chimay*). Usually, a small spoonful of dry *Duxelles** and chopped parsley is added. This mixture is also used to stuff different vegetables (which are then sprinkled with breadcrumbs, basted with melted butter and browned), and to fill small vol-au-vents, barquettes, tartlets, etc.

FORCING. FORÇAGE—Process of growing vegetables and fruit under glass in order to ripen them before their time. These products are then named 'forced' products.

The distinguishing quality of these fruits and vegetables is their rarity and their high price. Good cooks seldom buy them. They prefer to eat these different products in their season.

FORCING BAG (U.S. Pastry bag). POCHE—Funnel-shaped bag which can be fitted with nozzles (French *douilles*) of different shapes and diameters. These nozzles are made in various sizes, with large or small apertures which can be plain or fluted, so that creamy mixtures can be piped in a wide range of decorative designs.

FORELEG HAM. JAMBONNEAU—The French word *jambonneau*, sometimes translated 'foreleg ham', or in the U.S.A. *Picnic ham*, refers to the portion below the ham or shoulder of both fore and hind legs of the pig. See HAM.

FORESTIÈRE (A LA)—Method of preparation of small cuts of meat and poultry. This dish is garnished with morels, lean larding bacon cut in large squares and diced potatoes fried in butter. (See GARNISHES.)

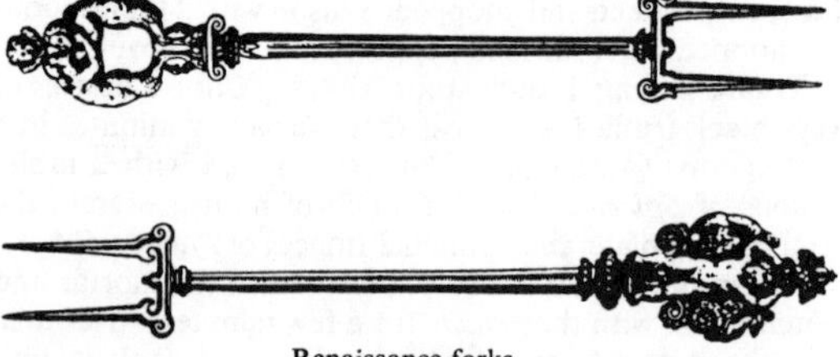

Renaissance forks

FORK. FOURCHETTE—A table utensil designed to pick up meat and other food. It is of very ancient origin as it is mentioned in the Old Testament, in Samuel, but it served first of all as a ritual instrument to grip pieces of meat destined for sacrifices; only later was it used in the kitchen. According to the eleventh century Italian scholar, Damiani, forks were introduced into Venice by a Byzantine princess and thence spread through Italy. They are mentioned in 1379 in an inventory of the French king, Charles V, and Edward II of England had a favourite, Piers Gaveston, who is recorded as having eaten a pear with a fork in the early fourteenth century, but these instances do not mean that forks were in general use. In fact, eating with forks did not become at all fashionable until the seventeenth century.

Jean Sulpice in his *Libellus de moribus in mensa servandis* (*Traité de civilité*), translated into French by Guillaume Durand in 1545, writes as follows on how a well-educated guest should behave at table: 'Take the meat with three fingers and do not fill your mouth with too big pieces. Do not keep your hands for long on the dish.'

Erasmus in his *Treatise on manners* published in 1530 also gives good advice, but does not mention forks. 'Be careful not to be the first to put your hands in the dish. What you cannot hold in your hands you must put on your plate. Also it is a great breach of etiquette when your fingers are dirty and greasy, to bring them to your mouth in order to lick them, or to clean them on your jacket.' He adds, 'It would be more decent to use the tablecloth.' This was not considered impolite in those days.

Ann of Austria (1601–1666) who, it is said, had very beautiful hands, did not hesitate to put her fingers into the dish. This is described in an amusing disrespectful verse by a chronicler of her time, who was present at a dinner given in her honour by the Président de Maisons.

Loret tells us in the *Muse historique* that Louis XIV (1643–1715), whose dinners, small and great, were always organized down to the minutest ceremonial detail, did not usually have a fork at table.

In the seventeenth century, use of the fork, which was originally two-pronged, then three-pronged, and later four-pronged, spread from Italy and Spain into France and England. An English traveller named Thomas Coryate is credited with bringing the use of the fork to England after a trip to Italy in 1608. When he came back, after seeing people eating with forks in Italy, he wrote, 'Forks are made of iron or steel; noblemen eat with silver forks. I have gone on using a fork even now that I am back in England. This has occasioned more than one joke and one of my intimate friends did not hesitate to apply to me in the middle of a dinner the adjective "Furciferous".' While in Paris that same year Coryate noted that the fork was unknown even among the nobility but when he returned in 1612, he remarked that the fork was more frequently used in good society, though not yet amongst the common people. Hérouard in the *Journal of Louis XIV* speaks of the Dauphin beating the table with his fork and spoon.

Modern forks are made in many sizes and many metals, as well as in plastics and woods. Etiquette as to the proper way of holding and using a fork, and in which hand, varies.

FORK LUNCHEON. DÉJEUNER À LA FOURCHETTE—A meal taken towards the middle of the day.

FOUR MENDICANTS. QUATRE MENDIANTS—Dessert made up of figs, raisins, nuts and almonds, whose colours recall those of the four mendicant orders.

FOUR RED FRUITS. QUATRE FRUITS ROUGES—Strawberries, cherries, red currants and raspberries.

FOUR SPICES. QUATRE ÉPICES—A much used mixture, for which, formerly, each purveyor had a special formula; the most usual is the following:

$1\frac{1}{8}$ cup (125 grams) white pepper, $1\frac{1}{2}$ tablespoons (10 grams) powdered cloves, $3\frac{1}{2}$ tablespoons (30 grams) ginger, 4 tablespoons (35 grams) grated nutmeg.

FOUR YELLOW FRUITS. QUATRE FRUITS JAUNES—Oranges, lemons, bitter oranges and citrons.

FOURDERAINE—A home-made liqueur which used to be common in the north of France and is still sometimes found there. The hedge sloes used in making it are picked after the first frost when they are ripe. This liqueur is prepared in the same way as cassis.

FOX. RENARD—Animal ranking as vermin; its flesh, very tough and with an extremely unpleasant 'wild' taste, is, however, sometimes eaten, after the animal has been skinned and the flesh soaked in running water or boiling water.

FRANCHE-COMTÉ—Franche-Comté is a mountainous region in the western part of the Belfort Gap.

Surrounded as it is by regions abundant in edible products and famous wines, the inhabitants have always been accustomed to eating well. In the north are Lorraine and Alsace; in the south Savoy, including the Bugey, pre-eminently in a place of fine cuisine. To the west, it borders on Burgundy, Bresse and Champagne. To the east its immediate neighbour is Switzerland where good eating is also the rule. The geographical position of

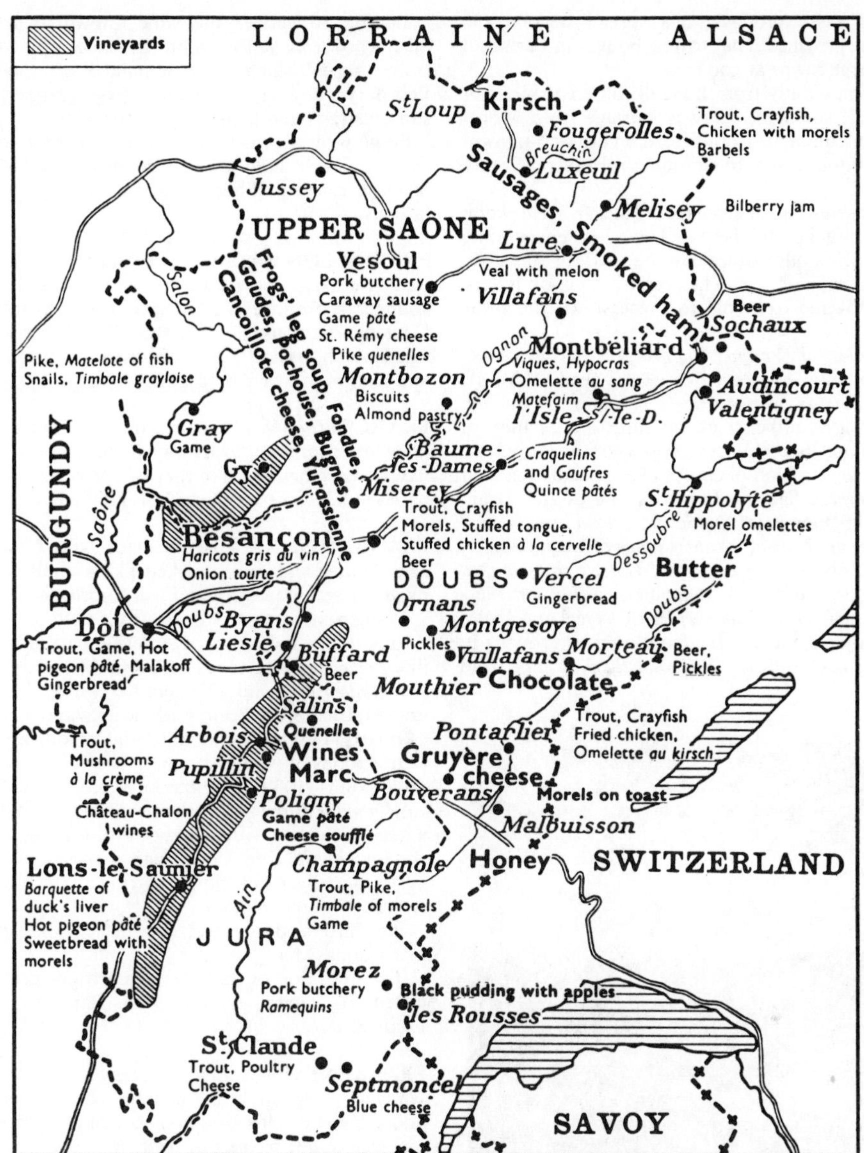

Gastronomic map of Franche-Comté

Franche-Comté has therefore inclined its inhabitants to be great gastronomes.

A variety of excellent foods is produced in this province.

In Franche-Comté, and particularly in the Jura, the beef cattle are famous for their well flavoured meat and high quality milk from which are made cheese and other dairy products, the fame of which stretches beyond the frontiers of this province.

In the orchards of Franche-Comté, excellent fruit, particularly stone fruit, is grown.

This part of France has an abundant variety of game.

In the rivers, streams and ponds, numerous kinds of fish are found in great quantities. The inhabitants cook them in delicious ways, notably in succulent stews. Special praise for their delicacy is given to the *Saulon carp*, *red mullet*, *pike l'Ognon*, *Doubs* and *Dessoubs trout* and *Breuchin salmon trout*, the flesh of which is very well flavoured. In the Breuchin there are also beautiful *crayfish* to be found.

Cheeses from Franche-Comté are well known, such as *Septmoncel*, which some knowledgeable people consider a rival to Roquefort, *Comté* cheese, a kind of Gruyère which some people prefer to Swiss Gruyère, la *Concoillotte*, also known as *Fromagère*, and *Fromage fort*.

Culinary specialities of Franche-Comté—Foremost among the specialities are: a kind of *Maize porridge*, of which the inhabitants of Franche-Comté are very fond; *Potée franc-comtoise*, which is prepared like *potée** from other regions, but its characteristic is the addition of *Morteau sausage; Frogs' leg soup; Panada** (which is a dish like a soup with bread and butter boiled to a pulp); *Cherry soup;* and the whole range of soups made with fresh vegetables.

All pork butchery is excellent in Franche-Comté. The

reputation of these products has spread beyond the frontiers of the province. They can be bought in Paris and many other large towns at good shops.

Smoked ham, mainly from Luxeuil, different kinds of small and large sausages, caraway sausage from Montbozon and stuffed tongue from Besançon are well-known.

The most famous dishes to be found in Franche-Comté are:

Various *Fish stews* made from freshwater fish with white or red wine, onions and herbs; *Meat braised in wine.* Though different kinds of meat can be used for this dish, generally it is made of beef. The secret is to cook it very slowly in a covered casserole to preserve all the meat juices.

Pike quenelles of Vesoul; Jugged hare à !a franc-comtoise; Cheese fondue; Pain d'écrivisses (see LOAVES); *Marrow* (squash) *au gratin; Cheese potatoes; Morels on toast; Onion tourte;* rather thick and nourishing pancakes called *Matefaim* (i.e. hunger appeasers); *Ramekins; Fritters; Flamusse*, a kind of cheese tart specially made in Burgundy; *Sèche*, a flat bread made with eggs and sugar; *Craquelins** of Baume-les-Dames; *Almond pastry and biscuits* (cookies) of Montbozon; *Viques* of Montbéliard; *Malakoff* of Dole; *Quiche comtoise; Galette de goumeau* of Saint-Amour; *Gaufres de chanoinesses* of Baume-les-Dames; *Chestnut cakes; Pain d'épice* of Vercel and Dôle; the local fruit jams, paste made from quinces growing in Baume-les-Dames; *Bilberry and whortleberry jam* from Melisey.

Franche-Comté (*French Government Tourist office*)

Wines and liqueurs of Franche-Comté—Rare wines of a very special character are produced in Franche-Comté. Connoisseurs appreciate their bouquet and their colour. There are first of all the wines from Arbois, with a colour like the skin of an onion, and the yellow wine which is like certain Rhine wines. There are also white and sparkling wines from the Jura. There are the wines of the Côte-de-Mouchard at Lons-le-Saunier; and there are the wines of Château-Chalon, Salins, Armires, Pupillin, Poligny and Etoile. Coming back to Besançon there are the wines of Port-Lesney in the Jura, and the wines of Buffard, Byans, Liesle, Trois-Châtels, Miserey, Mouthiers and Vuillafans in the Doubs.

During November the wine known as frost-nipped (also known as yellow wine) is made. This is prepared from grapes which have remained on the plant. In February a dessert wine is made from grapes dried in the sun on straw, and kept through the winter.

Some well known liqueurs are also made in Franche-Comté. The distilleries at Ornans and at Montgesoye produce excellent liqueurs. Kirsch from Fougerolles is famous.

FRANCILLON SALAD—This title is often given to a Japanese salad the recipe for which was given by the younger Alexandre Dumas in a play performed at the Comédie-Française entitled *Francillon.* The recipe for this salad which, basically, is composed of mussels, potatoes and truffles will be found under SALAD.

FRANCOLIN—Wild bird resembling a partridge, found in warm countries, especially in Sicily and Greece. Its flavour is something like that of partridge, and it is prepared in the same way (see PARTRIDGE).

FRANGIPANE—A mixture made with flour, yolks of eggs, butter and milk, cooked like a chou (cream puff) pastry. Used in poultry and fish forcemeat.

Frangipane cream—This cream is used in the preparation of different desserts or sweets and cakes and is made like *French pastry cream* (see CREAM).

Ingredients. 1 cup (250 grams) sugar, $1\frac{3}{4}$ cups (250 grams) sifted bread flour, 4 whole eggs and 4 yolks of egg, $1\frac{1}{2}$ quarts ($1\frac{1}{2}$ litres) milk boiled and flavoured with vanilla (2 teaspoons of vanilla extract), 50 crushed macaroons, 7 tablespoons (100 grams) butter, a pinch of salt.

Method. Put the sugar, the sieved flour and the salt into a heavy saucepan with a flat bottom. Add the eggs. Mix all the ingredients thoroughly with a spoon. Add the milk very gradually. Cook slowly stirring all the time. Let cook for two to three minutes.

Put into a dish. Add the butter and the crushed macaroons. Mix.

The invention of this cream is attributed to an Italian called Frangipani, who lived in Paris at the time of Louis XIII.

FRANKENTAL—A black grape also known as *Black Hamburg*, originating in Germany. The fruit is very large and juicy. For this reason Frankental grapes are often included in gift baskets of fruit.

FRASCATI (A LA)—Garnish for meat dishes. It consists of thin slices of *foie gras*, asparagus tips, mushrooms and truffles. See GARNISHES.

FREEZING—See PRESERVATION OF FOOD.

FRICANDEAU—Rump (topside) of veal. Also describes a dish made of loin of veal (*noix de veau*) larded, braised or roasted (see VEAL, *Noix de veau*).

The name is also applied to slices or fillets of fish, mainly those of sturgeon and fresh tunny (tuna fish). The fish are braised in a fish stock.

FRICASSÉE—In modern French usage, the word *fricassée* applies almost exclusively to a method of preparing poultry in a white sauce.

In earlier times (and to this day in English-speaking countries), the term denoted various kinds of stew; stew made with white or brown stock and made not only from poultry but from meat, fish and vegetables.

Nowadays, a fricassée of poultry is prepared in very much the same way as a *blanquette**, a dish usually made with veal or lamb.

Fricassée of chicken à la berrichonne. FRICASSÉE DE POULET À LA BERRICHONNE—Brown in butter ½ pound (250 grams) of new carrots, whole if they are small, quartered if they are large.

When the carrots are nicely browned, remove them from the pan and, in the butter in which they were fried, brown the pieces of a jointed chicken (a chicken cut up for fricassée).

As soon as these pieces are a good colour, add 1 cup (2 decilitres) of boiling water or white stock; add the carrots and a bunch of mixed herbs. Season. Cover and cook for 30 minutes.

Pour off the chicken stock, add to it 5 tablespoons of cream and 2 yolks of egg with a small pinch of fine sugar. Mix well and pour over chicken. Add a tablespoon of vinegar.

Warm the chicken in the sauce without bringing it to the boil.

Fricassée périgourdine—This is the name given in Périgord to the vegetables of a *pot-au-feu*. Before this is quite cooked, the vegetables are removed, drained, sliced, browned in butter or oil, sprinkled with flour, moistened with a little stock and then put back in the pot-au-feu to finish cooking.

The same name is given to a mixture of aromatic vegetables which in a raw state are cooked in butter or oil with garlic and ham. This fricassée is used in various soups.

FRINGALE (hunger pang)—This word comes from the ancient Norman '*faim-valle*' which meant *faim de cheval*, or a sudden, commanding and even painful hunger.

FRITOT—A type of fritter made with small pieces of meat and poultry (collops of poultry, lamb or veal sweetbreads, brains, calves' heads etc.).

These pieces of meat and poultry are marinated in advance. Begin by soaking the pieces of meat for half an hour in oil, lemon juice (or vinegar) with mixed chopped herbs. Just before serving, the meat should be dipped in a light batter and fried in deep fat.

Drain the fritters. Season with salt and arrange them on a dish covered with a napkin. Garnish with fried parsley and quartered lemons. Tomato sauce, or any other suitable sauce, should be served in a sauce-boat.

A number of recipes are given under the heading *fritot* in the section devoted to hot hors-d'oeuvre. See HORS-D'OEUVRE.

Small pieces of meat and poultry prepared *à la Villeroi* are also called *fritot*.

FRITTER. BEIGNET—Some authors say that the French name of this dish—*beignet*—which describes any object dipped in batter and fried in smoking-hot, deep fat (lard, oil, clarified butter or vegetable fat) comes from the Celtic word meaning swelling.

The batter for coating various food substances varies according to the nature of these foods. See BATTER.

There is another variety of fritter which is made of a paste like the *Chou paste* and which are normally called *Soufflé fritters* or, in French, *Pets de nonne*. Some people find the latter expression too coarse and refer to them as *Soupirs de nonne**.

There is a third variety which is made of yeast dough, similar to brioche pastry, see *Vienna fritters*, below.

There is a fourth variety, *Cream fritters* and, finally, the fifth, *Waffle batter fritters* (see WAFFLE), which can be used as *croustades** for garnishes.

La marchande de beignets. Painting by Gérard Dov (*Uffizi, Florence*)

FRITTERS FOR HORS-D'OEUVRE AND SMALL ENTRÉES—These fritters, the recipes for which are given below, should be served with tomato or other sauce, passed separately.

Anchovy fritters I. BEIGNETS D'ANCHOIS—Trim and de-salt anchovy fillets. Spread them on one side with hard boiled yolks rubbed through a sieve and mixed with a little butter and chopped parsley. Roll them up, dip into a light batter and deep fry. Serve on a napkin, garnished with fried parsley.

Anchovy fritters II. BEIGNETS D'ANCHOIS—De-salt, trim and dry the anchovy fillets. Sandwich them two by two with finely pounded fish forcemeat, flavoured with anchovy purée and mixed with a little chopped parsley. When required, dip fillets into batter and deep fry.

Artichoke fritters. BEIGNETS D'ARTICHAUTS—See HORS-D'OEUVRE, *Hot hors-d'oeuvre*.

Aubergine (egg-plant) fritters. BEIGNETS D'AUBERGINES—Peel the aubergines, cut into round slices and marinate for an hour in oil, lemon juice, chopped parsley, salt and pepper. Dip into batter and deep fry.

Beef fritters. BEIGNETS DE BOEUF—See HORS-D'OEUVRE, *Hot hors-d'oeuvre*.

Fritters

Brain fritters, lamb's or calf's. BEIGNETS DE CERVELLES D'AGNEAU, DE VEAU—Cook the brains in *court-bouillon**, cut into small slices and marinate in oil, lemon juice and chopped parsley. When required, dip into batter and deep fry.

Brussels sprouts fritters. BEIGNETS DE CHOUX DE BRUXELLES—Marinate Brussels sprouts (half cooked in salted water, drained, dipped in cold water and thoroughly dried), in oil, lemon juice and chopped parsley. When required, dip into batter and deep fry.

Cardoon (edible thistle) or chard fritters. BEIGNETS DE CARDONS, DE CARDES—Cardoons or chards cooked, marinated and treated as described above.

Cauliflower or broccoli fritters. BEIGNETS DE CHOUX-FLEURS, DE BROCOLIS—Divided into flowerets, marinated and cooked as above.

Celery fritters. BEIGNETS DE CÉLERI—Cook, marinate and prepare as described above. Celeriac (i.e. turnip-rooted celery) or ordinary celery may be used.

Chicken fritters. BEIGNETS DE VOLAILLE—Chicken left-overs, poached or braised and cut into small slices. Marinate these slices in oil, lemon juice and chopped parsley. Dip into batter and deep fry.

Chicken liver fritters. BEIGNETS DE FOIES DE POULETS—Cut the livers into a *salpicon**, brown briskly in butter, add diced mushrooms, also tossed in butter, and blend with thick *Béchamel sauce* (see SAUCE). When the mixture is cold, divide into small (25 gram) pieces and roll into balls.

Dip into batter and deep fry at the last moment.

Egg fritters. BEIGNETS D'OEUFS—Prepare a *salpicon** composed of hard boiled eggs, mushrooms and truffles (and lean ham, for meat fritters) and blend with thick *Béchamel sauce*, or, for meat fritters, thick *Velouté sauce* (see SAUCE). Spread the mixture on a metal sheet and allow it to cool, then divide it into small pieces. Roll into little balls. When required, dip into batter and deep fry.

Egg fritters à la duxelles. BEIGNETS D'OEUFS À LA DUXELLES—Cut hard boiled eggs across into six round slices each. Sandwich them two by two, having first spread them with a teaspoon of *duxelles**. When required, dip them into batter and deep fry.

Egg fritters à la reine. BEIGNETS D'OEUFS À LA REINE—Make a flat, thin omelette, allow it to cool and cut into square or lozenge shaped pieces. On each piece of omelette put a small tablespoon of chicken purée bound with thick *Velouté sauce* (see SAUCE) mixed with chopped truffles. Sandwich the pieces two by two. Dip into batter and deep fry.

Endive fritters. BEIGNETS D'ENDIVES—Braise the endives (broad-leaved chicory), dry well and cut in two lengthways. Marinate for 30 minutes in oil, lemon juice and chopped parsley. When required, dip into batter and deep fry.

Fish, crustacea, shell-fish and fruits de mer fritters. BEIGNETS DE POISSONS, CRUSTACÉS, COQUILLAGES, FRUITS DE MER—Recipes for these various kinds of fritters will be found under the heading HORS-D'OEUVRE. See HORS-D'OEUVRE, *Hot hors-d'oeuvre:* various *fish fritters; Soft roe fritters, Mussel fritters.*

Fish fritters (pickled or smoked fish). BEIGNETS DE POISSONS MARINÉS, FUMÉS—Proceed as described for *Anchovy fritters II.* Fritters can be made of different kinds of fish, such as herring fillets, smoked eel, sardines in oil, smoked salmon, tunny in oil, etc.

Foie gras fritters à l'ancienne. BEIGNETS DE FOIE GRAS À L'ANCIENNE—Make thin unsweetened pancakes. Spread with purée of foie gras mixed with diced truffles and flavoured with brandy. Roll the pancake into scrolls. Cut these scrolls into 2 or 3 pieces. Dip in light batter and deep fry.

Foie gras and truffle fritters. BEIGNETS DE FOIE GRAS AUX TRUFFES—Prepare a *salpicon** of foie gras (cooked) and truffles. Blend this *salpicon* with very thick, greatly concentrated, Madeira flavoured *Demi-glace* (see SAUCE). Allow to cool. Divide into small parts. Wrap each part of this *salpicon* in a piece of pig's caul or a paper-thin slice of salt pork, previously soaked in cold water. When required, dip into batter and deep fry. Serve *Périgueux sauce* separately (see SAUCE).

Jerusalem artichoke fritters. BEIGNETS DE TOPINAMBOURS—Cook, marinate, dip into batter and deep fry.

Marrow (zucchini or Italian marrows) fritters—As *Aubergine fritters.*

Meat fritters (various meat salpicons). BEIGNETS DE SALPICONS DE VIANDES—Prepare a *salpicon**, blend it with a sauce, white or brown, depending on the type of meat chosen (cooked meat leftovers: lamb, beef, mutton, pork, veal, poultry). Add diced truffles and mushrooms to the *salpicon.* Spread on a metal sheet and allow to cool. Divide into small pieces, roll each into a ball, dip into batter and deep fry.

Calf's mesentery fritters. BEIGNETS DE FRAISE DE VEAU—Cook the calf's mesentery in a *court-bouillon**, drain, dry, marinate and prepare like *Brain fritters.*

Mushroom fritters. BEIGNETS DE CHAMPIGNONS—Prepare a *salpicon** of cultivated mushrooms (add diced ham, if desired), blend with *Béchamel sauce* (see SAUCE), divide into small pieces, roll into balls, dip into batter and deep fry.

Oyster fritters à la normande—See OYSTERS.

Potato fritters I. BEIGNETS DE POMMES DE TERRE—Bind a *salpicon** of boiled potatoes with *Béchamel sauce* (see SAUCE). Spread the *salpicon* on a dish and leave until cold.

Divide into small parts and shape each into a ball. At the last moment, dip in a light batter and fry in deep fat. Serve arranged in a heap on a folded napkin.

Potato fritters II. BEIGNETS DE POMMES DE TERRE—Grate or mince raw potatoes, dry well and season with salt, pepper and grated nutmeg. Bind with yolks of egg. Divide into small parts. Dip in a light batter, deep fry at the last moment and serve on a folded napkin.

Salsify fritters. BEIGNETS DE SALSIFIS—Cook the salsify, cut into little chunks, marinate, dip into batter and deep fry.

Sorrel fritters. BEIGNETS D'OSEILLE—See recipes for *Spinach fritters.*

Spinach fritters I. BEIGNETS D'ÉPINARDS—Steep spinach leaves for a few minutes in oil, lemon juice, salt and pepper. Take them four at a time, pressing the leaves together. When required, dip into batter (light batter) and deep fry.

Spinach fritters II. BEIGNETS D'ÉPINARDS—Prepare *Quenelle forcemeat* (see FORCEMEAT) and put a thin layer of it on large spinach leaves, previously steeped in oil, lemon juice, salt and pepper. Roll them up and, when required, dip into batter and deep fry.

Sweetbread fritters (lamb's or calf's). BEIGNETS DE RIS D'AGNEAU, DE VEAU—Braise the sweetbreads in a *court-bouillon**. Marinate them for 30 minutes in oil, lemon juice and chopped parsley. When required, dip into batter and deep fry.

Tomato fritters. BEIGNETS DE TOMATES—Cut raw tomatoes into quarters, remove seeds, marinate, dip into batter and deep fry.

Tongue fritters, ox (beef) or calf's. BEIGNETS DE LANGUE DE BOEUF, DE VEAU—Cook and cool the tongue and cut into small slices. Marinate, dip into batter and deep fry.

Truffle fritters. BEIGNETS DE TRUFFES—Cut raw truffles into thick slices, steep in brandy with salt, pepper and spices, dip into batter and deep fry.

Vegetable-marrow (squash) fritters—See HORS-D'OEUVRE, *Hot hors-d'oeuvre.*

Vine tendril fritters. BEIGNETS DE VRILLES DE VIGNE—Put the tendrils to steep in oil, lemon, salt and pepper. Taking a few at a time, dip into batter and deep fry.

SWEET (DESSERT) FRITTERS. BEIGNETS D'ENTREMETS

Acacia blossom fritters. BEIGNETS D'ACACIA—Cut off stalks, sprinkle the bunches of blossoms with sugar, pour over a little rum or brandy and leave to steep for 30 minutes.

At the last moment, dip into batter.

Fry in very deep, sizzling hot fat. Drain, sprinkle with sugar and serve on a paper doyley or a napkin.

Apple fritters. BEIGNETS DE POMMES—Core the apples with a corer before peeling them. Cut them across in slices, about ⅛ inch thick. Steep for half an hour in brandy, kirsch or rum.

Drain, dip into batter and deep fry.

Drain, put on a baking tray, sprinkle with fine sugar and glaze in a very hot oven. Arrange in a crown on a napkin covered dish.

Apricot fritters. BEIGNETS D'ABRICOTS—Divide the apricots in half and steep them in sugar and liqueur.

Finish cooking as described in the recipe for *Crystallised fruit fritters.*

Banana fritters. BEIGNETS DE BANANES—Peel the bananas and divide in half lengthways, steep in sugar and liqueur.

Finish as described in the recipe for *Crystallised fruit fritters.*

Blossom and flower fritters. BEIGNETS DE FLEURS—Using acacia, elder and marrow blossoms, lilies and violets, divide these flowers into bunches, or, depending on their nature, snip off stalks and leave whole or separate into petals.

Steep in sugar and the liqueur chosen for 30 minutes, then finish cooking as described in the recipe for *Acacia blossom fritters.*

Cherry fritters. BEIGNETS DE CERISES—Stone the cherries. Steep them in sugar and liqueur (kirsch or cherry brandy).

Finish as described in the recipe for *Fresh fruit fritters.*

Cherry soufflé fritters. BEIGNETS SOUFFLÉS AUX CERISES—Make the fritters as described in the recipe for *Soufflé fritters I.* After cooking, garnish with stoned cherries, cooked in syrup, combined with a little cherry jam, and flavoured with kirsch.

Chestnut fritters. BEIGNETS DE MARRONS—Prepare vanilla flavoured *Chestnut purée.** Taking pieces the size of a walnut, wrap them in leaves of unleavened bread (Matzos) dipped in water. Dip into batter and finish as described in the recipe for *Fresh fruit fritters.*

Cold fritters, called Krapfen. BEIGNETS FROIDS, DITS KRAPFENS—Prepare and deep fry the fritters as described in the recipe for *Vienna fritters.*

As soon as they are cooked, drain them and drop into a hot, light syrup, flavoured as desired. When they are well steeped, strain and serve cold.

Cream fritters. BEIGNETS DE CRÈME—Prepare a custard cream as indicated under CREAMS.

Spread this cream or custard on a buttered metal baking sheet in a layer ¾ inch thick. Leave to cool.

Dip into batter and finish off as described in the recipe for *Crystallised fruit fritters* or *Fresh fruit fritters.* Custard fritters are sometimes coated with egg and breadcrumb before frying. In that case they go into the category of croquettes. They are also called *Fried creams.*

Fritters à la créole. BEIGNETS À LA CRÉOLE—Take 24 dates, slit them on one side and through this opening remove the stones. Stuff each date with a hazel-nut sized piece of sweetened rice mixed with finely chopped orange peel and flavoured with curaçao.

Enclose each date in a very thin piece of *Vienna fritter* dough. Proceed as described in the recipe for *Vienna fritters.*

Fritters à la Creppazi. BEIGNETS À LA CREPPAZI—Prepare *Sweet pancakes* (see CRÊPE) of a rather large diameter. Lay them on the table and coat with a light layer of *French pastry cream* (see CREAMS) flavoured with kirsch and mixed with crushed macaroons.

Put the pancakes on top of each other until the layer of pancakes is about ¼ inch thick.

Cut these layers into 1½ inch square pieces. Dip into batter and finish as described in the recipe for *Fresh fruit fritters.*

Crystallised fruit fritters. BEIGNETS DE FRUITS GLACÉS—Using apricots, pineapple, peaches, pears and apples, either peel them or leave them as they are, depending on their nature, and—also depending on their nature—divide in halves, quarters, segments or cut into slices.

Put the fruit into a dish, dust with sugar, sprinkle with brandy, kirsch, rum or any other liqueur and leave to steep for 30 minutes.

Drain the fruit, dry, dip into batter and deep fry in smoking hot fat.

Drain, dry in a cloth, arrange on a baking tray or a low dish, sprinkle with fine sugar and glaze either in a very hot oven or under a grill.

Arrange on a napkin or a paper doyley, in a heap or a ring.

Currant fritters. BEIGNETS DE GROSEILLES—As *Strawberry fritters.*

Date fritters. BEIGNETS DE DATTES—Stone the dates. Stuff each one with very thick *French pastry cream* (see CREAMS), a knob about the size of a hazel-nut, flavoured with kirsch or some other liqueur.

Dip the dates in light batter and deep fry. Drain the fritters. Arrange them in a clump on a napkin. Dust with fine sugar.

Fig fritters. BEIGNETS DE FIGUES—Peel the figs and quarter them. Steep them for 30 minutes in brandy or some other liqueur and sugar.

At the last moment, dip them in light batter and deep fry.

Fresh fruit fritters. BEIGNETS DE FRUITS—Using cherries, strawberries, raspberries, red currants, tangerines and oranges, proceed to deal with the fruit as required, stoning and hulling the berries, dividing oranges and tangerines into segments and trimming them.

Sprinkle all this fruit with sugar and leave to steep in the liqueur chosen for 30 minutes.

Drain, dip into batter and deep fry as described above.

Drain, dry, arrange in a heap on a napkin or a paper doyley and sprinkle with fine sugar.

Fruit jelly fritters I. BEIGNETS DE MARMELADES—Spread the jelly in a thin layer on a moist baking pan.

Allow to cool. Then cut as desired and finish as described in the recipe for *Fresh Fruit Fritters.*

Fruit jelly fritters II. BEIGNETS DE MARMELADE—Wrap the fruit jelly in round pieces of unleavened bread (Matzos) soaked in water.

Finish as described in the recipe for *Fresh fruit fritters.*

Mont-Bry fritters. BEIGNETS MONT-BRY—Prepare sweetened semolina as for a dessert (sweet course) and cool it by spreading it on a buttered metal sheet in a layer ⅓ inch (1 centimeter) thick.

Cut into small rectangles. Coat these rectangles with thick apricot jam mixed with a fine *salpicon** of walnuts and figs and flavoured with rum. Dip into batter and deep fry.

Nanette fritters. BEIGNETS NANETTE—Cut a stale brioche into small round slices.

Spread these slices with *French pastry cream* (see CREAMS) mixed with a *salpicon** of crystallised fruit steeped in kirsch. Sandwich the slices two by two and leave them to steep in kirsch.

Dip into a light batter and finish as described in the recipe for *Crystallised fruit fritters* or *Fresh fruit fritters.*

Peach fritters. BEIGNETS DE PÊCHES—Choose ripe peaches, divide in half, peel, put into a dish, sprinkle with sugar and kirsch, rum or brandy and leave to steep in a cool place for an hour.

Dry the halved peaches, dip in batter and fry in very hot deep fat.

Drain the fritters, put them on a baking tray, sprinkle with fine sugar and glaze in a hot oven or with a salamander. Serve in a heap on a napkin-covered dish.

Pear fritters. BEIGNETS DE POIRES—Proceed as described in the recipe for *Apple fritters.*

Pineapple fritters. BEIGNETS D'ANANAS—Cut the pineapple in round slices, divide each slice in half, sprinkle with sugar and steep in liqueur (kirsch or rum).

Finish as described in the recipe for *Crystallised fruit fritters.*

Plum fritters. BEIGNETS DE PRUNES—Steep some halved greengages or plums for an hour in kirsch, brandy, rum or quetsch and sugar.

Drain them, dip them in batter and fry in deep fat.

Drain the fritters. Arrange them on a plate, sprinkle with fine sugar and glaze in a hot oven or with a glazing iron.

Note. These fritters may also be prepared without glazing. As soon as they are fried and a good golden brown, they should be drained, set in a mound on a napkin and sprinkled with fine sugar.

Plum fritters à l'agenaise. BEIGNETS DE PRUNES À L'AGENAISE—Stick together two by two halves of greengages that have been soaked in liqueur and sugar, each coated with a small spoonful of plum purée flavoured with kirsch.

Just before they are wanted, dip the plums in batter and fry in deep fat. Sprinkle with fine sugar and serve on a napkin.

Polenta fritters. BEIGNETS DE POLENTA—Using sweetened polenta cooked in milk, prepared as *Rice fritters.*

Raspberry fritters. BEIGNETS DE FRAMBOISES—Remove stems, sugar lightly, sprinkle with a little kirsch or with brandy distilled from raspberries. Drain, dip in batter. Fry in very hot fat, drain, sprinkle with sugar and serve on a napkin.

Rice fritters. BEIGNETS DE RIZ—Prepare sweetened rice, as for a dessert course. Allow it to cool, spread it in a thick layer, ¾ inch thick. Cut into small square, rectangular or lozenge-shaped pieces. Dip into light batter.

Finish off as described in the recipe for *Cream fritters.*

Rice fritters with various fillings. BEIGNETS DE RIZ FOURRÉS—Prepare the fritters as described in the preceding recipe, filling them with jam, jelly or a *salpicon** of various fruit.

Rice cream fritters. BEIGNETS DE RIZ À LA CRÈME—Prepare sweetened rice, spread it in a layer and leave to cool.

Cut this rice into round pieces about 1½ inches in diameter.

Sandwich these little circlets together with a layer of a rather thick *French pastry cream.* See CREAMS.

Dip the fritters into a batter and fry in a very hot fat.

Drain the fritters and arrange them in a heap on a napkin covered dish. Just before serving, sprinkle with sugar.

Semolina fritters. BEIGNETS DE SEMOULE—Prepare sweetened semolina and proceed as described in the recipe for *Rice fritters.*

Shrove-Tuesday fritters (Alsatian cookery). BEIGNETS DE MARDI-GRAS—Prepare *Noodle paste** with the addition of butter. Roll out to a thickness of ⅛ inch. Cut into all sorts of shapes with a pastry cutter. Deep fry in sizzling oil. Drain in a napkin. Sprinkle with sugar mixed with cinnamon.

Soufflé fritters

Soufflé fritters I (or Pets de nonne). BEIGNETS SOUFFLÉS (PETS DE NONNE)—Into a saucepan with a flat bottom put one quart (1 litre) of water, ¾ cup (200 grams) of butter, 1½ teaspoons (10 grams) of salt, and ½ cup (120 grams) of sugar and bring to the boil. Remove the saucepan from fire. Pour in 5½ cups (625 grams) of sieved flour. Mix well. Put the saucepan back on the fire. Dry off the paste by stirring with a wooden spoon until it comes away from the walls of the saucepan and becomes slightly oily.

Remove from fire and add 12 to 14 eggs, one at a time, stirring vigorously.

With a spoon take up dollops of this paste, the size of a walnut or a hazel nut, depending on the type of fritter puff required, and drop them one at a time into hot, deep fat, but not smoking.

Gradually heat the fat to cook the fritters through and to make them a fine light golden colour.

Drain, arrange on a napkin in a heap, and sprinkle with fine sugar.

When the fritters are cooked, fill them as indicated in individual recipes, with various custards, creams, jams, etc.

Soufflé fritters II. BEIGNETS SOUFFLÉS—Prepare 1½ cups (250 grams) of *Chou paste* (see DOUGH) without sugar. With a spoon divide the paste into portions the size of a small walnut. Drop one after the other into hot but not boiling fat.

Cook until the paste has risen and the fritters are crisp on the outside and golden coloured. Drain well on a cloth, season and serve on a napkin.

Strawberry fritters. BEIGNETS DE FRAISES—Hull the strawberries and steep them in liqueur. Finish as described in the recipe for *Fresh fruit fritters.*

Stuffed fritters, called surprise fritters. BEIGNETS FOURRÉS, EN SURPRISE—Prepare the fritters as described in the recipe for *Soufflé fritters*.

Drain them, make a small slit on the side and fill them, using a forcing (pastry) bag with *French pastry cream* (see CREAMS), jam, fruit purée or *salpicon**, as indicated.

Tangerine or orange fritters. BEIGNETS DE MANDARINES, D'ORANGES—Divide the tangerines or oranges into sections, trim them, steep in sugar and liqueur and finish as described in the recipe for *Fresh fruit fritters*.

Vienna fritters or Dauphine fritters. BEIGNETS VIENNOIS, BEIGNETS DAUPHINE—*Ingredients.* 3¾ cups (500 grams) sieved flour, ¾ cup (200 grams) butter, 6 eggs, ⅝ ounce (20 grams) yeast, 2½ teaspoons (15 grams) salt, 1½ tablespoons (25 grams) sugar, ⅓ cup to ½ cup (1 decilitre) milk.

Method. Combine the above ingredients to make a paste as described in the recipe for *Brioche dough, ordinary**.

Roll out the pastry to a thickness of ⅛ inch.

On this rolled out piece of pastry, at regular intervals, allowing quite a bit of space between them, put in little spoonfuls—the size of a walnut—of the filling indicated: cream, custard, *salpicon** of fruit, etc.

Dip a pastry brush in water and moisten the edges around this filling. Cover with a second piece of rolled out pastry, of the same size and thickness as the first.

Press down with the back of a round biscuit punch to seal the pastry of each fritter. Stamp out the fritters with a round cutter, about 2 inches in diameter.

Lay them out on a baking tray covered with a cloth sprinkled with flour.

Leave to rise in a warm place for 30 minutes.

Drop the fritters into very hot deep fat and cook until they are well done and acquire a fine golden colour.

Drain, arrange on a napkin and sprinkle with fine sugar.

FRITTO-MISTO (Italian cookery)—This dish is called in France '*friture à l'italienne*'.

It should be made up of a great many different items, some fried in deep fat, others sautéed in butter.

A *fritto-misto* is prepared from the following ingredients: pieces of calves' head, brain, spinal bone-marrow (of sheep and calves), testicles, lamb's feet, rice and egg croquettes, fried bread, collops (slices) of sautéed calves' liver.

All these items, some fried in flour and egg batter, others in egg and breadcrumbs, are either fried in deep fat or sautéed in butter.

Fritto-misto, prepared in this way, makes an unusual and tasty luncheon dish.

In France the name *fritto-misto* is applied to a dish made up entirely of calves' head fritters served with tomato sauce.

FROG. GRENOUILLE—*Batrachia* of which there are about 20 species. Among those to be found in France are the *green* or *common frog*, the *rusty* or *mute frog*, so-called because the male has no voice-box.

In the United States there is a very large species called the *bull-frog* or *bellowing-frog*. This creature is twice the size of the types indigenous to Europe.

Frog-meat, which is no more than a tit-bit, is nevertheless easily digestible.

Method. Trim the frogs, that is to say, skin them and remove the breast, retaining only the legs which alone are edible. Cut off the feet. Skewer the legs and immerse them in very cold water. Change the water every two hours to whiten and swell the flesh. Dry the legs thus prepared and cook them according to one or other of the recipes set out below. Usually three pairs per serving are allowed.

Frogs' legs à l'anglaise. GRENOUILLES À L'ANGLAISE—Season the frogs' legs with salt and pepper. Flour them and dip in breadcrumbs *à l'anglaise**. Sauté in butter. Serve them on a long dish on a bed of *Maître d'hôtel butter* (see BUTTER, *Compound butters*). Serve boiled potatoes separately.

This dish is called *à l'anglaise* solely because this is the name given to foodstuffs dipped in egg and breadcrumbs and fried. It is well known that frogs' legs are not appreciated in England.

Frogs' legs à la béchamel. GRENOUILLES À LA BÉCHAMEL—Season the frogs' legs with salt and pepper. Put them in a frying pan with a little butter and a tablespoon of white wine. Cover and cook over a high flame.

Add a few tablespoons thick *Béchamel sauce* (see SAUCE) mixed with some fresh cream.

Simmer for a few moments. At the last minute, add a teaspoon of butter. Serve in a pyramid on a platter.

Frogs' legs au blanc. GRENOUILLES AU BLANC—Proceed as for *Frogs' legs à la béchamel*.

Frogs' legs as a border, au gratin. GRENOUILLES EN BORDURES, GRATINÉES—Prepared like *Frogs' legs à la Mornay*, but served as a garnish.

Frogs' legs in cream. GRENOUILLES À LA CRÈME—Cook the frogs' legs as for *Frogs' legs à la béchamel**. Boil some fresh cream and moisten the frogs' legs with a few tablespoons of this cream. Boil down (reduce) over a hot flame and arrange in a pyramid on a platter.

Curried frogs' legs. GRENOUILLES À L'INDIENNE—Sauté the frogs' legs in butter. Serve them in a border of curried rice. Pour *Curry sauce* over the frogs. See SAUCE.

Fried frogs' legs. GRENOUILLES FRITES—Soak the frogs' legs in a *marinade** for half an hour, as for *Frogs' legs fritters*, and proceed in the same way as for *Frogs' legs fritters*. See HORS-D'OEUVRE, *Hot hors-d'oeuvre*.

The frogs' legs may also simply be dipped in flour and fried in the usual way.

Frogs' legs fritters. BEIGNETS DE GRENOUILLES—See HORS-D'OEUVRE, *Hot hors-d'oeuvre*.

Frogs' legs au gratin. GRENOUILLES AU GRATIN—Season the frogs' legs. Sauté them quickly in smoking hot butter.

Put them on a round dish covered with a *Cream sauce* (see SAUCE), surrounded by a border of mushrooms cut into rather thick strips. Cover with cream sauce. Sprinkle with breadcrumbs. Pour on melted butter, and brown.

Frogs' legs à la lyonnaise. GRENOUILLES À LA LYONNAISE—Season the frogs' legs and dip them in flour. Sauté in butter over a very high flame.

When they are well browned, add 2 tablespoons of finely sliced onion lightly browned in butter. Sauté the frogs' legs and onions together. Sprinkle with chopped parsley. Heap on a platter, covered with a sauce made by heating a little vinegar in the cooking butter.

Frogs' legs à la meunière. GRENOUILLES À LA MEUNIÈRE—Season and flour the frogs' legs. Put them in a frying pan and sauté them in butter.

Heap them on a platter. Sprinkle with chopped parsley. Squeeze a few drops of lemon juice over them. Pour on the cooking butter, which has been heated until it turns brown. If necessary, add a little fresh butter. Serve at once.

Frogs' legs à la Mirepoix. GRENOUILLES À LA MIREPOIX—Season and flour the frogs' legs. Sauté them in butter in a frying pan. When they are cooked, add 2 tablespoons of vegetable *mirepoix** which has been slowly cooked in butter until tender.

Cook these ingredients over a very high flame and mix well. Heap on a serving dish. Pour over the mixture 2 tablespoons of concentrated meat stock and sprinkle with chopped parsley.

Frogs' legs à la Mornay. GRENOUILLES À LA MORNAY—Cook the frogs' legs gently in a little white wine, butter and lemon juice. Drain them and dry them with a cloth.

Serve them on a round dish lined with *Mornay sauce* (see SAUCE) and surrounded with a border of *Duchess potatoes* (see POTATOES).

Cover with *Mornay sauce* to which the pan juices have been added. Sprinkle with cheese. Pour on melted butter. Brush the border with beaten egg yolk. Brown in the oven or under the grill (broiler).

Frogs' legs à la niçoise. GRENOUILLES À LA NIÇOISE—Proceed as for *Frogs' legs à la mirepoix* substituting *Tomato fondue à la niçoise** for the *mirepoix*.

Frogs' legs with chopped parsley. GRENOUILLES AUX FINES HERBES—Season the frogs' legs with salt and pepper. Dip in flour. Sauté in butter in a frying pan over a high flame.

When they are cooked and well browned, pile them in a pyramid on a platter. Sprinkle them with chopped parsley. Squeeze the juice of a lemon over them and pour on the butter in which they have been cooked.

Frogs' legs à la poulette. GRENOUILLES À LA POULETTE—Cook the frogs' legs gently in a little white wine, with butter and a squeeze of lemon juice. Season with salt and pepper. Add a small onion and a *bouquet garni**.

As soon as the liquid comes to the boil, add peeled, sliced mushrooms. Cover and simmer.

Drain the frogs' legs and the mushrooms. Strain the stock and boil it down. Thicken with yolks of egg and cream, as for *Poulette sauce* (see SAUCE).

The sauce should be fairly thick. Put the frogs' legs and mushrooms back in the sauce and heat. At the last minute, add a heaped tablespoon of fresh butter, chopped parsley and a squeeze of lemon juice. Heap on a platter.

Frogs' legs prepared in this way can be served in a pie-crust or a vol-au-vent. They are then called *timbales* or *vol-au-vents* of frogs' legs *à la poulette*.

Frogs' legs sautéed à la provençale. GRENOUILLES SAUTÉES À LA PROVENÇALE—Sauté the frogs' legs in a frying pan, in butter or oil, as for *Frogs' legs à la lyonnaise*. At the last moment, add a little crushed garlic and chopped parsley. Heap on a platter.

FROMAGE D'ITALIE—A dish made from pig's liver. See OFFAL OR VARIETY MEATS.

FROMAGE GLACÉ—In former times, plain ices moulded into conical shapes were called *fromage glacé* in France.

The name *fromage bavarois* was used for the cold sweet made from a mixture of custard and whipped cream, which is now called *bavarois* (see BAVARIAN CREAM).

FROMAGER—To add grated cheese (in large or small quantities) to a sauce, a stuffing or any kind of dough, or sprinkling it over food to be browned in the oven. The cheeses most commonly used for this purpose are Parmesan and Gruyère.

FROMENTEAU—A variety of table grapes.

FRONTIGNAN—A small town of the Hérault district which has given its name to a very heavy type of muscatel wine.

Fruit for dessert

FRUIT—Botanically speaking fruit is the ovary of any growing plant. In current usage, however, 'fruit' refers only to those ovaries which may be eaten as dessert.

Some fruits, in fact, are eaten as vegetables. Examples of these are egg-plant (aubergines), pumpkins, marrows, gourds, cucumbers, olives, tomatoes etc.

In terms of calories some of the commoner fruits have little food value, except for those with a high starch, oil or sugar content. However, it is from fruit that we get, in a readily assimilated form, essential minerals as well as all the precious health-giving vitamins.

Even the water in fruit has a part to play. Because of it, fruit is an excellent thirst quencher, often available when cooling drinks are not.

Dried fruit. FRUITS SECS—Included under this heading are naturally dry fruits such as almonds, hazelnuts, walnuts, etc., rich in fats and albumen. Also included are artificially dried fruits (apricots, cherries, figs, apples, pears, prunes, raisins, etc.) which are eaten without further preparation. All these provide very concentrated nourishment. When they are soaked and cooked, although they have not quite all the qualities of fresh fruit, they do, up to a point, provide a useful substitute.

Fruit ices. GLACES AUX FRUITS—For these ices, the basic syrup consists of 4 cups sugar to 2 cups of water boiled 5 minutes and cooled. This gives an approximate density of 18° to 22° when measured on a saccharometer. To this cold syrup various fruit pulps or juices are added.

Fruit juices. SUCS (JUS) DE FRUITS—Fruit juices, obtained by cooking fruit with a little water or by squeezing it, are very popular, especially as drinks for persons suffering from feverish illnesses.

Fruit juices are also extracted commercially. Most of these drinks are excellent, especially those sterilized by some means other than boiling. They have considerable food value, comparable with that of milk.

Fruit mould. PAIN DE FRUITS—Coat a charlotte mould with a thick layer of jelly (made of the same fruit as the loaf or mixture to be used in the centre).

When this layer of jelly sets well, fill the middle of the mould with a fruit *bavarois* mixture, prepared in advance in the usual manner (see BAVARIAN CREAM) but without adding any cream. Cover with a layer of jelly. Chill on ice and serve on a napkin-covered dish.

Pickled fruits. FRUITS CONFITS AU VINAIGRE—Pour vinegar into glass or stone pickling jars; add enough fine sugar to turn the mixture into a syrup which is sharp without being too sour. Add the fruit to be pickled to the syrup. After a few weeks the fruit will be thoroughly impregnated with the syrup and will be ready for eating.

Pickled fruit may be used for the same purpose as fruit preserved in brandy, but is more commonly served as a condiment.

Fruit salad. FRUITS RAFRAÎCHIS—*Ingredients* (for 10 people). 6 peaches, 6 apricots, 6 greengages, 3 ripe pears, 2 apples, 4 bananas, 1 cup (125 grams) of raspberries, 1 cup (125 grams) of white and black grapes, 1 cup (125 grams) of small strawberries, 24 fresh almonds, 1 cup (3 decilitres) of kirsch and/or maraschino, 5 or 6 tablespoons of fine sugar.

Method. Peel the peaches, pears and apples and cut them into little pieces. Peel the bananas and cut them into strips. Stone the apricots and greengages and cut them up.

Mix all the fruit in a bowl. Add two-thirds of the strawberries and raspberries. Decorate with the grapes. Sprinkle the sugar on top and pour on the liqueur. Gently shake the dish so that the various fruits are properly mixed. Put the bowl into a larger bowl containing crushed ice. Leave it to soak for an hour.

Transfer the fruit salad to a decorative glass bowl (or a special double container). Surround it with crushed ice. Decorate the top of the fruit salad with the remaining strawberries, raspberries, grapes and almonds. (The almonds must be blanched and halved.)

Note. The ingredients of a fruit salad vary according to the season. All kinds of fruit may be used, such as pineapples, oranges, nectarines, mirabelle plums, cherries, etc. It may also be made from fruit preserved in syrup.

Instead of sweetening it with sugar, syrup may be poured on to the fruit salad, and any liqueur may be used for flavouring. Fruit salad can be served as a dessert (sweet) course or as a salad course.

Fruit salad à la créole. FRUITS RAFRAÎCHIS À LA CRÉOLE —A *macédoine** of fruit made from bananas, pineapples and oranges finely sliced, sprinkled with rum and sugar and left to stand in ice. It is served in a glass bowl (or a special double container) on a bed of pineapple ice cream. At the last moment, pour on lightly whipped sweetened fresh cream flavoured with rum. Decorate the top with orange segments with all the inner skin cut away and with blanched pistachio nuts.

Fruit salad with kirsch. FRUITS RAFRAÎCHIS AU KIRSCH—In the preparation of this sweet, all the fruits in season are used: strawberries, cherries, peaches, apricots, grapes, almonds, etc., with stalks, stones, skins and so on removed. Some are sliced, others left whole.

The mixed fruit is served in a silver or glass bowl, sprinkled with sugar, mixed without bruising and with kirsch poured over it. It is then embedded in a larger bowl full of crushed ice.

Instead of sugar, the fruit salad may be sweetened with a very heavy syrup.

Fruit salad à la maltaise. FRUITS RAFRAÎCHIS À LA MALTAISE—A *macédoine** of fruit made from oranges, bananas, cherries, and pineapples left to soak with sugar and curaçao.

Serve in a glass bowl or special double container on a bed of orange ice cream. Cover with whipped cream. Decorate with segments of orange from which all the inner skin has been removed.

Fruit salad à la normande. FRUITS RAFRAÎCHIS À LA NORMANDE—Put in a dish with crushed ice a *macédoine** of fruit consisting of russets, or tart apples, fresh pineapple, and bananas; let this mixture soak in sugar and calvados.

Serve in a glass bowl or special double container. Cover with slightly beaten fresh cream which has been sweetened with sugar and flavoured with calvados.

Fruit salad à l'occitanienne. FRUITS RAFRAÎCHIS À L'OCCITANIENNE—Place in layers, in a silver bowl, sliced pears, black and white grapes and peeled figs, cut into round slices. Sprinkle with sugar and pour on some *Blanquette de Limoux** and a little brandy. Surround the bowl with ice mixed with a little kitchen salt, so that the fruit may be slightly congealed.

At the last minute cover with *Chantilly cream* (see CREAMS). Decorate with grapes.

Fruit salad Tsarina (Czarina). FRUITS RAFRAÎCHIS TZARINE—Put mixed fruit, whole or sliced as appropriate, soaked with sugar and kummel on top of a layer of pineapple ice cream.

Cover with *Chantilly cream* (see CREAMS), flavoured with kummel. Decorate with crystallised violets and lozenge-shaped pieces of angelica. This sweet (dessert) should be served in a glass bowl.

Fruit sauces—See SAUCE, *Dessert sauces.*

Sugar-coated and marzipan fruit. FRUITS DÉGUISÉS—In confectionery, small fruit (strawberries, black-currants, cherries, gooseberries, plums, etc.), either fresh or preserved in brandy, can be coated with *Fondant icing* (see ICING) approximating to the natural colour of the fruit.

Marzipan fruits are a kind of *petit four** made from very thick fruit purée mixed with almond paste or sometimes with concentrated jam. These mixtures are moulded into the shape of various fruits and covered with caramel sugar. They are usually served in little paper cases.

FRUIT KERNEL. NOYAU—Softer (usually edible) part within hard shell of nut or stone fruit, body of seed with husk, etc.

Fruit kernel liqueur. CRÈME DE NOYAUX—A liqueur which has fruit kernels as a basis. See LIQUEUR.

FRUIT STONE CRACKER. ENOYAUTEUR—An implement for cracking the stones of certain fruits such as cherries, without crushing them completely.

FRUITARIAN. FRUGIVORE—A person who lives exclusively on fruit and vegetables.

Such a person believes that man should feed only on that which can be eaten in the natural state in which it grows.

FRUITERY. FRUITERIE, FRUITIÈRE—A *Fruiterie* is a special storage place for fruit. *Fruitière* is the name given to a cheese factory usually situated in the mountains near pastures.

FRUMENTY. FROMENTÉE—A porridge made from wheat flour.

FRYING—See DEEP FRYING, and CULINARY METHODS, *Sauté.*

FRYING PAN. POÊLE—Kitchen utensil, usually made of iron, shallow, widening out at the top, with a long handle, used for frying food. The ordinary frying pan is round in shape.

A fish frying pan is oval in shape and a pan for roasting chestnuts is perforated on the bottom.

FUCHSINE—A dye sold in the form of purplish scales, sweetish in taste and somewhat unpleasant in smell. It is sometimes used as artificial colouring for wines and foodstuffs.

FULBERT-DUMONTEIL — Fulbert-Dumonteil, a French writer, born at Vergt in the Dordogne on April 10th, 1830, was a great gastronome. He wrote charming articles on the art of cookery which were published in the form of a chronicle in various journals, notably the old *Figaro*. These articles were for the most part collected in one volume, under the title of *La France gourmande*.

FUMET—In cookery, this name is given to a number of different liquids which are used to flavour or give body to stocks and sauces. *Fumets* are prepared by boiling foodstuffs of one kind or another either in stock or in wine of some sort.

Fumets should not be confused with essences, extracts or concentrates.

Chicken fumet, FUMET DE VOLAILLE—Strictly speaking, this is a kind of chicken soup, made by boiling down very considerably a chicken stock which has been prepared in the usual way (see STOCK).

This fumet is used to add flavour to various poultry dishes which are served with a sauce.

Fish fumet. FUMET DE POISSON—This is a stock made from the bones and trimmings of fish, the flesh being prepared separately. This fish stock is very much reduced. It is used with white wine in the cooking of certain fish, and also in the preparation of special white or brown fish sauces.

For the preparation of fish *fumet*, see STOCK.

Game fumet. FUMET DE GIBIER—This is a game stock (made with the carcases and trimmings of different game) which is reduced (boiled down) to a more or less concentrated consistency, according to the flavour desired.

Pâté fumet—See PÂTÉ.

Truffle fumet. FUMET DE TRUFFES—This *fumet*, used to enhance the flavour of certain sauces, is made by boiling down (reducing) almost to nothing a stock made by simmering truffle peelings in Madeira (or any other heavy wine). This stock is usually made when the truffles themselves are being used for some other purpose.

Fruit Salad

GADELLE—This is the name used in Western France for the red currant, which is called *gade* in Normandy.

The vineyards of Gaillac (*French Government Tourist Office*)

GAILLAC—Small town in the Tarn district whose white wines enjoy a great reputation. These are sold as young wines in Paris but are strongly laced with spirits to enable them to travel. Some of these wines, processed like champagne, are very popular in France.

GALANTINE—A dish made from boned poultry or meat, stuffed and pressed into a symmetrical shape. Galantines are cooked in a gelatine stock.

Does the word come, as some authorities believe, from the Gothic root '*gal*', *jelly*, appearing first perhaps in the form '*galatine*' and later as '*galantine*'? We do not think so. We believe rather that this term must derive from the words '*géline*' or '*galine*' which, in Old French, meant chicken, for this dish was first made with poultry, and later, that is to say towards the end of the seventeenth century, with other types of bird, cuts of meat and even fish, as shown by what used to be called a '*sous presse*' of fish, which was a form of galantine.

Nowadays, galantines are made from other meats besides poultry, but strictly the word 'galantine' without qualification denotes galantine of poultry.

There are many ways of preparing this cold dish. Here first is the recipe from the chapter on *cold entrées* in Carême's *Le Cuisinier parisien*.

Galantine of chicken I (Carême's recipe). GALANTINE DE POULARDE À LA GELÉE—*The forcemeat.* 'Chop ½ pound veal (*noix de veau*) with 1 pound fat bacon and ½ pound cooked ham (*noix de jambon cuit*). Mix in 1 teaspoon spiced salt, 2 yolks of egg, 2 tablespoons of chopped herbs with the same quantity of truffles. Mix well and place in an earthenware dish.

'Peel 1½ pounds very ripe truffles. Cut each truffle into quarters. Take a good, red pickled tongue. Skin and cut lengthwise into six slices only. Cut into thick fingers 1 pound raw fat ham, fresh pork fat or calf's udder. (This last is preferable.)

The chicken. 'Singe, pluck and bone a medium-sized plump chicken. When it is boned, open it out on a cloth. With a knife cut away half the meat of the breast and thighs. Use the pieces thus removed to line the bird wherever there is so little flesh that the skin is almost showing through, so that the flesh may be evenly distributed. Season with an appropriate amount of spiced salt. After boning the chicken, weigh it. If it weighs 2 pounds season with 4 *gros* (½ ounce or 1 tablespoon) of spiced salt per pound.

'Spread out on the chicken half the forcemeat and lay upon it half the truffles, tongue and ham fat, making sure that the colours present a mottled effect. Season lightly with spiced salt. Cover the whole with half the remaining forcemeat and lay on top the truffles and fat from the pickled tongue with a little added seasoning. Cover with the remaining forcemeat.

'Now fold the chicken to approximate to its original shape, sewing it up with a trussing needle so that all the garnish is contained in the chicken, which should be moulded into a round or slightly oval shape.

'Having completed this operation, wrap slices of fat bacon round the chicken. Fold a piece of muslin round the whole, tying both ends tightly with string. Tie a piece of string round the middle of the chicken to keep it in shape. Then tie in two more places to the right and left of the first, making sure not to draw tightly.

'Brown strips of fat bacon in an oval or round casserole. Place the galantine in it and surround with four onions, four carrots, a large bunch of parsley and spring onions. Season with thyme, laurel, basil and four cloves. Add the bones of the chicken and four knuckles of veal or two calves' feet, enough stock or chicken broth to cover the galantine, then a glass of dry Madeira or good white wine and two tablespoons of old brandy. Cover the whole with a round piece of buttered paper and cook over a high flame. Then simmer slowly for three hours and remove from the stove.

'An hour later, carefully lift the galantine out of the casserole. Lay it breast downwards on a slightly curved earthenware platter and squeeze it gently, still wrapped in the muslin, to remove any little moisture left in it.

'Cover with a lid and place on top an 8 pound weight, in order to flatten and spread the chicken.

'Next, strain the jelly through a fine sieve. Remove all fat and leave it to settle for a full quarter of an hour and clarify by one of the methods described under JELLY.

'When the galantine is cold, uncover it, dry it gently with a cloth and remove all string.

'If necessary, pat it into shape, then cover it very carefully all over with a white glaze.

'Place the galantine on an entrée dish. Arrange a rosette of jelly on the top, surround with chopped jelly and then with rounds of jelly cut with a pastry cutter ⅓ inch in diameter, and serve.'

Another method of preparing this galantine is mentioned by Carême. 'Dice some truffles and blanched bacon or udder, pickled tongue and blanched pistachio nuts, mix all these ingredients to make chicken quenelle forcemeat, and serve as a garnish with the chicken.'

Galantine of chicken II. GALANTINE DE POULARDE—*Ingredients. For the galantine:* 1 chicken weighing 4 pounds (2 kilos), ½ pound (250 grams) finely minced pork; ½ pound (250 grams) finely minced veal; a generous ¼ pound (150 grams) each of fat bacon, York ham (lean, cooked ham), pickled tongue; 6 truffles (150 grams); 2 tablespoons (25 grams) pistachio nuts; ⅓ cup (1 decilitre) brandy; 2 eggs; salt, pepper, spices.

For the stock or jelly: 2 calves' feet; 1 pound (500 grams) fresh bacon rind; 5 pounds (2 kilos 500 grams) fleshy knuckle of veal; 2 carrots; 1 onion; 2 leeks; 1 *bouquet garni**; 5 quarts (litres) white stock; 1½ cups (4 decilitres) Madeira; salt.

Method. Singe and pluck the bird in the normal way. It is unnecessary to draw it at this stage. It is simpler to do this after the chicken has been boned.

Remove the feet and pinions. Slit the chicken along the back and with a small very sharp knife bone it without tearing the flesh. (This operation, which at first sight seems awkward, is actually fairly simple. It is necessary only to follow the joints of the chicken and to work inwards towards the carcase, shaving off the flesh as close to the bone as possible. This first boning operation separates the carcase from the body of the chicken, leaving them both whole.) Now remove the bones from the legs, thighs and wings, still being very careful not to tear the skin.

Spread out the chicken on the table, and cut away the breast and the greater part of the fleshy portions of thighs and wings. Cut these pieces into neat squares which will be used for the *salpicon** or rich meat ragoût in which this galantine is served.

The forcemeat. Normally, this forcemeat is made of finely chopped lean pork and veal in equal quantities.

Pound this forcemeat in a mortar, seasoning it with salt, pepper and spices. (To obtain a very fine forcemeat, it is advisable to rub the mixture, after pounding, through a sieve.)

The salpicon. Take the lean pieces cut away from the chicken; the fat bacon cut neatly into squares of about ⅜ inch; the cooked lean ham, and the pickled tongue cut up in the same way; the coarsely diced truffles; and the blanched pistachio nuts.

Place these ingredients in an earthenware dish, add the forcemeat and two eggs and the brandy, and mix thoroughly, adding seasoning if necessary.

Preparation of the galantine. Knead all the forcemeat into a ball and lay it on the chicken, which should be well spread out on the table. (From time to time, the hands should be dipped in water to make it easier to work the forcemeat.) Spread this forcemeat evenly over the chicken, forming it into a rectangular shape. Fold over this rectangle of forcemeat the parts of the chicken skin which project at the sides and ends.

Take a coarse linen cloth, dip it in water and wring it out, then spread it flat on the table. Place it so that a flap about ten inches wide hangs over the edge of the table.

Place the galantine lengthwise on this cloth, about four inches from the edge of the table, breast upwards.

Wrap the galantine in the cloth as tightly as possible. Tie both ends of the cloth securely. Tie the galantine with string in three places to keep it in shape. Done up in this way, it should look like a bundle 9 inches long and approximately 4 inches wide.

(Another method is to sew up the slit in the chicken before wrapping it; this precaution, however, is unnecessary if the skin is carefully folded over the forcemeat to prevent it from oozing out.)

Method of cooking. The stock, made from the ingredients listed above, is prepared according to the recipe for *jelly* (see JELLY). To the ingredients listed, add the carcase and giblets of the chicken, with the exception of the liver.

Cook this stock for 1½ hours before putting in the galantine. Lay the galantine in the stock and simmer gently for 1 hour and 45 minutes.

Remove the galantine from the stock. Let it stand for 15 minutes before unwrapping it.

Remove the cloth. Rinse the cloth in lukewarm water and wring it thoroughly. Spread it on the table and lay the galantine upon it. Carefully wrap the galantine in the cloth as before, taking care to keep the slit part of the chicken underneath.

Tie up the galantine. Press it on a slab covered with a wooden board with a weight on top. Allow it to cool for at least 12 hours.

Note. The galantine can be kept for several days, if it is stored in a cool place.

It is served garnished with its own jelly, which must be clarified by the usual method. (See JELLY.)

Other galantines—By the same method as that indicated for galantine of chicken, galantines of other poultry may be prepared, e.g. young turkey, Nantes duckling, guinea-fowl, pigeon. Also by the same method, but altering the ingredients of the stuffing according to the bird used, galantines may be made of various game birds such as pheasant, partridge, grouse, hazel-grouse etc.

The recipes for these various galantines are given in alphabetical order under the name of each game-bird.

Galantines may also be prepared according to the method used by pork-butchers, that is to say that, instead of wrapping them in a cloth, they are put in special rectangular metal or earthenware moulds. To improve the flavour of these galantines, a certain amount of *foie gras* may be added to the stuffing. Diced *foie gras* may also be added to the *salpicon.**

Galantine of jellied eels. GALANTINE D'ANGUILLE À LA GELÉE—Prepare the eel according to the instructions for cold stuffed eels (see EEL). Cook it in a fish stock. Drain it. Allow it to cool under a weight. Unwrap the galantine, cover it with the half-set jelly. Place it on a long dish (either flat or raised on a slice of buttered sandwich bread cut lengthwise. Garnish with chopped jelly (jelly strained and clarified) made from the eel stock.

GALATHÉE—A species of shell-fish similar to the freshwater crayfish. The parent species of this shell-fish, the *galathée grêle*, is common on the European shores of the Atlantic and in the Mediterranean. *Galathée* is prepared as indicated for lobster and crayfish. (See LOBSTER and CRAYFISH.)

GALAZYME, GALACTOZYME—Frothy milk, slightly fermented and with a very small alcohol content. See KÉFIR.

GALETTE (FRENCH TWELFTH CAKE)—Round cake made from flaky pastry. The galette is the symbolic cake eaten on Twelfth Night in most of the provinces north of the Loire, notably in the region of Paris.

South of the Loire, notably in the South of France, the Twelfth cake is made from yeast dough in the form of a crown. In both cakes, the symbolic bean is baked in the dough. This is not always, as it used to be, a real bean, but is sometimes a small porcelain model either of a baby emerging from a bean or of some other figure.

Flaky-pastry galette. GALETTE FEUILLETÉE—Roll out flat some flaky-pastry dough and cut from it a round piece between 6–7 inches in diameter. Place this round piece of pastry on a slab. Crimp the edges and brush over with egg; mark out the top in lozenge-shaped segments. Bake in a hot oven.

Small orange galettes. PETITES GALETTES ORANGINES—Place in a circle on the table 2 cups (250 grams) of sieved flour. In the centre of the flour, place ½ cup (120 grams) of sugar, ⅔ cup (150 grams) of butter, a pinch of salt, the peel of two oranges rubbed on lumps of sugar and 6 yolks of eggs. Mix these ingredients and work in the flour. Knead this dough into a ball and allow it to stand for a few hours in a cool place.

Roll out the dough to a thickness of ⅛ inch. Cut into rounds with a fluted cutter 2 to 2½ inches in diameter. Place the rounds of dough on a buttered baking sheet. Brush them with egg beaten with a pinch of sugar.

Bake in a hot oven (425° F.) for 6–8 minutes.

Potato galettes. GALETTES DE POMMES DE TERRE—These galettes, which can be made either of potatoes prepared as for *Duchess potatoes* (see POTATOES) or with potatoes cut into thin discs, are used as a garnish for various dishes, and are sometimes served topped with tiny pieces of meat, poultry or fish.

Rich galette. GALETTE FONDANTE—*Ingredients.* 2½ cups (300 grams) bread flour; 1 cup (250 grams) butter; 1 egg and 1 yolk; 1 teaspoon (5 grams) salt; 1 heaping tablespoon (20 grams) sugar; ⅓–½ cup (1 decilitre) fresh cream; vanilla.

Method. Work the flour with 3 tablespoons (50 grams) of the butter; add the eggs, cream, salt and sugar. Leave the dough to stand for 10 minutes.

Knead the dough and add the remaining butter. Roll out and fold the dough four times as is done for *Flaky pastry* (see DOUGH). Brush the galette with egg. Lattice it with a knife. Cook in a hot oven and sprinkle it, while hot, with powdered sugar.

Savoury galettes. GALETTES SALÉES—Knead 2 cups (250 grams) of sieved flour with ⅔ cup (150 grams) of butter, ½ cup (8 tablespoons) of cold milk and 1½ teaspoons (10 grams) of salt. Allow this dough to stand for two hours.

Roll it out very thin on the floured table. Prick the rolled out dough with a fork. Cut it into rounds of 2 to 2½ inches in diameter. Place these rounds on a buttered baking sheet and brush with milk to which a lot of salt has been added. Bake in a very hot oven (450° F.) for 6 to 8 minutes.

As soon as the galettes are out of the oven brush them again with salted milk.

Galette de Plomb—*Ingredients.* 2⅔ cups (300 grams) sieved flour, ¾ cup (200 grams) butter, 1 whole egg, 1 yolk, 1 teaspoon (5 grams) fine sugar, 1 tablespoon (15 grams) table salt, 1 to 2 tablespoons milk or cream.

Method. Sieve the flour on to a marble slab or pastry table; make a well in the centre. Dissolve the table salt and sugar in a tablespoon of milk or cream and pour into the well. Knead the butter until it is quite malleable, cut it up into very small pieces and dot these about in the circle of flour. Beat together on a plate with a fork, the egg and the yolk, as for an omelette. Work the butter and the flour until the mixture is very short. This is done by rubbing the hands together with the mixture of flour and butter between them.

Continue to shorten the dough in this way until the butter is entirely broken up into infinitesimal particles. This done, spread out the dough, taking care to scrape the pastry table or slab to remove the mixture of milk, salt, sugar and flour which always sticks to it because of the moisture.

Pour the beaten egg and yolk over the dough and work it in the same way as before, but pressing the hands more and more tightly together as the kneading proceeds.

The ingredients in the dough should moisten it sufficiently to hold it together. The pastry should be fairly limp. If it is a little too firm, add, just before the end, the second tablespoon of milk or cream. (The amount of moistening required may vary with the type of flour used.)

When the dough is thoroughly kneaded, cover it with a damp cloth and put it in a cool place. Let it stand for half an hour. At the end of this time, take the dough, flatten it on the table with the palm of the hand, flour it lightly, and fold it into three. Roll it into a ball. Flatten it into a round shape about an inch thick. Crimp the edges with the back of a knife.

Place the galette on a lightly buttered baking sheet and surround it with a tart-ring buttered in advance. Brush the top of the galette with the beaten egg and trace on it either lozenges as for the flaky pastry galette or rosettes as for *Pithiviers cake.** This last is the characteristic design for the *Galette de Plomb.*

Bake for 20 to 25 minutes in a moderate oven (350°F.). The *Galette de Plomb* is eaten lukewarm or cold.

Galettes de Plomb—Arrange in a circle on the table 2 cups (250 grams) of sieved flour. Place in the middle of the circle 2 whole eggs, 4 tablespoons of double (thick) cream, 2 tablespoons of sugar, a pinch of salt. Knead this thoroughly into a dough. Let it stand for 2 hours.

Divide the dough into pieces, each the size of a small egg. Roll these pieces into balls. Place these balls of dough on a buttered slab. Flatten them slightly with the floured base of a tumbler. Brush with egg. Score with the tip of a knife. Bake in a very hot oven (450° F.) for 8 to 10 minutes.

GALICIEN—This sweet (dessert), which is a type of cake, was created, it is said, in Paris, at the Pâtisserie Frascati which has now disappeared. It was situated on the corner of the Boulevard Richelieu and the Rue Richelieu. This pastry-shop was built on the site of what was during the years 1796 to 1799 (the Directory) one of the most famous gaming-houses in Paris.

Ingredients. 2 cups (500 grams) fine sugar, 3 cups (375 grams) sifted bread flour, 16 eggs.

Method. Whisk together in a pan, on the edge of a low fire, the sugar and the eggs. After this mixture has tripled in volume in the pan, add the sieved flour away from the flame. Stir in carefully. Pour this mixture into a large shallow sloping sided cake tin. Bake in a fairly hot oven (400° F.). Leave to cool.

Slice the cake across. Spread on each half a layer of *Butter cream* (see CREAMS) flavoured with pistachio nuts. Put the two halves together, exerting a little pressure to joint them firmly. Spread the cake with apricot jam. Ice with a *Pistachio icing* (see ICING) and decorate with more of the pistachio-flavoured butter cream, using a forcing (pastry) bag. Sprinkle on top finely chopped pistachio nuts.

GALICHONS—Also called *calissons*. Little iced cakes made with pounded almonds, a speciality of Aix.

GALINGALE. SOUCHET—Common name of the plant *Cyperus* whose tubers are edible and known in French as *amandes de terre*.

GALL. FIEL—A secretion of the liver commonly called bile in humans. It is a very bitter greenish substance. The gall-bladder is attached to the liver. In drawing poultry or winged game, the gall-bladder must always be removed with the greatest care to avoid its breaking and giving a bitter flavour to the bird. Only pigeon liver contains no gall.

GALLIMAUFRY. GALIMAFRÉE—A chicken stew from medieval cookery. Taillevent, in his book *Le Viandier*, gives the following recipe:

'For gallimaufry, take roast chickens or capons, cut into sections and afterwards fry in bacon or goose fat. When this is done, add wine and verjuice and, for spices, put in ground ginger and, to thicken it, treacle-mustard, and a moderate quantity of salt.'

Gallimaufry (another recipe)—'Take a leg of mutton freshly cooked, and chop it as finely as possible in a dish of onions. Stew these ingredients with a little verjuice, butter, and ground white ginger mixed together and seasoned with salt.' (Old recipe.)

The word gallimaufry is now used in a disparaging sense, and means a badly cooked stew made from scraps.

GALLON—A liquid measure used in most English-speaking countries including America. It is equivalent to about $4\frac{1}{2}$ litres (U.S.A. $3\frac{3}{8}$ litres).

GAMAY—A village in Burgundy which has given its name to a vine. The *petit gamay* is one of the most prolific vines in Burgundy.

Although this vine is not of as fine a quality as the *pinot*, Gamay grapes are much sought after for their yield, which is always fairly high.

The grapes of the Gamay vine are sometimes used with those of the *pinot*, but the grapes of the *pinot* are used by themselves in the best wines.

In districts to the west of the Côte d'Or and in the Beaujolais, Mâconnais and Lyonnais districts, the grapes of the Gamay vine, used by themselves, make wines of excellent quality, for instance, those named *Moulins-à-vent* and *Les Thorins*. See BURGUNDY.

GAMBRA—A type of partridge of central European origin. All the recipes for partridge may be used in the preparation of this bird for the table. See PARTRIDGE.

GAME. GIBIER—The term game applies to all wild animals and birds which are hunted and eaten.

Gibier, the French word for game, comes from *gibecer* which, in old French, meant hunting. *Gibecer* in turn derives from the Latin adjective *gibbosus*, meaning hunchback. This word was used to describe the various animals killed in the chase for the following reason: To carry home the game they killed, huntsmen were equipped with a bag, pouch or box, which they usually carried on their backs. Thus equipped, they had the appearance of hunchbacks. Thus arose the word *gibecer*, followed by its derivative *gibecière* for the huntsman's bag or pouch. From the word *gibecière* it was an obvious step to the word *gibier*, 'that which was carried', and it was not long before the word was firmly established in the language.

Game can be divided into three categories:

(1) Small birds, none larger than the quail or the thrush.

Game (Frans Snyders)

(2) Game proper which can be sub-divided into winged game (landrail or corncrake, woodcock, partridge, pheasant, etc.) and ground game (wild rabbit and hare).

(3) Large game or venison (roebuck, deer and wild boar).

'Game', writes Brillat-Savarin, 'is a healthy, warming and savoury food, fit for the most delicate palate and easy to digest. In the hands of an experienced cook, game can provide dishes of the highest quality which raise the culinary art to the level of a science.

'There is game of all sorts. Certain types of game from Périgord will not have the same flavour as similar game killed at Sologne. Whereas a hare killed round and about Paris will make dull eating, a leveret from the Haut Dauphiné or the Burgundy district will be more deliciously flavoured than any other of its kind.'

Note. In Britain there is a close season for most game, i.e. a period when game may not be shot and killed. Several birds are protected all the year round, including blackbird, bustard, cygnet, heron, landrail, lapwing, lark, quail, rail, swan and swift.

Digestibility of game—Small game birds, some of which are cooked undrawn, are usually eaten fresh, 'while the gun is still smoking.' They are as digestible as poultry. The thrush, however, is an exception, being very highly flavoured.

Ground game, hare in particular, is classed among the red meats. It is rich in constituents which, even when the game is fresh, are more harmful to the digestion than those of butcher's meat, and considerably more so when the game has been hanging for a long time.

The same is true of venison. The meat of young roebuck, whether shot or trapped, is the most readily digestible especially if it has not been marinated too long.

The meat of game worn out by the chase is much more harmful and less digestible. Such game must always be marinated for a long time. The meat of old animals (ten-point stag, full-grown boar) is very tough.

Whether or not game birds should be drawn is a controversial question. Nevertheless, it is normal practice not to draw birds with slender tapering beaks, such as the corncrake (U.S. Sora-type rail) or thrush, and those with long, slender beaks, such as the woodcock.

Game fumet—See FUMET.

GAME-BAG. Carnier—Bag or net used to hold game.

GAMMELÖST—A Norwegian cheese which can be eaten all the year round.

GANDER. Jars—See GOOSE.

GANGA—Hazel-grouse found in the Pyrenees.

GANTOIS (Flemish pastries)—Arrange in a circle on the table 1⅝ cups (200 grams) of sieved bread flour. Place in the centre 1 cup (150 grams) of refined brown sugar, 10 tablespoons (15 grams) of butter, 2 medium sized eggs; a teaspoon of ground cinnamon, ½ teaspoon ground cloves, a pinch of salt and a little (¼ teaspoon) bicarbonate of soda, enough to cover a sixpence.

Knead, and when the flour and other ingredients are thoroughly mixed, work the dough with the palm of the hand. Let the dough stand in a cool place for an hour.

Divide the dough into five parts. Roll out each part into a round ⅛ inch thick. Place on a buttered baking sheet and bake in a moderate oven (375° F.) until golden brown. Let the pastries cool on a wire cake-tray.

Spread each round with a thin layer of greengage jam. Place the rounds one on top of the other. Trim them and cover the whole completely with concentrated apricot jam. Coat the cake all over with a mixture, made by thoroughly mixing in a small earthenware bowl ¼ cup (30 grams) of icing sugar, 2–3 tablespoons (25 grams) of blanched and ground almonds, the candied peel of one orange (approximately 2 tablespoons) finely diced and the white of an egg.

When the cake is covered with this mixture, sprinkle sugar over it and brown it in the oven.

Let it cool before serving.

GAPERON—A cheese from Limagne which can be eaten from September to July.

GARBURE—This magnificent broth of the Béarnais district may be said, along with pickled goose (*confit d'oie*), which itself is one of the ingredients of the broth, to epitomise all the cookery of this region of France. At the same time, the name *Garbure* is not only applied to that dish, which is the jewel in the gastronomic crown of the province of Béarn, but to many other broths or rather soups. Their common characteristics are the slices of bread covered with various savoury spreads, browned in the oven or simmered in fat in the stock-pot, and served with the soup.

If certain authorities are to be believed, the word *garbure* comes from the Spanish *garbias* which means stew. This etymological conjecture is probably correct since a *garbure* is rather a *pot-au-feu* than a broth, but it is challenged by Simin Palay in his very interesting book *La Cuisine en Béarn:*

'Where does this term come from? The root is surely *garbe*, a sheaf or bunch. It is certainly a bunch of vegetables which provides the basic stock of the *garbure:* cabbage, thyme, garlic, parsley, marjoram, French beans, peas . . . Moreover, (in Béarn) the term '*garburatye*' is used to designate any collection or mixture of fresh green vegetables. It seems pointless to me therefore to look elsewhere for the derivation of this word, since its full meaning is implicit in the word *garbe*.'

Here is Simin Palay's recipe for the classic *garbure:*

'Boil water in an earthenware pot glazed on the inside (cast iron or iron pots spoil the delicacy of the flavour). When it is boiling, throw in potatoes, peeled and cut into thick slices. Add other fresh vegetables in season; haricot or broad beans, peas or French beans. Season with salt and pepper. Red pepper may be used in place of white pepper. Flavour with garlic, a sprig of thyme, parsley or fresh marjoram. Leave it to cook, making sure that the water is constantly on the boil. Take, in addition, some tender green cabbages. Shred them as finely as possible into strips, cutting across the width of the leaves, after having removed such portions as are too tough.

'Once the rest of the ingredients are thoroughly cooked, throw the cabbage into the boiling stock. Cover the pot to keep the cabbage leaves green and, half an hour before serving, put in a piece of pickled meat: *lou trébuc;* the fat adhering to this will be sufficient. If pork is used, a little goose fat will enhance the flavour. Cut stale wholemeal bread into thin slices and add to the stock and vegetables.

'The mixture must be thick enough for the ladle to stand up in it, when set in the centre of the tureen.'

'It is possible to make a good *garbure*,' writes Simin Palay, 'without *trébuc;* nevertheless it is necessary to put in the cold water a piece of ham bone, or a sausage or, at the very least, lean bacon (thin flank). White cabbage may be used instead of green cabbage.

'For an everyday *garbure*, it is usual to make do with a piece of bacon or ham fat, or bacon chopped with crushed garlic.

'According to season, a few slices of pink swede (rutabaga) or roast chestnuts are added. In winter, dried beans only being available, these have to be cooked in advance. They must be drained after cooking, as their water would destroy the characteristic flavour of the *garbure*.

'To thicken the broth, the beans are sometimes crushed and rubbed through a sieve.

'It goes without saying that the meat is served separately from the broth, either by itself or with the vegetables, like the boiled beef of a hot-pot. Some cooks brown the *trébuc* in a pan before putting it in the stock. In this case the necessary fat must be added, but the fat in which the *trébuc* was browned should not be used.

'A good *goudale* (see GOUDALE) is an indispensable finish to every garbure.'

GARDE-MANGER—*Garde-manger*, in French, means, primarily, a storage-place, cool and well-aired, in large eating-houses where the food required for the preparation of meals is stored.

In this store-room special equipment is set up, such as ice-chests or refrigerators in which are stored meat, poultry, game, fish and other provisions.

Further, it is in this store-room, which is always next to the kitchen itself, that all the cold buffet is prepared and all the preparatory work done on raw foodstuffs, such as boning and jointing butcher's meat, drawing and trussing poultry and gutting fish.

The name *garde-manger* is also used in France to designate the man whose special duty it is to supervise this part of the work of a large kitchen.

The term *garde-manger* is used too for what in English is usually called a meat-safe; a small cupboard the sides of which are made of wire-mesh. Meat-safes are less widely used nowadays as they have been replaced more or less everywhere by gas or electric refrigerators.

Finally *garde-manger* can also mean an ordinary larder.

GARDEN WARBLER. BECFIGUE—This bird is found in great numbers in the south of France, particularly in Provençe. It is called *béguinette* locally.

The garden warbler was greatly praised by Brillat-Savarin, who, with some exaggeration, no doubt, put it in the first place among the small birds.

This bird, he said, 'gets at least as plump as robins and ortolans and nature has given its flesh a slight bitterness and an unique flavour, so exquisite that they engage, gratify and stimulate all the degustatory powers. If the garden warbler were the size of a pheasant it would certainly be worth the price of an acre of land.'

The poet Martial gives this advice for spicing the warbler well:

'If by good fortune you come by a garden warbler with a fat tender rump, if you would do the right thing, dredge it with pepper.'

For the preparation of the garden-warbler and other similar birds, Brillat-Savarin gives rather a curious recipe, particularly as it requires no cooking whatsoever. Here s this recipe, dictated to Brillat-Savarin by the great gastronome, Canon Charcot:

'Take a nice little fat bird by the beak, sprinkle it with a little salt, take out the gizzard, pop it adroitly in your mouth, bite, cut off the bit quite near your fingers and chew quickly. The result will be a fairly abundant flow of juice to inundate the whole organ and you will experience a delight unknown to the common people lacking refined taste.'

It would appear that an essential passage was left out of this recipe, for, however fine and delicate a bird a garden warbler may be, it does not seem possible to eat it absolutely uncooked.

There are a great number of other recipes for preparing these little birds. In addition to the recipes given elsewhere in this book for *Ortolans**, here are some others:

Garden warblers à l'arlésienne. BECFIGUES À L'ARLÉSIENNE—Fill the middle of a round loaf of bread, hollowed out as a *croustade**, buttered and baked in the oven, with St. George's agarics (see MUSHROOMS), briskly sautéed in butter.

On the mushrooms put 6 drawn and trussed warblers. Season with salt and pepper. Sprinkle with melted butter. Cook quickly in a very hot oven and serve in the bread croustade.

Garden warblers in the manner of Father Fabri. BECFIGUES À LA FAÇON DU PÈRE FABRI—Put a piece of foie gras the size of a walnut, studded with a piece of truffle, inside each warbler.

Brown briskly in sizzling butter, simply to set the surface.

Line an ovenproof dish with a layer of *à gratin forcemeat* (see FORCEMEAT) and put the birds on this, pressing them down into the forcemeat. Cover the birds with a few tablespoons of a fine *salpicon** of mushrooms tossed in butter. Sprinkle with a few drops of fine champagne brandy and 2 tablespoons of melted butter. Cook in a hot oven.

Garden warblers à la landaise. BECFIGUES À LA LANDAISE—Wrap each warbler in a vine leaf and a thin rasher of bacon. Put the warblers on metal skewers, three birds to a skewer, separated from each other by croûtons of bread lightly fried in butter.

Put them in a long fire-proof dish, season with salt and pepper, sprinkle with butter, or, better still, *foie gras* fat. Cook quickly in a hot oven.

At the last moment, pour over the birds a little armagnac, previously heated, with fresh peeled grapes and a teaspoon of dissolved meat jelly added to it.

Garden warblers à la piémontaise. BECFIGUES À LA PIÉMONTAISE—Heat butter in a sauté pan and lightly brown some shredded rashers of bacon, previously blanched and drained. In the same fat, sizzling hot, cook the warblers.

Arrange the little birds in a pie dish (or a timbale) on a foundation of very smooth *Risotto with truffles.* See RICE.

Dilute the pan juices with a little Madeira, add a few tablespoons of thickened brown veal gravy and pour over the birds.

Garden warblers à la polenta (called à la romaine). BECFIGUES À LA POLENTA—Put a fairly stiff layer of *Polenta with cheese* (see POLENTA) into a round ovenproof dish.

With the back of a wet spoon press as many hollows in this layer of polenta as there are birds.

Into each hollow put one garden warbler, briskly tossed in butter just to brown them lightly.

Pour over the birds the butter in which they were browned, having added a little previously burnt brandy to it. Cook in a very hot oven. Serve in the same dish.

Roast garden warblers. BECFIGUES RÔTIS—Prepare like *Roast ortolans* (see ORTOLAN).

GARFISH (SNIPE EEL). Orphie—The garfish, or sea eel, has dry, lean flesh, poisonous at certain times. Prepare like *Conger eel* (see EEL).

Garlic

GARLIC. Ail—A perennial plant, distinguished by its strong smell, cultivated for its bulb. It is also called *poor man's theriac* and *herbe aux aulx* ('garlic herb').

In the country, some people consider garlic as a very powerful anthelmintic and also as an antifebrile.

Aristophanes wrote that the athletes used to eat garlic to put themselves on their mettle in their exercises at the stadium.

Virgil said that garlic is the right food to maintain the strength of the harvest reapers.

Pliny, the naturalist, maintained that garlic is a cure for consumption.

Celsius cited it as a cure for fever.

Hippocrates classed garlic among the sudorific drugs and adds: 'garlic is hot, laxative and diuretic, but it is bad for the eyes'.

Dioscorides made a great case in its favour as an anthelmintic (a cure for intestinal worms).

The prophet Mohammed said: 'In cases of stings and bites by poisonous animals, garlic acts as a theriac. Applied to the spot bitten by viper, or sting of scorpion, it produces successful effects.'

In Cayenne garlic is used against bites of certain snakes.

In his *Eléments d'histoire naturelle* published in 1792, Millin claimed that 'garlic is a preventive against the plague.'

Bernardin de Saint-Pierre said: 'garlic, the smell of which is so dreaded by our little mistresses, is perhaps the most powerful remedy in existence against the vapours and nervous maladies to which they are subject.'

Alfred Franklin in *La Vie d'autrefois* says:

'In the sixteenth century, the Parisians did not neglect to eat garlic with fresh butter during the month of May and were quite convinced that this rustic diet strengthened their health for the whole year.'

In the sixteenth century, certain doctors, says Dr. Félix Brémond in his *Dictionnaire de la table*, 'condemned themselves to constant carrying of several cloves of garlic in their pockets to protect themselves, and their patients, from the bad air and epidemic diseases.'

Garlic butter. Beurre d'ail—This butter, which is used as a supplementary ingredient in sauces, forcemeats, or in the preparation of cold hors-d'oeuvre, is made by pounding together 4 cloves of garlic, peeled, blanched and drained and ¼ pound of fresh butter. Pass the mixture through a fine sieve.

Garlic capons. Chapons à l'ail—This is the name given, in the south-west of France, to crusts of bread which are rubbed with raw garlic, seasoned with oil, vinegar, salt and pepper and added to green salads, especially to curly chicory.

Chopped or grated garlic. Ail haché, rapé—To chop garlic is, in fact, an incorrect term, as garlic is more often grated or pounded in the mortar than chopped. Grated garlic is added to a great number of dishes. It is advisable, when adding it as a condiment to ingredients fried in butter, cooking fat or oil, to add it to all these different things only at the last moment and, above all, not to allow it to fry at all, as this would render the dishes too pungent.

The expression '*a point of garlic*' (chopped or grated) means the very small quantity of garlic which can be held on a point of a knife.

Garlic forcemeat. Farce d'ail—This forcemeat is used for the preparation of cold hors-d'oeuvre and for various other dishes. Pound equal quantities of yolks of hard boiled eggs and blanched cloves of garlic in a mortar. Add to this mixture half its volume of fresh butter, blend and pass through a fine sieve.

Garlic oil. Huile d'ail—Blanch thoroughly 15 cloves of garlic, drain them and pound in a mortar to a fine paste. Add 1⅓ cups (3 decilitres) of olive oil. Pass through a muslin cloth.

This oil is used for seasoning salads.

It can also be made by adding grated garlic to olive oil which is then passed through a cloth under a press.

Powdered garlic. Poudre d'ail—Dry peeled garlic cloves slowly in an oven. When the cloves are quite dry, pound them in a mortar and put to dry once again in the oven. Pound them again until they are reduced to a fine powder. Pass through a sieve. Pound the pieces left in the sieve again and sift once more.

Put this powder into jars, seal and keep in a dry place.

Garlic purée. Purée d'ail—Blanch cloves of garlic and cook them in butter in a covered pan. Add a few spoons of very thick *Béchamel sauce* (see SAUCE). Blend and pass through a sieve.

This purée is used as a supplementary ingredient for certain sauces and forcemeats.

Garlic sauce. Sauce à l'ail—Name sometimes used to describe *aioli**.

Garlic soup. Soupe à l'ail—This soup, the recipe for which will be found under SOUPS AND BROTHS, is very popular in the whole of the south of France.

Garlic toast. Rôtie à l'ail—This is a speciality of the south-west of France. This is how it is made:

Toast lightly slices of wholemeal bread. Spread them with *garlic purée.** Sprinkle with grated breadcrumbs and olive oil. Brown briskly in the oven.

GARNISHES. Garnitures—Garnishes are numerous and important to French cuisine. They are sometimes named after the man who originated them, or for an occasion, or for a place, or for many other reasons.

Garnishes consist of various trimmings added to a dish or placed around meat, chicken, fish, etc., or served at the same time on a separate dish. Some garnishes are complicated and are made only by professionals; others are adaptable to the domestic kitchen.

Garnishes must always blend with the flavour of the basic dish. They may consist of one or several elements, and are termed *Simple* or *Composite*.

Simple garnishes: These consist of a single element, most commonly a vegetable, braised, tossed or blended in butter, a cereal (rice, etc.) or a farinaceous food (tarts, croûtons, etc.).

Composite garnishes: These garnishes are made from a number of ingredients, varying according to the basic dish. These ingredients must not only blend in flavour with the main dish but with one another.

Certain composite garnishes are often called *ragoûts* (*ragoûts financières*, *Godard*, *Toulouse*, etc.). The various components of these ragoûts are generally disposed separately around the dish but they may also be mixed.

The garnishes listed in this section for quick reference are mainly composite, that is to say each one is made up of several ingredients. The component parts are merely named and very brief directions given. More detailed recipes for individual parts of the garnishes will be found under the entries listed in alphabetical order.

ARRANGEMENT OF GARNISHES:

Large cuts of meat, poultry, game—If there is no risk of their being spoilt by the stock or gravy of the main dish, the garnishes should be disposed round the main dish in separate groups.

The main meat should never be completely hidden by the garnish. If it is small, it is advisable to raise it on a croûton of fried bread or some other foundation.

This type of arrangement, being somewhat complicated, should be used only for formal banquets where invariably dishes are presented to each guest and served by a waiter, and is only appropriate to certain garnishes made up of a large number of ingredients, such as *Financière*, *Godard*, *Toulouse* or *Tortue*.

To meet the needs of present-day service at table, which is much speedier than it used to be, it has become necessary to adopt simplified methods of garnishing.

This simplification has in no way affected the basic culinary preparations, but it has reduced to a minimum the decorative trimmings, so much in fashion in the past.

Thus, even at great banquets, large hot joints, etc., are very often served to the guests already carved and arranged without decoration. Gravy and garnishes are served separately at the same time.

On the other hand, certain vegetable garnishes must invariably be served separately. This applies especially to purées of vegetables or dried vegetables, to green vegetables in butter, which would become limp in the stock or gravy of the main dish, and finally to *pastas* and cereals (rice, semolina, etc.).

The stocks, gravies and sauces appropriate to each garnish are listed under the various garnishes.

The dressing should be very lightly sprinkled over the main dish. The remainder is served in a sauceboat.

Generally, garnishes set out round the main dish should not be sprinkled with dressing; especially those garnishes made of fresh vegetables with butter, vegetables browned in butter or those served *au gratin* or any deep fried garnish.

Braised vegetables only should have the dressing poured over them.

Meat served in individual portions: Cutlets, escalopes, chops, noisettes, medallions, small fillets, fillet-steaks, suprême of chicken, sautéed chicken—Apart from certain very special dishes, to which attention is drawn under the appropriate heading, these small cuts of meat may be served with any of the garnishes indicated for large cuts.

It is advisable to prepare these garnishes in smaller shapes and quantities so that they may be in better proportion to the individual portions.

All the garnishes should be placed around or along the sides of the main dish.

If sautéed, these portions should be served with their own gravy. For grills it is always preferable to serve the gravy separately.

The garnishes of individual portions may be served with sauce or not, according to the principles applicable to large cuts.

Cold dishes—Details of the ingredients and arrangement of garnishes for these dishes are given under the heading COLD FOODSTUFFS.

The quantities of garnish to be used depend upon the main dish, but they vary also according to the composition of the menu as a whole.

The various ingredients of a composite garnish must always be sufficient in number to serve all the guests.

The quantities used in the preparation of garnishes, whether simple or composite, should be calculated at approximately $\frac{1}{4}$ pound (125 to 150 grams) for each guest.

Soups and broths—These garnishes may consist of a single item or may be composite; some, such as tapioca and other similar ingredients, are cooked in the soup itself; others are prepared separately and added to the soup at the last moment, or, where appropriate, served separately.

SIMPLE GARNISHES:

For main meat dishes and for small individual portions:

Artichokes: Hearts or quarters, stewed, braised or sautéed. Hearts, stuffed, sprinkled with breadcrumbs and browned. Purée of hearts, served separately.

Artichokes, Japanese: Sautéed; fried; in cream.

Broad beans (fresh): In butter, in cream, purée, with savoy; served separately.

Brussels Sprouts: Sautéed.

Cabbage, green or red: Braised, stuffed with forcemeat, rolled into balls, or stuffed with small slices of meat, rolled into sausages (see PAUPIETTES).

Carrots, glazed: In gravy; with Vichy sauce.

Cauliflower: Sautéed, coated with *Mornay sauce* (see SAUCE), in knobs, sprinkled with breadcrumbs and browned.

Celery or Celeriac: Stewed, braised.

Cèpes: à la bordelaise; With chopped herbs; *à la provençale;* with cream (served separately).

Chestnuts: Stewed, braised.

Corn-on-the-cob, green: In butter; in cream; served separately.

Cucumbers: Cut pear-shaped, stewed in butter; in thick slices, stuffed.

Egg-plant (aubergines): In cream, served separately.

Endive: Braised, in butter or cream, with gravy or juice (served separately).

Fennel (bulbous): Braised, stewed.

French (string) beans: In butter; in cream; purée.

Fungi: Cultivated mushrooms, chanterelles, morels, flap-mushrooms St. George's agaric, orange-milk agaric, etc. Sautéed, and cooked in various other ways.

Gourd (Pumpkin): Quartered, stewed in butter, braised, stuffed, cooked in cream.

Hop panicles: In butter or cream; served separately.

Kidney-beans (*flageolets*) (*fresh or dried small*): In butter or cream, purée; served separately.

Ladies' fingers: In cream, in gravy; served separately.

Lentils: In butter; purée; served separately.

Lettuce: Braised; stuffed.

Macaroni: Prepared in various ways; served separately.

Mixed beans: Mixture of French beans and small kidney beans (*flageolets*), fresh or dried; served separately.

Noodles and other pasta of the same type: Prepared in various ways; served separately.

Onions: Glazed; stuffed.

Peas: A la française; cooked with lettuce leaves; *à la paysanne;* purée *St. Germain*; served separately.

Potatoes: Boiled; *Anna:* cut oval and cooked slowly in clarified butter; croquettes; *fondants;* fried in different ways; covered with breadcrumbs and browned; fried with minced onions previously browned; shaped as nuts and browned in butter; *Parisienne;* sprinkled with parsley.

Red beans: A la bourguignonne; in gravy, purée; served separately.

Rice: Cooked in fat; curried; pilaf; risotto croquettes (served separately); in cream.

Sauerkraut.

Spinach: Whole or as a purée, in butter, in cream, in gravy, served separately.

Sugar-peas: Served separately.

Tomatoes: Stuffed in various ways; sprinkled with cheese or breadcrumbs and browned; grilled; sautéed.

Turnips: Glazed; stuffed.

White beans: In butter; *à la bretonne*, in cream, in gravy, *à la maître d'hôtel*, purée; served separately.

Simple garnishes for poultry:

Artichokes: Hearts or quartered whole artichokes; stewed, braised, sautéed; with poultry pot-roasted, sautéed or cooked in a casserole for drumsticks or breasts of poultry.

Hearts in cream with pot-roasted, poached or sautéed poultry; with drumsticks or breasts of poultry.

Hearts, stuffed with braised or pot-roasted poultry; braised in white stock for poached poultry.

Cèpes: With braised or pot-roasted poultry, sautéed chicken or chicken casserole; with drumsticks or breasts of poultry.

Chestnuts: Braised or stewed, with braised or pot-roasted poultry; with braised or pot-roasted young turkey; with pot-roasted pigeon.

Lettuce: Braised with braised, pot-roasted, poached or stewed poultry; braised or pot-roasted young turkey; braised or pot-roasted pigeon.

Mixed vegetables: Glazed carrots, in gravy, or *à la Vichy;* cauliflower sautéed, sprinkled with cheese or breadcrumbs and browned; sauerkraut; braised fennel; broad beans in butter or cream; glazed turnips; glazed onions; French beans in butter or cream; peas cooked in various ways; salsify, sautéed or in cream; sautéed tomatoes; Jerusalem artichokes in butter, etc. All these vegetables may be served with braised, pot-roasted or poached poultry, sautéed chicken or chicken casserole, cutlets, breasts or fillets of chicken as indicated in the detailed recipes for garnishes.

Mushrooms: Cooked in a white stock with poached poultry, with drumsticks or breasts of poultry; mushrooms cooked in a brown stock with braised, pot-roasted, sautéed or casseroled poultry, drumsticks or breasts of poultry; pot-roasted pigeon, pot-roasted guinea-fowl.

Noodles and other pasta: With braised or pot-roasted poultry; with chicken, sauté or casserole; with pot-roasted turkey.

Pilaf: With pot-roasted poultry; sautéed chicken or casserole chicken; drumsticks, breasts of poultry, with pot-roasted turkey.

Rice: Cooked in fat; with poached poultry.

Risotto: With braised or pot-roasted poultry; with chicken, sautéed or cooked in a casserole, with drumsticks or breasts of poultry.

Turnips: Glazed with braised poultry; with Nantes duckling, braised or pot-roasted.

Young Corn-on-the-cob: In butter or cream with braised, pot-roasted or poached poultry, with sautéed or stewed chicken; with cutlets, breasts or fillets of poultry; with pot-roasted guinea-fowl.

Garnishes for eggs: Like all other basic foods, eggs, especially soft boiled or poached in the ordinary way or in moulds, may be served with a great variety of garnishes. Detailed recipes for those garnishes and instructions for setting them out on the dish are to be found among the recipes for egg dishes. See EGGS.

Garnishes for fish: Braised fish, whole or in thick slices, is garnished according to the instructions set out for main meat dishes.

Poached fish, that is fish cooked in a *court-bouillon*, whole or sliced, is invariably garnished with boiled or steamed potatoes and with fresh parsley. The dressing is a sauce of some kind, served separately. To this standard garnish are sometimes added further ingredients such as very small fried fish, minute croquettes, or shells filled with various garnishes, etc.

Small fish, or fillets poached in a little *court-bouillon*, are served with various garnishes, simple or composite. Details of these garnishes are given with the recipe for the fish in question.

Small fish and their garnishes are normally covered with the sauce prescribed for them, unless they are fried in the conventional way or in flour, milk and butter (*à la meunière*) or sprinkled with cheese or breadcrumbs and browned.

Grilled fish, whole or sliced, is garnished as a rule with boiled potatoes, slices of lemon cut with a fluted knife, and fresh parsley. Some types of grilled fish have special garnishes. Details of these are given with the recipe for the fish in question.

Fried fish is invariably garnished with fried parsley and halved or quartered lemons.

It was once normal practice to substitute Seville oranges for lemons as a garnish for fried fish.

COMPOSITE GARNISHES:

A l'africaine—Description which applies to a garnish consisting of black potatoes (potatoes the pulp of which is dark bluish in colour—see POTATOES), cut to look like marbles, blanched in salt water and cooked in butter, and braised zucchini or little marrows.

Serve with rice cooked in fat stock lightly flavoured with saffron.

Agnès Sorel—*Salpicon** of pickled tongue, mushrooms and truffles with little mounds of white rice.

Sauce: Stock of the main dish blended with Madeira and a *demi-glace sauce* (see SAUCE).

Uses: For large cuts of meat, poultry and eggs.

Albigeoise—Potato croquettes prepared as for *Duchess Potatoes* (see POTATOES) mixed with lean chopped ham. Small tomatoes stuffed with chopped mushrooms (*duxelles*) fried with chopped onion in butter and mixed with breadcrumbs, garlic and chopped parsley.

Sauce: A *demi-glace sauce* flavoured with tomato (see SAUCE).

Uses: For large and small cuts of meat.

Albuféra—Small tartlets garnished with truffles shaped with a ball-scoop (the size of a pea) and forcemeat balls of the same shape made from chicken stuffing. Cock's kidneys, mushrooms, pickled tongue, shaped as cocks' combs are placed on top of each tartlet.

Sauce: Albuféra sauce (see SAUCE).

Uses: For poached chicken. Chickens thus prepared are stuffed with rice mixed with a *salpicon** of *foie gras* and truffles.

Algérienne I—Sweet potato croquettes. Small tomatoes stewed in oil.

Sauce: Clear veal stock flavoured with tomato.

Uses: For large or small cuts of meat; poultry.

Algérienne II—Croquettes of rice and sweet peppers. Thick slices of egg-plant (aubergines).

Sauce: Clear veal stock flavoured with tomato.

Alsacienne—Braised sauerkraut; poached Strasbourg sausages cut into rounds; boiled potatoes.

Sauce: Veal stock or a thin *Demi-glace sauce* (see SAUCE).

Uses: For large cuts of meat; poultry, especially goose and duck.

Ambassadrice—Cocks' combs, cock's kidneys; sautéed mushrooms; sautéed chicken livers; shredded truffles.

Sauce: Stock of the main dish blended with Madeira and thickened veal gravy.

Uses: For small cuts of meat and poultry.

Américaine—Small slices of crayfish or lobster tails cooked *à l'américaine.*

Sauce: Sauce à l'américaine (see SAUCE) to which must be added the concentrated stock of the fish used for the main dish. See *Brill à l'Américaine.*

Uses: For fish.

A l'ancienne I—Forcemeat balls of chicken and truffles; lamb sweetbreads; truffles shaped as olives; mushrooms; fresh crayfish cooked in a fish *court-bouillon.**

Sauce: Suprême sauce (see SAUCE) to which has been added a fine vegetable pulp (*mirepoix**), flavoured with Madeira.

Uses: For calf's sweetbreads, poached or braised poultry, vol-au-vent, hot pâtés, savoury tarts.

Garnish à l'ancienne round a saddle of veal

A l'ancienne II—Little savoury nests made of *Duchess potatoes* (see POTATOES) fried and filled with calf's kidneys diced and sautéed in butter and diced mushrooms, the filling bound with thickened veal gravy; stuffed braised lettuce; small potato balls browned in butter; French (string) beans in butter.

Sauce: Braising liquor or pot-roast juices.

Uses: For large braised or pot-roasted cuts of meat, loin and saddle of veal in particular.

A l'ancienne III—Small pastry boats garnished with a *salpicon** of soft roes blended with a *Normande sauce* (see SAUCE); truffles trimmed to look like olives; mushrooms; fresh-water crayfish cooked in a *court-bouillon.**

Sauce: Thickened pan juices of the main dish blended with a Madeira-flavoured *Velouté* (see SAUCE) based on fish stock and cream to which a fine vegetable *mirepoix** is added.

Uses: For baked or poached fish.

A l'anglaise I—Carrots cut in 2-inch oval lengths and medium-sized onions cooked with leg of lamb; mashed turnips also cooked with the leg of lamb, drained and mashed (pulped).

Sauce: Butter sauce (see SAUCE) with capers in vinegar added, served separately.

Uses: For poached leg of lamb.

A l'anglaise II—Carrots and turnips cut in 2-inch oval lengths, celery hearts (all these vegetables cooked with chicken); French (string) beans and cauliflower, boiled.

Sauce: Butter sauce (see SAUCE) with capers in vinegar added, served separately.

See CHICKEN, *Chicken à l'anglaise.*

A l'anversoise—Hop shoots in cream; potatoes cut to look like olives, deep fried in butter, or: Small artichoke hearts stewed in butter, filled with hop shoots in cream; *chicory* (*endive*) *à la flamande.**

Sauce: Roast gravy or clear veal gravy.

Uses: For large or small cuts of meal, poultry.

Armenonville—Garnish for small pieces of meat, calf's sweetbreads, etc., composed of small *Anna potatoes* (see POTATOES), morels in cream and tartlets filled with a *salpicon** of cocks' combs and kidneys.

A la banquière—Chicken quenelles; mushrooms; shredded truffles.

(According to the nature of the main dish, the components of this garnish are either prepared separately or mixed in a ragoût.)

Sauce: Banquière sauce (see SAUCE).

Uses: For poultry and calves' sweetbreads poached or braised *à blanc**; vol-au-vent.

Béatrix—Morels sautéed in butter; glazed carrots; braised quartered artichokes; browned new potatoes.

Sauce: Diluted meat juices from the cooking pan.

Uses: For small cuts of meat.

A la Beauharnais—Very small artichoke hearts filled with *Béarnaise sauce* (see SAUCE) to which sieved tarragon leaves have been added at the end; small potato balls browned in butter.

Sauce: Pan juices of the main dish diluted with Madeira and veal stock, plus chopped truffles.

Uses: For small cuts of meat.

Beauvilliers—Small spinach kromeskies (prepared by filling pancakes with spinach, rolling them, cutting them into rounds, dipping them into frying batter and frying them in deep fat at the last moment); small tomatoes stuffed with cooked brain purée browned with breadcrumbs; salsify cut into neat rounds, sautéed in butter.

Sauce: Braising stock.

Uses: For large cuts of meat, braised.

A la bénédictine—Very small tartlets or pastry boats garnished with *Brandade of salt cod* (see COD) with chopped truffles added.

Sauce: White wine sauce if accompanying fish; *Cream sauce for eggs.* See SAUCE.

Uses: For fish or coddled or poached eggs.

A la Berrichonne—It consists of braised cabbage, small onions, chestnuts and rashers (strips) of lean bacon.

Uses: For meat, principally mutton, served in big cuts.

A la Biarrotte—*Grilled cèpes* (see MUSHROOMS) and *Duchess potato cakes* (see POTATOES) used as a foundation for meat.

Uses: Garnish for meat served in small portions.

Bonne-femme I—For poultry: a garnish which must be cooked with the chicken in the stew-pan, made of potatoes trimmed into small oval lengths, small onions, lean larding bacon and mushrooms, if desired.

Bonne-femme II—For fish: thinly sliced mushrooms which must be cooked with the fish.

A la bordelaise I—For large joints; *cèpes* sautéed *à la bordelaise* (see MUSHROOMS); potatoes cut to look like olives and cooked slowly in clarified butter.

Sauce: Gravy of the roast.

A la bordelaise II—Small quartered artichokes stewed in butter; potatoes thinly sliced when raw and sautéed in butter; fried onion rings; fried parsley.

Sauce: Pan juices of main dish diluted with white wine and veal or chicken stock.

Uses: For jointed (cut up) poultry.

A la boulangère—Potatoes thinly sliced, or quartered; onions thinly sliced (these ingredients, mixed, must always be cooked with the main dish).

Sauce: Gravy of the roast.

Uses: For shoulder, leg and other cuts of mutton and lamb, and occasionally for poultry.

A la bouquetière I—Glazed carrots and turnips trimmed into very small oval lengths or shaped with a ball-scoop; peas and French (string) beans, diced, boiled separately, and blended with butter; cauliflower divided into flowerets and boiled, covered as they are set out on the dish with *Hollandaise sauce* (see SAUCE) or melted butter; new potatoes (or potatoes cut to look like little olives) browned in butter.

Dispose these vegetables round the main dish in separate groups.

Sauce: Gravy of the roast.

Uses: For large and small cuts of meat.

A la bouquetière II—Very small artichoke hearts simmered in butter, filled alternately with carrots and turnips; buttered French (string) beans; small bunches of asparagus tips, held upright by a ring of carrots; cauliflower, divided into flowerets, covered with *Hollandaise sauce* (see SAUCE); potatoes, cut to look like olives and sautéed in butter.

Sauce: Gravy of the roast.

Uses: For large and small cuts of meat.

A la bourgeoise (sometimes called à la mode)—Glazed carrots (cut in oval lengths) and onions, cooked with the meat; sometimes braised fresh vegetables such as celery, lettuce, etc. are added.

Sauce: Braising liquor of the main dish.

Uses: For large braised cuts of meat, notably beef rump braised *à la bourgeoise* (see BEEF), but this garnish may be used with braised ox tongue, veal (*noix de veau*) or leg of lamb or mutton.

A la bourguignonne I—Small glazed onions; whole or quartered mushrooms, sautéed in butter; salt (pickled) pork, diced, blanched and browned.

Sauce: *Bourguignonne sauce* (see SAUCE). This garnish, generally served with braised meat, should be added to the main dish a little while before it is completely cooked.

Uses: For large cuts of meat, especially beef.

A la bourguignonne II—Exactly the same as the previous garnish, but without the pork.

Sauce: Red wine sauce (made with vegetable or fish stock with a little fresh butter added at the last minute).

Uses: For braised fish.

A la brabançonne I—Braised chicory; *potatoes fondante.**

Sauce: Thickened veal gravy.

Uses: Large cuts of meat.

A la brabançonne II—Little tartlets garnished with Brussels sprouts simmered in butter, covered with *Mornay sauce* (see SAUCE), sprinkled with breadcrumbs and browned; potato croquettes.

Sauce: Thickened veal gravy.

Brancas—*Anna potatoes* (see POTATOES) cooked in individual moulds and turned out, *Chiffonnade of lettuce with cream*, quite dry (see LETTUCE).

Sauce: Thickened veal stock or a *Demi-glace* (see SAUCE).

Uses: For small cuts of meat, white meat, especially poultry.

A la bretonne I—Dry white beans or small kidney beans, cooked in meat stock and blended with *Bretonne sauce* (see SAUCE).

Sauce: Roast pan juices or veal gravy flavoured with tomato.

Uses: For large cuts of meat (especially leg of lamb) pot-roasted or roasted.

A la bretonne II—*Purée bretonne* (see PURÉE).

Sauce: Gravy of the roast.

Uses: For large cuts of meat.

A la bretonne III (for fish)—Leeks, onions, celery and mushrooms, cut in thin strips and cooked slowly in butter until they are very tender and added to the main fish dish before it is fully cooked.

The sauce for fish *à la bretonne* is made with a *Velouté* base (see SAUCE) and cream.

Uses: For a baked or poached fish.

Brillat-Savarin—Little nests made of *Duchess potatoes* (see POTATOES), fried and hollowed to hold a *salpicon** of foie gras and truffles blended into a concentrated *Demi-glace sauce* (see SAUCE). Asparagus tips (arranged if desired on tartlets).

Sauce: A thin *Demi-glace sauce* for large cuts. Stock of the main dish flavoured with white Malaga wine, a third veal stock and two thirds Chicken *velouté* (see SAUCE), for small cuts.

Uses: For large and small cuts of meat.

A la bruxelloise—Brussels sprouts in butter; *Potatoes fondante** or potatoes cut to look like olives and cooked slowly in clarified butter.

Sauce: Clear veal gravy or a thin *Demi-glace sauce* (see SAUCE).

Uses: For large and small cuts of meat.

Camérani—Small tartlets filled with *purée of foie gras;** shredded truffles; slices of pickled tongue shaped as cocks' combs; *macaroni à l'italienne.*

Sauce: Suprême sauce (see SAUCE) to which the reduced pan juices have been added.

Uses: Poultry and poached calf's sweetbreads.

A la cancalaise—Lenten garnish composed of oysters and shrimps' tails in *Normande sauce* (see SAUCE).

A la cardinal—Fish garnish composed of little *coquilles cardinal*, mushrooms, slices of truffle.

Little carrot timbales—PETITS PAINS DE CAROTTES—Prepare the carrots in the same way as for *Carrot timbale* (see CARROTS). Fill little buttered custard cups or dariole moulds with this preparation. Cook in a moderate oven in a pan of hot water or *bain-marie.**

Castiglione—Large mushrooms filled with risotto mixed with chopped lean ham, sprinkled with breadcrumbs and browned; rounds of egg-plant (aubergines) sautéed in butter (to be used as canapés); strips of poached bone-marrow.

Sauce: Stock of the main dish flavoured with white wine to which chopped shallots and veal stock have been added. (Butter should be added to this sauce after it has been reduced.)

Uses: For small cuts of meat.

A la catalane—Aubergine (egg-plant), coarsely diced, sautéed in oil; *Rice pilaf* (see PILAF).

Sauce: A *Demi-glace sauce* (see SAUCE) flavoured with tomato.

Uses: For large cuts of meat.

Cavour—Small baked rounds of polenta made with cheese (to be used as canapés); large grilled mushrooms filled with purée of chicken liver; shredded truffles.

Sauce: Veal stock flavoured with Marsala or tomato.

Uses: For small cuts of meat, especially sautéed escalopes (U.S. cutlets) of veal and breaded calf's sweetbreads.

A la chalonnaise—Small tartlets garnished with cocks' kidneys blended with a concentrated *Velouté sauce* (see SAUCE); cocks' combs *à la Villiers;* slices of truffles; mushrooms.

Sauce: Suprême sauce (see SAUCE).

Uses: For poultry, calves' sweetbreads poached or braised in a white stock.

Chambord—Large and small fish quenelles; mushrooms; fillets of sole; soft roes sautéed in butter; truffles cut to look like olives; fresh-water crayfish cooked in a *court-bouillon**;* small fried croûtons.

Sauce: Red wine sauce (see SAUCE).

Uses: For large braised fish.

A la chanoinesse—Very small carrots in cream mixed with coarsely chopped truffles. Used as a filling for tartlets.

Sauce: Pan juices diluted with sherry and veal stock.

Uses: For calves' sweetbreads, *Suprême of chicken* (see CHICKEN), coddled or poached eggs.

A la châtelaine—Artichoke hearts filled with chestnut purée mixed with rice, sprinkled with breadcrumbs and browned; braised lettuce; potato balls, browned in butter.

Sauce: Thickened veal gravy, or diluted pan juices, of the main dish.

Uses: For large cuts of meat.

Chervil (leaf). PLUCHES DE CERFEUIL—All traces of stalk and fibre should be removed from the leaves of chervil. Almost all soups with a base of whole or puréed vegetables should have chervil added at the end—one teaspoon to every quart (litre) of soup. Because of the very delicate aromatic flavour of this herb, the leaves must be added to the soup at the last moment, when the soup is off the boil.

Chiffonnade—Finely shredded lettuce leaves and sorrel stewed slowly in butter. This *chiffonnade* is used in a great many different soups.

A la chinonaise—Small rolls of green cabbage stuffed with sausage meat, braised; potatoes sprinkled with chopped parsley.

Sauce: A *Demi-glace sauce* (see SAUCE).

Uses: For large cuts of meat.

Chipolata—Braised chestnuts; small glazed onions; chipolata sausages; mushrooms.

Sauce: A *Demi-glace sauce* (see SAUCE) or the braising stock of the main dish.

Sometimes lean bacon, coarsely diced, blanched and browned in butter with braised carrots, is also served.

Uses: For large cuts of meat, poultry, braised, poached or stewed.

Choron—Potato balls browned in butter; artichoke hearts filled with peas (or asparagus tips) done in butter.

Sauce: Béarnaise sauce (see SAUCE) flavoured with tomato in a ring round the main dish, and thickened gravy.

Uses: For small cuts of meat, fried or grilled.

Chou-paste balls (for soup garnish). PROFITEROLES—Using *Chou paste* (cream puff pastry, see DOUGH) in a forcing bag (pastry bag) with a round nozzle, squeeze out on to a baking sheet little balls each the size of a nut. Bake in the oven (375° F.) for 20–25 minutes.

Stuff the balls with a purée or whatever other ingredient is appropriate, according to the recipe for the soup in which they are to be served. Heat up the balls. Serve them separately at the same time as the soup.

A la clamart I—Artichoke hearts filled with peas in butter. Potato balls browned in butter.

Sauce: Veal stock blended with *Demi-glace sauce* (see SAUCE).

Uses: For large or small cuts of meat.

A la clamart II—See *St. Germain garnish II.*

A la clermont—Rolls of green cabbage stuffed and braised; rectangular slices of salt (pickled) pork cooked with the cabbage; potatoes.

Sauce: A *Demi-glace sauce* (see SAUCE) or the braising liquor.

Uses: For large cuts of meat.

Cock's kidneys as garnish. ROGNONS DE COQ—Wash in several waters ¼ pound (125 grams) of firm, white cocks' kidneys. Put them into a small saucepan with ½ cup (1 decilitre) of water, a pinch of salt, 2 tablespoons (25 grams) of butter and a few drops of lemon juice.

Start cooking over a good heat; as soon as the liquid begins to boil turn the heat very low and cook, covered, for 10 to 12 minutes, taking care to avoid boiling.

Use according to the recipe.

A la Conti—Small croquettes of purée of lentils (rolled into balls); potatoes cut to look like olives, fried in butter.

Sauce: Pan juices diluted with Madeira and *Demi-glace* (see SAUCE).

Uses: For small cuts of meat.

Crêpes (for soup garnish)—Place in an earthenware dish 1 cup (125 grams) of sieved flour and 1 teaspoon (5 grams) of table salt. Add two whole eggs, mix well, and dilute the mixture with 1¼ cups (2½ decilitres) of boiled milk.

Make the pancakes in the usual way, and use them as appropriate. Clear soup may be used instead of milk in the preparation of this garnish.

Croûtes garnished and browned à l'ancienne. CROÛTES GARNIES ET GRATINÉES À L'ANCIENNE—Take a long thin French loaf. Cut it into slices about 1½ inches thick. Scoop out about three quarters of the bread to make nests. Brush with butter or fat from a *pot-au-feu;* toast them lightly in the oven. Chop or sieve the vegetables from the *pot-au-feu;* add grated cheese and garnish the bread with little mounds of this mixture. Place these *croûtes* on a baking sheet and sprinkle with grated cheese. Moisten with a few drops of the fat and brown. Arrange on a paper doyley. Serve with clear soup.

Croûtons—Dice slices of sandwich loaf or French loaf into cubes approximately ¼ inch across. Fry them in butter (preferably clarified butter) just before serving.

Allow 2 ounces (60 grams) of fried bread for every quart (litre) of soup.

A la Cussy—Artichoke hearts filled with mushroom purée, sprinkled with breadcrumbs and browned; cock's kidneys; shredded truffles.

Sauce: Sauce flavoured with Madeira or Port.

Uses: For small cuts of meat. Poultry, whole or jointed.

A la daumont—Tails of fresh-water *crayfish à la Nantua** (in scallop shells or pastry boats); large *fish quenelles* (see QUENELLES), decorated with truffles; fillets of sole decorated with truffles cut in fancy shapes; slices of truffle; mushrooms cooked in *court-bouillon.**

Sauce: Normande sauce (see SAUCE) with *Crayfish butter* (see BUTTER, *Compound butters*).

Uses: For large baked fish.

A la Dauphine—*Potatoes à la Dauphine.**

Sauce: Roast pan juices or clear veal gravy.

Uses: For large or small cuts of meat.

A la demi-deuil—Food prepared *à la demi-deuil* is covered with a *Suprême sauce* (see SAUCE) and garnished with truffles.

Uses: Especially for poached poultry and veal braised *à blanc.*

A la deippoisse—Mussels (shelled) in white wine; tails of fresh-water crayfish, grey or pink (shelled); mushrooms.

Sauce: White wine sauce (see SAUCE).

Uses: For fish poached in white wine.

A la Dubarry—A garnish for large or small cuts of meat. It consists of cauliflower shaped into balls, masked with *Mornay sauce* (see SAUCE) sprinkled with grated cheese and browned.

A la duchesse. *Duchess potatoes* (see POTATOES) in different shapes according to the nature of the main dish.

Sauce: Thickened veal or roast pan juices.

Uses: For large or small cuts of meat.

Duroc—New potatoes (very small), browned in butter.

Sauce: Chasseur sauce (see SAUCE) cooked in the frying-pan used for the main dish.

Uses: For small cuts of meat and poultry, sautéed.

Duxelles—Chopped mushrooms, browned in butter and oil mixed with chopped onions and shallots, moistened with white wine, with chopped parsley added.

Uses: For small cuts of meats.

Favart—Chicken quenelles seasoned with chopped tarragon, tartlets or rich pastry filled with a *salpicon** of mushrooms (cèpes) in cream.

Sauce: A thick *Velouté* (see SAUCE) of chicken with *Crayfish butter* (see BUTTER, *Compound butters*).

Uses: For poultry, veal sweetbreads.

A la favorite—Small artichokes (or quarters of artichokes) braised; lettuces stuffed and braised; mushrooms cooked in butter filled with mixed diced vegetables; small *Anna potatoes* baked in individual moulds and turned out—See POTATOES, *Anna potatoes for garnish.*

Sauce: Thickened veal gravy, a *Demi-glace sauce* (see SAUCE) or the diluted pan juices of the main dish.

Uses: For large and small cuts of meat.

A la fermière—Artichoke hearts filled with a *fondue** of mixed vegetables; braised lettuces.

Sauce: A *Demi-glace sauce* (see SAUCE).

Uses: For large cuts of meat.

A la financière—Chicken or veal quenelles; cocks' combs and kidneys; mushrooms; shredded truffles (and sometimes stoned and blanched olives, and fresh-water crayfish).

Sauce: Financière sauce (see SAUCE).

Uses: For large and small cuts of meat; calves' sweetbreads; poultry; vol-au-vent, etc.

A la flamande—Green cabbage (rolled) stuffed and braised; carrots and turnips trimmed into large oval shapes and glazed; potatoes. Diced pork fat and slices of sausage cooked with the cabbage are sometimes added to this garnish.

Sauce: A *Demi-glace sauce* (see SAUCE); veal gravy or the diluted pan juices of the main dish.

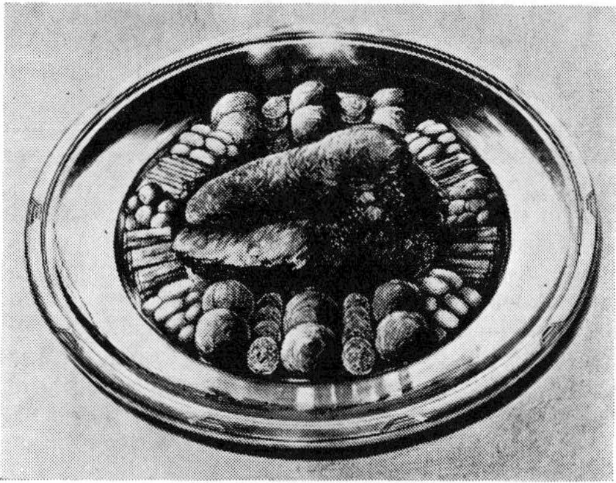

Garnish à la flamande round a fillet of beef

Uses: For large and small cuts of meat.

A la forestière—Morels sautéed in butter; potato balls browned in butter; sometimes salt (pickled) pork, diced, blanched and fried in butter is added to this garnish.

A la française—Small nests made from *Duchess potatoes* (see POTATOES), dipped in egg and breadcrumbs fried and hollowed out, filled with diced mixed vegetables; bunches of asparagus tips; braised lettuces; flowerets of cauliflower, coated with *Hollandaise sauce* (see SAUCE).

Sauce: A thin *Demi-glace sauce* (see SAUCE) or clear veal gravy.

Uses: For large cuts of meat.

A Frascati garnish round a fillet of beef

Frascati—Large baked mushrooms, some filled with a *salpicon** of truffles, others with buttered green asparagus tips; small slices of *foie gras* sautéed in butter.

Sauce: A *Demi-glace sauce* flavoured with port (see SAUCE).

Uses: Garnish for large cuts of meat.

A la gauloise I—Tartlets filled with cocks' kidneys; cockscombs fried *à la Villeroi;* mushrooms; truffles.

Sauce: Pan juices of the main dish diluted with white wine.

Uses: For small cuts of meat; jointed (cut up) poultry.

A la gauloise II—Pastry-boats filled with a *salpicon** of truffles and *mushrooms à la crème: potato croquettes;* fresh-water crayfish cooked in a *court-bouillon.**

Sauce: Matelote sauce (see SAUCE).

Uses: For large baked or poached fish.

Glazed carrots for garnish—See CARROTS.

Glazed Italian marrow (zucchini) garnish — See ITALIAN MARROW.

Glazed onions for garnish. OIGNONS GLACÉS—Skin *little*, uniform-sized onions. Fry them very lightly in butter in a shallow pan. Sprinkle with a little sugar and season.

Moisten with stock (or water, if the garnish is required for a Lenten dish) so that the liquid does not quite cover them.

Simmer gently with a lid on until the liquid has completely disappeared.

Note. If, after this reduction of liquid, the onions are not yet cooked, add a few tablespoons of hot stock and finish cooking and glaze, without stirring them.

Godard—Large decorated *quenelles;* small veal or poultry quenelles with truffles; sheep's sweetbreads, braised and glazed; cocks' combs and kidneys; small whole truffles (or cut to look like olives); mushroom caps.

When this garnish is for a substantial second course, veal sweetbreads stuffed with bacon and braised may be substituted for the sheep's sweetbreads. (For fuller information, see the recipe for *Chicken à la Godard.*)

Sauce: Godard sauce (see SAUCE).

Uses: For large cuts of meat, poultry.

Gorenflot—Braised red cabbage (coarsely shredded); rounds of Saveloy sausage (cooked with the cabbage); *Potatoes à la ménagère.*

Sauce: Braising stock.

Uses: For large braised cuts of meat.

Gouffé—Little nests of *Duchess potatoes* (see POTATOES) fried and hollowed out to hold morels cooked in cream; asparagus tips in butter.

Sauce: Stock of the main dish blended with Madeira and thickened veal gravy.

Uses: For large and small cuts of meat.

Gratin dauphinois. Gratin of potatoes à la dauphinoise. GRATIN DE POMMES DE TERRE À LA DAUPHINOISE—Slice thinly 2 pounds (1 kilo) of potatoes. Season with salt and pepper and put them in an earthenware oven dish previously rubbed with garlic and butter. Sprinkle grated cheese on the potatoes, spread out in the dish in even layers.

Pour over this a mixture of 2 eggs and 2 cups (6 decilitres) of boiled milk, a little salt and a dash of grated nutmeg.

Sprinkle with grated cheese and dot the top with butter.

Bring to the boil on the stove and complete the cooking by baking in the oven for about 40 minutes.

Serve in the baking dish.

The garlic and grated nutmeg may be omitted if desired, though, strictly speaking, they form an essential seasoning of this dish.

Gratin of potatoes à la savoyarde. GRATIN DE POMMES DE TERRE À LA SAVOYARDE—This is prepared as for *Gratin dauphinois,* substituting clear stock for the milk.

Helder—Potato balls browned in butter; *Béarnaise sauce* (see SAUCE), traced in a circle on the meat; very thick *Tomato fondue** placed in the middle of the *Béarnaise sauce.*

Sauce: Meat juices of the main dish blended with thickened veal stock.

Uses: For small sautéed cuts of meat.

Henry IV—Artichoke hearts filled with *Béarnaise sauce* (see SAUCE) with very concentrated veal gravy added; potato balls browned in butter; shredded truffles.

Sauce: Stock of the main dish blended with Madeira and thickened veal stock.

Uses: For small cuts of meat.

A la hongroise I—Large knobs of cauliflower coated with *Mornay sauce* (see SAUCE), seasoned with paprika, sprinkled with breadcrumbs and browned under the grill; *Potatoes fondante.**

Sauce: A thin *Demi-glace sauce* (see SAUCE).

Uses: For large and small cuts of meat.

A la hongroise II—*Duchess potato nests* (see POTATOES) garnished with knobs of cauliflower coated with *Mornay sauce* (see SAUCE) to which is added chopped onion, simmered in butter and seasoned with paprika.

Sauce: Pan juices of the main dish blended with cream, seasoned with paprika and thickened with a little *Velouté* or *Béchamel* (see SAUCE).

Uses: For small cuts of meat.

A la hongroise III—Pilaf of rice, diced tomatoes simmered in butter.

Sauce: Hongroise sauce (see SAUCE).

Uses: For poultry, poached or sautéed.

Japanese garnish—See JAPONAISE, A LA.

A la jardinière—Glazed carrots and turnips in small oval shapes (or rounded with a ball-scoop), peas; French beans; small kidney-beans in butter (all these vegetables disposed round the dish in separate groups).

Little knobs of cauliflower, coated with *Hollandaise sauce* (see SAUCE) or melted butter are sometimes added.

Sauce: Pan juices or clear veal gravy.

Uses: For large and small cuts of meat.

Jessica—Tiny artichokes cooked in butter, stuffed with a *salpicon** of bone-marrow cooked with shallots morels, sautéed in butter; *Anna potatoes* (see POTATOES) baked in individual moulds and turned out to act as canapés for the food to be served.

Sauce: Allemande sauce (see SAUCE) increased by a third with concentrated veal stock and essence of truffles.

Uses: For *Suprême of chicken* (see CHICKEN), veal escalopes (U.S. cutlets), coddled or poached eggs.

Joinville—*Salpicon** of shrimps, truffles and mushrooms, blended into a *Velouté sauce* or a *Normande sauce* (see SAUCE); sliced truffle.

Sauce: A *Normande sauce* with shrimp butter.

Uses: For baked fish.

Julienne—Prepared by cooking vegetables slowly in butter until they are very tender: carrots, turnips, leeks, onions, celery—all cut like matchsticks. When these vegetables are thoroughly cooked, clear meat stock is added. If a vegetarian soup is required, water is added instead of stock. To this mixture cabbage and lettuce hearts, similarly cut, are also added, as well as fresh peas and one or two spoonfuls of shredded sorrel. See SOUPS AND BROTHS.

A la languedocienne—Cèpes sautéed in butter or oil; egg-plant (*aubergines*) in rounds or coarsely diced, fried in oil; potatoes cut to look like olives and cooked slowly in clarified butter.

Sauce: A *Demi-glace* (see SAUCE) flavoured with tomato.

Uses: For large and small cuts of meat, poultry.

A la lorraine—Red cabbage braised in red wine; *Potato fondantes.**

Sauce: A diluted *Demi-glace* (see SAUCE) or braising stock; in addition horseradish sauce served separately or grated horseradish.

Uses: For large cuts of meat, particularly braised cuts.

A la lyonnaise—Medium sized stuffed onions, braised; *Potato fondantes.**

Sauce: Lyonnaise sauce (see SAUCE).

Uses: For large cuts of meat.

Macédoine—A mixture of vegetables boiled separately beforehand, drained and tossed in butter; carrots and turnips diced or shaped with a ball-scoop; diced French (string) beans; small kidney beans; peas, etc. Cauliflower flowerets may be added.

Sauce: Gravy of the roast or clear veal gravy.

Uses: For large or small cuts of meat.

Maillot garnish round a ham

Maillot I (also called Porte-Maillot)—Glazed carrots and turnips in small oval lengths (or shaped with a ball-scoop); French (string) beans in butter; braised lettuces. (These vegetables, disposed round the dish in separate groups, are sometimes interspersed with little glazed onions and knobs of cauliflower sprinkled with melted butter.)

Sauce: Demi-glace sauce flavoured with Madeira (see SAUCE).

Uses: For large cuts of meat, especially ham.

Maillot II—Coarsely shredded carrots and turnips, simmered in butter in covered pan; French (string) beans in butter.

A la maraîchère—Carrots trimmed into large oval lengths, glazed; small glazed onions; thick slices of stuffed and braised cucumber; quartered cooked artichokes simmered in butter in a covered pan.

Sauce: Strained braising liquor, with all fat removed.

Uses: For large braised cuts of meat.

A la maréchale—Asparagus tips in butter; sliced truffles. Ingredients prepared *à la maréchale* are dipped in a mixture of two thirds breadcrumbs and one third finely chopped truffles.

Sauce: Maître d'hôtel butter (see BUTTER, *Compound butters*) or *Châteaubriand sauce* (see SAUCE).

Uses: For *Suprême of chicken* (see CHICKEN), escalopes (U.S. cutlets) of veal, sweetbreads and sometimes fillets of fish.

A la Marigny—Small artichoke hearts filled with corn kernels in cream; potato balls, browned in butter.

Sauce: Pan juices of the main dish diluted with white wine and thickened veal stock.

Uses: For small cuts of meat.

A la marinière—Shelled mussels cooked in white wine, shelled tails of fresh-water crayfish.

Sauce: Marinière sauce (see SAUCE).

Uses: For fish.

Marivaux—Oval nests made of *Duchess potato mixture* (see POTATOES), browned in the oven, filled with a mixture of finely chopped carrots, celery, artichoke hearts and mushrooms, simmered in butter in a covered pan, blended with a *Béchamel sauce* (see SAUCE), sprinkled with Parmesan cheese and breadcrumbs and browned; French (string) beans in butter.

Sauce: A thin *Demi-glace sauce* (see SAUCE) or thickened veal gravy.

Uses: For large cuts of meat.

A la marocaine—Little mounds of rice pilaf, lightly seasoned with saffron (to be used as canapés); diced baby marrows (U.S. zucchinis) sautéed in oil; sweet peppers stuffed with chicken forcemeat, braised.

Sauce: Pan juices diluted with tomato juice.

Uses: For *Noisettes* of mutton or lamb.

A la mascotte—Artichoke hearts in slices, sautéed in butter; potatoes trimmed into very small oval lengths browned in butter; sliced truffles.

Ingredients prepared *à la mascotte* are usually served in a deep pie-dish or in earthenware dishes.

Sauce: Pan juices diluted with white wine and thickened veal stock.

Uses: For small cuts of meat, poultry.

Masséna—Artichoke hearts garnished with strips of poached bone-marrow.

Sauce: Marrow-bone sauce (prepared by diluting the juices left in the pan in which the marrow has been cooked. (See SAUCE.)

Uses: For small cuts of meat.

Massenet—Anna potatoes baked in individual moulds and turned out (see POTATOES, *Anna potatoes for garnish*); small artichokes filled with a *salpicon** of bone-marrow; French (string) beans in butter.

Sauce: Meat juices of the main dish or a *Demi-glace sauce* flavoured with Madeira (see SAUCE).

Uses: For large or small cuts of meat.

Matelote—Small glazed onions; mushrooms; small croûtons fried in butter.

Sauce: Matelote sauce with red wine (see SAUCE).

Uses: For fish prepared *en matelote.*

Matignon—Artichoke hearts stuffed with a *Matignon fondue**, sprinkled with breadcrumbs and browned; stuffed braised lettuces.

Sauce: Madeira or *Port wine sauce* (see SAUCE).

Uses: For large and small cuts of meat.

Melba—Very small tomatoes filled with a *salpicon** of chicken, truffles and mushrooms, blended in a *Velouté sauce* (see SAUCE), sprinkled with breadcrumbs and browned; braised lettuce.

Sauce: Thickened veal gravy flavoured with port.

Uses: For small cuts of meat.

Mentonnaise—Thick slices of small vegetable marrows (zucchinis) stuffed with tomato-flavoured rice; small cooked artichokes simmered in butter in covered pan; potatoes cut to look like olives and cooked slowly in clarified butter.

Sauce: Thickened veal gravy or a *Demi-glace sauce* (see SAUCE).

Uses: For large and small cuts of meat.

Mikado—Small mounds of curried rice to be used as canapés. Small tartlets filled with soya bean shoots in cream.

Sauce: Curry sauce with soya added (see SAUCE).

Uses: For *Suprême of chicken,** escalopes (U.S. cutlets) of veal.

Milanaise III—*Macaroni à l'italienne;* cooked ham, moulds (darioles) turned out.

Sauce: Veal stock flavoured with tomato.

Uses: For large cuts of meat.

Milanaise II—Semolina *gnocchi* (cut in lozenges and rectangles) sprinkled with cheese and browned. See *Gnocchi à la romaine.*

Sauce: Thickened veal stock flavoured with tomato.

Milanaise III—*Macaroni à l'italienne;* cooked ham, pickled tongue, mushrooms and truffles cut into strips and blended in concentrated veal stock flavoured with tomato, making a coarse *julienne.**

This *julienne* is either mixed with the macaroni or arranged in a circle round it.

Uses: For meat served in individual portions, especially veal cutlets (U.S. chops) in breadcrumbs.

Mirabeau—Stoned olives; anchovy fillets; blanched tarragon leaves. Served especially with grilled steaks. Water-cress and occasionally match-stick potatoes are also included in this garnish.

Sauce: Anchovy butter (see BUTTER, *Compound butters*).

Uses: For small cuts of meat.

A la moderne—*Chartreuses* of vegetables; small individual (dariole) moulds are filled with alternate layers of cooked vegetables cut in small balls or dice (carrots, turnips, French string beans and peas). These are sealed in with *forcemeat** and cooked in a pan of hot water (*bain-marie*) for 30 minutes. They are turned out for serving.

Mont-Bry—Little cakes of spinach cooked in Parmesan cheese (to be used as canapés); cèpes in cream.

Sauce: Pan juices of the main dish blended with white wine and thickened veal stock.

Uses: For small cuts of meat.

Montpensier—Green asparagus tips in butter; sliced truffles (or 'match-stick' truffles).

Sauce: Stock of the main dish blended with Madeira and thickened veal stock.

Uses: For small cuts of meat, jointed (cut up) chicken.

Nanette—Small cooked artichoke hearts cooked in butter in a covered pan, filled with *Lettuce chiffonnade à la crème;** mushrooms simmered in butter and filled with a *salpicon** of truffles blended with a concentrated *Demi-glace sauce* (see SAUCE).

Sauce: Pan juices of the main dish flavoured with Marsala and blended with *Chicken velouté* (see SAUCE), cream and white chicken jelly.

Uses: Lamb cutlets (U.S. chops), escalopes (U.S. cutlets) of veal or calf's sweetbreads.

Nantua—Fresh-water *crayfish tails à la Nantua.** This ragoût is arranged in shells, pastry-boats or tartlets, or set on the dish surrounding fish cooked in white wine; shredded truffles are sometimes added.

Sauce: Nantua sauce (see SAUCE).

Uses: For fish.

Nichette—Grilled mushrooms filled with grated horse-radish; *ragoût* of cocks' combs and cocks' kidneys, blended in bone-marrow sauce.

Sauce: Marrow sauce (see SAUCE).

Uses: For small cuts of meat, or *suprêmes*.

A la niçoise I—Small skinned tomatoes, simmered in butter; very small vegetable marrows (zucchini) braised; small artichokes stewed in butter; potato balls browned in butter.

Sauce: Thickened veal gravy flavoured with tomato or pan juices of the main dish flavoured with tomato.

Uses: Large and small cuts of meat, poultry.

A la niçoise II—Small tomatoes simmered in butter with a little chopped garlic; French (string) beans in butter; new potatoes browned in butter, or potatoes cut to look like olives and cooked slowly in clarified butter.

Sauce: As above.

A la niçoise III—Tomato fondue *à la niçoise;* blanched green or black olives; anchovy fillets; capers.

When served with baked fish, the tomato *fondue* is cooked in the same dish; for grilled fish, it is prepared separately.

Uses: For fish.

Ninon—*Duchess potato nests* (see POTATOES) filled with a *salpicon** of cock's combs and kidneys blended in a *Velouté sauce* (see SAUCE); asparagus tips in butter.

Sauce: Marrow sauce (see SAUCE).

Uses: For small cuts of meat.

Nivernaise—Carrots trimmed in small oval lengths; small glazed onions.

Sauce: A *Demi-glace sauce* (see SAUCE) or, if the main dish is braised, the braising stock.

Uses: For large cuts of meat.

Normande—Oysters, trimmed and poached; mussels; shrimps; mushrooms; shredded truffles; fresh-water crayfish cooked in a *court-bouillon**; fried breaded gudgeon; bread croûtons fried in butter.

Sauce: Normande sauce. See SAUCE and, for further details of this dish, the recipe for *Sole à la normande.*

Uses: For fish.

Olives for garnish—See OLIVES.

A l'orientale I—Small tomatoes stuffed with rice lightly flavoured with saffron; okras (ladies' fingers) cooked in butter; sweet peppers, skinned and simmered in butter in a covered pan.

The large cuts of meat served with this garnish must not be either interlarded with or wrapped in bacon.

Sauce: Tomato sauce with butter (see SAUCE).

Uses: For large and small cuts of meat.

A l'orientale II—Pilaf of rice turned out of little conical moulds; cooked okra (ladies' fingers); small tomatoes stuffed with a tomato *salpicon.**

Sauce: As above.

A la paloise—Potato balls browned in butter; French (string) beans in cream.

Sauce: Paloise sauce (see SAUCE).

Uses: For small cuts of grilled meat.

A la parisienne I—*Potatoes à la parisienne;** braised lettuce.

Sauce: Pan juices of the main dish diluted with white wine and veal stock.

Uses: For large and small cuts of meat, poultry.

A la parisienne II—As above, using quartered artichokes instead of lettuce.

Parmesan Génoise—Mix in a bowl 2 yolks of eggs seasoned with a little grated nutmeg, 2 stiffly beaten whites of egg, $\frac{1}{4}$ cup (35 grams) of sieved flour, $\frac{1}{2}$ cup (60 grams) of grated Parmesan cheese.

Spread the mixture on sheets of paper on a buttered baking tin. It should be 3 inches thick. Bake in a very slow oven and allow it to cool; cut up into any shape desired.

Uses: Garnish for soups.

Pasta and cereals (soup garnish)—$\frac{1}{2}$ cup (60 grams) of Italian *pasta* or vermicelli should be used for each quart (litre) of soup; cooking time varies from 8 to 14 minutes according to the size and quality of the *pasta* used.

$\frac{2}{3}$ cup (80 grams) of *Pastina* or *pasta beads* should be used for each quart (litre) of clear soup. Cooking time is 22 to 25 minutes.

Use approximately $\frac{1}{2}$ cup (70 grams) per quart (litre) of clear soup of tapioca, sago or salep. Cooking time is 20 minutes.

3 tablespoons (50 grams) of rice should be used for every quart of clear soup. After pouring boiling water over it, the rice should be cooked in the clear soup for 25 minutes.

A la persane—Rounds (or long slices) of egg-plant (aubergines) sautéed in oil; onion rings fried in oil; *fondue** of tomatoes with peppers (to decorate the other garnishes).

Sauce: Pan juices of the main dish or mutton or lamb stock flavoured with tomato.

Uses: Cutlets (U.S. chops) and *noisettes of mutton* or *lamb*.

A la piémontaise—Croquettes of risotto (mixed with a *salpicon** of truffles, mushrooms, pickled tongue and ham) shaped to look like corks.

Sauce: A rather thin tomato sauce.

Uses: For large cuts of meat.

A la portugaise—Tomatoes stuffed with chopped mushrooms *à la duxelle**; potatoes cut to look like olives and cooked slowly in clarified butter.

Sauce: Veal gravy or a *Demi-glace sauce* (see SAUCE) flavoured with tomato.

Uses: For large cuts of meat.

Prince Albert—Whole truffles simmered in butter in a covered pan.

The fillet of beef prepared according to this recipe is stuffed with *foie gras*. See BEEF, *Fillet of beef à la Prince Albert*.

Sauce: Gravy of the main dish flavoured with Madeira or port; thickened veal stock.

Uses: For fillet of beef.

A la princesse—Asparagus tips in butter or cream; truffles in slices or diced.

Sauce: Allemande sauce (see SAUCE).

Uses: For poultry, calves' sweetbreads, small vol-au-vents, tartlets.

Printanier (garnish for soup)—Cut carrots and turnips in fine strips about 1 inch long. Blanch these vegetables and boil them in clear stock. When they are almost cooked, add peas and French beans cut into lozenges, which have been boiled and well drained.

Put these vegetables in the boiling clear soup.

Note. Asparagus tips and small young kidney-beans may be added.

The carrots and turnips may also be shaped with a small ball-scoop or diced.

A la printanière—New carrots and turnips cut in small oval lengths, cooked in white stock and tossed in butter; peas; asparagus tips in butter.

Sauce: Clear veal stock.

Uses: For large and small cuts of meat and poultry.

A la provençale—Egg-plant (aubergines) cut in chunks, stuffed with *fondue** of tomatoes, sprinkled with bread-crumbs and browned; French (string) beans in butter; potatoes cut to look like olives and cooked slowly in clarified butter.

Sauce: Thickened veal stock, flavoured with tomato, and chopped tarragon.

Uses: For large and small cuts of meat.

Quenelles (garnish for soups)—Little balls about the size of a white bean rounded or fluted.

According to the recipe followed, they may be made of fine poultry, game or fish forcemeat (see QUENELLES).

Force through a pastry horn or forcing-bag (pastry bag) and arrange in a buttered pan. Ten minutes before serving, cover with boiling salt water and simmer them slowly. If no other garnish is used, 35 to 40 of these balls should be used to every quart (litre) of clear soup. If other garnishes are used, 20 quenelles per quart (litre) will be sufficient.

For certain soups, the balls are shaped in a teaspoon and sometimes stuffed with a *brunoise** of vegetables.

Rachel—Slices of bone-marrow, poached, drained, grilled and set on top of the piece of meat, which itself is set on artichoke hearts simmered in butter.

Sauce: Bordelaise sauce (see SAUCE).

Uses: For small pieces of grilled meat.

Ravioli—Prepare the ravioli as described in the recipe for ravioli, but make very small. Fill them with chicken, foie gras or any other delicately flavoured forcemeat. Simmer the ravioli, drain and add to clear soup at the last moment.

Régence garnish round veal sweetbreads

Régence—Large quenelles decorated with truffles, small chicken quenelles, slices of foie gras sautéed in butter, cocks' combs, mushrooms, thick slices of truffles (or truffles cut in ovals). For detailed instructions for the preparation of this dish see the recipe for *Chicken à la régence**.

Sauce: Allemande sauce (see SAUCE).

Uses: For cuts of white meat, calf's sweetbreads, poultry, savoury flans and tarts, vol-au-vent.

Réjane — Nests made of *Duchess potatoes* (see POTATOES), fried, hollowed out and filled with leaf-spinach in butter; quartered artichokes simmered in butter; slices of bone marrow, poached and drained.

Sauce: Braising stock.

Uses: For veal sweetbreads, braised.

Renaissance—A variety of spring vegetables, disposed round the dish in individual groups. (These vegetables are separately glazed, braised, tossed in butter or fried, as appropriate.)

Sauce: Gravy of the roast or clear veal gravy.

Uses: For large cuts of meat.

Richelieu—Medium-sized stuffed tomatoes, sprinkled with breadcrumbs and browned; braised lettuce; potatoes cut as for small chips and cooked slowly in clarified butter or new potatoes fried in butter.

Sauce: Thickened veal stock or a rather liquid *Demi-glace sauce* (see SAUCE).

Uses: For large cuts of meat.

A la romaine—Individual *Spinach timbales à la romaine;* individual *Anna potatoes for garnish* (see POTATOES) turned out of uniform moulds.

Sauce: Rather liquid tomato sauce or thickened veal gravy flavoured with tomato.

Uses: For large cuts of meat.

Romanov—Cucumber stuffed with chopped mushrooms (*à la duxelle**) sprinkled with breadcrumbs and browned and cut in thick slices; *Duchess potatoes* (see POTATOES), filled with a *salpicon** of celeriac and mushrooms in a *Velouté sauce* (see SAUCE), sprinkled with grated horseradish.

Sauce: A *Demi-glace sauce* flavoured with Madeira (see SAUCE).

Uses: Garnish for large and small cuts of meat.

Rossini—Thick slices of truffle; slices of foie gras sautéed in butter.

Sauce: Stock of the main dish blended with Madeira and thickened veal gravy.

Uses: Garnish for small cuts of meat.

Royale—This garnish for soup is prepared from a mixture, generally consisting of a clear meat stock variously flavoured, thickened with eggs, or of a purée of some kind, similarly thickened with egg.

Put this preparation in small cylindrical moulds (darioles) and cook in a *bain-marie** (pan of hot water) in a 350°F. oven until firm. When completely cold, turn out the moulds on to a cloth and dice neatly or cut into lozenges, squares or, with a pastry cutter, into rounds, stars, leaves, etc.

Royales are especially used as garnishes for clear soups. Occasionally, they are used in thick soups, but not often.

The measures given below are for 1½ quarts (litres) of clear soup.

Royale of asparagus tips. ROYALE DE POINTES D'ASPERGES —Boil ½ cup (75 grams) of asparagus tips hastily in salt water and add 5 or 6 leaves of young spinach. Drain; add 1½ tablespoons of *Béchamel* (see SAUCE), 2 tablespoons of clear meat stock and pass through a sieve. Blend in 4 egg yolks and cook as for other *royales*.

Royale of carrots, called à la Crécy. ROYALE DE CAROTTES, DITE À LA CRÉCY—Cook slowly in butter 1 medium sized carrot, sliced and seasoned with salt and a little sugar. Add 2 teaspoons of *Béchamel sauce* (see SAUCE), 2 tablespoons of cream, and put through a sieve. Blend in 4 egg yolks; pour into a buttered mould; cook in a *bain-marie** (pan of hot water) in a moderate oven (350°F.) until firm.

Royale of celery. ROYALE DE CÉLERI—Cook in butter 3 tablespoons (75 grams) of stick celery finely shredded; add a tablespoon of *Béchamel sauce* (see SAUCE), 2 tablespoons of clear meat stock and blend in 4 egg yolks. Cook in a double saucepan.

Royale of chicken purée. ROYALE DE PURÉE DE VOLAILLE —Pound to a fine pulp 2 tablespoons (50 grams) of cooked white meat of poultry; add 2 tablespoons of *Béchamel sauce* (see SAUCE), 2 tablespoons of cream and strain. Blend in 4 egg yolks. Poach as for other *Royales*.

Royale of game purée. ROYALE DE PURÉE DE GIBIER—Pound to a fine pulp 2 ounces (50 to 60 grams) of flesh of ground game (hare or roebuck) or of winged game (partridge or pheasant) as required. Add 1½ tablespoons of *Demi-glace sauce* (see SAUCE), 3 tablespoons of clear meat stock and strain. Blend in 1 whole egg and 2 yolks. Pour into a mould and poach like other *royales*.

Royale of fresh pea purée. ROYALE DE PURÉE DE POIS FRAIS—Blend two heaped tablespoons of fresh pea purée with 4 tablespoons of clear meat stock. Season with salt and a little sugar. Blend in 1 whole egg and 2 yolks. Pour into a mould and poach like other *royales*.

Royale of tomato purée. ROYALE DE PURÉE DE TOMATES —Thin ⅓ cup (1 decilitre) of very red concentrated tomato purée with 4 tablespoons of clear meat stock. Season with salt and sugar; thicken with 4 egg yolks; poach as for other *royales*.

Plain royale. ROYALE ORDINAIRE—Put a large pinch of chervil into ⅔ cup (1½ decilitres) of boiling clear meat stock and leave it to infuse for 10 minutes. Beat as for an omelette 1 whole egg and 2 yolks; blend the eggs little by little into stock; strain, skim and pour into a buttered mould. Cook as other *royales*.

Sagan—Risotto as a foundation for the garnishes; mushrooms stuffed with purée of brain mixed with a *salpicon** of truffles.

Sauce: Stock of the main dish blended with Madeira and thickened veal gravy.

Uses: For escalopes of veal (U.S. veal cutlets) or veal sweetbreads, *suprêmes of chicken* (see CHICKEN).

Saint-Germain I—Rather thick purée of green peas, usually served separately.

Sauce: Clear veal stock.

Uses: Large and small cuts of meat.

Saint-Germain II—Cooked artichoke hearts simmered in butter garnished with purée of green peas. This garnish is sometimes referred to as *Clamart*.

Saint-Saëns—Little fritters of truffles and foie gras; cocks' kidneys; asparagus tips.

Sauce: A *Suprême sauce* (see SAUCE) flavoured with essence of truffles.

Uses: For *suprêmes* of poultry.

A la sarde—Cork-shaped croquettes of rice cooked with cheese: mushrooms sautéed in butter; French (string) beans in butter.

Sauce: Rather thin tomato sauce or veal gravy flavoured with tomato.

Uses: For large cuts of meat.

A la sarrasine—Small buckwheat cakes, browned in butter; little rice tartlets, filled with *fondue** of tomatoes with sweet peppers added. On each tartlet one or two fried onion rings are placed.

Sauce: A rather thin *Demi-glace sauce* (see SAUCE).

Uses: For large cuts of meat.

Sauerkraut. CHOUCROUTE—Wash and drain the sauerkraut; squeeze it dry and simmer it in clear soup or white stock.

Semolina gnocchi (garnish for soups) (Hungarian cookery). GNOCCHI DE SEMOULE—Put 5 tablespoons (75 grams) of butter in a bowl and work it with a spatula. During this process, add an egg, ½ cup (65 grams) of semolina and 2 teaspoons of flour. Season with salt and a pinch of grated nutmeg. Work vigorously with a spatula until the mixture is slightly frothy. Leave it to stand for a hour.

With this mixture make some large oval balls shaped with a tablespoon. Place these as they are made into a buttered pan. Add boiling water and leave to simmer for 20 minutes.

Serge—Very small quartered cooked artichokes simmered in butter; coarsely shredded ham simmered in Madeira.

Ingredients prepared *à la Serge* are dipped in a mixture of breadcrumbs and chopped truffles and mushrooms.

Sauce: A *Demi-glace sauce* (see SAUCE) flavoured with essence of truffles.

Uses: Escalopes of veal (U.S. veal cutlets) or calf's sweetbreads.

Spun eggs. OEUFS FILÉS—For a quart (litre) of soup, beat an egg as for an omelette; strain it through muslin. Put it in a fine strainer held over a frying pan containing boiling clear stock. Move the strainer back and forth over the stock.

Drain the threads of egg thus prepared and add them to the soup.

A la strasbourgeoise—Braised sauerkraut; thin rectangles of salt (pickled) pork cooked with the sauerkraut; slices of foie gras sautéed in butter.

Sauce: Reduced pan juices of the main dish.

Uses: For braised or pot-roasted poultry.

A la sultane—Canapés of chicken forcemeat (shaped as cutlets) (U.S. chops) on which the *suprêmes* (chicken breasts) are placed; very small tartlets filled with purée of truffles with pieces of blanched pistachio nut on top; cock's combs.

Suprêmes prepared *à la sultane* are dipped in a mixture of breadcrumbs and chopped truffles.

Sauce: Suprême sauce (see SAUCE) very slightly seasoned with curry-powder.

Uses: For *suprêmes of chicken* (see CHICKEN).

Tomatoes (soup garnish). TOMATES—Peel small, very

firm tomatoes; remove liquid and pips; dice the flesh into squares ¼ inch across and add these to boiling clear meat stock. Leave them to simmer for 7 minutes and drain them just before adding them to the soup.

Tortue—Little veal *quenelles;* stoned olives; mushrooms; sliced truffles and gherkins; fresh-water crayfish cooked in a *court-bouillon*;* fried yolks of eggs; heart-shaped pieces of fried bread; small collops (pieces) of tongue and calves' brains.

Sauce: Tortue sauce (see SAUCE).

Purpose: For calf's head.

A la toscane—Thick macaroni, diced, mixed with a purée of foie gras; coarsely diced truffles sautéed in butter.

Ingredients prepared *à la toscane* must be dipped in a mixture of breadcrumbs and grated Parmesan cheese.

Sauce: Thickened veal gravy.

Uses: For escalopes (U.S. cutlets) of veal or calves' sweetbreads; breasts of chicken.

A la toulousaine, also called à la Toulouse—Chicken quenelles; cocks' combs and kidneys; braised lamb or calves' sweetbreads; mushrooms; shredded truffles.

The elements of this garnish are arranged in separate groups and sometimes include chicken livers sautéed in butter.

Sauce: Allemande sauce (see SAUCE).

Uses: For calves' sweetbreads, poultry, savoury pies, tarts, vol-au-vents.

A la trouvillaise—Shrimps. shelled; mussels; mushrooms.

Sauce: Shrimp sauce.

Uses: For fish.

Truffles. TRUFFES—This garnish is only very occasionally added to soups.

Shred fresh truffles into fine strips or, if preferred, dice them into ⅓ inch squares. Put these truffles in the boiling soup, but only at the last minute. The heat of the soup is sufficient to cook the truffles.

A la tyrolienne—Tomatoes cut into quarters, cooked slowly in butter until very tender; onion rings fried in oil.

Sauce: Thickened veal gravy with butter added.

Uses: For grilled cuts of meat or poultry.

A la Valenciennes—Rice cooked in meat stock (or plain boiled rice) mixed with a *salpicon** of sweet peppers.

Sauce: Pan juices of the main dish diluted with white wine or tomato-flavoured thickened veal gravy.

Uses: For small cuts of meat, poultry.

A la Valois—Thinly sliced potatoes and slices of artichoke hearts sautéed together in butter. (This garnish is served in the *terrine* in which the meat is cooked.)

Sauce: Pan juices of the main dish diluted with white wine, and buttered veal gravy.

Uses: For small cuts of meat.

Au vert-pré—Match-stick potatoes; watercress.

Sauce: Maître d'hôtel butter (see BUTTER, *Compound butters*).

Uses: For small cuts of meat and poultry, grilled.

Victoria—Small tomatoes stuffed with purée of mushrooms; quartered artichokes simmered in butter.

Sauce: Meat juices of the main dish blended with Madeira or port and thickened veal stock.

Uses: For small cuts of meat.

A la viennoise—Whites and yolks of hard boiled egg, chopped separately; anchovy fillets; stoned olives; rounds of lemon with rind and skin removed; capers; chopped parsley. All these ingredients are disposed round the dish in separate groups.

Sauce: Brown butter (see BUTTER, *Compound butters*).

Uses: For small cuts of meat, poultry.

This garnish is especially suitable for cutlets (U.S. chops) and escalopes (U.S. cutlets) of veal, breasts of poultry, dipped in breadcrumbs and sautéed in butter. This garnish can also be served with fillets of fish, chiefly brill (U.S. flounder) and sole.

Vladimir—Cucumbers cut in small oval lengths and simmered in butter; very small vegetable marrows (zucchinis), coarsely diced, sautéed in butter.

Sauce: Stock of the main dish blended with sour cream, seasoned with paprika, and with grated horse-radish sprinkled on top .

Uses: For small cuts of meat.

GARUM—A type of condiment, much used as a spice in ancient Roman cookery. It is generally agreed that this condiment could not have been anything other than the pickling brine derived from salting sea-water fish—scomber or mackerel in particular—and squeezing them to extract the liquid.

The best known, which was that extracted from scomber, was called *garum nigrum.* It was put in little pots, as mustard is nowadays, and each guest flavoured it to his own liking, one with vinegar (*oenogarum*); another with water (*hydrogarum*); another with oil (*oleogarum*).

The *garum piperatum* was, as its name indicates, strongly flavoured with pepper.

GASCONY—This ancient province, which once included the Landes, the Basque country, the Chalosse, Condomois, Armagnac, Comminges, Couserans, Lomagne, Astarac and Bigorre districts and part of the Bordelais and Bazadais districts, has always been a land of high gastronomic repute.

The inhabitants have maintained the cult of good eating in the departments which have been formed within the boundaries of Gascony—Hautes-Pyrénées, Gers, Landes, part of the Basses-Pyrénées, Haute-Garonne, Lot-et-Garonne and Tarn-et-Garonne.

It would appear that it was in this province favoured by the god of feasting that the magnificent dish called *Gallimaufry** was created, the dish for which Taillevent, master-chef of King Charles VII, gave the recipe and the name of which, no one quite knows why, has become a synonym for a bad stew.

The good things of this province are many, and it would be difficult to enumerate them all in this brief review. Among the foods which cause the mouth of every food lover to water are the *hams* of the Landes and of Ossau, hams which are eaten raw, like those of Parma, or which are used in fricassées of various kinds, *goose livers* and *duck livers*, *buntings*, *preserves of goose* and of *pork*. Here are to be found the savoury *oysters* of Cap Breton and here, the splendid *potted meats* and *pâtés* and truffled *foie gras* of the Gers, the Landes and the Lot-et-Garonne. (See map on next page.)

GASTRONOME—A slightly pedantic term, dating back to the beginning of the nineteenth century, signifying experts in gastronomy.

Genuine connoisseurs in matters of good food are satisfied with the name 'gourmand' which, though normally translated as 'greedy', has no derogatory overtones in French.

Brillat-Savarin believed that he could detect the true gastronome by means of what he called '*les éprouvettes gastronomiques*' ('little gastronomic tests').

'We mean by this expression,' he used to say, 'foods renowned for their flavour and of such indisputable

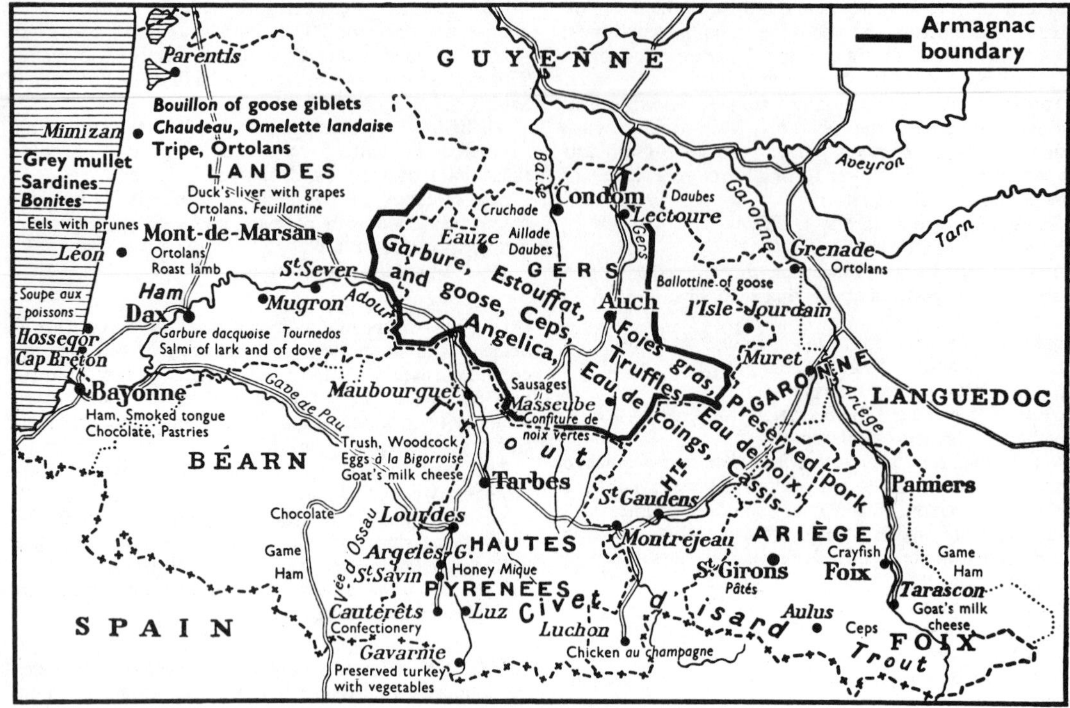

Gastronomic map of Gascony

excellence that their mere appearance must evoke, in a man of well-ordered character, all the powers of the palate; so that all those in whom, in such circumstances, no spark of desire, no ecstatic radiance reveals itself, may justly be marked down as unworthy of the honour of the occasion and of all the pleasures attached thereto.

'Each time a dish of a distinguished and well-reputed flavour is served, the guests should be studied attentively, and all those whose expressions do not reveal enchantment, should be marked down as unworthy'.

An ostentatious host of the type cited by Brillat-Savarin, who was rich, with an income of 30,000 francs might offer his guest 'a seven pound chicken stuffed with Périgord truffles so as to turn it into a completely round ball,' or 'quails, stuffed with truffles and bone-marrow served on toast spread with butter flavoured with basil', or again—magnificent dish—'a pheasant in prime condition, "tufted" ' (which is a culinary error) 'laid on a rôtie "à la Sainte-Alliance".'

In the home of a host of 'middling wealth' in Brillat-Savarin's time, the following menu was served to guests:

'A thick round of veal interlarded with fat bacon and cooked in its own juice;

'A farm turkey-cock stuffed with Lyonnais chestnuts;

'Fat cage-bred pigeons, basted and cooked in the appropriate manner;

'Eggs "à la neige";

'A dish of sauerkraut supported on a crown of sausages, smoked Strasbourg bacon.'

It took robust guests to digest such 'little test' meals as this. There are few such guests to be found today, and if there are, they would no doubt be offered a better balanced and much less heavy menu.

Today, the satisfaction of guests is evinced in the most discreet manner possible, however magnificent may have been the dish which they have just savoured. Reserve of manner, moreover, seems to have met with the approval of Brillat-Savarin for, at the end of his *Méditation* on the little tests, he says: 'A very witty woman told me that she recognized a gourmand by the way he stressed the word "good" in his sentences: "Here's a good thing, here's a very good thing," and so on; she asserts that the *gourmand* infuses into this succinct monosyllable a note of truth, sweetness or enthusiasm which a graceless palate could never attain.

'The validity of the little tests,' says Brillat-Savarin, 'is relative, and must be appropriate to the faculties and habits of various classes of society. Taking everything into account, the little test must be calculated to evoke admiration and surprise; it is a power-gauge which must be differently calibrated for different levels of society.

'Thus the little test designed for a small householder of the rue Coquenard would not be appropriate for a civil servant, and would not even be worthy of notice at a dinner of chosen guests given by a financier or a minister of state.'

But if, nowadays, we no longer rely on Brillat-Savarin's 'little tests' to establish the genuine qualities of a gastronome, it is no less true that there are still true and false gastronomes.

The true gastronome, while esteeming the most refined products of the culinary arts, enjoys them in moderation, and, for his normal fare, seeks out the simplest dishes, those which, moreover, are the most difficult to prepare to perfection. While he is not himself a practitioner of the culinary art, he knows enough of its methods to be able to pass judgment on a dish and to recognise, more or less, the ingredients of which it is composed.

The false gastronome is always a gross eater, fat and proud of it, who is almost totally ignorant in matters of cookery.

It is the false gastronome who believes in 'the tricks of the trade', in secrets handed down from mother to daughter regarding the preparation of certain dishes, in the enormous amount of time required, according to him, to prepare and cook a meal properly, in the need to order long in advance to ensure good service, in short, in the incompatibility of good cooking with modern technical and scientific progress.

The Gourmand (*Boilly*)

GASTRONOMICAL CUSTOMS — Gastronomical customs vary according to the period and the country.

The narrow-minded gastronome admits as orthodox only the usages and seasonings to which he is accustomed, and considers those who have a different conception of the art of eating quite barbarous.

In America it is quite usual to add sugar to a salad. Heresy! Abomination! exclaim certain French authorities, who nevertheless think it nothing out of the ordinary to add slices of sweet beetroot to a salad of *mâche* (lamb's lettuce or corn salad). In Germany and in England, sweet cooked fruit is often served with the meat, and the same critics denounce this depraved and barbarous taste; yet they would permit a garnish of chestnut purée (which is nothing but a purée of fruit much sweeter than some cooked apples or cranberries), or seasoning a haunch of venison with redcurrant jelly or regaling themselves with *caneton à l'orange* or *cailles aux racines* or other savoury dishes garnished with sweet fruits.

In any case gastronomic usages are not the same everywhere in France, and the description of each province found in this dictionary in alphabetical order shows this clearly. Not only are the culinary preparations different but the way the food is served and the arrangement of the meals vary. Thus in Flanders it is the established custom to serve soup at the beginning of the principal meal of the day. In other regions the habit of drinking a *trou de milieu* or, in Normandy, a *trou Normande* has persisted.

The *trou de milieu* consists of serving, in the middle of the meal, generally before the service of the roast, small glasses of spiritous liqueurs of various kinds; *cognac*, *armagnac*, *marc*, *quetsche*, *calvados*, *kirsch*, etc. In the south-west of France, where this custom used to be traditional, it was the young daughter of the house who offered the guests these liqueurs placed on a great silver tray.

In modern practice, although the custom of the *Trou de milieu* still persists in some parts, the *sorbet*, still made with a base of liqueur or liqueur wine, has for the most part taken its place.

GAUDES—The name given in Franche-Comté, Burgundy and other districts to a kind of maize-flour porridge or pudding somewhat similar to the Italian *polenta*, or to hasty-pudding.

Franche-Comté gaudes. GAUDES DE FRANCHE-COMTÉ—Pour into a saucepan containing 3½ quarts (3½ litres) of salted boiling water, 3 cups (500 grams) of maize-flour which has been mixed in cold water to a smooth consistency. Mix well. Cook this pudding, stirring it constantly with a large wooden spoon, until it is thick.

Add 7 tablespoons (100 grams) of butter. Serve this hasty-pudding hot.

Sometimes this pudding, after it is cooked, is poured into small bowls where it is left to cool. It is then cut into slices which are heated in butter and sprinkled with fine sugar.

The *gaudes* may also be served cold, in which case the maize-flour mixture is poured into round moulds. When the gaudes have cooled, they are turned out of the moulds and eaten with sugar.

Here is another recipe for gaudes, given by Dr. Perron, a native of the Franche-Comté:

'First we stir the maize flour, moistened with cold water, very carefully to avoid lumps or, as is sometimes said, to prevent the mixture from being gritty.

'When the mixture is smooth enough, we set it to cook over a moderate heat, and stir constantly with a ladle or large wooden spoon, so that it does not stick, taking care always to stir in the same direction. As the mixture thickens in the cooking, we pour milk into it to thin it down. After an hour and a half of simmering, the *gaudes* are cooked; let us salt them first *avara manu* (with a sparing hand); then, with your permission, we will add several spoonfuls of good cream, and there will be a delicious porridge.'

GAULOISE (A LA)—A name used in particular for a garnish served with clear soup, consisting of cocks' combs and kidneys. See SOUPS AND BROTHS.

This name is also used for a garnish served with large and small vol-au-vents, or pies, having cocks' kidneys as their chief ingredient, with pickled tongue and truffles added. This filling is blended in *Suprême sauce* (see SAUCE) flavoured with Madeira.

Thirdly, the name *gauloise* is used for little cakes made of *Pain de Gênes* (see CAKE, *Genoa cake*) mixture cooked in special moulds (*moules à diplomates*), spread with apricot jam and grilled chopped almonds.

GAYETTES (Provençal cookery)—A type of flat sausage, with pork liver and fresh bacon, encased in pork-caul, or salt pork cut paper thin and cooked in the oven.

These are generally served cold, as an hors-d'oeuvre. See *Pork liver gayettes**.

GAZELLE—This animal,which is a kind of antelope, is to be found in northern and western Asia and in Central Africa.

The meat of the gazelle which, however it is cooked, must first be left to stand in a mild marinade, is very good to eat. All the recipes appropriate to roebuck and venison are suitable for gazelle. See ROEBUCK and VENISON.

GAZPACHO (Spanish Cookery)—This dish is a soup-salad made of fresh cucumber, tomatoes, with peel and pips removed, sweet peppers thinly sliced, and little round slices of bread moistened with water.

These ingredients, except the cucumber and bread, are sliced and seasoned with a dressing prepared as follows: Pound in a mortar 2 cloves of garlic; season with salt, pepper and a little cumin. Blend with oil and vinegar; add a little finely sliced shallot, chopped chervil and a cup of iced water. Leave to soak for half an hour. Ten minutes before serving, add thinly sliced cucumber, slices of bread, more water, if necessary, and cubes of ice. Serve very cold.

GEANS (GUIGNES) CHERRIES—A species of cherry which may be red, black or white. They are firm and fairly sweet.

A great many varieties are grown in France.

Geans are mainly used in France to make a liqueur called *guignolet*, which is a speciality of the town of Angers.

GEBIE—A small shell-fish, whitish in colour, found in French coastal waters. This shell-fish, which can be cooked like shrimps, is used mainly as bait for large fish.

GELATINE—An amorphous, colourless solid, without smell, which swells in water and, when mixed in hot water, forms a viscous substance which turns to jelly when the mixture is cold, provided that it has not been allowed to boil for too long.

Gelatine is produced by the action of heat upon a substance contained in bones, cartilage and tendons. It is used in the preparation of jellies.

Leaf gelatine. GRÉNÉTINE—A very pure and transparent form of gelatine used in pharmacy and cookery.

GELOSE—Synonym of agar-agar. A viscous substance extracted from certain marine algae. Much used in Japan in the preparation of fruit and other jellies. Now in use in various branches of the food industry.

GENDARME—A French popular name for pickled herring. This name is also given to a type of sausage, dry and very hard, which is made in Switzerland and bears some slight resemblance to a herring in appearance.

GENEVOISE SAUCE—This sauce, originally called *Génoise*, is served only with fish. It is flavoured with red wine. (See SAUCE.)

GENISTA (BROOM). GENÊT—The botanical name for a number of plants of the broom family. They have butterfly-like flowers.

Broom buds are sometimes pickled in vinegar and used as a substitute for capers.

GENOESE. GÉNOISE—In cookery in former times, *Génoise* was the name of a sauce served only with fish cooked in a *court-bouillon** (salmon and salmon trout in particular). Nowadays, this sauce is called *Genevoise.*

In confectionery, cakes made from a Genoese mixture are called Genoese cakes.

Genoese cake I. PÂTE À GÉNOISE—*Ingredients.* 2 cups (500 grams) fine sugar; 3¾ cups (500 grams) sieved flour; 1 pound (500 grams) butter; 16 eggs; a pinch of salt; one vanilla bean.

Method. Place in a copper basin the sugar, eggs, salt and a vanilla bean. Set the pan on the stove over a very gentle heat and beat the ingredients with a whisk. This may equally be done in a large double boiler. When the mixture begins to foam and rise well up in the pan, remove it from the stove and continue whisking until it is cold. Now, still beating the mixture, add the flour, using a dredger, and the butter, which should be melted and tepid.

Pour this mixture into sloping sided baking tins or into fairly deep square tins, as desired.

Bake in a 375°F. oven for 40–45 minutes. This will make 3–4 cakes, depending on size.

Genoese cake II. PÂTE À GÉNOISE À L'ANCIENNE—*Ingredients.* 2 cups (500 grams) sugar, 3¾ cups (500 grams) sieved flour; 1¼ cups (180 grams) fresh almonds; 1 heaped tablespoon (20 grams) bitter almonds; ⅓ cup (300 grams) butter; 12 eggs; a small pinch of salt.

Method. Pound the almonds to a fine powder in a mortar (after blanching them). Put them in a bowl and mix in 2 eggs.

Add the sugar, the flour and 5 whole eggs, broken in one at a time. Beat all these ingredients with a wooden spoon for 5 minutes. Add to this mixture 5 egg yolks, then the melted butter, and finally the beaten whites of the remaining eggs.

Put the mixture into buttered sloping sided baking tins or in a deep cake tin or on to a baking sheet with a rim. Bake in a hot oven.

Apricot Genoese cake. GÉNOISE À L'ABRICOT—Bake a Genoese cake. Slice it horizontally into 3 layers of equal thickness. Rub some apricot jam through a sieve and flavour it with kirsch. Spread a layer of this jam on one layer of cake. Cover this with the middle slice. Now spread the middle slice with the apricot jam. Set the last slice carefully on top of the other two. See that the edges of the cake fit together as neatly as possible.

Spread the cake on top and sides with apricot jam and ice it with a *fondant icing* (see ICING) flavoured with kirsch.

The cake may be sprinkled with blanched and chopped pistachio nuts or with chopped browned almonds, according to taste.

It may also be decorated with crystallised fruits or *Royal icing* (see ICING).

Apricot Genoese cake may also be finished with nothing more than a coating of apricot jam, boiled down to a very stiff consistency, so that it will give a shining finish to the cake without being absorbed by it.

In the same way Genoese cake may be coated with other jams.

Genoese cake with chocolate filling

Genoese cake with chocolate filling. GÉNOISE FOURRÉE AU CHOCOLAT—Take a round Genoese cake. Slice it horizontally into 3 layers of equal thickness. Spread a layer of *Chocolate butter cream* (see CREAMS) on one slice of cake. Cover this with another slice. Spread this second slice with the butter cream. Lay the last slice on top of the other two. Press gently on the cake to stick the three parts firmly together. Spread apricot jam on top and sides and sprinkle chocolate hundreds and thousands all over it.

Genoese cake with mocha cream. GÉNOISE FOURRÉE AU MOKA—This cake is made like Genoese cake with chocolate filling, except that, instead of chocolate butter cream, coffee butter cream is put between the layers. Apricot jam is then spread on the top and sides of the cake and it is iced with *mocha fondant* (see ICING).

Genoese cake with filling à la normande. GÉNOISE FOURRÉE À LA NORMANDE—Take a round Genoese cake. Slice it horizontally into 2 layers of equal thickness. Moisten the halves with calvados. Spread one half with very thick apple jam mixed with half its weight of *French pastry cream* (see CREAMS) flavoured with calvados. On top of this slice and filling, place the other half of the cake. Spread apricot jam on the top and sides. Ice it with fondant (see ICING) flavoured with calvados. Decorate the top of the cake with quartered apples cooked in syrup, halves of almonds, and lozenges of angelica.

Gentian

GENTIAN. GENTIANE—A general name given to several species of plants.

The large gentian or yellow gentian as well as other flowers of this family are used in the preparation of certain apéritifs. *Gentiane*, a digestive liqueur, is distilled from the gentian in France and Switzerland and has a distinctive taste much prized in these countries.

The enormous, bitter-tasting root of the gentian is decocted either by soaking or infusion—¼ to ½ ounce per quart (8 to 15 grams per litre).

GEOPHAGIST (Earth-eater). GÉOPHAGE—Either because of depravations following upon nervous disorders, or through necessity, certain American Indians in times of scarcity used to eat a type of clay soil. This soil has no food value, and serves only to create an illusion of satiety.

In different parts of Asia, Africa and America, there are whole tribes of geophagists. The yellow races are especially addicted to this peculiar custom, although it has been observed also in several peoples belonging to other ethnic groups. Geophagists are to be found, in fact, in almost all latitudes: in Guiana, Siberia, Venezuela, New Caledonia, the Cameroons and Siam.

In Java and Sumatra, the clay which provides a feast for the inhabitants undergoes some preparation in advance. According to Hekmeyer, it is mixed into a paste with water after all foreign bodies, such as sand and stones and other hard matter, have been removed. It is then rolled out into thin cakes and baked in an iron pan over a charcoal fire.

GEORGETTE—A name for certain foods, potatoes in particular, which are stuffed with a *ragoût** of fresh-water crayfish tails. Kitchen lore has it that this method of serving potatoes was first used at the Paillard Restaurant, a famous Parisian eating-house, now no longer in existence.

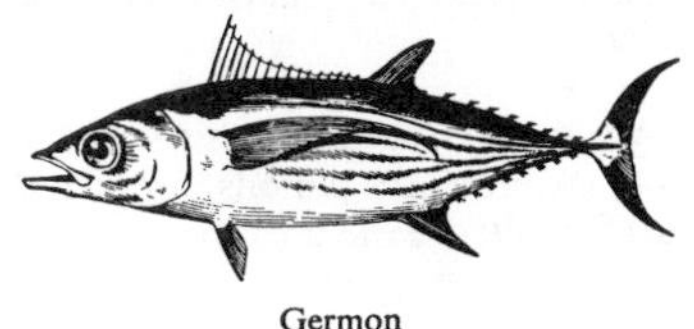

Germon

GERMON—Common name for tunny (tuna) sometimes also called white tunny, because of its fairly close resemblance to that fish.

The *common germon*, which is to be found in the Mediterranean, has white flesh which makes quite good eating. All recipes suitable for tunny (tuna) may be used for germon. In U.S.A. the Pacific coast *albacore* is a white meat tunny (tuna fish).

GÉROMÉ—See CHEESE.

GEX CHEESE—See CHEESE.

GHERKIN. CORNICHON—Gherkins are very young fruits of certain varieties of cucumber. They are gathered green and scarcely developed for preservation in vinegar. They are used as a condiment.

Gherkins in vinegar (cooked). CORNICHONS AU VINAIGRE (À CHAUD)—Trim and rub the gherkins and soak them in salt for 24 hours. Drain them on a sieve, and wipe them well with a cloth, one by one.

Put them in a large basin, and cover them with vinegar which has been boiled in a copper pan. Leave for 10 hours in the vinegar.

Put the vinegar back to boil, adding some fresh vinegar, allowing a pint (½ litre) for 3 quarts (litres) of boiled vinegar, and pour this boiling vinegar on the gherkins.

Drain them, put them in jars or pots with the aromatics and condiments listed above. Cover them with the vinegar. Seal the pots or jars hermetically and keep in a cool place.

Gherkins in vinegar (uncooked). CORNICHONS AU VINAIGRE (À CRU)—Rub the gherkins vigorously with a cloth, or brush them, to remove the down which covers them.

Put them in a basin and cover them with sea salt. Leave them in the salt for 24 hours.

Drain the gherkins. Wash them in vinegar water. Drain and wipe them one by one.

Arrange them in a glass jar, or in a stoneware pot, strewing here and there some little white onions, chilis, sprigs of thyme, fragments of bay leaf, tarragon sprigs and cloves.

Cover with wine vinegar. Seal the pots hermetically. Keep in a cool place.

Gherkins prepared in this way can be eaten at the end of 4 to 5 weeks.

Fresh salt gherkins à la russe. CORNICHONS FRAIS SALÉS À LA RUSSE—Wash 24 fresh little gherkins in lukewarm water without trimming them. Leave them to get cool in a large basin of cold water. Drain them well; wipe them. Put them in a jar, in layers, putting between each layer blackcurrant leaves and little sprays of fennel.

On the last layer of gherkins, which ought to reach ¾ inch below the top of the receptacle, put some little shavings of horse-radish, and a layer of blackcurrant leaves. Press the leaves down.

Pour salt water over the gherkins, which has been boiled and allowed to cool.

Put a little round wooden dish on top of the gherkins to keep them in the pickle. Leave to soak for 24 hours. Gherkins, which in Russia are called *ogurtzy*, are used as an hors-d'oeuvre.

GIBLETS. ABATIS—In cookery, this word means the head, the neck, the heart, the pinions, the feet, the gizzard and the liver of poultry, as well as the cocks' combs and kidneys.

The giblets of turkeys and large chickens are used for making ragoûts, and are also sometimes used to improve the taste of stocks and clear soups.

The cocks' combs and kidneys and the livers of fowl are often used for garnishes of various classic dishes such as *financière*, *Toulouse*, and *ambassadrice*, or other dishes of a similar type. See COCKS' COMBS.

The livers of geese and ducks are not considered as giblets. These are expensive delicacies and require special preparation.

Authors of cookery books do not all agree as to the nutritive value of giblets. Actually, these can be made into excellent dishes and do not deserve the somewhat sweeping criticisms of Dr. Félix Brémond, who declared in his witty *Dictionnaire de la table* that, 'There is the same difference between the people who eat chicken and those who are satisfied with giblets, as between passengers travelling inside the omnibus and those on the open top deck, for in travelling, as in eating, there are clients of first and second class.'

According to this judgment Victor Hugo was an upper deck traveller in his tastes!

Erroneously, the word *abatis* (*giblets*) which, logically, should be reserved for parts of poultry, is sometimes used to define various entrails of slaughtered animals, more commonly known as *Offal* (*Variety meats*).

Methods of preparing poultry giblets—The giblets of turkeys and geese are the ones which are most frequently used for ragoûts.

Giblets of other poultry, such as chickens, table-fowl and spring chickens are also used for improving the taste of stocks.

Before being used in any manner whatsoever, the giblets should be thoroughly washed and trimmed. Proceed in the following manner: singe the neck, the head and the pinions, and remove all feathers carefully.

Scald the feet, peel off the outer skin which covers them and pare off the ends of the spurs.

Slit the gizzard on the curved side, open it and remove the inner bag, taking care not to break it (this bag is full of grit).

Remove the gall bladder from the liver and trim off the upper part of the heart.

The pinions, head and neck of turkeys, geese and ducks should sometimes be scalded to make plucking easier. For this, plunge them into boiling water and pluck immediately.

The giblets of various kinds of poultry are all prepared in a similar manner. We are, therefore, restricting ourselves here to giving recipes only for turkey giblets, which are bigger in size. Depending on how tender they are, it will be sufficient to increase or reduce the period of cooking.

As a general rule, as will be seen from reading the recipes which follow, we recommend moistening with water for all the ragoûts. We consider that this is better than moistening with stock or other flavoured broths because it does not obscure the flavour of the basic meat of the ragoût. Only stocks made of the same kind of meat as that which forms the basis of the ragoût should be used, or of meats which cannot affect the taste. A chicken ragoût, therefore, should be moistened with chicken or veal stock, but never with lamb or mutton stock.

In addition to the recipes given below all those given for lamb, mutton, veal or chicken ragoûts, can also be applied to giblets. See RAGOÛTS.

Note. The livers of fowls (those of duck, turkey, goose and chicken) should not be added to the various giblet ragoûts earlier than ten minutes before removing from the fire.

Mostly, however, these livers are used separately, sautéed, cooked on skewers, in pilaf or risotto or prepared in some other way. See OFFAL OR VARIETY MEATS.

Duck and chicken giblets. ABATIS DE CANARDS ET DE POULETS—These are prepared like *turkey giblets* (see below).

Giblet soup—See SOUPS AND BROTHS.

TURKEY GIBLETS. ABATIS DE DINDE:

Turkey giblets à l'anglaise I. ABATIS DE DINDE À L'ANGLAISE—*Ingredients.* One large set (or two small) of giblets: head, neck, pinions, gizzard, liver, feet—approximately 1½ pounds (700 to 800 grams); 2 medium large onions (250 grams); 2 large potatoes (500 grams); *bouquet garni** (a sprig of parsley, thyme and half a bay leaf); 1 tablespoon each of chopped parsley and chervil; salt, pepper.

Method. Scald the head, the neck, the pinions and the feet and remove all feathers. Slit and clean the gizzard, remove the gall bladder from the liver; cut up the giblets into uniform pieces.

Slice the onions; cut the potatoes into rounds.

Prepare the *bouquet garni* and separately chop the parsley and the chervil.

Put half the onions and the potatoes into a shallow pan, (a deep heavy frying or sauté pan). Sprinkle with half the chopped parsley.

On this layer of vegetables put the pieces of giblets, all except the liver, which will only be added at the last moment.

Cover with the rest of the onions, the potatoes and chopped parsley; put the *bouquet garni* in the middle, season with freshly ground salt and pepper; pour in enough water to cover everything.

Put on high flame. As soon as it begins to boil fast, draw the pan away to the edge of the burner, cover and keep it simmering moderately but continuously for 45 minutes. 10 minutes before serving add the liver.

Serve the giblets in a shallow dish, or a pie-dish, taking care not to break the pieces. Sprinkle with chopped chervil and serve.

Turkey giblets à l'anglaise II. ABATIS DE DINDE À L'ANGLAISE—This method differs little from the preceding.

In spite of the wide-spread prejudice in restaurants and in *grande cuisine*, simple dishes such as *ragoûts*, *fricassées* and others of the same category are more often prepared with less complication than at home.

In classic French cookery, the pieces of giblets, after a preliminary cooking with sliced onions and potatoes, are taken out, put in another shallow pan, covered with about 20 blanched small onions and the same number of new potatoes (or, if these are not available, old potatoes cut down to as nearly the same size as possible) and with the juice in which they were cooked passed through a fine strainer and poured over them.

Turkey giblets bonne femme. ABATIS DE DINDE BONNE FEMME—*Ingredients.* One large set (or two small) of giblets approximately 1½ pounds; 1 generous tablespoon (25 grams) of butter (or fat); 5 slices (100 grams) of lean bacon (free of salt); 10–12 very small onions (100 grams); 24 small new carrots (300 grams) or 3 large carrots cut to size of new carrots; a heaped tablespoon (25 grams) of flour; a wineglass (1 decilitre) of white wine; a *bouquet garni**, a clove of garlic, 5 cups (1¼ litres) of water, salt, pepper.

Method. Follow the instructions given in the recipe for *Turkey giblets à la bourgeoise.*

Turkey giblets à la bourgeoise. ABATIS DE DINDE À LA BOURGEOISE—*Ingredients.* One large set (or two small) of giblets—approximately 1½ pounds; 1 generous tablespoon (25 grams) of butter (or fat); 5 slices (100 grams) of lean bacon (freed of salt); 10–12 very small onions (100 grams); 24 small new carrots or 3 large carrots cut to size of new carrots (300 grams); a large tablespoon (25 grams) of flour; a wineglass (1 decilitre) of white wine; a *bouquet garni**, a clove of garlic; 5 cups (1¼ litre) of water; salt, pepper.

Method. Prepare the giblets as indicated in the first paragraph of the recipe for *Turkey giblets à l'anglaise I.* Cut the bacon into small square pieces and *blanch** it. Peel the little onions and the new carrots; peel the clove of garlic and chop it. Prepare the *bouquet garni**.

Put the butter (or fat) to heat in a shallow pan. Add the bacon and brown it lightly.

Remove it, put on a plate, in its place in the pan put the little onions and fry until golden. Drain and put with the bacon. In the same pan put the pieces of giblets (except for the liver which will be added at the last moment).

Season with salt (allowances must be made for salt content of the bacon). Brown on a high flame, turning with a spoon to ensure even cooking. As soon as the giblets are nicely browned, add chopped garlic and immediately sprinkle with flour.

Stir to blend well and, as soon as the flour begins to brown, which happens very quickly on a high flame, moisten with white wine and leave to reduce for a few minutes. Complete the moistening with enough water or stock to cover.

Add the *bouquet garni*, pieces of bacon, small onions and carrots. Taste and add salt and pepper, if necessary; cover the pan with its lid and as soon as it begins to boil fast, draw away to the edge of the stove, or put it in the oven, and leave to finish cooking on a moderate heat for 45 minutes. 10 minutes before serving, add the liver. Arrange the pieces of turkey giblets in a shallow dish or in a pie-dish and put the garnish (without damaging it) around it. Pour the sauce over the whole.

Turkey giblets à la bourguignonne. ABATIS DE DINDE À LA BOURGUIGNONNE—*Ingredients.* One large set of turkey giblets (or two small ones) approximately 1½ pounds; 1 generous tablespoon (25 grams) butter (or fat); 5 slices (100 grams) de-salted lean bacon; 10–12 very small onions (100 grams); ¼ pound (100 grams) of cultivated mushrooms; a tablespoon of flour; 2 cups (½ litre) of red wine; a *bouquet garni**; a clove of garlic; 2 cups (½ litre) of water or stock; salt, pepper.

Method. Follow the instructions given in the recipe for *Turkey giblets à la bourgeoise.*

Turkey giblets chasseur. ABATIS DE DINDE CHASSEUR—Season the giblets with salt and pepper and fry them in a shallow pan using oil and butter in equal proportions; drain and keep hot.

In the same pan, put ¼ pound (120 grams) thinly sliced mushrooms and replace on high flame; add 2 chopped shallots, moisten with half a glass of white wine and reduce.

Add ⅓ cup (1 decilitre) of *tomato sauce* (see SAUCE) and ⅞ cup (2 decilitres) of thickened brown veal stock.

Put the giblets back into this sauce; re-heat without boiling and, at the last moment, add a tablespoon of chopped parsley, chervil and tarragon.

This dish should not be too thick. The tomato sauce is sufficient to give it the desired consistency. One may, however, in a domestic kitchen, where the various flavoured stocks are not readily available, sprinkle the giblets with flour, moisten with water and strengthen this with a meat extract or tomato purée.

Turkey giblets with chipolata sausages. ABATIS DE DINDE À LA CHIPOLATA—*Ingredients.* One large set (or two small) of turkey giblets—approximately 1½ pounds; a generous tablespoon (25 grams) of butter (or fat); 5–6 very small onions (50 grams) previously blanched and glazed; 24 chestnuts, peeled and three quarters cooked in stock with a pinch of sugar and 1 tablespoon of butter; 8 little chipolata or link sausages cooked in the oven; 3 slices (50 grams) of lean bacon, freed from salt, cut into square pieces, blanched then browned lightly; a tablespoon of flour, a wineglass (1 decilitre) of white wine; a *bouquet garni**; 5 cups (1¼ litres) of water, salt, pepper.

Method. Follow the instructions given in the recipe for *Turkey giblets à la bourgeoise.* The cooked chestnuts should not be added to the ragoût until 15 minutes before serving.

Turkey giblets à l'écossaise. ABATIS DE DINDE À L'ÉCOSSAISE—Follow the recipe for *Turkey giblets bonne femme* with the following Brunoise garnish: a large 'bed' of finely shredded carrots, celery and onions half cooked in butter and 1 cup (2 decilitres) of hulled barley, previously soaked in warm water and cooked in salted water for 35 minutes.

Turkey giblets à la fermière. ABATIS DE DINDE À LA FERMIÈRE—Follow the recipe for *Turkey giblets à la bourgeoise* but replace the garnish given for that recipe by 2 cups (4 decilitres) of *Vegetable fondue.* See FONDUE.

Fricassée of turkey giblets (early French recipe). ABATIS DE DINDE EN FRICASSÉE AU BLANC—Take one or two sets of turkey giblets, which include the wings, the feet, the neck, the liver and the gizzard; scald and pluck them all, put into a saucepan with 2 tablespoons of butter, a sprig of parsley, a scallion, a clove of garlic, 2 cloves, thyme, bay leaf, basil and some mushrooms; put on the fire and add a good pinch of flour; moisten with water or stock; season with salt and coarsely ground pepper; cook to reduce and thicken the sauce; when you are ready to serve, remove the herbs, add gradually 3 yolks of egg blended with 3 tablespoons of cream, bind with this liaison without bringing to the boil. A dash of vinegar or lemon juice may be added to the *roux*, before binding the sauce.

Turkey giblets fried in batter. ABATIS DE DINDE EN FRITOT—Cook the giblets in stock. (Giblets left over from making consommé can be used for this dish.)

Drain them and allow to cool; season with a tablespoon of oil, a few drops of vinegar or lemon juice, chopped parsley, salt and pepper. Soak the giblets in batter (mixture of 5 tablespoons (75 grams) of flour, one tablespoon of oil, ⅓ cup (1 decilitre) of warm water, salt and pepper, adding, after letting the mixture stand for a while, one white of egg beaten until stiff).

Batter is made in different ways, depending on the purpose for which it is intended. See DOUGH.

Fry the giblets in deep fat, smoking hot. Drain, sprinkle with very fine dry salt, and arrange them on a napkin. Garnish with fried parsley and quarters of lemon. Serve tomato sauce separately.

Turkey giblet ragoût (Basic method). ABATIS DE DINDE EN RAGOÛT À BRUN—Cut the neck, the pinions and the gizzard into regular pieces. Cut up the feet, too, if they are being used with the giblets.

Put the giblets into a shallow pan in which butter (or other fat) has previously been heated. Cook, stirring from time to time, sprinkle with flour, and brown lightly. Add a little crushed garlic (if the recipe includes this condiment). Moisten with stock or water, having first added some white wine, as prescribed. Add a *bouquet garni**. Bring to the boil, season, cover the pan with a lid and cook for 30 to 35 minutes. Strain the pieces of giblets, trim them and carefully remove all bone splinters and put the boned giblets back in a clean pan.

Garnish with the prescribed vegetables, according to the recipe chosen, (the vegetables having previously been blanched, then fried lightly, if necessary).

Pour over the juices left in the pan, having passed them through a sieve, removed surplus fat and added tomato purée, according to recipe.

Bring to the boil, cover and finish cooking in the oven; 10 minutes before serving, add the liver.

Serve in a dish, taking care not to break the pieces of giblets or the vegetables.

Note. The moistening of brown giblet ragoûts is usually done with veal and chicken broth or light stock. They could also be moistened with just water. In some cases the moistening can be supplemented by a small quantity of tomato purée.

Turkey giblets with turnips. ABATIS DE DINDE AUX NAVETS—'Take two sets of turkey giblets, open the gizzards to empty them; scald the pinions and the necks to pluck them and singe them, cut into pieces and wash under a running tap, then drain. Put a piece of butter with half a pound of bacon cut into large dice into a saucepan; when it is fried, put in the giblets to colour them a little; sprinkle with a little flour and moisten with stock or water; add an onion stuck with four cloves, salt, pepper, and a *bouquet garni*;* cut the turnips to look like large olives, put them with some butter and sugar into a saucepan to brown lightly; moisten with the sauce in which the giblets were cooked; add the turnips to the giblets, cook to reduce the sauce to the desired consistency; simmer gently on the edge of the stove to allow fat to rise, which you will then remove. Taste to see if there is enough salt, remove the *bouquet* and the onions stuck with cloves; serve hot.' (from *La Grande Cuisine simplifiée*, by Robert, Paris, published by Audot, 1845.)

Note. The giblets of turkeys and other fowl can be prepared in the same manner with mushrooms, celeriac, artichoke hearts, cucumbers and all sorts of other vegetables.

Turkey livers. FOIES DE DINDES—All recipes for chicken livers are suitable for the livers of turkeys and young turkeys.

Turkey livers are sometimes very large and delicately flavoured. They are very similar to duck and goose livers and the same methods of preparation can be applied to them as to the livers of duck and goose.

Young pigeon livers. FOIES DE PIGEONNEAUX—Usually the pigeon liver, which contains no gall, is left inside the bird if it is to be braised, stewed, pot-roasted or roasted.

All recipes for chicken livers are suitable for pigeon livers.

GIGOT (MANCHE DE)—A small metal appliance attached to the bone or 'handle' of the leg of mutton after cooking so as to keep it steady while carving.

GIGUE—See HAUNCH.

GILD. DORER—In cookery some types of pastry and other preparations are brushed with egg (gilded or glazed) before browning in the oven.

GIMBLETTE—See RING-BISCUIT.

GIMLET. FORET—A steel point used to penetrate wood and casks and also used by wine-waiters to uncork bottles.

GIN—A spirit, distilled from grain (barley, wheat, oats) and flavoured with juniper berries.

GINGER. GINGEMBRE—Root-stock of a tropical plant which grew originally in Bengal and Malabar. It is sold in two forms. *Grey ginger* has the stronger smell and comes in tubercles $1\frac{1}{2}$–4 inches long and $\frac{1}{3}$–$\frac{2}{3}$ inches thick, covered with a greyish-yellow skin and well-defined rings. *White ginger* is sold skinned and cut up into smaller pieces.

It is used as a condiment; jam is also made with ginger.

GINGER-BEER—See BEER.

GIRAFFE. GIRAFE—A ruminant African mammal. Its flesh is edible.

GIRAUMONT—West Indian pumpkin. Its flesh is sweet and delicate, sometimes with a musky flavour. It is eaten raw in salads like cucumber, or cooked with other types of gourd and pumpkin. See GOURD and PUMPKIN.

GIRDLE (U.S. GRIDDLE). GALETTOIRE—Flat iron pan without an edge or with a very shallow edge, used for baking pancakes of wholemeal flour called *galetons*, i.e. drop scones or girdle cakes (U.S. griddle cakes).

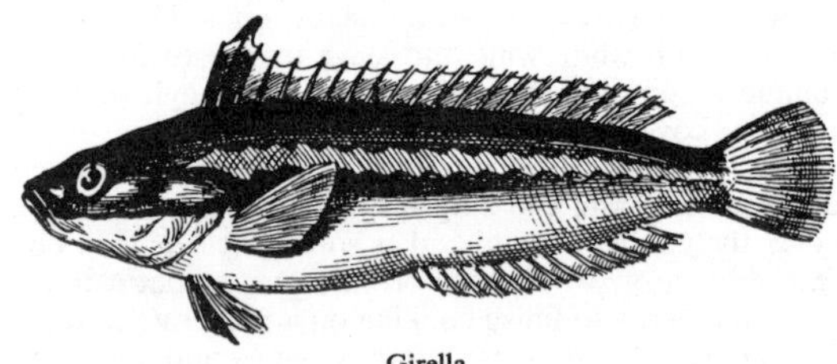

Girella

GIRELLA. GIRELLE—A small, graceful seafish. It is exquisitely coloured and has no scales.

The *common girella* is violet with an orange stripe; the *red girella*, a rich scarlet, the *Turkish girella*, green with turquoise blue stripes. These are all Mediterranean fish.

The girella is used mainly in *bouillabaisse**, but it can be served fried. Its flesh is fairly delicate.

GIZZARD. GÉSIER—Third digestive pouch in birds. In birds of prey, it has a membraneous lining. In grain-eating birds, it is very muscular and thick.

GLAÇAGE—There is no single English equivalent for this word. It is used for several quite distinct operations for which there are various terms in English.

In its proper sense, *glacer* means to *freeze* a liquid until it turns to ice. Thus a creamy or other mixture may be put in a freezer with salt, salt-petre and natural ice to make *une glace*, that is to say, an *ice cream or water ice* (see ICE CREAMS AND ICES).

But *glaçage* is also used for culinary operations

carried out in an excessively hot oven. In this sense *glaçage* means *browning* or *glazing*.

A braised cut of meat, poultry or game is *glacé* (browned or glazed) by being subjected to intense heat in the oven after basting in its own reduced stock.

The meat is said to be *browned* if served hot, and *glazed* (with jelly) if served cold.

Further, *glaçage* is used for *glazing* in another sense, and here also a 'hot' rather than a 'cold' operation is involved. It is applied to fish, eggs or anything else covered with a white sauce of some kind.

Glaçage can mean *glazing*, in the sense of sprinkling sweets and confectionery with icing sugar and subjecting them to intense heat. This last form of *glaçage* is also applied to certain vegetables, notably carrots, turnips and onions.

The term *glaçage* is applied also to the *icing* of cakes.

GLACIÈRE—In French, the term *glacière* has two meanings. It means ice box or refrigerator; it is also used for a sugar-dredger or metal container with pierced lid used to sprinkle icing sugar on cakes.

Old bottles and old champagne glasses

GLASS AND GLASSES. VERRE, VERRERIE—Ever since glass was invented it has been used to make receptacles to contain and store drinks and foodstuffs. Glass utensils were used side by side with the pottery which had served the same purpose since ancient times, but glass, which by its transparency allowed the liquid inside to be seen, was preferred for flagons containing drinks and for drinking vessels, because it afforded pleasure to the eye at the same time as the pleasure to the palate. There exist, in museums and privately, rich collections of bottles, carafes and drinking vessels of every period and every country as well as innumerable specimens of glasses and bowls.

When glass-makers were sufficiently masters of their technique to be able to seek an artistic effect, objects made of glass sometimes became purely ornamental, and were used for their luxurious effect on the table.

GLUCOMETER. GLUCOMÈTRE, GLYCOMÈTRE — A graduated hydrometer, used for the instantaneous assessment of the sugar-content of liquids. Special glucometers are used for measuring the sugar-density of wines and syrups.

GLUCOSE—Glucose is a sugar found in its natural state in many different fruits, and in particular in grapes.

It is made industrially by heating starch of one kind or another with various acids. This produces first dextrins and then an impure form of glucose itself.

Commercially two forms of glucose are used, viscous and semi-solid.

Glucose has many industrial uses, notably to increase the sugar content of wine and beer. It is also used in confectionery in the manufacture of syrup and jam. French law demands that when glucose is used in this way, the fact must be indicated on the label.

GLUTEN—An albumenous substance in flour.

When flour is kneaded under running water, a paste is first formed, then—the starch having been gradually washed away—a greyish elastic dough is produced. This is the gluten.

It is because of its gluten content that flour can be made into bread.

Ordinary bread contains 7% of gluten.

Gluten dough, bread and biscuits. PAINS, PÂTES, BISCUITS DE GLUTEN—These products, manufactured especially for diabetics, have a quantity of gluten added. Gluten bread still retains an average of 40% of starch while potatoes contain only 23%. These 'low' starch products are not recommended, except in very mild cases of diabetes, since they contain such a high proportion of starch. In cases where the starch content has been appreciably reduced, the product no longer bears any real resemblance to bread.

Glass tableware (*Steuben*)

GLYCERINE—A colourless, sweetish, syrupy liquid, a by-product of soap manufacture. It can be extracted from most fats.

Glycerine can be used in industrial confectionery without injury to health. It is also regarded as a valuable substitute for sugar in the sweetening of diabetic foods.

GNOCCHI—This dish, made from flour or semolina, can be prepared in two ways, either from *chou paste* (see DOUGH) made with milk or from a semolina porridge.

Gnocchi can also be made from potatoes. These various dishes, of Italian or Austro-Hungarian origin, can be served as a hot hors-d'oeuvre or as a separate course.

Gnocchi au gratin (Austro-Hungarian cookery)—Make a *Chou paste* (see DOUGH) in the usual way, using milk instead of water. When it is ready add 2–3 ounces of grated Parmesan for every pound of paste.

Put the paste in a large forcing-bag with a round nozzle. Force it through by pressing with the hand. The *gnocchi* must be dropped into a pan of boiling salted water, and each one should be the size of a small walnut.

Simmer the *gnocchi* for a few minutes. As soon as they rise to the surface of the water, drain them and put them on a cloth to dry.

Put them in a gratin dish lined with a layer of *Mornay sauce*, which is a *Béchamel sauce* (see SAUCE) with grated cheese added. Cover them with the same sauce. Sprinkle grated cheese on the top and pour on melted butter. Brown them in a slow oven.

Gnocchi à la romaine—Into a quart (litre) of boiling milk, shake, through a dredger, ½ pound (250 grams) of semolina. Season with salt, pepper and grated nutmeg. Mix well and cook for 20 minutes.

Remove the mixture from the stove and add 2 egg yolks. Spread it out evenly on a moistened slab so that it is about ⅓ inch thick. Leave it to cool. Cut it into shapes with a pastry-cutter 2 inches in diameter, or into lozenges with a knife.

Put the *gnocchi* on a buttered dish which is lined with grated cheese (Gruyère or Parmesan). Sprinkle the *gnocchi* with the same cheese; pour melted butter over the dish and bake in a slow oven.

Potato gnocchi (German cookery). GNOCCHI DE POMMES DE TERRE—Boil 2 pounds (1 kilo) of potatoes in salt water. Drain and dry in the oven. Rub them quickly through a fine sieve. While it is still hot, add to this purée 2 whole eggs, 2 yolks, 3 tablespoons (50 grams) of butter, ½ cup (150 grams) of flour. Season with salt, pepper and grated nutmeg. Mix.

Cut this mixture into pieces each the size of a walnut. Roll the pieces into balls. Flatten them gently, pressing on them with the back of a fork so that they have ridges along the top. Simmer them in salted boiling water. Drain them. Put them in a dish in layers, sprinkling a little grated cheese on each layer. Pour melted butter over them and brown in the oven.

Semolina gnocchi as soup garnish—See GARNISHES.

Goats in the Camargue (*French Government Tourist Office*)

GOAT. CHÈVRE—Goats are raised especially for dairy production. Goat's meat when the animal is still too young for breeding has an agreeable flavour, although always tougher than mutton. But as a rule only animals which are old and worn out by milking are slaughtered. The meat is as nutritive as mutton, but its smell *sui generis* is disagreeable. Goat is eaten particularly in Spain, in Italy and in the south of France, but for reasons which have nothing to do with gastronomy. In the high mountains goat's meat is dried in the fresh air; this is the *bindenfleisch* of the *canton des Grisons*.

He-goat. BOUC—The flesh of the male goat is not really fit for food: it is tough and has a very unpleasant smell.

Male goats' flesh can be eaten only when the animals are very young: from six weeks to four months.

GOAT'S BEARD. BARBE-DE-BOUC—A plant greatly resembling salsify. It is, in fact, wild salsify, of which several varieties are known. The tender shoots of some are eaten like asparagus, the roots of others are prepared like *scorzonera* (*black salsify*). See SALSIFY.

There is a variety of goat's beard which has for a long time been cultivated in Belgium called *witloof*, which in France is called endive.

The shoots of goat's beard, when they are pale as a result of etiolation (i.e. a process of excluding light), can be prepared as *chard**.

GOBLET. GOBELET—A round, wide-mouthed drinking vessel, which used to be made of silver or silver-plate.

Antique goblets are often exquisitely engraved. Small silver wine-tasters are also called *gobelets* in French, though the more usual name for them is *tâte-vin* (wine taster).

The goblet service. SERVICE DU GOBELET—At the French court, *serving the goblet* was one of the most important ceremonies of the Royal Household.

The master of the goblet, who was the head functionary of the Royal kitchens, was in sole charge of the household bread, fruit and linen for the royal table.

(BLACK) GOBY. GOBIE—A fish known in colloquial French as the *goujon de mer*. It is to be found in all the oceans, and some kinds are also found in large rivers. This tiny fish, which has very delicate flesh, is usually eaten fried, like river gudgeon.

GODARD—A garnish for certain meat dishes served as a second course, and for poultry entrées. It is made up of quenelles, cocks' combs and kidneys, pickled tongue, lambs' sweetbreads, truffles and mushrooms. See GARNISHES.

GODIVEAU—A delicate forcemeat from which quenelles are made.

The etymology of this word is uncertain. Scheler suggests that it derives from the Old French verb '*goder*' which means to make '*godinettes*'. But we do not know the meaning of '*godinettes*', nor even whether it does in fact belong to the vocabulary of the kitchen.

Other writers, and Lacam in particular, believe that *godiveau* derives from the old word *godebillaux;* this seems strange, as *godebillaux* has always been used to designate all the tripe of animals slaughtered for butcher's meat.

In justification of this etymology, Lacam says that formerly '*godebillaux*' meant a kind of pie filled with meat balls made of chopped veal and *béatilles*. Béatilles are tit-bits such as cock's combs and kidneys, lambs' sweetbreads etc., made into a stew.

Godiveau forcemeat can be prepared in different ways. See FORCEMEAT AND STUFFING. In addition to the recipes given elsewhere, here is the one given by Carême for this forcemeat.

Godiveau with chives (Carême's recipe). GODIVEAU À LA CIBOULETTE—'Trim 1 pound of fillet of veal and 1 pound 8 ounces of suet. Chop the veal finely and mix in the fat. After the whole has been finely chopped, add one ounce (2 tablespoons) of spiced salt, a pinch of nutmeg and 4 eggs. Chop for several minutes.

'Pound the *godiveau* in a mortar, so that not a single fragment of veal or fat is to be seen. Next, remove it from the mortar and place it on ice or in a cool place for a couple of hours. Now, divide the mixture into two parts and pound each part separately, moistening little by little with pieces of washed ice each the size of an egg. This will make the *godiveau* very firm and smooth.

'Put it in a large bowl and pound the rest in the same way, putting it in the bowl when it is ready, with two spoonfuls of *Velouté* (see SAUCE) and one of chives chopped very fine. This mixture is used like forcemeat.'

Carême goes on to explain the role played by the ice in this preparation:

'This ice helps remarkably in binding and giving body to the *godiveau*, which is what gives it its perfect and most desirable smooth softness.'

'Our ancestors,' he says further, 'made their *godiveau* on the chopping board, that is to say, they never pounded it, in order, so they said, to keep it soft. Pounding it, on the other hand, they said, caused it to lose something of this quality.

'These are indeed the words of hidebound men, for it is impossible that a *godiveau* should attain on the chopping board that degree of perfection of which it is capable.

'When it is finished in the mortar, it retains all the oily juices which are its distinctive characteristic.'

GODWIT. BARGE—A marsh bird, also found along river banks and near the sea shore, commonly called *oyster-catcher* (cricket-teal).

The two varieties, the *Black tailed godwit* and the *Bar tailed godwit* are found in Europe. In America there is the large *Marbled godwit* and the small *Hudsonian godwit*.

All the recipes given for *woodcock** can be applied to godwit.

GOELAND—Colloquial French name for large seagulls. The flesh of this bird, which is oily, leathery and unpleasant in flavour, used to be eaten as Lenten fare. Its eggs are edible. It is prepared in the same way as *bustard*, which is cooked like domestic goose or duckling.

GOÉMON—Colloquial name for a type of seaweed of which there is a large number of varieties. According to legend, it is from a kind of goémon that salangane swallows extract the glutinous substance with which they make their nests.

GOGUES (Angevin cookery)—Chop finely equal quantities of onions, spinach, beet and lettuce. Season these vegetables with salt and leave them to absorb the seasoning for 12 hours. Next day cook the vegetables in lard until they are very soft.

At the same time, finely dice some fat bacon equal in weight to the mixed vegetables. Cook the bacon a little, then add it to the vegetables. Season the ingredients with pepper, salt, and allspice. Add enough pigs' blood to make a rather thin mixture.

Mix all these ingredients thoroughly and wrap them in thin pieces of beef. Each piece (*gogue*) should be 8 inches long. Secure the ends. Simmer the *gogues* in salt water for 2½ hours.

Drain the *gogues* and leave them to cool.

When they are quite cold, slice them, toss them in butter in a frying pan, browning them slightly on both sides.

GOGUETTE—This name used to be given to a kind of flat sausage made from a highly spiced pork stuffing.

GOLD. OR—Precious non-rusting metal sometimes used in the Middle Ages in thin leaves for wrapping some pastes and certain roast birds. Gold is still used for this purpose in the Far East.

GOLDEN ORIOLE. LORIOT—A small European bird, cooked in the same way as *lark**.

GOOD KING HENRY (ALLGOOD, ENGLISH MERCURY). BON-HENRI—Plant commonly found in wild places frequently growing against walls. It is also called wild spinach.

The leaves are cooked like spinach, but they should be cooked in two waters and the first, very green and bitter, should be thrown away.

The young shoots are sometimes eaten like asparagus.

Geese (Hautes-Pyrénées) (*French Government Tourist Office*)

GOOSE. OIE—All the species of geese which are used as food in Europe are the issue of the wild goose (*ancer segetum*).

In France two varieties of geese are raised, referred to as the *petite* and the *grosse*.

The smaller breed goose (*petite*), which is the most popular, weighs about 6 pounds (3 kilos) on the average; after methodical fattening they attain the weight of 10 pounds (5 kilos) and are excellent roasting birds.

The common goose can be treated in any way suitable for poultry in general and for turkey in particular. The common goose, which differs essentially from the big fatted goose, is also referred to in aviculture as *grey* or *barnyard goose*.

The big breed goose (*grosse*) is a heavy bird, weighing 10 pounds (5 kilos) on the average and reaching 20 to 24 pounds (10–20 kilos) after fattening.

Geese of this type are found mainly around Toulouse, where they are bred, and in the Garonne basin. This bird is usually called the *Toulouse* goose; the *Strasbourg* goose is a species of the same breed.

This bird carries its body almost perpendicularly; its behind, called 'artichoke', drags on the ground even before the fattening process. The skin covering its breast is loose and slack, forming a lappet, or wattle, which constitutes a veritable fat store.

It is this variety of goose that is used in the south-west of France for the *Confit d'oie*.

The Toulouse bred geese, after methodical fattening, also provide the livers which are made into those famous *pâtés de foie gras with truffles*, produced in Toulouse, in the Gers, the Landes, in Strasbourg and other parts of France.

The Toulouse variety of geese, however flavoursome its flesh, is used only for making the *Confit d'oie* and cannot be treated by any of the culinary methods applied to its cousin, the common goose.

The *confit* and various other specialities made of preserved goose of the Toulouse species are excellent, but by far the most delicate part of this bird is, of course, the liver, especially when an intensive cramming, coupled with total immobilisation, have enlarged this organ to the state of complete fatty degeneration.

From time immemorial the raising of geese has been practised in France and the birds were greatly esteemed by all France's neighbours.

For many centuries the goose was considered the best of poultry; indeed, it was regarded as so rare and dainty a dish that it was served before the kings.

In Paris, *rôtisseurs* (caterers in cooked viands) principally sold roast geese, hence the name of *'oyers'* by which they were, for many years, described in their statutes.

These oyers, with all their shops concentrated in the same district, have given their name to a street where they lived, which was called *rue aux Oues*. In later years this etymology went astray and the street acquired the rather strange name of *rue aux Ours*, which it still bears.

In England the goose has always been greatly appreciated and on Michaelmas Day it used to be the custom to serve roast goose, prepared in the traditional English way, stuffed with sage and onions. This tradition goes back to the sixteenth century and Alfred Suzanne in his book *La Cuisine Anglaise*, described its origins as follows:

'The 29th September, Michaelmas Day, is the anniversary of a great naval victory won by the English against the Spaniards. Queen Elizabeth was at table when the news of the sinking of the Spanish Armada was brought to her.

'The principal dish that day was roast goose, to which the Queen, it is said, was particularly partial, and in an excited outburst of patriotism and . . . . gourmandism, she decreed that this glorious occasion be commemorated by serving roast goose on the day every year.'

In our time the goose is not nearly so popular, which seems very strange as its flesh, when young of course, is good eating.

The flesh of adult geese is no doubt rather tough and requires prolonged cooking, usually braising, but the flesh of young goose is very tender and delicate. In Northern France, where the common goose is more appreciated than in the South, it is customary to expose the birds to cold for a time during winter, to freeze the flesh and make it tender.

In his book *L'Ancienne Alsace à table*, Charles Gérard wrote: 'The bird itself is nothing, but the art of man has turned it into an instrument which produces marvellous results, a kind of living greenhouse in which the supreme fruit of gastronomy is grown.'

The foie gras is indeed the 'supreme fruit of gastronomy', especially when prepared as it is done in Strasbourg or Toulouse, but the flesh of a young goose, or *gosling*, as the bird is called up to 7 months old, is not to be despised and a great many gastronomes rank it very high.

A young goose, like the duck, can be recognised by the pliability of its underbill.

Goose à l'alsacienne. OIE À L'ALSACIENNE—Stuff the goose with sausage meat. Truss it for roasting and pan-roast it in butter.

Arrange the goose on a long dish. Garnish with sauerkraut, braised separately in the usual manner (see SAUERKRAUT) with the fat given out by the goose during cooking added to it.

Put on the sauerkraut, alternating them, pieces of lean bacon (cooked with the sauerkraut) and poached Strasbourg sausages. Dilute the pan juices with white wine and veal stock and pour over the goose.

Note. The goose, after having been browned in butter or goose fat, can also be cooked with sauerkraut.

Goose à l'anglaise (English style). OIE À L'ANGLAISE—Stuff the goose with a stuffing prepared in the following manner:

Bake 2 pounds (1 kilo) of big, unpeeled onions in the oven and allow to cool. Peel and chop, adding to them an equal weight of crustless bread, soaked and pressed out. Season this forcemeat with $1\frac{1}{2}$ teaspoons (10 grams) of salt, a pinch of pepper, a little grated nutmeg and 3 tablespoons of chopped fresh (or dried) sage.

Truss the goose for roasting, and roast in the oven or on a spit. Arrange on a long dish. Spoon over some diluted pan juices and serve with apple sauce, cooked without sugar, or only very slightly sweetened.

Ballottine and galantine of goose. BALLOTTINE, GALANTINE D'OIE—Prepare like *Galantine of chicken** using boned goose, fine pork or chicken forcemeat, truffles, pickled tongue and ham cut in dice or thin strips.

Ballottine of goose is usually served cold, the liquor in which it was cooked being made into jelly, but it can also be served hot accompanied by a garnish.

Goose à la bourguignonne. OIE À LA BOURGUIGNONNE—Prepare, either stuffed or not, as for *Chicken à la bourguignonne**.

Braised goose with various garnishes. OIE BRAISÉE—Prepare, either stuffed or not, like *Braised turkey* (see TURKEY).

Goose à la chipolata. OIE À LA CHIPOLATA—Prepare, pan-roasted or braised, as *Turkey à la chipolata**.

Civet of goose. CIVET D'OIE—Prepare like *Civet of hare* (see HARE) using goose cut into uniform pieces.

Confit d'oie I—Bleed the goose, pluck and singe it and leave until quite cold before cutting. Slit open the back completely, clean out the bird and remove the liver, taking great care not to damage it. (The liver can be used separately for making *terrines* and pâtés.) Divide the goose into four pieces. Leave the bones adhering to these pieces intact to prevent the flesh losing its shape too much during cooking in the fat.

Salt the pieces of goose, put them into a large earthenware pot and leave in a cold place for 24 hours or longer.

When the pieces of goose are thoroughly impregnated with salt, take them out, brush off the salt which covers them and wipe with a cloth.

Put to cook in a mixture of goose fat and lard (or in goose fat alone), previously clarified in a large pan. Cut the goose fat into small pieces, put into a deep pot, moisten with a few tablespoons of water and add a muslin bag containing several cloves of garlic, a few cloves, and some peppercorns. Do not put the pieces of goose in the fat until this is three quarters melted. Cook on a moderate heat for about an hour.

Test with a big needle to make sure the goose is done. The juice which comes out of the hole pricked by the needle should be perfectly clear, which indicates that the cooking is complete.

Drain the pieces of goose and trim them, that is remove

the carcase bones. Pour a thick layer of the fat in which the goose was cooked, clarified and strained, into a big earthenware jar, glazed on the inside. When this fat is completely solidified, put in the pieces of goose, neatly and in such a way as to prevent them touching the wall of the jar.

Cover the pieces of goose with warm goose fat.

Leave to rest for 2 days. Strain into the pot some hot fat to seal any holes which may have occurred. When this new layer of fat is well congealed, pour a layer of lard over it and, when this is set, put a circle of greaseproof paper on top, pressing it down to make it adhere. Cover the top of the jar with a double thickness of paper and tie with string.

Note. Confit d'oie prepared in this way will keep for a very long time (from one season to another).

Confit d'oie can also be tinned (canned), the tins (cans) being placed in boiling water, as usual. The quality will be just as good as of the *confit* made in an earthenware jar, with the added advantage that it will keep much longer.

Confit d'oie II—Cut the goose into quarters and rub the whole surface with spiced salt, prepared by mixing the following ingredients: 2 pounds (1 kilo) of salt, $\frac{1}{5}$ ounce (6 grams) of saltpetre, 4 crushed cloves, 2 pounded bay leaves, a good pinch of pounded thyme.

Put the pieces of goose into an earthenware pot, glazed on the inside. Cover with spiced salt. Leave to steep in this seasoning for 24 hours.

Take the pieces of goose out of the salt. Shake off surplus salt and wipe the pieces carefully.

Put them into a big pot in which the goose fat has been left to melt slowly. Cook on a low heat for about an hour and a half.

Test the pieces of goose with a thick straw; if the straw penetrates the flesh easily, the cooking is just right.

Drain the quarters, put them into a big earthenware jar glazed on the inside. Strain the hot fat over them, making sure the meat is covered completely.

When quite cold and the goose fat has become congealed, pour a layer of lard, about half an inch thick, over the surface. The lard is denser in consistency and this operation will ensure that the *confit* will keep for a long time.

Prepared in this way, fat pieces of goose will keep in a perfect state for a very long time, on condition that the jars are kept in a cool dry place.

When taking pieces of goose out of the jar for use, care must be taken to see that the remaining pieces are completely covered by the fat.

Note. Confit d'oie is one of the best specialities of Languedoc and Gascogne. This *confit* is one of the absolutely essential ingredients for the *garbure**, the most characteristic of Béarn dishes.

'Leg of preserved goose,' says Simin Palay, who wrote a book on Béarn cookery, 'is a dish which is always ready should a relative or a guest arrive unexpectedly. An old country saying assures us:

'Lou qui a coèche d'auque a hourrup de bi,
Que pot embita parent ou besi'

which means:

'He who has a goose leg and a little wine can safely invite relatives or neighbours.'

In Languedoc *confit d'oie* is used for the preparation of *Cassoulet**.

The *confit*, however, is not used solely as an element of garnish for the *garbure** or *cassoulet*. It can also be served on its own, hot or cold, with or without garnish. Here are some recipes for serving it hot:

Confit d'oie, Basque. CONFIT D'OIE À LA BASQUAISE—Heat the quarter of goose in its own fat, drain and garnish with cèpes, cooked in a mixture of oil and goose fat (in equal proportions) and, at the end of cooking, mix with chopped parsley and garlic.

Confit d'oie à la béarnaise—Heat the pieces of goose in their own fat and drain. Fry some thin slices of raw potato in goose fat, sprinkle with a tablespoon of chopped parsley mixed with a pinch of pounded garlic at the end of cooking and use as garnish for the goose.

Confit d'oie with green cabbage. CONFIT D'OIE AUX CHOUX VERTS—Prepare the green cabbage as described in the recipe for *Braised cabbage* (see CABBAGE). When nearly done, add a piece of goose with all the fat adhering to it. Arrange the piece of goose on a round dish. Surround with the cabbage. Garnish with boiled potatoes (or potatoes cooked with the cabbage).

Confit d'oie with kidney beans. CONFIT D'OIE AUX HARICOT BLANCS—Add the piece of goose to beans cooked *à la bretonne* (see BEANS), simmer for a few minutes and serve in a timbale.

Confit d'oie with lentils. CONFIT D'OIE AUX LENTILLES—Cook a quart (litre) of lentils with the usual aromatics. Drain when cooked, and put to simmer with a few tablespoons of thickened brown veal gravy. 25 minutes before serving add the piece of goose. Heat gently with a lid on.

Confit d'oie with peas, or à la landaise. CONFIT D'OIE AUX PETITS POIS, DIT À LA LANDAISE—Put a piece of *confit d'oie*, having first removed the surplus fat covering it, into a casserole containing peas prepared in the following manner.

Melt some goose fat in an earthenware casserole and fry in it 8 small onions and 2 tablespoons of Bayonne ham cut in small dice. Add a quart (litre) of freshly shelled peas. Cook the peas in the fat for five minutes. Sprinkle a tablespoon of flour, cook for a few moments, stirring with a wooden spoon, moisten with $\frac{3}{4}$ cup ($1\frac{1}{2}$ decilitres) of water and season with a little salt (very little, allowing for the salt in ham) and a teaspoon of sugar. Add a *bouquet garni** consisting of parsley, chervil, thyme and bay leaf; cook with a lid on for 40 minutes. Put in the piece of goose and finish cooking together with a lid on for 25 minutes.

Confit d'oie à la périgourdine, also called à la sarladaise—Prepare as *Confit d'oie à la béarnaise* with a garnish of sautéed potatoes (sliced raw and fried in goose fat) mixed with slivers of truffles at the end of cooking.

Goose en daube capitole. OIE EN DAUBE CAPITOLE—Stuff the goose with a *fine forcemeat* (see FORCEMEAT) mixed with foie gras and diced truffles. Truss and braise in the usual way. When the goose is nearly done, strain the braising liquor through a fine strainer.

Remove trussing string and put the goose back into the braising pan with $\frac{1}{2}$ pound (250 grams) of small mushrooms, $\frac{1}{2}$ pound (250 grams) of stoned blanched olives, and $\frac{1}{2}$ pound (250 grams) of small chipolata sausages tossed in butter. Pour in the braising liquor and finish cooking in a low oven.

Goose à la flamande. OIE À LA FLAMANDE—Braise the goose (stuffed or not as the case may be) in the usual manner. Arrange it on a big, long dish. Surround with *garnish à la flamande**, composed of small balls of green braised cabbages, carrots and turnips cooked in stock, boiled potatoes cut in biggish chunks, and pieces of fat bacon cooked with the cabbage. Reduce (boil down) the braising liquor, strain and pour over the goose.

Goose frittons or grattons. FRITTONS, GRATTONS D'OIE—This is a culinary name for the residue which remains in the pot after the melting of goose fat.

Minute fragments of flesh, which are trimmed off the

quarters of goose while preparing *confit d'oie*, are sometimes added to this residue.

The frittons are drained and pressed, to extract all the fat contained in them, then seasoned with salt and left to get cold.

Frittons are eaten as hors-d'oeuvre. They can be pressed into a block by moulding them in a bowl or some other receptacle.

Goose giblets and pinions. ABATIS, AILERONS D'OIE—Prepare as *Turkey giblets and pinions*. See GIBLETS.

Goose livers. FOIES D'OIE—Livers of geese which have not been fattened, that is of roasting geese, are prepared as for liver of all other poultry.

They can be cooked on skewers, sautéed with mushrooms, in Madeira, with truffles, pilaf, risotto, etc. They can be used as a garnish for eggs prepared in different ways or various entrée dishes.

They are also used for preparing *forcemeat à gratin**.

Foie gras, i.e. liver of fattened geese, can be prepared in innumerable ways, both hot and cold. See FOIE GRAS.

Goose pâté, cold. PÂTÉ FROID D'OIE—Using goose meat prepare like *Chicken pâté, cold**. See PÂTÉ, *cold pâtés*.

Goose pâté, hot. PÂTÉ CHAUD D'OIE—Prepare, using goose meat, like *Chicken pâté, hot*.

Goose ragoûts. RAGOÛTS D'OIE—Prepare using goose meat cut in uniform pieces.

These ragoûts can be garnished in various ways They can be made *à la bourgeoise*, *à la chipolata*, with celeriac with turnips, chestnuts, olives, etc. See RAGOÛT.

Goose ragoût à la bonne femme. RAGOÛT D'OIE À LA BONNE FEMME—Cut a medium sized goose into uniform pieces. Season them with salt and pepper and put into a sauté pan in which two good tablespoons of clarified butter (or goose fat) have been heated. Add a big onion and a carrot, cut into quarters. Brown the pieces of goose and the vegetables well.

When the pieces of goose are nicely coloured, sprinkle in 2 tablespoons of flour and fry this flour, stirring the ragoût on the fire. Add a small crushed clove of garlic, moisten with half a glass of white wine and add 2 cups (4 decilitres) of stock. Add a *bouquet garni**, cook for 40 minutes, keeping the pan uncovered.

Drain the goose on a sieve placed over a bowl. Trim the pieces of goose and put into the cleaned pan. Add ½ pound (250 grams) of small onions. lightly tossed in butter, ½ pound (250 grams) of lean bacon, cut into small square pieces, scalded and fried lightly, and 2 pounds (1 kilo) of potatoes, cut down to pieces of uniform size (or quartered), distributing these ingredients evenly over the goose. Skim off surplus fat from the sauce, add 2 tablespoons of *tomato purée** and pour it over the goose. Put on the stove for a moment, cover the pan and cook in a hot oven—without stirring—for 45 minutes.

Roast goose. OIE RÔTI—This method of cooking is suitable only for very young and tender geese, qualifying for the title of *goslings*.

The goose can be roasted in the oven or on a spit, and should be left a little underdone.

Roast goose à l'anglaise is stuffed with sage and onions. See *Goose à l'anglaise*.

In England, stuffed roast goose used to be served for the traditional Michaelmas night dinner.

Smoked breast of goose. POITRINE D'OIE FUMÉE—This preparation, which is made in Alsace and in Germany, can be found in shops ready for use.

Smoked breast of goose is eaten cold, like smoked ham; it is also used as an ingredient of *Cabbage potée* and as garnish for sauerkraut.

Stuffed goose necks. COUS D'OIE FARCIS—This dish, which makes an excellent hors-d'oeuvre (and is eaten as a sausage) is prepared in various regions of south-western France when *confit d'oie* is being made.

This is how it is made: Bone the necks, leaving a lot of the skin covering the breast attached to them.

Using the flesh taken off the bones, make a forcemeat, adding some minced pork, mixed, to give the composition more flavour, with a small quantity of goose liver and truffles, cut in small dice. Season this forcemeat and stuff the necks. Put the necks to cook in goose fat, then keep in earthenware jars as pieces of *confit d'oie*.

Note. Stuffed goose necks are generally served cold, as a hors-d'oeuvre, but they may also be served hot, as pieces of *confit d'oie*. They can be prepared in any way suitable for *confit d'oie*.

Goose terrine. TERRINE D'OIE—This is prepared, using slices or thin strips of goose meat and fine pork forcemeat, mixed with goose forcemeat, as *Turkey terrine*. See TERRINE.

Goose tongues. LANGUES D'OIE—In Béarn, the tongues of big geese, which are used for making *confit*, are prepared separately.

'The tongues,' says Simin Palay, 'cooked on a grill, are usually left to the children. It is merely a "pastime", as the pieces are not big. When I was a child I often lamented the fact that we never killed more than half a dozen at a time.' (*La Cuisine en Béarn*.)

Goose à la mode de Visé, also called à l'instar de Visé (Flemish cookery). OIE À LA MODE DE VISÉ, À L'INSTAR DE VISÉ—Cook a young goose, that *has not yet started laying*, in white stock spiced with two heads of garlic.

Drain, cut into pieces, put the pieces into a sauté pan, sprinkle with goose fat and simmer with a lid on until ready to serve.

Meanwhile prepare a *Velouté sauce* (see SAUCE), mixing flour with goose fat for the *roux** and using the liquor in which the goose was poached for diluting it. Keep on simmering this *velouté* for an hour; it should be rather thick. Make a liaison with 4 yolks of eggs as for *Chicken fricassée**. Strain the sauce, add to it a few tablespoons of cream and a good spoonful of *garlic purée** (using the garlic cooked with the goose).

Drain the pieces of goose dry and put into the sauce. Heat well and serve heaped on a dish.

GOOSEBERRY. GROSEILLE—A large berry, green in colour or streaked with red. In French the gooseberry is called *groseille à maquereau* because it is used in the preparation of a sauce which, traditionally, is served with mackerel.

In France, gooseberries are mainly grown in Normandy and other northern districts.

GORENFLOT CAKE—The name of a sweet made of *baba** dough baked in a hexagonal mould. This cake was first made at the Maison Bourbonneaux in the middle of the nineteenth century. It was called Gorenflot by its creator, in memory of the hero of Alexandre Dumas' play *La Dame de Monsoreau*.

GORGONZOLA—Italian cheese. See CHEESE.

GOUDALE—A *garbure** soup to which red or white wine is added. Simin Palay, in his *Cuisine en Béarn*, says that a *goudale* is the traditional conclusion to every *garbure*. The bread and vegetables of this broth having been eaten, the diner pours into his plate a generous cup of red or white wine, mixes it with the soup left at the bottom of the plate, and drinks it.

The *goudale* is considered in Béarn to be a sovereign remedy for illness, if a local proverb is to be believed:

'*Goudal plâ adoubado.*
'*Tiro un escut de la pocho deu médicin.*'

('A well-made *goudale* keeps a coin from the doctor's pocket'.)

GOUFFÉ (JULES)—One of the greatest chefs of the nineteenth century.

Born in Paris in 1807, he felt himself to have a talent for cookery from his early youth. His father, an established pastry-cook in the Saint-Merri quarter, taught him the basic principles of cookery. It was then that Carême, hearing of the talent of the young Gouffé—who at 17 was already showing promise in the decoration and presentation of set pieces—took him into his kitchens at the Austrian Embassy in Paris. Carême turned him into a model craftsman, a celebrity of his day.

In 1840, Jules Gouffé set up on his own in the Faubourg Saint-Honoré; his restaurant became one of the best in Paris.

In 1855 he retired, but went back to work in 1867, encouraged by those famous gourmets, Dumas the elder and Baron Brisse. This pair of epicures offered him the post of head chef at the Jockey Club. It was at this time that Gouffé began work on his *Livre de Cuisine*, a magnificent book which deserves a place in every library of cookery, side by side with Carême, Plumerey, Urbain Dubois, Emile Bernard, Escoffier, etc.

A few lines from the master's preface will suffice to show the importance of his work:

'Having, from my earliest youth, embarked upon a career of cookery, I saw much, observed much, practised much in every sense of the word. I am not one of those who declare that French cookery—that part of our national heritage of which we have reason to be proud—is lost today and that it will never recover. The good and true things never die. No doubt there may be periods of decline, but sooner or later, with hard work, intelligence and good will, there must be a recovery.

'If, thanks to the reforms and the methods which I propose, I find that in a few years' time everyone, whatever his rank in society, is eating as well as he possibly can; that, on the one hand, household cookery is at last being carried on with care, economy and comfort; and on the other hand, the *grande cuisine* goes forward under progressive conditions, with that good taste and brilliance which is so appropriate to a century of enlightenment and luxury like our own; then I shall have truly attained the goal which I have set myself . . . I shall feel myself well paid for all my pains.'

In 1872, Jules Gouffé published *Le Livre de Pâtisserie*, then *Le Livre des Conserves*.

In 1875 *Le Livre des Soupes et des Potages* was published. This was the crowning point of a whole life-time devoted to remarkable work in the field of cookery.

Gouffé died at Neuilly in 1877.

GOUGELHOF OR GOUGELHOPF—
See KUGELHUPF.

GOUGÈRE (Burgundian pastry)—This pastry, which is said to have originated at Sens, is made not only in Burgundy but also at Troyes and in Champagne, as well as other districts of France.

Here is the recipe:

The dough. Place in a thick, flat-bottomed saucepan 1 cup (2½ decilitres) of water, ½ cup (100 grams) of butter and 1 teaspoon (8 grams) of salt. As soon as the water is boiling, move the saucepan away from the flame and add 1½ cups (200 grams) of sieved flour. Mix, then dry the dough over a high flame, stirring it with a wooden spoon, like *chou paste** until it comes away easily from the sides of the saucepan.

Remove the pan from the stove and beat into the mixture 5 whole eggs, put in one by one, 1 cup (100 grams) of Gruyère cheese, finely diced, and a pinch of white pepper.

Making the cake. With a tablespoon, scoop out pieces of dough, each the size of an egg. Put them straight into a buttered pie-dish, one against the other in a circle. Smooth the circle on top and round the inside with the back of a spoon. Brush with beaten egg. Sprinkle with very finely diced cheese. Bake in a slow oven.

The more usual way to serve a *gougère* is cold, but it may also be served hot as hors-d'oeuvre.

GOUGNETTES (Lot cookery)—A *gougnette* is a type of doughnut. Prepare a dough from 3¾ cups (500 grams) of flour, 5 eggs, ⅓ cup (75 grams) of sugar and 1 package (10 grams) dried or compressed yeast. Leave it to rise for about an hour.

Roll out the dough with a rolling pin on a floured table. Shape flattened dough into small thin loaves.

Cut them into 2 inch pieces.

Fry the pieces in very hot fat. Drain the *gougnettes* when they are crisp and evenly browned. Sprinkle with sugar, and arrange in a pyramid on a napkin.

GOULASCH (Hungarian cookery)—Goulasch (sometimes called gulyas) is generally a kind of beef stew made with diced onions and seasoned with Hungarian paprika.

Several kinds of goulasch are made in Hungary, and recipes for them are given under BEEF.

Goulasch soup (Hungarian broth)—Dice coarsely ¾ pound (300 grams) of beef sirloin, trimmed and with all fat removed.

Brown this meat in butter in a casserole (U.S. soup kettle) with 2 tablespoons of finely chopped onions.

Season with salt and a large pinch of paprika. Add a little cummin and a small crushed clove of garlic.

When the meat is well browned all over, sprinkle a generous tablespoon (10 grams) of flour over it. Mix and let it cook for a minute or two, but without allowing it to brown.

Add 1½ quarts (litres) of plain clear soup. Bring it to the boil. Let it cook slowly for about 3 hours.

An hour before serving, add to the broth 2 diced potatoes. Serve with bread *croûtons** fried in butter.

GOURD. COURGE—Gourd is the name given to many species of the *Cucurbitaceae* family. *C. pepo* include the summer and autumn pumpkins (yellow gourds), the vegetable marrows, and various summer squashes. *C. maxima* include the North American winter squashes. *C. moschata* include the Canada or cushaw, Quaker or Japanese squashes (or pumpkin).

Gourds are one of the oldest vegetables known to man although it is doubtful if any of the many kinds which grow today could be identified with any of the original species. The word *gourd* is reserved in North America for the decorative inedible variety. Winter and summer squash as well as pumpkin are grown on a very large scale. Winter squash can often be used in place of pumpkin.

GOURILOS—See CHICORY.

The gourmand (*Collection of J.-J. T. de Lusse*)

GOURMAND, GOURMANDISM—Many people take the word *gourmandise* to be synonymous with *gluttony*.

Brillat-Savarin is sternly critical of this interpretation. 'Authorities who thus interpret *gourmandise* have completely forgotten social *gourmandise* which combines the elegance of Athens, the luxury of Rome and the delicacy of France. Such *gourmandise* orders with discernment, supervises with wisdom, savours with enthusiasm, judges with profundity. It is a precious attribute which may well be esteemed a virtue, for it is the source of our purest delights.

'*Gourmandise* . . . is a passionate, rational and habitual preference for all that flatters the palate.

'*Gourmandise* is the enemy of excess; every man who gives himself indigestion or gets drunk, runs the risk of no longer being a true gourmand.

'Daintiness (*friandise*) is an essential part of *gourmandise*, for daintiness is the same kind of discrimination applied to light, delicate tit-bits such as preserves, pastries and sweets . . . '

From the social point of view, the advantages of gourmandism are innumerable. 'It is *gourmandise*,' continues Brillat-Savarin, 'which stimulates the transport from pole to pole of wines, spirits, sugar, spices, pickles, savouries, indeed provisions of every kind, down to eggs and melons.

'It is this which affords a livelihood to the industrious multitude of cooks, confectioners, pastrycooks and other diversely named purveyors of food, who, in their turn, rely for the satisfaction of their needs on workers of all kinds. This gives rise, always and everywhere, to a wealth of economic activity, of which even the most lively mind cannot calculate the extent nor assess the value.

'*Gourmandise*,' adds Brillat-Savarin, 'is a great source of fiscal revenue. It contributes towards city tolls, customs dues, indirect taxation. Dues are paid on everything we eat. There is no public treasury which the *gourmand* does not support.

'*Gourmandise* is one of the greatest benefits of society. It is responsible for the gradual spread of that spirit of conviviality which every day brings together people of different social levels, welds them into a single whole, enlivens conversation and rubs off the corners of conventional social inequality . . . When it is shared, it has the most important influence imaginable on the happiness of a marriage.

'The husband and wife are called to the table by the shared need. They remain there to gratify it. In the course of the meal each shows to the other those little marks of consideration which spring from the desire to please. The agreeable atmosphere of a shared meal contributes much to a happy life.'

Joining issue with the Church, which puts *gourmandise* among the seven deadly sins, Brillat-Savarin says: 'If nations were capable of gratitude, the French should have erected a temple and altars to *gourmandise*.' (*Physiologie du Goût*.)

GOURMET—Formerly, the word *gourmet* was never used in the inexact sense which is current nowadays.

The *gourmet*, whose full title was '*courtier-gourmet-piquer*', was not a *gourmand*, in other words a connoisseur of good things, but rather a sworn official, charged with the duty of tasting wines and spirits. Taster-grooms were once part of a confraternity. Nowadays they are organised into syndicates.

GRAHAM BREAD—A kind of wholemeal bread made from a mixture of different cereal flours. This bread was invented in 1840 by an American, Silvester Graham.

GRAIN—A small weight used in former times. It weighed approximately a twentieth of a gram.

GRAMOLATES OR GRAMOLATAS—A kind of sherbet made from a *granité** mixture. See ICE CREAMS AND ICES.

GRAND-MAÎTRE—Under the old French monarchy, the *grand-maître*, who was also called *souverain maître de l'hôtel du roi* (supreme major-domo to the Sovereign) was chief of all the officers of the royal kitchens.

GRAND VENEUR—A brown sauce, served only with ground game and venison. See SAUCES, *Brown sauces*.

GRANITÉS—A type of sherbet. No Italian meringue is added to this mixture, as is done with ordinary sherbet mixture. (See ICE CREAMS AND ICES.)

GRAPE. RAISIN—Fruit of the vine.

The stem of the grape bunch, more or less ligneous according to the species, contains a little free acid and tannin.

The seeds contain a tannin, a resinous substance, an essential oil and volatile acids which come into play later in the development of the bouquet.

The pulp is held in place by very thin membraneous cell walls (hardly ½% of the weight of the fruit) so thin that the weight of the juice is just about equal to that of the pulp; it consists mainly of sugar in proportions which vary according to the type of plant and the year, sometimes rising as high as 23½% of sugar in weight, that is, 260 grams per litre of must, corresponding to 15% of alcohol in volume; in a good year most choice types give comparable figures; the aramon (a Mediterranean vine plant) gives only 14%.

Dessert grapes. RAISINS DE TABLE—These are the best French varieties of dessert grapes:

Black Alicante: Ripe at the end of October. Very large bunches with elliptical fruit of dark purplish-black colour. Very good fruit.

Golden Chasselas of Fontainebleu: Ripe in the second fortnight of September. Large bunches with round fruit, large, pearly white colour. Very good fruit.

Napoleon or Bicane Chasselas: Ripe in the second fortnight of October. Bunch shaped like an elongated cone. Large fruit, a little marked with yellow. Very good fruit.

Rose Chasselas: Ripe in the second fortnight of September. Fairly large bunches with large round fruit, rosy pink in colour. Exquisite fruit.

Vibert Chasselas: Ripe in the first fortnight of September. Large bunches. Large round fruit, rather close set, amber-white in colour. Very good fruit.

Frankenthal: Ripe in the second fortnight of October. Enormous bunch with fruit a little ovoid in shape Very large, blue-black in colour. Very good fruit (hot house).

Gamay: Ripe at the end of July and August. The bunches of this species are quite large. The grapes are round, medium-sized and black in colour. Good fruit.

Long Black Spanish: Ripe in the first fortnight of October. Long bunches with quite large grapes, a little elongated, dark black in colour. Quite good. Used mainly for decorating baskets of fruit.

Royal Madeleine: Ripe in the second fortnight of August. Quite large bunches; grapes round, medium sized, pearly white in colour. Very good fruit.

White Muscat: Ripe in October. Large, rather compact bunch. Fruit round and white in colour. Very good fruit with rather musky flavour.

For the varieties of grapes used to make wine see WINE.

Keeping grapes—The system used at Thomery, for the Chasselas grape, consists of cutting off the bunch, with a piece of the main stem attached, before it is quite ripe, and soaking the thick stem in a bottle half filled with water.

Dried grapes. RAISINS SECS—Gathered when perfectly ripe and generally dried in the sun. The principal commercial types in France are:

Raisins coming mainly from the Midi, gathered very ripe, plunged into a wash of boiling water and ash, then dried in the sun on their stalks.

Sultanas, large fruit, practically seedless and with a muscat flavour.

Currants, coming mainly from the Greek islands, small, seedless, washed with ash and stripped from their stalks.

Dried grapes are used in cookery, pastry-making and confectionery. They can still be used to make wine after being soaked.

Grape jelly. CONFITURE DE RAISINS—Like *Currant jelly II*, using ½ pound (250 grams) of sugar to 1 pound (500 grams) of grape juice. See JAMS AND JELLIES.

GRAPEFRUIT. PAMPLEMOUSSE—Citrus fruit the size of a very big orange or larger, pale yellow in colour. The Chinese are in the habit of eating this fruit at the beginning of a meal as an aperitif and this custom was copied by the Americans when they acclimatised the fruit in their country.

It is served prepared in the following manner:

Cut the fruit in two horizontally with a very sharp knife (a special knife is used for this purpose), make a circular incision around the white substance found in the middle of the fruit and remove this substance. Slide the knife into each section of the fruit to loosen the pulp from the skin surrounding it. Sprinkle with fine sugar.

Note. Grapefruit prepared in this way is eaten with a spoon.

It can be flavoured with liqueur and served on ice.

GRAPPA—Piedmontese marc-brandy in which a sprig of rue is infused.

GRASS SNAKE. COULEUVRE—Non-poisonous snake. The common grass snake is sometimes eaten in France under the name of *anguille des haies* (hedge eel). Prepared in the same way as *Eel**.

GRASSHOPPER. SAUTERELLE—Orthopterous, herbiverous insect, often constituting a positive plague to agriculture. Grasshoppers are greatly relished by African natives who eat them in the most diverse forms, boiled, roasted, grilled, salted, dried and reduced to a paste. Moses permitted the Hebrews to eat four different species, described in Leviticus.

GRATER. RÂPE—Utensil with rough surface, pierced with holes, used to reduce to a coarse powder certain vegetables, fruits or other commodities (cheese, nutmeg, almonds, etc.).

GRATERON—A common French term for rennet.

GRATIN—The term *gratin* means the thin crust formed on the surface of certain dishes when they are browned in the oven or under the grill.

It is extended to denote a certain method of preparation. Thus we speak of *Macaroni au gratin*, *Sole au gratin*. See CULINARY METHODS.

Gratin languedocien—Half cook in oil, in a frying pan, 4 egg-plants (aubergines), peeled and cut into slices of equal thickness and seasoned with salt and pepper. Cook in oil, also, 12 halves of tomato seasoned with salt and pepper.

When both the egg-plants and tomatoes are ready, arrange them in alternate layers in a baking dish.

Cover the whole with a mixture of breadcrumbs and chopped garlic and parsley. Sprinkle with olive oil. Bring the dish to the boil on the stove, and then bake slowly in the oven until the top is well browned.

GRATTONS OR GRATTERONS—These names are given in certain regions of France, especially in the south-west, to the residue of the melted fat of pork, goose or turkey. This residue, also sometimes called *frittons*, is salted while it is still hot and eaten cold as an hors-d'oeuvre.

Grattons must not be confused with *rillettes* which are prepared by pounding in a mortar a mixture of fat and lean pork, which has been cooked slowly beforehand.

Grattons (speciality of the Île Bourbon). GRATTONS À L'ÎLE DE LA RÉUNION (ÎLE BOURBON) are prepared as follows:

Take the skin of a young pig (it is best to take it from the back), leaving on it ¾ inch of fat. Cut it into pieces 3¼ inches square. Score the fat without reaching the skin with criss-cross lines, making little squares about 3 inches across. Put the pieces of skin in a pan with some melted fat. Leave them to cook very slowly for at least 3 to 4 hours. When the skin is tender and transparent, raise the heat and cook for a further half hour to three quarters of an hour, until the pieces of skin bubble up and become crisp. They should swell up like fritters. Remove them from the pan with a perforated spoon or skimmer and put them in a dish. Sprinkle with table salt. This dish should always be cooked uncovered.

GRAVENCHE—A fish of the salmon family which is found mainly in Lake Geneva. This fish closely resembles the *féra* with which it is often confused. It can be distinguished from the *féra*, however, by the more definite curve of its back and the lighter colouring of its scales.

The *gravenche* is usually much smaller than the *féra*. Its flesh is fairly firm and delicate but has much less flavour than that of the *féra*.

All recipes suitable for *féra* and river trout may be used for *gravenche*. See FÉRA and TROUT.

GRAVES—See BORDEAUX, *Wines of Bordeaux*.

Grayling

GRAYLING. OMBRE COMMUN—Rather rare fresh-water fish resembling trout, from which it differs by its bigger and more brilliant scales, smaller snout, an enormous dorsal fin of bluish-grey colour and the absence of orbitosphonoid. Its sides are silvery, sometimes tinged with pink or purple and flecked with dark spots.

The flesh is very delicate and has a slight flavour of thyme. It is prepared like TROUT.

GRECQUE (A LA)—Strictly speaking, dishes *à la grecque* should be of Greek origin in their method of preparation. In practice this is seldom the case. Though it sometimes happens that a dish called '*à la grecque*' on a restaurant menu really is of Greek origin, more often than not the name is given to dishes of French origin.

Among the dishes called '*à la grecque*' are *Artichokes à la grecque** and other vegetables prepared in the same way.

GREENGAGE. REINE-CLAUDE—Plum whose skin is a yellowish green, lightly tinted with red on the side of the fruit exposed to the sun. See PLUM.

GREENHOUSE, HOTHOUSE. SERRE—Building made of glass where plants are raised in artificial heat. The products (vegetable or fruit) of cultivation under glass always have less flavour than plants cultivated in the open air.

GRENACHE WINE—The word *Grenache* comes from the Italian *granaccio* which means large grains, and refers to a grape used in the preparation of a cooked wine. This grape grows scarcely anywhere but in the South of France.

Grenache wines are very sweet and intoxicating. Both white and red wines are made from this grape, but especially red wines.

The best known are those of the East Pyrenees (Banyuls, Port-Vendres, Collioure, Rivesaltes).

GRENADIER—A fish, called *Grenadier* in France because of the shape of its head which is reminiscent of a French Grenadier's cap. It is never more than 16 inches long, and its white flesh is quite delicate. It is served poached with half-melted *Maître d'hôtel butter* (see BUTTER, *Compound butters*); boiled (hot or cold) with various sauces; *à la boulangère*, with sliced potatoes and onion rings. (See COD.)

GRENADINS—Strictly, grenadins are little slices of fillet (sirloin) of veal cut in the shape of triangles or rectangles which are interlarded with best larding bacon and braised.

Braised veal grenadins. GRENADINS DE VEAU BRAISÉS—Using fillet (sirloin) or under-fillet (top of the leg) of veal, cut narrow, rather thick escalopes, each one weighing about 3½ ounces.

Flatten them gently. Trim them and stud them with thin strips of larding bacon or salt pork.

Brown in butter fresh crackling (or bacon rind), a medium-sized onion, a carrot cut into thin slices and the trimmings of the veal. Lay the *grenadins* very flat in the pan and brown them lightly.

Cover and cook gently on a low flame for 15 minutes.

Moisten with ⅝ cup of white wine; boil down the stock almost completely. Add a little water to this thick stock. Bring to the boil. Cover and bake in a slow oven for about 45 minutes, basting from time to time.

Drain the *grenadins*. Lay them on a dish. Strain the stock, and pour a few tablespoons over the *grenadins*. Brown them in the oven, basting frequently.

Dilute the cooking stock in the pan with clear veal stock or *consommé**. Scrape the sides of the pan and stir the fragments into the gravy.

Strain this gravy through a fine sieve. Remove fat. Boil down if necessary. Pour over the *grenadins*.

Note. Serve braised veal grenadins with all the garnishes suitable for veal chops, escalopes, fillet of veal or *fricandeaux**. *Grenadins* are, in fact, small *fricandeaux*.

Among the garnishes best suited to this dish are the following: *bouquetière; bourgeoise**; glazed carrots; braised celery; braised endive; chicory; spinach; *fermière**; *jardinière**, braised lettuce; *macédoine; nivernaise**, green peas; *printanière**; purée of fresh or dried vegetables; quartered artichokes or artichoke hearts. See GARNISHES.

Poultry grenadins. GRENADINS DE VOLAILLE—The term *grenadin* is extended to include collops of white meat of large poultry, especially turkey. This dish is prepared in the same way as veal *grenadins*.

GRÉSILLER—This means, in French cookery, to shrink or shrivel by heating. The real meaning of the word *grésiller* is to patter. It is applied also to foodstuffs which in cooking make a pattering sound like falling hail.

GRESSIN—See BREAD, *Diet bread*.

GRIBICHE—A cold sauce served in particular with cold fish. It is an oily sauce made of the yolks of hard boiled eggs, oil and vinegar, seasoned with mustard. To this mixture are added capers and chopped gherkins, chopped parsley, chervil and tarragon, and whites of hard boiled eggs cut into short match sticks. See SAUCE, *Cold sauces*.

GRIDIRON, GRILL. GRIL—This kitchen implement has a very long history. It is a contemporary of the spit. The cooking of meat on a spit is far older than the preparation of foodstuffs in earthenware or bronze containers.

The metal gridiron was certainly one of the first implements used by our remote ancestors for cooking meat.

GRIGNON—A piece of dry bread, baked very hard, which can be nibbled (*grignoté*). The name *grignon* is also given to the end crust of a long or round loaf. It is also called *quignon*.

GRILL-ROOM—A restaurant where, as its name implies, only grilled meats are served. This type of restaurant was started in England, but there are a great many of them in Paris, and some of the large French provincial towns, and they are common in U.S.A.

In most of these grill-rooms there is a bar where drinks, cocktails especially, are served.

GRILLARDIN—This is the name given by the French to the chef who, in large restaurants, is concerned entirely with the grilling or broiling of various types of food.

GRILLETTES—This was the name given in former times to thin slices of fresh pork fried in butter or fat.

GRILLING, BOILING. GRILLADE—A method of cooking food by putting it on a gridiron over embers, or, in modern stoves, under a broiler (grill), more or less hot as required.

In former times, grilling was always accomplished on an open wood or charcoal fire. Nowadays, foods may be grilled by gas or electricity, and, thanks to the scientific development of this type of apparatus, the art of grilling or broiling has reached perfection.

GRILSE. SAUMONEAU—Name for a young salmon that has been only once to sea. Before it goes to sea the salmon is called a parn.

All the methods of preparation given for large salmon are applicable to the young fish.

Grimod de la Reynière (1758–1838)

GRIMOD DE LA REYNIÈRE—A famous gastronome, born in Paris in 1758, died in 1838. His father, who was Farmer General, was himself the son of a pork butcher.

Grimod de la Reynière, barrister-at-law, did not devote much time to his profession. He preferred sessions at the table to sessions in the Palace of Justice. The first edition of his *Manuel des Amphitryons* came out in 1808, and the series *Almanacs des Gourmands* were published between 1803 and 1812.

These books are rather scarce today. They are oddities in several respects, but they can hardly be regarded as interesting from the strictly culinary point of view.

'Grimod de la Reynière,' says Carême, 'was familiar with the *ancien régime*, and lived through the horrors of the Revolution. After the reign of terror, he considered it both necessary and wise to write his *Manuel des Amphitryons*, so as to instruct the new rich in the conventions and properties which they must observe.

'His *Almanac des Gourmands* is full of flashes of gastronomy and wit. Doubtless, he had some good influence on the science of cookery, but he played no part in the rapid progress which modern cookery has made since the renaissance of the art.'

Grimod de la Reynière was able to consecrate his authority in the eyes of his contemporaries, by setting up his 'jury of tasters', who used to award to this or that dish a kind of academic certificate called '*légitimation*.'

This jury of tasters met at fixed intervals at the home of the celebrated gastronome who lived in the Champs-Elysées. There, in solemn fashion, they tasted the dishes sent to Grimod de la Reynière by tradesmen who sought publicity, by making known to their ordinary customers (who paid spot cash for their food) the judgment, always favourable, pronounced by this gastronomic Areopagus.

The jury of tasters, however, soon had to give up its sittings—because some of its judgments aroused protest. Grimod de la Reynière was even accused of interested partiality!

GRIND. ÉGRUGER—To reduce to powder. This term is used especially of sea salt, ground in a mortar or mill.

GRISETTE. COUCOUMELLE—Edible mushroom, a sub-species of Amanita which has no ring. See MUSHROOMS.

GRISSINI—Long sticks of hard baked bread varying in length from 10–30 inches.

Grissini are of Italian origin. They can be bought at large bakeries.

GROG—A drink containing rum or some other spirit, lemon, sugar and hot water.

GROS-BLANQUET—A variety of pear with a greenish-yellow skin. It is quite sweet, but rather gritty in texture.

GROUSE. TÉTRAS—A game bird of the order *Galliformes*, of which there are several varieties.

The largest bird of this family is the *Capercaillie*, a superb creature, the largest game bird, with very delicate flesh.

Quite common in countries of Northern Europe, it is only rarely found in France. It is prepared like pheasant or ordinary grouse.

The *Black grouse*, a bird about the size of the pheasant and cooked in the same way, the French *Gelinotte* (hazel grouse or hen), the English *Red grouse* or *Scotch grouse*, and the *Ganga* or pin-tailed grouse which is found in the South of France and Algeria, all belong to the same family. The latter bird, whose flesh is extremely delicate, is the size of a good partridge. It is usually spit-roasted but may be prepared in any way suitable for the *Gelinotte*.

This bird should not be confused with the bird from the same region called *Ganga-cata*, or *Gelinotte des Pyrenées*, which is equally good to eat, but smaller in size.

All these birds have very good flesh, but they have a pronounced pine flavour, the leg meat in particular; so normally the legs are not served.

In North America there are many species including *Ruffed grouse* (Partridge), *Blue grouse*, *Sage grouse*, *Sharp-tailed grouse* and *Prairie chicken*.

This game is much prized in England and in U.S.A. It is scarcer in France, where it is known as *gelinotte* (*Hazel grouse* or *Hazel hen*), a bird of much poorer quality than the British or American grouse.

Young grouse is best roasted but may be cooked in the same way as *Hazel grouse**.

Marinated grouse (Roman cookery). TÉTRAS MARINÉ—'Make a good marinade using white wine. After having cleaned out your bird (and usually the skin is removed also), marinate it for three or four days.

'Dress it in bacon fat (that is to say, bard it). Braise it, adding a good *mirepoix** of vegetables lightly cooked in butter, a *bouquet garni*, veal stock and the marinade.

'Allow to cool in its cooking liquid; remove all grease

from this to clarify it, then reduce (boil it down) to the point where it can be moulded into a border. In the middle of this border, turned out of its mould on to the serving dish, put the sliced meat of the grouse.

'Serve separately on a napkin slices of buttered toast.' (Recipe of B. Farrep.)

GROUX OR GROUS—A Breton name for a thick gruel made from buckwheat flour.

GRUYÈRE—A valley in the Swiss canton of Fribourg after which Gruyère cheese is named. See CHEESE.

GUAVA. GOYAVE—The fruit of the guava-tree, a bush which grows in the tropical regions of America and Asia.

There are several species of guava, some are pear-shaped, others orange-shaped. There is one type which is shaped like a fig.

The pulp of the guava is somewhat insipid. It is usually eaten raw, but can be stewed or made into jam, jelly or paste.

GUDGEON. GOUJON—The gudgeon is a small fish which is to be found on the sandy bottom of all the lakes and rivers of Europe. Gudgeon live in shoals. There are various kinds.

The parent species, the *Common gudgeon*, is the one found in large numbers in the rivers of France.

Another kind is found particularly in the Somme and yet another in the Danube. One species, *Gremille*, is found in almost all French rivers, especially the Seine and the Moselle, and is called in French, *Goujonnière* or *Perche goujonnière*. See POPE.

The flesh of the gudgeon is very delicate. This fish is usually eaten fried, like the smelt.

Gudgeon en manchon. GOUJON EN MANCHON—Coat the bodies of the gudgeon only with egg and breadcrumbs, leaving the heads and tails uncoated; deep fry. These are used as a garnish for braised fish. Other small fish can be sprinkled with breadcrumbs in this way before frying.

GUIGNETTE—A name given in some parts of France to the *sand piper*, a bird of the snipe family.

All recipes for snipe are suitable for this bird. See SNIPE.

In some parts of France the name *guignette* is applied to a mollusc, the *littorine*, found in French coastal waters.

Guinea fowl

GUINEA-FOWL. PINTADE, PINTADEAU—A genus of bird of the *Gallinaceae* family which includes several species. The bird is a native of Africa and was known to the Romans, who called it *Numidian hen* or *Carthaginian* (*Carthage*) *hen*. The flesh of young guinea-fowl is delicate and recalls that of pheasant.

The guinea-fowl often figures on the menus of banquets and wedding receptions as *Bohemian pheasant*, a name which, it must in truth be said, is somewhat exaggerated.

Guinea-poults, which are found on the market in France towards the end of July, are excellent. They can be prepared in any way suitable for pheasant or partridges.

Fully grown guinea-fowls are prepared—hot or cold—in any way suitable for chicken.

Guinea-fowl liver. FOIE DE PINTADES—All recipes for chicken livers are suitable for guinea-fowl livers. These are also used as an ingredient in stuffings.

GUINEA PIG. COCHON D'INDE—Domestic rodent of South American origin. Its flesh is edible, but it is chiefly used for laboratory experiments.

GUINGUETTE—Guinguette is the name given to a French suburban place of refreshment with music and dancing. Some etymologists believe that this name derives from *guinguet*, a type of grape cultivated in the Paris suburbs. A rather sour wine was made from these grapes and this was mainly drunk in taverns on the outskirts of Paris.

GULL. MOUETTE—A seabird whose flesh is leathery with an unpleasant taste, but whose eggs are edible.

GULYAS—See GOULASCH.

GUM. GOMME—This term is applied to any of a number of very diverse substances which flow either naturally or by inducement from the stems of certain plants. When mixed with water these substances have adhesive properties. The stems of the plants exude gum when they are punctured by insects or when incisions are made in them.

One of these gums, *gum tragacanth*, is used in cookery. It is also used in the preparation of medicinal pastes and in the manufacture of syrup gum.

It is said that some resinous gums were used as condiments by the Romans.

Gum arabic. ARABIQUE (GOMME)—Gum arabic is the product of secretion of various species of acacia trees.

It is found in the form of yellowish or reddish fragments, soluble in water, contact with which gives them a viscous consistency. This property renders it useful in pharmaceutics and in cookery, for the preparation of mucilages.

Gum arabic is the basis of jujube, marshmallow and liquorice paste. Its contribution to the art of cookery and confectionery is extremely important.

Syrup gum. SIROP DE GOMME—Crush 1 pound (500 grams) of gum arabic. Put it to soak for 24 hours in a pint ($\frac{1}{2}$ litre) of cold water. Add this solution of gum to a syrup made with 4 pounds (2 kilos) of sugar, 1 quart (litre) of water boiled to 220°F. Boil the mixture. Skim it. Filter it when quite cool and store in bottles.

GURNEAU—French name for a species of gurnet. It is found in the Mediterranean, in British coastal waters and in the Baltic.

All recipes for gurnet are suitable for this fish (see GURNET).

GURNET. GRONDIN—This European fish, which is of the trigla family, is often sold in France as *red mullet*, but erroneously, since though quite delicate in flavour, this fish cannot be compared with the true red mullet.

Guinea-fowl à la languedocienne (*Robert Carrier*)

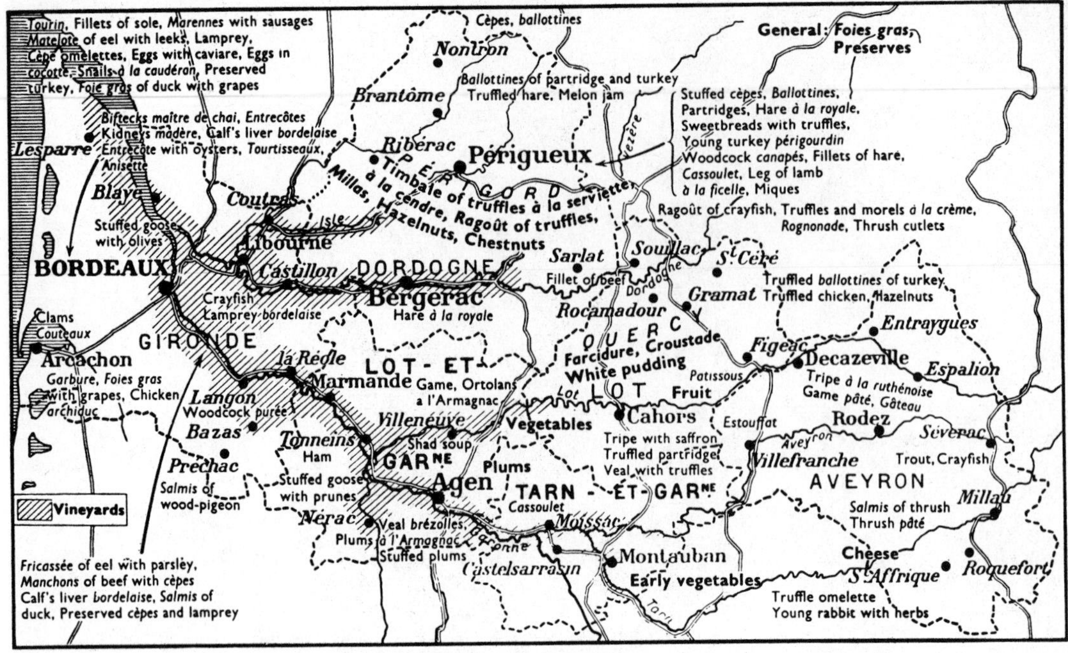

Gastronomic map of Guyenne

The gurnet is callet '*grondin*' (grunter) in French because of the grunting sound it is said to make when it comes out of the water. It is quite different in shape from the true red mullet. It is only in colour that certain species of trigla can be compared with the mullet.

There are various types of gurnet. Among those to be found in France are the *Red gurnet*, whose scales are a beautiful clear red or rose colour; the *Cuckoo gurnet*, red in colour; the *Trigle lyre*, whose back is a beautiful clear red with silvery and rose-coloured belly and sides; the *Grey gurnet*, grey with whitish spots on back and flanks; the *Shining gurnet*, also called the *Long-finned gurnet*, which is the largest of the species (it can be as much as 24 inches in length) coloured yellowish-pink along the back, pinkish white on the belly. The shining gurnet, when its fins are outspread, has the appearance of a butterfly, with delicately tinted 'wings' ranging from blue to deep purple.

Gurnet is quite good to eat. Its flesh is white and flaky.

All recipes for *Red mullet* (see MULLET) are suitable for gurnet. Gurnets can be fried, grilled or cooked in butter *à la meunière**. They can be stewed or cooked in white wine and they are used in *bouillabaisse**.

GUYENNE—This vast province has been divided into the Departments of the Gironde, Dordogne, Lot, Aveyron, Lot-et-Garonne and Tarn-et-Garonne.

As in the case of Gascony, which is discussed elsewhere, the *cuisine* of this region is dominated by two flavours; truffles of Périgord and Lot and garlic, which is used liberally in most of the local dishes.

In the forefront of local products in this region is the celebrated Roquefort cheese, which enjoys a world-wide reputation.

Next among the good things to eat must be mentioned the truffles of Périgord and Lot, the geese and duck livers which, in this epicurean district, are potted or made into pâtés, the *confit d'oie* of Montauban, the lamb of Pauillac and all the succulent partridge, woodcock and thrush pâtés made almost everywhere in the region, but especially in the little town of Limogne, which deserves its fame as a centre of delicious cooking.

Among the special local dishes of Guyenne those deserving of special mention are:

Estouffat of haricot beans; Lampreys à la bordelaise*; Tripe with saffron; Tripe à la Ruthénoise; Leg of lamb à la ficelle; White pudding quercinois; Stuffed chicken; Potted truffles; Cèpes à la bordelaise; Millas* girondin; Agen prunes; Hearth-cake**.

This region is also famous for its wines. These are discussed at length in the section entitled BORDEAUX.

The magnificent broths and pots-au-feu of this district include the *Garbure Gasconne* and, no less delectable, the *Chandeau* and the *Tomato tourin.*

Most famous of the fish dishes of Guyenne are *Matelotes of lampreys and eels* and *Trout à la meunière**.

Exclusive to this region are: *Oyster sausages; Bunting en caisses; Old fashioned galimaufry; Foie-gras with grapes; Jugged mountain hare; Tripe à la landaise; Leg of lamb à la gasconnade; Stuffed chicken*—which the good French King Henry IV wished that all his subjects could eat on Sundays!—*Alicuit of goose or chicken; Stuffed goose hearts; Roast wood-pigeon; Woodcock salmi* and finally, the dish extolled by Marcel Prévost the *Christmas estouffat.*

Among the sweets of the district are: *Tourtisseaux; Cruchade gasconne* and *Lou pasti.*

Lastly, the *feuillantines* of Gers and the *Gâteau à la broche* must not be forgotten.

We must not end this list without a brief reference to the excellent red and white wines of the district, notably those of Portet, Chalosse, Pouillon, etc., and above all to the *eau de vie* of Armagnac.

GYMNÈTRE—A species of fish which tastes rather like fresh cod.

The *gymnètre faux*, which is found in the Mediterranean is about 18 inches long, very flat, silver in colour with red fins. All recipes for cod are suitable for this fish. See COD.

HADDOCK. ÉGLEFIN—A sea-fish of the cod family, but smaller than the true cod. This fish is also known in France as *aiglefin*, *égrefin*, *morue noire* (black cod), *morue Saint-Pierre* and in Newfoundland as *âne* or *ânon*.

In England this fish is split, opened out and smoked. Fresh haddock is white and delicate. All recipes for cod are suitable for fresh haddock. See COD.

Smoked haddock

Smoked haddock is very popular in England and the U.S.A., and of recent years it has also become popular in France. As soon as it is caught, the fish is split lengthwise, lightly rubbed over with salt, hung by the tail and left to smoke for 24 hours. Smoked haddock keeps fresh for several days.

Cod and haddock, when they are fresh, lend themselves to a great number of culinary treatments and suitable recipes will be found under BASS, BRILL, EEL, WHITING, TUNNY-FISH, TURBOT.

Baked haddock

Baked haddock à l'irlandaise. AIGREFIN AU FOUR À L'IRLANDAISE—Stuff a haddock with suet stuffing. Truss it in an S-shape. Make slight incisions on the sides. Put in a buttered baking pan. Season with salt and pepper. Moisten with ⅝ cup (1½ decilitres) of Madeira. Cover with a buttered paper.

Bake in the oven basting frequently. Untie the fish, arrange on a very hot dish and sprinkle with the pan juices.

Serve *Oyster* or *Shrimp sauce* separately. See SAUCE.

Curried haddock. HADDOCK À L'INDIENNE—Bone, skin and dice the fish. Cook chopped onion in butter in a pan Add the haddock. Cook for 5 minutes. Add a fairly thin *Curry sauce* (see SAUCE). Cover and simmer for 10 minutes. Pour into a deep dish. Serve *Rice à l'indienne** separately.

Grilled haddock. HADDOCK GRILLÉ—Brush the fish with oil or melted butter. Cook it slowly under the grill.

Serve with melted butter and boiled potatoes or with *Maître d'hôtel butter* (see BUTTER, *Compound butters*).

Haddock with paprika. HADDOCK AU PAPRIKA—Proceed as for *Curried haddock*, substituting paprika sauce (*Hungarian sauce*) for curry. See SAUCE.

Poached haddock. HADDOCK POCHÉ—Put the fish in slightly salted boiling water. Simmer *without bringing to the boil* for 6 to 10 minutes according to the size of the haddock.

Serve with melted butter and boiled potatoes.

Note. Haddock can also be poached in milk.

HAGGIS (Scottish Cookery)—Haggis may be regarded as the national dish of Scotland. It is in that part of the United Kingdom only that this somewhat unusual dish is fully appreciated.

Robert Burns wrote a poem 'To a Haggis' which is very popular in the Highlands. When this dish is served at certain large banquets in Scotland, it is accompanied by an escort of pipers.

Here is the recipe for this robust dish given by Alfred Suzanne in his book *La Cuisine anglaise.*

'To make a haggis, take a sheep's stomach, clean thoroughly and turn inside out.

'Take the heart, liver and lungs of a sheep. Boil all these for half an hour in salt water. Take out the offal and mince very finely, except for part of the liver which must be allowed to get quite cold so that it can be grated.

'Spread the mince on a table and season with salt, pepper, nutmeg, cayenne pepper and chopped onion.

'Add the grated liver, a handful of oatmeal and a pound of chopped beef suet. Now fill the stomach with the mince, a little more than half full, leaving plenty of space at the top to prevent it from bursting during cooking.

Add a glassful of good gravy. Prick the haggis here and there with a large needle and sew up the opening. Place in a large pan with plenty of water and boil for 3 hours.

'It sometimes happens that the bladder bursts during cooking and spills out its contents. To avoid this, wrap the haggis in a napkin, as though it were a galantine, before putting it into boiling water.'

Haggis is normally served wrapped in a well starched napkin and whisky is the traditional drink which goes with it.

HAKE—A seafish called *merlan* (whiting) in Provence, *colin* (cod) in Paris and *saumon blanc* (white salmon) on some French menus. Its flesh is tender, white, flaky and easy to digest. When dried, it is called *merluche* (stockfish).

All recipes for cod are suitable for hake. See COD.

HALBRAN. ALBRAN—Name given to very young wild duck. When a little older it is called duckling, then duck. It is cooked like *duck**.

HALCYON (Kingfisher). ALCYON—The name of this bird comes from the Greek *alkuon* (formed of *als*, the sea, and *kuon*, one who nurses its young). According to a Greek legend the halcyon built its nest on the waves of the sea. Halcyone, or Alcyone, was the wife of Ceyx, who perished in a shipwreck. When Halcyone found his body on the shore, she threw herself into the sea. Halcyone and Ceyx were changed into the birds that bear her name, which are fabled to keep the waters calm while they are nesting. Hence the expression 'Halcyon days'.

This bird, remarkable for its brilliant blue plumage, with varying shades of red on the breast, is the Australian version of our kingfisher, or laughing jackass. From Australia the species has spread to Cochin-China, China and Japan.

The halcyons built their nests with the aid of a gelatinous substance secreted during laying period by their crops. These nests are much esteemed by the Chinese, who are very fond of them. In their dried state they are imported into Europe and are greatly prized at the best tables, where they are known as *birds' nests*.

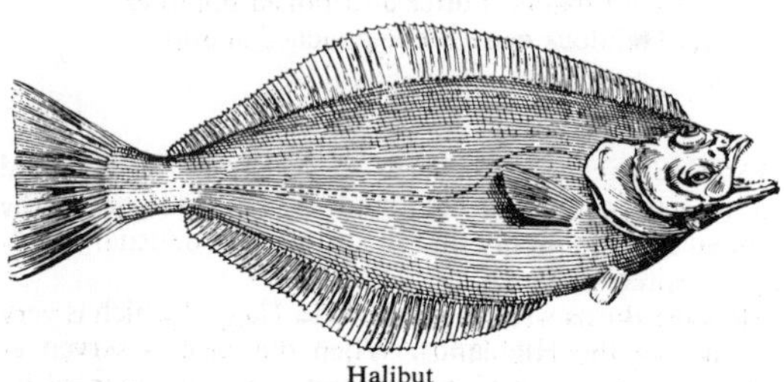

Halibut

HALIBUT. FLÉTAN—A large flat fish found in northern waters. The body is more elongated in shape than other flat fish, the eyes are on the right side and the mouth is large. A halibut can be as much as ten feet long and weighs between 300 and 400 pounds (150 and 200 kilos).

The firm white flesh of halibut is greatly valued as food, and all recipes given under BRILL may be used for this fish.

HAM. JAMBON—Strictly, a ham is a leg of pork, salted and smoked. In current usage, however, the term is also applied to the shoulder of pig which is cured in the same fashion. This cut, though excellent, is nevertheless a good deal less delicate than the leg.

In French cookery the term *jambon* not only means 'ham' but is also applied to a leg of fresh pork. This cut can be cooked in a great many ways either whole or divided into smaller cuts. It is also used as an ingredient of stuffing and in various manufactured pork products. See PORK.

So great has been, and still is today, the role of ham and all forms of salt pork in the history of food, that a special Ham Fair is held regularly in Paris and some other large French cities.

The Ham Fair which, in former times, was held during the three days preceding Good Friday, and which was then called *Foire du lard* (the Bacon Fair), was held in the square in front of Notre-Dame. The canons used to lease the ground to the butchers and pork-butchers. The site was changed several times. In 1813, the fair was transferred to the Quai des Grands-Augustins. Here it remained until 1832, when it was moved to Faubourg Saint-Martin. Then, in 1848, it was transferred to the Boulevard Bourdon. At the end of the Second Empire it was moved, for the last time, to the Boulevard Richard-Lenoir, where it is still held today.

The salting and smoking of pork to produce ham is of French origin. It was, in fact, the Gauls, great devotees of pig meat and very efficient pig-breeders, who first became renowned for the salting, smoking and curing of the various cuts of pork.

At that period, France was covered with immense forests in which innumerable herds of pigs wandered, feeding on the vegetation without cost to the Gauls for whom they were a valuable asset. Such was the skill of the Gauls in the curing of hams that they became suppliers of ham to Rome and indeed to the whole of Italy.

This, according to reliable documentary evidence, is how the Gauls cured their hams:

After salting them, they subjected them for two days to the smoke of certain selected woods. Then they rubbed them with oil and vinegar and hung them up, to dry and preserve them.

The Gauls ate ham either at the beginning of a meal to sharpen their appetites or at the end to induce thirst, for salt meat was already at that time regarded as the most effective 'spur of Bacchus'.

A great many different kinds of salt and smoked ham are obtainable in France. Almost every region has its own local ham. Pigs bred in France being generally excellent, most of these local hams are extremely good.

Among the best known French hams are: the *Jambon de Bayonne*, cured at Orthez, but known the world over as *Jambon de Bayonne*. This ham is eaten raw, as an hors-d'oeuvre. It is also used in cooking in various ways, but unlike York ham or other lightly smoked hams, it must not be boiled. *Jambon de Bayonne* is served with eggs cooked in various ways and, finally, it forms an ingredient of various sauces and *ragoûts*. The *Jambon de Toulouse* is merely salted and dried. It is eaten raw like the *Jambon de Bayonne*, and is also used in cooking.

There are a large number of salted and smoked hams called in France *Jambons de campagne*. Among these are the hams of Brittany, Morvan, Burgundy, Montagne-Noir (Cévennes), Lorraine, Alsace, Touraine, Limousin, Auvergne, the Vosges, Savoy, etc. Almost all these hams are eaten raw, or may be used in cooking, like the *Jambon de Toulouse*. Some may be boiled like York ham.

French cooking hams, similar to English cooking hams, are *Jambon blanc* or *Jambon demi-sel* also known as *Jambon de Paris*. This ham, which is either not smoked at all or only very lightly smoked, is sold by all French pork-butchers under the name of *Jambon glacé*.

American hams (Preserved). JAMBONS D'AMÉRIQUE—Excellent hams are cured in the United States. Almost all American hams exported to Europe, however, and particularly to France, are cooked and preserved.

Baked York ham (*Pig Industry Development Association*)

English hams. JAMBONS D'ANGLETERRE—English hams are usually described on French menus as *York ham,* but a distinction can and must be made between the various methods of processing. This is indicated by their trade mark.

York ham, which is smoked (lightly or heavily), is usually boiled. It is served either hot or cold. When hot, a special sauce is served with it, flavoured with Madeira, sherry, port, etc. York ham can also be boiled and finally baked in the oven, covered with brown sugar, spice and cloves.

Raw York ham, thinly sliced and sautéed in butter, is often served with eggs.

German, Czechoslovakian and Hungarian hams. JAMBONS D'ALLEMAGNE, DE BOHÊME, DE HONGRIE—The best known is Mainz ham which, like Westphalian ham, is mostly eaten raw, but may also be boiled whole and served before the main course. Other well known German hams come from Hamburg, Gotha and Stuttgart.

The best Czechoslovakian ham is Prague ham; it is also cooked whole, and makes a delicious prelude to the main course. It is also served cold.

Excellent smoked hams are made in Hungary.

Italian hams. JAMBONS D'ITALIE—The best known of Italian hams is Parma ham. This is usually eaten raw as an hors-d'oeuvre and is one of the most delicate of hams. It can be used in cooking, though it must not be boiled like York ham, but cut into thin slices or diced and sautéed in butter or fat. Cooked in this way it can be served with eggs, various meat dishes, poultry or risottos.

There are other kinds of Italian ham which are either boiled whole and eaten hot or cold, or used in the same way as Parma ham.

Spanish hams. JAMBONS D'ESPAGNE—Asturias ham is the best known of Spanish hams. It is a mild ham, very delicate in flavour, and is eaten hot or cold, after having been boiled like York ham. It is also used in cooking, like the hams of Bayonne and Toulouse.

Salted and smoked ham. JAMBON DE PORC SALÉ ET FUMÉ—Salted and smoked hams, whether of French or foreign origin, after having been boiled as described, provide an intermediate course (remove) much prized by connoisseurs. These boiled hams are also served cold.

Boiled and cold hams of various kinds are to be found in all the pork-butcher shops of Paris and the big provincial towns. In these shops are to be found, apart from the *Jambon de Paris* (*jambon glacé*), boiled hams boned and moulded with jelly, smoked hams, boiled hams, boiled rolled hams, Dijon hams prepared with parsley and the foreleg hams of Paris, Reims, Strasbourg, Nancy etc.

The curing of ham, which is now a great industry, involves two main operations, salting and smoking.

The hams are either salted in brine or dry salt or they may be rubbed over with dry salt, saltpetre and sugar and left for three days well covered with this mixture. After this they are put into brine, then washed, brushed and dried and finally smoked in special chambers, starting with a light smoke which grows denser as the operation proceeds.

Cooked, i.e. York, Prague, Bayonne or Westphalian ham makes one of the best removes in French cuisine.

It is difficult to say which ham is the best, but it can be said that, for delicacy of taste the first place goes to sweet Bohemian ham, known as 'Prague ham', if served hot, and to York ham, if served cold.

Nevertheless, York ham, as well as ham produced in France, which has a great deal in common with English ham, is also excellent served hot.

Method of cooking—Poaching. Ham should be soaked in cold water for at least 6 hours before cooking. It is then scrubbed, boned at the chump end and put into cold water to cook, without any seasoning or aromatics.

As soon as boiling is properly established, draw the pan to the corner of the stove and leave to poach, simmering very gently so that the water just shivers, allowing 20 minutes cooking time per pound of York, Hamburg or Paris ham. Bohemian and Spanish ham requires a little less cooking time.

If the ham has to be served cold, leave it to cool in the same water in which it was cooked. If it is to be served hot, drain it, trim, that is remove the skin, and glaze.

Cold ham is served with jelly.

Hot, it is served with vegetables, most frequently spinach, and with Madeira or other wine sauce.

Glazing. Having poached the ham as described, remove the skin. Put the ham into a pan, sprinkle with icing sugar and brown in the oven or under the grill.

The sugar, upon caramelising, forms a sort of light glaze on the surface of the ham, which not only makes its appearance more appetising, but also renders it more flavoursome. (See illustration on next page.)

The ham can also be glazed by following the method given for braised meats. See CULINARY METHODS.

Jambonnière or braising pan for ham (*Larousse*)

Braising. Soak the ham as described above and poach very gently—so that boiling is hardly perceptible.

Remove 40 minutes before it is completely cooked. Skin it and put into a braising pan which is just big enough for it. Add $2\frac{1}{2}$ cups (5 decilitres) of Madeira or any other liqueur wine (port, sherry, Frontignan, Lunel, Marsala etc.).

Cover with a lid and cook in the oven from 45 minutes to an hour. Glaze the ham as described above. Arrange

Ham glacé (*Robert Carrier*)

on a serving dish; put a paper frill or a special metal *manche* around the knuckle. Garnish the ham as described in the recipe, or serve the garnish and the appropriate sauce separately.

Garnishes and sauces suitable for York and other hams served hot. Alsacienne (Madeira sauce); Berrichonne (Madeira sauce); Brabançonne (Madeira sauce); chipolata (Madeira sauce); braised celery or celeriac (Madeira sauce); glazed cucumbers in big chunks (Madeira sauce); chicory (Madeira sauce); leaf or chopped spinach (Madeira sauce); Flamande (Demi-glace sauce); Hongroise (Demi-glace sauce); macédoine (Demi-glace sauce); Nivernaise (Demi-glace sauce); noodles with Noisette butter (see BUTTER) (Madeira, Sherry or Port sauce); garden peas or other green vegetable dressed with butter or cream (Madeira sauce, or wine-flavoured Cream sauce); various fresh or dried vegetable purées (Demi-glace sauce, flavoured with Madeira or other liqueur wine); romaine (Marsala sauce). See GARNISHES, SAUCE.

Ham à l'alsacienne I. JAMBON À L'ALSACIENNE—Braise the ham and glaze it as described under *Cold ham.* Garnish with braised sauerkraut, Strasbourg sausages and boiled potatoes.

Ham à l'alsacienne II. JAMBON À L'ALSACIENNE—Heat some cooked York ham, cut into thin slices, in a few tablespoons of stock without allowing it to boil. Serve on a foundation of braised sauerkraut.

Garnish with Strasbourg sausages and boiled potatoes.

Ham à la bayonnaise. JAMBON À LA BAYONNAISE—Poach a well desalted Bayonne ham in water until three quarters cooked.

Take out of the pan, remove skin and trim off surplus fat (on the surface only).

Put it into a braising pan and finish braising in Madeira. Glaze and arrange on a long dish. Separately, serve *Rice pilaf* (see PILAF), with chopped tomatoes, small button mushrooms and little chipolata sausages fried in butter. Hand round *Madeira sauce* (see SAUCE) based on the braising liquor.

Burgundian ham with parsley (cold). JAMBON PERSILLÉ DE BOURGOGNE—This dish is a must on an Easter luncheon table in Burgundy. This is how it is prepared:

Wash the ham and desalt it. Blanch it thoroughly, drain, skin and cut into big uniform pieces.

Put these pieces of ham into a big pan with 1 pound (500 grams) of veal knuckle cut into round slices, two calves' feet, boned, blanched and tied with string, and a very big *bouquet garni** consisting, in addition to the usual herbs, of chervil and tarragon, and ten peppercorns (tied in a piece of muslin). Season with a little salt. Add enough dry white wine to cover all the meat. Bring to the boil on a high flame, then reduce heat, cover and simmer gently, on a low and sustained heat, to obtain a very clear stock, which will be used for making the jelly to accompany the ham.

When the ham is very well cooked, drain it, flake with a fork and put into a salad dish, pressing it down well.

Strain the liquor through a napkin. Add a good tablespoonful of tarragon vinegar. When it begins to coagulate, add two tablespoons of chopped parsley.

Pour this jelly over the ham. Leave in a cool place until cold. It is advisable to prepare this dish the day before it is required.

Ham in Chambertin. JAMBON AU CHAMBERTIN—Cook the ham (York or Prague) in water until three quarters done. Drain, trim and skin.

Put on to braise in a braising liquor based on Chambertin. When cooked, drain the ham and glaze.

Arrange on a big long dish. Surround with small glazed onions and button mushrooms fried in butter.

Strain the braising liquor and pour over the ham.

Cold ham. JAMBON FROID—Poach the ham in water as described under *Salted and smoked ham.* If the ham is to be served whole leave it to cool in its poaching liquor, then trim, remove skin, cover with liquid *aspic jelly**.

If, on the other hand, it is to be moulded, then bone it, trim, remove skin and put it into a special mould and leave to cool under a press.

Prepared in this manner, cold ham is either served plain, as it is, or decorated in one way or another.

Ham mousse

Cold ham mousse. MOUSSE FROIDE DE JAMBON—Pound finely in a mortar 1 pound (500 grams) of cooked lean ham (York or French) adding 1 cup (2 decilitres) of cold thick *Velouté sauce* (see SAUCE). Rub through a sieve.

Put this purée into a bowl, season, stand it on ice and stir with a wooden spoon for a few minutes, adding, little by little, $\frac{3}{4}$ cup ($1\frac{1}{2}$ decilitres) of liquid jelly. At the last moment carefully fold in 2 cups (4 decilitres) of half-whipped cream. Pour this mixture into a jelly-lined mould and leave on ice to set.

Turn out on to a dish, or a buttered bread *croûton*, and garnish with jelly.

Ham à la crème. JAMBON À LA CRÈME—Cook a York or Prague ham in salted water until two thirds done, skin, then braise in a Madeira *mirepoix**. When the ham is braised, drain and glaze.

Cook down the braising liquor by two thirds, add $2\frac{1}{2}$ cups (5 decilitres) of fresh double cream. Reduce this sauce by one third, strain and serve with the ham, which should be placed on a long dish.

Ham en croûte. JAMBON EN CROÛTE—See *Prague ham in pastry à l'ancienne.*

Ham glacé Reine Pédauque (Cold buffet dish). JAMBON GLACÉ REINE PÉDAUQUE—Cut the pope's eye (U.S. eye of the round) of a York ham, poached in Meursault wine and left until cold, into thin slices. Put these slices together again, sandwiching them with a layer of foie gras purée mixed with diced truffles, reshaping the ham into its original form. Coat the ham thus reconstituted with port-flavoured *chaud-froid sauce* (see SAUCE). Decorate with truffles, glaze with port-flavoured aspic jelly, arrange on a long dish and surround with jelly *croûtons.* (Illustrated on next page.)

Ham with lettuce, chicory and endives. JAMBON AU LAITUES, AUX ENDIVES, À LA CHICORÉE—Braise the ham (York or French) in Madeira, garnish with halved

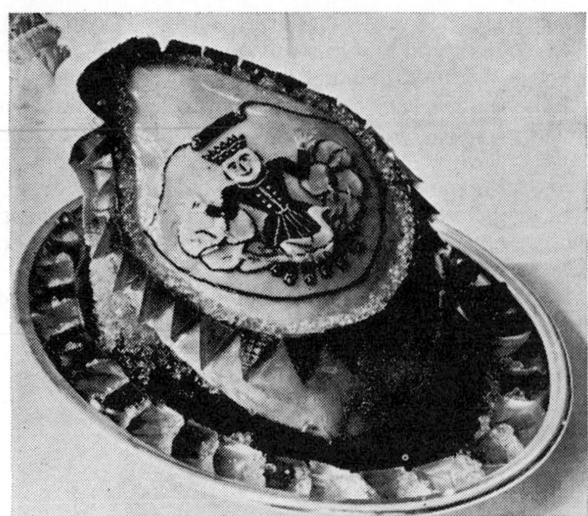

Ham glacé Reine Pédauque (*Larousse*)

braised lettuces (or chicory or endive) and serve Madeira-flavoured *Demi-glace sauce* separately (see SAUCE).

Ham au madère. JAMBON AU MADÈRE—Ham which, having been boiled until it is three parts cooked, is then braised in Madeira stock. See *Ham à la bayonnaise*.

Ham à la maillot. JAMBON À LA MAILLOT—Desalt the ham, wrap it in a cloth, put in a big braising pan and cover with cold water.

Simmer gently, with hardly perceptible boiling.

When the ham is cooked, drain it and skin. Put it into a small braising pan with a grid, add a pint ($\frac{1}{2}$ litre) of Madeira, cover and simmer for half an hour.

Take the ham out of the pan and glaze.

Arrange on a big dish. Garnish with big glazed carrots cut into balls, French (string) beans, small onions glazed in stock and braised lettuce, all these vegetables being disposed in separate groups. Serve Madeira sauce (see SAUCE) separately.

Ham in pastry, or Ham turnover with foie gras and truffles. JAMBON EN CHAUSSON: CHAUSSON DE JAMBON AU FOIE GRAS ET TRUFFES—Braise a Prague or other ham in Madeira, port or sherry.

When the ham is cooked, take out the pope's eye and the round, (U.S. eye of the round), trim them and cut each into 8 or 10 slices of uniform thickness.

Put these slices of ham on an oval-shaped piece of rolled out *Lining pastry* (see DOUGH) on a foundation of a *Duxelles** mixture and chopped truffles, alternating with layers of foie gras, tossed in butter, and slivers of truffles. Cover the ham with a layer of *Duxelles* mixture and chopped truffles, put another piece of rolled out lining paste on top and seal and pinch up the edges. Brush the top with beaten egg, make a few light incisions, make a hole in the middle to allow steam to escape and bake in a hot oven for about 45 minutes.

Arrange the ham in pastry on a serving dish. Through the hole in the middle pour into it a few tablespoons of *Port sauce* (see SAUCE) and serve the rest of the sauce separately.

Note. Ham in pastry can be prepared with various garnishes, such as *Ragoût à la financière*, *Ragoût à la Godard*, morels fried in butter, spinach or any other braised vegetable.

Another variation is to place the ham and its garnish on a round piece of pastry, which is then folded over thus forming the classic turnover.

Ham pie. PÂTÉ DE JAMBON—Using thin slices of ham (York or French), *Fine forcemeat* (see FORCEMEAT) and truffles, prepare as *Veal and ham pâté*. See PÂTÉ.

Prague ham in pastry à l'ancienne. JAMBON DE PRAGUE EN PÂTE À L'ANCIENNE—Poach the ham in water until it is two thirds done. Drain, skin and glaze.

Ham in pastry (*Robert Carrier*)

Prague ham in pastry à l'ancienne (*Larousse*)

When cold, put it, glazed side down, on a big piece of rolled out *Lining pastry* (see DOUGH), spread with a layer of fine *mirepoix** of vegetables, softened in butter and mixed with dried *Duxelles mixture** and chopped truffles.

Enclose the ham in the pastry and seal the edges.

Turn it and put into a buttered baking tin, placing it sealed side down. Brush the top with beaten egg and decorate with pieces of pastry cut out in fancy shapes. Make a hole in the middle to allow steam to escape and bake in a hot oven for about 45 minutes.

Put the ham on a serving dish. Through the hole in the middle pour into it a few tablespoons of *Périgueux sauce* (see SAUCE).

Note. This dish is sometimes served under the name of *Jambon sous la cendre* (ham under ashes), which appears to be a misnomer for there is nothing in its preparation to justify this.

Instead of enclosing the ham in a piece of lining paste (fine or common), it can sometimes be covered with a simple flour and water paste, in which case the dish is less flavoursome. The flour and water crust is not edible.

Ham with sauerkraut. JAMBON À LA CHOUCROUTE—The same as *Ham à l'alsacienne*. Separately, serve *Demi-glace sauce* (see SAUCE) or a sauce based on some Alsatian wine.

Ham with spinach. JAMBON AUX ÉPINARDS—Braise the ham (York or French) in Madeira. Serve it with leaf spinach cooked in butter, or chopped spinach cooked with gravy. Serve *Demi-glace* or *Madeira sauce* separately (see SAUCE).

York ham à la financière. JAMBON D'YORK À LA FINANCIÈRE—Braise the ham in Madeira, in the usual manner.

Glaze and arrange on a serving dish. Surround with *Financière garnish* (see GARNISHES). Skim off surplus fat from the braising liquor, reduce (cook down) strain and pour over the ham.

HAMBURGER STEAK, BEEF (Austro-Hungarian cookery). KEFTEDES—This dish is made from minced beefsteak browned in butter or fat. Similar 'steaks' are made from minced veal, poultry and game. Here is a Hungarian recipe for hamburger steak:

'2 pounds (1 kilo) of lean finely minced beef or veal; 10 rashers (strips) (200 grams) of bacon, chopped separately.

'Mix the beef or veal with the bacon and add to it 200 grams of crustless bread soaked in milk and squeezed out. Season with salt, pepper and grated nutmeg.

'When all the ingredients are well mixed, divide the mixture into pieces of equal weight. Shape each piece into a steak 2½ to 3 inches in diameter and ⅝ inch thick. Flour the "steaks".

'Fry them in fat at the last moment. When they are cooked dip them in concentrated meat stock. Serve with mashed potatoes or any other vegetable.'

Hamburger steak (German cookery). KEFTEDES DE BOEUF—Proceed as for *Hamburger steak also called à l'allemande* (see BEEF), but leave out the chopped fried onions put on top of the steak at the last moment.

Hamburger steaks à la berlinoise. KEFTEDES DE BOEUF À LA BERLINOISE—Mince finely ¾ pound (300 grams) of tender lean beef and 2½ ounces (75 grams) of fat bacon (or salt pork). Add 1½ cups (75 grams) of soft bread soaked in milk and squeezed dry. Season with salt, pepper and nutmeg and mix thoroughly.

Divide the mixture into 4 parts. Shape each piece so that it is round and flattish. Dip in flour and fry quickly in boiling lard. Brown the steaks well on both sides. Serve the steaks on a round dish and pour a *Demi-glace sauce* (see SAUCE) over them.

Game hamburger steaks. KEFTEDES DE GIBIER—Remove fat and sinews from the game. Mince finely, adding a tablespoon of onion browned in butter. Divide the mince into pieces of equal size and pat into little round or oval shapes. Dip in flour and fry in butter. Serve with an appropriate sauce and garnish.

Poultry hamburger steaks. KEFTEDES DE VOLAILLE—Proceed as for *Game hamburger steaks*, substituting poultry for game.

HAMMERHEAD SHARK. MARTEAU—A type of porbeagle. Its flesh, which is oily and leathery, is salted and eaten in some parts of the world.

HANGING. MORTIFIER—A process for tenderising butcher's meat or game by leaving it to hang for a longer or shorter period.

Hang meat on a hook in a cool, well-ventilated, very dry place.

HARE. LIÈVRE—A wild rodent with dark flesh, highly flavoured and excellent to eat. The mountain hare is more delicate than that of the plains. German hares are of poorer quality than French.

The male hare is called a *buck* and the female a *doe*. In France a young leveret up to 3 months is called a *financier;* up to 6 months a *trois-quarts* and at a year a *capucin* or *lièvre pit*. Young hares can be recognised by the fact that their ears tear easily and by a little rounded prominence on a bone under the leg joint which disappears as it grows older.

Hare can be eaten fresh, as soon as it is shot, or, if it is left to get cold, two or three days after killing, depending on the time of the year. It must never be eaten 'high'.

How to choose a hare. A hare is always tender in its first year. As it grows older its flesh becomes tough and stringy, but the female, in its second year, is still tender.

First year hares can be recognised by their slender paws and by the smoothness of their coat which, in older hares becomes slightly wavy and shows traces of greying.

In a young hare, the claws, hidden under the fur of the paws, are invisible. With age, the claws grow and project very slightly beyond the fur.

French hares. The best are those of Beauce, Brie, Normandy, Champagne and Touraine.

The hares of Northern France and Brittany are of inferior quality. This is due to the nature of the soil, which is poor feeding ground for hares.

The hares of Beauce, Brie and Champagne, have golden coats, the colour of ripe corn.

The hares of Normandy and Touraine are usually small, with tan coats, darker than those of Beauce, Brie and Champagne.

The hares of Brittany are also small, and have very dark tan coats mottled with black.

Many of the hares of Southern France are of fine quality, especially those of Périgord and Gascony, though these are seldom to be found on sale in Paris.

Hare à l'allemande. LIÈVRE À L'ALLEMANDE—For this dish, the saddle and haunch of the hare are used, if not the whole animal. Roast the hare in the usual way and pour sour cream into the roasting pan. Strain the sauce through a fine strainer and serve separately. Sometimes this sauce is poured over the hare. See also *Saddle of hare à l'allemande**.

Ballottine of hare (cold). BALLOTTINE DE LIÈVRE—Made of slices of hare, lean ham, pickled tongue, pork fat, foie gras, truffles and hare stuffing, in the same way as *Galantine of chicken.* See GALANTINE.

Ballottine of hare à la périgourdine (hot). BALLOTTINE DE LIÈVRE À LA PÉRIGOURDINE—Bone a hare of between 3 and 6 months old. Spread it on a fine cloth covered with thin slices of pork fat. Season with spiced salt and pour brandy over it. (Once it is boned, the hare may be put in a marinade.) Cover the hare with a layer of game stuffing made from the flesh of a leveret with chopped truffles added. On top of this stuffing put alternate thin strips of hare, cut from the thighs and browned in butter, strips of foie gras and slices of truffles. Season and pour brandy over these ingredients. Cover them with a layer of *à gratin game stuffing* (see FORCEMEAT). Fold the hare into a roll and tie with string. Braise it in a Madeira braising stock, made from shin of veal, the bones and trimmings of the hare and the leveret, and the usual pot vegetables. Cook for about an hour and a half. Drain the hare and remove the string. Brown in the oven. Reduce (boil down) the braising liquor, strain, add some shredded truffles and pour over the ballottine.

Civet of hare. CIVET DE LIÈVRE—Skin and draw a hare of between 3 and 6 months old. When drawing it, collect the blood and put it aside with the hare's liver, removing the gall-bladder.

Joint the hare, cutting the body into 3 or 4 pieces, according to the size of the hare. Put these pieces of hare in a dish. Season with salt, pepper, thyme and powdered bay leaf. Add a sliced onion. Moisten with 2 or 3 tablespoons of oil and a tablespoon of brandy. Leave the hare in this marinade for 3 hours. (The hare should be no more than coated with this marinade. No red or white wine should be added to it.)

For a medium-sized hare brown in butter 7 ounces (200 grams) of lean bacon, cut into squares and parboiled. When it is browned, remove from the pan and, in the same butter, brown two medium-sized quartered onions.

Add 3 tablespoons of flour. Cook, stirring constantly with a wooden spoon until the flour is a golden colour.

Now add the pieces of hare, well dried. Brown them in the roux, stirring constantly.

Moisten with enough red wine just to cover the hare. Add a *bouquet garni** to which has been added a clove of garlic. Cover the pan. Simmer slowly for 45 minutes to an hour.

Drain the pieces of hare. Scrape off any fragments of skin or bone clinging to them. Clean out the saucepan and put in the hare. Add the fried lardoons (bacon), 24 small braised onions and 24 small mushrooms tossed in butter.

Add the marinade to the cooking stock. Strain and pour over the hare. Cover the pan. Cook in a moderate oven (350°F.) for about 45 minutes.

A few minutes before serving, the chopped liver may be added to the civet and the sauce may be thickened with the hare's blood mixed with 3 or 4 tablespoons of fresh cream.

Serve the civet in a pie dish or other deep dish. Garnish with slices of bread cut into the shape of hearts, fried in butter.

Civet of hare au chaudron. CIVET DE LIÈVRE AU CHAUDRON—This dish is prepared in the same way as *civet of hare*, except that the hare is cooked in a pot hanging from a hook in the chimney of an open wood fire. Further, the sauce is thickened with kneaded butter and flour—$\frac{1}{4}$ pound (125 grams) of butter and 2 tablespoons of flour for a hare of between 3 and 6 months old.

This civet is garnished with coarsely diced belly of pork, blanched, and browned in butter, and small onions.

Civet of hare à la flamande. CIVET DE LIÈVRE À LA FLAMANDE—Brown the pieces of hare in butter. When they are a good colour, sprinkle with 2 tablespoons of flour. Cook the flour for a few seconds, stirring with a wooden spoon.

Moisten with a quart (litre) of red wine to which has been added the hare's liver rubbed through a sieve, with the hare's blood and $\frac{2}{3}$ cup (2 decilitres) of vinegar. Season with salt and pepper. Add 3 tablespoons (30 grams) of brown sugar and a large *bouquet garni**. Cover and cook for 12 minutes. Add 4 medium-sized onions (500 grams) finely sliced and tossed in butter. Complete the cooking in the oven, keeping the pan covered.

When the pieces of hare are cooked, drain and trim them and put them in a frying pan. Rub the sauce with the onions through a fine sieve. Pour the sauce over the hare and simmer for a few minutes, covered.

Serve the civet in a pie dish or other deep dish. Surround with slices of bread cut into the shape of hearts, fried in butter and spread with redcurrant jelly.

Civet of hare à la lyonnaise. CIVET DE LIÈVRE À LA LYONNAISE—Proceed as for ordinary *Civet of hare*, replacing the mushrooms in the garnish by chestnuts cooked in stock and browned.

Hare cutlets. CÔTELETTES DE LIÈVRE—There are three quite different ways of preparing hare cutlets.

(1) Make a croquette forcemeat using scraps of hare, mushrooms and truffles, blended with a thick brown or white sauce. Leave to cool. Shape into cutlets. Cook the cutlets in clarified butter. Serve them plain or garnished, like chicken cutlets. Serve a game sauce separately.

(2) Chop finely the raw flesh of a hare. Add a quarter of its weight of bread, soaked and squeezed dry, and the same quantity of butter. Season well. Shape the mixture into cutlets. Flour them. Fry in clarified butter.

Arrange in a circle on a round dish. Garnish to taste. Serve with a *Demi-glace sauce* (see SAUCE) based on concentrated game stock.

(3) Using raw hare, make a forcemeat of bread boiled to a pulp and butter (see FORCEMEAT). Put it into buttered cutlet moulds. Poach. Turn out the cutlets. Serve them on round pieces of bread fried in butter. Garnish to taste. Pour over them a brown or white sauce based on concentrated game stock.

Fillets of hare. FILETS DE LIÈVRE—Fillet a raw saddle of hare so that the meat comes away in long slices. Remove the tendons. Interlard with best lardoons. Season. Put the fillets in a baking dish. Pour melted butter and a little brandy over them and bake in a moderate oven.

Serve each fillet on a slice of bread fried in butter. Garnish according to the recipe used. Mask with a sauce suitable for ground game.

Note. The *filets mignons*, that is to say the slender strips of meat inside the saddle, can be prepared in the same way as the larger fillets. Usually, however, they are left with the larger fillets. All garnishes and sauces for *saddle of hare* are suitable for fillets.

In some restaurants, very grand entrées are made with fillets of hare. For instance, they are folded into crescent shapes and poached as indicated above. They are then presented on a foundation of *Mousseline* forcemeat (see FORCEMEAT) made from the remaining meat of the hare. Hare prepared in this way is served with garnishes such as *financière*, *périgourdine*, *Rossini*, etc. (see GARNISHES). All these entrées, which it must be repeated are in the realm of *grande cuisine*, are served with a *Demi-glace sauce* (see SAUCE), based on concentrated stock made from the bones and trimmings of the hare.

Fillets of hare en chaud-froid. FILETS DE LIÈVRE EN CHAUD-FROID—Stud the fillets with truffles. Fold into the shape of crescents. Stew in Madeira. Leave them to cool. Mask with a brown or white *Chaud-froid sauce* (see SAUCE) based on concentrated stock.

Decorate with truffles, the whites of hard-boiled eggs or some other garnish. Glaze with jelly. Serve them in a silver or glass dish. Pour over them very clear jelly stock flavoured with Madeira or some other heavy wine.

Fillets of hare in cream. FILETS DE LIÈVRE À LA CRÈME—Interlard the fillets. Steep them for an hour in a marinade of brandy, oil, salt, pepper and spices. Proceed as for *Saddle of hare à l'allemande**.

Fillets of hare à la Lucullus. FILETS DE LIÈVRE À LA LUCULLUS—Decorate the fillets of hare with pickled tongue and truffles cut in the shape of cocks' combs and dipped in white of egg. Fold them into crescent shapes. Stew slowly in brandy and butter.

Drain the fillets. Arrange them in a round flaky pastry crust filled with a *salpicon** of truffles and foie gras blended with a *Demi-glace sauce* (see SAUCE) based on concentrated game stock.

Fillets of hare sautéed with truffles. FILETS DE LIÈVRE SAUTÉS AUX TRUFFES—Cut the fillets into slices. Season and brown them quickly in butter, taking care that they keep their pinkish colour.

Drain and put in a serving dish. In the cooking butter, toss a dozen or so thick strips of truffle so that they are barely cooked. Put the truffles on the slices of hare. Pour a little Madeira into the cooking pan and add a few tablespoons of *Demi-glace sauce* (see SAUCE) based on concentrated game stock. Pour this sauce over the pieces of hare.

Pâté of hare. PÂTÉ DE LIÈVRE—Bone a hare. Set aside the breast meat, the *filets mignons** and the loins. Remove the gristle from these parts and interlard them with best lardoons. Season with *spiced salt*. Steep in a brandy marinade, adding equal quantities of fine strips of fresh ham (not smoked), fresh pork fat and quartered truffles.

With the rest of the meat make a forcemeat, as described in the recipe for *Game forcemeat* (see FORCEMEAT). Rub through a sieve. Bind with the blood of the hare set aside for this purpose.

Take a special oval or rectangular hinged mould. Grease it with butter. Line with *Pastry dough* (see DOUGH). Cover the dough with thin slices of larding bacon. Line the bottom and sides of the mould with a layer of hare forcemeat. Arrange the meats, truffles, etc., alternating them on this foundation of forcemeat.

Cover with a layer of forcemeat. Continue to fill the mould with alternate layers of meat and forcemeat, finishing with a layer of forcemeat. Cover with a thin slice of pork-fat. Put a layer of rolled-out pastry on top of this, pressing the edges of the dough together to seal the pâté. Flute the edges with pastry pincers. Decorate the top with motifs cut out of the dough. Make a hole in the middle of the pâté to allow the steam to escape during baking. Brush with beaten egg.

Bake in the oven allowing 15–20 minutes per pound (35 minutes per kilo).

Leave the pâté to cool in the mould. When it is cold pour a few tablespoons of Madeira flavoured meat jelly into it, so as to fill any gaps. If the pâté is to be kept for any length of time, substitute a mixture of butter and lard for the jelly.

Hare pâté must be made at least 24 hours before serving.

Potted hare. TERRINE DE LIÈVRE—Made from strips of hare, pork fat, foie gras, truffles and hare stuffing, in the same way as *Potted duck* (see TERRINE).

Roast legs of hare. CUISSES DE LIÈVRE RÔTIES—Take the legs of a hare. Remove the tendons. Stud the legs with best larding bacon to form rosettes. Roast them. Serve with *Poivrade sauce* (see SAUCE) and *Chestnut purée**.

Note. All recipes for saddle of hare are suitable for the legs.

Saddle of hare. RÂBLE DE LIÈVRE—For a *baron* of hare the whole body of the hare from the base of the neck to the tail is used, but very often the saddle alone, that is the portion of the trunk which ends at the top of the thigh, is served.

This is one of the most delicate parts of the hare. Before cooking it (and there are many different ways of preparing saddle of hare) it is advisable to remove all the thin membrane which covers the flesh.

According to the recipe, the saddle may or may not be interlarded with lardoons. Sometimes, it is merely barded with a thin slice of pork fat. In some cases, it is studded with truffles.

We do not recommend putting the saddle of hare in a marinade, especially in the case of a young animal. In certain special cases, which are indicated in the recipes given below, the hare may be marinated, but only for a short time and almost always in a marinade made from uncooked ingredients only (see MARINADE).

Generally, saddle of hare is roasted and, in this case, is always served with a *Poivrade sauce* (see SAUCE) and a *Purée of chestnuts* (see CHESTNUTS). The sauce and chestnuts are always served separately.

Saddle of hare à l'allemande. RÂBLE DE LIÈVRE À L'ALLEMANDE—Interlard the saddle with best lardoons. Steep for 2 hours in a raw *marinade**.

Put the marinade vegetables in a medium-sized roasting pan. Dry the saddle of hare thoroughly and lay it on top. Roast in a hot oven. When the saddle is almost cooked, take out the vegetables. Pour the marinade over the hare and add 1 cup (2 decilitres) of cream.

Put the saddle on a serving dish. Squeeze some lemon into the cream sauce and strain the sauce. Pour it over the hare. Serve redcurrant jelly or unsweetened apple sauce separately.

Saddle of hare au chambertin. RÂBLE DE LIÈVRE AU CHAMBERTIN—Interlard the saddle. Roast in the oven, taking care that it retains its pinkish colour.

Fry a slice of bread and spread it with *à gratin game forcemeat* (see FORCEMEAT). Lay the saddle on top. Garnish with mushrooms cooked in butter, small strips of belly of pork, parboiled and fried in butter, and truffles cut into thick strips. Mask with *Chambertin sauce* (see SAUCE), to which the pan juices, diluted with red wine, have been added.

Saddle of hare, roast. RÂBLE DE LIÈVRE RÔTI—Interlard the saddle. Roast in a hot oven for 18 to 20 minutes, or on a spit, allowing an extra 2 to 5 minutes.

Serve the hare on a long dish. Garnish with a bunch of

watercress and half a lemon. Make a border of slices of lemon and beetroot cut with a fluted knife and arranged alternately. Serve separately the diluted cooking juices or a rather thin *Poivrade sauce* (see SAUCE).

Hare soufflé. SOUFFLÉ DE LIÈVRE—Made, with hare, in the same way as *Soufflé of poultry*. See SOUFFLÉ.

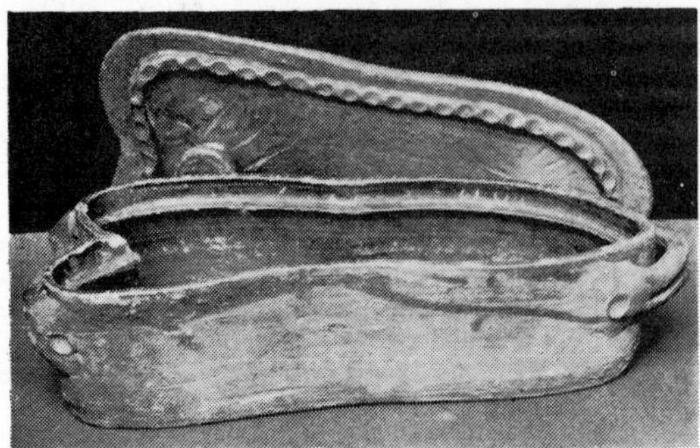

17th century terrine for preparing hare à la royale

Stuffed hare à la périgourdine or à la royale (Périgord cookery). LIÈVRE FARCI À LA PÉRIGOURDINE, À LA ROYALE —In the Périgord region this dish bears the high-sounding title of *Hare à la royale*. This magnificent dish must not be confused with a dish of the same name, which was looked upon for a very long time in Paris as a kind of culinary masterpiece, though it was, in fact, nothing more than a rather mediocre hare hash strongly flavoured with shallots and garlic. In any event, this dish had no claim to the epithet '*royale*' which was given to it by certain pseudo-gastronomes at the end of the nineteenth century.

This is how *Hare à la royale* is prepared in Périgord.

When drawing the hare, collect all the blood carefully and set it aside to bind the stuffing which will be used later.

Crush the paws of the hare. Remove the tendons. Interlard the fillets and legs with best lardoons.

Meanwhile prepare the stuffing as follows:

Chop the liver, heart and lungs of the hare. Add to this about 7 ounces (200 grams) of raw goose foie gras and 3½ ounces (100 grams) of fresh pork fat.

Add to this mixture 2 cups (100 grams) of bread soaked in clear soup and squeezed dry, a tablespoon of chopped onion, cooked very slowly in butter until tender and left to cool, a soupçon of pounded garlic, 5 ounces (150 grams) of chopped truffles and a pinch of chopped parsley. Bind this stuffing with the blood of the hare kept in reserve for this purpose. Season well.

Stuff the hare with this mixture. Carefully sew up the skin so as to hold the stuffing in. Truss the hare.

Braise the hare in a very little white wine for about two hours, basting frequently. At the last moment, brown the hare in the oven.

Drain and untie the hare. Put it on a long dish. Add to the braising stock a few tablespoons of *Demi-glace sauce* (see SAUCE) based on concentrated game stock and 2 tablespoons of Armagnac. Strain and add 5 ounces (150 grams) of shredded or diced truffles. Pour this sauce over the hare.

Note. Hare à la royale is often braised in red wine.

Stuffed hare à la périgourdine (cold). LIÈVRE ÉTOUFFÉ À LA PÉRIGOURDINE—Bone a hare, slitting it along the back, before drawing it, so that the skin of the belly remains intact. Draw it and cut off the legs and shoulders.

Set aside the liver, heart, kidneys and blood. Keep the blood in a bowl, with a spoonful of vinegar to prevent it from clotting.

Using the boned meat of the thighs and shoulders, some lean veal, fresh pork and pork fat, make a game stuffing (see FORCEMEAT). Add to this stuffing a quarter of its weight of *à gratin stuffing* (see FORCEMEAT), made from the liver, heart and kidneys of the hare with an equal quantity of raw foie gras. Bind this stuffing with 2 eggs. Season well. Add spices and 2 tablespoons of brandy.

Season the hare with *spiced salt* (see SALT) and sprinkle with a little brandy. Put a layer of stuffing on top. In the middle of the stuffing lay alternate thin strips of lean veal browned in butter, thin strips of foie gras seasoned with spiced salt and moistened with brandy, lardoons of pork fat (or blanched salt pork) and pieces of truffle. Cover with a layer of stuffing. Add further layers of meat and stuffing.

Fold the hare into shape and sew it up. Wrap it in a fine cloth. Tie it in the shape of a *ballottine**. Put the hare to cook in a game jelly stock flavoured with Madeira. This stock should be prepared in advance, using the bones and trimmings of the hare, a knuckle of veal, fresh pork skin (or bacon rinds) and a calf's foot, boned and blanched. Simmer very gently for about an hour and a half. When the hare is cooked, drain and unwrap it. Put it back in the cloth, wrapping it tightly. Cool under a weight. Next day, unwrap the hare. Glaze with jelly. Arrange it on a long dish or on a long slice of bread. Surround with a border of jelly croûtons.

Stuffed hare à la périgourdine en cabessal or chabessal. LIÈVRE FARCI À LA PÉRIGOURDINE EN CABESSAL—The hare is stuffed with a stuffing of fillet of veal, fresh pork and ham, seasoned with salt, pepper, spices, shallots and garlic. Having stuffed the hare, sew up the skin of the belly. Bard it and braise in red wine in a large round pie-dish. In order to cook it in this way the hare must be tied into the shape of a ring. Prepared in this way the hare is said to be *en cabessal* or *chabessal*. The *cabessal* was the name given to the folded ring of soft cloth which women wore on their heads to support pails or jars of water.

When the hare is braised, bone it almost completely. (The bones will come away easily, after long cooking.) Pound the hare's liver with garlic and blend it into the sauce. Add the hare's blood and a little vinegar.

This method of preparing hare or leveret is very popular in Périgord, and is also used in the Aveyron region.

HARICOT OF MUTTON. HARICOT DE MOUTON—This dish, which is a mutton stew made with turnips and potatoes, should more properly be called *halicot of mutton*. Although in English *haricot* is the more usual term, it is, in fact, a corruption of the French *halicot*, from *halicoter* (to chop very finely). See MUTTON.

HASH. HACHIS—A hash is usually made from 'left-overs' or scraps of beef, mutton, pork, veal, poultry, fish or shellfish, and, in France, is prepared in various ways.

For a hash, it is desirable to dice the meat very small, rather than mince or chop it. In this way, the hash will taste better and look more appetising.

French hashes are usually blended with white or brown sauces.

Hashes made from left-overs of roast or pot-roasted meat must not boil after the sauce has been added, but should merely be warmed up over a low flame. Hashes made from boiled or braised meat, on the other hand, should simmer on the stove for a while.

Hashes of all kinds are served in pie dishes or piled inside a border of *Duchess potatoes* (see POTATOES). In this case the hash is usually sprinkled with breadcrumbs and browned. Hash may also be served in a border of pilaff or risotto.

Sometimes hash is served in a pie-dish as a garnish with hard boiled, poached or coddled eggs.

Boiled beef hash I. HACHIS DE BOEUF—Dice very finely 2 cups (500 grams) of boiled beef scraps. Put them in a pan and bind with $\frac{3}{4}$ cup ($1\frac{1}{2}$ decilitres) of *Demi-glace sauce* (see SAUCE). This must not be too thick.

Cover and bring to the boil. Cook in the oven for 25 minutes. Stir from time to time while cooking and add a few tablespoons of *Demi-glace* if the sauce appears too thick. Serve in a deep dish or pie-dish.

Boiled beef hash II. HACHIS DE BOEUF—Cook 2 tablespoons chopped onion slowly in a frying pan with tablespoon of butter until very tender. Sprinkle with 1 tablespoon of flour. Brown. Add 1 cup (2 decilitres) of veal stock or soup (or, if neither is available, a little meat concentrate mixed with water).

Season and bring quickly to the boil stirring all the time. Then simmer for 15 minutes.

Dice the boiled beef very finely and add it to the mixture. Proceed as indicated in the previous recipe.

Curried beef hash I. HACHIS DE BOEUF À L'INDIENNE—Proceed as for *Roast beef hash*. Bind the diced meat with curry sauce. Serve in a border of rice. Serve *Curry sauce* (see SAUCE) separately.

Curried beef hash II. HACHIS DE BOEUF À L'INDIENNE—Put 2 tablespoons of chopped onion in a pan with a tablespoon of butter. Cook slowly until the onion is very tender. Sprinkle with a teaspoon of curry powder and a tablespoon of flour. Add 1 cup (2 decilitres) of white stock or broth. Mix well. Cook for 15 minutes.

Add the finely diced beef. Serve in a border of rice with *Curry sauce* (see SAUCE).

Beef hash with herbs. HACHIS DE BOEUF AUX FINES HERBES—Proceed as for *Roast beef hash*. Just before serving sprinkle with a tablespoon of chopped parsley and a tablespoon of chopped chervil.

Beef hash à la hongroise. HACHIS DE BOEUF À LA HONGROISE—Proceed as for *Roast beef hash**. Bind the diced meat with *Hungarian sauce* (see SAUCE).

Beef hash à l'italienne. HACHIS DE BOEUF À L'ITALIENNE—Proceed as for roast beef hash. Bind with *Italian sauce* (see SAUCE). This is made from chopped mushrooms browned with chopped onions or shallots with *Demi-glace sauce* (see SAUCE) added.

Beef hash à la languedocienne. HACHIS DE BOEUF À LA LANGUEDOCIENNE—Proceed as for *Roast beef hash**. Add 2 tablespoons of chopped parsley and a little grated garlic.

Serve on a buttered earthenware plate on a layer of sliced egg-plant (aubergines) sautéed in oil or butter. Smooth the surface of the hash. Surround with a very thick *Tomato fondue**. Sprinkle with breadcrumbs and cheese. Pour melted butter over it and brown.

Beef hash à la lyonnaise. HACHIS DE BOEUF À LA LYONNAISE—Proceed as for *Beef hash à la languedocienne*, binding the diced meat with *Lyonnaise sauce*. See SAUCE.

Serve the hash in a pie dish or on a flat dish with a border of *Duchess potatoes* (see POTATOES). Decorate the top with fried onion rings.

Beef hash à la Parmentier. HACHIS DE BOEUF À LA PARMENTIER—Proceed as for *Roast beef hash**. Serve in large partly scooped out baked potatoes.

Sprinkle with breadcrumbs. Pour melted butter over them and brown in the oven.

Beef hash à la polonaise. HACHIS DE BOEUF À LA POLONAISE—Proceed as for *Roast beef hash**. Serve in a pie dish. Garnish with poached eggs. Edge the dish with *Tomato sauce* (see SAUCE).

Beef hash with poached eggs. HACHIS DE BOEUF AUX OEUFS POCHÉS—Proceed as for *Boiled beef hash II*.

Serve in a pie-dish or other deep dish. Garnish with well-drained poached eggs. If desired, cover with *Tomato sauce* (see SAUCE).

Beef hash à la portugaise. HACHIS DE BOEUF À LA PORTUGAISE—Proceed as for *Roast beef hash**. Bind with *Tomato sauce* (see SAUCE).

Cover the bottom of a flat earthenware dish with slices of tomato tossed in butter or oil. Spread the hash over the tomatoes. Cover with a further layer of tomatoes cooked in the same way. Sprinkle with breadcrumbs. Pour melted butter or oil over the top. Brown in the oven.

The hash may be seasoned with a soupçon of garlic.

Beef hash with potatoes. HACHIS DE BOEUF EN BORDURE—Proceed as for *Roast beef hash**.

Pile the hash in the middle of a buttered earthenware dish, surrounded by a border of *Duchess potatoes* (see POTATOES). Sprinkle with breadcrumbs and grated cheese. Brush the border with beaten egg. Pour on melted butter and brown.

Beef hash with mashed potatoes. HACHIS DE BOEUF À LA PURÉE DE POMMES DE TERRE—Mix $1\frac{1}{2}$ cups (300 grams) of finely diced boiled beef with 1 cup (200 grams) of *Potato purée** (this must not be too thick). Season.

Put the hash in a buttered earthenware dish. Cover with a thin layer of mashed potatoes. Smooth the surface, sprinkle with breadcrumbs and grated cheese. Pour melted butter over the top and brown.

Note. This hash can be prepared in the same way with purée of white or red haricot beans, lentils or split peas.

Roast beef hash. HACHIS DE BOEUF—Dice the beef very finely. Bind with boiling *Demi-glace sauce* (see SAUCE). Heat it in a double saucepan. Serve in a pie dish.

Fish hash. HACHIS DE POISSONS—Use finely diced pieces of cooked fish (cod, turbot, brill, sole or salmon). Bind with vegetable-based *Velouté*, *Béchamel*, or any other sauce suitable for fish (see SAUCE).

Fish hash may be served on its own but usually it is used as a filling for pastry-boats, large or small *vol-au-vents**, tartlets, etc.

Hash of ground game. HACHIS DE GIBIERS DE POIL—Made from left-overs of braised game, venison, roast roebuck, deer or wild goat. Bind with a brown stock to which *Espagnole sauce* with game essence, *Demi-glace sauce* or Madeira, has been added (see SAUCE).

Hash of winged game. HACHIS DE GIBIERS DE PLUME—Made from left-overs of game, braised, pot-roasted or roast (pheasant, hazel-grouse, partridge). These are cooked in a white stock which is thickened with *Allemande sauce*, *Béchamel* or *Velouté* (see SAUCE), the sauce having been previously cooked down with concentrated game stock. They can also be cooked in brown stock, to which a *Demi-glace*, *Madeira* or *Salmi* sauce are added.

This hash is most commonly used as a filling for *vol-au-vents**, pies or tartlets, and can also be served on fried bread.

Lobster and shell-fish hash. HACHIS DE HOMARD—Made from lobster or any other similar shell-fish, finely diced, warmed up and mixed with *Velouté*, *Béchamel* or any other sauce (see SAUCE) suitable for fish and shell-fish, served hot. Shell-fish hash may be served on its own, but usually it is used as a filling for pastry-boats, large or small *vol-au-vents**, tartlets, etc.

Mutton or lamb hash. HACHIS DE MOUTON, D'AGNEAU—Use roast, braised or boiled left-overs of lamb or mutton and proceed as for *Beef hash**.

All recipes for beef hash are suitable for mutton or lamb hash.

Pork hash. Hachis de porc—Made from left-overs of roast, braised or boiled pork. Proceed as for *Beef hash*, if a brown stock is used, or use a white stock and follow the recipe for *Veal hash.*

Poultry hash. Hachis de volaille—Use left-over pieces of braised, stewed, pot-roasted or roast poultry. This dish is usually made with a white stock, as described in the recipe for *Veal hash à l'allemande*, but it may also be made with brown stock as described in the recipe for *Beef hash.*

Poultry hash *à blanc* has *Allemande*, *Béchamel*, *Cream* or *Velouté* sauce (see SAUCE) added. It must be heated in a double saucepan.

Note. Poultry hash, whether a white or brown stock is used, is often served with poached or coddled eggs. It can be used as a filling for large or small *vol-au-vents*, tartlets and other pastry cases, and also as a stuffing for artichoke hearts or mushrooms. These are sprinkled with bread-crumbs and browned. They are served as a garnish for main dishes.

Sweetbread (veal or lamb) hash. Hachis de ris de veau, d'agneau—This can be made with a white or brown stock. Dice the sweetbreads very small and proceed as for veal or poultry hash.

Veal hash. Hachis de veau—Use left-over pieces of braised, stewed, pot-roasted or roast veal. Using a brown stock, proceed as described in the recipe for *Beef hash**.

Veal hash à l'allemande. Hachis de veau à l'allemande—Dice the veal very finely. Bind with *Allemande sauce* (see SAUCE). Heat in a double saucepan.

Serve in a pie-dish or, if desired, in a pie-crust or *vol-au-vent.*

Veal hash à la béchamel. Hachis de veau à la béchamel—Proceed as for *Veal hash à l'allemande*, using a *Béchamel sauce* (see SAUCE).

Veal hash with cream sauce. Hachis de veau à la crème—Proceed as for *Veal hash à l'allemande**, using a *Cream sauce* (see SAUCE).

Veal hash à la Mornay. Hachis de veau Mornay—Bind the hash with a *Béchamel sauce* (see SAUCE). Serve it in a round dish in a border of *Duchess potatoes* (see POTATOES). Cover with *Mornay sauce* (see SAUCE); sprinkle with grated cheese. Pour on melted butter and brown.

HÂTEREAU—An old French word for little balls of pork liver similar to *gayettes.* See GAYETTES.

Nowadays, this is the name given to a hot hors-d'oeuvre or a light main course made of small pieces of food, dipped in egg and breadcrumbs and fried, then skewered and coated with a sauce of some kind.

HATTELLE OR HÂTTELETTE—Old French words for small birds, giblets, etc., roasted on skewers. It is derived from '*Hâtelet*' or '*attelet*' (skewer).

HAUNCH. Cimier—Hind quarters of the ox and of certain wild animals. This word, which is little used for the ox, is applied particularly to deer.

For detailed recipes see ROEBUCK or VENISON.

The French also use the words *gigue* and *cuissot* to describe haunch of game.

HAUT-BRION—A Bordeaux wine of great repute. The Château Haut-Brion, which is in the Pessac commune, is therefore in the Graves and not the Médoc district. According to the list drawn up in 1855 by the Bordeaux Chamber of Commerce, this is the only Graves wine given a 'First growth' classification. The other 'first growth' Bordeaux wines are Château-Lafite, Château-Margaux, and Château-Latour.

HAUT-SAUTERNES — White Bordeaux wine. See SAUTERNES.

HAWFINCH. Gros-bec—A European seed-eating bird. It is known in France as *gros-bec*, *casse-noix* or *pinson royal.* It is usually roasted for eating.

HAWKSBILL TURTLE. Caret—A kind of aquatic tortoise, native of the warm American and Indian seas. It furnishes the valuable tortoiseshell of commerce; its flesh is not worth eating but its eggs are highly esteemed.

HAY BOX OR FUELLESS COOKER. Marmite norvégienne—An ordinary pot, when its contents have been brought to the boil, is enclosed in an insulating box, that is to say, embedded, in materials which are bad heat conductors. In this way, the temperature drops very slowly, remaining at 70°C (158°F.) even after 5 or 6 hours or, with the most up-to-date equipment, even longer. In this way, food can be cooked without supervision and without the use of fuel once it has been brought to the boil.

Hazel-grouse

HAZEL-GROUSE. Gelinotte—This bird is also known as wood-grouse and ruffled-grouse. Hazel-grouse lives in woods. There are two species, one a native of Europe, the other of Asia.

The common hazel-grouse, which is on sale in France during the winter months, is a bird about the size of a partridge, whose plumage, which is reddish in colour, is speckled with brown, black, white and grey.

The hazel-grouse, which was once very common in France, especially in Alsace, the Ardennes and the Pyrenees, is rarer nowadays, and the greater number of hazel-grouse sold in France come from Russia, and are frozen. The best come from Vologda, Archangel and Kazan. The flavour of these birds is in no way spoilt by refrigeration.

The meat of the hazel-grouse is white and tender, but tastes rather strongly of fir-cones, which some people find unpleasant. This flavour can be made less strong by soaking the hazel-grouse in milk for some time before cooking.

All the recipes given for *partridge* are suitable for hazel-grouse. See PARTRIDGE.

Hazel-grouse à l'allemande. Gelinotte à l'allemande—Truss a hazel-grouse for the table. Season it; heat a spoonful of butter in a saucepan and put in the hazel-grouse. Cover it. Brown it all over. When the bird is three-parts cooked, drain it, remove the breasts and cut them into thin strips. Put them back on the bird, taking care to restore it to its original shape. Cover the hazel-grouse with a *Béchamel sauce* (see SAUCE) mixed with sour cream. Sprinkle it with breadcrumbs, and pour on a little melted butter. Let it brown a little in the oven. Serve a *Demi-glace sauce* separately (see SAUCE).

Casserole of hazel-grouse à la polonaise. Gelinotte en casserole à la polonaise—Stuff the hazel-grouse with *à gratin* stuffing for game (see FORCEMEAT), flavoured with one or two crushed juniper berries. Truss for the table. Cook it in butter in an earthenware casserole. At the last moment, after removing the string, pour over it 3 tablespoons of game stock (or of concentrated thickened veal stock) and a little lemon juice; then add browned melted butter with a handful of freshly grated bread-crumbs fried in it.

Chaud-froid of hazel-grouse. GELINOTTE EN CHAUD-FROID—Prepared in white or brown stock, as for *Chaud-froid of partridge* (see PARTRIDGE).

Hazel-grouse à la crème. GELINOTTE À LA CRÈME—Wrap larding bacon round the hazel-grouse and truss it. To lessen the taste of fir-cones, soak it for an hour in milk before cooking.

Heat a large tablespoon of butter in an earthenware casserole and place the hazel-grouse in it. Brown the bird well in the butter. Put the casserole in the oven, uncovered. Cook in a very hot oven 425°F., basting frequently, for about 18 minutes.

Remove the hazel-grouse from the casserole. Remove string and larding bacon. Put it back in the casserole. Pour over it ½ cup (1 decilitre) of fresh thick cream. Complete the cooking in a slow oven (325°F.), basting frequently.

Grilled hazel-grouse. GELINOTTE GRILLÉE—Slit the hazel-grouse, trussed for the table, along the back. Open it and remove most of the small bones. Gently flatten the bird, season it with salt and paprika, brush with melted butter, cover it all over with freshly grated breadcrumbs and cook under the grill on a gentle heat. Brown it well on all sides.

Put the hazel-grouse on a round dish. Garnish with watercress and surround it with a border of half-slices of lemon cut with a fluted edged knife, and slices of gherkin.

Serve either with *Maître d'hôtel butter** (see BUTTER, *Compound butters*), with *Diable* or with any other sauce suitable for grilled poultry and wildfowl. See SAUCE.

Hazel-grouse à la hongroise. GELINOTTE À LA HONGROISE—Cook in butter, in an earthenware casserole, 2 table-spoons of chopped onion seasoned with paprika. Put the hazel-grouse, trussed for the table, in the casserole. Cook it in the oven, with a gentle heat. When it is almost cooked, remove the string and put it back in the casserole, pouring over it 4 tablespoons of cream. Season with paprika. Complete the cooking, basting the bird frequently with the cream.

Hazel-grouse loaf. PAIN DE GELINOTTE—This is prepared like *partridge loaf.* See LOAVES, *Winged game loaf.*

Hazel-grouse mousse, hot or cold. MOUSSE DE GELINOTTE—This is made from fillets of hazel-grouse in the same way as quail. See QUAIL.

Pâté of hazel-grouse and potted hazel-grouse. PÂTÉ, TERRINE DE GELINOTTE—Pâtés of hazel-grouse or potted hazel-grouse are prepared in the same way as pâtés of partridge and potted partridge.

Roast hazel-grouse. GELINOTTE RÔTIE—Wrap the bird in larding bacon and truss. Cook it in a hot oven for 15 to 18 minutes, and on the spit for 18 to 20 minutes. Add a little water to the roasting pan to make a gravy. Serve with the bird in a sauce boat.

In England, bread sauce, fried breadcrumbs and potato crisps are usually served with this game.

Salmi of hazel-grouse. GELINOTTE EN SALMIS—This is prepared in the same way as *Salmi of woodcock*. See WOODCOCK.

Hazel-grouse soufflé. SOUFFLÉ DE GELINOTTE—Made from raw meat of hazel-grouse, in the same way as *Partridge soufflé*. See PARTRIDGE.

Suprêmes of hazel-grouse. SUPRÊMES DE GELINOTTE—Remove the breasts from an uncooked hazel-grouse. Trim and bone them. Flatten them carefully, season with salt and pepper and cook in butter. Lay them on a dish, garnish as indicated in the appropriate recipe, and serve them with the sauce recommended. See GARNISHES.

All recipes given for cooking and serving *suprêmes* of chicken and game birds are suitable for *suprêmes* of hazel-grouse. See CHICKEN.

HAZEL-NUT. NOISETTE—The fruit of the hazel-nut or cob-nut bush, which grows all over Europe. This nut is rich in oil and pleasant to taste. Hazel-nuts are used in confectionery.

Cultivated hazel-nuts are called filberts.

Hazel-nut butter—See BUTTER, *Compound butters.*

HEADY. CAPITEUX—Adjective applied to wines which 'go to one's head', that is wines which are generous and rich in alcohol.

HEART. COEUR—See OFFAL OR VARIETY MEATS.

HEARTH-CAKE. FOUACE—This is an old form of pastry, like a *galette* of fine wheaten flour. It is made of un-leavened dough and was originally baked not in the oven but under the ashes in the hearth (*focus*); hence its name. Hearth-cake is made in all the provinces of France.

Hearth-cake makers from Lerné have acquired a universal reputation, thanks to the novel *Gargantua;* though actually the cake they made is very ordinary. It was a sort of bread made with best white flour which was first cooked under the ashes, but later baked in the oven. In the sixteenth century the guild of hearth-cake makers consisted largely of inhabitants of Lerné.

In almost all the houses of the market-town of Lerné, there was an oven to cook the hearth-cakes. Some of these ovens, hewn in the rocks, still exist, and some of them go back to the eleventh century.

The original recipe was certainly modified, as Rabelais indicates a composition of 'best flour enlarged with good yolks of egg and butter, good saffron and good spices and water.' (*Gargantua, XXXIII.*)

Rightly esteemed, these little cakes were known for miles around and created an important trade, which was a source of income for the inhabitants of Lerné who encouraged the manufacturing of the hearth-cake to keep up the reputation of their products. There was never a market fair or an assembly in the districts of Chinonais, Loudonois, or Saumurois without vendors of hearth-cakes.

The sale of these cakes was such that in order to satisfy their clients hearth-cake vendors had to bring whole cartloads.

The fashion for Lerné hearth-cakes, of which the peasants from Chinonais were so fond, continued until the end of the eighteenth century.

E. Johanneau, who published an edition of the works of Rabelais with interesting commentaries, tells the story of his trip to Lerné in September 1821.

In this village he was given 'Galettes, called hearth-cakes which have a high reputation in this part of the country.'

Since 1821, the trade in these cakes has become negligible at Lerné, and soon only their memory will remain. Since they have fallen into such undeserved disfavour, it is well to recall what Rabelais said about them:

'Notez que c'est viande céleste, manger à déjeuner, raisins avec fouache fraische.'

'It is heavenly fare to lunch on grapes and fresh baked hearth-cakes.'

Hearth-cakes are still made in the Auvergne, but in quite a different way from these famous hearth-cakes.

Auvergne hearth-cakes. FOUACES D'AUVERGNE—*Ingredients.* 3¾ cups (500 grams) flour; ⅜ cup (100 grams) butter; 1 package (⅗ ounce) (15 grams) yeast; 3 eggs; cognac, a little glass; orange water, a few drops; ⅓ cup (1 decilitre) of milk.

Method. Work all ingredients together in a bowl. Leave for 12 hours. Set out like a crown on buttered paper. Brush with yolk of egg. Bake in moderate oven (350°F.).

HEDGEHOG. HÉRISSON—An insect-eating mammal, regarded by some people as very good to eat.

HELVELLE—A type of fungus which grows in Europe in damp grass, or in upland woods at the base of trees, especially fir trees.

Most types of *helvelle* are edible. They are sometimes called monks' morels, baby morels. The best of them is the crinkled *helvelle*, which tastes somewhat like the true morel.

HÉMIONE—A wild animal found in Asia. It is akin to the donkey and horse. For suitable recipes, see DONKEY and HORSE.

HEMLOCK. CIGUE—Name of a number of poisonous plants of the *Umbelliferae* family. The poisonous qualities of some of these plants have been greatly exaggerated. The *Great hemlock* (which might be confused with parsley) is in fact hardly poisonous. It seems improbable that Socrates should have been poisoned with the juice of this plant alone.

The *Little hemlock* is distinguished from parsley and chervil, with which it could be confused, by its thicker and larger leaves which are marbled with black or violet on the lower side and on the edges, and particularly by the unpleasant smell which is released when the leaves are rubbed. Some poisonous effects are attributed to it, but as with the preceding species, its poisonous qualities are exaggerated.

HERB-BENNET. BENOÎTE—The roots of this plant, which gives out a smell of cloves, possess stimulating and tonic properties.

Its yellow leaves, picked before the appearance of the flowers, are sometimes eaten in salad.

HERB-IVY. IVE—A species of chive. It is used in the flavouring of salads and sauces.

HERBS. HERBES—A large number of aromatic plants used in the kitchen come under the general heading of herbs.

Among the most common are chervil, tarragon, chive and parsley. Herbs are also used as trimmings in salads. See AROMATIC PLANTS.

Herb broth. POTAGE AUX HERBES—A refreshing soup made with leeks and pot herbs. See SOUPS.

Fines herbes—In French *fines herbes* usually means chopped parsley. In former times the term was more properly used to signify mixed chopped herbs. In old-style cookery, chopped mushrooms and truffles were mixed in with the herbs.

To prepare an aromatic mixture of herbs, use chopped chervil, chives, tarragon, parsley, fennel and other chopped aromatic plants.

Pot vegetables or 'herbs'. HERBES POTAGÈRES—Generally, 6 vegetables only are included among the pot herbs. They are: orach (rarely found), spinach, lettuce, sorrel, seakale-beet and purslane. All these vegetables are used in the preparation of soups and broths, but this list of 6 is a somewhat arbitrary selection, as there are many other vegetables equally suitable for the pot.

Turtle herbs. HERBES À TORTUE—A mixture of aromatic herbs of which the main ones are basil, marjoram, savory and thyme.

These herbs are used in the flavouring of turtle soup, and also in turtle sauce which is served with calves' head. See SAUCE, *Tortue sauce*.

HÈRE—French term for a stag between 18 months and 2 years old; that is to say, from the time that bumps appear on its forehead to the time when the antlers are fully formed.

HERMETICAL SEALING. HERMÉTIQUE—When a lid or stopper of a container fits so exactly that the container is rendered airtight, it is said to be hermetically sealed. Casseroles and saucepans can be made almost airtight by using flour and water paste to seal them.

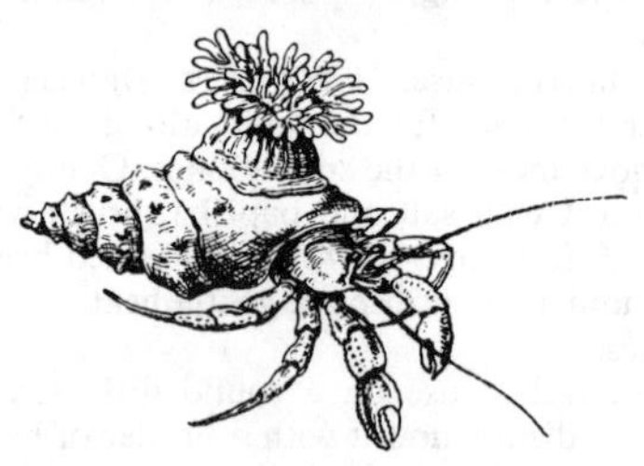

Hermit-crab

HERMIT-CRAB. BERNARD-L'ERMITE—This crustacean, the scientific name for which is *pagurian*, has one extremely interesting characteristic. Nature having neglected to give it a hard shell except just round the middle, to protect itself from its enemies, it creeps into shells of molluscs, abandoned by the rightful owner.

Alexander Dumas the elder, writing about this crustacean in his *Dictionnaire de la cuisine*, says that 'the Creator, who had started to dress him as a lobster, was disturbed, or became absent-minded in the middle of the job, and finished him dressed as a slug.

'And so, to protect those parts of its body which are vulnerable and so tempting, as soon as it sees a shell which fits its size, it eats the owner of the shell and proceeds to take its place, while it is still warm.'

Hermit-crab can be cooked in the same way as shrimps. Having been taken out of the shell, it is cooked in salted *court-bouillon** flavoured with thyme and bay leaf. It can also be cooked simply in sea water.

One can also, after having cleaned the hermit-crab, sprinkle it with butter and cook it in its borrowed shell under the grill or bake it on hot coals.

HERMITAGE WINE—See ERMITAGE.

HERRING. HARENG—A type of fish of which the parent species is the *common herring* which has bluish scales along its back and silvery sides and belly.

These fish, which are found in the North Sea, are prodigiously fertile. Every year, in March, they migrate from the Polar seas to the Atlantic coastal waters of France or the Channel, where they congregate in immense shoals.

The herring fisheries in the Channel extend from the Pas de Calais to the mouth of the Orne. The fishing season lasts from the middle of October to the end of December. Boulogne can firmly claim to be the real centre of the French herring industry.

The fresh herring is among the most delicately flavoured of fish. It can be cooked in a great many different ways. See below.

For countless ages, the herring, especially herring caught in the Channel, has been used for food by man.

Those of our ancestors who lived towards the end of pre-historic times, especially those who inhabited the temperate regions which later became Central and Southern Europe, certainly fed on the fish which then teemed in the rivers, lakes and streams. Tribes living on the coast also ate whatever sea-fish they could catch to supplement such forest game as wild ox, urus, stag, antelope, ibex and badger.

The most abundant of sea-fish at that time was herring.

In some of the inlets worn away by the sea on the French, Portuguese and Danish coasts, there are caves, in which vestiges of the meals eaten by our pre-historic ancestors have been found. These consist mainly of fish and shell-fish and there are herring bones among them.

Dressing of fresh fish. Cut them through the gills leaving the hard and soft roes. Scale, wash and dry thoroughly.

According to the way in which they are to be cooked, slit them along the back and sides, fillet them or, if they are to be stewed, braised or grilled, leave them whole.

Salt herrings. Fillet them. To remove the salt, soak them in milk or a mixture of equal parts of milk and water. Drain, dry and trim them and cook according to the recipe.

Smoked herrings. Fillet, skin and trim them. Soak, if necessary, to remove salt. Cook according to the recipe.

Bloaters and kippers. Grill or fry them as they are.

FRESH HERRINGS. HARENGS FRAIS:

Devilled grilled herrings—Slit the herrings along back and sides. Coat them with mustard. Season them. Sprinkle with white breadcrumbs, and oil and cook slowly under the grill.

Serve with *Mustard sauce* or *Ravigote sauce*. See SAUCE.

Fillets of herrings à l'anglaise. FILETS DE HARENGS À L'ANGLAISE—Fillet and trim the herrings. Dip them in egg and breadcrumbs and deep-fry in boiling fat.

Serve with *Maître d'hôtel butter* (see BUTTER, *Compound butters*) mixed with boiled, mashed soft roes.

Fried herrings. HARENGS FRITS—Slit the herrings along back and sides. Dip them in milk and flour and deep-fry in boiling fat.

Drain them. Dry them in a cloth. Season with salt and serve on a napkin-covered dish, garnish with fried parsley and quartered lemons.

Grilled herrings. HARENGS GRILLÉS—Gut, scale and dry the herrings. Slit along back and sides. Coat them with oil or melted butter. Season and cook slowly under the grill.

Serve with *Maître d'hôtel butter*, mustard sauce or any other sauce suitable for grilled fish. See BUTTER, *Compound butters;* SAUCE.

Herrings à la boulangère. HARENGS À LA BOULANGÈRE—Grease an oval earthenware dish liberally with butter. Lay 6 herrings in the dish and sprinkle with salt. Surround with 2 thinly sliced medium sized potatoes (300 grams) and one medium sized onion (100 grams).

Season with salt, pepper, a little thyme and powdered, bay leaf. Pour 2–3 tablespoons of melted butter over the dish. Add enough water to cover. Bring it to the boil on the stove, then cook in the oven, basting from time to time. Sprinkle with chopped parsley and serve in the cooking dish.

Herrings à la meunière. HARENGS À LA MEUNIÈRE—Proceed as for *Féra à la meunière*.

Marinade of fresh herrings (Hors-d'oeuvre). HARENGS FRAIS MARINÉS—Steep 12 soft-roed herrings in salt for 6 hours. Dry them with a cloth. Put a layer of finely sliced onions and carrots in an oval earthenware dish with sprigs of parsley and thyme, half a bay leaf, a few pepper corns and one or two cloves. Lay the herrings in this dish.

Pour over the herrings a mixture of equal parts of white wine and vinegar. This should not quite cover them. Put another layer of sliced onions and carrots on top. Cover the dish with oiled paper. Bring to the boil over the stove. When the liquid is bubbling all over, cover the dish and simmer slowly for 15 minutes.

Leave the herrings to cool in the stock.

Sautéed herrings à la lyonnaise. HARENGS SAUTÉS LYONNAISE—Slit the herrings along back and sides. Season and dip in flour. Sauté them on one side in butter in a frying pan. Turn the herrings over and add 3–4 tablespoons of finely sliced onions previously lightly fried in butter.

Finish cooking the onions and herrings together. Arrange on a long dish. Pour the butter and onions over the dish. Sprinkle with chopped parsley. Pour a little vinegar into the pan and warm in the cooking butter. Pour this over the fish.

Soft herring roes. LAITANCES DE HARENGS—Remove the soft roes from fresh herrings. Use any recipe indicated for carp soft roes. See SOFT ROES.

Stewed herrings in white wine. HARENGS ÉTUVÉS AU VIN BLANC—Cut the herrings into thick slices. Put them in a buttered dish and season with salt. Moisten with 1 cup (2 decilitres) of white wine; season with salt and pepper. Dot with butter cut into small pieces.

Bring to the boil over a very high flame. Cover and simmer for 8 to 10 minutes.

Drain the herrings. Arrange them on a long dish. Simmer the cooking liquor to evaporate some of the liquid, add butter and pour over the herrings.

SALT HERRINGS. HARENGS SALÉS—In the Boulogne fisheries, herrings are either salted at sea or in port. Salt herrings are processed industrially by the following method:

The Boulogne herring fleet trawls in the North Sea from June to October. The trawlers are at sea for long periods at a time and, therefore, the fish are salted on board, as soon as they are caught. The herrings are put down in barrels with alternate layers of salt. The barrels are then hermetically sealed.

Fishing vessels operating in the Pas de Calais and the Channel ports put into port each day as soon as the nets are hauled in.

The fish is transported from the boat to the salting sheds. After it has been mixed with salt in a long wooden trough it is thrown into cement vats. The salt mixes with the moisture from the herrings to form a brine with a salt-density of 25°. The fish must remain steeped in this brine for at least ten days, to ensure its preservation.

SMOKED HERRINGS. HARENGS FUMÉS—There are two ways of smoking fish, 'hot' and 'cold'.

In 'cold' smoking, the fish is hung some way away from the fire and is smoked at a temperature of about 77°F.

In 'hot' smoking, the fish is hung close to the fire and is partially cooked.

'Cold' smoking is carried out almost exclusively in France, notably in Boulogne. The fuel used is always wood, preferably beech, and sawdust. Resinous wood should be avoided, as it imparts an unpleasant flavour to the fish.

'Hot' smoking is scarcely ever used except in the preparation of bucklings, which are much in demand in Alsace.

Smoked herrings are processed in the following way: The herring is salted to a greater or lesser degree according to the type of smoked herring required. Pickled smoked herrings must be salted for at least eight days. Slightly salted or mild smoked herrings are made from fresh herrings salted for 24 to 48 hours. Bloaters are salted for a few hours only.

Once they are salted, the herrings are strung on rods threaded through their gills and are put to drain on trolleys or racks, then set up in the smoking chimneys.

In modern smokeries, the racks are fitted into the chimney, thus avoiding a great deal of handling.

When the herrings are in the chimney, a beechwood fire is lit. This produces a powerful draught, which dries the herrings, and at the same time draws off any excess oil. Next, the fire is damped with beech sawdust and chips. This causes the fire to send off a dense smoke which smokes the herring and gives it its special flavour.

When the herrings have been sufficiently smoked, they are removed from the chimney and taken to the smokery workshops. There girls sort and grade them, and crate the sound ones according to size and quality.

Generally, very large herrings (808) are crated in twenties, weighing from 8 to 10 pounds (4 to 5 kilos) according to season. Medium herrings (1010) are packed in batches of twenty-five, weighing from 7 to 8 pounds (3 kg 500 to 4 kilos). Small herrings (1212) are also packed in batches of twenty-five and weigh from 7 to 8 pounds (3 kg 500 to 4 kg). Smoked herrings are also packed in wooden barrels which hold from 60 to 100 fish, according to size.

Bloaters are made from herrings which are very slightly salted and smoked. They do not keep for any length of time, and should be eaten without delay, like fresh fish.

Kippers are lightly smoked herrings slit from top to bottom and opened out. In recent years, kippers have become very popular in France.

Fillets of fresh and salt herring are very much sought after. Skilled girls cut off the head and tail of the herring, slit it open, bone, and skin it. In this way fillets are obtained of which every part can be eaten, and there is no waste whatsoever. 7 ounces (200 grams) of fillets are packed in little wooden boxes, or parcels of 2 pounds (1 kilo) of fillets are made up.

Irish smoked herrings. HARENGS SAURS À L'IRLANDAISE—Wash and dry the herrings. Cut off the heads. Split the fish in half lengthwise. Spread them out very flat in a deep dish. Cover them with whisky and set light to them. When the whisky has all burnt away and the flame extinguished, the herrings are ready for eating.

Smoked fillets of herring in oil. FILETS DE HARENGS SAURS MARINÉS À L'HUILE—Fillet 24 smoked herrings. Trim the fillets. Soak them in milk for 2 hours to remove salt. Drain, and dry them in a cloth. Put them in a pie-dish in layers, with alternate layers of finely sliced onions, little sprigs of thyme and broken-up bay leaves. Place on top the soft and hard roes of the herrings. Cover with olive oil. Leave them to soak for 24 hours.

Smoked fillets of herring with soft roes. FILETS DE HARENGS SAURS AUX LAITANCES—Fillet several smoked, soft-roed herrings. Remove the skin. Bone them as completely as possible. Cut each fillet into strips. Put the fillets in a pan with enough milk almost to cover them. Leave them to soak for half an hour, or longer if the herrings are very salty.

Rub the soft roes through a sieve, collecting the purée in a bowl underneath. Add a teaspoon of mustard, $\frac{1}{2}$ cup (1 decilitre) of oil (stirring it in a little at a time) and a little vinegar. Add further seasoning if necessary.

Drain the fillets of herring and dry them in a cloth. Arrange them in hors-d'oeuvre dishes. Pour the soft roe sauce over them and sprinkle with chopped parsley.

HIPPOCRAS—A spiced aromatic wine much enjoyed by our ancestors. It was so called because it was filtered through a bag of a type said to be invented by Hippocrates, the great physician who lived in the fifth century B.C.

Properly speaking Hippocras was a type of *apéritif* similar to the vermouths and quinquinas made nowadays, rather than a table-wine. Our forebears, in fact, drank it before meals or, if it was served at table, right at the end of the meal.

Arnaud de Villeneuve, famous thirteenth century physician, gives a number of different recipes for this spiced wine.

In one recipe he recommends bringing the wine to the boil and then putting in it a sachet containing, for 3 litres of wine, 3 ounces each of the following spices: cubeb, cloves, nutmeg and raisins. Boil the wine until it is reduced by a third of its volume. Then add sugar.

In another recipe, Arnaud de Villeneuve suggests that the wine should be spiced with a mixture of cinnamon, ginger, paradise nuts, cloves, sugar and a pinch of musk.

Hippocras was drunk cooled or even iced whenever possible.

This wine remained popular for a very long time. It was still in fashion in the eighteenth century. Presents of it were made to the King and to foreign nobility.

Here is a more recent recipe for Hippocras:

Put 3 cups (700 grams) of sugar in a saucepan with 2 cups (4 decilitres) of water. Add the following spices: 4 teaspoons (10 grams) of ginger, 2 cloves, $\frac{1}{4}$ (or 2 teaspoons) of ground nutmeg, 2 tablespoons (15 grams) of cinnamon and the zest of 2 Seville oranges.

Boil this syrup for a few minutes. Add 2 quarts (litres) of old wine (white or red). Leave the mixture on the stove until the surface turns white. Now pour it into a large jug and leave it to infuse for 30 minutes. Strain through muslin and bottle.

HIPPOPOTAMUS. HIPPOPOTAME—A large amphibious pachyderm whose flesh is much sought after for food by the African natives.

HOCCO—A type of gallinaceous bird of which there are a dozen species to be found in the equatorial regions of Central America. They are similar to the European turkey. A certain number are bred in the poultry-runs of France. It is to be hoped that, in time, they will be bred in Europe on a wider scale, as they are considered by those who have eaten them to be delicious.

The flesh of this bird, which is very white, is quite exquisite. In his *Souvenirs d'émigration*, Brillat-Savarin mentions this kind of wild turkey and remarks upon its succulent flesh. It is cooked in the same way as turkey.

HOG-FISH. RASCASSE—Fish oblong in shape and rather high-backed, with a large and spiny head. It has spikes, whose prick is poisonous, on its dorsal fins. Its colouring is varied, but mostly it is greyish with black markings. The Provençal fishermen know the hog-fish under such names as *scorpion*, *crapaud* (toad) or *diable de mer* (sea-devil).

The flesh of the hog-fish is tough. It is not used other than for *bouillabaisse* or similar fish soups.

HOG'S FAT. PANNE—The fat which covers the pig's kidneys and fillets.

It is used for making fine forcemeats and black (blood) puddings.

Rendered down it produces superior quality lard which in French is called *axonge*.

HOG'S HEAD CHEESE or PORK BRAWN. FROMAGE DE TÊTE DE PORC—A kind of *galantine** made from hog's head.

HOLLANDAISE—The name of a hot sauce made with yolks of egg and butter (see SAUCE). It is served with eggs, fish and vegetables.

In former times fish '*à la hollandaise*' was served with melted butter.

HOLLY. HOUX—A bush of the ilex family. In some countries, notably Corsica, holly berries are roasted and powdered and are used to make a drink similar to coffee.

Butcher's-broom or Knee-holly. HOUX-FRELON, PETIT-HOUX—A European plant used in pharmacy under its botanical name of ruscus. Its root has diuretic properties. The young shoots of the plant are edible and can be cooked in the same way as asparagus.

Paraguayan holly—See MATÉ.

HOLLYHOCK. ALCÉE—Plant originating in Lebanon where it is commonly known as *Rose-mallow*. It has an appreciable nutritive content. A very nourishing starch flour is obtained from its roots.

HONEY. MIEL—A sweet liquid manufactured in the sac of the worker bee from the nectar secreted in certain flowers and introduced by the insect into the cells of the hive. Honey was the chief sweet food of ancient times when cane sugar was a rarity.

The carbohydrates in honey are made up of a mixture of glucose, levulose and a little saccharose. It also contains a little mannite, organic acids and fragrant ethers, as well as a small quantity of bee-glue, a resinous substance which makes up the walls of the cell.

Several grades of honey are sold commercially:

(1) *Virgin or superfine honey*, extracted from the combs by exposure to the sun or gentle heat.

(2) *Common or yellow honey*, extracted under greater heat.

(3) *Brown honey*, extracted by pressure under heat.

Honey is a very rich and concentrated food (100 g = 321 calories). Its effect is very similar to that of sugar but it is generally more readily assimilated. Apart from this, it is indicated or prohibited medically in the same cases as sugar, and in particular must be forbidden to diabetics. Honey is slightly laxative.

In diet, especially that of children, it can take the place of sugar in almost all its uses, though there are people who find it indigestible.

The quality, consistency, aroma and flavour of honey varies according to the place where it has been gathered, that is to say according to the type of flowers most widespread in the region. The best is made from the nectar of labiates (thyme, mother of thyme). Narbonne honey owes its distinctive flavour to the nectar of rosemary. The most highly reputed honey is that of Hymethus in Greece, and in France that of Narbonne, Gâtenais, Champagne and Savoy. Spring honey is always superior to autumn honey.

Certain plants impart a distinctive flavour to honey which is sometimes unpleasant (for instance, honey gathered from pines, which has a resinous taste). Honey made from the nectar of poisonous plants such as belladonna can itself be poisonous.

HONGROISE (A LA)—Dishes prepared *à la hongroise* are always cooked in a cream sauce seasoned with paprika. Eggs, fish, meat (other than pork products), poultry, etc., can be prepared *à la hongroise*. Recipes for these dishes are given in alphabetical order under appropriate headings.

HOP. HOUBLON—A hardy plant grown in many countries.

The cones of the female plant are used in the brewing of beer.

Hop shoots. JETS DE HOUBLON—In French cookery, the name *jets de houblon* is given to the edible flowers of the male plant, or panicles. The edible tip of the panicle is broken away from its woody stem in the same way as green asparagus tips.

Hop shoots are boiled in salt water, with a few drops of lemon juice. Once they are cooked they can be treated in a number of different ways:

In butter. Toss for a few seconds in butter.

In cream. Toss in butter and simmer in fresh cream.

In gravy. Toss in butter. Simmer for a few seconds in concentrated brown veal stock.

Hop shoots may be served as a vegetable or a garnish with various dishes. In particular they are used as a garnish with eggs (omelette with hop shoots, etc.).

In Belgium, where this vegetable is much prized, hop shoots, when they are served as a vegetable, are always garnished with poached eggs arranged in a circle on top and interspersed with croûtons of bread cut in the shape of cocks' combs and fried in butter.

In U.S.A. hop panicles or 'shoots' are not sold in the market, but there are some large hop producing regions where they may be found.

HORN. CORNE—Little horn utensil, as its name indicates, used in the kitchen or for cake-making to scrape up the preparations in mortars or in basins, or on marble slabs.

HORS-D'OEUVRE—By definition, these snacks are additional to the menu. They should therefore be light and very delicate, especially when served before a rather heavy menu consisting of a number of courses.

With a light luncheon, the hors-d'oeuvre may be somewhat more substantial and nourishing.

There are two main types: *cold* hors-d'oeuvre and *hot* hors-d'oeuvre.

Cold hors-d'oeuvre, usually served with luncheon, are of two kinds: those which can be bought ready for the table and those which require some preparation at home.

Formerly, hot hors-d'oeuvre were called *entrées volantes* or *petites entrées*. They generally formed part of the dinner menu, and were served after the soup. Hot hors-d'oeuvre can, however, be served at luncheon at the same time as cold hors-d'oeuvre.

Nowadays, it is customary to serve a rich variety of hors-d'oeuvre at the beginning of a luncheon. This practice, which was originally much in fashion in restaurants, has now spread to private households.

It will be appreciated that for the guests to be able to eat such a variety of snacks at the beginning of a meal

Hors-d'oeuvre vegetables (*Robert Carrier*)

without overloading their stomachs, these must be very light and delicate.

France has also adopted a custom imported from Russia, of serving hors-d'oeuvre in a special way, as *Zakuski.*

The *Zakuski* is a kind of meal-before-the-meal, entirely made up of hors-d'oeuvre, washed down with liberal draughts of wine and liqueur. Formerly, in Russia, this was served in an ante-chamber adjoining the dining room.

In France, the custom has been somewhat modified. Under the name of *Zakuski* or *Hors-d'oeuvre à la russe,* these snacks are arranged on trays and served to the guests at the table itself.

PRESENTATION OF COLD HORS-D'OEUVRE—These snacks must be presented elegantly. The lady of the house must not only supervise their presentation, but must co-operate in it and put herself out to devise original and graceful decorative effects.

Here are a few hints to help the hostess.

(1) *The dishes.* Apart from special hors-d'oeuvre sets, china or glass plates and dishes or antique gold or silver plate may be used.

Old rustic-style plates, pottery or silver porringers, crystal bowls, etc. can be used very effectively.

(2) *The garnishes.* Garnishes, though purely decorative, *must all be edible.*

There is a great variety of such garnishes. Tastefully chosen and arranged, they give a very attractive appearance to the hors-d'oeuvre. The most common garnish is parsley, which must be very green and curly. This parsley can be used in sprigs or chopped, as required.

Hors-d'oeuvre can also be garnished with chervil, tarragon, water-cress and lettuce hearts. As a contrast to these greenstuffs, half slices of lemon and beetroot can be used. Beetroot is also used diced, cut into matchsticks and in other ways.

Finally, the decoration of hors-d'oeuvre can be varied by using any of the following: capers; gherkins; red pomegranate seeds; hard boiled eggs (halved, quartered or chopped); small pickled onions; large onions sliced into rings or chopped; small kidney-beans; French (string) beans; green peas; asparagus tips; boiled carrots and turnips; radishes; black radish; the leaves and stalks of leeks; yellow, red and green peppers; mushrooms; truffles, etc.

To achieve greater variety in form and colour, flowers can also be used. Nasturtiums (whose leaves are also edible), borage, violets, chrysanthemums and daisies all enhance the decorative effect.

PRESENTATION OF HOT HORS-D'OEUVRE—Unless otherwise stated under the entry relating to a particular item, hot hors-d'oeuvre are always served straight on a dish, a folded napkin or a paper doily, garnished with fresh or fried parsley according to their nature. Fried hors-d'oeuvre such as fritters, *cromesquis**, croquettes, etc., may be served in nests of match-stick potatoes.

COLD HORS-D'OEUVRE. HORS-D'OEUVRE FROIDS—

Basic components of cold hors-d'oeuvre—A cold hors-d'oeuvre can consist of one ingredient only or of several ingredients, generally cut into dice, seasoned, with an oil and vinegar dressing or with a mayonnaise sauce. Compound butters (see BUTTER), forcemeats, special pureés and *salpicons** may also be added.

The following are the most usual hors-d'oeuvre.

Aceto-dolce—See *Sour-sweet pickles,* below.

Cold hors-d'oeuvre

Allumettes—See *Pastry straws,* below.

Anchovies. ANCHOIS—No matter what dish salted anchovies are finally used for, it is necessary first of all to free them from salt and to prepare them in the following way:

(*a*) *For different mixtures* (compound butters, stuffings, purées, *salpicons** sauces, etc.): Wash the anchovies, free them from salt in cold water, cut into fillets; clean the fillets and dry them. The method of preparation after this varies according to the particular dish for which they are intended.

(*b*) *For hors-d'oeuvre and different garnishes:* Free the anchovies from salt and cut them into fillets as above. Scrape the fillets and clean them well to ensure that all the scales have been removed. Dry them lightly in a cloth.

Cut the fillets into small strips or leave them whole, according to the dish for which they are intended.

Arrange anchovy fillets in a regular pattern on a deep dish or terrine. Cover them with olive oil. Put the lid on. Keep in a cool place. Use as indicated.

Anchovies and hard boiled eggs I. ANCHOIS ET OEUFS DURS—Make a mixture of two thirds hard boiled eggs and one third anchovies freed from salt. Cut the anchovies into fillets and then into small dice. Season with oil, vinegar, salt, pepper and finely chopped herbs or with mayonnaise.

Anchovies and hard boiled eggs II. ANCHOIS AUX OEUFS DURS—Proceed as for *anchovies in oil.* Garnish with the yolks and the white of hard boiled eggs (chopped separately), with capers and with chopped parsley.

The dressing, garnish and decoration of marinated anchovy fillets can be infinitely varied. Apart from the additional ingredients mentioned above, a variety of other items can be used, e.g. lettuce *chiffonnade**, olives, beetroot, lemon, chervil, tarragon, etc.

Anchovies à la grecque. ANCHOIS À LA GRECQUE—Put fresh anchovies, cleaned and dried in a cloth, into salt for two hours. Free them from salt. Shake them individually to ensure that all the salt falls off. Sear for one minute only in smoking oil.

Drain the anchovies and arrange in layers in a terrine. Each layer should be sprinkled with a bit of thyme, sweet bay, coriander and pepper grains.

Make a *Fish court-bouillon II* (*à la grecque*) (see COURT-BOUILLON) and pour while still boiling over the anchovies. Marinate the anchovies in this *court-bouillon* for 24 hours.

Serve the anchovies in an hors-d'oeuvre dish. Sprinkle them with the marinade, garnish with round slices of peeled lemon and sprinkle with freshly chopped fennel.

In France this dish is also known as *Escabèche d'anchois à la grecque*.

Anchovies à la normande. ANCHOIS À LA NORMANDE—Arrange the marinated anchovy fillets on a *salpicon** of rennet apples seasoned with mayonnaise.

Surround with a border of beetroot cut into very small dice. Dress with a thin trickle of oil.

Norwegian anchovies (Kilkis). ANCHOIS DE NORVÈGE—These can be bought ready prepared. Arrange the anchovies on an hors-d'oeuvre dish; surround them with half slices of lemons, cut with a fluted cutter, and with fresh parsley. Sprinkle with several tablespoons of their marinade.

Norwegian anchovies or Kilkis can also be used in all ways indicated for anchovies in brine.

Anchovies in oil. ANCHOIS À L'HUILE—Free anchovies from salt. Cut into thin strips. Arrange on an hors-d'oeuvre dish, criss-cross or in some other pattern. Garnish with capers and chopped parsley. Dress with a thin trickle of oil.

Anchovies à la russe. ANCHOIS À LA RUSSE—Arrange marinated anchovy fillets on a salad made of cooked potatoes and good sharp apples, cut into very small dice.

Surround with a border of chopped chives and grated horse-radish, arranged in separate rows. Dress with a thin trickle of oil.

Anchovy salads, various. SALADES D'ANCHOIS—Anchovy fillets in oil or with hard boiled eggs accompanied by a salad.

Anchovy salad can be served with a great variety of dishes: lettuce *chiffonnade**, boiled potatoes cut into fine slices or into dice, celeriac cut into a fine *julienne**, etc.

It is essential that these various additions only act as accompaniments; the anchovy must always dominate the dish.

Anchovy scrolls. PAUPIETTES D'ANCHOIS—Free anchovy fillets from salt, scrape and dry in a cloth. Flatten the fillets and coat them with a thin layer of fish purée or any other mixture suitable for cold hors-d'oeuvre. Roll the fillets up into scrolls.

Arrange the scrolls in an hors-d'oeuvre dish; garnish with the yolks and the whites of hard boiled eggs (chopped separately), capers and chopped parsley. Dress with a thin trickle of oil.

Bargeman's anchovy scrolls. PAUPIETTES D'ANCHOIS BATELIÈRE—Stuff the scrolls with tunny (tuna fish) purée blended with mayonnaise. Arrange them two by two in small baked *barquette* shells. Garnish with a *salpicon** made with hard boiled eggs and gherkins, seasoned with mayonnaise. Arrange on a paper doyley and garnish with fresh parsley.

Monselet anchovy scrolls. PAUPIETTES D'ANCHOIS MONSELET—Fill the scrolls with a stuffing made with the yolk of hard boiled eggs. Arrange each scroll on a round canapé of bread, toasted on both sides and covered with *anchovy butter* (see BUTTER, *Compound butters*).

Surround the scrolls with a ring of capers. Put a small sprig of tarragon in each scroll.

Arrange on a paper doyley and garnish with fresh parsley.

Anchovy scrolls à la Niçoise. PAUPIETTES D'ANCHOIS À LA NIÇOISE—Fill the scrolls with *Tarragon butter* (see BUTTER, *Compound butter*).

Hollow some very small raw tomatoes. Marinate them and fill them two thirds with a fish purée chosen from the recipes given specially for cold hors-d'oeuvre. Place the scrolls in the tomatoes on a foundation of fish purée.

Decorate to taste. Arrange on an hors-d'oeuvre dish. Dress with a trickle of oil.

Vatel anchovy scrolls. PAUPIETTES D'ANCHOIS VATEL—Stuff the scrolls with *Anchovy butter* (see BUTTER, *Compound butters*) to which chopped tarragon has been added.

Make small patty cases of puff pastry. Fill these cases two thirds with a *salpicon** of marinated tunny (tuna fish) and truffles seasoned with mayonnaise. Put one scroll on each patty. Put a sliver of truffle on each scroll. On each sliver of truffle put a dot of butter mixed with the yolk of hard boiled eggs.

Arrange on a paper doyley and garnish with fresh parsley.

Artichokes

Artichokes. ARTICHAUTS—Small artichokes, quartered artichokes and hearts of artichokes, prepared according to the methods described under the heading ARTICHOKE, can be used as ingredients of a variety of hors-d'oeuvre.

Artichokes Baron-Brisse. ARTICHAUTS BARON-BRISSE—Cut the hearts of artichokes into thin slices and cook them lightly. Throw them for a few moments into boiling oil, moving them around all the while. Moisten with a few tablespoons of *Tomato essence* (see ESSENCE). Add some lemon juice, salt, pepper, parsley and chopped chervil. Boil everything together for a few minutes.

Let cool. Arrange on an hors-d'oeuvre dish with rounds of peeled lemon.

Artichokes à la croque-au-sel. ARTICHAUTS À LA CROQUE-AU-SEL—Name given to a dish of young raw artichokes. The only accompaniment is salt.

Artichokes à la grecque. ARTICHAUTS À LA GRECQUE—Trim according to instructions (see ARTICHOKE) 20 small very tender artichokes. Flavour with lemon and plunge one after the other into a liquid prepared as follows.

Boil together for five minutes in a casserole $2\frac{1}{2}$ cups (5 decilitres) of water, $\frac{1}{2}$ cup (1 decilitre) of olive oil, the juice of a lemon, a pinch of salt, 10 seeds of coriander, the same number of peppercorns and a large *bouquet garni* composed of parsley, thyme, bay leaf, celery and fennel, to make a well flavoured *court-bouillon**.

Cook the artichokes in this liquor for 18 to 20 minutes. Take the artichokes out of the liquor and keep in a cool place. Arrange on an hors-d'oeuvre dish or in a glass dish and serve as cold as possible—iced if desired.

This hors-d'oeuvre keeps fairly well, particularly if the artichokes are put in a narrow pickling jar and kept in a very cool place.

Another way of preserving artichokes is described in the article on ARTICHOKE, *pickling of artichokes*.

Artichokes à la poivrade. ARTICHAUTS À LA POIVRADE—Name given to a dish of small young artichokes eaten raw. Diners prepare their own sauce consisting of *Vinaigrette* (see SAUCE) strongly flavoured with pepper.

Artichokes à la vinaigrette. ARTICHAUTS À LA VINAIGRETTE—This is another name for *Artichokes à la poivrade.*

Note. Often, boiled artichokes, either hot or cold, accompanied by a *Vinaigrette sauce* (see SAUCE), are also served under this name.

Garnished artichoke hearts. FONDS D'ARTICHAUTS GARNIS—Prepare and cook very small artichoke hearts according to the usual method (see ARTICHOKE).

Drain and dry the artichokes. Garnish them with vegetable salad, asparagus tips, different *salpicons**, etc.; season with mayonnaise or *à la vinaigrette**.

Artichoke hearts may be garnished with different purées. Caviar is also a good garnish for artichoke hearts and so are many other items used generally as garnishes for cold hors-d'oeuvre.

Arrange the hearts in an hors-d'oeuvre dish. Decorate with fresh parsley, hard boiled eggs, chopped up jelly, etc.

Artichoke hearts à la grecque. FONDS D'ARTICHAUTS À LA GRECQUE—Proceed as indicated for *Artichokes à la grecque* above, using very small artichoke hearts or large hearts cut into slices.

Artichoke hearts à la tartare. FONDS D'ARTICHAUTS À LA TARTARE—Cook artichoke hearts in *White Court-bouillon II* (see COURT-BOUILLON); drain, dry and cut into very regular slices. Arrange them in an hors-d'oeuvre dish with *Tartare sauce* (see SAUCE).

Garnish with a border of the yolks of hard boiled eggs and chopped parsley, arranged in separate rows. Surround with half slices of cooked beetroot, cut with a fluted edged knife.

Quartered artichokes. QUARTIERS D'ARTICHAUTS—Very tender quartered artichokes are prepared as an hors-d'oeuvre following the instructions given for artichoke hearts and whole artichokes.

Assiette anglaise—An assortment of different kinds of cold meat arranged on a plate or dish.

As a rule this assortment consists of York ham, pickled tongue, entrecôte, fillet or roast beef.

Garnish the meat with chopped jelly, watercress and gherkins.

Assiette anglaise is mainly served for luncheon.

Assorted hors-d'oeuvre. ASSIETTE ASSORTIE; ASSIETTE VOLANTE—Name of a dish containing an assortment of different kinds of hors-d'oeuvre, mainly salted items, all cut into very small slices.

In ancient times this dish was called *Assiette volante* and consisted of a wide choice of items.

Barquettes—Small oval-shaped patties made of pastry, baked blind (empty), garnished with different fillings (see BARQUETTES).

All preparations mentioned in this section on cold hors-d'oeuvre can be used as garnishes for barquettes.

The following are just a few examples, which can be infinitely varied. All recipes given for filling patties, *canapés* and tartlets apply to barquettes.

Barquettes are generally served on a paper doyley. On the menu they are often called *'frivolités'*, a name originally given them by Escoffier.

Bagration barquettes. BARQUETTES BAGRATION—Garnish the barquettes with a thin layer of cold *Chicken purée* (see CHICKEN). Cover this purée alternately with very thin round slices of breast of chicken and truffles. Spoon into the barquettes some half-set jelly.

Beauharnais barquettes. BARQUETTES BEAUHARNAIS—Garnish the barquettes with a *salpicon** of breast of chicken and truffles. Cover this garnish with a layer of mayonnaise, to which a purée of tarragon, as well as some gelatine, has been added. Decorate with tiny pieces of truffles and cover with jelly.

Marivaux barquettes. BARQUETTES MARIVAUX—Fill the barquettes with a *salpicon** made of shrimps and mushrooms, blended with gelatine-strengthened mayonnaise. Decorate with rounds of hard boiled eggs and chervil. Coat with jelly.

Barquettes à la cancalaise—Garnish the barquettes with a *mousse* made from whitings or other white fish. Poach, drain and trim some oysters. Lay these oysters on the *mousse* in each barquette and spoon over some jelly.

Barquettes à la normande—Garnish the barquettes with a *salpicon** made of fillets of sole, mussels and truffles.

Coat the barquettes with a white meatless *Chaud-froid sauce* (see SAUCE). Put on each boat a poached oyster and two shelled crayfish tails. Spoon over some jelly.

Barquettes with different garnishes—Items which can be used as garnishes for pastry boats include anchovy in *salpicon** or anchovy scrolls; smoked eel; beetroot; special compound butters for hors-d'oeuvre; caviar; pickled cucumber; prawns, shrimps, crayfish; foie gras; pickled herrings; lobster and crawfish; different vegetables in *salpicon** or cut into round slices; poached mussels; olives; hard boiled eggs; plovers' eggs; red and green peppers; different sausages; marinated tunny; tomatoes; truffles.

The following serve as decorations for these various pastry boats: capers; gherkins; beetroot; chopped jelly; hard boiled eggs; fresh parsley; chervil; tarragon; lettuce.

Beef. BOEUF:

Salad of ox muzzle. MUSEAU DE BOEUF EN SALADE—Blanch, cool and drain the muzzle. Scrape and wash. Make a white *Court-bouillon**. Boil the muzzle in it and leave it to cool in the pot.

Drain and wipe dry. Cut into very thin slices. Season with a very strong *Vinaigrette sauce* (see SAUCE) to which onion and chopped parsley have been added.

Arrange on an hors-d'oeuvre dish. Decorate with tiny rings of raw onions and, if desired, chopped hard boiled eggs.

This hors-d'oeuvre can be bought ready-made.

Salad of ox tongue. PALAIS DE BOEUF EN SALADE—Proceed as for *Salad of ox muzzle* as above.

Smoked beef. BOEUF FUMÉ—Cut the meat into very thin slices. Serve in an hors-d'oeuvre dish or on a plate. The meat can be arranged flat or rolled into a cornet. Garnish with parsley. Smoked beef is also used as a garnish for canapés.

Beetroot. BETTERAVE—Beetroot can be bought cooked in greengrocers' shops. If prepared at home it should be baked in a very slow oven. Beetroot is mainly used for salads.

Peel the beetroot and cut it into thin round slices. Arrange the slices in an hors-d'oeuvre dish. Season with oil, vinegar, salt and pepper. Sprinkle with chopped parsley.

Beetroot cassolettes—See BEETROOT.

Beetroot à la crème. BETTERAVE À LA CRÈME—Cut the beetroot into fine matchsticks. Season with a *Mustard cream sauce* (see SAUCE). Serve in an hors-d'oeuvre dish.

Beetroot and hard boiled eggs. BETTERAVE ET OEUFS DURS—Take equal quantities of beetroot cooked in the oven and hard boiled eggs cut into dice. Season as for anchovies and hard boiled eggs.

Beetroot à la normande. BETTERAVE À LA NORMANDE—Cut beetroot and good tart apples into slices and arrange alternately on an hors-d'oeuvre dish. Surround with a ring of chopped chives. Season with *Vinaigrette sauce* (see SAUCE) made with cider vinegar.

Beetroot salad. SALADE DE BETTERAVE—Beetroot salad is served with a *Vinaigrette* or with a *Cream sauce* (see SAUCE) as indicated above. Serve in an hors-d'oeuvre dish or in a salad bowl.

Bouchées—See *Patties* below.

Brioches: Small garnished brioches. BRIOCHES MIGNONNES GARNIES—Take very small *Brioche à tête**, empty three quarters and fill with any of the garnishes usually served with pastry boats, tartlets and other similar preparations.

Cabbage, green. CHOUX VERTS—Prepare in the same way as *Red cabbage*, below.

Cabbage, red. CHOU ROUGE—Trim and wash a medium sized cabbage. Cut it into very fine small strips. Put these strips into a dish and pour 1½ cups (3 decilitres) of boiling vinegar on them. Mix well and leave for 5 hours. Drain and season with oil, salt and pepper.

Red cabbage can also be blanched before it is steeped in the vinegar.

Canapés—Small garnished pieces of toast make a very dainty hors-d'oeuvre. They can also be served like sandwiches for tea or during an evening's entertainment.

There are two ways of serving garnished toast.

First method. Take a sandwich loaf. Cut the crusts off. Cut into thin slices. Cut the slices with a biscuit cutter into small pieces of various shapes and forms.

Toast these shaped slices of bread on both sides without browning.

When the toast is cool spread it on one side only with a compound or plain butter or with any other suitable preparation according to the kind of toast desired.

Garnish the toast accordingly. Instructions for decorating can be found at the end of the description of these canapés. Arrange the pieces of toast on a paper doyley, napkin, plate or dish, mixed or separate.

Second method. Toast lightly on both sides large slices of a sandwich loaf cut according to taste. When cool spread with butter or any other suitable preparation. Garnish accordingly. Cut into canapés of various shapes with a biscuit cutter or with a knife. Decorate in keeping with the garnish.

Note. If a great many canapés of the same kind are to be served, the second method is to be recommended. The pieces of toast can also be made of black bread with the rind cut off or with ordinary brioche (baked, unsweetened, in a rectangular tin if possible).

In addition to the recipes listed below, canapés may be prepared in an infinite number of ways. As garnish all sorts of different preparations can be used—different kinds of meat, fish, vegetables, truffles, mushrooms, etc., all cut into thin slices or made into *salpicons**.

As decoration for canapés the following are used: hard boiled eggs (either the yolk and white separated or the whole egg cut into slices), capers, gherkins, olives, beetroot, cucumber, truffles, mushrooms, parsley, chervil, tarragon, etc.

All recipes for preparations to be served with canapés, such as compound butters, suitable purées, and special spreads, are given below in their alphabetical order.

Anchovy canapés—See ANCHOVY.

Aurora canapés. CANAPÉS À L'AURORE—Use a round-shaped unsweetened brioche loaf. Spread with yellow butter. Garnish with a thin round slice of smoked salmon, put a round of beetroot in the middle, sprinkle with a pinch of minced yolk of a hard boiled egg and surround with a border of yellow butter.

Canapés à la bayonnaise—Slice a square or round sandwich loaf, spread the slices with parsley butter and garnish with very thin slices of Bayonne ham.

Canapés à la bordelaise—Slice a round or square sandwich loaf. Spread the slices with *Shallot butter*, garnish with a *salpicon** made of cooked *cèpes* and lean ham and surround with a border of *Paprika butter* (see BUTTER, *Compound butters*).

Canapés with caviar. CANAPÉS AU CAVIAR—Slice a sandwich loaf, brown loaf or unsweetened brioche; whichever base you choose for your canapés, the slices should be round. Spread with *Caviar butter* (see BUTTER, *Compound butters*) or with fresh butter. Surround with a fairly high border of caviar butter. Garnish the centre with fresh caviar. Sprinkle with a pinch of chives.

These canapés can also be made with pressed caviar, but they will not be nearly so delicate.

Crayfish canapés. CANAPÉS AUX ÉCREVISSES—Follow the recipe for *Shrimp canapés*, using *Crayfish butter* (see BUTTER, *Compound butters*) and crayfish tails instead of prawns.

Canapés à la danoise—Slice a dark rye loaf of rectangular shape, spread with *Horseradish butter* (see BUTTER, *Compound butters*), garnish with thin strips of smoked salmon alternating with fillets of herring, separate each bit of fish by a little fresh caviar and surround with a border of chopped chives.

Harlequin canapés. CANAPÉS ARLEQUIN—Slice a sandwich loaf. Spread the slices with a compound butter or some other kind of spread, garnish with separate bunches of different chopped preparations, such as yolks and whites of hard boiled eggs, smoked tongue, ham, truffles, parsley, etc. Surround with a thin border of compound butter.

These canapés can be garnished with a mixture of different preparations. The garnish is generally prepared last and therefore all the left-overs of special canapés can be used up for this dish.

Herring canapés. CANAPÉS AUX HARENGS—Use the recipe for *Anchovy canapés* (see ANCHOVY), substituting *Herring butter* (see BUTTER, *Compound butters*) and fillets of herring for the anchovy.

These canapés can be garnished with different kinds of herrings.

Canapés à la hollandaise—Slice a sandwich loaf. Spread the slices with a purée of soft herring roes, garnish with fillets of herring arranged in a criss-cross pattern, fill each opening with chopped yolks of hard boiled eggs and surround with a border of chopped parsley.

Canapés Laguipière—Use *Ordinary brioche bread* (see BRIOCHE), non-sweetened, sliced and cut into lozenge (diamond) shapes, spread with *Truffle butter* (see BUTTER, *Compound butters*); garnish with slices of breast of chicken, decorate the points of the lozenges with separately chopped pickled or smoked *tongue* (see OFFAL OR VARIETY MEATS) and chopped truffles; surround with a border of yellow butter.

Canapés à la livonienne—Slice a dark rye loaf of rectangular shape, spread the slices with *Horseradish butter* (see BUTTER, *Compound butters*), garnish with slivers of herring fillets alternating with thin ribbons of good tart apples, brush lightly with oil and surround with a border of chopped chives.

Lobster canapés. CANAPÉS AU HOMARD—Follow the recipe for *Prawn canapés*, substituting *Lobster butter* (see BUTTER, *Compound butters*) and pieces of lobster.

Monselet canapés. CANAPÉS MONSELET—Trim slices of sandwich loaf into oval shapes, spread with yellow butter, garnish with a border of tiny round slices of breast of chicken, alternating with tiny rounds of pickled or smoked tongue. Fill the centre with a *salpicon** of truffles and surround with a border of yellow butter.

Mont-Bry canapés. CANAPÉS MONT-BRY—Slice unsweetened *Ordinary brioche* (see BRIOCHE), rectangular in shape; spread with herring butter (see BUTTER, *Compound butters*), garnish with fillets of herring, alternating with evenly cut strips of beetroot and gherkins cut in a similar shape; surround with a border of chopped yolks of hard boiled eggs.

Canapés à la moscovite—Slice a square-shaped black rye loaf, spread the slices with *Horseradish butter* (see BUTTER, *Compound butters*), surround with a border of butter mixed with the coral of spiny lobsters, fill the centre with fresh caviar and decorate with shrimp tails in a rosette.

Canapés à la nantaise—Slice sandwich bread thin and trim the slices in long oval shapes, spread with *Sardine butter* (see BUTTER, *Compound butters*), garnish with fillets of sardines in oil from which all the bones and skin have been carefully removed, garnish with sardine butter in such a way as to make the canapés look like fish.

Canapés Ninon—Trim slices of sandwich bread into oval shapes, spread with *Printanier butter* (see BUTTER, *Compound butters*), garnish with a border of very small thin rounds of breast of chicken, alternating with rounds of truffles. Fill the centre with lean ham cut into very small dice.

Canapés à la parisienne—Slice a sandwich loaf of rectangular shape, spread the slices with butter mixed with pounded chervil, garnish with very small thin slices of breast of chicken, coated with gelatine-strengthened mayonnaise and decorated with truffles and tarragon leaves. Surround with a border of chopped jelly.

Canapés à la printanière—Trim slices of sandwich loaf into rounds, spread with *Montpellier butter* (see BUTTER, *Compound butters*), garnish with leaves of water cress, alternating with thin round slices of carrots cooked in clear stock. Spoon over a thin layer of meat jelly and surround with a border of chopped yolks of hard boiled eggs.

Canapés à la reine—Trim slices of ordinary unsweetened *Brioche** into rounds, spread the rounds with *Truffle butter* (see BUTTER, *Compound butters*), garnish with a *salpicon** made of breast of chicken, decorate with a lozenge-shaped slice of truffle and surround with a border of yellow butter.

Russian salad canapés. CANAPÉS À LA RUSSE—Slice any shape of sandwich loaf, spread the slices with butter *aux fines herbes*, surround with a border of yellow butter, fill the centre with *Russian salad*, decorate with truffles, cover with a thin coat of jelly.

Shrimp canapés. CANAPÉS AUX CREVETTES—Slice a rounded sandwich loaf or cut out rounds from square slices. Spread the slices with *Shrimp butter* (see BUTTER, *Compound butters*), garnish with shrimp tails arranged in a rosette. Surround with a border of shrimp butter or with chopped parsley.

Smoked eel canapés. CANAPÉS À L'ANGUILLE FUMÉE—Slice a round-shaped sandwich loaf, spread with *Mustard butter* or with *Horseradish butter* (see BUTTER, *Compound butters*), garnish with thin round slices of smoked eel and surround with yolk of hard boiled eggs and chives, chopped separately.

Canapés with spiny lobster. CANAPÉS DE LANGOUSTE—Follow the recipe for *Shrimp canapés*, using *Spiny lobster butter* (see BUTTER, *Compound butters*) and slices of spiny lobster or spiny lobster cut into dice.

Canapés with pickled tongue. CANAPÉS À L'ÉCARLATE—Slice a sandwich loaf, spread the slices with *Paprika butter*, garnish with thin slices of pickled or smoked tongue or with tongue cut into very small dice. Surround with a border of *Paprika butter* (see BUTTER, *Compound butters*).

Canapés à la Véron—Slice a square-shaped black rye loaf, spread the slices with *Horseradish butter* (see BUTTER, *Compound butters*), garnish with thin slices of Bayonne ham, surround with a border of the yolks of hard boiled eggs and parsley chopped up, in equal proportions.

Canapés with York ham. CANAPÉS À LA YORKAISE—Slice a sandwich loaf, spread the slices with *Chivry butter* (see BUTTER, *Compound butters*), garnish with thin slices of York ham and surround with a border of chopped parsley.

Carolines—Small éclairs made of unsweetened *Chou paste* (see DOUGH), garnished to taste with a great many different preparations such as *mousses* or *purées* made of shrimps, prawns, crayfish, lobster, spiny lobster, foie gras, salmon, sole, poultry, game, etc. The éclairs are coated with a *Chaud-froid sauce* (see SAUCE) in keeping with the filling and glazed with jelly. Arrange them on a paper doyley.

Caroline éclairs can also be filled with salpicons blended with a *Chaud-froid sauce* (see SAUCE), or with mayonnaise or jelly. They can also be garnished with fresh caviar.

When served in restaurants or hotels the filling of the éclairs should always be made clear on the menu, e.g. *Caroline with foie gras*, *Caroline with salmon*, *with caviar*, etc.

Caviar—The word 'caviar' generally indicates fresh caviar, i.e. the roe of one of the members of the sturgeon family.

Salted and pressed caviars are also on the market, but their flavour is not so good as that of the real caviar.

Fresh caviar is served in its original container surrounded by crushed ice or in special containers which must also be surrounded by ice.

Caviar should be delicately handled. It should be served with special spoons made of crystal or ivory.

Caviar is usually served with thin slices of rye bread lightly buttered, or with a kind of Russian pancake called *blini* (see BLINI).

Lemon and chopped chives must be provided when serving caviar and each diner helps himself according to taste.

Caviar barquettes or tartlets. BARQUETTES, TARTELETTES AU CAVIAR—Use very small barquettes or tartlets. Garnish with fresh caviar. Serve on a paper doyley.

Small brioches with caviar. PETITES BRIOCHES AU CAVIAR—Use very small *Brioches à tête** made from unsweetened dough. Hollow out the brioches and fill with fresh caviar. Serve on a paper doyley.

Celeriac. CÉLERI-RAVE—Cut into dice, cook quickly, drain, season with oil and vinegar, mayonnaise or mustard.

Celery à la grecque. CÉLERI À LA GRECQUE—Trim and wash the celery, cut the celery hearts into quarters and prepare in the same way as *Artichokes à la grecque*.

Cherries in vinegar, also called preserved cherries. BIGARREAUX AU VINAIGRE—Choose very firm white heart cherries. Cut their stalks by two thirds.

Put the cherries in an earthenware jar. Sprinkle with tiny pieces of thyme and bay leaf.

Season some vinegar with salt and two cloves. Bring to the boil. Pour over the cherries. Cover the jug with a lid. Keep cool. Leave to infuse for 15 days.

Serve the cherries in an hors-d'oeuvre dish. Sprinkle with the marinade.

Cherries preserved in vinegar are served separately as hors-d'oeuvre or with cold or hot meat dishes.

Chicken Reine—Breast of chicken, truffles, and mushrooms cut into dice, seasoned with oil, vinegar, salt and pepper, or with mayonnaise. The ingredients can also be blended with a *White chaud-froid sauce* (see SAUCE).

Salt cod. MORUE:

Curried salt cod. ESCALOPES DE MORUE À L'INDIENNE—Free the cod thoroughly from salt. Cut $\frac{1}{2}$ pound (250 grams) of fillets of cod into thin narrow slices. Wash, and dry the slices in a cloth. Flour lightly and cook quickly in boiling oil.

Take the fish out of the pan. Cook two tablespoons of finely minced onion in the pan, sprinkle in a tablespoon of curry powder, moisten with $\frac{3}{4}$ cup ($1\frac{1}{2}$ decilitres) of white wine and a little lemon juice and add a little crushed garlic. Allow to boil for a few minutes before putting the slices of cod into this *court-bouillon**. Bring to the boil again, cover and remove from the heat.

Allow to cool, arrange in an hors-d'oeuvre dish and surround with slices of lemon cut with a fluted cutter.

Cod tonges à la madrilène. LANGUES DE MORUES À LA MADRILÈNE—Cook an unpeeled clove of garlic in oil. Toss the cod tongues in this oil, which must be very hot.

Pour over the tongues a sufficient quantity of vinegar to cover them. Season with thyme, powdered bay leaf and red Spanish pepper.

Cook in an open pan for 12 minutes. At the last moment sprinkle in a generous amount of freshly chopped fennel.

Leave to cool in the stock. Arrange in an hors-d'oeuvre dish.

Marinated cod tongues. LANGUES DE MORUES MARINÉES—Free the cod tongues from salt. Fry quickly in olive oil.

Moisten the tongues with white wine *Court-bouillon** but add just enough to cover them. Cook slowly for 12 minutes.

Put the tongues and the cooking liquor into a terrine. Leave to cool.

Arrange in an hors-d'oeuvre dish. Sprinkle with chopped parsley.

Crayfish. ÉCREVISSES—Crayfish tails cut into dice, seasoned with oil, vinegar, salt and pepper, or with a mayonnaise.

Cucumbers. CONCOMBRES—Cut fresh cucumbers into small dice, put them in a dish and sprinkle them with salt. Season with salt, pepper, vinegar and oil.

Cucumber à la grecque. CONCOMBRES À LA GRECQUE—Cut the cucumber into chunks and proceed as for *Artichokes à la grecque*, but cook only for 10 or 12 minutes.

Cucumber salad. CONCOMBRES EN SALADE—Peel the cucumbers and cut them lengthwise into very thin slices.

Put them on a cloth, sprinkle them with fine salt and leave them to render their liquor for 30 minutes. Drain, dry, and season with oil, vinegar, pepper, parsley and chopped chervil.

Cucumber stuffed with vegetable salad. CONCOMBRES FARCIS À LA PRINTANIÈRE—Cut a large cucumber into uniform chunks and blanch in salted water. Drain, dry, and hollow out to give them the shape of *cassolettes*. Fill with a vegetable salad: carrots, turnips, French (string) beans cut into dice, and peas, blended with a thick mayonnaise.

Arrange the pieces of stuffed cucumber on an hors-d'oeuvre dish and sprinkle with oil and vinegar.

Éclairs à la Karoly—Stuff éclairs with a game purée, coat with a *Brown chaud-froid sauce* (see SAUCE) and glaze over with jelly. Serve on a paper doily.

Eel. ANGUILLE—For the general method of cleaning and cooking, see EEL. Various dishes which can be served as hot or cold hors-d'oeuvre, particularly *Eels au vert**, are also described in the section EEL.

Commachio eel. ANGUILLE DE COMMACHIO—This kind of salted and smoked eel is only used as hors-d'oeuvre. Serve in an hors-d'oeuvre dish.

Eel à l'indienne. ANGUILLE À L'INDIENNE—Proceed as for *Eel à l'italienne*. Moisten with a *court-bouillon** seasoned with curry powder. Put into a terrine with the liquid. This dish must be completely cooled before it is served.

Arrange eels on an hors-d'oeuvre dish; garnish with quartered pimentos and thin slices of raw tomatoes which have previously been sprinkled with salt to render their liquor. Finally sprinkle the whole dish with the liquor in which the eel has been cooked.

Eel à l'italienne. ANGUILLE À L'ITALIENNE—Take an eel weighing approximately $1\frac{1}{2}$ pounds (700 to 800 grams) before it is skinned. Cut it into 2 inch pieces.

Thread the pieces, separated by bay leaves, on small wooden skewers.

Put all the skewers in an oiled pan. Season and sprinkle with oil. Cook for 12 minutes in the oven. Drain and remove the pieces of eel from the skewers. Arrange them in a terrine.

Put 1 cup (2 decilitres) of vinegar and $\frac{1}{2}$ cup (1 decilitre) of water into the dish in which the eel has been cooked. Add a lump of sugar, 4 cloves and a pinch of salt. Let this *court-bouillon** boil for 5 minutes. Pour it over the eel. Cover the terrine and put it into a very cool place. Leave for two or three days before serving.

Arrange on an hors-d'oeuvre dish and cover with the jelly which has formed in the terrine. This dish keeps for quite a long time, if the terrine is kept in a cool place.

Jellied eel in Chablis. ANGUILLE AU VIN DE CHABLIS, EN GELÉE—Cut small eels into pieces. Cook the eel in a concentrated fish stock prepared with Chablis. Drain the eel, put the pieces into a small terrine. Clarify the liquid in which the eel has been cooked and cover the pieces in the terrine with this. Let this dish get very cold on ice.

Another way of arranging these jellied eels is to arrange the pieces and let them set in aspic jelly in a round mould.

Eel marinated in red wine. ANGUILLE MARINÉE AU VIN ROUGE—Proceed as described for eel marinated in white wine, but use red wine for the *Court-bouillon*.

Eel marinated in vinegar. ANGUILLE MARINÉE AU VINAIGRE—Proceed as described for *Eel marinated in white wine* but use vinegar instead of white wine for the *Court-bouillon*.

Eel marinated in white wine. ANGUILLE MARINÉE AU VIN BLANC—Cut the eel into regular pieces. Mince onions and cook in butter until they are very soft. Line a shallow pan with these onions and put the eel on them. Cover the eel with *Court-bouillon XII**. Add a large *bouquet garni**. Cook for twenty minutes. Cool the eel in its liquor and serve on an hors-d'oeuvre dish.

Eel à l'orientale. ANGUILLE À L'ORIENTALE—Proceed with eel, cut into pieces, as for *Red mullet à l'orientale*.

Smoked eel (Kiel). ANGUILLE FUMÉE DE KIEL—Cut the eel into fillets or into very thin slices. Arrange on an hors-d'oeuvre dish. Garnish with fresh parsley and half slices of lemon cut with a fluted cutter.

Smoked eel canapés—See *Canapés*.

Eel in verjuice. ANGUILLE AU VERJUS—Cut the eel in pieces. Chop up onions and cook them gently in butter. Line the bottom of a flat pan with these onions and place the pieces of eel on top. Season. Add a *bouquet garni*. Moisten with verjuice and white wine in equal quantities. Finish the dish as for *Eel marinated in white wine*.

Hors-d'oeuvre (*Robert Carrier*)

Eggs—Oeufs:

Hard boiled eggs. Oeufs durs—Cut into dice or slice, season with oil, vinegar, salt and pepper or with mayonnaise.

Stuffed eggs. Oeufs farcis—Boil the eggs hard. Cut into halves. Take out the yolks and mix these with whatever preparation is used as stuffing. Another way of stuffing eggs is to cut a little off at both ends so that they can stand. Carefully take the yolks out without breaking the white. Stuff the eggs to taste. Arrange them standing up looking like little barrels.

Salads and *salpicons** can be used as stuffings for eggs.

Decorate the halved eggs or the little barrel-shaped eggs, glaze over with jelly; arrange on an hors-d'oeuvre dish or on a plate garnished with curly parsley.

Egg stuffing à la moscovite. Farce d'oeufs à la moscovite—Pound two hard boiled eggs. Add 2 tablespoons of thick mayonnaise, 1 tablespoon of finely chopped onions, cooked until completely tender in oil, and 1 tablespoon of chopped parsley. Season with salt and paprika and mix well.

Plovers' or lapwings' eggs. Oeufs de pluvier, de vanneau—Boil the eggs hard. Peel two thirds of the eggs. Put the part of the egg which is left in the shell on a bed of water cress. The cress should be made to look like a nest. The merits of this hors-d'oeuvre lie mainly in the rarity of the eggs and their high price. Lapwings' eggs appear on the market in France round about Easter. Very high prices are often obtained for those first on sale.

Escabèche of various fishes (Spanish and Provençal cooking). Escabèche de poissons divers—Smelts, mackerels, whitings, red mullets, etc., are washed, cleaned and dried in a cloth. Then they are dipped in flour and fried in olive oil until both sides are lightly coloured. They are arranged in a deep dish and a boiling *court-bouillon** is poured over them. This is prepared as follows:

The oil in which the fishes were fried is heated until it begins to smoke, and the following ingredients are added: $1\frac{1}{4}$ cups ($2\frac{1}{2}$ decilitres) of oil, 5 cloves of unpeeled garlic, an onion and a carrot, both medium-sized and cut into thin rounds. All these ingredients are fried together for a few minutes before the following are added to complete the marinade: $\frac{3}{4}$ cup ($1\frac{1}{2}$ decilitres) of vinegar, $\frac{1}{4}$ cup ($\frac{1}{2}$

decilitre) of water, a sprig of thyme, half a bay leaf, some parsley, three pimentos, salt and pepper. This marinade is cooked for 10 to 12 minutes before it is poured over the fish, which is left to soak in it for 24 hours. The fish should be served cold with the marinade.

Fanchonettes—See *Patties, Fanchonette patties*, below.

Fennel roots. FENOUIL BULBEUX—Peel and wash the bulbous part of the fennel; cut into halves or quarters; serve plain with *Vinaigrette sauce* handed separately.

Fennel roots à la grecque. FENOUIL BULBEUX À LA GRECQUE—Cut the bulbous roots into halves or quarters and proceed as indicated for *Artichokes à la grecque*.

Figs, fresh. FIGUES FRAÎCHES—Serve as they are. Arrange the figs on vine leaves or, preferably on small fig leaves.

French (string) beans. HARICOTS VERTS—Cook in salt water, drain, cut into dice, season with oil and vinegar, salt and pepper, or with mayonnaise.

Frogs' legs. GRENOUILLES—See recipes for the general preparation of dishes with *Frogs' legs**.

Frogs' legs à la grecque. GRENOUILLES À LA GRECQUE—Cook frogs' legs in a *Court-bouillon I (à la grecque)**.

Leave to cool in their cooking stock.

Serve in an hors-d'oeuvre dish or in a glass bowl; garnish with rounds of peeled lemon.

Frogs' legs à la parisienne. GRENOUILLES À LA PARISIENNE—Cook frogs' legs in white wine to which a squeeze of lemon has been added; season with salt and pepper.

Drain the frogs' legs and dry them in a cloth. Cover with *Mayonnaise III* (see SAUCE).

Serve in an hors-d'oeuvre dish on diced potato salad. Garnish with chopped hard boiled eggs (the yolk and the white are chopped separately) and parsley.

Frogs' legs with pimentos. GRENOUILLES AUX PIMENTS DOUX—Cook the frogs' legs as described in the recipe for *Frogs' legs à la parisienne* above. Add finely cut red and green peppers. Add vinegar or lemon juice to the cooking stock and at the last minute dress with a trickle of oil.

Allow to cool. Serve in an hors-d'oeuvre dish or in a crystal bowl.

Frogs' legs à la vinaigrette. GRENOUILLES À LA VINAIGRETTE—Poach the frogs' legs as described in the recipe for *Frogs' legs à la parisienne* above.

Drain the frogs' legs, season with oil, vinegar, pepper, salt and chopped parsley. Sprinkle some of the reduced (concentrated) cooking stock over the dish.

Serve in an hors-d'oeuvre dish, in a crystal bowl, or in a salad bowl.

Gherkins. CORNICHONS—Gherkins in vinegar are served cut into dice.

Goose, smoked. OIE FUMÉE—Cut the breast into very thin slices indeed. Arrange on an hors-d'oeuvre dish with fresh parsley.

Ham (Bayonne, Parma, Westphalia, Ardennes, Toulouse). JAMBONS—Cut the raw ham into very thin slices; arrange in slices or rolled into cornets in an hors-d'oeuvre dish. Garnish with fresh parsley.

Herrings. HARENGS—Cut into small dice fillets of smoked herrings, freed from salt and washed. Season with an oil and vinegar dressing or with mayonnaise. Hard boiled eggs, cut into dice and sprinkled with chives or chopped onions, may be added to the herrings.

Fillets of salted herrings. FILETS DE HARENGS SALÉS—Remove the fillets of six salted herrings; skin them and free them from salt by soaking in milk and water. Drain them, dry in a cloth and arrange in a terrine. Put rounds of blanched onions on them and add thyme, bay leaf and cloves. Pour 1 cup (2 decilitres) of vinegar over the fillets and marinate them in this mixture for five hours. Cover with oil and keep in a cool place.

Serve in an hors-d'oeuvre dish; garnish with capers, gherkins and lemon.

These fillets can also be prepared in a *court-bouillon**, or they can be dressed with a mayonnaise. Finally they can be used as a garnish for canapés, but for this purpose they must be thoroughly dried on a cloth.

Fillets of smoked salted herring. FILETS DE HARENGS SAURS—Remove the fillets of smoked salted herrings; skin them, free them from salt in milk and water. Drain, dry in a cloth, arrange in a terrine, put blanched rounds of onions on them, sprinkle with thyme, add a bay leaf and some cloves, cover with oil; keep cool.

Arrange in an hors-d'oeuvre dish, garnish with hard boiled eggs, chopped parsley, and rounds of fluted lemon slices.

Note. Fillets of smoked and salted herring prepared in this way can be dressed with mayonnaise. They can also be used as garnish for canapés.

The soft and hard roes are steeped in oil and served with the fillets.

Fillets of smoked and salted herrings can be bought ready prepared.

Herrings à la livonienne. HARENGS À LA LIVONIENNE—Choose large smoked herrings. Remove the fillets, skin and trim them. Keep the heads and tails. Cut the fillets into dice and add an equal quantity of potatoes and good, tart apples, also cut into dice.

Season with oil, vinegar and pepper; add chopped parsley, chervil, tarragon and fennel. Mix well.

Arrange on an hors-d'oeuvre dish in the shape of herrings and complete by adding the heads and tails.

Fresh herrings, marinated. HARENGS FRAIS MARINÉS—Take six herrings with soft roes. Divide each into four pieces. Arrange in a buttered or oiled pan.

Make *Court-bouillon XII**, pour over the herrings and bring quickly to the boil. Cover and cook for 10 to 12 minutes.

Put into a terrine with the cooking stock. Let cool before serving.

Arrange in an hors-d'oeuvre dish. Sprinkle with some of the stock; decorate with the vegetables cooked in the *court-bouillon*, and thin rounds of lemon cut with a fluted cutter.

Fresh marinated herrings can also be prepared whole.

Herrings à la portugaise. HARENGS À LA PORTUGAISE—Cut herrings into large pieces and cook in 1 cup (2 decilitres) of *Tomato fondue**.

Serve as above.

Smoked herring à la russe. HARENGS FUMÉS À LA RUSSE—Take the fillets of six smoked herrings, soak them in milk or cold strained tea, skin and cut crosswise into thin slices. Arrange in an hors-d'oeuvre dish, giving them their original shape. Season with several tablespoons of *Vinaigrette sauce* (see SAUCE) to which chervil, tarragon, fennel and chopped shallots have been added. It is also usual to add 2–3 tablespoons of sour cream to the dressing.

Kilkis or Norwegian anchovies—Arrange on an hors-d'oeuvre dish or serve in the original container. See under *Anchovies* above.

Leeks à la grecque. POIREAUX À LA GRECQUE—Choose large tender leeks. Use the white part only. Cut into pieces 2½–3 inches long; blanch and cook as indicated for *Artichokes à la grecque*.

Lobster, spiny lobster and other shellfish. HOMARD, LANGOUSTE, CRUSTACÉS—Cut into dice, season with oil and vinegar, salt and pepper, or with mayonnaise.

Mackerel, marinated. MAQUEREAUX MARINÉS—Serve in an hors-d'oeuvre dish or in the original container.

Marinated mackerel can also be prepared at home. Choose very small fish and proceed as for *Marinated smelts*.

Melon—The serving of melons is a very simple matter. Cut them in half, drain the water and take the seeds out. Cut in slices. Serve on a dish covered with green leaves. Surround with crushed ice.

Small preserved melons. PETITS MELONS CONFITS—Proceed with very small melons as indicated in the recipe for *Gherkins in vinegar* (see GHERKINS).

Leave to soak for 10 days before serving. Serve in an hors-d'oeuvre dish or in an earthenware jar.

Mortadella. MORTADELLE—Cut the mortadella into thin slices. According to their diameter, divide the slices in two or cut into quarters. Arrange on an hors-d'oeuvre dish, flat or rolled into cornets. Garnish with fresh parsley.

Mousse Fanchon—This is a very dainty hors-d'oeuvre. In France it is also called *mousse mignonne*. It consists of various kinds of *mousses*.

Take very small cylindrical moulds or other shaped moulds, coat them with jelly, fill them with the various *mousses* and decorate them with minute bits of truffles or other items used generally in the decoration of hors-d'oeuvre. Put in the refrigerator.

Turn out the moulds just before serving. Put them on canapés of sandwich bread spread with a compound butter in keeping with the *mousse*. Arrange on a paper doyley.

Mousses Fanchon can also be served on tartlets or on artichoke hearts.

Mulberries. MÛRES FRAÎCHES—Serve plain in a fruit dish or on a plate covered with green leaves.

Red mullet à l'orientale or red mullet with saffron. ROUGETS À L'ORIENTALE, AU SAFRAN—Choose very small fish. Season with salt and pepper; roll in flour; deep-fry in hot oil.

Arrange the fish on an oiled baking dish. Cover with *Tomato fondue**, spiced with a little bit of saffron, fennel, thyme, powdered bayleaf, some grains of coriander, garlic and chopped parsley. Bring to the boil. Cover the dish and finish the cooking in the oven for 6–8 minutes.

Serve the fish in an hors-d'oeuvre dish (unless the fish has been cooked in a long earthenware or china dish) with slices of peeled lemon. Sprinkle with chopped parsley.

Mushrooms. CHAMPIGNONS—Cook in a white *Court-bouillon III** mushrooms cut into small dice, season with an oil and vinegar dressing, or with mayonnaise.

Marinated cèpes and mushrooms. CÈPES, CHAMPIGNONS MARINÉS—Use very small white firm mushrooms. Parboil for four minutes in salted boiling water. Drain and dry the mushrooms. Put them in an earthenware dish and cover them with a boiling marinade, prepared as follows:

For 2 pounds (1 kilo) of mushrooms, boil together for 10 minutes $2\frac{1}{2}$ cups (5 decilitres) of vinegar, $\frac{3}{4}$ cup ($1\frac{1}{2}$ decilitres) of oil, 3 crushed cloves of garlic, 2 parsley roots, half a bay leaf, a twig of thyme and a little fennel, a teaspoonful of coriander, 6–8 peppercorns.

Leave the mushrooms in the marinade for four to five days. Serve in an hors-d'oeuvre dish.

These mushrooms can be bottled in the prescribed marinade. Bottling jars of one quart (litre) capacity must be boiled for 35 minutes; those of a pint (half litre) capacity only need 25 minutes.

Mussels. MOULES—Cook in white wine. Shell, dry, season with oil and vinegar, salt and pepper or with mayonnaise.

Mussels à la ravigote. MOULES À LA RAVIGOTE—Cook and drain large mussels. Put them in a terrine. Season with *Vinaigrette sauce* (see SAUCE) to which hard boiled eggs, parsley, chervil, tarragon and chopped gherkins have been added. Arrange on an hors-d'oeuvre dish or in small crystal bowls.

Mussel salad. SALADE DE MOULES—Prepare the mussels as for *Mussels à la marinière**. Shell them. Dress with oil, vinegar, pepper and *fines herbes*. Serve in an hors-d'oeuvre dish.

Mussels à la tartare. MOULES À LA TARTARE—Prepare some large mussels *à la marinière*. Shell them and arrange in an hors-d'oeuvre dish or glass bowl. Mask with *Tartare sauce* (see SAUCE). Surround with half-slices of lemon cut with a fluted knife.

Olives—Arrange on an hors-d'oeuvre dish without dressing them.

Black olives. OLIVES NOIRES—These can be bought ready for the table and are served without dressing. Arrange on an hors-d'oeuvre dish.

Stuffed olives. OLIVES FARCIES—Use olives freed from salt. Choose large stoned olives. Stuff with a suitable compound butter. The most usual stuffing for olives is *Anchovy butter** (see BUTTER, *Compound butters*). Arrange the stuffed olives on an hors-d'oeuvre dish and dress with a few spoonfuls of oil.

Stuffed olives can also be bought.

Onions. OIGNONS—Cut raw into dice, blanch, drain, season with oil, vinegar, salt and pepper, or with mayonnaise.

Onions à la grecque. OIGNONS À LA GRECQUE—Prepared like *Artichokes à la grecque**.

Onions à l'orientale. OIGNONS À L'ORIENTALE—See ONION.

Oysters (*Mac Fisheries*)

Oysters. HUÎTRES—Oysters are usually eaten raw (see OYSTERS). There are a number of recipes for serving oysters as a cold hors-d'oeuvre. The most famous are *Oysters à l'andalouse*, *Oysters in barquettes (pastry boats)*, *Oysters with caviar*, *The gastronome's oyster*, and *Marinated oysters*. (See OYSTERS.)

Pastry straws. ALLUMETTES:

Anchovy pastry straws. ALLUMETTES AUX ANCHOIS—Proceed as for *Hot anchovy allumettes*. Serve cold.

Caviare pastry straws. ALLUMETTES AU CAVIAR—Prepare pastry as for *Allumettes**. Cover with a thin layer of fish stuffing and cook in the oven. Cool and cover with fresh caviar.

Norwegian pastry straws. ALLUMETTES À LA NORVÉGIENNE—Prepare the pastry as for *Allumettes**. Cover with a thin layer of a *salpicon** of hard boiled eggs, blended with a *Béchamel sauce* (see SAUCE). Bake in the oven; let cool and garnish with Norwegian anchovy fillets.

Parisian pastry straws. ALLUMETTES À LA PARISIENNE—Prepare the pastry as for *Allumettes**. Coat with a thin layer of *Chicken mousseline forcemeat* (see FORCEMEAT) and bake in the oven.

Cool, garnish with thin strips of breast of chicken alternating with slices of truffles and pickled tongue. Glaze with jelly.

Vladimir pastry straws. ALLUMETTES VLADIMIR—Prepare the pastry as for *Allumettes**, coat with a thin layer of pike stuffing and crayfish butter. Bake in the oven. Leave to cool, garnish with small slices of smoked salmon, alternating with slices of truffles. Glaze with jelly.

Patties. BOUCHÉES—Very small patties made of puff pastry garnished with different *mousses*:* prawns, shrimps, crayfish, foie gras, game, poultry, etc.

Fanchonette patties. BOUCHÉES FANCHONETTE—Make very small patties of puff pastry. Garnish with a salad made of breast of chicken and a *salpicon** of red and green peppers seasoned with mayonnaise. Put a fairly thick slice of truffle on each patty.

Small patties can be garnished in the same way as canapés, tartlets, and other similar preparations.

Sweet peppers. PIMENTS DOUX—Skin the peppers, open them and take the seeds out. Cut into sticks and season with oil, vinegar, salt and pepper. Arrange in an hors-d'oeuvre dish, sprinkle with chopped parsley, garnish with thin rings of raw onion.

Small green peppers. PETITS PIMENTS VERTS, POIVRONS—Proceed as indicated for *sweet peppers.*

Pickles—Arrange in an hors-d'oeuvre dish or serve in the original container.

Pissalat (condiment)—This can be bought ready-made.

To make it yourself pickle for eight days a mixture of small shad, herrings, sardines and anchovies (the anchovies preponderating). Then rub through a sieve and dilute with some spoonfuls of the brine in which the fish were pickled. Add some cloves and put into jars. Seal well and keep in a cool place.

Pissalat condiment can be used as it is, or with oil added to it.

Potatoes. POMMES DE TERRE—Cooked in water, cut into dice, or sliced, seasoned with oil, vinegar, salt and pepper, or with mayonnaise.

Printanière—See *Spring vegetables*, below.

Radishes. RADIS:

Black radishes. RADIS NOIRS—Scrape the radishes and cut them into thin slices; sprinkle them with salt and leave them to render their liquor for 30 minutes. Dry and arrange in an hors-d'oeuvre dish.

Slices of black radish can be served as they are or you can add a little *Vinaigrette sauce* (see SAUCE). In Russia, black radish is generally served with a sour cream dressing.

Red and white radishes. RADIS ROSES, RADIS GRIS—Scrape the radishes, cut the green part short, wash and arrange in an hors-d'oeuvre dish. Serve with salt and fresh butter.

Red radishes are often used to decorate cold dishes and salad arrangements.

Rollmops

Rollmops—Fillets of herring, marinated and strongly spiced. They are stuffed with a gherkin, rolled up and secured with a little wooden stick. Rollmops are served on an hors-d'oeuvre dish decorated with rounds of onions.

Rolls, garnished. PETITS PAINS GARNIS—Choose very small oblong-shaped rolls made with butter. Similarly shaped rolls made from *ordinary brioche dough* (see DOUGH) can also be used. Fill them *à la française*, or *à la russe*.

A la française: Cut open on one side only. Spread with butter (either ordinary butter or mustard butter). Garnish with thin slices of breast of chicken (or other poultry), ham, pickled tongue, fillet of beef, smoked salmon or similar items according to taste.

Various purées or foie gras can also be used as stuffing.

A la russe: Take a round slice off the top of the rolls. Empty the rolls through this opening without breaking the crust. Fill the roll with a purée, a salad, or a *salpicon**.

Whatever filling is used, arrange the rolls on a paper doyley, or on a napkin.

Rolls *à la française* are served at luncheon or as sandwiches.

Rolls *à la russe* should always be very small. They belong to a Russian hors-d'oeuvre, i.e. *zakuski.*

Salami—Cut into thin slices, arrange on an hors-d'oeuvre dish, garnish with fresh parsley.

Salmon à la canadienne. SAUMONS À LA CANADIENNE—Cut the salmon in squares and sauté it in oil. Season with salt and paprika.

Add okra pods (ladies' fingers) which have been poached separately. Moisten with white wine and lemon juice. Cover with a lid and simmer for a few seconds. Leave to cool.

Arrange in an hors-d'oeuvre dish. Garnish with red and green peppers, peeled and cut into dice. Pour a little olive oil over the dish.

Fresh salmon can be served as an hors-d'oeuvre following the instructions given for different sorts of fish as hors-d'oeuvre.

Salmon paupiettes à l'impériale. PAUPIETTES DE SAUMON À L'IMPÉRIALE—Flatten very thin narrow slices of salmon, season, coat lightly with a thin layer of pike forcemeat with a little shallot and some chopped parsley added to it, roll it up into the shape of a *paupiette** and secure with string.

Put the paupiettes into an oiled pan, packing them in fairly tightly. Moisten with a few tablespoons of white wine and a squeeze of lemon juice. Season and add a little bouquet of fennel. Simmer very slowly with the lid on.

Drain the paupiettes, untie and place each one on a

very small artichoke heart, cooked in a white wine stock. Arrange in an hors-d'oeuvre dish, sprinkle with the stock in which the paupiettes have been cooked, add a little olive oil and a few spices. Decorate with capers, half slices of lemon cut with a fluted cutter and fresh parsley.

Salmon paupiettes au vert. PAUPIETTES DE SAUMON AU VERT—Prepare the paupiettes as in the preceding recipe. Cook them according to the instruction for *Eels au vert**.

Smoked salmon. SAUMON FUMÉ—Cut the smoked salmon into very thin slices. Arrange on an hors-d'oeuvre dish, flat or rolled into cornets. Garnish with fresh parsley.

Smoked salmon Boston style. SAUMON FUMÉ À LA BOSTONAISE—Cut ¼ pound (125 grams) of smoked salmon into very thin short strips. Add ¼ pound (125 grams) of cooked mushrooms and one green and one red peeled pepper (75 grams of each) cut in the same way. Season with mayonnaise mixed with a very little *Tabasco sauce* (American commercial product). Arrange on an hors-d'oeuvre dish, surround with the chopped yolks and whites of hard boiled eggs and sprigs of parsley. Sprinkle with chopped parsley and serve.

Smoked salmon à la moscovite. SAUMON FUMÉ À LA MOSCOVITE—Roll very small slices of smoked salmon into cornets. Fill the cornets with fresh caviar. Arrange the cornets in a circle on a round crystal plate. Decorate with the chopped yolks and whites of hard boiled eggs, parsley and capers.

Sardines in oil. SARDINES À L'HUILE—Arrange on an hors-d'oeuvre dish, dress with oil, garnish with capers and fresh parsley.

Sardine purée. PURÉE DE SARDINES—Put a dozen well boned sardines which have been kept in olive oil into a mortar. Pound together in the mortar with 4 yolks of hard boiled eggs. Pass through a fine strainer and use for cold or hot hors-d'oeuvre.

Sausages, various. SAUCISSONS—Among the large number of different sausages which can be bought ready in French shops and served as hors-d'oeuvre are the following: Arles, Bologna, Brittany, Florence, Frankfurt, Dutch, Hungary, Lorraine, Luchon, Lyon, Milan, Nancy, Rennes, Strasbourg, Toulouse, Verona.

They are all cut into thin round slices and arranged on an hors-d'oeuvre dish with fresh parsley.

Goose liver sausage. SAUCISSON DE FOIE GRAS—Cut into thin round slices and arrange on an hors-d'oeuvre dish with fresh parsley.

Saveloys (sausage). CERVELAS—Cook various kinds of saveloys and let cool. Cut into thin slices and serve like other sausage.

Sheep's trotters à la vinaigrette. PIEDS DE MOUTON À LA VINAIGRETTE—Cook the sheep's trotters in the usual way (see OFFAL, VARIETY MEATS); drain, bone and cut into very small pieces. Season the meat, while it is still hot with oil, vinegar, salt, pepper, onions and chopped parsley. Arrange in small salad bowls or in an hors-d'oeuvre dish.

Shellfish, mixed. FRUITS DE MER—Different kinds of shellfish served raw.

Shrimps. CREVETTES—Shrimps' tails, cut into dice, seasoned with oil, vinegar, salt and pepper, or with mayonnaise.

Shrimp salad. SALADE DE CREVETTES—Shell the shrimps; put them in a deep glass dish. Cover the tails with mayonnaise. Garnish the dish with lettuce, leaving the centre free; put rounds of hard boiled eggs in the middle.

Sigui, Smoked. SIGUI FUMÉ–Cut smoked sigui into very thin slices, arrange on an hors-d'oeuvre dish and garnish with fresh parsley. You can also use smoked sigui for filling barquettes, canapés, tartlets, etc.

Smelts in marinade. ÉPERLANS MARINÉS—Clean and dry 24 carefully chosen smelts. Roll them in flour and fry them in boiling oil so that they quickly colour on both sides. Season.

Drain the smelts; arrange them in a deep dish, put rounds of blanched onions on them and sprinkle with thyme and bay leaf; add peppercorns and cloves. Cover with cold concentrated vinegar. Leave the smelts for 12 hours in this marinade. Serve in an hors-d'oeuvre dish.

Sour-sweet pickles (Aceto-dolce)—Different kinds of vegetables and fruits are preserved in vinegar. They are then put in a syrup of must and honey spiced with mustard.

Arrange in an hors-d'oeuvre dish or serve in the original jar.

Sprats—Take the heads and the tails off the fish and skin them. Arrange on a plate and sprinkle with chopped shallots and parsley; moisten with oil and vinegar; leave to steep for several hours in this marinade before serving. Arrange on an hors-d'oeuvre dish; garnish with fresh parsley.

Spring vegetables

Spring vegetables (Printanière)—French beans cut into dice, carrots and turnips cut into very small squares, peas and asparagus tips are all cooked in water, drained and seasoned with oil, vinegar, salt and pepper.

Tartlets, garnished. TARTLETTES GARNIES—Garnished tartlets are prepared and filled in the same way as barquettes; the only difference lies in their shape. Tartlets are baked in small round tins with plain or fluted borders.

Toast, garnished. TOASTS GARNIS—All recipes for garnished canapés can be used for garnished toast.

Tomatoes. TOMATES—Peel and seed the tomatoes. Cut them into dice or into slices. Sprinkle with salt, leave them to stand for a while, then season with oil, vinegar, salt and pepper.

Tomatoes à l'antiboise. TOMATES À L'ANTIBOISE—Choose nice red, uniform, small tomatoes. Take out the seeds without breaking the flesh. Leave them for one hour in oil, vinegar, salt and pepper. Garnish them with a mixture of chopped tunny (tuna fish) in oil, hard boiled eggs, capers, parsley, chervil and tarragon blended with a strongly flavoured mayonnaise to which anchovy essence has been added. Arrange on an hors-d'oeuvre dish or on a plate, sprinkle with the marinade and garnish with fresh parsley and half slices of lemon cut with a fluted cutter.

Tomatoes à la vinaigrette. TOMATES À LA VINAIGRETTE—Skin the tomatoes, take the seeds and water out without breaking them. Cut into slices or into quarters. Put on a towel, cover with salt and leave them to render their liquor for one hour.

Arrange in an hors-d'oeuvre dish, sprinkle with oil and vinegar, chopped parsley, chervil and tarragon. Sprinkle with freshly ground pepper and garnish with thin little rounds of raw onion, if liked.

Stuffed tomatoes

Stuffed tomatoes. TOMATES FARCIES—Choose and prepare the tomatoes as described in the recipe for *Tomatoes à l'antiboise*. Garnish them with a compound butter, a purée, Russian salad, or a *salpicon**.

Tongue, pickled smoked. LANGUE ÉCARLATE, FUMÉ—Cut into thin slices and serve in an hors-d'oeuvre dish.

Trout à l'orientale. TRUITES À L'ORIENTALE—Prepare and cook very small trout as indicated for *Red mullet à l'orientale* above. Arrange on an hors-d'oeuvre dish.

Trout, marinated. TRUITES MARINÉES—Cook very small trout in *Court-bouillon XII**. Leave them to cool in their cooking stock. Arrange in an hors-d'oeuvre dish. Pour the stock over the fish. Garnish with slices of lemon, seeded and peeled, and fresh parsley.

Truffles. TRUFFES—Cut truffles cooked or raw into dice or strips, season with oil, vinegar, salt and pepper or with mayonnaise. Truffles can also be blended with jelly or with a *Brown chaud-froid sauce* (see SAUCE).

Tunny (Tuna-fish). THON—Marinate in oil, cut into dice, season with oil, vinegar, salt and pepper, or with mayonnaise.

Tunny (tuna fish) à la nantaise. THON À LA NANTAISE—Cut tunny (tuna) fish in oil neatly into round slices. Cover the slices with a thin coating of *Horse-radish butter* (see BUTTER, *Compound butters*), arrange two by two in a circle on a small round plate, alternating with rounds of cooked beetroot. Garnish the centre of the plate with a salad of mussels and potatoes. Sprinkle with chives and chopped tarragon.

Tunny (tuna fish) in oil. THON À L'HUILE—Arrange canned tunny (tuna fish) on an hors-d'oeuvre dish, dress with oil and garnish with capers or fresh parsley.

Vegetable boats, garnished. BARQUETTES DE LÉGUMES GARNIES—Pieces of vegetables, mainly beetroot and cucumber, which are shaped like boats, hollowed out and then garnished in different ways.

All the fillings given for barquettes also apply as garnishes for vegetable boats. The most usual garnish for this kind of hors-d'oeuvre are caviar, vegetable macédoine, purées, butter compounds, *salpicons** of shellfish, or other kinds of fish and of poultry.

Vegetable julienne. JULIENNE DE LÉGUMES—Cook the following fine *julienne** slowly in oil in a covered pan. ½ cup (100 grams) of the white part of leeks, ½ cup (100 grams) of celery and 4 tablespoons (50 grams) of onions. Season.

When three quarters cooked add 4 tablespoons (50 grams) of raw mushrooms also cut into *julienne* strips. Blend with fresh cream or with mayonnaise, or leave as it is, according to what other dishes you are serving.

Watercress canapés. CANAPÉS AU CRESSON—Slice a sandwich loaf. Spread with a butter made like *Tarragon butter* (see BUTTER, *Compound butters*), substituting watercress leaves for the tarragon; garnish with leaves of blanched watercress and surround with a border of chopped hard boiled eggs.

Whitebait, marinated. NONATS MARINÉS—Put the fish in a deep dish. Cover with a boiling marinade made with white wine. Cover and leave to cool before serving. Arrange in an hors-d'oeuvre dish, sprinkle with chopped parsley and surround with half slices of lemon cut with a fluted cutter.

Whitebait salad. SALADE DE NONATS—Put a twig of thyme, a bay leaf and some salt into a pot of water. Bring to the boil, put the fish in and boil for one minute. Drain, arrange in a salad bowl or an hors-d'oeuvre dish, and sprinkle with some *Vinaigrette sauce* (see SAUCE).

Zampino—Boned and stuffed pigs' trotters—a dish found ready for cooking. Cook and leave to cool. Cut into very thin slices. Arrange on an hors-d'oeuvre dish, garnished with parsley. Zampino can be bought ready cooked in shops selling Italian produce.

HOT HORS-D'OEUVRE:

Allumettes—Allumettes are puff pastry rectangles, spread with a suitable mixture and baked in the oven.

Make puff pastry. Roll out to thickness of ⅛ inch and cut into ribbons 3 inches long.

Spread with a cold forcemeat, generally made of poultry or fish, and add garnish appropriate to the recipe.

Cut the ribbons into rectangles about 1 inch wide. Put on a baking sheet. Bake in the oven for 12 to 15 minutes. Arrange on a napkin and serve very hot.

Allumettes with anchovies I. ALLUMETTES AUX ANCHOIS—*Spread: Fish forcemeat* (see FORCEMEAT) with *Anchovy butter* (see BUTTER, *Compound butters.*)

Garnish: Fillets of anchovy.

Allumettes with anchovies II. ALLUMETTES AUX ANCHOIS—*Spread: Salpicon** of fillets of anchovies and hard boiled eggs blended with a thick *Béchamel sauce* (see SAUCE).

Garnish: Fillets of anchovy.

Allumettes à l'andalouse—*Spread: Poultry forcemeat* (see FORCEMEAT) seasoned with paprika, mixed with a *salpicon** made of lean ham and onions cooked in butter, also seasoned with paprika.

Allumettes à la chalonnaise—*Spread: Poultry forcemeat* (see FORCEMEAT) to which diced cock's combs and kidneys, mushrooms and truffles have been added.

Allumettes Chavette—*Spread: Fish forcemeat* (see FORCEMEAT) with *Crayfish butter* (see BUTTER, *Compound butters*).

Garnish: Crayfish tails and truffles.

Allumettes à l'écarlate—*Spread: Veal forcemeat* (see FORCEMEAT) to which a *salpicon** of pickled or smoked tongue has been added.

Allumettes à l'écossaise—*Spread:* Purée of haddock blended with a thick *Béchamel sauce* (see SAUCE).

Allumettes à la florentine—*Spread:* Spinach cooked in butter, blended with a thick *Béchamel sauce* (see SAUCE), to which grated cheese has been added. At the last minute sprinkle with Parmesan cheese and brown in the oven.

Anchovy tarts with pissalat. TOURTE D'ANCHOIS AU PISSALAT—Roll out *lining pastry* (see DOUGH) to a thickness of ¼ inch.

Line a large tart tin with this pastry, crimp the edges. Free fillets of anchovy from salt, dry them well in a cloth and cover the pastry with them in a criss-cross pattern. Sprinkle a large spoonful of finely chopped onions over the anchovies and distribute 20 black olives over them. Dress with three tablespoons of olive oil mixed with two tablespoons of *pissalat.** Cook in a slow oven. Serve very hot.

Anchoyade I—Scrape fillets of anchovy and free from salt, steep them for several minutes in olive oil to which chopped garlic and ground pepper have been added.

Arrange the anchovy fillets on fairly large pieces of crust, cut from the lower part of home-made bread.

Crush the fillets on to the bread by pressing them with other pieces of bread cut into squares which are then removed. The diners eat these square pieces one after the other as they get impregnated with anchovy.

Moisten the crusts of bread with the oil in which the fillets have soaked and grill.

This Provençal dish is known in the Bouches-du-Rhône district under the name of *quichet*.

Anchoyade II—Free fillets of anchovy from salt. Pound, moistening with a few spoonfuls of olive oil and vinegar.

Spread this purée on large slices of bread. Cover the purée with slices of hard boiled eggs and minced onions. Add a few drops of olive oil, season with freshly ground pepper and heat lightly in the oven.

Attereaux—This name is given to the method of cooking on skewers, in which the ingredients, instead of being grilled, are coated with a sauce and dipped into egg and breadcrumbs and fried.

Method. All the ingredients are first cooked, then cut into uniform pieces. Any ingredient used for *attereaux* must be quite cold before it is put on a wooden or metal skewer. The different ingredients used are garnished according to their nature with mushrooms, truffles, etc.

The sauce must be thick and almost cold.

When the skewer is full and coated with sauce it is left to get quite cold before it is dipped into egg and breadcrumbs. *Attereaux* are fried just before serving, drained and dried, arranged on a napkin and garnished with fresh parsley.

Note. If wooden skewers are used in the preparation of *attereaux*, they must be taken out when the cooking is finished and replaced by silver skewers for serving.

It is better, in the preparation of *attereaux*, to use short metal skewers instead of wooden ones. This does away with the necessity of replacing the skewers after cooking.

In ancient times *attereaux* were served as an *entrée volante* or small entrée. They were then not served on a napkin arranged on a plate, but in a circle on a crust of fried sandwich bread, or on a foundation of rice.

All kinds of meat, fish, crustaceans, and an infinite variety of other things, cut into small square pieces, can be used for *attereaux.*

The sauce can be white or brown, made from meat, fish or vegetable stock, according to the principal ingredient of the *attereaux*. This ingredient determines the name given to the *attereaux* on the menu.

Attereaux à l'écarlate—*Ingredients:* pickled or smoked tongue, mushrooms, truffles.

Coating: thick *Velouté sauce* (see SAUCE) with tomato purée added.

Attereaux à la Villeroi—*Ingredients:* brains, cock's combs or combs of other birds, foie gras, sweetbread, cock's kidneys, etc. The dish may be completed with the usual additions such as mushrooms, truffles, artichoke hearts, pickled tongue, ham, etc. Poultry or other cold meat can be used in the same way.

Coating: Villeroi sauce (see SAUCE).

Attereaux of brain à l'ancienne. ATTEREAUX DE CERVELLE À L'ANCIENNE—*Ingredients:* poached brain, mushrooms, truffles.

Coating: Villeroi sauce (see SAUCE).

Attereaux of brain à l'italienne. ATTEREAUX DE CERVELLE À L'ITALIENNE—*Ingredients:* poached brain, ham, mushrooms.

Coating: Duxelles sauce (see SAUCE).

Attereaux of brain à la mirepoix. ATTEREAUX DE CERVELLE À LA MIREPOIX—*Ingredients:* poached brain, ham.

*Coating: mirepoix** of vegetables blended with *Villeroi sauce* (see SAUCE).

Attereaux of chicken livers à la duxelles. ATTEREAUX DE FOIES DE VOLAILLE À LA DUXELLES—*Ingredients:* Chicken livers browned lightly in butter, mushrooms.

Coating: Duxelles sauce (see SAUCE).

Attereaux of cock's combs à l'ancienne. ATTEREAUX DE CRÊTES DE COQ À L'ANCIENNE—*Ingredients:* cock's combs stuffed *à la duxelles**, ham, mushrooms.

Coating: Villeroi sauce (see SAUCE) with tomatoes.

Attereaux of lobster. ATTEREAUX DE HOMARD—*Ingredients:* lobster, mushrooms, truffles.

Coating: Villeroi sauce (see SAUCE) or a *shellfish butter* (see BUTTER, *Compound butters*).

Attereaux of oysters. ATTEREAUX D'HUÎTRES — *Ingredients:* poached oysters, mushrooms.

Coating: Villeroi sauce, based on fish stock (see SAUCE).

Attereaux of Parmesan, also known as à la royale and à la princesse. ATTEREAUX AU PARMESAN—Cook a stiff semolina with Parmesan. Spread out to cool on a baking sheet in ¼ inch layer. When quite cold, cut into circlets 1 inch in diameter. Put these circlets on the skewers, alternating with rounds of Gruyère cheese. Coat with egg and breadcrumbs, but do not coat with any sauce.

Attereaux of sweetbreads. ATTEREAUX DE RIS D'AGNEAU, RIS DE VEAU—*Ingredients:* sweetbreads, mushrooms, truffles.

Coating: Villeroi sauce (see SAUCE).

Attereaux of various vegetables. ATTEREAUX DE LÉGUMES—*Ingredients:* Cooked or parboiled vegetables, such as artichoke hearts, carrots, celeriac, pumpkin, etc. One of these or various combinations can be used.

Coating: thick *Béchamel sauce* (see SAUCE).

Barquettes, garnished. BARQUETTES GARNIES—Oval-shaped tartlets lined with different kinds of pastry: puff pastry, ordinary lining (pie) pastry, etc., baked blind and filled with different ingredients.

Method. When preparing the pastry, roll it out to a thickness of about ⅛ inch. Stamp the dough out with a fluted oval pastry-cutter into as many pieces as you need for your barquettes. Butter barquette baking tins. (These can be plain or fluted.) Put the cut-out pieces of pastry into the moulds, pressing well down so that it clings to all sides of the tins.

Prick the part of the pastry lining the bottom of the tins to prevent blistering. Put into each tin a piece of greaseproof paper and fill the tins with dried peas or rice.

Bake in a moderate oven (375°F.) for 12 to 15 minutes. Remove the paper and the peas or rice. Take the pastry out of the tins, brush over with egg and put back into the oven for a few minutes to dry, leaving the oven door open.

Note. This way of preparing pastry is called *baking blind* (unfilled). The only reason for filling the tartlets with dried vegetables or cereals (which are taken out after cooking and can be used again) is to keep the pastry uniformly hollow.

Fillings for barquettes. The ingredients of the fillings vary according to the recipe chosen. The most usual are purées, ragoûts and *salpicons**. You can also fill barquettes with all the garnishes given for patties, crusts, tartlets, etc.

Once filled, serve the barquettes as they are, or sprinkle with fried breadcrumbs or grated cheese and brown the top under the grill, or decorate as indicated in the recipe.

Serving of barquettes. Cover a round dish with a napkin or a paper doyley and arrange the barquettes on it; garnish with parsley.

Note. Barquettes can be served as a small *entrée* or *entrée volante.* In this case they should be baked in slightly bigger moulds than for hors-d'oeuvre.

Barquettes à l'américaine—

*Garnish. Salpicon** of spiny lobster and *Lobster à l'américaine**. Fill the barquettes, sprinkle with fried breadcrumbs and put in the oven for a short time.

Barquettes with anchovies. BARQUETTES AUX ANCHOIS—Free anchovy fillets from salt; cut mushrooms and onions into dice and cook slowly in butter. Blend all together with a *Béchamel sauce* (see SAUCE). Bake the barquettes blind and fill them with the above *salpicon.* Sprinkle with breadcrumbs fried in butter and drained. Put for a few minutes into a very hot oven. Arrange on a napkin.

Barquettes à la bouquetière—

Garnish. Blend mixed vegetables with a *Béchamel* or a *Velouté sauce* (see SAUCE). Fill the barquettes and put on each a small bouquet of asparagus tips.

Barquettes with chestnuts. BARQUETTES AUX MARRONS—Use best lining pastry (*Fine pastry dough*—see DOUGH) and bake cases for barquettes or tartlets blind (unfilled) as indicated above. Fill with *Chestnut purée**. Pile the purée into a dome and smooth the surface. Sprinkle with grated Parmesan cheese. Pour melted butter over it and brown in a hot oven.

Barquettes with mussels. BARQUETTES DE MOULES—

Garnish. Prepare *mussels à la poulette**, sprinkle fried breadcrumbs over them, fill the barquettes and put in the oven for a few moments.

Barquettes with oysters. BARQUETTES D'HUÎTRES—

Garnish. Poach the oysters and drain; cover with *Oyster sauce* (see SAUCE). Brown in a very hot oven.

Barquettes with shrimps. BARQUETTES DE CREVETTES—

Garnish. Make a ragoût of shrimp tails. Fill the barquettes. Spoon over some *Mornay sauce* (see SAUCE). Sprinkle with cheese. Brown the top under the grill.

Beurrecks à la turque I—Cut ½ pound (250 grams) of Gruyère cheese into dice, mix with ½ cup (1 decilitre) of thick almost cold *Béchamel sauce* (see SAUCE) and leave to get quite cold.

Divide the mixture into small portions (about 40 grams) and mould into cigar shapes.

Make some ordinary noodle paste, roll out wafer thin, enclose each portion of cheese mixture in an oval piece of noodle paste, dip in egg and breadcrumbs and fry just before serving. Arrange on a napkin.

Beurrecks à la turque II—Make the mixture of cheese and *Béchamel sauce* as in the above recipe.

Make ordinary noodle paste, roll out wafer thin, cut into round pieces, put the cheese and béchamel mixture on the pastry and fold it like a turn-over. Dip in egg and breadcrumbs and fry at the last minute.

Blini (Russian cooking)—Blini are a kind of pancake made with yeast. They are very popular in Russia.

Blini are often served with fresh caviar sprinkled with melted butter, or with sour cream.

First method. Dilute ½ ounce (7 to 8 grams) of yeast in 1 cup (2 decilitres) of warm milk. Mix, do not let curdle, pass through a strainer. Sieve 1 cup (125 grams) of fine white flour and 1 cup (150 grams) of buckwheat flour and mix together with a pinch of salt. Put in a bowl and add the liquid. Mix in the yolks of three eggs. The paste should have the consistency of pancake batter and care should be taken to keep it light.

Leave to rise in a warm place for 2 hours.

Add two beaten whites of egg and 1¼ cups (2½ decilitres) of whipped cream.

Cover and leave to rise for 20 minutes.

Second Method. Prepare a yeast batter using 2 cups (250 grams) of sifted flour, ½ ounce (15 grams) of yeast, and 1¼ cups (2½ decilitres) of warm milk.

Leave to rise in a warm place for 2 hours.

Add 1 cup (125 grams) of flour, a pinch of salt, 2 yolks of egg and ¾ cup (1½ decilitres) of warm milk.

Mix. Add 2 beaten whites of eggs.

Cover and leave to rise for 30 minutes.

Third method. Put into a bowl 1¾ cups (250 grams) of buckwheat flour and 5/6 ounce (25 grams) of yeast. Moisten with 1 to 1½ cups (2 to 3 decilitres) of warm water; leave to ferment in a cool place for 4 hours.

Add 1 cup (125 grams) of fine white flour, a pinch of salt, 2 small yolks of egg and ¾ cup (1½ decilitres) of warm cream.

Mix; add 2 firmly beaten whites of egg and half their volume of whipped cream. Leave to rise for 20 minutes.

Blini can also be made of rice flour or maize (corn) flour.

Cooking of blini. In France, blini are cooked in the same way as ordinary pancakes (*crêpes*).

In Russia, blini are fried in special little cast-iron frying pans, divided into flat 'nests', in which up to half a dozen small, absolutely uniform sized, individual pancakes can be cooked at once.

Blini are served in Russia very hot, with melted butter, sour cream, chopped hard boiled eggs in melted butter, caviare, smoked salmon, *kilki*, salted herring, and other similar 'fishy' foods.

Blini with carrots. BLINI AUX CAROTTES—Add purée of carrots to the blini batter. Put a tablespoonful of carrots previously cut into dice and cooked in butter into a buttered frying pan and pour the *blini* mixture over it. Continue as usual.

Blini with caviar. BLINI AU CAVIAR—Prepare the blini according to one of the methods described above.

Serve piping hot with fresh caviar, melted butter and sour cream.

Blini with eggs. BLINI AUX OEUFS—Before putting the *blini* mixture into the buttered frying pan, sprinkle into the pan a spoonful of chopped hard boiled eggs.

Cook the *blini* in the usual way.

Lithuanian blini. BLINI LIVONIENS—Mix in a bowl 4 tablespoons of flour and 4 whole eggs. Add little by little 4 glasses of milk, a pinch of salt and a pinch of sugar.

Incorporate 4 beaten whites of egg and 4 tablespoons of whipped cream.

Cook the *blini* in the usual way.

Brioches, garnished. BRIOCHES GARNIES—These brioches must be very small. They are often served as patties.

Method. Baking: The dough used for garnished brioches is ordinary unsweetened brioche dough. Bake the brioches in very small fluted moulds in the shape of *Brioches à tête**. See BRIOCHE.

Leave them to cool. Remove the heads (keep them to serve as lids). Scoop out the brioches taking care not to break them. Dry them for a few minutes in the oven with the door open. Fill according to instructions.

Garnish. Small *Brioches à la tête* may be filled with the same ingredients as given for patties. When garnished put the heads back on the brioches to serve as lids and put in the oven for a few seconds.

Small garnished brioches can be used as an accompaniment for large dishes of various kinds, in which case they should be baked in very small moulds.

Brochettes—Prepare brochettes according to the recipes given in their alphabetical order in different articles on brochettes. See SKEWER, BEEF, *Fillet of beef on skewers*, MUTTON, *Fillets of Mutton on skewers*.

Brochettes served as an hors-d'oeuvre should be very much smaller than those prepared for an entrée.

Brochettes de Parme—This is another name for *Attereaux au Parmesan.* (See *Attereaux* in this section.)

Brochettes of sweetbreads. BROCHETTES DE RIS D'AGNEAU, RIS DE VEAU—Parboil or braise lamb or calf sweetbreads, cut into square pieces and put them on metal skewers, alternating with rectangles of lean blanched bacon or lean ham and, if desired, with cooked, sliced mushrooms.

Brush the brochettes over with melted butter, roll in fine breadcrumbs and grill on a moderate heat.

Caissettes (small garnished cases)—In former times paper cases were used. Nowadays these are replaced by round or oval receptacles made of oven-proof china, glass or metal.

The cases are filled with ragoûts, *salpicons** or similar ingredients. Recipes for these are given elsewhere; they are the same as for *barquettes*, patties, pies, tartlets, etc.

According to the nature of the garnish used the cases are sprinkled with breadcrumbs or grated cheese and put under the grill. Alternatively, they may be sprinkled with well-drained fried breadcrumbs, and then simply put in the oven. A third possibility is to decorate the cases with truffles, mushrooms, etc.

Canapés or garnished toast. CANAPÉS, TOASTS GARNIS—Cut the canapés from a sandwich loaf, having first removed the crust. Shape them, as required, into squares, rectangles, ovals or rounds.

Toast the slices on both sides, butter them or spread them with whatever ingredient is indicated in the chosen recipe (forcemeat, scrambled eggs, purées, *salpicon**, etc.).

Garnish the canapés as indicated, sprinkle with freshly grated breadcrumbs, fried breadcrumbs or grated cheese, according to the garnish used and grill them or brown them quickly in the oven.

Arrange on a paper doyley or on a napkin and decorate with very green curly parsley.

Garnishes for canapés are numerous. Apart from those given in the recipes which follow, you can use all those indicated in the section on *croûtes**.

Canapés with bloater. CANAPÉS AU BLOATER—For bloater canapés the sandwich loaf should be cut into roundels. Heap the bloater purée, to which *Béchamel sauce* (see SAUCE) and butter have been added, on the round slices of bread and heat in the oven.

Alternatively, garnish the canapés as indicated above but sprinkle them with grated Parmesan cheese and then brown them in the oven.

Canapés with hard boiled eggs. CANAPÉS AUX OEUFS DURS—Make rectangular pieces of toast. Make a *salpicon** of hard boiled eggs blended with a *Béchamel sauce* (see SAUCE). Spread this on the toast and cover each piece with two roundels of hard boiled egg. Fry breadcrumbs in butter and drain well, sprinkle on the canapés and brown lightly in the oven.

Canapés with scrambled eggs. CANAPÉS AUX OEUFS BROUILLÉS—Make roundels of toast. Cover with scrambled eggs arranged in a dome. Sprinkle with grated Parmesan cheese and brown quickly in the oven.

Canapés à la florentine—Toast slices of sandwich bread. Parboil some spinach, drain and rub through a sieve. Blend with a thick *Béchamel sauce* (see SAUCE) and spread on the toast.

Sprinkle with grated Parmesan cheese. Brown quickly in the oven.

Canapés with Gruyère cheese. CANAPÉS AU FROMAGE DE GRUYÈRE—Spread the canapés with a layer of thick *Béchamel sauce* (see SAUCE) to which grated Gruyère cheese and a pinch of cayenne have been added. Scatter diced Gruyère cheese over the canapés covered with the *Béchamel* and brown quickly in the oven.

Canapés can be made in the same way with Cheshire, Edam or Parmesan cheese.

Canapés with ham. CANAPÉS AU JAMBON—Cut the sandwich loaf into oval shaped slices. Make a *salpicon** of York ham or Prague ham and blend it with a concentrated *Demi-glace sauce* (see SAUCE) to which chopped parsley has been added. Spread the *salpicon* on the toast.

Fry slices of ham quickly in butter and put one on each canapé. Sprinkle with breadcrumbs fried in butter.

Canapés with sardines. CANAPÉS AUX SARDINES—Cut rectangular pieces of bread and toast. Cover with fillets of sardines. Heat for a few moments in the oven. Arrange on a napkin.

Alternatively, make a purée of sardines in oil, mixed with hard boiled eggs, rub the mixture through a sieve and add a little English mustard. Spread this on the canapés and arrange on them fillets of sardines in oil.

Sprinkle with breadcrumbs fried in butter and well-drained. Put in the oven for a few minutes. Season with a pinch of cayenne and serve.

Canapés Victoria—Make a *salpicon** of lobster or spiny lobster, truffles and mushrooms all cut into very small dice, blended with a thick *Béchamel sauce* (see SAUCE) and finished off with *Shellfish butter* (see BUTTER, *Compound butters: Shrimp butter*).

Spread the toast with this *salpicon.* Fry breadcrumbs in butter, and drain well. Sprinkle on the canapés and put them in the oven for a few moments.

Cannelons, garnished. CANNELONS GARNIS—Cannelons can be of rectangular shape or made as cornets.

Rectangular. Roll out puff pastry in rectangles measuring $1\frac{1}{2}$ by 4 inches.

Using a forcing (pastry) bag with a plain nozzle make a line of some kind of cold forcemeat or other mixture in the middle of the rectangles of puff pastry. Moisten the border all around the forcemeat and cover with another rectangle of puff pastry. Brush over with egg and bake in the oven.

Cornets. Cut the dough into straight ribbons and roll around special 'funnels' as explained in the section for pastry cornets. See CORNETS.

When the cornets are baked, take the funnels out and fill the cornets. A variety of ingredients could be used as filling, such as *salpicons**, meat purée, fish or crustacean purée, etc.; the purées should be rather thick.

All the garnishes given for *barquettes*, patties, *cassolettes*, and similar dishes can be used for cannelons.

Cassolettes—*Cassolettes* are individual glass, metal or porcelain containers. The most usual ingredients for cassolettes are purées, ragoûts, *salpicons** and similar preparations.

Cassolettes without a border. Fill the cassolettes with the preparation indicated.

Sprinkle with breadcrumbs fried in butter and drained, or, according to the recipe used, with grated cheese. Brown for a few moments in the oven.

Cassolettes with a border of Duchess potato. Use a forcing (pastry) bag with a plain or fluted nozzle and pipe a thin border of *Duchess potato mixture* (see POTATOES) round the edge of the cassolette.

Fill the cassolettes with the preparation indicated, sprinkle with breadcrumbs fried in butter and drained, or with grated cheese, and brown in the oven.

Cassolettes topped with Duchess potato. Prepare the cassolettes as indicated in the above recipe. Fill as described, cover with a layer of *Duchess potato*, pressing down on the edges to seal in the contents. Brush the top with egg. Brown in the oven.

Cassolettes with border and covered with puff pastry. Put a narrow band of ordinary puff pastry round the rim of the cassolettes.

Fill the cassolettes with the desired preparation, which should be cold or lukewarm.

Cover the cassolettes with a round of puff pastry. Press well on to the border. Decorate the top of the cassolettes with flower-shaped ornaments or other motifs made from puff pastry. Brush over with egg and bake in the oven for 10 to 12 minutes.

Cassolettes ambassadrice—Make the lid and a border for the cassolettes, using *Duchess potatoes* (see POTATOES).

Garnish. Ragoût of chicken livers.

Put for a few minutes in the oven.

Cassolettes bouquetière—Make the border of the cassolettes with *Duchess potatoes* (see POTATOES).

*Garnish. Macédoine** of vegetables with cream.

Put in the oven. When taking out of the oven put on each cassolette a spoonful of asparagus tips cooked in butter and a little knob of cauliflower.

Cassolettes à la florentine (with meat)—Use *Duchess potatoes* (see POTATOES) to make the top of the cassolettes.

Put a large tablespoon of spinach leaves cooked in butter at the bottom of the cassolettes. Put on the spinach a tablespoon of *salpicon** of chicken blended with a *Velouté sauce* (see SAUCE). Brown in the oven.

Cassolettes à la gauloise—Use *Duchess potatoes* (see POTATOES) to make the border of the cassolettes.

*Garnish. Salpicon** of cock's combs and kidneys, truffles and mushrooms blended with a *Velouté sauce* (see SAUCE).

Brown in the oven. When taking out of the oven put a *Cock's comb fried à la Villeroi** on each cassolette.

Cassolettes with lobster or spiny lobster. CASSOLETTES AU HOMARD, À LA LANGOUSTE—Make the border or top of whatever preparation you desire.

*Garnish. Salpicon** of lobster or spiny lobster blended with cream and finished off with *shellfish butter* (see BUTTER, *Compound butters: shrimp butter*). Brown in the oven.

Cassolettes marquise—Make the border of the cassolettes of puff pastry.

Garnish. Ragoût of *Crayfish tails à la Nantua** to which diced truffles and mushrooms have been added. Bake in the oven.

Cassolettes Régence—Make the border of the cassolettes using *Duchess potatoes* (see POTATOES).

*Garnish. Salpicon** of breast of chicken and truffles cooked in a *Velouté sauce* (see SAUCE).

Bake in the oven. When taking out, put a large slice of truffle on each cassolette and cover this with a small bouquet of asparagus tips cooked in butter.

Cassolettes Sagan (without a border)—

*Garnish. Salpicon** of truffles and mushrooms cooked in *Velouté sauce* (see SAUCE). Sprinkle with grated Parmesan cheese.

Brown in the oven. When taking out, put on each cassolette a very small slice of calf's brain sautéed in butter.

Cassolettes of sweetbread. CASSOLETTES DE RIS D'AGNEAU, RIS DE VEAU—These can have a border or they can be served plain.

*Garnish. Salpicon** of sweetbread blended with a *Velouté sauce* (see SAUCE), to which truffles and mushrooms can be added if desired. Sprinkle with fried breadcrumbs. Brown in the oven.

Cassolettes à la vénitienne (without a border)—Line the bottom of the cassolettes with macaroni *à l'italienne* cut into dice. Put on the macaroni a tablespoon of ragoût of sweetbreads, truffles and mushrooms, if desired. Sprinkle with fried breadcrumbs. Brown in the oven.

Choux (U.S. cream puffs)—Using ordinary *Chou paste* (see DOUGH), make small choux (cream puffs), the size of a pigeon's egg.

After the choux (cream puffs) are cooked, split the sides open and fill with whatever preparation is indicated in the recipe used.

Heat for a few moments in the oven. Arrange on a napkin.

If the choux are small enough they can be used as a garnish for large dishes; they can also be served as savouries.

Choux can be filled with all the preparations recommended for barquettes, cassolettes, tartlets and other similar dishes.

Choux with cheese. CHOUX AU FROMAGE—

Garnish. Cream made with cheese. Choux with cheese can be filled with a cream made with Cheshire, Gruyère or Parmesan cheese.

Choux à la maraîchère—

*Garnish. Salpicon** of carrots, leeks, celery—all cooked in butter and blended with a thick *Béchamel sauce* (see SAUCE).

Choux à la Nantua—

Garnish. Purée of crayfish to which chopped truffles have been added.

Choux à la royale—

Garnish. Purée of truffles with cream.

Choux à la Saint-Hubert—

Garnish. Purée of game blended with a *Demi-glace sauce* (see SAUCE) based on concentrated game stock.

Choux à la strasbourgeoise—

*Garnish. Salpicon** of foie gras and truffles blended with a concentrated *Demi-glace sauce* (see SAUCE).

Choux à la toulousaine—

Garnish. Salpicon of sweetbreads, cock's combs

and cock's kidneys, mushrooms and truffles blended with an *Allemande sauce*. (See SAUCE.)

Choux au vert-pré—

Garnish. Purée of green beans, green peas and asparagus tips blended with cream.

Cierniki (Polish cookery)—Mix in a terrine ½ pound (250 grams) of pressed white cheese, 1 cup (125 grams) of sifted flour, 3 tablespoons (50 grams) of melted butter and 3 eggs. Season with salt, pepper and grated nutmeg. Blend all these ingredients with a spatula and gradually work in a further ½ cup (75 grams) of flour.

Experiment with poaching a small spoonful of this composition in boiling water. If the mixture is not thick enough add a little more flour; if it is too thick, lighten it with a tablespoon or two of cream.

Sprinkle flour on a table and roll the mixture out on it; shape into small galettes 1½ to 2 inches in diameter and ⅓ inch thick.

Poach the galettes for 15–18 minutes in boiling water, drain them, arrange them in a pie dish and pour melted butter over them.

Cock's Combs. CRÊTES DE COQ—

Attereaux of cock's combs à l'ancienne—See ATTEREAUX in this section.

Fritot of cock's combs—See FRITOT in this section.

Cock's combs Villeroi. CRÊTES DE COQ VILLEROI—Drain the cock's combs cooked in a white *Court-bouillon** and put them in a lukewarm *Villeroi sauce* (see SAUCE).

Take them out and dip one by one in finely grated breadcrumbs. Each cock's comb must be covered all over. Dip into beaten egg and once again in breadcrumbs.

Fry at the last moment. Heap on a napkin (or arrange in a nest of straw potatoes). Garnish with fried parsley.

Serve with a separate *Tomato sauce* or *Périgueux sauce* (see SAUCE).

Stuffed cock's combs Villeroi. CRÊTES DE COQ FARCIES VILLEROI—Choose very large cock's combs. Cook. Open them on the fleshy side without cutting right through.

Stuff them with a little forcemeat. Complete the cooking and serving as in the preceding recipe.

Cock's combs can be stuffed with all kinds of different preparations, such as forcemeats, or purées of mushrooms, foie gras, different vegetables, *Duxelles**, *Brunoise**, *Portugaise**, etc.

Cock's kidneys. ROGNONS DE COQ—Cook the kidneys in a *white court-bouillon I* (see COURT-BOUILLON) as described in the recipe for *Kidneys as a garnish.* Then follow any of the recipes for cock's combs in this section.

Colombines—Line buttered tartlet tins with a *Semolina mixture* flavoured with Parmesan cheese.

Fill the tins with a *salpicon**, a purée or any other mixture generally used for barquettes, patties and other similar dishes. Cover with a thin layer of semolina.

Dip the tins into warm water and turn out the tartlets.

Dip the tartlets in egg and breadcrumbs and deep fry them at the last minute. Arrange on a napkin and serve with fried parsley.

If these tartlets are made in very small tins, they can also be used as a garnish for large dishes.

Craquelins—These are *croquettes* prepared with stuffed pancakes (*crêpes*). This hors-d'oeuvre is better known under the name of *pannequet.*

Crayfish. ÉCREVISSES—Small crayfish, cooked *à la nage*, *à la marinière*, or *à la liégeoise*, can be served as hot hors-d'oeuvre. Crayfish tails are often used as the main ingredient for certain hot hors-d'oeuvre such as fritters (*à la Nantua*), croquettes, stuffed potatoes (*Potato Georgette*), rissoles, soufflés or tartlets.

Cromesquis—See *Kromeskies* in this section.

Croquets—A variety of croquettes made of pasta, macaroni, spaghetti, etc.

Begin by poaching the pasta in salted water, drain and cut into dice. Then blend with a thick *Béchamel sauce* (see SAUCE) and add grated cheese.

This preparation can be finished off with lean ham or scarlet tongue cut into *julienne** strips. Serve with *Tomato sauce* (see SAUCE).

Croquettes—Croquettes served as hot hors-d'oeuvre are composed of one or several preparations cut into small dice (or, in certain cases, chopped). They are blended with a white or brown sauce based on meat, fish or vegetable stock. See CROQUETTES.

Beef croquettes I. CROQUETTES DE BOEUF—Shape according to taste.

Ingredients. Minced boiled beef, blended with a beaten egg, with chopped parsley added.

Serve with *Tomato sauce* (see SAUCE).

Beef croquettes II—Shape according to taste.

*Ingredients. Salpicon** of boiled beef, mushrooms and lean ham, blended with a concentrated *Demi-glace sauce* (see SAUCE).

Serve with *Piquant sauce* (see SAUCE).

Beef croquettes III—Shape according to taste.

*Ingredients. Salpicon** of boiled beef and lean ham, blended with a thick *Béchamel sauce* (see SAUCE).

Serve with *Tomato sauce* (see SAUCE).

Beef croquettes IV—Shape according to taste.

Ingredients. Two-thirds *salpicon** of boiled beef, one-third rice cooked in meat stock.

Serve with *Tomato sauce* (see SAUCE).

Beef croquettes V—

Ingredients. Salpicon of corned-beef (pressed beef) blended with a *Demi-glace sauce* or with a *Béchamel sauce* (see SAUCE).

Serve with *Tomato sauce* (see SAUCE).

Note on beef croquettes made of left-overs. An infinite variety of preparations can be made by adding to the boiled beef any number of different ingredients: Spinach, lettuce, celery or other chopped vegetables, grated cheese, chopped onion stewed in butter, *tomato fondue*, purées of fresh and dried vegetables, *mirepoix** of vegetables, bread soaked in *bouillon** or in milk, etc.

Bone marrow croquettes. CROQUETTES D'AMOURETTES—Shape to look like corks.

*Ingredients. Salpicon** of bone marrow and mushrooms blended with an *Allemande sauce* (see SAUCE).

Serve *Tomato sauce* (see SAUCE) separately.

Brain Croquettes. CROQUETTES DE CERVELLE—Shape according to taste. Prepare like *Bone marrow croquettes*, using instead a *salpicon** of sheep's or calf's brain.

Cod croquettes. CROQUETTES DE MORUE—Shape into balls. These are also called fishballs or fishcakes.

Ingredients. Two-thirds cod, which should be cooked, drained, and cut into pieces, mixed with one-third *Duchess potatoes* (see POTATOES) blended with a thick *Béchamel sauce* (see SAUCE).

Serve with *Tomato sauce* (see SAUCE).

Cress croquettes. CROQUETTES CRESSONNIÈRE—Shape according to taste.

Ingredients. Purée of watercress to which *Duchess potatoes* (see POTATOES) have been added. Blend with a *Velouté sauce* flavoured with mixed herbs (see SAUCE).

Fish croquettes. CROQUETTES DE POISSONS DE DESSERTE—Shape according to taste.

Ingredients. A *salpicon** composed solely of the fish prescribed, blended with *Béchamel* or *Allemande sauce* (see SAUCE).

Serve a sauce in character with the fish used for the croquettes.

These croquettes are usually served in the shape of balls. They are also known as fishballs or fishcakes. If they are described as such on the menu, *Duchess potato mixture* (see POTATOES) should be added to the ingredients and the croquettes should be served with *Tomato sauce* (see SAUCE).

Mushrooms and truffles cut into dice can also be added to the ingredients of fish croquettes.

Foie gras croquettes à la Périgueux. CROQUETTES DE FOIE GRAS À LA PÉRIGUEUX—Shape into little flat cakes.

*Ingredients. Salpicon** of foie gras and truffles, blended with a very strong *Demi-glace sauce* flavoured with Madeira, or, if desired, with *Allemande sauce* (see SAUCE).

Serve with *Périgueux sauce* (see SAUCE).

Foie gras croquettes à la reine. CROQUETTES DE FOIE GRAS À LA REINE—Shape into little flat cakes.

*Ingredients. Salpicon** of foie gras, bound into *Allemande sauce* (see SAUCE).

Serve with *Suprême sauce* (see SAUCE) with dropped truffles added.

Game croquettes. CROQUETTES DE GIBIER—Shape according to taste.

*Ingredients. Salpicon** of game left-overs, mushrooms and truffles, blended with a very concentrated *Demi-glace sauce* (see SAUCE).

Serve with a *Demi-glace sauce* based on concentrated game stock.

On the menu, name the croquettes after the game which is predominant in their preparation, e.g., *Pheasant croquettes*, *Venison croquettes*, etc.

To use up left-overs of different kinds of game, croquettes can be prepared from a mixture of them.

Lobster croquettes I. CROQUETTES DE HOMARD—*Ingredients. Salpicon** of lobster to which mushrooms and truffles chopped into dice have been added, blended with a thick *Béchamel sauce* (see SAUCE).

Serve with *White wine sauce* (see SAUCE).

Lobster croquettes II. CROQUETTES DE HOMARD—*Ingredients. Salpicon** of lobster, mushrooms and truffles, blended with *Allemande sauce* (see SAUCE), finished with a *Crustacean butter* (see BUTTER, *Compound butters: Shrimp butter*).

Serve with *Lobster sauce* (see SAUCE).

Lobster croquettes III. CROQUETTES DE HOMARD—*Ingredients.* Two-thirds *salpicon** of lobster, one-third rice cooked in meat or fish stock.

Serve with *Lobster sauce* (see SAUCE) made with white wine.

Note. This method of preparation applies to all crustaceans. It is a practical way of using up left-overs of which there are not sufficient to make it worth while serving them by themselves.

If there is not a sufficient quantity of left-overs, potato purée or rice can be added to the *salpicon.*

Macaroni croquettes valentinoise. CROQUETTES DE MACARONI VALENTINOISE—Shape into little rectangles.

*Ingredients. Salpicon** of big macaroni, blended with a thick *Béchamel sauce* (see SAUCE) to which grated cheese has been added.

Spread the macaroni on a shallow dish, making the layer $\frac{1}{3}$ inch thick. Add a layer of *salpicon à la Nantua* to which truffles cut into dice have been added. Cover with a second layer of the macaroni mixture. Leave to cool.

Divide into portions. Dip into egg and breadcrumbs and fry. Finish as described in the recipe under CROQUETTES. Serve with *Nantua sauce* (see SAUCE).

Meat croquettes (made with various meat left-overs). CROQUETTES DE VIANDES—Shape according to taste.

*Ingredients. Salpicon** of the meat blended with *Allemande sauce*, *Demi-glace sauce* or *Tomato sauce*, depending on the meat used. (See SAUCE.)

The *salpicon* can be finished off with mushrooms and truffles, smoked or pickled tongue or ham cut into dice.

Montrouge croquettes. CROQUETTES MONTROUGE—Shape to look like very small eggs.

Ingredients. Mushroom purée blended with yolks of eggs, mixed with chopped lean ham.

These croquettes are mainly used as garnish and should therefore be very small. If they are used as garnish for a fish dish, the chopped ham must be left out.

Mussel croquettes. CROQUETTES DE MOULES—Shape according to taste.

*Ingredients. Salpicon** of mussels and mushrooms, blended with thick *Béchamel* or *Allemande sauce*, based on fish stock. See SAUCE.

Serve with *White wine sauce* (see SAUCE).

Noodle croquettes. CROQUETTES DE NOUILLES—Shape according to taste.

Prepare, cook and serve as *Macaroni croquettes*, using ordinary or small noodles instead of macaroni.

Oyster croquettes à la normande. CROQUETTES D'HUÎTRES À LA NORMANDE—Shape into flat little cakes.

*Ingredients. Salpicon** of poached oysters, mushrooms and truffles blended with *Allemande sauce* (see SAUCE).

Serve with *Normande sauce* (see SAUCE).

Oyster croquettes Victoria. CROQUETTES D'HUÎTRES VICTORIA—Shape into flat little cakes.

*Ingredients. Salpicon** of lobster, mushrooms and truffles blended with *Béchamel sauce* (see SAUCE). Put in the middle of each croquette a poached oyster coated with *Allemande sauce* (see SAUCE) and finished with a *Crustacean butter* (see BUTTER, *Compound butters: Shrimp butter*).

Serve with *Lobster sauce* (see SAUCE).

Potato croquettes. CROQUETTES DE POMMES DE TERRE—Shape according to taste.

Potato croquettes are usually served without sauce.

Potato croquettes Dauphiné—See POTATOES, *Dauphiné potatoes.*

Potato croquettes à la florentine.—CROQUETTES DE POMMES DE TERRE À LA FLORENTINE—Shape according to taste.

Ingredients. Two-thirds of *Duchess potatoes* (see POTATOES) mixed with one-third of spinach cooked in butter and $\frac{1}{2}$ cup (50 grams) of grated Parmesan cheese for each $2\frac{1}{2}$ cups (500 grams) of potato and spinach mixture.

Potato croquettes à la niçoise. CROQUETTES DE POMMES DE TERRE À LA NIÇOISE—Shape according to taste.

Ingredients. Duchess potatoes (see POTATOES) mixed with 1 cup (2 decilitres) of thick *Tomato fondue à la niçoise** for each $2\frac{1}{2}$ cups (500 grams) of potato.

Potato croquettes with Parmesan cheese. CROQUETTES DE POMMES DE TERRE À LA PARMESANE—*Ingredients. Duchess potatoes* (see POTATOES) with grated Parmesan cheese. For each $2\frac{1}{2}$ cups (500 grams) of purée add $\frac{1}{2}$ cup (50 grams) of cheese.

Potato croquettes can also be made with Cheshire cheese or with Gruyere cheese.

Poultry croquettes. CROQUETTES DE VOLAILLE—Shape according to taste.

Ingredients. Salpicon of poultry meat, mushrooms and truffles, blended with *Allemande sauce* (see SAUCE).

Serve with *Demi-glace sauce*, *Périgueux sauce* or *Tomato sauce* according to taste. See SAUCE.

Printanière croquettes—Shape according to taste.

Ingredients. Spring vegetables blended with *Béchamel sauce* or *Allemande sauce* (see SAUCE).

Serve with a *Cream sauce* (see SAUCE) to which parsley and chervil have been added.

Rice croquettes. CROQUETTES DE RIZ—Shape according to taste.

Ingredients. Rice cooked in meat, fish or vegetable stock, plain or with grated cheese added.

Serve with *Tomato sauce* (see SAUCE).

Rice croquettes à l'américaine. CROQUETTES DE RIZ À L'AMÉRICAINE—Shape according to taste.

Ingredients. Rice cooked in fish stock to which a *salpicon** of *Lobster à l'américaine* has been added.

Serve with *Américaine sauce* (see SAUCE).

Curried rice croquettes. CROQUETTES DE RIZ À L'INDIENNE—Shape according to taste.

Ingredients. Rice cooked in a meat, fish or vegetable stock to which is added a *salpicon** of onions, cooked in butter until soft and blended with a few tablespoons of *Curry sauce* (see SAUCE).

Rice croquettes à la piémontaise. CROQUETTES DE RIZ À LA PIÉMONTAISE—Shape according to taste.

Ingredients. Risotto à la piémontaise. (See RICE.)

Serve with *Tomato sauce* (see SAUCE.)

Spiny lobster croquettes. CROQUETTES DE LANGOUSTE—Shape according to taste.

Ingredients. As for *Lobster croquettes*, using a *salpicon** of spiny lobster instead of lobster.

Vegetable croquettes (various). CROQUETTES DE LÉGUMES—Shape according to taste.

*Ingredients. Salpicon** of vegetable (cooked), blended with *Béchamel sauce* (see SAUCE).

Serve with a *Tomato* or *Cream sauce* (see SAUCE).

Vegetable croquettes are usually made from artichoke hearts, carrots, celeriac or French beans.

Croquettes can equally well be prepared using a *macédoine** of vegetables.

Croquettes à la viennoise—Shape into small rectangles.

Ingredients. Salpicon of lamb sweetbreads, lean ham, mushrooms and chopped onions, cooked in butter until they are quite soft, and blended with a thick *Velouté sauce* (see SAUCE) seasoned with paprika.

After the croquettes are fried, arrange in a circle and garnish the centre with a heap of fried onions.

Serve with *Tomato sauce* (see SAUCE), seasoned with paprika.

Croustades—Small hors-d'oeuvre croustades, to be filled with different garnishes, are made of *Duchess potatoes* (see POTATOES), rice, semolina, or lining paste (see DOUGH).

Method 1. *Croustade made of duchess potatoes.* Make a very thick *Duchess potato* mixture. Roll out on a floured table to a thickness of about 1¼ inches.

Using a round, plain pastry-cutter, cut out pieces with a diameter of 1½ to 2 inches.

Dip in egg and breadcrumbs twice.

With the help of a round pastry-cutter smaller than the one used before, mark out the lid of the croustade, by pressing on it.

Fry the croustades. Remove the lids. Hollow out the croustades very carefully. Fill as directed by the recipe chosen and cover with their lids.

Serve the croustades on a napkin or on a paper doyley.

Method 2. *Croustades made of rice or semolina.* Prepare as described in the recipe for *Duchess potato croustades*, using rice or semolina cooked in a meat, fish or vegetable stock, bound with yolks of eggs, spread on a slab and left to cool.

Method 3. *Croustades made of lining paste* (*tart pastry*). Line croustade moulds with lining paste, following the directions given for barquettes. Bake the pastry blind (unfilled). Garnish as described in the recipe chosen.

Croustades à l'alsacienne—Make the croustades using *Duchess potatoes* (see POTATOES).

Garnish. Braised sauerkraut. Put on each croustade a slice of ham and a roundel of poached Strasbourg sausage.

Croustades à l'anversoise—Make the croustades using *Duchess potatoes* (see POTATOES).

Garnish. Hop shoots with cream.

Croustades à la bretonne—Make the croustades using *Duchess potatoes* (see POTATOES).

Garnish. Purée of *Kidney beans à la bretonne* (see BEANS).

Croustades à la forestière—Make the croustades using *Duchess potatoes* (see POTATOES). Cut out with an oval pastry-cutter.

Garnish. Morels sautéed with parsley. Put on each croustade a small rectangle of blanched lean bacon browned in butter.

Croustades à la grecque—Make rice croustades and cut into oval shapes.

*Garnish. Tomato fondue à la grecque**. Put on each croustade 3 onion rings, dipped in frying-batter and fried.

Croustades à la marinière—Make the croustades using *lining paste* (see DOUGH).

Garnish. Ragoût of *Mussels à la marinière**.

Croustades à la Montrouge—Make the croustades using *lining paste* (see DOUGH).

Garnish. Purée of mushrooms with cream.

Croustades à la napolitaine—Make the croustades using *lining paste* (see DOUGH).

*Garnish. Spaghetti a la napolitaine**.

Croustades à la nivernaise—Make the croustades using *Duchess potatoes* (see POTATOES).

Garnish. Very small glazed carrots. Put on each croustade a bouquet of very small glazed onions.

Croustades à la toulousaine—Make the croustades using *lining paste* (see DOUGH).

Garnish. Ragoût of cock's kidneys and forcemeat blended with *Suprême sauce* (see SAUCE). Put on each croustade a small slice of calf's sweetbread, a slice of truffle and a cock's comb.

Croustades vert-pré—Make the croustades using *Duchess potatoes* (see POTATOES).

Garnish. Mix in equal parts French (string) beans cut into dice, peas and asparagus tips blended with butter.

Croustades Vichy—Make rice croustades.

*Garnish. Carrots à la Vichy**.

Note. Apart from all the special recipes given for croustades they can also be made according to all the recipes given for barquettes (pastry boats) and similar dishes

Croûtes, garnished. CROÛTES GARNIES—Using a biscuit cutter cut slices of stale sandwich loaf into rounds with a diameter of 1½ to 2¼ inches, and ¾ inch thick.

With a round biscuit cutter, of a smaller diameter than the one used before, mark the top of the crusts firmly but without cutting right through.

Fry the crusts in butter until golden brown. Drain and hollow out.

Garnish according to the selected recipe.

Alternately, instead of frying the crusts in butter, spread them with butter and brown them in the oven.

Croûtes à l'ambassadrice—

Garnish. Purée of breast of chicken (or other poultry)

in a *Velouté sauce* (see SAUCE). Put on each croûte a large slice of truffle and on the truffle a small bouquet of *mirepoix** of vegetables.

Anchovy croûtes. CROÛTES AUX ANCHOIS—Cut slices of a sandwich loaf in round or rectangular pieces. Fry them quickly in sizzling butter. De-salt anchovy fillets and cut into thin strips. Put these strips on the croûtes.

Sprinkle with breadcrumbs fried in butter and seasoned with cayenne. Put for a few moments in a very hot oven.

Arrange on a napkin or on a paper doyley. Garnish with fresh parsley.

Croûtes with bone-marrow. CROÛTES À LA MOELLE—

Garnish. Bone-marrow cut into dice and poached. Sprinkle with a little chopped shallot. Pour some concentrated and thickened veal stock on the croûtes and brown in the oven. At the last moment, put on each croûte two or three nice slices of bone-marrow. Sprinkle with chopped parsley.

Croûtes Brillat-Savarin—

*Garnish. Salpicon** of hard boiled eggs, mushrooms and truffles blended with a *Béchamel sauce* (see SAUCE). Make a criss-cross pattern of anchovy fillets on each crust. Sprinkle with fried breadcrumbs; brown.

Croûtes cardinal—

*Garnish. Salpicon** of lobster and truffles blended with a *Béchamel sauce* (see SAUCE) finished with *Lobster butter* (see BUTTER, *Compound butters*). Sprinkle with breadcrumbs and brown. When ready, put on each crust a slice of lobster and 2 slivers of truffles.

Cheese croûtes. CROÛTES AU FROMAGE—

*Garnish. Salpicon** of Gruyère cheese. Season with paprika and grated nutmeg.

Sprinkle grated cheese and melted butter on the croûtes and brown.

Croûtes à la Clamart (Vegetarian recipe)—

Garnish. Purée of fresh peas (see PEAS) diluted with fiesh cream.

Devilled croûtes. CROÛTES À LA DIABLE—

*Garnish. Salpicon** of York ham and mushrooms blended with a very strong *Demi-glace sauce* (see SAUCE), seasoned with a pinch of cayenne. Sprinkle with fried breadcrumbs; brown.

Croûtes Dubarry—

Garnish. Flowerets of cauliflower cooked in butter. Coat with *Mornay sauce* (see SAUCE), sprinkle with grated cheese and brown.

Croûtes à la livonienne—

Garnish. Purée of soft roes of smoked herring with the addition of *Béchamel sauce* (see SAUCE). Put on each croûte a spoonful of *salpicon** of fillets of smoked herrings and good, tart apples. Sprinkle with fried breadcrumbs and brown.

Croûtes à la lyonnaise—

Garnish. Boiled beef cut into small dice and sautéed in butter, and mixed with an equal quantity of onions cut into dice and tossed in butter. Sprinkle with breadcrumbs, pour butter over the croûtes and brown. Then pour some drops of lemon juice or vinegar on them and sprinkle with chopped parsley.

Mushroom croûtes. CROÛTES AUX CHAMPIGNONS—

Garnish. Ragoût of small *mushrooms à l'allemande.*

Mushroom croûtes are usually made from small, round crusty rolls (Emperor rolls). Scoop out the rolls, butter them and brown them in the oven. Mushroom crusts can also be made from French (Joko) bread cut into croûtes and prepared in the same way as the rolls.

Tourte de champignons à la crème is also sometimes called *Mushroom croûte.*

Croûtes à la paysanne I—

Garnish. Coarsely chopped vegetables cooked in butter until soft. Sprinkle with grated cheese and brown.

Croûtes à la paysanne II—

Garnish. Stock pot vegetables chopped and mixed with grated cheese. Finish as in the previous recipe.

Croûtes à la provençale—

Garnish. Tomato fondue à la provençale (see FONDUE). Put on each croûte 4 black, stoned olives, each surrounded by a fillet of anchovy. Sprinkle with fried breadcrumbs. Heat in the oven. Sprinkle with chopped parsley.

Croûtes à la reine—.

*Garnish. Salpicon** of poultry, truffles and mushrooms, blended with a thick *Velouté sauce* (see SAUCE), sprinkled with fried breadcrumbs. Brown in the oven.

Croûtes à la rouennaise—

Garnish. Gratin forcemeat (see FORCEMEAT) made, whenever possible, of *Rouen duckling livers* (see DUCK). Heat for a minute in the oven. Put a grilled mushroom on each croûte. Fill the hollow of the mushroom with a little very thick *Bordelaise sauce* (see SAUCE).

Croûtes with skate liver. CROÛTES DE FOIE DE RAIE—

*Garnish. Salpicon** of skate liver (cooked in a *court-bouillon**). Pour melted butter seasoned with salt and pepper and a squeeze of lemon juice over the *salpicon.* Put in the oven. Arrange the croûtes with the liver on a dish, sprinkle with chopped parsley, squeeze a few drops of lemon juice over the croûtes and at the last minute pour a little brown butter on them.

Crusts with soft roes. CROÛTES AUX LAITANCES—

Garnish. Soft roes of fresh herrings. Sprinkle with fried breadcrumbs and put in the oven.

Croûtes à la zingara—

Garnish. Ham, smoked or pickled tongue and truffles cut into strips blended with tomato-flavoured *Demi-glace sauce* (see SAUCE).Put on each garnished croûte a little round slice of heated ham and on each piece of ham a grilled mushroom. Sprinkle with chopped parsley.

Note. Apart from the above recipes, recipes given for barquettes, cassolettes, etc., can be applied to garnished croûtes.

Cutlets (Compound), (U.S. Chopettes). CÔTELETTES COMPOSÉES—Make the preparation for croquettes composed of the ingredients indicated in the chosen croquette recipe.

Spread a layer of this preparation on a flat dish, leave to cool completely and divide into portions of 2 to 3 tablespoons (50 to 70 grams).

Dip into egg and breadcrumbs and shape into the form of cutlets (chops).

Fry in clarified butter or sauté in butter, depending on recipe. Arrange in the shape of a crown. Add appropriate garnish.

Stick a piece of raw macaroni on each cutlet and dress each such piece of macaroni with a tiny paper frill.

Serve with an appropriate sauce.

These cutlets can be used as a garnish for large dishes. If served in this way they should be very small.

Note. All the directions given for making croquettes also apply to these cutlets, which differ from croquettes only in their shape.

These cutlets can also be made from purée of poultry, game, fish, etc., and can be dipped in egg and breadcrumbs and sautéed in butter.

Cutlets which have purées as a basic ingredient can have a filling of plain or compound *salpicon** blended with a very thick sauce.

Dartois—*Dartois* are similar to *allumettes**. Their difference lies in the fact that the garnish in a *dartois* is enclosed in two bands of puff pastry, and that these bands are not cut into rectangles until after the cooking is finished.

Method. Roll the puff pastry out as for *allumettes*, cut into bands and put on a moistened baking tray.

Spread the middle of the band with the chosen garnish, which must be cold, leaving $\frac{1}{3}$ inch clear on each side.

Put on each garnished band of pastry another band of pastry of the same length and width but a little thicker than the bottom one. Moisten the border of the lower band with water and press the upper band on to this border. Make a few light cuts along the edges. Brush with egg and score the surface lightly; mark into divisions to make subsequent cutting easier. Bake in a hot oven for 20 to 25 minutes; cut into rectangles about an inch long. Arrange on a napkin.

Garnish. All preparations and forcemeats given in the recipes for *allumettes* can be used for *dartois*. They can also be garnished with *salpicons** of meat, poultry, fish, etc., blended with white or brown stock.

Anchovy dartois (Sausselis). DARTOIS AUX ANCHOIS—*Garnish. Anchovy forcemeat.* See FORCEMEAT. Decorate with anchovy fillets, cover with a layer of puff pastry and bake in the oven.

Dartois à la florentine—

Garnish. Spinach cooked in butter, blended with *Béchamel sauce* (see SAUCE) to which grated cheese has been added.

Dartois Grimod de la Reynière—

Garnish. Fine pike forcemeat (see FORCEMEAT) with *Crayfish butter* (see BUTTER, *Compound butters*). Decorate with crayfish tails and sliced truffles.

Dartois Laguipière—

*Garnish. Salpicon** of calf's sweetbreads and truffles to which is added a *brunoise** of vegetables, blended with thick *Velouté sauce* (see SAUCE).

Dartois Lucullus—

*Garnish. Salpicon** of foie gras and truffles blended with a concentrated *Demi-glace sauce* (see SAUCE).

Dartois à la reine—

*Garnish. Salpicon** of poultry, truffles and mushrooms blended with *Velouté sauce* (see SAUCE).

Sardine dartois. DARTOIS AUX SARDINES—Made like *Anchovy dartois*, using well-trimmed fillets of sardines in oil instead.

Tunny (Tuna fish) dartois. DARTOIS AU THON—Made like *Sardine dartois*, using finely cut-up slices of tunny in oil.

Eggs mignons. OEUFS MIGNONS—This is the name given to very small egg-shaped cases made of *Duchess potato mixture* (see POTATOES). They are dipped in egg and breadcrumbs, deep fried, hollowed out and filled in various ways.

Method. Make a *Duchess potato* mixture and leave until quite cold. Divide into portions of 1 tablespoon (30 grams). Roll these portions in flour and shape to look like eggs. Roll them in egg and breadcrumbs twice. Fry in hot, deep fat, then drain the 'eggs' and dry them.

Make a small round opening in the top. Hollow out the 'egg' completely through the opening, without breaking the crust. Fill the eggs with the selected preparation. Arrange them on a napkin-covered dish or in a nest of straw potatoes. Garnish with fried parsley.

Eggs mignons d'Aigrefeuille. OEUFS MIGNONS D'AIGREFEUILLE—

Garnish. Purée of poultry finished with *Crayfish butter* (see BUTTER, *Compound butters*).

Eggs mignons à l'andalouse. OEUFS MIGNONS À L'ANDALOUSE—

Garnish. Purée of foie gras to which grated orange peel has been added.

Eggs mignons Beauharnais. OEUFS MIGNONS BEAUHARNAIS—

Garnish. Purée of poultry finished with *Tarragon butter* (see BUTTER, *Compound butters*).

Eggs mignons à la cévenole. OEUFS MIGNONS À LA CÉVENOLE—

*Garnish. Chestnut purée**, mixed with a purée of onions.

Eggs mignons à la Clamart. OEUFS MIGNONS À LA CLAMART—

Garnish. Purée of fresh peas with cream.

Curried eggs mignons. OEUFS MIGNONS À L'INDIENNE—

*Garnish. Salpicon** of poultry blended with *Curry sauce* (see SAUCE).

Eggs mignons à la nivernaise. OEUFS MIGNONS À LA NIVERNAISE—

*Garnish. Fondue** of carrots and onions cut into dice blended with veal stock.

Eggs mignons à la normande. OEUFS MIGNONS À LA NORMANDE—

Garnish. Oyster ragoût à la normande.

Eggs mignons à la royale. OEUFS MIGNONS À LA ROYALE—

*Garnish. Salpicon** of French (string) beans and asparagus tips, blended with butter.

Note. In addition to the garnishes mentioned above, all the garnishes given for *barquettes* (pastry boats), patties, *croustades*, etc., can be used for eggs mignons.

Fondants (croquettes)—The French call very small croquettes *fondants*. They are made of (*a*) different vegetable purées, or (*b*) cream preparations made with cheese.

(*a*) Prepare the purée of the selected vegetables and add to it an appropriate sauce. The sauce should be very thick. The proportion of sauce to vegetable purée should be one to three.

Divide the purée into small portions (50 grams each). Roll in flour and coat with egg and breadcrumbs as for croquettes. Shape to look like eggs or pears.

Fry just before serving. Drain. Arrange on a napkin. Garnish with fried parsley.

These croquettes can be made from any one vegetable purée or a combination of purées. The basic purée must, however, always weigh two-thirds of the whole preparation.

(*b*) Prepare a very thick unsweetened *French pastry cream* (see CREAMS) with grated cheese added.

Spread the cheese cream on a slab to a thickness of about $\frac{1}{3}$ inch. Leave to cool. Cut into rectangles or any other shape. Dip into egg and breadcrumbs. Finish as for vegetable croquettes.

Argenteuil fondants. FONDANTS ARGENTEUIL—*Ingredients.* Asparagus purée with *Béchamel sauce* (see SAUCE).

Cheese fondants. FONDANTS DE FROMAGES—*Ingredients.* A creamy cheese mixture made of Brie, Camembert, Cantal, Cheshire, Gruyère or Dutch cheese.

Fondants Crécy—*Ingredients.* Purée of carrots with *Béchamel sauce* (see SAUCE).

Fondants with foie gras Taillevent. FONDANTS DE FOIE GRAS TAILLEVENT—*Ingredients.* Purée of foie gras and purée of the white meat of poultry; *Allemande sauce* (see SAUCE).

Fondants with foie gras and truffles. FONDANTS DE FOIE GRAS AUX TRUFFES—Purée of foie gras and purée of truffles with a very concentrated *Madeira sauce* (see SAUCE).

Meat fondants. FONDANTS DE VIANDE—Prepare in the same way as *Fondants à la reine*, using different kinds of meat purées, as indicated in various recipes, and blending these purées with a sauce appropriate to the meat.

Fondants à la Nantua—*Ingredients.* Purée of sole with *Béchamel sauce* (see SAUCE) and *Crayfish butter* (see BUTTER, *Compound butters*).

Fondants with poultry liver or à la rouennaise. FONDANTS DE FOIES DE VOLAILLE À LA ROUENNAISE—*Ingredients.* Purée of poultry liver with *Rouennaise sauce* (see SAUCE).

Fondants à la reine—*Ingredients.* Purée of poultry, to which mushrooms and truffles cut into very small dice have been added, blended with an *Allemande sauce* (see SAUCE).

Fondants Vladimir—*Ingredients.* Purée of calf's sweetbreads mixed with purée of truffles, blended with *Allemande sauce* (see SAUCE).

Fondants à la Yorkaise—*Ingredients.* Purée of ham with *Béchamel sauce* (see SAUCE).

Fritots—Fritots are a kind of fritter, the commonest ingredients of which are offal (or variety meats), poultry, left-overs of fish and shellfish.

Beef fritots. FRITOTS DE BOEUF—Cut boiled beef into square pieces of 1½ inches. Finish as for *Bone-marrow fritots.*

Bone-marrow fritots. FRITOTS D'AMOURETTES—Cook the bone-marrow in a white *court-bouillon**. Divide into pieces 2¼ inches long. Marinate the pieces, dip them in batter and deep fry. Arrange the fritters on a napkin. Garnish with fried parsley. Serve with *Tomato sauce* (see SAUCE).

Fritots of sheep's and calf's brains—FRITOTS DE CERVELLE D'AGNEAU, DE VEAU—Cut the brains into thick slices and cook in a *Court-bouillon**. Then marinate and finish as *Bone-marrow fritots.*

Fritots of cock's comb. FRITOTS DE CRÊTES DE COQ—Cook the cock's combs in a white *Court-bouillon**. Marinate and finish as *Bone-marrow fritots.*

Calf's head fritots. FRITOTS DE TÊTE DE VEAU—Cook the calf's head in white *Court-bouillon I**. Marinate and finish as for *Bone-marrow fritots.*

Fritots of cooked fish. FRITOTS DE POISSONS DE DESSERTE—Divide the pieces of fish into pieces. Marinate them, dip in frying-batter and finish as *Bone-marrow fritots.*

Fritots of calf's (or sheep's) foot. FRITOTS DE PIEDS DE MOUTON, DE VEAU—Bone the calf's (or sheep's) foot. Cook in white *Court-bouillon I** and marinate. Finish as described in the recipe for *Bone-marrow fritots.*

Frog's legs fritots. FRITOTS DE GRENOUILLES—Trim the frog's legs. Put them in an uncooked *marinade** and leave for half an hour, dip in frying-batter and finish as described for *Bone-marrow fritots.*

Fritots of cold meat. FRITOTS DE VIANDES DE DESSERTE—Boiled or braised left-overs of lamb, mutton or veal can be used. Marinate and finish as described for *Beef fritots.*

Fritots of calf's mesentery. FRITOTS DE FRAISE DE VEAU—Cook and marinate the mesentery and finish like *Bone-marrow fritots.*

Mussel fritots. FRITOTS DE MOULES—Prepare in the same way as *Oyster fritots.*

Oyster fritots. FRITOTS D'HUÎTRES—Poach the oysters in their water. Drain, dry, marinate and dip in frying-batter. Finish as for *Bone-marrow fritots.*

Fritots of cold poultry. FRITOTS DE VOLAILLE DE DESSERTE—Left-overs of poached or braised poultry are best. Remove all the bones. Cut into very small regular pieces. Marinate and dip into frying-batter. Finish as for *Bone-marrow fritots.*

Sweetbread fritots. FRITOTS DE RIS D'AGNEAU—Braise lamb's sweetbreads and marinate. Finish like *Bone-marrow fritots.*

Vegetable fritots. FRITOTS DE LÉGUMES—Cut into quarters or into long pieces vegetables such as cardoon or salsify (which should be cooked in a white *Court-bouillon**), or artichokes and asparagus (which should only be blanched). Whichever way the vegetables are cooked, they should be marinated before being dipped in frying-batter. They are finished in the same way as *Bone-marrow fritots.*

Fritters. BEIGNETS—Fritters served as hors-d'oeuvre or small entrées can be made from a variety of ingredients—meat, poultry, fish and cooked vegetables—dipped in the batter and fried.

Different kinds of batter can be used—unsweetened ordinary *chou paste*, *brioche dough* (see DOUGH) and special *frying-batter* (see BATTER).

Method 1. *With frying-batter:* Whatever ingredients you use, they should be cooked first and then cut into slices, square pieces or any other shape desired.

Some recipes require the basic ingredient to be left to soak for half an hour in oil, lemon juice or vinegar, chopped parsley, salt and pepper.

At the last minute, dip the pieces one by one into a light batter, put them in very hot fat, deep-fry them until they are a good colour, dry them on a cloth, season with very fine dry salt and arrange them in a heap on a napkin-covered dish.

For fritters incorporating forcemeat, mince, purées or various *salpicons*, prepare the ingredients as directed in the recipe and leave until quite cold. Divide into small portions, shape into balls, corks, rissoles, flat round cakes, etc. Roll in flour. At the last minute dip in batter and finish as described above.

Method 2. *With chou paste* (*Soufflé fritters*). Prepare *Chou paste I** (see DOUGH). Add whatever ingredients are indicated in the recipe.

Divide the paste with a spoon into pieces as small as a hazelnut or as large as a walnut, depending on the ingredients. Drop one by one into hot, but not boiling, oil.

Cook on a high flame until the fritters are nicely shaped, dry and golden brown.

Drain on a paper or linen towelling, sprinkle with very fine dry salt and serve on a napkin-covered dish.

Anchovy fritters I. BEIGNETS D'ANCHOIS—Roll anchovy fillets into rings and put them on thin round slices of bread, about 1½ inches in diameter.

Sandwich these rounds together two by two, dip them in frying-batter, and fry just before serving.

The rounds of bread can be coated with a layer of fish forcemeat or spread with *Anchovy butter* (see BUTTER, *Compound butters*).

Alternatively, spread the rounds of bread with a *salpicon** of hard boiled eggs and fillets of anchovies blended with a spoonful of *Béchamel sauce* (see SAUCE). Finish in the usual way.

In all the recipes bread can be replaced by small savoury pancakes.

Anchovy fritters II. BEIGNETS D'ANCHOIS—Soak unleavened bread (matzos) in cold water and cut into small circlets. Put a little *salpicon** made of anchovies and hard boiled eggs blended with *Béchamel sauce* (see SAUCE) on each circlet. Seal the fritters like turnovers, dip in frying-batter and finish as indicated above.

Artichoke fritters. BEIGNETS D'ARTICHAUTS—Trim very tender artichokes and divide into quarters. Lay them on a dish and dress with a trickle of oil and a squeeze of lemon juice. Season with salt and pepper. Leave to marinate for 30 minutes.

Just before serving, dip the artichokes in frying-batter and fry them. If the artichokes are a little hard, blanch them lightly before putting them into the marinade.

Bernois fritters. BEIGNETS BERNOIS—Cut some Gruyère cheese into roundels of 1¼ inches in diameter. Make a thick *Béchamel sauce* (see SAUCE) and add minced ham to it. Coat the roundels of cheese with this sauce and sandwich together in pairs. Finish the fritters in the usual manner.

Beef fritters à la lyonnaise. BEIGNETS DE BOEUF À LA LYONNAISE—Make beef hash *à la lyonnaise* (see HASH), using beef left-overs.

Divide the mince into pieces the size of a walnut. Dip in frying-batter and fry.

Fish fritters. BEIGNETS DE POISSONS—Use left-over braised or poached fish. Cut into slices or square pieces and marinate for 30 minutes in oil, lemon juice, chopped parsley, salt and pepper.

Dip the pieces one by one in frying-batter and finish in the usual manner.

Fritters à la florentine. BEIGNETS À LA FLORENTINE—Prepare ½ pound (250 grams) of spinach purée, making it as dry as possible. Add 1 cup (2 decilitres) of thick *Béchamel sauce* (see SAUCE) and 2 to 3 tablespoons of grated cheese.

Leave to cool, divide into balls the size of a pigeon's egg, roll in flour, dip in frying-batter and finish in the usual manner.

Herring fritters. BEIGNETS DE HARENGS—Use marinated herrings. Drain and dry on a cloth, coat with a thin layer of fish forcemeat and roll.

Dip the herring rolls in frying-batter and finish in the usual way.

Fritters of marinated herrings. BEIGNETS DE HARENGS MARINÉS—Make a *salpicon** of marinated herrings and fish forcemeat and spread it on pancakes (*crêpes*) made without salt. Roll the pancakes, cut into uniform pieces, dip in frying-batter and finish in the usual way.

Lucullus fritters. BEIGNETS LUCULLUS—Cut truffles into thick slices, coat with a purée of foie gras and sandwich together in pairs. Dip in frying-batter and finish in the usual manner.

In France these fritters are also known as *Fritters à la périgourdine*.

Meat fritters. BEIGNETS DE VIANDES—Use braised or poached left-overs of meat. Cut into squares, slices or any other shape.

Marinate for 30 minutes in oil, lemon juice, chopped parsley, salt and pepper.

Dip the pieces one by one in frying-batter. Finish in the usual manner.

Mussel fritters à la duxelles. BEIGNETS DE MOULES À LA DUXELLES—Choose large mussels, cook them in white wine, take them out of their shells, dry well, cover with a teaspoon of thick *Duxelles sauce* (see SAUCE).

Dip in frying-batter. Finish in the usual manner.

Pasta fritters. BEIGNETS DE PÂTES—Prepare *macaroni à l'italienne** (cut into dice), shell-shaped pasta, noodles or vermicelli. Leave to cool. Divide up into portions the size of a pigeon's egg.

Dip in frying-batter and finish in the usual manner.

Rice fritters. BEIGNETS DE RIZ—Cook the rice and mix with Parmesan cheese. Divide into portions the size of a pigeon's egg. Dip in frying-batter. Finish in the usual manner.

Polenta and semolina fritters are prepared in the same way as rice fritters.

Soft roe fritters. BEIGNETS DE LAITANCES—Poach the soft roes in *Court-bouillon XV**. Drain them and put in a marinade of oil, lemon juice or vinegar and chopped parsley. Take them out, dip in frying-batter and fry in the usual way.

Soufflé fritters. BEIGNETS SOUFFLÉS—Prepare *Chou paste* (see DOUGH) without sugar. Divide with a spoon into pieces the size of a hazelnut. Drop one by one into hot, but not boiling, oil. Cook over a high flame until the fritters are nicely shaped, dry and golden in colour.

Drain on paper or linen towellmg and serve on a napkin-covered dish.

Soufflé fritters with anchovy I. BEIGNETS SOUFFLÉS AUX ANCHOIS—Prepare 1½ cups (250 grams) of *Chou paste* (see DOUGH) and add 2 tablespoons of *salpicon** of de-salted anchovies.

Proceed as for *Soufflé fritters*.

Soufflé fritters with anchovy II. BEIGNETS SOUFFLÉS AUX ANCHOIS—Make the fritters as directed for *Soufflé fritters*.

As soon as they are cooked and drained, stuff them with anchovy cream using a forcing (pastry) bag with a plain nozzle.

Soufflé fritters à la hongroise. BEIGNETS SOUFFLÉS À LA HONGROISE—Make 1½ cups (250 grams) of batter for *Soufflé fritters*. Add 3 tablespoons of chopped onions cooked in butter and season with half a teaspoon of paprika.

Soufflé fritters à la parmesane I, or cheese soufflé fritters. BEIGNETS SOUFFLÉS À LA PARMESANE, BEIGNETS AU FROMAGE—Prepare 1½ cups (250 grams) of *Chou paste* (see DOUGH), add ½ cup (50 grams) of grated Parmesan cheese and season with a little grated nutmeg.

Soufflé fritters à la parmesane II. BEIGNETS SOUFFLÉS À LA PARMESANE—Make the fritters as indicated for *Soufflé fritters*.

As soon as they are cooked and drained, stuff them with *Cream sauce I* (see SAUCE) to which Parmesan cheese has been added.

Soufflé fritters à la toscane. BEIGNETS SOUFFLÉS À LA TOSCANE—Proceed as indicated for *Soufflé fritters à la parmesane*, adding chopped lean ham and truffles to the *Chou paste* (see DOUGH).

Sweetbread fritters. BEIGNETS DE RIS D'AGNEAU, DE VEAU—Braise or poach the sweetbreads. Cut into square pieces. Marinate for 30 minutes in oil, lemon juice, chopped parsley, salt and pepper.

Dip the pieces in frying-batter. Fry them and finish in the usual manner.

Truffle fritters. BEIGNETS DE TRUFFES—Cover large slices of truffle with poultry purée and sandwich together in pairs.

Dip in frying-batter. Finish in the usual way.

Vegetable fritters. BEIGNETS DE LÉGUMES—Vegetables for fritters must be cooked or parboiled, according to their nature. Cut them into pieces, slices or strips.

Marinate the cut vegetables for 30 minutes in oil, lemon juice or vinegar, chopped parsley, salt and pepper.

Dip one by one in frying-batter. Fry in the usual manner.

The best vegetables for fritters are artichokes, white asparagus tips, Brussels sprouts, cauliflower, salsify, tomatoes.

Vegetable-marrow (U.S. squash) flower fritters. BEIGNETS DE FLEURS DE COURGES—Dip the flowers one by one into a light frying-batter and fry.

Vegetarian fritters à la printanière. BEIGNETS VÉGÉTARIENS À LA PRINTANIÈRE. Make 2 cups (250 grams) of vegetable *macédoine** and blend with 1 cup (2 decilitres) of a thick *Béchamel sauce* (see SAUCE). Leave to cool. Finish in the usual manner.

Vegetarian fritters à la romaine. BEIGNETS VÉGÉTARIENS À LA ROMAINE—Blanch some spinach, chop and simmer it in butter. Blend 2 cups (250 grams) of this spinach with 1 cup (2 decilitres) of thick *Béchamel sauce* (see SAUCE) and add 3 tablespoons of grated cheese. Leave to cool. Finish in the usual manner.

Kromeskies. CROMESQUIS—Kromeskies are generally made of the same ingredients as croquettes, and can be made as meat or Lenten dishes. They can also be made of other preparations such as mince, purée or forcemeat.

Kromeskies, like croquettes, can be made from all kinds of left-overs of meat, fish or vegetables.

Method 1. *A la française*—Prepare the ingredients as for croquettes according to the recipe chosen. Let this get quite cold.

Divide the preparation into portions of about 2 tablespoons (60 to 70 grams).

Roll these portions in flour and shape them into corks or into rectangles.

At the last moment dip the kromeskies into frying-batter and drop them one by one into a pan of boiling fat.

Fry until golden brown. Drain the kromeskies, dry in a cloth and sprinkle with salt.

Arrange in a heap on a napkin and garnish with fried parsley.

Serve with an appropriate sauce.

Method 2. *A la russe*—Prepare according to the recipe chosen and divide into pieces as directed above.

Wrap each portion in a very thin piece of pig's caul, and shape like a cork.

Dip into frying-batter and finish as indicated above.

Method 3. *A la polonaise*—Proceed as directed in the preceding recipe, using large thin unsweetened pancakes (*crêpes*) instead of caul.

Method 4. *A l'ancienne*—Wrap each portion in a thin layer of *Duchess potatoes* (see POTATOES). Wrap this in an unsweetened pancake (*crêpe*) and finish as directed in the preceding recipes.

Note. Kromeskies are generally served with a *Tomato sauce* (see SAUCE) or any other suitable sauce.

As kromeskies are very much like croquettes we give only a few special recipes. They are made, as far as the basic ingredients are concerned, in every way like croquettes, for which the recipes are given above.

Kromeskies à la bonne femme. CROMESQUIS À LA BONNE FEMME—*Wrapping*. Frying-batter.

Ingredients. *Beef hash à la lyonnaise* (see HASH).

Kromeskies à la carmélite. CROMESQUIS À LA CARMÉLITE—*Wrapping*. Pancakes; frying-batter.

Ingredients. Salt cod pounded with garlic, oil and cream to which chopped truffles have been added.

Serve a *White wine sauce* (see SAUCE) separately.

Kromeskies à la florentine. CROMESQUIS À LA FLORENTINE —*Wrapping*. Pancakes (*crêpes*); frying-batter.

Ingredients. Thick *Béchamel sauce* (see SAUCE) to which grated Parmesan cheese and spinach cooked in butter have been added.

Note. When the kromeskies are made of preparations which are difficult to divide into portions and to shape into corks or rectangles, as for instance, in the case of *Kromeskies à la florentine*, proceed in the following way: coat the pancakes with *béchamel*, then add the spinach. Roll the pancakes, cut them into pieces and dip the pieces of stuffed pancake in frying-batter. Finish as directed above.

Kromeskies à la mirepoix. CROMESQUIS À LA MIREPOIX—*Wrapping*. Pancakes (*crêpes*); frying-batter.

Ingredients. *Mirepoix** of vegetables, blended with a *Velouté sauce* or a *Béchamel sauce* (see SAUCE). If a meatless *mirepoix* is used it should be blended with a *Béchamel sauce*; if minced raw ham is added to the *mirepoix* a *Velouté sauce* should be used for blending. In either case serve *Tomato sauce* (see SAUCE) separately.

Kromeskies Saint-Hubert. CROMESQUIS SAINT-HUBERT—*Wrapping*. Caul (paper-thin slices of salt pork), frying-batter.

Ingredients. *Salpicon** of game blended with a *Demi-glace sauce* (see SAUCE) based on concentrated game stock.

Serve *Saint-Hubert sauce* separately.

Kromeskies with various vegetables. CROMESQUIS DE LÉGUMES—*Wrapping*. Pancakes (*crêpes*); frying-batter.

Ingredients. *Salpicon** of cooked vegetables blended with a *Béchamel sauce* (see SAUCE).

The most usual vegetables for this dish are artichoke hearts, asparagus, carrots, salsify and celeriac.

Kromeskies à la Vladimir. CROMESQUIS À LA WLADIMIR —*Wrapping*. *Duchess potatoes* (see POTATOES), pancakes (*crêpes*), frying-batter.

Ingredients. *Salpicon** of fillet of sole, truffles and crayfish tails blended with a thick *Velouté sauce* (see SAUCE), based on fish stock.

Serve *Normande sauce* (see SAUCE) separately.

Mazagrans—*Moulded mazagrans*. Butter some tartlet tins, line them with a thin layer of rolled out *Duchess potato* mixture (see POTATOES).

Fill the tartlets with a *salpicon** or any other preparation indicated in the recipe. The garnish should be quite cold.

With a fluted biscuit-cutter cut small circles of the potato mixture, brush with egg, and cover each tartlet with one of these circlets. Brush again with egg and brown in a very hot oven.

Take the mazagrans out of the tins when they are ready and arrange on a napkin.

Large mazagrans. Line some deep fireproof plates with rolled out *Duchess potato* mixture.

Fill with a *salpicon** or other cold preparation. Cover with another layer of the potato mixture. Decorate with rolled out pieces of *Duchess potato* mixture cut in fancy shapes. Bake in a moderate oven. Serve in the same plate in which the mazagran is baked.

Unmoulded mazagrans. Roll out a layer of *Duchess potatoes*. Cut it into pieces, using a round, fluted biscuit cutter about 2 inches in diameter.

Put these circlets on a buttered baking tray. Fill with a *salpicon** or any other suitable cold preparation, putting on each circlet a piece the size of a walnut.

Cover with a second circlet of *Duchess potatoes*. Seal the edges and brush with egg.

Put in a very hot oven to colour. Arrange on a napkin.

Note. All garnishes, *salpicons*, or other preparations given for patties, croustades, rissoles, tartlets, etc., can also be used for *mazagrans*.

Médaillons—The only difference between *médaillons* and *croquettes* is their shape. Médaillons are shaped like small flat cakes. They are made of the same preparations as croquettes and left until quite cold. Dip them in egg and breadcrumbs and sauté in clarified butter.

Arrange in a circle. Garnish with fried parsley.

Note. Médaillons are served with a sauce appropriate to the basic ingredients. They can also be garnished with vegetables blended with butter or with a fairly thick vegetable purée. See CROQUETTES.

Oysters. HUÎTRES—There are quite a few ways of serving cooked oysters as a hot hors-d'oeuvre, including

Oysters à l'américaine, *Attereaux of oysters*, fritots, patties, oysters on skewers, fried oysters, etc. The recipes are all to be found under OYSTER.

Pannequets—Pancakes served as *pannequets* in an hors-d'oeuvre are made from unsweetened *Pancake batter* (see CRÊPES).

Anchovy pannequets. PANNEQUETS AUX ANCHOIS—Cut the pancakes into rectangles.

Garnish. Pike forcemeat with anchovy butter. See FORCEMEATS AND STUFFINGS.

Pannequets à la brunoise—Roll the pancakes and fry them.

Stuff with a *brunoise** of vegetables cooked in butter, blended with *Béchamel sauce* (see SAUCE).

Cheese pannequets (Cheshire, Gruyère or Parmesan). PANNEQUETS AU FROMAGE—Cut the pancakes into rectangles.

Garnish. Cream cheese. Sprinkle with grated cheese and brown.

Pannequets à la florentine—Cut the pancakes into lozenge shapes.

Garnish. Spinach cooked in butter blended with *Béchamel sauce* (see SAUCE), to which grated cheese has been added. Sprinkle with more grated cheese and brown.

Pannequets à la grecque—Rolled pancakes.

*Garnish. Salpicon** of braised mutton, egg-plant (aubergines) sautéed in oil and pimentos, blended with *Tomato sauce* (see SAUCE) seasoned with paprika.

Dip in egg and breadcrumbs and fry.

Note. These pannequets are often made from very small pancakes spread with the prescribed forcemeat, folded in two and browned under the grill.

Fried pannequets in breadcrumbs. PANNEQUETS PANÉS ET FRITS—Prepare the pancakes and stuff them as described below under *Stuffed pannequets*.

Roll them into scrolls, cut into short pieces, dip in egg and breadcrumbs and fry at the last moment.

Pancakes prepared in this way are also known in France under the name of *croquettes* or *craquelins*.

Fried pancakes can also be done in a different way. Instead of dipping in egg and breadcrumbs, dip them in frying-batter. In that case they are known under the name of *Cromesquis à la polonaise*.

Apart from the recipes given here, pancakes can be stuffed with all kinds of other preparations, purées, *salpicons**, creams, etc., as given in recipes for pastry boats (*barquettes*), patties, canapés, tartlets and other small dishes of the same kind.

Pannequets à la hongroise—Rolled pancakes.

Garnish. Salpicon of onions and mushrooms cooked in butter until very soft, seasoned with paprika and blended with a *Béchamel* or *Velouté sauce* (see SAUCE).

Pannequets à l'italienne—Rolled pancakes.

Garnish. Duxelles (see SAUCE), to which lean chopped ham, blended with a very thick *Tomato sauce* (see SAUCE), has been added.

Dip in egg and breadcrumbs and fry.

Pannequets à la ligurienne—Make very small pancakes and fold in two.

*Garnish. Salpicon** of anchovies and hard boiled eggs blended with *Tomato fondue**, seasoned with tarragon.

Sprinkle with breadcrumbs and brown.

Pannequets à la Saint-Hubert—Cut the pancakes into rectangles or into lozenge shapes.

Garnish. Purée of ground game with a *Demi-glace sauce* (see SAUCE), based on concentrated game stock.

Pannequets à la strasbourgeoise—Cut the pancakes into rectangles.

Garnish. Purée of foie gras to which chopped truffles have been added.

Stuffed pannequets. PANNEQUETS FOURRÉS—Make the pancakes in the usual manner—big and very thin.

Spread the pancakes on a table, coat with a thin layer of the selected forcemeat.

Roll them up and cut each roll into two or three pieces.

Put the pieces on a baking tray and heat them in the oven.

Arrange on a napkin or a paper doyley.

Note. Stuffed pancakes can also be shaped differently. Instead of rolling them up, put two together and cut with a biscuit-cutter into rectangles, squares, lozenges or circles.

You can also make very small pancakes. After spreading with the selected filling, fold them in half or into quarters.

The pancakes can be sprinkled with breadcrumbs or grated cheese and grilled lightly. For further recipes see CRÊPES.

Small pâtés. PETITS PÂTÉS GARNIS—Small pâtés are prepared in the following way. Make a layer of puff pastry or any other pastry. This should be approximately $\frac{1}{4}$ inch thick. Cut with a round or oval pastry-cutter, with a plain or fluted edge. The diameter of the circlets should be about 2 inches.

Collect all the remains of the dough, roll them out into another layer, which should be a little thinner than the first layer. Cut the same number of shapes out of it as out of the first layer. Put the second lot of circlets on a moistened baking tray.

Slightly moisten the edges with water. Put in the centre of each circlet a portion—the size of a hazelnut—of filling: forcemeat, minced meat or any other preparation according to the recipe chosen.

Cover with the circlets cut out of the first layer of pastry. Press the dough with the back of a small biscuit-cutter, so that the two circlets stick together. Brush with egg and put in a hot oven for 12 to 15 minutes.

Small square or rectangular pâtés can be made in the same way.

In addition to the recipes given below, small pâtés can be filled with all the ingredients given for pastry boats (*barquettes*), patties, tartlets, etc.

Small fish pâtés. PETITS PÂTÉS DE POISSONS—These can be made in any shape.

Garnish. Forcemeat of pike, whiting or any other fish, or a *salpicon** of cooked fish, blended with a thick *Velouté sauce* (see SAUCE) based on fish stock. If desired, mushrooms and truffles cut into small dice can be added to the *salpicon*.

Small game pâtés with gravy. PETITS PÂTÉS DE GIBIER AU JUS—Proceed as indicated in the recipe for small pâtés with gravy, but use a *salpicon** of game instead of forcemeat.

Small meat pâtés. PETITS PÂTÉS DE VIANDES—Any shape.

Garnish. As for *Small pâtés à la Saint-Hubert*, replacing the purée of salpicon of game by any kind of meat.

Small pâtés with *salpicon* can also be made in moulds as described for *Small pâtés with gravy*.

Small mutton pâtés. PETITS PÂTÉS DE MOUTON À L'ANGLAISE—Line deep tartlet moulds with lining paste (pastry dough).

Fill with small dice of mutton, half lean half fat, season with salt and pepper and sprinkle with chopped herbs.

Make some puff pastry and give it eight turns. Cover the pâtés with little circlets of this. Brush with egg and make a little opening in the middle of each little pie.

Bake in a very low oven for 35 minutes. As you take the pâtés out of the oven pour into each 2 teaspoons of *Demi-glace sauce* (see SAUCE).

Small poultry pâtés with gravy. PETITS PÂTÉS DE VOLAILLE AU JUS—As described in the recipe for *Small pâtés with gravy*, using a *salpicon** of poultry.

Small pâtés with anchovy. PETITS PÂTÉS AUX ANCHOIS—Make the small pâtés, cutting them out with a round pastry-cutter.

Garnish. Fish forcemeat with anchovy butter to which a *salpicon** of anchovy fillets has been added. (See FORCEMEATS AND STUFFINGS.)

Small pâtés with gravy. PETITS PÂTÉS AU JUS—Line small pastry moulds with *Lining paste* (see DOUGH).

Fill them with a *salpicon** of forcemeat, mushrooms and truffles blended with a strong *Demi-glace sauce* (see SAUCE).

Cover each mould with a round of puff pastry. Stick the rims together firmly. Put on each cover a small ring of puff pastry cut out with a fluted pastry-cutter of a smaller diameter than the lid.

Pierce a small round hole in the middle of the lid. Brush with egg and bake in a hot oven for 15 to 18 minutes.

Take the pâtés out of the moulds. Arrange them on a dish. Pour into each pie a few drops of thickened veal juice piping hot.

Small pâtés with gravy can be prepared in the same way using all kinds of other meat.

Small pâtés à l'andalouse. PETITS PÂTÉS À L'ANDALOUSE—Make the small pâtés, cutting them out with a round pastry-cutter.

Garnish. Sausage meat to which a *salpicon** of pimentos cooked in butter and chopped onions lightly fried in butter has been added.

Small pâtés à la charcutière. PETITS PÂTÉS À LA CHARCUTIÈRE—Small round pâtés.

Garnish. Sausage meat to which chopped parsley has been added.

Small pâtés à la duxelles. PETITS PÂTÉS À LA DUXELLES—

Garnish. Pork forcemeat to which an equal part of dry *duxelles* has been added.

Small pâtés au gastronome. PETITS PÂTÉS AU GASTRONOME—Small oval pâtés.

*Garnish. Salpicon** of cock's comb, pickled or smoked tongue, truffles and mushrooms, blended with a strong Madeira-flavoured *Demi-glace sauce* (see SAUCE).

Small pâtés à la lyonnaise. PETITS PÂTÉS À LA LYONNAISE—Small square pâtés.

Garnish. Finely chopped braised or boiled beef to which chopped onions, cooked in butter until soft and blended with concentrated veal gravy, have been added.

Small pâtés à la moscovite. PETITS PÂTÉS À LA MOSCOVITE—Make a *Coulibiac* dough (see COULIBIAC); cut into circlets of approximately 3 inches in diameter.

Put a piece of *Pike forcemeat* (see FORCEMEAT) the size of a walnut in the middle of each circle.

Put a little cooked semolina on the forcemeat and, on top of this, a slice of any kind of raw white fish. Season with salt and spices. Fold the dough over towards the centre from the sides, making small oval-shaped pies. Press the rims together and crimp the edges. Make a very small opening in the middle.

Put on a tray in a warm place and leave to rise for 30 minutes. Brush with egg and bake in a hot oven for 25 minutes.

Just before serving pour into the opening of each pie a little concentrated *Demi-glace sauce* (see SAUCE) to which chopped parsley and lemon juice have been added.

Small pâtés à la reine. PETITS PÂTÉS À LA REINE—Small round pâtés.

Garnish. Poultry purée to which chopped truffles, blended with a thick *Velouté sauce* (see SAUCE), have been added.

Small pâtés à la Saint-Hubert. PETITS PÂTÉS À LA SAINT-HUBERT—Make small round pâtés.

Garnish. Game purée blended with a *Demi-glace sauce* (see SAUCE) based on concentrated game stock.

Small pâtés à la strasbourgeoise. PETITS PÂTÉS À LA STRASBOURGEOISE—

Garnish. Purée of foie gras to which chopped truffles have been added.

Garnished patties. BOUCHÉES GARNIES—Patties are made of puff pastry baked blind (empty) and garnished with a meat, fish or vegetable *salpicon**.

Method. Making the patties—Roll out puff pastry six times. Now roll out for use to a thickness of about $\frac{1}{4}$ inch and with a round fluted pastry-cutter cut out circlets $2\frac{1}{2}$ inches in diameter. Cut as many pieces as you need patties.

Put these circlets, turning them, on a slightly moistened metal tray.

Brush with egg, mark the lid by pressing each circlet with a pastry-cutter but taking care not to cut right through. The pastry-cutter for the lids should have a diameter of $1\frac{1}{4}$ inches.

Bake the patties in a hot oven. Remove the lids and scoop out the soft part from the interior of the patty.

These patties can vary in size depending on how they are to be finally served. They can be made oval or square in shape, though this is rarely done.

Very small, hollowed out and variously filled *brioches* are also called *patties.*

Filling the patties. Generally the filling for patties consists of a simple or compound meat, fish or vegetable *salpicon*, blended with white or brown stock.

Patties can also be filled with purées of meat, fish or vegetables.

Apart from these all the fillings recommended for *barquettes*, *croûtes*, tartlets and similar dishes can also be used for patties.

Very small patties can be used as a garnish for large dishes of various kinds. Slightly bigger patties can be served as small entrées.

The patties should be filled or garnished at the very last moment. Just before filling, put them in the oven for a few seconds. Better still, if at all possible, arrange the cooking so that garnishing can take place the minute they come out of the oven. This makes a tremendous difference to the flavour. The same applies to all kinds of pastry dishes filled with a *salpicon* or other hot garnish.

Patties à l'américaine. BOUCHÉES À L'AMÉRICAINE—

*Garnish. Salpicon** of spiny lobster or *Lobster à l'américaine**.

Patties à la bénédictine. BOUCHÉES À LA BÉNÉDICTINE—

Garnish. Salt cod pounded with garlic, oil and cream to which truffles cut into dice have been added. Cover the patties with slices of truffle.

Patties à la bouquetière. BOUCHÉES À LA BOUQUETIÈRE—

Garnish. Vegetable *macédoine**, blended with *Béchamel* or a *Velouté sauce* (see SAUCE).

Patties à la Clamart. BOUCHÉES À LA CLAMART—

Garnish. Purée of fresh peas with cream.

Crayfish patties. BOUCHÉES AUX ÉCREVISSES—*Garnish.* Ragoût of crayfish tails bound with *Nantua sauce* (see SAUCE).

Patties à la Crécy. BOUCHÉES À LA CRÉCY—

Garnish. Purée of carrots cooked in vegetable stock.

Patties à la dieppoise. BOUCHÉES À LA DIEPPOISE—*Garnish. Salpicon** of mussels and prawns blended with a *White wine sauce* (see SAUCE).

Patties à la financière. BOUCHÉES À LA FINANCIÈRE—*Garnish. Salpicon à la financière**. Cover with sliced truffles.

Patties à la julienne. BOUCHÉES À LA JULIENNE—*Garnish.* Vegetables cut into matchsticks, stewed in butter, blended with cream.

Patties with lobster, spiny lobster, or other crustaceans. BOUCHÉES AU HOMARD, À LA LANGOUSTE—*Garnish.* A *salpicon** of the chosen crustacean, blended with *Béchamel* or *Velouté sauce* (see SAUCE) based on fish stock and finished with *Crustacean butter* (see BUTTER, *Compound butters*).

Patties Montglas (square shape). BOUCHEÉS MONTGLAS—*Garnish. Montglas salpicon* of lamb sweetbreads, cock's combs and kidneys, truffles and mushrooms, blended with a Madeira-flavoured *Demi-glace sauce* (see SAUCE). Top with small slices of foie gras and slices of truffles.

Patties with mussels. BOUCHÉES AUX MOULES—*Garnish.* Mussels with *Allemande sauce* or *Poulette sauce* (see SAUCE).

Patties with oysters. BOUCHÉES AUX HUÎTRES—*Garnish.* Poached oysters, drained and de-bearded, with *Normande sauce* (see SAUCE) made with white wine.

Patties à la périgourdine. BOUCHÉES À LA PÉRIGOURDINE—*Garnish. Salpicon** of truffles and foie gras, blended with Madeira-flavoured *Demi-glace sauce* (see SAUCE).

Patties with poultry. BOUCHÉES DE VOLAILLE—*Garnish. Salpicon** of poultry or purée of poultry with cream.

Patties à la reine. BOUCHÉES À LA REINE—*Garnish.* Purée of poultry with cream of *Salpicon à la reine** (composed of diced poultry, mushrooms and truffles).

Patties à la Saint-Hubert. BOUCHÉES À LA SAINT-HUBERT—*Garnish.* Purée of game or *salpicon** made from the meat of ground game. The shape of these patties should be oval.

Sévigné patties. BOUCHÉES SÉVIGNÉ—*Garnish. Salpicon** of chicken quenelles with truffles cooked in *Velouté sauce* (see SAUCE). Put half a heart of braised lettuce on each patty.

Patties with shrimps. BOUCHÉES AUX CREVETTES—*Garnish.* Ragoût of shrimp tails with *shrimp sauce* (see SAUCE).

Patties with soft roes. BOUCHÉES AUX LAITANCES—*Garnish.* A *salpicon** of soft roe with cream or with *Velouté sauce* (see SAUCE).

Patties with truffles. BOUCHÉES AUX TRUFFES—*Garnish. Salpicon** of truffles stewed in butter with cream, or with Madeira or any other similar wine.

Piroghi (Russian cooking). PIROGUI—This is Russian for pies of various kinds. Pirog can be made from different doughs, chou paste, pancake batter, puff pastry, etc. They can be filled with a variety of mixtures such as meat, poultry, game, fish, vegetables, rice, cheese. See PIROGHI.

Pirozhki. PIROJKI—This Russian word is the plural of *pirozhok*—a diminutive of *piroghi*—i.e., small pie or patty, filled with all kinds of different ingredients. See PIROGHI.

Pomponnettes—A kind of rissole made in the shape of a very small pouch.

Make some best quality *Lining paste* (see DOUGH). Roll out to a thickness of $\frac{1}{8}$ inch, cut with a round, fluted pastry-cutter 3 inches in diameter.

Fill the middle of each of these circles of pastry with a portion of purée or any other preparation, the size of a walnut. Lightly moisten the rim of the dough and fold in towards the middle to make the shape of a small pouch.

At the last minute fry in deep fat over a hot flame.

Drain and arrange on a napkin.

Pomponnettes can equally well be made from left-over puff pastry.

All fillings given in the recipes for rissoles can be used for pomponnettes.

Stuffed potatoes. POMMES DE TERRE FOURRÉES—Potatoes can be stuffed with all kinds of different mixtures. After they have been baked in the oven and two-thirds of their pulp has been scooped out they can be filled with *Oyster Ragoût à la cancalaise*, with *Crayfish ragoût à la Nantua** or with a *Salpicon** of poultry (*à la Maintenon*).

Quiche lorraine—A kind of flan filled with a cream garnished with thin slices of lean bacon and served piping hot. The method of preparing quiches is described under QUICHE.

Ramekins. RAMEQUINS—A kind of tartlet with cream cheese. This name is also given to a small pastry made of chou paste to which cheese is added. For their preparation see RAMEKINS.

Rastegaï—This is a Russian patty, made of yeast dough (see DOUGH) and sealed only at the ends. Divide the yeast dough into 150 gram (5 ounce) pieces, roll into balls, allow to stand for 8–10 minutes, then roll out into circlets. Put a tablespoon of whatever filling is desired—minced beef with chopped eggs and onion, fish forcemeat or chopped mushrooms are the most popular fillings for this type of patty (see FORCEMEAT)—and crimp up the ends, making a boat-shaped patty, leaving the middle unsealed and the filling exposed. Hence the name, which in Russian means 'unbuttoned'. Leave to stand for 10 minutes then bake in a hot oven. When ready, brush the rastegaïs with melted butter and put in the middle garnish appropriate to the filling. Thus, a fish rastegaï should have a slice of cooked salmon or sturgeon, a mushroom rastegaï a teaspoon of small pickled cèpes, or slices of hard boiled egg, etc. Fish rastegais are served as an accompaniment to *Ukha*, i.e. clear fish soup, meat rastegaïs to strong beef consommé, mushrooms rastegaïs to mushroom consommé.

Ravioli—Small pasta envelopes filled with different purée stuffings and poached. Serve in a clear soup with grated cheese. See RAVIOLI.

Ravioli à la lithuanienne—See VARENIKI in this section.

Rissoles—Name given to small pastries of various shapes (round, oval, rectangular or turnovers). Rissoles are made from a variety of doughs, including lining paste (pastry dough), left-over puff pastry or ordinary brioche pastry.

They are filled mainly with croquette ingredients. The filling should only be put on the pastry when it is quite cold. For the method of preparation see RISSOLES.

Generally speaking rissoles should be fried, but sometimes they are baked in the oven.

Cinderella rissoles. RISSOLES CENDRILLON—Make the rissoles using *Brioche dough* (see DOUGH) in the shape of turnovers.

*Garnish. Salpicon** of poultry and truffles blended with a purée of foie gras.

Farm rissoles. RISSOLES À LA FERMIÈRE—These rissoles are made from *Lining paste* (see DOUGH) cut into circlets.

Garnish. Salpicon of equal quantities of ham and *mirepoix** of vegetables cooked in butter, blended with a rich *Demi-glace sauce* (see SAUCE).

Foie gras rissoles. RISSOLES AU FOIE GRAS—Choose your dough according to taste and shape it as you please.

Garnish. Purée of foie gras to which chopped truffles can be added, if desired.

Pompadour rissoles. RISSOLES POMPADOUR—Roll out left-over puff pastry and cut into rounds.

*Garnish. Salpicon** of pickled or smoked tongue, truffles and mushrooms blended with a *Demi-glace sauce* (see SAUCE).

Rissoles à la bohémienne—Using *Brioche dough* (see DOUGH) make the rissoles in the shape of turnovers.

*Garnish. Salpicon** of foie gras and truffles blended with a rich *Demi-glace sauce* (see SAUCE).

Rissoles à la chalonnaise—Using left-over puff pastry make round-shaped rissoles.

*Garnish. Salpicon** of cock's combs and kidneys, truffles and mushrooms, blended with a thick *Velouté sauce* (see SAUCE) based on chicken stock.

Rissoles à la dauphine—Using *Brioche dough* (see DOUGH) make the rissoles in the shape of turnovers.

Rissoles incorporating all kinds of garnishes, *salpicons**, etc. are served under this name.

The name of the main ingredients should appear on the menu, e.g., *Foie gras rissoles à la dauphine*, *Lobster rissoles à la dauphine*, etc.

Sausages. SAUCISSES—Small chipolata sausages, Strasbourg, Frankfurt and Vienna sausages can be served as hors-d'oeuvre.

Devilled chipolata sausages. SAUCISSES CHIPOLATAS À LA DIABLE—Cook the chipolata sausages under a grill. Put each sausage on a rectangular slice of sandwich bread, fried in butter and spread with mustard.

Sprinkle with fried breadcrumbs, season with a little cayenne and put in the oven for a minute.

Arrange on a round dish; garnish with fresh parsley.

Sausages à la duchesse. SAUCISSES À LA DUCHESSE—Fry the sausages quickly in butter. Make oval *Duchess potato cakes* (see POTATOES); brown in the oven and put one sausage on each potato cake.

Add white wine and *Demi-glace sauce* (see SAUCE) to the butter in which the sausages were cooked; boil down, add some more butter and pour this sauce over the sausages. Sprinkle with chopped parsley and serve in a round dish.

Frankfurt, Strasbourg and Vienna sausages. SAUCISSES DE FRANCFORT, DE STRASBOURG, DE VIENNE—Poach the sausages in boiling water for 10 minutes. Drain them, arrange on a dish and serve with grated horseradish handed separately.

Sausages à l'italienne. SAUCISSES À L'ITALIENNE—Proceed as for *Sausages à la duchesse*.

Pour very thick *Italian sauce* (see SAUCE) over the sausages.

Sausages à la languedocienne. SAUCISSES À LA LANGUEDOCIENNE—Fry the sausages quickly in butter.

Cut an aubergine (egg-plant) into thick round slices. Dip the slices in flour and fry in oil. Put one sausage on each slice of fried aubergine.

Put a spoonful of *Tomato fondue** seasoned with a little chopped garlic on the sausages. Sprinkle with fried breadcrumbs, put in the oven for a minute, sprinkle with chopped parsley and serve.

Sausage à la lyonnaise. SAUCISSON CHAUD À LA LYONNAISE—Poached saveloy sausage served with hot potato salad.

Saveloys are often made with truffles and also with pistachio nuts added.

Sausages à la maltaise. SAUCISSES À LA MALTAISE—Fry the sausages quickly in butter.

Cut a sandwich loaf into thick rectangular pieces. Hollow out and fry in butter. Put one sausage on each piece of fried bread.

Add white wine to the butter in which the sausages were fried, stirring well. Season with a little chopped shallot. Make a rich *Demi-glace sauce* (see SAUCE). Blanch some orange peel, drain, cut into very thin strips and add to the demi-glace sauce. Pour this sauce over the sausages.

Serve in a round dish.

Sausages à la tyrolienne. SAUCISSES À LA TYROLIENNE—Cook the sausages under the grill.

Cut a sandwich loaf into thick rectangular pieces. Hollow them out and fry in butter. Garnish with a spoonful of *Tomato fondue**. Put one sausage on each piece of fried bread.

Fry onion rings in oil and put two on each sausage.

Sausages à la zingara. SAUCISSES À LA ZINGARA—Fry the sausages quickly in butter.

Grill some mushrooms and fill with a *julienne** of lean ham, scarlet tongue, truffles and mushrooms, blended with tomato-flavoured *Demi-glace sauce* (see SAUCE).

Put one sausage on each garnished mushroom. Sprinkle with chopped tarragon.

Scallop shells, garnished. COQUILLES GARNIES—With the aid of a forcing (pastry) bag, with a plain or fluted nozzle, make a thin border of *Duchess potatoes* (see POTATOES) round the edge of the scallop shell. You can also use thin roundels of boiled potatoes to make a rim. If true scallop shells are not available, metal, earthenware and other oven-proof shells can be used.

Put a spoonful of the prescribed sauce on the bottom of the shell. Garnish, according to the recipe chosen, with collops (pieces) of fish or anything else.

Spoon over some more of the same sauce.

Sprinkle with breadcrumbs or grated cheese, depending on the ingredients used, and with melted butter.

Put the shells into a baking-dish, filled half-way up with warm water, and brown in a very hot oven.

Note. When scallop shells are *gratiné* (sprinkled with breadcrumbs and grated cheese and browned in the oven) or glazed (heated quickly in hot oven), the shells can be prepared without a potato border.

The function of the border is mainly to contain the ingredients of the garnish. Incidentally, the border can be made of all kinds of different preparations, which go well with the main ingredient of the garnish. You can, for instance, make a rim of chicken, veal or fish forcemeat for the shells; alternatively you can pipe a border of spinach, rice, etc.

The shells can also be made without breadcrumbs or glazing. In which case, if they are made with a border of Duchess potato, they should be baked quickly in the oven, to give the purée a good colour before the garnish is added.

After the shells have been coated with a sauce, gratiné or glazed, they can be decorated with different items—truffles, mushrooms, asparagus tips, etc. Care should be taken to use only decorations which are in harmony with the basic ingredients.

Scallop shells of bone-marrow à la duxelles. COQUILLES D'AMOURETTES À LA DUXELLES—Make a border of *Duchess potatoes* (see POTATOES).

Garnish. Slices of bone-marrow and mushrooms. *Duxelles sauce* (see SAUCE).

Sprinkle with breadcrumbs and melted butter and brown the top. After cooking, sprinkle a few drops of lemon juice on the shells and garnish with chopped parsley.

Scallop shells of brains à l'allemande. COQUILLES DE CERVELLE À L'ALLEMANDE—Make a border of *Duchess potatoes* (see POTATOES).

Garnish. Slices of lamb's or calf's brain; *Allemande sauce* (see SAUCE).

Glaze in the oven.

Scallop shells of brains à l'aurore. COQUILLES DE CERVELLE À L'AURORE—Make a border of *potato purée**.

Garnish. Brains, mushrooms, *Aurore sauce* (see SAUCE).

Sprinkle with grated cheese, pour melted butter over the shells and brown.

When cooked, sprinkle with chopped, hard boiled eggs and chopped parsley. Pour round a ring of *Tomato sauce* (see SAUCE).

Scallop shells of brains à la duxelles. COQUILLES DE CERVELLE À LA DUXELLES—Prepare in the same way as *Scallop shells of bone-marrow à la duxelles*, using slices of brains instead of bone-marrow.

Scallop shells of brill Mornay. COQUILLES DE BARBUE MORNAY—Make a border of *Duchess potatoes* (see POTATOES).

Garnish. Slices of cooked brill with *Mornay sauce* (see SAUCE).

Sprinkle with cheese, pour melted butter over the shells and brown.

(In U.S.A. grey sole or flounder can be substituted for brill.)

Scallop shells of brill à la trouvillaise. COQUILLES DE BARBUE À LA TROUVILLAISE—Make a border of *Duchess potatoes* (see POTATOES). Brown the border before garnishing.

Garnish. Slices of brill, mussels, shrimps' tails, *Shrimp sauce* (see SAUCE).

These shells are not glazed, but they should be decorated with small mushroom heads.

(In U.S.A. flounder, grey sole and shrimps are successful substitutes in this recipe.)

Scallop shells of crayfish. COQUILLES D'ÉCREVISSES—Make a rim of *Duchess potatoes* (see POTATOES).

Garnish. Ragoût of *Crayfish tails à la Nantua**.

Finish as for *Scallop shells of shrimps.*

These shells, which are mainly used as a garnish for fish dishes, should be very small.

Scallop shells of eggs au gratin. COQUILLES D'OEUFS AU GRATIN—Make a border of *Duchess potatoes* (see POTATOES).

Garnish. Hard boiled eggs cut into large dice, *Mornay sauce* (see SAUCE).

Sprinkle with cheese and brown in the oven.

Scallop shells of fish. COQUILLES DE POISSONS—Prepare these shells as described in the recipes given for *Scallop shells of brill, shrimps, crayfish, skate liver, lobster, oysters, soft roes* and *mussels.*

Fill the shells with garnishes and sauces, as directed in the recipe. The sauces used most often for fish in scallop shells are the following: *Aurore, Béchamel, Shrimp, Duxelles, Lobster, Hungarian, Curry, Italian, Mornay, Nantua, Niçoise, Normande,* and *White wine sauce.* See SAUCE.

According to the recipe chosen, scallop shells of fish are sprinkled with breadcrumbs or with grated cheese, or they are simply glazed.

Note. For all these dishes of fish in scallop shells, you can use up left-overs of boiled or braised fish such as perch, cod, coalfish, whiting, hake, skate, salmon, sole, trout, turbot, etc.

Scallop shells of left-overs. COQUILLES À LA MÉNAGÈRE—Make a border of plain *potato purée**.

Garnish. Minced left-over pieces of boiled beef blended with *Tomato sauce* (see SAUCE).

Sprinkle the shells with breadcrumbs and brown in the oven.

Left-overs in shells can also be prepared with minced mutton or veal. If minced veal is used, blend with a thick *Velouté sauce*, or, if not available, with a *Béchamel sauce* (see SAUCE).

Scallop shells of lobster. COQUILLES DE HOMARD—Make a border with *Duchess potatoes* (see POTATOES).

Garnish. Pieces of lobster or *salpicon** of lobster with *Béchamel sauce, Lobster sauce* or *Mornay sauce* (see SAUCE).

Sprinkle the shells with grated cheese and brown the top.

Scallop shells of meat. COQUILLES DE VIANDES—For the preparation of these shells follow the directions given for *Scallop shells of bone-marrow, brains* and *poultry.*

For shells filled with various kinds of meat, left-overs of boiled, braised or roast lamb, mutton, beef or veal can be used.

Scallop shells of mussels. COQUILLES DE MOULES—Prepare them as described in the recipes for *Scallop shells of oysters* or *Scallop shells of soft roes.* You can also prepare mussels in shells by following any of the recipes for fish in shells in general.

Scallop shells of oysters à la diable. COQUILLES D'HUÎTRES À LA DIABLE—Make a border of *Duchess potatoes* (see POTATOES).

Garnish. Poached oysters, drained and bearded. Thick *Béchamel sauce* (see SAUCE) made with the water in which the oysters have been poached, seasoned with a pinch of cayenne.

Sprinkle the shells with fried breadcrumbs. Brown.

Shells with oysters cooked in this way are often simply known as *Oysters à la diable.*

Scallop shells of oysters Mornay. COQUILLES D'HUÎTRES MORNAY—Make a border of *Duchess potatoes* (see POTATOES).

Garnish. Poached oysters, drained and de-bearded. *Mornay sauce* (see SAUCE).

Sprinkle with grated cheese, pour butter over the shells and brown.

Scallop shells of poultry. COQUILLES DE VOLAILLES—This name is given especially to shells with a basic ingredient of chicken or table-fowl. In principle the white meat only should be used. In ordinary home kitchens, where these shells are served mainly to use up left-overs, all parts of the poultry can be used.

Scallop shells of poultry à l'allemande. COQUILLES DE VOLAILLE À L'ALLEMANDE—Make a border of *Duchess potatoes* (see POTATOES).

Garnish. Slices of white poultry meat with *Allemande sauce* (see SAUCE).

Glaze in a hot oven.

Scallop shells of poultry Monselet. COQUILLES DE VOLAILLE MONSELET—Make a border of *Duchess potatoes* (See POTATOES).

Garnish. Slices of white meat of poultry and artichoke hearts. *Mornay sauce* (see SAUCE).

Sprinkle with grated cheese and brown in the oven. After taking out of the oven, garnish each shell with two slices of truffle alternating with sliced artichoke hearts cooked in butter.

Scallop shells of poultry princesse. COQUILLES DE VOLAILLE PRINCESSE—Make a border of *Duchess potatoes* (see POTATOES).

Garnish. Slices of white poultry meat. *Allemande sauce* (see SAUCE).

Do not glaze. Just before serving, put on each shell two slices of truffle and a bouquet of asparagus tips cooked in butter.

Scallop shells of poultry Rossini. COQUILLES DE VOLAILLE ROSSINI—Make a border of *Duchess potatoes* (see POTATOES) and brown before adding the garnish.

Garnish. Slices of white poultry meat and truffles. Thick *Madeira sauce* (see SAUCE).

Just before serving, put on each shell a slice of foie gras sautéed in butter and a slice of truffle.

Scallop shells of poultry with smoked or pickled tongue. COQUILLES DE VOLAILLE À L'ÉCARLATE—Make a border of *Duchess potatoes* (see POTATOES); brown before the garnish is added.

Garnish. Slices of white poultry meat and smoked or pickled tongue. *Allemande sauce* (see SAUCE).

Do not glaze, but sprinkle the shells just before serving with chopped tongue.

Scallop shells of shrimps. COQUILLES DE CREVETTES—Make a border of *Duchess potatoes* (see POTATOES).

Garnish. Ragoût of *Shrimps' tails à la béchamel* or *au velouté* finished with *Shrimp butter* (see BUTTER, *Compound butters*).

Sprinkle with grated cheese, pour melted butter over the shells and brown.

Scallop shells of skate liver and brown butter. COQUILLES DE FOIE DE RAIE AU BEURRE NOIR—Make a border of *Duchess potatoes* (see POTATOES) and brown before adding the garnish.

Garnish. Slices of cooked skate liver.

Sprinkle with pounded parsley, and a few drops of lemon juice. At the last moment pour brown butter over the shells (see BUTTER, *Compound butters*).

Scallop shells of skate liver à la polonaise. COQUILLES DE FOIE DE RAIE À LA POLONAISE—Dress and garnish as directed for *Scallop shells of skate liver and brown butter.*

Sprinkle with the chopped yolks of hard boiled eggs and chopped parsley.

Brown fine breadcrumbs in *Noisette butter* (see BUTTER, *Compound butters*) and pour over the shells.

Scallop shells of soft roes à la florentine. COQUILLES DE LAITANCES À LA FLORENTINE—Make a border of *Duchess potatoes* (see POTATOES).

Garnish. Slices of soft carp roes or herring roes arranged on a layer of spinach cooked in butter, *Mornay sauce* (see SAUCE).

Sprinkle with grated cheese and brown the top.

Scallop shells of sweetbreads. COQUILLES DE RIS D'AGNEAU—Prepare these shells with lamb's sweetbreads as described in the recipes for *Scallop shells of bone-marrow, brains,* or *poultry.*

Small soufflés. PETITS SOUFFLÉS—These are made in *cassolettes* from all the different mixtures described in the section on SOUFFLÉS.

Small soufflés à l'américaine. PETITS SOUFFLÉS À L'AMÉRICAINE—Fill the *cassolettes* with alternate layers of the mixture used for *Lobster soufflé* or *Spiny lobster soufflé* and *salpicon** of lobster or spiny lobster *à l'américaine.*

Finish in the ordinary way as described in the section on SOUFFLÉS.

Small soufflés à l'aurore. PETITS SOUFFLÉS À L'AURORE—Garnish the *cassolettes* with the mixture for *Chicken soufflé* (see SOUFFLÉ) and add concentrated tomato juice.

When the soufflés come out of the oven sprinkle them with the chopped yolk of hard boiled eggs and chopped parsley.

Small crayfish soufflés à la Nantua I. PETITS SOUFFLÉS D'ÉCREVISSES (À LA NANTUA)—Rub through a sieve ¼ pound (125 grams) of white fish (whiting, cod or sole) cooked in butter.

Add to this purée ¾ cup (1½ decilitres) of *Crayfish purée* blended with a thick *Béchamel sauce* (see SAUCE). Season with a little cayenne. Blend with three yolks of egg and, at the last minute, work three stiffly beaten whites of egg into the mixture.

Small crayfish soufflés à la Nantua II. PETITS SOUFFLÉS D'ÉCREVISSES (À LA NANTUA)—Prepare the mixture as described in the preceding recipe.

When putting it into the *cassolettes* arrange alternate layers of a *salpicon** of crayfish tails with truffles.

Finish as described in the preceding recipe.

Small crayfish soufflés with Parmesan. PETITS SOUFFLÉS D'ÉCREVISSES AU PARMESAN—Fill the *cassolettes* with a layer of *Parmesan soufflé mixture* (see SOUFFLÉ). On this put a spoonful of *Crayfish tail ragoût à la Nantua**. Cover with another layer of *Parmesan soufflé mixture.*

Finish as described in the preceding recipes.

Small oyster soufflés à la cancalaise. PETITS SOUFFLÉS AUX HUÎTRES, DITS À LA CANCALAISE—Poach 12 oysters taken out of their shells in their own juice. Drain them and dry them in a cloth.

Reduce (boil down) their cooking stock and add ¾ cup (1½ decilitres) of thick *Béchamel sauce* (see SAUCE). Strain this sauce. Blend with three yolks of egg, add the oysters cut in two and, at the last minute, the three beaten whites of egg.

Finish as described in the preceding recipes.

Small soufflés à la princesse. PETITS SOUFFLÉS À LA PRINCESSE—Fill the *cassolettes* with alternate layers of *chicken soufflé mixture* (see SOUFFLÉ) and a *salpicon** of truffles and asparagus tips.

Finish as described in the preceding recipes.

Small soft roe soufflés. PETITS SOUFFLÉS DE LAITANCES—Poach, cool and drain well the soft roe of carp or other fish. Rub through a fine sieve. To each ¼ pound (125 grams) of this purée add ¾ cup (1½ decilitres) of thick *Béchamel sauce* (see SAUCE).

Blend with three yolks of egg and, at the last minute, add the three beaten whites of egg.

Finish as described in the preceding recipes.

Subrics—*Subrics* are similar to small croquettes except that they are not dipped in egg and breadcrumbs and fried in deep fat, but are cooked in butter in a shallow pan.

For their general preparation see SUBRICS.

Brain and bone-marrow subrics. SUBRICS DE CERVELLE, D'AMOURETTES—Poach calf's brain, drain, and cut into large dice. Put into a terrine.

Add ¼ cup (half a decilitre) of *Allemande sauce* or *Béchamel sauce* (see SAUCE), one egg beaten as for omelette; season with salt, pepper and nutmeg.

Mix carefully so as not to crush the brain. Finish as described under SUBRICS.

Serve *Tomato sauce* separately (see SAUCE).

Note. Instead of calf's brain an equivalent amount of sheep's brains or ox brains can be used.

Subrics made of sweetbreads and bone-marrow are prepared in exactly the same manner.

Brain subrics à l'italienne. SUBRICS DE CERVELLE À L'ITALIENNE—Cut the brains into dice and blend with two eggs beaten as for an omelette with a tablespoon of flour, salt, pepper and nutmeg.

Add two tablespoons of grated Parmesan cheese. Finish as described under SUBRICS.

Serve *Tomato sauce* separately (see SAUCE).

Subrics à la florentine—Make a preparation for *subrics* with spinach and finish off with ⅜ cup (60 grams) of grated Parmesan cheese.

Finish as described under SUBRICS.

Subrics of goose liver. SUBRICS DE FOIE GRAS—Put ⅜ cup (50 grams) of sifted flour into a bowl. Add an egg beaten as for an omelette and 2 or 3 tablespoons of thick cream. Season with salt and pepper and mix.

Cook ½ pound (250 grams) of goose liver, cool and cut into dice. Mix carefully into the above preparation.

Finish as described under SUBRICS.

Serve *Périgueux sauce* separately (see SAUCE).

Subrics à la ménagère—Take ½ pound (250 grams) of cold braised or boiled beef cut into small dice. Add a tablespoon of chopped onion, cooked in butter until very soft, and a tablespoon of chopped parsley.

Blend this mixture with two eggs beaten as for an omelette and one tablespoon of flour. Season with salt, pepper and nutmeg. Mix well.

Finish as described under SUBRICS.

Subrics can be prepared in the same way using all kinds of cold cooked meat and fish.

Poultry liver subrics. SUBRICS DE FOIES DE VOLAILLE—Cook chicken (or other poultry) liver in butter, cool and cut into dice. Blend with two eggs, beaten as for an omelette, a tablespoon of flour, salt, pepper and nutmeg.

Finish as described under SUBRICS.

Rice subrics à la piémontaise. SUBRICS DE RIZ (À LA PIÉMONTAISE)—Blend 2 cups (250 grams) of cheese risotto with two eggs beaten as for an omelette. Add 1-2 tablespoons of lean, chopped ham and mix.

Finish the subrics in the usual manner.

Serve *Tomato sauce* separately (see SAUCE).

Semolina subrics. SUBRICS DE SEMOULE—Proceed as for *Rice subrics*, using semolina cooked in a clear stock or in milk.

Semolina *subrics* can also be made without chopped ham.

Sweetbread subrics. SUBRICS DE RIS DE VEAU, D'AGNEAU —Proceed as described for brain *subrics*, using a *salpicon** of sweetbreads instead.

Talmouse—This can be made in many different ways but it should always have cheese as a basis.

Line fluted tartlet tins with fine *lining paste* (see DOUGH) and fill with whatever cheese preparation is prescribed in the recipe chosen. Brush with egg, sprinkle with Gruyère cheese, cut into dice and bake in a slow oven. Take the talmouse out of the tins and arrange on a napkin.

Talmouses which have *Ramequin dough* (see RAMEKIN) as a basis are often filled, after they are cooked, with a cream cheese mixture.

Talmouses à l'ancienne I—Roll out some left-over puff pastry to a thickness of ⅛ inch. Cut into squares of 2½ inches. Coat with a thin layer of *Cheese soufflé mixture* (see SOUFFLÉ) made with not too much white of egg.

Put very small dice of Gruyère cheese on each talmouse. Lift its four corners so as to enclose the filling. Put these turnovers on a baking sheet.

Bake in a slow oven and serve on a napkin.

Talmouses à l'ancienne II—Roll out fine *lining paste* (see DOUGH). Cut with a round, fluted biscuit-cutter. The pieces should be 3 inches in diameter and ⅛ inch thick.

Make some *Chou paste* (see DOUGH) with cheese and put on each round of dough a portion the size of a walnut.

Brush over with egg, sprinkle with very small dice of Gruyére cheese, moisten the edge of the dough and fold over like a tricorn. Brush with egg a second time. Bake in a slow oven. Arrange on a napkin.

Talmouses à la pâtissière—Line fluted tartlet tins with fine *lining paste* (see DOUGH).

Fill with a cheese *Chou paste* (see DOUGH) piped through a forcing (pastry) bag. Brush over with egg, sprinkle with very small dice of Gruyère cheese and bake in a slow oven.

Take the *talmouses* out of their tins, fill the little *choux* with a cream cheese mixture piped through a forcing bag. Serve on a napkin.

Saint-Denis talmouses. TALMOUSES DE SAINT-DENIS—Recipe from *Cuisinier gascon*, Amsterdam 1747.

'Make ordinary puff pastry; make a preparation of cream cheese and drain well; work it thoroughly with your hands; add as many eggs as the cheese will absorb, a grain of salt, and a pinch of flour; when this is all well mixed, put a layer of the cheese mixture on the rolled-out puff pastry and fold over both layers. Brush over with egg, bake in the oven and serve.'

This kind of talmouse is very similar to a cheese *quiche*.

Spinach talmouses. TALMOUSES AUX ÉPINARDS—Prepare the talmouses as described previously and fill them with a *Spinach soufflé* (see SOUFFLÉ) to which grated cheese has been added.

Finish the talmouses as described in the preceding recipes.

Garnished tartlets and other little hot pastry hors-d'oeuvre

Garnished tartlets. TARTELETTES GARNIES—The preparation of garnished tartlets is the same as for barquettes from which they only differ in their shape. These tartlets can be prepared from all kinds of doughs but are as a rule made from fine *lining paste* (see DOUGH).

Method. Line some round or fluted tartlet moulds as described in the section on BARQUETTES. Bake the tartlets 'blind'.

Take the tartlets out of their baking tins and finish as described in the recipe. Arrange them on a napkin.

In addition to the garnishes given in the recipes which follow, all garnishes given for barquettes and similar dishes can be used for tartlets.

Agnès Sorel tartlets. TARTELETTES AGNÈS SOREL—*Garnish.* Line the bottom of the tartlets with a layer of *Chicken purée**. Surround with a border of very small slices of breast of chicken and pickled or smoked tongue. Put a mushroom head in the middle.

Put in the oven for a short while. After the cooking, spoon some *Allemande sauce* (see SAUCE) on the mushrooms.

Argenteuil tartlets. TARTELETTES ARGENTEUIL—*Garnish. Poultry purée.* Cover at the last minute with asparagus tips cooked in butter.

Béatrix tartlets. TARTELETTES BÉATRIX—*Garnish. Mushroom purée.* Make a border of shrimp tails. At the last minute put on each tartlet a poached oyster. Cover with *Normande sauce* (see SAUCE).

Curried tartlets. TARTELETTES À L'INDIENNE—*Garnish. Prawn ragoût* made with curry. Put on each tartlet a teaspoon of *Rice à l'indienne**.

Tartlets à l'écossaise. TARTELETTES À L'ÉCOSSAISE—*Garnish. Salmon purée* (see PURÉE). Cover with Mornay sauce (see SAUCE). Sprinkle with grated cheese; brown. At the last moment put on each tartlet a piece of sliced truffle.

Tartlets à la japonaise. TARTELETTES À LA JAPONAISE—*Garnish.* Chinese artichokes with cream. Sprinkle with fried breadcrumbs. Put in the oven.

Metternich tartlets. TARTELETTES METTERNICH—*Garnish. Salpicon* of sweetbreads and truffles seasoned with paprika. Put on each tartlet a small slice of calf's brain. Cover with *Hungarian sauce* (see SAUCE).

Tartlets à la mirepoix. TARTELETTES À LA MIREPOIX—*Garnish. Mirepoix** of vegetables cooked in butter with a *salpicon** of ham blended with rich veal gravy, covered with a thin layer of *Chicken forcemeat* (see FORCEMEAT), cooked in the oven.

Printania tartlets. TARTELETTES PRINTANIA—*Garnish.* Morels with cream. Sprinkle with fried breadcrumbs. Put in the oven. When cooked, put on each tartlet a teaspoon of asparagus tips cooked in butter.

Regina tartlets. TARTELETTES REGINA—*Garnish. Salpicon** of mushrooms and truffles with cream. Sprinkle with fried breadcrumbs. Put in the oven. When the cooking is finished put on each tartlet a very small slice of sweetbread sautéed in butter.

Garnished timbales. TIMBALES GARNIES—This name covers a variety of small dishes; though they are similar in shape their ingredients differ a great deal.

Use buttered dariole moulds. Decorate with tiny motifs of truffle, scarlet tongue or lean ham. Alternatively, sprinkle with chopped truffle or chopped tongue. Line evenly with a layer of fine forcemeat of poultry, fish or anything else suitable, $\frac{1}{3}$ inch thick.

Fill the middle with a cold *salpicon** prepared according to the recipe selected, or with any other preparation from a suitable recipe.

Cover the garnish with a layer of the same forcemeat as the one chosen for lining the inside of the mould; cook in the oven standing in a pan of water for 15 to 18 minutes. Leave in the moulds for a few minutes before taking out.

Cylindrical or six-sided dariole moulds can be used.

Garnished timbales are often masked with a sauce in character with the main ingredient; or the sauce is served separately.

These timbales can be served as they are on a dish by themselves or on a napkin. They can also be served on round croûtons of bread fried in butter, or on artichoke hearts.

Apart from the recipes which follow, small timbales can be garnished in the same way as *Barquettes, Croquettes, Croustades,* etc.

Timbales à l'amiral—Decorate the buttered moulds with truffles. Line them with fine *Fish forcemeat* (see FORCEMEAT).

Fill with a *salpicon** of crayfish tails, oysters and truffles blended with a *Velouté sauce* (see SAUCE) based on fish stock and finished with *Crayfish butter* (see BUTTER, *Compound butters*). Cover with the fish forcemeat, poach and serve with *Normande sauce* (see SAUCE).

Bagration timbales. TIMBALES BAGRATION—Sprinkle the buttered moulds with chopped truffles and chopped, pickled or smoked tongue.

Line them with a fine *Chicken forcemeat* (see FORCEMEAT).

Fill with macaroni cut into small dice, blended with cream to which a *salpicon** of truffles and chopped tongue has been added.

Finish in the usual manner.

Serve with *Suprême sauce* (see SAUCE).

Beauvilliers timbales. TIMBALES BEAUVILLIERS—Line buttered moulds with an unsweetened *Brioche dough* (see DOUGH). Bake and leave to cool.

Empty the brioches leaving a crust of $\frac{1}{8}$ inch thickness.

Warm the crusts slightly in the oven. Fill them at the last moment with a *salpicon** of breast of chicken and truffles blended with *Allemande sauce* (see SAUCE).

Put on each timbale a bouquet of asparagus tips cooked in butter.

Serve on a napkin.

Timbales à l'épicurienne—Sprinkle the buttered moulds with breadcrumbs; line them with a layer of rice, cooked in meat stock, to which chopped truffles have been added. This layer should cover the walls of the moulds very evenly and be about $\frac{1}{8}$ inch thick.

Fill with a *salpicon** of lamb sweetbreads, truffles and scarlet tongue blended with a *Mushroom purée.**

Cover the *salpicon* with a layer of the rice cooked in meat stock. Cook these small timbales for 8 minutes in an oven, without putting them in a *bain-marie* (a pan of hot water). Leave them to settle a little before turning out.

Serve with *Tomato sauce* (see SAUCE).

Timbales à la fermière—Butter the moulds and coat with a *Brunoise** of vegetables cooked in butter.

Line with a thin layer of *forcemeat**.

Fill with a *macédoine** of vegetables mixed with a thick *Béchamel sauce* (see SAUCE).

Finish as usual.

Serve with a light *Demi-glace sauce* (see SAUCE).

Timbales à la milanaise—Butter the moulds. Line with macaroni cooked in water, drained and dried.

Lay the macaroni in a spiral shape against the walls of the moulds. Cover them with a thin layer of fine *Chicken* or *Veal forcemeat* (see FORCEMEAT).

Fill with a *salpicon** of pickled or smoked tongue, lean ham, truffles and mushrooms, blended with a rich tomato-flavoured *Demi-glace sauce* (see SAUCE).

Finish as usual. Serve with tomato-flavoured *Demi-glace sauce.*

Timbales à la Montrouge—Decorate the buttered moulds with lean ham and line with fine *Chicken forcemeat* (see FORCEMEAT).

Garnish with a *salpicon** of chicken mixed with a *Mushroom purée**.

Finish in the usual manner. Serve with *Allemande sauce* (see SAUCE).

Timbales à la nantuatienne—Decorate the buttered moulds with crayfish tails and truffles.

Line them with a fine *Fish forcemeat* (see FORCEMEAT) or with *Crayfish butter* (see BUTTER, *Compound butters*).

Fill with *Crayfish purée* to which a *salpicon** of crayfish tails has been added.

Finish in the usual manner. Serve with *Nantua sauce* (see SAUCE).

Timbales à la piémontaise—Decorate the buttered moulds with pickled or smoked tongue and truffles cut into very small dice.

Fill with *Risotto* (see RICE) made with saffron to which a fine *julienne** of white truffles has been added at the last minute.

Finish in the usual manner. Serve with *Tomato sauce* (see SAUCE).

Timbales à la polonaise—Butter the moulds and line the bottom and sides with strips cut from thin unsweetened pancakes (*crêpes*).

Line with a light layer of *Chicken forcemeat with cream* (see FORCEMEAT).

Fill with a purée of brains to which chopped truffles have been added.

Finish in the usual manner. Serve with *Allemande sauce* (see SAUCE).

Timbales à la printanière—Cook some carrots, turnips and French (string) beans. Leave to cool and cut into short narrow strips. Decorate the buttered moulds with these vegetables.

Line with a thin coating of *Quenelle forcemeat* (see FORCEMEAT).

Fill with a *macédoine** of vegetables blended with *Béchamel sauce* (see SAUCE).

Finish in the usual manner. Serve with a light *Demi-glace sauce* (see SAUCE).

Timbales à la Rossini—Decorate the buttered moulds with truffles. Line them with fine *Chicken* or *Veal forcemeat* (see FORCEMEAT).

Fill with a *salpicon** of foie gras and truffles blended with a rich *Demi-glace sauce* (see SAUCE).

Finish in the usual manner. Serve with a *Demi-glace sauce* flavoured with truffle essence.

Timbales à la Saint-Hubert—Decorate the buttered moulds with chopped truffles and chopped, pickled or smoked tongue. Line them with *Game forcemeat* (see FORCEMEAT).

Fill with a *salpicon** of game to which truffles and mushrooms have been added. Blend with a *Demi-glace sauce* (see SAUCE) based on concentrated game stock.

Finish in the usual manner. Serve with a *Demi-glace sauce* based on concentrated game stock.

Valesniskis polonais—Work in a terrine $\frac{1}{4}$ pound (125 grams) of white, pressed cream cheese. Add $\frac{1}{4}$ pound (125 grams) of well-softened butter. Season with salt, pepper and grated nutmeg; add one egg and mix.

Divide this mixture into portions of 1 to $1\frac{1}{2}$ tablespoons (50 to 70 grams). Put each portion on a small, thin, unsweetened pancake (*crêpe*). Fold the pancake over and dip in butter. Deep-fry in very hot fat, drain and sprinkle with fine salt. Arrange on a napkin. Garnish with fried parsley.

Lithuanian varéniki. VARÉNIKI LITHUANIENS—Chop a large onion finely and cook in butter. When the onion has turned a golden colour add $\frac{1}{4}$ pound (125 grams) of raw fillet of beef and $\frac{1}{4}$ pound (125 grams) of raw, finely chopped beef kidney fat. Season with salt, pepper and nutmeg. Brown the meat, then blend with two spoonfuls of thick *Béchamel sauce* (see SAUCE) and add a tablespoon of chopped parsley.

Make a *Noodle paste**. Cut into squares of $2\frac{1}{4}$ inches and put in the middle of each square a portion of the above preparation as for ravioli.

Poach these varéniki in salted boiling water for 15 to 18 minutes. Drain, put in a round pie-dish and sprinkle with melted butter.

Varéniki à la polonaise—Make a *Noodle paste**. Roll out and cut with a round pastry-cutter into pieces 2 inches in diameter.

Fill with cream cheese.

Cover each circlet of paste with another of the same size. Press lightly with a pastry-cutter of a slightly smaller diameter than the first one. (This helps to make the two circlets of pastry stick together.)

Poach these varéniki in salted boiling water for 15 to 18 minutes.

Drain and arrange in a round pie-dish. Sprinkle with melted butter.

HORSE BUTCHERY. HIPPOPHAGIE—The slaughter of horses for human consumption.

Horseflesh, forbidden in Mosaic law, was eaten from time immemorial in Tartary and northern lands. For centuries it has been the principal food of the Gaucho Indians of South America.

For a very long time the Teutons, too, lived on horsemeat. Indeed they continued to do so until their conversion to Christianity.

The people of Paris have always eaten horsemeat, in spite of numerous eighteenth-century police ordinances forbidding its sale in the hope of 'preventing those diseases which the consumption of such meat cannot fail to induce.'

In spite of the fact that horsemeat was in use during the critical revolutionary period, the order prohibiting its sale was re-enacted in 1803, and again in 1811.

There followed special orders permitting the use of horsemeat as animal food, for the animals in the zoo in particular. The interdict was finally revoked about 1830. This followed reports by Parmentier and Parent-Duchatelet, arising out of the publicly expressed views of Baron Larrey, who had used horsemeat extensively to feed his wounded men during the Napoleonic wars.

After the battle of Eylau, being entirely cut off from supplies on the Isle of Lobau, he made soup of it in the breastplates of the dismounted cavalry, and seasoned it with gunpowder in place of salt. More provident than the rest, he had kept a little salt for himself, and was thus able to invite Marshal Massena to share his hot-pot.

At the instigation of Geoffroy-Saint-Hilaire, there followed an ardent propaganda campaign in favour of horsemeat. This was crowned with success when on February 6th, 1865, a horsemeat banquet was held at the Grand Hotel. In the following year, on 9th July, another horsemeat banquet took place, at the establishment of Lemardelay, a Paris horse-butcher.

Since then, horsemeat has become more and more popular, and the number of horse-butchers greatly increased.

A variety of recipes in the BEEF section can be used for horsemeat.

HORSE-CHESTNUT. MARRON D'INDE—A seed fruit, very rich in starch. Once the acid has been extracted from it, the horse-chestnut can be made into flour suitable for human consumption.

HORSE PARSLEY. MACERON—Common name for a herbaceous plant of the umbelliferous group. This herb has a very strong aromatic fragrance similar to that of parsley. It grows wild by the roadside and in ditches, especially in cool and shady places.

The common horse parsley is fairly prolific in the South of France. In former times, the root of this plant was eaten. The tender leaves of the horse parsley are used in cooking as a substitute for parsley.

HORSERADISH. RAIFORT—Plant originating in the East, growing wild and cultivated. Its cylindrical root, brown outside, white inside, has a sharp and piquant flavour and a very penetrating smell. This root is used grated as a condiment.

Horseradish butter. BEURRE DE RAIFORT—See BUTTER, *Compound butters.*

Canapés of horseradish à l'anglaise. CANAPÉS DE RAIFORT À L'ANGLAISE—Spread thin slices of black bread with butter to which English mustard and chopped chives have been added. Cover with grated horseradish and surround with a border of chopped, hard boiled egg yolks.

Grated horseradish. RAIFORT RÂPÉE—Wash and peel a root of horseradish. Grate on a cheese grater. Serve as it is in an hors-d'oeuvre dish as accompaniment to boiled meat or cold meat.

Horseradish sauce or Albert sauce (hot). SAUCE AU RAIFORT DITE ALBERT SAUCE—Cook in 1 cup (2 decilitres) of white consommé 4 teaspoons of grated horseradish. Add 1¼ cups (2½ decilitres) of melted *Butter Sauce II.* See SAUCE.

Cook down. Put through a sieve. Bind with 2 egg yolks. Add a teaspoon of mustard blended with 2 teaspoons of wine vinegar.

Serve with boiled or braised beef.

Horseradish sauce (cold). SAUCE AU RAIFORT—Mix grated horseradish with breadcrumbs soaked in milk and squeezed as dry as possible. Season with salt and sugar. Add thick cream and vinegar.

HOSPICE DE BEAUNE—Name given to a famous wine harvested in the domain of the Hospice.

HOTCH-POTCH. HOCHEPOT—This is a corruption of the name given in France to a fatty broth made from pigs' ears and tails, breast of beef, breast and shoulder of mutton, salt bacon and mixed sliced vegetables, mainly cabbage, carrots, onions, leeks and potatoes. See SOUPS.

There is also a spiced oxtail stew which is called a hotch-potch. The recipe is given under OFFAL OR VARIETY MEATS, *Oxtail en hochepot.*

The French *hochepot* may derive from the verb *hocher*, to shake. Meats of various kinds cooked in a sauce are *shaken* in the pot to prevent them from sticking.

On the other hand, not all dishes cooked in casseroles, pots and braising pans are called hotch-potches, although in each of these cases the pan must be shaken during cooking.

Some authorities on cookery acknowledge this anomaly, and suggest that *hotch-potch* merely implies a certain method of preparation, like *salmi** or *civet** (game stew). It follows, they go on to suggest, that one may properly write on a menu such titles as *Hotch-potch of game* or *of poultry*, which seems to us to be carrying things a little too far.

Hotch Potch (Scottish Cookery)—A Scottish national soup prepared as follows.

Put in a stewing pot 2 pounds (1 kilo) of boned shoulder of mutton tied together and 2 pounds (1 kilo) of rump of beef. Pour enough cold water on the meat to cover it properly. Bring to the boil; remove scum, add salt and simmer for two hours on the side of the stove. Put a celeriac cut into quarters into the pot, add a small cabbage, a large onion with two cloves, the white part of four leeks, tied together into a bundle, 2 turnips, 4 carrots and 1 clove of garlic. Simmer all together for 35 minutes. Add 1 cup (200 grams) of potatoes cut into uniform pieces, ⅓ pound (150 grams) of French (string) beans cut into large dice, 5 tablespoons of fresh white beans, one lettuce cut into quarters, a handful of kidney beans taken out of their pods and a handful of fresh peas. Finish the dish by cooking all these ingredients together on a very small flame.

HUSK. GRUAU—The part of the wheat in which the grain is encased. It is the most nourishing part of the wheat and the richest in gluten. The husk is also the toughest part of the wheat. In the first stage of milling it is very coarsely ground, unless the millstones are tightly pressed one against the other.

At the second grinding, the husks are ground finer to produce wholemeal flour from which wholemeal bread is made.

The outer casings of oats, separated from the grain by a special milling process, are also called husks. (Oat husks cannot be used in the making of bread.) When the husks are removed from barley and the grain is smoothed it becomes pearl barley.

The French word for husk, *gruau*, is also given to a very small *pasta*, made from potatoes, which looks like sago. It is used in a kind of porridge (*bouillies**), soups and sweets (desserts). See SOUPS AND BROTHS.

HYDROMEL—A drink made from honey, much used by the Greeks and Romans. Plain hydromel is simply a solution of honey in water (64 grams per litre). Vinous hydromel (mead) is the result of the alcoholic fermentation of honey diluted with five times its volume of water. It has an alcohol content of 11° to 13°.

Hydromel may be made according to the following recipe:

Heat a hectolitre (approximately 109 quarts) of water to 122°F. in a copper kettle, little by little, add to this water 100 pounds (50 kilos) of honey.

Gradually raise the temperature of the water to boiling point, taking care to skim the liquid constantly.

Pour it into a vat and leave it to cool.

When it is quite cold, transfer it to a barrel where it must be left to ferment for 5 to 6 weeks.

Draw off the hydromel.

Spirits can be distilled from hydromel.

It can also be used in the manufacture of vinegar.

HYDROMETER. ARÉOMÈTRE—Instrument for measuring density. Hydrometers are principally used for the comparison of liquid densities at a constant weight and variable volume. These instruments, on being placed in the liquid under examination, by a simple reading of their graduated stems, show the density for a given temperature. Special tables enable necessary adjustments to be made when operating at a different temperature. There is a great number of these instruments in existence (syrup-gauge, salinometer, acidimeter, alcoholometer, etc.). Only the Gay-Lussac centesimal alcoholometer is legal in France.

HYSSOP. HYSOPE—A small plant with a pungent aromatic smell and a slightly bitter flavour. It is used in the distillation of a number of liqueurs.

IBEX. Bouquetin—A type of wild goat which lives in the high mountains. This game is becoming increasingly rare in Europe.

ICE CREAMS AND ICES. Glaces—Flavoured ices have been made since the very earliest times, and it is generally recognised that the Arabs and the Chinese knew the art of making iced sweets, especially water ices (sherbets).

It was the Chinese, it is said, who taught the art of ice cream making to the Indians, the Persians and the Arabs.

Ice creams and water ices were introduced into France, about the year 1660, by a Sicilian named Francisco Procopio. Some ten years later, he opened a café in Paris, in the Rue des Fossés-Saint-Germain-des Prés (now the Rue de l'Ancienne Comédie). It was here that Procopio (who had changed his name to the more Gallic-sounding Procope) sold variously flavoured ice creams and water ices to the Parisians, who at once acquired a taste for these sweets, which were still a novelty to them.

Other Parisian *limonadiers* quickly followed Procope's example, and soon there were so many of them that, in 1676, it was necessary to give statutory recognition to their corporation and to authorise its members officially to sell ice creams and water ices. It is said that there were in Paris, at that time, two hundred and fifty *limonadiers* who were selling ices.

But, until about the middle of the eighteenth century, ices were only sold in Paris in the summer. In 1750, Procope's successor, a man by the name of Buisson, started making ices all the year round. His competitors at once followed suit.

The ices so much enjoyed at this time were of poor quality. It was not until about 1776 that ices more delicate in flavour began to be made. These ices had more body than those of earlier times and could therefore be moulded into different shapes. It was about this time, too, also in Paris, that *fromages*, as well as a number of frozen desserts, some of which are still made today, were invented.

Although in former times it was the custom to cool drinks with ice or snow, this practice was not introduced into France until the seventeenth century, and even then it was only adopted by persons of great refinement.

In the *Dictionnaire de Monnet*, printed in 1636, the word *glacière* (ice-chest) does not even appear. Nevertheless, some 40 years later the custom of drinking iced wines was so general in France, that any departure from it was much frowned upon, if one may judge from what Boileau, among others, says in his *Repas Ridicule:*

Mais qui l'aurait pensé? Pour comble de disgrâce,
Par le chaud qu'il faisait, nous n'avions point de glace.
Point de glace, bon Dieu! Dans le fort de l'été,
Au mois de juin . . .

'The worst of disasters. But who would have thought it?
'In spite of the heat, we had no ice.
'No ice, good God! At the height of the summer,
'In the month of June . . .'

At the end of the eighteenth century, the manufacture of ices developed considerably, especially in Paris. The number of establishments which sold ices never ceased to grow in number. This was the age which saw the triumph of the ice-bombes. It was soon the invariable custom to serve a *bombe glacé* at the end of any formal meal, and the savouring of ices at the cafés of the Palais-Royal had by this time become very fashionable.

The same was true of the first Empire. At this period, thanks to the Italian ice cream manufacturers, of whom there were many in Paris at this time, ice cream and water ices of various kinds improved still further in quality. It was at this time, too, that ices began to be made from a basic mixture of egg yolks and syrup, which led to the creation of more elaborate sweets. These soon began to take the place of cylindrical ice cream blocks at formal dinners.

Pratti and Tortoni became famous all over the world for the exquisite delicacy of their ices.

It was under the Second Empire that someone invented the 'Surprise omelette', sometimes called *Omelette à la Norvégienne*. This remarkable sweet, with a centre of cold fruit, ice cream and a hot crust of meringue browned in the oven, was cleverly devised to produce a gastronomic paradox, a ball of ice in a piping hot casing. (See EGGS, *Omelette à la Norvégienne*.) Under the Second Empire, too, *coupes*, *mousses*, and *parfaits* were first made.

In our own time, the manufacture of ices, especially those with a base of whipped cream, has reached the highest point of perfection. There has also been great progress in the perfecting of the various appliances used in the preparation of iced sweets (desserts).

Iced sweets are made for the most part from a basic mixture of egg yolks and syrup (bombe mousse base), now sold ready-made in food shops. In France great industrial concerns, such as the Société Gervais, brought ice creams within the reach of everybody at a comparatively low cost.

General method for the preparation of ices:

Using a freezer. Having prepared the appropriate mixture (for syrup ice or cream ice), pour it into a metal freezer, already lodged in a bucket containing alternate layers of chipped ice, salt and saltpetre, allowing for 40 pounds (20 kilos) of ice, 6 pounds (3 kilos) of salt and 1 pound (500 grams) of saltpetre. This mixture should be well pressed down in the bucket. Replace the lid and start to churn, and continue until freezing is accomplished.

If a hand-manipulated freezer is used (though these are rare nowadays), close it tightly. Turn it up first one way and then the other by the handle attached to the lid. This operation throws some of the mixture against the sides of the freezer so that it solidifies by being forced up against the ice and chemicals in the bucket. It is therefore necessary from time to time to scrape the sides of the freezer with a special spatula and mix the frozen ice cream with the rest. During the freezing process, stir the mixture thoroughly from time to time with the spatula so that it remains smooth and creamy.

Using a refrigerator. For home use ice cream mixtures can be frozen quickly and easily in a household refrigerator or deep freeze. A refrigerator does not produce the perfect texture that an ice cream freezer can produce, but if the mixture is frozen quickly satisfactory results can be obtained.

Presentation of ices—Ice cream and water ice mixtures processed in a freezer can be presented in different ways. They can be shaped with a ball-scoop, served in shells or in special glasses, or—still shaped with a ball-scoop—formed into a pyramid on a dish covered with a folded napkin or paper doyley.

Ice cream and water ices can also be transferred, after freezing, to special moulds. These moulds, which are usually conical in shape, are hermetically sealed and placed, with their contents, in a bucket where they are packed round with chopped ice and salt.

To ensure that the ices are quite firm when they are turned out of the moulds, they should be left in the ice-bucket for at least an hour.

Turning-out of ices—To turn out ices (syrup ice, cream ice or water ices) which have been left to harden into different shapes, proceed thus: run cold water in a rapid stream over the mould. Dip the mould for a second into warm water. This will warm the mould slightly and detach the ice cream from the sides. Now, tip the mould upside down on to a dish covered with a folded table napkin and lift it up carefully, leaving the ice cream in the centre of the dish.

Fancy ices in small moulds—These ices are prepared in the same way as those shaped in large moulds.

These little fancy moulds (which are hinged and made of tin) are available in a variety of shapes, such as fruit, vegetables, human and animal figures, etc.

When these moulds are filled, their edges are sealed with butter. They are then pressed down into a bucket of crushed ice and salt, like other types of ice cream moulds.

ICE CREAM AND WATER ICE MIXTURES—These mixtures are of three kinds: those with a syrup base, which are used in the preparation of water ices flavoured with fruit juices, essences of liqueurs; those with a custard base, made from a mixture of egg yolks, sugar and milk; and, thirdly, those with a mousse base.

Mixture for fruit ices. GLACE AUX FRUITS—Rub the fruit (peeled in advance if necessary) through a fine sieve. Add to the purée thus obtained an equal quantity of cold *sugar-syrup* (4 cups water, 2 cups sugar boiled 5 minutes and cooled); add lemon juice, more or less according to the nature of the fruit purée. Mix all these ingredients on ice, testing where possible the sugar content of the mixture with a saccharometer. Fruit ices are made from a mixture registering a standard density of 18° to 22°.

Note. Fruit ices may also be prepared thus:

Pound the fruit to be used, in a mortar, with 1⅓ cups (300 grams) of sugar to every pound (500 grams) of fruit.

Rub through a fine sieve. Add to this mixture as much water as is required to bring it to the right density. (This must be tested with a saccharometer.)

Mixture for ices flavoured with liqueurs and essences. GLACES AUX LIQUEURS, AUX ESSENCES—This mixture is made by adding to cold *sugar-syrup* (see SYRUP) a larger or smaller quantity of the liqueur or essence desired. Usually, ⅓ to ½ cups (1 decilitre) of liqueur is required for every quart (litre) of syrup. A little lemon juice is always added to this mixture.

These are the basic ingredients of ices flavoured with Anisette, Armagnac, Crème de cacao, Curaçao, Cherry brandy, Kirsch, Rum, Maraschino, or any other liqueur.

As in the case of fruit ices, this mixture whenever possible must be tested with a saccharometer, which should register between 18° and 22°.

Ice cream mixture (custard). GLACE À LA CRÈME—Place in a saucepan 1⅓ cups (300 grams) of fine sugar and 10 egg yolks. Work this mixture with a spatula until it reaches ribbon consistency, that is to say, when it drops off the spatula like a ribbon.

Blend into this mixture little by little a quart (litre) of boiling milk (flavoured with vanilla or some other flavouring).

Cook this cream on the stove, stirring it until it sticks to the spoon. It must not, however, be allowed to come to the boil or the mixture will curdle.

Rub the cream into a bowl through a fine conical sieve. Stir it from time to time until it is quite cold.

Note. The mixture most commonly used is made of 1¾ cups (400 grams) of sugar and 8 egg yolks to 1 quart (litre) of milk. This is a very good recipe. It produces a firm, creamy ice, not too sweet, to which may safely be added a liquid flavouring (brandy, rum, kirsch, chartreuse or any other) without risk of spoiling its consistency. By using less milk and making up the liquid content with fresh cream, an ice cream of smoother texture can be obtained.

A drier and firmer ice can be made by using less sugar and fewer egg yolks. If, however, too little sugar or too few eggs are used, the result will be a disappointingly tasteless mixture.

In no circumstances should less than 1⅓ cups (300 grams) of sugar and 6 yolks of egg be used. Even these quantities will not yield an ice of good quality.

Mousse (bombe) mixture. PÂTE À BOMBE—For 32 egg yolks, 1 quart (litre) of syrup (in the proportions of 2 cups sugar and 1½ cups water boiled to 220°F., or until the syrup spins a fine thread from a spoon).

Place the syrup and the yolks of egg in a double saucepan (double boiler). Put the double saucepan on the stove, over a high flame. From time to time stir the mixture with a whisk. When the mixture reaches the consistency of thick cream, rub it through a fine sieve into a bowl. Next, whisk the mixture until it is quite cold. It should now be light, frothy and whitish in colour. It is then ready for an addition of an equal quantity of whipped cream. Extracts, liqueurs, purées of fruit are also added at this point.

This mixture can be kept in a stone jar or in a porcelain freezer and should be left in a bucket of ice without salt.

Recipes are given for a number of different ices, in the following order:

Plain fruit ices with a syrup base; Plain ice creams; Fancy ices (including *bombes, iced coupes, melbas, mousses, Neapolitan ice cream, parfaits*); **Water ices** (*granités, gramolates*—for recipes for water ices see separate section on SHERBETS); **Iced desserts** (*sweets*).

PLAIN FRUIT ICES WITH A SYRUP BASE. GLACES SIMPLES, AUX FRUITS, AU SIROP—

Apricot ice. GLACE À L'ABRICOT—Equal quantities of fresh apricot pulp or purée and syrup. The juice of 2 lemons is added to every quart (litre) of this mixture. (Density: 18° to 19°—see SUGAR.)

Banana ice. GLACE À LA BANANE—Proceed as for pineapple ice, using syrup and banana purée. Add lemon juice. Flavour with kirsch or rum. (Density: 20° to 21°—see SUGAR.)

Cherry ice. GLACE AUX CERISES—Soak 2 cups (½ litre) of crushed stoned cherries for 1 hour in 2 cups (5 decilitres) of syrup. Soak pounded kernels with the cherries. Add a few drops of lemon juice and a little kirsch. Rub through a fine sieve. (Density: 20° to 21°—see SUGAR.)

Lemon ice. GLACE AU CITRON—Soak the rind of 3 lemons for 2 hours in 2 cups (½ litre) of cold syrup. Add the juice of 4 lemons (and, if desired, the juice of 2 oranges). Strain. (Density: 21° to 22°—see SUGAR.)

Melon ice. GLACE AU MELON—Proceed as for *Apricot ice*, using melon pulp rubbed through a fine sieve. Add a little brandy to the mixture.

Orange ice. GLACE À L'ORANGE—Proceed as for *Tangerine ice* with the peel and juice of 4 to 5 oranges and the juice of 1 lemon. (Density: 20° to 21°—see SUGAR.)

Peach ice. GLACE À LA PÊCHE—Proceed as for *Apricot ice*, using peach pulp. (Density: 18° to 19°—see SUGAR.)

Pear ice. GLACE À LA POIRE—Pound in a mortar 2 cups (500 grams) of fine sugar with 2 cups (500 grams) of peeled and cored pears stewed until very soft. Add the juice of a lemon. Rub through a sieve. Add enough filtered water (approximately 2 cups) to bring the sugar density to 21° to 22° (see SUGAR).

Pineapple ice. GLACE À L'ANANAS—Soak 2 cups (½ litre) of finely pounded pineapple (fresh or tinned) for 2 hours in 2 cups (½ litre) of syrup. Add a little lemon juice and kirsch. (Density: 18° to 20°—see SUGAR.)

Plum ice. GLACE AUX PRUNES—Proceed as for *Apricot ice*, using purée of plums.

Raspberry ice. GLACE À LA FRAMBOISE—Proceed as for *Strawberry ice*, using crushed raspberries.

Redcurrant ice. GLACE À LA GROSEILLE—Add 2 cups (½ litre) of redcurrant juice to 2 cups (½ litre) of syrup. Add only a few drops of lemon juice, as the fruit is acid enough. (Density: 19° to 20°—see SUGAR.)

Strawberry ice. GLACE AUX FRAISES—Add 2 cups (½ litre) of crushed strawberries (fresh or preserved) to 2 cups (½ litre) of cold syrup. Add further the juice of 2 lemons and of 2 oranges. Put through a sieve. (Density: 16° to 18°—see SUGAR.)

This ice may also be prepared as follows: pound together 2 quarts (1 kilo) of strawberries and 2 cups (500 grams) of fine sugar. Add the juice of 2 lemons and of 2 oranges. Rub through a sieve.

Add to this mixture enough filtered water (2 cups) to bring the mixture to a density of 16° to 18° (see SUGAR).

Tangerine ice. GLACE À LA MANDARINE—Infuse the peel of 4 tangerines in 3 cups (7½ decilitres) of boiling syrup. When the mixture is cold, add the juice of 6 tangerines, 2 oranges and 1 lemon. Strain. (Density: 20° to 21°—see SUGAR.)

PLAIN ICE CREAMS. GLACES SIMPLES À LA CRÈME:

Almond ice cream. GLACES AUX AMANDES—Add to a quart (litre) of boiled milk ⅞ cup (100 grams) of fresh almonds and 5 bitter almonds, blanched and pounded fine with a few tablespoons of water. Infuse for 25 minutes.

Use this milk to prepare custard cream as described in the recipe for *Ice cream mixture*. Freeze the ice cream in the usual way.

Chocolate ice cream. GLACE AU CHOCOLAT—Add to a quart (litre) of boiled milk flavoured with vanilla, 1⅞ cups (250 grams) of grated chocolate, dissolved in 1 cup (2 decilitres) of water.

The chocolate being sweet in itself, only 1 cup (250 grams) of sugar should be used instead of the 1⅓ cups (300 grams) indicated in the instructions for *Ice cream mixture*.

Coffee ice cream. GLACE AU CAFÉ—Infuse 1½ cups (50 grams) of freshly roasted and ground coffee in a quart (litre) of hot, boiled milk for 25 minutes. Use this milk to prepare the cream according to the instructions for *Ice cream mixture*.

This ice cream can also be prepared by adding to the milk 1 cup (2 decilitres) of very strong liquid coffee.

Hazelnut ice cream. GLACE AUX AVELINES—Proceed as for *Almond ice cream*, substituting for the almonds ⅞ cup (100 grams) of hazelnuts, slightly roasted, and pounded.

Pistachio-nut ice cream. GLACE À LA PISTACHE—Pound together ⅝ cup (75 grams) of blanched pistachio nuts and 2½ tablespoons (25 grams) of blanched fresh almonds. While pounding, add a few tablespoons of milk.

Put this paste to infuse in a quart (litre) of boiling milk. Use this milk to prepare the cream according to the instructions for *Ice cream mixture*.

Plombières ice cream. GLACE PLOMBIÈRES—*The mixture*. Pound thoroughly in a mortar a scant 2 cups (300 grams) of blanched fresh almonds and 2 tablespoons (20 grams) of blanched bitter almonds. Mix with milk. Add 1½ quarts (litres) of scalded cream.

Strain this mixture, pressing it down in the strainer to extract all the milk.

Stir 10 yolks of eggs thoroughly with 1⅓ cups (300 grams) of sugar in a saucepan. Add the milk to this mixture.

Heat this cream of egg, milk and sugar on the stove without bringing it to the boil as for *Custard cream** (see CREAMS). Remove it from the stove and stir it vigorously for 3 minutes. Rub it through a sieve. Freeze this mixture in a freezer, stirring it from time to time with a spatula. When the mixture is partly frozen, add 1 pint (6 decilitres) of whipped cream. Continue the freezing process.

Drain off any water in the bucket and immerse the freezer once more. Cover it completely with ice and salt and leave it for 2 hours.

Scoop out the ice cream with a ball-scoop and arrange the balls in a pyramid on a dish covered with a folded napkin. Pour apricot jam over the ice cream.

Chestnut Plombières ice cream. GLACE PLOMBIÈRES AUX MARRONS—Mix with a quart of hot *Custard cream* (see CREAMS) 1 cup (250 grams) of chestnut purée (made from skinned chestnuts cooked in milk). Rub this mixture through a fine sieve. Freeze. When it is firm and smooth, mix in 1 pint (½ litre) of whipped cream, and flavour it with 5 tablespoons of maraschino.

Put this mixture in a cylindrical ice cream mould. leave it in the ice-bucket for an hour and a half.

Praline ice cream. GLACE AU PRALINÉ—Add to a quart (litre) of vanilla custard cream, prepared as described in the recipe for *Ice cream mixture*, ¼ pound (125 grams) of *praline** of burnt almonds, pounded, rubbed through a sieve or put through a grinder.

The same method is used for burnt hazelnuts, walnuts, pistachio ground nuts or peanuts.

Tea ice cream. GLACE AU THÉ—Prepare the cream in the usual way with a mixture of 1 quart (7½ decilitres) of milk and 1½ cups (3 decilitres) of very strong, strained tea.

The same method is used for the preparation of ice creams flavoured with peppermint, lime-flower or verbena infusions.

Vanilla ice cream. GLACE À LA VANILLE—Proceed as for *Ice cream mixture*, using milk in which a vanilla pod has been infused for 20 minutes or to which 1 tablespoon of vanilla extract has been added.

Walnut ice cream. GLACE AUX NOIX—Proceed as for *Almond ice cream*, using ⅝ cup (100 grams) of pounded walnuts.

Ice cream without eggs (American recipe). GLACE SANS OEUFS—Boil together 1 quart (litre) of milk, 1 quart (litre) of cream and 1 cup (250 grams) of sugar.

Bind with 4 tablespoons (45 grams) of corn starch. Rub through a hair sieve. Let it cool, stirring often.

Flavour with vanilla, lemon or orange zest, coffee, chocolate, liqueurs, etc. Freeze in the usual way.

FANCY ICES:

BOMBE ICES. BOMBES GLACÉES—In former times, *bombes* were made of water ice or ice cream mixtures and were shaped in spherical moulds. This is how they got their name. To make them more interesting in appearance, the ice was arranged in concentric layers in the mould. Nowadays, *bombe* ices are much more delicate in flavour, being made from the *mousse* (*bombe*) *mixture* described under the section on ICE CREAM AND WATER ICE MIXTURES.

Moulds for bombe ice creams—A *bombe* should be made of two different ice cream mixtures, one to line the mould (this is usually a plain ice cream or a fruit or water ice), the other, which fills the casing, is made from a *mousse* (*bombe*) *mixture*. *Bombes* are made in conical moulds, slightly rounded at the top. The moulds have tight-fitting lids and are hermetically sealed with butter. They should be left to stand in ice and salt for 2 hours.

Bombe Aida—Line the mould with tangerine ice. Fill with *mousse* (*bombe*) *mixture* (see above) flavoured with vanilla and kirsch.

Bombe l'algérienne—Line the *bombe* mould with tangerine ice. Fill with pineapple ice, to which pieces of crystallized pineapple steeped in kirsch have been added.

Bombe Alhambra—Line the mould with vanilla ice cream. Fill with strawberry-flavoured *mousse* (*bombe*) *mixture* (see above). After turning out, surround the *bombe* with large strawberries steeped in kirsch.

Bombe American. BOMBE AMÉRICAINE—Line the mould with strawberry ice cream. Fill with *mousse* (*bombe*) *mixture* (see above) flavoured with tangerine. Decorate the *bombe* with pistachio ice cream put through a forcing (pastry) bag. See *Tangerine ice* for preparing the syrup for the mixture.

Apricot bombe—See APRICOT.

Bombe Bourdaloue—Line the mould with vanilla ice cream. Fill with *mousse* (*bombe*) *mixture* (see above) flavoured with *praline*.

Bombe Bourdaloue—Line the mould with vanilla ice cream. Fill with *mousse* (*bombe*) *mixture* (see above) flavoured with anise. Decorate the *bombe* with crystallized violets.

Bombe cardinal—Line the mould with ice cream flavoured with strawberry and raspberry. Fill with vanilla *mousse* (*bombe*) *mixture* (see above) flavoured with *praline*.

Bombe Chateaubriand—Line the mould with apricot ice. Fill with *mousse* (*bombe*) *mixture* (see above) flavoured with vanilla, mixed with crystallized (candied) apricots, diced and steeped in kirsch.

Bombe dame-blanche—Line the mould with vanilla ice cream. Fill with *mousse* (*bombe*) *mixture* (see above) flavoured with almond milk.

Bombe dauphinoise—Line the mould with pineapple ice. Fill with whipped cream flavoured with green chartreuse.

Bombe diplomate—Line the mould with vanilla ice cream. Fill with *mousse* (*bombe*) *mixture* (see above) flavoured with maraschino, mixed with crystallized fruit steeped in liqueurs.

Bombe Doria—Line the mould with pistachio ice cream. Fill with *mousse* (*bombe*) *mixture* (see above) flavoured with vanilla, mixed with pieces of *marrons glacés* (see CHESTNUT) steeped in curaçao.

Bombe duchesse—Line the mould with pineapple ice. Fill with *mousse* (*bombe*) *mixture* (see above) flavoured with pears and kirsch.

Bombe Francillon—Line the mould with coffee ice cream. Fill with *mousse* (*bombe*) *mixture* (see above) flavoured with fine champagne brandy.

Bombe Gismonde—Line the mould with *praline ice cream.* Fill with *mousse* (*bombe*) *mixture* (see above) flavoured with aniseed, and a *praline* made with filberts. See PRALINE.

Bombe Grimaldi—Line the mould with vanilla ice cream. Fill with *mousse* (*bombe*) *mixture* (see above) flavoured with kummel. Decorate the *bombe* with crystallized (candied) violets and halved pistachio nuts.

Bombe Héricart—Line a large, shallow mould with strawberry ice cream. Fill with *mousse* (*bombe*) *mixture* (see above) flavoured with champagne brandy, with whole strawberries from strawberry jam dotted about here and there.

Bombe impératrice—Line the mould with redcurrant ice. Fill with *Rice à l'impératrice** mixed with diced crystallized (candied) fruit steeped in liqueur.

Bombe Médicis—Line the mould with pear ice cream. Fill with *mousse* (*bombe*) *mixture* (see above) flavoured with peach, and pieces of peach steeped in kirsch.

Bombe Monselet—Line the mould with tangerine ice. Fill with *mousse* (*bombe*) *mixture* (see above) flavoured with port and mixed with candied orange peel cut into little pieces and steeped in champagne brandy.

Bombe Montmorency—Line the mould with kirsch ice. Fill with *mousse* (*bombe*) *mixture* (see above) flavoured with cherry brandy, mixed with cherries steeped in kirsch.

Nelusko ice cream—A *mousse* (*bombe*) *mixture* (see above), enclosed in a layer of ice cream flavoured with *praline**.

Bombe Nesselrode—Line the mould with vanilla ice cream. Fill with *mousse* (*bombe*) *mixture* (see above) to which a purée of *marrons glacés* (see CHESTNUT) flavoured with kirsch has been added.

Bombe succès—Line the mould with apricot ice. Fill with *Chantilly cream* (see CREAMS) flavoured with kirsch, mixed with diced apricots.

Bombe tutti-frutti—Line the mould with strawberry ice. Fill with *mousse* (*bombe*) *mixture* (see above) flavoured with vanilla, and with a *salpicon** of crystallized fruit steeped in liqueur.

Bombe Véronique—Line the mould with pistachio ice cream. Fill with chocolate-flavoured *mousse* (*bombe*) *mixture* (see above) mixed with diced candied orange peel steeped in champagne brandy.

ICED COUPES OR SUNDAES. COUPES GLACÉES—These are a delicious composite sweet with ice cream as their main ingredient. They are served in glass or silver ice-cups, and for this reason they are known as *coupes* in France.

The glasses are usually filled with one or more kinds of ice cream and decorated on top with fresh or crystallized fruit, or with *Chantilly cream* (see CREAMS).

Preparation of coupes

Sundaes may be presented in a great many different ways. The *coupe Jacques* may be regarded as the classic sundae, the model for all others. See also SUNDAES.

Apricot coupe. COUPE GLACÉE AUX ABRICOTS—Put two tablespoons of fresh (or canned) sliced apricots, steeped in kirsch, into a champagne glass or ice-cup.

Top with a layer of apricot ice cream. Smooth down the surface. Decorate with half an apricot, steeped in kirsch, and fresh, halved, blanched almonds. Sprinkle with a few drops of kirsch.

Cherry coupe. COUPE GLACÉE AUX CERISES—Put two substantial tablespoons of stoned cherries which have been steeped in cherry brandy and sugar in the bottom of the ice-cups or champagne glasses. Cover with cherry ice.

Decorate the ices with fine cherries and fresh halved almonds.

Coupe Crapotte. COUPE GLACÉE CRAPOTTE—Fill champagne glasses or ice-cups three quarters full with a smooth layer of peach ice cream. Arrange on top a mixture of equal quantities of alpine strawberries and raspberries, previously steeped in kummel and chilled.

Cover the fruit with a layer of whipped cream piped through a forcing (pastry) bag with a fluted nozzle.

Decorate the top with fresh blanched almonds and crystallized violets. Arrange the glasses on a tray covered with a paper doyley.

Coupe Jacques—Fill champagne glasses or ice-cups with equal quantities of lemon ice and strawberry ice, with a space between. Put in the middle of the glass a heaped tablespoon of fresh fruit steeped in kirsch. Decorate with crystallized cherries and halved fresh almonds. Sprinkle on top a few drops of kirsch.

Peach coupe. COUPES GLACÉES AUX PÊCHES—Put a good tablespoon of a *salpicon** of raw peaches, steeped in some liqueur in the bottom of champagne glasses or ice-cups. Cover with peach ice cream or water ice or ice cream flavoured with some other flavouring. Smooth down the surface of the ice cream. In the middle of the goblet put a ripe peach, peeled and chilled on ice. Sprinkle with kirsch or any other liqueur.

ICED MELBAS:

Peach Melba. PÊCHES MELBA—This sweet, first made in London by Escoffier, is known the world over. It is made by lining a silver dish with a fairly thick layer of the very best vanilla ice cream, and placing on top peeled peaches which have been steeped in a syrup flavoured with vanilla, and left until they are quite cold. The peaches are then covered with *Raspberry purée**.

Many other kinds of fruit may be served in the same way. For instance, large fresh strawberries steeped in sugar or kirsch; pears (halved or quartered) stewed in vanilla-flavoured syrup, and chilled; nectarines (peeled, stewed in syrup and chilled), etc.

Pear Melba. POIRES MELBA—Poach the pears in vanilla-flavoured syrup. Drain and dry them. Arrange in a glass dish or a timbale on a foundation of vanilla ice cream and cover with *Raspberry purée**.

NEAPOLITAN ICE CREAM OR ICE GÂTEAU. BISCUITS GLACÉS— These ices are made of ice cream mixture shaped in special moulds. Layers of ice cream are alternated with layers of water ices of different colours and flavours in the moulds.

These moulds, which are made in the form of rectangular boxes, are left to freeze in ice and salt in the usual way, or placed in a deep freeze.

When the block of ice cream is taken out of the mould, it is cut into neat slabs. These slabs are presented in special waxed paper cases, and served either unadorned or decorated with plain ice cream piped through a forcing bag, according to the type of ice cream used.

Neapolitan ice cream, 'Comtesse-Marie'. BISCUIT COMTESSE-MARIE—This is made in a special square mould (called a *Comtesse-Marie* mould). The mould is entirely lined with strawberry ice cream and this ice cream casing is filled with sweet vanilla-flavoured whipped cream.

Turn the ice out of the mould into a special waxed paper case. Decorate with large strawberries steeped in kirsch, and with sweet whipped cream.

ICED PARFAIT. PARFAIT GLACÉ—In former times the term *parfait* was used exclusively for an iced sweet flavoured with coffee.

Nowadays, *parfaits* are made from all kinds of ices. They differ from *bombes* only in that they are not encased in a coating of plain ice cream.

Ingredients and method. Mix 32 egg yolks in a quart (litre) of syrup (4 cups sugar, 2 cups water boiled to 220°F. or 28° density, strained and cooled).

Cook this mixture over a low flame like a custard. Strain it through a fine sieve, and whisk it on ice until it is quite cold.

Flavour it with ½ cup (1 decilitre) of rum or brandy and blend in a quart (litre) of cream, stiffly beaten.

Put the mixture in a *parfait* mould. Leave it in ice and salt for 2 to 3 hours, or place in a deep freeze.

This mixture can be flavoured with coffee, chocolate, *praline**, vanilla and many other flavourings.

SUNDAES—See *Iced coupes.*

WATER ICES—See *Sherbets.*

Gramolates—A kind of *granité* (see below) served between main courses, like sherbets. They are also served as refreshments in the course of an evening's entertainment.

Granités—These ices, which are presented in special glasses, are served, like sherbets, between main courses at dinners.

They are made from fruit syrups, with a density of not more than 14° by the syrup glucometer.

They are frozen in an ice cream freezer or may be put in a deep freeze. Unlike other types of ice, they are not stirred during freezing. As their name suggests, *granités* should have a somewhat granular texture.

SPOOMS—This sort of ice is merely a *sherbet** with a sugar density of 20°. When it is frozen, Italian *meringue** is added to the mixture. Half the volume of syrup required for sherbet is used in this case.

Spooms are made from fruit juices or wines, such as champagne, muscatel, Frontignan, sherry, port, etc.

They are served in glasses, like sherbets.

ICED DESSERTS OR SWEETS. ENTREMETS GLACÉS—Sweets or desserts of this kind may either be served in addition to ice cream or they may include ice cream in their composition. The first of these two kinds of iced sweet is not frozen but merely set on ice so that it may be served very cold. Among these sweets are *Bavarian creams**, *Charlottes Russes**, fruit salads flavoured with liqueurs, various jellies including fruit moulds, puddings, *Rice à l'impératrice**, stewed *Suédoise of fruit**.

Recipes for these sweets are given in other parts of the book in alphabetical order. Other iced sweets are made from fruit served with an ice cream of one kind or another. Pineapples, tangerines, oranges, melons and other fruit may be served in this way.

Iced apples à la normande. POMMES GLACEÉS À LA NORMANDE—Scoop out some large, sound cooking apples without damaging the skins. Immerse the hollowed out apples for a few minutes in boiling syrup, so that they are slightly cooked.

From the pulp, make either a plain ice cream or a *mousse* (*bombe*) *mixture* (see above). Flavour this with calvados.

If the apples are filled with mousse mixture, chill them in plenty of ice and salt for about 2 hours.

If they are filled with plain ice cream, freeze the mixture first and fill the skins just before serving.

Iced pears belle angevine. POIRES BELLE ANGEVINE—Cut each pear at the stalk end, core it, scoop out some of the flesh without damaging the skin and pour boiling syrup over the fruit.

At the last moment, fill the pear with kirsch-flavoured *Iced pear mousse* (see below) or with ordinary pear ice made out of the scooped out flesh.

Arrange the pear on a napkin-covered dish on a block of ice, or on a foundation of nougat.

Iced cherry mousse. MOUSSE GLACÉE AUX CERISES—Add an equal volume of cherry purée to a syrup of 230°F. Incorporate firm *Chantilly cream* (see CREAMS) to twice the combined quantity of cherry and syrup.

Fill the ice moulds with this preparation and freeze in the usual manner.

Iced grapefruit (filled). PAMPLEMOUSSE GLACÉ—This sweet can be prepared in the same way as iced tangerines and oranges, by filling the skins with a plain ice or *mousse* (*bombe*) *mixture* (see above) made from the pulp.

Iced Marquises. MARQUISES GLACÉES—*Marquises* are made from a mixture similar to that used in the preparation of *granités* but are frozen to a somewhat stiffer consistency.

The mixture is flavoured with kirsch and should register 17° on the syrup glucometer.

At the last moment, mix in for every quart (litre) of the syrup, 2 cups (4 decilitres) of very stiffly beaten *Chantilly cream* (see CREAMS) mixed with a purée of strawberries or some other fruit.

Marquises are served in little glass goblets.

Iced melon (filled). MELON GLACÉ—Slice off the top of a large cantaloupe melon, near the stem. Remove all liquid and seeds.

Using a large spoon, scoop out all the pulp, being careful not to damage the rind. Using this pulp, make a water ice or ice cream flavoured with kirsch.

Just before serving, fill the melon with this ice. Serve the melon on a napkin, or in a large glass dish, surrounded with crushed ice.

Iced melon filled à la Chantilly. MELON GLACÉ À LA CHANTILLY—Prepare the melon as indicated above. Cook the pulp with sugar and rub it through a fine sieve. When it is quite cold, mix it with stiffly beaten *Chantilly cream* (see CREAMS) flavoured with kirsch. Sprinkle the inside of the melon rind with sugar and kirsch and leave to stand. Now fill the rind with the mixture.

Stand the melon in an ice-bucket for 2 hours.

Melon frappé—Two melons must be used in the preparation of this sweet. Using the pulp of one of them, make a *granité** flavoured with kirsch.

Slice off the top of the second melon near the stem. Remove all liquid and seeds. Using a spoon, scoop out all the pulp, being careful not to damage the rind. Steep the pulp on ice in Frontignan, port, sherry, kirsch, maraschino, curaçao, etc.

Before serving, put the shell of the melon in an ice-bucket until it is very cold. At the last moment, fill the shell with alternate layers of the *granité* and the iced flesh of the second melon.

Put the top back on the melon. Serve on a napkin or in a glass dish, surrounded with crushed ice. Or serve in the centre of a hollowed-out block of ice.

Iced mousses or mousselines. MOUSSES, MOUSSELINES GLACÉES—Iced mousse or mousseline may be made in two different ways, using either syrup or custard cream.

Ingredients for the syrup. This is prepared by adding to thick syrup (4 cups sugar, 2 cups water boiled to 220°F. and cooled) an equal quantity of fresh fruit pulp. To this mixture is added an equal quantity of very stiff *Chantilly cream* (see CREAMS).

Ingredients for the cream. Make a custard using 2 cups (500 grams) of sugar, 16 yolks of egg, and 1 pint ($\frac{1}{2}$ litre) of milk. Leave to cool. Add to this custard 1 pint ($\frac{1}{2}$ litre) of fresh cream, $\frac{3}{4}$ ounce (20 grams) of powdered gum tragacanth and the required flavouring (vanilla, orange or lemon rind, various liqueurs, etc.). If the mousse is made with fruit, add to the cream mixture a pint ($\frac{1}{2}$ litre) of fresh fruit pulp.

Beat the mixture on ice until it is very frothy. Put the mixture into moulds lined with white paper. Seal them hermetically and leave to stand in ice and salt for 2 to 3 hours according to the size of the tubs.

Peaches cardinal. PÊCHES CARDINAL—Stew the peaches in a syrup flavoured with vanilla. Leave until quite cold. Drain them. Put them in a silver dish on a fairly thick layer of strawberry ice cream. Cover them with iced red-currant jelly, flavoured with kirsch, and scatter some little wild strawberries on top.

Iced pears, filled. POIRES DUCHESSE GLACEÉS—Scoop out, without damaging the skins, some large, sound, well-shaped pears. Using the pulp, prepare a *mousse* (*bombe*) *mixture* (see above). Immerse the hollowed-out pears for 5 minutes in boiling syrup. Drain them and leave to cool. Fill them with the mousse mixture. Put them to chill in an ice-bucket with plenty of ice and salt for 2 hours.

Iced pineapple. ANANAS GLACÉ—Choose a large pineapple, regular in shape, with the plume of its tufted top left on.

Remove the tufted top by a clean cut about ¾ inch below the crown. Keep it to use as a lid.

Carefully remove all the flesh, leaving on the walls and on the bottom of the unbroken rind a thickness of pulp of about ½ inch. Dust the pineapple shell inside with two tablespoons of sugar, sprinkle with two tablespoons of kirsch and leave to saturate in a cold place for about 2 hours.

Just before serving, fill the unbroken pineapple rind with pineapple ice cream prepared from the pulp removed earlier, with shredded pineapple steeped in kirsch added to it.

Iced pineapple

Put the pineapple on a napkin or a block of ice, slightly hollowed out in the middle, and replace the tufted crown on top.

Iced pineapple à la bourbonnaise. ANANAS GLACÉ À LA BOURBONNAISE—Slice off the top of a large fresh pineapple. Keep this part with its leaves intact to cover the pineapple later.

Very carefully, so as not to break the skin, scoop out all the flesh of the pineapple. Core it, and cut the remainder into little cubes. Sprinkle with rum and sugar and stand it on ice.

At the same time, make a rum ice cream.

Before serving, sprinkle the inside of the scooped out shell with rum and sugar and embed it in an ice-bucket to chill. At the last moment, fill the shell with alternate layers of pineapple cubes and rum ice cream.

Cover it with the top of the pineapple. Serve on a dish covered with a napkin or in a bowl, surrounded with crushed ice.

Iced pineapple à la créole. ANANAS GLACÉ À LA CRÉOLE—Scoop out the pineapple as indicated above. Fill with an *Iced mousse** made from the pulp of the pineapple alternating with layers of chopped crystallized fruit steeped in rum.

When this is done, replace the top of the pineapple. Serve it on a round dish covered with a napkin, or on a block of ice.

Iced pineapple à la Chantilly. ANANAS GLACÉ À LA CHANTILLY—Proceed as described in the recipe for *Iced pineapple* above, replacing pineapple ice cream by a mixture of vanilla ice cream with whipped cream added to it.

Arrange the pineapple on a napkin or on a block of ice and replace the tufted top. (See picture on next page.)

Iced pineapple à la parisienne I. ANANAS GLACÉ À LA PARISIENNE—Prepare a *Banana ice cream* in the usual manner. Flavour this ice cream with champagne brandy.

Cut the top of the pineapple off neatly and scoop out three quarters of the pulp, without damaging the rind. Cut the scooped out pulp into small dice and put it to steep in a bowl with ¼ pound (125 grams) of small, wild strawberries and ¼ pound (125 grams) of black grapes, sugar and champagne brandy. Keep this fruit, as well as the pineapple shell, in a cool place until ready to serve.

At the last moment, fill the pineapple rind with banana ice cream, alternating in rows with fresh fruit. Sprinkle each layer of fruit with a spoonful of fresh, blanched, finely shredded almonds. Finish with a layer of ice cream and cover with the tufted top.

Put on a block of ice, slightly hollowed out in the middle. The pineapple can also be arranged simply on a napkin-covered dish.

Serve *Apricot sauce* (see SAUCE) laced with kirsch at the the same time.

Iced pineapple à la parisienne II. ANANAS GLACÉ À LA PARISIENNE—Scoop out the pineapple as indicated above. Fill with alternate layers of strawberry ice cream and a *salpicon** of pineapple pulp, diced and steeped in kirsch.

Serve on a round dish or block of ice.

Ice puddings. POUDINGS GLACÉS—Ice puddings can be made in an infinite number of ways. They are called ice puddings because, generally, they are shaped in pudding-basin moulds, though sometimes they are made in *bombe* moulds.

In the making of ice puddings the special moulds are lined with tightly packed wafers, or with sponge fingers steeped in liqueur as for a *Charlotte Russe**. They can also be lined with finely sliced Genoese cake cut into thin strips.

This casing can be filled with whatever ice cream is preferred though, almost always, a *mousse* (*bombe*) *mixture* is used. The pudding can be made more attractive by using different coloured layers of variously flavoured ice cream for the filling.

Ice puddings may also be made from a mixture similar to that used in a *Bavarian cream**.

Ice puddings are frozen with a great deal of ice or placed in the deep freeze.

Ice pudding capucine. POUDING GLACÉ CAPUCINE—Make a *Genoese cake** in a charlotte mould. Leave it until it is completely cold. Scoop out the cake almost completely, being careful not to break the crust. Fill it with alternate layers of iced tangerine mousse and iced mousse flavoured with kummel. The mousses must be prepared and iced in advance (see ICED MOUSSE).

Cover the Genoese cake with its own top layer. Surround it with ice and salt in a bucket and leave it for an hour, or place in a deep freeze.

Place it on a stand of clear sugar, decorated with flowers and ribbons of spun sugar. Pipe some *Chantilly cream* (see CREAMS) through a forcing bag on the cake.

Iced punch à la romaine. PUNCH GLACÉ À LA ROMAINE—Iced punch is served between main course, like sherbets and *granités*.

Ingredients and method. To a pint (½ litre) of syrup (density: 22°) or 2 cups sugar plus 1 cup water cooked to 220°F. add enough dry white wine or dry champagne (approximately 1 cup) to reduce the density to 17°. Add to this mixture a little lemon and orange rind and the juice of 2 oranges and of 3 lemons. Leave it to stand, covered, for an hour.

Strain the syrup and bring it to a density of 18°.

Ice this mixture in a freezer until it is rather stiff. Add a quarter of its volume of Italian *meringue**, made from 2 whites of egg and scant ½ cup (100 grams) of sugar.

Just before serving, mix in ½ cup (1 decilitre) of rum. Serve like sherbet.

Iced pineapple à la Chantilly (*Robert Carrier*)

Iced soufflés. SOUFFLÉS GLACÉS—These soufflés are prepared using either a mixture similar to that used for iced cream mousses, or a fruit mixture.

Ingredients and method for fruit iced soufflés. Whisk 10 whites of egg to a stiff foam. Add 2 cups (500 grams) of sugar cooked with 1 cup of water to a density of 370° measured by a syrup glucometer or to 240°F. (See SUGAR, *Cooking of sugar*). Put this mixture in a bowl and chill. Add a pint (½ litre) of whatever fruit purée is desired and a pint (½ litre) of cream beaten very stiff.

Moulds for iced soufflés. Large soufflés are served in an ordinary soufflé dish, surrounded by a white paper frill tied with string or stuck together with butter. The frill should be about 1¼ inches deeper than the dish. Fill the dish until the soufflé is flush with the frill. Put it in a bucket of ice and salt or in a deep freeze.

Small soufflés are served in the same way, either in little metal cases or in frilled paper cases. They, too, should be put to freeze in a bucket of ice and salt, or placed in a deep freeze.

Before serving remove the paper frills from the dish or cases.

Iced tangerines and oranges. MANDARINES ET ORANGES GLACÉES—Neatly slice off the top of the fruit near the stem. Scoop out the pulp carefully so as not to damage the skins.

Just before serving, fill the skins with a plain tangerine or orange ice made from the fruit pulp.

Cover with the top of the fruit and serve them on a napkin.

ICHTHYOPHAGY. ICHTYOPHAGIE—The practice of eating nothing, or almost nothing, but fish. Ichthyophagy is mainly practised among seaboard peoples. A fish diet is said to be less nourishing than a meat diet, but there are no substantial grounds for this view. Fish has been credited with aphrodisiac properties. It is also said to stimulate the brain. This has never been proved, in spite of the anecdote of the two dervishes, so charmingly related by Brillat-Savarin. These properties were attributed to fish because of a misguided belief that it contains a high proportion of phosphorus. In fact there is less phosphorus in fish than in butcher's meat, less even than in some vegetables. Fish on the whole is very easily digested. As a result it gives the impression of being less filling than some other foods, and so is not much in favour with manual workers.

Iced petits fours (*Larousse*)

ICING. GLACES DE SUCRE—Sugar icing, which may be prepared with or without cooking, is used in confectionery of all kinds. Pastries, cakes, and *petits fours** of various kinds may all be decorated with icing.

Blackcurrant icing. GLACE AU CASSIS—Mix ¼ cup (½ decilitre) of blackcurrant juice with ½ cup (1 decilitre) of syrup cooked to 250°F. (hard ball stage). Add enough icing sugar to produce a fairly stiff paste. Mix. This icing must be warmed slightly before use.

Usually, this icing is coloured with a little liquid carmine.

Using the same method, icing may be made with strawberries, raspberries, redcurrants and other red fruit.

Chocolate icing. GLACE AU CHOCOLAT—Place in a bowl 4 squares (125 grams) of unsweetened, softened chocolate.

Add a few tablespoons of lukewarm syrup, boiled to short thread stage.

Add icing sugar. This icing must be used at once.

Coffee icing. GLACE AU CAFÉ—Add to a pint (½ litre) of very strong coffee (coffee essence) enough icing sugar to make a fairly stiff paste. This icing must be used at once.

Fondant icing. GLACE AU FONDANT—Put in a basin 5 pounds (2½ kilos) of lump sugar. Add 1½ quarts (litres) of water and 5 teaspoons (100 grams) glucose or 1 teaspoon cream of tartar.

Cook over a high flame, skimming from time to time, until the sugar has reached 240°F. or soft ball stage (see SUGAR, *Cooking of sugar*).

Pour the sugar on to a marble slab. Let it cool a little. Work it with a spatula by folding the edges towards the centre until it is white and very smooth.

Put the fondant in a bowl. Cover with a damp cloth and leave it in a cool place.

To use the fondant. Soften a few tablespoons of the mixture in a small saucepan over a low flame, stirring constantly. Add a little syrup cooked to short thread stage. Flavour it with any appropriate liqueur, or add a little coffee essence or melted chocolate.

Colour the fondant with carmine or any other vegetable colouring, or if preferred, leave it white.

Lemon icing—GLACE AU CITRON—Made with the rind and juice of lemons, as for *Orange icing.**

Orange icing. GLACE À L'ORANGE—Put the peel of 2 oranges in ½ cup (1 decilitre) of syrup cooked to the hard ball stage (see SUGAR) and let it stand for 15 minutes. Add to this syrup the strained juice of the fruit. Put the mixture in a bowl. Add icing sugar. Proceed as for other kinds of icing.

This icing may be coloured with a little liquid carmine and a yellow vegetable dye. The icing must be used at once.

Royal icing. GLACE ROYALE—Put 2 whites of egg in a small bowl. Add to these whites enough icing sugar to make a fairly stiff paste, though it must be soft enough to spread easily on cakes and pastry.

Mix, without working the eggs and sugar too hard.

Royal icing for desserts or sweets. GLACE ROYALE—This is prepared in the same way as ordinary royal icing with whites of eggs and very fine icing sugar. Add to the mixture 6 to 8 drops of lemon juice and work with a spatula for 8 to 10 minutes. When the icing is ready, cover it with damp paper. Keep it in a cool place.

Strawberry fondant icing. GLACE AU FONDANT À LA FRAISE—Cook sugar to soft ball stage (240°F.) (see SUGAR, *Cooking of sugar*). Add a little strawberry juice and a few drops of lemon juice.

Pour it on a marble slab and work it with a spatula until it is very smooth. Put it in a bowl.

Using the same method, fondant icing may be made with raspberry juice, lemon (rind and juice), or orange (rind and juice), or from the pulp or juice of other kinds of fruit.

Icing flavoured with rum and other liqueurs. GLACE AU RHUM—Put in a bowl ½ cup (1 decilitre) of syrup cooked to soft ball stage (see SUGAR), ¼ decilitre of rum and a teaspoon of lemon juice.

Add icing sugar. Mix. Use at once.

Icing made in this way may be flavoured with other liqueurs.

IGUANA. IGUANE—The iguana is a kind of lizard very scarce except in the tropics. Iguanas are to be found in both hemispheres, but the American species are not to be found elsewhere.

In spite of its size, which precludes its assimilation with European lizards—though it is akin to these in its habits, and is almost as graceful and no less agile—the iguana should be included among those harmless animals which are worthy of preservation.

Its flesh is among the foods most highly prized by the *gourmets* of Central and South America.

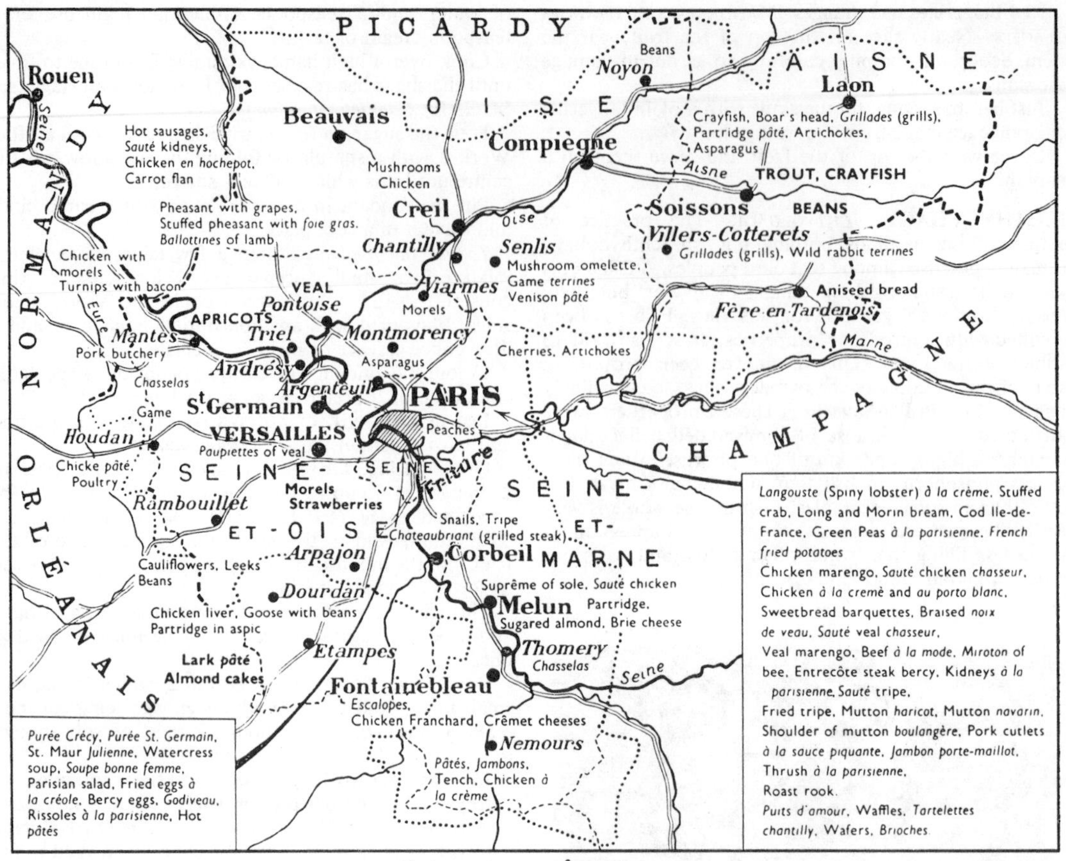

Gastronomic map of Île-de-France

ÎLE-DE-FRANCE—It is often said that Paris, the symbol and home of the whole gastronomic tradition of the Île-de-France, does not possess culinary specialities which are peculiarly her own.

According to those who express this opinion (and we regard them as very ill-informed), Paris is nothing more than a kind of cross-roads or rather a melting-pot in which all the varied regional dishes of the provinces of France and other European countries are thrown together and deprived of all local character.

Many gastronomes bluntly assert that Parisian cookery is banal and insipid or, worse still, that it simply does not exist, and that Paris should be omitted from the gastronomic map of France.

Such people take no account of the magnificent work which has been and is still being carried out by the master-chefs of truly Parisian restaurants. They totally disregard the rich store of special dishes—genuine culinary 'specialities' in the fullest sense of the term—added to the Parisian repertoire by a distinguished line of chefs from Carême to Escoffier. These are not the only great names overlooked—there were also Gouffé, Urbain Dubois, Philéas Gilbert, Marguery, Paillard, Mourier, Nignon and a host of others.

It is astonishing to find it stated in all, or almost all, works on French regional cookery that, apart from deep-fried foods and fish stewed in wine with onions and herbs (*matelote**), Paris has no culinary 'specialities'.

This is all the more amazing since there are to be found throughout the Île-de-France region foodstuffs which, in the opinion of connoisseurs, are of unrivalled excellence.

In fact it is hardly possible that the cuisine of Paris and its environs should be banal and characterless, when we consider that in this vast city there are the best cooks and most skilful *cordons bleus* of all France. Paris abounds with foodstuffs imported from abroad and brought in from every corner of France, not to mention the produce of the fertile soil of the Île-de-France, and the livestock reared in all the departments around Paris, which provide it with savoury fish, delicate poultry, every kind of game and a host of other delicious things.

The finest vegetables are grown in the Île-de-France, and the most delicately flavoured fruit is picked in the orchards of Paris. Here is a list of just a few of the gastronomic delights to be found in the Île-de-France, and in the Paris region in particular: *Argenteuil asparagus*, which with that of *Lauris* has the reputation of being the best in France; *Clamart green peas;* the *French beans of Bagnolet;* the *cauliflower of Arpajon;* the *carrots of Crécy-sur-Morin; Laon artichokes and asparagus;* the *white beans of Soissons*, or more accurately of *Noyon;* the *lettuces of Versailles;* the fragrant *morels* of the woods of *Verrières, Viarmes and Rambouillet;* the cultivated mushrooms of the Paris region, called *champignons de Paris;* the magnificent pot-vegetables grown at *Bagneux*, *Châtillon*, *Saint Denis* and other places in the area; onions, small and large, leeks, cabbages, carrots, turnips, cucumbers, shallots, various salads, spinach, sorrel, chervil, parsley, parsnips, horseradish, beetroot.

The fruits of the Paris orchards have a great reputation, some are even famous: the *Chasselas of Fontainebleau* (those from the *king's vine-arbour*), of *Thomery and*

Les Halles (*French Government Tourist Office*)

Andrézy; the *peaches of Montreuil;* the *strawberries of the Bièvre valley;* the *Héricart* strawberry which the barrow-men call *Ricart*, and many other sweet-smelling fruits which melt in the mouth, such as pears, apples, plums, figs, apricots and nectarines.

Excellent meat is sold in Paris. What is more, the Paris butchers are true artists, and their cuts are flawless. Pontoise veal, called *river veal*, is as tender and as delicate as any to be found.

In the woods and forests around Paris, in the regions of Versailles, Marly and Saint-Germain-au-Laye, there is an abundance of excellent game.

The poultry of Houdan is held in high repute for its delicate flavour. The freshwater fish caught in the Seine, the Marne, the Oise and the Aisne are especially delicious.

Very good cheeses are made round about Paris, among which are *Coulommiers, Brie, Brie de Melun,* and the fresh cream cheese known as the *Crèmet of Fontainebleau,* which rivals the famous fresh cream cheeses of Saumur and Angers and the fresh *Gervais.*

Parisian viticulture is virtually non-existent. We recall, a little wryly, the legendary '*petit bleu*' of Suresnes immortalized in the song by Paulus: '*En revenant de Suresnes,*' and the wines of *Argenteuil* and *Montmartre,* where the vine figures only, so to speak, in a decorative capacity.

Nevertheless, on the hillsides of the Marne, which are an extension of the neighbouring Champagne vineyards, grapes are gathered which produce 'little' table wines which are fresh and pleasant to taste.

In the Aisne and Oise districts, excellent cider is brewed, and among the liqueurs distilled in the Paris region there is one, the *Noyau de Poissy,* which enjoys a great and long-established reputation.

Culinary specialities of the Île-de-France—The following soups were invented in Paris, in Parisian restaurants by Parisian chefs; they may therefore be classed with absolute certainty among the culinary specialities of Paris and the Paris region: *Crécy, St. Germain, Parisien, Bonne-Femme, Cressonière, Santé, Bonvalet, Compiègne, Cormeilles, Briard, Parmentier, Soissonnais, Argenteuil, Ambassadeurs, Balvet, Faubonne, Germiny* (invented by Dugléré at the *Café Anglais*), *Darblay, Longchamp, Saint-Cloud.*

Among the pork specialities of the Paris region are: *Andouillettes* (chitterling sausages); *Boudins noirs et blancs* (black and white puddings); *Petit-salé; Veau piqué* (mis-named since it is not made from veal but from pork); *Friands parisiens; Pâté de foie de cochon* (pig's liver pâté); *Fromage de tête de porc* (pork brawn); *Roulade de tête de porc; Hure de porc à la parisienne* (boar's head *à la parisienne*); *Pâté de porc de Paris; Rillons* and *Rillettes; Cervelas* or *Saucisson à cuire* (saveloy or cooking sausage); *Jambon glacé de Paris* (glazed Paris ham); *Côtes de porc à la charcutière* (ribs of pork *à la charcutière*); *Pieds de porc à la parisienne* (pig's trotters *à la parisienne*).

Among the dishes made from meat are: Beef *miroton;* Shoulder of mutton *à la boulangère; Entrecôte Bercy* and *Entrecôte marchand de vin;* the celebrated *Navarin* of mutton, and the old *Halicot* of mutton with turnips, now (mistakenly in the French view) called *Haricot* of mutton; Fillet of beef *à la béarnaise* (*béarnaise* sauce having been created at Saint-Germain-en-Laye); Rib of veal *à la bonne femme;* Calves' tendons *à la paysanne;* the old-fashioned *Fricandeau;* Calves' head *du Puits Certin*; Sauté of veal *chasseur;* Mutton chops *Champvallon;* Sheeps' trotters *à la poulette; Épigrammes* of mutton, lamb, etc. (breast of mutton or lamb with a mutton or lamb chop, both fried in egg and breadcrumbs).

Among the special poultry and game dishes of Paris are: *Sauté* chicken *Bercy, Boivin-Champeaux, Chasseur, Durand, fines herbes, Lathuile, Parmentier;* Spring chicken *en cocotte, à la Clamart, à la bonne-femme, à la diable;* Squab *à la crapaudine, en compote, en papillotes;* Duckling *nantais* with turnips, green peas; Duckling *rouennais à la presse, Timbale* of duckling *voisin; Gibelotte* of young rabbit; young Garenne rabbit *chasseur;* Pheasant *à la Sainte-Alliance,* a majestic creation from the hands of Brillat-Savarin; Snipe *à la fine champagne,* and *à la Riche;* Wild duck *à la presse.*

Vol-au-vents, flans and tarts filled in many different ways have for a very long time been regarded as culinary specialities of Paris.

Special Parisian fish (sea and freshwater) and shellfish dishes are: Lobster *à l'américaine;* the various *matelotes* of eels and freshwater fish, for example *Matelotes Moulin de la Râpée* and *à la canotière; Eel à la tartare;* Carp *à la canotière, Bouillabaisse à la parisienne* (doubtless disapproved of by natives of Marseilles, but excellent all the same, and invented by a Parisian master-chef); Whiting *Bercy, Colbert, au gratin;* all manner of dishes made of sole, brill, turbot, sea-perch, etc., Brill *Dugléré,* Young turbot *au plat,* Sole *à la normande,* Sole *Marguery,* Turbot *à la parisienne,* Spring lobster *à la parisienne, Coquilles Saint-Jacques à la parisienne,* Frogs' legs *à la poulette.*

The sauces in the Paris repertoire are very numerous. Among the brown sauces may be mentioned: *Charcutière, Chasseur, Colbert, Diable, Hachée, Moelle* (bone-marrow) and *Robert.*

Among the white sauces the following are perhaps the best known: *Béarnaise, Bercy, Bonnefoy, Chantilly, Choron, Fayot, Laguipière, Marinière, Mousseline, Moutarde* (mustard), *Poulette, Ravigote, Riche* and *Véron.*

Here is a random selection of some other Parisian specialities: Green peas *à la française, à la parisienne,* the *Matelote de Beauvais,* the partridge *pâtés* of Laon, the poultry *pâtés* of Houdan, the lark *pâtés* of Étampes, the *Échaudés, puits d'amour, oublies,* the Paris *brioche,* the aniseed bread of Fère-en-Tardenois, the stuffed pears of Provins, the cakes of Compiègne and Étampes, the green walnuts of Faucaucoure, the barley-sugar of Moret and the sugared almonds of Melun.

IMPÉRATRICE (A L')—A name applied to various dishes and cakes. Among these is *Rice à l'impératrice,* a cold dessert, a recipe for which is given under RICE.

IMPERIAL. Impériale—A variety of plum.

IMPERIAL. Impériale—A large bottle holding about $1\frac{1}{2}$ gallons, which is used for Bordeaux wines and for spirits.

IMPÉRIALE (A L')—A name applied to various dishes garnished with truffles, foie-gras, cocks' combs and kidneys, and other similar garnishes.

IMPROMPTU—An improvised meal which would be described as a pot-luck meal in English.

INCISING. Inciser—The making of light incisions with a very sharp knife in the skin of fish which are to be grilled or fried.

INFUSE. Infuser—To steep herbs or other flavouring in boiling liquid, until the liquid absorbs the flavour.

Milk used in the preparation of creams and custards is flavoured by infusing vanilla, cinnamon or lemon or orange rind in it.

Wine used in the preparation of sauces is flavoured by the infusion of mushroom peelings, truffles or any kind of herb.

INSECTS, EDIBLE. Insectes comestibles—Considering the prodigious number of insects which, for the most part, feed on the greenstuffs which are also eaten by man and his flocks and cattle, one cannot help being surprised that in the west, even in times of famine, no one dreams of eating them.

They are usually objects of disgust among western

peoples who do not, however, hesitate to eat prawns and other shell-fish. On the other hand, the Arabs and other peoples of Africa and Asia look upon certain insects as great delicacies, and are amazed at our taste for shell-fish.

The Hebrew tribes ate insects, long before St. John the Baptist was forced to feed exclusively on locusts and other creatures of the same kind. In Leviticus (II, 21-22), Moses enumerates the animals which the Hebrews were permitted to eat. Among these he mentions four insects which St. Jerome in his Latin translation calls *locusta, bruchus, ophimachus* and *attacus*.

The *locusta*, it seems, must have been the locust, but naturalists have been unable to identify the other three.

Several other insects, such as *white ants*, are used as food by savage tribes.

In ancient times, the Greeks prized grasshoppers very highly, especially the larvae.

The Chinese, too, greatly enjoy eating certain insects, and feast upon the chrysalis of the silk-worm. Some gourmets even today appreciate grasshopper and bumble bees as accompaniments to apéritifs or cocktails.

INTERLARDING. PIQUAGE DES VIANDES—Certain cuts of meat, such as fillets of beef, leg of veal, etc., are interlarded with best pork fat cut into small neat lardoons. In the same way poultry, calf's sweetbreads, veal chops and, less commonly, large fish such as carp, sturgeon, etc., are interlarded with very small lardoons.

To interlard a fillet of beef. First trim the meat, that is to say, skin it and remove all tendons. Next, using a larding needle threaded with a lardoon, thread it into the fillet, following the grain of the meat. The depth of the stitch is determined by the length of the lardoon. Each lardoon must project ⅜ inch on each side.

Having thus made a first transverse row with the lardoons, thread the second row of lardoons through the meat, alternating them with the first. Make sure that the lardoons always project over the meat by the same length. Keeping the spacing even, thread as many double rows of lardoons into the meat as its length requires. Where the meat is narrower, fewer lardoons are required.

Finally, the fillet being completely interlarded, trim the lardoons so that the ends are of equal length. Tie the fillet crosswise to keep it round in shape. Put it on a spit or, if it is to be roasted in the oven, in a roasting pan fitted with a grid.

To interlard a fricandeau or leg of veal.* Trim the joint as indicated in the appropriate section under VEAL. Next, interlard as indicated for fillet of beef.

To interlard saddles of mutton, roebuck, baron of hare, haunch of venison, etc. Proceed as indicated above, adapting the thickness of the lardoons to the size of the meat, and varying the space between the rows, according to the size of the cut.

Interlarding of small cuts of meat, calf's sweetbreads, etc. Interlard with best lardoons chops, escalopes, *grenadins* and medallions of veal for braising. These lardoons must be cut very fine and the needle used must be proportionately small.

Small round portions of meat may be interlarded by threading the lardoons into them in the form of a rosette. This method can also be used for beef and mutton *filets mignons*. Calf's sweetbreads can be interlarded so that the lardoons form a rosette or with alternate rows of lardoons as for fillet of beef. Calf's sweetbreads, before interlarding, must be soaked in water, blanched, cooled under running water, and left to get quite cold under a weight.

Interlarding of poultry and game. Only large poultry for braising is interlarded. To make this operation easier, singe with a rather hot flame the part of the breast to be interlarded, or dip it in boiling water to make the flesh more firm.

Only old game for braising, such as partridge, pheasant or hazel-grouse, is interlarded. Proceed as for poultry, using very small lardoons.

IRIDESCENT SEAWEED. IRIDÉE—A kind of edible seaweed remarkable for its variegated colouring. It is eaten raw in salad or cooked like French beans.

IRISH STEW (English Cookery)—This dish really belongs to the Irish culinary repertoire. It is mutton stewed in white stock with potatoes and sliced onions. See MUTTON.

IRON. FER—This metal is part of the mineral content of organic matter, a minimum of which is present in most fresh food.

IRRORATEUR (Spray Gun)—A piece of apparatus, invented by Brillat-Savarin, which was used to perfume rooms, especially the dining room.

Speaking of this apparatus—of which there is probably not a single example now left in existence—Brillat-Savarin writes in the preface to *La Physiologie du Goût:* 'There is another day whose memory is, I think, dear to me, and that is the day on which I submitted to the Council of the Society for the Encouragement of National Industries my *irrorateur*, a piece of apparatus invented by me, which is none other than a compressor spray which can fill a room with perfume.

'I had brought the spray with me, in my pocket. It was well-filled. I turned on the tap and, with a hissing sound, out came a sweet-smelling vapour which rose right up to the ceiling and then fell in tiny drops on the people present and on their papers.

'It was then that I witnessed, with indescribable pleasure, the heads of the wisest men in the capital bending under my "irroration". I was enraptured to note that the wettest among them were also the happiest.'

The sprays used nowadays to purify and clean the air of public places, such as restaurants, theatres and concert halls, serve the same purpose as Brillat-Savarin's *irrorateur*.

ISIGNY—A small town in Calvados where some of the best butter in France is made.

ISINGLASS (Gelatine) FOR SWEETS (Desserts). COLLE DE POISSON CLARIFIÉE—'Take a one-ounce sheet of gelatine; after cutting it into small pieces, wash it, put it in a pan with eight glasses of filtered water and two ounces of sugar. Put it on the fire.

'As soon as rapid boiling is established, put the pan on the side of the fire in such a way as to keep it boiling.

'Take care to remove the scum as it rises and when the reduction produces a good glass of gelatine, strain it through a napkin into a clean vessel.

'The proper clarification of the sugar and the gelatine can be considered the secret of success of attractive fruit and liqueur jellies.' (Carême.)

ITALIAN MARROWS, COURGETTES (U.S. zucchini). COURGETTE—Variety of gourd with short fruits. These courgettes are also known under the name of *courgeron*, *coucouzelle*, and *zuchetti*. In U.S.A. they are called *Italian squash* or *zucchini*.

The courgettes have a very delicate taste.

Method of preparation. According to the use to which they are put, the courgette is or is not peeled. When the vegetable is to be fried it is peeled, cut up into thick rounds or little sticks, soaked in milk, then drained, and rolled in flour, and deep fried in boiling oil.

Italian marrows, courgettes (U.S. zucchini) à la créole—Peel the courgettes; remove the seeds. Cut them into dice. Put them in a pan with some good fat; lightly brown the courgettes in the fat; put on the lid; cook slowly on a low heat; add salt; stir often. Crush them with a spoon; reduce them as it were to jam. When all their moisture has evaporated, let them acquire a golden colour before serving.

Glazed Italian marrow, courgettes (U.S. zucchini) garnish. COURGETTES GLACÉES—Divide the courgettes in quarters; trim them into lozenge shapes, of even size; blanch for a few minutes and drain.

Put them in a sauté-pan with two tablespoons of butter, a pinch of salt, and a little sugar. Cover with cold water.

Bring to the boil; cover, and cook gently on the corner of the stove, until the liquid has almost entirely disappeared. Sauté the courgettes in the remaining liquor so that they are coated with it.

Italian marrow, courgettes (U.S. zucchini) à la grecque (hors-d'oeuvre)—Divide the courgettes into small slices without peeling them, or if you like, trim them into lozenge shapes. Put them into a court-bouillon prepared in the manner described for *Artichokes à la grecque**. Finish in the same way.

Italian marrows, courgettes (U.S. zucchini) à l'indienne—Prepare the marrows in the same way as for *Glazed Italian marrow*. Simmer them in butter. Season with salt and a strong pinch of curry powder.

When they are cooked, pour over some tablespoons of *Béchamel sauce* (see SAUCE); mix without breaking the courgettes.

Italian marrow, courgettes (U.S. zucchini) à la mentonnaise—Prepare the courgettes in the way described for *Italian marrow à la niçoise**.

Stuff the halved courgettes with their chopped pulp, to which an equal quantity of spinach, blanched, drained, chopped and simmered in butter, has been added. Add a little Parmesan cheese to the stuffing, a little garlic and some chopped parsley.

Sprinkle with browned breadcrumbs; pour some olive oil over the courgettes and brown in the oven.

Italian marrows, courgettes (U.S. zucchini) à la mingrélienne (Russian cookery). COURGETTES FARCIES À LA MINGRÉLIENNE—Peel the courgettes; cut them into slices 2 inches thick; remove the seeds, blanch and drain them.

Prepare the following stuffing: blanch some rice, drain it, put it under the cold tap, and drain again. Add to this rice some chopped mutton (rather fat), chopped onion melted in butter, chopped fennel, a little garlic, salt and pepper. Mix well.

Fill the courgettes with this stuffing, rounding the top. Arrange in a buttered sauté-pan, packing them in fairly tightly. Moisten with tomato-flavoured veal stock. Start cooking on top of the fire, and then cook gently in the oven with the lid on. Baste the dish with its own juice during the cooking.

Italian marrows, courgettes (U.S. zucchini) à la niçoise I—Pare the courgettes, cut them into thin slices; salt them, wipe them with a cloth, sprinkle with flour and sauté them in a pan in oil, on a strong flame.

Put them in a dish, alternating them with skinned and seeded tomatoes, which have been sliced and lightly fried in oil.

At the last moment, pour 2 tablespoons of boiling oil over them, in which some garlic and chopped parsley have been rapidly browned.

A little sliced onion, browned in oil, can also be added to this dish.

Courgettes à la niçoise II

Italian marrows, courgettes (U.S. zucchini) à la niçoise II—Divide the courgettes in half lengthways. Make a circular incision $\frac{1}{8}$ inch from the edge in the pulp, and make seven or eight little cuts in the middle of the pulp.

Season the courgettes with salt, set them on a cloth and leave them to get rid of their excess moisture. Dry them and cook them gently in oil, without letting them brown too much. Drain them.

Take out three quarters of the pulp, without damaging the skin.

Chop the pulp; add two thirds of its weight of risotto flavoured with Parmesan and 2 tablespoons of rather thick tomato purée, flavoured with a touch of grated garlic.

Stuff the halved courgettes with this mixture. Smooth the stuffing with a fork, giving it a lightly domed shape.

Put the courgettes in an oiled gratin dish. Sprinkle them with breadcrumbs; pour over some oil. Brown gently in the oven.

At the last moment surround them with a few tablespoons of good veal gravy and sprinkle with chopped parsley.

Italian marrows, courgettes (U.S. zucchini) à la provençale—Cut the courgettes into thick slices, cut either crossways or lengthways, without peeling them. Salt them, dry them, and sprinkle with flour. Sauté them in oil in a frying pan.

Arrange them in layers in a gratin dish, alternating the courgettes with rice cooked in stock and tomatoes lightly fried in oil in a pan, with sliced onions, and parsley and chopped garlic.

Smooth the surface of the dish, cover with grated cheese and brown in the oven at a moderate temperature (375°F.).

Italian marrow, courgette (U.S. zucchini) salad. COURGETTES EN SALADE—Divide the courgettes into quarters, lengthways. Blanch them in boiling salt and water for 6 to 8 minutes. Drain and wipe them on a cloth.

Put them in a salad bowl; pour over them a few tablespoons of *Vinaigrette sauce* (see SAUCE). Sprinkle abundantly with chervil and chopped tarragon.

This salad can be served with mayonnaise.

LOBSTER A LA PARISIENNE (*La Méditerranée*)

(*From Curnonsky:* Cuisine et Vins de France)

PETITS-FOURS AND SAVOURIES

Italian marrows, courgettes (U.S. zucchini) sautéed. Courgettes sautées—Peel the courgettes; cut them in round slices, not too thick; flour them; sauté them in oil or butter in the frying pan.

ITALIAN PASTES (Pasta products). Pâtes alimentaires—Dried wheaten flour preparation, mostly made from *Durum* wheat. The flour is well-kneaded into a stiff dough and forced through specially perforated cylinders from which it comes out in various shapes, known by different names (*macaroni, spaghetti, vermicelli, crescioni, ditalini, fedelini, ravioli, reginette, strichetti, tagliarini, tagliatelli, tortellini,* etc.). They are made by kneading vigorously from 68-72 pounds (34 to 36 kilos) of hard (red) wheat with 10 to 15 quarts (litres) of boiling water. After kneading, the paste is introduced into a bronze cylinder, equipped with a die, and pressure is then applied to it by a hydraulic press. A fan is usually placed near the outlet of the die, to begin the drying process which ends in the drying oven. The small pasta products are cut as they emerge from the cylinder by means of a circular knife; the others are produced in different lengths. Egg pasta can be made by adding dry or fresh eggs to the mixture; the slightly yellow colour of ordinary pasta is due to the addition of turmeric or to various chemical colouring matter.

The food value of pasta products is very great; 3½ ounces (100 grams) of pasta products corresponds to about 5 ounces (150 grams) of bread.

For preparation of home-made noodles, see NOODLES.

ITALIENNE (A L')—A name given to various dishes made of meat, poultry, fish and vegetables. In all these dishes finely-diced or chopped mushrooms are used.

The name *à l'italienne* is also given to a method of preparing macaroni or other pasta. See MACARONI.

IVA—A name given in some districts of France to the yarrow and to a type of gentian.

IVOIRE (A L')—a method of preparation used especially for poultry. See CHICKEN, *Chicken à l'ivoire.*

IVROGNE DE MER—A small fish with red scales found in the Atlantic, and in the Mediterranean and Adriatic. Its flesh is tough, but it is nevertheless edible.

IZARD. Isard—The name given to the wild goat of the Pyrenees. For methods of cooking it see ROEBUCK.

Italian pasta: *Spaghetti alla Bolognese*

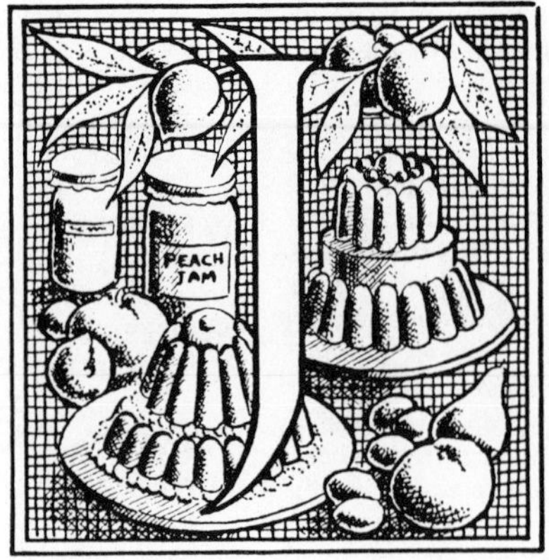

JALOUSIES—Little cakes made of flaky pastry.

Method I. Roll out a piece of *Flaky pastry dough* (see DOUGH) and cut it into slices about 3 inches wide.

Leaving a margin of ⅓ inch at either end, spread on each slice of dough a layer of *Almond paste** flavoured with vanilla.

Decorate the top with twisted strips of dough to make a criss-cross pattern. Secure this by pressing down at each end of the slice a narrow strip of dough moistened with a little water so that it sticks firmly. Crimp the edges. Brush with beaten egg. Bake in a medium oven; when cooked spread apricot jam on top. Cut into pieces of equal size.

Method II. Roll out a piece of flaky pastry, cut it in half and trim the halves into lengths 4 inches wide.

Place one of these lengths on a slightly moistened baking sheet. Brush the edges of the dough with water. Spread with apricot or other jam, leaving a border. Fold the second length of dough in two, lengthwise. Using the back of a large knife, carefully cut the folded dough into strips of equal width, leaving a border at each end. Open out the dough and lay it carefully on the slice spread with jam. Press the edges to join them. Trim the edges neatly and crimp them.

Brush the top with beaten egg. Bake in a medium oven (375°F.) for 25 to 30 minutes. Take the tart out of the oven, spread jam on it and sprinkle little sugar crystals round the edge.

Cut the tart into strips about 1½ inches wide. Leave them to cool on a wire tray.

JAMS AND JELLIES. Confitures, Gelées—A preparation of fruit for which the legal definition in France is as follows: 'Products constituted solely of refined or crystallized sugar and fresh fruits or juice of fresh fruits, or preserved in some way other than by drying' (decree of 25th September, 1925). They must contain a maximum of 40 per cent moisture, and in consequence hold 60 per cent of dry extract, of which 55 per cent must be sugar. (Fruit already contains 5 to 7 per cent dry extract.)

Only those products which correspond to this definition have a right to be labelled *pure fruit, pure sugar*.

The law authorises the mixing of fruits (in practice, apple juice is used a great deal, particularly for jellies), on condition that the fruit used in the highest proportion is put first on the label.

Marmalades must correspond to the same definition as jams, but the dry extract can fall as low as 55 per cent, and the use of brown sugar, or sugar which has already been used for crystallizing fruit, is authorised.

If tartaric acid or citric acid is added, the label must contain the word: *Fantaisie.* When artificial essences are added, the word *Fantaisie* or *Arôme artificiel* (artificial flavouring) must appear on the lable. When colouring matter is added, this must be indicated.

A product made with essences, acids and colouring matter cannot bear the name of a fruit, and can only be sold under the name of *Produit artificiel* (artificial product) with, if necessary, the mention of pure sugar.

Jams made of fruit or of mixtures of fruit, or marmalades made with syrup which has been used to preserve fruits (syrup containing about 5 per cent glucose) must bear the following mention: *Au sirop de fruits confits* (made with preserved fruit syrup).

Jams, all of which are obtained from an invariable basis of fruit and sugar, consist of various categories, which are:

1. *Jams* proper, made by cooking stoned fruit with sugar. Apricots, cherries, strawberries, oranges, plums, etc., are used and, according to its kind, the fruit is prepared whole or halved.

2. *Jellies*, made only with the juice of fruits and sugar;

3. *Marmalades*, prepared with strained fruit pulp and sugar.

4. Jams made with a multiple base, such as the *raisines*, or other similar preparations.

Jam-making—The quantity of sugar used varies according to the fruit in question. Sugar is used not only to sweeten the preparation, but to preserve it. When rather watery fruits with slight acidity are used, sugar must be introduced in a quantity to equal that of the fruit.

For fruits of more substance, containing mucilagineous matter, the quantity of sugar should be reduced. The quality of sugar used should be the best.

Too much sugar oversweetens the jam, noticeably diminishes the flavour of the fruit, and risks rapid crystallization. On the other hand, jams or jellies prepared with an insufficient quantity of sugar are in danger of fermenting, or, if they have been overcooked, of lacking all flavour.

We recommend, therefore, the following specific instructions, to be found below under the speciality headings.

Cooking. This cannot be properly done without an untinned copper or aluminium utensil.

The time taken to cook the jam depends upon the intensity of the heat to which it is submitted. It cannot be precisely measured.

The cooking period is divided into two phases: during the first the evaporation of the moisture contained in the fruit takes place. The process of dehydration is complete when the steam rising from the pan is less dense and the surface begins to seethe rather than to bubble. Then the real cooking begins, effected at greater or less speed according to whether the fruit is watery or easily jelled.

During this first phase, the skimming takes place, which consists in removing all the impurities which rise to the surface with the aid of an untinned copper skimming-ladle.

Once the evaporation has taken place, the cook must follow very closely the progress of the cooking, which from then on will be very rapid. He will put the skimming-ladle very frequently into the pan and see whether, on lifting it out each time, the drops of jam drop off easily or more slowly. As soon as these drops collect in the centre of the skimmer and slide slowly off, the jam can be considered to be ready. It is cooked to a degree called *jelling* (32°-33°C. and 235°F. on the sugar thermometer).

Potting, sealing and conservation. As soon as the jam has achieved the stage known as *jelling*, remove the pan from the fire.

Allow the jam to cool for some minutes. Fill the pots, remembering to heat them gradually beforehand so as to prevent them from cracking.

Put the pots on a table and leave them till the following day. Then cover the surface of the jam with a glycerine paper or paraffin wax and seal with a double paper tightly tied with string.

Gum a label on the pots indicating the type of jam and store in a very dry place.

Failures in jam-making and remedies.

The jam remains runny. There is a lack of pectin. Add some apple jelly.

The jam crystallizes. The fruits are insufficiently acid. Cook again, adding lemon juice, or tartaric or citric acid.

The jam develops mould. The jars are inadequately sealed. Remove the mould and cover with melted paraffin wax.

The jam ferments. The cooking has been insufficient; cook again.

Recipes for jams and jellies are given below; recipes for marmalade will be found under the separate heading MARMALADE.

JAMS. CONFITURES:

Apricot jam I. CONFITURE D'ABRICOTS—For 2 pounds (1 kilo) of apricots which are ripe, net weight stoned, 1½ pounds (750 grams) of preserving sugar.

Put the sugar in a pan with ½ cup (1 decilitre) of water. Let the sugar dissolve; boil for 5 minutes and skim.

Add the apricots. Cook till the *jelling* stage is reached, as described under *Cooking of jam.* Finish in the same way, adding at the last moment some of the apricot kernels which have been previously shelled and divided in two.

Apricot jam II. CONFITURE D'ABRICOTS—For 2 pounds (1 kilo) net weight of apricots, 3½ cups (800 grams) of sugar, ½ cup (1 decilitre) of water.

Put the fruit, sugar and water in a pan. Let the sugar melt, stirring all the time on a gentle heat.

Raise the heat and continue to cook until the *jelling* stage is reached. Add the peeled apricot kernels. Finish as directed above.

Cherry jam I. CONFITURE DE CERISES—For 2 pounds (1 kilo) of stoned cherries, use 2 pounds (1 kilo) of sugar and ½ cup (1 decilitre) of water. Proceed in the same way as for *Apricot jam I.*

If the cherries are very sweet, only 3 cups (750 grams) of sugar are used for every 2 pounds (1 kilo) of fruit.

Cherry jam II. CONFITURE DE CERISES—2 pounds (1 kilo) cherries; 2 pounds (1 kilo) sugar; 1 pint (½ litre) gooseberry juice; ½ cup (1 decilitre) water. Dissolve the sugar and water and boil for 5 minutes. Add the cherries and the gooseberry juice. Cook and finish in the usual way.

The addition of gooseberry juice makes for more rapid cooking and a more fragrant jam as well.

Chestnut jam. CONFITURE DE MARRONS—See CHESTNUTS.

Melon jam. CONFITURE DE MELON—For 2 pounds (1 kilo) of melon, net weight, after removing rind and seeds, 3 cups (750 grams) of fine sugar.

Cut the rosy flesh of the melon into little pieces. Put these in a large basin in successive layers, sprinkling each layer with sugar.

Leave to stand in a cool place for 3 or 4 hours.

Put the contents of the basin into a pan and cook to the *jelling* stage as described above.

Orange jam. CONFITURE D'ORANGES—For 2 pounds (1 kilo) of orange purée, 2 pounds (1 kilo) of sugar, ½ cup (1 decilitre) water and 1½ cups (3 decilitres) of apple juice.

Choose oranges of the same size, sound and with a thick skin. Prick them here and there rather deeply with a little pointed stick; put them in a pan of boiling water and leave to cook rapidly for 30 minutes.

Drain them, put them under a running cold tap for 12 to 15 hours (or soak them in a basin of cold water, renewing the water frequently, for 24 hours). This rather prolonged operation has as its object the removal of bitterness from the orange rind and to soften it more completely.

Drain the oranges, divide them into quarters, remove the pips and fine skins, and pass through a sieve.

Dissolve the sugar with ½ cup of water in a pan. Boil for a few moments, and skim. Add the purée of oranges, and the apple juice. Finish in the same way as the recipes above.

Peach jam. CONFITURE DE PÊCHES—Proceed with stoned and skinned peaches in the same way as for *Apricot jam.*

Pineapple jam. CONFITURE D'ANANAS—For 2 pounds (1 kilo) of fresh pineapple (net weight, after removing the outside and hard core), 3 cups (750 grams) of sugar, ½ cup (1 decilitre) of water.

Cut the pineapple into small, even, square pieces.

Dissolve the sugar and water and cook it to the ball stage (240°F.), then put in the pineapple chunks.

Cook the jam as usual until it reaches the *jelling* stage. Finish in the usual way.

Raspberry jam. CONFITURE DE FRAMBOISES—Remove stems from raspberries. Choose ripe but firm fruit. Put in a copper pan. Cover with sugar cooked to 240°F. For each pound of fruit take one pound of sugar.

Heat gently on a small flame or in a double cooker so that the sugar thoroughly penetrates the fruit. Remove from the fire.

Next morning drain the raspberries very carefully without crushing them, put the syrup back on the fire. Add an equal quantity of currant juice. Cook this syrup until it coats a silver spoon. Put the raspberries in it; bring to the boil.

Pot the jam. Cover with a layer of currant jelly. When the jam is absolutely cold, cover the pots.

Rhubarb jam. CONFITURE DE RHUBARBE—For 2 pounds (1 kilo) of rhubarb (net weight, with outer fibres removed): 3¼ cups (800 grams) of sugar; ½ cup (1 decilitre) of water.

Skin the stems of some rhubarb, chosen young and

either red or green according to whether one wishes to obtain a jam of one or the other colour, and divide into pieces 1½ to 2 inches (4 to 5 centimetres) long.

Wash the pieces, drain them, and put them in with the sugar which has been dissolved with water and boiled for a few minutes.

Draw the pan to one side of the fire and cover it. Leave it for 10 minutes so that the rhubarb softens.

Return the pan to full heat and cook stirring all the time until the jam reaches the *jelling* stage.

Finish in the usual way.

Strawberry jam. CONFITURE DE FRAISES—2 pounds (1 kilo) strawberries (net weight); 3 cups (750 grams) sugar; ½ cup (1 decilitre) water.

Put the sugar in a pan with the water; let it dissolve and cook to the ball stage (240°F.), taking care to skim well.

Put the strawberries, stalks removed, in the sugar. Keep the pan on the side of the fire for a few minutes.

When the juice from the strawberries has thinned the sugar to a syrupy consistency, drain the fruit through a silk strainer.

Cook the syrup again in the pan until it reaches 240°F. once more.

Put the strawberries back in the pan and cook for 5 or 6 minutes, just to the point at which the jam reaches the *jelling* stage (220°F.). Finish in the usual way.

The best kinds of strawberry used in France for jam are *Héricart*, very fragrant, *noble*, *sharpless*, and, among the white varieties, *gemma* and *mirabilis*.

The strawberries must be selected for perfect unblemished ripeness. It is advisable not to wash them unless absolutely necessary. In this case they should be well-drained and dried before cooking.

Tomato jam. CONFITURE DE TOMATES—2 pounds (1 kilo) of drained tomato pulp; 2 pounds (1 kilo) of sugar; ½ cup (1 decilitre) of water; 1½ cups (3 decilitres) of apple juice; one vanilla pod.

Put the sugar in a pan with the water and the vanilla pod. Let it dissolve and then cook to the ball stage (240°F.).

Put the tomato pulp in a pan. This is prepared by working the tomatoes through a sieve.

Cook on a lively heat stirring all the time with the skimmer until the jam reaches the *jelling* stage.

Finish in the usual way.

Instead of apple juice, gooseberry juice may be used. The addition of this juice is necessary to supply the jelling element to the tomatoes so that the jam sets properly.

Watermelon jam. CONFITURE DE PASTÈQUES—For 2 pounds (1 kilo) of watermelon, net weight after removing rind and seeds; 3 cups (750 grams) of fine sugar.

Proceed in the same way as for *Melon jam*.

JELLIES. GELÉES:

Apple jelly. GELÉE DE POMMES—This jelly, like nearly all the preparations of the same kind, is made by cutting good cooking apples into slices without peeling them or removing the pips. The fruit should be ripe and perfectly sound.

Put them in a preserving pan; moisten with a quart (litre) and a half of water for every 2 pounds (kilo) of fruit. As soon as the apples are cooked, turn them out into a jelly-bag placed over a large basin.

Add 3 cups (750 grams) of sugar for every quart (litre) of juice, which must be obtained without pressure, and put this to cook in a pan until it begins to jell. This stage is reached when a drop of jelly is made to fall from the skimmer onto a plate and it remains a drop without spreading.

Do not pot until the jelly is lukewarm, and wait till the following day before covering the pots.

Bitter orange jelly (Carême's recipe). GELÉE DE BIGARADES—After having taken the rind off two sound bitter oranges as thinly as possible, press over it the juice of five lemons and filter the whole through a straining-bag. Mix this fruit with 1¾ cups (14 ounces) of sugar and 1½ ounces of *isinglass**. Finish and pour the jelly into a mould as usual. Leave on ice or in the refrigerator to set properly.

Turn out on to a round dish or a glass fruit bowl.

Cherry jelly. GELÉE DE CERISES—For a quart (1 litre) of cherry juice: 3¼ cups (850 grams) of sugar, 1½ cups (3 decilitres) of apple juice, ½ cup (1 decilitre) of water.

Proceed in the same way as for *Currant jelly**.

Currant jelly I. GELÉE DE GROSEILLES—This jelly is prepared using two thirds of redcurrants and one third of white. 1 cup (125 grams) of raspberries are added as well to each 2 pounds (kilo) of currants.

Crush the currants and raspberries together, and strain them through a cloth which is wrung at both ends.

Dissolve the sugar, slightly moistened with hot water, allowing 2 pounds (1 kilo) for each quart (litre) of fruit juice. Cook to the *jelling* stage on a good heat.

Currant jelly II. GELÉE DE GROSEILLES—Add the currants and the raspberries to the sugar which has been dissolved in a pan allowing 2¼ cups (600 grams) of sugar for every 2 pounds (kilo) of fruit.

Allow the fruit to swell, keeping the pan on the corner of the stove. Then boil quickly until the *jelling* stage is reached. Strain the jelly and decant into pots.

Redcurrant juice can also be obtained in the following way: put the currants in a pan with the raspberries. Add a glass of water for every 2 pounds (kilo) of fruit. Keep on the edge of the stove, that is to say at a low temperature, until the skins burst and the juice comes out. Strain juice as described above.

Currant jelly III. GELÉE DE GROSEILLES—Put 8 pounds (4 kilos) of currants, half red and half white, in a copper pan with 2 pounds (1 kilo) of raspberries. Moisten with a quart (litre) of water, put on a lively heat. Stir with the skimmer to prevent the fruit sticking to the bottom of the pan.

Boil for 8 minutes.

Pour out the contents of the pan on to a horsehair sieve, set over a large basin. Add 2¼ cups (600 grams) of sugar to the sieved juice, for every 2 pounds (kilo) of juice.

Dissolve into a syrup. Strain through a silk tammy. Cook on a lively heat until the syrup reaches 28° (220°F.) on the syrup thermometer.

Bar-le-Duc currant jelly. GELÉE DE GROSEILLES DE BAR-LE-DUC—Choose large red or white currants. Pick them over and remove the pips with the help of a goose's feather cut to a sharp point. Put the currants on plates.

For 2 pounds (1 kilo) of fruit prepared in this way, make a syrup of 38° (250°F.).

Put the currants into the syrup. Boil gently and cook to 245°F.

Orange jelly. GELÉE D'ORANGES—Rub the zest of 10 or 12 fine oranges with ½ cup (100 grams) of lump sugar. Add this sugar, which has absorbed the fragrant oil of the oranges, to a quart (litre) of apple juice, obtained as described for *Apple jelly**.

Add to this mixture the strained juice of 10 or 12 oranges and 4½ cups (900 grams) of lump sugar. Add as well, but this is a matter of taste, 3½ ounces (100 grams) of crystallized orange peel, which has been soaked in lukewarm water and shredded into fine strips.

Cook the jelly to the *jelling* stage and finish in the manner already described.

Quince jelly. Gelée de coings—Cut the quinces, which should be chosen for ripeness, into slices, having peeled them first; put them into a basin of cold water as soon as sliced.

Then put them into a copper pan with water in the proportion of 1 quart (1 litre) of water for 1 pound (500 grams) of fruit. Cook them without stirring. As soon as the fruit is cooked turn them out on to a sieve and drain.

Put the juice obtained into a pan and add 3¼ cups (800 grams) of sugar for each quart (litre) of liquid. Dissolve the sugar. Cook on a lively heat until the jelly has reached the *jelling* stage.

JAMBE DE BOIS SOUP—This was the name given, in former times, to a clear soup whose principal ingredient was a piece of leg of beef on the bone. When it was ready, the meat fell away from the bone (it was as though a wooden leg was floating in the soup), hence its name.

JAMBON—See also **HAM.**

Jambon de Prague sous la cendre—Name which is often used in menus to describe ham (Prague, York or other) cooked in pastry.

JAPONAISE (A LA)—A number of different dishes are called *à la japonaise*. Most of them have this in common, that Chinese (in French, called Japanese) artichokes are included in the ingredients. *Francillon salad* is sometimes called *Salade à la japonaise*. It is made from mussels, potatoes and truffles, and was invented by Alexandre Dumas the younger. See SALADS, *Mixed* (*combination*) *salads*.

The term *japonaise* is also applied to an iced *bombe* made of peach ice cream filled with tea-flavoured mousse.

JARDINIÈRE (A LA)—The name given to a garnish which, by definition, is made of fresh vegetables, carrots and turnips (shaped with a ball-scoop, plain or fluted, cut with a hollow, tubular cutter, or diced), green peas, small kidney beans, French beans (diced or cut into lozenges), cauliflower, etc. Each of these vegetables is cooked separately, some boiled, others glazed. They are disposed round the main dish in separate groups. This garnish is served with roast, stewed or braised meat and pot-roasted poultry. See GARNISHES.

JASMIN—A plant containing a powerfully scented substance which is used in oriental cookery and confectionery.

JAY. Geai—This bird is regarded as a delicacy when it is young. The full-grown birds may also be eaten, but they must be boiled before roasting. These jays differ from the jays of North America. European jays have a pinkish brown body, white rump, black tail, white patch on wings, black and white crown feathers, blue and black wing coverts.

JELLY. Gelée—A jelly is, first of all, a clear meat or fish stock which solidifies when cold, by virtue of the gelatinous substances contained in it.

In former times, meat and fish jellies were prepared with hartshorn. Nowadays, these jellies are prepared in a more natural way, by including gelatinous bones in the stock or by adding a quantity of gelatine to it. It is this preparation which used to be called *aspic*.

Gelatine should not be used to excess in the preparation of meat jellies. Whenever possible it should be left out altogether, and this is possible where the stock is made from naturally gelatinous parts of the meat, such as veal knuckles and calves' feet, fresh bacon rind and poultry.

In jam-making, the name *jelly* is given to a preserve, made from fruit juice and sugar, which, by a careful control of temperature in cooking, is reduced to the required consistency. Jelly may be made from quinces, strawberries, raspberries, gooseberries, currants, apples and other fruits containing pectin. (See JAMS AND JELLIES.)

Certain sweets are also called jellies. These are made from various fruit juices with sugar and a variable quantity of gelatine added, or made by the old method, with calf's foot jelly.

Finally, jellies are made from fresh and dried vegetables, and cereals. These jellies are mainly used as invalid foods. Recipes for them are given further on in this section and elsewhere in this volume.

Clarification of jellies—Jelly stocks, whether they have a meat, fish or vegetable base, after they have been prepared according to the appropriate instructions and have been reduced, with or without gelatine, to the desired consistency, must always be clarified, to ensure perfect transparency.

Instructions for clarification of jelly stocks are given under ASPIC. Methods for clarifying meat, fish and vegetable stocks are also given in the article on CULINARY METHODS.

Chopped jelly. Gelée hachée—Chopped jelly is used as a garnish for cold dishes. To obtain the best results, place the jelly on a cloth spread out on the table. The cloth must first be dipped in cold water and wrung out thoroughly. Chop the jelly, more or less finely as required, with a large knife.

The chopped jelly must be arranged round the dish with a spoon and not, as is often done, squeezed through a forcing bag (pastry bag) as, treated in this way, the jelly tends to lose its colour and become cloudy.

Set pieces in jelly. Attelets de gelée—These set pieces, which were much used in former times to enhance the appearance of a cold dish, have now almost disappeared, although, on occasions, they still appear as a feature of a cold buffet.

Jelly triangles. Croûtons de gelée—These *croûtons** or triangles are used to provide a decorative border for a cold dish.

They are made from very stiff jelly which is first cut into strips about 2 inches wide and then shaped into elongated triangles to produce a dog's tooth effect.

The jelly may also be cut into other shapes, using pastry-cutters.

MEAT JELLIES. Gelées de viande:

Meat jelly stock—*Ingredients.* for 5 quarts (litres) of jelly:

Nourishing ingredients. 4 pounds (2 kilograms) beef (leg), 3 pounds (1 kilogram 500 grams) knuckle of veal, 3 pounds (1 kilogram 500 grams) veal and beef bones sawn in small pieces, 3 calves' feet (boned and blanched, with the bones ground), ½ pound (250 grams) bacon rinds.

Aromatic ingredients. 2 large carrots (250 grams), 2 medium-large onions (200 grams), 3 leeks (75 grams), 3 stalks of celery (50 grams), bouquet of herbs, salt and pepper.

Liquid. 8½ quarts (litres) of water.

Method. Put the beef, the veal (tied with string) and the bones in a pan and brown slightly in butter.

Transfer the meat and bones to a large stock-pot, brown them further with the carrots, onions and leeks.

Pour in the water.

Rinse the pan in which the meat and bones were first browned with a little water, and add the juice to the ingredients in the stock-pot. Bring it to the boil, skim it and add the calves' feet and bacon rinds, tied with string, and the bouquet of herbs. Season. Simmer gently for about 5 to 6 hours.

Strain this stock through muslin or a fine strainer. To turn it into aspic jelly, clarify it in the usual way.

Chicken jelly stock—Use the same method of preparation as for ordinary jelly adding, over and above the basic ingredients, a pullet, browned in the oven in advance or, alternatively, 3 pounds (1 kilogram 500 grams) of chicken carcase and giblets, also browned in advance in the oven.

When this jelly stock is intended as a garnish for galantine, the galantine takes the place of the pullet and should be cooked in the stock.

Fish jelly stock—This stock is made in the same way as concentrated fish stock, from the following basic ingredients and flavouring: for 5 quarts (litres): 1 pound (500 grams) fish bones and trimmings of turbot, brill or sole (U.S. flounder or haddock) or an equivalent quantity of fish such as whiting, gurnet, weever, etc.; 2 medium-sized onions (250 grams) finely sliced, mushroom peelings, celery, parsley roots, thyme, laurel.

This stock may be made with water but it is better made with fish *fumet** prepared in advance.

Fish jelly stock with red wine—More often than not, this stock is that used in cooking the various fish served in red wine jelly (salmon, salmon trout, brown trout, carp, etc.).

It may also be prepared like ordinary fish jelly, with the same basic ingredients and flavourings, to which should be added equal parts of red wine (Burgundy or Claret) and fish *fumet**.

Game jelly stock—The same method is used as that given for ordinary jelly. Use the same basic ingredients, adding about 2½ pounds (1 kilogram 200 grams) of game carcases and trimmings which have been previously browned in the oven. Add celery, thyme, bay leaf, and 8 to 10 juniper berries to the usual flavourings.

White jelly stock—Made from the same basic ingredients and flavourings as ordinary jelly, but without browning the meat or bones.

VEGETABLE JELLIES. GELÉES DE LÉGUMES—These jellies, which are prepared from various dried vegetables, cereals and fresh herbs, are used particularly as invalid foods. Pectose is a constituent of all these vegetables. In unripe fruit and vegetables, it is present in an insoluble state but, as the fruit or vegetable ripens, it changes into soluble pectin.

Fresh bean jelly. GELÉE DE FÈVES FRAÎCHES—Put some ripe, shelled beans in a saucepan. Add a little water, cover tightly and cook. From time to time, while they are cooking, add a little water so that the liquid level in the pan remains steady.

When the beans are cooked, turn them out into a sieve held over a dish. Press the vegetables gently to extract all the juice. The juice thus obtained makes a jelly with a very high albumen content.

In the same way, jellies can be extracted from small kidney-beans, French (string) beans, green peas and various other fresh vegetables.

DESSERT (SWEET) JELLIES. GELÉES D'ENTREMETS—Sweet jellies are made with a base of powdered gelatine or French leaf gelatine dissolved in water or (rarely) from calves' foot jelly plus sugar and water. For 1 quart of jelly, dissolve 2 tablespoons (2 ounces) of powdered gelatine in 1 cup cold water. Add 2 cups boiling water, ⅔ cup sugar, ¼ teaspoon salt. This base is flavoured either with liqueur or a dessert wine or a fruit juice.

For liqueur jellies, the liqueur is added after clarifying the jelly. ⅓ cup (1 decilitre) of liqueur is used to 3 cups (9 decilitres) of jelly stock.

Jellies made from juicy fruits. Use lemons, oranges, tangerines, pineapple, grapes, etc. The filtered juice of the fruit is added to the dissolved gelatine.

Muscovite jelly. GELÉE À LA MOSCOVITE—This jelly is made in the usual way, flavoured with liqueur or fruit juice, and poured into a hinged mould, called a 'Muscovite' mould. This mould must be completely airtight, as in the preparation of ice cream.

The special feature of this jelly is that it is covered with a thin coating of frost.

Red fruit jellies. Cherries, strawberries, raspberries, redcurrants, etc. Only very ripe fruit should be used. Put the fruit through a fine sieve. Add 1 to 1½ cups (3 decilitres) of water to 2 cups (500 grams) of juice, according to the pectin content of the fruit.

Filter this fruit juice, and add it in two stages to the calves' foot jelly or the gelatine, dissolved in advance, to ensure a jelly of the right consistency.

Russian jelly. GELÉE À LA RUSSE—This sweet is made like other jellies, with various flavourings. It is whisked on ice until it begins to set. It must be poured into a mould as quickly as possible, and put on ice to set. Turn out on a napkin.

Stone fruit. Apricots, nectarines, peaches, plums, etc., are often used as a garnish with different fruit jellies.

The jelly itself may also be made from these fruits.

Method. Dip the fruit in boiling water and peel. Cook it slowly in syrup. Leave the fruit in the syrup until cold. Make the jelly from the syrup and clarify in the usual way.

Generally, fruit jellies should be flavoured with kirsch, maraschino or some other liqueur.

Swedish fruit jelly. GELÉE DE FRUITS À LA SUÉDOISE—Fruit jelly, garnished after it is put in the mould, with various kinds of fruit which have been cooked in syrup and thoroughly drained.

Various wine jellies. Champagne, Frontignan, Madeira, Marsala, port, sherry, etc. 1½ cups (3 decilitres) of wine should be used to every 3⅓ cups (7 decilitres) of jelly stock.

PASTE JELLIES OR PÂTES (Confectionery)—These confections are made by mixing fruit or flower pulp with sugar.

Apple paste jellies. PÂTE DE POMMES—'Choose good, sound, cooking apples, peel them and remove core. Put into a pan with water and cook, turning with a wooden spoon from time to time, until they have been softened by the cooking. Remove, strain the juice into a bowl leaving the apples in the sieve until cold, then rub the pulp through a sieve, put on the fire and reduce (cook down) by half. Remove from heat, transfer from the pan into an earthenware or a glazed china bowl—a precaution which cannot be stressed too much.

'Clarify the same amount of sugar, cook it to small crack degree (310°F.), take the pan off the fire, pour in the apple pulp, stir the mixture thoroughly with a wooden spoon and place on a low heat. Allow to heat until the mixture shivers very slightly, stirring all the time, until you begin to see the bottom of the pan. Then proceed to pour into moulds as described (below).' (*Le Confiseur Moderne.*)

Apricot paste jellies. PÂTE D'ABRICOTS—'Choose sound, ripe apricots, stone them, put into a pan with water, stand on the fire and, as soon as boiling is established, remove and drain. Rub through a sieve at once to extract all pulp, collecting it in a bowl. You can throw away the skin as being useless. Weigh the pulp and evaporate it to reduce by half. Take out of the pan and transfer into an earthenware or china bowl. Clarify the same quantity of sugar as you have pulp and cook to small crack degree (310°F.). Pour the pulp into it, stirring with a wooden spoon. When the mixture is smooth, stand the pan on a low fire again stirring all the time until the bottom of the pan can be seen easily, then remove from heat.

'Put moulds of different shapes (round, heart-shaped, etc.) on a tinned metal sheet, fill them with the apricot and sugar confection, taking care to smooth the surface with a knife. When the moulds are filled, dust them with sugar and put them into a fairly hot drying-oven. Two days later take the confections out of the mould, turn them out on to a sieve, dust with sugar on top, leave in a drying-oven for a day, then store in tins with well-fitting lids, placing the confections in rows and putting a sheet of white paper between each layer.' (*Le Confiseur Moderne.*)

Cherry paste jellies. PÂTE DE CERISES—'Choose 12 to 15 pounds of very ripe red cherries. Remove stalks and stones, putting them into a bowl as you do so, then transfer into a pan and put on the fire. Bring them to the boil several times, stirring with a wooden spoon. Rub through a sieve to extract all pulp, collecting it in a bowl. Then reduce (boil down) by half in a pan, pour into a china bowl and weigh the pulp. Clarify the same weight of sugar, cook to ball degree (250°F.), add the cherry pulp and proceed as described in the recipe for *Apricot jellies.*' (*Le Confiseur Moderne.*)

Grape paste jellies. PÂTE DE VERJUS—'Pick good green grapes off the bunches and put into a silver basin with a little water. Bring to the boil on a high flame. When the grapes swell and burst strain the juice into a bowl, leaving the grapes to drip. Then rub them through a sieve, collecting the pulp in a bowl. Put it into a pan, set on a low flame, reduce (boil down) by half and weigh. Weigh out the same amount of sugar, cook to small ball degree (240°F.), take off the fire, pour in the grape pulp and add four ounces of apple pulp per pound of grape pulp. Mix well and proceed to make the jellies as described above ' (*Le Confiseur Moderne.*)

Greengage paste jellies. PÂTE DE REINES-CLAUDES—'Pick the greengages when they are very ripe. Stone, put into a pan with a little water, set on the fire and bring to the boil once. Strain the juice, leaving the greengages on the sieve to cool. When they are cold, rub them through the sieve, weigh the pulp and, allowing the same amount of sugar, proceed as described above.' (*Le Confiseur Moderne.*)

Mirabelle paste jellies. PÂTE DE MIRABELLES—'Choose sound mirabelles, peel, stone them and put into cold water. Place them on the fire in a pan, stirring with a wooden spoon until they are cooked. Drain, leave in a sieve until cold, then rub them through, reduce the quantity by half by evaporation, and pour from the pan into a china bowl. Weigh the pulp. Weigh out the same amount of sugar, cook it to small crack degree (310°F.), pour the pulp into it, stirring with a wooden spoon to mix, and proceed to make the jellies as described in the recipe for *Apricot paste jellies.*' (*Le Confiseur Moderne.*)

Peach paste jellies. PÂTE DE PÊCHES—'Proceed as above using the following ingredients: 4 pounds of peaches and 3 pounds of sugar.' (*Le Confiseur Moderne.*)

Pear paste jellies. PÂTE DE POIRES—'Prepare as *Apple paste jellies*, using the pulp of juicy pears.' (*Le Confiseur Moderne.*)

Quince paste jellies. PÂTE DE COINGS—'Choose very ripe quinces, cut into quarters, remove the skins and pips, put into a pan with water and place on the fire to soften. Drain, and proceed as described in the recipe for *Apricot paste jellies.*' (*Le Confiseur Moderne.*)

Raspberry paste jellies. PÂTE DE FRAMBOISES—'Choose ripe raspberries, rub through a sieve to extract the pulp. Put on the fire and cook down to reduce this pulp by half. Weigh, add the same amount (by weight) of sugar, cooked to ball degree (250°F.), and proceed to make the jellies as described above.

'*Note.* Strawberry jellies are made in the same way as raspberry jellies.' (*Le Confiseur Moderne.*)

Violet paste jellies. PÂTE DE VIOLETTES—'Take 2 pounds of clean violets, reduce to pulp by bruising in a mortar and add the juice of two lemons.

'Cook 2 pounds of sugar to ball degree (250°F.), take the pan off the fire, add the bruised violets and a pound of apple jelly, mix, and proceed to make the jellies as described above.

'*Note.* Various other flowers, such as orange blossom, roses, etc., can be made into jellies in a similar manner.' (*Le Confiseur Moderne.*)

JERBOA. GERBOISE—Small rodent about the size of a squirrel. It is to be found in all parts of Europe. It is prepared for the table like squirrel. Found in south-western U.S.A. and Mexico, under the name of *kangeroo-rat* or *pouched mouse.*

JERUSALEM ARTICHOKE. TOPINAMBOUR—Plant originating in North America and imported into France at the beginning of the seventeenth century. Jerusalem artichokes, also known as *artichauts du Canada* and *poires de terre*, were not much liked at the start, but were rehabilitated, like the potato, by Parmentier.

They are at their best on the borderline of winter and spring.

Jerusalem artichokes are firm in consistency. They resemble real artichokes to some extent in flavour and may be substituted for them in certain preparations. They have a pleasant taste, but one that soon palls.

Jerusalem artichokes à l'anglaise. TOPINAMBOURS À L'ANGLAISE—Peel the artichokes, divide them in quarters and cut the quarters to look like 'pigeon's eggs'. Cook gently in butter. Season and stir in a few tablespoons of rather thin *Béchamel sauce* (see SAUCE). Simmer for a few minutes. Serve in a deep dish.

Before being simmered in butter the artichokes may be lightly blanched in salted water.

Jerusalem artichokes in butter. TOPINAMBOURS AU BEURRE—Cut to look like 'pigeon's eggs'. Cook in butter like *Château potatoes* (see POTATOES). Serve in a deep dish.

Jerusalem artichokes à la crème. TOPINAMBOURS À LA CRÈME—The artichokes are cut to look like 'pigeon's eggs' and simmered gently in butter. When they are almost cooked, cover with boiling fresh cream. Finish cooking as slowly as possible. Season.

Add at the last moment a few tablespoons of fresh

cream. *Jerusalem artichokes à la crème* may also be prepared with rather thin *Béchamel sauce* (see SAUCE).

Fried Jerusalem artichokes. TOPINAMBOURS EN FRITOT—Cut the artichokes in rather thick slices; stew them in butter and season them. Just before serving, dip them in light batter and fry in smoking hot fat or oil.

Purée of Jerusalem artichokes. PURÉE DE TOPINAMBOURS—Peel the artichokes, cut in thin slices and simmer them in butter and a little water in a covered pan. Rub through a sieve. Heat this purée and add to it a sufficient quantity of potatoes to give it the required consistency. Add a few tablespoons of boiling hot milk (or cream) and 2 or 3 tablespoons of fresh butter.

Salad of Jerusalem artichokes. SALADE DE TOPINAMBOURS—Made like *Potato salad* (see SALAD).

Soufflé of Jerusalem artichokes. SOUFFLÉ DE TOPINAMBOURS—Made, using purée of Jerusalem artichokes, like *Potato soufflé* (see SOUFFLÉ).

JERUSALEM MELON. ABDELAVIS—Ordinary Egyptian melon, the sweet, juicy and succulent flesh of which is much valued. It possesses the property of quenching thirst. Its seeds are used for making sedative and tranquillising drinks. Its flesh is used in the manufacture of excellent ices, bombes, etc. It is eaten like melon.

JESSE—A fish to be found in almost all the rivers of Europe, rather similar in shape to the carp. It turns yellowish when cooked. It is fairly delicate but has too many bones. Jesse is cooked in the same way as carp.

JÉSUITE—A small pastry made of left-overs of *Flaky pastry dough* (see DOUGH).

Method. Roll out the dough. Cut it into lengths of 6 inches wide. Spread half the length with almond paste. Cover with the remaining length. Sprinkle with *praline**. Cut into triangles. Bake in a moderate oven (375°F.).

JÉSUS—A type of pork-liver sausage made in Switzerland and the Franche-Comté.

JOHANNISBEERKUCHEN (German cookery)—A red-currant tart *à l'allemande*. See TARTS, *Fruit tart à l'allemande*.

JOHANNISBERG—A village of Hesse-Nassau, in Prussia, where two special vines are grown, the large Riesling and the small Riesling. A very famous dry white wine is made from the grapes of these vines.

John Dory

JOHN DORY. SAINT-PIERRE—Fish, also called Dorée and known to the French as *Saint-Pierre*. It is very oddly shaped, oval in form, and very flat, with a very large spiny head. Its skin is very thick and it is covered with very small scales.

The first dorsal fin consists of nine spines held together by a membrane which ends in a very long filament.

Noticeable on flanks of the fish is a large blackish mark, round in shape, surrounded by a light grey circle.

The flesh of the John Dory is very delicate and rivals the turbot and sole. In U.S.A. the Atlantic fish, the *Porgy*, called *Scup* in New England, could be used for John Dory recipes.

It may be cooked whole, and in this form may be grilled, braised or poached in a *court-bouillon**, but most often it is filleted and then cooked in the same way as fillets of *brill**, *turbot** or *sole**.

The John Dory is also used as an ingredient of *bouillabaisse*.

Fillets of John Dory Pierre Chapelle. FILETS DE SAINT-PIERRE PIERRE CHAPELLE—Fillet a raw medium-sized John Dory. Season the fillets with salt and pepper and coat with egg and breadcrumbs. Use the skin and bones to prepare a white wine fish stock. Use this stock for a rice pilaf made of $\frac{1}{2}$ cup (125 grams) of rice tossed in butter with chopped onions, and cooked (in the stock) for 18 to 20 minutes. In another pot cook 4 tablespoons (50 grams) of chopped onions gently in butter. Add 4-6 large tomatoes, peeled, squeezed (to remove seeds) and chopped. Season with salt, pepper, garlic and 1 teaspoon of curry. Cook together for 20 minutes. Cook the fillets of fish in butter. Set them on a long dish on top of the pilaf. Surround with the tomatoes cooked in curry.

JOINTING. DÉPEÇAGE—The action of cutting up meat, poultry, etc. (see CARVING).

JOINVILLE (A LA)—The name of a special dish made with fillets of sole. See SOLE, *Fillets of sole Joinville*.

Joinville pastry. GÂTEAU DE JOINVILLE—*Ingredients*. 2 cups (250 grams) sieved flour; 1 cup (200 grams) butter; milk, sufficient to moisten the dough; pinch of salt.

Method. Using these ingredients, make a dough as for flaky pastry *galette**. Leave it to stand for a time.

Roll out the dough and cut out two squares of equal size. Spread one of these squares with raspberry jam and cover with the other square. Press the edges together and crimp them. Prick the top of the pastry. Do not brush with egg. Bake in the oven (400°F.) for 25 to 30 minutes. When the pastry is ready, take it out of the oven and sprinkle with sugar.

JUDAS-TREE. GAINIER—Judean tree which also grows in southern Europe, North America and Asia. Its strongly scented flowers are pickled in vinegar like capers.

JUICE. JUS—The French use the term *jus* in a somewhat wider sense than the English 'juice'.

Jus is used:

(1) As in English, of the juice squeezed out of food-stuffs, whether animal or vegetable, e.g., herbal juice, orange juice, lemon juice, meat juice, etc.

(2) Of the gravy of a roast made by diluting the juices of the roasting pan or dripping pan (in the case of spit roasts), with clear soup, water or any other suitable liquid, and then boiling it until all the goodness in the pan has been absorbed into the stock.

(3) Of meat juice, extracted by pressing slices of lightly grilled beef in a special press. This juice is taken as a tonic.

(4) Of *coulis** or brown stock, thickened or clear, of various kinds of meat, especially veal. This type of *jus* is really a gravy.

Recipes are given under STOCKS, *Veal stock*.

Apple juice. JUS DE POMMES—This is made from apple pulp. See APPLE, *Apple Pectin*.

Orange, Seville orange or lemon juices. JUS D'ORANGE, BIGARADE, CITRON—These juices have many uses in the kitchen, especially in confectionery and the preparation of sweets. They are extracted by squeezing the fruit either by hand or by means of a squeezer. The flavour of all these juices is accentuated and enhanced if a little grated rind is added before straining.

Pineapple juice. JUS D'ANANAS—Pound fresh pineapple pulp in a mortar. While pounding, mix in a few tablespoons of plain sugar syrup.

Strain the pulp through muslin. This juice, like all other fruit juices, is used in the preparation of sweets.

Red fruit juices. JUS DE FRUITS ROUGES—Made from strawberries, raspberries, redcurrants or cherries. Rub the raw fruit through a fine sieve.

Herb juices. JUS D'HERBES VERTES—Made from various raw herbs (watercress, chervil, parsley, tarragon, etc.) pounded in a mortar and strained through cloth.

Meat juice. JUS DE VIANDE—This is extracted by putting slices of lightly grilled beef into a special press. The juice dripping from the press must be collected in a cup standing in a bowl of hot water.

Jujube: (a) Flower; (b) Fruit

JUJUBE—The fruit of the jujube tree of Syrian origin. It grows in warm climates including the South of France. This ovoid fruit is about the size of an olive, covered with a smooth, leathery, red skin. The pulp is yellowish, mild and sweet. It has a long stone.

Dried jujubes are used to sweeten medicines. They are among the fruits soothing to the throat and chest. They are used in infusions, decoctions and in the form of paste, etc.

JULIENNE—This term is used in French cookery to designate:

(1) A clear vegetable soup made from clear consommé. To this stock is added a mixture of finely shredded vegetables cooked very slowly in butter until they are tender (see SOUPS AND BROTHS, *Consommé julienne*).

(2) Any foodstuffs coarsely or finely shredded. Thus one may say *julienne* of breast of chicken, *julienne* of mushrooms, *julienne* of truffles, *julienne* of gherkins, etc.

JUNIPER BERRIES. GENIÈVRE—The berries of a bush which grows wild in woods and mountain gullies.

Juniper berries are used to add flavour to marinades. They are also used as seasoning with certain foods (sauerkraut, thrushes, blackbirds, etc.).

Juniper berries are also used in the distillation of gin.

JUNIPER WINE. GENEVRETTE (VIN DE GENIÈVRE)—A medicinal drink made from juniper berries. See BEVERAGES, *Juniper Hippocras*.

This name is also given to a wine which used to be made in the Gâtinais district from absinthe and juniper seeds.

JUPITER'S BEARD. JOUBARBE—A name given to several plants with fleshy leaves. Among these are the houseleek or wild artichoke (see ARTICHOKE), and the white stonecrop which is edible, its leaves being mainly eaten in salad.

JURANÇON—A small town in the Basses-Pyrénées, ¾ mile from Pau. A very fine wine is made there which, it is said, was greatly prized by King Henry IV of France.

History, or rather legend, relates that when the king was born, his grandfather, the King of Navarre, after having rubbed the baby's lips with a clove of garlic, made him swallow a few drops of *Jurançon*. The royal infant having come through this gastronomic, or rather bacchic, ordeal very creditably, his grandfather, in a frenzy of enthusiasm, cried: 'You are a real Béarnais.'

White *Jurançon* is a full-blooded and intoxicating wine. With age, it acquires a strong flavour of Madeira.

A red *Jurançon* is also made, but it is less popular than the white. These wines are made by mixing the grapes of several different vines in the vat. Strangely enough, the grapes of the *Jurançon* vine are not among them.

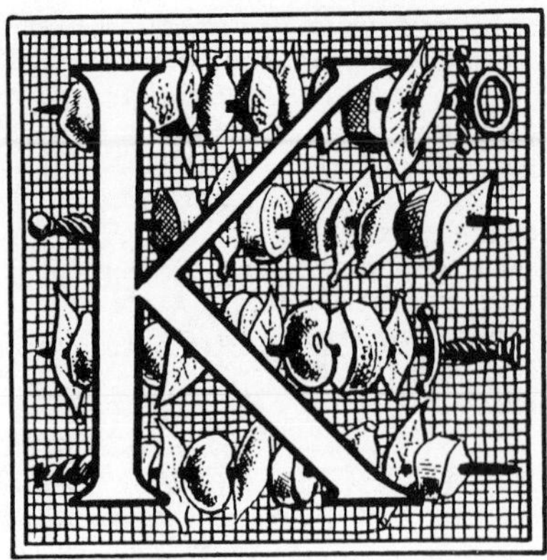

KALTSCHALE (Russian cookery)—This is a fruit salad moistened, more liberally than is common in France, with liqueur, wine or syrup.

Method. Take a selection of mixed fresh fruit such as apricots, pineapple, peaches, strawberries, raspberries, melon and water-melon. Where necessary, skin the fruit. Then cut it all up into small, fairly thick slices. Put the fruit into a silver bowl pressed down into a bucket of crushed ice. Bring to the boil a bottle of champagne, a pint of red Bordeaux wine, half a cup of Madeira, with 2 or 3 tablespoons of sugar and a pinch of ground cinnamon. Chill this mixture on ice and then pour it over the fruit. Chill again and serve.

Kaltschale with strawberry purée. KALTSCHALE À LA PURÉE DE FRAISES—Embed a silver bowl in crushed ice. Fill it with fruit as indicated above. Make a purée of strawberries as follows: rub through a fine sieve 2 pounds (1 kilo) of very ripe strawberries and ½ pound (250 grams) of redcurrants. Dilute this purée with a quart (litre) light sugar syrup and half a bottle of champagne previously brought to the boil and chilled. Pour over the fruit and serve chilled.

KANGAROO. KANGOUROU—The flesh of this Australian mammal is edible.

KASHA (Russian Cookery)—Kasha is the Russian for cooked buckwheat.

There are several ways of preparing buckwheat, all easy and successful.

Ingredients. 1 pound (500 grams) buckwheat, 1 teaspoon salt, 1 ounce (30 grams) butter.

(1) Sort the buckwheat to pick out any black grains—these are not bad but still covered with the hard husk which people find unsightly. Roast the buckwheat in a frying-pan, without grease or liquid, until the grains acquire a light golden colour. Put into an oven-proof dish, season with salt, add an ounce of butter or more, and pour in just enough boiling water to cover. (The amount of butter may be increased—there is even a popular saying in Russia which proclaims that buckwheat 'can't be spoilt by too much butter'.) Bake in a slow oven for 2½ or 3 hours. It should have a thin crust but the grains should fall apart easily.

(2) Using the same proportions, put the buckwheat in a double saucepan, add salt and melted butter, put in enough cold water to cover, stir and cook on a low heat for 3 hours.

(3) Wash the buckwheat, scald with boiling water and immediately pour off the liquid. Put in a saucepan with salt and butter, cover with boiling water, bring to the boil, stir and transfer into a double saucepan and cook for 3 hours.

KASHA CROÛTONS (Russian cookery)—

Method. Soak 1 pound (500 grams) of crushed buckwheat in warm water until it forms a thick porridge. Season this porridge with salt and put it in a large earthenware pot.

Put it in a hot oven and bake for 2 hours. Remove the thick crust formed on the surface. Scoop out all the porridge not sticking to the sides of the pan. Put it in a bowl. Add a piece of butter about the size of an egg. Mix well with a spatula. Press the porridge between two saucepan lids to make a 'dough' ⅛ inch thick. Cut it into shapes with a plain, round pastry-cutter. Brown the rounds in clarified butter.

Serve with the soup, separately. These buckwheat croûtons are served with *Shchi*, *Borshch* and other soups.

Kasha with mushrooms. KASHA AUX CHAMPIGNONS—Prepare the *buckwheat kasha* as indicated above, adding to it, before putting it in the oven, sliced mushrooms tossed in butter.

Serve in the cooking pot. Serve fresh butter separately.

Kasha with Parmesan. KASHA DE SARRASIN AU PARMESAN—Make the buckwheat porridge as indicated above. When it is baked, remove the crust from the top and use part of the soft porridge to line a buttered boat-shaped silver dish, or a deep gratin dish. Sprinkle the porridge with grated Parmesan cheese and melted butter. Spread another layer of porridge on top and sprinkle with grated Parmesan and melted butter. Fill the dish with layers of porridge, grated Parmesan and melted butter. When it is full, smooth the surface, sprinkle with Parmesan and melted butter and brown in the oven. Serve melted butter and rich *estouffade** gravy separately.

Polish kasha. KASHA POLONAIS—Pick over ½ pound (250 grams) of barley. Blanch and hull it. Simmer it gently in 3 quarts plus 1 cup of milk (3 litres) and a piece of butter about the size of an egg. Stir until the barley is fully cooked. Remove it from the stove. Add ½ pound (250 grams) of butter, 6 eggs beaten as for an omelette and half a glass (cup) of sour cream.

Put this mixture in a buttered Charlotte mould. Bake in a hot oven. Wrap the mould in a napkin and serve the kasha in it. Serve double cream separately.

Semolina kasha. KASHA DE SEMOULE—Pour 1 pound (500 grams) of Smolensk semolina on a slab. Beat 2 eggs as for omelette and pour over the semolina. Mix well so that the semolina is thoroughly moistened. Leave the mixture to dry in a very moderate oven. Put through a food mill or strainer.

Boil in a pan 2 quarts plus ¾ cup of milk with ½ pound (250 grams) of butter. Pour in the semolina. Season. Simmer gently, stirring frequently. Put into a silver serving dish and brown in a hot oven. Serve melted butter separately.

Like *Polish kasha,* this dish is a kind of hasty-pudding.

KEBAB (Turkish cookery)—This name is used in Turkey for various dishes whose principal feature is skewered meat.

The skewers are of metal or wood. The meat—mutton, lamb or buffalo—is cut into squares, seasoned with pepper, salt, thyme and powdered bay leaves. Square pieces of mutton fat are placed on the skewer between the pieces of meat. In Turkey, mutton fat takes the place of bacon. The skewered meat is grilled over hot embers, and is served plain, with lemon or with various garnishes.

Kebab galette. KEBAB EN GALETTE—Cut into thick squares a boned shoulder of lamb. Steep the pieces in milk and boil them. Place them on skewers with squares of green pepper, tomato, onion and bay leaves between. Sprinkle with powdered thyme. Grill over hot embers.

Take the pieces off the skewers. Arrange them on a *galette** (thin cake) made of wheaten flour. Cover with finely sliced onions previously browned in butter. Moisten with brown gravy and cover with another wheaten *galette,* which should be piping hot.

Shish-Kebab, which is the Turkish name for skewered mutton cooked in this way, is also served with pilaf of rice or with chick peas and raw finely sliced onions.

Tchevir me kebab—Place on an upright spit some thin slices of mutton, alternating with pieces of mutton fat. This spit turns itself in front of an upright grill.

As the meat is cooked the pieces are slit lengthwise and taken off the spit one after the other. This is served with yoghourt, pilaf of rice, etc.

KÉFIR—Fermented milk of Caucasian origin. Strictly it should be made of camel's milk but, in practice, it is made from cow's milk, skimmed or not according to taste. Fermentation is induced by means of *kéfir* bacteria. When the bacteria have been added to the milk it is put in bottles with patent stoppers and kept for a period in a hot cupboard. After a day, mild *kéfir* is obtained. This is slightly laxative. After two days, medium *kéfir* is obtained. This is not laxative. Strong *kéfir* is obtained after three days of fermentation. It is slightly constipating and contains 2.5 per cent of alcohol.

Kéfir has a rather sour taste. It is frothy and contains a greater or lesser proportion of alcohol according to the period of fermentation. The casein shows signs of peptorisation in the form of thin flakes. *Kéfir* is easily digestible and is often recommended for invalids.

KEFTES-KEBABS (Turkish cookery)—Made from small slices of raw meat (mutton, veal or buffalo), skewered, grilled and served with pilaf of rice and the gravy of roast meat.

KETCHUP or CATSUP—Strictly, ketchup is a condiment rather than a sauce in the proper sense of the word. It is manufactured commercially and much used in England and North America. It is also made in home kitchens.

Mushroom ketchup or catsup. KETCHUP AUX CHAMPIGNONS—Put in a salting jar layers of fresh sliced mushrooms (about ⅓ inch in depth) and sprinkle each layer with table salt, pepper and allspice.

Leave the mushrooms in the salt for 5 or 6 days in a cool place.

Press the mushrooms to extract all the juice. Boil this juice. Season with pepper, thyme, bay, ginger, marjoram and a little tomato paste.

Leave it to cool. Filter and bottle.

Tomato ketchup. KETCHUP AUX TOMATES—Cut up 8 pounds tomatoes (unpeeled), 6 medium onions, 2 red sweet peppers and 2 cloves garlic. Cover with water and boil gently until the vegetables are soft. Strain through a cloth or sieve. Tie in a bag 1 hot red pepper, 2 bay leaves, 1 tablespoon each celery and mustard seed, 1 teaspoon of peppercorns and 1 stick cinnamon, and add with 1 tablespoon of salt to the juice. Boil down the juice by half, stirring frequently. Add ½ cup brown sugar, ½ cup white sugar and 2 cups vinegar and continue simmering 15 to 20 minutes or until sauce is thickened to the desired point. Seal in hot sterilized jars or bottles. This makes approximately 5 quarts.

KETMIE—A plant, the fruit of which is edible and known as *okra, gumbo* or *ladies' fingers.* See OKRA.

KHLODNIK (Polish and Russian cookery)—A kind of iced soup, very popular in Poland, its country of origin, and in Russia.

It is made as follows:

Wash and blanch 4 large handfuls of tender beetroot leaves. Chop finely. Add to these a handful of finely chopped, blanched and drained chervil, tarragon, chive, fennel and shallot.

Put these herbs in a silver dish embedded in chopped ice, and moisten them with a pint (½ litre) of cucumber brine. Add the same amount of kvass, a drink very popular in Russia (see KVASS). Just before serving, season the soup with salt and a pinch of fine sugar. Add the following garnishes: 48 crayfish tails; 1 pound (500 grams) of diced, braised sturgeon, 4 or 5 spoonfuls of diced, fresh cucumber. Add 1½ cups (3 decilitres) of sieved sour cream and one or two pieces of ice. Serve separately quartered hard boiled eggs, sprinkled with finely chopped chervil and fennel.

KID. CHEVREAU, CABRI—Young goat, slaughtered before being weaned.

The meat of the kid is not very substantial but it is not unwholesome, as some people believe.

In butchery sucking kids 30 to 40 days old are called *tétards,* the others, 3 or 4 months old, are called *broutards.*

All the methods of preparation given for very young lamb are applicable to kid (see LAMB). As the meat is rather tasteless it has to be well seasoned.

KIDNEYS. ROGNON—Pig's and sheep's kidneys have the shape of a haricot (shell) bean; like those of man, calf and ox kidneys are multi-lobed.

Calf's and lamb's kidneys, which are included in offal (variety meats), are delicate and sought-after foodstuffs. Pig's kidneys, a little richer and with a sweetish taste, are less well thought of; ox and sheep's kidneys are tough and often taste of urine.

Ox (beef) kidney. ROGNON DE BOEUF—Ox (beef) kidney is generally served sautéed. It can be prepared in all the ways indicated for *Calf's kidneys.* See OFFAL OR VARIETY MEATS, *Ox and calf's kidneys.*

In England, ox kidney is used for making *Beefsteak and kidney pies** and *Beefsteak and kidney puddings* (see PUDDINGS).

Cock's kidneys. ROGNON DE COQ—These are used mainly as an ingredient in garnishes, but they may also be used, cooked in various ways, as hot hors-d'oeuvre or small entrées, in the same way as *cock's combs**.

To prepare a garnish, wash firm, white cock's kidneys in several waters. Put them into a small saucepan with water, a pinch of salt, a little butter and a few drops of lemon juice.

Start cooking over a good heat; as soon as the liquid begins to boil put the pot on the side of the stove (turn the heat very low) and cook, covered, for 10 to 12 minutes, taking care to avoid boiling.

Use according to the recipe.

Kidneys sautéed with Madeira. ROGNONS SAUTÉS AU MADÈRE—Calf's or sheep's kidneys sliced and sautéed in butter. Madeira is poured into the cooking pan and this sauce is diluted with *Demi-glace sauce* (see SAUCE). See OFFAL or VARIETY MEATS.

KILKIS (NORWEGIAN ANCHOVIES)—A tiny fish found mainly in northern European waters. It is preserved like the anchovy. Tallinn is the chief centre for the processing of these fish, which are very well liked in Russia. They are served as an hors-d'oeuvre. See HORS-D'OEUVRE, *Hot hors-d'oeuvre*.

KIMALI BUREK (Turkish and Russian cookery). KIMALI BEURRECK—A kind of stuffed pancake rolled into the shape of a cigar, filled with forcemeat or some other filling, and fried. See HORS-D'OEUVRE, *Hot hors-d'oeuvre*, *Beurrecks à la turque*.

KINGFISH. TASSARD—A type of large fish, *scombe-romerus*, found in all oceans. There are many different species.

The flesh is firm and white and it is prepared in the same way as tunny fish.

KIPPER—These, strictly called *kippered herrings*, are herrings which are slit open and smoked.

Kippers are very good to eat. They are usually grilled and served with melted butter or *Maître d'hôtel butter* (see BUTTER, *Compound butters*). They can also be boiled.

See HERRINGS.

KIRSCH—This spirit, with a very strong bouquet, is chiefly manufactured in eastern France and in Germany. It is distilled from ripe fermented wild cherries.

Kirsch is highly prized by connoisseurs. It is used a great deal for flavouring in confectionery and sweets.

The finest kirsch comes from Alsace. Black Forest kirsch also enjoys a great reputation.

KISEL—A Russian sweet made from all kinds of berries. It is served in a Charlotte mould with thick cream and can be eaten either hot or cold.

KISSING-CRUST. BAISURE—A bakery term describing the pale soft crust where one loaf has touched another in baking.

KITCHEN EQUIPMENT. BATTERIE DE CUISINE—This term covers all the utensils used in the kitchen for the preparation and cooking of food. These utensils, of various shapes, are made of copper or other metals, such as nickel, aluminium or bimetals, silver-plated copper, iron, cast-iron, bronze, sheet-iron, wrought iron, etc., of special fire-proof earthenware or china, or in hardened glass, such as pyrex, which, of course, is also fire-proof.

We know very little about the first kitchen utensils. The Egyptians, the Assyrians and the Persians principally used earthenware and brazen vessels, big-bellied in shape, with and without handles. They also used the spit and, for cooking cakes and biscuits, they had baking dishes rather like those we use nowadays.

The Jews did not generally use earthenware vessels for cooking purposes; most of their pots and pans were made of metal. To extract the meat from the big pots in which food destined to be offered to God was prepared, they used a big two-pronged fork, the forerunner of our table fork, which did not make its appearance until the seventeenth century.

The Greeks, for their culinary preparations, used greatly improved bronze, iron or silver vessels. They also had some in earthenware. Almost all these vessels were of conical shape and therefore not very deep. They were almost always provided with lids and either handles or detachable rings.

Among the principal kitchen utensils used by the Greeks was the *chytra*, a sort of earthenware marmite used for cooking meats and stews. It was apparently in these utensils that the famous Spartan broths were prepared. Or perhaps this almost historical dish was made in the *kakkabi*, which, too, was a fairly large three-legged pot. The Greeks also had another pot, which can be considered as the prototype of the earthenware casserole which we use nowadays for the *pot-au-feu*. This, filled with cooked fruit (probably cooked in wine and sweetened with honey), was carried to the altar of the god, Bacchus, on the third day of the feast of Anthesteria, the famous festival in honour of Dionysius.

The Greeks also had bronze casseroles which in shape resemble those now in use. For cooking meat and fish cut in pieces they had a kind of pan similar to the type which in France today is called *coupe lyonnaise* and which the Greeks called *têganon* (Mod. *tigáni*—frying pan). In order to place all these metal or earthenware receptacles on the fire, the Greeks used a triangular support, the tripod that is still in use to this day in country kitchens.

Kitchen utensils used by the Romans were similar to those of the Greeks. It is also a known fact that Greek cooks brought the art of cooking to Rome.

The Romans, sensual, voluptuous people, with a great love of luxury in all things, made kitchen utensils not only of bronze but also of silver. Among the treasures of Bosco-Reale, which are kept at the Louvre, various kitchen utensils of this type can be seen.

Kitchen utensils used by the Romans included the *clibanus*, an earthenware utensil, with holes pierced in it, which was used for cooking various dishes, mainly pastry, in hot ashes, *craticula*, a grill for cooking meat and fish on the glowing embers, and the *apala*, a sort of pie-dish, with cavities of varying sizes hollowed out in it used for cooking eggs, which seems to prove that the Romans knew all about poached eggs.

The Gauls and the Gallo-Romans had earthenware and metal kitchen utensils somewhat similar to those of the Greeks and the Romans; at any rate, Greek and Roman cookery by this time had become much simpler. The Celts knew nothing about the refinements and sumptuousness of cookery of the days of Imperial Rome and, consequently, their pots and pans were entirely rudimentary.

It is only with the coming of the Merovingian era that kitchen utensils began again to improve. Some specimens of these utensils have survived until our days, and we can see for ourselves the magnificent bronze vessels in which the dishes which were then popular were prepared.

From reading Charlemagne's *Capitularies*, it seems

evident that in the eighth and ninth centuries French kitchen utensils were improved still further.

This improvement of cooking utensils went even further from the twelfth to the sixteenth centuries. After successive crusades a great number of richly worked metal utensils—*ewers, salvers, cauldrons*—were brought to Europe and served as models for the artisans of the West in the manufacture of magnificent utensils.

In French museums and private collections can be seen, for example, cooking pots in engraved bronze or artistically beaten copper ware, wrought iron pot-hangers, which are veritable works of art, magnificent kitchen forks, which in those days were called *roables* in French, turning gridirons, big-bellied pots and kettles, the *acoste-pot* (old version of the *accote-pot*, 'tilt-pot'), and other kitchen implements which are all excellent examples of ironmongery.

To show what a collection of kitchen utensils in the sixteenth-century manor house was like, we cannot do better than reproduce an extract from an inventory made in 1530 at the château of La Mothe-Chandenier:

'In the kitchen of the aforesaid château of La Mothe:

'18 silver dishes and 18 *escuelles* (medieval version of *écuelle*—bowl) bearing the coat of arms which the late Master and the late Lady brought with them from Javarzay when they came here to the château of La Mothe.

'The following utensils were found in the said kitchen:

'Six large dishes, three small and ten bowls, all utensils engraved with the late Master's coat of arms;

'One pot-hanger;

'Two beaten iron cookers;

'One big iron spit;

'Then two more smaller spits;

'One iron fish slice, one grid;

'*Item*, one big cooking pot (marmite);

'*Item*, one big cast-iron pot with perforations;

'*Item*, another iron pot of one seillée (a measure of capacity);

'*Item*, two big three-seillée cauldrons, without rims;

'*Item*, another cauldron—two-seillées capacity;

'*Item*, another, of one seillée;

'*Item*, two small half-a-seillée cauldrons;

'*Item*, two big round brazen pans of about four seillées each;

French kitchen and table utensils of the Middle Ages and the Renaissance: 1. Trencher (16th century); 2. Lidded cup (14th century); 3. Copper pot with two handles (9th century); 4. Metal jug (15th century); 5. Knife (16th century); 6. Marmite with two handles (14th century); 7. Copper kettle (15th century); 8. Copper ewer with its oriental-style stand (9th century); 9. Pitcher sculpted in the decoration of the Saint-Benoit church in Paris; 10. Two-branched candlestick (16th century); 11. Cauldron (15th century)

'*Item*, plus another round two-seillée pan (with a piece broken off);

'One wooden press for pressing capons;

'Two iron spoons;

'One small skimmer;

'One round bronze pan with a long handle for cooking fish;

'Two old dripping pans;

'One small metal mortar and pestle;

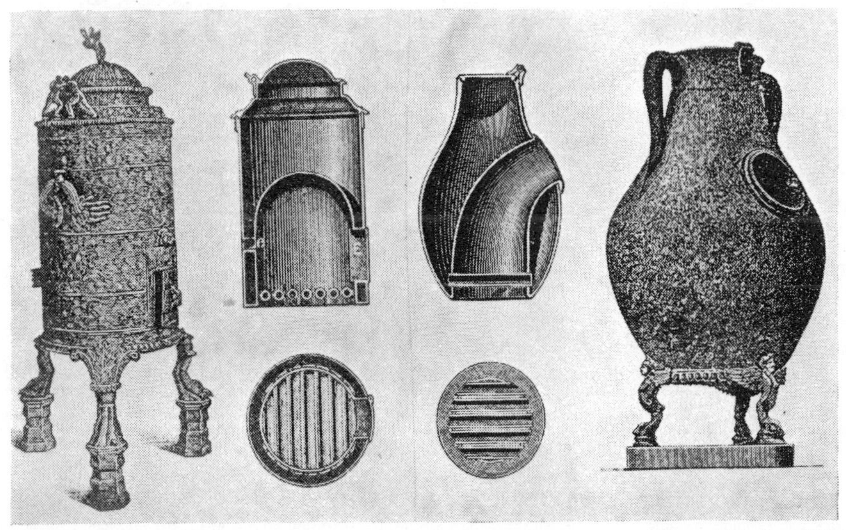

Water heaters found in the excavations at Pompeii provided with pipes to make the best possible use of the heat of the fire-place

Classic French pots and pans: 1. Casserole russe; 2. Sauté pan (plat à sauter); 3. Frying pan (Sauteuse); 4. Petite casserole russe; 5. Round cocotte; 6. Oval copper cocotte for cooking chicken en cocotte; 7. Small copper cocotte for game; 8. Stew pan (Marmite à ragoût); 9. Large stock pot (Grande marmite); 10. Double saucepan (marmite) for steaming potatoes; 11. Braising-pan (Braisière)

(*Photograph Larousse*)

Classic French pots and pans: 1. Copper fish kettle (Poissonière); 2. Saucepans (casseroles) for bain-marie; 3. Braising (Braisière) pan for fillet of beef; 4. Round stew pan (Bassine or Rondin à ragoût); 5. Copper pan (Plaque d'office); 6. Pan for cooking ham (Jambonnière); 7. Turbot kettle (Turbotière); 8. Fish pan (Plaque à poisson)

(*Photograph Larousse*)

'Three iron frying pans with long handles;

'A table on two trestles;

'One old bench with bar back;

'One cupboard with two glass doors, which can be locked with a key;

'Another old cupboard, for keeping plates and dishes, with two glass doors, which can be locked with a key;

'Six big copper candlesticks;

'Six other medium-size candlesticks;

'One deep copper basin for washing hands;

'Two deep bronze candlesticks, in the shape of a cup;

'In the larder near the said kitchen:

'Was found three long shelves, but there was no meat there except for one piglet, which was kept for the Master in case he wanted it while he was here.

'The following bottle-ware:

'Barrel of Gascony wine;

'Pitcher with a spout;

'Half-litre mugs;

'One stone mustard pot, for making mustard, etc.;

'One small table for making pastry'.

Our ancestors used many other utensils in addition to those mentioned in the inventory quoted above.

They knew, among others, the horse-hair sieve or tammy, which, it is said, was invented by the Gauls and which, strangely enough, although a most useful utensil, is not always found in modern private kitchens. They also had among their kitchen-ware the following utensils (and we give here the names which were then in use): the *couloir*, a sort of large strainer with a handle, which was used for draining foods; the *rastels* or *rastelrier*, sort of iron hooks on which food was hung; pots and kettles of all sizes; *tartières* (baking tins); a whole range of pans, each used for a different purpose; skillets, saucepans, frying pans, etc.; the *féral*—a large metal vessel used as a water container; the *becdasne*—a pot with a handle and a long curved spout; *funnels*, mostly in copper; the *esmieure*, a grater used for grating nutmeg and cheese. The nutmeg was greatly valued in those days, as we know. 'Do you like nutmeg? They put it in everything', Boileau was to write a few hundred years later.

In the kitchens of those times they also used gridirons, mortars, spice grinders, various ladles which were called *potlouches* and *poches; minchoirs*, long-bladed knives which were used for slicing pork fat into rashers; meat mincers and various other utensils which are still in use in the present day.

Tin-plating of pots and pans was already known at that time.

Tin-plating, it is said, was discovered in 100 B.C. In the Homeric era tin, along with silver, gold and bronze, was considered to be one of the precious metals. History tells us that the Aedui, the people who inhabited ancient Gaul, the capital of which was Bibracte (a town which was situated near Autun), invented metal plating and it is thanks to this discovery that vessels and kitchen utensils were made in such a way that tin, applied on copper, could not be distinguished from silver.

There are many gastronomes or, at any rate, people who fancy themselves to be such, blind followers of the old cuisine and its methods, who deplore the fact that, owing to the inevitable law of progress, kitchen equipment is becoming improved and transformed.

These gastronomes still protest against the disappearance of the archaic spits or such other utensils formerly used in the kitchen. They are even capable of lamenting the passing of those inconvenient charcoal kitchen ranges—the stoves about which Carême complained when he said: 'The coal is killing us!' These were the old-fashioned *paillasses*, laboriously kept up, where, in live charcoal embers, stews and braised dishes simmered and sometimes caught fire.

In 1849, Michel Chevalier wrote in the *Magasin Pittoresque:* 'The improvement of household utensils has more to do with real freedom than is generally realised, for it contributes a great deal to freedom from drudgery in the home, which matters no less to human happiness than liberty in a public place. One utensil may free the servants from one type of arduous or unhealthy task, another allows one person to do the work of three and, consequently, frees two from domestic drudgery'.

Modern kitchen equipment—Modern kitchen equipment either in domestic or institutional kitchens does not exclude such utensils as well-sharpened knives, wire whisks, saucepans, frying pans, casseroles, braising pans, kettles and strainers, but it does include many inventions which in recent years have contributed much to making culinary operations easier and have taken the drudgery out of cooking.

The kitchen in many modern homes is the centre of family living, especially in the ever-increasing number of areas where domestic service does not exist. This means that the kitchen must be an attractive room to be in, as well as an efficient place in which to produce meals. Such a room includes in many cases a dining area, either a table or counter space. The basic requirements, the stove and the refrigerator, are designed for appearance as well as usefulness, but besides these appliances there are many others designed for home use which make the preparation of food not only easy but enjoyable. Included in an ever-expanding list of such appliances are electric beaters, electric blenders for chopping, pulverizing and puréeing, pressure cookers, machines for slicing and shredding vegetables, rôtisseries, thermostatically-controlled frying pans, garbage disposal units, automatic dish washers and home freezers. All this equipment does not assure good food. On the contrary, gourmets agree that much in texture and flavour can be sacrificed to the speed and efficiency of many of the modern gadgets.

Kitchens in small restaurants and inns are usually an elaboration of a domestic kitchen, but the modern kitchen designed for large hotels, restaurants and institutions may be compared to a factory. Here the utensils are tools of the trade and are built on a large scale and of sturdy materials. The kitchen is divided into many departments, each of which will have its head chef and assistants. There may be departments for baked goods, soups, roasts, fish, salads and hors-d'oeuvre, vegetables, desserts, beverages; in some kitchens these departments will be further subdivided; in others they will be combined. All these departments are under the direction of a manager or head chef who is responsible for the whole operation. On his staff there are usually one or more dietitians to plan the menus. Kitchen engineers, trained in the field, design kitchens of various types and specifications depending on circumstances, but each one must meet public health requirements which are today more rigid than heretofore and more closely controlled. Specifications for a modern kitchen designed in the U.S.A. to feed 2,000 people a day, but capable of feeding 5,000, include the following equipment:

3 electric ranges
3 compartment steamers
2 240-gallon tilting kettles used for soups and vegetables
2 undercounter refrigerators

1 bakers' revolving tray oven
2 cooks' tables with sinks
1 60-quart electric mixer
2 salad preparation tables
Salad refrigerator (80 cubic feet)
Fish refrigerator
80-quart electric mixer
Mobile flour bin
Room refrigerators for meat
Room refrigerator for vegetables and dairy products
Room refrigerator for frozen foods
Baker's refrigerator (50 cubic feet)
'Pass-through' refrigerator (80 cubic feet), which can be filled from the kitchen side and opened on the serving side
5 10-quart tilting pans used for soups and sauces
Hot food table
Refrigerated cold table
Milk dispenser
Cream dispenser
Tea urn
Coffee urn
Electric juice dispenser
Electric ice maker.

Added to these utensils used in the preparation of food, there are many machines for serving food and for disposing of garbage and for washing dishes. These include:

Food warmers
Heated plate dispensers
Garbage disposers
Dishwashing and drying machines
Silver burnisher.

Many hotels catering to a luxury clientele will have charcoal broilers and rôtisserie spits rotating before open fires. Another machine now in use is the deep-heat oven and the broiler that cooks meat in an extremely short time by infra-red and violet rays.

KITCHEN TEAM. Brigade de Cuisine—In a hotel or restaurant this term applies to the staff of a kitchen.

In principle, a kitchen team of a relatively important establishment, a team which takes its orders from a chef, referred to as the *gros bonnet* ('big-hat') in professional jargon, consists of a *sauce chef*, who is considered to be the deputy head of the team; an *entremettier*, who has charge of the preparation of soups, vegetables and sweet courses; a *rôtisseur* who, in addition to various roasts, also prepares fried dishes and grills, and, finally, a *garde-manger* (larder chef) who has charge of all the supplies, raw and cooked, and prepares cold dishes such as *galantines*, *terrines*, *pâtés*, *mousses*, etc. He also prepares the jellies, sees to the cutting up of meat, fish, poultry, game, etc., and does all the cold hors-d'oeuvre relevant to the kitchen service.

According to the importance of the establishment, kitchen assistants, called *commis*, are attached to the chef of each section.

If the establishment is a very important one, and the work therefore more considerable, some of these sections (each team service is called a section, or *partie*, in France), are doubled. Thus the sauce section might have a second service in charge of a special chef—the fish chef. *Entremets* becomes a separate section, still with a chef at its head, usually the soup chef, called *potagiste* or *potager*. The *rôtisserie* (the section in charge of roasts) may be supplemented by a cook who would have the charge of all grills and would, therefore, be called the *grillardin.*

In an establishment of still greater importance, the roasting section, in addition to the roast chef proper and the *grillardin*, would also have a *friturier* (fryer), a noun which probably does not exist in any dictionary but is accepted in culinary terminology and means exactly what it says.

Equally, the *garde-manger* (supplies service), in addition to the actual head of this extremely important section, might be supplemented by the inclusion of other chefs, each with his own speciality; one might have the charge of hors-d'oeuvre, the other of meat, etc.

In a really big restaurant, where the teams work under a chef and an assistant chef, there are also special teams dealing with pastry which consist of a *chef pâtissier* and several assistants, a *chef confiseur* and a *chef glacier*.

In addition, the teams of many restaurants have an *annonceur*, the man who actually 'announces' the order, who, in kitchen slang is known as the *aboyeur* ('barker').

The art of managing the kitchen team of a big restaurant or hotel is a difficult one. A chef in charge of a kitchen must not only be a man who knows his job—his art, we should say—inside out, but he must also have the qualities of an ideal administrator. The time is long past (if it ever existed at all) when kitchens were run in big establishments without some system of accounting. Today, more than ever, the kitchen of a restaurant or a hotel must be well organised, everything must be foreseen and carried out in such a way that the dishes, whilst being excellent in quality, cost only what they should cost and no more.

In a modern establishment the kitchen is a department which must not show a loss. It must show a profit.

No doubt in certain cases the preoccupation of getting this profit does have a detrimental effect on the quality of the dishes. Of this type of establishment we can only say that they are open to criticism and not fit to keep up the prestige of French cookery.

At the end of the nineteenth century and at the beginning of the present one there were a great number of *chefs de cuisine* (famous *gros bonnets*), who had charge of kitchen teams: M. Prat, who for a long time had charge of the kitchens at the Grand-Hotel in Paris; Jean Giroix, who for a long time directed the kitchen at the Hôtel de Paris in Monte Carlo; Leopold Mourier, who, after having directed the kitchen of the Maire restaurant—now no more—became the *grand maître* of various famous restaurants, such as the Café de Paris, Armenonville, the Pré-Catelan, Fouquet, etc.

The great Escoffier, who died in 1935, was first the chef of the Petit Moulin-Rouge, then took charge of the no less famous kitchens of the old Maire restaurant, then the Grand-Hotel at Monte Carlo and the Savoy in London. He finished his active career at the Carlton Hotel in London. Philéas Gilbert was the author of the best culinary works of our time. Other illustrious names include Tony Girod, Ninlias, Argentier, Prosper Drenault, Prosper Salles and Deland.

It is impossible for us to give the names of all the *gros bonnets* of the past who have rendered the culinary art illustrious. We can only mention chefs of the great private houses, such as Urbain Dubois, Émile Bernard, Armand Goufé, Joseph Favre and Gastilleur, some of whom had charge of the Imperial and Royal kitchens of princes' homes and other society homes.

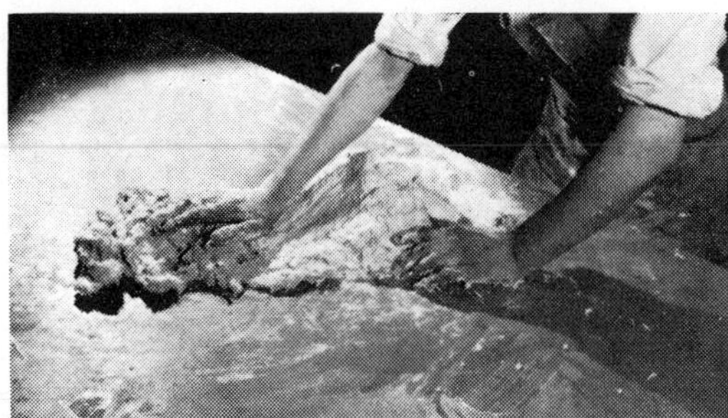

Kneading dough (*Larousse*)

KNEADING OF DOUGH. FRAISAGE—This operation consists of breaking up the dough once it has become elastic, by working it with the palm of the hand. The object of handling the dough in this way is to obtain a perfect mixture of all the ingredients.

KNIFE. COUTEAU—A cutting instrument, consisting of a handle and a blade.

Kitchen knives—For the various culinary operations it is essential to have good tools, and in particular very good knives.

Each of the knives has its proper use. In order of size they are: vegetable knife for peeling vegetables; knife for cutting fish fillets, with a larger blade; slicing knife, a tool with a fairly large blade with which it is possible to slice raw or cooked meat perfectly; straight-bladed chopper, a tool with which it is not only possible to break bones of a certain size, but also to hash up meat in the same way as with the four-bladed chopper; the carving knife, which is used for cutting bards of fat pork or bacon and which resembles a little the so-called 'English' knife used to carve large joints of beef and hams, but which, instead of having a rounded point, is sharply pointed.

We must also mention the knife used for boning meat, which is used more especially in butchery but can be used in cooking.

Among the cutting tools which it is necessary to have in a well-ordered kitchen, are the following: the cleaver, a fairly large instrument with which a carcase can be cut in half; the chopper, with which it is possible to crack the hardest bones; the chopping knife, which is made with one, two or four blades; and, finally, the whole series of small knives used for chopping vegetables, particularly potatoes, for peeling and paring vegetables, and those for cutting potatoes into ribbons; knives for opening oysters and, finally, tin-openers, which can be included among cutting tools.

Little tools, such as knives with a fluting device or one for scraping lemon zest, should be mentioned; little instruments for cutting ravioli; special knives for cutting grapefruit; scissors for jointing chicken; the cutlet beater; the butcher's saw; and, finally, the scraper for the butcher's table.

Table knives should be of excellent quality, which means with good cutting blades in pure steel. Many table knives are made today in stainless steel. Their principal advantage is that they do not stain. For serving fruit, knives are made in silver plate. For fish, special utensils are made of silver plate and are used to cut up the fish once served.

KNIFE REST. PORTE-COUTEAU—Utensils of various shapes, in cut glass or silver, on which the knife is placed to prevent soiling the tablecloth.

KNUCKLE. SOURIS—Small, fleshy muscle on the leg of mutton, a piece much appreciated by connoisseurs who would not exchange it for a slice from the middle of the leg.

KOHLRABI. CHOUX-RAVES—These are not, properly speaking, roots, but a swelling of the stem above ground in the form of a plump, pithy ball. Some varieties have quite a delicate flavour. All the recipes given for *turnips** and for *celeriac** may be used for this vegetable.

Kohlrabi à la paysanne. CHOU-RAVE À LA PAYSANNE—Cut the kohlrabi into slices. Cook them in lard in which some chopped onion has been softened. Add some fresh breast of pork and season with salt. Moisten with white wine and stock in equal proportions.

KOUMISS—Fermented mare's milk, originally made in Turkestan and Tartary, rather similar to *kéfir*. The ferment used is prepared by working ½ pound (250 grams) of barm (brewer's yeast) and ¼ pound (125 grams) of flour with a little honey and a glass of milk. Next day, 3 quarts, plus 1 cup (3 litres) of milk are added to this leaven. It contains a great deal of carbonic acid gas and from 1.65 per cent to 3.23 per cent of alcohol.

Kugelhupf

KUGELHUPF OR SUGLHUPF (Alsatian pastry)—It is said that Queen Marie Antoinette was very fond of this pastry, which contributed a great deal to the fashion in her day for sweets made from risen dough. These were no longer made, as they had been until the middle of the eighteenth century, with leaven but with barm (brewer's yeast), which had been in use for a very long time in Austria and Poland.

Some authorities, however, believe that it was Carême who popularised this pastry in Paris, when he established himself as a pastry-cook. It is said that he was given the recipe by M. Eugène, at that time master chef of Prince Schwartzenberg, the Austrian Ambassador.

Another writer on cookery states that the first *pâtisserie* to make *kugelhupf* in Paris was that under the direction of a man named Georges who, in 1840, set up as a pastry-cook in the Rue de Coq. His shop was swallowed up by the extension of the *Magasins du Louvre*.

Ingredients. 3¾ cups (500 grams) sieved flour; 1 cup (200 grams) butter; 6 tablespoons (90 grams) fine sugar; 4 eggs; a scant ounce (25 grams) yeast (or 1 large yeast cake), ½ ounce or 15 grams in summer; ½ cup (50 grams) currants; 1½ teaspoons (10 grams) salt.

Method. Make the dough according to the instructions for *brioche dough* (see DOUGH), but making the dough a little less firm.

Butter a large *kugelhupf* mould and line the sides with shredded almonds. Half-fill this mould with dough. Leave the dough to rise in a warm place, until it has risen above the sides of the mould.

Bake in a hot oven (400°F.) for 40 to 45 minutes.

KULICH (Russian cookery)—A cake made from risen dough. It is made in Russia for the ceremonial Easter dinner. This cake is decorated, after it has been baked and cooled, with a cluster of artificial roses.

KUMMEL—A liqueur flavoured with cummin (the German for cummin is *kummel*). It is made by adding alcohol to a cummin syrup which causes the sugar (which is less soluble in water containing alcohol) to form crystals on the sides of the bottle.

KUMQUAT—A kind of tiny orange shaped like an elongated olive. This fruit, which is nowadays sold in all food stores in France, is eaten raw, like oranges and tangerines.

Like oranges this fruit can be made into salads or marmalade.

It is also used in cooking as a garnish for certain dishes, notably pot-roasted or braised duck.

It can be pickled in vinegar like cucumbers or small melons.

KVASS—A slightly gaseous, mild alcoholic drink similar to beer. It is made in Russia by adding fermented yeast to a must of rye flour mixed with a little sprouted barley. It is sometimes flavoured with leaves of mint or juniper berries.

Kulich

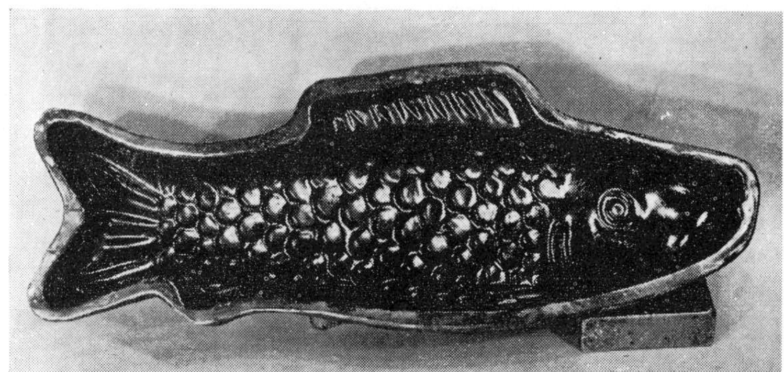

Mould for first of April kugelhupf

LABRUS. Labre—A European sea fish also called wrasse. It is remarkable for its brilliant colouring, but it is tasteless and limp in texture. It is served fried or may be used as an ingredient of *bouillabaisse**.

LACHE—A small sea fish. It is very delicate to eat and rather scarce. It is cooked in the same way as the smelt.

LACRIMA-CHRISTI—A wine made from grapes grown on the slopes of Vesuvius. It is rather sweet and delicate.

LACTARY. Lactaire—A fungus of the agaric type. It contains a white or coloured milky juice. Some lactaries are poisonous, others are edible, though of rather poor flavour in spite of the fact that one type is called *Delicious*.

LACTIC ACID. Lactique—An acid present in sour milk and certain fermented substances. It is an antiseptic and is particularly effective in preventing putrefaction. A primitive method of preserving meat was to immerse it in sour milk.

LACTIC FERMENTS. Lactiques—These are microbes which are very widespread and of many kinds. When they are introduced into milk the lactose (milk sugar) molecules are split and lactic acid is produced. It is these microbes which breed on the teats of cows in cowsheds and in dairies, which cause the curdling of milk and are one of the agents in the production of cheese.

Sour milk is produced either by introducing indigenous ferments into the milk or by using ferments imported from the Balkans, Egypt and the Caucasus. These latter, being adapted to higher temperatures, produce a larger quantity of lactic acid. See CHEESE, KÉFIR, KOUMISS, YOGHOURT.

LACTOMETER. Lactomètre—A graduated densimeter which shows the density of milk, from which the cream content can be calculated.

LADIES' FINGERS—See OKRA.

LADLE. Poche—Large spoon with cup bowl and a long handle used mainly for serving liquid dishes.

LAGOPUS. Lagopède—The lagopus or Pyrenean partridge has tawny plumage with thin black streaks in summer. In winter it turns almost completely white, except for touches of black on the tail. It is because of its winter plumage that this bird is sometimes called snow partridge.

This bird is much sought-after for the table, in spite of its slightly bitter flavour, which is due to the fact that it feeds on birch-shoots, myrtle berries and other mountain berries.

All recipes for grouse (which belongs to the same family as the lagopus) are suitable for this bird. See GROUSE.

LAGUIPIÈRE—Laguipière, who was born in the middle of the eighteenth century and died in 1812, was one of the great masters of French cookery. Carême described him as 'the most remarkable chef of our times.' Carême's tutor in all branches of cookery was, in fact, the great Laguipière, who accompanied Murat to Naples and later followed him to Russia and froze to death at Vilno (now Vilnius) during the 1812 retreat from Moscow.

At the beginning of his book, *Le Cuisinier Parisien*, Carême wrote the following words about his great master: 'Awake! Shade of Laguipière. Listen to the voice of a pupil, a friend, a devotee!' (Carême, who was somewhat grandiloquent, never failed to express his feelings with great force). 'Your talents were extraordinary and earned you the hatred of those who ought to have admired your noble striving for perfection. You should have died in Paris, surrounded by the reverence evoked in all of us by the memory of your great work . . . Laguipière, accept the pious homage of a faithful disciple. I couple my works with your name. I have cited you with pride in all my books, and, today, I invoke your memory and dedicate to you my finest work.'

It is regrettable that so learned a practitioner of the art of cooking as Laguipière should not have left any written record for posterity of his culinary teachings.

LAITIAT—This is the name given in the Franche-Comté to a refreshing drink made by steeping wild fruit in whey.

LAMB. Agneau—Young ovine animal before it is a year old. In U.S.A. called 'spring lamb.'

After the age of one year, when the animal has already grown its first two nippers (incisor teeth of herbivorous animals), it is called a *yearling*. When the first permanent teeth appear, the animal becomes a *ram* or a *ewe*.

In the culinary sense lamb is known in two forms: firstly, the *milk-fed* (or baby) *lamb*, the animal which has not yet been weaned and has not yet been put out to graze. The best lamb of this type is Pauillac lamb. Secondly, *yearling lamb* or *salt meadow lamb*, that is, a young sheep which has not yet reached its full growth.

Good quality lamb can be recognised by the width of its loins, which should be well covered with flesh, and by the whiteness of its fat, which should be firm and abundant, especially round the kidneys.

Its freshness can be judged from the firmness of its legs and the colour of the kidneys, which should be pale pink.

Baby or milk-fed lamb is generally sold whole, with its pluck. It is also sometimes sold in quarters.

Lamb should be eaten at its freshest. This meat does not keep for very long.

Ordinary lamb and milk-fed lamb is sold in butchers' shops and, in France, in poultry shops (especially milk-fed lamb). Ordinary lamb is divided into cuts almost like mutton.

The best parts are: the legs, the saddle and the loins. The neck, breast and shoulder are principally used for making *blanquettes*, *fricassées*, ragoûts and sauté dishes.

The *legs* are generally used for roasting. They are served as they are, plain or with a garnish most frequently consisting of vegetables—baked, dressed with butter, or braised.

The *shoulder*, whether boned or not, is prepared in the same manner as legs.

Two legs are called a *double*. When the saddle, and sometimes a part of the loins, is left with the legs, then such a joint is called a *baron*. A quarter is half this joint.

The best way to prepare these various joints is to roast or pot-roast them.

The loins can also be cooked whole (on the spit or in the oven) but they are usually cut into cutlets, which can be grilled or fried and served plain or with various garnishes.

All lamb variety meats (or cuts of edible offal) are delicate in flavour. They are prepared as beef or veal variety meats (offal).

Lamb plays an important part both in classical French cookery and in home cookery. It lends itself to an infinite number of treatments. Baby or milk-fed lamb is divided into cuts in the same way as ordinary lamb: *baron*, *loin*, *double*, *shoulder*, *leg*, *quarter*, *saddle*.

All these cuts can be served with garnishes recommended for ordinary lamb and for mutton. Bearing in mind the particularly delicate flavour of this meat, however, it is advisable to serve it grilled, pot-roasted or as a roast, with its own juice—thickened or clear—as the only accompaniment.

Other parts of milk-fed lamb are used for *blanquettes*, ragoûts and sauté dishes.

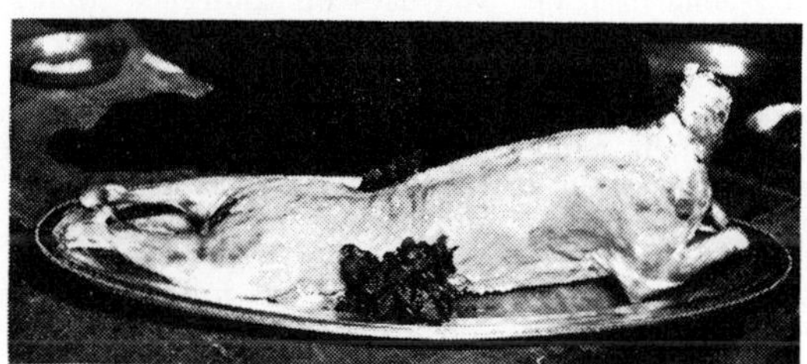

Pauillac lamb

BABY OR MILK-FED LAMB OR YEANLING. AGNEAU DE LAIT, AGNELET:

Leg of baby or milk-fed lamb in pastry à la périgourdine. GIGOT D'AGNEAU EN PÂTE À LA PÉRIGOURDINE—This is a method of preparation for leg of baby or milk-fed lamb.

Trim the leg and remove most of the bone. Cook in a hot oven for 10 minutes to brown it. Allow to cool. Cover completely with 1 pound of sausage meat, mixed with uncooked goose liver, amounting to one-third of its weight, rubbed through a sieve, together with 2 diced truffles, the whole bound with an egg. Wrap the leg in a sheet of salt pork or a piece of pig's caul, previously soaked in cold water.

Put the leg on an oval-shaped sheet of rolled out pastry. Cover with another sheet of the same pastry. Seal the edges of the pastry by crimping them. Make a hole in the middle of the pastry to allow steam to escape. Brush the top of the pastry with beaten egg, and put it on a baking sheet.

Cook in a moderate oven (350°F.) for an hour and a half.

When removed from the oven, pour through the hole in the top $\frac{3}{4}$ cup ($1\frac{1}{2}$ decilitres) of *Périgueux sauce* (see SAUCE). Serve on a napkin-covered dish.

This sort of hot pie can also be made with a boned and rolled leg of lamb.

Fried loin of baby or milk-fed lamb à la viennoise. CARRÉ D'AGNEAU FRIT À LA VIENNOISE—This method of preparation is only suitable for loin of milk-fed (or baby) lamb.

Divide the loin in halves. Marinate for one hour in oil, lemon juice, salt, pepper and chopped parsley. Drain the pieces of lamb and dry, dredge in flour and dip in egg and breadcrumbs. Fry in clarified butter or deep fry in sizzling fat. Serve on a napkin, garnished with fried parsley and quarters of lemon.

Baby or milk-fed lamb or yeanling à la kurd. AGNEAU (AGNELET) À LA KURDE—This recipe was given to us by Roland Dorgelès. It is rather an original one. The author of *Les Croix de Bois* declares that, prepared in this manner, baby or milk-fed lamb is excellent.

'On the banks of the Euphrates, where I lived among camel drivers and Bedouin, I discovered a dish which I did not know before . . . . Take a small milk-fed lamb, one of those little lambs which the nomad shepherds carry about like babies. You clean it out, season the inside and stuff with a forcemeat made from its liver, heart and lungs. You mix this forcemeat generously with rice half-cooked with fat, in which you have incorporated dry, not sweet, apricots, which have been cooked in the gravy. Then you serve it with the gravy from which the fat has been skimmed off.

'This is what is called *Yeanling à la kurd*.'

No doubt the addition of apricots to this dish may appear a little eccentric to certain gastronomical purists (and you may count me as one) but let us not forget that many people relish venison with redcurrant jelly.

Roast baby or milk-fed lamb. AGNEAU DE LAIT RÔTI—This method of preparation is most suitable for small-sized lambs. Dress the skin over the knuckles and shoulders. Truss the lamb to give it its proper shape. Put on a spit, season with salt and pepper, brush with melted butter and roast before a brisk fire, allowing 18 to 25 minutes per pound.

Take off the spit, put on a big, long dish, garnish with bunches of watercress and quarters of lemon.

Dilute the pan juices with a little stock and serve with the lamb.

Note. Roast lamb is generally served with mint sauce. It is garnished with various vegetables. Lamb can also be roasted in the oven.

Grilled shoulder of baby or milk-fed lamb. ÉPAULE D'AGNEAU DE LAIT GRILLÉE—Trim shoulder, make a few slits on both sides, season and brush with melted butter.

Grill under a moderate flame for 20 to 25 minutes.

Sprinkle with white breadcrumbs; then brush with melted butter and put under the grill or broiler to colour.

Arrange on a long dish. Serve garnished with watercress.

Baby or milk-fed lamb stuffed with rice. AGNEAU DE LAIT FARCI AU RIZ—Stuff the lamb with half-cooked rice pilaf (see PILAF), to which the animal's liver, heart, sweetbreads and kidneys, cut into small slices, briskly fried in butter and seasoned, have been added.

Sew up the opening, truss as described in recipe for *Roast baby or milk-fed lamb*. Cover the back with strips or rashers of bacon tied in place; put on a spit and roast before a lively fire, allowing 18-25 minutes per pound.

Remove from the spit, take off the bacon and cut away trussing string. Put on a big, long dish, garnish with watercress and quarters of lemon. Serve the pan juices, diluted with a few tablespoons of stock, with the lamb.

Roast baron of lamb

LAMB. AGNEAU:

Baron of lamb. BARON D'AGNEAU—The cut comprising the two legs and the saddle.

This joint (or cut), is roasted on a spit or pot-roasted, but may also be served as a roast in its own juice.

When it is served as a remove (separate course), it is accompanied by a garnish of vegetables (either disposed around the joint or served separately), and with its own juice, left as it is or thickened into a gravy, depending on the nature of the garnish.

Average cooking time. 15 to 18 minutes per pound.

Garnishes suitable for baron of lamb. Various green vegetables dressed with butter or cream; braised vegetables; *à la anversoise*, *à la bouquetière*, *bretonne*, *clamart*, *dauphine*, *duchesse*, *jardinière*, *macédoine*, *parisienne*, *Anna potatoes* and potatoes prepared in various other ways (see POTATOES); *provençale*, *renaissance*, *Richelieu*. For the preparation of all these, see GARNISHES.

Blanquette of lamb. BLANQUETTE D'AGNEAU—This method of preparation is often described as *fricassée**.

Soak the pieces of lamb and dry well. Fry quickly in butter without allowing to brown. Season, sprinkle with 2 tablespoons of flour, blend on the fire, add white stock and garnish as above. Bring to the boil, simmer under a lid from 45 minutes to an hour.

Transfer into another pan. Add small onions and mushrooms. Add the sauce and blend in yolks of egg as described above.

Blanquette of lamb à l'ancienne. BLANQUETTE D'AGNEAU À L'ANCIENNE—This is made of shoulder and ribs of yearling or salt meadow lamb. Cut 4 pounds of lamb into uniform pieces. Soak for an hour in water, blanch, dip in cold water to cool, and dry.

Put into a shallow pan; add enough white stock (or a light pot-au-feu broth—see SOUPS AND BROTHS) just to cover the meat. Add 2 medium-sized carrots (150 grams) cut in quarters, 2 medium-sized onions—one studded with a clove—and a *bouquet garni* consisting of a sprig of parsley, a stalk of celery, 2 leeks, a sprig of thyme and a bay leaf. Season with salt.

Bring to the boil, remove scum and cook under a lid from 45 minutes to 1 hour.

Remove the pieces of lamb, trim them, i.e. remove small pieces of bone and skin which have become detached during cooking. Put the lamb into a shallow pan with 12 small onions (200 grams) previously cooked in *court-bouillon**, and the same amount of cooked mushrooms.

Make a *roux** of 4 tablespoons (60 grams) of butter and 5 tablespoons (70 grams) of flour, add strained stock in which the lamb was cooked, simmer this sauce for 15 minutes, skim, strain, and pour over the lamb.

Simmer gently for 20 to 25 minutes. At the last moment, blend in 4 yolks of egg mixed with 4 tablespoons (7 decilitres) of cream, a dash of lemon juice and a pinch of grated nutmeg. After completing this liaison, keep the *blanquette* hot but do not allow to boil.

Note. Alternatively, cook the lamb in stock, put into a shallow pan with onions cooked in *court-bouillon** and the mushrooms. Keep hot under a lid. At the last moment pour over some *Velouté sauce* (see SAUCE) prepared of the stock in which the lamb was cooked, blended, as usual, with yolks of eggs, cream and lemon juice, reduced to the desired consistency and strained through a tammy cloth.

Lamb's brains—See OFFAL OR VARIETY MEATS.

Lamb's breast. POITRINE D'AGNEAU—This is generally used, whether boned or not, for making ragoûts or sauté dishes.

It can also be made into *épigrammes** and is also used instead of beef to prepare peasant soups. See SOUPS AND BROTHS, *Mutton broth*.

Lamb's breast à l'anglaise. POITRINE D'AGNEAU À L'ANGLAISE—Cook the breast as in the recipe for *Lamb's breast à la diable* and allow to get cold under a press. Cut into rectangular pieces. Dip these pieces in beaten egg and breadcrumbs. Fry in clarified butter. Arrange on a long dish, dot with dabs of half-melted *Maître d'hôtel butter* (see BUTTER, *Compound butters*).

Lamb's breast à la diable. POITRINE D'AGNEAU À LA DIABLE—Braise the breast or cook it in a little white stock. Drain, remove all the rib bones. Allow to cool under a press. Cut into rectangular pieces. Spread these pieces with mustard with a pinch of cayenne pepper added to it. Dip in melted butter and breadcrumbs. Sprinkle with butter and cook on a low grill.

Arrange in a circle on a round dish. Garnish with watercress. Serve *Diable sauce* (see SAUCE) separately.

Épigrammes of lamb's breast. POITRINE D'AGNEAU EN ÉPIGRAMMES—Braise a lamb's breast or poach it in very little white stock. Drain, bone and cool under a press.

Cut into heart-shaped pieces of uniform size. Dip in egg and breadcrumbs.

At the same time dip in egg and breadcrumbs a number of lamb chops, similar in shape and size to the pieces of breast.

Cook the chops and the pieces of breast under a low grill or flame (or, if you prefer, sauté them both in butter).

Arrange in a crown on a long dish. Decorate end bones with paper frills. Put the garnish recommended in the middle of the dish. Pour on the épigrammes a few tablespoons of *Demi-glace sauce* (see SAUCE), or the stock left over from braising the breast, boiled down and strained.

Garnishes suitable for épigrammes of lamb. All those recommended elsewhere for lamb chops or noisettes.

Breast of lamb fried in batter. POITRINE D'AGNEAU EN FRITOT—Braise, bone, cool under a press and cut the breast of lamb into small, square pieces. Steep for an hour in oil, lemon juice, chopped parsley, salt and pepper.

Then dip the pieces in a light batter and deep fry. Drain, dry, season with finely ground salt. Arrange on a napkin in a pyramid, garnish with fried parsley and serve with tomato sauce.

Breast of lamb in breadcrumbs with various garnishes. POITRINE D'AGNEAU PANÉE—Cook in clarified butter pieces of breast, dipped in egg and breadcrumbs, as described in the recipe for *Breast of Lamb à l'anglaise.*

Arrange in a crown on a round dish. Fill the middle of the dish with the garnish indicated. Surround with a border of thickened veal gravy.

Garnishes suitable for breast in breadcrumbs. Green vegetables blended with butter or cream; purées of various vegetables; spinach—leaf or purée; rice pilaf or risotto; various pasta products with butter or *à l'italienne**; new potatoes in butter; *carrots, glazed** or *à la Vichy**, etc.

Stuffed breast of lamb. POITRINE D'AGNEAU FARCIE—Slit the pieces of breast to form pockets. Fill them with finely pounded forcemeat bound with an egg (see FORCEMEAT). Sew up the opening. Wrap the pieces in thin rashers (strips) of bacon. Braise them, as usual, in a small quantity of liquid.

Drain the pieces of breast. Unwrap and glaze. Arrange on a round dish. Garnish as indicated. Sprinkle with strained pan juices.

Stuffed breast of lamb can be served with all the garnishes recommended for pieces of braised lamb or mutton.

Lamb chops. CÔTELETTES D'AGNEAU—*Rib lamb chops* are cut from the rib roast. In France they are called *côtelettes* and in England they are called *cutlets.*

Loin lamb chops are cut from the loin and are known in French as *côtes.* In England they are known as *lamb chops.*

Chops are most often grilled but all the preparations recommended in the following recipes are suitable for rib chops (cutlets) or lamb chops cut from the loin. They can be served with any of the garnishes recommended for *Mutton chops**. Most frequently these garnishes consist of a green vegetable dressed with butter, such as beans, peas, asparagus tips, etc.

Chops are best taken from yearling lambs. The best are those bred in salt meadows.

Lamb chops à l'ancienne. CÔTELETTES D'AGNEAU À L'ANCIENNE—Fry the chops in butter. Arrange in a crown on a round dish. Garnish the middle with a ragoût made of lamb's sweetbreads, cocks' combs and kidneys, truffles and mushrooms, bound with *Velouté sauce* (see SAUCE) with cream. Dilute the pan juices with Madeira, sherry or other similar wine, add a little light *Demi-glace sauce* (see SAUCE) and pour over the chops. Garnish the bones with paper frills.

Lamb chops à l'anglaise. CÔTELETTES D'AGNEAU À L'ANGLAISE—These are prepared in two ways:

Grilled. Season the chops, dip in melted butter and breadcrumbs and grill or broil.

Arrange on a round dish. Garnish with grilled strips or rashers of bacon, potatoes *à l'anglaise* (i.e., boiled in water) and watercress.

Sautéed. Dip in beaten egg and breadcrumbs and sauté in clarified butter. Arrange in a crown on a round dish and sprinkle with *Noisette butter* (see BUTTER, *Compound butters*).

Lamb chops in aspic jelly. CÔTELETTES D'AGNEAU À LA GELÉE—Braise a large lamb loin, neatly trimmed, in very little *court-bouillon**. Allow to cool in its own strained juices.

Drain and cut into chops. Dry them and glaze with jelly. (The pan juices left over from braising the cutlets should be added to the jelly before its clarification.)

Arrange the chops in a turban, on a round dish. Garnish with chopped jelly.

These chops in jelly can be garnished with hard boiled eggs cut into quarters and lettuce hearts, or with mixed salads.

They can be served with *Mayonnaise* or *Tartare sauce* or, as is customary in England, with *Mint sauce.* See SAUCE, *Cold sauces.*

Finally, instead of cooking the loin whole and then cutting it, the chops can be prepared as described in the recipe for *Chaud-froid of lamb chops.*

Bar-man lamb chops. CÔTELETTES D'AGNEAU BAR-MAN—Grill the chops. Arrange on a round dish. Garnish with whole, grilled tomatoes and mushrooms. Put a rasher (strip) of grilled bacon on each cutlet. Garnish with watercress.

Lamb chops in breadcrumbs, garnished. CÔTELETTES D'AGNEAU PANÉES GARNIES—Dip the chops in egg and breadcrumbs if they are to be fried, and in butter and breadcrumbs if they are to be grilled.

Depending on the method chosen, fry in clarified butter, making both sides golden, or cook under the grill on low heat.

Arrange in a dish. Surround with the recommended garnish.

All the garnishes recommended for fried lamb chops are applicable to lamb chops in breadcrumbs.

Lamb chops (cutlets) Brossard. CÔTELETTES D'AGNEAU BROSSARD—Dip the chops into beaten egg and breadcrumbs mixed with chopped truffles.

Sauté in butter. Arrange in a crown on a round dish. Garnish the middle of the dish with mushrooms stewed in cream. Put a border of buttered *Demi-glace sauce* (see SAUCE) around the chops.

Lamb chops Champvallon. CÔTELETTES D'AGNEAU CHAMPVALLON—Choose lower ribs from yearling or salt meadow lamb, cut fairly thick. Proceed as with *Mutton chops Champvallon.* See MUTTON.

Chaud-froid of lamb chops. CÔTELETTES D'AGNEAU EN CHAUD-FROID—Braise the chops (cut fairly thick) in very little liquid. Leave to get cold under a press in the stock in which they were braised, strained and with surplus fat removed.

When they become quite cold, drain, trim, cover with *Chaud-froid sauce*, prepared in the usual manner, using the pan juices in which the cutlets were cooked (see SAUCE).

Decorate with pieces of white of hard boiled eggs, truffles, pickled tongue, etc. Glaze with liquid jelly and leave in a cold place to set.

Lay the chops in a circle on a round dish. Garnish with chopped jelly. Serve with mint sauce. *Chaud-froid* of lamb chops can be served with a vegetable salad or some other mixed salad.

Alternatively, instead of putting the cutlets flat on a dish, you can arrange them in a crown and garnish the centre of the dish with a mixed salad, dressed with mayonnaise stiffened with gelatine, moulded in a dome shape. The lamb chops can be coated with various *chaud-froid* sauces, white or brown. See SAUCE.

Lamb chops Conti. CÔTELETTES D'AGNEAU CONTI—Coat the chops on both sides with a *mirepoix** of vegetables finely chopped and cooked in butter. Dip in breadcrumbs and fry in clarified butter. Arrange in a crown on a round dish, alternating with slices of ham cut in triangles, fried in butter. Garnish the centre of the dish with a fairly thick *Purée of lentils**. Surround with a border of *Demi-glace sauce* (see SAUCE).

Lamb chops in crépinettes. CÔTELETTES D'AGNEAU EN CRÉPINETTES—Prepare as *Mutton chops in crépinettes.* See MUTTON.

These chops can also be prepared by simply frying them in butter before wrapping in pieces of thin salt pork or pig's caul, instead of braising them.

Lamb chops Dubarry. CÔTELETTES D'AGNEAU DUBARRY—Grill or fry the chops and garnish with cauliflower divided into flowerettes, covered with Mornay sauce (see SAUCE), sprinkled with Parmesan cheese. Brown in the oven or under a grill.

Lamb chops à la financière. CÔTELETTES D'AGNEAU À LA FINANCIÈRE—Fry the chops; add Madeira to the pan and finish off the sauce with *Demi-glace sauce* (see SAUCE).

Arrange the chops in a circle in a puff-pastry shell (not too raised) and garnish the middle with a *Ragoût à la financière**—quenelles, cocks' combs and kidneys, mushrooms and truffles, blended in a *Demi-glace sauce* reduced (boiled down) with Madeira.

If there is no time to make a pastry shell, the chops can be arranged in a crown, putting each on a heart-shaped croûton fried in butter.

Lamb chops à la française. CÔTELETTES D'AGNEAU À LA FRANÇAISE—'Fry 12 cutlets, put them under a press; when they are cold, coat with chicken quenelle forcemeat.

'Put them on a metal sheet greased with clarified butter and glaze with egg. Cook in the oven, painting them with melted butter—using a brush from time to time. Leave until nicely golden.

'Prepare a *croustade** from a piece of bread about 4 inches in diameter, scooped out in the middle and fried in deep fat. Put this *croustade* in the middle of an entrée dish, place the cutlets around it and fill the middle with fried lamb's sweetbreads and truffles. Glaze and serve.' (*Grande Cuisine Simplifiée*, by Robert, 1845.)

Lamb chops with garnish. CÔTELETTES D'AGNEAU SAUTÉES GARNIES—Season the chops. Sauté them in butter. Arrange them in a crown on a round dish. Garnish with vegetables (or any other garnish) recommended below. Dilute the pan juices left over from frying with white wine (or other wine), add *Demi-glace sauce* (see SAUCE) or veal stock, boil down, strain and pour over the chops.

Garnishes suitable for lamb chops. Green vegetables dressed with butter or cream; various braised vegetables; potatoes prepared in various ways; purées of fresh or dried vegetables; various pasta products; rice, risotto and, in general, all the garnishes, simple or mixed, recommended for small fillet steaks, tournedos, escalopes of veal, noisettes and medallions of mutton or lamb.

Grilled lamb chops garnished with various vegetables. CÔTELETTES D'AGNEAU GRILLÉES GARNIES DE LÉGUMES—Season the cutlets, brush with melted butter or oil. Cook under a moderate flame. Arrange on a round dish. Garnish with the chosen vegetables. Put paper frills on end bones.

Grilled lamb chops served with rice

Grilled chops can be garnished with various green vegetables, dressed with butter or cream (asparagus tips, French beans, kidney beans, young broad beans, garden peas, etc.); potatoes prepared in different ways; braised vegetables (celery, lettuce, endive, etc.); purées of fresh vegetables; small marrows (zucchini) or aubergines (U.S. egg-plant) cut in dice and sautéed in butter or oil; tomatoes lightly sautéed in butter or oil; Brussels sprouts or cauliflower sautéed in butter; cucumbers (cut into uniform pieces) steamed in butter; artichoke hearts fried lightly in butter, etc.

Lamb chops à l'italienne—See *Mutton chops à l'italienne.*

Lamb chops Maintenon—See *Mutton chops Maintenon.*

Lamb chops à la maréchale. CÔTELETTES D'AGNEAU À LA MARÉCHALE—Dip in egg and breadcrumbs and fry in clarified butter.

Arrange the chops in a crown, put on each chop a sliver of truffle heated in butter. Garnish with asparagus tips dressed with butter. Put a border of *Demi-glace sauce* (see SAUCE) with Madeira and butter around the chops.

Lamb chops à la mexicaine. CÔTELETTES D'AGNEAU À LA MEXICAINE—Fry the chops in butter. Arrange in a crown on a round dish. Garnish the middle with bananas cut in slices, dipped in batter and fried at the last moment. Pour over the chops a sauce made of their pan juices in the following manner:

Add to the pan juices (for 6 chops) 2 tablespoons of wine vinegar. Pour in 1 cup (2 decilitres) of thickened brown veal stock. Simmer to thicken. Add to it the peel of 1 orange, finely shredded, blanched, rinsed in cold water to cool and well-drained.

Minute lamb chops. CÔTELETTES D'AGNEAU À LA MINUTE—Beat the chops flat and season. Sauté as briskly as possible in sizzling butter.

Arrange in a crown. Pour over the butter left over in the pan with a dash of lemon juice and some chopped parsley added to it.

Lamb chops Montrouge. CÔTELETTES D'AGNEAU MONTROUGE—Dip in egg and breadcrumbs. Fry in clarified butter. Arrange in a crown on a round dish. Garnish the middle with fairly thick *mushroom purée.** Put a border of buttered *Demi-glace sauce* (see SAUCE) around the chops.

Lamb chops Paul Mounet. CÔTELETTES D'AGNEAU PAUL MOUNET—Fry the chops in goose fat. Arrange them in a crown, alternating with rows of fried heart-shaped croûtons. Pour over the pan juices finished off in the following manner:

Put into the pan in which the chops were fried—for 6 chops—2 tablespoons of Bayonne ham, finely shredded, blanched, drained and dried; when the ham is lightly browned (without becoming shrivelled up) add 2 spoonfuls of fresh shredded cèpes or mushroom caps and sauté lightly. Then add 2 cloves of garlic, also finely chopped; dilute with a tablespoon of wine vinegar, add ⅞ cup (2 decilitres) of tomato-flavoured *Demi-glace sauce* (see SAUCE); cook for 5 minutes. Pour over the chops.

Lamb chops in papillotes. CÔTELETTES D'AGNEAU EN PAPILLOTES—Prepare as described in the recipe for *Veal chops en papillotes*. See VEAL.

Lamb chops, instead of being fried, can be braised, allowed to get cold in the juices in which they were braised and then put into buttered papers.

In this case, the pan juices left over from braising will be used for moistening the *duxelles**.

Lamb chops à la parisienne. CÔTELETTES D'AGNEAU À LA PARISIENNE—Dip the chops in beaten egg, then in breadcrumbs mixed with chopped truffles.

Cook in clarified butter. Arrange in a crown in a round dish.

Garnish the middle of the dish with mushrooms cooked in cream and around the chops put a border of asparagus tips dressed with butter. See ASPARAGUS.

Lamb chops Périnette. CÔTELETTES D'AGNEAU PÉRINETTE —Dip the chops in egg and breadcrumbs mixed with finely chopped cooked ham. Fry them in clarified butter.

Arrange in a crown alternating with rows of young marrows (zucchini) cut in long slices and fried in oil. Garnish the middle of the dish with a *Tomato fondue**, mixed with sweet pimentos, cut in large dice and fried in oil.

Lamb chops à la portugaise. CÔTELETTES D'AGNEAU À LA PORTUGAISE—Fry the lamb chops in butter. Arrange on a round dish. Garnish with very small, stuffed tomatoes, cooked in the oven or under a grill to brown the top. Dilute the pan juices left over from frying the chops with white wine, add a light *Tomato purée* (see SAUCE), with a finely chopped or pounded clove of garlic blended in, and pour this sauce over the chops.

Lamb chops princesse. CÔTELETTES D'AGNEAU PRINCESSE —The following two methods of preparation are described by this name:

(1) Dip the chops into egg and breadcrumbs, fry them in clarified butter, arrange in a circle on a round dish. Garnish with little bunches of asparagus tips, dressed with butter, and coarsely shredded truffles. Serve separately *Allemande sauce* (see SAUCE) based on concentrated mushroom stock.

(2) Cook the chops in butter. Arrange in a circle. Cover with *Allemande sauce* based on concentrated mushroom stock. Put a sliver of truffle on each chop and garnish the middle of the dish with asparagus tips dressed with butter. Dilute the pan juices with Madeira, add ¾ cup thickened brown stock and pour over the chops.

Lamb chops à la romaine. CÔTELETTES D'AGNEAU À LA ROMAINE—Fry the chops in butter. Arrange in a crown on a round dish, alternating with rows of heart-shaped croûtons of bread fried in butter. Garnish the middle of the dish with small potato balls, cooked in butter and tossed in concentrated meat stock. Pour over the chops *Romaine sauce* (see SAUCE) to which the pan juices left over from frying the chops, diluted with 2 tablespoons of wine vinegar, have been added.

Lamb chops Rossini. CÔTELETTES D'AGNEAU ROSSINI— Fry in butter. Arrange the chops on a dish. Put on each chop a slice of *foie gras* fried in butter and two or three slivers of truffle tossed in butter. Dilute the pan juices left over from frying the chops with Madeira (or any other similar wine), add some *Demi-glace sauce* (see SAUCE), boil down, strain and pour over the chops.

Lamb chops à la rouennaise. CÔTELETTES D'AGNEAU À LA ROUENNAISE—Fry the chops in butter. When half-cooked, add to the pan—for 6 chops—2 tablespoons of chopped onion cooked lightly in butter and a teaspoon of chopped shallots. Drain the chops. Arrange in a crown in a round dish, alternating with rows of heart-shaped croûtons fried in butter. Pour over the following sauce:

Dilute the pan juices left over from frying with 1¼ cups (3 decilitres) of *Demi-glace sauce* (see SAUCE). Boil for 5 minutes. Take off the fire and bind the sauce with 3 chicken livers rubbed through a fine sieve, uncooked and blended with 2 tablespoons of calvados. Heat without allowing to boil. Put the sauce through a strainer. Heat it again without allowing to boil and blend in 2 teaspoons of butter.

Lamb chops à la sarladaise. CÔTELETTES D'AGNEAU À LA SARLADAISE—Grill or fry the chops in butter. Arrange in a ring on a layer of potatoes *à la sarladaise* (*Anna potatoes* mixed with slivers of truffles—see POTATOES). Pour around the potatoes several tablespoons of *Périgueux sauce* (see SAUCE).

Lamb chops soubise. CÔTELETTES D'AGNEAU SOUBISE— Grill or fry. Arrange in a crown. Garnish with a fairly thick *Soubise purée* (see PURÉE).

Lamb chops Talleyrand. CÔTELETTES D'AGNEAU TALLEYRAND—Sauté the chops in butter. Arrange in a crown. Garnish the middle of the dish with a fairly thick *Soubise purée* (see PURÉE). Pour over the chops a sauce prepared in the following manner:

In the butter left over in the pan from frying the chops, lightly fry mushrooms cut in dice, and truffles also cut in dice; dilute with 2 tablespoons of sherry and add ½ cup of thick fresh cream. Simmer for a few moments. Pour over the chops.

Lamb chops à la Toulouse. CÔTELETTES D'AGNEAU À LA TOULOUSE—Braise the chops. Remove them from the pan and glaze in the oven. Boil down the stock to brown gravy and add to it 2 tablespoons of Madeira.

Arrange the chops in a slightly raised puff-pastry shell (or in a circle on croûtons fried in butter) and garnish them, in the centre, with *ragoût à la Toulousaine** (quenelles, cocks' combs and kidneys, lamb's sweetbreads, or small escalopes of calf's sweetbreads, truffles and mushrooms) in a very thick *Allemande sauce* (see SAUCE). Sprinkle the chops with the pan juices only. Put paper frills on end bones.

Lamb chops à la turque. CÔTELETTES D'AGNEAU À LA TURQUE—Fry the lamb chops in butter. Arrange in a circle on a round dish. Garnish the middle of the dish with *Rice pilaf à la turque* (see PILAF). Dilute the pan juices with stock and *Tomato sauce* (see SAUCE), add a pounded clove of garlic and pour over the chops.

Lamb chops Villeroi—See *Mutton chops à la Villeroi.*

Crépinettes of lamb. CRÉPINETTES D'AGNEAU—Prepare like crépinettes of pork using lamb *salpicon**. See PORK, *Crépinettes of pork*.

Crépinettes of lamb à la périgourdine. CRÉPINETTES D'AGNEAU À LA PÉRIGOURDINE—Flatten and trim 6 lamb cutlets, season them with salt and pepper and braise. Allow to cool in the pan juices.

In the meantime, prepare 1 cup (200 grams) of finely pounded *Pork forcemeat* (see FORCEMEAT), add to it ½ cup (100 grams) of *foie gras* and 2 truffles (50 grams) cut in dice; mix well.

Drain the chops and dry them off. Coat on both sides

with a layer of the above forcemeat. Wrap each cutlet in a thin piece of pig's caul or salt pork, making sure that it is entirely closed.

Brush the crépinettes with melted butter, press into breadcrumbs and cook under a low flame.

Lamb curry

Lamb curry. CARI D'AGNEAU—Follow directions for *Curried mutton*, using baby or spring lamb, reducing the cooking time slightly, allowing for the tenderness of the meat. See MUTTON.

Lamb cutlets—These are cut from the best end of neck (U.S. shoulder). Prepare by following recipes for lamb chops.

Double of lamb. DOUBLE D'AGNEAU—This is a joint comprising the two legs of the animal. You can either roast or pot-roast it. It is garnished with vegetables and served with its own gravy, clear or thickened, depending on the type of vegetable chosen.

Cooking time. 18 to 20 minutes per pound.

All the garnishes recommended for the baron are suitable for a double of lamb.

Filets mignons of lamb. FILETS MIGNONS D'AGNEAU—These are the small pieces of lean meat (U.S. tenderloin) which are found on the bone of the saddle. In general, these small fillets are left with the big fillets of the saddle when the saddle is boned, but they can also be prepared separately. See MUTTON, *Filets mignons of mutton.*

Fillets of lamb (U.S. loin of lamb). FILETS D'AGNEAU—This name defines half of the saddle of fully-grown lamb boned, rolled and secured with string.

It can be roasted, pot-roasted or braised.

All the methods of preparation given for *Loin of lamb* or for *Shoulder of lamb* are applicable.

Fricassée of lamb. FRICASSÉE D'AGNEAU—This is the same as the second recipe for *Blanquette of lamb* above.

Lamb's head à l'écossaise. TÊTE D'AGNEAU À L'ÉCOSSAISE—Singe and carefully clean the lamb's head. Cut into two, lengthwise. Leave to soak thoroughly in cold water.

Remove the brains, which are cooked separately in *court-bouillon**.

Cook the two halves of the head in water with carrots, onions and celery as a *pot-au-feu**. (Cooking time about 2 hours.)

Drain the head, put it in an oven-proof dish, brush with melted butter and put in a very hot oven.

Serve with a white sauce (see SAUCE) to which a tablespoon of chopped and blanched sage and the brains cut in small dice have been added.

Stuffed lamb's head à l'anglaise. TÊTE D'AGNEAU FARCIE À L'ANGLAISE—Scald the lamb's head and remove all bones. Fill it with a stuffing *à l'anglaise*, made of chopped suet and breadcrumbs, well-seasoned and mixed with forcemeat made from minced lamb's liver and bacon. See FORCEMEAT.

Wrap the lamb's head in a napkin and secure both ends of the napkin with string.

Brown sliced bacon rinds, carrots and onions in butter in a braising pan. Put in the head. Add a *bouquet garni** and a clove. Braise for half an hour.

Serve with *Pascaline sauce* prepared as follows:

Toss 1 medium-large onion (125 grams) chopped, in 2 tablespoons of butter, moisten with 1 cup (2 decilitres) of white wine. Boil down and add 1½ cups (3 decilitres) of white sauce. Bring to the boil; bind with 2 yolks of egg and, at the last moment, add a small tablespoon of chopped, blanched parsley, a dash of lemon juice and a pinch of cayenne pepper.

Lamb kidney—See OFFAL OR VARIETY MEATS.

Leg of lamb. GIGOT D'AGNEAU—The best way to prepare the leg of a fully-grown lamb is to roast, pot-roast or braise it. This joint, when it is big, can also be boiled, according to the English method.

Roast, pot-roast or boiled leg of lamb can be served with all the garnishes recommended for leg, baron, double or shoulder of mutton.

The leg of baby or milk-fed lamb (Pauillac or Toulouse lamb) is either roasted or pot-roasted.

Cooking time for a leg of lamb. From 18 to 25 minutes per pound.

Roast leg of lamb is served garnished with watercress and quarters of lemon and accompanied by its own gravy.

It can also be served, as is customary in England, with *Mint sauce.* See SAUCE, *Cold sauces.*

Leg of lamb à l'anglaise. GIGOT D'AGNEAU À L'ANGLAISE—Season the leg of a fully-grown lamb, trim it and bone it almost completely. Wrap it in a napkin, lightly buttered and sprinkled with flour. Secure with string.

Put it into boiling water, salted in the proportion of 1 teaspoon per quart (8 grams of salt per litre), with 2 quartered carrots, 2 medium-sized onions, one stuck with a clove, and a *bouquet garni* consisting of a sprig of parsley, thyme and a bay leaf, as well as a clove of garlic.

Cook the leg, simmering gently, and allowing 15 to 18 minutes per pound.

Drain the leg. Unwrap it and arrange on a long dish. Put the vegetables around it. Serve with *Butter sauce II* (see SAUCE), with 2 teaspoons of capers and a sauceboat of the strained stock in which the leg was cooked added to it.

Leg of lamb boiled *à l'anglaise* can be served with a purée of turnips or celery which has been cooked with the leg. Mashed potatoes or purée of white beans can also be served with the leg of lamb.

Leg of lamb à la bonne femme. GIGOT D'AGNEAU À LA BONNE FEMME—Prepare, using leg of fully-grown lamb, as described in the recipe for *Leg of mutton à la bonne femme*. See MUTTON.

Leg of lamb à la bordelaise. GIGOT D'AGNEAU À LA BORDELAISE—Cook in a casserole a leg of lamb in a mixture of butter and oil. When one-third done, put 2 cups (600 grams) of tiny potato balls and ½ pound (250 grams) of fresh cèpes or button mushrooms lightly tossed in oil, into the casserole. Season. Cook in a slow oven. When the leg and the garnish are cooked, sprinkle with *Noisette butter* (see BUTTER, *Compound butters*) in which 4 tablespoons of breadcrumbs with a good tablespoon of chopped parsley and garlic have been fried.

Parslied leg of lamb (*Robert Carrier*)

Lamb on skewers or brochettes (*Robert Carrier*)

Leg of lamb à la boulangère. GIGOT D'AGNEAU À LA BOULANGÈRE—Prepare like *Shoulder of mutton à la boulangère*. See MUTTON.

Braised leg of lamb with various garnishes. GIGOT D'AGNEAU BRAISÉ—Prepare like *Braised shoulder of lamb* below and serve with all the usual garnishes suitable for braised, pot-roasted or roast mutton or lamb.

Leg of lamb en chevreuil. GIGOT D'AGNEAU EN CHEVREUIL—Prepare, using leg of fully-grown lamb, as described in the recipe for *Leg of mutton en chevreuil.* See MUTTON.

Parslied leg of lamb. GIGOT D'AGNEAU PERSILLÉ—This is a leg of fully-grown or baby or milk-fed lamb, cooked in the oven or on a spit. When cooked, it is coated with fresh breadcrumbs mixed with chopped parsley. Press well to make this mixture adhere evenly all over the joint and put the leg back in the oven until the surface turns golden. Arrange on a long dish, garnish with watercress and lemons cut in half. Serve its own gravy separately.

In the south-west of France chopped garlic is added to the parsley and breadcrumbs mixture.

Pot-roasted leg of lamb with various garnishes. GIGOT D'AGNEAU POÊLÉ—This is a leg of lamb trimmed and pot-roasted in a casserole in butter or other fat, but without adding any liquid.

When the leg is cooked, put it on a long dish, surround with the garnish desired (all garnishes recommended for baron, double, or loin of lamb). Pour over the pan juices, diluted with white wine and thickened brown stock.

Roast leg of lamb. GIGOT D'AGNEAU RÔTI—Trim the leg at the knuckle end, loosen the flesh around the knuckle; remove most of the bone. Tie this part of the leg with string.

Cook on a spit or in the oven allowing 15 to 25 minutes per pound.

Arrange the leg on a long dish, garnish with a bunch of watercress. Serve with diluted pan juices, keeping a little fat in them, and halves of lemons.

Mint sauce is usually served with roast leg of lamb.

Lamb's liver. FOIE D'AGNEAU—This is generally used with the rest of the lamb's pluck to prepare a special dish called *fressure*.

All recipes for calves' liver can also be used for lamb's liver. See OFFAL OR VARIETY MEATS.

Loin of lamb. CARRÉS D'AGNEAU—Loin of yearling lamb is roasted. All the garnishes recommended for *baron* or *double* of lamb are applicable to this cut. They are served with their own juice, clear or thickened into a gravy, depending on the nature of the garnish. They are also served, as is the custom in England, with mint sauce.

Cooking time for roast loin of lamb. 15 to 18 minutes per pound (22-25 minutes per kilo). Baby or milk-fed lamb loins, which are not very big, are usually pot-roasted in butter or grilled.

Loin of lamb (U.S.)—See *Fillets of lamb.*

Loin of lamb à la beauharnais. CARRÉ D'AGNEAU À LA BEAUHARNAIS—Trim the loin, season, brush with melted butter and grill or broil under a gentle heat. When it is nearly cooked, sprinkle with white breadcrumbs and finish cooking under the grill or broiler to brown the surface.

Put the meat on a long dish, garnish at each end with *Noisette potatoes* (see POTATOES) scooped out with a potato baller to look like hazel nuts (or very small new potatoes cooked in butter), and on the sides with little artichoke hearts boiled in *court-bouillon** and sautéed in butter, filled with *Beauharnais sauce* or *Béarnaise* finished off with a purée of tarragon. Surround the loin with a border of buttered *Demi-glace sauce* (see SAUCE).

Loin of lamb à la bonne femme. CARRÉ D'AGNEAU À LA BONNE FEMME—Trim the loin of lamb and brown it in butter in a *cocotte* (earthenware fire-proof casserole). Put into the *cocotte* 12 small onions, previously tossed in butter, 12 lightly fried bacon strips or rashers and a cup of tiny potato balls (250 grams). Season, sprinkle with 2 tablespoons of butter, cook in a slow oven (325°F.) and serve in the same *cocotte*.

Loin of lamb à la bordelaise. CARRÉ D'AGNEAU À LA BORDELAISE—Pare and trim the loin and brown it lightly in a mixture of butter and oil in equal proportions, in a *cocotte**. Add cèpes or cultivated mushrooms fried in oil and potatoes cut down to look like small olives. Season and cook in a slow oven (325°F.). At the last moment, add several tablespoons of brown stock mixed with tomato purée and flavoured with a crushed clove of garlic. Sprinkle with chopped parsley. Serve in the *cocotte**.

Loin of lamb à la boulangère. CARRÉ D'AGNEAU À LA BOULANGÈRE—Trim the loin. Prepare in an earthenware dish as *Shoulder of lamb à la boulangère.*

Loin of lamb à la Clamart. CARRÉ D'AGNEAU À LA CLAMART—Trim the loin of baby or milk-fed lamb and pot-roast it in butter. When cooked, add to the casserole 2 cups ($\frac{1}{2}$ litre) of fresh garden peas prepared *à la française*. (See PEAS). Leave to simmer for 5 minutes under a lid.

Loin of lamb in a cocotte à la maraîchère. CARRÉ D'AGNEAU EN COCOTTE À LA MARAÎCHÈRE—Trim a loin of lamb and brown it in butter in an earthenware dish. Put into the *cocotte* 24 small potatoes carefully peeled to the same size and tossed in butter, 2 handfuls of salsify (150 grams) cooked in *court-bouillon** and tossed in butter, and 24 Brussels sprouts lightly blanched and tossed in butter.

Finish cooking everything together. At the last moment, add 4 tablespoons of thickened brown stock. Serve in the *cocotte*.

Grilled loin of lamb. CARRÉ D'AGNEAU GRILLÉ—Trim the loin. Make a few surface incisions in the skin, season, brush with melted butter and grill (or broil) under a low flame until both sides are nicely golden.

Arrange on a long dish, garnish with watercress and serve with half-melted *Maître d'hôtel butter*. (See BUTTER, *Compound butters.*)

Loin of lamb à la languedocienne. CARRÉ D'AGNEAU À LA LANGUEDOCIENNE—Trim the lamb and brown it lightly in butter (or goose fat) in an earthenware dish. Add 2 small onions tossed in butter with 12 small, square pieces of smoked ham, 6 cloves of blanched garlic and $\frac{1}{2}$ pound (200 grams) of small white cèpes or button mushrooms fried in oil. Season. Cook in a slow oven, basting frequently. Sprinkle with chopped parsley and serve in the dish in which it was cooked.

Loin of lamb la Varenne. CARRÉ D'AGNEAU LA VARENNE—Bone a trimmed loin of baby or milk-fed lamb completely. Beat it to flatten slightly, season with salt and pepper, dip in beaten egg and cover with breadcrumbs, pressing down well to make the crumbs adhere. Cook the loin in clarified butter, making both sides a nice golden colour.

Arrange on a round dish on a foundation composed of a *salpicon** of culvitated mushrooms *à la crème.* Sprinkle with *Noisette butter.* (See BUTTER, *Compound butters.*)

Loin of lamb maharajah. CARRÉ D'AGNEAU MAHARADJAH—Trim loin of milk-fed lamb and pot-roast in butter.

When half-cooked, add 3 tablespoons (75 grams) of chopped onion lightly cooked in butter. Season with salt, a teaspoon of curry powder and a clove of garlic. Cook with a lid on.

Arrange on a round dish. Garnish with *Rice pilaf* (see PILAF) and small tomatoes cooked in oil. Dilute the pan juices with $\frac{3}{4}$ cup ($1\frac{1}{2}$ decilitres) of white wine, add 1 cup (2 decilitres) of fresh cream, simmer and pour over the curry.

Loin of lamb Monselet. CARRÉ D'AGNEAU MONSELET—Trim loin of baby or milk-fed lamb and cook under a grill. When it is nearly cooked, sprinkle with fresh grated breadcrumbs and put back under grill to turn golden.

Put on a foundation of *Anna potatoes* (see POTATOES), not too thick. Garnish with quarters of small artichokes cooked in butter. Surround with a border of buttered *Demi-glace sauce* (see SAUCE).

Loin of lamb à la niçoise. CARRÉ D'AGNEAU À LA NIÇOISE—Trim a loin of lamb and brown in butter in an earthenware *cocotte**. Add zucchini or a marrow, peeled, cut in large dice and tossed in butter, a large peeled tomato, cut into square pieces with the seeds taken out and fried in oil, and about 20 small new potatoes, correctly peeled and cut down to a uniform size. Season with salt and pepper. Cook in a slow oven (300°F.). Sprinkle with chopped parsley. Serve in the *cocotte*.

Loin of lamb with noodles. CARRÉ D'AGNEAU AUX NOUILLES—Trim the loin of lamb and cook it in butter in a *cocotte*. When it is nearly cooked, remove from the *cocotte*; put noodles, freshly boiled in salted water, drained and tossed in *Noisette butter* (see BUTTER, *Compound butters*), into the *cocotte*. Put the loin back. Finish cooking together in the oven. At the last moment, sprinkle with a few tablespoons of thickened brown stock.

Loin of lamb Parmentier. CARRÉ D'AGNEAU PARMENTIER—Brown a trimmed loin of lamb in butter. Put in a pan 1 cup (250 grams) of potatoes cut in dice. Season and sprinkle with melted butter. Finish cooking everything together in a slow oven (300°F.). Arrange on a round dish. Dilute the pan juices with white wine, add thickened veal stock and pour over the loin. Sprinkle with chopped parsley.

Loin of lamb à la périgourdine. CARRÉ D'AGNEAU EN CRÉPINE À LA PÉRIGOURDINE—Trim the loin of milk-fed lamb and cook in butter until three-quarters done. (The loin can also be boned before cooking.) Allow to cool.

Coat on both sides with a finely minced pork forcemeat mixed with diced truffles. Wrap the meat in a thin piece of pig's caul (previously soaked in cold water). Make sure the fat covers the meat completely. Spread with melted butter, cover with white breadcrumbs, sprinkle with butter and grill on a low fire or broil. Put the meat on a dish, garnish with small potato balls cooked in butter. Serve *Périgueux sauce* separately. See SAUCE.

Pot-roasted loin of lamb with various garnishes. CARRÉ D'AGNEAU POÊLÉ—Trim the loin of lamb and cook in butter. When half-cooked, add the vegetable chosen as garnish and finish cooking together or, if the particular vegetable should be prepared entirely separately, finish cooking the meat by itself.

Arrange the meat in a round dish. Surround with garnish. Dilute the pan juices with white wine, blend in thickened brown stock and pour over loin.

The pot-roasted loin of lamb may, as stated above, after having been cooked separately, be garnished with one or other of the garnishes recommended for the baron or the double of lamb.

The following garnishes can be added to the loin during cooking: artichokes (hearts or quarters); aubergines (egg-plant), in large dice, previously tossed in butter or oil; new carrots, half-cooked in butter and water; cèpes, fried in oil or butter; various types of mushrooms; Brussels sprouts; marrows (zucchini), cut in large dice; Chinese artichokes, half-braised; half-cooked turnips; glazed small onions; potatoes diced, cut down to the size of olives or shredded into straws; salsify, cooked in *court-bouillon**, drained and tossed in butter.

Pot-roasted loin of lamb can also be garnished with the following: pasta products, prepared in various ways; purées of fresh or dried vegetables; rice pilaf or risotto; *fondue* of tomatoes, *soubise*, etc.

Médaillons of lamb. MÉDAILLONS D'AGNEAU—Another name for *Noisettes of lamb*. See below.

Mignonnettes of lamb. MIGNONNETTES D'AGNEAU—This name is often used (we do not advocate its use, as it sounds somewhat precious) for *Lamb noisettes*.

Minced lamb. HACHIS D'AGNEAU—Prepare as *Beef hash**.

Lamb moussaka. MOUSSAKA D'AGNEAU—This is prepared with minced lamb and aubergines (egg-plants) like *Mutton moussaka*. See MUTTON.

Lamb noisettes. NOISETTES D'AGNEAU—Very delicate pieces of meat taken from the rib or loin of lamb. They are trimmed into round, rather thick little fillets. Their weight varies between $2\frac{1}{2}$ to 3 ounces (70 to 90 grams).

Lamb noisettes à l'algérienne. NOISETTES D'AGNEAU À L'ALGÉRIENNE—Proceed as described in the recipe given for *Tournedos à l'algérienne*. See BEEF.

Lamb noisettes Armenonville. NOISETTES D'AGNEAU ARMENONVILLE—Sauté the noisettes in butter, arrange on little foundations of *Anna potatoes* (see POTATOES), garnish with morels in cream and cocks' combs and kidneys. Serve with a sauce made of the pan juices, diluted with white wine and thickened veal stock.

Lamb noisettes Béatrix. NOISETTES D'AGNEAU BÉATRIX—Sauté the noisettes in butter, put on fried croûtons, garnish with morels or other mushrooms fried in butter, very small quarters of artichokes cooked in butter under a lid, small, glazed carrots and new potatoes in butter. Serve with a sauce made from the pan juices, diluted with sherry and thickened veal stock.

Lamb noisettes Beauharnais. NOISETTES D'AGNEAU BEAUHARNAIS—Sauté the noisettes in butter. Put on fried croûtons. Garnish with very small artichoke hearts filled with thick *Béarnaise sauce* (see SAUCE) with a purée of tarragon added to it, and tiny potato balls. Serve with a sauce made from the pan juices diluted with Madeira and *Demi-glace sauce* (see SAUCE), with chopped truffles added to it.

Lamb noisettes Carignan. NOISETTES D'AGNEAU CARIGNAN—Sauté the noisettes in butter and put on a foundation of *Anna potatoes* (see POTATOES).

Garnish with very small quarters of artichokes stewed in butter and asparagus tips dressed with butter. Put between each noisette a very small 'egg', made of *Duchess potato mixture* (see POTATO), dipped in egg and breadcrumbs, fried, hollowed out and filled with a purée of *foie gras* with truffles. Serve with a sauce made from the pan juices diluted with port and *Demi-glace sauce* (see SAUCE).

Lamb noisettes chasseur. NOISETTES D'AGNEAU CHASSEUR—Sauté the noisettes in a mixture of butter and oil. Arrange on a dish. Serve with a sauce made from the pan juices diluted with *Chasseur sauce*. See SAUCE.

You can also, as soon as the noisettes are fried, remove them and put into the same pan (for 8 noisettes) $\frac{1}{4}$ pound

(125 grams) of chopped mushrooms and a teaspoon of chopped shallots; dilute with white wine and moisten with veal stock and a little *Tomato sauce* (see SAUCE).

Lamb noisettes Cussy. NOISETTES D'AGNEAU CUSSY—Sauté the noisettes in butter and arrange on fried *croûtons*. Garnish with little artichoke hearts, filled with mushroom purée and sprinkled with breadcrumbs, and cock's kidneys. Serve with a sauce made from the juices diluted with Madeira and *Demi-glace sauce* (see SAUCE).

Lamb noisettes Duroc. NOISETTES D'AGNEAU DUROC—Proceed as for *Lamb noisettes chasseur*. Garnish with very small potato balls fried in butter. Sprinkle with chopped tarragon.

Lamb noisettes à l'italienne. NOISETTES D'AGNEAU À L'ITALIENNE—Sauté the noisettes in oil. Arrange on fried croûtons and put on each noisette a little slice of lean ham fried in oil. Serve with a sauce made from the pan juices diluted with *Italian sauce* (see SAUCE).

Lamb noisettes Melba. NOISETTES D'AGNEAU MELBA—Sauté the noisettes in butter, arrange on fried croûtons, garnish with braised lettuce hearts or very small tomatoes stuffed with a mixture of chicken, truffles and mushrooms, bound with *Velouté sauce* (see SAUCE) and browned in the oven or under a grill. Serve with a sauce made from the pan juices diluted with Madeira and *Demi-glace sauce* (see SAUCE).

Lamb noisettes Montpensier. NOISETTES D'AGNEAU MONTPENSIER—Sauté the noisettes in butter, arrange on fried croûtons and garnish with coarsely shredded truffles fried in butter and asparagus tips in butter. Serve with a sauce made from the pan juices diluted with Madeira and *Demi-glace sauce* (see SAUCE).

Lamb noisettes Nichette. NOISETTES D'AGNEAU NICHETTE—Grill the noisettes, put each on a *Duchess potato cake* (see POTATOES) cooked in the oven until golden, and garnish with cocks' combs and kidneys. Put a grilled mushroom filled with grated horseradish on top of each noisette. Serve with *Marrow sauce* (see SAUCE).

Lamb noisettes à la niçoise I. NOISETTES D'AGNEAU À LA NIÇOISE—Sauté the noisettes in oil, put *Garnish à la niçoise** around. Serve with a sauce made from the pan juices diluted with white wine and tomato-flavoured veal stock.

Lamb noisettes à la niçoise II. NOISETTES D'AGNEAU À LA NIÇOISE—Sauté the noisettes in oil, put on a dish, garnish with very small new potatoes tossed in butter and French beans in butter. Put on each noisette a spoonful of *Tomato fondue**. Serve with a sauce made from the pan juices diluted with white wine and tomato-flavoured veal stock.

Lamb noisettes Rivoli. NOISETTES D'AGNEAU RIVOLI—Sauté the noisettes in butter, arrange on *Anna potatoes* (see POTATOES) and serve with a sauce made from the pan juices diluted with Madeira and *Demi-glace sauce* (see SAUCE) with truffles added to it.

These can be served in *cocotte*.

Lamb noisettes Saint-Germain. NOISETTES D'AGNEAU SAINT-GERMAIN—Proceed as described in the recipe for *Tournedos Saint-Germain*. See BEEF.

Sautéed noisettes of lamb. NOISETTES D'AGNEAU SAUTÉES—Trim the noisettes and flatten them lightly. Season and sauté as briskly as possible in clarified butter, in oil, or in a mixture of butter and oil, depending on the recipe.

Arrange in a dish, garnish and serve with sauce indicated in the recipe.

Note. Sautéed noisettes are sometimes served on croûtons fried in butter or on various other garnishes as foundations.

Garnishes and sauces for them will be found in the recipes which follow. In addition to these recipes, all those given elsewhere for tournedos or médaillons of beef, as well as those indicated for lamb or mutton cutlets, can be applied to noisettes.

The stocks and gravies most commonly used in cooking are based on veal, chicken or beef. These stocks, although very palatable when they are prepared under the right conditions, have not got the special taste of mutton or lamb stock.

In the home, when there is an occasion to prepare noisettes of mutton or lamb, a stock can also be made of the pieces trimmed away and the bones. To make this stock, proceed as described in the recipe for *Thickened veal stock*. See STOCKS.

Lamb noisettes à la turque. NOISETTES D'AGNEAU À LA TURQUE—Sauté the noisettes in butter, garnish with *Rice pilaf à la turque* (see PILAF) and aubergines (egg-plant) cut in large dice and fried in oil. Serve with a sauce made from the pan juices diluted with tomato-flavoured veal stock.

Lamb noisettes à la Valencienne. NOISETTES D'AGNEAU À LA VALENCIENNE—Sauté the noisettes in butter, put each one on a little mound of *Rice à la Valencienne**. Serve with a sauce made from the pan juices diluted with white wine and tomato-flavoured veal stock with a pounded clove of garlic added to it.

Lamb noisettes garnished with vegetables. NOISETTES D'AGNEAU GARNIES AUX LÉGUMES—Sauté the noisettes in butter (or grill them), garnish with the vegetables recommended and, if the noisettes are sautéed, sprinkle them very lightly with a sauce made from the pan juices, diluted and reduced, or with a thickened *Demi-glace sauce* (see SAUCE).

Note. The following vegetables are mainly used for garnishing noisettes: quarters of hearts of artichokes; aubergines (egg-plant), sautéed or fried; fried cèpes and other mushrooms; braised endive; kidney beans in butter; sautéed brussels sprouts; cucumbers, cut into uniform pieces and cooked in butter; Chinese artichokes stewed; stewed gumbos (okra); French beans in butter; braised lettuce; peas in butter or *à la française**; asparagus tips in butter, etc.

The noisettes can also be garnished with purée of fresh vegetables, such as chicory or spinach, or a purée of leguminous plants.

Some of these garnishes, depending on their nature, should be served separately.

Pascaline of lamb. PASCALINE D'AGNEAU—Plumerey, who continued Carême's work, gives a recipe for this rather complicated dish. He says that he wrote this recipe under the dictation of the old Controller of the Prince de Conti's household and that he himself never tried it out. Here it is:

'Take 4 lambs' heads. See that they are perfectly scalded, put them to soak, as well as the 4 sets of brains and 4 tongues. Take 3 lambs' livers, which you mince with half of fresh bacon, *fines herbes*, salt, pepper and spices, to make it into forcemeat; and 12 lambs' feet which you cook with the tongues. Cook them in a *court-bouillon*.

'You also cook the brains, but separately, in a *white court-bouillon;* when the tongues and the brains are cooked, you cut them into large dice with mushrooms, and shape them into 12 croquettes.

'Now take the 4 blanched heads of lamb and fill with the forcemeat; sew them up securely; put on top of them several slices of lemon; cover with bacon and cook them in a good casserole (by "cooking in a good casserole" Plumerey means cooking in a covered casserole on a bed of vegetables).

'Have a dozen larded lambs' sweetbreads ready; keep the throats; prepare a smooth sauce (*Velouté*—see SAUCE), into which you have put 2 handfuls of mushrooms, reduce it and bind with 6 yolks of eggs. Then, take the heads out of the casserole, drain, remove thread, arrange on a long dish, nose part facing outwards; cut each foot in two and put 3 of them between each head; pour over the sauce and put around them the 12 fried croquettes, 12 larded lambs' sweetbreads and 12 croûtons of bread cut to look like cocks' combs (fried in butter); throw the lamb's throats with mushrooms into the sauce and cover the heads with it.'

Alexandre Dumas père, who wrote a gastronomical dictionary, gives for the preparation of *Pascaline of lamb* the following recipe, totally different from that given by Plumerey:

Pascaline of lamb à la royale. PASCALINE D'AGNEAU À LA ROYALE—'The custom of serving a lamb whole on Easter Sunday was kept in France until the time of Louis XV and even Louis XVI. This is how the dish, the origin of which appears to go back to the agapes of the early Christians, was prepared:

'The neck of a six-month-old lamb was boned; the breast bone was sawn through and the shoulder bone broken and fastened to it with string (that is to say, the shoulder bones were trussed to the breast); the two shank bones of the legs were also broken and fastened in the same manner.

'It was stuffed with a forcemeat of pounded lamb, yolks of hard boiled eggs, stale breadcrumbs and chopped *fines herbes* and seasoned with four spices.

'The lamb's flesh was carefully larded and put to roast before a big fire; it was served whole, as a remove (separate course), after the soup, either with a green sauce or on a ragoût of truffles cooked in ham jelly.'

Pâté of lamb à la périgourdine—See PÂTÉ.

Lamb pie à la languedocienne. TOURTE D'AGNEAU À LA LANGUEDOCIENNE—This is prepared as an ordinary puff-pastry pie (see DOUGH), with a filling of small lamb noisettes sautéed in butter, salsify cooked in *court-bouillon IX** cut into pieces and tossed in butter, sliced mushrooms, stoned and blanched olives—all these ingredients being put into a pastry-lined dish on a layer of finely pounded *pork forcemeat* (see FORCEMEAT). Dot with a few dabs of butter. Cover with a piece of rolled out pastry, brush with egg and bake in the oven (400°F.) for 40 or 45 minutes. At the last moment, pour into the pie a few tablespoons of reduced *Demi-glace sauce* (see SAUCE), flavoured with Madeira.

Lamb pilaf. PILAF D'AGNEAU—This is prepared like *Mutton pilaf.* See PILAF.

Lamb's pluck—See OFFAL OR VARIETY MEATS.

Quarter of lamb. QUARTIER D'AGNEAU—This name defines a joint comprising the leg and half the saddle, It is mainly taken from baby or milk-fed (Pauillac) lamb. and is usually roasted. All the garnishes recommended for the baron or the saddle of lamb are applicable to quarter of lamb.

Lamb ragoût. RAGOÛT D'AGNEAU—This method of preparation is mainly used for fully-grown lamb. The parts which are most suitable for this dish are lower ribs, the neck, shoulder and breast.

Ragoût of lamb à l'anglaise. RAGOÛT D'AGNEAU À BLANC (À L'ANGLAISE)—Put into a pan, in alternate layers, 1½ pounds (750 grams) of lamb cut in square pieces and 3 medium (500 grams) potatoes, sliced, mixed with 2 medium-sized onions, chopped. Season and add a *bouquet garni**. Pour in enough water (or light stock) to cover the meat. Cook fairly briskly with a lid on.

Heap in a deep dish. Sprinkle with chopped parsley.

Ragoût of lamb à la bonne femme. RAGOÛT D'AGNEAU À LA BONNE FEMME—Brown 1½ pounds (750 grams) of lamb in clarified fat; season with salt, pepper and a pinch of sugar.

Sprinkle with 2 tablespoons of flour and brown lightly. Moisten with 3½ cups (¾ litre) of water, add a *bouquet garni** and half a crushed clove of garlic.

Cook with a lid on for 40 minutes. Drain the pieces of lamb, trim them and put them back in the pan.

Add 2 cups (500 grams) of small potato balls and 12 small onions lightly fried in butter (use new potatoes and onions when in season). Cook with a lid on from 40 to 45 minutes. Serve in a dish.

2 tablespoons of tomato sauce can be added.

Note. All the recipes given for ragoût of mutton can be used for ragoûts of lamb. See MUTTON.

Rib roast of lamb (U.S.)—See *Loin of lamb.*

Saddle of lamb. SELLE D'AGNEAU—The saddle of a yearling (spring) lamb can be prepared by roasting, pot-roasting or braising it, like *Saddle of mutton.* (See MUTTON.) All the garnishes recommended for mutton can be applied to it.

The saddle of baby or milk-fed lamb is either roasted or pot-roasted. Usually, this saddle remains attached to the two legs of the animal, which constitutes the joint known as the baron of lamb.

Lamb sauté. SAUTÉ D'AGNEAU—This is prepared from the same parts of the animal as are used for ragoûts.

To make the sauté dishes, for which the ingredients are only browned, fried with very little fat, and, when off the fire, sprinkled with their pan juices diluted, it is best to use neck and shoulder, boned and cut in small square pieces.

Cut 3 pounds (1½ kilos) of boned lamb into square pieces. Brown in butter in a pan with a carrot and an onion cut in quarters. Season.

When the lamb is nicely brown, remove with a perforated spoon, put into a sauté pan with the garnish indicated in the recipe chosen.

Dilute the pan juices with ⅝ (2 decilitres) cup of white wine (or other wine, depending on recipe), and add 1½ cups (4 decilitres) of thickened brown stock and ⅜ cup (1 decilitre) of tomato purée, strain through a fine strainer and pour over the lamb.

Add a *bouquet garni** and finish cooking with a lid on in the oven for 25 minutes.

Heap in a shallow platter. Boil down (reduce) the sauce, if necessary, and pour over.

Lamb sauté à l'ancienne. SAUTÉ D'AGNEAU À L'ANCIENNE—Bone and cut the lamb as above into pieces and sauté in butter. Put into a pan with ¼ pound (125 grams) of lamb's sweetbreads (soaked, blanched and half-cooked in butter); ½ pound (250 grams) of small mushrooms, lightly tossed in butter, and ¼ pound of cocks' combs and kidneys, cooked in a white *court-bouillon**. Moisten with the pan juices diluted with ⅝ cup (2 decilitres) of Madeira, to which 1-1½ cups (3 decilitres) of *Velouté sauce* (see SAUCE) and ⅝ cup (2 decilitres) of thick fresh cream have been added, simmer for 5 minutes, well-seasoned and strained. Leave to simmer gently for 20 minutes.

Heap in a shallow platter. Garnish with heart-shaped croûtons fried in butter.

Lamb sauté with artichokes. SAUTÉ D'AGNEAU AUX ARTICHAUTS—Fry in butter or oil 1½ pounds (750 grams) of neck or shoulder of lamb, boned and cut in square pieces. Season with salt and pepper and cook until done.

Heap in a shallow platter; decorate with 4 artichoke hearts, blanched and cut in large dice, or sliced and fried in butter or oil.

Dilute the pan juices with one wine glass (1 decilitre) of white wine, reduce (boil down); add ⅞ cup (2 decilitres) of thickened veal stock and pour over the sauté. Sprinkle with chopped parsley.

Lamb sauté with aubergines (egg-plant). SAUTÉ D'AGNEAU AUX AUBERGINES—Cut 3 pounds (1½ kilos) of boned and trimmed lamb's neck into uniform pieces. Season with salt and pepper and cook in a sauté pan, in a mixture of butter and oil in equal proportions until nicely brown. When the lamb is cooked, heap in a shallow platter. Put on top 3 small aubergines (egg-plants) peeled, cut in small square pieces and fried in oil. Pour over the sauté the pan juices, diluted with white wine, moistened with 1½ cups of thickened brown veal stock and 4 tablespoons of tomato purée, flavoured with as much chopped garlic as can be held on the point of a knife, reduced (boiled down) and strained. Sprinkle with chopped parsley.

Lamb sauté with cèpes, morels, St. George's agaric. SAUTÉ D'AGNEAU AUX CÈPES, MORILLES, MOUSSERONS—Proceed to cook the lamb as described in the recipe for *Lamb sauté with aubergines*. Replace the latter by ½ pound (250 grams) of cèpes, morels or St. George's agarics, fried—separately—in butter or oil.

Lamb sauté chasseur. SAUTÉ D'AGNEAU CHASSEUR—Proceed as described in the recipe given for *Veal sauté chasseur*.

Lamb sauté à la crème. SAUTÉ D'AGNEAU À LA CRÈME—Season the lamb, boned and cut into square pieces, with salt and paprika and fry in butter.

When it is done, and sufficiently browned, heap on a shallow platter. Dilute the pan juices with 1 cup (2½ decilitres) of cream. Boil down one-third, add 2½ tablespoons (40 grams) of butter, strain and pour over the lamb.

Lamb sauté aux fines herbes. SAUTÉ D'AGNEAU AUX FINES HERBES—Proceed as described in the recipe for *Lamb sauté à la minute*, adding 1 tablespoon of chopped shallots and 2 tablespoons of a combination of chopped parsley, chervil and tarragon, to the sauce.

Lamb sauté à l'indienne. SAUTÉ D'AGNEAU À L'INDIENNE—Proceed as described in the recipe for *Veal sauté à l'indienne*. See VEAL.

Lamb sauté à l'italienne. SAUTÉ D'AGNEAU À L'ITALIENNE—Proceed as described in the recipe for *Lamb sauté à la minute*. Dilute the pan juices with white wine and *Italian sauce* (see SAUCE).

Lamb sauté à la minute. SAUTÉ D'AGNEAU À LA MINUTE—Cut a boned neck or shoulder of lamb into small uniform pieces. Sauté on a lively fire in butter or oil.

As soon as the pieces of lamb are cooked and sufficiently browned, put in a dish, sprinkle with chopped parsley and a dash of lemon juice and pour over the pan juices, diluted with a wine glass (1 decilitre) of white wine and thickened veal stock.

Lamb sauté with mushrooms. SAUTÉ D'AGNEAU AUX CHAMPIGNONS—As in the recipe for *Lamb sauté with cèpes, morels and St. George's agarics*, but use cultivated mushrooms, correctly peeled and fried in butter (whole, if they are small; sliced, if they are big).

Lamb sauté with paprika (à la hongroise). SAUTÉ D'AGNEAU AU PAPRIKA (À LA HONGROISE)—Cut into square pieces 3 pounds (1½ kilos) of boned lower ribs (or shoulder) of lamb. Brown in ¼ pound of butter. As soon as they are nicely coloured, put in a pan 2 medium onions, chopped. Season with salt and a scant tablespoon of paprika. Sprinkle in 2 tablespoons of flour. Moisten with ⅞ cup (2 decilitres) of white wine. Boil down (reduce), add 1½ cups (3 decilitres) of white stock or strained broth and 2 tablespoons of tomato purée. Add a *bouquet garni**. Cook with a lid on for 30 minutes. Take the pieces of lamb out with a perforated spoon, put into a pan with ½ pound (250 grams) of mushrooms, sliced and lightly tossed in butter. Add 1 cup of fresh cream, seasoned with paprika, to the sauce, boil down, strain and pour over the lamb. Simmer gently with a lid on for 25 minutes. Heap on a shallow platter.

Lamb sauté Parmentier. SAUTÉ D'AGNEAU PARMENTIER—Proceed to cook the meat and the sauce as described in the recipe for *Lamb sauté with aubergines*. Replace the latter with 4 large, long potatoes, cut in dice and fried in butter or oil.

Lamb sauté à la printanière. SAUTÉ D'AGNEAU À LA PRINTANIÈRE—Proceed as in the recipe for *Veal sauté à la printanière*. See VEAL.

Lamb sauté with tomatoes. SAUTÉ D'AGNEAU AUX TOMATES—Proceed as described in the recipe for *Lamb sauté with artichokes*. Replace the latter by 8 small tomatoes, peeled, with the seeds taken out, and cooked in butter or oil.

Note. A grated clove of garlic can be added.

Shoulder of lamb. ÉPAULE D'AGNEAU—All the recipes given for shoulder of mutton are applicable to shoulders of full-grown young lamb. They can be boned and stuffed before cooking.

Shoulder of baby or milk-fed lamb and Pauillac lamb should not be boned. These are principally grilled or roasted and can be served with various garnishes.

Shoulder of lamb à l'albigeoise. ÉPAULE D'AGNEAU À L'ALBIGEOISE. Bone the shoulder and stuff with forcemeat made of sausage meat and minced pig's liver in equal proportions, flavoured with chopped garlic and parsley and well-seasoned. Roll the shoulder and secure with string.

Fry it lightly until golden in sizzling goose fat in an earthenware casserole. Surround with potatoes in quarters (or whole new potatoes) and 12 lightly blanched cloves of garlic. Season, sprinkle with a little goose fat and cook in the oven. At the last moment, sprinkle with chopped parsley. Serve in the dish in which it was cooked.

Shoulder of lamb à la boulangère. ÉPAULE À LA BOULANGÈRE—Bone, season on the inside, roll and secure with string. Cook for 30 minutes in an oval-shaped earthenware fireproof dish, in which 3-4 tablespoons of butter have previously been heated.

Surround with 3 medium-large potatoes (600 grams) cut into long slices (or cut into quarters) and 3 medium-size onions (300 grams), finely chopped and lightly fried in butter (or 20 small onions similarly tossed in butter). Season the garnish, sprinkle with the butter left over in the pan and finish cooking in the oven, basting frequently. At the last moment add 4 tablespoons of thickened brown gravy.

Braised shoulder of lamb with various garnishes—ÉPAULE D'AGNEAU BRAISÉE—Bone a shoulder of a yearling or spring (salt meadow) lamb. Season inside, roll into a long roll and secure with string.

Put into a braising pan bacon rinds, 2 carrots and 1 onion—all finely chopped and lightly fried in butter.

POTATOES. Potatoes stuffed with tomato and mushrooms, French petits pois

(*From Curnonsky:* Cuisine et Vins de France)

POULTRY. *Above:* Chicken with rice, sauce Suprême *Below:* Goose with chestnut stuffing

(*Nézard-Debillot*).

(*From Curnonsky:* Cuisine et Vins de France)

Put the shoulder of lamb on top. Season. Leave to cook under a lid for 10 minutes. Moisten with ½ cup (1½ decilitres) of white wine, boil down, add 1 cup (2½ decilitres) of thickened brown gravy and 4 tablespoons (1 decilitre) of tomato purée; put in a *bouquet garni** and the trimmed off scraps and the bones, crushed into tiny pieces and tossed in butter. Cover with a lid and cook in the oven at 350°F. for an hour or an hour and a half, depending on the size of the shoulder.

Drain the shoulder. Glaze it in the oven. Arrange on a long dish. Surround with the recommended garnish. Heat the pan juices left over from braising, remove fat, reduce, if necessary, strain and pour over the shoulder.

Garnishes suitable for braised shoulder of lamb—All the garnishes indicated for the baron, the double, the loin and the saddle of roast or braised mutton, and, principally, beans or *Bean purée à la bretonne* (see PURÉE).

Some of the garnishes of this joint, for example, the so-called *bourgeoise**, should be cooked with the shoulder.

Shoulder of lamb à la catalane or with pistachio nuts. ÉPAULE D'AGNEAU À LA CATALANE (EN PISTACHE)—See MUTTON, *Shoulder of mutton à la catalane.*

Shoulder of lamb à la gasconne. ÉPAULE D'AGNEAU À LA GASCONNE—Stuff the boned shoulder with a stuffing or forcemeat made of 1½ cups of raw ham (fat and lean), 2 cups of stale bread (without crusts) soaked in stock and squeezed out, 2 tablespoons of chopped onion, 1 clove of garlic slivered and 2 tablespoons chopped parsley, bound with an egg and well-seasoned.

Brush with goose fat and brown lightly in the oven.

Put into a braising pan with coarsely shredded, blanched, green cabbage, 2 quartered carrots, 1 onion stuck with a clove and a *bouquet garni**. Moisten with slightly fat stock. Cook in the oven for 45 minutes. Add quartered potatoes and finish cooking together for another 45 minutes.

Roast shoulder of lamb. ÉPAULE D'AGNEAU RÔTIE—The shoulder of a fully-grown salt meadow lamb is usually boned, rolled and secured with string before being put to roast in the oven or on a spit. It is garnished with watercress and its gravy is served separately.

The shoulder of baby or milk-fed lamb is not boned. It should be roasted in the oven or on a spit on a brisk fire. Garnish with watercress and serve the gravy separately.

Rolled shoulder of lamb (Carême's recipe). ÉPAULE D'AGNEAU EN BALLOTTINE—'Bone two shoulders of lamb to the shank bone; season with salt, pepper and nutmeg and stuff it with a finely pounded forcemeat.

'With a butcher's needle thread a string through to the end of the shoulder in such a way as to make it serve as a draw string. Lard each shoulder with lardoons of bacon, working them in in the shape of a rosette. Put into a casserole trimmings from the shoulders and veal scraps, 1 carrot, 2 onions, a *bouquet garni**, and cover with rashers (strips) of bacon; moisten with bouillon and a good glass of white wine to cover the larded shoulders and cook for 1½ hours. Take care to glaze the larded shoulders gradually; drain, remove string, arrange on a dish and garnish with small glazed carrots and onions, or braised lettuce or celery; strain the pan juice and remove surplus fat, reduce, pour some over the rolled shoulder of lamb and serve the rest separately.

'One can also serve some purée with a rolled shoulder of lamb, according to taste, but I recommend serving it separately as, served on the dish, it always makes a bad effect.'

Lamb on skewers. BROCHETTE D'AGNEAU—Prepare, using pieces of lean cuts of lamb from the neck or lower ribs and pieces of bacon, as described in the recipe for *Brochette of veal.* See VEAL.

Sliced lamb. ÉMINCÉS D'AGNEAU—Prepared of best cuts of yearling or spring (salt meadow) lamb, pot-roasted or braised. See MUTTON.

Lamb's sweetbreads—See OFFAL OR VARIETY MEATS.

Timbale of lamb à l'ancienne. TIMBALE D'AGNEAU À L'ANCIENNE—Line a Charlotte mould with pie pastry. Put in it little lamb's noisettes braised in *court-bouillon**, lamb's sweetbreads cooked in butter, truffles and mushrooms, the whole blended with *Velouté sauce* (see SAUCE) diluted with cream and flavoured with Madeira (reserve a few tablespoons), alternating with layers of macaroni cooked in water, cut in large pieces, blended with cream, butter and grated cheese. These fillings must be completely cold before being put into the pie dish. Cover the dish with a pastry lid, decorate the top with pastry leaves, etc.; make an opening in the middle to allow steam to escape and brush over with beaten egg. Bake in a hot oven (400°F.) 40 to 45 minutes. Just before serving, pour into the pie through the opening in the top, a few tablespoons of the *Velouté sauce.*

Lamb's trotters (feet). PIEDS D'AGNEAU—These are prepared as *Sheep's trotters (feet).* See OFFAL OR VARIETY MEATS.

Vol-au-Vent of lamb with truffles and mushrooms. VOL-AU-VENT D'AGNEAU AUX TRUFFES ET CHAMPIGNONS—Fill a *vol-au-vent** case as soon as it is out of the oven, with a ragoût, moistened with white or brown thickened stock, made of braised thin *noisettes* of lamb, lamb's sweetbreads cooked in butter and sliced truffles and mushrooms.

LAMBALLE—This is a name given to various dishes. It is most commonly applied to a meat broth made by adding clear soup with tapioca cooked in it to a purée of fresh peas (peas *à la Saint-Germain*). See SOUPS AND BROTHS, *Potage Lamballe.*

LAMBICK—A highly intoxicating Belgian beer, rather sour in taste. See BEER.

Lamprey

LAMPREY. LAMPROIE—There are three types of edible lamprey: the lamprey-eel or sea-lamprey, the lampern or river lamprey and the lamprey proper.

The lamprey-eel is the most highly prized. It is to be found particularly in the Atlantic and the Mediterranean.

It is similar to the eel in general appearance, but different from it in a number of particulars: its skin is yellowish with brown markings, its dorsal fins are spaced along its back, and it has seven bronchial orifices which form two vertical lines on either side of its neck.

In spring, the lamprey-eels migrate to the mouths of rivers. They are to be found in large numbers in the Loire, the Rhône and the Gironde.

The flesh of the lamprey is delicate but, being very fatty, it is somewhat indigestible.

Lampreys of medium size are the most sought after, especially those caught in the mouths of rivers.

Trimming. Scald the fish so that the skin can be easily removed. According to the manner in which it is to be cooked, cut it into thick slices or leave it whole. Prepare according to the selected recipe.

Lamprey dishes. The lamprey can be cooked in a great many different ways. Most commonly it is stewed in wine (*en matelote*) flavoured with the blood of the lamprey. In addition, all recipes for eels are suitable for lampreys. See EEL.

Lamprey à la bordelaise (Bordeaux cookery). LAMPROIE À LA BORDELAISE—Bleed a medium-sized lamprey. Keep the blood aside to flavour the sauce. Scald the fish and scrape off the skin. Remove the central nerve. (To do this, cut off the tip of the lamprey's tail, make an incision round the neck below the gills and, through this opening, catch hold of the nerve and pull it out.)

Cut the fish into slices 2 inches thick. Butter a pan and line it with sliced onions and carrots. Put in the slices of lamprey. Add a *bouquet garni** and a clove of garlic. These should be put in the middle of the dish. Season with salt and pepper. Moisten with enough red wine to cover the fish. Boil hastily for 12 minutes.

Drain the slices of lamprey. Cook 12 slices of white leek in butter with 4 tablespoons of raw diced bacon in a covered pan. Put the slices of lamprey in a pan alternating with slices of white leek. Make a *roux** of flour and butter. Moisten with the cooking stock of the lamprey. Cook this sauce for 15 minutes. Strain and pour over the lamprey. Simmer very slowly until the fish is cooked. Serve the lamprey in a round dish. Pour the sauce over it having mixed in the blood kept in reserve. Garnish with slices of bread fried in butter.

LAMPSANA, NIPPLEWORT. LAMPSANE—A plant of the endive family, similar to the sow-thistle. Its leaves are eaten raw in salad. (Cooking turns them bitter.)

LANGUE DE CHAT (CAT'S TONGUE) (Pastry)—In the view of some experts, this biscuit derives its name from its shape—thin, flat and narrow, somewhat like a cat's tongue in appearance.

Langues de chat, which are crisp, dry biscuits, can be made, or rather flavoured, in various ways. Only biscuits made according to the recipe given below, however, can properly be called *langues de chat.*

These biscuits keep for quite a long time and are usually served with certain liqueurs and sparkling wines. They are also served with iced sweets (desserts) and used as an ingredient of various puddings.

Langue de chat I—Work together, in a bowl, 1 cup (250 grams) of fine sugar and 1½ cups (2½ decilitres) of fresh cream. Add 2 cups (250 grams) of sieved cake flour, a tablespoon of vanilla-flavoured sugar or 1 teaspoon of vanilla extract and, when the mixture is quite smooth, 5 stiffly beaten whites of egg.

Rub a metal baking sheet with pure wax or line with heavy waxed paper and, using a forcing (pastry) bag with a round nozzle, pipe the mixture to make little strips about an inch apart so that they will not run into one another during baking.

Bake in a hot oven (400°F.) for about 8 minutes.

Langue de chat II—*Ingredients.* ½ cup (125 grams) butter; ½ cup (125 grams) sieved cake flour; 6 tablespoons (100 grams) fine sugar; 1½ tablespoons (25 grams) vanilla-flavoured sugar (7 tablespoons fine sugar and 1 teaspoon of vanilla extract may be substituted for these last two ingredients); 2 eggs.

Method. Cream the butter in a warmed bowl. Add the sugar and vanilla flavoured sugar. Work the mixture for two minutes, then mix in the eggs, one at a time. Lastly, add the sieved flour.

Pipe this mixture on to a baking sheet as indicated above.

Ambialet, Tarn (*French Government Tourist Office*)

LANGUEDOC, ROUSSILLON, COMTE DE FOIX—The land of Oc (Languedoc) is a district which for centuries has had a tradition of fine cooking. Its people have always been connoisseurs of good food and have gloried in a well-furnished table. Not only have they provided substantial dishes in abundance, such as the famous *cassoulet** of Castelnaudary and the *Daube Languedocienne*, but also subtly flavoured and delicate appetisers such as the magnificent *pâté de foie gras* with truffles, gem of the Languedoc culinary repertoire, which has made famous throughout the world the names of Toulouse, Cazères, Albi and other cities where for so long these exquisite delicacies have been made.

In Languedoc, the Roman and Arab influence which gradually determined the character of its cooking are still recognizable. In the province, *Gallia Narbonensis* under the Romans, was invented the ragoût of mutton with white beans which was, in all probability, the prototype of that robust dish known the world over as *cassoulet.*

The Languedoc larder is well stocked. In the south-western provinces of France are to be found excellent fatstock and succulent poultry and good winged and ground game. The finest *foie gras* is made from goose and duck liver and their indispensable foil, the truffle, that 'subterranean empress', as it was called by the Marquis de Cussy.

To these delicacies must be added excellent salt-water and freshwater fish. Among the latter are the trout of the icy Pyrenean streams, the perch, bream, tench, pike, etc., which are found in abundance in the Garonne, Ariège, Tarn and Aude rivers. The Languedoc kitchen gardens are well stocked with vegetables and its orchards with delicious fruit. Languedoc also has its vineyards and produces excellent wine.

Culinary specialities. With such natural resources, it is no wonder that the cuisine of Languedoc is excellent and that the region has a large number of succulent specialities.

Here, first, are some typical Languedoc broths and soups: *Pot-au-feu à la poule farcie* (stuffed chicken hot-pot); *Soup au farci; Pot-au-feu albigeois* (with stuffed goose neck); *Pot-au-feu carcassonnais* (with ribs of beef, neck of mutton, lean bacon, stuffed cabbage and, over and above the usual pot-vegetables, white beans); *Ouillade catalan; Braou bouffat de Cerdagne; Bouillinade des pêcheurs* (Roussillon); *Bouillabaisse Catalane* (which is nothing like the *bouillabaisse* of Marseilles); *Soupe aux poissons de Sète* (fish soup); *Soupe aux clovisses* (cockle soup); *Soupe à l'ail* (garlic soup); *Soupe à la courge* (pumpkin soup); *Soupe aux choux* (cabbage soup); *Soupe aux tomates* (tomato soup); *Tourin;* and, finally, though this dish is more commonly associated with the Béarnais district, the magnificent *garbure*.

Among the *hors-d'oeuvre* of the area are: Black Mountain and Ariège ham; Sausages of Luchon, Toulouse, the Black Mountain and Ariège; *Frittons* or *grattons* of pork, goose and turkey; Dried *fèche* with radishes of the Tarn; *Melsat* of Dourgne; little tongues of the Tarn; Anchovy *pâté* of Collioure; little pâtés of Pézenas or Béziers (which are also eaten as a dessert); *anchoiade;* fresh white beans *à la croque-au-sel;* fresh figs.

Among the special egg dishes of Languedoc are: Omelettes *à la cansalado;* Omelettes made with ham, blood, wild asparagus tips, hop shoots (called *omelette à la Saint-Jean*), agaric, peppers, pine-kernels, garlic, tomatoes and Quercy truffles; Poached or fried eggs with ham, tomatoes, egg-plant (aubergines), garlic; Poached or fried eggs *à la cansalado.*

The following dishes are made from salt-water and freshwater fish, shell fish of all kinds, snails and frogs: Cod *à l'ailloli;* Ragoût of cod *à la carcassonnaise;* Cod *à la persillade* (with parsley); *Brandade* of cod; Cod *bouillabaisse;* Shad *à la persillade;* Stuffed shad on the spit; Lamprey *en matelote; Fricandeau* of tunny (tuna) fish *à la catalane*, with olives or anchovy; Chopped tunny (tuna) *à la palavasienne;* River trout *à la meunière;* River trout in *court-bouillon;* small fry in *court-bouillon;* Eel *à la catalane;* Elver fry; Pike on the spit; *Matelotes* of various freshwater fish; *Civet* of spiny lobster (Roussillon); Freshwater crayfish in *court-bouillon;* Mussels *à la ravigote;* Mussels *à la catalane;* Mussels with rice; Cockles *à la persillade;* Snails *à la languedocienne, à la lodévoise, à la narbonnaise, à la sommeroise; Mourguettes à la meridionale;* Frogs legs *à la persillade.*

Here are some of the meat, poultry and game dishes of Languedoc: *Daube* of beef *à l'albigeoise, à la carcassonnaise; Estouffat* of beef *à la catalane;* Veal slices with agaric; Roll of veal *en papillote;* Veal *en persillade; Ragoût* of veal with olives; Chump-end of veal with salsify; *pistache** of mutton; *Gasconnade* of mutton; Braised leg of mutton with salsify; *Ragoût* of mutton with white beans; Leg of mutton with garlic; Luchon salted ewe; Toulouse quarter of lamb *à la persillade; Blanquette*

Gastronomic map of Languedoc

of lamb; Cutlets of sucking lamb *en culotte;* Leg of lamb with agaric; Galimaufry of pork; Ribs of pork *à la persillade;* Ribs of pork *en papillote; Lumbet* of pork with potatoes; *Cassoulets* of Carcassonne, Castelnaudary and Toulouse; *Estouffat* of white beans of Carcassonne; *Saupiquet arigeois* (with white beans); Roast sucking pig with piglet skin; Tripe *à l'albigeoise;* Tripe *à la mode narbonnaise; Cabassols* (Hérault); *Manouls* (Hérault); Tripe with saffron; The *petarram* of Luchon; Lamb's pluck *à la languedocienne;* Lamb's sweetbread pie with salsify; Calves' head with olives; Calves' brain *en papillote;* Veal kidneys *à la catalane;* Fricassée of chicken; Poultry pie with agaric, salsify, mushrooms and truffles; Stuffed chicken; Truffled capon; Capon *à la carcassonnaise** (stuffed with sausage, olives, chicken livers; the neck stuffed with garlic bread, roasted on the spit); Truffled young turkey; Young turkey with olives; Duck *à la bigarade;* Duck with olives; *Salmi** of duck; Pigeon *à la catalane; Compote* of pigeon; Pigeon in blood; Goose with chestnuts; *Ragoût* of goose with celery; *Salmi* of guinea-fowl; *Alicuit* of chicken, turkey and goose; *Sanguette* of chicken; Turkey livers with capers, olives or sautéed with garlic and lemon; *Foie gras* of duck or goose with capers, grapes, truffles, Frontignac wine, in pies, charcoal-grilled, potted or made into Toulouse, Cazères and Luchon *pâtés de foie gras* with truffles; Pickled goose and duck; Partridge *à la catalane; Salmi* of partridge; partridge with cabbage; *salmi* of larks; larks *en caisse;* small birds baked in a pie; bunting *en caisse; salmi* of thrush; Teal *à la bigarade;* hare *au saupiquet,* civet of hare; civet of izard (Pyrenean mountain goat); *pâté* of young rabbit with truffles from Arboces; hare *pâté.*

Finally, here are some of the vegetable dishes, sweets and preserves made in Languedoc: *Gratin** of tomatoes and aubergines (egg-plant); Aubergine (egg-plant) stuffed *à la catalane;* Agarics sautéed with garlic; *Cèpes à la persillade;* Green peas with ham; Salsify deep-fried with sugar; Stuffed cabbage; Green cabbage sautéed and stewed; French (string) beans with tomato sauce.

The biscuits of Bedarieux: honey croquettes of Narbonne; grape tart; the *touron* of Limoux; Montpellier pie; Limoux cake; the dry pepper cakes of Limoux; the *Alleluias* of Castelnaudary; the ring-biscuits and *janots* of Albi; the flaky pastry of Carcassonne; the *rauzel* of Carcassonne; the *flaunes* or *flauzonnes* of Lodéve; the heart-cakes of Tarn; the *bras de Vénus* of Narbonne; pancakes (*pescajous*); *oreillettes* ('rabbits' ears'); pickled plums; the crystallized fruit of Carcassonne.

Drinks—To go with the dishes listed above, to wash down this sumptuous *cassoulet* or that marvellous *daube* or a dish of hare *au saupiquet,* connoisseurs will find in Languedoc and Roussillon very fine wines which, though doubtless they cannot rival the genuine vintages of Burgundy, Bordeaux or the Rhône, yet have the priceless virtue of blending admirably with the local dishes.

Here are the principal wines:

Red wines of the Narbonne and Minervois districts: Clos Grand-Quatourze; Château de Levrette; Clos-Saint-Crescent; Cruzy; Château de Vergel; Château de Fontarèche; Manoir de Combestrenières; Château de Montrabech.

Red wines of the Corbières and Roussillon districts: Château de Serame; Domaine de Nouvelle; Saint-Georges; Château Saint-Lucie; Clos Val-Marie Romanée; Château de l'Esparron.

Rosé wines: Rosés de la Croix-Blanche de Bessan; de Saint-Jean; de Saint-Colombe (Salces).

White wines: La Clape (Clos Moyan); Picpoul (Clos Rouquette); Picpoul (Château de la Barale); Picpoul (Château de Fontarèche); Picpoul (Domaine de la Commère); Clairette du Clos de la Rouquette; Grenache blanc du Château de l'Esparron.

Heavy wines: Grenache du Château de Serame; Muscat du Frontignan; Rancio du Rousillon du Château de l'Esparron.

Sparkling wines: Blanquette de Limoux; Royal Languedoc du Château des Cheminières; Gaillac.

LANGUEDOCIENNE (A LA)—A name given to a number of different dishes mostly served with a garnish of tomatoes, aubergines (egg-plant) and cèpes. The sauce served with dishes prepared *à la languedocienne* is flavoured with garlic.

LAPWING. VANNEAU—Bird of passage with crested head; it is considered very good to eat and its eggs ('plovers eggs') are much sought after. The lapwing is cooked like plover.

LARD. SAINDOUX—Cooking fat obtained from the methodical melting down of pork fat. This fat, well prepared and free from all impurities and admixtures, is excellent and is used in certain regions of France, notably the south-west, for the greater part of their culinary preparations, in place of butter or oil.

Preparation. Cut the fat in very small square pieces and put them in a deep pot with ½ cup (a decilitre) of water for each pound (500 grams) of fat.

Start cooking over a good heat, stirring with a wooden spoon.

Allow to cook over a gentle but sustained heat, stirring often, until the fat is completely melted and well cooked. At this point the pieces of pork fat will appear very well fried and crisp while the liquid part will be very clear and will give off no more steam.

As soon as it is ready, strain through a very fine strainer, or through a closely-woven cloth.

Put into pots, which should be filled to the top, the fat setting as it cools.

When the fat is completely set, cover the pots with paper, tie with string, and put them in a cool, dry place. The lard will keep for several months.

After the melting process is complete the strained pork fat leaves a residue that is considered very good to eat in the districts of France where lard is used.

Lard gras (pork fat)—The fat of pork lying between the skin and the flesh which is found all along the chine.

This fat, usually eaten fresh, is in two layers.

The first layer, which is next to the flesh, is used chiefly in the preparation of lard. It is called melting fat. The second layer, next to the skin, is firmer and melts less readily. It is used in various ways in pork-butchery and also for barding. It is known as hard fat.

Lard maigre—This is the fat of the pig's belly. It is streaked with muscular tissue. It can be salted or smoked.

In France this fat is better eaten fresh but in England and in U.S.A. it is smoked and known as bacon, or salted and known as salt pork.

LARDING. LARDER—Threading lardoons of varying thickness into large cuts of meat, by means of a larding-needle.

Larding fat. LARD À PIQUER—Pork fat used for interlarding meat.

This fat must be white, firm and dry.

In summer it must, if possible, be kept on ice before being cut into lardoons. The purpose for which the lardoons are used determines their length and thickness.

To make them, first cut the fat into rectangular slabs. When measured across, these slabs should correspond to the desired length of the lardoons.

Lay these slabs flat on a table, skin downwards. Now slice the fat evenly. With the flat of the knife smooth the surface of the fat, and then slice horizontally to obtain the lardoons.

These lardoons must be kept in a cool place until they are needed. Larding-needles of different thicknesses are available for threading the lardoons into the meat to be cooked.

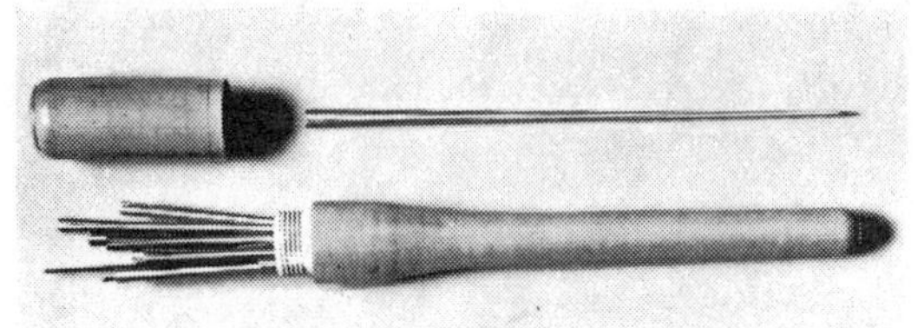

Larding needles (*Coutellerie André*)

LARDING-NEEDLE. LARDOIRE—An implement used for larding cuts of meat, poultry and game.

LARDOONS. LARDONS—Strips of larding fat of varying lengths and thickness, threaded into meat, poultry and game by means of a larding-needle.

In French, the name *lardon* (lardoon) is also used of coarsely or finely diced bacon of varying thickness, blanched and fried, which is added to certain dishes such as *civet* of hare, *ragoût of beef à la bourguignonne* etc., and to a number of garnishes.

LARK. ALOUETTE, MAUVIETTE—Bird, of which numerous species are known, including the calandra and crested lark.

The lark has a very delicate flesh but, in some countries, it is in great demand more as an aviary bird than as food, by reason of its varied and harmonious song.

In France, larks are eagerly sought for the preparation of lark pâté, greatly esteemed by all gastronomes. See PÂTÉ, *pâtés de Pithiviers*.

Although the lark is found in Asia and in Africa, it seems to belong more to northern parts of Europe. Larks abound in Provence, in Languedoc, in the plains of Champagne and Bourgogne, as well as in the steppes of southern Russia.

In France, the meadow lark (*alouettes des champs*) is always referred to as *mauviette* when it is used for the table.

In former times, this savoury bird was called *mauvis*, which derives from the Latin *mala avis*, meaning bad bird. It is strange that the qualification *mauvais* (bad) should have been applied to a bird which is extremely delicate to eat.

Larks à la bonne femme. MAUVIETTES À LA BONNE FEMME—Prepared in a casserole in the same way as *Thrushes à la bonne femme**.

Larks in breadcrust. MAUVIETTES EN CROÛTE—Slit the birds along the back and bone them. Stuff them with a piece of foie gras about the size of a small nut. Press in a piece of diced truffle. Fold the birds back into shape. Place the birds in a buttered casserole, pressing them closely one against the other so that they keep their shape in cooking. Season. Pour on melted butter. Cook for 5 minutes in a very hot oven.

Drain the larks. Scoop out a round loaf. Butter the inside and line with *à gratin forcemeat* (see FORCEMEAT). Brown in the oven. Put the larks in the crust and finish cooking them in the oven for 8 minutes. Pour over them a few spoonfuls of Madeira-flavoured concentrated *Demi-glace* sauce (see SAUCE). Put the 'pie' on the dish covered with a napkin and serve.

Larks en caisses. MAUVIETTES EN CAISSES—Proceed as for *Thrushes en caisses**.

Larks à la minute. MAUVIETTES À LA MINUTE—Slit the larks along the back. Open them. Flatten them gently. Season with salt and pepper. Fry quickly in a frying pan using very best butter. Place each bird on a slice of bread fried in butter, and serve on a round dish. Pour a little *fine champagne* (liqueur brandy) and *Demi-glace sauce* (see SAUCE) into the roasting pan and stir. Pour this sauce over the larks.

Lark pâté, cold. PÂTÉ FROID DE MAUVIETTES—Made with boned larks stuffed in the same way as cold *Partridge pâté*. See PÂTÉ.

Lark pâté, hot. PÂTÉ CHAUD DE MAUVIETTES—Made with boned larks stuffed with foie gras and truffles, in the same way as *hot quail pâté*. See PÂTÉ.

Larks à la piémontaise. MAUVIETTES À LA PIÉMONTAISE—Stuff each lark with a piece of *à gratin forcemeat* (see FORCEMEAT) about the size of a small nut. Cook them quickly in butter. Serve them in a deep, round, earthenware dish on a bed of *polenta** made with cheese. Press the birds down into the polenta. Pour on melted butter. Bake in the oven for 5 minutes. Sprinkle with a few tablespoons of game stock flavoured with Marsala.

Pilaf of larks. PILAF DE MAUVIETTES—Cook the larks quickly in butter. Arrange them in a circle on a bed of *Rice pilaf* (see PILAF).

Pour over the birds a few tablespoons of game essence flavoured with Madeira.

Larks with risotto. MAUVIETTES AU RISOTTO—Proceed as for *Pilaf of larks*. Serve the larks on a bed of *Risotto* (see RICE).

LASAGNE. LAZAGNE—Italian *pasta* cut in the shape of wide ribbons. It is cooked in the same way as *Macaroni**.

LATEX—The milky sap of a number of plants. The *galactodendron* of Colombia is drunk and used in cooking in the same way as milk.

LATOUR (Vin de Château Latour)—This wine is classified as one of the first growths of this region. It is made in the vineyards of Pauillac and the Gironde.

Latticed apple flan

LATTICED FLAN OR TART. GRILLÉ—A flan or tart pastry shell filled with fruit, cream or other filling, covered with narrow criss-cross strips of pastry.

LA VARENNE—A great chef who lived in the seventeenth century. La Varenne began his career as kitchen minion or *marmiton* in the home of the Duchesse de Bar, sister of Henry IV of France.

The King, author of the legendary '*Poule au pot*', observing that La Varenne was a bright lad, entrusted him with certain negotiations in an affair of the heart. As a result of this, he made such a great fortune (it is said that he came to hold a position akin to that of a Minister of State) that the Duchess remarked jestingly to him one day: 'You have done better by carrying my brother's "*poulets*" (amorous notes) than by larding mine.'

But La Varenne also had great talents as a chef. He was the author of the very first systematically planned books on cookery and confectionery. These books are now exceedingly rare, but they have been consulted for centuries and contain recipes which can still be used today. Here are their titles: *Le Pâtissier français* (first edition 1653); *Le Confiseur français* (1664); *Le Cuisinier français* (first edition 1651, published by Pierre David at Lyons, now virtually unobtainable); and, lastly, also published at Lyons by Jacques Carnier in 1725, the book entitled *L'École des ragoûts*.

LAVARET—A fish of the salmon family to be found in all very deep lakes. There are also salt-water lavarets which periodically run to the rivers. Four separate breeds are to be found in French rivers and lakes. The most sought-after is that of Lake Le Bourget.

This fish is very delicate. All recipes for river trout and salmon trout are suitable for lavaret. See TROUT.

LAYON. COTEAUX DU LAYON—The vineyards of Anjou are to be found on these slopes. Some of the best white wines of the Maine-et-Loire department come from the grapes grown in vineyards on these slopes on the right bank of the Layon river.

LEAF CHERVIL. PLUCHES DE CERFEUIL—See GARNISHES, *Chervil.*

LEAKAGE. COULAGE—Loss of liquor from a cask.

LEAVEN. LEVAIN—Sour wheat paste which has begun to ferment and which is in a fit state to induce fermentation, and thus cause kneaded dough to rise. The term leaven is often used instead of barm (brewer's yeast).

LEBERKNODELN OR SOUP WITH LIVER BALLS (Hungarian cookery)—See SOUPS AND BROTHS.

LEBER-SUPPE OR MINCED LIVER SOUP (Hungarian cookery)—See SOUPS AND BROTHS.

LECITHIN. LÉCITHINE—A fat containing phosphorus which is found in yolks of egg, brain, etc.

LECKERLIE (Swiss pastry)—A type of spiced biscuit, rectangular in shape and about ⅛ inch thick.

Ingredients. 10 tablespoons (150 grams) fine sugar; ¾ pound (350 grams) honey; 4 cups (500 grams) sieved cake flour; 2 tablespoons (30 grams) chopped fresh almonds; 2½ tablespoons (50 grams) chopped candied lemon or orange peel; 1 teaspoon (5 grams) bicarbonate of soda; 2½ tablespoons (20 grams) spices (cloves, nutmeg and ginger).

Method. Arrange the flour in a ring on the table. Put the honey in the centre of the ring. Work with a spatula. Add all the other ingredients and knead well.

Put the mixture on square baking trays. (These must be well buttered.) Bake in the oven. Cut into small rectangles and brush with milk just before taking out of the oven.

Leeks (*Kollar*)

LEEK. POIREAU—Hardy biennial plant, the origins of which go back a very long way, which has never been found in its wild state and is believed to be a cultivated variety of oriental garlic.

The principal French varieties are: *Gros du Midi* (summer variety), *Very long winter* (Paris), *Long Mezières Very big Rouen leek*, *Monster of Carentan* and *Giant of Verrières*.

The Egyptians held the leek in very great esteem. Nero had leek soup served to him every day. It is known that Nero was anxious to have a clear and sonorous voice for delivering his orations. The Romans, it is said, attributed to leeks the property of imparting and keeping up the sonority of the voice.

This plant, which is mainly used as a condiment for the stock-pot or as an ingredient of home-made soups, can also be prepared in various ways as a vegetable on its own.

Leeks à la béchamel. POIREAUX À LA BÉCHAMEL—Trim off the leeks leaving only the blanched lower part, parboil for 5 minutes in salted water and drain. Stew them in butter and arrange in a timbale or a round dish.

Cover with not too thick *Béchamel sauce*. See SAUCE.

Boiled leeks. POIREAUX À L'ANGLAISE—Trim off the roots of the leeks and the greater part of the green ends, leaving only the blanched lower part, take off the outside skin and wash them. Tie them in bunches like asparagus and cook in boiling salted water.

Drain and dry them, serve on a folded napkin or in a perforated asparagus dish. Garnish with fresh parsley. Serve melted butter separately.

Braised leeks. POIREAUX BRAISÉS—These can be prepared with meat stock or as a Lenten dish.

As a Lenten dish. Trim 12 large leeks leaving only the blanched lower part, cut into uniform chunks and put into a sauté pan in which 3 tablespoons of butter have been heated. Season with salt and pepper. Moisten with 5 tablespoons of water, cover the pan and simmer for about 40 minutes. Put the leeks into a vegetable dish. Sprinkle with the braising liquor to which a good tablespoon of butter has been added.

With meat stock. Proceed as above but moisten the leeks with clear meat stock.

Leeks with melted butter or other sauces. POIREAUX AU BEURRE FONDU—Boil in water and serve separately melted butter or any other sauce, such as *Cream, Hollandaise, Mousseline, Vinaigrette.* See SAUCE.

Leeks à la crème. POIREAUX À LA CRÈME—Put the blanched lower part of the leeks into a buttered sauté pan. Season and cook gently for 15 minutes with a lid on. Moisten with fresh cream in sufficient quantity to cover the leeks. Cover and simmer gently for 30 minutes. Put into a vegetable dish. Add a few tablespoons of fresh cream to the pan juices and pour over the leeks.

Deep-fried leeks. POIREAUX EN FRITOT—Trim the leeks leaving only the white part, cut into uniform chunks, parboil in salted water for 8 minutes and marinate for 30 minutes in oil, lemon juice, salt and pepper.

When required, dip in a light batter and fry in smoking hot deep fat.

When they become golden and crisp, drain them, dry, season with fine salt, arrange in a heap on a folded napkin or on a paper doyley and garnish with fried parsley

Leeks au gratin. POIREAUX AU GRATIN—Trim the leeks leaving only the white part, parboil in salted water and cook gently in butter in a covered sauté pan. Put into a buttered oven-proof dish, sprinkle with grated cheese (Parmesan, for preference), pour over some melted butter and brown the top in a slow oven, or under a low grill.

Leeks à la grecque. POIREAUX À LA GRECQUE—White part of the leeks cooked in a *court-bouillon** consisting of water, oil and lemon juice, spiced with coriander. See HORS-D'OEUVRE, *Cold hors-d'oeuvre.*

Leeks Mornay. POIREAUX MORNAY—Cook the white part of the leeks in butter. Put them into a fire-proof dish on a layer of *Mornay sauce* (see SAUCE). Sprinkle with grated cheese and melted butter and brown the top in the oven.

Velouté or cream of leek. VELOUTÉ, CRÈME DE POIREAUX —Recipes for these soups will be found in the section entitled SOUPS AND BROTHS.

Leeks à la vinaigrette. POIREAUX À LA VINAIGRETTE—Cook the white parts of the leeks in salted water. Drain and dry them, arrange in an hors-d'oeuvre dish and season with oil, vinegar, salt and pepper.

LEFT-OVERS. RESTES—The art of dishing up left-overs passes very often for the heights of culinary science. We cannot subscribe to this opinion. We consider, on the contrary that in any house where there are abundant left-overs the administration of the kitchen is very bad.

If the left-overs after a meal are considerable it is clear that the food was either carelessly provided in too large a quantity, or was badly prepared, and not to the taste of the guests.

Sometimes, however, foodstuffs are served in large quantity on purpose—when, for example, they will be served at a subsequent meal as cold meat. It is also done with roast meat or poultry or braised meat (*boeuf à la mode* for example), when it is intended to reheat these meats to serve them again.

LEGUMIN. LÉGUMINE—A proteid substance resembling casein found in pulses (peas, beans, lentils). It is less well assimilated than animal protein, and combines with chalk to form an insoluble deposit. For this reason pulses cannot be satisfactorily cooked in hard water.

Lemons growing in the Côte d'Azur (*French Government Tourist Office*)

LEMON. CITRON—The fruit of the lemon tree, very acid and highly scented, is originally from India, but grows out of doors in the Mediterranean region and extensively in California, U.S.A.

The juice and the zest of lemons are used in cooking to flavour and season a great number of dishes. Various creams, puddings and sauces are flavoured with the zest (the outside part of the skin). The juice is used to enhance the flavour of certain dishes and to season salads and mayonnaise instead of vinegar.

Fried or grilled fish is garnished with halves or quarters of lemon. The lemon is almost a 'must' for oysters.

This fruit is used a great deal in distilling.

For the use of lemon as a flavouring for *Bavarois, Custard cream* (see CREAMS), *Mousses, Puddings, Sauces,* see these words in their alphabetical order.

Lemon custard. CRÈME AU CITRON—Make a *Custard cream* (see CREAMS) using milk which has been boiled with lemon zest. Pass the custard cream through a very fine strainer or silk tammy.

Lemon jam. CONFITURE DE CITRON—Blanch the skins of 24 lemons. When they are half-cooked drain them; chop up half the lemon skins, and rub them through a sieve. Cut the rest up into thin strips. Mix these ingredients and moisten with the juice of 8 lemons. Add an amount of sugar equal in weight to the lemon skins. Cook in a copper pan in the same way as other jams.

Lemon manqué. MANQUÉ AU CITRON—Use lemon-flavoured sugar for the mixture and add diced crystallized citron to it or add ½ teaspoon lemon extract.

When the *manqué* is baked and turned out, mask it completely with whites of egg whisked stiff with sugar. Frost with icing sugar. Sprinkle pistachio nuts on top. Dry in the oven but do not brown.

Note. Crystallized apricots or aniseed or caraway, or grilled nuts or currants can be used to make the manqué. The flavouring should blend with the ingredients used. See general recipe for MANQUÉ.

Preserved lemon peel. ÉCORCE DE CITRON CONFITE (CITRONNAT)—Blanch the pieces of fresh lemon peel, from which the pith has been removed with the help of a spoon. In this way only the outside of the skin (zest) is used. Drain the pieces and put them in syrup. Leave them all night in the syrup (see SYRUP).

The next day cook the syrup until it measures 25 degrees on the saccharometer or until it drops in a short thread from the spoon. Put back the peel. Leave to soak in syrup overnight and repeat the operation for several days, cooking the syrup for the last time to the point of crystallization (245° to 250°F.).

Lemon soufflé

Lemon soufflés. CITRONS SOUFFLÉS—Prepared in the same way as *Orange Soufflé*. See SOUFFLÉ.

Lemon Syrup. SIROP DE CITRON—Soak the zest of 12 fine lemons in their own juice. Prepare a quart (litre) of hot sugar syrup measuring 36 degrees (245° to 250°F.) on the saccharometer. Add the juice and zest to this syrup. Leave it for 5 to 6 days. Filter. (See SYRUP.)

Lemon zest. ZESTE DE CITRON—Lemon zest is used to flavour creams and other preparations for sweets by grating the skin with a lump of sugar. The sugar becomes impregnated with the essential oil of the lemon and is then put in the preparation to be flavoured.

Milk can also be flavoured with lemon zest and used to moisten creams and custards. The zest which is used to flavour certain culinary preparations is prepared in this way:

Remove the zest from the fruit with a sharp knife. According to the use to which it is to be put, chop the zest finely, or slice it into fine strips. In the latter case, blanch the lemon *julienne*, drain and dry it.

LEMONADE. CITRONNADE, LIMONADE—A drink consisting of lemon juice, sugar and water.

Lemonade I. CITRONNADE—Dissolve ½ pound (250 grams) of lump sugar in a quart (litre) of filtered water. Add the juice of two lemons to the syrup, and the zest. Leave to infuse for 3 hours in a cool place.

Strain through a fine strainer. A siphon of Seltzer (soda) water, or fresh water, can be added to the lemonade. Serve cold in glasses and put a slice of lemon in each glass.

Lemonade II. LIMONADE CUITE—Cut a lemon into thin slices. Remove the seeds. Infuse for an hour in a pint (½ litre) of boiling water. Add 5 teaspoons (25 grams) of sugar.

Fizzy lemonade. LIMONADE GAZEUSE—This lemonade is usually artificially made and aerated with carbonic acid gas, like manufactured soda water, and sold in bottles or siphons.

LEMON-SOLE. LIMANDE-SOLE—The name lemon-sole is a corruption of the French *Limande-sole*. This fish is really a kind of dab but, unlike the dab and other flat fish such as flounder and plaice, it is elongated and oval in shape, and is thus somewhat similar to a sole in appearance.

Some authorities assert that lemon sole is very little inferior in quality to the sole, but this opinion is not shared by gastronomes, who, with good reason, find this fish comparatively stringy and tasteless. It corresponds to the *Yellowtail flounder* in U.S.A.

All recipes for *Brill** and *Sole** are suitable for lemon-sole.

LENT. CARÊME—Forty days fast imposed by the Catholic religion, from Ash Wednesday till Easter. This period of fasting in the early Church had excellent physical effects by imposing on the digestive system, worn out by gastronomic excess during the winter season, a salutary rest.

Brillat-Savarin tell us that towards the middle of the eighteenth century the normal regime in bourgeois families consisted of four meals:

Breakfast, taking place before nine in the morning, consisting of bread, cheese, fruit, sometimes a pâté or cold meat. (The habit of drinking coffee had not yet penetrated into provincial life.)

Dinner, which took place between twelve and one, with soup, the boiled meat of the pot-au-feu, with vegetable accompaniments according to the season.

Around four o'clock there was a light meal enjoyed as a rule by the ladies of the household and the children.

Supper was at eight o'clock, with *entrée*, roast, side-dishes, salad and dessert.

During Lent breakfast was suppressed, meat was excluded from the menu at dinner, and in the evening supper was replaced by a meal which contained no eggs, butter, or anything of a live nature.

The real test of culinary art was, according to this genial gastronome, to create a rigorously apostolic meal which had all the appearance of an excellent supper.

The battle between Carême (Lent) and Mardi-Gras (from a 17th century print)

Little by little, the Church relaxed its original severity and permitted the use of butter and eggs and, later, the flesh of 'cold-blooded' animals, such as fish and, still later, certain aquatic game considered to be cold-blooded, such as the spoon-bill, pintail, scoter-duck, moorhen, coot, teal, water-rail, curlew, heron, godwit and sand-piper.

A Lenten meal could also include an impressive list of sumptuous removes, *entrées* and roasts.

Understood in these terms the Lenten diet does not differ from normal diet, from the health point of view.

LENTIL. LENTILLE—A pulse (leguminous seed), originally from central Asia where it was cultivated in pre-historic times. There are numerous varieties. This vegetable contains more protein than any other. 3½ ounces (100 grams) provide 337 calories.

Cooking of lentils. Proceed exactly as for dried white beans (see BEAN). Like these, lentils must be soaked, but not for long, in cold water before cooking. If lentils are soaked for too long, they begin to germinate, which renders them, if not actually poisonous, at least more difficult to digest.

After cooking in meat or vegetable stock, lentils can be prepared in any way suitable for dried white beans.

LENTISK. LENTISQUE—A bush of the same family as the turpentine tree. It is grown in the Greek Archipelago. Its fruit yields an edible oil. A resin known as *mastic* is collected from its trunk by making incisions in it. This resin is used to flavour the spirit known as *Raki.*

LÉOGNAN—A red wine made from the grapes grown in the commune of Léognan, in the Graves region. The wines of this region, though not officially classified, are of fine quality. They are very smooth and have a distinctive and very delicate aroma.

Among the excellent wines made in the Gironde commune are *Château Haut-Bailly*, *Haut-Brion Larrivet*, *Château Carbonnieux*, *Domaine de Chevalier* and *Château Brown-Léognan.*

LEOVILLE—A red Bordeaux wine classed among the second growths of the great Médoc wines.

Léoville-Lascases, *Léoville-Poyferré* and *Léoville-Bartou*, which are made in the commune of Saint-Julien, are highly prized by connoisseurs.

LEPIOTA. LÉPIOTE—A species of fungus of which a number of varieties are edible, the best known in France being the cultivated *lepiota*, also known as the *coulemelle.*

LEPISOSTEUS (Gar-Pike). LEPIDOSTÉE—The peculiarity of this fish is that it has very hard, pebbly scales, so that it is encased in a veritable suit of armour.

It is to be found in the rivers and lakes of Central America. Its flesh is fairly delicate. All recipes for *pike** are suitable for this fish.

LESSER CELANDINE. FICAIRE—A plant whose leaves are sometimes eaten, being first blanched. They are cooked in the same way as *spinach**.

LETTUCE. LAITUE—A plant which grows wild all over Europe, in the Caucasus and in India.

It has been cultivated in Egypt and China from time immemorial.

The word lettuce comes from the Latin *lactuca*, for lettuce, when it is cut, exudes a milky juice.

In ancient times, the lettuce was looked upon as a sacred plant (it figures in the Passover ritual of the Hebrews at the same time as the Paschal lamb). It was brought into favour in ancient Rome by Antonius Musa, physician to the Emperor Augustus.

Galen asserts that this plant cured him of stomach disorders when he was young. He adds that, in his old age, lettuce brought him restful sleep.

Among the Romans, lettuce was usually served at the end of the evening meal. Under the Emperor Domitian, the fashion changed and it became customary to serve lettuce at the beginning of the meal, which caused the poet Martial to write:

'How comes it that this food which our ancestors ate only as a dessert is now the first that is put before us?' To this question of Martial's there is a simple answer. The Romans regarded lettuce, especially when dressed as a salad, as an appetiser, and so took to serving it as an hors-d'oeuvre.

The juice of the lettuce, especially of the poisonous variety, is a narcotic somewhat similar to the opium of the East.

Lettuce is in season all the year round, except in winter.

All the common varieties of lettuce can be eaten raw, in salads.

In cookery, cabbage lettuces are mainly used, but cos lettuces can also be cooked. Lettuce can be braised, like endive.

Braised lettuce in meat stock. LAITUES BRAISÉES AU GRAS—Trim the lettuces by removing the tough green outer leaves. Parboil them for 5 minutes in salt water. Cool them under running water. Squeeze the leaves to extract all the cooking water. Tie two or three lettuces together.

Butter a pan and line it with bacon rind, sliced onions and carrots. Lay the lettuces in this pan. Cover with rather fat stock. Bring to the boil. Cover and cook in a moderate oven for 50 minutes.

Drain the lettuces. Untie them. Cut each lettuce in half, lengthwise. Trim the leaves at both ends and fold each half in two. Put them in a buttered pan. Boil down (reduce) the cooking stock, strain it through a fine strainer (sieve) and pour over the lettuces.

Note. Lettuces prepared in this way can be served as they are, as a vegetable or as a garnish for various main dishes, or may be cooked further with various sauces as indicated below.

Vegetarian braised lettuce. LAITUES BRAISÉES AU MAIGRE—Proceed exactly as stated above, omitting the bacon rind. Moisten with water instead of stock.

Lettuce with bone-marrow. LAITUES À LA MOELLE—Arrange some braised lettuces in a circle in a round dish or shallow pie-dish, alternating with slices of bread fried in butter. Put on top of each lettuce two slices of poached beef marrow. Add a little *Demi-glace sauce* (see SAUCE) to the braising stock. Reduce (boil down) the stock. Add butter. Strain and pour over the dish. Sprinkle a little chopped parsley on top of each slice of marrow.

Lettuce in browned butter. LAITUES AU BEURRE NOISETTE—Braise the lettuces as indicated above. Halve them and roll them. Arrange them in the form of a rosette on a dish. Just before serving, pour a few tablespoons of *Browned butter* (see BUTTER) over them.

Chiffonnade of lettuce for cold dishes. LAITUES EN CHIFFONNADE—Shred very finely some trimmed and washed lettuces. Squeeze them to extract all moisture.

Season with oil, vinegar, salt and pepper.

Note. This *chiffonnade* is used mainly to decorate salads and mayonnaise of fish, shell fish or poultry.

Chiffonnade of lettuce in butter for garnishing. LAITUES EN CHIFFONNADE AU BEURRE—Shred very finely 4 trimmed and washed lettuces. Put them in a pan with 2 tablespoons of butter. Season with table salt. Moisten with ½ cup of clear soup. Cover and simmer gently. Use as indicated in the recipe for whatever main dish is to be served with this garnish.

Chiffonnade of lettuce with cream as garnish. LAITUES EN CHIFFONNADE À LA CRÈME—Prepare and cook finely shredded lettuce as for the preceding recipe.

When the lettuce is soft, moisten it with ¾ cup (1½ decilitres) of cream.

Simmer for a few minutes. Serve as garnish with a suitable main dish.

Lettuce Colbert (Vegetarian cookery). LAITUES COLBERT—Cook the lettuces in butter in a covered pan. Drain and halve them. Fold the halves into heart shapes.

Squeeze them gently. Dip them in egg and breadcrumbs. Deep-fry just before serving.

Arrange them in a circle on a round dish. Cover them with *Maître d'hôtel butter* (see BUTTER, *Compound butters*).

Deep-fried lettuce. LAITUES EN FRITOT—Braise the lettuces as indicated above. Fold the quarters. Put them in a dish. Season with oil, lemon juice, salt and pepper. Leave them in this marinade for 30 minutes. Just before serving, dip them in a light batter. Deep-fry. Serve on a napkin, garnished with fried parsley.

Lettuce au gratin (in white sauce). LAITUES AU GRATIN—Arrange halved braised lettuces in a gratin dish. Pour *Mornay sauce* (see SAUCE) over them. Sprinkle with grated cheese. Pour on melted butter and brown.

Lettuce in gravy. LAITUES AU JUS—Braise some lettuces as indicated above. Halve them. Put them in a buttered pan. Sprinkle with a few tablespoons of well-seasoned brown veal stock. Simmer. Arrange the lettuces in a ring, alternating with slices of bread fried in butter. Boil down the cooking stock. Add butter to it and pour it over the dish.

Lettuce à la hollandaise. LAITUES À LA HOLLANDAISE—Arrange on a round dish, alternating with slices of bread fried in butter, halved lettuces braised in a vegetable stock. Cover with *Hollandaise sauce* (see SAUCE, *Cold sauces*).

Lettuce à l'italienne. LAITUES À L'ITALIENNE—Proceed as for *Lettuce in gravy*, using *Italian sauce* (see SAUCE) instead of gravy.

Lettuce Mornay. LAITUES MORNAY—See *Lettuce au gratin* (*in white sauce*).

Lettuce purée. PURÉE DE LAITUE—Rub through a fine sieve lettuces braised in meat or vegetable stock. Heat the purée. To give it body, add a few tablespoons of concentrated and strained *Béchamel sauce* (see SAUCE). Season. Mix and add butter.

Note. Mashed potatoes can be added to this purée just as they can be added to the purées of all watery vegetables.

Lettuce salad—See SALAD.

Lettuce soufflé. SOUFFLÉ DE LAITUE—Made with purée of lettuce in the same way as *Endive soufflé* (see ENDIVE).

Stuffed lettuce. LAITUES FARCIES—Blanch the lettuces. Cool them under running water and squeeze them dry. Slit them in half without cutting the stump. Season them inside. Fill each lettuce with a fine *forcemeat** mixed with *duxelles**. Each piece of mixed forcemeat should be the size of an egg. Close up the lettuces and tie them. Braise them.

Note. Stuffed lettuce can be served as a vegetable (arranged in a circle on a round dish with fried bread between and covered with any suitable sauce) or may be used as a garnish.

Lettuce stumps. MOELLE DE LAITUE—The stumps of cos (romaine) lettuces which have gone to seed are mainly used. These stumps, after trimming, are cooked like asparagus, or in any of the ways suitable for artichoke stalks or endive stumps.

LEVERET. LEVRAUT—A young hare, between 2 and 4 months old. Up to the age of 2 months, a young hare is called a *levretaut* in France. See HARE.

LIAISON—See THICKENING.

LIARD—The French use this term (which means a small coin) to denote foodstuffs cut into thin, flat, round slices which look like old coins. The term applies especially to potato crisps.

LICHIA. LICHE—A fish which has much in common with the tunny (tuna fish), and which grows to quite a considerable size. The *Lichiamia* which is found in the deeper parts of the Mediterranean reaches up to 3 feet in length.

This fish is cooked in the same way as tunny. See TUNNY (*tuna fish*).

LIÉGEOISE (A LA)—A method of cooking, applied to various foodstuffs. Its characteristic feature is the use of juniper flavouring. See OFFAL OR VARIETY MEATS, *Calf's kidneys à la liégeoise;* THRUSH, *Thrushes à la liégeoise.*

LIGHTEN. DÉTENDRE—In cooking or confectionery, to make a mixture lighter by the addition of eggs or some liquid.

LIGHTS. MOU—In the tripe-trade this term is used to designate the lungs of certain animals. For the preparation of lamb's and calf's lights, see OFFAL OR VARIETY MEATS.

LIMANDELLE—A flat fish, also called *cardine* or *mère de sole*. It has a comparatively elongated oval body (10 to 14 inches long) with fragile, shaded scales. Its eyes are placed on the left side which is pale yellow with brown shading. Its blind side is white. It is very good to eat. All recipes for *plaice** and *brill** are suitable for this fish.

LIME. LIMON—A thin-skinned citrus fruit.

Lime-tree. TILLEUL—Tree of which there are several species in Europe. The scented flowers are used in infusion for their soothing and anti-spasmodic properties. The American species (*Tilia Americana*) is called a linden tree.

The flowers are also used in pastry-making and confectionery to flavour creams, ices and sweets (desserts) of various kinds.

LIMONADIERS—This was the name given in France in former times to sellers of non-alcoholic drinks, the equivalent of café proprietors today. In the Middle Ages the only alcoholic drinks available were beer, hippocras (mead), sweet or heavy wines. Anyone was free to stock and sell wines, without seeking permission of any authority. In the sixteenth century, spirits began to be widely used. They were sold by the small glassful at vinegar shops.

It was the Italians, many of whom followed Catherine de Medici into France, who introduced a number of entirely new drinks. Among these were lemonade, orangeade, bitter citron cordial, frangipane water, sherbets, rosolio cordial, *populo*, etc. The drink which undoubtedly found most favour with the public was lemonade, since the name *limonadiers* stuck to shopkeepers who sold a great many other drinks as well.

LIMOUSIN—See MARCHE AND LIMOUSIN.

LIMOUSINE (A LA)—A method of preparing red cabbage.

Cuts of meat and poultry garnished with red cabbage cooked in this way are also called *à la limousine*.

LIMOUX (Blanquette de)—A sparkling wine, fairly heavy, made at Limoux in the Aude district.

LING. LINGUE—A fish of the Cod family, also called sea-burbot or long cod. It is fished in the same latitudes as cod. It is quite good to eat and is usually salted like cod. It is prepared in the same way as *cod** or codling.

In U.S.A. the name *ling* is sometimes given to the freshwater burbot.

LINNET. LINOT-LINOTTE—A small edible bird which feeds on linseed or hempseed. It is rather tasteless. It is prepared in the same way as *lark**.

LION—Lion meat, though edible, is seldom used in cookery. It is rather tasteless and must be steeped in an aromatic marinade before cooking.

All recipes for beef are suitable for lion.

LIQUEUR—A name given to various composite alcoholic drinks. Nowadays these are almost all made from a mixture of spirits and syrups.

There are innumerable liqueurs with many different names. Their alcoholic content varies.

Liqueurs can be made in the home. Their quality varies according to the spirits or alcohol used.

All home-made liqueurs are made by steeping fruit and other basic ingredients in alcohol or spirits. The best spirits to use are 70° proof. Liqueurs made in this way are often called ratafias.

Acacia liqueur or ratafia I. LIQUEUR, RATAFIA D'ACACIA—Remove stalks from some acacia flowers and steep 3½ ounces (100 grams) of the flowers in a quart (litre) of spirits, preferably white, proof 88°.

Leave to infuse for a month, keeping the container hermetically sealed, in a warm place.

At the end of a month, add ½ cup (125 grams) of sugar and stir from time to time until all the sugar is dissolved. This takes about a fortnight. Filter through filter paper and bottle.

Acacia liqueur or ratafia II (Old recipe). LIQUEUR, RATAFIA D'ACACIA—Put 7 ounces (200 grams) of acacia flowers in a deep dish with alternate layers of fine sugar. Steep for 24 hours.

Moisten this mixture with a cup (¼ litre) of water and strain. Add to it a syrup made with ⅔ cup (1½ decilitres) of water and the remainder of the sugar (3 cups are needed in all). Finally, add 1½ cups (60 centilitres) of spirits.

Leave to steep for a few months. Filter and bottle.

Angelica liqueur or ratafia. LIQUEUR, RATAFIA D'ANGÉLIQUE—*Ingredients.* 2 pounds (900 grams) of angelica; 2 pounds (900 grams) lump sugar; 6 quarts (5 litres) of spirits; 2 tablespoons or ½ ounce (15 grams) cinnamon; 1¼ teaspoons (3 grams) nutmeg; 1 clove; 1 pint (½ litre) filtered water.

Method. Place the sticks of angelica cut into small pieces, the sugar, the spirits, and other ingredients listed above, in a large jar, which can be hermetically sealed.

Strain through a fine strainer over a large bowl. Press the pieces of angelica to extract all the juice.

Filter the liqueur through filter paper.

Bottle, cork well, and keep bottles in a moderate temperature, in a cupboard rather than a cellar.

Anise or anisette liqueur or ratafia I. LIQUEUR, RATAFIA D'ANIS (ANISETTE)—Put into a quart and 3 ounces (1 litre) of spirits 1 ounce (30 grams) of green, crushed anise, ½ teaspoon (7 grams) of cinnamon, 2 tablespoons or ½ ounce (15 grams) of coriander. Infuse for a month.

Add 500 grams of sugar dissolved in a little water. Filter and bottle.

Anise liqueur or ratafia II. LIQUEUR, RATAFIA D'ANIS II—Make a syrup of 3 pounds (2 kilograms 500 grams) of sugar and 1 quart (litre) of water. Strain this syrup through muslin.

At the same time, dissolve, in ½ ounce (15 grams) of spirits 70° proof, 1/10 ounce (3 grams) essence of Chinese anise, 1/60 ounce (½ gram) essence of Seville orange neroli, 1/60 ounce (½ gram) essence of cinnamon, 1/6 ounce (5 grams) essence of anise, 1/30 ounce (1 gram) essence of nutmeg, 1/30 ounce (1 gram) tincture of vanilla.

Mix all these ingredients thoroughly. Add 1 quart plus 1 cup (1 kilogram 50 grams) alcohol 85° proof, then the syrup indicated above. Leave to stand for 24 hours. Filter and bottle.

Anise liqueur III or cream of aniseed (Old recipe). LIQUEUR OU CRÈME D'ANIS—3½ ounces (100 grams) whole aniseed, 4⅜ quarts (4 litres) spirits 37° proof.

Infuse for 6 days and strain through muslin.

Add 6 pounds of sugar (3 kilos) dissolved in 2 quarts (litres) of water.

Leave to stand for several days, that is to say until the liqueur is clear. Strain through a muslin bag.

Apricot liqueur. LIQUEUR D'ABRICOTS—*Ingredients.* 30 apricots; 4 quarts (litres) white wine; 2 pounds (1 kilo) sugar; 1 quart (litre) 58° proof spirits; 1½ tablespoons or ⅓ ounce (10 grams) cinnamon.

Method. Put the apricots in a large basin. Moisten with the white wine.

Bring to the boil. When the wine comes to the boil, add the sugar, the cinnamon and the spirits of wine.

Take the basin off the fire. Cover it. Leave it to infuse for 4 days. Strain, filter and bottle. Cork the bottles tightly. Keep in a dry place.

Blackcurrant liqueur I. LIQUEUR DE CASSIS—*Ingredients.* To 1 quart (litre) of spirits take 2 pounds (1 kilo) blackcurrants, 1½ pounds (750 grams) of crystallized sugar in lumps or powdered, 1 clove, 1/30 ounce (1 gram) cinnamon pods (Ceylon cinnamon is preferable to Chinese cinnamon). To give a stronger flavour, add about 10 little blackcurrant leaves, the greenest available, taken from the tops of the branches.

Method. Put the herbs (clove, cinnamon and blackcurrant leaves) at the bottom of a bowl. On top lay the blackcurrants, picked and well crushed by hand.

When the blackcurrants are crushed, pour the spirits over them. Mix, add the sugar and mix again. Put the mixture in a stone jar and seal. Keep the jar in a warm place (in the sun if possible) for at least a month to ensure a thorough infusion. At the end of this time strain the liqueur through a sieve over a bowl. Extract all liquid by squeezing the pulp in a coarse linen cloth.

Filter and bottle the liqueur.

In no circumstances should water be added to help dissolve the sugar, since this would lower the alcohol content of the liqueur. If the liqueur is too strong, add plain syrup to make it less potent.

To make a plain syrup the usual proportions are 2 cups (500 grams) of sugar to 2 cups (500 grams) of water. Dissolve cold.

Blackcurrant liqueur II (Old recipe). LIQUEUR DE CASSIS II—Infuse together for 15 days, in a jar, 2 pounds (1 kilo) blackcurrants, 1 teaspoon (2 grams) each of cloves and of cinnamon, 3¼ quarts (3 litres) of spirits and 1½ pounds (750 grams) of sugar.

Take care to mix these ingredients every day, during the fortnight. At the end of this time, strain through muslin, filter and, when it is perfectly clear, bottle. The sugar need not be added until after filtering.

Carnation liqueur or ratafia. LIQUEUR, RATAFIA D'OEILLETS—Steep for a month, in 1 quart (litre) of alcohol at 39° proof, ½ pound (250 grams) of carnation petals. Spice with a clove and ½ teaspoon (7 grams) of cinnamon. Filter.

Add a syrup made from 2 cups (500 grams) of sugar and 2 cups (500 grams) of water. Filter once more. Bottle.

Cherry liqueur or ratafia. LIQUEUR, RATAFIA DE CERISES—Crush 8½ pounds (4 kilos) of Montmorency cherries with the stones. Put them in a bowl and leave to ferment for 4 days.

Add 4⅝ quarts (4 litres) of alcohol, 38° proof spirit, and 2 pounds (1 kilo) of sugar. Put the mixture in a jar and leave to infuse for a month. Squeeze through muslin.

Filter and bottle.

Cherry liqueur or ratafia, Grenoble style. LIQUEUR, RATAFIA DE CERISES À LA FAÇON DE GRENOBLE—Infuse in 2 quarts, 6 ounces (2 litres) of brandy: ¼ pound (125 grams) of blanched cherry stone kernels; ⅓ ounce (10 grams) of peach blossom or leaves; 1 teaspoon (2 grams) of cinnamon; 10 to 12 cloves.

When the brandy is thoroughly impregnated with the aroma of these ingredients, pour it over 2 quarts, 6 ounces (2 litres) of cherry juice with 1 pound (500 grams) of sugar dissolved in it. Mix. Filter and bottle.

Liqueur or ratafia of cherry stones. LIQUEUR, RATAFIA DE NOYAUX DE CERISES—This can be made from the stones of cherries used for jam-making.

Wash the stones. Dry them. When they are quite dry, crush them.

Put them to infuse in alcohol, allowing 2 pounds (1 kilo) of stones to 1 quart, 3 ounces (1 litre) of spirits.

Proceed as indicated in the previous recipe.

Citron liqueur or ratafia. LIQUEUR, RATAFIA DE CÉDRAT—Made with the peel and juice of citrons, in the same way as *Orange ratafia*. See below.

Coffee liqueur (Old recipe). LIQUEUR DE CAFÉ—To obtain this, take 3 pounds (1½ kilograms) of best moka coffee. Roast carefully; grind very fine. Infuse the coffee in 10 quarts (9 litres) of brandy or, better still, 5½ quarts (5 litres) of alcohol 58° proof and 4½ quarts (4 litres) of water. After 10 days of infusion, distil in a *bain-marie* (double boiler) to obtain 5½ quarts (5 litres). If a stronger flavour of coffee is desired, fresh coffee can be infused in the liqueur. Next, dissolve 5 pounds (2½ kilos) of sugar in 2¾ quarts (2½ litres) of water and add this to the liqueur. Leave to stand overnight and filter next day.

Curaçao liqueur. LIQUEUR DE CURAÇAO—*Ingredients.* 1⅔ ounces (50 grams) bitter orange peel; 1¼ teaspoons (2½ grams) cinnamon; 1 ounce (30 grams) Pernambuco bark; 1 clove; 1 quart 3 ounces (1 litre) of pure wine alcohol, 79° proof; 1 pound (500 grams) of sugar; 2¼ cups (½ litre) of water.

Infuse the orange peel, Pernambuco bark, cinnamon and clove for 3 weeks. Make a syrup of the sugar and water and pour it over these ingredients.

Filter and bottle. If necessary, colour with carmine and caramel.

Dantzig liqueur. LIQUEUR DE DANTZIG—This liqueur is sold as *Eau-de-vie de Dantzig*. It is made from sweetened 85° proof grain spirits with water added. It is flavoured with various herbs.

The characteristic feature of this liqueur is that it has tiny specks of gold leaf floating in it.

Fennel liqueur. LIQUEUR DE FENOUIL—This is made from fennel stalks in the same way as *Angelica liqueur*.

Grande-Chartreuse—The liqueur of the Grande-Chartreuse, generally called *Chartreuse*, is one of the most famous liqueurs now being made. It is produced by the distillation of herbs gathered in Alpine regions. This liqueur is named after the monastery of the *Grande-Chartreuse* where it was first manufactured by the monks.

Juniper liqueur or ratafia. LIQUEUR, RATAFIA DE GENIÈVRE—Make a syrup of 8 pounds (4 kilos) of sugar dissolved in a little water. With this syrup, moisten 4⅝ quarts (4 litres) of juniper berries placed in a stone crock with 4⅝ quarts (4 litres) of alcohol.

Seal and leave to infuse for 15 days, taking care to shake the crock from time to time after the first 3 or 4 days.

Strain the liqueur through a muslin bag. Bottle.

This liqueur is good only when it has been kept a very long time.

Lemon liqueur or ratafia. LIQUEUR, RATAFIA DE CITRON—Made with the peel and juice of lemons, in the same way as *Orange liqueur*.

Orange liqueur or ratafia. LIQUEUR, RATAFIA D'ORANGES—*Ingredients.* 6 oranges; 1 quart 3 ounces (1 litre) of brandy or pure white spirits of wine; 1 pound (500 grams) of lump sugar; ½ teaspoon (1 gram) of cinnamon; ½ teaspoon (1 gram) of coriander.

Method. Peel the oranges carefully, so that none of the white pith is mixed with the outer rind. Chop the rind finely.

Squeeze the juice of the oranges into a jar. Add the sugar to the juice.

Add the chopped rind, a little cinnamon and a little coriander. Pour the spirits over this mixture. Mix all together. Leave to infuse for 2 months.

Filter and bottle.

Orange blossom liqueur or ratafia. LIQUEUR, RATAFIA DE FLEURS D'ORANGER—Made from the petals of orange blossom in the same way as *Carnation liqueur*.

Liqueur or ratafia of peach and apricot stones. LIQUEUR, RATAFIA DE NOYAUX—Made from peach and apricot stones or a mixture of the two.

Half-fill a stone crock with whole stones. Fill up with white alcohol.

Leave to infuse for 1½ months, placing the crock either in the sun or in a hot place.

Now take out a quarter of the stones. Crack them and put the shells and kernels back in the crock. Leave them to infuse for another 15 days.

Draw off the liqueur. Add an equal quantity of water with 5 ounces of sugar per pound (300 grams per kilo) dissolved in it.

After 10 days, filter and bottle.

Peppermint liqueur (Old recipe). LIQUEUR DE MENTHE—For 5½ quarts (5 litres): 5 pounds (2½ kilos) of white sugar. Dissolve on the stove in 2 quarts (1¾ litres) of water. Add 2 quarts 6 ounces (2 litres) of alcohol, 58° proof, then 1/30 ounce (1 gram) of essence of mint.

Leave for 30 days. Filter through filter paper.

Persico or persicot—Alcoholic liqueur, made of eau-de-vie, peach stone almonds, sugar and aromatic substances. It is used for flavouring pastry desserts.

Quince liqueur or ratafia (quince water) I. LIQUEUR, RATAFIA DE COINGS (EAU DE COINGS)—Cut the quinces into quarters. Remove pips. Grate the quinces without peeling them.

Put the grated quinces into a bowl. Cover and leave to stand in a cool place for 3 days.

Squeeze through muslin. Add to the quince juice an equal quantity of spirits. To every quart (litre) of this mixture, add 1⅛ cups (300 grams) of sugar, a clove and a small piece of cinnamon. Infuse in a jar for 2 months.

Strain through a muslin bag. Bottle.

Quince liqueur or ratafia II. LIQUEUR, RATAFIA DE COINGS II—Prepare the quince juice as for the previous recipe. To every 1½ quarts (1½ litres) of juice add a pint (½ litre) of alcohol, 85° proof. Add ¼ teaspoon (10 centigrams) of cloves, 1 teaspoon (2 grams) of Ceylon cinnamon, a pinch of ground mace and 1 or 2 teaspoons (50 centigrams) of bitter almonds.

Leave the mixture to infuse for 2 months. Then add a syrup (cold) made from ½ pound (250 grams) of sugar dissolved on the stove in ⅓ cup (20 centilitres) of water.

Filter and bottle.

Raspberry liqueur or ratafia. LIQUEUR, RATAFIA DE FRAMBOISES—Put 2 pounds (1 kilo) of very ripe raspberries in a jar. Cover with 4⅜ quarts (4 litres) of spirits. Cork the jar and leave to infuse for 2 months, putting the jar in the sun whenever possible.

Add to the liqueur 1 pound (500 grams) of sugar, barely moistened to dissolve it.

Filter and bottle.

Tangerine liqueur or ratafia. LIQUEUR, RATAFIA DE MANDARINE—Proceed as for *Orange liqueur*, using the peel and juice of tangerines.

Vanilla liqueur or ratafia. LIQUEUR, RATAFIA À LA VANILLE—Infuse 3 vanilla pods in a quart (litre) of spirits for 15 days. Mix with a very thick syrup. Filter and bottle.

Verbena liqueur or ratafia. LIQUEUR, RATAFIA DE VERVEINE—Made with verbena leaves in the same way as *Vanilla liqueur*.

Violet liqueur or ratafia. LIQUEUR, RATAFIA DE VIOLETTES—Made with violets in the same way as *Carnation liqueur*.

Walnut liqueur or ratafia (walnut water or cordial). LIQUEUR, RATAFIA DE NOIX (BROU, EAU DE NOIX)—Split in half 20 green walnuts and put them in a jar with 1½ quarts (litres) of spirits. Cork tightly.

Leave this mixture to infuse for 6 weeks in a cool place, taking care to shake the jar from time to time.

Strain through a cloth. Mix in a syrup made from 1 pound (500 grams) of sugar and 1 cup (¼ litre) of boiled water. Add a little cinnamon and a pinch of coriander.

Leave to infuse for another month. Strain and bottle.

Walnut liqueur or ratafia (Walnut water or cordial à la carmélite). LIQUEUR, RATAFIA DE NOIX (BROU, EAU DE NOIX À LA CARMÉLITE)—Proceed as indicated in the previous recipe, using 100 green walnuts and ½ tablespoon (4 grams) of cloves. The walnuts must be unripe so that they can be pierced with a thick pin.

When the mixture has infused for 2 months, add 4 pounds (2 kilos) of sugar.

Proceed as indicated in the previous recipe.

LIQUEUR OR DESSERT WINES. VINS DE LIQUEUR—This name is given to any wine which is both sweet and intoxicating. Among these wines, which are mainly drunk as *apéritifs*, and used in cooking and confectionery, the following are well known: *Frontignac, Muscatel, Lunel, Grenache, Banyuls, Madeira, Malaga, Malmsey, Marsala, Port, Sherry, Lacrima-Christi.*

LIQUORICE. RÉGLISSE—Plant of the *Leguminoceae* family found mainly in Spain and Sicily; its rhizome contains a sweet substance, and when soaked or infused in water in the ratio of 2 ounces to 1 quart (60 grams to 1 litre), provides a sweet and pectoral drink.

Solidified liquorice comes from a watery extract obtained by strong pressure which is then evaporated to a solid consistency. It is black in colour, and it is usually moulded into cylindrical sticks, glossy when broken, sweet tasting, a little bitter and sharp, to an extent soluble in water when pure.

LITCHI OR LICHEE. LETCHI—This fruit, which seems to be of Chinese origin, is also cultivated in India, the Philippine Islands and other countries of the Far East. It has the appearance of a berry, about the size of a cherry, with a large stone. The pulp is white, sweet and musky in flavour. It has a thin hard and scaly shell which comes away easily from the fruit. The shell is greenish at first, then it turns pink, and finally, when fully ripe, red.

Litchis or Lichees

For export, the fruit is usually left to dry in its shell. It then turns black like a prune, is very sweet with a slightly acid flavour, and is called *Lichee* or *Litchi nuts.* The Litchi tree is grown as a garden tree in south Florida and California in U.S.A.

LITRON—An old French liquid measure. An old bushel measured about 13 litres and a litron was a sixteenth of a bushel.

LITTLE BUSTARD (FIELD DUCK). CANEPETIÈRE—Migratory European wild bird of the wader family.

LIVER. FOIE—The liver is the largest and most important of the glands attached to the digestive organs.

The livers of slaughtered animals, poultry and game are all used in cookery, as are also those of one or two fish, such as the turbot and skate. See OFFAL OR VARIETY MEATS.

LIVESTOCK. BÉTAIL—This word is used to describe all the animals, particularly animals intended for food, raised on cattle-breeding farms.

Erroneously this word is also applied to small farmyard animals, various types of poultry and hutch rabbits.

The only animals which should come under this heading are bullocks, oxen, cows, calves, sheep, lambs and pigs.

LLAMA. LAMA—A ruminant mammal found in Peru. It is edible and is cooked in the same way as *beef**.

LOACH. LOCHE—A name given to several European freshwater fish, all long in shape and barbed.

There are three types: the *common loach*, a delicate fish found in mountain streams; the *spined loach* or *groundling*, a small fish found in rivers and streams, about the size of a gudgeon, and rather leathery; the *rockling*, about the same size as the other two, but less delicate in flavour. The loach is eaten fried, *en matelote* or *à la meunière*.

LOAVES. PAINS—The word *pain* is a culinary term which applies to dishes, served cold or hot, made of a forcemeat placed in a special mould and poached in a *bain-marie**, in the case of a dish being served hot, and set in a mould, lined with aspic jelly and chilled, in the case of a dish being served cold.

This type of entrée was very popular in old culinary practice but is not done much nowadays. It has been replaced by *mousses**, which are also prepared hot or cold.

The various ingredients used for the forcemeats are, as indicated in individual recipes, liver (*foie gras*), game meat (winged and ground game), poultry and vegetables, as well as fish and crustaceans.

FISH AND SHELL-FISH LOAVES. PAINS DE POISSONS, CRUSTACÉS.

Pike loaf (hot). PAIN DE BROCHET—Dice 1 pound (500 grams) of pike flesh (net weight, after cleaning the fish).

Season with 1 teaspoon (6 grams) of salt, a pinch of white pepper and a little grated nutmeg. Pound in a mortar into a fine paste.

Remove the fish from the mortar and in its place put in 1¼ cups (200 grams) of *Flour panada* (see PANADA). After pounding the panada thoroughly, add to it ½ pound (250 grams) of butter. Blend by pounding together.

Put the pike back in the mortar and pound vigorously to obtain a perfectly smooth mixture.

Add, still pounding, one whole egg and, one by one, 4 yolks of egg.

Remove the forcemeat from the mortar, rub it through a fine sieve, transfer into a bowl and stir with a wooden spoon until very smooth.

Butter a plain round mould and fill with this mixture.

Cook the loaf in a *bain-marie** (pan of hot water), in the oven, from 45 to 50 minutes, depending on the size of the mould.

Turn out on to a serving dish, either straight on to the dish or on a fried croûton of bread. Serve with the garnish and sauce as indicated in the recipe.

Various fish loaves (hot). PAINS DE POISSON—Using carp, salmon or turbot flesh, prepare as described in the recipe for *Pike loaf.*

The forcemeat can also be prepared as described in the recipe for *Mousseline forcemeat*, for fish mousse and mousseline (see FORCEMEAT).

Garnishes and sauces: Cancalaise (poached oysters) and *Normande sauce; Américaine* (slices of spiny lobster) and *American sauce; Cardinal* (slices of spiny lobster or lobster, truffles and mushrooms) and *Cardinal sauce; Normande* (mussels, oysters, crayfish, mushrooms, truffles) and *Normande sauce; Trouvillaise* (shrimps' tails, mussels, mushrooms) and *Shrimp sauce.* See GARNISHES, SAUCES.

Shell-fish loaves (hot). PAINS DE CRUSTACÉS—Prepare a *lobster, spiny lobster, crab* or any other shell-fish forcemeat, as described in the recipe for *Forcemeat with panada and butter* (see FORCEMEAT), pour into a well-buttered, plain round mould with a hole in the middle and poach in the oven in a *bain-marie**.

Turn out on to a round dish. Serve with the garnish indicated and pour over a sauce appropriate to the garnish.

Garnishes and sauces. All the garnishes and sauces recommended for fish are applicable to shell-fish loaves.

FOIE GRAS LOAVES. PAINS DE FOIE GRAS—In the old days the foie gras loaves (today replaced by foie gras mousses and mousselines) were prepared using *panada** as an element of liaison. This type of liaison is no longer used nowadays and a much more delicate composition is obtained and the binding of the mixture is assured by using meat jelly. Here is an old recipe for this type of entrée:

Jellied foie gras loaf (*Carême*)

Jellied foie gras loaf (Carême's recipe). PAIN DE FOIE GRAS À LA GELÉE—In this recipe Carême only speaks of fattened capon liver, but this entrée can also be made from fattened goose liver.

'Trim a pound of fat capon liver, which you have previously soaked in water.

'Weigh out six ounces of panada and the same amount of butter or grated bacon fat.

'Begin to pound the panada, then add butter to it. Take this mixture out of the mortar and proceed to pound the liver into a perfectly smooth paste.

'Add the panada and pound together for a good quarter of an hour, adding 5 yolks of egg, one ounce of spiced salt, two tablespoons of *fines herbes* tossed in butter (by *fines herbes*, Carême meant a mixture of chopped mushrooms, truffles, shallots and aromatic herbs) and one of *Velouté sauce* (see SAUCE).

'When the whole has been well blended, rub it through a quenelle-mixture sieve and put this forcemeat into a bowl.

'Add two ounces of blanched, diced udder, two of pickled tongue and two of truffles (two ounces of pistachio nuts can also be added).

'Transfer the mixture into a cylindrical-shaped mould, lined with thin rashers (strips) of bacon, in such a way as to have the whole inside surface covered completely.

Press down the mould with a napkin to make the forcemeat take shape. Cover with more bacon rashers and stand the mould in a casserole four inches larger than the mould. Pour enough boiling water into the casserole to cover the mould completely (that is to say, the water should reach to within $\frac{1}{8}$ inch of the rim). Place on red coals and put some glowing coals on the lid as well, to ensure that the water maintains the same temperature—almost boiling—all the time. (Or you can cook the loaf in a slow oven in a *bain-marie**.)

'A good two hours later take out the mould (an hour later if the cooking is done in the oven) and put it on ice or in a cold place. When the loaf is quite cold, heat the mould on the stove just to loosen it and turn out the loaf on to a casserole lid.

'Remove the bacon rashers covering the loaf, and spoon over some warm, clear jelly on top and all round.

'Put the loaf on an entrée dish, the bottom of which should be lined with some liquid jelly, and set; garnish the edges of the dish first with chopped jelly, then with jelly croûtons and decorate the top with jelly.'

GAME LOAVES. Pain de gibiers.

Ground game loaf (hot). Pain de gibier de poil—This is prepared, using the flesh of leveret, hare or deer, like *Chicken loaf* (*hot*).

Ground game loaf in jelly. Pain de gibier de poil à la gelée—Like *Winged game loaf in jelly.*

Winged game loaf (hot). Pain de gibier de plume—This is made, using the meat of woodcock, pheasant, partridge, like *Chicken loaf* (*hot*). The garnish and sauces suitable for hot game loaf are: mushrooms and *Demi-glace sauce* (see SAUCE) based on buttered, concentrated game stock reduced (simmered down) to the consistency of a *fumet**; *chipolata sausages* with buttered *Demi-glace; Rossini* (escalopes of liver and truffles) and *Demi-glace sauce* based on a truffle *fumet; truffles* and *Demi-glace* based on truffle *fumet.*

Winged game loaf in jelly. Pain de gibier de plume à la gelée—Prepare like *Foie gras loaf in jelly*, replacing the liver by 1 pound (500 grams) (net weight) of game meat, as indicated.

VEGETABLE LOAVES. Pain de légumes—These loaves are usually made, using braised vegetables, mixed with eggs beaten as for an omelette, poured into a buttered plain mould and poached in a *bain-marie**.

By following the recipe given for *Endive loaf* (see ENDIVE) various other vegetable loaves can be made: artichoke, aubergine (egg-plant), carrot, cauliflower, turnip, etc.

This type of loaf, made in large moulds, is served as a small entrée. They usually have a sauce, generally a cream sauce, poured over them.

Small vegetable loaves are used as a garnish for meat and broiled, braised or poached poultry. They can also be used for garnishing fish dishes or poached or soft-boiled eggs. Some recipes are given below.

Small cauliflower loaves. Petits pains de chou-fleur—Prepare a cauliflower purée (bound with yolks of egg), pour it into small buttered dariole moulds and cook in the oven in a *bain-marie**.

Small lettuce loaves. Petits pains de laitues—Using lettuces, braised, chopped and bound with egg, prepare as *Small spinach loaves.*

Various other vegetable loaves or vegetable purées such as carrot, mushrooms, endive, Brussels sprouts, chicory, tomato, etc. can be prepared in the same manner.

Small spinach loaves à la romaine. Petits pains d'épinards à la romaine—Prepare a leaf spinach purée, tossed in *Noisette butter* (see BUTTER, *Compound butters*), mixed with diced anchovy fillets, and bound (1 pound or 500 grams of spinach) with 2 eggs beaten as for an omelette. Pour the mixture into buttered dariole moulds and cook in a *bain-marie** (pan of hot water).

LOBSTER. Homard—A large sea-water crustacean similar in shape to the crayfish. There are two main types, the one to be found in European waters, the other in American waters.

The shell of the lobster is smooth. Its claws are armed with pincers of unequal size. One is large and oval in shape, the other more slender and elongated.

The lobster found in European waters is of a rich, dark blue colour tinged with purple. Its joints are orange and its feelers, which are as long as its body, red.

The lobster reaches full growth very slowly. At five years old, it is about 5 inches long, having shed its tail some twenty times in the course of this period. Later it grows very much larger, attaining 12 to 14 inches in length and weighing up to 10 pounds.

The female lobster carries its eggs in the tail. The French have a special name, *paquette*, for the female lobster with fully-formed eggs, and connoisseurs assert that it is when the eggs are formed and not laid that the flesh of the female lobster is at its most delicate and savoury.

The American lobster lives only on the Eastern coast of North America, running from Labrador to North Carolina, although the most important sources are off the coast of Nova Scotia and the state of Maine. According to United States fisheries authorities, the five-year-old lobster measures about $10\frac{1}{2}$ inches and has moulted 25 times. It is a dark mottled green when caught.

The flesh of the lobster is more highly flavoured than that of the spiny lobster or crayfish.

There are many different ways of preparing lobster. It can be eaten hot or cold like the spiny lobster (see SPINY LOBSTER).

Lobster à l'américaine. Homard à l'américaine—Any well-informed gastronome will recognise the ingredients and preparation of this dish as of Provençal origin. Raw lobster sautéed in oil and the use of tomatoes are characteristic features of Mediterranean cookery, and indeed tomatoes were scarcely known anywhere else until the nineteenth century. Furthermore, recipes for crayfish (in those days there was some confusion as to the distinction between freshwater and sea-water crayfish) similar to that for *Lobster à l'américaine* are to be found in old French recipe books.

Towards the middle of the nineteenth century, this dish was called *Lobster à la provençale* (Gouffé). The name *Lobster à l'américaine* was applied at that time to a dish made from poached lobster.

A certain confusion had arisen over these two names. *Lobster à la provençale*, simpler to prepare and less subtle in flavour, usurped both the name and the position of *Lobster à l'américaine.*

There is still some doubt as to who invented the name *Lobster à l'américaine*, the dish itself having been known for a very long time.

Was it some anonymous cook, as the master-chef Escoffier would have us believe, who, having known the dish in Nice, exported it to America whence it was subsequently reimported into France? Was it some *restaurateur*, perhaps Fraisse of Noêl and Peter's Res-

Lobster (*Robert Carrier*)

taurant, who gave this name to the dish in honour of some transatlantic patron?

It must be said, however, that there are many experts who assert that this method of cooking lobster originated in Brittany, and that the name *à l'américaine* is nothing but an error of transcription, the proper form being *à l'armoricaine*.

We share this view and are convinced that this dish came to us from Armorica (Brittany), and that the name, if not transposed, was at least adjusted by the master-cooks of Paris.

This does not in any way run counter to the view that, at the same period, Provençal cooks were preparing lobsters and spiny lobsters (especially spiny lobsters) in the Provençal fashion, that is to say in a *coulis** of tomatoes flavoured with onion, garlic and parsley.

Method. Take a hen lobster weighing 2 pounds (1 kilo). Cut the tail into neat slices following the marks of the joints. Split the carcase in two, lengthwise. Crack the shell of the claws. Remove all the gritty substance near the head. Remove and keep the coral and the water of the lobster. These will be used at the end to thicken the sauce. Season the portions of the lobster with salt and pepper.

Heat 4 to 6 tablespoons of olive oil in a pan. Put the pieces of lobster in the pan and brown quickly on both sides. Remove them from the pan.

Put 2 tablespoons of finely chopped onion in the pan. Cook it slowly until it is very tender, stirring frequently.

When the onion is almost cooked, add 2 chopped shallots. Stir with a wooden spoon to mix thoroughly.

Put 2 coarsely chopped tomatoes (peeled, squeezed and with seeds removed) into the pan. Add a touch of garlic, a tablespoon of chopped parsley and tarragon.

Lay the pieces of lobster on this foundation of herbs and vegetables. Moisten with ½ cup (a decilitre) of dry white wine, ½ cup (a decilitre) of fish *fumet** and 4 tablespoons of brandy. Season with cayenne pepper.

Bring the mixture to the boil. Cover the pan. Cook on the stove or in the oven for 20 minutes.

(1) (2) Cut off the claws

(3) Cut off the tip of the tail

(4) Split the carcase in two

(5) (6) Cut the head in two and remove gritty substance

How to cut up a lobster for Lobster à l'américaine (*Larousse*)

Drain the pieces of lobster. Pick out the flesh from the claws and the tail.

Serve in the halves of the shells on a long dish. Keep warm while the sauce is being made.

The sauce. Boil down the pan juices by half. Add the coral and the water of the lobster, pounded and mixed with butter. Whisk over a high flame.

Remove the pan from the fire and, still whisking to ensure a smooth and creamy sauce, add 6 tablespoons (100 grams) of butter cut into tiny fragments.

Season with a little cayenne pepper and a squeeze of lemon juice. Pour this sauce, piping hot, over the lobster. Sprinkle with chopped parsley.

Note. The above method can be varied.

Some cooks leave out the chopped onion and tarragon. Others add a certain amount of fine vegetable *mirepoix** to the lobster. We consider this to be a most inappropriate addition. *Mirepoix* should only be used with shell-fish when it is prepared *à la bordelaise**.

Finally, the lobster sauce may be strained before the butter is added.

Lobster aspic. ASPIC DE HOMARD—Take a mould (this may be conical, round, plain or embellished with decorative motifs). Line it with jelly and lay in it collops (thick slices) of lobster interlaced with strips of truffle, decorated with jelly.

Fill the mould to the top with clear white fish jelly. Leave it on ice to set.

Turn out the aspic on to a dish. It can either be put straight on to the dish or may be served on a round slice of buttered sandwich bread. Decorate with jelly.

Boiled lobster. HOMARD BOUILLI—Proceed as for *Lobster à la nage* (see below).

This dish is served hot with one or other of the sauces usually served with boiled fish or shell-fish. When it is eaten cold, it should be served with any sauce suitable for cold fish or shell-fish.

Lobster à la bordelaise. HOMARD À LA BORDELAISE—Generally, small lobsters only are prepared in this way. These small lobsters are called *Demoiselles of Cherbourg or Dieppe.* If they are very small, the lobsters are cooked whole. If they are big, they are split in half, lengthwise.

Large lobsters can be prepared *à la bordelaise* by splitting them into sections as for lobster *à l'américaine.*

To prepare lobster in this way, proceed as for *Crayfish à la bordelaise.* See CRAYFISH.

Lobster Brillat-Savarin. HOMARD BRILLAT-SAVARIN—Boil a large lobster in a white wine *court-bouillon XII**.

Drain. Cut off the tail and shell it. Cut the flesh into fairly thick slices. Put them to simmer in a rather thick *Américaine sauce* (see SAUCE), which has been prepared separately, adding to it some of the *court-bouillon* in which the lobster was cooked, boiled down almost to a jelly.

Shell the claws and the carcase. Chop the flesh into a coarse *salpicon**. Add equal quantities of *salpicon* of cooked truffles and mushrooms. Simmer all these ingredients in a *Curry sauce* (see SAUCE) made with the rest of the lobster *court-bouillon.*

Cook slowly in oil very small marrows (zucchini), cut into thick slices—the same number as there are lobster slices.

To serve. Place the slices of lobster and marrow alternately in a ring inside a baked flan-crust. Put the *salpicon* in the middle and cover with *Américaine sauce.* On top of each slice of lobster, put a large thick strip of truffle.

Lobster cardinal. HOMARD CARDINAL—Put the lobster in a boiling *Court-bouillon XII**. Boil until it is cooked. Drain the lobster. Let it cool a little. Split it lengthwise. Remove the flesh from the tail and cut it into collops (slices) of equal thickness. Cut off the claws and take out the flesh. Dice this flesh to make a *salpicon**. Add to this *salpicon* an equal quantity of diced cooked mushrooms and half the quantity of diced truffles. Bind the *salpicon* with a *Lobster sauce* (see SAUCE).

Fill the halves of the lobster shell with the *salpicon.* Place on top the collops interspersed with strips of truffles. Pour on some *Lobster sauce.* Sprinkle with grated cheese and melted butter.

Place the halves of a lobster on a baking sheet close together and brown them quickly in the oven.

Serve on a napkin, garnished with curly parsley.

Lobster en chemise. HOMARD EN CHEMISE—Kill a lobster by plunging it in boiling water. Season with salt and pepper. Baste with oil or melted butter. Wrap it in a double thickness of oiled grease-proof paper and tie it with string.

Put the lobster thus parcelled up on a baking sheet. Bake in a hot oven for 40 to 50 minutes for a medium-sized lobster.

Untie the lobster and serve it as it is in the paper in which it has been cooked.

Suitable dressings are half-melted *Maître d'hôtel butter* (see BUTTER, *Compound butters*), or any sauce usually served with grilled fish: *Américaine, Béarnaise, Bercy, Bordelaise, Hongroise, Indienne, Ravigote.* See SAUCE.

Lobster in cream. HOMARD À LA CRÈME—Cut up the lobster as for *Lobster à l'américaine**. Sauté the portions in butter. Drain off the butter. Pour 3 tablespoons of brandy into the pan and mix with pan juices. Add $2\frac{1}{2}$ cups (5 decilitres) of cream. Season with salt and a touch of cayenne pepper. Cover the pan and simmer.

Serve the lobster in a pie-dish (in or out of its shell). Cook down the cooking sauce to half its volume, add 3 tablespoons (50 grams) of butter and a few drops of lemon juice and strain through muslin. Pour this sauce over the lobster.

Lobster croquettes. CROQUETTES DE HOMARD—Made from lobster *salpicon** in the same way as plain croquettes. If desired a *salpicon* of mushrooms and truffles may be added. See HORS-D'OEUVRE, *Hot hors-d'oeuvre, croquettes.*

Lobster à la franco-américaine. HOMARD À LA FRANCO-AMÉRICAINE—This method of cooking lobster, for which recipes are given by several authorities on cookery, is a variant of the recipe for *Lobster à l'américaine.*

Take two medium-sized live lobsters and kill them by plunging them in boiling water. Cut off the claws and crack them in order that, after cooking, the flesh can be easily taken out.

Split the lobsters in half, lengthwise. Drain the carcases and scrape them out, keeping the coral and the liquid contained in them.

Put 4 tablespoons of oil in a pan and heat in it 2 tablespoons of chopped onion and 1 tablespoon of chopped shallot. Put the lobsters in the pan. Season with salt and freshly ground pepper.

Pour over the lobsters $1\frac{1}{2}$ cups (3 decilitres) of rather thin *Tomato sauce* (see SAUCE). Boil for 5 minutes. Add 2 small glasses of brandy. Cover the pan and bake in the oven for 16 to 18 minutes.

Drain the lobsters. Put them on a serving dish and keep warm.

Strain the sauce. Put it back in the pan. Add the liquid and coral, 2 tablespoons of meat essence, half a glass of Madeira, 2 tablespoons of blazing brandy and one or two small chopped sweet peppers. Cook down this sauce and add butter to it. Pour it over the lobsters.

Grilled lobster. HOMARD GRILLÉ—Take a live medium-sized lobster and plunge it into boiling salt water for 3 minutes. This will kill it instantly and make the flesh firmer.

Drain it. Split it in two, lengthwise. Season and pour melted butter over it. Grill it on a moderate heat.

Crack the claws so that the flesh can be easily removed, then serve the lobster on a napkin garnished with fresh parsley.

Serve separately one or other of the sauces usually served with grilled fish. Melted butter, *Maître d'hôtel butter* or *Ravigote butter* can also be served with grilled lobster. See BUTTER, *Compound butters.*

Lobster Henri Duvernois. HOMARD HENRI DUVERNOIS—According to the size of the lobster, either split it lengthwise or joint it as for *Lobster à l'américaine.* Season with salt and paprika. Brown it in butter.

As soon as the lobster is well-browned, take it out of the pan. Add to the cooking butter 4 heaped tablespoons of *julienne** of leeks and 4 of mushrooms tossed in butter.

Put the lobster back in the pan. Moisten with $\frac{2}{3}$ cup ($1\frac{1}{2}$ decilitres) of sherry and 2 tablespoons of brandy. Reduce, add fresh cream, cover with a lid and simmer.

Put the lobster on a long dish. Garnish with a pilaf of rice arranged along each side of the dish. Reduce the cooking sauce, add 2 tablespoons of butter and pour it over the lobster.

Lobster kromeskies. CROMESQUIS DE HOMARD—This dish is served as a hot hors-d'oeuvre or as a light main course. It is made from lobster *salpicon** either plain or with a *Velouté* or *Béchamel sauce* (see SAUCE), to which diced truffles and mushrooms have been added. For further details see HORS-D'OEUVRE, *Hot hors-d'oeuvre.*

Lobster à la marinière. HOMARD AU COURT-BOUILLON À LA MARINIÈRE—In the main, very small lobsters are used for this dish. Proceed as for *Crayfish à la marinière.* See CRAYFISH.

Lobsters cooked in this way are often called *Lobsters à la nage.*

Lobster Mornay. *Homard Mornay*—Proceed as for *Lobster cardinal,* substituting *Mornay sauce* (see SAUCE) for *Lobster sauce.*

Lobster Mornay in scallop shells (hot). COQUILLES DE HOMARD MORNAY—Proceed as for *Brill in scallop shells** or any other fish in scallop shells, using a *salpicon** and thick slices of lobster coated with *Mornay sauce* (see SAUCE). Brown in a very hot oven.

Note. As with all other scallop shells, whether filled with poultry, fish or other ingredients, the shells should be decorated with a border of *Duchess potato mixture* (see POTATOES) piped through a forcing (pastry) bag with a fluted nozzle, before they are filled.

Hot lobster scallop shells can also be made with other sauces such as *Cardinal, Nantua, Normande, White wine sauce* (see SAUCE).

Cold lobster mousse. MOUSSE DE HOMARD FROIDE—Add to a *mirepoix** some dry white wine and 3 tablespoons of brandy which had been set alight. Cook the lobster in this and leave it to cool in it. Drain the lobster and take it out of its shell. Pound the flesh finely in a mortar, adding little by little for every 2 cups (500 grams) of flesh (net weight) the equivalent of 1 cup (2 decilitres) of cold *Velouté sauce* (see SAUCE) based on fish stock. Rub this mixture through a sieve. Put the purée thus obtained in a pan on ice. Stir it with a spatula for a few minutes. Add 4 to 5 tablespoons of cold *Fish aspic jelly* (see ASPIC) and about 1 cup (2 decilitres) of fresh slightly whipped cream. Season.

Line a plain mould with fish jelly. Fill it with the lobster mousse and decorate with truffles or some other garnish. Put it on ice to set.

Turn the mousse out on to a serving dish. It may either be put straight on the dish or on a slice of thickly buttered sandwich bread. Surround the mousse with chopped jelly and a border of jelly croûtons.

The lobster mousse mixture may also be served in a glass or silver bowl and covered with fish aspic jelly. A *salpicon** of lobster and truffles may be added to the mixture.

Cold lobster mousselines (mousses served in individual portions). MOUSSELINES DE HOMARD FROIDES—These are made from the same mixture as *Cold lobster mousse.* Serve the mixture either in small cylindrical moulds lined with jelly and decorated with truffles or in little silver or porcelain cups.

Note. Lobster *mousselines* can be served as hors-d'oeuvre or as a light main course, or may be used as a garnish with large cold fish.

Lobster à la nage

Lobster à la nage (cold). HOMARD À LA NAGE—Proceed as for *Lobster à la nage (hot).* Leave the lobsters to cool in the *court-bouillon*.* Serve them in the *court-bouillon.* Serve separately a *Mayonnaise sauce* or *Tartare sauce* (see SAUCE, *Cold sauces*), a French dressing or any other sauce usually served with cold fish or shell-fish.

Lobster à la nage (hot). HOMARD À LA NAGE—Make a white wine *court-bouillon XII*.* In this stock boil some small lobsters of the type known as *demoiselles of Cherbourg or Dieppe.*

Serve these lobsters hot in the *court-bouillon.* Serve separately a special sauce suitable for poached fish.

Lobster Newburg. HOMARD À LA NEWBURG—*Ingredients.* 2 live lobsters weighing about 1 pound (400 to 500 grams) each, $\frac{3}{4}$ cup (175 grams) of butter, 1 cup (3 decilitres) of sherry, 1 cup (3 decilitres) concentrated fish stock, 1 cup (3 decilitres) *Velouté sauce* (see SAUCE), $1\frac{1}{3}$ cups (4 decilitres) cream, salt, paprika.

Method. Wash the lobsters and joint them as for *Lobster à l'américaine.* Remove the coral and keep for use later. Season the lobsters with salt and paprika. Heat 5 tablespoons (75 grams) of butter in a pan. Brown the lobsters in it. Turn the lobster pieces over to brown them on both sides. Cover the pan and cook for 12 minutes.

Drain off the butter and add the sherry. Cook down over a high flame. Add the fish stock and the *Velouté,* keeping the pan covered, simmer gently for 20 minutes.

Take out the pieces of lobster and arrange them in a deep dish or a silver bowl. (The tail pieces may be shelled.)

Boil down the sauce, add the cream, and test the sauce. When it coats the back of a spoon, add the coral, previously rubbed through a fine sieve and blended with the rest of the butter. Mix the sauce quickly by whisking. Pour over the pieces of lobster.

Note. This dish is also sometimes called *Lobster sauté à la crème*. This name is, in fact, the more intelligible of the two, since it indicates one of the principal ingredients of the sauce.

Lobster à la parisienne. HOMARD À LA PARISIENNE—Cut into collops (slices) of equal thickness the tail of a medium-sized lobster, cooked in a *court-bouillon* and cooled. Coat these collops with gelatine-strengthened mayonnaise. Decorate them with strips of truffle dipped in the half-set mayonnaise jelly, and glaze with jelly.

Arrange the collops as a border on a round dish. For the centre of the dish turn out a mould lined with jelly, filled with vegetable salad mixed with the rest of the lobster, diced, with diced truffles in mayonnaise jelly added. Garnish with chopped jelly.

The collops may also be served coated with jelly in a glass dish, as a border to *Salad à la parisienne** which should be piled up into a small dome in the middle.

Cold lobster à la parisienne or à la russe. HOMARD FROID À LA PARISIENNE, À LA RUSSE—Proceed according to the recipe for *Spiny lobster à la parisienne or à la russe*. See SPINY LOBSTER.

Lobster pilaf. PILAF DE HOMARD—Coarsely dice the flesh of boiled lobsters or cut it into collops (pieces). Brown it lightly in butter.

Line a domed mould with *pilaf* of rice (see RICE), and fill it with the *salpicon** of collops of lobster. Turn out the mould on a serving dish. Surround with *Lobster sauce* (see SAUCE) or any other sauce suitable for shellfish.

The pilaf may also be served in the following way: put the pilaf in a bowl. Place in the centre the *salpicon* of lobster mixed with lobster sauce or any other sauce desired.

Lobster risotto. RISOTTO DE HOMARD—Proceed as for *Lobster pilaf.* Fill a ring mould with risotto. Turn it out, and heap *salpicon** or collops (pieces) of lobster in the middle.

Lobster salad (*Mac Fisheries*)

Lobster salad. SALADE DE HOMARD—See SALAD, *Lobster salad.*

Cold lobster with various sauces. HOMARD FROID AVEC SAUCES DIVERSES—Boil the lobster in a *court-bouillon**. Leave it to cool. Split it in two, lengthwise. Crack the shell of the claws so that the flesh can be taken out easily.

Serve on a napkin and garnish with fresh parsley or lettuce hearts.

Serve with mayonnaise sauce or any other cold sauce, such as *Gribiche*, *Rémoulade*, *Tartare*. See SAUCE, *Cold sauces.*

Lobster in scallop shells (cold). COQUILLES FROIDES DE HOMARD—This dish is usually made from scraps.

Line the scallop shells (or shells made of silver or porcelain) with shredded lettuce seasoned with salt, pepper, oil and vinegar. On this foundation, put a lobster *salpicon**, also seasoned with a French dressing and sprinkled with chopped chervil and parsley.

Put in each shell one or two thick slices of lobster. Cover with mayonnaise. Decorate the top with fillets of anchovy, capers and olives. Garnish with lettuce hearts and quartered hard boiled eggs.

Lobster in scallop shells à la parisienne. COQUILLES DE HOMARD À LA PARISIENNE—Proceed as for *Lobster in scallop shells* (*cold*), using vegetable salad dressed with mayonnaise or French dressing instead of lettuce. Decorate with strips of truffle, capers, lettuce hearts and quartered hard boiled eggs.

Lobster in scallop shells vert-pré. COQUILLES DE HOMARD VERT-PRÉ—Line the shells with shredded water-cress leaves in a French dressing. Place on top the *salpicon** and collops (slices) of lobster. Coat with green mayonnaise. Decorate with round slices of gherkin and chopped yolks of hard boiled eggs. Surround with a border of French beans boiled in salt water, drained, diced and seasoned with a French dressing.

Lobster soufflé. SOUFFLÉ DE HOMARD—Finely pound in a mortar 10 ounces or approximately $1\frac{1}{2}$ cups (300 grams) (net weight) of cooked lobster. Rub through a fine sieve. Add to the purée 1 cup (2 decilitres) of *Béchamel sauce* (see SAUCE) previously cooked with a little of the lobster stock. Season with salt, pepper and grated nutmeg. Blend in 4 egg yolks. At the last minute, add 4 stiffly beaten whites of eggs.

Put the mixture in a buttered soufflé dish. Cook in a slow oven for 25 to 30 minutes. Serve immediately.

Note. Little lobster soufflés can be served as an hors-d'oeuvre or light main course. These are made from the same mixture as lobster soufflé, but are cooked in little buttered cups or cases.

Lobster on the spit. HOMARD À LA BROCHE—Plunge a large live lobster into boiling salt water for a few seconds. (This is done to ensure that the lobster is killed instantly.)

Put the lobster on a spit. Season it with salt, pepper, thyme, and powdered bay leaf. Baste it with melted butter or oil with a dripping pan or other suitable dish underneath. Put into the pan a few tablespoons of dry white wine and two tablespoons of butter. Cook in front of a very hot fire. Baste frequently during cooking. A lobster weighing 3 pounds ($1\frac{1}{2}$ kilograms) needs to be cooked for 40 to 45 minutes.

Remove the lobster from the spit. Arrange it on a long dish. Serve the juice collected in the dripping pan separately.

Lobster on the spit can be served with spicy sauces such as *Béarnaise*, *Curry*, *Ravigote* (see SAUCE).

Lobster thermidor. HOMARD THERMIDOR—Split a live lobster in two, lengthwise. Crack the shell of the claws and pick out the meat. Season both halves of the lobster with salt. Pour oil over them and roast them in the oven for 15 to 20 minutes.

Dice the lobster flesh coarsely. Make a stock of white

Lobster thermidor

wine, fish *fumet** and meat gravy, flavoured with chervil, tarragon and chopped shallots. Boil it down to a concentrated consistency. Add to this concentrated stock a little very thick *Béchamel sauce* (see SAUCE) and some English mustard.

Boil this sauce for a few seconds, then whisk in fresh butter (one-third of the volume of the sauce).

Line the two halves of the carcases with a little of this sauce. Fill them with the flesh of the lobster, cover with the remainder of the sauce, sprinkle with grated Parmesan and melted butter and brown quickly in the oven.

Note. This is the recipe for *Lobster thermidor* given to us by M. Tony Girod, for very many years master chef of that famous Parisian restaurant, the Café de Paris.

This dish is often prepared in a different way. The tail of the lobster is split in half and grilled, then the flesh is cut into thick slices and put back in the shells which have been coated with a little cream sauce seasoned with mustard. They are covered with the same sauce and browned in the oven.

LOCUST OR CAROB TREE. CAROUBE—A leguminous plant which grows in the East, and in the Mediterranean. The long pod contains numerous seeds and a rather insipid sweet pulp.

LOIN. CARRÉ—The front part of a hindquarter of beef, mutton, lamb, pork or veal with the flank removed.

LONGCHAMP—A broth fundamental to Parisian cooking. It is made by cooking shredded sorrel and vermicelli in clear soup (*consommé*) and adding a purée of fresh green peas. See SOUPS AND BROTHS.

LONGE—Strictly this French term should refer only to the top part of the loin of veal. See VEAL.

It is, however, inaccurately extended to refer to the same part of any slaughtered animal.

LONZO (Corsican cookery)—This pork-product which is eaten raw as an hors-d'oeuvre, like raw salt ham, is made from boned fillet of pork. This is steeped in brine with herbs and then dried. It is served in very thin slices.

LOQUAT OR JAPANESE MEDLAR. NÈFLE DU JAPON—The fruit of the Japanese *biwa*. This fruit looks something like a small plum. Its seeds are enclosed in a large stone. Loquats ripen in Provence from April onward. They are quite sweet, slightly tart, and refreshing.

LORDS AND LADIES (also known as cuckoo-pint and wake-robin). PIED-DE-VEAU—Common name for wild arum, the tuberous roots of which contain edible fecula.

LORRAINE—Lorraine is a district of high gastronomic repute. Here the connoisseur of good cooking will savour innumerable exquisite dishes, and, moreover, he will find white, red and rosé wines, all delightful though some are more fragrant than others.

The dishes of Lorraine are, for the most part, substantial. The people of Lorraine like their meals to be filling. Heading the list of the culinary specialities of what was once the ancient province of Lotharingie is the magnificent *potée* which, one can truly say, is the national soup of this region. But there are many other dishes in the gastronomic repertoire of Lorraine, all of the robust type. Washed down with the exquisite wines of the Moselle, Meurthe-et-Moselle and Meuse districts, they combine to make a perfect gastronomic symphony.

First of all there is the *quiche*, a dish which goes back centuries in the gastronomic history of Lorraine. This is an exquisite tart made with eggs, cream and lean bacon. This *quiche*, which typifies the cuisine of Lorraine, is also called *féouse*.

Quiche lorraine

Another characteristic local dish is the *Tourte à la Lorraine*. This tart is made with two kinds of meat, veal and pork. These are first steeped with herbs in a marinade and then baked together on a bed of savoury egg custard in a pie crust of fine pastry.

From the long list of the culinary specialities of this province, where it is a point of honour to eat well, we select *Ramequins; Kneppes; Oeufs à l'escargot* (eggs with snails); *Choucroute* (sauerkraut) *à la messine; Tourte aux oignons* (onion tart) which is similar to the Strasbourg onion tart; *pâtés; Quenelles de foie de veau* (calves' liver forcemeat balls); *Civet de porc frais* (civet of fresh pork) and a whole series of local pork products, the finest being the famous *Black pudding* of Nancy. Not to be overlooked are the potted meats and *pâtés de foie gras* of Lorraine, which all connoisseurs affirm rival in delicacy even those of the neighbouring Alsace.

But it is impossible to cite the full honours list of Lorraine cooking, for the table of this ancient province is laden with riches. A local writer, Auricoste de Lazarque, devoted a tome of some 300 pages to the gastronomy of his homeland, but even this fascinating and detailed book does not tell the whole story.

Auricoste de Lazarque speaks with fervent eloquence of the *Matelote* of Metz; *Crayfish à la mode de Boulay; Frogs' legs à la mode de Riom; Partridge with cabbage à la Lorraine* and the *Daube** of goose. He also gives details of the *Soupe au lard du Lorraine* and the *Soupe au boudin* (black pudding soup). He gives local recipes for *Sucking pig in aspic; Ham au foin;* the *Pâté of goose of Rupt-de-Mad; Soupe dorée; Meillat* or *Miot; Rouyats* (or *pâtés* of apples); *Chaudée*, which is a kind of apple

Gastronomic map of Lorraine

tart; *Chemitrés* (a kind of waffle) and a hundred other delicious dishes which are fundamental to the cooking of Lorraine.

A great many delicate pastries are made in Lorraine. Among these are the *Macaroons* and *Bergamotes* of Nancy; the *Madeleines* of Commercy; the *Kugelhupf* (similar to that of Alsace); *Nancy cake;* the *Nonettes* of *Remiremont; Aniseed bread* and *Mirabelle plum tart.* There are, too, the *Myrtle jams;* the famous *sugar-almonds* of Verdun, and many other sweet dishes, each more exquisite than the next.

Among the wines of this region are:

From Moselle: the red wines of Vir (Château-Salins), Aucy, Ars, Jussy, Sarrebourg, and the white wines of Thionville.

From Meurthe-et-Moselle: the red wines of Pagny, Thiaucourt and Guétrauge; the wines from the slopes of Liverdun, Essey-la-Côte and Bayon; the white wines of Bruley.

From the Vosges: the red wines of Mirecourt, Vittel, Bulgnéville, Lamarche, Neufchâteau, Coussey and Charmes.

From the Meuse: the *pineau de Bar*, the red wines of Apremont, Liouville, Loupmont, Woinville, Vaneville, Vigneulles-Saint-Julien, Champougny, Vaucouleurs, Vignot, Sampigny, Buxières, Montsec-Hattonchâtel. The red, white and rosé wines of Creüe, near Saint-Michel, the red wines of Montmédy.

The Mirabelle and Quetsch liqueurs must also be mentioned, and the excellent local light and dark ales.

Finally, there are the cheeses—Gérardmer cheese, admirable partner to the loca lwines, the Lorraine cheese made from scalded curds, and the *Fromgey*, a kind of white cheese, which locally is spread on a slice of bread and sprinkled with chopped onions and shallots.

LOTUS—In ancient Egypt the tuberous stump of white lotus was eaten, grilled or boiled. The pink lotus, on the other hand, being regarded as a sacred plant, was forbidden food.

LOUBINE—A French local name for the grey mullet. See MULLET.

LOUISE-BONNE—A variety of pear. See PEAR.

LOVAGE. Livèche—A herb of the angelica family, much used in Roman cookery. The young leaves, ribs and leaf stalks are eaten like celery. The seeds are used in confectionery.

LOVE-IN-A-MIST. Poivrette—Common name for the cultivated nigella (see NIGELLA).

LUMPY. Grenu—Stuffing or dough are said to be lumpy when they are not thoroughly kneaded and smooth.

LUNEL WINE—A muscatel wine made in the Hérault commune, round about Lunel. Lunel, which contains 15 to 20 degrees of alcohol, is a sweet dessert wine.

LUPIN—A pulse (leguminous plant) used as fodder. Its bitter seeds can only be eaten after soaking in water.

LUTE. Lut—A paste which hardens as it dries. It is used to seal containers hermetically. Almond lute is made by mixing powdered almonds, from which the oil has been extracted, with starch paste. In cooking a flour and water paste is used, which is also called *repère* or *repaire*.

LYONNAIS—This region, though small, comprising as it does only two departments, those of the Loire and the Rhône, nevertheless, deserves a place in the first rank for its excellent cuisine. Lyons can in fact be regarded as the gastronomic capital of France.

Although the Lyonnais district is more industrial than agricultural, it is not poor in foodstuffs. It has a few fertile plains, notably those of Forez and Roannais, and market gardening is carried out on a wide scale in the area. There is an abundance of good quality potatoes as well as excellent onions, such as those of Roanne, which are used in the preparation of a large number of special dishes, for example the famous *Tripe à la lyonnaise*, a dish renowned all over the world.

In the Lyonnais plains many other vegetables are grown. Fruit production is also an important industry, and some fruit, such as the apricots of Ampuis and the salades of the Île Barbe have a well-deserved reputation. So, too, have the very sweet chestnuts which come from the many chestnut trees that flourish on the mountain-sides in this region.

The neighbouring regions converge on Lyons, a town of the highest gastronomic repute for its superb cuisine—with many excellent foodstuffs, such as the succulent poultry of Bresse, which is unquestionably the best in France.

In the Lyonnais district excellent meat is to be found. Pigs, bred in large numbers in this area, provide Lyons with the material for the many pork products made there which enjoy a world-wide reputation.

The game of this region is also of fine quality.

The many different fish caught in the Loire, the Saône and the Rhône, as well as in the local ponds, are all excellent.

And, worthy accompaniment of all the dishes made in the Lyonnais district from the excellent local products, are the wines drunk by the gourmets of this food-loving region: the delicious Beaujolais, and those of the neighbouring Burgundy and of the vineyards of the Rhône.

Specialities of Lyonnais—In the front rank of the culinary specialities of this region is the Lyons sausage, which is world-famous.

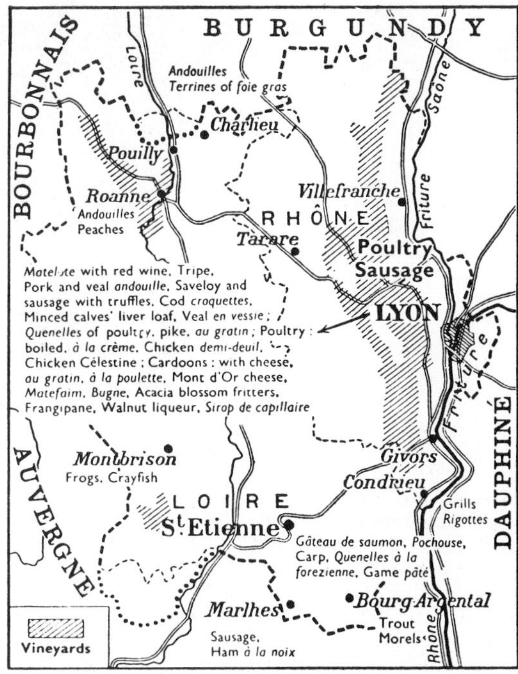

Gastronomic map of Lyonnais

Other dishes which have been made in Lyons for generations and which have earned the admiration of the whole world include: *Pike au bleu; Quenelles (fish balls) of pike à la lyonnaise; Gratin of crayfish tails; Matelot of Loire and Saône fish; Omelette à la lyonnaise; Black pudding with apples; Tripe à la lyonnaise; Poached Saveloy with pistachio nuts and truffles; Roulade of pig's head; Charlieu chitterlings; Ham with walnuts; Marlhes sausage; Chicken en demi-deuil;* and the celebrated *Poached chicken de la mère Filloux; Chicken à la crème; Chicken en vessie* (chicken sausages); *Chicken célestine; Veal en vessie* (veal sausages); *Cardoons au gratin.*

Among the special sweets of this region are *Bugnes lyonnaises* (a special type of fritter); *Acacia blossom fritters* and *Frangipane;* the substantial *Matefaim* (a type of pancake); and *Pumpkin cake.*

The best-known cheese of the region is *Mont d'Or.*

MACARONI—A farinaceous food, originally from Italy (some authorities give Naples as its place of origin), where it has been eaten for centuries. Macaroni, like all other *pasta*, is extremely nourishing.

The cooking of macaroni—Put 2¾ quarts (2½ litres) of water in a pan adding salt in the ratio of 1½ teaspoons per quart (10 grams per litre). Bring it to the boil and put in 5 ounces (150 grams) of macaroni, broken into six to eight pieces, according to the length of the macaroni.

Boil very fast for 16 to 20 minutes according to the thickness of the macaroni. Macaroni, like all pasta products, must not be overcooked. Remove the saucepan from the stove. Cover it and leave the *pasta* to swell in the water for a few minutes.

Drain the macaroni. Put it back in the saucepan. Evaporate all moisture by leaving it on the stove for a few seconds. This is necessary to get rid of any water absorbed by the macaroni during cooking.

When the macaroni is cooked, proceed according to the recipe used.

Macaroni à l'anglaise—Boil the macaroni as indicated above. Heap on a serving platter. Serve butter separately. The guests will help themselves to it when the macaroni is on their plates.

Macaroni à la béchamel—Boil the macaroni as indicated above. Add several tablespoons of *Béchamel sauce* (see SAUCE). Season. Mix. Just before serving, add 3 tablespoons of butter. Heap on a serving platter.

Macaroni with butter. MACARONI AU BUERRE—Boil the macaroni as indicated above. Drain it. Put it back in the saucepan. Evaporate all moisture. Add 4 to 5 tablespoons (60 to 80 grams) of fresh butter, cut into small pieces. Season. Toss so that the butter is well-mixed in. Heap on a serving platter.

Macaroni with cheese. MACARONI AU FROMAGE—This is another name for *Macaroni à l'italienne*.

Macaroni with cream. MACARONI À LA CRÈME—Boil the macaroni until it is three-parts cooked. Drain it. Put it back in the saucepan and evaporate all moisture on the stove. Moisten with 1 cup (2 decilitres) of boiled fresh cream. Simmer slowly for 10 to 12 minutes. Season with a pinch of salt and a little grated nutmeg. Remove the pan from the stove and mix in 4 tablespoons (60 grams) of butter cut into small pieces. Heap on a serving platter.

Macaroni à la créole—Proceed as for *Macaroni à l'italienne*. Make a coarse *salpicon** of sweet peppers (green and red), very small vegetable marrows (zucchini) tossed in oil, tomatoes tossed in oil and a touch of garlic. Bind with cheese. Mix this *salpicon* with the macaroni.

Macaroni croquettes. MACARONI EN CROQUETTES—These are made in the usual way (see CROQUETTES) using macaroni, boiled in salt water, drained, diced and blended with *Allemande sauce* or *Béchamel sauce* (see SAUCE).

Macaroni à la fermière—Proceed as for *Macaroni à l'italienne*. Serve in a deep, round dish alternating with layers of *Vegetable fondue à la fermière* (carrots, turnips, celery, onion, leek, finely sliced and cooked slowly in butter until very tender).

Macaroni au gratin (*The Cheese Bureau*)

Macaroni au gratin—Proceed as for *Macaroni à l'italienne*. Serve in an ovenware dish lined with butter and grated cheese. Sprinkle the top of the macaroni with mixed breadcrumbs and grated cheese. Pour melted butter over it. Brown in the oven.

Macaroni in gravy. MACARONI AU JUS—Boil the macaroni until it is three-parts cooked. Drain it. Put it in a saucepan with 1 cup (2 decilitres) of brown veal or beef gravy. Cover and leave to simmer slowly for 12 to 15 minutes.

Heap on a serving platter. Pour over it 2 tablespoons of concentrated brown gravy.

Macaroni à l'italienne—Boil the macaroni as indicated above. After draining and evaporating, add ⅝ cup (60 grams) of grated cheese (a mixture of Gruyère and Parmesan) and 4 tablespoons (60 grams) of butter cut into small pieces. Season with salt and a little grated nutmeg. Toss to mix thoroughly. Heap on a serving platter. One kind of cheese only need be used, though a mixture of Parmesan and Gruyère gives better results.

The amount of butter and cheese used may vary according to taste.

Macaroni à la Lucullus—Proceed as for *Macaroni à l'italienne*. Serve in a dish with alternate layers of a coarse *salpicon** of foie gras and truffles blended in a very concentrated *Madeira sauce* (see SAUCE). Decorate the top of the macaroni with strips of truffle.

Macaroni à la milanaise—Proceed as for *Macaroni à l'italienne*. Add 2 to 3 tablespoons of *Demi-glace sauce* (see SAUCE) flavoured with tomato, and 2 to 3 tablespoons of *Milanaise* garnish (coarsely shredded ham, pickled tongue, mushrooms and truffles).

Mix well and heap on a serving platter.

Macaroni à la mirepoix—Make a *mirepoix** of vegetables, rather coarsely diced, cooked slowly in butter until very tender and blended with cheese. It should be a quarter of the weight of the macaroni. Mix the *mirepoix* with the cooked macaroni.

Put the mixture in an ovenware dish lined with butter and grated cheese. Sprinkle the top of the macaroni with cheese. Pour butter over it. Brown in the oven.

Macaroni à la Nantua—*Macaroni à l'italienne* served in a pie crust of lining pastry baked blind (empty) with alternate layers of *Crayfish tails à la Nantua**.

Macaroni à la napolitaine I—Proceed as for *Macaroni à l'italienne*. Add ½ cup of *Tomato sauce* (see SAUCE) to the macaroni. Mix. Serve in a deep round dish. Sprinkle with grated cheese.

Macaroni à la napolitaine II—Take some thick macaroni and break into short sticks before cooking. Boil in salt water until the macaroni is only three-parts cooked. Drain and mix with butter.

Put the macaroni in an oven-proof round dish lined with butter and grated cheese, with alternate layers of *Estouffade of beef* cooked in advance and rubbed through a sieve. See BEEF, *Braised beef*. Sprinkle the layers with grated cheese. Warm over a low heat and serve in the dish.

Macaroni à la piémontaise—Proceed as for *Macaroni à l'italienne*. After adding the butter and cheese, add raw white truffles, peeled and cut into thin slivers. Mix and serve in a deep round dish.

The white truffles being very finely sliced (they should be cut with a special slicer) are cooked by the heat of the macaroni.

Macaroni with seafood. MACARONI AUX FRUITS DE MER—Proceed as for *Macaroni à l'italienne*. Serve in a deep round dish with alternate layers of seafood *ragoût**.

Macaroni à la sicilienne—Proceed as for *Macaroni à l'italienne*. Add, at the same time as the butter and cheese, a few tablespoons of purée of chicken livers mixed with *Velouté sauce* (see SAUCE). Serve in a deep round dish.

Macaroni with tomato sauce. MACARONI À LA TOMATE—Proceed as for *Macaroni in gravy*, substituting tomato sauce for the gravy.

Macaroni with truffles. MACARONI AUX TRUFFES—At the same time as the butter and cheese mix in coarsely-shredded truffles tossed in butter. Serve the macaroni in a deep, round dish. Decorate the top with strips of truffles.

MACAROON. MACARON—A small round dry pastry made of almond paste, sugar and white of egg.

The origin of this pastry is unknown. It certainly goes back a long way, for, by the seventeenth century, the macaroons of Nancy already enjoyed a great reputation.

Some authorities suggest that this little biscuit was invented in Italy, and from there came to France, where it was readily appreciated by connoisseurs, and was subsequently mass-produced.

Very delicately-flavoured macaroons are made in various parts of France. Those of Nancy are considered the best. They have been made for nearly two centuries by successive generations of the same family, and are known as the macaroons of the *Macaroon Sisters*.

In the eighteenth century in France, it became the custom in many convents for the nuns to make macaroons. The nuns of the Convent of the Visitation of Our Lady at Melun made these and other sweetmeats which, it seems, were much appreciated in the locality.

It may be seen from the municipal accounts that when, in 1748, the Court was at Fontainebleau, the Dauphin and his wife went to visit the Convent of the Visitation of Our Lady at Melun, and that, at the *Porte de Bière* the procession was addressed by the Mayor, who offered the visitors a ceremonial bottle of wine with a basket of biscuits, macaroons, sugar-sticks and other sweetmeats.

Plain macaroons. MACARONS ORDINAIRES—Pound in a mortar 7 ounces or ⅞ cup (200 grams) of blanched almonds (4 of which should be bitter almonds) moistened with the white of an egg. As soon as the almonds are well-pounded, add ⅝ cup (150 grams) of sugar to them. Mix with the pestle. Add half a white of egg, then, still mixing with the pestle, add ⅝ cup (150 grams) of sugar and the other half of the white of egg.

The mixture must be rather soft but not runny. If necessary at this stage, add a further half white of egg and mix in thoroughly.

Pipe the mixture on to a sheet of rice paper. Each macaroon should be 1¼ to 1½ inches in diameter, and should be wide enough apart to prevent them from running into one another in baking.

Sprinkle with icing sugar and bake in a 350°F. oven for 20 minutes or until the macaroons are a rich golden colour.

Crisp macaroons. MACARONS CROQUANTS—Pound in a mortar with a little white of egg 1½ cups (250 grams) of blanched almonds. When the almonds are thoroughly pounded, add 1 cup (250 grams) of sugar flavoured to taste. Mix well. Add to the mixture 1 cup (250 grams) of sugar and enough white of egg to make a fairly soft but not runny paste. Put small heaps of this mixture about the size of a small walnut on rice paper. Bake in a 350°F. oven, without opening the door, for 18 to 20 minutes.

Hazel nut macaroons. MACARONS AUX NOISETTES—Hazel nuts, whites of egg and sugar are used for these macaroons. The hazel nuts are not blanched. The method is the same as for plain macaroons.

Pine kernel macaroons can also be made in the same way.

Note. In accordance with a regulation regarding the naming of foodstuffs, the above biscuits may no longer commercially be called *macaroons* in France.

Montmorillon macaroons. MACARONS DE MONTMORILLON—These macaroons, which are different in appearance from other macaroons (they are in the shape of a ring, the paste being piped through a fluted nozzle), are a speciality of Vienna.

Niort macaroons. MACARONS DE NIORT—Pound in a mortar 1¼ cups (375 grams) of blanched almonds with 5 whites of egg and 2 cups (500 grams) of sugar. Transfer the mixture to a small saucepan and dry out on the stove. Add 4 teaspoons (25 grams) of crystallized angelica, finely chopped.

Proceed as indicated above.

Macaroons à la parisienne. MACARONS À LA PARISIENNE—Pound in a mortar ½ pound (250 grams) of blanched almonds with 4 whites of egg. Add 1½ cups (375 grams) of fine sugar and a little vanilla. Mix well. Put the mixture in a bowl and blend in 2 more whites of egg. Whisk the mixture. Pipe on to rice paper. Sprinkle with sugar and bake as indicated above.

Soft macaroons. MACARONS MOELLEUX—Pound in a mortar ½ pound (250 grams) of almonds with ½ pound

(250 grams) of lump sugar. Pound into this mixture with the pestle enough double (thick) cream and white of egg to make a paste which is soft but not runny.

Put the mixture on sheets of rice paper and bake as indicated above.

MACE. MACIS—The dried shell of the nutmeg. Its flavour is midway between that of nutmeg and cinnamon. It is used to flavour marinades, brines and sauces.

MACÉDOINE—A mixture of raw or cooked fruit or vegetables. It can be served either hot or cold.

The name *macédoine* is derived from Macedonia, the country formed by small states which were conquered by Alexander the Great.

MACÉDOINE OF FRUIT. MACÉDOINE DE FRUITS:

Macédoine of fruit, chilled (Fruit salad). MACÉDOINE DE FRUITS RAFRAÎCHIS—Put in a glass or silver bowl all kinds of fruit in season, such as pears (quartered or sliced), bananas (peeled and sliced), apricots (sliced), strawberries, raspberries (whole), fresh almonds (blanched), etc. Mix well.

Pour a heavy sugar syrup over the fruit, or sprinkle each layer of fruit with fine sugar. Flavour with a few teaspoons of kirsch, maraschino, or other liqueur.

Embed the bowl of fruit in a bucket of crushed ice. Leave to chill for 2 hours.

Macédoine of fruit in jelly. See JELLY, *Dessert Jellies.*

MACÉDOINE OF VEGETABLES. MACÉDOINE DE LÉGUMES:

Macédoine of vegetables with butter. MACÉDOINE DE LÉGUMES AU BEURRE—Shape carrots and turnips into balls with a ball scoop or dice them finely. Dice French beans or cut them into lozenges. Dice green asparagus tips. Boil each of these vegetables and some green peas separately in salt water.

Warm the vegetables together. When the vegetables are still hot, blend in butter. Season. Serve in a vegetable dish.

Cold macédoine of vegetables. MACÉDOINE DE LÉGUMES FROIDS—Prepare, boil and mix in a bowl the same vegetables as in the recipe for *Macédoine of vegetables with butter.* Dress either with oil, vinegar, salt and pepper or with mayonnaise.

This dish can be eaten either as a salad or an hors-d'oeuvre, and should therefore be served either in a salad bowl or in hors-d'oeuvre dishes, as required.

Macédoine of vegetables with cream. MACÉDOINE DE LÉGUMES À LA CRÈME—Prepare and boil the same mixture of vegetables as above. Blend in fresh cream.

Macédoine of vegetables in jelly. MACÉDOINE DE LÉGUMES À LA GELÉE—This type of *macédoine*, which is usually served with mayonnaise mixed with concentrated jelly stock, is set in a mould lined with jelly. It is also known as *Aspic of vegetables.*

MACKEREL. MAQUEREAU—A long, slender, salt-water fish. Its scales are small and smooth. Its back is steely blue or greenish, its belly an opalescent silvery white. It is fatty and savoury, and is eaten fresh, smoked, salted or soused. In French, young mackerel are called *sansonnets.*

Mackerel à l'anglaise. MAQUEREAU À L'ANGLAISE—Cut the fish into thick slices. Poach in a *court-bouillon** flavoured with fennel.

Serve separately a rather liquid gooseberry purée.

Mackerel à la boulonnaise. MAQUEREAU À LA BOULONNAISE—Cut the mackerel into thick slices. Poach in a *court-bouillon** with a lot of vinegar. Drain and skin. Arrange on a long dish. Surround with shelled, poached mussels. Cover with *Butter sauce* (see SAUCE) moistened with a little of the mackerel and mussel cooking stocks.

Mackerel with browned butter I.—MAQUEREAU AU BEURRE NOISETTE—Poach the mackerel (sliced or filleted) in a *court-bouillon**. Put it on a serving dish. Pour lemon juice over it. Just before serving, pour on 2 to 3 tablespoons of butter heated in a pan until it is nut-brown.

Mackerel with browned butter II—MAQUEREAU AU BEURRE NOIR—Cut the mackerel into thick slices or fillet it. Poach in a vinegar *court-bouillon**. Drain. Put on a serving dish. Dry it a little in the oven. Sprinkle with chopped parsley and capers. Pour a little lemon juice or vinegar over it. Just before serving, pour on 2 tablespoons of butter heated in a frying pan until it is a very dark brown.

The mackerel can also be prepared as follows:

Put it on a serving dish. Dry in the oven and sprinkle with capers. Pour a little lemon juice or vinegar over it. At the last minute pour on browned butter as indicated above, with 2 tablespoons of parsley leaves fried in it.

Mackerel Colbert. MAQUEREAU COLBERT—Slit the fish along the back. Open it and remove the bone. Season with salt and pepper. Dip in egg and breadcrumbs. Deep-fry. Serve with *Maître d'hôtel butter* (see BUTTER, *Compound butters*).

Mackerel in court-bouillon. MAQUEREAU AU COURT-BOUILLON—Poach the fish, whole or sliced, in a *court-bouillon** of water, vinegar or lemon juice, seasoned with salt and flavoured with thyme and bay leaves.

Drain. Serve on a napkin, garnished with fresh parsley. Serve with one of the following sauces: *Butter, Parsley, Hollandaise, Lobster, Ravigote, Venetian.* See SAUCE.

Fillets of mackerel à la dieppoise. FILETS DE MAQUEREAU À LA DIEPPOISE—Poach the fillets in white wine. Drain them. Arrange on a long dish surrounded by a *Dieppoise garnish* (see GARNISHES). Cover with *White wine sauce* (see SAUCE), with the cooking liquor of the mussels and fillets added to it. Sprinkle the garnish with chopped parsley.

Fillets of mackerel with egg-plant (aubergines). FILETS DE MAQUEREAU AUX AUBERGINES—Season the fillets and fry them in butter as for *Mackerel à la meunière.* Put them on a serving dish. Surround with round slices of egg-plant fried in butter. Squeeze lemon juice over the fillets. Pour on the cooking butter, piping hot.

Fillets of mackerel à la florentine. FILETS DE MAQUEREAU À LA FLORENTINE—Cook the fillets in a very little white wine. Stew leaf spinach in butter. Put it on a long dish. Arrange the fillets on this bed of spinach. Cover with *Mornay sauce* (see SAUCE) with the cooking stock added to it. Sprinkle with grated cheese and melted butter and brown the top in the oven or under a grill.

Fillets of mackerel au gratin. FILETS DE MAQUEREAU AU GRATIN—Proceed as for *Sole au gratin**.

Fillets of mackerel with various garnishes. FILETS DE MAQUEREAU—Cook as indicated above. Put on a serving dish. Surround with one or other of the following garnishes: cèpes sautéed in oil; thick slices of mushrooms cooked in butter; pieces of cucumber cut into small, oval chunks, cooked in butter; very small vegetable marrows (*courgettes* or *zucchinis*) cut into rounds and sautéed in butter or oil; tomatoes sautéed in oil or butter, flavoured with garlic if desired; potatoes, coarsely diced, sautéed in butter.

Pour lemon juice over the fillets and the cooking butter, piping hot.

Fillets of mackerel à la lyonnaise. FILETS DE MAQUEREAU À LA LYONNAISE—Cook ½ cup sliced onions very slowly in butter until tender. Moisten with 2 tablespoons of vinegar. Line a long dish with 2 tablespoons of this mixture. Season the fillets and lay them on top of the onions. Cover the fish with remaining onions. Moisten with ½ cup (½ decilitre) of white wine. Sprinkle with breadcrumbs. Dot with tiny pieces of butter. Bake in the oven. Sprinkle with chopped parsley.

Fillets of mackerel à la piémontaise. FILETS DE MAQUEREAU À LA PIÉMONTAISE—Season the fillets and dip in egg and breadcrumbs. Fry in butter until they are a good colour on both sides.

Serve on a long dish on a foundation of risotto.

Surround with a border of rather liquid *Tomato fondue**.

Fillets of mackerel à la vénitienne. FILETS DE MAQUEREAU À LA VÉNITIENNE—Cook the fillets in white wine with chopped shallots and chervil. Drain. Put on a serving dish. Cover with *Venetian sauce* (see SAUCE) to which the reduced (concentrated) pan juices have been added.

Fillets of mackerel in white wine. FILETS DE MAQUEREAU AU VIN BLANC—Fillet the mackerel and trim the fillets. Season with salt and pepper. Put in a buttered baking tin. Moisten with concentrated white wine fish *fumet**. Bake in the oven for 8 to 10 minutes. Drain the fillets. Put them on a serving dish. Reduce the pan juices and use as basis for *White wine sauce* (see SAUCE). Pour the sauce over the mackerel and serve.

Fried mackerel. MAQUEREAU FRIT—This is especially suitable for small mackerel. Dip in cold, boiled milk. Flour lightly. Deep-fry in very hot fat. Drain, dry on a cloth and season with very dry table salt. Serve on a napkin, garnished with fried parsley and lemon.

Grilled mackerel. MAQUEREAU GRILLÉ—Snip off the tip of the mackerel's jaws. Slit the fish along the back. Open it and cut the bone in two places without separating the halves. Season. Baste with melted butter. Grill slowly.

Shape the mackerel in its original form. Serve it on a hot plate. Pour on half-melted *Maître d'hôtel butter* (see BUTTER, *Compound butters*).

Any sauce suitable for grilled fish, e.g., *Bordelaise*, *Provençale*, *Saint-Malo* (see SAUCE) can be served with mackerel.

Mackerel à la livornaise. MAQUEREAU À LA LIVORNAISE —Proceed as for *Bass à la livornaise*. See BASS.

Mackerel à la meunière. MAQUEREAU À LA MEUNIÈRE—Proceed as for *Bass à la meunière*. See BASS.

Mackerel à l'orientale. MAQUEREAU À L'ORIENTALE—Especially suitable for small mackerel. Proceed as for *Red mullet à l'orientale*. See HORS-D'OEUVRE, *Cold hors-d'oeuvre*.

Mackerel soft roes. LAITANCES DE MAQUEREAU—Proceed as for soft roes of *Carp* or *Herring*. See SOFT ROES.

Soused mackerel. MAQUEREAUX MARINÉS—Usually served as a cold hors-d'oeuvre. Proceed as for *Soused herrings*. See HERRINGS, *Marinade of fresh herrings*.

MÂCON WINE—The name of Mâcon is known the world over, thanks to the excellent wines made from the grapes grown around this town in the Saône-et-Loire department.

The *Côte mâconnaise* extends along the slopes which run almost parallel to the right bank of the Saône between Tournus and the boundary of the Rhône department.

The Mâconnais wines, known as Mâcon wines, are full-bodied and very smooth, with a delicate and quite distinctive aroma. These wines when bottled deteriorate fairly quickly. The bottles become lined with a filmy deposit, so that after a few years thev take on the colour of *pelure d'oignon* (onion skin).

The prime vintages of the Mâconnais district are those of Thorins, Moulin-a-Vent and Romanèche.

Not far from Mâcon, in the Mâconnais region, are the *communes* of Fuissé and Solutré, whose vineyards produce the white wines of Pouilly, very delicate and fragrant.

Highly prized white wines are also made in the *communes* of Vergisson, Loché and Chaintré. See BURGUNDY.

MÂCONNAISE—A wine-cask in use in the Mâconnais district. It holds about 212 litres (231.8 quarts).

This name is also applied to a bottle, containing 80 centilitres (28 ounces) which is used for Mâconnais wines.

MÂCONNAISE (A LA)—A name given to various meat dishes, flavoured with red wine.

MADDER-WORT. GARANCE—A plant used in dyeing, from which a kind of beer can be brewed. It is prepared as follows:

Wash the madder-wort roots and chop them coarsely. Place them in a large container. Moisten them liberally with cold water. Add sugar and a little yeast. Leave to ferment for five to six days. Strain and bottle. Seal carefully. This plant is also known as *Dyer's madder*.

MADEIRA CAKE (English pastry-making)—Sift 4½ cups of sifted flour with ½ teaspoon of salt. Cream 2 cups of butter and 2 cups of sugar. Beat 10 egg yolks until light and corporate them into the butter mixture. Sift the flour gradually into the batter. Add ½ teaspoon lemon extract and the grated rind of ½ lemon. Beat the egg whites stiff and fold into batter. Line 1 long or 2 ordinary bread tins with buttered paper or heavy wax paper. Pour the batter into the pans and sprinkle the surface with sugar. Bake 1¼ hours at 300°F. Small slices of candied citron are placed on the surface of the cake after the first 15 minutes of baking.

MADEIRA WINE. VIN DE MADÈRE—This wine, which if made from grapes grown on the island of Madeira in the Atlantic Ocean, is one of the finest of fortified wines.

Various types of wine are made in Madeira, such as Malmsey, Muscatel, Dry Madeira, etc. These wines are made from the grapes of vines which are said to have been imported into Madeira from Cyprus in about the fifteenth century. Funchal, the capital of the island, is the storehouse of these famous wines.

Madeira is a tonic and an exhilarating wine. It is drunk as an *apéritif* before meals and is used a great deal in cooking.

Madeira pie. CROÛTE AU MADÈRE—A fruit pie served with apricot sauce flavoured with Madeira.

Madeira sauce. SAUCE AU MADÈRE—A demi-glace sauce cooked down with Madeira. See SAUCE.

Madeira sherbets. SORBETS AU MADÈRE—Sherbets served in sherbet glasses with Madeira poured over them just before serving.

MADELEINE—A small cake whose ingredients are flour, butter, eggs and sugar.

A chronicler of the history of pastry-making says that the great pastry-cook, Avice, when he was working for Prince Talleyrand, invented the madeleine. 'He had the idea of using *tôt-fait** or *quatre-quarts** mixture for little cakes baked in an aspic mould. M. Boucher and Carême approved the idea. He gave the name of madeleines to these cakes.' (Lacam, *Mémorial de la pâtisserie.*)

Other authorities, however, hold that far from having been invented by Avice, these little cakes were known in France long before his time. They believe that they were first made at Commercy, and were brought into fashion about 1730, first at Versailles and then in Paris, by Stanislas Leczinski, father-in-law of Louis XV, who was very partial to them.

The recipe for *Madeleines* remained a secret for a very long time. It is said that it was sold for a very large sum to the pastry-makers of Commercy who made of this great delicacy one of the finest gastronomic specialities of their town.

Commercy madeleines

Commercy madeleine. MADELEINE DE COMMERCY—Work together in a bowl 2½ cups (625 grams) of fine sugar; 5 cups (625 grams) of sieved cake flour; 12 eggs; 1½ teaspoons (5 grams) of bicarbonate of soda; the grated rind of a lemon; a pinch of salt.

When this mixture is very smooth, add to it 1¼ cups (300 grams) of melted butter. Mix well.

Put this mixture in special buttered madeleine moulds. Bake in a very slow oven.

Plain madeleines. MADELEINES ORDINAIRES—*Ingredients.* 1 cup (250 grams) fine sugar; 2 cups (250 grams) sieved cake flour; 1 cup (250 grams) melted butter; 4 eggs; a pinch of salt; vanilla or other flavouring.

Method. Put the sugar, flour, eggs, salt and flavouring into a bowl. Work with a spatula until the mixture is smooth. Add the melted butter.

Butter and flour the required number of madeleine moulds. Put in the mixture. The moulds should be two-thirds full. Bake in a 375°F. oven for 15 to 20 minutes.

MADERIZED. MADÉRISÉ—Certain white wines acquire with age a flavour of Madeira. These are said to be maderized.

The term *madérisé* in modern French parlance also applies to the unpleasant bottle smell of a wine kept for too long a period.

MADRILÈNE (A LA)—A name usually given to a clear soup (generally served cold or even chilled) which is flavoured with tomato juice. See SOUPS AND BROTHS, *Consommés.*

The name is also applied to various other dishes, all of which are flavoured with tomato juice.

MAGISTÈRES—The name given to a number of nourishing soups, the name and recipes for which were invented by Brillat-Savarin, author of *La Physiologie du goût.*

'The first of the *magistères*', says Brillat-Savarin, 'is made as follows:

'Take six large onions, 3 carrots, a handful of parsley. Chop all these ingredients and put them in a pot to warm and brown with a piece of good fresh butter.

'When the mixture is just right, throw in 6 ounces of candied sugar, 20 grains of pounded amber, with a slice of toast and 3 bottles of water. Boil for three-quarters of an hour and add fresh water to make up the small amount lost through evaporation, so that 3 bottles full of liquid remain.

'While all this is going on, kill, pluck and draw an old cock. Pound it, *flesh, bones and all*, in a mortar with an iron pestle. Chop 2 pounds of carefully chosen beef.

'When this is done mix the two meats, adding the necessary quantity of salt and pepper.

'Put the mixture in a saucepan over a high flame, so that the heat penetrates right through, and from time to time add a little fresh butter so that the mixture is well browned without sticking to the pan.

'When it is seen to be browned, that is, when the stock begins to brown, strain the soup which is in the first saucepan. With this, moisten little by little the mixture in the second saucepan, and, when it is all mixed in, boil it for three-quarters of an hour so that the surface of the liquid ripples throughout. Care must be taken to add hot water from time to time so that the liquid level remains constant. At the end of this time, the operation is complete, and the result is a potion whose beneficial effect is certain as long as the invalid, however exhausted he may be, is still able to digest food.'

Brillat-Savarin goes on to explain how the *magistère* should be given to the invalid.

'On the first day he should be given a cup every three hours until he settles down for the night; on the following days, a large cup in the morning only and the same amount in the evening, until the three bottles are used up. The invalid should be kept on a light though nourishing diet, such as legs of poultry, fish, sweet fruit and jam.

'Towards the fourth day the invalid should be able to return to normal life.

'This *magistère*,' Brillat-Savarin points out, 'is intended for robust and dynamic characters and for people who generally wear themselves out by burning up their energies.'

The master suggests another *magistère* made from shin of veal, pigeons and crayfish, intended for 'the weak and the infirm'.

MAGPIE. PIE—Very common bird in France sometimes eaten in the country. The flesh is very dry and is used mainly for stock. Young magpies are a little more tender and more edible.

MAIA—The name given in the Balkans to milk soured by previous fermentation and used as a leaven in the preparation of yoghourt.

MAILLOT—See GARNISHES.

MAINE—See ORLÉANAIS.

MAINTENON (A LA)—See MIXTURES, *Maintenon mixture.*

MAISON—The term '*maison*' is often abused in restaurants. All too often one reads: *Sole* (or some other fish) *maison, Chicken maison,* etc.

The epithet *maison*, in its origin and in the minds of *restaurateurs* who use it honestly, indicates that the dish in question has been made by the *restaurateur* himself or his staff, following a recipe which he can claim as his own.

Nevertheless, the term does lack precision. It would be more satisfactory to say '*de notre maison*' or '*à la manière de notre maison*', since '*maison*' as it stands is vague enough for unscrupulous restaurateurs to offer as a '*Tarte maison*', for instance, a pastry which comes from a '*maison*' other than their own, from a wholesale confectioner, in fact! This does not mean, of course, that the wholesale product is inferior, but, in such a case, the epithet is pretentious and likely to mislead the consumer.

There would be no great harm in this, were it not that more serious abuses may arise from it, when, for instance '*maison*' is applied to a product whose name implies its place of origin. '*Fine maison*', i.e. *Fine champagne* (a liqueur brandy) would be suspect, because, by law, the designations '*cognac*' and '*fine champagne*' are reserved exclusively, under pain of prosecution and severe penalties, for brandies made in *Cognac* or within the official boundaries of the *Fine Champagne* region. Thus, the expression '*fine maison*' is a purely fanciful one. It suggests to the consumer a *fine champagne* which the '*maison*' has imported for its own exclusive use, from the *Fine Champagne* region. In fact, it merely enables the *restaurateur* to sell, without risk of prosecution, adulterated brandy, made from spirits which might come from anywhere.

MAISON DU ROI (ROYAL HOUSEHOLD)—Under the old French Monarchy, this was the name given to all the departments and personnel of the court. Chief among these departments was the *Bouche du Roi* (Royal Kitchens), which was made up of a truly amazing number of functionaries.

MAITRANK—This drink is very popular in Germany. It is made up of the words *mai* (May) and *trank* (drink), indicating that it is made in the spring.

It is prepared from young, fragrant, asperula shoots. This plant is also known as woodruff.

Method. Put some young asperula shoots in a large soup tureen. Moisten with a bottle of white Rhine wine and 2 to 4 tablespoons of brandy. Cover the tureen and leave to infuse for half an hour. Add $\frac{1}{2}$ cup (100 grams) of sugar dissolved in a little water. Mix.

This drink can also be made with white Alsace wine or white Graves.

MAÎTRE D'HÔTEL—Nowadays, the title of *maître d'hôtel* is reserved for the man in charge of the dining room in a hotel or restaurant. He is assisted by a large or small team of senior, junior and assistant waiters.

Formerly this title was used also of a hotel proprietor, but only in the provinces.

In the past, in royal, princely, and other noble households, the office of *maître d'hôtel* was always held by persons of the highest rank, sometimes princes of the blood royal. Although at that time the office was a sinecure, the *maître d'hôtel* was, at least nominally, in charge of all departments of the royal household, whether of king or prince, including the kitchens, the cellars and all the major and minor functionaries and servants.

The *maître d'hôtel* of a modern restaurant or a great private establishment today must have a very extensive range of technical knowledge.

A *maître d'hôtel* worthy of the name must be a chef in every sense of the word. He must have qualities of leadership which will enable him to command the corps under his direct authority, and to command with courtesy. He must be a first class administrator and—no less important—a tactful diplomatist.

He must be thoroughly familiar not only with all the details of the special work of the dining room, but also that of the kitchens and cellars.

He must be a subtle psychologist. He must be able to talk to the clients—in several languages—politely but not obsequiously. He must be able to advise his clients, to guide them in their choice of dishes, the wines to go with them and the fruit to follow.

These are the qualities which the modern *maître d'hôtel* must possess. If he is no longer a *grand seigneur*, as were the important personages who filled this office in the great royal households, he is usually a man of distinction, good education and, most essential, a master of his art, for service at the table is as much an art as cooking.

MAÎTRE D'HÔTEL BUTTER. BEURRE À LA MAÎTRE D'HÔTEL—A seasoned butter served with grilled meat or fish, fried fish and other dishes. It is prepared by creaming fresh butter with chopped parsley, lemon juice, salt and pepper. See BUTTER, *Compound butters*.

MAIZE—See CORN.

MALAGA—A sweet wine made in Andalucia. It enjoys a very great reputation. There is white Malaga, which is a golden colour, and red Malaga.

Malaga wine is used in cooking and confectionery.

MALAXER—A French word meaning to knead a substance in order to soften it.

MALIC ACID. MALIQUE—An organic acid present not only in apples, but in most fruit and some vegetables.

MALLOW. MAUVE—A plant whose leaves, which contain a viscous substance, are used as an emollient in poultices and infusions.

The flowers are among those which are soothing to chest troubles. The leaves can be eaten in salad or as a vegetable, like spinach.

MALMSEY (MALVOISIE) WINE. VIN DE MALVOISIE—This famous wine made in Madeira, Cyprus and the Canary Islands, is named after a vine originating in the Greek island, Malavosia. The transplanted vine yields a slightly musky wine, sometimes a little bitter, more or less heavy and, occasionally, perfectly dry.

This wine, which is very similar to Frontignac, is drunk as an apéritif. It is also used a great deal in cooking in the preparation of sweets, and to flavour certain sauces, instead of Madeira and other heavy wines.

MALT—Barley prepared for brewing by steeping, germination or kiln-drying. See BEER.

Malt extract. EXTRAIT DE MALT—A concentrated infusion of germinated barley which is made into syrups or crystals. It is used as a food, especially (because of its enzyme content), to moisten porridges for very young babies.

MANCHE—In French cookery, the projecting bone of a cutlet is called a *manche*.

MANCHETTE—A paper frill for the projecting bones of cutlets or joints. See PAPILLOTE.

MANCHON (Pastry)—This is a name for:

(1) A small cake made of flaky pastry and baked in a mould in the shape of a muff.

(2) A *petit four* biscuit made of almond paste rolled out rather thin, baked for a few seconds in the oven, then rolled on a wooden handle to make a kind of little muff.

When these *manchons* are cold they are filled with butter cream flavoured with *pralines**. Each end of the biscuit is then dipped into very finely shredded green almonds.

MANGE-TOUT—A sugar pea or bean of which the pod is eaten as well as the seeds. They are cooked in the same way as French beans. See BEANS, *French (string) beans.*

MANGO. MANGUE—The mango-tree, of which the mango is the fruit, is of East Indian origin. It is cultivated in the East Indies, Cayenne, Malaya, China, the island of Mauritius in the Indian Ocean, and in southern Florida and California in U.S.A.

The mango is an oblong fruit about the size of a big pear. It is green in colour, turning orange-yellow when ripe with a rosy blush on the side exposed to the sun.

The flesh is orange-yellow in colour, similar to that of a carrot. It is pleasant in flavour but a little acrid and therefore does not appeal to all tastes.

Besides being eaten raw, mangoes can also be made into jam and thick 'mango fool'.

Mangoes are used in the preparation of Indian chutney, a pickle with a very great reputation, which is used as a condiment.

MANICLE—A vine grown in Bugey. It yields a 'muddy' (*épais*) wine. Brillat-Savarin says that this vine was planted by the Romans.

MANIER (TO WORK)—A French culinary term for working a mixture by hand. In cookery, it is used mainly for the operation which consists in thoroughly mixing a quantity of flour with a variable quantity of butter or other fat. This mixture is used to effect a rapid thickening of sauces, gravies and stews, and is called kneaded butter.

MANQUÉ (Pastry)—A cake very popular in Paris. It was invented, so it is said, as a result of a mistake. The story runs thus:

One day, the chief baker of the *Maison Félix*, a famous Paris confectioner, was preparing a *biscuit de Savoie* mixture.

The whites of egg had been badly whisked and were lumpy. The *patron*, observing this, said to his chief baker: 'The cake is a failure!' ('*Le gâteau est manqué!*'). The baker, not wishing to waste the mixture, had the idea of adding a certain amount of butter and of making a cake which he covered with *pralines**. The new cake was offered for sale and was bought immediately by a customer, who, a few days later, came back to the *Maison Félix* and demanded a cake similar to that which she had bought on the last occasion. She praised it for its succulence but said she did not know what it was called.

The baker was questioned. He, recalling the incident of the spoiled mixture, replied at once that this cake was *un manqué*, and that he could make another like it.

And thus was created the cake which achieved fame overnight, and for the manufacture of which a special mould was made, called, naturally, a *moule à manqué.*

At first, the *manqué* mixture was made with the same ingredients and in the same way as the *Biscuit de Savoie.* Since that time the composition of the dough has changed. The recipe for *manqué* cake as it is made today is given under SPONGE CAKE.

Ingredients. 2 cups (250 grams) sifted cake flour; $1\frac{1}{2}$ cups (375 grams) fine sugar; $\frac{1}{2}$ cup (125 grams) butter; 9 eggs; a small pinch of salt; vanilla.

Method. Work in a mixing bowl the yolks of egg with the sugar, vanilla and salt. When the mixture is light and fluffy, add the melted butter, the flour, then, stirring gently, the stiffly beaten whites of egg. Fill a *brioche** mould with this mixture. (This was the mould originally used for the *manqué*, before the invention of the special mould.) Bake in a slow oven. Sprinkle the cake with *pralines** and decorate the top with a piece of crystallized fruit.

MAPLE. ÉRABLE À SUCRE—A true native to South America, and cultivated in the United States and Canada. The trunk of this tree, tapped in the spring, yields abundant sap which can be fermented or made into vinegar, but which is usually eaten in the form of syrup (maple syrup) or sugar (maple sugar).

A maple-tree can yield, in 24 hours, as much as 60 pounds (30 kilos) of sap containing 4 pounds (2 kilos) of sugar.

Several varieties of maple yield sugar.

MARAÎCHÈRE (A LA)—A method of preparation applied especially to large roast or braised cuts of meat. The main ingredients are carrots, small onions, braised stuffed cucumbers, salsify, artichokes, *château potatoes* (see POTATOES).

MARASCHINO. MARASQUIN—A liqueur made chiefly in Zara in Dalmatia. Its main ingredient is a type of black cherry called *marasca* in Italy.

The cherries are pounded and the stones crushed (which is not the case with kirsch). Honey is added and the mixture is left to ferment. The mixture is then distilled and sugar is added.

MARBLED. PERSILLÉ—Meat is said to be marbled when it is flecked with tiny particles of fat. This marbling only occurs in meat of the finest quality.

In French the term *persillé* is also applied to various green-veined cheeses. The cheese called *Persillé de Savoie* can be eaten from May to January.

MARC—The residue of various fruits and vegetables after pressing. The word is often used as an abbreviation for *marc eau-de-vie*, a spirit distilled from the husks of grapes. It can also mean the residue of substances like tea or coffee from which the goodness has been extracted by boiling, steeping or lixiviation.

MARCHE AND LIMOUSIN—Geographically and historically these two ancient French provinces are distinctly different one from the other.

Gastronomically, however, they can be regarded as one, for not only are they neighbours but they share the same produce and the same culinary specialities.

The province of Limousin, a region of hihg gastronomic repute, is now divided into the departments of Corrèze and Haute-Vienne. It is said that in this province the famous *Hare à la royale* was created.

Corrèze must take a very high place in the gastronomic hierarchy of France. It is in this Department that the town of Brive is situated. Here *Potted foie gras* and *Pâtés de foie gras* are made which enjoy a very great reputation.

Limoges, too, must be given a privileged place among the most gastronomically famous cities in France, not only because of its admirable cooking, but also because,

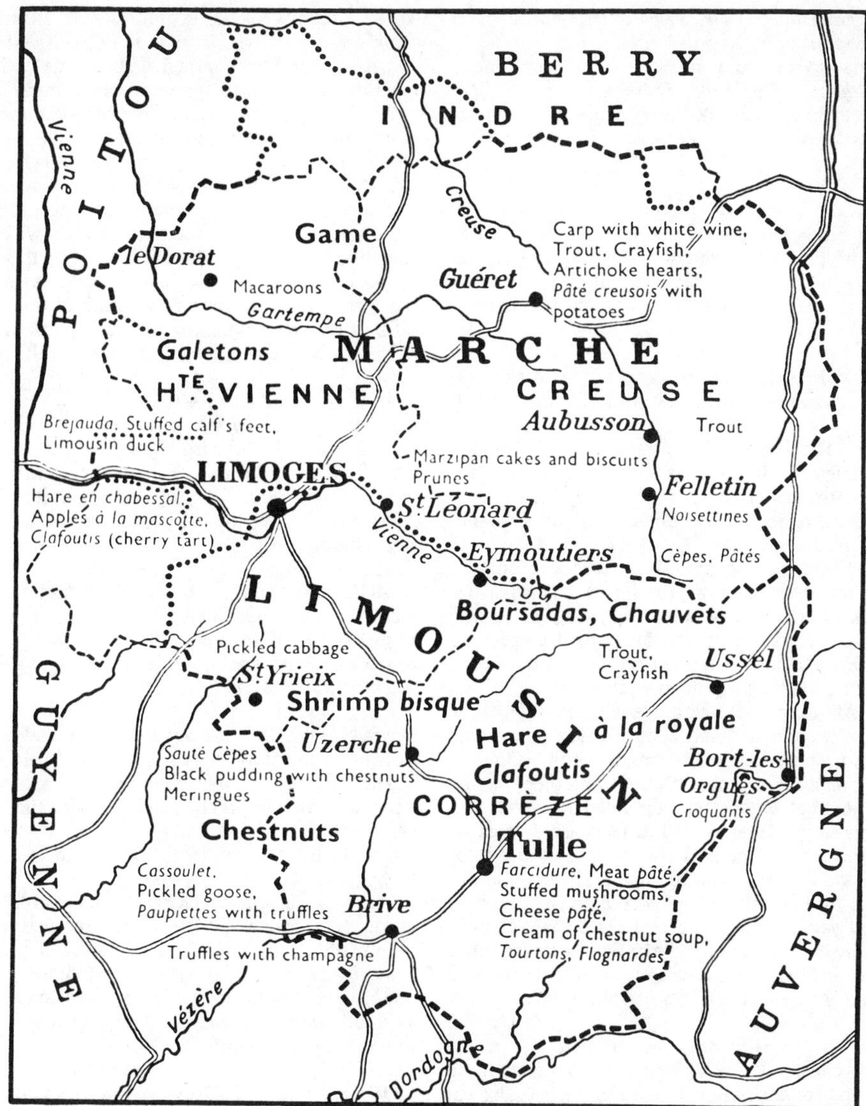

Gastronomic map of Marche and Limousin

more than any other, it has contributed beautiful china to the refinements of the table.

In these two ancient provinces are to be found foodstuffs of every kind and all of the highest quality.

Stock-rearing in this region produces magnificent meat. The cattle of Limousin are famous, as are its pigs, from which excellent pork products are made.

Ground and winged game abound in the Marche and Limousin provinces.

Freshwater fish, carp, perch, pike and others fill the rivers, lakes and ponds of the region. The trout of Vienne, Maulde and Vézère are very delicate in flavour. Crayfish abound in the waterways. Notable, too, are the salmon of Vézère.

The market-gardens produce excellent vegetables. There is an abundance of fruit, especially chestnuts.

In the woods and fields of this region, all kinds of fungi are to be found, in particular cèpes and morels.

Excellent cheeses are made in the Marche and Limousin provinces.

The slopes of Argentat and Queyssac in Corrèze produce very pleasant little wines. The Rosé wines of Chabanais, Etagnat, Saint-Brice, Verneuil and Aise, in the Vienne Valley, have a great local reputation.

Culinary Specialities. Soupe bouillie d'avoine (oat porridge); *Soupe au pain de seigle* (Rye-bread soup); *Soupe au choux* (cabbage soup); *Soupe Bréjauda* (a soup made from cabbage and bacon. With this soup the people of Limousin make *Chabrol*, that is to say that they add to the last few spoonfuls of soup left in the plate, half a glassful of red wine).

Farcidures (balls made from buckwheat flour mixed with sorrel and beetroot and wrapped in cabbage leaves. These are sometimes made rather small and cooked in cabbage soup). *Trout à la meunière; Matelotes of fish à la Corrèze; Crayfish in court-bouillon; Broccana* (meat *pâtés*, made from sausage meat and veal); *Hare au Cabessal* or *Chabessal* (this dish, which is the great culinary speciality of the region, is known among connoisseurs as *Hare à la Royale*). *Cèpes* stuffed *à la corézienne; Farcidure of fried potatoes; Chou farci* (Stuffed cabbage).

Among the sweets and desserts are the famous Limousin *Clafoutis, Flognarde, Fruit tart, Cheese pâté, Tourtons* (buckwheat *galettes*), the *Macaroons* of Dorat; the *Croquants* (biscuits) of Bort-les-Orgues; the *Meringues* of Uzerches.

MARÉCHALE (A LA)—A method of preparing escalopes, wings and breasts of poultry and other small cuts. Meat and poultry prepared in this way are dipped in egg and breadcrumbs and fried in butter. These small cuts are usually garnished with green asparagus tips and truffles.

MARÉE—The French collective name for all the sea-water fish, crustaceans and seafood sold in a fish-market.

MARENGO—The name of the battle in which Napoleon Bonaparte defeated the Austrians on the 14th June, 1800. This battle has given its name to a chicken dish which was cooked on the battlefield itself by Dunand, chef to Napoleon.

Bonaparte, who, on the day of a battle, ate nothing until after it was over, had gone forward with his general staff and was a long way from his supply wagons. Seeing his enemies put to flight, he asked Dunand to prepare dinner for him. The master-chef at once sent men of the quartermaster's staff and ordnance corps in search of provisions. All they could find were three eggs, four tomatoes, six crayfish, a small hen, a little garlic, some oil and a saucepan. Using his bread ration, Dunand first made a *panade** with oil and water, and then, having drawn and jointed his chicken, browned it in oil, and fried the eggs in the same oil with a few cloves of garlic and the tomatoes. He poured over this mixture some water laced with brandy borrowed from the General's flask and put the crayfish on top to cook in the steam.

The dish was served on a tin plate, the chicken surrounded by the fried eggs and crayfish, with the sauce poured over it. Bonaparte, having feasted upon it, said to Dunand: 'You must feed me like this after every battle.'

The originality of this improvised dish lay in the garnish, for chicken '*à la Provençale*', sautéed in oil with garlic and tomatoes, was known in Paris under the Directory (1796-1799). Dunand was well aware that the crayfish were out of place in this dish, and so he later substituted wine for the water and added mushrooms. But one day, when he had served the dish improved in this way, Bonaparte said angrily: 'You have left out the crayfish. It will bring me bad luck. I don't want any of it.'

Willy-nilly, the crayfish garnish had to be restored, and it has remained to this day the traditional garnish for the dish.

For detailed recipes see CHICKEN, and also *Veal sauté marengo*.

MARENNES—A small port in the Charente-Maritime district where, in vast beds (at La Tremblade), magnificent white and green oysters are bred.

MARES-TAILS. PRÊLE—Common plant of the fields, especially in damp places, hard stemmed and rich in silica. In their first week of growth the young shoots, not yet silicious, are edible and can be used like asparagus. The Romans valued them and the habit of eating them is maintained in certain regions. They are also pickled in vinegar.

MARGARINE—Cooking fat, made from the most soluble parts of beef and veal fat, purified by heating and decanting and churned with a little cream. A little vegetable oil is added (ground-nuts, sesame or coconut).

This type of margarine is intended especially for pastry-making, etc. The type called table margarine and used in household cooking is made entirely from vegetable fat. These margarines can be used in place of all other fats in cooking. Unfortunately in France, margarine has too often been used to adulterate butter, which has given rise to stringent regulations controlling the sale of this product. The margarine, cut in the shape of a cube, must bear the inscription 'Margarine' on at least four sides of its wrapping. Only the trade mark and the name of the manufacturers may be printed on the packet.

MARIGNAN (Pastry)—This cake is very popular in Paris. It is made as follows: Bake a *Savarin** in a *manqué* mould. When the cake is ready, soak it in syrup flavoured with liqueur to taste. Cut two horizontal channels on top of the cake. Decorate them with *Meringue à Marignan**. Cover the cake with apricot jam, leaving the meringue plain.

MARIGOLD. SOUCI—Name of several plants, among them the cultivated marigold whose yellow flowers are sometimes used to colour butter. The full-blown buds of the marsh marigold are sometimes pickled in vinegar, masquerading as capers.

MARINADE—A seasoned liquid, cooked or uncooked, in which foodstuffs, notably meat and fish, are steeped.

The purpose of a marinade is to season the food steeped in it by impregnating them with the flavour of its condiments. It also softens the fibres of some kinds of meat a little, and enables fish and meat to be kept rather longer than is generally possible.

The time during which foodstuffs should be left in a marinade depends upon their size and texture.

In winter large cuts of meat and venison can be left in a marinade for 5 to 6 days. In summer, on the other hand, they should not be steeped for longer than 24 to 48 hours, except in the case of large cuts of venison which require longer steeping.

COOKED MARINADES. MARINADES CUITES.

Preservation of cooked marinades—These marinades can be kept for quite a long time provided they are brought to the boil every other day in summer and every four days in winter. Each time the marinade is boiled a little wine and vinegar should be added to it.

Cooked marinade for meat and venison—Brown very slightly in oil the vegetables and herbs indicated for *Uncooked marinade*.

Add white wine and vinegar, and simmer gently for 30 minutes.

Season the meat with salt and pepper. Put it in a bowl and cover with the marinade, which must be quite cold. Keep in a cool place.

Note. As in the case of raw marinades, this marinade can be seasoned with coriander and juniper. When it is used for large cuts of venison, it can also have a little rosemary added.

Cooked marinade for mutton, called 'en chevreuil'. MARINADE EN CHEVREUIL—Proceed as indicated above, adding juniper and rosemary.

Red wine marinade for meat. MARINADE AU VIN ROUGE—Proceed as indicated above, using red wine instead of white wine. Leave to steep for 2 hours.

UNCOOKED MARINADES. Marinades crues.

Uncooked marinade I (for meat and game)—Slice 1 medium-sized (50 grams) carrot; 6 tablespoons (75 grams) of onion; 1½ tablespoons (15 grams) of shallots; 2 tablespoons (25 grams) of diced celery and a clove of garlic. Put half these vegetables in a deep dish. This dish must be just large enough to contain the meat. Add a sprig of chopped parsley, a few shreds of thyme and bay leaf, 6 to 8 peppercorns and a clove.

Season the meat with salt and pepper and put it in the dish. Cover the meat with the rest of the vegetables. Moisten with 3 cups (6 decilitres) of dry white wine and 1¼ cups (2½ decilitres) of oil.

Keep in a cool place. Turn the meat over frequently so that it is thoroughly impregnated with the flavour of the herbs.

Note. When this marinade is to be used for venison, 6 coriander seeds and 6 crushed juniper berries should be added.

Uncooked marinade II (for large cuts of meat)—Season the cut (haunch, rib, shoulder, etc.) with salt, pepper and spices. Put it in a bowl. Cover with an onion and a carrot, sliced. Add 2 crushed cloves of garlic, a sprig of parsley and thyme, a quarter of a bay leaf and a clove. Moisten with cooking wine (dry white wine or red wine). Add a few drops of brandy. Cover with a plate, face downwards, and leave to steep in a cool place for 6 hours (or longer, in cool weather). Turn the meat over from time to time so that it is thoroughly impregnated with the marinade.

The meat is then moistened with this marinade when braised.

Uncooked marinade III (for small individual portions of meat, or for poultry, fish, etc.)—Season the meat, poultry or fish with salt and pepper before putting it in the marinade. Lay the pieces in a deep dish. Sprinkle with finely sliced onions or shallots, coarsely chopped parsley, shreds of thyme and bay leaf and garlic, if desired. Pour oil over this mixture and a squeeze of lemon juice.

Leave to steep for 2 hours, turning over frequently.

Uncooked marinade IV (for garnishes to be served with pâtés, potted meats, galantines, etc.)—Season the garnish indicated with salt, pepper and spices. Pour on white wine, brandy and oil. Leave to steep in this marinade for 2 hours.

MARINIÈRE (A LA)—A method of preparing mussels and other shell-fish. See MUSSELS. This name is also applied to certain dishes made of fish cooked in white wine and garnished with mussels. See *Brill à la marinière*.

MARIVAUX—See GARNISHES.

MARJORAM. Marjolaine—A plant of the *Labiate* family. This aromatic herb, which is used in cookery, flowers in the middle of summer.

MARMALADES. Marmelades—Recipes are given below for various fruit marmalades. For general instructions on jam-making, see JAM.

Apple marmalade. Marmelade de pommes—Put the peeled and quartered apples into a copper pan. Moisten with a few tablespoons of water. Cook on the stove, over a gentle heat.

Rub the apples through a sieve set over a large basin. Return the purée thus obtained to the pan, with the liquor in which it has been cooked. Add 1¼ cups (300 grams) of granulated sugar for every pound (500 grams) of pulp. Mix and boil the marmalade, stirring all the time with the skimmer.

To determine whether the marmalade is cooked let a little drop from the skimmer on to a plate. If this remains in a blob, without spreading out, the marmalade is cooked.

Apricot marmalade. Marmelade d'abricots—2 pounds (1 kilo) stoned apricots (net weight); 3 cups (750 grams) sugar; ½ cup (1 decilitre) water.

Soften the apricots moistened with the water for 20 minutes on the fire, stirring them with a copper or wooden spatula.

Rub through a sieve. Put the pulp obtained in this way into a pan with the sugar.

Cook to the jelling stage. Finish as described above.

Fig marmalade. Marmelade de figues—Peel some figs which should be ripe but firm, and slice them.

Prepare a syrup made of ¾ cup (200 grams) of sugar for every 2 pounds (kilo) of fruit and a little water. Boil the syrup for a few minutes and put the sliced figs into it. Boil until the jelling stage is reached.

Melon marmalade. Marmelade de melon—Remove the rind of the melons and the seeds, and pass the pulp through a sieve.

Add a fourth part of sugar per pound of pulp, if this is very sweet, or more if it is less sweet. Boil till it sets.

Orange marmalade. Marmelade d'oranges—Blanch 10 oranges in boiling water for 25 to 30 minutes. The oranges should be pierced in several places with a pointed stick.

Put them under the cold tap for some time.

Divide them in quarters, remove the seeds, the pith and the fibrous parts, then rub through a wide-meshed wire sieve.

Add an equal quantity of preserving sugar to the pulp and a third of the weight of the pulp in apple juice, obtained in the manner described for *Apple jelly* (see JAM). Boil in the usual way.

Peach marmalade. Marmelade de pêches—Prepared with peaches in the same way as *Apricot marmalade.*

Pear marmalade. Marmelade de poires—Prepared with quartered pears in the same way as *Apple marmalade.*

Plum marmalade. Marmelade de prunes—Prepared with plums in the same way as *Apricot marmalade.*

Quince marmalade. Marmelade de coings—Prepared in the same way as *Apple marmalade*, using quinces.

MARMELADE—In French this term is applied to fruit stewed for a very long time until it is reduced to a thick purée.

MARMITE—A metal or earthenware covered pot, with or without feet, depending on whether it is used for cooking in the hearth or on the stove.

Straight-sided *marmites* for stove-cooking can have a capacity of as much as 200 quarts (litres). These very large pots have a tap fitted near the base.

Cooking pots of this size or even larger are often required in large establishments such as hospitals, etc. They may be either fixed or swinging, and should be made with a false bottom so that their contents are heated by steam.

There are special types for medium or high pressure.

Large swinging *marmites* are balanced in such a way as to ensure their stability at all angles. Pots of this type intended for use on board ship have a concave lip to prevent spilling in heavy seas.

There is also a type of double cooking pot called a

marmite. In this pot the water in the bottom is heated by vapour passing through a coil of copper tubing. In this type of pot special baskets are used for cooking rice, fish, meat, etc.

MARMITE (PETITE)—The name of a clear savoury broth, a type of hot-pot, cooked and served in an earthenware pot.

This broth was invented in Paris and is much prized by gourmets. See PETITE MARMITE and SOUPS AND BROTHS.

MARMOT. Marmotte—A rodent about the size of a large cat. It lives at high altitudes (in the Alps and the Pyrenees). Marmots grow very fat towards the end of the autumn. In the winter they hibernate and live on their fat. Their flesh, which has a very pronounced musky flavour, is edible after long steeping in a marinade.

MAROILLES—A small town of northern France which has given its name to a cheese, also known as Marolles. See CHEESE.

MAROUETTE—A type of rail which is very good to eat.

It is said that King Charles X of France gave orders that, even if he were in council with his Ministers, he should be immediately informed whenever a flight of *marouettes* was sighted.

This bird is prepared in the same way as *quail**.

MARQUER—In French cookery, this term covers all operations connected with the preparation of foodstuffs prior to cooking.

'Food fully prepared, and put in a saucepan, when nothing remains but to cook it.' This is how Plumerey defines this cooking term. '*Marquer*', however, is generally used in a more limited sense, meaning to place food in a buttered or greased pan lined, where appropriate, with pork skin and carrots and onions cut into rings.

MARQUISE (PEAR)—The name of a variety of pear which is very tender and sweet. This fruit, which is pyramid-shaped, is in season in France from November to December.

MARRONS GLACÉS—See CHESTNUT.

MARSALA—A dessert wine made in Italy from grapes grown in Sicily. This wine, which has something in common with sherry and Madeira, contains about 24% of alcohol.

It is drunk as an aperitif before meals, and is also used in cooking and pastry-making.

MARSEILLAN—A wine generally known as *Pelure d'oignon* (onion skin). It is made at Marseillan, a little town in the Hérault district.

MARSHMALLOW. Pâte de Guimauve—This confection contains no real marshmallow, in spite of its name. It is made of egg whites.

MARTAGON—A variety of Alpine lily, also found in Russia, where the bulbs are used for food.

MARTINIQUE—An island in the Lesser Antilles colonised by the French in the seventeenth century and renowned for its rum, which is considered the best in the world. Sugar-cane is grown extensively in this part of the world, and rum is one of the products of sugar-cane.

Martinique coffee has a great reputation. This island also produces cocoa and fine spices.

MARTIN-SEC—A variety of pear in season in France from November to January. It is ovoid in shape and of medium size. Its skin is russet in colour. The pulp is gritty and rather dry, but quite sweet.

MARTIN-SIRE—A variety of pear in season in France in November. It is rather large and elongated. Its skin is yellowish with grey flecks. The pulp is firm and quite sweet. This pear is also known as *rouville*.

MARZIPAN. Massepain—Marzipan is made from ground almonds, sugar and whites of egg. It can be coloured and flavoured and made into *petits fours** of different shapes. These little fancy biscuits are known in France as *massepains*.

Marzipan is also used to make little sweets in the form of fruit, vegetables, etc.

Marzipan is of very ancient origin. It would seem that, as with most little cakes and sweets, it was made originally by some order of nuns.

On the subject of this little sweetmeat Dr. Cabanès, who wrote a great many books of anecdotes, had a curious story to tell in which Balzac features.

'At the beginning of March, 1844, a sudden rumour began to circulate that the author of *La Comédie Humaine* (Balzac) had set himself up as a confectioner.

'No one talked of anything else on the Stock Exchange, in the foyer of the Opera, at the Théâtre-Français, and in all the cafés on the Paris boulevards.

'Several thousands of copies of a curious circular had just made their appearance in Paris. It read as follows:

Issoudon Marzipan!

"Gentlemen,

"I have just opened a shop at 38 bis Rue Vivienne to exploit this product which, in the province of Berry, enjoys a reputation almost a hundred years old. The most remarkable novelist of our era speaks of it thus in one of his works:

> 'This worthy woman was given the recipe by those most famous nuns to whom we owe Issoudon marzipan, one of the greatest creations of French confectionery, and which no master-chef, cook, pastrycook or confectioner has been able to imitate. M. de Rivière, French Ambassador in Constantinople, ordered large quantities every year for the seraglio of the Sultan Mahmoud.'—H. de Balzac.

"This unique sweetmeat, which to this day has been made only for the rich man's table, will now come within the reach of many more people by virtue of our new selling policy. Issoudon marzipan costing from 60 francs to 5 francs will be on sale to the people of Paris. In order to popularise the extraordinary qualities of this sweetmeat, slices of it will be sold for 50 centimes in the shop."

'This proclamation bore no signature. It might therefore have been inferred that it came from the pen of Balzac or that of a friend, editor or colleague. No one else had ever thought of the idea of launching a confectioner's shop with a paragraph from a novel.

'After making enquiries, Balzac, though he did not go to the length of taking a hand in the work, patronized the confectioner's shop in the Rue Vivienne.

'For a fortnight, there were long queues of curious visitors and, though there were few takers at 60 francs, the 50-centime slices were sold in large numbers.

'Then Paris turned its attention to other matters and the sale of marzipan sweets slumped.'

According to this story it seems certain that marzipan sweets, if they were not actually invented in the province of Berry, were once very popular there, and that those of Issoudon enjoyed a great reputation.

It must be added that this sweet, for marzipan is a sweet rather than a pastry, is very popular in Flanders and indeed all over Belgium, where marzipan of the finest quality is manufactured industrially.

Marzipan is a paste made from almonds and sugar. Like biscuits (cookies), marzipan sweets are made all the year round. They can be varied according to the fruit in season by using different jams with them, as will be seen below.

Old recipes for marzipan sweets: The following recipes are taken from the *Confiturier royal*, published by Claud Prud'homme in 1732.

Plain marzipan sweets. MASSEPAIN COMMUN—'Take 3 pounds of sweet almonds. Peel them in hot water. Drain and dry them. After this, pound them in a marble mortar, pouring white of egg over them from time to time to prevent them from becoming too oily.

'When the almonds are pounded to a smooth paste, cook 1½ pounds of sugar to the feather stage. Next, put in your almonds and blend all the ingredients with a spatula, carefully scraping the sides of the pan to prevent sticking, which may occur even though the pan is taken off the stove. You will know that your paste is ready if none sticks to the back of your hand when you touch it. Next, take the paste out of the pan and put it on a pastry board. Sprinkle it with fine sugar on both sides. Leave to cool.

'To work on it, roll it out to a moderate thickness. Cut your shapes out of the paste with biscuit-cutters. Press them down slightly with the tip of your finger on to sheets of rice paper, to bake them. Expose them to heat on one side only. Next, ice them on the other side (see below) and then cook in the same way.

'They can be made round, oval, fluted, heart-shaped, etc. You can also make your paste very moist and squirt it through a syringe. Your marzipan sweets will have as many special names as they have shapes, though they will differ from one another only in shape and the manner in which they are iced, as will be seen below.'

Iced marzipan. MASSEPAIN GLACÉ—'When your marzipan sweets, cut round, long, oval or fluted, are baked and ready on one side, gently lift them off the paper with a knife. Then ice them on the unbaked side in one of the two following ways:

'Take water scented with orange blossom or some other flavouring, or cooked fruit juice, according to the type of marzipan sweets you wish to make. Mix in little by little some fine powdered (icing) sugar, stirring the mixture well until it is as thick as porridge. Take out some of this icing with a knife and spread it neatly on your marzipan sweets. Then, put them back on the rice paper and warm them gently in the oven to set the icing. Put them in a tin for use when required.

'The other type of icing is made with the white of an egg and fine sugar only, or mixed with some cooked fruit pulp, working and using as indicated above. You can make both types of icing at the same time, so as to distinguish between differently shaped sweets by icing them differently.'

Royal marzipan sweets. MASSEPAIN ROYAL —'The paste is the same as for the first kind. Take a piece and stretch it out on the table to about the thickness of a finger. Cut the strip into as many pieces as will make a ring around your finger. Press the ends firmly together so that they will not come apart. Dip these rings in white of egg into which a little apricot jam has been mixed, then, dip them in fine sugar. Blow on them to shake off surplus sugar. Put them on rice paper to bake on both sides in the oven, as they have been iced top and bottom.'

Modern recipes for marzipan sweets:

Plain marzipan sweets. MASSEPAINS ORDINAIRES—Pound in a mortar, moistening from time to time with a little cold water, ½ pound (250 grams) of blanched sweet almonds and 4 or 5 bitter almonds.

As soon as the almonds are reduced to a smooth rather stiff paste, put them in a copper pan with 1 pound (500 grams) of fine sugar, a pinch of powdered vanilla and a few drops of orange-blossom water. Mix well over a low flame, stirring with a wooden spoon until the mixture is thoroughly dried. Now, put it back in the mortar and work well with the pestle until it becomes very smooth. To make it even smoother, put it on the table and work by hand, mixing in a small handful of fine sugar sifted through a hair sieve.

Roll out the paste to a thickness of ⅜ inch. Put it on a sheet of rice paper, cut it into squares, rectangles or any other shape. Put these shapes on a baking sheet covered with paper. Dry in a very cool oven.

Soft marzipan sweets. MASSEPAINS DITS MOELLEUX—*Ingredients.* 1 pound (500 grams) almonds, 1 pound (500 grams) sugar, ½ pound (250 grams) *Royal icing* (see ICING), 10 whites of egg, 10 drops essence of bitter almonds or ½ teaspoon almond extract.

Method. Proceed as indicated above. Pipe on to buttered paper in various shapes or in rings. Sprinkle with sugar. Bake in a moderate oven.

Marzipan sweets. MASSEPAINS—Pound finely in a mortar 1 pound (500 grams) of blanched almonds with 1⅞ cups (450 grams) of sugar and ¼ cup (50 grams) of vanilla-flavoured sugar, adding little by little the whites of 4 eggs.

Leave this mixture to stand for a few minutes. Roll it out to a thickness of ⅛ inch. Cut out the sweets with differently shaped pastry-cutters. Ice with rather liquid *Royal icing* (see ICING) flavoured with a few drops of orange-blossom water or orange extract. Put on a baking sheet. Bake in a slow oven.

Marzipan sweets à la russe. MASSEPAINS À LA RUSSE—Work together in a bowl ¾ cup plus 2 tablespoons (100 grams) of sieved cake flour and 2¾ cups (375 grams) of fine sugar, adding eight whites of egg, two at a time.

Working the mixture well, add ¾ pound (375 grams) of ground almonds and ½ pound (250 grams) of candied orange peel, finely chopped. Pipe the paste on to buttered and floured baking sheets. Bake in a hot oven. Lift the sweets off the baking sheet while they are still hot.

MASCOTTE (A LA)—The name of a garnish served with small cuts of meat and poultry. It consists of quartered artichoke hearts sautéed in butter, small potatoes cut into the shape of olives and cooked in butter, and truffles.

MASCOTTE—A cake made by filling a Genoese cake with *Mocha butter cream* (see CREAMS) mixed with finely pounded roasted hazel-nuts. The Genoese cake is iced with this cream.

MASKING. NAPPER—Masking is the covering of food with its appropriate sauce after it is dished up for serving.

MASSÉNA (A LA)—The name of a garnish served with small cuts of meat, *tournedos* steaks and fillets. It consists of artichoke hearts filled with thick *Béarnaise sauce* (see SAUCE) and strips of poached beef bone-marrow.

MASSILLONS—A *petit four** of almond paste in the shape of a tartlet.

Ingredients. ¼ pound (125 grams) blanched almonds, ½ pound (250 grams) fine sugar, ¼ pound (125 grams) butter, 6 whites of egg, ⅞ cup (125 grams) cornflour (cornstarch), vanilla.

Method. Pound the almonds with 2 whites of egg, the sugar and the vanilla. Rub this mixture through a sieve. Put it in a bowl and work it, adding the rest of the whites of egg to make it very frothy. Add the butter, melted, then dredge in the cornflour (cornstarch). Mix thoroughly.

Fill little buttered tartlet cases with this mixture. Bake in a hot oven. As soon as they are taken out of the oven, spread the tartlets with apricot jam and ice with kirsch-flavoured *Fondant icing* (see ICING).

MASTIC—A resin which exudes in the form of pale yellow tears from incisions made in the mastic-tree. These tears are floury on the surface, having an aromatic and resinous flavour. Mastic comes mainly from the island of Chios. It is chewed in the East and is also used in the spirit known as *Raki**.

Silver vessel for the preparation of an infusion of maté. The hollow stem serves as a drinking straw. Its base is a perforated hollow ball which serves as a strainer

(*Larousse*)

MATÉ—A plant sometimes known as *Paraguay tea.* Its leaves, which are rich in caffein, are used in the preparation of an infusion which is both a stimulant and a tonic.

This drink, which is relatively cheap, is much used in Peru, Chile, the Argentine, Brazil, Bolivia, Paraguay, etc.

In South America, maté tea is made in a somewhat eccentric fashion. The powdered maté is placed in hollowed-out gourds which have been dried and decorated. These are called *matés* in some countries and *culha* in Brazil. Boiling water is poured over the powder. The tops are then replaced on the gourds. The drinkers take it in turns to suck the tea contained in the gourds through a special straw known as a *bombilla.*

This infusion is also made in containers of precious metal, with a *bombilla* of the same metal through which the tea is drunk.

Maté can be prepared in different ways. It is best in an infusion, prepared as follows:

Put in a teapot ⅞ ounce (25 grams) of maté (leaves or powder). Pour on a quart (litre) of boiling water. Leave to infuse in a hot place for at least 10 minutes. Strain.

Drink hot or cold, with or without sugar, according to taste.

Note. The infusion of maté, which must always be carried out in a hot place, can be prolonged beyond 10 minutes.

Some authorities go so far as to assert that this plant only yields up all its properties after long simmering and that it should be left to infuse (with the teapot standing on the stove or in a basin of boiling water) for an hour.

As in the case of tea, maté can be flavoured in various ways. Thus lemon juice, rum, kirsch, etc., may be added to it. Finally, after straining, the leaves or grounds can be stirred once or twice into hot water, producing a second and third drink which is still quite pleasant.

MATEFAIM—A name given in certain regions of France, notably the Loire, Ain and Jura, to a rather coarse but very nourishing type of pancake which, as its name indicates, appeases or dulls the edge of appetite.

MATELOTE—A *matelote* is the name given in French cooking to a fish stew made with white or red wine.

Strictly, *matelotes*, which are also called *meurettes* or *pochouses* according to district and method of preparation, should be made from freshwater fish.

Only the dish known as *matelote à la normande* is made from sea fish, mainly sole, conger eel and gurnet. This *matelote* is moistened with cider and thickened with a *Velouté sauce* based on fish stock (see SAUCE) and fresh cream.

The term *matelote* is also loosely and improperly applied to dishes made of veal and poultry. We confine ourselves merely to mentioning this misnomer. We cannot recommend that it should be used in the drawing-up of menus.

Most *matelotes* of freshwater fish should be garnished, in addition to the small onions and mushrooms, which must always be cooked with the fish, with freshwater crayfish cooked in a *court-bouillon**, and with heart-shaped pieces of fried bread.

With some types of *matelote* such as *pochouse* and *matelote à la tourangelle*, in addition to the garnishes mentioned above which are virtually indispensible, lardoons of belly of pork are cooked with the fish at the same time as the small onions and mushrooms.

The method used in the preparation of most *matelotes* is indicated below under *Matelote à la canotière.*

Matelote à la bourguignonne or matelote de meunier—This *matelote* is none other than that known as *meurette.* It is made from all kinds of freshwater fish: small carp, pikerel, eel, barbel.

All these fish, cut into chunks, are put in a copper cauldron on a foundation of finely sliced carrots and onions, sprigs of parsley, thyme, bay leaves and crushed cloves of garlic. The mixture is moistened with good red wine, blazing Burgundy marc-brandy is added and the sauce is thickened with butter and flour kneaded together. Garnish with bread cut into squares, fried in butter, and rubbed with garlic.

Matelote à la canotière—Made with carp and eel.

Butter a deep frying pan. Line with ⅝ cup (150 grams) of finely sliced onion and 4 cloves of garlic, crushed. Put in 3 pounds (1 kilo 500 grams) of fish cut into pieces of equal thickness. Put a large *bouquet garni** in the middle of the pan. Moisten with a quart (litre) of dry white wine. Bring to the boil, add ½ cup (1 decilitre) of brandy, set it alight and cook with the pan covered.

Drain the pieces of fish. Put them in another pan. Add ⅝ cup (125 grams) of small cooked mushrooms and ⅝ cup (125 grams) of small glazed onions. Moisten with the stock in which the fish has been cooked, reduced by boiling to two-thirds of its volume. Thicken with butter and flour kneaded together, allowing 5 tablespoons (60 grams) of flour and 6 tablespoons (100 grams) of butter to every quart (litre) of stock and finally add ⅝ cup (150 grams) of butter. Simmer gently. Serve the *matelote* in a deep, round dish or bowl. Garnish with fried gudgeon, dipped in egg and breadcrumbs with the head and tail uncovered, and freshwater crayfish cooked in a *court-bouillon**.

Matelote à la marinière—Made with a mixture of freshwater fish. Proceed as for *Matelote à la canotière*, moistening the stew with white wine. Thicken the sauce with a *Velouté sauce* (see SAUCE) made by moistening a white *roux* of butter and flour with concentrated fish stock. This stock is made from the heads and trimmings of the fish moistened with white wine and flavoured with onions, parsley, thyme and bay leaves.

Garnish the *matelote* with small glazed onions, mushrooms, freshwater crayfish and heart-shaped pieces of fried bread.

Matelote à la meunière—Made with one kind of fish only (usually eel) or with several different kinds of fish. Proceed as for *Matelote à la canotière*, moistening the fish with red wine. Thicken the sauce with butter and flour kneaded together.

Garnish the *matelote* with freshwater crayfish and pieces of bread fried in butter.

Matelote à la normande—Made with salt-water fish cut into thick slices. Moisten the fish with cider. Add calvados and set alight. Thicken with *Velouté sauce* (see SAUCE) based on concentrated fish stock. Bring the sauce to the required consistency by adding thick fresh cream, allowing ⅝ cup to a quart (1½ decilitres to a litre) of sauce.

Garnish with mushrooms, mussels, poached oysters, crayfish, and small heart-shaped pieces of bread fried in butter.

Matelote called pochouse—Made from all kinds of freshwater fish. Moisten with red wine. Add blazing brandy. Thicken with butter and flour kneaded together.

Garnish with coarsely diced belly of pork, mushrooms and small glazed onions (these ingredients must be cooked with the fish), and bread cut into squares, rubbed with garlic, buttered and toasted in the oven.

MATIGNON—A *fondue**of vegetables served as a garnish with a large number of dishes. See also GARNISHES.

Lean matignon. MATIGNON AU MAIGRE—Stew gently in butter 3 small carrots (125 grams) diced; 2 tablespoons (50 grams) of celery; 2 tablespoons (25 grams) of finely sliced onions. Add half a bay leaf and a sprig of thyme. Season with salt and a pinch of sugar.

When the vegetables are very tender, moisten with ½ cup (1 decilitre) of Madeira. Boil down to an essence.

Matignon with meat. MATIGNON AU GRAS—Prepared as indicated above, with the addition of 3½ ounces (100 grams) of lean raw ham cut into very small thin slices.

MAYONNAISE—A cold sauce of which the basic ingredients are egg yolks and oil blended into an emulsion. For recipes, see SAUCE, *Cold sauces*.

'Culinary purists,' writes Carême in his *Cuisinier parisien: Traité des entrées froides*, 'are not in agreement regarding the name. Some say *mayonnaise*, others *mahonnaise* and others *bayonnaise*.

'I will admit that these words may be current among common cooks, but for my part, I protest that never in our great kitchens (and that is where the purists are to be found) are these three words ever pronounced. We always refer to this sauce by the name of *magnonaise*.

'But how is it that M. Grimod-de-la-Reynière, a man of logic and wit, could not see at first glance that *magnonaise*, derived from the verb *manier* (to stir), was the most appropriate name for this sauce, which owes its very being to the unremitting stirring which it undergoes in the course of preparation? I am more than ever convinced of this when I consider that it is only by working the liquid ingredients together (as may easily be seen from the detailed recipe for this sauce) that a very smooth, creamy sauce is finally produced; a sauce which is very appetising and unique of its kind, since it is totally unlike all other sauces, which are produced by reduction over heat.'

However logical Carême's justification for the exclusive use of the term *magnonaise* may seem, we are not by any means convinced that it should take the place of the usual form, *mayonnaise*.

Mayonnaise, in our view, is a popular corruption of *moyeunaise*, derived from the very old French word *moyeu*, which means yolk of egg. For, when all is said, this sauce is nothing but an emulsion of egg yolks and oil.

If all sauces *stirred* for a longer or shorter period, on or off the stove, required a name deriving from the word *manier*, then a great many would come under this heading, for instance, *Béarnaise* and *Hollandaise*.

MAYONNAISES—The term *mayonnaise* is used of cold dishes made from fish, shell-fish or poultry, covered with mayonnaise sauce and garnished with lettuce hearts, hard boiled eggs, anchovy fillets, olives and capers.

Fish mayonnaise. MAYONNAISE DE POISSONS—Made from various kinds of fish, cooked and cut into small slices, in the same way as *Lobster mayonnaise* (see below).

Lobster mayonnaise. MAYONNAISE DE HOMARD—Boil a lobster in a *court-bouillon** and leave to cool. Take the meat of the tail and the claws out of the shell and cut into pieces of equal thickness. Season with salt, pepper, oil, vinegar (or lemon juice), chopped parsley and chervil.

Dice the rest of the lobster separately and season in the same way.

Take the outer green leaves of a number of lettuces (setting aside the hearts for garnishing). Shred them coarsely and dress.

Take a round dish, a salad bowl or other glass bowl, line it with shredded lettuce, dome the lettuce slightly. Put the diced lobster on this and arrange the slices on top. Cover with mayonnaise.

Decorate the mayonnaise with fillets of anchovy, olives and capers, and surround with quartered hard boiled eggs and lettuce hearts.

Poultry mayonnaise. MAYONNAISE DE VOLAILLE—Proceed as for *Lobster mayonnaise*, using cooked poultry (usually poached chicken) cut into small slices.

This mayonnaise can also be made with the chicken jointed and skinned, especially when a small bird is used.

Mayonnaise of Dublin Bay prawns. MAYONNAISE DE LANGOUSTINES—Prepared in the same way as *Lobster mayonnaise*, using the tails of Dublin Bay prawns.

Note. Mayonnaise of all kinds of shell-fish, crabs, shrimps, crayfish tails, etc., can be made in the same way.

Spiny lobster mayonnaise. MAYONNAISE DE LANGOUSTE—Instead of arranging the spiny lobster slices on a dish or in a salad bowl, they may be served in their shell (cut in two, lengthwise). In this case, too, they should be arranged on bed of dressed shredded lettuce.

Mayonnaise of fillets of sole à l'ancienne with a border of jelly. MAYONNAISE DE FILETS DE SOLES À L'ANCIENNE, SUR BORDURE DE GELÉE—Poach fillets of sole in a very little white wine. Leave them to cool. Trim into rectangles. Cover with gelatine-strengthened mayonnaise.

Fill a turban (ring) mould with fish aspic jelly. Turn it out on to a round dish. Fill the centre of this jelly border with a salad of potatoes, artichoke hearts and diced truffles dressed with gelatine-strengthened mayonnaise.

Arrange the fillets of sole on top of the jelly.

MAZAGRAN—In France this is the name given to cold coffee served in a glass, but the word is often applied to hot coffee when it is served in a glass.

The word also means a kind of tartlet lined with *Duchess potatoes* (see POTATOES), filled with a *salpicon** or any other preparation, and baked in the oven.

MAZARIN—Fill a plain round baking tin 2 to 2½ inches in depth with best *Genoese mixture* (see DOUGH). Bake the cake and allow it to cool. Scoop out the middle, making a funnel-shaped cavity which does not quite reach the bottom. Ice the cone removed from the cake with pale pink fondant icing.

Fill the well of the cake with chopped crystallized fruit (angelica, candied orange and lemon peel, stem ginger, etc.), with a little syrup and thick apricot purée added. Flavour with kirsch. Cover the cake with apricot jam. Cover the well with the iced core and decorate with crystallized fruit.

MEADOW-SWEET. REINE DES PRÉS—Plant of the *Rosaceae* family whose tender leaves and flower tips, put to infuse in wine or hydromel, communicate to them an agreeable taste; they are used in making certain types of vermouth.

MEAL. REPAS—A grouping together of various kinds of nourishment taken at a fixed and traditional time.

Preparation for a meal. MISE EN PLACE—In large kitchens this covers all the preparatory operations involved in the cooking of a meal. The preparation of a meal in large establishments, private as well as commercial, is conducted on a grand scale, which the ordinary housewife cannot hope to emulate.

All the same it is useful, in a small as well as a large establishment, to prepare the various ingredients required for the meal in advance, methodically and with care.

That is to say, before starting on the cooking, it is wise to peel the vegetables, tie the *bouquets garnis**, etc. When all these small tasks are done, and all the operations preceding the actual cooking completed, the work of cooking is much simplified.

MEAT. VIANDE—The word *viande* derives from the Latin *vivenda*—which maintains life—and was, until the seventeenth century, like the word 'meat' in English, synonymous with foodstuff in general. Cynegetic (hunting) language, preserving an archaic tradition, keeps up this meaning in the words *viandis* and *viander* to describe pasture or the action of pasturing where wild beasts are concerned. Today in French, and almost exclusively in English, the meaning is restricted to the muscular flesh of edible animals.

When a piece of meat is examined closely it is seen to be formed of small reddish fibres enclosed in a thin skin; these fibres are grouped into bundles, and their covering skin, thickening, forms the tendons; certain muscles are surrounded or separated from other groups by thicker coverings of tendon tissue, the mucous membranes. Round about the muscular masses and sometimes between their bundles of fibre, there can be seen deposits of fat varying in quantity.

The connective tissue which holds them together and forms the tendons and muscular fibres is broken down in cooking and then attacked by the gastric juices; but these last leave intact the corresponding tissue in raw meat and it is broken down only in the intestines.

As for its composition, muscular tissue is formed from albumens and fats; there are only traces of carbohydrates (except in horsemeat, which is richer in glycogen and glucose than the meat of other animals); it contains a large proportion of water (sometimes as much as 70 per cent in certain cuts), mineral salts, among which phosphorus and iron are the most important, and gelatine.

As with all albumens, muscular tissue coagulates in heat from 70° to 80°C. (158° to 176°F.).

Muscular flesh also contains some soluble substances called extractives, because they are found in the extract obtained from the evaporations of their solutions, substances of which some can be identified by chemical means while others remain unknown; they belong to the chemical group of purines, which relates them to the alkaloids in coffee, tea and chocolate; as is the case with these latter, they are transformed by heat into tasty and aromatic substances; these act as stimulants to the digestive system, the nervous system and the heart.

Freshness of meat—Immediately after slaughter meat is slightly acid because of the presence of lactic acid in the muscular tissue, and hard as a result of stiffening in death. In this state it can be used for methods of preparation that involve long cooking, like *pot-au-feu;* for all other purposes it must be 'hung', that is to say, kept for a day or two in a cool place, according to the season, for a certain degree of decomposition to take place. This is due to the action of soluble ferments which exist in the muscles as in all organic tissue and which soften the fibres by the phenomenon of autolysis (spontaneous decomposition). This autolysis, if it is allowed to proceed to its extreme limits (for example, a small piece of meat removed in aseptic conditions and kept sterile in a hermetically sealed receptacle) will continue to the point of complete liquefaction. This process must not be confused with the putrefaction due to bacteria.

The longer it is hung, the more tender the meat becomes. In some places, for example, in Vienna, everything is sacrificed to tenderness and meat is eaten that has been hung for seven or eight days.

Quality of meat—Variable proportions of fat are found in different kinds and cuts of meat. It may be found around or between the muscular fibres or even in the middle of them, between the bundles of fibre, in very well-nourished animals.

The choicest cuts always have some fat, which is very desirable in cooking, but this should not be excessive. Analyses show that nutritional value in terms of calories depends chiefly on the fat content, since the latter contains more calories than do albumens, but instructions based on such facts should not be followed to the letter, since few people eat very fatty pieces and would normally leave them on the side of the plate.

Generally, meat that is only moderately fat is easier to digest than meat with a very high fat content.

The dark meats (*viandes noires*) of game and venison contain more extractives, and even toxic substances (when the animal has been hard-hunted or when the flesh is very 'high'); they are usually more difficult to digest than butcher's meat.

Red meats are those of adult animals (bullock, cow, bull, sheep, horse, donkey, mule); they can be digested and tolerated by most, provided their use is not abused.

The way in which the animals are fed has a great effect on the quality of the meat.

Meat extract. EXTRAIT DE VIANDE—Meat extracts are only stock that has been concentrated by heat or in a vacuum; they contain part of the extractive substances of the meat, some mineral salts and, above all, the same aromatic ingredients (celery, etc.) which give stocks their savoury taste.

There are a great many of these extracts on sale; they should be regarded as condiments which permit any liquid to be given approximately the same flavour as beef stock.

Meat juice. JUS DE VIANDE—The name juice or 'gravy' properly belongs to the liquid which escapes from a piece of meat during cooking, and which is served with roast meats.

There exist commercial substitutes for this juice, very similar to meat extracts.

Meat pulp—Describes meat which has been pulped, that is to say, scraped while raw. The meat, which has the appearance of a homogeneous paste, is used for additional nourishment in special diets.

MEAT CLEAVER. FEUILLE—An implement used to split carcases in half. It is also used in the kitchen for cutting up meat for stews, etc.

MEATBALLS (German and Austrian cookery). KLÖSSE—Very popular in Austria and Germany, klösse are a kind of round ball made of different forcemeats.

These meat balls are boiled in salt water, thoroughly drained and served on a dish with browned buttei and fried breadcrumbs poured over them.

Meatballs à la viennoise. KLÖSSE À LA VIENNOISE—Dice finely 1 pound (500 grams) of sandwich bread. Toss in butter until golden. Place in a deep dish. Pour on a few tablespoons of boiling milk and leave to soak. Add ½ pound (250 grams) of finely diced lean ham tossed in butter, ¾ cup (175 grams) of chopped onion, cooked slowly in butter until very tender, and a tablespoon of chopped chervil and tarragon. Add 2 tablespoons of flour and 3 or 4 eggs beaten as for an omelette. Season with salt, pepper and nutmeg. Mix thoroughly.

Divide this mixture into pieces each weighing about 1½ ounces (50 grams). Shape these pieces into balls. Dip the balls in flour.

Poach the meatballs in salt water for 10 to 12 minutes. Drain them. At the last minute brown a handful of breadcrumbs in browned butter and pour over the meatballs.

MÉCHOUI (Arab cookery)—The Arabic word *méchoui* means roasted. Arab roasts are made with various animals such as gazelle, sheep, *moufflon* (wild sheep), young camel or lamb. The animal must always be very fat.

'The cooking demands very special care, for a *méchoui* cannot be perfect unless it is constantly basted with melted butter and roasted slowly on red hot charcoal embers which must be kept at the same temperature the whole time. Care must also be taken that the meat is not charred outside and raw inside.

'A *méchoui* is perfectly cooked when, on pricking it with a large needle, no drops of pink juice exude through the puncture. Care must be taken that the kidneys are properly cooked. These are the most precious part of the roast. A successful *méchoui* must be of a fine golden-brown colour and the meat must be well roasted and crackling. This is how it is done:

'Kill, skin and eviscerate a sucking lamb. Impale it from head to tail on a pointed wooden spit.

'Tie the shoulders to the neck with string. Stretch the legs out to the full length of the spit, binding them with a strip of linen. Season well with salt and pepper. Rest each end of the spit on a stone or Y-shaped support on which the spit can be turned. Near the spitted carcase, dig a hole a metre (40 inches) in length and 50 centimetres (20 inches) in depth. Lay a wood fire and light it. Place the lamb about 50 centimetres (20 inches) from the fire. Rotate the spit slowly so that the whole lamb is exposed to the embers. Using a brush, baste with melted butter.

'When it is cooked, take it off the spit. Lay it on a dish. Place it in the middle of the table. According to tradition, the diners must abandon the use of knives and forks. Custom requires that the *méchoui* should be eaten with fingers, the guests tearing off the flesh as desired. The host must serve himself first and must pluck out the kidneys to offer to his guests.

'When the *méchoui* is all eaten, the servants pass round the ewer containing warm water scented with rose-leaves, so that the guests may rinse their hands.

'The whole beauty of this dish lies in the incomparable flavour of the crackling skin and browned flesh. So that it may lose none of the delicacy which makes it so much sought-after by gourmets, it must be speedily dismembered as soon as it appears on the table. If it is left to get cold, the skin, firm and crackling at the outset, grows soft very quickly. One should therefore never forget to provide the guests with hot plates for a *méchoui*.

'In different regions of Morocco and Tunisia, the *méchoui* differs only in the method of cooking. It is braised in a glazed earthenware oven.' (L. Isnard, *L'Afrique gourmande*.)

MEDALLION. MÉDAILLON—This is a name applied to various foodstuffs which must, by definition, be cut in the shape of medallions, that is to say, round or oval.

Strictly speaking, the word is synonymous with *tournedos** when applied to small cuts of beef, with *collops** when applied to slices of mutton, veal or large poultry.

The term is extended to designate collops of foie gras served hot or cold.

MEDLAR. NÈFLE—The fruit of the medlar tree, a rosaceous plant, which grows wild in all the temperate regions of Europe.

The medlar is a very tart fruit which can only be eaten when it is thoroughly ripe and soft, when it has quite a pleasant flavour of wine.

MÉDOC—A region in the heart of the Gironde. The well-known wines of Médoc have a character all their own. They are distinguished by a slight tartness quite unlike that of any other wine, by their delicacy, their aroma, their smoothness, and a bouquet which improves even after long years of keeping.

These wines are full-bodied without being highly intoxicating. When they are new, they are of a beautiful garnet colour. With maturity they turn to a burnt ruby. See BORDEAUX wines.

MEHLSUPPE (German cookery)—For this soup made from flour, known also as sweet-and-sour soup, see **SOUPS AND BROTHS.**

MELBA—See GARNISHES.

MELILOT—A fragrant herb which, in country districts, is used to stuff a freshly killed rabbit to flavour the meat.

The dried leaves and flowers are used to flavour marinades and stews. It is also used in the making of Gruyère cheese.

Melissa

MELISSA. MÉLISSE—A plant of Mediterranean origin, known also as lemon-balm. It has oblong, light green, slightly velvety leaves. It smells rather like lemon.

Melissa cordial. EAU DE MÉLISSE—A spirit distilled from melissa. The best-known *melissa cordial* is that of Carmes, made by infusion of spirits of kidney vetch and spirits of melissa.

Slit or crush the various ingredients. Put them with the alcohol in the steam chamber of a distilling apparatus. Leave to infuse for 4 days in a cool place, then distil to obtain 4,500 grams of spirits.

MELON—The fruit of a number of herbaceous plants of the species *Cucumis melo*. It is of Asian origin and was first transplanted to Italy, then to France well before the sixteenth century. The melon was known in early times and was much prized by the Greeks and Romans.

Generally speaking, melon is eaten raw and in its natural state, either at the beginning of the meal as an hors-d'oeuvre (eaten thus it is at once refreshing and appetising) or at the end, as a fruit.

Melon

As an hors-d'oeuvre it is often seasoned with salt and spiced with ginger. As a dessert it is sprinkled with sugar, though a great many connoisseurs consider that the only admissible seasoning is salt, often with pepper added.

Choosing a melon is a delicate undertaking. A connoisseur would not dream of leaving it to anyone else to choose a melon for his delectation. He smells the fruit lingeringly, he taps it lightly to discover whether it is well-fleshed or hollow. He looks to see whether it has round its stem that 'crown' which indicates that the melon is perfectly ripe and whether or not it is sweet.

Chilled melon with Frontignan wine. MELON RAFRAÎCHI AU FRONTIGNAN—Take a large cantaloup melon. Make a circular incision round the stem. Remove the top and scoop out the seeds.

Embed the melon in a bowl full of crushed ice. Sprinkle inside with one or two tablespoons of sugar and pour into it 1 to 1½ cups (2 or 3 decilitres) of Frontignan wine (or any other dessert wine). Replace the top of the melon and leave to chill thoroughly. Serve in a bowl full of crushed ice.

Note. Melon prepared in this way is not cut into slices. The pulp is served *en coquilles*, that is to say, shell-shaped pieces are scooped out with a large silver spoon.

Chilled melon prepared in this way can be flavoured with Grenache, Madeira, Marsala, Muscatel, port, sherry, Tokay, etc.

Chilled melon e.. surprise or melon à la parisienne. MELON RAFRAÎCHI EN SURPRISE (MELON À LA PARISIENNE) —Scoop out a large cantaloup melon as indicated for *Iced melon.* Dice the scooped-out pulp, or cut it into small pieces. Add to these pieces of melon various fruits in season; pineapple, apricots, peaches, pears, cherries, plums, oranges, bananas, apples, grapes, etc., cut into pieces, coarsely diced or merely stoned, as appropriate. Add sugar and moisten with kirsch or maraschino or or any other liqueur, as for *Fruit salad**.

Fill the melon with this mixture. Embed it in a large bowl filled with crushed ice. Leave to chill thoroughly before serving. The melon may also be served on a napkin.

Sometimes the melon is cut in half and the fruit salad served in one of the halves.

Crystallized melon. MELON CONFIT—In high-grade industrial confectionery, whole melons are treated in this way. They are crystallized in their rind and are sometimes very large.

In household kitchens, melons can be crystallized in slices or cubes. Proceed as follows:

Cut into slices of equal size a cantaloup melon which is not over-ripe. Skin the slices and remove the seeds. Put in a bowl. Sprinkle with sugar. Leave the melon to steep in the sugar for a few hours. Drain. Keep the juice. Put the melon in cold water and leave overnight.

Next day pour the melon juice into a pan. Add enough water and sugar to make a syrup with a density of 14° as measured on a saccharometer. Put the slices of melon in this syrup and boil them. Put the melon covered with its syrup in an earthenware bowl and leave to stand overnight. Next day, drain the pieces of melon, taking them out with care so as not to break them. Boil the syrup on the stove until it is reduced to 16° density. Pour the syrup over the melon. Repeat this operation several times, reducing the syrup each time until it reaches a density of 32°. In French confectionery this process is called *façon*.

When the melon has undergone the required number of *façons*, drain it and dry it. Keep it in a very dry place.

Fresh melon. MELON AU NATUREL—Generally, before serving, melon should be well chilled. If possible, it is desirable to leave it on ice for an hour or two before serving.

If the melon is to be served as an hors-d'oeuvre, each guest will season it himself with salt and sometimes pepper or with fine sugar. It can also be spiced with ground ginger. When melon is served as a dessert, it is advisable, if it is fragrant and rich in flavour, either to eat it plain or to sweeten it with fine sugar.

Note. Melon, in common with other fruit, must not be sliced with an ordinary steel knife. Whether for slicing or eating, a silver, silver-plated or stainless steel knife should be used. Often, the guests eat the pulp with a silver spoon.

Iced melon. MELON GLACÉ—Take a large cantaloup melon. Cut out a circle of rind round the stem. Using a silver spoon, scoop out the melon, leaving only a thin layer of pulp on the rind.

With the pulp make a melon ice cream in the usual way (see ICES AND ICE CREAM). Just before serving, fill the melon rind with the ice cream. Place in a bowl or serve on a napkin.

Melon jam. CONFITURE DE MELON—Proceed as for *Apricot jam* (see JAM).

Melon pickled in vinegar. MELON CONFIT AU VINAIGRE—For this, choose small, not very ripe melons. Cut into pieces of equal thickness, and proceed as for gherkins pickled in vinegar. See GHERKIN.

Note. Melon in vinegar is used in the same way as gherkins, as an accompaniment to boiled meat and cold meat.

Small green melons are generally used.

The rind of large melons can be pickled in the same way. Remove the outer skin only, and dice.

MELON DE MALABAR—The name given in France to the Siamese pumpkin. This pumpkin, which is quite tasty, is cooked in the same way as ordinary pumpkin. See PUMPKIN.

MELONGÈNE—French name for the aubergine (egg-plant). See AUBERGINE.

MELTING-HOUSE. FONDOIR—This is where the melting of fats and tallow from slaughterhouses takes place.

MENDIANTS—Common name for a dessert made of almonds, figs, hazel-nuts and raisins, whose colours recall the dress of the four Roman Catholic mendicant Orders.

MENTONNAISE (A LA)—A method of cooking certain foodstuffs, especially rock-pool fish. The characteristic ingredients are tomatoes, black olives and garlic seasoning. See GARNISHES.

MENUS—A menu is a sheet of paper or cardboard on which is written, in a specific order, the names of all the dishes which are to be served in succession at a given meal.

The idea of providing a 'bill of fare', which in old French was called an *escriteau*, is not new. But these old lists were not, strictly speaking, menus, that is to say, cards placed on the table itself as is customary nowadays.

Here, for instance, is a list of dishes which were served on the occasion of the marriage of a Counsellor and Master in Ordinary of the Counting House in 1571. This curious document, preserved in the archives of the Northern Department of France, is entitled:

'Bill of fare for the nuptial supper of Master Baulde Cuvillon.'

First Course

Salads of various kinds
Flesh of *prinsel* with parsley and vinegar (savoury preserves)
Mutton broth
Fricassée of gosling
Spring chickens with spinach
Cold *saille*
Pigeons *à la Trimoulette*
Roast joint of mutton
Roast breast of veal
Small pastries with hot sauce
Roast roebuck
Dainty pâté
Spring chickens in aspic
Sweetened mustard

Second Course

Venison broth
Roast capon
Orange salad
Roast pheasants
Roast rabbits
Roast spring chickens, some stuffed, others larded
Chériots
Roast quails
Roast *crousets*
Smoked tongues
Boulogne sausages
Pheasant pâtés
Pâté of Meaux ham
Crousets pâtés
Turkey or peacock pâté
Venison pâté
Leg of lamb *daube*
Capon in aspic
Roast swan
Sweetened mustard
Olives

Dessert

Mousse tart
Apple tart
Chervil tart
Jam tart
Cream flan
Gohière
Waffles
Pâté of pears
Clove apples

Pears in mead
Sartelles pears
Angelots
Morbecque cream
Green walnuts
Fresh fruit
Ample jelly
Cheese

A great many menus of this kind are to be found in the archives of large French towns, but most of them are no more than the accounts of the money spent in buying the food to be served at such and such a great feast.

The 'bill of fare' and *escriteau* were, in reality, merely working menus, instructions of a sort whose sole object was to indicate to the kitchen staff of a royal or princely household the order in which the various courses should succeed one another at a great dinner. Considering the amplitude of these working menus it will be readily understood that it would be difficult, if not impossible, to place these immense pieces of cardboard on the table for the information of the guests.

The individual menu, as we know it today, did not come into use until the early nineteenth century, at the time of the first Restoration in France, and it is almost certain that it was born in the celebrated restaurants of the Palais-Royal which at that time was the gastronomic centre of Paris.

In these eating-houses, some of which had been founded in the last years of the previous century, it was customary to show at the door enormous posters on which were inscribed the names of the dishes provided by the establishment. One or two of these poster-menus have come down to us, notably that of the ancient *Rocher de Cancale*, one of the most celebrated restaurants of the time, and that of the equally famous *Hôtel des Américains*. This last restaurant was most highly praised by Grimod de la Reynière and Brillat-Savarin.

As soon as the individual menu came into being, every effort was made to render it more and more artistic and elaborate. The greatest artists did not consider it beneath their dignity to illustrate it with their own hands, so that a large number of these little cards were afterwards much sought after by collectors of rarities, and often bought at a very high price.

Other individual menus, though less artistic, were also sought after by collectors. These menus, though often written out by hand on plain cards, recorded meals which have become historic, meals enjoyed by famous guests who, themselves, were to become a part of history.

Sixteenth century menu—This menu is taken from a *Mémoire* on the preparation of an *escriteau* for a banquet.

Ragoûts: Woodcock *à la Quesat*—Capons *pèlerins*—Stuffed roebuck—Civet of venison with turnips—Rabbit *à la grenade*—Lion of white capon—Stuffed birds—Goslings with Milanese cheese—Partridge *à la tonnelette*—Partridge *à l'orange*—Partridge with capers—Wood pigeon *en poivrade*—Pickled teal—*Soleil* of white capon—Venison with turnips—White jelly, decorated, shredded, moulded—Chitterlings in jelly—Jelly *angelots*—*Orissan* in jelly—Quails with bay leaves—Roebuck with Milanese cheese—Roebuck head—Salt venison frumenty—Sheep's tongues *à la vinaigrette*—Mock hedgehog—Goslings in Malmsey wine—Peacocks in their feathers—Devilled trotters with sturgeon—Spring chickens in vinegar—Boar with chestnuts—Veal sausages—Tench *à la lombarde*—Amber jelly, plain and fancy—Jelly shield—Jelly escutcheon—Jelly fountain.

Roasts: Larks—Bitterns—Capons—Herons—Young rabbits—Side of beef—Partridge—Plovers—Boar—Doves—Woodcock—Quail—Roebuck—Pheasant—Rabbit—Young hare—Goslings—Young pigeons Chickens—Teal.

Salads: White—Green—Hop shoots—Olives—Pickled purslane—Lemon—Pomegranate—Lettuces—Samphire—*Bon-Chrétien* pear.

Final course: Saveloys—Mainz ham—Pâtés of artichokes, capon, ox-tongue, ox-feet, sheep's feet, teal—Small hot *choux* pastries—Rissoles—Pickled cucumbers—Rosemary snow—Rosemary cream—Apples *au gatelin* *Étrier* of plums—Tarts, old style, with cream, beef bone-marrow, plums—Cream gâteau—*Gâteau joyeux*—Boar's head—*Pâtés à la tonnelette* with woodcock, quince, chestnuts, apples, chickens—Venison pâtés—Cheese tarts—Asparagus—Blancmange—Frumenty cream—*Baudrier* of apples—Fritters—*Tarte angoulousée*—*Tarte d'Angleterre*—*Tarte fanaide*—Chopped apple tart—White wine tart—Flaky pastry—Italian gâteau.

Seventeenth century menu—Under Louis XIV, the menus were magnificent. Doubtless, not all the dishes which figured in the five obligatory courses which made up the gala banquets were perfectly executed, nor were they as varied as they should have been. Nevertheless, there were many of them, if one may judge from the menu of the dinner offered by Mme. la Chancelière to Louis XIV in 1656 in her Château of Pontchartrain.

Here is the menu:

First course: Eight potted meats and vegetables and sixteen hot hors-d'oeuvre.

Second course: Eight important intermediate dishes called broths. Sixteen entrées of fine meats.

Third course: Eight roast dishes and sixteen vegetable dishes cooked in meat stock.

Fourth course: Eight *pâtés* or cold meat and fish dishes and sixteen raw salads, with oil, cream and butter.

Fifth and last course: Twenty-four different kinds of pastries—twenty-four jars of raw fruit—twenty-four dishes of sweetmeats—preserves, dried and in syrup and jams.

There were, in all, 168 garnished dishes or plates, not counting the various foodstuffs served as dessert.

Eighteenth century menu—Here, as a curiosity, is a menu whose originality, it is true, is due to exceptional circumstances. It is that of a meal which Marshal the Duc de Richelieu offered to all the princes and princesses and the members of their suites taken prisoner by him during the Hanoverian war. President Hénault tells us how the menu for this memorable supper was drafted by the Duc de Richelieu himself. Its peculiarity lay in the fact that it was made up entirely of one kind of meat, namely beef, because, on that particular day, there was nothing in the Marshal's larder but a carcase of beef and a few root vegetables.

'My Lord,' said Rullières to the Marshal, somewhat anxiously observing that the Duc de Richelieu wished to offer supper to a large number of guests, 'there is nothing in the kitchens except a carcase of beef and a few roots . . .'

'Very good,' said the Marshal, 'that is more than is needed to provide the prettiest supper in the world.'

'But, my lord, it would be impossible . . .'

'Come, Rullières, calm yourself, and write out the menu that I am about to dictate to you.'

And the Marshal, seeing Rullières more and more alarmed, took the pen out of his hand and, seated in his secretary's place, wrote the following menu which, later, was brought into the collection of Monsieur de la Popelinière.

SUPPER MENU

Centrepiece

The large silver-gilt salver with the equestrian figure of the King, the statues of Du Guesclin, Dunois, Bayard, Turenne. My silver-gilt plate with the arms embossed and enamelled.

First course: Tureen: A tureen of *garbure gratinée,* made of beef consommé.

Four hors-d'oeuvre: Palate of beef *à la Saint-Menehould*—Little pâtés of chopped fillet of beef with chives—Kidneys with fried onion—Tripe *à la poulette* with lemon juice.

To follow the broth: Rump of beef garnished with root vegetables in gravy. (Trim these vegetables into grotesque shapes on account of the Germans.)

Six entrées: Oxtail with chestnut purée—Civet of tongue *à la bourguignonne—paupiettes* of beef *à l'estouffade* with pickled nasturtium buds—fillet of beef braised with celery—Beef rissoles with hazel-nut purée—Beef marrow on toast (ration bread will do).

Second course: Roast sirloin (baste it with melted bone-marrow)—Endive salad with ox-tongue—Beef *à la mode* with white jelly mixed with pistachio nuts—Cold beef gâteau with blood and Jurançon wine. (Don't make a mistake!)

Six final dishes: Glazed turnips with the gravy of the roast—Beef bone-marrow pie with breadcrumbs and candy sugar—Beef stock aspic with lemon rind and pralines—Purée of artichoke hearts with gravy (beef) and almond milk—Fritters of beef brain steeped in Seville orange juice—Beef jelly with Alicante wine and Verdun mirabelles.

To follow, all that is left in the way of jams or preserves.

And, as a coda to this majestic menu (which we should like to regard as authentic and of its period, although in some respects it strikes us as somewhat odd!), the Marshal added:

'If by any unhappy chance, this meal turns out not to be very good, I shall withhold from the wages of Maret and Roquelère (his maître-d'hôtel and master-chef, no doubt) a fine of 100 pistols. Go, and entertain no more doubts!

Signed: RICHELIEU'

This menu, strange as its composition may seem, is perfectly orthodox. Structurally, it obeys all the rules which were in force at this period concerning the organisation of important meals.

Nineteenth century menu—Here is a menu of a historic dinner. This dinner, known as the dinner of the 'Three Emperors', was served on June 7th, 1867, at the Café Anglais, which no longer exists.

Among the illustrious guests who attended this dinner were Alexander II, Czar of all the Russias, the Czarevich (the future Alexander III) and the King of Prussia who afterwards became the Emperor William I.

This dinner, it is said, cost 400 francs a head.

MENU

Soups:

Impératrice—Fontanges

Intermediate course:

Soufflé à la Reine

Fillet of sole *à la vénitienne*

Collops of turbot *au gratin*

Saddle of mutton with *purée bretonne*

Entrées:

Chickens *à la portugaise*

Hot quail *pâté*

Lobster *à la parisienne*

Champagne Sherbets

Rôts:

Duckling *à la rouennaise*

Canapés of bunting

Final course:

Aubergines à l'espagnole

Asparagus

Cassolettes princesse

Iced *bombe*

Fruit

Wines:

Madère retour des Indes, 1846

Sherry 1821

Château-Yquem 1847

Chambertin 1846

Château-Margaux 1847

Château-Latour 1847

Château-Lafite 1848

Composition of a banquet menu—Generally speaking, the menu of a great banquet should be made up as follows:

A soup. Often for an important dinner two soups are served, one clear and one thick.

Hot hors-d'oeuvre. This type of dish is more often than not omitted at great dinners.

Cold hors-d'oeuvre. In former times, these were, so to speak, obligatory at great dinners. They are now no longer served in the evening, but only at luncheons at the beginning of the meal.

Intermediate fish courses. These consist as a rule of large fish braised and served with various garnishes and sauces, or poached, with special sauces served separately.

Intermediate meat, poultry or game courses. Usually the intermediate course consists of a large cut of meat, beef, mutton or lamb, roast or braised and garnished with vegetables.

Less commonly, a large bird is served as an intermediate course.

A cut of venison can also be used for this purpose. It should be served with chestnut purée and a special venison sauce.

Very rarely, winged game is served as an intermediate course. Usually it is presented as an *entrée* or *rôt.*

Entrées. The number of dishes which can be served as *entrées* is very great.

To ensure efficient service at an important dinner, there should be not more than one *entrée*, and this should be chosen from among those which are easy to serve.

Very seldom, in a well-planned menu, is a cold dish such as aspic, *chaud-froid*, mousse, mould, *pâté de foie gras*, galantine of chicken, etc., served as an *entrée.* These dishes belong more properly in the category of cold *rôts.*

The *rôt* is usually poultry or winged game. Less commonly, a cut of venison is served as a *rôt.* Even more rarely, roast red meat is served, such as fillet, rib or sirloin. This rule holds not only for large dinners but also for those where there are only a small number of guests. Such cuts should only be served as *rôts* at intimate dinners where the laws governing the composition of a menu may be transgressed. At the family table full licence is permitted.

To follow, or even to be served with the *rôt*, there must be a salad. At a large dinner it is advisable to keep to plain salads called *salade en saison*, but a composite salad may also be served. Recipes for these salads are to be found under SALAD.

Cold rôt. This is the name given to a cold dish served after the hot *rôt*. The cold *rôt* is most commonly either a *Pâté de foie gras* with truffles or a foie gras in aspic. Salad should not be served with this delicate dish.

The following may also be served as cold *rôts:* Spiny lobster prepared *en bellevue*, *à la parisienne* or *à la russe;* jelly with a border of collops of various shell-fish; mousses or moulds of foie gras or ham; galantines of various types of poultry or winged game; freshwater crayfish served *en buisson* and, finally, most of the cold fish, meat or poultry dishes given in this volume.

Entremets. In former times this term covered not only the vegetable side dishes which must always be served after the roast, but also the various sweets which nowadays form the dessert, but which usually appear on menus under the name of *entremets*. (Nowadays, this word is virtually synonymous with sweet or dessert.)

In former times, at a large dinner, several vegetable dishes were served. In current practice, it is usual to serve one kind of vegetable only, and this is much more satisfactory. The second part of the *entremets*, the *douceur* (sweet) as it was formerly called in France, is made up more often than not of *bombes**, *mousses** or iced *parfaits**. Other hot or cold sweets can also be served, such as apricots *Condé*, pear flans *Bourdaloue*, puddings made with cream or fruit, peaches *impératrice**, various Bavarian creams, fruit salad with liqueurs, chestnut or strawberry *mont-blanc*, creams in moulds, fruit jellies, etc.

In France the correct procedure is to serve the sweet after, not before, the cheese.

MERCUREY—This wine, which is made from grapes grown in the commune of Mercurey in the Saône-et-Loire district, is classified as a first growth of the Chalon slopes.

It is similar to the wines of the Beaune slopes, but is a little less sweet. It contains 12° to 13° of alcohol.

MÈRE DE SOLE—A fish also called in France *cardine* or *limandelle*. It is cooked in the same way as plaice. See PLAICE.

MÈRE GOUTTE—A wine made from the juice extracted from the grapes when they are first crushed, and before they are put in the press.

MERGA (Arab cookery)—This is the name of the sauce served with *couscous**. This sauce is made from the cooking stock of the meat served with the couscous, and can be made either mild or strong. Strong merga is spiced with red pepper.

MERINGUE—A small pâtisserie made from white of egg and sugar.

Historians of cookery say that this little pâtisserie was invented in 1720. This invention (if invention it was, for it seems clear that whites of egg were used in pastry-making before this period) is attributed to a Swiss pastry-cook called Gasparini, who practised his art in Mehrinyghen, a small town which was in the State of Saxe-Coburg-Gotha, according to some authorities, and in Switzerland according to others.

The first meringues made in France were served in Nancy to King Stanislaus who, it is said, prized them highly.

It was he, no doubt, who gave the recipe for this sweetmeat to Marie Leczinska, who also enjoyed it very much. Queen Marie-Antoinette had a great liking for meringues as well. Court lore has it that she made them herself with her own royal hands at the Trianon, where she also made *vacherins* for which a similar mixture is used.

Up to the beginning of the nineteenth century, meringues were shaped in a spoon as the pastry forcing-bag had not yet been invented.

Ingredients. 12 whites of egg, 1 pound (500 grams) fine sugar, 1½ teaspoons (10 grams) table salt, flavouring to taste.

Method. Whisk the whites to a stiff foam. When they have risen well, add the salt and sugar.

Fill a forcing-bag (with a plain round nozzle) with this mixture, and pipe the meringues in the desired shape and size on to buttered and floured baking sheets.

Sprinkle with sugar. Bake in a very low oven.

After taking the meringues out of the oven, press the base of each one with the thumb to make a little hollow. Keep in a dry place.

Border of meringue with Chantilly cream. BORDURE DE MERINGUES À LA CHANTILLY—Take some oval meringues, half of them white, flavoured with vanilla, half pink, flavoured with strawberry or raspberry essence.

Arrange them in a circle, sticking them together with boiled sugar. Put them in a ring to form a border on a round dish. Just before serving, fill the middle of the dish with *Chantilly cream* (see CREAMS) flavoured with vanilla or fruit juice.

Meringue croquembouche or pyramid. CROQUEMBOUCHE DE MERINGUES—Using small oval or round meringues made in different colours and differently flavoured, make a pyramid by joining them together, with sugar boiled to crack degree (275°F.) (see SUGAR). Alternate the colours in forming the pyramid.

Meringue crust. MERINGUE—A raw or cooked sweet, once it is made, may be covered with meringue mixture and put in the oven to bake the meringue crust.

Italian meringues. MERINGUE À L'ITALIENNE—Proceed as for plain meringues, using the cooked meringue mixture called *Italian meringue*. See MIXTURES, *Italian meringue mixture*.

Meringue à Marignan—Cook 1 pound (500 grams) of sugar dissolved in a little water. Add to the sugar liqueur to taste (kirsch, maraschino or any other). Cook a little longer to bring it back to the ball degree (see SUGAR). Pour this sugar on to 5 stiffly beaten whites of egg.

Marignan meringue is usually decorated with a long strip of crystallized angelica stuck at each end like the handle of a basket.

Swiss meringues. MERINGUES SUISSES—*Ingredients.* 6 whites of egg, 1 pound (500 grams) icing sugar, 3 drops acetic acid or ½ teaspoon lemon juice, vanilla, a pinch of salt.

Method. Work the sugar with 2 whites of egg, the acetic acid, vanilla and salt.

When the mixture is very white and smooth add the 4 remaining whites of egg, whisked to a stiff froth. Mix well. Pipe as indicated above. Bake in the oven.

Swiss meringues are decorated with crystallized fruit and sprinkled with sugar of different colours.

MÉROU—Common name for a fish found in Mediterranean coastal waters. A *mérou* can be as much as 40 inches in length. It is rather a tasteless fish.

All recipes for tunny are suitable for *mérou*. See TUNNY.

MERVEILLE—The name of a French pastry made from dough cut into different shapes and deep-fried.

Method. Make a dough with 3¾ cups (500 grams) of sifted flour, ⅔ cup (150 grams) of butter, 4 teaspoons (20 grams) of sugar, 4 eggs and a small pinch of salt. Leave this dough to stand for an hour. Roll it out to a thickness of ⅛ inch. Cut it into various shapes with fluted pastry-cutters. Deep-fry in boiling fat. Drain. Sprinkle with vanilla-flavoured sugar. Arrange in a heap on a napkin.

MESCAL—An alcoholic drink tasting of bitter almonds. It is made in Mexico and South America from the *maguey* (Mexican agave).

MESENTERY OF CALF. FRAISE DE VEAU—Membrane which envelopes the intestines of the calf. This is cooked like *calf's head.* See OFFAL OR VARIETY MEATS.

MESSIRE-JEAN—A French variety of pear which ripens in autumn. It is of medium size. Its skin is russet in colour with a greyish tinge. It is rather gritty in texture, but very fragrant.

METS—The French apply this term to any food prepared for the table. It derives from the Latin *missus.*

MEUNIÈRE (A LA)—A method of cooking fish. Fish cooked *à la meunière* is seasoned, lightly floured and fried in butter. Serve on a long dish. Squeeze a few drops of lemon juice over it. Sprinkle with parsley and pour on the cooking butter, piping hot.

MEURETTE—The name of a *Matelote à la bourguignonne.* See MATELOTE.

MEURSAULT—A great white Burgundy classified among the wines of the Beaune slopes.

The prime first growths among Mersault wines are: the *Perrières, dessus* and *dessous.*

The first growths are: the white *Santenots,* the *Genevrières, dessous;* the *Charmes, dessus;* the *Bouchères;* the *Tessons;* the *Goutte-d'or.*

MIGNONNETTE—Coarse-ground pepper is known in France as *mignonnette.*

In former times, this was the name given to a muslin sachet containing red pepper, nutmeg, coriander, cinnamon, ginger and cloves.

This aromatic sachet was dipped for a few moments in the cooking pot to season the food. It could be used several times.

MIGNOT—A celebrated restaurateur of the seventeenth century.

He was immortalized, in a manner of speaking, by Boileau who, in his satire *La repas ridicule* called him a poisoner.

'*Car Mignot, c'est tout dire, et dans le monde entier*
Jamais empoisonneur ne sut mieux son métièr.'

'For Mignot, I need say no more, and in the whole world
'Never did a poisoner know his job better.'

Mignot who, it is said, was a cook of some talent and a conscientious restaurateur, was much enraged by such criticism and took his complaint to court. His suit was rejected and he resolved to take vengeance himself. At that time, he was making a kind of dry pastry much prized by Parisians. He conceived the idea of wrapping these little cakes in a sheet of paper upon which, at his own expense, he had printed a violent satire on Boileau written by his enemy, the Abbé Cottin.

The success of these pastries, which were called *biscuits Mignot,* was enormous. All Paris wanted to taste them so as to be able to savour, at the same time, the verses in which Cottin slated Boileau. The rage of Mignot subsided somewhat when he discovered that, far from doing him any harm, Boileau's couplet had contributed to his greater prosperity.

MIGRAINE—Wine made from grapes grown in the neighbourhood of Auxerre.

MIKADO—See GARNISHES.

MILANAISE (A LA)—Food prepared *à la milanaise* is generally dipped in egg and breadcrumbs mixed with grated Parmesan cheese, and fried in clarified butter.

This name also designates a method of preparing macaroni (see MACARONI), and a garnish for cuts of meat made from macaroni with cheese, coarsely shredded ham, pickled tongue, mushrooms and truffles, all blended in tomato sauce.

This garnish is also used with *Timbale à la milanaise**.

MILANESE CAKE. MILANAIS—Heat on the stove, as for a Genoese cake, 1 cup (250 grams) of castor (fine) sugar and 6 eggs until the mixture begins to rise. When the mixture begins to get hot, add ⅞ cup (200 grams) of melted butter and 1⅝ cups (200 grams) of sieved cake flour. Flavour with ½ cup (a decilitre) of anisette liqueur.

Pour the mixture into ornamental round baking tins. Bake in a medium oven. Turn out the cakes. Spread with apricot jam and ice with aniseed-flavoured *Fondant icing* (see ICING).

MILK. LAIT—An opaque white alkaline liquid with a yellowish or bluish tinge secreted by the mammary glands.

The milk content varies according to the type and breed of animal, its state of health and the diet on which it has been reared.

Milk has great nutritive value. An average quart (litre) of milk provides 690 calories, which corresponds approximately to ½ pound (240 grams) of sirloin beef.

Normally, milk is easy to digest, especially for children. Adults with good digestions can also assimilate milk quite easily, provided they do not take it to excess. There are no poisonous elements in milk, nor is there any risk of it causing any form of irritation in the alimentary canal. In fact, because of the lactic acids formed by the action of the digestive juices always present in the intestines, milk is a valuable internal antiseptic.

In spite of the fact that it is a liquid, milk should always be regarded as a food and not as a drink. It should be *eaten* rather than *drunk.* That is to say it should be sipped and swallowed slowly. Taken in this way, it coagulates in little fragments in the stomach, and these can be dealt with readily by the digestive juices. On the other hand, if it is gulped down it forms a large indigestible clot in the stomach, and the digestive juices have difficulty in breaking it down. For the same reason, milk is more digestible in the form of broths and porridges because, mixed with carbohydrates, the clot breaks up into fragments more readily. Even persons suffering from enteritis can take milk in this form.

Condensed milk. LAITS CONDENSÉS—Milk collected with the utmost care, with or without added sugar, is evaporated in a vacuum at 60 per cent. so as to reduce its water content by 40 to 50 per cent.

Sweetened condensed milk keeps better, once the tin is opened, than unsweetened milk. It has the consistency of thick cream.

Dried milk. LAITS DESSÉCHÉS—Milk, usually partly skimmed, is evaporated very rapidly by passing through heated cylinders. Powdered milk keeps very well. The partial skimming of the milk makes it less likely that the powder will turn rancid. This milk, suitably diluted, can be given to young babies.

Fermented milk. LAITS FERMENTÉS—All agricultural communities make use of fermentation to preserve milk and alter its flavour. Apart from spontaneous coagulation, due to the action of the lactic microbes, which produces curds, and curdling by means of rennet, which is the basis of cheese making, there are many other types of fermented milk. Examples of these are the *Dahdi* of India, the *Mazyn* of Armenia, the *Huslanka* of the Carpathians and Bukovina, the *Laban Zebadi* of Egypt, the *Yoghourt* of Bulgaria and the *Taetta* of Scandinavia. This latter is a runny, viscous milk to which vegetable juices are added to prevent coagulation.

All these types of sour milk are produced by the action of lactic ferments of varying degrees of purity and obtained from a number of different sources.

*Kefir** and *koumiss** are due to the combined action of the lactic ferments and barm (brewer's yeast) which produces lactic acid, alcohol, and carbonic acid which renders the milk frothy.

MILL. MOULIN—A small machine used to pulverise certain foodstuffs such as coffee, breadcrumbs, pepper, block salt, etc.

MILLAS OR MILIASSE—This is a name given in the Languedoc region to a kind of porridge or hasty-pudding made either with maize flour (cornmeal) or with a mixture of wheaten flour and maize flour.

The name of this dish would seem to come from the word *millet*, the common French name for some types of grain grown in the south of France, especially in the Landes. One, called *millette*, a small-grained variety of maize, was originally used to make this porridge.

Though the true *millas* is made in Languedoc, very similar porridges are made in various parts of south-eastern and south-western France, though, in different areas, they are given different names.

This type of porridge is called *cruchade* in Guyenne and Gascony; *broye*, *gaudines* or *verbilhou* in Béarn; *pous* or *rimotes* in Périgord; *gaudes* in Franche-Comté.

Polenta, which is made in Corsica and in Provence, is a porridge or hasty-pudding of the same type as *millas*.

The *millas* of Languedoc is a dish in rustic style. Formerly in the countryside of this region it was eaten like bread with certain dishes cooked in gravy, such as beef *daube*, civet of hare, etc.

When used in this way, the *millas*, when it is quite cold, is cut into square or rectangular slices, then browned in fat in a frying pan, or toasted on the grill.

In Languedoc, various sweets are made from *millas*.

Cherry millas. MILLAS AUX CERISES—Put a layer of hot *millas* in a buttered pie-dish. It must be freshly cooked with sugar added and flavoured with kirsch. Smooth the *millas* carefully. Part-cook in syrup some stoned cherries. Drain and steep in kirsch. Spread them on top of the *millas*. Cover with another layer of *millas*. Smooth the surface carefully. Make a border of cherries, prepared as indicated above. Sprinkle with crushed macaroons. Pour on melted butter. Brown in a slow oven.

A *millas* sweet (dessert) can be made in the same way using various kinds of cooked fruit such as apricots, bananas, peaches, pears, apples, plums, etc.

Fried millas. MILLAS FRIT—Cut the *millas* into neat slices of equal thickness. Flour the slices and brown them lightly in butter or fat, in a frying pan. Prepared in this way *millas* can be used in place of bread with various dishes in gravy.

Millas with frittons. MILLAS AUX FRITTONS—In Languedoc this type of *millas* is made on the day when, according to the local phrase, the housewife '*fait le cochon*' (cooks the pig). The porridge is cooked in the cauldron used to clarify the fat of the pig. At the end of the cooking, the *frittons* (the residue of the pork-fat after melting) are added to the *millas*.

When it is ready, the porridge is poured on to a floured linen cloth and left to cool. It is then sliced into squares or rectangles before being fried or grilled.

Millas with grape jam. MILLAS AU RAISINÉ—Spread slices of *millas* each with a heaped tablespoon of *raisiné* (grape jam, see RAISINÉ). Arrange them in a circle on a round dish. Sprinkle the slices with crushed macaroons. Pour on melted butter. Brown gently in the oven.

Proceeding in the same way, the *millas* may be spread with other types of jam or thick purée.

Lot-et-Garonne millas. MILLAS DE LOT-ET-GARONNE—In this region, this kind of *millas* is called a *rimote* and also a *cruchade*.

Pour water into a rather large pan and bring to the boil. When it is boiling, flavour with lemon essence and orange flower water.

Sprinkle into the boiling liquid freshly milled maize flour (cornmeal) as for a cream, until a thick porridge is produced. Pour into shallow plates.

Rimotes are eaten hot, sprinkled with sugar. When they are cold, they can be cut into quarters, browned on both sides in a frying pan and sprinkled with sugar.

Millas with sugar. MILLAS AU SUCRE—Cut the layer of *millas* into square or rectangular slices. Heat butter in a frying pan and put the slices of *millas* to cook in it. (In Languedoc pork or goose fat is used for this purpose.) Brown the slices on both sides. Drain. Arrange on a serving dish. Sprinkle liberally with fine sugar flavoured with vanilla or lemon rind.

Toasted millas. MILLAS GRILLÉ—Spread the slices of *millas* with fat or butter. Toast them gently under the grill.

Mille feuilles

MILLE-FEUILLE—A pastry very much in vogue in Paris. As its name (*mille-feuille*, a thousand leaves) indicates, it is made by arranging thin layers of flaky pastry one on top of the other with layers of cream or some other filling in between.

Mille-feuille pastry can be baked in the form of a large sweet, decorated in various ways, or, as is customary in Paris *pâtisseries*, in small individual portions, by cutting the flaky pastry into pieces 2 inches wide and laying them one on top of the other, sandwiched together in the same way with cream or some other filling.

Large mille-feuille. GROS MILLE-FEUILLE—Roll out the *Flaky pastry* (see DOUGH) and fold it in three on itself 6 times. The rolled-out pastry should be about ⅜ inch thick. Cut out of this circles of the required size (6 to 7 inches in diameter). Put these circles of flaky pastry on a baking sheet. Dredge with sugar. Bake in a hot oven. Leave to cool, trim and spread each circle with *French pastry cream* (see CREAMS) or with any other sweet cream. Mount the circles one on top of the other to produce a cake 7 to 8 inches deep. It must be very regular in shape. Ice it with plain meringue which must be carefully smoothed with a knife. Sprinkle with sugar and put the cake in the oven for a few moments to set the meringue.

Decorate the top of the cake according to taste.

Note. Large *mille-feuilles*, after being covered with a thin layer of meringue, may be sprinkled on the top and sides with dried sultanas and currants and pistachio nuts either whole or chopped.

When these large *mille-feuilles* are intended to be used for a cold buffet (they are particularly suitable for this purpose), they can be further decorated with sugar ornaments arranged as a border on top of the cake and with plumes of spun sugar.

But this type of decoration for large cakes is hardly ever used nowadays. Most commonly, *mille-feuilles* are made square and simply sprinkled with icing sugar.

Mille-feuille can also be filled with any kind of confectioner's cream or various rather thick, fruit purées or jams, in alternate layers.

The layers of a large *mille-feuille* can also be spread with very thick *Chantilly cream* (see CREAMS) flavoured with vanilla or some other flavouring. In this case the cream must not be spread on the layers until the very last moment.

Small mille-feuille. PETIT MILLE-FEUILLE—Individual portions are made in the same way as large *mille-feuilles*, but the square layers, spread with cream or some other filling, are laid one on top of the other, and cut into pieces 2 inches wide. The top is left plain.

MILLER'S THUMB. MEUNIER—Common name for a freshwater fish, also known as a *bull-head.* It is eaten fried.

MILLET—A cereal grain which is one of several species of panic-grass. There are two main edible varieties, the *common millet* and what is now called *Italian or German millet*.

This plant has been cultivated from very ancient times, the common millet in the Egypto-Arab countries and the 'Italian' variety in Japan. Millet was cultivated in India in prehistoric times. The Romans used it to make a kind of milk porridge, made from the grains after removing the husks. It is still used in this way by some African tribes.

MILLIASSOUS (Pastry)—Put in a bowl 7⅝ ounces or approximately 1½ cups (200 grams) of flour made from small millet, 3 cups (400 grams) of castor (fine) sugar and 8 eggs. Work this mixture thoroughly. Add the finely chopped rind of 2 lemons. Moisten with 7 cups (1½ litres) of boiling milk and mix well.

Fill small plain round buttered baking-tins with this mixture. Bake in a hot oven for about 20 to 30 minutes.

MIMOSA SALAD—This salad can be made from a very wide variety of ingredients. To justify its name to some extent, a mimosa salad, after having been put in a salad dish or crystal bowl, must be sprinkled with coarsely chopped yolks of hard boiled egg.

MINCEMEAT—Mincemeat takes rather a long time to prepare, owing to the fact that it must steep for a month in Madeira, rum or brandy.

Mince pie is also popular in the United States, but the mincemeats differ.

Meat is not an ingredient of English mincemeat. In the United States meat (beef or venison) is almost always included, although several recipes for mock (meatless) mincemeat exist, some using green tomatoes and others more closely resembling the English variety.

English mincemeat—1 pound of finely chopped suet; 1 pound of currants; 1 pound of seeded raisins, chopped; 1 pound of apples, chopped; 2 cups of sugar; ½ pound of sultanas; 4 ounces chopped, mixed candied fruit peel; ¼ cup of brandy or rum; juice and rind of 1 lemon; 1 teaspoon each of cinnamon, nutmeg, clove and mace.

Combine ingredients. Pack closely in a jar. Cover tightly. Yields 4 to 5 pounds mincemeat.

American mincemeat—Put the following ingredients in a large bowl: 1 pound of minced beef suet; 1 pound of sirloin of beef cooked and finely diced; 1 pound of stoned and minced raisins; 1 pound of currants and sultanas, cleaned and washed; 1 pound of rennet apples, peeled and chopped; 5 ounces of candied citron, finely diced; 3½ ounces candied orange peel, chopped; the chopped rind of an orange and the juice; 1 pound of yellow (light brown) moist sugar; 1 ounce of mixed spices; 2½ teaspoons of salt; a half-bottle of brandy; ½ cup of rum; ½ cup of Madeira.

Mix all the ingredients thoroughly. Leave the mixture to steep for a month in a cool place. During this time, stir every 8 days.

Mincemeat fritters. BEIGNETS DE MINCEMEAT—Moisten rounds of rice paper by dipping them in water. Fill them with mincemeat and shape into balls. Just before serving, dip them in batter and deep-fry. Serve in a heap on a napkin with apricot sauce flavoured with rum.

Mincemeat omelette, or Christmas omelette. OMELETTE DE MINCEMEAT (OMELETTE DE NOËL)—Beat the eggs, adding a few tablespoons of fresh cream, a little rum, grated lemon rind, and sugar.

Make the omelette with butter and, just before folding it over, fill it with a few tablespoons of mincemeat, heated with fresh cream.

Sprinkle the omelette with sugar, pour plenty of rum over it, set alight and serve.

Mincemeat rissoles. RISSOLES DE MINCEMEAT—Proceed as for plain rissoles. See RISSOLES.

Mincemeat vol-au-vents. BOUCHÉES DE MINCEMEAT—Bake small vol-au-vents. While they are still hot, fill them with mincemeat with fresh cream added.

Mince pie—'This little pie', wrote Suzanne, French historian of English cookery, 'is especially esteemed and popular in England. This, with the legendary plum-pudding, presides as master at the gargantuan love-feast of Christmas. Its absence from a Christmas dinner would be looked upon as a breach of the traditional rules and customs.'

To make the pies, line some large, deep, buttered tartlet tins with plain lining dough or with flaky pastry trimmings. Fill with one of the mincemeats indicated above. Cover with a thin layer of *Flaky pastry* (see DOUGH). Press the edges together. Make a hole in the centre of each pie to allow the steam to escape. Brush with egg. Bake in a hot oven. Serve the mince pies hot.

MINCERS AND CHOPPERS—HACHOIRS—Today, in butchers' shops and restaurant kitchens, precision implements are used for mincing and chopping. Many of them are electrically operated.

In French private kitchens, one of the implements used is the four-bladed, double-handled chopper. An ordinary meat chopper can be used, too, though this is really intended for chopping bones.

Chopping boards are now sometimes made of cross-grained plywood, like the chopping blocks described under CHOPPING.

MINERAL WATERS. EAUX MINÉRALES—It seems probable that some natural mineral water is produced by the disintegration of the rocks under intense heat in the bowels of the earth. This water is sometimes hot when it reaches the earth's surface (thermal water), sometimes cold. Each mineral spring has its own special properties which seems to be almost unrelated to its chemical composition, since two springs very close together can have different properties.

Minestrone

MINESTRA—An Italian word for a thick soup. The best-known of Italian *minestras* is *minestrone*, for which a recipe is given under SOUPS AND BROTHS.

Minnow

MINNOW. VAIRON—Small freshwater fish whose bronze-coloured back has olive lights; it is often substituted for the gudgeon in *fritures* of small fish; its flesh is, however, less fine and more bitter in taste than that of the gudgeon. Prepared in the same way as gudgeon. See GUDGEON.

MINT. MENTHE—A fragrant plant of which there are a great many varieties. Those most commonly used in France are *menthe pouliot*, *menthe crépue* (curly mint) or *menthe rouge* (red mint). Peppermint is a variety of histamint used in dispensary. It is cultivated in England. It has a four-sided stem which is green or reddish. It contains an oily essence (essence of peppermint) from which crystals of camphor mint or menthol can be extracted.

Mint, which is used a great deal in infusions, is also an ingredient in a large number of liqueurs. It is also used in cooking, especially in England.

Spirits of mint is made by steeping 1,000 grams of fresh mint leaves in 3,000 grams of alcohol 80° proof for 3 days and distilling it by condensation.

Mint sauce (English cookery). SAUCE-MENTHE—This sauce, which in England is an almost indispensible adjunct to hot or cold lamb, is made by moistening with ⅝ cup (1½ decilitres) of vinegar and 4 tablespoons of water, 1⅝ ounces (50 grams) of finely shredded mint leaves put in a bowl with 3 tablespoons (25 grams) of castor (fine) sugar, a pinch of salt and a little pepper. See SAUCE, *Cold sauces*.

MIQUES DE MAÏS (Périgord cookery)—Make a fairly stiff dough with ½ pound (250 grams) of maize flour (cornmeal), 1⅞ cups (250 grams) of sifted flour, a heaped tablespoon of pork fat, a pinch of salt and a glass of tepid water.

When this dough is well kneaded, break it into small pieces (100 grams each). Shape the pieces into balls by rolling them in the hands, which should be floured.

Drop these dough balls into a saucepan full of salted boiling water. Poach like forcemeat balls. Turn them over once or twice so that they are fully cooked.

When they are ready (after 25 to 30 minutes' boiling), strain the *miques*, put them on a cloth and keep them warm.

Note. Miques are eaten as bread. In the countryside around Périgord, they are an almost indispensible accompaniment to certain dishes such as *salé aux choux* (pickled pork with cabbage), civet of hare or rabbit, etc.

They can also be served as a sweet (dessert) by frying them in butter and sprinkling with sugar.

MIRABEAU (A LA)—This garnish is served mainly with grilled meat. It consists of strips of anchovy fillets arranged in a criss-cross pattern on the meat, stoned olives, blanched tarragon leaves and anchovy butters.

MIRABELLE—A small plum, golden yellow in colour, with a very penetrating smell. It is sweet in taste. It is eaten stewed, made into jam and preserved, and used in the manufacture of a spirit. It is also used in confectionery.

Mirabelle plum flan. FLAN AUX MIRABELLES—Proceed as indicated for *Apricot flan*. See TART.

Mirabelle tarts and tartlets. TARTES ET TARTELETTES AUX MIRABELLES—Proceed as indicated for *Apricot tarts and tartlets*. See TARTS AND TARTLETS.

MIRBANE—The name given to an artificial essence of bitter almonds. It is a yellow liquid with a very powerful smell. It is used in perfumery and occasionally in inferior confectionery.

MIREPOIX—This mixture, which can be made with or without meat, is used in meat, fish and shell-fish dishes to enhance their flavour.

Mirepoix with meat. MIREPOIX AU GRAS—Dice, more or less coarsely, as appropriate to the dish, 2 small carrots (150 grams); ½ cup (100 grams) of onions; ¼ cup (50 grams) of celery; and 3½ ounces (100 grams) of raw ham or blanched belly of pork.

Heat 2 tablespoons (30 grams) of butter in a saucepan and put all these ingredients to cook in it. Add a sprig of thyme and a quarter of a bay leaf. Cover and simmer slowly until the vegetables are very tender.

Mirepoix is added to certain sauces, notably *Espagnole sauce* (see SAUCE), to enhance the flavour. It can also be added to various types of braised or pot-roasted meat or poultry.

Vegetable mirepoix. MIREPOIX AU MAIGRE—This *mirepoix* is often called *brunoise.* It is used mainly in the preparation of shell-fish *à la bordelaise.* (See CRAYFISH). It is also used as an additional ingredient in some white sauces.

Dice extremely finely 2 small carrots (150 grams), ½ cup (100 grams) of onions and ¼ cup (50 grams) of celery.

Put these vegetables to cook slowly in butter. Season with salt and a pinch of powdered thyme and bay leaf. Cook until the vegetables are very tender.

MIRLITONS DE ROUEN—A small pastry in the form of a tartlet which is a speciality of Rouen confectionery.

Ingredients. ½ pound (250 grams) flaky pastry dough, 4 yolks of egg, 3 tablespoons (50 grams) sugar, ¼ pound (125 grams) butter, 1 pod vanilla, ½ tablespoon orange blossom water (U.S. ½ teaspoon each of vanilla and orange extract).

Method. Make flaky pastry in the usual way. See DOUGH.

Mix in a bowl the sugar, the yolks and the vanilla (the part taken from the inside of the pod). Add the butter, heated until it is nut-brown in colour, and the orange blossom water. Line tartlet tins with flaky pastry. Fill two-thirds full of the mixture indicated.

Sprinkle with fine sugar and bake in a hot oven for about 15 minutes.

MIROIR (AU)—A descriptive term used especially of eggs baked in the oven so that the white forms a polished film over the yolk. It is also more loosely applied to other dishes which have a mirror-bright finish. See EGG, *Baked eggs au miroir*.

MIROTON—A type of stew made from cooked meat flavoured with onions.

This definition does not, however, explain the etymology of this name, which is several hundred years old.

In a number of old French recipe books this dish is called *mironton*, a name which seems to indicate that the name of this stew is contemporary in origin with the nursery rhyme '*Marlborough-s'en-va-t-en-guerre*' ('Marlborough goes to war'), which has the refrain '*Mironton-mironton-mirontaine*'. This would place it in the eighteenth century.

This method of preparing scraps of meat must go back further than this date, but it was only then that the name *mironton* (later corrupted to *miroton*) was given to it.

In former times, moreover, the word *miroton* or *mironton* was used not only of a meat dish but also designated dishes made with fruit.

For the preparation of *miroton* see BEEF, *Miroton of beef*.

MISSEL-THRUSH. DRAINE—A species of thrush called missel-thrush because it feeds on mistletoe berries. Its plumage is darker than that of the common thrush, and it is longer. It is cooked in the same way as thrush. See THRUSH.

The bird is also called *Jocasse* in French.

MISSION HAUT-BRION WINE—The Mission Haut-Brion is a vineyard in the Gironde in the Persac commune. A red Graves which enjoys a high reputation is made from its grapes. The Mission Haut-Brion is distinct from Haut-Brion, a magnificent wine made from grapes grown in a vineyard separated only by a narrow path from the Mission.

The Mission Haut-Brion vineyard is one of the oldest in the Bordeaux region.

MITAN (MIDDLE-CUT)—An old French word, a synonym of middle. It is used in cooking for the middle-cut of salmon.

MITE. CIRON—Common name for all the animalcules which live in food matter, in cheese for instance, or in vegetable refuse.

MITONNER—A French cooking term meaning to simmer bread for a long time in soup.

MIX. DÉLAYER—To blend various ingredients thoroughly into a homogeneous mixture.

MIXTURES. APPAREIL:

Cream cheese mixture for hot hors-d'oeuvre à la russe. APPAREIL TVAROGUE—This is prepared from pressed creamed cheese, mixed with an equal quantity of fresh butter, blended until it is very smooth. See TVOROG.

Dauphine potato mixture. APPAREIL À POMMES DE TERRE DAUPHINE—*Duchess potatoes* (see POTATOES) mixed with *Chou paste*, see DOUGH (cream puff pastry), prepared without sugar, in the proportion of just over one part of chou paste to three parts of duchess potatoes.

Duchess potato mixture. APPAREIL À POMMES DE TERRE DUCHESSE—Potato purée bound with eggs. See POTATOES.

Mixtures for kromeskies and croquettes. APPAREILS À CROMESQUIS, À CROQUETTES—In principle, these mixtures, which are similar for both preparations, are composed of one or several ingredients, cut into a *salpicon**, i.e. into small dice, blended for a white mixture with *velouté* with yolks of egg added to it, or with *béchamel* for a brown mixture with very rich demi-glace (meat jelly) or thickened brown gravy. See CROQUETTES AND KROMESKI.

Maintenon mixture. APPAREIL À MAINTENON—Mixture of *Soubise purée* and thick *Béchamel* (see SAUCE), bound with yolks of egg, incorporating sliced or shredded mushrooms cooked in butter, at times supplemented with truffles and *Pickled tongue* (see OFFAL OR VARIETY MEATS).

Matignon mixture. APPAREIL À MATIGNON—Vegetables cut in thin slices, stewed in butter with ham; diluted with Madeira. See MATIGNON.

This is used as a supplementary ingredient for various mixtures; also for braised and fried dishes *à la Matignon.*

Mirepoix mixture. APPAREIL À MIREPOIX—Vegetables cut *en brunoise**, the degree of fineness depending on the final use for which it is intended, lightly cooked in butter, with lean smoked ham (or lean bacon), according to recipe, cut in very small dice, added to it. See MIREPOIX.

This is used as a supplementary ingredient for sauces,

forcemeats and various mixtures; it is also used for braised and fried dishes *à la Mirepoix*.

Semolina mixture for hot pies à la russe (Semolina kasha)—See KASHA.

MIXTURES FOR SWEET DISHES:

Bavarois mixture. APPAREIL À BAVAROIS—A mixture of English custard combined with dissolved gelatine, variously flavoured, with whipped cream added to it. See BAVAROIS.

Butter cream mixture. APPAREIL À CRÈME AU BEURRE—This mixture which is used in the preparation of various cold pastry desserts (coffee gâteau, praline, chocolate gâteaux, etc.), is made either using syrup (boiled to 220°F.), yolks of egg and fresh butter, or custard to which fresh butter has been added while it was still warm. See CREAMS.

Caramel cream mixture. APPAREIL À CRÈME AU CARAMEL—A mixture of eggs, sugar, milk and the flavouring chosen, cooked in a *bain-marie**, in a mould coated with light caramel. See CUSTARD, *Caramel custard.*

Chou paste or cream puff pastry mixture. APPAREIL À PÂTE À CHOU—This mixture is used not only for making cakes of various kinds (cream buns, éclairs, Saint-Honoré, etc.) but also for the preparation of various dishes, such as *beignets soufflés* (soufflé fritters), *gnocchi, profiteroles*, etc. See DOUGH.

Condé mixture. APPAREIL À CONDÉ—*Ingredients.* ½ pound (250 grams) of chopped almonds, 3 cups (375 grams) of icing or confectioner's sugar, whites of egg, powdered vanilla bean.

Method of preparation. Put the icing sugar, almonds and vanilla into a bowl. Moisten with white of egg, in sufficient quantity to make an easily spreadable, non-runny paste. Put it in the oven while the articles which are to be coated are cooking. See CONDÉ.

This mixture is used for icing various dessert pastries.

French pastry cream mixture. APPAREIL À CRÈME PÂTISSIÈRE—Cream cooked to rather a firm consistency, made by diluting yolks of egg blended with flour and granulated or castor sugar with boiled milk flavoured as desired. See CREAMS.

Crème Saint-Honoré mixture. APPAREIL À CRÈME SAINT-HONORÉ—Mixture of *French pastry cream* and whites of egg beaten into a stiff foam, added while it is still cooking (see CREAMS). Used for various sweet dishes.

English custard mixture. APPAREIL À CRÈME ANGLAISE—This custard is made of 2 cups (500 grams) of sugar, 16 yolks of egg, 1 quart (litre) of boiled milk (flavoured as desired). It is cooked on the stove, stirring constantly, until the first sign of boiling.

This custard, for sweet dishes, which is also known under the name of *English sauce*, can be served independently, but is more often served as an accompaniment to various desserts, in particular to puddings.

Depending on the final use for which it is intended, it can be blended with gelatine, dissolved in a little cold water allowing 1¾ to 2 ounces French sheet gelatine to 1 quart or 2 to 2½ tablespoons powdered gelatine to 1 quart (20 to 25 grams per litre).

This custard is served hot or cold, as indicated in the recipe. See CREAMS.

Custard mould mixture. APPAREIL À CRÈME RENVERSÉE—Mixture prepared like English custard, using for 1 quart (litre) of milk, boiled and flavoured as desired, 4 whole eggs and 7 yolks of egg, and ¾ cup (200 grams) of castor (fine) sugar blended together.

Fruit soufflé mixture. APPAREIL À SOUFFLÉ AUX FRUITS—Cook 1 cup (250 grams) of sugar in a copper pan to crack condition, 280°F. At the end of cooking, add 1 cup (200 grams) of fruit pulp (apricots, strawberries, cherries, etc.) rubbed through a sieve.

Bring the syrup to 250°F. See SUGAR, *Cooking of sugar*.

Pour the syrup gradually on 5 whites of egg whisked into a very stiff froth. Pour the mixture into a soufflé dish and bake like an ordinary soufflé.

Meringue mixture. APPAREIL À MERINGUE ORDINAIRE—Whisk 8 whites of egg into a very stiff froth, stiff enough to hold a large coin without it sinking into the mass; add 2 cups (500 grams) of slightly moistened granulated or castor sugar to the mixture, folding it in gently with a wooden spoon.

The proportion of whites of egg for the meringue can be increased. Up to 12 whites of egg for 2 cups (500 grams) of sugar can be used.

Italian meringue mixture. APPAREIL À MERINGUE ITALIENNE—Whisk 8 whites of egg until very stiff. Add to them, when they are well whisked, a syrup made of 2 cups (500 grams) sugar and 1 cup of water cooked to 238°F.

Pour this syrup in a thin thread on the whites of egg whisking vigorously throughout this operation. This may be done with some electric beaters.

Italian meringue mixture en génoise. APPAREIL À MERINGUE ITALIENNE EN GÉNOISE—Put 2 cups (500 grams) of castor (fine) sugar and 8 whites of egg into a copper pan. Blend these ingredients keeping them on a hot plate (or on hot cinders) whisking all the time until the mixture reaches a consistency when it can be held on the whisk.

This meringue can be kept in a bowl for a time. Cover it with a circle of paper.

MOCHA. MOKA—A variety of coffee-bean grown in Mocha in Arabia. These beans, which are very fragrant, are roasted rather less than those of Réunion Island and Martinique which are blended in the coffee commonly used in France.

Coffee made from pure mocha is generally served in special cups, smaller than those used for ordinary coffee.

Mocha cake. GÂTEAU MOKA—This cake is made by covering round, square or rectangular layers of cake made from best Genoese mixture with butter cream flavoured with mocha. Put one layer of cake spread with mocha cream on top of the other.

Ice with mocha-flavoured fondant icing or mocha-flavoured butter cream. Decorate the iced cake by piping the icing or cream used through a fluted nozzle on to the sides and top.

Mocha cream. CRÈME AU MOKA—A custard flavoured with coffee essence. Butter cream can also be flavoured with mocha.

French pastry cream used for filling *choux* and *éclairs* may be flavoured with mocha coffee. See CREAMS.

Mocha is sometimes added to *Chantilly cream.*

Mocha essence. ESSENCE DE MOKA—Made with unadulterated roasted mocha coffee by infusion in the same way as any other coffee essence.

Proceed as follows:

Put in the upper compartment of a large coffee filter 7 ounces (200 grams) of freshly roasted and ground coffee. Pour on to this coffee, a little at a time, 2½ cups (5 decilitres) of very strong coffee which should be prepared in advance and poured on hot but not boiling.

During this process the filter should stand in hot water.

Coffee essence can also be made with skimmed milk, but only if it is to be used to flavour creams or ice cream mixtures. To make this essence, proceed as follows:

Completely skim 2½ cups (5 decilitres) of milk. Bring to the boil. Put in 7 ounces (200 grams) of roasted coffee, still hot and crushed with a rolling-pin. Cover the container with a cloth. Leave to infuse for 15 minutes.

Mocha ice cream. GLACE AU MOKA—Ice cream flavoured with mocha coffee. See ICE CREAMS AND ICES, *Coffee ice cream.*

MOCHATINE CAKES. MOKATINE—This diminutive is used of individual portions of mocha cake or *petits fours** made from best Genoese mixture, filled with mocha-flavoured butter cream and iced with mocha-flavoured fondant icing.

MOCK TURTLE SOUP (English cookery). POTAGE FAUSSE TORTUE—A soup made with calf's head. See SOUPS AND BROTHS.

MODE (A LA)—This name is given mainly to large cuts of braised beef. See BEEF, *Top of rump à la mode.*

MOISTENING. MOUILLEMENT—Moistening is the process of adding a liquid of some kind to a dish such as *ragoûts*, stews, braised meat, fish or poultry, etc.

The term *moistening* can also be applied to the liquid, broth, clear soup, stock, wine, etc., used in this way.

MOLASSES. MÉLASSE—A thick brownish substance which is the residue of sugar refining. It will not crystallize. Sugar-beet molasses, which retains 50% of sugar, has an unpleasant taste and smell. It is mainly used in cattle feeding. Deodorised and purified, it is used in distilling.

Sugar-cane molasses, on the other hand, has quite a pleasant smell and taste, and is used in the distillation of tafia, generally known as rum, a name once used only of the spirit distilled from cane-juice, the natural juice of the sugar-cane.

MOLLUSC. COQUILLAGES—Univalve or bivalve edible mollusc. Nearly all are of marine origin; the snail is the one terrestrial mollusc that is eaten.

Many types are eaten raw, simply sprinkled with a little lemon juice or vinegar: molluscs are used as a garnish for numerous dishes, especially for fish.

Some molluscs can cause poisoning and infectious diseases (see MUSSELS) but the majority of those caught in clear water can be consumed without danger.

Oysters hold first place by reason of their delicate taste and substance. They are easily digested and have the advantage of being able to be consumed alive. It is possible to eat a very large quantity of oysters without loss of appetite; an equivalent quantity of meat with a far lower nutritive value would bring about satiety; the quantity of diluted sea water which they contain is a mineralizing element of the first order. See OYSTERS.

Mussels, perhaps richer in food value than oysters, are rather more difficult to digest.

They are usually eaten cooked.

Among the other shell-fish, scallops deserve a place apart. They have a flavour approaching that of lobster. See SCALLOPS.

MONACO—Monaco consommé is a clear chicken broth thickened with arrowroot, with a special garnish of small rounds of a cake mixture made with cheese.

Monaco cream soup is a cream of chicken soup served with the same garnish indicated above.

MONBAZILLAC—This white wine, which is very rich and somewhat similar to Sauternes, is made from grapes grown at Monbazillac, a small commune in the Dordogne five miles from Bergerac. A ministerial decree of May 1936 lays down the boundaries of the Monbazillac vineyards. Wine grown beyond these boundaries may not bear the name Monbazillac.

MONSELET—The nineteenth century author Charles Monselet was born at Nantes in 1828 and died in Paris in 1888. He was one of the well-known writers of his day.

He was also a great gastronome, or more exactly, a poet of gastronomy, for he wrote a number of pleasant poems on the good things of the table.

He published several gastronomic works, among which the *Almanach des Gourmands*, the *Lettres gourmandes* and *La Cuisinière poétique* are worthy of mention. He also wrote a large number of sonnets on cooking.

Charles Monselet was more a man of the eighteenth century than of his own day. Victor Hugo once said of him: 'When I write to Charles Monselet at the Quai Voltaire, I always feel like addressing the envelope to M. de Voltaire, Quai Monselet.'

MONSELET (A LA)—A name given to a great many dishes.

The distinctive feature of these dishes is that the ingredients include artichoke hearts and truffles, with potatoes fried in butter where appropriate.

MONT-BLANC—See CHESTNUTS.

MONT-BRY—See GARNISHES.

MONT-CENIS CHEESE—See CHEESE.

MONTE-CRISTO—Montpensier Gâteau is often called by this name.

The recipe for this cake is given under MONTPENSIER.

MONTGLAS—*Salpicon à la Montglas* is made from foie gras, pickled tongue, truffles and mushrooms blended in *Demi-glace sauce* (see SAUCE) flavoured with Madeira. This *salpicon* is used as a filling for very small vol-au-vents, tartlets and other pastry cases.

MONTMAUR—Pierre de Montmaur was a great French scholar and a distinguished Hellenist.

He was born in about 1576 at Bétaille, a village of Bas-Limousin between Tulle and Brive. He was quite brilliant, and above all he had a prodigious memory.

He became Professor of Greek in Paris in 1623, and died on September 7th 1648.

He was mean, parasitic (a sponger as we would say today) and also a slanderer. Because of this he made a lot of enemies. Among these was Ménage, a French literary figure (1613-1692), tutor to Marc de Sévigné, who averred that Montmaur had above all been a teacher of adulation and cookery.

'He gave his lessons in flattery in the morning and his cookery lessons in the evening.'

Ménage said that Montmaur, in his theories of cookery, gave an inflated importance to the position of chef. He advocated that anyone who aspired to become an expert in this important branch of human knowledge should first study the science of government, medicine, painting, astrology, architecture and arithmetic, and gave specious and absurd reasons for this.

'It is necessary for the chef to consider with care the place, the time, the guests and the host; it is necessary for him to be able to direct a meal as though he were directing a battle. He has to be versed in chemical analysis, so as to distinguish between wholesome and dangerous foodstuffs, and those more or less resistant to the action of heat. He has to be able, like a painter, to make attractive designs and blend colours with skill, and so on.'

MONTMORENCY—A name given to a variety of cherry cultivated in the neighbourhood of Paris.

MONTMORENCY (A LA)—This name is given to various dishes, cakes or sweets, all of which have cherries added to them in one form or another.

For example: Duck *à la Montmorency*;

Aiguillettes (thin slices of breast) of Rouen duck with cherries, called Montmorency;

Cherry ice cream, called Montmorency;

Iced mousse with cherries, called Montmorency;

Cherry tarts and tartlets, called Montmorency.

Border of cream à la Montmorency. BORDURE DE CRÈME À LA MONTMORENCY—Fill a turban (ring) mould with rich custard flavoured with kirsch and cook in a saucepan of water.

Leave to cool. Turn out on a round dish.

Fill the middle with stoned cherries, poached in syrup and flavoured with kirsch. Mask with *Chantilly cream* (see CREAMS) shaped into a dome and decorated with large stoned cherries cooked in syrup.

Montmorency cake. GÂTEAU MONTMORENCY—Cook some stoned cherries in syrup. Drain and mix with cherry jam flavoured with kirsch.

Using best Genoese mixture, make a round cake. Spread with the cherry mixture. Cover the cherries with Italian meringue. Smooth the meringue and decorate with meringue piping.

Sprinkle with icing sugar. Brown in the oven. Decorate the top of the cake with cherries, lightly sprinkled with sugar.

MONTPELLIER BUTTER. BEURRE DE MONTPELLIER—A fancy butter, coloured green, used in the presentation and decoration of cold dishes. This butter is perfectly edible, but it is intended primarily for decoration rather than for food, properly speaking. See BUTTERS, *Compound butters.*

MONTPENSIER—See GARNISHES.

MONTPENSIER FLAN OR CAKE—*For the dough.* 2 cups minus 2 tablespoons (250 grams) of sifted flour, ½ cup (125 grams) of sugar, ½ cup (125 grams) of butter, 2 whole eggs.

For the filling. 4 ounces (125 grams) blanched almonds, 1 cup (250 grams) granulated sugar, 3½ tablespoons (50 grams) of butter, a pinch of vanilla or 1 teaspoon (5 grams) vanilla extract, 1 cup (2 decilitres) water, 5 whites of egg.

Method. Sieve the flour and arrange it in a ring on the table. Put the sugar, butter and eggs in the middle. Mix quickly and, when the dough is of a good consistency, knead into a ball. Leave the dough to stand while the filling is prepared as follows:

Pound the almonds as finely as possible in a mortar adding the water. Put them in a bowl. Add the sugar, vanilla and the butter previously melted. Mix well and, at the end, add the whites of egg beaten to a stiff foam. The whites should be added a little at a time and should be completely absorbed into the mixture.

Shaping and baking. Roll out the sweetened dough with a rolling-pin, having sprinkled it lightly with flour to prevent it from sticking to the table. Lay the dough on a flan ring 8 to 10 inches in diameter. Press it well down into the ring with the thumb, making sure that it is firmly attached to the sides. A pie tin may be used as a substitute for the ring and baking sheet. In this case the tart is served in the tin.

Trim the edge of the circle with a knife. Put the ring on a white metal baking sheet. Prick the bottom of the flan with the point of a knife (or a fork).

Pour the filling into the flan. Sprinkle with fine sugar and bake in a slow oven for 45 minutes.

A few seconds before the flan is cooked, turn it out. Put it back in the oven to brown the sides. Sprinkle once more with fine sugar, and leave to cool before serving.

MONTRACHET—Montrachet is one of the great white wines of the Côte d'Or. Among these wines, which are made from grapes grown at Puligny-Montrachet, the best is first growth Montrachet, sometimes called Grand Montrachet.

Other first growths are: Chevalier-Montrachet; Bâtard-Montrachet (which shares the vineyard with Chassagne); Bienvenue-Bâtard; Combettes; Blagny Blanc; Champ Canet.

MOOSE OR ELK. ORIGINAL—The largest member of the deer family. The flesh of Canadian moose is comparable to venison. It is prepared like deer.

MOQUE (Belgian confectionery)—Put 3¾ cups (500 grams) of sieved flour in a ring on the table. In the middle put 4 or 5 crushed cloves, a pinch of bicarbonate of soda, a pinch of salt, ⅜ cup (100 grams) of moist brown sugar, the same weight of molasses and 1¼ cups (300 grams) of butter.

Mix thoroughly, working in the flour a little at a time. Roll the dough into the shape of a long sausage. Stand it in a cool place and leave it for several hours.

Next day, cut the dough 'sausage' into slices ⅛ inch thick. Put these rounds of dough, spaced out a little, on a buttered baking sheet.

Bake in a moderate oven.

MORAY. MURÈNE—All the histories of ancient Rome speak with enthusiasm of this fish. Wealthy gourmets of imperial Rome, it is said, bred moray, whose flesh grew more succulent in the magnificent breeding-grounds which were maintained at great expense.

It is probably as a result of one or two isolated incidents, much exaggerated in the telling, that the legend grew up that slaves were thrown as food to the moray.

The moray, which is somewhat similar to an eel in appearance, is a carnivorous fish of extreme voracity.

In cookery, the moray is prepared in the same way as eel. See EEL.

MOREL. MORILLE—The name of a fungus which is one of the best growing in France. It is to be found in the spring on the fringe of woods. There are various species, the most highly prized being the little black pointed morels found in mountainous country.

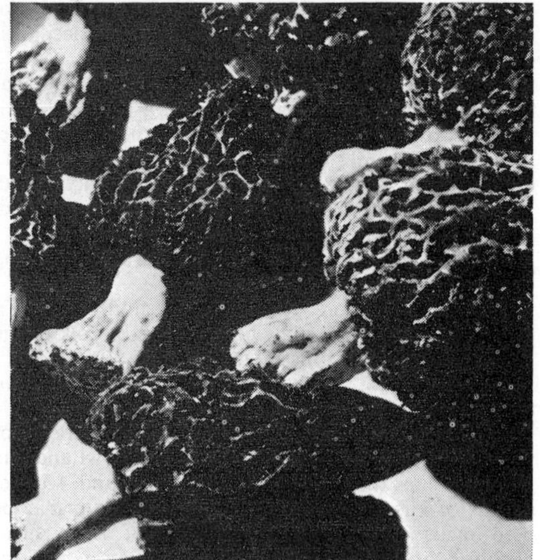

Morels (*Kollar*)

To prepare for cooking, trim, wash in several waters and very carefully remove any dirt in the interstices of the honeycombed caps.

Simmer them in butter in a covered pan in the same way as cèpes.

When the morels are large, divide them in halves or quarters before cooking.

Morels can also be fried without first simmering them in butter. In this case they must be thoroughly dried after washing.

MORELLO CHERRY. GRIOTTE—This species of cherry is dark red or almost black. It has a tough skin. The pulp, which is red, is firm, sweetish, but sometimes bitter.

All recipes for the preparation of cherries are suitable for morello cherries. See CHERRY.

MORINGA—The Ben-nut tree, or the Horseradish tree, a shrub native of Egypt.

The fruit of this tree, about the size of hazel-nuts, yield an oil greatly valued in perfumery.

The pods, when fresh and very ripe, are edible. They are called *desert dates*. They are added to food to enhance its taste.

MORNAY (A LA)—A method of preparing certain food, principally fish. All dishes *à la Mornay* are covered with *Mornay sauce* (see SAUCE).

MORTADELLA. MORTADELLE—A large type of sausage of Italian origin. The mortadella of Bologna has the highest reputation. Mortadella sausages are also made in France, notably in Lyons and Paris. These are excellent.

Mortadella is not one of the pork products which can be made in household kitchens. It is an industrial product and is sold by all French pork-butchers. It is served as an hors-d'oeuvre.

MORTAR. MORTIER—A kind of bowl made of marble, stone, metal or wood in which forcemeats and other mixtures are pounded or mixed with a pestle made of hard wood.

MOSCOVITE—Sweets *à la moscovite* are prepared in various ways.

Cold *moscovites* are similar to *bavarois* (*Bavarian creams*)*. Moscovites, however, are different in that they are usually made in a hexagonal mould with a hinged lid and embedded in crushed ice and salt.

The name *moscovite* is also used of an iced *bombe** with kummel and almonds, and of an ice pudding flavoured with vanilla and also made in a hexagonal mould. In this case the ice cream is made with a hole in the centre which is filled with fresh fruit and *Chantilly cream* (see CREAMS).

Moscovite jellies are made with fruit or liqueurs in a hermetically sealed mould and embedded in ice and salt. The distinctive feature of these jellies is that they are covered with a frosting of rime.

Fruit moscovite. MOSCOVITE AUX FRUITS—Rub through a fine sieve enough of whatever fruit is selected to produce $2\frac{3}{8}$ cups (8 decilitres) of pulp. Add $2\frac{1}{4}$ cups (300 grams) of fine sugar and $\frac{2}{3}$ ounce (20 grams) of gelatine dissolved in water. Mix well and put it to set on ice, stirring constantly. Flavour with kirsch.

When it begins to set, add 2 cups (6 decilitres) of very stiffly whipped fresh cream. Mix.

With this mixture, fill a moscovite mould. Close it, and, to ensure that it is hermetically sealed, rub a little butter round the rim of the lid.

Put the mould in a bucket or bowl on a bed of crushed ice sprinkled with coarse salt. Surround and cover with crushed ice and salt. Wrap in a cloth. Leave to stand for 2 hours. Turn out like a plain ice cream.

Note. Proceeding as indicated above, moscovites can be made using apricots, pineapple, cherries, strawberries, peaches, pears, etc. They can also be frozen in a deep-freeze.

This sweet can also be flavoured with various liqueurs.

MOSTELLE—A fish of the gade family, found mainly in the Mediterranean. This fish is very delicately flavoured. It is scarcely possible to eat it except in the places where it is caught, as it deteriorates when transported.

All recipes for whiting are suitable for *mostelle.*

MOTHER OF VINEGAR. MÈRE DE VINAIGRE—A thick, corrugated film which forms during the acidulation of wine, as a result of the action of *mycoderma aceti.*

MOUFFLON. MOUFLON—A name given to various breeds of wild sheep.

The *European moufflon*, which is the parent stock of the domestic sheep, is mainly found in Sardinia and Corsica, where it is known as *mufione* or *mufoli.*

The *African 'cuffed' moufflon* is about the size of an ordinary sheep.

The *American moufflon*, also called *mountain ram*, is a slender animal with very long legs. Its horns, which in the male are very large and thick, come right down to the eyes, and form an almost complete spiral. Its coat, short and wiry, is brown in colour. All these animals are edible. Their meat is very similar to that of the chamois.

Before cooking in any way, moufflon meat must be steeped for a long time in an aromatic marinade. It can be roasted and made into a *ragoût** or civet. All recipes for mutton and roebuck are suitable for moufflon.

MOULD. MOULE—A hollow receptacle made in different materials and different shapes, used in cooking and confectionery.

MOULDING. MOULAGE—The process of putting a liquid or semi-liquid in a mould, whose shape it takes when it sets or thickens either by congealing or cooking.

In former times, moulded plinths were much used for the presentation of cold dishes, but this practice has almost disappeared today.

MOULIN-A-VENT—A red Burgundy wine. It is made from grapes grown in the Mâcon district in the vineyards of the communes of Thornis, Moulin-à-Vent and Romanèche. Mâconnais red wines are full-bodied, very smooth with a most delicate aroma. They deteriorate rather quickly when bottled, depositing a film on the inside of the bottle. After only a few years they change in colour to what is known as 'onion-skin'.

MOUSSACHE—Manioc flour used in the manufacture of tapioca.

MOUSSAKA—A dish of Rumanian origin, now made also in a number of Eastern countries. For a recipe see MUTTON, *Moussaka of mutton.*

MOUSSES—In cooking and confectionery this term is used of a number of very different dishes, mostly served cold and even iced, though a few can be eaten hot.

SAVOURY MOUSSES. MOUSSES D'ENTRÉES.

Mousse of fish—See FISH, *Fish mousse.*

Mousse of foie gras—*Method.* Pound with a white of egg in a mortar, 4 ounces (125 grams) of raw chicken or veal with no skin or gristle. Rub through a fine sieve.

Put this mixture in a bowl and add 4 ounces (125 grams) of raw foie gras and 1⅝ ounces (50 grams) of raw truffles, both rubbed through a sieve. Season.

Mix these ingredients on ice, working with a spatula and blending in, a little at a time, ½ cup (a decilitre) of thick cream.

At the last moment, add 2 stiffly beaten whites of egg. Put in a soufflé dish, cover, and cook standing in a pan of water for 25 to 30 minutes.

Serve with this mousse *Madeira* or *Perigueux sauce* (see SAUCE).

Note. This dish is sometimes called *Soufflé of foie gras.* It is served as an hors-d'oeuvre or light entrée.

Cold foie gras and poultry mousses—See FOIE GRAS and CHICKEN.

Cold quail mousse—See QUAIL.

DESSERT MOUSSES. MOUSSES D'ENTREMETS.

Chocolate mousse

Chocolate mousse—MOUSSE AU CHOCOLAT—Make *Chantilly cream* (see CREAMS) using 3 cups (6 decilitres) of fresh cream.

Meanwhile melt 7 ounces (200 grams) of vanilla-flavoured (bitter-sweet) chocolate with 4 tablespoons of hot water over a gentle heat until it forms a smooth paste. Add to this paste 1½ cups (200 grams) of fine sugar and 6 tablespoons of water. When it is thoroughly mixed, bring to the boil, then leave to stand until quite cold, before adding the cream.

Take the same precautions as when incorporating stiffly beaten whites of egg.

Note. To give more body to the Chantilly cream, a small quantity of very stiffly beaten white or yolk of egg may be added to it, if necessary.

Fruit mousses. MOUSSES DE FRUITS—Here, as an example, is a recipe for *Apricot mousse.*

Rub through muslin 1 pound 6 ounces (625 grams) of very ripe apricots. Collect the purée in a bowl and mix with it 2 cups (250 grams) of icing sugar and 4 tablespoons of kirsch. Instead of icing sugar, syrup may be used made with 1 cup (250 grams) of lump sugar dissolved in a few spoonfuls of hot water, boiled for 2 minutes and left to get quite cold before it is added to the apricot purée.

Take a mould with a cover which can be hermetically sealed. Line with fine white paper.

Whisk ½ pint of thick fresh cream until it is stiff enough to fill the gaps between the struts of the beater. Mix this cream with the apricot purée.

Put this mixture in the prepared mould, covering with a disc of white paper. Close the mould and seal round the rim with butter. (In contact with the ice the butter will harden. The mould being thus hermetically sealed, there can be no seepage of salt water.) Place the mould in a container on a deep bed of ice, salt and saltpetre. Surround with layers of ice and saltpetre and cover with the same mixture.

Leave to chill for 2 hours.

Just before serving, wash the mould, dry it, turn out the mousse and remove the paper.

Following this same recipe, mousses can be made with various kinds of fruit, such as pineapple, cherries, peaches, pears, plums, etc.

Note. The term *mousse* is also used to describe sweet jellies made with fruit or flavoured with liqueurs. These jellies are whisked on ice until they begin to set. They are then poured into jelly moulds and left to set on ice.

Mousses made in this way can also be served in salad bowls or other glass bowls.

Iced mousses. MOUSSES GLACÉES—These are iced sweets, usually made from *bombe mixture.* See ICE CREAMS AND ICES.

MOUSSEAU—A type of French bread made from wheaten flour.

MOUSSELINE—A name given to various preparations, most of which have a large or small quantity of whipped cream added to them.

This term is in particular used of little moulds made from various pastes enriched with cream (poultry, game, fish, shell-fish, foie gras). These are shaped in little moulds or served in paper cases.

These *mousselines* are served hot or cold. If cold, they are also known as small *aspics.*

Mousseline is also used as an adjective to denote a sauce enriched with whipped cream (thus: *mayonnaise mousseline, hollandaise mousseline*). It is also used of the paste or forcemeat used to make fish-balls and mousses.

The term *mousseline* is much used in confectionery to designate certain cakes and pastries made of delicate mixtures (e.g. *Brioche mousseline*).

MOUSSELINE—This cake is made as follows:

Work together $2\frac{1}{4}$ cups (300 grams) of fine sugar, 8 yolks of egg and a little powdered vanilla. When the mixture is very frothy, add to it $\frac{3}{4}$ cup (250 grams) of cornflour (cornstarch) and sifted cake flour mixed in equal parts, and 8 very stiffly beaten whites of egg.

Put this mixture in Genoese cake tins, buttered and dusted with sugar. Bake in a moderate oven.

Note. Mousseline cakes may be filled with various creams, with vanilla, coffee, chocolate or other flavouring. They are iced with liqueur-flavoured icing.

MOUTARDELLE—A kind of horseradish, which is eaten in the same way as horseradish.

MOYEU—Old French word for the yolk of an egg. Some culinary authorities aver that the word *moyeunnaise* was derived from *moyeu* and was later corrupted into *mayonnaise*. Other authorities question this etymology, and believe that *mayonnaise* comes from *Mahon* and that following the victory of Port-Mahon Marshal the Duke of Richelieu thus named the cold sauce made with yolk of egg and oil (see SAUCE).

There are authorities, Carême among them, who hold that the famous cold sauce should really be called *magnonnaise*.

MUGWORT. BARBOTINE—Name sometimes given in *tansy*, a plant which is also called *herbe aux vers* in French (worm herb), because of its anthelmintic properties.

In the north of France, this aromatic plant is used for flavouring certain cakes and dishes.

In the olden days, tansy or mugwort was used in England for flavouring ale.

MULBERRY. MÛRE—The fruit of the mulberry tree, which the Romans are said to have prized highly. It is sweet but rather tasteless, and is seldom eaten raw. A syrup is made from it and its juice is used to colour wines.

The fruit of the bramble or wild mulberry is stewed and used in jams and jellies. A syrup is also made from it which has a slightly tart flavour.

MULE—Mule meat is highly prized, except when it is musky in flavour. All recipes for horsemeat are suitable for mule.

GREY MULLET. MUGE, MULET—A fish found in coastal waters. This fish has a protuberance in the middle of the lower jaw which corresponds to an indentation in the upper jaw. Its body is elongated, with rather narrow flanks. It is covered with large broad scales. There are a number of varieties, the most common being the *striped mullet* and the *grey mullet*.

In France this fish is sometimes called *poisson sauteur* (leaping fish), because of its great agility. Flattening itself on the surface of the water and spreading its tail in a brusque movement, the mullet leaps sideways to great heights.

The flesh of this fish is white, fatty, delicate and easy to digest. All recipes for bass are suitable for grey mullet. See BASS.

Botargo is made mainly from the roe of this fish.

RED MULLET. ROUGET—The name *Rouget* is given in French to quite different types and species of sea fish which have nothing in common except their red colouring.

Two sorts may be distinguished: first, red mullet, which have two barbels on their lower jaw; second, gurnets, recognisable by their large bony heads as well as their three pectoral rays. The Mediterranean *rouget*, which is of the mullet type, has a red back and flanks and belly that are pink and silver without longitudinal bands; its head is heavy and has two barbels on the lower jaw; its tail is cankerous. The white flesh is very fine and delicate.

The American mullet is the most important food fish in southern U.S.A. It is marketed from $\frac{1}{2}$ to 5 pounds.

Those who really enjoy red mullet eat it grilled and accompanied by *Maître d'hôtel butter* (see BUTTER) or one of the special sauces for grilled fish.

For many of these connoisseurs this fish must be cooked without being cleaned out first and even without having its scales removed. It is sometimes known as *Bécasse de mer* (sea woodcock) a name which suggests that its inside may be eaten.

Red mullet à la Bercy. ROUGET À LA BERCY—Make a few shallow cuts across the mullet if it is scaled; season with salt and pepper, brush with oil and cook in the grill at a gentle heat.

Set on a serving dish. Cover with half-melted *Bercy butter* (see BUTTER, *Compound butters*).

Red mullet à la bordelaise. ROUGET À LA BORDELAISE—Make a few shallow cuts across the back of the mullet. Brush with oil, season and grill under a gentle heat.

Set on a long dish; garnish with fresh parsley and lemon and serve *Bordelaise sauce* (see SAUCE) made with white wine separately.

Red mullet en caisse. ROUGET EN CAISSE—Grill the red mullet (or sauté it in butter). Put it into a rectangular paper case, or aluminium foil, oiled and dried in the oven, the bottom coated with *Duxelles sauce* or any other suitable sauce. Coat the fish with the same sauce. Cover with breadcrumbs, sprinkle with oil or melted butter. Put in the oven for a few moments.

Note. Mullet *en caisse* may be made by following the instructions given above, in the following styles: *à la bordelaise**, *à la duxelles**, *à l'italienne**, *à la moelle**, *à la niçoise**, and *à la provençale**.

Red mullet with fennel. ROUGET AU FENOUIL—Put the mullet, with a few light incisions, across the back and seasoned with salt and pepper, into a fireproof dish, lined with 2 tablespoons (25 grams) of chopped onions gently cooked in oil, mixed, after they are cooked, with $1\frac{1}{2}$ tablespoons of chopped fresh fennel.

Cover with breadcrumbs; sprinkle with a little oil. Cook in the oven at a gentle heat. When cooking is finished sprinkle over a little lemon juice and chopped parsley.

Fillets of red mullet à l'anglaise. FILLETS DE ROUGET À L'ANGLAISE—Fillet the mullet raw. Trim the fillets, season with salt and pepper; flour them; coat in egg and breadcrumbs.

Cook in butter, browning them on both sides. Set on a serving dish with *Maître d'hôtel butter* (see BUTTER) on top.

Fried red mullet. ROUGET FRIT—Using red mullet make a few light incisions and proceed as described in recipe for *Fried bass*. See BASS.

Red mullet au gratin. ROUGET AU GRATIN—Cooked like *Sole au gratin*. See SOLE.

Grilled red mullet. ROUGET GRILLÉ—Score, season, oil

and grill the mullet on a gentle heat, as for *Grilled bass* (see BASS) Serve with *Maître d'hôtel butter* (see BUTTER) or with one of the special sauces for grilled fish (see SAUCE).

Red mullet à l'indienne. ROUGET À L'INDIENNE—Sauté in oil the mullet lightly scored across the back, seasoned and floured.

Set on a serving dish. Pour *Curry sauce* (see SAUCE) over it. Surround with little heaps of tomatoes cooked in butter. Serve *Rice à l'indienne** separately.

Red mullet à l'italienne. ROUGET À L'ITALIENNE—Score the mullet, season it and sauté it in butter (or grill it).

Set on a serving dish the bottom of which is lined with *Italian sauce* (see SAUCE).

Coat with the same sauce; cover with breadcrumbs, sprinkle with melted butter and brown in the oven for a few minutes. Sprinkle with chopped parsley.

Red mullet à la meunière. ROUGET À LA MEUNIÈRE—Proceed as for *Bass à la meunière**.

Red mullet à la moelle. ROUGET À LA MOELLE—Grill the mullet and serve it with *Marrow sauce* handed separately (see SAUCE).

Red mullet à la Nantaise. ROUGET À LA NANTAISE—Grill the mullet, seasoned with salt and pepper and brushed with oil. When grilled take the liver from the fish, taking care not to tear it.

Add this liver, crushed, to the following sauce, which will have been prepared separately.

Reduce (simmer down) ¾ cup (1½ decilitres) of white wine to which has been added a tablespoon of finely chopped shallot. Add a little dissolved meat glaze, a little butter and some lemon juice. Put this sauce in a flat dish. Set the mullet upon it. Surround with half-slices of lemon with fluted edges.

Red mullet à la niçoise I. ROUGETS À LA NIÇOISE—Season the mullet with salt and pepper, flour lightly and brown quickly on both sides in oil in a frying pan. Put them in a long fireproof dish, the bottom of which has been lined with a layer of tomatoes cooked to a pulp and flavoured with tarragon. See TOMATOES.

Put on top of the mullet anchovy fillets cut into thin strips. Cover with breadcrumbs; sprinkle with olive oil. Cook in the oven for 6 to 8 minutes. When taking the fish from the oven set on each a round of peeled lemon.

Red mullet à la niçoise II. ROUGETS À LA NIÇOISE—Season one mullet with salt and pepper, brush with olive oil and grill under a gentle heat.

Set on a long dish the bottom of which has been spread with a layer of tomatoes cooked to a pulp and flavoured with tarragon. Put on the fish fillets of anchovies cut into thin strips and rounds of lemon.

Note. Red mullet à la niçoise is often garnished with black olives (unstoned) and also with capers.

Red mullet à l'orientale—See HORS-D'OEUVRE, *Cold hors-d'oeuvre*.

Red mullet en papillote. ROUGET EN PAPILLOTE—Grill the mullet; enclose it between two layers of *Duxelles sauce* (see SAUCE) in a sheet of paper cut heart-shaped and oiled. Close up the paper, put it on a dish, put it in the oven for a few moments to make it puff up. Serve immediately.

Red mullet à la provençale. ROUGET À LA PROVENÇALE—Prepared as for *Bass à la provençale*. See BASS.

Red mullet with shallots. ROUGET À L'ÉCHALOTE—Put the mullet, with a few light incisions down the back and seasoned with salt and pepper, in a fireproof dish, spread with a layer of chopped shallots cooked almost dry in white wine. Sprinkle over 2 tablespoons of dry white wine. Dot with small pieces of butter. Begin cooking on the stove, then cook in the oven at a moderate temperature, basting frequently. Sprinkle over chopped parsley and a little lemon juice. Serve in the dish in which it was cooked.

MULLIGATAWNY HOT-POT (Creole cookery). MOULOUCOUTANI, BOUILLON DE FEU—A very highly spiced dish which contains curry-powder and a special curry paste. This dish, which has a great deal of sauce, is served in soup plates, with creole rice served separately.

Method. Take a fairly young chicken. Put it to brown very slightly in a pan with fat. Remove it and keep hot. In this fat, cook a saucerful of finely chopped onions. Do not brown. Cook also a large fresh tomato, chopped. When these ingredients are very tender, add a heaped tablespoon of Indian curry-powder, garlic, thyme, parsley and ginger thoroughly pounded together in a mortar. Stir this mixture several times. Joint (cut up) the chicken as for *Chicken sauté** and put it in the pan with the other ingredients. Allow the chicken to become coated with the mixture, then moisten little by little with clear chicken stock prepared the day before. Shortly before serving, mix a spoonful of curry paste in a little of this stock and pour into the sauce. Simmer gently for at least 4 hours.

MUSCADEL. VIN DE MUSCAT—A sweet dessert wine made from muscat grapes.

MUSCADELLE—A winter pear with a musky flavour.

MUSCADET—A wine made in the vineyards of the lower Loire. It has something of the flavour of muscadel.

MUSCAT—White or black grapes with a musky flavour.

MUSETTE (EN)—In former times this was the name given to a shoulder of beef boned, rolled in the form of a bladder and braised. This joint, rolled in the same way, was also called *en ballon*.

MUSHROOMS. CHAMPIGNONS—Cryptogamus plants, devoid of chlorophyll, of which there are a great number of species, some edible, others poisonous. We should remember that apart from their botanical characteristics *there is no empirical means of distinguishing the good from the bad;* that the blackening of a silver object or of an onion provides absolutely no guarantee, and even if it is possible to make certain fungi safe for consumption by a preliminary boiling in salted water or vinegar (to the detriment of their flavour), this proceeding is without avail for fungi which contain amanita-toxin, the most deadly of all.

It is wise, therefore, if one has no knowledge and no experience of identifying mushrooms, to be satisfied with cultivated mushrooms, which are found at all greengrocers and markets and are perfectly safe, and which are anyway one of the best species.

As far as wild mushrooms are concerned, if one wishes to gather them, it is necessary to learn to identify the edible kinds, recognised as such in the locality, and at the same time to recognise the dangerous species, fairly easy if one does not burden oneself with the whole gamut of scientific classification.

In fact, one can make an arbitrary division of mushrooms into three groups: on the one hand, the species which are very poisonous and dangerous, then those which are not only edible, but really of excellent flavour and worth cooking, and between these two groups the immense quantity of mushrooms which are, some suspect, some edible, but without gastronomic interest, except for those passionate devotees whose attention we should direct to the treatises of experts so that they may distinguish, among the Lepiotae, the Russulae, the Lactarius, the Hydnums, the Clavaires, etc., the suspect from the edible.

The consumption of these species would only be of interest if their nutritive value had been clearly demonstrated, which is not the case. Certainly analyses indicate an impressive proportion of albuminous substances and of mineral salts, a special sugar, trehalose, and a little lecithin; unfortunately most of these substances are without value, either because they are not assimilable in this particular form, or because the cellulose which encloses them is not soluble by the digestive juices.

It follows that mushrooms can hardly be considered as food, but more as a condiment, a role which classic cookery has always allotted to them.

Among the dangerous mushrooms the following should be recognised:

Amanita phalloides (L'AMANITE PHALLOIDE, ORONGE VERTE OU ORONGE CIGUË) the most dangerous of all, nearly always mortal. The mushroom has a rounded cap which later flattens out, dirty green in colour, fading to a yellowish brown, sometimes bluish, sometimes a paler yellow. It has white gills, a white ring, a long stem, narrower at the top, swollen at the base, in the form of a cup enclosed in a sheath or volva, which is only seen on digging it out of the ground. The spores are colourless.

Amanita verna (L'AMANITE VERNA, PRINTANIÈRE) which is probably only a variety of Amanita phalloides, has a cap of the same form, white, shining, dotted with the remains of the volva; white flesh, white gills, a white ring around the stalk which has a tendency to drop away.

Both these species are particularly poisonous and are responsible for the majority of deaths from eating mushrooms.

Amanita pantherina (L'AMANITE PANTHERINA, FAUSSE GOLMOTTE) has first of all a rounded cap, then becoming curved, then flattening out. The colour is variable, brown, greyish-red, the colour of dead leaves, sometimes dark yellowish green, almost always covered with scales (the debris of the volva) which sometimes disappear after prolonged rain. White gills, white ring, a white stalk, whose swollen base buried below ground bears two or three circular ridges. Not found in U.S.A.

Amanita muscaria (L'AMANITE MUSCARIA, TUE-MOUCHES FAUSSE ORONGE). Its cap, of the same form as the preceding species, is a brilliant vermillion red or orange red covered with whitish debris from the volva, except after heavy rain, white gills, a white ring; the base of the stem, underground, is covered with white scales.

Amanita citrina (L'AMANITE CITRINE) is less poisonous than the preceding species. It has even been the subject of rehabilitation and is eaten in certain areas, but it should be regarded at least as suspect. This fungus has a citron yellow cap, or greenish yellow, sometimes almost white, covered with the debris of the yellowish volva.

The gills are white, the stalk is fairly tall, swollen at the base. There is a white ring which does not become detached.

Apart from *Amanita verna*, these species appear particularly in summer and autumn in the woods.

Besides these poisonous species the Amanita group includes some highly esteemed mushrooms, *Amanita caesarea* (*oronge*), *Amanita rubescens* (*golmotte*), and *Amanitopsis fulva* and *A. vaginata* (*Coucoumelle*).

Amanita caesarea (L'ORONGE) is a magnificent mushroom, rather rare; it has in the first place the form of an egg as long as it is enclosed in the volva, then, when this tears, the red or orange cap appears, first domed, then convex, never covered with scales, but sometimes one can see the traces (two or three fragments) of the volva. The cap is gleaming, sometimes a little slimy in damp weather, is easily detachable and reveals very white flesh. The gills are large, *yellow*, never attached to the stem; the stalk is cylindrical, yellow, swollen at the foot, surrounded with a white volva; a yellow ring, which tends to drop off. Found in the woods at the end of summer and in autumn. Occasionally found in Massachusetts and New York in U.S.A.

Poisonous mushrooms: 1. Amanita citrina (suspect); 2. Volvaria gloiocephala (suspect); 3. Amanita phalloides (deadly); 4. Amanita verna (deadly); 5. Amanita muscaria (poisonous); 6. Amanita pantherina (poisonous)

Amanita rubescens (LA GOLMOTTE, warty caps) has a convex cap which later on becomes flatter, brownish red, wine-coloured, more or less dark, presenting whitish or whitish-yellow scales. The flesh is pinkish or white, turning to pink when in contact with the air, the stalk is hollow, thick, yellow or whitish pink, with a deepening wine-coloured tinge at the base. The gills are white or pinkish. Found in clearings from the end of spring until autumn.

Amanitopsis fulva and **Amanitopsis vaginata** (U.S.A. **Sheathed Amanitopsis**) (COUCOUMELLE, grisette, tawny grisette). This has a domed cap, then spreading out, grey, lead-coloured, yellowish brown, or beige, usually free of debris from the volva, but sometimes bearing large white patches of volva. It never has a ring on the stalk. The stem is slender, white or slightly coloured, hardly swollen at the base which remains enclosed by the persistent volva, white or coloured. The gills are white, and are never joined to the stalk. It is found particularly in autumn.

As well as the *Amanitae*, here are some spring mushrooms:

Morel, Morchella esculenta (MORILLES) whose various varieties do not lend themselves to any confusion with dangerous species, and are among the most sought after mushrooms. They have a rounded or oval shape, beige, greyish or almost black according to the species, the cap indented with honeycombing; the stalk is often shorter than the cap. Morels are found in spring in clearings and copses. In U.S.A. they are found in sandy soil during warm weather in May and June.

Blewits (MOUSSERON VRAI) Tricholoma species; convex cap, often wavy at the edges, matt, smooth, creamy in colour, sometimes greyish, pinkish or lilac coloured; the stem is short, thick, cylindrical, full; the gills are sinuous, white or cream, joined to the stem. The blewit grows in rings (fairy rings) in the spring in meadows, on the borders of woods; it is found sometimes, but rarely, in autumn. In U.S.A. this species, known as *Masked Tricholoma* is found from September to freezing weather in thin woods and open grassy places.

Fairy ring champignon; Marasmus oreades (FAUX MOUSSERON) is sometimes found in spring but more often in autumn; it grows in circles in dry meadows and pastures, on the edges of paths. The cap is yellow, thin, without much substance, with a central prominence, smooth at the edges; the gills are whitish, uneven, fairly wide apart, and not joined to the stalk. This mushroom, which is never attacked by insects, is sought for its aroma. In U.S.A. it is found from May to October.

Boletus (LES BOLETS) are found in spring and autumn. There are numerous species. Instead of gills they have fleshy tubes on the underside of the cap, white or yellowish, sometimes red, turning to a greenish hue in time, when they are detachable from the cap in the same manner as the choke of an artichoke when cooked. According to the species, the cap is light or dark brown, sometimes very dark brown; the thick stalk, substantial, white or brown, never has a trace of red in the edible species; the white flesh does not turn green when it comes in contact with the air. Even though there are edible species with red tubes, one would do well to avoid them, in spite of the fact that the most suspect cèpe, *Boletus satanas*, only gives rise to serious indigestion; there is one cèpe of a pale yellow colour which without being poisonous is uneatable on account of its bitterness.

The mushrooms that follow are only found in summer and autumn.

Psalliota arvensis (PRATELLE, horse mushroom) has a globular cap of a rosy tint, which later spreads out, thick and white, a strong stem, thickened at the base, rosy white gills, white flesh, yellowing a little when in contact with the air, and a large double ring which distinguishes it from the following:

Lepiota procera (COULMELLE, the Parasol mushroom) has an ovoid cap, becoming rounder and finally spread out, domed in the centre, brown or brownish grey, a hollow stem, rather tall; the gills are numerous, and stand away from the stalk; the flesh is rather soft and insubstantial and white, turning pink or reddish in the air.

Cantharellus cibarius (CHANTERELLE, GIROLLE) has a form in the shape of a cup, with a frilled edge, and thick swollen vein-like gills, the colour of yolk of egg, dark or paler (according to humidity); the stalk fleshy, short, sometimes non-existent. This mushroom cannot be confused with any other. In U.S.A. the *chanterelle hygrophorus* (Hygrophorus miniatus) is found from June to September in clusters, in bogs or on dry hillocks. It closely resembles the French *girolle*.

The craterelle, called sometimes in France the horn of plenty or trumpet of death, belongs to the chanterelle family, *Cantharellus tubiformis*, and appears in the woods at the end of summer and in autumn. The mushroom is in the form of a horn, with vein-like gills and frilled edges, nearly black on top, and dark grey on the underside, smooth on top, slightly veined on the underside. The stem is tubular, ash grey or black. Unattractive and tough as it is, this mushroom is sought for as a condiment on account of its smell which recalls that of the truffle. In U.S.A. *Cantharellus floccosus* is found from July to September in woods. Characteristics are the same as the *craterelle*. Many edible and poisonous mushrooms not mentioned here are found in U.S.A. Novices are urged to use only *field mushrooms*, *coral fungi*, *morels* and *puffballs*. Cultivated mushrooms are very widely marketed and are government supervised.

Mushroom poisoning—Leaving aside the mushrooms which are suspect and can produce serious indigestion, there exist two types of poisoning according to the type of poison contained in the fungi.

Muscarine poisoning (Amanita muscaria, A. pantherina, etc.) resembles atropine intoxication.

The start is rapid (1 to 4 hours after eating). It is characterised by an indefinable malaise, rapidly followed by colic, vomiting, diarrhoea, stomach cramps, abundant salivation, followed by nervous disorders (delirium, excitement, fainting, reeling, dilation of the pupils) followed by prostration.

Avoid the use of alcohol which dissolves the poison, and attempt to empty the stomach by administering vomitives (luke-warm water, soapy water, never ipecac); the patient must be kept warm, given frictions, made to inhale ether. The recovery often occurs in one or two days, the convalescence is short. There are, nevertheless, more serious cases, even fatal (20 per cent of cases for *Amanita pantherina*).

Phalline poisoning (more correctly, Amanita-toxin) is much more serious; it is above all caused by *Amanita phalloides* and *Amanita verna.* The beginning of the symptoms is much more delayed (12 to 24 hours after eating, sometimes more), and they manifest themselves by fainting fits, great pain, burning stomach, cramp in various parts of the body; intestinal disturbances take the appearance of cholera symptoms, with incessant vomiting, diarrhoea, often bleeding, pain, cold sweats, cold extremities. The stomach is hypersensitive, and rejects everything, the liver is enlarged and painful. The symptoms occur, reach a crisis, are followed by periods of calm.

The mind is not affected until the final period, when the

pulse slows down, breathing becomes difficult, the patient turns yellow, and then prostration and collapse ensue, all these symptoms manifesting themselves over two or four days at least, lasting sometimes for eight or ten; death follows in 60 per cent of cases; if a recovery is possible it still necessitates a long convalescence.

The emptying of the stomach, which must always be attempted by means of vomitives and stomach douches, has only a small chance of success, the poison being already absorbed.

We must apologise for introducing a rather terrifying picture in a work dedicated to gastronomy, but when one thinks of the too frequent fatal accidents which occur every year from eating poisonous mushrooms, one cannot too often sound a note of warning.

Preparation of mushrooms.

Cultivated mushrooms. CHAMPIGNONS DE COUCHE—Choose 1 pound (500 grams) of very white mushrooms, remove the earthy bottom of the stalk. Wash quickly in a lot of water and as minutely as possible. Drain the mushrooms and dry them. Slice off the stalks on a level with the caps. Pare the caps neatly or groove them by cutting minute and regular incisions.

When one is dealing with cultivated mushrooms which are fresh and firm, it is best neither to groove or even less to attempt any kind of embellishment when peeling them, but simply to pare them neatly. It is, however, common practice in restaurant cookery and in bourgeois cookery to groove them.

Throw them into a boiling liquor called *Blanc à champignons* prepared in the following way: Boil together ½ cup (1 decilitre) of water, 2 tablespoons (40 grams) of butter, the juice of half a lemon and 1 teaspoon (6 grams) of salt. Boil the mushrooms in this liquor for 5 minutes. Turn out into an earthenware vessel with the liquor.

The court-bouillon having once served to cook the mushrooms is used for various preparations: it is added to white sauces, such as *velouté*, *supreme*, *allemande*, *white wine*, etc. It can also be used to prepare hors-d'oeuvre cooked in a marinade.

Another method. Pare the mushrooms or groove them as directed, and rub them with half a lemon; put them in a pan in which a little butter has been melted.

Season with a pinch of salt; moisten with two tablespoons of white stock or with Madeira wine (according to their ultimate use) and simmer with the lid on for 8 minutes. Use according to instructions.

Prepared in this way mushrooms are less white but of better flavour.

Recipes suitable for cultivated mushrooms:

Mushroom barquettes (hot hors-d'oeuvre). BARQUETTES AUX CHAMPIGNONS—Fill puff-paste barquettes with a ragoût of mushrooms cooked in cream, or *à la poulette*. See HORS-D'OEUVRE, *Hot hors-d'oeuvre*.

Mushroom bouchées or patties.—See PATTY SHELLS.

Mushrooms cooked in butter. CHAMPIGNONS AU BEURRE—Slice them into two or three pieces according to their size; season with salt and pepper; sauté them in a frying pan in butter over a lively heat. Transfer to a vegetable dish.

This recipe is applicable to cèpes, field mushrooms, chanterelles, morels, blewits and *oronges* (*Amanita caesarea*).

Mushrooms cooked in cream I. CHAMPIGNONS À LA CRÈME—Slice the mushrooms, season them and simmer them in butter for 8 to 10 minutes.

Cover with boiling cream (½ pint of cream to ½ pound mushrooms) and leave to cook until the cream is almost completely boiled down.

Mushrooms cooked in cream

Add a little fresh cream and stir it in.

This recipe can be applied to cèpes, morels and oronges (*Amanita caesarea*) and to field mushrooms.

Mushrooms cooked in cream II. CHAMPIGNONS À LA CRÈME—Simmer in butter and add some tablespoons of *Cream sauce* (see SAUCE).

Mushroom croquettes and kromeskies—See CROQUETTES AND KROMESKIES.

Mushroom croûte I. CROÛTE AUX CHAMPIGNONS—Simmer the mushrooms in butter. Add a few tablespoons of *Allemande sauce*, or *Béchamel sauce* (see SAUCE) if the dish is to be cooked *au maigre*. Mix together.

Arrange this preparation in a round bread roll which has been hollowed out, buttered and gilded in the oven. Heat for a moment.

This recipe applies to cèpes, clavaires, etc.

Mushroom croûte II. CROÛTE AUX CHAMPIGNONS—Simmer the mushrooms in butter. Dust lightly with flour and moisten with fresh cream. Season. Cook very gently for 12 minutes. Add butter, and finish in the same way as the recipe above.

Little mushroom croûtes (hot hors-d'oeuvre). PETITS CROÛTES AUX CHAMPIGNONS — Prepare a *Mushroom purée**, and fill bread rolls which have been scooped out, or spread on biscuits (crackers).

Mushroom essence—See ESSENCES.

Mushrooms aux fines herbes. CHAMPIGNONS AUX FINES HERBES—The same as *Mushrooms cooked in butter* with the addition of chopped parsley.

This recipe is applicable to cèpes, field mushrooms, chanterelles, morels, blewits, oronges (*Amanita caesarea*).

Mushroom forcemeat or duxelles. FARCE DE CHAMPIGNONS, DUXELLES—This stuffing is usually prepared with cultivated mushroom stalks and peelings, the caps being used for other purposes, but it can be made with other types of mushroom.

Cook gently some chopped onion in a mixture of butter and oil in a casserole, to which a little chopped shallot is added when the onion is almost cooked. Put in the stalks and peelings of the mushrooms which have been chopped up and pressed to extract the moisture. For 1 pound (500 grams) of mushrooms use 4 tablespoons (50 grams) of onion, 2 tablespoons (25 grams) of shallot, 3 tablespoons (50 grams) of butter, 4 tablespoons (50 grams) of oil.

Cook on a lively heat until all the moisture has evaporated. Season with salt and pepper. Add finally a teaspoon of chopped parsley.

Duxelles prepared in this way is used as an element in a large number of preparations.

Mushroom fumet. FUMET DE CHAMPIGNONS—This is the term given to the liquor in which mushrooms have cooked. The liquor is reduced (boiled down) to about a quarter of its original volume.

Mushroom garnish. GARNITURE DE CHAMPIGNONS—Mushrooms which have been sautéed, grilled or cooked in a *blanc à champignons* are added to countless preparations such as *blanquettes, fricassées, escalopes, noisettes* (small slices of fillet, loin, or leg of lamb, pork, etc.), *tournedos*, chicken, sweetbreads, fish, eggs, etc.

Mushrooms à la grecque (cold hors-d'oeuvre). CHAMPIGNONS À LA GRECQUE—Choose very small mushrooms. Cooked in the same way as for *Artichoke à la grecque.*

Grilled mushrooms. CHAMPIGNONS GRILLÉS—Choose large even-sized mushrooms, remove the stalks. Wash them, wipe them, soak them in butter or oil, season, and grill under a gentle heat.

Set on a round dish with *Maître d'hôtel butter* (see BUTTER, *Compound butters*) or as they are, or use according to the directions of the recipe.

Mushrooms à la hongroise. CHAMPIGNONS À LA HONGROISE—Prepared in the same way as *Cèpes à la hongroise* (see below).

Mushroom julienne. JULIENNE DE CHAMPIGNONS—Trim, wash, wipe and pare the mushrooms. Cut them into *julienne** strips, thick or thin according to the use to which they will be put. Season and simmer in butter.

Mushroom ketchup—An English condiment made and sold commercially. It is used in English cookery to season sauces and as a condiment with cold meat. It is prepared as follows:

Peel, trim and wash some fresh mushrooms. Slice them finely. Put them in layers in an earthenware bowl, sprinkling each layer with fine salt. Cover the bowl and leave to macerate for three days in a cool place. Skim each day.

Strain the juice through a stout cloth. Measure the liquid. Put it in a saucepan. Add the following spices for every litre (quart plus 3 ounces) of juice: $\frac{1}{3}$ ounce (10 grams) of fennel-flower, 1 tablespoon (8 grams) of ground mace, $3\frac{1}{2}$ teaspoons (10 grams) of ground ginger, 1 teaspoon (3 grams) of cayenne pepper, 1 teaspoon (3 grams) of grated nutmeg, 1 teaspoon (3 grams) of powdered cloves.

Cook until the liquid forms a syrup. Pour into small bottles. Cork and seal.

Mushrooms à la lyonnaise. CHAMPIGNONS À LA LYONNAISE—The same as *Mushrooms cooked in butter* with chopped onion melted in butter.

Set in a vegetable dish, sprinkle with drops of lemon juice, and chopped parsley, and pour over the mushrooms the hot butter in which they were cooked. All edible mushrooms can be prepared in this way.

Mushrooms in Madeira or in other liqueur wines (garnish). CHAMPIGNONS AU MADÈRE—Sauté the mushrooms in butter. Drain them, deglaze the sauté-pan with the wine indicated; reduce (boil down); add a few tablespoons of thick *Spanish sauce* (see SAUCE); reduce by half and strain through a sieve. Put the mushrooms back into this sauce.

Cultivated mushrooms, field mushrooms, morels, etc., are prepared in this way.

Use according to instructions in the recipe.

Mushrooms in marinade (hors-d'oeuvre). CHAMPIGNONS MARINÉS—Cèpes and cultivated mushrooms can be prepared in a marinade.

See HORS-D'OEUVRE, *Cold hors-d'oeuvre, Marinated cèpes.*

Mushroom omelette. OMELETTE AUX CHAMPIGNONS—Slice the mushrooms thinly, or cut them into dice. Season and sauté in butter.

Add to the beaten eggs and make the omelette in the usual way. See EGGS.

Mushrooms prepared in this way can be used to garnish fried eggs, poached eggs or soft boiled eggs.

All kinds of mushrooms can be used in this way.

Mushroom patties (hot hors-d'oeuvre or garnish). TARTELETTES AUX CHAMPIGNONS—Prepare the mushrooms by cooking them in cream, or in a *Poulette sauce* (see SAUCE). Put the mixture in little short-pastry tarts which have been baked blind beforehand. Sprinkle with dried breadcrumbs or with breadcrumbs fried in butter and drained, or with grated cheese. Brown in the oven.

These patties can also be prepared with mushrooms cut in *julienne*, or in dice, sautéed in butter and combined with a brown or white sauce.

Mushrooms à la poulette I. CHAMPIGNONS À LA POULETTE—Simmer in butter. Add a few tablespoons of *Poulette sauce* (see SAUCE). Set in a vegetable dish, sprinkle with chopped parsley.

Cultivated mushrooms, field mushrooms, cèpes and morels are prepared in this way.

Mushrooms à la poulette II. CHAMPIGNONS À LA POULETTE—Drain the mushrooms as soon as they have been softened in butter. Put a spoonful of flour in the sauté-pan. Mix it and moisten with bouillon or white stock; reduce (boil down) and combine with one or two egg yolks. Finish the sauce with cream and butter, season, and pass through a sieve.

Mushroom powder. POUDRE DE CHAMPIGNONS—Trim and clean the mushrooms (cultivated or other mushrooms). Slice them. Put them on a baking sheet on layers of paper and dry very slowly in the oven or near an open fire. When they are perfectly dry pound them in a mortar, and pass through a fine sieve. The powder is used to flavour various preparations such as ragoûts, sauces and stuffings.

Preserved mushrooms (au naturel). CONSERVES DE CHAMPIGNONS—Sterilize the mushrooms as soon as they have been gathered. Peel them, scrape and wash them in several waters until they are tender. Drain, leave to cool, and put into glass jars. Sterilize by cooking just under the boiling point (212°F.) for an hour and a quarter.

See also HORS-D'OEUVRE, *Cold hors-d'oeuvre, Marinated cèpes.*

Mushroom purée. PURÉE DE CHAMPIGNONS—Prepare in advance $\frac{2}{3}$ cup (2 decilitres) of *Béchamel sauce* (see SAUCE), add to it $\frac{1}{3}$ cup (1 decilitre) of cream and stir it over heat until the quantity is reduced to $\frac{2}{3}$ cup (2 decilitres). Pass through a metal sieve or purée in a blender 1 pound (500 grams) of fresh mushrooms which have been cleaned, and collect the purée into a pan stirring it over heat until all the moisture has evaporated. Add the béchamel, a pinch of salt, a little white pepper, and a little grated nutmeg and stir over the fire for a further few minutes. Take off the fire; stir in 3 tablespoons (50 grams) of butter.

Mushroom rissoles—See RISSOLE.

Mushroom salad. SALADE DE CHAMPIGNONS—Only freshly gathered mushrooms are employed in this way (agarics, morels, or, failing these, cultivated mushrooms).

Trim them, wash them rapidly, wipe them, and cut them up finely, seasoning with oil, lemon juice or vinegar, salt, pepper and chopped herbs. Put in a salad bowl.

One can also apply a salad dressing to little cultivated mushrooms which have been pared and cooked in a *blanc de champignon*, and serve as an hors-d'oeuvre.

Mushroom salpicon. SALPICON DE CHAMPIGNONS—The mushrooms are cut into dice, big or small, according to the use to which they are put, and cooked in butter.

Little mushroom soufflés. PETITS SOUFFLÉS AUX CHAMPIGNONS—Make the soufflé preparation with mushroom purée according to the method given for all soufflés with a vegetable purée base.

Put the preparation into little soufflé dishes. Cook in the oven. See SOUFFLÉ.

Cream of mushroom soup. POTAGE CRÈME DE CHAMPIGNONS—See SOUPS AND BROTHS, *Mushroom velouté soup.*

Mushrooms sous cloche. CHAMPIGNONS SOUS CLOCHE—Choose mushrooms of medium size; trim, wash, remove the stems; season them. Put each one on a round slice of bread, which has been fried in butter or toasted, gills uppermost. Fill each cap with a little *Maître d'hôtel butter* (see BUTTER, *Compound butters*) and a few drops of cream. Set on a round gratin dish. Cover with a glass cloche of the same diameter as the plate. Cook on top of the stove at a low temperature for 15 to 18 minutes.

This recipe is suitable only for cultivated mushrooms.

Stuffed mushrooms. CHAMPIGNONS FARCIS—Choose mushrooms of the same size and weight for this garnish; remove the stalks by breaking them away from the cap. Wash the caps and wipe them.

Arrange them on an oiled or buttered baking tray, season them, moisten them lightly with oil or melted butter and set in the oven for five minutes.

Stuff each cap with a solid spoonful of *duxelles**, arranging the duxelles in the form of a little mould. Dust with fine dried breadcrumbs; sprinkle with oil or butter and brown in the oven.

Mushrooms can be filled with various preparations such as *brunoise** or *mirepoix**, different purées, lean stuffings, risotto, various *salpicons*, etc., in the manner indicated for all those vegetables which are stuffed and browned in the oven. (See GRATIN).

Mushroom tart. TOURTE AUX CHAMPIGNONS—Prepare the mushrooms by cooking them *in cream* or in a *Poulette sauce* (see SAUCE). Arrange in an open tart pastry case (or shell) of *Pâte feuilletée* (see DOUGH).

Mushrooms on toast (hot hors-d'oeuvre). TOASTS AUX CHAMPIGNONS—Grill the mushrooms or sauté them in butter. Arrange them on toast cut in rectangles or rounds, grilled or fried. Sprinkle with fried breadcrumbs. Put in the oven for a moment. Season with freshly ground pepper; sprinkle with chopped parsley. Serve on a napkin.

Mushroom vol-au-vent. VOL-AU-VENT AUX CHAMPIGNONS—Fill a vol-au-vent case with a ragoût of mushrooms cooked in cream or in a *Poulette sauce* (see SAUCE).

Recipes suitable for cèpes and other varieties:

Cèpes à la béarnaise. CÈPES À LA MODE BÉARNAISE—Trim, wash and wipe the cèpes, and dry them by putting them under the grill (broiler) or putting them in the oven.

Insert small pieces of raw garlic into the caps, in the same way as garlic is inserted into a leg of mutton. Season with salt and pepper. Grill them.

Arrange them on a hot plate; cover them at the last moment with a mixture of breadcrumbs fried in very hot oil and chopped parsley.

Cèpes à la bordelaise. CÈPES À LA BORDELAISE—Trim and wash the cèpes and simmer them in butter and lemon juice. Drain them and sponge them. Cut them into slices if they are very large, leave them whole if they are small. Put them in a pan in which some oil has been heated. Season with salt and pepper. Sauté on the fire allowing them to brown slightly.

At the last moment, add for each pound (500 grams) of cèpes the chopped-up stalks, two teaspoons of chopped shallot, 2 heaped tablespoons of freshly grated breadcrumbs, and finally a teaspoon of chopped parsley.

Arrange the cèpes in a dish, sprinkle over them a little lemon juice, and some chopped parsley.

This is how cèpes *à la bordelaise* are prepared in Paris restaurants. In Bordeaux and in south-west France, the cèpes are not seasoned with shallots but with chopped garlic, as in the case of cèpes *à la provençale*, and breadcrumbs are not added to the preparation.

In that same region, cèpes prepared *à la bordelaise* are never browned; they are sometimes cooked in oil, not in a frying pan but in an earthenware casserole.

Cèpes cooked with cream I. CÈPES À LA CRÈME—Cèpes which are white-fleshed and firm are cooked in this way. According to their size they are cut into slices or left whole.

Put the cèpes into a pan in which some butter has been heated. Season with salt and pepper, and simmer them in the butter.

When they are cooked, cover them with fresh boiling cream ($\frac{1}{2}$ pint cream to $\frac{1}{2}$ pound mushrooms). Cook until the cream has almost disappeared.

At the last moment add 3 to 4 tablespoons of fresh cream. Mix. Arrange the cèpes in their sauce in a dish.

A tablespoon of chopped onion which has been lightly fried in butter can be added to the cèpes when they are simmering in butter.

Cèpes cooked with cream II. CÈPES À LA CRÈME—Simmer the cèpes in butter. Moisten with a *Cream Sauce* (see SAUCE) which is not too thick. Cook for a further few minutes. Finish with a little fresh cream.

Cèpes au gratin. CÈPES AU GRATIN—Trim, wash and remove the stalks from some cèpes chosen for their size and firmness. Season with salt and pepper; simmer them in a little butter.

Arrange them in a fireproof dish which has been buttered or oiled, caps downwards. Put on to each cap a good tablespoon of stuffing prepared with the chopped stalks, mixed with breadcrumbs, chopped onion lightly fried in oil or butter, parsley, chopped garlic and seasoning. Press the stuffing into the caps so that it adheres to them properly; sprinkle with grated dried breadcrumbs, and pour over each cap a little melted butter (or oil). Brown gently in the oven.

Cèpes à la grecque (hors-d'oeuvre). CÈPES À LA GRECQUE—Choose small cèpes which are not yet fully grown. Cook them in a *court-bouillon** as for *Artichokes à la grecque**.

Grilled cèpes. CÈPES GRILLÉS—Large white-fleshed cèpes are prepared in this way. Make superficial cuts in the domed caps. Season with salt and pepper. Brush over with oil or melted butter. Cook them under the grill at a moderate temperature.

Serve them with *Maître d'hôtel butter* (see BUTTER, *Compound butters*) separately or placed on the cèpes.

Cèpes à la hongroise. CÈPES À LA HONGROISE—Cook 1 cup (500 grams) of cèpes in butter with 2 good tablespoons of chopped onion (which has been cooked beforehand in butter). Leave them whole if they are small, slice them if they are large. Season with salt and paprika pepper. Cover with boiling cream or with a *Cream sauce* (see (SAUCE) which is not too thick. Cook until the cream is almost entirely reduced.

Add a little butter at the last moment.

Cèpes with Indian sauce. CÈPES À L'INDIENNE—Sauté 1 pound (500 grams) of small cèpes in butter, after paring, washing and drying them. When they are cooked, add

2 tablespoons of chopped onion which have been cooked in butter. Mix while shaking the pan. Simmer gently, and at the last moment add a few tablespoons of *Indian sauce* (see SAUCE).

Cèpes in marinade (hors-d'oeuvre). CÈPES MARINÉS—Little cèpes cooked in a marinade. See HORS-D'OEUVRE, *Cold hors-d'oeuvre.*

Cèpes à la provençale. CÈPES À LA PROVENÇALE—Cook in the same way as for *Cèpes à la bordelaise*, but replacing the shallot with finely chopped onion and adding a little crushed garlic.

Smothered or stewed cèpes I. CÈPES ÉTUVÉS—Choose 1 pound (500 grams) of fresh cèpes of even size. Trim the earthy part of the stem; wash them rapidly, drain and wipe dry. Slice off the stalks on a level with the cap; leave the caps whole or divide them in two if they are too large. Wipe them.

Put them in a pan with a large tablespoon of butter, some drops of lemon juice and a pinch of salt. Simmer with the lid on for 5 minutes.

Turn out into an earthenware terrine with their liquor. Use according to the instructions in the recipe.

Smothered or stewed cèpes II. CÈPES ÉTUVÉS—Wash and trim the cèpes, sponge them, oil them lightly and put them for a few minutes under the grill to make them give off their liquor.

Morels. MORILLES—Trim them, wash them in several waters, and very carefully remove any dirt in the interstices of the honeycombed caps.

Stew them in butter in the same way as cèpes.

When the morels are large, divide them in halves or quarters before cooking.

Morels can also be fried without first stewing them in butter. In this case they must be thoroughly dried after washing.

Chanterelles, blewits, oronges (Amanita caesarea)—All these mushrooms are initially prepared according to the methods prescribed for cèpes and morels. If they are cooked as soon as picked they can be fried in oil or butter without any further treatment save for thorough washing and drying in a cloth.

After being treated in this way, all these mushrooms can be prepared in the ways described above.

MUSHROOM BED. CHAMPIGNONNIÈRE—Place given over to the cultivation of mushrooms, nearly always established in old pits.

MUSK-DEER. CHEVROTIN—Small wild deer found in India, Tibet and also in Africa. It is hunted for its musk, the product secreted in an abdominal pocket. The animal is edible when young.

In the kitchen, all the preparations suitable for *Kid* can also be applied to it. See KID.

MUSLIN BAG. NOUET—A bag used in cooking. Anything to be cooked or infused in liquid and later taken out can be put in one of these bags, which is knotted or tied with string, thus flavouring the liquid without leaving any solid particles in it.

MUSSEL. MOULE—An edible mollusc found in all the oceans of the world, especially in cold regions.

There are two main species of mussel, the *common mussel*, which is the most widespread, and which has a long shell with a very slight roughness along the back, and the *Provence mussel*, with a larger shell, sharper along the edges, which is found at Biarritz, at Bidassoa and on the Mediterranean seaboard. The Provence mussel is bred in salt-water pools along this sheltered coast, at Toulon and Marseilles. It is a little tougher and less highly prized than the common mussel.

A distinction must also be made between wild mussels, gathered in their natural beds and on rocks, and cultivated mussels bred on wooden hurdles. In places exposed to the pounding of the waves, wild mussels are small and leathery; those found in slimy places are uneatable. On the other hand, a number of natural beds in France produce very good mussels (Villerville, Dives, Port-en-Bessin, Quiberon). The mussel-beds of Isigny, which are permanently under water, have to be dredged. These mussels, which can be up to 4½ inches in length and are very curved in shape, enjoy a great reputation under the name of *caïeu d'Isigny*.

Breeding on hurdles produces tender and delicately flavoured mussels. They remain small but are very plump. Hurdle-bred mussels can generally be distinguished from wild mussels by the following characteristics: in the hurdle-bred mussel the edge of the shell opposite the hinge (the frontal edge) is always slightly convex, whereas with wild mussels found in French coastal waters it is always slightly concave.

Poisoning and allergy—Mussels cause skin eruptions and digestive disturbances to some people. Anyone with this kind of sensitivity should avoid eating them.

Mussels gathered in polluted water can spread typhoid infection if they are eaten raw, as is sometimes the case in Provence, but as they are almost always cooked the dangerous microbes are thus destroyed.

On the other hand, a poison secreted by certain diseased mussels cannot be destroyed by cooking, and may cause serious illness and sometimes death. At the very first onset of the symptoms, while the doctor is on his way, purgatives and emetics must be given.

It was once thought that, to avoid the danger, it was enough to put a piece of silver in the cooking water and discard the mussels if the coin turned black. This, however, is not an adequate precaution, because the coin will in fact turn black when the mussels are not very fresh and give off hydrogen sulphide which is not in itself poisonous. The poison in question does not turn silver coins black. A useful precaution is to add a pinch (3 grams) of bicarbonate of soda to every litre of cooking water. This is sufficient to destroy the poison. A little vinegar, added as seasoning, also has a beneficial effect.

It must not be thought either that mussels taken from the hulls of ships covered with copper plating are unhealthy because they contain copper salts. These mussels should, however, be rejected because harbour water is impure and contaminated, and mussels collected in this way often smell of sewage.

Mussels à la bordelaise. MOULES À LA BORDELAISE—Cook in white wine, with a sliced onion, parsley, thyme and bay leaf (as for *Mussels à la marinière*), 2 quarts (litres) of mussels, trimmed, scraped and washed. When the mussels split open, drain them. Put them in a bowl or deep dish after having removed one shell from each mussel. Keep hot.

Make 1 cup (2 decilitres) of vegetable *mirepoix** by cooking the vegetables slowly in butter until very tender. Just before it is ready, add ¾ cup (1½ decilitres) of *Velouté sauce* (see SAUCE). Strain the stock in which the mussels were cooked and moisten the *mirepoix* with it. Add 1 cup (2 decilitres) of fresh cream and 2 tablespoons of tomato purée. Boil down this sauce and whisk in 3 tablespoons (50 grams) of fresh butter, a squeeze of lemon juice and the necessary seasoning. Pour this sauce, boiling hot, over the mussels. Sprinkle with chopped parsley.

Mussels in cream. Moules à la crème—Cook 2 quarts (litres) of mussels as for *Mussels à la marinière**. Put them in a bowl and keep hot.

Strain the stock in which the mussels were cooked and add it to 1½ cups (3 decilitres) of *Béchamel sauce* (see SAUCE). Mix a few tablespoons of fresh cream into this sauce and simmer until it is quite thick.

Finish with 4 tablespoons of cream and a tablespoon of butter. Season and strain through muslin. Bring this sauce to the boil and pour over the mussels.

Curried mussels. Moules au currie (à l'indienne)—Proceed as for *Mussels à la hongroise*, substituting for the paprika indicated in this recipe, a teaspoon of curry powder.

*Rice à l'indienne** is served with mussels prepared in this way.

Fried mussels. Moules frites—Steep shelled mussels for 30 minutes in a marinade of oil, lemon juice and chopped parsley, after having cooked them as for *Mussels à la marinière*.

Just before serving, dip the mussels in a light batter and deep-fry in boiling fat.

Drain and dry in a cloth. Serve in a heap on a napkin, garnished with fried parsley.

Mussels as a garnish—Wash the mussels in several changes of water. Scrape. Cook them in white wine, with sliced onions, parsley, thyme and bay leaves.

Drain and shell them. Use as indicated in the selected recipe.

The cooking stock of the mussels is added to the sauce after having been reduced and strained through muslin.

Mussels à la hongroise. Moules à la hongroise—Cook the mussels as for *Mussels à la marinière*, seasoning them with paprika. Serve in a bowl. Strain the cooking stock through a fine strainer. Cook slowly in butter, until very tender, ½ cup (100 grams) of chopped onions seasoned with a teaspoon of paprika. Moisten with the stock.

Add 3 spoonfuls of *Béchamel sauce* (see SAUCE) and a little fresh cream. Cook until quite thick. Add 2 tablespoons of butter to this sauce. Strain and pour, boiling hot, over the mussels.

Mussels à la marinière I. Moules à la marinière—Line a buttered saucepan with 2 tablespoons of chopped shallot. Add one or two sprigs of parsley, a sprig of thyme and a quarter of a bay leaf. Put in 2 quarts (litres) of mussels, trimmed, scraped and washed.

Add 2 tablespoons of butter cut into very small pieces. Moisten with 1 cup (2 decilitres) of dry white wine. Cook, covered, over a very high flame.

As soon as the mussels are fully opened, drain them. Remove one shell from each, and put them in a bowl. Keep hot. Take the parsley, thyme and bay leaf out of the saucepan. Add 3 tablespoons of butter to the stock. Mix well and pour over the mussels. Sprinkle with chopped parsley.

Mussels à la marinière II. Moules à la marinière—Put in the buttered pan chopped onion (instead of shallot), chopped parsley, a sprig of thyme and a shred of bay leaf.

Lay the mussels on top. Moisten with dry white wine. Season with freshly-ground pepper. Cover and cook hastily. Drain the mussels. Put them in a bowl and keep hot.

Add to the stock 3 to 4 tablespoons of *Velouté sauce* (see SAUCE), based on fish stock, and a squeeze of lemon. Add butter, and mix. Pour this sauce over the mussels. Sprinkle with chopped parsley.

Mussels à la poulette. Moules à la poulette—Cook 2 quarts (litres) of mussels as indicated for *Mussels à la marinière*. Drain and put in a bowl.

Decant the cooking stock. Strain and boil down. Add it to 1½ cups (3 decilitres) of *Poulette sauce* (see SAUCE) based on concentrated fish stock. Add butter to this sauce and a squeeze of lemon juice, and pour over the mussels. Sprinkle with chopped parsley.

Mussels in a border (ring) of rice. Bordure de moules au riz—Scrape and wash a quart (litre) of mussels. Put them in a saucepan with 2 tablespoons (25 grams) of butter, a finely sliced onion, a sprig of thyme, a quarter of a bay leaf and a pinch of pepper. Moisten with ¾ cup (1½ decilitres) of white wine. Bring to the boil. Cover and simmer gently for 5 to 6 minutes. Shell the mussels. Put them in a frying pan. Boil down the stock. Thicken with a tablespoon each of butter and flour kneaded together. Boil for a few seconds. Add more butter. Strain and pour over the mussels. Add a tablespoon of chopped parsley. Heat without boiling. Prepare a *Pilaf of rice** separately. Put it in a buttered border (ring) mould. Press it down well. Just before serving, turn it out on a round dish. Put the *ragoût* of mussels in the middle of the rice border.

Risotto with mussels. Risotto de moules—Prepare the mussels as indicated for *Mussels à la poulette*. Shell them. Strain the cooking sauce and add butter. Put the mussels back in their sauce. Pile this *ragoût* in the middle of a border of risotto (prepared in the usual way). See RICE.

Mussel sauce. Sauce aux moules—A white wine sauce made with the concentrated and strained cooking stock of the mussels, with shelled mussels added.

Mussel soup. Soupe aux moules—Cook the mussels as for *Mussels à la marinière*. Drain and shell. With the cooking stock make a thin *Velouté sauce* (see SAUCE). Enrich this *velouté* with a few tablespoons of fresh cream. Add butter. Rub through a sieve. Put the shelled mussels in it.

MUSTARD. Moutarde—The name of various plants whose seeds are used in the preparation of the condiment known as mustard. The most commonly used are the *white mustard*, with reddish-yellow seeds, *black mustard*, with smaller blackish-red seeds (the leaves of this plant are sometimes used in salad) and *wild mustard* whose oily seeds are mainly used to adulterate the other two varieties.

Mustard was known to the Romans. Imported into Gaul by them, it quickly gained favour as a condiment.

There are a great many formulae for mustard, differing with each manufacturer. English mustard is usually sold as a fine powder (it is a mixture of black and white mustard, with curcuma added). It is mixed with water first before use. French mustards, which are sold in the form of paste, are made with a mixture of white and black powdered mustard seed, often with herbs added. It is mixed with verjuice (Dijon mustard) or unfermented wine (Bordeaux mustard). In Italy, Cremona mustard contains crystallized fruit.

Leaf or Chinese mustard. Moutarde de Chine—This is an herbaceous plant, used in cooking like spinach, of which two varieties are cultivated in France. They are the *moutarde de Chine à feuille de chou* (Brassica juncea) (cabbage-leaf variety) and the *moutarde de Chine frisée* (Brassica erispifolia) (curly variety). They are in season from October into the winter.

This vegetable has rather a strong smell.

Mustard sauce. Sauce moutarde—This sauce is

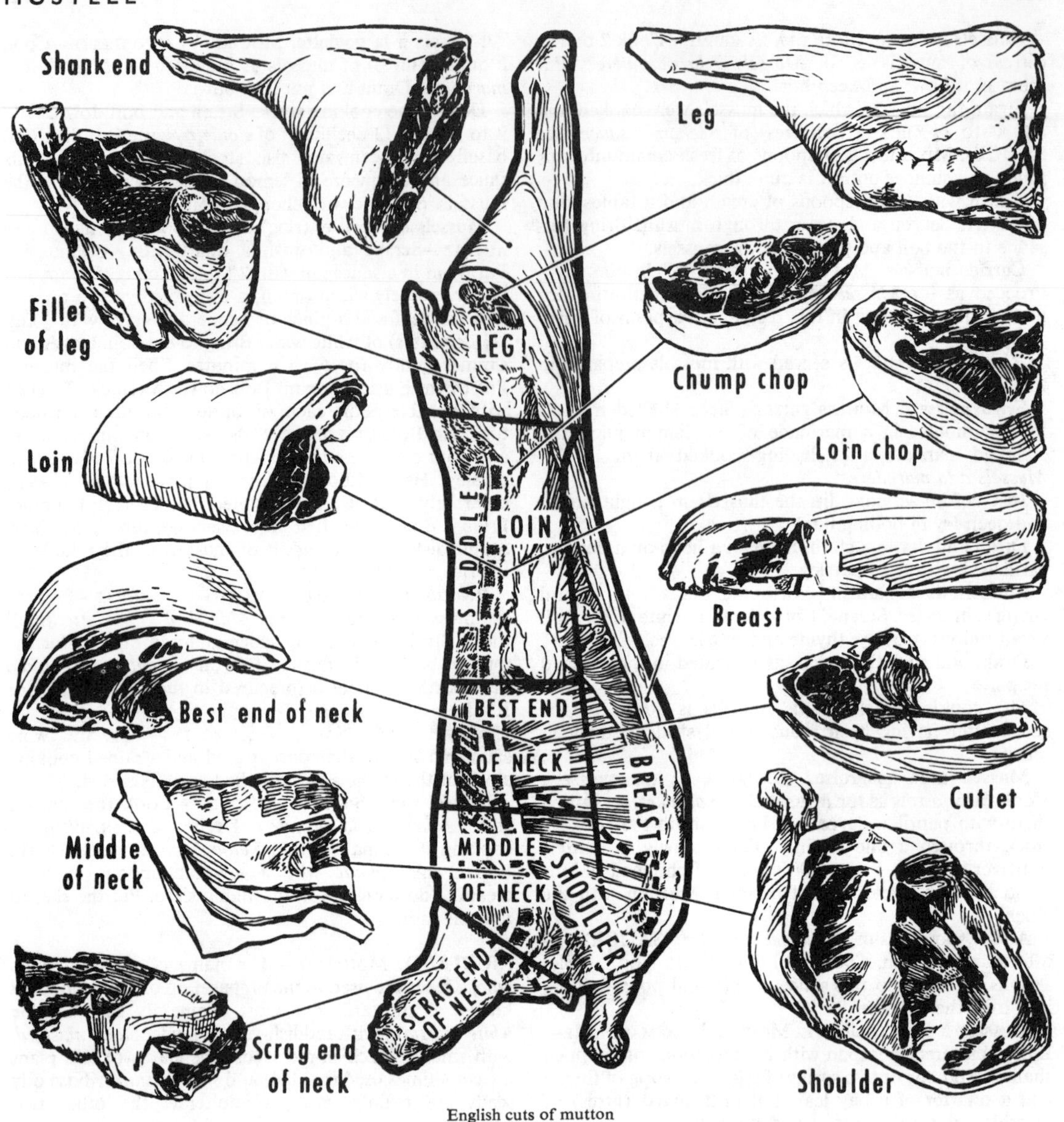

English cuts of mutton

usually served with fish. It is made by adding mustard to *Butter sauce* (see SAUCE). One tablespoon is used to 1¼ cups (2½ decilitres) of sauce.

MUSTÈLE—This fish, which is found mainly in the Mediterranean and which the Italians call *galea* or *pesce moro*, is somewhat similar to the burbot. Its liver is highly prized by connoisseurs. All recipes for *Burbot** and *Cod-burbot** are suitable for this fish.

MUTTON. Mouton—Mutton, somewhat fatter and darker in colour than beef, has much the same properties as other red meat. It is believed to be a little more digestible, though this depends on the cut.

In France *salt meadow* mutton is highly prized. This comes from sheep pastured on the coast where aromatic plants are prolific. The English cross-breed (Southdown cross-breed) is also well liked for its fat and tasty meat, as well as the Dishley cross-breed which provides small legs and large cutlets. In some districts mutton tends to taste of wool-grease. In Africa and several Asian countries sheep are bred with especially large tails. This fat takes the place of butter in the cooking of meat in Moslem communities.

Best quality mutton is bright red, close-grained and firm. It has a great deal of fat which is white and firm and evenly spread over the muscular tissue and in the tissue itself. A fleshy leg of mutton has a thick layer of fat at the base. In second-grade mutton, there is less fat. The meat is less red and firm. In third-grade mutton there is only a very thin layer of fat on the kidneys and noneon the surface of the meat.

In France the cuts of mutton, as with beef, are divided into three categories for sale.

First category: Leg, rib, fillet, chump cutlets (U.S. English lamb chops), loin cutlets (U.S. loin chops).

Second category: Shoulder, chuck, neck cutlets (U.S. rib chops).

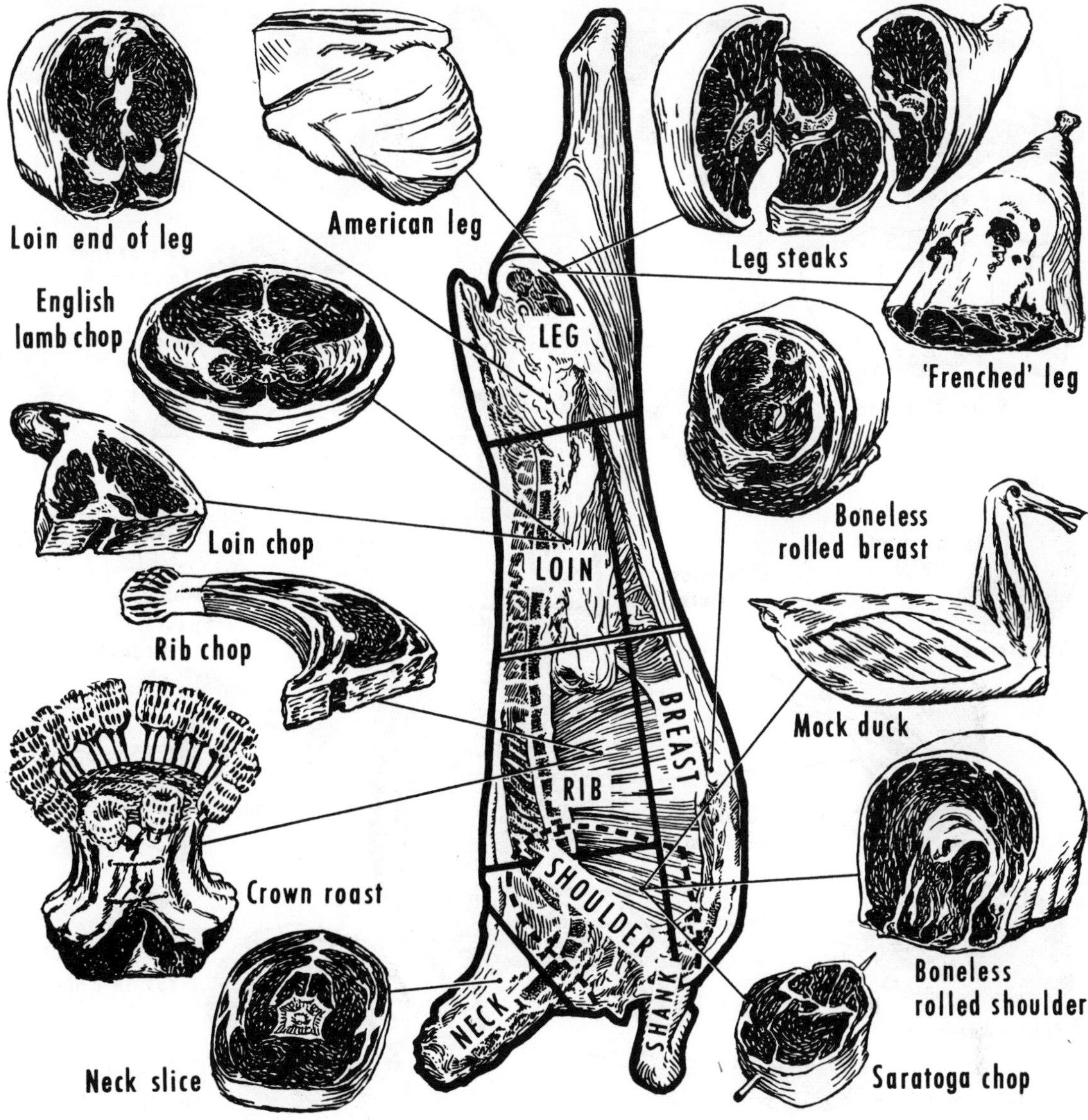

American cuts of mutton

Third category: Flank, neck, breast and shin.

Baron of mutton. BARON DE MOUTON—A cut comprising the entire hind-quarters of the sheep, that is to say the saddle and the two hind legs.

Salt meadow lamb and Pauillac lamb are usually cut in this way. Barons of mutton are less commonly found.

These large cuts, which are always roasted, are served as an intermediate course (see CULINARY METHODS, *Roasting*). They are served with a garnish of vegetables and their own gravy, slightly thickened, according to the nature of the garnish.

Cooking time: in the oven, 15 minutes per pound; *on the spit*, 18 to 20 minutes per pound.

Garnishes for baron of mutton: Bouquetière; Bretonne; Clamart; Dauphine; Duchesse; Jardinière; Potatoes Château, Fondantes, with parsley, *Anna* or prepared in some other way; *Portugaise; Provençale; Renaissance; Richelieu.* See GARNISHES and POTATOES.

Mutton or lamb brains—See OFFAL OR VARIETY MEATS.

Breast of mutton. POITRINE DE MOUTON—This part of the sheep is used mainly in the preparation of *ragoûts.*

In addition, all recipes for breast of lamb are suitable for breast of mutton. This cut is especially suitable for *épigrammes.* See LAMB, *Breast of lamb en épigrammes.*

Further, the breast may be used with the neck in the preparation of *Mutton broth* (see SOUPS AND BROTHS).

Grilled breast of mutton (Carême's recipe). POITRINE DE MOUTON GRILLÉE AU NATUREL—'Take two fine well-fleshed breasts of mutton. With a single stroke of the knife remove the part of the bone above the gristle. Tie the breasts. Put them in an oval casserole with 2 carrots, 2 onions and a *bouquet garni**. Moisten with good clear soup (enough to cover the meat). Bring to the boil. Skim and cook for $2\frac{1}{2}$ hours. Drain the breasts and put them in a press. When they are cold, trim them and gently take off the skin without touching the fat. Round the meat on the side where the gristle is. Saw off the bones, if they are too long, at the lower edge of the breast. Dip

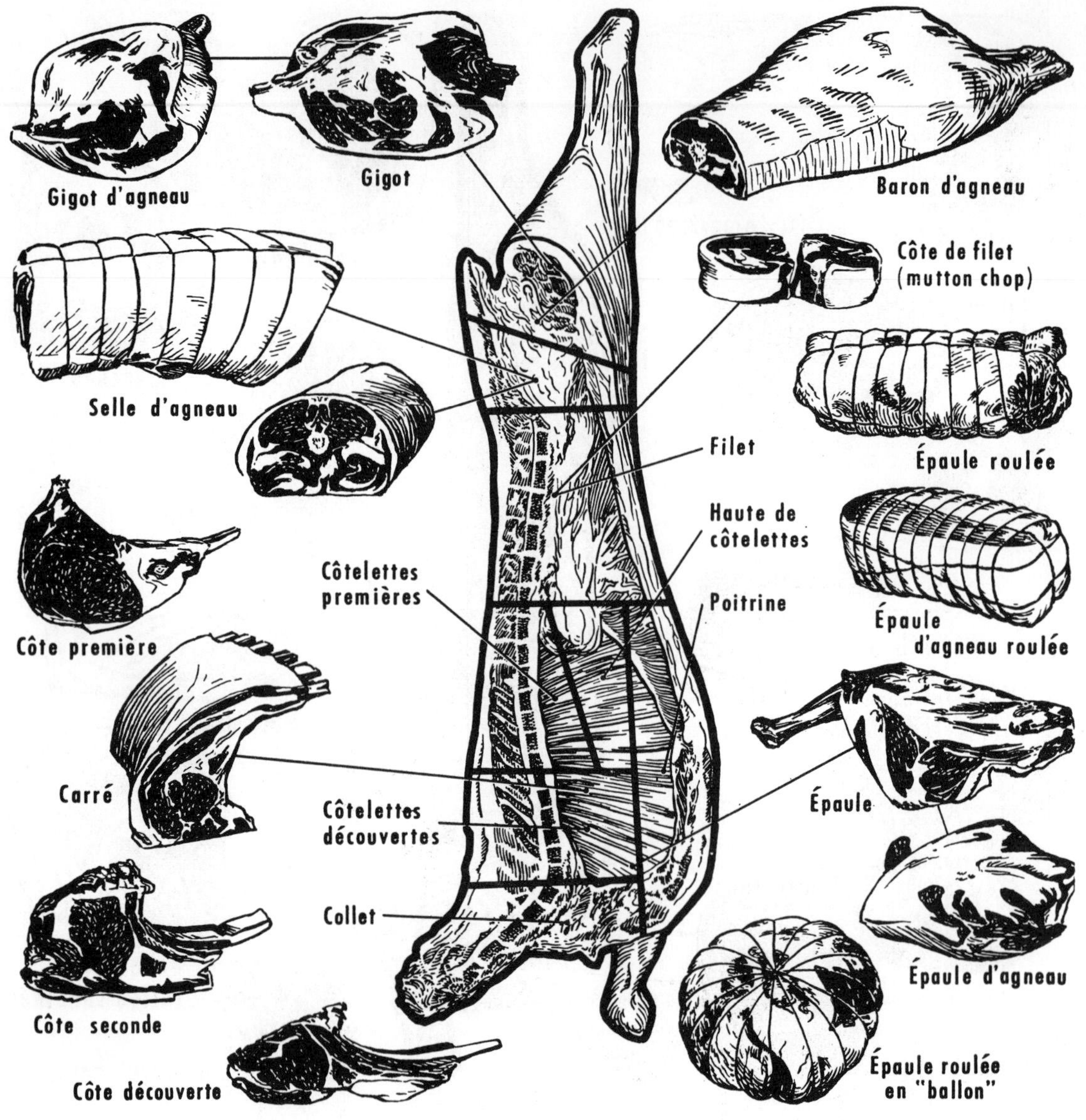

French cuts of mutton

them in melted butter. Grill over a gentle heat, making sure that they are a good colour and that, while grilling, they are gradually warmed through. Serve.'

Prepared in this way, grilled breast of mutton is served with *Diable sauce* (see SAUCE) or any other sauce especially suitable for grilled meat.

Grilled breast of mutton in breadcrumbs (Carême's recipe). POITRINE DE MOUTON PANÉE GRILLÉE—After having prepared two breasts of mutton as indicated in the previous recipe, and having left them to cool, cut each breast into 6 pieces. Trim these pieces, leaving the bone as in a cutlet. Dip them in melted butter and breadcrumbs. Grill them until they are a good colour and serve with a fine *Poivrade sauce* (see SAUCE).

Stuffed breast of mutton à l'ariégeoise. POITRINE DE MOUTON FARCIE À L'ARIÉGEOISE—Cut open a breast of mutton to form a pouch. Season inside. Stuff with a rather thick stuffing made of breadcrumbs dipped in clear soup and squeezed, chopped raw ham, lean and fat, and chopped parsley and garlic. Bind with eggs and season well. Sew up the opening in the breast.

Put the meat in a buttered braising pan, lined with fresh pork skin (or bacon rinds), onions and carrots cut round. Add a *bouquet garni**. Cover and cook gently on the stove for 15 minutes. Moisten with $\frac{3}{4}$ cup ($1\frac{1}{2}$ decilitres) of dry white wine. Boil down. Add 3 tablespoons of tomato purée and $1\frac{1}{2}$ cups (3 decilitres) of thickened brown stock. Cover and cook in the oven for 45 minutes to an hour.

Drain the meat. Serve on a large, long dish.

Surround with a garnish of stuffed cabbage (rolled into balls) and potatoes cooked in clear stock and butter.

Skim all fat off the braising stock. Boil down and strain. Pour over the dish.

Mutton broth (English cookery)—A broth made with the breast and neck of mutton, a mixture of coarsely chopped pot vegetables and pearl barley. See SOUPS AND BROTHS.

Mutton chops. CÔTELETTES DE MOUTON ANGLAISES—Mutton chops (U.S. English lamb chops) are cut from the fillet of mutton. They are cut very thick ($1\frac{1}{2}$ to 2 inches).

Roll the end of the chop inwards and fix with a skewer.

Mutton chops are always grilled. They are served plain as a rule, garnished with parsley, though any of the garnishes suitable for mutton cutlets may be served with these chops.

Mutton cutlets (U.S. chops). CÔTELETTES DE MOUTON—The cutlets are cut from the rib. According to the part from which they are taken, they have different names.

Chump cutlets (U.S. loin chops) are taken from the covered part of the rib.

These cutlets must be cut rather thick. They are trimmed by cutting off the end of the bone and paring away the narrow strips of meat on either side of this bone, as well as excessive fat along the top.

After trimming, the cutlets are flattened slightly.

Chump cutlets are usually grilled, since this method of cooking suits them best. They may, however, be sautéed or braised.

The *neck cutlets* (U.S. rib chops) are those cut from the uncovered part of the rib. These cutlets are prepared in the same way as chump cutlets, but generally they are sautéed or braised.

Untrimmed cutlets are taken either from the covered or uncovered part of the rib. The French call them *bouchères.*

The term *undressed* is also applied to a cutlet whose bone-meat, after having been detached from the bone and folded back on itself, is kept in this shape by the bone.

Fillet cutlets (U.S. sirloin chops) are not taken from the rib. They are cut from the saddle of mutton, split in two, lengthwise.

Mutton cutlets (chops) à l'albigeoise. CÔTELETTES DE MOUTON À L'ALBIGEOISE—Sauté the cutlets in oil. Arrange in a circle. Garnish the middle of the dish with sliced cèpes sautéed in oil and flavoured with garlic. Dilute the pan juices with white wine poured into the pan and heated. Season with a touch of garlic. Add fairly thin *Tomato sauce* (see SAUCE). Pour this sauce over the cutlets. Sprinkle with chopped parsley.

Mutton cutlets (chops) à l'anglaise. CÔTELETTES DE MOUTON À L'ANGLAISE—Season with salt and pepper. Dip in egg and breadcrumbs. Fry in butter.

Garnish with potatoes or green vegetables tossed in butter.

Mutton cutlets (chops) à la bouchère. CÔTELETTES DE MOUTON À LA BOUCHÈRE—This is the name given to neck cutlets (U.S. rib chops), whose bone is not scraped, and to cutlets of which the meat on the bone is cut away and rolled back. These cutlets are grilled.

Braised cutlets (chops) with various garnishes. CÔTELETTES DE MOUTON BRAISÉES—These cutlets (chops) should be cut rather thick. Season. Put in a buttered frying pan lined with pork skin, finely sliced onions and carrots. Cover and cook gently for 10 minutes. Moisten with white wine and a few tablespoons of thickened brown gravy. Boil down. Add a *bouquet garni**. Cover and cook in the oven for 45 minutes to an hour according to the size of the cutlets. Drain the cutlets. Serve on a round dish. Garnish with the vegetables indicated. Reduce the braising liquor, strain it and pour it over the cutlets.

Mutton cutlets (chops) à la bretonne. CÔTELETTES DE MOUTON À LA BRETONNE—Sauté in butter. Arrange in a circle. Garnish the middle of the dish with white beans or small kidney beans *à la bretonne* (see BEANS). Dilute the pan juices with a little clear stock. Pour it round the cutlets.

Mutton cutlets (chops) à la bruxelloise. CÔTELETTES DE MOUTON À LA BRUXELLOISE—Sauté in butter. Garnish with Brussels sprouts sautéed in butter. Pour white wine and *Demi-glace sauce* (see SAUCE) into the pan. Heat and serve with the cutlets.

Mutton cutlets (chops) à la cévenole. CÔTELETTES DE MOUTON À LA CÉVENOLE—Braise the cutlets in the usual way, uncovered, with very little stock. When they are three-parts cooked, put in the saucepan 18 chestnuts, three-parts cooked, 18 small glazed onions, and 12 small lardoons of belly of pork, blanched and fried. Finish cooking all together. 5 minutes before removing from the stove, add 12 small chipolata sausages, cooked in butter. Arrange the cutlets in a circle on a round dish. Put the other ingredients in the middle. Pour on the braising stock. Carrots cut into uniform pieces can be added to the garnish.

Mutton cutlets (chops) Champvallon. CÔTELETTES DE MOUTON CHAMPVALLON—Season 6 neck cutlets (U.S. rib chops) and brown them quickly in butter on both sides. Line an earthenware dish with 3 tablespoons of sliced onions cooked in butter without browning. Lay the cutlets on top. Pour white stock or water into the pan in which the cutlets were fried and heat. Moisten the cutlets and onions with this stock. Add a *bouquet garni** and half a clove of crushed garlic. Bring to the boil on the stove, then cover and put in the oven. Cook for 35 minutes.

Put on the top of the cutlets 2 cups (500 grams) of potatoes cut into thin round slices. Season the potatoes. Moisten a little if necessary, and finish cooking in the oven, basting frequently.

Remove the *bouquet garni.* Sprinkle with chopped parsley and serve as it is.

Mutton cutlets (chops) chasseur. CÔTELETTES DE MOUTON CHASSEUR—Sauté the cutlets (chops) in butter. Drain them. Put in the frying pan (for 6 cutlets) 1 tablespoon of chopped shallots and 6 sliced mushrooms. Brown for a few seconds over a very hot flame. Moisten with $\frac{2}{3}$ cup ($1\frac{1}{2}$ decilitres) of white wine. Boil down. Add $1\frac{1}{4}$ cups ($2\frac{1}{2}$ decilitres) of thickened brown stock and a tablespoon of *Tomato sauce* (see SAUCE). Boil for a few seconds. Add 2 teaspoons of chopped chervil and tarragon and a tablespoon of butter. Arrange the chops in a circle on a round dish and pour the sauce over them.

Mutton cutlets (chops) en chaud-froid and in jelly. CÔTELETTES DE MOUTON EN CHAUD-FROID (À LA GELÉE)—Proceed as indicated for *Chaud-froid of lamb chops* and *Lamb chops in aspic jelly.*

Note. Mutton cutlets are rarely served cold. It is usually lamb cutlets which are served in this way.

Mutton cutlets (chops) à la Clamart. CÔTELETTES DE MOUTON À LA CLAMART—This dish can be prepared in two ways.

(1) *Grilled* or *sautéed* and garnished with *petits pois à la française* (young peas cooked in butter with onions and shredded lettuce) or, sometimes, green peas simply tossed in butter.

(2) *Braised.* Brown the cutlets on both sides in butter. Put in the pan (for 6 cutlets) a quart (litre) of newly shelled peas, a shredded lettuce, 12 small onions, all these ingredients previously mixed with 5 tablespoons (75 grams) of butter, salt and a pinch of sugar.

Add a *bouquet garni** of parsley and chervil. Moisten with 4 tablespoons of slightly thickened brown veal stock. Cover and cook for 45 minutes to an hour.

Arrange the cutlets in a circle on a round deep dish. Pile the peas in the middle.

Mutton cutlets (chops) en crépinettes à l'ancienne. CÔTELETTES DE MOUTON EN CRÉPINETTES À L'ANCIENNE—Cut the cutlets (chops) rather thin and chop off the end of the bone. Braise them. Leave to cool in their stock. Drain and dry in a cloth. Coat them on both sides with fine stuffing mixed with diced truffles, well seasoned and flavoured with a few drops of brandy. Wrap each cutlet in a piece of pig's caul (or thin slice of salt pork), dipped in cold water. Dip the cutlets in melted butter and breadcrumbs. Baste with melted butter. Grill slowly.

Arrange the cutlets in a circle on a round dish. Garnish the middle of the dish with rather thick mushroom purée (see MUSHROOMS). Serve with a *Périgueux sauce* (see SAUCE) made with the braising stock of the cutlets.

Curried mutton cutlets (chops). CÔTELETTES DE MOUTON AU CURRIE—Sauté the cutlets in oil. Arrange in a circle on a round dish. Cover with *Curry sauce* (see SAUCE) to which the diluted pan juices left from cooking the cutlets have been added. Serve *Rice à l'indienne** separately.

Mutton cutlets (chops) à la duxelles. CÔTELETTES DE MOUTON À LA DUXELLES—Sauté the cutlets in butter (or a mixture of equal parts of oil and butter). Drain them. Serve on a round dish. Pour white wine into the cooking pan. Add *Duxelles sauce* (see SAUCE). Boil for a few seconds. Pour this sauce over the cutlets. Sprinkle with chopped parsley.

Mutton cutlets (chops) à la fermière. CÔTELETTES DE MOUTON À LA FERMIÈRE—In an earthenware casserole, fry in butter lower-rib cutlets (loin chops) cut rather thick and seasoned with salt and pepper. Put in the casserole (for 6 cutlets) 1½ cups (3 decilitres) of *Fondue of vegetables à la fermière* and 4 or 5 tablespoons of fresh green peas. Season. Moisten with ¾ cup (1½ decilitres) of white wine. Boil down. Add 1 cup (2 decilitres) of brown stock, slightly thickened, and a small *bouquet garni**. Cook for 20 minutes. Add about 20 small potatoes trimmed into pear shapes. Cover and finish cooking in the oven for about 45 minutes. Serve as they are, in the casserole.

Grilled mutton cutlets (chops). CÔTELETTES DE MOUTON GRILLÉES—Trim the cutlets. Flatten them slightly. Baste with melted butter (or oil). Season. Cook under the grill. Serve the cutlets on a very hot, round dish. Decorate the bones with paper frills. Garnish with watercress.

Grilled mutton cutlets (chops) à l'anglaise. CÔTELETTES DE MOUTON À L'ANGLAISE—Season. Dip in melted butter and breadcrumbs. Grill slowly. Garnish to taste.

Grilled mutton cutlets (chops) in breadcrumbs. CÔTELETTES DE MOUTON GRILLÉES PANÉES—Baste the cutlets with melted butter. Season. Coat both sides with freshly made breadcrumbs. Pour on melted butter. Cook under the grill. Serve on a very hot dish, garnished with watercress. Decorate the bones with cutlet frills.

Mutton cutlets (chops) à la hongroise. CÔTELETTES DE MOUTON À LA HONGROISE—Season the cutlets with salt and paprika. Sauté in butter. When they are browned on both sides, put in the frying pan (for 6 cutlets) 2 tablespoons of chopped onion cooked slowly in butter until very tender and seasoned with paprika. Finish cooking all together. Serve the cutlets in a circle on a round dish. Heap potatoes sautéed in butter in the middle (or any other vegetable tossed in butter).

Pour ½ cup (a decilitre) of white wine into the frying pan. Add 2 cups (4 decilitres) of thick fresh cream. Simmer until quite thick. Blend in 2 teaspoons of butter. Pour this sauce over the cutlets.

Mutton cutlets (chops) à l'italienne. CÔTELETTES DE MOUTON À L'ITALIENNE—Sauté in a mixture of oil and butter. Take the cutlets (chops) out of the pan. Put them on a round dish. Put in the pan (for 6 cutlets) 1½ cups (3 decilitres) of *Italian sauce* (see SAUCE). Add 2 tablespoons of very finely diced lean cooked ham. Add a tablespoon of butter and 2 teaspoons of chopped parsley. Pour this sauce over the cutlets.

Mutton cutlets (chops) Maintenon. CÔTELETTES DE MOUTON MAINTENON—Fry the cutlets (chops) in butter on one side only. Drain and dry in a cloth. Put on the cooked side a heaped tablespoon of *Maintenon mixture* (see MIXTURE): a *Soubise* (see PURÉE) with shredded truffles, mushrooms and pickled tongue added. Smooth this mixture carefully into a dome. Heat some butter in a baking tin and lay the cutlets in it. Sprinkle with breadcrumbs. Pour on melted butter. Brown in the oven.

Arrange the cutlets in a rosette on a round dish. Decorate the bones with cutlet frills. Serve *Périgueux sauce* (see SAUCE) separately.

This dish can also be prepared as follows:

Braise the cutlets in a very little stock. Leave to cool under a weight in the strained braising stock. Drain, trim and heap *Maintenon mixture* (see MIXTURE) on one side. Finish cooking as indicated above. (The *Périgueux sauce* is made with the cooking stock.)

Minced mutton cutlets (chops) sautéed and garnished. CÔTELETTES DE MOUTON HACHÉES, SAUTÉES, GARNIES—Cut the medallion of lean meat out of the cutlet (chop) without touching the fat part on the bone. Mince the meat finely, adding to it a third of its weight of butter. Season with salt and pepper. Using this minced meat, reshape the cutlet medallion. Sauté in butter. Serve on a round dish. Garnish with any vegetables tossed in butter.

Minced mutton cutlets (chops) in breadcrumbs, sautéed. CÔTELETTES DE MOUTON HACHÉES, PANÉES, SAUTÉES—Prepare the cutlets as indicated above. After reshaping them, dip in egg and breadcrumbs. Sauté in butter.

Garnish with vegetables tossed in butter.

Mutton cutlets (chops) à la niçoise. CÔTELETTES DE MOUTON À LA NIÇOISE—Sauté the cutlets in oil. Drain and arrange in a circle on a round dish. Fill the middle with small potatoes fried in butter (preferably new potatoes). Round the edge of the dish arrange alternately French beans in butter and small tomatoes stewed in butter, with spaces between. Pour a little white wine into the cooking pan. Add a sauce composed of one-third thickened brown gravy and two-thirds tomato sauce. Season with a touch of garlic and butter. Pour this sauce over the cutlets. Sprinkle with chopped parsley.

Mutton cutlets (chops) Parmentier. CÔTELETTES DE MOUTON PARMENTIER—Sauté the cutlets in butter. When they are well browned on both sides, put in the pan diced potatoes three-parts cooked in butter. Finish cooking all together. Arrange the cutlets in a circle. Heap the potatoes in the middle. Pour white wine and a few spoonfuls of stock into the cooking pan. Heat, and pour this sauce over the dish. Sprinkle with chopped parsley.

Mutton cutlets (chops) Pompadour (Carême's recipe.) CÔTELETTES DE MOUTON POMPADOUR—'After having prepared the cutlets in the same way as those called *à la Soubise* (Braised) do not heat them but coat with a concentrated *Soubise purée* (see PURÉE). Coat the purée once with breadcrumbs. Dip in egg, then dip in breadcrumbs a second time. Brown in clarified butter. Arrange on a dish. Put a *macédoine** in the middle. Reduce the pan juices and pour over the dish.'

Mutton cutlets (chops) à la provençale. CÔTELETTES DE MOUTON À LA PROVENÇALE—Sauté the cutlets in oil. Arrange on a dish. Garnish with small tomatoes stewed in butter (or oil), sautéed mushrooms and blanched olives.

Pour white wine into the cooking pan. Add tomato-flavoured veal stock with a touch of garlic added. Pour this sauce over the dish.

Mutton cutlets (chops) à la Réforme. CÔTELETTES DE MOUTON À LA RÉFORME—Season the cutlets. Baste with butter. Coat with white breadcrumbs mixed with a third of finely chopped lean ham. Sauté in butter. Arrange on a dish. Garnish with the white of a hard boiled egg, 2 cooked mushrooms, a small truffle, a gherkin and a small slice of pickled tongue. All these ingredients must be cut into short, rather thick strips and mixed.

Pour *Poivrade sauce* (see SAUCE) into the cooking pan. Heat and pour over the shredded mixture only. Serve with redcurrant jelly.

Mutton cutlets (chops) à la russe. CÔTELETTES DE MOUTON À LA RUSSE—Leaving the fat on the bone, cut out the medallion of meat of each cutlet. Prepare a mince as for *Beefsteak à la russe* (see BEEF). Reshape the cutlets. Dip in egg and breadcrumbs. Sauté in clarified butter.

Arrange in a circle on a round dish. On each cutlet place a little mound of onions fried in butter. In the middle of the dish heap sautéed potatoes.

Serve separately a *Sour cream sauce* prepared as follows: Pour the sour cream into the pan in which the cutlets have been cooked. Enrich this cream with a few tablespoons of *Demi-glace sauce* (see SAUCE). Cook down and strain.

Mutton cutlets (chops) sautéed in breadcrumbs. CÔTELETTES DE MOUTON SAUTÉES, PANÉES—Season the cutlets. Dip in egg and breadcrumbs. Sauté in butter.

Arrange on a round dish. Serve as they are, simply with the cooking butter poured over them, or garnished with vegetables.

Mutton cutlets (chops) sautéed with garnish. CÔTELETTES DE MOUTON SAUTÉES, GARNIES—Sauté the cutlets in butter so that they remain pinkish inside.

Arrange on a very hot dish. Pour dry white wine into the cooking pan and add a few tablespoons of thickened brown gravy. Heat and pour over the dish.

Garnishes for sautéed mutton cutlets. All those indicated for medallion of mutton. They can also be garnished with purées of various vegetables, especially *Purée bretonne**; green vegetables tossed in butter or cream; potatoes cooked in various ways; various cheese pastes; risotto.

Mutton cutlets (chops) Soubise. CÔTELETTES DE MOUTON SOUBISE—Serve *Soubise purée* separately. See PURÉE.

Stuffed cutlets (chops), with various garnishes. CÔTELETTES DE MOUTON EN PORTE-FEUILLE—Take some rather thick cutlets. Make an incision in the thickest part of the meat.

Pull the edges a little apart to form a pouch. Season the cutlets. Fill with a *Quenelle forcemeat* (see FORCEMEAT) mixed with diced mushrooms and truffles tossed in butter. Close up the pouch in the cutlets and cover with a thin strip of pork fat (or bacon rasher), securing it with string. Brown the cutlets in butter on both sides. Moisten with slightly thickened brown stock. Braise the cutlets. When they are cooked, drain them and remove the pork fat. Glaze them. Arrange in a circle on a round dish. Garnish as indicated. Boil down and strain the cooking stock and pour over the dish.

Note. Prepared in this way, cutlets can be garnished with vegetables, tossed in butter or braised, and served with garnishes such as chipolata, *forestière*, *financière*, etc. See GARNISHES.

They can also be garnished with vegetable purées, pasta prepared in different ways, risotto, etc.

Mutton cutlets (chops) La Varenne. CÔTELETTES DE MOUTON LA VARENNE—Cut the medallions out of 6 cutlets. Finely chop this meat with a third of its weight of dry *Duxelles**, 2 tablespoons of butter, 2 teaspoons of chopped parsley, salt and pepper. Reshape the cutlets with this mixture, putting them back on the bone. Dip the cutlets in egg and breadcrumbs. Sauté in clarified butter. Arrange in a circle on a round dish. Fill the middle of the dish with very thick *Mushroom purée**, made with the addition of 3½ ounces (100 grams) of diced truffles tossed in butter. Make a sauce of a few tablespoons of *Demi-glace sauce* cooked with Madeira. Add butter and strain. Pour over the dish.

Mutton cutlets (chops) à la villageoise. CÔTELETTES DE MOUTON À LA VILLAGEOISE—Braise and leave to cool in their stock. Make a *Soubise* (see PURÉE) with very concentrated veal stock, and sliced mushrooms sautéed in butter added. Heap some of this mixture on one side of each cutlet. Proceed as for *Mutton cutlets Maintenon.*

Mutton cutlets (chops) à la Villeroi. CÔTELETTES DE MOUTON À LA VILLEROI—Braise the cutlets and leave to cool in their stock. Drain and trim. Dip in *Villeroi sauce* (see SAUCE) and in egg and breadcrumbs. Just before serving, cook in clarified butter. Drain them. Arrange in a circle on a paper doyley. Garnish with fried parsley. Serve *Périgueux sauce* or *Tomato sauce* (see SAUCE) separately.

Civet of mutton. CIVET DE MOUTON—Brown in butter in a frying pan 24 small onions and 7 ounces (200 grams) of belly of pork, diced and blanched.

When these ingredients are browned, take them out of the pan and, in the same fat, brown thoroughly 1½ pounds (750 grams) of lower mutton cutlets (U.S. rib chops), boned and trimmed into squares. Season with salt, pepper and spices. When these pieces of mutton are well browned, add a crushed clove of garlic and sprinkle with 2 spoonfuls of flour. Cook until the flour is golden-brown. Moisten with equal parts of red wine and clear stock. Add a *bouquet garni** and 2 tablespoons of brandy. Cover and cook in the oven for an hour.

Drain the mutton on a sieve. Put the pieces back in the pan. Add the lardoons, the small onions and 24 small mushrooms previously tossed in butter. Strain the sauce and pour it over the mutton. Cover and cook in the oven for an hour.

Note. The sauce of this civet is thickened with the blood of a chicken or rabbit.

Curried mutton. RAGOÛT DE MOUTON À L'INDIENNE (CURRIE DE MOUTON)—Dice 3 pounds (1 kilo 500 grams) of lean mutton (neck chops or shoulder) into pieces 1½ inches square. Brown the mutton in lard with ¾ cup (150 grams) of chopped onions. Season with salt and a teaspoon of curry powder. Brown for a few seconds on the stove. Add a clove of garlic, crushed. Sprinkle with 3 tablespoons (45 grams) of flour. Mix. Moisten with clear stock (or water), just enough to cover the meat. Add a chopped tomato, peeled, with the seeds removed, and a *bouquet garni**. Cover and cook for 1½ hours.

Take out the bouquet. Put the meat in a bowl. Pour on the sauce (boiled down if necessary), flavoured with a squeeze of lemon. Serve *Rice à l'indienne** separately.

Note. Curried mutton can also be prepared in the same way as *Chicken curry**.

It is also possible, still preparing it in the French way as indicated above, to moisten it with coconut milk instead of clear soup. This milk is made by diluting a grated coconut with its own milk mixed with water (or ordinary milk) and then forcing this pulp through muslin.

Mutton daube à l'avignonnaise. DAUBE DE MOUTON À L'AVIGNONNAISE—Cut into square pieces weighing 3 ounces (90 grams) each a boned leg or shoulder of mutton. Following the grain of the meat, interlard each piece with a thick lardoon seasoned with salt, pepper and spices.

Steep this mutton for 2 hours in a marinade of red wine, oil, finely sliced carrots and onions, crushed garlic, parsley, thyme and bay leaves.

Line a deep earthenware dish with thin slices of pork fat in layers. Intersperse each layer with 2 tablespoons of chopped onion, belly of pork and fresh pork skin, diced and blanched, and a little crushed garlic. Put the pieces of mutton on top. Season with salt, pepper, thyme and powdered bay leaf. In the middle of the meat put a large bouquet of parsley stalks with a piece of dried orange peel. Moisten with the strained marinade, adding enough clear stock to cover the meat. Put slices of pork fat on top. Cover the dish. Seal hermetically with flour-and-water paste. Cook slowly and evenly in the oven for 5 hours.

Éclanche of mutton. ÉCLANCHE DE MOUTON—This is the old French word for shoulder of mutton.

Épigrammes of mutton. ÉPIGRAMMES DE MOUTON—*Épigrammes* of mutton are made with a piece of the breast (braised or boiled), trimmed in the shape of a heart, dipped in egg and breadcrumbs, and sautéed in butter (or grilled), and a grilled mutton chop.

Épigrammes can be garnished with different vegetables. For a recipe, see LAMB, *Breast of lamb en épigrammes.*

Filets mignons of mutton en chevreuil (venison style). FILETS MIGNONS DE MOUTON EN CHEVREUIL—Proceed as for *Beef filets mignons en chevreuil* (*venison style*). See BEEF.

Grilled filets mignons of mutton. FILETS MIGNONS DE MOUTON GRILLÉS—Flatten the fillets slightly. Season. Baste with melted butter (or oil). Coat with breadcrumbs. Pour melted butter over them. Grill slowly. Serve with *Maître d'hôtel butter* (see BUTTER, *Compound butters*) or any other sauce suitable for grilled meat.

Fillet of mutton (U.S. Sirloin roast). FILET DE MOUTON—This is the name given to the half-saddle, split lengthwise.

This cut, after boning, is rolled and tied. (The fillet can, after trimming, also be interlarded with best pork fat.) It can be roasted, pot-roasted or braised, as for rib or shoulder. All garnishes for rib or shoulder are suitable for fillet of mutton.

Note. The term *filets mignons* (of mutton or lamb) is used of the two thin slivers of meat found under the saddle.

Fillets of mutton on skewers. BROCHETTES DE FILET DE MOUTON—Cut a well-trimmed loin of mutton or lamb into pieces about ¼ inch thick. Thread these pieces of mutton on skewers alternating with blanched pieces of lean bacon. Season, dip into melted butter, cover with white breadcrumbs, sprinkle with melted butter and grill.

Note. In addition to pieces of bacon, which are the usual accompaniment of things cooked on skewers, sliced mushrooms, lightly tossed in butter, can also be added.

Proceeding as described above, various dishes on skewers, such as chicken livers, lamb's sweetbreads, or escalopes of calf's sweetbreads, fillets of beef, mutton, lamb or veal, fillets of various fish (for the latter omit the bacon) fillets of chicken, etc., can be prepared. Lean bacon can be replaced by square pieces of smoked bacon, which does not need to be blanched.

Fillets of mutton in red wine. FILETS DE MOUTON AU VIN ROUGE—Cut the fillets (from top leg or sirloin) into little square pieces. Season with salt and pepper. Cook quickly in sizzling butter, keeping slightly underdone on the inside. Drain. Using the same butter, toss (for 6 pieces of mutton fillet) ¼ pound (125 grams) of rather thickly sliced mushrooms. Take the mushrooms out of the pan and put them with the meat.

Pour 1½ cups (3 decilitres) of red wine into the pan. Boil down (reduce), add a few tablespoons of thickened brown veal stock, simmer to a concentrated consistency, blend in some butter, strain and pour over the fillets of mutton and the mushrooms.

Haricot or halicot of mutton. HARICOT (HALICOT) DE MOUTON—A mutton ragoût whose name, which is of very ancient origin, is no doubt derived from the old French *halicoter* (to cut into tiny morsels). It is also very likely that the French word for bean derives from the same source, its Mexican name being similar in sound.

There are recipes for this dish which date back to a time before the vegetable bean (*haricot*) was generally known. In one of the oldest formulae given by Taillevent, the following recipe for this dish is given.

'Put them all raw to fry in lard, cut into tiny pieces with sliced onions and some beef broth, verjuice, parsley, hyssop and sage, and boil all together, with fine-powdered spices.'

Thus in former times haricot (or halicot) of mutton was made without haricot beans. The only garnish was turnips, potatoes and onions.

Haricot of mutton is made like a *ragoût* of mutton with potatoes, and has nothing in common with the *ragoût of mutton* with white haricot beans for which the recipe is given below.

Mutton hash. HACHIS DE MOUTON—Mutton hash is made from cooked meat, braised or roasted, in the same way as *Beef hash.* See BEEF.

Mutton head—See OFFAL OR VARIETY MEATS, *Sheep's head.*

Mutton hindquarter. DOUBLE DE MOUTON—This cut is made up of the two hind legs of the animal. They are not split. The hindquarter is usually roasted and served as an intermediate meat course.

All garnishes and sauces indicated for *Baron of mutton* can be served with hindquarter mutton.

Mutton kidneys—See OFFAL OR VARIETY MEATS.

Leg of mutton à l'anglaise I. GIGOT DE MOUTON À L'ANGLAISE—Take a leg of mutton. Trim and cut off the end of the bone. Wrap in a buttered and floured cloth. Plunge into a pan full of boiling salt water. Add 4 medium-sized carrots, cut to look like big olives, 6 medium-sized onions (one studded with 2 cloves), a *bouquet garni** and 2 cloves of garlic. In the same pan put a dozen large tender turnips, quartered and tied in a cloth.

Boil steadily, allowing 30 minutes per pound of meat. Drain and unwrap the leg of mutton. Put it on a serving dish. Surround with the carrots and onions.

With it, serve the turnips, rubbed through a sieve and a butter sauce made with the cooking stock of the mutton with 2 tablespoons of capers added. See SAUCE.

Skim and drain the rest of the stock and serve at the same time in a sauceboat.

Leg of mutton à l'anglaise II. GIGOT DE MOUTON À L'ANGLAISE—Proceed as indicated above, substituting a purée of celery for the purée of turnips. (Like the turnips, the celery must be cooked with the mutton.)

Mashed potatoes cooked with the mutton can be served in place of turnips or celery.

Note. Leg of mutton cooked strictly according to the English method should be served with a purée of turnips only.

These turnips must be cooked with the meat.

Carême, in his *Traité des grosses pièces de mouton*, advises glazing the leg after boiling with the usual ingredients. He also advises garnishing with cauliflower covered with a very smooth *Espagnole sauce* (see SAUCE).

He adds that all kinds of vegetables and sauces can be served with leg of mutton cooked in this way.

'It is a strange error on the part of many chefs,' he concludes, 'to suppose that English gourmets will eat this leg only if served with boiled carrots and turnips. What the English like best is to see the juice coming from the leg when they slice it.'

Leg of mutton à la bonne femme. GIGOT DE MOUTON À LA BONNE FEMME—Proceed as indicated for *Shoulder of mutton à la bonne femme.*

Leg of mutton à la bordelaise. GIGOT DE MOUTON À LA BORDELAISE—'Take a leg of mutton which has been hung until very tender. Bone it, except for the projecting bone. Stuff with ham and fillets of anchovy from which all salt has been removed, and also with chopped parsley, 2 shallots and a clove of garlic, chopped and blanched. Tie the leg to keep in all the stuffing. Brown lightly in butter. Moisten with a bottle of good red Bordeaux wine. Add 2 carrots, 3 onions (1 studded with 2 cloves), a *bouquet garni** of thyme, bay leaves and basil. Cover and stew slowly, but in such a way as to reduce the stock to a *Demi-glace* (see SAUCE). Cook for 1½ hours. Have ready 1½ quarts (litres) of perfectly skinned cloves of garlic. Boil in a lot of water. Drain. Cool under running water and sauté in the best butter. Keep them hot. Drain the leg of mutton. Put it on a serving dish. Cook down (reduce) the stock with 2 tablespoonfuls of *Espagnole sauce* (see SAUCE).

'After taking out the vegetables and the *bouquet garni*, strain the stock through muslin. Pour over the joint. Dress the garlic with a spoonful of *Allemande sauce* and a small pinch of Cayenne pepper. Serve in a sauceboat or silver bowl.' (A. Carême.)

Leg of mutton à la boulangère. GIGOT DE MOUTON À LA BOULANGÈRE—Proceed as for *Shoulder of mutton à la boulangère.*

Braised leg of mutton. GIGOT DE MOUTON BRAISÉ—Proceed as for *Braised shoulder of mutton.*

Leg of mutton à la bretonne. GIGOT DE MOUTON À LA BRETONNE—Roast a leg of mutton. Serve with it the diluted pan juices with a little fat left in them. Garnish with white haricot beans, small kidney beans *à la bretonne*, or *Purée of haricot beans à la bretonne* (see BEANS). The garnish must be served separately.

Leg of mutton en chevreuil (venison style). GIGOT DE MOUTON EN CHEVREUIL—Bone the chump end of a leg of mutton and fix the bone into the smaller end so that it projects. Completely skin the meat and interlard with best lardoons, as for a haunch of roebuck.

Put the leg to steep in a special marinade (see MARINADE). Leave it in this marinade for some time. The period of maceration depends on the tenderness of the meat and the weather (2 days in summer and 4 to 5 days in winter).

Dry the leg of mutton in a cloth. Roast it. Serve *Roebuck sauce* or *Poivrade sauce* (see SAUCE) separately.

Roast leg of mutton. GIGOT DE MOUTON RÔTI. Bone the chump (U.S. loin) end of the leg. Roast on the spit for 20 to 25 minutes per pound; in the oven for 20 to 22 minutes. Serve the diluted pan juices with it.

Note. It is customary to stud the leg near the projecting bones with 2 or 3 small cloves of garlic.

Cold leg of mutton is cooked in the same way as roast leg of mutton. It is served plain, garnished only with watercress.

Leg of mutton de sept heures or à la cuiller. GIGOT DE MOUTON DE SEPT HEURES (À LA CUILLER)—Trim the leg and cut off the end of the bone. Braise in the usual way, but cook for a long time at a moderate temperature.

After cooking, this mutton should be so tender that it can be cut with a spoon.

Serve with the braising liquor, strained and reduced.

Note. All garnishes indicated for braised rib or shoulder of mutton are suitable for leg of mutton *à la cuiller.*

Leg of mutton à la Soubise. GIGOT DE MOUTON À LA SOUBISE—Trim the leg of mutton. Braise in the usual way. When it is half-cooked, drain it. Strain the braising stock. Put the leg back in the braising pan. Surround with 4 pounds (2 kilos) of parboiled quartered onions. Pour on the braising stock. Finish cooking all together.

Drain the onions. Crush them in a saucepan, and add ½ pound (250 grams) of rice cooked in clear chicken soup. Simmer for 10 minutes. Rub the onions through a fine sieve (or through a tammy cloth, pressing hard). Heat this purée, and add butter to it at the last moment. Glaze the joint. Put it on a serving dish. Pour over it a few tablespoons of stock, strained and boiled down, if necessary. Serve the braising stock and the *Soubise* (onion purée) separately.

Note. The leg can also be braised in the usual way, with the *Soubise* prepared separately as indicated in the recipe for this purée. See PURÉE.

Mutton and lamb's liver, heart and spleen. FOIE, COEUR ET RATE DE MOUTON—These parts constitute what is called the *pluck.*

Sheep and lamb pluck is used mostly in ragoûts.

Moussaka of mutton (Rumanian cookery). MOUSSAKA DE MOUTON—*Ingredients prepared in advance.* Using cooked mutton make 2 pounds (1 kilo) of mince.

Cook in oil 6 egg-plants (aubergines) halved lengthwise and lightly scored with a knife. Scoop out the pulp of these egg-plants and chop it. Keep the skins to line the mould.

Cook in oil 2 egg-plants (aubergines) peeled and cut into thick round slices.

Add the chopped aubergines to the mutton mince, and add also ⅞ cup (125 grams) of chopped mushrooms tossed in butter, 6 tablespoons (75 grams) of chopped onions cooked very slowly in butter until tender, a tablespoon of chopped parsley, a touch of garlic, and ½ cup (a decilitre) of *Espagnole sauce* (see SAUCE) strongly flavoured with tomato. Season with salt, pepper and spices.

Bind with 2 or 3 eggs. Mix thoroughly.

Final preparations for the moussaka. Completely line a large buttered charlotte mould with the aubergine skins, purple side downward. Fill this mould with alternate layers of mince and round slices of fried aubergine. Press these ingredients well down into the mould. Cover with aubergine skins. On top of the skins lay a sheet of buttered greaseproof paper. Stand the mould in a pan of water and cook the *moussaka* in the oven for an hour.

Let it stand for a few minutes before turning out on to a serving dish.

Note. If aubergines are not available the moussaka may be made with very small vegetable marrows (zucchini). However, as a matter of strict principle, this dish should be made with aubergines.

For individual portions served in a restaurant, the *moussaka* is usually made in a large rectangular mould. It can also be made in a deep earthenware dish, which should also be lined with aubergine skins.

Navarin of mutton. NAVARIN DE MOUTON—A type of *ragoût* garnished with different vegetables.

Navarin of mutton with potatoes. NAVARIN DE MOUTON AUX POMMES DE TERRE—This is the name given to *Ragoût of mutton à la bonne femme* cooked without belly of pork. See below.

Navarin of mutton printanier. NAVARIN DE MOUTON PRINTANIER—The chuck and shoulder of mutton cut into pieces each weighing about 2 ounces (60 grams). Season with salt, pepper and a pinch of fine sugar (this sugar, turning to caramel in the pan and later dissolved by the stock, gives just the right flavour to the sauce).

With 2 tablespoons of fat skimmed off stock or of butter, brown the pieces thoroughly, then sprinkle with about 2 tablespoons of flour. Mix and brown lightly in the oven. Next, add enough tepid water to cover the meat. Bring to the boil, stirring constantly, to ensure that the *roux** is well blended into the stock. Before bringing to the boil add also 4 medium-sized tomatoes, squeezed and chopped (or, failing these, tomato purée), a clove of crushed garlic, and a *bouquet garni**. Cover and simmer gently (preferably in the oven) for an hour. At the end of this time, remove the pieces of meat and strain the sauce. Rinse the saucepan in hot water to detach bone splinters and improve the quality of the sauce. Put all the ingredients and the sauce back in the pan. Bring to the boil once more and add 12 small onions, 16 quarters of small carrots, the same number of turnips cut to look like olives and 20 small new potatoes. Continue cooking, still very slowly (bearing in mind that vegetables cook slowly in sauce), for an hour.

About 25 minutes after bringing to the boil, add 1½ cups of large freshly shelled peas and a cup (100 grams) of French (string) beans. Finish cooking the *navarin*, still simmering very gently.

At the last moment, skim all fat off the *navarin* and serve in a bowl or deep round dish.

Noisettes of mutton Armenonville

Noisettes of mutton. NOISETTES DE MOUTON—Strictly these small pieces should be cut from the *noix* of the leg, since *noisette* is the diminutive of *noix*. In practice, however, these very delicate cuts which provide entrées very much prized by connoisseurs, are almost always taken nowadays from the fillet (loin) or even the rib of the animal.

Noisettes cut from the rib are more regular in shape than those cut from the loin.

These cuts may be either sautéed or grilled, and can be served with all garnishes suitable for *Mutton cutlets* and *Noisettes of lamb*. See LAMB.

Noisettes of mutton Armenonville. NOISETTES DE MOUTON ARMENONVILLE—Sauté the *noisettes* in butter. Set each one on a small *Anna potato* (see POTATOES) cooked in a tartlet.

Garnish with cocks' combs and cocks' kidneys, alternating with the *noisettes* and morels in cream piled in the middle of the dish. Dilute the pan juices with white wine. Heat and pour over the meat.

Noisettes of mutton Nichette. NOISETTES DE MOUTON NICHETTE—Grill the *noisettes*. Put each one on a bed of browned *Duchess potatoes* (see POTATOES). On top of each *noisette* put a large grilled mushroom. In the middle of the dish heap morels sautéed with chopped parsley.

Pour concentrated veal gravy enriched with butter round the dish.

Noisettes of mutton à la tyrolienne

Noisettes of mutton à la tyrolienne. NOISETTES DE MOUTON À LA TYROLIENNE—Sauté the noisettes in butter. Set each on a small *Anna potato* (see POTATOES). Decorate the top of each *noisette* with a spoonful of *Tomato fondue**. Fill the middle of the plate with fried onion rings. Pour the cooking stock over the *noisettes*.

Mutton pie (English cookery)—See PIE.

Pistache of mutton or mutton à la catalane (Languedoc cookery). PISTACHE DE MOUTON (MOUTON À LA CATALANE)—Made from boned shoulder of mutton or part of the leg. The distinctive feature of this dish is that it is garnished with a considerable amount of garlic. See *Shoulder of mutton à la catalane*.

Ragoût of mutton. RAGOÛTS DE MOUTON—*Ragoûts* are made with the shoulder, neck, neck chops and breast of the sheep.

These different parts of the meat are trimmed, boned if necessary, and all cut into neat pieces weighing 3 to 3½ ounces (90 to 100 grams).

Ragoûts may be prepared in white or brown stock. Different vegetables, fresh or dried, and rice or barley are served with them.

Ragoût of mutton à l'anglaise I (Irish stew). RAGOÛT DE MOUTON À L'ANGLAISE—Cut into neat pieces of equal size, 1½ pounds (750 grams) of mutton. Put these pieces in a saucepan, in alternating layers, with 2 cups (500 grams) of sliced potatoes and 1 cup (200 grams) of sliced or chopped onions. Put a *bouquet garni** in the middle of the pan. Season with salt and pepper. Moisten with enough water just to cover the meat and potatoes.

Bring to the boil. Cover the pan. Cook in a hot oven for about an hour. Remove the *bouquet*. Serve in a bowl or deep dish.

Note. This stew has no thickening other than the potatoes, which in cooking should thicken the stock sufficiently.

Ragoût of mutton à l'anglaise II (Irish stew). RAGOÛT DE MOUTON À L'ANGLAISE—Prepare the stew as indicated in the previous recipe, but using only half the quantity of potatoes and onions. Boil the stew hastily for 35 minutes.

Drain on a sieve. Put the pieces of meat back in the saucepan. Cover with 1¾ cups (400 grams) of potatoes cut into ovals and 24 small parboiled onions. Pour strained cooking stock over all these ingredients. Cover and cook in the oven for 35 to 40 minutes. Serve in a bowl or deep dish.

Ragoût of mutton with barley. RAGOÛT DE MOUTON À L'ORGE. Use the same ingredients and procedure as for *Ragoût of mutton with white haricot beans*, leaving out the belly and substituting for the beans ⅝ cup (150 grams) of pearl barley, previously cooked in salt water for an hour. The cooking water of the barley should be used to moisten the *ragoût*.

Ragoût of mutton with red beans. RAGOÛT DE MOUTON AUX HARICOTS ROUGES—Proceed as for *Ragoût with white haricot beans*, substituting for the white beans the same quantity of red beans, three-parts cooked in red wine.

Ragoût of mutton with white haricot beans

Ragoût of mutton with white haricot beans. RAGOÛT DE MOUTON AUX HARICOTS BLANCS—This *ragoût*, which must not be confused with haricot of mutton, is prepared as follows:

Brown in fat ¼ pound (125 grams) of belly of pork, diced and blanched. Take these lardoons out of the pan and, in the same fat, brown 1½ pounds (750 grams) of mutton cut into square pieces and seasoned with salt and pepper.

Dust flour over the *ragoût* and proceed as indicated for the first stage of *Ragoût of mutton à la bonne femme*.

Drain the mutton. Put the pieces back in the pan. Add 2 cups (½ litre) of white beans, three-parts cooked, and the browned lardoons. Skim all fat off the sauce. Strain and pour over the *ragoût*.

Cover and cook in the oven for 1½ hours.

Ragoût of mutton à la bonne femme. RAGOÛT DE MOUTON À LA BONNE FEMME—Cut into square pieces 1½ pounds (750 grams) of mutton. Season with salt and pepper and brown with a quartered onion in fat. When the pieces of mutton are well browned, pour off some of the cooking fat. Add a pinch of fine sugar (this sugar, turning into caramel, will give the necessary colouring to the sauce), and 2 tablespoons of flour. Mix. Add a small clove of garlic, crushed. Moisten with a quart (litre) of water (or clear stock). Add 3 tablespoons of tomato purée, or ¾ cup (100 grams) of fresh, pulped tomatoes, and a *bouquet garni**. Cover and cook in the oven for an hour.

Drain the pieces of mutton on a sieve. Trim the pieces, that is to say remove the skin and splinters of bone separated during cooking. Put the meat back in the pan. Add 1¾ cups (400 grams) of potatoes cut to look like big olives, 24 small glazed onions and ¼ pound (125 grams) of belly of pork cut into little squares, blanched and browned. Skim all fat off the sauce. Strain and pour over the *ragoût*. Bring to the boil. Cover and cook in the oven for an hour. Serve in a bowl or round dish.

Ragoût of mutton with celeriac. RAGOÛT DE MOUTON AU CÉLERI-RAVE—Proceed as indicated for *Ragoût of mutton à la bonne femme*, substituting for the garnish indicated an equal quantity of celeriac cut into large oval pieces and parboiled.

Ragoût of mutton with chick-peas, à la catalane. RAGOÛT DE MOUTON AUX POIS CHICHES (À LA CATALANE)—Proceed as for the first stage of *Ragoût of mutton à la bonne femme*, using a little more tomato purée and seasoning liberally with crushed garlic. Put the pieces of mutton back in the pan. Add chick-peas, cooked separately in the usual way. Strain the sauce and pour it over the dish. Finish cooking in a slow oven.

Ragoût of mutton with kohl-rabi. RAGOÛT DE MOUTON AUX CHOUX-RAVES—Proceed as indicated for *Ragoût of mutton with celeriac*, substituting kohl-rabi, cut to look like big olives and parboiled, for celeriac.

Ragoût of mutton with macaroni, à la milanaise. RAGOÛT DE MOUTON AU MACARONI (À LA MILANAISE)—Proceed as for the first stage of *Ragoût of mutton à la bonne femme*, using a larger quantity of tomato purée and cooking the meat completely in one stage.

Put the pieces of mutton, drained and trimmed, in a flat earthenware dish. Cover with macaroni, half-boiled in salt water, drained, cut into lengths of 2½ inches, and then cooked in butter. Thoroughly mix grated Parmesan into this macaroni. Pour over this the sauce strained through a fine sieve, sprinkle with melted butter, and brown slowly in the oven.

Ragoût of mutton à la niçoise. RAGOÛT DE MOUTON À LA NIÇOISE—Bone and cut into square pieces 1½ pounds (750 grams) of shoulder of mutton. Brown in oil. When the meat is well browned, sprinkle flour over it. Add 2 cloves of garlic, crushed.

Moisten with ⅝ cup (1½ decilitres) of white wine. Boil down (reduce). Add enough clear stock to cover the meat, 4 tablespoons of tomato purée and a *bouquet garni**. Cook for one hour. Drain the meat and trim it. Put the pieces back in the pan. Add about 30 small new potatoes and 12 small browned onions. Strain the sauce and pour it over the mutton. Cover and cook in the oven for 45 minutes. Without stirring the *ragoût*, add to it 4 very small vegetable marrows (zucchini), peeled, coarsely diced and browned in oil. Cook in a slow oven for 15 minutes.

Ragoût of mutton à la paysanne. RAGOÛT DE MOUTON À LA PAYSANNE—Proceed as for *Ragoût of mutton à la bonne femme*, cooking the meat with carrots, turnips, onions and potatoes, quartered instead of being cut to look like olives.

This ragoût is also made with carrots, turnips, onions and celery cut into triangles and tossed in butter, and potatoes cut to look like olives.

Ragoût of mutton printanier. RAGOÛT DE MOUTON PRINTANIER—This is another name for *Navarin of mutton printanier*.

Ragoût of mutton with rice. RAGOÛT DE MOUTON AU RIZ—Proceed with the same ingredients as for *Ragoût of mutton with barley*, substituting for the barley ⅝ cup (150 grams) of rice, added to the ragoût 30 minutes before serving.

Rib of mutton. CARRÉ DE MOUTON—Most commonly the rib of mutton is divided into cutlets. It can also be roasted or braised whole, and garnished with vegetables. It should be served as intermediate course. A rib of mutton should not include more than 8 to 9 cutlets (chops) starting from the chump.

Preparation of a whole rib: Sever at the chuck. Remove the thin parchment-like skin which covers the meat. Remove the backbone. Loosen the tips of the cutlet (chop) bones. Bard the skinned meat with pork fat tied on with several lengths of string.

Rib of mutton à l'ancienne (Carême's recipe). CARRÉ DE MOUTON À L'ANCIENNE—'Cut two ribs of mutton from the fillet (loin) to the fourth cutlet (rib) from the neck.

'Completely remove all the skin covering the fillet, after having removed the backbone, and trim the fillet. Detach to the width of a thumb the meat covering the ribs at the top end. Saw through one bone of each pair of cutlets so that the remainder are only 2½ inches long. Interlard one of the ribs with best square lardoons. Thread sprigs of parsley into the other.

'Put the ribs in a marinade composed of an onion cut into rings, parsley, thyme, bay leaf, salt, pepper and half a glass of good oil.

'Three-quarters of an hour before serving, put it on the spit. Wrap in a sheet of buttered paper. Baste frequently. Five minutes before serving, unwrap, glaze, serve and pour clear stock over it.'

Rib of mutton à la boulangère. CARRÉ DE MOUTON À LA BOULANGÈRE—Proceed as for *Shoulder of lamb à la boulangère*. See LAMB.

Rib of mutton à la bretonne. CARRÉ DE MOUTON À LA BRETONNE—Roast the rib in the oven or on the spit. Serve with *white beans* or small *kidney beans à la bretonne*. Serve the gravy of the roast separately. See BEANS.

A *Purée bretonne** can also be served with rib of mutton.

Rib of mutton, braised with various garnishes. CARRÉ DE MOUTON BRAISÉ—Put the rib, trimmed, barded and tied, in a buttered braising pan lined with pork skin and a sliced onion and carrot which have been tossed in butter. Add a *bouquet garni*. Season. Cover and cook gently for 15 minutes. Moisten with ⅝ cup (1½ decilitres) of white wine. Boil down (reduce) to an essence. Moisten with 1½ cups (3 decilitres) of thickened veal gravy or clear soup. Cover and cook in the oven for 45 minutes to an hour, according to the size of the joint (cut).

Drain the rib. Glaze it. Put on a long dish. Garnish as indicated. Pour over it the reduced and strained braising stock with the fat skimmed off.

Garnishes for rib of mutton. Most garnishes indicated for *Baron of mutton* are suitable for this cut. It can also be garnished (these garnishes are very suitable for the rib) with purées of fresh or dried vegetables, especially pulses (lentils, dried beans, etc.), risotto and *pasta* prepared in different ways.

As appropriate, these garnishes are arranged round the meat or served separately.

Cold rib of mutton. CARRÉ DE MOUTON FROID—Roast the rib in the oven or on the spit, and leave until cold.

Trim. Glaze with jelly. Serve on a long dish. Garnish, at each end of the dish, with bunches of watercress and, along the sides, with chopped jelly.

Note. In England it is customary to serve mint sauce with cold lamb or mutton. See SAUCE, *Cold Sauces*.

Rib of mutton à la Maintenon. CARRÉ DE MOUTON À LA MAINTENON—Proceed as for *Saddle of mutton à la Maintenon*.

Rib of mutton à l'orientale. CARRÉ DE MOUTON À L'ORIENTALE—Trim a rib of mutton and braise in the usual way. Drain it. Serve on a long dish. Garnish along the sides with small tomatoes stuffed with a *salpicon** of sheep's (lamb's) liver, sautéed in butter, blended with thick brown gravy with a *salpicon* of sweet peppers cooked in oil added to it, and with small artichokes filled with a *salpicon* of onions cooked in butter until very tender and braised. Garnish each end of the dish with saffron-flavoured *Pilaf of rice**. Serve with the braising liquor.

Roast rib of mutton. CARRÉ DE MOUTON RÔTI—Trim all skin from the rib. Bard with pork fat and tie the joint. Roast in the oven or on the spit. When it is ready, the inside of the meat should be pinkish in colour.

Serve on a long dish garnished with watercress. Serve with its pan juices, with surplus fat skimmed off.

Cooking time: in the oven, 25 minutes per pound.
on the spit, 28 to 30 minutes per pound.

Roast rib of mutton with various garnishes. CARRÉ DE MOUTON RÔTI—Prepare and cook as indicated in the previous recipe. Serve on a long dish. Surround with the garnish indicated. Serve separately the pan juices, clear or slightly thickened, according to the nature of the garnish.

Garnishes suitable for roast rib of mutton: All those indicated for *Baron of mutton*.

Saddle of mutton. SELLE DE MOUTON—This cut is most commonly roasted and sometimes braised. It provides an intermediate meat course.

To roast a saddle of mutton, allow 20 to 22 minutes per pound in the oven, and a few minutes more on the spit.

It is served surrounded by the desired garnish and with the pan juices, clear or thickened, depending on the nature of the garnish. All garnishes indicated for *Rib* or *Leg of mutton* are suitable for saddle of mutton.

Cold saddle of mutton. SELLE FROIDE DE MOUTON—Proceed as for *Roast leg of mutton*, served cold.

Saddle of mutton à la Maintenon. SELLE DE MOUTON À LA MAINTENON—Trim a saddle of mutton cut near the upper leg. Braise it until it is three-parts cooked. Strain the stock and leave the meat to cool in it.

Drain the saddle and cut thin long slices inside the saddle, leaving the overhang on either side. Put these slices back inside the saddle with layers of *Maintenon* mixture between (see MIXTURES, *Maintenon mixture*), all pressed close together, so as to reshape the saddle. Cover with *Soubise* purée bound with egg. Put the saddle on an oval dish. Sprinkle with breadcrumbs and pour on melted butter. Pour round the saddle a few tablespoons of the strained braising stock. Cook in a slow oven until the top of the saddle is lightly browned. Serve with it the braising stock, strained and boiled down (reduced).

Note. Saddle of mutton *à la Maintenon* is usually garnished with braised vegetables.

Shoulder of mutton en ballon or en musette. ÉPAULE DE MOUTON EN BALLON (EN MUSETTE)—Bone the shoulder. Season inside. Instead of rolling it lengthwise as indicated for *Braised shoulder of mutton*, shape it into a ball. This type of rolled mutton is called '*en ballon*' or '*en musette*'. Braise the shoulder in the usual way. Drain and untie.

Shoulder of mutton en ballon or en musette

Glaze. Serve on a round dish, garnishing according to the recipe selected. Pour the braising stock over it.

Note. Shoulder of lamb *en ballon* may be stuffed.

Shoulder of mutton à la bonne femme I. ÉPAULE DE MOUTON À LA BONNE FEMME—Bone the shoulder and season. Stuff with sausage meat. Roll lengthwise and tie. Half-cook it in butter (or lard). Put it in an earthenware or copper dish lined with 2½ cups (600 grams) of potatoes cut to look like big olives (or new potatoes neatly peeled), ¾ cup (150 grams) of small half-cooked onions and 5 ounces (150 grams) of pork lardoons, blanched and fried. Season these ingredients well. Pour on butter or fat. Add a *bouquet garni**. Cook in a moderate oven, basting frequently. Serve as it is.

Shoulder of mutton à la bonne femme II. ÉPAULE DE MOUTON À LA BONNE FEMME—Trim a shoulder of mutton. Cut off the end of the bone, but do not bone the meat. Brown it in butter in an oval earthenware dish. When the shoulder is lightly browned all over, remove it from the dish. In the same butter, lightly brown 5 ounces (150 grams) of pork lardoons (blanched and drained) and about twenty small onions. Take these ingredients out of the dish and put back the shoulder of mutton. Surround with 2½ cups (600 grams) of potatoes, quartered, the small onions and the lardoons. Pour butter over the dish. Season. Cook in the oven, basting frequently.

Shoulder of mutton à la boulangère. ÉPAULE DE MOUTON À LA BOULANGÈRE—Bone the shoulder, season inside. (Roll lengthwise, if desired.) Tie. Cook for 30 minutes. Surround with 2½ cups (300 grams) of sliced onions, or about 20 small onions, tossed in butter. Season these ingredients. Pour the cooking butter over them. Finish cooking in the oven, basting frequently. Just before serving, add a few tablespoons of thickened brown gravy.

Shoulder of mutton à la bourgeoise. ÉPAULE DE MOUTON À LA BOURGEOISE—Bone the shoulder. Stuff it if desired. Braise. When the joint is half-cooked, drain it. Put it in another braising pan (or in a deep oval earthenware dish) with 6 small carrots (200 grams), cut to look like big olives, half-cooked in butter; 20 small glazed onions (150 grams); 5½ ounces (175 grams) of coarsely diced belly of pork, blanched and browned. Moisten with the strained cooking stock. Cover and finish cooking all together in the oven.

Braised shoulder of mutton with various garnishes. ÉPAULE DE MOUTON BRAISÉE—Bone the shoulder. Season inside with salt and pepper. Roll lengthwise and tie.

Put the shoulder in a buttered braising pan lined with pork skin (or bacon rinds), carrots and onions sliced round and tossed in butter. Surround the shoulder with the bones and trimmings of the shoulder cut into small pieces and tossed in butter. Add a large *bouquet garni**. Season. Cover and cook gently for 15 minutes. Moisten with 1 cup (2 decilitres) of dry white wine. Reduce. Add 2 cups (4 decilitres) of thickened brown stock and 3 tablespoons of *Tomato sauce* (see SAUCE). Bring to the boil.

Cover and cook in the oven for about 1½ hours. Drain and untie the shoulder. Glaze in the oven. Put it on a long dish. Surround with a suitable garnish. Boil down the braising stock, remove surplus fat, strain and pour over the meat.

Suitable garnishes for braised shoulder of mutton. All garnishes indicated for *Braised rib of mutton*, especially *Bretonne* garnish, various vegetable purées (dried vegetables in particular), risotto, and pasta prepared in various ways.

Shoulder of mutton à la bretonne. ÉPAULE DE MOUTON À LA BRETONNE—Bone and braise. Garnish with *white haricot beans* or small *kidney beans à la bretonne* (see BEANS), or with a purée of white haricot beans *à la bretonne*. Pour the strained braising stock over the shoulder.

Shoulder of mutton with red cabbage à la flamande. ÉPAULE DE MOUTON AUX CHOUX ROUGES, À LA FLAMANDE—Bone the shoulder. Stuff if desired. Roll lengthwise and tie. Braise until half-cooked. Line a deep earthenware dish with red cabbage prepared *à la flamande* (see CABBAGE) but which is only half-cooked. Lay the shoulder on this bed and cover with more red cabbage. Cover and cook slowly in the oven.

When the shoulder is ready, drain and untie it. Put it back in the dish on top of the cabbage. Pour over it a few tablespoons of gravy.

Shoulder of mutton à la catalane or en pistache. ÉPAULE DE MOUTON À LA CATALANE (EN PISTACHE)—Bone the shoulder, roll lengthwise and tie. Put it in a saucepan lined with a large slice of raw ham (not smoked), a sliced onion and carrot.

Season. Pour over it 2 tablespoons of goose fat (or lard). Cover and cook gently on the stove for 25 to 30 minutes. Take the shoulder and the slice of ham out of the pan. Put two tablespoons of flour in it. Brown this flour. Moisten with 1 cup (2 decilitres) of white wine. Add 2 cups (4 decilitres) of brown stock (or clear soup). Mix well. Strain. Put the joint and the slice of ham, diced, back in the saucepan. Add 50 blanched cloves of garlic and a *bouquet garni** containing a piece of dried orange peel. Moisten with the cooking stock. Cover and cook in a moderate oven for about an hour.

Drain and untie the shoulder. Put on a round dish. Pour over it the sauce and the cloves of garlic.

Note. The sauce for *pistache* of mutton can also be thickened with breadcrumbs.

Shoulder of mutton à la chipolata. ÉPAULE DE MOUTON À LA CHIPOLATA—Bone and braise. Proceed as for *Shoulder of mutton à la bourgeoise*, garnishing with chipolata sausages. (See GARNISHES.)

Shoulder of mutton in jelly. ÉPAULE DE MOUTON EN GELÉE—Bone the shoulder. Stuff with a *Fine forcemeat* (see FORCEMEAT) mixed with lean diced ham with one or two eggs to bind it. Roll lengthwise and tie. Put the shoulder in a stock mixed with *mirepoix**. Cook for an hour. Drain the meat. Leave it to cool under a weight. Untie. Skim off surplus fat from the stock. Mix in a little concentrated and strained aspic jelly. Pour over the meat. Leave to cool. Put the shoulder in an earthenware dish on a foundation of jelly set hard. Cover completely with half-set jelly. Leave until quite cold. Serve in the earthenware dish.

Shoulder of mutton with rice. ÉPAULE DE MOUTON AU RIZ—Bone. Roll lengthwise and tie. Braise until three-parts cooked, moistening with a fair amount of rather thin stock. Drain. Put it in another saucepan. Add 7 pounds (500 grams) of parboiled rice. Moisten with the strained stock. Finish cooking all together.

Stuffed shoulder of mutton, braised. ÉPAULE DE MOUTON FARCIE BRAISÉE—Bone the shoulder. Season inside. Stuff with fine pork stuffing mixed with $\frac{3}{4}$ cup (150 grams) of chopped onions cooked in butter until very tender, a tablespoon of chopped parsley. (These quantities are for 1 pound, i.e. 500 grams, of stuffing.) Season well with salt, pepper and spices. Roll the shoulder lengthwise and tie. Braise as indicated in the recipe for *Braised mutton with various garnishes*.

Serve the shoulder on a long dish. Garnish as indicated in the above-mentioned recipe. Pour on the braising stock, boiled down (reduced) and strained.

Stuffed shoulder of mutton en daube à la bourguignonne. ÉPAULE DE MOUTON FARCIE EN DAUBE À LA BOURGUIGNONNE—Bone the shoulder. Stuff it with fine pork stuffing, adding to this a chopped onion cooked slowly in butter until very tender, 2 or 3 tablespoons of dry *duxelles**, and some chopped parsley.

Roll the shoulder into a ball (*en ballon* or *en musette*, see above). Braise in red wine. When it is half-cooked, drain and untie. Put it in a deep round earthenware dish. Add 1 cup (200 grams) of mushrooms tossed in butter, 20 small glazed onions (150 grams), $\frac{1}{4}$ pound (125 grams) of coarsely diced belly of pork, blanched and browned. Moisten with the strained cooking stock. Add 2 tablespoons of blazing brandy. Cover the dish. Seal with flour-and-water paste. Cook in the oven for 45 minutes to an hour, according to the size of the shoulder.

Shoulder of mutton with turnips. ÉPAULE DE MOUTON AUX NAVETS—Bone the shoulder. Stuff if desired. Roll lengthwise and tie. Braise until three-parts cooked. Drain. Put the shoulder in another saucepan with 2 pounds (1 kilo) of tender turnips, cut to look like big olives and browned in butter, and 30 small onions (250 grams) also browned in a frying pan.

Skim all fat off the braising stock. Strain and pour over the dish. Finish cooking all together.

Sliced mutton. ÉMINCÉS DE MOUTON—Prepared with cooked mutton, in the same way as *Sliced beef* (see BEEF).

Braised sheep's tails (Carême's recipe). QUEUES DE MOUTON BRAISÉES—'Take 12 medium-sized tails. Soak in cold water for an hour. Pour boiling water over them. Line a saucepan with mutton trimmings, a *bouquet garni**, 2 onions, 2 carrots. Cover with thin strips of belly of pork. Tie the tails in pairs. Moisten with good clear soup. Cook for $1\frac{1}{2}$ hours. Drain the tails and put them in a press. Skim all fat off the stock; boil down almost to a jelly. When the tails are cold, trim them and heat slowly in the stock, reducing this slowly to a liquid jelly. Turn the tails over and over so that they are thoroughly impregnated with this liquid jelly. Serve them like cutlets, with *Espagnole sauce* (see SAUCE), boiled down (reduced) to half its volume.'

Grilled sheep's tails (Carême's recipe). QUEUES DE MOUTON PANÉES GRILLÉES—'After having prepared a dozen sheep's tails as indicated in the previous recipe and having trimmed them, dip them in melted butter and breadcrumbs. Grill until they are a good colour. Serve with *Hachée sauce* or a thin *Tomato sauce* (see SAUCE).'

Sheep's tongues—See OFFAL OR VARIETY MEATS.

Sheep's trotters—See OFFAL OR VARIETY MEATS.

MYRTLE. MYRTE—A fragrant evergreen shrub common all over Europe. Myrtle berries were used in place of pepper among the ancients. They were used in cookery and even gave their name to a stew, *Myrtalum*. There was also a spiced wine made from myrtle (*Myrtidanum*).

The pepper myrtle has leaves similar to those of the bay tree. Its powdered berries are known as Jamaican pepper.

NAGE (A LA)—A method of preparing certain shellfish, notably freshwater crayfish, spiny lobsters and small lobsters. These are cooked in a *court-bouillon** flavoured with herbs. Shellfish prepared in this way can be eaten cold or hot, and are served in this *court-bouillon.* See CRAYFISH, LOBSTER, SPINY LOBSTER.

NALESNIKI (Russian cookery)—A kind of *kromesky** made from a mixture of white cheese and butter. This mixture is used to fill a pancake made without sugar. The pancake is then dipped in butter and deep-fried.

NANTAIS—Nantes duckling sometimes appears on French menus simply as *Nantais.* See DUCKLING.

NANTAIS (Pastry)—A small almond biscuit.

Put 4 cups (500 grams) of sieved cake flour in a circle on the table. In the middle place ¾ cup (125 grams) of almonds pounded in a mortar, 1¾ cups (250 grams) of fine sugar, ½ pound (250 grams) of butter, 3 eggs and ½ cup (a decilitre) of kirsch. Work this dough in the usual way. Leave to stand in a cool place.

Roll out the dough. Cut it into circlets with a round, fluted pastry-cutter. Put the biscuits on a baking sheet. Brush with egg. Dust with sugar mixed with chopped almonds. Bake in a moderate oven.

Nantes cookies. PETITS PAINS DE NANTES—Put 7 tablespoons (100 grams) of softened butter into a bowl with 7 tablespoons (100 grams) of castor sugar, a pinch of salt, ½ teaspoon of baking powder and the rind of one lemon or orange grated on to the sugar. Mix these ingredients well until a creamy consistency is reached. Then, whisking vigorously, incorporate 2 whole eggs and, last of all, 1 cup (125 grams) of sieved cake flour.

Put the mixture into tartlet tins, buttered and sprinkled with finely shredded, well-dried almonds. Bake in a moderate oven.

Turn out the cookies on to a wire tray. Brush the top with apricot jam, then ice with maraschino-flavoured fondant icing and sprinkle with pink sugar.

NANTUA (A LA)—This name is given to various dishes, all of which are garnished with freshwater crayfish tails or, where appropriate, covered with crayfish purée.

NAPKINS. SERVIETTES DE TABLE—Table napkins should be folded simply, and should not present the fanciful and pretentious shapes that they used to be given.

NAPOLITAIN—Napolitains are large cakes which, like *Breton* and *Savoie* cakes, *mille-feuilles* and *croquembouche*, were once used to decorate elaborate buffets.

In former times it was customary to place at each end of a table set for a large dinner-party either an imposing decorated pastry or a heap of crayfish or other shellfish. This practice has now been abandoned; and although *napolitains* are still made, they are now usually small.

The name of this cake suggests that it was created in Naples, but was this, in fact, the case? Or must we, as would seem more probable, ascribe its invention to Carême, who, as is generally known, at the time when he was making great set pieces, invented a certain number of large and magnificent pastries to which he himself gave the names which they bear today? It is a question to which no certain answer can be given.

Ingredients. For a large napolitain: 2¼ cups (365 grams) blanched sweet almonds; 1 tablespoon (12½ grams) blanched bitter almonds; 1¼ cups (175 grams) fine sugar; ½ pound (250 grams) butter; 4 cups (500 grams) sieved cake flour; 1¼ cups (30 grams) sugar flavoured with lemon (or any other flavouring); a pinch of salt.

Method. Pound the almonds in a mortar with a little white of egg to bind them.

When the almonds are pounded to a fine paste, add the fine sugar, the flavoured sugar, the butter and flour.

Pounding constantly, add as many whole eggs as are required to make a very smooth and rather stiff paste. Take this paste out of the mortar and leave to stand for a while in a cool place.

Roll out the paste. Cut it into square, round or hexagonal pieces. With a pastry-cutter 2 inches in diameter, cut out the middle of each piece, except for two which will serve for the top and bottom layer of cake.

Bake these layers of pastry in a hot oven.

When the layers are quite cold spread each one with a different fruit purée or jelly.

Put the layers one on top of the other, using an uncut layer to form the base, with alternate layers of jam or jelly. Cover with the other uncut layer. When the cake is built up, coat with golden apricot jam and pipe with royal icing.

Note. In former times, *napolitain* cakes were decorated with motifs in almond paste or flaky pastry baked without browning.

NARBONNE—Narbonne, a town in the Aude district, may be regarded as one of the capitals of French viticulture, for it is in the Narbonne region that many of the ordinary table wines are made.

NARCISSUS. NARCISSE—The bulbs of this plant are edible and are used for food in some regions. They are cooked in the same way as Jerusalem artichokes.

NARWHAL. NARVAL—A cetacean found in Arctic seas. It has a unique defensive weapon in the form of the left canine tooth which can be up to 20 feet in length. This weapon, believed to belong to the fabulous unicorn, changed hands at very high prices in the Middle Ages, for it was believed to have the power of divining poisons.

Nowadays, the narwhal is chiefly used for the oil processed from its fat. The flesh is eaten by the people of Greenland, probably when no other food is available.

NASTURTIUM. CAPUCINE—Edible and decorative plant. Its flowers and leaves are similar to watercress in taste. It used, at one time, to be called *Mexican cress* and *Jesuits' cress* because it was brought into Europe by the Jesuits.

Nasturtium flowers are used in salads. The leaves when young can also be used in salads, like cress. The buds and the seeds, when they are still tender, are pickled in vinegar like capers.

NATURISM, NATURIST. NATURISME, NATURISTE—A doctrine which preaches the return to nature, with regard to clothing as well as food.

Naturism prescribes a much more rigorous diet than vegetarianism. According to the apostles who preach this regenerative doctrine, diet must be made up entirely of raw fruit and vegetables, with some relaxation which permits the seasoning of these natural foods and the preparation of cereal porridges.

NAVARIN—This name is used expressly for a *ragoût** of mutton made either with small onions and potatoes or—and in this case the dish must be described as *à la printanière*—with different vegetables such as carrots, turnips, small onions, new potatoes and green peas. See MUTTON.

The term *navarin* is sometimes wrongly applied to *ragoûts* of shell-fish or poultry. This name, we must repeat, should only be used of mutton dishes or, in exceptional cases, lamb.

NEAPOLITAN SLICES. TRANCHES NAPOLITAINES—These are mass-produced Neapolitan ice creams sold in cafés and some restaurants. They are made of alternate layers of plain ice cream and mousse mixture, cut into slices from a larger block.

NECTARINE—A smooth-skinned variety of peach. This fruit is eaten raw, like the peach, and can be cooked like peaches. It is also called *Brugnon* in French. See PEACHES.

NEEDLE. AIGUILLE—

Larding needle. AIGUILLE À PIQUER—Small-size larding needle pointed at one end and pronged at the other, used for piercing and larding various substances with thin strips of bacon. It is with a larding needle that we stud fillet of beef, calf's sweetbreads, small pieces of meat, poultry and winged game and different cuts of venison, with pieces of bacon, pork or ham fat.

Trussing needle. AIGUILLE À BRIDER—A steel pin pointed at one end and pierced at the other. A trussing needle is used for trussing poultry and game.

NEF (Ship)—This name was given in France to a piece of goldsmith's work made in the form of a ship, which contained cutlery, napery, etc., used at the royal table, such as the salt cellar, the great carvers and the table napkins in scented sachets.

All persons—even princesses—passing by the royal *nef* had to salute it.

NÉGUS—Wine spiced with sugar, lemons and nutmeg.

NEIGE DE FLORENCE—An extremely delicate *pasta* product, which is used in clear soup. This pasta, which the guests themselves put into their *consommé* in their soup-plates, is presented in the form of flakes, pure white and very light. Hence its name, 'Florentine snow'.

NELUSKO—Iced *petits fours* which are made as follows:

Take some cherries in brandy. Drain them. Put them on a napkin to dry them slightly. Make a *Fondant icing* (see ICING) and warm it gently. While it is being warmed in a *bain-marie**, slit each cherry and stone it. Put the cherries back on the napkin with the hole upward. Fill the cherries with a little *Bar-le-Duc* red currant jam (that is to say, without pips). To do this drain off the syrup from the jam and use the currants only. (A forcing bag may be used for this operation.) Flavour the fondant icing, which must remain thick, with a little of the brandy from the cherries. Heat the fondant.

Using a skewer and taking care to keep the hole in the cherries upward, dip them in the icing. This must be very thick because, in melting, it will turn to liqueur. The thicker it is, the more liqueur and the better the sweet.

The dipping must be carried out quickly, for the stoned cherries filled with Bar-le-Duc red currant jam are very moist, and the moisture, which cannot be retained in the fruit, will immediately mix with the icing and melt it.

As soon as the *neluskos* are cold, put them in fluted paper cases or, better still, in silver paper cases, since the syrup always manages to ooze through paper.

NEMOURS (Tartlets)—These small tartlets are prepared as follows. Line tartlet tins with *Flaky pastry dough* (see DOUGH). Put a little mirabelle jam at the bottom of each one. On top of the jam, pipe some *Chou paste* (see DOUGH). Bake in a hot oven. Sprinkle with icing sugar.

NÉROLI—A volatile oil extracted from orange-blossom.

This oil is used in confectionery, and in the manufacture of some liqueurs.

NÉROLI (Pastry)—Pound in a mortar ¾ cup (125 grams) of blanched almonds with 3 eggs. Add 1½ cups (200 grams) of fine sugar, the candied peel of 3 oranges chopped fine, and ¼ cup (½ decilitre) of orange-blossom water or 1 teaspoon orange extract. Work this mixture thoroughly with the pestle.

Put the mixture in a bowl. Add 5 tablespoons (60 grams) of melted butter and 3 tablespoons (30 grams) of cornflour (cornstarch). Mix well.

Fill small buttered tins with this mixture, sprinkle with chopped almonds and bake in a moderate oven.

NESSELRODE—An iced sweet, usually known as *Iced Nesselrode pudding*. See PUDDING.

NESTS. NIDS—In cookery, edible nests are made in various ways. They are used for the presentation of small tit-bits.

Potato nests are like little baskets (round or oval, according to the shape of the mould in which they are cooked) made with match-stick potatoes, which are put in small wire baskets shaped like nests, and deep-fried in boiling fat.

In these nests, fried food of various kinds is served or, after lining them with pancakes, various *ragoûts** may be served in them.

See QUAIL, *Quails in a nest*.

Swallows' nests. NIDS D'HIRONDELLES—Nests built by salanganes. They are much sought after by Chinese gourmets.

The nests of salanganes, incorrectly called sea-swallows, have given rise to the most extraordinary views regarding their nature. The one most widely believed was that the birds used regurgitated seaweed to build them after having partially digested it.

Nowadays it is known that the salangane builds its nest with its saliva. Just before the mating season, the bird's saliva glands become greatly enlarged and secrete a thick viscous glutinous liquid containing 90 per cent of a protein which is insoluble in water.

The nests, constructed in layers, placed one on top of the other, are font-shaped and are attached to the sides of rocks in almost inaccessible grottos on the coast of Annam, in Java, and on one or two islands of the Malay Archipelago.

Collecting these nests is an extremely painful and dangerous occupation, and only the high price paid for the nests can explain the risks taken by men engaged in 'hunting the nests'.

Before being sold for food, the nests undergo complicated processing. They are washed several times in hot water, kneaded with groundnut oil which is then washed out in a further bath of hot water. The nests are then very carefully cleared with pincers of all down and feathers.

Particularly enjoyed by gourmets of China, swallows' nests are generally eaten in the form of soup. After being dipped in hot water they are added to carefully clarified beef or chicken broth and cooked for at least half an hour in a double saucepan. For every bowl of soup of 10 to 13 ounces (300 to 400 grams), a nest weighing ¼ to ½ ounce (8 to 15 grams) is required. See SOUPS AND BROTHS, *Consommé with birds' nests*, and SWALLOW.

NETTLE OR TIE—A weed, with stinging hairs on leaves full of formic acid, which provokes skin eruption. Some species of this plant such as *White dead nettle* and *Blind nettle*, or *Lamium album*, are edible, used like sorrel, as a vegetable or in soups.

NEUFCHÂTEL CHEESE—See CHEESE.

NIÇOISE (A LA)—A method of preparing various dishes, all of which have tomatoes among their ingredients. They are usually flavoured with garlic. See MULLET, *Red Mullet à la niçoise*.

NIGELLA. NIGELLE—The name given to a number of plants of the *Renunculus* family, whose seeds are used as a spice. Some varieties have aromatic and pungent seeds which can be used instead of pepper. Nigella is sometimes known as *fennel flower* or *devil-in-the-bush*.

Cultivated nigella is used as a spice in Egypt.

Damascene nigella, sometimes known as *Venus' hair* because of its thread-like leaves, has seeds which are used in the East to sprinkle on bread and cakes.

NIGHTSHADE. NORELLE—Undeservedly, this plant (*Solanum nigrum*) is reputed to be poisonous. Parmentier, the French agriculturist (1737-1813), long since proved that it was used for food in certain regions. In the West Indies the leaves are eaten like spinach and are called *brèdes*. For recipes, see SPINACH.

NITROGEN. AZOTE—Colourless, tasteless, scentless permanent gas forming 78.1 per cent of the atmosphere; it enters into the composition of many of the substances used as food. See ALBUMINOIDS.

NIVERNAIS AND MORVAN—The culinary repertoire of this ancient province, which roughly corresponds with the Nièvre department of today, has no dishes in the grand manner. This does not mean, however, that the Nivernais table is without merit, nor that in this part of the country lovers of good food, even if they confine themselves to local dishes, cannot enjoy good meals.

The foodstuffs produced in this area are, in fact, all excellent. The livestock bred here produce meat of the highest quality. Cattle reared and nurtured in the rich plains of the Loire (Charolais cattle, locally bred) are especially prized for the fine quality of their meat.

Sheep bred in this area are of the very best. For delicacy of flavour, they rival those reared in the Bourbonnais and Berry districts.

The pigs of the Nivernais province are equally excellent, and very good poultry is bred here. That of Morvan is especially delicate.

Succulent winged and ground game is fairly abundant in this region.

In the rivers and small lakes of the Nivernais and Morvan province fish of all kinds abound. These provide the materials for exquisite *matelotes**. River trout and crayfish are plentiful.

The kitchen gardens and orchards also yield very good products. Pot vegetables in the strict sense, such as carrots and onions, are especially flavoursome, and it is because of the fine quality of its vegetables that the name *Nivernais* is given to one of the principal and best garnishes for meat dishes in the classic culinary repertoire.

The best known cheese of the region is that called *fromage sec* (dry cheese) which is made by drying white cheese in straw baskets, draining them well and dusting them with pepper.

Excellent table wines are made in the Nivernais region. Some of the white and red wines, though they cannot be compared in bouquet with the great wines of the neighbouring Burgundy, are nevertheless excellent.

The white wines of Pouilly-sur-Loire, the *Muscadet*, the *Blanc-fumé* and the *Tannay*, are very pleasant wines, especially the *Pouilly*, with quite a pronounced taste of gun-flint.

Among the red wines of the region are: *Charité*, *Chaulgnes*, *Saint-Benin-d'Azy*.

Culinary specialities—*Cabbage soup with pork fat; Nivernais hot-pot; Mixed vegetable soup, country style; Chitterlings and baby chitterlings of Clamecy; Saveloy; Cooking sausage (with garlic); Beursaudes (pork greaves); Morvan smoked ham; Black puddings with wild thyme; Griaudes; Matelotes of Loire fish; Fricassée of pike; River trout à la meunière; Freshwater crayfish in court-bouillon; Nivernaise omelette* (a flat omelette, filled with sorrel, ham and chives); *Beef daube* (made with a lot of carrots); *Grilled beef à la marinière* (similar to charcoal grilled beef); *Veal stewed in red wine; Grenadins of veal of Corbigny; Tripe à la morvandelle* (similar to *tripe à la mode de Caen*); *Pig's liver with onions; Eel galette; Griaude galette; Chicken en barboille* (chicken in red wine, the sauce thickened with chicken's blood); *Rabbit en barboille; Civet of hare* (in the Nivernais district turnips are added to the civet); *Saupiquet des Amognes; Potato pâté; treuffes* (potatoes) *en tourtière* (baked in a pie-dish); *Leek tart* (a kind of *flamiche*); *Dandelion salad with bacon; Grapiaux* (large pancakes cooked in melted pork fat).

Among the Nivernais sweets, pastries and confectionery are: *Flamusse aux pommes* (a special kind of apple flan); *Pâté aux poires* (pear paste); *Sour milk fritters; Galettes aux griaudes; Croquets (petits fours) of Nevers and Prémery; Nougatines of Nevers; Barley-sugar of Morvan; Négus* (a kind of soft caramel); *Marzipan sweets of Decize.*

NIVERNAISE (A LA)—The name of a garnish served mainly with intermediate meat courses. It is made up of carrots cut to look like olives and small glazed onions.

NOISETTE (Butchery)—Strictly, the term *noisette* designates a small individual portion of meat, particularly a small round slice cut from the fillet, rib or leg of mutton or lamb.

A *noisette*, as its name suggests, must be round in shape. Its average weight should be from 2 to 3 ounces (70 to 90 grams).

For the preparation of *noisettes*, see LAMB and MUTTON.

More loosely, the term *noisette* is used of a small slice of veal fillet or a little round slice of fillet of beef.

NOISETTE POTATOES—Potatoes shaped to look like hazel-nuts with a ball scoop (see POTATOES), cooked in butter, slightly browned.

NOISETTE SAUCE—See SAUCE.

NOISETTINES (Pastry)—Small cakes made by putting together two oval layers of short pastry with *Frangipane cream* flavoured with hazel-nuts.

They can also be made of large round layers of short pastry filled with hazel-nut cream.

NONAT—There is some doubt as to whether this tiny Mediterranean fish is a separate species or, according to a view quite widely held, merely the fry of the goby. It has not yet been possible to decide the point, but what everyone unanimously recognises is that the *nonat* is an exquisite delicacy. Unfortunately it can only be eaten in places close to its fishing grounds.

The best way of preparing nonats is deep-frying. They can also be prepared as an hors-d'oeuvre, and are used as a garnish for omelettes.

Fried nonats. NONATS FRITS—Dip them in flour. Shake gently in the frying basket to get rid of excess flour, and plunge them for about a minute in deep fat, which should be as hot as possible. As soon as they are crisp, drain, season with dry table salt, and arrange them in a heap on a napkin, garnished with fried parsley.

NONNETTE (Iced gingerbread)—A small round gingerbread which is made industrially. The chief centres for the manufacture of *nonnettes* are Dijon and Reims.

NONPAREILLE—This is the name given in France to small capers pickled in vinegar.

The same name is given to coloured granulated sugar used to decorate sweets and cakes.

There is also a French variety of pear called *nonpareille*. It is large, ripens in the autumn, and is somewhat tart in flavour.

NOODLES. NOUILLE—A pasta made with flour, eggs and water. Noodles can be eaten fresh or dried.

Dried noodles or very small noodles. NOUILLES SÈCHES, NOUILLETTES—These can be bought ready-made. They are poached in salt water as described for freshly made noodles and macaroni. After poaching they are prepared like the latter.

Note. Dried noodles are served by themselves or are used as garnish for meat, fish, eggs, etc. When noodles are used as garnish, they are more often than not prepared with butter or gravy.

Generally speaking pasta should not be poached in a bouillon or in gravy as that toughens them without improving their flavour.

However, you may, if you like, cook the pasta three-quarters in salted water, drain them and then simmer them gently for a few minutes in a bouillon.

Fresh noodles. NOUILLES FRAÎCHES—Fresh noodles can be bought ready-made in food stores, in large towns at least. But in France, especially in Alsace, housewives make them at home, as indicated below.

Ingredients. ¾ cup (500 grams) sifted flour; 3 whole eggs and 6 yolks; 2 teaspoons (12 grams) of salt and 2 to 4 tablespoons of water. The pasta is more delicate if only yolks of eggs are used. This depends on what the noodles are to be used for; in some cases they are made with whole eggs.

Method. Sieve the flour. Arrange it in a circle on the table. Put the salt and the water in the middle. Dissolve the salt and add the eggs and the yolks. Mix the flour a little at a time with the eggs. Knead thoroughly to make sure that the flour is well mixed and to ensure a homogeneous and smooth mixture.

Note that the pasta must be very firm. Wrap in a thin cloth to prevent it from drying, and leave to stand for at least an hour, until it loses its elasticity. When a large quantity of noodles is required, it is desirable to make them several hours beforehand. It is then easier to cut them into strips.

Making the noodles. Divide the dough into pieces about the size of an egg and roll into balls. Roll out each piece into the shape of a large pancake, which should be no more than $\frac{1}{16}$ inch thick.

Spread the rolled-out dough on baking sheets covered with sheets of paper or, if more convenient, folded in half over a string line. Leave to dry for 50 minutes. Next, lightly dust each 'pancake' with flour. Roll them and cut into whorls $\frac{1}{16}$ inch wide. Spread them out on a baking sheet.

(These are very fine noodles, but if the noodles are required for garnishing they should be cut about ⅛ inch wide.)

Fresh noodles à l'alsacienne. NOUILLES FRAÎCHES À L'ALSACIENNE—Prepare the noodles as indicated for *Noodles with butter.*

Put the noodles in a pie-dish and sprinkle on the top a handful of noodles which have been put raw in a frying pan and lightly browned in butter.

Boiled fresh noodles. NOUILLES AU NATUREL—Plunge into 2½ quarts (litres) of boiling water, with 1½ teaspoons (10 grams) of salt per quart (litre), ½ pound (250 grams) of fresh noodles.

Boil fast for 8 to 10 minutes.

Drain the noodles. Put them in a shallow pan and evaporate all their excess moisure over a low flame. Serve in a well-heated deep round dish.

Fresh noodles in butter. NOUILLES FRAÎCHES AU BEURRE—Cook the noodles in salted water and drain. Put them in a pan and dry them slowly on the stove.

Cut 4 to 5 tablespoons (60 to 80 grams) of butter into small pieces so that the butter will melt quickly and blend more easily. Add to the noodles and mix well. Season. Serve in a pie-dish.

Fresh noodles with brown butter. NOUILLES FRAÎCHES AU BEURRE NOISETTE—Cook the noodles in salted water and drain. Dry them and put them in a warm dish. Heat 5 to 6 tablespoons (60 to 80 grams) of butter in a frying pan until it has taken a nut-brown colour. Pour it over the noodles and mix gently with a fork.

Fresh noodles au gratin. NOUILLES FRAÎCHES AU GRATIN—Cook the noodles in salted water as described in the recipe for *Noodles in butter*.

Drain the noodles. Add 2 ounces (60 grams) of mixed Gruyère and Parmesan cheese and 3 tablespoons (50 grams) of butter. Season with salt and pepper and a little grated nutmeg. Spread the noodles evenly on a dish, buttered and sprinkled with grated cheese.

Put grated cheese on the noodles and sprinkle a little melted butter over it. Brown the noodles in a hot oven.

Fresh noodles with gravy. NOUILLES FRAÎCHES AU JUS—Cook and drain the noodles and sprinkle them with several tablespoons of thick brown veal gravy, with beef gravy or any other slightly strengthened meat gravy.

Leave to simmer for a few minutes on the side of the stove and serve in a pie-dish.

Fresh noodles à l'italienne. NOUILLES FRAÎCHES À L'ITALIENNE—Cook the noodles in the usual way. Drain and finish them off with butter and grated cheese as described in the recipe for *Noodles au gratin* but do not brown them. Serve the noodles in a pie-dish.

Note. This dish can be made with Parmesan cheese only or with Gruyère cheese only, but the mixture of both cheeses gives a better result.

Fresh noodles à la lyonnaise. NOUILLES FRAÎCHES À LA LYONNAISE—Prepare the noodles as described in the recipe for *Noodles with butter*. Arrange them in a pie-dish and garnish the top with 3 tablespoons of finely minced onions fried in butter.

Fresh noodles à la milanaise. NOUILLES FRAÎCHES À LA MILANAISE—Cook the noodles, drain them and finish them as described in the recipe for *Macaroni à la milanaise**.

Fresh noodles à la napolitaine. NOUILLES FRAÎCHES À LA NAPOLITAINE—Cook the noodles, drain them and finish the dish as described in the recipe for *Macaroni à la napolitaine**.

NOQUES (Alsatian cookery)—Work to a paste, in a warmed bowl, ½ pound (250 grams) of butter seasoned with salt, pepper and a touch of grated nutmeg, adding 2 whole eggs and 2 yolks, 1 cup plus 2 tablespoons (150 grams) of sieved flour and a stiffly beaten white of egg. Divide this mixture into parts, each about the size of a hazel-nut. Poach in boiling salt water. Drain. Serve in a deep round dish, sprinkled with grated Parmesan and browned butter.

Noques are also served in soup.

Noques à la viennoise (Austrian sweet or dessert)—These *noques* are a kind of small *quenelle**, similar to *Eggs à la neige* (see EGGS, *Snow eggs*), but less delicate, although they can be made lighter if desired by beating the whites of egg used instead of leaving them as they are. Like *Eggs à la neige*, these *noques* are served with vanilla-flavoured custard.

Ingredients—¼ pound (125 grams) butter; 6 tablespoons (100 grams) of sugar; ⅞ cup (100 grams) of sieved flour; 9 eggs; 1 pod vanilla or 1 teaspoon vanilla extract; 2 cups (½ litre) milk; ½ cup (1 decilitre) double cream; a pinch of table salt.

Method—Put the butter in a bowl and work with a spatula until it is smooth and creamy.

When it is reduced to a paste, work in a pinch of salt (3 grams), a little sugar (2 tablespoons) and 5 yolks of egg, added one by one. Next, add half the double cream.

Beat all the ingredients together vigorously. When the mixture is very fluffy, whisk with an egg-whisk in place of the spatula. While beating with the egg-whisk, sprinkle in the flour in a fine spray. When this is thoroughly mixed, beat a white of egg to a stiff foam and blend it into the mixture. At the end, mix in one by one 3 plain whites of egg (that is to say, whites which have not been beaten to a foam).

The *noques* are poached in sweetened milk in exactly the same way as *Eggs à la neige*.

Poach the *noques* without bringing the liquid to the boil. (If the milk is allowed to boil, this causes the *noques* to swell unduly.) While they are poaching, turn them over gently with a skimmer, then, when they are ready, drain them on a dish.

To make the custard which goes with the *noques*, use the milk in which they have been poached, with the double cream and 4 yolks of egg added. Beat the yolks and the cream with an egg-whisk, and when they are well mixed, blend in the boiling sweetened milk. Thicken this custard by heating it on the stove for a few seconds, but do not let it boil. As soon as the custard thickens, strain it through a fine sieve on to the *noques*.

This sweet can equally well be served cold or hot.

NORMANDE (A LA)—A method of preparation used mainly for fish braised in white wine, especially sole.

The usual garnish for these fish, which are coated with *Normande sauce* (see SAUCE), comprises poached oysters, shelled shrimps, mushrooms, strips of truffle, fried gudgeon (or smelt), freshwater crayfish in *court-bouillon**, and lozenge-shaped pieces of bread fried in butter. Often, poached and shelled mussels are added to this garnish.

See SOLE, *Sole normande*.

In quite a different way from that used for fish, small cuts of meat, and chicken, can be prepared *à la normande*. These, after they are cooked, have cider poured over them. The sauce is enriched with a little calvados.

Some species of winged game, especially partridge, can be prepared *à la normande*. See PARTRIDGE.

There are also in pastry-making a large number of preparations called *à la normande*.

NORMANDY—Normandy is a province of high gastronomic repute, and the Normandy table can be regarded as one of the best in all the provinces of France.

This is readily understandable when one considers that Normandy produces excellent butter and cream and that, in all the characteristic dishes of the region, this butter and cream are used, if not prodigally, at least in sufficient quantity to ensure that the food is deliciously flavoured.

Moreover, the larders of this province are among the most richly stocked in the country.

The stock, cattle and sheep, nurtured on its rich pastures, provide high-grade meat. Its salt-meadow sheep are particularly good.

The orchards of Normandy are magnificent, and fruit production is a very important industry. Normandy apples have a great reputation.

Normandy is well provided with sea fish. Its coastal waters provide an abundance of sole, brill, turbot, mackerel and a good many other delicate fish.

The Seine shad and the salmon and trout of Bresles and the Arques are extremely delicate fish.

There is no lack of shell-fish. There are the white

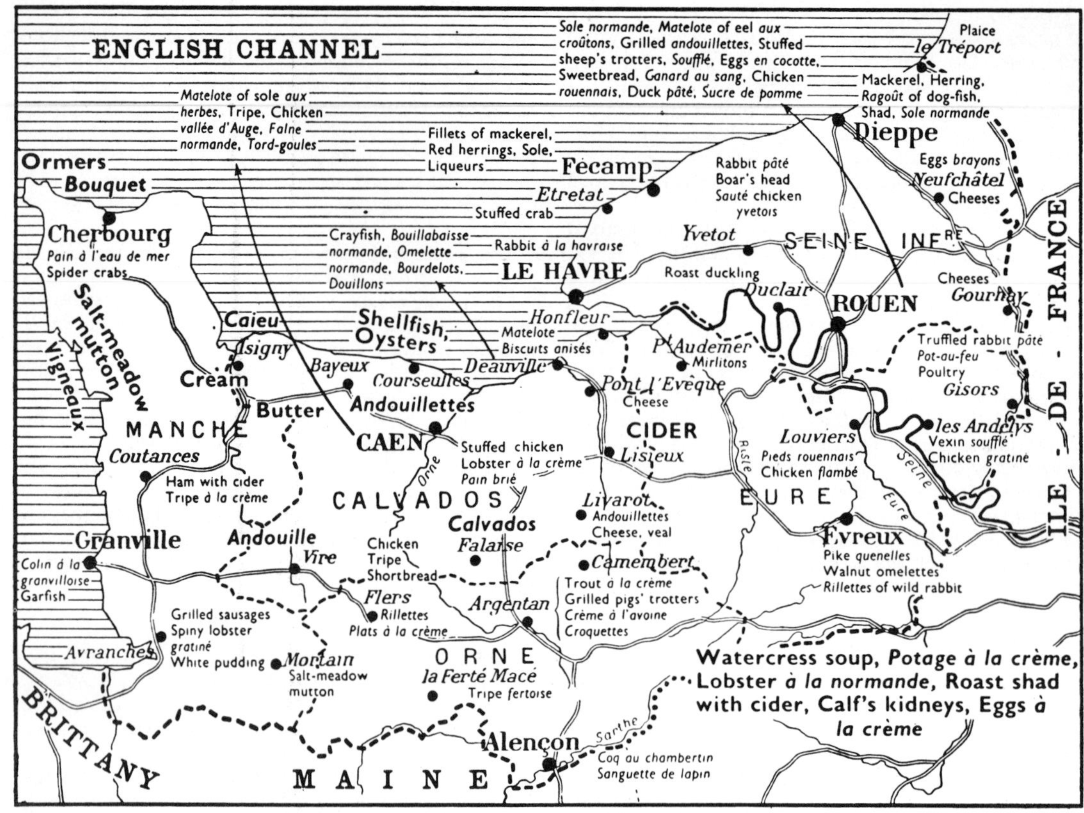

Gastronomic map of Normandy

oysters of Dives, Luc-sur-mer and Courseulles, the mussels from the natural mussel-beds, which are as fat as one could wish; clams; *fleons* (*donax*); cockles. Giant mussels, called *caieu*, are found at Isigny, and there are the *ormiers* (or haliotis) of the Cap de la Hague; the winkles or periwinkles and also the prawns (*bouquet*) of Cherbourg; and the *demoiselles* (small lobsters) of Caen, Cherbourg and Dieppe.

The milk and cream of Normandy have a well-deserved reputation. The most famous butter is that of Isigny. The butter sold in the markets of Cormeilles (Eure) and Neufchâtel (Seine-Inférieure) is also of very good quality.

The winged and ground game shot in Normandy is highly prized.

Admittedly, this region has no vineyards. Wine, moreover, is not much drunk by its people. They have, however, excellent cider and perry to drink with the special dishes of their province. The cider of the Auge Valley has the highest reputation. The pears of Clécy, Alemon, Argentan, Ecouche and Domfront are highly prized.

And among the good things of this region, we must not forget to mention the cider spirit called *Calvados*, and also the celebrated Benedictine liqueur made at Fécamp.

Culinary specialities—First of all it must be observed that the distinctive feature of a large number of the dishes of Normandy is that they are cooked in cream. Another characteristic of cooking in this region is that it is done with a special fat called *graisse normande*, which is made by melting together and clarifying equal quantities of pork fat and suet, flavoured with pot vegetables and herbs and seasoned with salt and pepper. This fat gives a special flavour to food cooked in it.

Among the culinary specialities of this region are: *Soup normande;* the famous *Madame Poulard omelette, Omelette aux coques; Matelote normande*, made with salt-water fish; the true *sole normande*, which is a way of stewing soles in cream, and which has nothing in common with the *sole à la normande* served in Paris restaurants; *Sole à la dieppoise* (and other sea fish prepared in the same way); *Mussels à la marinière; Seine shad stuffed and baked; Tripe à la mode de Caen* and *Tripe à la mode de la Ferté-Macé; Sheep's trotters à la Rouennaise; Casserole of veal in cream; White pudding of l'Avranchin; Duckling à la Rouennaise*, which is prepared in different ways in Rouen and Duclair; *Wood partridges flambés*, which are a great speciality of the Hostellerie du Cheval Blanc (White Horse Inn) at Vire, and the famous *Poulet à la crème* (chicken in cream) called *vallée d'Auge*.

Among the vegetables let us single out for special mention French (string) beans in cream and salsify *à la normande*.

The pork products of Rouen, Vire and other places, such as the chitterlings of Vire and the baby chitterlings of Caen, black and white puddings, sausages, etc., are excellent.

The cheeses of this region have a high reputation. The best known are: *Pont-l'Evêque*, *Camembert*, *Livarot*, *Neufchâtel*, *Bondon*, *Gournay*, and the famous small double-cream cheeses among which is the celebrated Gervais *petit suisse*.

Among the sweets and confectionery of Normandy are *Terrinée* which is also called *Tord-goule;* Normandy *Bourdelots* (apple turnovers), made by cooking whole apples in a coating of pastry; *Douillons*, made in the same way with pears; *Galette normande; Fouace* (hearth cake) *of Caen; Roulettes of Rouen; Mirlitons of Rouen and*

A farmhouse in Normandy
(*French Government Tourist Office*)

Pont-Audemer; delicious *Normandy shortbread; Duchesses de Normandie; Norelles, Boulots, Rivets* and *Chemineaux;* and finally the famous *sucres de pomme*, whose reputation is several centuries old.

NORVÉGIEN (Pastry)—Pound in a mortar 1½ cups (250 grams) of sweet almonds and 1 tablespoon (10 grams) of blanched apricot kernels, with 4 whole eggs. When the almonds are pounded to a smooth paste, add 2 cups plus 2 tablespoons (280 grams) of fine sugar. Blend this mixture thoroughly.

Put the mixture in a bowl and add ⅞ cup (200 grams) of softened butter. Work with a spatula until the mixture is frothy; then, still stirring, add 5 teaspoons (25 grams) of cornflour (cornstarch) and a small glass of kirsch.

Put the mixture into round buttered moulds lined with buttered paper. Bake in a moderate oven.

NORVÉGIENNE (A LA)—This name is given to various preparations in cookery and confectionery, but it is more precisely used for a kind of surprise pudding, ice cream inside a piping hot casing. This sweet, invented, it is believed, by an American physicist called Rumford (1753—1814), is called *Omelette à la norvégienne*.

The same name is also applied to certain methods of presenting cold fish or shellfish, such as salmon, lobster and spiny lobster.

NOUGAT—A sweet made with roasted almonds (or walnuts) and honey (or syrup).

According to some authorities the word nougat is of Spanish origin. What is certain is that it derives from the Latin *nux*, nut (walnut) for it would appear that originally this sweet was made mainly with walnuts, whereas nowadays it is generally made with almonds and sugar, honey being substituted occasionally for the latter. Industrially, it is made with hazel-nuts or pistachios.

There are a great many kinds of nougat; hard or soft, white or coloured. White nougat is usually made industrially; the Montélimar nougat enjoys a great reputation.

In home confectionery, a type of nougat is also made. See below the recipe for *White nougat*.

In the South of France, the oil-cake made from the residue of walnut oil is called *nougat*.

White nougat. NOUGAT BLANC—Cook together to the small crack degree (260°F.) ½ pound (250 grams) of honey and an equal quantity of sugar. Add a tablespoon of orange-blossom water, or ½ teaspoon orange extract, and a stiffly beaten white of egg.

Melt over a gentle flame, stirring, and bring the sugar to the ball degree (246°F.).

Now add 1 pound (500 grams) of sweet almonds, blanched, dried, chopped and heated.

Put this mixture in a flat baking tin lined with sheets of rice-paper. Cover with sheets of the same paper. Place on top of the nougat a wooden board with a 2 pound (kilo) weight on it. Leave until lukewarm. Cut into squares or other shapes.

Note. Nougat with filberts, hazel-nut, pine-kernels or pistachio nuts can be made in the same way.

NOUGATINE CAKES—Put into a deep square well buttered baking tin (about 3 inches in depth) some best *Genoese cake mixture** flavoured with vanilla. Bake this cake and leave to cool.

Cut the cake into squares and slice each of these squares across into 3 or 4 layers. Spread *Praline cream* (see CREAM) on each of these layers. Build them up by putting the layers one on top of the other, and ice with *Chocolate fondant icing* (see ICING).

Note. These cakes can be made separately in small square pieces instead of making them out of one large cake.

NUT. NOIX—The name for a number of different types of fruit with a woody outer casing and a soft inner skin enclosing an edible kernel.

NUT-GALL. NOIX DE GALLE—Eastern peoples eat fleshy nut-gall. It is about the size of a lady apple, and grows on a species of sage bush.

In some places a nut-gall is eaten which grows on a species of ground-ivy.

Nutmeg

NUTMEG. MUSCADE—The seed of the nutmeg tree, which grows in warm countries and is similar in appearance to the pear tree.

The nutmeg is oval in shape, rounded, greyish brown in colour, usually with a whitish coating of milk of lime. It contains 25 per cent of fat (nutmeg butter), volatile oil, acid and starch. It is an aromatic spice, stimulating to the palate, and is used a good deal in cooking.

OATMEAL. GRUAU D'AVOINE—Oats with the husk removed. The oats, after the grain has been separated from the chaff, are ground. This oatmeal is used in broths and porridge, which are very appetizing.

Oatmeal porridge—See PORRIDGE.

Oatmeal soup. POTAGE AU GRUAU D'AVOINE—Pour into 1 quart (litre) of stock 4 tablespoons of oatmeal. Mix well and allow to simmer gently for 30 minutes. At the last moment, add 3 tablespoons (50 grams) of fresh butter and blend well. This soup can also be made with milk or water.

Cream of oatmeal soup. POTAGE CRÈME D'AVOINE—Boil the oatmeal as described in the recipe for *Oatmeal soup*. Strain through a coarse muslin cloth and bind with yolks of egg, cream and fresh butter.

Oatmeal soup au naturel. POTAGE À L'AVOINE AU NATUREL—Soak crushed oat grains in warm water. Put them into a saucepan, add plenty of water, season with salt and cook, simmering very gently, for 4 hours.

Strain the liquid through a muslin bag, bind with a few tablespoons of cream or milk and a little fresh butter.

OATS. AVOINE—Cereal, the grain of which excels all others as fodder for horses, cattle and poultry.

It is also used as food for men in the form of fine flour (oatmeal), slightly coarser groats and also flattened into what is known as rolled or flaked oats. It is used for porridge (Scots porridge) and for soups.

Roast oat grains have a smell which strongly resembles that of vanilla.

Because of its low gluten content, oatmeal flour does not produce malleable paste when mixed with water; it is, therefore, not a bread crop.

Sweetened cream of oats gruel. BOUILLIE À LA CRÈME D'AVOINE SUCRÉE—This dish is recommended mostly for children, the aged and the invalids. To ensure that this gruel is smooth, the oatmeal should be diluted, little by little, with cold liquid, then poured into sweetened boiling liquid (usually milk). Allow to cook for 10 minutes, stirring with a wooden spoon.

OBA—A species of mango from Gabon (Africa) of which the fruit is called *ibas;* it contains a white oily almond which can be used in its natural state to prepare *pain de dika;* it tastes like cocoa.

The mango from Gabon was introduced into Europe in 1855.

OBLADE—A Mediterranean fish, somewhat similar to bream. See BREAM.

It is cooked *à la meunière*, fried or boiled.

OCCA, OKA-PLANT, OXALIS—This plant was introduced from South America into England in 1829. It is extensively cultivated in Peru and Bolivia and grows very well in England and Wales. It grows wild in the forests of France. It has edible tubers which are washed, parboiled in salted boiling water and then prepared in different ways; *au beurre* (lightly fried), *à la crème*, in gravy, etc.

OCTOPUS. POULPE—Marine cephalopod mollusc, known in Brittany under the names of *pieuvre* and *minard;* tough-fleshed, eatable after prolonged beating.

Octopus provençal. POULPE PROVENÇALE—Clean an octopus and leave it for as long as possible in running water. Drain it; beat it hard with big sticks so as to soften the flesh, which is always rather leathery.

Cut up the tentacles into chunks of equal size, and the middle of the creature also, having removed the eyes and mouth and discarded them. Blanch these bits of octopus; drain and wipe them and cook them lightly in oil with some chopped onion. Simmer for a few moments. Pour in half a bottle of dry white wine and an equal quantity of water. Add a *bouquet garni* and a crushed clove of garlic.

Cook for a long time, the saucepan covered, until the pieces are quite tender.

Sprinkle with chopped parsley. Serve in a deep dish.

Octopus with rice. POULPE AU RIZ—Prepare the chunks of octopus as in the preceding recipe. When the octopus is two-thirds cooked, put in the casserole ½ pound (250 grams) of rice. Season with a pinch of saffron. Continue cooking for another 20 or 25 minutes.

Note. Octopus may also be cut in pieces, deep-fried in oil and served with spinach.

OEBITHERA. ONAGRAIRE, ONAGRE—Herbaceous plant, one species of which, the *Evening primrose*, has edible roots. These roots are prepared like salsify.

OFFAL (G.B.) OR VARIETY MEATS (U.S.A.). ABATS DE BOUCHERIE—These terms define various parts of the carcase, some relevant to the tripe trade, others to the meat trade. The offal or variety meats for beef, mutton and lamb, pork and veal are as follows:

Beef. White: Feet and belly (generally used in the preparation of tripe), tripe, brains.

Red: Lights, heart and liver (the tongue and the kidneys are left as part of the carcase; instructions for the preparation of tongue are, however, included here).

Mutton and Lamb. Kidneys, tongue, brains, feet, animelles, stomachs (the pluck, i.e., heart, liver and lung of these animals are sold in butchers' shops).

Pork. Kidneys, liver, brains, trotters and head. All

the pig's entrails are used in the pork butchery trade. The intestines are used as containers in the manufacture of sausages, saveloys, dried sausages and black (blood) puddings. The pig's blood is used in the manufacture of black puddings.

Veal. Lights, heart, liver, mesentery, amourette (or spinal marrow), head, sweetbreads, trotters (the kidneys remain as part of the carcase).

BEEF OR OX OFFAL OR VARIETY MEATS. ABATS DE BOEUF—In the U.S.A., all parts of beef are called beef, whereas in England only the best cuts are called beef and the less choice are termed ox. Example: Rump of beef, Fillet of beef; Ox liver, Ox tongue.

Beef amourettes (Ox pith). AMOURETTE DE BOEUF—In French the name *amourette* defines the spinal marrow. The spinal marrow of beef or ox is used in the kitchen, and even more so the spinal marrow of calves.

All the methods of preparation given elsewhere for the *Calf* (*veal*) *amourettes* (which are more delicate in flavour than those of beef or oxen) are applicable to the amourettes of beef or ox.

Beef or ox brains. CERVELLE DE BOEUF—*Method of preparation.* Soak the brains at least 4 hours in cold water. Clean well; remove all the membranes which cover the brains. Soak once again in cold water to make quite white. Put into boiling strained *court-bouillon*, prepared in advance, of water, sliced carrots and onions, a dash of vinegar or lemon juice, salt, a sprig of thyme, and a bay leaf. Cook for 20 to 25 minutes.

Drain and prepare as described in appropriate recipes.

If the brains are not to be used at once, keep in the *court-bouillon* in which they were cooked.

All the recipes given in this section for the preparation of *Calf's brains* can be applied to ox brains.

Beef or ox feet. PIEDS DE BOEUF—These are not used except as a garnish for tripe cooked *à la mode de Caen.*

Beef or ox heart. COEUR DE BOEUF—Prepared like *Calf's heart**.

Beef or ox kidneys. ROGNONS DE BOEUF—This variety meat or piece of offal, which is mediocre in taste, and often tough, can be prepared as described in the recipes given in this section for *Calf's* (*veal*) *kidneys.*

Beef or ox liver. FOIE DE BOEUF—Beef or ox liver, although less inferior in flavour, can be prepared as described in the recipes given for *Calf's* (*veal*) *liver.*

Beef or ox muzzle. MUSEAU DE BOEUF—This can be prepared as described in most of the recipes given for ox tongue. More often, muzzle is served cold, seasoned with oil and vinegar dressing, as hors-d'oeuvre.

For this method of preparation, cook the muzzle, previously soaked in salted water, from 6 to 8 hours.

When it is cold, cut it into thin slices, season with oil, vinegar, salt, pepper and chopped fine herbs. This salad is often sprinkled with chopped onion.

Beef or ox palate. PALAIS DE BOEUF—This piece of offal (variety meat) is not much used in the kitchen nowadays. In the olden days it was, on the contrary, very popular.

Method of preparation. Soak the palate for a long time in cold water. Blanch it, allow to cool, and drain. Remove the skin which covers it.

Cook it in a white *court-bouillon*, like *Calf's head.*

Beef or ox palate fried in batter. FRITOT DE PALAIS DE BOEUF—Cut the palate, cooked and allowed to cool as described above, into uniform pieces. Marinate for 1 hour in a mixture of oil, lemon juice and chopped parsley. When ready, soak in a light batter and deep-fry in sizzling fat. Arrange on a napkin; garnish with fried parsley. Serve tomato sauce separately.

Beef or ox palate au gratin. PALAIS DE BOEUF AU GRATIN—Cook the palate as above and slice. Arrange in a crown on a round buttered dish. Cover with *Duxelle sauce* (see SAUCE), sprinkle with grated breadcrumbs and brown the top.

Beef or ox palate à la lyonnaise. PALAIS DE BOEUF À LA LYONNAISE—This is prepared of ox palate, cooked as described above, cut into thick slices like *Tripe à la lyonnaise.*

Beef or ox palate à la poulette. PALAIS DE BOEUF À LA POULETTE—Put the palate, cooked as described above, and cut into thick slices or escalopes, to simmer with cooked, sliced mushrooms.

Ox-tail. QUEUE DE BOEUF—The caudal appendage of the ox's body is a very tasty bit. It is used for making various soups, particularly *Ox-tail soup* (see SOUPS AND BROTHS). It can also be prepared independently in a great many ways.

Ox-tail is normally sold in butcher's shops completely skinned, but there are some dishes which require unskinned ox-tail, for instance for the preparation of boned, stuffed ox-tail.

Generally speaking, before being cooked in any way, either in soups, or braised, the ox-tail is cut into uniform chunks, varying in size depending on the final use for which they are intended.

The same applies to unskinned ox-tail, except in cases when, before being boned and stuffed, it has to be left whole.

Cut into pieces, the ox-tail (whether skinned or not) is usually braised. The braising is usually done *à brun*, as indicated for this type of dish (see CULINARY METHODS, *Braising in brown gravy*). Ox-tail can be served with all the garnishes recommended for braised top of rump.

Among the garnishes, the following are the most suitable for ox-tail: *Berrichonne*, *Bourgeoise*, *Bourguignonne*, *Chipolata sausages*, *Compote*, *Fermière*, *Flamande*, various fresh, buttered, braised or glazed vegetables, *Maraîchère*, braised chestnuts, *Macaroni à l'italienne* (or other pasta products), *Nivernaise*, fresh noodles, *Piémontaise*, purées of various vegetables (fresh or dried), *Tortue*.

Depending on its nature, the garnish is either disposed around the ox-tail or served separately in a timbale. After the ox-tail has been arranged on a serving dish, its braising liquor should be reduced, strained and poured over it.

Braised stuffed ox-tail. QUEUE DE BOEUF FARCIE BRAISÉE—Soak a whole, unskinned ox-tail in cold water. Bone it carefully, without damaging the skin. Spread it on the table, season with salt, pepper and spices and fill along the entire length with some forcemeat (finely pounded pork *forcemeat** is the most suitable), mixed with chopped onion lightly fried in butter and chopped parsley, and bound with an egg. Reshape the tail, sew up the slit side, wrap in a cloth and tie with string as a long ballottine.

Braise in brown gravy as described in the recipe for *Braised top of rump* (see BEEF).

Stuffed ox-tail can be accompanied by all the garnishes recommended above for ox-tail cooked in pieces.

Instead of rolling the stuffed ox-tail into a long ballottine, as a galantine, it can be twisted into a ring and tied with string to keep that shape.

Grilled ox-tail Sainte-Menehould. QUEUE DE BOEUF GRILLÉE SAINTE-MENEHOULD—Cut the ox-tail into rather big chunks and cook in a stock-pot as a *pot-au-feu**.

Drain the pieces of ox-tail, bone them without

damaging, and cool under a press in the strained liquid in which they were cooked. Drain, spread with mustard slightly flavoured with cayenne pepper. Sprinkle with melted butter, roll in fresh breadcrumbs and cook under a low grill.

Serve separately some rather spiced sauce, such as *Diable*, *Piquante*, *Poivrade*, etc.

Ox-tail en hochepot. QUEUE DE BOEUF EN HOCHEPOT—Cut the ox-tail, whether skinned or not, into uniform chunks. Put into a stock-pot with 2 raw pig's trotters, each cut into 4 or 5 pieces, and a whole raw pig's ear.

Add enough water to cover, bring to the boil, remove scum and simmer gently for 2 hours.

Add a small cabbage cut in quarters and blanched, 3 carrots and 2 turnips, in quarters or cut into small uniform pieces, and 10 small onions. Simmer gently for 2 hours.

Drain the pieces of ox-tail and the pig's trotters. Arrange them on a large, deep, round dish. Put the vegetables in the middle. Surround with grilled chipolata sausages and the pig's ear cut into strips. Serve boiled potatoes separately.

Beef tongue (*Larousse*)

Beef or ox tongue. LANGUE DE BOEUF—Ox tongue can be used fresh or salted.

If used fresh, after having been soaked in cold water for several hours, trimmed and skinned (that is, removing the skin that covers it), the tongue is either braised or poached.

Before cooking the tongue by either of these methods, it is a good idea to steep it in salt for about 24 hours. This preliminary seasoning adds to its taste.

Braised: The tongue is prepared in the same manner as a piece of braised beef, and can be accompanied by all sorts of garnishes recommended for this dish (*Bourgeoise*, *Bourguignonne*, *Sauerkraut*, *Milanaise*, etc.). See recipes below.

Poached: The tongue is poached like top of rump and accompanied by the same garnishes as this dish.

Salted: The tongue is poached and, in this case, principally served cold as *Langue à l'écarlate*, or hot with various vegetables, mainly vegetable purées.

Beef or ox tongue à l'alsacienne. LANGUE DE BOEUF À L'ALSACIENNE—Poach the tongue (soaked, skinned and trimmed) in stock with the usual aromatic bouquet until it is half-cooked. Finish cooking it with separately prepared sauerkraut and lean bacon, following the usual method. See SAUERKRAUT.

Drain the tongue. Arrange it on a big long dish, on a bed of sauerkraut. Surround with thin slices of bacon and Strasbourg sausages poached for 10 minutes in boiling water. Serve with boiled potatoes.

Beef or ox tongue à la bourgeoise. LANGUE DE BOEUF À LA BOURGEOISE—Braise the tongue in the usual way. (See BEEF, *Braised beef.*) When it is nearly cooked, remove from saucepan. Strain the stock in which the tongue was boiled through a fine strainer. Put the tongue back into the pan. Add *Bourgeoise garnish:* half-cooked carrots (cut to uniform size), little glazed onions (half-cooked), pieces of larding bacon lightly fried in butter. Pour the strained stock over the tongue. Finish cooking everything together in a moderate oven (350°F.).

Braised beef or ox tongue with various garnishes. LANGUE DE BOEUF BRAISÉE—Braise the tongue slowly in the usual manner. Drain, arrange on a big long dish. Surround with the garnish specified (or, if preferred, serve the accompaniments separately). Strain the stock, remove surplus fat, boil down the sauce to thicken it, pass through a strainer and pour over the tongue.

Garnishes for braised tongue: Bourguignonne, Bruxelloise, Cévenole; Chipolata sausages, braised chicory, buttered spinach purée fermière, Flamande, jardinière, macédoine, Milanaise, Nivernaise; noodles (or other pasta with an Italian sauce), *purées of fresh or dried vegetables, various green vegetables braised or dressed with butter; risotto.* See GARNISHES.

Depending on the chosen method of preparation, the sauce is made with white wine, red wine or Madeira.

Beef or ox tongue à la diable. LANGUE DE BOEUF À LA DIABLE—Cut braised or poached cold tongue crossways into rather thick slices. Spread these slices with mustard; dip in melted butter and breadcrumbs and sprinkle with melted butter. Grill under a gentle fire, browning on both sides. Arrange on a round dish. Serve with *Diable sauce* (see SAUCE).

Cold beef tongue

Braised beef or ox tongue with various sauces. LANGUE DE BOEUF BRAISÉE—Braise the tongue in the usual manner. Serve it with one of the following sauces: *Mushroom*, *à la chasseur*, *Lyonnaise*, *Madeira* (or other wine sauces), *Piquante*, *Poivrade*, *Tomato sauce*, etc. See SAUCE.

Beef or ox tongue au gratin. LANGUE DE BOEUF AU GRATIN—Cut braised cold tongue into slices, not too thin. Arrange the slices in the shape of a circle on a round buttered dish, alternating with rows of thin slices of lean boiled ham. Put some cooked mushrooms on the tongue. Pour over *Duxelle sauce* (see SAUCE) to which has been added the juices in which the tongue was cooked. Sprinkle with breadcrumbs and melted butter; put under a grill or in the oven to brown the top.

Pickled (scarlet) beef or ox tongue. LANGUE DE BOEUF À L'ÉCARLATE—Soak the trimmed tongue for several hours in cold water, drain and dry. Prick it all over and rub thoroughly with a mixture of salt and saltpetre (sodium nitrate).

Put the tongue into a wooden or earthenware container. Cover with pickling brine, prepared as described below and allowed to cool. Put on a wooden lid, pressing down well, and leave in the brine for six days in the summer and eight days in the winter.

Pickling brine for ox tongue. Into a large saucepan

Preparation of tripe à la mode de Caen (*Robert Carrier*)

pour in 6 quarts (5 litres) of water with 5 pounds ($2\frac{1}{4}$ kilo) of sea salt (coarse salt), 5 ounces (150 grams) of saltpetre, 2 cups (300 grams) of brown sugar, a sprig of thyme, a bay leaf, 12 juniper berries and 12 peppercorns.

Boil for a few minutes. Allow to cool completely before pouring over the articles to be pickled.

Method of cooking ox tongue. Having allowed the tongue to pickle, drain it, soak in cold water for several hours to free it from salt.

Boil it in water *without any seasoning or condiments* from 2 to 3 hours, depending on size.

Tripe. GRAS-DOUBLE—The best parts of beef or ox stomachs. It is sold fresh, blanched (pickled), uncooked and cooked. If uncooked, it requires 3 to $3\frac{1}{2}$ hours of cooking in a *Salt water court-bouillon V* (see COURT-BOUILLON). Blanched or pickled tripe requires 1 to 1½ hours of cooking in salted water.

Tripe en blanquette. GRAS-DOUBLE DE BOEUF EN BLANQUETTE—Brown lightly two large tablespoons of chopped onion with 2 large tablespoons (50 grams) of butter.

Sprinkle with a heaping tablespoon of flour and add 3 cups (6 decilitres) of stock. Mix, allow to boil for a few minutes.

Add to this sauce 1½ pounds (750 grams) of cooked tripe, cut into square pieces. Season with salt and pepper, add a *bouquet garni** and allow to cook, uncovered, for an hour and a half.

Just before serving, bind with 2 yolks of egg mixed with 2 tablespoons of cold water; blend well, add 2 tablespoons of fresh butter, a tablespoon of chopped parsley and several drops of lemon juice. To serve, heap high on a serving platter.

Tripe à la bourgeoise. GRAS-DOUBLE DE BOEUF À LA BOURGEOISE—Brown lightly 12 small onions in 2 tablespoons (50 grams) of butter. Sprinkle with a heaping tablespoon of flour, allow to brown slightly, moisten with 3 cups (6 decilitres) of stock. Mix, boil for a few minutes.

Put in a saucepan 1½ pounds (750 grams) of cooked tripe cut into square pieces. Season, add a *bouquet garni**, allow to boil fast.

Add 24 small new carrots, lightly *blanched** and the same number of small half-cooked onions; cover the saucepan and cook for an hour and a half.

Serve in a dish; sprinkle with chopped parsley.

Tripe à la fermière. GRAS-DOUBLE DE BOEUF À LA FERMIÈRE—Brown lightly 4 tablespoons of chopped onion and 4 tablespoons of young diced carrots in 2½ tablespoons (50 grams) of butter. Sprinkle with 2 tablespoons of flour, allow to colour slightly, add 3 cups (6 decilitres) of stock and boil for a few minutes.

Add cooked tripe seasoned with salt and pepper; cover and cook 1½ hours.

Ten minutes before serving, add 2 tablespoons of sliced cultivated mushrooms fried in butter.

Fried tripe in breadcrumbs. GRAS-DOUBLE DE BOEUF, FRIT PANÉ—Cut the cooked tripe into little square or rectangular pieces; season with salt and pepper; dip them in beaten egg and breadcrumbs and fry in fat or oil.

As soon as it turns golden and becomes crisp, drain, arrange on a napkin and serve with *Diable*, *Piquante*, *Rémoulade*, *Tartare*, *Tomato* or any other spiced sauce (see SAUCE).

Grilled tripe à l'espagnole. GRAS-DOUBLE DE BOEUF À L'ESPAGNOLE—Cut 1½ pounds (650 grams) of cooked and well-drained tripe into uniform square pieces of approximately 3 inches. Marinate it for one hour in 4 tablespoons oil, 1 teaspoon lemon juice, 1 teaspoon salt, 3 to 4 pepper corns and 1 tablespoon chopped parsley.

Drain the pieces; cover them with breadcrumbs and grill under a gentle flame.

Arrange the tripe in a crown, alternating with rows of halved tomatoes fried in oil; in the centre put onions sliced in rounds and fried in oil.

Tripe à la lyonnaise. GRAS-DOUBLE DE BOEUF À LA LYONNAISE—Cut the tripe, previously cooked and well drained, into thin strips. Fry in a pan in sizzling butter or lard.

Season; add 4 large tablespoons of chopped onion previously fried (in butter or lard).

Mix and cook together until the tripe is nicely browned. Heap on a serving platter. Add a dash of vinegar heated in the frying pan; sprinkle with chopped parsley.

Tripe à la mode de Caen. TRIPES À LA MODE DE CAEN—In Paris and several other big cities in France one can find *Tripes à la mode de Caen*, cooked and ready to serve, frequently of excellent quality, which is easily explained, as these dishes are prepared in large quantities by first-rate specialists.

But this dish being very easy to make, we think it would be a good idea to give a detailed recipe for its preparation.

As tripe is usually sold cleaned, washed and blanched, all that remains is to stew it slowly in a *marmite* or a casserole, with aromatics and moistening. The cooking takes a long time, about 10 to 12 hours in a slow oven.

Tripe will be better and will stay whiter after cooking if it is prepared in a special *marmite*, a sort of earthenware utensil, with a very small opening, which is used principally in Normandy. One can, however, if no such pot is available, cook the tripe in an ordinary casserole or in an earthenware fireproof dish. What is of the greatest importance in the cooking is to make sure that it is done in a hermetically sealed utensil, in a moderate but sustained heat.

The hermetic sealing of the utensil can be achieved by covering it, before putting on the lid, with a strip of flour-and-water paste. This paste is not edible; its purpose consists entirely of forming, along with a layer of fat, a protective coating under which the tripe, cooking without bubbling, remains very white. This paste is prepared by kneading some ordinary flour with hot water. Slow and regular heat can be obtained by using a baker's or a pastry-cook's oven. But let us hasten to add that this dish can be prepared in an ordinary casserole and can very well be cooked in an ordinary oven.

Ingredients. The essential basic ingredients include ox mesentery, represented in kind by all the parts of which it is composed: the honeycomb or reticulum, the psalterium or manyplies, rennet or reed and the belly.

To these should be added a gelatinous substance provided by the feet and fatty matter, which is to form a protective layer above the liquid. This fatty matter is fat taken off beef cut in slices.

The net weight of the basic ingredients of this dish should be 4½ pounds (2 kilos), and the following ingredients are then added:

1 whole ox or calf's foot; 1 pound (500 grams) beef fat; 5 medium large onions (600 grams); 5 medium large carrots (500 grams); 4 leeks (300 grams); *bouquet garni* (with the accent on thyme and bay leaf); 4 cloves garlic; 2 teaspoons (15 grams) salt; ¼ teaspoon (4 grams) pepper; ¼ teaspoon (2 grams) allspice.

In principle, the liquid used should be cider, strengthened with a few spoonfuls of calvados or other spirits with a cider base. But, as it often happens that tripe prepared with cider turns dark, it would be best to use plain water.

The amount of liquid should be sufficient for the tripe to be completely submerged. The quantity, therefore, will depend on the type of utensil used.

Method of preparation. Line the bottom of the special *marmite* or casserole with onions and carrots cut into uniform pieces.

On top of these vegetables put the ox foot, boned and cut into pieces, as well as its bone, split into two, lengthways. Add the tripe, cut into square pieces of 2 to 3 inches. Bury the garlic, *bouquet garni* and the leeks tied in a bunch, among the pieces of tripe. Season with salt, freshly ground pepper and spices.

Cover the whole with beef fat cut into slices and flattened, and pour in enough water to cover.

Put the paste lid, rolled out rather thick, on the casserole, so as to seal the top as hermetically as possible.

Put in the oven and cook until the paste is well set. As soon as this paste is done, cover the utensil and leave in a slow oven for about 10 hours.

To serve. Remove the paste lid. Take out the layer of fat. Drain the tripe, remove the vegetables, the *bouquet garni* and the bunch of leeks, and all the bones, both large and small.

Put the tripe into a serving dish; strain the gravy, take off surplus fat and pour the gravy over the tripe.

Keep hot in a *bain-marie* until ready to serve.

Serve on very hot plates or in little earthenware bowls.

Tripe à la polonaise I. TRIPES DE BOEUF À LA POLONAISE —*Blanch** the tripe, drain, allow to cool and put into boiling water to cook for 4 or 5 hours, with a garnish of vegetables as for *pot-au-feu**.

Drain the tripe and cut into slices.

Meanwhile, prepare a *julienne* of mixed vegetables; celery, parsley root or parsnips and carrots, and boil it in strained tripe stock until the vegetables are done. Add the tripe to the vegetables. Season with salt and pepper; add a little powdered sweet marjoram. Blend in some *Kneaded butter* (see BUTTER, *compound butters*). Bring to the boil. Serve in a flat dish.

Tripe à la polonaise II. GRAS-DOUBLE DE BOEUF À LA POLONAISE—Fry the cooked tripe, cut in thin strips, in butter until it is nicely brown.

Arrange in a dish, sprinkle with chopped hard boiled yolks of egg and parsley; dress with a dash of vinegar or lemon juice and pour on the butter from the pan, in which ½ cup (50 grams) of breadcrumbs have been browned.

Tripe à la portugaise. GRAS-DOUBLE DE BOEUF À LA PORTUGAISE—Cut 1½ pounds (750 grams) of tripe, previously cooked and drained, into little square pieces. Put them in a saucepan with 3 decilitres of *Tomato fondue à la portugaise**.

Allow to simmer with a lid on for 20 minutes.

Arrange on a dish, sprinkle with chopped parsley.

Tripe à la poulette I. GRAS-DOUBLE DE BOEUF À LA POULETTE—'Cut the tripe into pieces one inch square; keep hot in a double boiler or *bain-marie* with a little butter and meat jelly; have some light *Allemande sauce* (see SAUCE) to which you have added some lightly fried blanched chopped parsley. Mix half of it with the tripe; add juice of one lemon; heat on a dish; cover with the rest of the *allemande* into which you put ½ pound (250 grams) of peeled mushrooms.' (From Carême and Plumerey.)

Tripe à la poulette II. GRAS-DOUBLE DE BOEUF À LA POULETTE—Cut cooked and drained tripe into small square pieces. Put them on to simmer for a few minutes in 1½ cups (3 decilitres) of *Poulette sauce* (see SAUCE); add 12 mushrooms lightly cooked and a spoonful of chopped parsley. Heap on a serving dish.

Tripe à la provençale. GRAS-DOUBLE DE BOEUF À LA PROVENÇALE—Proceed as described in the recipe for *Tripe en blanquette*, using shredded bacon fat or pork fat instead of butter and, after having bound the sauce with yolks of egg, add a few leaves of basil pounded with bacon fat or pork fat.

LAMB OR MUTTON OFFAL OR VARIETY MEATS.

ABATS D'AGNEAU, DE MOUTON:

Animelles (U.S. Fry)—This is a culinary term for the testicles of male animals, in particular those of lambs and sheep. In the past *animelles* were very much in vogue in France, Spain and Italy.

This is a delicate piece of offal (variety meats) and there are many recipes for preparing it, some of which are given below.

Before preparing them in one manner or another, scald, skin and soak the animelles in cold water for 2 to 3 hours.

Animelles (U.S. Fry) in cream sauce. (ANIMELLES À LA CRÈME—Cut in thin slices. Season with salt and pepper. Cook in butter. As soon as they are cooked, add a few tablespoons of *Cream sauce* (see SAUCE) and simmer gently. At the last moment, add a little cream and some fresh butter. Mix well.

Prepared in this manner, the animelles are mostly used as a garnish for patties, pies and vol-au-vent dishes. When they are intended to be used as a garnish for these various dishes, mushrooms and truffles can be added to them.

Fricassée of animelles (U.S. Fry). ANIMELLES EN FRICASSÉE—Slice the animelles into escalopes and cook in *Court-bouillon XII**. Drain, put into a shallow pan with cooked, sliced mushrooms (or left whole, if they are small). Add *Poulette sauce* (see SAUCE). Simmer gently without allowing to boil. At the last moment, add some fresh butter.

Fried animelles. ANIMELLES DE MOUTONS FRITES—'Choose 3 fresh sheep's (mutton) animelles, remove the skin and cut each into 8 pieces of uniform size. Put into an earthenware bowl with salt, pepper, 2 teaspoons of tarragon vinegar, 2 teaspoons of olive oil, a little thyme, half a bay leaf, a sliced onion and a few sprigs of parsley. Cover the bowl; after one hour they should give out their liquid. Drain, put back into the bowl with the rest of the ingredients, and sprinkle with the juice of half a lemon. Before serving, drain on a cloth, pressing lightly, dredge with flour and fry until golden. Arrange in a heap on a napkin and garnish with fried parsley.' (Plumerey's recipe.)

Animelles (U.S. Fry) fried in batter. ANIMELLES FRITES—Cut the animelles into broad but thin slices. Marinate for one hour in oil, lemon juice, chopped parsley, salt and pepper.

When required, dip them into light batter (see BATTERS). Fry, arrange on a napkin, garnish with fried parsley. Serve *Tomato sauce* (see SAUCE) separately.

Fried animelles (U.S. Fry) with mushrooms. ANIMELLES SAUTÉES AUX CHAMPIGNONS—Scald, skin and thoroughly soak the animelles, then slice and dry.

Sauté on a brisk flame in sizzling butter and finish off as described in the recipe for *Calf's kidney sautéed with mushrooms**.

Animelles (U.S. Fry) à la vinaigrette. ANIMELLES À LA VINAIGRETTE—Cook the animelles in *White court-bouillon* like calf's head. Serve with *Vinaigrette sauce* (see SAUCE).

Sheep's (mutton) or lamb's brains. CERVELLE DE MOUTON, D'AGNEAU—All the methods of preparation given for ox (beef) as well as calf's brains can be applied to sheep's and lamb's brains.

Before being prepared in any manner whatsoever, the brains must be soaked, the membranes covering them removed, and the brains must be cooked in *Court-bouillon III**.

Sheep's (mutton) brains fried in batter. CERVELLE DE MOUTON EN FRITOT—Like *Calf's brains fried in batter.*

Sheep's (mutton) brains à la bordelaise. CERVELLE DE MOUTON À LA BORDELAISE—Cut the brains, cooked in *court-bouillon III** into not-too-thin slices. Dredge with

Kidneys on skewers. How to open kidneys and how to skewer them

flour and brown lightly in clarified butter. Arrange in a crown, alternating with rows of oval-shaped croûtons of bread fried in butter. Add a few tablespoons of *Bordelaise sauce with red wine* (see SAUCE).

Sheep's (mutton) brains à l'indienne. CERVELLE DE MOUTON À L'INDIENNE—Like *Calf's brains à l'indienne.*

Sheep's (mutton) brains with red wine. CERVELLE DE MOUTON AU VIN ROUGE—Like *Calf's brains with red wine*, or *à la bourguignonne*.

Sheep's head. TÊTE DE MOUTON—Usually only the tongue and brain of the sheep are used in cookery, though sheep's head can be prepared in the same way as lamb's head. See LAMB.

Lamb kidneys. ROGNONS D'AGNEAU—These are prepared like *Sheep's kidneys*. See below.

Sheep's (mutton) kidney à l'anglaise. ROGNON DE MOUTON À L'ANGLAISE—Slit on the bulging side and open without actually separating the two halves completely, having previously removed the skin covering the kidney. Put on a skewer to keep the kidney open (2 pieces of kidney per skewer). Season with salt and pepper, brush with melted butter, dip in breadcrumbs and grill. Arrange on a long dish, garnish with grilled rashers of bacon, boiled potatoes and watercress. Put a pat of *Maître d'hôtel butter* (see BUTTER, *Compound butters*), the size of a walnut, on each kidney.

Kidneys *à l'anglaise* can also be prepared without being dipped in butter and breadcrumbs.

Sheep's (mutton) kidneys Carvalho. ROGNONS DE MOUTON CARVALHO—Remove the thin skin covering the kidneys. Cut in two, lengthways. Season the halved kidneys and sauté them as briskly as possible in sizzling butter.

Arrange the halved kidneys in a crown on a round dish, placing them on croûtons of the same shape as the kidneys, fried in butter.

Put on each half of a kidney 2 thin slices of truffle and a mushroom cap fried in butter.

Lace the pan juices with Madeira, dilute with *Demi-glace* (see SAUCE), add butter, strain and pour over the kidneys.

Sheep's (mutton) kidneys au gratin. ROGNONS DE MOUTON AU GRATIN—Sauté quickly the halved kidneys, seasoned with salt and pepper, in butter over a brisk flame, just to stiffen them.

Arrange these halved kidneys on sausage stuffing or forcemeat mixed with a third of its weight in dry *Duxelles** which has been piped in a circle on a round, buttered dish (the kidneys being placed bulging side up and slightly pressed into the forcemeat). Put on each half of kidney a cooked mushroom and surround the base with forcemeat studded with slices of uncooked mushrooms. Pour over *Duxelles sauce* (see SAUCE). Sprinkle with breadcrumbs and melted butter. Brown in a very hot oven.

Remove from oven, squeeze on a few drops of lemon juice and sprinkle with chopped parsley.

Sheep's (mutton) kidneys sautéed with mushrooms or with various wines. ROGNON DE MOUTON SAUTÉ AUX CHAMPIGNONS—Like *Calf's kidney sautéed with mushrooms* and *Calf's kidney sautéed with various wines.*

Sheep's (mutton) kidneys on skewers. BROCHETTES DE ROGNONS DE MOUTON—Sheep's kidneys cut into small slices, square pieces of lightly fried bacon, and often sliced mushrooms tossed in butter are placed and cooked on skewers. See *Calf's kidney on skewers.*

Kidneys Turbigo

Sheep's (mutton) kidneys Turbigo. ROGNONS DE MOUTON TURBIGO—Divide the kidneys in halves and fry briskly in butter. Arrange in a circle on a round dish. In the middle of the circle of kidneys put some peeled mushrooms fried in the butter in which the kidneys were done. Between each half of kidney put 2 chipolata or small link sausages, grilled or fried in butter, and on each of these halves place a mushroom cap fried in butter.

Add some white wine to the pan juices with tomato-flavoured *Demi-glace* (see SAUCE), blend and pour this over the kidneys and the garnish.

Sheep's (mutton) kidneys au vert-pré. ROGNONS DE MOUTON AU VERT-PRÉ—Prepare *Sheep kidneys on skewers.* Arrange on a long dish, garnish with potato straws and watercress. Place a pat of *Maître d'hôtel butter* on the kidneys (see BUTTER, *Compound butters*).

Lamb's liver. FOIE D'AGNEAU—Lamb's liver is rarely prepared by itself. It forms a part of the animal's pluck which is used for ragoûts.

Lamb's liver can be cooked on skewers as *Calf's liver on skewers*, or it can be fried in butter like *Calf's liver à l'anglaise*.

Lamb's pluck à l'anglaise. FRESSURE D'AGNEAU À L'ANGLAISE—Slice the lamb's liver, heart, spleen and lungs (the two latter having previously been blanched for 10 minutes in salted water).

Slice the lamb's sweetbreads. Season with salt and pepper and dredge all the above ingredients in flour. Fry in a shallow pan in clarified butter. Drain and arrange on a round dish. Put a tablespoon of flour into the pan in which the pluck was fried and cook for a few moments to brown lightly; add one wine glass (1 decilitre) of Madeira, then a few tablespoons of veal stock and a few drops of *Harvey sauce* (English spice sauce). Pour this sauce over the pluck.

Lamb's tongues. LANGUES D'AGNEAU—Lamb's tongues are generally braised. They can also be cooked in white *court-bouillon** like *Calf's tongue* and treated in the same way.

Braised lamb's tongues can be served with a garnish of vegetables, dressed with butter, or braised. They can be served as a ragoût, with mushrooms, with chipolata or link sausages, with young carrots, *à la bourguignonne**, etc. They can also be prepared in the following manner: grilled *à la diable*,* fried in butter, in buttered papers (as rib chops of veal) *à la Sainte-Menehould** (as pig's trotters), in *crépinettes*, etc.

Lamb's sweetbreads. RIS D'AGNEAU—Most of the recipes given for *Calf's sweetbreads* can be used for lamb's sweetbreads.

Method of preparation. Soak the sweetbreads and put them into a pan. Moisten with a few tablespoons of white stock; add a teaspoon of butter and a few drops of lemon juice. Cover and simmer for 25 minutes.

Leave to cool in strained stock in which they were cooked and proceed as indicated in the selected recipe.

Lamb's sweetbreads are used as a garnish for vol-au-vent, patty shells, raised pies, timbales, various decorative borders, etc.

They can also be served fried with various garnishes: *à la crème*, on skewers, *en attereaux*, in scallop shells, fried in batter, *à la poulette*, *à l'indienne*, as kromeskies or croquettes, *à la hongroise*, with pilaf, etc.

They are also used as garnish for eggs, and for small entrée dishes of meat, chicken, etc.

For these dishes, see *Calf's sweetbreads* in this section.

Hot pâté of lamb's sweetbreads à l'ancienne. PÂTÉ CHAUD DE RIS D'AGNEAU À L'ANCIENNE—Line the walls and bottom of a buttered, low, hot pâté mould with pastry for lining pie dishes (see DOUGH).

Cover the bottom and the sides of the baking dish with a fairly thick layer of *Forcemeat à la crème**.

On this forecemeat put a layer of lamb's sweetbreads half-cooked in butter, slices of mushrooms lightly fried in butter, and thick slices of truffles. Cover these ingredients with another layer of forcemeat, follow with another layer of sweetbreads, mushrooms and truffles and finish off with a layer of forcemeat.

Cover the pâté with a piece of rolled-out pastry and seal the edges thoroughly. Make an opening in this pastry lid to allow steam to escape. Decorate the top with small pastry decorations and brush with beaten egg. Bake in a good moderate oven (375°F.) from 45 minutes to an hour, depending on the thickness of the pastry.

Put the pâté on a round dish. Through the opening in the top pour in several spoonfuls of *Allemande sauce* (see SAUCE), flavoured with truffles.

Lamb's sweetbreads pilaf. PILAF DE RIS D'AGNEAU—Prepare like *Chicken liver pilaf* (see PILAF) replacing the latter by lamb's sweetbreads cooked in butter (having previously soaked them in cold water and blanched them).

Vol-au-vent of lamb's sweetbreads with truffles and mushrooms. VOL-AU-VENT DE RIS D'AGNEAU AUX TRUFFES ET CHAMPIGNONS—Prepare the vol-au-vent case as usual (see VOL-AU-VENT).

Just before serving fill the case with a ragoût of lamb's sweetbreads braised in *court-bouillon**, with sliced truffles and mushrooms in very hot *Allemande sauce* (see SAUCE).

Serve on a napkin-covered dish.

Note. Ragoûts of lamb's sweetbreads intended for filling vol-au-vent cases (or other similar dishes) can be cooked either in a white or brown stock.

In addition to truffles and mushrooms, which constitute the compulsory garnish, so to speak, these ragoûts can further be supplemented with various ingredients such as quenelles, cocks' combs and kidneys, brains in large dice, sliced artichoke hearts, etc. In all this mixed filling, the lamb's sweetbreads must, of course, be the predominating ingredient.

Sheep's (mutton) tongues. LANGUES DE MOUTON—These can be prepared in various ways. Before cooking in any way, they must be soaked in cold water and scalded for skinning.

Braised sheep's (mutton) tongues with various garnishes. LANGUES DE MOUTON BRAISÉES—Braise in a very little stock in the usual way. Arrange on a round dish. Surround with a suitable garnish. Pour the braising stock, reduced and strained, over the dish.

Note. All garnishes indicated for *Braised shoulder or rib of mutton* are suitable for braised sheep's (mutton) tongues.

Sheep's (mutton) tongues en crépinettes. LANGUES DE MOUTON EN CRÉPINETTES—Braise the tongues. Leave them to cool in their stock. Cut them in half and enclose each half in fine pork stuffing with truffles. Wrap each one in a piece of pork caul.

Baste the *crépinettes* with melted butter. Dip in breadcrumbs. Grill slowly. Serve with *Périgueux sauce* (see SAUCE).

Devilled sheep's (mutton) tongues. LANGUES DE MOUTON À LA DIABLE—Braise the tongues and leave to cool in their stock. Cut them in half and spread each half with mustard seasoned with a touch of cayenne pepper. Baste with butter. Dip in breadcrumbs. Pour butter over them. Grill slowly. Serve with *Diable sauce* (see SAUCE).

Fritot of sheep's (mutton) tongues. LANGUES DE MOUTON EN FRITOT—Braise the tongues (or poach them in very little liquid). Leave them to cool in their stock. Drain. Cut into rather thin slices. Steep them for an hour in a marinade of oil, lemon juice, chopped parsley, salt and pepper.

At the last moment, dip in a light batter. Deep-fry in boiling fat. Serve on a napkin, garnished with fried parsley. Serve *Tomato sauce* (see SAUCE) separately.

Sheep's (mutton) tongues au gratin. LANGUES DE MOUTON AU GRATIN—Braise the tongues. Cut them in half, lengthwise. Put them in an ovenware dish masked with *Mornay sauce* (see SAUCE). Decorate each half tongue with a cooked mushroom. Cover with Mornay sauce. Dust with breadcrumbs. Pour on melted butter. Brown slowly. Sprinkle with chopped parsley.

Sheep's (mutton) tongues à la hongroise. LANGUES DE MOUTON À LA HONGROISE—Half-cook the tongues in clear soup. Drain. Skin them. Cook slowly in a frying pan until very tender (for 6 tongues) $\frac{1}{2}$ cup (100 grams) of chopped onion. Put the tongues on top.

Season with salt and paprika. Cover and stew. Moisten with $\frac{3}{4}$ cup ($1\frac{1}{2}$ decilitres) of white wine. Boil down.

Moisten with a rather thin *Velouté sauce* (see SAUCE). Cover and cook. Serve in a deep round dish. Pour the sauce, strained or not as desired, over the tongues.

Sheep's (mutton) tongues à l'italienne. LANGUES DE MOUTON À L'ITALIENNE—Braise and simmer in *Italian sauce* (see SAUCE).

Pickled sheep's (mutton) tongues. LANGUES DE MOUTON À L'ÉCARLATE—Wash the tongues. Put them in brine, as for *Pickled ox tongue.* Do not leave them in the brine for more than 3 or 4 days. Cook in the same way as ox tongue.

Note. These tongues can be served hot with any garnish (especially with purée of lentils or chestnuts), or with green or red cabbage, in which the tongues should be simmered.

They can be served cold, like ox tongue, after having been coloured with carmine or caramel.

Sheep's (mutton) tongues à la poulette. LANGUES DE MOUTON À LA POULETTE—Cook the tongues in white stock. Drain and slice. Proceed as indicated for *Sheep's trotters à la poulette.*

Skewered sheep's (mutton) tongues. LANGUES DE MOUTON EN BROCHETTES—Braise the tongues. Leave to cool. Slice neatly. Fix these pieces of tongue on metal skewers. In between each piece put a slice of mushroom tossed in butter and a little square piece of bacon, lightly browned.

Baste with butter. Coat with breadcrumbs. Pour butter over them. Grill slowly.

Serve with *Piquante sauce* made with the braising stock of the tongues or with *Diable sauce* (see SAUCE).

Sheep's (mutton) tongues à la vinaigrette. LANGUES DE MOUTON À LA VINAIGRETTE—Cook in a white stock, as for *Calf's head.* Drain and skin. Serve on a napkin. Garnish with fresh parsley. Serve, separately, *Vinaigrette sauce* (see SAUCE), capers, onions and chopped parsley.

Sheep's (mutton) and lamb's trotters. PIEDS DE MOUTON, D'AGNEAU—Before preparing in any manner, sheep's trotters (which can be bought in the shops already blanched) must be boned, singed and the little tufts of hair between the cleavage in the hoof removed.

Then, immediately, cook in a light white *Court-bouillon** and proceed as described in the given recipe.

Sheep's (mutton) trotters en blanquette. PIEDS DE MOUTON EN BLANQUETTES—This is the same as *Sheep's trotters à la poulette* (see below) to which, in addition to the mushrooms, small onions cooked in a veal or chicken consommé are also added.

Sheep's (mutton) trotters in crépinettes à la périgourdine. PIEDS DE MOUTON EN CRÉPINETTES À LA PÉRIGOURDINE—Braise the trotters. Allow to cool in their braising stock. Drain. Put half of each trotter between two layers of finely minced truffled forcemeat. Wrap in pieces of pig's caul or paper-thin slices of salt pork. Brush with melted butter, dip in breadcrumbs and grill under a gentle flame. Serve separately the pan juices in which the trotters were braised, boiled down with a wine glass of Madeira, strained and with a few diced truffles added.

Croquettes of sheep's (mutton) trotters. CROQUETTES DE PIEDS DE MOUTON—These are prepared with a *salpicon** of sheep's trotters mixed with mushrooms and truffles, and bound with *Allemande sauce* (see SAUCE) like ordinary croquettes. See HORS-D'OEUVRE, *Hot hors-d'oeuvre.*

Fried sheep's (mutton) trotters. PIEDS DE MOUTON FRITS —Marinate for 30 minutes in oil, lemon juice, chopped parsley, salt and pepper, halved sheep's trotters, previously cooked in white *Court-bouillon**, drained and dried.

When needed, dip into batter. Deep-fry in sizzling fat. Arrange on a napkin, garnish with fried parsley. Serve *Tomato sauce* (see SAUCE) separately.

Fried sheep's (mutton) trotters à l'ancienne. PIEDS DE MOUTON FRITS À L'ANCIENNE—Cook the trotters in white *Court-bouillon** or braise. Drain, dry, split, and cover each half with a layer of finely pounded stuffing or forcemeat mixed with chopped truffles. Put the halves together, sandwiching tightly. Wrap in a piece of pig's caul or a paper-thin sheet of salt pork. Leave to marinate.

When required, dip in batter and fry. Serve *Périgueux sauce* (see SAUCE) separately.

Sheep's (mutton) trotters à la hongroise. PIEDS DE MOUTON À LA HONGROISE—Prepare like *Sheep's trotters à la poulette* (see below), with finely chopped onion slightly browned in butter and seasoned with paprika.

Sheep's (mutton) trotters à la poulette. PIEDS DE MOUTON À LA POULETTE—Bone the trotters completely, cooked in white *Court-bouillon**. Put into a shallow pan with, for 12 trotters split in half, $\frac{1}{2}$ pound (250 grams) of cooked mushrooms sliced if large, whole if small. Add 4 tablespoons of white stock and the same amount of mushroom stock. Reduce (boil down) almost entirely.

Add $1\frac{1}{2}$ cups (3 decilitres) of *Velouté sauce* (see SAUCE) and 3 tablespoons of cream. Simmer for 5 to 6 minutes.

Bind the sauce, at the last moment, with a liaison of 3 or 4 yolks of egg mixed with 3 or 4 tablespoons of cream. Simmer the trotters but avoid boiling. Add 3 tablespoons of butter, a dash of lemon juice and a tablespoon of chopped parsley. Mix well. Serve heaped on a platter.

Sheep's (mutton) trotters à la rouennaise I. PIEDS DE MOUTON À LA ROUENNAISE—Blanch the trotters whole. Braise them in a good strong stock. Drain and remove all bones. Fill the inside with sausage meat mixed with a lightly browned chopped onion, chopped parsley and the stock left over from the braising, reduced and strained.

Dip the trotters in egg and breadcrumbs. Just before serving, deep-fry in sizzling fat. Arrange on a napkin, garnish with fried parsley.

Sheep's (mutton) trotters à la rouennaise II. PIEDS DE MOUTON À LA ROUENNAISE—Braise the trotters. Divide in halves. Sandwich them between two layers of stuffing or of forcemeat prepared as described in the preceding recipe, wrap in pieces of pig's caul or paper-thin slices of salt pork, enclosing the whole surface. Brush with melted butter, roll in breadcrumbs and grill under a low flame.

Sheep's (mutton) trotters à la vinaigrette—PIEDS DE MOUTON À LA VINAIGRETTE—Cook the trotters in a white *Court-bouillon**. Drain and bone completely. Season while hot with oil, vinegar, salt, pepper and finely chopped herbs.

This salad (which is served as an hors-d'oeuvre) is generally flavoured with chopped spring onions.

PORK OFFAL OR VARIETY MEATS. ABATS DE PORC:

Pig's bladder. VESSIE DE PORC—This part of the animal, after careful washing, is blown up and dried and then used as a casing for big sausages. It is also used for wrapping lard.

Pig's bladder is also used in the kitchen for wrapping ducks and other poultry prepared *en chemise.* See DUCK.

Pig's brains. CERVELLE DE PORC—Pig's brains can be prepared in any way suitable for *Calf's brains.*

Smoked pig's cheek (bath chap). JOUE DE PORC FUMÉE—This part of the animal is much prized in England. Smoked pig's cheeks (bath chaps) are boiled in water and generally eaten cold, like ham.

Pig's ears. OREILLES DE PORC—Pig's ears are mainly used in the preparation of various pork butchery products, chiefly for brawn or head cheese.

They can also be served separately, as a small entrée. Having been boiled in a *court-bouillon** as for Pig's feet (trotters), or braised, pig's ears can be prepared as follows:

Boiled pig's ears. OREILLES DE PORC BOUILLIES—Singe the ears, clean the inside thoroughly and boil them in salted water, allowing $1\frac{1}{4}$ teaspoons (8 or 9 grams) of salt per quart (litre) with carrots, an onion studded with a clove and a *bouquet garni**. Simmer gently for about 50 minutes.

Drain the ears and prepare as indicated in individual recipes.

Having been boiled in this manner, pig's ears can be treated in various ways, for instance: coated with batter and fried in deep fat, *à la lyonnaise* (cut into coarse *julienne** strips and fried in butter with sliced onions), *à la vinaigrette* (see *calf's head*), etc.

Braised pig's ears with various garnishes. OREILLES DE PORC BRAISÉES—Singe 4 pig's ears and clean the inside thoroughly. Blanch for 5 minutes in boiling water. Drain and cut each in half, lengthways.

Put these halved ears, laying them down flat, into a buttered sauté pan, on a foundation of bacon rinds and sliced onions and carrots. Put a *bouquet garni** in the middle of the dish. Cover and cook on the top of the stove. Moisten with 1 cup (2 decilitres) of white wine, reduce (boil down) completely, add 2 cups (4 decilitres) of thickened brown veal gravy and cook in the oven, with a lid on, for 50 minutes.

Drain the ears, arrange on a serving dish and garnish as indicated in the recipe. Boil down the braising liquor, strain it and pour over the ears.

Pig's ears au gratin. OREILLES DE PORC AU GRATIN—Braise the ears and cut in two, lengthways. Put them into a buttered oven-proof dish. Surround with sliced mushrooms. Cover with gratin sauce (made of *Duxelles mixture** and the liquor left from braising the ears). Sprinkle with grated breadcrumbs and melted butter. Brown the top slowly in the oven. Take out of the oven, squeeze a few drops of lemon juice over the ears and sprinkle them with chopped parsley.

Grilled pig's ears. OREILLES DE PORC GRILLÉES—Boil or braise the ears and cut in two, lengthways. Coat with melted butter and breadcrumbs. Sprinkle with melted butter and grill gently. Serve a well spiced sauce separately.

Note. Grilled pig's ears are generally accompanied by mashed potatoes, served separately.

Grilled pig's ears Sainte-Menehould. OREILLES DE PORC GRILLÉES SAINTE-MENEHOULD—Boil the pig's ears in a spiced *court-bouillon** like pig's feet. Drain and cool under a press. Cut in two, coat with melted butter and white breadcrumbs and cook either under the grill or in the oven.

Pig's ears à la hongroise. OREILLES DE PORC À LA HONGROISE—Boil the pig's ears as described above and cut into uniform pieces. Melt some butter in a sauté pan, soften in it (for 2 ears) $\frac{1}{2}$ cup (100 grams) of onions cut in small dice, seasoned with salt and paprika, and put in the pig's ears. Cook, covered, for 10 minutes. Add 4 tablespoons of mushrooms cut in large dice and tossed in butter. Moisten with 2 cups (4 decilitres) of *Velouté sauce* (see SAUCE).

Cook with a lid on for 15 minutes. At the last moment, add 3 tablespoons of butter.

Stuffed pig's ears. OREILLES DE PORC FARCIES—Prepare like *Calf's ears Villeroi.*

Pig's feet (trotters). PIEDS DE PORC—Tie the pig's feet two by two, boil in stock, prepared after the fashion of a meat stock, aromatised with carrots, onions and a *bouquet garni**; drain, straighten, by placing between two thin boards tied with string, and cool under a press.

When cold, cut each trotter in two, lengthways, brush with butter or lard and grill gently. Pig's feet are usually accompanied by mashed potatoes served separately.

Note. Pig's feet can be braised. They are cooked in this way when they are intended for preparing a *salpicon** or when they are used as an element of various garnishes.

Boiled pig's feet can also be prepared in any way suitable for *Calf's feet.*

Pig's feet Sainte-Menehould. PIEDS DE PORC SAINTE-MENEHOULD—This is a special way of cooking pig's feet, so that a particular softening of the bones is obtained, to such an extent that the bones can easily be crunched.

Cook the feet (the cooking has to be prolonged and simmering done so gently that boiling is almost imperceptible) and leave them whole, i.e. do not cut them in halves. Brush them with melted butter and coat with white breadcrumbs. Sprinkle with melted butter or lard and cook in the oven until golden.

As in the case of grilled pig's feet, this dish is also accompanied by mashed potatoes served separately.

Truffled pig's feet I. PIEDS DE PORC TRUFFÉS—Cook the pig's feet (either boil or braise them) and bone completely. Cut the flesh into large dice. Mix this *salpicon** with fine pork forcemeat to which some diced or chopped truffles have been added. Season this forcemeat with salt, pepper and spices and add a dash of brandy.

Divide into 3 ounce (100 gram) parts and shape them into *crépinettes**, pointed at one end. Put two or three fine truffle slices on each *crépinette* and wrap in a piece of pig's caul.

Brush with melted butter, coat with grated breadcrumbs and grill gently. Serve with mashed potatoes.

Truffled pig's feet II. PIEDS DE PORC TRUFFÉS—Braise the pig's feet in Madeira-flavoured stock. Leave in the braising liquor until cold, then drain and bone. Cut half of the flesh into as many pieces as there are feet to be served. Chop the rest, mix with fine truffled forcemeat and add the braising liquor, reduced (boiled down) and strained.

Pork intestine. INTESTIN DE PORC—The small intestine, known in French pork butchery trade as *menus* or *menuises*, is used for making various kinds of sausages and black puddings. The caecum, which is also called *sac* or *poche* in French, is used for making *andouilles* and other sausages.

The colon, which is also called *chaudin*, and the rectum, which is known under the names of *rosette*, *boyau gras* or *fuseau*, is used for the same purposes.

Pig's kidney. ROGNON DE PORC—Prepare in the same way as *Calf's kidney.*

Pig's lights (lungs). MOU DE PORC (POUMON DE PORC)—The pig's lights, or lungs, are not very substantial. They acquire a certain nutritive value—but not much—from the garnish and sauces which accompany them.

They are used by pork butchers in making pork pâtés de foie, and in cookery for making stews in the same way as *Lamb's or Calf's pluck.*

Blanquette of pig's lights. MOU DE PORC EN BLANQUETTE—Cut the lights into pieces, season and cook as described in the recipe for *Tripe en blanquette.*

Ragoût of pig's lights. MOU DE PORC EN RAGOÛT—Beat the lungs to expel all air from them and cut into small (40 to 50 gram) pieces.

Season with salt and pepper and fry in butter or lard, stirring frequently so that all the pieces get nicely browned.

Sprinkle with flour and let this flour colour slightly in the oven, not on the top of the stove, where it might catch.

Moisten with white stock; add a little crushed garlic and a *bouquet garni**.

Cook in the oven from one hour to an hour and a half. Drain the pieces, trim them, put into another casserole with the garnish indicated. Strain the sauce over the lights, cover and cook in the oven from 20 to 30 minutes. Heap on a serving dish.

Pig's lights à la bonne femme. MOU DE PORC À LA BONNE FEMME—Cut 2 pounds (1 kilo) of lights into pieces, season with salt and pepper and fry in butter or lard.

Sprinkle in 2 tablespoons of flour, moisten with 6½ cups (1½ litres) of white stock or water, add a *bouquet garni** and a crushed clove of garlic. Bring to the boil, then cook in the oven for an hour and a half.

Drain the pieces, trim them, put into another casserole with 12 small, glazed onions, ¼ pound (125 grams) of bacon, cut in dice, scalded and fried lightly, and 1¾ cups (400 grams) of potatoes, in quarters or cut to look like large olives. Cook in the oven from 25 to 30 minutes. Heap on a serving dish.

Pig's lights en civet, or in red wine. MOU DE PORC EN CIVET (AU VIN ROUGE)—Proceed as described in the recipe for *Pig's lights à la bonne femme*. Moisten with a quart (litre) of red wine and 2 cups (½ litre) of white stock. Add small glazed onions, ¼ pound (125 grams) of diced and fried bacon, and ¾ cup (125 grams) of raw mushrooms, sliced or cut into quarters. Cook in the oven for 25 minutes. Thicken the ragoût with 1 cup (2 decilitres) of pig's blood.

Pig's lights à la ménagère. MOU DE PORC À LA MÉNAGÈRE—Fry the lights in butter or lard. When half-cooked, add 2 big onions and 2 carrots cut into quarters.

Moisten with 1 cup (2 decilitres) of white wine, reduce (boil down), add a crushed clove of garlic and a *bouquet garni**.

Add 6 cups (1½ litres) of white stock (or water) and cook in the oven for an hour.

Add 4 to 5 potatoes (50 grams), cut into quarters and leave to cook in the oven for 30 minutes.

Pig's lights à la provençale. MOU DE PORC À LA PROVENÇALE—Cut the lights as described above and fry in oil. Add 2 crushed cloves of garlic and a big *bouquet garni** consisting of thyme, bay leaf, parsley and basil.

Dilute with 1 cup (2 decilitres) of white wine and reduce (boil down). Moisten with one cup (2 decilitres) of thickened veal stock and 4 cups (8 decilitres) of light *Tomato sauce* (see SAUCE). Cook in the oven for 1½ hours.

Drain the pieces, trim them and put into another casserole with ½ pound (250 grams) of black olives. Strain the sauce over them and cook in the oven for 25 minutes. Heap on a serving dish, and sprinkle with chopped parsley.

Note. Fresh tomatoes, peeled, seeded and coarsely chopped, can be used instead of tomato sauce.

Pig's liver. FOIE DE PORC—Pig's liver is mainly used as a forcemeat ingredient for various pork butchery products, such as pork brawn and *gayettes*. It can also be served hot cooked in various ways. All the recipes given for *Calf's liver* are applicable to it.

Pig's liver gayettes (Provençale cookery). GAYETTES DE FOIE DE PORC—Cut 7 pounds (500 grams) of pig's liver and the same amount of fresh fat bacon (or pig intestine fat) into very small dice. Add 2 cloves (10 grams) of finely pounded garlic. Season with 3 teaspoons (20 grams) of salt, ⅛ teaspoon (2 grams) of freshly ground pepper and a little spice. Mix.

Divide this forcemeat into 3 ounce (100 gram) parts. Wrap each in a piece of pig's caul (or fat pork), well softened in water. Secure with string.

Put the *gayettes* into a greased pan. Sprinkle with a few tablespoonfuls of lard (fat). Cook in the oven from 25 to 30 minutes. The *gayettes* are generally served cold as an hors-d'oeuvre.

Pig's snout. GROIN DE PORC—This part of the animal is mainly used for preparing brawn.

It can also be cooked like *pig's ears* or *trotters*, allowed to cool and grilled like trotters.

Pig's spleen. RATE DE PORC—This part of the viscera is rather mediocre in taste. It is mainly used in pork butchery for making ordinary sausages.

In cookery, the spleen, together with the lungs and the heart, can be made into a stew.

Pig's stomach. ESTOMAC DE PORC—The hog's stomach or paunch is used, after it has been washed thoroughly and cooked for a long time, only for making sausages.

Pig's tails. QUEUES DE PORC—These are usually grilled, as *Pig's feet* (*trotters*).

Singe and clean the tails. Cook them as described in the recipe for *Pig's ears*. Cool under a press to straighten them. Coat with melted butter and breadcrumbs. Grill gently. Serve mashed potatoes separately.

Stuffed, braised pigs' tails with various garnishes. QUEUES DE PORC FARCIES, BRAISÉES—Bone the pigs' tails completely in such a way as to obtain long bags, taking care not to tear the skin. Stuff with fine pork or other forcemeat, truffled if desired. Secure with string and braise in very little liquid in the usual manner.

Drain, put on a serving dish and surround with the garnish indicated. Reduce the braising liquor, strain and pour over the tails.

Note. All the garnishes recommended for sautéed, pot-roasted or braised meat, served in small portions, are applicable to stuffed, braised pigs' tails.

Stuffed, grilled pigs' tails. QUEUES DE PORC FARCIES, GRILLÉES—Stuff the tails and braise as described above, or cook them in stock as indicated for *Pig's ears*. Cool under a press.

Brush with melted butter, coat with grated breadcrumbs and grill gently.

Serve with mashed potatoes.

Pig's tongue in jelly (*P.I.D.A.*)

Pig's tongue. LANGUE DE PORC—Pig's tongue can be prepared in any way suitable for *Calf's tongue*.

After pickling in brine, pig's tongue can be prepared as *Ox-tongue à l'écarlate*.

Pig's tongue is also used as an ingredient for potted heads (head cheese) and head brawn.

VEAL OFFAL OR VARIETY MEATS. ABATS DE VEAU:

Veal amourette. AMOURETTE DE VEAU—This is calf's spinal marrow. Calf's amourette is principally used, that of oxen (beef) more rarely.

This substance has a very great similarity to brains.

Before preparing it in any manner, the amourette must be soaked in cold water and all membranes covering it must be removed.

After careful washing, boil it as you would brains, in *court-bouillon*. Then proceed to follow any of the recipes given for *Brains*.

The amourette, cut into little pieces, after having been cooked in *court-bouillon*, can be used as a garnish for pie dishes, raised pies, vol-au-vent and other similar dishes.

It can also be served as hors-d'oeuvre, with oil and vinegar dressing, or with mayonnaise.

Calf's brains. CERVELLE DE VEAU—1 pound (500 grams) of calf's brains serves 4 people. Soak the brains in cold water for 1 hour. Remove the skin and any traces of blood. Unless otherwise specified in a particular recipe, simmer them (do not boil) in *Court-bouillon III** to which a tablespoon of vinegar has been added for 15 to 20 minutes. Drain and plunge in very cold water and allow to cool. Drain and dry. Follow succeeding recipes for final preparation.

Calf's brains à l'allemande. CERVELLE DE VEAU À L'ALLEMANDE—Cook the brains in *court-bouillon** as above and drain; cut into three or four uniform slices and dip in flour.

Sauté these slices in butter until nicely browned. Arrange on croûtons of bread fried in butter and cover with *Allemande sauce* (see SAUCE).

Calf's brains à la bourguignonne. CERVELLE DE VEAU À LA BOURGUIGNONNE—Proceed as described in the recipe for *Calf's brains à l'allemande* but use *Bourguignonne sauce* instead of *Allemande*. See SAUCE.

A *Bourguignonne* garnish can also be added. See GARNISHES.

Calf's brains in browned butter I. CERVELLE DE VEAU AU BEURRE NOIR—Cut the brains, cooked in *court-bouillon* and drained as above, into uniform slices; arrange them on a dish, season and sprinkle with 3 to 4 tablespoons of butter, browned in a shallow pan, having added to it, at the last moment, a tablespoon of chopped parsley. Add a dash of vinegar heated in the same pan after the butter has been poured off.

Calf's brains in browned butter II. CERVELLE DE VEAU AU BEURRE NOIR—Season and flour the slices of brains, fry them lightly in butter in a shallow pan, arrange on a dish and finish off as described above.

Calf's brains in noisette butter. CERVELLE DE VEAU AU BEURRE NOISETTE—Season and flour the slices of brains, brown lightly in a shallow pan, arrange on a dish, sprinkle with chopped parsley, add a dash of lemon juice and pour over a few tablespoons of *Noisette butter* (see BUTTER, *Compound butters*), browned lightly in a pan.

Fried calf's brains à l'anglaise. CERVELLE DE VEAU FRITE À L'ANGLAISE—Cut the cooked brains in slices and marinate for 25 minutes in 2 tablespoons of oil mixed with lemon juice, salt, pepper and chopped parsley.

Dip the slices in slightly beaten egg and breadcrumbs; fry in 2 to 3 inches of very hot fat; drain and arrange on a napkin with fried parsley. Serve *Tomato sauce* (see SAUCE) separately.

Calf's brains fried in batter. CERVELLE DE VEAU EN FRITOT—Cut into square, uniform pieces 1 pound (500 grams) of calf's brains, which have been boiled in *court-bouillon* and allowed to get cool. Soak for 25 minutes in a mixture of oil, lemon juice, chopped parsley, salt and pepper. Dip the pieces of brains in *Light frying batter VI* (see BATTER) and deep-fry in sizzling fat. Drain, dry, season with fine salt. Arrange on a napkin in the shape of a pyramid; garnish with fried parsley. Serve *Tomato sauce* (see SAUCE) separately.

Fried calf's brains à la provençale. CERVELLE DE VEAU SAUTÉE À LA PROVENÇALE—Proceed as described in the recipe for *Calf's brains à l'italienne*, but instead of using Italian sauce, put some *Tomato fondue** in the middle of the dish.

Garnish with black olives and sprinkle with chopped tarragon.

Fried calf's brains à la romaine. CERVELLE DE VEAU FRITE À LA ROMAINE—Prepare the brains as described in the recipe given for *Calf's brains à l'anglaise**.

Arrange in a circle, put some leaf spinach cooked in butter in the middle, place a rolled anchovy on each slice of brains and sprinkle with a few tablespoons of *Noisette butter* (see BUTTER, *Compound butters*).

Calf's brains au gratin. CERVELLE DE VEAU AU GRATIN—Put slices of calf's brains cooked in *court-bouillon* and drained as described above and coated with a few spoonfuls of *Duxelles sauce* (see SAUCE) into a fireproof dish. Put on each a slice of cooked mushroom.

Cover with *Duxelles sauce*, sprinkle with white breadcrumbs, then with melted butter, and brown the top in a slow oven. Sprinkle with chopped parsley and add a dash of lemon juice.

Calf's brains à la hongroise. CERVELLE DE VEAU À LA HONGROISE—Cut a pair of cooked brains into slices. Season with paprika, sprinkle with flour and fry lightly in butter.

Arrange in a crown on croûtons of bread fried in butter.

Put in the middle a mixture of diced mushrooms, hard-boiled eggs and truffles, all tossed in butter.

Put on each slice a small sliver of ham heated in butter. Pour some *Paprika sauce* (see SAUCE, *Hungarian sauce*) over the middle of the dish and sprinkle with chopped parsley.

Calf's brains à l'indienne. CERVELLE DE VEAU À L'INDIENNE—Cut the cooked brains into slices and fry lightly in butter. Arrange in a crown with some *Rice à l'indienne** and cover the brains with *Curry sauce* (see SAUCE).

Calf's brains à l'italienne. CERVELLE DE VEAU À L'ITALIENNE—Cut the cooked brains into regular slices; season, sprinkle with flour and fry lightly in oil, or oil and butter in equal proportions.

Arrange in a circle and cover with *Italian sauce* (see SAUCE).

Calf's brains in jelly. CERVELLE DE VEAU À LA GELÉE—Blanch 1 pound of calf's brains, previously soaked and skinned, in salted water for 5 minutes. Put them to cook into a saucepan with $1\frac{1}{2}$ to 2 cups (4 decilitres) of jellied meat stock. Allow to boil for 5 minutes. Leave to cool in the pan.

Then drain the brains, divide in halves, dry and put into a glass or a silver dish, pour over the pan juices, clarified and strained through a napkin. Put on ice to set.

Cold jellied calf's brains. CERVELLE DE VEAU EN CHAUD-FROID—Cook 1 pound (500 grams) of calf's brains as described in the recipe for *Calf's brains in jelly*.

Allow to cool in the liquid in which they were boiled. As soon as they are quite cold, drain, divide in halves, dry them without damaging them, and coat them with *White chaud-froid sauce* (see SAUCE).

Cold jellied calf's brains à la parisienne. CERVELLE DE VEAU EN CHAUD-FROID À LA PARISIENNE—Prepare the brains as described in the preceeding recipe and garnish, when arranging them, with *Parisian salad* (see SALAD).

Calf's brains loaf à l'ancienne. PAIN DE CERVELLE DE VEAU À L'ANCIENNE—Cook 1 pound (500 grams) of calf's brains, of medium size, in butter. Pound in a mortar after adding 2 tablespoons (50 grams) of butter and ½ recipe (100 grams) of *Frangipane panada* (see PANADA).

Season with salt, pepper and ground nutmeg and add two eggs, pounding well to achieve a smooth mixture.

Pass through a fine sieve, blend with a spoon and put into a buttered mould.

Cook in a pan of hot water or *bain-marie*, in the oven, from 25 to 30 minutes. Allow to rest for 5 minutes before turning out.

Put the loaf on a round dish; surround with mushrooms cooked in *Court-bouillon IX**; pour over 1 cup (2 decilitres) of *Allemande sauce* (see SAUCE), and decorate with a dozen slivers of truffles.

Calf's brains en matelote. CERVELLE DE VEAU EN MATELOTE—Boil 1 pound (500 grams) of calf's brains in 3 to 4 cups (8 decilitres) of *Court-bouillon with red wine (XIV)**; prepared in advance. Drain, divide into escalopes (thick slices), put into a shallow pan with 24 small glazed onions and 24 small mushrooms fried in butter.

Reduce (boil down) the *court-bouillon* by half, blend in 3 tablespoons (50 grams) of *Kneaded butter* (see BUTTER, *Compound butters*), strain and pour over the brains.

Allow to simmer for a few moments, without boiling.

Arrange on a dish, garnish with heart-shaped croûtons of bread fried in butter.

Calf's brains à la poulette. CERVELLE DE VEAU À LA POULETTE—Cut the cooked brains into thick slices and cook for a few moments, without allowing to boil, in *Poulette sauce* (see SAUCE). Heap in a shallow platter.

Brain stuffing or forcemeat. FARCE DE CERVELLE—Cook a brain in a *court-bouillon*. Drain it. Rub through a fine sieve. Put the purée in a double saucepan and heat it. According to the recipe used, add a little butter, cream, *Béchamel* or *Velouté* sauce.

This stuffing is used to fill small vol-au-vents, tarts or tartlets, barquettes, etc.

Calf's ears braised à la mirepoix. OREILLES DE VEAU BRAISÉES À LA MIREPOIX—Blanch four calf's ears for 8 minutes. Cool them in cold water, drain, trim, dry and thoroughly clean the inside.

Put into a saucepan, cover with ¾ to 1 cup of mirepoix*, add a *bouquet garni**, season with salt and pepper, add a wineglass of white wine and cook to thicken.

Add 1½ cups of slightly thickened brown veal stock and cook in the oven with a lid on for an hour and a half.

Drain the ears, remove with the aid of a spoon the skin which covers the thin part on the inside and on the outside. Beat this part flat and slit it.

Arrange the ears on a round dish (each could be placed on a croûton of bread fried in butter); strain the pan juices, remove surplus fat and pour over the dish.

Braised calf's ears Mont-Bry. OREILLES DE VEAU BRAISÉES MONT-BRY—Cook the ears as described in the recipe for *Calf's ears braised à la mirepoix*.

Drain them, put each one on a little *Anna potato cake* (see POTATOES), garnish with four lettuce hearts braised in the juice. Strain the pan juices, remove surplus fat, pour over the ears and serve.

Fried calf's ears I. OREILLES DE VEAU FRITES—Cook the ears as described in the recipe for *Calf's ears braised à la mirepoix*, drain, allow to cool, divide into uniform pieces, dip in beaten egg and breadcrumbs and deep-fry in sizzling fat.

Arrange in a pyramid, decorate with fried parsley and serve with the pan juices, strained and finished off as *Diable* or *Piquante* sauce (see SAUCE).

Fried calf's ears II. OREILLES DE VEAU FRITES—Cut the ears into strips, leave to soak in batter and finish off as described above.

Fried calf's ears III. OREILLES DE VEAU EN FRITOT—Cook the ears in a flour-and-water stock; drain them; wipe them; cut each one into 8 or 10 pieces of regular shape and size.

Marinate for 30 minutes with oil, lemon juice, chopped parsley, salt and pepper.

At the last moment dip into a light batter and fry in smoking hot deep fat.

Serve in a mound on a table napkin; garnish with fried parsley. Serve *Tomato sauce* (see SAUCE) separately.

Grilled calf's ears à la diable. OREILLES DE VEAU GRILLÉES À LA DIABLE—Cut the braised ears in two, lengthways, put them under a press for a few moments, spread them with mustard, sprinkle with melted butter, dust with white breadcrumbs and cook on both sides under a gentle grill. Serve *Diable sauce* separately (see SAUCE).

Calf's ears à la hongroise. OREILLES DE VEAU À LA HONGROISE—The ears having been cooked in a flour-and-water *court-bouillon**, cut them into uniform pieces and put them into a sauté pan in which ½ cup (100 grams) of finely diced onions (for every 2 ears), seasoned with salt and paprika, have been cooked in butter. Stew the ears for 10 minutes. Add 4 tablespoons of mushrooms cut into large dice and lightly cooked in butter. Stir in 2 cups (4 decilitres) of rather thin *Velouté* or *Béchamel sauce* (see SAUCE). Cook covered for about 15 minutes. At the last moment, add 3 tablespoons of butter.

Calf's ears à l'indienne. OREILLES DE VEAU À L'INDIENNE—Cook in flour-and-water *court-bouillon**. Cut into squares and treat like *Calf's feet â l'indienne**.

Calf's ears à l'italienne. OREILLES DE VEAU À L'ITALIENNE—'Prepare and cook the calf's ears as described in the recipe for *Calf's ears braised à la mirepoix**, but instead of slitting them, cut the tendons to round off the end, and dress the inside with a mixture of truffles, mushrooms and calf's tongue cut up very small, and bound with two spoonfuls of thick *Financière sauce* (see SAUCE). Bring the whole to the boil and serve with an *Italian sauce*.' (From Carême and Plumerey.)

Calf's ears en tortue. OREILLES DE VEAU EN TORTUE—Cook the ears as described in the recipe for *Calf's ears braised à la mirepoix** but replacing white wine by Madeira.

Drain, arrange on fried croûtons, surround with the garnish *en tortue* (see GARNISHES); strain the pan juices, skim off fat and finish off as described for *Tortue sauce* (see SAUCE). Pour over the dish and serve.

Calf's ears stuffed en tortue. OREILLES DE VEAU FARCIES EN TORTUE—The ears, having been carefully soaked, should be two-thirds cooked in a flour-and-water *court-bouillon** like *Calf's head*.

Stuff them with a *forcemeat** composed of one half fine pork forcemeat and one half veal forcemeat, with the addition of diced truffles, the whole bound with eggs.

Finish cooking the ears in a Madeira-flavoured braising stock.

Finish off as for *Calf's head en tortue.*

Calf's ears Villeroi. OREILLES DE VEAU VILLEROI—Cook the ears as described in the recipe for *Calf's ears braised à la mirepoix* and drain.

Trim, fill the inside with a finely pounded *Chicken forcemeat* (see FORCEMEAT), dip in *Villeroi sauce* (see SAUCE), then in breadcrumbs, and fry.

Arrange on a napkin with fried parsley and serve with *Tomato* or *Perigueux sauce* (see SAUCE).

Calf's feet. PIEDS DE VEAU—After having been soaked in cold water, boned and blanched, the feet are cooked in a *court-bouillon* (see *Calf's head*) and are then treated in different manners, as sheep's feet.

They can be fried in a shallow pan or in deep fat: cut into uniform pieces, marinate for an hour in oil, lemon juice, chopped parsley, salt and pepper; dip into a light batter at the last moment and deep-fry in sizzling fat.

All the recipes given for *Calf's head* can be used for *Calf's feet.*

Calf's feet à l'indienne. PIEDS DE VEAU À L'INDIENNE—Cook as in the recipe for *Calf's feet** and serve with *Rice à l'indienne**, the feet covered with *Curry sauce* (see SAUCE).

Calf's feet à l'italienne. PIEDS DE VEAU À L'ITALIENNE—Cut cooked calf's feet into uniform pieces and put into *Italian sauce* (see SAUCE).

Calf's feet with tartare sauce. PIEDS DE VEAU À LA TARTARE—Cut into uniform pieces, dip in egg and breadcrumbs, deep fry and serve *Tartare sauce* (see SAUCE, *Cold sauces*) separately.

Calf's feet à la vinaigrette. PIEDS DE VEAU À LA VINAIGRETTE—Prepared like *Calf's head in oil.*

Calf's head. TÊTE DE VEAU—Before being cooked in any manner, calf's head should be boned and soaked for a long time in cold water. It should then be blanched, cooled and cut into pieces, or—depending on the method of preparation—it can be left whole. Then it is cooked in a *White court-bouillon* (see below). It is only when calf's head is being cooked *à l'anglaise* that it does not have to be boned. In this case, after a long soaking and blanching, it is cooked in *White court-bouillon.* Whatever method of preparing the calf's head is chosen, it should always be served with the tongue sliced and the brains cooked separately in *White court-bouillon* and cut in slices. The brains can also be pounded and blended with the cold sauce to be served with calf's head.

White court-bouillon for calf's head. BLANC POUR CUIRE LA TÊTE DE VEAU—Mix flour with cold water, using a heaped tablespoon per quart (litre) of water, until smooth. Pass this mixture through a fine strainer. Pour into a saucepan, big enough to take the head, either whole or divided in halves, or cut into pieces. Season with 1 teaspoon (6 grams) of salt and add one tablespoon of vinegar per quart (litre) of water. Bring to the boil; add a large onion studded with two cloves and a good *bouquet garni* consisting of a sprig of parsley, thyme and bay leaf. When this stock is boiling, put in the calf's head wrapped in a fine muslin cloth.

Add ½ pound (250 grams) of beef (or veal) fat, chopped and soaked in cold water. This fat, upon melting, will form a protective layer over the calf's head and will prevent it from going black.

Calf's head à l'anglaise. TÊTE DE VEAU À L'ANGLAISE—Cook the calf's head in *White court-bouillon* as above, whole or split in half, but without boning.

Arrange the head on a napkin and serve with a piece of boiled bacon and *Parsley sauce* (see SAUCE).

Calf's head à la bonne femme. TÊTE DE VEAU À LA BONNE FEMME—Boil the calf's head in *White court-bouillon*, cut into uniform pieces and simmer gently in a *Demi-glace* (see SAUCE) with pieces of bacon, lightly browned in butter, glazed mushrooms, olives and small onions. Heap on a platter.

Calf's head Caillou. TÊTE DE VEAU CAILLOU—For 6 persons, cook half a blanched calf's head, cut into 6 pieces, as well as half the calf's tongue, in a large saucepan. (Cooked in this way in a *marmite*, the calf's head is less white, but has more flavour.) The head should only be three-quarters cooked. The final cooking must take place in the sauce.

Melt 3 tablespoons of butter and fry one large chopped onion without allowing it to brown, adding 2 tablespoons (50 grams) of lean smoked ham cut into little pieces. Sprinkle in 3 heaped tablespoons of flour, brown lightly, blend with 2½ cups (5 decilitres) of stock. Add 2 tablespoons of *Tomato sauce* (see SAUCE), a *bouquet garni* consisting of 2 sprigs of parsley, one small clove of garlic, one sprig of thyme, a quarter of a bay leaf and a stalk of celery. Mix well and cook for 20 minutes.

Put the calf's head and the tongue, cut into 6 slices, into a sauté pan, add 48 peeled chestnuts, half-cooked in consommé, 48 large, stoned olives, and 12 cultivated mushrooms, with the stalks removed, skinned and washed. Add one wine glass (1 decilitre) of Madeira. Simmer for 10 minutes. Cover with the strained sauce and cook under a lid for 35 minutes.

Arrange the calf's head and the chestnuts on a large shallow dish. Garnish with little escalopes of brains, rolled in slightly beaten egg and breadcrumbs and fried in butter, and with heart-shaped croûtons fried in butter.

Calf's head in crépinettes. TÊTE DE VEAU EN CRÉPINETTES—Cut 1 pound (500 grams) of calf's head (cooked in *White court-bouillon*) into average-size pieces. Add to this a third of its weight in mushrooms, diced and lightly fried in butter, and 4 teaspoons of truffles in small dice. Blend this mixture with *Madeira sauce* (see SAUCE) based on truffle essence and greatly reduced. Add some diced calf's tongue and brains. Allow to cool.

Divide this mixture into parts of 2 tablespoons (50 grams) each. Enclose each of these parts in 3 tablespoons (100 grams) of finely-minced pork forcemeat. Roll each into the shape of a flat sausage. Wrap a piece of caul in salt pork, cut paper-thin, moistened with cold water.

Smear the wrappings with melted butter or other fat, roll in white breadcrumbs, sprinkle with melted butter and grill under a gentle flame. Serve with *Périgueux sauce* (see SAUCE) or with any other sauce recommended for grilled meats.

Calf's head à la financière. TÊTE DE VEAU À LA FINANCIÈRE—Cut the head, boiled in *White court-bouillon* and well drained, into 2 inch pieces. Stew in Madeira. Arrange in a dish. Cover with *Financière garnish* (see GARNISHES), to which pieces of calf's tongue, cut into slices or dices, and brain sliced into escalopes have been added.

Fried calf's head. TÊTE DE VEAU FRITE—Cut the head into square pieces. Marinate for 1 hour in oil, lemon juice, salt, pepper and chopped parsley.

Dip the pieces of head into a light batter (see BATTER) and, at the last moment, deep-fry in sizzling fat.

Arrange on a napkin, garnish with fried parsley. Serve with tomato sauce or any other sauce recommended for calf's head.

Calf's head fried in batter. TÊTE DE VEAU EN FRITOT—This is the same recipe as that for *Fried calf's head.*

Fried calf's head à la piémontaise. TÊTE DE VEAU FRITE À LA PIÉMONTAISE—Cut the calf's head cooked in *White court-bouillon* into small square pieces. Slice the tongue and the brains similarly. Marinate for 1 hour in oil, lemon juice, salt, pepper and chopped parsley.

At the last moment, dip into a light batter and deep-fry in sizzling fat.

Drain on a cloth, season with finely ground salt. Arrange in a heap surrounded by a border of *Risotto à la piémontaise* (see RICE).

Pour a few tablespoons of a not too thick *Tomato sauce* (see SAUCE) over the risotto.

Calf's head Godard. TÊTE DE VEAU GODARD—This is prepared like *Calf's head à la financière.*

In the olden days, calf's head Godard used to be served whole and almost always stuffed. (See *Stuffed calf's head à l'ancienne.*)

Calf's head with Gribiche sauce. TÊTE DE VEAU SAUCE GRIBICHE—Cut the calf's head and the tongue, cooked in *White court-bouillon,* into uniform pieces. Arrange the well-drained head on a napkin. Garnish with escalopes of tongue and slices of brains, cooked separately in *court-bouillon.* Garnish with fresh parsley. Serve *Gribiche sauce* separately (see SAUCE, *Cold sauces*).

Calf's head à l'italienne. TÊTE DE VEAU À L'ITALIENNE—This is cooked calf's head cut into square pieces put into *Italian sauce* (see SAUCE). Serve in a dish and sprinkle with chopped parsley.

Calf's head à la lyonnaise. TÊTE DE VEAU À LA LYONNAISE—Put the calf's head, cooked in *White court-bouillon,* and cut into pieces, into an ovenproof dish, lined with a layer of thinly sliced onions, lightly fried in butter and mixed with chopped parsley. Cover with *Lyonnaise sauce* (see SAUCE). Sprinkle with breadcrumbs and melted butter. Brown the top lightly in the oven.

Calf's head à l'occitane (Languedoc cookery). TÊTE DE VEAU À L'OCCITANE—Cut half a well-soaked calf's head into 8 uniform pieces. In the same *court-bouillon* cook half a calf's tongue and poach the brains separately in a well-spiced *court-bouillon* (see *Court-bouillon V*). Put 3 tablespoons of chopped onion, lightly fried in butter, into a shallow fireproof dish and add one clove of garlic towards the end of cooking.

Put into this dish, which you will have placed in a pan of boiling water, the pieces of calf's head, as well as the sliced tongue and the brains. Garnish with black olives (black olives should not be stoned), 2 peeled tomatoes, from which the seeds have been pressed out, cut into little pieces and tossed in oil, and 2 hard boiled eggs, cut into rather thick slices. Season with salt and pepper. Put on the calf's head 3 tablespoons (75 grams) of butter divided into tiny dabs, $\frac{1}{4}$ cup of oil, juice of half a lemon and 2 teaspoons of chopped parsley. Heat in a pan of water keeping the dish covered. Just before serving, baste the calf's head well with the sauce.

Calf's head in oil. TÊTE DE VEAU À L'HUILE—Served on a napkin, with slices of tongue and brains, garnished with fresh parsley. Serve *Vinaigrette sauce* (see SAUCE) separately.

Calf's head with olives. TÊTE DE VEAU AUX OLIVES—Cut the head into pieces. Put into a shallow pan with some *Demi-glace* (see SAUCE) or rich meat stock laced with Madeira. Add stoned and blanched olives. Allow to simmer slowly.

Calf's head à la portugaise. TÊTE DE VEAU À LA PORTUGAISE—Cut the boiled calf's head (as well as the tongue) into square pieces. Cook gently in a not too thick *Tomato fondue à la portugaise**.

Arrange on a dish. Put on top calf's brains cut into little slices. Sprinkle with chopped parsley.

Calf's head à la poulette. TÊTE DE VEAU À LA POULETTE—Boil in *White court-bouillon;* cut into little slices. Prepare as described in the recipe for *Sheep's trotters à la poulette.*

Calf's head à la ravigote. TÊTE DE VEAU À LA RAVIGOTE—Put the calf's head, together with the tongue cooked in *court-bouillon**, drained and cut into square pieces, into a dish. Cover with *Ravigote sauce* (see SAUCE). Garnish with slices of brains.

Hot calf's head with various cold sauces. TÊTE DE VEAU CHAUDE—Arrange the head on a napkin with slices of tongue and brains. Garnish with fresh parsley. Serve with various cold sauces, such as: *Aïoli, Gribiche, Mayonnaise, Ravigote* (or *Vinaigrette*), *Rémoulade, Tartare, Vincent* (see SAUCE, *Cold sauces*).

Hot calf's head with various hot sauces. TÊTE DE VEAU CHAUDE—Slice the calf's head (cooked in *White court-bouillon* and drained), arrange on a napkin, with slices of tongue and brains, garnish with fried parsley and serve with various sauces such as: *Caper, Fines herbes, Hungarian, Ravigote,* as white sauces; *Charcutière, Diable, Fines herbes, Piquante, Robert,* etc., as brown sauces. The calf's head can also be arranged in a dish, cut in small square pieces, with one of the above mentioned sauces poured over it.

Stuffed calf's head. TÊTE DE VEAU FARCIE—Boil the calf's head in white *court-bouillon,* divide in half, or cut into pieces; cut the lean parts neatly into slices of 2 to 3 inches.

Arrange these pieces of calf's head inside the head with a stuffing made of chopped minced veal, *panada** and cream and a mixture of chopped dried mushrooms, chopped hard boiled eggs and chopped parsley. (Press in this forcemeat in a dome shape.) Put the pieces of head, stuffed side up into a buttered ovenproof dish, with several tablespoons of white stock. Sprinkle with breadcrumbs and melted butter. Poach and brown the top in a slow oven, the dish being put in a pan half-filled with hot water.

Serve separately a well-spiced sauce, such as *Piquante, Poivrade, Tartare, Ravigote* or *Béarnaise* (see SAUCE).

Note. Calf's head can also be served with one of the garnishes which usually go with *Braised calf's head* (*Financière, Godard, Tortue,* etc.).

Stuffed calf's head à l'ancienne. TÊTE DE VEAU FARCIE À L'ANCIENNE—*Preliminary preparation.* Boil a boned calf's head in a *White court-bouillon* until three-quarters done. Drain and dry the head. Remove the ears, which will be cooked separately and put back on the head when serving it. Spread the head, skin side down, on a damp wrung out napkin, stretched taut on the table. Remove some of the lean flesh inside the head, patch the hole made in the skin by the removal of the ears, with a thick slice or rasher of bacon. Season with salt, pepper and allspice. Fill with a *forcemeat** made of minced veal, *panada** and cream, adding a mixture made of the lean flesh taken out of the head (trimmed and diced), the tongue and some truffles.

Enclose this stuffing in the skin completely. Sew up the opening. Wrap in the napkin and mould the head into its original shape. Secure with strings.

Method of preparation. Brown some pieces of bacon rinds, carrots and sliced onions in butter in a braising pan, and put in the calf's head. Put around it some slices of knuckle, previously browned in butter. Add a large *bouquet garni.* Simmer under a lid, on the top of the stove, for 15 minutes. Add $1\frac{1}{2}$ cups (3 decilitres) of Madeira and reduce (boil down). Add 2½ cups (5 decilitres) of thickened veal stock. Put the ears into the saucepan, wrapped in a piece of muslin cloth to be able to take them out easily. Bring to boil. Finish cooking in a slow oven with a lid on. Before the cooking is complete, remove the ears, which consist of more delicate flesh and are, therefore, cooked sooner.

Serving. Drain the head. Unwrap it and arrange on a large long dish. Fix the ears in their place by means of small skewers.

Surround the head either with *Financière* or *Godard garnish* (see GARNISHES) arranged in bunches.

Add calf's brains, cooked in *court-bouillon* and sliced.

Strain the pan juices, remove surplus fat, reduce and pour over the calf's head.

Calf's head à la Tertillière. TÊTE DE VEAU À LA TERTILLIÈRE—Cook the head in *White court-bouillon*, drain, cut into pieces and put into a shallow pan with (for half a head cut into 10 pieces) ¼ pound (150 grams) pickled tongue, ¼ pound (150 grams) of cooked mushrooms, 6 small truffles (150 grams), all coarsely shredded, and 1¾ cups (3½ decilitres) of *Madeira sauce* (see SAUCE) with truffle essence. Allow to cook gently for 30 minutes. At the last moment, add a teaspoon of finely shredded, blanched and drained lemon peel.

Arrange on a dish. Garnish with halves of hard boiled eggs and little slices of calf's brains.

Calf's head en tortue. TÊTE DE VEAU EN TORTUE—In the olden days, the serving of calf's head *en tortue*, a large entrée demanding a certain number of garnishes, was carried out in a most decorative manner. Nowadays, more often than not, this dish is served in a *timbale* and the various garnishes, which were once disposed in separate groups around the calf's head served on a fried croûton, are put in a mixed ragoût over it.

This garnish is made of the following ingredients: little *quenelles* of minced veal (see FORCEMEAT); cocks' combs and kidneys, cooked mushrooms, stoned, stuffed, poached olives, slivers of truffles and escalopes of calf's tongue. To this ragoût, stewed with Madeira and blended with *Tortue sauce* (see SAUCE), at the last moment are added gherkins, cut in little uniform pieces. Once the head is arranged on a dish, dressed with the garnishes and *Tortue sauce*, it is decorated on the top with small fried eggs, little slices of calf's brains, cooked in *court-bouillon**, dressed crayfish, also cooked in *court-bouillon*, and heart-shaped fried croûtons.

Pieces of calf's head, after having been slowly cooked in *Tortue sauce*, can also be arranged on a round dish, each on a croûton of bread fried in butter, with the garnishes disposed all around.

Finally, calf's head can be served whole, stuffed and cooked in braising stock spiced with *Turtle herbs* (see HERBS).

In the olden days, not only were little quenelles of veal and chicken forcemeat added to this dish, but also large mosaic quenelles, that is quenelles decorated with truffles, braised larded calf's sweetbreads and many other garnishes.

Calf's head à la toulousaine. TÊTE DE VEAU À LA TOULOUSAINE—Cut the cooked head into square pieces. Put in a dish with pieces of tongue and brains. Add *Garnish à la toulousaine**. Heat, cover with *Allemande sauce* (see SAUCE) based on mushroom essence. Garnish with slivers of truffle.

The head can also be served, cut in neat round pieces, on a dish—each piece on a circular croûton fried in butter—with the garnish put around in separate groups. Pour over *Allemande sauce*.

Calf's head à la vinaigrette. TÊTE DE VEAU À LA VINAIGRETTE—Prepared like *Calf's head in oil**.

Calf's heart à l'anglaise I. COEUR DE VEAU À L'ANGLAISE—Cut the calf's heart into slices about ¾ inch thick. Remove the little clot of blood which forms in the centre, between the compartments. Season with salt and pepper, brush with melted butter, roll in freshly grated breadcrumbs. Grill under a gentle flame. Arrange in a round dish, alternating with grilled slices of bacon. Garnish with boiled potatoes. Dot the slices of heart with dabs of half-melted *Maître d'hôtel butter* (see BUTTER, *Compound butters*).

Calf's heart à l'anglaise II. COEUR DE VEAU À L'ANGLAISE—Cut into slices and fry in butter as described in the recipe for *Calf's liver à l'anglaise I.*

Casserole of calf's heart. COEUR DE VEAU EN CASSEROLE—Season the heart with salt and pepper. Put into an earthenware casserole, in which three tablespoons of butter have been heated. Cook it in a moderate oven from 30 to 35 minutes, basting frequently with the gravy.

At the last moment, baste with a few tablespoons of thickened veal stock. Serve in the casserole in which it was cooked.

Casserole of calf's heart à la bonne femme. COEUR DE VEAU EN CASSEROLE À LA BONNE FEMME—Brown the calf's heart in sizzling butter in an earthenware fireproof casserole as described above. Put into the casserole very small potatoes, small glazed onions and lean rashers (slices) of bacon, fried in butter. Cook all the ingredients together. Finish off as described in the preceding recipe.

Casserole of calf's heart can be garnished with various vegetables, some of which may be cooked with the heart, or added to the casserole; others may be added after the heart is cooked.

Roast calf's heart. COEUR DE VEAU RÔTI—Season calf's heart with salt and pepper; sprinkle with olive oil and a dash of lemon juice. Leave to soak for 30 minutes in this seasoning. Wrap in a sheet of pork fat or in a piece of pig's caul. Put it on a spit. Roast on a spit before a brisk fire for 35 minutes (or bake 1½ to 2 hours in the oven). Serve with diluted pan juices poured over.

Sautéed calf's heart. COEUR DE VEAU SAUTÉ—Cut the heart into thin small slices. Season with salt and pepper. Toss as quickly as possible in sizzling butter and finish cooking as described in the recipe for *Calf's kidney sauté à la bordelaise*.

Sautéed calf's heart can be prepared with a *Mushroom sauce*, *Chasseur sauce*, *Madeira* or other wine sauce (see SAUCE).

An alternative, after having tossed it in butter, is to add rice pilaf or risotto to it.

Stuffed calf's heart with various vegetables. COEUR DE VEAU FARCI AVEC LÉGUMES—Open the heart without separating the halves completely. Remove the clot of blood which forms in the middle. Season with salt and pepper and fill with finely minced pork *forcemeat** or other stuffing. Wrap it in a sheet of salt pork; cut paper-thin or in a piece of caul or in thin slices of bacon, and secure with string. Put into a casserole, sprinkle with melted butter, season and cook in a slow oven for about an hour.

Arrange the heart on a round dish. Garnish with the vegetables indicated. Dilute the pan juices with some dry white wine, blend in some thickened veal stock, reduce, add some butter, pour over the heart and serve.

Calf's kidneys. ROGNON DE VEAU—When a calf's kidney has to be cut into slices or escalopes (for frying or grilling) it is advisable to cut off all fat and remove membranes. If it is to be cooked whole, in a casserole or otherwise, it is trimmed less drastically, so as to leave a light coating of fat around it.

Calf's kidney à la Bercy. ROGNON DE VEAU À LA BERCY —Cut the kidney across into slices $\frac{3}{8}$ inch thick. Brush them with melted butter, season and dip in breadcrumbs. Grill under a brisk flame. Serve with *Bercy butter* (see BUTTER, *Compound butters*).

Calf's kidney à la bordelaise. ROGNON DE VEAU À LA BORDELAISE—Skin the kidneys and cut them open without dividing the halves completely. Put two skewers through each kidney to keep the shape. Season, spread with butter, sprinkle with breadcrumbs and grill under a brisk flame (cooking the open side of the kidney first).

Arrange on a round dish, garnish with slivers of marrow, poached in salted water and drained. Pour a border of *Bordelaise sauce* around the kidneys (see SAUCE).

Casserole of calf's kidney. ROGNON DE VEAU EN CASSEROLE—Cook the kidney whole (taking some of the fat off) seasoned with salt and pepper, in an earthenware casserole in which 2 tablespoons of butter have been heated. At the last moment, baste with 2 tablespoons of thickened veal gravy. Serve as it is, in the casserole in which it was cooked.

Casserole of calf's kidney à la bonne femme. ROGNON DE VEAU EN CASSEROLE À LA BONNE FEMME—Put some butter into an earthenware fireproof casserole and cook 3 slices or rashers of bacon in large dices and 4 small onions. Remove these from the casserole and in the same butter toss a whole kidney (with the fat partly taken off) just to stiffen it. Add the diced bacon and the onions, put around the kidney a dozen small new potatoes (or old potatoes cut down to the size of olives) three-quarters cooked in butter in a shallow pan.

Season with salt and pepper. Cook in the oven uncovered. At the last moment baste with 4 tablespoons of veal stock. Serve in the same casserole in which it was cooked.

Sometimes mushrooms lightly tossed in butter are added to the garnish of the kidney.

Grilled calf's kidney. ROGNON DE VEAU GRILLÉ—Slit the kidney lengthways without dividing into halves. Put two metal skewers through it to keep it open. Season, brush over with melted butter. Cook under a grill. Serve with *Maître d'hôtel butter* (separately or on the kidney), *Bercy butter*, or any other sauce specially recommended for grills. One can, before grilling the kidney, dip it in breadcrumbs. See BUTTER, *Compound butters*.

Calf's kidney à la liégeoise. ROGNON DE VEAU À LA LIÉGEOISE—Cook the kidney as described in the recipe for *Casserole of calf's kidney*. At the last moment, put in the casserole 4 crushed juniper berries, 2 tablespoons of gin which has been set ablaze and $1\frac{1}{2}$ tablespoons of thickened veal stock. Serve just as it is.

Calf's kidney with pilaf. ROGNON DE VEAU EN PILAF— Prepared like *Calf's liver with pilaf*.

Calf's kidney Pithiviers (Carême's recipe). PITHIVIERS AUX ROGNONS—'Prepare a demi-litron of puff pastry. When it has had eight turns, divide in two parts, giving two-thirds of the volume to one of the parts, which you then roll out big enough to cut out a circle from it nine inches in diameter.

'Incorporate whatever pieces are left over from the circle of pastry with the rest of the puff pastry, roll it out to form a circle seven inches in diameter and put on a tinned copper baking sheet.

'Then lightly moisten the edges of this piece of pastry, put on the kidney filling, spread it evenly to within a finger's width of the edges, cover with the second pieces of rolled-out puff pastry and press well round the edges to seal them. Flute the edges by cutting round with the point of a knife at a distance of eight *lignes* (see WEIGHTS AND MEASURES) from the edge of the filling. Brush the top lightly with beaten egg, then cut out a leaf or a rosette.

'Set in a lively oven. When it is nicely coloured, put it nearer the mouth of the oven, so that the pastry can dry off without acquiring any more colour. After baking for three-quarters of an hour, sprinkle evenly with fine sugar for glazing.'

(*Kidney filling*. Chop finely half a roast calf's kidney. Mix with eight ounces of pounded almonds, six of castor sugar, four of best butter, two of macaroons, shredded rind of one lemon, a grain of salt, four yolks of egg and four tablespoonfuls of whipped cream.)

Calf's kidney sautéed à la bordelaise. ROGNON DE VEAU SAUTÉ À LA BORDELAISE—Skin the kidney and cut into small escalopes. Season with salt and pepper. Sauté briskly in sizzling butter, remove the kidneys and keep hot.

Add a wineglass (1 decilitre) of white wine to the casserole. Put in a tablespoon of finely chopped shallots. Reduce, then add 1 cup ($2\frac{1}{2}$ decilitres) of brown thickened veal stock. Add the pan juices left over from frying the kidneys. Reduce the gravy to the desired consistency. Put the kidneys into the sauce with 2 tablespoons of diced beef marrow, poached and well drained. Mix, serve in a dish sprinkled with chopped parsley.

Calf's kidney sautéed with mushrooms. ROGNON DE VEAU SAUTÉ AUX CHAMPIGNONS—Cut the kidney into small slices, season with salt and pepper and sauté briskly in sizzling butter. Remove, put on a plate and keep hot.

In the same butter fry 4 sliced mushrooms. Remove the mushrooms and add to the kidney.

Into a saucepan pour a wineglass (1 decilitre) of Madeira, reduce, add $\frac{2}{3}$ cup ($1\frac{1}{2}$ decilitres) of thickened brown veal stock or *Demi-glace* (see SAUCE) and the juices left over from the kidney. Cook down by a good third.

Put the kidneys and the mushrooms into this sauce, which should be quite thick. Add 1 tablespoon of butter. Shake the pan to mix well. Heap on a platter.

Sautéed calf's kidney with various wines. ROGNON SAUTÉ AU VIN—Prepare as described above (with or without mushrooms) and replace Madeira by another wine: white wine (chablis, sauternes, graves or other), red wine (Burgundy, Bordeaux, Côtes du Rhône, or others), Alsatian wine, Rhine wine, etc.

Calf's kidneys on skewers. ROGNON DE VEAU EN BROCHETTE—Skin the kidneys and cut into uniform pieces. Season with salt and pepper. Put on metal skewers, alternating with rows of small square pieces of bacon, lightly fried in butter. Dip in breadcrumbs and grill under a brisk flame. Serve with *Maître d'hôtel butter*, *Bercy butter* or a special sauce recommended for grills (see BUTTER, *Compound butters*, and SAUCE).

Calf's liver à l'anglaise. FOIE DE VEAU À L'ANGLAISE— Cut the calf's liver into thin slices, season with salt and pepper, dredge lightly with flour and fry very quickly in sizzling butter. Brown on both sides. Arrange on a dish with thin rashers (slices) of bacon, also fried in butter in the same pan as the liver.

Serve with potatoes cut down to the same size, boiled in salted water and well drained, or with steamed potatoes.

Sprinkle with chopped parsley and a few drops of

lemon juice and pour over the butter in which the liver was cooked.

Calf's liver à l'anglaise can also be prepared by grilling the liver and the bacon, garnishing the dish with boiled potatoes and dabbing the dish with *Maître d'hôtel butter* (see BUTTER, *Compound butters*).

Calf's liver Bercy. FOIE DE VEAU BERCY—Slice, season, dredge with flour and grill. Arrange on a round dish. Serve with *Bercy butter* (see BUTTER, *Compound butters*).

Calf's liver à la bordelaise. FOIE DE VEAU À LA BORDELAISE—Slice, season, dredge with flour and fry in butter. Arrange on a round dish in alternate rows with slices of ham fried in butter. Serve with *Bordelaise sauce* (see SAUCE).

Calf's liver à la bourgeoise. FOIE DE VEAU À LA BOURGEOISE—Lard the liver with thick lardoons of bacon strips of fat (¼ inch square and 2 to 3 inches long) seasoned with pepper, spices and chopped parsley. Sprinkle with brandy. Secure with string. Braise like *Top of rump à la bourgeoise* (see BEEF).

Calf's liver à la bourguignonne. FOIE DE VEAU À LA BOURGUIGNONNE—Proceed using sliced calf's liver as described in the recipe for *Entrecôte à la bourguignonne* (see BEEF).

Calf's liver à la créole. FOIE DE VEAU À LA CRÉOLE—Cut the liver in slices and lard with small pieces of larding bacon. Leave to marinate in a few drops of oil. Dust lightly with flour. Brown on both sides in fat and leave in the corner of the pan. In the same pan, fry lightly 1 teaspoon of finely chopped onion, then add the same quantity of chopped parsley, breadcrumbs and salt; blend as much tomato purée as can be held on the point of a knife with a tablespoon of white wine and add to the pan. Remove the slices of liver, put on each a little of the mixture in the pan. Heat a dish, put a knob of butter at the bottom and arrange the slices of liver on this dish. Pour over the sauce, which should be thick. (Creole recipe.)

Calf's liver à l'espagnole. FOIE DE VEAU À L'ESPAGNOLE—Cut in slices, season, dredge with flour and fry in butter. Arrange on a bed of *Tomato fondue à la Niçoise** garnish with fried onion rings and fried parsley.

Calf's liver à l'italienne. FOIE DE VEAU À L'ITALIENNE—Cut into thin slices. Season with salt and pepper. Fry briskly in sizzling butter. Serve with *Tomato sauce* (see SAUCE).

Calf's liver à la lyonnaise. FOIE DE VEAU À LA LYONNAISE—Cut into thin strips. Season, dredge with flour, fry briskly in butter (or butter and oil mixed). Arrange in a dish. Fry lightly sliced onion in butter and put on top of the liver; add a few tablespoons rich veal stock or meat jelly. Sprinkle with a dash of vinegar heated in the same pan and sprinkle with chopped parsley.

Calf's liver with pilaf. FOIE DE VEAU EN PILAF—Cut the liver into square pieces, season and dredge with flour. Fry briskly in butter. Serve in a dish with *Rice pilaf* (see PILAF). Sprinkle with a little veal stock, flavoured with *Tomato purée* (see SAUCE) and boiled down to thicken.

Calf's liver à la provençale. FOIE DE VEAU À LA PROVENÇALE—Cut in slices and proceed as given in the recipe for *Calf's brains à la provençale*.

Roast calf's liver. FOIE DE VEAU RÔTI—Lard the liver with lardoons of bacon (strips of fat ¼ inch wide and 2 inches long) seasoned with pepper, spices and chopped parsley and sprinkle with brandy. Wrap in a caul (or thin sheet of salt pork), previously soaked in cold water, and tie with string.

Cook on a spit or roast in the oven from 13 to 15 minutes per pound. Dilute the pan juices with white wine or clear veal stock, pour over the liver and serve.

Calf's liver on skewers. FOIE DE VEAU EN BROCHETTES—Cut the liver into pieces 1½ inches square and ¼ to ½ inch thick. Fry these pieces in butter quickly just to stiffen them. Put them on metal skewers, alternating with rows of lean bacon cut to the same size and fried lightly. Brush with melted butter and dip in breadcrumbs. Grill and serve with *Maître d'hôtel butter* (see BUTTER, *Compound butters*), or serve with one of the sauces specially recommended for grills, such as *Diable*, *Piquante*, *Bordelaise* (see SAUCE).

Mushrooms, cut into thick slices and lightly tossed in butter, can also be added to the liver.

Calf's liver soufflé. SOUFFLÉ DE FOIE DE VEAU—Pound 500 grams (1 pound) of braised calf's liver in a mortar or purée in electric blender with 4 tablespoons (75 grams) of butter and 1 cup (2 decilitres) of very thick *Béchamel sauce* (see SAUCE). Bind with 3 yolks of eggs and 4 tablespoons (½ decilitre) of double cream; season with salt, pepper and nutmeg. Pass through a sieve, rubbing through with a wooden spoon. At the last moment, add 3 very stiffly beaten whites of egg.

Pour into a buttered soufflé dish. Bake in the oven like an ordinary soufflé (see SOUFFLÉ).

Calf's lungs or lights. MOU DE VEAU—Calf's lights contain little nourishment and are rarely sold in the U.S.A. It is recommended, before preparing them in one form or another, to beat them vigorously to expel the air contained in them.

Then immediately cut into uniform pieces and prepare according to the recipe chosen. They are usually prepared in a ragoût and always accompanied by a plentiful garnish.

Calf's lungs à la bourgeoise. MOU DE VEAU À LA BOURGEOISE—Calf's lungs can be prepared as *Ragoût à la bourgeoise*, that is to say, with a garnish of carrots, small onions and lardoons. See *Stewed calf's lungs* for method.

Calf's lungs à la poulette. MOU DE VEAU À LA POULETTE—Cut in small pieces, simmer in butter in covered pan and finish cooking as described in the recipe for *Sheep's trotters à la poulette*.

Stewed calf's lungs. CIVET DE MOU DE VEAU—Cut the lungs into small (50 gram) pieces. Season with salt and pepper. Brown in butter.

When the pieces are nicely brown, sprinkle in two heaped tablespoons of flour. Allow the flour to cook for a few moments, stirring it. Add enough red wine (undiluted red wine or half wine and half stock) to cover the lungs. Add a good *bouquet garni** and a crushed clove of garlic and mix. Cook in a moderate oven with a lid on for an hour and a half.

Remove the pieces of lung, put them into a shallow pan with ½ pound (250 grams) of lean bacon, diced, blanched, and fried in butter; ½ pound (250 grams) of mushrooms, sliced if they are big, whole if small; 24 small fried onions. Strain the pan juices and pour over the whole. Continue to cook in the oven for 30 minutes.

Serve in a dish. Garnish with heart-shaped croûtons of bread fried in butter.

Calf's mesentery. FRAISE DE VEAU—This is a fold of peritoneum which attaches part of the intestinal canal to the posterior wall of the abdomen. It is not sold in the U.S.A.

Fried calf's mesentery. FRAISE DE VEAU FRITE—Drain the mesentery cooked in a special *court-bouillon* (see recipe for *Calf's head*). Dry, cut in square pieces, season the pieces and dip in lightly beaten egg and breadcrumbs and, at the last moment, deep-fry in sizzling fat.

Arrange on a napkin, garnish with fried parsley. Serve separately a spiced sauce such as *Diable*, *Piquante*, etc. (see SAUCE).

Calf's mesentery à la hongroise. FRAISE DE VEAU À LA HONGROISE—Cut the mesentery into uniform pieces, fry briskly for a few minutes in butter, sprinkling them with a good pinch of paprika.

Serve in a dish with *Hungarian sauce* (see SAUCE).

Calf's mesentery à l'indienne. FRAISE DE VEAU À L'INDIENNE—Cut the mesentery into uniform slices, put them for a few moments into *Curry sauce* (see SAUCE).

Calf's mesentery à la lyonnaise. FRAISE DE VEAU À LA LYONNAISE—Cook the mesentery as described above, cut it into thin strips and proceed as described in the recipe for *Tripe à la lyonnaise*.

Calf's mesentery à la poulette. FRAISE DE VEAU À LA POULETTE—Cook the mesentery as above, cut into uniform pieces and proceed as described in the recipe for *Tripe à la poulette*.

Calf's sweetbreads. RIS DE VEAU—There are two glands taken from calves. The long one is taken from near the throat and the rounder one, which is distinctly preferable, is taken from near the heart. Allow 2 sets for 4 people.

Method of preparation. Soak the sweetbreads in cold water until they become white.

Put into a saucepan, cover with salted cold water and put the saucepan on a fire. Stir frequently with a wooden spoon.

At the first sign of boiling, cool under running water.

Drain the sweetbreads, trim, put under a press between two cloths, under a board with a weight on top.

With a larding needle insert into the sweetbreads strips of bacon, stud with pieces of truffles, tongue, ham, or leave them as they are, according to the use for which they are intended.

After this preparation, the sweetbreads can be cooked according to whatever recipe is chosen.

Calf's sweetbreads à l'anversoise. RIS DE VEAU À L'ANVERSOISE—Braise in white stock, serve with *Anversoise garnish* (see GARNISHES) and the pan juices, with a little veal stock added and reduced (boiled down) to the desired consistency.

Attereaux of calf's sweetbreads—See ATTEREAUX.

Calf's sweetbreads à la banquière. RIS DE VEAU À LA BANQUIÈRE—Braise in white stock, as described in the recipe below; serve with *Banquière garnish* (see GARNISHES).

Calf's sweetbreads braised in brown stock. RIS DE VEAU BRAISÉS À BRUN—Put the calf's sweetbreads, prepared as described above, into a shallow pan with butter, in which 1 tablespoon of diced salt pork or bacon rinds have been browned, and add thinly sliced onions and carrots. Season and add a *bouquet garni**.

Cook gently in the covered pan, add a few tablespoons of white wine, reduce to a glazed condition, add a few tablespoons of brown veal stock.

Escalopes of calf's sweetbreads served in a pastry case *(Robert Carrier)*

Finish cooking as described in the recipe for *Calf's sweetbreads braised in white stock* but glaze for a little longer.

Serve and garnish as indicated in a particular recipe.

The liquid used for the moistening of the sweetbreads should be very thick.

Calf's sweetbreads braised in white stock. RIS DE VEAU BRAISÉ À BLANC—Put the blanched, cooled and pressed sweetbreads (larded, studded or left plain, according to recipe) into a shallow pan in which some bacon rinds have been browned in butter, with finely sliced carrots and onions. Season and add a small *bouquet garni**.

Stew under a cover on a gentle fire. Add a few spoonfuls of white stock. Bring to the boil, cover, cook in the oven from 35 to 45 minutes, basting frequently with the juices.

As soon as the sweetbreads are cooked, glaze them very lightly (if the recipe calls for such glazing) by exposing them for a few minutes, uncovered, to the heat of the oven, and by basting them with the fat of the pan juices. Remove the sweetbreads, strain the pan juices. Serve and garnish as indicated in the recipe.

Calf's sweetbreads Clamart. RIS DE VEAU CLAMART—Braise in brown stock. Serve with *Clamart garnish* (or with green peas and butter) and the pan juices poured over (see GARNISHES).

Calf's sweetbreads in crépinettes—See CRÉPINETTES.

Escalope of calf's sweetbreads à l'ancienne

Escalopes of calf's sweetbread à l'ancienne. ESCALOPES DE RIS DE VEAU À L'ANCIENNE—Cut the sweetbreads into fairly round, rather thick slices, and braise in white stock as in recipe above. Arrange on the inner edge of a large puff pastry shell. Fill the centre with a ragoût of cock's combs and cock's kidneys, truffles and mushrooms, blended with *Velouté sauce* (see SAUCE) made with chicken stock reduced with cream and flavoured with Madeira. Put a sliver of truffle on each escalope.

Escalopes of calf's sweetbreads in breadcrumbs. ESCALOPES DE RIS DE VEAU PANÉES—Cut the escalopes as described above. Dip in lightly beaten egg and breadcrumbs.

Fry them in *Clarified butter* (see BUTTER, *Clarification of butter*). Serve with garnish and sauce recommended in the recipe. The escalopes can sometimes be coated with various substances such as mushrooms, ham, chopped parsley or truffles, grated Parmesan, *mirepoix**, etc.

Escalopes of calf's sweetbread in butter. ESCALOPES DE RIS DE VEAU AU BEURRE—These escalopes (thick slices) are usually prepared of sweetbreads which had been blanched and cooled under a press.

Cut the sweetbreads into 3 or 4 escalopes each, depending on thickness. Season the escalopes, dredge with flour and sauté in butter.

Serve with garnish and sauce recommended in the recipe.

Fried escalopes of calf's sweetbreads in Allemande sauce. ESCALOPES DE RIS DE VEAU SAUTÉES À L'ALLEMANDE—Fry in butter, arrange on fried croûtons, serve with *Allemande sauce* (see SAUCE).

Escalopes of calf's sweetbreads au gratin. ESCALOPES DE RIS DE VEAU AU GRATIN—Braise and slice the sweetbreads, arrange in a circle on a buttered dish, surround with sliced mushrooms, cover with *Duxelles sauce* (see SAUCE), sprinkle with breadcrumbs and brown the top.

When ready, sprinkle with a little lemon juice and chopped parsley.

Escalopes of calf's sweetbreads à l'italienne. ESCALOPES DE RIS DE VEAU À L'ITALIENNE—Fry escalopes of braised sweetbreads in oil. Pour over *Italian sauce* (see SAUCE).

Escalopes of calf's sweetbreads à la maréchale. ESCALOPES DE RIS DE VEAU À LA MARÉCHALE—Dip in slightly beaten egg and breadcrumbs and fry in butter; garnish with slivers of truffles and cooked asparagus tips dressed with butter. Sprinkle with the butter left in the pan in which the escalopes were cooked.

Escalopes of calf's sweetbreads à la milanaise. ESCALOPES DE RIS DE VEAU À LA MILANAISE—Coat with a mixture of grated cheese and breadcrumbs, finish off as described in the recipe for *Veal chops à la milanaise**.

Escalopes of calf's sweetbreads Rossini. ESCALOPES DE RIS DE VEAU ROSSINI—Fry in butter, complete as described in the recipe for *Tournedos Rossini* (see BEEF).

Escalopes of calf's sweetbreads Saint-Germain. ESCALOPES DE RIS DE VEAU SAINT-GERMAIN—Cut a heart sweetbread (soaked, blanched and cooled under a press) into four uniform escalopes.

Season these escalopes with salt and pepper, dredge with flour and fry in butter.

Arrange each on a little cake of *Anna potatoes* (see POTATOES). Put on each escalope a trickle of very thick *Béarnaise sauce* (see SAUCE) and in the centre of this spot of *Béarnaise* put a very small spoonful of meat jelly. Add a little butter to the pan juices, boiled down to thicken, and spoon around the escalopes.

Note. Escalopes of calf's sweetbreads can be grilled instead of being fried in butter.

Escalopes of calf's sweetbreads with truffles

Escalopes of calf's sweetbreads with truffles. ESCALOPES DE RIS DE VEAU AUX TRUFFES—Cook the escalopes in butter. Arrange each one on a crouton of bread fried in butter. Put on each escalope 3 or 4 slivers of truffle heated in butter. Garnish the middle of the dish with *Noisette potatoes* (see POTATOES). Add some Madeira and veal stock to the pan juices, reduce (boil down) and pour the sauce over the escalopes.

Escalopes of calf's sweetbreads Villeroi. ESCALOPES DE RIS DE VEAU VILLEROI—Braise and slice the sweetbreads, coat with *Villeroi sauce* (see SAUCE), dip in breadcrumbs and fry.

Arrange in a ring on a napkin, garnish with fried parsley. Serve *Périgueux sauce* or *Tomato sauce* separately (see SAUCE).

Calf's sweetbreads à la fermière. RIS DE VEAU À LA FERMIÈRE—Braise in brown stock, as described above. When half-cooked add *Garnish à la fermière**. Finish cooking together, serve with its own juices.

Calf's sweetbreads à la financière. RIS DE VEAU À LA FINANCIÈRE—Stud with pieces of truffle and *Tongue à l'écarlate*. Braise in brown stock, serve with *Financière garnish* and *Financière sauce* with the pan juices added (see GARNISHES and SAUCE).

This is usually served either on fried croûtons or in a pie crust.

Grilled calf's sweetbreads. RIS DE VEAU GRILLÉS—Rinse, blanch, cool and press the sweetbreads. Brush with melted butter, season and grill under a moderate flame. Serve and garnish as indicated in the recipe.

If the sweetbreads are too big, divide them horizontally in halves before grilling them.

Grilled calf's sweetbreads with various garnishes. RIS DE VEAU GRILLÉ—Garnish with braised or buttered vegetables; purées of green or dried vegetables (the purées are usually served separately), fried mushrooms, grilled or sautéed tomatoes, spinach, braised chicory, noodles, risotto, etc.

According to the garnish chosen, serve with *Maître d'hôtel butter*, or one of the sauces specially recommended for grills; *Diable*, *Italian*, *Marrow*, *Piquant*, *Robert*, etc. (see BUTTER, *Compound butters*, and SAUCE).

Calf's sweetbreads à la japonaise. RIS DE VEAU À LA JAPONAISE—Braise in brown stock as in above recipe. Serve with *Japanese garnish** and the reduced (boiled down) pan juices (see JAPONAISE, *A la*).

Calf's sweetbreads à la jardinière. RIS DE VEAU À LA JARDINIÈRE—Braise in brown stock as in above recipe; serve with *Jardinière garnish* (see GARNISH) and the pan juices reduced (boiled down).

Calf's sweetbreads à la macédoine. RIS DE VEAU À LA MACÉDOINE—Braise in brown stock, as described above. Serve with garnish *à la macédoine* (see GARNISHES).

Calf's sweetbreads à la Nantua I. RIS DE VEAU À LA NANTUA—Braise in white stock, without larding (see above). Scoop about two-thirds out of the top part. Fill with *Crayfish à la Nantua**, substituting, if necessary, 2 small lobsters for the crayfish and garnish the main part of the sweetbreads with this mixture.

Cover with *Allemande sauce*, sprinkle with breadcrumbs, glaze lightly in the oven. Arrange on croûtons, garnish with very small patty shells filled with the crayfish sauce and slivers of truffles. Serve with *Suprême sauce*, to which *Crayfish butter* is added. See SAUCE and BUTTER, *Compound butters*.

Calf's sweetbreads à la Nantua II. RIS DE VEAU À LA NANTUA—Braise in white stock as in above recipe; garnish with crayfish tails, shrimps or pieces of lobster meat and slivers of truffle; cover with *Suprême sauce* (with the cooked down pan juices) to which *Crayfish butter* has been added. See SAUCE and BUTTER, *Compound butters*.

Calf's sweetbreads à la périgourdine. RIS DE VEAU À LA PÉRIGOURDINE—Braise in brown stock, as above; garnish with truffles cut in thin slices or diced. Serve with *Madeira sauce* (see SAUCE) made with reduced (boiled down) pan juices.

Poached calf's sweetbreads. RIS DE VEAU POCHÉS—Prepare the sweetbreads as described above and put into a saucepan. Cover with white stock. Bring to the boil, remove scum and simmer gently for 35 to 40 minutes, depending on size. Drain the sweetbreads and strain the stock.

Serve and garnish as described in the recipe used.

Calf's sweetbreads poêlé. RIS DE VEAU POÊLÉS—Prepare the sweetbreads as described above. Heat a generous tablespoon of butter in a shallow frying pan, put in sweetbreads, season and cook under a lid on a gentle heat from 35 to 40 minutes.

Garnish and serve as described in a particular recipe.

Calf's sweetbreads à la princesse. RIS DE VEAU À LA PRINCESSE—Poach or braise in white stock as in above recipes; serve with *Princess garnish* (see GARNISHES) and white *Allemande sauce* (see SAUCE) made with the reduced (boiled down) pan juices.

Calf's sweetbreads with various purées. RIS DE VEAU AUX PURÉES—Braise in brown stock, as above; serve separately with purée of any of the following vegetables: artichokes, asparagus, aubergines (egg-plants), carrots, mushrooms, cucumbers, kidney beans, French beans, lentils, onions, green peas, soubise. See PURÉE.

Calf's sweetbreads Régence. RIS DE VEAU RÉGENCE—Stud with slivers of truffle; braise in white stock as above. Serve with *Regency garnish* and *Allemande sauce* made with concentrated pan juices (see GARNISHES and SAUCE).

Roast calf's sweetbreads. RIS DE VEAU RÔTIS—Prepare sweetbreads as described above. Lard them with strips of fat bacon, or leave plain. Season, wrap in a sheet of salt pork or in a piece of caul and put on a spit.

Cook over a brisk fire for 35 minutes.

Serve and garnish as described in a particular recipe.

Soufflé of calf's sweetbreads. RIS DE VEAU SOUFFLÉ—Braise sweetbreads in white stock as described above and hollow out. Prepare the scooped out pieces as a soufflé (see SOUFFLÉ) and fill the hollowed-out parts with it. Bake in a slow oven from 12 to 15 minutes. Arrange on a croûton. Serve with garnish and sauce recommended in recipe.

Calf's sweetbreads Talleyrand. RIS DE VEAU TALLEYRAND—Stud with truffles, braise in brown stock as described above, serve with *Talleyrand sauce* (see SAUCE) made with reduced (concentrated) pan juices.

Calf's sweetbreads Toulouse or Toulousaine. RIS DE VEAU TOULOUSE, TOULOUSAINE—Poach or braise in white stock as above. Serve with *Toulouse garnish* and *Allemande sauce** made with reduced (concentrated) pan juices (see GARNISHES and SAUCE).

Calf's sweetbreads with various vegetables. RIS DE VEAU AUX LÉGUMES—Braise in brown stock as above, garnish with various buttered or braised vegetables: young carrots, mushrooms, celery, cèpes, chicory, cucumbers, endives, young beans, shoots of young hops, kidney beans, French beans, lettuce, sweet corn, morels, glazed onions, green peas and reduced (boiled down) pan juices.

Calf's tongue. LANGUE DE VEAU—All the methods of preparation given for beef or ox tongue: braised, with various garnishes; grilled, *à la diable;* fried, with Italian sauce, etc., can be used for cooking calf's tongue.

Calf's tongue, cooked in a special *court-bouillon* (see recipe for cooking *Calf's head*), is always served with calf's head.

POULTRY OFFAL OR VARIETY MEATS—See also GIBLETS.

Chicken livers. FOIES DE VOLAILLE—These are prepared

skewered, in pilaf or risotto, sautéed and are served with various garnishes, etc.

They are also used as garnishes and as an ingredient of various forcemeats, particularly of *Forcemeat à gratin**.

Chicken livers on skewers à l'indienne. BROCHETTE DE FOIES DE POULET À L'INDIENNE—Cut the trimmed livers into 3 or 4 pieces. Season with salt and pepper. Fry them quickly in sizzling butter.

Thread these pieces of liver on metal skewers in rows, alternating with blanched bacon cut in rather thick square pieces and thickish slices of mushrooms, both lightly tossed in butter.

Dip the skewers with the ingredients threaded on them in the butter left in the pan from frying the liver, then roll in freshly grated breadcrumbs and grill on a brisk fire. Serve with *Rice à l'indienne** and a *Curry sauce* (see SAUCE).

Duck livers. FOIES DE CANETON—Duck livers are prepared in the same way as those of other poultry: on skewers, in a pilaf, as a risotto, sautéed with various garnishes. They are also used as an ingredient in forcemeats, especially for *Forcemeat à gratin.**

For hot and cold duck *foie gras* recipes, see FOIE GRAS.

OFFICINAL PASTILLES. PÂTES OFFICINALES—Substances of a firm consistency (small aromatic confections, usually hard gums or jelly jujubes), which do not stick to the fingers and are composed of gum and sugar dissolved in water, flavoured with aromatic flavourings or medicaments, transparent, if they have been moulded and brought to the right consistency by a slow process of evaporation and dried in a drying oven, and opaque, if they have been evaporated in too high a temperature and stirred with a wooden spoon. 'Sugared pastilles' are covered with a light coating of crystallized sugar, which increases their keeping quality.

OGNONNADE OR OIGNONADE—A stew containing a large proportion of onions. The term also applies to finely chopped onion, melted in butter or cooked in white wine.

OIL. HUILE—A fat which is liquid at normal temperatures. There are animal and vegetable oils but vegetable oils are more common. Oil does not mix with water but can be emulsified. It is soluble in alcohol, ether, benzine, etc.

In industry oils are divided into two categories, siccative or quick-drying oils (which thicken but do not turn rancid when exposed to the air), and non-siccative oils, which tend to turn rancid when exposed to the air, but do not thicken.

Oil of sweet and bitter almonds. HUILE D'AMANDES DOUCES (ET AMÈRES)—Extracted from almonds put in linen bags and subjected to pressure. This oil is used in confectionery.

Cotton-seed oil. HUILE DE COTON—Extracted from cotton seed. Now that this oil can be purified and rendered colourless, it is used in cookery. It is used chiefly as an ingredient of vegetable cooking fats or oleomargarine.

Ground-nut oil (peanut oil). HUILE D'ARACHIDES—A clear, non-siccative oil extracted from peanuts. It is tasteless and odourless. It is used as a table oil by people who prefer an oil entirely without taste.

Olive oil. HUILE D'OLIVE—The oil *par excellence*,

Pounding olives to extract olive oil (after Stradanus)

since etymologically the word 'oil' is derived from 'olive'. There are different grades of olive oil.

Pure oil is extracted cold from the finest fresh olives, which are simply crushed. This oil has a distinctive flavour, is greenish in colour and keeps fresh for a long time.

Second grade oil is extracted by pressure under heat. It is white in colour and becomes rancid more quickly (when exposed to the air).

Third grade oil (lubricating oil), is extracted from windfalls or fermented or preserved olives. It is often treated with sulphate of carbon, and then neutralized and rendered odourless. This oil is intended only for industrial use, but is all too often used for adulteration.

Connoisseurs distinguish between the various 'vintages' of olive oil, and hold the oil of Provence in particularly high esteem.

Palm oil. HUILE DE PALME—This oil is solid at normal temperatures. It is used in cooking by Africans. It is chiefly used in the manufacture of soap.

Poppy-seed oil. HUILE D'OILLETTE—Extracted from the seeds of the black, white or purple poppy. A quick-drying oil, which is used a great deal as a table oil in northern France and in Paris because of its lack of taste. It is generally called *huile blanche* in France.

Sesame oil. HUILE DE SÉSAME—Extracted from the seeds of the sesame plant, grown in warm climates. It has a rich nutty flavour. It is non-siccative. It is a staple food in India and the Orient and is growing increasingly popular in the Western world in preparing confectionery and baked goods.

Shell-fish oil. HUILE DE CRUSTACÉS—Pound finely in a mortar the trimmings and shells of crustaceans of which the flesh has been used for some other purpose. While pounding, add olive oil, equivalent in weight to the shells. Pound thoroughly with the pestle so as to obtain a smooth mixture. Rub the mixture first through a fine sieve and then strain through coarse muslin. This mixture is used to season mayonnaise and other cold sauces. It is also used as a seasoning in shell-fish and fish salads and in the preparation of cold hors-d'oeuvre.

Walnut oil. HUILE DE NOIX—A quick-drying oil. The pure oil extracted cold from dried walnuts is used in cookery. It has a very pronounced nutty flavour, well-liked by some people but disliked by those who are unaccustomed to it. Walnut oil extracted under heat is not edible.

OILLE—In the olden days the name *oille* was applied to a kind of *potée* made of various meats and vegetables.

The word *oille*, according to some authorities, comes from the Spanish *olla*. It seems more reasonable, however, to presume that this word was derived from *oule*, which in the south-west of France is used to describe an earthenware pot in which this dish is prepared.

There are three kinds of *oilles:*

The first is the old French soup which, in the days of Louis XIII, was called *Grand-ouille* and which is the *Ouille-en-pot* mentioned in the letters of Madame de Maintenon.

The second is *Olla-podrida*, a complicated dish of foreign origin. Spanish ambassadors served this dish as a part of the diplomatic representation and official ceremonial. Protocol decreed that this soup be served for a dinner given for a Spanish Grandee.

The third is *Oille-moderne à la française.*

Here is the method of preparing this *oille*, according to an old recipe:

'Take a plump chicken and two big pigeons. Trim and clean them and stuff with a forcemeat composed of crustless bread soaked in stock, blended with 8 yolks of egg, a white onion baked on hot coals, and 3 chopped artichoke hearts, the whole seasoned with a few leaves of chervil and a pinch of grated nutmeg. Sew up the 3 birds, to keep in the forcemeat, and truss them, to prevent deformation during cooking. Take an earthenware pot, put into it 6 or 8 pounds of beef cut into thin slices, a veal knuckle, cut into 4 pieces, 3 onions, a parsnip, 2 carrots, 2 turnips, 2 white leeks tied with 2 stalks of purslane, orach and chard. On this foundation put the stuffed birds. First heat on a very hot coal fire, then place the pot on a moderate heat, remove scum and leave to simmer gently. After 5 hours' cooking, cut crusts of slices of bread, toast them lightly on a low heat, put into an *oille* serving dish or some other big silver dish, moisten with stock and simmer until they begin to stick to the bottom of the dish. Arrange the chicken and the pigeons (but none of the other meat) on the toasted bread, untruss the 3 birds, strain the stock to remove fat and pour over the *oille*.'

OIORBA DE SCHIMBEA (Rumanian cookery)—This tripe soup is prepared in the following manner: Cook the tripe, cleaned and scalded, in a white *court-bouillon**, well flavoured with onions, cloves, peppers and vinegar.

Drain the tripe, cut into *julienne** strips, put into a casserole with one or two shredded pimentos, pour in the strained liquor, boil for a few minutes and bind with a liaison of yolks of egg and butter.

OISEAUX SANS TÊTE—Name given in some regions to stuffed fillets of various meats, particularly beef.

Oiseaux sans tête 'Loose vinken' (Belgian cookery)—Beat slices of beef until very thin. Season, put a little sausage meat, or, if preferred, a small piece of lean blanched bacon in the middle, roll up the slices and tie with string.

Fry these rolls brown in butter or lard, with sliced onions. When they are nicely browned on all sides, sprinkle with flour, moisten either with beer or stock in sufficient quantity just to cover the stuffed rolls. Cook gently with a lid on and serve in the same dish.

OKRA OR LADIES' FINGERS. GOMBO, GOMBAUT—A plant of the mallow family, very prolific in South American and southern United States, West Africa and India where it is cultivated and eaten as a vegetable.

There are a number of different species, most of them edible. In most cases, it is the pods which are eaten, but one species, from New Guinea, has sorrel-like leaves which are eaten like sorrel.

The best-known variety with edible pods is known as *okra* or *gumbo* or in the Near East and France as *bamia.* Another variety, commonly called the royal marshmallow, whose flowers are like those of the holly-hock, bears a juicy fruit called *nafé* in France; it is used in the preparation of a poultice for the chest.

Okra or ladies' fingers, when they are young with tender seeds, are eaten fresh. They can also be dried and kept for a long time; they look like haricot (white) beans and should be steeped in warm water before use.

However they are to be prepared, okra should always be slightly blanched first in salt water.

Okra braised with bacon. GOMBOS BRAISÉS AU GRAS—Chop onions and cook in butter until very tender. Put the onions in a shallow buttered saucepan, lined with slices of lean bacon, previously blanched. Blanch and drain the okra and lay them on the onions. Cook as described in the recipe for *Okra in butter*.

Arrange slices of bacon in the shape of a ring on the dish in which they are to be served. Place the okra in the middle.

Okra

Okra in butter. GOMBOS AU BEURRE—Blanch and drain the okra. Put them in a buttered frying pan. Season with salt and pepper. Add a few tablespoons of consommé or water. Cover and cook slowly. Cooked in this way, okra is used as a garnish for eggs cooked in various ways, for braised fish, for individual servings of meat or for poultry. If okra is to be served with meat or poultry, the pan juices should be added just before the end of cooking. Okra in butter may also be served as a separate vegetable.

Okra in cream. GOMBOS À LA CRÈME—Cook the okra as for *Okra in butter*. When they are ready, cover with a *Cream sauce* (see SAUCE). Let them simmer for a few minutes. Serve in a deep dish.

Okra à la créole. GOMBOS À LA CRÉOLE—Prepare the okra as for *Okra in tomato sauce*, seasoning them with saffron. Serve in a round dish with a border of rice, cooked with meat stock.

Fried okra. GOMBOS AUX FRITOTS—Blanch the okra. Drain and dry them with a cloth. Soak them for half an hour in oil, lemon juice, chopped parsley, salt and pepper. Dip them in frying batter (see BATTER) and deep-fry. Serve on a napkin, garnished with fried parsley and lemon.

Okra in tomato sauce. GOMBOS À LA TOMATE—Brown the okra lightly in a frying pan in which 1 large onion (150 grams), chopped fine has been slowly cooked in oil until tender. Add 2 pounds (1 kilo) of okra, 4 tomatoes, peeled, seeded and coarsely chopped. Season. Add a clove of garlic. Cover and cook slowly for 45 minutes.

Okra à la turque. GOMBOS À LA TURQUE—For this dish use the dried okra, called *bamia*. These are usually to be found dried in oriental food stores.

Each pod is the size of a haricot (white) bean. Steep them for at least 12 hours in cold water. Drain them. Brown in oil, for every 2 pounds (kilo) of okra, ½ cup (100 grams) of lean diced mutton and 1 medium-sized onion (100 grams), chopped. Add the okra and brown lightly. Moisten with a few spoonfuls of clear soup or water. Season. Add a pinch of cayenne pepper. Cover and cook slowly.

OLÉO-MARGARINE—Artificial product, made in imitation of and as an alternative to butter. It was invented by the French chemist Mège-Mouriès, who was commissioned by Napoleon III to seek a butter substitute during a period of acute shortage. It is usually referred to simply as margarine.

Gathering olives at St. Jean de Fos, Hérault
(*French Government Tourist Office*)

OLIVE—The olive is probably a native of eastern Mediterranean countries, but is now grown throughout the Mediterranean regions, as well as in tropical and sub-tropical areas. It has been cultivated for hundreds of years and is recorded as grown in Egypt in the seventeenth century B.C. They are also grown in South Australia. They were introduced in the seventeenth century by Jesuit missionaries into Mexico and California where they are very abundant.

The fruit is primarily exploited to extract its oil; the Latin term (*olea*) applies exclusively to olive oil (see OIL).

The olives, which are hard-stoned berries, are used as condiment, seasoning and hors-d'oeuvre in two forms:

Green olives: picked unripe, treated with hot weak alkali (potassium or ash solution), which removes their bitter taste, and then pickled in spiced brine.

Black olives: picked ripe, washed in several waters, put into boiling brine, without the alkali treatment, then dried and pickled in oil.

The species of olives known in French as *picholines* are cultivated specially for the table. They are big, of elongated form and reddish-black colour.

Olives with anchovy butter. OLIVES AUX BEURRE D'ANCHOIS—Wash and dry five salted anchovy fillets. Cut them, pound in a mortar and add 4 tablespoons (60 grams) of butter. Mix, season with pepper and rub through a sieve. Stone the olives and stuff with this butter with the aid of a paper forcing (pastry) bag.

Olives for garnish—Stone the olives with a special utensil or a knife, or buy stoned olives. Blanch them, drain and rinse in cold water.

Put in to simmer with the dish for which the garnish is intended.

Stuffed olives for garnish—Stone some big olives, blanch for 3 minutes, rinse in cold water and drain.

Stuff with a *quenelle forcemeat* (see FORCEMEAT) mixed with *fines herbes* or chopped truffles, depending on the nature of the dish.

OLIVET CHEESE—See CHEESE.

OLLA-PODRIDA—A Spanish soup in a very grand style, somewhat similar to the *Hoche-pot flamand*, which is also a soup served as a grand 'spread'.

The French translation of the word is *Pot-pourri.* This term, in the olden days, was used to describe not a soup, but a stew, made of various meats.

The word *Olla-podrida* is rarely used nowadays to describe this national soup, which is also called *Puchero* or *Cocido.*

Here is an idea of the ingredients required for an *olla-podrida* intended for twenty guests with healthy appetites. First the nutritive basis: 4 pounds (2 kilos) of beef (brisket or forequarter flank), 1 pound (500 grams) of shoulder of mutton, 1 pound (500 grams) of breast of mutton, 1 pound (500 grams) of uncooked ham, 1 pound (500 grams) of salt pork, 2 each of pig's ears, feet and tails, one chicken (tender and plump), 2 partridges (when in season), 6 chorizos (Spanish sausages).

Vegetables: 4 medium-large carrots (400 grams), 8 big leeks (white only), 2 big onions, a cabbage, 2 heads of lettuce, 8 potatoes and (absolutely essential ingredient) 1 pound (500 grams) of chick-peas (garbanzos), well soaked; as well as garlic, salt, pepper and a large *bouquet garni**.

Put all the meat, except the chicken, partridge and the chorizos, into a pit pot. Cover with plenty of cold water. Season with salt (making allowances for the salt content of some of the meats). Bring to the boil, remove scum and add crushed garlic and the *bouquet garni.* Put in the chick-peas (previously well soaked in cold water). Cook for 2 hours. Add the various roughly sliced vegetables, except the potatoes, which (similarly sliced) should be put into the soup only 35 minutes before serving.

Simmer gently for 2 hours. As cooking progresses, take out the meats which are done; some being more tender than others will require less time.

Arrange all the meats and the vegetables on a big dish and serve the soup in a soup tureen.

OMELETTES—See EGGS.

OMNIBUS—In restaurant terminology (Paris restaurants particularly) this name is applied to the *commis*, or chef's assistant, or waiter, whose work consists, at the time of serving, of passing on the orders to the kitchen and fetching from the kitchen whatever is indicated on the order. *Omnibus* is a kind of apprentice.

ONAGER. ONAGRE—Wild ass which in Persia is considered highly prized game. This is the wild ass of the Bible.

ONION. OIGNON—Biennial plant, native of Asia and Palestine, which has been cultivated from earliest times. This vegetable of the *Liliaceae* family was so greatly prized in Egypt that it was worshipped.

The bulb has many concentric coats (and country people believe that their number and thickness increase to herald a hard winter); it contains a strong and acrid sulphuretted essence, which causes watering of the eyes and rubefaction of the skin but disappears in the cooking process; its taste is pungent.

Chopped onion. OIGNONS HACHIS—Peel the onion, cut in half, cut each half into very thin slices without separating them from the root, then make 5 to 6 horizontal cuts through the whole thickness of the onion.

Now cut the onion again vertically. You will thus have minute dice which will need very little chopping to obtain finely chopped onion.

The onion, fresh chopped, can be used as it is.

If prepared in advance, to 'revive' it it should be tied in a corner of a cloth and placed under a cold water tap. Then squeeze the onion in the cloth to drain it well and spread it in a saucer.

Proceed in the same way if very white chopped onion is required, as an accompaniment for calf's head or any dish *à la vinaigrette.*

Fried onions. OIGNONS FRITS—Cut medium-sized onions into round slices about $\frac{1}{8}$ inch thick. Shake out the slices into rings. Season with salt, dredge with flour and fry in smoking hot oil. Drain the onions, dry on a cloth and sprinkle with salt.

Note. Fried onions are used as a garnish, particularly for *Entrecôte à la tyrolienne* and *Chicken sauté à la bordelaise.*

Onions fried in batter. OIGNONS EN FRITOT—Cut the onions into round slices, as described above. Shake out the slices into rings. Season with salt and pepper and sprinkle with oil and lemon juice. Leave to marinate in this seasoning for 30 minutes.

At the last moment, dip the onion rings into a light batter and fry.

Onions fried in this way are used as a garnish.

Glazed onions. OIGNONS GLACÉS—*White:* Skin *small* button onions. Put them into a shallow pan and add enough white stock almost to cover them. Add butter, allowing $\frac{1}{4}$ pound (125 grams) per quart (litre) of liquid. Season and simmer with a lid on. At the last moment, turn the onions in their liquor, cooked down to a glaze—so that they can be coated with this glaze all over.

Brown: Heat some butter in a shallow pan and put in the onions. Season with salt and a pinch of castor (fine) sugar. Cook, covered, on a moderate heat, in such a way as to allow the onions to cook and acquire their colour at the same time.

Glazed onions for garnish—See GARNISHES.

Onions à la grecque (Hors-d'oeuvre). OIGNONS À LA GRECQUE—Skin small uniform-sized onions. Blanch them, dip in cold water and drain. Cook in a *court-bouillon** as indicated for *Artichokes à la grecque**. Leave to cool in the *court-bouillon.*

Onions à l'orientale (Hors-d'oeuvre). OIGNONS À L'ORIENTALE—Choose medium-sized onions, blanch them thoroughly in salted water and remove three-quarters of the inside.

Stuff with a composition prepared by mixing chopped onion (using the scooped out parts), half its weight of rice cooked in stock, *Tomato fondue**, cooked with oil and flavoured with garlic, and sweet pimentos, stewed in butter and chopped. Season with saffron. Stuff the onions with this forcemeat, piling it into a dome. Put the onions into an oiled dish, sprinkle with oil, bake slowly in the oven and leave to get cold before serving.

Onion purée or soubise—See PURÉE.

Onion soup. SOUPE À L'OIGNON—See various recipes for the preparation of this soup in the section entitled SOUPS AND BROTHS.

Stuffed onions. OIGNONS FARCIS—Peel medium-sized onions, taking care not to damage the first white layer. Cut transversally, at the stalk end, at about three-quarters of their height. Blanch thoroughly in salted water, plunge into cold water and drain.

Remove the inside, leaving a thickness all round of two layers of onion skins.

Chop the scooped out part finely and mix with some forcemeat (pork, veal, beef or mutton).

Stuff the onions with this mixture, put them into a buttered sauté pan, moisten with a few tablespoons of slightly thickened brown veal gravy, bring to the boil with a lid on and finish cooking in the oven, basting frequently, to glaze the onions. A few moments before removing from the oven, sprinkle the surface with a little grated, toasted or fresh breadcrumbs and brown the top.

Note. This method is mainly applied to sweet Spanish onions.

These onions may be served separately, as a vegetable, but are principally used as a garnish.

Stuffed onions à la catalane. OIGNONS FARCIS À LA CATALANE—Prepare the onions as described above. Stuff them with a mixture of chopped onion, rice cooked in meat stock, sweet pimentos, stewed in oil and chopped, and hard boiled eggs—the whole well blended, seasoned and spiced. Put the stuffed onions into a well-oiled oven-proof dish. Pour in enough stock to cover the onions half-way and cook gently in the oven. A few moments before removing from the oven, sprinkle with white breadcrumbs and brown the top.

Stuffed onions à la duxelles, called à la parisienne. OIGNONS FARCIS À LA DUXELLES (À LA PARISIENNE)—Prepare the onions as described above. Stuff with a mixture of chopped onions, *Duxelles** and chopped, lean, cooked ham. Braise in the usual manner.

Stuffed onions à l'italienne. OIGNONS FARCIS À L'ITALIENNE—Prepare the onions as described above. Stuff them with a risotto, mixed with chopped onions and chopped, cooked, lean ham. Braise in the usual manner. A few moments before removing from the oven, sprinkle with grated Parmesan and brown the top.

ONOPORDON—A genus of coarse thistle-like herbs of the composite family. One species is a wild artichoke, also called *Onopordum*, which grows on hillsides and roadsides.

The leaf receptacles of this plant are eaten as cultivated artichokes. The stalks are also eaten as cardoons and the roots as salsify.

ONOS. APHIE—A type of fish caught in the Mediterranean which is also called *rockling*.

Some doctors maintain that the flesh of the rockling is very indigestible. This was not so in the opinion of the ancients who, justly, greatly appreciated this fish for its very nourishing flesh. It is prepared like whiting.

OPHIDIUM. DONZELLE—A small Mediterranean fish similar to the eel. It is sometimes known in France as *demoiselle* and *girelle* (potter's wheel). This fish is used as an ingredient of *bouillabaisse**.

OPOSSUM—A marsupial, reaching the size of a hare, which abounds in certain regions of North America. The flesh is edible and resembles that of rabbit.

ORACH OR ORACHE. ARROCHE—Common name of several species of plants frequently cultivated in gardens, among them a type called *Mountain spinach*, the leaves of which are eaten, cooked like spinach. In U.S.A. this is called *French spinach* or *Sea-purslane.*

ORANGE—Citrus fruit. The tree producing it is an evergreen and there are many species of the same family *Rutaceae*, including the *Orange tree* proper (*Citrus sinencis*), *Citron* or *Lemon trees* (*Citrus medica*), the *Sour* or *Bitter orange tree* (*Citrus aurantium*), the *Lime* (*Citrus aurantifolia*) and the *Grapefruit tree* (*Citrus maxima*), and the *Bergamot orange tree* (*Citrus bergamia*), from which an oil is extracted for use in confectionery and perfumery.

The blossom of the orange tree has a very pleasant smell and the fruit is the sweet orange. The tree is a native of China and Cochin-China.

The *Bitter orange* (*bigarade*) is a native of India.

The Bergamot orange, which has never been found in the wild state, appears to be a result of cultivation.

The Greeks and the Romans did not know the sweet orange, but they did perhaps know the bitter orange. The Sanscrit name of this was *Nagrunga*, from which the Italian words *Naranzi* and *d'Aranzi*, the Latin terms (of the Middle Ages) of *Arantium*, *Arangium*, and later, *Aurantium*—which produced the French word *Orange*—were all derived.

The crusaders brought bitter oranges from Palestine into Italy. The Arabs introduced it into Spain and the south of France, as well as into East Africa.

Nice has been trading in bitter oranges since 1332.

A historic orange tree, planted in 1422, by Eleonora de Castille, the wife of Carlos III, the King of Navarra, came into the possession of the Constable of Bourbon, was confiscated with all his possessions in 1552 and later graced first the gardens of Fontainebleau, under the name of Lord High Constable, then the gardens of Versailles. It died in 1858.

The sweet orange tree is classified as a native of China and the Chinese consider oranges wild fruit. Vasca da Gama brought a root of this tree into Portugal and it is from this tree, preserved in Lisbon, at the home of Count de Saint-Laurent, that all the oranges of Portugal, Spain, Provence, etc., have come.

As this tree does not always reproduce itself faithfully from seed, de Candolle thinks that it could be a variety of bitter orange tree, which supervened a long way back.

There is a considerable trade in sweet oranges throughout southern Europe. The best of this fruit comes from the Azores, Malta, Portugal, Southern Italy, Sicily, the Balearic Islands and Valencia.

Algerian oranges are also very famous, as are those cultivated in the Nice region.

Oranges are grown commercially on a very large scale in the United States, principally in California, Florida, Louisiana and Texas.

Orange blossom and leaves. FLEURS, FEUILLES D'ORANGER—The flowers and the leaves of orange trees (particularly those of the bitter orange, which are more strongly scented) are used as an infusion.

The essential oil of orange flowers is called *Neroli;* that of the bitter orange is called *Essence de petit-grain.* It is used for scenting creams, custards, pancake batter, etc.

Orange blossom water. EAU DE FLEUR D'ORANGER—Orange blossom water has a very subtle fragrance and is used in pastry-making and confectionery for aromatizing various preparations.

Orange blossom water is manufactured industrially.

Orangeade—Very refreshing beverage made by adding the juice of one or several oranges to sweetened water.

To improve the taste of the orangeade a little curaçao can be added to it; a little brandy, rum or some other spirit can also be added to accentuate the taste.

This beverage should be served as cold as possible, preferably iced.

Orangeat—French name for finely-chopped, candied orange peel.

Orange cake. GÂTEAU À L'ORANGE—This cake is made of Genoese pastry mixture, flavoured with orange, and is usually called *orangine.*

Candied orange peel. ÉCORCE D'ORANGE CONFITE—Candied orange peel is used in pastry-making and confectionery. It is prepared in the following manner.

Scrape the orange rind with a spoon to remove all the white pith lining it on the inside, blanch and put into syrup. Leave in the syrup for 24 hours. On the following day, drain, cook the syrup to 25°, or until it threads from the spoon, and put in the rind. This constitutes *façon* in confectionery terms. Repeat this operation several times bringing the sugar to the desired degree of crystallization at the last boiling.

Orange compote. COMPOTE D'ORANGES—Divide the oranges into segments; remove skin and pips and put into a bowl. Pour over them 20° or 22° syrup (1½ cups sugar to 2 cups of water) flavoured with orange peel. (The syrup should be boiling.) Cover the bowl. Leave to steep in the juice in a cold place. Serve in a fruit dish.

Orange cream. CRÈME À L'ORANGE—Custard cream flavoured with orange peel.

Orange fritters. BEIGNETS D'ORANGES—Prepare like all fruit fritters, using orange segments. See FRITTERS, *Dessert* (*sweet*) *fritters.*

Glacé orange segments. QUARTIERS D'ORANGE GLACÉS—Trim the orange segments, that is to say remove all the white pith covering them, taking care not to damage the thin skin in which the pulp is contained. Put them in the oven for a few moments to dry.

Spike the orange segments on a cocktail stick or a needle and dip them, one by one, into sugar cooked to crack degree. Leave them to cool on a wire mesh or a metal sieve. Put each segment into a little frilly paper case.

Note. It is of orange segments prepared in this manner that orange *croquembouches** are made. They are also used for decorating sweet dishes.

Orange granité. GRANITÉS GLACÉES À L'ORANGE—This is served like sherbet. See ICE CREAMS AND ICES, *Granités.*

Orange ice and iced mousse. GLACE ET MOUSSE GLACÉE À L'ORANGE—Orange ice is made of sugar syrup, flavoured with orange, in the same way as all other water ices. (See ICE CREAMS AND ICES.) This ice is set in special forms, or served in glasses, or *en rocher*, like all other ices. It can also be served in scooped-out orange peel.

Orange iced mousse is prepared using orange-flavoured mousse (bombe) mixture and set in iced biscuit moulds.

This mousse is often served under the name of *Biscuit glacé à l'orange.* It is also used as an ingredient of mixed ice *bombes.*

Orange jelly. GELÉE À L'ORANGE—This is a jelly to be served as a sweet course (not to be confused with the *Orange jelly preserve*) which is set in special moulds or served in cups of orange peel.

Orange jelly is prepared as all other fruit jellies (see JELLY) and is usually flavoured with a few drops of curaçao.

Orange jelly (preserve). GELÉE D'ORANGE—This is made of juice of sweet oranges in the usual manner. See JAMS AND JELLIES.

Orange liqueur—See LIQUEUR.

Orange marmalade. MARMELADE D'ORANGES—As described in recipes for other fruit marmalades. See MARMALADE.

Bitter orange marmalade. CONFITURE (MARMELADE) DE BIGARADES—Prepare like *Orange marmalade* (see MARMALADE), using bitter oranges.

Orange pudding. POUDING À L'ORANGE—See PUDDINGS, *Lemon, Tangerine or Orange soufflé pudding.*

Orange salad. SALADE D'ORANGE—The word *salad* is incorrectly used in this case, as not a single particle of salt enters into the preparation of this dish. But as it has become common usage to call this dish by this name, we shall conform.

Peel the oranges and remove all the pith covering them.

Cut into round slices ⅛ inch thick and remove all pips. Arrange them in a fruit dish (this dish, to justify its name, is often served in a salad bowl). Sprinkle with castor (fine) sugar and a little curaçao, or any other liqueur, such as rum, brandy or kirsch, and serve.

Bitter orange salad. SALADE DE BIGARADES—This is served as a sweet course. Prepare, using bitter oranges, as *Orange salad.*

Again, the word *salad* is here used in an unorthodox sense, for this dish is more of a compote and requires no oil, vinegar or salt. However, bitter oranges, as well as sweet oranges, can be used in real salads.

Orange sherbet. SORBET À L'ORANGE—See ICE CREAMS AND ICES, *Sherbets.*

Orange soufflé. SOUFFLÉ À L'ORANGE—Using orange-flavoured soufflé mixture, prepare like any other cream soufflé (see SOUFFLÉS).

Striped oranges. ORANGES RUBANÉES—Choose big oranges and scoop out the pulp taking care not to damage the skins. Using this pulp make a clear orange jelly; meanwhile, prepare a *Bavarois** mixture keeping it as white as possible, to contrast with the red of the orange jelly.

Fill the orange peel cups with these two compositions, putting them in alternate, well-marked layers. Do not pour any jelly or bavarois mixture into the orange skins, until the previous layer is completely set. This result is easily achieved if the orange peel cups are placed into a pan filled with crushed ice. Chill.

Cut each orange peel cup into quarters and serve in a fruit dish.

Oranges in syrup (Turkish cookery). ORANGES AU SIROP—Remove the yellow part of the peel of Jaffa oranges (big oranges without seeds). Remove the pith covering the oranges and shred the peel into thin, long *julienne** strips. Poach the oranges in thick, slightly caramelised syrup. Leave the oranges in this until the syrup thickens once more.

Towards the end of cooking, put in the shredded rind.

Orange wine. VIN D'ORANGE—The word 'wine' is incorrectly applied to this beverage, which, however, is excellent and very refreshing. It is prepared in the following manner:

Choose very ripe oranges, peel them and cut into slices transversally. Press them to extract all the juice.

For every 4 quarts (litres) of this juice add 2 pounds (1 kilo) of sugar. Bottle, cork, tie with string and leave to ferment.

ORANGE MILK AGARIC. ORONGE—Common name for a mushroom of the *amanita* genus. See MUSHROOMS.

ORANGINE—Genoese pastry, flavoured with candied orange peel, cut transversally into three layers, sandwiched with *French pastry cream* (see CREAM) and iced with *Fondant icing* (see ICING).

Method. Cut a *Genoese cake**, flavoured with candied orange peel and baked in a flan ring (U.S. cake pan) with rather high sides, into three layers. Cover each with a layer of orange-flavoured *French pastry cream* (see CREAM). Reshape the cake. Ice with orange-flavoured *Fondant icing* (see ICING). Decorate with candied orange peel of small green Chinese oranges preserved in brandy.

Note. This *gâteau* can also be made by putting round Genoese cakes, each baked in a flan ring in layer cake tins of different dimensions, one on top of another, sandwiching with orange-flavoured *French pastry cream.*

ORCHIS—Name of various European and Asiatic orchids, the roots of which contain flour used for the preparation of salep.

OREILLER DE LA BELLE AURORE (The Pillow of Belle Aurore)—In his book, *La Table au pays de Brillat-Savarin,* Lucien Tendret gives a recipe for this grandiose game pie, which, he says, was one of Brillat-Savarin's favourite dishes.

'At midday', wrote Tendret, 'we would sit at table, drink Côte-Grèle wine, from Brillat-Savarin's vineyard, and eat the traditional pie, square shaped and for that reason called *l'Oreiller de la Belle Aurore* after Brillat-Savarin's mother, Claudine-Aurore Récamier.'

Lucien Tendret's recipe for this pie was modified by Philéas Gilbert, and it is this version that we quote below:

'In a pie in which game is the principal element the flavour of game meat must be the predominating flavour and the addition even of the smallest quantity of *panada**, advocated by Tendret, is superfluous. A *panada* (of which there are various kinds) has its uses and is even essential in certain forcemeats in which it acts as a binding agent, an element affecting liaison, but not in this case.

'Bone marrow fat, indicated by Tendret as part of the composition, does not go at all well in a cold pie and can with advantage be replaced by fat goose liver. The same applies to calf's sweetbreads included in the filling, which is more suitable as an ingredient of a hot pie. Finally, the actual method of preparing the paste is somewhat confused and we prefer to interpret it rather than carry it out to the letter.'

Method. 'Choose a plump, tender pheasant, bone it, having first cut off the drumsticks; season with a good pinch of *spiced salt* (see SALT) and put into an earthenware casserole with 5 tablespoons of fine champagne brandy and the same amount of Madeira.

'Take a big fat goose liver, remove all sinews and stud it generously with quarters of fresh, peeled truffles. Season with spiced salt and put it with the pheasant. Leave to marinate for one hour, turning both the pheasant and the liver from time to time.

'Cut into big dice $\frac{3}{4}$ pound (350 grams) of wild rabbit meat, the flesh from the drumsticks (which should previously be skinned), 5 ounces (150 grams) of fillet of pork, 5 ounces (150 grams) of round of veal and 14 ounces (400 grams) of fresh fat bacon. First pound each of these ingredients separately, then put them all into the mortar, with 7 ounces (200 grams) of raw goose liver and $1\frac{1}{2}$ to 2 tablespoons (40 or 50 grams) of spiced salt (depending on temperature). Continue to pound until all the ingredients have blended into an absolutely homogeneous mixture, adding, little by little, two eggs beaten as for an omelette. Rub the forcemeat through a sieve into a bowl, add $3\frac{1}{2}$ ounces (100 grams) of fresh, finely chopped truffles and keep in a cool place. When ready to use, add the marinated pheasant and goose liver to the forcemeat.

'Meanwhile, bone two woodcocks, which should be just right for use. Keep the trail.

'Sauté in butter $3\frac{1}{2}$ ounces (100 grams) of chicken livers, as well as the livers of the pheasant and the woodcocks. (These should be fried very lightly, just enough to stiffen them.) Add a teaspoon of chopped shallot, a pinch of spiced salt and 2 tablespoons (20 grams) of fresh mushroom parings. Put on the fire for 2 minutes and dilute with two tablespoons of Madeira.

'Pound first these livers in a mortar, then the woodcock meat. Combine these two ingredients, add $3\frac{1}{2}$ ounces (100 grams) of raw goose liver, 2 to 3 slices (50 grams) of finely shredded bacon, the trail of woodcocks, a pinch of spiced salt, a fresh, peeled truffle (about 2 ounces, 60 grams) and continue to pound in a mortar until the mixture is perfectly smooth. Rub through a sieve and keep by.

'Using $4\frac{3}{4}$ cups (600 grams) of sieved flour, 2 teaspoons (12 grams) of salt, $1\frac{1}{2}$ cups (3 decilitres) of water and 2 tablespoons (30 grams) of butter, prepare semi-puff pastry, allowing five-and-a-half turns.

'When ready, roll out two-thirds of the pastry into 12-inch-square sheets. Line the middle of this rolled-out piece of pastry with thin bacon rashers (slices), covering about 7 square inches of the surface and, therefore, leaving a border of pastry about 5 inches to use to enclose the filling. Spread half of the first forcemeat on the bacon rashers in an even layer.

'Spread the pheasant on the table (skin downwards), cover with half of the woodcock forcemeat, put the goose liver on top and cover with the rest of the forcemeat. Bring the edges of the pheasant's skin and flesh together, so as to enclose the liver and to form a kind of slightly flattened galantine. Place this galantine on the layer of forcemeat spread on the pastry. Cover completely with the other half of the forcemeat and on top of that lay a few thin rashers of bacon.

'Sprinkle with a pinch of spiced salt, add a small pinch of crushed bay leaf and a little powdered dry thyme.

'Roll out the rest of the pastry into a sheet about 7 inches square, rolling it out a little thinner than the first piece. Pinch up the edges of the first piece of pastry all round the filling. Cover with the second piece of pastry and, by pressing with the fingers, seal up the edges, having first carefully moistened them with water to make the pastry adhere. Trim away surplus pastry, crimp the edges all the way around and decorate the four sides with pieces of rolled-out pastry cut in fancy shapes (crescents, circles, lozenges), which are made to adhere by moistening the pastry slightly. Decorate the top with pastry leaves, cut out with a special cutter or knife, trace the veins on them and lay on the top of the pie slightly overlapping them.

'Put three square scallop-edged pieces of pastry, each of a different size, placed one on top of the other, in the middle of the pie and make a hole in the centre to allow steam to escape during cooking.

'Brush the pie on top and all round with beaten egg. As a precautionary measure, surround the pie with a piece of buttered greaseproof paper, which should be fastened with string all round and can be removed after the pie has been in the oven for three-quarters of an hour.

'Put into a hot oven, keeping a regular heat (particularly in the hearth), that of the vault always being sufficient, considering the rather prolonged cooking time. Allow from 15 to 16 minutes per pound (30 to 32 minutes per kilo).

'When cooked and the pastry is no more than warm, pour ⅝ cup (1½ decilitres) of very good game liquid aspic jelly through the hole in the top.

'This pie should be prepared at least 24 hours in advance.' (Philéas Gilbert.)

ORGANT. WILD MARJORAM. ORIGAN—An aromatic herb, possessing a pungent smell and slightly bitter taste, somewhat similar to sweet marjoram.

ORGEAT—A beverage made from an emulsion of almonds, with sugar. In the past this was made out of barley decoction.

Orgeat syrup. SIROP D'ORGEAT—This beverage is thus called because, in the olden days, it was prepared from a barley emulsion to which an almond decoction was added.

This syrup is nowadays made only out of almonds. Here is a formula: 2 pounds (1 kilo) of almonds including 30 to 40 bitter almonds, 5 cups (1 kilogram 200 grams) of sugar, 3½ cups (800 grams) of water or milk and 4 teaspoons (15 grams) of tartaric acid (cream of Tartar).

Method. Scald the almonds for a few moments in boiling water to loosen the skin, blanch, wash and pound into a fine paste. Squeeze out the oil, reduce the rest to a powder, mix with enough water to make it into a liquid paste and leave to stand for 24 hours. Add the rest of the water and dissolve the tartaric acid, which has the property of precipitating casein, in the emulsion.

Filter through paper. Dissolve the sugar, either cold or on a low heat, and add to the emulsion.

ORIENTALE (A L')—Term applied to the preparation of various ingredients (fish, eggs, vegetables) cooked with tomatoes, flavoured with garlic and sometimes spiced with saffron.

ORLÉANAIS—This ancient province of France can be classed among the gastronomical centres of the country, by virtue of the succulent game pâtés made there.

The gastronomical resources of Orléanais are great and all the produce—agricultural and livestock—is of the highest quality.

In Perche, cattle is raised, producing meat of excellent quality. The region specialises in raising very big sheep, which are perhaps less delicate than the smaller ones raised in Sologne.

In Beauce excellent poultry is raised. The best comes from Romorantin, Selles-sur-Cher, Montargis and Dreux.

Sologne produces the best game in the country and Sologne winged game is considered the best in France.

Loire fish (carps, pike, shad) is famous for its delicate flavour and is used in the preparation of delicious *matelotes*.

Loire salmon is a highly prized fish and crayfish abound in the waterways of this region.

Val-de-Loire (as the beautiful Loire valley is called) is extremely fertile. The produce of its admirable market gardens and orchards are choice and in great demand. Vendôme asparagus is greatly prized on all the French markets.

Beauce wheat produces one of the best quality flours to be found in France.

At Boynes, near Pithiviers, saffron is grown. And among the food products of this region, we must not neglect to give particular mention to wine vinegar (made of pure wine) which has for centuries been produced at Orléans and which is famous throughout the world.

The vineyards of Loiret, situated near the hillsides of Val-de-Loire, produce light and highly esteemed wines. The best of these come from Meung, Beaugency and Sully.

Excellent little wines are produced in Loir-et-Cher, especially in Blaisois, and in Cher and Vendôme hillside vineyards.

Finally, excellent cider is made in Orléanais, in the Perche region.

Gastronomic map of Orléanais

Culinary specialities—Among the culinary specialities of this region we must, first of all, mention the celebrated, the delicious, Pithiviers *Lark pâté,* magnificent pâtés which have been made for 200 years, according to an old recipe, in the shop of master-pastrycook Gringoire. We must also dwell on the whole range of other succulent pies made for centuries in this region: the *Chartres pâtés,* made of partridge or lapwing; *Étampes and Blois lark pies; Gien thrush pâtés; Dreux wild rabbit pâtés; Beaugency rabbit pâtés; Anet pâtés,* etc.

The Orléanais gastronomical repertoire, however, is not limited to these game pâtés. There are in this region many other excellent culinary specialities, of which the following are the best known: *Blois and Vendôme rillettes* (potted mince) and *greaves;* the succulent *Jargeau andouilles* and various other exquisite local pork products; *Pike à la marinière; Pike in saffron* (Gâtinais-grown saffron); *Baked carp; Matelote of eel; Braised beef à la beauceronne; Boiled leg of Sologne mutton; Calf's mesentery à la blasoise; Young rabbit à la solognote; Terrine of hare; Stuffed potatoes; Stuffed cabbage; Croûte aux champignons de Montargis.*

Orléanais can be justly proud of its puff pastries with almonds, universally known as *Pithiviers almond cakes;* the famous *'demoiselles Tastue'* tart, made in Lamotte-Beuvron; *Beaugency fruit pâté, Sully, Montoire and Romorantin crisp biscuits;* the *Orléans quince marmalade;* and, last but not least, although it is not a culinary speciality but a natural product, we must mention the exquisite *Gâtinais honey.*

ORLY (A LA)—Method of preparation applied mostly to fish. For this, the fish is generally filleted, the fillets are skinned, dipped into a light batter, fried in deep fat and accompanied by tomato sauce served separately. See WHITING, *Whiting Orly.*

ORTOLAN OR GARDEN BUNTING—This small bird enjoys a high reputation as a table delicacy.

The ortolans are found in central and southern Europe. They are quite plentiful in the south of France, particularly in Landes, a region which specialises in fattening them, and also in Spain, Italy and Greece.

Ortolans can be prepared in any way suitable for *Garden warblers* or *Larks.*

Generally speaking, gastronomes hold the opinion that the only way to cook this bird is to roast it in the oven or on the spit and insist that it should not be cooked in anything but its own fat.

Ortolans à la Brissac—'Cut a ham pope's eye, from the part where the lean merges with the fat, into 24 little squares (depending on the number of ortolans you have) the size of little bacon rashers which accompany the ortolans and are called *temoins* ("witnesses"). Prior to this, you should de-salt the piece of ham completely. Thread the ortolans on very thin skewers, interspersing with pieces of ham, put them on a spit, placing them back to back; the back being the fattest part of the bird, it loses less of its fat in this position. Cook before a clear, lively fire basting continuously with clarified butter.

'When nearly cooked, sprinkle with breadcrumbs and do not baste any more, to allow the birds to colour nicely. Take off the skewers, arrange on a dish and add small croûtons of bread to the ham. Peel two small baskets of mushrooms, slice them and sauté in a glass of Aix oil until they acquire a pale golden colour, add half a dozen sliced truffles and drain off all the oil; add a piece of concentrated meat jelly about the size of a walnut, a tablespoon of *Espagnole demi-glace* (see SAUCE) and a dash of lemon juice, pour in the middle of the ortolans and serve.' (Plumerey's recipe.)

Ortolans à la Carême—'Stuff the ortolans, boned through the back, with a little foie gras encrusted with a piece of truffle. Wrap each one in a piece of muslin cloth and tie with string at both ends. Plunge them into boiling port. Poach for 5 minutes. Drain and unwrap.

'Arrange each in a tartlet case, baked blind and filled with a *salpicon** of lamb's sweetbreads, truffles and mushrooms, bound with chicken *Velouté sauce* (see SAUCE) reduced (cooked down) with the port and a little cream.'

Ortolans in cases à la royale. ORTOLANS EN CAISSE À LA ROYALE—Bone the ortolans through the back. Stuff each one with a piece of foie gras, encrusted with a slice of truffle, seasoned with spiced salt and sprinkled with brandy.

Reshape the ortolans. Brown them quickly in butter. Put each one into a small frilly paper case (or into individual oven-proof porcelain dishes) on a spoonful of truffles shredded into *julienne** strips. Sprinkle with melted butter, cook in the oven for 5 or 6 minutes and serve as they are.

Cold Ortolans. ORTOLANS FROIDS—All the methods of preparation given for quails, thrushes and larks are applicable to ortolans, but, we repeat, all these recipes are given just for the record, for ortolan, whether it is to be served hot or cold, should be prepared in the simplest manner, and true connoisseurs of this delicate game will not have it otherwise than roasted.

Ortolans à la landaise—This recipe was supplied by Félix Campagné, Hôtel de France, at Pau.

'In the course of a few delightful car outings in the immense wilderness of Landes, my friends and I had the occasion each to consume half a dozen ortolans. These ortolans, in their turn, were preceded by a good half-dozen other copious dishes.

'The good woman who kept the inn where we were in the habit of savouring these dainties trussed them with great skill and simply put them into little cases made out of very white school paper. They were arranged in rows in a dripping pan and the dripping pan stood in a big open fire-place before a great log fire. We used to crowd around the glowing embers and watch them cook in their own melting fat.

'Each one of us could, seeing them, leave them to be cooked to his taste. We salted and spiced them with just one turn of the pepper mill and ate them with the fingers. That was divine.'

Ortolans à la périgourdine—Heat 2 tablespoons of butter in an earthenware casserole and put in 6 ortolans, trussed in the usual manner. Brown them quickly in the sizzling butter. Cover with a dozen rather thick slices of truffles. Season with salt and pepper. Cover the casserole with a lid and cook in the oven for about 8 minutes, basting the birds with a good tablespoon of armagnac which has been set alight. Serve in the same casserole.

Ortolans à la provençale—'Twenty ortolans would be enough for an entrée. Cut 24 oval-shaped croûtons about two *lignes* (a ligne is about $\frac{1}{12}$ inch) thick; hollow out a thickness of one *ligne* on one side, put an ortolan on each such croûton, then place into a sauté pan, in which you have put two *lignes* of best olive oil, spiced with half a pounded clove of garlic. Put on the stove to heat the oil with the croûtons and the ortolans, then set in the oven.

'As soon as the croûtons begin to colour lightly,

remove the pan from heat, drain them on a cloth to wipe off oil and arrange on a dish. Separately, prepare a truffle *ragoût** and *Parisian sauce* (see SAUCE, *Cold sauces*), add to it anchovy butter (made from two completely de-salted anchovy fillets), put in a tablespoon of cold olive oil and the juice of half a lemon, pour in the middle of the dish containing the ortolans and serve.' (A. Carême.)

Roast ortolans. ORTOLANS RÔTIS—Truss the ortolans in the usual manner and wrap in vine leaves.

Put them in rows, packing them in fairly tightly, into a pan moistened with a little salted water.

Roast in a very hot oven for about 5 minutes.

Arrange each on a croûton fried in butter. Serve with lemon halves.

Note. Cooked in this way in the oven, in a moistened pan, the birds don't lose their fat, greatly enjoyed by the gastronomes who like this game.

Ortolans on skewers. BROCHETTE D'ORTOLANS—Wrap the ortolans, trussed in the usual manner, in thin rashers of fat bacon. Thread on skewers, 4 birds to a skewer, separating from each other with little croûtons, cut to look like cocks' combs and lightly fried in butter. Put the skewers into a roasting pan in which a little butter has been heated. Cook briskly in a hot oven for about 5 minutes.

Arrange the skewers on a long dish. Garnish with watercress and quarters of lemon. Pour the pan juices over the birds.

ORVAL OR CLARY. SAUGE SCLARÉE, ORVALE—Variety of sage used in the manufacture of Turin Vermouth.

OSTRICH. AUTRUCHE—The flesh of this bird, forbidden to the Jews and the Moslems, was much valued by the Romans. The second Apicius dedicated a special sauce to it.

An ostrich, on the average, gives about 60 pounds (30 kilograms) of meat and 40 pounds (20 kilograms) of fat.

OTTER. LOUTRE DE RIVIÈRE—A carnivorous water mammal. Its flesh, which is oily and leathery, has a horrible taste.

OUBLIE (WAFER)—Furetières defines the oublie as a 'thin round wafer cooked between two irons.' According to him, the word *oublie* is a corruption of *oblaye*, derived from *oblata*, which used to define non-consecrated Eucharist host. It used to be called *oblée* or *oublie*.

The most famous of these wafers were made in Lyons and it is in this town that they were first rolled into a cone. In Paris they used to be flat and insipid.

In the beginning, these wafers, made out of any pastry remnants, were left to bakery boys—it was their profit. On winter evenings they would offer them to the passer-by and sell them from door to door; they sold 7 or 8 of these wafers at a time and this was called '*une main d'oublies*' (a handful of wafers).

The wafer-vendors played with their clients, casting dice for their wares. Towards the middle of the eighteenth century these vendors were called '*marchands de plaisir*', because their cry was '*Voilà le plaisir.*'

Here is a recipe for making these wafers.

Oublies à la parisienne (Parisian wafers)—*Ingredients.* 2 cups (250 grams) of sieved cake flour, 1¼ cups (150 grams) of castor (fine) sugar, 2 eggs, 4 tablespoons (65 grams) of melted butter, 3½ cups (7 decilitres) of milk, flavouring, orange-blossom water, lemon rind.

Method. Blend the flour, sugar, eggs and flavouring together in a bowl. When the mixture has been worked into a smooth paste, add the milk, little by little; then melted butter and, last of all, grated lemon rind.

Heat the wafer irons and grease them evenly, pour in a spoonful of the above mixture and cook on a very lively fire, turning the irons. Take out the cooked wafer, roll it into a cone, round a conical piece of wood, or, if you prefer, leave it flat.

OUILLAT OR TOURRI (Béarn cookery)—'Put a chopped onion to cook in fat or olive oil in an earthenware casserole. When the onion colours, add some crushed garlic and cook. Pour in enough hot water. Add a bouquet of thyme and parsley, season with pepper and salt, simmer for half an hour, then strain on to slices of bread.

'Water in which French beans, dried peas, broad beans and asparagus were cooked is sometimes used for this purpose. An egg and a dash of vinegar can be added at the moment of straining into the soup tureen. Grated Gruyère cheese can be substituted for egg. When in season, tomatoes, peeled and sliced, are put to cook with the onion.' (Simin Palay.)

OVEN. FOUR—An oven is an enclosed space which can be brought to a high temperature and into which dishes are put to cook. Cooking in the oven has been known for a very long time. The *baker's oven* is still today constructed almost in the same way as in ancient times (see BAKERY). A *pastry oven* is a little smaller and has certain special characteristics (see PÂTISSERIE). The oven for cooking is usually part of the whole cooking range (or *stove**), though separate ovens are also sometimes used. The great progress which has been made in our time in the construction of ovens consists mainly in the use of metals, insulating materials, and double walls. Such walls are a great economy and assure perfect regularity of heat. Further advances are the use of other combustibles than wood, such as gas, oil, steam and electricity for baker's and pastry-cook ovens. The most modern and practical kitchen stoves are those heated by gas or electricity.

OVERLAP. IMBRIQUER—Overlapping is sometimes used for decorative effect in the garnishing of dishes. For instance, little strips of truffle can be laid one against the other and set in jelly to decorate certain cold dishes. The effect is reminiscent of tiling.

OX—See also BEEF and OFFAL OR VARIETY MEATS.

Ox-belly (Tripe). GRAS-DOUBLE DE BOEUF—This part of the offal comes from the animal's paunch. It is generally sold cooked and can be prepared in various ways.

For all recipes for preparing ox-belly, see section entitled OFFAL OR VARIETY MEATS.

Ox brain—See OFFAL OR VARIETY MEATS.

Ox-cheeks. JOUES DE BOEUF—Boned and trimmed ox-cheeks are used for preparing pot-au-feu. Some people, including some butchers, claim that stock made from ox-cheeks has more taste than that made of a piece of rump. This opinion is somewhat foolhardy. Its fleshy bits are quite good indeed, but they cannot compare in flavour to other parts of the animal, such as silverside (flank and leg), palate or top of rump.

Ox-cheeks can be braised or made into stews. They can also be prepared like *Pickled tongue*. See OFFAL OR VARIETY MEATS.

Ox heart, Ox-muzzle, Ox-palate, Oxtail—See OFFAL OR VARIETY MEATS.

Oxtail Soup—See SOUPS AND BROTHS.

Ox (beef) tongue—See OFFAL OR VARIETY MEATS.

Ox tripe. TRIPES DE BOEUF—This term applies equally to the ox-belly and the tripe itself. See OFFAL OR VARIETY MEATS.

OXFORD SAUCE (English cookery)—This sauce is served with cold venison. The ingredients are red currant jelly, port, chopped shallot, grated orange and lemon rind, orange and lemon juice, mustard and powdered ginger.

OXYMEL—A sort of a syrup made from a mixture of honey and vinegar. It is obtained by cooking one part of vinegar with 4 parts honey.

Oyster seller, Paris
(*French Government Tourist Office*)

OYSTER. HUÎTRE—A bivalve mollusc usually eaten raw.

The oyster has been known to man from the earliest times. Nevertheless there is no positive evidence that the Egyptians and Assyrians ever ate this delicious mollusc. It seems to have been unknown to the Jews. At any rate there is no mention of it in the Bible. On the other hand, the Celts gathered oysters and fed on them abundantly.

The Greeks prized oysters very highly. They knew how to prepare them in a number of ways. They were especially fond of Hellespont (Dardanelles) oysters. It is, moreover, well known that the people of Greece used oyster shells for casting their votes. The voter inscribed his choice with a sharp point on the white mother-of-pearl of the shell.

The Romans, too, were great lovers of oysters. They particularly prized those gathered in the Lucrine Lake, and after these, the oysters of Brindisi, Taranto and Circeo. It is said that they seasoned their oysters with *garum**.

In France, right up to the beginning of the nineteenth century, it was thought that the coastal oyster beds were inexhaustible. So much so that the Ordinance of 1681, which was enacted to protect mussels, left the oyster fisheries free from control. Moreover, a royal decree of 23rd April, 1726, still permitted the use of the iron-toothed dragnet. This policy was so completely mistaken that, during the whole of the years 1750, 1751, 1752 and 1753 it was necessary to forbid the gathering of oysters all over Arcachon Bay. In 1754 and 1759, it became necessary to prohibit the gathering of oysters with rakes and even by hand, each year between 1st April and 31st October. Similar measures had to be taken in Brittany.

In spite of these precautions, the devastations of the natural oyster beds continued in all coastal areas, until in 1840 it became necessary to call in a naval vessel at Arcachon to guard the oyster beds in the bay! But the beds, once depleted, could not be replenished by 'spontaneous generation'. Moreover, if a few beds remained, they declined in conditions of stagnation which were as harmful to them as the pillage which had gone before.

The Administration of Fisheries eventually realized that new oysters would have to be brought to the depleted beds.

It was then that Coste, the true father of the oyster industry, went to Lake Fusaro and became initiated into the methods by which the Italians maintained a supply of excellent oysters. The man-made oyster beds of Tarento consisted of stakes tied together with ropes from which were suspended traps in the form of small faggots. The stakes and faggots were encrusted with oysters of every size. The saleable oysters were put on the market. The smaller ones were put into osier baskets to attain full growth.

On his return to France, Coste succeeded in stocking the Bay of Saint-Brieuc with oysters collected at Cancale (on the English Channel) and Tréguier (Côte de Nord). He replenished the Thau pool and the Bays of Toulon and Brest with British oysters. The Concarneau reserve came into being, and finally model beds were built up at Arcachon (in the Cès, at Crastorbe and then at Lahillon).

The American Indians ate large quantities of oysters. Oyster fisheries and farming represent a large industry in North America today.

Nutritive value of oysters—Raw oysters contain vitamins, phosphorus salts, chalk, iron, copper and manganese in a readily assimilable form. They also contain a very high proportion of iodine and are sometimes eaten to combat anaemia.

Green American oysters (different from the Marenne oyster) have been used in the treatment of anaemia with results equal to those obtained from calves' liver.

The risk of infectious diseases being spread through the water contained in oysters is small, provided they are bought from a conscientious supplier who has made it his business to know where they come from.

Tradition has established the hygienic rule that oysters may not be eaten during the warm months of the year—that is to say, when there is no 'r' in the month.

Oysters on the Atlantic coasts are 'in season' from September to May, although the idea that they are inedible during the summer months, the breeding period, is erroneous. Pacific coast oysters are sold all year long.

Various types of oyster—There are two main types, the *wild oyster*, which has a very pronounced sea-water flavour, and the *cultivated oyster*. In the cultivation of oysters, *seed-oysters* are affixed to tiles and reared in farms some way out to sea. When they have reached a certain size, they are transferred to the fattening beds which are always situated at the mouth of a river, the mixture of fresh and sea water being essential to induce over-growth of the liver in which the fattening consists.

The green Marenne oysters owe their colouring to the algae and microscopic diatoma which live in the fattening pools in which they are embedded.

This colouring was an accidental discovery. During the siege of La Rochelle, some oysters were thrown into the old salt marshes. When they were fished out again, everyone was astonished at their green colour. After a good deal of hesitation, it was decided that they should be tasted and it was noticed that, far from being spoiled, they had acquired a more delicate flavour.

The name *Portuguese oyster* is given to a sub-variety of oyster whose proper name is *gryphaea*. Since it has become customary to bed and treat them like the Marenne oysters, their flavour has improved noticeably, though they are still not comparable with genuine oysters.

Oysters can be prepared in a great many different ways. They can be served as hot or cold hors-d'oeuvre. They can be used in the preparation of elegant and elaborate garnishes, and excellent soups and sauces can be made from them.

Choose 12 deep halves of oyster shells as regular in shape as possible. Wash them thoroughly, and fill them with *Tomato mousse*, doming it a little. Put 2 oysters on each shell. Mask with half-set jelly and leave to set.

Arrange the oysters in a bed of snow or crushed ice on a round dish.

Attereaux of oysters—See HORS-D'OEUVRE, *Hot hors-d'oeuvre*.

Oysters in barquettes. HUÎTRES EN BARQUETTES—Poach the oysters. Drain and remove the beards. Mask them with glazing mayonnaise. Decorate with truffles and the roe of a spiny lobster (crayfish). Mask with jelly.

Set them in pairs in little barquettes baked 'blind' (unfilled). Garnish to taste with Russian salad, any vegetable mousse or other hors-d'oeuvre filling.

Serve the barquettes on a paper doyley. Garnish with very green curly parsley.

Oyster barquettes à l'américaine. BARQUETTES D'HUÎTRES À L'AMÉRICAINE— Bake some barquettes 'blind' (unfilled). Fill each one with a tablespoon of *Américaine sauce* (see SAUCE). Place on top of each boat 2 or 3 poached, drained and trimmed oysters. Sprinkle with fried breadcrumbs, and seasoned with a touch of cayenne pepper.

Oyster barquettes à la Nantua. BARQUETTES D'HUÎTRES À LA NANTUA—Fill the cooked barquettes with a tablespoon of *ragoût* of *Crayfish tails à la Nantua**. Put 2 poached oysters on top of each boat. Coat with *Nantua sauce* (see SAUCE). Sprinkle with grated cheese. Brown quickly in the oven.

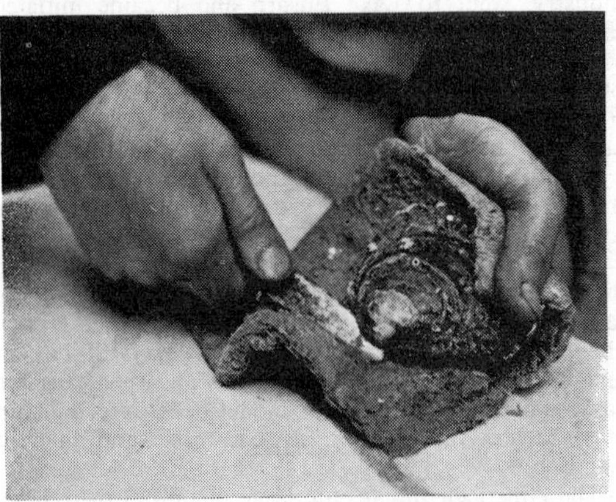

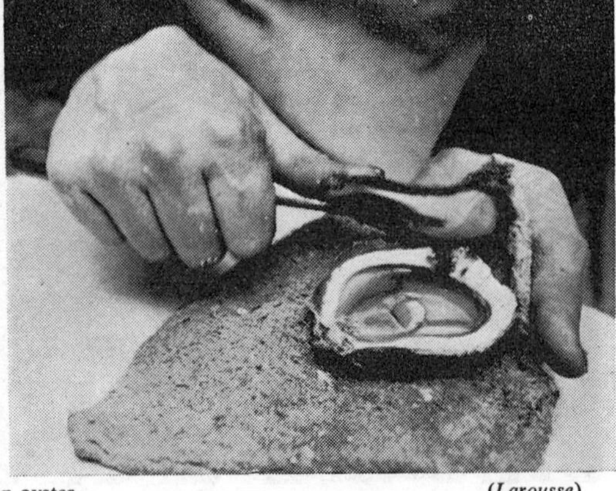

How to open an oyster (*Larousse*)

Oysters à l'américaine I. HUÎTRES À L'AMÉRICAINE—Put the oysters in the deep halves of their shells. Lay them on a baking sheet lined with cooking salt. Squeeze a few drops of lemon juice on each oyster and season with a touch of cayenne pepper.

Sprinkle with fried breadcrumbs. Pour over them melted butter seasoned with lemon, salt and pepper. Brown in a very hot oven.

Serve on a napkin, garnished with fresh parsley.

Oysters à l'américaine II. HUÎTRES À L'AMÉRICAINE—Put the oysters back in the deep halves of their shells. Cover with *Américaine sauce* (see SAUCE) with the concentrated liquor of the oysters added. Serve on a napkin; garnish with fresh parsley.

Oysters à l'andalouse. HUÎTRES À L'ANDALOUSE—Poach 24 oysters in their own liquor. Drain them. Dry in a cloth. Remove the beards and leave them to cool.

Decorate each one with a little sliver of truffle, making them stick with jelly, then spoon over the decorations some half-set jelly and leave till they are quite cold.

Oyster barquettes à la normande. BARQUETTES D'HUÎTRES À LA NORMANDE—Fill the barquettes with a *salpicon** of crayfish tails, mussels and mushrooms blended in a *Normande sauce* (see SAUCE). Put 2 poached oysters on top of each boat. Mask with *Normande sauce*. Put a strip of truffle on top of each barquette.

Oyster bouchées—See HORS-D'OEUVRE, *Hot hors-d'oeuvre. Patties with oysters.*

Oysters with caviar. HUÎTRES AU CAVIAR—Bake 'blind' (empty) some little round tartlet shells, using *Fine lining paste* (see DOUGH). Fill each one with a teaspoon of fresh caviar. Place on top a single shelled oyster.

Arrange the tartlets on a paper doyley. Garnish with fresh parsley. Serve lemon with this dish.

Note. The tartlets must be filled at the last moment, and the oysters opened and shelled just as they are about to be served. Oysters and caviar can also be served in well-washed oyster shells.

Oyster coquilles—See HORS-D'OEUVRE, *Hot Hors-d'oeuvre, Scallop shells of oysters.*

Oysters à la florentine (*Robert Carrier*)

Oysters à la crème. HUÎTRES GRATINÉES À LA CRÈME—Detach oysters from shell, remove beards and put a tablespoon of cream in each shell with the oyster. Sprinkle with a little melted butter and Parmesan cheese and grill under a fairly high flame.

Oyster croquettes—See HORS-D'OEUVRE, *Hot hors-d'oeuvre, Croquettes.*

Devilled oysters—See below, *Grilled oysters.*

Oysters à la florentine. HUÎTRES À LA FLORENTINE—Fill the deep halves of the oyster shells with a layer of spinach cooked in butter. Put an oyster on top of each one. Cover with *Mornay sauce* (see SAUCE). Sprinkle with cheese. Brown in the oven.

Fried oysters. HUÎTRES FRITES—Poach, drain and remove the beards from the oysters. Dip them in milk and flour them. Shake off any excess flour. Deep-fry them in boiling fat. Drain and dry on a cloth. Season with fine salt. Serve on a napkin arranged in a clump. Garnish with lemon and fried parsley.

Fried oysters Colbert. HUÎTRES FRITES COLBERT—Poach, drain and remove the beards of the oysters. Dip them in egg and breadcrumbs. Fry them at the last moment. Arrange them in a heap on a napkin. Garnish with lemon and fried parsley. Serve *Maître d'hôtel butter* separately (see BUTTER, *Compound butters*).

Oyster fritot—See HORS-D'OEUVRE, *Hot hors-d'oeuvre, Fritot.*

Oyster fritters à la normande. BEIGNETS D'HUÎTRES À LA NORMANDE—Poach the oysters. Leave them to cool in their own liquor. Drain them. Wipe them with a cloth. Dip them one by one in *Villeroi sauce* (see SAUCE) with chopped truffles and vegetables added. Dip them in batter. Deep-fry in very hot fat over a hasty flame until the fritters have swelled to their full extent and are a fine golden colour.

Drain them on a cloth. Season with very dry fine salt. Arrange them in a heap on a napkin.

Oysters for garnishing. HUÎTRES POUR GARNITURES—Shell the oysters. Poach them in their own liquor.

Remove the pan from the fire as soon as the liquor begins to boil. Drain and trim the oysters and proceed according to the recipe used.

Note. If the oysters are not to be used at once, keep them hot in their own strained liquor. Care must be taken to see that they do not boil. The oyster liquor is strained and added to the sauce.

The gastronome's oyster. HUÎTRES DU GASTRONOME—Poach the oysters. Drain them. Remove the beards and leave to cool. Coat them with a *Chaud-froid sauce à la hongroise* based on vegetable stock (see SAUCE). Cover with jelly.

Cook some tiny artichoke hearts in a white *court-bouillon**. Steep them in oil and lemon juice. Just before serving, fill these with a salad of crayfish tails and diced truffles dressed with gelatine-strengthened *mayonnaise* (see SAUCE, *Cold sauces*). Put an oyster on top of each one.

Arrange the artichoke hearts on a round dish. Garnish with chopped jelly.

Oysters au gratin I. HUÎTRES AU GRATIN—Fill the deep halves of oyster shells with a layer of *duxelles**. Put an oyster on each shell and a mushroom on top of each oyster. Cover with *Duxelles sauce* (see SAUCE), with the oyster liquor added. Sprinkle with breadcrumbs. Pour on melted butter seasoned with salt and pepper and a few drops of lemon. Brown in a very hot oven. After they have been taken out of the oven, squeeze on a few drops of lemon juice. Sprinkle with chopped parsley. Serve on a napkin, garnished with fresh parsley.

Oysters au gratin II. HUÎTRES AU GRATIN—Proceed as for *Oysters à l'américaine I.*

Grilled oysters, also called devilled oysters. HUÎTRES GRILLÉES, À LA DIABLE—Poach, drain and remove the beards of the oysters. Skewer them on little metal skewers.

Pour melted butter seasoned with lemon, salt and pepper over the oysters. Dip them in fine breadcrumbs seasoned with a little cayenne pepper. Grill under a low flame. Serve in the same way as *Oysters on skewers.* Serve *Diable sauce* separately (see SAUCE).

Oysters as cold hors-d'oeuvre. HORS-D'OEUVRE FROIDS—However sumptuous or delicate the manner in which this mollusc may be prepared, the true connoisseur values nothing so much as a plain, raw, absolutely fresh oyster.

Oysters must not be opened until just before serving, and are best served very cold. It is therefore advisable, whenever possible, to lay the oysters as soon as they are opened on a bed of crushed ice. Eaten in this way, with the midday or evening meal, the oyster provides a healthy and delicious hors-d'oeuvre. Its dressing is usually simple, consisting of lemon juice or shallot vinegar with coarsely ground pepper.

Slices of buttered brown or white bread are usually served with fresh oysters.

Oysters as hot hors-d'oeuvre. HORS-D'OEUVRE CHAUDS—There are a great many recipes for cooked oysters, the best known of which are given in this section.

However oysters are to be prepared, they must always first be poached in their own liquor.

To poach oysters. Open the oysters. Prise them away from the shells without tearing the flesh.

Put the oysters in a pan, with their own liquor strained through muslin.

Bring to the boil. As soon as the liquid begins to bubble, remove the pan from the stove.

Cooked oysters are often served in the deep halves of their shells. If they are to be glazed or sprinkled with cheese and browned, the shells must be embedded in a layer of salt spread on a baking sheet, to keep them upright.

Glazing and browning must be accomplished very quickly, to prevent the oysters from becoming tough.

Marinated oysters. HUÎTRES MARINÉES—Shell the oysters. Put them in a marinade of white wine, oil and lemon juice, well seasoned with herbs and prepared in advance.

Bring the oysters to the boil and remove at once from the stove. Pour the stock and oysters into a bowl. Leave them until they are quite cold.

Serve them in hors-d'oeuvre dishes with the marinade.

Oysters à la Mornay. HUÎTRES À LA MORNAY—Line the deep halves of the oyster shells with *Mornay sauce* (see SAUCE). Put an oyster on top of each one. Cover with the same sauce. Sprinkle with grated Parmesan. Pour on melted butter. Brown in a very hot oven. Serve on a napkin, garnished with fresh parsley.

Oysters à la polonaise. HUÎTRES À LA POLONAISE—Put the oysters back in the deep halves of their shells. Sprinkle with chopped yolks of hard boiled egg and chopped parsley. Warm in the oven. Just before serving, pour a tablespoon of browned butter with fried bread-crumbs over each oyster.

Oysters on skewers. BROCHETTES D'HUÎTRES—Skewer poached oysters on little metal skewers with slices of cooked mushroom in between.

Pour melted butter seasoned with lemon juice and pepper over them. Dip them in fine breadcrumbs. Grill under a low heat.

Serve on a long dish. Surround with a border of fluted half-slices of lemon. Garnish with parsley.

Sprinkle with melted *Maître d'hôtel butter*, or with one of the sauces especially suitable for grilled fish (see BUTTER, *Compound butters*, and SAUCE).

Oyster soufflés. HUÎTRES SOUFFLÉES—Pound in a mortar 12 raw oysters. Mix in little by little the white of one raw egg.

Rub through a sieve. Put this mixture in a bowl and stir it on ice. Mix in an ounce (30 grams) of *Fine pike forcemeat* and about 1 cup (2 decilitres) of thick fresh cream. See FORCEMEAT.

Put half a tablespoon of this mixture in each oyster shell. On top of this forcemeat, put a poached and drained oyster. Cover with a layer of soufflé mixture. Smooth it, doming it slightly.

Bake in the oven for 6 to 8 minutes.

Oyster soup. SOUPE AUX HUÎTRES—Open 24 oysters and shell them. Put the oysters in a pan. Pour on them their liquor, strained. Add 1 cup (2 decilitres) of white wine.

Bring them to the boil. As soon as the liquid begins to boil, turn the flame very low. Skim. Add 1 cup (2 decilitres) of cream, ½ cup of crushed biscuit crackers, 6 tablespoons (100 grams) of butter, cut into tiny fragments. Season. Spice with a touch of cayenne pepper. Mix. Pour the soup into a tureen. Serve crushed crackers separately.

Oysters Villeroi. BROCHETTES D'HUÎTRES VILLEROI—Poach and drain the oysters. Cover them with *Villeroi sauce* (see SAUCE). Skewer them on little metal skewers. Fry them just before serving. Drain them. Serve on a napkin, garnished with parsley.

OYSTER-CATCHER. HUÎTRIER—A wader, sometimes called sea-magpie. The flesh of the young bird is quite delicate. It is prepared in the same way as plover.

OYSTER PLANT—See SALSIFY.

PACARET—This word, which is a variation of *Pascarete*, is used to define wine of the Jerez district of Spain. The name of the wine is derived from the name of the small town of *Paxarete* or *Pajarete* in the Jerez sherry-producing district. The grapes gathered there yield very sweet juice, which is treated with brandy to prevent it fermenting and results in the *Paxarete* or *Pajarete* liqueur wine. This used to be much in vogue in England in the eighteenth century.

PAELLA—A Spanish rice dish which has gained international fame. Different regions of Spain vary the paella according to the local produce. Vegetables, meat, chicken and sausage, characterise the paellas of interior Spain; places such as Valencia and Barcelona specialize in combining sea foods with chicken and vegetables in the rice base. The name of the dish comes from the iron frying pan with two handles, the paella, in which the rice is cooked and served. The following is a Valencian paella:

Heat 3 tablespoons of oil in a deep iron frying pan with 2 cloves of garlic, finely chopped. Add 2 onions, chopped and 2 sweet red peppers, diced. Add to this a small chicken cut in small pieces, bones and all, and ½ pound of pork, ham or beefsteak cut in small dice. Brown the meat and then add 4 small tomatoes, peeled and quartered. Stir in 1½ pounds of rice and cook gently for 5 minutes. Cover with well-seasoned stock to which a pinch of saffron has been added. Add 1 cup of shelled peas and 1 cup of fresh kidney beans and, if possible, several artichoke hearts. Cook 10 minutes more and then add 1 pound of cod, whiting or hake, cut in small pieces, a lobster or crayfish, also cut in small pieces, ½ pound of shrimp or prawns, a pint of mussels or small clams, thoroughly washed. Boil hard for 5 minutes and simmer for 15 more, adding more stock as necessary. The rice should be moist but not soupy. When the rice is cooked, place the paella in the oven for a few minutes. Chopped parsley is added before serving. Small inkfish or squid and garlic sausages may also be added to the above ingredients. The inkfish are usually fried in the oil before adding the rice and the garlic added after the meat has been browned.

PAILLASSE—French name for a charcoal fire which was used in kitchens of long ago to prepare dishes which needed prolonged cooking, especially braised meat.

Meat also used to be grilled on glowing embers in a sort of bucket-shaped brick brazier.

The term *paillasse* is also used to define the layer of glowing charcoal embers spread out on the grill.

PAILLETTES—Thin flakes of metal used in the wine and spirit industry (Danziger Goldwasser, etc.), and in confectionery (*palets d'or*).

PAINS—This is a French culinary term which applies to dishes, served cold or hot, made of a forcemeat placed in a special mould and poached in a *bain-marie* (pan of hot water), in the case of a dish being served hot, and set in a mould, lined with aspic jelly and chilled, in the case of a dish being served cold.

This type of entrée was very popular in the old culinary practice but is not done much nowadays. It has been replaced by mousses which are also prepared hot or cold.

The various ingredients used for the forcemeats are, as indicated in individual recipes, liver (*foie gras*), game meat (winged and ground game), poultry, vegetables, as well as fish and crustaceans. For recipes see LOAVES.

PAK-CHOY. PÉ-TSAÏ—A variety of cabbage imported from China. See CHINESE CABBAGE.

PALATE OF OX—See OFFAL OR VARIETY MEATS, *Ox-palate*.

PALETS DE DAMES—Little dry *petit fours* (fancy biscuits) which are prepared in the following manner:

Into a hot bowl put 1¾ cups (250 grams) of fine sugar, then 6 eggs, one by one, and stir well with a wooden spoon. When the mixture is frothy add, stirring all the time, 2 cups (250 grams) of sieved cake flour.

Put on a baking sheet, buttered and lightly sprinkled with flour. Bake in a hot oven. When baked, glaze with *Water icing* (Confectioners' frosting).

Note. Palets de dames (which are sometimes written *palais*) can be flavoured with vanilla, lemon or orange rind or any other flavouring.

PALETTE-KNIFE. AMASETTE—A small utensil used in pastry-making for picking up paste.

PALMAE. PALMIER—The name of a large family of trees, of which the fruit (dates), the nuts (coconut), the terminal shoots (cabbage palm), sago (the pitch or interior of the stem) and the sap (palm wine) are used in cookery.

Palm hearts. COEURS DE PALMIER—The hearts or tender shoots of palms are cooked like asparagus. Peel the stalks completely and boil in salted water. Serve hot with various white sauces or cold *à la vinaigrette*.

Palm hearts can also be prepared in various other

ways: *à la crème*, stewed in butter, in gravy, *au gratin*, with Parmesan cheese, *à la polonaise*, and in general in any way suitable for *Asparagus** or *Cardoons**.

Palm oil—See OIL.

PALM NUT. NOIX DE PALME—Fruit of the Eléis of New Guinea, varying from about the size of a hazel nut to that of a walnut. Palm oil is extracted from these nuts

PALMIER (Pastry)—This small pastry, a Paris speciality, is prepared in the following manner:

Take some puff pastry which has had three turns. Give it another three turns on a table sprinkled with icing sugar instead of flour.

Roll out to a thickness of ⅛ inch and cut into strips 12 inches wide.

Bring the two ends of these strips together towards the centre and fold in two, lengthways.

Leave these strips to settle for a few moments, then cut them across into pieces ¼ inch thick.

Put these pieces of pastry flat on a baking sheet, placing them at a little distance from each other. Bake in a hot oven (400°F.).

PALOURDE—Name given to a kind of squash (vegetable marrow) in some parts of France.

PALUS—Vineyards planted on the alluvial tracts of land in the Bordeaux region and on the estates bordering on the banks of the Garonne, Dordogne and Gironde.

PANADA. PANADE—This name applies to two differene preparations: one is a kind of soup or pappy meal, mada of bread, stock, milk or water and butter; the other , paste of flour, bread, toast (*biscottes*) or various faecula used for binding meat or fish forcemeats.

A. Flour panada for forcemeat. PANADE POUR FARCE À LA FARINE—Put 1½ cups (3 decilitres) of water into a saucepan, add 5 tablespoons (50 grams) of butter and ⅓ teaspoon (2 grams) of salt and, when it boils, pour in 1⅓ cups (150 grams) of sieved flour. Mix well on the fire stirring with a wooden spoon. Cook like chou paste, i.e. until the mixture thickens leaving the sides of the pan clean.

Put into a buttered dish, spread in an even layer, cover with a piece of buttered paper and leave until quite cold.

Uses: For all sorts of quenelle forcemeats.

B. Frangipane panada. PANADE À LA FRANGIPANE—Put 1 cup (125 grams) of sieved flour and 4 egg yolks into a pan. Mix well, stirring with a wooden spoon. Add 6 tablespoons (90 grams) of melted butter and season with ⅓ teaspoon (2 grams) of salt, pepper and a pinch of grated nutmeg.

Stirring all the time, dilute the mixture with 1¼ cups (2½ decilitres) of boiling milk, poured in little by little.

Cook for 5 or 6 minutes, beating vigorously with a whisk.

Leave until cold, as above.

Uses: For chicken and fish forcemeats.

C. Bread panada. PANADE AU PAIN—Soak 4½ cups (250 grams) of white crustless bread in 1½ cups (3 decilitres) of boiled milk until it absorbs all it can. Blend the mixture, dry off a little on the fire, stirring all the time, as described in the recipe for *Panada A*.

Leave until quite cold, as described above.

Uses: For fish forcemeats.

D. Potato Panada. PANADE À LA POMME DE TERRE—Season 1½ cups (3 decilitres) of milk with ⅓ teaspoon (2 grams) of salt, a pinch of pepper and a soupçon of grated nutmeg. Boil until it has been reduced by one-sixth, then put into this milk 4 teaspoons (20 grams) of butter and 1 cup (250 grams) (net weight) of boiled potatoes, peeled and thinly sliced. Cook gently for 15 minutes. Blend well to obtain a perfectly smooth mixture.

Use this panada while it is still warm.

Uses: For big, white meat *quenelles*.

E. Rice panada. PANADE AU RIZ—Cook 1 cup (200 grams) of Piemonte rice in 3 cups (6 decilitres) of white stock, to which 4 teaspoons (20 grams) of butter have been added (allowing about 50 minutes' cooking time in the oven). Blend the rice well with a spoon to obtain a smooth mixture.

Leave until cold, as described in the recipe for *Panada A*.

Uses: For various forcemeats.

PANCAKES—See CRÊPES.

PANETIÈRE—A small sideboard dresser, with lattice work, usually carved and decorated, in which, in some regions of France, bread is kept.

PANETIÈRE—Method of preparation applied to various articles (lambs' sweetbread, chicken livers, cocks' combs and kidneys, etc.), or to small birds, which, after cooking, are placed in round loaves, scooped out as *croustades** and baked golden in the oven.

PANETONE (Italian cake)—*Ingredients.* 3¾ cups (500 grams) of sieved flour, ½ cup (130 grams) of butter, ½ cup (80 grams) of brown sugar, 3 eggs and 4 yolks of egg, ⅝ ounce (175 grams) dried or compressed yeast, 3 teaspoons (18 grams) of salt, 2 tablespoons (30 grams) of castor (fine) sugar, 2½ tablespoons (30 grams) of sultanas, 2½ tablespoons (40 grams) of candied citron peel cut in small dice.

Method. The dough: Spread the flour in a circle, make a well in the middle and put in the salt, eggs, brown sugar, diluted in a little warm water, 5 tablespoons (80 grams) of butter (just softened), and yeast. Begin by mixing these ingredients, adding a few tablespoons of warm water, little by little. Then incorporate the flour, a little at a time. When the moistening is complete, stir the dough vigorously (just as for a brioche) until it *acquires body*, that is to say becomes elastic and does not stick to the hands.

At this moment, spread it in not-too-thick a layer and sprinkle with castor (fine) sugar, add 2 yolks of egg and the rest of the butter softened into a paste, scatter sultanas and candied citron peel on top and blend in all the ingredients, kneading the dough for a few minutes. Finally, roll into a ball, put into a buttered and floured baking tin and stand in a warm place to allow the dough to ferment. This fermentation takes rather a long time; it is assumed to be just right when little air bubbles appear on the surface. You can then proceed to bake. Using the 2 remaining yolks of egg, diluted with a few teaspoons of water and mixed with a pinch of flour and the same amount of icing sugar (or very fine castor sugar), brush the top copiously, mark the top with a crossways incision and sprinkle with granulated sugar. Bake in the oven, in moderate but sustained heat.

PANICUM. PANIC—Old Latin name for one of the millets. *Panicum miliaceum* is milled into flour in Italy, which is used to prepare a kind of meal, with milk or stock.

PANIER—Wicker-work basket with a handle. In cookery and pastry-making various substances are fashioned to look like wicker-work baskets.

Potato paniers. PANIERS EN POMMES DE TERRE—These baskets, used for arranging various fried objects, are made out of potatoes cut in thin ribbons and fried in deep fat.

Pulled sugar paniers. PANIERS EN SUCRE TIRÉ—These baskets are used for arranging petits fours, especially iced petits fours. Bombes, mousses and iced cakes are also served in them.

These are often extremely decorative pieces, carried out by pastry-cooks and confectioners who are real artists.

PANNEQUETS—Pancakes spread over the whole surface with some composition, such as cream, jam, marmalade or any other mixture, then rolled or folded in four, sprinkled with icing sugar or crushed macaroons and glazed in the oven or under a grill. For the preparation of batter, see DOUGH, *Crêpe batter* (*sweet*).

These pancakes can also be spread with savoury mixtures, especially cream cheese. Such pancakes are served as a hot hors-d'oeuvre or as a small entrée. See also HORS-D'OEUVRE, *Hot hors-d'oeuvre*.

HORS-D'OEUVRE AND SOUP PANNEQUETS. PANNEQUETS DE HORS-D'OEUVRE:

Anchovy pannequets. PANNEQUETS AUX ANCHOIS—Spread the pancakes (made of unsweetened batter) with thick *Béchamel sauce* (see SAUCE) mixed with anchovy purée and some de-salted anchovy fillets, cut in large dice. Fold the pancakes in flour. Put into a buttered, oven-proof dish, sprinkle with breadcrumbs, fried in butter and drained and put in a very hot oven or under a grill for a few moments.

Pannequets with crayfish, called à la Nantua. PANNEQUETS AUX ÉCREVISSES, À LA NANTUA—As pannequets with shrimps, using *Nantua purée* and diced crayfish tails.

Note. These pancakes can be sprinkled with grated Parmesan, instead of fried breadcrumbs and browned in the oven or under a grill.

Pannequets Mornay—Spread the pancakes with a *salpicon** of ham and mushroom bound with *Béchamel sauce* (see SAUCE). Roll them. Arrange on a buttered fire-proof dish, cover with a thin layer of not-too-thick *Mornay sauce* (see SAUCE), sprinkle with grated Parmesan and melted butter and brown the top quickly.

Pannequets à la reine—Spread the pancakes with *Chicken purée* mixed with truffles cut in small dice. Roll the pancakes and cut each roll into 2 lozenges. Cover each with a tablespoon of chicken *Velouté sauce* (see SAUCE) cooked with cream. Sprinkle with grated Parmesan and brown the top.

Pannequets with shrimps, or other shellfish. PANNEQUETS AUX CREVETTES—Prepare as *Anchovy pannequets*, spreading the pancakes with shrimp or other shellfish purée, mixed with a *salpicon** of the chopped tails of the crustacean indicated.

Pannequets with soft roes. PANNEQUETS AUX LAITANCES—Spread the pancakes with a *salpicon* of soft roes and mushrooms bound with *Velouté sauce* (see SAUCE), based on a fish stock and cooked with cream. Roll the pancakes, sprinkle the rolls with grated Parmesan and melted butter and brown the top.

Pannequets for soup garnish. PANNEQUETS (GARNITURES DE POTAGE)—Make some very thin pancakes (see CRÊPES). Fill each one with a basic forcemeat or add, as appropriate, dry diced mushrooms (*duxelles*), chopped truffles, cooked diced vegetables (*mirepoix*). Cover with another pancake. Cut round with a fluted cutter. Add to boiling clear soup at the last minute.

Pannequets la Varenne—Spread the pancakes with *duxelles** mixed with a fine *salpicon** of ham, bound with a thick *Velouté sauce* (see SAUCE). Sprinkle with grated Parmesan and brown on top.

SWEET PANNEQUETS. PANNEQUETS D'ENTREMETS:

Pannequets with apples—See APPLE, *Crêpes stuffed with apples*.

Apricot pannequets. PANNEQUETS D'ABRICOTS—Spread the pancakes with a mixture composed of diced apricots bound with *French pastry cream* (see CREAM) and mixed with the apricot kernels, blanched, chopped and sprinkled with kirsch. Roll up the pancakes, cut each roll into two lozenges, put on a baking sheet, sprinkle with icing sugar, glaze in a very hot oven and serve on a napkin-covered dish.

Pannequets à la cévenole—Spread the pancakes with *Chestnut purée** mixed with fresh double cream and flavoured with kirsch. Finish off as described above.

Pannequets à la créole—Spread the pancakes with a *salpicon** of pineapple bound with rum-flavoured *French pastry cream* (see CREAM). Finish off as described above.

Pannequet with various fruit. PANNEQUETS AUX FRUITS—Prepare using *salpicon** of fruit (bananas, cherries, strawberries, peaches, pears, apples, etc., cooked in syrup) bound with *French pastry cream* or *Frangipane* (see CREAMS). Finish off as described above.

Jam pannequets. PANNEQUETS AUX CONFITURES—Spread the pancakes with jam. Roll (or fold in four) and finish off as described above.

Pannequets with pineapple—See PINEAPPLE.

Pannequets au praliné—Spread the pancakes with a *praliné* (either almond or hazelnut), bound with *French pastry cream* (see CREAM), flavoured with kirsch or other liqueur. Roll up the pancakes, cut each roll into two lozenges, put on a baking sheet, sprinkle with finely crushed macaroons and glaze.

PANOUFLE—French butchery term for the under part of the top of sirloin.

PANTIN (Petit)—A small oval or rectangular-shaped patty, usually filled with a fine pork forcemeat, which may or may not be truffled.

PANTLER. PANETIER—Officer in charge of the pantry or bread office and master dispenser of the bread.

The Lord Pantler (*Grand Panetier*) was the officer of the French Royal Household who had jurisdiction over all the bakers of the capital and over all the officers of the pantry (Royal and common). Under Louis XIV his function consisted of 'placing the King's knife and fork on ceremonial occasions, assisted by Esquire-trenchants, and to taste the dishes set before the King.'

In England in the Middle Ages the Pantler had to put the salt cellar and the knives on the table. The pantler's office was amalgamated with the office of master dispenser of the bread, and was allowed as hereditary to the Beauchamps of Elmley, afterwards Earls of Warwick.

In France the Pantler had under his command 24 gentlemen-servants each quarter (with a token surety of 700 pounds in 1661). His coat of arms bore the insignia of his office—the *nef* (a vessel-shaped gold or silver receptacle in which the King's salt cellar, cutlery, etc. were kept) and the *cadenas*.

PANURE—French culinary term applied to the coating of breadcrumbs adhering to some substance either by means of melted butter or beaten eggs.

This coating of breadcrumbs, after cooking (fried in deep fat or cooked in butter) should be of a fine golden colour and slightly crusty.

PAPAYA OR PAWPAW. PAPAYER—Tree found extensively in the Malay Archipelago, India, Cochin-China, Réunion Island, Tahiti, Senegal, Gabon, Guinea and Martinique. Its fruit is sweet and easily digestible owing to its enzyme content.

PAPILLOTE—Term which applies firstly to paper frills used for putting on various dishes, particularly on end bones of lamb, mutton, and veal cutlets, suprêmes of chicken, cutlet-shaped croquettes, etc.

Secondly, it is used to describe small joints (principally chop end of veal) which, after preliminary cooking, are enclosed in a sheet of oiled white paper cut in the shape of a heart, and put in the oven, where the paper covering the meat swells under the action of heat. See *Veal chops en papillotes*.

Thirdly, it once described sweets wrapped in gold or silver paper. These sweets used to be very popular in the past, but are not in vogue any longer. They were pulled like crackers and there was a piece of paper inside with an inscription of a poem or motto.

PAPRIKA—Hungarian name for sweet pepper. Powder made from this pepper is red in colour, has a slightly pungent taste and is used as a condiment. It is also used as seasoning for goulash, the Hungarian national dish.

PARADISE NUTS. MANIGUETTE, GRAINE DE PARADIS—An aromatic and acrid condiment much used in former times. Nowadays, it is sometimes used to adulterate pepper.

PARAFFIN. PARAFFINE—Hydrocarbon resulting from the distillation of petroleum, which exists both in solid and liquid form. Solid paraffin has no culinary uses. It is, however, used for making bases or supports for various dishes, for as stearin it ensures the solidity of lard, for sealing jam jars and other similar receptacles and, in the form of paraffin-treated paper, as isolating substances for various tinned (canned) foods.

Liquid paraffin does not go rancid and it even possesses the strange property of imparting the same resistance to rancidness of other fatty matter with which it is mixed. This property has led to its widespread exploitation in industry.

Mixed with olive oil, or walnut oil (in the proportion of 10 per cent) it will make it keep from one year to another; it can then be recovered by cooling (for liquid paraffin is more expensive than olive oil). The use of liquid paraffin in the manufacture of chocolates also prevents rancidity and ensures keeping quality, giving these sweets, once very constipating, slightly laxative properties.

PARASOL MUSHROOM. COULEMELLE—Edible mushroom with a ring but without a volve.

The *Parasol mushroom* is one of the largest edible mushrooms, sometimes as large as a dinner plate. It contains a great deal of moisture, and needs to be cooked very rapidly by frying or grilling, or it will be tough and leathery.

PARFAIT—In the olden days the term *parfait* applied only to an iced sweet based on a coffee cream.

Nowadays, this term is applied to an ice made of single flavour mousse (bombe) mixture set in plain moulds, without lining them with the ice mixture, as is done in the case of *bombes*. See ICE CREAMS AND ICES.

On the menu one can, therefore, describe light ices made out of variously flavoured mixtures, as parfaits.

PARFAIT-AMOUR—Liqueur flavoured with grated citron peel, coriander and cinnamon. Also called *citron liqueur*.

Paris-Brest
(*Maison Desmeuzes. Photograph Larousse*)

PARIS-BREST (Pastry)—The name of a Paris speciality, a pastry made of *chou paste*, forced through a forcing (pastry) bag in the form of a crown, sprinkled with grated or chopped almonds.

After baking, this crown-shaped pastry is slit open and filled with *Praline butter cream* (see CREAMS).

PARISIEN (Gâteau)—This gâteau, which used to be called *Polonais*, was made in the following manner:

Prepare a fine sponge mixture using 1 cup (250 grams) of sugar, ½ cup (65 grams) of sieved flour, 7 tablespoons (65 grams) of cornflour (cornstarch), 7 yolks of egg, 7 stiffly beaten whites of egg, a grain of salt and vanilla or lemon peel. See DOUGH, *Sponge cake, batter*.

Butter a plain round tin with a hole in the middle, sprinkle with sugar and cornflour (cornstarch) and fill up to three-quarters with the cake mixture. Bake in a slow oven for 40 minutes.

Lift the cake out of the tin and leave to cool on a wire tray or a sieve. Cut into layers ⅓ inch thick. Spread each layer with a coating of *Frangipane cream* (see CREAMS) and sandwich together, reshaping the cake. Put a piece of sponge cake on the bottom of the hollow part and fill the centre with a *salpicon** of crystallized fruit bound with frangipane or very thick apricot jam. Cover the top of the hole with another piece of sponge cake. Coat the top and the sides with diluted apricot jam and cover with Italian meringue. Pipe meringue decorations on top. Sprinkle with icing sugar. Bake in a slow oven just to make the meringue golden. Serve with kirsch-flavoured apricot jam.

Note. This gâteau can also be made by sandwiching several layers of sponge cake, spread with frangipane cream and sprinkled with diced crystallized fruit. The gâteau is then covered with Italian meringue and baked golden in the oven.

PARISIENNE (A LA)—Name of a garnish the elements of which vary sometimes, but should always include *Potatoes à la parisienne*.

This garnish is served with meat and poultry.

PARMENTIER (Antoine-Auguste)—Economist and agronomist, born in 1737, died in 1817, who wrote numerous works on food and to whom we owe the popularisation of potatoes, scorned as food in France before his time.

PARMENTIER—Method of preparing various dishes, which always include potatoes in one form or another. See SOUPS AND BROTHS, *Purée of potato soup Parmentier;* and under BEEF, *Boiled beef sauté Parmentier.*

PARMENTIÈRE—Name sometimes given to potato.

PARMESAN—Italian cheese made in the Parma region. See also CHEESE.

Parmesan straws. PAILETTES AU PARMESAN—Give ten turns to puff pastry. Work it on a table sprinkled with very finely grated Parmesan, add a little cayenne pepper.

As soon as all the cheese has been absorbed by the paste, roll it out in ribbons of 4 inches long and ⅛ inch thick.

Cut these bands into small sticks of ⅛ inch width.

Put these little sticks on a buttered baking tray. Cook in a very hot oven.

Arrange on a napkin. Serve piping hot.

Note. Cheshire and Gruyère cheese straws are prepared in the same way as Parmesan straws.

In France Parmesan straws are also called *Paillettes dorées.* Cheese straws are often served as a garnish for clear soups.

PARMESANE (A LA)—Term applied to a great many preparations which invariably include Parmesan cheese, usually grated.

PARR. TOCAN—Name for very young salmon, less than one year old.

PARROT FISH. PERROQUET DE MER—One of the numerous species of coral fish.

PARSLEY. PERSIL—Hardy biennial plant used as a flavouring in cookery.

There are four edible varieties of parsley: *common* parsley, *curly-leaved* parsley, *Neapolitan*, or *celery-leaved* parsley and *Hamburg* or *turnip-rooted* parsley, the fleshy roots of which are eaten as celeriac.

In culinary preparations parsley is used in several forms: in *sprigs*, mixed with other aromatic plants, especially thyme and bay leaf (see BOUQUET GARNI); *chopped* or *rough-chopped*, in which case it is added to the dish at the end of cooking; sometimes even sprinkled on the dish ready for serving; *en pluches*, i.e. picked off leaf by leaf, blanched in salted boiling water, drained and added to the dishes at the end of cooking or fried quickly in butter and poured over dishes served with browned butter; and *fried in deep fat* until crisp and used as a garnish for fried dishes.

Fresh parsley, picked over and washed, is also used for garnishing cold dishes.

Parsley roots are used as a condiment.

Rough-chopped parsley. Pick over and wash the parsley and chop it coarsely.

Chopped parsley. Pick over, wash and dry the parsley. Put together in a tight bunch; cut it first, then chop as quickly as possible, either with a kitchen knife or with a multiple-blade chopping knife.

When parsley is not to be used immediately after chopping it is advisable, to keep it fresh for several hours, to tie it in a corner of a cloth and wash it by leaving it under a running tap. Dry it well by twisting the cloth and put into a small receptacle.

Fried parsley. Wash the parsley well, dry it and pick off in little sprigs. Put it in a wire basket, plunge into a frying kettle full of sizzling fat. Keep it in the fat for a few moments, then dry on a cloth.

Parsley en pluches. Wash the parsley and pick off leaf by leaf, then blanch or fry, as required.

PARSNIP. PANAIS—Root vegetable used as condiment, particularly for flavouring stocks. It can also be served as a vegetable.

Parsnips can be prepared in any way suitable for *Carrots* and *Kohl-rabi.*

Rock partridge

PARTRIDGE. PERDREAU, PERDRIX—Name covering several genera of the game bird family *Phasianidae*, all of which are edible.

Partridges were introduced into France in the fifteenth century by René, King of Naples, who brought several pairs from the island of Scio for breeding in Provence.

The principle species found in France is the *Common* or *Grey partridge*, brownish grey in colour, speckled with white on the back, ash coloured on the breast. The male has a brown spot.

Red-legged partridge is bigger than the common species, brownish, slightly darker on the back, grey breast, red below, with pure white neck and red bill and legs. It is mainly found in the South of France.

The *Rock partridge* and the *Snow partridge* or Lagopus are also to be found in France.

The American partridge can now be obtained on the market in France in its frozen state.

Ballottine of partridge with various garnishes. BALLOTTINE DE PERDREAU—Bone the partridge and stuff with foie gras, truffles and game forcemeat, as described in the recipe for *Ballottine of pheasant.* See PHEASANT.

Wrap the partridge in a piece of cloth (muslin for preference) and tie with string. Cook it for 45 minutes in very little Madeira-flavoured braising liquor, made from the bones and scraps pared off the partridge, a veal knuckle and the usual aromatic vegetables.

Drain the ballottine, unwrap and glaze in the oven. Arrange on a serving dish and surround with the garnish recommended. Reduce (cook down) the braising liquor, strain and pour over the ballottine.

Note. Ballottines of partridges can be served with all the garnishes recommended for pan-roasted or braised pheasant, woodcock and other winged game.

Jellied ballottine of partridge. BALLOTTINE DE PERDREAU À LA GELÉE—Prepare like *Ballottine of partridge.* Cook the ballottine in Madeira-flavoured liquid game jelly.

When cooked, drain and cool under a light press. Arrange in an oval-shaped terrine or a glass dish. Clarify the jelly in the usual manner and pour over the ballottine. See JELLY.

Partridges with cabbage. PERDRIX AUX CHOUX—Partridges which are generally used for this dish must not, of course, be too old, as they would then be hard and tough. Some gastronomes even maintain that to prepare this dish the cabbage must be cooked with an old partridge, which—after it has communicated its flavour to the cabbage—is replaced by a young partridge, roasted in the oven and put into the cabbage for a few moments to mingle the flavours. This method of procedure, of course, is rather extravagant. Besides, if the partridge used is not too old, excellent results can be achieved and the bird, being braised with the cabbage, retains all its flavour.

Brown two partridges carefully in the oven (having larded the breasts). Put them into a casserole in which half a big cabbage has been cooked with a piece of lean bacon, an uncooked sausage, 2 big carrots and the usual aromatics. When the time comes, remove the bacon and the sausage and finish cooking the partridge and the cabbage. The cooking takes about 2 hours.

Untruss and arrange the cabbage in a deep round dish or in a *timbale.*

Put the partridge on it, garnish with the bacon cut in rectangles, the sausage and the carrots cut in round slices. Baste with a few tablespoons of good gravy.

Note. The partridge can also be served in the following manner: Butter a round *timbale*, line it with round slices of carrot and sausage and rectangles of bacon. Cover this garnish with a layer of cabbage. Put the untrussed partridge in the middle and cover with the rest of the cabbage, pressing down carefully with a skimmer. Set in the oven for 5 minutes to heat.

Turn out the timbale on to a round dish. Pour a few tablespoonfuls of *Demi-glace sauce* (see SAUCE) based on a game *fumet**, or some brown veal gravy around the cabbage.

The same method of preparation can be applied to pheasant, hazel-grouse or guinea-fowl.

Casserole of partridge (or partridge in cocotte). PERDREAU EN CASSEROLE, EN COCOTTE—Prepare like *Casserole of pheasant* (see PHEASANT) making allowances for cooking time according to the size of the partridge.

Casserole of partridge à l'ancienne. PERDREAU EN CASSEROLE À L'ANCIENNE—Stuff the partridge with foie gras and truffles, cut in large dice, seasoned and sprinkled with a dash of brandy. Truss and bard the partridge. Put it into a casserole in which a good tablespoon of butter has been heated. Season and sprinkle with butter. Cook in the oven. When three-quarters cooked, add to the casserole a dozen cocks' kidneys, cooked in Madeira, and 4 mushrooms cut into big pieces or some small white mushrooms. Moisten with ½ cup (a decilitre) of Madeira and 1 cup (2 decilitres) of fresh cream. Finish cooking, basting frequently. Untruss the partridge and remove the barding. Serve in the same casserole.

Partridge à la catalane, called en pistache (Languedoc cookery). PERDREAU À LA CATALANE, EN PISTACHE—Stuff the partridge with a forcemeat made of its chopped liver, freshly grated, untoasted breadcrumbs, chopped lean ham, parsley and garlic and bound with an egg. Truss the partridge, bard it, season and put into an earthenware casserole in which 3 tablespoons of butter, or—more of a local note—goose fat, has been heated. When the partridge acquires a nice golden colour, remove it from the casserole. Put into the casserole a large tablespoon of raw ham cut in dice. Sprinkle with 2 tablespoons of flour. Cook the flour for a few moments. Moisten with ¼ cup (½ decilitre) of dry white wine and ½ cup (1 decilitre) of stock. Add a tablespoon of tomato purée, a *bouquet garni* composed of parsley, thyme and bay leaf and a small piece of orange peel. Cook for 10 minutes. Remove the ham and the *bouquet garni* and strain the sauce. Put the partridge into the casserole with the ham and the *bouquet garni* and pour in the sauce. Bring to the boil, cover and simmer for 10 minutes. Add 12 cloves of garlic, previously boiled in salted water and drained. Finish cooking together, simmering gently for 35 minutes. Remove the *bouquet garni* and serve the partridge in the casserole in which it was cooked.

In western Languedoc this sauce is usually thickened with breadcrumbs.

Partridge in chambertin. PERDREAU AU CHAMBERTIN—Stuff the partridge, if desired, and prepare as described in the recipe for *Woodcock au chambertin**.

Partridge à la champenoise. PERDREAU À LA CHAMPENOISE—Stuff the partridge with a fat goose liver (foie gras), cut in large dice, seasoned and sprinkled with a tablespoon of brandy. Truss as for an entrée and pot roast in butter. When three-quarters done, add 8 peeled mushroom caps and finish cooking together. Drain the partridge, untruss and arrange on a croûton, fried in butter and spread with a layer of *Forcemeat à gratin**. Dilute the pan juices with 1¼ cups (2½ decilitres) of champagne, add some fresh cream, simmer until the sauce thickens, blend in some butter, strain, add 3 tablespoons of fresh truffles, shredded into a fine *julienne** and lightly tossed in butter, and pour over the partridge.

Chartreuse of partridge. CHARTREUSE DE PERDRIX—Pluck, draw and singe two partridges. Truss them and lard the breast with thin lardoons of bacon fat.

Brush them with butter, season and colour on all sides in a hot oven for 7 or 8 minutes.

Put some bacon rinds and sliced carrots and onions on the bottom of a deep casserole.

Put in a layer of cabbage, blanched, well drained and seasoned.

Place the partridges on the cabbage. Add 6 to 7 ounces (200 grams) of lean scalded bacon, a small uncooked sausage, a medium-sized carrot cut into quarters, an onion studded with a clove and a *bouquet garni.**

Cover all the ingredients with another layer of cabbage, blanched, well drained and seasoned with salt and pepper.

Moisten with the pan juices left over from colouring the partridges, diluted with 4 cups (8 decilitres) of stock.

Bring to the boil on the stove, then put in the oven and cook with a lid on from 1½ hours to 2 hours, depending on how tender the birds are.

Before the cooking is complete, remove the bacon and the sausage, to avoid their being overcooked, if they are left in the casserole until the end.

Preparation of the chartreuse. The chartreuse of partridge (or any other game) is, in fact, a variation of partridge with cabbage and differs mainly in its more decorative and elaborate arrangement.

The arrangement requires great attention to detail. It needs, in addition to the lean bacon and the sausage cooked with the cabbage, the following ingredients, which should be prepared separately, while the partridges are cooking: 2 young turnips (100 grams), cut with a small vegetable tube into little sticks, 1¼ inches long, and cooked in stock; 3 medium to small carrots (150 grams), cut and cooked in a similar way; a handful (150 grams) of French beans cooked in salted water, drained and dressed with butter; 5 tablespoons of big fresh garden peas, cooked in salted water and well drained; and 5 tablespoons (75 grams) of *Quenelle forcemeat II* (see FORCEMEAT).

Remove the partridge, untruss and cut each into quarters.

Drain the cabbage. Remove the vegetables, the *bouquet garni* and the bacon rinds and keep all these ingredients hot.

Butter a big charlotte mould generously.

Decorate it with little turnip and carrot sticks, placing them in rows, separated from each other by a row of big peas.

Cover these vegetables with a thin layer of *Veal forcemeat à la crème* (see FORCEMEAT). The object of this is to solidify the vegetable garnish.

Line the mould with well-drained and pressed-out cabbage.

On this cabbage, distributing them evenly, place the pieces of partridge and the lean bacon, trimmed and cut into small rectangles.

Cover the partridges and the lean bacon with the rest of the cabbage, again making sure that it is well pressed.

Cover the whole with a layer of veal forcemeat and smooth the forcemeat evenly.

Put the mould, thus filled, into a pan half-filled with boiling water.

Cook in a slow oven for about 40 minutes.

Let the chartreuse stand for 5 minutes before turning it out. Turn it out on to a round dish.

Garnish the top with a sausage, skinned, cut in round slices, and arranged in a circle.

Chartreuse of partridge poult. PERDREAU EN CHARTREUSE—In classical cookery of the highest order, this chartreuse is made of young partridges, which are roasted, jointed (divided into pieces) and arranged in a mould or a *timbale*, on a foundation of braised cabbage, cooked with old partridges to give them more flavour. See *Chartreuse of partridges* above.

Chaud-froid of partridge. CHAUD-FROID DE PERDREAU—Roast the partridge in the oven, allow to cool and joint (cut into portions).

Skin the pieces and trim them.

Cover with *Brown chaud-froid sauce*, based on a concentrated game stock (see SAUCE). Decorate with pieces of truffles, whites of hard boiled egg and pickled tongue and glaze with jelly.

Arrange in a glass dish on a foundation of well-set jelly. Cover completely with semi-liquid jelly (flavoured with Madeira or other liqueur wine).

Chill well on ice.

Note. The chaud-froid of partridge can also be served on a buttered croûton, as described in the recipe for *Chaud-froid of chicken* (see CHICKEN) and garnished with chopped jelly.

Partridge à la chipolata. PERDREAU À LA CHIPOLATA—Truss the partridge as for an entrée. Cook in a casserole. When it is nearly cooked, untruss and replace in the casserole. Add *Chipolata garnish* (see GARNISHES) and simmer gently.

Note. After being cooked the partridge can also be arranged on a round dish, placed on a croûton fried in butter, and surrounded with chipolata garnish. Dilute the pan juices with Madeira and concentrated game stock and pour over the partridge.

Partridge à la crapaudine. PERDREAU À LA CRAPAUDINE—Prepare as *Pigeon à la crapaudine**.

Serve with *Diable sauce* to which some game *fumet** has been added, or with *Périgueux sauce* (see SAUCE).

Partridge à la crème. PERDREAU À LA CRÈME—Prepare as *Pheasant en cocotte with cream**, making allowances for cooking time, depending on the size of the bird.

Crépinettes of partridge. CRÉPINETTES DE PERDREAU—These are prepared as *Chicken crépinettes** replacing chicken meat by that of partridge.

They should be made a little smaller than chicken crépinettes and the forcemeat should always be truffled. They are cooked on a low grill.

They are usually served with *Chestnut purée**, but they can be served with any of the garnishes recommended for *Crépinettes of pork*. See PORK.

Crépinette of partridge Brillat-Savarin. PERDREAU EN CRÉPINE BRILLAT-SAVARIN—Split the partridge along the back, as for grilled chicken. Remove all the small bones from the inside. Flatten slightly and season with salt and spices. Fry the partridge quickly in butter, not to cook it, but merely to stiffen the flesh.

Coat on both sides with *Foie gras forcemeat* (see FORCEMEAT) mixed with truffles and wrap in a piece of pig's caul (or pounded fat pork).

Arrange on a foundation of lentil purée. Simmer a few tablespoons of game *fumet** with Madeira, strain, add a little butter and pour around the dish.

Crépinette of partridge à la périgourdine. PERDREAU EN CRÉPINE À LA PÉRIGOURDINE—Truss the partridge as for an entrée, slit open the back and remove all the small bones from the inside (leaving only the drumsticks and the bones of the pinions). Flatten the partridge slightly, season with salt and pepper, and fry it quickly in butter just to stiffen the flesh.

Put the partridge on a layer of *Fine pork forcemeat* (see FORCEMEAT), mixed with a *salpicon** of foie gras and truffles and enlivened with a tablespoon of brandy which has been set alight, all of this spread on a piece of pig's caul (or pounded pork fat) big enough to enclose the partridge and the forcemeat. Put a layer of the same forcemeat over the partridge and cover it well. Wrap the whole in the piece of pig's caul.

Brush the crépinette with melted butter, dip in freshly-ground breadcrumbs and cook on a low grill until both sides are golden.

Arrange the crépinette on a round dish. Surround with a ragoût of truffles and mushrooms in Madeira-flavoured game *fumet**.

Jellied partridge en daube. PERDREAU EN DAUBE À LA GELÉE. See PHEASANT. *Daube of pheasant in jelly.*

Estouffade of partridge. PERDREAU EN ESTOUFFADE—Truss the partridge as for an entrée, season it, brush with butter and roast until golden in the oven.

Put into an oval-shaped earthenware *cocotte**, on a foundation of a *mirepoix** of vegetables, well softened in butter. Cover the partridge with a layer of the same *mirepoix** of vegetables. Sprinkle with melted butter and add 2 tablespoons of burnt brandy. Put the lid on and seal it with flour-and-water paste. Cook in a hot oven from 25 to 30 minutes. Serve as it is.

Estouffade of partridge à la cévenole. PERDREAU EN ESTOUFFADE À LA CÉVENOLE—Stuff the partridge with *Fine pork forcemeat* (see FORCEMEAT) mixed with one-third of its weight of *Forcemeat à gratin** and a tablespoon of chopped truffles. Truss as for an entrée. Season with salt and pepper and brown quickly in butter just to stiffen it. Untruss, put into an earthenware casserole, surround with a garnish of 12 choice chestnuts, three-quarters cooked in concentrated veal stock, 6 mushrooms, tossed in butter (cultivated mushrooms, small cèpes, or any other) and 6 lardoons of breast of pork, scalded thoroughly and fried in butter. Moisten with 4 tablespoons of concentrated game stock (or concentrated brown veal gravy) flavoured with some Madeira. Sprinkle with a tablespoon of burnt brandy. Put the lid on the casserole and seal it with flour-and-water paste. Cook in a hot oven from 40 to 45 minutes. Serve as it is.

Partridge à la financière. PERDREAU À LA FINANCIÈRE—Cook the partridge in butter in an earthenware *cocotte.* When it is nearly cooked, untruss it and put back in the *cocotte* with *Garnish à la financière**, bound with 4 tablespoons of Madeira-flavoured game stock.

Finish cooking in a slow oven. Serve in the same *cocotte.*

Note. Instead of cooking and serving the partridge in a *cocotte*, it can be pot roasted in butter, then arranged on a round dish, placed on a croûton fried in butter and spread with *Forcemeat à gratin**, and surrounded with the various elements of *financière* garnish disposed in separate groups.

Partridge à la forestière. PERDREAU À LA FORESTIÈRE—Stuff the partridge with *Forcemeat à gratin**. Truss it as for an entrée and fry it in butter just to stiffen it. Take out of the casserole. Put into the casserole a small teaspoon of chopped shallot, then replace the partridge and surround it with 1 cup (150 grams) of sliced mushrooms, 12 lean lardoons, scalded and tossed in butter, and 4 to 6 tablespoons of potato, cut in dice and tossed in butter. Finish cooking together in the oven with a lid on.

When the partridge is cooked, untruss it, baste with 3 tablespoons of game *fumet** (greatly concentrated game stock) and serve in the same casserole.

Galantine of partridge. GALANTINE DE PERDREAU—Bone the partridge and prepare as described in the recipe for *Galantine of pheasant* (see PHEASANT).

Grilled partridge à la diable. PERDREAU GRILLÉ À LA DIABLE—Split the partridge on the back, open it out and flatten slightly. Brush with melted butter, season with salt and pepper and cook under a moderate grill (4 minutes each side). Brush with melted butter and dip in freshly grated breadcrumbs.

Put the partridge back under the grill and finish grilling gently, basting frequently with melted butter.

Arrange the partridge on a round dish. Decorate with watercress and a lemon quarter at each end.

Garnish the edges of the dish with fluted-edged half-slices of lemon, and thin slices of gherkins. Serve *Diable sauce* separately (see SAUCE).

Note. Grilled partridges can also be served with *Maître d'hôtel butter* (see BUTTER, *Compound butters*).

Partridge à la mirepoix. PERDREAU À LA MIREPOIX—Stuff the partridge with *Game forcemeat à gratin* (see FORCEMEAT) mixed with diced truffles. Truss it as for an entrée. Fry quickly in butter just to stiffen it. Remove trussing. Cover with a fine *mirepoix** of vegetables, gently cooked in butter and diluted with a little Madeira. Wrap the partridge in a piece of pig's caul (or pork fat).

Cook it in very little Madeira-flavoured braising stock.

Drain the partridge, unwrap and arrange on a croûton, fried in butter, spread with *Forcemeat à gratin** and browned under a grill.

Add 3 tablespoons of Madeira and one tablespoon of burnt brandy to the braising liquor, reduce (cook down), strain and pour over the partridge.

Partridge à la moldave (Moldavian style). PERDREAU À LA MOLDAVE—Split open the partridge, flatten it, season, dip in egg and black breadcrumbs, mixed with a little powdered coriander. Sauté in clarified butter until both sides are golden.

Arrange on a round cake made of potato pulp (having baked the potatoes in the oven), mixed with a *brunoise** of carrot, celery and mushrooms (binding this mixture with yolks of egg, shaping it into a pancake, dredging with flour and frying in butter).

Pour a ring of concentrated veal gravy around the partridge. Squeeze out a few drops of lemon juice on the partridge and sprinkle it with a tablespoon of *Noisette butter* (see BUTTER, *Compound butters*).

Partridge Monselet. PERDREAU MONSELET—Stuff the partridge with foie gras and truffles in large dice. Truss it, season and cook in butter in an earthenware cocotte. When half-cooked, add two artichoke hearts, sliced and tossed in butter and, last of all, a medium-sized truffle, cut in thick slices. Moisten with 3 tablespoonfuls of game *fumet** and a tablespoon of burnt brandy. Cover the cocotte and leave to sweat in the oven for 3 minutes. Serve as it is, in the same cocotte.

Partridge mousses and mousselines. MOUSSES, MOUSSELINES DE PERDREAU—Using boned partridge prepare like *Quail mousses**.

Partridge à la normande. PERDREAU À LA NORMANDE—Truss the partridge as for an entrée and brown it in butter. Put into an earthenware casserole on a foundation of cooking apples, peeled, sliced and tossed in butter. Surround the partridge with similarly treated apples. Moisten with fresh cream. Cook in a hot oven under a lid.

Serve as it is, in the same casserole.

Cold partridge pâté. PÂTÉ FROID DE PERDREAU—Prepare like *Cold pheasant pâté* (see PHEASANT).

Hot partridge pâté. PÂTÉ CHAUD DE PERDREAU—Using boned partridges, *Forcemeat à gratin*, foie gras and truffles, prepare like *Hot Woodcock pâté* (see WOODCOCK).

Partridge à la Périgueux. PERDREAU À LA PÉRIGUEUX—Stuff the partridge with truffles as described in the recipe for *Truffled partridge.* Cook it gently in butter in an earthenware casserole. When three-quarters cooked, add twenty or so rather thick slices of truffles, seasoned with salt, pepper and a pinch of spices. Sprinkle with $\frac{3}{4}$ cup ($1\frac{1}{2}$ decilitres) of Madeira-flavoured game *fumet** and a tablespoon of burnt brandy. Serve as it is, in the same casserole.

Roast partridge. PERDREAU RÔTI—Cover the partridge with a vine leaf, then with a thin rasher (strip) of bacon fat, in such a way as to enclose the breast completely. Keep this bacon fat in place by tying it with string.

Roast the partridge in the oven from 18 to 20 minutes, or on a spit from 20 to 25 minutes.

Untruss the partridge, arrange it on a serving dish, on a croûton of bread fried in butter (or in the fat collected in the dripping pan), spread with a layer of *Game forcemeat à gratin* (see FORCEMEAT) and brown lightly on top.

Garnish with watercress and half a lemon. Serve with pan juices left from cooking the bird.

Salmis of partridge. SALMIS DE PERDREAU—Using roast partridge, underdone and cut into joints, prepare as *Salmis of woodcock* (see WOODCOCK).

Partridge sautéed with truffles. PERDREAU SAUTÉ AUX TRUFFES—Choose a big plump partridge and cut up into joints, as in the case of *chicken sauté.* Season with salt and pepper and sauté briskly in butter (in a sauté pan). Remove the partridge joints, arrange them on a croûton, fried in butter, spread with *Forcemeat à gratin* and browned on top.

Toss a dozen rather thick slices of truffles quickly in butter and season with salt and pepper. Cook the truffles very lightly, taking care not to let them dry up. Put them on the partridge. Dilute the pan juices with Madeira, add a few tablespoons of *Brown game stock* (see STOCK), cook down (reduce), blend in a little butter, strain and pour over the partridge.

Partridge soufflé. SOUFFLÉ DE PERDREAU—Mainly old partridges are prepared in this way. The soufflé mixture is made from partridge meat in the same manner as *Woodcock soufflé*.

Partridge à la Souvarof. PERDREAU À LA SOUVAROF—Stuff the partridge with foie gras and truffles, cut in large dice, seasoned with salt and pepper and sprinkled with a dash of brandy. Truss it as for an entrée. Brown quickly in butter, just to stiffen it. Put into an oval-shaped earthenware cocotte. Surround with 3 truffles cut in large pieces, or whole truffles, peeled and seasoned.

Moisten with ½ cup (1 decilitre) of Madeira-flavoured game *fumet**, to which the pan juices left from frying the partridge, diluted with Madeira, have been added. Sprinkle with a dash of brandy.

Cover the cocotte with its lid and seal it with flour-and-water paste. Cook the partridge in a hot oven for 40 minutes. Serve as it is, in the same *cocotte*.

Stuffed partridges in aspic. PERDREAUX FARCIS À LA GELÉE—Slit the partridges along the back, bone, open them out and season with spiced salt. Stuff each with truffled game forcemeat (see FORCEMEAT), placing in the middle of it a piece of foie gras, encrusted with a peeled truffle, seasoned with spiced salt and sprinkled with brandy.

Reshape the partridges. Truss them, wrap each one in a thin rasher of bacon fat (or a piece of pig's caul) and cook in a little Madeira-flavoured aspic jelly, prepared in advance in the usual manner, using the carcases and scraps trimmed off the birds, a veal knuckle and fresh bacon rinds (the latter in sufficient quantity to give the jelly, when cold, the desired consistency). See JELLY.

When the partridges are cooked, drain them, unwrap, untruss and dry on a cloth. Put into an oval-shaped *terrine* and leave until cold.

When they are quite cold, cover completely with the jelly, clarified in the usual manner. See JELLY, *Clarification*.

Chill thoroughly before serving.

Stuffed partridges in aspic (tinned or canned). PERDREAUX FARCIS À LA GELÉE—Bone the partridges partly, opening on the back. Stuff them with a big piece of raw fat goose liver, encrusted with one or two medium-sized truffles, peeled, seasoned with spiced salt and sprinkled with brandy, and enclosed in a layer of truffled fine pork forcemeat. Truss the partridges as for an entrée, wrap each in a thin rasher of bacon fat (or a piece of pig's caul). Put them, packing them in fairly tightly, into a sauté pan on a foundation of chopped fresh bacon rinds, carrots and onions and the giblets and carcases of the birds, all lightly tossed in butter. Moisten with Madeira (or any other liqueur wine). Cook gently, with the lid on, for 10 minutes. Moisten with good strong jelly, prepared separately, using the usual basic meats, calves' feet and fresh bacon rinds, but no gelatine, and cook in the oven from 30 to 35 minutes.

Drain the partridges, remove barding and trussing string, and dry the birds on a cloth.

Put each into an oval-shaped tin-plated can, breast downwards, and leave to cool.

When the partridges are quite cold, cover with the jelly in which they were cooked, clarified in the usual manner. See JELLY, *Clarification*.

Leave until quite cold. Solder the tins (cans). Put them to boil in water for 45 minutes, making sure that during this operation boiling does not cease for a single moment.

Take the tins out of the water, put them on the table and leave to cool, placing them in such a way that the partridges are breast downwards. Mark the tin (can) on the top to make sure it is breast side up when you open it.

Terrine of partridge. TERRINE DE PERDEAU—Prepared like *Potted pheasant* (see PHEASANT).

Timbale of partridge. TIMBALE DE PERDREAU—Prepared like *Timbale of woodcock* (see WOODCOCK).

Truffled partridge (Roast). PERDREAU TRUFFÉ (RÔTI)—Choose a big plump partridge and bone it partly, opening it on the back, near the neck (the bird having been cleaned from the front). Through this opening, stuff it with about 3½ ounces (100 grams) of pork fat, studded with pieces of truffle, and 2 to 3 ounces (60 to 80 grams) of truffles cut in quarters. Truss the partridge and wrap it in a thin slice of bacon fat. Roast it in a slow oven from 30 to 35 minutes, or on a spit from 35 to 40 minutes.

Serve either with the diluted pan juices or with *Périgueux sauce* (see SAUCE), to which the diluted pan juices have been added.

Note. The truffling of game or poultry should be done at least 24 hours in advance. This will render the flesh more flavoursome and more delicious.

When the bird is being cooked on a spit, it is also a good idea to cover it completely with a piece of buttered greaseproof paper. This paper is removed a few minutes before taking the bird off the spit, so as to brown it.

Truffled partridge, like all other truffled winged game, can also be cooked in a casserole or a cocotte.

Partridge à la vigneronne. PERDREAU À LA VIGNERONNE—Truss the partridge as for an entrée and cook it in butter in a casserole or a cocotte. When it is cooked, untruss it. Put into the casserole 24 peeled and seeded grapes. Add 3 tablespoons of game *fumet** and a tablespoon of burnt brandy. Simmer with a lid on for 5 minutes. Serve as it is, in the same casserole in which it was cooked.

PASKHA (Russian sweet or dessert)—This dish used to be an essential part of the Easter table in Russia.

Press out any excess moisture from 3 pounds of cream (U.S. cottage) cheese, blend with ½ cup of sour cream, ¼ pound butter, 1 teaspoon salt, ½ to ⅔ cup of sugar (previously rubbed with a vanilla bean, or substitute 1 teaspoon of vanilla extract), 2 tablespoons finely grated lemon rind, 2 ounces chopped almonds and 5 tablespoons seedless raisins. When the mixture is very smooth, place in a muslin or napkin-lined receptacle (traditionally pyramid shaped) which will allow the mixture to drain. Put a weight on top and leave in a cool place.

To serve, turn out on a dessert dish and decorate with fresh or frozen berries, chopped pistachio nuts or crystallized fruit.

PASSARELLE—French name for dried muscatel grapes, prepared in the Frontignan region as well as in Smyrna and Damascus.

The process of turning these grapes into raisins is called *passerillage* or *passarillage*.

PASSE-CRASSANE—A variety of very fragrant winter pear.

PASSE-POMME—Name given to three varieties of apple which ripen in August: *White*, *Red* and *Jerusalem*.

PASSE-TOUT-GRAIN OR PASSE-TOUS-GRAINS—Name of a red Burgundy wine made from mixed (Pinot) and Gamay (common Burgundy) grapes, without any special selection. All the vintage wines, on the other hand, are made from selected quality grapes.

PASSION-FRUIT. Barbadine—Edible fruit of the passion-flower tree or giant granadilla, used as a dessert.

PASTA—See ITALIAN PASTES, MACARONI, NOODLES, RAVIOLI and SPAGHETTI.

PASTE—See DOUGH and PASTRY.

PASTEURISATION—Process of heating a liquid up to a temperature between 70° to 80°C. (131° to 158°F.) then cooling quickly. Pasteurisation arrests development of certain bacteria and increases the duration for which the product can be kept, without assuring complete sterilisation.

Pastillage (*Maison Morat*)

PASTILLAGE—Paste which was much in demand in the past for decorating big pastry and confectionery creations, as well as pillars and ornaments used for dressing big cakes. This paste was made from icing sugar, powdered starch, gum tragacanth and water. Pastillage is not used a great deal nowadays.

Passe-Crassane pears (*Wide World*)

PASTILLE—A small round confection made from dissolved sugar and water, poured hot, drop by drop, on to a cold marble slab. The sugar is usually flavoured with various aromatic flavourings. In the present day pastilles are manufactured almost entirely in factories.

General rules for making pastilles—(1) Choose very white, well grained and odourless sugar. Having pounded it into powder and sifted through a horsehair sieve, extract the finest part by means of a silk sieve. This powder, being too fine, has the drawback of making the pastilles too heavy and compact and less shiny.

(2) Dilute the sugar with the desired aromatic essence and a sufficient quantity of water. Use a small silver pan, if possible, as it is both clean and will not communicate any unpleasant taste to the mixture.

(3) Watch the sugar carefully while it is on the fire, stirring from time to time when the mixture begins to simmer.

(4) Make sure that the paste is not too liquid for pouring; should that be the case, take the mixture off the fire and stir with a wooden spoon until it acquires the desired consistency.

(5) Make sure that the flavourings used, which are the juices pressed out from various kinds of fruit, are fresh and smell as they should.

Coffee pastilles. Pastilles au café—Prepare 3 pounds of finest quality sugar as described above. Bring ¼ cup (25 grams) of powdered coffee to the boil several times in a pint (½ litre) of water. Pour the decoction through a straining bag in which a piece of gelatine has been put to make the grounds settle.

When the liquid is cold, strain and use for diluting the sugar, then proceed to pour the pastilles.

Jasmin pastilles. Pastilles au jasmin—Having pounded and sifted 4 pounds of sugar, put it into a china bowl and dilute with 2 ounces (65 grams) of jasmin essence, adding water, until it forms a paste. Then roll and make into pastilles.

Mignonette, jonquil and tuberose pastilles are made in a similar manner using the same quantity of the essence of these flowers per pound of sugar.

Orange blossom pastilles. Pastilles à la fleur d'oranger—Pound 4 pounds of very white superfine sugar in a marble mortar. Sift it through a horsehair or silk sieve to extract the finest part, which can be kept for other uses.

Put the rest of the sugar remaining in the sieve into a china bowl and dilute with good double orange blossom water, using a wooden spoon for the purpose, pouring a little water on at a time and stirring continuously until the paste is quite firm. If too much water has been added and the paste has become too liquid, thicken it with a little powdered sugar (some of which should always be kept in reserve for such an emergency).

To test whether the composition has reached the desired degree, take a little of it with a wooden spoon, hold it up and if it becomes detached by itself it is just right.

Put 4 ounces (125 grams) of this paste into a small pan with a long spout. Put on the stove, heat the paste until it becomes liquid, stirring with a wooden spoon. Remove from heat when the paste is just about to boil and, stirring it a few more times, begin to pour on to tin-plated metal sheets in the following manner:

Hold the pan with your left hand and, tipping the spout very gently, pour the paste which comes over the edge with the aid of half a knitting needle, fixed in a small piece of wood, held in your right hand, moving the saucepan and the needle in such a way as to make the paste drop on the metal sheet in the shape of little buttons (which are called pastilles).

(*Note.* There are special droppers for shaping boiled sugar drops.)

Take care to space the pastilles properly when pouring them and to pour the same quantity of paste for all of them.

Leave for an hour, then take off the metal sheets, put on a paper-covered sieve and put in a warm place for a day (longer than that would diminish the aroma).

Rose pastilles. PASTILLES À LA ROSE—Pound 4 pounds of best sugar in a marble mortar, sift through a horsehair sieve into a china bowl, dilute with attar of roses until it forms a fairly thick paste, pour from the pan with a knitting needle to drop the pastilles, as described above. (*Le Confiseur moderne*, 1821.)

PASTIS (Béarn cake)—'Put 12 eggs with a spoonful of orange blossom water, a small glass of brandy, 3 cups (400 grams) of castor (fine) sugar, a little milk and 6 tablespoons (100 grams) of melted butter and whisk vigorously.

'Add a little baker's yeast to the mixture and stir, adding flour until the paste is sufficiently thick.

'Blend the dough well, roll into a loaf in the bowl, sprinkle with flour, cover with a cloth and leave, near the fire, until the next day.

'Put the dough into a buttered tin and bake in a hot oven.' (*Simin Palay: La Cuisine en Béarn.*)

PASTRY. PÂTE—See also DOUGH.

Pastry dough for hot or cold pâtés (pies). PÂTE ORDINAIRE —*Ingredients.* 7½ cups (1 kilo) of sifted flour, ½ pound (250 grams) of butter, 2 whole eggs, 2 tablespoons (30 grams) of salt, about 2 cups (4 decilitres) of water. (The quantity of water may vary depending on the quality of flour used. The better the quality of flour, the more water it can absorb.)

Method. Spread the flour in a circle on the board and put the salt, water, eggs and butter in the middle.

Mix in the usual manner and knead the paste to make it smooth and homogeneous. Roll into a ball, wrap in a cloth and keep in a cool place until required for use.

Note. Pâte or pie pastry, like all pastry, should be prepared at least 12 hours before it is to be used. A *well-rested* pastry (and the pastry made according to this recipe can rest up to 24 hours) is easier to work and takes on less colour during baking.

Common brioche pastry dough. PÂTE À BRIOCHE COMMUNE—Some pâtés (pies), especially those made in the shape of oval or rectangular patties or turnovers, are shaped by hand, that is without a mould, and are made either out of unsweetened common brioche pastry or out of short pastry. Recipes for both these types of pastry will be found in the section entitled DOUGH.

Lard pastry dough. PÂTE AU SAINDOUX—*Ingredients.* 7½ cups (1 kilo) of sifted flour, ½ pound (250 grams) of warm, melted lard, 2 whole eggs, 2 cups (4 decilitres) warm water and 2 tablespoons (30 grams) of salt.

Prepare in the same manner as ordinary pastry dough (see above). Use for big cold pâtés (pies).

Puff pastry cases (patty shells). BOUCHÉES FEUILLETÉES—Roll out puff pastry to a thickness of about ⅛ inch (see DOUGH).

Cut this pastry out with a fluted-edged pastry cutter, about 4 inches in diameter.

Turn these pastry circles and put them on a baking sheet, moistened with a brush.

Paint with beaten egg. Make a circular incision in the centre to form the future lid (with the aid of a plain, round pastry cutter); leave to stand for 10 minutes and bake in the oven (400°F.) from 12 to 15 minutes.

Remove the lids and fill the bouchées as indicated in the recipe.

Puff pastry shells. CROÛTES DE BOUCHÉES FEUILLETÉES—Prepared with puff pastry rolled out six times and which has been allowed to rest. Roll out this pastry to a thickness of ¼ inch. Using a round, fluted pastry cutter, cut out pastry rounds 2½ inches in diameter.

Put these on to a wet baking sheet, turning them over. Using a simple round cutter, 1¼ inches across, dipped in hot water, mark out the lids of the little pieces of pastry. Mark the edges with a knife.

Cook the croûtes in a hot oven. When these are taken out of the oven, remove the lids. Fill them with whatever preparation is indicated.

Pastry sticks—See ALLUMETTES, STRAWS.

PASTRY CREAM, FRENCH. CRÈME PÂTISSIÈRE—Custard made of eggs, sugar, flour, milk and flavouring, which is used in pastry-making as filling for various cakes, such as *choux, éclairs, baton de Jacob.* See CREAMS. This preparation is also known as *Confectioner's custard.*

PASTRY CRIMPER (PINCER). PINCE—Tool used for pinching the edges of pies, tarts, etc.

PASTRY CUTTER. COUPE PÂTE—Instrument used to cut sheets of pastry into round or oval shapes. They operate in the same way as punches, and they exist in series in various sizes and progressions. They are either plain or fluted.

PASTRY WHEEL. GAUFREUSE—Small pastry tool of hardwood, used in place of metal pastry pincers to crimp the edges of tarts and pastries.

PÂTE—Pâte is a general term used for pastry doughs, bread doughs, sweet pastes and batters. For recipes, see DOUGH and PASTRY.

PÂTÉ (Pie)—A pastry case consisting of a bottom, sides and top, containing a filling of meat, fish, vegetables or fruit.

In principle, the word *pâté* should apply only to meat or fish dishes enclosed in *pastry* (lining paste, puff pastry, or any other) and baked in the oven.

The term, however, is also used to describe any preparation put into a pie dish lined with rashers (strips) of bacon and baked in the oven. The correct name for this type of dish is *terrine*, and they should always be referred to as such, but common usage has applied the term *pâté* to these preparations, which, by the way, are always served cold, whereas the real pâtés can be served hot or cold.

There is a great number of pâtés. One can rarely find a town in France which cannot boast of having a speciality of this kind and some of these pâtés (or terrines) enjoy a great reputation.

Preparation of Pâtés (or pies):

Lining the mould. Choose a hinged mould, round, oval or rectangular, depending on the nature of the pâté in question, and butter it carefully.

Take three-quarters of the pastry (prepared in advance and well rested). Roll into a ball, roll out with a pin, then fold in the shape of a *calotte* (flattened dome).

Roll out this *calotte*, unfold and repeat the same

process, rolling it in the opposite direction to a thickness of $\frac{1}{8}$ inch.

Unfold the *calotte* of pastry and put in the middle of a mould (placed on a metal baking sheet). Press the pastry down all round the walls of the tin, taking care to see that it is pressed evenly all the way to the bottom and rises about $\frac{3}{8}$ inch above the edge of the tin, to form a sort of rim, which will later be sealed with a pastry lid.

Filling the pâté (or pie). Line the bottom and the walls of the pâté (pie) with very thin rashers (strips) of bacon.

Over the bacon, put a thin layer of the prescribed forcemeat. Smooth this layer of forcemeat carefully, to ensure that it is even all over.

Now fill the pâté (pie) with the ingredients indicated: thin slices or escalopes of veal (browned in butter), diced or sliced poultry or game meat, fresh pork (prepared in the same manner as the veal), ham, etc., alternating with bacon cut in thin slivers, or truffles, either cut in uniform pieces, or left whole if they are small, but always peeled and previously steeped (as should be all other garnish, by the way) in brandy with spiced salt.

All this filling should be sealed down with a small quantity of the above forcemeat and put into the pâté in layers.

Cover the last layer of forcemeat with a thin rasher of bacon.

Sealing the pastry. Roll the remainder of the pastry into a round or oval-shaped piece, of the same diameter as the opening of the pâté. Moisten the edges of the rim with water, put the rolled-out pastry lid on top and seal the edges, pressing lightly with index finger and thumb. Crimp the edges neatly with a pastry crimper.

Decorate the top with pieces of lining paste (or rough puff paste) cut out in fancy shapes, and brush the top with beaten egg.

Make a hole or a *chimney* in the middle. Butter a piece of thin cardboard, roll it into a tube and place in the hole. (This chimney provides an outlet for steam during cooking.) Brush the top with beaten egg once again.

Baking of pâté (pie). Put the pâté into a hot oven and leave to bake, allowing 18 to 20 minutes per pound (35 to 40 minutes per kilo).

Final operations. Leave the pâté until completely cold. Pour a few tablespoons of melted butter (or warm lard) through the hole in the middle to fill up any gaps in the forcemeat, or, if the pâté is intended for immediate consumption, pour into it some meat, chicken or game jelly, depending on the nature of the pâté. (The jelly should be semi-liquid.)

Do not turn out until the butter or the jelly, which have been poured in, are cold, and, therefore, sufficiently solidified. Keep in a cool place until ready to serve.

Note. The above method of preparation for meat, poultry or game pâtés (pies) is also applicable to fish or shellfish pâtés (pies).

Hot or cold pâté fumets—These fumets are made from the bones, skins and parings of poultry or game used in the preparation of the pâté (or pie). See STOCK.

These bones and parings are lightly fried in butter with a *mirepoix** of vegetables, moistened with white wine (or liqueur wine, depending on the nature of the preparation), then boiled down, moistened with veal stock or gravy, or *Demi-glace sauce* (see SAUCE) and cooked to the consistency of an essence and strained.

HOT PÂTÉS (Pies). PÂTÉS CHAUDS—Recipes are given below for fish and shellfish, game and poultry pâtés.

FISH AND SHELLFISH PÂTÉS (Pies). PÂTÉS DE POISSON, DE CRUSTACÉS:

Hot eel pâté (pie). PÂTÉ CHAUD D'ANGUILLE—Cut boned eel fillets into thin slices about $2\frac{1}{2}$ inches long. Stud them with truffles or, if preferred, with de-salted anchovy fillets. Marinate for 2 hours in white wine, brandy, oil, salt, pepper and dried *fines herbes* (chopped parsley, tarragon and chives).

Fry the fillets briskly in butter and sprinkle with chopped shallots.

Line an oval-shaped mould with ordinary pastry dough, cover the walls and the bottom with a layer of *Pike forcemeat* (or other fish forcemeat, see FORCEMEAT) mixed with diced truffles.

Fill the pâté with the eel escalopes, alternating with layers of pike forcemeat and pour the marinating liquor over the top. Cover with another layer of forcemeat, sprinkle with melted butter and put on a piece of rolled-out pastry as a lid. Decorate the top of the pâté with pieces of rolled-out pastry cut in fancy shapes. Make a hole in the middle to allow steam to escape.

Bake in a moderate oven from $1\frac{1}{2}$ to 2 hours, depending on the size of the pâté.

At the last moment, through the opening in the top, pour in a few tablespoons of *Demi-glace* or *Velouté sauce*, based on fish stock (see SAUCE).

Note. Instead of adding a *salpicon** of truffles to the forcemeat, diced mushrooms, tossed in butter and sprinkled with chopped *fines herbes**, can be put into it.

Eel pâté can be garnished inside with shelled crayfish tails, in which case *Crayfish sauce* (see SAUCE) is poured in at the end.

The pâté can also be filled simply with the fish, covering each layer of eel escalopes with a layer of truffle slivers.

Eel pâté to be served cold is prepared in the same manner. When it is cold, pour a few tablespoons of fish aspic jelly (made from the bones and parings of eel) into it, or, if the pâté has to be kept for some time, a few tablespoons of melted, almost cold butter. See EEL.

Hot lamprey pâté (pie) à la bordelaise. PÂTÉ CHAUD DE LAMPROIE À LA BORDELAISE—Prepare as *Hot eel pâté** using fillets of lamprey and *Fish forcemeat* (see FORCEMEAT) mixed with chopped parsley and chives. Put a layer of the white part of leeks, sliced and lightly cooked in butter, and a layer of truffle slivers between each layer of lamprey fillets.

Hot salmon pâté (pie). PÂTÉ CHAUD DE SAUMON—Prepare in an oval-shaped mould, lined with *Fine lining paste* (see DOUGH) as *Hot eel pâté*, using slices of salmon, *Pike forcemeat* (see FORCEMEAT), truffles and other garnish.

Hot salmon pâté (pie) en pantin. PÂTÉ CHAUD DE SAUMON EN PANTIN—Prepare using sliced salmon, pike forcemeat, truffles and other garnish, putting all these ingredients into the pâté in alternate layers, on an oval-shaped mould, lined with *Fine lining paste* (see DOUGH).

When all the ingredients have been put in, cover with a rolled-out piece of pastry, seal and crimp up the edges.

Decorate the top with pieces of rolled-out pastry cut in fancy shapes, brush with beaten egg, make a hole in the middle to allow steam to escape and bake in a slow oven as an ordinary pâté.

Note. This hot pâté can be made of common brioche pastry dough (as for a coulibiac), instead of lining paste.

Also, instead of making it in the traditional '*pantin*' (crescent) shape, it can be made as a turnover, that is to say a disc of rolled-out pastry folded over to form a semi-circular pastry or pâté.

Hot salmon pâté (pie) à la russe I. PÂTÉ CHAUD DE SAUMON À LA RUSSE—'I shall give you the details', says Carême, 'of this hot pâté as I have seen it made in the house of the Russian Ambassador (Prince Kurakin), by his Russian cook.

'*Manner of procedure*. Having cut a small fillet of salmon into slices, season with *fines herbes**, salt, pepper and grated nutmeg. Dredge a small *Strasbourg foie gras*, cut in slices, in the same seasoning and herbs. Chop 12 hard boiled yolks of egg. Line the pâté mould as usual for a hot pâté, garnish the walls and the bottom with rice cooked in good chicken stock (the rice, as well as the rest of the garnish, should be cold). Put in a layer of salmon slices, sprinkle with chopped yolks, cover with slices of foie gras and follow up with a sprinkling of yolks. Repeat the process again with the same filling of salmon and foie gras. Pour over some butter flavoured with *fines herbes** (in which the foie gras and the salmon have been tossed). Cover the rest with a layer of rice and finish making the pâté as usual. Bake it for an hour and a half and serve at once.

'*Note*. The Russian cook put no sauce in, but it seems to me that a good concentrated *Demi-espagnole** will give more taste and will render this strange ragoût more delicate.' (*Traité des entrées chaudes de pâtisseries*, by Carême.)

Hot salmon pâté (pie) à la russe II—See COULIBIAC.

Hot sole pâté (pie). PÂTÉ CHAUD DE SOLES—Prepare as *Hot eel pâté* in an oval or rectangular mould, lined with *Fine lining paste* (see DOUGH), using fillets of sole, *Fish forcemeat* (see FORCEMEAT), truffle and other garnish.

Note. This pâté can be made by filling it with rolled fillets of sole, stuffed with truffled fish forcemeat.

Hot spiny lobster and other shellfish pâté (pie). PÂTÉ CHAUD DE LANGOUSTE—Prepare as *Hot eel pâté* replacing the eel by slices of the shellfish in question. The forcemeat used for this pâté should have some compound butter, flavoured and coloured with the appropriate shellfish, added to it.

This pâté is usually made in an oval or rectangular *pantin* (crescent) shape.

Hot turbot pâté (pie). PÂTÉ CHAUD DE TURBOT—Prepare as *Hot eel pâté*, in an oval or rectangular mould, replacing the eel by fillets of turbot.

Note. Proceeding as described in the recipe for *Hot eel pâté* and other recipes, pâtés can be made of all kinds of fish, such as brill, pike, cod, carp, sturgeon, eel-pout, whiting, grayling, salmon, trout, etc.

All these pâtés can be served cold.

HOT GAME PÂTÉS (Pies). PÂTÉS CHAUDS DE GIBIER.

Hot blackbird pâté (pie). PÂTÉ CHAUD DE MERLES—Prepare as described in the recipe for *Hot thrush pâté (pie)* below.

Hot hare pâté (pie). PÂTÉ CHAUD DE LIÈVRE—Prepare as *Hot rabbit pâté* (pie) below, using sliced hare meat, *Game forcemeat* (see FORCEMEAT) and truffles.

Hot lark pâté (pie) I. PÂTÉ CHAUD DE MAUVIETTES—Using boned larks, stuffed with foie gras or *Forcemeat à gratin* and truffles, prepare as *Hot Quail pâté (pie)* below.

Hot lark pâté II or Dijon roussotte. PÂTÉ CHAUD D'ALOUETTE, DIJONNAIS ROUSSOTTE—For 6 persons take 18 larks, ¾ pound (350 grams) of fresh pork fillet, 4 ounces (120 grams) of fat pork, 3½ ounces (100 grams) of cooked ham.

Bone the larks, leaving only the leg bones (keeping all the trail) and put them to marinate for 2 days in brandy, Madeira, salt, pepper and spices.

Cut the pork fillets and the fat pork into large dice and brown lightly on a high flame. Leave until quite cold, then pound in a mortar, incorporating the cooked ham, 5 or 6 good truffles and the larks' trail, lightly fried in butter. Taste, add seasoning, if necessary, and rub through a fine sieve.

Reshape the larks, stuffing with a little forcemeat, a piece of truffle and a piece of foie gras.

Line a mould or a pan (*bain-marie** type) with very fine *lining paste* (see DOUGH). Cover the paste with very thin rashers (slices) of bacon, spread a little forcemeat on the bottom and put in the larks, placing them in rows and interspersing each row with a thin layer of forcemeat. Put on a pastry lid (without making any hole in the centre, as for other pies). Scatter 2 or 3 pieces of fresh butter on the top and bake in a slow oven for about one hour and a quarter. Turn out and serve as it is.

Note. This pâté can be served cold. In this case, intersperse the larks with good pieces of truffled foie gras and, when the pâté is cold, pour in some good game aspic jelly.

The larks can, of course, be replaced by thrushes, quails, etc. This pâté is also known as *Pâté Racouchot*.

Hot pheasant pâté (pie). PÂTÉ CHAUD DE FAISAN—Prepare, using jointed roast pheasant (kept very underdone) as described in the recipe for *Hot woodcock pâté (pie)*.

Hot quail pâté (pie) with truffles. PÂTÉ CHAUD DE CAILLES AUX TRUFFES—Line a low round mould with *Fine lining paste* (see DOUGH). Coat the walls and the bottom with *Forcemeat à gratin**. Fill with boned quails, stuffed with foie gras and truffles, rolled into little ballottines and half-cooked in Madeira-flavoured braising stock. Fill the middle of the mould (the quails being arranged in a circle) with truffles lightly tossed in butter. Cover with a pastry lid and finish making the pâté in the usual manner. Bake in a moderate oven for about an hour.

Before serving, pour into the pâté a few tablespoons of *Demi-glace sauce* (see SAUCE) having added to it the liquor left from braising the quails.

Note. This type of pâté is usually made in shallow moulds; it is a *croustade** more than a *pâté* and is usually described on the menus as *Croustade of quails*.

Hot rabbit pie (pâté) with truffles. PÂTÉ CHAUD DE LAPEREAU AUX TRUFFES—Slice the fillets of two young rabbits and brown them briskly in butter without actually cooking them.

Take the flesh of the shoulders and legs off the bones, prepare a fine forcemeat and add to it half its weight of pork forcemeat.

Line an oval or round mould with *Fine lining paste* (see DOUGH) and spread the walls and the bottom with a layer of the forcemeat.

Fill the pâté with slices of rabbit meat putting them in rows, covering each row with slivers of truffles, lightly tossed in butter, and a layer of the forcemeat.

Cover with a pastry lid and finish making the pâté as described above. Bake in a moderate oven from one hour to one hour and a quarter, depending on size.

Thrush or blackbird pâté (pie). PÂTÉ DE GRIVES, DE MERLES—Prepare, using boned and stuffed thrushes and blackbirds as described in the recipe for *Lark pâté* or *Woodcock pâté*.

Hot thrush pâté (pie) à l'ardennaise. PÂTÉ CHAUD DE GRIVES À L'ARDENNAISE—Bone and stuff the thrushes with juniper-flavoured game *Forcemeat à gratin*, as *Hot quail pie*, but without the truffles. Put a piece of lean bacon, lightly fried in butter, between each thrush.

Just before serving pour into the pâté a few tablespoons of concentrated game stock (made of the carcases and parings of thrushes), flavoured with juniper berries.

Hot thrush pâté (pie) à la cévenole. PÂTÉ CHAUD DE GRIVES À LA CÉVENOLE—Prepare as *Hot quail pâté*, using boned thrushes stuffed with *Forcemeat à gratin**. Garnish the pâté with braised chestnuts (half-cooked) and lean rashers (strips) of bacon, scalded and fried lightly.

At the last moment pour into the pâté a few tablespoons of Madeira-flavoured game *fumet**.

Hot woodcock pâté (pie) with truffles. PÂTÉ CHAUD DE BÉCASSES AUX TRUFFES—Line an oval-shaped pie mould with fine lining paste. Coat the walls and the bottom with a layer of game *Forcemeat à gratin**, mixed with the livers and the trail of the birds, rubbed through a sieve.

Put in the breasts of 2 woodcocks, roasted and kept very underdone. Bone the legs, pound the flesh in a mortar and add to the forcemeat.

Cover with thick slices of truffles, lightly tossed in butter and over these spread a layer of forcemeat. Cover the pâté with a piece of rolled-out pastry, finish making it in the usual manner, and bake in the oven for about an hour.

Note. This pâté can also be made of boned woodcock, stuffed with foie gras and truffles, as described in the recipe for *Hot chicken pâté (pie)*.

Hot pâtés (pies) of wood-pigeon, partridge and other game. PÂTÉ CHAUD DE PALOMBE, PERDREAU—Using the meat of the game chosen, prepare as pheasant or woodcock pie.

HOT MEAT PÂTÉS. PÂTÉS DE VIANDES DIVERSES.

Hot beef pâté (pie) à la parisienne. PÂTÉ CHAUD DE BOEUF À LA PARISIENNE—Line a round or oval-shaped pie mould with *Fine lining paste* (see DOUGH) as usual. Coat the bottom and the walls with a *quenelle forcemeat* (see FORCEMEAT) made of a mixture of beef and veal—half-and-half. Fill the pâtés with thin slices of fillet of beef, previously marinated for one hour in white wine and brandy with *fines herbes** and chopped shallots, seasoned with salt, pepper and spices, fried quickly in butter until they are half-cooked and left to get cold.

Put these slices of beef into the pâté in layers, scattering some sliced mushrooms, fried in butter, on each layer. Put on a layer of forcemeat, sprinkle with melted butter, cover with a piece of rolled-out pastry and finish making the pâté in the usual manner. Bake in a slow oven from one hour to an hour and a quarter.

Before serving, pour into the pâté a few tablespoons of *demi-glace**, reduced (boiled down) with the marinating liquor.

Hot calf's sweetbreads pâté (pie) à l'ancienne. PÂTÉ CHAUD DE RIS DE VEAU À L'ANCIENNE—Line an oval-shaped, rather low, pie dish with *Fine lining paste.* Coat the bottom and walls with a layer of *godiveau* (veal forcemeat) *à la crème* mixed with chopped truffles (see FORCEMEAT).

Put on the bottom a layer of truffles and mushrooms, sliced and lightly fried in butter. On this garnish put two calf's sweetbreads, half-braised in a *court-bouillon**. Cover with truffles and mushrooms. Sprinkle with melted butter. Put on the pastry lid and finish making the pâté as described above. Bake in a moderate oven from 45 minutes to an hour, depending on the size of the pâté.

Before serving, pour into the pâté a few tablespoons of *Velouté sauce* (see SAUCE) cooked with cream.

Note. This pâté can also be filled with calf's sweetbreads, sliced and lightly fried in butter.

Lamb pâté (pie) à la périgourdine I. PÂTÉ D'AGNEAU À LA PÉRIGOURDINE—Line a pâté mould with pastry as described above. Cover the walls with a mixture of finely pounded *Veal and pork forcemeat* (see FORCEMEAT).

Fill the dish with alternate rows of lamb's sweetbreads half-cooked in butter, slices of *foie gras* and slivers of truffles, lightly fried in butter. End with a layer of forcemeat. Cover with a piece of rolled-out pastry as described. Bake for 45 minutes to an hour.

When cooked, pour into the pâté a few tablespoons of *Périgueux sauce* (see SAUCE).

Hot lamb pâté (pie) à la périgourdine II. PÂTÉ D'AGNEAU À LA PÉRIGOURDINE—Prepare as in previous recipe, but replace lamb's sweetbreads by little escalopes of loin or fillets of lamb, briskly fried in butter for just long enough to stiffen them.

Hot lamb sweetbreads pâté (pie). PÂTÉ CHAUD DE RIS D'AGNEAU—Prepare as *Hot calf's sweetbreads pâté*, using lamb's sweetbreads, blanched and lightly fried in butter.

Hot Anglo-French mutton pie. PÂTÉ CHAUD DE MOUTON ANGLO-FRANÇAIS—'Having trimmed the fillets of four loins of mutton, cut and trim into slices and season on both sides with salt, coarsely ground pepper and nutmeg. Then warm slightly eight ounces of Isigny butter, add two tablespoons of parsley, twice the amount of mushrooms and the same quantity of truffles, all finely chopped, and a blanched and chopped shallot (this mixture used to be known in old culinary practice as *fines herbes*).

'Line the pie dish as usual (with fine lining paste), dip the fillets into the butter *aux fines herbes* and, one by one, put them in the pie dish, arranging them in a circle. Fill the middle with the best, correctly peeled, cooked, white mushrooms, sliced truffles or artichoke hearts, or some escalopes of lamb's or calf's sweetbreads. Sprinkle the rest of the butter *aux fines herbes* on top.

'Finish making the pâté in the usual manner and put in a lively oven. Bake for an hour and a half. When ready to serve, remove the bacon rasher and the two bay leaves (put in the pie under the piece of pastry forming the lid), cover with mutton *demi-glace* blended with some mushroom or truffle essence and add the juice of one lemon.

'Or you can remove surplus fat from the hot pâté and pour over a good *espagnole* with mushrooms, truffles, artichoke hearts and lamb's sweetbreads, or tomato sauce.' (A. Carême.)

Hot pork pâté (pie) à la hongroise. PÂTÉ CHAUD DE PORC À LA HONGROISE—Line a round or oval-shaped pie mould with *Fine lining paste* (see DOUGH). Coat the walls and the bottom with some *godiveau* (veal *forcemeat**) spiced with chopped chives and seasoned with paprika.

Line the bottom of the pâté with a thick layer of onions and mushrooms, cut in small dice, cooked gently in butter, seasoned with salt and paprika and bound with a few tablespoons of *Velouté sauce* (see SAUCE).

On this garnish put thin slices of pork, previously marinated and browned quickly in butter. Cover with a layer of *godiveau*; put on a piece of rolled-out pastry as a lid and finish making the pâté in the usual manner. Bake in a slow oven for an hour or an hour and a quarter.

Just before serving, pour a few tablespoons of *Paprika sauce* (see SAUCE, *Hungarian sauce*) into the pâté.

Note. This type of pâté is usually served as a *croustade**.

Hot fillet of veal pâté (pie). PÂTÉ CHAUD DE FILET DE VEAU—Proceed as for *Hot beef pâté (pie) à la parisienne*, using slices of veal and quenelle *forcemeat**.

HOT POULTRY PÂTÉS. PÂTÉS DE VOLAILLES.

Hot chicken pâté (pie) I. PÂTÉ CHAUD DE POULARDE EN PANTIN—This pâté is made in the shape of a '*pantin*' (crescent) using a boned fowl, stuffed with a fine *Foie gras forcemeat* (see FORCEMEAT), slivers of chicken meat and truffles, rolled into a *ballottine*, half-cooked in chicken stock and left to get cold.

Put this fowl on an oval-shaped rolled-out piece of pastry, covered with bacon rashers (strips). Cover with another piece of rolled-out pastry and seal the edges.

Decorate the top of the pâté with pieces of pastry cut out in fancy shapes. Brush with beaten egg, make one or two holes to allow steam to escape. Bake in a moderate oven from 1½ to 2 hours depending on the size of the pie.

Just before serving pour into the pâté a few tablespoons of brown chicken stock flavoured with truffle *fumet** or *Chicken velouté sauce* cooked with cream (see SAUCE).

Note. You can also, instead of pouring the sauce into the pâté, which makes the cutting difficult, serve the sauce separately.

Hot chicken pâté II. PÂTÉ CHAUD DE POULARDE—Prepare the pâté in an oval, round or rectangular mould, following the instructions given for the preparation of pâtés.

Fill with slices or fillets of fowl, fried in butter, chicken or quenelle *forcemeat**, truffles and other garnish.

Cover the pâté, decorate the top, brush with beaten egg and bake in a moderate oven.

Note. Pâtés prepared of various kinds of poultry, whether baked in moulds or shaped into 'crescents' can also be served cold.

Rouen duckling pâté. PÂTÉ DE CANETON ROUENNAIS—Prepare in a 'pantin' (crescent) shape, as *Lark pâté*, or in a mould, as *Woodcock pâté*, using boned duckling, stuffed with *Forcemeat à gratin**, foie gras and truffles.

Hot Rouen duckling pâté (pie) à la rouennaise. PÂTÉ CHAUD DE CANETON DE ROUEN À LA ROUENNAISE—Roast a plump Rouen duckling keeping it very underdone. Cut the breast into not-too-thin slices. Skin the legs, remove bones, pound the flesh in a mortar and rub it through a sieve. Add to it three times its weight of *Forcemeat à gratin** and some diced truffles. Add the blood pressed out of the duckling's carcase to the forcemeat. Season it well and add 2 tablespoons of calvados which has been set alight.

Choose an oval-shaped mould (either a hinged mould or one with low sides), line it with *Fine lining paste* (see DOUGH), mixed with truffles shredded into a fine *julienne** during rolling, and coat the walls and the bottom with a layer of poultry meat or *Quenelle forcemeat* (see FORCEMEAT).

Fill the pâté with slices of duckling, alternating with layers of truffled forcemeat à gratin and sliced mushrooms and truffles, lightly tossed in butter. End with a layer of poultry meat forcemeat, cover with a piece of rolled-out pastry and finish making the pâté in the usual manner.

Bake in a moderate oven from one hour to one hour and a quarter, depending on the size. At the last moment pour into the pâté a few tablespoons of *Rouennaise sauce* (see SAUCE).

Hot foie gras and truffle pâté (pie). PÂTÉ CHAUD DE FOIE GRAS AUX TRUFFES—In principle this type of pâté is made by filling a pie crust baked blind (empty), lined with a layer of *Purée of foie gras* or *Forcemeat à gratin**, with a whole goose liver (foie gras), cooked in port, sherry, or other liqueur wine. The pâté is garnished with truffles, sliced and fried lightly in butter; and a few tablespoons of sauce, flavoured with port or other liqueur wine and mixed with the concentrated liquor left from cooking the liver, is poured in.

Prepared in this manner the hot foie gras pâté is really a sort of a *timbale* and is often described as such on the menu.

Hot foie gras pâté can also be prepared as *Hot chicken pâté*. The liver is half-cooked with port (studded with truffles or not, as the case may be), placed in a mould, lined with *Fine lining paste* (see DOUGH), coated with a layer of foie gras or other forcemeat, covered with a piece of rolled-out pastry and finished as described in the general instructions on making pâtés.

After baking, a few tablespoons of *Demi-glace sauce* cooked with truffle *fumet** are poured into the pâté (see SAUCE).

Note. Like all hot pâtés for which we give recipes in this section, the foie gras pâté described above can be served cold. A few tablespoons of semi-liquid aspic jelly should be poured into it when it is quite cold.

Hot pâtés (pies) made of various kinds of poultry. PÂTÉS CHAUDS DE VOLAILLES—These pâtés (pies) can be made of turkeys, geese, pigeons, guinea-fowls, etc., by following the recipe given for *Hot chicken pâté (pie)*.

These birds are used either whole, boned and stuffed, or sliced.

COLD PÂTÉS (PIES). PÂTÉS FROIDS—These pâtés and pies, made of various meats, poultry, game, fish and shellfish, are mostly prepared as hot pâtés (pies). They are made either in moulds or '*en pantin*', that is to say, 'crescents' shaped by hand.

When cold, either chicken, game or fish aspic jelly, depending on the nature of the pâté, or—if the pâté has to be kept for some time—melted butter or lard, are poured into it through the hole in the top.

Generally speaking, cold pâtés (pies)—whatever they are made of—should be prepared at least 12 hours before they are required for the table.

All the pastes, forcemeats and *fumets** indicated for the preparation of hot pâtés, can also be used for making cold pâtés.

Amiens duck pâté. PÂTÉ DE CANARD D'AMIENS—These pâtés enjoy a justly merited reputation, for they are excellent.

'At present there are two kinds of pâté made in Amiens: pâté of boned duck and pâté made of duck which has not been boned. In the original recipe the duck was not boned. In our time, in an effort to improve the pâté, boning was introduced.

'The duck pâté is made without a mould; it is shaped by hand.

'Here is a recipe for pâté, for which the duck is not boned, as it was made in Amiens towards the middle of the last century.

'*The preparation of paste: Ingredients.* 3¾ cups (500 grams) of sifted flour, ¼ pound (125 grams) of lard, 1 tablespoon of olive oil, 1 whole egg, 1½ teaspoons (10 grams) of fine salt and about 1½ tablespoons of water.

'*Method.* Spread the flour on a board in a circle, make a well in the middle and put in the salt. Break the egg into it and dissolve the salt with it, then add olive oil. Knead the lard, if it is hard, and mix with the liquid part of the ingredients in the middle of the flour. Rub the lard and the flour together, without moistening at all. When the paste is well mixed, spread it on a marble slab and sprinkle with cold water. Keep it on the firm side. Collect all together into one lump and leave the paste to rest in a cool place for at least 2 hours before using. (This paste is not edible; it has the great advantage of changing very little in baking.)

'*The preparation of the duck.* Only very young ducklings, which take very little cooking time, should be used for these pâtés.

'The duck having been killed, plucked, cleaned out and singed, remove carefully any innards which may have been left in. Cut off the pinions a little below the first joint from the shoulder.

'Cut off the feet at the joint. Season the duck with spiced salt, inside and outside. Slice a little breast of pork, previously scalded, and soften it in a little fat on a low fire. When the pork is nicely fried, remove it and fry the duck, on a low fire, turning to brown on all sides. Drain the duck on a dish and leave to cool before making the pâté.

'*Preparation of the forcemeat.* Forcemeat *à gratin* is always used for this pâté. This forcemeat is composed, depending on supplies available, either of calf's or chicken livers. It goes without saying, of course, that the duck's liver will be kept and added to this forcemeat.

'*Ingredients.* 1 pound (500 grams) of calf's or chicken livers, 5 ounces (150 grams) shredded fat bacon, 1 medium-sized onion, 3 teaspoons (15 grams) of spiced salt, a few fragments of thyme and bay leaf and 2 chopped shallots.

'*Method.* Render down the fat bacon on a low fire and fry in this fat the liver or livers, trimmed and cut in large dice. When the livers are fried, add the onion and shallots and season with spiced salt, thyme and bay leaf. Cover and leave for a minute or two on the edge of the stove. Remove from fire and leave to get cold, then pound in the mortar and rub the forcemeat through a fine sieve.

'When the paste, the forcemeat and the duck are ready, proceed to make the pâté.

'*The preparation of the pâté.* Divide the paste into two equal parts. Using half the paste, roll it out into an oval-shaped piece one centimetre thick. This piece of paste should be a little longer and wider than the duck. Put this piece of paste in the middle of a baking sheet or baking tin, slightly moistened with a little cold water to make the paste adhere. Spread the middle of it with a quarter of the forcemeat, place the fried and cold duck in the forcemeat and season again with spiced salt and cayenne pepper. The cayenne pepper seasoning should be light, for, although the pâté must be condimented, it must not be uneatable. The duck, therefore, will be lying on its back on a bed of forcemeat *à gratin.* Cover the duck with the rest of the forcemeat, putting it on the bird in such a way as to enclose it completely.

'Put another oval-shaped piece of rolled-out paste over the duck, seal the edges, crimp up the sides with a pastry-crimper and decorate the top with pieces of paste cut out in fancy shapes. Make a hole in the centre, to allow an outlet for steam.

'Brush the pâté with beaten egg. Bake in a hot oven from an hour and a quarter to an hour and a half, depending on size.' (M. Dumont-Lespine's recipe.)

Various fish pâtés (pies) (cold). PÂTÉS DE POISSONS—These pies are made in exactly the same way as those which are intended to be served hot. They can be shaped as '*pantins*' (crescents) or made in moulds lined with fine lining paste. See *Eel pâté (pie).*

Pâté of foie gras with truffles. PÂTÉ DE FOIE GRAS AUX TRUFFES—*The forcemeat.* Pound finely in a mortar (for a pâté for 10 persons) ¾ pound (375 grams) of lean pork, 1 pound (475 grams) of fresh bacon and 5 ounces (150 grams) of raw goose liver parings. Season this forcemeat with 5 teaspoons (25 grams) of *Spiced salt* (see SALT) and rub through a sieve.

Foie gras. Stud a big, pared goose liver (or two small livers) generously with pieces of truffle, seasoned with spiced salt. Marinate this liver in brandy and Madeira and season with spiced salt.

Preparation of pâté. Line a round or a hinged mould with *Lining paste* (see PASTRY DOUGH) made with butter or lard.

Coat the walls and the bottom of the mould with a layer of the forcemeat, to which a tablespoon of brandy and liquor left from marinating the liver have been added. Put the liver in the middle of the mould. Cover with a layer of forcemeat, piling it up in a dome. Place on top a rasher (slice) of bacon and a small bay leaf.

Cover with a piece of rolled-out pastry, seal and crimp up the edges. Decorate the top with pieces of pastry cut out in fancy shapes. Make a hole in the centre. Cut some pastry rings with a fluted-edged pastry cutter, superimpose several of them one on top of another and put around the hole. Brush with beaten egg.

Bake in a moderate oven, allowing 30 minutes per pound.

Leave the pâté to cool in the mould. When it is just warm, pour either some warm laid into the pâté (if it is to be kept for some time), or some Madeira-flavoured aspic jelly.

Note. The pâtés are cut in different ways, according to their shapes. Foie gras pâtés made in round moulds can be served in slices, cut from top to bottom. Bigger pâtés can be served in scallop shells, as follows: Remove the pastry lid, scrape off the surface fat layer and ladle out the pâté with a big silver spoon dipped into hot water. Scoop up enough pâté each time just to fill a shell. Put the filled shells on a plate.

Arrange the empty pâté crust on a napkin-covered dish, placing the pastry lid on it upside down. Garnish the lid with a layer of chopped jelly. Dispose the scallop shell of foie gras on it, piling them up in a heap.

Rectangular-shaped pâtés, which is the type most commonly found in shops, are cut in slices, which are then halved if they are too big, and arranged, overlapping slightly, on a long dish, covered with a napkin.

Ham pâté (pie). PÂTÉ DE JAMBON—This is made in an oval-shaped mould, like *Veal and ham pâté (pie)*, the recipe for which will be found below, using forcemeat indicated in that recipe, mixed with chopped lean ham, or *panada* and butter forcemeat, also mixed with chopped ham, and slices of raw ham. When the pâté (pie) is cold, pour into it some Madeira-flavoured aspic jelly. The use of truffles in this pâté (pie) is optional.

Lark pâté en pantin. PÂTÉ D'ALOUETTES EN PANTIN—Bone the larks completely and stuff with *Forcemeat à gratin** studded with a piece of truffle. Wrap each lark in a thin rasher (slice) of bacon.

Roll out a rectangular piece of lining paste, cover it with a thin bacon rasher, spread with a layer of forcemeat (truffled, if desired) and lay the larks on top. Cover the larks with a layer of forcemeat and over the forcemeat put a thin rasher of fat bacon.

Thin down the edges of the rolled-out piece of pastry with a rolling-pin, bring the edges together and seal them. Put the pâté upside down on a baking tray. Make one or two little holes to allow steam to escape during baking, brush with beaten egg and bake in a moderate oven.

Leave the pâté to get cold. Pour into it some game aspic jelly, or, if the pâté is not to be eaten at once, some melted butter.

Pithiviers lark pâté. PÂTÉ D'ALOUETTES—For this pâté the larks can be boned or left whole, according to taste.

Whether the larks are boned or not, stuff each with a little *Forcemeat à gratin**, one large cube of fresh goose liver (foie gras) and a medium-sized truffle. Season the larks with spiced salt, wrap in thin bacon rashers (slices) and lay them out side by side on a rolled-out piece of pastry, spread with a thin layer of forcemeat. Cover the larks with the same forcemeat and finish making the pâté, giving a square form (these pâtés are shaped by hand). Leave to rest for a night and bake on the following day. When the pâté is cold, pour into it some *Aspic jelly**.

To serve, cut the pâté into small rectangular pieces in such a way as to make sure that each piece contains a whole lark. Do away with the crust surrounding the sides of the pâté and serve only the top and bottom crust.

Partridge pâté (pie). PÂTÉ DE PERDREAU—Prepare in an oval or rectangular mould like *Woodcock pâté*.

Pheasant pâté. PÂTÉ DE FAISAN—Using boned and stuffed pheasant, prepare like *Woodcock pâté*.

This pâté can also be made using a boned pheasant, cut into thin slices. The pâté is lined with these thin slices alternating with rows of slivers of foie gras and truffles, the whole sealed down with *Game forcemeat* (see FORCEMEAT).

Pâtés (pies) made out of various kinds of poultry. PÂTÉS DE VOLAILLES—These pâtés can be made out of fowl, chicken, turkey, pigeon, or guinea fowl, boned, stuffed with appropriate forcemeat, foie gras and truffles, or with the flesh of the appropriate bird cut in thin slices, with foie gras, truffles and forcemeat, as described in the recipe for *Cold veal and ham pâté*. They can be shaped into '*pantin*' (crescents) by hand or baked in oval or rectangular moulds, lined with fine lining paste.

Veal and ham pâté (pie). PÂTÉ DE VEAU ET JAMBON—*The filling*. 10 ounces (300 grams) of lean veal, 10 ounces (300 grams) of lean pork, 7 ounces (200 grams) of ham, 1 pound (500 grams) of *Fine forcemeat* (see FORCEMEAT), 7 ounces (200 grams) of fat bacon, $\frac{1}{2}$ cup (1 decilitre) of Madeira and 3 to 4 teaspoons (20 grams) of *Spiced salt* (see SALT).

Preparation of the pâté (pie). Remove all sinews from the veal (taken from the chump end of loin) and cut into little strips about 4 inches long. Prepare the pork and the ham in a similar manner and put all these meats into a bowl. Season with spiced salt. Sprinkle with Madeira and leave to steep for several hours.

To heighten the taste of these ingredients, they can be sprinkled with a small quantity of *fines herbes** and chopped shallots.

Lining the mould. Line the mould (round, oval or rectangular in shape) with *pastry dough* or *lining paste* (see PASTRY DOUGH), prepared in advance and left to rest for some time.

Cover this paste on the walls and the bottom with thin rashers (slices) of fat bacon and coat with a layer of *fine forcemeat*.

Fill the pâté (pie) with veal, pork and ham in alternate rows, sealing them down with a thin layer of forcemeat.

Add some truffles cut in quarters, in whatever quantity desired. Finish off with rather a thick layer of forcemeat.

Roll out the rest of the paste into a circle of the same diameter as the opening of the mould. Put it over the pâté (pie) and seal the edges, pinching them between the index finger and the thumb.

Finish by crimping all the edges with a pastry-crimper.

Brush the top with beaten egg and decorate with pieces of pastry rolled out very thin and cut in fancy shapes.

Make a hole or a chimney in the middle. Roll a piece of buttered cardboard and put it into the hole. The object of this chimney is to hasten the cooking process and to prevent the pie walls from subsiding.

Brush with beaten egg once again.

Baking of the pâté (pie). Set the pâté in the oven and leave it there for about an hour and a quarter.

Final operations. Leave the *pâté* until it is completely cold. Through the hole in the middle pour into it some melted butter or lard, to seal any gaps. When this butter is solidified completely, turn out the pâté. If the pâté is to be eaten immediately, a few tablespoons of aspic jelly can be poured into it.

Woodcock pâté (pie). PÂTÉ DE BÉCASSES—Bone the woodcock completely and stuff with *Forcemeat à gratin** mixed with the chopped trail of the birds, pieces of foie gras and truffles. Reshape the woodcocks. Put them, wedging them in tightly one against another, into an oval mould, lined with pastry and bacon rashers (slices) and coated on the walls and bottom with *Game forcemeat* (see FORCEMEAT), truffled if desired. Cover with a layer of forcemeat. Place a rasher of bacon on this forcemeat. Cover with an oval-shaped piece of rolled-out pastry, seal and crimp the edges and decorate the top with pieces of rolled-out pastry cut out in fancy shapes. Make a hole in the centre, brush with beaten egg and bake in a moderate oven.

When the pâté is quite cold, pour into it some aspic jelly based on a game *fumet**.

PATELLA. PATELLE—Name applied to various gastropod molluscs. They are univalve, edible and known also by the name of *limpets*. They are eaten raw, like clams.

PATIENCE DOCK. PATIENCE—Name of various plants of the *Rumex* genus, among them *Herb Patience*, which has a bitter root, used in making depurative and anti-scorbutic decoctions. The leaves and petioles of the *Alpine dock*, known also as *Monk's rhubarb*, are eaten in the Alps, the Pyrenees and in the Auvergne, in soups and cooked as a vegetable. Rhubarb sorrel, which was already known as a pot herb in the times of antiquity, is mentioned by Horace.

PÂTISSERIE—French name for various preparations made of pastry, generally baked in the oven. The term also applies to the art of the pastry-cook, as well as to the place where pastries are made and sold.

We should have to go far back into the distant past to find the origins of pastry-making, but what has definitely been established is the fact that the Greeks began it; there are documents surviving to this day which mention the different kinds of pastries which delighted the palates of the gastronomes of the time. Bourdeau, in his *Histoire de l'Alimentation*, even attributes the invention of plum pudding to the Greeks.

In the Middle Ages in France the pastry-cooks were called *oubleyeurs*, after *oublie*, a sort of wafer cooked in irons, or gaufre moulds, which was their main product.

Until the Middle Ages the pastry-cooks were not governed by any laws except customs of the trade, but in 1268, Etienne Boileau in his *Livre des Métiers* laid down rules and statutes, which made provisions for relations between the masters and the workers (or valets) and fixed the duration of the apprenticeship, and the rise in salaries, not forgetting the fines incurred in the event of an infraction of the statutes. The preamble stated: 'Whoever wishes to become an *oubleyeur* in the city of Paris may do so freely and openly, provided he

A pastry-cook's shop in the eighteenth century, from Diderot's *Encyclopédie*. Victuals can be seen hanging from the ceiling; there is also the butcher's block (No. 8), which shows how much the pastry-cooks competed with the pork butchers

knows the trade, has the wherewithal and keeps to the usages and customs of the trade.'

These statutes were modified from century to century, embodying ever more restrictive clauses and the terms and conditions for obtaining the Master's certificate becoming more and more in favour of the Treasury and the King.

Rabelais in his *Fourth Book of Pantagruel* (Chapter 59) enumerates some of the pastries which were in great vogue at the time, such as big *Puff pastry*, *Gâteaux*, *Carves*, *Casse-museaux* (small cream buns), *Brides à veaux*, *Caillebotte* (curd cake), *Poupelins* ('baby dolls'), *Macaroons*, *Quince pies*, 20 kinds of tarts, 16 kinds of *tourtes**, etc.

As the years went by, numerous disagreements arose between the pastry-cooks, the bakers and the pork butchers, all accusing each other of trespassing on each other's trades. In the seventeenth century the bakers added the sale of small cakes to their trade. The pastry-cooks protested, started a court case and the Lieutenant-General of Police issued an order forbidding the master bakers to encroach on the trade of the said community of pastry-cooks. Later, another dispute arose in connection with Twelfth Night cakes†, which the bakers were in the habit of offering to clients who brought their bread to be baked in their ovens. They were forbidden to do so, but nevertheless continued to bake and offer these cakes. In 1794, however, the Twelfth Night cakes aroused the wrath of the Revolutionaries, who seemed to see liberticide tendencies in this mock-royal bean kingship.† The result was the following decree issued by Nicolas Chambon: 'It has come to my notice through the Revolutionary Committee that there are still some pastry-cooks who permit themselves to bake and sell Twelfth Night cakes. Taking into consideration that the pastry-cooks who do so have no other intentions but to destroy liberty and taking into consideration that certain persons may even have ordered this, no doubt with the aim of preserving the superstitious custom of the former aristocratic feast, the guilty pastry-cooks should be unmasked and suspended and an end should be put to the orgies at which they dare to fête the shadow of the tyrant.' That good Jacobin forgot that no decree or order on earth could possibly eradicate a time-honoured custom, let alone abolish a gourmand tradition.

The pastry-cooks were not greatly upset by this, and with some presence of mind overcame the difficulty by substituting Liberty cakes for Twelfth Night cakes, complete with Phrygian cap traced with the point of a kitchen knife on their golden surface. The bakers' annual generosity continued until 1914, then came the war with its hard restrictions and that was the end—this time without any decrees of the Twelfth Night cakes being offered to the clients.

The main dispute between the pastry-cooks and the pork butchers, ending in a long court case, arose in connection with a ham pâté made by a man called Noël. The pâté in question was a ham, cooked as usual and enclosed in pastry. The pork butchers, quite rightly, maintained that as the crust did not adhere to the ham it could not be considered a pie. It is true that only raw ingredients enclosed in pastry and cooked at the same time as the pastry can be considered as pies. The pork butchers, therefore, won their case.

From the beginning of the nineteenth century French pastry-making made great strides forward with Carême, the creator of large display or show pieces and of numerous elements of what is called '*pâtisserie de main*'. He perfected the existing cakes and created new ones, such as the *Croquembouche*, *Mille-feuille*, *Sultanes*, decorated with pulled sugar, etc. This was also the epoch of great *pâtissiers*, such as Rouget, Leblanc, Jacquet, Félix and Lesage, the great specialist of display pieces. Later, towards 1844, came the Julien dynasty, founders of cake shops in the Bourse, Favart and Boulevard des Italiens, prolific creators to whom we owe such cakes as *Trois-frères*, *Savarin*, *Gorenflot*, *Regent*, *Richelieu* and *Paris-pâté*. Along with them, the cake shops of Seugnot, Bourbonneux, Quillet, Chiboust, Frascati, Petit (almost all of which have now disappeared) vied with each other. All these houses specialised in the creation of numerous cakes, such as *Bourdaloue*, *Saint-honoré*, *Napolitain*,

Châteaubriand, *Cussy*, *Ambroisie* (or Genoese cake) and many others, forgotten now in the never-ceasing search for novel delicacies created by the admirable modern pastry-cooks.

† Twelfth Night cake—a decorated cake which used to be prepared for and eaten on the Feast of the Epiphany (January 6th). Usually a bean (or, in later years, a silver coin) was baked in the cake. The person getting this at the Twelfth Night feast was accepted as King for the occasion.

PÂTISSIÈRE (NOIX)—French culinary term for the chump end of the loin of veal, which is situated in the fillet. It is sometimes called round of veal.

PATRONNET—French name for a pastry-cook's young apprentice.

PATTIES. Petits pâtés:

Small hot patties. Petits pâtés chauds—As their name indicates, small hot patties are the diminutive versions of big hot entrée pies and pâtés. They are served as hors-d'oeuvre and as small entrées.

'Small patties,' said Carême, 'are perfect only when eaten straight out of the oven. If they are allowed to get cold and are then reheated, they lose some of their quality.'

Richelieu, who, as is well known, was a great gastronome (the invention of mayonnaise is attributed to him), said that to eat excellent small patties 'one should have an oven in the pocket of one's waistcoat.'

In days gone by patties used to be sold in the streets of Paris to the accompaniment of the cry: 'Piping hot! Piping hot!' These patties, perhaps, did not have much taste, but, being eaten piping hot, they delighted those who consumed them.

Today, some bakers and caterers still sell a sort of patty, filled with sausage meat or a *salpicon** of pork, but instead of being round or oval in shape, they are rectangular. They are known as '*friands*'.

In the section devoted to hot hors-d'oeuvre, various recipes for the preparation of patties will be found.

Little Russian patties. Petits pâtés à la russe—These little patties are served as an accompaniment to soup, and are made of *Puff pastry* or common *Brioche dough* (see DOUGH). They can be filled with various compositions, especially various fish forcemeats, principally salmon.

PAUCHOUSE OR POCHOUSE—A kind of *Matelote à la bourguignonne** made of all freshwater fish. Moisten with red (or white) wine, set alight with brandy and blend with kneaded butter. Garnish with diced breast of pork and small onions, which should be cooked with the fish. Serve with bread croûtons, buttered, dried in the oven and rubbed with garlic.

PAUILLAC—Commune of the department of Gironde where the famous Pauillac milk-fed lambs are raised. See LAMB.

PAUNCH (Belly)—See OFFAL OR VARIETY MEATS.

PAUPIETTES—Thin slices of beef or other meat, stuffed with some forcemeat, rolled into paupiettes (i.e. into the shape of big corks) wrapped in a thin rasher (slice) of bacon and braised in very little liquid. Paupiettes are served with a vegetable garnish. See BEEF, *Paupiettes of beef*.

Paupiettes can also be made out of fillets of fish. See SOLE, *Paupiettes of sole*.

Paupiettes of lamb à la créole. Paupiettes d'agneau à la créole—Cut some lamb (taken from the leg or the shoulder) into escalopes, flatten them well and spread with a *Fine pork forcemeat* (see FORCEMEAT) mixed with chopped onion, fried in butter, with half its weight of sweet pimentos cut in very small dice.

Roll the escalopes into paupiettes and tie them with string. Put into a sauté pan in which ½ cup (100 grams) of chopped onion has been softened in butter. Brown the paupiettes with the onion.

Add 2 peeled, seeded and chopped tomatoes. Season with salt and pepper and add a *bouquet garni**, a pinch of garlic and a small piece of lemon rind. Cook in the oven, uncovered, for 45 minutes.

Drain the paupiettes. Arrange them on a round dish. Garnish the middle of the dish with *Rice à la créole**. Boil down (reduce) the pan juices, strain and pour over the paupiettes.

Paupiettes of veal à la grecque, also called Boucon à la grecque. Paupiettes de veau à la grecque, Boucon à la grecque—*Method.* Beat the veal escalopes, cut rather longer than they are wide, to flatten them well; season with salt and pepper and sprinkle with chopped chervil, tarragon and chives.

Put a very thin slice of ham on each escalope. Roll the paupiettes and tie with string.

Put them, packing them in tightly, into an earthenware casserole buttered and lined with sliced onions and mushrooms. Sweat (cook gently) with a lid on.

Moisten with a few tablespoons of Cyprus wine, simmer, add some good veal stock and braise in the oven. When the paupiettes are nearly done, add some sliced truffles.

Serve with the braising liquor.

PAVÉ—Term describing a cold dish composed of some sort of a mixture (most frequently, a mousse), set in a special square or rectangular mould, coated with jelly and decorated with truffles, etc.

The name *pavé* also applies to certain square-shaped cakes, made of Genoese (or sponge) layers, sandwiched with a butter cream of sorts, as well as to spice cake.

Pavé of chicken à l'écarlate. Pavé de volaille à l'écarlate—Coat a plain, square mould with very clear chicken aspic jelly, flavoured with Madeira. Decorate the mould on the inside with little circlets of pickled tongue, thin slices of chicken breast and round slivers of truffles (alternating the colours). Spoon a little aspic jelly over the decorations to seal them.

Fill the mould with alternate layers of chicken mousse and pickled tongue mousse (both mousses bound with aspic jelly). Put some slivers of truffles between each layer.

Cover with a layer of chicken aspic jelly and chill on ice.

Turn out the pavé on to a round dish. Surround with round, even slices of pickled tongue, decorated with slivers of truffle and glazed with jelly. Garnish with chopped jelly.

Pavé of foie gras à la king. Pavé du roi, au foie gras—This pavé is not made of mousse set in a square mould. It is composed of a big, fat goose liver, generously studded with truffles, enclosed in *Fine lining paste* (see DOUGH), rolled out in a circle and shaped into a '*pantin*', i.e. 'crescent', decorated on top with fleurs-de-lys cut out of paste. It is, in fact, a kind of foie gras pie fashioned by hand instead of being baked in a mould.

When this pie is cold, some port-flavoured jelly is poured into it.

Pavé of foie gras with truffles (cold). PAVÉ DE FOIE GRAS AUX TRUFFES—Line a square or rectangular mould with jelly flavoured with sherry (or other liqueur wine), decorate with slivers of truffles and fill with *Foie gras mousse* (see MOUSSE) and slices of foie gras and truffles, putting them into the mould in alternate layers. Cover with a layer of jelly. Chill on ice. Turn out on to a serving dish and garnish with chopped jelly.

Pavé of pheasant or other game à la Saint-Hubert. PAVÉ DE FAISAN À LA SAINT-HUBERT—This dish is made in a square or rectangular-shaped mould, using pheasant (or other game) mousse, slices of the appropriate game and slivers of truffles, prepared as described in the recipe for *Pavé of foie gras with truffles.*

Pavé of salmon à la Nantua. PAVÉ DE SAUMON À LA NANTUA—Coat a square-shaped mould with fish aspic jelly, decorate with *Crayfish tails dipped in Nantua chaud-froid sauce** and slivers of truffles, and fill with *Salmon mousse* bound with aspic jelly (see FISH MOUSSE).

Cover the mousse with a layer of jelly and chill on ice.

Turn out on to a round dish. Garnish with little *barquettes* baked blind (empty) filled with crayfish tails, covered with Nantua chaud-froid sauce and glazed with jelly. Put a little chopped jelly between each tartlet.

Pavés of soles or other fish. PAVÉS DE SOLES—Prepare as *Pavé of salmon* using sole mousse, fillets of sole, cooked in white wine and well drained, and slivers of truffles.

These pavés are decorated with truffles, round slices of hard boiled yolks of egg, blanched tarragon or chervil leaves, lobster coral, etc.

They can be garnished, in addition to fillets of soles and truffles, with slices of lobster or spiny lobster, crayfish tails, poached oysters, well dried, glazed with aspic jelly, etc.

SWEET PAVÉS. PAVÉS D'ENTREMETS:

Chocolate pavé. PAVÉ AU CHOCOLAT—Sandwich Genoese or chocolate sponge layers together with *Chocolate butter cream* (see CREAMS), making sure the cake layers are not too thick. Trim the sandwich, giving it a square shape. Ice with chocolate icing.

Note. As in the case of all cakes filled with butter cream, the pavés should be put in the ice box for a time to allow the cream to set.

Coffee pavé. PAVÉ AU MOKA—Prepare as *Chocolate pavé*, using *Coffee butter cream* (see CREAMS) and *Coffee icing* (see ICING).

Fruit pavé. PAVÉ AUX FRUITS—Spread Genoese sponge layers with vanilla-flavoured butter cream, putting a layer of various fruit, cooked in syrup, well drained and chopped into a *salpicon** on the cream. Sandwich the layers of cake, pressing down to make the layers adhere. Trim the cake to give it an even, square shape. Ice with kirsch-flavoured *Fondant icing* (see ICING). Decorate with crystallized fruit, angelica lozenges and almonds.

Hazelnut pavé. PAVÉ AUX NOISETTES—Prepare as *Chocolate pavé*, using burnt hazelnut butter cream and kirsch-flavoured icing.

Praliné pavé. PAVÉ AU PRALINÉ—Prepare as *Chocolate pavé*, using *Burnt almond butter cream* (see CREAMS) and kirsch-flavoured icing.

Small rice pavés à la cévenole. PETITS PAVÉS DE RIZ À LA CÉVENOLE—Prepare the pavés as described in the recipe for *Rice pavés with fruit*, using a purée of *Marrons glacés** or vanilla-flavoured *Chestnut purée**. Deep-fry and arrange in a pyramid.

Small rice pavés à la créole. PETITS PAVÉS DE RIZ À LA CRÉOLE—Spread the pavés, prepared as described above, with a *salpicon** of pineapple, cooked in syrup, cut in very small dice and bound with stewed apricots. Deep-fry and arrange in a pyramid.

Small rice pavés with fruit. PETITS PAVÉS DE RIZ AUX FRUITS—Cook ½ cup (125 grams) of sweetened rice (see RICE). When it is cooked and bound, spread it on a buttered pan in a layer ⅛ inch thick. Cover the surface with a little butter to prevent crust from forming and leave the rice to cool.

Turn out the rice and cut into an even number of rectangular pieces, 1½ inches wide and about 2½ inches long. Spread half of these rectangles on one side only with a layer of stewed fruit: apricots, chestnuts, peaches, apples, or any other. Cover the remaining rectangles with rice, then dip in egg and breadcrumbs, making the breadcrumbs adhere and shaping the pieces into straight-sided pavés.

Deep-fry in smoking hot fat, drain, arrange in a pyramid on a napkin-covered dish and serve with a fruit sauce, flavoured with kirsch (or any other liqueur).

Small rice pavés à la normande. PETITS PAVÉS DE RIZ À LA NORMANDE—Spread the pavés, prepared as described above, with stewed apples. Fry and arrange in a pyramid.

Small rice pavés Pompadour. PETITS PAVÉS DE RIZ POMPADOUR—Spread the pavés, prepared as described above, with a *salpicon** of crystallized fruit, cut in very small dice and bound with a few tablespoons of rum-flavoured *French pastry cream* (see CREAMS). Fry and arrange in a pyramid.

Small semolina pavés. PETITS PAVÉS DE SEMOULE—Prepare like *Rice pavés*, using sweetened, cooked semolina.

Note. We give only a few recipes for these *pavés.* One can, however, vary them endlessly, by spreading with various jams, stewed fruit and *salpicons**.

They can also be spread with variously flavoured French pastry cream.

PAVIE—Firm-fleshed peach, similar to a Clingstoen with the pulp adhering to the stone.

PAYSANNE (A LA)—Method of preparing butcher's meat and poultry, which are usually braised and accompanied by a garnish composed of carrots, turnips, onions and celery sliced and lightly cooked in butter, pieces of lean bacon, scalded and fried and potatoes cut down to a uniform small size.

PEA. POIS—Plant thought by some to have originated in western Asia and derived from the wild pea. According to whether the pod is tender or parchment-lined, the peas are classified as *edible-podded* or *shelling peas.* According to their size, peas are either tall or dwarf. The most esteemed French varieties, which are eaten 'green', before they reach complete maturity, i.e. when they are still *petits pois* (small peas), are *pois de Clamart* and *pois Michaux.* The late varieties are preserved by means of drying. Whole *dried peas,* of greyish yellow colour, are preferred in France to *split peas* which are of a greyish green colour.

Cultivated by the Hebrews, Persians, Greeks and later the Romans, peas are now found throughout most of the world. This vegetable is very rich in nitrogen and mucilage, contains a strong proportion of oxalic acid and has a pleasant taste recalling a little that of chestnuts.

Garden peas (*Claire*)

FRESH GARDEN PEAS. Pois frais:

Boiled peas. Petits pois à l'anglaise—Cook the peas in boiling salted water as quickly as possible, keeping the saucepan uncovered.

Drain and dry off by tossing them in a saucepan on the fire. Put into a serving dish. Serve fresh butter separately.

Peas à la bonne femme. Petits pois à la bonne femme—Melt some butter in a saucepan and brown lightly 12 small onions (new, when in season) and ¼ pound (125 grams) of lean bacon cut in dice and scalded. Remove the onions and the bacon from the pan.

Add 2 tablespoons of flour to the butter and cook for a few minutes, stirring with a wooden spoon. Dilute with 1 cup (2 decilitres) of white stock. Boil for 5 minutes. Put one quart (litre) of fresh garden peas into this sauce, add the small onions, the diced bacon and a *bouquet garni** and simmer with a lid on.

Peas in butter. Petits pois au beurre—Cook the peas in salted boiling water. Drain them and dry off by tossing in a saucepan on a brisk fire. Season with a pinch of castor (fine) sugar. Dress with fresh butter divided into tiny pieces, allowing ¼ pound (125 grams) of butter per quart (litre) of shelled garden peas.

Peas à la crème. Petits pois à la crème—Boil the peas in water, drain and toss in a pan on the fire for a few moments to dry off surplus moisture. Cover with boiling fresh cream. Simmer until the liquid is reduced by half and season with salt and a pinch of sugar. Add 2 tablespoons of fresh cream, blend well and serve in a *timbale*.

Peas with fennel. Petits pois au fenouil—Boil the peas in salted water with a good bunch of fresh fennel, tied with a string. Drain, dress with butter and, at the last moment, add a tablepoon of chopped fennel. Serve in a *timbale*.

Peas à la fermière. Petits pois à la fermière—Cook 1 pound (500 grams) of very small new carrots with 12 small onions, as described in the recipe for *Glazed carrots* (see CARROTS). When the carrots are half-cooked, add to the pan 4 cups (8 decilitres) of freshly shelled garden peas, one head of lettuce shredded into a coarse *julienne** and a *bouquet garni** composed of parsley and chervil. Season with salt and sugar. Moisten with 2 tablespoons of water. Simmer with a lid on. Add butter at the last moment.

Peas à la française. Petits pois à la française—Choose a deep saucepan, big enough to contain the peas and all the garnish, put into it one quart (litre) of fresh garden peas, a lettuce heart shredded into a chiffonnade*, 12 small onions (new, if in season), a *bouquet garni** composed of parsley and chervil, ¼ pound (125 grams) of butter, 1⅔ teaspoons (10 grams) of salt and 4 teaspoons (20 grams) of sugar. Stir to mix all the ingredients.

Add 3 to 4 tablespoons of cold water. Bring to the boil, then simmer gently with a lid on. At the last moment, when the peas are cooked, remove the *bouquet garni**, take the pan off the fire and add 3 or 4 teaspoons of fresh butter. Mix and serve in a *timbale*.

Peas with ham (Languedoc cookery). Petits pois au jambon—Cut a medium-sized onion into quarters and brown with 4 ounces (125 grams) of lean, raw (*not smoked*) ham in butter (in Languedoc goose fat is used). Add one quart (litre) of fresh shelled garden peas to the pan. Toss them lightly in the butter, sprinkle in a tablespoon of flour and cook for a few minutes. Moisten with 1½ cups (3 decilitres) of water, season with salt and sugar, add a small *bouquet garni** and simmer with a lid on from 45 to 50 minutes. Remove the *bouquet garni* and serve in a *timbale*.

Peas with lettuce. Petits pois aux laitues—Prepare as *Peas à la française*, using tied lettuce heads and omitting the small onions.

When the peas are cooked, drain the lettuces and cut into quarters. Put these on the peas. Finish off with some fresh butter and serve in a *timbale*.

Peas with mint. Petits pois à la menthe—Proceed as described in the recipe for *Peas with fennel**, substituting fresh mint for the fennel. Serve the peas in a *timbale*, dress with butter and put some scalded mint leaves on top.

Peas à la paysanne. Petits pois à la paysanne—Prepare, using big fresh garden peas, like *Peas à la française**, with coarsely shredded lettuce and onions cut in quarters. When the peas are cooked, effect a liaison with kneaded butter, allowing 2 tablespoons (30 grams) of butter and 1 tablespoon (10 grams) of flour per quart (litre) of peas.

Note. Peas à la paysanne are often called *à la bonne femme*.

Purée of fresh garden peas, called Saint-Germain. Purée de pois frais, dite Saint-Germain—Cook the peas as described in the recipe for *Peas à la française*, drain them and rub through a fine sieve.

Heat this purée, add the liquor left from cooking the peas, boiled down and strained, and, at the last moment, blend in fresh butter, allowing ¼ pound (125 grams) per quart (litre) of purée. For this purée big peas are used, which must, however, always be absolutely fresh.

Note. This purée can also be made using peas boiled in salted water and well drained.

DRIED PEAS. Pois secs—Three kinds of dried peas are used in the kitchen: *split peas, yellow peas* and *chick-peas*.

Yellow peas are only used in some parts of eastern France and almost always as a purée. This purée is often served in Germany as an accompaniment to sauerkraut. Yellow peas can also be cooked in the same manner as dried white beans.

Chick-peas, dried whole, come from a plant of the family *Leguminosae*, which in France is also called *pois chiche* or *pois cornu*.

Split peas are more commonly used in France, served mainly as a purée.

To cook split peas. Soak the split peas in water just to soften them, that is , do not leave them soaking too long.

Put them into a saucepan and cover with water, allowing 3 cups (1½ litres) of water per 1 pound (500 grams) of split peas. Add a ham knuckle and a coarse *mirepoix** composed of a carrot, a medium-sized onion and 2½ ounces (75 grams) of scalded lean bacon—all these ingredients cut in large dice and softened in butter. Add a *bouquet garni** consisting of parsley, thyme, bay leaf and the green part of 3 leeks. Season, bring to the boil and simmer gently with a lid on for about an hour and a half. A few leaves of lettuce can also be added as a garnish for split peas.

Split pea purée. PURÉE DE POIS CASSÉS—Cook the split peas as described above and rub through a sieve or force through a coarse tammy cloth. Heat the purée, stirring it with a wooden spoon. Dilute with a few tablespoons of the liquid left over from cooking the peas, strained through a fine strainer. Take off the fire and, just before serving, add butter.

Note. If this purée is served as a vegetable or garnish, a few tablespoons of fresh cream can be added to it.

Split pea soup or Potage aux croûtons. POTAGE DE POIS CASSÉS—Soup made of split peas, cooked as described above and rubbed through a sieve. See SOUPS AND BROTHS, *Purée of split pea soup.*

EDIBLE-PODDED OR SUGAR PEAS. POIS MANGE-TOUT, PRINCESSES—These are peas the pods of which have no parchment lining; they can therefore be eaten seed, pod and all.

Break the pods (having topped and tailed them) into two or three pieces. Proceed to cook them in any way recommended above for fresh garden peas.

Dessert peaches

PEACH. PÊCHE—The peach is the fruit of the peach tree of the family *Rosaceae*, said to have originated in China and introduced into Europe, through Persia, about 2,000 years ago, and is one of the best and most delicious fruits to be found in France.

There are two principal types of peaches: peaches with a downy skin, that is slightly hairy, this category itself being divided into *peaches* proper, fruit with a juicy flesh and a free stone, and *clingstone*, fruit with a firmer flesh adhering to stone.

The smooth-skinned hairless peaches have a firm flesh and a cling stone. *Nectarines*, with a melting, fragrant flesh, are usually described as a species of a smooth-skinned peach.

Peaches grown against a sheltered wall are finer, bigger, juicier and more fragrant than those grown in the open.

Peaches grown in Montreuil, Bagnolet and Fréjus are considered the best in France. Peaches are cultivated on a big scale in the Pyrenées-Orientales and in the Rhône valley. They are to be found on the market from July to the end of September.

Peaches are eaten raw as a dessert fruit, or cooked, and in the latter form they enter into the making of a vast number of sweets and pastries.

Peaches are used in a great many confectionery preparations. Various excellent beverages are also made from peaches; highly flavoured brandies and liqueurs are distilled from them.

The following can be classed among the best varieties of French peaches: *Amsdem*, a round fruit, slightly flattened, of medium size, with red flush and mottling, with a greenish-white, juicy flesh of good flavour; *Early Croncels*, a big ovoid fruit, amber coloured with purplish flush, with a delicate flesh and pleasant flavour; *Felignies* (end of August) medium-sized fruit, yellow with crimson flush, creamy white flesh of very good flavour; *Victoria*, round medium-sized fruit, yellow with crimson flush, white melting flesh tinted next stone, very good; *Hale's early*, medium-sized fruit, slightly flattened, flushed and mottled, very juicy flesh of good flavour; *France*, big round fruit with very downy skin, yellow and crimson in colour, with white flesh, slightly tinted next stone, very good; *grosse mignonne*, very big almost round fruit, skin flushed with purple, white juicy flesh, very melting and sweet; *Reine des vergers*, big, slightly elongated fruit, crimson-purplish flush, white flesh, slightly pink next stone, melting and sweet; *admirable yellow* or *apricot peach*, a round fruit, with orange tinted yellow skin, very good white juicy flesh; *Venus' breast*, big round fruit with a nipple on the top, crimson flush, rather fine, semi-melting flesh, quite good in flavour.

Peaches Bourdaloue. PÊCHES BOURDALOUE—Halve the peaches, peel and poach in vanilla-flavoured syrup. Drain and dry them. Arrange in a flan case, baked blind (empty) on a foundation of *Frangipane cream* (see CREAMS), not too thick and mixed with crushed macaroons.

Cover the peaches with a layer of the same cream. Sprinkle with crushed macaroons and a little melted butter and glaze quickly in the oven.

Note. This dessert can also be made without covering the peaches with *Frangipane cream* (see CREAM). They should then be decorated with crystallised cherries, lozenges of angelica and halved almonds.

Instead of frangipane cream the flan case can also be filled with sweetened semolina, bound with eggs and butter and flavoured with kirsch.

A *salpicon** of crystallised fruit, steeped in some liqueur, can be added to either of the above compositions.

Chilled peaches with raspberries. PÊCHES RAFRAÎCHIES AUX FRAMBOISES—Poach some choice peaches in vanilla-flavoured syrup. Chill on ice. Just before serving arrange in a glass fruit dish, cover with a purée of fresh raspberries, diluted with a little of the syrup in which the peaches were cooked, boiled down and laced with a few drops of kirsch. Scatter some fresh raspberries on top.

Peaches Colbert. PÊCHES COLBERT—Using halved peaches, poached in vanilla-flavoured syrup, prepare like *Colbert Apricots* (see APRICOT).

Compote of peaches. COMPOTE DE PÊCHES—Peel the peaches (plunge them into boiling water for a moment first, then peel immediately). Poach them, whole or halved, in vanilla-flavoured 18° syrup. See SYRUP.

Serve hot or cold.

Peaches Condé. PÊCHES CONDÉ—Using halved peaches, poached in vanilla-flavoured syrup, prepare like *Condé apricots* (see APRICOT).

Peach coupe—See ICE CREAMS AND ICES.

Peach croûte. CROÛTE AUX PÊCHES—Prepare, using halved or quartered peaches, cooked in vanilla-flavoured syrup and drained, as described in the recipe for *Apricot croûte**.

Crystallised peaches. PÊCHES CONFITES—Prepare like *Crystallised apricots* (see APRICOTS).

Peaches in brandy. PÊCHES À L'EAU-DE-VIE—Prepare like *Apricot comfits in alcohol* (see APRICOTS).

Peach flambée Brillat-Savarin. PÊCHES FLAMBÉES BRILLAT-SAVARIN—Prepare as many little *savarins** (crown-shaped) as you have halves of big peaches.

Arrange the *savarins* (soaked in syrup) in a circle on a round ovenproof dish. Put into each *savarin* a tablespoon of very thick *French pastry cream* (see CREAMS), mixed with a *salpicon** of crystallised fruit, steeped in kirsch or maraschino.

Separately, poach the halved and peeled peaches in vanilla-flavoured syrup. Drain and dry them. Arrange on the *savarins*. Sprinkle with crushed macaroons and a little melted butter. Brown lightly in the oven.

At the last moment, just before serving, sprinkle with kirsch and set alight.

Serve with apricot sauce, made by diluting apricot jam with the syrup in which the peaches were cooked, heating it and straining.

Peaches flambée au kirsch. PÊCHES FLAMBÉES AU KIRSCH—Peel the peaches and poach them in vanilla-flavoured syrup. Drain and arrange in a dessert dish. Pour over a few tablespoons of the syrup in which they were cooked thickened with arrowroot just before serving. Sprinkle with heated kirsch and set alight.

Note. Instead of serving all the peaches together in one dish, they can be arranged in individual silver or fire-proof china *cassolettes*.

Pêches flambées can be similarly prepared with other spirits: armagnac, brandy, calvados, rum, etc.

Peach flan

Peach flan or tart. FLAN, TARTE AUX PÊCHES—Prepare as described in the recipe for *Apricot flan or tart*, using halved or quartered peaches. See TART.

Peach fritters—See FRITTERS.

Peaches in Frontignan. PÊCHES AU FRONTIGNAN—Peel the peaches and cook in vanilla-flavoured syrup. Drain them and arrange in a dessert dish. Reduce the syrup by two-thirds, add several tablespoons of Frontignan wine and pour over the peaches. Serve hot or cold.

Peach ice—See ICE CREAMS AND ICES.

Peaches à l'impératrice. PÊCHES À L'IMPÉRATRICE—Peel the peaches, halve and poach in vanilla-flavoured syrup. Drain and dry.

Arrange them in a glass dish or a silver dessert dish filled up to two-thirds with *Rice à l'impératrice**, chilled in a refrigerator.

Cover the peaches with a layer of raspberry or strawberry jelly.

Peach jam—See JAMS.

Penelope peaches. PÊCHES PÉNÉLOPE—Poach the peaches in syrup, strongly flavoured with vanilla, and allow to cool in this syrup.

Prepare an iced strawberry mousse in the usual manner: 35° of syrup, sugar cooked to large pearl (222°F.) mixed with an equal quantity of strawberry pulp and twice its volume of whipped *Chantilly cream* (see CREAM) whisked very stiff.

Fill individual shallow round moulds with this mousse, seal hermetically and chill for 2 hours.

Just before serving, turn out the strawberry mousse into low round glass fruit dishes.

Arrange the peaches, drained, dried and chilled in a refrigerator, on this mousse.

Garnish the middle with fresh chilled strawberries. Cover with a film of sugar cooked to 'pearl degree'. Serve with *Zabaglione** flavoured with *Parfait-amour** liqueur.

Peach pulp (raw). PULPE DE PÊCHES (CRUE)—Rub the flesh of the peaches through a fine sieve. Add to the pulp a third of its weight of castor (fine) sugar. Mix well. Flavour with liqueur.

This pulp is used for covering chilled fruit, as a compote and for certain cold sweets (desserts), such as charlottes, fruit moulds, puddings, etc.

Peaches à la Madame Récamier. PÊCHES MADAME RÉCAMIER—René de Beauvoir gave the following recipe for this dish in *Monde Illustré* (May 1857), dictated by Chevrier, the illustrious maître d'hôtel of the early nineteenth century:

'Madame Récamier,' says Chevrier, 'had lost all interest in food and we could see her fading away. No one dared to disobey the doctor's orders for her—a diet. Very well, I said to myself, she likes peaches—I'll serve her some in my own way.

'And I put one, the best I could find, to cook in a *bain-marie**; I smothered it with exquisite sugar syrup, poured some cream over it—and there it was.'

Peaches with rice and meringue. PÊCHES MERINGUÉES AU RIZ—Proceed as described in the recipe for *Apricots with rice and meringue*, using halved peaches, poached in vanilla-flavoured syrup.

Ring (border) of peaches à la Chantilly (Cold sweet or dessert). BORDURE DE PÊCHES À LA CHANTILLY—Bake a *Vanilla-flavoured custard* (see CUSTARD) in a ring mould; leave until cold and turn out on to a round dish. Halve 6 peaches, poach in vanilla-flavoured syrup, drain, dry and arrange these halves in the middle of the ring.

Cover the peaches with vanilla-flavoured whipped cream, piling it up in a dome. Decorate with crystallised cherries and halved pistachio nuts.

Peach soufflé. SOUFFLÉ AUX PÊCHES—Using peach purée, mixed first with sugar syrup cooked to crack degree (260°F.), then with whites of egg, whisked into a stiff froth, prepare as indicated in the recipe for *Fruit soufflés*. See SOUFFLÉ.

Note. Peach soufflés can also be made using a cream composition, mixed with peach pulp and pieces of peaches cooked in vanilla-flavoured syrup, well drained and dried.

Peaches Sultana. PÊCHES SULTANE—Poach whole (or halved) peaches in vanilla-flavoured syrup and leave until quite cold.

Drain them and arrange in a silver *timbale*, or glass dessert dish, on a foundation of *Pistachio ice cream* (see ICE CREAMS AND ICES). Cover with syrup, flavoured with attar of roses. Pour on a film of sugar cooked to pearl degree (220°F.).

Peaches in red wine à la bordelaise. PÊCHES AU VIN ROUGE, DITES À LA BORDELAISE—Halve 4 peaches and peel them. Sprinkle with sugar and leave to stand for an hour.

Boil 1½ cups (3 decilitres) of red (Bordeaux) wine with 8 lumps of sugar and a small piece of cinnamon bark, in a copper pan.

Put the halved peaches to poach in the wine.

When the fruit is cooked, drain and arrange in a glass dish. Boil down the syrup, pour over the peaches and leave to get cold.

Serve with slices of brioche, sprinkled with sugar and glazed in a hot oven.

PEACOCK. PAON—This magnificent bird used to be esteemed by gastronomes in as much as it constituted a rarity.

Today, the peacock, although still greatly admired for its ornamental qualities, has lost its gastronomical value.

In the Middle Ages it held pride of place at great State banquets and provided occasion for knights to take their solemn oaths.

Its cooking needed all the skill of an experienced master-cook. The bird was skinned carefully, the skin was treated and dressed, the tail spread in a fan, the head with its crest was wrapped in a piece of linen, constantly moistened with water during roasting. The feet and the beak were gilded, and the bird, dressed in full feather, was carried to the table in a solemn procession. At great feasts it was served either buried under flowers or with flames shooting out of its beak (this effect being achieved by putting a piece of cotton dipped in spirit or a piece of camphor in its beak).

The bird, in all its splendour, was set before the master of the house or the most distinguished guest present, only the noblest of guests having the right to carve it, and only if they could do it with such skill as to allow each guest, however many there might be at table, to have a piece.

This operation was accomplished amid the praise and approval of the guests, acknowledging the knight-trenchant's skill, who, fired with enthusiasm, would rise and with his hand on the dish, take an oath vowing to be worthy of the eulogies, either by being the first to raise his standard on a town which was about to be besieged, or by leading a lance attack upon the enemy . . .

He took the oath by reciting this sacred formula: 'I vow to God, the Holy Virgin, the Ladies and the Peacock . . .' to accomplish this or that deed of valour.

Then each knight, receiving his piece, would make his vow to the peacock—and failure to carry it out would be a blot on his escutcheon.

For culinary preparation of peacock, see PHEASANT.

PEANUT. ARACHIDE—Plant originating from America which is cultivated in all hot countries. Its pods, which bury themselves in the earth after fecundation to mature the seeds, produce nuts which are eaten either raw or roasted. They are also known under the names of *earth-nuts*, *ground-nut* and *monkey-nut*. The nutrition value of the peanut is considerable.

Peanut oil and *peanut butter* are made from this nut. The latter can be eaten in sandwiches or on pieces of toast, accompanied by lettuce leaves, garden cream, chervil and tarragon, or on gingerbread, with jam or jelly.

Peanut oil—See OIL, *Ground-nut oil*

Peanut paste. PÂTE D'ARACHIDE—This is prepared using blanched peanuts in the same way as *Almond paste*. See ALMONDS.

'Beurré Clairgeau' pears (*Wide World*)

PEAR. POIRE—Fruit of the pear tree of the family *Rosaceae* which does not seem to have been known in the distant past. It was cultivated by the Romans and Pliny mentions 38 varieties of it, whilst Virgil only mentions three. Today, a whole volume would be required to enumerate them.

There are various shapes of pears: the *bézy*, which looks like an egg, the *bergamotte*, which looks like a ball, the *chrétien*, which looks like a quince, the *calabash*, which looks like a bludgeon, the *colmar*, which looks like a spinning top, the *doyenné*, which looks like a barrel, etc.

A qualification is usually added to indicate the quality of the flesh (beurré, melting, firm, gritty, etc.), the ripening time, etc.

Among the varieties meant for the table the following can be listed, in order of their appearance on the French market:

From 15th June: *Saint-Jean*, a small green pear of mediocre taste.

Beginning of July: *Doyenné de juillet*, small, with a good flavour.

July: *Beurré Giffard*, bulbous yellow with russet patches; *Docteur Jules Guyot*, big, pyriform, pale yellow with russet patches and slight red flush, with fine juicy flesh.

August and September: *Williams* (the Bartlett in U.S.A.), which appears around the 15th August, big, oval, golden yellow with russet dots and marbling and faint red stripes, with fine, slightly musky flavour; these pears do not keep and last until about the 15th September.

September: *Beurré d'Angleterre*, olive green, with brown patches, blets very quickly; *Beurré Hardy*, big, russet with dark red flush, with very delicate flesh of faint pink tinge, tender and transparent, with rose water flavour.

End of September: *Louise-Bonne*, big, yellow with red flush and prominent red spots, the flesh is white, very melting, sweet and delicious. This pear will keep for two months.

October: *Doyenné blanc*, skin tinged with a little cinnamon russet; the flesh is very melting, not gritty, with a vinous flavour, keeps well; *Duchesse d'Angoulême*, big, yellow with conspicuous russet dots and patches, melting flesh, extremely sweet with a fine aroma; keeps until the end of January. *Doyenné de Comice*, big, bulbous, pale green with fine russet and occasional red flush, with exquisite flesh, the most esteemed of pears. *Beurré Clairgeau*, beautiful yellow colour with bright red flush, but mediocre in flavour; the flesh is firm, not melting and faintly musky. *Beurré Diel*, big, dull yellow with slightly brown flush; the skin is rough, with large russet dots and slight russet. The flesh is juicy but a little gritty at the core.

End of October and November: *Crassane*, medium-sized, flat and round, green with brownish dots and patches, pleasant slightly astringent flavour, keeps until April. *Passe-Crassane*, which ripens towards All Saints Day, big, round, flattened flesh often a little gritty, with a musky flavour; keeps until April. *Beurré d'Aremberg*, bulbous, round, uneven, fairly smooth yellow skin with small russet patches and brown red flush, flesh sweet and juicy with a characteristic aroma, a little gritty at the core; keeps until the end of March. *Doyenné d'hiver*, the shape of a big fig, rough skin, pea-green fading to yellow green, with russet patches and marbling, slightly acid flavour, but due to improved methods, this pear is definitely classified in England as having a rich, sweet and musky flavour; keeps until April. *Bergamotte*, big, flattened, round, rough yellowish green skin, dotted and striped with russet and a little red flush; the flesh is often gritty but very fragrant, keeps until the end of June.

The following can also be added to the above varieties: *Catillac*, dull yellowish green with brown red flush, with firm, sweet and aromatic flesh (this pear cooks a deep red). *Poire de curé*, longish in shape, green and russet in colour, less aroma. *Bon chrétien d'hiver*, big and green and used as a purely decorative element in fruit baskets. *Belle angevine*, an enormous pear of a magnificent yellowish green colour dotted with crimson, but the flesh is firm and tasteless.

Dessert pears, i.e., pears which are eaten raw, are sub-divided into *summer pears* (from July to September), *autumn pears* (from October to December) and *winter pears* (from December to May).

Cooking pears generally have a firm flesh, sometimes a little granular and often a little tart. These ripen from December to May and can only be eaten cooked, in a compote or prepared in some other manner.

Perry pears are the pears which are used for making *perry* or *pear cider*.

Dessert pears, one of the best dessert fruit, are usually eaten raw, out of hand, but can also be cooked and in this form enter into the preparation of a great number of sweets (desserts) and pastries, such as flans, tarts, pies, iced mousses, charlottes, etc.

Excellent preserves are also made of dessert pears. They can be crystallised like any other fruit, whole or quartered. They are then partly dried in the oven and flattened on one side—these dried pears can be found in the shops and are called *poires tapées* in France.

Baked pears, also called Poires en douillon and Poires cartouches. POIRES EN RABOTTE—Peel and core the pears, half-cook in butter and wrap each in a piece of *Fine lining paste* (see DOUGH). Put on top of each pear a circlet cut out of the same paste with a fluted-edged pastry cutter. Brush with beaten egg and bake in a hot oven for 25 minutes, or longer, if the pears are big.

Note. The *douillons* or baked pears can also be prepared without peeling the pears and half-cooking them in the oven before enclosing in pastry.

Pears Bourdaloue. POIRES BOURDALOUE—Cut the pears in half, if they are of medium size, or in quarters if they are big, trim and poach in vanilla-flavoured syrup.

Put these pears in a flan case (baked pie shell), filled with *Frangipane cream* (see CREAMS) and proceed as described in the recipe for *Peaches Bourdaloue*. See PEACH.

Pears Brillat-Savarin. POIRES BRILLAT-SAVARIN—Poach 8 pear halves in vanilla-flavoured syrup. Drain them, dry and arrange in a circle on a *Genoese cake**, cut into two layers and sandwiched together with fairly thick, rum-flavoured stewed pear mixture. Decorate with crystallised cherries and lozenges of angelica. Heat in the oven. Pour over some rum-flavoured, thinned-down apricot pulp. Serve with rum-flavoured *Custard cream à l'anglaise* (see CREAM) thickened with arrowroot.

Cardinal pears. POIRES CARDINAL—Poach the pears in vanilla-flavoured syrup. Allow them to cool, drain, arrange in a glass fruit dish or in a *timbale*, cover with kirsch-flavoured, sweetened *Raspberry purée** and sprinkle with chopped almonds.

Pear charlotte. CHARLOTTE DE POIRES—Prepare, using stewed pears, as described in the recipe for *Apple charlotte*. See CHARLOTTE.

Pear compote. COMPOTE DE POIRES—Prepare, using whole pears, if they are small, halved or quartered, if they are big, as described in the recipe for *Peach compote*. See COMPOTE.

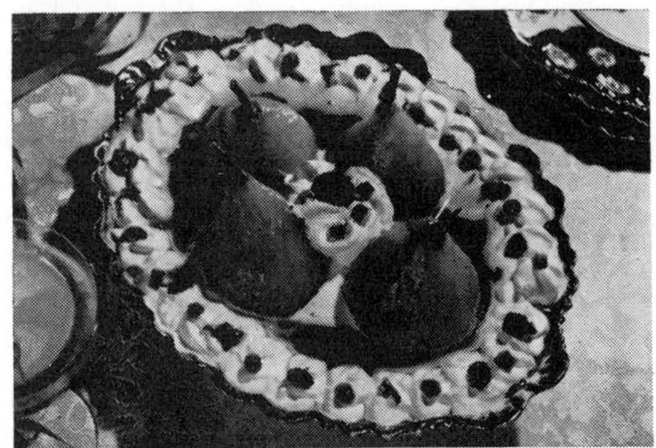

Pears Condé

Pears Condé. POIRES CONDÉ—Prepare, using pears cooked in syrup, like *Condé Apricots* (see APRICOTS).

Pear croûtes. CROÛTES AUX POIRES—Prepare using halved or quartered pears, poached in vanilla-flavoured syrup, as described in the recipe for *Apricot croûtes**.

Pear flambée au kirsch. POIRES FLAMBÉES AU KIRSCH—Prepare, using whole or halved pears, cooked in vanilla-flavoured syrup, like *Peach flambée au kirsch**.

Pear fritters—See FRITTERS.

Pears Hélène. POIRES HÉLÈNE—Poach the pears in vanilla-flavoured syrup and arrange on vanilla-flavoured ice. Serve *Hot chocolate sauce* (see SAUCE) separately.

Pear ice and iced mousse—See ICE CREAMS AND ICES.

Iced pears Mourier. POIRES GLACÉES MOURIER—Take Crassane pears, peel them down to as uniform a size as possible and poach in syrup, strongly flavoured with vanilla. Drain and chill on ice.

Pears à l'impératrice (*Robert Carrier*)

Arrange in a meringue flan case (meringue shell), filling the middle with kirsch-flavoured *Iced pear mousse* (see ICE CREAMS AND ICES).

Pipe some whipped cream over the mousse through a forcing (pastry) bag and decorate with glacé cherries, angelica lozenges and almonds.

Pears à l'impératrice. POIRES À L'IMPÉRATRICE—Using pears (whole or halved), poached in vanilla-flavoured syrup, proceed as described in the recipe for *Peaches à l'impératrice*. See PEACH.

Pear Melba—See ICE CREAMS AND ICES.

Pears with rice and meringue. POIRES MERINGUÉES AU RIZ—Proceed as described in the recipe for *Apricots with rice and meringue**, using halved or quartered pears poached in vanilla-flavoured syrup.

Ring (border) of pears Chantilly. BORDURE DE POIRES CHANTILLY—These cold sweets (desserts) are made using quartered pears, cooked in syrup like *Border of peaches à la Chantilly*. See PEACH.

Pears with semolina. POIRES À LA SEMOULE GRATINÉES—Peel the pears, cut into quarters and cook in a light vanilla-flavoured syrup. Drain them, arrange in a circle in a buttered oven-proof dish on a thick layer of semolina, cooked as described in the recipe for *Semolina pudding**.

Sprinkle with crushed macaroons and melted butter. Brown the top in a slow oven and serve in the same dish.

Pear soufflé. SOUFFLÉ AUX POIRES—Prepare like a *Cream soufflé*, using a cream composition mixed with pear pulp and a *salpicon** of crystallised pears, steeped in kirsch. See SOUFFLÉ.

Pear tarts. FLANS, TARTES AUX POIRES—Prepare, using sliced or quartered pears, like any fruit flan or tart. See TART.

Timbale of pears d'Aremberg. TIMBALE DE POIRES D'AREMBERG—Butter a charlotte mould and line it with slightly firm *Brioche dough* (see DOUGH). Fill the mould with quarters of pears, half-cooked in vanilla-flavoured syrup, putting them in rows alternating with stewed apricots.

Cover the *timbale* with a piece of rolled out brioche dough sealing the edges thoroughly. Make a small hole in the middle to allow steam to escape. Bake in a hot oven for about 45 minutes.

Turn out on to a serving dish and pour over kirsch-flavoured *Apricot sauce* (see SAUCE).

Timbale of pears à la suédoise. TIMBALE DE POIRES À LA SUÉDOISE—Prepare like *Timbale of pears d'Aremberg* replacing the stewed apricots by *French pastry cream* or *Frangipane cream* (see CREAMS).

PEARL. PERLÉ—Pearl-like. Hulled and polished barley is called pearl barley. See BARLEY.

A degree of the boiling of sugar is also called *pearl degree* (230°F.). See SUGAR.

PEC—French word used only in the expression *hareng pec*, i.e. freshly-salted herring, barrelled without being smoked.

PECCARY. PÉCARI—A species of South American wild pig. Its flesh is much prized but sometimes has a musky flavour. Peccary is prepared like young *Wild boar**.

PECTEN. PEIGNE—Genus of bivalve molluscs of the family *Pectinidae* with rounded shells, divided into grooves radiating from the middle of the hinge, the most important species being the scallop.

In many respects scallops can be compared to oysters, but, while oysters are stationary, stuck to the rocks, scallops are mobile, rising and whirling on the surface of the water.

In the past, the pilgrims to the shrine of St. James at Santiago de Compostela always wore the 'palmer's cockle' (*Pecten jacobaeus*) on their shoulder, having gathered them on the seashore. Thus this mollusc first acquired in French the name of *peigne Saint-Jacques* and later became merely Saint-Jacques. See SCALLOPS, *St. Jacques scallops*.

PECTIN. PECTINE—Mucilaginous substance occurring as a constituent in certain fruits (quince, apples, oranges, lemons, etc.) and vegetables (split peas, lentils, etc.) which causes their pulp, when boiled with sugar in the presence of sufficient acid, to set as a jelly. The skin and pips of the above-mentioned fruit contain a great deal of pectin and should, therefore, be used in the preparation of jellies.

PEDIMENTS. SOCLES—For a very long time ornamental pediments played a great part in the serving of cold dishes, important sweet dishes, etc.

In modern practice their use has little by little been completely abandoned.

PEEL. ÉCALURE—The name given to the outer skin, whether hard or soft, of some fruit and vegetables.

PEELING. ÉPLUCHAGE—The action of removing the skin of fruit or vegetables. Not all vegetables are peeled

Pediments for cold dishes, after Carême

Some green vegetables, such as sorrel, spinach and watercress are *stripped*, that is to say, pulled off their stalks. In stripping, all faded leaves are discarded. Other vegetables such as peas are *shelled*.

The process of preparing French beans and runner beans for the pot is known as *stringing*. (When they are young they are simply topped and tailed.)

PÉGOT—Sticky coating which covers Roquefort cheese.

PELAMYS THYNNUS (BONITO). PÉLAMIDE—A genus of fish related to the tunny. It only differs from the latter by its more elongated body, a longer and more pointed muzzle and a big jaw.

The prototype of the species of the common pelamys is the *Sardinian pelamys* or *red-backed bonito*.

This fish, which reaches a length of 27 inches, is silvery with light blue tints on the back. It is found in the Mediterranean and in the Atlantic and can be prepared in any way suitable for tunny. See TUNNY.

PELICAN—Large web-footed water fowl, with a large naked pouch or gular sac, which hangs from the long bill, serving as a temporary storage place for fish. They live mainly in freshwater lakes and lagoons, but there are a few marine species, like the Chilean and the Brown pelicans.

Their flesh is oily and tough but is, nevertheless, eaten in some countries.

PEL'MENI (Siberian). PELLMÈNES SIBÉRIENS—A kind of ravioli with a filling of beef, or a mixture of beef and pork. The pel'meni are generally served in soup, like *Ravioli in brodo*. They can be served boiled with a dollop of sour cream. The Siberians like a mustard and vinegar dressing with them.

Ingredients. 1 egg (or 2 yolks), 2½ tablespoons of cold water, ½ lb. flour, 1½ teaspoons salt, ¼ teaspoon pepper, ¾ lb. meat (the best mixture is half beef, half lean pork), 1 small onion, 2½ pints stock or water.

Using egg, water, flour and salt make pastry as for noodles (see NOODLES).

Mince the pork and the beef together with an onion, season with salt and pepper, add one or two tablespoons of cold water and mix well.

Roll out the pastry very thin, cut out small circles with a pastry cutter or a sherry glass. Put a little of the minced meat filling on each circlet of pastry, crimp up the edges, forming rather a plump semi-circle, and join the two tapering ends together, pinching quite hard to make them stick. You will now have a little round pastry. Sprinkle a wooden board lightly with flour and put your pel'meni on it.

If served as a main dish allow at least 15 small pel'meni per portion; if they are intended merely as a soup, to be followed by another dish, allow seven or eight.

The pel'meni look much nicer if made quite small. Do not put in too much filling, allowing a little space between the meat and the pastry, in which delicious juices collect.

Pel'meni can be prepared a day or two in advance and kept in a refrigerator (but they must be laid out so as not to touch each other). This is a Siberian speciality and Siberians maintain that the pel'meni taste much better for a preliminary freezing.

To cook. Drop the pel'meni, a couple at a time, into boiling stock, bring to the boil and simmer gently for about 10 minutes. They are ready as soon as they float up to the surface. Sprinkle with chopped parsley and serve.

If the pel'meni are served not as a soup, but as an independent dish, boil them in water for 10 minutes as described, take out with a perforated spoon and serve at once with melted butter or sour cream.

Alternatively, boil the pel'meni in salted water for three minutes, drain, fry in butter until pale golden on both sides and serve.

PELURES—French culinary term for usable parings, such as truffle or mushroom parings.

PEMMICAN—North American Indian cake of dried and pounded meat mixed with melted fat, a food product famous since the early expeditions to North America, which is no longer in demand nowadays.

Pemmican had the advantage that it could be kept for a long time, was absolutely wholesome and was condensed to take little space.

It is said that it was made from the meat of the bison (North American wild ox, now almost completely extinct), or from venison.

The rump of the animal was cut into thin slices, dried in the sun and pounded finely.

This meat powder was then mixed with melted fat in the proportion of two parts meat to one part fat, and enclosed in bags made from the animal's skin.

Two pounds of pemmican was enough for the daily ration of a working man.

Pemmican was eaten as it was, raw, or boiled in water.

PÉNIDE—French term for sugar cooked with a decoction of barley, then poured on an oiled marble slab and twisted, like a cord, with oiled hands. This manipulation renders the sugar opaque, wherein lies its difference from barley sugar, which is left transparent and, moreover, is no longer made with a barley decoction.

PENNYROYAL. POULIOT—A kind of wild mint with a strong, pungent flavour, sometimes used as a condiment in cookery.

PEPPER. POIVRE—Fruit of the pepper plant, a genus of vine-like shrubs, a native of the Indian Archipelago. It is now extensively cultivated throughout the whole of tropical Asia and equatorial America.

Pepper was one of the first spices to be introduced into Europe. It was used by Hippocrates in his prescriptions.

The berries are picked before they are ripe. There are two kinds of pepper in commerce: *black pepper*, with a greenish-black wrinkled surface, and *white pepper*, which is the same seed freed from the skin and the fleshy part of the fruit; it is less pungent and less aromatic than black pepper.

Ground pepper rapidly loses its flavour and aroma; it is therefore advisible always to grind it as and when required. A *pepper mill* is used for this purpose. These are made in various shapes and of various materials depending on whether they are intended for the kitchen or for the table. By using a pepper mill one avoids the possible substitutes and adulterations which pepper sold in ground form undergoes, such as admixtures of ground 'grains of paradise' (*Amomom cardamomum*) and such inert additions as ground date stones, etc.

Pepper is a much used condiment, entering into almost all the culinary preparations; it is an excitant and a stimulant, and its abuse must therefore be avoided.

Red pepper or pimento. PIMENT—*Capsicum frutescens* has many varieties and is a native of America. It is now cultivated in all warm parts of the world. Dried and ground it becomes, according to the variety, *Cayenne pepper*, *Chili powder*, *Paprika* and *Red pepper*.

All these various kinds of peppers are used mainly as condiments.

Red pepper (pimento) paste (Creole cookery). PÂTÉ DE PIMENTS—This can be brought in delicatessen shops ready for use, but it can also be made at home.

Pound long, strong red peppers (having removed the seeds), with a little onion, ginger and salt, finely in a mortar. Put this thick paste into a jar with a well-fitting lid and cover it with best oil. Leave to macerate. This paste will keep indefinitely, as long as there is a protective layer of oil on top.

Sweet peppers. PIMENTS DOUX—The big *Sweet peppers* or *Pimentos*, which are cultivated in Spain, Italy, the South of France and in the United States, are used in cookery and are served (red or green) as hors-d'oeuvre, as vegetable and as a salad.

It is for this latter variety that the recipes which follow are intended.

Sweet peppers fried in batter. PIMENTS DOUX EN FRITOT—Choose small-sized peppers, put them under a grill for a few moments to loosen the skin, peel and remove seeds. Stuff them with a *salpicon** composed of onions and mushrooms, softened in butter and bound with a little tomato sauce, mixed with some chopped garlic and parsley. Leave the peppers to macerate for an hour in oil, lemon juice, salt and pepper.

A few minutes before serving, dip the peppers one by one in a light batter (see BATTER).

Fry in smoking hot deep fat; drain on a cloth, season with very fine dry salt and arrange in a heap on a napkin-covered dish. Garnish with fried parsley. Serve with *Tomato sauce* (see SAUCE).

Sweet peppers au gratin. PIMENTS DOUX GRATINÉS—Peel the peppers, remove seeds and cook in butter. Line the bottom of an oven-proof dish with *Mornay sauce* (see SAUCE), mixed with a good tablespoonful of chopped onion softened in butter. Put in the peppers, cover with *Mornay sauce*, sprinkle with grated cheese and melted butter and brown the top in a slow oven.

Sweet peppers or pimentos with black olives (Creole cookery). PIMENTS, PIMENTOS DOUX AUX OLIVES NOIRES—Put 4 big green peppers under a grill just to make peeling them easier. Remove seeds, then shred the pimentos into fine *julienne** strips and season with a few tablespoons of *Vinaigrette sauce* (see SAUCE).

Arrange this *julienne* as a border in an hors-d'oeuvre dish and fill the middle with small black olives, marinated in oil.

Sweet peppers à l'orientale. PIMENTS DOUX À L'ORIENTALE—Peel the peppers, remove seeds and cut into large dice. Put into a casserole in which, for 1 pound (500 grams) of peppers, ½ cup (100 grams) of chopped onion has been softened in oil, without allowing it to colour. Add a pinch of garlic. Moisten with ¾ cup (1½ decilitres) of stock and simmer gently for 35 minutes.

Sweet peppers à la petite russienne (Russian cookery). PIMENTS DOUX À LA PETITE RUSSIENNE—Cut 24 green sweet peppers open at the stalk end. Remove the seeds. Parboil the pepper slightly and stuff with a forcemeat prepared in the following manner:

Chop coarsely two handfuls of sorrel leaves, 4 peeled and seeded tomatoes, 3 sweet Spanish onions, 3 green peppers and a stalk of fennel. Put these vegetables into a saucepan in which a little olive oil has been heated. Heat and at the first sign of boiling drain in a sieve to remove excess liquid from the forcemeat.

Fill the peppers with this forcemeat mixed with a little rice, parboiled in salted water and drained.

Put the peppers into an oiled sauté pan, packing them in fairly tightly. Moisten with some tomato purée, which should not be too thick. Add the juice of two lemons and 1 cup (2 decilitres) of olive oil. Cook for 25 minutes. Transfer into a deep dish and leave until cold.

Note. These peppers are served as hors-d'oeuvre, which in Russia are called '*zakuski*'.

Sweet peppers à la piémontaise. PIMENTS DOUX À LA PIÉMONTAISE—Peel the peppers, remove seeds and cook in stock for 15 minutes. Butter an oven-proof dish and put in the peppers in rows, alternating with rows of cheese *risotto**. Finish with a layer of peppers. Sprinkle with grated Parmesan cheese and melted butter and brown the top gently in the oven.

Sweet pepper purée—see PURÉE.

Ragoût of sweet peppers à l'espagnole. RAGOÛT DE PIMENTS DOUX À L'ESPAGNOLE—Peel 6 peppers, remove seeds, cut into quarters and put into a sauté pan in which ½ cup (100 grams) of finely sliced onion has been softened in oil. Season with salt and red pepper. Add a clove of pounded garlic, sprinkle in a spoonful of flour and moisten with 1½ cups (3 decilitres) of stock and 2 tablespoons of tomato purée. Simmer gently for 35 minutes. Serve in a vegetable dish or timbale. Sprinkle with chopped parsley.

Sweet pepper salad à la créole. SALADE DE PIMENTS DOUX À LA CRÉOLE—Mixture of sweet peppers and boiled rice, seasoned with oil, vinegar, salt and paprika. See SALAD, *Sweet pimento salad à la créole*.

Sweet peppers à la turque. PIMENTS DOUC FARCIS À LA TURQUE—Peel the peppers, open them at the stalk end and remove seeds. Parboil for five minutes and stuff with a forcemeat composed of two-thirds cooked, chopped mutton and one-third rice, boiled in stock, seasoned with salt and pepper, flavoured with a little garlic and bound with 4 tablespoons of tomato purée.

Put the peppers, packing them in rather tightly, into a sauté pan on a foundation of chopped onions lightly fried in oil. Moisten with a few tablespoons of light *Tomato sauce* (see SAUCE). Bring to the boil on the stove, then cook in the oven with a lid on from 30 to 35 minutes. Serve in a *timbale* (vegetable dish) with the pan juices poured over.

Sweet peppers à la vinaigrette. PIMENTS DOUX À LA VINAIGRETTE—Choose small sized peppers and cut them into quarters or slices. Arrange in an hors-d'oeuvre dish. Season with oil, vinegar, salt and pepper. Sprinkle with chopped parsley and chervil.

Note. Sweet peppers prepared as an hors-d'oeuvre may be garnished with finely sliced young onions, tomatoes in small quarters, chopped hard boiled eggs and other ingredients normally used as hors-d'oeuvre garnish.

Black bass perch)

PERCH. PERCHE—A genus of freshwater fish.

The *common* or *river* perch is considered in France one of the best freshwater fish.

It can be recognised by its closely spaced dorsal fins, with hard spines in the first, its hard scalloped scales, sticking closely to the skin, and its bright colours:

olivaceous above, golden yellow below, with six transverse brown bars. River perch reaches a length of 14 inches and attains a weight of 4 pounds. Its flesh is quite delicate and easily digestible.

The young of the species, called *perchettes* in French, are generally fried in deep fat; the medium-sized perch are prepared *à la meunière* and the very big can be stuffed and prepared like *Shad**.

The name of perch is also given to other different species of spiny-finned freshwater fish, such as *Silver perch, Black bass, Trout-perch,* etc.

Black bass, also of North American origin, has been acclimatised in French waters for some years past. Its flesh is white, delicate and has few bones. In flavour it resembles river trout a little and can be prepared in any way suitable for this fish. See TROUT.

The American *perch-trout* also now acclimatised in French waters, is prepared like river trout.

'Bass' is derived from '*Barse*', an old English name for the perch.

PERCOLATOR. PERCOLATEUR—A big coffee pot with a filter used for making black coffee in big quantities. See COFFEE.

PERDRIX—In French culinary terminology the word *perdrix* is used to describe old partridges.

These can be used only for preparing game forcemeats and purées. When they are not too tough, they can also be used for galantines, terrines and pâtés as well as for making game stocks, *fumets** and gravies.

They can also, provided always that they are not too old and that therefore their flesh is not too dry, be stewed with cabbage or used for chartreuse of partridge. Tender old partridges can be prepared in any way suitable for young partridge.

PÉRIGOURDINE (A LA)—All dishes prepared *à la périgourdine* include a garnish of truffles, to which *foie gras* is sometimes added.

PERLOT—Name used in Manche for a small oyster.

PERRY. POIRÉ—Fermented beverage, made in the same way as cider, using pear juice.

The most famous perry is made in Normandy, from Coq pears.

PERSILLADE—Culinary term for chopped parsley, often mixed with varying quantities of chopped garlic, which is added to certain dishes at the end of cooking. The term also applies to left-over meat, fried in butter, cooking fat or oil and sprinkled with *persillade.* Thus we have the household expression *Persillade de boeuf,* which means *Beef sauté with chopped parsley.*

PERSILLER—French term which means to sprinkle a dish with chopped parsley.

PERSIMMON. KAKI—The fruit of a tree of Japanese origin. It has been cultivated for centuries in Japan and China. It is cultivated commercially in France, Italy, Spain and other Mediterranean countries and, in the U.S.A., in the South and in California. It is rather like a tomato in appearance. As it ripens, it turns from yellow to red. It is a soft, sweet fruit, quite pleasant in taste.

Iced persimmon à la créole. KAKIS GLACÉS À LA CRÉOLE—Cut a hole in the fruit round the stalk. Scoop out the pulp without breaking the skins. Sprinkle kirsch or some other liqueur inside the scooped-out fruit. Leave them to steep for an hour in a cool place.

Just before serving, fill them with pineapple ice to which the persimmon pulp has been added after having been rubbed through a fine sieve.

Persimmon à l'impératrice. KAKIS À L'IMPÉRATRICE—Steep the scooped-out fruit in liqueur, as in the previous recipe. Dice the pulp finely and mix it with *Rice à l'impératrice**. Fill the scooped-out fruit with this mixture.

Persimmon jam. CONFITURE DE KAKIS—Made from very ripe fruit in the same way as *Apricot jam.* See JAM.

Persimmon with kirsch. KAKIS AU KIRSCH—Take very ripe persimmons. Cut a hole in each of them. Sprinkle with sugar and pour kirsch into them. Serve on a bed of ice shavings.

Stewed persimmon. COMPOTE DE KAKIS—Made from very ripe fruit, in the same way as stewed apricots. See APRICOTS.

PESTLE. PILON—Wood, metal or porcelain instrument used for pounding in a mortar.

PETITS FOURS (Cakes)—Name adopted for many kinds of small fancy cakes and biscuits.

Petits fours (*Claire*)

The name, according to Carême, who has described a great many *petits fours,* comes from the fact that, in principle, they are baked in a slow oven, after the big cakes have been baked and the temperature of the oven has gone down considerably.

There are two kinds of *petits fours.* The first includes all the little fancy biscuits (cookies), *tuiles, palets de dames,* macaroons, shortbreads, etc. The second covers the iced *petits fours,* generally small *Genoese cake** fancies dipped into *Fondant icing* (see ICING).

There are other *petits fours* which belong more in the realm of confectionery than pastry-making, such as

Iced petits fours

candied fruit sold in the shops in France under the name of *Fruits déguisés*, as well as marzipan fruits, moulded in different shapes and coloured.

PETITE MARMITE—The *petite marmite* is one of the best specialities of Paris restaurants. This method of serving consommé was invented in Paris some eighty years ago.

This presentation of a soup in the earthenware receptacle in which it was cooked, was an enormous success at once and the vogue for '*petite marmite*' soup spread to all the restaurants of the old world and the new.

The *petite marmite*, however, must not suffer from any mediocrity. It must contain all the ingredients which go to make up this dish, i.e. lean pieces of meat, oxtail, poultry, marrow bones and all the usual aromatic stock-pot vegetables, with the addition of little cabbage balls. This consommé is usually served with small pieces of toast, spread with bone marrow, rusks sprinkled with stock-pot fat and dried in the oven, or thin slices of French bread dried in the oven and (as is done in most restaurants) sprinkled with grated cheese.

For the method of preparation of the *petite marmite*, see SOUPS AND BROTHS, *Clear soups*.

PETITS-PIEDS—French menu term used to describe all the small birds, such as blackbirds, thrushes, ortolans, larks, etc.

PETITS POIS—Culinary term for fresh garden peas.

PETS DE NONNE—See FRITTERS, *Soufflé fritters*.

PFANNKUCHEN (*Austrian pastry*). FAN-KOUKE—Roll out ordinary *Brioche dough* (see DOUGH) to a thickness of $\frac{1}{8}$ inch. Cut pieces with a plain pastry cutter, about 3 inches in diameter. In the middle of these rounds put a spoonful of rather thick apricot purée. Moisten the edges with water. Cover with rounds of the same size and seal by pressing the edges firmly together.

Put the *pfannkuchen* on a floured cloth and leave in a warm place to rise.

Fry them, drain and immerse in hot rum syrup.

PFLAUMENKUCHEN (German pastry)—Plum tart made in the German way. See TARTS, *Fruit tart à l'allemande*.

PHEASANT. FAISAN—*Phasianus* is the Latin name of this magnificent and succulent bird, which the ancients called the *bird of Phasis*, the river of Colchide which separated Europe from Asia.

The bird of Phasis, originally a native of the Caspian region, has multiplied in Europe, in game preserves, without losing anything of its distinctive flavour, which is essentially that of a wild bird.

Brillat-Savarin, who prized this bird very highly, tells us in his *Variétés* that the 'pheasant is an enigma to which only experts have the key, and they alone can savour it in all its excellence.'

But he adds, and we must admit here that we are not entirely of his opinion, that the pheasant, like the snipe, does not reach its 'apogee of delicacy' until it begins to decompose. 'This bird, when eaten within three days of its death, is in no way distinguished. It has neither the delicacy of a chicken nor the aroma of a quail.

'Eaten at precisely the right moment, its flesh is tender, sublime and highly flavoured, for it has at once something of the flavour of poultry and of venison.

'This ideal moment is when the pheasant begins to decompose. Then its aroma develops in an oily essence which requires a little fermentation to reach perfection, like the aroma of coffee which manifests itself only through roasting.

'When the pheasant has reached this point, and not before, it should be plucked and it should be interlarded with care, the freshest and finest lardoons being used.'

Brillat-Savarin, who was, without doubt, a great gastronome (perhaps greater as a theorist than as a practitioner, as his contemporaries said), is wrong, wholly wrong, when he says that a young pheasant should be interlarded. This bird must not be interlarded; barded certainly, but not interlarded.

But he is right when he says that it is not unimportant to avoid plucking the pheasant too soon, because careful experiment has proved that birds preserved in their feathers have much more aroma than those left stripped for a long time, either because exposure to the air robs them of some of their aroma, or because (in the case of unplucked birds) some of the oil in the feathers is absorbed into the flesh and gives it added flavour.

The common pheasant is now found all over Europe, as far away as Siberia. Various breeds have sprung from the original Phasis species.

Among these breeds, the following provide the best eating: the *common pheasant*, the *golden pheasant* and the *silver pheasant*. The common pheasant, almost alone, is used for the table. The other breeds are rather for ornament.

True connoisseurs of this most savoury bird prefer the hen-pheasant to the cock. The distinctive features of the cock-pheasant are the shape of its tail, which is longer than its whole body, and its neck feathers, which are iridescent and shot with blue and green. The hen, on the other hand, has a short tail, and its plumage is very much less brilliant in colouring than that of the cock.

A yearling pheasant can be distinguished from an old bird by the first wing-tip feather, which is pointed in a young bird and rounded in an old one. When the upper part of the pheasant's beak is pliable to the touch, then one can be certain that it is a yearling bird.

HOT PHEASANT DISHES. FAISANS CHAUDS:

Pheasant à l'alsacienne. FAISAN À L'ALSACIENNE—This is the name given to *Pheasant with sauerkraut*, prepared as indicated in the recipe below.

Pheasant à l'américaine. FAISAN À L'AMÉRICAINE—Slit a pheasant along the back. Open and flatten gently. Season with salt and pepper. Sauté quickly in butter on both sides. Coat both sides with freshly made breadcrumbs (these breadcrumbs should be seasoned with a touch of cayenne pepper). Grill the pheasant slowly. Put it on a round dish. Cover with slices of grilled bacon. Garnish with grilled tomatoes and mushrooms, bunches of watercress and potato crisps. Serve *Maître d'hôtel butter* separately (see BUTTER, *Compound butters*).

Pheasant à la bohémienne. FAISAN À LA BOHÉMIENNE—Slit along the front. Draw the pheasant and remove the breastbone. Stuff with a small (cold) foie gras, studded with truffles, seasoned with salt and paprika and cooked for 15 minutes in Madeira.

Truss the bird, with the legs pressed tightly against the breast. Cook in a casserole or ovenware dish in butter for about 45 minutes.

Just before serving, pour 2 tablespoons of blazing brandy over the pheasant, and a few tablespoons of game essence. Serve it as it is, in the cooking dish.

Pheasant with cabbage. FAISAN AUX CHOUX—Proceed as for *Partridge poult with cabbage**.

In restaurants this dish is prepared by braising the cabbage with an old pheasant. The cabbage is served, however, with a tender young pheasant pot-roasted in butter.

Casserole of pheasant. FAISAN EN CASSEROLE, EN COCOTTE—Truss the pheasant with the legs pressed tightly against the breast. Cook in butter in an earthenware casserole. When it is cooked, pour a little brandy over it, and 2 to 3 tablespoons of game stock.

Casserole of pheasant with mushrooms. FAISAN EN CASSEROLE AUX CHAMPIGNONS—Prepare the pheasant as for *Casserole of pheasant*. When it is half-cooked, add a dozen mushrooms without the stalks. Finish cooking all together. Finish as for *Casserole of pheasant*.

Pheasant en chartreuse. FAISAN EN CHARTREUSE—Brown a pheasant in the oven and proceed as indicated for *Chartreuse of partridge*. See PARTRIDGE.

Pheasant en cocotte. FAISAN EN COCOTTE—This is another name for *Casserole of pheasant* for which the recipe is given above. In former times this dish was garnished with large mushrooms without their stalks and potatoes trimmed into small pear shapes. This garnish was cooked with the pheasant.

With or without this garnish, proceed as for *Casserole of pheasant*.

The term *en cocotte* does not imply that food prepared in this way must be served with some kind of garnish. It merely indicates the method of cooking, which is actually a kind of pot-roasting in a fireproof earthenware dish (cocotte). *Pheasant en cocotte* can be served with various garnishes but in this case it is desirable to indicate the garnish by the name of the dish. See GARNISHES.

Pheasant en cocotte with cream. FAISAN EN COCOTTE À LA CRÈME—Truss the pheasant with the legs pressed against the breast. Cook in butter until three-parts cooked. At this point, pour on 1¼ cups (2½ decilitres) of fresh cream. Finish cooking, basting the pheasant frequently with the cream. Just before serving, add a squeeze of lemon juice.

Sour cream may be used for this dish.

Pheasant croquettes. CROQUETTES DE FAISAN—Proceed as for *Chicken croquettes**, using a *salpicon** of pheasant, truffles and mushrooms blended in white or brown sauce.

Pheasant cutlets. CÔTELETTES DE FAISAN—These are made with the breast of the bird, cut off before cooking, as for *Chicken côtelettes**, and all recipes and garnishes for these are suitable for pheasant cutlets.

These small cuts are often called '*suprêmes*'.

Pheasant à la géorgienne. FAISAN À LA GÉORGIENNE—This dish belongs to the old Russian culinary repertoire. It may seem somewhat eccentric in composition, but it is, in fact, excellent, especially if a fat pheasant is used.

Truss *en entrée*, that is to say with the legs pressed against the breast, a fine hen-pheasant. Bard it.

Put it in a casserole with about 30 fresh shelled and skinned walnuts. Moisten with the juice of 3 oranges and 1½ pounds (750 grams) of grapes squeezed and strained, a glass of malmsey and the same amount of a very strong infusion of green tea. Add 3 tablespoons of butter. Season with salt and pepper. Cover the pheasant and cook in this mixture for about 45 minutes. Drain. Untruss and remove barding. Brown it. Put it on a round dish surrounded with fresh walnuts. Pour on the cooking stock, strained through muslin, reduced (cooked down) with a few spoonfuls of brown stock added, or, better still, game essence.

Grilled pheasant. FAISAN GRILLÉ—This method is generally used for very young pheasant. Slit the bird along the back. Open and flatten gently. Season with salt and pepper. Coat with butter. Dip in breadcrumbs. Grill slowly, as for *Grilled chicken diable*. See CHICKEN.

Grilled pheasant is served with devilled sauce (*Diable sauce*) or *Périgueux sauce* (see SAUCE).

Pheasant à la languedocienne. FAISAN À LA LANGUEDOCIENNE—Joint a raw pheasant. Season with salt and pepper. Make a *mirepoix** of carrots, onions, celery and lean raw ham seasoned with salt, pepper, powdered thyme and bay leaf. Cook it slowly until very tender. Put the pheasant in the pan with the *mirepoix*. Brown the pheasant. When it is well browned, sprinkle with 2 tablespoons of flour. Cook the flour until it is golden in colour. Moisten with 1½ cups (3 decilitres) of red wine. Mix well. Add a few tablespoons of clear stock and a small *bouquet garni**. Cover and cook for 35 minutes.

Drain the jointed pheasant. Put it in an earthenware (or ovenware) porcelain dish with 8 small mushrooms and a dozen thick strips of truffle. Pour on 2 tablespoons of brandy. Moisten with the sauce, strained, with butter added. Put the lid on the baking dish. Seal the edges with flour-and-water paste. Stand in water and cook in the oven for 35 minutes. Serve in the baking dish.

Pheasant à la normande. FAISAN À LA NORMANDE—Brown the pheasant in butter and put it in an oval ovenware dish or casserole lined with a layer of peeled sweet apples, sliced and lightly browned in butter. Surround the pheasant with apples prepared in the same way. Cook in a slow oven. Just before serving, pour fresh cream and a little calvados over it.

Hot pheasant pâté—See PÂTÉ, *Hot pâtés*.

Pheasant à la périgueux. FAISAN À LA PÉRIGUEUX—This is really truffled pheasant, pot-roasted instead of roasted. It is served on a slice of sandwich bread fried in butter and surrounded by large *forcemeat** balls made from game stuffing with truffles.

Serve *Périgueux sauce* separately (see SAUCE) with the cooking stock of the pheasant added to it.

Pheasant pie with truffles. TOURTE DE FAISAN AUX TRUFFES—Proceed, using pheasant, as indicated for *Woodcock pie with truffles**.

Pheasant purée. PURÉE DE FAISAN—Usually, this purée is made from pot-roasted pheasant or pheasant scraps. It is used for filling small vol-au-vents, barquettes, or tartlets. Proceed as indicated for *Purée of woodcock*. See WOODCOCK.

Roast pheasant. FAISAN RÔTI—Truss and bard the breast with a large slice of pork fat. Tie the fat with string. Baste the pheasant with melted butter. Season. Roast in a hot oven for about 30 minutes. If the pheasant is roasted on the spit, allow a few minutes longer for cooking.

Untruss the pheasant. Put it on a long dish on a slice of fried bread, spread with *à gratin forcemeat* (see FORCEMEAT) if desired. (The stuffing should be made with the chopped liver of the pheasant.) Garnish with watercress and lemon. Serve the cooking stock, diluted, with it.

Pheasant à la Sainte-Alliance. FAISAN À LA SAINTE-ALLIANCE—'Take a pheasant, hung until it is perfect to eat. Pluck it and interlard it carefully with the freshest and firmest pork fat you can find.

'Take two woodcocks. Bone and draw them and make two piles, one of the meat, the other of the entrails and livers.

'With the meat, make a stuffing by chopping it with steamed beef bone-marrow, a little grated pork fat, pepper, salt, *fines herbes**, and a quantity of good truffles, enough to stuff the pheasant completely.

'Take care to put in the stuffing in such a way that none falls out. This is sometimes difficult when the bird is rather old. Nevertheless, there are various ways of achieving this end. One is to cut a slice of bread and tie it on to the bird with a string, so as to seal its breast.

'Cut a slice of bread which overlaps the laid-out pheasant from neck to tail by two inches. Next take the liver and entrails of the woodcock. Pound in a mortar with two large truffles, an anchovy, a little grated pork fat and a piece of good fresh butter.

'Toast the bread and spread this paste evenly on it. Put this under the pheasant, prepared as indicated above, so that the bread will be thoroughly impregnated with the roasting juice.

'When the pheasant is cooked, serve it, elegantly couched on the slice of bread. Surround with Seville oranges, and look forward with an easy mind to the outcome.' (Brillat-Savarin, *Physiologie du goût.*)

Salmis of pheasant. SALMIS DE FAISAN—Roast the pheasant in the oven or on the spit until it is three-quarters cooked. Joint it. Trim the pieces and skin them. Put them in a buttered pan. Cover with 1 cup (150 grams) of mushrooms tossed in butter (whole if they are small, colloped if they are large) and 5 ounces (150 grams) of truffles, shredded. Pour on ½ cup of *Espagnole sauce*, based on concentrated game stock (see SAUCE). Keep hot, *taking care not to allow it to come to the boil.*

Chop the carcase and the trimmings. Put them to brown slightly in a pan in which ½ cup of *mirepoix** has been cooked. Moisten with the cooking stock of the pheasant, diluted with 1 cup (2 decilitres) of white wine. Cook down. Moisten with ¾ cup (1½ decilitres) of *Espagnole sauce* based on concentrated game stock. Cook for 15 minutes. Strain the sauce through a fine strainer, pressing with the back of a spoon so as to extract all the juice from the meat and vegetables. Strain this sauce once more through muslin. Reduce (cook down). Add 2 tablespoons of blazing brandy and 4 tablespoons of butter. Mix and pour over the pheasant. Heat, *taking care not to allow to come to the boil.*

To serve. Drain the pheasant. Arrange the joints in a pyramid on a round dish on a slice of bread fried in butter, spread with game *à gratin forcemeat* (see FORCE-MEAT) and browned in the oven. Put the mushrooms and truffles on top. Pour the sauce, piping hot, over the dish.

Instead of serving the salmis on a large slice of bread, it may be put in a deep dish or a shallow bowl. Pour its sauce over it and garnish with slices of fried bread cut into heart shapes and spread with game *à gratin* forcemeat.

Salmis of pheasant in red wine. SALMIS DE FAISAN AU VIN ROUGE. Proceed in every particular as indicated above, moistening with red wine instead of white wine.

Pheasant sauté. FAISAN SAUTÉ, SAUTÉ DE FAISAN—Pheasant is seldom prepared in this way. A tender young pheasant can, however, be sautéed.

Joint the bird. Season with salt and pepper. Sauté in butter slowly, taking care not to dry the pheasant.

Serve the jointed bird on a round dish. Pour over it the cooking stock diluted with white wine or any other wine, according to the recipe, flavoured with a little concentrated game or veal stock, with butter added.

Pheasant à la Souvarov. FAISAN À LA SOUVAROV—Stuff the pheasant with a coarse *salpicon** of foie gras and truffles seasoned with salt, pepper and spice, and with brandy poured over it.

Truss the bird with the legs pressed against the breast. Bard it. Cook in butter until three-quarters cooked. Untruss and untie the barding.

Put it in an oval earthenware dish with twelve medium-sized truffles, tossed in butter.

Moisten with the cooking stock diluted with Madeira. Add 1 cup (2 decilitres) of *Demi-glace sauce*, based on concentrated game stock with a little brandy (see SAUCE).

Cover the dish. Seal with flour-and-water paste. Finish cooking in the oven for 15 to 18 minutes.

Suprêmes of pheasant. SUPRÊMES DE FAISAN—Cut off the wings and breasts of the pheasant before cooking (these are the *suprêmes*). Poach them or sauté in butter, and serve with various sauces and garnishes.

The breasts of pheasants are seldom prepared in this way, though all recipes for *Suprêmes of chicken* (see CHICKEN) are suitable for *Suprêmes of pheasant.*

Truffled pheasant. FAISAN TRUFFÉ—Pheasant is truffled in the same way as young turkey.

Ingredients for a medium-sized truffled pheasant. ¾ pound (350 grams) of fresh pork suet and ½ pound (250 grams) of truffles.

In the oven, cook for 50 to 55 minutes (medium oven), on the spit, for 55 minutes to an hour.

The bird must be truffled at least 24 hours before cooking.

COLD PHEASANT DISHES. FAISANS FROIDS.

Pheasant aspic à l'ancienne. ASPIC DE FAISAN À L'ANCIENNE—Truss a pheasant with the legs pressed against the breast. Pot-roast in butter keeping the meat slightly pinkish in colour. Cut off the breasts. Separate the mignon fillets (underpart of breast meat) from the *suprêmes.* Cut each *suprême* in 3 thin *aiguillettes.*

Spread one side of these *aiguillettes* thickly with pheasant purée made from the legs and some foie gras, blended with a little concentrated game stock, flavoured with a little liqueur brandy, with a third of its weight of whipped cream added. Dome the purée slightly on top of the *aiguillettes* of pheasant. Cover them with *White chaud-froid sauce* based on game stock (see SAUCE).

On top of each one put a strip of truffle dipped in jelly. Glaze with game jelly. Line an aspic mould with jelly and put in the *aiguillettes.* Decorate with collops cut from the mignon fillets and with strips of truffle.

Fill the mould with very clear game jelly. Leave to set in a refrigerator or cooler.

Turn out the aspic straight on to a round dish or on to a slice of bread cut to the size of the mould, and buttered.

Surround the aspic with chopped jelly and a border of rounds of jelly (shaped with a pastry-cutter).

Ballottine of pheasant in jelly (Carême's recipe). BALLOTTINE DE FAISAN À LA GELÉE—'Take a Strasbourg foie gras. Soak in cold water and blanch. Cut each half into 4 fillets and trim.

'Pound 2 of these fillets in a mortar with the trimmings and the meat of a red partridge with an equal weight of pork fat. Season the mixture very well. Add 2 yolks of eggs and *fines herbes* tossed in butter. Pound the lot thoroughly. (By '*fines herbes*', Carême means cultivated mushrooms.)

'Rub the stuffing through a *quenelle* sieve. Carefully bone a well hung, fat partridge. Lay it on a cloth and season very well.

'Lay on top of it half the stuffing, and then 3 fillets of foie gras, interspersing these with halved truffles. Add as much spiced salt as required. Cover the whole with half the remaining stuffing.

'Lay on top the rest of the foie gras and the halves of truffle. Season and cover with the rest of the stuffing.

'Fold the pheasant into shape. Wrap in a cloth. Tie and cook in jelly stock flavoured with Madeira, to which have been added the bones and trimmings of the pheasant and partridge.

'Leave the *ballottine* to cool under a light weight. Glaze with jelly in the usual way.'

Chaud-froid of pheasant
(*French Government Tourist Office*)

Chaud-froid of pheasant. FAISAN EN CHAUD-FROID—Truss a pheasant with the legs pressed against the breast. Cook in butter, taking care that the meat remains pinkish. Joint the bird. Skin the pieces and trim them.

Coat with *Brown chaud-froid sauce* (see SAUCE) prepared in the usual way, with game stock flavoured with essence of truffles. Decorate these pieces of pheasant with truffles cut into fancy shapes, the whites of hard boiled eggs and other decorative motifs. All these must be dipped into half-set jelly before they are put on the pheasant. Glaze the joints of pheasant with jelly. Chill in a refrigerator or cooler.

Line a round dish with a slice of buttered sandwich bread. Arrange the pheasant on it, with the legs on the platform of bread and the breast and wings on top. Surround the pheasant with chopped jelly (use a spoon for this; if the jelly is piped it may be discoloured). Make a border of rounds of jelly, cut out carefully with a pastry cutter. As with all *chauds-froids* of poultry or winged game the pheasant *en chaud-froid* can be served in a glass bowl or deep round silver dish, and coated with very clear jelly. In fact, this is the very best way of serving this dish.

Daube of pheasant in jelly. FAISAN EN DAUBE À LA GELÉE—Slit a pheasant along the back and bone it. Season inside. Stuff with a forcemeat made of lean veal, *à gratin game stuffing* (see FORCEMEAT) and foie gras, with 3 tablespoons of game essence and 2 tablespoons of brandy added. Season this stuffing well and bind with 1 or 2 yolks of egg. Spread the stuffing evenly on the pheasant and put in the middle half a raw foie gras studded with 4 large raw quarters of truffle. Season with spiced salt and pour on a little brandy. Fold the pheasant into shape. Truss with the legs pressed against the breast. Bard with a thin slice of pork fat. Pot-roast in Madeira for 45 minutes to an hour.

Drain the pheasant. Untruss and remove the pork fat. Put it in an oval earthenware dish into which it fits exactly. Moisten with the cooking stock with 2½ cups (5 decilitres) of jelly added (game jelly for preference). The stock must be strained without removing the fat.

Leave to cool thoroughly for at least 12 hours. Before serving (in the earthenware dish) skim off the film of fat on the surface of the jelly.

Galantine of pheasant in jelly. GALANTINE DE FAISAN À LA GELÉE—Proceed as for *Ballottine of pheasant in jelly.*

Pheasant loaf à l'ancienne—See LOAVES, *Winged game loaf.*

Pheasant pâté. PÂTÉ DE FAISAN—Completely bone a large pheasant. Set aside the wings and breasts to be cut into thin slices and steeped in brandy. With the rest of the meat prepare a stuffing as indicated under FORCEMEAT. Season the stuffing, flavour with a little brandy and bind with an egg. Line an oval pâté mould (a mould with a hinged lid) with *ordinary* or *fine lining pastry* (see DOUGH), and cover this with thin slices of pork fat.

Put a layer of stuffing at the bottom of the mould. On this stuffing arrange some of the slices of breast alternating with thin slices of foie gras and quartered truffles. Cover these with a layer of stuffing and continue to fill the mould in this way to within ⅛ inch of the rim, ending with a layer of stuffing. On top of this last layer, put half a bay leaf. Fold inward the overlapping ends of the pork fat. Cover the pâté with an oval layer of rolled-out pastry which must be pressed down at the edges. Pink the edges with pastry pincers to form a coxcomb design. Make a round hole in the middle of the pâté for the escape of steam. Decorate the top with motifs cut with a pastry cutter from a thinly rolled out layer of dough. Brush the top of the pâté with egg. Bake in a moderate oven for 1¼ hours, or longer if the pâté is large.

Leave to cool without turning out. When it is cold, pour in half-set jelly.

Pheasant pâtés (like all cold pâtés) must be prepared at least 24 hours before using.

In addition to those listed above, other ingredients may be used, such as thin slices of lean cooked ham or pickled tongue; thin slices of fresh pork fat, etc.

Another way of preparing the pâté is to dice coarsely the slices of pheasant and other whole ingredients and mix them with the stuffing.

Potted pheasant. TERRINE DE FAISAN—This is made with the same ingredients as those indicated for *Pheasant pâté:* thin slices of breast of pheasant, foie gras, truffles, game stuffing.

With these ingredients, fill a round or oval bowl (lined with thin slices of pork fat) in alternate layers. On top of the last layer of stuffing put a thin slice of pork fat. Cover the bowl, sealing the edges with flour-and-water paste. Stand in water and cook in the oven for an hour to an hour and 45 minutes, according to the size of the bowl. Leave the mixture to cool under a light weight.

Next day, that is to say when the potted pheasant is quite cold, turn it out. Dry it with a cloth, then put it back in the bowl which must, meanwhile, have been lined with a layer of lard ⅛ inch thick. The lard must be well set before the mixture is put into the bowl. Pour lard which is almost cold on top of the mixture so that it is completely covered and the edges sealed with lard.

Thus encased in fat, the potted pheasant will keep for several days. If it is to be eaten at once, concentrated game jelly may be used instead of lard.

Preserved pheasant with foie gras and jelly. CONSERVE DE FAISAN AU FOIE GRAS À LA GELÉE—Prepare the pheasant as indicated for *Daube of pheasant in jelly.* Drain, untruss and remove barding. Dry well in a cloth.

Put it in a tin just large enough to take the whole of it. Cover with very clear jelly (made from the cooking stock and clarified), flavoured with Madeira or some other heavy wine. Solder the tin. Mark the lid with a touch of solder. Put it in a pan with enough water to cover the tin. Boil. Leave to boil *steadily* for an hour and a quarter. Take the tin out of the pan. Put it upside down on a table so that the breast of the pheasant is glazed with jelly. Leave to get cold.

Pheasant Prince Orloff in jelly. FAISAN PRINCE ORLOFF À LA GELÉE—Bone a pheasant, leaving the bones in the wing tips and lower part of the leg. Season the pheasant inside, and stuff with a forcemeat made of the boned meat of another pheasant, trimmed and minced, with an equal quantity of fresh chopped pork fat and a quarter of its volume of cooked foie gras coarsely diced, and diced truffles. Season the mixture well and flavour with a spoonful of brandy.

Fold the pheasant into shape and sew it up. Baste with melted butter. Wrap in a fine cloth and tie with several lengths of string. Put the pheasant, trussed in this way, in a braising pan lined with fresh pork skin, and carrots and onions cut into rounds and tossed in butter. Moisten with game stock, made separately from the bones and trimmings of the two pheasants. Cover and cook slowly for a quarter of an hour.

Drain the pheasant. Unwrap it, then wrap it again after washing the cloth in hot water and wringing it out. Tie and leave until it is quite cold.

When the pheasant is very cold (it can be prepared the day before it is required), unwrap it. Dry it well in a cloth and coat it completely with a *White chaud-froid sauce* (see SAUCE), made with the cooking stock of the pheasant. Decorate the breast of the bird with truffles and the whites of hard boiled egg cut round or into fancy shapes. Highlight with jelly flavoured with Madeira. Serve the pheasant on a long dish, on a slice of sandwich bread, cut to the size of the pheasant and spread with melted butter. Surround with 8 truffles, cooked in Madeira, scooped out and filled with purée of foie gras. Separate the truffles with a spoonful of chopped jelly, and make a border of jelly cut into triangles.

(Instead of a dish an oval glass bowl may be used for serving the pheasant, which should then be coated with jelly.)

Pheasant with sauerkraut or à l'alsacienne. FAISAN À LA CHOUCROUTE, À L'ALSACIENNE—Truss the pheasant with the legs pressed tightly against the breast. Cook in butter, keeping the meat pinkish inside. Put in a braising pan in which sauerkraut has been cooked in the usual way, flavoured with game essence and goose fat, with the customary garnish of belly of pork (fat bacon) and saveloy. Cook in the oven for 25 minutes.

Put the pheasant on a long dish, on a bed of sauerkraut, surround with the saveloy and with the fat bacon cut in rectangles.

PHOSPHORUS. PHOSPHORE—Phosphorus is a chemical element which is a constituent of animal tissues, including the brain, and forms a major part of bone material; in combination with albumen (nuclein) or the fats (lecithin), it enters into the composition of the muscles, the glands and the nerve tissues.

Generally speaking, the food we eat contains too great a proportion of phosphorus substances, a great part of which is eliminated. It would appear that the substance which is easiest to assimilate is vegetable phosphorus matter.

PHYSALIS PERUVIANA—Botanical name for *Cape gooseberry.* See also STRAWBERRY TOMATO (*Physalis alkekengi*).

PHYTOLACCA—A genus of shrubs, one species of which, *Phytolacca decandra*, is known as *Virginian poke weed* or *Pokeberry*, *Pigeon berry*, *Red-ink plant*, *Vermilion plant* or *Dyer's grapes*. The shoots and young leaves of this plant are sometimes eaten in the southern states of the U.S.A., like spinach or asparagus, but the seeds and roots are poisonous. The berries have a staining juice.

PICARDAN—Variety of Languedoc vine plant, producing muscat wines.

PICARDY. PICARDIE—This region of France, according to some authorities, is the least favoured from the gastronomical point of view.

'In Picardy', Alphonse Karr wrote some sixty years ago, 'I was served a leek flan. It would have been awful, had one been able to eat it.'

Although 'leek flan' or *flamique*, which enjoys great popularity in Picardy—and in the Champagne region as well—is not a dish of transcendent quality, it is not so bad as the author of *Les Guêpes* will have us believe.

In addition, there are many other culinary specialities in the Picardy region repertoire which a true gastronome would not disdain, such as, for example, the magnificent duck pâtés of Amiens and Abbeville.

The Picardy larder is well stocked. The market gardening industry of the region produces very good vegetables.

Magnificent vegetables are grown in the Amiens area, most of which are exported to England, where they are particularly appreciated.

Cattle raised for food in the Picardy pastures produces meat of the first quality. The Baie-de-Somme salt meadow sheep are famous. Picardy pork is also excellent and is made into exquisite pork butchery products.

Although the coast of Picardy does not stretch very far, sea fish, crustaceans and shellfish are found in great abundance. Cockles, which are called *hénons* locally, are found in prodigious quantities in Baie de la Somme.

Excellent fish is found in the River Somme.

As for game, this region abounds in birds of passage: wild duck, teal and gargney, and sometimes even bustards, or wild geese—game which, as is well known, is becoming more and more rare in France. Thrushes, too, are found in Picardy in vast numbers.

Excellent cheeses are made in Picardy, some of which, such as those of Maroilles, which are usually referred to as *Marolles*, and those of Mouchelet, are very famous.

Cider is the local drink, but a lot of beer is also drunk in this region.

Culinary specialities—Excellent pork butchery produce of all kinds: *Andouilles*, *Andouillettes**, various small *Sausages*, *Black puddings*, *Smoked ham*, etc.

Tripe soup, which is made as an ordinary *pot-au-feu** using pork offal and parings, muzzle, ears, liver, heart. spleen, etc.; *Pumpkin soup; Frogs' legs soup; Leek soup; Flamiques* or *Flamiches*, a kind of country flan made of leeks, onions and marrows; various fish *Pâtés; Amiens* and *Abbeville duck pâté; Caqhuse*, a fresh piece of braised pork; *Potato flan; Potato pie*.

The following are among the sweet and confectionery specialities of Picardy: *Apple tart, Péronne shortbreads, Vitalons*, a kind of *quenelles* made of batter and poached in sweetened, aromatised milk; *Gâteau battu; Plum tart; Taliburs aux pommes*, similar to *Douillon Normand; Bissale*, made of buttered bread dough; and the Amiens, Abbeville and Ham *Macaroons* and *Biscuits*.

edges well together. Knock up (turn up) and scallop the sides, decorate with pieces of the same pastry, rolled out and cut in fancy shapes, brush with beaten egg and bake in a slow oven from 45 minutes to an hour.

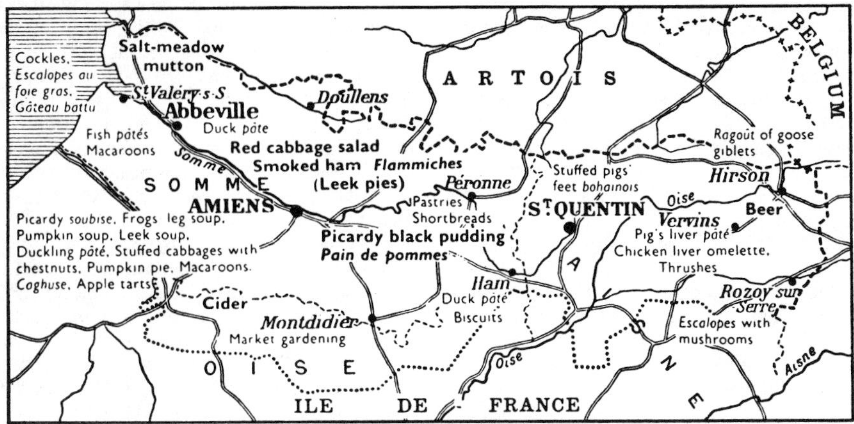

Gastronomic map of Picardy

PICAREL—French name for small Mediterranean fish, which is prepared like anchovy.

PICCALILLI—A pickle, originally East Indian, of chopped vegetables in vinegar, mustard and spices. This product is found in the shops ready for use.

PICHOLINE—French name for big green table olives.

PICKEREL. BROCHETON—Young pike. It can be prepared in any manner given for large pike (see PIKE), and is used mainly for *matelotes** and freshwater fish stews.

PICKLED. À L'ÉCARLATE—Pork or beef are pickled by steeping for a longer or shorter period in brine with saltpetre added, and then boiled.

The addition of saltpetre to the brine causes the meat to turn red. It is, therefore, known in France as pork or beef *à l'écarlate* (scarlet meat).

PICKLES—Gherkins, cucumbers and various vegetables pickled in vinegar and spices. This product is found in the shops ready for use, and is often bottled in the home.

PICNIC. PIQUE-NIQUE—A meal taken in the open, or a meal to which each participant contributes a dish.

PICQUEPOUL OR PICPOUILLE—Variety of vine plant grown in Gers, from which Armagnac is distilled.

PIE OR PÂTÉ—An article of food, consisting of a pastry crust with various kinds of filling. See also TART and PÂTÉS.

Apple pie à l'anglaise. PÂTÉ DE POMMES À L'ANGLAISE—*Ingredients.* 3¾ cups (500 grams) of sifted flour, 1½ cups (350 grams) of butter, 2 tablespoons (25 grams) of castor (fine) sugar, 2 yolks of egg, 1 cup (2 decilitres) of water and 1½ teaspoons (10 grams) of salt.

Method. Put the flour in a circle on the board, make a well in the middle, put into it the salt and the sugar and dissolve these ingredients with water. Add the yolks. Mix the pastry without kneading too much. Roll into a ball and leave to stand in a cool place for 2 hours.

The apples. Cut them into quarters, remove core, peel and cut into thick slices. Put into an English pie dish, piling them up into a dome. Sprinkle with castor (fine) sugar mixed with a little powdered cinnamon.

Pastry lid. Wet the edges of the pie dish and put a border of pastry around them. Brush this over with a little water and cover with a lid of pastry, pressing the

Beefsteak pie—See BEEF.

Beefsteak and kidney pie—See BEEF.

Chicken pie. PÂTÉ CHAUD DE POULET À L'ANGLAISE—Joint a medium-sized chicken. Sprinkle the joints with finely chopped shallots, onion, mushrooms and parsley and season with salt and pepper.

Put these pieces of chicken into an English pie dish lined with thin seasoned slices of veal on the bottom and walls.

Arrange the joints, putting in first the legs, then the wings and breast. Cover with 5 ounces (150 grams) of bacon cut into thin rashers (slices). Add 4 halved yolks of hard boiled eggs.

Pour in chicken stock to cover the ingredients up to three-quarters.

Wet the edges of the pie dish and put round a band of pastry. Brush this over with a little water and cover with a lid of puff pastry, press the edges well together, knock up (turn up) and scallop the sides, make a hole in the centre and brush over with beaten egg. Bake in a moderate oven for an hour and a half.

When the pie is cooked, pour in a few tablespoons of concentrated chicken gravy.

Hot guinea fowl pie. PÂTÉ CHAUD DE PINTADE—Prepare as *Hot chicken pâté* (see PÂTÉ), using a boned guinea fowl, stuffed with foie gras and truffles (fine truffled forcemeat).

This pie can also be prepared using cooked and jointed guinea fowl, as described in the recipe for *Duckling pie à la rouennaise* (see DUCK).

Mince pies. GÂTEAUX DE NOËL—These pies are especially popular in England. They are, wrote Suzanne, 'the cakes which, with the traditional plum pudding, are pre-eminent among the dishes of the copious Christmas Dinner.'

These pies are made by filling with mincemeat small deep tartlets made of pie crust or flaky pastry. The tartlets are covered with a thin roof of flaky pastry with a hole pricked in the middle. They are brushed with egg, baked in a hot oven, and served hot. Here is a French recipe for mince pies:

Mincemeat. Prepare and leave to soak for 6 to 8 days the following ingredients:

4 tablespoons (100 grams) of finely chopped fillet of beef, 2 tablespoons (50 grams) of pickled tongue very

finely diced, 2 tablespoons (50 grams) of chopped fat bacon, ½ cup (100 grams) of sultanas, ½ cup (100 grams) of currants, carefully cleaned, ⅓ cup (50 grams) of almonds, freshly blanched and chopped, ⅓ cup (50 grams) of brown sugar, a pinch of mixed spices, the grated rind of a lemon and the juice. Mix these ingredients together, adding half a glass of brandy.

Special pie crust. 3¾ cups (500 grams) of sieved flour, 1½ cups (100 grams) of beef suet, 7 tablespoons (100 grams) of butter, 1 egg, 1½ teaspoons (10 grams) of salt, ⅓ to ½ cup (about 10 centilitres) of water. Knead all these ingredients into a rather firm dough. Leave it to stand, then roll it out and fold it into three. Repeat this operation twice more. Divide the dough into small pieces and line deep buttered tartlet tins with the pieces, making sure the dough is evenly spread. Fill each tartlet with mincemeat and cover with a pastry lid. The pies should be sealed at the edges with pastry pincers. Brush the tops of the pies with milk and sprinkle lightly with brown sugar. Cook in a fairly hot oven.

Hot mutton pie (English cookery). PÂTÉ CHAUD DE MOUTON À L'ANGLAISE—This pie is made in a special pie dish and is covered with lining pastry. It is made with mutton in the same way as *Steak pie*. See BEEF.

Small mutton pies or mutton patties. PETITS PÂTÉS DE MOUTON À L'ANGLAISE—Line rather deep tartlet tins with ordinary *Lining paste* (see DOUGH).

Fill with mutton, half fat half lean, cut in small dice, seasoned with salt and pepper (the latter in a generous proportion), and sprinkled with chopped *fines herbes**.

Cover with a lid of *Puff pastry* (see DOUGH), sealing the edges thoroughly.

Brush the top with beaten egg and make a small hole in the middle of the pies.

Bake in a moderate oven for 40 minutes.

When baked, pour into each patty a tablespoon of not-too-thick *Demi-glace sauce* (see SAUCE).

These patties are generally eaten hot, but can also be eaten cold.

Pigeon pie. PÂTÉ CHAUD DE PIGEON À L'ANGLAISE—This is made in an English pie dish, the bottom and walls of which should be lined with thin rashers of smoked bacon. Sprinkle these rashers of bacon with finely chopped shallots and put in the pigeons, each cut in four pieces, seasoned with salt and pepper and sprinkled with chopped parsley. Add a hard boiled egg yolk, cut in half, for each pigeon.

Pour in some light brown gravy to about half-way. Wet the edges of the pie dish and put a border of pastry around them. Brush this over with a little water and cover with a lid of puff pastry, press the edges well together, knock up (turn up) and scallop the sides, make a hole in the centre and brush over with beaten egg. Bake in a moderate oven for an hour and a half.

Take out of the oven and pour into the pie a few tablespoons of gravy.

Hot pigeon pie à la languedocienne. PÂTÉ CHAUD DE PIGEON À LA LANGUEDOCIENNE—Proceed as described in the recipe for *Hot pigeon pie with mushrooms and truffles*, replacing the last two ingredients by a garnish composed of salsify (cooked in a *court-bouillon**, cut into little sticks and fried in butter), stoned and blanched olives, small button mushrooms, sliced chicken livers sautéed in butter and lean bacon, cut up, well scalded and fried.

Before serving put into the pie a few tablespoons of concentrated brown veal gravy.

Note. This type of pie is usually made as a *croustade**, that is to say in the manner of English pies, cooked in a pie dish and covered with a piece of rolled-out pastry.

Hot pigeon pie with mushrooms and truffles. PÂTÉ CHAUD DE PIGEON AUX CHAMPIGNONS ET AUX TRUFFES—Line a low round mould with *Fine lining paste* (see DOUGH).

Coat the walls and the bottom with truffled *Quenelle forcemeat* (see FORCEMEAT). Put the truffles and mushrooms, sliced and lightly tossed in butter, on the bottom of the pie dish. On this put two pigeons, each cut in four pieces and browned in butter. Cover with truffles and mushrooms. Sprinkle with melted butter. Cover with pastry, finish making the pie in the usual manner and bake in the oven for about one hour.

At the last moment, pour into the pie a few tablespoons of chicken *Velouté sauce* (see SAUCE) cooked with cream and flavoured with Madeira or any other wine.

Pork pie—See PORK.

Raised pie cooked blind (mixed entrée). CROÛTE DE GRANDE TIMBALE CUITE À BLANC—Butter the interior of a large charlotte mould, and decorate the sides with details made with a *Noodle paste**.

Make some short pastry into a ball. Roll out the ball into a round about 8 inches in diameter. Sprinkle the round of pastry lightly with flour and fold it in half. Take the points of this half-circle and draw them together in such a way as to form a kind of dome. Roll it out once to make an even thickness of about ⅛ of an inch. Put the dome in the bottom of the mould. Press on the bottom and round the sides to make the paste adhere to the mould and rise gently up the sides, without disturbing the noodle paste decorations.

Line the bottom and the sides of the mould with a fine buttered paper and fill it up with dried raw beans or other articles in the same way as for a *Flan case**. Put a dome-shaped piece of paper on top of the dry filling, and put a thin sheet of pastry on top of this, joining the edges together with the pastry lining, by gently pressing with the fingers. Make the rim of the pie by pinching this border with pastry pincers both inside and out. Moisten lightly the part forming the lid with water, and put decorative details on it arranged in a regular manner, cut from a thin sheet of pastry, leaves, roses, made with a special pastry cutter or with a knife.

Put on top of the lid 3 or 4 rounds of pastry, cut with a circular, fluted, pastry cutter and emptied to make circles. Stick these circles of paste together and make an opening in the middle to allow for the escape of steam during the cooking. Gild the outside of the pie and cook in the oven at a good moderate heat for 30 to 35 minutes.

When the pastry is cooked, take off the lid. Remove the paper and the provisional filling; gild the interior with egg and let it dry for a few minutes at the mouth of the oven. (The pie can be immediately turned out of its mould and dried off in a warm place.) Fill it with whatever preparation is indicated.

Raised pies, or *timbales*, cooked blind in this way, are used for a great number of mixed entrées. They can be filled after cooking with various *ragoûts**, simple or complex, or with fillings such as *Financière*, *Grimaldi*, *Joinville*, *Milanaise*, *Napolitaine*, *Toulousaine*, or things of the same nature. Most often, these *timbales* are filled with macaroni which is arranged in layers alternating with a ragoût composed of various elements combined with a white or brown sauce. See TIMBALE.

PIÈCES MONTÉES—In old-fashioned culinary practice much use was made of decorative pieces, which were often made of inedible ingredients. They were frequently monumental affairs and have now disappeared so far as cookery is concerned, although they still survive to a certain extent in pastry-making.

PIED-DE-CHEVAL—A variety of large oysters, not greatly esteemed in Europe.

PIÉMONTAISE (A LA)—Garnish served with meat and poultry. It is composed of *timbales* of risotto, mixed with blanched, shredded truffles. The risotto can be served in a mound with the meat or poultry.

PIERRY—Name of a vineyard on the Epernay slope, producing grapes from which excellent champagne is made.

PIG—See PORK.

PIGEON, SQUAB—PIGEONNEAU—Granivorous bird of which there are many domestic and wild species. The principal of these are *rock-pigeons* or *carrier-pigeons*, from which, it is considered, the domesticated varieties evolved, the *ring-dove* or *wood-pigeon* whose flesh is much esteemed by gastronomes, and *turtle-dove* or *passenger pigeon.*

In French culinary language the word pigeon rarely figures on the menu. The word *pigeonneau* (squab) is used instead. This applies to a very young and really tender bird, which can be prepared in many different ways.

Unlike other birds, pigeon's liver contains no gall. It is therefore customary to leave the liver inside the bird when dressing it.

It is drawn and prepared for cooking like all other domesticated birds. Pigeons should be barded before being roasted on a spit or cooked in a casserole or a *cocotte.*

Casserole of pigeon (squab) or pigeon en cocotte. PIGEONNEAU EN CASSEROLE, EN COCOTTE—Prepare like *Casserole of chicken* or *Chicken en cocotte.* See CHICKEN.

Pigeon (squab) à la catalan (Catalan style) or en pistache. PIGEONNEAU À LA CATALANE, EN PISTACHE—Proceed as described in the recipe for *Partridge à la catalane*.*

Cold pigeons (squabs). PIGEONS FROIDS—Pigeons and squabs can be prepared in any way suitable for poultry, particularly for spring chickens and grain-fed poulets. See CHICKEN.

Cold pigeons can be prepared as *Ballottines; en Chaud-froid; Daube à la gelée; Galantine; Mousse; Mousselines; Loaf; Pie* and *Terrine.*

Compote of pigeon (squab) I. PIGEONNEAU EN COMPOTE—Brown the pigeon in butter and drain. Dilute the pan juices with ½ cup (1 decilitre) of white wine; boil down by two-thirds, add ¾ cup (1½ decilitres) of *Demi-glace sauce* (see SAUCE) and strain.

Put the pigeon back in the casserole with 12 small, glazed onions, 12 mushrooms and 2 tablespoons (50 grams) of fat bacon cut in dice, scalded and fried. Cover with the sauce, bring to the boil, cover the casserole and cook in the oven from 25 to 30 minutes.

Arrange the pigeon on a serving dish, surround with garnish and pour the sauce over it.

Compote of pigeon (squab) II. PIGEONNEAU EN COMPOTE—Fry some fat bacon, cut in dice and scalded, in a tablespoon of butter. Add blanched onions and mushrooms. Fry together, then drain all this garnish.

Brown the pigeon in the same fat, remove, put a tablespoon of flour into a casserole, moisten with ½ cup (a decilitre) of white wine, reduce, add 1 cup (2 decilitres) of white stock and reduce by one-third.

Put the pigeon and its garnish back in the casserole, add a *bouquet garni** and cook with a lid on for 25 to 30 minutes.

Pigeon (squab) à la crapaudine. PIGEONNEAU À LA CRAPAUDINE—Split the pigeon horizontally, from the tip of the breast to the wings.

Open it, flatten slightly, spread with melted butter and season with salt and pepper.

Grill slowly until both sides are golden.

Arrange the pigeon on a round dish.

Decorate the border of the dish with a row of gherkins cut in round slices or in some other way.

Serve *Diable sauce* separately. See SAUCE.

Pigeon (squab) à la diable. PIGEONNEAU À LA DIABLE—Prepare as described in the recipe for *Chicken à la diable*.*

Fried pigeon (squab). PIGEONNEAU EN FRITOT—Prepare like *Chicken fritot*.*

Grilled pigeon (squab) à la Saint-Germain. PIGEONNEAU GRILLÉ À LA SAINT-GERMAIN—Split the pigeon open, remove most of the bones from inside, flatten slightly, season with salt and pepper, spread with melted butter, cover on both sides with freshly grated breadcrumbs, sprinkle with butter and grill slowly.

Arrange the pigeon on a round dish. Put some rather thick *Béarnaise sauce* (see SAUCE) on both sides and garnish with *Potatoes à la parisienne*.* Cook down a few tablespoons of veal gravy, add some butter to it and pour around the pigeon.

Pigeon (squab) à la Maître-Jacques (old recipe). PIGEONNEAU À LA MAÎTRE-JACQUES—'Bone 2 pigeons completely. Season with salt, pepper and spices and stuff with the following forcemeat: add 4 tablespoons (50 grams) of chopped onion softened in butter, ½ cup (100 grams) of dried *Duxelles** (parings and stalks of chopped mushrooms), 2 spoonfuls of chopped parsley, the chopped livers of the pigeons, 1 egg, a tablespoon of brandy, salt and pepper to 5 ounces (150 grams) of fine pork *forcemeat*.* Roll the pigeons into *ballottines** and wrap each in a very thin, very big escalope of veal seasoned with salt, pepper and spices. Tie the pigeons as ballottines. Put into a casserole on a foundation of bacon rinds, carrots and onions chopped and fried in butter. Simmer on the stove with a lid on for 15 minutes. Moisten with a glass of Madeira, boil down (reduce) and add a few tablespoons of thickened brown veal gravy in sufficient quantity to cover the pigeons. Cook in the oven for 30 minutes. Drain the ballottines and remove the string. Put them into an oval-shaped earthenware cocotte. Add 1 pound (500 grams) of mushrooms, sliced and tossed in butter, and 20 thick slices of truffles. Strain the braising liquor, cook down, add 3 good tablespoons of burnt brandy (fine champagne), and pour over the pigeons. Seal the lid of the cocotte with flour-and-water paste. Cook in the oven for 40 minutes and serve in the cocotte.

Pigeon (squab) à la minute. PIGEONNEAU À LA MINUTE—Split the pigeon in half and remove all small bones. Flatten slightly, then fry quickly in sizzling butter. When the pigeon is almost cooked, add a tablespoon of chopped onion, lightly fried in butter. Finish cooking together.

Arrange the pigeon on a round dish. Dilute the pan juices with a dash of brandy, add a little dissolved meat jelly and half a tablespoon of chopped parsley and pour over the pigeon.

Pigeon (squab) mousse and mousselines. MOUSSE, MOUSSELINES DE PIGEONNEAU—Prepare like *Chicken mousse* and *mousselines.* See CHICKEN.

Pigeon (squab) with olives. PIGEONNEAU AUX OLIVES—Prepare like *Duckling with olives.* See DUCK.

Pigeon (squab) en papillote. PIGEONNEAU EN PAPILLOTE—Split the pigeon in half, lengthways, bone the halves partially, season with salt and pepper and fry in butter quickly just to stiffen them. Wrap each half in a piece of buttered greaseproof paper, cut in the shape of a heart, spread with *Duxelles** and lined with a slice of ham, as described in the recipe for *Veal cutlets en papillote**. Close the *papillote* securely and cook in the oven.

Hot pigeon (squab) pâté (pie) with mushrooms and truffles—See PIE.

Pigeon (squab) with peas I. PIGEONNEAU AUX PETITS POIS—Fry 2 ounces (60 grams) of diced and blanched fat bacon and 12 small onions in butter. When done, remove these ingredients from the sauté pan.

In the same butter brown a pigeon trussed as for an entrée. Remove the pigeon. Dilute the pan juices with white wine and thickened veal gravy. Replace the pigeon in the sauté pan. Add 2 large cups (4½ decilitres) of peas, a *bouquet garni**, the small onions and the lardoons. Season and finish cooking together.

Pigeon (squab) with peas II. PIGEONNEAU AUX PETITS POIS—Truss the pigeon as for an entrée and brown in butter. Prepare *Peas à la française** and put the pigeon into the same casserole. Moisten with the diluted pan juices and an equal amount of water. Finish cooking together.

Hot pigeon (squab) pie (English style)—See PIE, *Pigeon pie*.

Pigeon (squab) à la Richelieu. PIGEONNEAU À LA RICHELIEU—Split the pigeon down the back and open it out. Remove most of the bones from the inside. Dip the pigeon in egg and breadcrumbs and fry in clarified butter until both sides are golden. Arrange on a serving dish, garnish with slivers of truffle and put some softened *Maître d'hôtel butter* on top. See BUTTER, *Compound butters*.

Roast pigeon (squab). PIGEONNEAU RÔTI—Truss and bard the pigeon, season on the inside and roast on a spit from 22 to 25 minutes, or in the oven from 18 to 20 minutes.

Arrange on a long dish. Garnish with watercress. Serve diluted pan juices separately.

Salmis of pigeon (squab). PIGEONNEAU EN SALMIS—Proceed as described in the recipe for *Salmis of woodcock* (see WOODCOCK).

Pigeon (squab) stewed with blood, also called Pigeon stew with blood (Old recipe). PIGEONNEAU ÉTUVÉ AU SANG, DITE AUSSI ÉTUVÉE DE PIGEON AU SANG—'Bleed two pigeons from the pigeon run, keeping all the blood and adding half a spoonful of vinegar to it to prevent it from coagulating.

'Pluck, draw, singe and split the pigeons in half.

'Season with salt and pepper and brown in a casserole with a tablespoon of grated bacon fat.

'As soon as they are browned on both sides, remove and keep hot in the oven.

'Into the casserole in which the pigeons were browned put in 24 small young onions and ¼ pound (125 grams) of lean bacon, cut in large lardoons and blanched.

'Fry a pale golden colour and sprinkle in a spoonful of flour.

'Cook for a moment, then moisten with 2 cups (4 decilitres) of good red wine and 1 cup (2 decilitres) of stock or water.

'Season and add a *bouquet garni** and a little chopped garlic. Put the pigeons into this gravy and simmer for 45 minutes.

'Two minutes before serving, thicken with the blood kept for this purpose.

'Serve in a large round dish, garnish with 8 croûtons of home-made bread fried in butter and pour the gravy over the pigeons.'

Pigeon (squab) Villeroi. PIGEONNEAU VILLEROI—Split the pigeon in half, lengthways. Remove most of the bones and flatten the pigeon halves slightly. Season and cook in butter (or braise). Leave to get cold under a press.

Dip in *Villeroi sauce* (see SAUCE), dip in egg and breadcrumbs and fry when required. Arrange on a napkin-covered dish and garnish with fried parsley. Serve *Périgueux sauce* (see SAUCE) separately.

PIKE. BROCHET—Freshwater fish with a long body, large flat jaw, mouth stretching to the eyes and armed with numerous strong teeth. The back is slightly flattened and dark green, the belly white, the sides have golden glints and the fins are reddish. Pike likes fresh water, whether fast flowing or calm, where it devours enormous quantities of fish. Its white, firm flesh is greatly esteemed. Pike milt and roe are slightly toxic, especially during spawning season (February to April). In U.S.A. the best-known species of pike are *Common pike*, *Muskellunge* and *Pickerels*.

Pike au beurre blanc. BROCHET AU BEURRE BLANC—In the Anjou, as well as in the Nantes region, there are numerous recipes for preparing *Beurre blanc*, an exquisite sauce, which is almost a must for serving with pike and Loire shad. Here are some local recipes for the preparation of this dish:

First recipe—Prepare a *Court-bouillon** as usual and boil it for about half an hour. Put the pike into warm *court-bouillon*. As soon as boiling is once again established, draw the fish kettle to the edge of the stove and leave to poach for 25 to 30 minutes. Then take the fish kettle off the fire.

While the fish is poaching, boil down the vinegar. Add to it 2 or 3 chopped shallots, a pinch of salt and a little freshly ground pepper (just one turn of the mill). Allow to boil down by half and remove to the corner of the stove. (At this stage it is important to avoid too great a heat).

Soften a good piece of butter on a plate and incorporate it, little by little, in the reduced vinegar, beating vigorously with a whisk. The sauce will become frothy without being liquid and acquire the whiteness which is its feature.

At this moment, drain the pike, arrange it on a long, very hot dish and pour the *beurre blanc* over it, having added a little fresh, chopped parsley to it at the last moment.

Second recipe. Cook a 1½ pound (750 gram) pike in very little *court-bouillon* made of white wine, water, and the usual vegetables, seasoning and aromatics. When the fish is cooked, drain it, arrange on a long, very hot dish and cover with *beurre blanc* prepared in the following manner: put a chopped shallot and a pinch of salt into a saucepan, moisten with two tablespoons of water and one tablespoon of vinegar and boil down by two-thirds.

Remove the pan to the edge of the stove and little by little, stirring all the time, add to it approximately 5 to 7 ounces (150 to 200 grams) of the finest, freshest butter. Sprinkle with chopped parsley.

Third recipe. For 8 persons allow a 4 pound (2 kilo) pike. Open it, clean it very thoroughly, cut off the fins and tail, wash carefully in several waters, dry, sprinkle with fine salt and leave for a quarter of an hour. Wash again, put into a fish kettle surrounded with fresh cut parsley, 2 sliced onions, 2 quartered shallots, 2 cloves of garlic, 8 to 10 chives, or the green of one leek, a branch of fresh thyme, one small bay leaf, a few slices of carrot, some fine salt and ground pepper. Sprinkle with sprigs of parsley, pour in enough white wine to cover and leave to marinate for one hour.

About three-quarters of an hour before serving put the fish kettle on a brisk fire. At the first sign of the surface beginning to 'shiver' or ripple gently, draw aside and keep near boiling point.

Separately, put a tablespoon of chopped shallot into a saucepan, add a good pinch of freshly ground pepper and a good glass of best quality white wine vinegar (this is *very important*) and not just any commercial vinegar with a brutal taste. Cook down gently by three-quarters. Take 2 pounds of the best fresh butter, perfectly dried, of that lovely straw colour and delicious creamy taste, and chop it into small pieces.

Strain the concentrated vinegar. Put it into a strong copper pan with a tablespoon of shallots, very finely chopped and lightly squeezed with the flat of the knife, add a few pieces of butter and put over a high flame. Stir all the time with a wooden spoon and little by little add two-thirds of the butter. As soon as a light white *mousse* is formed, remove from the fire but do not stop stirring. Add the rest of the butter, stir until it has been absorbed and keep hot without allowing the sauce to boil. Season to taste. The sauce should be creamy.

To serve, drain the pike as soon as it is cooked, wipe it on a cloth, put on a long, deep, very hot dish. Cut the skin deftly along the backbone, slip the point of the knife under the incision, quickly remove the main bone in one movement, holding the head with the left hand. Reshape the fish, stir the *beurre blanc* a couple of times just to make sure the shallots are well mixed, spread over the pike and serve.

Fourth recipe. Prepare a *court-bouillon* made of water, a large onion, a sliced carrot, one cup (⅛ litre) of vinegar, salt, peppercorns, a sprig of parsley, thyme and a bay leaf. Allow to cook for 20 minutes.

Put a 4 or 5 pound pike, carefully scaled, cleaned and washed, into this composition. Keep on a low fire with the water just simmering for 20 or 25 minutes.

Meanwhile, put 2 medium-sized chopped shallots, 2 tablespoons of vinegar, some salt and freshly ground pepper into a flat-bottomed saucepan. (When adding salt, bear in mind that the butter may be salted.) Then add the butter cut in large dice.

Put the sauce on a brisk fire and keep stirring with a wooden spoon until the surface whitens slightly. Remove the saucepan from the fire and continue to stir.

When ready to serve, drain the fish, dry on a cloth, put on a long hot dish (white china for preference), cover the pike with *beurre blanc*, sprinkle with chopped parsley and serve very hot. (Recipe from *Phare de la Loire*.)

Fifth recipe. Le beurre blanc de ma tante. Take a live pike. Give it a blow on the head, then scale and clean it out. A delicate operation: one slit under the gills, otherwise no cuts at all, as the pike must remain intact.

Cook the fish in a fish kettle in *court-bouillon* made of new white wine, water and a sprinkling of vinegar, with a sprig of thyme, bay leaf, parsley, carrot cut in very thin slices, onion, a clove of garlic, black peppercorns and coarse salt.

When the *court-bouillon* is ready put it on a lively fire. When you see it boiling and when it begins to diffuse a delicious aroma, put in the pike.

The cooking must not take longer than a quarter of an hour. Take a fork, carefully introduce it into the flesh of the fish; if the fork penetrates it easily your pike is cooked to a turn.

Then remove the fish kettle from the fire without uncovering, so that your pike becomes completely imbued with the *court-bouillon*.

The sauce is the most delicate part of the operation. Take a good pan for making sauces. Put into it a tablespoon of chopped shallot, a pinch of ground pepper, a tablespoon of flour and some butter; ½ pound (250 grams) will be sufficient for a 3 pound pike. Add a tablespoon of vinegar. Put the sauce thus prepared on the fire taking care to stir from time to time with a wooden spoon. When the butter melts, the liaison is achieved by adding a ladleful of previously prepared *court-bouillon*. Allow to simmer.

To serve, take the pike out of the fish kettle and put it on a long china dish. Pour over the sauce, very hot. Then mix some of the sauce with 3 or 4 tablespoons of well beaten fresh cream, and put it around the fish. Finally, sprinkle with chopped parsley and finely grated lemon rind.

Pike au bleu. BROCHET AU BLEU—This method is mainly used for small pike.

Put the pike into a *court-bouillon** prepared as described in the recipe for *Blue trout*. See TROUT.

Drain the fish, arrange on a napkin and garnish with fresh parsley. Serve with boiled potatoes and melted butter or one of the other sauces specially recommended for poached fish.

Braised fillets of pike with various sauces and garnishes. FILETS DE BROCHET BRAISÉS—Take the fillets off a large uncooked pike. Trim the fillets, remove bones and skin. Cut the fillets into slices of uniform size (or, according to circumstances, leave them whole). Cook them in very little concentrated fish stock. Drain, dry, arrange on a serving dish, surround with the garnish recommended and pour over a sauce that goes with the garnish adding to it the liquor in which the fish was cooked, greatly concentrated.

Note. All the sauces and garnishes recommended for *Brill*,* *Sole** and young *Turbot** are suitable for fillets of pike.

Pike cutlets I. CÔTELETTES DE BROCHET—Using *Pike forcemeat* (see FORCEMEAT) shape in little, buttered moulds having the form of cutlets and poach. Arrange the cutlets on a serving dish, placing them either straight on the dish or putting each cutlet on a heart-shaped croûton, or on a puff pastry foundation. Serve with the garnish and sauce indicated in the recipe. (All the sauces and garnishes recommended for poached fillets of sole are applicable to these cutlets.)

Pike cutlets II. CÔTELETTES DE BROCHET—Prepare a croquette mixture, using a *salpicon** of cooked pike as the main ingredient, with truffles and mushrooms added. These cutlets, which are really a variety of croquettes, are deep fried like croquettes. See CROQUETTES.

Pike mousse—See FISH MOUSSE.

Pike mousselines. MOUSSELINES DE BROCHET—These are made of *Mousseline forcemeat* (see FORCEMEAT) poached in small dariole moulds. See MOUSSELINES.

Pike quenelles. QUENELLES DE BROCHET—Prepare 10 ounces (300 grams) bread *panada* (using 1 cup of milk and 3 cups of soft breadcrumbs) or a flour *panada* (using ½ cup hot water, ¼ cup butter and ½ cup flour) well in advance, so that it is cold when needed for use.

Pound finely 1 pound (500 grams) of pike flesh, carefully boned and skinned, with 2 teaspoons (12 grams) of salt, a pinch of pepper and a little grated nutmeg.

Remove the fish and leave on a plate. Pound the

Pike quenelles *en croustade*

panada until it is reduced to a completely smooth pulp, put the fish back into the mortar with 200 grams of butter and continue to pound until the three elements are combined into a homogeneous mixture. Then add, one at a time, 2 whole eggs and 4 yolks and rub through a sieve.

Transfer the resulting forcemeat into a bowl, stir with a wooden spoon to blend well and taking a piece the size of a hazelnut, drop it into salted water to poach. This is to test the seasoning and the texture of the forcemeat and to rectify them, if necessary.

There are special moulds for these quenelles and all that has to be done is to butter them and fill with forcemeat. When no such moulds are available, mould the quenelles in a large spoon and put them in rows into a buttered sauté pan. They can also be piped through a forcing (pastry) bag and cut off in 1½ inch lengths. Allow 2 ounces (60 grams) of forcemeat for one quenelle. Cover the quenelles with salted boiling water, allowing 1½ teaspoons (10 grams) of salt per quart (litre). Cover and poach on the edge of the burner for 10 minutes, keeping the water just simmering. Make sure that the poaching is complete just at the right time so that the quenelles are ready when needed for serving, or only a few minutes before.

Drain the quenelles on a cloth, arrange in a crown on a dish and serve with the sauce and garnish indicated in the recipe.

Note. The use of an electric blender can greatly facilitate this process.

Pike quenelles à la crème. QUENELLES DE BROCHET À LA CRÈME—Pipe the quenelles through a forcing (pastry) bag with a plain nozzle, or mould them with a large spoon, into a buttered sauté (sauce) pan. Cover with boiling salted water. Poach for 10 minutes, simmering so gently that the boiling is imperceptible.

Drain the quenelles and dry on a cloth. Arrange them in a round dish, placing each on a croûton fried in butter. Pour over boiling *Cream sauce* (see SAUCE).

Pike quenelles à la florentine. QUENELLES DE BROCHET À LA FLORENTINE—Poach in salted water, drain and dry. Arrange in an oven-proof dish on a bed of spinach leaves cooked in butter and seasoned with salt, pepper and grated nutmeg.

Cover with *Mornay sauce* (see SAUCE), sprinkle with grated cheese, pour over some melted butter and brown the top quickly in the oven.

Pike quenelles à la lyonnaise. QUENELLES DE BROCHET À LA LYONNAISE—These are made of *Pike forcemeat à la lyonnaise* (see FORCEMEAT), moulded with a spoon or shaped by hand and poached in salted water.

When the quenelles are poached, drain them and put into a sauté pan containing some rather thin *Espagnole sauce* (see SAUCE). Add, for 12 quenelles of medium size, 36 cooked mushrooms, 36 stoned blanched olives, and 24 rather thick slices of truffles.

Simmer for 10 minutes with a lid on, without turning the quenelles. After such simmering, the quenelles should swell.

Arrange in a pyramid, or in a flan crust baked blind (baked tart shell).

Pike quenelles à la lyonnaise

Quenelles of pike mousseline—See QUENELLES.

Quenelles of pike princesse—See QUENELLES.

Roast pike à la mode de Bugey. BROCHET RÔTI À LA MODE DE BUGEY—Stuff a pike with a forcemeat made of whiting mixed with diced truffles bound with *Cream sauce* (see SAUCE) and finished off with *Crayfish butter* (see BUTTER, *Compound butters*).

Put the pike on a spit, brush with melted butter; season with salt and pepper and roast before a lively fire. When it is nearly cooked, baste with fresh cream.

Arrange on a long dish, surround with little *barquettes*, some filled with *Crayfish tails à la Nantua** and others with *Truffles à la crème**. Add some fresh cream to the pan juices, cook down, strain and pour over the fish.

The same recipe can be used for salmon, salmon trout and char.

PIKE-PERCH. SANDRE—Type of fish of the *Percidae* family found mostly in the watercourses of central and eastern Europe. In France it is found only in the Doubs and the Saône. Its flesh is very white, flaky and very delicate in taste. All the cooking methods given for perch are applicable to the pike-perch.

PILAF, PILAU OR PILAW—This method of preparing rice originated in the East.

Rice prepared in this manner may be served without any garnish, but some ingredients are usually added to it, such as shrimps, chicken livers, lobster or various other shellfish, lamb's or sheep's sweetbreads, kidney, poultry, meat, etc.

Rice pilaf or pilaw. RIZ PILAF—Cook lightly in 6 tablespoons (100 grams) of butter, without allowing to colour, 1 cup (100 grams) of chopped onion. When it is cooked add 1 pound (500 grams) of Patna rice.

Stir this rice over the heat until all the grains are lightly cooked, then add a quart (litre) of *pot-au-feu* broth or white stock. Season, cook in the oven, the pot covered, and *without disturbing*, for 18 to 20 minutes.

When the rice is cooked, mix with it 3 tablespoons (50 grams) of butter cut into small pieces.

Rice pilaf (Turkish cookery). RIZ PILAF—Soak the rice for an hour or two in strongly-salted water; drain it and cook for a few minutes, without colouring it, in plenty of butter.

Add a *bouquet garni** and pour in twice its volume of

SALAD VEGETABLES

(*From Curnonsky:* Cuisine et Vins de France)

SAUCE. A white sauce *(Robert Carrie*

liquid. Allow to cook, covered, without disturbing, until little holes form on the surface of the rice.

It is sometimes mixed with cooked chick-peas, currants and pine kernels.

Chicken liver pilaf. PILAF DE FOIES DE VOLAILLE—Put the rice into a round buttered mould. Fill the middle with chicken livers, sliced and sautéed in butter. Finish as described in the recipe for *Shrimp pilaf* (see SHRIMP). Turn out the pilaf on to a round dish and pour around it a few tablespoons of *Demi-glace sauce* (see SAUCE), adding to it the butter in which the chicken livers were cooked.

Foie gras pilaf. PILAF DE FOIE GRAS—Arrange the rice on a round dish in a circle. Fill the middle with slices of foie gras sautéed in butter. Pour over them the pan juices diluted with Maderia and moistened with *Demi-glace sauce*. See SAUCE.

Truffle slivers, sautéed in butter, can be added.

Pilaf with mussels. PILAF DE MOULES—Cook the mussels as indicated for *Mussels à la poulette**. Shell them. Moisten with a few tablespoons of their cooking sauce. Pile them inside a border of *Rice pilaf*. Pour a few tablespoons of *Poulette sauce* (see SAUCE) round the border.

Mutton pilaf I. PILAF DE MOUTON—There are various ways of preparing this dish.

Restaurant method. Sauté in butter 1 pound (500 grams) of lean coarsely diced mutton. Season with salt and pepper. Drain and keep hot.

Pour $\frac{3}{4}$ cup ($1\frac{1}{2}$ decilitres) of wine into the frying pan. Heat and stir. Add 1 cup (2 decilitres) of *Demi-glace sauce* (see SAUCE) or thickened veal stock or brown stock made from the bones and trimmings of the mutton and $\frac{1}{2}$ cup (a decilitre) of *Tomato purée**. Bring to the boil. Put the mutton into this sauce. Heat *without bringing to the boil.*

Butter a deep round dish lined completely with *Rice pilaf* (see above). Take away most of the mutton sauce and pour the meat, with the rest of the sauce, into the dish. Cover with rice. Turn out on a round dish. Pour the sauce over the rice.

Mutton prepared as indicated above can also be served in a border of pilaf rice. This is made by filling a buttered turban (ring) mould with rice, pressing down well before turning out. Pour the sauce over the dish.

Another method is to bone the mutton and cut it into neat pieces. Braise in a very little tomato-flavoured stock. Serve in a border of rice pilaf as indicated above.

Mutton pilaf II (Turkish cookery). PILAF DE MOUTON—Make a *ragoût** of mutton in the usual way, flavouring it strongly with tomatoes and spicing with a little ginger (or, if preferred, with saffron) and a touch of garlic.

When the mutton is almost cooked, drain it. Put it in another saucepan with sweet peppers, peeled and coarsely diced. Add parboiled rice. Moisten with the strained cooking stock. Finish cooking all together. Serve in a bowl or deep round dish.

Sheep's (mutton) kidney pilaf. PILAF DE ROGNONS DE MOUTON—This is made with kidneys cut in slices. See OFFAL OR VARIETY MEATS, *Calf's liver pilaf*.

Veal pilaf. PILAF DE VEAU—Prepared with fillet (U.S. sirloin) of veal cut into small square pieces and sautéed in butter, in the same way as *Mutton pilaf*.

PILCHARD—Small fish of the *Clupeidae* genus, sold mainly tinned (canned) in spiced oil like sardines.

PILOT-FISH. FANFRE—A fish somewhat similar to mackerel. It is cooked in the same way. The pilot-fish is quite tasty, but indigestible.

PIMENTO—See PEPPER.

PINCER—French culinary term which describes the operation of browning certain substances in fat. It is applicable mainly to browning meat and vegetables before adding stock or any other liquid to them.

'*Pincer*' also applies to the operation of pinching up the edges of pies, tarts, etc.

PINCH. PINCÉE—The term pinch frequently occurs in this book and it corresponds to about 5 grams (less than a teaspoon) in the case of salt and about 2 grams ($\frac{1}{8}$ teaspoon) in the case of pepper or mixed spices.

The term *pinch*, however, is used only in application to quick seasoning; seasoning for dishes requiring prolonged cooking must be expressed in more precise quantities.

PINE SEED (Nut). PIGNON—The kernels of pine cones, which in taste resemble almonds and have various uses in cookery and confectionery.

This nut is known as *pignoli* in cookery.

PINEAPPLE. ANANAS—Herbaceous hardy perennial plant, rather similar to aloes in the structure of its leaves, although they are less thick than those of the latter plant. The flowers, bluish in colour, produce an ovoid globular fruit, yellowish in colour when ripe.

The pineapple is a native of America; it has, however, naturalized admirably in Asia and Africa, where it is generally cultivated.

Pineapple contains a strong proportion of sugar (more than 15 per cent), citric and malic acids and a ferment called *bromeline* very close to pepsin and papain (vegetable pepsin). It is a ferment which can be dissolved in proteinic substances and which acts very energetically on albumin contained in white of egg, in meat and in milk, which it curdles to begin with.

This ferment appears to be destroyed by heating and it is not present in sterilised, tinned pineapple. The juice of fresh pineapples, on the other hand, possesses definite digestive properties and they are, therefore, more suitable at the end of a meal consisting of a substantial portion of meat.

When it is quite ripe this fruit of the *ananas*, called pineapple or sugar-loaf, has a very pleasant smell. It makes an exquisite sweet (dessert). Its firm, melting flesh, of a clear yellow colour, contains an abundance of fragrant juice in which the flavours of the apple, the strawberry and the peach seem to mingle all at once.

Pineapple is eaten as it is, plain, or is used for preparing various sweet dishes, ices, sherbets, jams, cakes and very refreshing drinks.

A sort of wine is made from fermented pineapple juice. When distilled, this wine produces a very pleasant liqueur.

Pineapples, preserved in syrup, can be found in shops and, when they are of good quality, can replace fresh pineapples, but they will not, however, equal fresh pineapples in fragrance and delicacy of flavour.

Pineapple à la bavaroise. ANANAS À LA BAVAROISE—Hollow out and prepare a large pineapple as described in the recipe for *Iced pineapple* (see ICE CREAMS AND ICES).

Fill it with a *Pineapple cream à bavarois* with grated pineapple, steeped in kirsch, added to it. See BAVAROIS.

Pineapple Bourdaloue. ANANAS BOURDALOUE—Proceed as described in the recipe for *Apricots Bourdaloue**, replacing the halved apricots by half-slices of pineapple.

Or else arrange the half-slices of pineapple in a baked flan case (or shell) made of sweet pastry, lined with *Frangipane cream* with some crushed macaroons added to it (see CREAMS).

Dust with crushed macaroons, sprinkle with melted butter and glaze in the oven.

Pineapple compote. COMPOTE D'ANANAS—Peel a fresh, perfectly ripe, sound pineapple. Remove the eyes, which penetrate a little into the flesh beneath the rind.

Divide the pineapple in halves, lengthways, remove the hard core and cut each half into regular slices.

Put these slices to cook in a light syrup, plain or flavoured with vanilla.

When the pineapple is cooked, arrange in a fruit dish, sprinkle with its syrup laced with kirsch or rum (or allow to cool in a bowl and use as described in individual recipes). Pineapple compote is served cold.

Instead of dividing the pineapple in halves, one can leave it whole. In that case, the core must be removed with the aid of a special corer and the pineapple cut into round slices.

The pineapple can also be cooked whole, according to various recipes.

Pineapple Condé. ANANAS CONDÉ—Arrange about 20 half-slices of fresh pineapple cooked in syrup, or tinned pineapple, in a shallow oven-proof dish, three-quarters filled with *Dessert rice* (see RICE).

Decorate with glacé cherries cut in halves and lozenges of angelica.

Heat in a very moderate oven (325°F.) and serve with *Apricot sauce* (see SAUCE) laced with kirsch, either poured over or separately.

Or you can, alternatively, arrange the half-slices of pineapple on a border of *Dessert rice* prepared as described in the recipe for *Condé apricots* (see APRICOT).

Pineapple fritters. BEIGNETS D'ANANAS—Cut a fresh or tinned pineapple into slices. Dust these slices with sugar, sprinkle with kirsch or rum and leave to steep for half an hour.

Proceed as described in recipes for *Fruit fritters* (see FRITTERS).

Pineapple fritters à la Carême. BEIGNETS D'ANANAS À LA CARÊME—Slice the pineapple and leave to steep as described in the preceding recipe.

Dry the slices, coat them with a thin layer of very thick apricot jam and stick them together in pairs.

Dip into a light batter. Fry in deep fat. Serve on a napkin.

Pineapple ice cream. GLACE À L'ANANAS—Add to half a litre of syrup, prepared as described for fruit ices, half a fresh shredded or grated pineapple. Leave to steep for 2 hours.

Pass this mixture through a sieve and flavour it with kirsch.

Measure it with a syrup gauge and rectify until it registers from 18° to 20°.

Chill in a freezer, as usual. See ICE CREAMS AND ICES.

Put in a special mould or, according to directions, in little fancy moulds, in wine glasses, goblets or sundae glasses.

Iced pineapple—See ICE CREAMS AND ICES.

Pineapple with vanilla ice cream. COUPES GLACÉES À L'ANANAS À LA VANILLE—Fill dessert glasses with vanilla ice cream and pineapple cut in dice and steeped in kirsch.

Decorate with pineapple cut in lozenges and sprinkle with kirsch.

Pineapple à l'impératrice. ANANAS À L'IMPÉRATRICE—Proceed as described in the recipe for *Apricots à l'impératrice**, replacing the latter by half-slices of pineapple cooked in syrup.

Or, prepare the pineapple as described for *Iced pineapple* (see ICE CREAMS AND ICES).

Fill it with *Rice à l'impératrice**, with diced pineapple scooped out of the rind and steeped in kirsch added to it.

Put to set in a cold place or on ice and serve like *Iced pineapple.*

Pineapple manqué. MANQUÉ À L'ANANAS—Add to *Manqué** mixture some diced crystallized pineapple. Bake and turn out the cake. Ice with *Fondant icing* (see ICING) flavoured with pineapple. Decorate the top with pieces of crystallized pineapple.

Pineapple pancakes (crêpes). CRÊPES FOURRÉES, PANNEQUETS À L'ANANAS—Prepare *pannequets**. Coat them with thick apricot jam, with pineapple cooked in syrup and cut into minute dice added to it. Roll up the pancakes.

Glaze in the oven as described in the recipe for *pannequets.*

Alternatively, coat the pancakes with *French pastry cream* (see CREAMS) with a grated pineapple added to it.

Finish as indicated in the recipe for *pannequets.*

Pineapple à la piémontaise. ANANAS À LA PIÉMONTAISE—Proceed as described in the recipe for *Pineapple Condé*, replacing dessert rice by a layer of *Polenta** bound with egg and flavoured with vanilla.

Alternatively, arrange the half-slices of pineapple, cut rather thick and cooked in syrup, on crescent-shaped polenta croquettes.

Pineapple with rice. ANANAS AU RIZ—Proceed as described in the recipe for *Apricots with rice**, replacing the halved apricots by half-slices of pineapple in syrup.

Pineapple and rice with meringue. ANANAS MERINGUÉ AU RIZ—Proceed as described in the recipe for *Apricots and rice with meringue** using slices of pineapple poached in vanilla-flavoured syrup.

Pineapple sauce—See SAUCE.

Pineapple savarin. SAVARIN À L'ANANAS—Prepare a *savarin**. Saturate it with syrup and flavour with kirsch or rum. Arrange it in a round dish and garnish with half-slices of pineapple cooked in syrup, or fill the middle with pineapple cooked in syrup and cut in large dice. Serve hot or cold.

Pineapple surprise. ANANAS EN SURPRISE—Scoop out and prepare a large pineapple as described in the recipe for *Iced pineapple* (see ICE CREAMS AND ICES).

Fill it with a *macédoine** composed of the scooped-out pineapple pulp cut in thin slices, strawberries, peaches, apricots, fresh blanched almonds and, in general, with all kinds of fruit, whether red coloured or not, sliced or left whole, according to their nature, all previously steeped in kirsch and castor (or powdered) sugar.

Put the pineapple upright in a dish filled with crushed ice and leave to chill for 2 hours before serving.

Serve like *Iced pineapple.*

Pineapple tart. CROÛTE À L'ANANAS—Proceed as described in the recipe for *Fruit tart* (see TART) using, instead of mixed fruit, only pineapple cut in half-slices for the border and in large dice for the interior.

Decorate with cherries and angelica and finish off as described in the recipe for *Fruit tart.*

Pineapple tart à la royale. CROÛTE À L'ANANAS À LA ROYALE—Arrange a border composed of half-slices of pineapple and slices of *savarin**.

Fill the middle with a thick *French pastry cream* (see CREAMS) mixed with a grated pineapple flavoured with kirsch. Sprinkle with crushed macaroons. Decorate with crystallized fruit.

Pineapple tourte—See TOURTE, *Apricot tourte.*

PINEAU OR PINOT—Variety of grapes, black and white, with small tight berries, used exclusively for making the best Burgundy wines.

PINÉE—French word for first quality dried cod.

PINION OR POULTRY WING. AILERON—The terminal segment of a bird's wing, also called wing tip.

The pinions of large birds which, in principle, are classed as *giblets*, can be made into a great number of dishes. See GIBLETS.

The word pinion also means the bones which support the fin rays of fish.

All the recipes which follow are intended for pinions of turkeys or turkey-poults, but they are suitable for preparing pinions of other big poultry.

Pinions of turkey à l'anglaise. AILERONS DE DINDONNEAU À L'ANGLAISE—See GIBLETS, *Turkey giblets à l'anglaise.*

Pinions of turkey à la bourgeoise. AILERONS DE DINDONNEAU À LA BOURGEOISE—See GIBLETS, *Turkey giblets à la bourgeoise.*

Turkey pinion broth. POT-AU-FEU AUX AILERONS DE DINDONNEAU—This is prepared like ordinary broth with stuffed turkey pinions. See SOUPS AND BROTHS, *Pot-au-feu.*

Pinions of turkey chasseur. AILERONS DE DINDONNEAU CHASSEUR—Cut the pinions each in two pieces. Season them with salt and pepper. Fry them in butter. Finish cooking as described in the recipe for *Chicken sauté chasseur**.

Consommé with pinions I. CONSOMMÉ AUX AILERONS—Prepare a chicken *consommé** as usual. Bone and stuff the pinions with a *Quenelle forcemeat* (see FORCEMEAT). Put the pinions into the consommé to cook.

Pass the consommé through a muslin cloth and serve with trimmed pinions.

Rice cooked in consommé is sometimes added to this soup.

Consommé with pinions II. CONSOMMÉ AUX AILERONS—Prepare meat stock as usual. Trim 6 pinions, put in a muslin bag and cook in the stock.

Strain the stock and serve with the pinions, removing all the little bones from them which have come loose during cooking.

Serve bread, cut into small pieces and dried in the oven at the same time.

Carrots and leeks, cooked in stock and cut into little pieces are sometimes added to this soup.

Fricassée of turkey pinions. AILERONS DE DINDONNEAU EN FRICASSÉE—Cook the pinions, stuffed as described above, until two-thirds done in chicken or veal stock. Remove them and put into a sauté pan with small onions and mushrooms half-cooked in chicken or veal stock. Moisten with *Velouté sauce* (see SAUCE) made from the stock in which the pinions were cooked. Finish cooking together, simmering gently. At the last moment, bind the sauce with yolks of eggs and cream, as described in the recipe for *Fricassée of chicken* (see CHICKEN).

Turkey pinions à la niçoise. AILERONS DE DINDONNEAU À LA NIÇOISE—Season the pinions with salt and pepper. Fry briskly in a mixture of butter and oil. Remove when nicely golden. Into the same pan put (for 6 pinions) 4 tablespoons (50 grams) chopped onion, fry lightly, add 3 peeled, chopped tomatoes, with the seeds taken out, and as much grated garlic as can be held on the point of a knife. Cook for 5 minutes, put the pinions back in the pan, add a *bouquet garni**, moisten with ¾ cup (1½ decilitres) of dry white wine, season, bring to the boil, cover and simmer for 20 minutes. Add 24 black olives and the same number of small button mushrooms. Finish cooking, simmering gently for 15 minutes. Sprinkle with chopped tarragon.

Turkey pinions en tortue. AILERONS DE DINDONNEAU EN TORTUE—Bone 12 turkey pinions in such a way as to shape them into pockets. Stuff with a *Quenelle forcemeat* (see FORCEMEAT). Secure the opening with thread. In a shallow pan fry thinly sliced carrots and onions in bacon fat and add the pinions. Season with salt and as much allspice as can be held on the point of a knife. Put in a *bouquet garni**; sprinkle with melted butter and put on a brisk fire. Brown both sides of the pinions lightly. Moisten with a glass of Madeira. Leave to reduce (boil down) completely. Add a few tablespoons of thickened brown veal gravy and braise in a slow oven, uncovered.

Remove the pinions with a perforated spoon, put into another pan with *Tortue garnish* (see GARNISHES). Add herbs *à tortue* to the braising pan juices, boil down, strain and pour over the pinions. Leave to simmer for a few minutes. Arrange the pinions on a serving dish with the garnish around them. Add supplementary garnish: gherkins cut in small uniform pieces, fried yolks of egg, dressed crayfish, heart-shaped croûtons fried in butter. Pour the sauce over the pinions.

Stuffed turkey pinions in aspic jelly. AILERONS DE DINDONNEAU FARCIS À LA GELÉE—Stuff the pinions with a finely pounded pork *forcemeat** with diced truffles added to it (or a forcemeat made of minced pork, *foie gras* and truffles). Wrap each in a piece of muslin and secure with string. Cook them in a stock made from Madeira-flavoured meat jelly or in a rich broth flavoured with Madeira. Drain, cook and put into a glass or earthenware dish. Clarify the liquid jelly in which they were cooked in the usual manner and pour over the pinions. See JELLY.

Stuffed braised pinions of turkey. AILERONS DE DINDONNEAU FARCIS, BRAISÉS—Singe and pluck 6 turkey pinions. Bone them carefully, so as not to damage the skin.

Stuff them with any forcemeat you like (finely pounded pork forcemeat, chicken forcemeat, quenelle forcemeat, or any other). Wrap each one in a thin rasher of bacon and secure with thread.

Melt some butter in a sauté pan, brown lightly some bacon rinds, 1 medium-small onion (50 grams) and 1 medium-small carrot (50 grams) cut in thin round slices. Arrange the pinions on these. Add a *bouquet garni**. Season with salt and pepper. Simmer under a lid on top of the stove for 15 minutes.

Moisten with 1 cup (2 decilitres) of dry white wine (or Madeira, according to recipe), boil down and add 2 cups (4 decilitres) of brown chicken or veal gravy. Bring to the boil. Cook in the oven with a lid on for 40 minutes. Remove the pinions, unwrap them and glaze in a hot oven. Arrange them on a round dish. Pour over them the pan juices in which they were braised, with fat skimmed off, boiled down and strained.

After having been braised as described above, the pinions can be completed with various garnishes.

Stuffed turkey pinions in chaud-froid sauce. AILERONS DE DINDONNEAU FARCIS EN CHAUD-FROID—Cook the stuffed pinions in liquid aspic jelly laced with Madeira. Allow to cool in the stock. Drain and dry well.

Cover with white or brown *Chaud-froid sauce* (see SAUCE), depending on the nature of the dish. Glaze the pinions with a jelly.

Arrange on a dish and garnish with chopped jelly.

Pinions in *Chaud-froid sauce* can be decorated with truffles, tongue *à l'écarlate*, white of hard boiled eggs, etc.

You can, instead of arranging them on a dish (putting them either straight on the dish or placing each on a croûton of bread spread with butter), place them into a glass dish and cover with jelly. You can also, according to an old recipe, arrange them in a pyramid, with a cone-shaped croûton as a central support.

Stuffed turkey pinions with chipolata sausages. AILERONS DE DINDONNEAU FARCIS CHIPOLATA—Prepare like *Turkey giblets with chipolata sausages*. See GIBLETS.

Stuffed turkey pinions à la fermière. AILERONS DE DINDONNEAU FARCIS À LA FERMIÈRE—Stuff the pinions with a finely pounded forcemeat made of a mixture of chopped onions, cooked in butter until transparent, and chopped parsley. Braise the pinions until half done. Remove them, put into an earthenware casserole. Cover them with garnish *à la fermière* (carrots, turnips, celery and onions, cut *en paysanne** and lightly fried in butter). Remove fat from the pan juices, reduce, strain and pour over the ingredients in the casserole. Finish cooking in the oven with a lid on.

Stuffed turkey pinions fried in batter. AILERONS DE DINDONNEAU FARCIS EN FRITOT—Stuff and cook the little pinions as described above. Strain the stock in which they were cooked and leave them to cool in it.

Drain and marinate for half an hour in oil, lemon juice, salt, pepper and chopped parsley.

At the last moment, dip them in a light batter (see BATTER) and deep fry in sizzling fat.

Drain, dry, season with very dry finely ground salt and arrange on a napkin (or a paper doyley). Garnish with fried parsley and quarters of lemon. Serve with tomato or other sauce.

Stuffed turley pinions à la périgourdine. AILERONS DE DINDONNEAU FARCIS À LA PÉRIGOURDINE—Stuff the pinions with *foie gras* and diced truffles (to which a little pork forcemeat can be added), season with salt, pepper and spices and sprinkle with brandy.

Wrap in rashers (strips) of bacon. Braise in stock laced with Madeira. When three-quarters cooked, remove, unwrap, put into an earthenware dish with (for 6 pinions) 4 to 5 truffles (200 grams) in quarters. Skim the fat off the stock in which the pinions were braised, reduce, strain and pour over them. Stew in the oven for 15 minutes.

Stuffed turkey pinions Sainte-Menehould. AILERONS DE DINDONNEAU SAINTE-MENEHOULD—Stuff the pinions as described and braise in white wine or in clear veal stock. Drain and cool under a press.

Brush with butter, dip in toasted breadcrumbs (or in freshly grated breadcrumbs), sprinkle with melted butter and grill on a low heat until both sides are golden.

Serve either with *Diable sauce* or with *Sainte-Menehould sauce* (made from the stock in which the pinions were braised). See SAUCE.

Grilled pinions *Sainte-Menehould* can be served with various vegetables, cooked in water and dressed with butter, or with purées of vegetables. As in the case of *Pig's trotters Sainte-Menehould*, mustard should be served with these pinions.

Stuffed turkey pinions à la Soubise. AILERONS DE DINDONNEAU FARCIS À LA SOUBISE—Stuff and braise the pinions as described above. Drain and glaze. Arrange on a round dish. Sprinkle with reduced pan juices. Serve *Soubise purée* separately (see PURÉE).

PINTAIL (DUCK). PILET—A variety of wild duck. Prepare like wild duck or spoonbill or shoveller duck. See DUCK.

PIPÉRADE—Local dish consisting of cooked tomatoes and peppers to which eggs are added one by one to obtain a fluffy purée.

PIPIT—Small edible bird which can be prepared in the same way as larks.

PIPKIN. HUGUENOTE—An old-fashioned cooking pot with or without little feet.

PIQUEPOULT—Wine made in the Gers Department from which Armagnacs are distilled.

PIQUETTE—Wine of second or third pressing obtained by flooding husks of grapes with unsweetened warm water. It is a light, refreshing drink which does not travel and is used either for home consumption or for distilling purposes. Common usage has also extended the word to mean 'mediocre wine'.

PIROGHI OR PIROZHKI. PIROGUI—In Russian the name *piroghi* means pies large enough to be cut into portions. *Pirozhki*, meaning little pies, are small enough to be eaten out of hand.

Carrot pirozhki. PIROGUI AUX CAROTTES—Roll out puff pastry to a thickness of about ¼ inch and cut into circles 4 inches in diameter.

Shred the carrots into a *brunoise**, cook in butter, mix with chopped hard boiled eggs, parsley and chives, bind with thick *Béchamel sauce* (see SAUCE) and put a spoonful of this mixture on each circlet of pastry.

Moisten the edges of the pastry and bring them together, enclosing the filling and giving the pirozhki an oval shape. Put them on a baking sheet, brush with beaten egg and bake for 18 minutes in a hot oven.

Serve on a napkin-covered dish arranged in a pyramid.

Caucasian pirozhki. PIROGUI CAUCASIEN—Spread a thin layer of cheese-flavoured *Chou paste* (cream puff pastry) on a baking sheet.

Bake in the oven. Turn put the sheet of pastry on to a table, divide into two parts and sandwich them together, having first coated them with a light layer of thick *Béchamel sauce* (see SAUCE), to which some grated cheese and cooked sliced mushrooms have been added.

Cut into rectangles 2½ inches long and 1¼ inches wide.

Cover these rectangles completely with cheese-flavoured *Béchamel sauce* and coat with breadcrumbs.

Fry in smoking hot deep fat. Drain and serve on a napkin-covered dish.

Cream cheese pirozhki. PIROGUI AU FROMAGE—Butter dariole moulds and line them with unsweetened *Common brioche dough* (see BRIOCHE). Fill with cream cheese (cottage cheese), cover with a circlet of the same paste and seal the edges.

Leave to rise in a warm place for 30 minutes.

Bake in a hot oven from 20 to 25 minutes. Turn out and serve on napkin-covered dish.

Fish pirozhki. PIROGUI AU POISSON—Proceed as described in the recipe for *Game pirozhki*, replacing the game meat by chopped cooked white fish.

Game pirozhki. PIROGUI AU GIBIER—Prepare *Puff pastry* (see DOUGH), roll it out to a thickness of ⅛ inch, cut into little circlets about 3 inches in diameter.

Put a tablespoon of game hash, mixed with chopped hard boiled eggs, cooked buckwheat or rice cooked in meat stock.

Moisten the edges of the pastry, cover with another circlet of puff pastry of the same size and thickness. Brush with beaten egg, bake in a hot oven from 18 to 20 minutes and serve on a napkin-covered dish.

Moscow pirozhki. PIROGUI À LA MOSCOVITE—Roll out unsweetened *Common brioche dough* (see BRIOCHE) into small oval pieces, about 2½ inches wide and 4 inches long.

Put on each of these some filling, the size of a walnut, prepared in the following manner:

Chop and mix ¼ pound (125 grams) of white flaked fish, 2½ ounces (75 grams) of cooked visiga (dry spinal cord of the sturgeon) and 2 hard boiled eggs. Season.

Moisten the edges of the dough slightly and enclose the filling by bringing the edges together and sealing them. Keep in a warm place to rise for 25 minutes. Bake in a hot oven for 20 minutes.

Butter is served with these *pirozhki.*

Polish pirozhki. PIROGUI POLONAIS—Roll out puff pastry to a thickness of ¼ inch and cut into oval-shaped pieces about 2½ inches wide and 4 inches long.

Put on each some filling, the size of a walnut, prepared in the following manner:

Sauté gently 4 tablespoons (50 grams) of chopped onion in butter, add ½ pound (250 grams) of veal udder and ½ pound (250 grams) of lean veal, cut in small dice and also fried in butter. Season with salt, pepper and nutmeg and leave to cool before using.

Proceed as described in the recipe for *Moscow pirozhki.*

Smolensk pirozhki. PIROGUI DE SMOLENSK—Roll out puff pastry to a thickness of ¼ inch and cut it into small pieces 2¾ inches square.

Put on each some filling, the size of a walnut, prepared in the following manner:

Heat in butter ¼ pound (125 grams) of cooked semolina, add 4 chopped hard boiled eggs, a tablespoon of chopped parsley and a tablespoon of chopped onions fried in butter, although the latter is optional. Season with salt, pepper and nutmeg, mix well and allow to cool before using.

Cover with pieces of rolled-out pastry of the same size. Brush with beaten egg and bake in a hot oven from 18 to 20 minutes.

Pirozhki with truffles. PIROGUI AUX TRUFFES—Cut cooked truffles into thick round slices. Cover with thick *Béchamel sauce* (see SAUCE) and leave until cold.

Sandwich these between two *blini** circlets, cut out with a pastry cutter, and press down well to seal the edges.

Dip in beaten egg, roll in breadcrumbs and, just before serving, fry in clarified butter. Serve on a napkin-covered dish.

Pirozhki with various vegetable filling. PIROGUI AUX LÉGUMES—Proceed as described in the recipe for *Carrot pirozhki,* replacing carrots by a *salpicon** of various vegetables cooked in butter and bound with *Béchamel sauce* (see SAUCE).

The filling of vegetable *pirozhki* may be supplemented by buckwheat or rice cooked in stock or water.

Visiga pirozhki. PIROGUI AU VÉSIGA—Roll out puff pastry to a thickness of ¼ inch and cut into circlets 4 inches in diameter.

Put on each some of the following mixture:

Cook ¼ pound (125 grams) of visiga (dry spinal cord of the sturgeon) in white stock, 4 parsley roots and a stalk of celery.

Drain the visiga, chop it, as well as the parsley roots and the celery, add 2 chopped hard boiled eggs and a tablespoon of chopped parsley. Bind with 3 tablespoons of thick *Béchamel sauce* (see SAUCE), season with salt, pepper and nutmeg and leave to get cold before using.

Moisten the edges of the pastry, fold in the shape of a turnover, press with the back of a dough knife to seal well, brush with beaten egg and bake in a hot oven from 18 to 20 minutes.

PISSALADIÈRE—A kind of flan (tart) made mainly in the Nice region, filled with onions, anchovy fillets and black olives.

PISSALAT (Provence cookery)—Condiment which is found ready for use in the shops.

It is made by rubbing through a sieve the young 'fry' of various fish of the herring family (principally anchovies), previously pickled in brine for 8 days. The purée is diluted with a few tablespoons of the brine in which the fry were pickled, spiced with cloves, decanted into jars with well-fitting lids and kept in a cool place.

This condiment is used as it is or diluted with oil.

PISTACHE (EN)—This term is used in the south-western part of France, mainly in the Catalan country, to describe a special method of preparing leg of mutton. The outstanding feature of this dish is that its only garnish consists of cloves of garlic. See MUTTON.

Pigeons and partridges can also be prepared '*en pistache*'.

PISTACHIO. PISTACHE—Seed of the *Pistacia vera,* a deciduous tree, native of the Levant, which, it is said, was brought to Rome by Vitellius. It yields an edible nut, about the size of an olive, brown-reddish in colour, with a thin husk, inside which a ligneous membrane is found; this is easily separated into two halves and contains a very pale almond enclosed in a reddish skin.

Pistachio nuts have a sweet and pleasant flavour and are used as a flavouring in cookery, pork butchery, pastry-making and confectionery.

PISTOLE—Name of a variety of plums of the perdrigon genus, which are stoned, flattened and dried in the sun like prunes.

PISTOU (Italian cookery)—This soup, the recipe for which is given in the section headed SOUPS AND BROTHS, is made of various vegetables and thick vermicelli. Its main characteristic is that the liaison is affected by using pounded garlic with basil and grilled tomatoes mixed with oil.

PITHIVIERS (Gâteau)—This gâteau is a speciality of Pithiviers. It is made of *Puff pastry* (see DOUGH) and almond paste, which can be prepared from the following ingredients: ⅓ cup (50 grams) of blanched almonds, 6 tablespoons (50 grams) of fine sugar, 3½ tablespoons (50 grams) of butter, 3 eggs and ½ cup (½ decilitre) of rum.

Pound the almonds in a mortar, adding one egg.

When they are reduced to a fine paste, put into a bowl, add castor (fine) sugar and butter and blend the mixture, stirring with a wooden spoon until very smooth.

Add two eggs one by one and flavour with rum.

Roll out half the puff pastry into a round piece 8 inches in diameter and $\frac{1}{16}$ inch thick.

Turn the pastry and put on a moistened metal sheet.

Spread this piece of pastry with the almond paste, leaving about ⅜ inch of the edges all round uncovered. Roll out the rest of the pastry into a circle of the same diameter as that forming the bottom of the gâteau.

To seal, moisten the bottom piece of pastry around the edges and cover with the second piece of pastry, taking care to turn it.

Press well all round to seal the edges properly, brush with beaten egg and leave to rest for 5 minutes. With the point of a knife mark the top with faint lines in the shape of a rosette and bake in the oven from 25 to 30 minutes.

Two minutes before taking it out of the oven, sprinkle the gâteau with very fine sugar and put to glaze in the hottest part of the oven.

PLAFOND—French word for tinned copper metal baking sheets, which were used in the olden days for browning small pieces of meat.

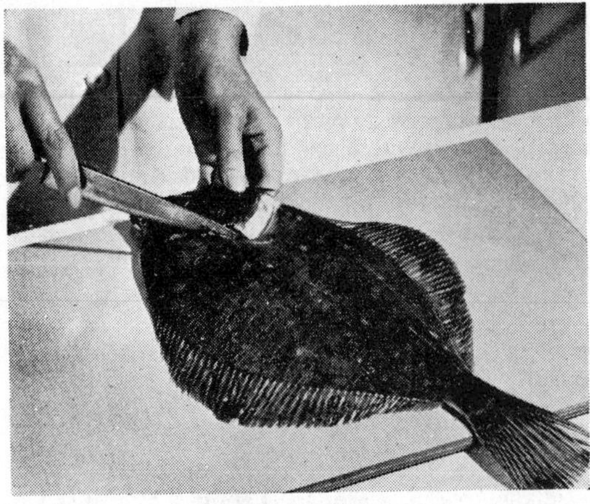

Remove head

Make an incision down the back base

Cut into fillets

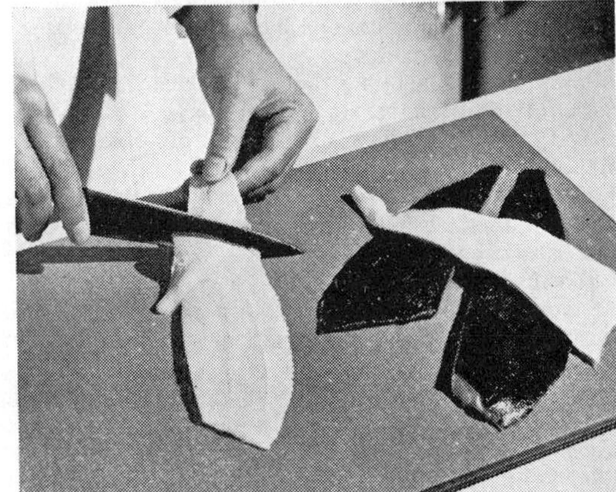

Skin

How to fillet plaice

(*photographs Mac Fisheries*)

PLAICE (U.S. FLOUNDER OR FLUKE). CARRELET, PLIE FRANCHE—Sea water fish, which is flat, diamond-shaped with rounded angles; the two eyes are set on the left side of the head The left side is brownish with rounded or oval spots, red or orange. Plaice have 5 or 6 bony tubercles well marked between the eyes. The reverse side is white.

This fish, though of medium quality, is not without merit, provided it is perfectly fresh.

Boiled plaice with various sauces. CARRELET BOUILLI—Only large plaice are used in this way, cooked whole, or cut into slices.

Cook them in a *court-bouillon* consisting of water, milk, salt, and lemon slices, in the same way as for brill.

Drain the plaice. Lay it on a napkin, and garnish with fresh parsley. Serve with plain, boiled potatoes in a separate dish, and hand one of the sauces which are normally served with boiled fish.

Plaice à la bonne femme. CARRELET À LA BONNE FEMME—Proceed as for *Brill à la bonne femme**.

Plaice Dugléré. CARRELET DUGLÉRÉ—Proceed with a large plaice cut into slices in the same way as for *Bass Dugléré**.

Chef's lore maintains that it was for plaice that Dugléré (then chef of the one-time Café Anglais) invented this method of preparation, which in actual practice is used for bass, brill and chicken-turbot.

Fried plaice. CARRELET FRIT—Use only a little plaice and cook in the same manner as *Fried brill.* See BRILL.

Plaice à l'indienne. CARRELET À L'INDIENNE—Cut up a large plaice into even slices. Season them with salt and pepper and put them in a pan on a base of chopped onions, already softened in butter, and seasoned with curry powder.

Stew the plaice with the lid on. Sprinkle it with curry powder, pour over it 2 decilitres of white wine (for 750 grams of fish). Reduce the liquor, and cover with a *Béchamel sauce* (see SAUCE) which is not too thick. Cook for a further 15 minutes on a low heat.

Grilled fillets of plaice

Place the pieces of fish in a dish, cover them with the reduced sauce to which butter has been added, flavoured with a little lemon juice. Serve with *Rice à l'indienne** dished separately.

Plaice à la niçoise. CARRELET À LA NIÇOISE—Make some light incisions in the plaice. Season with salt and pepper. Paint it with oil. Grill it under a gentle heat.

Put it on a serving dish on a layer of tomatoes softened in butter seasoned with garlic and chopped tarragon. Lay a grid of anchovies on top of the fish, and sprinkle with capers. Surround it with green olives which have been stoned and blanched, or black olives unstoned. Sprinkle with chopped basil.

As well as the methods indicated above for cooking plaice, all those given elsewhere for brill, turbot and sole are applicable.

PLATES

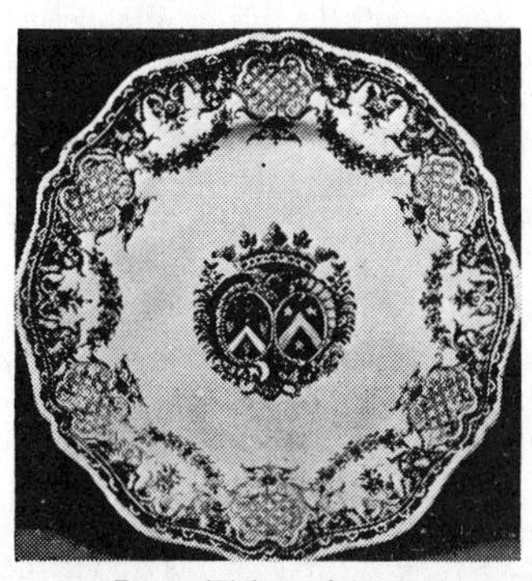

Rouen (Eighteenth century)

Moustier

Moustier

Old Sèvres — Old Sèvres — Sèvres (Empire period) — Sèvres (Fontainebleau service)

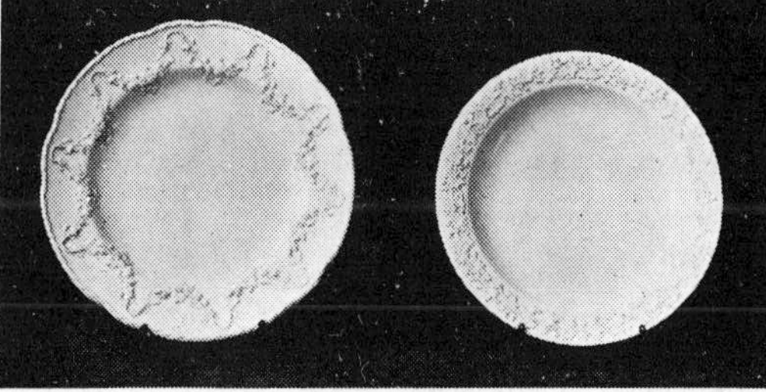

Wedgwood: meat and dessert plates

PLAISIR—French word for a small wafer or *oublie*, rolled into a cone. See OUBLIE.

PLANTAIN—Young leaves of this plant are used in salads.

PLANTAIN TREE. FIGUIER D'ADAM—A type of banana tree. See BANANA.

PLASTRON—Ventral part of the shell of turtles. This part, as well as the dorsal one, after being taken out of the horny plate or shell, is used for making turtle soup.

PLATE. ASSIETTE—A small table utensil, mostly of porcelain or china nowadays, of various materials in the past. The centre of the plate is called the *well* and the border, which forms the band around the hollow part, is called the *rim*. This band is also sometimes referred to as the *shoulder*.

The Greeks had two types of plates; the first, *tryps*, were quite big and could serve as a dish; the other, *tryblion*, was smaller.

The Romans had plates in pottery, glass, silver and even gold. The common people, though, often had to make do with wooden bowls.

In the Middle Ages, the individual plate disappeared. It was replaced by a round slice of bread which was called a *trencher*. After the meal this bread was distributed to the poor.

At the end of the fifteenth century everybody wanted to have silver plates and dishes. Juvenal des Ursin sorrowfully protested against this abuse.

In the sixteenth and seventeenth centuries plates became magnificent works of art, in which gold, enamel and even precious stones were combined. There exist today wonderful plates, which were made by the enamellers of Limoges. On the plates of Bernard Palissy, plants, shells and animals can be seen worked in relief.

Although the greater part of the plates in precious metals and enamels are of the same size as present day plates (about 8 inches in diameter), we are rather inclined to believe that they were more show pieces than table utensils in daily use.

The modern plate is more modest as far as the materials from which it is made are concerned. Nevertheless, plates manufactured at Sèvres come very near to the art of gone-by days. It is true, these are not within the reach of everybody, and only people of means can afford the luxury of such a service.

The faience of Moustiers, remarkable for its decorative qualities and the purity of its enamel, was for a long time attributed to the factories of Rouen. Several writers of the eighteeneth century: Piganiol de la Force, Abbé Delaporte, Fournay, etc., praised them in their writings, which makes it all the more difficult to understand the total oblivion into which they have fallen. Monsieur Riocreux, keeper of the Sèvres museum of ceramics, was the first to have traced the history of this faience, and a few years later Baron C. Davillier published an excellent work on the history of Moustiers and Marseilles faience and porcelain.

It was at the end of the seventeenth century that Pierre Clérissy, coming from a family of potters, managed to create in Moustiers a pottery industry, which according to Davillier must have brought him a fortune, to his descendants ennoblement, and to his town a century of prosperity. His nephew, who succeeded him in 1728 and bore the same name, was elevated by Louis XV in 1743 and took the title of Seigneur de Trévans. He was appointed secretary of the king's chancellery in 1847 by the Parliament of Provence, when he joined forces with Joseph Fouque, the skilled artist, and handed over his factory to him. The factory by now employed no less than 28 painters and remained the first and most important of all those soon to be established by his competitors at Moustiers and in several neighbouring localities. Its products at this time enjoyed a well-merited reputation, which they maintained for a long time, for Abbé Delaporte, in his *Voyageur français*, published in Paris in 1788, speaks of it in these terms:

'There is in the little town of Moustiers a factory of faience which is considered the best and finest in the kingdom.'

Other factories in the south of France included those at Marseilles; some of the factories, notably those of Savy (placed under the protection of the King's brother, Compte de Provence, later Louis XVII), of Robert and of the widow Perrin, produced remarkable pieces, decorated with landscapes and still life, painted in various colours with great perfection.

The decoration of plates offers a great variety of subjects and anecdotal curiosities. The décor of Italian plates, or *majolica*, is extremely varied. At the beginning, the ornaments were mixed with figures, then scenes reproduced from the works of great masters began to take precedence, often taking up the whole surface of the well and the shoulder. And, finally, the central motive was framed with so-called grotesque ornaments. At Nevers, at first Italian influence is felt, later we find white decorations on Persian blue background; still later, the Chinese style. Nevers also produced popular anecdotal china plates, particularly so-called 'patronymic' plates, bearing the name of the person for whom they were destined as wedding presents, with a figure of his or her patron saint painted on it, plates bearing professional emblems and, finally, plates made during the whole of the revolutionary period, with mottos and symbols.

Historical events have often been represented on popular plates. The conquest of Algeria, depicting military scenes, such as *The Award of the Croix d'Honneur; The Consuls of Damascus congratulating Abd el-Kader on his intervention on the side of the Lebanese maronites massacred by the Turks; The Syrian maronites welcoming French troops*, and episodes from the 1914 War. Puzzle pictures and Béranger songs must also be mentioned as decorations of popular plates.

The Rouen plates have had several styles of decoration: the *lambrequin* design, that is, a design composed of symmetrical patterns, repeated or alternating, and converging towards the centre of the plate; the design inspired by the rococo style, armorial bearings, and couplets, with the music carefully noted down. Floral pieces, in fresh and brilliant colours, decorate the Strasbourg plates.

Decoration of plates is in fact a very active branch of art even in our modern times.

PLATINE—French name for a small low baking pan.

PLEUROTE—Genus of fungi, one species of which, *Argouane* or *Pleurote du panicaut*, is edible and excellent.

PLOMBIÈRE (ICE)—Iced sweets. See ICE CREAMS AND ICES.

PLOVER. Pluvier—A genus of wading birds of which there are several species: the *great plover* is about the size of a lapwing or peewit and, like them, it haunts marshlands and water-meadows near the sea. The *golden plover* is the size of a turtle dove and its plumage is speckled with yellow.

Plovers are considered excellent game and some gastronomes insist that they should be cooked undrawn. This tradition is an old one: in the sixteenth century, according to Lucien Tendret, only three kinds of birds (larks, turtle doves and plovers) used to be roasted without 'breaking into them.'

Plover can be prepared in any way suitable for WOODCOCK*.

PLUCHES—French name for the leaves of certain plants, such as *chervil* and *parsley*. These leaves are generally used raw (chervil leaves being put into some soups). In some cases the leaves are blanched in boiling water.

PLUCK. Issues—The lights, heart and entrails of slaughtered animals. See OFFAL OR VARIETY MEATS, *Lamb's pluck à l'anglaise*.

The French word *issues* is also wrongly used for the giblets of poultry.

The expression *issues de table* was used formerly to designate the last tit-bits served at the end of a great banquet. These included sweets, sugared almonds, crystallized fruit, and other delicacies which went with the sweet. Sometimes these were not served at the table but in a room next to the dining room.

PLUM. Prune—Fruit of the plum tree, of the family *Rosaceae*.

It is cultivated a little everywhere in Europe. There is an infinite variety of plum trees in France which all produce sweet tasting fruit.

Among the best of these fruits are the greengage (*reine-claude*) which ripens at the end of July and whose flesh is very sweet and well flavoured, the golden greengage (*reine-claude dorée*) which ripens towards the end of August; the *mirabelle*, a small round plum, yellow in colour streaked with red, the flesh very well flavoured, which is fully ripened at the end of August; the late *mirabelle*, which ripens from the end of September to October; the large damson of Tours, a plum which is dried; the musk damson; the violet, white and black damsons; the Saint Catherine; the early yellow; the *kirke*, large globular fruit, dark violet in colour, ripe at the end of August; the *de Monsieur* (thus named in honour of Monsieur, brother of King Louis XIV, who, it is said, greatly appreciated this fruit), a large fruit with lobes of unequal size, amber and carmine, ripe at the end of July and in August; the violet *perdrigon*, plump fruit coming to maturity in September; the *quetsche*, the fruit from which the famous liqueur is made, and which is also used for compotes, jams and in pastry-making, ripe in August; the plum of Ente or Agen, medium-sized fruit, pinkish violet in colour, which ripens in September; the Golden Drop Plum (*prune goutte d'or*), a large, oval, yellow fruit with red streaks, ripening at the end of September.

All these varieties of plums are eaten in France in their natural state, as fresh fruit. They can also be used to make compotes, jams and a great number of pastries.

Plums Bourdaloue. PRUNES BOURDALOUE—Large greengages are used in this way. Proceed as for *Apricots Bourdaloue**.

Plums in brandy. PRUNES À L'EAU-DE-VIE—Wipe some greengages; prick them two or three times with a big needle. Weigh the fruit. Make a syrup of sugar in the ratio of 1 cup (250 grams) of sugar and ¼ cup (¼ tumbler) of water to each 2 pounds (kilo) of fruit and cook to 105°C. (220°F.).

When the syrup is ready, immerse the plums in it. Let them boil twice before touching with the skimmer.

Drain and put them in a jar.

Let the syrup cool completely. Add to it some good quality 90° alcohol in sufficient quantity to obtain a liqueur of 45°. Strain the liquid through a muslin. Fill the jar with it. Cork and secure firmly. Allow to soak well before using.

Candied plums. PRUNES CONFITES—Prepared as for *Candied apricots*. See APRICOT.

Compote of plums—See COMPOTE, *Plum compote*.

Plums Condé. PRUNES CONDÉ—Large greengages are used most of all for this recipe. Proceed as for *Condé apricots* (see APRICOT).

Plums flambé Lorraine. PRUNES FLAMBÉES À LA LORRAINE—Cook lightly in a vanilla syrup some stoned mirabelle plums. Drain them. Put them in little oven-ware dishes of metal or porcelain. Pour over a little syrup bound with arrowroot. Sprinkle with hot Quetsche. Set alight when serving.

Plum fritters—See FRITTERS.

Plum fritters a l'agenaise—See FRITTERS.

Plum jam. CONFITURE DE PRUNES—Allow 1½ cups (350 grams) of sugar for 1 pound (500 grams) of stoned fruit. For the cooking proceed as for *Apricot jam*. See JAM.

Ice and iced mousse of plums. GLACE, MOUSSE GLACÉE AUX PRUNES—The same procedure as for *Ice* or *Iced mousse of apricots*. See ICE CREAMS AND ICES.

Plum soufflé Lorraine. SOUFFLÉ AUX PRUNES À LA LORRAINE—Prepared with a mixture of 7 ounces, i.e., almost a cup (200 grams) of mirabelle plums, ½ pound (250 grams) of sugar cooked to a heavy syrup, and 5 egg whites, beaten to a very stiff foam, with the addition of preserved plums cut in dice, soaked in plum brandy. To cook proceed as for sweet soufflés. See SOUFFLÉ.

Alsatian plum tart—See TART, *Fruit tart à l'alsacienne*.

POACHING. POCHAGE—Method of cooking meat, poultry, fish, etc., in a clear spiced and flavoured stock, or in water. See CULINARY METHODS.

Poached eggs. OEUFS POCHÉS—The eggs selected must be very small and very fresh, and there should be one for each person.

Prepare the eggs as described in the recipe for *Poached eggs*. See EGGS.

POCHARD. AYTHYA—A species of duck, known as *pochard*, *pockard* or *poker* (the female of which is known as dunbird).

A fully-grown male pochard has a bright red head and neck, the back and breast, partly a dull black, partly ash grey with thin black stripes; the sides are similarly striped, the lower region of the abdomen is black, the bill is dark blue, the culmen and the tip are black, the tarsus and the scutes blueish and the eyes are orange-red. The plumage of the female of the species, even in the spring, is infinitely less brilliant.

This species frequently nest in the marshy plains of Holland, Northern Germany and Belgium and cross France twice a year during winter migrations. They are then keenly pursued by sportsmen for the succulence and the distinctive taste of their flesh which is greatly prized by the connoisseurs.

All the methods of preparation given for wild duck can be applied to pochard. See DUCK.

POCHETEAU—French name for rays or skates with pointed elongated muzzles. For culinary preparation of this fish, see RAY OR SKATE.

POCHOUSE—The *pochouse* (also written *pauchouse* is a *matelote** made of all sorts of freshwater fish, with eel predominating, which should be cooked with white wine and thickened with kneaded butter, as the *Matelote à la meunière**.

The indispensable ingredients of the pochouse garnish are lean bacon, cut in large dice, scalded and fried in butter, sliced or diced mushrooms and small glazed onions. This matelote is served with square croûtons of home-made bread, dried in the oven, or fried golden in butter, and rubbed with garlic. It is prepared in the following manner:

Cut the fish into uniform chunks and put into a buttered sauté pan on a foundation of onions and carrots cut in round slices. Season and put a big *bouquet garni** containing a clove of garlic in the middle. Pour in enough dry white wine to cover the fish.

Bring to the boil, then cover and simmer from 20 to 25 minutes.

Drain the pieces of fish. Put them into another sauté pan with diced bacon, mushrooms and small onions.

Thicken the liquor in which the fish was cooked with kneaded butter, strain and pour over the fish. Simmer for a few moments. Just before serving add a few tablespoons of fresh cream.

Pochouse de Verdun-sur-le-Doub—Obtain fish of different kinds: the superior kinds (eel, pike, lote) and lower quality fish (carp, barbel, chub and bream).

Put them in chunks into a tinned copper cauldron and pour in a glass of ordinary white Burgundy wine, so that the pieces of fish are well covered.

For a *pochouse* requiring 4 or 5 pounds of fish, you will need garlic, *a lot of garlic*, ¼ pound (125 grams) of bacon cut into lardoons, thyme, bay leaf, enough salt and a good dose of pepper (begin by grilling the bacon).

Knead ½ pound (250 grams) of fresh butter mixed with flour, for thickening the sauce.

Put the butter in 12 minutes before serving.

The cooking should take from 30 to 45 minutes. At first boil fast, then simmer for 12 minutes, after the butter has been added.

To serve, take the chunks out one by one, put them on a dish on a foundation of croûtons of bread fried in butter and rubbed with garlic. Strain the sauce over the fish.

Take care not to stir the chunks of fish during cooking; be content with just shaking the pan.

Avoid cooking the hard roes of pike, barbel and chub.

POD. Cosse—Vessel enclosing certain leguminous seeds: pea-pod, bean-pod, etc.

Poêle (pan) for crêpes, fish and ordinary frying (*Larousse*)

POÊLAGE—Method of cooking applied to various substances, which are cooked *à l'étuvée**, i.e., in a covered pan with butter or other fat. See CULINARY METHODS, *Pot-roasting*.

POÊLON—An earthenware utensil or a pan made of copper or some other metal, with a long handle. Such aluminium or copper pans are used for cooking sugar.

POGNE DE ROMANS—Cake which is a kind of sweet brioche and is prepared in the following manner: sift 6 cups (500 grams) of sifted cake flour and spread it on the table in a circle. In the middle of this circle put 1¼ teaspoons (8 grams) of salt, a tablespoon of orange blossom water, or ½ teaspoon orange extract, ⅞ ounce (25 grams) of yeast, ½ pound (250 grams) of softened butter and 4 eggs. Mix all the ingredients well, working the dough vigorously to give it body. Add 2 more eggs, one by one and, finally, without stopping to knead the dough, incorporate 1½ cups (200 grams) of castor (fine) sugar, putting it in little by little. Put this dough into a small bowl, sprinkled with flour, cover and keep in a warm place from 10 to 12 hours.

Turn out the dough on to a board and pummel it to arrest fermentation. Divide into two parts, mould into balls, shape the top (as in the case of ordinary brioche). Put the cakes into buttered baking tins, leave the dough to rise for another half an hour in a warm place, brush with beaten egg and bake in a moderate oven (the *pogne* can be eaten hot or cold). It can be served with red currant jelly.

POISSONNIER—French word for the chef of an important restaurant who is in charge of all fish dishes, with the exception of fried or grilled fish, which are the domain of the *rôtisseur* or the *grillardin*. *Poissonnier* also means fishmonger.

POITOU—The Poitou gastronomic folklore extends to several departments (Vendée, Vienne, Deux-Sèvres, Maine-et-Loire). The culinary specialities are in fact local dishes, as they are everywhere, varying in detail according to tastes in different places.

This region is particularly favoured in so far as food supplies are concerned. The cattle raised in Parthenay and Bressuire furnish perfect meat, mutton is of good quality and the pork, owing to the good pig food, is of excellent flavour.

Poultry farming produces a whole range of birds: turkeys, capons, table fowl, guinea-fowl, and in the cantons of Chef-Boutonne and Sauzé-Vaussay ducks are raised for the production of foie gras. The *Civray Pâté de foie gras* is famous; *Confit de canard* is also made here.

Ground game is of high repute, as well as winged game (partridges, woodcock, snipe, quail, rail, and field-ducks) and the water-fowl, which abounds here.

Coastal parts of Vendée abound in excellent fish. Almost every kind of shell-fish is found there. The Portuguese oysters of Tranche and Groin-du-Cou, the mussels from the Aiguillon mussel-farms and the spiny lobsters (crayfish) of the island of Yeu are greatly prized. The rivers provide a great variety of freshwater fish, the brooks and streams furnish crayfish and the marshes abound in eels and frogs.

The land of Poitou is fertile and produces an abundance of onions (very famous), artichokes, garden peas, Marac haricot beans (shell beans), Niort cauliflowers and Vendée green cabbages.

The wooded district north-west of Poitou produces choice chestnuts and Vienne equally good walnuts.

Among the cheeses made in this district are *La Mothe Saint-Héraye*, *Saint-Loup*, *Goat cheese*, *Vienne chabichou*, etc.

Local butter, without equalling the quality of that of Charente, is excellent.

Culinary specialities—Among the typical local dishes is *Potée à la tête de porc*, which furnishes both a soup and the main course; the pig's head is cut into pieces and eaten sprinkled with sea salt and a dash of vinegar. Among the fish dishes are: *Grilled eels of Saint-Trojan; Bouilleture*, a *matelote** of eel in red wine, with prunes added to the garnish; *Chaudrée*, a kind of fish stew—its main feature being the great variety and freshness of the fish used; the *Cotriade*, a kind of bouillabaisse, which is not specifically a Vendée dish, but is made all along the coast, particularly in the canton of Noirmoutier. *Frogs' legs à la luçonnaise* are first soaked for an hour in vinegar-flavoured water, then drained, dried, dredged with flour, fried in *Noisette butter* and served with fried cloves of garlic.

Among meat dishes, the *Vendée fressure* deserves a mention; it is the pluck, including the pig's lungs, liver, heart and spleen, chopped and mixed with congealed pig's blood. The whole is then cooked with chopped fat bacon, slowly and for a long time. It is usually eaten cold.

Pâté de Pâques, or Easter pie, is long, crescent shaped and filled with balls of hashed meat, hard boiled eggs, and slices of pork, chicken or rabbit, sautéed in butter and left to get cold. The *Vendée pie* is made of fillets of wild rabbit and forcemeat of the same animal's flesh, mixed with an equal quantity of pork, half cooked and chopped. *Easter loaf* or '*Galette piquante*' is made of bread dough mixed with butter, sugar, eggs and orange blossom water, and shaped into a cob.

Vegetable dishes include the *Chouée*, which is green cabbage boiled in salted water, drained and pressed, with a lot of butter added to it; *Mogettes*, French beans cooked in the ordinary way and dressed with butter and cream; the *Far* (or *farci*), which is composed of different vegetables, such as Swiss chard leaves, spinach, leeks, and cabbage, first cooked in salted water, then drained, pressed, chopped and stewed for a long time in a pan with pork fat, onion and diced bacon. Finally, beaten eggs and cream are added to the mixture.

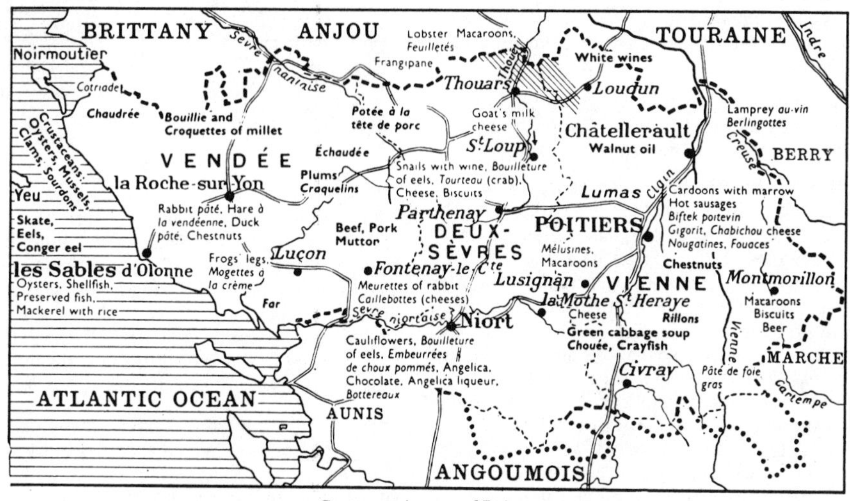

Gastronomic map of Poitou

Notable sweets and pastries include the *Tourteau fromagé*, cream cheese or goat cheese reduced into a fine paste, to which a quarter of its weight of flour, fine sugar, butter, yolks of eggs, whites beaten into a stiff froth, and flavourings are added. It is then put into a mould, allowed to ferment, and baked in the oven. The *Fouée* ('faggot'), a circlet of bread dough, covered with cream, melted butter or oil, which used to be baked in a blazing oven; *Bottereaux de Langon*, a sort of *oreillettes* deep-fried in oil; *Plum pies*. The following are among very famous local products: *Montmorillon macaroons and biscuits*, *Lusignan mélusines and macaroons*, *Parthenay biscuits*, *Châtellerault caramels*, *Niort angelica*.

Beverages. The little local wines are excellent—the red wines of Foye-Monjault and the white wines of Loudun (Saint-Léger, Montbrillan, Pounançay, Ternay).

In the Deux-Sèvres, near Parthenay, excellent Brézé and Bourgueil wines are made from locally grown grapes. The white wines of Thouars (Bilaizais, Ligron, Taizé) and the red (Pompois) are somewhat similar to the wines of Saumur. The wines of Mareuil-sur-Lay are greatly appreciated in Vendée.

The Montmorillon beer enjoys a great reputation, and angelica liqueur is made in Niort.

POIVRADE. Method of preparing certain meats, mainly ground game. See ROEBUCK, SAUCE.

The name also applies to small young artichokes which are eaten *à la croque-au-sel* (that is with salt as the only accompaniment).

POIVRON—French common name for red pepper or pimento.

POLENTA—Piedmont form of maize (corn) meal porridge. It is made simply of maize flour dried in the open and not in the oven, as for *gaudes* (hasty puddings).

Polenta can also be made of chestnut flour, as is done in Corsica.

Polenta is used as a garnish for garden-warblers and other similar small birds; this is a traditional north Italian dish and was a great favourite of Napoleon I.

To cook polenta. Bring one quart (litre) of water to the boil, add salt, allowing 2½ teaspoons (15 grams) per quart (litre) and sprinkle in the maize flour gradually, stirring with a wooden spoon. Cook from 25 to 30 minutes. Add, for the above quantity of polenta, about 4 tablespoons (from 60 to 70 grams) of butter and ¾ cup (75 grams) of grated Parmesan cheese.

Spread the polenta, cooked as described above, on a moistened baking tray in an even layer. When cold, cut the polenta into square or lozenge-shaped pieces.

Fry these pieces golden brown in butter, arrange on a round dish and sprinkle with grated cheese and *Noisette butter*. See BUTTER, *Compound butters*.

Polenta can be used as a garnish for various meat and fish. Various dishes can be made of polenta. To prepare these dishes proceed as described in the recipes for *Semolina soufflés*, *timbale*, etc. See SEMOLINA.

Polenta fritters—See FRITTERS.

Polenta pudding (Sweet)—See PUDDING.

Thrushes or other small birds with polenta. Grives à la polenta—Prepare polenta with cheese as described above. Pour it into a buttered, oven-proof dish, spreading the polenta in a layer 1¼ inches thick.

With the aid of a spoon dipped in water indent as many 'nests' as there are thrushes (or other birds). Sprinkle with grated cheese. Half roast the birds in the oven and put one in each little cavity. Sprinkle with a little melted butter. Finish cooking in the oven. Dilute the pan juices left over from roasting the thrushes with white wine and pour around the dish.

POLONAISE (A LA)—Method of preparing certain dishes. See ASPARAGUS, CAULIFLOWER.

POLYPODIUM. Polypode—A species of edible ferns. See FERN.

POLYPORUS. Polypore—A very big species of fungi (reaching a weight of up to 40 pounds), growing generally at the foot of old oak trees and on the ground. These giant mushrooms are edible but the flesh is rather tough. They are found mainly in Germany, Hungary, Italy and more rarely, in France.

POMEGRANATE. Grenade—The fruit of the common pomegranate tree which is believed to be of North African origin. It is used widely in France.

Pomegranates can be eaten raw like other fruit, but generally it is the juice only which is used. From this juice, the very popular *grenadine* syrup is made. Pomegranates are also used in the preparation of ices and jellies, and a type of alcoholic drink is made from this fruit.

POMFRET. Brème de mer—Fish (*Brama rayi*) which is also known as *Ray's bream* and *sea-bream*, and is found in the North Atlantic and Pacific Oceans. Pomfret is also the name of flat fish found in the Indian Ocean.

POMMARD—This wine, which is produced in the little commune of Côte-d'Or (Côte de Beaune), is classed among the finest growths of Burgundy wines.

POMPE OR GIBASSIER (Provence cake)—*Pompe* is the traditional cake which is eaten in Provence at the '*gros soupa*' on Christmas Eve. It is also called *gibassier* ('gibbous'), because of the lumps on its surface.

The '*gros soupa*' is the meal which precedes the midnight mass. As the fast entails abstinence from meat, this meal almost invariably consists of Lenten dishes, some of which are a 'must', so to say, such as *Cod en rayte* or *en brandade* and *Cardoons in cream.*

'The dessert is by no means the least attraction of this traditional meal and consists mainly of locally manufactured *nougat*, dates, and—above all—the *pompe* or *gibassier*, another local product, the whole washed down liberally with the customary mulled wine.

'Here is the recipe for this cake:

'*Ingredients.* 1 pound (500 grams) of bread dough leaven, 1 pound (500 grams) of brown sugar, 4 pounds (2 kilos) of flour, 6 eggs, half a tumbler of best oil (about ½ cup) and finely grated rind of one lemon and one orange.

'*Method.* Spread the flour on a board in a circle, make a well in the middle and put into it the leaven with the brown sugar, oil and half the eggs. Mix well, incorporating the flour little by little. Knead the dough well and add the rest of the eggs one by one. This dough should be quite soft.

'Leave to rise for about 6 hours in a warm temperature, then beat it out, divide into pieces of about 6 to 7 ounces (200 grams), shape into crowns and put on boards sprinkled with fine bran.

'Keep in a warm place, as this dough takes a long time to rise.

'Bake in a lively oven. When ready, take out of the oven and moisten the surface of each cake with a cloth dipped in a mixture of pure water and orange blossom water.' (A. Caillat.)

POMPONNETTES—These small preparations are served as hors-d'oeuvre. See HORS-D'OEUVRE, *Hot hors-d'oeuvre.*

PONT-L'ÉVÊQUE CHEESE—See CHEESE.

PONT-NEUF (Pastry)—Line buttered tartlet tins with *Puff pastry* (see DOUGH). Fill with *Frangipane cream* (see CREAM) mixed with crushed macaroons. Put two thin strips of puff pastry criss-cross fashion on each tartlet. Bake in a moderate oven. When ready, remove from oven and sprinkle with fine sugar.

Pope

POPE. Gremille—A fish of the perch family, sometimes called ruff. It is a freshwater fish found in most of the rivers of France, especially in the Seine and the Moselle. The pike perches of the middle western section of U.S.A. are very similar.

The flesh is quite delicate. All the recipes for perch may be used in the preparation of this fish (see PERCH). It is used especially in fish stews (*matelotes**).

POPPY. Coquelicot—A very common plant in cornfields, the petals of which are used to dye certain liquids. The leaves, in spite of being slightly narcotic, are sometimes used as a vegetable like spinach.

The white poppy is cultivated principally for the extraction of poppy seed oil. The aromatic seeds were used in pastry-making in times of antiquity (they were known to the Egyptians earlier than 1500 B.C.), and are still used in many regions for sprinkling cakes and bread.

PORCELAIN. Porcelaine—Fine kind of earthenware. It owes its name to the *cowrie*, or *porcelain-shell*, which in old French was called *pourcelline* or *pourcellaine* and in Italian and Latin *porcellana* or *porcellina.*

There are two kinds of porcelain: *hard-paste* or *Chinese porcelain* and *soft-paste* or *French porcelain.*

Hard-paste porcelain dates back to the Han period, 206 B.C. The best period was during the reign of Ch'eng Hua, 1465-1487 (Ming dynasty). From China the industry spread to Japan in the sixteenth century.

For a long time Chinese and Japanese porcelain aroused the admiration of connoisseurs and the envy of European potters.

Soft-paste porcelain does not owe its name to the degree of hardness of the actual paste but to its weak resistance to high temperature and to the softness of its glaze, easily scratched by steel. It is highly probable that its discovery is due to a Rouen earthenware maker by the name of Poterat.

A century earlier, however, in 1585, a first attempt, soon to be abandoned, was made in Florence. At the end of the seventeenth century the first pottery works producing soft-paste porcelain was established at Saint-Cloud. In the eighteenth century rival establishments sprang up in Paris, Lille, Chantilly and, finally, under the patronage of Madame de Pompadour and Louis XV, at Vincennes, which in 1753 became the Royal pottery works. In 1756 it was transferred to Sèvres where it is active to this day.

This small workshop, in which Orry and Fuloy were able to establish themselves, thanks to the patronage of Madame de Pompadour, produced far better results than were achieved before that in France or abroad, in spite of the competition set up by Meissen in Saxony, where hard-paste porcelain has been made since 1709, following the discovery of kaolin clay deposits in the region. The problem of manufacturing porcelain similar to that made in China and Japan which had for so long occupied the minds of potters, was solved, and that period saw the rise of numerous potteries in Germany. Potteries were also established in Austria, Holland, Denmark, Russia, Switzerland and Italy. Finally, in 1776, kaolin deposits were found in France, first at Alençon, then at Saint-Yrieux, near Limoges. It was then that Sèvres began to modify its production and potteries were opened all over France, in Limoges, Paris, and other places.

The pottery industry was neglected for a time but, in our time, beautiful porcelain is once again in favour.

The Sèvres porcelain factory, with its workshops and laboratories, has made important improvements in the manufacturing process and the decoration of the porcelain.

PORCUPINE. PORC-ÉPIC—Animal, whose rather fat flesh is good to eat, especially when young.

PORK. PORC—A domestic pachyderm which is not usually referred to by this name until after slaughter. The male is called a *boar*, the female a *sow*, the castrated animal is called *fig* or *stag* and the young animal is called *piglet*, *porker* or *sucking pig*.

Pork is fat and firm and has more red meat than white (it only acquires this colour when the animal is killed by complete bleeding). It is more difficult to digest than other meat, but, on the other hand, is more assimilable.

There are three principal breeds of pigs which have produced the many species which exist in Europe: the *Asiatic*, *Neapolitan* and *Celtic*.

The *Asiatic breed*, with small straight, pointed ears, has been used for cross-breeding, as it was considered that it produced bacon of soft and inferior quality.

The *Neapolitan breed*, with pointed, horizontally placed ears, without cross-breeding and living mostly in the open, has retained its purity of strain.

The *Celtic breed*, with long, wide, lop ears, which formerly inhabited Gaul and the British Isles, has, as a result of cross-breeding, undergone various changes in various regions of France. So much so that today there is a great variety of species, including the following: *Alsace*, *Anjou*, *Bayonne*, *Bresse*, *Brittany*, *Bugey*, *Champagne*, *Charolais*, *Craon*, *Corsican*, *Landes*, *Lauraguaise*, *Limousin*, *Lorraine*, *Manche*, *Marche*, *Nevers*, *Normandy*, *Périgord*, *Picardy*, *Rouergue*, *Vendée*, etc.

Among the different breeds which we have enumerated above, five can be singled out:

The *Normandy breed*, with a lean body and saddle-back, which gives superior quality flesh; *Craon* or *Anjou breed*, raised in the Loire basin; *Lorraine breed*, raised mainly in the Departments of Meurthe and Moselle, greatly prized for the quality of its flesh and bacon; the *Périgord breed*, which produces pigs with a very highly developed sense of smell, used for finding truffles; the *Bresse breed*, black pigs with a white band encircling the middle of the body.

Among the English cross-breeds, all of which have been introduced into France, is the *Yorkshire*, white or yellowish skinned pigs, which produce the famous hams. Other principal breeds of British pig include: *Large White Ulster*, *Large Black*, *Tamworth*, *Wessex Saddle-back*, *Berkshire*, *Gloucester Old Spots*, *Lincoln Curly-coated*, *Cumberland*, *Essex*.

Pork is eaten either fresh or cured. Its flesh lends itself particularly to salting, smoking and many other processes of pork butchery. The joints most frequently eaten fresh are *chine* (*U.S. loin*), *fillet*, *chops* and *ham*.

Pork andouilles and andouillettes (sausages). ANDOUILLES, ANDOUILLETTES DE PORC—These big pork sausages are made of the big intestine and the stomach of the pig, cut into strips and mixed with lardoons of pork fat. These sausages are salted and can be kept for a long time.

The most famous *andouilles* are those made in Vire and in Brittany. They are eaten as hors-d'oeuvre, cut into thin slices like saveloys and other sausage.

They can also be served hot. For this they should first be boiled in slightly salted water, allowed to cool, then grilled and served with mashed potatoes or other vegetable.

The best *andouillettes* come from Troyes, Nancy, Tours, Strasbourg, Lyons, Cambrai, Caen and, last but by no means least, Paris, as made by the best pork butchers in the capital.

All these varieties of *andouillettes* are treated in the same way, i.e. they are grilled and served with mashed potatoes or other vegetables.

Before being put under the grill, the *andouillettes* should be slashed slightly and brushed with melted butter.

They can also be fried in butter or lard.

Home-made andouilles. ANDOUILLES DE MÉNAGE—Soak big, fat pig's intestines in cold water and wash well.

Drain, dry on a cloth, cut into thin strips and put into a bowl with half their weight of lean bacon, cut into very small pieces.

Add a glass of white wine and chopped onion, shallot and parsley. Season with salt, pepper and spices, mix well and leave to marinate in this seasoning for several hours. Fill big pig's intestines, well soaked and washed, with this mixture.

Cook and finish off as described in the recipe for *Nancy andouilles*.

Nancy andouilles. ANDOUILLES DE NANCY—Soak $1\frac{1}{2}$ pounds (750 grams) of pork belly and $1\frac{1}{2}$ pounds (750 grams) of calf's mesentery in cold water. Wash them carefully and put to cook in salted water for 2 hours. Drain, rinse in cold water, dry on a cloth and cut into very small pieces.

Put into a bowl, season with salt, pepper and spices, moisten with 1 cup (2 decilitres) of white wine and add $\frac{1}{2}$ cup (100 grams) of chopped mushrooms lightly fried in butter with chopped onion, shallot and parsley. Chopped truffles can also be added.

Fill big pig's intestines (thoroughly soaked and washed) with this mixture.

Form the *andouilles* by twisting the intestine at intervals of 6 to 8 inches.

Prick the *andouilles* with a big needle and plunge them into a big pan of boiling water. Season with salt and add sliced onions and carrots, 2 cloves of garlic and a good *bouquet garni**.

As soon as boiling is established, draw the pan to the corner of the stove, cover with a lid and simmer very gently for 2 hours.

Take the pan off the fire and leave the *andouilles* in the liquid in which they were cooked until almost quite cold.

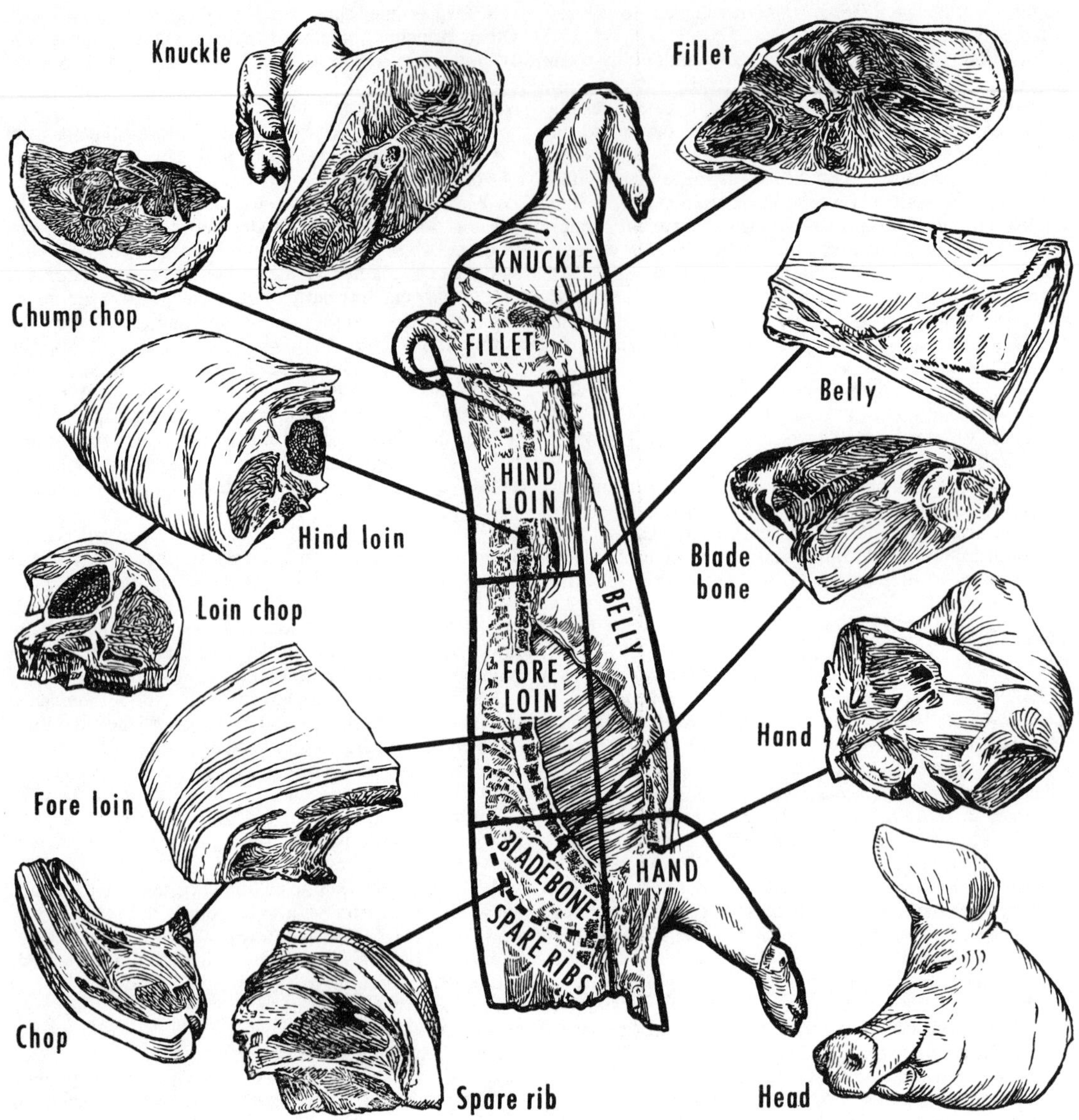

English cuts of pork

Drain, put in a shallow baking pan, cover with a board, put a weight on top and leave in a cool place until quite cold.

To serve, slash the *andouilles* with a few very light incisions, grill and serve with mashed potatoes.

Fine pork andouillettes. ANDOUILLETTES FINES DE PORC —Cook a calf's mesentery, cut into big square pieces, and half of its weight of lean bacon, similarly cut, in a quart (litre) of meat stock, to which an onion studded with a clove and a good *bouquet garni** have been added. Season and bring to the boil. Then cover with a lid and simmer very gently for about 2 hours.

Drain the meats and chop coarsely, put into a bowl, add ½ cup (100 grams) of chopped mushrooms, lightly fried with chopped onions, shallots and parsley and bound with a few tablespoons of concentrated stock.

Add 6 raw yolks of egg and mix all the ingredients well. Stuff this mixture into pig's intestines, well soaked and washed, and tie the *andouillettes* into pieces of 4 inches. Cook and finish off as described in the preceding recipes.

Pig's blood. SANG DE PORC—This is almost solely used for making black puddings. It can also be used for clarifying jellies, and as an element of liaison for red wine sauces of the *civet* type.

Blood pudding—See *Black pudding* in this section.

Breast of pork. POITRINE DE PORC—This part of the animal is used fresh for making *ragoûts*. It can also be boned and grilled, after some of the fat has been removed.

In its salted or smoked state it provides bacon, which is used in numerous culinary preparations.

Carbonnades of pork. CARBONNADES DE PORC—The word *carbonnades*, which in the past applied to all meat cooked on a grill ('*sur des charbons ardents*', i.e. *on glowing coals*) today only applies to thin slices of pork cut from the neck end, as well as lean parts of top

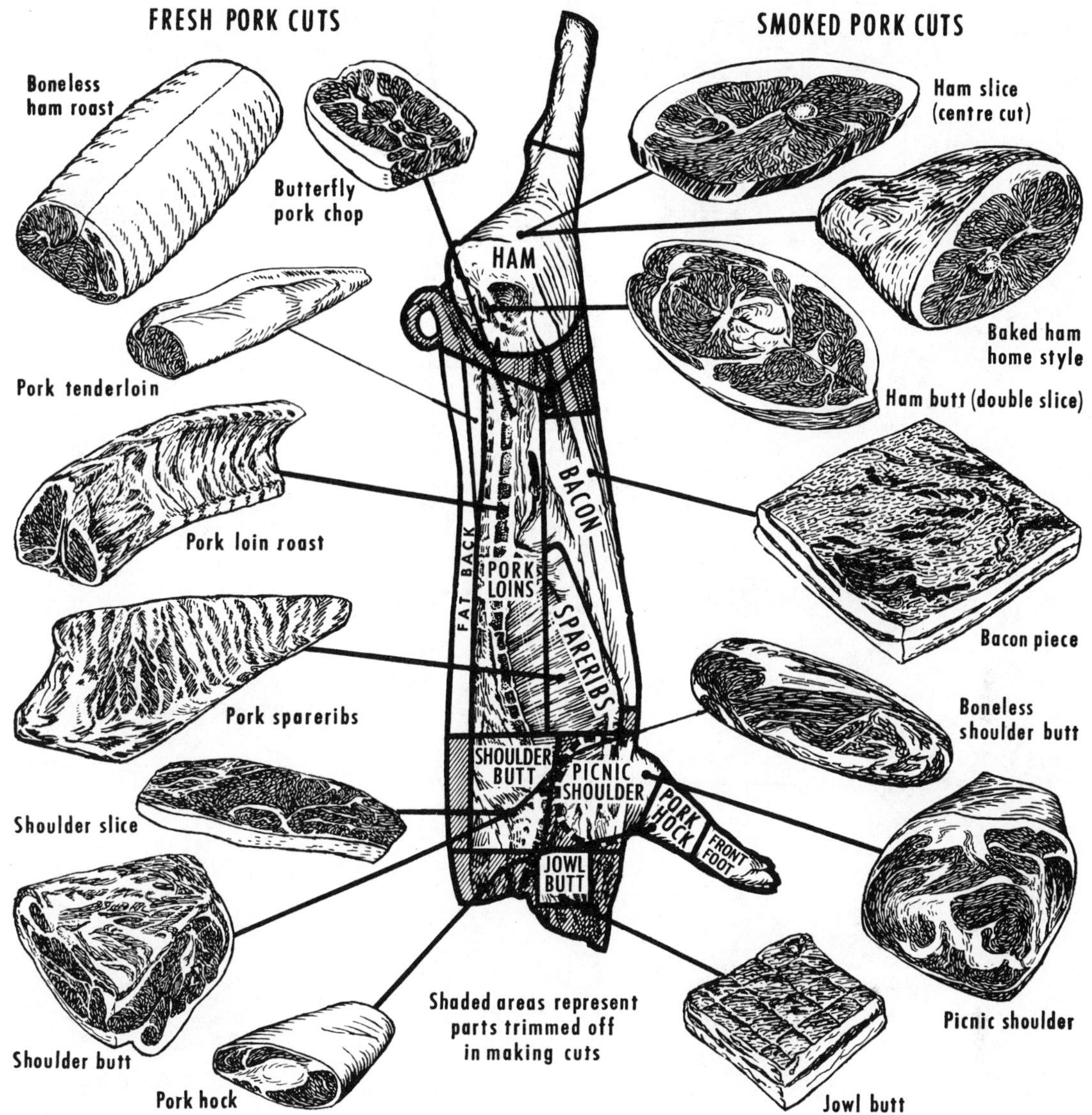

American cuts of Pork

of rump, which, to justify their name, are grilled on hot coals.

The term *carbonnades* also applies to thin slices of pork braised like *Carbonnades of beef à la flamande*. See BEEF.

Grilled carbonnades of pork (which are generally dipped in butter and breadcrumbs before cooking) and sautéed carbonnades can be served with all the garnishes recommended for veal or pork chops.

Chine of pork. ÉCHINE DE PORC—By definition this is a cut taken from the back of the animal, which includes part of the backbone and surrounding flesh. In some regions of France it is also called *échinée* and *épinée*.

The term is principally used to describe that part of the chine which is located next to the neck.

All the methods of preparation given for loin and fillet of pork are suitable for chine. This cut is also used (either boned or not, as the case may be) for making stews.

After cutting it into slices, it can also be grilled or sautéed in the same way as pork chops and, generally, all methods of preparing chops can be applied to chine. Prepared in this way and grilled they are usually called *carbonnades*.

Chine of pork can be half or fully salted and in this form used as an ingredient of *potées* and *estouffades*. This cut is not marketed in the U.S.A.

Pork chops à l'alsacienne. CÔTES DE PORC À L'ALSACIENNE —Season the chops and sauté them in butter or lard, or braise them. Arrange them in a turban on a round dish. Fill the middle of the dish with sauerkraut, prepared in the usual manner. Put on this sauerkraut, piled up into a dome, some poached Strasbourg sausages. Garnish the dish with boiled potatoes. Pour over the chops some of the diluted pan juices, or, if the chops are braised, some of the strained braising liquor.

Pork chops à l'ardennaise. CÔTES DE PORC À L'ARDENNAISE—Sauté the chops in butter or lard. Arrange in a turban. Put in the middle of the dish some potatoes

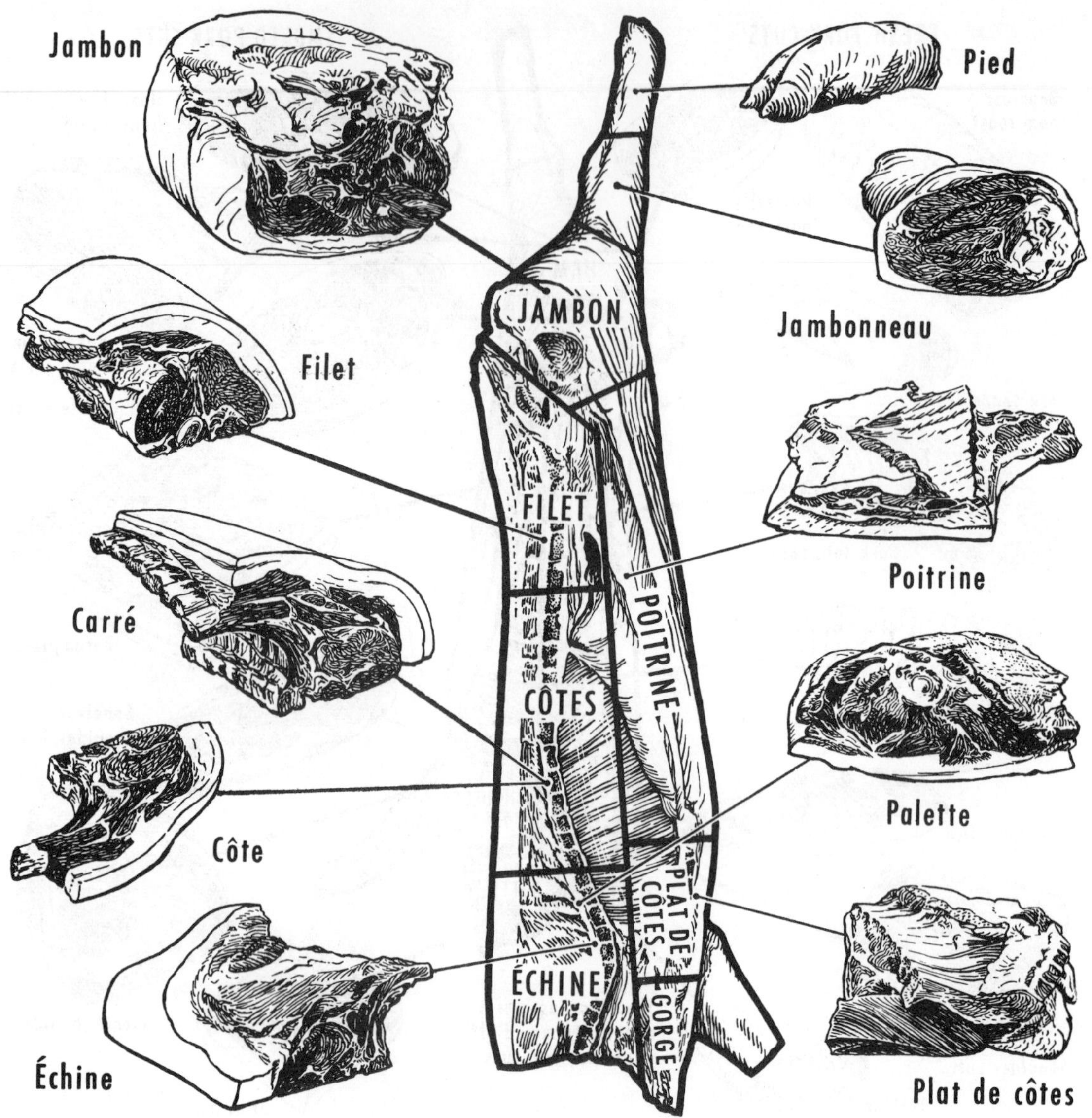

French cuts of pork

sautéed in butter and mixed with diced, fried bacon, and chopped onion lightly fried in butter.

Dilute the pan juices with white wine, add a few crushed juniper berries, moisten with *Demi-glace sauce* (see SAUCE), strain and pour over the chops.

Pork chops à la bayonnaise. CÔTES DE PORC À LA BAYONNAISE—Insert some slivers of garlic into the meaty part of the chops. Season with salt, pepper and powdered thyme and bay leaf, sprinkle with oil and a dash of vinegar. Leave them to marinate in this seasoning for an hour. Sauté briskly in lard in an earthenware dish. When the chops are nicely browned on both sides, surround with small, new potatoes, tossed in lard, and sliced cèpes sautéed in oil. Finish cooking everything together in the oven. Sprinkle with chopped parsley.

Braised pork chops with various garnishes. CÔTES DE PORC BRAISÉES—Cut the chops a little on the thick side. Braise and garnish them in the same way as *Veal chops**.

Pork chops charcutière. CÔTES DE PORC CHARCUTIÈRE—This dish, which is found ready for use in pork butcher's shops in Paris as well as in most provincial towns, is prepared differently in restaurants.

This is how it is made in a restaurant: Flatten the chops slightly, season, coat with melted butter, dip in breadcrumbs and grill gently. Arrange in a crown, fill the middle of the dish with mashed potatoes and, separately, serve *Charcutière sauce* (see SAUCE) which is Robert sauce to which, at the last moment, gherkins —shredded into a coarse and short *julienne**—are added.

Pork chops *charcutières* (whether breadcrumbed or not) after having been fried in lard are put to simmer in *Charcutière sauce* to which some sliced gherkins have been added. (See illustration opposite.)

Fried pork chops with garnish. CÔTES DE PORC SAUTÉES GARNIES—Trim and flatten 4 loin pork chops lightly. Season with salt and pepper and put them to cook in a

Pork chops charcutière (*Robert Carrier*)

sauté pan in which a tablespoon of butter or lard has been heated.

Cook the chops on a lively heat. Brown well on both sides. When they are cooked, remove from the pan, surround with the garnish indicated in the recipe and pour over the pan juices, diluted as indicated in the recipe and strained through a fine sieve or strainer.

Pork chops à la gasconne. CÔTES DE PORC À LA GASCONNE—Marinate the pork chops as described in the recipe for *Pork chops à la bayonnaise*, then fry them quickly in butter or goose fat, just to stiffen them.

Put into the sauté pan 6 peeled and slightly blanched cloves of garlic for each chop.

Cover the pan and finish cooking on a low fire. When the chops are nearly cooked, add 8 stoned and blanched olives (per chop). Arrange the chops in a crown. Put the garnish in the middle of the dish. Dilute the pan juices with half a glass of white wine, add a few tablespoons of thickened veal gravy, boil for a few moments and pour over the chops. Sprinkle with chopped parsley.

Grilled pork chops. CÔTES DE PORC GRILLÉES—Season loin chops with salt and pepper, brush them with melted butter, oil or lard and cook under a moderate grill.

Arrange on a round dish and garnish with watercress.

Note. Grilled pork chops are served as they are, plain, or with a garnish of vegetables, most often with mashed potatoes.

Pork chops à la milanaise. CÔTES DE PORC À LA MILANAISE—Beat loin pork chops flat, season with salt and pepper, coat with egg and breadcrumbs and proceed as described in the recipe for *Veal chops à la milanaise**.

Pork chops Pilleverjus. CÔTES DE PORC PILLEVERJUS—Flatten slightly and trim loin chops. Season them with salt and pepper.

Fry in lard in a sauté pan. When both sides are nicely browned, put into the sauté pan (for 4 chops) 4 tablespoons of finely chopped onion, three-quarters cooked. Add a *bouquet garni**, cover the sauté pan and cook on a low heat for 35 minutes.

Shred a young cabbage heart into a *julienne** and cook in butter or lard, with a lid on and as slowly as possible. As soon as the cabbage is done, moisten it with a few tablespoons of cream and simmer for a few moments, stirring all the time.

Arrange the chops on a round dish on a foundation of the cabbage *julienne*. Garnish with boiled potatoes.

Dilute the pan juices left over from cooking the chops with a good tablespoon of vinegar, add 3 tablespoons of gravy and pour over the chops.

Grilled pork chops garnished with apple rings

Pork chops with Robert sauce. CÔTES DE PORC SAUCE ROBERT—Season the chops and grill them. Serve *Robert sauce* (see SAUCE) and mashed potatoes separately.

Or: Sauté the chops in butter (or lard). When they are half-cooked, put into the sauté pan (for 4 chops) ½ cup (100 grams) of finely chopped white onions.

Drain the chops and arrange them on a dish.

Dilute the pan juices with 1 cup (2 decilitres) of white wine. Boil down almost completely. Add 1½ cups (3 decilitres) of *Demi-glace sauce* (see SAUCE). Boil for 5 minutes.

Remove from fire, add a pinch of sugar and a good teaspoon of mustard to the sauce, mix and pour over the chops.

Note. In a home kitchen, where, generally, neither veal stocks, gravies nor *Demi-glace* are available, proceed in the following manner: Dilute the pan juices with white wine, add some meat stock, boil for a few minutes, then bind with a tablespoon of butter kneaded with flour and add a tablespoon or two of *Tomato purée**.

Alternatively, proceed as follows:

Having cooked the chops, remove them from the pan. Into the same butter (or lard) put a tablespoon or two of flour, mix and cook the flour lightly. Moisten with white wine and stock, blend well, and cook for a few minutes.

Pork chops à la vosgienne. CÔTES DE PORC À LA VOSGIENNE—Sauté the chops in lard (or butter); when half done add a tablespoon of chopped onion lightly fried in butter (a tablespoon per chop). Finish cooking together on a gentle heat.

Arrange the chops in a crown. Fill the middle of the dish with stoned mirabelles, cooked without sugar.

Dilute the pan juices with vinegar and white wine, add some concentrated veal stock and pour over the chops.

Pork crépinettes. CRÉPINETTES DE PORC—*Crépinettes* or small flat sausages are made of *Fine pork forcemeat* (see FORCEMEAT) (or sausage meat) mixed with chopped fine herbs and flavoured with brandy.

The forcemeat is divided into 3 to 3½ ounce (90 or 100 gram) pieces, each of which is then wrapped in a piece of pig's caul, previously soaked in cold water, and moulded into a rectangular shape.

The *crépinettes* are coated with butter and freshly sifted breadcrumbs, sprinkled with melted butter and grilled gently.

Note. Grilled *crépinettes* are usually served with mashed potatoes. They can also be served with various vegetables dressed with butter.

Cinderella pork crépinettes

Cinderella pork crépinettes. CRÉPINETTES DE PORC CENDRILLON—These *crépinettes* are made of fine truffled pork forcemeat. Put a good tablespoon of *salpicon** of pig's feet, mixed with truffles and mushrooms, cut into dice and bound with greatly concentrated veal stock, in the middle of each *crépinette*.

Cinderella *crépinettes* are grilled and served with *Périgueux sauce* and mashed potatoes.

Note. In the past Cinderella *crépinettes* used to be cooked in the hearth, wrapped in buttered greaseproof paper, in hot ashes. The ashes were changed several times during the cooking of the *crépinettes*, which lasted from 20 to 25 minutes.

In the present time, *crépinettes* made of truffled forcemeat and enclosed in an oval-shaped piece of pie pastry, are often served under the name of *Crépinettes Cendrillon* (i.e. *Cinderella crépinettes*).

These *crépinettes in pastry*—for this is how they should be described—are baked in the oven like ordinary small hot pies.

Pork fat. LARD—The adipose tissue of the pig.

In French, the term *lard*, which is sometimes used of fat of animals other than pig, usually means fresh raw pork fat. The French equivalent of the English 'lard' is *saindoux*.

Fillet (U.S. Tenderloin) of pork. FILET DE PORC—The fillet (tenderloin) of pork is the part of the animal from the first ribs to the leg. It is the part which in the case of veal or mutton is called *saddle*.

The pig's back, or saddle, is generally cut in half, lengthways.

The fillet of pork can be prepared in any way suitable for the loin.

Escalopes and noisettes as well as *filets mignons*, are cut from boned fillets of pork, and are prepared in any way suitable for chops.

Roast or pot-roasted fillet of pork is often referred to in French as *longe*.

Pork fricadelles. FRICADELLES DE PORC—Prepare, using pork meat, in the same way as *Beef fricadelles*. See BEEF.

Pork gelatine. COLLE DE COUENNES—Soak 6 pounds (3 kilos) of fresh pork skins in cold water. Put them in a casserole, cover with water; bring to the boil; drain. Put the skins under the cold tap, scrape them, wash them; put them back in the casserole, cover with water. Boil, skim; simmer for 6 or 8 hours, skimming often.

Pass the contents of the pan through a strainer into a basin; leave to cool. When it is cold and has set, remove all the fat from the surface and rub the gelatine with a cloth dipped in boiling water so as to remove every trace of fat.

Add this gelatine to the prepared stock. See JELLY.

Ham—See HAM.

Hand of pork. JAMBONNEAU—Cook in the same way as ham (see HAM, *Smoked and salted ham*) until the flesh comes away from the bones. Reshape it by wrapping tightly in a cloth, leave to cool in the liquid it was cooked in, grease slightly and roll in breadcrumbs.

Pork hash. HACHIS DE PORC—Prepare like *Beef hash*, using left-over pieces of pork. See BEEF.

Potted head (head cheese). HURE DE PORC—This is generally sold in pork butchers' shops ready for the table. In times gone by it used to be made in the country. Here is an old recipe for *Potted head à la pistache:*

Potted head (head cheese) à la pistache (Home recipe). HURE À LA PISTACHE—Clean and scrape a pig's head, remove the tongue, brains and all the fat part of the throat and cut off the ears. Put the head, ears and tongue and 2 calf's tongues to steep in brine for 3 or 4 days. Drain. Wrap the head in a cloth and put into a braising pan, together with the ears, also wrapped, and cook gently in the usual manner (CULINARY METHODS

Potted head cheese: In the middle large Lyon potted head, on either side small Paris potted heads, whole and cut (*Larousse*)

Braising) for 4 or 5 hours. Add the tongues two hours later. Take off the best piece of skin and spread it on a napkin. Cut the fleshy part of the head into strips, as long and as big as possible, rejecting all pieces tinged with blood.

Sprinkle this meat with *Four-spices** and chopped shallots. Lay out these strips, without allowing them to get cold and arranging them in such a way as to mix the various meats as well as possible. Scatter a few pistachio nuts here and there. Fold the skin over these bits and pieces, wrap tightly in a napkin tying it securely with string. Put back to cook. Bring the braising liquid to the boil, then draw away to the edge of the burner, so that it just simmers. One hour later, drain, remove string, put the contents of the napkin into a brawn mould. Put a weight on top to press down well and leave until quite cold.

Potted head (head cheese) with truffles. HURE DE PORC AUX TRUFFES—As above, adding raw truffles cut into strips.

Leg of pork (ham). JAMBON—French and imported hams are listed under the entry entitled HAM. Leg of pork can be eaten fresh, salted or smoked.

Braised fresh leg of pork. JAMBON DE PORC FRAIS BRAISÉ—This joint is treated in the same way as *Braised noix de veau* (chump end of the loin). Allow from 20 to 25 minutes cooking time per pound. See CULINARY METHODS, *Braising*.

Fresh braised leg of pork can be accompanied by any of the garnishes recommended for braised meat. The braising liquor is boiled down, the surplus fat is removed from it; it is then strained and poured over the leg.

Note. A few hours before putting fresh leg of pork to braise, season it with salt flavoured with powdered thyme and bay leaf.

Roast leg of pork. JAMBON DE PORC FRAIS RÔTI—Trim the leg of pork, that is to say, remove bone up to the knuckle and skin it. A few hours before roasting the leg cover it with salt. Then wipe and roast in the oven, allowing 30 minutes to the pound, or on a spit, allowing 45 minutes to the pound. Serve the leg with the pan juices diluted with white wine or Madeira. Any of the garnishes recommended for roast meat can be used.

Stuffed pig's leg or Zampino (Italian speciality). JAMBE DE PORC FARCIE, ZAMPINO—Soak the leg in cold water for 3 hours and scrape the skin thoroughly. Prick in a few places with a trussing needle. Wrap in a fine cloth and tie at both ends and in the middle. Put the *zampino* into a braising pan and cover with cold water. Bring to the boil, then simmer for 3 hours.

The *zampino* is served hot, with potato or lentil purée. It can also be served cold, cut in slices like sausage.

Pig's liver. FOIE DE PORC—All recipes for calf's liver are suitable for pig's liver, though it is mainly used as an ingredient in stuffings. See OFFAL OR VARIETY MEATS.

Roast leg of pork

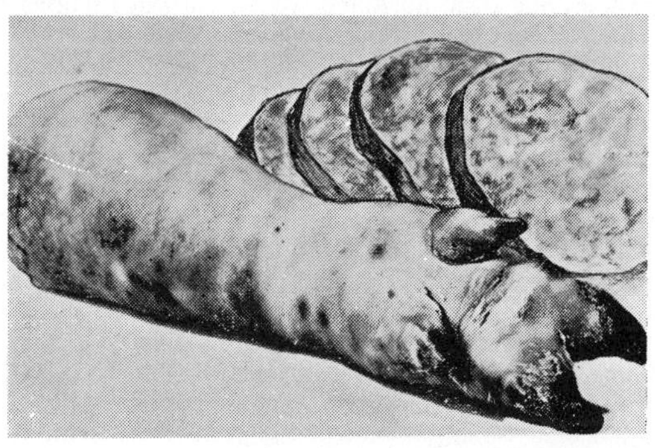

Zampino (Stuffed pig's leg) (*Larousse*)

Loin of pork. CARRÉ DE PORC—This cut can be roasted or pot-roasted. It is usually accompanied by its own gravy, suitably diluted, and most often with a garnish composed of potatoes prepared in various ways (especially mashed potatoes) or a purée of dried vegetables, or fresh braised vegetables (celery, chicory, endives, lettuce, etc.).

Cooking time for this joint is calculated at 25 minutes per pound if roasted in the oven, and 40 minutes if roasted on a spit.

Note. It is advisable, before roasting or pot-roasting a loin of pork (as well as all other pork joints cooked in the same way) to season it, several hours before cooking, with salt mixed with powdered thyme and bay leaf. Seasoned thus in advance, the flavour of fresh pork is rendered more delicious.

Cold loin of pork. CARRÉ DE PORC FROID—Cold loin of pork is generally served with a green salad, potato salad, or red cabbage salad. It is usually accompanied by mayonnaise sauce and pickled gherkins.

Loin of pork à l'alsacienne. CARRÉ DE PORC À L'ALSACIENNE—Season the loin of pork in advance and cook in the oven until three-quarters done.

Finish cooking with sauerkraut, prepared separately in the usual manner (see SAUERKRAUT) and with the usual garnish (lean smoked bacon, Strasbourg sausages).

Drain the loin. Arrange on a large oval-shaped dish. Garnish at two ends with sauerkraut, surround with sausages and bacon cut in rectangles and serve with boiled potatoes.

Note. Loin of pork *à l'alsacienne* can also be made by simply roasting (or pot-roasting) the loin and serving it surrounded with sauerkraut. Pour over the pan juices left over from roasting the loin.

Loin of pork à la bonne femme. CARRÉ DE PORC À LA BONNE FEMME—Season the loin of pork in advance and put it into an earthenware dish in which several tablespoons of butter or lard have been heated.

Roast the loin in the oven until half done, browning it nicely. Put into the roasting pan, for a loin weighing about 2 pounds (one kilo), 1 pound or 2½ cups (500 grams) of potatoes, cut to look like large olives or into quarters and 24 small onions, fried in butter or lard. Season the garnish, add a *bouquet garni** and finish cooking together in the oven, basting frequently. Take out of the oven, sprinkle with chopped parsley and serve in the same dish in which it was cooked.

Loin of pork à la boulangère. CARRÉ DE PORC À LA BOULANGÈRE—Trim the loin of pork and proceed as described in the recipe for *Shoulder of lamb à la boulangère*. See LAMB.

Loin of pork with green cabbage, or with Brussels sprouts. CARRÉ DE PORC AUX CHOUX VERTS, AUX CHOUX DE BRUXELLES—Roast or pot-roast the loin. Arrange it on a serving dish. Surround with a garnish of braised green cabbage, or Brussels sprouts, boiled in water, drained and tossed in the fat in which the loin was cooked. Pour over the pan juices left from roasting the loin.

Loin of pork with red cabbage. CARRÉ DE PORC AUX CHOUX ROUGES—Roast or pot-roast the loin of pork as described above. Arrange it on a serving dish. Surround with red cabbage braised separately.

Loin of pork à la chipolata. CARRÉ DE PORC À LA CHIPOLATA—Season the loin of pork in advance and pot-roast it. Arrange it on a serving dish. Surround with *Chipolata garnish* (see GARNISHES), composed of braised chestnuts, small glazed onions, chipolata sausages and glazed carrots, although the carrots are optional. Pour over the pan juices left from cooking the loin.

Loin of pork à la limousine. CARRÉ DE PORC À LA LIMOUSINE—Roast or pot-roast the loin. Garnish with *Red cabbage à la limousine*, braised with mashed chestnuts. See CABBAGE.

Pour over the pan juices left from roasting the loin.

Roast loin of pork

Roast loin of pork. CARRÉ DE PORC RÔTI—Trim and season the loin in advance. Roast it in the oven allowing 25 minutes per pound, or on a spit allowing 40 minutes per pound.

Arrange on a serving dish. Garnish with watercress. Serve with the pan juices, suitably diluted.

Note. It is customary in certain parts of France to serve roast loin of pork with unsweetened apple purée.

Roast loin of pork à la languedocienne. CARRÉ DE PORC RÔTI À LA LANGUEDOCIENNE—Twelve hours before roasting the loin, insert into it some pieces of garlic cut into little strips. Season it with salt and spices and sprinkle with oil. Leave to marinate in this seasoning. Roast in the oven or on a spit. Serve with its own gravy.

Roast loin of pork à la provençale. CARRÉ DE PORC À LA PROVENÇALE—Twelve hours before roasting the loin insert into it some sage leaves. Season with salt and powdered thyme and bay leaf. Cover with crushed cloves of garlic and pour over a few tablespoons of olive oil.

Roast the loin in the oven (putting the cloves of garlic into the roasting pan), arrange on a serving dish and pour over the pan juices.

Roast loin of pork garnished with orange

Roast loin of pork with various sauces and garnishes. CARRÉ DE PORC RÔTI—Roast the loin in the oven. Arrange on a serving dish. Surround with the garnish indicated (or dish up the garnish separately in a *timbale*) and serve with the sauce recommended.

All the garnishes which are suitable for meat courses (lamb, beef, mutton, veal) can be served with loin of pork.

Roast loin of pork (whether garnished or not) can be served with various sauces, such as: *Charcutière*, *Mustard*, *Piquante*, *Robert*, *Tomato*, etc. See SAUCE.

Loin of pork with sauerkraut—See *Loin of pork à l'alsacienne.*

Roast loin of pork à la soissonnaise. CARRÉ DE PORC RÔTI À LA SOISSONNAISE—Trim the loin of pork, season it in advance and roast it in an oval-shaped earthenware dish, cooking it only until it is three-quarters done.

Add some kidney beans, cooked separately in the usual manner. See BEANS.

Finish cooking in the oven, basting the loin frequently. Serve in the same dish.

Pork offal or variety meats. ABATS DE PORC—The major part of pork offal is used as ingredients for various products known in U.S.A. as variety meats or cold cuts and in England as preparations of pork butchery: brawn (U.S. head cheese), sausages, etc.

The feet (trotters), brains, liver, kidneys and the head—especially the ears—can be prepared as independent dishes by following the instructions given in the recipes for veal and mutton offal or variety meats. All recipes for preparing pig's ears and trotters will be found under OFFAL OR VARIETY MEATS.

Pork pie

Hot pork pie. PÂTÉ CHAUD DE PORC À L'ANGLAISE—Line the wall and the bottom of a pie dish with thin slices of raw ham. Put into this dish, in alternate layers, 1 pound (500 grams) of slices of fresh pork, seasoned with salt, pepper and powdered thyme and bay leaf and sprinkled with dried *Duxelles mixture**, and chopped parsley and sage, 2 cups (500 grams) of raw potatoes, cut in thin round slices and ½ cup (100 grams) of chopped onion.

Moisten with ¾ cup (1½ decilitres) of water, cover with a lid of *Lining paste* or *Puff pastry* (see DOUGH), as described in the recipe for *Beefsteak pie* (see BEEF). Brush the top with beaten egg, crimp up the edges and bake in a moderate oven for about 2 hours.

Piglet. PORCELET—This name applies to a young pig up to the age of two months. In culinary parlance it is called *sucking* or *suckling pig*.

Suckling pig, whether stuffed or not, is usually roasted on a spit. It is best to roast it in such a way as to make the skin golden and crisp. Cooking time for a medium-sized suckling pig varies between 1½ and 2 hours. If the animal is stuffed, the cooking time should be increased by a quarter of an hour for each pound (500 grams) of stuffing.

Suckling pig can also be braised, or boiled—as is done in Russia—in which case it can be served either hot or cold, in aspic.

Black pudding (U.S. blood pudding). BOUDIN—A large sausage made of pig's blood and suet enclosed in an intestine.

According to some historians, black pudding, as we know it today, is one of the few Assyrian dishes which have come down to us still greatly resembling those made by the pork butchers of Tyre, who, it is said, excelled in this type of preparation.

The preparation of black puddings has greatly improved in the course of the centuries and nowadays, although many people assure us that things are not what they used to be, the black puddings which are made today are vastly superior to those of our grandparents' time.

Black pudding is the traditional French dish served at supper after the Christmas midnight mass. Enormous quantities of both black and white puddings are eaten at this meal. The black pudding enters the menu, however, mainly as a symbolic dish and the Christmas dinner generally includes many other traditional dishes, such as truffled turkey, goose stuffed with chestnuts, and, of course, foie gras with truffles, served in a *terrine**, in jelly or in a pie crust. There is yet another typical dish served at this nocturnal meal, and that is plum pudding, which comes from the Anglo-Saxon world, although some authors claim, and we think they are right, that this dish was known to the ancient Greeks.

A great number of recipes for the preparation of black and white puddings are given in this section. In addition to these, we quote that composed by Achille Ozanne, cook and poet:

'Préparez des oignons, hachés menus, menus,
Qu'avec autant de lard sur un feu doux l'on passe,
Les tournant tant, qu'ils soient d'un beau blond devenus,
Et que leur doux arome envahisse l'espace . . .
Mêlez le tout au sang, puis, bien assaisonnez,
De sel, poivre et muscade, ainsi que des épices;
Un verre de Cognac; après: vous entonnez
Dans les boyaux de porc, dont l'un des orifices
Est d'avance fermé, et dès qu'ils sont remplis,
Ficelez l'autre bout, et dans l'eau frémissante
Plongez tous les boudins! Ces travaux accomplis,
Egouttez-les après vingt minutes d'attente.'

'Chop the onions, finely, finely,
Toss them in an equal amount of fat on a low fire,
Stirring them, until they are a beautiful golden colour,
And their fragrance pervades all round . . .
Blend them with blood then season well with
Salt, pepper, nutmeg and the spices;
A glass of brandy and then you stuff the mixture
Into a pig's intestine, one end of which
Has previously been sealed. As soon as this is filled,
Tie up the other end and into simmering water
Plunge the black pudding! Once this is done,
You give them twenty minutes, and drain.'

The most famous type of black pudding in France is made at Nancy, but many other regions produce black puddings, which, without enjoying the same renown as those of Lorraine, are nevertheless extremely flavoursome and merit better acquaintance.

Black puddings can be made using blood of animals other than pig, but any addition to pig's blood, or even its complete substitution by the blood of ox, calf or sheep, produces black puddings of mediocre quality and amounts to a fraudulent act.

Black puddings can be made from the blood of various fowls, rabbits, and all sorts of wild animals such as deer, wild boar, etc., but these puddings can only be made if the blood of these animals can be obtained, and they must therefore be blooded, as is done with the domestic pig.

In France the name *boudin* also applies to various preparations made out of poultry and game, which are really no more than quenelles.

A great variety of black and white puddings are made in France. Each region has its special *boudin.* Among the most famous are the black and white puddings of Nancy, Metz, Strasbourg, Lyons (a city which has always been known for the excellence of its pork products), Dijon, Rouen, Pau, Albi, Toulouse, Auvergne, Limousin, Roussillon, Berry, Brittany, Flanders and, last but not least, those made in Paris.

Black pudding and white pudding (U.S. blood sausage and white sausage). BOUDIN DE PORC—These pork sausages are generally found in the shops ready for use. They can be grilled or cooked in the oven, as well as fried in butter or lard.

The *black* pudding is made of pig's blood and fat.

The *white* pudding is a sausage made of white pork meat and fat.

Black puddings (U.S. blood sausage). BOUDINS NOIRS DE PORC—Into a large bowl put 2 pounds (1 kilo) of fresh hog's fat, cut in large dice and half-melted, 2 cups (400 grams) of chopped onion, fried lightly in lard (without allowing it to colour), 5 teaspoons (40 grams) of salt, a good pinch of freshly ground pepper and a good pinch of spices. Add 4 cups (8 decilitres) of pig's blood and 1 cup (2 decilitres) of fresh cream.

Mix all these ingredients properly. Fill pig's intestines with this mixture, without stuffing them too much, as the mixture swells during cooking and may cause the casings to burst. Tie the black puddings into the desired lengths, or leave whole, as the case may be.

Lay them out on a wicker tray and plunge this tray with the black puddings on it into a big pan of boiling water. Drain the pan to the side of the burner and poach the black puddings at a temperature of 90°C. (190°F.) for about 20 minutes. As the black puddings begin to rise to the surface, prick them with a pin to let out air contained in them, which otherwise when heated may cause the casings to burst.

Drain the black puddings. Leave them to get cold on the wicker tray, covered with a cloth to prevent their drying up too much.

After having been thus treated, black puddings are grilled in the following manner:

Make a few shallow incisions on both sides and grill very gently on a moderate fire. Serve mashed potatoes separately.

Black puddings (U.S. blood sausage) à l'anglaise. BOUDINS NOIRS À L'ANGLAISE—Prepare as ordinary black puddings, adding to the mixture 1 pound (500 grams) of rice well cooked in stock, or an equal quantity of pearl barley, also cooked in stock and seasoning the mixture with plenty of spices.

These are grilled like ordinary black puddings.

Black puddings (U.S. blood sausage) à la flamande. BOUDINS À LA FLAMANDE—Prepare using mixture similar to that for ordinary black puddings (blood sausage), adding to it $1\frac{1}{4}$ cups (200 grams) of brown sugar, 1 cup (120 grams) of currants and the same amount of sultanas, picked over, washed, allowed to swell in warm water and drained well.

These black puddings are grilled in the usual way and served with *Apple marmelade* (*Applesauce*)*.

Black puddings (U.S. blood sausages) with apples, called à la normande. BOUDINS NOIRS AUX POMMES, DITS À LA NORMANDE—Cut the black puddings into uniform little chunks and sauté in butter in a frying pan.

When they are lightly browned, add cooking apples, peeled, sliced and cooked in butter, allowing 1 pound (500 grams) of apples per 2 pounds (kilo) of black puddings.

Sauté the apples and the black puddings for a few moments. Serve in a deep dish.

White puddings (U.S. sausage). BOUDINS BLANCS DE PORC—Chop finely together 1 pound (500 grams) of lean pork and $1\frac{3}{4}$ pounds (800 grams) of fresh pork fat.

Pound this mixture in a mortar, adding to it $3\frac{1}{2}$ ounces (100 grams) of butter (or, which would make the white puddings even more flavoursome, an equal quantity of raw fat goose liver).

Rub this mixture through a sieve, put into a bowl and stir with a wooden spoon adding, one by one, 4 whole eggs, $\frac{1}{2}$ cup (100 grams) of chopped onion fried lightly in butter without allowing it to colour, and 1 cup (2 decilitres) of fresh cream.

Season with 5 teaspoons (30 grams) of salt, a good pinch of white pepper and a pinch of spices. Mix well.

Fill pig's intestines (casings) with this mixture and poach as described in the recipe for black puddings.

Grilled white puddings (sausage). BOUDINS BLANCS GRILLÉS—When the white puddings are quite cold, prick them (do not make incisions with a knife) on both sides, wrap each in a piece of buttered greaseproof paper and cook gently under a grill. Serve mashed potatoes separately.

Bacon rinds (or pork skin). COUENNE DE PORC—Bacon rinds or pork skin are used in a great number of culinary preparations.

They are used mainly as an element of garnish for braised meats and, along with calves' feet, as the gelatinous element in preparing jellies.

Pork skin, boiled in well spiced stock, can also be prepared as *ballottines* or *roulades*, which are served cold.

Salt pork. PETIT SALÉ DE PORC—This term covers various joints of pork pickled in brine. Forequarter-flank, cutlets, ears, knuckles, pig's snout, etc., can be treated in this way.

Wash the pork in plenty of water, then put into brine and leave from 3 to 6 days, depending on the season.

These cuts are boiled in water and served hot, with potato salad.

In cookery the term *petit salé* applies to salt chine of pork, which is simply boiled and served with various vegetables, most frequently with boiled or braised cabbage or mashed potatoes.

This cut is also used as an ingredient for *potée.*

Boiled salt pork à l'anglaise. PORC SALÉ BOUILLI À L'ANGLAISE—Boil a piece of salt pork (shoulder or breast) in water with the usual vegetables and 6 parsnips.

Arrange the pork on a round dish. Surround with the vegetable garnish. Serve pease-pudding separately, which is prepared in the following manner:

Blend together in a bowl 2 cups (500 grams) of rather

a thick purée of split peas (yellow peas, for preference), 6 tablespoons (100 grams) of butter, 3 whole eggs, salt, pepper and grated nutmeg.

Put this purée into a buttered pudding basin and cook in the oven in a *bain-marie.*

Note. Instead of putting the mixture into a pudding basin, it can be put in a scalded, buttered and floured cloth, tied and cooked with the pork.

Purée of yellow split peas can be served with *Boiled salt pork à l'anglaise* instead of pease-pudding.

Pork sausages. SAUCISSES DE PORC—Pork sausages, whether they be long or flat, are made of the forcemeat called *sausage meat,* which can include various ingredients.

Sausages which are not made of pork, as well as sausages of foreign origin (Cambridge sausages, Frankfurt sausages, etc.) are dealt with under SAUSAGE.

Sausage meat. Chop separately equal quantities of lean pork having removed all sinews, and fresh pork fat. Pound this forcemeat in a mortar to varying degrees of fineness, depending on the type of sauage for which they are intended. Season with spiced salt, allowing from 2 to 3 teaspoons of salt per pound (25 to 30 grams per kilo) of forcemeat.

Or: Use half-fat, half-lean pork, remove all sinews and chop finely. While the pork is being chopped, season with salt in the same proportions as above.

Or: Although this is rather a rare combination—chop lean beef and neck end of pork in equal proportions.

Making sausages. When the forcemeat is ready, stuff pig's intestines with it, using a special utensil. To facilitate this operation, incorporate a little cold water in the forcemeat while mixing it or, better still, 1 whole egg per pound of meat.

Truffled sausage meat. Prepare as above adding 5 ounces (150 grams) of fresh truffles, cut in small dice, to the forcemeat.

Note. Truffled sausages are mostly made of forcemeat to which not diced truffles, but truffle parings have been added. We cannot deplore this practice too strongly.

Sausages with red or green cabbage. SAUCISSES AUX CHOUX ROUGES, CHOUX VERTS—Grill the sausages or poach them in white wine. Arrange them in a round dish on a bed of braised green cabbage, or red cabbage prepared as described in the recipe for *Red cabbage à la flamande.* See CABBAGE.

If the sausages are poached, as for instance sausages in white wine, add the liquor in which they are cooked to the cabbage braising liquid.

Sausages à la catalane (Catalan style). SAUCISSES À LA CATALANE—Fry in lard in a sauté pan 2 pounds (1 kilo) of big sausage twisted into a coil. When it is nicely browned, remove from the pan.

Into the same fat put in 2 tablespoons of flour and colour lightly. Moisten with white wine and meat stock, add a tablespoon of tomato purée and mix well. Cook for 10 minutes and strain this sauce.

Put the sausage back into the sauté pan. Add 24 blanched cloves of garlic and a *bouquet garni**, to which a small piece of bitter orange rind has been added. Pour the sauce over the sausage. Cover and simmer gently for 30 minutes.

The sauce can be thickened with white breadcrumbs instead of flour.

Chipolata sausages. SAUCISSES CHIPOLATAS—Long sausages made in very small-sized casings. These are divided into small pieces from 1½ to 2 inches long.

They are used as a garnish for various dishes and can be grilled, fried in butter or poached in white wine.

Country sausages I. SAUCISSES DE CAMPAGNE—Stuff pig's intestines with a forcemeat composed of two parts lean beef and one part lean fresh bacon, seasoned with 3½ teaspoons (40 grams) of salt, ¼ teaspoon (4 grams) of pepper, ⅛ teaspoon (2 grams) of pounded pimento, a pinch (1 gram) of saltpetre and a clove of garlic, per pound (kilo) of forcemeat, making the sausages from 4 to 5 inches long.

When the sausages are ready they are put to dry on the top part of the oven or smoked lightly.

They are poached in boiling water or stock from 10 to 12 minutes.

This type of sausage is used mainly as an element of garnish for potées.

Country sausages II. SAUCISSES DE CAMPAGNE—Prepare using forcemeat composed of two parts of lean pork and one part of firm bacon fat, seasoned as above and flavoured to taste with savoury, coriander, marjoram, thyme, bay leaf, and moistened with ¼ cup of red wine per pound (1 decilitre per kilo).

Stuff small ox intestines with this forcemeat. Join the sausages two by two and dry in a dry place.

These sausages are poached in water or are cooked in *potées.*

Pig's liver sausage. SAUCISSES DE FOIE DE PORC—This is made in beef intestine casings using forcemeat composed of three parts of pork (fat and lean) and one part of pig's liver, previously parboiled, seasoned with spiced salt, allowing from 2½ to 3 teaspoons of *Spiced salt* (see SALT) per pound (25 to 30 grams per kilo) and mixed with 2 tablespoons of pig's blood.

Divide into lengths of 4 to 5 inches. Poach in water like black puddings.

Note. Pig's liver sausage is grilled like black pudding. It can also be cooked in the oven, in a frilly paper case.

Shoulder of pork. ÉPAULE DE PORC—Fresh shoulder of pork is used in the same way as chine. Bone and roll the shoulder, then roast, pot-roast or braise it. It can be served with all the garnishes suitable for loin of pork. The shoulder can also be cut into pieces and made into stews. Salted shoulder of pork is used as an ingredient for potées.

Boned, salted and smoked shoulder of pork is prepared like leg.

Pork skin. COUENNE—Thick hard skin of pork. Used in *charcuterie* to make *Fromage de tête* (brawn); in cooking, as a foundation for braises. See GRATTONS.

Cold pork slices. ÉMINCÉS DE PORC—Prepare, using left-over pork, cut into thin slices, as described in the recipe for *Sliced beef.* See BEEF.

This dish is usually served with *Charcutière* or *Robert sauce* (see SAUCE) and accompanied by mashed potatoes or a purée of any other starchy vegetable.

Pork stew. RAGOÛT DE PORC—Pork is seldom cooked as a stew. The cuts most suitable for this method of preparation are the shoulder, chine and breast and care should be taken in removing all surplus fat.

Sucking pig, suckling pig—See *Piglet.*

Stuffed suckling pig à l'occitane. PORCELET ÉTOFFÉ À L'OCCITANE—Clean out the suckling pig (through a short incision on the belly) and bone it, leaving only the leg bones.

Season inside with salt and spices, sprinkle with brandy and leave to marinate for a few hours.

Stuff it with the following mixture:

Slice the pig's liver, and an equal quantity of calf's liver, into small slices. Season and brown briskly in sizzling butter, just to stiffen them. Drain and put in a dish.

In the same butter, brown—again, as quickly as possible—the heart and the kidneys of the suckling pig, cut into small slices, as well as 4 to 6 ounces of lamb's sweetbreads, soaked, parboiled, rinsed in cold water and sliced.

Drain all these ingredients and put together with the liver.

Add 3 tablespoons of butter to the same pan and lightly fry 1 cup (200 grams) of finely chopped onion without allowing it to colour. When the onion is well softened, add 3 tablespoons of chopped shallots and 1 cup (2 decilitres) of dried *Duxelles**. Fry for a few moments, then add a pinch of pounded garlic. Moisten with dry white wine, reduce, and add 2 cups (4 decilitres) of rich veal broth.

Bring to the boil, add 3 ounces (150 grams) of fresh bacon rinds, cooked and cut in small square pieces, and green olives, stoned and blanched. Cook for a few minutes. Put the above ingredients into this sauce. Heat, without allowing the sauce to boil, stir and leave this ragoût to cool.

When it is cold, mix it with sausage meat, bind with eggs, season well, add some chopped parsley and a dash of brandy and blend.

Stuff the suckling pig the day before it is to be cooked and leave it until the last moment in a marinade made of oil, brandy, sliced carrots and onions, parsley, thyme, bay leaf, crushed cloves of garlic and spices.

Cooking. Truss and skewer the suckling pig and sew up the opening. Put it into a long braising pan on a foundation of bacon rinds, carrots and onions cut in round slices (those used for the marinade, with the addition, if necessary, of fresh carrots and onions, also cut in thick, round slices; it is advisable to put in quite a lot of these vegetables, taking into consideration the fact that they are used as a garnish). Sprinkle with lard, cover with a lid and cook gently on the top of the stove until the vegetables begin to brown.

Moisten with 1½ cups (3 decilitres) of dry white wine. Reduce (boil down) this liquid. Add a few tablespoons of thickened, brown veal gravy and a good *bouquet garni**. Cook in the oven; when done, the skin of the suckling pig should be golden and crisp.

Serving. Drain the piglet, untruss and put on a serving dish. Garnish all round with small pork crépinettes *aux fines herbes* and small black puddings fried in butter. Add the onions and carrots from the braising pan. Pour over the strained braising liquor.

Serve with a purée made of mashed celeriac and potatoes in equal proportions.

Note. Instead of braising the piglet with round slices of onions and carrots, it can be garnished with medium sized whole onions and carrots cut down to a uniform size, disposing them around the dish along with black pudding and *crépinettes.*

The stuffing should be of an adequate consistency (which is achieved by binding it with egg) to ensure that when the suckling pig is cut, it does not spill out but remains intact, together with the cut slice.

PORKER. GORET—This is the name given to a piglet which, having reached the age of six months, is no longer a suckling pig.

PORPOISE. MARSOUIN—The smallest of the puffing cetaceans. It is valuable mainly for the oil extracted from it. The porpoise is edible, though oily. In former times it was sold in Paris during Lent. It is prepared in various ways and eaten in Scotland, Iceland and Newfoundland.

PORRIDGE (English cookery)—A popular food, made of specially treated oatmeal and water. Porridge is greatly appreciated in Scotland, Ireland and throughout England. Here is the recipe:

Boil a quart (litre) of water with 2½ teaspoons (15 grams) of salt.

As soon as boiling is established, pour about 3 cups (300 grams) of oatmeal into it in a steady rain. Stir all the time, until the porridge acquires the desired consistency.

Leave to simmer for 20 minutes, stirring from time to time.

Serve with cold milk or cream.

Each person at table is left to season porridge to his or her taste.

Porridge or hasty-pudding. BOUILLIE—Bring salt water to the boil in a pan. Pour in maize flour (corn meal) (or a mixture of maize and wheaten flour) to obtain a fairly thick mixture. Cook on a moderate heat, stirring frequently with a wooden spoon, until the mixture is very thick. Add a few tablespoons of pork fat. Mix well.

While it is still hot, pour this porridge on to a coarse linen cloth and spread it out in a layer of about 1 inch thick. Leave to cool. When it is quite cold, cut it into squares or rectangles, and proceed as indicated in the selected recipe.

Arrowroot porridge—See ARROWROOT.

Buckwheat porridge—See KASHA.

Maize porridge or las pous (Périgord cookery). BOUILLIE DE MAÏS DITE LAS POUS—This bouillie or porridge, which in Périgord is also called *rimotes*, is somewhat similar to the *gaudes* of Franche-Comté and also to polenta, as it is made in Italy, Corsica and Provence.

The *bouillie*, which is eaten instead of bread with certain dishes, such as salt pork with cabbage and jugged hare, and is also served as a soup, is prepared generally like *polenta**.

It can also be eaten as a sweet course. For this, when the maize is cooked, pour it into a baking pan or some other fairly shallow receptacle, spread it in an even layer and allow to cool. Then cut into uniform pieces, dip in flour and fry in lard or butter. Arrange on a round dish and sprinkle with sugar.

Béarn millas. MILLAS DU BÉARN—This porridge, which in this region is also called *paste, pastel, gaudines* and *yerbilhou*, is prepared in the same way as *broye*. See BROYE.

Périgord millas or las pous. MILLAS PÉRIGOURDIN, LAS POUS—Proceed in the usual way with a mixture of equal quantities of maize (corn meal) and wheaten flour.

If the porridge is too thick it can be made lighter with a little hot milk.

This *millas* can be made more delicate by the addition of a little fresh butter just before the porridge is ready.

Dr. Bircher-Benner's müsli. BOUILLIE CRUE DU DOCTEUR BIRCHER-BENNER—This is not strictly speaking a porridge, because it is not boiled at all, but its consistency is so mushy that it has the appearance of porridge.

Attaching great importance to the nutritive value of raw food, Dr. Bircher-Benner prescribed this mixture as a breakfast and supper dish. At lunch time he allowed various cooked foods and even meat, in addition to raw vegetables and fruit served as an hors-d'oeuvre.

The *müsli* is prepared overnight in the following manner: soak 2 or 3 tablespoons of rolled oats in cold water for 12 hours. On the following morning, drain and mix with condensed milk, raw grated unpeeled apples, or with any other fruit in season, sometimes with grated carrots. Then, add honey and lemon juice. The taste of this concoction is far from unpleasant.

PORRINGER. ÉCUELLE—A bowl made of wood, earthenware or metal to hold an individual portion of food. In the Middle Ages it was usual for two people to share a porringer, hence the French expression: '*Manger à la même écuelle*' (which means roughly to live in one another's pocket).

PORT. PORTO—Portuguese wine, made from grapes, grown in the upper Douro valley of Portugal, fortified at the time of the vintage and shipped from Oporto. It is sweet and soft, and in France it is sometimes drunk as an aperitif. It is used in preparing sauces.

PORT-SALUT—Cheese made from scalded curds of a fairly firm texture. See CHEESE.

PORTER—English beer, very strong and very dark, almost black.

PORTUGAISE—*Tomato fondue* made with butter or oil and flavoured with onion, garlic and parsley. See TOMATO.

PORTUGUESE OYSTER. GRYPHÉE—A type of mollusc. See OYSTERS.

POSSET—Hot drink made of milk and white wine or beer.

POT-AU-FEU—Essentially French method of cooking a broth which provides at one time soup, meat and vegetables. See SOUPS AND BROTHS.

POT-ROASTING. POÊLAGE—This is a method of slow cooking by steam. A casserole with a tightly fitting lid is used. The food is cooked in butter or fat and flavoured with vegetables which have been cooked slowly in butter until very tender.

Pot-roasted meat, poultry or fish must be basted frequently during cooking. When it is ready, take it out of the casserole. Serve on a dish or, where appropriate, in a *cocotte**. Remove most of the cooking fat.

Dilute the juices in the casserole with wine or stock as indicated in the recipe. Boil for a few seconds. Strain and pour over the dish.

Pot-roasting à la Matignon. Brown lightly in butter the meat or fish to be pot-roasted. Cover with a thick layer of *Matignon* or *Fondue** of root vegetables (see MATIGNON). Wrap in buttered grease-proof paper and cook in the oven in a braising pan, or on the spit. After cooking, unwrap, place on a dish, surround with appropriate garnishes and pour on the stock to which the *matignon* has been added before straining.

Braising à la matignon can also be carried out by lining the braising pan with the *fondue* of root vegetables and placing the meat, fish or poultry, which should be liberally basted with butter, on top.

POTASH. POTASSE—Oxide of potassium. Alkaline substance which plays an important role in nutrition.

POTASSIUM NITRATE—See SALTPETRE.

POTATOES. POMMES DE TERRE—Tuber-bearing plants, native of South America, introduced into France, as an ornamental plant, towards 1540.

It was probably in 1539 or in 1540 that the potato was brought from Quito in South America, first into Spain, where it was cultivated in Galicia, and later from North America into England.

In 1563 Sir John Hawkins is said to have introduced the potato into England, but its cultivation was neglected there and it was reintroduced in 1586 by Sir Francis Drake. Sir Walter Raleigh grew potatoes in Ireland.

Potatoes (from left to right across dish): Duchess, Parisienne, Croquettes, Straw potatoes

In 1593, Gaspar Bauhon praised it and engaged several farmers around Lyons and the Vosges region to grow it, but in 1630 the Parliament of Besançon, from fear of leprosy, forbade the cultivation of potato.

The potato must have been introduced into Lorraine in 1665, for on the 28th June 1715 the Court of Nancy issued a decree exacting a tithe, which was only payable after 50 years of cultivation.

In 1597, the botanist Gérard, who received some potatoes direct from Virginia, gave the following discription of this crop: 'These tubers are nourishing as well as a pleasant dish, equal in wholesomeness and salubrity to the batata (sweet potato), whether they be baked in hot ashes, or boiled and eaten with oil, vinegar or pepper, or prepared in any other way by the hands of an able cook.'

Francis Bacon (in his essay on the *History of Life and Death*) sings high-sounding praises to it, as a health-giving and fortifying food.

In 1619 potato figures among the foods to be served at the Royal table in England. It did not, however, become an article of import until 1662.

In Scotland it has been cultivated since 1683—and in open fields, for the first time, by Thomas Prentice in 1728.

It was introduced into the Low Countries in 1588 by Clusius, who got it from Gérard.

The English introduced it into Flanders during the wars against Louis XIV.

In France the potato was still considered suspect in 1771; it was said to be unfit for human consumption and dangerous, because of its weakening properties. It was Parmentier who rehabilitated it. In 1771, in a thesis, which was hailed by the Besançon Academy, he listed it among the vegetables which could be used in times of food shortage along with horse-chestnuts, acorns, and the roots of bryony, iris, gladioli and couch-grass. In 1773 he published his work entitled *Chemical examination of potato, wheat and rice* and began his research into the panification of potato flour.

In 1787, during a period of scarcity, he obtained the

concession of 50 arpents (an old French measure roughly equivalent to an acre) of poor land in the Sablon plain; the cultivation proved successful, contrary to all expectations, and a short while later Parmentier was able to offer King Louis XVI a bouquet of potato flowers, which set a fashion for this plant.

We know the methods to which he resorted to arouse the covetousness of the Parisians: the field was closely guarded during the day by soldiers of the Garde Française, but was left unsupervised during the night.

Parmentier had his precursors—and he never denied this: Turgot acclimatised potatoes in the Limousin; Lavoisier, on the advice of Parmentier, cultivated them in his lands in Fréchines, in Vendôme; Larouchefoucauld-Liancourt in Beauvais, Chalaire in the Boulogne region in 1763; Dottu, the great agriculturist of Villers-Bretonneux, in Picardy from 1766.

Denigration gave place to a period of enthusiasm and a craze for the potato flower, which was used as a decorative design for plates. After its popularisation, thanks to Parmentier, the potato became one of the staple foods at the beginning of the nineteenth century. It is suitable for people of all ages and all temperaments. In its most digestible form, namely mashed, the potato is one of the first vegetables to be given to infants after weaning and to convalescents permitted solid food.

Potato contains a lot of water (about 77 per cent); it neither loses nor gains by being cooked in water and retains its water content during the period of intestinal digestion. It therefore provides a great deal of bulk and satisfies hunger easily. It is perfectly digestible, however, the fecula becoming almost entirely dissolved in the intestine.

Weight for weight, potato contains two and a half times less carbohydrates than bread, which makes it a highly desirable food in diets for diabetics, as 40 grams ($1\frac{1}{3}$ ounce) of bread can be replaced by 100 grams ($3\frac{1}{2}$ ounces) of potato, all the more desirable considering the fact that it is rich in potassium and therefore constitutes a highly alkaline food.

To avoid the loss of mineral salts, and in particular of potassium salts, it should not be boiled in too much water (or at least the water in which it is boiled should be kept for soup). This loss is decreased by cooking in fat, such as butter, lard or oil. The best method of cooking potato to preserve the maximum of its mineral elements and the maximum of its taste, is to bake it in the ashes or in the oven. More potato is lost that way when it is peeled after baking, but the taste is incomparably better and it makes it possible to eat potatoes without salt, should this be necessary.

The potato plays a very important part throughout Europe as an article of food.

Among the numerous varieties of potato which are cultivated in France, the following are considered the best: *Jaune longue de Hollande* (Dutch yellow long), longish, sausage-shaped, very regular and almost devoid of eyes; *Rouge longue de Hollande* (Dutch red long); *Sausage*, *Marjolin* or *Quarantaine; Quarantaine de Noisy; Magnum bonum; Pousse debout; Institut de Beauvais; Shaw; Early rose.*

We must also mention *Black potato*, or rather purple potato, called *négresse* in French, if only by way of its being a gastronomical curiosity.

Potatoes à l'anglaise. POMMES DE TERRE À L'ANGLAISE—Peel the potatoes down to as uniform a size as possible and either boil them in salted water or steam them. *Potatoes à l'anglaise* are used as a garnish for boiled fish and some meat dishes.

Anna potatoes, also called potato cake with butter. POMMES DE TERRE ANNA, GALETTE DE POMMES DE TERRE AU BEURRE—Peel some long yellow (or Idaho) potatoes, trim them to shape into big uniform-sized cylinders. Slice them thinly with a knife or an automatic slicer, wash and dry.

Put them into a special straight-sided dish with a lid, intended for this purpose, with plenty of clarified butter.

Arrange the potato slices in uniform overlapping layers.

Fill the dish with rows of potato slices, season each layer and sprinkle with clarified butter.

Cover the dish, start cooking on the stove, then put into a very hot oven and cook from 30 to 35 minutes.

When three-quarters cooked, turn the potato cake upside down to colour the other side.

Turn the cake out on to the lid of the dish, drain off the butter and arrange on a round dish.

Note. If a special utensil is not available, these potatoes can be cooked in an ordinary sauté pan with a very flat bottom.

Anna potatoes for garnish. POMMES DE TERRE ANNA—Proceed as described in the previous recipe for *Anna potatoes*, piling the potatoes into well buttered, tinned-copper dariole moulds and using round slices of potato of the same diameter as the mould used.

Put the moulds to cook in the oven, standing them in a pie dish, or to activate the cooking process and to ensure a better colour, put them into a baking pan containing very hot deep fat.

Turn out and use as indicated in the recipe.

Anna potatoes (home method). POMMES DE TERRE ANNA—Peel the potatoes as uniformly as possible, slice them in thin round slices, wash, dry and season.

Heat some butter in a frying pan and put in the potatoes.

Sauté them in the butter until they are all completely impregnated with butter. Shape into a big cake, pressing them with the back of a fork.

Brown on one side on a moderate heat, toss the cake like a pancake to turn it; if you are apprehensive of your chances of success with this operation, which does demand a certain amount of skill, place a dish over the frying pan upside down and turn the pan quickly with the right hand, holding the dish with the left.

Slide the cake back into the pan from the dish, finish cooking and brown the other side.

Annette potatoes. POMMES DE TERRE ANNETTE—Cut the potatoes into thin *julienne** strips, wash, dry, season and fill with them a well buttered casserole and bake in the oven as described in the recipe for *Anna potatoes.*

Note. This dish, which is a variation of Anna potatoes, can also be cooked in a frying pan, like a pancake.

Potatoes cooked in the ashes. POMMES DE TERRE SOUS LE CENDRE—Wash big long potatoes. Dry them and bake in hot ashes with glowing embers on top.

Wipe the potatoes, arrange on a napkin and serve with fresh butter.

Potatoes baked in the oven. POMMES DE TERRE AU FOUR—Wash the potatoes, dry them and bake in a hot oven. Serve them as they are, arranged on a folded napkin, and serve fresh butter separately.

Potatoes with bacon. POMMES DE TERRE AU LARD—Fry 4 ounces (125 grams) of bacon, diced and blanched, in a sauté pan in 2 tablespoons of butter (or lard, or goose fat). Add 10 small onions.

Remove the bacon and the onions. Put a tablespoon of flour into the pan, allow it to colour slightly; moisten with $1\frac{3}{4}$ cups ($3\frac{1}{2}$ decilitres) of stock (or water), season, add a *bouquet garni** and bring to the boil.

Put 2 cups (500 or 600 grams) of potatoes, cut to look like olives (or into quarters), the bacon and the onions into this sauce.

Bring to the boil, cover the pan and cook in a slow oven.

Serve in a vegetable dish and sprinkle with chopped parsley.

Potatoes with basil. POMMES DE TERRE AU BASILIC—Cook the potatoes, cut down to a uniform size, in butter, keeping the pan covered and not allowing them to colour much. When ready, sprinkle with coarsely chopped fresh basil, allowing a good tablespoon for a pound (500 grams) of potatoes.

Potato baskets. PANIERS DE POMMES DE TERRE—This dish is not suitable for making at home. It requires a very great quantity of fat for deep-frying, especially if tall baskets or baskets with handles are envisaged.

The baskets are made by weaving fine potato ribbons, cut off slices of potatoes about $\frac{1}{8}$ inch thick, over little sticks stuck in crumb.

These baskets are fried in very hot deep fat, as described in the recipe for *Potato nests.*

Potatoes à la basquaise (Basque style). POMMES DE TERRE À LA BASQUAISE—Choose big long potatoes and hollow them out lengthways. Parboil for 5 minutes, drain and dry. Stuff them, filling them up well, with garlic-flavoured *Tomato fondue**, mixed with a *salpicon** of sweet pimentos cooked in butter (or oil), chopped Bayonne ham and chopped parsley.

Butter (or oil) a deep *à gratin* dish, put the potatoes into it, season, sprinkle with melted butter (or oil), heat on the stove, then finish cooking in a slow oven.

When the potatoes are done, scatter some breadcrumbs on top, sprinkle with butter and brown the top.

Pour on a few tablespoons of thickened brown veal gravy.

Potatoes à la berrichonne. POMMES DE TERRE À LA BERRICHONNE—Peel 1 pound (500 grams) of potatoes cutting them down to a uniform size to look like large olives, as for *Château potatoes.* Put them into a sauté pan in which 2 tablespoons of chopped onion and $3\frac{1}{2}$ ounces (100 grams) of diced and scalded bacon have been fried together in a tablespoon of butter. Brown lightly, pour in enough stock to cover the potatoes, season, add a *bouquet garni** and cook with a lid on.

Serve in a vegetable dish, sprinkled with chopped parsley.

Black potatoes, also called négresses or pommes de Madagascar. POMMES DE TERRE NOIRES, DITES NÉGRESSES, POMMES DE MADAGASCAR—This variety of potatoes is remarkable only for its colour, which after cooking is not really black, but rather a dark purple.

These potatoes are used mainly as an element of mixed salads and cold hors-d'oeuvre.

They can, however, be prepared in most of the ways suitable for ordinary potatoes.

Boiled potatoes. POMMES DE TERRE BOUILLIES—Wash the potatoes, put them into a saucepan, cover with water, season with coarse salt and cook, keeping up light but sustained boiling until done.

Drain the potatoes, peel and use as indicated in the recipe: Creamed; *Lyonnaise, Maître d'hôtel,* in salad, sautéed, etc.

Note. Potatoes cooked in this way are also called *Jacket potatoes.*

Potato borders. BORDURES DE POMMES DE TERRE—These borders are made of *Duchess potato mixture.*

It is piped through a forcing (pastry) bag with a plain or fluted nozzle around the edges of round or oval dishes, depending on the nature of the preparation, brushed with beaten egg and browned lightly in the oven.

Note. Potato border can also be made by moulding *Duchess potato mixture* by hand.

Potatoes à la boulangère (garnish). POMMES DE TERRE À LA BOULANGÈRE—These potatoes are usually put to cook around a joint of meat baked in the oven, as described in the recipe for *Shoulder of lamb à la boulangère.* See LAMB.

They can also be cooked separately, in a baking pan, in the oven.

Potatoes in butter (garnish). POMMES DE TERRE AU BEURRE—Cut the potatoes to look like large olives, or if new potatoes are used, peel them correctly.

Wash, drain, put into a sauté pan in which some butter has been heated, season with salt and sauté to impregnate them with scalding butter.

Cook in the oven or on the stove until the potatoes acquire a fine golden colour. Shake the pan from time to time during cooking.

Arrange in a vegetable dish and sprinkle with chopped parsley.

Note. These potatoes are also called *Château potatoes.*

Potato cakes. GALETTES DE POMMES DE TERRE—These can be prepared in several ways.

(*a*) Using *Duchess potato mixture,* shaped into round or oval cakes, brush with beaten egg and cook in the oven until golden.

(*b*) Prepare the potato cakes as above. Dredge them in flour and fry until pale golden in clarified butter.

(*c*) Make small or large potato cakes, as described in the recipe for *Anna potatoes,* making them thinner.

Finish off as indicated in individual recipes, putting different ingredients between each layer of potatoes, such as: *brunoise* or *mirepoix* of vegetables, sliced mushrooms, spinach cooked in butter, chopped ham, various vegetables thinly sliced and cooked in butter, truffles, etc.

Note. These potato cakes can be made big or small depending on the final use for which they are intended. When small, they are used as a garnish, or as foundations for escalopes, medallions, noisettes, tournedos, etc.

Little potato cakes (Carême's recipe). PETITS PAINS DE POMMES DE TERRE—'Peel a dozen good kidney potatoes, baked in the ashes. Remove all the reddish parts and use only the white flesh; weigh out 12 ounces of this and pound with 4 ounces of Isigny butter. When this mixture becomes smooth add to it 4 ounces of castor sugar, two of sieved flour, 2 yolks of egg and a grain of salt. Pound everything together into a perfectly smooth paste. Take the paste out of the mortar, put on a lightly floured board, roll and cut into four parts. Roll each part, making it twice its original length, then cut into little balls the size of a walnut, give them the shape of little boats, and place them one by one on a buttered baking sheet. Brush with beaten egg and bake in a moderate oven.'

Château potatoes. POMMES DE TERRE CHÂTEAU—See *Potatoes in butter.*

Note. Château potatoes constitute a traditional garnish for grilled Chateaubriand steak.

Potatoes Chatouillard. POMMES FRITES CHATOUILLARD—Cut the potatoes into ribbons, peeling them off spiral-fashion, $\frac{1}{8}$ inch thick. See CHATOUILLARD.

Cook like *Soufflé potatoes.* Drain, season and arrange on a napkin or around grilled meat.

Potatoes copeaux. POMMES FRITES COPEAUX—Like *Chatouillard potatoes* but cut into irregular ribbons.

Crainquebille potatoes. POMMES DE TERRE CRAINQUEBILLE—Put some very big, long, correctly peeled potatoes into a sauté pan, on a foundation of chopped onion fried in butter.

Pour in enough stock to cover the potatoes half-way.

Season with salt and pepper, add a *bouquet garni** with a clove of garlic added to it, place on each potato a slice of tomato with the seeds taken out and sprinkle with melted butter. Bring to the boil on the stove, then cook in the oven. A few moments before taking out of the oven, sprinkle with white breadcrumbs and brown the top.

Potatoes à la Crécy, also called à la Vichy. POMMES DE TERRE À LA CRÉCY, À LA VICHY—Prepare like *Anna Potatoes*, putting a layer of *Carrots à la Vichy** between each layer of potato.

Potatoes à la crème. POMMES DE TERRE À LA CRÈME—Boil the potatoes in water, peel them when cooked, cut into rather thick round slices and put into a sauté pan. Cover with boiling milk (or boiling fresh cream). Cook briskly until the liquid is reduced. Season with salt, pepper and grated nutmeg. At the last moment, add a few tablespoons of fresh cream.

Potato curly crisps (U.S. chips). POMMES FRITES COLLERETTES—Like *Fried potatoes* (*Potato crisps*), but cut with a fluted cutter.

Potato croquettes

Potato croquettes. CROQUETTES DE POMMES DE TERRE—Divide *Duchess potato mixture* into small (40 or 50 gram) pieces. Mould into the shape of corks rolling them in flour.

Dip in egg and breadcrumbs and fry in very hot deep fat.

Use as indicated in the recipe.

Note. Potato croquettes can be moulded into various shapes.

Potato croquettes Chevreuse. CROQUETTES DE POMMES DE TERRE CHEVREUSE—As above, adding some chopped chervil to the duchess potato mixture.

Potato croquettes à la lyonnaise. CROQUETTES DE POMMES DE TERRE À LA LYONNAISE—As above, adding some chopped onion lightly fried in butter and chopped parsley to the duchess potato mixture.

Potato croquettes à la parmesane. CROQUETTES DE POMMES DE TERRE À LA PARMESANE—As above, adding some grated Parmesan cheese to the duchess potato mixture.

Potato croquettes à la périgourdine. CROQUETTES DE POMMES DE TERRE À LA PÉRIGOURDINE—As above, adding some chopped truffles to the duchess potato mixture.

Potato croustades (Hors-d'oeuvre or entrée volante). CROUSTADES DE POMMES DE TERRE—These *croustades** are made of duchess potato in the following manner:

(*a*) Roll out *Duchess potato mixture* to a thickness of about 1 inch and with a pastry cutter cut out little circlets about 2¼ inches in diameter.

Dip in egg and breadcrumbs. Mark the middle of each circlet with a pastry cutter about 1¼ inches in diameter, pressing the cutter in only to penetrate one-third of the circlet's thickness.

Fry in very hot deep fat. Drain on a cloth, remove the small circle forming the lid and hollow out the *croustades* without breaking them.

Fill them as indicated in the recipe.

Note. These *croustades* are used as hot hors-d'oeuvre or as a garnish for meat, poultry and fish.

(*b*) Line some generously buttered, fluted, small brioche tins with *Duchess potato mixture*. Put in a layer of purée thick enough to give resistance to the walls yet not too thick to leave no room for the filling.

Brush the inside of the *croustades* with beaten egg and cook golden in the oven.

Turn out of the tins very carefully, brush the outside with beaten egg and put in the oven for a few moments. Fill as indicated in the recipe. The same uses as above.

(*c*) Mould duchess potato mixture on a round, buttered dish in such a way as to obtain a *croustade* deep enough to contain the filling indicated.

Decorate the edges of this *croustade* by piping some mixture through a forcing (pastry) bag with a plain or fluted nozzle. Fill as indicated in the recipe.

Note. These *croustades* can be made small or big depending on the final use for which they are intended. They are used as a foundation for meat, poultry, fish, etc., served in small pieces and accompanied by a sauce.

(*d*) Shred the potatoes into *julienne* strips (as described in the recipe for *Annette potatoes*) and line with them a well-buttered dish for cooking *Anna potatoes*.

In the middle of the potatoes put a cast iron form (rather like a layer-cake tin), buttered on the outside.

Press hard on this to make the potatoes go up the walls of the dish and to form a lining layer ½ inch thick.

Fill the inner mould with deep-frying fat.

Cook the *croustade* in the oven like *Annette potatoes*.

When it is cooked, remove the inner mould, press down the potatoes with a fork on the walls and the bottom and brown the inside part lightly.

Turn out on to a round dish very carefully and fill as indicated in the recipe.

Note. These *croustades* can be made big or small.

They can also be made without the inside mould, by simply pressing the potatoes, when half cooked, against the walls of the dish. This latter method, however, does not give such good results.

Dauphine potatoes. POMMES DE TERRE DAUPHINE—Mix *Duchess potatoes* with one-third of their weight of unsweetened common *Chou paste* (see DOUGH). Leave until cold.

Divide into small (40 or 50 gram) pieces. Shape into balls, roll in flour and fry in very hot deep fat.

Drain, dry, sprinkle with salt and arrange in a heap on a napkin or in a potato nest, or use as a garnish, as indicated in the recipe.

Note. These potatoes can be moulded into different shapes. They can also be dipped in egg and breadcrumbs before deep-frying.

Potatoes à la dauphinoise, also called Gratin de pommes à la dauphinoise. POMMES DE TERRE DAUPHINOISE—Slice 1 pound (500 grams) of potatoes very finely, put them in a bowl and moisten with 1½ cups (3 decilitres) of boiled milk with a beaten egg added to it.

Season with salt, pepper and grated nutmeg. Add ½ cup (50 grams) of grated Gruyère cheese and mix.

Put these potatoes into an earthenware dish, buttered and rubbed with garlic.

Potatoes à la dauphinoise (*Claire*)

Sprinkle with grated Gruyère cheese, scatter 1½ tablespoons (25 grams) of butter in tiny pieces over the top, wipe the edges of the dish carefully and bake in a slow oven for 45 minutes. Serve in the dish in which the potatoes are cooked.

Potato fritters; scallops garnished with Duchess potatoes

Duchess potatoes. POMMES DE TERRE DUCHESSE—Duchess potato mixture is prepared in the following manner:

Cut 1 pound (500 grams) of yellow, peeled potatoes into thick slices or into quarters. Boil them briskly in salted water. Drain, put in the oven for a few moments to evaporate excessive moisture and quickly rub through a sieve.

Put the purée into a saucepan, dry off for a few moments on the fire, turning with a wooden spoon; add 3 tablespoons (50 grams) of butter, season with salt, pepper and a little grated nutmeg, bind with a whole egg or two yolks and mix.

Spread the purée on a buttered metal sheet, leave until cold, then shape as indicated in the recipe.

Note. When this mixture is intended for borders to be piped through a forcing bag, it is used while still hot. It can in such a case be not so thick as when it is intended for croquettes or to be served as duchess potatoes proper.

Duchess potatoes for garnish. POMMES DE TERRE DUCHESSE—These potatoes are prepared from *Potato purée* described below. It is moulded by hand into various shapes or forced through a bag on to a buttered baking sheet.

As soon as the purée has been piped through, brush with beaten egg and put in the oven to colour. Use as indicated in the recipe.

Potatoes with fennel. POMMES DE TERRE AU FENOUIL—Like *Potatoes with basil*, replacing the latter by fresh chopped fennel.

Potato fondantes. POMMES DE TERRE FONDANTES—Cut the potatoes to uniform size to look like small eggs. Put them into a buttered sauté pan. Cover and cook gently on the top of the stove. Turn them carefully one at a time—just once during the cooking.

When cooked, golden on the outside and very soft inside, arrange them in a vegetable dish.

They can also be prepared as follows:

Cook the potatoes, cut as described, in lard. When they are done, drain off the lard and replace it by butter.

Dry sliced potatoes in a cloth before frying (*Claire*)

Fried potatoes. POMMES DE TERRE FRITES—This is the most popular form of potatoes eaten; also the least digestible. If the frying is carried out correctly, at the right temperature, the potatoes should be crisp, very pleasant to the taste and easier to digest; if the frying is badly done and the potatoes are impregnated with fat, they become indigestible.

Fried potatoes can be cooked in cooking fat or oil; they are immersed in deep fat at a temperature of 180°C. (356°F.) (beginning to smoke); this temperature is at once lowered to 160°C. (320°F.) then to 150°C. (302°F.) by the introduction of cold potatoes into it. The potatoes acquire a golden colour when the fat is reheated to 175° to 180°C. (347° to 356°F.).

Cut very finely (straw potatoes) and immersed into special fat heated to 190°C. (374°F.), they cause the temperature of the fat to fall in five minutes' cooking time to only 177°C. (350°F.).

Under the entry entitled DEEP-FRYING all instructions relative to the clarification of the fat in which the potatoes are cooked are given, as well as all information dealing with utensils, pans, etc., which are used for deep-frying.

Fried potatoes, or potato crisps (U.S. chips). POMMES FRITES CHIP, EN LIARDS—Cut the potatoes into the shape of corks. Cut them into very thin round slices with a knife or potato slicer. Soak in cold water for 10 minutes. Drain, dry on a cloth and fry in very hot deep fat. Drain and season.

Note. These potatoes are often used as an accompaniment to roast game *à l'anglaise.*

Fried potatoes Pont-Neuf. POMMES FRITES PONT-NEUF—Cut the potatoes into pieces $\frac{1}{3}$ inch thick and $2\frac{1}{2}$ inches long.

Fry in boiling fat.

Potato fritters—See FRITTERS.

Gastronome potatoes, also called potatoes à la Cussy. POMMES DE TERRE GASTRONOME, POMMES DE TERRE CUSSY—'Take big yellow potatoes, cut off the two ends, to be able to cut them with a special cutter (called in French, a *colonne*) into cork-shaped chunks, about 1 inch in diameter. Cut them into slices one *line* ($\frac{1}{4}$ inch) thick, putting them into water as you cut them. Dry on a cloth to absorb all water.

'Put them into a big pan with half a pound of hot clarified butter, so that they cook gently, colouring without sticking to the pan or drying up. In the meantime, slice six or eight truffles, toss them in butter with a tablespoon of Madeira and a piece of chicken jelly the size of a walnut. When the potatoes are cooked and acquire a fine golden colour, remove them from the fire, add the truffles and the juice of half a lemon and serve piping hot.

'We owe this side dish to the late Monsieur de Cussy, a fine gourmet and former administrator of Napoleon's palace.' (Plumerey's recipe.)

Note. This method of preparing potatoes is somewhat similar to the one called '*à la sarlandaise*'.

Potatoes Georgette. POMMES DE TERRE GEORGETTE—These are principally served as a hot hors-d'oeuvre. Choose medium-sized potatoes, bake in the oven and cut a circle on one side.

Through this opening scoop out three-quarters of the pulp.

While still hot fill them with *Crayfish à la Nantua**.

Heat the potatoes in the oven and serve in a folded napkin.

Potatoes in gravy. POMMES DE TERRE AU JUS—Cut the potatoes into quarters and put into a sauté pan with butter. Pour in enough clear brown veal gravy to cover. Season, cover with a lid and cook in the oven. Serve in a vegetable dish.

Grilled potatoes. POMMES DE TERRE GRILLÉES—Choose big, long potatoes and cut them lengthways into slices $\frac{1}{3}$ thick. Parboil them in salted boiling water for 4 minutes. Drain and dry on a cloth. Brush with oil or melted butter. Cook under a low grill (or broiler). Arrange on a round dish and top with half melted *Maître d'hôtel butter.* See BUTTER, *Compound butters.*

Hashed browned potatoes (American cookery). POMMES DE TERRE HACHÉES BRUNES À L'AMÉRICAINE—Boil the potatoes in salted water, drain well and chop up roughly.

Fry them in butter in a frying pan, allowing them to brown thoroughly. Season with salt and pepper. Give them the shape of a turnover, allow to colour and serve on a long dish.

Chopped onions fried in butter are sometimes added to this dish.

Potatoes à la hongroise. POMMES DE TERRE À LA HONGROISE—Soften 6 tablespoons (75 grams) of chopped onion in butter in a sauté pan. Season with $\frac{1}{2}$ teaspoon of paprika. Add one peeled, seeded and roughly chopped tomato.

Put in a pound (500 grams) of long potatoes cut into rather thick round slices. Season with salt. Moisten with meat stock in just sufficient quantity to cover the potatoes. Bake in the oven. Sprinkle with chopped parsley.

Jackson potatoes. POMMES DE TERRE JACKSON—Another name for *Potatoes au gratin.*

Potatoes à la landaise. POMMES DE TERRE À LA LANDAISE—Fry $\frac{1}{2}$ cup (100 grams) of diced onions and 5 ounces (150 grams) of Bayonne ham, cut into $\frac{1}{3}$ inch square dice, in goose fat (or lard). When the onions and the ham are nicely browned, add 1 pound (500 grams) of potatoes cut in large dice. Season with salt and pepper. Cook with a lid on, stirring from time to time. At the last moment, add a tablespoon of chopped garlic and parsley.

Potato loaves. PAINS DE POMMES DE TERRE—Bake some big floury potatoes in the oven and scoop out the pulp with a spoon. Rub this pulp through a metal sieve as quickly as possible.

Put the purée thus obtained into a saucepan with butter, allowing 6 tablespoons (100 grams) of butter per 4 cups (kilo) of purée, salt, pepper and grated nutmeg. Stir this purée on the fire for a few moments to dry off excessive moisture, then remove from heat and add one whole egg and 4 yolks.

Divide this composition into 2 tablespoon (60 gram) pieces, mould them into small boat-shaped cakes slit in the middle. Put on a baking sheet, brush with beaten egg and cook in a very hot oven until golden.

Potatoes Lorette. POMMES DE TERRE LORETTE—Divide *Dauphine potato mixture* into small (40 to 50 gram) parts, shape into crescents and fry in deep fat, without dipping in egg and breadcrumbs.

Potatoes à la lyonnaise. POMMES DE TERRE À LA LYONNAISE—Prepare as described in the recipe for *Sauté potatoes.* When three-quarters cooked, add 4 tablespoons of onions, sliced and fried in butter.

Finish cooking together, shaking the pan frequently to mix well.

Serve in a vegetable dish, sprinkled with chopped parsley.

Macaire potatoes. POMMES DE TERRE MACAIRE—Choose big potatoes, bake in the oven, cut in two and scoop out the pulp with a fork. Mash this pulp incorporating in it several tablespoons of butter, allowing $3\frac{1}{2}$ ounces (100 grams) of butter per 6 cups (kilo) of pulp. Season with salt and pepper.

Put the potato pulp into a frying pan in which some butter has been heated. Spread in a flat cake. Fry golden on both sides. Serve this flat cake on a round dish.

Maire potatoes. POMMES DE TERRE MAIRE—The same as *Potatoes à la crème.*

Potatoes à la maître d'hôtel. POMMES DE TERRE À LA MAÎTRE D'HÔTEL—Boil the potatoes in salted water. Peel and slice them. Put them into a sauté pan and cover with boiling milk. Add 2 or 3 tablespoons of butter, season and cook until the liquid is reduced.

Sprinkle with chopped parsley and serve in a vegetable dish.

Potato matches (U.S. potato sticks). POMMES FRITES ALLUMETTES—Cut the potatoes into little sticks $\frac{1}{8}$ inch wide and $2\frac{1}{2}$ inches long.

Fry in very hot deep fat in order to obtain crisp golden potatoes.

Drain, dry and season with fine, very dry salt.

Arrange in a heap on a napkin or on a special paper doyley.

Boiled new potatoes (*Pommes de terre au naturel*)

Potatoes with mint. POMMES DE TERRE À LA MENTHE—Boil new potatoes with a sprig of mint. Serve in a vegetable dish and put a green mint leaf on each potato.

Potatoes Mont-Doré. POMMES DE TERRE MONT-DORÉ—Prepare creamy mashed potatoes mixed with grated cheese, heap in a dome in a buttered fire-proof dish, sprinkle with grated cheese, pour on some melted butter and brown the top.

Potatoes mousseline. POMMES DE TERRE MOUSSELINE—Bake the potatoes, remove pulp and rub it through a sieve. Stir this pulp in a pan on the fire, adding to it, for 6 cups (1 kilo) of pulp, ½ pound (250 grams) of butter and 4 yolks of egg. Season with salt, pepper and grated nutmeg. Remove from fire and add 1 cup (2 decilitres) of whipped cream. Pile in a dome in a buttered fire-proof dish, sprinkle with melted butter and brown the top quickly in the oven.

Note. This purée can also be put into a flan case, made of lining paste, baked blind (baked pie shell).

Potatoes nature or au naturel. POMMES DE TERRE NATURE, AU NATUREL—One or other of these names is often given boiled potatoes (*Potatoes à l'anglaise*).

Potato nests. NIDS DE POMMES DE TERRE—Shred the potato into fine *julienne** strips, as described in the recipe for *Straw potatoes.*

Wash, dry and use them for lining special moulds or wire baskets.

Press the potatoes well against the walls of the wire baskets. Trim away any overlapping parts, close the baskets and plunge them into very hot deep fat.

Take out of deep-frying pan, turn out, drain and season. Arrange the nest on a napkin and fill as indicated in the recipe.

Noisette potatoes (garnish). POMMES DE TERRE NOISETTE—With a round vegetable scooping spoon, scoop out pieces of potato the size and shape of cobnuts (hazel nuts).

Fry them in butter in a sauté pan, season and cook until golden all over.

Serve in a vegetable dish or use as indicated in the recipe.

Potatoes à la normande. POMMES DE TERRE À LA NORMANDE—Cut a pound (500 grams) of potatoes into thin round slices. Wash them, dry on a cloth, season with salt and freshly ground pepper and put into a

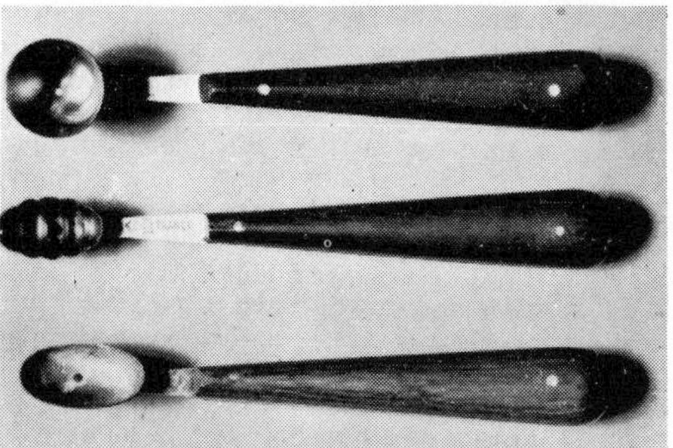

Spoons for scooping out potatoes and for cutting out noisette potatoes (*Larousse*)

buttered sauté pan in layers, alternating with the shredded white part of 2 big leeks and 2 to 3 tablespoons of chopped parsley.

Add a *bouquet garni**. Add enough white veal stock, meat stock or water—if the dish is intended to be served as Lenten fare—to cover the potatoes. Scatter 3 tablespoons (50 grams) of butter in tiny dabs.

Bring to the boil on the stove, cover with a lid and cook in the oven. Serve in a vegetable dish.

Potato pancakes. CRÊPES DE POMMES DE TERRE—Peel, wash and dry the potatoes, then put them through a mincer. Dab the pulp obtained with a cloth, put it into a bowl, season with salt, pepper and grated nutmeg and add, for 1 pound (2 to 3 medium size or 500 grams) of potatoes, 2 eggs beaten with ½ cup (a decilitre) of milk and 50 grams of *Noisette butter*. See BUTTER, *Compound butters.*

Using this composition make the pancakes in the usual manner, keeping them a little thicker than for stuffed or sweet pancakes.

Serve the pancakes on a very hot round dish.

Note. Some cheese can also be added to the composition.

Potatoes à la parisienne

Potatoes à la parisienne (garnish). POMMES DE TERRE À LA PARISIENNE—Like *Noisette potatoes*, but smaller in size. As soon as the potatoes are cooked, toss them in greatly concentrated veal gravy or dissolved meat jelly. Sprinkle with chopped parsley.

Parmentier potatoes. POMMES DE TERRE PARMENTIER—Cut potatoes into pieces about ⅓ inch square. Cook them in butter. Serve in a vegetable dish and sprinkle with chopped parsley.

Note. These potatoes are more often cooked with the meat with which they are served.

Parsley potatoes. POMMES DE TERRE PERSILLÉES—Boil the potatoes, drain well and add melted butter and chopped parsley. Serve in a vegetable dish.

Note. Potatoes with bacon (POMMES DE TERRE AU LARD), the recipe for which is given elsewhere in this section, are often served under this name.

Potatoes à la paysanne. POMMES DE TERRE À LA PAYSANNE—Cut the potatoes into very thin round slices. Put them into a buttered sauté pan in alternate layers with chopped sorrel quickly cooked in butter (using about a tenth part of sorrel to nine parts of potatoes), mixed with pounded chervil and a pinch of grated garlic. Season with salt and pepper, add meat stock (or water, if the dish is to be served as Lenten fare), scatter over some tiny dabs of butter and cook in the oven.

Potato purée. PURÉE DE POMMES DE TERRE—Cut potatoes into thick slices or quarters and cook them in fast boiling salted water.

Drain, put in the oven for a few moments to evaporate surplus moisture and rub through a sieve, pressing down with a wooden masher, with vertical, not horizontal, strokes.

Put the purée into a pan, put on the stove and blend in from 2½ to 3 ounces of very fresh butter per pound of purée.

Lighten to the desired degree by adding a few tablespoons of boiling milk, stir vigorously with a wooden spoon and serve in a vegetable dish.

Note. The purée should not be allowed to boil after butter has been added to it. If it has to be kept for a while before serving, it should be kept hot in a *bain-marie**. It must, however, be borne in mind that this dish is at its best freshly made.

Potato purée à la crème. PURÉE DE POMMES DE TERRE À LA CRÈME—As above, replacing milk by fresh cream.

Potato purée au gratin. PURÉE DE POMMES DE TERRE AU GRATIN—Prepare the purée as described above. Add some grated cheese to it, put into a buttered fire-proof dish, smooth the surface, working it into a slight dome shape, sprinkle with grated cheese and melted butter and brown the top.

Potato purée soup. Potage purée de pommes de terre—See SOUPS AND BROTHS, *Purée of potato soup Parmentier*.

Potato quenelles à l'alsacienne, called floutes (Alsatian cookery). QUENELLES DE POMMES DE TERRE À L'ALSACIENNE, DITES FLOUTES—Prepare 4 cups (500 grams) of very fine potato purée. Add to it 2 whole eggs and about ½ cup (75 grams) of unsifted flour in order to obtain a fairly firm paste. Season with salt, pepper and grated nutmeg.

Shape into balls, roll to look like corks, or mould with a soup spoon.

Drop the quenelles one by one into a pan of salted boiling water.

Poach from 8 to 10 minutes. Drain the quenelles and put into a buttered dish.

At the last moment, pour over some piping hot *Noisette butter* (see BUTTER, *Compound butters*) in which a handful of fine, freshly grated breadcrumbs have been fried lightly.

Potato quenelles with Parmesan cheese. QUENELLES DE POMMES DE TERRE AU PARMESAN—Prepare the quenelles as described in the above recipe. After poaching, put them into a dish, buttered and sprinkled with grated Parmesan cheese. Sprinkle with grated Parmesan, spoon over some melted butter and brown the top in a very hot oven.

Rissole potatoes. POMMES DE TERRE RISSOLÉES—Another name for *Sauté potatoes*.

Roast potatoes. POMMES DE TERRE RÔTIES—Choose big, long potatoes, peel them correctly and put into a sauté pan in which some butter (or lard) has been heated. Season with salt. Cook in the oven, basting frequently, until golden all over.

Potatoes Saint-Flour. POMMES DE TERRE SAINT-FLOUR—Line the bottom of a deep, fire-proof dish with a layer of green cabbage braised in fat (cooked slightly crisp). Over the cabbage put a layer of potatoes cut in rather thick round slices, mixed with lean bacon, diced, scalded and fried. Season with salt and pepper. Moisten with stock, flavoured with a little crushed garlic. Sprinkle with grated cheese. Cook in a slow oven.

Potato salad—See SALAD.

Potatoes à la sarlandaise. POMMES DE TERRE À LA SARLANDAISE—Prepare like *Anna potatoes*, putting the potatoes into the special tall-sided dish in layers, alternating with rows of thinly sliced truffles.

Potatoes—roast; noisette; sauté; mashed and boiled *à l'anglaise*; fried

Sauté (sautéed) potatoes I. POMMES DE TERRE SAUTÉES—Cut freshly boiled, peeled, potatoes into uniform round slices.

Heat some butter in a frying pan and put in the potatoes. Season.

Fry until golden, shaking the pan frequently to ensure even browning.

Serve in a vegetable dish and sprinkle with chopped parsley.

Sauté (sautéed) potatoes II. POMMES DE TERRE SAUTÉES À CRU—Cut 1 pound (500 grams) of uncooked Dutch potatoes into very thin slices, wash, dry on a cloth and season.

Cook in a frying pan in butter. Shake the pan frequently to ensure even cooking and to give all the potatoes a nice golden colour.

SHELL-FISH. *Above:* Oysters Mornay, Grilled lobster, Crab à l'armoricaine. Oysters on toast *Below:* Mixed shell-fish, Lobster Thermidor (*Prunier*)

(*From Curnonsky:* Cuisine et Vins de France)

SALAD NICOISE. (*Robert Carrier*)

Serve in a vegetable dish and sprinkle with chopped parsley.

Sauté (sautéed) potatoes à la provençale. POMMES DE TERRE SAUTÉES À LA PROVENÇALE—Prepare using either raw or boiled potatoes like *Sauté potatoes I or II.* At the last moment, add a good tablespoon of chopped parsley and garlic.

Note. These potatoes can also be cooked in oil instead of butter.

Potatoes à la savoyarde. POMMES DE TERRE À LA SAVOYARDE—Prepare like *Potatoes à la dauphinoise,* replacing the milk by white stock.

Potato soufflé—See SOUFFLÉ.

Soufflé potatoes (or puffed potatoes). POMMES DE TERRE SOUFFLÉES—Choose uniform-sized potatoes, peel and trim them.

Cut them lengthways into slices, ⅛ inch thick, wash and dry on a cloth.

Plunge into deep fat, which should be hot, but not too hot.

Heat the fat gradually and cook the potatoes until they begin to rise to the surface. Drain in a frying basket.

Just before serving, plunge them into a second pan of very hot deep fat.

Drain the potatoes, which should be greatly puffed up, spread them on a cloth and sprinkle with salt. Serve on a napkin.

Note. This method of cooking potatoes was discovered by accident. It is claimed that the discovery took place at Saint-Germain-en-Laye, when the railway (which was inaugurated in 1837 and stopped at Pecq) was brought to this place.

The train had great difficulty in clambering up the final slope and had to have several goes at it. The proprietor of the restaurant in which the Company was giving lunch to its guests had prepared some fried potatoes for the appointed time, let them get cold and then, taken by surprise by the unexpected arrival of the party, only had time to plunge them into boiling fat quickly and, to his amazement, saw them puff up.

The famous analytical chemist Chevreul, who was informed of this phenomenon, studied it experimentally and established the conditions under which it occurred and could be reproduced at will.

It is perhaps the only time that a train being late had happy consequences!

Soufflé potatoes require double cooking and fat which can be brought to a very high temperature without burning, which is best achieved with beef suet. The potatoes should first be plunged into fat at a temperature of 180°C. (356°F.) contained in a big pan (which reduces the degree of cooling); this temperature falls to 135°C. (275°F.) in 2 minutes. After 7 minutes—the time needed for cooking through slices ⅛ inch thick—the temperature falls to 120°C. (248°F.). The potatoes are then cooked and soft. They are taken out, the heat is increased and the potatoes are reimmersed, a few at a time, in hot fat which should register at least 190° to ensure *puffing up*. At this temperature the surface of the slices is transformed into a waterproof skin, which will swell as a result of the volatilization of the water contained inside.

Steamed potatoes. POMMES DE TERRE À LA VAPEUR—Steam the potatoes as described in the recipe for *Potatoes à l'anglaise*, in a special steamer.

Straw potatoes. POMMES FRITES PAILLE—Cut the potatoes into very thin *julienne** sticks. Wash and dry on a cloth.

Fry in hot deep fat. Drain in a frying basket. Just before serving, plunge into smoking hot fat.

Stuffed potatoes I. POMMES DE TERRE FARCIES—Bake big, long potatoes in the oven and scoop out two-thirds of the pulp. Rub the pulp through a sieve and mix with various other ingredients if desired, such as *duxelles**, *fines herbes**, grated cheese, chopped ham, *mirepoix**, chopped onion softened in butter, various chopped meats, etc. Season well, add butter and fill the potato skins with this pulp.

Sprinkle with grated cheese or breadcrumbs, pour on a little melted butter and brown the top.

Or: Peel some very big, long potatoes. Cut them to look like stout cylinders, slice off the ends to make them all the same height, say about 2 inches.

Hollow out with a round vegetable scooping spoon, to form a cavity capable of containing from 2 to 3 tablespoons (40 to 60 grams) of *forcemeat**.

Blanch quickly in fast boiling salted water, drain, dry, arrange in a well-buttered sauté pan and season.

Stuff with the filling indicated, either through a forcing (pastry) bag or with a spoon. Smooth the top layer of the filling into a dome shape.

Moisten the potatoes with meat stock (without covering them).

Bring to the boil on the stove, cover the sauté pan and cook in a slow oven from 35 to 40 minutes.

Remove the potatoes carefully, arrange them in a fire-proof dish, sprinkle with breadcrumbs and melted butter and brown the top in the oven.

Reduce (boil down) the pan juices left over from cooking the potatoes, skim off surplus fat, strain and pour over the potatoes.

Stuffed potatoes II. POMMES DE TERRE FOURRÉES—This dish is more of a small entrée than an hors-d'oeuvre. If they are served as such, it is advisable to use potatoes that are not too big.

Method. Bake medium-sized, uniform-shaped potatoes. Cut a circular opening on one side and keep the cut-out pieces to use as lids for stuffed potatoes.

Scoop out three-quarters of the pulp, taking care not to damage the skin.

Stuff the potatoes with the filling indicated.

Depending on the nature of the dish, sprinkle the top with breadcrumbs or grated cheese and brown the top, or merely replace the cut-out circles as lids.

Serve on a folded napkin.

If the stuffed potatoes are to be browned later, it is better to cut them in half, lengthways, instead of hollowing them out through a circular opening.

Stuffed potatoes à la cancalaise. POMMES DE TERRE À LA CANCALAISE—Prepare like *Stuffed potatoes I. Filling:* Poached oysters, mushrooms, *White wine sauce.* See SAUCE.

Stuffed potatoes à la cantalienne. POMMES DE TERRE À LA CANTALIENNE—*Filling:* Pulp scooped out of the potato, mashed and mixed with two-thirds of its weight of braised, chopped cabbage.

Sprinkle with grated cheese and brown the top.

Stuffed potatoes à la chasseur (Hunter style). POMMES DE TERRE CHASSEUR—*Filling:* Sliced chicken livers and mushrooms, sautéed in butter, *Chasseur sauce.* See SAUCE.

Stuffed potatoes with cheese. POMMES DE TERRE AU FROMAGE, GRATINÉES. *Filling:* The pulp scooped out of the potatoes, seasoned and with butter added to it.

Sprinkle with grated cheese and brown the top.

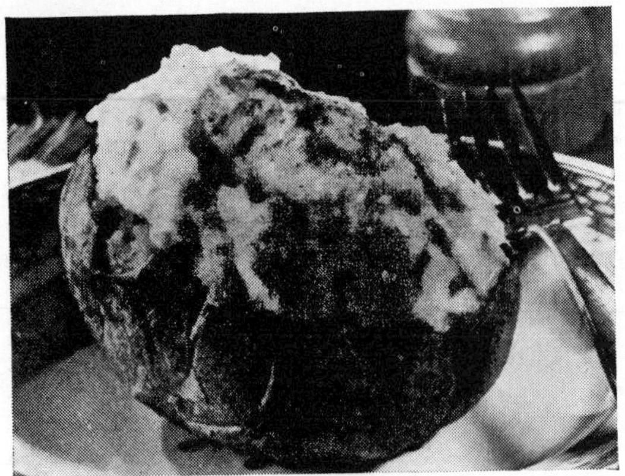

Stuffed potato with cheese

Stuffed potatoes à la duxelles. POMMES DE TERRE FARCIES À LA DUXELLES—Prepare like *Potatoes stuffed with sausage meat* and stuff with a *Duxelles mixture**.

Stuffed potatoes fermière. POMMES DE TERRE FERMIÈRE—*Filling:* Pulp scooped out of the potatoes, mashed and mixed with two-thirds of its weight of chopped stock-pot vegetables.

Sprinkle with grated cheese and brown the top.

Stuffed potatoes à la florentine. POMMES DE TERRE À LA FLORENTINE—*Filling:* Spinach cooked in butter. Cover with *Mornay sauce* (see SAUCE), sprinkle with grated cheese and brown the top.

Stuffed potatoes à la hongroise. POMMES DE TERRE À LA HONGROISE—*Filling:* Pulp scooped out of the potatoes, mashed with a fork, mixed with one-third of its weight of chopped onion gently fried in butter and seasoned with paprika.

Stuffed potatoes Maintenon. POMMES DE TERRE MAINTENON—*Filling: Salpicon** of breast of chicken, pickled tongue, truffles and mushrooms bound with *Soubise**.

Sprinkle with grated cheese mixed with breadcrumbs and brown the top.

Stuffed potatoes à la ménagère. POMMES DE TERRE FARCIES À LA MÉNAGÈRE—Prepare like *Potatoes stuffed with sausage meat* and stuff with chopped meat left-overs.

Note. The chopped meat (beef or mutton) (lamb) can be mixed with a third of their weight of fine forcemeat or sausage meat.

Stuffed potatoes princesse. POMMES DE TERRE PRINCESSE—*Filling: Asparagus tips à la crème**. Cover the potatoes with slivers of truffles.

Stuffed potatoes à la provençale. POMMES DE TERRE À LA PROVENÇALE—*Filling: Salpicon** of marinated tunny (tuna fish) and hard boiled eggs, bound with *Tomato fondue**.

Sprinkle with breadcrumbs and brown the top.

Potatoes stuffed with sausage meat. POMMES DE TERRE FARCIES CHARCUTIÈRE—Prepare as described in the second method of the recipe for *Stuffed potatoes I.* Fill with sausage meat stuffing, mixed with chopped parsley (and, if desired, chopped onions lightly fried in butter).

Note. These potatoes can also be stuffed with sausage meat mixed with the pulp of cooked potatoes, as described in the first method of the same recipe.

Stuffed potatoes soubise. POMMES DE TERRE SOUBISE—*Filling:* Thick *Soubise purée* (see PURÉE) with cream.

Sprinkle with breadcrumbs and brown the top.

Stuffed potatoes à la Vichy. POMMES DE TERRE À LA VICHY—*Filling: Carrots à la Vichy**.

Sprinkle with breadcrumbs and brown the top.

Stuffed potatoes Yorkshire style. POMMES DE TERRE À LA YORKAISE—Bake the potatoes in the oven and fill with chopped York ham and mushrooms bound with *Béchamel sauce* (see SAUCE), mixed with chopped onion lightly fried in butter and seasoned with a little paprika.

Potato subrics. SUBRICS DE POMMES DE TERRE—Cut the potatoes into small dice, parboil in salted water for 2 minutes, drain, dry, then cook lightly in butter in a covered pan.

Remove from heat and bind these potatoes with thick *Béchamel sauce* (see SAUCE), allowing $1\frac{1}{4}$ cups ($2\frac{1}{2}$ decilitres) of sauce per $2\frac{1}{2}$ cups (500 grams) of potatoes.

Add 3 yolks and 1 whole egg to the mixture. Season with salt, pepper and grated nutmeg and mix.

Heat some clarified butter in a frying pan and, taking a spoonful of the mixture at a time, drop into the hot butter, taking care to allow some space for the subrics to spread during cooking and to prevent their sticking to each other.

Turn the subrics, with a palette knife, to make both sides golden. Arrange in a serving or a vegetable dish. Serve *Cream sauce* (see SAUCE) separately.

Potatoes à la toulousaine. POMMES DE TERRE À LA TOULOUSAINE—Cut the potatoes into quarters and brown them lightly in a sauté pan with two-thirds goose fat and one-third oil.

Season, sprinkle with flour, add a tablespoonful of chopped garlic and parsley.

Pour in enough stock (or water) to cover the potatoes. Stir, bring to the boil, cover with a lid and cook in the oven.

Serve in a vegetable dish and sprinkle with chopped parsley.

Potatoes à la Vichy. POMMES DE TERRE À LA VICHY—Name sometimes given to *Potatoes à la Crécy.*

Potatoes voisin. POMMES DE TERRE VOISIN—Prepare like *Anna potatoes*, sprinkling each layer of potatoes with grated cheese.

Potatoes Yvette. POMMES DE TERRE YVETTE—Name under which *Annette potatoes* are sometimes served.

POTÉE—By this French term is understood, in general, all preparations cooked in an earthenware pot; but in particular the word *potée* describes a kind of soup made with pork and vegetables, mostly cabbage and potatoes, of which *Cabbage Soup* is the most characteristic.

Potée Lorraine—Line the bottom of an earthenware vessel with pieces of pork skin or bacon rind. Place on top some fresh pork fat, a knuckle of ham or bladebone of pork, carrots, turnips, little bunches of leeks and a whole cabbage previously blanched. Barely cover with cold water. Cook for 3 hours. Half an hour before taking it from the fire, a large sausage, well pricked, is put in. Plain boiled potatoes may also be added at the moment of serving.

POTTED CHAR (English cookery)—A fish conserve formerly held in great esteem in England, where it was eaten at breakfast. It is made in this way:

Cook the char in a prepared vegetable stock and let them cool in the liquid.

Remove all skin and bones and arrange the fillets of fish, well drained, in shallow earthenware pots. Cover with clarified butter and set in the oven for quarter of an hour. Allow to get quite cold. Add a few more spoonfuls of clarified butter if necessary so that the fish is completely covered.

Potted char, kept in a cool place, will keep for 2 weeks.

Note. In U.S.A., *char* is the name given to certain types of red-fleshed trout. Trout may be used in this recipe.

POUILLARD—Name given to a young partridge. It is prepared in the same way as a fully grown partridge.

POULE-AU-POT—Pot-au-feu prepared with beef and a stuffed chicken. See SOUPS AND BROTHS, *Pot-au-feu à la béarnaise*.

POULETTE (A LA)—Method of preparing a diversity of ingredients, notably offal (variety meats). Previously cooked, these are moistened with a *Velouté sauce* bound with egg yolks and with cream and usually garnished with little onions and mushrooms. It is a sort of fricassée. See OFFAL OR VARIETY MEATS, *Sheep's trotters à la Poulette;* MUSHROOMS, *Mushrooms à la poulette*.

POULTRY—See CHICKEN.

POUPELIN—This *gâteau*, which was very popular in former days, is made by cooking *chou paste* (see DOUGH) in a plain round mould. Three-quarters of the pastry spilling outside the mould during cooking, all that is left is a sort of outer crust, which is filled, once it has cooled, with *Chantilly cream* (see CREAMS), fruit mousse or ice cream.

POUPETON—Method of preparing certain butcher's meats, which are rolled one inside the other into a kind of meat roll. These pieces are generally braised.

POUSSIN—See CHICKEN, *Spring Chicken*.

POUSSOIR—Small machine used in pork butchery, with which the minced meats are pressed into the gut to make sausages.

By means of this gadget, too, air is prevented from entering the gut, an essential condition of perfect sausage making.

POUTINE—Tiny undeveloped fish (larvae or post-larvae or 'fry') of various kinds, mainly the early stages of sardines and anchovies. They are treated in the same way as *Nonats**.

PRAIRE—The popular name in France for the clam, a bivalve mollusc, most often eaten raw like oysters but which may also be cooked like mussels. See CLAMS.

This shellfish is found on the sandy Atlantic coasts of France and also in the Mediterranean.

It is also known as *Coque rayée* in the bays of Cancale and St. Malo, and as *Rigadelle* down the length of the Atlantic Coast from St. Brieuc to Lannion.

PRALIN—A preparation used by pastrycooks, made in the following way:

Ingredients. $\frac{3}{4}$ cup (100 grams) almonds, $\frac{1}{2}$ cup (100 grams) sugar, half a pod of vanilla (or 1 teaspoon vanilla extract) added along with the almonds.

Method. Put the sugar and vanilla in a copper pan. Melt over a good heat until it is brown; add the almonds previously browned in the oven. Mix together.

Pour into a greased baking tin, cool, then pound in a mortar as finely as possible.

Mushrooms à la poulette (*Robert Carrier*)

PRALINÉ (CAKE)—Cake made with layers of *Genoese pastry** or almond paste, separated by a layer of *Praline butter cream*, covered on the surface with a layer of the same cream and sprinkled with chopped almonds.

Praline butter cream is made by adding 4 tablespoons of powdered pralines to 1 cup of *Butter cream.* See CREAMS.

PRALINE (CONFECTIONERY)—A very delicate sweet which is nothing more than an almond covered with a coating of cooked sugar, variously flavoured and coloured.

PRALINER—To add praline to a custard, ice cream mixture or mousse.

PRATELLE—A variety of mushroom, large and pinkish, cultivated in beds.

PREIGNAC—This white wine, which is held in esteem, comes from a district of the same name in the Gironde.

PRÉ-SALÉ—Young sheep fattened in meadows bordering the sea (Brittany, Vendée, Guyenne), rich in aromatic pasture, which communicates great delicacy to the flavour of the flesh. For culinary preparation see MUTTON.

PRESENT—Dutch cheese, also known under the name of Edammer Kaas.

PRESENTATION OF DISHES—Dressage des plats—To *present a dish* is to arrange food on a serving dish in accordance with certain accepted rules, e.g., a joint of meat surrounded by its appropriate garnish.

In former times (and this usage persisted up to the end of the nineteenth century) the presentation of dishes was somewhat elaborate. There was no question of serving either hot or cold dishes except in some decorative or even architectural form.

There are many fine drawings of these masterpieces of culinary architecture in the works of Carême.

During the twentieth century, both at large and small dinner parties, a radical change has come about in the presentation of dishes, which is now as simple as possible. For the presentation of hot dishes, it is no longer customary to serve them on beds of rice or bread or in borders of *pasta* such as noodles, or fried bread motifs and skewered tit-bits.

As regards cold dishes, they are generally served straight on the dish on a layer of jelly and surrounded by a suitable garnish or jelly motifs or, and this is perhaps the best way of serving them, in glass or crystal bowls, completely covered with very clear jelly.

Aspics, *mousses*, *moulds* and other moulded dishes are sometimes set on a slice of sandwich bread (cut to the shape of their base) and surrounded with a border of jelly, but they are more commonly served straight on the dish, decorated with jelly, or in a glass bowl.

It is usual to serve cold fish and shellfish as simply as possible. Fish is generally served on a napkin and surrounded by the appropriate garnish interspersed with sprigs of curly parsley, or, where appropriate, skinned, trimmed and masked with jelly and decorated with whatever jelly is indicated in the recipe.

This simplification in the serving of cold dishes, especially sweets (desserts), was recommended by Carême himself, who urged the use of crystal bowls (which are now almost *de rigueur* for this purpose).

In the 'introductory discourse' to the *Cuisinier parisien*, Carême says that, for the presentation of these dishes which, in his day, were set on more or less elaborate plinths, he had furnished manufacturers with 'several models of bowls for sweets, some of which should be presented in crystal containers.' He advised the cooks of his own day to 'stand jelly sweets on ice to set', which is now current practice.

'In general', wrote Carême, 'I would wish to see these new bowls carried out in future in handsome silverware. They would do honour to the goldsmiths and silversmiths of France.'

PRESENTOIR—Dish on which a tureen, vegetable dish, etc. rests.

PRESERVATION OF FOOD. Conserve—The art of preserving food is extremely ancient, but it is only since the beginning of the nineteenth century that it has moved out of the empirical realm into the scientific.

Since the earliest times man has tried to guard against famine by preserving foods during their season of abundance: in particular, meat obtained by hunting.

It is quite certain that the only means for preserving food in prehistoric times was by drying. This method is still employed today, particularly in Switzerland, where beef is preserved (*Bindenfleisch*) in the Grisons, by being dried solely in the strong pure air.

But when man once knew how to use fire to cook meat, he very soon used it for curing it. This was the first scientific method of preserving. Having noticed the effect that fire had on meat, an effect which altered its substance, made it more tasty and above all easier to masticate, the possibility dawned on primitive man of delaying its decomposition by smoking it. This method of preserving, assisted it is true by a preliminary salting, is still used today, and it is in this manner that all hams and all smoked meats that are eaten raw or cooked are prepared and preserved.

Freezing also played a part in preserving meat in those remote days.

There was also preservation of food by salting, but only in regions near the sea where rock salt was found.

Fruit and vegetables were first preserved by drying in the sun or at the fire.

Later on, recourse was made to the system of enveloping food substances in fat. Although rather imperfect, this procedure is still used today to preserve, for a limited period, meat which had first been cooked in fat, put in stoneware pots and covered entirely with fat, which once congealed makes an almost completely airtight cover.

The basic methods of preserving food, i.e., canning, freezing, salting and dehydrating are still in use, but modern methods have revolutionized the processes. The preservation of food in the home as well as in the factory is very important to the whole subject of food.

CANNING—Canning is a process of hermetically sealing food for future use. The process was invented in 1795 by a Frenchman, Nicholas Appert. In 1810 a patent was taken out in England for Appert's method and from there it quickly spread to America where lobsters and salmon were the first foods canned. In 1823 Thomas Kensett, an American, invented the tin can for packing all kinds of food, including meat, poultry, fish, vegetables and fruit. Glass containers, earthenware jars and tin cans are now all used in both commercial and home canning.

Canning is basically a process whereby the action of moulds, yeasts and bacteria that spoil fresh food is stopped by subjecting them to high heat long enough to stop the action. Most vegetables as well as poultry, meat and fish are home-processed in pressure canners under a 10 pound pressure at 240°F. (115°C.). Most fruits and tomatoes and pickled vegetables are processed in a boiling water bath. Several varieties of containers are used; all are equipped with covers or seals and directions to make the containers air-tight. With the advent of home freezers, canning of poultry, meat and fish is quite rare, but canning of vegetables and fruit is very common. Following are directions for the home canning of representative vegetables.

HOME CANNING OF VEGETABLES

Vegetable	*How to prepare*	*Process time (in minutes) at 10 pounds pressure*	
		Pint jars	*Quart jars*
ASPARAGUS.	Wash, remove scales. Cut into pieces 1 inch long. Mix buds with stalk pieces (or use whole stalks). Pack into jars. Pack tightly without crushing. Add hot water, leaving ½ inch headspace. Add salt, ½ teaspoon to a pint, 1 teaspoon to a quart. Adjust lids. Process.	25	35
GREEN BEANS, FRENCH STRING BEANS.	Wash. Snip off ends. Cut into 1-inch lengths. Wash again. Pack tightly, without crushing, into jars. Add hot water, leaving ½ inch headspace. Add salt, ½ teaspoon to a pint, 1 teaspoon to a quart. Adjust lids. Process.	20	25
SHELL OR LIMA, HARICOT BEANS.	Shell. Blanch in hot water for 3 to 5 minutes, depending on maturity. Cool. Pack into jars to within 1 inch of top. Add hot water, leaving ½ inch headspace. Add salt, ½ teaspoon to a pint, 1 teaspoon to a quart. Adjust lids. Process.	35	45
BEETS, BEETROOTS.	Cut off tops, leaving 1 inch of stem and all of roots. Wash. Cover with boiling water. Boil until skins slip off easily. Skin and trim. Cut large beets into slices or quarters. Pack tightly without crushing into jars. Add hot water, leaving ½ inch headspace. Add salt, ½ teaspoon to a pint, 1 teaspoon to a quart. Adjust lids. Process.	25	35
CARROTS.	Wash carrots thoroughly. Slice or leave whole, depending on maturity. Add hot water, leaving ½ inch headspace. Add salt, ½ teaspoon to a pint, 1 teaspoon to a quart. Adjust lids. Process.	20	25
CORN Cream style.	Husk, remove silk, and clean carefully. Blanch 5 minutes in boiling water. Cool. Cut from cob at about centre of kernel with sharp knife. Scrape cob with knife. To each quart of corn add 1 pint boiling water. Bring to a boil. Pack hot into pint jars. DO NOT USE QUARTS. Fill, leaving 1 inch headspace. Add ½ teaspoon salt. Adjust lids. Process.	85	—
CORN Whole kernel.	Husk, remove silk, and clean carefully. Cut from cob to get most of kernels, but not deep enough to cut into cob. Pack loosely into jars. Fill to within 1 inch of top. Add boiling water, leaving 1 inch headspace. Add salt, ½ teaspoon to a pint, 1 teaspoon to a quart. Adjust lids. Process.	55	65
GREENS (Spinach, Chard, Beet tops, Dandelions).	Select tender, young leaves from freshly picked greens. Cut off roots, discard wilted leaves and tough stems. Wash thoroughly in two or more changes of water. Lift greens from water with a fork. (Do not pour water off.) Heat until greens are wilted, using just enough water to prevent sticking. Pack hot and loosely into jars, cutting through the pack several times with a sharp knife, to loosen. Fill jars with hot water or with blanching liquid, leaving ½ inch headspace. Add salt, ½ teaspoon to a pint, 1 teaspoon to a quart. Adjust lids. Process.	70	100
PEAS (Green).	Shell and wash peas. Cover with boiling water and bring to boil. Pack hot into jars. Fill with hot water. Leave 1 inch headspace. Add salt, ½ teaspoon to a pint, 1 teaspoon to a quart. Adjust lids. Process.	35	40
PEPPERS.	Wash. Cut out stem end. Remove seeds and cell walls. Blanch for 3 minutes in boiling water until soft and flexible. Fold and pack closely, filling jars. Add hot water, leaving ½ inch headspace. Add salt, ½ teaspoon to a pint, 1 teaspoon to a quart. Add 1 tablespoon of vinegar to a pint, 2 tablespoons to a quart. Adjust lids. Process.	35	40

HOME CANNING OF VEGETABLES – *continued*

Vegetable	*How to prepare*	*Process time (in minutes) at 10 pounds pressure*	
		Pint jars	*Quart jars*
POTATOES, White.	Wash, peel, and trim. Cut large potatoes into ½ to 1 inch cubes. Leave small ones whole. Place potatoes in weak brine —3 tablespoons salt to 4 quarts water—until ready to pack. Blanch 5 minutes in boiling water. Rinse and pack closely into jars. Add hot water, leaving ½ inch headspace. Add salt, ½ teaspoon to a pint, 1 teaspoon to a quart. Adjust lids. Process.	30	40
VEGETABLE MARROWS, Zucchini, Summer squash.	Wash. Cut into size desired. Blanch 1 minute in hot water. Pack loosely into jars. Add hot water used for blanching, leaving ½ inch headspace. Add salt, ½ teaspoon to a pint, 1 teaspoon to a quart. Adjust lids. Process.	30	40
SQUASH, Winter or Pumpkin, strained.	Wash. Remove seeds, cut up. Steam or bake until soft. Scrape pulp from shell. Mix to a thick paste with water. Pack into jars, leaving ½ inch headspace. Add salt, ½ teaspoon to a pint, 1 teaspoon to a quart. Adjust lids. Process.	70	90
SQUASH, Cubed.	Wash. Remove seeds, cut up, and peel. Cut into ½ to 1 inch cubes. Add just enough water to cover, and bring to a boil. Pack hot into jars. Add hot water, leaving ½ inch headspace. Add salt, ½ teaspoon to a pint, 1 teaspoon to a quart. Adjust lids. Process.	55	75

Home canning of fruit and tomatoes—Most fruits are canned in syrup of varying degrees of sweetness. A *Light syrup* contains 3 cups of water and 1 cup of sugar; a *Medium syrup* contains 2 cups of water and 1 cup of sugar; a *Heavy syrup* contains 1 cup of sugar and 1 cup of water. Once the containers are packed and the lids adjusted the fruit or tomatoes are processed in a boiling water bath (212°F., 100°C.), the length of time depending on the fruit. Following is a table of representative fruits and directions for processing tomatoes.

HOME CANNING OF FRUIT AND TOMATOES

Fruit	*How to prepare*	*Process time (in minutes) for boiling water bath (212°F.)*	
		Pint jars	*Quart jars*
APPLES.	Wash. Peel and core. Cut into sizes desired. To prevent darkening, drop into gallon of water containing 2 tablespoons salt and 2 tablespoons vinegar. Drain. Cook in light syrup 5 minutes. Pack hot into jars. Cover with boiling syrup. Adjust lids. Process.	20	25
	For applesauce: Wash, quarter, and core apples. Add a little water and cook until soft. Put through food mill or sieve to remove skins. Sweeten to taste. Reheat to boiling. Pack hot into jars. Adjust lids. Process.	10	10
BLUEBERRIES Hot pack.	Pick over and wash carefully. Blanch by putting approximately 2 quarts of berries into a square of cheesecloth formed into a bag and dipping them in boiling water 15 to 30 seconds. Spots of juice on cloth indicate finish point. Cool. Pack into jars as tightly as possible. Adjust lids. Process. *Note.* This method results in a better-looking pack with less liquid.	15	20
Cold pack.	Pick over and wash fruit carefully. Pack, without crushing, into clean jars. Fill with medium syrup, leaving headspace. Adjust lids. Process.	15	20

HOME CANNING OF FRUIT AND TOMATOES – *continued*

Fruit	*How to prepare*	*Process time (in minutes) for boiling water bath (212°F.)*	
		Pint jars	*Quart jars*
CHERRIES.	Stem and wash fruit. Remove pits (stones). Pack into jars, settling fruit by shaking jars. Fill with hot syrup, making sure no air remains in jar. Use heavy syrup for sour cherries, medium for sweet. Adjust lids. Process. *Note.* Cherries for pies and tarts may be canned without syrup—use only water.	15	20
PEACHES, NECTARINES, APRICOTS.	Wash. To peel, dip peaches in boiling water for a minute or two. Cool. Remove skin and cut in halves. Take out pits (stones). Slice if desired. Place peaches in gallon of water containing 2 tablespoons salt and 2 tablespoons vinegar. Drain. Pack tightly without crushing. If packing halves, cut pit cavity down. Fill with hot medium syrup and add ⅛ teaspoon of ascorbic acid per quart. Adjust lids. Process.	25	30
PEARS.	Peel, cut in halves, core. To prevent darkening, place in gallon of water containing 2 tablespoons salt and 2 tablespoons vinegar. Pack cold, core side down. Cover with medium syrup and add ⅛ teaspoon of ascorbic acid per quart. Adjust lids. Process.	25	30
RASPBERRIES, BLACKBERRIES.	Wash, drain and pick over berries. Pack carefully and tightly without crushing. Cover with hot medium syrup. Adjust lids. Process.	15	20
RHUBARB.	Wash rhubarb and cut into ½ inch pieces. Add ½ cup sugar to each quart and let stand several hours to draw out juice. Bring to a boil. Pack hot into jars. Cover with syrup. Adjust lids. Process.	10	10
STRAWBERRIES.	Wash and hull berries. Add ½ cup sugar to each quart of fruit. Bring slowly to a boil. Remove from fire and let stand overnight. Bring quickly to a boil. Pack hot into jars. Cover with boiling syrup. Adjust lids. Process.	15	20
TOMATOES AND TOMATO PRODUCTS Hot pack.	Select ripe, firm, uniform tomatoes. Wash to loosen skins. Dip into boiling water for 1 minute, then quickly dip into cold water. Cut out stem ends and peel. Cut up and bring to a boil. Cook until all are heated through, stirring frequently. Pack into jars, filling to top. Add salt, ½ teaspoon to a pint, 1 teaspoon to a quart. Adjust lids. Process in boiling water bath.	10	10
Cold pack.	Prepare tomatoes as above, but cut them into pieces convenient for passing into the jar. Pack the jar tightly, pressing down with fingers to press out ½ to 1 cup of juice per pint jar. Add salt, ½ teaspoon to a pint, 1 teaspoon to a quart. Adjust lids. Process.	35	45

CURING (Domestic)—The curing of meat is an ancient practice. Cato the Censor gives a recipe for the salting of ham which goes back to 200 B.C. In England, by the fourteenth century, it was indeed a sign of poverty to be without bacon. Until the middle of the nineteenth century bacon and ham could only be cured in the winter. Then, when a method of cooling curing cellars with ice was introduced, curing began to be carried out all the year round. Mechanical refrigeration, introduced in Britain in 1877, was the beginning of the modern curing industry, which revolutionized the whole approach.

The success of home curing largely depends on the extent to which unspecialised premises can be adapted for the purpose.

The ideal curing room should have a temperature of between 38° and 50°F., a free circulation of fresh cool air and a means of darkening, as light has a bad effect on the fat of the meat. Most cellars are even in temperature and, provided they are not too damp, are suitable for mild-curing salting.

For *drying* the best room is one which keeps a temperature of about 60°F., preferably with a current of air. The ceiling of a large kitchen at the point furthest away from the fire, or of a passage leading from the kitchen, is good for this purpose. Rooms in which there is a hot water tank may be used, if the meat is not placed too near the source of heat.

For storage the essentials are absence of light and steady though not necessarily low temperature. (Most attics are too hot in summer and subject to variations in temperature, which lead to condensation on the surface of the bacon or ham and in time produce slime and other evils. Cellars are often too damp and lack adequate air circulation.) A good larder or unheated ground-floor room facing north is best.

The equipment for home curing need not be elaborate but should include a boning knife, a carving knife, scales for weighing meat, a large basin or tub for brining head and trotters, a curing trough, shelf or floor, depending on the type of cure, and max/min thermometer.

For *dry salting* a stone or brick floor or slate shelf will be needed. If a 'box' cure is contemplated, a strong box with pieces of wood and weights; for *pickle curing*, tubs or barrels are suitable. It must be remembered that the meat will float in the pickle and boards with weights (large clean stones will do) must be provided as a cover.

For a combination of dry and pickle cures, a stone or lead trough is ideal, preferably with a plug hole for drawing off the liquor, but wooden troughs and basins may be used.

When the meat is being dried, meat hooks and strong twine will be needed and, for storage, greaseproof paper and clean muslin or calico.

Curing ingredients—The preservation of meat consists partly of drying the meat and partly of impregnating it with a sufficiently high concentration of salt and saltpetre (sometimes sugar as well).

Salt is the really essential ingredient in curing. Saltpetre is not a substance required for human nutrition and, except in small concentrations, could be regarded as an irritant or a weak poison, like many other preservatives. Common salt differs in being a necessary ingredient of the human diet, yet in high concentrations it can become an irritant or even a poison. Sugar has none of the objectionable qualities of the other preservatives and is supposed to help keep the meat soft by counteracting the hardening effects of saltpetre.

Curing ingredients also include vinegar (mostly acetic acid), pepper (the essential oil probably has a preservative effect), beer, wines and spirits (alcohol being the preserving agent) and wood smoke in which are found formaldehyde, alcohols, tars, creosote, etc.

Fruits, berries, spices, etc., have practically no preservative effect, apart from some of the acids or essential oils contained in them, and their main function is to add flavour to the cured product.

Cleansing—The first operation in treating a fresh cut is to cleanse it by dipping it for a short time in a strong brine. This has several advantages: it is rapid and allows the full cure to be carried out at once. It provides the wet salt surface which starts the penetration of salt into the meat without the laborious process of rubbing. This brine can be watered down after cleansing and used for the light pickling of small cuts or offal (variety meats).

The brine is prepared by dissolving 13 pounds of salt and 4 ounces of saltpetre in 5 gallons of boiling water. Mix thoroughly, strain through a cloth and cool to 50°F. or even lower before using.

The loin should be immersed for 10 minutes, until clean. The ham will require longer, about an hour, and while in the brine the large veins should be squeezed from the hock end to the fillet end. After cleansing, place the cut skin-side upwards to drain, but do not allow to dry.

Pickling—Dilute above quantity of brine by adding it to 1½ gallons of water. Stir well and use as a pickling brine for head, trotters, tongue, etc.

Salting—Weigh the meat and allow one-tenth of its weight of salt. The amount of saltpetre required is one-fortieth of the weight of salt. Thus for 10 pounds of meat to be cured, 1 pound of salt and 0.4 ounces of saltpetre will be needed.

Owing to the small amount of saltpetre the mixing should be very thorough. To ensure this, use dry, sieved salt. Divide it into three equal parts and add to each the appropriate amount of crushed and sieved saltpetre. Mix each pile of salt and saltpetre thoroughly and sift the mixture, but do not mix the three piles of curing mixture, as one will be used for rubbing in, one for sprinkling and the last for sprinkling at the time of rebedding.

Drain the cleansing brine from the cut and, using one-third of the curing mixture, rub thoroughly first on the skin side, forcing some of it down the shank of the ham, then rub the flesh side lightly.

Prepare a bed of salt about 2 inches thick and press down the cut or cuts into it, skin side down. Sprinkle lightly with a third of the curing mixture. Cover all the cuts entirely with 1 or 2 inches of salt, taking care to pack the salt tightly at the sides. (The meat tends to shrink and draw away from the salt, causing the surface to become dry and the salting uneven.)

After five days, break the pack, remove any discoloured salt and repack the cut, sprinkling as before with the remainder of the curing mixture.

The cuts should be kept in salt for varying periods, depending on their thickness (ham is usually kept in salt 6 to 7 days per 1 inch of thickness) and, in the case of several cuts being cured, care should be taken to repack the salt after each removal of meat.

Washing and maturation—Remove meat from the salt bed, wash the surface in cold water, or leave the ham or bacon in the room where it has been salted for a further period of 2 to 4 weeks, to enable the salt and saltpetre to go on penetrating, until enough curing mixture has been absorbed to prevent the growth of undesirable bacteria. During this period the maturation begins and continues through the subsequent operations of drying, smoking and storage. After this preliminary maturation, wash off excess salt from the surface of the ham, soaking it in a little cold water overnight, if necessary.

Drying—Hang the meat in a warm place with a temperature of about 60°F., not exceeding 70°F. As the drying proceeds, a white surface layer of crystalline salt appears, but if the washing has been thorough, this is not excessive. Where it is difficult to obtain dry storage conditions it is particularly important to remove this surface salt, as it attracts moisture.

Smoking—This should be considered as an alternative method of drying. In addition, however, smoking introduces preservatives and flavouring substances into the meat. Smoking should be carried out at a temperature below 90°F., otherwise the fat will melt, and it is essential to ensure that sufficient moisture has been removed from the bacon or ham.

Storage—This should be, as far as possible, in the dark, at a temperature of about 60°F., but it does no harm to store at temperatures down to 32°F., provided variations are avoided. Should the temperature of the meat surface at any time be below the dewpoint, a film of moisture will be deposited and the value of the drying process will be partly lost.

If bacon and hams can be kept under dry conditions, they may be hung up without any covering. Added protection is supplied by wrapping the meat in paper or cloth and surrounding with some substance which will take up moisture from the air, such as kiln-dried salt (so long as it does not come into actual contact with the meat), slaked lime, charcoal, wood ashes, malt culms, dried oat hulls or oat meal (provided it is free from mites). Cured meat may be stored by hanging up in clean linen or calico bags, lime washing the bags two or three times. (With acknowledgement to the Controller of Her Majesty's Stationery Office. Part of this article is taken from *Bulletin No. 127* of the Ministry of Agriculture and Fisheries.)

DEHYDRATION—Evaporation of water from foods is another time-honoured technique which has a modern development, but except in time of war when dehydrated foods are used extensively because of the small shipping space they take, foods processed by canning or freezing are much more acceptable both for reasons of flavour and of keeping qualities. Comparatively few dehydrated foods are sold extensively. Exceptions to this are dried fruits (raisins, prunes, apricots, peaches, pears, etc.), milk (dried to a soluble powder which is used for reconstituted milk in liquid form and for cake and bread 'mixes') and potatoes. Dried whole eggs can be successfully used and egg whites can be dried and used for meringues and icings.

FREEZING—Frozen foods when properly processed resemble the fresh variety more closely than foods preserved by any other method, although no preserved food can claim equality with absolutely fresh food. Freezing in ice is an ancient practice, but the modern method of quick freezing plays a major role in gastronomy in both commercial and domestic areas. To have complete success, food must be used when at its peak, packaged so as to exclude all air and frozen as quickly and as thoroughly as possible. Such food is stored at 0°F. (—18°C.) and is usually cooked before thawing.

Home freezers are used for storage of commercially frozen products, produce of the garden, orchard or farm, breads, pies, cakes and ice creams, dairy products and pre-cooked meat and vegetable dishes. Well planned use of a home freezer is a great boon to the modern housewife. Home freezers are in widespread use in the U.S.A. and are becoming increasingly popular in England and in France. Most frozen foods should be consumed within one year of being processed. Some foods do not retain their good quality that long. The following should not be stored in a freezer longer than four months: ham, bacon, duck, goose, rich fish (salmon, turbot, haddock, cod, etc.), offal (variety meats) or sausage.

Meat, poultry, fish, and game—Properly aged and trimmed cuts of meat are packed in heavy 'freezer' paper. Pork should be used within 4 months but other meats (beef, veal and lamb) may be kept a year. If the package is neither heavy nor tight enough, freezer 'burn' will develop.

Poultry—Chicken, ducks, wild game and rabbits to be cooked whole should be cleaned and trussed before freezing. Giblets are wrapped in freezer paper and stored in the body cavity. Small birds and fowl may be cut up (jointed) and wrapped in small packages.

Fish—Fish should be chilled, cleaned and washed before freezing. Small fish are frozen whole; large fish are cut into steaks or filleted. It is important to freeze fish as soon after it is caught as possible.

Vegetables—Some vegetables freeze more successfully than others. All vegetables must be blanched by boiling water or steam before freezing. Following is a representative list of vegetables with instructions for home processing and freezing. The vegetables are packed in airtight containers of plastic, pliofilm or specially treated paper.

HOME FREEZING OF VEGETABLES

Vegetables	*Preparation*	*Blanching time in boiling water*	*Processing*
ASPARAGUS.	Select young, tender stalks. Sort according to thickness of stalk. Wash and discard tough sections. Leave in lengths to fit package or cut into pieces.	Small stalks, 2 minutes; medium, 3 minutes; large, 4 minutes.	Blanch, cool, drain and pack. When packing, spear alternate tips and stem ends.
LIMA BEANS, HARICOT BEANS, KIDNEY BEANS.	Select well-filled pods. Beans should be ripe but not starchy or mealy. Shell, wash and sort according to size.	Small, 2 minutes; medium, 3 minutes; large, 4 minutes.	Blanch and cool. Pack into containers, seal and freeze.
FRENCH (STRING) BEANS.	Select young, tender beans, wash, cut off stem and tips. Leave whole, slice or cut into pieces.	3 minutes.	Blanch, cool and drain. Pack, seal and freeze.
BEETS.	Select beets not more than 3 inches across. Wash and sort according to size. Trim tops, leaving ½ inch of stems. Cook in boiling water until tender—small beets 25 to 30 minutes, medium size 45 to 50 minutes. Cool, peel, cut into slices or cubes.	—	Pack, seal and freeze.
BROCCOLI.	Select tight, compact, dark-green heads with tender stalks. Wash, peel stalks and trim. To remove insects, soak for ½ hour in a solution made of 4 teaspoons salt to 1 gallon cold water. Split lengthwise so heads are not more than 1½ inches across.	3 minutes.	Blanch, cool and drain. Pack leaving no head-space. Seal and freeze.

HOME FREEZING OF VEGETABLES – *continued*

Vegetables	*Preparation*	*Blanching time in boiling water*	*Processing*
CARROTS.	Select tender carrots. Remove tops, wash and peel. Leave small carrots whole. Cut others into ¼ inch cubes, thin slices or strips.	Whole carrots (small), 5 minutes; diced or sliced, 2 minutes; strips, 2 minutes.	Blanch, cool and drain. Pack, seal and freeze.
CAULIFLOWER.	Select firm, tender, snow-white heads. Break or cut into pieces about 1 inch across. Wash well. If necessary to remove insects, soak for 30 minutes in a solution made of 4 teaspoons salt to 1 gallon cold water. Drain.	3 minutes.	Blanch, cool and drain. Pack leaving no head-space. Seal and freeze.
CORN (Maize).	*Whole kernel and cream style:* Select ears with plump, tender kernels and thin, sweet milk. More mature corn should be frozen cream style. Husk ears, remove silk and wash. Blanch, cool and drain. Whole kernel—cut kernels from cob at about two-thirds the depth of the kernels. Cream style—cut kernels from cob at half the kernel depth, scrape cobs with back of knife to remove juice and heart of kernel.	5 minutes.	Pack, seal and freeze.
	On the cob: Husk, remove silk, wash, and sort according to size.	Small ears, 7 minutes; medium, 9 minutes; large, 11 minutes; Seal.	Blanch, cool thoroughly and drain. Pack ears in containers or wrap in moisture vapour-resistant material. Seal and freeze.
GREENS.	Select tender leaves. Wash well. Remove tough stems and imperfect leaves.	Beet greens, Kale, Chard, Mustard greens, Turnip greens, 2 minutes; Collards, 3 minutes; Spinach, 1½ minutes.	Blanch, cool thoroughly and drain. Pack, seal and freeze.
MUSHROOMS.	Wash and trim. Soak 5 minutes in 2 cups water with 1 teaspoon lemon.	Steam 3 minutes for small or sliced mush-rooms, 5 minutes for whole.	Cool, pack, seal and freeze.
OKRA (Ladies' fingers).	Select young tender green pods. Wash thoroughly. Cut off stems.	Small pods 3 minutes; large pods 4 minutes.	Blanch, cool and drain. Leave whole or slice cross-wise. Pack, seal and freeze.
PEAS.	Select plump, firm pods with sweet, tender peas. Shell and sort out tough or im-mature peas.	1½ minutes.	Blanch, cool and drain. Pack, seal and freeze.
PEPPERS Green and hot).	*Green peppers:* Peppers frozen without heating are best for use in uncooked foods. Blanched peppers are easier to pack and good for use in cooking. Select firm, crisp, thick-walled peppers. Wash, cut out stems, cut in half and remove seeds. If desired, cut in strips or rings.	Halves, 3 minutes; slices, 2 minutes.	Blanch, cool and drain. *Unblanched* peppers — pack, leaving no head-space. Seal and freeze. *Blanched* peppers—pack leaving ½ inch headspace.
	Red peppers: Wash and stem peppers.	Halves, 3 minutes; slices, 2 minutes.	Pack into small contain-ers, leaving no headspace. Seal and freeze.
PUMPKIN.	Select full-coloured, mature pumpkin. Wash, cut into quarters or smaller pieces and remove seeds. Cook pieces until soft. Remove pulp from rind and mash it or press it through a sieve.		Cool, pack, seal and freeze.
SQUASH, WINTER.	Select firm, mature squash. Wash, cut in pieces and remove seeds. Cook pieces until soft. Remove pulp from rind and mash or press through sieve. Cool.		Pack, leaving ½ inch head-space. Seal and freeze.

HOME FREEZING OF VEGETABLES – *continued*

Vegetables	*Preparation*	*Blanching time in boiling water*	*Processing*
TOMATO JUICE.	Wash, sort and trim, and cut up the tomatoes. Simmer for 5 to 10 minutes. Press through a sieve. If desired, add 1 teaspoon salt to each quart of juice for seasoning.		Fill containers, seal and freeze.

Fruits—Some fruits such as apples, apricots and peaches darken when frozen. To prevent this the fruit is packed in a sugar syrup and a little ascorbic acid (Vitamin C) is added. Following is a representative list of fruits that can be frozen. A 40 per cent syrup contains 3 cups of sugar and 4 cups of water. A 50 per cent syrup contains 4¾ cups sugar and 4 cups of water. A 60 per cent syrup contains 7 cups of sugar and 4 cups of water. Containers are pint or quart containers of glass, treated paper or plastic.

HOME FREEZING OF FRUITS

Fruits	*Preparation*	*Processing*
APPLES.	Select crisp, firm apples. Wash, peel and core. Slice medium apples into twelfths, large-sized into sixteenths. Use 40 per cent syrup (3 cups sugar, 7 cups water). For a better quality product add ½ teaspoon (1000 milligrams) ascorbic acid to each quart of syrup. Slice apples into ½ cup syrup in container.	Pack well and cover with syrup. Leave headspace, seal and freeze.
APPLESAUCE.	Select full-flavoured apples. Wash, peel if desired, core and slice. Add ½ cup of water to each quart of apples. Cook until tender. Cool and strain. Sweeten to taste with ¼ to ¾ cup of sugar for each quart of sauce.	Pack into containers, leave headspace, seal and freeze.
APRICOTS.	Select firm, ripe, uniformly-coloured fruit. Sort, wash, halve and pit (stone). Peel and slice if desired. If not peeled, heat in boiling water ½ minute to keep skins from toughening during freezing. Cool and drain. Use 40 per cent syrup. To keep from darkening, add ¾ teaspoon (1500 milligrams) ascorbic acid to each quart of syrup.	Pack, cover with syrup, leave headspace. Seal and freeze.
	Crushed or Purée: Use fully-ripe fruit. For crushed apricots, heat in boiling water ½ minute, cool and peel. Pit (stone) and crush. For purée, pit (stone), quarter and press through a sieve; or heat apricots in small amount of water and press through sieve. With each quart of prepared apricots mix 1 cup of sugar. Add ¼ teaspoon (500 milligrams) ascorbic acid dissolved in ½ cup water to fruit before adding sugar.	Pack, leaving headspace. Seal and freeze.
BERRIES (except blueberries and strawberries).	Select firm, fully ripe juicy berries. Sort, wash and drain well. Do not wash raspberries unless necessary.	Pack berries into containers and cover with 40 per cent or 50 per cent syrup, depending on sweetness of fruit. Leave headspace. Seal and freeze.
BLUEBERRIES	Select full-flavoured, ripe berries. Sort, wash and drain. If desired, steam for 1 minute and cool immediately. Preheating in steam aids in tenderizing the skin.	Pack berries into containers and cover with cold 40 per cent syrup. Leave headspace. Seal and freeze.
CHERRIES (Sour).	Select bright red, tree-ripened cherries. Stem, sort and wash. Drain and pit (stone).	Pack cherries into containers and cover with cold 60 per cent syrup. Leave headspace. Seal and freeze.
CRANBERRIES.	Select firm, deep-red berries with glossy skins. Stem and sort. Wash and drain.	Pack berries into containers. Leave headspace. Seal and freeze.

HOME FREEZING OF FRUITS – *continued*

Fruits	*Preparation*	*Processing*
PEACHES AND NECTARINES.	Select firm, ripe, well-coloured fruit. Wash, pit (stone) and peel. Cut into halves, quarters or slices. Use 40 per cent syrup. To prevent darkening, add ½ teaspoon ascorbic acid (1000 milligrams) for each quart of syrup. Place fruit in cold syrup in container—starting with ½ cup syrup to a pint container. Press fruit down and add syrup to cover, leaving headspace.	Seal and freeze.
PLUMS AND PRUNES.	Select firm, tree-ripened fruit. Wash. Leave whole, cut in halves or in quarters. Pack cut fruit into containers. Cover fruit with cold 40 per cent or 50 per cent syrup depending on tartness of fruit. For improved quality, add ½ teaspoon (1000 milligrams) ascorbic acid to a quart of syrup.	Leave headspace. Seal and freeze.
RHUBARB.	Select firm, tender, well-coloured stalks with good flavour and few fibres. Wash, trim and cut into 1 or 2 inch pieces or in lengths to fit the package. Heating in boiling water for 1 minute and cooling promptly helps retain colour and flavour.	Pack either raw or pre-heated rhubarb into containers, and cover with cold 40 per cent syrup. Leave headspace. Seal and freeze.

PRESS. PRESSE—Culinary instrument serving to extract by pressure fruit juice or the juice from the carcase of a fowl or of a piece of cooked meat.

According to their use (juice press, lemon squeezer, etc.) these presses take various forms.

PRESS. FOULER—Passing a purée or some other substance through a strainer while pressing on the food with a large wooden spoon.

PRESSED BEEF—See BEEF, *Pressed beef.*

PRESSURE COOKER. MARMITE À PRESSION—A hermetically sealed cooking pan with a lid. In this type of saucepan the pressure forces the temperature up to as much as 130°C. (266°F.) whereas, in an ordinary saucepan, it cannot rise above 100°C. (212°F.). The cooking of meat and vegetables can be speeded up considerably by this means.

PRÊTRE—Small regional sea fish of France, about the size of a smelt, about 4 to 7 inches long, with a silvery star-shaped mark on its sides. Its flesh is quite delicate.

PRETZEL—German and Alsatian savoury biscuit, baked in the shape of a loose knot, hard, sprinkled with salt and cumin seeds. Pretzels are served with beer.

Prepare separately the paste and the liquid for cooking the pretzels.

(1) *Paste.* Allow 1 cup (¼ litre) of water for 3½ cups (500 grams) of flour, ⅔ ounce (20 grams) of yeast, 2½ teaspoons (15 grams) of salt and 4 teaspoons (10 grams) of caraway seed. Make a stiff paste and knead it well. Leave to rise for half an hour in a warm place, covered with a cloth.

(2) *Liquid.* 2 cups (½ litre) of water, 2 teaspoons (30 grams) of bicarbonate of soda, 1¼ teaspoons (5 grams) of carbonate of ammonia.

Shape the paste into pretzels and plunge them into the boiling liquid. They will fall to the bottom of the pan. When they rise to the surface, take them out, put on a baking sheet, sprinkle with coarse sea salt and bake in the oven. They should be brushed with beaten egg and sprinkled with cumin seeds.

PRICKLY PEAR. FIGUIER DE BARBARIE—A cactus with edible fruit, which is generally eaten raw but can be stewed.

PRIMEUR—Fruit, vegetable or any other foodstuff obtained before the normal season of its maturity.

PRIMROSE. PRIMAVÈRE—Fresh leaves of this plant can be eaten in salad; the flowers serve to decorate the salad.

PRINCE ALBERT—See GARNISHES.

PRINCESSE (A LA)—Name used for various preparations, in ordinary cookery and pastry-making.

The garnish known as *Princesse*, composed of green asparagus tips and truffles, is chiefly used to accompany *Suprêmes of chicken.* See CHICKEN.

PRINTANIER. PRINTANIÈRE—A mixture of vegetables, scooped out in the shape of little balls with a special vegetable baller or cut into dice or lozenges, cooked separately in water and dressed with butter.

The term *à la printanière* is applied to various dishes, but mainly to meat entrées garnished with early or mixed vegetables.

Profiteroles

PROFITEROLE (Pastry)—Little balls of *chou paste* (see DOUGH) piped through a forcing (pastry) bag.

These little éclairs may, after cooking, be filled with various substances: game or other purée, cheese mixtures, etc.; or with sweet custards, jams, etc.

Profiteroles, filled with vanilla custard and iced with caramelised syrup, are used for making *Croquembouches* and *Gâteaux St. Honoré*.

Profiteroles with a savoury filling are used to garnish soup.

Profiteroles are usually forced through a forcing (pastry) bag with a plain round nozzle on to a baking tin. They are brushed with egg and baked in a moderate oven.

Garnish the *profiteroles* with *French pastry cream* (see CREAM) or sweetened whipped cream. Arrange in a pyramid on a dessert platter and pour over *Chocolate sauce*. See SAUCE.

PROVENÇALE (A LA)—Describes certain preparations characterised by the use of tomato and garlic mixed, and sometimes of garlic alone.

tiny fish fry, with *nonats* (a minute Mediterranean fish), in the region of Nice; *Pistou*, which contains French (string) beans, potatoes, tomatoes and vermicelli, and is finished with an *aillade* of basil and grated cheese.

Fish: *Bouillabaisse; Bourride*, a kind of *bouillabaisse* made with white fish, without saffron seasoning. Part of the soup serves to soak slices of bread put in a dish; the rest, with 2 tablespoons of *aïoli* and an egg yolk per person, is used to prepare a sauce which is poured over the slices of bread.

Fish is eaten with *aïoli*, a kind of mayonnaise made with garlic purée, allowing, per person, 5 large cloves of garlic (10 grams), an egg yolk, salt, ½ cup (1 decilitre) of oil and a little lemon juice. This sauce is really only the accompaniment of the *aïoli* (a Marseilles dish com-

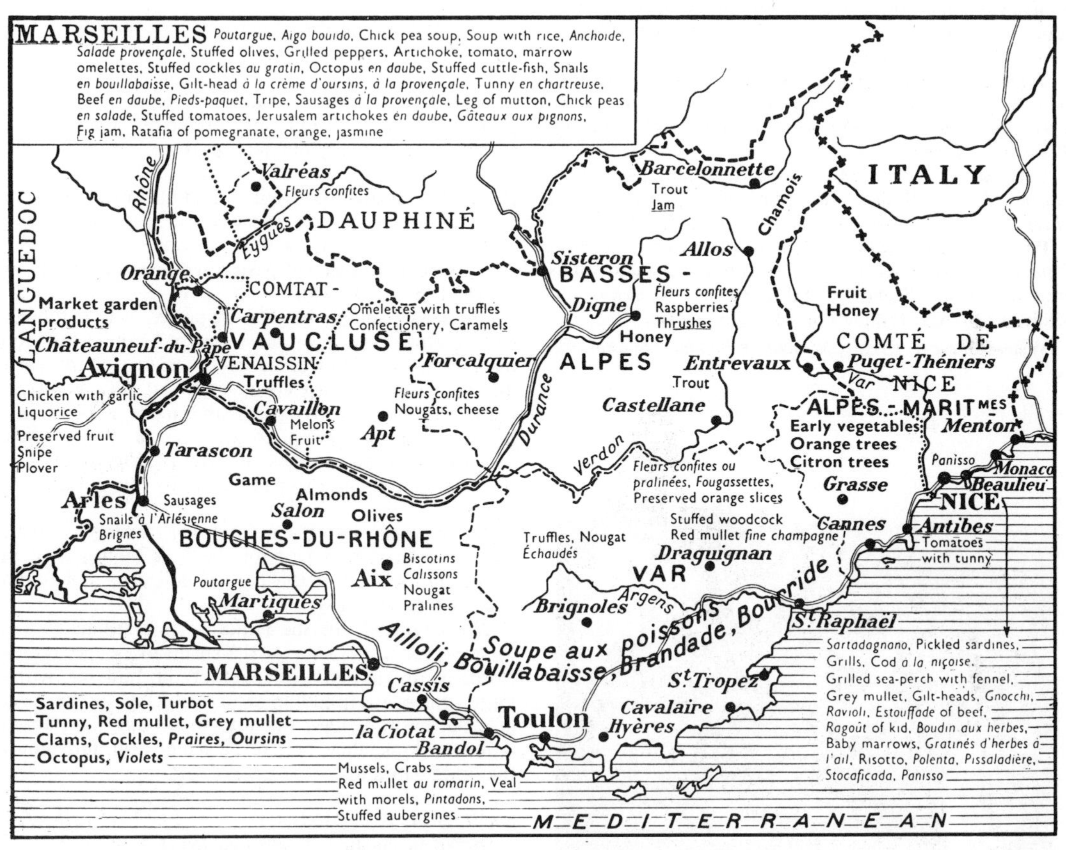

Gastronomic map of Provence

PROVENCE, COMTÉ DE NICE—Provence! Word evocative of sunshine, of exuberance, of the joy of good living, which can be extended to include the region of Nice, a part of France rich in culinary specialities.

Garlic is the base of almost all the Provençal dishes, but it must be remembered that the Midi garlic has not such a strong taste or such a bitter flavour as that of the northern districts.

So long is the list of Provençal dishes that we can only indicate briefly how they are made up.

Principal Provençal soups: *Garlic; Aïgo-sacu* (a kind of *bouillabaisse* with white fish, the fish used being eaten with *aïoli* or other sauce); *Conger*; *Aigo-bouido* with poached eggs; *Mariage*, a very thick soup made of beef, mutton or chicken stock and rice, with *poutine* made of

prising boiled salt cod, snails, carrots, French (string) beans and potatoes).

Dried salt cod en rayte; Grilled red mullet with fennel; Sartadagnano (a macédoine of little fish cooked in oil in the frying pan, pressed together in cooking so that they can be turned like a pancake, sprinkled with hot vinegar on the plate).

Stockfish, belonging more particularly to the region of Nice, is dried salt cod, hard as wood, and needing long soaking before use; a sort of stew the ingredients of which, along with the stockfish, include intestines, onions and leeks, garlic, sweet pimentos, aromatic plants, potatoes and black olives (*stocaficada*).

Esquinado of Toulon, crabs cooked in vinegar and water, dressed and mixed with an equivalent quantity of mussels; then the crab shells are refilled with the mixture. sprinkled with breadcrumbs and browned.

The *Poutine* and the *Melet* are used to prepare savoury purées, such as *Pissalat*, *Tapenade*, etc. The *Pissaladiére*, a speciality of Nice, is a sort of open tart of ordinary pastry or bread dough filled with chopped onions cooked in oil, covered with fillets of anchovy and black olives.

Pan bagna is a slice of bread moistened with olive oil and covered with anchovy fillets, thin slices of tomato and capers.

Panisso is a porridge of chick-peas or corn meal cooled in very small saucers and fried in oil. It is eaten sprinkled with sugar.

Meat: *Beef en daube; Leg of mutton Avignonnaise; Pieds paquets* of the Pomme district; *Gayettes* (sort of sausages made of pig's liver); *Sou-fassum*, a kind of stuffed cabbage cooked in an ordinary pot-au-feu or with mutton, a speciality of the Grasse-Antibes region; *Liver à la moissonneuse.*

Vegetables and cereals: *Stuffed marrow (squash) flowers; Swiss chard au gratin; Tart of soft fruits in the Nice style; Stuffed baby marrows (zucchini); Ravioli, Cannelloni, Capelletti.*

Cheeses: *Strong cheese* of Mont-Ventoux; *goats' milk cheese* of the Alpilles, the Maures and the Esterel; *sheeps' milk cheese* of Banon, Brousse, Valdebleou.

Pastry and Specialities: *Gâteaux—Gibassier, Fougasse, Pompe* (this last particularly for Réveillon, the Christmas morning feast); *Bugnes* of Arles, *Biscuits (cookies)* and *Calissons* of Aix, *Praline flowers* from Grasse.

Wines: *Blanc de Cassis, Muscat de Bandols, Roquevaire.*

Puyrémas, Vaucluse (*French Government Tourist Office*)

PRUNE. PRUNEAU—A red or purple plum, dried in the sun or in the oven, after which treatment it will keep for a long time in a perfect state. Most plums can be dried, but particularly the plum of Ente, or Agen, the Large Damson of Tours, the Catherine plum and the Imperial.

The Perdrigon plum, when it has been peeled, stoned, dried in the sun and flattened, is commercially known under the name of *Pistole*. The same plum, unpeeled, unstoned, scalded, then dried in the shade, is called a *Brignole* or *Pruneau fleuri.*

In France the most renowned prunes are those of Agen and of Touraine.

At the present day excellent Californian prunes are to be found. Their flesh, however, is less delicate than that of French prunes.

Prunes are most often cooked in a *compote*. Cooked and stoned prunes are used for the preparation of various sweets, such as cakes, puddings, soufflés, tarts, etc.

Compote of prunes (Stewed prunes). COMPOTE DE PRUNEAUX—Soak the prunes in cold water. When they have swollen sufficiently, drain them. Put them in a saucepan, cover with cold water. Add ½ cup (125 grams) of sugar for 1 pound (500 grams) of fruit. Flavour with lemon or orange rind, vanilla or cinnamon.

Cook gently for about an hour.

Compote of prunes with red or white wine. COMPOTE DE PRUNES AU VIN ROUGE, BLANC—The same as above, substituting red or white wine for water.

Prune tart and tartlets—See TARTS AND TARTLETS.

PUCHERO (Spanish cookery)—A sort of stew made of different kinds of meat and vegetables.

PUDDING. POUDING—Name given to numerous dishes, both sweet and savoury, served hot or cold, which are made up in many different ways.

BOILED PUDDING—Boiled pudding can be served either as an entrée or a sweet course (dessert).

It is made by putting some savoury or sweet filling into a rolled-out piece of pastry, wrapped in a cloth and poached in boiling water.

Grease a pudding basin with butter, before filling it with mixture. The basin must always be quite full, so if the mixture does not come up to the top of the basin, fill the basin up with crusts of bread. Tie a scalded, floured cloth over the basin and make a pleat in it before tying with string, to give the pudding room to rise. Tie the corners of the cloth over the top of the basin; this enables the basin to be lifted easily in and out of the water.

Put the basin into a pan containing enough water to cover the basin and boil for the time indicated in the recipe. Do not allow the pan to boil dry; add boiling water when necessary.

When cooked, lift the pudding from the pan, allow to stand for a moment for the steam to escape, remove cloth, gently loosen the edges of the pudding with a knife, unless the pudding is to be served in the basin, give the basin a slight shake to make sure the pudding is not sticking, then reverse on a hot dish and remove the basin carefully.

SAVOURY PUDDINGS—

Beefsteak pudding (English cookery)—

Suet pastry for the pudding. Mix 2 pounds (1 kilo) of sieved flour with 1¼ pounds (600 grams) of suet (having first removed the skin and strings from the suet and shredded it finely), a good pinch of salt and about 1 cup (2 decilitres) of water. The mixture should be a smooth and soft dough.

Preparation of the pudding. Using two-thirds of the pastry line a buttered pudding basin or a round-bottomed mould. In this pastry lined basin arrange in layers 3 pounds (1½ kilo) of beef, cut in slices a little less than ½ inch (one centimetre) thick, season with salt, pepper and grated nutmeg and sprinkled with chopped onion and parsley. Moisten with water in sufficient quantity to cover the meat. Roll out the rest of the pastry, cover the pudding and seal the edges.

Cooking of the pudding. Tie a scalded, floured cloth over the top, not forgetting to make a pleat in the cloth to allow the pudding to rise, and put to cook in a pan of boiling water, for 3 hours if fillet of beef is used, for 4 hours if the meat is taken from some other part of the animal. Keep the water boiling constantly, adding more boiling water if necessary.

Beefsteak and kidney pudding (English cookery)—This is made like *Beefsteak pudding*, using slices of beef and beef kidney.

Beefsteak and oyster pudding (English cookery)—This is prepared in the same way as *Beefsteak pudding*, adding uncooked oysters to the filling.

Chicken puddings à la Richelieu. BOUDINS DE VOLAILLE À LA RICHELIEU—Line small, oval or rectangular, well-buttered moulds with *Fine chicken forcemeat* (see FORCEMEAT). Fill these moulds with a *salpicon** of breast of chicken, truffles and mushrooms, blended with very thick *Allemande sauce* (see SAUCE). Cover with another layer of chicken forcemeat, which should be well smoothed over with the blade of a knife dipped in cold water.

Poach these *quenelles* (for these 'boudins' are no more than stuffed *quenelles*) in the oven, placing the moulds in a pan of hot water. Turn out of the moulds, dry, dip in egg and breadcrumbs and fry until light golden in clarified butter.

Arrange the little puddings in a circle on a round napkin-covered dish, packing them in fairly tightly. Garnish the middle of the dish with fried parsley. Serve *Périgueux sauce* or *Suprême sauce* with diced truffles added to it. See SAUCE.

Chicken puddings can also be prepared in the following manner: Roll the chicken forcemeat, which should be of a fairly firm consistency, into little cylinders. Poach them. Slit open these large *quenelles* on one side, stuff with the *salpicon** indicated and close the opening. Dip in egg and breadcrumbs and fry in clarified butter.

Game pudding (stuffed). BOUDINS DE GIBIERS—Prepare, using various game *forcemeat** and suitable *salpicon**, as described in the recipe for *Chicken puddings à la Richelieu.*

Mutton pudding (English cookery). POUDING DE MOUTON—Proceed as for *Beefsteak pudding.*

SWEET (DESSERT) PUDDINGS—

English almond pudding. POUDING AUX AMANDES À L'ANGLAISE—Cream together ½ cup (125 grams) of butter and ⅝ cup (150 grams) of sugar in a basin. Add 1½ cups (250 grams) of almonds, blanched and chopped finely. Season with a pinch of salt. Add a teaspoon of orange flower water or ½ teaspoon orange extract, 2 whole eggs and 2 yolks and 4 tablespoons of thick fresh cream. Blend well.

Pour into a pudding basin. Cook in a *bain-marie* (pan of hot water) in a slow oven, and serve in the same dish.

American pudding. POUDING À L'AMÉRICAINE—Put in a basin 1¾ cups (75 grams) of breadcrumbs, ¾ cup (100 grams) of unsifted flour, ⅝ cup (100 grams) brown sugar and 2½ ounces (75 grams) of chopped beef marrow. Add 3½ ounces (100 grams) of crystallized fruits cut in dice and a little finely shredded orange and lemon peel.

Bind with one whole egg and 3 yolks; add a little cinnamon and grated nutmeg and a small glass of rum or brandy. Mix well.

Pour the mixture into a buttered, floured mould. Cook in a *bain-marie* (pan of hot water). Serve rum flavoured *Zabaglione** separately.

English apple pudding. POUDING DE POMMES À L'ANGLAISE—Line a pudding basin with suet pastry (see DOUGH, *Dumpling dough*), rolled out to a thickness of ¼ inch.

Fill with cut up apples, adding sugar and a flavouring of grated lemon rind and powdered cinnamon. Put on top of the pudding a flat piece of pastry, joining it carefully at the edges. Wrap the basin in a cloth, tied very firmly, and put it into a saucepan of boiling water. Keep the water constantly boiling; cook for about two hours. Turn out on to a round dish.

Note. The pudding may be made in the same way with pears instead of apples.

Biscuit pudding or Lady finger pudding. POUDING DE BISCUITS—Put into a saucepan ½ pound (250 grams) of crumbled sponge finger biscuits and moisten with 2 cups (2 decilitres) of boiling milk sweetened with ¾ cup (150 grams) of sugar.

Put this mixture over the heat, stirring with a wooden spoon. Add 1¼ cups (150 grams) of currants and 5 ounces of crystallized fruits cut in dice, soaked in kirsch. Add 3 yolks of eggs and ½ cup (125 grams) of melted butter, and finally, 3 stiffly beaten egg whites.

Fill with this mixture a round mould which has been buttered and sprinkled with breadcrumbs.

Cook in the oven in a *bain-marie* (pan of hot water). Serve with *Apricot sauce* (see SAUCE), handed separately.

Brazilian pudding. POUDING BRÉSILIEN—Prepared with the same mixture as for *Tapioca pudding*. Put into a plain mould coated with caramel. Poach in a *bain-marie* (pan of hot water). Serve as it is, without sauce or any other accompaniment.

French bread pudding. POUDING AU PAIN À LA FRANÇAISE—Soak 4 cups (300 grams) of breadcrumbs in a quart (litre) of boiled milk with vanilla and ½ pound (250 grams) of sugar.

Put the mixture through a sieve. Add 4 whole eggs and 6 yolks. At the last moment fold in 4 stiffly beaten egg whites.

Fill with this mixture a plain mould buttered and sprinkled with fine breadcrumbs.

Cook in the oven in a *bain-marie* (pan of hot water). Let the pudding rest a few moments before turning it out of its mould. Set it on a round dish. Serve with *Custard sauce**, *Zabaglione**, or fruit sauce, separately or poured over the pudding.

German bread pudding. POUDING AU PAIN À L'ALLEMANDE—Soak 4 cups (300 grams) of breadcrumbs in a quart (litre) of Rhine wine or Moselle to which has been added 1¼ cups (200 grams) of brown sugar and a little cinnamon.

Put this mixture through a sieve; add 4 whole eggs, 6 yolks and 1⅛ cups (150 grams) of melted butter. Finally, incorporate 4 stiffly beaten egg whites.

Put the mixture in buttered moulds sprinkled with breadcrumbs. Cook in the oven in a *bain-marie* (pan of hot water).

Serve with fruit sauce flavoured with kirsch or any other liqueur.

German bread and fruit pudding. POUDING AU PAIN ET AUX FRUITS À L'ALLEMANDE—Put in a basin 3 cups (150 grams) of bread cut in small dice and fried in butter. Pour on this bread 1¼ cups (2½ decilitres) of boiled milk. Let it soak in well. Add 2 cooked apples cut in small dice, 1⅔ ounces (50 grams) of candied orange peel cut in small dice, ⅓ cup (50 grams) of ground almonds and the same quantity of raisins, stoned, put to swell in water and drained.

Add 5 tablespoons (75 grams) of sugar, a little grated lemon peel and 3 egg yolks. Mix all these ingredients

German bread and fruit pudding (*Claire*)

well together and finally add to them 3 stiffly beaten egg whites.

Fill with this mixture a buttered pudding basin. Cook in the oven in a *bain-marie* (pan of hot water) for 45 minutes.

Let the pudding rest before turning it out of its mould. Set it on a round dish. Coat it with a white wine sauce made with 1 cup (2 decilitres) of wine and 2 tablespoons of apricot jam.

Bread pudding with red wine. POUDING AU PAIN AU VIN ROUGE—Prepared in the same way as *German bread pudding* but replacing the white wine by red wine.

Cabinet pudding. POUDING DE CABINET—*Ingredients.* 5 ounces (150 grams) of sponge finger biscuits (lady fingers), 2 tablespoons of crystallized fruits cut into dice, 2 tablespoons of stoned and cleaned raisins, 2 cups (6 decilitres) of mixture for baked *Vanilla custard* (see CUSTARD), 1 large tablespoon (20 grams) of butter, a small glass of kirsch, a small glass of maraschino, 1⅓ cups (4 decilitres) of *Vanilla-flavoured custard cream.* See CREAM.

Method. Butter a plain cylindrical mould, and arrange in it alternate layers of the sponge fingers broken up and soaked in liqueur and the raisins also soaked in liqueur. Fill up the mould with the baked custard mixture prepared in the usual way. See CUSTARD.

Put the mould in a pan two-thirds full of hot water; cook in a *bain-marie** (pan of hot water) in the oven for 30 minutes.

Let the pudding rest a little before turning out of the mould. Serve on a round plate and pass *Custard cream* (see CREAM) separately.

Note. Cabinet puddings can be prepared with all sorts of flavours. They can be served with *Zabaglione** or different fruit sauces.

Chestnut soufflé pudding. POUDING SOUFFLÉ AUX MARRONS—Rub through a fine sieve 2 pounds (1 kilo) of chestnuts, peeled, cooked in a light vanilla-flavoured syrup and well drained.

Add to the purée, stirring with a wooden spoon, ⅔ cup (150 grams) of sugar and 6 tablespoons (100 grams) of butter and dry out over heat.

Remove from heat, add 8 egg yolks and fold in carefully 6 stiffly beaten egg whites. Cook in a *bain-marie* (pan of hot water).

Serve with *Custard sauce** flavoured with vanilla, or *Apricot sauce* (see SAUCE) flavoured with kirsch.

Chocolate pudding. POUDING AU CHOCOLAT—Soften in the oven 3 tablets (4 ounces) of semi-sweet chocolate (125 grams). Work by hand in a cloth 10 tablespoons (150 grams) of butter until very soft, put it in a basin previously scalded with boiling water, and beat with a wooden spoon. When it is creamy in consistency add ½ cup (75 grams) of castor (powdered) sugar and ¼ cup (25 grams) of vanilla sugar; or ¾ cup granulated sugar plus 1 teaspoon vanilla extract. Beat to a froth, then add 8 egg yolks, one by one, and the chocolate beaten to a fine paste with a little of the butter and sugar mixture added to make it easier to incorporate, 5 tablespoons (40 grams) of sifted flour and 4 tablespoons (40 grams) of potato flour.

Put this mixture in a round or oval buttered and floured mould, of about 1½ quarts (12 decilitres) in capacity.

Poach in a *bain-marie** (pan of hot water) for about 45 minutes. Let the pudding rest before turning it out of the mould on to a round dish and pouring chocolate-flavoured *Custard sauce** over it.

Clermont pudding (cold). POUDING CLERMONT—Add to a *Bavarian cream mixture** flavoured with rum a quarter of its volume of chestnut purée, and for every quart (litre) of the mixture ¼ pound (125 grams) of broken-up *marrons glacés.* Put the mixture into a mould greased with sweet almond oil and put on ice or in a deep-freeze to set. Serve in the mould wrapped in a napkin, with a liqueur flavoured fruit sauce.

Diplomat pudding (cold). POUDING DIPLOMATE—Decorate the bottom of an oiled mould with crystallized fruit, then fill it with alternate layers of sponge finger (lady finger) crumbs soaked in kirsch or other liqueur and a *Bavarian cream mixture** flavoured with vanilla.

Put on each layer of sponge biscuits some currants and sultanas (seedless raisins) which have been put to swell in warm syrup and well drained, and, here and there, a spoonful of apricot jam. Put on ice or in a deep-freeze to set. Wrap the mould in a napkin. Serve with a fruit and liqueur sauce.

Diplomat pudding with fruit (cold). POUDING DIPLOMATE AUX FRUITS—Prepared as described in the preceding recipe with the addition of layers of various fruits, peeled, sliced and soaked in sugar and liqueur.

Set the pudding on a serving dish; surround the base with fruit cooked in syrup and well drained.

Fruit pudding. POUDING DE FRUITS—Put in a *bain-marie* (pan of hot water) a plain buttered mould. Pour into this mould a few tablespoons of custard mixture prepared as for *Cabinet pudding* but made with 6 whole eggs and 6 yolks to each quart (litre) of milk and with the addition of one-third of fruit purée.

Cook this layer of custard until it is set, then put on top a layer of the same fruit used for the purée, previously cut up and soaked in sugar and liqueur.

Pour over the fruit another layer of custard, and continue to fill the mould with alternate layers of fruit and custard, cooking the layer of custard each time.

Finish cooking in the *bain-marie* (pan of hot water) over a gentle heat.

Let the pudding rest a few minutes before turning it out of the mould. Serve with a fruit sauce flavoured with kirsch or any other liqueur.

Note. Fruit puddings can be prepared with apricots, nectarines, peaches, pears, apples, etc.

Lemon, tangerine or orange soufflé pudding. POUDING SOUFFLÉ AU CITRON, À LA MANDARINE, À L'ORANGE—Prepare the same mixture as for *Saxon pudding.* Flavour with lemon, tangerine or orange. Cook in a *bain-marie* (pan of hot water). Serve with *Custard sauce** flavoured with lemon, tangerine or orange.

Macaroni pudding. POUDING AUX NOUILLES—Prepared in the same way as *Semolina pudding*.

Marrow pudding. POUDING À LA MOELLE—Melt in a *bain-marie* (double boiler saucepan) ½ pound (250 grams) of marrow and 1⅝ ounces (50 grams) of beef suet. Let the mixture cool a little. Beat in a basin with 1½ cups (200 grams) of sugar; add ⅔ cup (80 grams) of bread, soaked in milk and squeezed out, 3 whole eggs and 8 yolks, 7 ounces (200 grams) of chopped crystallized fruit, ⅓ cup (50 grams) of stoned raisins and ½ cup (80 grams) of sultanas (seedless raisins). Mix well together.

Fill with this mixture a buttered and floured mould. Cook gently in a *bain-marie* (pan of hot water).

Serve with a *Zabaglione**, flavoured with rum.

Nesselrode pudding I (cold). POUDING NESSELRODE—Add to a quart (litre) of *Custard sauce**, ½ pound (250 grams) of fine chestnut purée, 4 ounces (125 grams) each of candied orange peel and crystallized cherries cut in dice, and soaked in Malaga; 4 ounces (125 grams) each of currants and sultanas (seedless raisins), picked over, set to swell in warm water and then soaked in Malaga.

Add to this custard an equal amount of whipped cream flavoured with maraschino.

Put this mixture in a large charlotte mould with a lid, having lined the base and sides with white paper. Close the mould and, to seal it hermetically, fill in the lid opening with butter. Put the mould in ice and salt to set, or place in a deep-freeze.

Turn out the pudding on to a serving dish. Take off the paper covering it and surround the base with *marrons glacés*.

Note. This pudding was invented, as was the following one, it is said, by Monsieur Mouy, chef to the Comte de Nesselrode.

Nesselrode pudding II. POUDING NESSELRODE—Put through a fine sieve 40 good chestnuts peeled and cooked in a light syrup (of 16°) with a vanilla pod.

Mix the chestnut purée with custard sauce made from 8 yolks of eggs, a scant cup (200 grams) of sugar and 1 quart (8 decilitres) of fresh boiled cream. Flavour this mixture with ½ cup (1 decilitre) of maraschino and strain through a cloth.

Freeze this mixture in an ice cream freezer, and as soon as it sets add to it 1½ cups (3 decilitres) of whipped cream and a scant cup (100 grams) of currants, carefully picked over and cleaned, and ½ cup (100 grams) of stoned raisins, both previously cooked in a heavy syrup of 30°.

Plum pudding—A sweet which is served in England and in the United States at Christmas time and called *Christmas pudding*.

Ingredients (for a pudding to serve 15 to 20 persons): 1 pound (500 grams) of suet (net weight, after skinning, etc.), 5½ cups (300 grams) of fresh breadcrumbs, 2⅓ cups (300 grams) of sifted flour, ¾ cup (150 grams) of stoned Malaga raisins, 1¼ cups (150 grams) of best currants, 1 cup (150 grams) of sultanas (seedless raisins), ¼ pound (125 grams) of candied citron, ¼ pound (125 grams) of candied orange peel, ½ cup (150 grams) of stoned prunes, 2 cups (250 grams) of peeled and grated cooking apples, 1 cup (150 grams) of blanched and chopped almonds, 1½ cups (250 grams) of brown sugar, the grated rind and juice of one orange and one lemon, 4 whole eggs, 4 cups (8 decilitres) of rum, 3 tablespoons (20 grams) of mixed spices (cinnamon, nutmeg, ginger), 1⅔ teaspoons (10 grams) of salt.

Method. Remove all skin and fibre from the suet and chop it finely. The chopping is rendered much easier if the suet is sprinkled with a third of the flour indicated.

Other preliminary operations are as follows: stone the raisins, and pick over the currants and sultanas carefully. The sultanas and currants can easily be cleaned by rubbing them in a cloth with a tablespoon or two of flour—in addition to the flour allowed above—and then washing them.

The prunes, after being stoned, should be chopped with a knife or put through a mincer. (This addition of prunes to the plum pudding is optional. We advise it, nevertheless, as apart from their good flavour, the prunes also give the pudding mixture a richer darker colour.)

The apples should be peeled and grated or chopped.

The candied citron and orange peel should be cut in minute dice. The almonds are blanched and chopped.

The orange and lemon peel is grated as usual and the juice is pressed out and strained through a muslin bag.

Mixing of ingredients. Put the suet and all the rest of the above ingredients, except the eggs, into a big basin. The eggs are added shortly before the pudding is put on to cook. Stir until the mixture is smooth, then add a quarter of the rum indicated above.

Cover the basin with a cloth and leave in a cool place.

Stir the mixture every day, adding a few tablespoons of rum each time.

(The mixture can be left to stand for a fortnight and longer before the plum pudding is cooked. In England this preparation is done at least a month before Christmas.)

Moistening the plum pudding. On the last day, that is to say a little while before cooking the pudding, add the eggs. Stir the pudding to ensure perfect blending. If the mixture is too thick and difficult to stir, soften it a little by adding a few tablespoons of milk, or—more strictly in conformity with the English tradition—with stout. Put the mixture into special basins, greased with butter and sprinkled with flour. If no such pudding basins are available, wrap the mixture in buttered, floured cloths (previously scalded).

Cooking the plum pudding. Put the pudding into a big saucepan of boiling water. Boil for at least 6 hours.

To serve. Remove the pudding from the saucepan and leave to stand for a few minutes before turning out. Remove the cloth and turn out the pudding on to a round dish.

Sprinkle the pudding with tiny pieces of sugar. Heat the rum, pour over the pudding and set it alight when ready to serve.

There are other variants of serving plum pudding. It can be set alight with kirsch, brandy or whisky; it can be served with rum-flavoured *Zabaglione** or with hot custard.

In England it is often served with *Brandy butter*, which is prepared as follows:

Heat a bowl and put into it ⅞ cup (200 grams) of butter. Beat the butter to turn it into a paste, adding to it a tablespoonful of castor (fine) sugar and ¼ cup (half a decilitre) of brandy. Whisk vigorously to make the mixture frothy. This butter is served cold.

Note. The making of plum pudding is simple and easy. This sweet (dessert), which is one of the most nourishing dishes, has the advantage that it can be made well in advance and keeps for a long time. Thus one can have an excellent sweet course ready in reserve.

Pumpkin pudding (Gâteau of gourd). GÂTEAU DE POTIRON—Prepare as for *Purée of pumpkin soup* (see SOUP), pressing the purée vigorously to remove the water. For each cup (500 grams) of purée add 2 cups (½ litre) of milk, ⅓ cup (100 grams) of sugar and 3 tablespoons (60 grams) of butter and bring to the boil. Now add 2 tablespoons of potato flour blended with a little water; stir, then simmer for 30 minutes, stirring from time to time. Take from the heat and cool a little, then add 3 yolks of eggs and flavouring (orange flower water or ½ teaspoon orange extract or vanilla). Beat the 3 egg whites stiffly and fold them into the mixture, then turn it into a buttered mould. Cook for 45 minutes in a slow oven.

Rice pudding. POUDING AU RIZ—Wash ½ pound (250 grams) of rice, blanch and drain it and put it in a saucepan; pour in a quart (litre) of milk previously boiled with ⅝ cup (150 grams) of sugar, half a pod of vanilla or 2 teaspoons vanilla extract (or other flavouring according to taste) and a pinch of salt. Add 3 tablespoons (50 grams) of butter.

Put to cook over the heat. As soon as boiling begins, cover the pot and cook the rice in the oven, at a low heat (*and without stirring*) for 25 to 30 minutes.

Remove from heat, add 8 egg yolks, mix with care so as not to break the grains of rice, then add 7 or 8 stiffly beaten egg whites.

Fill with this mixture buttered moulds sprinkled with fine breadcrumbs.

Cook in the oven in a *bain-marie* (pan of hot water).

Serve *Custard sauce**, *Zabaglione** or a liqueur-flavoured fruit sauce separately.

Chocolate rice pudding. POUDING AU RIZ AU CHOCOLAT —Prepared and cooked in a mould or pudding dish as for *Rice pudding*, but with the addition of 1⅝ ounces (50 grams) of semi-sweet chocolate melted for every pound (500 grams) of rice pudding.

English rice pudding I. POUDING AU RIZ À L'ANGLAISE—Prepare the mixture as described in the recipe for *Rice pudding* with ¾ cup (180 grams) of rice, a quart (litre) of milk flavoured to taste, 3½ tablespoons (50 grams) of sugar, 6 tablespoons (80 grams) of butter and a small pinch of salt. Keep the rice rather firm. Bind the mixture with 3 whole eggs.

Put into a pudding dish and cook in the oven in a *bain-marie** (pan of hot water).

When it is cooked, sprinkle the pudding with sugar and glaze.

English rice pudding II. POUDING DE RIZ AU PLAT, DIT À L'ANGLAISE—Prepare milk rice in the usual way. Add to it 3 tablespoons (50 grams) of butter and 3 whole eggs. Mix and pour into a buttered pudding dish.

Put to cook in the oven, in a *bain-marie* (pan of hot water) for 25 minutes. At the last moment sprinkle with sugar and glaze.

Sago pudding. POUDING AU SAGOU—Prepared as described in the recipe for *Semolina pudding*, using sago.

Saxon pudding. POUDING SAXON—In a saucepan beat 6 tablespoons (100 grams) of butter to a cream with a wooden spoon. Add 6 tablespoons (100 grams) of sugar and ⅞ cup (100 grams) of sieved flour. Moisten with 1½ cups (3 decilitres) of boiled milk and mix.

Bring this mixture to the boil, stirring all the time with a wooden spoon, until it is firm and dry like chou pastry.

Remove from heat, add 5 egg yolks, then carefully fold in 5 stiffly beaten egg whites.

Fill with the mixture a plain buttered mould. Cook in a slow oven in a *bain-marie* (pan of hot water). Serve with a *Zabaglione** or *Custard sauce**.

Scotch pudding. POUDING ÉCOSSAIS—Put in a basin 9 cups (500 grams) of freshly made breadcrumbs; moisten with a little boiled milk.

Add ¾ pound (375 grams) of finely chopped beef marrow, ½ cup (125 grams) of sugar, 1 cup (125 grams) of currants, ¾ cup (125 grams) of sultanas (seedless raisins), ¾ cup (125 grams) of raisins, 6 ounces (175 grams) of chopped crystallized fruits.

Put in 4 eggs and 4 tablespoons of rum and beat well together.

Put this mixture in a large plain mould, well buttered, filling to not more than ½ inch from the top.

Cook in a *bain-marie* (pan of hot water) in the oven for an hour. Serve with *Zabaglione** or *Custard** flavoured with Madeira.

Semolina pudding. POUDING À LA SEMOULE—Sprinkle ½ pound (250 grams) semolina gradually into a quart (litre) of boiling milk with ½ cup (125 grams) of sugar, a pinch of salt, 6 tablespoons (100 grams) of butter and flavouring added to it. Mix well. Cook in a low oven for 25 minutes. Turn the mixture out of the basin, incorporate 6 egg yolks, 5 tablespoons (75 grams) of butter and, finally, 4 stiffly beaten egg whites.

Butter a mould, sprinkle it with semolina and fill it with the pudding mixture.

Poach in a *bain-marie* (pan of hot water) in a moderate oven (350°F.). It is cooked when the composition becomes a little elastic to the touch.

Let the pudding rest for a few minutes before turning out.

Serve *Custard sauce**, *Zabaglione** or liqueur flavoured fruit sauce separately.

English suet roll pudding. POUDING ROULÉ À L'ANGLAISE —An hour before it is needed, prepare a suet pudding pastry made with 3¾ cups (500 grams) of sifted flour, 4¼ cups (300 grams) of very dry beef suet, 3 tablespoons (50 grams) of sugar, 2½ teaspoons (15 grams) of salt and 1 cup (2 decilitres) of water.

Roll out this pastry into a rectangle about ¼ inch thick.

Spread on this strip of pastry some jam or marmalade and roll up into a sausage.

Wrap the sausage in a buttered and floured cloth and tie it. Put to cook in boiling water (or steam) for an hour and a half.

Drain the pudding, unwrap it, cut it into slices about ¾ inch thick and arrange the pieces in a circle. Serve with fruit sauce.

Sweet potato pudding. POUDING DE PATATES AU PLAT—Peel 6 to 7 sweet potatoes (750 grams), cut into rather thick slices and boil in water with a pinch of salt.

As soon as they are cooked, drain, put in the oven just to dry off excess of moisture and rub through a small mesh metal sieve.

Put this purée into a bowl. Add ½ cup (125 grams) of sugar and 3 whole eggs and blend, stirring with a wooden spoon.

When the mixture is quite smooth, moisten with a pint (half a litre) of milk boiled with a vanilla bean, or add 1 teaspoon vanilla extract after boiling. Mix, then pour the mixture into a buttered English pudding dish, or into any other oven-proof china receptacle.

Put the dish into a pan half filled with hot water. Bring to the boil on the stove, then cook in a slow oven for 35 minutes (if the oven is too hot cover the pudding to prevent it browning too quickly).

Five minutes before taking out of the oven, sprinkle with sugar and glaze the top, placing the dish in the hottest part of the oven. Serve in the same dish.

Note. This pudding can be served hot or cold. It can be flavoured with kirsch, rum, orange, lemon, etc.

Tapioca pudding. POUDING AU TAPIOCA—The same method of preparation as for *Semolina pudding*, using tapioca.

Vermicelli pudding. POUDING AU VERMICELLE—The same method of preparation as for *Semolina pudding*, using vermicelli.

PUFFER—A sort of fritter made with a batter whose base is flaked oats, which is worked with warm water, sugar, a little salt and eggs as wanted, and flavoured with cinnamon. They are cooked in butter in a frying pan.

PUITS D'AMOUR (pastry)—Using *Flaky pastry* (see DOUGH) that has been rolled and turned six times, cut out with a fluted cutter rounds of 2 to 3 inches in diameter.

Put half of these on a lightly moistened baking sheet, keeping them a little apart from each other. Cut out the centres of the other pastry rounds with the aid of a plain or fluted cutter, so as to make 'crowns', whose sides are about ⅓ inch wide.

Moisten round the tops of the pastry rounds on the baking tin and set one of the cut-out crowns on each. Place them with precision and press them gently so that the two stick together. Brush the top of the upper crowns with egg and cook for about 15 minutes in a medium oven (375°F.). Once they are cooked draw the baking tin to the front of the oven without taking it right out and powder the pastry cases lightly with icing sugar. Put them for a moment in the hottest part of the oven to melt this sugar, which will form a glaze; take them out and put on a rack to cool.

These pastries look like puff pastry cases. When they are quite cool, they are filled with *Confectioner's custard* (see CREAM, *French pastry cream*) with the aid of a spoon, or better still a forcing (pastry) bag, or alternatively with very thick gooseberry jelly.

PULP. PULPE—The soft and fleshy parts of fruit or vegetables reduced to a moist paste by rubbing through a sieve.

PULQUE—A drink which has some relation to cider. The *agave* from which this drink is made was cultivated on a large scale in the empire of the ancient Aztecs.

Pumpkins at Les Halles, Paris
(*French Government Tourist Office*)

PUMPKIN. POTIRON, COURGE—Pumpkin is the name of a gourd belonging to the *Cucurbita maxima* family. In England the name is used to describe a variety of gourds, known in the U.S.A. as *Squash*. The French *potiron* is the same as the American pumpkin, a gourd having an orange-coloured flesh which has a distinctive and sweet flavour. In France it is used to make soup, jam and a dessert (sweet). In U.S.A. almost its only use in the culinary line is as a filling for pies.

Pumpkin compote—See COMPOTES.

Pumpkin au gratin. COURGE AU GRATIN—Pare the pumpkin, divide into quarters of medium size. Blanch for a short time in boiling salt water; drain and dry.

Arrange the pieces on a gratin dish, which has already been buttered and sprinkled with grated cheese. Sprinkle with more cheese, pour on some melted butter, and brown in a warm oven.

This dish can be prepared by alternating the slices of pumpkin in the dish with slices of onion which have already been melted in butter. It could be prepared with North American winter squash.

Pumpkin (*Sougez*)

Gratin of pumpkin with rice. GRATIN DE COURGE AU RIZ—Put the slices of pumpkin which have been first simmered in butter into a gratin dish which is well buttered and sprinkled with grated cheese. Put alternate layers of pumpkin and rice, the latter already cooked in unskimmed stock. Sprinkle with grated cheese and pour melted butter over the dish. Brown in a warm oven. This could be made with North American winter squash.

Pumpkin jam. CONFITURE DE COURGE—Prepared with very ripe pumpkin in the same way as *Apricot jam.* See JAM.

Pumpkin au jus. COURGE AU JUS—Divide the pumpkin into quarters or into lozenge-shaped pieces. Blanch for a few minutes in boiling salted water. Drain, dry and put in a sauté pan with a few spoonfuls of reduced veal stock. Simmer for 25 minutes with the lid on.

Pumpkin pudding—See PUDDING.

Pumpkin purée. PURÉE DE COURGE—Divide the pumpkin into quarters, and cook slowly in butter with the lid on, having seasoned first with salt and a pinch of sugar.

When the pumpkin is very soft, put it through a sieve. Heat the purée and add, off the fire, a little butter.

To obtain a purée with a better consistency, add one-third of its weight in potato purée. The purée can be finished with fresh cream or concentrated meat stock, and can be made with pumpkin or any of the North American winter squashes.

Pumpkin salad. SALADE DE COURGE—Pare the pumpkin;

divide it into quarters. Blanch in salt water; put under the cold tap; drain; dry. Season with oil, vinegar, or with lemon juice, and salt and pepper.

Pumpkin soufflé. SOUFFLÉ DE COURGE—Bind 2 cups (250 grams) of pumpkin purée flavoured with sugar and vanilla, with 3 egg yolks. Add 3 egg whites beaten stiff.

Turn out into a buttered soufflé dish and cook in the usual way. See SOUFFLÉ.

Pumpkin soup.—See SOUPS AND BROTHS, *Purée of pumpkin soup.*

Sweet-sour pumpkin (à l'allemande) (Cold hors-d'oeuvre). COURGE À L'AIGRE-DOUX, À L'ALLEMANDE—Pare the pumpkin, cut it into square pieces or trim into lozenge shape, and put the pieces in a jar, strewing each layer with fragments of cinnamon, cloves, thyme, bay and grated nutmeg. Cover with vinegar which has been boiled with 5 ounces (150 grams) of cinnamon per 35 ounces (litre) and allowed to cool.

Cover the jar and leave to soak for 10 to 12 days.

PUNCH—A drink said to have originated among English sailors, and which, about 1552, consisted of a simple mixture of cane spirit and sugar, heated.

On the 25th October, 1599, Sir Edward Kennel, commander-in-chief of the English navy, offered to his ships' companies a monster punch which he had prepared in a vast marble basin. For his concoction he used 80 casks of brandy, 9 of water, 25,000 large limes, 80 pints of lemon juice, 13 quintals (1,300 pounds) of Lisbon sugar, 5 pounds of nutmeg and 300 biscuits, plus a great cask of Malaga.

A platform had been constructed over the basin to shelter it from the rain, and the serving was done by a ship's boy who sailed on this sea of punch in a rosewood boat. To serve the 6,000 guests one ship's boy had to be replaced by another several times, each one finding himself intoxicated by the fumes from the lake of alcohol at the end of a quarter of an hour.

Iced punch. PUNCH GLACÉ—Prepare a mixture similar to that for *Punch Marquise*. While the wine is hot, add to it 5 tablespoons (20 grams) of tea and infuse.

Strain through a silk strainer. Add an orange and a lemon, peeled and cut in slices, and 1 cup (2 decilitres) of hot rum. Set alight, allow to cool, strain, add water if too syrupy and freeze like a water ice.

Kirsch punch. PUNCH AU KIRSCH—Infuse 6 tablespoons (25 grams) of tea for 8 minutes in a quart (litre) of boiling water. Pour this infusion, straining it, into a punch-bowl with 1 pound (500 grams) of lump sugar. Stir with a silver spoon to dissolve the sugar.

Add three-quarters of a quart (litre) of kirsch. Set alight and serve in punch glasses.

Punch Marquise—Put in a copper pan a quart (litre) of Sauternes (or any other rather sweet white wine), ½ pound (250 grams) of sugar and the rind of a lemon tied in muslin with a clove in the middle. Dissolve the sugar. Heat the wine to the point where a fine white froth rises to the surface. Pour the mixture into a punch-qowl. Add 1 to 1¼ cups (2½ decilitres) of cognac. Set alight. Serve in punch glasses with a thin slice of lemon in each glass.

Rum punch. PUNCH AU RHUM—Prepare an infusion of tea in the same way as for *Kirsch punch*. Pour this infusion into a punch bowl with sugar and some thin slices of lemon. Add ¾ quart (litre) of rum. Set alight.

PURÉE—A preparation obtained by mashing and sieving certain foodstuffs. Any kind of food, whether from the animal or the vegetable kingdom, can be reduced to a purée after having been cooked.

According to the uses for which they are intended purées are made of varying consistency. Those to be served as a vegetable or a garnish are kept to a thickish consistency; those meant to make soup are kept rather lighter.

Some vegetables, being too watery to make a sufficiently thick purée, have a complementary thickening ingredient added to them, most frequently another more floury vegetable, a cereal or a thick sauce.

Meat purées of all kinds and fish purées have the addition of sauce, brown or white according to the nature of the purée and well reduced.

The use of a kitchen blender greatly facilitates the making of purées.

PURÉES OF FISH, CRUSTACEANS AND MOLLUSCS. PURÉES DE POISSONS, CRUSTACÉS ET MOLLUSQUES:

Anchovy purée (cold). PURÉE D'ANCHOIS—Pound in a mortar 2 ounces (50 grams) of anchovy fillets de-salted and well cleaned, with the yolks of 4 hard boiled eggs and 3 tablespoons of butter. Rub through a fine sieve.

According to the individual recipe the purée can be completed with chopped herbs or other savoury additions.

Use as garnish for various hors-d'oeuvre, to stuff hard boiled eggs, artichoke bottoms, olives, etc.

Anchovy purée (hot). PURÉE D'ANCHOIS—Add 2 tablespoons of anchovy purée to ¾ cup (1½ decilitres) of thick *Béchamel sauce* (see SAUCE). Strain through a cloth. Heat and add butter at the last moment.

According to the individual recipe this purée can also include hard boiled eggs and chopped parsley.

Use as filling for pastry cases, fritters, rissoles, etc.

Herring purée. PURÉE DE HARENGS—Prepared like *Anchovy purée*, replacing anchovies with de-salted herring fillets. The same uses.

Mussel purée. PURÉE DE MOULES—This purée is prepared in the same way as *Oyster purée* and is used in the same way.

Oyster purée. PURÉE D'HUÎTRES—*Hot.* Pound in a mortar 24 oysters which have been poached in their liquor and well drained. Strain this purée. Add to it 1½ cups (3 decilitres) of *Béchamel sauce* (see SAUCE), which has had the oyster liquid added to it and has then been cooked down, mixed with cream and strained through a cloth.

Use like *Shrimp purée.*

Cold. Crush in the mortar 24 oysters, poached and well drained, with 4 yolks of hard boiled eggs and 2 tablespoons of butter. Put through a fine strainer.

Salmon purée. PURÉE DE SAUMON—*With fresh salmon.* Put through a sieve ½ pound (250 grams) of salmon flesh (cooked in butter). Heat this purée; bind it with 1 cup (2 decilitres) of thick *Béchamel sauce* (see SAUCE). Season. Add butter at the last moment.

Used for garnishing eggs, pastry cases and shells, bread, etc.

With smoked salmon. Put through a sieve ½ pound (250 grams) of smoked salmon. Add to this purée 4 yolks of hard boiled eggs, rub through a fine sieve, add 3 tablespoons (50 grams) of butter and mix well.

Use for canapés, pastry shapes and various hors-d'oeuvre.

Sea-urchin purée. PURÉE D'OURSINS—Clean the sea-urchins, remove the yellow substance which adheres to the inside of the shell. Add this substance to some thick *Béchamel sauce* (see SAUCE) which has been mixed with some cream, allowing one quart (litre) of sauce to 36 sea-urchins. Mix well. Put through a fine strainer.

The same uses as for *Shrimp purée.*

Shrimp purée. PURÉE DE CREVETTES—Pound finely in a mortar the shells of the shrimps (or prawns or other crustaceans), whose flesh is being otherwise used.

Add this purée to an equal quantity of thick *Béchamel sauce* (see SAUCE) which has been mixed with cream. Put through a cloth, pressing with a wooden spoon.

Use as a complementary ingredient of sauces, forcemeats, etc. for fish and crustaceans and for hot hors-d'oeuvre.

Tunny (U.S. tuna fish) purée. PURÉE DE THON—Like *Anchovy purée.* The same uses.

GAME PURÉES. PURÉE DE GIBIER:

Game purée I. PURÉE DE GIBIER—Pound in a mortar, with half of its weight of rice cooked in consommé, the flesh of any game bird or animal cooked and cut up small.

Put through a fine sieve. Add this purée to some rich *Brown sauce* (see SAUCE) made with the cooking juices of game. Mix well over the heat, season and add butter.

Game purée II. PURÉE DE GIBIER—The game being well pounded, add to it some thick lentil purée. Finish as above.

Use as a garnish for poached or soft boiled eggs, or as a filling for omelettes, stuffing for vegetables and garnish for pastry shells.

MEAT AND POULTRY PURÉES. PURÉE DE VIANDES:

Beef purée. PURÉE DE BOEUF—Pound in a mortar 1 pound (500 grams) of braised beef, carefully trimmed and with all gristle removed. Add this purée to 2 cups (4 decilitres) of concentrated *Brown sauce* (see SAUCE). Mix over heat, stirring with a wooden spoon. Strain through a fine sieve or a cloth.

Use as a filling for various pastries, *pasta** and ravioli, stuffing for vegetables (onions, tomatoes, artichoke bottoms, etc.) veal or beef olives, etc.

This purée may be bound with egg.

Brain purée. PURÉE DE CERVELLE D'AGNEAU, DE VEAU—Rub cooked lamb's or calf's brain through a fine sieve. Add this purée to some *Béchamel* or *Velouté sauce* (see SAUCE), which has been mixed with cream, allowing 1 cup (2 decilitres) of sauce per set of brains. Mix over the heat, season and put through a fine sieve or cloth.

Use as garnish to poached eggs or soft boiled eggs, as a forcemeat for fowl, as filling for pastry cases, tartlets, artichoke bottoms, mushrooms, etc.

Brain purée, and in general all white meat purées, may have diced truffles, mushrooms or ham added to them, or may be enriched by *duxelles** or mixed vegetables cooked in butter.

Calf's liver purée. PURÉE DE FOIE DE VEAU—Pound in a mortar 1 pound (500 grams) of calf's liver cut in pieces, sautéed in butter (just enough to seal it), seasoned and cooled.

Rub the liver through a fine sieve.

Use in the same way as *Forcemeat à gratin**.

Chicken purée (cold). PURÉE DE VOLAILLE—Pound in a mortar the flesh of a poached chicken. Turn this purée into a bowl, add to it a few tablespoons of very thick fresh cream, season and put it through a fine strainer. Mix till very smooth.

Use for cold hors-d'oeuvre, canapés and pastry cases.

Chicken purée (hot). PURÉE DE VOLAILLE—Pound in a mortar the boned and trimmed flesh of a chicken, poached in chicken stock.

Rub this flesh through a fine sieve. Heat in a sauté pan. Bind it with one-third of its weight of thick *Chicken velouté sauce* (see SAUCE). Season, and at the last moment add butter and fresh cream.

Use as garnish with poached and soft boiled eggs, in pastry shells, and small cases made of other crusts and to stuff certain vegetables such as artichoke bottoms, cucumbers, tomatoes, mushrooms, etc.

Chicken liver purée—See FORCEMEAT, *A gratin poultry liver forcemeat.*

Foie gras purée. PURÉE DE FOIE GRAS—*Hot.* Mix some thick *Chicken velouté sauce* (see SAUCE) with twice the volume of cooked *foie gras* (truffled or not, as desired) which has been rubbed through a fine sieve. Mix well over the heat and bind with egg yolks.

Used to garnish pastry shells and tartlets, as stuffing for various vegetables such as artichoke bottoms, mushrooms, etc. (in this case white breadcrumbs are added).

Cold. Rub some cooked *foie gras* through a fine sieve. Work till very smooth.

Use for cold hors-d'oeuvre and for cold eggs, poached or soft boiled.

Sweetbread purée. PURÉE DE RIS DE VEAU—Prepared with braised sweetbread as described in the recipe for *Brain purée.* The same uses.

Veal purée. PURÉE DE VEAU—Prepared with braised veal in the same way as *Beef purée.* This purée is bound with *Chicken velouté sauce* or *Béchamel sauce* (see SAUCE). The same uses.

VEGETABLE PURÉES. PURÉES DE LÉGUMES:

Artichoke purée I. PURÉE D'ARTICHAUTS—Simmer in butter 6 large artichoke bottoms, half cooked in a flour-and-water *court-bouillon** and sliced. Add to them 1 cup (2 decilitres) of *Béchamel sauce* (see SAUCE) and finish as above. Use as a vegetable or garnish for meat or poultry.

Artichoke purée II. PURÉE D'ARTICHAUTS—Add to the artichoke bottoms put to cook in butter 1 medium-sized potato (200 grams) cut in thick slices. Moisten with $\frac{3}{4}$ cup ($1\frac{1}{2}$ decilitres) of consommé. Cook together. Finish the purée as above.

The same uses as the preceding purée.

Green asparagus purée. PURÉE D'ASPERGES VERTES—Prepared, with green asparagus, as in the preceding recipe.

White asparagus purée. PURÉE D'ASPERGES BLANCHES—Cook the asparagus tips in salt water, drain and rub through fine sieve. Heat this purée, then remove from heat and add a little fresh butter.

This purée being of a thin consistency, a quarter of its weight of *Potato purée** may be added to it. Or, depending on its final use, one-third of its volume of thick *Béchamel sauce* (see SAUCE) may be added.

The uses are the same as for *Artichoke purée.*

Aubergine (egg-plant) purée. PURÉE D'AUBERGINES—Simmer in butter in a covered pan 4 aubergines (egg-plant), peeled, sliced and cut in rounds. Add 1 medium-large potato (250 grams) in slices. Moisten with $\frac{3}{4}$ cup ($1\frac{1}{2}$ decilitres) of consommé. Season. Cook gently. Rub through a fine sieve and finish the purée as described in the recipe for *Artichoke purée.* The same uses.

Broad bean purée. PURÉE DE FÈVES FRAÎCHES—Rub 1 pound (500 grams) of broad beans (U.S. white beans) cooked in salted water and seasoned with a sprig of savory through a fine sieve.

Heat this purée and bind it with butter or cream.

Alternatively, cook the beans like *Peas à la française**, rub through a fine sieve and bind the purée with butter or cream.

To make a thicker consistency the beans may be

augmented by a quarter of their volume of potatoes, added during cooking.

Use as garnish to eggs, small cuts of meat and poultry.

Fresh flageolet bean purée. PURÉE DE FLAGEOLETS FRAIS—Prepared with fresh flageolet beans cooked in water in the same way as for *Broad bean purée*, and used in the same way.

French (string) bean purée. PURÉE DE HARICOTS VERTS—*Hot*. Rub through a sieve 1 pound (500 grams) of French (string) beans, cooked in salted water and drained. Heat this purée and bind with butter or cream.

Used as garnish for eggs, small cuts of meat, poultry, or as a vegetable.

Cold. Rub through a fine sieve some French (string) beans, cooked in salted water and drained. Bind this purée with thick mayonnaise.

Use as filling for artichoke bottoms, tomatoes and pastry cases, and, by itself, as garnish for cold dishes.

Breton white bean purée. PURÉE DE HARICOTS BLANCS À LA BRETONNE, DITE PURÉE BRETONNE—White haricot (U.S. shell) beans are cooked in a meat stock (see BEANS), drained, bound with *Bretonne sauce* (see SAUCE) and rubbed through a sieve.

Use as garnish for roast, baked or braised meat, especially mutton. It is also served as a vegetable.

White bean purée or Purée soissonnaise. PURÉE DE HARICOTS, DITE À LA SOISSONNAISE, PURÉE SOISSONNAISE—White haricot (shell) beans cooked in water or in a meat stock and rubbed through a sieve when they are still hot. Stir the purée over the heat, adding 6 tablespoons (100 grams) of butter for each 2 cups (500 grams) of purée. Dilute if necessary with a few tablespoons of boiling milk or the water in which the haricots were cooked.

Use in the same way as *Breton white bean purée*. See also SOUPS AND BROTHS, *Purée of white haricot bean soup*.

Dried bean purée. PURÉE DE FLAGEOLETS SECS—Prepared in the same way as *Dried haricot bean purée* and having the same uses.

Dried haricot (shell) bean purée (white or red). PURÉE DE HARICOTS—Rub through a fine sieve dried white or red haricot beans cooked in stock or water. (See BEANS, *Dried beans*). Heat this purée and bind with fresh butter.

Use as garnish for large or small cuts of meat, particularly mutton.

Beetroot purée. PURÉE DE BETTERAVES—*Hot*. Rub through a fine sieve 2 large beetroots cooked in the oven (as for salad beetroots) and peeled. Put this purée to heat in a sauté pan. Add to it 1 cup (2½ decilitres) of concentrated rich *Brown sauce* (see SAUCE). Season; bring to the boil, stirring with a wooden spoon. At the last moment add 2 teaspoons of butter.

The purée may also be thickened with concentrated *Béchamel sauce*. See SAUCE.

Use as garnish to small pieces of game meat.

Cold. Add to the cold beetroot purée 1 cup (2 decilitres) of very thick mayonnaise.

Use as filling for canapés, boat-shaped pastry cases and hors-d'oeuvre tartlets.

Carrot purée. PURÉE DE CAROTTES—Simmer 1 pound (500 grams) of carrots in butter in a covered pan until they are very tender (new carrots should be used if possible). Bind with *Béchamel sauce* (see SAUCE). Finish like *Artichoke purée*.

Use as garnish for small or large cuts of meat. It is also served by itself as a vegetable.

Cauliflower purée. PURÉE DE CHOU-FLEUR—Cook the cauliflower in water and rub through a fine sieve. Heat the purée. Bind it with a third of its volume of *Béchamel sauce* (see SAUCE). Add some butter at the last moment.

To make a thicker consistency a small quantity of potatoes may be added.

Use as a garnish for eggs, small pieces of meat, and sweetbreads. This purée can also be served as a vegetable.

Celery purée. PURÉE DE CÉLERI—Simmer in butter in a covered pan celery stalks or celeriac, previously blanched in salted water. Finish as described in the recipe for *Artichoke purée*.

This purée can be thickened with concentrated *Béchamel sauce* (see SAUCE), or with a relative amount of potato cooked with the celery.

Use as a garnish with eggs and with large or small cuts of meat; is also served as a vegetable.

Chestnut purée. PURÉE DE MARRONS—This purée is mainly used as accompaniment to game meats and venison. See CHESTNUT.

Cucumber purée. PURÉE DE CONCOMBRES—As *Artichoke purée*, using cucumbers, peeled, sliced and cooked in butter in a covered pan.

Used as garnish with salmon steaks, cooked in butter or *court-bouillon**, and with small cuts of meat.

Garlic purée. PURÉE D'AIL—Blanch lightly in salted water 10 garlic cloves (50 grams). Drain and stew them for 15 minutes in butter without letting them colour. Add 1 cup (2½ decilitres) of thick *Béchamel sauce* (see SAUCE). Rub through a fine sieve. Heat and add a teaspoon of butter.

This purée is used as garnish for small cuts of sautéed meat (most of all *noisettes* or mutton or lamb cutlets), poached eggs and hot hors-d'oeuvre.

Jerusalem artichoke purée. PURÉE DE TOPINAMBOURS—Cook the Jerusalem artichokes in butter in a covered pan. Put them through a fine sieve. Heat the purée and bind it with butter or cream.

For a thicker consistency, potato purée to the amount of one-half or one-third the volume of the artichoke purée may be added.

Japanese artichoke, root chervil and salsify purées are made in the same way.

Used as garnish for eggs, small cuts of meat and game meat.

Lentil purée. PURÉE DE LENTILLES—As *Haricot bean purée*, using lentils cooked in stock or water.

Used as garnish with large and small cuts of meat and a variety of game.

Lettuce purée. PURÉE DE LAITUES—Rub through a fine sieve some lettuces braised in stock or water. Heat this purée, and bind it with butter or cream.

Used as garnish with eggs or small cuts of meat, sweetbreads, poultry, etc.

Note. Chicory, endives, the leaves of red or white beet or other similar vegetables may be made into purée in the same way.

Marrow or gourd (U.S. squash) purée. PURÉE DE COURGE, DE POTIRON—A purée of marrow or gourd may be served as a vegetable or as garnish and as a soup (see SOUPS AND BROTHS, *Purée of marrow soup*).

Baby marrow (zucchini) purée. PURÉE DE COURGETTES—Prepared in the same way as *Aubergine purée*. The same uses.

Mushroom purée. PURÉE DE CHAMPIGNONS—Trim, wash and dry 1 pound (500 grams) of firm, white cultivated mushrooms and rub them through a sieve as rapidly as possible (peel them if they are not white enough).

Add this purée to 1 cup (2 decilitres) of *Béchamel sauce* (see SAUCE) which has been thickened in a pan with a few tablespoons of cream. Boil down for a few moments over a good heat, season and strain through a cloth. Heat the purée once more, remove from heat and incorporate 3 tablespoons (50 grams) of butter.

Use as garnish for meat, chicken and fish, and to stuff artichoke bottoms, eggs, fillets of fish, etc.; it is also used as filling for pastry shells and canapés served as a hot hors-d'oeuvre or small entrée.

Onion soubise I. PURÉE D'OIGNONS, DITE SOUBISE—This purée, which is used as a garnish for meat, can be prepared in two ways:

Blanch 2 pounds (a kilo) of sliced onions thoroughly in salted water. Five minutes before draining them add ½ pound (250 grams) of rice. Drain these ingredients, hold under a cold water tap to cool, dry and season with salt, white pepper, grated nutmeg and a pinch of sugar.

Put, pressing down well, into a casserole with fairly high sides (the so-called Russian casserole), lined completely with thin rashers of fat bacon. Moisten with white stock in sufficient quantity to cover the onions. Bring to the boil on the stove, then cook in the oven with a lid on.

Take the onions and the rice out of the casserole (without touching the bacon rashers). Rub through a sieve, pressing with a wooden spoon.

Reheat the purée. At the last moment, add to it 10 tablespoons (150 grams) of butter and ½ cup (a decilitre) of fresh double cream. Blend.

Or: Blanch 2 pounds (a kilo) of sliced onions thoroughly and stew gently in butter, without allowing them to take on any colour.

Add 1 quart (a litre) of very thick *Béchamel sauce* (see SAUCE). Season with salt, white pepper and grated nutmeg. Simmer gently, stirring frequently. Rub through a sieve, pressing with a wooden spoon. Finish cooking the purée as above.

Onion soubise II. PURÉE SOUBISE—Blanch 1 pound (500 grams) of onions sliced, drain them and put to cook in the oven (without a lid) with 3 tablespoons (50 grams) of butter, a pinch of salt, a pinch of white pepper and a pinch of fine sugar.

When the onions are done, without getting coloured, add 2 cups (4 decilitres) of thick *Béchamel sauce* (see SAUCE), blend, and cook in the oven with a lid on for 30 minutes.

Rub through a sieve and finish off the purée with 3 tablespoons (50 grams) of butter, whitening it, if necessary, with several tablespoons of cream.

Prepared in this way, the soubise is thinner in consistency and is mainly served as a sauce for grilled meat.

Chick-pea purée. PURÉE DE POIS CHICHES—Prepared like *Split pea purée.*

Fresh pea purée. PURÉE DE POIS FRAIS—Rub through a fine sieve some fresh garden peas cooked in water or *à la française* (see PEAS). Heat this purée and add butter at the last moment.

Used as garnish for eggs, small cuts of meat, sweetbreads and poultry. It is also served as a vegetable and as a soup. See SOUPS AND BROTHS, *Purée of fresh pea soup.*

Split pea purée. PURÉE DE POIS CASSÉS—Like *Dried haricot bean purée*, using split peas cooked in stock or water.

Use as garnish for large and small cuts of meat, braised or roast goose, ham and venison.

Sweet pepper purée. PURÉE DE PIMENTS DOUX—Peel the peppers, remove seeds, cook in butter, then pound them finely in a mortar with half their weight of thick *Béchamel sauce* (see SAUCE). Rub through a sieve, reheat and add some butter.

This purée is used as a garnish for grills, and for poached or soft boiled eggs.

Potato purée—See POTATOES.

Pumpkin purée—See PUMPKIN.

Spinach purée. PURÉE D'ÉPINARDS—Cook the spinach in salted water. Drain it, cool it in cold water, drain it anew and squeeze as dry as possible. Rub through a fine sieve then heat it and bind it with butter and cream.

Use as garnish with meat, and poached or soft boiled eggs. May also be used as a vegetable.

Tarragon purée. PURÉE D'ESTRAGON—*Hot:* Blanch rapidly in salted water 3 cups (250 grams) of fresh tarragon leaves. Drain, cool in cold water, drain again, squeeze as dry as possible and rub through a fine sieve.

Add this purée of herbs to 1 cup (2 decilitres) of thick *Béchamel sauce* (see SAUCE). Heat well, add butter, season and mix well.

Used as filling for mushrooms, artichoke bottoms and pastry shells, or as garnish for large or small cuts of meat, chicken, eggs or fish.

Cold: Bind the tarragon purée, prepared as above, with very thick mayonnaise. See also TARRAGON.

Used as an ingredient of cold hors-d'oeuvre.

Note. Watercress, chervil, parsley or other herb purées, hot or cold, are prepared in the same way.

Tomato purée—See SAUCE.

Truffle purée. PURÉE DE TRUFFES—Rub through a fine sieve ½ pound (250 grams) of fresh truffles, raw or cooked. Mix this truffle pulp with 1 cup (2 decilitres) of *Béchamel sauce* (see SAUCE) which has been cooked with fresh cream.

Boil for a few moments. Strain through a cloth.

Used as filling for the pastry cases and little shells of bread, potato crust, etc., which accompany elaborate dishes, and as stuffing for artichoke bottoms, mushrooms, etc., as well as a liaison for various sauces.

PURÉE-PRESSER. PASSE-PURÉE—Kitchen utensil, of which there are many types, used for pressing through purées of meat, fish, vegetables or fruit.

PURSLANE OR PUSSLEY. POURPIER—A weed of both hemispheres. There are two principal varieties of purslane: the *Common* or *Winter Purslane*, cultivated for its large leaves, and the *Garden Purslane* or *Rosemoss.*

Ordinarily the leaves of common purslane are eaten in salad, but they may also be cooked and served with butter or cream or in their own juices, like French beans.

Finally, purslane leaves may be preserved in vinegar and used as a condiment.

QUAIL. CAILLE—This word comes from the old Flemish word *Quakele*. Quail is a bird of passage, a native of hot countries. It comes to Europe in the spring and returns to hot climates at the beginning of winter.

The common quail (*Coturnix Vulgaris*) is the only species which comes to Europe but there are many exotic varieties of quail in Asia and the Indian Archipelago.

There is a bird called American quail belonging to the American partridge family. It is a little bigger than the common quail and its flesh has a delicate flavour. It can be found on the markets in France in the winter. It can be prepared in any manner suitable for ordinary quail.

In September and October the quails begin to migrate to Africa and India. In the spring they cross the Mediterranean in enormous blocks—covering the whole distance without stopping—and come to France. There they are trapped alive and put into cages for systematic fattening.

Charles Jobey says that the quail 'belongs to the highest aristocracy of the bird world' and this is true in so far as wild quail is concerned, but applies much less in the case of quail bred for food. No doubt quail which have been fattened in a cage by the modern process are not without flavour, but a real connoisseur of delicate game will not be content with that.

There are a great many recipes for the preparation of this bird. It should never be allowed to get high. In addition to the recipes given below for the preparation of quail, it can also be prepared by following any of the recipes given for *Partridge**.

Quails in cases (cold). CAILLES EN CAISSE—Prepare the quails as described below in the recipe for *Chaud-froid of quails*.

Arrange each bird in an oval-shaped paper case or fine porcelain dish. Surround with a border of chopped jelly.

Quails in cases (stuffed). CAILLES EN CAISSE—Bone the quails. Stuff each with a little (25 grams) of *Forcemeat à gratin** (adding to it the quails' livers) and mixing in some chopped truffles. Reshape the birds again to give them their proper form and wrap each in a piece of buttered greaseproof paper. Put them into a buttered pan, placing them in tightly against each other. Sprinkle with a little melted butter, cover with a lid and cook in the oven from 15 to 18 minutes. Remove the birds from the sauté pan and, after taking off the papers, put each into an oval-shaped paper case, brushed with oil and dried in the oven. Dilute the pan juices with Madeira, moisten with a little concentrated game stock and pour over the quail. Put the cases back in the oven for 5 minutes, then serve on a napkin-covered dish.

Quails in cases à l'italienne. CAILLES EN CAISSES À L'ITALIENNE—Prepare the quails as described in the recipe for *Quails in cases* (stuffed). Put a spoonful of *Italian sauce* (see SAUCE) into each case before putting in the birds. Finish cooking as described in the recipe for *Quails in cases*.

Quails in cases à la Lamballe. CAILLES EN CAISSES À LA LAMBALLE—Prepare the quails as described above. Before putting in the birds, line the cases with a *julienne** of mushrooms and truffles blended with cream. Dilute the pan juices with port, add some fresh cream and pour this sauce over the quails.

Quails in cases à la mirepoix. CAILLES EN CAISSES À LA MIREPOIX—Prepare the quails as described above. Add some vegetable *Mirepoix** to the pan juices and pour over the birds.

Quails in cases Mont-Bry. CAILLES EN CAISSES MONT-BRY—Prepare the quails as described above, replacing *à gratin forcemeat* by *Chicken forcemeat* (see FORCEMEAT) mixed with chopped truffles. Dilute the pan juices left over from cooking the birds with champagne and brown veal gravy. Place the quails into cases and garnish with a *ragoût** of cocks' combs and kidneys.

Quails in cases à la Périgueux. CAILLES EN CAISSES À LA PÉRIGUEUX—Prepare the quails as described above. Arrange them in cases, put a thick slice of truffle on each one and pour over *Périgueux sauce* (see SAUCE), to which the pan juices left over from cooking the birds, diluted with Madeira, have been added.

Quails in cases à la strasbourgeoise. CAILLES EN CAISSES À LA STRASBOURGEOISE—Bone the quails and stuff them with a *salpicon** of foie gras and truffles, seasoned with salt and a pinch of spices and sprinkled with a few drops of brandy. Wrap the birds in buttered papers and cook as described in the recipe for *Quails in cases*. Arrange in paper cases, put a thick slice of truffle on each and cover with *Périgueux sauce*. See SAUCE.

Quails in cases à la vigneronne. CAILLES EN CAISSES À LA VIGNERONNE—Bone the quails leaving the legs and the wings intact. Stuff with foie gras and truffles (in large dice), sprinkled with brandy and well seasoned. Reshape the quails, wrap each one in a piece of muslin and tie with string.

Put to cook in jelly stock (made out of a veal knuckle and the quails' bones and trimmings) and add some white Bordeaux wine.

When the quails are cooked, drain them and cool thoroughly under a light press. Unwrap, coat with

Quails in cases à la vigneronne

Brown chaud-froid sauce (see SAUCE) prepared with a part of the liquor in which the quails were cooked. Glaze with jelly (made out of the rest of the liquor and flavoured with Madeira).

Arrange the quails, each in an oval-shaped frilly paper case, or in little individual silver dishes. Put on each quail a large round slice of truffle and top this with three large grapes.

Casserole of quails (or quails in cocotte). CAILLES EN CASSEROLE, EN COCOTTE—Put into each quail a piece of butter, the size of a cob-nut, kneaded with a little salt and pepper. Truss the birds. Put them into an earthenware casserole (or cocotte) in which some butter has been heated. Season and cook in the oven from 12 to 15 minutes. At the last moment add a dash of brandy and baste with a few tablespoons of game stock.

The quails may be wrapped in a vine leaf or in a thin rasher (slice) of bacon. Quails cooked in this way may be served with croûtons fried in butter, either spread with *à gratin forcemeat* (see FORCEMEAT), or not, according to taste.

Casserole of quails à la bonne femme. CAILLES EN CASSEROLE À LA BONNE FEMME—Cook the quails in a casserole with a garnish composed of diced potatoes (tossed in butter) and diced bacon (blanched). Finish cooking as described in the recipe for *Casserole of quails*.

Casserole of quails with grapes. CAILLES EN CASSEROLE AUX RAISINS—Clean out and singe 6 quails. Pluck them, truss and wrap each in a vine leaf and thin rasher (slice) of fat bacon. Put the quails into a sauté pan in which a good tablespoon of butter has been heated. Put the pan in a hot oven and cook for 8 minutes. Take the quails out of the pan, remove trussing string and arrange them in an earthenware oven-proof dish. Add 60 large fresh grapes, peeled and seeded. Sprinkle with the fat given out by the birds. Put the dish in the oven, uncovered, for 5 minutes.

At the last moment, that is exactly at the moment of serving, sprinkle the birds with their pan juices, diluted with 2 tablespoons of brandy and 4 tablespoons of brown veal gravy. Cover the cocotte, put it on a napkin and serve at once.

Chaud-froid of quails. CAILLES EN CHAUD-FROID, CHAUD-FROID DE CAILLES—Bone 10 quails completely and stuff with game *Forcemeat à gratin**. In the middle of the forcemeat put a piece of uncooked foie gras studded with a piece of truffle, seasoned with salt and spices and sprinkled with brandy. Reshape the quails, wrap each in a piece of muslin and tie both ends with string, in such a manner as to make little *ballottines*.

Put these ballottines into a sauté pan on a foundation of fresh bacon rinds (pork rind), carrots and onions—all chopped and fried in butter. Cover the birds, with their bones and trimmings previously tossed in butter. Moisten with $1\frac{1}{4}$ cups ($2\frac{1}{2}$ decilitres) of Madeira. Reduce (boil down) this liquid almost completely. Add some veal stock simmered with a few tablespoons of *Aspic jelly* (see JELLY). Bring to the boil, cover the sauté pan, then cook in a hot oven for 20 minutes.

Drain the quails, put them into a flat terrine. Strain the liquor in which the birds were cooked and pour over them. Leave to cool in this liquor.

Drain the quails again, unwrap, and dry thoroughly. Cover completely with half-set jelly. Keep on ice until (see SAUCE), which should be made out of the liquor left over from cooking the quails in the usual manner and flavoured with Madeira or some other wine.

Decorate the quails with pieces of truffles and the white of hard boiled eggs. Glaze with jelly and chill.

Arrange the quails in a crown in a deep, round dish. Cover completely with half set jelly. Keep on ice until ready to serve.

Note. Quails *en chaud-froid* prepared as above can be arranged in different ways. In old culinary practice, when, generally speaking, the arrangements were rather elaborate and when all cold dishes included a great deal of purely decorative elements, quails *en chaud-froid*—and other small game prepared in a similar manner—were mounted on moulded stearin pedestals and ornamented with jelly shapes on skewers and even with wax figurines. This type of arrangement is no longer popular. We confine ourselves to serving quails *en chaud-froid* straight on the dish, merely surrounding them with chopped jelly, or putting the quails into a glass or crystal dish and covering them with a clear and succulent jelly.

The quails can also be served individually, each in an oval-shaped frilly paper case on a foundation of chopped jelly, or in porcelain, glass or silver dishes.

Quails en chemise. CAILLES EN CHEMISE—Stuff the quails with *Forcemeat à gratin**. Truss them as for an entrée and enclose each one in a piece of small intestine. Tie up the piece of intestine at both ends and wrap the quails in a piece of muslin, which should also be tied at both ends. Put the quails to poach from 15 to 18 minutes in boiling clear stock. Drain, remove the muslin and serve the quails in a *timbale**, wrapped in their '*chemises*', sprinkled with a few tablespoons of the liquor in which they were cooked. At the same time serve *Rouennaise sauce* (see SAUCE) with some concentrated game stock, cooked down to the consistency of a *fumet**, added to it.

Quails with cherries. CAILLES AUX CERISES—Cook the quails (trussed as for an entrée) in butter in a casserole or an earthenware cocotte. When three-quarters done add 12 stoned cherries for each quail.

Either cooked or fresh cherries can be used. In the latter case, they should be treated in the following manner: Stone the cherries, put them into an ovenproof dish and cook in a low oven, without any liquid except the juice rendered by the fruit.

Cold quails. CAILLES FROIDES—In addition to various recipes in this section, all the methods of preparation given for cold partridge are suitable for cold quail. See PARTRIDGE.

Devilled quails. CAILLES GRILLÉES À LA DIABLE—Split the quails down the back and flatten them slightly. Brush with melted butter, season with salt and freshly ground pepper and dip in white breadcrumbs. Grill the quails on both sides under a low heat. Arrange on a round dish and garnish with a border of sliced lemon and gherkins.

Serve with *Diable sauce* (see SAUCE) flavoured with concentrated game stock cooked down to the consistency of a *fumet**.

Quails à la financière (stuffed) I. CAILLES À LA FINANCIÈRE—Prepare and cook the quails as described in the recipe for *Quails in cases* (stuffed). When they are cooked, sprinkle with a few tablespoons of *Demi-glace sauce* (see SAUCE) and glaze in the oven, placing each bird on an oval-shaped croûton fried in butter. Surround with *Garnish à la financière**. Put a thick slice of truffle on each quail. Dilute the pan juices with Madeira, add some *Demi-glace sauce* (see SAUCE) based on game *fumet** and pour over the birds.

Quails à la financière II. CAILLES À LA FINANCIÈRE—Proceed as described in the above recipe and arrange the quails with their garnish in a puff pastry shell or in a *timbale* made of pie lining paste (pastry dough), baked blind (unfilled).

Quails à la financière with a rice border. CAILLES À LA FINANCIÈRE EN BORDURE DE RIZ—Prepare the quails and the garnish as described in the recipe for *Quails à la financière* and serve them in a rice border. See BORDER.

Quails à la gourmande. CAILLES À LA GOURMANDE—Stuff the quails with a mixture of butter, lean ham and chopped truffles and cook them in butter. Dilute the pan juices with champagne and chicken stock. Add some fresh truffles shredded into a *julienne**. Arrange the quails on a round dish, placing them on a foundation of large mushrooms stewed in butter and filled with a *salpicon** of foie gras. Heat the sauce until piping hot and pour over the birds.

Quails à la grecque. CAILLES À LA GRECQUE—Truss the quails as for an entrée and cook in butter. Arrange in a pyramid on a foundation of *Rice à la grecque** and pour over the pan juices left over from cooking the quails, diluted with game stock concentrated to the consistency of *fumet**.

Grilled quails à la duchesse. CAILLES GRILLÉES À LA DUCHESSE—Grill the quails as described in the preceding recipe. Arrange them on small *Duchess potato cakes* (see POTATOES), garnish with asparagus tips dressed with butter, and surround with a ring of *Demi-glace sauce* (see SAUCE), based on a game *fumet**, with butter added to it.

Grilled quails à l'indienne. CAILLES GRILLÉES À L'INDIENNE—For 12 quails prepare the following mixture in a bowl: $1\frac{1}{4}$ cups (300 grams) of butter, blended into a paste, 1 tablespoon of curry powder, 1 tablespoon of Mulligatawny paste, $\frac{1}{2}$ tablespoon of Worcestershire sauce, $\frac{1}{2}$ tablespoon of Harvey sauce, 2 teaspoons of unsweetened chutney, $\frac{1}{4}$ teaspoon of paprika and salt. All these ingredients must be blended into a highly seasoned paste, which, however, must not burn the tongue. Remove the breastbone and put a little of the paste into each bird. Sear the quails quickly in the oven, then cool them under a light press. Coat the outside of each quail with the same paste and grill. When they are nicely brown, finish cooking in the oven. Prepare a *Game forcemeat* border (see FORCEMEAT), put the rice in the middle, arrange the quails on top, pour over a little of the sauce and serve the rest separately. Hand straw potatoes at the same time.

Rice for the garnish. Brown some chopped shallots lightly and moisten with the stock in which the rice is to be cooked. Season with curry powder, Mulligatawny paste and paprika. Leave to cook for a moment, then strain through a fine strainer. Pour this stock over the rice, bring to the boil, add a good piece of butter, cover and cook in the oven for 20 minutes.

Indian sauce. Fry 2 onions and 2 cloves of garlic lightly in butter. Add a little curry powder and 2 diced cooking apples. Moisten with brown veal stock, leave to cook, then pass through a sieve, pour into a saucepan and taste the sauce to make sure the flavour is good. Pour over the quails. (Recipe by M. A. Menager, chef to King Edward VII of England.)

Jellied quails à la périgourdine. CAILLES À LA PÉRIGOURDINE, À LA GELÉE—Bone and stuff the quails with *à gratin game forcemeat* (see FORCEMEAT), foie gras and truffles, allowing quite a lot of truffles. Reshape the quails, wrap each one in a piece of muslin and tie at both ends. Poach from 20 to 25 minutes in liquid game jelly, flavoured with Madeira (or any other wine), prepared in advance in the usual manner. (See JELLY.) Leave the quails to cool in their liquor. Drain, unwrap and dry on a cloth. Put them into an oval-shaped terrine or into a glass bowl. Clarify the jelly in the usual manner and pour over the quails. Chill thoroughly before serving.

Quails à la limousine. CAILLES À LA LIMOUSINE—Arrange the quails, grilled as described above, on a foundation of artichoke hearts, cooked in a *court-bouillon**, simmered in butter and filled with a *Chestnut purée**. Pour round the border a ring of *Demi-glace sauce* (see SAUCE) based on concentrated game *fumet** with butter added to it.

Quails Lucullus. CAILLES LUCULLUS—Bone the quails, put into each bird an ounce (25 to 30 grams) of uncooked foie gras, seasoned with salt and spices and studded with a small peeled truffle. Put the quails into a sauté pan and cook as described in the recipe for *Quails in cases.* Arrange in a fairly low pie pastry shell filled with a *ragoût** of *Truffles à la crème**. Dilute the pan juices with Madeira, add some brown veal stock, reduce (boil down) by half and, at the last moment, pour over the birds.

Minute quails. CAILLES À LA MINUTE—Open the quails down the back and remove the small bones from the inside. Beat lightly to flatten. Season with salt and pepper and sauté the birds briskly in butter, browning them slightly on both sides. When done, sprinkle with a little chopped onion fried in butter and chopped parsley. Put some thinly sliced mushrooms (one per quail) into the sauté pan to brown, add a dash of brandy, moisten with some game *fumet** and brown veal stock, boil for a few moments, add a dash of lemon juice and pour this sauce over the birds.

Quails à la Monselet. CAILLES À LA MONSELET—Half bone the quails. Stuff them with a *salpicon** of truffles and foie gras. Wrap each bird in a piece of muslin and poach in Madeira-flavoured game stock made from the quails' bones and trimmings. Drain the birds, unwrap, put into an earthenware cocotte or into a silver casserole with a garnish composed of sliced artichoke hearts tossed in butter, cultivated mushrooms and thick slices of truffles. Strain the liquor in which the quails were cooked, add an equal quantity of thick fresh cream, cook down and pour over the birds. Cover the cocotte and put in a slow oven for 5 minutes. Serve in a cocotte.

Cold quail mousse. MOUSSE FROIDE DE CAILLES—Truss 12 quails as for an entrée and braise them in Madeira-flavoured stock, with the usual vegetables and truffle and mushroom trimmings added to it. Allow the quails to cool in the braising liquor.

Drain and bone them completely, taking care to preserve the wings intact, as they will be used for garnishing the mousse.

Using the trimming, bones and skins of the quails, prepare a *Brown chaud-froid sauce*. See SAUCE.

Separately, prepare game stock jelly, flavoured with Madeira or some other wine. See JELLY.

The mousse mixture is prepared as follows:

Pound the rest of the quails' flesh finely in a mortar, adding to it 6 ounces (180 grams) of cooked foie gras and 3 or 4 tablespoons of the chaud-froid sauce. When this mixture is quite smooth, take it out of the mortar and rub through a fine sieve. This process can be accomplished with an electric blender.

Transfer the mixture into a bowl. Stir vigorously, keeping the bowl on ice and adding a dash of brandy, 2 or 3 tablespoons of concentrated liquid game jelly and 1¼ cups (2½ decilitres) of fresh cream very stiffly whipped. Blend carefully.

Line the bottom and the walls of a mousse mould with a layer of game jelly. Arrange a border on the bottom of alternating rows of thick slices of truffles (cooked in Madeira) and half of the quails' wings, cooled under a press and coated with the chaud-froid sauce. Fill the mould with the mousse mixture to within the width of one finger from the edge. Lay the remaining wings on top, alternating with rows of truffle slices and finish off with a layer of game jelly, filling the mould right up to the top.

Leave the mousse on ice (or in a refrigerator) until it sets completely. Then, turn out on to a round dish—either straight on the dish or on a buttered croûton. Surround with chopped game jelly and put a border of small pieces of jelly, cut in the shape of wolf's teeth, around the edge of the dish.

Note. Instead of putting the quail mousse into a mould, it can be put into a glass or silver dish on a layer of well-set jelly. In that case, pile the mixture into a dome, garnish with quails' wings coated with the chaud-froid sauce and slivers of truffles and pour half-set jelly over the top.

The mousse, set in a mould, can also be turned out into a glass or crystal dish, which should be stood in another receptacle filled with crushed ice.

Quails in a nest

Quails in a nest. CAILLES AU NID—Bone the quails, stuff with *Game forcemeat à gratin* (see FORCEMEAT) mixed with chopped truffles, wrap each bird in a small piece of muslin and make into a roll. Poach for 18 minutes in a stock prepared from the bones and trimmings, with clear veal stock and Madeira. Drain the quails, unwrap, press in a cloth to give them their proper shape and glaze lightly in the oven. Arrange them in a nest of *Straw potatoes*, prepared as described in the recipe (see POTATOES), lined inside with a salted batter pancake and filled with a *ragoût** of cocks' kidneys, small button mushrooms and truffles, blended with a few tablespoons of *Financière sauce* (see SAUCE) to which the liquor left over from poaching the quails has been added. Put the rest of the *ragoût* on top.

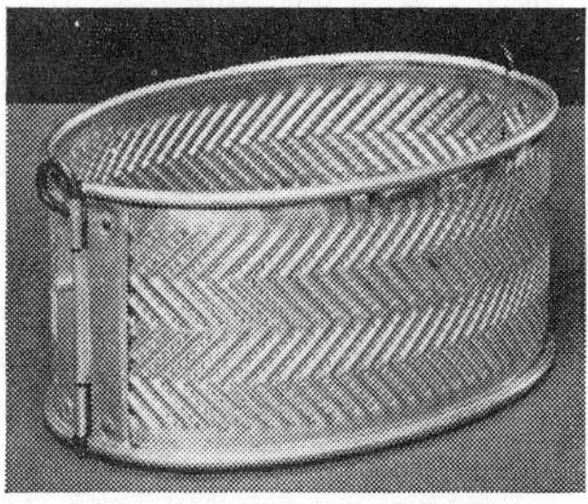

Hinged mould for quail pâté

Quail pâté. PÂTÉ DE CAILLES—Bone the quails completely. Stuff each one with a piece of *Forcemeat à gratin** about the size of a hazelnut and the same amount of foie gras, studded with a piece of truffle, the whole well seasoned with salt and spices and sprinkled with a dash of brandy. Wrap each quail in a very thin rasher (slice) of bacon.

Line a hinged oval or rectangular pâté mould with a fine pie pastry, then line the inside with thin rashers of bacon and cover the bottom and the walls of the mould with a layer of finely pounded forcemeat made of veal and lean and fat pork in equal proportions, bound with an egg, well seasoned, sprinkled with a little brandy and mixed with diced truffles. Over this forcemeat, on the bottom of the mould, put a layer of *Game à gratin forcemeat* (see FORCEMEAT). On this forcemeat, put in half of the stuffed quails, pressing down well. Cover with another layer of forcemeat, put in the rest of the quails and follow with a layer of forcemeat. Cover this with a layer of truffled forcemeat, flatten it and cover with a layer of thin rashers of lean bacon on top and cover with a piece of rolled out pastry, as usual. (See PÂTÉ, *Cold pâtés.*) Decorate the top with pieces of pastry cut in fancy shapes; see that they adhere properly, make a hole in the middle to allow steam to escape and brush the top with beaten egg. Bake in a hot oven for about an hour and a half.

When cooked, leave the pâté to cool and, when completely cold, pour some liquid game aspic jelly through the hole in the top.

Quails with peas. CAILLES AUX PETITS POIS—Cook the quails in a casserole as described in the appropriate recipe. Have ready a pint (½ litre) of fresh garden peas, cooked in butter, and some small young onions. Put the peas into the cocotte at the last moment and leave the whole to simmer together without allowing it to boil.

Quails petit-duc. CAILLES PETIT-DUC—Split the quails on the back and season with salt and paprika. Sprinkle with melted butter and dip in white breadcrumbs. Grill them and arrange each one on a little cake of *Anna potatoes* (see POTATOES), baked in tartlet tins. Put a large grilled mushroom, filled with grated horseradish, on each quail. Heat a few tablespoons of game *fumet**, add some Madeira and butter and pour over the birds.

Quails with rice. CAILLES AU RIZ—Truss the quails as for an entrée, season and cook in butter. Arrange them in a pyramid on a foundation of a rice *pilaf** to which the butter left in the pan after cooking the quails has been added. Add a dash of brandy to the pan juices, moisten with concentrated brown veal stock or concentrated game *fumet**. Pour over the quails.

Quails with rice (stuffed). CAILLES AU RIZ—Prepare and cook the quails as described in the recipe for *Quails in cases*.

Arrange them on a foundation of rice *pilaf**. Dilute the pan juices with brown veal stock, simmer for a few moments and pour over the quails.

Quails with risotto. CAILLES AU RISOTTO—Proceed as described in the recipe for *Quails with rice*, replacing the rice pilaf by *Risotto with cheese**.

Quails with risotto à la piémontaise. CAILLES AU RISOTTO À LA PIÉMONTAISE—Arrange quails cooked in butter on *Risotto à la piémontaise**, mixed with finely sliced white truffles. Dilute the pan juices with concentrated brown veal stock and pour over the quails.

Roast quails. CAILLES RÔTIES—Wrap the quails first in vine leaves, then in thin rashers of bacon and secure with string. Roast on a spit before a lively fire from 12 to 15 minutes (or in the oven, from 10 to 12 minutes). Arrange each quail on a garnished canapé. Garnish with watercress and quarters of lemon. Dilute the pan juices and serve the resulting sauce separately.

Quails à la romaine. CAILLES À LA ROMAINE—Heat some butter in an earthenware casserole and brown the quails all over. Add fresh peas, which have been prepared separately in the following manner: Fry some finely chopped young onions in butter with lean diced ham. Add freshly shelled peas. Season with salt and a pinch of sugar. Cover and cook from 35 to 40 minutes.

With the peas covering the quails, cover the casserole and finish cooking together in the oven. Serve in the same casserole.

Quails Saint-Mars. CAILLES EN COCOTTE SAINT-MARS—Put the quails, trussed as for an entrée, into a sauté pan. Cover them with a *julienne** of fairly coarsely shredded carrot, onion and celery, lightly fried in butter and moistened with double veal stock flavoured with sherry. Season and cook without a lid. Drain the quails, untruss and arrange in an earthenware cocotte (or a silver plate casserole). Cover with a *julienne** of coarsely shredded truffles and mushrooms. Pour the pan juices over the *julienne**. Sprinkle with 2 tablespoons of brandy and dot with small pieces of butter. Cover the cocotte and seal the lid with flour-and-water paste. Cook in the oven, in a *bain-marie** from 15 to 18 minutes.

Quails à la Souvarof. CAILLES À LA SOUVAROF—Stuff the quails with a *salpicon** of foie gras and truffles seasoned and sprinkled with a dash of brandy. Truss as for an entrée. Fry briskly in butter for 6 minutes. Put into an earthenware cocotte in which some truffles have previously been cooked, allowing two truffles per quail. Season with salt and pepper. Dilute the pan juices with Madeira, moisten with *Demi-glace sauce* (see SAUCE) based on game *fumet**. Simmer for a few moments and pour over the quails. Add a dash of brandy. Cover the cocotte, seal the lid on and cook in the oven for 12 minutes.

Quails à la Talleyrand. CAILLES À LA TALLEYRAND—Split the quails open, flatten them lightly and season. Coat on both sides with a thin layer of *Vegetable mirepoix**, mixed with a good tablespoon of lean, chopped, cooked ham and chopped truffles. Wrap each quail in a piece of pig's caul or a sheet of salt pork. Sprinkle with melted butter and roll in fresh breadcrumbs. Grill the quails on a low flame and arrange on puff pastry tartlets, baked blind (empty) and filled with mushroom purée. Serve with *Périgueux sauce* based on a game *fumet**. See SAUCE.

Quail terrine. TERRINE DE CAILLES—Bone the quails, stuff with foie gras, truffles and finely pounded game forcemeat and proceed as described in the recipe for *Terrine of pheasant*. See PHEASANT and TERRINE.

Tinned (canned) quails in jelly. CONSERVES DE CAILLES À LA GELÉE—*Forcemeat ingredients.* $\frac{1}{2}$ pound (200 grams) fine pork minced, $\frac{1}{4}$ pound (100 grams) *Forcemeat à gratin**, $\frac{1}{2}$ pound (200 grams) of cooked foie gras, 3 ounces (80 grams) of truffles (net weight), brandy, salt, pepper and spices.

Liquor for stewing. Strong meat jelly stock made from beef, a veal knuckle, calf's feet, chicken, fresh bacon rinds and the usual vegetables and aromatics, 2 cups (4 decilitres) of Madeira.

Method. Truss the quails as for an entrée. Remove the backbone and the breastbone and spread the quails flat on the table. Season and sprinkle with brandy.

Inside each quail put a piece of the forcemeat, the size of an egg. Each piece of forcemeat should have a piece of foie gras in the middle, which, in turn, is studded with a quarter of a truffle.

Reshape the quails and wrap each one in a piece of buttered paper. Put them, packing them in tightly, into a buttered sauté pan. Cover with the bones and trimmings, which should previously be tossed in butter.

Moisten with 1 cup (2 decilitres) of Madeira and bring to the boil. Cover with a sheet of buttered paper. Cook in the oven, without a lid, for 25 minutes. (To make sure whether the birds are done, test the quails gently with the point of a trussing needle: if no blood comes out, the birds are cooked.) Allow to cool in the braising liquor.

Drain the quails, untruss, unwrap and dry them. Put them into tins, breast downwards.

Cover the quails with liquid jelly, to which the diluted braising liquor has been added and which has been clarified in the usual manner. See JELLY.

When the jelly is quite cold, solder the lids of the tins. Mark the lids and put the tins into a big pan. Cover with cold water. Put a weight on the tins so as to make sure they are well submerged.

Give them one hour and 10 minutes of *uninterrupted* boiling for tins containing one quail and one hour 15 minutes for tins containing 2 quails.

Drain the tins, put them on the table flat and separated from each other, placing them marked side up. Leave until quite cold.

QUARTER. QUARTIER—Part of an object divided in the ordinary way into four.

The quarter of the forepart of beef includes the shoulder and the sides.

The hindquarter is made up of the thigh and sirloin.

In French butchery a 'fifth' quarter is spoken of to describe all the inedible parts of the slaughtered animal: skin, horns, hoofs and tallow.

QUASI—Piece from the rump of veal.

QUASSIA-AMARA—A bitter decoction from the wood, bark or root of a South American (Surinam) tree, used for apéritifs and medicines.

QUATRE-QUARTS (Four Quarters)—Household cake mixture, made up of equal quantities of eggs, flour, butter and sugar. (English Pound Cake.)

Beat together in a bowl $\frac{1}{2}$ cup (125 grams) of sugar with either 2 large eggs or 3 small ones until the mixture becomes white and frothy.

Add 1 cup (125 grams) of sifted flour, then $\frac{1}{2}$ cup (125 grams) of melted butter. Flavour the mixture to taste with orange blossom water, orange or lemon peel or any liqueur, and pour it in a buttered mould. Cook in the oven at a gentle heat (350°F.) for 25 or 30 minutes.

QUENELLE—A sort of dumpling made with fish or meat forcemeat bound with eggs. According to certain culinary writers the word comes from the Anglo-Saxon *knyll*, meaning to pound, to grind, because the flesh of the meat or fish, before being turned into quenelles, must be pounded in the mortar.

Quenelles are made with all kinds of meat, poultry, game, fish and crustaceans.

They are made in different shapes, large and small. The most important is the quenelle prepared with the forcemeat called *godiveau* or *quenelle forcemeat*. See FORCEMEAT.

Quenelles, the small kind particularly, are used as an element in such garnishes as *Financière*, *Godard*, *Toulouse*, etc.

Large quenelles, which are generally decorated or embellished with truffles, pickled tongue, etc., are used as a more elaborate garnish for large braised fish or entrées.

They are also used to prepare tarts, *timbales* or other preparations of the same kind.

Quenelles of foie gras. QUENELLES DE FOIE GRAS—Pound a raw foie gras and rub it through a fine sieve.

As a separate operation pound half as much raw chicken flesh as there is foie gras, mixing in with it, little by little, half its weight of *bread panada**. Rub this forcemeat through a sieve.

Put it back in the mortar and pound again, adding to it, little by little, the purée of foie gras and 3 or 4 egg yolks. Season with salt, pepper and spices. Beat this forcemeat on ice.

Make the quenelles in the usual way (with a spoon or with a forcing bag) and poach them in salted water.

Quenelles of meat, veal, chicken, game. QUENELLES DE VIANDES, VEAU, VOLAILLE, GIBIER—Prepared in the same way as those for pike. See FORCEMEAT and PIKE.

Quenelles of pike mousseline. QUENELLES DE BROCHET MOUSSELINE—Made with *Mousseline forcemeat* (see FORCEMEAT). They are moulded in a tablespoon, laid in a buttered sauté pan and poached in boiling salted water from 8 to 10 minutes according to size.

The quenelles are then drained, dried and set on a round dish, each one placed on a croûton of bread fried in butter (or on puff pastry crusts). Garnish and sauce are according to the particular recipe. '*Mousseline*' quenelles may be prepared in the same way using other fish (whiting, brill, sole, salmon, trout).

Quenelles of pike princesse

Quenelles of pike princesse. QUENELLES DE BROCHET PRINCESSE—Set the quenelles on a border of pike *forcemeat** with truffles. Decorate the middle of the dish with asparagus tips. Coat with *Normande sauce*. See SAUCE.

QUICHE—The *quiche* or *kiche* (sometimes the word is spelt in this way) originates in Lorraine, although some writers claim that this kind of savoury custard tart belongs to German cookery, since in Germany the *quiche* is known under the name *kuchen*, from which the word *kiche* could have come.

There are several kinds of *quiche*. Each region of Lorraine or Alsace has its own, and each claims that this alone is the true one.

The name *quiche* is also used for some sweet custard tarts served as a sweet.

That these should be so called is wrong, because the real *quiche*, that of Lorraine, is always served as hors-d'oeuvre and never for the sweet course.

Quiche Lorraine

Method. In the past the quiche was made with a bread paste. Modern practice has substituted short crust or sometimes even puff pastry.

Line with ordinary short crust (see DOUGH, *Lining paste*) a pie dish or plate with fluted edges, 8 inches in diameter and well buttered. See that the pastry extends a little beyond the edges.

Put in the bottom of this flan case thin slices of streaky bacon, blanched and lightly fried in butter.

Fill the crust with a mixture composed of 4 eggs and 2 cups (4 decilitres) of thick fresh cream, seasoned with salt and well beaten.

Put on top, when the flan is filled, 2 teaspoons of butter divided up into tiny pieces.

Cook in the oven at moderate heat (375°F.) for 30 to 35 minutes. Serve very hot.

Note. Sometimes the flan pastry is enriched with thin slices of Gruyère cheese, which are set alternately with the bacon.

Quiche Lorraine (old recipe)—'Roll out as thinly as possible some bread dough.

'Put this sheet of paste on a metal dish with raised and fluted edges, sprinkled with flour.

'Put small pieces of very fresh butter all over the paste.

'Fill the pie dish with a mixture of thick cream and eggs well beaten together and seasoned with salt.

'Cook in a very hot oven for a maximum of 10 minutes.

'Serve very hot.'

Little quiches with cheese. PETITES QUICHES AU FROMAGE—Line some tartlet cases with short crust.

Put in the bottom of these cases some Gruyère cheese cut into very small pieces.

Fill them with a mixture of cream and eggs. Cook in the oven for 14 or 15 minutes. Turn out and set on a napkin. Serve very hot.

Little quiches with ham. PETITES QUICHES AU JAMBON—Proceed as in the last recipe, replacing the cheese by lean cooked ham cut up into small pieces.

QUIGNON—A big wedge of bread cut from one of the larger French loaves.

QUILLET (Pastry)—This sweetmeat was created in a Parisian *pâtisserie* which was managed for a long time by M. Charabot, one of the masters of French pastry-making. This is the recipe:

Put in a copper basin 2 cups (500 grams) of sugar, and 15 whole eggs, powdered vanilla and a very small pinch of salt. Beat this mixture with a whisk over a very gentle heat, without letting it get too hot.

When the mixture is half thickened remove it and continue to beat it away from the heat until it is almost cold. Then add to it 3¾ cups (500 grams) of sieved flour, sprinkled in a shower and 1 pound (500 grams) of melted butter.

Fill round cake tins with the mixture. Bake in the oven at a moderate heat. Cool the cakes and fill them with a butter cream made in this way:

Heat together in a saucepan ½ cup (1 decilitre) of milk, 1 cup of sugar, ¾ cup of water boiled to 220°F. (1 decilitre of 28° syrup), 1 cup (2 decilitres) of *orgeat** and a vanilla pod. Cook this mixture for a few moments, then pour it over 8 egg yolks in a basin. Blend well with a whisk. Reheat the mixture gently without allowing to boil. Cool. Pour into a bowl on to ½ pound (250 grams) of butter which has been put through a sieve. Mix well. Keep this butter cream in a cool place until it is needed.

Having filled the cake with the cream, pipe the same cream through a forcing (pastry) bag over the top, and decorate all round with sugar.

QUINCE. COING—Fruit of the quince, a common tree which used to be as well known as the apple and the vine. It has a tart and astringent flavour, a very sweet smell, and cannot be eaten raw. It is full of pectin and is used for jellies, jams, marmalade, syrups, and home-made liqueurs. See JAM, SYRUP.

Quince compote. COMPOTE DE COINGS—Cut ripe quinces into quarters. Trim the quarters; blanch them for a few minutes in boiling water. Drain them and cook them in a vanilla syrup. Arrange them in a dish or timbale. Pour over them the syrup in which they have cooked.

Quince jelly. GELÉE DE COINGS—Made with an equal weight of sugar and quince juice, like *Apple jelly*. See JAMS AND JELLIES.

Quince liqueur or ratafia—This liqueur is called *Quince water*. See LIQUEUR.

Quince marmalade. MARMELADE DE COINGS—Made in the same way as *Apple marmalade*. See MARMALADE.

Quince paste. PÂTE DE COINGS—Make some quince marmalade in the same way as *Apple marmalade* (see MARMALADE). Reduce (boil down) the marmalade to a good thick consistency. Put it on a shallow baking dish. Dry it in a warm oven. Cut the paste into square or rectangular slices. Dust them with crystallized sugar. Keep in a dry place.

QUINTAL—Name of a variety of cabbage.

Quinces (*Evereinoff*)

RABBIT. LAPIN—A small rodent of the hare family. The rabbit is of African origin. There are several breeds of rabbit. Those most commonly used for the table are the *Hutch rabbit* or *Domestic rabbit* and the wild rabbit, which comes into the category of ground game.

The fur of this rabbit is sometimes white, sometimes grey, or black and tan, or mottled.

The domestic rabbit should be eaten young, that is to say when it is from 3 to 3½ months old. A young rabbit, that is to say a tender rabbit, can be recognized by the following indications: a short neck, plump knees, and very flexible front legs, which can be bent about at will.

The warren rabbit, the typical species of wild rabbit, is prodigiously fertile.

Fulbert-Dumonteil, the well-loved poet of good eating, praised it in these terms:

'It provides a feast for countryman and labourer,' he says. 'It is the youngster's game. It is present on all festive occasions, be it a suburban wedding or a village christening. Its appetizing aroma pervades farmhouse and cottage alike.'

The flesh of rabbit is fairly white and somewhat less fatty than that of poultry. Its flavour depends a great deal on its feeding. It is more stringy and less delicate than white poultry, but quite as readily digestible.

Note. All recipes for young wild rabbit are suitable for domestic rabbit, and all recipes given below can equally well be applied to young wild rabbit.

Rabbit Coquibus. LAPIN COQUIBUS—Joint (divide into pieces) a rabbit and put it for a time in a marinade. Sauté it very quickly. Add 24 small young onions and the same number of strips of lean blanched bacon. Fry all these ingredients. Sprinkle with a heaped tablespoon of flour. Brown for a few seconds. Moisten with 1 cup (2 decilitres) of white wine, a few tablespoons of clear soup and the marinade, strained. Add a large *bouquet garni** consisting of parsley, thyme, bay leaves and savory. Boil for 15 minutes. Put 6 to 8 (400 grams) small new potatoes in the saucepan. Cover and cook for 45 minutes.

Fricassée of rabbit. GIBELOTTE—This fricassée, which is called *Gibelotte* in French, is made with white or red wine. See *Young wild rabbit en gibelotte*, below.

Rabbit sauté with curry. LAPIN SAUTÉ AU CURRIE—Proceed as for *Rabbit sauté with paprika*, substituting Indian curry powder for paprika. Serve *Rice à l'indienne** separately.

Rabbit sauté with paprika. LAPIN SAUTÉ AU PAPRIKA—Joint (divide into pieces) the rabbit and steep it in a marinade, in the usual way. Cook very slowly in butter, until tender, 1 medium-sized (100 grams) onion, sliced. Brown the rabbit in the same pan. Season with 2 teaspoons of paprika.

When the pieces of rabbit are well fried, sprinkle with a heaped tablespoon of flour. The flour should take on a golden colour but should not brown. Moisten with half a glass of white wine. Cook down and add enough clear stock just to cover the rabbit. Strain the marinade and add it to the stock. Dice coarsely 1 cup (150 grams) of mushrooms and put them in the pan. Cover and cook for 35 minutes. Add ½ cup of thick fresh cream. Keeping the pan covered, simmer for about 35 minutes until the rabbit is cooked. At the last moment, add a little more fresh cream.

YOUNG WILD RABBIT. LAPEREAU—The flesh of this rabbit is somewhat firmer than that of the hutch rabbit. It also has more flavour, though frequently it is spoiled by mustiness.

Blanquette of young wild rabbit. LAPEREAU EN BLANQUETTE—Cut the rabbit into neat sections and proceed as for *Blanquette of lamb*. See LAMB.

Boiled young wild rabbit à l'anglaise. LAPEREAU BOUILLI À L'ANGLAISE—Draw the rabbit by making a very small incision in the belly. Stuff it with a *Stuffing à l'anglaise* made from one-third veal or ox kidneys, one-third best veal fat or udder, one-third sandwich bread soaked in milk and squeezed dry. Add 1 egg to every pound (½ kilo) of stuffing. Season with salt, pepper and spices. Having stuffed the rabbit, sew up the opening and truss. Simmer it in salted water for about an hour. Serve *Caper sauce* separately. See SAUCE.

Young wild rabbit chasseur, or sauté with mushrooms. LAPEREAU SAUTÉ AUX CHAMPIGNONS, CHASSEUR—Joint the rabbit. Season with salt, pepper, thyme and powdered bay leaf and cook with mushrooms or *chasseur*, following the recipes given under LAMB, *Sauté of lamb chasseur*, or *with mushrooms*.

Young wild rabbit en gibelotte. LAPEREAU EN GIBELOTTE—This is prepared in exactly the same way as *Civet of hare* (see HARE) except that white wine is often used instead of red wine. It is also quite usual to add quartered potatoes or small potato balls to this *gibelotte*.

Potted wild rabbit or pâté. PÂTÉ OU TERRINE DE LAPEREAU—These preparations are made with boned rabbit stuffed with pork in the same way as *Potted hare* or *Pâté of hare*. See HARE.

Roast young wild rabbit. LAPEREAU RÔTI—Proceed as for *Roast hare*. See HARE.

Young wild rabbit sauté à la minute. LAPEREAU SAUTÉ À LA MINUTE—Skin, draw and joint the rabbit, taking care the bones do not splinter. Season with salt and pepper.

Brown it quickly in very hot butter in a heavy iron pan until all the pieces are a good colour. Shake the pan frequently and turn over the pieces so that they are cooked all through.

As soon as it is ready, put the rabbit in a pie dish and keep it warm.

Dilute the pan juices with ⅝ cup (1½ decilitres) of white wine. Add a chopped shallot. Boil down the sauce until it is very concentrated. Add thickened brown veal gravy.

Boil for a few seconds. Add a teaspoon of butter and a squeeze of lemon juice. Pour over the rabbit. Sprinkle with chopped parsley.

RABIOLE—A variety of kohl-rabi or turnip.

RABOTTE OR DOUILLON—A sort of fruit dumpling of Norman origin. The fruit, mostly apple or pear, is enclosed in a shortcrust pastry to make a *douillette* (a priest's overcoat), from which word comes its name. It is then cooked in the oven.

RACAHOUT—Mixture of starches which, according to Dorvault, must be made in the following proportions: 2 ounces (60 grams) each of cocoa, acorn flour and rice flour; 1½ ounces (45 grams) potato flour; ½ ounce (15 grams) salep; ½ pound (250 grams) white sugar; ⅛ ounce (5 grams) vanilla sugar. Prepared like drinking chocolate.

RACHEL—See GARNISHES.

RACLETTE—Variety of Swiss cheese fondue, speciality of the canton of Valais, made by holding a big piece of the local cheese to the fire and scraping off the softened part as it melts. The scraped-off cheese is put on a plate and eaten with potatoes in their jackets, not forgetting the accompaniment of the very heavy white wine of Valais.

RACOON. RATON-LAVEUR—Small wild animal, with longish grey fur, living in the forests of America. This animal is edible. It is cooked like wild rabbit.

RADISH. RADIS—Plant of the *Cruciferae* family, of which the root is edible. Cultivated in China, Japan and the Indies in the most remote areas, the radish is found now in all the temperate regions of Europe.

There are a great many varieties of radish. There are round, long, pink, black, white and purple radishes.

All the radishes are eaten raw as hors-d'oeuvre with butter and salt.

The tender leaves of pink radishes can also be eaten. Raw, they are put in salad; cooked, they are used like spinach.

Pink radishes may also be served hot, cooked like new turnips.

Black radishes. RADIS NOIRS—After having been peeled, black radishes are cut into rounds and put to soak in salt for half an hour.

The rounds are then washed and served in a radish dish.

Pink radishes in cream. RADIS ROSES À LA CRÈME—Peel the radishes and blanch in salted water. Drain and stew in butter. When they are cooked add the cream, allowing for 1 pound (500 grams) of radishes, 1½ cups (3½ decilitres) of cream. Boil down the cream by one-third. Serve in a deep dish.

Glazed pink radishes. RADIS ROSES GLACÉS—Peel the radishes, blanch them for 5 minutes in salted water, drain and cool in cold water.

Toss in butter over a good heat, sprinkling them with a little sugar. When they are lightly coloured moisten them with stock of water sufficient to barely cover them. Cook, covered, until they have absorbed all the liquid. At this point the radishes should be cooked and well glazed.

If they are still hard, add more liquid and boil down once more.

Pink radishes in gravy. RADIS ROSES AU JUS—Cook the radishes in salt water. When they are cooked drain them and moisten with a few tablespoons of meat juice reduced (cooked down) until it is thick and brown. Simmer gently.

Pink radishes poulette. RADIS ROSES À LA POULETTE—Cook the radishes as above, moistening them with *Poulette sauce*. Simmer gently in the sauce. See SAUCE.

RAGOT—Name given in France to a wild boar more than two years old.

RAGOULE—Common name for the agaric. This edible fungus is also known under the name of *barigoule*.

RAGOÛT—Ragoûts are made from meat, fowl or fish cut in pieces of regular shape and size, browned or cooked without colouring and with or without an accompaniment of vegetables.

The 'brown' ragoûts, of which the best-known type is the *Ragoût of mutton* or *Navarin* (see MUTTON), are prepared by frying the meat lightly, sprinkling with flour and adding stock, meat juices or water.

The uncoloured ragoûts—*à blanc*, or sometimes described as *à l'anglaise*, which must not be confused with *blanquettes* and *fricassées*, belong to the category of poached food. They have no thickening other than that created by the addition of potatoes to their preparation. Typical of these ragoûts is *Irish stew*.

Also included under the name of ragoûts are various garnishes, composed of one or more ingredients,bound with a white or brown liaison, with a meat or meatless stock, used in preparing entrées or to embellish fish, fowl, eggs and other preparations. See GARNISHES.

Method of cooking 'brown' ragoûts. Cut up the meat, whether boned or not, into neat pieces about 2 inches long. Brown them over a good heat in a sauté pan, in smoking hot clarified fat. Season with salt, pepper and a pinch of sugar (the addition of sugar giving the preparation a good natural colour).

As soon as the pieces of meat are browned, pour off three-quarters of the fat. Sprinkle with flour and let it colour a little, shaking the pot over the heat.

Stir in water, stock or meat juice; add a *bouquet garni** and, if the type of ragoût calls for it, crushed garlic and tomato sauce.

Cook, covered, in the oven or on a very low heat for 45 minutes to an hour.

Drain the pieces of meat; trim them, put them in another pot or in the same pot—cleaned—in which they were cooked, cover them with the specified vegetables and pour over the sauce, strained and with the fat removed.

Cook covered, simmering very gently, for 45 minutes to an hour according to the kind of meat being used. (Cooking in the oven is best.)

Serve in a dish or deep plate, putting the pieces of meat below and the vegetables on top. Pour the boiling hot sauce over all.

The method recommended above (trimming the drained pieces and putting them in another pot with the strained and de-greased sauce) gives a better-looking dish. In home cooking, this complication can be avoided and the accompanying vegetables can be put directly into the ragoût without changing pots.

Method of cooking for ragoûts 'à blanc' or 'à l'anglaise': Put the pieces of meat, cut in pieces as above, in a sauté pan, alternately with layers of potatoes cut in slices and chopped onions. Season with salt and pepper and put a *bouquet garni** in the centre.

Pour over water or stock in sufficient quantity to cover meat and vegetables. Start cooking on a good heat, then cover and cook in the oven or over a very low heat for about an hour and a half.

Serve in the same way as for the brown ragoût.

Ragoût à la banquière—Ingredients given in the recipe for *Banquière garnish*, mixed and bound with a good thick sauce. See GARNISHES and SAUCE.

Used as filling for pastry cases, *timbales*, pies, *vol-au-vent*, etc.

Ragoût à la cancalaise—Poached oysters, bearded; shrimps; *Normande sauce* to bind. See SAUCE.

Used as filling for pastry cases, *timbales*, pies, *vol-au-vent*, etc.

Ragoût of celeriac. RAGOÛT DE CÉLERI-RAVE—Celeriac cut to look like 'pigeon's eggs', stewed in butter and bound in a *Cream sauce*. See SAUCE.

Same uses as *Ragoût à la banquière**.

Ragoût à la cévenole—Composed of braised chestnuts, small glazed onions, and big dice of streaky (lean) bacon, blanched and lightly fried, the whole bound with the cooking liquor of the braised meat which this garnish should accompany—or with thick rich brown sauce, flavoured with Madeira.

Ragoût à la Chambord—See *Carp Chambord**.

Ragoût chipolata—Composed of braised chestnuts, small glazed onions, mushrooms and chipolata sausages. This ragoût, which is bound with rich brown sauce flavoured with Madeira, is used as garnish for large cuts of braised or oven-roast red meat.

Ragoût of cock's combs and kidneys. RAGOÛT DE CRÊTES ET DE ROGNONS DE COQ—This ragoût, used to garnish poultry, as filling for vol-au-vent or other pastry cases, for rice borders, etc., is made up of cocks' combs and kidneys cooked in a flour-and-water *court-bouillon** and bound with a white or brown sauce according to the type of preparation.

Ragoût à la financière—This ragoût, used to accompany meat and poultry, as well as for filling *timbales*, pies, vol-au-vent, rice borders and other mixed entrées, is made up of quenelles, cocks' combs and kidneys, truffles and mushrooms, completed sometimes with peeled olives and bound with *Financière sauce*. See SAUCE.

Ragoût à la Godard—See CHICKEN and GARNISHES.

Ragoût of lobster à la cardinal. RAGOÛT DE HOMARD À LA CARDINAL—Ragoût composed of a mixture of sliced, cooked lobster, and slices of cooked truffles and mushrooms bound with very thick *Cardinal sauce*. See SAUCE.

Used as filling for pastry cases, *timbales*, vol-au-vent, etc.

Ragoût à la marinière—Composed in principle of mussels cooked in white wine and taken out of their shells, and shelled shrimps, bound in a *Marinière sauce*. See SAUCE.

This ragoût is used to garnish braised fish or as filling for tarts, tartlets, *timbales*, *vol-au-vent*, etc.

It can be finished off with all sorts of shellfish cooked in white wine, with their shells removed.

Ragoût of molluscs. RAGOÛT DE COQUILLAGES—Prepared by binding shellfish (mussels, oysters, cockles, clams, etc.) cooked in white wine and shelled in a white sauce suitable to the nature of the dish.

Ragoût of mushrooms. RAGOÛT DE CHAMPIGNONS—Sliced sautéed mushrooms bound with *Velouté sauce* (see SAUCE) mixed with cream, or with brown sauce cooked down with Madeira. The same uses as above.

Ragoût Nantua I—Shell 40 medium-sized crayfish tails, previously cooked in *mirepoix**.

Put them in a sauté pan with a tablespoon of butter. Sauté for a moment over a good heat. Sprinkle with a tablespoon of flour, moisten with a spoonful of brandy and cover with fresh cream. Mix, cook over a gentle heat for 10 minutes, stirring often. At the last moment add 5 tablespoons (80 grams) of crayfish butter (see BUTTER, *Compound butters*) made of the scraps and shells of crayfish.

Ragoût Nantua II—Cook the crayfish tails for a moment in butter, moisten with brandy and cream and cook until it is reduced to half its quantity.

Add 1 cup (2 decilitres) of crayfish purée prepared with the scraps and shells and *Béchamel sauce*.

Crayfish tails à la Nantua are used to fill pastry cases, tarts, tartlets and vol-au-vent. They are also used to garnish egg and fish dishes of various kinds. Sometimes truffles cut in slices or little olive-shaped pieces are added to the ragoût.

Offal (variety meats) ragoût. RAGOÛT D'ABATS—Ragoût of this kind, used as a garnish for braised, poached or oven-roast poultry, and also to garnish entrées made with pastry, is made with white offal (variety meats), brains and lamb's or calf's sweetbreads, sliced or cut in dice, with or without the addition of mushrooms and truffles, and bound with brown or white sauce.

Ragoût à la périgourdine—Mix *foie gras* cut in large dice and sautéed briskly in butter, with truffles cut in dice in the same way and cooked very lightly in butter. Bind them with concentrated cooking juices of the fowl or game to be garnished, flavoured with Madeira or some other wine.

Used as garnish for oven-roasted or braised poultry or game, and also as accompaniment to egg dishes of various kinds, pilaf, risotto, various borders of garnish and entrées made with pastry.

Sea-food ragoût. RAGOÛT DE LANGOUSTE, CRUSTACÉS—Small slices of crawfish, lobster, prawns or shrimps, shelled, bound with a *Cream sauce* or *White wine sauce* (see SAUCE) and finished with *Shrimp or other crustacean butter*. See BUTTER, *Compound butters*.

Ragoût Talleyrand—Heat in a small sauté pan with a few spoonfuls of Madeira, ¼ pound (125 grams) of cock's kidneys cooked in flour-and-water *court-bouillon**, and ¼ pound (125 grams) of mushrooms also cooked in flour-and-water *court-bouillon*. Bind with ¾ cup (1½ decilitres) of *Chicken velouté sauce* (see SAUCE) mixed with cream, strained and with the addition of 2 large tablespoons of *mirepoix** of root vegetables and a tablespoon of truffles cut in very small dice.

Ragoût à la tortue—This ragoût is the special accompaniment of calf's head cooked *à la tortue*. It is composed of quenelles, mushrooms, stuffed olives, sliced truffles, gherkins cut in small olive-shaped pieces, slices of tongue and calf's brain, all bound with *Tortue sauce* (rich brown sauce with Madeira added, flavoured with turtle herbs, see HERBS) and completed with small fried eggs, heart-shaped pieces of bread fried in butter and crayfish cooked in *court-bouillon** (these last ingredients added to the garnish when it is being set round the dish). See OFFAL OR VARIETY MEATS, *Calf's head en Tortue*.

Ragoût à la toulousaine—Ragoût used to garnish poultry, vol-au-vent and other preparations served as entrées. Composed of chicken forcemeat quenelles, slices of lamb's or calf's sweetbreads, cock's combs and kidneys, mushrooms and truffles, the whole bound with *Allemande sauce*. See *Chicken Toulouse*.

Ragoût of truffles. RAGOÛT DE TRUFFES—Under this name is described a garnish of truffles cut in thick slices or big dice and bound with either *Rich brown sauce* flavoured with Madeira or with a *White sauce*. See SAUCE.

Ragoût of vegetables or Ragoût à la printanière. RAGOÛT DE LÉGUMES DIT À LA PRINTANIÈRE—Put in a well buttered sauté pan the following vegetables: 1 pound (500 grams) of new carrots, 12 little new onions, 3 medium-sized artichokes divided into quarters (blanched for 5 minutes in water with salt and lemon juice), and 2 lettuces, trimmed, blanched, divided in quarters and folded over as for braising. Pour over the vegetables either water or white stock, for a richer preparation, in sufficient quantity to just cover them. Season and start cooking over a good heat. Cook at boiling point for 8 minutes with the pot covered, then add a pint ($\frac{1}{2}$ litre) of freshly shelled peas and a dozen new peeled potatoes. Cook, covered, in the oven for 40 to 45 minutes. Set in a deep dish. Pour the cooking liquor, reduced and enriched with butter, over the vegetables.

Note. This ragoût can be made with all sorts of new vegetables: fresh kidney beans, new broad beans, courgettes (zucchini) cut in quarters, asparagus tips, either white or green, cucumbers cut into small chunks, French beans, new turnips, etc.

These ragoûts should be cooked in earthenware casseroles, in fireproof porcelain or bi-metal pots and served in the same utensil.

RAGUENEAU—Parisian pastrycook described by Cyrano de Bergerac in his *Voyage aux états de la lune*, and again by Edmond Rostand.

A pastrycook of renown, keeping shop near the Palais, as fat as was suitable for a shopkeeper whose sign carried the words: *Aux amateurs de haulte graisse*, his days were spent happily, and without any occurrence of note, between the supervision of his oven and the service of his clientele, which was composed of attorneys and lawyers, among whom had slipped in some hungry-looking writers.

Why did he have to begin to write? History suspects one Béis—an author today completely forgotten—of having maliciously drawn him into it.

The *pâtisserie* of Ragueneau became a sort of academy, where the pastries and tarts served as attendance tallies. Ragueneau set himself to write a Pindaric ode, then a tragedy: *Don Olibrius, l'Occiseur d'Innocents*.

He neglected his oven, neglected his clients; the effect on his business was such that he felt constrained to shut up shop.

Packing up his belongings into a miserable little cart, he set off for the Midi with his wife. At Béziers he sought out Molière, to whom he offered *Don Olibrius*. One may guess the response of the great humorist; but out of pity he offered the ex-pastrycook a modest part as a valet in his troupe. Ragueneau was as bad an actor as he was a writer and he had to resign himself to the function of a candle-snuffer.

These functions he carried out subsequently at Lyons until his death, leaving as his whole fortune a hat with holes in it and a washed-out cloak. Among his papers were found four hundred and fifty-six sonnets, eight tragedies, seven epithalamiums, four elegies, sixty-three odes and nineteen heroic plays.

RAIDIR—In English 'to stiffen' or 'seal'—a culinary term meaning to sear a foodstuff quickly in butter or other smoking hot fat.

RAIL. RÂLE—Name of two species of migrant waders, the *Rail* or in French 'king of quails', and the *Water-rail*, very inferior to the former. Prepared like *Quail*.

RAISINÉ—Jam made by reducing grape juice or must to a jellied consistency. Often another fruit is added, principally pears.

Simple raisiné. RAISINÉ SIMPLE—Choose very sweet grapes, either green or black, strip them from their bunches and keep only the perfectly sound fruit. Put them in a pot over a gentle heat, and crush with a wooden spoon. Rub through a sieve, gathering the juice in a basin. Pour half this juice into a rinsed out pan and cook over over a stong heat, skimming from time to time. When the liquid rises, add a little of the juice reserved in the basin, repeat this each time it rises. Do not stop stirring until the cooking is done, which will be when the *raisiné* is boiled down by two-thirds.

Raisiné de Bourgogne—Prepare the must as described above, add sugar if necessary, reduce (cook down) to half, then put in fruit (pears, quinces, apples, peaches, melon, etc.) peeled, seeded and cut into thin slices. Cook like the simple *raisiné* until the preserve is so thick that if taken between thumb and forefinger, it forms a gluey thread.

RAISINS. RAISINS DE MALAGA—These are made from dried muscat grapes and are eaten as dessert. They are also used in confectionery as an ingredient of cakes and puddings, and in cookery to garnish various dishes.

RAITON—Small-sized skate, usually cooked by frying. See SKATE.

RAKI—Alcoholic drink with a basis of plum or grape *eau-de-vie*, flavoured with aniseed and mastic.

RAMBOUR OR RAMBOURG—Variety of apples whose name comes from the Rambour (Somme) district, where they were first cultivated. This fruit ripens in August. There is a *White* and a *Red Rambour*.

RAMEKIN. RAMEQUIN—Formerly toasted cheese was served under this name. Nowadays ramekins are tarts or tartlets filled with creamed cheese; this designation having, however, different interpretations in different regions.

Small pastries made with cheese-flavoured *chou* pastry are called ramekins. Individual earthenware baking dishes are also called ramekins.

Cheese ramekin I. RAMEQUIN DE FROMAGE—Add to 3 cups (500 grams) of *chou* pastry made without sugar, called ramekin pastry (see DOUGH, *Gougère pastry*), $\frac{1}{2}$ cup (50 grams) of grated Gruyère and $\frac{1}{3}$ cup (50 grams) of Gruyère cut in small dice.

Pipe the paste on to a baking tin in the form of medium-sized *choux*, through a forcing (pastry) bag with a plain nozzle. Brush with egg. Put on top of each a pinch of Gruyère cut into very small dice. Cook in the oven at moderate heat (375°F.) for 12 to 15 minutes.

Note. The ramekins may also be made in the form of elongated *choux*.

If a forcing bag is not available they may be shaped with a spoon.

Cheese ramekin II (old recipe). RAMEQUIN DE FROMAGE —'Take some cheese, melt it with butter, onion, whole or pounded, salt and pepper, spread over some bread, pass the shovel from the hot fire above it and serve hot.'

Note. This recipe, an extract from an old instruction book, is closely comparable with that of *Welsh rabbit* which is given in its alphabetical order.

Ramekin (Mont-Bry's recipe). RAMEQUIN—'Put in a saucepan a cup of milk. Season with a good pinch of salt, a very small pinch of sugar and a very little white pepper. Add 1½ tablespoons (25 grams) of butter. Bring to the boil.

'As soon as the milk is boiling, put into the pot, which you will have taken off the heat, ¾ cup (100 grams) of sifted flour. Mix. Stir over the heat with a wooden spoon to dry out the paste, exactly as is done for *chou* pastry.

'When the paste is well dried, remove from heat and add 3 eggs, one by one, and ⅜ cup (50 grams) of Gruyère cheese cut in small dice.

'Put the paste into a forcing (pastry) bag fitted with a plain nozzle and squeeze it into *choux* on a baking tin. Brush with egg and put on top of each a pinch of Gruyère cut in very little dice. Cook in a low oven.'

RAMEREAU—In French, a young wood-pigeon. For its culinary preparation see PIGEON.

RAMPION. RAIPONCE—Plant cultivated in gardens, but also growing wild in the fields.

The root of rampion may be eaten raw or cooked. It is prepared like salsify.

The leaves can be eaten raw in salad or cooked like spinach.

RANCIO—Red or rosé wine of the Midi with Madeira-like taste. This wine is very sweet, and its taste is reminiscent of Spanish wines.

RÂPÉ—Abbreviation for *Fromage râpé* (grated cheese).

RASPBERRY. FRAMBOISE—The raspberry is the fruit of the raspberry bush which grows wild in woods or which can be cultivated in the garden. It is one of the most delicately flavoured fruits.

This berry, which is not to be confused with blackberry (or brambleberry) is most often eaten raw.

It can also be prepared in various ways—such as in jelly, jam, compote, sweet paste and liqueurs.

Distillation of raspberries results in very delicious brandy.

The following are the best cultivated varieties in France.

Belle de Fontaney; Perpétuelle de Billard; Merveille des Quatre-Saisons (red or white); *Hornet* or *Pilate* (non-climbing).

Raspberry Bavarian cream. BAVAROIS AUX FRAMBOISES—This is prepared in the same way as other Bavarian creams with the addition of pulped raspberries. See BAVARIAN CREAM.

Raspberry charlotte. CHARLOTTE AUX FRAMBOISES—Line a mould with sponge-fingers as for *Charlotte russe**. Fill the mould with a charlotte composition adding raspberry pulp (see CHARLOTTE). Put in the refrigerator. Turn out of mould on to a dish covered with a folded napkin or a lace doyley.

Raspberry compote. COMPOTE DE FRAMBOISES—Remove stems of very ripe large raspberries. Put in a glass fruit dish or silver bowl. Pour several tablespoons of boiling syrup (¾ cup sugar to 1 cup water) on the fruit.

Raspberry cream. CRÈME AUX FRAMBOISES—Add cooked raspberry pulp to custard made with a little arrowroot, or cornstarch.

Iced raspberry mousse or purée. MOUSSE, MOUSSELINE GLACÉE À LA FRAMBOISE—This is made from raspberry juice or pulp (fresh or tinned) like other iced fruit mousses and purées. See ICE CREAMS AND ICES.

Raspberry juice or pulp. JUS, PULPE DE FRAMBOISES—Proceed with fresh raspberries as described for *Strawberry pulp*. See STRAWBERRIES.

Raspberry desserts, etc. — See also CRÊPES, FLAN, FRITTER, ICE CREAMS AND ICES, JAMS, LIQUEUR, SAUCE, SOUFFLÉS, SYRUP, TART.

RASTEGAÏS (Russian cookery) — See HORS-D'OEUVRE, *Hot hors-d'oeuvre*.

RAT—Rodent which was elevated to the rank of comestible during the siege of Paris in 1870, and which is eaten in certain regions. The flesh of well-nourished rats can be, it seems, of good quality, but sometimes with a musky taste. Rats nourished in the wine stores of the Gironde were at one time highly esteemed by the coopers, who grilled them, after having cleaned out and skinned them, on a fire of broken barrels, and seasoned them with a little oil and plenty of shallot. This dish, which was then called Cooper's Entrecôte, would be the origin of the *Entrecôte à la bordelaise*.

RATAFIA—a liqueur obtained without distilling, by simple infusion. See LIQUEUR.

RATATOUILLE—Peel and slice 6 aubergines and 6 Italian marrows (courgettes), sprinkle with salt and leave covered with a weighted plate for 1 hour. Slice 2 large onions. Skin, remove pips and cut up 8 tomatoes. Slice 2 peppers very thinly, removing core and seeds. Chop 3 garlic cloves.

Heat 1 cup olive oil in a heavy pan, fry onion until slightly coloured, add the garlic. Cook for 5 minutes, then add aubergines, courgettes, peppers and tomatoes. Season with salt and pepper, add a bouquet garni and cook, covered, for an hour. This dish may be served hot or cold.

RATON—Pastry with a cream cheese basis.

RAVIER—Small dish varying in shape and material in which hors-d'oeuvre are served.

RAVIGOTE—White sauce, hot or cold, which must, as its name indicates, be highly seasoned. See SAUCE.

RAVIOLI— The name of this comes, say certain culinary writers, from the fact that in times past everything left over after the distribution of food for a meal on board ship was used to make it.

To justify this etymology, they say that until the beginning of the nineteenth century it was called *rabiole*, a word meaning something of little value.

Ravioli is made with *pasta* (see ITALIAN PASTES). After having been stuffed with various mixtures the pieces are poached in salted water, moistened with veal or beef gravy and sprinkled with cheese.

Method. Roll out the paste very thinly and cut out with a fluted cutter into little rounds or squares about 2 inches across.

Put in the middle of each piece of *pasta* a piece of the prescribed forcemeat about as big as a walnut, moisten the edges and fold it over like an apple turnover.

Or: Roll out the paste into a piece about 3 inches wide and as long as space permits.

Set on this rectangle of paste a row of little balls of forcemeat about ¾ inch apart. Moisten the edges of the paste and double them over, then cut out the ravioli into half-moons with the aid of a fluted pastry cutter.

A square sheet of thin pastry may have little balls of forcemeat set out on it ¾ inch apart, longways and crossways. Moisten the spaces between them. Cover with a second sheet of pastry the same size. Cut out the ravioli with a special wheel cutter.

Preparing ravioli (*Larousse*)

To poach ravioli. Plunge the ravioli into boiling salted water. Boil steadily for 8 to 10 minutes, according to size.

To serve. Drain the ravioli, set in layers on a gratin dish, which has been buttered and sprinkled with grated cheese. Pour a few tablespoons of veal or beef gravy over each layer and sprinkle with grated cheese. Reheat or brown crisply according to the recipe.

Ravioli forcemeats. FARCES À RAVIOLI—The fillings for ravioli are numerous, and meat and poultry left-overs may be used for them.

However, for a classic ravioli the forcemeat should be made with *Daube of beef* (see BEEF) that has been very well cooked, allowed to get cold and minced. Later the cooked ravioli is sprinkled with the cooking liquor of the *daube*.

First mixture. Chop finely ¾ cup (150 grams) of cold braised beef. Add 2 cups (150 grams) of spinach which has been blanched, drained and chopped, ¼ cup (50 grams) of brain purée, a tablespoon of chopped shallot, an egg, a pinch of salt, pepper and a little grated nutmeg.

Second mixture. Chop finely ¾ cup (150 grams) of cold braised or boiled beef. Add 2 cups (150 grams) of spinach that has been blanched, drained and chopped, ¼ cup (50 grams) of brain purée, 2 tablespoons of chopped onion lightly cooked in butter, ½ cup (50 grams) of grated Parmesan, a whole egg, a pinch of salt, pepper and grated nutmeg. Mix well.

Third mixture. Chop finely ½ cup (100 grams) of cooked veal, add 1½ cups (100 grams) of spinach that has been blanched, drained and chopped, ½ cup (100 grams) of brain purée, 1⅔ ounces (50 grams) of cream cheese pressed dry, ½ cup (50 grams) of grated Parmesan, a whole egg, a pinch of salt, pepper and grated nutmeg. Mix well.

Fourth mixture. Proceed with cold chicken meat as for the forcemeat with veal above, replacing the spinach with blanched, drained and chopped lettuce cooked lightly in butter.

Fifth mixture. Pound in a mortar 5 ounces (150 grams) of chicken livers sautéed in butter with a chopped shallot, a chopped clove of garlic and a pinch of salt. Add 1½ cups (100 grams) of spinach blanched, drained and chopped, a fillet of de-salted anchovy, 3 tablespoons (50 grams) of butter and a whole egg. Season with salt, pepper, grated nutmeg and a little basil. Mix well with the pestle and rub through a sieve.

Sixth mixture. Proceed with cold braised sweetbreads as for the chicken liver forcemeat, replacing the spinach by beetroot leaves blanched, drained, chopped and cooked lightly in butter.

Seventh mixture. Chop finely 4½ cups (300 grams) of blanched and well drained spinach. Put into a sauté pan in which has been heated 3 tablespoons (50 grams) of butter. Cook, stirring with a wooden spoon. Season with salt, pepper and a little grated nutmeg.

Sprinkle the spinach with a scant tablespoon of flour. Shake for a moment over a good heat and add ½ cup (1 decilitre) of milk.

Bring to the boil. Take the pot from the heat; add the yolk of an egg and ½ cup (50 grams) of grated Parmesan. Mix well.

RAY—See SKATE.

RÉCHAUD—Small portable stove.

Also a utensil designed to keep dishes hot when they are on the table. It is heated by hot water, flame or electricity.

RECUIRE (RE-COOK)—This expression is used for different kinds of pastry preparations where the mixtures are cooked in two operations: the first time in a bowl at a low temperature, as is done in making certain biscuits (hence their name), and a second time in the oven, with the mixture (*already cooked*), put into a special mould.

The term is also used in sweet making to define the operation of bringing to the desired point a syrup or jelly which after the addition of some watery fruit would have become *uncooked*.

RECUITE—Cheese made with whey.

RED MULLET—See MULLET.

RED NETTLE. ÉPIAISE DES MARAIS—The roots of this plant are edible and can be used in place of the Chinese artichoke.

REDSTART. ROUGE-QUEUE—Bird of passage, prized as game. Prepared like lark.

RED MULLET—See MULLET.

REDUCTION—Action of reducing the volume of a liquid by evaporation, particularly a sauce. They are reduced to increase their savour and also to make them thicker in consistency. A brown sauce which has been reduced is also more brilliant in appearance. See SAUCE. In the U.S.A. the process of reducing is known as 'boiling down'.

REDWING. MAUVIS—A small type of thrush.

REFRIGERATION. FRIGORIFIQUE—The process of freezing. Low temperatures can be produced by various means, the simplest being the use of freezing mixtures. (See PRESERVATION OF FOOD, *Freezing*.) These mixtures have a number of domestic uses including the preparation of ice creams and water ices.

For lower temperatures, it is necessary to use a refrigerator. Refrigerators generally work on the principle of the lowering of temperature, either through the expansion of a gas or the evaporation of a volatile liquid. There are a number of highly volatile liquids and gases which can be readily liquefied, for example, ammonia, carbonic acid gas, methyl chloride, etc. All these liquids give off a gas which is compressed to raise its temperature. It then passes through a condenser which absorbs the heat and liquefies the gas. Next, it passes through a pressure-reducing valve into an expansion chamber, thus producing the required lowering of temperature. The gas is then pumped back into the condenser, and the cycle begins again and is repeated indefinitely, as long as the motor-driven compressor is kept working.

Some refrigerators have no compressors. These work by absorption and are dependent upon the ratio of solubility to temperature in the interaction of ammonia and water. In an absorber cooled by water circulation, the greater part of the ammonia liquefies as though it had been sucked in by a pump. Next, the solution, thus enriched, passes into a distiller, heated by one of a number of methods (steam, gas or electricity). Here the ammonia is given off by the solution and collects in the enclosed chamber as though it had been compressed by piston-action. The expansion takes place at the outlet of the distiller, and causes a lowering of temperature, as with compressor refrigeration. This process is used especially in certain types of domestic refrigerator. In large industrial refrigerators, an intermediate cooler is generally used. This may be a system of ventilation or a non-freezing brine which circulates through the pipes laid in the cold-cupboard or refrigeration chamber.

Finally, mention must be made of a modern method of refrigeration in which the place of ice is taken by solidified carbonic acid gas. This is much less bulky than ice and has the further advantage of producing a lower temperature without any liquid condensation whatsoever.

REFRIGERATOR. Réfrigérateur—Apparatus, usually made in the form of a cupboard, working by gas or electricity, used to refrigerate and conserve foodstuffs.

RÉGALADE—To drink *à la régalade* is to drink from a bottle without letting it touch the lips, in such a way that the liquid is poured directly into the mouth.

RÉGENCE—See GARNISHES.

REGIONAL COOKING IN FRANCE. Cuisine régionale—The various French provinces have each their particular *cuisine*. However, it should be observed that the dishes with a regional name are not always authentically and exclusively regional.

Real culinary specialities are numerous in some regions of France. For convenience these have been treated as a separate study, giving the principal local dishes and main food products. This information will be found under ALSACE, ANJOU, ARTOIS, AUVERGNE, BRESSE, BRITTANY, CHAMPAGNE, LANGUEDOC, NORMANDY, PROVENCE, etc.

REINDEER. Renne—The flesh of this animal provides a well-thought-of venison inferior, however, to that of the roebuck or deer. Prepared in the same way as these last. See ROEBUCK.

REINE (QUEEN)—Qualifications applied in French to a category of chicken whose size is intermediate between *poulet de grain* and the fat hen or *poularde*.

The name is also given to a preparation of chicken purée or of a mixture of cut up chicken with mushrooms and truffles bound with an *Allemande sauce* or *Chicken velouté sauce*. This name is also given to a thick soup made with chicken purée.

REINETTE—See APPLE.

RÉJANE—See GARNISHES.

RÉJOUISSANCE—Name given in France to the bones that are weighed with the meat. The weight of these bones is strictly limited.

RELÂCHER—In French, culinary term meaning to add any liquid to a purée or a sauce to thin it to the desired consistency.

RELIEFS—In French, the left-overs of a meal, that which is not used at table.

Religieuse

RELIGIEUSE—This *gâteau*, which appears to have originated in Paris, is made with éclairs filled with coffee, chocolate or vanilla-flavoured cream, iced with fondant and superimposed one on top of the other, or with *choux* similarly filled and iced, rising in a pyramid one on top of the other.

Usually, the éclairs and *choux* are set on a base of sweet pastry and decorated with piped cream.

The name *religieuse* is also used for a pastry made by spreading a strip of puff pastry with a mixture of apple jam, apricot jam and currants and covering it with strips of pastry in a criss-cross pattern.

REMONTER—French culinary term meaning to add a condiment to a sauce or ragoût to heighten its taste, or to add alcohol to a wine to give it greater strength.

RÉMOULADE—Mayonnaise to which gherkins, capers, parsley, spring onions, chervil, chopped tarragon and anchovy essence are added.

REMOVE. Relevé—Dish which in French service *relieves* (in the sense that one sentry relieves another) the soup or the fish. This course precedes those called entrées.

RENAISSANCE (A LA)—Garnish of various new vegetables. The vegetables are arranged in little heaps around the pieces of meat that they accompany. These pieces, served as entrées, are generally roasts.

RENNET. Présure—Ferment having the property of coagulating the casein of milk.

Animal rennet. Présure animale—This substance, which comes from the abomasum or fourth stomach of calves, lambs and kids, is used to curdle the milk in the cheese industry. An extract, marketed commercially in liquid or paste form (solid rennet), is most often used for this purpose.

Vegetable rennets. PRÉSURES VÉGÉTALES—Substances contained in certain plants (thistle, yellow bedstraw, common fig, etc.) having the property of coagulating milk.

REPÈRE—Mixture of flour and egg white, used to stick together the sections of a decoration or to fix them to a dish. For this latter use it is advisable to heat the dishes (if metal) before sticking on decorations with *repère.*

The flour-and-water paste, which is used to seal casseroles and *marmites* during cooking, is sometimes erroneously referred to as *repère.*

Behind the scenes in a Paris restaurant
(French Government Tourist Office)

RESTAURANT—A public establishment where food is served. The origin of restaurants, as we know them, is not very old. In the eighteenth century one could eat only in the inns, which served at fixed times an equally fixed menu, or at the shops of the *traiteurs* (eating-house keepers) who could only sell whole pieces.

In 1765 a man named Boulanger, a vendor of soup in the Rue Bailleul, gave to his soups the name of *restaurants,* i.e. restoratives, and inscribed on his sign: 'Boulanger sells magical restoratives', a notice which he embellished with a joke in culinary Latin: *Venite ad me; vos qui stomacho laboratis et ego restaurabo vos.*

Wishing to augment his menus and unable to serve sauces or ragoûts, because he was not a member of the corporation of *traiteurs,* he had the idea of offering his clients sheep's feet in white sauce. The *traiteurs* did not fail to bring a lawsuit against him, which was a tremendous advertisement for our innovator and his sheep's feet. Finally, Boulanger won the case, a solemn judgment of Parliament having decreed that sheep's feet in white sauce were not a ragoût. This was a great triumph; all Paris rushed to Boulanger's to taste this extraordinary dish on the recommendation of Moncrif who raved about it. Louis XV himself had it served at Versailles, but the king, who was a real gourmand, did not share the enthusiasm of his lector.

It nevertheless remains true that Boulanger created, as Brillat-Savarin says, a profession which commands a fortune for all who pursue it with good faith, orderliness and skill.

After Boulanger the first restaurant worthy of the name was that which Beauvilliers founded in 1783—an establishment which, in view of the revolutionary activities of 1793, its founder felt himself obliged to close. Then followed the restaurant which Barthélémy, Maneille and Simon opened in 1786 at the Palais-Royal under the sign '*Aux Trois Frères Provençaux*', although they were neither brothers nor Provençal! This restaurant shut its doors in 1869, and it was in this house that Dugléré, Casimir Moisson and several other great *cuisiniers* of the nineteenth century carried out their first campaigns.

The progress in the culinary art which restaurants have brought about is immense. 'Connoisseurs', says Brillat-Savarin, 'have kept in mind the names of many artists who have shone in Paris since the introduction of the restaurants. One may cite Beauvilliers, Méot, Robert, Rose, Legacque, the brothers Véry, Henneveux and Baleine of the *Rocher de Cancale.* . . . Some of these establishments owed their prosperity to special attractions, as: *Le Veau qui tette* to sheep's feet (doubtless cooked *à la poulette*); *Les Frères Provençaux* to salt cod with garlic; *Véry* to entrées with truffles; *Robert* to specially ordered dinners; *Baleine* to the care he took to have excellent fish; *Henneveux* to the mysterious boudoirs on the fourth floor. . . .'

Under the Revolution, following the abolition of corporations and privileges, the restaurants multiplied, spreading good cheer, permitting everyone, as Brillat-Savarin says, to 'make, according to his purse or according to his appetite, copious or delicate meals, which formerly were the perquisite of the very rich'.

Among the principal restaurateurs of this far-away epoch we may cite the two Marseillaise brothers, whose name history has not preserved, who founded '*Le Boeuf à la Mode*', whose sign caricatured the fashions of the day; later to the Terrasse des Feuillants came Legacque, praised by Grimod de la Reynière, though this did not prevent him from doing bad business, while his contemporary and neighbour, Véry, had a brilliant success in spite of the criticisms of the *Almanach des Gourmands.* After having been entitled *Palais des Restaurants* and *Restaurant des Palais,* Legacque's establishment got into difficulties and ended up as a fixed-price restaurant in the Palais-Royal. In this same period Véfour founded the *Café de Chartres,* and Baleine, at the *Rocher de Cancale,* was host to Grimod de la Reynière's 'Jury of Tasters'. Carême declared him a second-class *traiteur,* and his neighbour Philipe finished by supplanting him.

In the new boulevards were established the *Café Hardy,* the *Café de Foy,* which later became the *Café Bignon,* and the *Café Anglais,* opened in 1802. How many others which have long since vanished could be mentioned! Bonnefoy who opened in the Rue de l'Échelle and then moved out to the Boulevard Montmartre; Bonvalet, who competed on the Boulevard du Temple with the *Cadran Bleu,* directed by Henneveux, and La Galiote; *Père Lathuile,* Avenue de Clichy, where the allies established their headquarters in 1815; the *Moulin Rouge,* Avenue d'Antin, where Escoffier began, *Paillard, Vachette-Brébant, Voisin;* the *Café de Paris,* the old one, which was situated on the boulevards, the *Café Riche,* the *Restaurant Marguery,* and others, too many to enumerate.

The brasseries, taverns and cafés in Paris where meals are served are today very numerous.

Certain catering establishments of very grand style are

Restaurant Tour d'Argent, Paris
(*French Government Tourist Office*)

also sometimes called 'café', although generally they are not prepared to serve little drinks like an ordinary café.

Among cafés which have now disappeared are the *Café Anglais*, the *Café Voisin*, the *Café Riche*, the *Café Tortoni*. Every day in Paris one or another of these houses disappears.

Some very old restaurants are changing and becoming 'Americanized', which seems a great pity. Some become 'cold buffet counters', others become 'automatic', others again become 'cafeterias'.

It is regrettable to see celebrated Parisian eating-houses thus disappear—or at least become transformed. French cooking has nothing to gain by these changes.

The wine shops, the *troquets*, as they are familiarly known, where it is possible to eat, are also very numerous in Paris. In some of these houses, frequented by workmen and people in modest employment, the cooking is excellent, because it is simple and honest. It is still possible to find in Paris some establishments of this kind where one may regale oneself with succulent boiled beef, savoury pork with cabbage or a beef '*bourguignon*' done in the old-fashioned way.

But among these restaurants snobbery has done its worst. The great gastronomes have proclaimed the merits of this or that '*petite boîte*' which they have 'discovered', where *the owner does the cooking herself* and where the stew is succulent . . .

The owners of some of these establishments have resisted the hyperbolic eulogies which were made on their cooking in the gastronomic pages of the big Parisian newspapers and have continued to serve their customers decently and give them honest table wines. But other 'wine merchants', drunk with these eulogies, have aspired to the *grande cuisine*, and there figure now on their menus dishes prepared 'as at Palavas-les-Flots' or 'à la mode de la mère Brigitte' or even 'according to the old recipe of Madame Suzon' and other pretentious titles which bedeck the worst mediocrities.

RETICULUM or HONEY-COMB. BONNET—Second stomach of the ruminants.

RÉVEILLON—Supper eaten after midnight mass on Christmas Eve and, by extension, the supper eaten on Saint Sylvester's night (New Year's Eve) at the moment of the change of date.

REVENIR (FAIRE)—This French culinary term indicates the action of browning various cookery ingredients in butter, fat or oil.

Browning meat or fish has for its object to seal and make firm the exterior, but not to cook it. When the complete cooking must follow this operation, the words used are *sauté* for meat and *étuver* or *fondre* for vegetables.

REVERDIR—The French cookery term meaning to replace green colour in vegetables which has been lost in blanching. The use of copper (which forms chlorophyl, an insoluble colouring matter) has been almost abandoned because of the metallic taste which it communicated to the food, and in the canning industry it is almost always spinach green which is used for this purpose.

The 're-greening' which consists of putting the blanched ingredient in a solution of copper sulphate has been alternately forbidden and permitted again.

RHINE—If a fairy tale of Alsatian folklore is to be believed, this country boasts a hundred and forty different wines. See the list of the most reputable Rhine wines and those of the Lower Rhine under ALSACE.

RHINOCEROS—Large, herbivorous, African and S. Asiatic pachyderm, very savage, whose flesh (mostly that of the young animals) is edible. It is preferred to that of the elephant by natives who consider hippopotamus meat to be even better.

RHUBARB. RHUBARBE—Plant originating in northern Asia, introduced into Europe in the fourteenth century. It was cultivated first by the monks as a medicinal plant, then as an ornamental plant.

The fleshy stems are eaten, either stewed in a *compote* or as jam. It can also be made into pies and tarts in the English style.

Rhubarb tart

Compote of rhubarb. COMPOTE DE RHUBARBE—Divide the stems into pieces 2 to 3 inches long. Peel them and remove strings. Arrange them in a low copper pot and pour over very thick syrup to half-cover them. Poach covered in the oven without stirring.

Serve in a compote dish. Pour the syrup over the pieces of rhubarb.

Rhubarb jam. CONFITURE DE RHUBARBE—Dissolve in a copper pot 3½ cups (800 grams) of sugar moistened with a few spoonfuls of water. Boil over a high flame for 8 minutes. Put in a generous 2 pounds (1 kilo) of rhubarb stalks, carefully stripped and cut up. Poach on a moderate heat with the cover on the pan.

When the rhubarb is nearly cooked remove cover, reduce heat and continue to cook, stirring all the time, until the rhubarb becomes quite tender and comes apart.

Put the jam in pots, cover them. Keep in a cool, dry place.

Rhubarb pie (English pastry). PÂTÉ DE RHUBARBE—Peel the tender stalks of rhubarb and cut them in pieces 1 to 1½ inches long. Arrange them in an English-type pie dish. Cover with sugar, add two or three tablespoons of water and cover with a piece of pastry laid over a strip of pastry on the rim of the dish. Sprinkle the pastry with sugar. Cook at moderate heat (375°F.) in the oven for about 45 minutes.

Note. The pie may also be brushed with egg before being put in the oven. When taken out it is sprinkled with sugar and glazed with a hot iron or salamander, or under the grill.

In England, where this pie is very popular, it is served with double cream, whipped cream or custard.

RHYTON—An antique drinking vessel in the form of a ram's horn, generally decorated with a goat's head, without any flat base, so that the drinker was obliged to empty it before putting it down.

RIBBON. RUBAN—Describes a mixture of sugar and egg yolks which, having been well beaten, forms folds rather like a ribbon that has been dropped from a height.

RIBEAUVILLE—White wine harvested at Ribeauville in the Haut-Rhin.

RICE. RIZ—A graminaceous grain, originating in India and China, introduced first of all into Egypt, then into Greece, where it was already highly prized at the time of Theophrastus. Its popularity spread to Portugal, then to Italy and America. In France Cardinal Fleury's first attempts in Auvergne were not a success.

Rice is very low in fat content; it is rich in gluten, but this does not give an elastic paste.

The peoples who rely on rice for their principal nourishment always use it in its rough state, never polished. The substitution of polished rice for rough results in the disease called beri-beri, study of which was the point of departure for the theory of vitamins, substances which, however imponderable, are indispensable to nutrition.

In normal commerce, rice is sold under various names, not always descriptive of its origin. The principal types are:

Carolina rice, long-grained, angular, white or slightly bluish, bright and shining;

Indo-Chinese rice, which, though smaller than Indian rice, is excellent and cooks perfectly without breaking up.

Java rice, with more elongated grains, flat, transparent, shiny.

Japanese rice, regular oval grains, hard, translucent with a dark mark at the centre, greyish-white, shiny.

Patna rice, with grains less hard, less transparent and less shiny, milky white and more cylindrical in form.

Roman rice, greyish-white grains, dull.

Piedmont rice, short rounded grains, very white and shining, greyish and opaque at the centre.

To cook rice. All the peoples for whom rice is the staple diet are careful never to stir it while it is cooking, and never to cook it too long (twenty minutes on the average), so that the grains remain whole. Overcooking, reducing the rice to a mash, has, to a great extent, contributed to the disfavour in which this foodstuff was held in France. At the time of the siege of Paris in 1870 to 1871 when there was a shortage of bread, enormous quantities of rice remained unused.

Boiled rice with butter. RIZ AU BLANC, AU BEURRE—Put into a saucepan with a flat, thick bottom ½ pound (250 grams) of rice which has been previously washed. Cover with cold water in sufficient quantity to cover completely. Season with salt. Blanch the rice for 15 minutes.

Drain, put into sauté dish with 5 tablespoons (80 grams) of butter in little pieces.

Risotto à la piémontaise

Mix carefully with a fork, cover with a lid and put in the oven for 15 minutes.

Note. Rice prepared in this way may be eaten as it is. It is mostly used as an accompaniment for eggs, poultry, fish, etc.

Rice à la créole. RIZ À LA CRÉOLE—Take 2 pounds (1 kilo) of Indian rice for 8 persons. Wash it in several waters. Put the rice in a thick pan with a little salt. Cover with two good fingers of cold water. Set to cook on a good heat. When it is well cooked, lower the heat or set the pot, covered, on a corner of the stove. It will continue to cook and will dry slowly. Allow an hour for cooking.

Rice croquettes—See CROQUETTES.

Rice au gras. RIZ AU GRAS—Blanch ½ pound (250 grams) of rice; drain it, toss in butter and add to twice its height in the pan some *pot-au-feu* broth or some rather fatty white stock. Bring to the boil. Cook, covered, in the oven, without disturbing it, for 20 minutes.

Rice à la grecque. RIZ À LA GRECQUE—Prepare the rice as for pilaf (see below), adding when it is cooked, for every pound (500 grams) of rice weighed uncooked, a chopped onion tossed in 2 tablespoons of butter, 3 tablespoons (50 grams) of sausage meat, divided into small pieces, ½ cup (50 grams) of lettuce leaves cut in thin strips and cooked in butter, 4 tablespoons of peas cooked in butter, and 4 tablespoons (50 grams) of red pimentos cut in dice and cooked in butter.

Mix this garnish with the pilaf rice, taking every precaution not to break the grains.

Rice à l'indienne. RIZ À L'INDIENNE—Blanch 1 pound (500 grams) of rice for 15 minutes in salted water, allowing 1½ teaspoons (9 grams) of salt to a quart (litre) of water, stirring from time to time with a wooden spoon.

Drain the rice, wash it several times in cold water, drain and put on a napkin laid on a baking tin or on a strainer. Fold over the edges of the napkin so as to enclose the rice. Put to dry in a warm place for 15 minutes.

Note. Rice prepared in this way is the essential accompaniment of all curry dishes.

It may also be served as accompaniment to other strongly seasoned dishes.

Rice pilaf—See PILAF.

Risotto à la milanaise—Prepare the risotto as in the following recipe. When it is cooked add a *Milanaise* garnish* (see GARNISHES) and a little rich brown sauce which has been strongly flavoured with tomato.

(Milanaise garnish is composed of pickled tongue, cooked lean ham, mushrooms and truffles, cut into fairly coarse *julienne** strips and bound with rich brown sauce flavoured with tomato.)

Risotto à la piémontaise—Cook lightly in butter, without allowing to colour, 8 tablespoons (100 grams) of chopped onion. When it is cooked add 1 pound (500 grams) of Piedmont rice.

Cook gently over a low heat and stir and shake until all the grains are well impregnated with butter. Pour in, to twice the height of the rice in the pot, some pot-au-feu broth or white stock. Repeat this five or six times, adding a fresh quantity of liquid only when the last lot has been absorbed by the rice. Cook the risotto, covered, for 18 to 20 minutes. Add to it, when it is cooked, 2 tablespoons of butter and ¾ cup (75 grams) of grated Parmesan.

Note. The risotto can be finished off with different ingredients, such as ham cut into dice and tossed in butter, mussels, fresh peas (which can be cooked with the rice) or black truffles, which are added to the risotto at the last moment.

DESSERT OR SWEET RICE. ENTREMETS AU RIZ—

Dessert or sweet rice for croquettes and puddings. RIZ POUR BORDURES, CROQUETTES, POUDINGS—Wash ¼ pound (125 grams) of rice, blanch it, drain and rinse in warm water.

Drain again and put it into a pot with 4 cups (8 decilitres) of milk previously boiled with the chosen flavouring, 5 tablespoons (75 grams) of sugar, 2 tablespoons (25 grams) of butter and a small pinch of salt. 1 teaspoon of vanilla or other extract may be substituted for vanilla powder or bean.

Begin cooking over a big flame, cover the pot and put to cook in the oven at a gentle heat for 30 minutes. *Do not disturb it during cooking*, because this would make it stick to the bottom of the pot.

Take the rice from the oven and add to it 6 egg yolks, mixing them in carefully with a fork. Add more sugar, if needed.

Use according to the recipe.

Note. Dessert rice is flavoured with vanilla, orange or lemon peel.

The proportions given in this recipe will provide 6 to 8 helpings. If the rice is to be served without fruit or other accompaniment the ingredients may be augmented.

It is possible also to cook the rice as above and on taking it out of the oven to bind it with 3 whole eggs. This method is less extravagant than the preceding, but the rice is less delicate.

Creamed rice. RIZ À LA CRÈME—Cook with 3 cups (6 decilitres) of milk (previously boiled with the chosen flavouring) 5 tablespoons (75 grams) of sugar, a small pinch of salt, and ½ cup (125 grams) of rice, blanched and drained.

When it is cooked add to it 1 cup (2 decilitres) of rather thick fresh cream and 2 tablespoons (25 grams) of butter.

Add a little more sugar if required. This preparation is used for making hot or cold sweets.

Rice flan or tart. FLAN, TARTE DE RIZ—Fill a short-crust flan case (pie shell) with dessert rice to within ⅛ inch of the edge. Sprinkle with sugar. Cook in the oven at a moderate heat for 25 to 30 minutes.

Note. This sweet may be served hot or cold. It may be made with rice that has been mixed with chopped-up crystallized fruit soaked in kirsch or other liqueur.

Rice flan or tart with apricots. FLAN, TARTE DE RIZ AUX ABRICOTS—Proceed as in the above recipe, but fill the flan case only three-quarters full. On the rice place halves of raw apricots, soaked in kirsch and sugar. Sprinkle with sugar. Cook in the oven at a gentle heat.

Spread the top of the flan with apricot jam diluted with a little syrup and strained.

Note. In the same way rice flans may be made with various other fruits such as: bananas (cut in rounds or sliced longways) and, in this case, arranged on the flan in a rosette), cherries, pears (in quarters and half-cooked in syrup), peaches (in halves, soaked in liqueur and sugar), apples, plums, etc.

Rice gâteau with caramel. GÂTEAU DE RIZ AU CARAMEL—Fill a large Charlotte mould, lined with caramelized sugar, with dessert rice. Cook in the oven in a *bain-marie* (pan of hot water) for 25 to 30 minutes.

Serve hot or cold.

Gâteau or flan of rice with meringue. GÂTEAU, FLAN DE RIZ—Fill a round buttered fireproof dish with dessert rice mixed with crystallized fruit, cut in dice and soaked in kirsch or other liqueur. Build up the rice into a cake about 1¼ to 1½ inches high. Cover the rice with ordinary meringue, smoothing it nicely all over.

Decorate the top of the flan with meringue piped through a forcing (pastry) bag. Sprinkle with sugar. Put into a very hot oven to colour the meringue lightly.

Garnish with strained apricot jam and gooseberry jelly.

Pears *à l'impératrice*, with rice *à l'impératrice* in the centre

Rice à l'impératrice. RIZ À L'IMPÉRATRICE—Prepare ½ cup (125 grams) of dessert rice flavoured with vanilla.

When it is almost cold, add 3 large tablespoons of chopped up crystallized fruit soaked in kirsch.

Incorporate 1 cup (2 decilitres) of thick custard, mix and add at the last moment 1¼ cups (2½ decilitres) of whipped cream.

Pour this mixture into a Charlotte mould (or a Bavarois mould) the bottom of which has been spread with gooseberry jelly to a depth of a little less than ½ inch.

Put to set on ice.

Serve wrapped in a napkin or turned out into a glass bowl.

Many fruit desserts are made with a basis of *Rice à l'impératrice*. See *Pears à l'impératrice*.

Rice in milk. RIZ AU LAIT—Wash ½ cup (125 grams) of rice and blanch it. Drain it, rinse in warm water and put it back, well drained, into a pot containing 4 cups (8 decilitres) of milk and a small pinch of salt.

Cook very slowly, with a lid on, for 25 to 30 minutes.

Add sugar if the rice is intended for a sweet, and if necessary lighten it with a few tablespoons of boiled milk.

This rice is served hot or cold, and if served as a dessert, is flavoured with vanilla, orange peel or lemon peel.

Rice Montmorency—Prepare $\frac{1}{4}$ pound (125 grams) of dessert rice flavoured with vanilla. Put into a glass bowl and decorate with banana slices alternating with cherries in syrup.

Rice pudding mould. PUDDING DE RIZ MOULÉ—Prepare rice as for pudding. Incorporate in it, after having thickened it with egg yolks, 3 egg whites, stiffly beaten.

Fill with this mixture a large Charlotte mould, buttered and sprinkled with blond breadcrumbs.

Put to cook in the oven, in a *bain-marie* (pan of hot water) for 20 to 25 minutes.

Leave for a few minutes before turning out of the mould.

Serve with fruit sauce, custard or *Zabaglione**.

Ring of rice with fruit. BORDURE DE RIZ AUX FRUITS—Fill a buttered ring mould with dessert rice. Cook in the oven in a *bain-marie* (pan of hot water) for 10 to 12 minutes.

Turn out of the mould on to a round dish. Fill the middle with various fruits cooked in syrup, cut in big dice and warmed in *Apricot sauce* flavoured with kirsch. See SAUCE.

Put on the rice border half apricots cooked in syrup. Decorate with lozenges of angelica and crystallized cherries. Pour over a few tablespoons of apricot sauce flavoured with kirsch.

This sweet is also known as *Apricot Condé.*

Rijspap or saffron rice. RIZ AU SAFRAN—This pudding is very popular in the Flemish countryside. It is made in this way:

Cook $1\frac{1}{2}$ cups (300 grams) of rice in two quarts (litres) of milk lightly sweetened with brown sugar. Continue cooking this mixture until the grains of rice can easily be crushed. At the last moment, to colour the rice, add a small pinch of saffron.

Turn out the rice into flat plates, spreading it out well. Allow to cool. Sprinkle with brown or white sugar.

Subrics of rice. SUBRICS DE RIZ—Prepare the rice as for rice pudding. Add to this rice chopped-up crystallized fruit soaked in liqueur. Spread evenly, about 1 inch thick, on a buttered baking dish. Dot the surface with butter to prevent the rice from getting dry. Allow to cool.

Cut out into rounds about 2 inches in diameter.

Put the subrics into a pan in which clarified butter has been heated; colour them on both sides.

Arrange the subrics in a crown on a round dish and put in the middle of each a teaspoon of gooseberry jelly or any other good firm jam.

Vanilla rice à la Bourbon (Creole cookery). RIZ VANILLÉ À LA BOURBON—Cook gently in a quart (litre) of milk 4 tablespoons of rice previously blanched and drained well, until it becomes a porridge; add sugar and vanilla to taste.

When the rice has cooled add 3 egg yolks. Beat the whites separately into a stiff foam and fold them into the rice before turning into a deep lightly buttered dish.

Bake in the oven for 20 minutes. Sprinkle with sugar and serve your soufflé in the dish in which it was cooked in the oven.

Rice water. EAU DE RIZ—Boil 1 tablespoon (20 grams) of rice in a quart (litre) of water until it is soft. Sweeten with $\frac{2}{3}$ ounce (20 grams) of liquorice or 2 ounces (60 grams) of quince syrup, replacing these with saccharine when sugar is forbidden.

RICHE (A LA)—Method of preparing fish, particularly sole. It was at the *Café Riche*, a Parisian establishment which has now disappeared, that Riche sauce was created. See SAUCE.

RICHEBOURG—One of the great red wines of Burgundy from the Beaune district. See BURGUNDY WINES.

RICHELIEU (A LA)—Name given to various preparations.

In the first place the word describes a garnish composed of stuffed tomatoes and mushrooms, braised lettuce and potatoes lightly roasted in butter.

The term *à la Richelieu* also applies to a method of preparing fillets of sole or other fish. The fillets are coated in egg and breadcrumbs, cooked in butter, served with maître-d'hôtel butter and garnished with truffles. The name '*Richelieu*' is also given to a large sweet pastry, made as described below.

RICHELIEU—*Ingredients.* 2 cups (450 grams) sugar, 2 tablespoons (50 grams) vanilla sugar, $2\frac{1}{2}$ cups (375 grams) almonds, $\frac{2}{3}$ cup (150 grams) butter, 16 eggs, $\frac{1}{2}$ cup (1 decilitre) maraschino. (2 teaspoons vanilla extract can replace the vanilla sugar.)

Method. Pound the almonds finely, adding to them 2 egg whites and a little sugar. Rub through a sieve into a basin with the sugar, the egg yolks and the maraschino and stir with a wooden spoon until the mixture becomes white.

Add the melted butter, then the sieved flour, which should be sprinkled in, and finally 10 egg whites, stiffly beaten. Mix.

Pour this mixture into shallow buttered moulds. Bake in a moderate oven (375°F.).

Sandwich the cake layers with apricot jam and frangipane cream. Ice with white fondant icing flavoured with maraschino. Decorate with angelica.

RIDDLE. CRIBLE—Kitchen utensil similar to a sieve, but with larger holes.

RIDGE CUCUMBER. AGOURSI—*Agoursi* is the French spelling of the Russian word *Ogurtsy.* This is a species of the *Cucurbitaceae* family. In Russia, where cucumbers are highly appreciated, they apply to this type of cucumber all the treatments which we apply to white cucumbers: braising, *à la crème*, fried in batter, *au gratin*, *à la Mornay*, etc.

In France, these cucumbers are most often eaten as pickles in the guise of condiment, as gherkins. Formerly, it was chiefly in this form that they were found in food shops, but they are now sold fresh in France, England and the United States.

RIGODON—This Burgundian dish, very popular in some parts of Basse-Bourgogne, is served as an entrée when it has ham or bacon in it (giving it some resemblance to the *quiche lorraine*) or as a sweet with the addition of fruit purée, making it more like a pudding. The *rigodon* is served either warm or completely cold, so that it can be made in large enough quantity to be dished up twice. This dish used to be made on the day the bread was baked (in the days when each household made its own bread) and was put in the oven as soon as the bread came out.

Method. Boil three-quarters of a quart (litre) of milk, add to it $\frac{1}{2}$ cup (150 grams) of sugar, a pinch of salt and half a vanilla pod (or 1 teaspoon vanilla extract), or some lemon rind (the Burgundian housewives replaced these flavours with a good pinch of cinnamon).

Cover the utensil, leave to infuse away from heat, and stir from time to time to make sure the sugar dissolves.

Cut in small dice 2 cups (125 grams) of stale brioche; put it in a dish and sprinkle with 5 or 6 tablespoons of the sweet, flavoured milk.

Chop finely 7 or 8 good dried shelled walnuts; add to this 3 crushed hazelnuts (in the season, the dried walnuts are replaced by fresh, doubling the quantity, but fresh or dry, walnuts must figure in rigodon).

Mix in a bowl 7 beaten eggs and 2 tablespoons of rice flour. Add the sweet, flavoured milk little by little, beating well with a whisk to ensure that everything is perfectly blended. Finally, add to the mixture the diced brioche and chopped nuts and mix well together.

Pour into a deep well buttered dish, and dot the surface with about 2 tablespoons (25 to 30 grams) of butter in small pieces, and cook in the oven at a good medium heat (350°F.).

Its accompaniment is, as has been said above, a purée of fruit in season, mirabelle plums, greengages, quinces, apples, etc.

Whatever the fruit, it is cooked to a jam in which the quantity of sugar is in proportion to the sweetness of the fruit used.

After cooking, this jam is strained through a cloth or simply through a strainer, and cooked down over a strong heat until it becomes very thick.

When the *rigodon* has been taken out of the oven, and when it has become no more than lukewarm, the jam is poured over and, with the aid of a spoon, spread over it very evenly.

When it is served cold the jam can be replaced by a purée of strawberries. Purée of peaches also goes very well with *rigodon.*

Rigodon with meat. RIGODON AVEC VIANDE—'Put into a basin 3 good tablespoons of flour (or rice flour). Add 7 eggs. Mix well. Pour in, stirring well, a quart (litre) of boiled milk, lightly salted. Add 7 ounces (200 grams) of cold boiled pork cut in very small dice (or an equivalent quantity of streaky bacon). Pour the mixture into a deep dish, well buttered. Put small pieces of butter here and there on the surface. Cook in a moderate oven. This flan is eaten just lukewarm or cold.' (Philéas Gilbert's recipe.)

RILLAUDS AND RILLETTES—A French preparation made of pork, both lean and fat, cut into very small pieces, gently cooked in lard with the usual seasoning and condiments, allowed to cool and pounded in a mortar.

Rillettes differ from *rillauds* or *rillons* in that the latter are not pounded after cooking.

Rillettes are made industrially almost everywhere in France. *Tours* and *Le Mans rillettes* are highly esteemed.

Goose and rabbit *rillettes* are made in the same way as pork *rillettes.*

Method. Cut up 5 pounds ($2\frac{1}{2}$ kilos) of fresh breast of pork into large dice.

Heat 1 ounce (30 grams) of lard in a pan, add diced pork, and cook lightly. Add half a cup of water. Cook gently till tender, stirring frequently to make sure that the meat does not stick to the bottom.

When the pieces of pork are cooked and nicely browned, drain them.

Chop these *rillons* finely, put them in a basin; add to them the fat from the cooking. Season with salt and pepper and mix.

Put the *rillettes* into small stone jars and allow to cool. When they are cold pour over a thin layer of lard. Cover with white paper.

Rillauds of Anjou—Cut some fresh breast of pork into pieces about 2 inches square. Season with coarse rock salt allowing $\frac{1}{2}$ ounce of salt per pound (30 grams per kilo) and leave for 12 hours.

The next day put the *rillauds* in a saucepan in which some lard (one-third of the weight of the pork) has been heated.

Cook gently for 2 hours. Put the pot over a good heat; add a little caramel (U.S. Kitchen Bouquet) and cook for a few moments.

Drain the *rillauds* and serve piping hot.

Rillettes of Angers—Melt gently 2 pounds (1 kilo) of pork fat cut into very small pieces. When it is golden in colour add 8 pounds (4 kilos) of fresh pork, both fat and lean, cut into dice, and $\frac{1}{4}$ pound (125 grams) of coarse rock salt. Cook gently for 5 to 6 hours. Beat the pieces with a wooden spoon to crush them a little. Put into pots. Allow to become cold.

Rillettes of Le Mans—Like the rillettes of Angers, made of pieces of goose and pork mixed.

Rillettes of Tours—Prepared as described in the first recipe using fresh collar (U.S. use shoulder butt) of pork, both fat and lean. Season with salt, pepper and spices. Pound finely. Put in pots. Cover with a layer of lard.

Rillons, rillauds, rillots—Prepare and cook pieces of breast of pork as indicated in the first part of the recipe for *rillettes.*

When the pieces of pork are cooked and well browned, drain them in a strainer, season with salt and pepper and serve hot or cold.

RIND. ÉCORCE—The outer skin of some stalks and fruit. The rinds of cinnamon, lemon and orange are used in a great many different ways in cooking.

RING—See BORDER.

RING-BISCUIT (Cooky). GIMBLETTE—Name given to various types of small biscuit which are always made in the form of a ring.

The word *Gimblette* comes from the Italian *cianbetta* which means *scalded.* This etymology implies that gimblettes should be scalded before they are put in the oven.

The best-known—and their reputation is centuries old—are those of Albi.

Orange ring-biscuits (cookies). GIMBLETTES À L'ORANGE —Grate half an orange rind on a lump of sugar; crush the sugar to a fine powder and mix it with more fine sugar so that the whole amount measures $\frac{3}{4}$ cup (6 ounces); pound thoroughly $\frac{3}{4}$ cup (4 ounces) of fresh almonds. Place in a circle, round this mixture, 2 cups (8 ounces) of sifted cake flour; put in the centre 1 teaspoon (4 gros) ($\frac{1}{2}$ package dried or compressed) yeast dissolved in a quarter of a tumbler of milk. Add $\frac{1}{4}$ cup (2 ounces) of butter, two egg yolks, a pinch of salt, the almonds and the orange-flavoured sugar. Knead all these ingredients in the usual way and leave the dough in a warm place for 5 to 6 hours to allow the yeast to ferment.

'Now break the dough and roll it into strips each the width of a little finger. When there are 5 or 6 strips made, cut them diagonally into pieces each $2\frac{1}{2}$ inches in length. Make these into little rings so that the joins are invisible.

'Having prepared the dough in this way, drop the rings into a large saucepan of boiling water. Stir it gently with a spatula to prevent the rings from sticking and to bring them to the surface. Drain them and drop them into cool water.

'When they are cold, drain them in a large sieve. Now toss them to dry them. Dip each one in a little beaten egg (2 eggs should be used in all) two or three times.

'Leave them to drain for a few minutes.

'Arrange them carefully on three lightly greased

baking-sheets and bake them in a slow oven until they are a good colour.

'In the same way, it is possible to make little plaited biscuits or little rolls about as long as a thumb.

'These ring-biscuits may be also flavoured with the rind of lemon, citron or Seville orange, or with aniseed, vanilla or orange-flower water'. (Carême's recipe.)

RISOTTO—Dishes with a rice basis. See RICE.

RISSOLE—Pastry (of different kinds, but mostly puff pastry) with filling of different sorts of forcemeat, often made in the shape of a turnover and generally fried in deep fat.

This dish, which may also be oven cooked, like small patties, is served as a hot hors-d'oeuvre or a small entrée. Rissoles of very small size can be used as garnish for large pieces of meat or poultry.

Rissoles, which used to be called *roinsolles*, were known in the thirteenth century. In those days they were simply a kind of pancake fried in the frying pan in butter or dripping. Later they came to be filled with chopped meat.

The author of the *Cris de Paris* (Cries of Paris) called rissoles '*denrées aux dès*' (dice food) because in the evenings after supper the workmen, the students and other people subject to very strict rules could hazard nothing more than these pastries in their games of chance.

Method. Roll out the pastry made according to instructions to a thickness of ¼ inch.

Using a round or oval, plain or fancy edged pastry-cutter, cut out the necessary number of pieces. (Note that, except for rissoles in the form of a turnover, it is necessary to have two pieces of pastry for each rissole.)

Fill these little pieces with a piece of the forcemeat the size of a walnut of the type indicated in the recipe.

Moisten the edges with water. Cover with a second piece of pastry in the same shape and size, or fold over in the form of a turnover. Press the edges together to seal them.

Fry at the last moment. Drain. Set on a napkin. Garnish with fried parsley.

For different recipes see HORS-D'OEUVRE, *Hot hors-d'oeuvre*.

RIVESALTES (Muscat de)—Very strong liqueur wine harvested at Rivesaltes, a small town in the Pyrénées-Orientales. This wine is highly flavoured.

ROACH. Gardon—The common name of a freshwater fish, of the carp family, something between the carp and the bream. In U.S.A. it is called 'golden shiner' minnow. Its fins are red. Its white flesh is quite delicate, but it has so many forked bones that it is difficult to eat. Roach is most commonly eaten fried.

ROAST. Rôt, Rôti—The French word *rôt* is the most general term and the most noble, according to M. de Courchamps (author of a cookery book) to describe not only roasted meat but also the course which follows the entrée. The roast can be a piece of meat (though this was always the entrée in the *grande cuisine* of past days), poultry or game, or, in France, even fried fish or a Lenten fish pâté. Roasts are always served on oval dishes.

The word *rôti* describes the actual piece of meat, poultry or game, cooked on the spit or in the oven and served hot.

ROASTING. Rôtissage—Method of cooking foodstuffs which must be done according to certain principles. See CULINARY METHODS.

ROASTING PAN. Plaque à rôtir—Kitchen utensil which must not be confused with the dripping pan used for placing under joints roasting on the spit.

The roasting pan is a tinned-copper (or some other fairly tough metal) pan, provided with a grid on which cuts of meats to be roasted in the oven are placed. It is important that the roasting joints should not lie in the fat or the gravy.

In some restaurants, which take pride in their work, roasting pans have special devices which permit the joint intended for roasting to be put on a spit.

ROB—Fruit juice thickened by evaporation to the consistency of honey.

ROBERT (Sauce)—According to certain culinary authors, this sauce, which is an accompaniment to pork chops and which is seasoned with vinegar, onions and mustard, was invented by a certain Robert Vinot, who, according to the legend on a print which bears his portrait, was a celebrated sauce maker at the beginning of the seventeenth century. For the recipe of this old sauce, see SAUCE.

ROBIN. Rouge-gorge—Small passerine, sometimes eaten *en brochettes* (on skewers). Prepared in the same way as larks. The European robin is half the size of the American robin.

ROCK PARTRIDGE. Bartavelle—A variety of red-legged partridge, but bigger than the latter. It is called *Alectoris graeca*—Greek partridge.

The female is smaller than the male and has lighter coloured plumage.

This partridge is very common in southern Europe and in the Alps from which it comes down in the winter. Its flesh is very good.

Nostradamus—a great sixteenth-century gastronome and literary figure (1503-66) wrote that this bird originated in Greece and that it was King René of Anjou who brought it to Provence. The seventeenth-century poet, Cyrano de Bergerac, said that 'Bartavelles are to partridges as cardinals are to grey friars . . .'

As for Grimod de la Reynière, he considers that 'the bartavelles deserve such profound respect that people should go down on their knees to eat them!'

All the recipes given for *Partridge** can be applied to rock partridge.

ROCKET (CRESS). Roquette—Strong smelling plant with sharp and piquant flavour. Its leaves are smooth and glabrous, the flowers white or pale yellow and it grows wild in the fields. It is used as seasoning in salads.

ROE—See SOFT ROES.

ROEBUCK (U.S. VENISON). Chevreuil—Wild European and Asiatic deer which is called *fawn* until 18 months old in both sexes, *pricket* or *yearling* up to 2 years old, then *brocket*. One can establish the age of the animal in the male by the number of tines on the antlers, and in the female by the burrs.

The meat of the young roebuck or roedeer is delicate especially if it has not been marinated; that of the old brockets, which is tougher, does need marinating, but not for long.

The meat of deer is also called venison. The same word applies in the U.S.A. to the meat of other horned animals, such, as elk, moose, reindeer or caribou.

Civet of roebuck (or venison). Civet de chevreuil—The parts of the roebuck used for this stew, which is made in the same way as *Civet of hare* (see HARE) are the shoulders, the neck, the breast and the upper part of the loin.

As one can seldom obtain the blood of the roebuck, it is replaced for the final liaison of the sauce, with hare's blood, or even that of rabbit.

Roebuck or venison chops or cutlets. CÔTELETTES DE CHEVREUIL—These chops or cutlets are taken from the loin. Trim them, beat them lightly. Season with salt and pepper and sauté in burning hot oil as quickly as possible in order to keep the centre of each cutlet still slightly pink.

Arrange them in the form of a crown alternating with croûtons of bread cut into heart shape and fried in butter. Dress them with the sauce indicated by the particular recipe and garnish accordingly. (See recipes below.)

The meaty part of the cutlet can be larded with fine lardoons or strips of salt pork inserted into the meat in the form of a star. If the chops or cutlets are taken from an old animal they can be marinated beforehand.

Roebuck cutlets with chestnuts

Roebuck or venison chops or cutlets with chestnuts. CÔTELETTES DE CHEVREUIL AUX MARRONS—Cook the chops or cutlets in the same way as for *Roebuck or venison chops or cutlets poivrade**. Arrange them in the form of a crown, alternating with croûtons fried in butter. Fill the centre of the dish with braised chestnuts. Pour over a *Poivrade sauce* (see SAUCE). Fix a paper frill on each cutlet.

Roebuck or venison chops or cutlets Conti. CÔTELETTES DE CHEVREUIL CONTI—Prepare the chops or cutlets in the same way as for *Roebuck chops or cutlets poivrade**. Arrange them in the form of a crown. Fill the centre of the dish with a *Lentil purée* (see PURÉE). Cover the cutlets with *Poivrade sauce*. See SAUCE.

The lentil purée can also be served separately.

Roebuck or venison chops or cutlets à la crème. CÔTELETTES DE CHEVREUIL À LA CRÈME—Season the chops or cutlets with salt and paprika. Sauté them quickly in butter. Drain them. Arrange them in the form of a crown with fried croûtons. Pour over them a cream sauce prepared in the following way: for 6 cutlets pour ⅓ cup (1 decilitre) of Madeira into the pan in which the cutlets have been sautéed. Scrape the pan to blend the juices of the meat with the wine, and then boil down. Add 1 cup (3 decilitres) of thick fresh cream. Boil for a few minutes. Add a little lemon juice, strain through a sieve. Serve with a chestnut purée passed separately.

Roebuck or venison chops or cutlets with grapes. CÔTELETTES DE CHEVREUIL AUX RAISINS—Sauté the chops or cutlets in oil. Arrange them in the form of a crown alternating with fried croûtons. Put some fresh grapes, which have been skinned and seeded, into the pan in which the cutlets have been cooked. The grapes should be soaked in a little cognac beforehand, allowing ten grapes per cutlet. Moisten with *Poivrade sauce* (see SAUCE), not too strong (or with rich brown stock). Pour this sauce over the cutlets.

Roebuck or venison chops or cutlets with juniper berries. CÔTELETTES DE CHEVREUIL AU GENIÈVRE—Sauté the chops or cutlets in oil or butter. Arrange them in the form of a crown, alternating them with croûtons fried in butter. Pour over them the juices released in the pan to which two tablespoons of gin have been added, moistened with ⅔ cup (2 decilitres) of fresh cream and ⅓ cup (7 decilitres) of *Poivrade sauce* (see SAUCE) with a few crushed juniper berries (one or two per cutlet), and some drops of lemon juice. Boil for a few moments; sieve.

Serve with a purée of apples only very slightly sweetened, passed separately.

Roebuck or venison chops or cutlets à la minute. CÔTELETTES DE CHEVREUIL À LA MINUTE—Sauté the chops or cutlets quickly in oil or butter. Sprinkle them while they are cooking with a large tablespoon of finely chopped onion (for 6 cutlets). Drain the cutlets, arrange them in the form of a crown with fried croûtons. Pour over them the juices from the pan to which 2 tablespoons of cognac have been added over the fire and ¾ cup (1½ decilitres) of *Poivrade sauce* (see SAUCE) or, failing this, with a rich brown stock. Season with a little lemon juice and add, off the fire, 5 tablespoons (75 grams) of butter. Garnish the centre of the dish with sliced mushrooms sautéed in butter.

Roebuck or venison chops or cutlets poivrade. CÔTELETTES DE CHEVREUIL POIVRADE—Sauté the chops or cutlets in oil or butter. Add a little wine vinegar to the juices in the pan and some *Poivrade sauce* (see SAUCE). Arrange the cutlets in the form of a crown alternating them with fried croûtons. Attach a paper frill to each cutlet bone.

Roebuck or venison chops or cutlets à la romaine. CÔTELETTES DE CHEVREUIL À LA ROMAINE—Sauté the chops or cutlets in oil. Arrange them in the form of a crown, alternating with croûtons fried in butter. Cover them with a *Romaine sauce* (see SAUCE) combined with the juices in the pan which have been de-glazed with a little white wine.

Serve with a chestnut purée handed separately.

Roebuck or venison chops or cutlets d'Uzès. CÔTELETTES DE CHEVREUIL D'UZÈS—Sauté the chops or cutlets quickly in oil. Arrange them in the form of a crown, alternating with heart-shaped croûtons fried in butter. Fill the centre of the dish with *Dauphine potatoes* (see POTATOES). Cover the cutlets with a sauce made in the following way: Scrape the bottom of the pan in which the cutlets have cooked and to which 4 tablespoons of wine vinegar have been added. Moisten with 1 cup (2½ decilitres) of rich brown veal stock and 1½ cups (3 decilitres) of cream. Boil down; add butter off the fire, and pass through a sieve.

To this sauce; add a tablespoon of orange rind, which has been cut neatly into tiny strips, blanched and drained, 2 tablespoons of almonds which have been peeled by dipping in hot water and dried in the oven, and 2 tablespoons of gherkins, cut into strips. Add a little orange juice and season with freshly ground pepper.

Roebuck or venison filets mignons. FILETS MIGNONS DE CHEVREUIL—In principle the term '*filets mignons*' denotes the thin tongue of meat which is found under the bone of the animal's saddle. These can also be cut from the big fillets of the saddle.

These fillets, after being trimmed and lightly beaten, are larded with thin lardoons or strips of salt pork and sautéed in butter or in oil or grilled, and served with *Poivrade sauce* (see SAUCE) and a purée of chestnuts.

The little fillets can also be subjected to the various methods of preparation prescribed for *Roebuck or venison chops or cutlets**.

Roebuck or venison hash. HACHIS DE CHEVREUIL—Prepared with cold roebuck or venison in the same way as *Mutton hash* (see MUTTON). The hash is moistened with a thick brown sauce made with rich game stock.

Haunch of roebuck or venison. CUISSOT, GIGUE DE CHEVREUIL—Trim the haunch, that is to say, remove the thin skin which covers it. Lard it with narrow strips of larding bacon or thin strips of salt pork. Roast it in the oven or on the spit, allowing 6 to 7 minutes per pound.

Serve separately a *Poivrade sauce* or any other sauce appropriate to furred game (see SAUCE), a chestnut purée and gooseberry jelly.

Loin of roebuck or venison. CARRÉ DE CHEVREUIL—This dish is hardly ever prepared with the whole loin. If one wishes to treat it whole it is cooked in the same way as saddle of roebuck, which means to say that it is roasted in the oven or on the spit, allowing 6 to 7 minutes per pound. The loin is accompanied by *Poivrade sauce* (see SAUCE) or with any other sauce appropriate to furred game or to venison, and with a purée of chestnuts.

Cutlets (chops) or noisettes of roebuck are taken from the loin. Noisettes can also be taken from the upper part of the haunch and also, but less often, from the fillets of the saddle.

Roebuck or venison noisettes. NOISETTES DE CHEVREUIL—These little cuts are taken from the loin, but can also be taken from the upper end of the haunch or from the saddle fillets.

The noisettes should be cut rather thick and in the form of a round or oval.

They are cooked in the same way as for *Roebuck or venison chops or cutlets**, and are accompanied by all the sauces and garnishes indicated for these.

Roebuck or venison pâté and terrine. PÂTÉ, TERRINE DE CHEVREUIL—Prepared with strips of roebuck or venison and game forcemeat in the same way as *Hare terrines* and *pâtés*. See PÂTÉ, TERRINE.

Saddle of roebuck or venison. SELLE DE CHEVREUIL—The word saddle applies only to that part of the animal which is found between the loin and the haunch. However, one can leave the two loins adhering to the joint cutting the ribs very short.

Remove the sinewy parts of the meat and lard it with strips of larding bacon or salt pork. Roast it in the oven or on the spit allowing 6 to 7 minutes per pound.

Serve with *Poivrade sauce* (see SAUCE) passed separately, or any other appropriate sauce for furred game, with chestnut purée and gooseberry jelly.

Roebuck or venison saddle à l'allemande. SELLE DE CHEVREUIL À L'ALLEMANDE—Trim and lard the saddle. Marinate for 12 hours in an uncooked marinade (see MARINADES). Dry the meat and put it in a rather narrow roasting tin on a foundation of the vegetables from the marinade. Allow 6 to 7 minutes a pound for roasting.

When it is properly cooked set it on a dish and keep warm. Add a little of the liquor from the marinade to the juices and vegetables in the baking tin. Reduce almost completely. Add $1\frac{3}{4}$ cups ($3\frac{1}{2}$ decilitres) of cream. Boil down by one-third. Add a tablespoon of dissolved meat glaze or double consommé. Pass the sauce through a strainer and serve with the joint.

Roebuck or venison saddle grand veneur. SELLE DE CHEVREUIL GRAND VENEUR—Lard the saddle with strips of larding bacon or salt pork. Roast it in the manner described above. Arrange it on a serving dish. Garnish with braised chestnuts and *Dauphine potatoes* (see POTATOES) arranged in clumps at each end of the dish.

Serve with *Grand veneur sauce* separately.

Sliced roebuck or venison with various sauces. ÉMINCÉS DE CHEVREUIL—Prepared with cold roebuck or venison in the same way as for *Sliced lamb* or *Beef* with various sauces.

Cover the slices of meat with *Poivrade sauce*, *Grand veneur sauce*, or *Chasseur sauce* (see SAUCE). Serve with a chestnut purée handed separately and gooseberry jelly.

ROGNONNADE—French term for a cut of veal to which the kidney has been left adhering. This piece is roasted or baked.

ROI DES CAILLES (KING OF QUAILS)—Popular name for the land rail. This bird was so called because it appeared at the same time as the quails and disappeared at the same time that they did. Formerly it was believed that it directed the quails in their flight. For cooking instructions see QUAIL.

ROLL OUT. ABAISSER—To spread out pastry or any other mixture (puff pastry, short pastry, sweet pastry, almond paste, etc.) with the aid of a rolling-pin in one uniform strip of varying thinness. In the case of a biscuit or sponge, we would not say that it is rolled but that it is divided in one or several slices of the same thickness, or *abaisses*. For the method see DOUGH.

ROLLMOPS—Name given to fillets of herrings prepared in a highly seasoned marinade, generally based on white wine, then rolled around gherkins and pinned with a wooden skewer to secure them. Rollmops are served as hors-d'oeuvre.

ROLY-POLY PUDDING—Pudding made of suet pastry spread with jam, rolled in the shape of a sausage, and cooked in water. See PUDDING, *English suet roll pudding*.

ROMAINE OR COS LETTUCE—Variety of lettuce with firm leaves, mostly eaten in salad. Legend says that it was Rabelais who imported this variety into France. It is called *Cos* in England.

ROMANÉE—A great wine from the commune of Vosnes-Romanée. There are three distinct types, the Romanée, the Romanée-Conti and the Romanée-Saint-Vivant.

ROMANOV—See GARNISHES.

ROOK. FREUX—A kind of crow, which is sometimes eaten after it has been skinned.

Rook pie. PÂTÉ DE CORBEAU—Rook pie, in spite of what the sceptics and the incredulous may think, is a dish which is not to be despised, if properly prepared. It should first be said that this pie is only prepared with fledglings straight from the nest. 'There are certain rules which it is absolutely necessary to follow to achieve a good result. First of all, the rooks are not plucked, the birds are drawn and only the breast is retained. The legs are tough and the carcase bitter.

'Having washed the breasts, they are left to soak in milk for 6 hours, they are then cut up and the pieces are arranged in a pie dish, and seasoned, sparing neither pepper nor spices. The bottom of the dish should be lined with some slices of beef. Strips of bacon are placed on top of the pieces of rook, and halved hard boiled eggs are distributed here and there. This pie is then covered with a sheet of pastry and put in the oven for an hour and a half.

When the pie is taken out of the oven a little good stock to which a small quantity of half-glaze is added, is poured into the pie.' (Alfred Suzanne, *La cuisine et la pâtisserie anglaise.*)

ROOT. RAVE—Name used for a category of vegetable plants, whose subterranean parts are swollen (see TURNIP). In cookery those mostly used are turnip, kohl-rabi, beetroot, carrot, celeriac and radish.

ROPINESS. GRAISSE DES VINS—A defection peculiar to white wines. It is encountered especially in the white wines of the Cher, Poitou, Orleans, and Champagne districts.

This generally occurs as a result of pressing the grapes as soon as they are gathered. The must enclosed in the vats ferments independently of the skin, pips and stalks, which provide the tannin need to clarify the must.

At the clarification stage, the gelatinous and albuminous elements remain in suspension, which leaves the wines cloudy.

At this stage, the remedy is to put tannin in the cask. This not only causes the sediment in the wine to settle, but also separates out the fish glue which has been added as a clarifying agent, and which will not be found in the next clarification.

The proportion of tannin to be used with ropy wine is 15 to 30 grams ($\frac{1}{2}$ to 1 ounce) per hectolitre (100 litres or approximately 109 quarts).

ROQUEFORT CHEESE—See CHEESE.

ROQUEVAIRE—Liqueur wine which is made at Roquevaire in the Bouches-du-Rhône.

ROQUILLE—French culinary term for orange peel. These skins are candied and used in confectionery.

ROSEMARY. ROMARIN—Rosemary is a perennial evergreen, reaching 5 feet in height, with narrow hard leaves, green above and greyish below, with a strongly aromatic smell. The leaves, fresh and dried, are used in seasoning.

ROSETTE—Name given to a special sausage of the first quality made in the Lyons district, which is eaten uncooked. See SAUSAGE.

ROSSINI—See GARNISHES.

ROSSOLL OR ROSOLIO—Liqueur formerly made from the sundew plant. See LIQUEURS.

ROTA—Wine from the north of Spain, much used in blending.

ROTENGLE—A freshwater fish, better known in France as *gardon rouge*. Its body is a little deeper and less elongated than the common roach. It has a bright red eye and its fins are red and pink. It is cooked like roach. See ROACH.

RÔTIE (TOAST)—Slice of bread baked or toasted.

Rôties (pieces of toast) are buttered and served with breakfast, tea, etc. The same name is given to canapés spread with forcemeat which are served with game birds, roasts in general and woodcock and snipe in particular (see WOODCOCK), and to small snacks made by putting an egg or some kind of spread on a slice of toasted or fried bread.

RÔTISSERIE—Part of the kitchen specially equipped for preparing roasts. It is also the word given to modern portable appliances designed to roast meat on a spit.

By extension the word also describes the work done by the chef in this special section, in the big catering establishments, a specialist in all the work of the *rôtisserie*.

The *rôtisseur*, as he is called, is employed not only in roasting but grilling and frying. It must be said, however, that in the most important establishments the *rôtisserie* is divided into three parts, each having a specialist in charge: the *rôtisseur* proper, the *grillardin* and the *friturier*.

Certain specialized places, where all kinds of spit-roasted poultry are cooked and sold, are also called *rôtisseries*.

ROUELLE—Cut of veal. This is a fairly thick slice across the leg.

ROUGAIL—A sort of condiment, very popular in hot countries, served with various dishes cooked in the Creole style.

This condiment, being highly spiced, stimulates the appetite. It is served daily at all meals with *Rice à la créole*.

Note. All the *rougail* recipes which are given below belong to the repertoire of Creole cookery.

Rougail of green apples. ROUGAIL DE POMMES VERTES—Cut in tiny dice 4 peeled green apples. Put them, as they are prepared, into a bowl of salted water.

Drain these apple dice; put them in a napkin and squeeze to extract all the water. Put them in a dish where you will have set a layer of pimentos and ginger, pounded smoothly with a little olive oil.

If the apples are not sharp enough add a squeeze of lemon juice.

Rougail of aubergines (egg-plants). ROUGAIL D'AUBERGINES—Take two new aubergines (egg-plants), boil them in salted water. In the meantime pound in a mortar a slice of onion, a piece of ginger the size of a gaming dice and a little pimento seasoned with salt. Put this mixture on a plate and dilute it with lemon juice and good olive oil. Take out the cooked aubergines, split them, scoop out the flesh, having removed the seeds, and add them little by little to this prepared sauce, mashing with a fork so that the aubergines are completely reduced to a paste. Turn into an hors-d'oeuvre dish.

Rougail of salt cod and tomatoes. ROUGAIL DE MORUE ET DE TOMATES—De-salt a small salt cod by soaking in cool water the evening before it is wanted. Remove all skin and bones. Dry with a cloth. Cut in small pieces. Flour and brown lightly in a pan with oil and fat. Push to one side of the pan. Place in it some chopped onions (three or more). Cook them well over a low heat so that they do not colour. Add 4 fresh tomatoes, peeled and with the seeds removed. Stew together gently. Pound some ginger, a close of garlic, some thyme, some parsley and a small pimento. Incorporate this mixture with the gently simmering cod. Cook for about 40 minutes, then put the pot (still covered) in the oven, and leave it for 20 minutes.

Serve rice separately.

Rougail of shrimps or prawns. ROUGAIL DE CREVETTES—Remove the heads and tails from some shrimps or prawns and fry them in fat. Shell them.

Crush with the pestle in a mortar half an onion with a small piece of ginger and pimento. Season with salt.

Add the shrimps, little by little, pounding all the time. When all is reduced to a paste, add two small tomatoes that have been cooked in the oven. Add the juice of a lemon. Mix well.

Turn the mixture into an hors-d'oeuvre dish.

This rougail is served alone or with fish curry.

Often, when the rougail is made, it is reheated with olive oil in a frying pan.

Rougail of raw tomatoes. ROUGAIL DE TOMATES CRUES—Pound a little onion with a piece of ginger the size of a walnut. Add peeled and seeded tomatoes. Mash all together. Incorporate some pimento and a squeeze of lemon juice. Serve in an hors-d'oeuvre dish.

This seasoning accompanies Creole dishes served with rice.

ROUGE DE RIVIÈRE—A French name for the shoveller duck. This bird, whose flesh is succulent, is nearly always roasted. See DUCK, *Wild duck.*

ROULADE, ROLL—Rolled piece of veal or pork.

A thin slice of meat spread with some kind of forcemeat and rolled into a sausage is also known as *roulade.*

This term is also applied to various preparations, mostly of pork or veal, made like galantines. Thus *roulade de tête de porc* describes a pig's head, boned, stuffed with a forcemeat of chopped-up pig's tongue, streaky bacon and other ingredients, rolled like 'boar's head' and cooked in a jelly stock (see the recipe for pig's head under PORK); *roulade de veau* describes a slice of *noix de veau* well fattened, spread with a forcemeat of some kind, mixed with meat cut in small dice, rolled into a galantine and braised or poached in white *court-bouillon**.

ROULÉ—Rolled-out sheet of biscuit (cake) mixture, spread with thick jam, then rolled. The top is sprinkled with praline and toasted almonds.

ROULETTE (Pastry wheel)—A small toothed wheel, in wood or metal, mounted free on a handle, and used to cut pastry.

ROUND (U.S.) OR SILVERSIDE (G.B.). GÎTE À LA NOIX—Part of the leg of beef. This cut includes in particular the tendons (part tendon, part membrane) and part of the femoral biceps, the gemellus muscle, the pyramidal and the crural square.

This cut is used chiefly in hot-pots. It may also be braised.

In Paris and other large French cities, this cut is sold larded, rolled and tied.

ROUSSELET, RUSSET PEAR—Summer pear, so named because its skin is russet colour. The flesh is sweet and well flavoured.

This pear is mostly preserved by drying.

ROUSSETTE—Name given to a kind of fritter in certain regions of France, which in other places is known as *merveille* or *oreillette.* It is made in this way:

Make a rather thick paste of 3¾ cups (500 grams) of sifted flour, 3 eggs, 3 tablespoons of milk, a teaspoon of orange blossom water, a small glass of *eau-de-vie* and a pinch of salt.

Gather up the paste into a ball, wrap it in a cloth and leave it to rest in a cool place for 3 hours.

Roll out into a thin sheet, and cut out with a plain round pastry cutter.

Drop into hot deep fat. Drain the *rousettes* when they are nicely browned and crisp. Sprinkle with sugar. Arrange in a mound on a napkin.

ROUSSILLON—See LANGUEDOC AND ROUSSILLON.

ROUSSIR—To turn in smoking hot butter, or other fat, a piece of meat or poultry, in order to colour it.

The word *roussir* cannot be translated in its proper sense, because the meats so fried must be golden rather than russet.

ROUX—Mixture of butter or other fatty substance and flour, cooked together for varying periods of time depending on its final use.

The roux is the thickening element in sauces.

There are three kinds of roux: white roux, blond roux and brown roux.

Brown roux is used to thicken rich brown sauces like *Espagnole* and *Demi-glace* (see SAUCE). It is made by cooking flour in clarified butter in the oven, gently and for a long time, stirring frequently. The clarified fat from a *marmite** may also be used, but in each case the proportions are equal amounts by tablespoons of flour and of butter or fat.

This *roux* should be of a good light brown colour. It can be kept for quite a long time.

Blond *roux* is made only with butter. The proportions of butter and flour are the same as for brown *roux.* It is cooked more rapidly and it is only made at the moment it is needed. Its colour should be a pale gold.

White *roux* is used for *Béchamel* and *Velouté* sauces and special thick soups.

It is made by cooking flour and clarified butter for 5 minutes over the heat and stirring constantly with a wooden spoon.

ROYALE—Moulded custard, variously flavoured, which is used as garnish in clear soup. See GARNISHES.

ROYALE (A LA)—Name given to different preparations, for example, to consommé garnished with custard shapes, and to various dishes, particularly of poultry, poached in very little liquid, coated with *Velouté sauce* reduced (cooked down) with cream and finished with truffle purée and various garnishes.

The same name is applied to sweets, hot and cold.

ROYAN—Sort of large sardine.

RUM. RHUM—Product of the distillation of cane sugar into fermented sugar, a name extended to the product of the distillation of molasses (formerly called tafia). The rum, colourless like all eau-de-vie, takes on a light colouration from a long sojourn in vats. Ordinary commercial rums are always artificially coloured. The strength of Martinique rum is determined at 50° to 55°, that of Jamaica sometimes as much as 75° to 80°, but this is reduced before sale.

Rum has much more 'impurity' than eau-de-vie made from wine. Its properties are those of other eaux-de-vie: it is particularly used for the preparation of grogs and punches.

RUMP. CULOTTE—The fleshy part of the haunch of beef, used in hot-pots. This cut can also be braised and made into ragoûts. See BEEF.

TOP OF RUMP. POINTE DE CULOTTE—A piece of beef taken from the rump. It is usually braised or poached. See BEEF.

RUSCUS. PRAGON—Plant similar to asparagus. The best known variety is *Butcher's Broom* or knee-holly. The young shoots are eatable and are used like hop shoots.

RUSH. JONC—Most types of reed belong to the rush family. The scented Indian rush, *rattan,* is used as a spice in the East.

RUSKS. BISCOTTES—Slices of special bread, cut from the loaf and re-baked in the oven.

Diet rusks. BISCOTTES DE RÉGIME—There are various types of rusks on sale in the shops, of different degrees of hardness and friability, sweet rusks and salty rusks, etc. There are also special types of rusks with salt content completely or partially extracted, as well as rusks enriched in gluten, or containing additional casein (legumen), but with reduced starch content; others, on the contrary, are very rich in starch but their content in gluten and nitrogenous elements is reduced to the minimum.

Paris rusks. BISCOTTES PARISIENNES—Pound 3 cups (500 grams) of sweet almonds and 2 tablespoons (20 grams) of bitter almonds in a mortar, moistening with 2 whites of egg and a spoonful of kirsch or other liqueur.

When the almonds have been reduced to a smooth paste, put it into a bowl and add to it 10 yolks of egg, one at a time, stirring well with a wooden spoon. Add 1 pound (500 grams) of castor (fine) sugar, a pinch of salt and, at the last moment, 8 whites of egg whisked into a stiff froth, which should be incorporated in the mixture, sprinkling it with 1⅓ cup (200 grams) potato flour. Pipe this mixture through a forcing bag on to buttered baking sheets or into wide moulds. Bake in the oven.

RUSSULA. RUSSULE—A fungus with white flesh and quite a pleasant flavour known in various regions of France as *russule*, *bordet vert*, *vert bonnet*, *palomet*, *berdanel*, *blavet* and *verdette*.

They are found in summer and autumn, on the edges of the woods, in fallow land and near birch trees, and are prepared like mushrooms. See MUSHROOMS.

RUTABAGA, SWEDE TURNIP—Turnip with yellowish flesh, edible but seldom used in France as foodstuff.

RYE. SEIGLE—The most important European cereal after wheat, originating in the region between the Austrian Alps and the Caspian Sea. Very hardy, very resistant to cold, earlier than wheat, rye grows in the worst soils.

Rye flour, rather greyish in colour, consists mainly of gluten-casein, has little agglutinative quality and darkens quickly. It can nevertheless be made into bread, which is brown in colour, has an agreeable taste and keeps fresh for a long time, but is more difficult to digest than white bread. Rye flour is used to make spiced bread and cakes.

Salad Vegetables

SABLAGE—In times past this word, which means 'sanding', was used to describe a kind of table decoration which was made with sands of different colours. The sand was spread on the tablecloth so as to form different designs—flowers, landscapes, coats of arms, monograms, etc.

This type of decoration has today been completely abandoned.

SABLÉ—A very delicate small biscuit or cake, originating in Normandy. It is made in this way: Make a circle of 3¾ cups (500 grams) of sifted flour on the kitchen table. Place in the middle of the circle 1¾ cups (400 grams) of butter, 6 egg yolks, ⅝ cup (150 grams) of sugar, the interior of a vanilla pod (or 1 teaspoon vanilla extract) and a pinch of salt.

First mix the butter, the sugar, the yolks, the vanilla and the salt, then amalgamate the flour. Finish the operation as quickly as possible.

Blend the ingredients by breaking up the paste with the palm of the hand. Form it once more into a ball and leave it to rest for an hour.

Roll out the paste to a thickness of ¼ inch. Cut with a pastry cutter into rounds about 5 inches in diameter. Divide these rounds into 4 wedges. Put on a buttered baking sheet and cook in the oven at a gentle heat (350°F.) from 18 to 20 minutes.

SACCHARINE—Commercial name for a crystalline chemical substance, soluble in water, with a very sweet taste, having a faint taste of bitter almonds and leaving a dryness in the throat. The sensation of sweetness that it provides is 250 to 300 times stronger than that of sugar, 5 centigrams being equivalent to a normal-sized piece of sugar. But it has no chemical analogy with sugar and has none of its nutritional value.

It is chiefly used to give an illusion of sweetness for diabetics, to whom sugar is forbidden.

SACCHAROMETER. PÈSE-SIROP—A hydrometer calibrated to give the specific gravity or density of sugar solutions. The hydrometer, calibrated to give the sugar content of meat and, consequently, the alcohol degree of the urine which it will produce is a *pèse-moût*, also called in English a saccharometer.

SACRISTAIN—Small puff pastry made in the shape of a paper twist.

SADDLE. SELLE, RÂBLE—In terms of butchery the French word *selle* describes the part of the hindquarters extending from the last ribs to the leg on both sides (mutton, lamb, roebuck).

The French word *râble* describes the fleshy part extending from the base of the shoulder to the tail of small domestic or wild animals (rabbits, hares), formed by the sacro-lumbar, long dorsal and transverse spinal muscles. In English cookery, where small animals are concerned, the word 'saddle' is applied to the hare only.

SAFFRON. SAFRAN—The dried stamens of the saffron or cultivated crocus, a bulb, originating in the East and introduced into Spain by the Arabs, cultivated in France, particularly in the Gatinais, since the sixteenth century. Saffron contains a volatile oil and a colouring substance. It is the indispensable condiment for *bouillabaisse*.

A good saffron should be a dark orange colour all over without white streaks; it is sometimes falsified with safflower (bastard saffron), which is redder in colour.

It is said that a dish is *safrané* (saffroned) when it contains saffron or when it is saffron coloured.

Saffron of the Indies—See CURCUMA.

SAGE. SAUGE—Name of various *Labiatae* of which there are some 500 species with a distinct perfume and with an aromatic, slightly bitter taste, among which are three French varieties, great sage (*grande sauge*), of ramose inflorescence, with thick, oblong, hairy leaves, ashy green in colour; the small Provençal sage (*petite sauge de Provence*), with smaller, whiter leaves and a more pronounced scent, which is the most highly esteemed species; and the Catalogne sage, which is even smaller. All these species are used in making flavoured vinegar.

Sage is used in cookery to flavour marinades and forcemeats, and is threaded into meat that is to be roasted; small birds are wrapped in it, thrushes particularly. It is also added during the cooking of certain green vegetables, beans, peas and broad beans particularly, to flavour them. Some sweet fritters are made with it. In certain parts of northern Europe the young shoots are eaten as a salad.

In England there are two indigenous sages, *Salvia verbenaca* which is very common and *Salvia pratensis* which is rare. Our culinary sage, *Salvia officinalis*, is not a native plant. The culinary sages, *Salvia officinalis*, the common garden sage and the white sage, *Salvia officinalis alba* are grown in the U.S.A., but not in sufficient quantity, so that tons of sage are imported every year.

SAGO. SAGOU—Floury extract of the marrow of various kinds of palm tree.

This yellowish flour, always tending to red or brown, is used for cooking and baking as a liaison element, and often also to prepare thick or thin soups and dishes that are highly recommended for special diets.

Sago consommé—See SOUPS AND BROTHS, *Consommé with sago*.

Sago pudding—See PUDDING.

Sago with red wine (Russian cookery). SAGOU AU VIN ROUGE—Blanch for 2 minutes ½ pound (250 grams) of sago, drain and cool.

Put to cook in a saucepan with a quart (litre) of red Bordeaux wine, ½ cup (125 grams) of sugar, a small pinch of salt, the peel of half a lemon and a good pinch of powdered cinnamon.

Cook over a low heat for 25 minutes and heap it on a dessert platter after having taken out the lemon rind.

This sago dish can also be made with white wine. It may be served cold.

SAIGNEUX—French butchery term for the neck of veal or mutton.

SAINTE-MENEHOULD—This district of the Marne is renowned for its excellent pork products (*charcuterie*), and particularly for its *Pigs' feet*, a much enjoyed gastronomic speciality.

SAINT-ÉMILION—Saint-Émilion, a small commune of the Gironde in the Libourne district, is celebrated all over the world for its wines, which, after the Bordelais, most nearly approach the wines of Burgundy. See BORDEAUX, *Wines of Bordeaux*.

ST. GEORGE'S AGARIC. MOUSSERON—A small mushroom which grows in the fields in the autumn and spring.

It is cooked in the same way as the cultivated mushroom, and mainly used to flavour stews.

In south-western France, this mushroom is dried. In this state it has to be steeped in water before use. See MUSHROOMS.

SAINT-GERMAIN—This word is mostly used to describe a thick soup made with fresh peas. See SOUPS AND BROTHS, *Purée of fresh pea soup*.

A purée of dried peas is also erroneously called Saint-Germain.

The term also applies to a garnish whose principal ingredient is fresh peas, prepared in any one of a variety of ways. See GARNISHES.

Finally, the word is used for a preparation of grilled fillets of fish served with *Béarnaise sauce*. See SOLE, *Fillets of sole Saint-Germain*.

Saint Honoré

SAINT-HONORÉ—This cake, a speciality of Parisian pastrycooks, is so called in memory of St. Honoré, who is considered to be the patron saint of pastrycooks and bakers—though it is impossible to say why, because nothing in the life of St. Honoré (who about 660 A.D. was Bishop of Amiens, and whose feast is celebrated on May 16th) seemed to destine him to a patronage so completely gastronomic.

The Saint-Honoré is made with two different kinds of pastry: *Fine lining paste* for the base and *Chou pastry* for the little iced *choux*, which are arranged in a crown on this base. See DOUGH.

To make the Saint-Honoré. With the rolled-out lining paste make a circle 7 to 8 inches in diameter and set it in a baking tin. Moisten the edges with a brush, then, using a forcing bag with a plain nozzle, pipe a thick ring of chou pastry round the damp edge. Bake this pastry in the oven. On a separate baking sheet make two dozen little round *choux* the size of walnuts. Brush with egg and cook in the oven (375°F.) for 15 minutes.

To cook the sugar and icing for the choux. Put into a copper pan 1 cup (250 grams) of sugar, some glucose as big as a walnut and 1 cup (2 decilitres) of water. Cook rapidly over a good heat to crack degree (reached when, the index finger being dipped into cold water and then into the syrup, the sugar will snap off in the teeth and will not stick). (See SUGAR.) Take the pot from the fire and dip the little choux into the sugar, icing their tops only.

To stick them to the outer edge of the pastry base, dip their bottoms into the sugar *very lightly*, and set them instantly on to the ring of chou pastry.

Cream filling for the Saint-Honoré. 3 cups (¾ litre) of *French pastry cream* (*Crème pâtissière*—see CREAMS). Heat it, and add to it while warm 6 leaves of gelatine (or 1 ounce of granulated gelatine) previously soaked in cold water and softened.

Beat 6 egg whites stiffly, sprinkling them lightly with sugar when stiff, to prevent them from separating.

Incorporate them rapidly into the pastry cream, and fill the inside of the Saint-Honoré with the resulting cream, using a forcing (pastry) bag and a large, fluted nozzle.

SAINT-JACQUES—See SCALLOPS.

ST. JOHN'S WORT (Hypercium). MILLEPERTUIS—A plant with an aromatic and resinous fragrance, bitter in taste, whose flowering tops are used in infusions. In former times, liqueurs were made from this plant.

SAINT-MICHEL (Pastry)—Cook a fine Genoese pastry mixture in a cake tin.

When it is cool, cut it into three equal-sized round layers. Spread each with a layer of butter which has been beaten with coffee essence. Put the cake layers one on top of the other. Cover the top and sides with vanilla-flavoured *Butter cream* (see CREAMS) and smooth it over. Sprinkle the cake with chopped roasted almonds, and decorate, through a forcing bag, with coffee-flavoured butter cream.

SAKÉ—Alcoholic drink used in Japan, obtained by fermenting rice. This drink is taken hot before the meal.

SALAD. SALADE—Dishes made up of herbs, plants, vegetables, eggs, meat and fish, seasoned with oil, vinegar, salt and pepper, with or without other ingredients.

In seasoning salads it is important to use good wine vinegar. No purpose is served by replacing this with lemon juice unless one is doubtful about the quality of the vinegar.

Brillat-Savarin, who gave only restricted space to vegetables in his gastronomic dissertations, made an exception for salad which according to him, 'freshens without enfeebling and fortifies without irritating'. Here he once again showed himself ahead of his time.

Green salad (*Robert Carrier*)

However, as Doctor Leclerc so rightly points out, certain salads, blanched by being cultivated in cellars or by being earthed up to keep out light and air, like Belgian endives, the chicory known as *barbe de capucin*, white dandelion leaves, etc., are almost entirely without mineral salts, chlorophyll and vitamins. As foodstuffs their contents are restricted to cellulose and water, which act as bulk, augmenting the bowel contents.

Salads are of two kinds, plain and combination (or mixed salads).

PLAIN SALADS. SALADES SIMPLES—Plain salads can be sub-divided into green salads, or salad in season, which are served raw, and salads of cooked vegetables consisting of a single kind of vegetable.

These salads, whether raw or cooked, are usually served with the roast, hot or cold.

Dressings for plain salads. ASSAISONNEMENTS—Dressings for plain salads are made with oil, wine vinegar, salt and pepper. They may also be seasoned in the ways shown below:

Anchovy—For celery, endives or cooked vegetables.

Take two de-salted fillets of anchovies, and rub through a sieve. Put them in the salad dish and add oil, vinegar and pepper.

Cream—For cabbage and romaine (cos) lettuces.

Mix 4 tablespoons of fresh cream, not too thick, with a teaspoon of wine vinegar (or lemon juice). Add salt and pepper.

Indian—For cooked vegetables.

Cook gently in a tablespoon of oil a tablespoon of onion, finely chopped. Sprinkle with a teaspoon of curry. Finish with oil, lemon juice, salt, pepper and a little crushed garlic.

Gasconne—For curly and other endives.

As for *Marseillaise* with the addition of crusts rubbed with garlic.

Bacon fat—For 'wild' chicory, red cabbage, corn salad, dandelion.

Render down 5 strips or rashers (100 grams) of not too lean bacon, cut in dice. Pour the fat on the salad which has been set in a hot salad dish and seasoned with salt and pepper. Add a tablespoon of vinegar heated in the frying pan.

Marseillaise—For early endive, 'wild' chicory and other endives.

Crush a clove of garlic in the salad bowl; add oil, vinegar, salt and pepper.

Mustard cream—For raw and cooked celeriac cut in *julienne* (thin strips), and endives.

Mix 2 tablespoons of mustard with 4 tablespoons of fresh cream; add a few drops of lemon juice, salt and pepper.

Rémoulade—For all salads, raw or cooked.

Rub through a sieve (or crush) 3 hard boiled egg yolks. Put in the salad bowl and blend, as for mayonnaise, with oil, vinegar, salt and pepper.

Paprika—For celery or for cooked vegetables.

Bake an onion in the oven and chop or mince it. Put it in the salad bowl and add oil, vinegar, salt and paprika.

Tomato juice—For cooked baby marrows (zucchini), potatoes, Jerusalem artichokes, etc.

Rub 2 raw tomatoes through a fine sieve. Boil down the juice by half and add oil, vinegar, salt and pepper.

Note on the seasoning of salads. Olive oil is the best for all salads. It can nevertheless be replaced, according to taste, by a good nut oil or vegetable oil.

Wine vinegar may also be replaced by lemon juice, by verjuice or by cider vinegar.

Complementary garnishes for plain salads—For green salads or salads in season, the most usual garnishes are aromatic herbs, such as chervil, chives, tarragon and, sometimes, parsley and savory. These herbs are used coarsely chopped or the leaves are picked from the stems and used whole.

The following herbs and vegetables are also used to garnish plain salads, raw or cooked:

Beetroot, baked in the oven, peeled, cut into rounds, in dice or in a *julienne* (thin strips); capers, whole or chopped; crusts of bread rubbed with garlic and seasoned with *vinaigrette;* gherkins, whole, in dice, rounds, *julienne* (thin strips), or chopped; borage flowers, nasturtiums or violets; hard boiled eggs cut in halves or quarters or chopped; peeled tomatoes cut in thin slices or quarters; truffles, raw or cooked, cut in thin slices, *julienne* or large dice.

It must be said, where some of these additional garnishes are concerned, notably truffles, that it is preferable not to be too lavish with them in plain salads, their role being chiefly to enrich the mixed (combination) salads which will be dealt with later.

Raw salads. SALADES SIMPLES (À SERVIR CRUES)—

	Dressing
'Wild' chicory (*Barbe du capucin*)	Mustard cream.
Chopped celery	Vinaigrette.
Celery in sticks	Rémoulade.
Celeriac	Mustard cream.
Curly or other endive	Vinaigrette, with garlic-rubbed crust, Rémoulade, Bacon fat.
Kohl-rabi, coarsely grated ...	Vinaigrette or Mayonnaise.
Red cabbage, cut in *julienne* ...	Rémoulade, Bacon fat, or Vinaigrette.
Green cabbage (the tender parts cut in *julienne*)	Mustard cream.
Cucumber cut in rounds and left to stand in salt	Vinaigrette or Cream.
Cress	Vinaigrette.
Watercress	Vinaigrette.
Chicory	Rémoulade.
Fennel	Bagnacaude (Anchovy).
Lettuces of all kinds	Vinaigrette.
Romaine or cos lettuce ...	Cream.
Corn salad	Bacon fat.
Turnip tops (greens)	Vinaigrette.
Samphire (rare in U.S.A.) ...	Vinaigrette.
Salad burnet	Vinaigrette.
Dandelion	Bacon fat.
Leeks (the green parts)	Vinaigrette.
Purslane	Vinaigrette.
Radish (the tender leaves and the radishes chopped) ...	Vinaigrette.
Rampion	Vinaigrette.
Rocket cress	Bacon fat.
Salsify (the stems or tender leaves)	Cream.
Soya bean shoots	Mustard.

Plain salads from cooked vegetables. SALADES SIMPLES (À SERVIR CUITES)—

	Dressing
Artichokes (bottoms)	Vinaigrette.
Aubergines (egg-plant) (rounds blanched in salt water) ...	Mustard cream.
Artichokes (white and green) ...	Vinaigrette or Mayonnaise.

Beetroot (in rounds), served always as hors-d'oeuvre ...	Mustard cream.
Celeriac (cut in *julienne*) ...	Mustard cream.
Sprouting broccoli	Vinaigrette.
Brussels sprouts	Vinaigrette.
Sea-kale	Vinaigrette.
Rutabaga or Swede turnip ...	Mustard cream.
Kohl-rabi	Mustard cream.
Red cabbage (cut in *julienne*) ...	Vinaigrette.
Green cabbage (as hors-d'oeuvre)	Vinaigrette.
Courgette (zucchini)	Vinaigrette.
Chinese artichoke	Rémoulade.
Spinach leaves (very lightly blanched)	Vinaigrette.
Broad beans	Vinaigrette with savory.
Haricot beans (shell beans) ...	Vinaigrette with chopped onion.
French (string) beans	Vinaigrette.
Kidney and other beans ...	Vinaigrette.
Lettuce (hearts, blanched and drained)	Vinaigrette.
Lentils	Vinaigrette.
Sweet potatoes	Vinaigrette.
Leeks (white parts cooked in water)	Mayonnaise.
'Mange-tout' peas	Vinaigrette.
Potatoes (cooked in water, cut up when hot and soaked in white wine)	Vinaigrette or Mayonnaise.
Salsify	Vinaigrette or Mayonnaise.
Parsnips	Vinaigrette or Mayonnaise.

Note. Dried vegetables as well as fresh farinaceous vegetables gain from being seasoned while still hot, even if the salad is to be served cold. Such salads are usually garnished with parsley, onion or chopped chives.

Potato salad

MIXED (COMBINATION) SALADS. Salades composées—Mixed (combination) salads must be sub-divided into several categories. The first, based on mixed cooked vegetables, is prepared in the same way as for a plain salad. Others contain a variety of ingredients, not only mixed vegetables, but also truffles, mushrooms, sliced fish, shellfish, poultry, tongue, ham, etc.

Mushroom salad with pepper and chicory

Some of these salads, by reason of their elaborate preparation, come into the realm of *grande cuisine*, and actually constitute cold entrées rather than salads in the ordinary sense.

In this last category are various mayonnaises, chicken salads *en bellevue*, etc.

Mixed salads with a base of vegetables only are served like plain salads with the roast, hot or cold. Salads with multiple ingredients, particularly those demanding a rather elaborate arrangement, are served by themselves or as an accompaniment to a very special cold dish, such as *chaud-froids*, ham mousse, chicken mousse, etc.

Dressings for mixed (combination) salads. Assaisonnements—All salads with a vegetable basis are dressed in the same way as plain salads. They are garnished with the additional ingredients given above, always with the exception of those with too strongly marked a character, such as grated garlic or garlic-rubbed crusts.

These salads are served in glass bowls. The various vegetables of which they are composed are arranged in separate groups, the colours arranged to contrast.

If the salads are dressed in advance in the kitchen and then mixed together, macédoine fashion, they are garnished, after having been arranged in a dome in the salad dish, with little heaps and bunches of vegetables, arranged decoratively.

When the dressing used is vinaigrette, the vegetables composing the salad can be seasoned separately and arranged in 'bouquets'.

Mixed (combination) salads with a multiple basis are often dressed with mayonnaise. According to the type of salad, and, even more, according to the way in which it is to be arranged and served, the mayonnaise is used in its normal creamy form or very thick and stiff.

Some of these salads are moulded in aspic. In this case they become cold entrées rather than salads.

In the home, even for quite important dinners, it is best to serve salads with the greatest possible simplicity.

To serve them in crystal bowls is very elegant. To suit the nature of the salad these dishes can be surrounded with crushed ice or 'snow'.

Albignac salad. Salade d'Albignac—The white meat of chicken finely sliced; raw white truffles in thin slices; black truffles cut in *julienne* (thin strips); shelled crayfish; celeriac cut in a fine *julienne*; lettuce hearts; hard boiled eggs; chervil; tarragon.

Put the celeriac dressed with mayonnaise in the middle of the salad bowl, arranging it in a dome.

Surround alternately with the chicken meat, seasoned with oil, lemon juice, salt and pepper; the crayfish seasoned with tomato ketchup and the white truffles sprinkled with olive oil and seasoned with salt and paprika.

Insert lettuce hearts and hard boiled eggs between each separate group of garnish.

Strew over the celeriac the *julienne* of black truffles. Sprinkle with oil and lemon juice when serving.

Ali-Baba salad. SALADE ALI-BAB—Sweet potatoes, cooked, peeled and cut in slices; baby marrows (zucchinis) cut in quarters, cooked in salted water and drained; tomatoes, peeled, drained, seeded and chopped; quarters of hard boiled eggs; nasturtium flowers; shrimps in mayonnaise with chopped parsley, chervil and tarragon.

Arrange the shrimps in mayonnaise in a dome, in a china or glass salad bowl. Surround with garnish as above.

Just before serving sprinkle the garnish with a few tablespoons of *Vinaigrette*.

Allemande salad. SALADE À L'ALLEMANDE—Cut 2 medium-sized boiled potatoes (300 grams) and 1 cup (125 grams) of rather tart eating apples into dice. Season with 4 tablespoons of mayonnaise. Arrange in a dome in a salad dish.

Garnish with slices of cooked beetroot and onions.

Put on top of the potatoes some trimmed salt herring fillets and gherkins cut in strips.

Sprinkle with chopped parsley. Just before serving pour a little oil and vinegar over the border garnish.

American salad I. SALADE AMÉRICAINE—Celeriac cut in *julienne* (thin strips), seasoned with *Vinaigrette*, arranged in a dome. Surround with round slices of potatoes and slices of tomatoes. Garnish with quartered hard boiled eggs. Put on top of the celeriac thin slices of onions. Sprinkle with chopped chervil and tarragon.

American salad II. SALADE AMÉRICAINE—Cucumbers cut in thin slices, previously soaked in salt then rinsed, and seasoned with *vinaigrette*. Surround with lettuce hearts, with slices of tomato and quarters of hard boiled eggs. Sprinkle the whole with a few tablespoons of *vinaigrette*.

This salad must be served very cold, even iced. Cabbage lettuce is often replaced with cos lettuce hearts and the salad can be sprinkled with chopped chervil and tarragon.

Andalusian salad. SALADE ANDALOUSE—Arrange in a dome in a salad bowl rice cooked in salted water, well drained and seasoned with oil, vinegar, salt and paprika, with the addition of chopped onion and parsley and a little grated garlic.

Surround with alternate heaps of sweet pimentos, peeled, seasoned and cut in *julienne* (thin strips), and quarters of tomatoes. Sprinkle with chopped chervil.

Argenteuil salad. SALADE ARGENTEUIL—Arrange in a dome in a salad bowl potatoes cut in dice, seasoned with mayonnaise with the addition of chopped chervil.

Put on top of these potatoes white asparagus tips (about 2 inches long) seasoned with oil and lemon. Garnish with a border of shredded lettuce and quarters of hard boiled eggs.

Arlésienne salad. SALADE ARLÉSIENNE—Potatoes in round slices; sliced artichoke bottoms seasoned with oil, vinegar, salt and pepper; chopped chervil and tarragon.

Arrange in a dome in a salad bowl; garnish with endives cooked in a flour-and-water *Court-bouillon**, cut in small quarters; tomatoes cut in quarters and large stoned olives.

Garnish the top of the salad with fillets of anchovies arranged in a criss-cross pattern.

Bagration salad. SALADE BAGRATION—Composed in equal parts of artichoke bottoms cut in thick strips; celeriac in short strips; chunks of macaroni, the whole seasoned with mayonnaise flavoured with tomato.

Arrange in a dome with white and yolk of hard boiled egg, truffle and scarlet tongue. Sprinkle with chopped parsley.

Beef salad à la parisienne. SALADE DE BOEUF À LA PARISIENNE—This dish, generally served as an hors-d'oeuvre, is described under BEEF, *Boiled beef, cold, à la parisienne.*

Beetroot salad. SALADE DE BETTERAVES—Cut cooked beetroot into a *julienne** or into thin round slices. Dress with *Vinaigrette.* Arrange in an hors-d'oeuvre dish. sprinkle with chopped parsley and garnish with small raw onion rings, if liked.

Beetroot salad à la crème. SALADE DE BETTERAVES À LA CRÈME—Cut the beetroot as above. Dress with *Mustard sauce à la crème.*

Beetroot salad à la polonaise. SALADE DE BETTERAVES À LA POLONAISE—Cut the beetroot in a *julienne* (thin strips); season with mustard to which has been added a few tablespoons of cream and lemon juice, salt and pepper. Arrange in a salad bowl. Sprinkle with grated horseradish and chopped hard boiled eggs.

Bressane salad. SALADE BRESSANE—This preparation, like *Chicken mayonnaise,* constitutes a cold entrée rather than a salad in the proper sense.

Garnish the bottom of a salad bowl with shredded lettuce seasoned with *Vinaigrette* and pressed down to line the bowl. On this lettuce arrange, placing them very symmetrically, thin slices of chicken, seasoned with oil, lemon juice, salt, pepper and chopped chervil.

Cover this chicken with mayonnaise mixed with concentrated tomato juice and seasoned with paprika. Decorate the top of the salad with sliced truffles. Surround with green and red peppers, peeled, sliced in *julienne* (strips) seasoned with *Vinaigrette*, with asparagus tips and quartered hard boiled eggs.

Brimont salad. SALADE BRIMONT—Mix in equal parts potatoes and artichoke bottoms cut in dice, with mayonnaise seasoned with curry.

Surround with crayfish tails and stoned olives seasoned with oil and vinegar, in small heaps separated from each other by quartered hard boiled eggs. Garnish the top of the salad with sliced truffles.

Calves' brain salad (Carême's recipe). SALADE DE CERVELLE DE VEAU—After the brains have been blanched in salted water to which vinegar and tarragon have been added, Carême says that they should be braised 'masked with thin slices of lemon flesh' and covered with bards of bacon fat, with stock and seasoning.

Once cold, the brains are cut in half and arranged in the following way, which constitutes a mayonnaise rather than a salad:

'Arrange them in a crown on an entrée dish, the bottom of which will have been lined with shredded lettuce seasoned as a salad. Garnish the brains with the same lettuce, then make an elegant border of eggs (hard boiled) and decorate with lettuce hearts and fillets of anchovies.

'At the moment of serving mask the brains with a ravigote mayonnaise'.

Cancalaise salad. SALADE CANCALAISE—Fill shell-shaped lettuce leaves with a good spoonful each of potatoes (cut in dice and mixed with mayonnaise).

Put on each lettuce 'shell' three oysters poached in their own liquor, drained, de-bearded and seasoned with oil, lemon juice and pepper. Put a slice of truffle on each oyster. Arrange the lettuce leaves in the form of a flower on a round dish.

This dish can be served as a cold hors-d'oeuvre.

Celeriac salad with cress. SALADE DE CÉLERI-RAVE À LA CRESSONIÈRE—Cut the celeriac in *julienne* (strips), blanch in salted water, drain and season with *Vinaigrette* or mayonnaise. Arrange in a salad bowl, alternately with bunches of cress.

Spiny lobster salad. SALADE DE LANGOUSTE—Like *Lobster salad*, but made with the flesh of spiny lobster.

Demi-deuil salad. SALADE DEMI-DEUIL—Made up of equal parts of potatoes and truffles cut in *julienne* (strips), seasoned with mustard and cream. Decorate with slices of truffles and round slices of potato set alternately in a border.

Doria salad. SALADE DORIA—Celeriac cut in *julienne* (strips) seasoned with mayonnaise, arranged in a dome. Cover with thin slices of white truffle. Garnish with separate heaps of asparagus tips and beetroot cut in a *julienne*. Sprinkle with hard boiled egg yolk and chopped parsley.

Dubarry salad. SALADE DUBARRY—Arrange in a shallow salad dish flowerets of cauliflower cooked in salted water and well drained. Garnish with radishes and shredded watercress. Season with a sauce made with oil, lemon juice, salt, pepper and chopped chives.

Favourite salad. SALADE FAVORITE—Arrange in a salad dish, in separate heaps, asparagus tips, shelled crayfish and sliced white truffles. Season with oil, lemon juice, salt and pepper. Sprinkle with chopped celery and herbs.

Flemish salad. SALADE FLAMANDE—Season together, with oil, vinegar, salt and pepper, chicory and potatoes cut in thick strips, with the addition of onions cooked in the oven and chopped. Arrange in a dome; garnish with fillets of salt herring. Sprinkle with chopped parsley and chervil.

Francillon or Japanese salad. SALADE FRANCILLON, DITE JAPONAISE—Made of an equal part of potatoes seasoned when hot (marinated in Chablis) and mussels cooked as for *Mussels marinière** with celery, and shelled. Arrange in the shape of a *calotte de savant* ('wise man's skull cap'). Decorate with sliced truffles. (Alexandre Dumas, the younger.)

This salad is usually served under the name of *Japanese salad*.

Fruit salad. SALADE DE FRUITS—Fruit salads come into the category of sweet dishes rather than that of salads. They are seasoned not with *Vinaigrette* but with sugar and a liqueur. See ORANGE, *Orange salad*.

Certain fruits made into a salad, but without liqueur, are served as an accompaniment to game and venison and also to duck. Sometimes the more acid fruits are made into salads seasoned with oil, vinegar, pepper and salt. These are eccentric dishes and not to be recommended.

Imperia salad. SALADE IMPÉRIA—Choose lettuce leaves that are as white as possible, regular in shape and hollow.

At the last moment fill each of them with a salad made up of equal parts of asparagus tips and fresh truffles.

Arrange these leaves flower fashion in shallow glass bowls.

Italian salad. SALADE ITALIENNE—Made of equal parts of the following ingredients: carrots, turnips and potatoes, cut in dice or shaped with a small vegetable cutter; asparagus tips in dice; peas. Mix these vegetables with mayonnaise. Arrange them in a dome in a salad dish. Decorate with fillets of anchovies, tomatoes, stoned olives and capers. Surround with quartered hard boiled eggs. Sprinkle with chopped chervil.

This salad can be set in aspic. Truffles may also be added to it, but this is contrary to the general principle.

Japanese salad. SALADE JAPONAISE—*Francillon salad* is often known under this name.

In Japan this salad is made with chrysanthemum flowers.

There is also a salad known as 'Japanese' which consists of pineapple, oranges and tomatoes cut in square pieces, seasoned with lemon juice, arranged in a salad bowl and sprinkled with cream that is just slightly sour. To garnish, surround with lettuce hearts.

Lobster salad. SALADE DE HOMARD—Line the bottom of a salad bowl, or other glass dish, with a layer of shredded lettuce, seasoned with oil and vinegar and arranged in a dome.

On top of this set the flesh of the lobster claws, shelled and cut into large dice, seasoned with oil and vinegar. On top of these diced pieces set the rest of the lobster meat, sliced and also seasoned with *Vinaigrette*.

Sprinkle with chopped chervil and tarragon; garnish with quartered hard boiled eggs and lettuce hearts.

Maharajah salad. SALADE MAHARADJAH—Season with oil, vinegar, curry and salt, some rice cooked in salted water, mixed with crab flesh cut into dice. Arrange in a dome in a salad dish. Surround with celeriac cut in dice, blanched and seasoned, with diced courgettes (zucchini or Italian marrows) blanched and seasoned, and quartered tomatoes.

Sprinkle with chopped egg yolk and chives.

Mikado salad. SALADE MIKADO—Arrange, in a dome in a salad dish, potatoes cut in dice and mixed with shrimps, both bound together with mayonnaise flavoured with soya sauce.

Garnish the top of the salad with chrysanthemum petals, blanched, drained and seasoned with oil, lemon juice, salt and pepper (choose small chrysanthemums).

Surround with a border of sweet pimentos, peeled and cut in a *julienne* (strips) and diced tomatoes. Sprinkle with chopped chervil.

Niçoise salad. SALADE NIÇOISE—Mix equal parts of potatoes and French (string) beans, both cut in dice. Season with oil, vinegar, salt and pepper. Arrange in a dome in a salad dish. Decorate with fillets of anchovies, olives and capers. Garnish with quartered tomatoes. Sprinkle with chopped chervil and tarragon.

Oriental salad. SALADE ORIENTALE—Season with oil, vinegar, salt, paprika and onion, finely chopped, some rice cooked in salted water and well drained. Arrange this rice in a dome in a salad dish. Surround with sweet peppers, peeled, cut in dice and seasoned, quartered tomatoes and black olives. Sprinkle with chopped chervil.

Parisian salad. SALADE PARISIENNE—In general this salad is nothing but a vegetable salad with the addition of cut-up spiny lobster or crawfish and truffles, seasoned with very thick mayonnaise, arranged in a domed mould (like *Russian salad*) coated with jelly and lined with thin slices of spiny lobster or crawfish and truffles.

This salad can also be served in a salad dish, all the ingredients mixed, seasoned with mayonnaise, decorated with truffles and garnished with quartered hard boiled eggs and lettuce hearts.

Pernollet salad. SALADE PERNOLLET—Mix shelled crayfish and diced truffles with mayonnaise.

Fill with this salad large shell-shaped lettuce leaves. Put on each leaf a few green asparagus tips seasoned with oil and lemon juice.

Arrange the leaves flower fashion on a round dish.

This dish is mostly served as an hors-d'oeuvre.

Sweet pimento salad à la créole. SALADE DE PIMENTS DOUX À LA CRÉOLE—Arrange in separate small mounds in a salad dish, sweet pimentos, green or red, peeled, seeded, well blanched in salted water and drained, and some rice cooked in salted water and drained. Put on each mound of rice slices of raw tomato and on the pimentos a teaspoon of chopped chives. Season with oil, vinegar, salt and paprika.

Port-Royal salad. SALADE PORT-ROYAL—Arrange on a shallow glass salad dish a mixture of potatoes, sliced eating apples and diced French (string) beans, all seasoned with mayonnaise. Coat the whole salad with a layer of mayonnaise. Surround with quarters of lettuce and quartered hard boiled eggs. Decorate the top with French (string) beans.

Rachel salad. SALADE RACHEL—Equal parts of celery, artichoke bottoms, diced or *julienne* (matchstick) potatoes, mixed with mayonnaise. Arrange in a dome in a salad dish. Garnish with green asparagus tips.

Raphael salad. SALADE RAPHAEL—Garnish the bottom of a salad dish that has rather high sides with shredded lettuce mixed with paprika-seasoned mayonnaise. Arrange around this lettuce, in separate small mounds, thinly sliced cucumber, previously sprinkled with salt and left to stand, white asparagus tips cooked in water and well drained, peeled tomatoes with their seeds removed divided into small quarters, small lettuce hearts and pink unpeeled radishes, cut in rounds. Season with a sauce made with olive oil, lemon juice, salt, pepper and chopped chervil.

Reine Pédauque salad. SALADE REINE PÉDAUQUE—Arrange, in a crown on a round dish, quarters of lettuce hearts. Coat these with a sauce made with thick fresh cream, oil, mustard, lemon juice, salt and paprika. Fill the middle of the dish with shredded lettuce seasoned with oil and vinegar. On top of this put stoned cherries. On each lettuce heart put a piece of peeled orange.

Rossini salad. SALADE ROSSINI—From Rossini's letter: 'What is going to interest you much more than my opera is the discovery I have just made of a new salad, for which I hasten to send you the recipe.

'Take Provence oil, English mustard, French vinegar, a little lemon juice, pepper and salt; whisk and mix all together. Then throw in a few truffles, which you have taken care to cut in tiny pieces. The truffles give to this seasoning a kind of nimbus to plunge the gourmand into an ecstasy'.

Russian salad. SALADE RUSSE—This salad, in modern restaurant practice, is made by adding to a mixed vegetable salad (seasoned with mayonnaise) pickled tongue, sausage, cooked mushrooms, lobster or crawfish meat and truffles, cut in dice or *julienne* (strips).

This salad is arranged in a dome in a salad dish and decorated with fillets of anchovies, truffles, scarlet tongue, capers, gherkins, etc.

In classical cookery, Russian salad, seasoned with very thick mayonnaise, is put into a domed mould lined with jelly and decorated. After having been well chilled (on ice) the salad is turned out on to a napkin.

German sauerkraut salad. SALADE DE CHOUCROUTE À L'ALLEMANDE—Sauerkraut cooked in consommé or water, piled in a dome in a salad dish; garnished with hard boiled eggs and rounds of beetroot. Season with *Vinaigrette.*

Shellfish salad. SALADE DE CRUSTACÉS—Made with the flesh of lobster or crawfish, crab, shrimps, etc.

Cut in slices, thick or thin, the tail of the prescribed crustacean, as well as the claws, if it be lobster. Cut in big dice the rest of the flesh when shelled. Season the whole with oil, vinegar, salt, pepper, chopped parsley and chervil.

On a base of shredded and seasoned lettuce set first the diced meat, then the sliced. Garnish with fillets of anchovies, capers, olives, quartered hard boiled egg and lettuce hearts. Sprinkle with chopped chervil and parsley.

Shrimp salad—See SHRIMP.

Shrimp salad à la dieppoise. SALADE DE CREVETTES À LA DIEPPOISE—Made like *Cancalaise salad,* replacing the oysters by shrimps and mussels seasoned with oil, vinegar and pepper.

This dish can be served as a cold hors-d'oeuvre.

Truffle salad—See *Rossini salad.*

Vegetable salad. SALADE DE LÉGUMES—In general principle this is made up of all sorts of fresh vegetables (carrots and turnips in dice or cut with a small vegetable cutter; French (string) beans in dice; asparagus tips; peas; potatoes in dice, etc.).

All the vegetables are seasoned together with oil, vinegar, salt and pepper, arranged in a dome in a salad dish, garnished with a floweret of cauliflower set on the summit and sprinkled with chopped parsley and chervil.

Note. In a restaurant the different ingredients of this salad are set in the salad dish in separate mounds. The seasoning, and thus the mixing, is done before the customer.

Watercress salad. SALADE CRESSONIÈRE—Composed of half watercress and half *Potato salad.* Sprinkle with chopped hard boiled egg and chopped parsley.

SALAD BURNET. PIMPRENELLE—A hardy perennial herb with slightly villous leaves which smell like cucumbers when crushed.

Salad burnet is available from June to November and in the following spring, and is mainly used as a condiment. The tender fresh leaves of this plant can also be used in salads like watercress.

SALAMANDER—Oven, generally gas heated, into which dishes are put to glaze or brown the surface very rapidly.

In French, the word also means breadcrumbs fried in butter which are sprinkled over certain preparations.

SALAMBÔ—A small cake made with *chou* pastry, filled with *French pastry cream* (see CREAMS) flavoured with kirsch; the top is iced.

SALAMI—Product of Italian *charcuterie* (pork butchery) eaten like mortadella.

The salami, or rather, salamis, because there are several kinds, are commercial products sold in food shops. The most renowned is that of Bologna.

In Germany and various northern countries of Europe the name is given to a variety of similar preparations.

SALANGANE—Sea swallow of the Far East whose nests, constructed of seaweed fixed with the birds' saliva, are highly esteemed by the gourmets of China. They are sold in Europe as *Swallows' nests.* See NESTS and SOUPS AND BROTHS, *Consommé with birds' nest.*

SALÉ—The French for salted or pickled foodstuffs, synonymous with *salaison.*

Petit salé—The name for a piece of *charcuterie* made with the first bone of the flank end of belly of pork on which a little meat has been allowed to remain; left to salt for 12 hours in a light brine and cooked with other pieces of boiled charcuterie.

The *petit salé* is served hot or cold as an hors-d'oeuvre.

The term *petit salé* is also used for pieces of collar or neck, which are lightly pickled in brine and used in *potées* or served by themselves, after having been poached in an aromatic stock.

SALEP—Edible substance which comes from Persia and Asia Minor, in the form of small tubers ½ to ¾ inch in diameter, strung together in bunches. Translucent, yellowish grey in colour, horny in texture, and gelatinous in flavour, the salep comes from the tubers of various species of orchis, taken up after the stalks of the plant have faded and dried in the sun; they contain a floury substance and gelatine, and constitute an easily digested foodstuff highly esteemed in the East.

Indigenous orchids, treated in the same way, provide a salep comparable in every way with that of the East. Prepared as a jelly or soup.

Salep jelly. GELÉE AU SALEP—Mix, without allowing to curdle, a teaspoon of salep in 1 cup (200 grams) of water; cook over a low heat, keeping at boiling point for 4 or 5 minutes. Add a little cinnamon and 4 tablespoons of tamarind or pineapple syrup and allow to get cold.

Salep soup. POTAGE AU SALEP—Mix, without allowing to curdle, a teaspoon of salep in 1 cup (200 grams) of unsalted vegetable stock; add a sprig of tarragon and a teaspoon of soya sauce. Thus prepared, says Doctor Leclerc, it has been possible to serve this soup as 'Birds' Nest Soup' to certain gastronomes—who were no doubt not very knowledgeable about the latter delicacy!

SALMIGONDIS—A ragoût of several sorts of meat reheated. Reheated poultry ragoût is called *capillotade.*

SALMIS—A dish often prepared, or at least finished off, at the table, and made mostly with game, two-thirds cooked.

The origin of salmis is very distant: some authors put it as far back as the fourteenth century and assure us that the *Canard à la sauce Dodine* of which Tallevent speaks in his *Viandier* was a kind of salmis. Others say that it was at the beginning of the eighteenth century that this dish was invented.

In any case it is only in the cookery books of the beginning of the nineteenth century that we find recipes for salmis. Carême, notably, speaks of this way of preparing birds and says in a very positive way that salmis may be made with red or white wine. This, however, is denied by many culinary writers today.

Duck *à la rouennaise*, one of the finest dishes of Normandy cooking, is a kind of salmis and made with red wine. In the same way it is also possible to class as salmis *Caneton en chemise*, *Canard sauvage* (*Wild duck*) or *Bécasse* (*woodcock*) *au Chambertin* and a good number of other preparations of birds which, before being finished in a special sauce, are two-thirds roasted.

Method. Cook the bird in question in the oven or on the spit, but only for two-thirds of the necessary time.

Divide into joints, remove the skin and trim the pieces. Arrange them in a buttered sauté dish with mushrooms and sliced truffles (salmis being a dish that is often finished off at the table before the guests, it is important to choose a decorative pan made of silver plate or some other good-looking metal). Sprinkle with a few tablespoons of *Demi-glace sauce* (see SAUCE) and cook over hot water for 30 minutes.

Put the carcases and trimmings of the bird, broken up, to heat in butter in a casserole; add the cooking juices from the roasting diluted with white wine. Add a few tablespoons of game-flavoured *Espagnole sauce* (see SAUCE, *Salmis sauce*). Let this sauce boil for a few moments, then strain it, pressing all the time, first through a strainer, then through a cloth. Boil it down, add butter and pour it over the pieces of bird and the garnish. Heat, *still without boiling*, 5 minutes more, and serve, either on a big, round *croûton* of bread spread with *Forcemeat à gratin** and put briefly in the oven, or on a round, deep dish. In the latter case surround with heart-shaped croûtons fried in butter and spread with *Forcemeat à gratin.*

This method of preparation is applicable not only to game birds (woodcock, wild duck, pheasant, partridge, etc.) but also to some kinds of poultry (duck, pigeon, guinea-fowl, etc.).

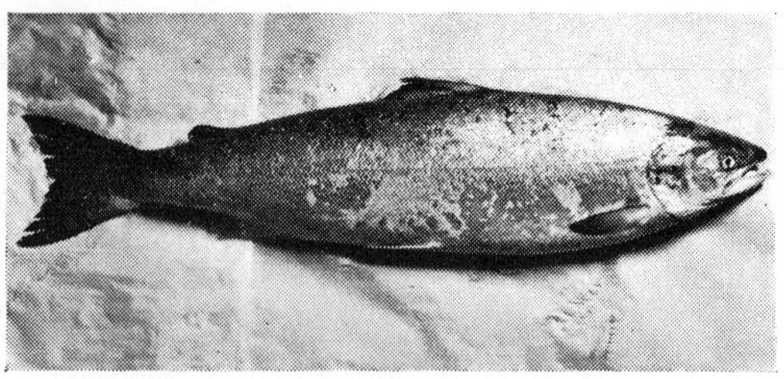

Salmon

SALMON. SAUMON—Migratory fish living in the sea but spawning in fresh water; at the time of spawning it makes its way up certain watercourses.

Salmon take no nourishment so long as they are in fresh water, so their flesh is at its driest and least good when they go down the rivers again to the sea.

Born in the rivers, the young salmon begins to develop there, not going far from its birthplace during the first few weeks. Then, following the flow of the river, it goes down to the depths of the sea, where, thanks to the abundant nourishment that it finds there, it rapidly develops in size.

The salmon's nourishment when it is in the deep sea consists mainly of the post-larvae of herrings and other fish.

The salmon can live without going to sea, as has been observed in Norway and Sweden where it inhabits certain freshwater lakes; during the winter and in spring it goes up the rivers to spawn. It returns to the lakes later to build itself up again, just as the salmon of other rivers return to the sea.

The same thing happens in certain Canadian lakes where the salmon hibernate. But these salmon develop much less rapidly than the salmon which travel to the sea, and the quality of their flesh is inferior to that of their fellows who have followed the natural law of their existence.

Salmon which have attained their maximum development measure 3½ to 4 feet in length and their weight ranges from 10 to 14 pounds. They achieve this size at the age of about six years.

In Scotland, salmon have been fished weighing up to 70 pounds. In the U.S.A. the Pacific coast salmon varies in weight from 6 to 60 pounds.

The flesh of salmon is conserved by drying, smoking or tinning (canning). The fish is cooked whole or cut in chunks or cutlets (steaks).

In France, whole or in pieces, salmon is most often poached in a flavoured *court-bouillon** and served hot or cold, with, in the case of the hot fish, one or other of the sauces normally served with fish cooked in *court-bouillon**, such as: *Anchovy*, *Butter*, *Caper*, *Shrimp*, *Lobster*, *Mousseline*, *Nantua*, *Ravigote*, *Venitienne*, etc.

Cold salmon is accompanied by cold sauces such as: *Mayonnaise*, *Tartare*, *Verte*, *Rémoulade*, *Vincent*, etc.

Salmon may also be braised whole (stuffed or otherwise), that is to say, cooked very slowly in fish *fumet** made with red or white wine. Prepared in this way various garnishes, plain or mixed, accompany the salmon.

Whole or cut into smaller pieces, it may also be cooked on the spit. This fish is excellent cooked in this way.

Côtelettes (cutlets or slices) of salmon are cooked in an infinity of ways. They are cooked in *court-bouillon* and served with the same sauces as those prescribed for salmon cooked whole or in sections; they are grilled, they are sautéed in butter and they are braised. Thus cooked they have the same garnishes as for large pieces or whole salmon.

Salmon may also be prepared in fillets, which are cooked whole, braised or otherwise, or cut in slices which are sautéed in butter and accompanied by a variety of sauces and garnishes.

The flesh of the salmon, which is pinkish and becomes bright pink when cooked, is extremely delicate. It is fatty and often a little indigestible.

Crimped salmon is so called from the treatment, certainly very barbarous, to which the fish is submitted immediately after its capture.

This practice consists of making a series of gashes in both sides of the flesh of the creature while it is still alive. These gashes are quite deep and about 1 inch apart.

The salmon is then hung up by its tail and is left to bleed—in agony—for some minutes. It is subsequently immersed in very cold water for about an hour.

This method of treating salmon is simply noted here without such usage being in any way recommended.

Court-bouillon for salmon—Put into a saucepan 3 quarts ($2\frac{1}{2}$ litres) of water; $\frac{1}{2}$ cup (1 decilitre) of vinegar (or lemon juice); 3 medium-sized carrots (300 grams) and 2 large onions (250 grams), both finely chopped; $\frac{1}{2}$ cup (50 grams) of parsley stalks; a bayleaf, a sprig of thyme and 1 tablespoon (30 grams) of rock salt. Boil very slowly for an hour. 10 minutes before taking it off the heat add 1 tablespoon (10 grams) of peppercorns. Strain through a fine sieve and cool before using.

To cook a whole salmon in a court-bouillon—Place the salmon on the grid of the fish-kettle. Cover with cold *court-bouillon*. Bring the liquid up to boiling point. Skim; turn the heat very low and let it poach without boiling.

To cook salmon côtelettes (cutlets or steaks) in court-bouillon. The *côtelettes* are cooked in *court-bouillon* prepared as above, but they are put into the liquid when it is already boiling. Cook over low heat without boiling.

To cook large cuts of salmon in court-bouillon. Proceed as for whole salmon.

Note. Salmon, whether whole, in large cuts or cutlets, may equally well be cooked in a *court-bouillon* prepared with half white wine and half water. This is flavoured with the same vegetables as are indicated for the ordinary *court-bouillon*, but they should first be cooked in butter before putting them in the liquor. This latter *court-bouillon* is used chiefly when the salmon is to be served cold and will be cooled in its cooking liquor.

HOT SALMON. Saumon chaud:

Salmon attereaux. Attereaux de saumon—Impale on metal skewers small pieces of salmon sealed in butter (having been previously marinated in oil, lemon juice, chopped parsley, salt and pepper) and sliced mushrooms. Coat in *Villeroi sauce* (see SAUCE), and when this is cold, cover with egg and breadcrumbs. Fry in deep fat and serve as they are, garnished with fried parsley and quarters of lemon. Alternatively they may be accompanied by various garnishes. See ATTEREAUX.

Boiled salmon with various sauces. Darne de saumon bouillie—Cook a chunk of salmon in *Court-bouillon.* Drain it and set it on a napkin (or a fish strainer). Garnish with fresh parsley and plain boiled potatoes. Serve with one or other of the sauces that accompany fish: *Anchovy, Butter, Caper, Cardinal, Shrimp, Curry, Diplomat, Hollandaise, Lobster, Laguipière, Mousseline, Mustard, Nantua, Noisette, Ravigote, Riche, Venetian, White Wine* (see recipes for these sauces under SAUCE).

Boiled salmon à l'anglaise. Saumon bouilli à l'anglaise—Cook the salmon (whole, in large cuts or in slices) in salted water (without herbs or condiments).

Drain it; serve it on a napkin (or on a fish grid). Serve with *Lobster sauce* or *Parsley sauce* (see SAUCE) and cucumber salad.

Braised salmon. Saumon braisé—Whole braised salmon may be prepared with or without stuffing. It is usually garnished with *Pike forcemeat* (see FORCEMEAT) to which truffles or a crustacean butter may be added.

The salmon is set on the well buttered grid of the fish-kettle. The bottom of the pan is lined with chopped carrots and onions, lightly tossed in butter. Fish *fumet** made with white or red wine is poured in to come half-way up the salmon. A *bouquet garni** and seasoning are added and the salmon is braised in the usual way. See CULINARY METHODS.

Once braised the salmon is drained, skinned, if necessary, and then glazed in the oven. It is set on a low dish, surrounded with the prescribed garnish and coated with a sauce prepared with its cooking liquor.

All the ways of preparing slices and chunks of salmon given elsewhere are applicable to whole, braised salmon.

Salmon Chambord. Darne de saumon Chambord—Cut from the salmon a rather thick slice. Braise it very slowly in *fumet** made with red wine (or white wine, as liked).

Drain the salmon; glaze it in a slow oven for a few minutes. Set on a serving dish and surround it with *Chambord garnish.* See GARNISHES.

Coat with *Genevoise sauce* (see SAUCE) made with the braising juices.

Côtelettes of salmon. Côtelettes de saumon—In French culinary terminology *côtelettes* of salmon describe the following:

(1) Salmon cutlets or slices which have been halved down the middle and trimmed into the shape of cutlets. These are cooked in butter, whether or not they are coated in egg and breadcrumbs, and served as they are, either sprinkled with a little of their cooking butter or accompanied by any one of a variety of sauces and garnishes.

(2) A sort of croquette, made with a croquette mixture (see HORS-D'OEUVRE, *Hot hors-d'oeuvre croquettes*), fashioned into the shape of cutlets, coated in egg and breadcrumbs and cooked in butter.

(3) A light dish served as hot hors-d'oeuvre or small entrée, in which a salmon quenelle mixture is put into cutlet-shaped moulds and poached.

Cutlets made of a forcemeat are coated with one of a variety of sauces and accompanied by some kind of garnish.

Côtelettes of salmon à l'américaine. Côtelettes de saumon à l'américaine—Half slices of salmon trimmed into cutlet shape, seasoned with salt and pepper and floured. Cook in half butter and half oil.

Drain the pieces; set them on a round dish. Put on top of each one a slice of lobster prepared *à l'américaine**. Garnish the middle of the dish with a *salpicon** of diced lobster (made with the rest of the lobster flesh). Coat with *Américaine sauce.* See SAUCE.

Côtelettes of salmon braised with red wine. CÔTELETTES DE SAUMON BRAISÉES AU VIN ROUGE, DITE À LA BOURGUIGNONNE—Cook the *côtelettes* in a fish *fumet** made with red wine. Drain them; set them on a serving dish (either directly on to the plate or on to heart-shaped croûtons of bread fried in butter).

Garnish with little mushrooms (which will have been cooked with the fish) and little glazed onions.

Boil down the cooking liquor and thicken it with kneaded butter (see BUTTER, *Compound butters); add* more butter and strain. Pour over the fish.

Note. Instead of mixing butter and flour into this sauce it may be thickened by adding two or three tablespoons of fish *Demi-glace sauce.* See SAUCE.

Côtelettes of salmon braised with white wine. CÔTELETTES DE SAUMON BRAISÉES AU VIN BLANC—Cook the *côtelettes* very slowly in fish *fumet** made with white wine.

Drain them, arrange them on a round dish in the shape of a crown. Decorate them with the required garnish. Coat with *White wine sauce* (see SAUCE) to which has been added (before straining) some of the cooking liquid, well boiled down.

Thus prepared, the *côtelettes* may be accompanied by one or other of the garnishes usually served with braised fish and coated with a sauce which will blend with the garnish.

Côtelettes of salmon à la florentine. CÔTELETTES DE SAUMON À LA FLORENTINE—The *côtelettes* are cooked very slowly in concentrated fish *fumet**. Drain and arrange them in a fire-proof dish on a layer of spinach which has been cooked, drained, dried, roughly chopped, simmered in butter, and seasoned with salt and pepper. Coat with *Mornay sauce.* See SAUCE.

Sprinkle with grated cheese and a little melted butter and brown well.

Côtelettes of salmon Mornay. CÔTELETTES DE SAUMON MORNAY—Prepared in the same way as *Côtelettes of salmon à la florentine*, but leaving out the layer of spinach.

Côtelettes of salmon with mushrooms à la crème. CÔTELETTES DE SAUMON AUX CHAMPIGNONS À LA CRÈME—Season the *côtelettes;* flour them; cook them in butter. When they are half-cooked put into the pan two or three mushrooms for each *côtelette;* finish cooking together.

Drain the pieces. Arrange them on a round dish (either directly on to the dish or set on heart-shaped croûtons of bread fried in butter). Set the mushrooms on top of the *côtelettes.* Coat with the cooking juices diluted with Madeira, with fresh cream and butter added and a tablespoon or two of fish *Velouté sauce* for thickening, the whole cooked down and strained.

Côtelettes of salmon with mushrooms and Madeira. CÔTELETTES DE SAUMON AUX CHAMPIGNONS AU MADÈRE—Cook the fish and mushrooms as above. Set on a round dish. Coat with a sauce made by diluting the cooking juices with Madeira and adding a few tablespoons of fish *Demi-glace sauce* (see SAUCE). This should be cooked down, then extra butter added and the sauce strained.

Côtelettes of salmon Pojarski. CÔTELETTES DE SAUMON POJARSKI—Mash $\frac{3}{4}$ pound (300 grams) of salmon flesh, adding $1\frac{1}{2}$ cups (70 grams) of breadcrumbs which have been soaked in milk and pressed as dry as possible and 5 tablespoons (70 grams) of fresh butter.

Season with salt, pepper and a pinch of grated nutmeg.

Divide up this mixture into six equal parts; shape each into the form of a cutlet (U.S. *chop*).

Cook these cutlets in clarified butter, so that they are nicely browned on both sides. Arrange on a serving dish; sprinkle with the cooking butter.

Note. Salmon cutlets Pojarski are usually accompanied by sautéed potatoes or a green vegetable tossed in butter and any of the sauces designed for fish.

Côtelettes of salmon with truffles. CÔTELETTES DE SAUMON AUX TRUFFES—Sauté the cutlets in butter. When they are almost cooked put into the pan some rather thick slices of truffles seasoned with salt and pepper. Finish cooking, with the pan covered, over a slow heat.

Arrange the cutlets on a round dish and set the truffle slices on top. Sprinkle with the cooking juices diluted with Madeira (or any other liqueur wine) to which have been added two tablespoons of *Demi-glace sauce* based on concentrated fish stock. See SAUCE.

Côtelettes of salmon with truffles and cream. CÔTELETTES DE SAUMON AUX TRUFFES À LA CRÈME—As above, but diluting the cooking juices with Madeira and fresh cream.

Côtelettes of salmon variously garnished. CÔTELETTES DE SAUMON HACHÉES, PANÉES—Prepare the cutlets as for côtelettes of *salmon Pojarski,* but coating them with egg and breadcrumbs.

Cook in clarified butter. Set in the form of a crown on a serving dish; fill the middle of the dish with the prescribed garnish and pour round about a sauce that will blend with the garnish used. Sprinkle the cutlets with *Noisette butter* (see BUTTER, *Compound butters*) and put paper frills on the ends.

Coulibiac of salmon. COULIBIAC DE SAUMON—*Ingredients for pastry.* 2 pounds (1 kilo) of *Ordinary brioche dough* (see DOUGH) made without sugar and kept rather firm so that it can be easily rolled out.

Sauté quickly and briefly in butter, $1\frac{1}{2}$ pounds (750 grams) of salmon cut in small slices. Season with salt and pepper. Allow to cool.

Cook in light consommé (or salted water) for $3\frac{1}{2}$ hours, 3 ounces (90 grams) of sturgeon notochord (the spinal cord of the sturgeon) which has been previously soaked in cold water for 5 hours. Drain this notochord and chop it roughly (after soaking the whole notochord produces about 500 grams).

Prepare a *kasha* or pudding of semolina in the following way: mix $1\frac{1}{4}$ cups (200 grams) of large grain wheat semolina with a beaten egg. Spread this semolina mixture in a baking tin and dry out in a slow oven.

Put the semolina through a coarse sieve. Cook it in consommé, drain it and allow it to cool.

Chop 3 hard boiled eggs, both white and yolks.

Toss in butter in which has previously been cooked 6 tablespoons (75 grams) of chopped onion, $\frac{3}{8}$ cup (100 grams) of cultivated mushrooms, chopped and pressed.

To make and cook coulibiac. Roll out the brioche paste into a rectangle 12 to 14 inches long and 8 inches wide. In the middle of this rectangle set the various ingredients of the filling, arranging them in layers one on top of the other—cooked semolina, slices of salmon, sturgeon notochord, hard boiled eggs and mushrooms, all these ingredients being quite cold. Finish with a layer of cooked semolina.

Close up the paste by folding over the edges from each side. The edges should be lightly damped with water before pressing together.

Put the *coulibiac* on a baking tin, turning it over so that the sealed side is on the bottom.

Put it in a warm place for the paste to rise for 30 minutes.

Brush the surface of *coulibiac* with melted butter; sprinkle it with breadcrumbs. Make an opening on top to let the steam escape.

Cook in the oven at a good heat for 45 minutes to 1 hour, according to the size of the *coulibiac*.

When taking the *coulibiac* from the oven pour into it, through the hole in the top, a few spoonfuls of melted butter.

Coulibiac is served as it is, without the accompaniment of a sauce.

Small coulibiacs of salmon. PETITS COULIBIACS DE SAUMON—Small coulibiacs, which are served as hors-d'oeuvre or light entrées, are made by filling with the same ingredients as above pieces of *Ordinary brioche dough* (See DOUGH) cut out with a round, fluted-edged pastry-cutter about 4½ inches in diameter.

Creamed salmon au gratin. BORDURE DE SAUMON CRÈME GRATIN—Made with left-over salmon like *Creamed cod au gratin.* See COD.

Croquettes and kromeskies of salmon. CROQUETTES, CROMESQUIS DE SAUMON—These are both made with a *salpicon** of cooked salmon mixed with diced truffles and mushrooms bound with *Allemande sauce* (or *Béchamel sauce*) (see SAUCE) in the ordinary way. See instructions under CROQUETTES and KROMESKIES.

Salmon Daumont. DARNE DE SAUMON DAUMONT—Braise a chunk of salmon, rather thick, in a fish *fumet** made with white wine.

Drain it and set it on a serving dish; surround with *Daumont garnish* (see GARNISHES). Coat with its cooking juices, buttered and strained. Serve *Nantua sauce* separately. See SAUCE.

Escalopes of salmon. ESCALOPES DE SAUMON—These escalopes are taken from fillets of salmon cut when raw, and should weigh about 3½ ounces (100 grams) each.

The escalopes are lightly flattened and trimmed if necessary so that they are oval in shape. They are cooked in butter or they may be poached in concentrated fish *fumet**.

All the ways described for preparing *côtelettes* and slices of salmon are applicable to the escalopes.

Salmon fillets. FILETS DE SALMON—This is the name given to thin slices of salmon cut from raw fillets. They are prepared like salmon cutlets, steaks and escalopes, but most frequently they are fried, either coated in egg and breadcrumbs or dipped in batter.

Orly of fillets of salmon with tomato sauce. ORLY DE FILETS DE SAUMON, SAUCE TOMATE—'Trim 14 fillets (see above) of salmon; put them in a bowl with salt, mignonette, a little grated nutmeg, 2 chopped shallots, parsley on its stalks, the juice of 2 lemons, ¼ cup of olive oil and a little thyme and bay leaf. Take care to move the fillets about in this seasoning and drain off the water they will exude; an hour before serving drain them on a white cloth and remove all the ingredients that have served to give them taste, including the mignonette; put a handful of flour on top and shake them about to dry them well, reshape them with the blade of a knife and dip them into four beaten eggs, to coat them and to ensure that they fry a good colour. At the moment of serving arrange them in the form of a crown and serve separately a light *Tomato sauce* (see SAUCE). (Plumerey's recipe.)

Note. In former times this word was spelt Horly and it is thus that Carême names this dish.

Salmon fritters. FRITOT DE SAUMON—Soak for 30 minutes in oil, lemon juice, chopped parsley, salt and pepper, some raw salmon cut into small slices or large dice.

Just before they are needed, dip these pieces in a light batter and fry them in deep fat.

Drain and dry on a cloth. Season with very dry fine salt. Set on a mound on a napkin. Garnish with fried parsley and lemon. Serve with *Tomato sauce* (see SAUCE) or any other sauce that is appropriate to fish.

Kedgeree of salmon. CADGERY DE SAUMON—Made with cooked flaked salmon, *Rice pilaf, Béchamel sauce* flavoured with curry and diced hard boiled eggs in the same way as *Turbot kedgeree**.

Mousse of salmon—See MOUSSES and MOUSSELINES.

Hot salmon pâté à la française. PÂTÉ CHAUD DE SAUMON À LA FRANÇAISE—'Cut a thick slice of salmon, remove the bone and the skin and stud it with truffles and de-salted anchovies. Next wash the flesh of a medium-sized pike and use it to make a *Quenelle forcemeat* (see FORCEMEAT). Wash the scraps remaining from the two fish and put them to cook in butter with chopped carrots and onions, parsley on its stems, thyme, bay leaf, a clove of garlic, two cloves and a small pinch of salt; pour over half a bottle of Chablis (*this constitutes a fish fumet*).

'Surround the salmon with light bards of bacon fat (thin slices of salt pork) and tie it; put it like this into the saucepan. Strain the fish stock at the end of three-quarters of an hour, during which it will have simmered gently; pour it over the salmon and give it 20 to 30 minutes longer. At the end of this time, drain it on a dish and allow it to cool. Strain the fish stock, remove all grease from it and reduce it, so that it can be used to make a *Financière sauce* (see SAUCE) which will be served with the hot pâté.

'You will have lined a mould with a pastry suitable for a hot entrée; spread the bottom and sides with the prepared pike forcemeat, to which will have been added two chopped raw truffles; slightly trim the salmon, put it into the pie and cover it with a sheet of pastry. Bake it in the oven for an hour, so that it will be perfectly cooked right through; at the end of this time take it out to serve it. Take off the pastry lid and the forcemeat which are masking the top of the salmon, and carefully remove all grease; garnish the top with a *ragoût* of soft roes, truffles, and mushrooms and coat with the prepared *Financière sauce.*

'Set on a dish covered with a folded napkin.

Note. 'If it were desired to serve the pâté cold, it would be prepared in the same way but the pastry lid would not be taken off. The fish stock would be more concentrated, half a glass of Madeira being added to it, and this would be poured into the pâté through the opening left in the pastry lid; this pâté would not then be served until twenty-four hours after it had been cooked.' (Plumerey's recipe, slightly modified.)

Salmon pilaf. PILAF DE SAUMON—Prepared with pieces of salmon sautéed in butter in the same way as *Pilaf of mutton.* See PILAF.

Note. Salmon pilaf can be garnished with mushrooms or truffles sautéed in butter. It is surrounded, once served, with a border of *Tomato sauce* (see SAUCE), tomatoes cooked till soft in butter or any sauce intended for fish.

It may also be garnished with shelled shrimps or crayfish. In this case the pilaf is surrounded with a border of *White wine sauce* or *Butter sauce* finished off with a prepared butter of the shellfish used.

Salmon à la princesse. DARNE DE SAUMON PRINCESSE—Cook a chunk of salmon very slowly in fish *fumet**. Drain it and set it on a serving dish. Garnish with green asparagus tips in butter. Coat with a sauce prepared with the cooking liquor with fish *Velouté sauce* (see SAUCE) added, then concentrated, enriched with cream and butter and strained. Put on top of the salmon slices of truffles heated in butter. Make a border of light fish glaze round the salmon.

Salmon quenelles. QUENELLES DE SAUMON—Salmon quenelles are prepared either with ordinary *Quenelle forcemeat* or *Mousseline forcemeat.* See FORCEMEAT.

They may be large or small. The latter are shaped with a tablespoon or poached in special moulds.

Small salmon quenelles are used as an element in garnishes.

Large salmon quenelles are served as a small entrée and in this case are themselves accompanied by various garnishes and coated with a sauce to blend with the particular garnish.

The large quenelles may have some kind of *salpicon** added to them.

Salmon quenelles, various sauces and garnishes. QUENELLES DE SAUMON—Poach the quenelles. Set them on a round dish (directly on to the dish or each one placed on an oval croûton of bread fried in butter).

Garnish with the prescribed garnish: mushrooms, shrimps, crayfish tails, lobster, spiny lobster in a *salpicon** or possibly vegetables in butter. Coat the quenelles with a sauce that will blend with the garnish.

Salmon risotto. RISOTTO DE SAUMON—Prepared like *Salmon pilaf**, replacing the pilaf rice by risotto.

Roast salmon. SAUMON RÔTI—Roasted whole or in large cuts.

Whole salmon are most often stuffed. When the fish is to be done in this way, season it and cover it with thin bards of bacon fat, holding these in place with a few turns of twine. Fix on the spit with the aid of skewers (alternatively—and this is the better system—the fish may be enclosed in a special spit made in the form of an oblong cage).

Cook the salmon before a hot fire. Baste it often during the cooking, allowing 15 to 18 minutes per pound (30 to 35 minutes per kilo).

Before taking the salmon off the spit, remove the bards and allow it to colour. Remove from the spit. Set on a serving dish. Serve with the cooking juices diluted with white wine and lemon juice.

Salmon in scallop shells. COQUILLES DE SAUMON—With the aid of a forcing (pastry) bag, fitted with a plain or fluted nozzle, pipe a thin border of thickened potato purée round the edge of some scallop shells (real shells or those made of metal or porcelain). Put into the bottom of each shell a tablespoon of the sauce indicated in the recipe and put on top the fish divided into small pieces, with the skin and bones carefully removed.

Add the garnish, if any.

Coat with the prescribed sauce; sprinkle with Parmesan cheese (if the recipe so demands) and a little melted butter. Brush the potato border with egg.

Place the scallops on a baking tin containing a little warm water and brown in a very hot oven.

Set the scallops on a napkin and garnish with fresh parsley.

Note. Instead of potato purée, chopped up boiled potatoes may be used for the border.

Salmon in scallop shells à la florentine. COQUILLES DE SAUMON À LA FLORENTINE—Put into the bottom of some scallop shells 2 tablespoons of spinach leaves simmered in butter; arrange on top some pieces of salmon. Coat with *Mornay sauce* (see SAUCE) and cover with grated Parmesan. Sprinkle with melted butter. Brown in the oven or under the grill.

Salmon in scallop shells à la Mornay. COQUILLES DE SAUMON À LA MORNAY—Arrange pieces of salmon in scallop shells. Coat with *Mornay sauce* (see SAUCE) and cover with grated Parmesan. Sprinkle with melted butter. Brown in the oven or under the grill.

Salmon in scallop shells à la provençale. COQUILLES DE SAUMON À LA PROVENÇALE—Arrange in scallop shells pieces of salmon, truffles, stoned olives and mushrooms. Cover with *Provençale sauce* (see SAUCE). Sprinkle with pale golden breadcrumbs and a little olive oil. Brown in the oven or under the grill, then set on each scallop an anchovy fillet curled into a ring, and some chopped parsley.

Salmon in scallop shells with shrimps. COQUILLES DE SAUMON AUX CREVETTES—Arrange on scallop shells pieces of salmon and shelled shrimps. Coat with *Mornay sauce* (see SAUCE) finished off with *Shrimp butter* (see BUTTER, *Compound butters*). Sprinkle with Parmesan and a little melted butter. Brown in the oven or under the grill.

Salmon in scallop shells à la Victoria. COQUILLES DE SAUMON À LA VICTORIA—Arrange in scallop shells pieces of salmon, truffles and mushrooms. Coat with *Nantua sauce* (see SAUCE). Sprinkle with Parmesan and melted butter. Brown in the oven, then place on each scallop a slice of truffle heated in butter.

Skewered salmon. BROCHETTES DE SAUMON—Impale on metal skewers pieces of salmon cut in neat squares, alternating them with mushrooms cut in rather thick slices and tossed in butter.

Season the skewered pieces with salt and pepper, pour over melted butter, coat with freshly made breadcrumbs and grill gently.

Set on a serving dish. Sprinkle with half melted *Maître d'hôtel butter* (see BUTTER, *Compound butters*), or serve this butter separately.

Garnish with fresh parsley and surround with half slices of lemon cut with fluted edges.

Note. One of the sauces recommended for grilled fish may be served separately with grilled skewered salmon.

Fried skewered salmon. BROCHETTES DE SAUMON FRITES—Prepare the skewers as above but sauté the pieces of salmon lightly in butter before impaling them. Coat the skewered pieces in egg and breadcrumbs.

Fry in deep fat, set on a napkin and garnish with fried parsley and quarters of lemon. Serve separately *Tomato sauce*, or any other sauce appropriate to fish. See SAUCE.

Salmon soufflé. SOUFFLÉ DE SAUMON—Prepared with cooked salmon rubbed through a sieve, mixed with *Béchamel sauce* (see SAUCE), bound with egg yolks and with stiffly beaten egg whites folded in at the last moment. See SOUFFLÉ.

Salmon steak à l'américaine. DARNE DE SAUMON À L'AMÉRICAINE—Cut from the middle of the salmon a slice about 2½ to 3 inches thick.

Season with salt and pepper. Set to cook in a buttered sauté pan the bottom of which has been lined with 2 tablespoons of *matignon** (fondue) of raw root vegetables.

Sprinkle with 4 tablespoons of melted butter. Begin cooking over a good heat. Cover the pan and cook in the oven, basting frequently with the butter, but without adding any liquid.

As soon as the salmon is cooked, take it out of the pan and keep it warm.

There will have been previously prepared a *Spiny lobster* or *Lobster à l'américaine**, following the usual method except that the spiny lobster or lobster must be left whole.

As soon as the spiny lobster is cooked, remove the shell from the tail and slice the latter into six equal slices.

Split the body in half, longways; take out all the flesh without breaking the half shells.

Dice this flesh, add to it an equal quantity of cooked, diced mushrooms and bind this *salpicon** with ½ cup (1 decilitre) of concentrated *Allemande sauce* (see SAUCE) to which chopped tarragon and chervil have been added.

Fill the half shells with this mixture. Smooth over the surfaces and sprinkle them with grated Parmesan and a little melted butter.

Put these half shells on a baking sheet and brown them in a very hot oven 10 minutes before serving.

The sauce. Add the *matignon* with which the salmon was cooked to the *Américaine sauce* (see SAUCE). Add 1½ cups (3 decilitres) of fish *fumet** and ½ cup (1 decilitre) of *Velouté sauce* (see SAUCE) and cook down by one-third over a good heat, stirring with a wooden spoon.

Finish off the sauce away from the heat, thicken it with the coral rubbed through a sieve and blended with 7 tablespoons (100 grams) of fresh butter. Add chopped parsley, chervil and tarragon, the juice of half a lemon and salt and pepper if necessary, and mix well with a whisk.

To serve the dish. Place the salmon, very hot, on a croûton of bread fried in butter, on a large oval dish.

Put at each end of the dish the half shells of spiny lobster. Place on each side of the salmon the slices of spiny lobster, each set into a little tartlet of fine pastry and lightly coated with *Américaine sauce.*

Coat the salmon with the rest of the sauce and serve immediately.

Salmon steak à l'anglaise. DARNE DE SAUMON À L'ANGLAISE—Slice of salmon coated in egg and breadcrumbs and cooked (pan broiled) in butter. Served with *Maître d'hôtel butter.* See BUTTER, *Compound butters.*

Fried salmon steaks. DARNE DE SAUMON FRITE—Cut the salmon in thin slices. Soak them in cold boiled milk. Flour them lightly. Fry in smoking fat (oil for preference).

Drain the slices when they are well coloured, arrange them on a napkin and garnish with fried parsley and quarters of lemon.

Grilled salmon steaks (*Mac Fisheries*)

Grilled salmon steak. DARNE DE SAUMON GRILLÉE—Season the salmon steak with salt and pepper. Brush with oil (or melted butter). Cook under the grill at a moderate heat.

Serve with *Maître d'hôtel butter* (see BUTTER, *Compound butters*) or any sauce recommended for grilled fish.

Darne of salmon à la meunière. DARNE DE SAUMON À LA MEUNIÈRE—Cut the salmon into slices, not too thick. Season these slices and sprinkle them lightly with flour. Cook in the frying pan in smoking hot butter.

Arrange the slices on a long dish, sprinkle them with chopped parsley and squeeze over a little lemon juice. At the moment of serving pour over the cooking butter, very hot. Surround with half slices of lemon with fluted edges.

Salmon steak à la Nantua. DARNE DE SAUMON À LA NANTUA—Cook a chunk of salmon, cut rather thick, in fish *fumet**. Drain it, set it on a serving dish and surround with shelled crayfish tails.

Coat with *Nantua sauce* (see SAUCE) to which the concentrated cooking juices of the fish have been added before straining.

Salmon steak poached in white wine, various garnishes. DARNE DE SAUMON POCHÉE AU VIN BLANC—Poach the salmon steaks, cut rather thick, in fish *fumet** made with white wine. Drain them and set them on a serving dish. Surround them with the prescribed garnish. Coat with *White wine sauce* (see SAUCE) prepared in the usual way, to which the concentrated cooking liquor of the fish has been added before straining.

Tronçon of salmon Philéas Gilbert

Tronçon of salmon Philéas Gilbert. TRONÇON DE SAUMON PHILÉAS GILBERT—Fill the inside of a large chunk of salmon, weighing 5 pounds (2 kilos 500 grams) with the following mixture: cook in butter 3 carrots and half a celery heart, these vegetables being cut in a short *julienne* (thin strips). When this *julienne* is cooked add to it 3 tablespoons of truffles and an equal quantity of mushrooms, also cut in *julienne.* Pour in ¾ cup (1½ decilitres) of sherry and cook down. Bind this *julienne* with a few tablespoons of very thick *Béchamel sauce* (see SAUCE) and season.

The fish being stuffed with this mixture, cover each end with a thin bard of bacon fat and tie securely so that the stuffing cannot escape.

Put it in a fish kettle (placed on the grid) lined with a chopped carrot and a chopped onion which have been cooked till soft in butter, some mushroom and truffle skins (from those used in the stuffing) and a good *bouquet garni**.

Season the salmon; pour over some melted butter and fill the pan with sherry to half-way up the fish. Start cooking over the heat, then put to cook in the oven, the fish-kettle covered, for 40 to 45 minutes.

When the salmon is cooked take it out of the pan. Skin the middle part, leaving only a thin strip of skin at either end. Keep the salmon warm in the oven; cover it with buttered heavy paper.

COLD SALMON. SAUMON FROID:

Cold whole salmon or cuts of salmon with various sauces and garnishes. SAUMON ENTIER, EN TRONÇONS (FROID)—Poach the salmon, whole or in large cuts, in *court-bouillon**. Leave to cool in the cooking liquor.

Drain the fish and wipe it dry. Set on a large dish,

directly on to the dish, or on a napkin or grid. Garnish with fresh parsley or with quartered hard boiled eggs and lettuce hearts.

Accompanying sauces—Cold salmon is usually served with cold sauces made with an oil and egg yolk base, such as:

Andalouse, *Chantilly*, *Gribiche*, *Mayonnaise*, *Ravigote*, *Rémoulade*, *Russian*, *Tartare*, *Vincent*, *Vinaigrette*, etc. See SAUCE, *Cold sauces*.

Garnishes for cold salmon—These are endlessly varied. They consist chiefly, apart from lettuce hearts and hard boiled eggs, of vegetable salads mixed with *Mayonnaise* (with the addition of gelatine) or *Vinaigrette*.

When cold salmon is served *à l'anglaise* it must be accompanied by cucumber salad.

The garnishes most often used with cold salmon (and, in general, with all cold fish) are the following:

Small aspics of crayfish tails or shrimps, of lobster or crawfish; various *salpicons; macédoines* of vegetables, etc.

Tartlets or barquettes made of fine pastry, cooked empty, filled with caviar, *macédoine* of vegetables, etc., various mousses or purées, various *salpicons*, etc.

Barquettes or cassolettes made of beetroot or cucumber, filled as above.

Small silver or *glass scallop shells* (or real scallop shells) with any of the fillings described above.

Artichoke bottoms (cooked in a flour-and-water *court-bouillon*) garnished with the same preparations used to fill *barquettes*, etc.

Stuffed hard boiled eggs, using mousses and purées of various kinds for filling.

Small tomatoes, scooped out, marinated and filled with salad, or some kind of mousse or purée.

Note. The garnishes enumerated above apply chiefly to salmon poached in a *court-bouillon**. Instructions will be found below for cold salmon cooked in a white wine fish stock.

Decorating cold salmon. When salmon is served cold—either a whole fish or a large cut, the skin is sometimes wholly or partially removed to expose the flesh and allow it to be decorated with truffles, beetroot, anchovies, sprigs of chervil, tarragon leaves, lobster coral, etc., which are fixed on the fish with half set jelly. This decoration is always rather vulgar and the true connoisseur would always rather serve the salmon in its natural state, that is to say covered with its own skin.

The same is true of *socles* (pedestals) and *tampons* (raised bases), formerly much used and nowadays almost completely abandoned.

Certainly, if the garnish surrounding the cold fish is on a generous scale, it is a good idea to raise the fish a little by placing it on a simple base of rice, moulded in a suitable shape.

This suggestion is made without any particular recommendation, because we think that really fine *cuisine* can and must dispense with these decorative excesses, so highly thought of in the past.

Note. Salmon poached in the ordinary *court-bouillon* may also be prepared with *Montpellier butter* (see BUTTER, *Compound butters*), and salmon steaks or chunks may be served in the same way.

Cold boiled salmon, with various sauces and garnishes. SAUMON BOUILLI FROID—Cook in *court-bouillon* (whole, in large cuts or slices); cool in the cooking liquor.

Drain the fish, dry it, set on a napkin and garnish with fresh parsley, with hard boiled eggs or lettuce hearts. Serve separately one or other of the sauces recommended for cold fish.

Cold salmon à l'anglaise

Note. In England it is usual to accompany salmon, particularly when it is served cold, with cucumber seasoned with *Vinaigrette* or plain, cut in thin slices.

Côtelettes of salmon in aspic. CÔTELETTES DE SAUMON À LA GELÉE—Prepared either by coating with fish aspic jelly half slices of salmon that have been cooked in a *court-bouillon**, cooled and drained, or by braising in a cooking base of fish aspic jelly made with white wine (or any other wine) slices of salmon trimmed into the shape of cutlets (U.S. chops).

These cutlets (*côtelettes*), once they are quite cool, are decorated with truffles or something of the same kind and glazed with the prescribed jelly. They are arranged in the form of a crown on a round dish and garnished with chopped jelly, or they may be put into a glass bowl and completely covered with the jelly.

Salmon cutlets may also be put into *barquettes* made of fine short crust pastry (cooked empty), on a layer of chopped jelly. Alternatively they may be set each on a *croûton* of bread cut into the same shape as the cutlet and covered with one of the compound butters. See BUTTER.

Côtelettes of salmon à la moscovite. CÔTELETTES DE SAUMON À LA MOSCOVITE—Braise the cutlets in an aspic jelly stock made with dry champagne. Coat them, once they are cold, with white *Chaud-froid sauce* (see SAUCE) with the addition of chopped chives, blanched and drained.

Set them in *barquettes* of fine lining dough pastry, cooked empty, garnished with a good tablespoon of fresh caviare.

Arrange the *barquettes* on a round dish on a napkin. Garnish with fresh parsley. Serve *Tartare sauce* separately. See SAUCE, *Cold sauces*.

Côtelettes of salmon à la Nantua. CÔTELETTES DE SAUMON À LA NANTUA—Cook the cutlets in an aspic jelly stock made with white wine. Allow them to cool.

Coat with *Chaud-froid sauce* that has been finished off with *Crayfish butter* (see BUTTER, *Compound butters*). Decorate each one with a broad thin slice of truffle and on top of this two crayfish (or shrimp) tails. Glaze the cutlets with jelly.

Set in a glass bowl on a layer of well set jelly; garnish the middle with *Crayfish mousse** formed into a dome. Decorate with crayfish tails and slices of truffle arranged in alternate layers.

Glaze with jelly; set well on ice.

Set the bowl on a dish covered with a napkin. Surround with powdered ice.

Côtelettes of salmon à l'orientale. CÔTELETTES DE SAUMON À L'ORIENTALE—Proceed, with half-slices of salmon, as for *Red mullet à l'orientale*. See HORS-D'OEUVRE, *Cold hors-d'œuvre*.

SOLE. *Above:* Paupiettes of fillets of sole normande *Below:* Fillets of Sole Marguery (*La Méditerranée*)

(*From Curnonsky:* Cuisine et Vins de France)

SOUP. Soupe de poisson *(Robert Carrier)*

Côtelettes of salmon à la parisienne. CÔTELETTES DE SAUMON À LA PARISIENNE—Put into the bottom of some scallop shells 2 tablespoons of vegetable salad mixed with mayonnaise. Arrange on top pieces of salmon sliced as neatly as possible. Coat with gelatine-strengthened mayonnaise.

Arrange round the edge of each scallop a little border of asparagus tips, pieces of carrot scooped out with a vegetable baller and French (string) beans cut in dice, all previously cooked in salted water and well drained.

Set a slice of truffle on top of each shell.

Côtelettes of salmon à la russe. CÔTELETTES DE SAUMON À LA RUSSE—Put into the bottom of some scallop shells a good tablespoon each of shredded lettuce seasoned with oil and vinegar. Set slices of salmon on top. Coat with gelatine-strengthened mayonnaise.

Decorate with very small lettuce hearts, quartered hard boiled eggs, olives, capers and anchovy fillets.

Galantine of salmon. GALANTINE DE SAUMON—This dish, known in old cookery under the name of *Sous-presse de saumon*, is prepared in same way as *Galantine* or *Ballottine of eel* (see EEL), with truffles, fillets of salmon and *Pike forcemeat*. See FORCEMEAT.

This galantine, rolled up in a linen cloth, is cooked in a strengthened fish stock or *fumet**. When cooked, it is untied and rolled up anew in a linen cloth which is firmly secured with twine, and the galantine is put to cool under light pressure.

Once cold, it is decorated with truffles or some other garnish of the same sort and glazed with jelly. It is served on a long dish and surrounded with chopped jelly, the edges of the dish being decorated with jelly croûtons.

Mayonnaise or some other cold sauce is served at the same time.

Glazed salmon Bellevue in aspic. SAUMON GLACÉ BELLEVUE, EN ASPIC—Cook the salmon (whole or in large cuts) in an enriched fish aspic stock (see JELLY). Allow to cool in its cooking liquor.

Drain the fish, skin without breaking the flesh; wipe with a napkin.

Coat with half set jelly (prepared with the liquor in which the fish was cooked, clarified in the usual way). Glaze it by applying several layers of this jelly until it is covered with a uniform coating.

Put the salmon on a long dish covered with a layer of firmly set jelly. Decorate with cut-out jelly shapes. Keep in a cold place until ready to serve.

Note. When a cut of salmon is being used it may be set in an oval glass bowl instead of in a long dish. Set this bowl in a block of ice or surround it with crushed ice.

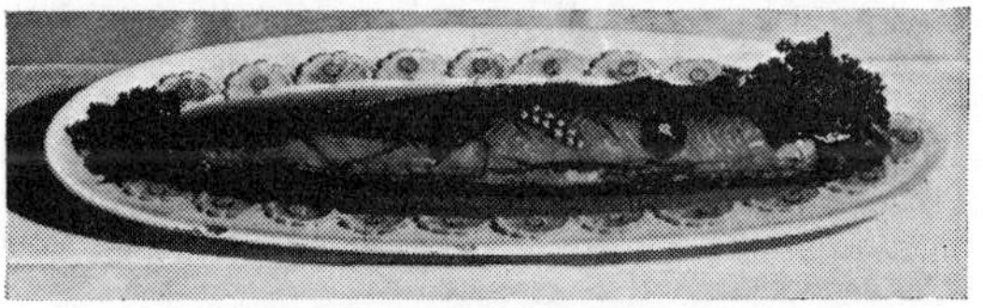

Glazed salmon au chambertin (*Larousse*)

Glazed salmon au chambertin. SAUMON GLACÉ AU CHAMBERTIN—Proceed as *Glazed salmon Bellevue in aspic*, using a fish aspic stock prepared with Chambertin.

Serve on a dish or in a glass bowl.

Glazed salmon côtelettes au chambertin. CÔTELETTES DE SAUMON GLACÉES AU CHAMBERTIN—Braise the salmon cutlets in Chambertin. Let them cool in the cooking liquor.

Finish off the cutlets as for *Côtelettes of salmon in jelly*.

Note. The cutlets may be prepared in the same way with champagne, Bordeaux, Alsace or Rhine wine, etc.

Glazed salmon à la champenoise. SAUMON GLACÉ À LA CHAMPENOISE—Like *Glazed salmon Bellevue in aspic*, using a fish sapic stock made with dry champagne.

Serve on a dish or in a glass bowl.

Glazed côtelettes of salmon with macédoine of vegetables. CÔTELETTES DE SAUMON GLACÉ MACÉDOINE DE LÉGUMES—Cut the salmon in thick slices ¾ inch thick and divide each one in half. Shape these halves in the form of cutlets (U.S. chops).

Arrange the cutlets in a buttered dish; season with salt and pepper. Pour over fish *fumet** made with white wine and add a squeeze of lemon juice. Poach gently, keeping the dish covered. Put to cool under pressure. Drain the cutlets; dry them and decorate them with truffles, tarragon leaves or something else of the same kind. Glaze them with jelly.

Arrange in the form of a circle on a round dish (directly on to the dish or on a shaped base of rice).

Garnish the middle of the dish with a vegetable salad mixed with very thick mayonnaise and shaped into a dome. Decorate the top of the salad with truffles, lobster coral, anchovy fillets, etc.

Surround the cutlets with jelly croûtons. Serve *Mayonnaise* separately. See SAUCE, *Cold sauces*.

Glazed salmon à l'impériale. SAUMON GLACÉ À L'IMPÉRIALE—Cook the salmon as for *Glazed salmon Bellevue in aspic*.

Decorate it, after it has been skinned, with truffles and the whites of hard boiled eggs cut in the form of scales. Coat with the jelly.

Set on a long dish, on a bed of rice or directly on to the plate.

Surround with a garnish composed of little *mousselines** of crayfish, *barquettes* of fine pastry filled with soft carp roes poached in white wine and coated with *White chaud-froid sauce*, based on fish *fumet**, and halved hard boiled eggs. See SAUCE.

Serve with *mayonnaise* mixed with truffle purée.

Glazed salmon Monselet. SAUMON GLACÉ MONSELET—Cook the salmon in the same way as for *Glazed salmon Bellevue in aspic*.

Decorate it, after it has been skinned, with truffles and lobster coral; glaze with jelly.

Set on a long dish either on a bed of rice or directly on a plate.

Surround with a garnish composed of very small artichoke bottoms filled with a salad of green asparagus tips and truffles, and small *Tomato mousses* decorated with tarragon leaves.

Serve with *mayonnaise* mixed with tomato juice.

Glazed salmon à la parisienne (*Larousse*)

Glazed salmon à la parisienne. SAUMON GLACÉ À LA PARISIENNE—Cook and cool the salmon (either whole or in a large cut) as for *Glazed salmon Bellevue in aspic*.

Decorate it with truffles and the other garnishes usual to this kind of arrangement, and glaze with jelly.

Set on a long or round dish.

Surround with a *Parisienne garnish* for cold fish (see GARNISH) arranged in little clusters, separated from each other by lettuce hearts and halved hard boiled eggs. Decorate with chopped jelly. Serve with mayonnaise.

Glazed salmon à la russe. SAUMON GLACÉ À LA RUSSE—Cook the salmon as for *Glazed salmon à la parisienne* and allow it to cool.

Drain, skin it, decorate with truffles, tarragon leaves etc., and glaze it with jelly.

Set on a long dish (on a bed of rice or directly on to the plate).

Surround with small Russian salads moulded in darioles lined with jelly, small *barquettes* made out of cucumber (blanched, well drained and marinated with oil, lemon juice, salt and pepper) and filled with caviare and quartered hard boiled eggs. Garnish the edges of the plate with jelly croûtons.

Salmon mayonnaise. SAUMON FROID EN MAYONNAISE—Put in the bottom of a salad dish (or any other deep dish) a layer of shredded lettuce seasoned with salt and pepper, oil and vinegar.

Place on this lettuce, piled up a little in the form of a dome, a mound of salmon either cut into fine slices, or simply flaked, the skin and bones having been removed.

Cover with mayonnaise. Smooth over the coating of sauce so as to obtain a perfectly regular form. Decorate with anchovies, capers, chervil or tarragon leaves, and stoned olives.

Surround with quartered hard boiled eggs and lettuce hearts.

Note. All the garnishes suggested elsewhere for cold fish may be used as garnish for *Salmon mayonnaise.*

Médaillons of cold salmon. MÉDAILLONS DE SAUMON FROID—Cut the salmon in slices; divide each of the slices in two; trim each of these slices into rounds or *médaillons.*

Cook and finish off according to any of the recipes given for *Côtelettes of salmon.*

Cold salmon with Montpellier butter. SAUMON FROID AU BEURRE DE MONTPELLIER—Cook the salmon, whole or in large cuts, in a fish aspic stock made with white wine, as for *Glazed salmon Bellevue in aspic.* Allow to cool in its cooking liquor.

Drain the fish; remove the skin from the central part, keeping only a narrow strip at each side. Wipe dry.

Cover the skinned part with *Montpellier butter* (see BUTTER, *Compound butters*). Smooth over this layer of butter. Decorate it with small pieces of truffles dipped in half set jelly, always keeping the design simple. Glaze with half set jelly (made with the liquor in which the fish was cooked).

Set the fish on a long dish, directly on to the plate or raised on a bed of rice or buttered *croûton* of bread.

Surround with a garnish composed of hard boiled eggs, lettuce hearts, croûtons spread with *Montpellier butter* and jelly or any other garnish chosen from among those enumerated above.

Cold salmon steak with various sauces and garnishes. DARNES DE SAUMON FROIDES—All the recipes given for cold cutlets of salmon can be applied to salmon steaks.

The steaks, cooked in *court-bouillon* and left to cool in the liquor, are set on a napkin, garnished with quartered hard boiled eggs, lettuce hearts or any other garnish suitable for cold fish, and served accompanied by some cold sauce (*Mayonnaise, Rémoulade, Tartare, Verte,* etc.; see SAUCE, *Cold sauces*).

SALMON TROUT. TRUITE SAUMONÉE—Trout with pink flesh. See TROUT.

SALPICON—In French cookery parlance a preparation made up of one or more ingredients cut in small dice and bound with a sauce, whether rich or plain, white or brown.

Salpicons, with other hors-d'oeuvre mixtures, are used to fill pastry *barquettes* and other tartlets, canapés, pastry cases, *croustades* or hollowed bread cases, rissoles and timbales. They may be made into kromeskies, cutlets and croquettes. They are used to stuff eggs, poultry, game, and fish as well as some cuts of meat.

Cold salpicons are seasoned with *Vinaigrette* or mayonnaise.

In pastry-making and confectionery salpicons of fresh or candied fruit are used.

Salpicon à l'américaine (hot)—Lobster or spiny lobster flesh *à l'américaine,* bound with *Américaine sauce.* See SAUCE.

Salpicon of anchovies (hot or cold). SALPICON D'ANCHOIS—De-salted anchovy fillets cut into uniform dice. Use hot or cold according to the particular recipe.

Salpicon of artichokes (cold). SALPICON D'ARTICHAUTS—Bind with mayonnaise thickened with jelly some artichoke bottoms cooked in flour and water *court-bouillon**, drained and dried and cut in dice.

Used to garnish eggs, fish, cold chicken, pastry boats and tartlets.

Salpicon of artichokes with cream. SALPICON D'ARTICHAUTS À LA CRÈME—Cut artichoke bottoms half cooked in flour and water *court-bouillon** into dice, large or small, according to the final use.

Finish cooking these artichokes in butter. Season them, bind with a few tablespoons of rather thick *Cream sauce.* See SAUCE.

This salpicon, like all the vegetables in the recipes which follow, may be bound with thick *Velouté sauce* (see SAUCE) instead of *Cream sauce.*

Used as garnish with eggs, barquettes and tartlets, with small cuts of meat, poultry, and with fish.

Salpicon of green asparagus (cold). SALPICON D'ASPERGES VERTES—Cut green asparagus in dice, large or small according to the final use. Cook in salted water.

Drain and dry; bind with thick mayonnaise.

Same uses as the *Salpicon of artichokes.*

Salpicon of aubergines in cream. SALPICON D'AUBERGINES À LA CRÈME—Cook in butter some aubergines cut in dice. Season, bind when cooked with *Cream sauce.* See SAUCE.

Same uses as the *Salpicon of artichokes.*

Salpicon of beetroot (cold). SALPICON DE BETTERAVES—Cut a beetroot, cooked in the oven and peeled, into dice. Season the salpicon with oil, vinegar, salt and pepper or with thick mayonnaise.

Salpicon à la bohémienne (cold)—The same mixture as in the recipe which follows (see below), bound with meat jelly.

Salpicon à la bohémienne (hot)—Mixture of *foie gras* and cooked truffles cut in dice; bound with *Madeira sauce* made with truffle essence.

This salpicon sometimes has the addition of a small quantity of diced onion stewed in butter and seasoned with paprika. Used for canapés, tartlets, poached eggs, etc.

Salpicon of brains (hot). SALPICON DE CERVELLE—Bound with *Allemande, Béchamel* or *Velouté sauce.* See SAUCE.

Salpicon cancalaise (hot)—Mixture of poached oysters and cooked mushrooms, bound with *Normande sauce* or *Velouté sauce,* based on concentrated fish stock. See SAUCE.

Salpicon cardinal (hot)—Mixture of diced lobster, truffles and mushrooms bound with *Cardinal sauce.* See SAUCE.

Salpicon of carrots à la crème. SALPICON DE CAROTTES À LA CRÈME—Cut in dice the orange part of some carrots. Put in a saucepan, cover with water, add 4 tablespoons (60 grams) of butter to each pint (½ litre) of water. Season with salt and a very little sugar. Cook till all the liquid is absorbed. Bind with *Cream sauce* (see SAUCE).

Same uses as the *Salpicon of artichokes.*

Salpicon of celeriac (cold). SALPICON DE CÉLERI-RAVE—Cook celeriac cut into dice in salted water. Drain, dry, bind with thick mayonnaise.

Same uses as the *Salpicon of artichokes.*

Salpicon of celeriac à la crème (hot). SALPICON DE CÉLERI-RAVE À LA CRÈME—Cut into dice a celeriac root. Cook in butter in covered pan. Season when cooked; bind with *Cream sauce.* See SAUCE.

Same uses as the *Salpicon of artichokes.*

Salpicon of cèpes à la crème. SALPICON DE CÈPES À LA CRÈME—Cut cooked cèpes in dice. Stew in butter. Bind with *Cream sauce.* See SAUCE.

Same uses as the *Salpicon of artichokes.*

Salpicon à la chalonnaise (hot)—Mixture of cocks' combs and truffles; bound with *Allemande sauce.* See SAUCE.

Salpicon chasseur (hot)—Mixture of chicken livers (cut in dice and sautéed in butter) and mushrooms, bound with concentrated *Chasseur sauce.* See SAUCE.

Salpicon of chicken livers. SALPICON DE FOIES DE VOLAILLES—Like *Salpicon of foie gras.*

Salpicon of cocks' combs (hot). SALPICON DE CRÊTES—Bound with *Allemande, Béchamel* or *Demi-glace sauce* (see SAUCE), or brown veal stock, concentrated and thickened.

Salpicon of crayfish. SALPICON DE CREVETTES—Bound with *Béchamel* or *Crayfish sauce* (hot); with *Vinaigrette* or *Mayonnaise* (cold). See SAUCE.

Salpicon of cucumbers (cold). SALPICON DE CONCOMBRES—Cut in big dice some cucumbers split in two, lengthways, and emptied of their seeds (they are removed with a spoon). Spread them on a cloth, sprinkle them with salt and leave them till they are translucent. Dry them, season with oil and vinegar or bind them with thick mayonnaise.

Same uses as *Salpicon of artichokes.*

Salpicon Cussy (hot)—Mixture of sweetbreads, truffles and mushrooms, bound with concentrated *Madeira sauce.* See SAUCE.

Salpicon cutlets. CÔTELETTES DE SALPICONS—These cutlets are made with a salpicon (fine mince) of various ingredients, to which mushrooms and truffles cut into dice are added and combined with an *Allemande* or a *Béchamel sauce.* See SAUCE.

This preparation is made into cutlet shape and then dipped in egg and breadcrumbs. They are then cooked in clarified butter.

Salpicon à la dieppoise (hot)—Mixture of crayfish, mussels and mushrooms; bound with *Normande sauce* or *White wine sauce I.* See SAUCE.

Salpicon à l'écarlate (hot)—Pickled tongue bound with *Demi-glace sauce.* See SAUCE.

Salpicon of hard boiled eggs. SALPICON D'OEUFS DURS—Bound with *Allemande, Béchamel, Cream* or *Velouté sauce* (hot); with *Vinaigrette* or *Mayonnaise* (cold). See SAUCE.

Salpicon à la financière (hot)—Mixture of quenelles, cocks' combs, cocks' kidneys, mushrooms and truffles; bound with concentrated *Financière sauce.* See SAUCE.

Salpicon of fish. SALPICON DE POISSON—Cooked fish bound with *Béchamel, Normande* or *White wine sauce I* (hot); with *Vinaigrette* or *Mayonnaise* (cold). See SAUCE.

Salpicon of foie gras—Bound with *Madeira, Port,* or *Sherry* sauce (see SAUCE) or game gravy (hot); in jelly (cold).

Salpicon of French (string) beans (cold). SALPICON DE HARICOTS VERTS—Like *Salpicon of green asparagus.*

Salpicon of French (string) beans à la crème (hot). SALPICON DE HARICOTS VERTS À LA CRÈME—Cut in dice, when raw, some French beans. Cook briskly in salted water, but keep fairly firm. Simmer in butter in covered pan. Bind with *Cream sauce.* See SAUCE.

Same uses as the *Salpicon of artichokes.*

Salpicons of fruit. SALPICONS DE FRUITS—These salpicons, usually made with fresh fruit cooked in syrup (apricots, cherries, peaches, pears, apples, plums, etc.) are used as filling or garnish for a great many pastries and sweet dishes. Salpicons may also be made from candied fruits, which are used in the same way.

Fruit salpicons should be soaked in liqueur.

Salpicon of game. SALPICON DE GIBIER—Bound with white or brown sauce, based on the game used (hot); bound with jelly (cold).

Salpicon of ham (hot). SALPICON DE JAMBON—Made with cooked ham.

Cut up the ham into small dice; bind with *Demi-glace sauce.* Various garnishes and forcemeats can be added. When cold used for canapés and other cold hors-d'oeuvre.

Salpicon of Jerusalem artichokes. SALPICON DE TOPINAMBOURS—Like the *Salpicon of artichokes,* made with Jerusalem artichokes cooked in salted water.

Salpicon à la Joinville (hot)—Mixture of crayfish, truffles and mushrooms bound with *Joinville sauce.* See SAUCE.

Salpicon of lobster. SALPICON DE HOMARD—Bound with *Béchamel, Lobster* or *Nantua sauce* (hot); with *Vinaigrette* or *Mayonnaise* (cold). See SAUCE.

Salpicon of meat. SALPICON DE VIANDES DE DESSERTE—Salpicons are made with various left-over meats (beef, veal, lamb, mutton, pork) cut in dice, large or small, according to their final use, and bound with brown or white sauce.

These salpicons are used to make croquettes and kromeskies or to fill pastry cases, hollowed crusts, etc.

Salpicon à la Montglas (hot)—Mixture of *foie gras,* pickled tongue, truffles and mushrooms, bound with concentrated *Madeira sauce.* See SAUCE.

Salpicon of mushrooms (cold). SALPICON DE CHAMPIGNONS—The mushrooms cooked, cut in dice, bound with thick mayonnaise.

Same uses as *Salpicon of artichokes.*

Salpicon of mushrooms and other fungi (hot). SALPICON DE CHAMPIGNONS DE COUCHE—Cut in dice the mushrooms, peeled and washed. Cook gently in butter, bind with *Cream sauce.* See SAUCE.

Same uses as *Salpicon of artichokes.*

Salpicon of mushrooms with Madeira (hot). SALPICON DE CHAMPIGNONS AU MADÈRE—Cook in butter the mushrooms cut in dice. Dilute the cooking juices with a little Madeira or other liqueur wine. Bind with concentrated rich *Brown sauce* (see SAUCE) based on mushroom stock. Same uses as *Salpicon of artichokes.*

Salpicon of mussels (hot). SALPICON DE MOULES—Bound with *Allemande, Poulette* or *White wine sauce* (hot); with *Vinaigrette* or *Mayonnaise* (cold). See SAUCE.

Salpicon of onion. SALPICON D'OIGNON—*White.* Cook the onions in butter, bind with *Cream sauce.* See SAUCE.

Brown. Bind the onions, once cooked, with concentrated rich *Brown sauce.* See SAUCE.

Salpicon à la périgourdine (hot)—Mixture of *foie gras* and truffles bound with concentrated *Madeira sauce.* See SAUCE.

Salpicon of potatoes (cold). SALPICON DE POMMES DE TERRE—With potatoes cooked in their jackets, peeled, cut into dice, large or small according to the final use, and mixed with *Vinaigrette* or *Mayonnaise.* See SAUCE.

Same use as *Salpicon of artichokes.*

Salpicon à la reine (hot)—Mixture of white chicken meat, mushrooms and truffles, bound with *Allemande sauce.* See SAUCE.

Salpicon à la royale (hot)—Mixture of truffles and mushrooms bound with chicken purée.

Salpicon à la Saint-Hubert (hot)—Game meat, bound with *Demi-glace sauce* (see SAUCE) cooked down with the pan juices left from cooking the game.

Salpicon of shrimps (hot). SALPICON D'ÉCREVISSES—Bound with *Béchamel, Shrimp* or *Nantua sauce* (hot); with *Vinaigrette* or *Mayonnaise* (cold). See SAUCE.

Salpicon of spiny lobster or crawfish. SALPICON DE LANGOUSTE—Like *Salpicon of lobster.*

Salpicon of sweetbreads (hot). SALPICON DE RIS D'AGNEAU, DE VEAU—Bound with *Allemande, Béchamel, Demi-glace, Madeira* or *Suprême sauce.* See SAUCE.

Salpicon of tomatoes I. SALPICON DE TOMATES—Peel the tomatoes and remove the seeds. Cut them in dice large or small according to their final use. Season with salt and lay on a cloth to yield some of their moisture.

Use as they are, or season with oil and vinegar.

Same uses as *Salpicon of artichokes.*

Salpicon of tomatoes II. SALPICON DE TOMATES—Cut the tomatoes in dice. Put them in a wire basket. Plunge them for a minute into boiling salted water.

Use as an auxiliary ingredient in soups, sauces and mixed salpicons.

Salpicon of truffles. SALPICON DE TRUFFES—Made with fresh truffles, raw or cooked in Madeira, or with tinned truffles.

Cut them into dice, large or small according to the final use. Season with salt and pepper, and, if necessary, with oil and lemon juice or leave them as they are for cold preparations.

For hot dishes, simmer them in butter or bind them in a few tablespoons of rich *Brown sauce* flavoured with Madeira, or, if more suitable, bind them with *Velouté* or *Cream sauce* (see SAUCE). Used *cold* as a garnish in hors-d'oeuvre, with eggs, fish, made-up salads; *hot* in *barquettes*, tartlets, etc., and as a supplementary ingredient in sauces, forcemeats, and various mixtures.

Salpicon of veal. SALPICON DE VEAU—Bound with *Allemande, Béchamel* or *Demi-glace sauce* or brown veal gravy (hot); bound with jelly (cold).

SALSIFY OR OYSTER PLANT. SALSIFIS—In culinary language the name of salsify, or oyster plant, is used not only for the root of the plant of the *Compositae* family which alone is entitled to it, but also for that of another plant of the same family which botanically is called *scorzonera.*

While one of these roots, that of the true salsify, is white outside, that of the scorzonera is blackish.

The flesh of these two roots is very similar in taste, and they are prepared in exactly the same way.

The word *scorzonera* comes from the Catalan *escorso*, which means *viper.* The plant was so called, it is said, because formerly, in Spain, it was used as a remedy for the bite of this dangerous snake.

The wild salsify, commonly known as Goat's Beard, should also be mentioned. It grows in the fields and in damp and rich pastureland. The young shoots of this plant can be eaten in salad and can also be prepared like spinach. The roots are eaten like those of scorzonera.

The stalks or tender shoots of salsify and scorzonera may also be prepared in various ways. They are mostly eaten raw in salad.

To cook salsify—Scrape the salsify roots; divide them into chunks $2\frac{1}{2}$ to 3 inches long. Plunge them as they are prepared into water with a little lemon or vinegar in it, to prevent them from turning black. Put to cook in a boiling flour-and-water *court-bouillon.* See COURT-BOUILLON, *Court-bouillon for vegetables.*

Cook, covered, over a gentle but steady heat, for about two hours. Put into a basin and keep in a cool place.

Drain and dry the salsify before preparing them in any manner.

Note. After having been cooked in this way the salsify can be treated in different ways. It is served by itself as a vegetable or used as a garnish.

When it is not to be used immediately, it can be kept in its cooking liquor, where it can be left for several days without deteriorating.

To cook leaves or shoots of salsify or oyster plant—Pick the tender shoots, wash them in plenty of water and cook in a flour-and-water *court-bouillon** for 40 minutes. Drain, dry and prepare according to the recipe.

Salsify in béchamel. SALSIFIS À LA BÉCHAMEL—Cut the salsify, cooked in flour-and-water *court-bouillon**, into chunks $1\frac{1}{2}$ to 2 inches long. Put them in a sauté pan, cover with rather thin *Béchamel sauce* (see SAUCE) and simmer. At the last moment add a few tablespoons of fresh cream.

Salsify prepared in this way is often described as *à la crème.*

Salsify au beurre noisette. SALSIFIS AU BEURRE NOISETTE—Cook the salsify in a flour-and-water *court-bouillon**, serve them piping hot in a deep dish sprinkled with a few tablespoons of *Noisette butter.* See BUTTER, *Compound butters.*

Salsify à la crème. SALSIFIS À LA CRÈME—Prepared like *Salsify in béchamel.*

Alternatively, the salsify, after being lightly cooked in butter, may be covered with fresh cream and simmered gently.

Salsify fritters. SALSIFIS FRITS, FRITOT DE SALSIFIS—Cook salsify roots in a flour-and-water *court-bouillon**, drain and cut in neat pieces. Put them in a deep dish, season with salt and pepper, sprinkle with chopped parsley, oil and lemon juice and leave them to soak in this marinade for 30 minutes.

Take them out of the marinade with a perforated spoon, dip them in a light batter and fry in smoking hot deep fat. Drain, arrange on a napkin, garnish with fried parsley and serve.

Salsify Mornay. SALSIFIS MORNAY—Stew the salsify in butter; put them in a gratin dish lined with a layer of *Mornay sauce* (see SAUCE). Coat with *Mornay sauce* and sprinkle with grated Parmesan. Pour over a little melted butter and brown in the oven.

Salsify à la polonaise. SALSIFIS À LA POLONAISE—Arrange in a shallow dish the salsify roots cooked in a white *court-bouillon**, as above, and stewed in butter. Sprinkle with chopped yolks of hard boiled eggs and parsley. At the last moment before serving pour over a little *Noisette butter* (see BUTTER, *Compound butters*) in which some freshly made breadcrumbs have been fried, allowing ½ cup (30 grams) of breadcrumbs to ½ cup (100 grams) of butter.

Salsify salad. SALSIFIS EN SALADE—Cook the salsify in a flour-and-water *court-bouillon**. Drain them, dry and cut into neat pieces. Set in a salad bowl, seasoned with oil, vinegar (or lemon juice), salt and pepper. Sprinkle with chopped parsley, chervil and tarragon.

Salsify sautéed au beurre. SALSIFIS SAUTÉS AU BEURRE—Sauté in very hot butter, browning them lightly, some salsify roots that have been first cooked in a flour-and-water *court-bouillon** as described above, drained, dried and cut in neat pieces. Season.

Salsify sautéed aux fines herbes. SALSIFIS SAUTÉS AUX FINES HERBES—As above, adding chopped parsley to the salsify at the last moment.

Salsify sautéed à la provençale. SALSIFIS SAUTÉS À LA PROVENÇALE—Sauté the salsify in a mixture of butter and oil (half-and-half). At the last moment add a tablespoon of chopped garlic and parsley.

Salsify in veal gravy. SALSIFIS AU BLOND DE VEAU, SALSIFIS AU JUS—Stew for a few moments in butter, browning them lightly, some salsify roots three-quarters cooked in a flour-and-water *court-bouillon**, as described above, drained, dried and cut in neat pieces. Moisten with a few tablespoons of veal gravy, not too thick.

Finish cooking the salsify in this gravy. Serve in a deep dish.

SALT. SEL—Sodium chloride, the first salt to be discovered by man, which has given its name to all analagous chemical products.

There are two sorts of salt: sea salt, which is distilled from sea-water, and rock salt, which is found in the earth in crystalline form.

Sea salt is the only mineral condiment that we add to our food, and it may be noted that the higher the vegetable content of the diet, the greater is the need of salt. This is true among animals as well; herbivorous creatures are greedy for salt but carnivorous animals have no desire for it.

The average consumption of salt, among people who do not abuse the use of this condiment, is about 8 to 10 grams a day. Foodstuffs (before salt is added) contain 1 to 1½ grams in an ordinary diet and the rest is added during cooking or at the table. Complete abstinence from salt has not been found possible even in the most austere monastic orders.

Some culinary practices influence the consumption of —or need for—salt. Boiling vegetables in a large quantity of water deprives them of a large part of their mineral salts, a deficiency which one instinctively corrects by adding salt at the table; potatoes cooked in hot ashes or in the oven have sufficient taste to be eaten without salt, while those cooked in a great deal of water are almost uneatable without this seasoning. Vegetables stewed in their own juices also need much less salt.

Different kinds of salt—Grey (rock) salt is less pure, but among its 'impurities' there are traces of valuable minerals such as arsenic; it is thus rational to use this for cooking and keep the white salt for the table.

Various brands of table salt are marketed; some, generally as the result of adding phosphate of lime, have the advantage that the salt keeps its powder form, whereas pure salt tends to return to its crystalline state under the action of humidity. Other products, chemically produced, contain a much weaker proportion of sodium chloride or are even made up entirely of different types of salt which have a taste more or less comparable with sea salt. These products are designed to give an illusion of salt to invalids on a salt-free diet.

Generally speaking these various products must be added to foodstuffs at the table, their taste being much weakened—or even disappearing altogether—if they are dissolved.

When making up a salt-free diet it is important to recognise that fruit, most vegetables and, with certain exceptions, cereals are the least rich in salt; meat and eggs have less than milk and that a salt-free diet demands a special bread with a genuinely low salt content or the replacement of bread in the diet by potatoes.

Celery salt. SEL DE CÉLERI—Fine salt flavoured with dried and powdered celery. This condiment, which is commercially prepared and marketed, is excellent.

Spiced salt (for forcemeats). SEL ÉPICÉ—Mixture of 2 pounds (1 kilogramme) of fine dry salt with 1¾ cups of white pepper and 1¾ cups of mixed spices.

SALT GRINDER. ÉGRUGEOIR—A small mortar or mill made of wood and used for grinding rock salt to powder.

SALTING. SALAISON—Operation which consists of treating meat, fish and various other substances with salt, or of immersing them in brine, to preserve them for a long time. See BRINE.

Meats and other foodstuffs which have been treated in this way are called *salaisons* in French.

SALTING TUB. SALOIR—Large bucket in which pieces of meat are put to be pickled in brine.

There are different sorts of salting tubs. One kind, a simple receptacle, is used in domestic kitchens to salt pieces of meat, mostly pork; others are great vats of wood, stone or cement, of various shapes, and which in different regions of France are called *baignoires*, *bagnons* or *barbantelles*.

Salting tubs in stone or cement are the best. Every one is provided with a cover, a sort of lattice-work frame, which fits inside the receptacle. On this are placed stones or other heavy objects, so that the substances put in the brine are completely immersed.

SALTPETRE—Potassium nitrate, nitre, a white crystalline salty substance, odourless, fresh tasting, piquant and a little bitter, easily soluble in hot water, less so in cold water. Used in the salting industries because it gives an agreeable red colour to meat, but only in small doses because it also toughens. (It is also used as a constituent of gunpowder.)

SAMOS—Sweet wine harvested on the island of the same name in the Greek Archipelago.

SAMPHIRE. BACILE—A hardy plant which grows on cliffs, by the sea. It is also known under the names of *Peter's cress* and *Sea-fennel* (see illustration on next page). It is grown in gardens, in dry and rocky soil. This plant is eaten principally as a salad.

It can also be cooked in butter or cream, like purslane, or pickled in vinegar like gherkins.

SAND EEL. ÉQUILLE—Common name for a small fish which is found on sandy beaches. It buries itself in the sand at low tide.

It is cooked in the same way as the smelt. See SMELT.

Sand eel is also called *lançon* in French.

SANDPIPER. MAUBÈCHE—A small edible water sparrow. It is cooked in the same way as snipe. See SNIPE.

Samphire

SANDWICH—Foodstuff composed of two slices of buttered bread with some edible substance between.

Is it John Montagu, Earl of Sandwich (who had this food served to him at the gaming table, so that he could eat while he gambled), to whom the invention of this form of foodstuff is due? That cannot be confirmed. All that can be said with certainty is that his name has been given to the preparation.

Since the most faraway times it has been the custom in the French countryside to give workers in the fields meat for their meal enclosed between two pieces of wholemeal or black bread. Moreover, in all the south-west districts it was customary to provide people setting out on a journey with slices of meat, mostly pork or veal cooked in the pot, enclosed, sprinkled with their succulent juices, between two pieces of bread. Sandwiches made with sardines, tunny fish, anchovies, sliced chicken and even with flat omelettes were known in France well before the word, coming from England, had entered into French culinary terminology.

To make sandwiches. Sandwiches are made with English-type bread or French bread, with ordinary bread or enriched bread, with black bread or with special little boat-shaped rolls made with brioche dough. The latter are mostly served at parties and in France are often called *petits pains fourrées.*

Sandwiches in brioche bread—Made like ordinary sandwiches, using little boat-shaped rolls made of brioche mixture (like English bridge rolls).

Sandwiches of French bread—Sandwiches in France are usually made from *petits pains*, i.e. crusty rolls, either round or sausage-shaped, split open, buttered and filled with the same fillings as for English-type bread.

Long French loaves are split and made into sandwiches in the same way.

Sandwiches with loaf bread—Spread with butter, which may, if desirable, be mixed with a little mustard, some slices of fairly dry bread, with the crusts cut off. On these slices of buttered bread put the meat required. Cover with another slice of buttered bread; press the two slices well together. Trim the sandwiches at the sides and cut into rectangles or triangles.

Sandwiches made with English-type bread may be filled with various kinds of meat, all cut into thin slices: *ham; tongue; mortadella; roast pork; pressed beef; chicken* or other poultry; *roast beef; roast veal*, etc.

They may also be filled with the following: *cucumbers* pickled in the Russian style, between two buttered slices of bread sprinkled with grated horseradish; *anchovies* and other filleted salt fish such as *herrings, kilkis, sprats*, etc.; *artichokes* (artichoke bottoms cut in small dice, mixed with hard boiled eggs, also cut in dice); *caviar*; *celeriac*, cut in dice and blanched; *cucumber; cress* or *watercress; shrimps* or *prawns, crayfish, lobsters, spiny lobster* (the butter mixed with a purée made from their shells); *lettuce* (the leaves left whole or shredded); *corn salad* (lamb's lettuce); *hard boiled eggs* (the eggs cut in slices or small dice); *sweet peppers; poutargue* (mullet roes); *sardines* or other fish preserved in oil or salt; *salmon; tomatoes* (sliced with the seeds removed and soaked in salt to remove their moisture); *truffles* (raw truffles cut in thin slices and seasoned).

Sweet sandwiches—Prepared with thin slices of stale brioche or Genoa cake. They are buttered or not according to what is used for the filling.

These sandwiches may be made with chopped up fruit, jam, thick custards, etc.

Toasted sandwiches—Prepared with lightly toasted, sliced tin loaf, French bread or split rolls.

The filling for these sandwiches is the same as for untoasted bread.

Alsatian sandwiches—SANDWICHS ALSACIENS—Fill with Strasbourg sausage, peeled and cut in slices, black bread spread with butter mixed with grated horseradish.

Antibois sandwiches. SANDWICHS ANTIBOIS—Fill with hard boiled eggs, capers and chopped gherkins, slices of toasted bread spread with butter mixed with chopped tarragon.

Basil sandwiches—SANDWICHS AU BASILIC—Fill with chopped hard boiled eggs, thin slices of toasted bread spread with butter to which chopped fresh basil has been added.

Bookmaker's sandwiches—SANDWICHS DU BOOKMAKER—Made with slices of bread with the crusts left on.

Butter these pieces of bread. Fill with a ½ inch thick grilled steak, seasoned with salt and pepper, and spread, when cold, with English mustard.

Dijon sandwiches. SANDWICHS DIJONAIS—Fill with diced hard boiled egg and parsley ham (a regional speciality of Dijon) some slices of French bread spread with butter mixed with Dijon mustard.

Foie gras sandwiches. SANDWICHS DE FOIE GRAS—Spread a slice of bread with a layer of *foie gras*, with or without truffles. Cover with another slice of bread.

These sandwiches can also be made by filling lightly buttered slices of loaf bread, crusty rolls or brioche mixture rolls (bridge rolls) with slices of truffled *foie gras*.

In principle, they should be made with unbuttered bread.

Perigourdine sandwiches. SANDWICHS À LA PÉRIGOURDINE—Fill with small slices of *foie gras* slices of toasted bread spread with truffle purée.

Tartare sandwiches. SANDWICHS À LA TARTARE—Spread slices of bread with a thick layer of minced raw beef mixed with half its weight of butter, chopped chives, salt and paprika.

SANGLER—To pack ice, or ice and salt, around a mould placed in a wooden receptacle, in order to freeze water ice or ice cream mixtures.

SANGRI—Stimulating beverage obtained by mixing Madeira with water, sugar and a little grated nutmeg.

SANGUINE—A dish known under this name in some districts of France, notably Berry, is called *sanquette* in the south-west.

Cook lightly in butter, in a pan, ½ cup (100 grams) of chopped white onions. When they are cooked and golden in colour, pour into the pan the blood of two chickens. Season, shake to mix well and cook like a pancake.

SANGUINE (Blood orange)—Variety of sweet orange with red flesh.

SANSONNET—Colloquial name for the starling, properly called *étourneau* in French, a bird considered edible and cooked like the lark. See LARK.

The same word is used in French for a small mackerel.

SAPID. SAPIDE—That which is savoury and agreeably excites the sense of taste.

SAPODILLA OR NASEBERRY PLUM. SAPOTILLE—Name of Malay origin given in Java and the East Indies to a fruit which in French is called *nèfle d'Amérique* or *sapotile*. Scientifically it is the *sapota achras*. It is about as large as a lemon; its exterior colour is greyish; the flesh is reddish-yellow, something like that of an apricot; the taste is delicious but this fruit can only be eaten where it grows.

SARACEN CORN (BUCKWHEAT). SARASSIN—Herbaceous plant, sometimes known in France as *blé noir* which is classed as a cereal. It prefers a granitic terrain and is grown more in Brittany than in any other part of France.

Unsuitable for making bread, its grain is used for porridges, *galettes* and pancakes. See BUCKWHEAT.

SARDINE—Migratory fish of the genus *Clupeidae*, which in some provinces of the north-west of France is called *cardeau* and *harenguet*, and, at Bordeaux, *royan*.

It is fished abundantly in Sardinia, and from there comes its name.

It is also fished along the coasts of Brittany, where the preservation of sardines in oil is done on a large scale.

In the Mediterranean region, particularly between Menton and Marseilles, the sardines fished are extremely delicate, and are eaten fresh, but cannot be sent long distances without deterioration.

Thus almost everywhere the fish is only known slightly salted or completely preserved in brine or, its most frequent form, tinned in oil.

When served fresh the sardine is presented in various ways.

Conserved in oil or salt the sardine is served as hors-d'oeuvre.

The recipes which follow are for fresh sardines unless otherwise stated. In U.S.A. young fresh herring can be substituted for the European sardine.

Sardines à l'anglaise—Open the fresh sardines and take out the bones. Coat the sardines with egg and breadcrumbs. Fry them in clarified butter. Cover with *Maître d'hôtel butter*, half-melted. See BUTTER, *Compound butters*.

Sardines à l'antiboise—Take off the heads of the fresh sardines, open them and take out the backbones. Coat with egg and breadcrumbs and fry in olive oil.

Arrange on a round dish in the form of a crown. Garnish the middle of the dish with tomato *fondue** seasoned with a little garlic.

Bouillabaisse of sardines (Provençal cookery). BOUILLABAISSE DE SARDINES—Scale, clean out, wash and wipe 1 pound (500 grams) of large fresh sardines.

Cook lightly in a saucepan with 3 tablespoons of oil, 2 tablespoons of chopped onion and a tablespoon of chopped leek.

Add 2 tomatoes, peeled, seeded and chopped, 2 crushed cloves of garlic, a pinch of salt, pepper, thyme, half a bay leaf, a little fennel and a small piece of bitter orange rind.

Pour in 3½ cups (7 decilitres) of water; add 2 medium-size potatoes (300 grams), cut in thick slices, and start cooking on a good heat.

Put in a pinch of saffron and when the potatoes are three-quarters cooked, put the sardines on top. Cover the pot and leave to cook briskly for 8 to 10 minutes.

Drain the sardines and potatoes and set them on a dish. Sprinkle with chopped parsley.

Pour the broth in another round deep dish lined with a dozen rather thick slices of French bread. Sprinkle this, too, with chopped parsley.

Serve both dishes at the same time.

Sardine butter. BEURRE DE SARDINES—Pound 2½ ounces (75 grams) of fillets of sardines in oil. Add 6 tablespoons (100 grams) of butter. Rub through a cloth.

Used cold for hors-d'oeuvre, hot for canapés, fried hollow crusts and pastry cases.

Dartois of sardines. DARTOIS AUX SARDINES—Like *Dartois of anchovies*. See HORS-D'OEUVRE, *Hot hors-d'oeuvre*.

Fried sardines. SARDINES FRITES—Cooked like *Fried smelts*. See SMELT.

Grilled sardines. SARDINES GRILLÉES—Brush the fresh sardines with oil. Season them. Cook under the grill at not too great a heat. Serve with *Maître d'hôtel butter*. See BUTTER, *Compound butters*.

Sardines in oil. SARDINES À L'HUÎLE—Sardines are found marketed commercially in this form. They are served as hors-d'oeuvre.

Sardines in paper cases au gratin. SARDINES EN CAISSES AU GRATIN—Arrange the fresh sardines, stuffed and cooked in white wine (see *Sardines with white wine*, below) in paper cases (oiled and dried in the oven) garnished with a good tablespoon of thick *duxelles**.

Add one or two tablespoons of *duxelles* and a tablespoon of tomato sauce to the liquor in which the sardines were cooked and spoon some of this sauce over them.

Sprinkle with breadcrumbs and melted butter and brown lightly in the oven. Put chopped parsley on top and arrange the paper cases on a napkin-covered dish.

Sardines in paper cases à l'italienne. SARDINES EN CAISSES À L'ITALIENNE—Prepare and cook the fresh sardines like *Sardines with white wine*.

When they are cooked set each one in a little rectangular paper case (previously rubbed with oil and dried in the stove) garnished on the bottom with a good tablespoon of chopped mushrooms.

Sardines in paper cases à la portugaise. SARDINES EN CAISSES À LA PORTUGAISE—Like *Sardines in paper cases au gratin*, replacing the *duxelles* with *tomato fondue**.

This preparation can be made with oil in place of butter.

Sardines en papillotes—Take off the heads and remove the bones of some large fresh sardines. Brush with oil, season and grill lightly.

Wrap each in a sheet of paper prepared in the same

way as for *Mullet en papillotes*, covering the fish with very thick *duxelles**.

Put the *papillotes* briefly in a very hot oven and serve at once.

Sardines en paupiettes—Choose large fresh sardines, scale, clean out and wipe the fish and then fillet them.

Lay the fillets quite flat on the table, skin downwards, and using a forcing (pastry) bag, pipe on to each a thin line of quenelle *Fish forcemeat* (see FORCEMEAT) or very thick *duxelles**.

Roll up the fillets *en paupiettes**, and put them in rows in a buttered sauté dish; pour over a little white wine, mushroom juice or fish stock, and cook very gently, covered, for 8 minutes.

Serve with *White wine* or other sauce (see SAUCE), or finish off according to the particular recipe.

Sardines au plat—Put the sardines, seasoned with salt, on a fireproof dish which has been buttered and sprinkled with chopped shallot; pour over, for 12 sardines, 4 tablespoons of dry white wine and a little lemon juice. Dot with little pieces of butter. Cook in the oven at a good heat for 8 to 10 minutes. Sprinkle with parsley.

Salted sardines (preserved). SARDINES SALÉES—Proceed, using fresh sardines, as described in the recipe for *Preserved anchovies*. See ANCHOVY.

Sardines with spinach à la provençale. SARDINES AUX ÉPINARDS À LA PROVENÇALE—Open the fresh sardines, take out the bones. Coat with egg and breadcrumbs. Fry in butter. Arrange on some leaf spinach tossed in *Noisette butter* (see BUTTER, *Compound butters*) and seasoned with grated garlic.

Sardines with white wine (stuffed). SARDINES AU VIN BLANC—Scale, clean and empty 12 large fresh sardines. Take off the heads and open the fish lengthways down the belly to take out the backbone.

Set the opened sardines on the table and stuff each one with a small quantity of quenelle *Fish forcemeat* (see FORCEMEAT). Close the sardines again, pressing lightly to stick them together and set in a buttered baking dish. Season with salt and pepper. Pour over ½ cup (1 decilitre) of white wine; start cooking on the top of the stove, then finish cooking in the oven for 8 to 10 minutes.

Drain the sardines and arrange them on a long dish. Add the strained cooking liquor of the sardines to some *White wine sauce* (see SAUCE) and just before serving, pour a few tablespoons of the sauce over the sardines.

SARGASSO. SARGASSE—Name of a seaweed eaten in Spain in the form of a salad.

SATYRION—Orchid with a goat-like smell whose tubers contain an edible, floury substance analagous to salep.

SAUCE—By this word is understood in a general way every kind of liquid seasoning for food.

Classed as sauces in the French *cuisine* are many preparations quite different from each other, not only in their taste and appearance but in the way they are made; the juices of roasted meats, *Vinaigrette* and its derivatives, *Hollandaise*, *Mayonnaise*, *Béarnaise*, gravy thickened with flour, with *fécule* (like potato—or cornflour), with blood, etc.

Sauces from the repertory of French cookery are considered the best it is possible to make. 'Be assured,' said Carême in his *Cuisinier parisien*, 'that no foreign sauce is comparable to those of our great modern *cuisine* (Carême was speaking of cookery at the beginning of the nineteenth century). I have been able to make comparisons: I have seen England, Russia, Germany and Italy and I have met, everywhere, our cooks occupying the highest posts in foreign courts.

'I will add to *our* Espagnole and to *our* Allemande (we underline the possessive pronouns to emphasise that these sauces are entirely French in origin) Suprême sauce, Tarragon sauce, Ravigote sauce, Vert-pré sauce, Béchamel sauce, Financière sauce, Périgueux sauce, Tortue sauce, Matelote sauce, Champagne sauce, Sauce à la régence (Regency sauce), Sauce à la bourguignotte (which has become Bourguignonne sauce), Sturgeon sauce, Poivrade sauce, Chevreuil (roebuck) sauce, Aigre-doux (sweet-sour) sauce, Piquante sauce, Salmis sauce, Tomato sauce, Leveret sauce thickened with blood, Parisienne sauce, Robert sauce, Raifort (horseradish) sauce, Magnonaise sauce (Carême thus designated mayonnaise), Provençale sauce, Crayfish butter sauce, Lobster sauce, Shrimp sauce, Oyster sauce, Anchovy butter sauce, Cream sauce, Sauce à la pluche, Butter or Bâtarde sauce and Caper sauce.

'We have Gallicised Italian sauce, Venetian sauce, Hollandaise sauce, Russian sauce, Polish sauce, Portuguese sauce and Milanese sauce . . . .'

Such is the nomenclature of the sauces of the French school of cookery at the beginning of the nineteenth century. Today the French culinary repertory includes almost two hundred recipes for sauces, brown and white, hot and cold (not including variations). It is in this order that they will be described, beginning with the basic, or great sauces, brown and white, followed by compound sauces, brown and white. Cold sauces and dessert sauces will be found at the end of this section.

BASIC OR GREAT SAUCES. SAUCES MÈRES, GRANDES SAUCES—These are so called because they are used in the preparation of many other sauces.

BROWN BASIC SAUCES. SAUCES BRUNES—

Demi-glace sauce or rich brown sauce—Cook down by two-thirds 2½ cups (5 decilitres) of *Espagnole sauce* (see below) to which 4 cups (8 decilitres) of clear brown stock have been added. At the last moment remove from heat, add ¼ cup (½ decilitre) of Madeira. Strain through a cloth.

Note. A handful of mushroom skins may be added during cooking.

Espagnole sauce I (based on meat stock). SAUCE ESPAGNOLE (GRASSE)—For 2½ quarts (litres): 4 quarts (litres) of warm, light brown stock and ⅞ cup (300 grams) of brown *roux*. Mix and boil over a brisk heat.

Reduce the heat, add a *mirepoix* made up of 1 medium-large carrot (125 grams) and 1 medium-small onion (75 grams) cut in dice and fried lightly, with 4 strips (75 grams) of streaky (lean) bacon also cut in dice.

Put in this *mirepoix* a sprig of thyme and half a bay leaf, but before adding it to the *mirepoix* pour off the bacon fat, dilute the pan juices with ½ cup (1 decilitre) of white wine and add to the sauce.

Cook the *Espagnole* very gently for 2½ hours, skimming frequently.

Put through a fine strainer, pressing the vegetables well to extract their juice. Put back in a pot and add 3 to 4 cups (6 to 8 decilitres) of stock.

Cook for 2½ hours, skimming frequently.

Strain the sauce into a basin. Stir with a wooden spoon until it is cold.

The next day put the Espagnole back to cook again after having added to it a quart (litre) of stock and a pint (½ litre) of tomato purée.

Mix well, cook very slowly for an hour, skim often,

A brown sauce (*Robert Carrier*)

so as to obtain a brilliant textured sauce. Remove all grease, strain through a cloth. Use according to the instructions in the particular recipe.

Espagnole sauce II (based on fish stock). SAUCE ESPAGNOLE (MAIGRE)—For 2½ quarts (litres):

Proceed as for the ordinary *Espagnole*, replacing the meat stock with fish stock, and fry the *mirepoix** in butter instead of lard. Add 1 cup (150 grams) of mushroom skins.

Finish off as for the ordinary *Espagnole*.

Tomato sauce I (based on meat stock). SAUCE TOMATE (AU GRAS)—Apart from its use as accompaniment to a great number of dishes, tomato sauce is used as an auxiliary ingredient in numerous preparations. It adds the final touch to most brown sauces and ragoûts.

For 2½ quarts (litres):

Ingredients. Principal element: 2 quarts (litres) of purée of tomatoes, or 6 pounds (3 kilos) of pressed fresh tomatoes; *Nutritive bases:* 5 strips (rashers) (100 grams) of streaky (lean) bacon cut in dice and blanched, 5 ounces (150 grams) of knuckle of ham, blanched; *Aromatic bases:* 1 medium-large carrot (100 grams) cut in dice, 1 medium-size onion (100 grams) cut in dice, a *bouquet garni*, an unpeeled clove of garlic; *Auxiliary bases:* 3 tablespoons (50 grams) butter, ½ cup (75 grams) flour; *Seasoning:* 1½ teaspoons (10 grams) salt, 4 teaspoons (20 grams) sugar, a pinch of pepper; *Liquid:* 1 quart (litre) white stock.

Method. Cook the bacon lightly in butter in a heavy-bottomed pot. Put into the pot the vegetables cut in dice. Cook them until they are quite soft.

Sprinkle with flour. Cook together till the flour colours, but not too much.

Add the tomato purée (or the fresh tomatoes, pressed and cut in quarters).

Put in the tomato the clove of garlic, the *bouquet garni* and the ham knuckle.

Add the liquid; season.

Bring to the boil, stirring. Cover the pot. Cook in the oven at a low heat for 2 hours.

Take out the *bouquet garni*, the garlic and the knuckle of ham.

Strain the purée through a cloth, pressing it with a spatula, or put it through a fine strainer.

Pour into a basin and whisk to make the sauce as smooth as possible. Butter the surface to prevent a skin forming.

Keep in a very cool place. Use as instructed.

Tomato sauce II (meatless). SAUCE TOMATE (AU MAIGRE —Proceed as in the preceding recipe, leaving out the bacon and ham knuckle and using water instead of stock.

Tomato sauce III (Coulis de tomate). SAUCE TOMATE AU NATUREL, COULIS DE TOMATE—Cook gently in butter a *mirepoix** composed of 4 tablespoons (50 grams) of shredded carrots and 4 tablespoons (50 grams) of shredded onion.

Add 3 pounds (1 kilogram 500 grams) of fresh tomatoes, pressed and cut in quarters.

Season with salt, a little sugar and a pinch of pepper. Add a small *bouquet garni**.

Stir over a good heat to blend the ingredients. When the mixture comes to the boil, cover the pot and cook in a slow oven.

Put through a fine strainer.

Boil down over a strong heat until the sauce thickens to the right consistency.

Use according to instructions.

Note. Tomato sauce, and *coulis* of tomatoes, can be made with tinned tomato purée.

WHITE BASIC SAUCES. SAUCES BLANCHES:

Allemande sauce—This sauce is often wrongly included among 'basic' sauces. Allemande, which in spite of its name is entirely French in origin, is a compound sauce. See COMPOUND SAUCES.

Béchamel sauce. SAUCE BÉCHAMEL—In modern practice this sauce is prepared quite differently from the way it used to be made. Formerly *Béchamel* was a *Velouté sauce* with cream blended into it, whereas nowadays it is made by stirring boiling milk into a *roux* of butter and flour.

Béchamel sauce I (based on meat stock). SAUCE BÉCHAMEL (GRASSE)—For 2½ quarts (litres) stir 2¾ quarts (litres) of boiling milk into 1 cup (325 grams) of white roux made of butter and flour. Mix well. Add 5 ounces (150 grams) of lean veal cut into dice, cooked in butter without colouring with 4 tablespoons (50 grams) of chopped onion. Season, add a sprig of thyme, a fragment of bay leaf and a little grated nutmeg. Simmer very gently for 45 minutes to one hour. Strain through a cloth.

Béchamel sauce II (meatless). SAUCE BÉCHAMEL (MAIGRE)—As above, leaving out the veal.

Suprême sauce. SAUCE SUPRÊME—The same applies here as to *Allemande sauce*.

Suprême sauce is a combined sauce, the recipe for which will be found below, under COMPOUND SAUCES.

Velouté sauce. VELOUTÉ, SAUCE BLANCHE GRASSE—For 2½ quarts (litres): stir 2¾ quarts (litres) of white stock made with veal or chicken (see STOCK) into 1 cup (325 grams) of pale blond *roux* made with butter and flour.

Blend well together. Bring to the boil, stirring with a wooden spoon until the first bubbles appear. Cook the *Velouté* very slowly for an hour and a half, skimming frequently.

Strain through a cloth. Stir until it is completely cold.

Note. Velouté is a great basic sauce, and it may be prepared in advance. Obviously it may also be made just before it is used.

As the white stock which is used for making it is seasoned and flavoured, it is not necessary to add other flavourings to this sauce. An exception may be made for skins and trimmings of mushrooms which may be added when available, this addition making the sauce yet more delicate.

Velouté sauce II (based on chicken stock). VELOUTÉ DE VOLAILLE—Made like ordinary *Velouté sauce*, using white chicken stock to stir into the blond roux.

Velouté sauce III (based on fish stock). VELOUTÉ DE POISSON, DIT VELOUTÉ MAIGRE—Made like ordinary *Velouté sauce*, replacing the veal or chicken stock with fish stock.

COMPOUND BROWN SAUCES. SAUCES COMPOSÉES, BRUNES:

African sauce (for small cuts of meat, pot-roasted chicken). SAUCE AFRICAINE—Cook in oil till soft ½ cup (100 grams) of onions cut in small dice. Add to this onion when it is cooked, 2 tomatoes peeled, drained and cut in dice and 2 green peppers, peeled and also cut in dice. Season with salt, paprika, a small clove of grated garlic, and a *bouquet garni*, composed of parsley, thyme, bay leaf and a sprig of basil. Cook for 10 minutes. Pour in ½ cup (1 decilitre) of white wine. Cook down. Add 1 cup (2 decilitres) of concentrated and thickened brown veal gravy.

Cook for 15 minutes.

Aigre-douce sauce (for small cuts of meat, white giblets). SAUCE AIGRE-DOUCE—Caramelize lightly in a small saucepan 3 lumps of sugar moistened with 3 tablespoons of wine vinegar. Pour in $\frac{3}{4}$ cup ($1\frac{1}{2}$ decilitres) of white wine. Add a tablespoon of chopped shallots. Cook down. Pour in $1\frac{1}{4}$ cups ($2\frac{1}{2}$ decilitres) of *Demi-glace sauce*. Boil for a few moments. Strain through a fine sieve or a cloth. Boil, add 2 tablespoons of stoned raisins which have been soaked in cold water and a tablespoon of capers.

Alboni sauce (English cookery) (for venison). SAUCE ALBONI—Reduce by two-thirds $\frac{1}{2}$ cup (1 decilitre) of white wine to which a tablespoon of chopped shallot, a sprig of thyme, a piece of bay leaf, a sprig of parsley and a pinch of paprika have been added.

Pour in 1 cup (2 decilitres) of *Demi-glace sauce* (see above) and 3 to 4 tablespoons of concentrated game stock, add 10 crushed juniper berries. Boil for a few moments, strain through a cloth, add at the last moment a tablespoon of redcurrant jelly and a tablespoon of pine kernels browned in the oven.

Aniseed sauce (for roast venison). SAUCE À L'ANIS—Put into a pan 2 large lumps of sugar and 3 tablespoons of wine vinegar.

Cook to a caramel. Add to this $\frac{1}{2}$ cup (1 decilitre) of white wine and add a teaspoon of green anise. When it has boiled, strain it.

Boil down the white wine by two-thirds and add to it $1\frac{1}{2}$ cups (3 decilitres) of concentrated and thickened brown veal gravy. Boil for a few moments and strain through muslin.

Bigarade sauce I (Old recipe). SAUCE À LA BIGARADE—'Take off in strips from top to bottom the peel of a bitter orange; take care to cut it very thin so that there will be no bitter taste, which there will be if you leave a little of the white pith. Trim the edge of each strip so that they may then be cut evenly in fine shreds. All the peel being thus cut, throw it into a little boiling water. After boiling for a few minutes drain and put it in a saucepan with enough very smooth *Espagnole* to sauce an entrée, a little game glaze, a pinch of mignonette and the juice of half a bitter orange. After having brought it to the boil several times, add a piece of fine butter'. (A. Carême, *L'Art de la cuisine française au XIXe siècle.*)

Bigarade sauce II (for duck or duckling, roasted or pot-roasted). SAUCE BIGARADE—Dilute the thick juices in the roasting pan with a stock prepared in the following way: cook to a pale caramel in a pan 4 teaspoons (20 grams) of sugar soaked in a tablespoon of wine vinegar. When the sugar begins to change colour, pour in 1 cup (2 decilitres) of brown veal gravy. Pour this mixture into the roasting pan and blend with the juices.

Cook this mixture for 5 minutes over a strong heat. At the last moment add the juice of an orange and a squeeze of lemon juice and strain through a cloth. Add 2 tablespoons of orange peel cut in a fine *julienne* (thin strips), blanched, cooled in cold water and drained.

Note. Ducks and ducklings *à la bigarade* are garnished with quarters of peeled and seeded oranges. They are surrounded with a border of half slices of oranges, cut with fluted-edged cutters.

Bigarade sauce can be flavoured with a very small quantity of curaçao added at the last moment.

One-third lemon peel cut in a fine *julienne* is sometimes added to the *julienne* of orange peel.

Bigarade sauce III. SAUCE BIGARADE—When the duck is cooked, dilute the thick juices in the roasting pan with a glass of white wine. Boil down. Pour in $\frac{3}{4}$ cup ($1\frac{1}{2}$ decilitres) of white stock or consommé. Boil for 5 minutes. Thicken with a teaspoon of potato flour or arrowroot blended with cold water. Add the juice of an orange and a squeeze of lemon juice. Strain and finish with a *julienne* (thin strips) of orange peel.

Bigarade sauce IV. SAUCE BIGARADE—Dilute the thick pan juices with $\frac{1}{2}$ cup (1 decilitre) of Madeira or port.

Pour in 1 cup (2 decilitres) of brown veal gravy. Boil down by one-third, thicken with a teaspoon of arrowroot or corn starch mixed with a few drops of wine vinegar and bring to the boil.

Add the juice of an orange and a squeeze of lemon juice, strain through muslin and finish off with orange peel cut in a fine *julienne* (thin strips).

Bigarade sauce V. SAUCE BIGARADE—Remove all grease, strain the braising juices of duck and boil down to the desired consistency.

Add the juice of an orange and a squeeze of lemon juice, strain through muslin and finish off with orange peel cut in a fine *julienne* (thin strips).

Bonnefoy sauce (for meat and grilled fish). SAUCE BONNEFOY—Proceed as for *Bordelaise sauce I* but use white wine.

This sauce can also be made with finely chopped shallot and used unstrained.

Bordelaise sauce I (for grilled meat). SAUCE BORDELAISE—Boil down by two-thirds 1 cup (2 decilitres) of red wine with a tablespoon of chopped shallot, a sprig of thyme, a piece of bay leaf and a pinch of salt.

Pour in 1 cup (2 decilitres) of *Demi-glace sauce* (see above). Boil down by one-third, remove from heat, add 2 tablespoons (25 grams) of butter and strain through a cloth.

Add at the last moment 2 ounces (25 grams) of beef marrow cut in dice, poached and drained, and 2 teaspoons of chopped parsley.

Note. Grilled meats served with *Bordelaise sauce* are usually garnished with round slices of beef marrow, poached and drained.

Bordelaise sauce II. SAUCE BORDELAISE—Prepare some concentrated red wine as in the preceding recipe, but cook it down only by half. Thicken with $2\frac{1}{2}$ tablespoons (40 grams) of *Kneaded butter* (see BUTTER, *Compound butters*). Boil for a few moments. Add meat glaze or meat extract equal in bulk to a walnut. Finish as in the preceding recipe.

Bordelaise sauce III (Old recipe). SAUCE À LA BORDELAISE—'Put in a saucepan 2 cloves of garlic, a pinch of tarragon leaves, the seeded flesh of a lemon, a little bay leaf and 2 cloves, a glass of Sauternes and 2 teaspoons of Aix oil (Provence olive oil), simmer all together over a low heat. Skim off all fat from this seasoning, add enough very smooth Espagnole to sauce an entrée, and 3 to 4 tablespoons of light veal stock. Boil down, add half a glass of Sauternes, still simmering. When the sauce reaches the right consistency, strain through a cloth. Just before serving, add a little butter and the juice of half a lemon'. (A. Carême, *L'Art de la cuisine française au XIXe siècle.*)

Bourguignonne sauce—See *Burgundy sauce*, below.

Bread sauce (Old recipe). SAUCE À LA MIE DE PAIN À L'ANCIENNE—'Chop a clove of garlic, a shallot and some parsley, put them in a saucepan with half a glass (cup) of white wine, cook down, then mix in 2 to 3 tablespoons of very fine breadcrumbs, a little good butter, a pinch of mignonette and grated nutmeg, 2 tablespoons of good consommé and 4 tablespoons of light veal stock. Boil down by half and add the juice of a lemon'. (A. Carême, *L'Art de la cuisine française au XIXe siècle.*)

Fried bread sauce (English cookery) (for small roasted birds). SAUCE AU PAIN FRIT—Put into 1¼ cups (2½ decilitres) of consommé 4 tablespoons (25 grams) of lean ham cut in very small dice and a tablespoon of finely chopped shallot. Bring to the boil; allow to simmer for 10 minutes.

At the last moment finish off with 1 cup (50 grams) of breadcrumbs fried in butter and a pinch of chopped parsley; heighten the seasoning with a few drops of lemon juice.

Breton or bretonne sauce I. SAUCE À LA BRETONNE—'Cut 6 large onions in rings, colour them in clarified butter. Drain them on a horsehair sieve, mix with two tablespoons of consommé and two good tablespoons of well beaten *Espagnole sauce*. Add a little sugar, a little butter and a little chicken glaze, then strain this sauce, pressing it through a fine cloth'. (A. Carême, *L'Art de la cuisine française au XIXe siècle.*)

Breton sauce II (to bind flageolet and haricot beans). SAUCE BRETONNE—See FONDUE, *Onion fondue.*

Brown gravy (English cookery) (for roast veal). SAUCE AU JUS COLORÉ—Add to 1 cup (2 decilitres) of *Butter sauce II*, ½ cup (1 decilitre) of good strong juices from the roast. Finish off with a few drops of Harvey sauce or Worcestershire sauce and ketchup.

Burgundy or Bourguignonne sauce or red wine sauce I (for eggs, meat, poultry). SAUCE BOURGUIGNONNE, SAUCE AU VIN ROUGE—Cook in butter 2 tablespoons of chopped onion.

Stir in 2½ cups (5 decilitres) of red wine, season, add a *bouquet garni** and cook down by two-thirds.

Add 1½ cups (3 decilitres) of *Espagnole sauce*, cook down by half and strain through a cloth.

Just before serving, add 3 tablespoons (50 grams) of butter.

Note. Bourguignonne sauce intended to accompany a piece of sautéed meat or poultry must be made in the sauté pan in which this was cooked. In this case the onion, previously cooked in butter till soft, is put into the sauté pan at the same time as the wine with which the thick, sticky pan juices are diluted. This onion may also be put to cook at the same time as the meat or bird.

Like all red wine sauces, *Bourguignonne sauce* may have a handful of mushroom skins added to it during cooking.

Burgundy or Bourguignonne sauce II (for poached eggs). SAUCE BOURGUIGNONNE—Boil down by a half a quart (litre) of red wine to which has been added a tablespoon of chopped shallots, a small *bouquet garni**, a pinch of salt and a little freshly ground pepper.

Thicken with 2½ tablespoons (40 grams) of *Kneaded butter* (see BUTTER, *Compound butters*). Simmer for a few moments, at the last moment add 3 tablespoons (50 grams) of butter.

Burgundy or Bourguignonne sauce III (for fish). SAUCE BOURGUIGNONNE—Prepare a fish *fumet** with a quart (litre) of red wine, bones and trimmings from the fish that is being prepared, a medium-sized chopped onion, a small *bouquet garni** and a handful of mushroom skins; season.

Strain the *fumet* through a fine strainer, boil down by half and finish with *Kneaded butter* (see BUTTER, *Compound butters*) as in the preceding recipe.

Note. If the fish *Bourguignonne sauce* is intended for is braised, keep ½ cup (1 decilitre) of red wine *fumet* to cook it in. This *fumet*, after the fish has been cooked, can be added to the sauce.

Burgundy or Bourguignotte sauce (old recipe) (for freshwater fish). SAUCE À LA BOURGUIGNOTTE—'Clean a medium-sized eel, cut it in chunks and put it in a saucepan with 2 onions, ½ pound (2 punnets) of chopped mushrooms, 2 cloves of garlic, 2 shallots, a *bouquet garni**, a pinch of powdered pepper, a pinch of *four spices**, 4 washed anchovies and half a bottle of Volnay. Cook down a little on a low heat, then strain this essence through a cloth, using pressure. Next add 3 to 4 tablespoons of well mixed *Espagnole sauce*, and ½ pound (2 punnets) of peeled mushrooms, with their stalks. Cook over a strong heat in the usual way, then pour in another glass of Volnay. When the sauce is cooked down to the right consistency, put it into a *bain-marie* (double boiler). At the moment of serving add some crayfish butter, 30 crayfish tails, and the same number of nice white little mushrooms.' (A. Carême, *L'Art de la cuisine française au XIXe siècle.*)

Chambertin sauce. SAUCE AU CHAMBERTIN—See *Burgundy sauce*. Use Chambertin to make the sauce.

Chambord sauce. SAUCE CHAMBORD—This sauce is simply a Genevoise sauce prepared with the cooking liquor of the fish used, and using red wine. See CARP, *Carp Chambord.*

Chapelure sauce (Bread sauce) (Old recipe). SAUCE À LA CHAPELURE—'Chop 2 shallots, cut up finely a little lean ham, put in a saucepan with 2 to 3 tablespoons of light veal stock and a pinch of mignonette, simmer over a low heat. When the sauce is cooked down, remove the ham and add 2 tablespoons of very fine breadcrumbs, a little fresh butter, 2 tablespoons of good consommé and the juice of a lemon. Boil for a few minutes and serve.' (A. Carême, *L'Art de la cuisine française au XIXe siècle.*)

Charcutière sauce I (for cuts of grilled or sautéed pork). SAUCE CHARCUTIÈRE—Cook till soft with a tablespoon of lard (or butter), 2 tablespoons of finely chopped onion; stir in 1 cup (2 decilitres) of *Demi-glace sauce.* Allow to boil for a few moments.

Add at the last moment 2 tablespoons of gherkins cut in a *julienne* (thin strips) or in dice.

The sauce may be strained before adding the gherkins.

Charcutière sauce II. SAUCE CHARCUTIÈRE—Proceed as above, but diluting the thick pan juices with a tablespoon of wine vinegar before adding the *Demi-glace sauce.* Finish with the gherkins.

Charcutière sauce III. SAUCE CHARCUTIÈRE—Dilute the cooked onion with a tablespoon of white wine, stir in *Demi-glace sauce* and add the gherkins and a teaspoon of mustard.

Charcutière sauce IV. SAUCE CHARCUTIÈRE—Sprinkle the cooked onion with a tablespoon of flour. Cook till golden. Dilute with a little wine or wine vinegar; stir in white stock (or water with the addition of meat glaze or meat extract). Boil for a few moments; finish as above.

Chasseur or Hunter sauce I (for small cuts of meat and sautéed fowl). SAUCE CHASSEUR—Sauté in butter ¼ pound (100 grams) of chopped mushrooms, season with salt and when they are three-quarters cooked add a tablespoon of finely chopped shallot.

Dilute with ½ cup (1 decilitre) of white wine, boil down by half, stir in ¾ cup (1½ decilitres) of *Demi-glace sauce* and ½ cup (1 decilitre) of *Tomato sauce.* Boil for a few moments. At the last moment add 2 tablespoons (30 grams) of butter and a tablespoon of chopped parsley, chervil and tarragon.

The mushrooms may also be sautéed in a mixture of butter and oil.

Chasseur or Hunter sauce II. SAUCE CHASSEUR—Chop the mushrooms, toss in butter with the chopped shallots and remove from sauté pan.

Put into the cooking butter a tablespoon of flour, cook gently till golden, dilute with ½ cup (1 decilitre) of white wine, then stir in 1 cup (2 decilitres) of consommé or white stock (or water with the addition of a little meat glaze) and a teaspoon of tomato purée.

Boil down, put back the mushrooms in the sauce and finish off as above.

Chateaubriand sauce I (for grilled meat). SAUCE CHATEAUBRIAND—Cook down by two-thirds ½ cup (1 decilitre) of white wine with a tablespoon of chopped shallot.

Add ¾ cup (1½ decilitres) of *Demi-glace sauce;* cook down by half.

Add, away from the fire, 6 tablespoons (100 grams) of fresh butter and a tablespoon of chopped tarragon. Season with a little cayenne and a few drops of lemon juice.

Mix well; do not strain.

Note. This sauce used to be always served with grilled *Chateaubriand steak.* Today this is usually served with *Béarnaise sauce.*

Chateaubriand sauce II. SAUCE CHATEAUBRIAND—Heat 2 tablespoons of meat glaze (or extract), mixed with a tablespoon of white stock (or water). Add 8 tablespoons (¼ pound) (125 grams) of fresh butter divided into tiny fragments, a tablespoon of chopped parsley and a few drops of lemon juice. Season with a little cayenne. Mix well.

Chaud-froid sauce, brown (for various meats). SAUCE CHAUD-FROID BRUNE—For 2½ cups (5 decilitres): put in a thick-bottomed saucepan 1¾ cups (3½ decilitres) of *Demi-glace sauce* and 1 cup (2 decilitres) of clear brown stock.

Boil down over a strong heat, stirring with a wooden spoon and adding, a little at a time, 2 cups (4 decilitres) of meat jelly.

Boil down until the sauce has the right consistency. Chill a small quantity of the sauce on ice; if it is not firm enough add a few tablespoons of jelly and cook down.

Remove from heat, add 2 tablespoons of Madeira, port, sherry or any other wine indicated in the recipe and strain. Stir the sauce until it is quite cold.

Note. To obtain a perfect coating the sauce must be poured over the meat when cold but not set.

Chaud-froid sauce, chicken. SAUCE CHAUD-FROID POUR VOLAILLES—Proceed as for the ordinary *Chaud-froid sauce*, replacing brown stock by chicken stock.

Flavour this stock with Madeira or other wine, or, according to its final use, with a few spoonfuls of *Truffle essence.* See ESSENCE.

Chaud-froid sauce, fish. SAUCE CHAUD-FROID POUR POISSON—Proceed as for ordinary *Chaud-froid sauce*, using *Espagnole sauce* based on fish stock, well skimmed, and replacing the brown stock by fish stock.

Chaud-froid sauce, game flavoured. SAUCE CHAUD-FROID, À L'ESSENCE DE GIBIER—Proceed as in the recipe for ordinary *Chaud-froid sauce*, replacing the brown stock by ½ cup (a decilitre) of game essence or *fumet** (previously prepared with the carcases and trimmings of the game being used).

Flavour the sauce with Madeira or other similar wine.

Note. For certain game, notably for thrushes, add to this sauce a few drops of cognac or Hollands gin.

Chaud-froid sauce with orange (for duck and duckling). SAUCE CHAUD-FROID À L'ORANGE—Proceed as for *Chaud-froid sauce I*, replacing the brown duck by ¾ cup (1½ decilitres) of duck *fumet** (previously prepared using the carcases and trimmings of the duck).

Concentrate this sauce more than usual so that it will not be made too thin by the addition of the orange juice.

Strain the sauce, add to it the juice of an orange, also strained, and 2 tablespoons of orange peel cut in a fine *julienne* (thin strips), blanched, cooled in cold water and drained.

Note. This sauce can also be used to coat various kinds of game. In this case the duck *fumet* is replaced by that of the game being used.

Chaud-froid sauce with tomatoes. SAUCE CHAUD-FROID À LA TOMATE—Boil down by one-third 2½ cups (5 decilitres) of tomato pulp to which 1¾ cups (3½ decilitres) of meat jelly have been added.

Strain, stir until completely cold.

Chaud-froid sauce with truffle essence. SAUCE CHAUD-FROID À L'ESSENCE DE TRUFFES—Prepare game flavoured *Chaud-froid sauce* with ½ cup (1 decilitre) of *Truffle essence.* See ESSENCE.

Chaud-froid sauce à la niçoise. SAUCE CHAUD-FROID À LA NIÇOISE—Proceed as for *Fish chaud-froid sauce.* Add to the sauce, finished and strained, a few drops of anchovy essence and a tablespoon of chopped tarragon.

Dried cherry sauce (Old recipe) (for venison). SAUCE AUX CERISES SÈCHES—'Peel and wash half a pound of dried cherries, pound them in a mortar and boil them in a saucepan with 2 tablespoons of sugar, 2 glasses of good Burgundy, quarter of a glass of wine vinegar, a pinch of coriander and a little lemon peel. After having simmered this seasoning for 20 to 25 minutes, mix with it 2 tablespoons of *Espagnole sauce* and the juice of a lemon. Reduce the sauce, stirring all the time over a strong heat, and then strain it through a cloth, using pressure.' (A. Carême, *L'Art de la cuisine française au XIXe siècle.*)

Colbert sauce (for grilled fish and meat and for vegetables). SAUCE COLBERT—Bring to the boil 3 to 4 tablespoons of meat glaze diluted with a tablespoon of white stock (or water).

Remove from heat and incorporate ¼ pound (125 grams) of butter, previously softened.

Season and add a little grated nutmeg and a pinch of cayenne. Add, stirring all the time, the juice of half a lemon, a tablespoon of chopped parsley and a tablespoon of Madeira.

Cranberry sauce (Anglo-American cookery) (for roast fowl, particularly turkey). SAUCE AUX AIRELLES—Put into a saucepan ½ pound (250 grams) of cranberries with 2½ cups (5 decilitres) of water. Cover the pan and cook them, for a few minutes, until the berries split, drain and rub through a fine sieve.

Put the purée in a saucepan, dilute with a few tablespoons of the cooking juice to make a thick sauce. Sweeten lightly. Heat thoroughly. Chill before serving.

Note. This sauce can be bought ready made, so that it can be served even when the fruit is out of season.

Diable or Devilled sauce I (for grilled chicken, etc.). SAUCE À LA DIABLE—Boil down by two-thirds ¾ cup (1½ decilitres) of white wine and a tablespoon of vinegar with a tablespoon of chopped shallot, a sprig of thyme, a quarter of a bay leaf and a good pinch of freshly ground pepper. Stir in 1 cup (2 decilitres) of *Demi-glace sauce.* Allow to boil for a few moments and strain.

Add at the last moment a teaspoon of chopped parsley and season with cayenne pepper.

Note. The wine can be boiled down with vinegar alone.

Devilled sauce can be served without being strained.

A small quantity of fresh butter may also be added, but be sure to remove the saucepan from heat before doing so.

Diable or Devilled sauce II. SAUCE À LA DIABLE—Prepare the wine and herbs as above. Pour in stock (or water to which meat glaze or extract has been added). Thicken with *Kneaded butter* (see BUTTER, *Compound butters*). Finish off as above.

Diable or Devilled sauce III (English cookery) (for grilled chicken, etc.). SAUCE À LA DIABLE—Boil down by half $\frac{3}{4}$ cup ($1\frac{1}{2}$ decilitres) of wine vinegar to which a tablespoon of chopped shallot has been added.

Stir in $1\frac{1}{4}$ cups ($2\frac{1}{2}$ decilitres) of *Espagnole sauce* and two tablespoons of tomato purée. Cook for 5 minutes. At the last moment add a tablespoon of Worcester sauce and a tablespoon of Harvey sauce, heighten the seasoning with a little cayenne and strain through a cloth.

Duxelles sauce (for eggs, small cuts of meat, fish, chicken). SAUCE DUXELLES—Stir in $\frac{1}{2}$ cup (1 decilitre) of white wine to dilute 2 tablespoons of chopped mushrooms prepared as *duxelles**. Cook down, stir in $\frac{3}{4}$ cup ($1\frac{1}{2}$ decilitres) of *Demi-glace sauce* and $\frac{1}{2}$ cup (1 decilitre) of tomato purée (see *Tomato sauce*, above). Boil for a few moments. At the last moment add a tablespoon of chopped parsley.

Note. In times past this sauce was known as *Sauce aux fines herbes.*

Espagnole demi-glace—This is a rich sauce, used as a basis for many other lesser sauces. After adding a specified quantity of clear stock (white or brown) to the basic stock and boiling it down methodically, the brown sauce becomes very thick—almost jellied. This can then be used in the preparation of a great number of different brown sauces.

In modern cookery, although *Espagnole demi-glace* is still used, it is often replaced by stock or brown veal gravy, brought to the right consistency by simply boiling it down or by thickening it quickly with potato flour or arrowroot. This latter method gives a very good result.

Financière sauce I (for sweetbreads, fowl, timbales, vol-au-vent, etc.). SAUCE FINANCIÈRE—Add to 1 cup (2 decilitres) of *Madeira sauce*, as it cooks, $\frac{1}{2}$ cup (1 decilitre) of truffle essence and strain.

Note. This sauce is rarely used by itself. Its most important function is to bind the *Financière garnish.* See GARNISHES.

Financière sauce II (Old recipe). SAUCE FINANCIÈRE—'Put into a saucepan some shredded lean ham, a pinch of mignonette, a little thyme and bay leaf, some mushroom and truffle trimmings and 2 glasses of dry Madeira. Cook down over a low heat and add 2 tablespoons of consommé and 2 tablespoons of well beaten *Espagnole sauce.* When this sauce is cooked down by half, strain it, then put it back on the fire, mixing in half a glass of Madeira. Boil down to the desired point and serve the sauce in a *bain-marie* (double boiler).

Note. When this sauce is intended for a game entrée, the chicken consommé is replaced by an appropriate game *fumet**. Add a little butter just before serving.' (A. Carême, *L'Art de la cuisine française au XIXe siècle.*)

Fines herbes sauce I (for small cuts of meat). SAUCE AUX FINES HERBES—Add 2 tablespoons of chopped parsley, chervil and tarragon to $\frac{3}{4}$ cup ($1\frac{1}{2}$ decilitres) of strained *Demi-glace sauce* or concentrated brown gravy. Add a few drops of lemon juice.

Fines herbes sauce II. SAUCE AUX FINES HERBES—Boil down $\frac{1}{2}$ cup (1 decilitre) of white wine with a handful of parsley, chervil and tarragon leaves. Add 1 cup (2 decilitres) of *Demi-glace sauce.* Finish off as for *Tarragon sauce.*

Fines herbes sauce III. SAUCE AUX FINES HERBES—Toss in butter a tablespoon of chopped shallot. Add $\frac{1}{2}$ cup (1 decilitre) of white wine, boil down and add 1 cup (2 decilitres) of stock. Thicken with $2\frac{1}{2}$ tablespoons (40 grams) of *Kneaded butter* (see BUTTER, *Compound butters*). Allow to boil for a few moments, strain; add, at the last moment, a tablespoon of chopped parsley, chervil and tarragon and a few drops of lemon juice.

Note. Formerly this *Fines herbes sauce* was made like the *Duxelles sauce* for which the recipe is given above.

Genevoise sauce (for fish, chiefly trout and salmon). SAUCE GENEVOISE—Cook gently in butter a *mirepoix** consisting of 2 tablespoons (50 grams) of diced carrot, 2 tablespoons (50 grams) of diced onion, a stick of celery, a sprig of thyme, a piece of bay leaf and 10 parsley sprigs.

Put into this *mirepoix* 1 pound (500 grams) of salmon head cut in small pieces (or an equal quantity of bones and trimmings of other fish).

Cook slowly with a lid on for 15 minutes.

Pour off the cooking butter (butter augmented with the oil from frying the salmon). Add to it 3 cups (6 decilitres) of good red wine and cook down by half.

Add $1\frac{1}{2}$ cups (3 decilitres) of *Espagnole sauce II based on fish stock.* Bring to the boil, skim and simmer over a low heat for an hour, skimming frequently and adding extra fish *fumet**, if necessary.

Strain the sauce through a fine strainer, pressing the ingredients to preserve as much of the flavour as possible. Remove all grease, put the sauce into a saucepan, dilute with a few tablespoons of fish *fumet* made with red wine and cook down by one-third to one-half according to the desired consistency.

Strain the sauce, remove from heat and incorporate 4 to 5 tablespoons (60 to 80 grams) of fresh butter and a teaspoon of anchovy essence.

Note. The delicate flavour of this sauce will be improved by adding, in the course of the cooking, a handful of mushroom skins.

When the fish it accompanies has been braised (with red wine) all or part of the braising liquor must be added to the sauce.

To obtain a brown and brilliant Genevoise sauce it is important that it should be stirred not with a whisk but with a wooden spoon when the butter is incorporated. This applies to all brown sauces with butter.

Note. This sauce was formerly known as *Génoise.* The recipe for this sauce follows below.

Génoise sauce with Bordeaux wine (Old recipe). SAUCE GÉNOISE AU VIN DE BORDEAUX—'Pour into a saucepan 2 glasses (cups) of red Bordeaux wine, add 2 to 3 tablespoons of herbs, composed of mushrooms, truffles, parsley and 2 shallots, all blanched and chopped, a pinch of *four-spices** (quatre-épices) and a pinch of finely ground pepper. Boil down almost completely, add 2 tablespoons of consommé, 3 to 4 tablespoons of *Espagnole sauce* and a glass of Bordeaux wine. Cook down to the desired consistency and transfer the sauce to a *bain-marie* (double boiler). At the moment of serving, blend in a little Isigny butter.' (A. Carême, *L'Art de la cuisine française au XIXe siècle.*)

Gooseberry sauce (English cookery). SAUCE AUX GROSEILLES—Put in a copper pan 2 cups ($\frac{1}{2}$ litre) of green gooseberries, topped and tailed, with $\frac{1}{4}$ cup ($\frac{1}{2}$ decilitre) of water and 5 tablespoons (75 grams) of sugar.

Cook and rub through a fine strainer.

Grand veneur sauce I (for venison). SAUCE GRAND VENEUR—Add to 1 cup (2 decilitres) of concentrated and strained *Pepper or Poivrade sauce II* (see below) 1 tablespoon of gooseberry jelly. Mix.

Grand veneur sauce II. SAUCE GRAND VENEUR—Finish

off *Pepper or Poivrade sauce II* (see below) with gooseberry jelly and 3 to 4 tablespoons of cream. Mix.

Grand veneur sauce III. SAUCE GRAND VENEUR—Add to *Pepper or Poivrade sauce II* (see below) a few tablespoons of hare's blood diluted with a little of the marinade of the game being used.

Hachée sauce I (for minced meat and other dishes made with left-overs). SAUCE HACHÉE—Cook with a tablespoon of butter, 2 tablespoons of chopped onion. When it is three-quarters cooked, add half a tablespoon of chopped shallot.

Stir in ½ cup (1 decilitre) of wine vinegar, boil down and add ¾ cup (1½ decilitres) of *Demi-glace sauce* (see above) and ½ cup (1 decilitre) of tomato purée. Simmer for a few moments. At the last moment add 1 tablespoon of chopped lean ham, 1 tablespoon of dry *duxelles**, a tablespoon of chopped capers and gherkins and a tablespoon of chopped parsley.

Hachée sauce II (Old recipe). SAUCE HACHÉE—'Pour into a saucepan 4 tablespoons of vinegar, add 2 tablespoons of chopped mushrooms, half this quantity of parsley, 2 chopped shallots, a little garlic, a fragment of thyme and bay leaf, 2 cloves, a good pinch of white pepper and a little grated nutmeg. Cook this seasoning over low heat; take out the bay leaf, thyme and cloves and add 4 tablespoons of consommé and ½ cup of *Espagnole sauce*. Cook down to the desired point and transfer it to a *bain-marie** (double boiler). At the moment of serving mix in a little anchovy butter, 2 small gherkins chopped very finely and some capers,' (A. Carême, *L'Art de la cuisine française au XIXe siècle*.)

Herb sauce (English cookery) (for boiled fish and joints). SAUCE AUX AROMATES—Put in a saucepan a chopped shallot, a sprig of thyme, a pinch of chives, a pinch of savory, a pinch of marjoram, a good pinch of sage, a good pinch of basil, 4 peppercorns and a little grated nutmeg.

Pour over these ingredients 1¼ cups (2½ decilitres) of boiling consommé. Cover the casserole and allow to infuse for 10 minutes. Strain through a fine strainer. Stir this infusion into a blond *roux* prepared in a saucepan with 2 tablespoons (25 grams) of butter and 2 tablespoons (30 grams) of flour. Mix, simmer for a few moments, strain and finish with a tablespoon of chopped, blanched chervil and tarragon and a squeeze of lemon juice.

Hunter sauce—See *Chasseur sauce*.

Italian sauce I (for small cuts of meat, fowl). SAUCE ITALIENNE—Prepare 1 cup (2 decilitres) of *Duxelles sauce* and add to it at the last moment a tablespoon of lean cooked ham in very small dice or chopped, and a tablespoon of chopped parsley, chervil and tarragon.

Italian sauce II (for grilled fish). SAUCE ITALIENNE—Proceed as in the foregoing recipe, but using *Espagnole sauce* based on fish stock to add to the *duxelles** and leaving out the ham.

Lyonnaise sauce I (for small cuts of meat, chiefly for left-overs). SAUCE LYONNAISE—Cook 3 tablespoons of finely chopped onion in a tablespoon of butter.

Moisten with ¼ cup (½ decilitre) of wine vinegar and an equal quantity of white wine. Boil down and add 1 cup (2 decilitres) of *Demi-glace sauce*. Cook at boiling point for a few moments.

According to the recipe, strain or serve as it is.

Note. A small quantity of tomato purée may be added.

Lyonnaise sauce II. SAUCE LYONNAISE—Cook the onion in butter. Sprinkle with a tablespoon of flour. Allow to colour lightly. Stir in wine vinegar and white wine, then stock. Finish off as above.

Madeira sauce I (for small cuts of meat). SAUCE AU MADÈRE—Add to 1 cup (2 decilitres) of concentrated *Demi-glace sauce* 3 tablespoons of Madeira.

Madeira sauce II. SAUCE AU MADÈRE—Sauté in butter the piece of meat being used. After having taken it out of the pot, dilute the cooking juices with a tablespoon of Madeira, then add 1 cup (2 decilitres) of stock (or water to which a little meat glaze or extract has been added). Bring to the boil. Thicken with 3 tablespoons (40 grams) of *Kneaded butter* (see BUTTER, *Compound butters*). Finish with 2 tablespoons of Madeira and strain.

Marrow sauce (for grilled meat, vegetables, poached eggs). SAUCE À LA MOELLE—Like *Bordelaise sauce*, but replacing the red wine with white wine.

Marrow sauce II (for grilled fish). SAUCE À LA MOELLE—Boil down ½ cup (1 decilitre) of white wine with a good tablespoon of chopped shallot. Season with salt and a little freshly ground pepper.

Add 2 tablespoons of concentrated and thickened brown stock or a tablespoon of meat glaze or meat extract; mix.

Incorporate, away from the heat, 6 tablespoons (100 grams) of butter divided up into tiny pieces and 2 ounces (50 grams) of marrow cut into small dice, blanched and drained.

Add a few drops of lemon juice and a tablespoon of chopped parsley.

Note. This sauce, a variant of *Bercy sauce*, is poured directly on the grilled fish.

Matelote sauce (for eel and freshwater fish). SAUCE MATELOTE—See *Red wine sauce*.

Mushroom sauce I (for small cuts of meat; sautéed poultry). SAUCE AUX CHAMPIGNONS—Sauté in butter ¼ pound (100 grams) of peeled mushroom caps (or large sliced mushrooms). Season them, pour in 1 cup (2 decilitres) of *Demi-glace sauce* finished off with a tablespoon of Madeira and simmer over a gentle heat, without allowing to boil.

If fresh mushrooms are not available, tinned (canned) mushrooms can be used.

Mushroom sauce II. SAUCE AUX CHAMPIGNONS—Sauté the mushrooms in butter. Take them out of the sauté pan. Put in the cooking butter a scant tablespoon of flour. Cook till pale golden colour.

Stir in 1½ cups (3 decilitres) of white stock or consommé and cook down by one-third. Put the mushrooms back in the sauce, heat without boiling and at the last moment add a tablespoon of Madeira.

Mustard sauce (for grilled meat, particularly for pig's trotters St. Menehould). SAUCE MOUTARDE—Cook gently in butter 4 tablespoons (50 grams) of finely chopped onion, season with salt, pepper, a pinch of thyme and powdered bay leaf.

Stir in ¾ cup (1½ decilitres) of white wine, boil down, add ¾ cup (1½ decilitres) of *Demi-glace sauce*. Boil down by one-third.

At the last moment incorporate a good teaspoon of Dijon mustard, a teaspoon of butter and a squeeze of lemon juice.

Strain the sauce or use it as it is, as desired.

Napolitaine sauce (Old recipe) (for game and venison). SAUCE À LA NAPOLITAINE—'Put in a saucepan a tablespoon of grated horseradish, a little chopped lean ham, a seasoned *bouquet garni*, a little mignonette and grated nutmeg and a glass of dry *Madeira*. Cook down over a very low heat, take out the *bouquet*, add 2 tablespoons of consommé and 4 tablespoons of *Espagnole sauce*. When the sauce is cooked down, strain it through a cloth and cook down again, mixing in, little by little, a glass of

Malaga and quarter of a pot of redcurrant jelly. At the moment of serving add a little butter and game glaze.

Note. To serve with entrées of braised fillets of beef and roasts served *à la napolitaine*, add some sultanas, picked over and washed, to the sauce. A little candied citron cut in small dice and blanched may also be added.' (A. Carême, *L'Art de la cuisine française au XIXᵉ siècle.*)

Noisette sauce. SAUCE NOISETTE—*Hollandaise sauce* with *Noisette butter* added. See BUTTER, *Compound butters.*

Orange sauce (for duck and teal, spit or oven roasted). SAUCE À L'ORANGE—After cooking the duck, dilute the cooking juices in the pan (the grease having previously been removed) with a glass of white wine. Boil down, add 1 cup (2 decilitres) of concentrated and thickened brown stock. Simmer for a few moments and add the juice of an orange.

Strain through muslin and add 2 tablespoons of orange peel cut in a fine *julienne* (thin strips), blanched and drained.

Oyster sauce or Brown oyster sauce (English cookery) (for grilled meat, meat pudding, grilled cod). SAUCE AUX HUÎTRES—Stir into a brown *roux* composed of 1½ tablespoons (20 grams) of butter and 2 tablespoons (15 grams) of flour, ½ cup (1 decilitre) of the liquor in which oysters were cooked and 1 cup (2 decilitres) of light brown stock.

Season very lightly, bring to the boil and cook for 10 minutes.

Strain, add 12 poached, de-bearded and sliced oysters, heighten the seasoning with a pinch of cayenne.

Pepper or Poivrade sauce I (for meat). SAUCE POIVRADE —Cook gently in butter ½ cup (1 decilitre) of vegetable *mirepoix**. When the vegetables are soft, moisten them with ¼ cup (½ decilitre) of wine vinegar and the same amount of white wine. Boil down by half.

Stir in 1 cup (2 decilitres) of *Espagnole sauce* (see above) and 1 cup (2 decilitres) of white stock. Cook very slowly but steadily for an hour. Skim the sauce from time to time and add a few tablespoons of white stock if the boiling down is too rapid.

A few minutes before straining the sauce add 5 crushed peppercorns.

Strain the sauce through a fine strainer, pressing well. Put back the sauce to boil for a few minutes after having added to it 3 or 4 tablespoons of stock. Strain.

Note. If the *Poivrade sauce* is to accompany marinated meat, add to it, in the course of cooking, a few tablespoons of the marinade.

If the recipe demands butter, add it just before serving.

Note. The characteristic of this sauce is its peppery taste blending with that of the various vegetables and aromatics and sharpened by the vinegar.

It is important, however, not to abuse this condiment. It must only be added to the preparation at the last moment. Pepper allowed to cook for a long time develops an acrid taste. This is a general rule. A small amount, added at the end of the preparation of a dish, always produces a better result than a very large quantity put in at the beginning.

The *mirepoix*, the recipe for which is given elsewhere, always includes a certain amount of thyme and bay leaf.

When the *mirepoix* is intended for a *Pepper or Poivrade sauce* the proportions of these herbs may be increased.

Pepper or Poivrade sauce II (for game). SAUCE POIVRADE AU GIBIER—Cook the *mirepoix** of vegetables in butter until they are soft, as in the preceding recipe, adding to them the trimmings of the game being used, cut in small pieces.

When everything is cooked, and a good, deep colour, moisten with wine vinegar and white wine and finish off as for the ordinary *Poivrade sauce*.

Note. The *mirepoix* may be cooked in oil instead of butter.

To heighten the fine flavour of Poivrade sauces, add to them in the course of cooking a handful of mushroom skins.

Pepper or Poivrade sauce III (Old recipe). SAUCE POIVRADE—'Put in a saucepan 2 chopped onions and 2 chopped carrots, add a little lean ham, a few sprigs of parsley, a little thyme and bay leaf, a good pinch of mignonette, a little mace, 2 tablespoons of good vinegar, and 3 to 4 tablespoons of consommé. Simmer this seasoning on a very low heat.

'When the cooking down is complete, add 3 to 4 tablespoons of consommé and ½ cup of well stirred *Espagnole sauce* (see above). Simmer for a few moments, strain the sauce, using pressure, and boil it down to the desired consistency. At the moment of serving add a little butter.' (A. Carême, *L'Art de la cuisine française au XIXᵉ siècle.*)

Périgueux sauce I (for small cuts of meat, fowl, game, timbales, vol-au-vent, etc.). SAUCE PÉRIGUEUX—Boil down by one-third 1 cup (2 decilitres) of *Demi-glace sauce* (see above) with 2 or 3 tablespoons of *Truffle essence.* See ESSENCE.

Strain. Add, away from the heat, 2 tablespoons of cooked truffles cut in small dice or chopped.

Note. After the truffles have been added the sauce must not be boiled again.

Périgueux sauce II. SAUCE PÉRIGUEUX—Cook gently in butter 2 tablespoons of raw truffles cut in dice; season with salt and pepper and drain.

Dilute the juices in the pan with a tablespoon of Madeira. Stir in 1 cup (2 decilitres) of concentrated and thickened brown stock. Simmer for a few moments. Strain. Put the truffles back in the sauce, add 2 tablespoons of Madeira and keep hot without allowing to boil.

Périgourdine sauce (for small cuts of meat, fowl, etc.). SAUCE PÉRIGOURDINE—A variant of *Périgueux sauce.* The only difference is that the truffles are cut in rather thick round slices.

Pine kernel sauce à l'italienne (Old recipe). SAUCE AUX PIGNOLES À L'ITALIENNE—'Put into a saucepan 2 ounces of brown or white sugar, 2 tablespoons of good vinegar, 2 tablespoons of light veal stock, a seasoned *bouquet*, a pinch of grated nutmeg and a pinch of mignonette. Simmer all together over a moderate heat. When the boiling down is complete, add 4 tablespoons of *Espagnole sauce* and a glass of red Bordeaux wine. When the sauce has boiled down to the desired point, strain it through a cloth, add a spoonful of the little white pine kernels which the Italians call *pignoli.* Just before serving make sure the *pignoli* boil for a second in the sauce.' (A. Carême, *L'Art de la cuisine française au XIXᵉ siècle.*)

Piquante sauce (for small cuts of meat and various left-over meat dishes). SAUCE PIQUANTE—Make 1 cup (2 decilitres) of *Devilled* (*Diable*) *sauce* with wine vinegar.

Add at the last moment a tablespoon of chopped gherkins and a tablespoon of chopped parsley.

Poor man's sauce I (for dishes made with left-overs). SAUCE PAUVRE HOMME—Colour lightly in a tablespoon of butter a good tablespoon of flour.

Moisten with ¼ cup (½ litre) of wine vinegar, boil down and stir in 1 cup (2 decilitres) of stock or water with a little meat glaze or extract, season and simmer for a few seconds.

At the last moment add a tablespoon of chopped and blanched shallots, a tablespoon of chopped parsley and 2 tablespoons of golden breadcrumbs.

Note. The shallot may be replaced by chives, or both may be used.

Poor man's sauce II. SAUCE PAUVRE HOMME—Fry in a tablespoon of butter 3 to 4 tablespoons of golden breadcrumbs. Moisten with ¼ cup (½ decilitre) of wine vinegar. Boil down; stir in stock. Simmer for a few moments and finish off with blanched and chopped shallots and onions and a tablespoon of chopped parsley.

Poor man's sauce III (English cookery). SAUCE PAUVRE HOMME—Colour lightly in butter 5 tablespoons (60 grams) of chopped onion. Moisten with ¼ cup (½ decilitre) of white wine and ¼ cup (½ decilitre) of wine vinegar.

Boil down by two-thirds, stir in ¾ cup (1½ decilitres) of consommé and thicken with 1 tablespoon (20 grams) of brown *roux*. Cook for 10 minutes.

At the last moment finish off with a teaspoon of capers, a teaspoon of chopped parsley and a little cayenne.

Port wine sauce I (for meat, fowl, foie gras). SAUCE AU PORTO—Proceed as for *Madeira sauce*, replacing the latter with port wine.

Port wine sauce II (English cookery) (for game birds, particularly wild duck). SAUCE AU PORTO—Boil down by half ½ cup (1 decilitre) of port to which half a tablespoon of chopped shallot, a sprig of thyme and a piece of bay leaf have been added.

Add the juice of an orange and half a lemon, as well as a pinch of grated orange rind.

Stir in 1 cup (2 decilitres) of concentrated and thickened brown veal stock; simmer for a few moments and strain.

Portugaise sauce I (for eggs, fish, meat and poultry). SAUCE PORTUGAISE—Cook lightly in a tablespoon of oil 2 tablespoons of finely chopped onion.

When it is cooked and golden in colour, add 4 medium-sized tomatoes, peeled, drained and coarsely chopped, and a little grated garlic. Season.

Begin cooking over a good heat, then cover the pot and cook very slowly, stirring from time to time, for 25 minutes.

Stir in ½ cup of concentrated and thickened brown stock; add a tablespoon of chopped parsley and a little freshly ground pepper and mix well.

Portugaise sauce can also be prepared with butter, although oil is more in keeping with the recipe.

Portugaise sauce II (Old recipe) (for braised or roasted fillet of beef, and for ham). SAUCE À LA PORTUGAISE—'Take off carefully two small pieces of lemon peel and the same amount of orange peel; put them into a saucepan, adding a teaspoon of coriander seeds, a teaspoon of sugar and a glass of Malaga. Simmer over a low heat, add 4 tablespoons of consommé and strain this seasoning through a cloth. Add enough *Espagnole sauce* to accompany an entrée. After having boiled down the sauce to the desired point, add a glass of Malaga. Boil down anew, then pour the sauce into a *bain-marie* (double boiler), add the juice of a lemon and a little butter.' (A. Carême, *L'Art de la cuisine française au XIXe siècle.*)

Provençal sauce (for eggs, fish, small cuts of meat, fowl, vegetables). SAUCE PROVENÇALE—Cook in oil until soft 4 tablespoons (50 grams) of chopped onion. Add 4 large peeled, drained and pressed tomatoes, a small clove of crushed garlic, salt and pepper. Cook for a few minutes over a good heat. Moisten with ¾ cup (1½ decilitres) of dry white wine. Boil down. Add 1¼ cups (2½ decilitres) of light veal stock. Cook for 15 minutes. Add a teaspoon of chopped parsley.

Ravigote sauce (Old recipe). SAUCE RAVIGOTE À L'ANCIENNE—'Chop an onion and cook it lightly in a little clarified butter. Add a glass of Chablis, a large spoonful of consommé, the juice of a lemon, a little garlic and shallot, a chopped gherkin, a spoonful of capers, some parsley roots, tarragon leaves, a small *bouquet garni*, a clove, a pinch of nutmeg and crushed peppercorns. Simmer for 20 minutes, strain through a silk strainer into a saucepan containing ¼ cup of boiling *Espagnole sauce*, and carefully remove all grease from this sauce. Boil down to the desired point, mix in a teaspoon of fine mustard and strain through a cloth. When ready to serve, blend in a little Isigny butter (fresh butter) and a spoonful of chopped chervil and tarragon.' (A. Carême, *L'Art de la cuisine française au XIXe siècle.*)

Red wine sauce I—See *Bourguignonne sauce I.*

Red wine sauce II (for eggs and fish). SAUCE AU VIN ROUGE—Cook till soft in butter ¼ cup (½ decilitre) of vegetable *mirepoix** seasoned with thyme and bay leaf.

Pour in 2½ cups (5 decilitres) of red wine, add a small clove of garlic, crushed, and a handful of mushroom skins. Boil down by half.

Add 1½ cups (3 decilitres) of *Espagnole sauce* (see above) and a few tablespoons of light stock (or *fumet** from the fish being cooked). Boil down by half.

Add, away from the heat, 3 tablespoons (50 grams) of butter, and a few drops of anchovy essence. Heighten the seasoning with a pinch of cayenne and strain.

Red wine sauce III (for fish). SAUCE AU VIN ROUGE—Cook the fish in a liquor prepared with ¼ cup (½ decilitre) of vegetable *mirepoix** cooked until soft in butter, 2½ cups (5 decilitres) of red wine, a clove of garlic and some mushroom skins.

Boil down the liquid by one-third. Thicken with 2½ tablespoons (40 grams) of *Kneaded butter*. See BUTTER, *Compound butters.*

Finish off as above with butter and anchovy essence.

Reform sauce (English cookery) (for mutton cutlets). SAUCE RÉFORME—Add to 1¼ cups (2½ decilitres) of ordinary *Poivrade sauce* (see above) a garnish composed of a gherkin, the white of a hard boiled egg, 2 cooked mushrooms, ⅝ ounce (20 grams) of scarlet (pickled) tongue and 1 small cooked truffle (10 grams), all cut in short strips.

After the garnish is added to the sauce, avoid boiling.

Régence sauce (Old recipe) (for sweetbreads, oven-roast or braised chicken). SAUCE RÉGENCE—'Cook without colouring in a saucepan with 3 tablespoons (50 grams) of butter, 1 cup (100 grams) of lean ham cut in big dice and an onion cut in quarters. When the onions are almost cooked, add a chopped shallot.

'Moisten with ½ cup (1 decilitre) of Graves, boil down by two-thirds and add 1 cup (2 decilitres) of chicken stock. Cook over a low heat.

'When the onions are cooked, rub them through a horsehair sieve, add 2 cups (4 decilitres) of *Demi-glace sauce* and ½ cup (1 decilitre) of chicken essence (concentrated chicken stock). Boil down until the sauce will coat the spoon. Strain through a cloth.' (A. Carême, *L'Art de la cuisine française au XIXe siècle.*)

Robert sauce I (for grilled meat, mostly grilled pork). SAUCE ROBERT—Cook till soft 2 tablespoons of finely chopped onion in a tablespoon of butter (or lard).

Moisten with ½ cup (1 decilitre) of white wine. Boil down and add 1 cup (2 decilitres) of *Demi-glace sauce* (see above). Simmer for a few seconds. At the last moment add a teaspoon of mustard. Strain or serve as it is, according to taste.

Robert sauce II. SAUCE ROBERT—Sprinkle the cooked onion with a spoonful of flour, allow to colour lightly, moisten with white wine and add stock. Finish off with mustard.

Robert sauce III (Old recipe). SAUCE ROBERT—'Cut 3 onions into small dice, cook till they are golden in clarified butter, drain and mix with some consommé and ¼ cup of *Espagnole sauce*. Boil down the sauce to the desired consistency, mix in a little sugar, a little pepper, a little vinegar and a spoonful of fine mustard.' (A. Carême, *L'Art de la cuisine française au XIXᵉ siècle.*)

Roebuck sauce I (for small cuts of meat). SAUCE CHEVREUIL—Boil down by one-third 1½ cups (3 decilitres) of ordinary *Poivrade sauce* (see above), adding in the course of cooking ¼ cup (½ decilitre) of red wine, poured in little by little, season with a little cayenne and strain through a cloth.

Roebuck sauce II. SAUCE CHEVREUIL—Proceed as in the above recipe using *Pepper or Poivrade sauce* for game (see above).

Roebuck sauce III (English cookery). SAUCE CHEVREUIL—Cook in butter until they begin to colour 2 tablespoons of chopped onion and 2 tablespoons (40 grams) of raw ham cut in small dice. Add a *bouquet garni**, pour in ⅓ cup (¾ decilitre) of wine vinegar and boil down almost to nothing.

Add 1 cup (2 decilitres) of *Espagnole sauce* (see above); boil for 25 minutes, skimming frequently.

At the last moment take out the *bouquet garni* and finish off the sauce with half a glass of port and a tablespoon of redcurrant jelly.

Romaine sauce I (for venison). SAUCE À LA ROMAINE—Cook to a pale caramel 3 large lumps of sugar. Moisten with a tablespoon of vinegar, add 1 cup (2 decilitres) of *Demi-glace sauce* (see above) and 4 tablespoons of game *fumet**. Simmer for a few minutes. Strain through a cloth. Add a tablespoon of pine kernels, roasted lightly in the oven, and a tablespoon of currants and sultanas, washed, soaked till swollen in warm water, and dried.

Romaine sauce II (Old recipe). SAUCE À LA ROMAINE—'Chop up the white part of a celery heart and put it in a saucepan with a good pinch of coriander, a pinch of sugar, a clove of garlic, a little basil, bay leaf and 2 glasses (cups) of champagne. Simmer over a low heat. When the celery is cooked, add 2 large tablespoons of consommé and ½ cup of *Espagnole sauce*. Boil down, pour in half a glass of champagne and boil down anew, strain the sauce, using pressure, and just before serving add a little butter and the juice of a lemon.' (A. Carême, *L'Art de la cuisine française au XIXᵉ siècle.*)

Rouennaise sauce (for duck; may also be served with poached eggs). SAUCE ROUENNAISE—Bring to the boil 1 cup (2 decilitres) of *Bordelaise sauce* (see above). Remove from direct heat, but keep the sauce hot, and add the liver of a Rouen duck, chopped finely (or sieved). Stir, season with salt, freshly ground pepper and a small pinch of spice. Strain through a cloth, pressing with a wooden spoon. Keep hot in the *bain-marie* (double boiler).

Note. This sauce may also be made with chicken livers.

Sainte-Menehoulde sauce (for grilled pork, chiefly pig's trotters). SAUCE SAINTE-MENEHOULDE—Cook till soft in a tablespoon of butter 2 tablespoons of finely chopped onion. Season with a pinch of salt and a little thyme and powdered bay leaf.

Moisten with ½ cup (1 decilitre) of white wine and a tablespoon of vinegar. Boil down completely. Stir in 1 cup (2 decilitres) of *Demi-glace sauce* (see above). Simmer for a few seconds over a good heat and at the last moment add a teaspoon each of mustard, chopped gherkins and chopped parsley and chervil. Heighten the seasoning with a pinch of cayenne.

Salmis sauce (for game birds prepared in salmis). SAUCE SALMIS—Cook till soft in butter ½ cup (1 decilitre) of vegetable *mirepoix**, together with the carcase, skin and trimmings (all chopped) of the game being cooked (previously roasted and jointed when hot). See WOODCOCK, *Salmis of woodcock*.

Moisten with ½ cup (1 decilitre) of white wine and boil down. Add 1 cup (2 decilitres) of *Demi-glace sauce* (see above) and a few tablespoons of game *fumet** or light stock.

Simmer for 25 minutes. Put through a fine strainer, using pressure. Put the sauce back in the pan with 1 cup (2 decilitres) of game *fumet** or light stock. Simmer for 20 minutes, skim and strain.

Pour this sauce over the pieces of game arranged in the sauté pan. Heat without boiling.

Note. This sauce must be thick enough to coat the pieces of game.

Salmis sauce with champagne (Old recipe). SAUCE SALMIS AU VIN DE CHAMPAGNE—'Put into a saucepan half a bottle of champagne, add the trimmings of 6 partridges prepared for a salmis, a piece of bay leaf, 2 shallots and 2 tablespoons of consommé and simmer this *fumet** for an hour. Strain it through a silk sieve and boil it down by half, add ¼ cup of *Espagnole sauce*.

'When this sauce is almost boiled down to the proper point, pour into it half a glass of champagne, and boil it down anew to the desired consistency, strain through a cloth and, at the moment of serving, blend in a little fine butter,

'*Note.* To make a salmis with Bordeaux use a bottle of Bordeaux wine in place of the champagne and for ordinary salmis make the *fumet* simply with stock, a shallot and a piece of bay leaf.' (A. Carême, *L'Art de la cuisine française au XIXᵉ siècle.*)

Salmis sauce with red wine. SAUCE SALMIS AU VIN ROUGE—Proceed as in the above recipe but using red wine instead of white.

Tarragon sauce I (for eggs, small cuts of meat, etc.). SAUCE À L'ESTRAGON—Boil down ½ cup (1 decilitre) of white wine with 2 tablespoons (10 grams) of tarragon leaves, roughly chopped. Add 1 cup (2 decilitres) of *Demi-glace sauce* (see above) (or thickened brown gravy). Allow to boil for a few moments; strain through a cloth.

At the last moment, add a tablespoon of chopped tarragon. (Garnish whatever is to be served with this sauce with tarragon leaves blanched for a moment in boiling salted water, cooled in cold water and drained.)

Note. This sauce can be made with bottled tarragon.

Tarragon sauce II. SAUCE À L'ESTRAGON—Sauté the meat (poultry, etc.) in butter. Drain, dilute the juices in the saucepan with ½ cup (1 decilitre) of white wine, add a handful of chopped tarragon, cook down, pour in stock (or water with meat glaze or extract added) and bind with *Kneaded butter*. See BUTTER, *Compound butters*.

Tarragon sauce III (for poached fowl). SAUCE À L'ESTRAGON—Put into the white stock in which the chicken was poached a good handful of tarragon.

Strain this stock, with all grease carefully removed, through muslin, boil it down and thicken with arrowroot (corn starch) or potato flour.

Note. This sauce can be finished off with chopped tarragon.

Poached fowl served with this sauce, or rather, thickened broth, is always garnished with blanched tarragon leaves.

Tortue sauce (for calf's head or other offal (U.S. variety meats) served 'en tortue'). SAUCE TORTUE—Bring to the boil in a small saucepan ½ cup (1 decilitre) of white wine. Add a sprig of thyme, quarter of a bay leaf, a sprig of crushed parsley, one or two sage leaves, a sprig of rosemary and a sprig of basil.

Cover the saucepan and allow to infuse over low heat without boiling, for 15 to 20 minutes.

Strain this infusion and add it to 1¼ cups (2½ decilitres) of *Demi-glace sauce* (see above) boiled down by half after having added to it ½ cup (1 decilitre) of tomato sauce, ½ cup (1 decilitre) of light stock and a handful of mushroom skins.

Simmer for an instant, add seasoning, including a pinch of cayenne and a little spice and at the last moment add 3 tablespoons of Madeira. Strain through a cloth.

Tortue sauce with Madeira (Old recipe). SAUCE TORTUE AU VIN DE MADÈRE—'Put into a saucepan a glass (cup) of dry Madeira, a little chopped lean ham, a pinch of mignonette, a pinch of pimento, a pinch of cayenne and a chopped shallot. Simmer over a low heat and add 2 tablespoons of consommé, ¼ cup of well stirred *Espagnole sauce* and a little tomato sauce.

'When this sauce is cooked down to the desired point, add to it a quarter of a glass of Madeira, bring to the boil once or twice, strain through a cloth and, just before serving, add a little Isigny butter (fresh butter).' (A. Carême, *L'Art de la cuisine française au XIXe siècle.*)

Venison sauce—See GRAND VENEUR SAUCE.

Venison sauce (Old recipe). SAUCE VENAISON—'Pour into a saucepan a glass of old Burgundy wine, 2 tablespoons of ordinary vinegar, 2 tablespoons of sugar, the flesh of half a lemon with its seeds removed, half a pot of redcurrants, cook down and add 2 tablespoons of *Espagnole sauce*. Cook down anew, mixing in at intervals a second glass of Burgundy. When the sauce is concentrated to the desired consistency, strain through a cloth.' (A. Carême, *L'Art de la cuisine française au XIXe siècle.*)

Victoria sauce (English cookery) (for venison). SAUCE VICTORIA—Add to 1¼ cups (2½ decilitres) of *Espagnole sauce* ¾ cup (1½ decilitres) of port and 3 tablespoons redcurrant jelly. Add 8 peppercorns, 2 cloves, a fragment of cinnamon and the peel of one orange.

Boil down by one-third, add the juice of an orange, heighten the seasoning with a little cayenne and strain through a cloth.

Yorkshire sauce (English cooking) (for braised ham and roast and braised duck). SAUCE YORKSHIRE—Cook a tablespoon of orange peel cut in a fine *julienne* (thin strips) in 1 cup (2 decilitres) of port.

Drain the peel. Add ¼ cup of *Espagnole sauce* and a tablespoon of redcurrant jelly to the port. Season with a pinch of powdered cinnamon and a pinch of cayenne and simmer for a moment. Add the juice of an orange and strain. Finish off with the orange peel cooked in port.

Zingara sauce (for small cuts of meat and poultry). SAUCE ZINGARA—To 1 cup (2 decilitres) of *Demi-glace sauce* (see above) cooked with a few tablespoons of tomato sauce and a few tablespoons of mushroom stock, add a *julienne** composed of a tablespoon each of lean cooked ham, scarlet (pickled) tongue and mushrooms and a heaped teaspoon of truffles. Season with a little paprika and keep warm without allowing the sauce to boil.

COMPOUND WHITE SAUCES: SAUCES COMPOSÉES, BLANCHES:

Aigrelette sauce with verjuice (Old cookery). SAUCE AIGRELETTE AU VERJUS—'Having washed 30 verjuice grapes, pound them and press out the juice through a cloth. Just before serving, have boiling in a saucepan 2 tablespoons of *Allemande sauce*, to which should be added a little chicken glaze, a little Isigny butter, a pinch of nutmeg and finely ground pepper and enough verjuice to render this sauce sharp and appetizing.' (A. Carême, *L'Art de la cuisine française au XIXe siècle.*)

Albert sauce (English cookery) (for braised beef). SAUCE ALBERT—Cook at boiling point for 20 minutes 4 tablespoons (75 grams) of grated horseradish moistened with ½ cup (a decilitre) of light consommé.

Add ¾ cup (1½ decilitres) of *Butter sauce II*, ½ cup (1 decilitre) of cream and ½ cup (20 grams) of fine breadcrumbs.

Boil down over a strong heat, stirring all the time. Strain, pressing with spoon. Put back in the saucepan, thicken with an egg yolk and season with salt and pepper.

Finish off, at the last moment, with half a teaspoon of English mustard diluted with a few drops of vinegar.

Albuféra sauce (for sweetbreads and poached or braised poultry). SAUCE ALBUFÉRA—Add 1 cup (2 decilitres) of *Suprême sauce* to 2 tablespoons of concentrated veal stock and a tablespoon of *Pimento butter*.

Allemande sauce I (or thick velouté) (for offal or U.S. variety meats, poached chicken, vegetables and eggs). SAUCE ALLEMANDE, VELOUTÉ LIÉ—For 2½ cups (5 decilitres): put into a pan with a thick, flat bottom, 2 egg yolks (3 if they are small) and 2 cups (4 decilitres) of light veal or chicken stock. Mix together. Add 2½ cups (5 decilitres) of *Velouté sauce;* mix with a whisk.

Begin cooking over a good heat, stirring with a wooden spoon to keep the sauce from sticking to the bottom of the pot.

Cook down carefully without boiling, until the sauce coats the spoon well.

At the last moment add 3 tablespoons (50 grams) of butter, rectify the seasoning and strain through a cloth.

Keep in the *bain-marie* (double boiler) until the moment of using (beat the sauce while it is in the *bain-marie* and butter the surface to prevent skin forming).

Note. Depending on its intended use and according to taste this sauce can be seasoned with a pinch of grated nutmeg and sharpened with a squeeze of lemon juice.

Allemande sauce II (fish). SAUCE ALLEMANDE—Proceed as in the preceding recipe, using fish stock or *fumet** in place of the stock and fish *Velouté sauce* in place of the *Velouté sauce* made with meat or poultry stock.

Allemande sauce III (mushroom flavoured). SAUCE ALLEMANDE AU FUMET DE CHAMPIGNONS—Proceed as in first recipe; add to the *Velouté sauce* a few tablespoons of the cooking juices of mushrooms.

Note. It is also possible to add to the sauce in course of cooking a good handful of mushroom skins and stalks.

Allemande sauce IV (truffle flavoured). SAUCE ALLEMANDE AU FUMET DE TRUFFES—As above. Replace the mushroom juices with *fumet** of truffles.

American sauce (for fish, crustaceans, eggs). SAUCE AMÉRICAINE—In principle this sauce is the product of preparing lobster or crawfish *à l'américaine*.

It is used to coat braised fish, poached eggs and boiled eggs.

Anchovy sauce I (for fish). SAUCE ANCHOIS—Add to 1 cup (2 decilitres) of *Normande sauce* (or *White wine sauce*) 2 tablespoons of anchovy butter (or a teaspoon of anchovy essence or paste). Strain.

Anchovy sauce II. SAUCE ANCHOIS—As above, using *Béchamel sauce* instead of *Normande sauce*.

Anchovy sauce III. SAUCE ANCHOIS—As above, using *Butter sauce* instead of *Normande sauce*.

Andalouse sauce (for eggs, fish, poultry). SAUCE ANDALOUSE—Add to 1 cup (2 decilitres) of thick *Velouté sauce,* ¼ cup (½ decilitre) of *Essence of tomato** (strongly-concentrated tomato purée). Add 2 tablespoons of sweet pimentos that have been peeled, braised and cut in dice, and a teaspoon of chopped parsley.

Note. This sauce may be seasoned with a little grated garlic.

Aurora sauce (for eggs, poultry, sweetbreads). SAUCE AURORE—Add to 1 cup (2 decilitres) of *Velouté sauce* ¼ cup (½ decilitre) of very thick tomato purée.

Finish off with 3 tablespoons (50 grams) of butter and strain.

Banquière sauce (for eggs, poultry, offal or U.S. variety meats, vol-au-vent). SAUCE BANQUIÈRE—Add to 1 cup (2 decilitres) of *Suprême sauce* ¼ cup (½ decilitre) of Madeira. Strain through a cloth. Finish off with 2 tablespoons of chopped truffles.

Bâtarde sauce (for boiled fish and vegetables). SAUCE BÂTARDE—See *Butter sauce*.

Béarnaise sauce (for grilled or sautéed meat, grilled fish). SAUCE BÉARNAISE—Put into a saucepan a good tablespoon of chopped shallot, 2 tablespoons of tarragon and chopped chervil, a sprig of thyme, and a fragment of bay leaf. Moisten with ¼ cup (½ decilitre) of vinegar and ¼ cup (½ decilitre) of white wine; season with a pinch of salt and a pinch of mignonette pepper. Boil down by two-thirds.

Allow to cool. Put into the pan 2 raw egg yolks mixed with a tablespoon of water.

Beat the sauce with a whisk over very low heat. As soon as the yolks begin to thicken, incorporate little by little and whisking all the time, ¼ pound (125 grams) of fresh butter.

Season the sauce, sharpen it if necessary with a squeeze of lemon juice and heighten the seasoning with a pinch of cayenne.

Strain. Finish off with a tablespoon of chopped tarragon and chervil. Keep warm in a *bain-marie* (double boiler).

Béarnaise sauce, tomato flavoured or Choron sauce (for grilled meat). SAUCE BÉARNAISE, SAUCE CHORON—Add to 1 cup (2 decilitres) of strained *Béarnaise sauce*, 2 good tablespoons of very concentrated tomato purée.

Beauharnais sauce (for grilled and sautéed meat and grilled fish). SAUCE BEAUHARNAIS—Add to 1 cup (2 decilitres) of strained *Béarnaise sauce* 2 good tablespoons of green *Tarragon butter*. See BUTTER, *Compound butters*.

Béchamel sauce with onion. BÉCHAMEL SOUBISE—Add *Onion purée* (*soubise*) to *Béchamel sauce*. See PURÉE and BASIC SAUCES.

Bercy sauce (for fish). SAUCE BERCY—Cook a tablespoon of chopped shallot gently in butter without letting it colour. Moisten with ½ cup (1 decilitre) of white wine and ½ cup (1 decilitre) of fish *fumet**.

Boil down by half; add 1 cup (2 decilitres) of *Velouté sauce* based on fish stock; cook at boiling point for a few moments over a good heat.

Add, away from the heat, 3 tablespoons (50 grams) of butter, finish off with a tablespoon of chopped parsley; do not strain through a cloth.

Note. Usually this sauce is made while the fish is cooked. See *Brill à la Bercy*.

Bontemps sauce (for grilled meat and poultry). SAUCE BONTEMPS—Cook in butter a tablespoon of finely chopped onion. Season with a pinch of salt and a little paprika. Pour in 1 cup (2 decilitres) of cider. Boil down by two-thirds.

Add 1 cup (2 decilitres) of *Velouté sauce*. Cook at boiling point for a few moments; remove from heat and incorporate 3 tablespoons (50 grams) of butter and a teaspoon of mustard and strain.

Brandade à la provençale (Old recipe) (for boiled fish, principally salt cod). SAUCE BRANDADE À LA PROVENÇALE —'Put into a saucepan 4 tablespoons of fish *Allemande sauce*, 3 egg yolks, a pinch of grated nutmeg, a pinch of finely ground pepper, a little pounded garlic, the juice of a large lemon and a little salt. After having mixed this seasoning perfectly, set the saucepan on some hot cinders, stirring all the time to obtain a perfectly thick and velvety sauce; then take it off the heat in order to mix in, spoonful by spoonful, 1½ glasses (cups) of good oil of Aix (Provençal olive oil). At the moment of serving add the juice of a lemon and a large tablespoon of chopped and blanched chervil, or tarragon, similarly chopped and blanched.' (A. Carême, *L'Art de la cuisine française au XIX*[e] *siècle*.)

Bread sauce (English cookery) (for poultry and roast game birds). SAUCE AU PAIN—Put into 2½ cups (5 decilitres) of boiling milk 1½ cups (80 grams) of freshly-prepared breadcrumbs. Add a small onion studded with a clove, 2 tablespoons (30 grams) of butter and a pinch of salt. Mix, bring to the boil and cook gently for 15 minutes.

At the last moment take out the onion and incorporate in the sauce ½ cup (1 decilitre) of cream. Beat smooth with a whisk.

Breton sauce (for eggs, fish, white meat, poultry, offal or variety meats). SAUCE BRETONNE—Prepare a fine *julienne** (thin strips) composed of half a medium-sized onion, the white of a leek and quarter of a celery heart. Season these vegetables with a pinch of salt and a little sugar; let them cook slowly till soft in a saucepan with a tablespoon of butter.

As soon as these vegetables are cooked, add 3 tablespoons of uncooked mushrooms, also cut in a *julienne*.

Moisten with ¼ cup (½ decilitre) of white wine. Boil down to almost nothing, add ¾ cup (1½ decilitres) of

Velouté sauce (which may be based on meat or fish stock, according to the final use). Cook at boiling point for a few moments over a strong heat, incorporate, at the last moment, 3 tablespoons (50 grams) of fresh butter and 2 tablespoons of rather thick fresh cream; do not strain.

Note. When Breton sauce is to accompany braised fish, the latter must cook in the *julienne* indicated above, moistened with a few tablespoons of fish *fumet** or white wine.

After the fish is cooked finish off the sauce as shown above.

Butter sauce I or Bâtarde sauce (for vegetables, boiled fish). SAUCE AU BEURRE, SAUCE BÂTARDE—Melt in a saucepan 1½ tablespoons (20 grams) of butter, add 2 tablespoons (20 grams) of flour, mix and moisten with 1¼ cups (2½ decilitres) of boiling salted water.

Stir the mixture vigorously with a whisk, add an egg yolk mixed with a good tablespoon of cold water.

Incorporate, stirring all the time and keeping the saucepan over a very low heat, 6 tablespoons (100 grams) of fresh butter divided into small pieces. Season the sauce and strain.

Note. This sauce may be sharpened with a few drops of lemon juice.

Butter sauce II (English cookery). SAUCE AU BEURRE À L'ANGLAISE—Proceed as above using 2 tablespoons (30 grams) of butter and 4 tablespoons (30 grams) of flour.

Do not thicken the sauce with egg yolk.

Butter sauce III (Old recipe). SAUCE AU BEURRE—'Put into a saucepan a small spoonful of flour and a little Isigny butter. After having amalgamated the flour with a wooden spoon, add half a glass of water or consommé, a little salt and grated nutmeg and the juice of half a lemon, stir in the seasoning over a brisk heat, and, as soon as it comes to the boil, remove the sauce, mixing in a good piece of Isigny butter; the sauce should then be velvety, very smooth and excellent to the taste.' (A. Carême, *L'Art de la cuisine française au XIXe siècle.*)

Note. In his *Traité des petites sauces*, Antonin Carême gives a great variety of white sauces deriving from this sauce. In modern practice all these sauces are prepared using *Allemande sauce* or *Suprême sauce* as their base, and their recipes are given in their alphabetical order.

Butter sauce with chervil (Old recipe). SAUCE AU BEURRE À LA PLUCHE DE CERFEUIL—'Bring to the boil in a saucepan 2 tablespoons of *Butter sauce* adding to it a little salt, pepper and grated nutmeg, the juice of half a lemon, a good piece of Isigny butter and 1½ tablespoons of blanched small chervil leaves.' (A. Carême, *L'Art de la cuisine française au XIXe siècle.*)

Caper sauce I (for boiled fish). SAUCE AUX CÂPRES—Add to 1¼ cups (2½ decilitres) of *Hollandaise sauce* 2 teaspoons of well-drained capers.

Caper sauce II. SAUCE AUX CÂPRES—Proceed as above, using *Butter sauce.*

Caper sauce III, English (for boiled fish). SAUCE AUX CÂPRES À L'ANGLAISE—Prepare English *Butter sauce;* finish it off with well-drained capers and a little anchovy essence.

Caper sauce IV, English (for boiled leg of mutton). SAUCE AUX CÂPRES À L'ANGLAISE—Prepare a white *roux* as for English *Butter sauce*, moisten it with the cooking broth of the mutton. Cook the sauce, strain it, finish off with the capers.

Note. Caper sauce made with water can be served with boiled leg of mutton. This sauce is also served with boiled rabbit.

Cardinal sauce I (for fish). SAUCE CARDINAL—Boil down by half 1 cup (2 decilitres) of *Velouté sauce* based on fish stock, and ½ cup (1 decilitre) of fish *fumet**.

Add ½ cup (1 decilitre) of cream, simmer for a few moments, remove from heat, add 3 tablespoons (50 grams) of lobster (or spiny lobster) butter, heighten the seasoning with a pinch of cayenne and strain through a cloth. Add a tablespoon of chopped truffles.

Note. When this sauce is used for fish garnished with slices of truffle, leave out the chopped truffles.

Cardinal sauce II. SAUCE CARDINAL—Proceed as above, replacing the *Velouté sauce* by *Béchamel sauce.*

Celery sauce (English cookery) (for boiled and braised poultry). SAUCE AU CÉLERI—Put into a sauté pan the trimmed hearts of 3 heads of celery. Add a *bouquet garni* and a small onion stuck with a clove; cover with light *consommé.* Cook slowly.

Drain the celery, pound it and sieve.

Put the purée into a saucepan; add to it an equal quantity of *Cream sauce*, dilute with a spoonful or two of the concentrated celery cooking liquor and mix well. Heat without allowing to boil.

Chantilly sauce (for poultry and white offal or U.S. variety meats). SAUCE CHANTILLY—Add to 1 cup (2 decilitres) of very thick *Suprême sauce* ½ cup (1 decilitre) of whipped cream.

White chaud-froid sauce I (for eggs, poultry, white offal or U.S. variety meats). SAUCE CHAUD-FROID BLANCHE—For 2½ cups (5 decilitres): put into a thick-bottomed sauté pan 1¾ cups (3½ decilitres) of *Velouté sauce* and ½ cup (1 decilitre) of mushroom *fumet**.

Boil down over a good heat, stirring with a wooden spoon and adding, a little at a time, 2 cups (4 decilitres) of chicken or veal jelly and ¾ cup (1½ decilitres) of cream.

Cook down until the sauce has the desired consistency and will coat the spoon.

To be certain of this consistency, chill on ice a small quantity of the sauce. If it is not firm enough add a few more tablespoons of jelly and cook down anew.

Strain the sauce and whisk until it is quite cold.

Note. Depending on its final use, *chaud-froid sauce* may be left as it is or flavoured with some wine such as Madeira, sherry, etc. The wine must be added to the sauce when it is almost cold.

White chaud-froid sauce II (for fish and shellfish). SAUCE CHAUD-FROID BLANCHE MAIGRE—Proceed as for *White chaud-froid sauce I* using *Velouté sauce* based on fish stock and fish aspic jelly in place of meat *Velouté sauce* and jelly; strain.

Chaud-froid sauce à l'allemande. SAUCE CHAUD-FROID À L'ALLEMANDE—Proceed as for *White chaud-froid sauce I*, replacing the *Velouté sauce* with *Allemande sauce.*

Reduce a little the proportion of cream added in the course of cooking so that the sauce is less thick in consistency.

Flavour with Madeira or other similar wine.

Chaud-froid sauce à l'andalouse. SAUCE CHAUD-FROID À L'ANDALOUSE—Prepare the sauce as for *Chaud-froid sauce I.*

Flavour it with sherry and add to it 2 tablespoons of orange peel cut in a very fine *julienne** (thin strips), blanched, cooled in water and drained.

Chaud-froid sauce à l'aurore. SAUCE CHAUD-FROID À L'AURORE—Add to *White chaud-froid sauce I* 3 tablespoons of concentrated tomato purée; strain.

Chaud-froid sauce à la banquière. SAUCE CHAUD-FROID À LA BANQUIÈRE—Add to strained *White chaud-froid sauce I* some finely chopped truffles and 3 tablespoons of Madeira.

Chaud-froid sauce Beauharnais. SAUCE CHAUD-FROID BEAUHARNAIS—Colour *White chaud-froid sauce I* before straining with 2 tablespoons of purée of green herbs (tarragon and chervil) blanched, cooled in water, drained and rubbed through a fine sieve.

Chaud-froid sauce, blonde. SAUCE CHAUD-FROID BLONDE —Add to *White chaud-froid sauce I* during cooking 2 tablespoons of blond chicken glaze and strain.

Chaud-froid sauce à l'écossaise. SAUCE CHAUD-FROID À L'ÉCOSSAISE—Add to *White chaud-froid sauce I*, finished and strained, 2 spoonfuls of fine *brunoise** of carrot, the white part of leek and celery, all cooked gently in light stock, a spoonful of scarlet (pickled) tongue and a spoonful of truffles cut in very small dice. Flavour with Madeira.

Chaud-froid sauce à la hongroise. SAUCE CHAUD-FROID À LA HONGROISE—Add to *White chaud-froid sauce I*, in course of cooking, 2 tablespoons of finely chopped onion, blanched, drained and cooked in a decilitre (½ cup) of white wine till no liquid remains. Season with a good pinch of paprika. Strain through a cloth.

Chaud-froid sauce à l'indienne. SAUCE CHAUD-FROID À L'INDIENNE—Proceed as above. Season the chopped onion with a small spoonful of curry; strain through a cloth.

Chaud-froid sauce à la Nantua. SAUCE CHAUD-FROID À LA NANTUA—Recommended for fish and crustaceans. Add to the ordinary *White chaud-froid sauce II* before straining 2 tablespoons of crayfish purée.

Finish off, after straining, with a tablespoon of chopped truffles.

Chaud-froid sauce à la royale. SAUCE CHAUD-FROID À LA ROYALE—Add to *White chaud-froid sauce I* before straining, 2 tablespoons of truffle purée diluted with a tablespoon of sherry.

Chaud-froid sauce à la sicilienne. SAUCE CHAUD-FROID À LA SICILIENNE—Add to the *White chaud-froid sauce I*, before straining, 2 tablespoons of pistachio nuts, blanched, pounded finely in a mortar, diluted with a little cream and put through a fine sieve.

Chivry sauce I (for eggs and poultry). SAUCE CHIVRY—Boil down ½ cup (1 decilitre) of white wine by half with a teaspoon of chopped shallot and a tablespoon of chopped chervil and tarragon.

Add 1 cup (2 decilitres) of *Chicken velouté sauce* and ½ cup (1 decilitre) of white stock; boil down by one-third.

Finish off with 2 tablespoons of *Printanier butter*. See BUTTER, *Compound butters*. Strain.

Chivry sauce II (for braised fish). SAUCE CHIVRY—Proceed as above replacing the *Chicken velouté sauce* with *Velouté sauce based on fish stock*, and the white stock by fish stock or *fumet**.

Choron sauce (for grilled and sautéed meat). SAUCE CHORON—The same as *Béarnaise sauce*, *tomato flavoured*.

Crayfish sauce I (English cookery) (for fish). SAUCE AUX QUEUES D'ÉCREVISSES À L'ANGLAISE—Proceed as for *Lobster sauce II*, *English*, below. Replace the lobster by crayfish tails cut in dice.

Crayfish sauce II (Old recipe). SAUCE AUX ÉCREVISSES—'Wash 50 medium-sized crayfish and cook them with half a bottle of Champagne, a chopped onion, a *bouquet garni*, a pinch of mignonette and a little salt. When your crayfish are cold, drain them and strain the cooking liquor through a silk strainer, boil down by half, then add ½ cup of *Allemande sauce*, boil down to the desired consistency and add half a glass of champagne. The cooking complete, strain the sauce through a cloth. At the last moment add a little glaze and best butter, then the shelled crayfish tails.

'Add to the sauce some crayfish butter made from the crayfish shells.' (A. Carême, *L'Art de la cuisine française au XIXe siècle*.)

Cream sauce (for vegetables, fish, eggs, poultry). SAUCE À LA CRÈME—Cook down by one-third 1 cup (2 decilitres) of *Béchamel sauce* to which has been added ½ cup (1 decilitre) of cream.

Remove from heat, add 3 tablespoons (50 grams) of butter and 4 tablespoons of cream and strain.

See also *English cream sauce*.

Curry or Indian sauce I (for eggs, poultry, mutton). SAUCE AU CURRIE, SAUCE INDIENNE—Cook till pale golden in 2 tablespoons (25 grams) of butter, ½ cup (100 grams) of chopped onion. When the onion is half-cooked add 2 roots of parsley and a chopped stick of celery, a sprig of thyme, half a bay leaf and a fragment of mace.

Sprinkle with 2 tablespoons (25 grams) of flour, and a small teaspoon of curry powder. Mix and colour lightly.

Stir in 2 cups (4 decilitres) of light stock or ordinary consommé, blend, bring to the boil and simmer very slowly for 40 minutes.

Strain the sauce through a cloth, pressing with a wooden spoon. Put back in the saucepan and reheat. At the last moment add to it ½ cup of fresh cream and a squeeze of lemon juice.

Note. The liquid for curry sauce can be three-quarters white stock and one-quarter coconut milk. See COCONUT.

Curry sauce II. SAUCE AU CURRIE—Cook ½ cup (100 grams) of chopped onion gently in butter.

Sprinkle in a teaspoon of curry powder, add a seeded and chopped tomato, a grated clove of garlic, a sprig of parsley, a sprig of thyme and a fragment of bay leaf.

Stir in 1½ cups (3 decilitres) of rather thin *Velouté sauce* (based on meat stock). Cook for 35 minutes, stirring frequently. Boil down by one-third, adding, in the course of cooking, ½ cup (1 decilitre) of cream.

Strain the sauce through a cloth, reheat it and, at the last moment, heighten the seasoning with a squeeze of lemon juice.

Curry sauce III (for poached eggs or shelled boiled eggs). SAUCE AU CURRIE—Cook ½ cup (100 grams) of chopped onions slowly in butter.

Sprinkle in a teaspoon of curry powder.

Stir in 1½ cups (3 decilitres) of *Béchamel sauce*, not too thick. Boil down over a strong heat, and strain through a cloth.

Heat and add, at the last moment, 3 tablespoons (50 grams) of butter.

Curry sauce IV (for fish and crustaceans). SAUCE AU CURRIE—Proceed as in the first recipe, replacing the consommé by fish stock or *fumet**.

Curry sauce à l'indienne (Old recipe). SAUCE AU CURRIE À L'INDIENNE—'Put into a saucepan a few slices of lean ham, a chopped onion, a *bouquet garni*, 2 punnets of mushrooms, chopped, 3 cloves, a good pinch of pimento, a pinch of cayenne pepper and a little mace. Add 4 tablespoons of chicken consommé, simmer over a very low heat, strain through a napkin and remove all grease. When it is somewhat cooked down mix in some *Allemande sauce;* when it is cooked down to the desired point, add a small infusion of saffron so as to colour it a nice yellow, then strain through a cloth. Just before serving put in a little butter and three punnets of small mushrooms.

'*Note*. Some people add small, very green gherkins cut to look like olives to this sauce'. (A. Carême, *L'Art de la cuisine française au XIXe siècle*.)

Diplomat sauce or Riche sauce (for fish). SAUCE DIPLOMATE, SAUCE RICHE—Finish off 1 cup (2 decilitres) of *Normande sauce* with 2 tablespoons of lobster butter. Add a tablespoon of brandy, heighten the seasoning with a pinch of cayenne and strain through a cloth.

Note. If this sauce is served separately, add to it at the last moment a tablespoon of truffles cut in dice and a tablespoon of lobster flesh cut in the same way.

Écossaise sauce I (for eggs, poultry and white offal or U.S. variety meats). SAUCE ÉCOSSAISE—Add to 1 cup (2 decilitres) of strained *Cream sauce*, ¼ cup (½ decilitre) of vegetable *brunoise** cooked in butter until soft, and adding some French (string) beans, cut in very small dice, to the usual vegetables.

Écossaise sauce II. SAUCE ÉCOSSAISE—Proceed as above. Replace the *Cream sauce* by *Allemande sauce.*

Écossaise sauce III. SAUCE ÉCOSSAISE—As above, with *White wine sauce.*

Egg sauce (English cookery) (for fish, chiefly haddock and cod). SAUCE AUX OEUFS À L'ANGLAISE—Stir 1¼ cups (2½ decilitres) of boiling milk into a white *roux* composed of 2 tablespoons (30 grams) of butter and 2 tablespoons (15 grams) of flour. Season with salt, white pepper and nutmeg. Bring to the boil and cook for 6 minutes. Finish the sauce with 2 hot hard boiled eggs cut in dice.

Egg and butter sauce (English cookery) (for large boiled fish). SAUCE AUX OEUFS AU BEURRE—Add to ¼ pound (125 grams) of melted butter seasoned with salt, pepper and a squeeze of lemon juice, 2 hot hard boiled eggs cut in large dice and a teaspoon of chopped and blanched parsley.

Egg sauce à l'écossaise. SAUCE AUX OEUFS À L'ÉCOSSAISE—Prepare the sauce as above. Add the egg whites cut in small strips, and, at the last moment, the yolks pressed into vermicelli-like threads through a strainer.

Mix very lightly so that the pieces of egg can be seen in the sauce.

English sauce or Sauce à l'anglaise (Old recipe) (for poultry). SAUCE À L'ANGLAISE—'Chop the yolks of 4 hard boiled eggs very finely, mix them, in a saucepan, with enough half-thickened *Velouté sauce* to sauce an entrée. Then add a pinch of pepper and grated nutmeg, the juice of a lemon and a little anchovy butter'. (A. Carême, *L'Art de la cuisine française au XIXe siècle.*)

English bread and butter sauce (Old recipe) (for roast game birds). SAUCE AU BEURRE ET AU PAIN À L'ANGLAISE—'Bring to the boil in ¼ cup of consommé 2 tablespoons of breadcrumbs, adding a small onion cut in two and a clove. Add a little salt, grated nutmeg and cayenne pepper. Simmer for 10 minutes, remove the onion and the clove, then mix in a tablespoon of *Butter sauce* and, just before serving, add a little best butter.' (A. Carême, *L'Art de la cuisine française au XIXe siècle.*)

English cream sauce. SAUCE CRÈME À L'ANGLAISE—Stir into a white *roux* made of 3 tablespoons (50 grams) of butter and 4 tablespoons (30 grams) of flour, 1¾ cups (3½ decilitres) of white consommé, 3 tablespoons of mushroom *essence** and ½ cup (1 decilitre) of cream. Mix together.

Fennel sauce I (Old recipe). SAUCE AU FENOUIL—'Pick over and wash some fennel, chop it and put a tablespoon into a saucepan containing ½ cup of boiling *Allemande sauce.* Add a little chicken glaze, a little butter, a pinch of nutmeg and the juice of a lemon.' (A. Carême, *L'Art de la cuisine française au XIXe siècle.*)

Fennel sauce II (English cookery) (for grilled or boiled fish, chiefly mackerel). SAUCE AU FENOUIL—Add to 1¼ cups (2½ decilitres) of English *Butter sauce* a large tablespoon of chopped and blanched fennel.

Fines herbes sauce (for fish). SAUCE AUX FINES HERBES—Add to 1 cup (2 decilitres) of *White wine sauce* ¼ cup (½ decilitre) of finely grated shallot. Strain through a cloth; at the last moment add a tablespoon of chopped chervil and parsley.

Foyot sauce (for grilled meat). SAUCE FOYOT—Add to 1 cup (2 decilitres) of strained *Béarnaise sauce,* 2 tablespoons of meat glaze.

French sauce (Old recipe) (for fish). SAUCE À LA FRANÇAISE—'Put into a saucepan some *Béchamel sauce based on fish stock.* When it is almost boiling, add a little garlic, a little grated nutmeg and mushroom *essence**. When it has boiled for a moment, and just before serving, add crayfish butter to give it a pinkish colour.

'*Note.* Shelled crayfish tails and small peeled mushrooms may be added to this sauce. I served this sauce for the first time in the house of Prince Paul de Wurtemberg.' (A. Carême, *L'Art de la cuisine française au XIXe siècle.*)

Freshwater fish sauce (English cookery). SAUCE WATERFISH—Cut 2 tablespoons (25 grams) of carrot and 1 tablespoon (15 grams) of parsley roots into a fine *julienne**. Add 2 teaspoons of shredded orange peel.

Put all together into a small saucepan, moisten with ½ cup (1 decilitre) of white wine and boil until the liquid is completely absorbed.

Moisten again with ½ cup (1 decilitre) of fish *court-bouillon** made with white wine; finish cooking and cook down until all liquid is absorbed.

Add 1¼ cups (2½ decilitres) of *Hollandaise sauce* to the *julienne.*

Finish off with a few leaves of blanched parsley.

Garlic sauce—See GARLIC.

Godard sauce (for sweetbreads and poultry). SAUCE GODARD—Boil down by half 1 cup (2 decilitres) of Champagne with 3 tablespoons of *mirepoix** of vegetables.

Add 1 cup (2 decilitres) of *Demi-glace sauce* and ½ cup (1 decilitre) of mushroom *essence**. Boil down by one-third and strain.

Greek sauce (for fish). SAUCE À LA GRECQUE—Cook together 2 tablespoons of onion and quarter of a celery heart, both chopped, in a tablespoon of butter. Add a *bouquet garni* composed of a stalk of fennel, a little thyme and bay leaf.

Moisten with ½ cup (1 decilitre) of white wine, add 10 coriander seeds and cook down by two-thirds.

Stir in ½ cup (1 decilitre) of *Velouté sauce based on fish stock* and ½ cup (1 decilitre) of cream. Boil down by one-third, finish off with 3 tablespoons (50 grams) of butter and strain.

Hollandaise sauce I (for vegetables, fish and eggs). SAUCE HOLLANDAISE—Boil down by two-thirds in a small saucepan ½ cup (1 decilitre) of water with a pinch of salt and a pinch of mignonette pepper (coarsely ground pepper).

Let the bottom of the saucepan cool a little, then add 5 raw egg yolks, beaten slightly with a tablespoon of water.

Beat up the sauce with a whisk over a very gentle heat. As soon as the yolks thicken to a creamy consistency add, little by little and beating all the time, 1 pound (500 grams) of melted butter, just lukewarm.

Add 2 tablespoons of water, a few drops at a time. Season the sauce, sharpen it to the desired point with a few drops of lemon juice and strain through a cloth. Keep in a *bain-marie* (double boiler).

Note. The water can be replaced with half water and half vinegar.

Hollandaise sauce can be made in a *bain-marie* (double boiler).

Hollandaise sauce II (Old recipe). SAUCE HOLLANDAISE—'Put into a saucepan 5 egg yolks, a little fine butter, salt, pepper and grated nutmeg; place the saucepan on a pan with some almost boiling water in it, or simply stand it over a very low heat. Stir the sauce constantly with a wooden spoon, and as it develops more and more body mix in small quantities of Isigny butter. After having added more than half a pound, mix in a spoonful of ordinary vinegar.' (A. Carême, *L'Art de la cuisine française au XIXe siècle.*)

Hollandaise sauce suprême (Old recipe). SAUCE HOLLANDAISE AU SUPRÊME—'Break 5 egg yolks into a saucepan, blend in a little best butter, salt, fine pepper, grated nutmeg, 2 tablespoons of *Allemande sauce* and 1 tablespoon of chicken glaze. Stir this sauce over a very low heat, and as it continues to thicken, add to it a little butter in 2 or 3 operations, taking care to stir all the time. At the moment of serving pour in a little good ordinary vinegar and add a good piece of butter.' (A. Carême, *L'Art de la cuisine française au XIXe siècle.*)

Horseradish sauce, hot (English cookery). SAUCE RAIFORT CHAUDE—Proceed as for *Albert sauce.*

Hungarian sauce I (for small cuts of sautéed meat, eggs, fish, offal or U.S. variety meats, and poultry). SAUCE HONGROISE—Cook in butter, without allowing to colour, 4 tablespoons of chopped onion. Sprinkle with a good pinch of paprika, season with a pinch of salt, moisten with ½ cup (1 decilitre) of white wine and add a small *bouquet garni.* Boil down by two-thirds.

Stir in 1¼ cups (2½ decilitres) of *Velouté sauce* based on either meat or fish stock. Simmer over a good heat for 5 minutes, strain through a cloth and finish off with 3 tablespoons (50 grams) of butter.

Hungarian sauce II. SAUCE HONGROISE—Cook the chopped onion in butter and sprinkle it with a tablespoon of flour and a good pinch of paprika. Moisten with ½ cup (1 decilitre) of white wine and add a small *bouquet garni.* Boil down by two-thirds. Stir in 1½ cups (3 decilitres) of light consommé or stock (or water to which a small quantity of meat glaze or extract has been added).

Cook very slowly for 25 minutes and finish off as above.

Hungarian sauce III. SAUCE HONGROISE—Stir the cooking liquor of 8 oysters into a white roux composed of a tablespoon of butter and a tablespoon of flour. Add ¾ cup (1½ decilitres) of mushroom or fish *fumet**. Cook very slowly for 20 minutes. Thicken with 2 egg yolks, strain through a cloth, finish off with 3 tablespoons (50 grams) of butter and add the oysters, poached, drained and de-bearded.

Indian sauce—See *Curry sauce.*

Ivoire sauce (for eggs, sweetbreads, poultry). SAUCE IVOIRE—Add to 1 cup (2 decilitres) of *Suprême sauce** 3 to 4 tablespoons of very concentrated brown veal gravy or a tablespoon of meat glaze.

Joinville sauce (for fish). SAUCE JOINVILLE—Add to 1 cup (2 decilitres) of *Shrimp sauce** a tablespoon of truffles cut in a fine *julienne** (thin strips).

Note. If the Joinville sauce is intended to coat braised fish, the *julienne* of truffles is not added to it because these must figure in the garnish.

This sauce is also prepared with crayfish butter, and sometimes with mixed shrimp and crayfish butter.

Laguipière sauce I (for fish). SAUCE LAGUIPIÈRE—Add to 1 cup (2 decilitres) of *Normande sauce* 2 tablespoons of chopped truffles infused in a tablespoon of Madeira.

Laguipière sauce II (Old recipe). SAUCE LAGUIPIÈRE—'Put into a saucepan ¼ cup of *Butter sauce,* add a tablespoon of good consommé, or even a little chicken glaze, a pinch of salt, some nutmeg and good ordinary vinegar or lemon juice, boil for a few seconds, then mix in a good piece of fine butter.

'This may be made with fish glaze instead of chicken glaze'. (A. Carême, *L'Art de la cuisine française au XIXe siècle.*)

Lobster sauce I (for fish). SAUCE HOMARD—Add to 1 cup (2 decilitres) of *White wine sauce** 2 tablespoons of lobster butter. Heighten the seasoning with a pinch of cayenne and strain through a cloth. Add at the last moment a tablespoon of lobster flesh cut in very small dice.

Lobster sauce II, English (for fish). SAUCE HOMARD À L'ANGLAISE—Add to 1¼ cups (2½ decilitres) of *Béchamel sauce* (see above), ½ teaspoon of anchovy essence or paste and 2 tablespoons (40 grams) of lobster flesh cut in dice. Heighten the seasoning with a pinch of cayenne.

Lyonnaise sauce III (Old recipe). SAUCE À LA LYONNAISE—'Blanch 4 large onions cut in dice and simmer them in clarified butter. When almost cooked, drain them on a horsehair sieve, then mix them with 2 tablespoons of game *fumet** and ½ cup of *Allemande sauce** (see above), stirring vigorously. When this is cooked down to the desired point, add a little chopped and blanched tarragon, the juice of a lemon, a little grated nutmeg, a little butter, and a little game glaze'. (A. Carême, *L'Art de la cuisine française au XIXe siècle.*)

Maître d'hôtel sauce (Old recipe). SAUCE À LA MAÎTRE D'HÔTEL LIÉE—'Put into a saucepan ⅓ cup of half-thickened *Velouté sauce**. Just before serving it should be boiling. Remove from heat, blend in a little glaze and some *Maître d'hôtel butter* prepared in the usual way (see BUTTER, *Compound butters*). Mix thoroughly'. (A. Carême, *L'Art de la cuisine française au XIXe siècle.*)

Maltaise sauce I (for boiled vegetables). SAUCE MALTAISE Add to 1 cup (2 decilitres) of *Hollandaise sauce* (see below) some blood-orange juice and a teaspoon of finely grated orange peel.

Maltaise sauce II. SAUCE MALTAISE—Proceed as above, using tangerine juice and peel.

Note. This sauce may be flavoured with a few drops of curaçao.

Marinière sauce (for fish, mussels, timbales, vol-au-vent). SAUCE MARINIÈRE—Prepare a *Bercy sauce* (with mussel cooking liquor). Thicken it with eggs yolks as for *White wine sauce.*

Morel sauce (Old recipe). SAUCE AROMATIQUE AUX MORILLES—'Put into a saucepan a pinch of rosemary, the same amount of sage, thyme and basil, quarter of a bay leaf, a clove, a little mignonette and a pinch of nutmeg. Add a chopped onion and 2 tablespoons of good consommé. Simmer for a few minutes, strain through a cloth, using pressure, put into it thirty sound and perfectly washed small morels. When boiling is established pour in enough *Allemande sauce** (see above) for an entrée and cook down to the desired point.

'Just before serving, blend in a little chicken glaze, a little fine butter, the juice of a lemon and a dessertspoon of chopped and blanched chervil'. (A. Carême, *L'Art de la cuisine française au XIXe siècle.*)

Mornay sauce I (for eggs and vegetables). SAUCE MORNAY—Boil down by one-third 1 cup (2 decilitres) of *Béchamel sauce** mixed with ½ cup (1 decilitre) of fresh cream.

Add ⅓ cup (40 grams) of grated Gruyère and Parmesan cheese, mix, incorporate 3 tablespoons (50 grams) of butter and strain.

Mornay sauce II (for chicken or eggs). SAUCE MORNAY

—Proceed as in the preceding recipe, replacing the cream with light chicken stock.

Mornay sauce III (for fish). SAUCE MORNAY—Proceed as above, cooking the *Béchamel sauce* with fish stock or *fumet** in which the fish was cooked.

Mousseline sauce or Sauce Chantilly (for fish and boiled vegetables). SAUCE MOUSSELINE, SAUCE CHANTILLY—Add to 1 cup (2 decilitres) of *Hollandaise sauce* at the last moment ½ cup (1 decilitre) of whipped cream.

Mousseuse sauce (for fish and boiled vegetables). SAUCE MOUSSEUSE—Put into a basin rinsed with boiling water and wiped dry, ½ pound (250 grams) of very fine butter softened to a creamy consistency and season with a pinch of salt.

Beat with a whisk, adding little by little 1 cup (2 decilitres) of cold water and a squeeze of lemon juice.

At the last moment add 2 or 3 tablespoons of whipped cream.

Note. This sauce is served cold.

Mustard sauce I (for boiled or grilled fish). SAUCE MOUTARDE—Add to 1 cup (2 decilitres) of *Butter sauce* a teaspoon of mustard and strain.

Mustard sauce II. SAUCE MOUTARDE—Proceed as above, replacing the *Butter sauce* by *Hollandaise sauce.*

Nantua sauce I (for eggs, fish, crustaceans). SAUCE NANTUA—Boil down by half ½ cup (1 decilitre) of *Béchamel sauce* to which the cooking liquor of crayfish and ½ cup (1 decilitre) of cream have been added.

Finish off with 3 tablespoons (50 grams) of crayfish butter (see BUTTER, *Compound butters*), a few drops of brandy and a pinch of cayenne; strain.

Nantua sauce II. SAUCE NANTUA—Heat ¾ cup (1½ decilitres) of crayfish purée and dilute to the desired consistency with 4 tablespoons (60 grams) of butter and a few tablespoons of cream. Heighten the seasoning with a pinch of cayenne; strain.

Normande (Normandy) sauce I (for fish). SAUCE NORMANDE—Mix in a saucepan 1 cup (2 decilitres) of *Velouté sauce* based on fish stock, ½ cup (1 decilitre) of fish *fumet** and ½ cup (1 decilitre) of mushroom cooking liquor. Boil down by one-third over a good heat. Add 2 egg yolks mixed with 2 tablespoons of cream.

Finish off with 3 tablespoons (50 grams) of butter and 3 tablespoons of cream; strain through a cloth.

Normande (Normandy) sauce II. SAUCE NORMANDE—Boil down by half 1 cup (2 decilitres) of fish *fumet** to which 2 tablespoons of mushroom skins have been added.

Add 1 cup (2 decilitres) of *Velouté sauce** based on fish stock and ½ cup (1 decilitre) of cream. Cook down by half. Finish by adding 3 tablespoons (50 grams) of butter and 4 tablespoons of cream. Strain through a cloth.

Onion sauce (English cookery) (for boiled mutton, poultry, braised game, rabbit, tripe). SAUCE AUX OIGNONS—Cook ½ cup (100 grams) of chopped onions in 1½ cups (3 decilitres) of milk with salt, pepper and nutmeg. Drain them as soon as they are cooked and chop again more finely.

Stir the milk in which the onions were cooked into a white *roux* composed of 1½ tablespoons (20 grams) of butter and 3 tablespoons (20 grams) of flour. Bring to the boil, add the onions and cook gently for 8 minutes.

Note. This sauce is always served poured over the meat it accompanies.

Oyster sauce I (for fish). SAUCE AUX HUÎTRES—Add to 1 cup (2 decilitres) of *Normande* or *White wine sauce* (incorporating concentrated oyster cooking liquor) 8 oysters, poached, drained and de-bearded.

Oyster sauce II, English (for boiled cod). SAUCE AUX HUÎTRES À L'ANGLAISE—Stir into a blond *roux*, composed of 1½ tablespoons (20 grams) of butter and 2 tablespoons (15 grams) of flour, ½ cup (1 decilitre) of oyster cooking liquor, ½ cup (1 decilitre) of milk and ½ cup (1 decilitre) of cream. Season with a very small pinch of salt, bring to the boil and cook for 10 minutes.

Strain through a cloth, add 12 poached, de-bearded and sliced oysters; heighten the seasoning with a pinch of cayenne.

Paloise sauce (for grilled meat and poultry). SAUCE PALOISE—Proceed as for *Béarnaise sauce*, replacing the tarragon by mint.

Parsley sauce I (English cookery) (for calf's head, boiled poultry and rabbit and braised veal). SAUCE PERSIL—Add to 1¼ cups (2½ decilitres) of *Butter sauce* a tablespoon of chopped and blanched parsley and a few drops of lemon juice.

Parsley sauce II (for mackerel and salmon). SAUCE PERSIL—Stir into 3 tablespoons (30 grams) of white *roux* 1¼ cups (2½ decilitres) of parsley-flavoured *court-bouillon* left from cooking the fish. Simmer for 8 minutes; strain.

At the moment of serving, finish off with a teaspoon of chopped parsley and a squeeze of lemon juice.

Piémontaise sauce (Old recipe) (for braised and pot-roasted chicken). SAUCE À LA PIÉMONTAISE—'Cut two large onions into very small dice, and cook them to a nice golden colour in clarified butter. Having strained them, cook them in some excellent consommé and remove all grease. Blend in enough *Béchamel sauce* to accompany an entrée and half a pound of Piedmont truffles cut in large dice, then 2 tablespoons of *pignoli* (pine kernels), white and clean. After the sauce has boiled for an instant, mix in a little chicken glaze, a little garlic butter and the juice of a lemon'. (A. Carême, *L'Art de la cuisine française au XIXe siècle.)*

Polonaise sauce (Old recipe). SAUCE POLONAISE—'Scrape a root of horseradish then grate half of it, put three spoonfuls of this into a saucepan with a spoonful of sugar. Dilute it little by little with half-thickened *Velouté sauce,** in sufficient quantity to accompany an entrée. When this sauce comes to the boil, add the juice of a lemon, a little glaze and some fine butter'. (A. Carême, *L'Art de la cuisine française au XIXe siècle.)*

Poulette sauce (for vegetables and poached offal or U.S. variety meats). SAUCE POULETTE—Add to 1 cup (2 decilitres) of *Allemande sauce* a tablespoon of chopped parsley and a few drops of lemon juice.

Princesse sauce (Old recipe). SAUCE PRINCESSE—'Add to ½ cup of boiling *Allemande sauce* some blanched chopped parsley, a pinch of grated nutmeg, a little chicken glaze, a little butter and the juice of a lemon'. (A. Carême, *L'Art de la cuisine française au XIXe siècle.)*

Printanière sauce (for eggs and poultry). SAUCE PRINTANIÈRE—Finish 1 cup (2 decilitres) of *Allemande sauce** with 3 tablespoons (50 grams) of green *Printanier butter*. Strain. See BUTTER, *Compound butters.*

Provençal garlic sauce (Old recipe). SAUCE À L'AIL À LA PROVENÇALE—'Simmer in a saucepan 4 cloves of garlic, a lightly seasoned *bouquet garni*, a pinch of mignonette pepper and 2 tablespoons of consommé. Boil down almost to the desired point, take out the garlic and the *bouquet* and then add ¼ cup of *Velouté sauce* and the beaten yolks of three eggs. After boiling for a few minutes, strain the sauce through a cloth, and at the moment of serving mix in a little butter and lemon juice'. (A. Carême, *L'Art de la cuisine française au XIXe siècle.)*

Ravigote sauce (for offal or U.S. variety meats and

poultry). SAUCE RAVIGOTE—Boil down by two-thirds 2 tablespoons of white wine and 2 tablespoons of vinegar to which have been added a chopped shallot, a sprig of thyme, a fragment of bay leaf, a sprig of parsley, a pinch of salt and a pinch of mignonette pepper (coarsely ground pepper).

Stir in 1 cup (2 decilitres) of *Velouté sauce** and ½ cup (1 decilitre) of mushroom cooking liquor. Boil down by one-third, finish off with 3 tablespoons (50 grams) of butter and 3 tablespoons of cream, heighten the seasoning with a pinch of cayenne and strain through a cloth.

Note. A brown sauce somewhat similar to *Piquante sauce* used to be served under the name '*ravigote*'.

Riche sauce (for fish)—See *Diplomat sauce* above.

Richelieu sauce (Old recipe). SAUCE RICHELIEU—'Cut 4 large onions into small dice, cook them till golden in clarified butter, drain on a horsehair sieve and cook in two large spoonfuls of consommé, adding a little sugar, a little grated nutmeg and some mignonette (coarsely ground pepper). When the onion is cooked, add ½ cup of *Allemande sauce*, a little chicken glaze and a little fine butter. Strain the sauce through a cloth, using pressure.

'At the moment of serving add a teaspoon of chopped and blanched chervil'. (A. Carême, *L'Art de la cuisine française au XIXe siècle.*)

Royal sauce (for poached eggs and boiled chicken). SAUCE ROYALE—Boil down by half 1 cup (2 decilitres) of *Chicken velouté sauce,** thinned with ½ cup (1 decilitre) of white chicken stock.

Add, in the course of cooking, ½ cup (1 decilitre) of cream, and, at the last moment, 2 tablespoons of raw truffles put through a sieve.

Finish off with 3 tablespoons (50 grams) of butter and a tablespoon of sherry. Strain.

Russian sauce (Old recipe) (for large cuts of beef). SAUCE À LA RUSSE—'Chop and blanch a tablespoon of parsley, chervil and tarragon, drain and mix them into some half thickened *Velouté sauce*, using enough of this to accompany an entrée. At the moment of serving, add a teaspoon of fine mustard, ½ teaspoon of sugar, a pinch of fine pepper and the juice of a lemon'. (A. Carême, *L'Art de la cuisine française au XIXe siècle.*)

Sage and onion sauce (English cookery) (for roast pork and goose). SAUCE À LA SAUGE—Chop 2 large onions, previously cooked in salted water and drained.

Put these onions into a saucepan with 2 cups (100 grams) of freshly grated breadcrumbs and 2 tablespoons (25 grams) of butter. Season with salt and pepper and add a tablespoon of chopped sage.

Cook for 5 minutes mixing well with a wooden spoon. At the last moment add 3 tablespoons of the pan juices.

St. Malo sauce I (for grilled fish). SAUCE SAINT-MALO—Moisten with ½ cup (1 decilitre) of white wine 2 tablespoons of chopped onion lightly cooked in butter without colouring. Garnish with a sprig of thyme, a piece of bay leaf and a sprig of parsley. Cook down by two-thirds.

Stir in ¾ cup (1½ decilitres) of *Velouté sauce* based on fish stock and ½ cup (1 decilitre) of *Espagnole sauce** based on fish stock. Thin down with ½ cup (1 decilitre) of mushroom *fumet** and boil down by one-third.

Put through a strainer, pressing well; finish off with a teaspoon of mustard, a few drops of Worcestershire sauce and a teaspoon of butter.

St. Malo sauce II. SAUCE SAINT-MALO—Add to 1 cup (2 decilitres) of *White wine sauce** 2 teaspoons of chopped shallot cooked in white wine until no moisture remains, a teaspoon of mustard and a few drops of anchovy essence or ½ teaspoon of anchovy paste.

Scotch egg sauce (English cookery) (for cod). SAUCE À L'ÉCOSSAISE—Stir 1 cup (2 decilitres) of boiling milk into a white *roux* composed of 2 tablespoons (30 grams) of butter and 2 tablespoons (15 grams) of flour. Season with salt and pepper and a little grated nutmeg. Mix well and bring to the boil.

Add the chopped whites of two hard boiled eggs, and, at the last moment, blend in the yolks, rubbed through a coarse sieve.

Shallot sauce. SAUCE À L'ÉCHALOTE—Another name for *Bercy sauce.*

Shrimp sauce I (for fish). SAUCE AUX CREVETTES—Finish off 1 cup (2 decilitres) of *Normande sauce* (or *White wine sauce*) with 2 tablespoons of shrimp butter, heighten the seasoning with a pinch of cayenne and strain through a cloth.

Note. If the sauce is served separately add to it, at the last moment, a tablespoon of shelled shrimps.

Shrimp sauce II, English (for fish). SAUCE AUX CREVETTES À L'ANGLAISE—Add to 1¼ cups (2½ decilitres) of *English butter sauce* ½ teaspoon of anchovy essence and 2 tablespoons (40 grams) of tiny shelled shrimps. Heighten the seasoning with a pinch of cayenne.

Soubise sauce (Old recipe). SAUCE SOUBISE—'Cut 4 onions in two, make four incisions from top to bottom down the onion, then cut them across and throw them into boiling water for a moment. Drain and put them into a saucepan with a good piece of Isigny butter and a little consommé. Simmer over a low heat. As soon as it is cooked, strain anew and pour into the saucepan with 4 tablespoons of concentrated consommé from which all grease has been removed. Add to this ½ cup of *Béchamel sauce*, a pinch of nutmeg, a little sugar and a little chicken glaze. Strain through a cloth, using pressure. Just before serving, blend in a little Isigny butter.' (A. Carême, *L'Art de la cuisine française au XIXe siècle.*)

Suprême sauce I (for eggs, poultry, offal or U.S. variety meats and vegetables). SAUCE SUPRÊME, VELOUTÉ À LA CRÈME—To make 2½ cups (5 decilitres): mix in a thick-bottomed saucepan 2½ cups (5 decilitres) of *Chicken velouté sauce* and 2 cups (4 decilitres) of light chicken stock. Boil down by half over a good heat, adding during the cooking 1½ cups (3 or 4 decilitres) of fresh cream.

When the sauce coats the spoon, incorporate, away from the heat, 3 tablespoons (50 grams) of fresh butter and strain. Keep in a *bain-marie* (double boiler) until needed.

Suprême sauce II (Old recipe). SAUCE AU SUPRÊME—'Put into a saucepan some *Allemande sauce* in sufficient quantity to accompany an entrée. When it is almost boiling and just before serving, add 3 to 4 tablespoons of chicken consommé and 2 small pats of Isigny butter.' (A. Carême, *L'Art de la cuisine française au XIXe siècle.*)

Talleyrand sauce. SAUCE TALLEYRAND—Cook down by half 1 cup (2 decilitres) of *Chicken velouté sauce* and 1 cup (2 decilitres) of light stock. As soon as boiling is established, add 4 tablespoons of fresh cream and ¼ cup (½ decilitre) of Madeira. Incorporate, away from the heat, 3 tablespoons (50 grams) of butter. Strain.

Add a tablespoon of vegetable *mirepoix** and a tablespoon of truffles and scarlet (pickled) tongue cut in very small dice.

Velouté sauce with green onions (Old recipe). SAUCE VELOUTÉE À LA CIVETTE—'Put into a saucepan ¼ cup of *Allemande sauce* and 2 tablespoons of tomato sauce, add a pinch of grated nutmeg, pepper and the juice of a lemon, allow to boil for a moment, then just before serving, blend in shrimp butter and a teaspoon of very finely chopped green onion.' (A. Carême, *L'Art de la cuisine française au XIXe siècle.*)

Venetian sauce I (for eggs and poultry). SAUCE VÉNITIENNE—Cook down by two-thirds ½ cup (1 decilitre) of vinegar to which a chopped shallot and 2 tablespoons of chopped chervil and parsley have been added.

Stir in 1 cup (2 decilitres) of *Allemande sauce*, finish off with 3 tablespoons (50 grams) of *Green butter* (see BUTTER, *Compound butters*), strain and add a tablespoon of chopped chervil and tarragon.

Venetian sauce II (Old recipe). SAUCE VÉNITIENNE—'Just before serving have boiling in a saucepan 2 tablespoons of *Allemande sauce*, mix in a good pinch of shredded tarragon leaves blanched and drained on a silk strainer, then a tablespoon of chicken glaze, a little Isigny butter, a pinch of grated nutmeg and a few drops of good tarragon vinegar.' (A. Carême, *L'Art de la cuisine française au XIXe siècle.*)

Véron sauce (for fish). SAUCE VÉRON—Cook the wine and herbs as for *Béarnaise sauce*. Stir in 1 cup (2 decilitres) of *Normande sauce* and 2 tablespoons of very concentrated brown veal gravy (or fish glaze). Heighten the seasoning with a pinch of cayenne, strain and add a tablespoon of chopped chervil and tarragon.

Victoria sauce (for fish). SAUCE VICTORIA—Prepare 1¼ cups (2½ decilitres) of *Lobster sauce*.

Add to it when finished 2 to 3 tablespoons of lobster flesh and truffles cut in very small dice.

Villeroi sauce (to coat foodstuffs to be fried à la Villeroi). SAUCE VILLEROI—Cook down until it will coat the back of the spoon 1 cup (2 decilitres) of *Allemande sauce* thinned with 4 tablespoons of light stock and mushroom *fumet**.

Strain and stir well until it is cold.

This sauce is used when almost cold to coat foodstuffs which are then dipped in a mixture of egg, oil and seasoning and breadcrumbed before being fried in deep fat.

Note. According to the recipe chosen, this sauce may be finished with truffle *essence**, *Tomato purée* or *Soubise purée*. See PURÉE.

Depending on its intended use, it may also have truffles, chopped mushrooms, *mirepoix** of vegetables, etc. added to it.

Villeroi sauce for fish is prepared with *Allemande sauce* based on fish stock.

White wine sauce I (for fish). SAUCE VIN BLANC—Boil down by two-thirds ¾ cup (1½ decilitres) of fish *fumet** (made with white wine).

Allow to cool a little and add 2 egg yolks, beat with a whisk over a low heat until it thickens, as for *Hollandaise sauce*.

As soon as the yolks begin to thicken add, little by little, ⅗ cup (150 grams) of melted butter, beating all the time.

Season, sharpen with a few drops of lemon juice, and strain through a cloth.

Note. Mushroom skins and stalks may be added to the sauce in the course of the cooking.

White wine sauce II. SAUCE VIN BLANC—Prepare 1 cup (2 decilitres) of *Hollandaise sauce* adding in the course of preparation ¼ cup (½ decilitre) of concentrated fish *fumet** (made with white wine). Season and strain through a cloth.

White wine sauce III (for fish to be glazed). SAUCE VIN BLANC—Boil down by half ½ cup (1 decilitre) of fish *Velouté sauce** to which ½ cup (1 decilitre) of fish *fumet** (made with white wine) has been added.

Add 2 egg yolks, cook for a few moments over a low heat, beating and incorporating, little by little, 4 to 5 tablespoons (60 to 80 grams) of butter divided into tiny pieces. Season and strain.

COLD SAUCES—Mayonnaise is the basis of a great number of cold sauces which are used for hors-d'oeuvre and cold entrées, and may be varied in an infinite number of ways. Some of the best known cold sauces are given below.

Aïoli or Beurre de Provence—Pound finely in a small mortar 5 cloves of garlic.

Add the raw yolk of an egg and a pinch of salt. Mix with the pestle.

Pour into the mortar, stirring all the time with the pestle 1¼ cups (2½ decilitres) of olive oil, put in little by little.

Add, from time to time, a few drops of lemon juice and a few drops of water to thin down a little the consistency of the sauce.

Anchovy sauce. SAUCE ANCHOIS—Pound together hard boiled eggs and anchovy purée or paste. Add oil, vinegar, and a little pepper.

Andalouse sauce. SAUCE ANDALOUSE—*Mayonnaise sauce* to which has been added one quarter of its weight of concentrated tomato juice and sweet pimentos, peeled, cut in dice and cooked in oil.

Apple sauce (English cookery) (for pork, duck and goose). SAUCE AUX POMMES—Cook the apples till they are soft with very little sugar. Flavour with a little powdered cinnamon.

Note. This sauce is commonly used as accompaniment to a roast in Germany, England, Belgium and Holland.

Cambridge sauce (English cookery) (for cold meat). SAUCE CAMBRIDGE—Pound together hard boiled egg yolks, anchovy fillets, capers, chives, chervil and tarragon. Add English mustard. Beat in oil and vinegar in the same way as for mayonnaise. Rub through a fine sieve or a cloth. Add chopped parsley and a pinch of cayenne.

Chantilly sauce (for asparagus and other boiled vegetables served cold). SAUCE CHANTILLY—Mayonnaise to which stiffly whipped cream has been added at the last moment.

Cingalaise sauce. SAUCE CINGALAISE—A fine *salpicon** of hard boiled egg yolks, sweet pimentos, tomatoes, boiled *courgettes* (zucchini), and cucumbers, seasoned with curry and salt and mixed with oil and lemon juice. Add chopped parsley and chives.

Collioure sauce. SAUCE COLLIOURE—Mayonnaise to which has been added essence or purée of anchovies and chopped parsley, with the additional seasoning of a little grated garlic.

Cressonnière sauce. SAUCE CRESSONNIÈRE—Season with oil, vinegar, salt and pepper, finely chopped watercress and finely chopped hard boiled egg yolks. Mix.

Cumberland sauce (English cookery) (for cold venison). SAUCE CUMBERLAND—Add to 1 cup (2 decilitres) of melted redcurrant jelly, a teaspoon of chopped shallot, blanched and drained, 2 tablespoons of orange and lemon peel, cut in a fine *julienne* (thin strips) and blanched, and a teaspoon of mustard. Add 1 cup (2 decilitres) of port, the juice of an orange and a lemon. Season with salt, ginger and cayenne.

Dijonnaise sauce. SAUCE DIJONNAISE—Pound together 4 hard boiled egg yolks and 4 teaspoons of Dijon mustard. Season with salt and pepper. Beat with oil and lemon juice like a mayonnaise.

Gribiche sauce (for cold fish and crustaceans). SAUCE GRIBICHE—Hard boiled egg yolks reduced to a paste, beaten up with oil and vinegar like a mayonnaise. Season with salt and pepper. Add chopped gherkins, capers, parsley, chervil and tarragon. Add the egg whites cut in a short *julienne* (thin strips).

Mayonnaise sauce (*Robert Carrier*)

Horseradish sauce. SAUCE RAIFORT—Mix grated horseradish and breadcrumbs soaked in milk and squeezed. Season with salt and sugar. Add thick fresh cream and, at the last moment, some vinegar.

Indienne sauce. SAUCE INDIENNE—Mayonnaise seasoned with curry and with chopped chives added.

Maltaise sauce (for asparagus). SAUCE MALTAISE—Mayonnaise to which the juice of a blood orange and a ***julienne*** (thin strips) of blanched, rinsed and dried orange peel have been added.

Mayonnaise sauce I. SAUCE MAYONNAISE—For $2\frac{1}{2}$ cups (5 decilitres): 3 egg yolks, $2\frac{1}{2}$ cups (5 decilitres) olive oil, 1 tablespoon vinegar or lemon juice, 1 teaspoon (5 grams) salt, $\frac{1}{8}$ teaspoon (50 centigrams) white pepper.

Method. Put into a bowl (or into the salad dish) the egg yolks free from any white of egg. Add the salt (very dry), the white pepper and a few drops of vinegar or lemon juice.

Mix these ingredients with a whisk, not beating too hard.

Add the oil, drop by drop at first, then in a thin trickle, beating constantly either with a whisk or with a wooden spoon.

Absorb, in this way, the whole of the oil into the mayonnaise.

Thin down the consistency of the sauce from time to time by adding a few drops of the vinegar or lemon juice.

As soon as the sauce is finished, incorporate, beating all the time, 2 or 3 spoonfuls of boiling water. This addition is to preserve the texture of the mayonnaise and prevent it from breaking down, or 'curdling', if it is to be kept for some time.

Note. If the foregoing instructions are followed, a light and smooth mayonnaise can be guaranteed.

To be sure of success in making this sauce, which is really very simple in spite of the difficulties it seems to have acquired in the eyes of many housewives, it is advisable to bear the following points in mind:

1. Keep to the exact proportions of egg and oil. The maximum amount of oil is 1 cup (2 decilitres) per egg yolk of medium size.

2. Use oil at room temperature, and if, in winter, the oil has coagulated, warm it very slightly before adding it to the yolks.

3. Add the oil drop by drop at the beginning. Then when the sauce begins to thicken a little, let it pour in a very thin trickle.

Mayonnaise sauce II (Old recipe). SAUCE MAYONNAISE —'Put into a medium-sized bowl 2 fresh egg yolks, a little salt and white pepper and a little tarragon vinegar. Stir this mixture quickly with a wooden spoon. As soon as it begins to thicken, blend in, little by little, a spoonful of Aix olive oil and a little vinegar, taking care to beat the sauce against the sides of the bowl.

'On this continued beating depends the whiteness of the mayonnaise. As it takes on more body, add more oil, a little more vinegar and, at the beginning, a little aspic jelly. It is essential to put these ingredients in a little at a time, to prevent curdling.

'You will need for this preparation 2 glasses (cups) of oil, half a glass of aspic jelly and enough tarragon vinegar to give an appetizing taste. To make it whiter, add lemon juice.' (A Carême, *L'Art de la cuisine française au XIXe siècle.*)

Mayonnaise sauce III (thick) (to bind mixed salads, and coat various foodstuffs). SAUCE MAYONNAISE—Add to 1¼ cups (2½ decilitres) of mayonnaise ½ cup (1 decilitre) of melted meat jelly. Mix well with a whisk.

Note. As soon as the jelly has been added to the mayonnaise, the sauce must be used promptly, because it will set very quickly. (This sauce is used in the same way as *White chaud-froid sauce.*)

Note. Thick or jelly-strengthened mayonnaise may be finished off with various flavourings or with any of the ingredients specified for the different mayonnaise sauces.

Mayonnaise sauce with anchovy. SAUCE MAYONNAISE À L'ANCHOIS—Add to 1¼ cups (2½ decilitres) of mayonnaise a teaspoon of anchovy essence or natural anchovy purée or paste. Mix well.

Mayonnaise sauce with caviare. SAUCE MAYONNAISE AU CAVIAR—Pound in a mortar 1 tablespoon (25 grams) of caviare. Add, pounding constantly, 3 tablespoons of mayonnaise. Strain this mixture through a fine sieve, add it to 1 cup (2 decilitres) of mayonnaise and blend well.

Mayonnaise sauce with cress. SAUCE MAYONNAISE AU CRESSON—Add to the mayonnaise, kept very thick, some chopped and pressed cress.

Green mayonnaise. SAUCE VERTE—Add some mayonnaise to a purée of green herbs (spinach, watercress, parsley, chervil, tarragon, all blanched, cooled in water and pounded in a mortar). Strain.

Mayonnaise sauce à la russe. SAUCE MAYONNAISE À LA RUSSE—Add to 1½ cups (3 decilitres) of mayonnaise 2 cups (4 decilitres) of liquid jelly and a tablespoon of vinegar. Mix briskly with a whisk, on ice, until the mixture takes on the character of a mousse. (Use for moulded vegetable salads.)

Mayonnaise sauce with shrimps. SAUCE MAYONNAISE AUX CREVETTES—Pound in a mortar 2 tablespoons (50 grams) of shrimps and 3 tablespoons of mayonnaise.

Put this mixture through a fine sieve, add it to 1 cup (2 decilitres) of mayonnaise, colour with a drop of carmine and mix well.

Mayonnaise sauce with tarragon. SAUCE MAYONNAISE À L'ESTRAGON—Add to the mayonnaise, kept very thick, some finely chopped, fresh tarragon.

Mint sauce (English cookery). SAUCE MENTHE—Pour over ⅜ cup (50 grams) of shredded or chopped fresh mint 2 cups (4 decilitres) of boiling vinegar. Season with salt, pepper and brown or white sugar.

Mousquetaire sauce. SAUCE MOUSQUETAIRE—Add to 2½ cups (5 decilitres) of mayonnaise 2 tablespoons of chopped shallot cooked in white wine till all liquid is absorbed, and a tablespoon of dissolved meat glaze. Add to the seasoning a pinch of cayenne.

Mustard and cream sauce. SAUCE MOUTARDE À LA CRÈME—Add one-third Dijon mustard to two-thirds very thick cream.

Season with a little lemon juice, salt and pepper. Mix well with a whisk to render the sauce a little frothy.

Niçoise sauce. SAUCE NIÇOISE—Chop up finely 2 pimentos, add 2 tablespoons of tomato purée and a few leaves of tarragon. Pass through a coarse sieve or tammy and add to half a pint of mayonnaise.

Orientale sauce. SAUCE ORIENTALE—A mixture of three parts very thick mayonnaise mixed with tomatoes cooked to a *fondue** in oil and seasoned with saffron, and a *salpicon** of sweet peppers.

Parisian sauce (for cold asparagus). SAUCE PARISIENNE—Pound in a bowl 2 small Gervais cheeses (*Petits suisses* or 2 ounces Philadelphia cream cheese). Season with salt and paprika. Beat with oil and lemon juice like a mayonnaise. Add a tablespoon of chopped chervil.

Provençal sauce. SAUCE PROVENÇALE—Season with oil, vinegar, salt and pepper a mixture of peeled, pressed and chopped tomatoes, hard boiled eggs, capers, gherkins and parsley, all chopped; flavour with a little garlic.

Ravigote sauce. SAUCE RAVIGOTE—Season with oil, vinegar, salt and pepper a mixture of capers, onions, chives, parsley, chervil and tarragon, all chopped.

Rémoulade sauce. SAUCE RÉMOULADE—Mayonnaise to which has been added mustard, anchovy essence, gherkins, capers, parsley and chervil, all chopped.

Note. Rémoulade sauce is also made, in home cooking, by seasoning with oil, vinegar, salt and pepper a mixture of hard boiled eggs, capers, gherkins and herbs, all chopped.

Russian sauce. SAUCE RUSSE—Add to some mayonnaise a quarter of its volume of a purée made with caviare and the creamy parts (coral, etc.) of a lobster, all pounded and rubbed through a fine sieve. Add mustard.

Sardalaise sauce. SAUCE SARDALAISE—Pound 6 hard boiled egg yolks with 2 or 3 tablespoons of thick fresh cream. Add to 1 cup of fresh sieved truffles.

Beat up this sauce with oil and lemon like a mayonnaise, season with salt and pepper and add a tablespoon of Armagnac.

Vinaigrette sauce (*Robert Carrier*)

Shallot sauce (for raw oysters and shellfish). SAUCE ÉCHALOTE—Vinegar to which has been added finely chopped shallot seasoned with salt and freshly milled pepper (or mignonette pepper).

Swedish sauce (for goose and cold pork). SAUCE SUÉDOISE—Mayonnaise to which apples cooked without sugar are added, seasoned with grated horseradish or mustard.

Tartare sauce. SAUCE TARTARE—Mayonnaise made with hard boiled egg yolks and with chopped chives added.

La Varenne sauce. SAUCE LA VARENNE—Mayonnaise to which dry *duxelles**, (made with oil) and chopped parsley and chervil, have been added.

Verdurette sauce. SAUCE VERDURETTE—Put into a bowl 6 tablespoons of chopped chives, boiled, cooled in water and drained, 2 finely chopped hard boiled egg yolks and 2 tablespoons of chopped chervil, tarragon and parsley. Add oil, vinegar, salt and pepper.

Vinaigrette sauce. SAUCE VINAIGRETTE, SAUCE À L'HUILE —As a general principle, salads are seasoned at table. This seasoning is made in the proportion of a tablespoon of vinegar to 3 tablespoons of oil. Salt and pepper are added in the usual proportions.

Separately prepared *Vinaigrette sauce* is served with asparagus, cauliflower, boiled fish, etc. It is also served with calf's head, but with the addition of chopped parsley and onion, and sometimes thickened with pounded calf's brain.

Vincent sauce. SAUCE VINCENT—Add to some mayonnaise a purée of green herbs (sorrel, parsley, chervil, watercress, chives and burnet) and some chopped hard boiled egg yolks (the chopped whites of the hard boiled eggs may also be added to this sauce).

DESSERT SAUCES. SAUCES POUR LES ENTREMETS—

Apricot sauce. SAUCE À L'ABRICOT—Rub a dozen ripe apricots through a fine sieve or crush in blender. Put the pulp thus obtained into a small copper pan and dilute it with 2 cups (5 decilitres) of light syrup. Bring to the boil, take off scum and remove from heat when the sauce coats the spoon. Pass through muslin bag or a fine strainer.

Flavour with a tablespoon of kirsch or any other liqueur, as indicated.

Note. Apricot sauce, which is used as an accompaniment to hot or cold sweets, can be served hot or cold, depending on the nature of these dishes. If served hot, it can be made smoother in texture by adding a very small quantity of fresh butter. When stewed, fresh, canned or bottled apricots are used, the syrup should be used for diluting the sauce.

Apricot sauce can also be made by diluting apricot jam with hot water. This sauce should be strained and flavoured, as described above.

Cherry sauce. SAUCE AUX CERISES—Prepared with fresh cherry pulp or cherry jam in the same way as for *Apricot sauce*.

The sauce is used as an accompaniment for hot or cold sweets.

Chocolate sauce I. CRÈME AU CHOCOLAT—Moisten ¼ pound (125 grams) of grated semi-sweet chocolate with 1 cup (2 decilitres) of lukewarm water. Work on a low heat until it boils. Cook for 15 minutes. Finally add ½ cup of thick fresh cream and a tablespoon of butter.

This sauce is usually served hot, but it can also be used cold.

Chocolate sauce II. CRÈME AU CHOCOLAT—Add softened sweet chocolate to a pint (½ litre) of custard cream, prepared according to the recipe for *Custard cream*. See CREAMS.

Custard sauces—See CREAMS, *Custard creams*.

Pineapple sauce. SAUCE À L'ANANAS—Use syrup in which pineapple has been cooked for another sweet course. Bring it to the boil and thicken with a teaspoon of arrowroot or cornstarch.

Pass this syrup through a silk sieve or through a muslin bag and then flavour it, according to directions of the recipe, with kirsch, rum or any other liqueur.

This thickened syrup is used for pouring over some sweet dishes, hot or cold, such as tarts, puddings, etc. It takes the place of apricot sauce, which is normally used for this purpose.

Raspberry sauce. SAUCE AUX FRAMBOISES—This is made in the same way as *Strawberry sauce*, substituting raspberries for strawberries.

Strawberry sauce. SAUCE AUX FRAISES—Use either strawberry jam or fresh strawberry pulp, diluted with syrup and flavoured with liqueurs.

SAUCEBOAT. SAUCIÈRE—Part of dinner service, in porcelain or metal, generally oval in form.

Silver sauceboats are often supplied with a double bottom which can be heated.

The saucisson
(*French Government Tourist Office*)

SAUCISSON—There is a great variety of saucissons, large sausages which are always served sliced, some made in France (and these are numerous and savoury) and others, equally numerous, made in other countries of Europe.

Among the best-known French *saucissons* which require no cooking, are those of Lyon, Arles, Lorraine, Brittany, Mortagne, Strasbourg and Luchon.

Among the large sausages made abroad, mention must first be made of those which come from Italy, such as those from Milan, Bologna and Florence, not forgetting (because this also is a kind of *saucisson*) the *mortadella* of Bologna.

Also included in this category are certain other kinds of *charcuterie:* for example salami (from Italy, Germany, Switzerland and other countries of Europe) and saveloys, made in France and elsewhere. But these last are not eaten raw.

The manufacture of these large sausages is strictly controlled in France. They may be made with pork meat only, lean and fat, to which there may sometimes be added, for certain specialities, beef, veal or mutton.

Any sausages containing horse, donkey or mule meat, or having a proportion of flour, must carry labels detailing these contents exactly.

Dried sausage, such as comes from Arles or Lyon, the *saucisson de ménage*, the *saucisson de montagne* and other sausage of the same type is eaten raw, as hors-d'oeuvre.

The saveloy sausage of Paris, Lyon, Nancy and other places is poached in water and eaten as hors-d'oeuvre, hot or cold.

Household or home-made sausage. SAUCISSON DE MÉNAGE, SAUCISSON VIEUX—This sausage is made in large pig's intestines with a forcemeat composed of lean pork meat, minced or chopped with a knife, seasoned with

3 tablespoons (45 grams) of salt, 1½ teaspoons (3 grams) of pepper, ½ teaspoon (1 gram) of peppercorns, ¼ teaspoon (1 gram) of saltpetre and enough chopped garlic to cover the point of a knife for every 2 pounds (kilo) of forcemeat.

Fill the skins, tie them longways and round, and hang in the drying place.

After three or four weeks the skin becomes pink and small white marks appear here and there on the surface, showing that the sausages have 'ripened' and are successful.

This sausage is eaten as it is, when it has become well dried.

Lyon sausage (dry). SAUCISSON DE LYON (SEC)—Ham made from fresh pork, carefully trimmed and with all fat removed, is used to make this sausage. This meat is chopped, and in the course of the chopping seasoned with 3 tablespoons (45 grams) of salt and 1 teaspoon (2 grams) of pepper for each 2 pounds (kilo) of meat.

There is then added, for every 2 pounds (kilo) of forcemeat, 4½ ounces (135 grams) of diced pork fat (the dice about ¼ inch square) taken from a very firm piece of pork fat which has been salted dry for 10 days.

Add to this mixture ½ teaspoon (1 gram) of white peppercorns and as much chopped garlic as will go on the point of a knife.

Press this mixture into big pig's intestine and tie at 18 inch lengths.

Tie up the sausages in the drying place and leave them for 48 hours.

Press the sausages at each end to solidify the contents of the skins, and re-tie them. String the sausages longways and crossways so as to make them very straight in shape.

Hang them in the drying place, where they must be left for three or four months, until they are very dry.

Note. Some beef, well trimmed and with all gristle, etc. removed, may be added to the pork. This addition hastens the drying of the sausages and does not harm the quality.

Lyon sausage is eaten raw as hors-d'oeuvre.

Parisian saucisson. SAUCISSON-CERVELAS DE PARIS—Made with a forcemeat similar to that described above, seasoned, for each 2 pounds (1 kilo) with 2 tablespoons (40 grams) of salt, 1 teaspoon (2 grams) of pepper, ½ teaspoon (1 gram) of pounded pimento (cayenne pepper), and a small pinch (1 gram) of saltpetre. Fill skins with this as described above. Divide into sections of equal length. Hang the sausages above the stove for a day or two so that they dry and redden in colour.

Prepare for the table by poaching in water.

Plain saucisson. SAUCISSON-CERVELAS ORDINAIRE—Trim carefully some lean fresh pork and remove all gristle. Chop roughly. Add, for every 10 pounds (5 kilos) of lean meat 2 pounds (1 kilo) of finely chopped, fresh pork fat.

Season this mixture with 1½ tablespoons (25 grams) of salt, 1 teaspoon (2 grams) of pepper and ½ teaspoon (1 gram) of saltpetre to each 2 pounds (kilo) of pork.

Blend the mixture well and press it into beef gut. Divide it into lengths of 8 to 12 inches, tying the ends of each sausage. Smoke lightly.

To cook. Poach in water or light stock for 30 to 45 minutes according to the size of the sausages.

These are served hot (usually accompanied by a potato salad) or cold.

SAUERKRAUT (Pickled cabbage). CHOUCROUTE—Finely shredded cabbage, which has fermented in brine flavoured with juniper berries. The fermentation, which deprives the cabbage of a part of its nutritive value, makes it more digestible. The indigestibility attributed to sauerkraut really derives from the salted or smoked and fat meats which normally accompany it.

Preparation of the cabbage—Remove the green and torn leaves surrounding the cabbage. Remove the stem. With the help of a slicing device or a knife with a large blade, slice the cabbage finely. Wash it well. Drain. Put the cabbage into a receptacle (earthenware crock) which has been lined with cabbage leaves or vine leaves. Arrange the cabbage in layers, pressed down, each layer sprinkled with sea salt (coarse salt) and strewn with juniper berries. Put a handful of sea salt on the last layer of cabbage, allowing 3 pounds (1500 grams) of salt for every 200 pounds (100 kilos) of cabbage.

Cover the surface with a cloth and set a round wooden cover on top of the cloth, the diameter of which is smaller than the aperture. Put a non-porous stone on top of the wooden lid.

The next day the water will rise above the lid under this pressure. See that this is always so. Keep the barrel or crock in an airy place. At the end of about 3 weeks when no more froth appears on top of the cabbage, the sauerkraut is ready. Replace the liquid with fresh water.

Note. Each time some cabbage is taken out, remove the liquid with a wooden bowl, and after taking the cabbage put back the cloth, the cover, and the stone, and add fresh water.

Sauerkraut as soup garnish. CHOUCROUTE POUR GARNITURE DE POTAGE—Wash, soak and press the sauerkraut, and put it in a white consommé to cook gently.

When it is cooked, drain it and add it to the soup.

Sauerkraut à l'alsacienne. CHOUCROUTE À L'ALSACIENNE—Soak 5 pounds (2 kilos 500 grams) of sauerkraut for a few hours in cold water (indispensable precaution if old sauerkraut is used, but useless on the other hand if the sauerkraut is fresh). Drain the sauerkraut by pressing it well between the palms of the hands to extract all the water. Then spread it out, so that it is not congealed into lumps. Season with salt and freshly ground pepper. Put the sauerkraut in a heavy pan lined with smoked bacon rinds, adding to the mass of cabbage 2 or 3 onions each stuck with a clove, 3 carrots quartered, a strong *bouquet garni**, 2½ ounces (75 grams) of juniper berries tied in a muslin bag. Add 10 ounces (300 grams) of blanched fat breast of pork, a slice of smoked pork (these being disposed in the sauerkraut) and 5 ounces (150 grams) of goose fat, or of lard.

Add enough white consommé to come to the top of the sauerkraut. Cover with bards of larding bacon. Set to boil on the stove and then put the braising pan in the oven for four hours. Remove the lean pork and the smoked pork.

When the sauerkraut is cooked, take the vegetables, the *bouquet garni** and the juniper berries out of the pan. Arrange the sauerkraut, well drained, either in a vegetable dish or in a deep platter.

Garnish with the smoked pork cut up into slices, the lean pork cut into rectangles, with thin slices of ham, poached Strasbourg sausages and smoked *cervelas* (saveloys). Add potatoes which have been pared into a neat shape and boiled, or serve these on a separate dish.

Note. Sauerkraut can, of course, be prepared with other garnishes. For instance, a salted brisket (U.S. corned beef) can be set to cook in the sauerkraut. (The brisket can also be half cooked in a white stock before being put in the sauerkraut.)

Smoked goose can be cooked in the sauerkraut, or a smoked loin of pork, or simply salt pork.

All these meats which are intended to impart their

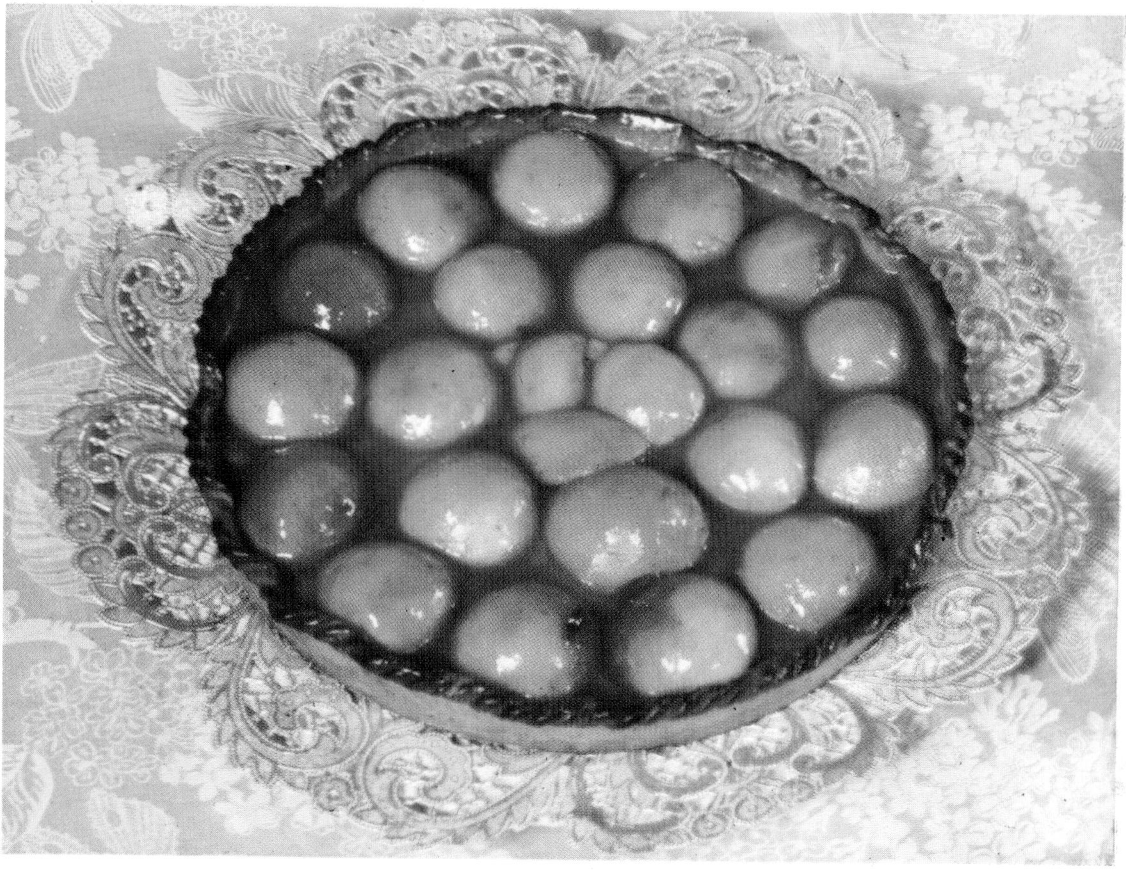

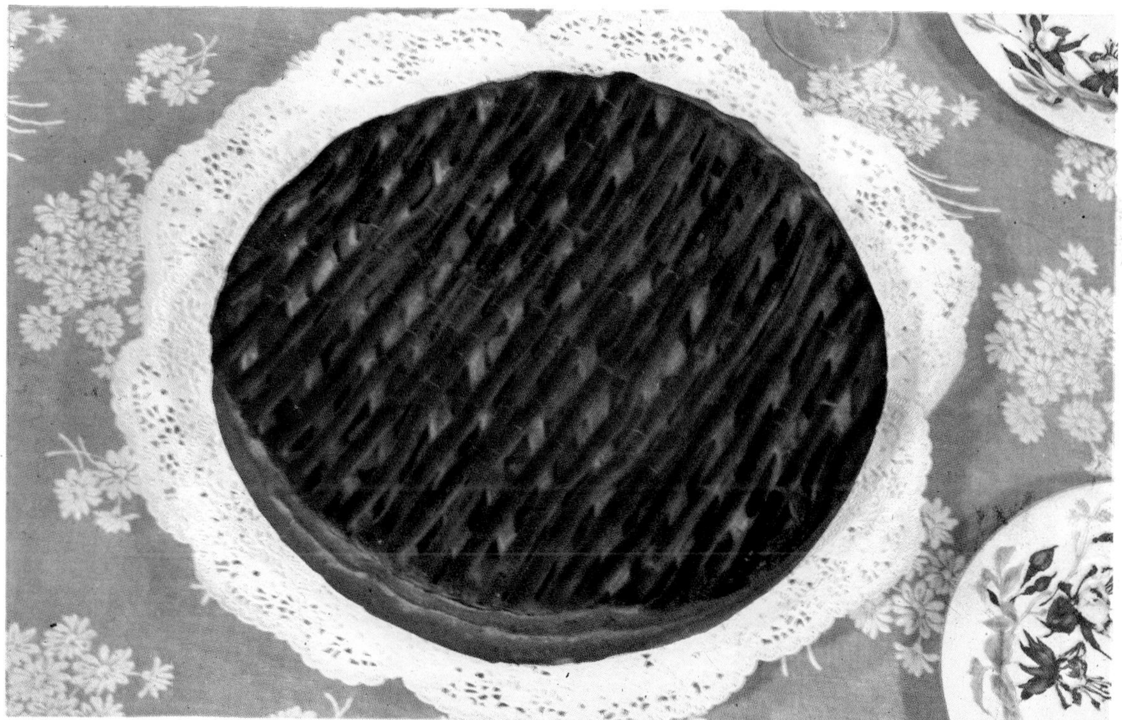

TARTS. *Above:* Apricot tart *Below:* Apple tart

(*From Curnonsky:* Cuisine et Vins de France)

(*Hotel Lutetia*)

VACHERIN

(*From Curnonsky:* Cuisine et Vins de France)

flavour to the sauerkraut must, as a rule, be removed from the braising pan before the cooking is completed (or they would be overcooked).

Sauerkraut prepared in the Frankfurt manner is very much the same as *à l'alsacienne*, but the Strasbourg sausages in the garnish are replaced by frankfurters.

It is customary in Alsace to accompany the sauerkraut with a dish of pease-pudding, as well as with the boiled potatoes.

Sauerkraut à la Strasbourgeoise. CHOUCROUTE À LA STRASBOURGEOISE—This name is given sometimes to *Sauerkraut à l'alsacienne*, for which the recipe is given above.

Sauerkraut garnish I. CHOUCROUTE POUR GARNITURE—Put 2 pounds (a kilo) of sauerkraut which has been rinsed, soaked in cold water, and thoroughly pressed, in a casserole with some lard, the bottom being already lined with bacon rinds, and sliced onions and carrots. Put a *bouquet garni** in the middle of the sauerkraut and a dozen juniper berries tied up in muslin. Moisten with a white consommé from which not all the fat has been skimmed. Cover with bacon rinds. Bring to the boil on top of the stove, and cook in the oven for 3 hours.

Sauerkraut garnish II. CHOUCROUTE POUR GARNITURE—Line a buttered casserole with slices of onion and carrot. Put the sauerkraut which has been first washed, soaked, and pressed, on to this base. Season and add a *bouquet garni** and a few juniper berries tied up in muslin. Moisten with water. Cover with a buttered paper. Cook in the same way as above.

Sauerkraut salad à l'allemande. CHOUCROUTE EN SALADE À L'ALLEMANDE—Cook the sauerkraut in a white consommé or in water with whole onions. Once the sauerkraut is cooked remove the onions and cut them into small dice.

Add them to the drained sauerkraut; season with oil, vinegar, salt and pepper. Mix well. Arrange in a salad bowl, the salad being piled into the form of a dome. Garnish with hard boiled eggs and rounds of cooked beetroot.

SAUPIQUET—In the Middle Ages the saupiquet was simply a wine sauce thickened with *pain hallé* (grilled bread or toast) which was served with roast rabbit, and also, like *Dodine sauce*, with waterfowl. Here is the recipe which Taillevent gives in the *Viandier* for this sauce:

'To make *saupiquet* for coney or other roast, toast some bread and put it to soak in some bouillon, melt bacon fat in a frying pan, put some onion cut up very small into it and fry it. To serve four, take 2 ounces of cinnamon, ½ ounce of ginger and ½ ounce of small spices, some red wine and some vinegar. Mix the bread and all the spices together and set to boil in a pan or in a pot, then pour over the roast.'

This sauce was, in fact, quite similar to one made today in the south-west of France which accompanies roast hare.

SAUR—French word used to describe a herring that has been both salted and smoked. The word was formerly *sauret* or *soret*. See HERRING.

SAUREL—A long fish resembling the mackerel and sometimes in England called *Horse mackerel*. Less positive in colour than the proper mackerel, it also lacks its false fins near the tail and has a row of spines on either side of the back. The flesh, of good quality, is not so fine as that of the real mackerel.

In U.S.A. the horse mackerel is the name applied to an Atlantic species of *Tuna fish*. The Atlantic *Bluefish* is also called sometimes *Horse mackerel* and more closely resembles the *Saurel*.

Prepared like mackerel.

SAUSAGE (SMALL SAUSAGE). SAUCISSE—This word comes from the Latin *salsisium*, from *salsus*, salted. This etymology seems to indicate that sausages can be made with all sorts of salt meats, which is of course true, but such preparations are only called sausages by extension, this word being applied more precisely to chopped pork meat packed into gut.

Sausages of all kinds are usually bought already prepared.

In France ordinary sausages, that is to say those made from fresh pork, are made both long and flat in shape. The flat sausages are called *crépinettes*.

Usually these small pieces of *charcuterie* are grilled. They can also be fried in butter or fat, or they can be boiled. This last method is chiefly used for 'dry' sausages or smoked sausages, such as those of Frankfurt, Strasbourg, Spain (*chorizos*), Vienna, etc. Recipes for sausages other than foreign sausages are given under the word PORK.

Augsburgerwürste. SAUCISSES D'AUGSBOURG—Made in beef gut, with a forcemeat of coarsely chopped lean pork mixed with bacon fat cut in small dice, seasoned with salt, pepper, cloves, nutmeg and saltpetre. These sausages, after having been dried are smoked lightly. They are poached in water.

Chorizos, red sausages. SAUCISSES ROUGES—These sausages are a Spanish speciality. They are made like *Country sausages* (see PORK), using pork forcemeat strongly flavoured with red pepper.

They are used as an ingredient of *potées*. They are most frequently cooked with *garbanzos*, i.e. chick-peas, stewed *à la mode d'Espagne* (Spanish style).

Flat sausages. SAUCISSES PLATES—Sausages wrapped in pig's caul (or pork fat); they are known under the name of *crépinettes* and are grilled or fried.

Frankfurt sausages or Frankfurterwürste. SAUCISSES DE FRANCFORT—Frankfurt sausages, a German speciality, are most often used to accompany sauerkraut. They are also served hot, as hors-d'oeuvre, with grated horseradish. They are made from a forcemeat composed of lean beef, trimmed of all fat, etc., and well beaten, and pork meat. Saltpetre is added to give a slightly pink colour. These sausages are tied together in pairs and smoked. They are poached in water.

Plunge the sausages into boiling water. Cover the pot, allow them to poach, boiling imperceptibly, for 10 minutes.

Drain and serve according to the recipe.

Gehirnwürste. SAUCISSES DE CERVELLE—Made in pork gut with a forcemeat consisting of equal parts of pork brains (cooked in salted and acidulated water) and pork meat (half fat, half lean), seasoned with salt, pepper and mace. These sausages, tied together in pairs, are poached for 5 minutes in boiling water, then cooled and cooked in butter.

Sausages for garnish. SAUCISSES POUR GARNITURES—Small sausages, called chipolatas, are used as a garnish. They are pricked lightly with the point of a needle and cooked under a grill or in the oven, as indicated in the recipe.

Grilled sausages. SAUCISSES GRILLÉES—Prepare like ordinary long or flat sausages.

The long sausage is sometimes divided into lengths of 5 to 7 inches. Sometimes it is left whole, whatever its length, in which case it is twisted into a coil and the shape is secured with the aid of two skewers put in crossways.

Grilled sausages should be cooked slowly on a moderate fire. They are generally served with mashed potatoes.

Grutzwürste. SAUCISSES AU GRUAU—Made in pork gut in 4 inch lengths with a forcemeat composed of wheat meal cooked in an aromatic stock and rather fat pork skin, cooked and chopped, seasoned with salt, pepper, mace and chopped lemon peel. Soak these sausages for 3 minutes in boiling water, drain and dry them and toss in butter.

Knackwürste. SAUCISSES CROQUANTES—Made in pork gut with a forcemeat composed of 5 parts of lean pork, 3 parts of beef and 2 parts of fresh pork fat, seasoned with salt, cumin, garlic and saltpetre.

The sausages are tied together in pairs. They are dried for 4 days, then smoked cold. They are poached for 10 minutes in water.

Knoblauchwürste. SAUCISSES À L'AIL—Sausage encased in pork gut made from a forcemeat composed of both fat and lean pork, seasoned with salt, pepper, spice and pounded garlic.

Kochwürstel or Mettwürste. SAUCISSES À BOUILLIR—Made in beef gut with a forcemeat consisting of lean pork meat and fresh pork fat, seasoned with salt, pepper and saltpetre. These sausages are poached in water.

Königswürste. SAUCISSES ROYALES—Made in pork gut with a forcemeat composed of equal parts of chicken and partridge meat. To this forcemeat are added chopped truffles and mushrooms. It is then bound with eggs, seasoned with salt, pepper and mace and flavoured with Rhine wine.

These sausages, which are rather large, are braised, then sliced when cold and served as hors-d'oeuvre.

Sausages à la languedocienne. SAUCISSES À LA LANGUEDOCIENNE—Twist 2 pounds (1 kilo) of Toulouse sausage into a coil and secure the shape with 2 crossed skewers. Heat 3 tablespoons of lard (or goose fat) in a sauté pan and put in the sausage. Add 4 chopped cloves of garlic and a *bouquet garni**. Cook with a lid on for 18 minutes. Drain the sausage, put it on a round dish and pour over the pan juices, treated in the following manner:

Dilute with 2 tablespoons of vinegar. Moisten with 1½ cups (3 decilitres) of *Demi-glace sauce* (see SAUCE) and ½ cup (1 decilitre) of tomato purée. Boil for a few moments. Add 3 tablespoons of capers pickled in vinegar and a tablespoon of chopped parsley to the sauce.

Long sausages. SAUCISSES LONGUES—Ordinary sausages, thus called to distinguish them from the flat sausages or crépinettes.

Madrilène sausages. SAUCISSES MADRILÈNES—Made in small beef gut with a forcemeat composed of veal, fresh pork fat and sardine fillets in oil. These sausages are tied into rings. They are poached for 10 minutes in light veal stock, then cooled and fried in butter.

Sausage meat—See PORK, *pork sausages.*

Nürnbergerwürste. SAUCISSES DE NUREMBERG—Made in pork gut with a lean pork forcemeat, seasoned with salt, pepper, thyme, nutmeg and marjoram, with the addition of bacon fat cut in small dice and flavoured with kirsch. They are tied up into 3½ ounce (100 grams) sections. These sausages are fried in butter.

Polnischewürste. SAUCISSES DE POLOGNE—Made in pork gut, in ½ pound (250 gram) sections, with a forcemeat composed of two-thirds lean pork and one-third of fat, seasoned with salt, pepper, pimento and cloves, and bound with pig's blood, allowing ½ cup to the pound (2 decilitres to kilo). These sausages are dried, then smoked. To serve, poach in water.

Rindfleischkochwürste. SAUCISSES DE BOEUF À BOUILLIR—Made with beef gut with a forcemeat composed of 3 parts of lean beef and 2 parts of fresh pork fat, seasoned with salt, pepper, coriander and saltpetre. These sausages are tied in pairs. They are dried for 48 hours. To serve, poach for 10 minutes in water.

Sausages with risotto. SAUCISSES AU RISOTTO—Cook chipolata sausages in butter and white wine. Put them in the middle of a *Risotto border* (see RICE), turned out on to a round dish. Add a tablespoon of meat jelly to the pan juices and pour over the sausages.

Sausages with risotto à la piémontaise. SAUCISSES AU RISOTTO, À LA PIÉMONTAISE—Cook the sausages as described above, adding to them, towards the end of cooking, some white truffles, cut in thin slices.

Put them in the middle of a *Risotto border* (see RICE) and pour over the pan juices.

In Italy, a small quantity of chopped green cabbage is added to the risotto during cooking.

Sausage roll. FRIAND—Puff pastry filled with pork sausage meat.

Smoked sausages. SAUCISSES FUMÉES—Prepare like *Country sausages* (see PORK) and put to smoke in a smoke-house for 2 days. Poach in water.

These sausages are used as an ingredient for potées. They are also served hot, as an hors-d'oeuvre.

Strasbourg sausages. SAUCISSES DE STRASBOURG—An Alsatian speciality. These sausages are made like smoked *Frankfurt sausages* and receive the same garnish. They are mainly used for garnishing sauerkraut.

Toulouse sausages. SAUCISSES DE TOULOUSE—Big sausages the forcemeat for which is chopped by hand. To cook: grill or fry as ordinary long sausages.

Vienna sausages. SAUCISSES DE VIENNE—An Austrian speciality, found ready-made in food shops. They are prepared like *Frankfurt sausages* and are accompanied by the same garnishes.

Sausages in white wine. SAUCISSES AU VIN BLANC—Cook long sausages in butter in the oven. Drain them and arrange on rectangular croûtons, fried in butter or toasted under the grill, allowing two sausages per croûton. Dilute the pan juices with white wine, add some *Demi-glace sauce* (see SAUCE) and butter and pour over the sausages.

Or: Brown 12 long sausages in butter in a sauté pan. Moisten them with ½ cup (1 decilitre) of dry white wine. Cook in the oven with a lid on.

Drain the sausages. Arrange them in pairs on croûtons fried in butter. Pour over the pan juices, prepared in the following manner: boil down the white wine by two-thirds, bind with a yolk of egg, add a dash of lemon juice, a good tablespoon of meat jelly and 4 tablespoons (60 grams) of butter and blend well.

Würstchen—Small sausages made in sheep's gut with a forcemeat composed of two parts lean pork, one part veal and one part of throat meat of pork, seasoned with salt, pepper, pimento and cardamon and mixed with Rhine wine. The sausages are tied together in bunches. They are poached for 3 minutes in salt water, then cooled and grilled.

Würste von Kalbsgekröse. SAUCISSES DE FRAISE DE VEAU—Made with pork gut from calf's mesentery, washed, blanched, cooked for a few moments in vinegar and then in an aromatic *court-bouillon**, chopped finely, seasoned with salt, pepper and nutmeg and bound, for every 2 pounds (kilo) with 2 eggs and ¾ cup (1½ decilitres) of fresh cream. Poach for 10 minutes, allow to cool and toss in butter.

SAUTÉ. SAUTER—To cook over a strong heat in fat or oil, shaking the pan and making whatever is in it 'sauter' or jump, to keep it from sticking to the bottom. See CULINARY METHODS.

SAUTÉ—This generic term applies to preparations made from meat, fowl, game or fish, cut up into pieces of equal size, which are sautéed, that is to say cooked over a good heat in butter, oil, or other fat.

Sautés differ from *ragoûts* in that the former are not sprinkled with flour before liquid is added, as is the case with ragoûts. A thickened liquid is added to the diluted pan juices.

Sauté of fish. SAUTÉS DE POISSONS—Fillet, raw, some large fish (perch, brill, cod, salmon, tunny, etc.). Trim the fillets and use the bones and scraps to make a *fumet** for the final sauce.

Cut the fillets in pieces 1 to 1½ inches long. Season these pieces and sauté them briskly in butter or oil. Drain them. Dilute pan juices with white or red wine, depending on the recipe. Add the prescribed sauce. Simmer for a few moments, add butter and strain through a cloth. Put the pieces of fish into this sauce and heat without allowing to boil.

Note. Various garnishes may be added to sauté of fish such as: mushrooms, aubergines (egg-plants), courgettes (zucchini), artichoke bottoms, tomatoes, truffles, etc. Sautéed fish may be browned or cooked without allowing to colour.

Sauté of game. SAUTÉS DE GIBIERS—Prepared with game meat or game birds. The recipes for these sautés are given under the words PHEASANT, RABBIT, PARTRIDGE.

Sauté of meat. SAUTÉS DE VIANDES DE BOUCHERIE—Lamb, pork and veal are chiefly prepared in this way, though the method may be applied to beef and mutton, bearing in mind that the latter, when cooked in this way (cut up into small square pieces), should remain a little pink inside, and should therefore not be allowed to boil in the accompanying sauce which is added after the pieces have been fried. See LAMB, BEEF, MUTTON, PORK, VEAL.

Sauté of poultry. SAUTÉS DE POULET—Recipes will be found under CHICKEN.

SAUTÉ PAN. SAUTOIR—Saucepan with a thick base and rather low sides used to sauté meat, vegetables, etc.

SAUTERNES—Commune of the Gironde, a district of Bazas, renowned for its sweet, white wines. The communes of Barsac, Preignac, Sauternes, Bommes and Fargues together make up the territory whose right to give to its wines the names of Sauternes has been recognized. See BORDEAUX, *Wines of Bordeaux*.

SAUVIGNON—Species of wine-producing vine cultivated in the Armagnac and the Bordelais. In the Sauternes district the Sauvignon gives some renowned wines.

SAVARIN—Cake made with a yeast mixture, soaked in flavoured syrup with rum or kirsch added.

Ingredients. 3¾ cups (500 grams) sifted flour, 1½ cups (375 grams) butter, 5 teaspoons (25 grams) sugar, ⅝ ounce (20 grams) yeast, 8 whole eggs, scant ½ cup (1 decilitre) warm milk, 1½ teaspoons (10 grams) salt.

Method. With these ingredients make a dough in the same way as for *Baba dough.* See BABA.

Moulding and cooking. Put the dough into a buttered ring mould of the type known as a 'Savarin mould', taking care to fill it not more than three-quarters full.

Let it rise in a warm place until the dough has risen to the top of the mould.

Savarin (*Larousse*)

Cook in a hot oven for 45 minutes. Allow to cool completely before turning out.

To serve. Soak the savarin in a rum syrup (or syrup flavoured with some other liqueur) prepared in the following way:

Syrup for the savarin. Melt over the heat 1 pound (2 cups) (500 grams) of sugar and a pint (½ litre) of water. Add ⅓ ounce (10 grams) of blanched aniseed, ⅙ ounce (5 grams) of cinnamon, a few grains of coriander and a fragment of mace (the outer covering of the nutmeg).

When the syrup is boiling, flavour it with 1 cup (2 decilitres) of rum or kirsch.

Put the savarin on a dish and sprinkle it with the hot syrup.

When the cake is well soaked, take it off the dish and sprinkle over a few more tablespoons of kirsch or rum just before serving.

Cherry savarin à la Chantilly. SAVARIN AUX CERISES À LA CHANTILLY—Stone 2 pounds (1 kilo) of Morello (dark) cherries, put them in a deep dish and sprinkle them with sugar. Put into the dish a dozen crushed cherry stones tied in a muslin bag.

When the cherry juice begins to run, cook them, covered, in this juice without additional liquid over a low heat. Allow to cool.

Prepare *Chantilly cream* (see CREAMS) flavoured with cherry brandy.

Drain the cherries and dry them, set them in the middle of a savarin cake, soaked in the cherry juice and flavoured with cherry brandy (or kirsch).

Cover the cherries with the *Chantilly cream*, piled into a dome. Decorate with some good cherries, reserved for the purpose.

Savarin à la crème—Fill the inside of a savarin, soaked and flavoured, with a pint (½ litre) of very thick *French pastry cream* (see CREAMS) mixed with ½ cup (50 grams) of crushed macaroons. This sweet can be served cold or hot. In the latter case the top of the cream is sprinkled with fine sugar and glazed with a glazing iron.

Savarins served hot should normally be accompanied by a fruit sauce (apricot, redcurrant, or strawberry), flavoured with kirsch or some other liqueur.

Savarin Montmorency—Remove the stalks and stones from 1 pound (500 grams) of English (pale red semi-sweet) cherries and poach them in 2 pints (1 litre) of light syrup. When they are cooked (after 4 minutes boiling), drain them and stew for a few minutes in a pan with ½ cup (1 decilitre) of kirsch, then use them to fill the middle of a savarin cake, previously soaked in the way described above.

SAVORY. Sarriette—Aromatic garden herb with a scent recalling that of thyme, used as seasoning.

SAVOURIES—In England this term describes a range of light preparations. Served right at the end of dinner, even after dessert, these might be called *post-oeuvre* as distinct from *hors-d'oeuvre*, served at the beginning of the meal.

Savouries, as has been said, are numerous, but the following are the principal ones (recipes are given in their alphabetical order): cheese straws, angels on horseback (oysters and bacon, grilled), cheese fritters, various foodstuffs cooked on skewers, *chou profiteroles* with cheese, fried Camembert, canapés, various foodstuffs on toast, devilled chicken legs and wings, cheese *condés*, fried cheese custard shapes, various croquettes and kromeskies, *diablotins**, rib bones of beef seasoned with mustard and cayenne and grilled, *paillettes* seasoned with Parmesan or paprika, cheese pancakes, tartlets and barquettes with various fillings, Welsh rarebit and other toasted cheese dishes, etc.

Wine tasting during the nineteenth century

SAVOURING. Dégustation—The palatal appreciation of the flavour of a solid or liquid. The savouring or 'tasting' of wines and spirits is a highly refined art, which demands great finesse of taste, but, above all, wide experience and a considerable sensory memory.

The preliminary operations consist of scrutinising the wine so as to judge its colour, detect any impurities and assess its limpidity and brilliance.

Next, the sense of smell must be brought into play to appreciate the aroma given off by the wine. The sense of smell is also initially associated with the sense of taste when tasting proper begins.

The sense of taste, though apparently exercised upon both solids and liquids, is in reality only effective with liquids, since the taste buds respond only to soluble substances.

These taste buds are dispersed throughout the mouth, some having specialized functions. Sourness is recognized with the tip of the tongue; sweetness with the flat of the tongue; under the tongue are the buds which respond especially to bitterness; tartness reacts upon the inner surface of the cheeks. Professional tasters put this specialized sensitivity to good use.

To savour a wine, for instance, a small sip is first taken. This is held in the front of the mouth against the teeth, while the tip of the tongue is gently moved back and forth to appreciate the sourness of the wine. Next, the head is tilted back a little and a deep breath is taken which is mixed with the liquid. At this point the aroma is savoured (this is given off by one of the essential oils contained in the skin of the grape and consequently depends upon the growth); this aroma is present in unmatured wines. It becomes more subtle and refined with maturity. Later the bouquet develops. This is present only in old wines and is due to the slow blending of the more volatile spirits, the ethers, aldehydes and essences of the wine. Finally, in these early stages, the taster takes note also of the special properties of the wine, the native tang, the standard flavour of the hybrid growths, the taste of cask, musk, sulphur, etc.

The wine is then spread over tongue and palate for about two seconds; at this point the taster will recognize the warmth of a full-bodied wine or its absence in a wine of less generous quality. He will experience a burning sensation if raw alcohol has been added. At the same time, the sweetness, smoothness and texture of the wine are appreciated, that is to say the proportion of sugar and tannin. Finally, the tartness and astringency are appreciated by rolling the wine against the cheeks.

At this point, professional tasters usually stop, spitting out the mouthful, since their vast experience enables them to judge a host of other subtle qualities in the wine.

There is something to be said, however, for swallowing the mouthful, provided that one is not obliged to taste too large a number of samples at the same session.

By swallowing slowly with the mouth closed, there are still further shades of taste to be distinguished. First of all some flavours which take about 10 seconds to develop, then the 'readiness' which arises from the fusion of aroma and bouquet, and finally the perfumed aftertaste which indicates that the wine 'ends well'.

The tasting of oil, butter and solid foods is carried out in the same way. It should be undertaken in the mornings on an empty stomach, or at least some considerable time after a meal. Above all, the taster *should not smoke* before tasting.

Haute Savoie, Château de Menthon
(French Government Tourist Office)

SAVOY. Savoie—The territory of the Savoy, jagged with mountains, offers only a restricted space for the cultivation of such crops as cereals, buckwheat and potatoes, but the gentler slopes of the Alps provide fine pasture lands which nourish livestock for meat and for dairy produce. The milk and cream used in the Savoyard kitchen are culinary ingredients of the highest order. On the hillsides which face the midday sun, vines are grown. Fine orchards are planted with cherry, plum,

Gastronomic map of Savoy

pear and cider apple trees. Walnut trees and chestnuts prosper. The clearings in the woods abound with sweet fragrant little strawberries, and the cool earth of the forests and meadows encourages the growth of mushrooms in summer.

Game, nourished by the aromatic herbs of the grasslands, is particularly good to eat; hares, partridges, quails and woodwock are plentiful. Excellent fish abounds in the cold waters of the lakes and rivers and torrents: carp, eel, perch, trout, char and burbot. Two delicious fish, the *lavaret* and the *féra*, are almost unique to the province. The crayfish are small but good. The bees provide excellent honey, that of Tarentaise in particular being renowned.

Culinary specialities—Savoyard cooking, done with ingredients of the highest quality, is good and healthy but a little heavy. There exist some special dishes.

Under the name of *Civet*, hare and pork are prepared with a very rich sauce in which spices and aromatics are combined with the blood of the animal, wine and fresh cream.

In this cheese-producing region *gratin* dishes are greatly relished: *gratins* of crayfish, cardoons and potatoes have a place of honour: the last differs from the *Gratin dauphinoise* in being made without milk.

The *Farçon* is another local potato dish which constitutes a sort of sweet pudding.

Rissoles of meat or other mixtures and preparations made with veal and lamb offal (U.S. variety meats): ears, sweetbreads, brains and liver are much appreciated.

Savoyard housewives are expert in the art of making sausages and pâtés; the hams of Celliers and Taninges, dried and smoked in the open air, are of high repute, as are the game pâtés of Bonneville.

Among the fish dishes must be mentioned the *Batter-fried perch* and *trout*, the *Blue salmon trout*, the *Trout meunière*, the *char* cooked in *court-bouillon*. The fishermen of Lac Léman prepared a fish soup analagous, by virtue of its accompanying sauce, to the *chaudrées*, *cotriades* and *bouillabaisses* of the sea coast.

As for vegetables, the general use of cardoons is notable. The *nouilles* (noodles) and *nouillettes aux oeufs* of Albertville and Chambéry have a high reputation. Nut oil is much liked both for cooking and salad dressings.

Cheeses are numerous and choice: *Chevrette*, *Reblochon*, *Vacherin*—which is an imitation of Gruyère—and *Tome de Sixt*, which is eaten very hard, several years after making.

The *Matefaim* is a sort of thick pancake which can be eaten with salt or sugar according to taste.

At Chamonix are made *Bonbons au miel des Alpes* (Alpine honey sweets), *Nougat* and good pastries; *Biscuits* are made at Thonon; *Chocolate* at Sallanches. At Saint-Genis-d'Aoste and at Taninges exquisite *Gâteaux de Savoie* are made according to the ancient tradition of the region.

Wines—The Savoy produces some pleasant wines. Among the white wines, fine and piquante, the most renowned in this region are those of *Roussette*, *Marétel*, *Chignin*, *Aïse*, *Conflans*, *Bossey*, *Frangy*, *Digny* and *Crépy*. The Aïse is often a sparkling wine. The red wines recall those of Beaujolais; the best-known is that of Montmélian, classed as fourth growth; then come the vineyards of Saint-Jean de la Porte, Conflans, Charpignat, d'Aigueblanche, Cantefort and Touvière. Cider is drunk in many of the cantons; Chambéry, Annecy and Rumilly make beer. In Savoy an excellent kirsch and a special *eau-de-vie* which is put in coffee are made. Among the liqueurs of the country the best-known is the vermouth of Chambéry.

SAVOY BISCUIT—See SPONGE CAKE, *Savoy sponge cake*.

SAVOYARDE (A LA)—Name given to two different preparations: (1) *Omelette à la Savoyarde*—pancake omelette filled with round slices of potato sautéed in butter and thin shavings of Gruyère (see EGGS); (2) Potatoes chopped up raw, mixed with grated Gruyère and consommé and cooked in an earthenware dish. See POTATOES.

SAXIFRAGES—Name of a number of fleshy-leaved plants, some of which can be used as vegetables or in soup.

SCABIOUS. SCABIEUSE—Name of several different plants, formerly used as depuratives. *Field scabious* has succulent leaves which may be eaten cooked or in salad. Scabious is prepared like spinach.

SCALD. ÉBOUILLANTER—To plunge any food into boiling water to harden it and facilitate peeling. (This process is also known as blanching.)

SCALE. ÉCAILLER—To remove the scales of a fish. This is part of the process of *dressing* a fish before cooking.

SCALLION OR SPRING ONION. CIBOULE—A plant closely related to the onion, but whereas the onion, when young, has leaves of a pale green tending to white at the bottom of the stem, those of the scallion or spring onion are dark green all the way down.

Scallions are found in the market in spring.

Chiefly eaten raw, chopped, for seasoning green salads.

SCALLOP. PÉTONCLE—A species of bivalve mollusc with ribbed rounded shells belonging to the *Pectinidae* family. It is commonly found in France on the Channel and Atlantic coasts and is called variously, Olivette, Vanette or Vanneau. Scallops are common on the American coasts, varying in size from very small (bay scallops) to some very large varieties. Found rarely on the Mediterranean coast, they are called *Pèlerines* or pilgrim shells.

SCALLOP SAINT-JACQUES. COQUILLE SAINT-JACQUES—Bivalve mollusc, commonly known as the pilgrim shell, and called in French *Coquille Saint-Jacques*.

This shellfish is prepared in various ways.

Before preparing scallops in any way, and after having washed and scrubbed them well, put them on a shelf of the stove (or in the oven at a very low heat), the rounded part downwards. Under the influence of the warmth they will open completely.

The flesh, as well as the little coral tongue, which is a great delicacy, is taken out. (Do not discard the shells. Scrub them and keep for future use for various scallop shell dishes.)

The flesh and the coral are poached in a *court-bouillon** made with white wine, well seasoned, and flavoured with onion, thyme and bay leaf.

Drain the scallops and they are ready to be treated according to the recipe.

In U.S.A., the scallops have no coral and are rarely sold in the shells. All but the hinge is discarded. The flavour of the coral tongue can be approximated by the addition of lemon juice.

Fried scallops. COQUILLES SAINT-JACQUES FRITES—Cook the scallops in *court-bouillon**, drain and slice. Marinate them for 30 minutes in oil, lemon juice and chopped parsley. Just before serving, dip them in a light batter and fry in smoking hot deep fat. Drain. Arrange on a napkin. Garnish with fried parsley and quarters of lemon.

Scallops fried in batter. FRITOT DE COQUILLES SAINT-JACQUES—Prepared like *Fried scallops*. Serve *Tomato sauce* separately. See SAUCE.

Fried scallops Colbert. COQUILLES SAINT-JACQUES FRITES COLBERT—Dip the white flesh of the scallops in egg and breadcrumbs. Fry in clarified butter. Heap on a serving dish, garnish with chopped parsley and serve with *Colbert butter*, handed separately. See BUTTER, *Compound butters*.

Scallops au gratin. COQUILLES SAINT-JACQUES AU GRATIN—Cook the scallops as described above, cut it in slices and set in scallop shells, on a layer of *Duxelles** with the chopped onion bound with tomato sauce. Place the coral on top of the scallop slices.

Coat with tomato-flavoured *Duxelles sauce*. Sprinkle with breadcrumbs and melted butter. Brown lightly in the oven. Serve on a napkin-covered dish.

Scallops au gratin à la dieppoise. COQUILLES SAINT-JACQUES AU GRATIN À LA DIEPPOISE—Set the scallops and coral in the deep shells, coated with *Dieppoise sauce* (see SAUCE), alternating them with mussels and shrimps. Coat with *Dieppoise sauce*. Sprinkle with breadcrumbs and melted butter. Brown quickly in the oven.

Scallops in mayonnaise. COQUILLES SAINT-JACQUES EN MAYONNAISE—Set the scallops, seasoned with oil and vinegar and sprinkled with chopped parsley, in the deep shells, lined with a little shredded and seasoned lettuce. Coat with mayonnaise. Decorate with the coral, fillets of anchovies and capers. Surround with lettuce hearts, quartered hard boiled eggs and stoned olives.

Scallops Mornay. COQUILLES SAINT-JACQUES MORNAY—Line the bottoms of the hollow scallop shells, which have been edged with a border of *Duchess potato mixture* (see POTATOES) piped through a forcing bag with a fluted pipe, with a spoonful of *Mornay sauce*. See SAUCE.

Put on top of this sauce the slices of scallop flesh and the coral. Coat with *Mornay sauce*. Sprinkle with grated cheese and melted butter and brown in the oven.

Scallops à la parisienne (*Larousse*)

Scallops à la parisienne. COQUILLES SAINT-JACQUES À LA PARISIENNE—Line the bottoms of the scallop shells with a good spoonful of a mixture consisting of chopped mushrooms lightly cooked in butter, onion, shallot, scallop 'beards' (all chopped), breadcrumbs, chopped parsley and *Velouté sauce* (see SAUCE) made with the *court-bouillon** in which the scallops were cooked. On this mixture place the scallop flesh and coral. Coat with some more sauce, thinned down a little. Sprinkle with browned breadcrumbs and melted butter. Brown in the oven.

Fried scallops à la tartare. COQUILLES SAINT-JACQUES FRITES À LA TARTARE—Prepare the flesh of the scallops as for *Fried scallops Colbert.* Serve *Tartare sauce* separately. See SAUCE, *Cold sauces.*

Note. Scallops fried in this way can be served with various sauces, such as *Béarnaise*, *Hongroise*, *Portugaise*, etc.

SCAMPI—See DUBLIN BAY PRAWNS.

SCARUS, PARROT-FISH. SCARE—Mediterranean fish with rather fine flesh which was particularly esteemed by the Romans. It is called parrot-fish because of its bright colours. Prepared in *court-bouillon*, *à la meunière* or fried.

SCHALETH, JEWISH. SCHALETH À LA JUIVE—*Method.* Prepare some ordinary *Noodle paste* as long in advance as possible, so that it is well 'rested' before using. See NOODLES.

Roll out this paste thinly, and line a large, metal, well-buttered basin. Fill this basin, to three-quarters of its capacity, with a sweet apple purée prepared in this way:

Cook down 1½ pounds (800 grams) of apple jam made in the ordinary way to which 5 ounces (150 grams) of raisins, cleaned and seeded, and ½ pound (250 grams) of currants and sultanas, picked over, washed and swollen in warm water, have been added. Add some very finely chopped orange and lemon peel (half a tablespoon of each), ½ cup (125 grams) of sugar and a little grated nutmeg. Bind with 5 whole eggs and 3 yolks (away from the heat); add ½ cup (1 decilitre) of Malaga. Mix.

Cover the basin with a layer of pastry. Make a hole in the middle to allow steam to escape. Cook in the oven for 50 minutes to one hour. Allow to stand for a few minutes before turning out.

SCHNITZEL. SCHNITZEN—Escalope (thin cutlet) of veal coated with egg and breadcrumbs and cooked in butter or fat is known by this name in Germany and Austria. See VEAL.

SCOLYMUS. SCOLYME—Plant of the *Compositae* family which is found in the south-west of France. The Spanish scolymus has an edible root which is eaten in the same way as salsify.

SCOTER-DUCK. MACREUSE—A genus of duck among which are Polar species which migrate to both the Old and New World. Their oily flesh is strong in flavour but edible, if the birds are young and properly cooked.

SCUM. ÉCUME—A froth which forms on the surface of a boiling liquid, or the skin which forms on top of a protein liquid such as soup, through the coagulation of soluble proteins when the liquid is cold.

SEA ANEMONES. ANÉMONES DE MER—Name commonly given to *Actinia* or starfish, edible molluscs which abound on the coasts of France, particularly on the Mediterranean side.

SEA-BASS. LOUP DE MER—A name given in some districts to the sea-perch.

In U.S.A. the *Sea-bass* of the eastern coast and the *Groupers* of the southern shores are very similar to the French *Loup de mer.*

Sea-bream

SEA-BREAM. DAURADE—A very delicately flavoured fish found in the Mediterranean end of the Gulf of Gascony and very occasionally in the English Channel.

The back of the sea-bream is bluish white or dark blue, the flanks, silvery-yellow, the belly white. The ancients called it *golden eyebrow* because of the brilliant golden crescent between its eyes. The French name for this fish is *daurade*. It is sometimes spelt *dorade*, but usually the name *dorade* is used in France for various types of salt-water fish with golden glints, which fishmongers sometimes pass off as genuine sea-bream, such as the *pagre*, the *boops*, the greyling and some other fish. Some fish (with reddish glints) are called *dorades rouges*.

Sometimes the true sea-bream is misspelt *dorade* in French. Sea-bream is best grilled *à la meunière* or *à la Dugléré*, or boiled and served with melted butter.

SEA-COW, MANATEE. LAMANTIN—The flesh of this herbivorous sea-mammal, which tastes something like pork, is much esteemed in the West Indies, as is the 'bacon' made from it.

SEA EEL—See EEL.

SEAFOODS. FRUITS DE MER—This name is applied to crustaceans and shellfish of various kinds, which are served together, raw or cooked. It is used, in particular, of a dish of raw shellfish served as an hors-d'oeuvre, such as oysters.

Seafoods, which sometimes include slices of various fish, can be cooked in a great many different ways. They can be made into *ragoûts**, flans (tarts), risottos, stuffings, etc.

Seafood risotto. RISOTTO AUX FRUITS DE MER—**Cook separately, in white wine, seasoned with the usual spices and herbs, 2 quarts (litres) of mussels and 1 quart (litre)**

of cockles or small clams. Drain these shellfish and remove them from their shells. Put them in a casserole with ½ pint (200 grams) of shelled prawns' tails (shrimps) and 4 shelled scallops, previously cooked in white wine. Add 2 cups (4 decilitres) of *Fish velouté sauce* (see SAUCE) which has been prepared separately by using the combined cooking liquors and a white *roux** of butter and flour. This sauce must be cooked for 25 minutes and should be very smooth. When it is cooked, add 5 spoonfuls of cream and simmer for a few minutes. Finally, add 2 tablespoons of butter and strain it.

The ragoût, with the *velouté* added to it, should be kept hot without boiling.

Meanwhile, prepare the risotto. Sauté gently an onion, chopped medium fine, in butter without letting it brown. Mix in ½ pound (250 grams) of rice, stirring well so that all the grains are well coated with butter. Add meat stock (twice the volume of the rice), not all at once, but in 5 or 6 stages. Each time allow the rice to absorb the liquid before pouring on any more.

Cover and cook for 15 to 20 minutes, stirring from time to time. At the last moment, add 3 tablespoons of butter and ½ cup (50 grams) of grated cheese.

Arrange the rice in a border on a large dish. Place in the centre the seafood ragoût and arrange on top the coral of the scallops (set aside for this purpose).

Note. In U.S.A., scallops are rarely sold in the shell. A little lemon juice can be substituted for the flavour of the coral. This recipe serves 10 people.

SEA HOG—See PORPOISE.

SEAKALE. CHOU MARIN—This plant, which is appreciated in England, is little known in France, although it was introduced into cultivation a long time ago: M. Massey cultivated it in the royal vegetable garden at Versailles in 1820.

Seakale takes the form of a strong root out of which grow leaf rosettes consisting of long thick stalks terminating in fringed rounded crests. These so-called leaves are pale in colour, almost white.

This vegetable, which grows wild on the coast of most of western Europe, provides a special product, the leaf stalks, whose taste when cooked has a nutty flavour.

Seakale is eaten in the same way as asparagus or cardoons.

Method of cooking. Trim and wash the seakale and tie it up 6 to 8 stalks at a time in a bundle. Cook in boiling salted water; drain; arrange on a napkin.

Serve with one or other of the sauces used to accompany boiled vegetables.

SEAL. PHOQUE—Marine mammal hunted for its skin and the oil which is extracted from its fat. Seal's flesh is eaten by the Eskimos who, it is said, are particularly fond of its liver, lungs, heart and blood, which they make into sausages.

SEA-PERCH. PERCHE DE MER—Name sometimes given to bass. See BASS.

SEA-SLUG. HOLOTHURIE—A creature rather like a worm. Some breeds are edible, among them the *tripang* found in Chinese waters which is said to be highly prized among the gastronomes of the Far East.

SEASONING. ASSAISONNEMENT—This word defines both the act of seasoning a dish with one of the special substances (salt, for instance) and this substance itself.

To season and to flavour is not the same thing. Whereas seasoning a preparation consists of a large or small amount of salt being added to it, flavouring a dish means enhancing its taste by the addition of condiments, aromatics and spices.

In the amusing little quotation given below, however, the word *seasoning* is used not only to include salt, but all sorts of other condiments.

In one of his *Essays*, Montaigne talks of a pheasant and a peacock served to the king of Thunes, when he disembarked at Naples for a meeting with the Emperor Charles, the seasoning of which cost a hundred ducats.

'When they were carved, not only the banqueting room, but all the other rooms in the palace, and even the streets outside, were filled with a very suave vapour which did not fade for some time.'

Sea-urchins (*Larousse*)

SEA-URCHIN. OURSIN—Popular name of the marine animals of the *Echinus* species, covered with spines, several species of which are edible.

The best are the *Green sea-urchin* and the *Black sea-urchin*. The latter, called by various names in various regions—*Sea-hedgehog*, *Sea-egg*, etc.—is found at low tide on rocks.

There are few recipes for preparing the sea-urchin. It is chiefly eaten, lightly boiled, exactly like an egg. Cook it in salted boiling water, drain, open by cutting with scissors on the concave side (where the sea-urchin's mouth is situated), drain it completely, throwing out the excremental part, then dip buttered sippets (morsels of bread) into the shell.

In the region of Marseilles, where sea-urchins are considered a delicacy, they are eaten out of the shell, as described, but uncooked. They are opened, washed (in sea water if possible) and buttered sippets are dipped into the yellow substance clinging to the walls of the shell.

It is said that sea-urchin has great restorative powers. Its taste, when cooked, is not unlike crayfish.

A very tasty cold sauce can also be made from sea-urchin's flesh. It is rubbed through a fine sieve and mixed with mayonnaise sauce.

Sea-urchin flesh can also be made into an excellent purée.

Sea-urchin purée. PURÉE D'OURSINS—Open 3 dozen sea-urchins previously well washed and remove the part resembling hard roe. Rub this substance through a sieve. Add an equal quantity of thick *Béchamel sauce.* See SAUCE.

Simmer for 5 minutes, then blend in 2 tablespoons of butter.

Note. This purée can be used for filling little tartlets or puff pastry vol-au-vent cases. It can also be spread on pieces of bread, lightly fried in butter. The pieces of bread are then sprinkled with grated cheese and put in a very hot oven to brown the top.

SEA WRACK, ROCK-WEED. FUCUS—A species of seaweed of the membraneous or filament type.

It is said that the inhabitants of Iceland, the Faroe Islands, Scotland, Norway, Denmark and North America use it for food. It is, however, only eaten in times of scarcity, except in Scotland, where the young stems of the tangle or sea-lettuce are sometimes eaten as a salad. This dish, however, has not found much favour with any visitors who have tasted it.

Matters are quite different in the Far East, especially in Japan where there is a flourishing industry in the by-products of seaweed in general and sea-wrack in particular. *Amanori* and *kombu,* for instance, are greatly prized for their gelatinous properties, though it must be said that these products are used more as condiments than as actual food.

SÉBILLE—A sort of saucer or small bowl usually made of wood. It is used in French cookery for beating eggs.

In large and important kitchens, parsley and other chopped ingredients set out for a particular dish are assembled in wooden *sébilles* of various capacities.

SELTZER-WATER. SELTZ, EAU DE SELTZ—Sparkling mineral water from Selters (Duchy of Nassau), sold in jars. *Artificial seltzer-water* is effervescent water charged with carbonic gas under pressure and sold in siphons.

SEMI-SPARKLING. MOUSTILLE—Certain red and white wines, which are not quite sparkling, have traces of effervescence. These are said to be semi-sparkling.

SEMOLINA. SEMOULE—Food made with cereals, mostly wheat, reduced to granules by coarse milling.

Semolina, particularly wheat semolina, is used to make groats, soups, puddings and various other dishes.

Semolina kasha (Russian cookery). KACHE DE SEMOULE —Mix on a baking tin 1½ cups (250 grams) of coarse semolina and one whole egg, beaten. Spread this mixture over the tin and dry it in the oven at a low heat.

Put the semolina through a coarse sieve; poach it for 20 minutes in consommé and drain it.

This *kasha* is used with *coulibiac* and various hors-d'oeuvre in Russian cookery.

Semolina pudding. POUDING DE SEMOULE—Shower 1½ cups (250 grams) semolina into 4¼ cups (1 litre) of boiling milk, sweetened and flavoured with vanilla. Add 2 tablespoons of butter and a pinch of salt. Mix well. Cook in the oven for 30 minutes.

Thicken, away from the heat, with 4 beaten eggs.

English semolina pudding. POUDING DE SEMOULE À L'ANGLAISE—Add to semolina prepared as for a pudding 4 egg yolks and ½ cup (1 decilitre) of fresh cream to each quart (litre) of the mixture.

Put this mixture in a buttered pie dish. Cook in the oven in a *bain-marie* (pan of hot water).

French semolina pudding—See PUDDING.

Semolina subrics. SUBRICS DE SEMOULE—Cook in a pint (½ litre) of consommé ⅝ cup (125 grams) of semolina; add 2 tablespoons of butter. When this mixture is quite cooked (25 minutes, covered, in the oven), bind it with 2 whole eggs and one extra yolk and ½ cup (50 grams) of grated cheese. Spread this mixture on a buttered baking tin. Butter the surface. Allow to cool. Cut out subrics with a round pastry cutter, about 2 inches in diameter. Fry on both sides in clarified butter.

Set in a crown and sprinkle with melted butter.

Note. To simplify the operation the subrics may be made in squares or rectangles.

In the same way subrics may be made of maize (polenta), rice, vermicelli, noodles and all kinds of cereals and their derivatives.

Semolina subrics (sweet). SUBRICS DE SEMOULE—Sprinkle ⅝ cup (125 grams) of semolina in a shower into a pint (½ litre) of milk previously boiled with ½ cup (100 grams) of sugar, half a pod of vanilla and a pinch of salt.

Add 2 tablespoons of butter and mix well. Cook in the oven, covered, for 25 minutes.

Remove from the heat and bind with 4 egg yolks. Turn the mixture into a baking tin in a layer ⅜ inch thick. Butter the surface and allow to cool.

Cut out in rings with a pastry cutter and fry on both sides in very hot butter. Arrange in a crown. Garnish the middle of each subric with apricot or redcurrant jelly.

SEPARATOR. ÉCRÉMEUSE—An implement used in dairies for separating the cream from the milk.

SEPT-OEIL—Name (Seven-eye) sometimes given to the lamprey. The spawn of this fish are also called *Sept-oeil.*

SERDEAU OR SERS-D'EAU—Official of the court of the King of France who received the dishes cleared from the table by the *maître d'hôtel.* Also the place to which these left-overs were taken and from which they were re-sold. Formerly at the court of France it was the custom to keep food always ready to serve to those whose duty or business brought them in touch with the king.

To this end dishes cleared from the royal table were brought to a special room or *serre,* which came to be called the *serre d'hôte,* and, by corruption, the *serdeau* (i.e. to be kept hot. A 'serre' is a hothouse).

Later, the custom of regaling the king's visitors fell into disuse and the left-overs, brought immediately to the *serdeau* as before, were sold by auction. This custom still existed at the time of Louis XIV and many Versailles households were cheaply provisioned in this way.

News-gatherers of the end of the eighteenth century were greatly amused by an adventure which happened at Versailles to an old gentleman whose state of fortune obliged him to make economies, and who was in the habit of making up his dinner from left-overs provided for him by the *serdeau* servants.

He had been called unexpectedly into a salon of the palace, when it was discovered that a very valuable snuff-box had suddenly disappeared without anybody having been seen to leave the room. To allay suspicion everybody present turned their pockets inside out, and, after a certain hesitation, the economy-minded courtier followed suit. One may imagine the burst of laughter that greeted the appearance of a piece of chicken that had been buried in his pocket, and which had been intended to constitute the poor gentleman's dinner.

The story appeared in all the papers after having acquired a number of embellishments.

SERRE—See CHEESE.

SERVICE—The word service used to mean a group of dishes composing one of the different parts of the meal. There were at least three services; after each service the table was cleared with the exception of the *dormants* or table centres and the *bouts de table,* on which were arranged the dishes for the next course.

The second sense of the word describes the manner of presenting the dishes to the guests; if the dishes are put on the table, each artistically arranged and set symmetrically, this is service *à la française.* Against this may be set service *à la russe,* now widely adopted, in which the dishes are passed in a pre-determined order to each guest, the meat being cut up in advance. Some details of these two kinds of service are given below.

Table service can also be taken to mean the *ensemble* of

objects which are used at table: linen, plates, glass and silver. In particular the utensils required to serve a special part of the meal are called services—e.g. coffee service, tea service, fruit service, etc.

In French the personnel of the restaurant who are responsible for serving meals are also called the *service*.

Service à la française and à la russe—The great *service à la française*, as it was practised during the First Empire and even more frequently during the Second, was only the continuation, in an already diminished form, of the ceremonial of the table observed under Louis XIV, which was called *le grand couvert*.

Because of its costly character this was only practised in the great houses, on grand occasions, and when it was brought into play it was a matter of pride for the host to give by this service—and sometimes by a certain degree of ostentation—an idea of his wealth and generosity; to leave his guests the memory not only of sensory pleasure but also an impression of a fine flowering of masterpieces of the art of the table.

A meal served *à la française* was divided in three quite distinct parts, which were the *services*. The first service consisted of the series of dishes inscribed on the menu from soup to roast, including the hors-d'oeuvre. The second comprised everything on the menu following the roast—cold second roasts and vegetables, continuing to the last item, the sweet dishes. The third service, completely independent of the kitchen, came from the pastry-cook, and there followed decorated pieces, various pastries, petits fours, sweets, ices and fruit; that which, in a word, constituted the dessert.

The order of the menu was regulated by the number of *entrées*, that is to say the dishes of the second service had to be equivalent in number to those of the first service and never adding up to an odd number. But there were certainly some deviations from the rule.

Thus in a menu in which there were 8 entrées, there had to be 2 soups, 2 large 'removes', 2 roasts, 2 cold pieces for the second roast, 2 side dishes and 2 vegetables (or 1 vegetable and a mixed salad).

Certain menus left by Carême (authentic menus for meals served principally at the table of the Prince Tallyrand) mention 32 and sometimes 48 entrées.

All the dishes for the first service were arranged on the table before the entry of the guests into the dining room, set, naturally, on *réchauds* (hot plates) to keep them hot and covered with cloche lids.

This magnificence, this satisfaction in the display of riches had its reverse side and presented various difficulties.

It is easy to understand how overloaded were the tables if to these covered dishes are added the great table centres, baskets of flowers, candelabras full of candles, set places, glass, etc. But the greatest inconvenience of this service, almost inevitably, was that in spite of the *réchauds* the last dishes of the series, however great the dexterity of the carving and the speed of serving, had become somewhat chilled, and no longer at their best. Moreover, it is equally evident that the guests could not try such a large number of dishes and must make a choice of one or two.

The service *à la russe*, popularised by Urbain Dubois round about 1860, is less rich, less representative and expressive of luxury, but it has the advantage of meeting in full the imperious demands of the table to 'serve hot'. The fundamental rule of this service is that everything should be organized in advance to this end. Here there is no more useless ornamentation, no more vulgar decoration; on the contrary, everything must be arranged so that the carving is done in the minimum time and the dish served to the guests before there is any change in its taste. By this method the guests help themselves—or have food served to them; but even though the carving is done in advance, the arrangement of the food on the dishes still demands correctness and an attractive appearance, especially when they are accompanied by a variety of different 'garnishes', which must always blend perfectly with the principal ingredient of the dish.

In service *à la russe* everything can be served piping hot if whosoever is in charge of the kitchen can calculate from the time for which the meal is fixed the moment at which he must begin to dish up, working out for this purpose the time taken in cooking and the exact instant at which the food must be presented to the guests, who may thus eat with the greatest possible enjoyment—always supposing that the unpunctuality of the guests themselves has not upset these calculations.

Obviously this rapid service, which proscribes all decoration or complicated arrangement of hot dishes, gives no scope to the culinary artist to exercise his talent in this respect.

However, there is nothing in service *à la russe* to exclude cold dishes which are not spoilt by waiting, such as various *chaud-froids*, decorated crustaceans in aspic, *fancy terrines*, glazed chickens, mousses in aspic, etc. In foodstuffs of this type the modern cuisine has made real progress in adopting a system of serving in bowls or deep dishes, so that there is no need for any supplementary preparation. Moulds have been completely abandoned.

In service *à la russe* the guests at a party are divided up into groups of 10 or 12 people, varying according to the total number, each group being served by one waiter, who is instructed in advance by the mistress of the house which guests to serve first and last.

At a ceremonial meal it is customary to serve all the ladies first, beginning at the right of the master of the house. Dishes are offered on the left-hand side of the seated person; the plate is put down and taken away on the right.

Wine is served on the right in the same order as the dishes, but the first drops are poured into the glass of the master of the house, so that small crumbs of cork do not fall into the glass of a guest.

On a less ceremonious occasion, where the master of the house carves and serves the food himself, the dishes, or the filled plates, should be passed round, beginning with the person on his right.

Service-berry

SERVICE-BERRY. ALISE—Fruit of various trees which should not be confused with sorb apple.

Wild service-tree as well as white-beam tree, commonly called shadbush, grows freely in the mountainous regions of Europe.

The Fontainebleau wild service-tree is found chiefly in the wooded parts along the banks of the Seine.

The fruit of wild service-trees has a very pleasant acid taste.

SERVIETTE, TABLE NAPKIN—A piece of linen to protect the clothing and to wipe mouth and fingers at table.

Its use is much less ancient than that of tablecloth or towel. Up to the fifteenth century one wiped one's fingers on the tablecloth or on the *doublier*, a second cloth, covered in its turn with a *longière*, yet a third, intended for this use; later came napkins or *touailles*, but they were few and generally attached to the walls. It was only in the sixteenth century that the use of the individual table napkin became general. At first it was kept over the left arm, then the fashion for starched ruffs made it necessary for them to be tied round the diners' necks.

At court, the king's napkin, wrapped up and placed in the *nef* (the golden vessel which contained his personal cruet and cutlery) was presented to him after his food had been tested, by the personage of the highest rank among those present, a prince of the blood royal or a high dignitary.

The Master of the Royal Household carried a rolled-up napkin over his left shoulder as an insignia of office.

SERVIETTE (A LA)—Describes a way of serving certain foodstuffs, notably truffles. Truffles *à la serviette* are certainly not cooked in a table napkin, but they are served in one, folded into a kind of pocket.

These truffles are cooked in Madeira or any other liqueur wine and set in a bowl or a silver dish which is placed, as has been said above, in a folded napkin.

Truffles cooked in hot ashes in the old-fashioned style are also served *à la serviette*.

Finally, potatoes cooked in their jackets in the oven or in hot ashes are also served *à la serviette*.

The latter form of cooking is almost impossible nowadays except in old kitchens where there is a coal or wood range providing ashes in which potatoes may be cooked.

Rice *à la serviette* is rice cooked for 15 minutes in salted water, drained, rinsed under the cold tap, and finished in a very low oven or special drying oven wrapped in a napkin. This recipe will be found under *Rice à l'indienne* in the section on RICE.

Finally, it should be said that folded napkins are used in serving certain dishes. It is on these napkins (or on pleated paper) that fried foods are set.

Folded napkins are placed under earthenware dishes and casseroles, or under metal dishes, under vol-au-vents and patties, and under the glass bowls in which cold jellied foods, mixed salads, iced sweets, etc., are served.

SESAME—Annual herbaceous tropical and subtropical plant, known to the ancient Greeks and Hebrews, the Egyptians and Persians, where its fruit or seeds have been used from time immemorial as a food grain and as oil.

These seeds, chiefly used to make *Halvah*, are also used for cakes, cookies (biscuits), and confectionery.

Industrially they are used to make an oil for oleomargarine, cosmetics and soap.

SET. Pris—Used in terms of cookery for liquids coagulated by heat (custards) or cold (ice creams and jellied preparations).

SETIER—Old French measure of capacity for grain equal to 152 litres or measure of capacity for liquids equal to 8 pints.

Demi-setier is a term used in Paris to mean a quarter of a litre.

SEYSSEL—Commune of the department of Ain where a well-known white wine of the same name is made.

SHAD. Alose—A migratory fish bearing some similarity to herring, but bigger in size. In the spring, the shad go up the rivers to spawn in fresh water.

There are two distinct species of shad: the *Allis shad* which is the more valued, and the *Waite shad* which is smaller and coarser.

The flesh of the shad, although a little heavy, is very delicate. The female is to be preferred to the male, but the latter are prized for their milt (soft roe).

If caught soon after spawning these fish have the tastiest of flesh. The only thing they can be reproached for is their numerous bones.

In U.S.A. a species of shad exists which is called *alosa menhaden*. Shad's roe is much prized in U.S.A.

Like all fish, the shad must be eaten very fresh. Its freshness can be recognized by its shiny skin and clear eye.

Note. In addition to the recipes given below, all those given for the preparation of sea-perch, cod, herring and mackerel can be applied to shad, whether cooked whole, sliced or in fillets.

Cleaning. Scrape off the scales and clean the fish inside. Wash it quickly, avoid letting it stay in the water; dry.

Keep the soft and the hard roes to prepare them as described in special recipes.

Shad Claudine. Alose Claudine—Cut the shad into slices of uniform thickness. Butter an ovenproof dish, line the bottom with chopped shallots cooked in white wine, uncooked mushrooms and chopped parsley. Put the slices of fish on top of these.

Moisten with a few tablespoons of white wine. Season, scatter a few small dabs of butter and bake in the oven, basting frequently. At the last moment, pour in $\frac{3}{4}$ cup ($1\frac{1}{2}$ decilitres) of thick fresh sour cream. Glaze in the oven.

Garnish with new potatoes tossed in butter.

Fried shad. Alose frite—Cut into slices, soak in milk, dredge with flour and deep-fry in sizzling fat.

Drain the shad and arrange on a napkin, garnished with fried parsley and quarters of lemon.

Fried shad Orly. Alose frite Orly—Marinate the fillets of shad (cut, if they are too big) in oil, lemon juice, chopped parsley, salt and pepper.

A few moments before serving, dip in batter and fry in deep fat. Serve with *Tomato sauce*. See SAUCE.

Fried shad à l'anglaise. Alose frite à l'anglaise—Cut shad fillets into slices; dip them in egg and breadcrumbs. Fry in the usual manner. Serve *Maître d'hôtel butter* separately (see BUTTER, *Compound butters*).

Grilled shad (whole). Alose grillée—Clean a medium-sized shad, scrape off scales, wash and thoroughly wipe it. Make a few regular, fairly deep incisions in the fleshy part of the back, on both sides. Season with salt and pepper and marinate for an hour in oil, lemon juice, parsley, thyme and bay leaf.

Cook under a grill, on moderate heat, for 30 minutes.

Arrange on a long dish; garnish the borders of the dish with half slices of lemon. Serve with *Maître d'hôtel butter* or with any other sauce suitable for grilled fish (see BUTTER, *Compound butters*, or SAUCE).

Grilled shad (in slices). Alose grillée—Cut the shad into slices $\frac{3}{4}$ inch thick, season, marinate in oil, lemon juice, parsley, thyme and bay leaf for 15 to 20 minutes;

grill for 12 to 15 minutes. Serve in the same manner as whole shad.

Shad with mushrooms, à la bonne femme. ALOSE AUX CHAMPIGNONS, À LA BONNE FEMME—Proceed as described in the recipe for *Brill à la bonne femme**.

Shad on plank (American cookery). ALOSE SUR PLANCHETTE—Put fillets of a medium-sized shad, taken off raw, trimmed and marinated for an hour in oil, lemon juice, salt and pepper, flat, skin side down, on a buttered plank. If a female shad is being cooked, place the roes in the middle of the fillets. Secure the whole with two big, heated, buttered skewers, the ends of which will be passed through the rings of the plank by crossing them over the fish.

Set to cook in the oven or, better still, under the grill. From time to time baste the fish with melted butter.

Put the plank on a long platter. Withdraw the skewers. Garnish with quarters of lemon and little sprigs of parsley.

Serve with *Maître d'hôtel butter*, or any other sauce which goes with grilled fish, and a cucumber salad.

Note. The cooking of certain dishes on planks, both fish and meat, is very popular in U.S.A. For this purpose an oak board is used, 14 inches long, 12 inches wide and 1¼ inches thick. These boards have a ring at each corner.

Usually, the articles which are put on the board to cook are surrounded by a border of *Duchess potatoes*, piped through a forcing (pastry) bag with a rose nozzle (see POTATOES).

Shad au plat. ALOSE AU PLAT—Choose a shad weighing about 1½ pounds (700 to 800 grams), coat the inside with 3 tablespoons (50 grams) of butter kneaded with a tablespoon of chopped parsley, a teaspoon of chopped shallots, salt and pepper.

Put in a long, buttered, ovenproof dish. Season with salt and pepper; sprinkle with ½ cup (1 decilitre) of white wine (or mushroom stock); scatter a few small dabs of butter; cook in the oven (375°F.) from 25 to 30 minutes.

Baste frequently during cooking; if the pan juices boil down too quickly, add a few drops of mushroom stock or water.

Serve in the dish in which the fish is cooked.

Stuffed shad à l'ancienne. ALOSE FARCIE À L'ANCIENNE—take a shad of average weight (about 2 pounds) and proceed as described in the recipe given for *Stuffed carp à l'ancienne* (see CARP).

Stuffed shad à la ménagère. ALOSE FARCIE À LA MÉNAGÈRE—Fill the shad with a stuffing prepared with a mixture of breadcrumbs, butter, lightly fried chopped onion, chopped parsley and chervil, all well seasoned.

Cook the shad as described in the recipe for *Shad au plat*.

Stuffed shad à la mode de Cocherel. ALOSE ÉTOUFFÉE À LA MODE DE COCHEREL—Stuff a shad weighing 4 pounds (2 kilos) with the following stuffing: Pound the flesh of whiting in a mortar, season with salt, pepper and grated nutmeg and add, whilst still pounding, for 10 ounces (300 grams) of whiting, one raw white of egg. Rub this forcemeat through a fine sieve; blend with a wooden spoon and add 1¾ cups (3½ decilitres) of fresh double cream, putting it in little by little; add 2 good tablespoons of chopped, blanched and drained spring onions, and one tablespoon of chopped parsley.

Wrap the shad in very thin bacon rashers, secure with string and put on skewers. Cook in front of brisk fire for about 45 minutes; a few minutes before removing the skewers, take off the rashers and brown the fish.

Arrange the shad in a large long dish; surround with the following garnish, arranged in separate groups: very small new potatoes cooked in butter; little quarters of young artichokes, blanched, drained and stewed in butter; little glazed new onions.

Dilute the juices left in the dripping pan with a glass of dry white wine, add 2 cups (4 decilitres) of cream, boil down, add butter, pass through a strainer and serve separately in a sauceboat.

Stuffed shad à la portugaise. ALOSE FARCIE À LA PORTUGAISE—Stuff the shad as described in the preceding recipe, but add some chopped mushrooms, lightly fried in oil, and a crushed clove of garlic to the stuffing.

Cook in oil in a fireproof dish; when half cooked add 1¼ cups (2½ decilitres) of *Tomato fondue* (tomatoes cooked to a pulp in butter, seasoned with garlic and chopped tarragon). Finish cooking everything together, basting frequently. A few moments before removing from the oven, sprinkle with breadcrumbs, add a dash of oil and brown lightly.

SHAD-BUSH. AMELANCHIER—A genus of service-tree covering several types of shrubs bearing edible fruit.

This fruit, which is slightly astringent and has a tart flavour, is better when slightly overripe. It is popular with children.

SHAGGY INK CAP. COPRIN—Edible mushroom characterized by black spores, from which its name derives. Prepared in the same way as cultivated mushrooms. This mushroom should only be eaten when very young, while the gills are still pink.

SHALLOT. ÉCHALOTE—A pot vegetable which, according to Candolle (French botanist 1806–1893) is merely a derivative of the onion, with a slight taste of garlic. Some people find the shallot more readily digestible than onion.

Shallot butter. BEURRE D'ÉCHALOTE—Pound finely in a mortar 3 ounces (100 grams) of shallot, blanched, cooled under running water, drained and squeezed. Add 3 ounces (100 grams) of fresh butter. Mix. Rub through tammy cloth or a hair sieve. This composite butter is used for cold hors-d'oeuvre preparations, especially canapés. It is also used as an additional ingredient in some sauces, and is served with grills.

Essence of shallot. ESSENCE D'ÉCHALOTES—Bring 1 cup (2 decilitres) of vinegar to the boil. Add 4 tablespoons (50 grams) of chopped shallot. Boil for 5 minutes. Strain through muslin. Essence of shallot can be made with white wine instead of vinegar.

SHARK. REQUIN—Name of a number of carnivorous fish whose size varies from a few inches to several yards long. The flesh of the shark, though very tough, is used as a foodstuff by the Lapps and by some negro peoples who are very partial to it.

Shark fins are much esteemed by the Chinese.

SHARPEN. AIGUISER—A term in pastry-making, used figuratively speaking of a cream or a liquid, which means sharpening it, rendering it acid, making it stimulating by adding lemon juice or citric acid.

The word is also used in the sense of spicing a dish strongly.

SHARPENING STEEL. FUSIL—A steel instrument used by butchers and cooks to sharpen their knives.

SHCHI—A Russian soup. See SOUPS AND BROTHS.

SHE-ASS. ÂNESSE—Female ass. Its milk in content comes nearer to human milk than that of any other domestic animal. See MILK.

Ass's milk was much valued in France for medicinal purposes since François I took it as a cure. All the courtisans hastened to imitate their king and that started the vogue for ass's milk.

SHEATH. GAINE—A type of wooden case bound with copper, nickel or leather in which butchers and cooks used to carry their knives. Such sheaths are no longer much in use today.

SHEEP—See MUTTON and LAMB.

Sheep's brains. CERVELLE DE MOUTON—All recipes for lambs' and calves' brains are suitable for sheep's brains. See OFFAL OR VARIETY MEATS.

Sheep's or lamb's kidney pilaf I. PILAF AUX ROGNONS DE MOUTON—Put the rice into a buttered border (ring) mould and turn out the rice border on to a round dish. Cover the rice with halved sheep's kidneys, sautéed in butter and finished as described in the recipe for *Kidney sautéed in white wine* (see OFFAL OR VARIETY MEATS).

Sheep's or lamb's kidney pilaf II. PILAF AUX ROGNONS DE MOUTON—Proceed as described in the recipe for *Shrimp pilaf II** garnishing the pilaf with sheep's or lamb's kidneys, sliced, fried in butter and finished as described in the recipe for *Kidneys sautéed in white wine* (see OFFAL OR VARIETY MEATS).

Sheep's liver. FOIE DE MOUTON—This liver is rather inferior in flavour. It can be cooked in the same way as calves' liver (see OFFAL OR VARIETY MEATS).

SHELL. ÉGRENER—To detach corn or other cereal grain from the stalk.

The French terms *écaler* and *écosser* also mean to shell. *Écaler* is applied to removing shells or husks of fruit and vegetables, shelling eggs and shell-fish. *Écosser* means to remove the shell or pod from peas and beans.

SHELL-FISH—See CRUSTACEANS.

SHEPHERD'S PURSE (Corn salad). BOURSE-À-PASTEUR—Common name for a plant which in French is also known as *Bourse-à-berger* and *Boursette* or *Bourcette*, often found in shady places. It is sometimes used in salads. If picked at flowering time, its taste is not unlike that of watercress. It is also called *Lamb's lettuce*.

SHERBETS. SORBETS—These ices, which in France are usually served between the main courses, take the place nowadays of the liqueurs which formerly used to be served in the middle of the meal and which in some parts of France were called *coup-du-milieu*, and in others *trou-normande*.

Sherbets are made from fruit, liqueurs and heavy wines. Here is the recipe most commonly used:

For a quart (litre) of sherbet. 1 pint (½ litre) of any sweet wine; the juice of 2 lemons and of 1 orange; and syrup (1 cup sugar and 2 cups water boiled 5 minutes, strained and cooled).

All sherbet mixtures must be made from a light syrup. The syrup glucometer should never register more than15°. Sherbets are iced as follows:

Pour the mixture into a freezer already embedded in ice. (The freezer may be operated by hand or by power.) Set the mechanism working. From time to time scrape the inside of the freezer to detach any sherbet sticking to the sides. This should not, however, be stirred into the rest of the mixture, as the sherbet, once it is frozen, should have a slightly gritty texture.

Stir in very gently some Italian *meringue** (a quarter of the volume of the sherbet) or, if preferred, the same amount of whipped cream, and whatever liqueur or dessert wine is desired.

Presentation of sherbets. The mixture should be removed from the freezer with a special conical scoop. Each portion should be set, point upwards, in a sherbet cup and then sprinkled with the same liqueur or wine as that used in the mixture.

SHERRY. XERES, JEREZ—Name given in England to the Spanish wine Xeres.

Sherry is a fortified wine, produced principally from the Palomino grape in the countryside surrounding Jerez de la Frontiera in Spain. There is a great variety of sherries ranging, in colour, from a pale gold to dark brown and, in taste, from very dry to sweet. The dry sherries include *Fino*, *Vino de Pasto*, *Manzanilla* and a darker, older variety called *Amontillado*. Slightly sweeter varieties include those called *Oloroso* and *Amoroso* and among the dark and quite sweet varieties are *Cream*, *Brown* and *East India*.

Spanish sherries, unlike many of their imitators, are subject to a very special process of fermentation, ageing and blending which make their product unequalled in the world.

Sherry cobbler—Iced drink prepared in this way: Put into a glass one-third filled with crushed ice, one tablespoon of sugar and 1½ tablespoons of curaçao. Fill up the glass with sherry. Add a slice of orange.

SHIN. JARRET—A part of the leg of an animal behind the knee-joint. It corresponds with the tibia-tarsal or radio-carpal bone in humans. The shin of veal is used in the preparation of stock. It can also be cut into sections and braised. See VEAL, *Knuckle of veal*.

SHIRR—To break eggs into a baking dish and cook them either in the oven or on top of the stove. See EGGS.

SHORTBREAD—Make pastry with 3¾ cups (500 grams) of flour, 1 cup minus 2 tablespoons (200 grams) of sugar, 1 pound (500 grams) of softened butter, 4 ounces (125 grams) of ground almonds, 3 egg whites and powdered vanilla.

Press out on to a buttered baking sheet through a forcing (pastry) bag fitted with a fluted pipe. Bake for 50 minutes in a 275°F. oven.

SHOULDER. ÉPAULE—The front leg of quadrupeds. Cuts from the shoulder of beef are braised or used in hot-pots.

Shoulder of veal is braised, pot-roasted or roasted. (It is usually boned and rolled into a long, tight bundle.) It is also used in sautés and *ragoûts*.

Shoulder of mutton and lamb, boned or whole, is cooked in the same way as the legs of these animals. It is also used in stews.

The shoulder of different types of venison is cooked in the same way as haunch of venison, but is more commonly used in *civets*.

SHOVELLER—See DUCK, *Wild duck*.

SHREDDER AND SLICER. MANDOLINE—A kind of plane, sometimes fluted, used for shredding or slicing vegetables, especially potatoes.

It is with an implement of this type that vegetables are shredded into matchsticks or straws or sliced very thin as for potato crisps.

SHRIKE. PIE-GRIÈCHE—Popular name of small perching bird of the family *Lanidae*. It can be prepared in any way suitable for lark.

SHRIMPS. CREVETTES—Little crustaceans very much in use for hors-d'oeuvre and garnishes.

The two principal European types are (1) the *Sword-shrimp* (*crevette rose*), the head of which is armed with a long-toothed beak; it becomes rosy when cooked, the flesh is white and firm; (2) the *Common shrimp* (*Crangon vulgaris*) which is smaller, with a smooth short beak, and which takes on a pinkish grey colour when cooked. The flesh, which is rather limp, is less appreciated than that of the sword-shrimp.

Cooking of shrimps. Put the shrimps alive into boiling salted water. Do not put in any other seasoning.

When possible, cook the shrimps in sea water which has been strained through muslin or through a fine sieve.

Cooked in this way and cooled, the shrimps are served as an hors-d'oeuvre. They are arranged in an hors-d'oeuvre dish, in crystal dishes or in stemmed glasses.

Shrimps in U.S.A. vary from the large size found off the southern shores, which average a dozen to the pound, to the tiny ones, averaging 40 to the pound. These small ones fished off the Alaskan and northern New England shores are less popular although very high in flavour.

Shrimp aspic. ASPIC DE CREVETTES—Arrange the peeled shrimps (which have been cooked in the manner described above) in a simple round mould, which has been lined with a clear aspic jelly, in layers leaving the centre of the mould free.

Fill the centre of the mould with a shrimp mousse made with the shrimp peelings or with a preparation made with common shrimps, according to the recipe for *Shrimp mousse* below.

Cover completely with aspic jelly which is almost set. Chill on ice or in the refrigerator.

Turn out of the mould and set on a round dish or in a crystal bowl.

Shrimp butter—See BUTTER, *Compound butters.*

Shrimp canapés—See HORS-D'OEUVRE, *Cold hors-d'oeuvre.*

Shrimp coquilles. COQUILLES DE CREVETTES—Made with peeled shrimps and *Béchamel sauce* (see SAUCE), to which shrimp butter is added, in the usual way.

Fried shrimps. CREVETTES FRITES—Plunge live shrimps, which have been trimmed, washed and well drained, into boiling oil. Drain, and season with fine salt; arrange them on a napkin; garnish with fried parsley.

Cold shrimp mousse. MOUSSE FROIDE DE CREVETTES—Cook the shrimps in a *mirepoix** in the same way as crayfish (see CRAYFISH). Peel some of the shrimps in order to have enough tails with which to decorate the mould. Pound the rest with the *mirepoix* in which they were cooked. Pass the mixture through a fine sieve.

Add to the purée thus obtained, a quarter of its volume of *Velouté sauce* (see SAUCE) based on fish stock which has been cooked down, and for every 2 cups (500 grams) of purée, add 1 cup (2 decilitres) of fish aspic. Finish this preparation at the moment of putting it into the mould with $1\frac{1}{4}$ cups ($2\frac{1}{2}$ decilitres) of cream, which has been whipped, but not whipped stiff.

Put the mousse in a mould lined with aspic and decorated with the shrimp tails (and if desired with some truffle decoration). Cover with aspic. Allow to get thoroughly cold. Turn out and arrange on a napkin or in a crystal bowl.

Shrimp pilaf I. PILAF DE CREVETTES—Cook the rice and add to it $\frac{1}{4}$ pound (125 grams) of peeled shrimps; mix carefully so as not to damage the rice grains.

Shrimp pilaf II. PILAF DE CREVETTES—Cook the rice and line a large, round, buttered mould with it.

On this rice put a ragoût of peeled shrimps (bound with *Shrimp sauce II*, see SAUCE). Cover with the rest of the rice, pressing lightly with the back of a spoon to pack the rice properly. Put in the oven for a few moments. Turn out on to a round dish and surround with a ring of *Shrimp sauce*.

Shrimp salad. SALADE DE CREVETTES—Season with vinaigrette or with mayonnaise some peeled shrimps. Arrange them in a dish. Decorate with quarters of hard boiled eggs and lettuce hearts.

Shrimp salad à la dieppoise—See SALAD.

Shrimp soup: cullis, cream or bisque. POTAGES AUX CREVETTES—Prepared with shrimps cooked in a *mirepoix* like the soups of a similar nature prepared with crayfish. See SOUPS AND BROTHS, *Purée of shrimp soup.*

SILK-COTTON TREE. FROMAGER—A tree, native to tropical Africa. Its trunk is of white wood, somewhat reminiscent of cheese in appearance. For this reason, it is called '*fromager*' in French. Oil is extracted from its fruit.

SILKWORMS (Chinese cookery). VERS À SOIE—This rather unusual foodstuff is, or at least was, very well thought of in the 'Celestial Empire', if we are to believe the account of a French missionary in China, Father Favaud:

'It is some centuries', he wrote, 'since our farmers in the Midi took up the production of silkworms, but I know they have never dreamed of using any of them for nourishment. In China it is not the same thing at all. During the long stay I have made in that country, I have often seen people eat silkworm chrysalids, and I have eaten them myself. I can state that they constitute an excellent stomachic, strengthening and refreshing at the same time, which delicate persons often use with successful results.

'The cocoons having been unwound, a certain quantity of the chrysalids are grilled in the pan so that the watery part runs right off. Their outer covering is then removed (this comes off by itself), and they are presented in the form of small yellow objects, rather like carp roes.

'These are fried in butter, fat or oil, and sprinkled with stock (chicken stock is the best).

'When they have boiled for five minutes they are crushed with a wooden spoon, and the whole mass is carefully stirred so that nothing is left in the bottom of the vessel. Some egg yolks are beaten, in the proportion of 3 to every 100 chrysalids, and poured over, and in this way a beautiful cream, golden yellow and of an exquisite flavour, is obtained.

'Thus this foodstuff was prepared for the mandarins and the wealthy. As for the poor, after having grilled the chrysalids and removed their outer covering, they fried the rest in butter or fat and seasoned them with a little salt, pepper or vinegar; or even ate them just as they were, with rice, content simply to have removed their outer covering.'

SILLERY—A renowned Champagne wine harvested in the country around the commune of Sillery in the department of the Marne.

SILVER. ARGENTERIE DE TABLE—This term describes all the utensils in silver (or silver-plated metal) used at table.

More specifically this applies to individual pieces of silver which go in to make up what is called the '*cover*', (U.S.A. 'place setting'), i.e. spoon, fork and knife, when the latter has a silver (or silver-plated) handle. See FORK and SPOON.

Table silver also includes other articles which in the olden days were called silver plate, articles of various shapes, such as round or oval dishes, large or small bowls, soup tureens, sauceboats, pie dishes, etc.

Among table silverware are also included decorative silver and silver-plate pieces, such as salvers, fruit baskets, pedestal dishes, etc.

16th-century ewer in rock crystal and silver

SILVER BIRCH. Bouleau blanc—In the spring this tree which grows in northern countries contains a great deal of sour-sweet sap which, when fresh, makes a very pleasant drink.

It is sometimes subjected to a fermentation process before being used. In U.S.A. this is called birch beer.

SILVERSIDE OR ATHERINE. Prêtre—Small regional sea fish of France about the size of a smelt, about 4 to 7 inches long, showing on its sides a silvery mark like a star. Its flesh is quite delicate.

SIMAROUBA—Tree native to Guiana whose bark is used for a bitter tonic.

SIMMER. Mijoter—To cook gently over a very low flame.

SIMMERING. Frémissement—The slight quivering of a liquid just before it comes to the boil. When *poaching* the liquid should be kept in this state all the time.

Some things, such as *pot-au-feu*, are cooked entirely by simmering.

SINGEING. Flambage—The process of rotating poultry and winged game, etc. over a spirit lamp or gas flame to burn off feathers and hair.

SINGER—French culinary term of unknown origin meaning to sprinkle with flour a *ragoût* or other preparation in order to thicken the sauce.

SIPHON—A sort of carafe in thick glass, often encased in wicker or metal, holding under pressure water that has been made effervescent with carbonic gas. Siphons are closed with a metal top provided with a lever which allows the liquid to escape. Some siphons allow Seltzer water to be made with the aid of capsules called sparklets.

SIRLOIN. Aloyau—This joint includes the lumbar region, starting from the last rib down to and including the top part of the pelvic basin (sacrum). The different parts are: the fillet, sirloin and rump-steak.

The sirloin, whole or divided transversally into pieces of varying weight, is roasted or braised.

When served as a roast, it is treated exactly as *contre-filet* or ribs of beef.

All the recipes for the preparation of sirloin, whole, or cut into pieces, will be found under BEEF.

SKATE OR RAY. Raie—Name of flat scaleless fish, flattened vertically, characterized by the development of pectoral fins in the form of wings, with a long and relatively thick tail.

The skin of the skate is covered with a viscous coating which continues to reform itself for 10 hours after death, so that it is possible by wiping the fish with a cloth and observing whether or not the coating reforms to judge how fresh it is. The skate is the only fish which gains from being slightly 'high', though this should not be allowed to get to the point where the smell alters.

The flesh of the skate is less digestible than that of white fish; the liver is sought after by certain connoisseurs.

In some European countries, notably in England, Belgium and Holland, the skate is found in the shops already skinned. This is not so in France.

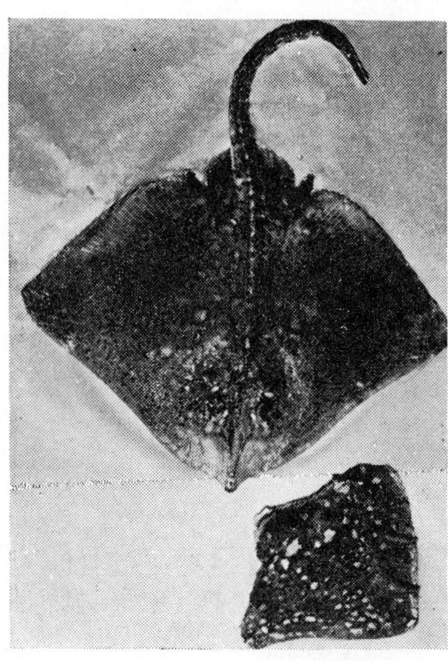

Whole skate and a 'wing' of skate

To cook skate. Cut up the skate in chunks or divide it into the two wings. Put the wings or pieces into a sauté pan and the central part or tail as well. Cover with water seasoned with 1 cup (2 decilitres) of wine vinegar to each quart (litre) of water and salt. Bring to the boil, skim, reduce heat and poach the fish gently.

Drain the skate. Remove the skin from both sides. Set on the serving dish. Serve according to recipe.

Skate au beurre noir. Raie au beurre noir—Proceed with skate cooked in *Court-bouillon**, drained and set on a serving dish as *Salt cod with brown butter*. See COD.

Skate au beurre noisette. Raie au beurre noisette—Prepared like *Salt cod with noisette butter* using skate cooked in *court-bouillon**. See COD.

Boiled skate with various sauces. Raie bouillie—Cook the skate in *court-bouillon**. Drain it. Set it on a napkin; garnish with fresh parsley. Serve with it separately one of the sauces suitable for boiled fish (*Melted butter*, *Bâtarde sauce*, *Cream sauce*, *Hollandaise sauce*, *etc.*). See SAUCE.

Fried skate. Raie frite—It is mostly small skate that are cooked in this way. Skin them, cut in chunks, or, if they are very small, leave them whole. Soak in cold, boiled milk; drain and flour them lightly. Fry in deep smoking fat. Drain, dry, season with salt, arrange on a napkin and garnish with fried parsley and lemon.

Skate au gratin. Raie au gratin—Usually prepared with the wings of small skates. Proceed in the same way as for *Sole au gratin*. See SOLE.

When using large skates, the fish must be cooked in *court-bouillon** before being coated with the *Au gratin sauce*.

Jellied skate. RAIE À LA GELÉE—Poach the wings of skate in fish stock with white wine. Let them cool in this liquor. Drain them and set on a serving dish. Make aspic jelly from the cooking liquor, clarify it and pour over the skate. See JELLY.

Skate liver. FOIE DE RAIE—Like burbot liver, the liver of the skate is very tasty. Usually it is poached with the skate and served with it.

It can also be served by itself in shells, and as fritters (pieces of skate liver poached, steeped in oil, lemon juice and parsley, dipped in butter and deep-fried in boiling fat).

Skate liver can also be served in scooped-out bread-crust or cooked in tarts and pâtés.

Skate liver croûtes. CROÛTE AU FOIE DE RAIE—Fill hollow crusts of fried bread with skate liver, cooked in a *court-bouillon** and sliced. Coat with *Mornay sauce* (see SAUCE), cover with grated cheese, sprinkle with melted butter and brown.

Skate liver fritters. BEIGNETS DE FOIE DE RAIE—Poach the skate liver in white wine. Allow to cool. Cut into little slices. Marinate these slices in oil, lemon juice, chopped parsley, salt and pepper. At the last moment dip into some light batter. Fry in smoking fat. Drain, season with salt, set on a napkin and garnish with fried parsley and lemon.

Skate à la meunière. RAIE À LA MEUNIÈRE—Use the wings of small skates in the same way a for *Sole à la meunière**.

SKEWER. BROCHETTE—A small spit, made of silver or other metal and sometimes of wood, on which various substances can be threaded before being grilled or fried.

Preparations cooked on skewers are called *brochettes* in French. Thus we have: *Brochette of chicken livers, Brochette of lamb's sweetbreads, Brochette of kidneys*, etc.

An infinite number of articles can be cooked on skewers.

See OFFAL OR VARIETY MEATS, *Calf's kidneys on skewers* and CHICKEN, *Chicken brochettes.*

SKIM. ÉCRÉMER, ÉCUMER, DÉPOUILLER—To skim cream from milk is expressed in French by the word *écrémer*. To remove with a spoon or skimmer all the scum which rises to the surface of a stock, sauce or ragoût is expressed by the words *écumer* or *dépouiller*.

SKIMMER. ÉCUMOIRE—A flat perforated spoon, used for skimming.

SKIN. PEAU—The skin forms one-fifth of the butcher's meat and is not normally used for food (except for the oxtail and muzzle).

The skin of sucking pig, of poultry and of winged game is eaten.

The skin of some aquatic birds is oily and has an unpleasant taste; it should, therefore, be taken off.

The skin of fruit contains valuable ferments and vitamins, but, being exposed to impurities, it should be peeled or washed carefully.

SKINNING. DÉPOUILLER—To remove the skin from ground game, e.g. *skinning a hare* (or rabbit).

Eels and conger eels are also said to be *skinned* when they are *stripped* for cooking.

SKIRRET. GIROLE, GIROLLE—Popular name for the mushroom which is known also as *chanterelle*. See MUSHROOMS.

SLAUGHTER. ABATAGE—The methods of killing the animals have a considerable influence on the appearance and the keeping quality of meat; they vary, however, according to the type of establishment and the type of animal slaughtered.

Slaughtering an ox in Egyptian times

In France, slaughtering, which should be preceded by an ante-mortem inspection of the livestock animal (on the hoof), should be carried out only after a period of rest of several days allowing the animals to recover from fatigue and ending with a day of complete fasting. These different rules are very rarely complied with. The animals which are bled before being stunned give a meat of better quality and a higher keeping quality. The cutting of the medulla will avoid the suffering of a prolonged agony. Immediately after the slaughter, the animals must at once be viscerated and undergo (this time compulsory), post-mortem inspection by a qualified inspector, at least in the slaughter houses of large towns.

In Great Britain, the law says that slaughtering can be carried out after 48 hours of resting and 24 hours of complete fasting. Regulations demand that all animals must be stunned humanely, the only exception being made in the case of kosher or Mohammedan butchers where the severing of the medulla is not recommended. Both ante- and post-mortem inspections are compulsory.

In the U.S.A., a high percentage of the slaughtering is centralized in a few very large slaughtering and packing houses, over which rigid control is exercised by the Department of Agriculture through ante- and post-mortem inspection of all animals. Every animal is stunned before butchering. Each state is responsible by law for local slaughter-houses under the Department of Health.

SLAUGHTER-HOUSE. ABATTOIR—An establishment where butchers kill animals for the market.

There are model slaughter-houses, like those of Chicago, the description of which has often tempted men of letters.

In large cities, the animals cannot be slaughtered except in public slaughter-houses which provide for reliable ante- and post-mortem inspection, which is impossible in the privately owned slaughter-houses, of which there are still too many in the country.

A modern slaughter-house consists of:

A common slaughter hall, well lit, well aired, well equipped for the washing and transport of meat, in which each butcher is given sufficient floor space to perform his work;

A refrigerator, which may or may not be preceded by a cold room, used as a salesroom;

Lairages and pens for the livestock, where the animals arrive by rail and from where they have only a short walk to the main slaughter hall;

A tripe-shop, with premises for washing and cleaning of viscera;

An inspection service with a well-equipped laboratory.

An industrial slaughter-house consists, mainly, of a building of several storeys: the animals are slaughtered on the top floor, to which they have access on foot; from there the carcase-meat on the one hand, and the by-products (blood, tallow, hide and various offals and scraps) on the other, are taken down to departments on lower floors by simple force of gravity—by means of chutes on rails, or sleeves.

In these slaughter-houses the workers specialize, each in one type of work, and a carcase passes through the hands of some fifty specialists; this contributes to increase of output since it is possible to slaughter up to 60 oxen an hour, thus lowering the manufacturing cost considerably; inspection is provided and all the work is done in extremely hygienic conditions.

The carcases are scrubbed, washed in hot water at 65°, from which they are sent to the refrigerator (dressed or not, as the case may be) after having passed from 16 to 24 hours in pre-refrigeration in the hanging rooms.

These industrial slaughter-houses are generally equipped with various installations which enable work to go on with processing and canning of meat.

SLEEVE-FISH. ENCORNET—Common name of the calamary. See CALAMARY.

SLIMNESS. MAIGREUR—Slimness, which is compatible with perfect health, should not be confused with emaciation. Some persons remain thin and do not put on weight, even if they eat a lot.

SLIVER. LÈCHE—A thin slice of bread or meat.

SLOE. PRUNELLE—Fruit of the sloe tree, also called the *blackthorn*, a tree found all over Europe.

The sloe, a tiny plum, dark blue in colour, is scarcely eatable, its flesh being very sour and sharp tasting.

In the Haute-Saône, there is a cultivated sloe which is used mainly in distilling and for making jams.

At Angers a much esteemed liqueur is made from sloes.

SMALL FILLETS. PETITS FILETS—Term applied to little round slices of fillet of beef (taken from the top or bottom end of the fillet or tenderloin).

Small fillets are cut into pieces weighing from 100 to 125 grams. They are grilled or fried in butter and, like beef *tournedos* (see BEEF), they can be served with various garnishes and sauces.

SMALLAGE. ACHE DES MARAIS—Wild plant (wild celery) which has been replaced in cookery by cultivated celery. It was used in cookery by the Romans.

This plant can be used as a salad.

SMELL. ODORAT—The sense of smell is active not only before a meal is taken, but also during the meal. The aroma released by fragrant parts of the food is inhaled and penetrates into the back-throat and into the nasal chambers.

It has been proved by experience that smell brings about the loosening of gastric secretion. In fact a strong secretion of gastric juices can be brought about by simply inhaling fragrant steam provided it comes from a nourishing substance such as meat bouillon. It can therefore be said that the smell of well cooked food aids the digestion.

SMELT. ÉPERLAN—This fish, says Rondelet, is so called (*éperlan*—pearly fish) 'for its beautiful, pure whiteness, comparable with that of the pearl'. The smelt is one of the most delicate of all freshwater fish. It is classed as a freshwater fish although it lives in the sea, because, like a good many other migratory fish, it spawns in fresh water. Nevertheless, smelts seldom run up river beyond the tide-line. Thus in the Seine, where this fish is now much less common than it used to be, smelts are seldom found beyond the Martet weir near Elbeuf. The greatest abundance of smelts is to be found near Caudebec, and it is for this reason that there are three smelts on the civic arms of this French town. Smelts are also fairly plentiful around La Mailleraye and Villequier.

These tiny fish usually migrate up river between February 20th and March 15th and this is also the best season for catching them. They are, however, to be found in these waters all the year round though, admittedly, less abundantly than during the spring run.

Freshly caught smelts have a fairly strong smell, similar to that of the violet. Some authorities, however, believe that smelts recall the scent of cucumbers rather than violets. One thing is certain, that this little fish is most delicate in flavour and that fried smelts are properly regarded as one of the finest of all fish dishes.

Method of preparation—Gut and wash the smelts, leaving them in water for as short a time as possible. Dry them and proceed according to the recipe.

Smelts à l'anglaise. ÉPERLANS À L'ANGLAISE—Slit the smelts along the back. Open out gently. Dip in egg and breadcrumbs and fry in clarified butter.

Put the smelts on a long dish. Pour over them half-melted *Maître d'hôtel butter*. See BUTTER, *Compound butters.*

Smelts en escabèche—See HORS-D'OEUVRE, *Cold hors-d'oeuvre, Escabèche of various fishes.*

Fried smelts. ÉPERLANS FRITS—Dip the smelts in salted milk and flour. Shake off excess flour and plunge into boiling deep fat.

Drain. Dry in a cloth. Season with very dry table salt. Arrange in a clump in a napkin with fried parsley and lemon.

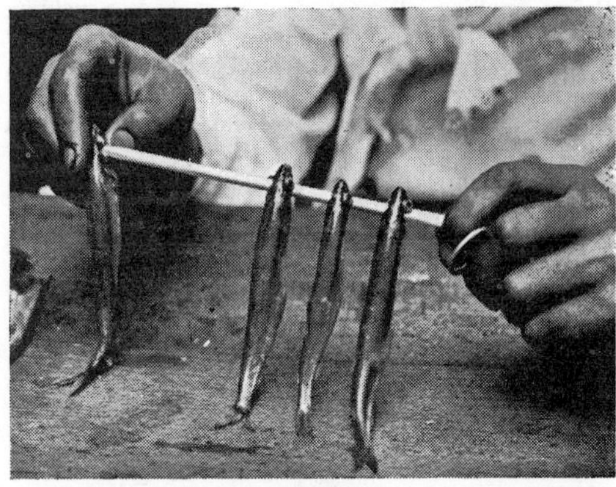

Skewering smelts

Fried smelts, skewered. ÉPERLANS FRITS EN BROCHETTES—Impale the smelts on metal skewers, 6 to each skewer, and deep-fry as indicated in the previous recipe.

Smelts au gratin. ÉPERLANS AU GRATIN—Arrange the smelts in a long ovenware dish, buttered and lined with chopped shallots cooked in white wine till the liquid is reduced to a coating in the pan. Put in a small cooked mushroom on top of each smelt. Surround with finely sliced mushrooms. Mask with *Mornay sauce* (see SAUCE). Sprinkle with breadcrumbs. Pour on melted butter. Cook in the oven and brown.

Grilled smelts. ÉPERLANS GRILLÉS—Slit the smelts along the back. Take out the bone. Season and flour. Baste with melted butter and grill hastily.

Serve on a long dish, garnished with fresh parsley and slices of lemon. Serve with *Maître d'hôtel butter* or some other sauce suitable for grilled fish.

Grilled smelts à l'anglaise. ÉPERLANS GRILLÉS À L'ANGLAISE—Gut the smelts. Slit them lengthwise along the back and take out the bone. Open them out gently.

Pour melted butter over them. Season with salt and cayenne pepper and dust with fresh breadcrumbs.

Grill fairly slowly. Turn the smelts over once during cooking, then serve on a dish on top of half melted *Maître d'hôtel butter* (see BUTTER, *Compound butters*).

Note. It may seem difficult at first sight to grill such a small fish as the smelt. In fact it is simple enough provided that the grill-pan and grid are perfectly clean and well greased with oil. Some hardware stores in France sell grills especially designed for smelts.

Cold marinade of smelts—See HORS-D'OEUVRE, *Cold hors-d'oeuvre, Smelts in marinade.*

Smelts on skewers. BROCHETTES D'ÉPERLANS—Clean out the smelts and thread them on metal skewers, allowing 8 to 10 small smelts per skewer and threading them through the eyes. Soak in milk. Dredge with flour lightly. Deep-fry in sizzling fat.

Drain the skewers, dry on a cloth and sprinkle with fine very dry salt.

Arrange on a napkin. Garnish with fried parsley and halves of lemons.

SMOKING. FUMAGE—A preserving process used especially for meat and fish. Woodsmoke is generally used, because of its drying and sterilizing properties. See PRESERVATION OF FOOD, CURING.

Sides of beef (especially rib and brisket), hams and other cuts of pork, sausages, poultry (goose in particular) and certain fish (herrings, salmon, eels, etc.), and some shellfish, can all be smoked.

Before smoking, all meat must be soaked in pickling brine. After it has been thoroughly wiped and dried, it is hung in a large chimney, not too near the fire, so that it may be dried right through. If the heat were too great, it would seal the meat and prevent the smoke from penetrating. For the same reason, the meat is very lightly smoked to begin with.

Some fish, such as herrings, are smoked without previous soaking. To get a suitable smoke, hardwood is used (oak, hornbeam), rather than wood of a resinous type. Green wood gives out more smoke than dry wood. Aromatic wood is often added to give an extra fragrance to the smoke, such as juniper with its berries, rosemary, laurel. Sometimes, though this is less common, spices are also added (liquorice, cloves, etc.).

Care is taken to change the position of the smoking meat from time to time, so that all parts may be thoroughly impregnated. The length of time needed to complete the process varies with the size of the meat or fish.

Smoking can be speeded up by injecting pickling brine flavoured with various spices into the meat.

Various types of smoking chambers are used in the smoking of foodstuffs. Some are smoking boxes which can be used in household kitchens. Others, used in large pork-butchers' establishments, are very elaborately constructed. They consist of several chambers through which the smoke, coming from a wood fire in the basement or on the ground floor of the building passes. Having passed through all the chambers in which the food to be smoked is hanging, the smoke escapes through an outlet in the ceiling of the last chamber.

SNAIL. ESCARGOT—The common name for a land gastropod mollusc. It was highly prized as food as far back as Roman times. The art of fattening snails is said to have been discovered by a Roman named Fulvius Lupinus.

Special snail pincers and fork for eating snails

In France, the vineyard snail is the most popular. As there are not enough of these to meet all demands another variety, the *petit-gris* of southern France is also used.

To avoid the risk of poisoning, snails must be deprived of food for some time before they are eaten, for they may have fed on plants harmless to themselves but poisonous to humans. Furthermore, it is advisable only to eat operculated snails, that is to say snails which have sealed themselves into their shells to hibernate.

Snail dish or escargotière

Snails à l'arlésienne. ESCARGOTS À L'ARLÉSIENNE—'Warm a little diced pork in a saucepan. Sprinkle with a little flour and moisten with a bottle of white wine. Add the snails, prepared in advance as follows:

'Take medium-sized snails, and soak them in tepid water. Next, blanch them with a handful of salt.

'Take them out of their shells. Drain them. Next, put them in the saucepan with a few cloves of garlic and plenty of herbs. Bring to the boil and leave to simmer slowly. When they are ready, drain them and put them back in their shells. Add a glass of Madeira and a pinch of cayenne pepper. Put the snails in the sauce and stir. Sprinkle with a little chopped parsley and the juice of a lemon.' (A. Helié's recipe.)

Snails à la bourguignonne. ESCARGOTS À LA BOURGUIGNONNE—Scrape away the chalky substance sealing the shells. Wash the snails in several waters and soak them for 2 hours with coarse salt, vinegar and a pinch of flour. Wash them again in a lot of water and blanch them for 5 minutes in boiling water. Drain and cool under running water. Take the snails out of their shells. Remove the black part at the end of the tail known as the *cloaca.*

Next put the snails in a saucepan. Moisten with equal parts of white wine and clear broth. The liquid should just cover the snails. Add carrots, onions, shallots and a large *bouquet garni.* Season with 1 teaspoon (8 grams) of salt to every quart (litre) of stock. Simmer for 3 to 4 hours. Leave to cool in the stock.

Boil the empty shells for 30 minutes in water with soda crystals added. Drain them, wash in cold water and dry. Put inside each shell a piece of butter *à la bourguignonne* prepared in advance. Each piece of butter should be about the size of a hazel-nut. Put the snails in the shells and seal with *Snail butter à la bourguignonne* (see BUTTER, *Compound butters*).

Put the filled shells in a dish with a little water at the bottom (or in a snail dish).

Sprinkle with a little fresh breadcrumbs. Warm in a hot oven. Serve as they are.

Snail broth. BOUILLON D'ESCARGOTS—Soak 24 snails thoroughly as indicated in the recipe for *Snails à la bourguignonne*. Break the shells and remove the snails. (Do not dip them in boiling water as this will wash away their natural gelatine.) Put them in a saucepan. Moisten with 3 litres (quarts) of water. Add 1 or 2 lettuces, a handful of purslane leaves and a little salt. (A piece of calf's head can also be added.) Skim. As soon as the broth is boiling steadily, lower the heat and simmer slowly for 3 hours. Add to the broth 30 grams of gum arabic dissolved in a glass of tepid water. Strain through muslin.

Snails à la chablaisienne. ESCARGOTS À LA CHABLAISIENNE—Proceed as indicated for *Snails à la bourguignonne*, pouring into each shell a few drops of white Chablis wine cooked with chopped shallot and parsley, enriched with meat essence and seasoned.

Put the snails back in the shells and seal with *Snail butter à la bourguignonne* (see BUTTER, *Compound butters*).

Snails Comtesse Riguidi. ESCARGOTS COMTESSE RIGUIDI —During the season when snails are unobtainable, said Grimod de la Reynière, cooks sometimes amuse themselves by cheating our palates by a not unpleasant imitation. A very fine stuffing is made either of game or fish, with fillets of anchovy, nutmeg, fine spices, *fines herbes*, bound with yolks of egg. Snail shells are thoroughly washed and warmed. Each one is filled with the stuffing and served piping hot.

Grimod de la Reynière, who in matters of cookery was somewhat romantic, tells us that 'these innocent deceptions never deceive a gourmet', but that nonetheless, as to the snails, 'many people prefer the imitation to the reality'.

Here is the recipe for *Mock Snails Comtesse Riguidi* 'Put into large well washed snail shells (from which, naturally, the unwanted sitting tenant has been evicted) little balls of lambs' sweetbread tossed in butter. Fill up the shell with a chicken cream stuffing and chopped truffles mixed together. Put the mock snails in an ovenware dish or a special snail dish. Sprinkle with breadcrumbs and cook for a few minutes in the oven.'

A quite popular variant of this delicate dish consists in filling the snail shells with cocks' kidneys cooked in white wine.

Snails à la poulette. ESCARGOTS À LA POULETTE—Soak the snails in a pan of boiling water, with a pinch of salt and some ashes. Boil for 5 minutes and then take out the snails. Take them out of their shells and put them in cold water.

Wash them with great care. Drain. Put the snails to boil in a *court-bouillon* with salt, pepper, thyme, bay leaves and parsley. At the end of an hour and a half, take the snails out of the *court-bouillon*. Drain them. Brown some chopped onions. Moisten with equal parts of white wine and water. When the liquid begins to boil, add a little *Allemande sauce* (see SAUCE). Put in the snails. Leave them for 5 to 7 minutes. Just before serving, blend in a little best quality butter and yolks of egg with a little lemon juice. Add a little more salt and pepper.

Snipe

SNIPE. BÉCASSINE—Migratory bird bearing great resemblance to the woodcock, but only about half the size of the latter.

This bird comes to France twice a year.

It can be prepared in any way suitable for woodcock, but the best method is roasting. In U.S.A. the *Wilson's snipe* or *American snipe* is almost identical.

Casserole of snipe. BÉCASSINES EN CASSEROLE—Truss the snipe, draw the heads round and run the beaks through the legs. Cover each with a rasher of fat bacon. Put them into a metal or earthenware casserole, in which some butter has been heated. Season and baste with butter. Cook in a hot oven for about 12 minutes. Put each bird on a small croûton fried in butter. Sprinkle with a tablespoon of brandy and 2 or 3 tablespoons of game *fumet**.

Croustade of snipe with truffles. CROUSTADE DE BÉCASSINES AUX TRUFFES—Bone the snipe. Stuff each one with a piece of *à gratin forcemeat* (see FORCEMEAT) about the size of a small egg, mixed with diced truffles, well seasoned and sprinkled with a little brandy. Brown lightly in butter for a few moments. Arrange in a deep round dish on a bed of *Quenelle forcemeat* (see FORCEMEAT) made with game. Cover with thin slices of truffles, seasoned and sprinkled with a little brandy. Put a strip of flaky pastry on the border of the dish. On this band of pastry, put a rolled-out cover of the same pastry and seal the edges. Decorate the top of the croustade with pieces of rolled-out puff pastry cut in fancy shapes. Make a hole in the middle. Brush with yolk of egg. Bake in a hot oven. At the last moment pour into the croustade a few tablespoons of greatly reduced *Demi-glace sauce* (see SAUCE) based on a concentrated game stock.

Hot snipe pâté Lucullus. PÂTÉ CHAUD DE BÉCASSINES LUCULLUS—Bone 6 snipe. Stuff with a *Fine panada forcemeat* (see FORCEMEAT) mixed with one-third of its weight of foie gras, as well as the chopped birds' trail.

Put this stuffing in a layer on the snipe laid out flat on a table. Put a piece of foie gras and a piece of truffle in the middle of each bird. Reshape the snipe in their original form and sprinkle with a few drops of brandy.

Line an oval-shaped mould for hot pâtés with pie pastry. Coat the inside of the pastry-lined mould with a layer of *Fine panada forcemeat* mixed with *à gratin forcemeat*, half-and-half.

Put the stuffed snipe into the pâté, packing them in tightly, and sealing them in with a layer of forcemeat similar to the one used for lining the pâté.

Finish with a layer of forcemeat and cover this with a rasher of fat bacon.

Cover with a piece of rolled-out pastry. Seal and crimp the edges. Decorate with rolled-out pieces of puff pastry cut in fancy shapes. Make an opening in the middle of this pastry lid to allow steam to escape. Brush with beaten egg.

Place the pâté on a baking sheet and set to bake in a moderate oven from 45 minutes to an hour.

Remove the pastry lid, cutting it carefully with a knife all around. Take off the bacon rasher covering the forcemeat. Unmould.

Pour into the pâté a ragoût of truffles (cut in thick slices) blended with a few tablespoons of Madeira flavoured, concentrated game stock.

Replace the pastry lid on the pâté. Put it in the oven for a few moments to heat thoroughly.

Serve on a dish covered with a folded napkin.

This pâté can also be served cold. In that case, pour into the pâté, when it is just warm, a few tablespoons of cold but liquid aspic jelly based on game stock and chill thoroughly.

GREAT SNIPE. Bécassin—This is the name commonly given to *cul-blanc*, a variety of snipe, which has distinctive white feathers on tail.

It is prepared in any way suitable for snipe, mainly roasting.

SNOW. Neige—In cooking, certain cold dishes are served on a bed of ice grated with a special grater. This grated ice is known as *neige*.

SNOWBALL. Boule de neige—Use a spherical mould. Line with chocolate ice cream. Fill with vanilla-flavoured *mousse mixture* (see ICE CREAMS AND ICES) and diced crystallized fruit steeped in Maraschino. When the ice is turned out, cover it entirely with *Chantilly cream* (see CREAMS), put through a forcing (pastry) bag with a fluted nozzle.

SNOW PARTRIDGE. Arbenne—A variety of grouse also called *Tibetan partridge*. They are found in the Valais (Switzerland), in Savoy and in Piedmont. For culinary purposes snow partridge is treated like grouse or partridge.

SOAKING. Trempage—Immersion in water, principally of dried vegetables. Used also to describe the moistening of some *gâteaux* with syrup. See BABA and SAVARIN.

SOBRONADE (SOUP)—Country soup, very popular in the Périgord countryside. It is made with both fresh and salt pork cut in large dice and a variety of vegetables: haricot beans, carrots, leeks, celery and root vegetables; together constituting what is a solid food rather than a soup in the ordinary sense. This is really a kind of *potée*.

SODA-WATER—Effervescent drink manufactured industrially. Soda-water, which is highly charged with carbonic gas, is added to syrups, fruit juices, whisky, etc.

SOFT ROE. Laitance, laite—The milt or sperm of the male fish, a smooth, white substance. It is a food rich in fat and phosphorus, and is easily digested.

Preparation of soft roes—Before they are cooked, soft roes must be cleansed in cold water and stripped of the little blood vessel that runs down one side.

They must then be poached for a very short time in a stock made from a little water, lemon juice and butter, seasoned with salt.

For some purposes, soft roes can be lightly floured and fried in very hot butter. This method of preparation is called *à la meunière*. Soft roes *à la meunière* are served on canapés, toast or in tartlets, barquettes, etc.

Soft roes of carp and other fish. Laitances de carpes—The soft roes of carp are perhaps the most delicate of all edible soft roes. Next in order of merit are the roes of herring and mackerel.

Soft roes can be cooked in an infinite number of ways. They can be served by themselves, as fritters, in tartlets or barquettes, on canapés, in small vol-au-vents, as hot or cold hors-d'oeuvre or as a light main dish. They can also be used as a garnish for braised or poached fish.

Soft roes à l'anglaise. Laitances à l'anglaise—Cleanse the soft roes. Poach them for 2 minutes in stock as indicated above. Drain them. Leave them to cool. Dip them in egg and breadcrumbs. Fry in butter, browning on both sides. Serve on a long dish, with half melted *Maître d'hôtel butter* on top and surrounded by fluted half slices of lemon. See BUTTER, *Compound butters*.

Soft roes in barquettes. Laitances en barquettes—Poach the soft roes in stock as indicated above. Drain and place in baked *barquettes* filled with a *salpicon** of mushrooms or some other suitable ingredient blended with *Velouté* or with *Béchamel sauce* based on fish stock. Spoon over some *Normande sauce* or some other white sauce based on fish stock. See SAUCE. Brown in a very hot oven.

Soft roes in browned butter I. Laitances au beurre noir—Poach the soft roes in stock as indicated above. Arrange them on a long dish. Garnish with capers and chopped parsley. Pour on a little lemon juice and a few spoonfuls of browned butter.

Soft roes in browned butter II. Laitances au beurre noir—Arrange the soft roes on a long dish. Garnish with capers, and pour over them a few drops of vinegar. Just before serving, pour on a few tablespoons of browned butter in which one or two tablespoons of shredded parsley have been fried.

Cold soft roes served with cold fish. Laitances froides—Poach the soft roes in white wine and lemon juice. Leave them to cool in this stock. Drain and dry them in a cloth.

If they are to be used as a garnish for cold fish, arrange them in barquettes of thin pastry baked blind (empty). Cover them with mayonnaise or some other cold sauce.

If the roes are to be used as an ingredient of a composite salad, put them, drained and dried, on top of the salad in a salad bowl, and season with oil, vinegar (or lemon juice), salt and pepper.

Soft roes on croutons—See FISH ROES, *Fish roes on toast*.

Soft roe fritters. Laitances en beignets—Poach the soft roes in stock as indicated above. Leave them to cool. Put them in a marinade of oil, lemon juice and chopped parsley. Just before serving, dip them in batter and deep-fry.

Serve on a napkin with fried parsley.

Soft roes as a garnish—Cleanse the soft roes in cold water. Put them in a casserole with a few tablespoons of water, a squeeze of lemon juice, a pinch of salt and a small knob of butter.

Bring them to the boil and then simmer very gently for 3 minutes.

Soft roes in mayonnaise. Mayonnaise de laitances—Poach the soft roes in salt water. Drain and dry in a cloth.

Fill a salad bowl with a mound of finely shredded lettuce, seasoned with oil, vinegar, salt and pepper, and drained. Place the soft roes on top.

Cover with mayonnaise. Surround with quartered hard boiled eggs and lettuce hearts.

Decorate the top of the mayonnaise with fillets of anchovy and capers.

Soft roes à la meunière. LAITANCES À LA MEUNIÈRE—Season the roes, dip them in flour and fry them in butter. Proceed thereafter as in recipe for *Fish à la meunière.*

Soft roes in noisette butter. LAITANCES AU BEURRE NOISETTE—Proceed as for *Soft roes in browned butter*, without the capers and chopped parsley, and substituting *Noisette butter* for *Browned butter* (see BUTTER, *Compound butters*).

Soft roes in scallop shells à la normande. LAITANCES EN COQUILLES À LA NORMANDE—Poach and drain the soft roes as indicated above. Put them in scallop shells surrounded by a border of *Duchess potato* (see POTATOES) previously lightly browned in the oven. Place on top an oyster, poached and drained, a cooked mushroom, a teaspoon of shrimps and mussels. Cover with *Normande sauce* (see SAUCE) and decorate each shell with a generous strip of truffle.

Soft roe tartlets. LAITANCES EN CAISSES—Proceed as for *Soft roes à la meunière**. Serve in baked tartlets. Brown a handful of breadcrumbs in the cooking butter and pour this over the roes. Add lemon juice and chopped parsley.

SOFTENING, BLETTING. BLET, BLETTE—Term used to define the state of overripeness (i.e. 'sleepiness') in certain kinds of fruit, preceding rotting.

In the case of some species of fruit (medlars, persimmons) the fruit does not attain the right state of ripeness, i.e. become edible, until it is bletted. In the case of other fruit (apples, pears, etc.), softening or overripeness is a sign of the beginning of decay.

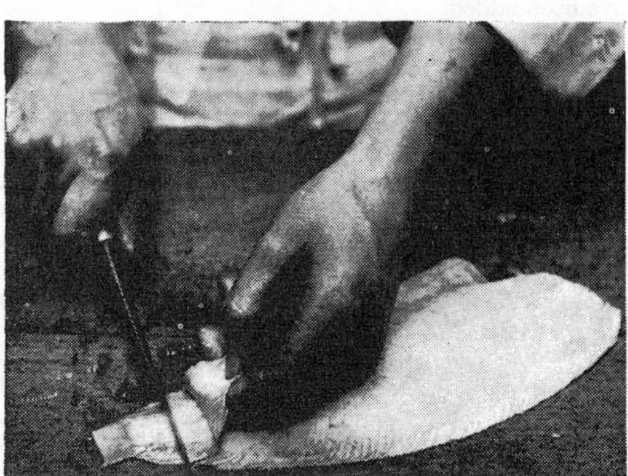

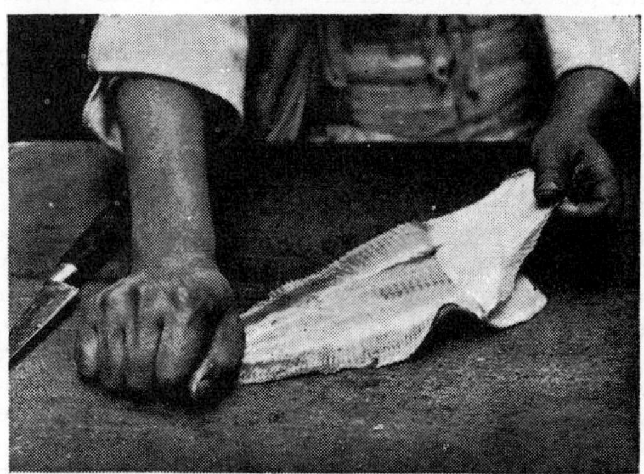

Preparation of sole *(Larousse)*

(1) To remove the skin make an incision near the tail

(2) Holding the fish down under the right hand, pull off the skin in one piece with the left hand

SOLE—The sole is a flat fish, in shape an elongated oval, almost completely surrounded by fins and covered with very small hard scales which are firmly attached to the skin. The colour of the skin varies according to the depth in which the sole is fished and varies from quite a dark brown to pale grey, but it is generally an olive brown with blackish irregular markings. The blind side of the sole is whitish in colour.

The eyes of the fish, placed on the right side (the brown side) are small and rather far apart; the mouth is arched, the teeth are fine and pointed and the lower jaw has short white barbels.

The sole is considered the best of the flat fish. Its flesh is white, firm, and delicate and is easily detached from the bones. It is easily digestible.

This sole, which is fished in most European waters, but not American waters, should not be confused with the fish known as lemon sole, which, though quite good to eat, is not to be compared with the true sole.

This fish can be prepared in an infinite number of ways. As well as the many ways of cooking it given here, it may have applied to it most of the recipes given for various other fish such as brill, plaice, lemon sole, whiting, etc.

Whole, the soles are prepared fried, boiled, poached, braised, *à la meunière* and grilled. Filleted, they may be prepared in every possible way.

Each of the recipes for whole soles given below is applicable to soles weighing about ¾ pound (from 350 to 400 grams), enough to serve two people, especially when the dish includes a fairly generous garnish.

Soles of medium size should be used for frying, baking in butter (*a la meunière*), or grilling, because these are usually served one to each guest.

Note. In order to facilitate the serving of whole soles, especially when they must be dished up with sauce and garnish, it is better to trim the fish to the edge of the fillets before cooking. Soles trimmed in this way appear smaller, but they are easier to serve.

If the backbone is broken before cooking it can be removed before serving.

The American 'sole' is not the same family as the English Dover sole and differs markedly in texture. However, *Lemon sole*, *Dab*, *Winter flounder* and *Grey sole* can be used in the following recipes.

Sole à l'américaine—Split the sole on the side from which the skin has been removed. Raise the fillets slightly and break the backbone in two or three places. Season the inside of the fish.

Poach the sole very gently in a white wine fish *fumet**. Drain it. Set it on a serving dish. Surround with a *salpicon** of lobster or spiny lobster prepared *à l'américaine* (see LOBSTER). Put two slices of lobster or spiny lobster on top of the sole. Coat with *Américaine sauce*, to which some concentrated *fumet* and butter have been added.

Note. This dish is often called *Sole à l'armoricaine*, since many people think that *Lobster à l'américaine* should really be *à l'armoricaine*.

Sole à l'amiral—Only very large soles with thick fillets are prepared in this way. For the recipes see *Brill à l'amiral* under BRILL.

Sole à l'anglaise—This name generally means a grilled sole accompanied by melted butter or *Maître d'hôtel*

butter (see BUTTER, *Compound butters*) and boiled potatoes, but can also be sole poached in salted water and milk, accompanied by melted butter and boiled potatoes.

The same name is finally applied to a sole boned when raw, coated in egg and breadcrumbs, cooked in clarified butter and served with rather soft *Maître d'hôtel butter*.

Sole à l'arlésienne—Poach the sole in *fumet**. Set it on a serving dish, and garnish with very small tomatoes peeled and cooked in butter, and sliced artichoke bottoms cooked in butter and their own juices and finished in a little cream.

To coat the sole, reduce (boil down) the cooking liquor and add a little fish aspic jelly and some concentrated tomato pulp, mixed with butter and a little grated garlic.

Attereaux of sole à l'ancienne. ATTEREAUX DE SOLES À L'ANCIENNE—Cut each fillet into 3 or 4 pieces of equal size. Season them and seal them in butter. Thread these pieces on a silver skewer, alternating them with truffles and mushrooms cut in slices. Dip the skewers into *Villeroi sauce* (see SAUCE). Allow to cool, then coat in egg and breadcrumbs and at the last moment fry in clarified butter. Serve on a napkin. Garnish with fried parsley and quarters of lemon.

Attereaux of sole à la moderne. ATTEREAUX DE SOLES À LA MODERNE—Prepare as above, but without dipping in Villeroi sauce. Serve *Tomato sauce* (see SAUCE) or other suitable sauce separately.

Sole with aubergines or egg-plant. SOLE AUX AUBERGINES —Cook the sole in butter *à la meunière*. Set it on a serving dish. Surround with round slices of aubergines (egg-plant) cooked in the pan with butter or oil. Sprinkle with chopped parsley, and a few drops of lemon juice and pour over the butter in which the fish was cooked, very hot.

Alternatively poach the sole in a *fumet**, over a very low heat. Drain, wipe and set it on a serving dish. Surround with round slices of aubergines cooked in butter. Coat with *White wine sauce*. Glaze in a hot oven.

The sole may be prepared with courgettes (Italian marrows or zucchini), cucumbers cut in oval chunks and simmered in butter, artichoke bottoms sliced and sautéed in butter, celeriac quartered and simmered in butter or sweet pimentos cut in large *julienne* (strips), cooked in butter or oil.

Drain off the cooking liquor. Boil it down by one-third and thicken with a tablespoon of kneaded butter. Add a good tablespoon of butter. Coat the sole with this sauce. Glaze in a hot oven.

Barquettes or tartlets of sole. BARQUETTES, TARTELETTES DE SOLES—Made with *salpicon** of sole, truffles and mushrooms, bound with a brown or white sauce.

Beignets of sole. BEIGNETS DE SOLES—Make a *salpicon** of sole, as for ordinary *croquettes*. Bind with *Velouté* or *Béchamel sauce* and allow to cool. See SAUCE.

Divide into small portions and roll each part into a ball. At the last moment dip each into a light batter and fry in deep fat. Serve in a mound, on a napkin, and garnish with fried parsley. Serve separately *Tomato sauce* or any other sauce suitable for fried fish.

Sole Bercy I—Put the sole on a long fireproof dish which has been buttered and sprinkled with chopped shallot and parsley.

Moisten with two tablespoons of white wine and a squeeze of lemon juice. Put on top of the sole a tablespoon of butter divided up into small pieces.

Cook the sole in the oven, basting often so as to glaze the fish nicely.

Sole Bercy II—Put the sole in a fireproof dish on a layer of chopped onions lightly cooked in butter without becoming too much coloured. Surround with 4 cultivated mushrooms, trimmed, sliced and sautéed in butter. Season. Moisten with four tablespoons of red Burgundy. Cook in the oven.

Drain off the cooking liquor. Reduce this by one-third and thicken with a tablespoon of butter worked together with flour; add a good tablespoon of butter. Coat the sole with this sauce. Glaze in a hot oven.

Sole à la bonne femme—Trim a medium-sized sole in the usual way, slit it longways along the skinned side and raise the fillets a little on each side to loosen the backbone.

Season inside and out and put into a buttered fireproof dish lined with a layer of chopped raw mushrooms and a pinch of chopped parsley.

Add ½ cup (1 decilitre) of white wine and a few drops of lemon juice. Dot the surface with 1 tablespoon (15 grams) of butter divided up into tiny pieces.

Bring to the boil, then put in the oven, cover and cook for 10 minutes.

Drain off the cooking liquor into a pan. Boil it down and thicken with a tablespoon of butter worked together with flour.

Coat the sole with this sauce. Glaze in a hot oven.

Sole à la bourguignonne—The same as *Sole with red wine*, the recipe for which is given below.

Sole à la bretonne—Put the sole, after seasoning it, on a buttered baking tin spread with ½ cup (1 decilitre) of *Vegetable fondue* (see FONDUE). Pour over ½ cup (1 decilitre) of fish *fumet** made with white wine. Cook, covered, in the oven, basting often.

Drain the fish; set it on a serving dish; coat with its cooking liquor to which 2 tablespoons of fresh cream have been added.

Brochettes of sole à la duxelles—Cut the fillets into square pieces of equal size. Sandwich them together two by two with a stuffing made of hard boiled egg yolks, breadcrumbs and chopped parsley. Thread them on skewers, alternating them with slices of mushrooms dipped in butter. Season and brush them with melted butter. Cover with white breadcrumbs. Grill. Set on a long dish on a layer of *Duxelles** bound with *Velouté sauce* (see SAUCE).

Sole cardinal—Stuff a boned sole with *Pike forcemeat* (see FORCEMEAT) mixed with *Lobster butter* (see BUTTER, *Compound butters*). Poach it in white wine that is scarcely boiling. Set on a serving dish. Garnish with slices of lobster or spiny lobster, or surround with a *salpicon** of one or other of these crustaceans. Coat with *Cardinal sauce* (see SAUCE) to which some of the concentrated cooking liquor has been added. Sprinkle with chopped lobster coral.

Note. It is mostly fillets of sole that are prepared in this way. The fillets are spread with the pike forcemeat and folded in two.

Sole Colbert—Split the sole along the side from which the skin has been removed. Raise the fillets so as to be able to loosen the backbone. Break the backbone in two or three places so that it may easily be removed after cooking.

Soak the sole in cold, boiled milk, flour it, coat it in egg and breadcrumbs. Raise the fillets and roll them back on themselves so as to leave the backbone free.

Fry the sole, drain it, remove the backbone. Fill the cavity with *Maître d'hôtel* butter (see BUTTER, *Compound butters*). Set on a long dish.

Croquettes and kromeskies of sole. CROQUETTES, CROMESQUIS DE SOLE—These small preparations which are served as a hot hors-d'oeuvre or a small entrée are made like ordinary croquettes, the recipe for which is given under HORS-D'OEUVRE, *Hot hors-d'oeuvre*.

Curried sole. SOLE À L'INDIENNE—Spread on a baking dish a layer of chopped onions cooked till soft in butter mixed with 2 to 3 tablespoons of tomatoes, peeled, pressed, chopped and also cooked in butter. Season with a teaspoon of curry. Set a sole on top and pour over it 2 tablespoons of mushroom stock. Poach in the oven.

Set the sole, well drained, on the serving dish (the fish having been trimmed and, if possible, the backbone removed).

Add to the cooking liquor 2 to 3 tablespoons of *Velouté* or *Béchamel sauce* (see SAUCE) based on fish stock and 3 tablespoons of thick fresh cream. Allow to boil for a few moments. Finish off with a teaspoon of butter and a few drops of lemon juice. Coat the fish with this sauce; serve Indian-style rice separately. See RICE, *Rice à l'indienne*.

Recipes given below for *Fillets of sole à l'indienne* can also be applied to whole sole.

Sole à la diplomate—Split the sole; raise the fillets, remove the backbone and stuff with a whiting forcemeat with cream and diced truffles. Poach the sole in a *fumet** that is scarcely boiling. Drain and dry; remove the side bones. Set on a long dish surrounded by a *salpicon** of lobster. Coat with *Diplomat sauce* (see SAUCE). Put on top of the sole four rather thick slices of truffles glazed with fish aspic jelly.

Sole dorée—See *Golden sole*.

Fillets of sole (*Larousse*)
(1) How to cut fillets of sole
(2) How to skin the fillets

Fillets of sole. FILETS DE SOLES—Fillets of sole, like those of other fish, are removed when raw, whatever method of cooking is subsequently employed.

According to their final use, the fillets are either left as they are and are simply flattened lightly, or rolled (after being slightly flattened).

All the methods of preparation given for the whole sole, as well as those given elsewhere for flat fish of various kinds, are applicable to fillets of sole.

These fillets can be served *à la meunière*, fried, boiled, poached and grilled. They are accompanied by various sauces and garnishes.

Fillets of sole can be rolled up to make *paupiettes*, recipes for which are to be found below.

Each of the recipes which follow require 8 fillets of sole.

Note. Fillets of sole cooked *à la meunière* or in a white wine *fumet* may also be garnished with aubergines (egg-plant), cucumbers (cut into 'pigeons' eggs' and cooked in butter), pimentos (peeled, cut in strips and stewed in butter or oil), tomatoes (halved and cooked in butter or oil) and other vegetables, cooked in butter or oil, braised, boiled or stewed in their own juices.

Instead of coating the fillets with *White wine sauce*, they may be covered with *Mornay sauce* and browned in the oven. See SAUCE.

Fillets of sole à l'américaine. FILETS DE SOLES À L'AMÉRICAINE—Poach the folded fillets in white wine. Drain them when they are cooked and finish off as described in the recipe for *Sole à l'américaine*.

Note. This dish is often served under the name of *Fillets of sole à l'armoricaine*.

Fillets of sole à l'ancienne. FILETS DE SOLES À L'ANCIENNE—Coat 8 lightly flattened fillets of sole with a thin layer of *Whiting forcemeat* (see FORCEMEAT) to which a third of its weight of dry *Duxelles** has been added. Fold the fillets. Coat them with egg and breadcrumbs. Cook in clarified butter. Arrange in a circle on a round dish, alternating them with little cutlets of whiting forcemeat (made in special moulds and poached). Garnish the middle of the dish with a *ragoût* composed of shrimps, mushrooms and truffles bound with fish *Velouté sauce*, mixed with cream and flavoured with Madeira. Sprinkle the fillets with a little *Noisette butter* (see BUTTER, *Compound butters*).

Fillets of sole à l'anglaise I. FILETS DE SOLES À L'ANGLAISE—Flatten and season the fillets of sole and coat them with egg and breadcrumbs. Cook in clarified butter. Set on a long dish. Cover with softened *Maître d'hôtel butter* (see BUTTER, *Compound butters*).

These fillets can be served with boiled or steamed potatoes.

Fillets of sole à l'anglaise II. FILETS DE SOLES À L'ANGLAISE—Fillets of sole poached in salted water and milk, served on a napkin or on a grid, with boiled potatoes and melted butter.

Fillets of sole à l'armoricaine. FILETS DE SOLES À L'ARMORICAINE—The same as *Fillets of sole à l'américaine*. It may be noted that under this name some authorities give a recipe in which the fillets, coated with *Américaine sauce*, are garnished with slices of lobster, poached oysters and soft herring roes poached in white wine.

Aspic of fillets of sole à la parisienne. ASPIC DE FILETS DE SOLES À LA PARISIENNE—Cook 8 large fillets of sole in a concentrated *fumet**, based on fish stock and made with white wine. Drain them and cool under pressure. Cut each into two pieces of equal size and coat with *White chaud-froid sauce* (see SAUCE). Decorate with cut-out pieces of truffle and glaze with jelly. Set in an aspic mould lined with fish jelly and decorated on the bottom and on the sides. The fillets should be arranged upright, one against the other. Fill the middle of the mould with a *Parisian salad* dressed with thick mayonnaise (see SALAD). Cover with a layer of fish jelly. Set on ice.

Turn out the aspic on to a round dish, either directly on to the dish or on a base of shaped rice or a buttered croûton of bread. Decorate with quartered hard boiled eggs and small lettuce hearts; surround with jelly croûtons.

Fillets of sole Bercy. FILETS DE SOLES BERCY—Proceed, using fillets, as for *Sole Bercy*.

Fillets of sole, boiled or poached. FILETS DE SOLES BOUILLIS, POCHÉS—Poach the fillets, left flat, in salted water and milk. Drain and set on a napkin or grid. Serve melted butter separately or some other sauce such as *Butter*, *Hollandaise or Cream sauce*.

Fillets of sole Boitelle. FILETS DE SOLES BOITELLE—Arrange in a circle in a buttered sauté pan the folded and seasoned fillets. Add 3 to 4 ounces (100 grams) of chopped mushrooms, 2 tablespoons of concentrated fish *fumet** and a squeeze of lemon juice. Poach, keeping the pan covered.

Arrange the fillets in a deep dish, put the mushrooms in the middle and pour over the pan juices to which 3 tablespoons (50 grams) of butter have been added.

Fillets of sole à la bonne femme. FILETS DE SOLES À LA BONNE FEMME—Using flat fillets of sole, prepare like *Sole à la bonne femme.*

Fillets of sole à la bordelaise. FILETS DE SOLES À LA BORDELAISE—Season the fillets, set them in a buttered fish kettle with slices of carrot and onion and a *bouquet garni**. Moisten with a glass of red Bordeaux. Poach for 8 minutes.

Drain the fillets and set them on a long dish with peeled mushrooms and small glazed onions.

Boil down the cooking liquor, adding to it 2 to 3 tablespoons of *Demi-glace sauce.* Beat butter into this sauce; strain and coat the fillets.

Border of fillets of sole à la dauphine. BORDURE DE FILETS DE SOLES À LA DAUPHINE—This dish is almost always served under the name of *Fillets of sole à la dauphine.*

Border of fillets of sole diplomate. BORDURE DE FILETS DE SOLES DIPLOMATE—Poach the fillets in a *fumet** made with white wine that is scarcely boiling. Drain, wipe and set on a moulded border made with *Whiting forcemeat* (see FORCEMEAT), alternating the fillets with slices of nice round truffles. Surround the border with a few spoonfuls of *Diplomate sauce* (see SAUCE). Fill the middle of the dish with a *salpicon** of lobster. Coat the fillets, which must be very white, and the truffles with the cooking liquor boiled down and buttered.

Fillets of sole à la bourguignonne. FILETS DE SOLES À LA BOURGUIGNONNE—Prepared like *Sole à la bourguignonne.*

Fillets of sole à la cancalaise. FILETS DE SOLES À LA CANCALAISE—Fold the fillets and cook them in a concentrated fish *fumet**, to which the liquor from oysters poached for the garnish has been added. Drain, dry and set them in the form of a circle. Fill the middle of the dish with peeled shrimps. Put two poached and de-bearded oysters on top of each fillet. Coat with *White wine sauce* to which some boiled down *fumet* has been added.

Fillets of sole cardinal (*Mac Fisheries*)

Fillets of sole cardinal. FILETS DE SOLES CARDINAL—The fillets are stuffed with pike or whiting forcemeat finished with lobster or crawfish butter and poached in fish *fumet** that is scarcely boiling.

Arrange the fillets on a dish in a circle, alternating them with slices of lobster or spiny lobster.

Coat with *Cardinal sauce* (see SAUCE) to which some of the concentrated *fumet** has been added. Sprinkle with chopped lobster coral.

Fillets of sole à la catalane. FILETS DE SOLES À LA CATALANE—Coat lightly flattened fillets with egg and breadcrumbs mixed with a little chopped parsley. Cook in half oil, half butter. Set on a long dish on a layer of *Tomato fondue** seasoned with a little garlic. Surround with diced aubergines (egg-plant) sautéed in oil. Put on top of each fillet a round slice of peeled lemon. Sprinkle with the cooking butter.

Fillets of sole with Chambertin or other red wine. FILETS DE SOLES AU CHAMBERTIN—Poach the fillets in a fish *fumet** made with the chosen red wine (Chambertin, Mâcon, Romanée, Vougeot, Corton or other fine red Burgundy) as for *Sole with red wine.*

The garnish for these fillets of sole is usually composed of mushrooms and small glazed onions. The whole sole or the fillets cooked with red wine may also be garnished with soft roes, mushrooms, truffles, shrimps or crayfish, pike quenelles, etc.

Fillets of sole chauchat (*Mac Fisheries*)

Fillets of sole Chauchat. FILETS DE SOLES CHAUCHAT—Cook the fillets (rolled) in butter and lemon juice, without letting them brown. Arrange them on a plate and cover with *Mornay sauce* (see SAUCE). Surround with a border of fried potatoes, sliced fairly thickly. Sprinkle with grated cheese, dot with butter and brown.

Fillets of sole Chivry. FILETS DE SOLES CHIVRY—Cook the fillets (rolled) with some chopped shallot and concentrated fish *fumet**. Drain and arrange in a circle on a round dish, alternating them with heart-shaped croûtons of bread fried in butter. Coat with *Chivry sauce* (see SAUCE). Pour round the fillets a border of blond fish jelly.

Fillets of sole, cold. FILETS DE SOLES FROIDS—Fillets of sole can be prepared as aspics (see ASPIC); rings (see BORDERS, *Cold rings*); glazed with Chambertin, Champagne or jelly; as a mayonnaise (like *Salmon mayonnaise*); as a salad (like *Lobster* or *Spiny lobster salad*). Cold sole can also be made into *pâtés* and *terrines.*

Fillets of sole with courgettes (zucchini) I. FILETS DE SOLES AUX COURGETTES—Cook the fillets, left flat, *à la meunière.* Arrange them on a long dish. Surround with *courgettes* (Italian marrow or zucchini) cut in thickish slices, cooked in the frying pan in butter or oil.

Sprinkle with chopped parsley and a few drops of lemon juice. Pour over the cooking butter, very hot.

Fillets of sole with courgettes (zucchini) II. FILETS DE SOLES AUX COURGETTES—Cook the fillets, folded, in fish *fumet** made with white wine. Set on a long dish; surround them with round slices of courgettes cooked in butter. Coat with *White wine sauce* (see SAUCE) to which some concentrated *fumet* has been added. Glaze in a hot oven.

Fillets of sole Crécy. FILETS DE SOLES CRÉCY—Poach the fillets, rolled, in fish *fumet**; drain them and arrange on a long dish.

Coat with a sauce made by boiling down the cooking liquid and adding 2 tablespoons of *Béchamel sauce* (see SAUCE) and 2 tablespoons of carrot purée.

Garnish with very small new carrots, glazed.

Fillets of sole Cubat. FILETS DE SOLES CUBAT—Cook the fillets, left flat, in mushroom stock and butter. Set them on a long fireproof dish. Coat with rather thick *Mushroom purée* (see PURÉE). Put two slices of truffle on each fillet. Coat with *Mornay sauce* (see SAUCE) and brown in the oven.

Fillets of sole Daumont. FILETS DE SOLES DAUMONT—Spread the sole fillets with fish *forcemeat* (pike or whiting) finished off with *Crayfish butter* (see BUTTER, *Compound butters*). Poach them in fish *fumet** that is scarcely boiling. Drain and dry.

Set on a round dish, each fillet placed on top of a large mushroom cap cooked in butter and filled with a *salpicon** of *Crayfish à la Nantua* (see CRAYFISH).

Coat with *Normande sauce*. Garnish with soft roes coated with egg and breadcrumbs and sautéed in butter.

Fillets of sole Dauphine. FILETS DE SOLES DAUPHINE—Poach the fillets, rolled, in Madeira which has had truffle and mushroom skins infused in it. Allow to cool, then drain them and mask with *Villeroi sauce* (see SAUCE) which has had some of the cooking liquor and *Crayfish butter* (see BUTTER, *Compound butters*) added. Coat with breadcrumbs; then, a few moments before serving, fry in clarified butter.

Drain and set on a moulded border of *Pike forcemeat* (see FORCEMEAT) cooked in a ring mould in a *bain-marie* (pan of hot water) and turned out on to a round dish.

Put in the middle of the dish a *ragoût** composed of cooked mushrooms, little pike quenelles, crayfish and sliced truffles, bound with thick *Velouté sauce*. Serve *Nantua sauce* separately (see SAUCE).

Fillets of sole à la dieppoise. FILETS DE SOLES À LA DIEPPOISE—Cook the fillets in a fish *fumet** that is scarcely boiling. Drain, dry and set them on a serving dish. Surround with a *Dieppoise garnish** (see GARNISHES) composed of mussels cooked in white wine and grey or pink shrimps, all shelled. Coat with *White wine sauce* (see SAUCE) to which boiled down cooking liquor from the fillets and from the mussels has been added.

Fillets of sole à la diplomate—See *Border of fillets of sole à la diplomate*.

Fillets of sole à l'espagnole—FILETS DE SOLES À L'ESPAGNOLE—Season the fillets with salt and paprika; flour and fry them in oil.

Set on a long dish on a bed of tomatoes that have been peeled, drained and chopped roughly, cooked in oil and seasoned with salt, paprika and a little garlic.

Put at each end of the dish some sweet pimentos, peeled, cut in strips and fried in oil, and place on top of the fillets a row of round slices of onion floured and fried in oil.

Fillets of sole à la fécampoise. FILETS DE SOLES À LA FÉCAMPOISE—Name sometimes given to *Fillets of sole à la trouvillaise*.

Fillets of sole à la florentine. FILETS DE SOLES À LA FLORENTINE—Cook the fillets in butter and lemon juice, without the addition of *fumet**. The fillets should be kept long, slightly flattened and seasoned.

Set on a long fireproof dish on a layer of leaf spinach blanched, drained and simmered in butter. Coat with *Mornay sauce* (see SAUCE). Sprinkle with grated Parmesan and a little melted butter. Brown in the oven.

Fillets of sole, fried. FILETS DE SOLES FRITS—Treated like other fried fish.

Fried fillets of sole are arranged in a mound on a napkin and garnished with fried parsley and lemon. They may also be cooked on metal skewers.

Fillets of sole en goujons

Fillets of sole en goujons. FILETS DE SOLES EN GOUJONS—Cut the fillets diagonally across in pieces ¾ inch wide. Dip these pieces in milk, drain and flour them shaking well to remove excess flour. Fry in deep fat (or oil, for preference).

Drain, salt and set in a mound on a napkin. Garnish with fried parsley and lemon.

Note. Sole fillets prepared in this way are often used as garnish for large braised fish.

Fillets of sole au gratin. FILETS DE SOLES AU GRATIN—Prepared using lightly flattened fillets, as *Sole au gratin*.

Fillets of sole, grilled. FILETS DE SOLES GRILLÉS—Flatten the fillets lightly and season them. Brush with oil or melted butter and cook under the grill at a moderate heat.

Set on a long, well heated dish. Surround with slices of lemon and small sprigs of fresh parsley.

Note. Grilled fillets of sole are usually accompanied by melted butter or softened *Maître d'hôtel butter* (see BUTTER, *Compound butters*). They may also be served with one of the sauces recommended for grilled fish.

It is also customary to serve boiled potatoes with grilled fillets of sole.

This simple but ever popular dish may also be accompanied by any kind of grilled vegetable, mushrooms, tomatoes, etc.

Fillets of sole à la hongroise. FILETS DE SOLES À LA HONGROISE—Put the fillets, folded and seasoned with salt and paprika into a sauté pan with 4 tablespoons (50 grams) of finely chopped onion cooked till soft in butter with a peeled, drained and crushed tomato, seasoned with paprika, added when the onion is almost cooked. Add 6 tablespoons of fish *fumet** made with white wine. Cover and cook all together. Drain the fillets, and arrange in a ring, alternating them with heart-shaped croutons of bread fried in butter. Pour over the fillets the cooking liquor, boiled down and mixed with 4 tablespoons of thick fresh cream, with butter and a squeeze of lemon juice added.

Note. Potatoes, cut to look like olives and cooked in butter and water, may be added to this dish, set in the middle of the ring.

Fillets of sole à l'indienne I. FILETS DE SOLES À L'INDIENNE—Divide each fillet into two pieces; fry in clarified butter a few moments before serving.

Prepare separately a *Curry sauce* based on fish stock (see SAUCE).

Set the fillets of sole on a bed of *Rice à l'indienne**. Pour the sauce around.

Fillets of sole à l'indienne II. FILETS DE SOLES À L'INDIENNE—Cut the fillets of sole into narrow strips. Tie each of these strips into a little knot.

Prepare separately the following *coulis*: Cook till soft in butter 2 tablespoons of chopped onion. Add, when the onion is cooked, a small eating apple, peeled and cut in dice, a medium-sized tomato, peeled and pressed, a little grated garlic, a sprig of thyme and powdered bay leaf. Sprinkle with curry. Pour in $\frac{3}{4}$ cup ($1\frac{1}{2}$ decilitres) of coconut milk or milk of almonds. Season. Cook for 10 minutes, stir in $\frac{3}{4}$ cup ($1\frac{1}{2}$ decilitres) of thick cream, bring to the boil and add a squeeze of lemon juice.

Put the little twists of sole fillets to cook in this sauce.

Serve in a deep dish with *Rice à l'indienne** handed separately.

Fillets of sole à la Jacques. FILETS DE SOLES À LA JACQUES—'Put in a deep saucepan some chopped onion that has previously been cooked till soft in butter, 1 cup (250 grams) of sliced potato and $1\frac{1}{2}$ cups (250 grams) of raw mushrooms also cut in slices.

'Pour in a little white wine and fish *fumet**. Season with salt and pepper and add a *bouquet garni**. Cook, boiling rapidly.

'When the potatoes are three-quarters cooked, put into the saucepan 8 fillets of sole, each cut in two. Add a small pinch of powdered saffron and cook briskly.

'Take out the fillets of sole, which should be cooked in 6 minutes; boil down the liquid if necessary.

'To serve, arrange the potatoes and mushrooms in a deep silver dish, put the fillets on top, sprinkle with the cooking liquor and chopped parsley and chervil.' (Azéma.)

Fillets of sole Joinville. FILETS DE SOLES JOINVILLE—Poach the fillets, folded, in *fumet** that is scarcely boiling. Drain and arrange them in a circle on a round dish, placing them with the points upwards instead of in the usual way. Fix on the tip of each fillet a peeled pink shrimp.

Put in the middle of the circle a *Joinville garnish* composed of shrimps, mushrooms and diced truffles, all bound with *Joinville sauce* (see SAUCE).

Coat the fillets with *Joinville sauce* to which has been added some of the concentrated cooking liquor. Put on each fillet a slice of truffle glazed with fish jelly.

Note. Formerly, fillets of sole prepared *à la Joinville* instead of being set in a circle directly on the plate as described here, were arranged in a circle on a moulded border of pike or other fish forcemeat. These fillets, instead of being coated with *Joinville sauce*, were left as they were, but each one was decorated with a large slice of truffle. The garnish was put into the middle of the moulded border.

Fillets of sole en julienne. FILETS DE SOLES EN JULIENNE—Prepared, fried, like the *Fillets of sole en goujons*, but the fillets are cut more finely.

Fillets of sole Marguery. FILETS DE SOLES MARGUERY—This is the recipe given by M. Mangin, who for some thirty years was head chef of the celebrated Restaurant Marguery, at the time when M. Marguery directed the establishment himself.

'Fillet two fine soles. Use the bones and trimmings to make a white wine *fumet**, flavoured with a little chopped onion, a sprig of thyme, quarter of a bay leaf and a little parsley. Season with salt and pepper. Simmer for 15 minutes. Add to this *fumet*, which should be strained and concentrated, the strained cooking liquor of a quart (litre) of mussels cooked in the usual way (using white wine).

'Place the fillets of sole, seasoned and lightly flattened, on a buttered baking dish. Sprinkle over a few tablespoons of the aforesaid *fumet*. Cover with buttered greaseproof paper and poach gently.

'Drain the fillets well. Set them in an oval dish and surround with a double row of shelled mussels and shrimps. Keep hot, covered, while the sauce is prepared.

'*The sauce*. Strain the *fumet* to which will have been added the cooking juices of the soles. Boil down by two-thirds. Remove from heat, allow the sauce to cool a little, then add 6 egg yolks. Whisk the sauce over a gentle heat, like a hollandaise, incorporating about $\frac{3}{4}$ pound (350 grams) of the finest butter, slightly melted. Season the sauce and strain. Coat with it the fillets and garnish. Glaze in a hot oven.'

Fillets of sole Marivaux. FILETS DE SOLES MARIVAUX—Poach the fillets, folded, in *fumet** that is scarcely boiling. Drain and set them on a round dish in the middle of a border of *Duchess potato mixture* (see POTATOES) piped through a forcing (pastry) bag, on top of a layer of chopped *Mushrooms cooked in cream** mixed with chopped truffles. Coat with a light *Mornay sauce* (see SAUCE). Brush the border with egg, sprinkle with grated Parmesan and brown in the oven.

Fillets of sole à la meunière. FILETS DE SOLES À LA MEUNIÈRE—Flat fillets fried in butter as for *Sole à la meunière*.

Fillets of soles Montreuil. FILETS DE SOLES MONTREUIL—Made with flat fillets in the same way as *Sole Montreuil*.

Fillets of sole Montrouge. FILETS DE SOLES MONTROUGE—Cook the fillets, folded, in butter, moistening them only with a few drops of white wine. Drain them. Set them on a long dish, and garnish with small peeled mushrooms, cooked in butter and bound with cream.

Coat the whole with a sauce made by adding to the cooking juices $\frac{1}{2}$ cup (1 decilitre) of *Mushroom purée* (see PURÉE), a few tablespoons of cream and some butter.

Fillets of sole Mornay. FILETS DE SOLES MORNAY—Cook the fillets, left flat, in *fumet** that is scarcely boiling. Set on a long dish, coat with *Mornay sauce* (see SAUCE), sprinkle with grated Parmesan and brown in the oven.

Fillets of sole Murat. FILETS DE SOLES MURAT—Cut the fillets of sole in strips; flour and sauté them in butter.

Sauté separately, for every 8 fillets, 2 medium-sized potatoes cut in dice and two half cooked artichoke bottoms cut in the same way.

When these are cooked mix the fillets with them and sauté all together over the heat for a few moments. Set in a deep dish. Put on top 8 slices of tomatoes, seasoned and sautéed in oil; sprinkle with chopped parsley; add a little meat glaze, and a squeeze of lemon juice and pour over a few tablespoons of *Noisette butter* (see BUTTER, *Compound butters*).

Fillets of sole with mushrooms. FILETS DE SOLES AUX CHAMPIGNONS.—Cook in a white wine fish *fumet** that is scarcely boiling, folded fillets of sole and two peeled mushrooms for each fillet. Set the fillets on a long dish with the mushrooms on top.

Boil down the cooking liquor with an equal quantity of fresh cream, add some butter, strain and pour over the fillets.

Note. These fillets may also be coated with *White wine sauce* (see SAUCE) with some concentrated *fumet* added before straining.

Fillets of sole with mussels. FILETS DE SOLES AUX MOULES—Poach the fillets, folded, in fish *fumet** and the cooking liquor of mussels. Set on a long dish. Surround with mussels cooked in white wine, shelled and wiped. Coat with *White wine sauce* (see SAUCE) to which some of the concentrated cooking liquor has been added.

Fillets of sole à la Nantua. FILETS DE SOLES AUX ÉCREVISSES, À LA NANTUA—Poach the fillets, folded, in a fish *fumet** that is scarcely boiling.

Drain, dry and set them in a circle on a round dish. Coat with *Nantua sauce* (see SAUCE) to which some boiled down cooking liquor has been added. Put a slice of truffle on each fillet.

Fillets of sole à la Nantua (old recipe). FILETS DE SOLES À LA NANTUA—Poach the fillets of sole very gently in white wine. Set them, well drained, on a moulded border made with *Pike forcemeat* (see FORCEMEAT) finished off with *Crayfish butter* (see BUTTER, *Compound butters*). Garnish the middle of the dish with a *ragoût* of *Crayfish à la Nantua**. Coat the fillets of sole with *Nantua sauce** (see SAUCE) to which some *fumet** has been added. Put a large slice of truffle on top of each fillet.

Fillets of sole à la normande

Fillets of sole à la normande. FILETS DE SOLES À LA NORMANDE—Poach gently in *fumet* the fillets, left flat. Set them on a serving dish when they have been well drained and surround them with a *Normande garnish* (see GARNISHES). Coat with *Normande sauce* (see SAUCE). Finish off as for *Sole à la normande*.

Fillets of sole à l'orientale. FILETS DE SOLES À L'ORIENTALE—Prepared, using flat fillets, like *Red mullet à l'orientale*. See HORS-D'OEUVRE, *Cold hors-d'oeuvre*. This dish is usually served cold, but it may be served hot.

Fillets of sole Orly. FILETS DE SOLES ORLY—Prepared as for *Whiting Orly**.

Fillets of sole with oysters. FILETS DE SOLES AUX HUÎTRES—Fold the fillets and cook them in fish *fumet**. Drain, dry and set them on a long dish. Put on top of each fillet 2 oysters poached in their own liquor and de-bearded. Coat with *Normande sauce* or *White wine sauce* to which some boiled-down *fumet* and oyster liquor have been added (see SAUCE).

Fillets of sole à la panetière. FILETS DE SOLES À LA PANETIÈRE—Fillet the sole when raw. Flatten and trim the fillets and fold them in two by doubling them over. Season with salt and pepper, flour and sauté them in butter.

Prepare separately a *ragoût** of mushrooms *à la crème*. Arrange the fillets in a crown on a thick, round slice of bread, cut from a large round loaf, hollowed out, buttered and crisped in the oven. Put the *ragoût* of mushrooms in the middle. Warm for a few moments in the oven and serve on a napkin-covered dish.

Fillets of sole Parmentier. FILETS DE SOLES PARMENTIER—Poach the fillets in *fumet** and drain them. Set each into half of a medium-sized potato baked in the oven and partly scooped out, as for *Georgette potatoes*. Coat the fillets with *Mornay sauce** (see SAUCE) to which some concentrated cooking liquor has been added. Sprinkle with grated Parmesan and melted butter. Brown in the oven and serve on a napkin.

Fillets of sole à la paysanne. FILETS DE SOLES À LA PAYSANNE—Prepared with folded fillets, like *Sole à la paysanne*.

Fillets of sole à la piémontaise. FILETS DE SOLES À LA PIÉMONTAISE—Sauté in butter the fillets, folded, seasoned and floured.

Set each on a croûton, cut out of a layer of *polenta** to the same size as the fillets and fried in butter.

Put on top of each fillet 4 slices of white truffles (Piedmont truffles) seasoned with salt and pepper and lightly sautéed in olive oil.

Pour around the fillets the cooking juices diluted with white wine, to which have been added a few tablespoons of tomato purée and butter.

Fillets of sole en pilaf. FILETS DE SOLES EN PILAF—Cut the fillets into little squares. Season and flour these pieces. Sauté briskly in butter and set them in the middle of a border of *Pilaf rice** prepared separately in the usual way. Serve *Tomato sauce* or *Curry sauce* separately. See SAUCE.

Fillets of sole sur le plat. FILETS DE SOLES SUR LE PLAT—This dish is most often prepared with a whole sole, but may be made with fillets. See *Sole sur le plat*.

Fillets of sole princesse. FILETS DE SOLES PRINCESSE—Poach the fillets, folded, in *fumet**. Set them on a long dish. Coat them with *Normande sauce* (see SAUCE) to which some of the concentrated cooking liquor has been added.

Garnish with very small fine pastry barquettes, filled with green asparagus tips bound with butter and slices of truffles dipped in fish aspic jelly.

Alternatively, the fillets may be coated with egg and breadcrumbs and sautéed in clarified butter.

Garnish with alternate clusters of asparagus tips in butter and diced truffles sautéed in butter and bound with a few drops of *Madeira sauce* (see SAUCE). Sprinkle the fillets with *Noisette butter* (see BUTTER, *Compound butters*).

Fillets of sole Riche. FILETS DE SOLES RICHE—*Riche sauce* is not so called because it is composed of particularly *rich* ingredients, but because it was a speciality of the famous Parisian Restaurant Riche, which has now disappeared.

This sauce was made, and is made still, with *Normande sauce* finished off with lobster butter and a few tablespoons of *Truffle essence*.

Poach the fillets, folded, in *fumet** that is scarcely boiling. Drain and arrange them in a circle. Garnish the middle with a *salpicon** of lobster flesh and truffles. Coat with *Riche sauce* (see SAUCE).

Fillets of sole Richelieu. FILETS DE SOLES RICHELIEU—Coat the fillets with egg and breadcrumbs and fry them in butter. Garnish with slices of truffles and cover with *Maître d'hôtel butter* (see BUTTER, *Compound butters*). Illustrated on next page.

Fillets of sole Saint-Germain. FILETS DE SOLES SAINT-GERMAIN—Flatten lightly 8 fillets, season them with salt

Fillets of sole Richelieu

and pepper, brush with melted butter and coat with freshly made breadcrumbs.

Sprinkle with butter and grill on both sides at a moderate heat, letting them colour lightly.

Set on a long dish. Surround with rather thick *Béarnaise sauce* (see SAUCE) and garnish with *Noisette potatoes* (see POTATOES).

Fillets of sole with shrimps. FILETS DE SOLES AUX CREVETTES—Cook the fillets, folded, in fish *fumet** made with white wine.

Drain and set them on a long dish. Surround with peeled shrimps.

Coat with *Shrimp sauce* to which some boiled down *fumet* left from the cooking has been added.

Fillets of sole Sylvette. FILETS DE SOLES SYLVETTE—Put 8 fillets in a sauté pan lined with 3 tablespoons of fine *mirepoix** cooked till soft in butter, composed of carrot, the white of leek, onion and celery cut in very small dice. Moisten with ½ cup (½ decilitre) of sherry. Cook, covered. When three-quarters cooked, add 4 tablespoons of mixed truffles and mushrooms cut in small dice.

Arrange the fillets, well drained, on a long dish. Garnish with very small tomatoes stuffed with a white fish purée, topped with crumbs and browned in the oven.

Boil down the cooking liquor, add to it a few tablespoons of fresh thick cream and butter and pour over the fillets.

Timbale of fillets of sole à l'ancienne. TIMBALE DE FILETS DE SOLES À L'ANCIENNE—Prepare a *Timbale pie crust* (see TIMBALE). Cook empty. When it is cooked, turn it out of the mould and allow it to become a nice golden brown all over.

Cook in concentrated *fumet** 12 *paupiettes of sole**, prepared with pike forcemeat finished off with lobster butter.

Prepare separately a *ragoût* made of poached and de-bearded oysters, shelled mussels cooked in white wine, slices of lobster, cooked mushrooms and slices of truffle. Bind this ragoût with fish *Velouté sauce* mixed with fresh cream, finished off with *Lobster butter* (see BUTTER, *Compound butters*) and a few drops of brandy.

Prepare also some macaroni bound with cream (this macaroni should be three-quarters cooked in salted water, drained, cut into short lengths, finished with fresh cream, seasoned and dressed with butter).

Filling the pastry. Put in the bottom of the pie crust, which must be filled while it is still quite hot, a layer of of macaroni. On top of the macaroni put half of the *ragoût** and on top of the *ragoût* six of the *paupiettes*. Cover with macaroni, add another layer of *ragoût* and the other six *paupiettes*. Finish with the rest of the macaroni, a row of truffle slices on top. Put back the 'lid' of the timbale and return it to the oven for a few moments. Serve on a dish covered with a napkin.

Timbale of fillets of sole Grimaldi. TIMBALE DE FILETS DE SOLES GRIMALDI—Prepared like *Timbale of fillets of sole à l'ancienne* with fillets of sole spread with truffled *fish forcemeat* (see FORCEMEAT), *ragoût* of *Crayfish à la Nantua**, slices of truffles and macaroni with cream.

Note. This *timbale* can also be made with *langoustines* (i.e. crayfish, scampi or Dublin Bay prawns) and sauce finished with *langoustine* butter instead of crayfish and crayfish sauce.

Timbale of fillets of sole à la normande. TIMBALE DE FILETS DE SOLES À LA NORMANDE—Prepared as above with *paupiettes of sole** spread with whiting forcemeat, poached oysters, mussels cooked in white wine, peeled shrimps, truffle slices and macaroni with cream.

Place on top of the pie, instead of a pastry lid. trussed crayfish and gudgeon coated in egg and breadcrumbs and fried.

Timbale of fillets of sole Victoria. TIMBALE DE FILETS DE SOLES VICTORIA—Prepared in a broad, rather shallow pastry crust that has been cooked empty.

Spread the fillets with *Pike forcemeat* (see FORCEMEAT) finished off with *Truffle purée** and cook them in concentrated fish *fumet** made with white wine.

Prepare separately a *ragoût** made of sliced spiny lobster or lobster, oysters, mushrooms and truffles bound with fish *Velouté sauce* mixed with cream and finished off with *Lobster butter* (see BUTTER, *Compound butters*) and brandy.

Put a few spoonfuls of *ragoût* in the bottom of the pie and arrange the *paupiettes*, well drained, in a circle on top. Fill up the middle with the rest of the *ragoût*. Coat with *Normande sauce* (see SAUCE) and put on top of each *paupiette* a slice of truffle dipped in fish aspic jelly.

Fillets of sole en torsade. FILETS DE SOLES EN TORSADE—Arrange flattened and seasoned fillets of sole in a buttered savarin mould. Place the fillets crossways, overlapping each other a little and leaving their ends just outside the mould.

Using a forcing (pastry) bag, fill the inside of the mould with some *Fish forcemeat* (see FORCEMEAT) (e.g. *quenelles*, *mousseline*, etc.), adding, according to the kind of forcemeat used, truffles, mushrooms or *Lobster or other crustacean butter* (see BUTTER, *Compound butters*). Tap the mould to settle the contents. Fold the ends of the fillets over the forcemeat and press them down to fix them in place.

Poach in a *bain-marie* (pan of hot water) in the oven. Take out of the oven, allow to rest for a few minutes, then turn out on to a round dish and serve with the prescribed sauce.

Fillets of sole à la trouvillaise. FILETS DE SOLES À LA TROUVILLAISE—Prepared like *Fillets of sole à la Dieppoise*, but coating the fillets with *White wine sauce* (see SAUCE) to which *Shrimp butter* (see BUTTER, *Compound butters*) has been added.

Turban of fillets of sole. TURBAN DE FILETS DE SOLES—Prepared in the same way as for *Fillets of sole en torsade*.

Fillets of sole à la vénitienne I. FILETS DE SOLES À LA VÉNITIENNE—Poach the fillets, folded, in *fumet**. Arrange in a ring, alternating them with heart-shaped croûtons of bread fried in butter. Coat the fillets with *Venetian sauce* (see SAUCE) to which some of the boiled down cooking liquor has been added.

Fillets of sole à la vénitienne II. FILETS DE SOLES À LA VÉNITIENNE—Plumerey, the successor of Carême, gives a different recipe for this preparation: 'The fillets of soles, folded, are poached in white wine, then drained wiped and arranged in a crown. The centre is garnished with a *salpicon** of lobster and truffles bound with *Venetian sauce*, without herbs but finished with *Lobster butter*, and fillets are coated with nice green *Venetian sauce* and garnished with chopped and blanched parsley.'

Fillets of sole Véron. FILETS DE SOLES VÉRON—Coat the fillets with egg and breadcrumbs and cook in clarified butter. Serve on a layer of *Véron sauce* (see SAUCE).

Fillets of sole Victoria. FILETS DE SOLES VICTORIA—Poach the fillets, folded, in *fumet** that is scarcely boiling. Drain and arrange on the serving dish in a circle. Garnish the middle of the dish with a *salpicon** composed of spiny lobster flesh and truffles. Coat with *White wine sauce* (see SAUCE) finished off with *Lobster or spiny lobster butter* (see BUTTER, *Compound butters*). Brown in a hot oven.

Vol-au-vent of fillets of sole. VOL-AU-VENT DE FILETS DE SOLES—Prepared with fillets or *paupiettes* of sole and a garnish of mushrooms and truffles (or other similar foodstuffs), in the same way as for *Chicken vol-au-vent*. See VOL-AU-VENT.

Fillets of sole Walewska. FILETS DE SOLES WALEWSKA—Poach the fillets, left flat, in fish *fumet* that is scarcely boiling. Set them on a long dish. Put on top of each fillet a slice of lobster or spiny lobster and a slice of raw truffle. Coat with *Mornay sauce* (see SAUCE) finished off with *Lobster or spiny lobster butter* (see BUTTER, *Compound butters*). Brown in a hot oven.

Fillets of sole with red wine. FILETS DE SOLES AU VIN ROUGE—Made with red wine like *Fillets of sole with Chambertin.*

Fillets of sole with white wine. FILETS DE SOLES AU VIN BLANC—Made, with the fillets folded and poached in a *fumet* made with white wine, like *Sole with white wine*.

Sole à la florentine—Trim the sole; poach it in fish *fumet** that is scarcely boiling. Drain and remove the backbone. Set the sole on a fireproof dish on a bed of leaf spinach, blanched, drained, pressed and simmered in butter. Coat with *Mornay sauce* (see SAUCE). Sprinkle with grated cheese and melted butter and brown in the oven.

Fried sole. SOLE FRITE—Soak the sole in milk; flour it. Plunge it into smoking hot fat (or oil if possible). Drain the sole as soon as it is a nice golden colour, and season with very dry salt. Set on a napkin or a strainer. Garnish with fried parsley and lemon.

Sole fritters. FRITOT DE SOLES—Marinate the fillets for 30 minutes with oil, lemon juice, chopped parsley, salt and pepper. At the last moment dip in a light batter and fry in deep fat. Arrange in a mound on a napkin. Garnish with fried parsley and lemon. Serve *Tomato sauce* separately (see SAUCE).

Golden sole. SOLE DORÉE—This rather high-sounding title describes quite a simple dish. The sole, floured, is cooked in clarified butter in the frying pan. Set on a long dish, put on top a row of lemon slices from which all the skin has been removed and sprinkle with *Noisette butter* (see BUTTER, *Compound butters*).

Sole au gratin I—Put in a long, buttered, fireproof dish lined with 2 to 3 tablespoons of dry *duxelles** a sole weighing about ¾ pound (300 grams). Season with salt and pepper.

Garnish with mushrooms cut in thin slices. Place on top of the sole 3 or 4 cooked mushroom caps. Coat with *Duxelles sauce* (see SAUCE) to which some concentrated fish *fumet** has been added. Sprinkle with breadcrumbs. Cook in a moderate oven in such a way that the fish is ready when it becomes nicely browned. Squeeze over a few drops of lemon juice.

Sole au gratin II—Put the sole, well seasoned, into a buttered fireproof dish lined with chopped shallot and parsley moistened with 2 tablespoons of white wine and a few drops of lemon juice. Dot little pieces of butter over the top. Cook in the oven for 5 minutes. Drain off the cooking liquor, boil down and add to it 4 tablespoons of *duxelles** (chopped mushrooms lightly cooked in butter with chopped onion and shallot). Add a teaspoon of tomato purée. Garnish the sole with mushrooms and pour the sauce over it. Sprinkle with breadcrumbs and melted butter. Brown in a hot oven.

Grilled sole. SOLE GRILLÉE—Make shallow incisions across the sole, season it, brush with oil or melted butter and cook under the grill, at a moderate heat.

Set on a long dish; surround with slices of lemon and small bunches of fresh parsley.

Serve with *Maître d'hôtel butter* or any other sauce suitable for grilled fish. See BUTTER, *Compound butters*.

Gulyas of sole. GULYAS DE SOLES—Cut the fillets into square pieces. Season and put them into a sauté pan in which (for 8 fillets) ½ cup (100 grams) of chopped onion seasoned with 1½ teaspoons of paprika have been cooked in butter. Sauté the pieces of sole quickly on each side, take them out of the sauté pan and put in 4 tablespoons of *Béchamel sauce* (see SAUCE), 2 tablespoons of *Tomato purée* and 1 cup (2 decilitres) of fresh cream. Simmer for a few moments. Put the pieces of sole back in the pan and cook for another 3 minutes. Set in a deep dish. Serve boiled potatoes separately.

Sole marchand de vin—Insert into a sole, with the fillets cut and raised a little, a piece of butter the size of a walnut seasoned with salt and pepper. Put the sole on a buttered baking dish sprinkled with a tablespoon of chopped shallot. Season, pour over ¾ cup (1½ decilitres) of red wine and poach in the oven.

Set the sole on a serving dish. Coat with a sauce made by cooking down the poaching liquor and adding to it a teaspoon of meat or fish glaze, 2 teaspoons of butter, a pinch of chopped parsley and a few drops of lemon juice.

Sole à la marinière—Poach the sole very gently in a fish *fumet** to which some chopped shallot has been added. Drain it and set it on a long dish. Surround with *Mussels à la marinière** removed from their shells and de-bearded. Coat with *Marinière sauce* (see SAUCE) to which some concentrated *fumet* has been added.

This dish is sometimes garnished with peeled shrimps.

Sole en matelote à la normande—Cut 2 large thick soles into uniform pieces. Season with salt and pepper and arrange the pieces in a sauté pan in which a chopped medium-sized onion has been cooked very gently without being allowed to colour. Pour over 1½ cups (3 decilitres) of dry white wine and a squeeze of lemon juice.

Cook for 10 minutes. Drain the pieces of sole and put them in a sauté dish. Put in at the same time some small mushrooms cooked in a flour-and-water *court-bouillon**, peeled shrimps and *Mussels à la marinière** removed from their shells. Pour over the whole a *Normande sauce* (see SAUCE) made in the usual way, incorporating the cooking liquor of both the soles and the mussels. Heat without allowing to boil.

Arrange the pieces of sole on a long dish. Garnish with the mussels, the shrimps and the mushrooms arranged in little groups. Set on top of each piece of fish thin slices of truffles heated in butter, and garnish with smelts coated in egg and breadcrumbs and fried, and croûtons of bread fried in butter.

Note. This dish may also be prepared using cider as the cooking liquid.

Sole à la ménagère—Put the sole in a fireproof dish on a layer of vegetables (carrots, onion, celery), chopped and cooked till soft in butter. Season with salt, pepper, a pinch of thyme and powdered bay leaf. Moisten with ½ cup (1 decilitre) of red wine. Cook, covered, in the oven. Drain off the cooking wine. Thicken this with a tablespoon of *Kneaded butter* (see BUTTER, *Compound butters*), then stir in extra butter. Coat the sole with this sauce. Glaze in a hot oven.

Sole à la meunière—Season and flour the sole and cook in butter in the frying pan.

Set on a serving dish. Sprinkle with chopped parsley and squeeze over a few drops of lemon juice. Pour over the hot cooking butter. Sometimes the serving of fish cooked *à la meunière* is decorated with slices, or half-slices, of lemon, rounds of radish, cut-out pieces of beetroot and sprigs of parsley. This kind of ornament is quite useless and not at all in keeping with the recipe.

Sole à la meunière, various garnishes. SOLE À LA MEUNIÈRE—Cook the soles as indicated above. Set on a long dish and surround with the required garnish. Finish off as in the preceding recipe. Soles prepared in this way may be garnished with the following:

Aubergines (egg-plant) cut in rounds and sautéed in butter; *cèpes* sliced and sautéed in butter (with the addition, if liked, of chopped shallot or a little garlic); sliced, sautéed *mushrooms* set on top of the fish; courgettes (Italian marrows or zucchini) used in the same way as aubergines; *potatoes* cut in large dice and sautéed in butter, set around the sole; *orange*, peeled and sliced, the sole having a few drops of orange juice instead of lemon juice squeezed over it with the cooking butter; *grapes*, peeled and sprinkled with butter; sliced *tomatoes*, sautéed in butter or oil, placed on or around the fish; *truffles*, cut in rather thick strips, at the last moment put to cook lightly in the butter in which the sole was cooked.

Sole meunière Mont-Bry—'Prepare in advance ½ pound (200 grams) of noodles cut very finely (dried noodles will not do for this purpose). Heat and peel 6 large tomatoes and press them to remove all seeds and juice. Add to these a medium-sized onion, chopped and cooked till golden in butter, a pinch of salt, a pinch of sugar and some crushed garlic, the size of a pea. Cover and cook gently.

'Prepare separately 3 soles weighing almost a pound (about 450 grams) each. Detach the fillets a little from the backbone (on the side from which the brown skin has been removed), season the soles with salt and pepper, toss them in flour and cook in clarified butter in the frying pan so that they are a nice golden brown on both sides.

'In another pan heat 5 or 6 tablespoons of clarified butter. Put in the noodles and sauté them until they are lightly fried and crisp.

'Set the soles on a heated long dish, squeeze over a little lemon juice, sprinkle a little chopped parsley over the surface, surround with the tomato and arrange the noodles in a mound at each end of the dish. Sprinkle the soles generously with *Noisette butter* (see BUTTER, *Compound butters*) and serve immediately so that when the dish arrives at the table the butter is still hot and frothy.' (Philéas Gilbert.)

Sole Montreuil—Poach the sole in *fumet** that is scarcely boiling. Set on a serving dish. Surround with potato balls (cut out with a vegetable baller), cooked in salted water. Coat the sole with *White wine sauce* and the potato balls with *Shrimp sauce* or any other pink sauce made with a crustacean butter (see SAUCE).

Sole Mornay—Cooked like *Brill Mornay**.

Mousse of sole. MOUSSE DE SOLES—Under this name are served small preparations made with the same mixture as for large *mousses*, but cooked in dariole moulds, silver or china *cassolettes* or goffered paper cases.

Note. Cold mousselines of sole are used to garnish large cold fish.

Sole with mushrooms. SOLE AUX CHAMPIGNONS—Prepared with whole sole in the same way as for *Brill with mushrooms* (see BRILL) or *Fillets of sole with mushrooms*.

Sole à la Nantua—Cooked in the same way as *Brill with crayfish à la Nantua**.

Sole à la niçoise—Season the sole; brush it with oil and grill. Set it on a serving dish and surround with a *Niçoise garnish* composed of tomatoes cooked till soft in butter with tarragon mixed with a little anchovy butter, black olives and capers, each of these being arranged in separate groups. Place on the sole anchovy fillets and slices of peeled lemons.

Note. Sole poached in white wine surrounded with a border of tomatoes cooked in butter with tarragon and black olives, coated with *White wine sauce* and garnished with anchovy fillets arranged in a criss-cross design, is often served under the same name.

Sole Noël—Poach the sole in the cooking liquor of mussels (or Chablis). Cook in the same baking dish 4 peeled mushroom caps.

Set the sole, well drained, on a fireproof dish, with the mushrooms on top.

Surround the fish with shelled mussels and shrimps.

Reduce (boil down) the cooking liquor. Thicken it with 2 egg yolks and beat in extra butter.

Coat the sole and its garnish with this sauce. Glaze quickly in a very hot oven. (Octave Vaudable's recipe.)

Sole à la normande—This dish, which has nothing in its composition to justify its name (some writers insist that it was created in Paris at the beginning of the nineteenth century by Philippe, who was at that time an established *restaurateur* in the Rue Montorgueil), is simply a *Sole au vin blanc* accompanied by a very complicated garnish, including ingredients, such as truffles, which have no fundamental place in Normandy cooking.

It seems, however, that this dish came from Normandy in the guise of *Stewed fish with cream*, being originally prepared with cider instead of white wine. To this dish the experts have added the rich garnish described below:

For a sole weighing about 14 *ounces* (400 *grams*): 4 oysters (poached and de-bearded), 12 mussels (cooked in white wine), a few (25 grams) peeled shrimps and 4 peeled mushrooms cooked in white wine. To these, which are set round the fish before the sauce is poured over, the following are added after the sauce: 6 slices of truffles (set in two rows on top of the fish), 4 fried gudgeon (coated in egg and breadcrumbs), 4 trussed crayfish (cooked in *court-bouillon**) and 4 lozenge-shaped croûtons of bread fried in butter.

The method of preparation is as follows:

Trim the sole, split it and raise the fillets a little from the skinned side. Break the backbone in two or three places so that it may more easily be removed after cooking. Poach in fish *fumet** made with white wine, scarcely boiling, to which the cooking juices of the mussels, the oysters and the mushrooms have been added.

Drain and wipe the fish and remove the backbone. Set on a long dish. Place on top or round the fish the garnishes first mentioned.

Coat with *Normande sauce* (see SAUCE) made with the *fumet* in which the fish was cooked. Add the other garnishes: the truffles, glazed with fish aspic jelly, the oysters and the mushrooms set in a straight line down the middle of the fish, the croûtons of fried bread in butter, alternating with the truffles on top of the fish, the fried gudgeon and the crayfish arranged on the sides of the dish. Coat the sole with sauce and pour a ring of light fish jelly, or meat aspic jelly around the fish.

Croûtons of fried bread are often replaced by small cut-outs of puff pastry. Frequently, too, the fried gudgeon are replaced by fried smelts.

Pâté of sole (hot and cold). PÂTÉS DE SOLES—Prepared like all other fish pies, using fillets of sole (generally spread with forcemeat and rolled in *paupiettes*), *Pike forcemeat* (see FORCEMEAT) or forcemeat made of any other fish, and truffles. See PÂTÉ.

When these pies are to be served hot, pour into them before serving a few tablespoons of fish *fumet** mixed with cream, or a few tablespoons of the accompanying sauce.

When served cold, a few tablespoons of *Fish aspic jelly* (see ASPIC) are poured in through the hole in the top made for the steam to escape. This should be done only when the pie is completely cold.

Paupiettes of sole. PAUPIETTES DE SOLES—Fillets of sole spread with a *Fish forcemeat* or some other mixture, rolled up and usually cooked slowly in a fish *fumet**. Sometimes *paupiettes* are cooked in butter.

Fillets of sole, also spread with some mixture, but folded in two before cooking instead of being rolled, are often, erroneously, referred to as *paupiettes of sole.*

All the garnishes and sauces used for fillets of sole are applicable to *paupiettes.*

Rolled *paupiettes* of sole are also served cold.

Paupiettes of sole Mont-Bry

Paupiettes of sole Mont-Bry. PAUPIETTES DE SOLES MONT-BRY—Spread fillets thinly with *Whiting forcemeat* (see FORCEMEAT). Roll them in *paupiettes.* Cook very gently in fish *fumet** made with white wine.

Drain the paupiettes and set each one in a tomato which has been cooked in oil and half-filled with risotto seasoned with saffron.

Coat the paupiettes with the cooking liquor concentrated and mixed with fresh cream and with chopped chervil and tarragon added.

Paupiettes of sole à la nissarde. PAUPIETTES DE SOLES À LA NISSARDE—Spread the fillets with *Pike forcemeat* (see FORCEMEAT) finished off with *Anchovy essence* (see ESSENCE) or purée and chopped parsley. Roll in *paupiettes.*

Poach the paupiettes in concentrated *fumet**, drain them and set each into half a courgette (Italian marrow or zucchini), cooked in butter and slightly hollowed out. Put on a round dish.

Boil down the cooking liquor, add tomato purée and butter, blend and pour over the paupiettes. Sprinkle with grated Parmesan and a few drops of oil. Brown in the oven.

Paupiettes of sole Paillard. PAUPIETTES DE SOLES PAILLARD—'Lay out on the table the flattened fillets of sole; season and spread them thinly with *Fish forcemeat* (see FORCEMEAT) finished off with *Mushroom purée**. Roll them into cork-shaped pieces. Put them into a sauté pan lined with chopped onions and mushrooms and a *bouquet garni** and moisten with *fish fumet** or dry white wine.

'Cook, covered, in the oven for 12 minutes.

'Drain the paupiettes, arrange them in a deep, buttered dish, cover and keep warm.

'Strain the cooking liquor through muslin, and to it add an equal quantity of mushroom purée, 2 egg yolks, and 1 cup (2 decilitres) of fresh cream. Bring just to the boil, whisking all the time, and adjust the seasoning.

'Coat the paupiettes with this sauce, glaze in a very hot oven and serve immediately.' (A. Deland, formerly head chef at the Restaurant Paillard.)

Note. At the Restaurant Paillard these *paupiettes* were served on artichoke bottoms.

Sole à la paysanne—For a sole weighing 12 ounces (350 grams): Cook gently in butter a carrot, an onion, a tender stick of celery, and the white part of a leek, seasoning them with salt and a pinch of sugar. Moisten these vegetables, after they have been cooked, with just enough warm water to cover them. Add to them a tablespoon of French beans cut in dice and a tablespoon of fresh green peas. Finish cooking all these vegetables together, boiling down the liquid a little.

Put the sole, seasoned with salt and pepper, into a buttered oval earthenware dish. Cover with the vegetable mixture and its cooking liquor. Poach the sole in this liquid, then drain off as much as possible and boil it down. Add, stirring well, 2 teaspoons of butter. Pour this sauce over the sole and glaze in a hot oven.

Note. This method of preparation is often described on menus as *Sole à la russe.* In fact, nothing in this dish justifies such an appellation, and it seems much more logical to present it under the title *à la paysanne*, which is justified by the use of vegetables cooked *à la paysanne.*

Pilaf of sole. PILAF DE SOLES—Cut the fillets of sole into small square pieces and sauté them in butter. Add sliced mushrooms, also sautéed in butter. Set in the middle of pilaf rice (see PILAF) shaped in a border mould. Coat the fish with *Tomato sauce* or *Normande sauce* (see SAUCE).

Sole sur le plat—Put inside a sole, whose fillets have been slightly raised, a little butter seasoned with salt and pepper. Put the fish in a buttered fireproof dish. Season with salt and pepper. Moisten with $\frac{1}{2}$ cup (1 decilitre) of fish *fumet** and a few drops of lemon juice, and dot small pieces of butter over the top of the fish.

Cook in the oven, basting frequently, until the liquor is reduced to a syrupy consistency and has given the sole a blond glaze.

Serve as it is, in the dish in which it was cooked.

Note. Sole sur le plat may be prepared in the same way replacing the *fumet* with a wine. Thus there may be *Sole sur le plat* cooked with Alsace wine, Chablis, Champagne (dry), Cassis, Sauternes, Monbazillac, Seyssel, Jurançon, Muscadet, *vin rosé* of Burgundy or Bordeaux and, finally, various red wines of Burgundy, Bordelais or other regions.

Poached sole, various sauces. Sole bouillie, pochée—Cook the sole in a stock or *court-bouillon** made of milk and water seasoned with salt. Drain and set on a perforated dish or on a napkin. Garnish with parsley and boiled potatoes. Serve melted butter separately, or any other sauce suitable for poached fish: *Hollandaise, Fines herbes, Lobster, etc.* (see SAUCE).

Sole à la portugaise—Put the seasoned sole into a long fireproof dish lined with cooked tomatoes mixed with chopped onion cooked in oil and seasoned with a little garlic; moisten with 2 tablespoons of fish *fumet** and 3 to 4 tablespoons of olive oil. Cook in the oven, basting often. Sprinkle the sole with breadcrumbs and brown lightly. Sprinkle over chopped parsley and a few drops of lemon juice.

Sole à la provençale—Sole cooked in the same way as *Sole à la niçoise* or *Sole à la portugaise* is often served under the name of *Sole à la provençale*. This is easily understood, if not altogether justifiable, since all these preparations include tomato and almost always in the form of *fondue*.

Put the sole, seasoned, into an oiled dish. Moisten with ½ cup (1 decilitre) of fish *fumet** seasoned with a little garlic. Sprinkle over the sole a tablespoon of oil and cook it in the oven. When it is almost cooked, surround with halved tomatoes, sautéed in oil, and set on top of fish 4 slices of peeled lemon. Sprinkle with breadcrumbs. Finish cooking in the oven. Sprinkle with chopped parsley. Serve in its cooking dish.

Purée of sole. Purée de soles—Cook the fillets of sole covered in butter and press through a fine sieve. Bind this purée with some *Béchamel sauce* or with *fish Velouté sauce* mixed with cream.

Note. This purée is used mostly as a filling for flaky pastry, patties, tartlets, barquettes, or other small preparations of the same kind.

Quenelles of sole—Sole is very seldom used to make quenelles. Quenelle fish forcemeat is usually made of pike or whiting.

Quenelle forcemeat made with sole is prepared in the same way as *Pike forcemeat*. See QUENELLE and FORCEMEAT.

These quenelles are served in a deep dish or flat plate; in the latter case they are generally set on cut-out pieces of puff pastry or oval croûtons of bread fried in butter. They are accompanied by one or other of the garnishes prescribed for fillets of sole and coated with sauce to blend with the rest of the dish.

Sole Richelieu—Prepared with a whole sole in the same way as *Fillets of sole Richelieu*. See above.

Risotto of sole—Made like *Pilaf of sole* with *Risotto* (see RICE) instead of pilaf rice.

Note. As well as mushrooms, which are the garnish for fish pilaf and risotto, shelled mussels and shrimps, or slices of any other crustacean may be added to these dishes.

Sole à la russe—See *Sole à la paysanne*.

Sole Saint-Germain—This method is mainly applied to fillets of fish.

Coat the sole with butter and breadcrumbs, sprinkle with melted butter, and put to cook on the grill, at a low heat. Set on a hot dish, surround with potatoes cut to look like olives and cooked in butter. Serve *Béarnaise sauce* (see SAUCE) separately.

Scallop shells of sole. Coquilles de soles—Prepared with fillets of sole cooked in butter like *Brill in scallop shells**.

Sole with shrimps. Sole aux crevettes—Prepared with the whole sole poached in a fish *fumet** that is scarcely boiling. Drain the sole; set it on a long dish. Surround with mussels cooked in white wine and removed from their shells and peeled shrimps. Coat with *White wine sauce* (see SAUCE). Serve as it is, or glaze in a hot oven.

Sole with red wine. Sole au vin rouge—Season the sole with salt and pepper. Put it in a baking dish on a layer of chopped onions and carrots which have been tossed in butter. Add a sprig of thyme, a piece of bay leaf and some mushroom skins (from the mushrooms used for the garnish, because, as a general rule, fish cooked with red wine is garnished with mushrooms and small glazed onions). Dot the top of the fish with tiny pieces of butter. Poach, covered, in the oven. Drain, dry, trim and remove the backbone. Set on a long dish. Coat with its cooking liquor finished off according to the instructions given elsewhere for *Red wine sauce for fish* (see SAUCE).

Note. Red wine used to poach fish may be any of a number of different vintages, Bordeaux, Burgundy, Côtes du Rhône, Touraine, etc. *Vin ordinaire* may also be used.

Sole with white wine. Sole au vin blanc—Poach the sole very gently in a *fumet** made with white wine.

Drain the fish, trim it, remove the backbone (to facilitate serving) and set on a long dish.

Coat with a *White wine sauce* prepared with the fumet in which the fish was cooked, according to one of the recipes given for this sauce (see SAUCE).

Serve as it is or glaze in a very hot oven.

SOLILEM OR SOLIMEME—This cake, Alsatian in origin, is prepared in the following way:

Ingredients. 3¾ cups (500 grams) of sifted flour; ¼ pound (125 grams) of butter; 2½ teaspoons (15 grams) of sugar; ½ ounce (15 grams) of yeast; ½ cup (1 decilitre) of cream; 4 eggs; 1½ teaspoons (10 grams) of salt.

Method. With a quarter of the flour, the yeast and a little warm water, make a paste and leave in a warm place to rise.

Add to this paste 2 eggs and ¼ cup (½ decilitre) of the cream. Add the rest of the flour and knead the dough.

Incorporate in this paste the butter, the rest of the cream and the eggs, put in little by little.

Beat the dough. It should be quite soft, and may have a little more cream added to it if it is too firm.

Half-fill with the dough a plain round mould, buttered with cold butter. Leave to rise for a while. Bake in the oven. Turn the cake out of the mould, cut in two layers, sprinkle each layer with melted, slightly salt butter. Put two pieces together. Serve very hot.

SOLOMON'S SEAL. Muguet angumeux—A plant found in the woods. The young shoots are edible, and prepared like asparagus. This plant is also known as *Sceau de Salomon* in French.

SOMMELIER—(1) Employee charged with the care of the cellars. (2) A member of a religious order concerned with the convent plates, linen, bread and wine.

In large restaurants the *sommelier* is in charge of the service of wines, and not only has to take charge of the wine in the cellar, but also the wine sold in the restaurant. The function of a *sommelier* in a large establishment demands extensive knowledge of wines. He must also understand how to choose wines to blend with particular foodstuffs.

A *somellerie* is either a group of persons engaged in looking after cellars and drinks in a royal household, or the place where the work of the *sommelier* is done, notably in monasteries and convents.

SOMMIER—Name formerly given to the servants of the kitchen, pantry and *sommelerie* in the palace of the French kings.

SORB-APPLE. SORBE—Fruit of the sorb, a tree of the *Rosaceae* family. Two varieties are known: The *Rowan* or *Mountain Ash*, whose fruits, much relished by thrushes, are highly astringent but used in some districts for distilling; and the *Sorb* or *Service tree* whose fruits become edible when overripe and serve to make a kind of cider.

SORGHUM. SORGHO—Cereal, native of Africa but long cultivated in southern Europe and China. It is a kind of millet. Its grain is used mostly to make porridges and flat cakes; the stalks, which serve for fodder, contain a high percentage of sugar and can be used to make a fermented drink.

SORREL. OSEILLE—A hardy perennial herb which dates back before 3000 B.C. and still grows wild today in Asia, Europe and North America. It is also cultivated.

In the thirteenth century it was listed as an English herb; it has long been used in the making of sauces and soups. The young under leaves of this plant, also called Sour Grass, are used as salad greens or as a vegetable.

Braised sorrel or sorrel purée. OSEILLE BRAISÉE, PURÉE D'OSEILLE—Put 2 pounds (1 kilo) of sorrel, picked over and washed in several waters into a big saucepan. Moisten with 2 cups (½ litre) of water and cook on a slow fire until it goes down in volume.

Drain the sorrel in a sieve.

Put it into another saucepan in which you have prepared a blond *roux** made of 4 tablespoons (60 grams) of butter and 2 tablespoons (30 grams) of flour. Mix well, add 3 cups (6 decilitres) of white stock, season with salt and a little castor (fine) sugar, cover the pan and cook in the oven for 2 hours.

Rub the sorrel through a fine sieve and put it back in the pan to reheat. At the last moment bind with a liaison of 3 whole eggs (or 6 yolks), beaten, mixed with ½ cup (1 decilitre) of cream, strained through a fine strainer and blended with 10 tablespoons (150 grams) of butter. Stir well.

Chiffonnade of sorrel. CHIFFONNADE D'OSEILLE—Pick over, wash and shred the sorrel into a fine *julienne**. Simmer gently in butter until all the water contained in the vegetable has evaporated.

Note. Chiffonnade of sorrel in butter is used as an element of garnish for various dishes. See SOUPS AND BROTHS; EGGS, *Sorrel omelette.*

Chiffonnade of sorrel with cream. CHIFFONNADE D'OSEILLE À LA CRÈME—Cook the chiffonnade on a slow fire until it goes down in volume, as described in the preceding recipe. When the liquid is completely evaporated, moisten the chiffonnade with a few tablespoons of fresh double cream. Simmer for a few minutes.

This is used for the same purposes as the sorrel chiffonnade cooked with butter.

Preserved sorrel. CONSERVE D'OSEILLE—Pick over, wash and cook the sorrel slowly as described above. Let it dry off thoroughly, extracting all the water contained in it. Compress it into a stone jar with a wide neck. Allow to cool. Pour a thick layer of clarified beef fat to seal it and keep in a cool place.

Note. Sorrel can also be bottled by putting it, after it is cooked, into jars or tins (cans) and treating them in a steriliser in the usual manner.

SOT-L'Y-LAISSE—This term, meaning 'a fool leaves it', is used to describe the small piece of flesh situated above the parson's nose of a chicken (or other fowl) which is considered a delicacy. In old French cookery '*ragoûts* of sot-l'y-laisse' are often mentioned.

SOUBISE—Purée of onions and rice used as an accompaniment to various cuts of meat, large and small. See PURÉE.

SOU-FASSUM (Nice cookery)—Stuffed cabbage made in the following way.

Blanch the cabbage as for *Whole stuffed cabbage* (see CABBAGE), and stuff with a forcemeat made up in this way: 1 pound (500 grams) of sausage meat, 7 ounces (200 grams) of streaky bacon cut in dice, blanched and fried, ½ cup (100 grams) of chopped onion, lightly cooked in butter, ½ pound (250 grams) of beetroot leaves blanched and chopped, 2 peeled and chopped tomatoes, 1 cup (125 grams) of fresh peas, chopped cabbage heart, 1 cup (100 grams) of blanched rice, chopped parsley, crushed garlic, salt and pepper.

Reform the cabbage, wrap it in muslin and cook for 3½ hours in mutton *pot-au-feu* (or ordinary *pot-au-feu*).

Serve the stuffed cabbage with *Tomato sauce* (see SAUCE).

SOUFFLÉS—Sweet and savoury, made of ingredients cooked to a purée, thickened with yolks of eggs and with stiffly beaten egg whites folded in, poured into a soufflé dish or into *cassolettes** and baked in the oven.

The same name has been extended to include quite different preparations, more like *mousses* or *mousselines*, served both hot and cold. The method of cooking the latter is given separately.

True soufflés are divided into two main categories: savoury soufflés, served as hors-d'oeuvre or small entrées and sometimes as a savoury, and sweet soufflés.

Small soufflés—These soufflés are made in *cassolettes** of fireproof porcelain, metal or oven-glass or in special goffered paper cases.

Method of preparation. Prepare the soufflé mixture according to the recipe. Turn the mixture into the buttered *cassolettes* filling these only three-quarters full. Smooth the surface of the soufflés.

Set the *cassolettes* on a baking sheet and cook in a low oven for 8 to 12 minutes.

Arrange on a napkin and serve immediately.

SAVOURY SOUFFLÉS. SOUFFLÉS DE CUISINE—*Method.* Prepare the basic ingredient, whether purée of meat, fish, crustacean or vegetable, or a *bouillie*.

Bind this ingredient, away from the fire, with 3 egg yolks for every 2 cups (250 grams) of the mixture.

Season quite strongly so as to compensate for the weakening effect of adding egg whites; mix.

At the last moment, and always away from the fire, incorporate 3 or 4 egg whites, stiffly beaten; mix quickly, but do not beat.

Fill a buttered soufflé dish with this mixture, filling only to within a finger's breadth from the top.

Smooth over the surface of the soufflé. Cook in a moderate oven for 20 to 25 minutes. Serve immediately.

Note. The same method is used to cook small soufflés. These are put into *cassolettes** of metal or fireproof porcelain.

Brain soufflé. SOUFFLÉ DE CERVELLE—Bind 1¼ cups (250 grams) of *Brain purée* (see PURÉE) with ¾ cup (1½ decilitres) of thick *Béchamel sauce* (see SAUCE). Season with salt, pepper and grated nutmeg.

Add 3 egg yolks, and, at the last moment, fold in 3 stiffly beaten egg whites.

Fill a buttered soufflé dish with the mixture. Finish off as in the above recipe.

Brain soufflé à la chanoinesse. SOUFFLÉ DE CERVELLE À LA CHANOINESSE—Prepare the mixture as above. Finish off with 2 ounces (60 grams) of grated Parmesan and 2 tablespoons of truffles cut in a fine *julienne* (thin strips).

Finish off as in the above recipe.

Note. Brain soufflés are often served as an hors-d'oeuvre and therefore cooked in *cassolettes** as for small soufflés.

Calf's liver or chicken liver soufflé. SOUFFLÉ DE FOIE DE VEAU, FOIES DE VOLAILLE—Pound in a mortar ½ pound (250 grams) of calf's liver cut into dice, sautéed in butter and drained, with 2 tablespoons (35 grams) of butter and ½ cup (1 decilitre) of thick *Béchamel sauce;* season.

Press through a strainer; add 2 yolks of eggs and, at the last moment, 3 beaten egg whites.

Finish off as in the preceding recipes.

Note. Chicken liver soufflé is prepared in the same way.

Cheese soufflé

Cheese soufflé. SOUFFLÉ AU FROMAGE—Stir into a white *roux*, composed of 3 tablespoons (50 grams) of butter and 4 tablespoons (60 grams) of flour, 1 cup (2 decilitres) of milk. Season with salt, pepper and grated nutmeg. Stir over a strong heat until boiling.

Remove from heat, add 2 ounces or ⅔ cup (60 grams) of grated Gruyère, 3 egg yolks and, at the last moment, 3 beaten egg whites.

Finish off as in the preceding recipes.

This mixture is also cooked in *cassolettes** and served as hors-d'oeuvre.

In the same way soufflés are made with Parmesan, Cheddar or Dutch cheese.

Chestnut soufflé. SOUFFLÉ DE MARRONS—Proceed, with chestnut purée, as for *Potato soufflé.*

Chestnut soufflé soubisé. SOUFFLÉ DE MARRONS SOUBISÉ—Prepare the basic mixture in the usual way, using two-thirds chestnut purée and one-third Soubise purée. See PURÉE.

Chicken soufflé. SOUFFLÉ DE VOLAILLE—Pound in a mortar 1½ cups (250 grams) of cooked chicken meat (the white meat for preference) with ⅓ to ½ cup of thick *Béchamel sauce*. Season and press through a sieve.

Allow to cool; add a good spoonful of butter and mix. Incorporate 3 egg yolks, then, at the last moment, 3 beaten whites. Finish off as in the preceding recipes.

Note. This recipe applies to chicken, pigeon, turkey and guinea fowl.

This soufflé mixture can be served in *cassolettes** as hors-d'oeuvre.

Chicken soufflé à la mirepoix. SOUFFLÉ DE VOLAILLE À LA MIREPOIX—Add to the mixture prepared as above ¼ cup of vegetable *mirepoix**. Finish off as in the preceding recipes.

Chicken soufflé with truffles (Soufflé à la reine). SOUFFLÉ DE VOLAILLE AUX TRUFFES, À LA REINE—Add to the mixture prepared as above 2 tablespoons of chopped truffles.

Chicory soufflé. SOUFFLÉ DE CHICORÉE—Dry out over the heat, stirring and shaking to prevent sticking, 2 cups (250 grams) of sieved braised chicory.

Add, away from the fire, 3 egg yolks and 8 beaten whites. Finish off as in preceding recipes.

Chicory soufflé with Parmesan. SOUFFLÉ DE CHICORÉE AU PARMESAN—Proceed as above, finishing off the mixture with 2 ounces (60 grams) of grated Parmesan.

Crayfish soufflé à la normande. SOUFFLÉ D'ÉCREVISSES À LA NORMANDE—Prepare the basic mixture in the same way as for *Shrimp soufflé.* Replace the latter by a similar quantity of crayfish.

Turn into a buttered soufflé dish, making alternate layers of the soufflé mixture and a *salpicon** of poached and drained oysters, truffles and mushrooms. Finish off as in the preceding recipes.

Fish soufflé. SOUFFLÉ DE POISSON—Cook the prescribed fish in butter, then press the flesh through a sieve. Add for every 1¼ cups (250 grams) ¾ cup (1½ decilitres) of thick *Béchamel sauce* (see SAUCE). Bind with the yolks of 3 eggs and incorporate, at the last moment, 3 or 4 beaten egg whites. Finish off as in the preceding recipes.

Note. This recipe applies to all fish. It can also be applied to left-overs of fish that has been cooked in butter or white wine.

Foie gras soufflé à la Périgueux—See MOUSSE, *Mousse of foie gras.*

Game soufflé. SOUFFLÉ DE GIBIER—Pound in a mortar ½ pound (250 grams) of cooked game with ¾ cup (1½ decilitres) of *Béchamel sauce* (see SAUCE) based on game *fumet**; season and sieve.

Add 3 egg yolks and, at the last moment, 3 stiffly beaten egg whites. Finish off as in the preceding recipes.

Chiefly served in *cassolettes* as hors-d'oeuvre.

Game soufflé à la Périgueux. SOUFFLÉ DE GIBIER À LA PÉRIGUEUX—Add to the above mixture 2 tablespoons of chopped truffles. Finish off in the usual way.

Ham soufflé. SOUFFLÉ DE JAMBON—Proceed, with ½ pound (250 grams) of lean cooked ham, as for *Game soufflé.*

Served chiefly in *cassolettes** as hors-d'oeuvre.

Ham soufflé à la strasbourgeoise. SOUFFLÉ DE JAMBON À LA STRASBOURGEOISE—Add to *ham purée* one third of its weight of *Pâté de foie gras* and a tablespoon of chopped truffles. Finish off as in the preceding recipes.

Soufflé à la hongroise—Prepare a mixture as for *Brain soufflé*, adding 2 tablespoons of chopped onion cooked till soft in butter and seasoned with paprika, and 2 tablespoons of mushrooms cut in dice and sautéed in butter. Finish off as in the preceding recipes.

Chiefly served in *cassolettes** as hors-d'oeuvre.

Jerusalem artichoke soufflé. SOUFFLÉ DE TOPINAMBOURS—Proceed, using a purée of Jerusalem artichokes, in the same way as for *Potato soufflé.*

Lettuce soufflé. SOUFFLÉ DE LAITUES—Proceed as for *Chicory soufflé*, replacing the latter by braised, chopped lettuces.

Grated Parmesan may be added, if liked.

Lobster soufflé. SOUFFLÉ DE HOMARD—Like *Shrimp soufflé*, replacing the shrimps with lobster purée.

Meat soufflé. SOUFFLÉ DE VIANDES—Proceed with the meat as for *Calf's liver soufflé.* Any meat may be used for this soufflé if it has been poached or braised, and according to the kind of meat *Béchamel sauce*, *Velouté sauce* or any other sauce that will blend with the meat is used to bind the purée.

Parmesan soufflé. SOUFFLÉ AU PARMESAN—Blend 5 tablespoons (75 grams) of sifted flour with 1 cup (2 decilitres) of boiled milk. Season with salt, pepper and grated nutmeg.

Stir over a good heat until boiling, then take off the heat and add 2 ounces (60 grams) of grated Parmesan, 4 teaspoons (20 grams) of butter, 3 egg yolks and 3 beaten whites.

Finish off as in the preceding recipes.

Also served in *cassolettes** as hors-d'oeuvre.

Potato soufflé. SOUFFLÉ DE POMMES DE TERRE—Bind 2 cups (4 decilitres) of potato purée with ¼ cup of cream. Season. Add 3 egg yolks and, at the last moment, 3 beaten egg whites. Finish off in the usual way.

Potato soufflé with cheese. SOUFFLÉ DE POMMES DE TERRE AU FROMAGE—As above, adding to the purée 2 ounces (60 grams) of grated Gruyère or Parmesan.

Potato soufflé à la hongroise. SOUFFLÉ DE POMMES DE TERRE À LA HONGROISE—As above, incorporating some chopped onion, softened in butter and seasoned with paprika, in the potato purée.

Sweet potato soufflé. SOUFFLÉ DE PATATES—Proceed with sweet potato purée in the same way as for *Potato soufflé*.

Shrimp soufflé (or other crustacean). SOUFFLÉ DE CREVETTES—Bind 1¼ cups (200 grams) of *Shrimp purée* (see PURÉE) (or purée made of some other crustacean) with ¾ cup (1½ decilitres) of thick *Béchamel sauce* (see SAUCE) to which the concentrated liquor left from cooking the shrimps has been added.

Add 3 egg yolks, and, at the last moment, fold in 3 beaten egg whites. Finish off as in the preceding recipes.

Note. Prawn, crayfish, lobster, spiny lobster and crab soufflés are prepared in the same way. A *salpicon** of shrimps or the flesh of the crustacean being used may be added to the mixture.

These soufflés are chiefly served as hors-d'oeuvre, cooked in *cassolettes**.

Spinach soufflé. SOUFFLÉ D'ÉPINARDS—Proceed as for *Chicory soufflé*, replacing the latter with an equal quantity of spinach, blanched, drained, pressed, chopped or sieved and simmered in butter. Finish off as in the preceding recipes.

Spinach soufflé à la florentine. SOUFFLÉ D'ÉPINARDS À LA FLORENTINE—Prepare the basic mixture as above, finishing with 2 ounces (60 grams) of grated Parmesan. Complete cooking as in the preceding recipes.

Spiny lobster soufflé. SOUFFLÉ DE LANGOUSTE—Like *Shrimp soufflé*, but using a spiny lobster purée.

Sweetbread soufflé. SOUFFLÉ DE RIS DE VEAU—Proceed, with calf's sweetbreads, as for *Calf's liver soufflé*.

Mostly served in *cassolettes** as hors-d'oeuvre.

Tomato soufflé. SOUFFLÉ DE TOMATES—Bind 1½ cups (3 decilitres) of thick *Tomato purée* with ½ cup (1 decilitre) of thick *Béchamel sauce* (see SAUCE). Remove from heat and add 2 ounces (60 grams) of grated Parmesan, 3 egg yolks and 3 beaten egg whites.

Finish off as in the preceding recipes.

Note. This soufflé may be made without the addition of grated Parmesan, or chopped tarragon may be added instead.

Truffle soufflé (Soufflé à la royale). SOUFFLÉ AUX TRUFFES, À LA ROYALE—Bind 5 ounces (150 grams) of truffle purée with ¾ cup (1½ decilitres) of *Béchamel sauce* made with *Truffle essence* (see ESSENCE). Season.

Add 3 egg yolks and, at the last moment, 3 beaten whites. Finish off as in the preceding recipes.

Chiefly served in *cassolettes** as hors-d'oeuvre.

Truffle soufflé with Parmesan. SOUFFLÉ AUX TRUFFES ET AU PARMESAN—Add to a Parmesan cheese soufflé mixture 2 ounces (60 grams) of truffles cut in a fine *julienne* (thin strips). Finish off as in the preceding recipes.

Mostly served in *cassolettes** as hors-d'oeuvre.

Soufflé of various vegetables. SOUFFLÉ DE LÉGUMES—Any vegetable, reduced to a purée, may be used to make soufflé. Before egg yolks are added, these purées should be dried out over heat and *Béchamel sauce* should be added as necessary, if they are too watery.

Proceed in the same way as for *Spinach soufflé* or *Chicory soufflé*.

Artichokes, asparagus, aubergines, carrots, celery, mushrooms, cauliflower, courgettes, turnips, etc., may be used to make soufflés in this way.

SWEET SOUFFLÉS. SOUFFLÉS D'ENTREMETS—Several kinds of basic mixtures are used for these soufflés, but they can be divided into two principal types: *cream-base* and *fruit-base*.

The cream-base mixtures are used for the greater number of soufflés, the basic mixture varying from recipe to recipe by the flavouring used and the ingredients added.

Soufflés are made in straight-sided containers of silver, fire-proof porcelain or oven-glass. Silver soufflé dishes are sometimes provided with an inner dish in which the soufflé is cooked. These utensils are buttered and sprinkled with fine sugar.

Soufflés are cooked in a moderate oven so that the heat penetrates right to the middle of the mixture.

A few moments before cooking is finished the top of the soufflé is sprinkled with sugar and it is glazed by being put in the hottest part of the oven.

The cooking time varies according to the size of the soufflé, but for the quantities given below should be 14 to 16 minutes.

Once cooked and glazed the soufflé *must be served without delay*.

Cream-base mixtures: Mixture A—Bring to the boil in a saucepan ½ cup (1 decilitre) of milk with 2 tablespoons (35 to 40 grams) of sugar and a pinch of salt.

Add 2 tablespoons (25 grams) of sifted flour, previously blended with a little cold milk. Flavour as required.

Cook, stirring, for 2 or 3 minutes.

Add, away from the fire, 2 egg yolks, and 2 teaspoons (10 grams) of butter, and, at the last moment, 3 stiffly beaten egg whites.

Mix quickly and fill the buttered and sugared soufflé dish. Smooth the surface of the soufflé. Put to cook in a moderate oven.

Two minutes before serving sprinkle with sugar to glaze.

Mixture B—Proceed in the same way as for *Mixture A*, replacing the flour with a teaspoon of potato starch. Finish off as above.

Mixture C—Beat free of lumps in a saucepan ½ cup (65 grams) of flour, ¼ cup (65 grams) of fine sugar, a pinch of salt, one whole egg and one egg yolk.

Stir in 1 cup (2 decilitres) of boiling milk and cook over the heat, stirring well to keep the mixture from sticking to the bottom. Flavour as required.

Add, away from the heat, 2 tablespoons (25 grams) of butter, an egg yolk, and at the last moment, 3 stiffly beaten egg whites. Finish off as above.

Mixture D—Put into a saucepan 2 tablespoons (25 grams) of sifted flour, 2 tablespoons (35 to 40 grams) of sugar and a pinch of salt.

Beat free of lumps with ½ cup (1 decilitre) of cold milk, add the required flavouring and cook for a few minutes over the heat, stirring all the time.

Add, away from the heat, 3 egg yolks and 2 teaspoons (10 grams) of butter, and at the last moment fold in 3 stiffly beaten egg whites.

Finish off as above.

Mixture E—In a saucepan blend ½ tablespoon (5 grams) of arrowroot with ½ cup (1 decilitre) of cold milk. Add 2 tablespoons (35 to 40 grams) of sugar and a pinch of salt. Bring to boiling point and cook for a moment, stirring all the time.

Add, away from the heat, 2 egg yolks and, at the last moment, 2 stiffly beaten egg whites.

Finish off as above.

This mixture is used in invalid cookery.

Mixture F—Put into a small saucepan 2 tablespoons (35 to 40 grams) of sugar, 3 egg yolks and a pinch of salt. Beat well with a spatula.

Stir in ½ cup (1 decilitre) of boiling milk. Keep over the heat until the first bubbles begin to appear, without ceasing to stir. Remove from the heat and, at the last moment, add 2 or 3 stiffly beaten egg whites. Finish off as above.

This recipe is also used in invalid cookery.

Note on flavouring soufflés. The flavour is added to the basic mixture during or after cooking. Vanilla pods and lemon, orange and mandarin peel are put in during cooking. Liqueurs are added away from the heat before incorporating egg whites.

Candied fruits, previously chopped, are also added just before folding in the egg whites.

Fruit-base mixtures—Add to 1 cup (250 grams) of sugar cooked to small crack degree (see SUGAR), 2 cups (200 grams) of purée of the required fruit. Allow to boil for a moment.

Pour this mixture on to 5 or 6 stiffly beaten egg whites, and mix quickly.

Turn into a soufflé dish buttered and sprinkled with sugar. Cook in the same way as described in the preceding recipes.

Note. Although soufflés of fresh fruit are made with a mixture like that described above, they may also be made with a cream-base mixture. In this case a very thick fruit purée is added to the mixture before incorporating the egg whites.

Almond soufflé. SOUFFLÉ AUX AMANDES—Fill a soufflé dish with a cream-base mixture in which milk of almonds has been used instead of ordinary milk, and to which 2 to 3 tablespoons of almonds, roasted in the oven and chopped, have been added. Cook in the ordinary way.

Fresh almond soufflé. SOUFFLÉ AUX AMANDES FRAÎCHES—As above, replacing the roasted almonds by fresh, blanched almonds. Cook in the ordinary way.

These soufflés should be glazed by sprinkling them with chopped almonds.

Ambassadrice soufflé. SOUFFLÉ AMBASSADRICE—Cream-base soufflé well flavoured with vanilla, with the addition of 2 crumbled macaroons and 2 to 3 tablespoons of fresh, blanched almonds flavoured with rum. Cook in the usual way.

Apple soufflé. SOUFFLÉ AUX POMMES—Proceed with stewed apples or apple jam as for *Apricot soufflé*.

Russian apple soufflé. SOUFFLÉ AUX POMMES À LA RUSSE—Add to stiffly beaten egg whites some thick apple purée (two-thirds apple purée and one-third egg white). Fill a soufflé dish with this mixture and cook in the usual way.

Apricot soufflé I. SOUFFLÉ AUX ABRICOTS—Fill a soufflé dish, buttered and sprinkled with sugar, with one of the cream-base mixtures flavoured with kirsch and with the addition of pieces of apricot cooked in syrup, well drained and soaked in kirsch. Cook in the usual way.

Apricot soufflé II. SOUFFLÉ AUX ABRICOTS—Proceed as above, using one of the cream-base mixtures with the addition of very thick apricot purée flavoured with kirsch. Cook in the ordinary way.

Apricot soufflé III. SOUFFLÉ AUX ABRICOTS—Fill the soufflé dish with apricot purée, made as described in the recipe for fruit-base mixtures and flavoured with kirsch. Cook in the ordinary way.

Note. In whatever way the apricot soufflé is cooked, a *salpicon** of candied apricots, soaked in kirsch or some other liqueur, should be added.

Alternatively, as the dish is filled, spoonfuls of very thick apricot jam may be put here and there into the soufflé mixture.

Cherry soufflé I. SOUFFLÉ AUX CERISES—Cream-base soufflé mixture flavoured with kirsch or cherry brandy, mixed with stoned cherries cooked in their own juice with sugar. Cook in the ordinary way.

Cherry soufflé II. SOUFFLÉ AUX CERISES—Fruit-base soufflé mixture made with cherry pulp according to the recipe for fruit-base soufflé mixture. Cook in the ordinary way.

Chestnut soufflé—See *Mont-Bry soufflé*.

Chocolate soufflé. SOUFFLÉ AU CHOCOLAT—Cream-base soufflé mixture to which ⅓ cup (50 grams) of grated chocolate, melted over a very low heat or dissolved with a little milk (or powdered cocoa) has been added. Cook in the ordinary way.

Cocoa soufflé—See *Chocolate soufflé*.

Coffee soufflé. SOUFFLÉ AU CAFÉ—Cream-base soufflé mixture with the addition of 4 or 5 tablespoons of coffee essence. Cook in the usual way.

Curaçao soufflé. SOUFFLÉ AU CURAÇAO—Cream-base soufflé mixture flavoured with orange peel and a small glass of curaçao. Cook in the ordinary way.

Hazelnut soufflé. SOUFFLÉ AUX AVELINES—Cream-base mixture to which 2 to 4 tablespoons of hazelnut praline has been added. Cook in the ordinary way.

Note. Soufflés made with almonds, hazelnuts, walnuts and pistachios are usually made without any flavouring. A little vanilla or a liqueur, preferably rum or kirsch, may, however, be added.

Lemon soufflé. SOUFFLÉ AU CITRON—Cream-base soufflé mixture flavoured with finely chopped lemon peel. Cook in the ordinary way.

Liqueur-flavoured soufflé. SOUFFLÉ AUX LIQUEURS—Proceed, using the required liqueur, as for *Curaçao soufflé*.

Note. To all liqueur-flavoured soufflés, in addition to the liqueur used in the basic mixture, sponge finger biscuits, cut into small squares and soaked in the same liqueur, may be added.

Mont-Bry soufflé. SOUFFLÉ MONT-BRY—Cream-base soufflé mixture mixed with one-third of its volume of chestnuts cooked in syrup and strongly flavoured with vanilla. Garnish with *marrons glacés* soaked in kirsch. Cook in the usual way.

Orange or mandarin soufflé. SOUFFLÉ À L'ORANGE, À LA MANDARINE—Cream-base soufflé mixture flavoured with the finely chopped peel of orange or mandarins. Cook in the ordinary way.

Coffee soufflé (*Robert Carrier*)

Palmyra soufflé. SOUFFLÉ PALMYRE—Cream-base soufflé mixture well flavoured with vanilla, mixed with small square pieces of sponge finger biscuits soaked in kirsch and anisette.

Peach soufflé. SOUFFLÉ AUX PÊCHES—Use one of the recipes given for *Apricot soufflé*, substituting peaches.

Pear soufflé. SOUFFLÉ AUX POIRES—Like *Apricot soufflé*, replacing the apricots by pears cooked in sugar and their own juice without any liquid.

Praline soufflé. SOUFFLÉ PRALINÉ—Cream-base soufflé mixture flavoured with vanilla, with 2 to 3 tablespoons of almond praline added. See PRALINE.

Note. When making this soufflé or the hazelnut soufflé, the praline may be put into the milk used to make the cream-base mixture.

Rothschild soufflé I. SOUFFLÉ ROTHSCHILD—Cream-base soufflé mixture to which 2 to 3 tablespoons of *salpicon** of candied fruits soaked in brandy, have been added. Cook in the usual way.

When the soufflé is almost cooked, decorate with crystallized cherries.

Rothschild soufflé II. SOUFFLÉ ROTHSCHILD—Cream-base soufflé mixture to which 2 tablespoons of *salpicon** of candied fruits, soaked in Danziger goldwasser, have been added. Cook in the usual way.

When the soufflé is almost cooked, decorate with large strawberries.

Strawberry soufflé I. SOUFFLÉ AUX FRAISES—Cream-base soufflé mixture mixed with wild strawberries or ordinary large strawberries soaked in sugar. Cook in the ordinary way.

Strawberry soufflé II. SOUFFLÉ AUX FRAISES—Cream-base soufflé mixture mixed with very thick wild strawberry pulp. Cook in the ordinary way.

Strawberry soufflé III. SOUFFLÉ AUX FRAISES—Strawberry pulp prepared as a fruit-base soufflé mixture. Cook in the ordinary way.

Tea soufflé. SOUFFLÉ AU THÉ—Cream-base soufflé mixture prepared with milk in which tea has been infused. Cook in the ordinary way.

Vanilla soufflé. SOUFFLÉ À LA VANILLE—Cream-base soufflé mixture flavoured with vanilla. Cook in the usual way.

Violet soufflé. SOUFFLÉ AUX VIOLETTES—Cream-base soufflé mixture flavoured with a few drops of essence of violets and with candied violets added. Cook in the ordinary way.

Note. In the same way soufflés may be made with other candied flowers such as roses and orange flower petals.

Walnut soufflé. SOUFFLÉ AUX NOIX—Cream-base soufflé mixture mixed with lightly grilled and chopped walnuts and flavoured with walnut juice. Cook in the ordinary way.

Note. This can also be made with fresh walnuts.

SOUPE—The French word *soupe* is used to describe not a liquid preparation, but various ingredients put into a *bouillon* or broth, whether made with fish or meat. Thus, for example, the croûtons of bread or the meat in the broth were *soupes.*

Nowadays in France the word *soupe*, as distinct from the more frequently used *potage*, is used to designate a peasant-style soup, of which the principal examples are *Cabbage soup*, *Garbure* and various thick vegetable soups, usually garnished with bread.

SOUPS AND BROTHS. POTAGES, SOUPES—In the seventeenth century the word *potage* did not have the same meaning as it has today. In those days this name was given to great big dishes of meat or fish boiled with vegetables:

'*Cependant on apporte un potage:*
Un coq y paraissait en pompeux équipage.'

'A *potage* is, however, brought in:
A cock is seen in it, in state.'
(Boileau, *Satire III*).

Potage à la jambe de bois

The old *Potage à la jambe de bois* is a good example of such a dish.

Prescribed and proscribed in turn, all in the interests of health, the soup is now what Grimod de la Reynière described so well when he said: 'It is to a dinner what a portico or a peristyle is to a building; that is to say, it is not only the first part of it, but it must be devised in such a manner as to set the tone of the whole banquet, in the same way as the overture of an opera announces the subject of the work.'

From this quotation, we can extract the essentials: the soup must be in perfect harmony with the whole menu.

At a family gathering, or at an intimate dinner, soup is served in a soup tureen, placed on the table, and the master or the lady of the house serves it to the guests.

At ceremonial dinners, especially of the kind where the menu includes two soups—a clear and a thick—this service is performed at a table placed not far from the dining table and the servants pass the plates to the guests. Whatever manner is adopted, soup must be served piping hot, in very hot plates.

There are soups which are based on meat stocks and soups made with water, with bread added to them, supplemented by vegetables, quenelles, *chiffonades**, pasta products, cereal starches and various other garnishings. See GARNISHES.

Depending on their consistency, soups can be classified into two big categories: *clear soups* and *thick soups.*

A clear soup is a *consommé* with various light garnishes added. The garnishings must be of the kind that go with the consommé. The latter itself can be defined as follows: meat stock brought to the extreme point of sapidity, specially prepared with this aim in view, or clarified and at the same time strengthened with lean chopped beef, diced aromatic vegetables and egg whites.

There are several kinds of thick soups. The liaison, or thickening, is obtained either naturally by the dissolving of the farinaceous principle of the ingredients used, or by an addition of *roux**, or some other element of liaison, such as cooked rice, bread boiled to pulp, purée of a starchy vegetable, etc. A great number of thick soups are bound with a liaison of yolks of egg and cream just before serving.

In this section thick soups are classified under three sub-headings: Cream, Purées and *Velouté*.

Pureé soups are either purées of feculent vegetables or leguminous plants, when the liaison is achieved naturally by the starch principles of these vegetables, or purées of crustaceans (bisques), fish, meat and vegetables, the liaison of which is obtained by the addition of a supplementary element.

In the *cream* soups (shell-fish, fish, meat and vegetable) the liaison is obtained by the addition of a certain quantity of *Béchamel sauce* (see SAUCE).

In *velouté* (whether shell-fish, fish, meat or vegetable) the liaison is obtained by the addition of *Velouté* (see SAUCE) and the final binding with yolks and cream.

In order to make this list of thick soups complete, the following should also be mentioned:

(1) *Thickened consommés:* these are ordinary or double consommés based on meat, fish or vegetable stock, to which yolks of egg and fresh cream are added at the last moment.

(2) *Compound or mixed thick soups:* these are made by mixing, in well-defined proportions, different kinds of soups which do not clash in flavour. These soups can, if desired, be thickened with yolks of egg and fresh cream.

(3) Special flour of various cereals; oatmeal, corn (maize), barley, rice, etc., diluted with meat or vegetable stock, which are sometimes called *bouillies* and are mainly given to children, can also be put in the category of thick soups. These soups can also be bound with yolks of egg and cream, as indicated.

Thickened consommés, mixed thick soups and the *bouillies* will not, however, be dwelt upon within the framework of this article. Following the section on *Thick velouté soups*, there is a section dealing with *Special purée and velouté soups*, then another on *Classical and regional soups* and, finally, *International soups and broths.*

CLEAR SOUPS. POTAGES CLAIRS: *Simple white consommé or grande marmite*—Ordinary meat stock made in a big stock-pot is called *simple white consommé.* We specify the big stock-pot, *grande marmite* to differentiate it from a soup called *petite marmite*, the recipe for which is given elsewhere in this book.

This simple consommé serves as a basis for all clear soups. If it is prepared with all the usual nutritive and aromatic elements, it should be very savoury.

The following cuts of meat are best for consommé: *Round* of beef and *silverside* (U.S. top and bottom round). These cuts make a savoury stock, but give rather dry boiled beef.

Leg of beef (comprising the whole of the upper tibial part, sold in transversal sections), shin, which also makes good stock.

Shoulder of beef (U.S. chuck): *shoulder blade, neck* and *ox-cheek* furnish cuts which also produce good stock. Boned ox-cheek makes quite good stock.

Various sub-divisions of the shoulder: *clod, chuck end* (U.S. arm and blade pot roast), the *gemellus muscle* (situated in front of the shoulder blade) and *macreuse**—all of which are cuts of the second category—produce good stock. To these various cuts butchers usually add, as 'make-weight', pieces of *knuckle, leg,* and other bony and gristly parts.

Rib of beef, which makes excellent stock, is subdivided into fore-ribs (five ribs situated in the shoulder part), and middle-rib, (four ribs from the eighth to the eleventh rib); and *chuck end of the clod* (three ribs).

The *top of sirloin*, and the *flank* which with the lower end of the breast (*gristle, middle* and *thick end*) constitute the *pis de boeuf.*

In addition to the basis cuts of meat mentioned above, it is a good idea to add chicken bones and giblets (previously browned in the oven) to the stock-pot, as this improves the stock.

Marrow bones (broken into chunks and each wrapped in a piece of muslin) can also be added. The cooked marrow can be extracted and spread on bread or toast.

Ingredients. For 5½ quarts (5 litres) of consommé: *Basic nutritive elements:* 4 pounds (2 kilos) of lean beef, 3 pounds (1 kilo, 500 grams) of beef knuckle (with bone).

Basic aromatics: 3 or 4 big carrots (750 grams), 2 or 3 turnips (400 grams), 1 parsnip (100 grams), 3 to 4 leeks (350 grams) tied in a bundle, 2 stalks of celery, one medium-sized onion with one or two cloves stuck in it, one clove of garlic, a sprig of thyme and a quarter of a bay leaf (optional).

Method. Tie the meat with string and put it into a big stock-pot (the earthenware kind are the best). Add 8 quarts (7 litres) of cold water.

Bring to the boil. When boiling is established a layer of slightly coagulated albumen forms on the surface. Remove this carefully, i.e. skim the stock-pot clean.

Season with 2 tablespoons (35 grams) of coarse salt.

Put all the vegetables indicated above into the stock-pot. Simmer very slowly, so that the boiling is hardly perceptible, for 5 hours.

Remove surplus fat carefully and strain the stock through a cloth (rinsed and wrung out) or through a very fine strainer.

Stock should not go on cooking for longer than 5 hours. As in this space of time—although it is quite long—it is impossible to extract by slow but constant boiling all the goodness out of the bones, they can be broken up and used for making first stock which should be boiled for a long time and can be used for adding to the stock-pot.

Or: Put the bones, broken into small pieces, into the stock-pot and cover with cold water. Bring to the boil, skim, add salt and simmer slowly for 2½ hours.

Then, into the *boiling stock* put in the meat, boned and tied with string.

Bring to the boil again, skim and season. Add the vegetables. Simmer slowly for about 4 hours.

Do not put in all the salt at the beginning; complete the seasoning at the end of cooking, if necessary.

To serve or use stock. Skim off fat and strain the stock. Use it for making soup, add to it sliced bread, various pasta products and other garnishings, as indicated in the recipe.

Use the meat and the vegetables as described in the recipe for *Boiled beef with root vegetables.* See BEEF.

Clarified consommé or consommé riche—*Ingredients,* for 2 quarts, 6 ounces (2 litres) of consommé:

Nutritive element: 1½ pounds (750 grams) of lean beef, chopped, with all sinews and gristle removed.

Aromatic elements: 1 large carrot (100 grams), ½ cup (100 grams) of white part of leeks.

Clarifying element: 1 raw white of egg.

Liquid: 3 quarts plus 1 cup (3 litres) of simple stock.

Method. Put the chopped meat, vegetables cut in very small dice and the white of egg into a saucepan. Mix and add cold or warm stock.

Bring to the boil, stirring constantly with a wooden spoon or with a whisk.

When boiling is established, draw the saucepan to the edge of the burner and simmer very slowly for an hour and a half.

To serve. Remove surplus fat and strain the consommé through a napkin.

Simple chicken consommé. CONSOMMÉ SIMPLE DE VOLAILLE—Proceed as described in the recipe for *Simple consommé,* adding to the nutritive elements indicated a small chicken, previously browned in the oven, or an equivalent quantity of chicken giblets and carcases.

Clarified chicken consommé. CONSOMMÉ DE VOLAILLES CLARIFIÉ—Proceed, using the same ingredients, as described in the recipe for *Clarified consommé,* adding to the beef 3 sets of chopped chicken giblets. It is also recommended to add a small chicken, previously browned in the oven, and the bones of a roast chicken, if available. To give the consommé the desired flavour, the addition of chicken is almost essential. The chicken can later be made up into various dishes.

Simple fish consommé. CONSOMMÉ SIMPLE DE POISSON—*Ingredients,* for 5½ quarts (5 litres) of consommé:

Nutritive elements: 3 pounds (1 kilo 500 grams) of pike (or other fish), 20 ounces (600 grams) of bones of sole (or other fish), 2 pounds (1 kilo) turbot (or other fish) head.

Aromatic elements: 1½ cups (300 grams) of chopped onions, 2 to 3 leeks (200 grams), a handful of parsley (80 grams), 3 tablespoons (30 grams) of chopped celery, a pinch of thyme (3 grams), one bay leaf.

Seasoning: 6 tablespoons (40 grams) of coarse salt.

Liquid: 5½ quarts (5 litres) of water, 3 cups (6 decilitres) of white wine.

Method. Proceed as described in the recipe for *Simple consommé.* Add onions cut in round slices and finely sliced leeks.

Boil slowly for 45 minutes.

To serve: Strain the stock through a napkin and use as indicated in the recipe.

Note. When resources allow it the proportion of fish can be increased. The fish, after cooking, can be used for making croquettes, or can be served in shells, *au gratin,* or any other way.

Clarified fish consommé. CONSOMMÉ DE POISSON CLARIFIÉ—For 2 quarts, 6 ounces (2 litres):

Nutritive elements: 1½ pounds (750 grams) of the flesh of pike or whiting (net weight, without bones or skins).

Aromatic elements: 6 tablespoons (75 grams) of chopped leeks, several sprigs of parsley (25 grams).

Clarifying element: 2 whites of egg.

Liquid: 4½ pints (2½ litres) of fish stock.

Method. Proceed as described in the recipe for clarified beef consommé. Simmer very slowly for 30 minutes.

To serve. Strain the consommé and use as indicated in the recipe.

Simple game consommé. CONSOMMÉ SIMPLE DE GIBIER—This can only be made in places where game is plentiful enough to be able to put it into the stock-pot in this way. Game which is too old to be cooked in any other way is used for this consommé.

Ingredients, For 4½ quarts (5 litres) of consommé:

Nutritive elements: 4 pounds (2 kilos) of shoulder and neck of venison, 2 pounds (1 kilo) of fore-quarter of hare, or an equivalent quantity of rabbit, one old pheasant, one old partridge.

Aromatic elements: 2 to 3 carrots (300 grams), 1½ cups (300 grams) of chopped onions, 3 leeks (300 grams), ¾ cup (150 grams) of chopped celery, several sprigs of parsley (50 grams), 2 cloves of garlic, 2 sprigs of thyme, one bay leaf, 1⅝ ounces (50 grams) of juniper berries, 3 cloves.

Seasoning: 2½ tablespoons (40 grams) of coarse salt.

Liquid: 5½ quarts (6 litres) of cold water.

Method. Brown all the game in the oven and put in the stock-pot. Add cold water and bring to the boil.

Skim, season, and add the vegetables, lightly browned in the fat rendered by the game. Add a *bouquet garni**, the juniper berries and the cloves in a herb bag.

Draw the stock-pot to the edge of the stove and simmer slowly for 3½ hours.

To serve. Remove surplus fat and strain the stock. Proceed to use as indicated in the recipe.

Note. The game which is served for making this consommé can be used for preparing patties, croquettes, hashes, etc., as well as for purée and *salpicon**.

Petite marmite—For 6 persons:

Nutritive elements: ¾ pound (400 grams) of top of rump, ½ pound (200 grams) of rib of beef, 3 ounces (100 grams) marrow bone, 2 sets of chicken giblets.

Aromatic elements: 2 to 3 small carrots (100 grams) 1 small turnip (75 grams), 2 to 3 leeks (75 grams) (white part only, cut in chunks), 2 small onions, quarter of a head of celery (about 50 grams), quarter of a small head of cabbage (about 100 grams).

Liquid: 4½ pints (2½ litres) of cold simple consommé.

Method. Put the meat, the marrow bone (wrapped in a piece of muslin) and the cold consommé into a small pan. Bring to the boil and skim.

Add carrots, turnips, cut down to uniform size and shape (blanching the vegetables, if they are old); leeks, cut in chunks and blanched; small onions lightly cooked on the stove; celery, blanched and cut into small pieces; cabbage, also blanched and rolled into a tight ball. Simmer very gently for 4 hours, adding a little stock from time to time, to make up for the loss of liquid by evaporation.

One hour before serving, add the chicken giblets.

To serve. Remove surplus fat, but bear in mind that petite marmite consommé should have a few light circlets of fat on the surface. Remove the marrow bone, unwrap and put it back into the pot.

Serve in the same pot with bread, sliced and dried in the oven, or with rusks.

Note. The chicken giblets can be browned in the oven before being put in the stock.

The cabbage, instead of being put to cook in the pot, can be cooked separately, in good, fat stock, and added to the consommé just before serving.

Petite marmite with chicken. PETITE MARMITE AVEC VOLAILLE—Proceed as described in the above recipe.

Add a small chicken, previously browned in the oven.

Serve in the same way as ordinary *Petite marmite.*

Pot-au-feu—A kind of home-made family soup, prepared in earthenware cast-iron or aluminium utensils in the same way as *Petite marmite.*

This preparation provides two dishes: the soup, which should be delicious (toasted bread, various pasta products, rice and, in general, all garnishings suitable for clear soups, are added to it), and meat and vegetables. These two dishes, simple as they are, are always greatly appreciated. Gherkins, samphire pickled in vinegar, coarse salt and mustard are served with boiled beef. *Tomato sauce,* grated horse-radish or *Horse-radish sauce* can also be served with it (see SAUCE).

Note. The classical *pot-au-feu* is made of beef and chicken, when available (or chicken giblets). In certain regions of France, however, it is customary to add veal, pork and sometimes mutton as well.

The chicken is sometimes replaced by duck or turkey.

Whatever meat is used for this dish, the method is the same. It is important only to make sure that these various meats are given long enough time to cook.

Pot-au-feu à l'albigeoise—*Method.* Prepare the pot-au-feu as described in the recipe for *Petite marmite*, but using the following nutritive elements: silverside (U.S. bottom round), veal knuckle, salted pork knuckle. When all the ingredients are nearly cooked, add a dry country sausage and, a few minutes before serving the soup, a quarter of *confit d'oie* (preserved goose).

This *pot-au-feu* should have plenty of vegetables, particularly cabbage.

Serve as described in the recipe for ordinary *pot-au-feu.*

Pot-au-feu à la béarnaise, called Poule-au-pot—Prepare the *pot-au-feu* as described in the preceding recipe adding a chicken stuffed with a forcemeat made of fresh pork and chopped Bayonne ham, mixed with chopped onion, garlic, parsley and chicken liver.

Serve as described in the recipe for ordinary *pot-au-feu.*

Pot-au-feu à la languedocienne—Prepare like ordinary *pot-au-feu*, adding a piece of fat bacon previously blanched and rinsed in cold water.

Serve as indicated in the recipe for ordinary *pot-au-feu.*

CONSOMMÉS WITH GARNISHES. CONSOMMÉS GARNIS—The recipes which follow have been worked out for five persons and are based on various kinds of consommés: beef, chicken, game, fish. The quantity of consommé required is 6¾ cups (1½ litres).

Under the heading GARNISHES, directions for the supplementary elements of these consommés will be found.

In some of these recipes the consommé has to be thickened with arrowroot, starch or tapioca. This liaison should be very light, just sufficient to give the consommé a mellow texture.

Consommé à l'alsacienne—Ordinary consommé. Add sauerkraut cooked in stock and Strasbourg sausages, poached, skinned and cut into round slices.

Consommé à l'ambassadrice—Chicken consommé thickened with tapioca, garnished with 24 small, truffled chicken *quenelles** and 12 small *profiteroles** filled with a purée of foie gras, and chervil leaves.

Note. All garnished consommés, thickened with arrowroot or tapioca, should be strained through a muslin cloth immediately after the liaison has been effected.

Consommé à l'américaine I—Proceed as described in the recipe for *Consommé à la madrilène II.* Serve cold in cups.

Consommé à l'américaine II—Chicken consommé thickened with arrowroot, garnished with gombos (okra or ladies' fingers) blanched in salted water, drained and cooked in stock tomatoes, peeled, pressed, cut into dice and cooked in stock and chervil leaves.

Consommé à l'amiral—Fish consommé thickened with arrowroot. Garnish with 24 small *quenelles** made of *Pike forcemeat* (see FORCEMEAT) flavoured with crayfish butter, 6 oysters poached, de-bearded and cut in half and 2 tablespoons of a *julienne** of truffles cooked in Madeira. Sprinkle with chervil leaves.

Consommé à l'ancienne—See *Consommé croûte au pot à l'ancienne.*

Consommé à la basquaise—Ordinary consommé garnished with 2 tablespoons of a *julienne** of sweet pimentos cooked in stock, 2 tablespoons of diced tomatoes cooked in stock and 4 tablespoons of rice cooked in stock. Sprinkle with chervil leaves.

Consommé Beauharnais—Chicken consommé thickened with arrowroot, garnished with *paupiettes** of lettuce, poached in stock and cut into round slices, asparagus tips and a *julienne** of truffles. Sprinkle with chervil leaves.

Consommé with birds' nests. CONSOMMÉ AUX NIDS D'HIRONDELLES—Prepare a good strong chicken consommé, clarify it and strain through a napkin.

Soak swallows' nests in cold water for 2 hours. When they swell and become transparent, clean them carefully, i.e. remove bits of egg shell and other foreign matter which they may contain, even though they have already been cleaned before being sold. Blanch these nests for 5 or 6 minutes and drain.

Put the nests into boiling consommé. Poach, keeping them on a gentle but sustained boil, for 45 minutes. Serve boiling hot. This soup is always served in cups.

Consommé Bizet—Chicken consommé thickened with tapioca, garnished with very small *Chicken quenelles* (see QUENELLES) mixed with chopped tarragon leaves. Sprinkle with chervil leaves.

Serve with very small *profiteroles** filled with a *brunoise** of vegetables.

Consommé à la bourgeoise—Ordinary consommé, garnished with stock-pot vegetables, carrots and turnips cut in small dice, diced potatoes, boiled in stock and chervil leaves.

Consommé Brancas—Ordinary consommé garnished with 2 tablespoons of *chiffonnade** of lettuce and sorrel, 2 tablespoons of vermicelli poached in stock, 2 tablespoons of *julienne** of mushrooms fried in butter and chervil leaves.

Consommé with bread—CONSOMMÉ AU PAIN—Serve boiling consommé with a plate of bread (long French) finely sliced and dried in the oven and with grated cheese.

Consommé Brillat-Savarin—Chicken consommé, thickened with tapioca, garnished with 2 tablespoons of *julienne** of breast of chicken, 2 tablespoons of savoury pancakes (crêpes) cut into lozenges, 2 tablespoons of chiffonnade of lettuce and sorrel and chervil leaves.

Consommé brunoise—Cut 2 to 3 small carrots (150 grams), 1 small turnip (100 grams), 2 to 3 leeks (75 grams) (white part), 2 tablespoons (25 grams) of chopped onion and 4 tablespoons (50 grams) of the white part of celery (diced small).

Season with salt and a pinch of sugar. Cook gently in 3 tablespoons (50 grams) of butter, with a lid on, for 25 minutes.

Moisten with 1½ cups (3 decilitres) of consommé and cook for an hour. 25 minutes before serving, add a tablespoon of fresh garden peas and a tablespoon of diced French beans.

To serve. Add 6 cups (1¼ litres) consommé. Boil for a few minutes, skim and sprinkle with chervil leaves.

Note. Fresh garden peas and French beans can be replaced by tinned (canned), in which case they are added only at the last moment, just before serving.

Consommé brunoise with various garnishes—Prepare the soup as described above. Add garnish, such as pasta products, tapioca, pearl barley, rice, semolina, vermicelli etc., which can either be cooked in the consommé itself, or separately.

Note. Consommé brunoise can also be served with very small poached eggs, quenelles, profiteroles, and ordinary *royale* (savoury custard, cut into slices and then into fancy shapes) or a *royale* of vegetables (see GARNISHES).

Consommé à la cancalaise—Fish consommé thickened with arrowroot, garnished with 24 small pike *quenelles**, 12 oysters, poached, de-bearded and cut in half, and chervil leaves.

Consommé Célestine—Chicken consommé thickened with tapioca, garnished with 2 tablespoons of small round slices of rolled pancakes, stuffed with chicken forcemeat, and chervil leaves.

Consommé chasseur—Game consommé, thickened with tapioca, garnished with 2 tablespoons of *julienne** of mushrooms, cooked in ¼ cup (½ decilitre) of Madeira wine, and chervil leaves. Serve with 20 small *profiteroles** filled with game purée.

Consommé aux cheveux d'ange—Ordinary consommé, garnished with 4 tablespoons of very fine, poached vermicelli.

Consommé with chicken giblets. CONSOMMÉ AUX ABATIS DE VOLAILLE—Prepare a pot-au-feu in the usual manner, put into it 4 chicken pinions (wing tips) and 2 necks, cut into 3 or 4 pieces and tied in a piece of muslin.

Serve the consommé with the pinions (wing tips) and the pot-au-feu vegetables cut into small pieces.

Consommé with stuffed chicken giblets. CONSOMMÉ AUX ABATIS DE VOLAILLE FARCIS—Prepare chicken consommé in the usual manner and poach in it 4 chicken pinions (wing tips), boned and stuffed with quenelle forcemeat.

Strain the consommé through a napkin and put the giblets into it.

In home cookery, this consommé is prepared using a full set of giblets, consisting of 2 pinions, neck (with a part of the head left attached), the skinned gizzard and 2 feet.

Usually, however, it is made only with pinions, stuffed or not, as the case may be. This consommé is frequently served under the name of *Consommé with chicken pinions*.

Consommé with chicken pinions (wing tips). CONSOMMÉ AUX AILERONS—Using chicken pinions proceed as described in the recipe for *Consommé with chicken giblets*.

Although chicken pinions are mainly used for this consommé, it can also be made of turkey and duck pinions.

Consommé with chicken pinions (wing tips) and rice. CONSOMMÉ AUX AILERONS AU RIZ—Prepare the consommé as described in the recipe for *Consommé with chicken giblets*. Add 2 good tablespoons of rice, blanched and cooked in stock.

Consommé à la chilienne—Chicken consommé garnished with rice cooked in stock and a *salpicon** of green pimentos, also cooked in stock sprinkled with chervil leaves. Serve *diablotins** at the same time.

Consommé à la Colbert—Chicken consommé garnished with a *brunoise** of all sorts of spring vegetables, 4 very small poached eggs and chervil leaves.

Consommé Colnet—Chicken consommé garnished with a *brunoise** of carrots and celery, lightly cooked in butter, *oeufs filés* (beaten egg, strained into the consommé through a fine strainer, to look like threads—see GARNISHES, *Spun eggs*) and chervil leaves.

Consommé Commodore—Fish consommé, thickened with arrowroot, garnished with clams, poached, debearded and cut in small pieces and diced tomatoes cooked in stock.

Consommé à la Crécy—Chicken consommé, thickened with tapioca, garnished with a *brunoise** of carrots, lightly cooked in butter, and chervil leaves.

Consommé with garden cress. CONSOMMÉ AU CRESSON ALÉNOIS—Add to a quart (litre) of boiling consommé, prepared in the usual manner, a handful of garden cress, having previously picked the leaves off the stalks, blanched them for a minute in salted water, drained and rinsed in cold water.

Consommé croûte au pot—Pot-au-feu consommé, garnished with the stock-pot vegetables (carrots, turnips, leeks and cabbage), cut in small uniform pieces.

Serve with hollowed-out crusts of bread dried in the oven, or sprinkled with stock-pot fat and browned lightly in the oven.

Consommé croûte au pot à l'ancienne—As above. Serve with hollowed-out crusts of bread, filled with chopped stock-pot vegetables and browned in the oven or under a grill.

Consommé Dalayrac—Chicken consommé thickened with tapioca, garnished with a *julienne** of breast of chicken, mushrooms and truffles.

Consommé aux diablotins—Chicken consommé thickened with tapioca. Serve with 24 round slices of bread, covered with cheese and browned as described in the recipe for *diablotins**.

Consommé à l'écossaise—Ordinary consommé, with pearl barley cooked in the consommé, garnished with a *julienne** of carrot, celery, and leek, lightly cooked in butter, and chervil leaves.

Consommé Edward VII—Chicken consommé, thickened with arrowroot, garnished with a *royale** of truffles, thin slices of *Chicken loaf* (cold) and asparagus tips. At the last moment, add a few tablespoons of port to the consommé.

Consommé à la flip—Chicken consommé, thickened with tapioca, garnished with a *julienne** of lettuce and leeks, lightly cooked in butter and dropped into the consommé, cooked ham, cut in *julienne** strips and chervil leaves.

Consommé Florence—Ordinary consommé, garnished with vermicelli cooked in stock. At the last moment put into the boiling consommé a *julienne** of uncooked truffles. Cover the saucepan and simmer without allowing it to boil.

Consommé à la florentine—Chicken consommé with *ouefs filés* (see GARNISHES, *Spun eggs*), 2 tablespoons of rice cooked in stock and chervil leaves.

Consommé Florette—Chicken consommé thickened with tapioca, garnished with a *julienne** of leek, lightly cooked in butter and dropped into consommé, and rice cooked in stock. Serve with very thick fresh cream and grated Parmesan cheese.

Consommé à la gauloise—Chicken consommé thickened with tapioca, garnished with very small, poached cocks' combs (if small cocks' combs are not available, cut ordinary ones into pieces), very small cocks' kidneys, pancakes cut into *julienne** strips and chervil leaves.

Consommé with gombos (okra or ladies' fingers) à l'orientale. CONSOMMÉ AUX GOMBOS À L'ORIENTALE—Fennel-flavoured chicken consommé, thickened with rice or potato flour, garnished with gombos (okra), blanched, drained and cooked in stock, and rice also cooked in stock and spiced with a pinch of cayenne pepper.

Consommé Grimaldi—Chicken consommé with tomato juice, garnished with a *julienne** of celeriac cooked in stock, tomato *royale** and chervil leaves.

Consommé à la hollandaise—Consommé seasoned with paprika, garnished with 2 tablespoons of small *Quenelles of calf's liver*, 2 tablespoons of bone marrow, cut in dice and poached in stock, and chervil leaves.

Consommé houblonnière—Ordinary consommé thickened with rice or potato flour, garnished with hop shoots, cooked in stock, and chervil leaves.

Consommé Hudson—Fish consommé with tomato juice, thickened with arrowroot, garnished with crab flesh, cut into small pieces, diced cucumbers cooked in stock and chervil leaves.

Consommé à l'impériale—Proceed as described in the recipe for *Consommé à la gauloise*, replacing the savoury pancakes by rice cooked in stock and adding some fresh garden peas, cooked in water and drained.

Consommé à l'infante—Chicken consommé thickened

with arrowroot. Serve with 24 small *profiteroles** filled with a purée of foie gras mixed with thick chicken *velouté* (see SAUCE).

Consommé à l'irlandaise—Ordinary consommé with a *salpicon** of mutton (cooked in the consommé), pearl barley, stock pot vegetables cut into small dice and chervil leaves.

Consommé à l'italienne—Chicken consommé, garnished with three kinds of *royale* (see GARNISHES), cut into dice or round slices: *royale* of chicken purée, *royale* of spinach purée and *royale* of tomato purée. Sprinkle with chervil leaves.

Consommé julienne—Cut 2 to 3 small carrots (100 grams), 1 small turnip (75 grams), 2 leeks (40 grams) (white part), 3 tablespoons (40 grams) of chopped onions and 3 tablespoons (40 grams) of tender celery into very thin sticks 1 inch long.

Season these vegetables with a pinch of salt and another of sugar. Soften in 3 tablespoons (50 grams) of butter, with a lid on, on a slow fire for 25 minutes.

Add ½ cup (50 grams) of cabbage heart, cut into *julienne** strips, blanched and drained, and a similarly shredded, medium-sized lettuce.

Cook everything together, with the lid on, for 45 minutes.

Moisten with 1½ cups (3 decilitres) of consommé and finish cooking, simmering gently, for 35 minutes.

25 minutes before serving, add ⅓ cup (25 grams) of sorrel shredded into a fine *chiffonnade** and a tablespoon of fresh garden peas.

To serve. Add 5½ cups (1¼ litres) of consommé, boil for a few seconds, skim, add chervil leaves.

Consommé julienne with various garnishes—This consommé, based on meat, fish or vegetable stock, can be served with the following garnishes: pasta products, pearl barley, rice, semolina, tapioca, vermicelli.

*Quenelles**, *profiteroles** or ordinary *royale** can also be added to it.

Consommé Léopold—Consommé thickened with semolina. At the last moment, add 2 tablespoons of a *julienne** of sorrel, lightly cooked in butter, and chervil leaves.

Consommé Leverrier—Chicken consommé, thickened with tapioca, garnished with various *royales** cut out in the shape of stars and sprinkled with chervil leaves.

Consommé with macaroni—CONSOMMÉ AU MACARONI—Ordinary consommé, garnished with macaroni, cut in very small pieces, three-quarters cooked in salted water, drained and finished off in the consommé. Serve grated cheese separately.

Consommé à la madrilène I—Chicken consommé with 1 cup (2 decilitres) of concentrated tomato pulp added to it, seasoned with a pinch of cayenne pepper.

This is mostly served very cold, and always in cups.

Consommé à la madrilène II—Prepare the consommé, adding to it during clarification 1½ cups (3 decilitres) of raw tomato pulp, rubbed through a sieve.

Strain the consommé through a muslin cloth, pressing lightly, and chill before serving.

Note. Sweet pimentos, cut in dice and cooked in stock, are often added to *Consommé madrilène*.

Consommé Mercédès—Chicken consommé, with ¼ cup (½ decilitre) of sherry and a pinch of cayenne pepper added to it, garnished with 2 tablespoons of cocks' kidneys, skinned and cut in very thin slices, 2 tablespoons of cocks' combs, split in two and cut into star shapes; and chervil leaves.

Consommé à la messine—*Petite marmite* consommé, with very small chipolata sausages, poached and skinned, and small cabbage rolls.

Consommé à la neige de Florence—Serve separately, as an accompaniment to the boiling consommé, *Neige de Florence*, which the guests add to their soup themselves.

Neige de Florence, a pasta product which is found in shops, is a substance presented in the shape of extremely fine white flakes.

Consommé Nesselrode—Game consommé with *profiteroles** filled with *Chestnut purée soubisée* (mixture of onion and chestnut purées) and a *salpicon** of mushrooms.

Consommé Nimrod—Game consommé, thickened with arrowroot, flavoured with 2 tablespoons of port, garnished with 4 tablespoons of very small quenelles made of game forcemeat mixed with chopped truffles.

Consommé with noodles. CONSOMMÉ AUX NOUILLES—Ordinary consommé with 2 to 3 ounces (70 to 90 grams) of fresh noodles, three-quarters cooked in water, drained and finished off in the consommé. Serve with grated cheese.

Consommé à l'Orléans—Chicken consommé thickened with tapioca, garnished with 4 tablespoons of very small quenelles made of three kinds of *Chicken forcemeat* (see FORCEMEAT): one with cream, one with tomato and one with pistachio nuts (or spinach). Add a sprinkling of chervil leaves.

Oxtail consommé or soup à la française. CONSOMMÉ QUEUE DE BOEUF À LA FRANÇAISE—Put 4 pounds (2 kilos) of oxtail, cut into uniform chunks, with 1 pound (500 grams) of veal knuckle into a stock-pot. Add 12 cups (3 litres) of white stock. Bring to the boil, skin, season, add the usual vegetable garnish and simmer gently so that boiling is hardly perceptible for 5 hours.

Strain the stock. Pour it into a pot into which you have put 13 ounces (400 grams) of lean beef and veal, chopped and browned in butter and sprinkled with a good tablespoon of arrowroot (cornstarch). Clarify, strain the stock through a muslin cloth or a fine strainer. Add the pieces of oxtail and 2 cups (250 grams) of carrots and turnips, scooped out to look like small, uniform balls and cooked in stock.

Note. This soup used to be called *Grand hochepot*. Instead of the carrots and turnips scooped out into balls, which it is usual to put in it nowadays, in bygone days thinly sliced carrots and turnips, stewed in fat stock, used to be added to it.

Consommé à la parisienne—Chicken consommé with a macédoine of vegetables, round slices of ordinary *royale* (see GARNISHES) and chervil leaves.

Consommé with pasta products. CONSOMMÉ AUX PÂTES D'ITALIE—Pour 2½ to 3 ounces (75 to 90 grams) of pasta products into 6 cups (1½ litres) of boiling consommé. Cook, keeping up slow but sustained boiling from 8 to 12 minutes, depending on the nature of the pasta.

Serve with grated cheese.

Consommé with pearl barley. CONSOMMÉ À L'ORGE PERLÉ—Ordinary consommé with ⅓ cup (75 grams) of pearl barley, washed in warm water, blanched and cooked in white stock for 2½ hours.

Blanched pearl barley can be cooked in the consommé.

Consommé Pépita—Chicken consommé with tomato juice, seasoned with paprika, garnished with a *Tomato royale* (see GARNISHES, *Royale*) cut in dice, peeled pimentos, diced and cooked in stock and chervil leaves.

Consommé aux perles—Pour from ¾ to 1 cup (100 to 125 grams) of *perles* into 6 cups (1½ litres) of boiling consommé. Cook on sustained heat from 20 to 25 minutes.

Consommé with plover or lapwing eggs. CONSOMMÉ AUX OEUFS DE PLUVIER, DE VANNEAU—Chicken consommé with poached plover or lapwing eggs.

Consommé with poached eggs. CONSOMMÉ AUX OEUFS POCHÉS—Consommé garnished with six small poached eggs.

Consommé princesse—Chicken consommé thickened with tapioca, garnished with very small chicken forcemeat *quenelles*, 2 tablespoons of green asparagus tips and chervil leaves.

Consommé Princess Alice—Chicken consommé thickened with tapioca, garnished with a tablespoon of a *julienne** of artichoke hearts, a tablespoon of a *chiffonnade** of lettuce, 2 tablespoons of fine vermicelli cooked in stock and chervil leaves.

Consommé printanier—Consommé with all kinds of spring vegetables added to it, sprinkled with chervil leaves.

Consommé printanier aux perles or au riz—As above. Reduce the proportion of vegetables and add *perles* or rice cooked in stock, sprinkle with chervil leaves.

Note. Poached eggs, *quenelles*, *profiteroles*, *royales*, etc., can also be served in *consommé printanier*.

Consommé with profiteroles. CONSOMMÉ AUX PROFITEROLES—Consommé thickened with tapioca, sprinkled with chervil leaves.

Serve *profiteroles** filled with some sort of a purée at the same time.

Consommé with quenelles. CONSOMMÉ AUX QUENELLES—Clear or thickened consommé garnished with chicken or other quenelles and sprinkled with chervil leaves.

Consommé Rachel—Chicken consommé, thickened with tapioca, garnished with very small chicken forcemeat quenelles, small lettuce rolls, filled with purée of chicken *à la crème*, and chervil leaves.

Consommé with ravioli. CONSOMMÉ AU RAVIOLI—thickened or clear consommé with 24 small ravioli, filled according to taste and sprinkled with chervil leaves.

Consommé à la reine—Chicken consommé thickened with tapioca, garnished with ordinary *royale* (see GARNISHES), a *julienne** of breast of chicken and chervil leaves.

Consommé à la Reine-Jeanne—Chicken consommé thickened with tapioca, garnished with very small chicken quenelles and chervil leaves.

Serve with *profiteroles**, filled with a chicken purée bound with almond milk.

Consommé with rice. CONSOMMÉ AU RIZ—Consommé to which from ¼ to ⅓ cup (60 to 80 grams) of rice, cooked in white stock, is added at the last moment.

Serve with grated cheese.

Consommé à la royale—Chicken consommé, thickened with tapioca, garnished with ordinary *royale**, cut in dice, in round slices or in any other way so long as it is done very neatly, and sprinkled with chervil leaves. See GARNISHES.

Consommé with sago. CONSOMMÉ AU SAGOU—Using sago, proceed as described in the recipe for *Consommé aux perles*.

Consommé à la Saint-Hubert—Game consommé, thickened with tapioca, garnished with a game purée *royale* and a *julienne** of mushrooms cooked in butter with Madeira.

Consommé with salep. CONSOMMÉ AU SALEP—Using salep, proceed as described in the recipe for *Consommé aux perles*.

Consommé with semolina. CONSOMMÉ À LA SEMOULE—Pour about ½ cup (75 to 90 grams) of semolina into 6 cups (1½ litres) of boiling consommé. Simmer on a sustained boiling from 18 to 20 minutes. Serve grated cheese separately.

Consommé à la strasbourgeoise—Consommé flavoured with a light infusion of juniper berries, thickened with rice or potato flour, garnished with 4 tablespoons of a *julienne** of red cabbage cooked in stock and a Strasbourg sausage, poached, skinned and cut in thin round slices. Serve with grated horse-radish.

Consommé au tapioca—Pour ½ to ¾ cup (from 80 to 100 grams) of tapioca in a rain into 6 cups (1½ litres) of boiling consommé. Stir to avoid formation of lumps and cook, keeping up sustained boiling, from 15 to 20 minutes. Serve with grated Parmesan cheese.

Consommé au vermicelli—Pour from 2½ to 3 ounces (75 to 90 grams) of vermicelli in a rain into 6 cups (1½ litres) of boiling consommé. Cook, keeping up sustained boiling, from 5 to 12 minutes, depending on the thickness of the vermicelli. Serve grated Parmesan cheese separately.

COLD CONSOMMÉS. CONSOMMÉS FROIDS—These consommés, intended for luncheons or suppers, are generally served in cups.

Their preparation is similar to that of hot consommés. They should be strongly flavoured and very clear.

Variously flavoured cold consommés can be made. Here are some of the more usual kind:

Celery-flavoured consommé. CONSOMMÉ À L'ESSENCE DE CÉLERI—Prepare 6 cups (1½ litres) of consommé in the usual manner. Clarify and add half a bunch of finely chopped celery. Strain through a napkin and chill before serving.

Consommé flavoured with game fumet. CONSOMMÉ AU FUMET DE GIBIER—Prepare as described in the recipe for *Game consommé*.

Tarragon flavoured consommé. CONSOMMÉ À L'ESSENCE D'ESTRAGON—About 6 minutes before straining the consommé, add to it 4 tablespoons (20 grams) of fresh tarragon leaves. Leave to infuse without boiling. Strain and serve as described above.

Tomato-flavoured consommé—See *Consommé à la madrilène*.

Truffle-flavoured consommé. CONSOMMÉ À L'ESSENCE DE TRUFFES—Add to the clarified consommé, 2 ounces (60 grams) of parings of fresh truffles. Strain, remove surplus fat and add 2 tablespoons of Madeira or port.

Consommé with various wines. CONSOMMÉ AU VIN—Clarify and strain the consommé and, when it is nearly cold, add to it various wines, such as Madeira, malmsey, Marsala, port, sherry, etc., allowing about ⅓ cup (8 to 10 centilitres) per quart (litre) of consommé.

THICK SOUPS. POTAGES LIÉS—*Cream*, *Purée and Velouté* soups are classed in this category. Cream soups are composed of a purée of shell-fish, vegetables, fish, or poultry, thickened with *Béchamel*.

Purées of starchy vegetables or leguminous plants are composed of vegetables rich in starch, such as sweet potatoes, potatoes, etc.; of leguminous plants, white or red dried beans, kidney beans, lentils, split peas, etc. These ingredients, being sufficiently rich in starch content, require no additional element for the purpose of liaison.

Purées of fresh vegetables, less rich in starch, are thickened with additional elements: cooked rice or a purée of some other vegetable, richer in starch content.

Meat, poultry or fish purées are composed of these various ingredients with the addition of supplementary liaison: rice, bread reduced to pulp, purées of leguminous plants or cereals.

Shell-fish purée soups, better known as *bisques*, which are thickened with rice, or according to the old method, with bread reduced to pulp, are also classified in this category.

Veloutés are also composed of some sort of a purée, bound with velouté and with a final liaison of yolks of egg and cream.

CREAM SOUPS. POTAGES CRÈMES—We class in this category soups, the basic element of which (vegetable, meat, fish or shell-fish purée) includes a certain quantity of *Béchamel* and is finished off with fresh cream.

Like all other thickened soups, cream soups can be garnished with pasta products, rice, barley, *perles*, tapioca, *julienne*, *brunoise*, *chiffonnade*, *quenelles*, *croûtons*, etc.

The recipes which follow have been worked out to serve 4 to 6 helpings.

Basic method of preparing cream soups (vegetable)—Shred and blanch the vegetable indicated and cook in butter, allowing 4 to 5 tablespoons (60 to 80 grams) of butter to 1 pound (500 grams) of vegetable.

Add 4 cups (8 decilitres) of *Béchamel* prepared by diluting a white roux, made of 2 tablespoons (35 grams) of butter and 3 tablespoons (45 grams) of flour, with 4¼ cups (8½ decilitres) of milk.

Simmer very gently from 12 to 18 minutes, depending on the nature of the vegetables used.

Rub through a sieve. Dilute with a few tablespoons of white consommé, or milk, if the soup is intended as Lenten fare. Heat and, at the last moment, blend in 2 decilitres of fresh cream.

Cream of artichoke soup. POTAGE CRÈME D'ARTICHAUTS—Cook eight big artichoke hearts, blanched and sliced, in butter. Add 4 cups (8 decilitres) of *Béchamel* and simmer gently for 12 minutes.

Rub through a sieve. Dilute with 1 cup (2 decilitres) of white consommé and heat to boiling point. Add seasoning if necessary. At the last moment, add 1 cup (2 decilitres) of fresh cream and a tablespoon of chervil leaves.

This can be made into a Lenten soup, by replacing consommé by milk.

Cream of asparagus soup (green). POTAGE CRÈME D'ASPERGES VERTES—As above, using green asparagus tips, blanched and cooked slowly in the *Béchamel*.

Cream of white asparagus, called Argenteuil. POTAGE CRÈME D'ASPERGES BLANCHES, DIT ARGENTEUIL—Using the tips of 2 pounds (1 kilo) of white asparagus, blanched and simmered in butter, in a covered pan, proceed as described in the recipe for *Cream of artichoke soup*.

Rub through a sieve as soon as the asparagus is put into the *Béchamel*.

Cream of barley soup I. POTAGE CRÈME D'ORGE—Wash 1¼ cups (300 grams) of pearl barley in several waters and soak it for an hour in warm water. Then, put into 4 cups (8 decilitres) of white consommé, add a sliced stalk of celery, bring to the boil and simmer gently for 2½ hours.

Rub through a sieve, dilute with a few tablespoons of consommé, heat and finish off with 1 cup (2 decilitres) of fresh cream. Add 2 tablespoons of pearl barley cooked in consommé.

The consommé can be replaced by milk.

Cream of barley soup II. POTAGE CRÈME D'ORGE—Using barley flour, proceed as described in the recipe for *Cream of oatmeal soup*.

Cream of bean soup. POTAGE CRÈME DE HARICOTS VERTS—Like *Cream of artichoke soup*, replacing the artichokes by 1 pound (500 grams) of French (string) beans, three-quarters blanched.

Cream of celery soup. POTAGE CRÈME DE CÉLERI—Using 2 bunches of celery, blanched and shredded, proceed as described in the recipe for *Cream of artichoke soup*.

Cream of chicken soup. POTAGE CRÈME DE VOLAILLE—Put a plump, tender chicken into a saucepan with 4 cups (8 decilitres) of white consommé. Season, add 2 leeks and a stalk of celery, tied in a bundle.

Bring to the boil, skim, cover and simmer gently.

When the chicken is cooked, drain and bone it. Keep the breast fillets for garnishing and pound the rest of the flesh finely in a mortar.

Rub this purée through a fine sieve. Mix it with 4 cups (8 decilitres) of *Béchamel*.

Heat to boiling point, lighten, if necessary, with a few tablespoons of the consommé in which the chicken was cooked, taste for seasoning. Strain through a sieve and, at the last moment, add ½ cup (1 decilitre) of fresh cream.

Dice the breast fillets and add to the soup.

Cream of chicory (U.S. endive) soup. POTAGE CRÈME D'ENDIVE—Slice the chicory and simmer it in butter in a covered pan without blanching. Finish off as described in the recipe for *Cream of endive soup*.

Cream of Chinese artichoke, Occa and Jerusalem artichoke. POTAGE CRÈME DE CROSNES, OXALIS, TOPINAMBOURS—Like *Cream of artichoke soup*, replacing the latter by 14 ounces (400 grams) of Chinese artichokes (or Occa, or Jerusalem artichoke), blanched and cooked in butter.

Cream of crayfish soup—See *Cream of shrimp soup*.

Cream of endive soup. POTAGE CRÈME DE CHICORÉE—Blanch, press and chop 1 pound (500 grams) of endives (choosing white and tender ones) and cook in butter.

Add 4 cups (8 decilitres) of *Béchamel sauce* (see SAUCE). Finish off as described in the recipe for *Cream of artichoke soup*.

Cream of leek soup, garnished with duchess potatoes

Cream of leek soup. POTAGE CRÈME DE POIREAUX—Shred and blanch 1 pound (500 grams) of leeks and cook them in butter in a covered pan.

Finish off as described in the recipe for *Cream of artichoke soup*.

Cream of lettuce soup. POTAGE CRÈME DE LAITUES—Using lettuce proceed as described in the recipe for *Cream of endive soup*.

Cream of lobster soup—See *Cream of shrimp soup*.

Cream of marrow soup. POTAGE CRÈME DE COURGETTES—Like *Cream of artichoke soup*, replacing the artichokes by 14 ounces (400 grams) of marrow, blanched and cooked in butter.

Cream of mushroom soup. POTAGE CRÈME DE CHAMPIGNONS—This soup is principally made of cultivated mushrooms or morels.

Slice the mushrooms, cook them in butter in a covered pan and proceed as described in the recipe for *Cream of artichoke soup.*

Cream of nettle soup. POTAGE CRÈME D'ORTIES—As *Cream of spinach soup*, replacing the spinach by young nettles.

Cream of oatmeal soup. POTAGE CRÈME D'AVOINE—Pour 3 tablespoons (150 grams) of oatmeal flour, diluted with 1 cup (2 decilitres) of cold milk, into 4 cups (8 decilitres) of boiling milk.

Stir until smooth, bring to the boil and simmer very gently for an hour and a half. Rub through a sieve. Re-heat.

At the last moment, add ½ cup (1 decilitre) of cream. The milk can be replaced by consommé.

Cream of rice soup I. POTAGE CRÈME DE RIZ—Cook 8 ounces of rice, blanched and drained, very gently for 45 minutes, in a pint of white consommé with a little butter.

Rub through a sieve and finish off as described in the recipe for *Cream of barley soup.*

Cream of rice soup II. POTAGE CRÈME DE RIZ—Using rice flour, proceed as described in the recipe for *Cream of oatmeal soup.*

Cream of shrimp (or other crustaceans). POTAGE CRÈME DE CREVETTES—Fry 4 tablespoons of *mirepoix** in butter, add to it 12 ounces of uncooked shrimps and sauté together. Season with salt and pepper, moisten with ¼ cup of white wine and a tablespoon of brandy which has been set alight. Cook for 5 minutes.

Pound the shrimps in a mortar (having kept a dozen shrimps' tails for the garnish).

Add 4 cups of *Béchamel.* Rub through a sieve.

Heat, dilute, if necessary, with a few tablespoons of white consommé, taste for seasoning and finish off with 1 cup of fresh cream.

Cream of spinach soup

Cream of spinach soup. POTAGE CRÈME D'ÉPINARDS—Cook 1 pound (500 grams) of spinach, blanched and pressed, in butter. Finish off with *Béchamel* as described in the recipe for *Cream of endive soup.*

Cream of spiny lobster soup—See *Cream of shrimp soup.*

Cream of watercress soup. POTAGE CRÈME DE CRESSON—Using 1 pound (500 grams) of watercress cooked in butter, proceed as for *Cream of endive soup.*

PURÉE SOUPS. POTAGES PURÉES—All the various purée soups described below can have pasta products, rice, tapioca, *perles*, pearl barley, *brunoise*, *julienne*, *chiffonnade*, etc., added to them.

All the recipes given below for vegetables and leguminous plants are intended for soups to be made with meat stock. These soups can also be prepared as Lenten fare by replacing stock by water and by using milk for the final liaison. Lean bacon, indicated as an ingredient for some of these soups, will, of course, be omitted from a Lenten soup.

The recipes which follow have been worked out to serve 5 or 6 helpings.

Purée of bean soup. POTAGE PURÉE DE FÈVES—Cook 1 pound (500 grams) of fresh shelled beans in 3 tablespoons (50 grams) of butter, with a branch of savory, a pinch of salt and ½ cup (1 decilitre) of water, keeping the pan covered. Rub through a fine sieve and finish off as described in the recipe for *Purée of celery soup.*

Purée of red haricot bean soup, called à la Condé. POTAGE PURÉE DE HARICOTS ROUGES, DITE À LA CONDÉ—Pick over and wash 2 cups (350 grams) of red haricot beans and put them into 7 cups (1½ litres) of cold water. Boil, skim, add 2½ teaspoons (15 grams) of salt, a medium-sized onion, studded with a clove, a quartered carrot, a *bouquet garni** and 2 ounces (50 grams) of lean bacon, cut in large dice, blanched and fried lightly. Add ¾ cup (1½ decilitres) of boiling red wine and leave uncovered to simmer very gently.

When the beans are quite done, drain them, remove the garnishing, and rub the beans through a fine sieve. Put the purée back into the pan, pour in the liquor, adding a few tablespoons of consommé if necessary. Strain, bring to the boil and blend in 4 tablespoons (60 grams) of butter.

Serve with small croûtons, fried in butter.

Note. The bacon may be omitted. In old culinary practice, this soup was made with game consommé and was sometimes garnished with rice, cooked in consommé, instead of croûtons.

Purée of white haricot bean soup, called Soissonnaise. POTAGE PURÉE DE HARICOTS BLANCS, DITE SOISSONNAISE—Using white haricot (shell) beans, proceed as described in the recipe for *Red haricot bean soup*, omitting the red wine.

Serve with small croûtons, fried in butter.

Purée of Brussels sprouts soup. POTAGE PURÉE DE CHOUX DE BRUXELLES—Proceed, using Brussels sprouts, as described in the recipe for *Purée of celery soup.*

Purée of carrot soup I, called Crécy. POTAGE PURÉE DE CAROTTES, DITE CRÉCY—Cook 3 to 4 tender carrots (500 grams) cut in thin slices, in 3 tablespoons (50 grams) of butter in a covered pan. Add 2 tablespoons of chopped onions, a pinch of salt and a pinch of sugar (if using old vegetables, parboil them, before cooking in butter).

When the carrots are quite soft, add a quart (litre) of consommé and ⅓ cup (100 grams) of rice. Simmer gently with a lid on.

Rub through a sieve, dilute with a few tablespoons of stock, heat, add 4 tablespoons (60 grams) of butter and serve with small croûtons fried in butter.

Purée of carrot soup II, called Crécy. POTAGE CRÉCY—Cook the carrots as described in the preceding recipe, replacing the rice indicated as a means of liaison by an equivalent amount of stale, crustless bread, or rusks dried in the oven. Finish off as described above.

Purée of cauliflower soup, called Dubarry. POTAGE PURÉE DE CHOU-FLEUR, DITE DUBARRY—Cook together 1¾ cups (400 grams) of cauliflower, blanched and drained, and 1½ cups (250 grams) of potatoes, cut in slices, in 3 cups (6 decilitres) of milk with a pinch of salt.

Rub through a sieve. Dilute with ½ cup (1 decilitre) of milk, heat and add 4 tablespoons (60 grams) of butter and a tablespoon of chervil leaves.

Serve with small croûtons, fried in butter.

The milk can be replaced by consommé.

Purée of celery soup. POTAGE PURÉE DE CÉLERI—Slice 2 cups (500 grams) of the white part of celery stalks (or the same amount of blanched celeriac) and cook in butter in a covered pan.

Moisten with a quart (litre) of stock, add 1½ cups (250 grams) of potatoes cut in quarters and simmer gently.

Rub through a sieve, dilute the purée with a few tablespoons of consommé, heat and blend in 4 tablespoons (60 grams) of butter.

Purée of chestnut soup. POTAGE PURÉE DE MARRONS—Shell and peel 1 pound (500 grams) of chestnuts and cook them in a quart (litre) of white consommé. Add a quarter of a head of celery cut up and cooked in 3 teaspoons (25 grams) of butter with a tablespoon of chopped onion.

Rub through a sieve, lighten with a few tablespoons of consommé or boiled milk, and finish off with fresh butter.

Serve with small croûtons, fried in butter.

Purée of chicken soup à la reine I. POTAGE PURÉE DE VOLAILLE À LA REINE—Put a tender chicken into a pan with 1 quart (litre) of white consommé. Garnish with the white part of leeks and a stalk of celery, tied in a bundle.

Bring to the boil, skim, add ⅓ cup (100 grams) of blanched and drained rice, cover and simmer gently.

When the chicken is cooked, drain and bone it. Pound the flesh finely in a mortar with the rice (leaving a part of the breast for garnish).

Dilute this purée with a few tablespoons of the consommé in which the chicken was cooked and rub through a sieve, pressing it through with a wooden spoon.

Put into a pan, heat to boiling point, and, if necessary, dilute with a few tablespoons of white consommé.

At the last moment, thicken with a liaison of 2 yolks of egg diluted with ½ cup (1 decilitre) of cream. Blend and incorporate from 4 to 5 tablespoons (60 to 80 grams) of butter.

Dice the breast fillets which were kept for the purpose, and add to the soup.

Purée of chicken soup à la reine II (Old recipe). POTAGE PURÉE DE VOLAILLE À LA REINE—'Take a *chopine* (half a litre) of consommé, put into it a piece of crustless bread the size of an egg and let it boil a few times. Pound finely in a mortar the breast of chicken cooked on a spit with 12 sweet almonds, 3 bitter almonds and 6 hard boiled yolks of egg. When the mixture has been well pounded, add the consommé, with the bread and a *demi-setier* (half a pint) of cream or good milk. Rub your sauce through a sieve, season and keep hot in a *bain-marie**.'

This recipe has been extracted from a sixteenth-century recipe book. Soup '*à la reine*' used to be served every Thursday at the Court of the Valois. Queen Marguerite de Valois, it is said, was very fond of it.

For a long time afterwards soups called '*à la reine*' were prepared from partridges or pigeons. These various soups were sometimes served poured over crusts crumbled and pulped in a plate.

Purée of chicory soup. POTAGE PURÉE D'ENDIVES—Cook a medium-size (400 grams) head of coarsely shredded chicory (U.S. endive) slowly in butter in a covered pan. Season with salt and a little sugar.

Add 1½ cups (250 grams) of potatoes, cut in slices. Moisten with 3 cups (6 decilitres) of consommé. Simmer, with a lid on for 30 minutes.

Rub through a sieve and finish off as described in the recipe for *Purée of celery soup*.

Soup purée Condé—See *Purée of red bean soup*.

Soup purée Conti—See *Puree of lentil soup*.

Soup purée Conti à la brunoise. POTAGE PURÉE CONTI À LA BRUNOISE—7 cups (1½ litres) of *Purée of lentil soup*, to which, at the last moment, 4 or 5 tablespoons of an ordinary *brunoise** and chervil leaves are added.

Soup purée Conti à la julienne. POTAGE PURÉE CONTI À LA JULIENNE—As above, replacing the *brunoise** by a *julienne**.

Purée of crab soup. POTAGE PURÉE DE CRABES—Like *Purée of crayfish soup*, replacing the crayfish by an equivalent quantity of crab.

Purée of crayfish soup or crayfish bisque. POTAGE PURÉE, BISQUE D'ÉCREVISSES—*Ingredients.* 18 crayfish, 6 tablespoons (100 grams) of butter, 1 cup (2 decilitres) of *mirepoix**, ½ cup (1 decilitre) of white wine, 2 tablespoons (2 centilitres) of brandy, ⅓ cup (80 grams) of rice, 1 quart (litre) of white consommé, ¾ cup (1½ decilitres) of fresh cream, salt, pepper, cayenne pepper, thyme, bay leaf, parsley.

For the garnish. 12 crayfish body shells filled with fish forcemeat; diced crayfish tails.

Method. Dress and wash the crayfish and put into the *mirepoix**, previously cooked in butter until soft.

Season with a pinch of salt and a little freshly ground pepper, add 2 sprigs of parsley, a sprig of thyme and a fragment of a bay leaf. Sauté the crayfish on a fierce fire until the shell turns red.

Moisten with brandy which has been set alight and the white wine. Boil down by two-thirds, add ½ cup (1 decilitre) of consommé and cook for 10 minutes.

Shell the crayfish, keeping the tails and 8 shells for the garnish.

Pound the crayfish shells finely in a mortar, adding to them the rice, cooked separately in 2 cups (4 decilitres) of consommé and the liquor left from cooking the crayfish. Rub this purée through a sieve, pressing it through with a wooden spoon.

Put the purée into a saucepan, dilute with the rest of the consommé, boil for a few seconds, strain through a fine strainer and keep hot in a *bain-marie** (double boiler).

At the last moment, add 5 tablespoons (80 grams) of butter divided into minute pieces and the fresh cream; blend, correct seasoning, if necessary, and flavour with a small pinch of cayenne pepper.

Pour into a soup tureen, garnish with the shells, filled with fish forcemeat and poached, and the diced tails kept for the purpose.

Note. Consommé can be replaced by fish stock or *fumet**.

Soup purée Crécy—See *Purée of carrot soup*.

Soup purée Crécy aux perles. POTAGE PURÉE CRÉCY AUX PERLES—7 cups (1½ litres) of *Purée of carrots à la Crécy* with 4 tablespoons of *perles*, cooked in stock, added to it.

Soup purée Crécy with rice. POTAGE PURÉE CRÉCY AU RIZ—7 cups (1½ litres) of *Purée of carrot soup à la Crécy* with 4 tablespoons of rice, cooked in stock, added to it.

Purée of garden cress soup. POTAGE PURÉE DE CRESSON ALÉNOIS—Pick over and wash ½ pound (250 grams) of garden cress, chop it and put to cook on the fire in a covered pan with 3 tablespoons (50 grams) of butter.

Moisten with 1 quart (litre) of good strong stock, add 1½ cups (250 grams) of potatoes, cut in thin slices and simmer gently.

Rub this purée through a sieve, lighten to the desired degree with stock and milk, add 3 good tablespoons of cream and a piece of fresh butter.

Fresh pea soup or Potage Saint-Germain with ham added *Robert Carrier)*

Pour into a soup tureen and garnish with leaves of garden cress, blanched in salted water and drained.

Soup purée with croûtons—See *Purée of split pea soup.*

Soup purée Dubarry—See *Purée of cauliflower soup.*

Soup purée Freneuse—See *Purée of turnip soup.*

Purée of game soup. POTAGE PURÉE DE GIBIER—Roast a pheasant or 2 partridges in the oven until three-quarters done, keeping them a little on the firm side.

Remove from cooking and brown ¾ cup (1½ decilitres) of *mirepoix** in the fat given out by the game.

Put the game and the *mirepoix* into a pan with 2 cups (200 grams) of lentils, three-quarters cooked.

Add a *bouquet garni**, season, moisten with a quart (litre) of ordinary consommé, or game consommé, if available. Bring to the boil, cover and simmer gently.

Drain the game and bone. Pound the flesh in a mortar adding the drained lentils.

Dilute the purée with the liquid left in the pan and rub through a sieve, pressing it through with a wooden spoon. Put back in the pan.

Heat, taste for seasoning (this dish should be well seasoned) and, at the last moment, add 5 tablespoons (80 grams) of butter.

Purée of Jerusalem artichoke soup. POTAGE PURÉE DE TOPINAMBOURS—Using Jerusalem artichokes, proceed as described in the recipe for *Purée of sweet potato soup.*

Purée of lentil soup à la Conti. POTAGE PURÉE DE LENTILLES À LA CONTI—Proceed, using lentils, as described in the recipe for *Purée of red haricot bean soup,* omitting the red wine.

Purée of lettuce soup. POTAGE PURÉE DE LAITUES—Proceed, using lettuce, as described in the recipe for *Purée of chicory soup.*

Purée of lobster soup or lobster bisque. POTAGE PURÉE, BISQUE DE HOMARD—Like *Crayfish bisque*, replacing the crayfish by an equivalent quantity of small lobsters, cut into pieces and sautéed with a *mirepoix**.

Garnish with diced lobster tails.

Purée of marrow soup—See *Purée of pumpkin soup.*

Soup purée Parmentier. See *Purée of potato soup.*

Purée of fresh pea soup, called Saint-Germain. POTAGE PURÉE DE POIS FRAIS, DITE SAINT-GERMAIN—Rub a quart (litre) of fresh peas, cooked quickly in salted water and drained, through a sieve.

Dilute the purée with 4 or 5 cups (8 or 10 decilitres) of white consommé. Bring to the boil and finish off with 4 tablespoons (60 grams) of fresh butter. Add 2 tablespoons of fresh garden peas, cooked in water and drained, and some chervil leaves.

Purée of split pea soup. POTAGE PURÉE DE POIS CASSÉS—Pick over and wash ¾ pound (350 grams) of split peas, soak them in cold water for 2 hours, and cook in 1½ quarts (litres) of cold water.

Bring to the boil, skim, season, add a *mirepoix** composed of 2 ounces (50 grams) of lean bacon, diced, blanched and fried lightly with 2 tablespoons of the red part of carrot and 1 tablespoon of onion cut in dice. Put in a *bouquet garni**, adding to it the green part of 2 leeks.

After cooking, rub through a sieve, put the purée

Purée of split pea soup, garnished with bacon

back into the pan, lighten with a few tablespoons of consommé and finish off with fresh butter and a tablespoon of chervil leaves.

Serve with small croûtons, fried in butter.

Note. This soup can also be prepared as a Lenten dish, by omitting the bacon and diluting the purée with milk.

Soup purée portugaise—See *Purée of tomato soup.*

Purée of potato soup Parmentier

Purée of potato soup Parmentier. POTAGE PURÉE DE POMMES DE TERRE, DITE PARMENTIER—Shred the white part of 2 leeks and lightly cook in 2 tablespoons (25 grams) of butter.

Add 3 cups (500 grams) of potatoes cut in quarters. Moisten with a quart (litre) of white consommé. Season and boil fast.

As soon as the potatoes are cooked, mash them and rub through a sieve. Lighten with a few tablespoons of consommé or cream and finish off with 4 tablespoons (60 grams) of fresh butter and a tablespoon of chervil leaves.

Serve with small croûtons, fried in butter.

Purée of sweet potato soup. POTAGE PURÉE DE PATATES—Peel and quarter 4 to 5 sweet potatoes (600 grams) and cook them in white consommé.

Rub through a sieve and lighten with 2 cups (½ litre) of consommé. Bring to the boil, stir and finish off by incorporating 4 tablespoons (60 grams) of fresh butter.

Serve with small croûtons fried in butter.

Purée of pumpkin soup I (based on meat stock). POTAGE PURÉE DE POTIRON AU GRAS—Peel and cut 1 pound (500 grams) of pumpkin into uniform pieces. Cook in 3 tablespoons (50 grams) of butter and 4 tablespoons of water in a covered pan. Season with a good pinch of salt.

When the pumpkin is quite soft, rub it through a fine sieve. Put the purée back into the pan, dilute it to the desired consistency with 3 to 4 cups (6 to 8 decilitres) of consommé, bring to the boil and finish off with 4 tablespoons (60 grams) of fresh butter.

Serve with small croûtons, fried in butter.

Purée of pumpkin soup II (Lenten). POTAGE PURÉE DE POTIRON AU MAIGRE—Cook the pumpkin as described in the preceding recipe.

Dilute the purée with boiling milk, adding to it 3 or 4 tablespoons of castor (fine) sugar. Finish off with butter.

Serve with small croûtons, fried in butter.

Purée of purslane soup. POTAGE PURÉE DE POURPIER—Proceed as described in the recipe for *Purée of garden cress soup*, replacing the cress by fresh purslane.

Soup purée à la reine—See *Purée of chicken soup.*

Soup purée Saint-Germain—See *Purée of fresh pea soup.*

Purée of shrimp soup or shrimp bisque. POTAGE PURÉE, BISQUE DE CREVETTES—Like *Purée of crayfish soup*, replacing the crayfish by an equivalent quantity of shrimps.

Soup purée soissonnaise—See *Purée of white haricot bean soup.*

Purée of spiny lobster soup or spiny lobster bisque. POTAGE PURÉE, BISQUE DE LANGOUSTE—Like *Purée of crayfish soup*, replacing the crayfish by an equivalent quantity of small spiny lobsters.

Purée of tomato soup

Purée of tomato soup I. POTAGE PURÉE DE TOMATES—Cook ¼ cup (50 grams) of sliced onion in butter in a covered pan. Add 1 pound (500 grams) of tomatoes, with the seeds pressed out and the flesh cut up. Season with salt and pepper and add one crushed clove of garlic and a *bouquet garni**.

Cook gently for a few moments, stirring all the time. Add ⅓ cup (100 grams) of rice, moisten with a quart (litre) of consommé, stir and simmer gently.

Rub through a sieve, put back in the pan, dilute with a few tablespoons of consommé, heat and, at the last moment, incorporate 4 tablespoons (60 grams) of butter. Add 2 tablespoons of rice cooked in consommé or in water.

Purée of tomato soup II. POTAGE PURÉE DE TOMATES—Sauté the onion in butter until soft, then fry the tomatoes in the same pan for a few moments. Sprinkle with 2 tablespoons of flour. Moisten with consommé and season. Garnish and finish off as described above.

Purée of turnip soup, called à la Freneuse. POTAGE PURÉE DE NAVETS, DITE À LA FRENEUSE—Cook 3 cups (500 grams) of sliced and blanched turnips gently in butter in a covered pan. Moisten with 1 cup (2 decilitres) of consommé and cook until three-quarters done.

Add 1½ cups (250 grams) of sliced potatoes, moisten with 2½ cups (5 decilitres) of consommé and finish cooking on a brisk fire.

Rub through a sieve and finish off as described in the recipe for *Purée of celery soup*.

VELOUTÉ SOUPS. POTAGES VELOUTÉS—These soups are composed of a *Velouté sauce*, based on vegetable, meat, fish or shellfish, cooked in *Velouté*, or, in the case of shellfish, added to the *Velouté* just before rubbing it through a sieve. After being rubbed through a sieve, these soups are thickened with a liaison of yolks of egg, cream and butter.

Veloutés can be served with all the garnishes indicated for cream and purée soups such as: pearl barley, *perles du Japon*, *printanière*, asparagus tips, *quenelles*, *royale*, tapioca. These garnishes are added to the soup after it has been put through a sieve and thickened.

The recipes which follow have been worked out to serve from four to six persons.

Method of preparation—For vegetable veloutés. Prepare a velouté using 4 tablespoons (80 grams) of white *roux** and 4 cups (8 decilitres) of ordinary white or chicken consommé, or white stock.

Add the vegetable indicated for this velouté, having first blanched it, if necessary, and cooked it in butter.

Simmer gently until the vegetable is cooked.

Rub through a sieve pressing it through with a wooden spoon.

Dilute the soup with a few tablespoons of white consommé. Heat to boiling point.

At the last moment, remove from heat, and thicken with a liaison of 3 yolks of egg and ½ cup (1 decilitre) of cream.

Blend in from 5 to 6 tablespoons (80 to 100 grams) of fresh butter.

For meat, poultry or game velouté. Prepare the velouté as described above.

Put in the meat, fowl or game into it to cook (the meat should be boned and tied with a string, the fowl or game trussed as for an entrée).

Simmer gently until the basic elements are quite done.

Drain this element, bone, if necessary, and pound in a mortar, keeping a small part of it as a garnish for the soup.

Dilute with white consommé and finish off as described in the preceding recipe.

For fish velouté. Using boned fish, proceed as described in the recipe above for meat, poultry or game velouté, using Lenten or fish stock for making the velouté, although it can also be made with meat or chicken stock.

For shellfish velouté. Cook the shellfish indicated with a *mirepoix**, then pound it in a mortar with the liquor in which it was cooked.

Add it to velouté, based on meat or fish stock.

Rub through a sieve and finish off as described above.

Compound butter, flavoured with the appropriate shellfish, is usually added to shellfish velouté soups.

Artichoke velouté soup. POTAGE VELOUTÉ D'ARTICHAUTS —Prepare 4 cups (8 decilitres) of *Velouté* based on white consommé. In this *Velouté* cook 8 artichoke hearts, blanched, sliced and simmered lightly in butter in a covered pan.

Rub through a sieve. Dilute with white consommé. Heat, thicken with a liaison of 3 yolks of egg and ½ cup (1 decilitre) of cream. At the last moment, incorporate from 6 to 8 tablespoons (80 to 100 grams) of butter.

Garnish with artichoke hearts, cooked in a *court-bouillon** and diced, and chervil leaves.

Asparagus velouté soup. POTAGE VELOUTÉ D'ASPERGES —Using the tips of 2 pounds (1 kilo) of asparagus, blanched and cooked in butter, in a covered pan, proceed as described in the recipe for *Artichoke velouté soup*.

This soup can be made of white or green asparagus.

Celery velouté soup. POTAGE VELOUTÉ DE CÉLERI—Like *Artichoke velouté soup*, using celery cooked in butter in a covered pan.

Chicken véloute soup I. POTAGE VELOUTÉ DE VOLAILLE —Prepare 4 cups (8 decilitres) of velouté.

Add a medium-sized, tender young chicken. Simmer gently.

Drain the chicken, bone it, keep a part of the breast fillets for garnish and pound the rest in the mortar.

Add this chicken purée to the velouté.

Rub through a sieve and finish off as described in the recipe for *Artichoke velouté soup*. Garnish with diced breast fillets.

Chicken véloute soup II. POTAGE VELOUTÉ DE VOLAILLE— Proceed to prepare the velouté and to cook the chicken as described in the preceding recipe.

When pounding the chicken meat, add to it 4 tablespoons (60 grams) of butter and ½ cup (1 decilitre) of fresh double cream.

Rub this purée through a horse-hair sieve. Thicken the velouté, strain and add the chicken purée to it. Finish off with fresh butter and cream.

Chicken velouté soup à l'écossaise. POTAGE VELOUTÉ DE VOLAILLE À L'ÉCOSSAISE—At the last moment, add 4 tablespoons of a fine *brunoise** of vegetables, softened in butter, and chervil leaves to the chicken velouté soup.

Chicken velouté soup à la Nantua. POTAGE VELOUTÉ DE VOLAILLE À LA NANTUA—Flavour *Chicken velouté soup* with crayfish butter. Garnish with shelled crayfish tails.

Chicken velouté soup à la portugaise. POTAGE VELOUTÉ DE VOLAILLE À LA PORTUGAISE—At the last moment, add to *Chicken velouté soup* 4 tablespoons of tomatoes, peeled, pressed out, cut into small square pieces and cooked in butter in a covered pan.

Chicken velouté soup sultane. POTAGE VELOUTÉ DE VOLAILLE SULTANE—Flavour the soup with pistachio butter and garnish with small quenelles made of *Chicken forcemeat aux fines herbes* (see FORCEMEAT).

Crayfish velouté soup. POTAGE VELOUTÉ D'ÉCREVISSES— Like *Shrimp velouté soup*, replacing the shrimps by 12 crayfish, cooked with a *mirepoix** and pounded in a mortar.

Finish off with *Crayfish butter* (see BUTTER, *Compound butters*).

Endive (U.S. chicory), spinach or lettuce velouté soup. POTAGE VELOUTÉ DE CHICORÉE, D'ÉPINARDS, DE LAITUE— Like *Artichoke velouté soup*, using one or other of these vegetables.

Frog velouté soup à la sicilienne. POTAGE VELOUTÉ DE GRENOUILLES À LA SICILIENNE—Proceed as described in the recipe for *Smelt velouté soup*, replacing the smelts with 48 frogs' legs, cooked in butter.

Finish off as described in the recipe for *Artichoke velouté soup*, flavouring it with pistachio butter.

Game velouté soup—See *Partridge velouté soup*.

Lobster velouté soup. POTAGE VELOUTÉ DE HOMARD— Like *Shrimp velouté soup*, using lobster cooked with a *mirepoix**.

Mushroom velouté soup, also called Pierre-le-grand. POTAGE VELOUTÉ DE CHAMPIGNONS, PIERRE-LE-GRAND— Like *Artichoke velouté soup*, using purée of cultivated mushrooms.

Some culinary authorities say that this soup should be made of a mixture of mushroom and grouse purée.

Oyster velouté soup. POTAGE VELOUTÉ AUX HUÎTRES—Prepare 4 cups (8 decilitres) of fish velouté, as described in the basic recipe. Add to it the water of 24 oysters.

Thicken the soup as described in the recipe for *Artichoke velouté soup*, and garnish it with poached and de-bearded oysters.

Partridge velouté soup. POTAGE VELOUTÉ DE PERDRIX—Prepare 4 cups (8 decilitres) of *Velouté* as described in the basic recipe.

Add 2 partridges, previously browned lightly in the oven. Simmer gently.

Drain the partridges, bone them and pound the flesh in a mortar, except for a part of the breast fillets, which should be kept for garnish. Add this purée to the velouté.

Rub through a sieve and finish off as described in the recipe for *Artichoke velouté soup.*

Garnish with the breast fillets, cut in dice.

Various game velouté soups are prepared in the same way, using wood-grouse, pheasant, hazel-grouse, etc.

Shrimp velouté soup. POTAGE VELOUTÉ DE CREVETTES—Prepare 4 cups (8 decilitres) of *Velouté* as described in the basic recipe for *Vegetable velouté.*

Method of preparation. At the time of passing this velouté through a sieve, add to it 1 pound (500 grams) of shrimps, cooked with a *mirepoix** and pounded in a mortar (having kept some shrimp tails for the garnish).

Finish off as described in the recipe for *Artichoke velouté soup*, but adding *Shrimp butter*, instead of ordinary fresh butter (see BUTTER, *Compound butters*).

Shrimp velouté soup à la normande. POTAGE VELOUTÉ DE CREVETTES À LA NORMANDE—As above. At the last moment, garnish with 12 shelled shrimp tails, 8 poached and de-bearded oysters and 8 small pike *quenelles**.

Smelt velouté soup I. POTAGE VELOUTÉ D'ÉPERLANS—Prepare the *Velouté*, as described in the basic recipe (using fish consommé, if desired).

Ten minutes before rubbing it through a sieve, add the fillets of ½ pound (250 grams) of smelts, previously cooked in butter, with a tablespoon of chopped onion, to the velouté. Drain the smelt fillets, pound them in a mortar, rub through a sieve and add to the velouté.

Strain and finish off as described in the recipe for *Artichoke velouté soup.*

Smelt velouté soup II, à la dieppoise. POTAGE VELOUTÉ D'ÉPERLANS À LA DIEPPOISE—As above, adding to the velouté a few tablespoons of the liquor in which mussels were cooked and garnishing the soup with 12 poached mussels and 12 shelled shrimps' tails.

Smelt velouté soup III, à l'indienne. POTAGE VELOUTÉ D'ÉPERLANS À L'INDIENNE—As above. Sprinkle the smelt fillets with a tablespoon of curry powder whilst cooking them with butter and chopped onion.

Spiny lobster and Dublin Bay prawn velouté soup. POTAGE VELOUTÉ DE LANGOUSTE, LANGOUSTINE—Like *Shrimp velouté soup*, using spiny lobster or Dublin Bay prawns cooked with a *mirepoix**.

SPECIAL PURÉE AND VELOUTÉ SOUPS—The recipes for these soups, based on purées or on veloutés with various garnishes, have been worked out to serve 4 to 6 persons.

Potage Ambassadeurs—Prepare 6 cups (1½ litres) of *Purée of fresh pea soup*, add to it 4 tablespoons of a *chiffonnade** of sorrel cooked in butter, 2 tablespoons of rice, poached in consommé, and chervil leaves.

This soup can also be made by adding a *chiffonnade* of mixed lettuce and sorrel.

Andalusian soup. POTAGE ANDALOUSE—Add to 6 cups (1½ litres) of *Tomato purée soup* 1¼ cups (2½ decilitres) of tapioca cooked in consommé.

Potage Apicius (old recipe)—'Reduce consommé by half for soup. Blanch 12 ounces of lasagne in salted boiling water. Drain and simmer for 20 minutes in half of the reduced consommé, with 4 ounces of best butter, a pinch of coarse ground pepper and a pinch of grated nutmeg. Reduce the breast of a fowl to purée, add to the lasagne and mix. Put a layer of the lasagne into a soup tureen, follow with a layer of big cocks' combs and kidneys, cooked in consommé, then add a plateful of small truffles, cut to look like olives, sautéed in butter with a little chicken jelly. Sprinkle with Parmesan cheese. Continue to superimpose these various elements in successive layers. Pour over the consommé left over from cooking the lasagne and serve.'

Potage d'Artois—Prepare 6 cups (1½ litres) of *White bean purée soup*, add to it 4 tablespoons of a fine *brunoise** of vegetables, cooked in butter until soft, and chervil leaves.

Potage Bagration I (based on meat)—Prepare 4 cups (8 decilitres) of *Velouté*, as described in the basic recipe for these soups. Add to it 1 pound (500 grams) of lean veal, cut in large dice and lightly fried in butter. Simmer gently.

Drain the veal. Pound it finely in a mortar and add to the *Velouté.*

Rub through a sieve and heat to boiling point.

Thicken with a liaison of 3 yolks of egg and ½ cup (1 decilitre) of cream. Add more seasoning, if necessary, and incorporate from 6 to 7 tablespoons (80 to 100 grams) of butter.

Garnish with macaroni, poached and diced. Serve grated cheese separately.

Potage Bagration II (based on fish)—Proceed as described in the preceding recipe, using *Velouté* based on fish stock and replacing the veal by ½ pound (250 grams) of fillets of sole, previously lightly fried in butter.

Potage Balvet, also called Jubilé—Prepare 6 cups (1½ litres) of *Purée of fresh pea soup*, dilute with a little consommé and add 4 tablespoons of stock-pot vegetables.

Potage bonne-femme I—Shred finely ½ cup (100 grams) of the white part of leeks and cook in butter in a covered pan. Moisten with 6 cups (1½ litres) of white consommé.

Add 1½ cups (250 grams) of sliced potatoes. Season and simmer gently.

At the last moment, add from 4 to 5 tablespoons (60 to 80 grams) of butter and some chervil leaves.

Serve with long French bread thinly sliced and dried in the oven.

The consommé can be replaced by water or milk.

Potage bonne-femme II—Cook the leeks in butter in a covered pan. Add 3 cups (6 decilitres) of a very thin potato purée and 6 cups (1½ litres) of consommé.

Add ¾ cup (150 grams) of sliced potatoes and simmer gently.

At the last moment, add 1 cup (2 decilitres) of cream, 4 tablespoons (60 grams) of butter and some chervil leaves.

Potage Camérani (old recipe)—'Soften slowly in butter 2 decilitres of a fine *brunoise** of vegetables, with a little turnip added to it.

'Add 12 chicken livers, trimmed and cut in very small dice. Season and brown on a brisk fire.

'Separately, and as quickly as possible, poach ¼ pound (125 grams) of Naples macaroni in salted water. Drain them, dress with butter and season.

'To serve, put the macaroni into a silver dish, buttered

and sprinkled with grated Parmesan cheese, alternating with layers of chopped chicken livers and sprinkling each layer with Parmesan.

'Heat for a few minutes on a low flame.'

Note. Though this dish belongs much more to that of entrées, we have placed it in the category of soups, to conform with an old usage.

Potage cultivateur—Cut 2 to 3 small carrots (150 grams), a small turnip (100 grams), 6 tablespoons (75 grams) of the white part of leeks (chopped) and 2 tablespoons (25 grams) of onions, into large dice.

Season with salt and a pinch of sugar. Cook in 3 tablespoons (50 grams) of butter in a covered pan.

Moisten with 6 cups (1½ litres) of white consommé and cook for 1¼ hours.

25 minutes before serving, add ¾ cup (150 grams) of sliced potatoes and 2½ ounces (75 grams) of bacon, cut in dice and well blanched.

In this soup the potatoes can be replaced by rice.

Potage Darblay—See *Potage julienne Darblay.*

Potage Faubonne—Add 4 tablespoons of a *julienne** of vegetables, cooked gently in butter, and some chervil leaves to 6 cups (1½ litres) of Saint-Germain purée soup (or split pea purée soup).

This soup can also be made of white bean or any other vegetable purée.

Some culinary authorities indicate a pheasant purée and a garnish composed of pheasant fillets and a *julienne** of truffles for this soup.

Potage fermière—Shred finely 2 to 3 small carrots (100 grams), 1 small turnip (75 grams), 6 tablespoons (75 grams) of the white part of leeks (chopped), 4 tablespoons (50 grams) of onions and ¾ cup (75 grams) of cabbage heart (shredded). Season these vegetables and simmer them slowly in 3 tablespoons (50 grams) of butter, in a covered pan.

Moisten with 4 cups (8 decilitres) of water in which white beans were cooked and 3 cups (6 decilitres) of white consommé. Cook for 1¼ hours.

At the last moment, add ½ cup (1 decilitre) of cream, 4 tablespoons of cooked white beans and some chervil leaves.

This soup can also be prepared as a Lenten dish, by omitting the consommé and using only water left over from cooking the beans.

Potage Fontanges

Potage Fontanges—Prepare 6 cups (1½ litres) of *Purée of fresh pea soup*, dilute with a little consommé and add to it 4 tablespoons of a *chiffonnade** of sorrel cooked in butter until soft, and some chervil leaves.

This soup is sometimes thickened with a liaison of yolks and cream.

Potage gentilhomme—Garnish 6 cups (1½ litres) of *Game purée soup* (based on lentil purée) with 4 tablespoons of small game quenelles.

Potage Germiny—Moisten 4 cups (200 grams) of sorrel, shredded into a *chiffonnade** and softened in butter, with 6 cups (1½ litres) of consommé.

At the last moment thicken with a liaison of 8 to 10 yolks of egg diluted with ½ cup (1 decilitre) of fresh cream. Add a tablespoon of chervil leaves.

Serve with long French bread, thinly sliced and dried in the oven.

Potage Jubilé—Another name for *Potage Balvet.*

Potage julienne à l'allemande—Prepare 4 cups (1 litre) of *Potage julienne.* At the last moment, thicken with a liaison of 4 yolks diluted with 1 cup (2 decilitres) of cream. Add from 6 to 7 tablespoons (80 to 100 grams) of butter and some chervil leaves.

Potage julienne à la cévenole—Prepare a quart (litre) of a light chestnut purée soup. Add to it a pint (½ litre) of a *julienne**, cooked in butter and consommé. Boil for 5 minutes. At the last moment, blend in 3 to 4 tablespoons (50 to 60 grams) of butter and sprinkle with a tablespoon of chervil leaves.

Potage julienne Darblay—Prepare 6 cups (1½ litres) of potato purée soup, dilute with a little consommé, add 4 tablespoons of a *julienne** of vegetables lightly cooked in butter.

Cook together, simmering gently for 10 minutes.

At the last moment, thicken with a liaison of 3 yolks diluted with ½ cup (1 decilitre) of fresh cream. Incorporate from 6 to 7 tablespoons (60 to 80 grams) of butter and add some chervil leaves.

Potage Lamballe—Add 3½ cups (7 decilitres) of rather thick consommé with tapioca to 4 cups (8 decilitres) of *Purée of fresh pea soup.*

Potage Longchamp—Add 3 tablespoons of a *chiffonnade** of sorrel, lightly cooked in butter, 2½ cups (5 decilitres) of consommé with vermicelli and some chervil leaves to 1 quart (litre) of *Purée of fresh pea soup.*

Potage Marigny—Like *Potage Fontanges.* Decrease the proportion of the *chiffonnade** of sorrel and add 2 tablespoons of garden peas and diced French (string) beans, cooked in water.

Oyster soup I. POTAGE AUX HUÎTRES—Prepare 6 cups (1½ litres) of *Velouté,* based on fish consommé, as described in the basic recipe for these soups, thicken with a liaison of 3 yolks diluted in ½ cup (1 decilitre) of cream and blend in some butter. Garnish it with 12 oysters, taken out of their shells and poached in their strained liquor. Add blanched and drained chervil leaves.

Note. The liquor drained out of the oysters should be added to the velouté.

This soup should be spiced with a pinch of cayenne pepper.

Oyster soup II. POTAGE AUX HUÎTRES—Make 6 tablespoons (80 grams) of white *roux** and dilute it with 4 cups (8 decilitres) of the liquid in which mussels were cooked (or concentrated fish stock), mixed with the liquor of 12 oysters. Mix and simmer gently.

Thicken with a liaison of 3 yolks diluted with ½ cup (1 decilitre) of cream. Finish off as described in the preceding recipe.

Potage paysanne—Shred finely 1 medium-large carrot (150 grams), 1 small turnip (75 grams), 4 tablespoons (50 grams) of the white part of leeks, 2 tablespoons (25 grams) of chopped onion, 2 tablespoons (25 grams) of celery and ¼ cup (25 grams) of shredded cabbage heart.

Season with salt and a pinch of sugar. Cook slowly in 3 tablespoons (50 grams) of butter in a covered pan.

Moisten with 6 cups ($1\frac{1}{2}$ litres) of white consommé. Cook for $1\frac{1}{4}$ hours.

25 minutes before serving, add $\frac{1}{2}$ cup (100 grams) of thinly sliced potatoes and 2 tablespoons of fresh garden peas. Lastly, add a tablespoon of chervil leaves.

Serve with long French bread, thinly sliced and dried in the oven.

Note. This soup can be prepared as a Lenten dish by replacing the consommé by water. In that case, add 4 tablespoons (60 grams) of butter before serving.

Potage Pierre-le-Grand (Peter the Great's soup)—See *Mushroom velouté soup*.

This soup can also be made by mixing mushroom and hazel-grouse purées.

Portuguese soup. POTAGE PORTUGAISE—Cook 6 tablespoons (75 grams) of chopped onion and $3\frac{1}{2}$ ounces (100 grams) of lean bacon, cut in small dice and blanched in butter in a covered pan.

Add 1 pound (500 grams) of tomatoes, with the seeds pressed out and cut in slices, a small *bouquet garni** and half a clove of garlic. Sauté for 10 minutes. Add $\frac{1}{3}$ cup (100 grams) of rice.

Moisten with 5 cups ($1\frac{1}{4}$ litres) of white consommé. Season and simmer gently for an hour.

Rub through a sieve, pressing through with a wooden spoon.

Heat the purée, dilute with a few tablespoons of consommé and incorporate in it from 4 to 5 tablespoons (60 to 80 grams) of butter. Add 4 tablespoons of rice, cooked in consommé.

Potage Raphael—This was classified by Carême as an Italian soup. He decreed a certain consommé for this soup, the costly preparation of which is no longer within the means at the disposal of a present-day kitchen. Without belittling the principles of classical teaching, it is quite possible to achieve good results by less expensive methods. Proceed as follows:

'Prepare a *petite marmite* in the usual manner (see above) and cook a small chicken in it. It should be very well cooked. Avoid using an old hen, as it invariably has an unpleasant taste.

'Bone the chicken completely, keep one fillet of breast, pound the rest of the meat in a mortar while still scalding hot and rub through a fine sieve. Collect the purée in a soup tureen, pour over a few tablespoons of strained consommé, cover and keep by.

'Allowing 2 quarts (litres) of the *petite marmite* consommé for 10 persons, skim off surplus fat and strain it through a napkin. Bring to the boil. Pour into it, in a rain, $\frac{5}{8}$ cup (100 grams) of coarse-ground semolina and simmer gently for 25 minutes. At the last moment, add the chicken purée, little by little, to the semolina, stirring it with a whisk. Add 20 small cocks' combs (or 10 medium-sized ones, cut in half), cooked in a light *court-bouillon**, as well as the breast fillet and two small truffles, shredded into a fine *julienne**.' (Philéas Gilbert.)

Potage Saint-Cloud—Soup made of *Purée of fresh pea soup*, called Saint-Germain, served with diced croûtons, fried in butter.

Potage santé—Prepare 6 cups ($1\frac{1}{2}$ litres) of a light *Soup purée Parmentier* and add to it 4 tablespoons of a *chiffonnade** of sorrel, lightly cooked in butter until soft.

Thicken with a liaison of 3 yolks, diluted with $\frac{1}{2}$ cup (1 decilitre) of cream.

Incorporate 7 tablespoons (100 grams) of butter and add some chervil leaves.

Serve with long French bread, thinly sliced and dried in the oven.

Potage Solférino—Cook in butter 6 tablespoons (75 grams) of the white part of leeks and 4 tablespoons (75 grams) of the red part of carrots, both shredded, in a covered pan, until tender.

Add 3 to 4 tomatoes (500 grams) pressed out and cut in slices; a small *bouquet garni** and, if liked, half a clove of garlic. Cook for 10 minutes.

Moisten with a quart (litre) of white consommé, add $1\frac{1}{2}$ cups (250 grams) of potatoes, cut in slices. Season and simmer gently.

Remove the *bouquet garni* and the garlic. Drain the vegetables and rub them through a sieve.

Add the liquor left in the pan to this purée and dilute it with a few tablespoons of consommé. Bring to the boil and skim the surface. At the last moment, add 6 to 7 tablespoons (80 to 100 grams) of butter.

Garnish with 2 tablespoons of small potato balls, scooped out with a vegetable baller and cooked in white consommé, and some chervil leaves.

Potage velours—Add a pint ($\frac{1}{2}$ litre) of consommé substantially thickened with tapioca to a quart (litre) of *Purée Crécy* (see above).

Potage Xavier—Prepare 6 cups ($1\frac{1}{2}$ litres) of *Cream of rice soup* (see above).

Thicken it, at the last moment, with a liaison of 3 yolks, diluted with $\frac{1}{2}$ cup (1 decilitre) of cream. Incorporate from 6 to 7 tablespoons (80 to 100 grams) of butter.

Serve with a chicken *royale* (see GARNISHES), cut in very small dice.

CLASSICAL AND REGIONAL SOUPS—We have grouped here various classical and regional soups of France.

Many of these soups have bread added to them.

The bread should be light and porous. It should have innumerable small holes, so as to be easily imbued with the soup. The bread should be stale, cut in slices of varying thickness, depending on the nature of the soup.

It is advisable to toast it or dry it in the oven. This slight torrefaction releases the aromatic properties of bread which communicates a pleasant flavour to the soup.

Soupe aigo-saou (Provençal cookery)—Put 2 pounds (a kilo) of white fish, cut into uniform pieces, a medium-sized sliced onion, 4 chopped tomatoes, 4 potatoes, cut in quarters, 2 cloves of garlic and a *bouquet garni**, composed of parsley, celery, thyme and bay leaf, into a saucepan. Season with 4 teaspoons (25 grams) of salt and a good pinch of pepper. Add 2 quarts (litres) of water and boil fast from 18 to 20 minutes.

Strain the soup into a tureen over slices of home-made bread, sprinkled with a dash of oil.

Arrange the fish and the potatoes on a dish; separately serve *aioli* or *rouille*, which is prepared as follows: pound a big clove of garlic with a red pepper in a mortar. Add a piece of bread (crumb, i.e. soft part only) the size of a walnut, soaked and pressed out.

Over the whole, little by little and stirring constantly, pour about $1\frac{1}{4}$ cups ($2\frac{1}{2}$ decilitres) of olive oil. Lastly, add a few tablespoons of fish stock to the mixture.

Soupe aigo à la ménagère (Provençal cookery)—Colour lightly a chopped onion and the white part of three leeks in oil. Add 2 tomatoes, seeded and chopped, 4 crushed cloves of garlic, a small branch of fennel, a piece of dried orange peel, a *bouquet garni**, 4 sliced potatoes and a small pinch of saffron. Add 2 quarts (litres) of water. Season with 3 teaspoons (20 grams) of salt and a pinch of pepper. Boil fast for a quarter of an hour.

Poach some eggs in this soup, allowing 1 per person. Drain the eggs, arrange them on a dish with the potatoes, which should be taken out of the saucepan and sprinkled with chopped parsley.

Strain the rest of the soup over slices of home-made bread arranged on a deep dish.

Soupe aigo bouido à la ménagère (Provençal cookery) —Boil 2 quarts (litres) of water into which you have put 15 crushed cloves of garlic, a *bouquet garni**, a sprig of sage, 1 cup (2 decilitres) of olive oil, 4 teaspoons (25 grams) of coarse salt and a pinch of pepper.

Pour this soup into a tureen over slices of bread sprinkled with chopped parsley.

Soupe aigo bouido with poached eggs (Provençal cookery)—Prepare the soup as described in the preceding recipe and poach the eggs in it. Arrange the eggs on slices of bread in a deep dish. Pour the soup over them and add a pinch of parsley leaves.

Soupe albigeoise—This soup is made not only in the Albi region but throughout the western part of France.

It is a kind of potée with beef (mainly rib of beef), salt pork, sausage and *confit d'oie* (preserved goose) as basic nutritive elements. The following vegetables are used for it: cabbage, carrots, turnips, leeks, onions, potatoes, and—as the principal flavouring—plenty of garlic.

Properly speaking, the *Potée albigeoise* differs very little from other French potées, the greatest of which is the Auvergne potée.

Arles soup. SOUPE ARLÉGEOISE—A potée prepared in the same manner as the Auvergne potée, that is to say, using cabbage, carrots, turnips, onions, leek and potatoes, in the way of vegetables, and salt pork, sometimes *confit d'oie* and a copious and succulent *farci*, as nutritive elements.

And as a predominant informing flavour, of course, plenty of garlic.

Black pudding water soup or bougras (Périgord cookery). SOUPE À L'EAU DE BOUDIN, BOUGRAS—This soup, greatly appreciated in Périgord, is usually prepared during Shrovetide, when pigs are slaughtered and delicious black puddings are made.

Bring the water in which the black puddings have been poached to the boil. For 2½ quarts (litres) of this water, add a head of curly green cabbage, cut into pieces and blanched, carrots, turnips, leeks, celery and onions in quarters. Simmer gently for 40 minutes. Add 2½ cups (400 grams) of potatoes cut in thick round slices and cook for another 35 minutes.

Fifteen minutes before serving, remove some of the vegetables with a perforated spoon, slice them, fry in fat, sprinkle with flour, moisten with a few tablespoons of stock and add to the soup. (This is called '*fricassée*' in Périgord and it is added to most soups.)

Pour the boiling soup into a tureen lined with thin slices of home-made bread.

Soupe à la bonne femme—Cook gently the finely shredded white part of 4 leeks in a covered saucepan, with 3 tablespoons (40 grams) of butter, without allowing the leeks to colour.

When the leeks are cooked and quite soft, add 3 quarts (litres) of ordinary consommé and bring to the boil.

Add 2 cups (350 grams) of potatoes cut in thin round slices. Bring to the boil, season and simmer gently.

At the last moment, when the soup is ready, remove the saucepan from heat and add 4 tablespoons (60 grams) of butter and a tablespoon of chervil leaves.

Soup with cabbage and miques (Périgord cookery). SOUPE AUX CHOUX ET AUX MIQUES—Put the cabbages into a saucepan and cover with water. Add a piece of salt, unsmoked ham (or a salt chine of pork), carrot, turnips, rape, onions studded with cloves, celery, garlic, a *bouquet garni** and the usual seasoning.

Using maize (U.S. corn) flour, make some *miques**.

A few minutes before serving the soup, take some of the vegetables out with a perforated spoon, fry them in fat, sprinkle with flour, moisten with a few tablespoons of stock and put back into the saucepan.

Serve the soup garnished with thin slices of bread and, on a separate dish, the ham (or chine of pork), placed on the cabbage and surrounded by maize flour *miques*.

Soupe à la farine (Alsatian cookery)—Pour 3 tablespoons of flour, diluted with cold consommé or water until quite smooth, into 1½ quarts (litres) of boiling consommé.

Season with salt, pepper and a pinch of grated nutmeg and mix well. Boil for 5 minutes. At the last moment, add ½ cup (1 decilitre) of fresh cream and 2 tablespoons of butter.

Fish soup with vermicelli à la marseillaise. SOUPE DE POISSON AU VERMICELLE À LA MARSEILLAISE—Sauté 2 good tablespoons of sliced onion in oil in a saucepan with a thick flat bottom. When the onion is cooked, sprinkle it with a tablespoon of flour and fry for a moment, stirring with a spoon.

Cover with 2 quarts (litres) of water. Add 6 pound (500 grams) of fish bones and trimmings cut up into very small pieces.

Season with salt and pepper. Add a tablespoon of pounded parsley, a fragment of bay leaf, a sprig of thyme, a little crushed garlic, 4 tablespoons of tomato purée and a good pinch of powdered saffron. Cook on a fairly high flame for about 20 minutes.

Strain the fish stock through a fine strainer. Bring it to the boil and pour into it 4 tablespoons of vermicelli. Poach for 10 minutes. At the last moment, add half a tablespoon of chopped parsley.

Soupe au fromage—See *Onion soup gratinée*.

Garlic soup à la provençale. SOUPE À L'AIL À LA PROVENÇALE—Put 2 quarts (litres) of water, 24 small cloves of garlic, a sprig of thyme, a clove, a branch of sage, 4 teaspoons (25 grams) of salt and a pinch of pepper into a saucepan. Boil fast for 20 minutes.

Strain the soup through a fine strainer and pour it into a tureen into which you have put about 20 small slices of bread, sprinkled with grated cheese and placed in the oven for an instant, just to melt the cheese, and with 2 tablespoons of olive oil poured over them. Let the bread swell properly, before serving.

Onion soup. SOUPE À L'OIGNON—Slice ½ pound (250 grams) of onions finely and fry in butter, cooking them through thoroughly but without allowing to colour too much

When the onion is nearly done, sprinkle it with 2 tablespoons (25 grams) of flour. Stir with a wooden spoon for a few moments. Add 2 quarts (litres) of white consommé or, if the soup is intended as a Lenten dish, an equal quantity of water. Cook for 25 minutes. Pour this soup (strained or not, as preferred) over slices of bread dried in the oven.

Onion soup gratinée, also called cheese soup. SOUPE À L'OIGNON GRATINÉE, SOUPE AU FROMAGE—Prepare like ordinary onion soup. Pour this soup (strained or not, as preferred) into an ovenproof earthenware or china bowl over slices of bread dried in the oven, arranged in the bowl in layers, each layer being covered with grated cheese. Sprinkle with grated cheese and a little melted butter. Put in the oven to brown the top.

Périgord soup 'sobronade'. SOUPE PÉRIGOURDINE 'SOBRONADE'—This dish constitutes a solid dish rather than a soup.

Put 1½ pounds (750 grams) of white beans, having previously soaked them in cold water, into a big saucepan. Cover with cold water. Add 1 pound (500 grams) of fresh pork (fat and lean) and ½ pound (250 grams) of ham cut into small square pieces. Bring to the boil and skim.

Add to the saucepan one or two turnips cut in thick slices (one-third of these sliced turnips previously fried in a pan, *fricassée* with chopped fat bacon), 3 carrots and a good stalk of celery, cut into quarters, an onion studded with 2 cloves, a *bouquet garni** and mixed chopped garlic and parsley. Season with salt and pepper and cook with a lid on.

After boiling for 20 minutes, add 1½ cups (250 grams) of potatoes cut in thick slices. Cook on a low heat for 1½ hours.

Pour this soup into a tureen over thin slices of stale bread.

Tourain périgourdin (Périgord cookery)—Fry ¾ cup (150 grams) of finely sliced onions in fat, colouring them slightly but not allowing them to brown. Sprinkle with a good tablespoon of flour, add 2 crushed cloves of garlic, moisten with a few tablespoons of boiling water and mix until smooth. This is called *fricassée*.

Cook 2 big, seeded tomatoes in 2 quarts (litres) of stock or water with salt and pepper. Drain the tomatoes, mash them and add to the stock. Add the *fricassée* to the stock. Simmer steadily for 45 minutes.

At the last moment, thicken this soup with a liaison of 2 yolks diluted with a few tablespoons of stock.

Pour into a soup tureen over big, thin slices of home-made bread.

Note. Like all onion soups, the Périgord *tourain* can be *gratinée*. To do this, pour it into a deep dish over slices of bread, each layer of which has been sprinkled with grated Gruyère cheese. Sprinkle the surface with grated cheese and slowly brown the top in the oven.

Spelt soup (Provençal cookery). SOUPE D'ÉPEAUTRE—Put 2 pounds (1 kilo) of mutton (shoulder or leg) into a saucepan. Cover with 3 quarts (litres) of water, bring to the boil and skim. Add an onion, studded with 2 cloves, 2 carrots, 1 turnip, 1 leek, 1 stalk of celery, 1 clove of garlic and season with salt.

Add 4 handfuls of spelt (a kind of chaffy wheat with small brownish grain). Simmer very gently for 3 hours.

Whiting soup à la bretonne. SOUPE DE MERLAN À LA BRETONNE—This soup is a kind of *Cotriade* (Breton bouillabaisse). It is prepared in the same manner as the latter, using whitings cut in chunks, potatoes and all the aromatic herbs characteristic of that dish. It can, in fact, be considered as a kind of bouillabaisse made without tomatoes, oil, garlic or saffron. See COTRIADE. (Illustrated on the next page.)

INTERNATIONAL SOUPS AND BROTHS:

Beer soup (German cookery). SOUPE À LA BIÈRE—Stir 1½ quarts (litres) of light beer into a *roux* of 3 tablespoons (50 grams) of butter and 4 tablespoons (60 grams) of flour. Season with salt, pepper and cinnamon. Add a teaspoon of sugar. Boil for a few minutes.

Bind with ⅔ cup (1½ decilitres) of thick cream and pour piping hot over slices of toast.

Onion soup (*Robert Carrier*)

Whiting soup à la bretonne (*Claire*)

Beetroot (U.S.A. beet) soup à l'allemande. POTAGE DE BETTERAVE À L'ALLEMANDE—Peel a big, raw beetroot, cut it into uniform chunks and bake it in the oven in a casserole with 3 tablespoons (50 grams) of butter and a pinch of salt.

Rub it through a fine sieve and add to the purée obtained one-third of its volume of potato purée, prepared as described in the recipe for *Purée of potato soup* (*Potage Parmentier*).

Dilute the soup to the desired consistency by adding to it the required quantity of consommé. Heat on a high flame, season and, at the last moment, add from 4 to 7 tablespoons (60 to 80 grams) of fresh butter. Serve croûtons fried in butter separately.

Beetroot soup à la russe. POTAGE DE BETTERAVE À LA RUSSE—Cut a medium-sized raw beetroot into *julienne** strips. Add one-third of its volume of onion and celery, also cut into *julienne** strips.

Soften these vegetables slowly in a casserole with 3 tablespoons (50 grams) of butter, a pinch of salt and a teaspoon of sugar.

When the vegetables are cooked, add 6 cups (1½ litres) of chicken consommé. Boil for 25 minutes. Skim off surplus fat and add chervil leaves to the soup. Serve croûtons fried in butter separately.

Polish borshch. POTAGE BORTSCH POLONAIS—Soften slowly in butter a *julienne** composed of one medium-sized onion, the white part of 2 leeks, ½ head (200 grams) of cabbage, 2½ cups (250 grams) of raw beetroot (U.S.A. beet), a stalk of celery and a parsnip. Cover with 2 quarts (litres) of white consommé.

Add a small duck browned in the oven, 1 pound (500 grams) of blanched brisket of beef and a piece of blanched lean bacon. Garnish with a *bouquet garni** containing, in addition to the usual herbs, some fennel and marjoram. Bring to the boil, skim, and simmer gently until all the meats are completely cooked, taking care to remove the duck and the bacon as soon as they are done.

Fifteen minutes before serving, add 8 small chipolata sausages to poach in the soup.

Remove all the meat garnish. Cut the breast of duck, the beef and the bacon into dice and the sausages into little round slices.

Add a tablespoon of *Mushroom essence* (see ESSENCE) to ½ cup (1 decilitre) of the juice of raw, grated beetroot and a tablespoon of chopped and blanched fennal and parsley to the soup.

Serve the meat garnish and a sauceboat of sour cream separately.

The sausages can be grilled instead of being poached in the soup.

The sour cream is often put in the soup, instead of being served separately.

Russian borshch. POTAGE BORTSCH À LA RUSSE—4 pints stock, 3 to 4 beetroots (U.S.A. beets), ½ pound fresh cabbage, 2 carrots, 1 parsnip, 2 stalks celery, ¼ pound boiled ham (optional), 6 Frankfurter sausages (optional), 1 large onion, 3 tablespoons tomato purée (or ¼ pound fresh tomatoes), 2 tablespoons vinegar, 1 tablespoon sugar, 1 to 2 bay leaves, sprig of dill, sprig of parsley, 1½ teaspoons salt, ½ teaspoon pepper, ¼ pint sour cream.

Method. Prepare stock. Clean and shred beetroot, carrots, parsnip, celery and the onion. Cut the root vegetables into slices first, then into little 'matchsticks'. The decorative appearance of the vegetables in borshch is very important. Put into a saucepan, add tomatoes or tomato purée, sugar and enough stock, with a little fat (if the stock has no fat, add 1 to 2 tablespoons butter) to cover the vegetables. Simmer for 15 to 20 minutes stirring from time to time and adding stock or water to prevent sticking. Add shredded cabbage, mix well and simmer another 15 to 20 minutes. Pour in all the stock, add salt and pepper to taste, bay leaf, 1 tablespoon vinegar, and simmer until the vegetables are done. Potatoes may be put in the borshch—whole if they are small, cut into chips if large. When the borshch is ready and just before serving, a few slices of boiled ham or sausages (of the Frankfurter type) can be added to it.

To give it its characteristic, attractive colour, keep one beetroot for last minute use. Rub it through a fine grater, cover with a cupful of stock, bring to the boil, simmer for 2 to 3 minutes with a teaspoon of vinegar and strain the liquid into the borshch. Sprinkle with finely chopped parsley and dill. Add the sour cream and serve. Mushroom patties or buckwheat croûtons may accompany the borshch.

Botvinya (Russian cookery). POTAGE BATWINIA—Boil 2 pounds (1 kilo) fish and leave to cool. Cook ¾ pound (350 grams) spinach and ½ pound (250 grams) sorrel separately and rub them through a sieve. Cut some fresh cucumbers into strips, grate some horseradish and chop some spring onions. Amalgamate the spinach and the sorrel purées, season with salt and pepper, add a little sugar, a teaspoonful of lemon zest and dilute with kvas.

To serve. Pour the botvinya into a tureen or straight into plates. Cut the fish into portions and put on a dish, garnish with fresh cucumbers, spring onions, horseradish and chopped dill. Surround the fish with cooked crayfish tails and lettuce hearts. Separately, serve ice cubes in a bowl, and a sauceboat of sour cream.

Camaro à la brésilienne—Truss a chicken as for an entrée and put it into an earthenware casserole. Cover with water. Bring to the boil, skim, season and add a *bouquet** composed of parsley, chervil and a medium-sized onion. Cook for 30 minutes.

Add 4 tablespoons of rice and cook, simmering gently for 2 or 3 hours, depending on the tenderness of the chicken.

Untruss the chicken. Put it back into the casserole and serve.

Cherry soup I (German cookery). SOUPE AUX CERISES—Put in a stewpan 1 pound (500 grams) of cherries, stoned, with 1 cup (2 decilitres) of hot water, a small piece of cinnamon bark and a small piece of lemon peel. Cook over a high flame for 8 to 10 minutes. Press the cherries through a fine sieve.

Dilute this purée with 1 cup (2½ decilitres) of Bordeaux wine which has been strained through muslin after having been boiled with the cherry stones crushed in a mortar. Mix, bring to the boil and bind with a teaspoon of potato flour blended with a little cold water.

Stir in a small spoonful of sugar and pour very hot into

the tureen: add some rusks broken into small pieces.

Cherry soup II. SOUPE AUX CERISES—Cook 1 pound (500 grams) of cherries, stoned, in a pot with water, cinnamon, lemon peel and 2 tablespoons (25 grams) of sugar. Boil for 4 minutes. Thicken with a teaspoon of potato flour blended with cold water.

Dilute with ⅔ cup (2 decilitres) of Bordeaux wine, previously boiled with the crushed cherry stones and strained.

Pour boiling hot into the tureen and serve at the same time pieces of rusk or slices of brioche lightly toasted.

Cherry soup III. SOUPE AUX CERISES—Melt 3 tablespoons (50 grams) of butter in a saucepan. Add 1 pound (500 grams) of cherries, stoned, 2 tablespoons (25 grams) of sugar, a little cinnamon and some lemon peel. Moisten with 1 cup (2 decilitres) of water. Boil for 8 minutes and pour on to slices of toast.

English chicken soup or chicken broth I. SOUPE AU POULET À L'ANGLAISE—Put into a deep stewpan or *marmite* a medium-sized chicken. Pour in 2 quarts (1¾ litres) of plain stock. Bring to the boil, skim, add salt.

Put in for flavouring an onion stuck with a clove, a bunch of herbs, and a stick of celery and add ½ cup (100 grams) of rice. Simmer very slowly till cooked.

Take out the chicken and cut it into small pieces. Put it back in the stewpan, having removed the onion and herbs. Add ¾ cup (1½ decilitres) of chopped vegetables cooked in butter and bring to the boil.

English chicken soup II. SOUPE AU POULET À L'ANGLAISE—Cook 1 cup (2 decilitres) of chopped-up mixed vegetables in butter until they are soft. Pour in 2 quarts (1¾ litres) of plain stock; then put in a medium-sized chicken cut up while raw into small pieces. Bring to the boil, skim.

Add ½ cup (100 grams) of rice and simmer slowly.

Chotodriec soup (Polish cookery)—Cut a cooked beet in thin rounds and put them in a tureen. Add 2 egg yolks cut in round slices, 2 tablespoons of peeled shrimps and thin slices of cucumber. Sprinkle with chopped fennel and chives. Pour over 1 quart (litre) of the juice of pickled cucumbers previously brought to the boil with a little yeast and mixed with a quart (litre) of sour milk. Season. Chill on ice before serving.

Clam soup with vegetables or Manhattan clam chowder (American cookery). SOUPE DE CLAMS AUX LÉGUMES—Cook gently in butter ½ cup (100 grams) of salt pork, cut in small dice. When the pork is almost cooked add a medium-sized onion cut in dice. Cook without allowing it to colour. Add 2 sticks of celery and one or two peeled green peppers, also cut in dice.

Sprinkle with a good tablespoon of flour (optional). Cook lightly, stirring all the time. Pour in 1½ quarts (litres) of light stock or water. Bring to the boil. Add 2 medium-sized tomatoes, peeled and with the seeds pressed out, cut in dice, and 2 medium-sized potatoes (300 grams) cut in slightly bigger dice. Season and cook briskly.

Now open 3 dozen hard-shelled clams, keeping their liquor. Trim these clams, putting aside the stomachs. Chop the trimmings and put them in a saucepan with the clam liquor and 1 cup (2 decilitres) of water. Cook for 15 minutes. Strain through a fine strainer and add this liquid to the soup. Put into the latter the soft parts of the clams cut into large dice. Bring to the boil, cover and leave them to poach on the lowest possible heat.

Finish the soup with a pinch of thyme, a spoonful of chopped parsley and ¼ pound (125 grams) of butter. Heat and serve with water biscuits (soda crackers) whole or broken.

New York clam chowder differs decidedly from New England clam chowder, which is a soup made with diced salt pork, onions, potatoes, clams and rich milk.

Cock-a-leekie (Scottish cookery). SOUPE AU COQ ET POIREAUX—Add to chicken broth (made with a medium-sized fowl), strained and skimmed of its fat, ⅞ cup (2 decilitres) of the white part of leeks cut into thin strips and simmered in butter and the flesh of the chicken cut in thin pieces.

Note. Although this recipe, with the further justification of its title, seems to demand a cockerel, the soup is most often prepared with a plump, tender hen.

Gulyas soup (Hungarian cookery). POTAGE GULYAS—This soup is made of beef cut into small pieces, onion and stock seasoned with *paprika*. It has either potatoes, cooked in the stock, or noodles added to it.

Gumbo or okra soup (American cookery). SOUPE AUX GOMBOS, SOUPE OKRA—Cook 2 chopped onions very lightly in 2 tablespoons of butter. Add 5 strips or rashers (75 grams) of bacon (or raw ham) cut in dice and cook for 3 minutes; then put in ½ pound (250 grams) of raw chicken flesh, cut in dice. Cook lightly, shaking the pot, until the pieces of chicken are quite firm. Pour in 1½ quarts (litres) of chicken stock, bring to the boil and cook gently for 25 minutes. Add 1 cup (150 grams) of chopped gumbos and 2 tomatoes, peeled, seeds pressed out, drained and crushed. Cook for 25 minutes.

Skim all fat from the soup, and before serving add 3 tablespoons of rice, boiled in salted water for 15 minutes and rinsed in cold water.

Note. This soup should be quite highly seasoned. It is sometimes finished off with a few drops of Worcestershire sauce.

Hare soup (English cookery). POTAGE AU LIÈVRE—Cut the forequarter and a leg of hare into pieces and cook in butter with 5 tablespoons of a *mirepoix** consisting of carrots, onion, white part of leeks, lean ham, a sprig of parsley and thyme and a bay leaf.

When all these ingredients are nicely browned, sprinkle them with 3 tablespoons (30 grams) of arrowroot or cornstarch. Brown the arrowroot lightly, add 2 quarts (litres) of ordinary stock, season and simmer gently for 2½ hours.

Remove the leg with a perforated spoon, bone it, cut in small dice and keep this *salpicon** hot. Moisten with a few tablespoons of strained stock. Add to it the hare's liver, cut into small slices and poach the liver lightly.

Take out the rest of the hare with a perforated spoon and bone it. Add the liver to the boned hare meat, pound together in a mortar and rub through a sieve.

Strain the stock and skim it for 25 minutes. Flavour it with 3 tablespoons of sweet marjoram, basil and rosemary infusion, add 4 tablespoons (60 grams) of butter and spice with a pinch of cayenne pepper.

Put the hare purée into a soup tureen and pour the stock over it. Mix well with a whisk. Add the hare *salpicon* to the soup and lace it with 4 tablespoons of port.

It is usual in England to add a tablespoon of redcurrant jelly to hare soup just before serving.

Hochepot à la flamande—Put 1 pound, 3 ounces (600 grams) of brisket of beef, 10 ounces (300 grams) of shoulder of mutton, 10 ounces (300 grams) of breast of mutton, 5 ounces (150 grams) of pigs' tails, 1 pound, 3 ounces (600 grams) of pig's feet, 10 ounces (300 grams) of pigs' ears and ½ pound (250 grams) of salted bacon into a big stock-pot.

Cover these meats with 3 quarts (litres) of water, season with 2 teaspoons (12 grams) of salt. Bring to the boil, skim and simmer gently.

After 2 hours of cooking add 2 medium-sized carrots

(200 grams), a medium-sized onion, 4 leeks (white part only), a head of cabbage and 3 big potatoes—slicing all these vegetables.

Continue to cook, simmering gently for about 2 hours.

Serve the bouillon of this soup in a tureen, garnishing it with a few vegetables. Separately, on a big dish, serve the meats and the rest of the vegetables. Add 12 chipolata sausages, which should be poached in the soup at the last moment.

Hungarian soup. POTAGE HONGROIS—Cut 1 pound (500 grams) of lean beef (taken from the top of contre-filet) into large dice and brown it in butter with ½ cup (100 grams) of chopped onion. Season with salt, a good pinch of paprika, a pinch (3 grams) of cumin and a pinch of garlic.

Sprinkle with 1½ tablespoons (20 grams) of flour. Cook this flour for a few moments, dilute with 2 quarts (litres) of ordinary stock, bring to the boil, and simmer gently.

After cooking for 1 hour, add ¾ cup (150 grams) of diced potatoes.

When serving, put 3 tablespoons of diced croûtons fried in butter into the soup.

Hungarian soup with liver dumplings. SOUPE AUX BOULETTES DE FOIE—Add to 1½ quarts (litres) of boiling consommé, liver dumplings prepared in this way:

Cook for a few moments, in lard or butter, ¾ cup (150 grams) of calf's or ox (beef) liver cut in small dice. Season and sauté over a high flame.

Pound the liver in a mortar and rub it through a sieve. Put the purée in a basin, stir until smooth and add to it 3 tablespoons (50 grams) of softened butter, 4 tablespoons (50 grams) of chopped onions cooked for a few moments in butter, 6 tablespoons (40 grams) of fresh breadcrumbs, a teaspoon of chopped parsley and 2 beaten eggs.

Season with salt, paprika and grated nutmeg. Mix well.

Using this mixture make dumplings or long quenelles of medium size, and poach them in the boiling consommé for 15 minutes.

Lithuanian soup. SOUPE LITHUANIENNE—Add to 1½ quarts (litres) of very light potato soup (without butter), half a celery heart, sliced into strips and cooked gently in butter. Cook for 30 minutes.

Add at the last moment 2 tablespoons of sorrel leaves cooked till soft in butter, ½ cup (1 decilitre) of sour cream and 3 tablespoons (50 grams) of fresh butter.

Garnish with 8 little squares of bacon (streaky bacon), 8 poached and skinned chipolata sausages and 4 fried egg yolks.

Liver soup or Maj leves (Hungarian cookery). SOUPE À LA PURÉE DE FOIE—Put into melted butter, in a saucepan, 4 tablespoons (50 grams) of onion, 3 tablespoons (50 grams) of carrot, 3 tablespoons (50 grams) of lean salt pork and a shallot, all finely chopped, a sprig of thyme and half a bay leaf.

When the vegetables are cooked, add ¾ cup (200 grams) of calf's or ox (beef) liver cut into dice. Season with salt, pepper and grated nutmeg and brown quickly. Sprinkle with 1½ tablespoons of flour. Stir in ½ cup (1 decilitre) of white wine and 1½ quarts (litres) of consommé. Cook for 25 minutes.

Drain the liver and vegetables and pound together in a mortar. Rub through a fine sieve. Add the cooking liquor, diluting it, if necessary, with a few tablespoons of consommé.

Bring to the boil and serve with small croûtons of bread fried in butter.

Livonian soup with klyotski (Russian cookery). POTAGE LIVONIEN AUX KLOSKI—Chop an onion and a handful (50 grams) of sorrel leaves finely and cook them in 3 tablespoons of butter in a covered pan. Add 1 pound or 2½ quarts (500 grams) of blanched, well pressed out spinach to these vegetables. Cook together for a few moments, then add 2 cups (4 decilitres) of *Béchamel sauce* (see SAUCE). Mix well and simmer gently for a quarter of an hour.

Rub this mixture through a sieve. Dilute this purée with a quart (litre) of ordinary stock. Put back into the saucepan for a quarter of an hour, skimming frequently.

At the last moment, finish off the soup with ½ cup (1 decilitre) of cream and 4 tablespoons (60 grams) of butter and serve it with klyotski (*quenelles*) prepared as follows:

Make 7 ounces (200 grams) of unsweetened *chou paste**, add to it a tablespoon of chopped, blanched and pressed out shallots, 1 ounce (25 grams) of chopped, lean, cooked ham and some (25 grams) very small croûtons fried in butter.

Take up a little of the mixture with a teaspoon and drop the *klyotski* into boiling water or stock. They are ready when they float up to the surface.

Mille-fanti soup (Italian cookery). SOUPE MILLE-FANTI—Add the following preparation little by little to 1½ quarts (litres) of boiling consommé:

Put into a basin ¾ cup (80 grams) of fresh breadcrumbs, ½ cup (50 grams) of grated Parmesan cheese and 2 beaten eggs. Season with salt, pepper and nutmeg and mix well.

Cover the soup and cook very slowly for 8 minutes. Stir with a whisk before serving.

Note. This soup, which is simply a kind of *panada* of cheese and egg, can be made with water in place of consommé.

Preparation of minestrone soup (*Claire*)

Minestrone (Italian cookery)—Melt in a saucepan 2 tablespoons (40 grams) of grated salt pork fat and add 3 strips or rashers (50 grams) of streaky bacon cut in small pieces, 2 tablespoons of chopped onion and the chopped white of a leek. Cook gently for 5 minutes. Pour in 1¾ quarts (litres) of water, season and bring to the boil.

Add 1 carrot, a turnip, a potato and a tender stick of celery cut in small pieces, the heart of a small cabbage similarly cut and 2 tomatoes peeled, with seeds pressed out, and chopped. Boil for 25 minutes. Add ½ cup (50 grams) of French (string) beans cut in dice, ½ cup (1 decilitre) of fresh peas and ⅓ cup (80 grams) of rice. Cook very gently for 45 minutes.

At the last moment add a tablespoon of grated salt pork fat crushed with 2 cloves of garlic, a tablespoon of chopped basil and a tablespoon of chopped parsley. Any vegetables in season may be put in minestrone.

Mock-turtle soup (English cookery)—Soak a calf's head in water, bone it and cook in white stock flavoured and seasoned with carrots, onion, celery, a *bouquet garni**, cloves, salt and pepper. Drain the head when it is cooked, cut off the ears (which are not used for this soup), trim the rest of the meat and put it under a press between two plates. When it is quite cold, cut it, either with a knife or a stamp cutter (punch), into square or round pieces. Keep these pieces hot in a little of the stock in which the calf's head was cooked, to be added to the soup at the last moment.

Separately, while the calf's head is cooking, in a saucepan prepare a clear brown gravy, made of slices of salt leg of pork, veal knuckle and a half-roasted chicken. Dilute this gravy with stock. When the meats are nearly done and the gravy is reduced, add the stock in which the calf's head was cooked. Garnish with stock-pot vegetables. Simmer gently for about 2 hours.

Strain the stock through a napkin. Thicken it with a little arrowroot diluted with cold stock. Add to it an aromatic infusion made by infusing some basil, spring onion, marjoram, thyme and bay leaf in Madeira or port.

Strain the soup through a muslin cloth and pour it into a soup tureen. Garnish with pieces of calf's head kept for this purpose and small quenelles made of ordinary forcemeat mixed with pounded, hard boiled yolks of egg.

Mulligatawny soup I—*Ingredients.* 2 quarts (litres) of water, 2 pounds (1 kilo) of mutton (a tin of mutton may be used), 2 onions, 2 carrots, 2 apples, 1 small turnip, a *bouquet garni*, 2 tablespoons of flour, 1 tablespoon of curry powder, the juice of ½ a lemon, salt.

Method. Remove the fat from the mutton and melt it in the saucepan. Have the apples and vegetables ready sliced, and when there is sufficient liquid fat to fry them, take out the pieces of fat, put in the vegetables and cook them for about 15 minutes. Sprinkle in the flour and curry powder, fry for a few minutes, then add the meat in small pieces, a teaspoon of salt, the herbs and water. When the compound boils, remove the scum as it rises, then cover and cook gently for about 3 hours. Strain, rub the meat through a wire sieve, and return to the saucepan. When boiling, add the lemon juice, season, and serve. Well-cooked rice should be handed round with this.

Note. The bones and remains of any kind of meat or poultry may be used instead of mutton.

Mulligatawny soup II (English cookery)—Cut a medium-sized chicken as for *fricassée** and cook it in 2 litres (quarts) of white stock with sliced carrot and a medium-sized onion, a *bouquet garni**, a sprig of parsley and 3 tablespoons of mushroom parings.

Separately, brown a medium-sized, chopped onion lightly in 3 tablespoons (50 grams) of butter. Sprinkle this onion with 1 tablespoon (20 grams) of cornflour and a small spoonful of curry powder. Moisten this mixture with the chicken stock and cook gently for 10 minutes.

Strain this thickened stock through a sieve, simmer it for 15 minutes, and, at the last moment, add to it 2 decilitres of cream.

Put the trimmed pieces of chicken into a soup tureen and strain the soup over them. Serve *Rice à l'indienne** separately.

Mutton broth (English cookery)—Cook in butter a coarse *brunoise** composed of a carrot, a turnip, 2 leeks (white part only), a good stalk of celery and a white onion. When this *brunoise* is done, cover it with 2 quarts (litres) of white stock.

Add 10 ounces (300 grams) of breast and neck of mutton and ⅓ cup (100 grams) of barley, previously well blanched. Simmer gently for an hour and a half.

Drain the mutton, bone it and cut into large dice. Put the meat back into the broth. Add a tablespoon of chopped and blanched parsley.

Mutton soup à la grecque (Greek style). POTAGE DE MOUTON À LA GRECQUE—Make 6 cups (1½ litres) of light *Split pea purée.*

In a big casserole fry in butter 1 pound (500 grams) of boned breast of mutton, cut in large dice, with 2 cups (4 decilitres) of *brunoise** of vegetables. Moisten with 3 quarts plus 1 cup (3 litres) of light stock (or water, if stock is not available). Season with salt and pepper. Bring to the boil, skim and simmer gently for an hour and a half.

Mix the *Split pea purée* and the mutton stock (leaving the pieces of mutton and the *brunoise* in it). Boil for a few moments.

Clear oxtail soup (English cookery). POTAGE OXTAIL CLAIR—Put 3 pounds (1 kilo 500 grams) of oxtail, cut in small chunks, into a stewpan, on a foundation of sliced carrots, leeks and onions. Sweat in the oven for 25 minutes.

Cover with 2½ quarts (litres) of stock made by cooking 3 pounds (1 kilo 500 grams) of gelatinous bones for 7 or 8 hours in 3¼ quarts (litres) of water. Season.

Simmer gently, so that the boiling is imperceptible, from 3½ to 4 hours.

Strain the soup and skim off surplus fat. Clarify by boiling it for an hour with 1 pound (500 grams) of chopped lean beef and the white part of two leeks, finely sliced, both these ingredients whisked with a raw white of egg.

Strain this stock through a napkin. Garnish with pieces of oxtail and 1½ cups (3 decilitres) of coarse *brunoise** of carrots, turnips and celery sweated in butter and dropped into the stock. Add a tablespoon of sherry.

Thick oxtail soup (English cookery). POTAGE OXTAIL LIÉ—Proceed as for *Clear oxtail.* When the broth has been strained, thicken it with 3 tablespoons (50 grams) of brown *roux** to each quart (litre) and 3 good tablespoons of *tomato purée*. Garnish with mixed vegetables cut up and cooked in butter as for clear oxtail soup. Flavour with sherry.

Oyster soup with okra (American cookery)—Put ⅜ cup (100 grams) of chopped pork fat into a thick-bottomed saucepan, and when the fat melts, add 1 cup (100 grams) of chopped onion and cook it gently without letting it colour. Next add 3 tomatoes peeled and cut in quarters, 10 okras, a small green pepper finely chopped, and 1 quart (litre) of white stock. Season with salt and pepper (a little curry powder may be added, if liked). Cook for 15 minutes, then put in 24 raw de-bearded oysters with their liquor, and poach them for a few moments. Thicken the soup with a little arrowroot.

Pistou soup I (Italian cookery). SOUPE AU PISTOU—Put in a saucepan, in 1½ quarts (litres) of boiling water, ½ pound (250 grams) of French (string) beans cut in dice, 3 potatoes cut in small pieces and 2 tomatoes peeled, with seeds pressed out and crushed. Season.

When the vegetables are almost cooked add a handful (100 grams) of spaghetti. Finish cooking very slowly.

In the meantime prepare the following mixture:

Pound in a mortar 2 cloves of garlic with several basil leaves. Add, still pounding in the mortar, 2 tablespoons of oil and, finally, 2 or 3 tablespoons of soup. Pour the soup into the tureen, adding to it the above mixture and 4 tablespoons of grated Parmesan.

This soup, of Genoese origin, is very popular in Provence.

Pistou soup II. SOUPE AU PISTOU—Cook gently in a tablespoon of butter a medium-sized onion and a leek cut in small pieces. Add 2 tomatoes peeled, drained and crushed.

Pour in 1½ quarts (litres) of stock or water, bring to the boil and add ½ pound (250 grams) of French (string) beans cut in dice and 3 potatoes cut in small pieces. Season.

Finish off as in the preceding recipe.

Note. The garlic paste prescribed for binding the pistou soup can also be prepared with grated salt pork fat. Sometimes halved tomatoes, well seeded then grilled, are also added.

Puchero soup (Spanish pot-au-feu). POTAGE PUCHERO—Prepare as for *Olla-Podrida**, but reduce considerably the quantity of basic ingredients, particularly the meats.

Rahm-suppe (German cookery)—Cook 3 tablespoons (50 grams) each of butter and flour together without colouring and stir in one quart (litre) of white stock and the same quantity of boiled milk. Put in a small onion stuck with a clove and a sprig of parsley, and season with a pinch of cumin, some grated nutmeg, 1 teaspoon (6 grams) of salt and 3 peppercorns. Cook for 45 minutes. Strain the soup and thicken it with 1 cup (2 decilitres) of sour cream, letting it boil for 1 minute. Serve with croûtons of bread fried in butter.

Rassol'nik (Russian cookery). POTAGE ROSSOLNICK—Prepare 2 quarts (litres) of slightly thickened chicken broth and add 1 cup (2 decilitres) of fresh cucumber juice. Cut some celery roots and large parsley roots (Hamburg parsley) into the shape of tiny carrots, cutting a cross in the base of each. Cut some pickled cucumbers into small chunks. Blanch all these vegetables well and add to the chicken broth. Cook gently for 40 minutes, keeping the soup well skimmed.

Finally, add 2 tablespoons of cucumber juice and bind with 2 egg yolks beaten in ½ cup (1 decilitre) of cream. Serve in the soup some very small dumplings made of chicken forcemeat and poached at the last moment.

Shchi (Russian cookery). POTAGE STSCHY—Cook in 2 tablespoons of butter until they are a pale golden colour 2 large chopped onions. Sprinkle these onions with 2 tablespoons of flour, cook for a few moments then stir in 2½ quarts (litres) of white stock and bring to the boil. Put into this soup ½ pound (250 grams) of brisket of beef cut into large dice, blanched for 10 minutes in salted water, drained and trimmed, and ½ pound (250 grams) of sauerkraut, coarsely chopped. Add a good bunch of herbs and cook very gently for about 3 hours. Finish off the soup at the last moment with ⅝ cup (1½ decilitres) of sour cream and a teaspoon of chopped blanched parsley.

Solyanka (Russian cookery). POTAGE SOLIANKA—Prepare 2 quarts (litres) of ham-flavoured consommé, and at the moment of serving add ½ pound (250 grams) of braised sauerkraut and a tablespoon of blanched parsley leaves.

Sour cream soup I (Hungarian cookery). SOUPE À LA CRÈME AIGRE—Add to 1½ quarts (litres) of thin white sauce an onion stuck with a clove, a *bouquet garni**, a pinch of powdered cumin and grated nutmeg. Cook for 20 minutes, skimming well. Rub through a fine sieve. Add ½ cup (1 decilitre) of sour cream and serve with croûtons of bread fried in butter.

Sour cream soup II. SOUPE À LA CRÈME AIGRE—Make a white *roux* of 3 tablespoons each of butter and flour. Stir in 1 quart (litre) of stock and a pint (½ litre) of boiled milk. Finish and garnish as above.

Sweet-sour soup, or Mehlsuppe, also called flour soup (German cookery). SOUPE AIGRE-DOUCE, SOUPE À LA FARINE—Cut up finely a medium-sized onion and the white parts of two leeks and cook them for a few moments in 2 tablespoons of butter. Sprinkle with two tablespoons of flour. Add 1½ quarts (litres) of stock or water and cook for 25 minutes. At the last moment stir in 1 cup (2 decilitres) of thick cream and a tablespoon of fresh butter.

Milanaise tripe soup, or Butséga. SOUPE AU GRAS-DOUBLE À LA MILANAISE—Cut in thin strips 1 pound (500 grams) of veal tripe, blanched, trimmed and drained. Put in a saucepan with a medium-sized onion and the white part of a leek, chopped and cooked with some salt pork fat cut into small dice. Cook for a few moments, sprinkle with a tablespoon of flour and stir in 2 quarts (litres) of stock (or water). Bring to the boil. Add two tomatoes peeled, with the seeds pressed out and cut in slices, the heart of a medium-sized cabbage cut in thin strips, ½ cup peas and a few broccoli heads. Season and cook briskly.

Turtle soup (English cookery). POTAGE À LA TORTUE—This soup is made from the large sea turtle, and is prepared with the bony carapace and plastron only, from which the outside shields (or thin hard shell) have been removed.

The carapace and plastron of the animal (bled after killing for as long as possible) are cut into pieces of equal size, blanched for a few minutes in boiling water, cleaned of the outer shields that cover them, put in a big stewpan with richly flavoured consommé, savoury vegetables and *turtle herbs* (see HERBS), and cooked like an ordinary broth for 6 or 7 hours. After cooking, the pieces of turtle are drained, boned, and cut into pieces about 1½ inch square and kept warm in some strained broth.

The liquor used to cook the turtle can be a stock made with the flesh of the interior of the animal, reinforced with some beef and chicken. The prepared soup is strained through a cloth, reheated and enriched with 1⅓ cups (4 decilitres) of Madeira (or sherry) to each quart (litre).

The aromatic herbs used for flavouring are basil, marjoram, sage, rosemary, savoury and thyme. Coriander and peppercorns are also added in a little muslin bag.

Just before serving, the pieces of turtle are put back in the soup.

Turtle soup (thick). POTAGE À LA TORTUE—This soup is made in the same way as described in the previous recipe. After it has been strained it is thickened with a *roux* of 2 tablespoons (30 grams) each of flour and butter, or with ½ cup (scant) of arrowroot to a quart (litre) of soup.

Ukha (Russian cookery). POTAGE OUKA—Prepare fish stock using sturgeon, tench or perch, well spiced with parsnip, celery, fennel and mushroom parings.

Separately, make small *paupiettes* of lavaret or whitefish and poach them and prepare ½ pound (250 grams) of *julienne** of parsnip, white part of leek and celery. Gently cook this *julienne* in butter, and when it is quite soft, moisten it with a few tablespoons of strained fish stock.

Clarify the fish stock, either with caviar or with chopped whiting, and strain through a napkin.

Add the fish paupiettes and the julienne of vegetables to the soup. Separately, serve a timbale of cooked buckwheat and a dish of small *rastegais*. See HORS-D'OEUVRE, *Hot hors-d'oeuvre*.

Veal soup with herbs (Dutch cookery). Soupe de veau aux herbes—Veal stock thickened with a white *roux* seasoned with aromatic herbs and garnished with *quenelles* or dumplings made with veal and chopped herbs.

SOUP LADLE. Louche—A deep spoon used to serve soup. Soup ladles are made in different sizes.

SOUPIR DE NONNE (NUN'S SIGH)—Name sometimes used for the soufflé fritter made of *chou* pastry commonly called *Pet de nonne*. See FRITTERS, *Soufflé fritters*.

SOUR. Aigre—Possessing an acid and piquant taste or smell.

SOUR-SWEET. Aigre-doux—Having a sweet and sour taste.

SOURIRE—French term meaning to simmer very gently. For example: '*Le pot-au-feu sourit*'.

SOUS-NAPPE (UNDER-TABLECLOTH)—The custom of putting a piece of thick flannel under the tablecloth should not be reserved for gala occasions. It should also be normal practice in the home.

Thus cushioned the table is more comfortable and utensils make no noise as they are set down.

SOUS-NOIX OF VEAL—Term used in French butchery to describe the under part or silverside of the leg of veal.

SOUVAROV—A kind of *petit-four* for which the recipe is as follows:

Make a paste with 5 cups (600 grams) of sifted cake flour, 1⅝ cup (400 grams) of butter, ⅞ cup (200 grams) of sugar and a little cream. Allow to rest. Roll out thinly. Cut out with a round or oval pastry cutter with fluted edges. Place the cut-out pastries on a baking sheet and cook in a fairly hot oven.

Sandwich the pieces of pastry together two by two, spread with very thick apricot jam and sprinkle with icing sugar.

SOUVAROV OR SOUVOROV (A LA)—This is sometimes spelt *Souwaroff* in cookery books. The name describes a method of preparing poultry and game birds.

A bird cooked *à la Souvarov* is done in an earthenware casserole with *foie gras* and truffles, sealed with a strip of dough round the lid. See CHICKEN, *Chicken Souvarov*, or PHEASANT, *Pheasant à la Souvarov*.

SOW. Truie—Female pig. See PORK.

Sow-thistle

SOW-THISTLE (U.S.A. MILKWEED). Laiteron—A plant which has something of the flavour of both lettuce and chicory. It contains a milky substance.

It is somewhat leathery, but, after boiling in salt water, can be prepared like spinach.

When the leaves are tender they can be used in salads.

In winter the roots are eaten, prepared in the same way as black and white salsify.

SOYA BEAN. Soja—Plant of the *Leguminosae* family, a native of China, now widely cultivated.

This plant has the great merit of being free from attack from insect pests, and it grows easily in dry country.

It is also the richest and the cheapest source of vegetable protein. Its further advantages are its fairly high fat content and extremely low starch content. Soya bean is in daily use in the East in one form or another.

Soya bean curd. Fromage de soja—Cook in water, without salt, freshly shelled soya beans. When they are almost cooked pour off the greater part of the water. Let them continue cooking until their skins are very tender. Then turn out into an earthenware basin and leave till the next day, when the preparation will have become jellied.

Reheat the beans and drain off the liquid, then rub the beans through a fine sieve. Add to the purée the drained-off cooking liquor.

This vegetable jelly is very rich in legumin, which differs from casein only in the products of its decomposition.

Add a little milk or yeast to produce fermentation and salt to taste. Drain on a sieve.

Separate the whole into cheeses of whatever size is desired and leave them to 'take' in the usual way.

Soya meat. Viande de soja—This preparation is too complicated to be made in the home, but needs industrial equipment.

This 'vegetarian meat' has the appearance and even the taste of cooked ham. It is used in sandwiches and for hors-d'oeuvre. It may also be eaten as it is, cold or reheated.

Soya milk. Lait de soja—The name for the mixture of cooking liquor and purée of soya beans before fermentation.

Soya sauce or extract. Sauce, extrait de soja—It is above all in the form of this condiment that Eastern peoples use soya.

This extract or sauce is used to heighten the flavour of various dishes. A few drops of the extract added to a vegetable soup make it more savoury.

It is also used to strengthen sauces and stews and as an addition to salad dressings.

SPAGHETTI—One of the most popular of Italian *pasta* products. It is made from wheat, like macaroni, but is solid not tubular. All the methods of preparing macaroni are applicable to spaghetti. See MACARONI.

Spaghetti à la napolitaine—This pasta, like all the rest is put to cook in plenty of boiling water, salted in the proportion of 1½ teaspoons (10 grams) to a quart (litre).

As soon as the pasta is cooked (9 to 12 minutes) drain it. Put it in a saucepan and hold it over the heat for a moment to dry off excess moisture. Season with salt and pepper and add, shaking the spaghetti in the pot, ½ cup (1 decilitre) of thick *Tomato sauce* (see SAUCE), an ounce (25 to 30 grams) of grated Parmesan and Gruyère mixed, and 3 tablespoons (50 grams) of butter to every ⅓ pound (150 grams) of pasta. Shake well to mix and serve in a deep dish or use to accompany meat or poultry, as required.

SPARKLET—A small ampoule containing liquid carbon dioxide, with which effervescent drinks can be made. See SIPHON.

SPARKLING. MOUSSEUX—Wines and certain other liquids processed like champagne are said to be sparkling when, on pouring, they produce a more or less abundant head.

Certain wines, white wines chiefly, are naturally sparkling. Among these are, or rather were, the wines of Gaillac and Limoux in France and those of Asti in Italy. Nowadays, however, almost all these wines are processed by the method used for champagne.

Certain red Guyenne and Burgundy wines can be made sparkling, also by the same process as champagne. These wines are not highly regarded by true gourmets, although there are among the red wines some which are naturally sparkling or rather semi-sparkling without having been treated by the champagne process. It is these natural wines which gourmets prefer.

SPATULA. SPATULE—Kitchen utensil made in steel, copper or wood.

SPECULOS (Belgian pastry)—Put on the kitchen table, forming a circle, 4 cups (500 grams) of sifted cake flour. Place in the centre of the circle a small pinch of salt, a teaspoon of bicarbonate of soda, 2 teaspoons of powdered cinnamon, 3 eggs, 4 finely crushed cloves, 2 cups (300 grams) of brown sugar and ½ pound (250 grams) of butter. Mix all these ingredients well together and, little by little, incorporate the flour. Press the dough together into a loaf and leave in a cool place until the next day.

Divide the dough into several pieces. Roll out each piece and mould in floured wooden moulds. Turn out on to lightly buttered baking sheets. Cook in a moderate oven.

SPETZLI (Alsatian cookery)—Mix together 4 cups (500 grams) of sifted cake flour, 4 eggs, 2 to 3 tablespoons of double (heavy) cream, salt, pepper and a pinch of grated nutmeg.

Drop this paste, bit by bit, with a spatula into a pan of salted boiling water, each piece being about the size of a small walnut. Poach.

Drain the spetzli, dry them on a cloth and toss them in butter in the frying pan.

Serve in a deep dish, sprinkled with *Noisette butter* (see BUTTER, *Compound butters*).

SPICE. ÉPICE—An aromatic substance such as pepper, cloves, etc., used to season culinary preparations. A complete list of spices is given under CONDIMENTS.

It is generally agreed that most spices and condiments used in cookery have the effect of stimulating the gastric juices.

The use of spices, especially in large quantities, in diets for persons suffering from stomach disorders is generally regarded as inadvisable.

The function of tasty substances, which enhance the flavour of food, is not to act directly on the gastric juices, but to stimulate the digestive processes by reflexes following their contact with the taste buds.

In the seventeenth century, says Franklin, spices were not used to excess to quite the same extent as in previous centuries, but the passion for perfumes which poisoned the French court from the sixteenth century up to the middle of the reign of Louis XIV did not even respect stews, pastries, liqueurs, etc. Orris-root, rose water, marjoram were all mixed into them and the chef always had musk and ambergris at hand.

Green walnuts were flavoured with rose water. 'Nulles', a type of cream, were seasoned with amber and musk. Pâtés and pies were flavoured with musk. Eggs were sprinkled with scented waters. Some dishes were even sprinkled with soot!

Fine spices. ÉPICES FINES—*Ingredients.* 5½ cups (700 grams) white pepper; 2½ cups (300 grams) red pepper; 1 cup minus 2 tablespoons (100 grams) mace; ⅓ cup (50 grams) each of nutmeg, cloves, cinnamon, bay leaves, sage, marjoram, rosemary.

Pound these ingredients in a mortar and mix them thoroughly. Rub through a fine sieve. Keep in tightly-stoppered bottles.

Mixed spices. ÉPICES COMPOSÉES—'Dry in the oven or a hot cupboard: thyme, bay leaves, basil, sage, a little coriander and mace. When these ingredients are perfectly dry, pound them in a mortar and sieve them. Add a third of fine pepper. Put them in a box with a tightly fitting lid in a dry place for use as required.' (Carême's recipe.)

Mixed spices (commercial). QUATRE ÉPICES, ÉPICES FINES—Most grocers sell mixed spices ready prepared.

Spiced salt. ÉPICE (SEL)—Spiced salt used for flavouring stuffings is made with 7 tablespoons (100 grams) of table salt, 2½ tablespoons (20 grams) of pepper and 8 teaspoons (20 grams) of *Fine spices* (see above).

SPICY. EXCITANT—Spicy foods are those which are strongly flavoured with condiments or which have a very pronounced flavour. Spicy foods act upon the taste buds in the mouth and stimulate the gastric juices. This function of condiments has been established by exact experiments.

Spider crab

SPIDER CRAB. ARAIGNÉE DE MER—Name given in France to various species of crustaceans allied to crabs. For culinary preparation see CRAB.

The name of spider crab is also commonly given in many coastal places in France to certain fish belonging to the weever genus.

SPIGOT. FOSSET—A wooden vent-peg inserted into the hole drilled in a wine cask to enable it to be tasted.

SPIKENARD. NARD—A spice, very much in favour in ancient times as an ointment, and in the Middle Ages as a condiment. It is still so used in Malayan cookery.

Indian spikenard (*Nardostachys jatamansi*) is the root of a Far-Eastern species of valerian, from which the above spice was derived. *American spikenard* (*Aralia racemosa*) has a powerful and pleasant fragrance, and bitter aromatic flavour.

SPINACH. ÉPINARDS—A pot vegetable cultivated for its leaves. It is of Persian origin. It was unknown to the Romans and transplanted to Europe by the Moors. It has been greatly improved by cultivation. Spinach contains a viscous substance by virtue of which it has laxative properties. It also contains potassium of oxalate and a fair amount of iron (though less than sorrel, leek and lettuce).

Method of preparation. Before cooking, spinach must be stripped, carefully washed and parboiled in a lot of boiling salt water. This parboiling must be carried out as quickly as possible. The spinach is then cooled under running water, drained thoroughly, squeezed to extract all moisture, and, finally, rubbed through a sieve or chopped.

When spinach is served whole (blended with butter or in any other way), after having been parboiled in boiling salt water, drained and dried, it must not be cooled under running water.

If very fresh garden spinach is used, it can be cooked as follows: strip, wash and put in a saucepan. For 1 pound (500 grams) of spinach (net weight) add 3 tablespoons (50 grams) of butter, ¼ cup (half a decilitre) of water and a pinch of salt. Cover and cook rapidly. When the spinach is cooked and all the moisture evaporated, add 3 tablespoons (50 grams) of fresh butter.

Spinach à l'anglaise. ÉPINARDS À L'ANGLAISE—Parboil the spinach rapidly in boiling salt water. Drain and dry in a cloth. Serve whole in a very hot dish. Serve fresh butter separately.

Spinach in butter. ÉPINARDS AU BEURRE—*Whole.* Heat a little butter in a pan. Add the spinach, parboiled, drained and dried in a cloth. Leave on the stove for a few minutes to evaporate all moisture. Season with salt and pepper and a pinch of nutmeg. Just before serving, when the spinach is perfectly dry, blend in butter, allowing 7 tablespoons (100 grams) of butter to 3 cups (500 grams) of cooked spinach.

Chopped. Parboil the spinach. Cool under running water. Drain, squeeze out as much moisture as possible. Chop coarsely and proceed as indicated above.

Purée. Parboil the spinach. Cool it under running water. Drain and dry in a cloth. Rub through a sieve and proceed as indicated above.

Spinach in browned butter. ÉPINARDS AU BEURRE NOISETTE—Using whole, chopped or sieved spinach, proceed as follows: Parboil and drain the spinach. Dry it thoroughly in a cloth. Heat butter in a pan until it is nut-brown in colour. Add the spinach. Season with salt, pepper and a touch of nutmeg. Mix. Serve in a deep round dish.

Spinach in cream. ÉPINARDS À LA CRÈME—Chop the spinach or rub through a sieve. Cook in butter in a pan. When all the moisture has evaporated, add fresh cream. Serve in a deep round dish. Surround with boiling hot fresh cream.

Spinach can also be served in this way using *Cream sauce* (see SAUCE) instead of fresh cream.

Spinach croquettes. CROQUETTES AUX ÉPINARDS—Make the croquettes in the usual way using the following mixture: Two-thirds of chopped spinach stewed in butter and one-third *Duchess potato mixture* (see POTATOES).

Fry the croquettes just before serving. Drain them. Serve on a napkin, garnished with fried parsley.

Croûtes of spinach au gratin. CROÛTES GRATINÉES AUX ÉPINARDS—Shape sandwich bread into deep hollow cases. Fry them in butter. Fill with spinach heaped up into a dome, prepared as indicated for *Spinach au gratin.* Sprinkle with grated cheese. Pour on melted butter. Brown in a very hot oven.

Spinach au gratin. ÉPINARDS AU GRATIN—Parboil and dry thoroughly 1 pound (500 grams) of spinach. Chop or leave whole. Simmer with 7 tablespoons (100 grams) of butter. Add ¾ cup (75 grams) of grated cheese. Season and mix. Put the mixture in a buttered ovenware dish. Sprinkle generously with grated cheese. Pour on melted butter. Brown in the oven.

Spinach can also be prepared in this way by adding a few tablespoons of *Cream sauce* (see SAUCE) after cooking in butter.

Spinach in gravy. ÉPINARDS AU JUS—Blanch and drain the spinach. Chop or rub through a sieve. Stew in butter until all moisture is evaporated. Add a few tablespoons of concentrated veal stock. Season. Serve in a deep round dish. Surround with a border of concentrated veal gravy.

Spinach pancakes. CRÊPES AUX ÉPINARDS—Blanch and drain the spinach and dry it in a cloth. Chop finely. To dry it further, simmer in butter. Add to the spinach an equal quantity of unsweetened pancake (*crêpe*) batter. Season with salt, pepper and nutmeg. Mix thoroughly. Make the pancakes in the usual way.

Spinach salad. SALADE D'ÉPINARDS—Plunge the whole spinach into boiling water, for a few seconds only. Cool under running water, drain, dry in a cloth. Put the spinach leaves in a salad bowl. Sprinkle with chopped hard boiled eggs. Dress with oil, vinegar, salt and pepper.

Spinach soufflé

Spinach soufflé. SOUFFLÉ AUX ÉPINARDS—Using chopped or sieved spinach cooked in butter, proceed as for *Endive soufflé.* See ENDIVE.

Subrics of spinach. SUBRICS D'ÉPINARDS—Parboil the whole spinach quickly in boiling salt water. Drain and dry in a cloth. Cook in butter until all moisture is evaporated. Take the pan off the stove and add, for 3 cups (500 grams) of spinach, ⅝ cup (1½ decilitres) of thick *Béchamel sauce* (see SAUCE), a whole egg, 3 yolks beaten as for an omelette, and 2 or 3 tablespoons of thick fresh cream. Season with salt, pepper and nutmeg. Mix. Heat clarified butter in a frying pan and pour the mixture into it, a spoonful at a time.

Take care that the *subrics* are separated from one another in the pan to prevent them from running together.

Fry for a minute, then turn them over to cook on the other side.

Serve on a flat or deep round dish. Serve cream separately.

Spinach with sugar. ÉPINARDS AU SUCRE—Parboil and drain the spinach. Dry in a cloth. Cook in butter until all moisture is evaporated. Sweeten slightly. Serve in a deep round dish. Shape into a dome. Cover with fresh cream, piping hot. Garnish with fried bread cut into sponge-finger shapes.

GIANT MEXICAN SPINACH. ÉPINARDS GÉANTS DU MEXIQUE—This vegetable derives from a shrub which is more than 7 feet tall. One plant yields from 2 to 3 pounds (1 kilo to 1,500 grams) of fleshy leaves each from 7 to 9 inches long.

The flavour of these leaves is midway between that of spinach and sorrel.

NEW ZEALAND SPINACH. TÉTRAGONE—This plant is one of the indigenous vegetables of New Zealand, having been brought back from that country by Captain Cook. It has long, thick, whitish-green leaves with a pleasant taste, which are prepared like ordinary spinach.

WILD SPINACH—See GOOD KING HENRY.

SPINY LOBSTER (SEA CRAYFISH OR ROCK LOBSTER). LANGOUSTE—A crustacean with a spiny shell, having two long antennae, greenish-brown in colour and with yellow markings on the tail.

Its oblong body, more barrel-shaped than that of the lobster, is divided into 6 shell plates and ends in a fan-shaped tail.

Spiny lobsters have no claws, as lobsters do, and their legs are all the same size and shape. Spiny lobsters vary in length from 12 to 20 inches.

Spiny lobsters are to be found in large numbers in the Atlantic and the Mediterranean.

Moroccan lobsters, too, have found their way into the continental market. They are known in France as the *Langouste royal.*

This shell-fish is very similar in shape to the spiny lobsters caught off the French coast, except that its body is somewhat flatter. It is of excellent quality.

Another variety of *langouste*, the Martinique lobster, is also to be found, in frozen condition, in French fish shops. These are very prolific in the West Indian Ocean and in the coastal waters of South America.

The spiny lobster of Florida measures 9 to 10 inches. A similar variety is caught off the Pacific coast.

Take a shallow buttered pan and place in it 1 pound (500 grams) of peeled, seeded and chopped tomatoes, 2 medium onions, sliced, a clove of garlic in its skin, half a bay leaf, a sprig of thyme, and a tablespoon of chopped parsley.

Lay the collops (slices) of spiny lobster on these vegetables. Season with salt and pepper. Pour on 2 tablespoons of olive oil, a glass (cup) of white wine, a small glass of Marsala and a small glass of brandy.

Cover and bring to the boil. Boil hastily for 20 minutes. Take out the lobster. Arrange it in a pie dish or other hollow dish. Boil down the sauce if necessary. Thicken it with the chopped coral, add a teaspoon of chopped parsley and a pinch of cayenne pepper. Bring to the boil and pour over the dish.

Spiny lobster butter. BEURRE DE LANGOUSTE—Made from the shells and trimmings of the spiny lobster. Pound these thoroughly. Add an equal weight of butter. Rub through a sieve. See BUTTER, *Compound butters.*

Spiny lobster cardinal. LANGOUSTE CARDINAL—Boil the spiny lobster in a *court-bouillon**. Drain it. Split it in two lengthwise. Shell it completely.

Cut each half of the tail into 6 to 8 slices of equal thickness and dice the rest of the flesh.

Put the diced flesh into a pan. Add neatly diced mushrooms and truffles and bind with *Béchamel sauce* (see SAUCE) with cream added. It should then be simmered down, blended with spiny lobster butter and strained before it is poured on to the spiny lobster.

Heat up this *salpicon** without letting it come to the boil. Fill the halves of the shell with it. Decorate the top of each shell with lobster collops alternating with strips of truffle.

(1) To cut open a spiny lobster begin with the tail

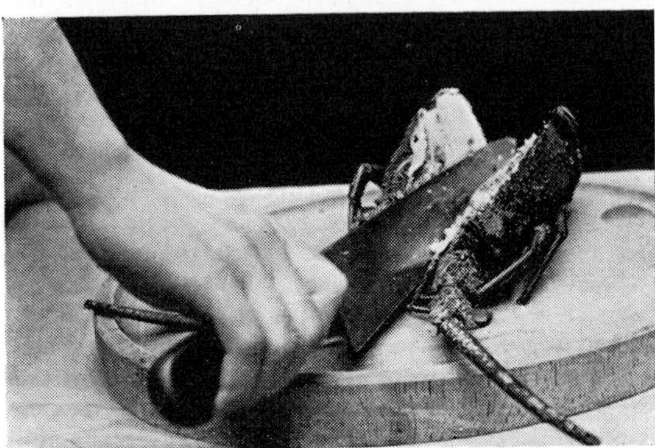

(2) Next split the head and thorax (*Larousse*)

Spiny lobster à l'américaine. LANGOUSTE À L'AMÉRICAINE—Proceed as for *Lobster à l'américaine**.

Spiny lobster aspic. ASPIC DE LANGOUSTE—Proceed as for *Lobster aspic**.

Boiled spiny lobster (hot or cold) with various sauces. LANGOUSTE BOUILLIE—Boil the spiny lobster in a *court-bouillon**, as for boiled lobster.

Serve *hot*, with a sauce suitable for poached or boiled fish or shell-fish; *cold*, with mayonnaise or some other cold sauce.

Spiny lobster à la bordelaise. LANGOUSTE À LA BORDELAISE—Proceed as for *Lobster à la bordelaise**.

Spiny lobster à la bourgeoise (Italian cookery). LANGOUSTE À LA BOURGEOISE—Take a live spiny lobster weighing approximately 1½ pounds (700 to 800 grams). Scrub it under the cold tap.

Cut it into neat slices as for *Lobster à l'américaine*. Set aside the coral and the creamy parts of the lobster.

Cover with *Béchamel sauce* to which spiny lobster butter has been added. Sprinkle with grated cheese. Pour on melted butter.

Put the halves of spiny lobster in a baking tin, lining them up straight, one next the other. Brown in a very hot oven. Serve on a dish covered with a napkin and garnish with fried parsley.

Collops of spiny lobster à l'andalouse. ESCALOPES DE LANGOUSTE À L'ANDALOUSE—Cook a spiny lobster in *court-bouillon** and leave to cool. Shell. Cut the tail into 10 collops (thick slices). Coat these collops with a *Chaud-froid sauce* (see SAUCE) with purée of red peppers and truffles. Glaze with jelly. Chill on ice.

Make a salad of the rest of the lobsters coarsely diced, diced truffles, green and red peppers, peeled, cooked and diced, and diced potatoes, seasoned with paprika mayonnaise mixed with thick jelly.

Make a dome of this salad in the centre of a round dish.

RÉVEILLON. *Top to bottom:* Corbeille of fruit, Roast turkey with chestnuts, Lobster, Black and white puddings, Foie gras in aspic, Zakouski, Oysters

(*From the original French edition of* Larousse Gastronomique)

VEAL. Rouelle of veal à la casserole (*Nézard-Debillot*)

(*From Curnonsky:* Cuisine et Vins de France)

Collops of spiny lobster à l'andalouse

This must be done as soon as the salad is seasoned, otherwise it will set too hard.

Surround the salad with as many *Tomato mousselines** as there are spiny lobster collops. Put a collop on top of each mould. Make a border of chopped jelly. Decorate the top of the salad with lettuce hearts and quartered hard boiled eggs.

Collops of spiny lobster à la parisienne. ESCALOPES DE LANGOUSTE À LA PARISIENNE—Cook a spiny lobster in *court-bouillon**. Leave to cool. Shell. Cut the tail neatly into collops. Cover the collops with jellied *mayonnaise* (see SAUCE).

Decorate the collops with truffles and carrots shaped with a small ball-scoop. Glaze with jelly. Chill thoroughly in a refrigerator.

Collops of spiny lobster à la parisienne

Arrange in a circle round a *Parisian salad* (see SALAD) seasoned with jelly mayonnaise and made into a dome in the centre of a round dish.

Decorate with round slices of hard boiled eggs and highlight them with jelly. In the centre of the dish, place a lettuce heart decorated with a hard boiled egg.

Coquilles of spiny lobster (cold). COQUILLES DE LANGOUSTE—Using spiny lobster, proceed as for *Cold lobster in scallop shells.* See LOBSTER.

Coquilles of spiny lobster (hot). COQUILLES DE LANGOUSTE—Made with spiny lobsters boiled in a *court-bouillon**, shelled, diced or cut into small collops. Proceed as for *Hot lobster in scallop shells* (see LOBSTER).

Spiny lobster in court-bouillon. LANGOUSTE AU COURT-BOUILLON—This is usually made with small spiny lobsters. Proceed as for freshwater crayfish in *court-bouillon.* See CRAYFISH, *Crayfish à la nage.*

Spiny lobsters cooked in this way are served hot. A suitable sauce is served separately. They can also be served cold, in which case they are usually called *Spiny lobsters à la nage.*

Spiny lobster in cream. LANGOUSTE À LA CRÈME—Proceed as for *Lobster in cream**.

Croquettes and kromeskis of spiny lobster. CROQUETTES, CROMESQUIS DE LANGOUSTE—Proceed as for any other *croquettes* or *kromeskis.* See HORS-D'OEUVRE, *Hot hors-d'oeuvre.*

Curried spiny lobster. ÉTUVÉ DE LANGOUSTE AU CURRIE—Sauté in butter in a frying pan 2 medium-sized spiny lobsters cut into slices as for spiny lobster *à l'américaine.* With the collops sauté ½ cup (100 grams) of chopped onion. Season with salt, pepper and 2 spoonfuls of curry.

When the collops are a golden colour (the onion must not be allowed to brown), moisten with 1½ cups (3 decilitres) of white wine. Add a *bouquet garni** and 2 peeled, pipped, crushed tomatoes. Cover the pan. Simmer until almost all the stock has evaporated.

Drain the collops of spiny lobster. Keep them warm. Remove the *bouquet garni* from the pan. Add 1 cup (2 decilitres) of *Béchamel sauce* (see SAUCE) and 1 cup (2 decilitres) of thick fresh cream. Mix. Boil for a few seconds.

Put the shelled spiny lobster collops back in the sauce Cover and simmer for 15 minutes.

Serve in a pie dish. Add to the sauce 2 teaspoons of butter and a squeeze of lemon juice. Pour over the collops.

Serve *Rice à l'indienne** separately.

Spiny lobster demi-deuil. LANGOUSTE DEMI-DEUIL—Boil 2 spiny lobsters in a white wine *court-bouillon**. (Drain and leave to cool.) Split them lengthwise. Shell them. Cut the tails into collops of equal thickness and dice the flesh of the body.

Warm up the diced flesh in a little Madeira, having added a *salpicon** of truffles and mushrooms blended in a little fish-based *Suprême sauce* (a thick fish-based *Velouté sauce* (see SAUCE) with fresh cream added). Put the *salpicon* in the shells and decorate the top with the tail collops. Mask with *Suprême sauce* and brown in a very hot oven. Warm some strips of truffle in white jelly fish stock and decorate the tops of the shells with them. Serve the spiny lobsters on a long dish.

Spiny lobster au gratin. LANGOUSTE AU GRATIN—Boil the spiny lobster in a *court-bouillon**. Split it lengthwise, shell it and cut it up as for *Spiny lobster Cardinal.*

Mix the *salpicon** with thick *Béchamel sauce* (see SAUCE) with butter added. Add to the *salpicon* an equal quantity of diced, cooked mushrooms.

Fill the halves of the shell with the *salpicon.* Arrange the collops on top. Cover with the remainder of the sauce. Sprinkle with grated cheese. Pour on melted butter. Brown.

Grilled spiny lobster. LANGOUSTE GRILLÉE—Proceed as for *Grilled lobster* (see LOBSTER).

Spiny lobster Mornay. LANGOUSTE MORNAY—This is another name for *Spiny lobster au gratin.*

Spiny lobster à la moscovite. LANGOUSTE À LA MOSCOVITE—Boil a large spiny lobster in a *court-bouillon**. Leave it to cool in the stock. Drain it. Make 2 incisions 1½ inches apart lengthwise in the shell. These should be shallow so as not to cut the flesh and should begin at the head and go towards the tail. Remove the part of the shell which has been cut. Remove the tail of the spiny lobster, being careful not to break it. Remove all the flesh and the creamy part from the body of the lobster.

Dice the flesh and add to it diced potatoes and diced truffles. Season with jellied *mayonnaise* (see SAUCE, *Cold sauces*). Stuff the shell with this salad.

Trim a slice of buttered sandwich bread into the form of a wedge and set the spiny lobster on it. Place on a large oval dish. Fill the well of the dish with very clear fish aspic jelly. Chill in a refrigerator or on ice.

Meanwhile, slice the tail of the spiny lobster into collops. Coat with a white *Chaud-froid sauce* based on fish *fumet**. See SAUCE. When this sauce has quite set, put a strip of truffle on top of each collop and glaze with jelly. Chill.

Arrange the collops on the spiny lobster shell, starting at the head and overlapping.

Surround with the following garnish:

Very small *barquettes** of thin lining pastry filled with fresh caviare; halves of hard boiled eggs decorated with strips of truffle and glazed with jelly; small artichoke hearts filled with vegetable salad, dressed with jelly mayonnaise (this salad would be domed and decorated on top with a round piece of truffle); lettuce hearts.

Run a decorated skewer between the eyes of the spiny lobster. Decorate with chopped jelly and surround the dish with rounds of jelly cut out with a pastry-cutter.

Serve with mayonnaise sauce mixed with the sieved roe of the spiny lobster.

Note. Instead of slitting the lobster along the top, it may be slit underneath. It can be filled with shredded lettuce salad instead of potato salad. In this case, little barquettes of cucumber or beetroot should be filled with the same salad and added to the garnish.

Spiny lobster mousse and mousseline. MOUSSE, MOUSSELINE DE LANGOUSTE—Served hot or cold and prepared in the same way as *Mousse and Mousselines of lobster*. See LOBSTER.

Spiny lobster à la nage. LANGOUSTE À LA NAGE—This method of preparation is especially suitable for small spiny lobsters. Proceed as for *Lobster à la nage**.

Spiny lobster à la Niçoise (cold). LANGOUSTE FROIDE À LA NIÇOISE—Boil a spiny lobster in a *court-bouillon**. Leave it to cool. Split it lengthwise and shell. Cut part of the flesh into 10 collops of equal thickness and dice the rest.

Add cooked diced potatoes, peas, French (string) beans and anchovy fillets (diced) to the diced flesh, and mix them into a salad with jellied mayonnaise. Fill the shells with this salad.

Arrange the halves of spiny lobster on a long dish. Put the collops on top. Cover these with jellied mayonnaise and decorate each one with rosettes of tarragon leaves.

Decorate the sides of the dish with tomatoes stuffed with a spoonful of the spiny lobster salad, alternating with cooked artichoke hearts filled with shredded lettuce seasoned with French dressing and decorated with fillets of anchovy and capers. At each end of the dish arrange halved hard boiled eggs and quartered lettuce hearts.

Serve separately a sauce made from mayonnaise mixed with a *Tomato fondue** cooked in oil and flavoured with anchovy essence.

Spiny lobster à la parisienne. LANGOUSTE À LA PARISIENNE —Proceed as for *Spiny lobster à la moscovite*, changing the presentation and garnish as follows:

Remove the tail and empty the shell. Fill with coarsely shredded lettuce salad. Put it on a buttered wedge of bread on a serving dish.

Cut the tail flesh into collops and arrange them on top of the spiny lobster shell. Decorate each one with a strip of truffle and glaze with jelly.

Garnish with artichoke hearts filled with a salad of vegetables and the diced flesh of the spiny lobster dressed with jellied mayonnaise; quartered or halved hard boiled eggs glazed with jelly (either plain or decorated with strips of truffles); quartered lettuce hearts.

Decorate the centre of the dish with chopped jelly and arrange rounds of jelly along the edge. Stick a decorated skewer between the eyes of the spiny lobster. Serve mayonnaise separately.

Spiny lobster pilaf and risotto. PILAF, RISOTTO DE LANGOUSTE—Proceed as for *pilaf and risotto of lobster*. See LOBSTER.

Spiny lobster à la russe. LANGOUSTE À LA RUSSE—Proceed as for *Spiny lobster à la moscovite*, changing the presentation and garnish as follows:

Coat the collops with jellied mayonnaise or a white *Chaud-froid sauce* (see SAUCE). Decorate with a dot of coral and two chervil leaves glazed with jelly. Arrange these collops on top of the spiny lobster (which should be stuffed with a coarsely shredded lettuce salad), and set on a wedge of buttered bread as for *Spiny lobster à la moscovite*.

Garnish with cylindrical moulds of Russian salad (containing no ham or tongue) dressed with jellied mayonnaise; halves of hard boiled eggs, decorated with truffles and glazed with jelly; lettuce hearts. Skewer the lobster. Serve with *Tartare sauce* (see SAUCE, *Cold sauces*).

Spiny lobster salad. SALADE DE LANGOUSTE—Using spiny lobster, proceed as for *lobster salad*. See SALAD.

Spiny lobster with various sauces (cold). LANGOUSTE FROIDE—Boil a spiny lobster in a *court-bouillon**. Leave it to cool. Serve on a napkin, garnished with fresh parsley or lettuce hearts. Serve with mayonnaise or any other sauce suitable for cold fish or shell-fish.

Spiny lobster on the spit. LANGOUSTE À LA BROCHE—Proceed as for *Lobster on the spit**.

Spiny lobster stew (Catalan and Languedoc cookery). CIVET DE LANGOUSTE—Cut the spiny lobster into collops and proceed as for *Spiny lobster à l'américaine*, increasing the amount of tomato and flavouring it strongly with garlic.

Brandy glasses

SPIRITS (EAUX-DE-VIE)—An alcoholic liquid with an alcohol content of between 16° and 17°. Strictly, *eau-de-vie* is the product of distilled wine (brandy), but the term is extended to cover spirits distilled from fruit and even cereals.

The *eau-de-vie* of Charentes, *cognac*, has a reputation equal to that of the greatest wines and is undoubtedly the first of all spirits. Its incomparable flavour is due to a special vine, the *folle blanche*, which also yields a sourish, insipid white wine. Its quality depends to a great extent on the growth. The first cognacs are made from the grapes grown in chalky vineyards known as *champagnes*. A distinction is made between *fines champagnes* (liqueur brandies) and *petites champagnes* and between

Armagnac *cave* at Condom, Gers
(*French Government Tourist Office*)

fins bois and *bons bois* cognacs, according to the origin of the wine distilled. In former times distillation was carried out in a very primitive still, heated over an open fire. This process was carried out in two stages. The *brouillis* collected first was distilled afresh over greater heat to arrive at the desired strength. The products were then graded.

Immediately after distilling, cognac which is 65° to 68° proof has scarcely any aroma. This develops by slow etherification and by mysterious internal changes while it is stored in casks, which lowers its strength and permits some evaporation of alcohol.

The manufacture and preparation of brandy casks demand particular care. After 25 years in a cask, a brandy loses about a third of its volume. It becomes slightly coloured and tart. Those incomparable brandies whose aroma lingers for several hours in the glasses into which they have been poured, are not to be bought in ordinary wine-shops but are used to make commercial products adulterated with younger spirits, after syrup and water have been added to reduce them to the commercial standard of 48°. Sometimes less orthodox methods are used, the brandy being adulterated with 'sauced' mixtures for which formulae are to be found in all distillers' manuals.

Here are a few sample formulae:

(1) Steep for 3 days in a litre of brandy: 60 grams of catechu, 10 grams of balsam of tolu and add 85 grams of ammonia.

(2) Steep for 3 days in a litre of brandy: 6 grams of vanilla, 80 grams catechu, 89 grams of tolu, 12 grams of sassafras, 1 gram of essence of bitter almonds and 100 grams of sugar.

These ingredients are added to 100 litres of unmatured *eau-de-vie* and rectified spirit, heated all together to blend the bouquets and cooled slowly.

The brandies of *Armagnac* are made from the vines of Gers called *picquepoul*, which is merely a variety of the *folle blanche* of Charentes. Their flavour is a little different from that of cognac. They are sold at a strength of 52°.

The wines of many other regions are distilled, but it is a notable fact that the prime growths usually do not yield fine brandies.

The marc of wines is also distilled after a little water has been added to it, as are the lees which remain at the bottom of the vats and casks. Some of these products enjoy a great reputation.

Cider (to which the marc is usually added), is distilled to produce the spirits known as *calvados*.

Spirits are also distilled from all fruit which is sufficiently abundant. It is first fermented, as with cider and wine. Thus, spirits are distilled from apricots, cherries, dates, figs, raspberries, mulberries, bilberries, mirabelles, pears, peaches, greengages, plums (quetsch, Slivovitz) and many other kinds of fruit.

True rum is distilled from sugar-cane juice but nowadays a distillation of molasses, once known as tafia, is also called rum.

Finally, the distilled grain of cereals, especially barley, yields spirits (Kornschnaps, whisky) sometimes flavoured with juniper berries (genievre, gin).

The analysis of spirits is concerned with the detection of minerals which should not be present, and with the proportion of impurities. This proportion should be 6 to 20 for rectified industrial spirits, 20 to 150 for 'medium taste' spirits. It is always more than 150 and can reach 300 in spirits of wine or fruit. This analysis is completed by the investigation of colouring matter, synthetic bouquets, saccharin and *dulcine*.

A spit (*Rôtisserie Reine-Pédauque*)

SPIT. Broche—Utensil on which meat, etc., can be roasted before a fire.

There are various types of spits. There is the kind on which the meat to be roasted is placed vertically and the kind on which it is placed horizontally.

Hand- or motor-operated mechanisms make the roasts turn slowly.

Many gastronomes do not recognise any roast as such except one cooked on a spit. They go even further and insist that the roasting must be done not before a coal but a wood fire.

It was in this manner that roasts were done in the olden days, in great houses as well as in modest ones.

Things are different now. Kitchen utensils have been greatly improved to be in line with present day requirements. This does not always meet with the approval of the gastronomical purists who would not hear of abandoning the old methods and who would like to make sure that only the archaic utensils of our fathers are used in the kitchen today.

No doubt a piece of meat, a fowl or a wild bird roasted the old-fashioned way, that is to say, on a spit, before a blazing fire of dry wood, had its charm and always tasted good, but conditions in the kitchen have changed and kitchen equipment had to be modified to come into line with modern needs. Gas and electric spits are very different from the spits used by our fathers, but they are nevertheless excellent and enable us to produce perfect roasts. And, no matter what some gastronomes who are so set on things of the past might say, joints roasted in the oven are also excellent, provided they are cooked with due care.

For these roasts (and this is the method now used almost universally) special utensils and devices are in use which allow the joint to be put on a spit before it is put in the oven, for raising it above the dripping or roasting pan.

SPLEEN. RATE—Ox (beef) spleen is sometimes used in pot-au-feu.

SPONDIAS—Indian tree whose edible fruit is known as a *hog apple*. The fruit of the spondias, which grows in many tropical regions, makes excellent preserves and a fermented drink.

SPONGE CAKES. BISCUITS—See also GENOESE CAKES.

Almond sponge cake. BISCUIT AUX AMANDES—Put 1¾ cups (330 grams) of sugar, 8 yolks of egg and a pinch of salt into a bowl and blend well with a wooden spoon.

When the mixture is frothy, incorporate ¾ cup (120 grams) of sweet almonds and 4 or 5 bitter almonds, blanched and pounded in a mortar into a smooth paste with a white of egg. Add a few drops of orange blossom water and blend well. Add 8 whites of egg whisked into a stiff froth and 1 cup (120 grams) of sieved flour.

Butter a sponge cake tin, sprinkle it with flour and pour in the cake mixture filling the tin only up to three quarters of its height. Bake in a moderate oven.

Turn out onto a wire cake tray and allow to cool. Cut into three layers of equal thickness. Coat one layer with apricot jam, the second with raspberry jelly and sandwich the layers together. Brush it with apricot jam, ice with *Vanilla flavoured fondant icing* (see ICING) and sprinkle with chopped pistachio nuts.

Sponge fingers (U.S. Lady fingers). BISCUITS À LA CUILLER—These biscuits are prepared of dough made of flour, sugar, yolks of egg, and stiffly beaten whites.

Sponge fingers are used in the preparation of many sweet dishes, such as *Charlottes russes*.

Method. Cream 1 cup (250 grams) of fine sugar and 8 yolks of egg in a bowl until the mixture forms a ribbon. Flavour with a teaspoon of orange blossom water, add 1½ cups (190 grams) of sieved flour and incorporate 8 whites of egg whisked into a stiff froth.

Blend the mixture, lifting it lightly with a spoon and folding in the whites gently so as not to cause them to subside.

Pipe this mixture on to sheets of strong paper through a forcing bag with a wide plain nozzle.

Sprinkle with fine sugar, lift the sheet of paper by the two ends to shake off surplus sugar.

Put the sheets of paper on a baking tray and bake in a 375°F. oven for 12 minutes.

Sponge finger mixture may be flavoured with grated orange or lemon rind or with vanilla.

Italian sponge cake. BISCUIT À L'ITALIENNE—*Ingredients.* 2 cups (500 grams) of fine sugar, 10 eggs, 1 cup (125 grams) of sieved flour, ¾ cup (125 grams) of sieved potato flour, 2 teaspoons (10 grams) of vanilla-flavoured sugar or 1 teaspoon of vanilla extract.

Method. Cream the sugar and the egg yolks, adding the yolks one by one.

Whisk the whites and fold them into the mixture.

Add the flour, potato flour, and vanilla-flavoured sugar, all previously mixed together on a sheet of paper. Blend well.

Pour the mixture into a charlotte mould, which has been buttered and dusted out with a mixture of icing sugar and potato flour in equal proportions.

Sponge cake manqué. BISCUIT MANQUÉ—The name of this sponge cake is rather strange, but the result is excellent. It is believed that it got its name for the simple reason that the pastry-cook responsible for its creation was making a classical cake mixture and, having failed, called the cake *manqué*!

Ingredients. 3¼ cups (400 grams) sieved flour, 2 cups (500 grams) of fine sugar, 18 yolks of egg, 1¼ cups (300 grams) of butter, 16 whites of egg whisked into a stiff froth, 3 tablespoons of rum.

Method. Cream the sugar and the yolks together in a bowl until the mixture turns white and frothy.

Add rum and flour and mix well. Then add stiffly beaten whites and, at the last moment, pour in melted butter, cooled.

Put the mixture in special *à manqué* cake tins which have been buttered and dusted out with flour.

Bake in a moderate oven (375°F.), for 40 to 45 minutes.

Punch sponge cakes. BISCUITS PUNCH—*Ingredients.* 3 cups (375 grams) of sieved flour, 2 cups (500 grams) of sugar, 12 egg yolks, 3 whole eggs, 8 whites of egg whisked into a stiff froth, 1⅓ cups (300 grams) of butter, half a spoonful of orange-flavoured sugar, half a tablespoonful of lemon-flavoured sugar and 3 tablespoons of rum (½ teaspoon of orange extract and ½ teaspoon of lemon extract may be used instead of the flavoured sugars).

Method. Cream together the sugar, the yolks and whole eggs in a bowl until the mixture becomes very light.

Add, stirring all the time, flavoured sugars, rum, flour, stiffly beaten whites of egg and, at the last moment, melted butter, cooled. Blend.

Put the mixture into buttered paper cases, or—depending on the final use for which the cakes are intended—into buttered flan rings or layer cake tins.

Bake in a moderate oven (375°F.).

Savoy sponge cake. BISCUIT DE SAVOIE—*Ingredients.* 1½ cups (185 grams) of sieved flour, 1 cup plus 2 tablespoons (185 grams) of potato flour, 2 cups (500 grams) of fine sugar, 14 yolks of egg, 14 stiffly beaten whites of egg, 1 tablespoon of vanilla flavoured sugar or 1 teaspoon vanilla extract.

Method. Cream the sugar and the yolks in a bowl until the mixture forms a ribbon. Add vanilla flavoured sugar, flour and potato flour mixed, and, at the last moment, fold in the whites of egg whisked into a stiff froth.

Put the mixture into Savoy cake tins, buttered and dusted out with potato flour, filling them only up to two-thirds. Bake in a slow oven (325°F.).

Note. Various other recipes for sponge cakes will be found under the entries entitled CAKE, GENOESE CAKE.

SPOOMS—See ICE CREAMS AND ICES.

SPOON. CUILLER—A utensil which has an oval or concave spherical form fixed to a handle (See COVER). Spoons used in cooking have various forms, and are made in different materials according to their particular uses: wooden spoons, spoons for sauces, basting spoons, soup ladles, etc.

SPRAT—Small sea fish 3 to 4½ inches long, a little smaller than the sardine and somewhat resembling the herring.

The back of this fish is blue-green and its sides are silvery with a gold band at spawning time.

Gastronomically it is not held in such high esteem as the sardine.

All the methods of preparation given for the *sardine** are applicable to the sprat. It is also preserved, smoked and salted.

SPRUCE BEER. SAPINETTE—Fermented drink, obtained from branches and cones of spruce, a native of America and Russia, which is also found in the north of France. These branches, etc. are boiled, then sugar, hops and yeast added when the beer is put into casks.

'SPURS OF BACCHUS'. ÉPERONS BACHIQUES—A metaphorical expression sometimes used on menus for the ensemble of small tit-bits making up a cold hors-d'oeuvre. It is used especially of salty tit-bits such as ham, sausages, saveloy and chitterlings, which, being highly seasoned, cause thirst. It is in this sense that Rabelais used the expression.

SQUAB—See PIGEON.

SQUASH (PATTYPAN). PÂTISSON—A member of the cucurbitaceae family, which, because of its shape, is called by various names in France such as *bonnet de prêtre*, *artichaut de Jérusalem*, etc. The best-known varieties are: American white, yellow and orange.

This and other squashes can be prepared in any way suitable for marrow and pumpkin.

Squash, hollowed out and blanched, can be used as a container for various dishes. The scooped out pulp is added to these dishes (stewed in butter or prepared in some other way).

SQUID—See CALAMARY.

SQUILL-FISH. SQUILLE—Crustacean known also as *sauterelle de mer* (sea-grasshopper) and *mante de mer* (sea mantis).

They are fished on the coasts of Spain and Italy and in the English Channel. They are prepared like lobsters and spiny lobsters.

SQUIRREL. ÉCUREUIL—A wild rodent. In some countries, it is highly esteemed as game. It is cooked in the same way as rabbit.

STALK. ÉGRAPPER—To remove grapes or other berries from their stalks.

STAMPPOT—This is a kind of national dish in Holland. It is made by serving smoked sausages on top of a hash of cabbage, potato and veal fat made into a raised bed on a round dish.

STAR ANISE. ANIS ÉTOILÉ—Common name of the badiane. Also known as Chinese anise.

Star anise

STAR OF BETHLEHEM. ORNYTHOGALE—Plant with edible roots, which are prepared as salsify.

STARCH. FÉCULE—In former times, all solids deposited by juices obtained by extraction were called starches, though they differed widely from one to another.

Nowadays, the term is used especially of pure starch powder or the white powdery starch deposit which separates out from water in which certain pounded vegetables (such as potatoes, manioc, sago, rice, etc.) are washed.

In cookery, four main types of starch are used to thicken sauces or make *coulis* and creams. These are: *local starches* contained in wheat, potatoes, corn (maize) and rice; *exotic starches*, salep, arrow-root, manioc, sago, yam, etc.; *pulse starches*, haricot (shell) beans, peas, lentils, etc.; *fruit starches*, extracted from chestnuts, bananas and sweet nuts.

For thickening soups, stocks and sauces, potato-starch and arrow-root (manioc starch) are mainly used. In the U.S.A. cornstarch is widely used.

Foods containing a high proportion of starch are said to be starchy.

STARLING. ÉTOURNEAU, SANSONNET—A bird similar to the blackbird, but smaller. The starling was much prized by the Romans. Nowadays in France it is cooked in the same way as the thrush. See THRUSH.

STEARIN. STEARINE—Neutral fat resulting from the combination of stearic acid with solid glycerine. It is found in varying proportions in edible fats, the quantity varying in relation to the point of fusion.

In former times stearin was much used in fashioning pediments and ornamental details. Nowadays this usage has been almost completely abandoned, even in culinary exhibitions.

STEEPING (MACERATION)—A culinary process consisting of soaking various foodstuffs in an aromatic liquid preparation.

During steeping, chemical changes occur both in the solid and the liquid. The nature and extent of these changes depend largely on the density of the liquid used and on the soluble elements in the solid.

When meat is steeped in brine, the salt penetrates the muscular tissue and the liquid absorbs a small proportion of the soluble protein in the meat. In the case of a marinade, the spices penetrate the solid in the same way.

When fruit is steeped in sweetened or diluted alcohol, the alcohol penetrates the fruit which yields up to the alcohol some of its juice.

When a solid is steeped in pure water or water with a little alcohol (the steeping of gentian, quassia, etc.) the soluble elements in the solid are absorbed into the water.

STERILIZE—To render sterile, to destroy germs and arrest fermentation in foodstuffs. Heat is the most effective agent of sterilization.

STERLET—A small sturgeon found in the Caspian Sea.

The sterlet is renowned for the delicacy of its flesh. It is eaten fresh, dried or salted. Its roe produces the finest caviare.

All the methods of preparation given for salmon, salmon trout and sturgeon are applicable to the sterlet. It is, however, mostly braised in white wine; but an essential condition of its preparation in Russia, and one which gourmets there insist must be observed, is that the sterlet shall be brought alive into the kitchen where it is to be cooked.

STICKLEBACK. ÉPINOCHE—A small river fish, insipid in flavour. It is usually deep-fried.

STOCKFISH—Dried Norwegian cod, differing very little in appearance from the more familiar *morue* (dried salt cod). It is very much liked in Germany, Belgium and Holland.

Stockfish is also eaten a great deal in the South of France, notably in Nice, where it is prepared to the recipe given below after having been soaked for a long time in water (3 days at least).

In Belgium, Holland and Germany it is soaked in lime water and afterwards cooked like ordinary salt cod.

Stockfish à la niçoise—Scrape the fish well after it has been soaked in cold water; remove the bone and cut into pieces of regular size.

Cook 3 large chopped onions for every 2 pounds (kilo) of stockfish, tossing them lightly in olive oil. When they are cooked, add 4 large tomatoes, seeded and chopped, 4 crushed cloves of garlic, a pinch of basil and a large *bouquet garni*. Season with salt and pepper. Cook for 20 minutes.

Add to these cooked vegetables the pieces of stockfish and sufficient boiling water to cover the fish. Cook, covered, for 50 minutes. Next add 2 large potatoes (400 grams), cut in thick slices and ½ pound (250 grams) of black olives and cook for another 30 minutes.

STOCKS. FONDS DE CUISINE—This term refers to many culinary preparations: fat or lean stock, or meat juices used for sauces, stews, and for braising.

Only a limited use is made of these *fonds* in practical day-to-day cooking. Stocks are mainly used to make sauces, broth and, for thickening, a quick *roux*.

For cooking in the grand manner it is good to have on hand stocks and other basic ingredients. Only these will allow you to work with ease and rapidity and obtain sauces with much better flavour.

Here are the necessary stocks: *broth*, *clear soup*, *veal stock*, *white* and *brown* (*thin* and *thick*), *juice* from *braised meat*, *poultry* and *game stock*, *fish stock* and *various jellies*.

These stocks, when boiled down and without the addition of any browning or starch, are used as flavouring, essence, and glaze.

When a certain quantity of *roux* or other binding element is added, these stocks become *Basic sauces*, from which many other sauces derive. See SAUCE.

White Stock is a broth which by definition has no colour. It has white meat and aromatic vegetables as a basis.

Brown Stock is made with beef, veal or poultry, which are first half-cooked in butter or fat, and always with the usual aromatic vegetables, also half-cooked in butter.

Fish Stock is prepared with the bones and trimmings of fish. The liquid consists of dry white wine and water in equal quantities; sometimes only white wine is used. The only aromatics added are sliced onions, parsley, thyme, bay leaf and lemon juice. Stalks and parings of mushrooms could be added to this, if available.

Vegetable Stock for vegetarian cooking is obtained by adding water to the following vegetables: carrots, onions and chopped celery slightly cooked in vegetable fat (or butter), flavoured with parsley, thyme, bay leaf and in some cases garlic.

Use of Stocks. White stock is used as liquid in white sauces and stews and for poached poultry. Brown stock is used as a liquid in brown sauces, for braising large cuts of meat and for dark stews.

Fish stock is used in the preparation of special fish sauces, such as *Normande sauce* (see SAUCE), a white wine sauce or a thin white sauce to be served with fish.

Fish stock can also be used to moisten fish when it is cooked whole or in slices before it is braised or poached.

Vegetable stock is used as a liquid for all preparations in vegetarian cooking.

Fish or stock concentrate. FONDS DE POISSON, FUMET DE POISSON—*Nourishing ingredients.* 5 pounds (2½ kilos) bones and trimmings of fish (sole, whiting, brill, sea perch, haddock, etc.).

Aromatic ingredients. One medium large onion minced (125 grams), ½ cup (150 grams) mushroom parings, a small bouquet of parsley, one sprig of thyme, half a bay leaf, 10 drops of lemon juice.

Seasoning. 1½ teaspoons (10 grams) kitchen salt.

Liquid. 2½ quarts (litres) of water, 1 pint (½ litre) of dry white wine.

Method. Put all the aromatics at the bottom of the stock pot. Cover these with the bones and trimmings of the fish. Moisten, season and add the lemon juice. Bring to the boil, skim, cook gently for 30 minutes. Strain through a muslin bag or fine sieve.

Fish stock with red wine or fish fumet with red wine. FONDS DE POISSON AU VIN ROUGE, FUMET DE POISSON AU VIN ROUGE—*Method.* Prepare as for ordinary fish stock using as liquid 1½ quarts (litres) of red wine and the same quantity of water. Strain through a muslin bag or fine sieve and use as directed.

Game stock. FONDS DE GIBIER—*Ingredients.* (For 2½ quarts (litres)): *Nourishing ingredients.* 2 pounds (1 kilo) shoulder, breast or other pieces of venison, 2 pounds (1 kilo) trimmings of hare or wild rabbit, one old partridge, one old pheasant, ⅛ pound (50 grams) fresh pork rind, 3 tablespoons (50 grams) dripping or butter.

Aromatic ingredients. One large carrot (150 grams), 1 large onion (150 grams), one *bouquet garni*, one sprig of sage, 10 juniper berries, 1 clove.

Seasoning. 1½ tablespoons (20 grams) salt.

Liquid. Three quarts (litres) of white stock or water, 1 pint (½ litre) of white wine.

Method. Tie the meat together and truss the feathered game; brush with dripping or butter and brown in the oven. Cut the vegetables into slices and brown in the stockpot with the rind. Add meat, moisten with stock obtained by the addition of white wine to the juice left in the roasting pan in which the meat and game have been browned. Add another pint of stock. Boil down to a jelly. Add the remainder of the stock. Bring to the boil, skim, season lightly, add sage, juniper berries and clove. Cook gently for 3 hours. Skim off all fat and strain through muslin bag or fine sieve.

This stock is used to make brown game sauces.

If left as it is, this stock can be used as sauce for small pieces of game tossed in butter.

Suitably boiled down it becomes game essence and can be used to flavour different game dishes.

The nourishing ingredients used in the preparation of this stock (venison, hare, partridge, etc.) can be used afterwards for an infinite variety of dishes, such as hash, stews and purées.

Light brown stock or estouffade. FONDS BRUN CLAIR, ESTOUFFADE—*Nourishing ingredients.* 5 pounds (2½ kilos) lean beef (leg of beef or shoulder), 5 pounds (2½ kilos), veal knuckle, 2 pounds (1 kilo) fleshy beef and veal bones (cut into small pieces); ½ pound (300 grams) fresh bacon rind, scalded, ½ pound (250 grams) ham knuckle blanched, 3 tablespoons (50 grams) of meat dripping (or butter).

Aromatic ingredients. 3 medium sized carrots (300 grams), 3 medium sized onions (300 grams), large *bouquet garni**, one clove of garlic.

Seasoning. 2 tablespoons (30 grams) cooking salt.

Liquid. Seven quarts (litres) thin white stock or water.

These quantities will give 5 litres (quarts) of stock.

Method. Bone the meat and cut it into fairly large pieces. (After cooking the meat can be used to make a hash.)

Break the bones into very small pieces. Cut carrots and onions into slices; half cook all ingredients in fat; add a pint (½ litre) of white stock and boil down to a jelly; add the same quantity of stock and boil down again. Add the rest of the stock. Bring to the boil and season lightly with salt. Simmer for 8 hours.

Skim off all fat from the stock; strain the whole through a muslin bag or fine sieve.

Light brown stock is used in brown sauces, stews, jellies, and in different ways of braising.

Stock of veal or other meat. FONDS DE VEAU, DE VIANDE —In the home this stock is prepared in the following way:

With the trimmings of veal or other butcher's meat prepare a meat stock, which can be used as a gravy for various dishes or as a liquid to dilute the pan juices of small pieces of meat. To make this stock, begin by cutting the meat in small pieces and sauté in butter allowing 1 carrot and 1 medium-sized onion, cut into dice, for ½ pound (250 grams) meat trimmings.

As soon as the ingredients begin to brown, sprinkle a tablespoon of flour on them. Let this flour get a golden colour while stirring with a wooden spoon. Add ½ cup (1 decilitre) of white wine. Boil it down. Add 1½ cups (3 decilitres) of meat broth. Cook slowly for 1 hour. Strain through a fine sieve.

Brown veal stock. FONDS BRUN DE VEAU, JUS BRUN DE VEAU—Ingredients for 5 quarts (litres):

Nourishing ingredients. 5 pounds (2 kilos 500 grams) boned veal shoulder, 5 pounds (2 kilos 500 grams) veal knuckle, 2 pounds (1 kilo) veal bones, 3 tablespoons (50 grams) drippings.

Aromatic ingredients. 3 medium-sized carrots (300 grams); 2 medium-sized onions (200 grams); 1 large *bouquet garni**.

Seasoning. 1½ tablespoons (20 grams) salt.

Liquid. Seven quarts (litres) white stock.

Method. Bone the meat, tie it up, brush with dripping, season and brown in the oven. Chop up the bones as small as possible. Cover the bottom of a large stock pot with vegetables cut in slices. Put the bones on top of the vegetables, then the meat, previously browned in the oven. Add *bouquet garni*, and cover the pot; simmer over gentle heat for 15 minutes. Moisten with a pint (½ litre) of white stock. Reduce to a jelly. Add the same quantity of stock once more. Boil down again. Then add the rest of the stock. Bring to the boil, skim, and season lightly with salt. Simmer for 6 hours. Skim off all fat and strain through a muslin bag or fine sieve.

Note. This really exquisite stock is the basis of *thin veal gravy.*

This stock if left as it is, that is to say without being thickened with arrowroot or starch, and without being boiled down, can be added to small pieces of meat or poultry previously tossed in butter or other fat.

Suitably boiled down, and thus made richer, and with a little butter added according to circumstances, this sauce is used for pieces of roast meat, with braised vegetables and also with other dishes.

It can be prepared more economically by using fresh trimmings and bones from beef, veal or poultry of which the meat has been used for other dishes.

The meat used as basis in this stock, as in all others, can of course be used in different ways after cooking. Excellent dishes can be made with these remainders.

The white stock used as liquid can be replaced by water. The result is of course not quite the same. If one wants to do this, a better way would be to prepare a broth with bones cut up very small and lightly coloured, cooking it for 6 to 8 hours. This would then be palatable enough as liquid for the aforementioned meat.

As the cooking of this stock takes a long time one must take care, in case the liquid boils down too fast, to add good stock or water from time to time. This applies to all stocks which need long cooking.

Thick veal stock, also known as thickened veal gravy. FONDS DE VEAU LIÉ, JUS DE VEAU LIÉ—*Method.* Boil down to three-quarters 2 quarts (litres) of brown veal stock. At the last moment thicken with 1½ tablespoons (15 grams) of arrowroot diluted with 3 tablespoons of clear cold veal stock. Strain through a muslin bag or fine sieve. Keep warm in *bain-marie** (double boiler).

This stock has many uses. It can be added to small pieces of butcher's meat or poultry previously tossed in butter, or it serves as gravy for roasts and pot roasts.

Tomato veal stock. FONDS DE VEAU TOMATÉ—*Method.* To 2 quarts (litres) of brown veal stock add 1 cup (2 decilitres) of tomato purée. Boil down by a quarter. Strain through a muslin bag or fine sieve.

White stock. FONDS BLANC—*Nourishing ingredients.* 3 pounds (1½ kilos) lean veal (shoulder); 4 pounds (2 kilos) veal knuckle; 4 pounds (2 kilos) poultry giblets; 4 pounds (2 kilos) or the equivalent weight in bones and trimmings.

Aromatic ingredients. 2 medium large carrots (250 grams); 2 medium large onions (200 grams); 3 to 4 leeks (150 grams); a medium-sized *bouquet garni**; 4 to 5 stalks (150 grams) of celery.

Seasoning. 2 teaspoons (30 grams) cooking salt.

Liquid. Seven quarts (litres) of water.

These ingredients will give 5 quarts (litres) of broth.

Method. Bone the meat and tie it up. Break the bones into small pieces. Put bones, meat and giblets in a stock pot. Add liquid. Bring to the boil, skim and season. Add vegetables and *bouquet garni.*

Cook slowly for 3½ hours. Remove fat and strain through a muslin bag or fine sieve.

(After cooking, the meat of the white stock can be used in different ways.)

White poultry stock. FONDS BLANC DE VOLAILLE—Proceed as for *White stock*, but reinforce the ingredients by a chicken or a much larger quantity of giblets or bones and trimmings.

(After cooking, the meat of the poultry can be used to make croquettes.)

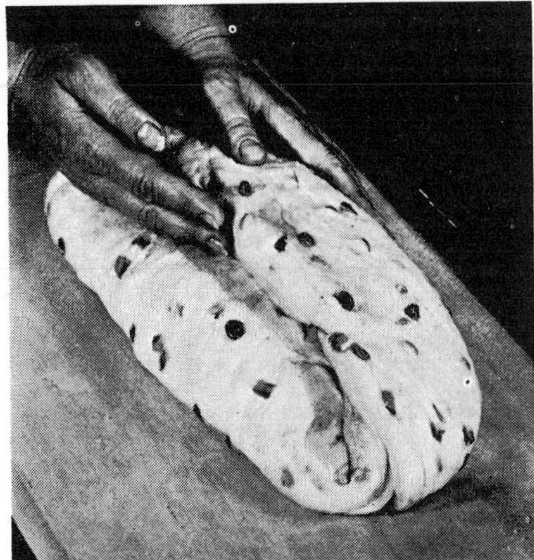

Making stollen

STOLLEN (German pâtisserie). *Ingredients*—7½ cups (1 kilo) sifted flour; 3 eggs; 1 pound (500 grams) butter; 2 ounces (60 grams) yeast; 6 ounces (200 grams) chopped almonds; 1½ cups (200 grams) currants; 1 cup (200 grams) candied orange and lemon peel; a pinch of powdered vanilla; ¼ cup (½ decilitre) of rum; 1¼ cups (2½ decilitres) warm milk; 5 or 6 powdered bitter almonds; 2 cups sugar.

Method. Put 5 cups (750 grams) of sifted flour into a deep dish; make a hollow in the middle and put in the yeast. Sprinkle the yeast with sugar and pour over the warm milk.

When the yeast begins to bubble mix all the ingredients into a homogenous paste. Cover this with a cloth and set near the fire.

While it rises wash the butter in water, then squeeze it to extract all moisture and dry it with a cloth.

Add the sugar and eggs, and work this butter until it becomes frothy. Add to it the rest of the flour, the currants, peel and other flavourings.

Blend together the dough and the butter mixture, adding a little milk but not too much, because this paste should be quite firm in consistency. Beat well then set it, covered, near the fire to rise.

Turn out on to a floured table top and form into a sort of thick loaf. Leave it to rise for 15 minutes, then put it on a buttered baking sheet and brush with melted butter.

Bake 1 hour at 350° F. Brush once more with melted butter when baked and sprinkle thickly with sugar.

The finished stollen (*Claire*)

STONECROP. Trique-madame—Very common plant of which the species often called *Orpine* has leaves somewhat resembling those of purslane, rather tasteless but edible as salad or cooked like purslane.

STONE-CURLEW. Oedicnème—A type of European *grallatoriae* bird comprising a dozen species. They are birds of medium size, similar to the plovers. Their meat is tasty. Stone-curlews are prepared like woodcock. See WOODCOCK.

STOPPER. Bouchon—The word *stopper* describes all objects, pieces of cork, glass, rubber or any other substance, usually round in shape, used for bottles, carafes and other receptacles, made of glass, china, metal or wood.

The matter of choosing corks for wine bottles is extremely important as it can affect the taste of wine. In this respect two things can go wrong: the wine may become tainted with the foul smell of bad cork or acquire a musty smell of mildew.

This deficiency in cork very often cannot be detected before manufacture and its effect on wine cannot be remedied. In cork-producing countries, however, for some years now it has been customary to cut cork boards into small cubes and 'corky' wine becomes more and more rare, because olfactive examination of the small pieces of cork enables specialists to sort out and eliminate those which are unfit for use. In the form of separate cubes the cork can be transported in much better ventilation conditions than in the case of boards and big pieces of bark. In the past it happened that cork, being transported in the hold of the ship in stale and foul air, often arrived at the cork factory in a deteriorated condition.

Corks should be made of fine bark, supple to the touch and without any defects.

Before using the corks put them through the following treatment:

Carefully sort to eliminate any which are not sound.

Place into a bucket and pour on boiling water. Leave to soak in this water for some time. This operation is intended not only to render the corks more flexible, but also to rid them of any impurities they may contain.

Drain them. Put on a sieve or a riddle and leave for an hour to dry thoroughly.

Soak them for 25 minutes either in good pleasant-tasting alcohol, brandy, or wine of the same nature for which the corks are intended.

In general, when bottling good quality wines, old corks should be avoided, unless they have been washed and scalded as described above, and only used when corking bottles containing wine for immediate consumption.

KITCHEN STOVE. Fourneau de cuisine—An apparatus made of masonry, or of cast iron, or of sheet metal, utilising the heat of a fire for the cooking of food either in the oven or on the heated top. Most modern stoves are heated with gas or electricity instead of with kerosene, wood or coal.

STRAINER. Passoire—Kitchen utensil used for straining sauces and other liquid preparations. The most practical strainer is the cone-shaped kind called *chinois*.

STRAINING BAG. Chausse—Funnel in felt or cloth used to clarify liquids, particularly syrups.

Straining of sauces and purées. Passage des sauces, des purées—Sauces are traditionally strained through a tammy-cloth (fine cheese-cloth), by two people, each holding one end of the cloth and twisting in opposite directions.

Two people are also needed to rub purées and other comparatively thick preparations through a tammy-cloth. Each person holds one twisted end of the cloth in the left hands and rubs the purée through, using a stout wooden spatula held in the right hand.

Some thin sauces can be strained, not through a tammy-cloth but through muslin, without twisting the material. In household kitchens a hair sieve is almost always used in place of a tammy-cloth, and a fine strainer in place of muslin.

STRAW-CASE. PAILLON—Straw wrapping in which bottles are transported. This straw, after treatment in boiling water, is also used for 'dressing' the bottles.

STRAWS. ALLUMETTES—Strips of puff pastry cooked in the oven, with different garnishes. See also ALLUMETTES.

Anchovy straws. ALLUMETTES AUX ANCHOIS—Coat the puff pastry with *Fish forcemeat* (see FORCEMEAT) blended with *Anchovy butter* (see BUTTER, *Compound butters*); garnish each strip with an anchovy fillet, trimmed and de-salted. Bake in the oven.

Straws à la chalonnaise. ALLUMETTES À LA CHALONNAISE—Coat the puff pastry with a *Chicken forcemeat* (see FORCEMEAT) blended with cream with a very finely chopped mixture of cocks' combs, mushrooms and truffles added to it. Bake in the oven.

Cheese straws. ALLUMETTES AU FROMAGE—Cheese straws, which are served as a cold hors-d'oeuvre and as an accompaniment to cheeses, are made of puff pastry with the addition of finely grated cheese during the last rolling out. The straws are then cut and put on a baking tray and sprinkled with grated Parmesan.

Crayfish straws. ALLUMETTES AUX CREVETTES—Coat the puff pastry with a finely minced *Fish forcemeat* (see FORCEMEAT) blended with *Crayfish butter* (see BUTTER, *Compound butters*) and with a finely chopped mixture of crayfish tails added to it. Bake in the oven.

STRAW (Potatoes). PAILLES—Potatoes cut longways, into very thin, almost *julienne** strips, like straw as their name implies, then deep-fried. See POTATOES.

STRAW WINES. VIN DE PAILLE—Wines made from grapes which are left to dry on straw mats for some time before being pressed.

STRAWBERRY. FRAISE—The strawberry, a plant of the rose family, is common throughout Europe. It only began to be cultivated in the thirteenth century.

Five or six species of strawberries were known. From these a number of varieties have been cultivated. Strawberries are classified in two groups: small strawberries of which the commonest variety is the ever-bearing strawberry, and large strawberries, which comprise a great many varieties. These are constantly being added to by crossings.

The most popular large strawberries in France are the following: *Héricart de Thury*, *Docteur Morère*, *La France*, *General Chanzy*, *President Carnot*, *May-Queen*, etc.

The European strawberry comes from the Haubois-strawberry: its flesh is firm and fragrant. A closely related species is the *Alpine strawberry*. The *perpetual strawberry* is a variety of this.

Varieties of large strawberries came from the United States and Canada (*Fragaria virginiana*), and from Chile, (*Fragaria Chiloensis*). They were imported into France by a naval officer named Freziers, and are still cultivated today in the region of Plougastel.

Pine strawberries (also called *common garden strawberries*) originating from Carolina are really hybrids of that species.

The strawberry must be eaten freshly gathered because it does not keep. It is used to make a soft drink and for the extraction of spirits. But above all strawberries are used for jam-making.

Strawberry Bavarian cream—See BAVARIAN CREAM.

Cardinal strawberries. FRAISES CARDINAL—Arrange well chilled strawberries in a glass fruit dish. Cover them with a sweetened purée of ripe raspberries. Sprinkle with fresh almonds finely chopped.

Strawberries in champagne. FRAISES AU CHAMPAGNE—Sugared strawberries are arranged in individual dishes or in a fruit dish and sprinkled with champagne. Chill thoroughly.

Strawberry compote I. COMPOTE DE FRAISES—Remove stems and clean strawberries. Put into dish. Add several tablespoons of boiling sugar syrup. Let the fruit soak for some time in this syrup. Serve hot or cold.

Strawberry compote II. COMPOTE DE FRAISES—Cook 1 cup (250 grams) of sugar and $\frac{3}{4}$ cup of water to the third degree (220°F.) (see SUGAR). Throw into this syrup 2 pounds (1 kilo) of large strawberries cleaned and with their stems removed. Let soak with lid on for ten minutes. Arrange on a fruit dish as required.

Strawberry Condé. FRAISES CONDÉ—Remove stems of large strawberries. Sugar the fruit and sprinkle with kirsch. Let it soak in a cool place.

Arrange in a pyramid in the middle of a border of rice. The rice must first be cooked in milk with sugar and vanilla and blended with yolks of egg. It is then moulded in a ring mould, cooked in a *bain-marie** (pan of hot water), cooled and turned out.

Serve with a sweetened purée of strawberries and raspberries.

Strawberries and cream. FRAISES À LA CRÈME—Remove stems, clean fruit, sugar, arrange in a glass dish or individual dishes and cover with thick fresh cream or with sweetened whipped cream.

Strawberries à la créole. FRAISES À LA CRÉOLE—Remove stems and clean the strawberries.

Cut off the top part of a pineapple. Through the opening, scoop out the flesh without damaging the outside. Cut out the core of the fruit, which is wooden and stringy. Cut the remainder of the flesh in dice. Dredge with sugar, sprinkle with kirsch or any other liqueur. Mix with the strawberries. Let them soak in a cold place.

Two hours before serving fill the pineapple with the mixture. Put the lid of the pineapple back. Seal the split with butter, stand the pineapple in a crystal dish or a silver bowl and surround it with crushed ice.

Strawberries Czarina. FRAISES TZARINE—Stand a silver dish on ice. Cover the bottom of the dish with a layer of pineapple ice cream. Arrange large strawberries on this ice cream, after they have been soaked in kummel and sugar and chilled.

Decorate with *Chantilly cream* (see CREAMS) by forcing it through a forcing (pastry) bag, with a large fluted nozzle. Sprinkle with candied violets.

Strawberry ice mixture. COMPOSITION AUX FRAISES POUR GLACES—Mix 2 cups ($\frac{1}{2}$ litre) fresh strawberries with a pint ($\frac{1}{2}$ litre) of syrup ($\frac{3}{4}$ cup sugar dissolved in $1\frac{1}{2}$ cups water). Add the juice of two lemons and of one orange. Add to this as much water as is necessary to obtain a mixture of 16° to 18° density measured by the saccharometer. If no such measuring device is at hand, let the $1\frac{1}{2}$ cups liquid include the fruit juices.

Strawberries à l'impératrice. FRAISES À L'IMPÉRATRICE—Prepare a dish of rice as for *Apricots à l'impératrice.**

Chill. Just before serving cover the rice with a pint (250 grams) of large strawberries sweetened with vanilla-flavoured or plain sugar.

Strawberry jam—See JAM.

Strawberries with liqueurs. FRAISES AUX LIQUEURS—Remove stems, clean strawberries and sugar them in a dessert dish or in individual glasses. Sprinkle with one of the following: kirsch, maraschino, cherry brandy, raspberry brandy, kummel, *fine champagne* (best cognac) or with some other liqueur. Serve very cold.

Strawberries à la maltaise. FRAISES À LA MALTAISE—Sugar small strawberries, add orange juice and a little curaçao; cool on ice. Just before serving put this mixture into baskets made of the oranges from which the juice has been extracted. Arrange on a dish covered with crushed ice.

Strawberries melba. FRAISES MELBA—At the bottom of a silver dish put a layer of vanilla ice. On this arrange very ripe strawberries. Cover with thick sugared strawberry purée. Pile ice round the dish.

Strawberry mousse—See ICE CREAMS AND ICES, *Mousses*.

Strawberry pulp for ices. PULPE DE FRAISES POUR GLACES—Rub very ripe strawberries through a fine sieve. To 2½ cups (5 decilitres) of this juice add 1 quart (litre) of sugar syrup at 35° measured by the saccharometer (4 cups sugar, 2 cups water boiled to 240°F.) and the juice of 1 lemon. Mix well. Churn in a freezer.

Strawberry pulp for ices, bottled. CONSERVE DE PULPE DE FRAISES POUR GLACES—Make a purée of fresh strawberries and pass through a very fine sieve. Add 1 cup (250 grams) of sugar to each 2 pounds (kilo) of fruit. Mix thoroughly and put in preserving jars. Close jars and place in a canning kettle. Cover with cold water. Let boil for 5 to 6 minutes. Let cool in canning kettle. Take jars out. Wipe and seal jars. Keep in cool place in a slanting position. This pulp may also be frozen and kept in a deep-freeze.

Strawberry ratafia—See LIQUEUR.

Strawberries Romanof. FRAISES ROMANOF—Stand a silver dish on ice. Arrange in this dish fine quality strawberries after they have been soaked in orange juice and curaçao and well chilled. Decorate with *Chantilly cream* (see CREAMS) (sweetened whipped cream) using a forcing (pastry) bag fitted with a large fluted nozzle.

Strawberry sauce—See SAUCE.

Strawberry soufflé—See SOUFFLÉ.

Strawberry tarts and tartlets—See TARTS AND TARTLETS.

Strawberries with various dessert wines. FRAISES AUX VINS DE LIQUEURS—Remove stems and clean strawberries. Dredge with sugar. Arrange in individual glass dishes or in a fruit dish. Sprinkle with Frontignac, muscadel, Madeira, sherry, port or marsala. Serve very cold.

STRAWBERRY TOMATO. ALKÉKENGE—Fruit originating in Mexico, which is better known under the name of *physalis*. The plant which produces it belongs to the same family as tomatoes and potatoes. In Mexico it is called Mexican tomato. Strawberry tomato grows very well in France, in the south and even around Paris. It is sometimes called husk tomato or winter cherry. The fruit is the size of a cherry, yellow in colour; its taste is sour-sweet. It is surrounded in a parchment-like calyx, which does not open, of a yellowish-grey colour. It is a fruit with seeds, not a stone fruit. The *physalis* are used in confectionery.

Strawberry tomato compote. COMPOTE D'ALKÉKENGES—*Ingredients.* 2 pounds (1 kilo) of strawberry tomatoes, 1 pound (500 grams) of sugar, 1 cup (2 decilitres) of water, peel of one lemon.

Method of preparation. Make a syrup of sugar and water, bring to the boil and throw in the strawberry tomatoes, having removed their calyxes. Allow to cook for 5 minutes.

Remove the fruit with a perforated spoon into an earthenware bowl and put the lemon peel in the middle. Put the syrup on to boil down and pour it over the fruit.

It is essential not to allow the lemon peel to boil with the compote as then the taste will be entirely changed.

Strawberry tomato

Glacé strawberry tomatoes in caramel. ALKÉKENGES GLACÉES AU CARAMEL—To make this, the fruit is opened and rolled in powdered gum arabic, then dipped into sugar syrup cooked to a degree of crack (310°F.). It is then taken out with a perforated spoon and put on a slab of marble or on a lightly greased metal sheet.

Glacé strawberry tomatoes in fondant icing. ALKÉKENGES GLACÉES AU FONDANT—The fruit is coated with *Fondant icing* (see ICING) white, pink or yellow, flavoured with kirsch, raspberry or pineapple essences.

To dip the fruit into fondant icing, the calyx has to be opened and turned back to form a stalk. The fruit is held by the end of the calyx and dipped into hot fondant icing, then drained and put on a tray sprinkled with icing sugar.

The fruits are then put into paper cases.

Strawberry tomato jam. CONFITURE D'ALKÉKENGES—*Ingredients.* 2 pounds (1 kilo) of strawberry tomatoes, 1½ pounds (750 grams) of loaf sugar, 3 cups (6 decilitres) of water.

Method of preparation. Make a syrup of the sugar and water and throw in the strawberry tomatoes with their calyxes removed. Bring to the boil. Remove scum as it forms. You must allow about 20 minutes of continuous boiling. At the end of this time, draw the pan away to the side of the stove, and leave the jam to cool a little.

Put into jars and seal like any other jam.

Strawberry tomato syrup. SIROP D'ALKÉKENGES—*Ingredients.* 3 pounds (1½ kilos) of strawberry tomatoes, 3 pounds (1½ kilos) of sugar, 1½ quarts (litres) of water.

Method of preparation. To make sure that the syrup keeps well, use only sound fruit.

Put the sugar and water into a red copper, not tinned, pan; put on the stove and bring to the boil. Drop the strawberry tomatoes in; allow to boil for 10 minutes and drain on a silk sieve or fine cheesecloth, placed over an earthenware bowl. Measure with a syrup gauge (it should register 28° or 220°F.). If the degree is lower than that, reduce the syrup. If it is above that, add a little water. Whisk a white of egg with 3 tablespoons (1 decilitre) of water and mix thoroughly in a basin with an egg whisk. Allow the syrup to clarify, leaving for 20 minutes on the side of the stove, simmering very gently.

Strain through a muslin bag. Heat the bottles gradually and pour in the boiling syrup. Cork the bottles and secure with string.

STRIP. EFFEUILLER—To take the leaves or petals of a plant off the stalk. Thus globe artichoke is stripped (if the heart only is to be used). Herbs, such as chervil and sorrel, are also stripped before use.

STRITZEL—In Austria the stritzel is the classic Christmas cake.

Ingredients. 7½ cups (1 kilo) sifted flour; ½ pound (250 grams) butter; 6 eggs; ¼ cup (60 grams) sugar; ½ ounce (15 grams) yeast; 2½ cups (5 decilitres) warm milk; ¼ pound (125 grams) sultanas and raisins; 2 lemons; 1½ teaspoons (10 grams) salt; a pinch each of grated nutmeg and powdered cumin.

Method. Make a dough with a quarter of the flour, a little milk, the yeast, the salt, the sugar, the nutmeg and a little butter. Allow to rise.

Break up the dough after having added to it the rest of the flour. Add the eggs, the rest of the butter, the raisins and the sultanas and work in the same way as for brioche pastry (see DOUGH), keeping the mixture fairly firm. Allow to rise again.

Break up the dough once more. Divide it into pieces—9 are needed to make a stritzel: 4 large, 3 medium and 2 small. Make all these pieces into 'tails' of the same length and make a plait of the 4 largest. Lay this plait on to a buttered baking sheet. Make another plait with the 3 medium sized tails and place this on top of the first. Twist the 2 smallest tails and set on top of the plaits. Stick the ends together neatly. Allow to rise a little.

Brush with egg; sprinkle with a little salt and some caraway seeds. Bake in a fairly hot oven.

STROGANOFF—See FILLET OF BEEF (U.S.A. TENDERLOIN) STROGANOFF.

STROMATEUS, RUDDERFISH. STROMATÉE—Fish of warm and temperate seas, inhabiting the Mediterranean where it is called *stromatée fiatole*, *lapuga* and *lippa*. Its flesh is very delicate and it is prepared in the same way as *Turbot*.

STRUDEL—The strudel is the national cake of Bavaria. It is made of noodle pastry with extra butter and rolled out as thinly as possible.

This sheet of pastry is divided into squares, each of which is spread with a mixture made of diced apples, butter, currants and chopped almonds, flavoured with cinnamon and a little brandy.

The edges of the strudels are moistened and the squares rolled and put into a buttered sauté dish. They are sprinkled with melted butter and browned. Then a little milk is poured into the dish and they are poached, covered, in the oven. The strudels are cooked when the milk has been absorbed. They are sprinkled with sugar when they come out of the oven, and eaten hot.

STURGEON. ESTURGEON—A large migratory fish, which lives in the sea and goes up rivers to spawn.

This fish was once very plentiful in certain French rivers. It is now rarely found there except in the Garonne. Nowadays, it is not often found outside Germany, Russia and the Balkans. In these countries sturgeons 6 to 7 metres long are quite often caught.

There are two breeds to be found in European waters, the *great sturgeon* (called in England the royal sturgeon), and the *common sturgeon*.

The *sterlet**, a fish much prized in Russia, is a breed of sturgeon caught particularly in the Volga.

In England, in the reign of Edward II, this fish was reserved for the royal table and a law was in force expressly forbidding its use elsewhere.

Now and then, though very rarely, sturgeons have been caught in the Seine as far down river as Paris. Carême saw a sturgeon caught at Neuilly Bridge. It was 2½ metres long, a metre in circumference, and weighed 100 kilograms (200 pounds). At an earlier period, history relates that two sturgeons were caught in Paris. One was presented to King Louis XV in 1758 and the other to King Louis XVI in 1782.

Although rather indigestible, sturgeon is quite tasty. Those caught in fresh water in the spring are the most sought after.

Sturgeons' eggs are made into *caviare*, a highly prized delicacy, which has always been expensive. See CAVIARE.

Vésiga is another product of the sturgeon. It is much used in Russian cookery. *Vésiga* is obtained by drying in a special manner the spinal marrow of the sturgeon.

In Russia, where the sturgeon is highly esteemed, it is eaten fresh or salted.

In France, sturgeon is less well liked. It is usually cut into steaks or rather thick slices or *fricandeau* which are braised like *fricandeau* of veal.

Sturgeon à la Brimont. ESTURGEON À LA BRIMONT—Fillet a medium-sized sturgeon. Trim the fillets. Thread fillets of anchovy into them. Put them in a baking dish lined with a *fondue** of vegetables cooked in butter (carrots, onions, celery finely sliced and cooked slowly in butter until very tender). Cover with 2 diced tomatoes, peeled and seeded by pressing, mixed with 4 large tablespoons of coarsely diced mushrooms. Surround with potatoes cut into little balls with a ball-scoop, half-cooked in salt water and drained. Moisten with ½ cup (1 decilitre) of dry white wine. Dot with 3 tablespoons (50 grams) of butter cut into tiny pieces. Bake in a slow oven, basting frequently. Five minutes before taking out of the oven, sprinkle with breadcrumbs and brown lightly.

Sturgeon in champagne. ESTURGEON AU CHAMPAGNE—Skin a medium-sized sturgeon. Trim it. Stud with truffles. Steep for an hour in a marinade of brandy, salt, spices and pepper.

Put the sturgeon in a fish kettle on a buttered grid. Moisten with fish *fumet* made with dry champagne, boiled down, and enriched, for 1 quart (litre) of stock, with 1 cup (2 decilitres) of fine *mirepoix* made of carrots, onions and celery, cooked slowly in butter until very tender.

Bring to the boil on the stove. Cook in a slow oven, basting frequently.

Drain the sturgeon. Glaze in the oven. Put it on a large dish. Surround with the garnish indicated. Cover with the cooking stock, enriched as follows:

Moisten the stock with 1¼ cups (2½ decilitres) of dry champagne. Cook down (reduce). Add 1¼ cups (2½ decilitres) of *Espagnole sauce* (see SAUCE) based on fish stock, carefully skimmed. Cook down. Season. At the last minute, add 3 ounces (100 grams) of butter. Strain.

Sturgeon braised in champagne can be served plain in its own juice, or with various garnishes. Among the most suitable garnishes are the following: *Chambord*, mushrooms, braised cucumbers, turtle, truffles.

Curried sturgeon. ESTURGEON AU CURRIE—Cook in butter, with 2 large sliced onions and a *bouquet garni**, a piece of fillet of sturgeon weighing about 1½ pounds (800 grams). Season with salt, pepper and 2 teaspoons of curry powder.

When the sturgeon is cooked, drain it and put it on a serving dish. Keep hot.

Dilute the pan juices with 1 cup (2 decilitres) of dry white wine. Cook down. Moisten with 1½ cups (3 decilitres) of *Velouté sauce*, based on fish stock. (See SAUCE). Season with 2 teaspoons of curry powder, mixed with 5 tablespoons of fresh cream. Boil for a few seconds. Add 3 tablespoons of butter. Strain this sauce and pour over the sturgeon. Serve *Rice à l'indienne** separately.

Fillets of sturgeon Boris. FILETS D'ESTURGEON BORIS—Fillet a raw medium-sized sturgeon. Trim the fillets. Steep for an hour in a marinade of oil, lemon juice, salt, paprika and spices.

Put them in an ovenware dish lined with 1 cup (2 decilitres) of dry *Duxelles** mixed with chopped chives. Moisten with 1 cup (2 decilitres) of dry white wine. Bring to the boil on the stove. Cover and cook in the oven for 10 minutes. Cover the fillets with coarsely shredded truffles. Pour the marinade over them. Moisten with 1½ cups (3 decilitres) of fresh cream. Dot with tiny pieces of butter. Finish cooking in a slow oven, basting frequently with cream. The cooking and glazing of the fish must take place simultaneously. Serve in the oven dish.

Fricandeau of sturgeon à la hongroise. FRICANDEAU D'ESTURGEON À LA HONGROISE—Brown a *fricandeau* or rather thick slice of sturgeon in butter with finely diced onions. Season with salt, paprika and a *bouquet garni**. Moisten with 1 cup (2 decilitres) of white wine. Cook down. Add 1½ cups (3 decilitres) of *Velouté sauce* (see SAUCE) based on fish stock. Finish cooking in a slow oven. Serve on a round dish. Add butter to the sauce and pour it over the fish. Serve with boiled potatoes.

Sturgeon steaks in cream. DARNES D'ESTURGEON À LA CRÈME—Skin the sturgeon and cut it into slices or steaks. Season with salt and paprika. Line a baking dish with chopped onion cooked slowly in butter until very tender. Lay the slices of sturgeon on top. Moisten with 1 cup (2 decilitres) of white wine. Bring to the boil on the stove. Bake in the oven for 15 minutes. Pour on thick fresh cream. Dot with tiny pieces of butter. Finish cooking in the oven, basting frequently.

SUBRICS—Small preparations served as hors-d'oeuvre, small entrée or garnish.

Subrics are a variety of *croquettes*, with the difference that they are never coated in egg and breadcrumbs. Moreover they are cooked in butter in a sauté pan and not in deep fat. Proceed as follows:

Bind the basic ingredient, cut into dice, with a mixture of *Allemande sauce* or *Béchamel sauce* (see SAUCE) and beaten egg. Season.

Using a spoon, divide this mixture into small portions (50 to 60 gram pieces) and cook in a frying pan or sauté pan in clarified butter. (Fat or oil may also be used.)

Keep the subrics apart in the pan so that they can spread without running into each other.

When they are nicely browned on one side, turn them over with a palette knife and cook them on the other side.

Drain the subrics, arrange them in a circle on a round dish and garnish with fried parsley.

Serve with the required sauce, or as they are.

Note. Some subric mixtures are bound only with egg, some have flour, cream or cheese added to them.

The name of this dish seems to have come from the fact that they used, long ago, to be cooked on the hot bricks of the fireplace. From '*sur briques*' came *subrics*.

Beef subrics à la ménagère. SUBRICS DE BOEUF À LA MÉNAGÈRE—Cut in small dice 1½ cups (300 grams) of left-over boiled beef. Put this beef into a basin and add 2 eggs beaten with a tablespoon of flour and ½ cup (50 grams) of grated Gruyère. Season with salt and pepper and mix well.

Heat in a frying pan equal quantities of butter and oil (or cooking fat). Put the beef mixture into the pan, spoonful by spoonful. Shape the subrics with the spoon, making them as regular as possible. As one side becomes cooked, turn them over with a palette knife.

Set on a hot dish and serve *Tomato sauce* or *Piquante sauce* separately (see SAUCE).

Note. In the same way subrics may be made from veal, chicken, pork, sweetbreads, brains, tongue, left-over fish, etc.

Foie gras subrics. SUBRICS DE FOIE GRAS—Cut 6 ounces (200 grams) of *foie gras* into dice of regular size. Bind with a mixture composed of 5 tablespoons (75 grams) of flour, one egg and 4 or 5 tablespoons of thick fresh cream. Season with salt, pepper and spices. Mix.

Cook as described in the recipe for *Beef subrics.* Serve on a napkin or paper doyley.

Potato subrics. SUBRICS DE POMMES DE TERRE—Break up with a fork the flesh of 6 large potatoes cooked in the oven in their skins. Bind this with an egg and a little *Béchamel sauce* (see SAUCE). Some grated cheese may be added if liked. Cook and serve like *Beef subrics.*

Semolina subrics—See SEMOLINA.

Spinach subrics—See SPINACH.

SUC—Liquid obtained by squeezing an animal or vegetable substance, or by boiling down some kind of juice.

Suc of meat. SUC DE VIANDE—This name is given to very much reduced consommé or to the juice which runs from roast meat; also to juice pressed from raw meat.

SUCÉES—A kind of *petits fours* made as follows:

Mix together in a basin 1 cup (250 grams) of sugar, ½ pound (250 grams) of butter, 1¼ cups (150 grams) of sifted cake flour and 5 egg yolks. Add to this mixture 5 ounces (150 grams) of candied fruit cut in very small dice. Fold in 5 stiffly beaten egg whites.

Make into a round shape on a buttered and floured baking sheet. Bake in a hot oven.

SUCKER. BARBIER—Common name applied to various types of fish which have either a cup-shaped sucker (*Lepadogaster de Gouan*), or a sharp spine on a fin (perch).

SUÉDOISE—A sweet dish made by arranging fruit (cooked in syrup), in layers in an aspic mould which is then filled with fruit or liqueur-flavoured jelly.

SUGAR. SUCRE—A sweet substance extracted from many plants; its chief sources are sugar cane, sugar beet, sugar maple and various species of palm. There are many types of sugar with varying molecular construction. The most important are *Sucrose* (cane sugar), *Levulose* (fruit sugar), *Maltose* (malt sugar) and *Lactose* (milk sugar).

From ancient times until the eighteenth century, honey took the place of sugar all over Europe. However, Le Grand d'Aussy (*Vie privée du français*), says, 'the origin of sugar is lost in the mists of time: India was propably the cradle of its manufacture; since the most faraway

Sugar model of the Merchandise Mart in Chicago, made by an American cook

times sugar cane has been known there in a wild state. The first writers who mention sugar described it as "Indian salt"; even the etymology of the word sugar seems to have derived from the Sanskrit work *sarkara* (in the Talmud *sakkara* and among the Mahrattas *sakar*), emphasizing the Indian origin of sugar.'

Crystallized sugar began to be brought from the East at the beginning of the eighteenth century. It came chiefly from Arabia by way of Alexandria. The greater part of this sugar was brought into Europe by the Italians. Some authorities, however, would have us believe that from the twelfth century onwards the Sicilians had introduced sugar cane to their island and began from about that time to manufacture sugar.

One certain fact is that the Portuguese prince, Dom Henrique, brought sugar canes from Sicily at the beginning of the fifteenth century and had them planted in the island of Madeira. From Madeira the Portuguese later took them to Brazil. At about the same time Spain followed the example of Portugal and introduced the cultivation of sugar cane to the kingdoms of Andalusia, Granada, Valencia and the Canaries.

Sugar, specifically white sugar, is mentioned in an account for the year 1333 from the house of Humbert, Dauphin of the Viennois. It is similarly mentioned in an order of King John dated 1353, where it is called *cabetin*. Eustache Deschamps, a poet who died about 1420, and several of whose manuscripts have been rediscovered, cites, among other housekeeping expenses incurred by a woman, the purchase of white sugar to make tartlets.

It was about 1420 that sugar began to be clarified. In 1471 a process for clarification was perfected by a Venetian.

For a long time, only apothecaries had the right to sell sugar. They considered this substance the first and most indispensable medicine. For this reason it was said of someone who lacked necessities that he was like an apothecary without sugar.

Sugar was one of the dearest of foodstuffs and was sold by the ounce. In spite of its price, it was used from the sixteenth century onwards to candy fruits and make different preparations.

Sugar melts at 160° C. (320° F.) and, on cooling, takes on a glossy appearance (barley sugar, candy sugar) but tends after a while to resume its crystalline structure: if it is heated further, it becomes a straw-colour, then brown, forming caramel at 180° C. (356° F.), becoming dark caramel at 190° C. (374° F.), black jack at 210° C. (410° F.): finally it decomposes.

Sugar is easily soluble in water which, when cold, can dissolve double its own weight of sugar. Solubility increases with rising temperature and saturated solutions would contain:

	C.	F.
64·18 per cent of sugar at	0°	(32°)
64·87 per cent of sugar at	5°	(41°)
65·56 per cent of sugar at	10°	(50°)
66·33 per cent of sugar at	15°	(59°)
67·09 per cent of sugar at	20°	(68°)
67·89 per cent of sugar at	25°	(77°)
68·70 per cent of sugar at	30°	(86°)
69·55 per cent of sugar at	35°	(95°)
70·42 per cent of sugar at	40°	(104°)
71·32 per cent of sugar at	45°	(113°)
72·25 per cent of sugar at	50°	(122°)
73·20 per cent of sugar at	55°	(131°)
74·18 per cent of sugar at	60°	(140°)
75·18 per cent of sugar at	65°	(149°)
76·12 per cent of sugar at	70°	(158°)
77·27 per cent of sugar at	75°	(167°)
78·38 per cent of sugar at	80°	(176°)
79·46 per cent of sugar at	85°	(185°)
80·61 per cent of sugar at	90°	(194°)
81·77 per cent of sugar at	95°	(203°)
82·97 per cent of sugar at	100°	(212°)

In solution in water, sugar raises both boiling point and density, thus providing a means of classifying sugar solutions and syrups as will be seen later.

Cane sugar—Sugar cane, originating in India and the West Indies and in America, is like a reed with a spongy marrow and grows to a height of six to nine feet. It is the source of about half the sugar produced commercially. The juice is pressed from the canes and is then subjected to a series of treatments to free it of impurities. The molasses is taken from the sugar leaving a yellow sugar, known in Great Britain as Demerara sugar. This sugar is crushed fine in the United States and is known as brown sugar. Further processes of refinement discolour the sugar and produce granulated, powdered, castor or fine sugar, icing or confectioners' sugar and lump sugar.

Beet sugar—In 1747 a German chemist, Marggraf, discovered sugar in beet juice. One of his followers, a French refugee named Achard, set up an experimental factory but had no financial success. His business failed but was started again in France at the instigation of Napoleon at the time of the Continental blockade. Manufacture of sugar by this method developed from that time until it became a big industry.

At first, sugar from beetroot was scorned. It was said to have a bad taste and to be less sweetening. It was alleged to have various defects and it was necessary for Chaptal to show, by irrefutable experiments, an absolute identity between the sugar from beet and sugar from cane before consumption of beet sugar became generally accepted. It is now almost as large a source of sugar as sugar cane.

Different sorts of sugar—Sugar loaves, which were very pure and had more sweetening power than ground sugar, are today more and more neglected: sugar cut into pieces of regular size is more convenient to use.

Powdered sugar is sugar in very fine grains sold ready to use.

Icing sugar is a powder sugar whose grains are so fine as to be almost intangible.

Sugar candy is manufactured by the crystallization of sugar syrup. The crystals are much larger than those obtained from crystallization which takes place more slowly at a lower temperature. This material, which always contains a certain proportion of invert sugar, is used in the manufacture of Champagne wines. Heated to the 'crack' degree, lightly coloured and acidulated, it is called *Barley sugar*, or *Apple sugar* if it is left transparent. If it is pulled it takes on a silky appearance (pulled sugar). True barley sugar used to be manufactured from a concoction of barley, although this is rarely done nowadays.

Food value of sugar—From the hygienic and dietetic point of view, it must first be emphasized that sugar is, with alcohol, the only chemically purified food in our diet. It is a reasonably pure carbohydrate, and 100 grams (3⅓ ounces) of sugar yield 393 calories. It is, therefore, a very concentrated foodstuff which is readily absorbed and does not leave any residue.

It is in many ways a valuable foodstuff but this does not mean to say that in all circumstances it is a good food.

Thanks to its rapid assimilation, sugar restores energy very quickly, though only for a limited time, in subjects exhausted by fatigue. This has been shown by trials made in different armies.

Its principal disadvantage is the absence in it of mineral salts, and its too rapid absorption.

It is necessary, therefore, to consider sugar as a condiment, a balancing food and something eaten occasionally.

For culinary purposes, sugar is used not only for confectionery and sweet preparations, but also in making sauces, ragoûts and other dishes. Sugar boiled to the caramel degree is used as colouring agent for soups, stocks and sauces.

The purists of the kitchen do not concede that anything should be coloured in this way, claiming, quite legimately, that the colouring of sauces and ragoûts should come about naturally without the addition of any foreign matter.

Sugar boiling—Before proceeding with sugar boiling, i.e. boiling carried to certain degrees, each of which has a name, which will be given later, it is necessary to prepare a syrup; that is to say a certain amount of sugar in a predetermined quantity of water. To begin with, then, a sufficient quantity of sugar for the work to be carried out is put into a saucepan or copper pan. Just enough water is added to melt the sugar. The usual proportions are 1¼ cups (2½ decilitres) of water to 2 pounds (1 kilo) of sugar.

The mixture is put on the fire, brought to the boil and skimmed carefully as the impurities of the sugar gradually come to the surface.

If this scum is allowed to stick to the side of the pan, it causes graining.

As soon as the boiling process produces small bubbles very close together, the evaporation of water is complete. At this precise moment, the sugar starts to cook and one has to watch it with care to stop it at the degree desired. During this process, the skin which forms on the side of the saucepan must be frequently removed.

A further method of preventing sugar graining during boiling is to add a spoonful of glucose for every pound of sugar.

Before arriving at the degree called caramel, the sugar passes through six different stages, which are designated by the following terms: *small thread*, *large thread*, *small ball*, *large ball*, *small crack*, *large crack*. Past this last degree the sugar becomes *caramel*.

The various sugar degrees can be determined by indications which after some careful practice can be easily recognised.

First degree: small gloss or small thread. Take between the thumb and the index finger a little of the sugar and stretch the two digits apart. Little threads forming between the two indicate that the sugar has arrived at the small thread degree.

Second degree: large thread. Continue boiling for a short while, then carry out the same test. This time it will be found that the threads are more numerous, longer and stronger, showing that the syrup is at the large thread degree.

Third degree: small ball. After the large thread degree the heat of the sugar is such that it is necessary before carrying out subsequent tests to dip the fingers into cold water placed ready at the side. For the less hardy, a little syrup dropped by spoon into cold water will indicate the degree.

Dip the tip of the index finger into the sugar and plunge it immediately into the water. Under the influence of the water, the sugar detaches itself from the finger forming a kind of glue which can be rolled into a soft ball, indicating that the sugar is at the soft ball degree.

Fourth degree: large ball. After a little more boiling carry out the preceding test again. The ball that is formed between the fingers is more resistant. This indicates that the sugar has arrived at the hard ball degree.

Fifth degree: small crack. After a little more boiling, dip the tip of the finger into the sugar and immediately into the cold water. A thin piece of sugar will fall off the finger which if put into the mouth will stick to the teeth. This indicates that the sugar has arrived at the small crack degree.

Sixth degree or hard crack. Once the sugar arrives at the degree indicated previously, it must be watched carefully for it will pass very rapidly into the last phase and change to caramel. The test is repeated as described above and as soon as the sugar detaches itself in thin films from the end of the finger dipped into cold water and breaks like glass, it has arrived at the large crack degree.

Once it arrives at this point, it needs only a few more seconds boiling over the fire to become caramel. In this form it is almost impossible to use it in the work of the pâtisserie or the confectionery establishment.

As soon as the desired degree is obtained, the saucepan must be taken away from the heat and the sugar kept in its condition over hot cinders or on the corner of the fire.

Some writers use the term *à la nappe* to designate a degree which precedes small thread. Others distinguish certain intermediate degrees between the *thread* degree and the *ball* degree, these being called *small pearl*, *large pearl*, *little soufflé* and *large soufflé*. At the *small pearl* degree the sugar boils, forming itself into small balls, like pearls. At the *large pearl* degree the pearls are better formed and better separated. At the *soufflé* degree small balls detach themselves from the skimmer when one blows across its holes after having dipped it in the syrup. In the *large soufflé* degree the bubbles are like snowflakes.

To identify these various degrees it is not unusual among professional practitioners to use a saccharometer or Baumé sugar weight-scale which indicates the degrees graduated from 0° to 44°. Below are given the degrees usually associated on the Baumé thermometer or saccharometer, and their equivalents in Fahrenheit and Centigrade terms.

Names	Density degrees	°F.	°C.
Gloss or thread	25°	215°	102·6°
Large gloss or large thread	30°	219°	104°
Small pearl	33°	220°	104·5°
Large pearl	35°	222°	106°
Soufflé (Blow)	37°	230°	110°
Large soufflé (Feather)	38°	232°	111°
Small ball	39°	230°–240°	110°–116°
Large ball	40°	246°–252°	119°–122°

The crack degree cannot be registered on the Baumé thermometer but various other degrees can be recognised on a special thermometer, graduating from 100°C. to 175°C. (212°F. to 347°F.). With this apparatus, which is used in the manufacture of confectionery, it is easy to distinguish one degree from another up to a point very close to caramel, as follows:

	°C.	°F.
Light crack	129°	264°
Medium crack	133°	271°
Hard crack	143°	289°
Extra hard crack	168°	334°
Caramel	180°	356°

The instructions given for the boiling of sugar must be observed very carefully. It must be repeated that the intervals separating the various stages in the cooking are very rapidly passed.

The sugar used to obtain a perfect boiling must be first grade.

Sugar syrup prepared cold. When sugar syrup prepared in advance is used, it is necessary to check the exact quantity of sugar and water that it contains. Here are two small tables which enable one to recognise both the quantity of sugar and the quantity of water by reference to the Baumé scale.

For one litre (35 ounces) of sugar solution.

Degrees Baumé	Weight of sugar
1°	20 g. or ⅔ oz.
2°	40 g. or 1⅓ oz.
3°	60 g. or 2 oz.
5°	120 g. or 4 oz.
10°	250 g. or 8 oz.
15°	500 g. or 16 oz.
21°	750 g. or 24 oz.
25°	875 g. or 28 oz.
27°	1,000 g. or 35 oz.
29°	1,225 g. or 41 oz.
31°	1,250 g. or 42 oz.

For 2 pounds 3 ounces of sugar (one kilo).

Degrees Baumé	Weight of water
32°	50 g. or 1¾ oz.
30°	70 g. or 2⅓ oz.
25°	100 g. or 3½ oz.
22°	130 g. or 4½ oz.
20°	150 g. or 5½ oz.
19°	170 g. or 6 oz.
18°	200 g. or 7 oz.

There are two other methods of classifying syrup, one of which is to note the temperature at boiling point, and the other to determine the density with a hygrometer giving the density based on water content.

There is also a special syrup-measuring apparatus from which a simple reading of the strength of the sugar solution can be taken .

The following points can also prove useful:

2 kilograms (4 pounds 6 ounces) of sugar melted cold, in a litre (35 ounces) of water measure 34°. The same melted hot would only measure 32°.

Anise sugar. SUCRE D'ANIS—Dry in a warm oven 50 grams (1⅔ ounces) of anise (wrapped in paper). Pound it finely in a mortar with 1 pound (500 grams) of sugar. Sieve through a silk strainer.

Put into a well-stoppered jar and keep in a dry place. (Anise sugar is used to make *petits fours*, as are all flavoured sugars.)

Cinnamon sugar. SUCRE À LA CANNELLE—Proceed in the same way as for *Vanilla sugar* (see below), replacing the vanilla by a thin stick of cinnamon.

Chop the cinnamon, adding to it a tablespoon of sugar; then pound all together with a second tablespoon of sugar. Put through a silk sieve. Then pound anew the cinnamon left in the sieve with another tablespoon of sugar and sift.

Clove sugar. SUCRE DE GIROFLE—Proceed as for *Anise sugar* with ⅔ ounce (20 grams) of cloves and 1 pound (500 grams) of sugar.

Ginger sugar. SUCRE DE GINGEMBRE—Proceed as for *Anise sugar* with 1 ounce or 4 tablespoons (30 grams) of ginger and 1 pound (500 grams) of sugar.

Icing sugars and pastillage — See ICING and PASTILLAGE.

Lemon peel sugar. SUCRE AU ZESTE DE CITRON—Cut off the peel of some lemons so as to have 2 ounces (60 grams). Dry this peel (in the shade) and chop it. Put into a mortar with 1 pound (500 grams) of lump sugar. Pound. Press through a silk sieve.

Orange sugar. SUCRE D'ORANGE—'Have some sweet Maltese oranges with very fine skin; grate the peel with lump of sugar, but lightly so as not to reach the white pith which is found immediately under the peel, because this is very bitter and spoils the fruit flavour.

'As the surface of the sugar becomes coloured scrape it with a knife to remove the peel which becomes stuck to it with repeated rubbing.

'Recommence the operation with the same care; then dry the sugar in a low oven or at the open door of a warm oven, and after having crushed it press it through a silk or horsehair sieve.

'For Seville orange, lemon, citron, or mandarine sugar proceed in the same way.' (Carême.)

Orange flower sugar. SUCRE DE FLEURS D'ORANGER—Proceed as for *Anise sugar* with ½ pound (250 grams) of orange flowers (whose petals have been dried) and 1 pound (500 grams) of sugar.

Orange peel sugar. SUCRE AU ZESTE D'ORANGE—Made with orange peel in the same way as for *Lemon peel sugar*.

Perfumed sugar. SUCRES ODORÉS—This is what Carême had to say about perfumed and flavoured sugars: 'The pastrycooks in the shops use distilled essences such as that of lemon and bergamot, rosewater, orange flower water and powdered orris, and these are used to flavour their sweet cakes and biscuits.

'But the true pastrycook in the house is bound to reject these perfumes and flavour his sweets, large and small, with the pleasant natural taste of orange, or citron, of Seville orange, or lemon, of orange flowers, or coffee, of vanilla, or green anise and saffron.'

Vanilla sugar. SUCRE VANILLÉ—Split 2 ounces (60 grams) of vanilla pods and chop them finely.

Put into a mortar with 1 pound (500 grams) of lump sugar. Pound finely. Press through a silk sieve.

SULTAN-HEN. POULE SULTANE—A web-footed aquatic bird, prepared for the table in the same way as the coot.

SULTANE—A large and elaborate pastry whose main characteristic is that it is set in the middle of a sort of cage of lattice-work sugar, generally surmounted by spun sugar plumes, or a huge spun sugar feather.

SULTANE (A LA)—Name applied to various preparations. *Velouté de volaille à la sultane* is a soup finished off with pistachio butter.

All dishes called *à la sultane* are characterised by the inclusion of pistachios (generally in the form of pistachio butter).

The name *à la sultane* is also used very often for sweets and pastries—for example *Apricots à la sultane*, and *Bavarois à la sultane*.

SUMMER-SNIPE OR SEA-LARK. ALOUETTE DE MER—A sort of plover of the order of waders, which the hunters call sandpipers. Its flesh is quite delicate. All the recipes given for woodcock are applicable to summer-snipe.

Raspberry sundae

SUMPTUOUS. SOMPTUEUX—That which is magnificent and which occasions great expense. In gastronomy sumptuousness is not always synonymous with culinary perfection.

SUNDAES (COUPES). COUPES GLACÉES—These are a delicious composite sweet with ice cream as their main ingredient. They are served in glass or silver ice-cups, and for this reason they are known as *coupes* in France.

The glasses are usually filled with one or more kinds of ice cream and decorated on top with fresh or crystallized fruit, or with *Chantilly cream*. See CREAMS.

Sundaes may be presented in a great many different ways. The *coupe Jacques* may be regarded as the classic sundae, the model for all others. Recipes for this and other *coupes* are given in the section on ICE CREAMS AND ICES.

Sundaes à la cévenole. COUPES GLACÉES À LA CÉVENOLE—Make 1 pint (½ litre) of *Vanilla ice cream* (see ICE CREAMS AND ICES). At the same time beat enough cream with sugar to make 1½ cups (3 decilitres) of *Chantilly cream** (see CREAMS). Break ½ pound (250 grams) of *marrons glacés* into tiny fragments and steep them for 30 minutes in a glass of kirsch.

To serve. Line the bottom of the ice cream glasses with the *marrons glacés*. On top of these, just before serving, put a very smooth layer of vanilla ice cream. Decorate the tops with *marrons glacés* and *Chantilly cream* piped through a forcing bag.

SUNDEW. ROSSOLIS—Aromatic plant whose leaves can be eaten as salad or cooked.

SUNFLOWER. HÉLIANTHI—Common name for the herbaceous Helianthus plant similar to the Jerusalem artichoke. It is grown in France for its long tubers. These can be eaten between November and the end of April. They taste like Jerusalem artichokes but their flavour is less pronounced. This vegetable is cleaned and cooked in the same way as salsify and Chinese artichoke.

SUPRÊMES—See CHICKEN, *Suprêmes of Chicken*.

All the methods of preparation given in that section are also applicable to suprêmes of partridge and other game birds.

SWALLOW. HIRONDELLE—In spite of the fact that swallows are protected birds in France they are still sometimes eaten in the guise of spit-roasted 'small birds'.

The nests of the *salangane* or Far-Eastern *sea-swallow*, which these birds make by regurgitating a gelatinous substance contained in their crops, are highly prized as food by the Chinese. (The jelly produced by the birds comes from the seaweed on which they feed.) So-called 'swallows' nests' are sold in Europe, but these are sometimes made from agar-agar.

Salangane swallows' nests are not used in China solely for the preparation of the celebrated birds' nest soup. They are also used as garnishes for various dishes, taking the place of cocks' combs and cocks' kidneys, mushrooms and truffles in composite *ragoûts**. See NESTS, *Swallows' nests*.

Swallows' nest soup—First make a chicken *consommé* (see SOUPS AND BROTHS) very rich in nourishing ingredients, and very clear.

Meanwhile, soak the nests for two hours in cold water in order to swell the sticky substance of which they are made. After it has been soaked, this substance should be transparent. Clean the filaments of the nests very carefully, removing all debris, such as feathers, shells and other impurities.

Blanch the nests in boiling water for 5 to 6 minutes. Bring the *consommé* to the boil and put in the nests.

Simmer gently for 45 minutes. During cooking, the nests disintegrate into thin gelatinous filaments. The sticky substance which held them together gives the soup its characteristic viscous texture.

In China, this soup is usually made with duck stock. It is generally served in tiny porcelain cups.

SWAN. CYGNE—A graceful, web-footed lamellirostrum, tame or wild. It ranked with the peacock in providing a sumptuous roast at state banquets in the Middle Ages. It was carefully plucked before being impaled on the spit and, after cooking, was dressed in its feathers and brought ceremoniously to the table with a piece of blazing camphor or wick in its beak.

Nowadays, swan is regarded as too oily and leathery for the connoisseur.

SWEDE (U.S. RUTABAGA). CHOUX-NAVETS—There are two varieties with swollen roots below ground, one the white turnip-rooted cabbage; the other, yellow, the swede, which is less used in ordinary cooking.

SWEETBREAD. RIS—Name of the thymus of calf and lamb. This organ, situated at the top of the breast, is in two parts, of which one, round in shape, is called in French the *noix*, and the other, more elongated and less regular is the throat sweetbread or *gorge*.

The flesh of the sweetbread is white and rather soft.

Sweetbreads are only found fully developed in young animals (calf, lamb and kid).

Chemical analysis of this substance shows that it contains three times more albumen and 4 to 5 times more gelatine than beef and only half as much fibre.

Calf's and lamb's sweetbreads are considered to be the most delicate products of butchery. The former make much appreciated entrées and the latter are used as garnish for a great many dishes (*brochettes*, little pastry cases, timbales, vol-au-vent, etc.). See OFFAL OR VARIETY MEATS.

Lamb's sweetbreads. RIS D'AGNEAU—Before being prepared in any manner, lamb's sweetbreads should be thoroughly soaked in cold water, blanched, cooled and dried.

They can then be braised, in white or brown gravy, or—according to the method of preparation chosen—fried in butter.

Lamb's sweetbreads are principally used as garnishes, by themselves or in combination with other ingredients.

To serve them as an independent dish, any of the recipes given for *Calf's sweetbreads* can be applied, in particular recipes for *Escalopes of calf's sweetbreads*. See OFFAL OR VARIETY MEATS.

Lamb's sweetbreads can be used for *attereaux**, on skewers, in scallop shells *au gratin*, with cream, as *kromeskis**, fried, *à la hongroise*, *à l'indienne*, with pilaf, *à la poulette*, with risotto, sautéed with mushrooms, *à la chasseur*, *fines herbes*, with Madeira, as hot pâté, *timbale*, raised (covered) pie, *vol-au-vent*.

SWEETEN. ADOUCIR—To reduce the acridity of a dish by prolonged cooking.

This term also applies to the operation which consists of diminishing the degree of saltiness in a dish by diluting it with water, milk or light stock.

SWEET POTATO. PATATE—Hardy plant with edible tubers resembling potatoes, native of India, now naturalised in all warm countries. Its taste is sweet and recalls a little that of artichoke.

There are many varieties of sweet potatoes; the best are *Virginian*, with yellow very tasty flesh, *White Spanish*, *Algerian*, *West Indian*, which is enormous and very floury, and the *Malaga pink*.

Different species of sweet potatoes cultivated in France are also very good.

Sweet potatoes (particularly Malaga pink), are made into very delicate jam. They can also be preserved in syrup, when they rather resemble *marrons glacés*.

In the regions where sweet potato is cultivated, the young leaves are eaten like spinach.

Baked sweet potatoes or sweet potatoes in jackets. PATATES EN CHEMISE, EN ROBE DE CHAMBRE—Bake in the oven and serve as they are with butter.

Boiled sweet potatoes with honey (Creole cookery). PATATES AU NATUREL AVEC MIEL—Boil the sweet potatoes in water, put them in the oven just long enough to dry them and serve on a napkin with a pot of honey.

Sweet potatoes à la crème. PATATES À LA CRÈME—Proceed as described in the recipe for *Potatoes à la crème**.

Sweet potato croquettes. PATATES EN CROQUETTES—Prepare like *Potato croquettes**.

Fried sweet potatoes. PATATES FRITES—Prepare like *Fried potatoes* (see POTATOES).

Fried sweet potatoes (Creole recipe). PATATES FRITES—Choose round, uniform-sized sweet potatoes. Boil them without salt. While still warm, cut into round slices ⅛ inch thick. Fry in a light-coloured very hot fat and serve sprinkled with vanilla-flavoured sugar.

Sweet potatoes au gratin. PATATES AU GRATIN—Proceed as described in the recipe for *Potatoes au gratin**.

Sweet potatoes à l'impériale, or Henri (American cookery). PATATES À L'IMPÉRIALE—'Butter a pie dish (or a shallow metal *timbale*) and put in sliced sweet potatoes, cooking apples and bananas, well mixed and seasoned with salt and paprika. Scatter small pieces of butter on top. Bake in a slow oven. Take out of the oven and cover with apricot or redcurrant pulp.'

Note. This dish is served as an accompaniment to meat, poultry or game.

Sweet potato purée. PURÉE DE PATATES—Prepare like *Potato purée**.

Sweet potato salad. SALADE DE PATATES—Prepared like *Potato salad* (see SALAD).

Stewed sweet potatoes. PATATES À L'ÉTUVÉE—Cut 3 to 4 sweet potatoes (500 grams) into uniform slices.

Put into a sauté pan with 3 tablespoons (50 grams) of butter, ½ cup (1 decilitre) of water and a pinch of salt.

Bring to the boil, cover and simmer for 30 minutes. Serve heaped in a vegetable dish.

SWEET POTATOES (Sweet dishes, desserts):

Sweet potato pudding (Creole cookery). GÂTEAU DE PATATES DOUCES—Take 5 good sweet potatoes. Boil them with their skins in unsalted water. When they are cooked take them out, peel and mash into a fine paste. Incorporate in this paste, stirring vigorously, some vanilla-flavoured sugar and a tablespoon of flour. Soften with a little milk. Break in 4 eggs, one by one. Keep one white of egg, which should be whisked into a stiff froth and folded into the mixture at the last moment to make it smooth and light. Add ¾ cup (150 grams) of Malaga raisins, previously steeped in rum and with the seeds taken out. Pour the mixture into a buttered charlotte mould. Cook for a few moments in a *bain-marie** (pan of hot water), then in the oven. Serve cold, as it is, or with English custard.

Sweet potato soufflé. SOUFFLÉ AUX PATATES—Using sweet potato pulp, bound with yolks of egg and mixed with stiffly beaten whites, prepare a soufflé, which can be served as a small entrée or as a sweet soufflé. See SOUFFLÉS.

SWIFT. MARTINET—A type of swallow. Its flesh is edible though rather tasteless.

SWISS CHARD, WHITE BEET, OR STRAWBERRY SPINACH. BETTE, BLETTE, POIRÉE À CARDE—Also known under the name of *chard* or *seakale beet*, this is a vegetable of the same type as beetroot, cultivated for its spinach-like leaves and broad white petioles and midribs. It is widely cultivated in France, particularly in the Lyons district, where this vegetable is greatly appreciated. It is found on the market from July to the first frosts.

Preparation of chards. Trim the chards (white ribs) keeping the green parts for another dish, scrape them and remove all stringy parts. Cut into 2½ to 3 inch chunks. Cook in a *court-bouillon for vegetables**. Drain and prepare as indicated in individual recipe.

The chards can also be boiled in salted water. Drain, immerse in cold water to cool, dry in a cloth, chop up and prepare like *spinach.*

Swiss chard à la béchamel. BETTES À LA BÉCHAMEL—Drain 1 pound (500 grams) of chards cooked in a *court-bouillon**. Put into a sauté pan with 1½ cups (3 decilitres) of not too thick *Béchamel sauce* (see SAUCE).

Simmer with a lid on for 5 minutes. Put into a vegetable dish. Add 5 tablespoons (80 grams) of butter to the sauce and pour it over the chards.

Swiss chard au blanc. BETTES AU BLANC—This is another name for *Swiss chard à la béchamel*, the recipe for which is given above.

Buttered Swiss chard I. BETTES AU BEURRE—Cook the chard (white ribs) in *court-bouillon**, drain and put into a sauté pan with 6 tablespoons (100 grams) of fresh butter for 1 pound (500 grams) of vegetables.

Simmer on a low heat with a lid on from 15 to 20 minutes. Serve in a vegetable dish, sprinkle with the butter in which it was cooked.

Buttered Swiss chard II. BETTES AU BEURRE—Trim the white ribs and cut into chunks. Blanch slightly in salted water, drain, immerse in cold water to cool. Drain again then put into a sauté pan with 1 cup (2 decilitres) of water and 6 tablespoons (100 grams) of butter for 1 pound (500 grams) of vegetables. Transfer into a vegetable dish and sprinkle with butter.

Swiss chard in cream. BETTES À LA CRÈME—Drain 1 pound (500 grams) of chards (white ribs) cooked in *court-bouillon**. Simmer for 5 minutes with 3 tablespoons (50 grams) of butter. Add 2 cups (4 decilitres) of boiling fresh cream and simmer to reduce by half. Transfer into a vegetable dish. Add 4 tablespoons (60 grams) of butter to the pan liquor and pour the sauce over the chards.

Swiss chard au gratin. BETTES AU GRATIN—Prepare *Swiss chard à la béchamel**; put into a fireproof dish on a layer of *Béchamel* and cover with the same sauce.

Sprinkle with grated cheese and melted butter and brown in a hot oven.

Swiss chard in gravy. BETTES AU JUS—Drain 1 pound (500 grams) of chard (white ribs) cooked in *court-bouillon**. Put into a sauté pan with 1½ cups (3 decilitres) of brown veal gravy. Leave to simmer under a lid for 10 minutes.

Transfer into a vegetable dish. Add 3 tablespoons (50 grams) of butter to the gravy and pour it over the chard.

Swiss chard à la hollandaise. BETTES À LA HOLLANDAISE—Trim and cut the chards (white ribs) into longish chunks. Tie into bundles as you would asparagus and cook in boiling salted water.

Drain, put on a serving dish for asparagus (with perforations to allow drainage) or on a napkin. Serve *Hollandaise sauce* (see SAUCE, *Cold sauces*) separately.

Chards prepared in this way can also be served with various other sauces, such as: melted butter, *Cream sauce*, *Maître d'hôtel sauce*, *Mousseline*, *Vinaigrette*, etc.

Swiss chard à l'italienne. BETTES À L'ITALIENNE—Prepared like *Swiss chard in gravy*, but replacing the veal gravy by *Italian sauce* (see SAUCE).

Swiss chard à la lyonnaise. BETTES À LA LYONNAISE—Prepared like *Swiss chard in gravy*, replacing the gravy by *Lyonnaise sauce*. See SAUCE.

Swiss chard à la milanaise. BETTES À LA MILANAISE—Cook the chards in salted water. Drain them, dry and prepare like *Asparagus à la milanaise**.

Swiss chard à la moelle. BETTES À LA MOELLE—Drain the chards, dry them and prepare like *Cardoons with marrow*. See CARDOON.

Swiss chard Mornay. BETTES MORNAY—Another name for *Swiss chard au gratin.*

Swiss chard à la polonaise. BETTES À LA POLONAISE—Cook the chards in salted water, drain, dry and prepare like *Asparagus à la polonaise.*

Chocolate-flavoured Swiss roll

SWISS ROLL. BÛCHE—Thin sponge cake baked in a special tin, then covered with jam or cream and rolled up like the French *Bûche de Noël.*

SWIZZLE STICK. MOUSSOIR—A little wooden or metal implement used to whisk chocolate and champagne.

SWORDFISH. ESPADON—This oceanic fish weighs sometimes as much as 600 pounds. Its flesh is white, fine and quite delicate. Recipes for tunny fish (fresh tuna fish) can be used for swordfish.

SYRINGE. SERINGUE—Instrument used in pastry-making instead of forcing bag and pipe when it is necessary to make decorations with a substance that is rather firm in consistency.

SYRUP. SIROP—Solution of sugar and water or sugar and fruit juice, concentrated to a sticky consistency. It can be hot or cold.

Almond syrup. SIROP D'AMANDES, SIROP D'ORGEAT—1 pound (500 grams) sweet almonds; 5 ounces (150 grams) bitter almonds; 6 pounds (3 kilos) white sugar; 7 cups (1 kilo 625 grams) distilled water; 1 cup (250 grams) orange flower water.

Blanch the almonds; pound them to a paste in a mortar

with ⅓ cup (75 grams) of sugar and ½ cup (125 grams) of water, and dilute little by little with the rest of the water; squeeze through a cloth, straining a little water through the residue so as to obtain 2½ cups (2,250 grams) of emulsion. Dissolve the sugar in this, in a *bain-marie* (double boiler). Add the orange flower water when the syrup is cold.

Blackcurrant syrup. SIROP DE CASSIS—Strip the blackcurrants from their stalks, crush them and press out the juice through a muslin bag. Weigh the juice and add sugar in the ratio of 3½ cups (900 grams) of sugar to 2 cups (500 grams) of juice.

Put this in a pan over a low heat, stirring all the time to prevent the sugar sticking to the bottom and to speed up melting.

Skim carefully and verify the degree of concentration which should be 31° (weighed boiling). Decant into bottles, cork, seal and keep in a cool, dry place.

Cherry, raspberry, gooseberry or mulberry syrup. SIROP DE CERISES, DE FRAMBOISES, DE GROSEILLES, DE MÛRES—Dissolve the sugar in the filtered fruit juice using, if possible, a copper pan (not tinned), set on the heat and strain as soon as the mixture begins to boil. The amount of sugar depends on the sweetness of the fruit juice, but in general 1½ cups of sugar to 2½ cups fruit juice is the best preparation.

Citric acid syrup. SIROP D'ACIDE CITRIQUE, SIROP DE LIMON—⅓ ounce (10 grams) citric acid, 1 quart (990 grams) plain syrup.

Dissolve by shaking and add ⅔ ounce (20 grams) of alcoholic tincture of lemon (lemon extract).

Coffee syrup. SIROP DE CAFÉ—With 1 pound (500 grams) of freshly ground coffee, make a very strong infusion. 8¾ cups (2 litres) of boiling water, strained twice over the very finely ground coffee, will give about 5½ cups (1¼ litres) of well flavoured coffee.

Put 5 pounds (2½ kilos) of sugar into a copper pan. Pour over the coffee infusion and melt over a low heat. As soon as the syrup begins to boil it should be removed.

Gum syrup. SIROP DE GOMME—3⅓ ounces (100 grams) white gum, washed; ⅔ cup (300 grams) white sugar; 1½ cups (340 grams) distilled water.

Dissolve the gum, then the sugar in the water. Heat to boiling point. Remove when the first bubbles appear and strain.

Orange syrup I. SIROP D'ORANGES—Make a cold syrup with sugar, melting 3½ pounds (1 kilo 750 grams) of sugar in a quart (litre) of water. Twenty-four hours are needed for the sugar to melt completely. Filter through a wet flannel.

To make orange syrup, melt 3½ ounces (100 grams) of citric acid in a little water and flavour it with orange extract.

This orange extract is obtained by soaking finely cut orange peel in alcohol. To double the strength of the extract, it can be reinfused with fresh orange peel after it has stood for a month. It is important to use only the coloured part of the skin, the white pith imparting a bitter taste.

Orange syrup can be prepared for instant use by rubbing the outsides of the oranges with sugar lumps until there is no more juice left in the skins.

For 6 oranges allow 4 pounds (2 kilos) of sugar, taking from this quantity sufficient pieces for rubbing the skins.

Melt all the sugar in 6½ cups (1½ litres) of cold water. Add ½ pound (250 grams) of citric acid.

Orange syrup II. SIROP D'ORANGES—Choose fine ripe oranges. Cut the peel off one or two of these very finely and put it on one side to flavour the syrup, then finish peeling the other oranges. Crush the pulp and squeeze out the juice in a damp cloth. Weigh the juice. Allow 3¼ cups (800 grams) of sugar for every 2 cups (500 grams) of juice. Set over the heat in a copper pot.

While this heats spread a damp cloth over a wooden frame. Put the orange peel on this. As soon as the syrup boils pour it over the peel. Cool before bottling.

Note. Lemon syrup can be made in the same way, but since lemon juice is much more acid than orange juice it is necessary to add an equal quantity of water and to use additional sugar.

Orgeat syrup. SIROP D'ORGEAT—Mix sweet and bitter almonds in the proportion of 5:1, that is to say 1½ pounds (750 grams) of sweet almonds and 5 ounces (150 grams) of bitter almonds.

Blanch them (by putting them for a few moments in boiling water, when the skins become easily detachable if rubbed between thumb and forefinger). Throw these almonds into cold water, drain them, then toss them in a cloth so as to remove all traces of moisture.

Pound the almonds in a marble mortar. The amounts indicated above should be divided into smaller parts, say 6 or 8, so that the pounding may be done more easily.

Allow, for 30 ounces (900 grams) of almonds, 5½ cups (1¼ litres) of water and 4½ pounds (2¼ kilos) of loaf sugar. Add ½ cup (100 grams) of sugar little by little to the almonds being pounded in the mortar, and, from time to time, a few drops of water. This prevents the almonds turning to oil.

When they are completely pounded, dilute the almonds to a paste by adding a little more than half of the total amount of water. Strain the paste thus diluted through a damp cloth. It is important to wring out the cloth thoroughly to extract all the almond milk.

Put back the residue in the mortar, pound it anew with about ¼ cup (50 grams) of sugar, then add the rest of the water. Strain this also through the cloth, squeezing out every possible drop of liquid.

Mix together the first and second pressings of almond milk and dissolve in it the rest of the sugar.

Pour into a pan and set over the heat, stirring frequently. Remove as soon as the first bubbles appear; this syrup must not be allowed to boil. Away from the heat add half a glass of orange flower water.

If the chosen flavouring is lemon, cut the lemon in slices and leave them in the syrup for a quarter of an hour.

Orgeat syrup can also be made in another way. Put the almond milk in a china bowl with the lump sugar broken up into small pieces. Set in a *bain-marie* (pan of hot water) and stir from time to time to hasten the melting of the sugar. As soon as the sugar is completely melted and the liquid is near boiling point, remove from heat. When the syrup is cold, flavour it with orange flower water poured on to the surface of the syrup; after a few moments mix and put into bottles. The syrup may be strained through a white cloth before bottling.

Plain syrup. SIROP DE SUCRE—To prepare cold, dissolve 7 cups (1,800 grams) of sugar in a quart (litre) of water. This syrup does not keep as well as the syrup prepared hot, which is made by adding 6 cups (1,650 grams) of white sugar to a quart (litre) of water heated just to boiling point. Strain and filter.

Redcurrant syrup. SIROP DE GROSEILLES—Boil 4 cups (1 kilo) of loaf sugar to 270° F. Rub raw redcurrants through a fine sieve. Add 2 cups (500 grams) of this juice to the sugar. When the syrup comes to the boil, leave it to stand to allow the scum to collect. Then skim it and cook the syrup to a density of 32° or until it measures 220°F.

TABLE CLOTH. NAPPE—A piece of linen used to cover the table for meals.

The table cloth has a long history and goes back to the early Middle Ages.

Up to the fifteenth century the table cloth was very wide and was folded in two so that it could be turned over. It was then known as the 'double cloth'. From this period, fashion decreed that table cloths should be of single width. They were often damascened or embroidered.

The table cloth played an important rôle in feudal ceremonial. It was perfectly acceptable for persons of different rank to dine at the same table, and it was usual for the master to take his meals with his servants, but the host's place alone had the distinction of being covered with a cloth, which set him apart from the others present at the table. If the table was entirely covered with a cloth, then the master's place was singled out from the rest in being covered with a special napkin.

It was not permitted to take food or drink from the cloth set before a person of superior rank, except by formal invitation.

When a nobleman received one of his vassals or a nobleman of somewhat inferior rank, while permitting him to eat off the same cloth, he would be careful to to preserve the social distinctions by having a small napkin set under his trencher.

One of the greatest affronts which could be levelled at a knight was to cut the table cloth to his right and to his left, to indicate that, having offended against the laws of chivalry, he was no longer accepted in the company of his peers.

Until the end of the fourteenth century, when the individual napkin had not yet come into use, the table cloth was covered with a 'runner', a very long narrow strip of linen laid along the edge of the cloth, which was used by the guests to wipe their fingers and mouths.

It was in the sixteenth century that table linen came into general use. At court, as in the homes of great noblemen, in bourgeois establishments, as in every hostelry, the tables were covered with cloths and each diner had his own napkin.

When Francis I, after his captivity in Spain, came to his good city of Bordeaux, Moreau de Villefranche tells us: 'Meats of all kinds in great abundance were served at tables covered with table cloths and napkins.'

At this period, luxury was carried so far that napkins were changed several times during a meal. The author of *L'Isle des Hermaphrodites*, a pamphlet directed against the court of Henry III, wrote: 'Afterwards, they brought him another napkin on a plate, for these were changed after each course, and even more often, as soon as a spot was noticed by anyone.' Since it must be admitted that at that period even persons of the greatest refinement (among them the minions of the King) ate somewhat uncleanly, it would seem that this lavish supply of napkins was not altogether pointless.

Even among the middle classes, this custom of changing napkins frequently during meals persisted for a long time. Montaigne noted and deplored the fact: 'I regret that a habit which I first saw practised by kings, should now have become widespread, so that our napkins are changed after each course like our plates.'

In the sixteenth century, the napkin which, in the fifteenth century, was merely placed on the shoulder or left arm, was tied round the neck to protect the fine muslin collars worn at that period. As the operation of knotting the two ends of the napkin was not an easy one for the diner to undertake himself, it was necessary to seek assistance from a fellow-guest, from which sprang the expression 'making both ends meet.'

It was at this period that table napkins began to be folded in different ways. This custom, however, was soon abandoned, but was to be adopted once more about three hundred years later, for, in the middle of the nineteenth century, it was popular for a time. In the sixteenth century, it was fashionable to fold napkins 'in the shape of divers fruits and birds.' It was also customary to perfume napkins and table cloths with rose water and other essences.

At this period table cloths were also treated in various ways to make them more decorative. They were goffered in different patterns and pleated like the ruffs worn round the neck. The author of *L'Isle des Hermaphrodites* tells us, in this connection, that a table cloth 'was pleated in such a way that it closely resembled some undulating river ruffled gently by a light breeze.'

Table linen which, in earlier centuries, was enriched with embroidery, often of gold or silver thread, completely changed its appearance in the sixteenth century. Its main decorative feature was that it was woven (by craftsmen known as *telliers* and *tisserands*) in such a way as to incorporate designs in the weave of the fabric itself.

It was at this period that damascene cloths and napkins began to be woven in France at Rheims and in Normandy, especially in the Caen area. These were as beautiful as those which had been made hitherto in Flanders and Venice.

It was a man called Graindorge who, it is said, had the idea of weaving chequered patterns and flowers into table linen. His son Richard made damascene cloth with human figures, animals and other designs. Finally, Michel, Richard's son, founded several factories for the production of damask table linen, so that its use spread throughout the kingdom.

TABLE DECORATIONS—Table decorations should not in any way impede the service or make it difficult for people to speak to or see one another.

The fashion for complicated decorations in *pâtisserie*, for candelabras, for monumental flower arrangements went out long ago; nowadays one or two low baskets or glass bowls of flowers make an elegant and practical décor. Centrepieces, mirrors with Japanese gardens arranged on them, are suitable for formal occasions. *Chemins de fleurs* in little crystal *jardinières*, long and narrow, arranged end to end to make a border of roses, violets or nasturtiums, look charming, as do sprays of autumn leaves on the tablecloth.

Bowls or baskets or fruit can replace floral decorations. Low fruit dishes, plates or baskets with handles that are easy to hold are preferable to symmetrical pyramidic arrangements on high dishes. Fruit should be arranged without too much fuss, interspersed if necessary with clusters of leaves, and should please the eye as well as the appetite.

A homely table setting, with brightly coloured linen and dishes, makes an informal meal very cheerful: glazed earthenware jugs, plates and dishes lend themselves to many decorative ideas. In general, one should avoid cluttering up the centre of the table, keep the decorations well balanced and use only utensils which are absolutely necessary for the meal.

Dishes, silver and glass, should be cleaned and polished so as to shine with all possible splendour. Place settings should be at least twelve inches apart. A thick flannel padding should be placed under the tablecloth. The fork should be placed at the left hand side of the plate, the spoon and knife at the right; the cutting edge of the latter should be turned inwards towards the plate. Glasses for water, wine, Madeira and champagne, are arranged either in a group or in a line, in the order of size. Carafes of water and *vin ordinaire* are grouped along the table alternately with the salt cellars and pepper pots.

TACAUD—Common French name for a variety of cod, also called *officier* and *monie borgne*.

The flesh is quite pleasant to eat but full of bones. All recipes given for cod can be applied to this fish. See COD.

TACON—Common French name for a young salmon. See SALMON.

TAILLEVENT—A famous cook who was the author of one of the oldest books on cookery.

Guillaume Tisel, called Taillevent, was born in 1326. From 1346 to 1350 he was head cook to Philippe VI de Valois. From 1355 to 1368 he was head cook and master of the kitchen to the Dauphin, the Duke of Normandy, and from 1368 to 1371 head cook to Charles VI: '*premier écuyer de cuisine et maistre des garnisons de cuisine de France*' (head cook and master of the garrisons of France).

Taillevent died in 1395 and it would seem that he wrote his *Viandier* between 1373 and 1380.

TAILLOIR, TRANCHOIR—Special slices of bread which in olden days took the place of plates; they were placed in turn on pieces of wood, coloured or plain, and on the slices of bread food was served. After each service, the bread was gathered up in baskets and distributed among the poor.

Nowadays, the word *tailloir* describes a wooden platter on which meat is cut up.

TALLEYRAND—Charles Maurice de Talleyrand-Périgord, celebrated statesman and diplomat, was born in Paris on the 13th February, 1734, and died in the same city on the 17th May, 1838. He was one of the greatest French gastronomes.

Talleyrand (1754–1838)

At the age of 21, he became abbot of Saint-Denis and in 1788 bishop of Autun, but high ecclesiastical office did not prevent him from leading a brilliant and dissipated worldly life. His lack of moral scruples and an extreme aptitude for diplomacy and intrigue enabled him to retain a high position throughout the Revolution, the Directory, the Empire and the Restoration, with only short periods of reversal of fortune.

While he was an important personage at court the luxury of his table and the splendour of his entertaining were celebrated. At the time of the First Empire he had as his cook the illustrious Carême. There is a story that one day the wife of Maréchal Lefèvre, whom Sardou made famous by the name of Madame Sans-Gêne, was present at one of Talleyrand's magnificent dinners. She exclaimed, 'Mon Dieu! you have given us such magnificent food. It must have cost you a lot of money.' 'Ah, madame, you are very kind; it is not a well-paid job,' replied Talleyrand.

The extravagance of Talleyrand's table was not entirely for the sake of pure gastronomical satisfaction; he believed that the pleasure he offered his guests at these receptions was an important element in the success of his diplomacy and intrigues. As he departed to negotiate at Vienna, where he hoped to secure important advantages for France, he said to Louis XVIII, 'Sire, I have more need of casseroles than of written instructions.'

He never let religious or moral scruples interfere with the pursuit of his career and personal pleasures; part of a letter written in 1791 to his friend the Duc de Lauzun demonstrates this side of his character. A bull of excommunication had been issued against several members of the clergy. Talleyrand, whose name was included, wrote ironically, 'You have heard the news: excommunicated. Come and dine to console me. Everyone refuses me fire and water; so we will eat nothing but glazed cold meats and drink only chilled wines.'

TALMOUSE—A kind of cheese tartlet, served as hors-d'oeuvre. See HORS-D'OEUVRE.

TAMARIND—Fruit of the tamarind-tree, a leguminous plant of the West Indies. The pods are filled with an acid juicy pulp which is used to prepare a *limonade* and can replace vinegar. Medicinally it has laxative properties.

TAMMY-CLOTH. ÉTAMINE—A piece of woollen material through which purées are rubbed by means of a spatula. It is also used for straining sauces and stocks.

TANGERINE. MANDARINE—The fruit of a species of orange-tree, originally from China. It is cultivated in the south-east of France, and in southern U.S.A. The tangerines of Nice and of Algeria are renowned.

The tangerine is a delicious fruit. It is usually eaten raw. Like the orange, it can also be treated in various ways in confectionery, in the preparation of cold sweets (desserts) and even in cooking.

Many recipes for oranges are suitable for tangerines. See ORANGE.

Tangerine tart or flan—See TARTS.

Iced tangerines. MANDARINES GLACÉES—Empty, without tearing the skin, tangerines of equal size. Make an ice cream mixture with the pulp of the tangerines (see ICE CREAMS AND ICES). Just before serving fill the skins of the tangerines with the ice cream.

Cover the skins with the tops which have been cut away.

Tangerines en surprise. MANDARINES EN SURPRISE—Empty the tangerines as indicated above. Fill with a heaped tablespoon of tangerine ice cream or Neapolitan ice cream flavoured with tangerine. On top of the ice, spread a layer of tangerine soufflé mixture. Sprinkle with icing sugar. Put in a very hot oven for a few seconds to brown.

Tangerines in syrup. COMPOTE DE MANDARINES—Prepared in the same way as *Orange compote**.

TANKARD OR BEER-GLASS. BOCK—Receptacle in glass or stoneware of half a litre capacity which is used for drinking beer.

Beer glasses generally have a handle. Those made of stoneware are often ornamented with designs in relief generally representing carousing scenes.

TAPIOCA—A farinaceous food extracted from the roots of cassava or manioc plant. It is very digestible and is used to thicken soups and broths, and make milk puddings.

TAPIR—Large mammiferous South American animal, rather resembling a pig. The flesh is highly thought of, and can be prepared like that of boar. See WILD BOAR.

A branch of tarragon

TARRAGON. ESTRAGON—A pot-herb used with chervil and chives to flavour green salads. Tarragon is also used to flavour some sauces. A liqueur is made from it.

Bottled tarragon. CONSERVE D'ESTRAGON—Press down well in champagne half-bottles some young sprigs of fresh tarragon, stripped, washed and dried in a cloth. Cork the bottles. (Cover with paper caps.) Tie string round the necks of the bottles. Put them, in straw wrappers, in a large pan (the bottom of the pan must also be lined with straw wrappers) or place them in a canning rack. Cover with cold water. Boil continuously for 40 minutes. Leave the bottles to cool in the pan. Drain and dry them. Keep in a cool place.

Treated in this way, tarragon can be kept for a very long time without losing any of its aroma. It is used in the same way as fresh tarragon.

Tarragon cream. CRÈME D'ESTRAGON—Boil, until almost completely dry, 1¼ cups (100 grams) of fresh crushed tarragon leaves, moistened with 7 cups (1½ litres) of dry white wine. Add 1¾ cups (3½ decilitres) of very thick *Béchamel sauce* (see SAUCE). Season. Boil for a few seconds. Rub through muslin. Heat the tarragon purée. At the last moment, add a little fresh butter.

This purée is used as a filling for small vol-au-vents, barquettes or canapés, and for stuffing certain vegetables, such as artichoke hearts, mushrooms, etc.

Dried tarragon. ESTRAGON SÈCHÉ—Strip and wash some large fresh branches of tarragon, recently picked. Dry the sprigs thoroughly in a cloth. Tie them into bunches of 6 to 8 with string.

Hang these bunches in a cool dry place and leave them until they are completely dried.

Dried tarragon is used in the same way as fresh or bottled tarragon.

Pickled tarragon. CONSERVE D'ESTRAGON AU VINAIGRE—Strip branches of fresh tarragon. Break into little sprigs. Wash in cold water. Dry thoroughly in a cloth. Put the sprigs in small bottles. Fill with very strong vinegar. Cork the bottles tightly. Tie with string. Keep in a cool place.

Tarragon purée. PURÉE D'ESTRAGON—*Hot.* Made with tarragon and very thick *Béchamel sauce* as indicated for *Tarragon cream.*

It can also be made by adding a purée of tarragon leaves (blanched, cooled under running water, drained, pounded in a mortar, rubbed through muslin) to twice its volume of mashed potatoes.

This purée is used as a filling for small vol-au-vents, canapés or other similar preparations.

It is also used to stuff certain vegetables: mushrooms, artichoke hearts, small tomatoes, etc.

Cold. Pound together in a mortar 1¼ cups (100 grams) of tarragon leaves, blanched, cooled and drained, with 6 yolks of hard boiled eggs. Add 2 tablespoons of fresh butter. Season. Rub through a hair sieve.

This purée is used in the preparation of various cold hors-d'oeuvre or to decorate cold fish.

Tarragon vinegar. VINAIGRE À L'ESTRAGON—Ordinary vinegar in which small tarragon shoots are steeped.

This vinegar is used to moisten sauces and in salad dressing.

TARTARE—Name given chiefly to a cold sauce, mayonnaise prepared with crushed hard boiled egg yolks and oil, with chopped chives added.

A la tartare is the name given to minced beef steak seasoned with salt and pepper, reshaped into a steak and served uncooked with a raw egg yolk on top, and, on the side, capers, chopped onion and parsley.

Fruit tart (*Robert Carrier*)

TART (FLAN). Tarte—The words tarte or 'tart' and 'flan' are often used interchangeably in England and France to designate a pastry filled with fruit, jam, custard or some other filling. The American term most often used for this confection is open or single crusted 'pie'. Almost all such dishes are cooked and served in the United States in a pie dish, whereas in England and France a metal flan or pastry ring, placed on a metal baking sheet, is used. For tarts and flans with savoury fillings, see FLANS. Recipes for sweet fillings suitable for desserts are given below. All recipes are suitable for baking in either an American pie dish or a flan ring.

In England the tart is often a two-crusted, fruit-filled dessert baked in a dish. This would be called a pie in U.S.A., whereas a tart would designate a small single-crusted pie which the French call *tartelette*.

Apple tart (flan) à l'alsacienne. FLAN DE POMMES À L'ALSACIENNE—Fill the flan crust with quartered small tart apples. Proceed as for *Apricot tart à l'alsacienne*, flavouring the custard with cinnamon.

Rectangular tarts to cut up in portions for restaurant use (*Larousse*)

Tart (flan) cases baked blind (unfilled). CROÛTES À FLAN CUITES À BLANC—These are made with a short pastry, fine or ordinary.

Roll out this pastry (200 grams) to a circle 9½ inches in diameter.

Transfer this sheet of pastry on to a circular, buttered baking tin. Let it fall into the tin, and press it round the inside of the tin. Pass the roller over the top of the tin which will cut off the excess pastry.

Make the rim of the tart out of the band of pastry rising up the sides of the tin. Lift it away from the edge and pinch it with the pastry pincers. Put the ring made in this way on a baking sheet. Prick the bottom of the tart (flan) with a knife which will prevent the pastry from bubbling up during the baking. Line the edge and bottom of the flan with a thin buttered paper. Fill it with dried beans, with rice or with dry cherry stones, or flour. Bake in the oven at a moderate temperature (375°F.) for 25 minutes.

Remove the buttered paper and whatever temporary filling has been used. Gild the border and interior of the tart (flan) with egg. Dry it for a few moments at the mouth of the oven. Fill with whatever filling is indicated by the recipe.

Alsatian tart. TARTE ALSACIENNE—*Ingredients.* 2 cups plus 2 tablespoons (250 grams) of sifted flour, 1 cup (250 grams) of castor (fine) sugar, ½ pound (250 grams) pounded sweet almonds, ¼ pound (125 grams) butter, 1 egg.

Method. Cream together the butter, sugar and egg. Add the flour and the almonds; mix. Roll out three quarters of the dough into a round piece ⅓ inch thick.

Roll out the rest of the pastry and cut it into thin strips.

Surround the round piece of pastry with one of these strips and arrange the others criss-cross on the top, fixing them together with water.

Fill each square space with a different kind of jam or marmalade. Cook in a moderately hot oven.

Apple tart (flan). TARTE AUX POMMES—Fill a flan case (pie shell) made of *Fine lining pastry* (*Pastry dough I*), *Sweet pastry* or *Flaky pastry* (see DOUGH) and sprinkled inside with fine sugar, with peeled eating apples, cut into quarters or thin slices.

Bake in a hot oven. When baked, coat the fruit either with apple jelly or apricot jam, strained and flavoured with liqueur.

Apple tart (flan) with lattice-work decoration. FLAN AUX POMMES GRILLÉ—Line a flan ring with short pastry. Fill with rather thick apple purée. Decorate the top with a latticed design made with thin strips of pastry. Press down well at the edges. Brush with egg. Bake in a hot oven.

Apple tart

Messina apple tart. TARTE AUX POMMES À LA MESSINE—Prepare a pastry case (pie shell) in the usual way. Fill with thin slices of sugared eating apples and seeded raisins.

Sprinkle with sugar and bake in the oven.

When the tart is ready, sprinkle with sugar mixed with cinnamon.

Apricot tart (flan). TARTE AUX ABRICOTS—Roll out a sheet of *Lining pastry* (*Pastry dough I*) or *Flaky pastry* (see DOUGH) ⅛ inch thick. Line a flan ring with this, and flute the edges. Place the tart on a metal baking dish and prick the pastry with a fork or point of a knife to prevent the pastry blistering in the heat. Sprinkle a little fine sugar over the pastry, and fill the tart with halves of apricots—fresh apricots or fruit preserved with or without sugar.

Cook in a moderate oven (375°F.) for about 30 minutes, then remove the flan ring and brush the whole of the tart with beaten egg. Put back in the oven for 5 minutes to finish cooking.

Once cooked put the tart on a cooling rack and coat

the fruit with a thin covering of transparent apricot jam or apricot purée. Set on top a few sweet almonds or apricot kernels.

Note. According to taste, the tart may simply be sprinkled with vanilla-flavoured sugar instead of using jam, but the latter method gives a better appearance. The tart must not be cooled on the baking sheet because the steam will escape too slowly and the pastry will lose its crispness.

Apricot tart (flan) à l'alsacienne. FLAN AUX ABRICOTS À L'ALSACIENNE—Fill the flan (tart) crust with halved apricots which have been steeped in kirsch and sugar. Just before putting the flan in the oven, pour into the crust a custard mixture thickened with a teaspoon of potato flour or arrowroot.

Cherry tart

Cherry tart (flan). TARTE AUX CERISES—Proceed as for *Apricot tart*, filling the pastry with stoned cherries.

When the tart is baked, cover with a film of red-currant jelly flavoured with raspberry or cherry jam strained and with a little kirsch or cherry brandy added.

Cherry tart à l'alsacienne

Cherry tart (flan) à l'alsacienne. FLAN AUX CERISES À L'ALSACIENNE—Proceed as for *Apricot tart à l'alsacienne*. Preserved cherries are sometimes used for this flan.

Tart of the Demoiselles Tatin. TARTE DES DEMOISELLES TATIN—Butter well a copper dish lined with tin and about 2½ inches deep. Put in a layer of fine sugar about ⅛ inch thick. Fill with peeled and quartered apples and on top of these put small pieces of butter and some more sugar.

Cover with a paper-thin sheet of *Fine lining pastry* (*Pastry dough I*) (see DOUGH).

Bake on a fire of wood charcoal covered with a 'country oven' (*four de campagne*), filled with glowing embers, for 20 to 25 minutes.

Take off the oven and make sure that the tart is cooked and the sugar well caramelised. If it is ready, turn it out on to a serving dish so that the pastry is on top. Serve hot.

Fig tart (flan). TARTE AUX FIGUES—Made with fresh figs, peeled and soaked in liqueur in the same way as *Strawberry tart*. Coat the fruit, once set in the pastry, with apricot jam, strained and flavoured with kirsch or some other liqueur.

Fruit tart à l'allemande. TARTE AUX FRUITS À L'ALLEMANDE—Under this heading comes a series of very good tarts of deservedly high reputation. Each has a special name according to the fruit used to make it.

Apfelkuchen or apple tart—Made like *Cherry tart*.

Aprikosenkuchen or apricot tart—Made like *Cherry tart*.

Erdbeerkuchen or strawberry tart—Differs from the preceding tarts in that the fruit is not cooked with the pastry. The tart shell is baked first and, when cold, filled with the strawberries, thickly sprinkled with sugar and coated with a thick layer of whipped cream, sweetened and flavoured with vanilla.

Himbeerkuchen or raspberry tart—Prepared in the same way as the above, substituting raspberries for strawberries.

Johanisbeerkuchen or redcurrant tart—Prepared like *Stachelbeerkuchen or gooseberry tart*.

Kirschenkuchen or German cherry tart—Roll out and turn some *Flaky pastry* (see DOUGH) six times, and roll it into a round sheet of the desired size about ⅛ inch thick. Set in a metal pie dish lightly moistened in the middle. Damp the edges of the pastry and pinch them to make a border.

Prick the pastry with a fork to keep it from blistering during cooking. Sprinkle over a little fine sugar and powdered cinnamon.

Arrange the stoned cherries (either fresh or preserved fruit) on the pastry. Bake in a moderate oven. While it cooks prepare a thick cherry syrup by cooking cherries and sugar together. Strain this syrup through a fine strainer, and when the tart is cold pour a good layer over the fruit. To finish off the tart make some fine bread-crumbs, sift and bake them to a pale golden colour in the oven. Sprinkle a good pinch of these breadcrumbs all over the tart.

Note. Do not forget to sprinkle sugar and powdered cinnamon over the tart *before* filling it with fruit.

Pflaumenkuchen or greengage tart—Made like *Kirschenkuchen*.

Stachelbeerkuchen or gooseberry tart—Bake the pastry shell empty in the oven. Throw the picked-over fruit into the same weight of sugar cooked to the 'crack' degree (see SUGAR). When this sugar is melted, strain out the fruit with a skimmer and boil down the juice until it begins to jelly. Take it from the fire and put back the fruit. Allow to boil together for a moment then pour all together into a basin. When this jam is quite cold, use it to make a thick layer in the tart, which should then be thickly coated with sweetened, vanilla-flavoured whipped cream.

Fruit tart (flan) à l'alsacienne. TARTE AUX FRUITS À L'ALSACIENNE—This tart is made chiefly with quetsch and mirabelle plums, apples and cherries. It is made like an ordinary fruit tart, but either ordinary custard or a light *French pastry cream* (see CREAMS) is poured over the fruit after it has been set in the pastry case (shell).

English fruit tart (pie). TARTE À L'ANGLAISE—Fill the special pie dish with cut-up apples (or other fruit), cover the fruit with white or brown sugar and put a little chopped lemon peel here and there. So that the tart will be nicely rounded, place an egg cup or saucer upside down on top.

Moisten with half a glass of water. Cover the tart with *Lining paste or Pastry dough II* (see DOUGH) made with an egg yolk, which should be fixed to a moistened band of pastry placed round the edge of the dish.

Brush the surface of the tart with water and sprinkle over fine sugar. Bake in the oven for 40 to 50 minutes.

Note. These tarts can also be flavoured with cinnamon or cloves. The top may be decorated with cut-out pieces of pastry and brushed with egg.

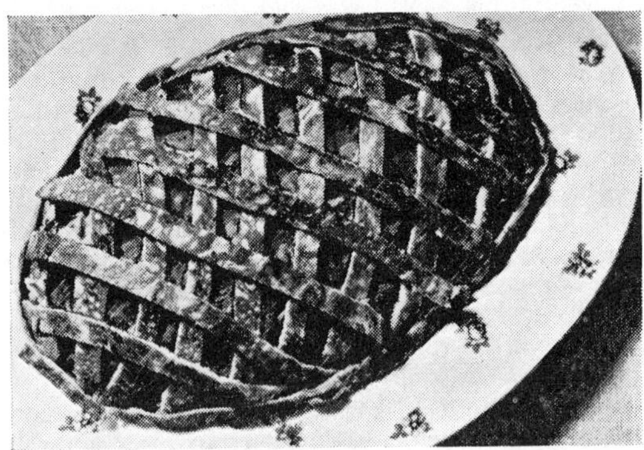

Linzertorte (*Claire*)

Linzertorte (Austrian tart). TARTE À L'AUTRICHIENNE—This Viennese pastry takes its name from the town of Linz in Austria.

It is a tart of *Lining paste* (*Pastry dough*) (see DOUGH) strongly flavoured with cinnamon, filled with strawberry jam and covered with criss-cross strips of pastry. *Linzertorte* proper is made from a special rich pastry which includes ground almonds, cinnamon, lemon juice and egg yolks in its composition.

Me'gin tart (Messina pastry). TARTE AU ME'GIN—Made like *Quiche Lorraine* with a mixture of eggs, a white cheese called *Fremgin*, well drained, and fresh cream.

Nectarine tart (flan). FLAN AUX BRUGNONS—Using halved nectarines, proceed as for *Apricot tart.*

Peach tart (flan). FLAN AUX PÊCHES—Proceed, using halved or quartered peaches, as for *Apricot tart.*

Pear tart (flan). TARTE AUX POIRES—Made with soft ripe pears, divided into small pieces lengthways, like *Apple tart.*

Pineapple tart (flan) I. TARTE À L'ANANAS—Prepare the crust with *Short pastry dough* or *Flaky pastry* like *Apricot tart* (see DOUGH). Bake this pastry case (shell) empty.

When it is ready, fill the shell with half-slices of pineapple cooked in syrup. Cover with apricot jam put through a fine sieve and flavoured with kirsch or rum.

Pineapple tart (flan) II. TARTE À L'ANANAS—Roll out a round or square of *Flaky pastry* (see DOUGH). Incise this lightly 1¼ inches from the edge. Set in the middle thin slices of pineapple (cooked or raw). Sprinkle with fine sugar. Brush the edges of the pastry with egg and bake in a hot oven. When cooked, coat the pineapple with apricot jam.

Plum tart (flan). TARTE AUX PRUNES—Made with greengages, mirabelles or quetsches like *Apricot tart.*

Plum tart à l'alsacienne. TARTE AUX PRUNES À L'ALSACIENNE—Made with quetsches in the same way as *Apple tart à l'alsacienne.*

Raspberry tart (flan). TARTE AUX FRAMBOISES—Made with raw raspberries as described in the recipe for *Strawberry tart.*

English rhubarb tart (pie). TARTE À LA RHUBARBE À L'ANGLAISE—Use a special English pie dish or a long deep dish of fire-proof porcelain.

Take 1½ pounds (750 grams) (net weight) of rhubarb, for preference the pale pink stalks from the middle of the rhubarb plant. Wash, dry, cut them into chunks 2 inches long and cut crossways after removing the thin skin.

Arrange the pieces of rhubarb in the dish in layers each of which should be sprinkled with a mixture of white and brown sugar, allowing 1 cup (125 grams) of each. Pour into the bottom of the dish 3 tablespoons of water, not more, since the rhubarb contains a lot of natural moisture. Roll out *Flaky pastry* scraps or *Tart pastry* (see DOUGH) into an oval shape ⅓ inch thick, a little bigger than the top of the dish. Use the trimmings to make a strip 1¼ inches wide and stick this to the edge of the pie dish. This is to facilitate fixing the pastry cover. Moisten lightly, place the sheet of pastry on top, and fix the edges to the strip of pastry below by pressing with the finger tips.

Brush lightly with egg. Pattern the edges with a fork, make a small opening in the middle to allow steam to escape and put in the oven at a good average, sustained heat.

Cooking time: 50 minutes.

This tart is eaten cold and is usually served with whipped cream sweetened and flavoured with vanilla.

Strawberry tart (flan). TARTE AUX FRAISES—Line the flan ring with *Lining pastry* (*Pastry dough I or II*) or short pastry dough (see DOUGH). Bake empty, then fill with raw strawberries, hulled and rolled in sugar. Coat with currant jelly flavoured with raspberry, or with cherry jam, strained and flavoured with kirsch.

Tangerine flan or tart. GÂTEAU (TARTE) À LA MANDARINE—*Ingredients.* ¾ cup (125 grams) blanched almonds; ½ cup (125 grams) fine sugar; 4 eggs; 2 candied tangerine peels; 2 drops essence of bitter almonds; vanilla; 1 tablespoon thick apricot purée.

Method. Pound the almonds finely in a mortar, adding the eggs one by one. Add the tangerine peel, very finely chopped, the sugar, the vanilla, the essence of bitter almonds and the purée, rubbed through a fine sieve. Mix well.

Line a flan (tart) tin with *Short pastry II* (see DOUGH). Spread a layer of tangerine purée on the bottom. Fill with the mixture prepared in the mortar. Bake in a moderate oven.

When the flan is cold, spread with apricot jam and garnish with splintered almonds. Put in the oven for a few seconds to brown the almonds.

TARTARIC ACID. TARTRIQUE—Acid found in a large number of fruits and which is extracted from the lees of wine.

It is used to prepare mineral drinks, a syrup and effervescent powders, and is also added to must which lacks acidity (its use is tolerated in this case, but not for wines which have to be acidulated, if necessary, with citric acid).

TARTLET. TARTELETTE—As its name indicates, a tartlet is a small tart. This small cake is of very ancient origin, and was already known in the sixteenth century when it was called a *flannet*, a word which is a diminutive of *flan*.

Tartlets are made in the same way as large tarts and are

filled in the same way, either with fruits of different kinds or creams or other mixtures.

Tartlets with savoury fillings are served as hors-d'oeuvre or small entrées. See HORS-D'OEUVRE, *Hot hors-d'oeuvre*.

Filling tartlets cooked empty (blind)

Tartlet cases or shells. Croûtes de tartelettes—These cases or shells are made in round pastry tins, either fluted or plain, and of various diameters, according to the nature of the preparation.

The tins are lined with either ordinary or fine short pastry, or with *Semi-flaky pastry* (see DOUGH) or with puff pastry left-overs, or with sweet pastry.

Apricot tartlets. Tartelettes aux abricots—Made in various shapes, round, oval, boat-shaped (*barquettes*), in moulds and in rings.

The rings or moulds are buttered and lined with very thin *Flaky pastry* or *Tart pastry* (see DOUGH), according to taste. The fillings and the baking are exactly the same as for tarts.

Cherry tartlets. Tartelettes aux cerises—Line tartlet moulds with *Lining pastry* (*Pastry dough I*) or *Flaky pastry* (see DOUGH). Prick the bottoms lightly with a fork. Fill with stoned cherries.

Cook in a hot oven (400°F.). Turn out the tartlets and coat the fruit with redcurrant jelly.

Tartlets may be made with cherries preserved in syrup.

Strawberry, raspberry, pear, apple, plum tartlets. Tartélettes aux fraises, framboises, poires, pommes, prunes—Made in the same way as the corresponding tarts, but using tartlet moulds.

TARTINE—Slice of bread spread with butter, jam or any other substance of the right consistency.

Swiss tartines. Tartines suisses—Roll out some *Flaky pastry* (see DOUGH) about ⅛ inch thick after it has been turned seven times. Cut this into rectangles 4 inches long and 2 inches wide. Set these pieces of pastry on a baking sheet, brush them with egg and bake in a hot oven (400°F.). When baked, sprinkle them immediately with fine sugar and glaze them in the oven. Cool on a cake rack.

Split these pastries on one side and fill the interior with a cream prepared in the following way:

Work together in a saucepan ⅜ cup (100 grams) of sugar, ⅓ cup (50 grams) of sifted flour and 4 egg yolks. Add a pinch of powdered vanilla or ½ teaspoon vanilla extract. Stir in 2 cups (4 decilitres) of milk and mix. Cook over heat, stirring constantly. Remove from heat and add 1½ tablespoons (25 grams) of butter and 3 stiffly beaten egg whites.

TASTE, FLAVOUR. Saveur—Sensation excited in certain organs of the mouth by contact with various substances. A classification of flavours has often been attempted, but as there is no standard of measurement such classifications remain vague and uncertain. It is possible to distinguish tastes that are sweet, acid, salty, sour and bitter, but the difficulty lies in establishing the demarcation between one type and another. These are far from being precise; the flavour of each substance comes, in fact, from the combination of a number of basic flavours.

Sweet, salty and sour tastes are generally better perceived when cold than when hot; some flavours, apparently opposed, may actually reinforce each other if they are combined in certain proportions; a sweet solution appears sweeter if a salty or sour solution diluted just to the point where it has no more taste of its own, is added to it; empiricists have always added a little salt to sweet dishes.

TASTING—See SAVOURING.

TÂTE-VIN—Silver or silver-plated cup, often decorated, used for examining and tasting wine.

TAVEL—A very popular red wine, harvested in Languedoc.

Branches of tea with flowers and fruits

TEA. Thé—Tea, the most universally consumed of all beverages, is derived from the leaves of *Thea sinensis*, a small tree which can reach the height of 30 feet. It is native to Assam, China and Japan. Tea was brought to Europe by the Dutch in 1610 and to England in 1644. It arrived in the U.S.A. in the early eighteenth century.

Tea-growing in China and Japan dates back to prehistoric times but it was not started in India and Ceylon until 1865. India and Ceylon are now the largest tea exporters in the world. The largest tea import to the United States comes from Japan and Formosa; England and Russia import enormous quantities from India and China respectively. China is the largest producer of tea but does not lead in the export trade.

Harvesting tea, from a Chinese painting

Tea is grown both in open fields and on terraced hillsides. It requires a warm climate with a very heavy rainfall (90 to 200 inches). For fine tea, the first one or two tiny leaves which appear on the end of each twig, during 'flushes' or growing periods, are plucked. The third and fourth leaves are used only in coarse teas. These pickings occur 10 to 25 times a year in Formosa and every 10 or 12 days in Ceylon. The principal difference in teas lies in the treatment of the leaves. Black tea comes from leaves that, partly dried, are piled up to ferment before being toasted. Green tea comes from leaves that have been fired immediately after harvesting and is unfermented. Oolong tea is semi-fermented.

The following are the principal teas:

India and Ceylon: Black—Pekoes (several sorts and grades), Souchongs and Congous. *Green*—(coloured) Gunpowder, Imperial, Young Hyson, Hyson (uncoloured) Hyson, Young Hyson.

China: Black—Congous, Canton, Pekoe, etc. *Green*—Gunpowder, Hyson, Young Hyson. *Oolongs*—Amoy, Foochow, etc.

Japan and Formosa: Green and Oolongs.

Infusions of tea contain aromatic ingredients, theine (identical with caffeine) and tannin; it is a pleasant stimulating drink which, taken in moderate quantities, aids the digestion and in hot countries constitutes one of the best ways to drink water, since this must necessarily be boiled before it is used.

To make tea. Tea is very delicate and must be kept in well-made containers in a dry place, well away from any food whose odours might contaminate it. The tea-pot, for the same reason, must be kept exclusively for its own purpose. Only pure water must be used to make it, and that as free from lime as possible. It is very important to heat the tea-pot first by rinsing it out with boiling water. When this has been done, the tea is put in in the ratio of one teaspoonful for each person, plus one, as it is said, 'for the pot'. The water must be absolutely boiling. The infusion is ready at the end of 5 or 6 minutes. After this time it becomes too strong, charged with tannin. That is why tea-pots which cut off contact between the tea-leaves and the infusion are to be recommended, as are tea-balls and tea-spoons. Certain brands of tea are sold in small muslin or paper sachets, each containing enough tea for one, two or several cups; these sachets are practical because they allow the tea to be made always to the same strength and check infusion at the right moment.

The name 'tea' is sometimes given to other infusions such as Jesuit's tea, Paraguay tea (see MATÉ), *thé St.-Germain*, *thé de santé* (health tea), a purgative, or Swiss tea, a healing lotion. In the same way the name beef tea is given to a preparation made from minced meat.

Tea ice—See ICE CREAMS AND ICES.

TEAL. Sarcelle—Wild palmiped, bird of passage with a light brown breast marked with black, white-bellied, with grey wings, white at the tips; its flesh is oily and generally little regarded. Teal is cooked like wild duck. See DUCK.

TENDON—Roped fibres, round or flat in form and varying in length, which finish off the muscular mass and constitute its means of attachment to the bone. Tendon fibres cannot be digested by the human intestines. In cooking they exude a certain amount of gelatine.

TERFEZIA—Large white African truffle, which is almost tasteless. It can be used like black truffle, but is most often eaten raw in salad.

TERRAPIN. Terrapène—Small turtle, originating in North America.

This variety of turtle is greatly prized by some Americans who, because of the shape of the faceted scales that cover its carapace, call it *Diamond-back*.

Only rarely is the terrapin found alive in France, and only the tinned form is eaten.

To cook terrapin. Put the turtle in a large bowl of fresh water and leave it there for a time, changing the water every half an hour.

Wash it and scald it by plunging it into a pot of boiling water.

Leave it in this water until the white skin which covers the head and feet can be taken off by rubbing with a cloth.

Cook the terrapin in boiling water without salt (or steam it). This cooking, which varies in time, depending on the size of the animal, should not exceed 45 minutes. If the flesh on the feet 'gives' under gentle pressure of the fingers, the terrapin is ready.

Once cooked, allow to cool. Remove the hard scales and with a knife detach the flat part, or pastron, from under the carapace. Remove also the feet; cut these into pieces about 4 centimetres in size and reserve them.

Remove the animal's liver, taking care not to puncture the gall bladder. Remove this gall bladder from the liver and cut off all the parts of the liver adjoining it. All these parts, the heart, the entrails and internal white muscles must be discarded.

Remove the eggs very carefully; put these in a saucepan with the feet, the sliced liver and the carapace cut into pieces of the same size as the feet. Season with salt, pepper and cayenne. Barely cover with water, bring to the boil, then finish cooking in the oven, at a gentle heat for 25 to 30 minutes.

TERRINE—Earthenware dish in which meat, game and fish are cooked. By extension the word *terrine* is also used to designate the food itself, for example, *Terrine of foie gras*, *of chicken*, etc.

Terrines of meat, fish, etc., must be completely cold before they are eaten. They can be kept for some days in perfect condition if they are put in a cool place.

Terrine of duckling. TERRINE DE CANETON—Bone a duckling completely. Remove all the flesh of the legs and breast.

Cut the breast into large dice. Put into a bowl with 3½ ounces (100 grams) of lean ham and 3½ ounces (100 grams) of bacon fat, cut in dice. Season with salt, pepper and spices; sprinkle with 2 tablespoons of brandy. Marinate for 2 hours.

Chop finely the flesh of the legs and add to it 5 ounces (150 grams) of lean pork meat, 5 ounces (150 grams) of veal and ½ pound (250 grams) of fresh pork fat, all finely chopped. Pound together in a mortar and season with spiced salt. Bind with 2 whole eggs; add 2 liqueur glasses of brandy. Rub through a sieve.

Put this forcemeat into the bowl where the *salpicon* of duckling has been marinating. Add the liver of the duckling cut into small pieces and quickly fried in very hot butter. Mix well.

Re-fill the skin of the duckling with this mixture and shape into a roll.

Put this roll into an oval terrine, lined with thin bards of bacon fat. Press the 'duckling' lightly to fit it well into the terrine.

Put the terrine in a baking tin half-filled with warm water. Cook in a hot oven, the terrine covered, for about an hour and a quarter. (The cooking time of terrines of poultry and other meats can be judged by the appearance of the fat that rises to the surface; if this fat is clear, the terrine is cooked. It can also be tested by inserting a long trussing needle into the meat. If this needle is hot when it comes out of the terrine the meat is cooked.)

Cool the terrine under pressure (a weight set on a cover cut to the shape of the terrine). The next day remove the fat which has risen to the surface and replace it with a layer of jelly (made from a knuckle, a calf's foot and the duckling giblets). It may also be turned out of the dish, wiped and replaced in the terrine after the jelly has been poured in and allowed to set. Some more jelly is poured on top and the terrine is cooled once more. Turn out before serving.

If the terrine is to be kept for several days, the jelly should be replaced by half melted lard.

TÊTE D'ALOYAU—In French butchery the part of beef found at the end of the rump.

TÊTE DE CUVÉE—The choice wine obtained from crushing the grape (*vin de goutte*) before the wine-press is used.

THICKENING. LIAISON—A culinary process designed to give body to a liquid food, sauce or broth.

Thickening with flour or starch consists of making a stable paste by heating. Thickening with yolk of egg or blood, which forms emulsions, must be effected at a temperature below 176°F. since the proteins curdle at a higher temperature.

Thickening with arrowroot. LIAISON À L'ARROWROOT—Pour into a pint (½ litre) of boiling stock or juice, 1 teaspoon (3 to 4 grams) of arrowroot, previously mixed with a few tablespoons of cold stock. Leave it on the fire for a few seconds. Mix and strain.

Thickening with kneaded butter. LIAISON AU BEURRE MANIÉ—This is a very quick method of thickening, mainly used to give the desired consistency to the sauces of stewed fish or *matelotes**.

To thicken a quart (litre) of liquid mix thoroughly ½ cup (75 grams) of flour with 6 tablespoons (100 grams) of butter.

Thickening à la meunière. LIAISON À LA MEUNIÈRE—A smooth mixture of flour and water. This is added to stocks and sauces to give them the consistency desired.

Thickening with a roux. LIAISON AU ROUX—A *roux* can be white, golden or brown, Usually it is made from butter and flour, but fat may be used instead of butter. See ROUX.

Thickening with tapioca for soups. LIAISON AU TAPIOCA POUR POTAGE—Bring to the boil 1½ quarts (litres) of clear soup (*consommé*). Sprinkle 3 tablespoons of tapioca into it. Boil for 18 minutes. Strain through muslin.

THISTLE. CHARDON—Wild plant from which globe artichokes and cardoons derive. Different kinds of wild thistle are eaten, some for their flower head like the artichoke, some for their stems and leaves, like the cardoon, some even for their roots.

THONINE—A species of tunny (tuna fish) found only in the Mediterranean. See TUNNY.

THONNÉ—A way of cooking veal. The meat is marinated for a long time before being cooked, with oil, lemon, thyme, bay leaf and spices.

THORINS—This wine, which is harvested in the department of Saône-et-Loire, is classed among the best Burgundies.

THOURINS OR TOURIN—Onion-based soup much favoured all over the South of France and in other parts of the country.

This preparation should not, however, be confused with *Soupe à l'oignon* (also called *Soupe à fromage*), eaten in Parisian night spots under the name of *gratinée*.

Method. Cook in butter, without allowing them to brown, 3 cups (300 grams) of finely chopped onions. When they are cooked and very lightly coloured (they should only be pale golden), sprinkle them with flour, stirring all the time with a wooden spoon.

Stir in 2 quarts plus 1 cup (2 litres) of boiled milk. Season with salt and freshly ground pepper. Cook very slowly for 25 minutes.

A few minutes before serving thicken the soup with 4 egg yolks beaten with 1½ cups (3 decilitres) of fresh cream, and add, at the last moment, 2 tablespoons of butter.

Serve with thin slices of French bread dried in the oven.

Thorins à la provençale—Prepare the soup as above. Before thickening it with the egg yolks and cream, add 2½ ounces (75 grams) of coarse vermicelli and poach this in the soup. Serve grated cheese separately.

THRUSH. GRIVE—A bird of medium size whose plumage is speckled with black or reddish spots.

There are various types of thrush. The *song thrush* makes excellent eating. It grows fat on grapes. The *missal thrush*, also called the *great thrush*, has less delicate flesh than the song thrush. The *redwing*, another thrush, is excellent game but the *fieldfare*, a native of northern Europe, is insipid in flavour.

Thrushes can be cooked in various ways. They are best roasted, and should be served on a slice of bread fried in the cooking fat. Although common in England and U.S.A., thrushes are rarely, if ever, eaten in these countries. In England it is classed as protected game.

Thrushes à l'ardennaise. GRIVES EN CROÛTE À L'ARDENNAISE—Bone, along the back only, 8 thrushes. Season with spiced salt (see SALT). Stuff each one with a little fine stuffing the size of a walnut. This stuffing should be enriched with chopped thrushes' livers, diced foie gras and truffles, all well seasoned, with a few crushed juniper berries added. Fold the thrushes back into shape. Wrap each one in a piece of pig's caul or salt pork. Place them, closely packed one against the other, in a pan containing the bones and trimmings of the birds, a carrot and onion, chopped medium fine, all browned in butter.

Sprinkle with melted butter. Braise in the oven for 12 minutes. Drain the thrushes. Remove wrapping. Put them in a large round bread crust which has been scooped out, buttered inside and browned in the oven. This crust should be lined with the following *gratin stuffing:* chicken livers browned in grated bacon fat; mushrooms, well seasoned and pounded in a mortar. These ingredients should be bound with strained yolks of egg.

Put the 'pie' in the oven for a few minutes. Just before serving pour over the thrushes a sauce made as follows: Moisten the boiled down braising stock with 1 cup (2 decilitres) of sherry. Boil down. Add 1 to 1½ cups (3 decilitres) of *Demi-glace sauce* (see SAUCE). Boil for a moment or two. Strain the sauce. Add rather thick slices of truffle, tossed in very hot butter.

Thrush à la bonne femme. GRIVES À LA BONNE FEMME—Truss and cook the birds in butter in an earthenware casserole with small pieces of larding bacon and diced fried bread. Sprinkle with a little brandy and pour on some game gravy. Serve in the casserole in which the thrushes were cooked.

Note. Strictly, all birds cooked *à la bonne femme* should be garnished with potatoes cut to look like olives, small onions, and larding bacon. These garnishes should be cooked with the poultry or game.

For small birds (quails, thrushes, larks, etc.) the *bonne femme* garnish consists only of small pieces of larding bacon and diced bread fried in the butter in which the bird has been cooked.

Thrush en caisses. GRIVES EN CAISSES—Bone the thrushes. Season them. Fill each one with a little *à gratin stuffing* the size of a walnut (see FORCEMEAT). Each of these little balls of stuffing should contain a small piece of foie gras and a little square of truffle. Remake the thrushes into their original shapes. Wrap each one in a strip of buttered greaseproof paper. Put them, closely packed one against the other, in a buttered pan. Cover the thrushes with their carcases and trimmings. These should first be tossed in butter with an onion and a finely sliced carrot. Pour over the dish ¾ cup (1½ decilitres) of Madeira. Cover and simmer for 10 minutes. Moisten with a few tablespoons of game stock. Braise them in the oven for 12 to 15 minutes.

Drain the thrushes. Remove the paper wrapping. Brown the thrushes. Serve them in frilled paper cases buttered and warmed, on a layer of sliced mushrooms and truffles tossed in butter. Pour over the birds the braising stock, strained and reduced. The thrushes can also be served in fireproof porcelain dishes.

Casserole of thrush or thrush en cocotte. GRIVES EN CASSEROLE, EN COCOTTE—Proceed as for *Casserole of quail* (see QUAIL).

Chaud-froid of thrush. GRIVES EN CHAUD-FROID—Made from thrushes, boned and stuffed with foie gras and truffles, as for *Chaud-froid of quail* (see QUAIL).

Thrushes with grapes. GRIVES AUX RAISINS—Cooked in a casserole as *Casserole of quails with grapes* (see QUAIL).

Thrushes au gratin. GRIVES AU GRATIN—Put inside each bird a piece of *à gratin game stuffing* (see FORCEMEAT), the size of a walnut, with the chopped giblets of the thrushes added. Flavour this stuffing with a few crushed juniper berries.

Truss the thrushes and brown them quickly in butter.

Take a buttered plate and spread on it a layer of gratin stuffing ⅛ inch thick. Press the thrushes gently into the stuffing. Coat them with rather thick *Duxelles sauce* (see SAUCE). Sprinkle with breadcrumbs, pour melted butter over them. Finish cooking by browning in a very hot oven.

Thrushes à la liégeoise. GRIVES À LA LIÉGEOISE—Put inside each bird a piece of butter the size of a walnut, with a few crushed juniper berries added. Place the thrushes in an earthenware casserole in which a little butter has been melted. Brown the thrushes in the butter. Sprinkle them with crushed juniper berries (2 berries for each bird). Cover and cook in the oven. Two minutes before taking the casserole out of the oven, cover each bird with a round piece of bread fried in butter. Sprinkle with a few drops of *genièvre* or gin.

Cold thrush pâté. PÂTÉ FROID DE GRIVES—Proceed as for *Cold woodcock pâté* (see WOODCOCK).

Hot thrush pâté. PÂTÉ CHAUD DE GRIVES—Bone the thrushes and stuff them with foie gras and truffles. Proceed as for *Hot woodcock pâté* (see WOODCOCK).

Thrush pie. TOURTE DE GRIVES À LA PÉRIGOURDINE—Bone the thrushes. Stuff each one with a little *à gratin stuffing* (see FORCEMEAT) the size of a walnut. Each of these little balls of stuffing should contain a small piece of foie gras with a piece of truffle embedded in it. Partly braise the thrushes in a Madeira-flavoured stock.

Allow them to get cold.

Put the thrushes in a thin pie crust lined with forcemeat covered with strips of truffle. Cover the thrushes with a thin layer of *à gratin* stuffing. Cover with a lid of thin pie crust. Seal the edges.

Decorate the top of the pie with little motifs of thin pastry. Brush with beaten egg. Bake in the oven for 40 to 45 minutes. After the pie has been taken out of the oven, pour into it a few tablespoons of *Salmis sauce* (see SAUCE).

Potted thrush. TERRINE DE GRIVES—Made from boned birds, stuffed with *foie gras* and truffles like other types of potted game. See TERRINE.

Roast thrushes. GRIVES RÔTIES—Wrap each bird in a thin strip of larding bacon. Spit them. Roast them in a hot oven for 10 to 12 minutes.

Serve each bird on a canapé of bread fried in butter. Dilute the gravy and serve separately.

THYME. THYM—Plant with small grey-green leaves and a pleasant, pungent smell, much used as a flavouring.

Wild thyme is a variety of the garden thyme.

THYMUS—A ductless gland situated in the upper part of the thorax in children and young vertebrates, which becomes atrophied in puberty.

In butchered animals it is called the *sweetbread* (calf, lamb) and constitutes a very delicate foodstuff. It should be eaten only in moderation or not at all, by sufferers from gout. For culinary preparations see OFFAL OR VARIETY MEATS.

TIERED PLINTH. GRADINS—In former times, carved wooden stands were used for the presentation of cold dishes, especially set pieces of confectionery. These stands were made in tiers. They were decorated with *pâte d'office*, almond paste, sugar motifs or icing sugar.

Nowadays, such plinths are made from sandwich bread, as, for example, for poultry *chaud-froids*. See CHAUD-FROID.

Carême tells us how tiered plinths were decorated in his day: 'Let us suppose, for example, that you wish to decorate a plinth with laurel leaves. You first cut out a laurel wreath in paper. Next you give the base of the plinth a light coating of icing, and stick the paper wreath to it. Now you cover the rest of the plinth with a medium grade of coarse sugar. When this is done, you remove the paper, after which you sprinkle the imprint of the leaves with pistachio-green sugar. Now, you have a laurel crown surrounding the base of the plinth.

'For a large, three-tiered set piece, each tier can be individually decorated. This creates a graceful and elegant effect.

'I have also sometimes embellished my tiers with laurel crowns made from biscuit pastry shaped like laurel leaves and coloured green, or with garlands of spun sugar. This last decoration has both brilliance and elegance.

'I have also created tiered plinths out of almond paste, moulded in basket moulds.'

But although he favoured the presentation of set pieces on plinths, Carême maintained that 'young practitioners' should not forget 'that plinths of German or Italian waffles, of *nougat*, of glazed *duchesse* cakes, of puff pastry, baked without filling or in the shape of fish scales, or in round or oval rings, of Genoese cake, or of nut toffee, are immensely effective and properly belong in the realm of the great pastry-making establishments.'

And, in the circumstances, Carême is right. All the different kinds of plinths he mentions in this list are made from edible substances. When all is said, wooden plinths, however decorative they may be, are nothing more than pieces of wood.

TIGER. TIGRE—The flesh of the tiger is sometimes eaten by natives.

'TILT-POT'. ACCOTE-POT—An old word which describes a small piece of iron which is put on the stove underneath the pot to *tilt* it.

TIMBALE—By definition this word (which comes from the Arab *thabal* meaning *drum*) means a small metal receptacle, round in shape and mostly intended to hold a beverage.

Timbales of this kind are chiefly made of silver, sometimes of gold, or sometimes of silver plate, and are of many kinds. Some are simple; others are ornamented.

The word *timbale*, which in early days was only applied to individual drinking cups, has taken on a much wider meaning, and is used to describe all sorts of bowls, of metal, earthenware and china, larger than those that our fathers used at table, which were of a size to serve two guests together (generally a man and a woman), so giving rise to the proverbial expression '*manger à la meme écuelle*' (eat at the same bowl).

These *timbales* of the new type were used chiefly to serve vegetables and food in sauce. In French culinary parlance today the same word is still used in the phrase *dresser en timbale* to describe the serving of some preparation in a large bowl, which may be a vegetable dish or *légumier*, although used for many other foodstuffs than vegetables. Thus in these *timbales-légumiers* are served scrambled eggs, food in sauce, purées, custards and other preparations, all to some extent liquid. *Dresser en timbale* in modern culinary parlance often means to heap the food on a platter in a pyramid shape, usually garnished.

Culinarily the word *timbale* means a preparation of any kind cooked or served in a pie crust.

Timbales of this kind are simply a sort of hot pie, which instead of being made in a special mould or dish, usually hinged, are made in a plain round mould with high sides. These moulds are sometimes embellished, that is to say, their sides are either goffered or decorated with motifs or different kinds.

These timbales are filled before cooking with forcemeat and meats of various sorts. Below will be found instructions for the various stages of preparation of a timbale in a mould with goffered sides. This is the true classic form of the timbale, of which a typical example is the *Timbale de macaroni* or *Timbale Milanaise*.

There are many other kinds of timbale which are not filled until after the crust has been cooked. In this case the crust is cooked *à blanc*, that is to say, empty. Among these are *Timbale of sole à la Grimaldi, Timbale de volaille à la royale, Timbale of lamb's sweetbreads à la périgourdine, Timbale of truffles à l'impériale*, and in the case of sweet timbales, *Timbale of apricots à la frangipane, Timbale of fruit à l'ancienne, Timbale of cherries à la Chantilly*, etc.

To meet the needs of the ordinary housewife, timbale cases are made in fireproof porcelain in the same shape and colour as the real pie-crusts.

But the true gourmand, is not satisfied with a timbale whose crust is not edible; when served with a real timbale, this gourmand enjoys not only the contents but the container too.

Large timbale case or crust (mixed entrée). CROÛTE DE GRANDE TIMBALE—Butter the interior of a large charlotte mould, and decorate the sides with little decorative shapes of *noodle paste**.

Roll some short pastry into a ball. Roll out the ball into a round 8 inches in diameter. Sprinkle the round of pastry lightly with flour and fold it in half. Take the points of this half-circle and draw them together. Roll it out once to make an even thickness of about $\frac{1}{8}$ inch. Put it in the bottom of the mould. Press on the bottom and round the sides to make the paste adhere to the mould and rise gently up the sides, without disturbing the noodle paste decorations.

Line the bottom and the sides of the paste with a fine buttered paper and fill it up with dried raw beans or other articles, as for a flan case or tart (see TART). Put a dome-shaped piece of paper on top of the dry filling, and put a thin sheet of pastry on top of this, joining the edges together with the pastry lining, by gently pressing with the fingers. Make the rim of the pie by pinching this border with pastry pincers. Moisten lightly the part forming the lid with water, and decorate with details, leaves, roses, etc., cut from a thin sheet of pastry, with a special pastry cutter or with a knife.

Put on top of the lid 3 or 4 rounds of pastry, cut with a circular fluted pastry cutter, with the middle cut out to make circles. Stick these circles of paste together and make an opening in the middle to allow for the escape of steam during the cooking. Gild the outside of the pie and cook in the oven at a good moderate heat for 30 to 35 minutes.

When the case is cooked, remove the lid. Take out the paper and dried beans; gild the inside with egg and let it dry in the oven for a few minutes.

Fill the timbale as desired.

Timbale cases cooked in this way are used as containers for a great variety of mixed entrées. They can be filled with ragoûts, with garnishes such as *Financière*,

Grimaldi, *Joinville*, *Milanaise*, *Napolitaine*, *Toulousaine* and others of a similar nature (see GARNISHES).

Most frequently, they are filled with macaroni arranged in alternate layers with a ragoût bound with brown or white sauce. See below.

Small timbales Agnès Sorel (Old recipe). PETITES TIMBALES AGNÈS SOREL—'Butter a dozen dariole moulds. Sprinkle into the interiors one-half truffles and one-half scarlet (pickled) tongue, both finely chopped.

'Prepare 1 pound (500 grams) of chicken forcemeat with cream; finish this off with a few tablespoons of *Soubise purée* (see PURÉE). With this forcemeat fill the moulds, taking care to leave a hole in the middle and to keep the forcemeat rather thick on the bottom and round the sides. Fill the hole in the middle with a *salpicon** made up of chicken and truffles bound with *Espagnole sauce* (see SAUCE) made with Madeira.

'Close the tops of the moulds with a layer of raw forcemeat. Set the moulds in a saucepan and pour in hot water to half way up the moulds. Poach the timbales near the front of the oven for 12 or 15 minutes. At the moment of serving turn the timbales out of their moulds; set them on a thin layer of forcemeat poached on the plate. Spoon over the forcemeat a little *Espagnole sauce* cooked with the trimmings and cooking liquor of the truffles.

'Send the surplus sauce to the table in a sauceboat.'

Timbale Brillat-Savarin—Hollow out a *Brioche mousseline** (cooked in a charlotte mould) to make a pie crust.

Brush this crust with apricot pulp flavoured with kirsch and heat in the oven. At the last moment fill it with alternate layers of quartered pears, cooked in vanilla syrup and well drained, and French pastry cream (see CREAMS) mixed with finely crushed macaroons.

Finish off by covering the top with pears mounted in a dome. Decorate with candied fruits. Heat at the entrance of the oven.

Serve separately some apricot pulp flavoured with kirsch.

Macaroni timbale à l'américaine. TIMBALE DE MACARONI À L'AMÉRICAINE—Prepare a timbale crust of *Fine lining paste* (see DOUGH) and bake it empty. Fill with alternate layers of macaroni cooked in water, drained and bound with Parmesan and butter, and a *salpicon** of *Lobster à l'américaine**.

Finish off by placing on top a row of sliced lobster and coat with *Américaine sauce* (see SAUCE).

Cover the timbale, heat for an instant in the oven and serve on a napkin.

Macaroni timbales à la milanaise. TIMBALES DE MACARONI À LA MILANAISE—Fill well-buttered dariole moulds, each of which has had a round slice of truffle placed on the bottom, with thick macaroni, cooked in salted water (left long and drained well, without cooling in cold water). Arrange this macaroni in spirals in the moulds. Line the interiors with a thin layer of *Quenelle forcemeat* (see FORCEMEAT); then fill with macaroni cut into small dice prepared *à la milanaise* (see MACARONI) and with a milanaise garnish added. This is made up of scarlet (pickled) tongue, cooked ham, truffles and mushrooms, all cut in *julienne*. Cover the timbales with a layer of quenelle forcemeat. Put into a *bain-marie* (pan of hot water) and poach in the oven (350°F.) for 18 to 20 minutes. Turn out the timbales on to a round dish. Pour into the bottom of the dish a few tablespoons of *Demi-glace sauce* flavoured with a little tomato and Madeira (see SAUCE).

Timbale of noodles. TIMBALE DE NOUILLES—Cook in salted water 1 pound (500 grams) of fresh noodles (or dried noodles). Drain them and put them into a sauté pan, season and toss for a few moments over the heat to dry out completely.

Add 4 egg yolks, mix together and fill with this composition a well-buttered charlotte mould. Press down well so that there are no little pockets of air. Cool.

Turn this noodle loaf out of its mould and coat it twice over with egg and breadcrumbs. Cut a circle on the top ¾ inch from the edge.

Fry the timbale in deep fat or oil, drain and remove the 'lid'. Through this opening scoop out two-thirds of the interior.

Fill the hollow according to the recipe.

Timbale of sole à l'américaine, or Timbale Monselet. TIMBALE DE SOLE À L'AMÉRICAINE—Prepare a timbale crust of *Fine lining paste* (see DOUGH) and bake it empty.

Fill with *Paupiettes of sole* cooked in white wine, cooked macaroni bound with butter and Parmesan and a *salpicon** of lobster prepared *à l'américaine*. Coat with *Américaine sauce* (see SAUCE).

Timbale of fillets of sole Grimaldi—See SOLE, *Fillets of sole*.

Small timbales of vegetables. PETITES TIMBALES DE LÉGUMES—To garnish cold meats, etc. Coat small dariole moulds with jelly based on fish or meat stock, according to the foodstuff that is to be garnished. Decorate these moulds with cut out pieces of truffle, hard boiled egg whites, scarlet (pickled) tongue and tarragon leaves. Fill with a vegetable salad bound with mayonnaise thickened with jelly. Pour a layer of jelly over the salad. Chill the timbales on ice or in a refrigerator and turn out at the last moment to garnish the meat or fish in question.

Note. Timbales of vegetables to garnish cold dishes (which can also be served as hors-d'oeuvre or small entrée) can be filled, rather than with a macédoine of vegetables, with a single vegetable—asparagus tips, French beans, little carrot balls, diced artichoke bottoms etc., dressed with vinaigrette or mayonnaise.

TINAMOU—Partridge-like bird native to South America. Efforts have been made to acclimatise it in France and have succeeded to the point where it can figure among French game birds.

All the recipes given for pheasant are applicable to tinamou.

TINPLATE. FER-BLANC—Tinplate is pressed iron covered with tin. A great many utensils used in cooking and confectionery used to be made from it, but in both large and small kitchens pots and pans made of aluminium, nickel, fireproof porcelain, heat-resisting glass, cast-iron, stainless steel, etc. are replacing many of these utensils.

TIRETTE—French butchery term describing a broad, flat tendon.

TISANE—This word comes from the Latin *ptisana*, barley water.

The *tisane* of Hippocrates was barley water; today the name tisane is applied to drinks for invalids prepared by soaking or infusion.

TISANE DE CHAMPAGNE—Name for a Champagne that is rather lighter than ordinary.

TOAST—A slice of bread, thick or thin, square or rectangular in shape, put under the grill or in an electric toaster and 'toasted' on both sides. It is sometimes served in a special holder called a toast-rack.

WINE. Treading the grapes, from a fifteenth century French tapestry

(*From the original French edition of* Larousse Gastronomique)

VEAL. Roast rib of veal

(Reine Pédauque)

TOBACCO. TABAC—Solanaceous plant, originating on the island of Tobago, the leaves of which are prepared in various ways and either smoked, taken as snuff or chewed.

Speaking only from the point of view of those who enjoy the pleasures of the table, we would say that smoking before a meal dulls the sense of taste; professional tasters are obliged to renounce it. Smoking during a meal is simply barbarian; tobacco smoke completely prevents one from savouring the dishes and annoys other people in those restaurants where this habit is allowed. Tobacco has its rightful place after a meal, when its aroma blends agreeably with that of coffee.

TOCANE—New Champagne made from the first pressing.

TODDY PALM. ARBRE À LIQUEUR—A species of palm tree, also known as milk tree. It grows in great numbers in the Moluccas (Spice Islands) and is in fact none other than sago palm. This palm tree produces sap during a part of the year, which is fermented into very strong alcoholic beverage much appreciated by the local inhabitants.

TOKAY—White wine originally harvested in Tokaj, Hungary. The name *Tokai* is also used for a variety of wine cultivated chiefly in Alsace. The so-called 'Tokay' wine of California is of very little worth.

TOMATO—Herbaceous plant of South American origin, of which there are many varieties, with red or yellow, round or oval fruit. Sometimes these fruits are called *pommes d'amour*—'love apples'.

Tomato fondue. FONDUE DE TOMATES—Tomatoes peeled, pressed, chopped and cooked till soft in butter, seasoned in various ways, usually with chopped garlic included. Tomato fondue is used as a garnish with various dishes, eggs, fish, meat, poultry, etc. They are also used to fill *bouchées* (patties), tartlets and croustades*.

Tomato fondue à la grecque. FONDUE DE TOMATES À LA GRECQUE—Put into a saucepan, in which 1 tablespoon (12 grams) of chopped onions have been cooked till soft in 2 tablespoons of oil, 6 peeled and roughly chopped tomatoes. Add two sweet pimentos, peeled and cut in very small dice. Season with salt and paprika and a little chopped garlic. Cook gently until the liquid from the tomatoes is well concentrated.

Tomato fondue à la niçoise. FONDUE DE TOMATES À LA NIÇOISE—Prepare the fondue as above. Season with a little garlic and add a teaspoon of chopped tarragon.

Tomato fondue à la portugaise. FONDUE DE TOMATES À LA PORTUGAISE—Like *Tomato fondue à la niçoise* but without the tarragon.

Tomato fondue à la turque. FONDUE DE TOMATES À LA TURQUE—Like *Tomato fondue à la grecque* but without the pimento.

Fried tomatoes. TOMATES FRITES—Heat and peel some tomatoes of medium size with firm flesh. Cut them in slices $\frac{1}{3}$ inch thick. Season these slices with salt and pepper. When ready dip them in a light batter and drop into smoking hot fat or oil.

Drain the tomatoes, set them on a napkin and garnish with fried parsley. Serve immediately, as they will quickly become limp.

Stuffed tomatoes (*Robert Carrier*)

Concentrated tomato glaze. SUC DE TOMATES CONCENTRÉ, GLACÉ DE TOMATES—Rub through a fine sieve 2 pounds (1 kilo) of raw tomatoes (without removing seeds or juice). Put to cook over a strong heat. When the pulp is reduced by half, strain through a very fine strainer.

Put back to cook once more. Strain again when it is well concentrated. Cook this pulp again until it is of a syrupy consistency.

Note. This glaze, when it has been reduced to the desired point, can be kept for a long time. It should be put in small pots of glass or china.

It is used to heighten the flavour of certain sauces and preparations such as stuffings, *salpicons**, salads, etc.

Gratin of tomato and aubergine (egg-plant). GRATIN DE TOMATES ET D'AUBERGINES—Prepared by arranging in layers in an oiled or buttered gratin dish, tomatoes and aubergines previously fried in butter or oil. Sprinkle with breadcrumbs, then with oil or melted butter. Brown in a moderate oven.

Grilled tomatoes. TOMATES GRILLÉES—Cut a circle off the top of the tomatoes on the stalk side and through this opening carefully remove the seeds. Season and brush with oil or melted butter. Grill at a low heat.

Note. The tomatoes may be halved before being grilled.

Tomato jam—See JAM.

Tomato ketchup or catsup—This English condiment, very highly spiced, is found ready-made in grocers and other foodshops. It is used in English cookery to season certain sauces and it accompanies cold meats. For recipe see KETCHUP.

Tomato loaf. PAIN DE TOMATES—Cook down some *Tomato purée* and when it is well thickened add 6 beaten eggs for every cup (500 grams) of the purée. Season with salt, pepper and a pinch of spice.

Fill a well-buttered plain round mould with this mixture. Poach in a *bain-marie* (pan of hot water) in a low oven.

Allow to rest for a few moments before turning out of the mould. Set on a round dish. Coat with *Tomato sauce* with added butter (see SAUCE).

Note. Tomato loaf is chiefly used as an accompaniment to meat, served in small dariole moulds.

Cold tomato mousse. MOUSSE FROIDE DE TOMATES—Cook gently in butter till soft 1 cup (500 grams) of tomato flesh (after peeling, pressing out seeds and juice and roughly chopping the tomatoes).

When the pulp has well dried out, add $\frac{1}{2}$ cup (1 decilitre) of *Velouté sauce* (see SAUCE) to which $1\frac{1}{2}$ tablespoons of powdered gelatine, softened in cold water, have been added.

Strain this mixture through a cloth. Put into a bowl, whisk until smooth, allow to cool and add half of its volume of half-whipped cream. Season, and heighten the seasoning with a little cayenne and a few drops of lemon juice. Mix well.

Pour this mixture into a glass dish or, when the tomato mousse is to be used as an accompaniment to cold dishes, into small dariole moulds lined with a layer of jelly.

Chill on ice or in the refrigerator.

Cold tomato mousselines. MOUSSELINES FROIDES DE TOMATES—Prepared with the same mixture as the above, but served in *cassolettes* of metal, china, glass or goffered paper, or moulded in small moulds lined with jelly.

These mousselines are served as cold hors-d'oeuvre or used as part of the garnish for a cold dish.

Fresh tomato pulp. PULPE DE TOMATES FRAÎCHES—This pulp (which should not be confused with tomato sauce or tomato purée) is quite often used in cookery. It is an ingredient of a number of made-up dishes, and, cold, is used to dress some salads. This pulp is also used to make tomato jam (see JAM).

It is made in the following way:

Wash $4\frac{1}{2}$ pounds (2 kilos 500 grams) of ripe, sound tomatoes, cut in slices and rub them through a sieve.

Put this pulp into a saucepan (or into a preserving pan if the pulp is to be used for jam) and boil for a few moments.

Strain through a cloth to get rid of the water completely. The thick pulp which remains in the cloth is used according to the instructions in the recipe.

Tomato purée—See SAUCE, *Tomato sauce*.

Tomato salad. SALADE DE TOMATES—Scald the tomatoes, peel them and remove the pips. Cut in slices, not too thick. Lay on a cloth folded in four, season with salt and leave for 30 minutes to yield their liquid.

Arrange in an hors-d'oeuvre or salad dish. Season with oil, vinegar, pepper and chopped parsley. This salad can also be made with the tomatoes cut in quarters.

Note. Tomato salad (which is normally served as an hors-d'oeuvre) may be sprinkled with various aromatic herbs, such as tarragon, fresh fennel, fresh basil, etc.

When served in hors-d'oeuvre dishes, the tomatoes may also be covered with thin slices of new onions.

Tomato sauce—See SAUCE.

Tomatoes sauté aux fines herbes. TOMATES SAUTÉES AUX FINES HERBES—Cut the tomatoes in two. Press the halves to extract the seeds and season with salt and pepper. Put into a frying pan in which some butter has been heated and fry lightly. Set on a round dish and sprinkle with parsley and with the cooking butter, very hot, in which a small quantity of freshly made breadcrumbs have been fried.

Tomatoes sauté à la lyonnaise. TOMATES SAUTÉES À LA LYONNAISE—Cook halved tomatoes in the frying pan as above. Set on a serving dish on a layer of chopped onions cooked in butter. Pour over the tomatoes, sprinkled with chopped parsley, the cooking butter to which 3 tablespoons of chopped onion, previously cooked in butter, have been added.

Tomatoes sauté à la provençale. TOMATES SAUTÉES À LA PROVENÇALE—Prepared in oil like *Tomatoes sauté aux fines herbes*, adding a little chopped garlic.

Tomato soufflé. SOUFFLÉ DE TOMATES—Prepare 3 cups (6 decilitres) of very thick *Tomato purée* (see SAUCE, *Tomato sauce*). Add to this $\frac{1}{2}$ cup of thick *Béchamel sauce* and 6 egg yolks. Season with salt, pepper and grated nutmeg.

Incorporate 6 stiffly beaten egg whites. Mix quickly.

Turn into a buttered soufflé dish filling only to within $\frac{1}{3}$ inch of the top. Smooth over the surface of the soufflé. Cook in the oven like an ordinary soufflé.

Soufflé tomatoes. TOMATES SOUFFLÉES—Empty without breaking some firm, regular-shaped tomatoes. Sprinkle them with oil or melted butter and cook in the oven for 5 minutes.

Allow to cool and fill them with tomato soufflé mixture made according to the recipe for *Tomato soufflé*.

Fill the tomatoes to the top, smooth the surface, sprinkle with grated Parmesan and cook in a slow oven for 10 minutes. Serve on a napkin.

Grated Parmesan may be added to the tomato soufflé mixture.

Stuffed tomatoes. TOMATES FARCIES—Choose medium sized tomatoes, regular in shape. Cut a circle round the stalk and open them. Press lightly to remove the juice and seeds and season the interior with salt and pepper.

Set in rows on an oiled baking tin; pour a few drops of

oil into each tomato and put into a very hot oven for 5 minutes.

Drain the tomatoes, stuff them, filling them well, with thickened *duxelles** seasoned with a little garlic and with the addition of lean ham cut in very small dice and a little freshly made breadcrumbs. Pile the stuffing in a dome. Set the tomatoes on an oiled baking tin. Put breadcrumbs on top and sprinkle with oil. Cook in the oven for 12 to 15 minutes.

Cold stuffed tomatoes. TOMATES FROIDES—These tomatoes are served as hors-d'oeuvre or used as garnish with various cold dishes. They are prepared as follows:

Empty small, round, firm tomatoes, without breaking the skin. Season with salt and pepper. Sprinkle with oil and a few drops of vinegar or lemon juice. Leave for an hour.

Fill the tomatoes with the prescribed mixture. Smooth over the surface, rounding it a little. Decorate the tops with truffles, hard boiled egg whites, tarragon or chervil leaves, or anything else normally used for decorating cold foodstuffs.

Cold stuffed tomatoes can be served as they are or coated with jelly.

Stuffed tomatoes à la bonne femme. TOMATES FARCIES À LA BONNE FEMME—Cut large tomatoes in two across the middle, remove the seeds and season with salt and pepper. Cook them very quickly in very hot oil in the frying pan and put them into an oiled dish. Stuff with sausage meat to which chopped onion, cooked till soft in butter, freshly made breadcrumbs and chopped parsley and garlic have been added. Cover with breadcrumbs and sprinkle with oil. Cook in a moderate oven.

Stuffed tomatoes à la languedocienne. TOMATES FARCIES À LA LANGUEDOCIENNE—Sauté quickly in oil in the frying pan halves of tomatoes seasoned with salt and pepper.

Stuff them with a mixture of sausage meat, chopped hard boiled egg yolks, chopped onion lightly cooked in oil and chopped parsley and garlic.

Place in an oiled gratin dish. Cover with breadcrumbs and sprinkle with oil. Cook gently in the oven.

Stuffed tomatoes à la niçoise. TOMATES FARCIES À LA NIÇOISE—Stuff the halves of tomatoes prepared as in the preceding recipe with a mixture of rice cooked in a meat stock, aubergine cooked in oil and chopped, breadcrumbs, chopped parsley and chopped garlic, the whole well seasoned and mixed.

Put the tomatoes in an oiled gratin dish; cover them with breadcrumbs and sprinkle with oil. Cook gently in the oven.

Stuffed tomatoes à la parisienne. TOMATES FARCIES À LA PARISIENNE—Cook whole tomatoes lightly in oil. Fill them with a fine forcemeat mixed with a *salpicon** of truffles and mushrooms, cooked in butter (see FORCEMEAT). Put into a buttered gratin dish. Cover with freshly grated breadcrumbs and sprinkle with melted butter. Cook gently in the oven.

Stuffed tomatoes à la piémontaise or à l'italienne. TOMATES FARCIES À LA PIÉMONTAISE, À L'ITALIENNE—Slice off the tops of some medium-sized tomatoes and press them to remove the juice and seeds, taking care not to break the skin. Season the inside. Stuff them, *before cooking*, with *Risotto* (see RICE) to which some concentrated *Tomato purée* has been added. Put the tomatoes on a buttered baking tin, sprinkle with melted butter and cook gently in the oven. Set them on a round dish, surround with *Tomato sauce* (not too thick—see SAUCE) and sprinkle with chopped parsley.

Stuffed tomatoes à la reine. TOMATES FARCIES AU SALPICON DE VOLAILLE, À LA REINE—Fill medium-sized tomatoes, seeded and lightly cooked in butter with a *salpicon** of poultry mixed with truffles and mushrooms in dice, bound with a thick *Velouté sauce* (see SAUCE).

Put the tomatoes on a buttered baking tin. Cover them with breadcrumbs and sprinkle with melted butter. Cook in the oven.

Tomatoes à la vinaigrette. TOMATES À LA VINAIGRETTE—Plunge some well-rounded tomatoes into boiling water, cool in cold water and dry them.

Peel them completely and, without breaking them, remove the seeds and juice.

Cut the tomatoes into very thin slices or, according to the use for which they are intended, into quarters.

Lay these slices, or quarters, on a napkin folded in four on the table. Season them with salt and leave them for 10 minutes in this seasoning.

Serve the tomatoes in an hors-d'oeuvre dish and sprinkle with a few tablespoons of *Vinaigrette* (see SAUCE).

Sprinkle with chopped parsley and, if liked, chervil and tarragon. Serve very cold.

TOMBER—This old French cookery term (literally 'to fall'), describes a way of cooking meat in a saucepan without any other liquid than that produced by the meat itself. The moisture must, after cooking is complete, be *tombé* (that is to say must fall or go down), to a syrupy consistency.

Tomber à glace—Phrase used when some substance, such as onion or shallot, is moistened during cooking with liquid which is then boiled down completely.

TONGS. PINCE—Name of various instruments of different shapes, according to the use for which they are intended. The following types of tongs are used at table: asparagus tongs, *escargot* tongs, sugar tongs, etc.

TONGUE CRESS—This species of cress (a plant of the family *Cruciferae*) which in France is called *alénois*, is also known as 'garden cress'. The word *alénois* is a corruption of *Orléanais*. This plant grows wild in France, but it is said that it is a native of Cyprus.

There are various species of garden cress: curly dwarf; golden, of which the leaves are of a pale green, yellowish tint; large leaf; and common cress.

It is usually eaten in salads, like watercress. It is the classic garnish for roast or grilled meat or poultry.

It can also be prepared in various ways like watercress.

Excellent soups can be made from this cress. See SOUPS AND BROTHS, *Consommé with garden cress*.

TORPEDO. TORPILLE—Large fish, somewhat resembling the skate, which is quite common in the Mediterranean. The flesh of the torpedo-fish is edible but mediocre. It is prepared like skate.

TOT. BOUJARON—A small measure of 6 centilitres (a dram) which was used for distributing rum to sailors.

TÔT-FAIT (Pastry)—Mix 2 cups (250 grams) of sifted cake flour, 1 cup (250 grams) of sugar, a small pinch of salt, a little grated lemon rind and 3 whole eggs in a basin with a wooden spoon.

When the mixture is smooth add ½ pound (250 grams) of melted butter. Blend.

Fill a buttered *manqué* mould with this mixture.

Cook in a moderate oven (375°F.) for 45 minutes. Turn out the cake and allow it to cool before serving.

TOUFFE—Stalks tied together in a bunch. Thus parsley arranged in a bunch is called a *touffe de persil*.

TOULOUSAINE (A LA)—Name given to various quite different preparations. It is mostly used for a *ragoût* bound with a white sauce used as an accompaniment to poached or roast poultry, or as filling for *croustades*, tarts and *vol-au-vent*.

TOUR DE FEUILLETAGE—French term for treatment (turns) given to pastry to make it flaky. See DOUGH.

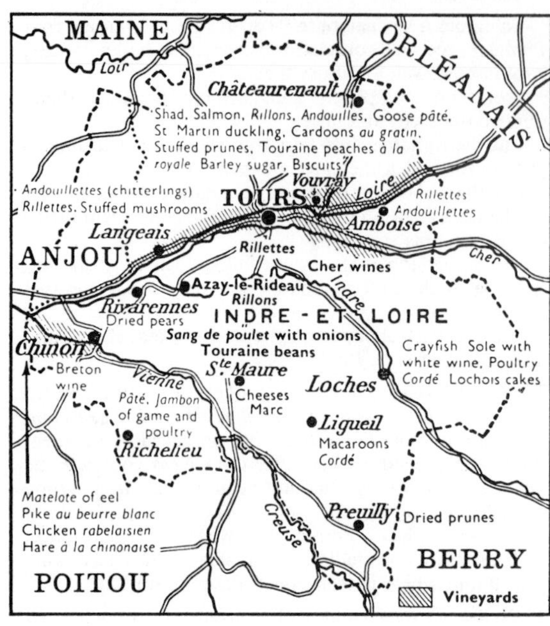

Gastronomic map of Touraine

TOURAINE—The Touraine, cradle of Gargantua, is the home of famous cooks.

Its meadows and fields, its woods and its waters provide food of the highest quality for the table: shad from the Loire, pike from the Cher, carp from the Indre, chicken, butter, veal, pork and, in the realm of vegetables, delicious mushrooms, abundant vegetables and exquisite fruit in plenty: Chasselas grapes from the slopes above the Loire, William pears, plums from Sainte-Catherine and Rochecorbon, eating apples from Azay-le-Rideau; and a whole range of delicious wines.

Culinary specialities—Touraine cookery is French cookery *par excellence*, wholesome, simple and admirably prepared, but it contains very few regional specialities. However, some old-fashioned dishes like *sang de poulet aux oignons* (chicken blood with onions), *rôtie au vin rouge* (roast meat with red wine) are still prepared in Touraine; they make there remarkable *fricassées* of chicken and *fritures* of fish, serve *cerneaux*, which are green walnuts, as hors-d'oeuvre and cook *hare à la chinonaise*.

The *charcuterie* is renowned, notably *rillettes* of Tours and *rillons*, *andouilles* and *andouillettes*, as well as similar products from Vouvray and Chinon. Richelieu has its *pâtés* and its *jambons* of game and poultry.

The sweetmeats of this district are *barley-sugar* and *biscuits* from Tours, *macaroons* from Cormery and Ligueil, cakes called *le Lochois* and *le Tourangeau*. Worthy of praise are the *stuffed prunes* of Tours and *dried prunes* of Preuilly and Huismes, the *dried pears* of Rivarennes and the traditional pastries: the *cordés*, *russerolles*, *fouaces*, and *cassemuse*.

Wines—Touraine produces delightful dry wines, at once strong and smooth, which rejoice the palate by an extremely agreeable aroma. The best growths among the white wines are the *pineau* grape of Vouvray, then Mont-Louis, Saint-Avertin, Rochecorbon, Candes and Saché; among red wines the *Bourgueil* with its aroma of strawberries and the *Breton* of Chinon which smells of raspberries.

Touraine kitchen, Plessis-les-Tours
(*French Government Tourist Office*)

TOURD—Mediterranean fish which is a type of wrasse. Its flesh is a little insipid.

TOURNE-BRIDE—Old word for a country inn established near a *château* where visitors' servants used to be lodged. Nowadays a name bestowed on certain modern restaurants to give them an antique charm.

TOURNEDOS—Small slices taken from the heart of the fillet of beef. This cut is sautéed or grilled and garnished in various ways. See BEEF, *Tournedos*.

TOURNÉE—Old name for *Allemande sauce* (see SAUCE).

TOURNER—Literally *to turn*, and describing in French the action of rounding off, while peeling, certain vegetables. Thus potatoes are 'turned' into the shape of olives, cobnuts, etc. Carrots, turnips and other pot-herbs are 'turned', and so are cultivated mushrooms, to peel and trim them to the right shape. Olives are also 'turned' when they are used as a garnish.

TOURTE—The word tourte, say some culinary writers, is derived from the Latin *tortus*, which means 'making round' thus indicating in a general way that the tourte should be round in shape.

The tourte is not made only as a meat course. There are also sweet tourtes, but these are really tarts, which also are usually round in shape. See also TART.

Tourtes as entrées. TOURTE D'ENTRÉE—The tourte served as an entrée, said Carême in his treatise *Entrées chaudes de pâtisserie*, 'is no longer sufficiently sumptuous to appear on our opulent tables because its shape is too common; even the bourgeois classes disdain it and eat only hot *pâtés* and *vol-au-vent*, where formerly the rich merchants and their families used to regale themselves with the humble tourte.

'But then these merchants did not pride themselves on being gastronomes. How times have changed! Our great cooks in the old days used to serve tourte at the tables of princes . . . . !'

Since Carême wrote these observations on the discredit suffered by the tourte in his days, this excellent hot entrée has come back into fashion, and now it is not only 'merchants' who regale themselves with it, but also the most fastidious gastronomes!

The recipe that Carême gave for making the tourte is as follows:

Tourte d'entrée à l'ancienne—'Make and roll out pastry as for a *Timbale**. Cut out a round about eight inches in diameter; place this on a small tray (metal baking tin); then make 36 to 40 *boulettes* (quenelles of *godiveau**, about the size of a pigeon's egg). Place half of these in the bottom of the tourte, keeping them an inch away from the edge. Set on top some slices of lamb's or calf's sweetbreads (cooked *aux fines herbes*), some mushrooms and some artichoke bottoms cut into eighths; then put on the rest of the *boulettes*, and, on top, the shelled claws and tails of four good crayfish, mushrooms and artichoke bottoms, taking pains to build up the top into a perfect dome.

'Next roll out some more pastry in the same way as for the bottom of the tourte and cut it into a round 9½ inches in diameter; it should be 2 *lignes* (⅛ of an inch) thick. Moisten lightly the edges of the first piece of pastry; cover this and its garnish with the large round piece of pastry and press the edges together all round almost as far as the *boulettes;* see that there is a little air inside the tourte when it is closed up (so that it will be plump and good-looking); however, take care that there is only a little air, otherwise the action of the heat in the oven may tend to make it come apart; this sometimes spoils the shape of the tourte. When this happens, and the pastry is already cooked, make a small hole with a large ordinary pin so that the air can escape.

'Next raise and press the edges of the lower piece of pastry over the edges of the second, so as to seal them as perfectly as possible; moisten the upper edge lightly and set on it a strip of puff pastry nine *lignes* (¾ inch) wide and not more than two good *lignes* (⅛ inch) thick, then fix and press down this strip.

'Having brushed the upper pastry lightly with egg, place in the middle a pretty rosette, at least six inches in diameter, made of rolled strips of the same pastry as the tourte, or even a little false top of puff pastry trimmings cut out in the old-fashioned way.

'Brush this false top with egg; surround the edges with a band of strong, buttered paper, to contain the whole thickness of the tourte, and put into a brisk oven; allow 1½ hours baking time.

'Once cooked cut a little lid three inches wide out of the top, pour a good Espagnole sauce into the tourte and re-cover.'

Tourte of truffles à la périgourdine. TOURTE DE TRUFFES À LA PÉRIGOURDINE—See TRUFFLES.

SWEET TOURTES. TOURTES D'ENTREMETS—To *make pastry*. Use puff pastry 'turned' six times. When the last turn has been given it should be 32 inches long. Make the band by cutting ⅛ inch off the edge of the pastry, then cut the band 1 inch wide.

Give one more turn to the rest of the pastry and from it cut out a base 8 inches in diameter. Set the base on a baking tin. Moisten lightly round the edges. Set the band of pastry on the moistened edge. Join the two ends of the band by pressing them together, having first cut them so that the band is made no thicker at this point. Brush the band with egg.

Fill the inside of the tourte with the composition or the fruits prescribed. Bake in a hot oven. At the last moment, sprinkle with icing sugar and glaze in the oven.

Note. Tourtes can be filled with all kinds of preparations, such as *French pastry cream*, *Frangipane*, jam or raw or cooked fruit (see CREAMS).

Some of these tourtes, mostly those made with jam, have the pastry base covered with a second piece cut to the same size, this being fixed to the moistened pastry band.

Tourtes may also be prepared by baking the pastry first and filling afterwards with fruit, cooked in vanilla syrup and well drained.

Apricot tourte I. TOURTE AUX ABRICOTS—With puff pastry rolled and turned 6 times, prepare a tourte crust as described above. Sprinkle fine sugar over the base, avoiding the band surrounding it. Fill the tourte with halves of well-ripened apricots. Brush the band with egg. Bake in a hot oven. Coat the apricots lightly with apricot jam diluted with a little syrup and strained.

Apricot tourte II (for home cooking). TOURTE AUX ABRICOTS—'Roll out some fine pastry; set it on a *tourtière* (the requisite pie-dish) lightly moistened in the middle. Cut it to the desired size, well rounded in shape. Prick the middle and moisten the edges, fixing on them a band of puff pastry 1 inch wide and ⅛ inch thick.

'Fill the tourte like a tart, but do not let the fruit touch the band of pastry, because this would prevent it from rising evenly during cooking. Brush the upper surface of this band with egg and mark it lightly with the edge of a kitchen knife.

'Bake for about 45 minutes in a moderate oven, and, 5 minutes before it is completely cooked, powder it lightly with icing sugar so that when it is put back in the oven the sugar glazes.' (Montbry.)

Tourte à la mode béarnaise—'Melt 1 pound (500 grams) of butter and pour it over 3½ ounces (100 grams) of yeast put into a bowl. Mix together.

'Add to the yeast 1 pound (500 grams) of sifted sugar, 12 eggs, a small glass of rum, a little grated lemon peel and a pinch of salt.

'Add to this mixture, which is rather liquid, enough flour to obtain a fairly firm mixture. Allow to ferment for 24 hours.

'Divide into small pieces and put them into buttered moulds. Bake in the oven.'

Corsican tourte. TOURTE CORSE—*Bouillie** of chestnut flour prepared like *polenta** with the addition of pine kernels, and dried fruits flavoured with anise, poured into a *tourtière** and baked in the oven.

Tourte with various fruits. TOURTE AUX FRUITS—Made like *Apricot tourte* with any kind of fruit, raw or cooked, whole or in halves, quarters or slices, according to their nature. Tourtes may be made with pineapple, cherries, nectarines, pears, apples, plums etc.

Tourtes made with strawberries or raspberries are filled with the fruit after the pastry is cooked.

TOURTEAU—French name for the large edible crab.

TOURTIÈRE—Pie-dish in which to make tourtes. Formerly tourtières were made of earthenware. Nowadays this utensil is made of metal. There are tourtières with plain sides and tourtières with goffered edges.

TRAGACANTH (Gum Dragon). ADRAGANTE—Gum provided by several species of plants. Tragacanth gum is mentioned in the writings of authors of the most ancient times.

Perfume-makers, confectioners and pastry-cooks use tragacanth gum to bind their oils or to give body to their pastes.

TRAIT—French term used by barmen preparing cocktails to describe a fixed quantity of liquor, usually about a spoonful.

To pour out with precision these small quantities of liquid the bottle is usually stoppered with a special metal cork. Turned upside down rapidly a bottle fitted with this cork allows only a little liquid to escape at a time.

The bottle is turned sharply up and down once for every *trait* required.

TRAITEUR—*Traiter*, or to treat, someone means in French to receive or welcome them to the table.

A *traiteur* is someone who provides meals for payment.

The *traiteur*, was in fact the predecessor of the *restaurateur*. During the eighteenth century people dined out at the *traiteur's*.

By the middle of the nineteenth century this term no longer had the same meaning as before. It had acquired a slightly derogatory sense, and was scarcely applied except to restaurateurs of the lowest class and wine merchants who provided meals. There still exist in Paris, in some of the populous districts, establishments whose signs carry the words: *Marchand des vins—Traiteur*.

In the eighteenth century, before the institution of the restaurants, not only were people obliged to buy whole joints, fowls, etc. from the traiteurs, but were even unable, when the latter were only food merchants, to eat on the premises.

It was in this epoch, says Brillat-Savarin (about 1770), that 'strangers had as yet very few resources in the way of good cheer . . . they were forced to have recourse to the innkeepers who were generally bad. . . . It was possible to go to the *traiteurs* but they could only sell whole pieces; and he who wished to entertain some friends had to order in advance, so that those who had not the good luck to be invited to some wealthy house left the great city without knowing the resources and delights of Parisian cuisine.' (*Physiologie du goût—Méditation XXVII.*)

It can be seen from this quotation from Brillat-Savarin that of the *traiteurs* of this period a certain number at least, if not all, provided meals in their establishments and were, in fact, restaurateurs of an early kind, long before the first restaurant, founded in 1765 by one Boulanger, was opened in the Rue des Poulies (a street situated near the Oratory of the Rue Saint-Honoré).

The establishment founded by Boulanger was not a 'restaurant' in the accepted sense of the word. Boulanger was still only a *traiteur*, and there existed in Paris at that time a great number of establishments similar to his.

TRANCHANT (Equerry)—This was the name, in former times, for the officer in charge of cutting meat at table. This office only existed in the great houses.

TRANCHE GRASSE (Top rump)—In French butchery the part of the leg of beef which extends the whole length of the *tende de tranche* (topside) as far as the rump.

Tranche au petit os is the middle of the silverside (rump).

TRANCHEUR—Waiter who, in a restaurant, is in charge of cutting meat.

TRANCHOIR, TRENCHER—Wooden dish on which meat is sliced. It was a slice of bread serving as a plate in the Middle Ages. These slices of bread were also called *tailloirs*.

TRAVAILLER—In culinary French this term is usually equivalent to 'beat'. It is much used in cookery and pastry-making.

To beat (or *travailler*) a sauce is to stir it with a spatula or wooden spoon to make it smooth, or mix it with a whisk to incorporate other substances.

A forcemeat or other similar mixture is also beaten (or *travaillé*) to render it homogeneous.

A paste or batter is beaten to ensure perfect blending.

Travailler is also used in French to indicate a change in the nature of something. Thus in speaking of wine it means to ferment. It is used also to describe a dough that rises.

TREFOIL (TRIFOLIUM). TRÈFLE—Type of leguminous plant of which one species is eaten as a vegetable in Iceland. Another, the marsh trefoil, has large smooth dark-green leaves rather resembling those of the broad bean. These leaves are bitter and are sometimes used instead of hops. The farinaceous root is edible; it is eaten like carrot.

TREMPER—Term used in the expressions *tremper la soupe* which means to soak slices of bread in soup, and *tremper le vin*, to mix wine with water.

TREMPETTE—A word derived from *tremper*, to soak, meaning a small slice of bread which has been dipped in a liquid.

TRESS. TRESSE—Design in which some pastries are made, called a plait or 'braid'. It is also called *natte* in French.

TRICLINIUM—Name for the special room in which the ancient Romans took their meals.

This is how, according to Mazoïs (*Palais de Scaurus*), the triclinium or dining room of the Romans was arranged:

'. . . As we were about to pass through the door of the ante-room which precedes the triclinium, a child, posted there for the purpose, warned us to enter with the right foot, so as not to bring in evil portents.

'. . . As soon as we had been announced slaves relieved us of our *bracae* (breeches) and our striped Gaulish *sagi* (military coats), and re-clothed us in fine robes to be worn only at the table.

'. . . We entered the triclinium; we were scarcely seated before Egyptian slaves came and poured cold water over our hands while others, having taken off our sandals, washed our feet and cleaned our toenails, even though the same service had already been performed for us in the bath. The triclinium or dining room is twice as long as it is wide and seems to be divided in two. The upper part is occupied by the table and couches; the lower is kept free for the service and for entertainment. Around the former part the walls are ornamented up to a certain height with costly paintings. The decoration of the rest of the room is noble and, at the same time, in keeping with its character; the pillars, festooned with ivy and vines, divide the walls into sections, each of which is bordered with fanciful ornament; in the centre of each panel there have been painted with admirable grace young fauns or bacchantes bearing *thyrsi*, vases, cups and all the paraphernalia of the feast. Above these columns runs a great frieze divided into twelve tableaux, each of which is surmounted by one of the signs of the Zodiac and represents the foodstuffs which are most sought after in the month to which the sign belongs; so that underneath Sagittarius have been painted shrimps, shell-fish and birds of passage, under Capricorn, lobsters, sea-fish, a wild boar and game birds; under Aquarius duck, plover, pigeons and water-rails, etc.

'Bronze lamps, suspended from chains of the same metal or supported by candelabras of rare workmanship, shed a bright light; slaves detailed to look after them were careful to cut the wicks from time to time and see that they did not lack oil.

'The table, made of cedar wood brought from the heart of Mauretania and prized above gold, rested on feet of ivory; it was covered with a massive tray of silver weighing five hundred pounds, ornamented with chasing and anaglyphs. The dining couches, enough for thirty persons, were of bronze, enriched with ornament in silver, gold and tortoiseshell; the mattresses of purple-dyed wool from Gaul and the rich feather-filled cushions were covered with brilliantly coloured materials, woven and embroidered with silk mixed with gold thread. Chrysippus told us that they had been made at Babylon and that they cost four million sesterces.

'The mosaic floor represented, by a curious caprice of the artist, all sorts of scraps of food, as though they had fallen naturally to the ground, so that at first glance it seemed not to have been swept since the last meal . . . At the end of the room there had been set up some Corinthian brass vases. This triclinium, the largest of four that Scaurus had in his palace, could easily hold a table with sixty couches, but it was seldom that so many guests met there, and when, on great occasions, there were five or six hundred people invited, they were received in the atrium. This dining room was reserved for autumn, winter and spring; the Romans made a study of the enjoyment of changing seasons.

'The service was regulated so that for each triclinium there were a great number of tables of different kinds, each with its own vases, dishes and servants.'

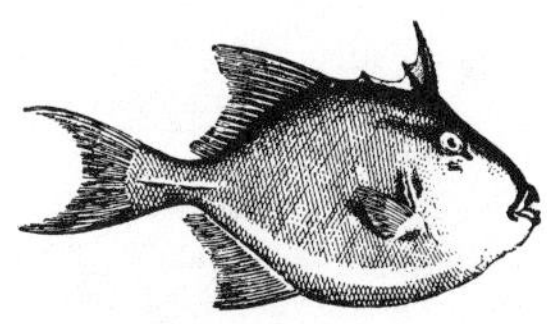

Triggerfish

TRIGGERFISH. BALISTE—Genus of fish distinguishable by their dorsal fin armed with a spine which is projected into an erect position when the fish is threatened with any danger.

This genus includes several species, all remarkable for their brilliant metallic colouring and thick granulous skin, which has the texture of armour.

Only one species of the genus is found on the French Mediterranean coast. These, when caught, are heard to make a grunting sound, resembling that of pigs. In U.S.A. the so-called pigfish is very abundant on the South Atlantic coast and averages about half a pound in weight.

The flesh is quite delicate and they are prepared like sturgeon or tunny (tuna fish).

TRIGLE, GURNARD—Species of fish, of which several varieties exist. See GURNET.

TRIM. PARER—To remove all parts which spoil the correct appearance of food.

Parer la marchandise ('to trim the goods') means to make a display of goods, featuring the best and concealing the others—those which are to be delivered to the customer.

TRIMMINGS. PARURES—This term applies to all the parts of meat—such as sinews, skin, etc., which are removed before the meat is cooked in one way or another.

Fresh meat trimmings, especially veal, beef and pork trimmings, are used for making stocks, which serve in preparing sauces. See STOCKS.

Mutton and lamb trimmings should only be used for making stocks intended for sauces to accompany these meats.

TRIPE. TRIPES—By this word is generally meant the stomach of ruminants used as foodstuff.

Other than those of ruminants, only tripes from certain butchered animals, such as pigs and sheep, are considered edible.

The latter are used in Provence for the preparation of *pieds-paquets à la marseillaise*, and in the south-west of France to make a dish known as *petarram*.

Pig's intestines are used on the one hand to enclose large and small sausages, *boudins* and saveloy, and on the other hand to make *andouilles* and *andouillettes*.

Rich in gelatine, tripe needs prolonged cooking and is not easy to digest, so that it has no place in the diet of the dyspeptic; its content of gelatine and nucleo-proteins means that it is also forbidden to sufferers from gout. For the preparation of tripe see OFFAL OR VARIETY MEATS.

The use of the first stomach of oxen (beef) is well-known; it is used for the famous *Tripes à la mode de Caen* and the no less celebrated *Gras-double à la Lyonnaise*.

'The origin of these dishes goes back far into the past. Athenaeus praised this dish. The father of Greek poetry, Homer, noted the excellence of tripe, prepared in honour of him whom Thetis made invulnerable by dipping him in the waters of the Styx.

'Rabelais tells us how Gargamelle gave birth to Gargantua after having eaten a huge dish of godebillios, and that, for him, is the occasion to inform us that "godebillios are the fat tripes of coiros; coiros are oxen fattened in the ox-stalls and guimo-meadows; guimo meadows are those that may be mowed twice a year".

'But well before Rabelais, William the Conqueror enjoyed tripe accompanied by Neustrian apple juice, and history, always at fault, even in small facts, has neglected to mention that a question of godebillios was the cause of the quarrel that cropped up between William the Bastard and Phillip I, King of France, a question which provoked a pleasantry by the latter to which the former replied by a promise as historic as it is threatening: "That he would come and be churched at Notre-Dame de Paris with ten thousand lances instead of candles."

'And thus, in the eleventh century, a gastronomic quarrel led to the invasion of the Norman Vexin. However, at this time the dreary *cuisine* of the Middle Ages had not known how to prepare tripe. It was only three centuries later that, in ancient Cadomum, was born a culinary genius, follower of Taillevent and precursor of Carême, Benoît, the great Benoît, who had the intelligence to substitute for the tastelessness of the original dish that which is at the heart of all good cooking, to wit, well-judged, carefully calculated seasoning.

'This was the cook who immortalised his district gastronomically, and it must be stated with regret that his fellow countrymen forgot to consecrate the memory of this local glory in bronze or marble, so generously erected to others who did not deserve it so much. Certainly Caen may congratulate herself on having given the light of day to Malherbe, to Segrais, to Choron (whose name is given to a tournedos) and to many other luminaries. She can be pleased with her title of "*cité litteraire et savante*", but what she should really pride herself on is to be the native land of Benoît and the eternal country of succulent tripe and frothing cider—"*ce suprême soulas, des grands gousiers normands*".

'On the tables of the most famous restaurants tripe comes on a fixed day, steaming in brown *terrines* fixed in silver heaters, whose luxury clashes with the rustic quality of the food. At the wine merchants', at the door of the dairy, a placard announces—tempting invitation—that the menu of the day includes tripe. There it is eaten from thick china plates. In humble homes to smell its robust savour means a delight and a feast to come. Beside a *terrine* of *tripes à la mode de Caen*, there is no more rank or condition or social hierarchy; this is a feast for all from the highest to the lowest.

'It cannot be denied that the preparation is long and laborious, and that a large quantity must be made in order to achieve the greatest succulence.

'But ancient tripe or *tripailles*, made famous by Athenaeus and Homer, godebillios exalted by the good Rabelais or modern *Tripes à la mode de Caen*, to which old Calvados adds its characteristic note, what does it matter what it is called or where it comes from, so long as the perfect succulence is there, so long as the squares of mesentery bathe in the golden juices, whose perfume whets the appetite, and a few bottles of the pure juice of Neustrian apples, the true Norman cider, father of golden drunkenness make their appearance at the same time?' (Philéas Gilbert.)

The detailed recipe for *Tripes à la mode de Caen* will be found under OFFAL OR VARIETY MEATS.

TRIPERIE—The sale of tripe, or the place in which it is sold.

As well as tripe of the ordinary kind, the *triperie* sells other kinds of offal (variety meats): calf's and sheep's head, brains, sweetbreads, udder, feet, tongue, hearts, liver, spleen and kidneys.

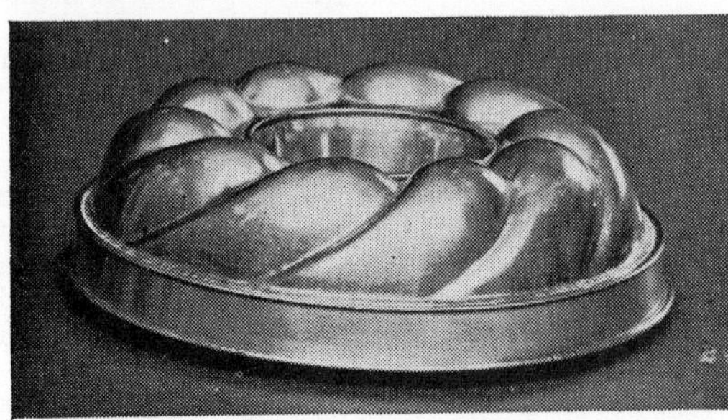

Mould to make Trois Frères

TROIS FRÈRES (Pastry)—Pastry created by the three Julien brothers, celebrated pastry-cooks of the nineteenth century, for which a special mould called the *moule à trois frères* was created.

Ingredients. 3 cups (500 grams) of rice flour; $2\frac{3}{4}$ cups (375 grams) fine sugar; $1\frac{3}{4}$ cups (400 grams) of butter; 2 ounces (60 grams) candied angelica cut in small dice; 15 whole eggs; 1 liqueur glass of maraschino; a pinch of salt.

Method. Put the sugar, the eggs and the salt into a copper pan. Cook this mixture by placing the pan in a *bain-marie** which is placed in turn in a sauté pan filled with hot water, and whisk until the composition becomes thick and frothy.

Add the rice flour, the melted butter and the maraschino.

Fill buttered and floured moulds with this mixture. Bake in a fairly hot oven.

Set the cakes on a base made of sweet pastry. Cover with apricot syrup and sprinkle with the chopped almonds and diced angelica.

TROGNON—Edible heart of a vegetable or fruit. *Trognons* of certain vegetables, notably those of chicory and cabbage can be prepared in various ways. See CHICORY.

TRONÇON (CHUNK)—French culinary term for a piece of foodstuff of any kind which is cut so that it is longer than it is wide. Used most of all to describe pieces cut from the middle of a large fish.

TROPIQUE—French term for the hottest part of the oven, by analogy with the regions north and south of the Equator which are the hottest parts of the earth.

TROU DU MILIEU OR COUP DU MILIEU—A glass of *eau-de-vie* or other liqueur which used to be drunk in the middle of a large and elaborate meal.

The coup du milieu was replaced by *sorbets* which are served at the same moment, that is to say between the entrée and the roast.

There are some people who are still faithful to this Bacchic practice, and one may yet see many a gastronome drink copious draughts of eau-de-vie in the middle of a meal.

Thus, for example, certain peoples of the North of Europe, notably the Swedes, drink eau-de-vie (aquavite) between courses.

Formerly at family dinners the liqueurs that were drunk as *Trou du milieu* were served by the young daughters of the house.

The *Trou normande* is the same thing as the *Trou du milieu* but the former must always be eau-de-vie distilled from apples.

TROUSSE—French word for the sort of sheath that holds the butcher's or cook's implements. The *trousse* is suspended from the apron string.

TROUT. Truite—Species of fish of the same group as the salmon, whose flesh, very delicate, is white, pinkish or 'salmon', according to the waters it inhabits.

In French fresh waters two kinds of trout are found: common trout (*Truite commune*, *Truite de rivière*, *de ruisseau* or *de torrent*) which live in running water. They correspond to the American mountain trout, *Dolly Vardens*, *Brook* or *Speckled trout*. The salmon trout (*Truit saumonée*, *Truite de mer* or *Truite de Dieppe*) are fish whose flesh is pink or 'salmon' and which, like the salmon, go up the rivers and correspond to the American *Brown* or *River trout*. Another variety of trout, called the *Rainbow trout*, also an anadromous species, is a native of California. It was imported into Europe some years ago and has now become acclimatized and is increasing rapidly; it is robust and does well in waters less fresh than those demanded by the common trout.

There are also lake trout which, living in very deep water, grow to a very large size, but their flesh is less delicate than that of river trout.

All methods of preparation given for fillets of sole or whiting are applicable to fillets of trout.

RIVER TROUT. Truites de rivière:

Blue trout. Truite au bleu—For this dish the trout must not only be absolutely fresh but actually alive.

Ten minutes before serving take the fish out of the water, despatch them with a blow on the head, empty and clean them; sprinkle them with vinegar, then plunge into a *court-bouillon** containing a high proportion of vinegar.

Cook as rapidly as possible, allowing 7 to 8 minutes for fish weighing about 5 ounces (150 grams) each.

Drain the trout; arrange on a napkin-covered dish and garnish them with fresh parsley. Serve separately melted butter or *Hollandaise sauce* (see SAUCE).

Blue trout (cold). TRUITES AU BLEU FROIDES—Prepared as above. Allow to cool in the *court-bouillon**. Serve on a napkin-covered dish, garnished with fresh parsley. Serve *Ravigote sauce* (see SAUCE) separately.

Boiled river trout with various sauces. TRUITES DE RIVIÈRE BOUILLIES—Cook the fish in *court-bouillon**. Drain them. Set on a table napkin. Serve with *Hollandaise sauce* or any other sauce suitable for boiled fish (see SAUCE).

River trout à la bourguignonne. TRUITES DE RIVIÈRE À LA BOURGUIGNONNE—Prepare like *River trout in red wine*, using red Burgundy. Garnish with mushrooms and small glazed onions. Coat with sauce prepared as in the recipe for *Trout in red wine*.

River trout Colbert. TRUITES DE RIVIÈRE COLBERT—Open the fish down the back and remove the central bone.

Coat the trout with egg and breadcrumbs. Fry in smoking hot deep fat or oil. When crisp and golden-brown, drain and set on a long dish. Put in the middle of each trout a tablespoon of *Colbert butter* (see BUTTER, *Compound butters*). At each end of the dish put a bunch of fried parsley.

River trout, cold. TRUITES DE RIVIÈRE FROIDES—All the methods of preparing cold *Salmon trout* are applicable to river trout. See below.

Fillets of river trout en papillotes à l'ancienne. FILETS DE TRUITES DE RIVIÈRE EN PAPILLOTES À L'ANCIENNE—Fillet the trout. Season the fillets and half cook them in butter. Put them, two by two, on one side of kitchen paper cut into the shape of hearts and oiled (in the same way as for veal cutlets *en papillotes*), on a layer of *duxelles** mixed with chopped truffles and bound with concentrated *Velouté sauce* (see SAUCE) based on fish stock. Cover the trout fillets with the same mixture. Close the *papillotes*, folding over the edges carefully. Cook in the oven so that they blow up. Serve as they are.

Fried trout

Fried trout. TRUITES DE RIVIÈRE FRITES—Chiefly small trout are prepared in this way. Proceed as for *Fried bass* (see BASS).

Grilled river trout. TRUITES DE RIVIÈRE GRILLÉES—Make shallow cuts on both sides of the back of the trout. Season, flour lightly, brush with oil or melted butter and cook on the grill at a gentle heat. Serve with *Maître d'hôtel butter* (see BUTTER, *Compound butters*) or any other sauce suitable for grilled fish (see SAUCE).

River trout à l'hôtelière. TRUITES DE RIVIÈRE À L'HÔTELIÈRE—Coat the trout with egg and breadcrumbs and fry. Set on a long dish on a mixture of *duxelles** and

Grilled trout garnished with Duchess potatoes

Maître d'hôtel butter (see BUTTER, *Compound butters*) in the ratio of one tablespoon of duxelles to every 6 tablespoons (100 grams) of butter. Put half slices of lemon with fluted edges along the sides of the dish.

River trout à la hussarde. TRUITES DE RIVIÈRE À LA HUSSARDE—Stuff 10 river trout with *Fish forcemeat* (see FORCEMEAT) mixed with chopped onion cooked till tender in butter allowing ½ cup (100 grams) of onion per pound (500 grams) of forcemeat. Season.

Put the trout in a baking tin, lined with ½ cup (100 grams) of finely chopped onions lightly cooked in butter without colouring. Add a small *bouquet garni*. Pour over 1 cup (2 decilitres) of dry white wine. Dot small pieces of butter over the top. Cook in the oven basting frequently.

Drain the trout, set on a serving dish, coat with the cooking liquor thickened with a little *Velouté sauce* (see SAUCE) based on fish stock, enriched with butter and strained. Glaze in a very hot oven.

Jellied river trout in red wine. TRUITES DE RIVIERE À LA GELÉE AU VIN ROUGE—Prepared like *Salmon glacé au chambertin**.

Note. In the same way jellied trout can be prepared using various wines: Barsac, Chambertin, Champagne, Chinon, Madeira and others.

Trout en matelote à la bourguignonne. TRUITES EN MATELOTE À LA BOURGUIGNONNE—Cut the trout into chunks, put them in a sauté pan lined with chopped onions and carrots lightly cooked in butter. Put in the middle of the pan a *bouquet garni**. Pour over enough red Burgundy to cover the trout. Season; cook, covered, for 10 minutes. Drain the trout and replace in the pan. Add small glazed onions and small mushrooms sautéed in butter. Pour over the cooking liquor thickened with *Kneaded butter* and strained (see BUTTER, *Compound butters*).

Simmer for 15 minutes. Serve the trout in a deep dish, garnished with croûtons fried in butter.

Trout en matelote à la normande. TRUITES EN MATELOTE À LA NORMANDE—Cook the trout as above, using white wine. Drain and put in a sauté pan with small mushrooms cooked in a flour and water *court-bouillon** and shelled crayfish. Pour over a *Normande sauce* (see SAUCE) made with the cooking liquor. Simmer gently. Serve the trout in a deep dish garnished with fried croûtons and crayfish cooked in *court-bouillon*.*

River trout en matelote à la tourangelle. TRUITES DE RIVIÈRE EN MATELOTE À LA TOURANGELLE—The trout are cut in two or in chunks, according to their size. Cook them in red wine (see MATELOTE). Set on a round dish. Garnish with small glazed onions, mushrooms and lardoons cooked with the fish, crayfish cooked in *court-bouillon** and heart-shaped croûtons fried in butter.

Trout à la meunière. TRUITES À LA MEUNIÈRE—Cook the trout in butter with a pinch of salt. When they are cooked, arrange them on a platter. Add the juice of one lemon and a little fresh cream to the butter in the pan. Warm it slightly and pour over the trout. Serve immediately.

Fillets of trout Orly. FILETS DE TRUITES ORLY—Prepared like whiting fillets (see *Whiting Orly.*)

River trout à la vauclusienne. TRUITES DE RIVIÈRE À LA VAUCLUSIENNE—Prepared like *Trout à la meunière*, replacing the butter with olive oil.

River trout au vert. TRUITES DE RIVIÈRE AU VERT—This recipe is mainly suitable for small trout. Proceed as for *Eels au vert**.

River trout in red wine I. TRUITES DE RIVIÈRE AU VIN ROUGE—Season the trout inside and outside with salt and pepper. Put in a baking tin lined, for every four trout, with one onion and one carrot, chopped and lightly cooked in butter. Pour over enough red wine almost to cover the trout. Start cooking on top of the stove, then cover and cook in a hot oven, for 10 minutes.

Drain the trout, wipe and set on a serving dish. Coat with a red wine sauce prepared as follows:

Strain the fish cooking liquor; thicken it with a tablespoon of *Kneaded butter* (see BUTTER, *Compound butters*), cook for a minute. Add 2 tablespoons of fresh butter. Strain.

River trout in red wine II. TRUITES DE RIVIÈRE AU VIN ROUGE—Put in a buttered baking tin the trout, seasoned with salt and pepper. Pour over separately prepared fish *fumet** made with red wine. Cook in the oven. Drain and wipe the trout. Set on a dish. Coat with the cooking liquor thickened with 1½ cups (3 decilitres) of *Espagnole sauce*, based on fish stock, enriched with butter and strained (see SAUCE).

River trout in white wine. TRUITES DE RIVIÈRE AU VIN BLANC—Prepared like *Brill in white wine**.

SALMON TROUT. TRUITE SAUMONÉE—This trout usually has pink flesh, hence its name. Trout with very pale flesh, sometimes even completely white, are also found and are no less excellent in quality.

All the methods of preparation, hot and cold, given elsewhere for salmon are equally applicable to salmon trout. In addition we give the following recipes, which are also applicable to salmon.

Salmon trout Beauharnais. TRUITE SAUMONÉE BEAUHARNAIS—Stuff a medium-sized salmon trout with *Fish forcemeat* (see FORCEMEAT) mixed with 4 tablespoons of *mirepoix** of vegetables (carrots, celery, onions in very small dice, cooked till soft in butter) for every ½ pound (250 grams) of forcemeat.

Put the trout on the grid of a buttered fish-kettle. Pour in fish *fumet** made with white wine, to reach half-way up the fish. Cook in the oven, basting frequently.

Set the trout on a serving dish. Garnish each end of the dish with *Noisette potatoes* (see POTATOES) cooked in butter, and the sides with very small artichoke bottoms cooked in butter and filled with *Beauharnais sauce* (see SAUCE).

Salmon trout Berchoux. TRUITE SAUMONÉE BERCHOUX—Stuff a salmon trout weighing about 4 pounds (2 kilos) with *Pike forcemeat à la crème* (see FORCEMEAT) to which chopped truffles have been added.

Put the trout on the buttered grid of a fish kettle the bottom of which is lined with chopped carrot and onion (one each of medium size) cooked till soft in butter, a good handful of mushroom peelings and a *bouquet garni**.

Pour in fish *fumet** made with white wine to reach half-way up the trout. Season and start cooking on top of the stove, then cover the fish kettle and cook in a slow oven for 40 minutes, basting the fish often during cooking.

Drain the trout, set it on a long dish, remove the central part of the skin so that the black parts of the flesh are seen, Sprinkle the fish with a few tablespoons of its cooking liquor, previously strained, and glaze lightly in the oven.

Surround the trout with the following garnish, the various elements of which should be grouped separately: 8 *barquettes** filled with carp roes and coated with *Normande sauce* (see SAUCE), 8 small croquettes made with *salpicon** of crayfish, mushrooms and truffles bound with *Fish velouté sauce* and fried, and 8 very small artichoke bottoms, half cooked in a flour-and-water *court-bouillon**, simmered in butter, filled with a large-diced *salpicon* of truffles bound with cream, sprinkled with grated Parmesan and browned.

Strain the cooking liquor. Add to this 1½ cups (3 decilitres) of *Velouté sauce* based on fish stock. Boil down over a strong heat, adding to the sauce, little by little, 1½ cups (3 decilitres) of thick fresh cream. Add butter to the sauce and strain. Pour a few tablespoons of sauce into the bottom of the dish. Serve the rest in a sauceboat.

Cold salmon trout

Cold salmon trout with various sauces. TRUITE SAUMONÉE FROIDE—Cook the trout in a *court-bouillon** as for salmon. Allow to cool in its cooking liquor. Drain and wipe. Set on a table napkin. Garnish with bunches of curly parsley. Serve with mayonnaise or any other cold sauce suitable for cold fish (see SAUCE).

Salmon trout en douillette. TRUITE SAUMONÉE EN DOUILLETTE—Fillet when raw a medium-sized trout. Season the fillets with salt and pepper and cook quickly in butter simply to seal them. Allow to cool.

Roll out some ordinary *Brioche dough* (see DOUGH) (made without sugar and kept rather firm) to make a piece of such a shape and size that the fillets can be placed on top.

Put in the middle of the dough a thin layer of *Pike forcemeat à la crème* (see FORCEMEAT). Place a fillet on this forcemeat. Cover the fillet with more forcemeat, to which some diced crayfish and truffles have been added. Put the second fillet on top of this and cover with another thin layer of forcemeat.

Put a rolled-out piece of brioche dough on top of the fish. Fix its edges to the edges of the bottom piece of dough. Make an opening in the middle of the dough to allow steam to escape. Put the *pâté* in a warm place to rise. Brush over the surface with melted butter and sprinkle with fine breadcrumbs. Bake in a moderate oven for 45 minutes.

Set the *pâté* on a long dish. At the last moment, pour

Glazed salmon trout au chambertin (*Robert Carrier*)

over a few tablespoons of melted butter. Serve *Nantua sauce* separately (see SAUCE).

Glazed salmon trout with Chambertin. TRUITE SAUMONÉE FROIDE AU CHAMBERTIN—Prepared like *Glazed salmon au chambertin* (see SALMON).

TROYES CHEESE—See CHEESE.

TRUELLE, TROWEL—A sort of spatula with a curved handle similar to a mason's trowel, used to serve fish and pastries.

TRUFFLAGE—French culinary term for adding of pieces of truffle to chicken or game.

TRUFFLE. TRUFFE—Subterranean fungus of which a number of varieties exist. The black truffle of Périgord and that of the Lot are the most highly esteemed. Truffles are also gathered in Dauphiné, Burgundy and Normandy and in various other regions in France, but all these are inferior in quality and have a less delicate aroma.

The food value of truffles, like other fungi, is problematical; it is difficult to digest because of its close texture.

The white truffle of Piedmont has a slight flavour of garlic which goes well with some dishes; it is most often eaten raw cut in very thin slices. (See WHITE TRUFFLE, following this section.)

To prepare truffles for use with poultry and game—Peel the truffles and cut them in quarters, or if they are not large, leave them whole. Season with salt, pepper, thyme, and powdered bay leaf. Put them to cook for 8 to 10 minutes in pork fat (which may be mixed with foie gras) previously prepared in the following way:

Pound 2 pounds (1 kilo) of fresh pork fat in a mortar with the trimmings of the truffles being used. If a more delicate mixture is desired add ½ pound (250 grams) of raw foie gras. Both fat and foie gras should be cut in large dice. Season with salt, pepper and a pinch of spice. Melt gently over a low heat and put through a fine strainer.

The truffles having been cooked in this truffled fat,

Cleaning truffles (*French Government Tourist Office*)

allow the mixture to cool before using it to 'truffle' the bird being used.

Tinned (canned) truffles. CONSERVE DE TRUFFES—Wash the truffles, scrubbing them under a jet of fresh water, after having previously soaked them in warm water.

Peel them, taking care to remove with the point of a knife all earth deposited in little holes and folds.

Season the truffles with very fine salt mixed with spice and pepper, and leave them in this seasoning for 2 hours.

Set to boil some Madeira wine, and add to it the truffle peelings and a pinch of salt.

Cover the infusion hermetically and leave to cool. Strain.

Put the truffles in one-litre tins. Pour over 1 to 1½ cups (2 or 3 decilitres) of Madeira. Seal the tins. Put them in a pot and cover completely with cold water. Set a weight on top to keep them covered with the water and bring to the highest possible boiling point, which should continue without interruption for 2¼ to 2½ hours, according to the size of the truffles.

Remove from the heat and allow to cool completely.

Note. Any tin (can) which, after boiling, is 'blown', should be considered doubtful and put under observation.

Boiling point can be raised by adding a good handful of salt to the water.

For ½ litre (pint) tins, allow one and a half hours.

For glass jars with special closures (there are innumerable systems, all very practical) the cooking time is the same, but jars or bottles must not be taken from the water until quite cold.

These jars and bottles must be wrapped in straw and set on a thick layer of straw placed in the bottom of the pot.

Truffles with champagne. TRUFFES AU CHAMPAGNE—Put well-cleaned truffles (which should be large and regular in shape) into a deep saucepan with, for every pound (500 grams) of truffles, 2 tablespoons of *mirepoix** of vegetables cooked in butter until soft. Add 1½ cups (3 decilitres) of champagne. Season. Cook, covered, for 15 minutes. Put the truffles into a deep dish (or put each into a little silver *cassolette*).

Sprinkle them with the pan juices, boiled down almost to nothing and mixed with a few tablespoons of thick brown veal gravy. Cover the dish (or *cassolettes*) and keep hot without allowing the liquid to boil for 8 to 10 minutes.

Note. It is customary to prepare truffles cooked in champagne or in any other wine without peeling them. It is nevertheless quite permissible—many people so preferring—to peel the truffles before they are cooked.

Truffles en chaussons (in turnovers). TRUFFES EN CHAUSSONS—Peel some medium-sized truffles and season with spiced salt. Wrap each in a thin rasher (slice) of fat bacon and place each one on a circlet of puff pastry. Moisten the edges of the pastry with water and fold over. Put on a baking sheet, brush with egg, make a little opening in the centre and bake in a hot oven for 18 to 20 minutes.

Truffles à la crème. TRUFFES À LA CRÈME—Stew gently in butter, 1 pound (500 grams) of truffles peeled and cut into thin slices, taking care not to let them dry out.

Season with salt and pepper. Sprinkle with a little brandy. Cover with boiling cream and boil for a moment Drain the truffles and put them in a deep dish. Boil down the cream and add to it for thickening 2 or 4 tablespoons of *Béchamel sauce* (see SAUCE). Add butter, season, strain through a cloth, then pour, boiling hot, over the truffles.

Truffles cooked in embers. TRUFFES SOUS LA CENDRE—Season with salt, pepper and spices, and sprinkle with a little brandy, some large, well cleaned truffles. Wrap each of these truffles first in a very thin bard of fat bacon, then in kitchen paper, sealing them into this paper hermetically by sticking the edges together with *repère* (a mixture of flour and egg white).

Put the truffles thus wrapped into a *tourtière* (metal pie-dish or tin plate) on hot ashes mixed with some glowing embers. Cover with cinders and embers.

Cook the truffles in the cinders for 40 to 45 minutes, then remove from the paper and serve, as they are, on a folded napkin.

Note. It is difficult nowadays to find houses, in towns at least, where there are wood fires and where, consequently, truffles could be cooked in this way. We have nevertheless included this rather archaic recipe because it might possibly be used in country places.

The title *Truffes sous la cendre* is also given to truffles cooked in a pie.

Truffle fritters. BEIGNETS DE TRUFFES—Cut some raw peeled truffles in thick slices. Soak them for an hour with brandy, salt, pepper, thyme and powdered bay leaf.

At the last moment, dip these truffle slices in a light batter and fry in clarified butter. Serve on a napkin.

Truffles for garnish. TRUFFES POUR GARNITURE—According to the type of dish to be garnished, the truffles are cut, raw, after being peeled, into thick or thin slices, large or small dice, quarters or oval shapes, to look like olives.

Cook them gently in butter, for a few minutes only until they are just cooked and no more, because truffles, especially when cut into small pieces or slices, must not be dried out in cooking.

Moisten the truffles with a few tablespoons of the wine indicated by the nature of the preparation, and keep hot, avoiding boiling.

Note. In principle, truffles used for garnish should cook with the foodstuff they are to accompany and should be put into the saucepan with it towards the end of the cooking time.

Instead of fresh truffles, whose season only lasts for a few months in winter, tinned truffles may be used. When using these truffles, which have usually been cooked twice already, before and after being tinned, it is not necessary to do more than heat them with the foodstuff they are to accompany.

Truffles with Madeira or other liqueur. TRUFFES AU MADÈRE—Proceed as for *Truffles with champagne*, replacing the latter with Madeira or other wine.

Truffles à la maréchale. TRUFFES À LA MARÉCHALE—'Remove the skins from 2 pounds of scrubbed, round truffles. Cut them in fairly thick round slices.

'Melt in a saucepan a quarter of butter and a piece of chicken glaze the size of an egg with 2 tablespoons of Madeira. Let all this boil a little but without letting it catch. Then sauté the truffles in it, and afterwards let them steam for 10 to 12 minutes. Sauté them a second time and leave them again, well covered. Above all, *do not let them fry*, but simply glaze lightly. When they are glazed, add 4 tablespoons of very fresh butter, a drop of lemon juice and some small bread croûtons (amounting to half the quantity of the truffles and cut to the same size as the truffles), fried in butter. Mix them well with the truffles and serve.' (Plumerey's recipe.)

Truffles in pastry à la périgourdine. TRUFFES EN PÂTE À LA PÉRIGOURDINE—Proceed as for *Truffles en chaussons* putting under the truffles small slices of raw foie gras seasoned with salt and pepper. Cook in the oven for 18 to 20 minutes.

Truffle purée. PURÉE DE TRUFFES—Rub ½ pound (250 grams) of raw truffles through a fine sieve. Add this truffle purée to 1½ cups (3 decilitres) of thick *Béchamel sauce* (see SAUCE) which has been diluted with a few tablespoons of fresh cream. Season, strain through a cloth, heat the purée and add butter at the last moment.

Note. Truffle purée is used to fill *bouchées* (patties), tartlets and other small preparations of the same kind, or to stuff vegetables, artichoke bottoms, mushrooms, etc.

Truffle rissoles à l'ancienne. RISSOLES DE TRUFFES À L'ANCIENNE—Cut some large peeled truffles in very thick slices. Season with salt, pepper and spices and sprinkle with brandy. Leave to soak for an hour.

Fold each truffle slice in a piece of ordinary *brioche paste.**

At the last moment, fry in deep fat or oil. Drain; set on a napkin.

Truffle rissoles à la Valromey. RISSOLES DE TRUFFES À LA VALROMEY—Sandwich together two by two broad thick slices of truffle with a slice of foie gras in between. Season with salt, pepper and spices; sprinkle with a little brandy.

Set each of these sandwiched slices on a round of puff pastry cut out with a fluted cutter, a little larger in diameter than the truffles. Cover with another round of pastry. Press the edges to stick them together.

Fry at the last moment. Arrange in a mound on a napkin; garnish with fried parsley. Serve *Périgueux sauce* separately (see SAUCE).

Truffle salad. SALADE DE TRUFFES—In principle this salad must be made only with raw truffles, chopped or cut in a *julienne* (thin strips), but in fact, except when truffles are in season, it is made with preserved truffles.

Nor, as a rule, is it truffle alone that is served in this salad. They are usually mixed either with boiled potatoes, cut in rounds or some other way (thus making a *Demi-deuil salad*) or chopped artichoke bottoms (constituting an *Impératrice salad*).

Truffle salad is seasoned with oil, lemon juice, salt and pepper, and should not, in principle, be flavoured with the aromatic herbs often used with other salads.

Sauté of truffles Brillat-Savarin. SAUTÉ DE TRUFFES BRILLAT-SAVARIN—Peel 12 large truffles which must be perfectly ripe, black, firm and regular. Cut each into 4 or 5 thick slices. Season with salt, freshly ground pepper and spice.

Just a few minutes before serving, sauté the truffles in quail fat, taking care not to fry them.

Drain them and set them in a low crust of puff pastry.

Dilute the cooking juices with Madeira, add a little concentrated veal stock, cook down and pour over the truffles.

Sauté of truffles à la provençale. TRUFFES SAUTÉES À LA PROVENÇALE—Peel the truffles and cut them in thick slices. Season them with salt and pepper.

Sauté for a few moments in a sauté pan in which there has been heated a few tablespoons of olive oil with an unpeeled clove of garlic. Avoid overcooking which makes truffles tough.

Truffles à la serviette. TRUFFES À LA SERVIETTE—This dish is so called not because of its method of preparation, which is, in any case, variable, but because of the manner of serving, which is in a napkin folded either in the 'artichoke' or the 'portfolio' style.

Truffles *à la serviette* are most often truffles cooked in Madeira, set in a deep dish or in silver *cassolettes*, and presented on or under a folded napkin.

It would be more logical to call by this name the truffles that are left unpeeled, poached in wine, drained and served on or under a napkin, like potatoes baked in their skins.

Truffles à la serviette cooked in Champagne. TRUFFES À LA SERVIETTE AU VIN DE CHAMPAGNE—'Take three pounds of truffles, the biggest you can find, round, smooth, firm and very black.

'Scrub them in two or three waters. When they are well drained, place them in a saucepan lined with bards of fat bacon and cover them in the same way.

'Cut in large dice a pound of ham which has been de-salted and the same quantity of fillet of veal and fresh bacon fat, and heat in butter in a saucepan, adding chopped carrots and onions, sprigs of parsley and little pieces of thyme, bay leaf, basil, half a clove of garlic and two cloves. Season with very little salt, white pepper, grated nutmeg and a pinch of spice. When these ingredients begin to colour lightly, pour in two bottles of sparkling champagne (Ay is the best). Bring to the boil, skim and simmer gently on the stove, without boiling down, then strain, using pressure, over the truffles. Cook the truffles for an hour before serving. Allow to boil gently for three quarters of an hour, then take off the fire and keep very hot, but without boiling. At the moment of serving drain and serve on a folded napkin in a silver dish; cover with a cloche to send very hot to the table.' (Plumerey's recipe.)

Small truffle soufflés. PETITS SOUFFLÉS DE TRUFFES—These soufflés, which are served as a hot hors-d'oeuvre, are made like ordinary soufflés (see SOUFFLÉ), using purée of truffles bound with egg yolks, to which stiffly beaten egg whites are added.

This mixture is put into *cassolettes** and cooked in the oven in the ordinary way.

Timbale of truffles. TIMBALE DE TRUFFES—Line a buttered *timbale* mould with rather low sides with ordinary *Lining paste* (see DOUGH). Cover the bottom and sides with thin strips of bacon fat. Fill to within ⅛ inch of the top with peeled raw truffles seasoned with salt, pepper and spices and sprinkled with brandy.

Moisten with a glass of Madeira and 3 tablespoons of very concentrated brown veal gravy. Cover the truffles with a bard of bacon fat. Cover the timbale with pastry.

Brush with egg. Cook in a hot oven for 50 to 55 minutes.

Turn out the timbale and set on a napkin.

Truffle tourte à la périgourdine. TOURTE DE TRUFFES À LA PÉRIGOURDINE—Spread on a round of fine pastry set on a baking tin a layer of raw foie gras cut in large dice, seasoned with salt, pepper and spices and sprinkled with brandy, covering the pastry to within ⅛ inch of the edge only.

Put on top of this foie gras some truffles, scrubbed, peeled, seasoned with salt, pepper and spices and sprinkled with brandy. On top of the truffles place small slices of seasoned foie gras.

Cover with a similar round of fine pastry and seal the edges. Decorate the top with small cut-out shapes of fine pastry. Make a small opening in the middle to allow steam to escape. Brush with egg. Cook in a hot oven for 40 to 45 minutes. When it is cooked, pour into the *tourte* a few tablespoons of *Demi-glace sauce* (see SAUCE) reduced with Madeira and truffle *essence**.

Tourte aux truffes is served hot, but can also be served cold.

WHITE TRUFFLES. TRUFFES BLANCHES—White truffles come chiefly from the North of Italy, principally from Piedmont. They are also called Piedmont truffles.

White truffles are also found in North Africa and in

some regions of France, but they are not at all like those which come from Italy either in aroma or texture.

The white truffle, which has a slight taste of garlic, is scarcely ever eaten other than raw, cut in thin slices.

When it is used as a garnish for hot dishes it is added at the very end of the cooking, and is not cooked itself other than by the heat of the foodstuff it accompanies. It is used in this way with *Risotto aux truffes blanches*. It is not added to this preparation until cooking is completely finished and, even then, when it is removed from heat.

White truffles cut in dice or thin slices are used to garnish egg dishes of various kinds, notably omelettes and scrambled eggs. Where these preparations are concerned, the white truffles are not added to the scrambled eggs until after they are cooked, but are put, raw, into the beaten egg before making the omelettes.

Finally, the white truffle is most often used in salad. This salad, like that made with black truffles, is seasoned with olive oil, lemon juice, salt and pepper.

White truffle risotto. TRUFFES BLANCHES AU RISOTTO—Cover with white truffles, peeled and cut into thin slivers and seasoned, a Parmesan risotto, set in a deep dish. Cover and keep hot for five minutes on a corner of the stove.

Sauté of Piedmont truffles. SAUTÉ DE TRUFFES DU PIÉMONT—'Take a dozen Piedmont truffles, well scrubbed; remove the skin carefully and cut them into very thin rounds; dissolve in a pot, on a low heat, some chicken glaze the size of an egg with four spoonfuls of oil, put in the truffles and season with a little white pepper, a little salt and a little grated nutmeg. Cover and cook over a good heat for 10 minutes, tossing them often (they need no more cooking), add a few pieces of fresh butter, the juice of half a lemon and serve.

'In Paris the oil is almost always replaced by butter, but nevertheless, oil is the true stamp of the Italian manner.

'At the outset of the preparation of *salmis* at the table, some noblemen rather like to cook the Piedmont truffles themselves. This is how they are prepared: Chop the truffles with a cucumber slicer; put in the bottom of a silver casserole a few spoonfuls of olive oil or butter, according to taste and some good glaze the size of an egg cut into small pieces. Place the truffles on top with some salt, white pepper and grated nutmeg. Sprinkle a few drops of oil over the truffles, or set a few pieces of fine butter on top.

'This silver casserole, its lid in place, is set on top of a spirit heater, set alight, set in front of the host, who with the aid of a spoon turns the truffles frequently, replacing the lid of the casserole each time.

'Seven to eight minutes are enough for the cooking; the *seigneur* adds the juice of a lemon and serves himself.' (Plumerey's recipe).

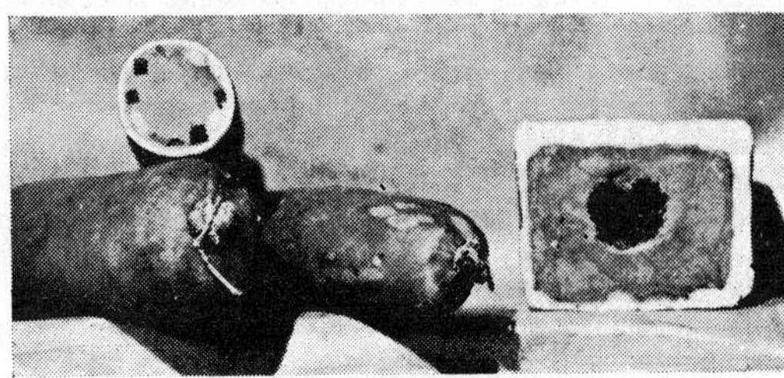

Truffled saucissons of foie gras and truffled pâté de foie gras

TRUFFLE. TRUFFER—To garnish or stuff with truffles. Used also to describe the action of studding a foodstuff with small pieces of truffle.

TRUIE DE MER (SEA-SOW)—A French name for *Hog-fish*, more usually called *Rascasse*.

TRUSS. BRIDER—To thread a string to secure the legs and wings of poultry and game with the aid of a strong needle, called a trussing needle.

The trussing of poultry and game is done in different ways depending on the nature of the finished dish.

For roasting, the legs are left outside, for braising, poaching or pot-roasting their end bones are worked under the skin.

Before being trussed, poultry and game should be dressed; that is plucked, cleaned and singed.

TUFTED LARK. HUPPE—A kind of lark whose flesh sometimes has a musky flavour. It is cooked in the same way as *lark**.

TUILES (Petits-fours)—Cream together in a bowl ½ pound (250 grams) of butter and 1¾ cups (250 grams) of fine sugar. Add 5 eggs, one by one, then 2 cups (250 grams) of sifted cake flour. Pipe this mixture on to a baking tin in rounds with the aid of a forcing (pastry) bag. Bake in the oven.

When they come out of the oven bend each one over a rolling pin so that they are given the shape of curved tiles (*tuiles*).

Tuiles with almonds. TUILES AUX AMANDES—Cream together in a bowl ½ pound (250 grams) of ground almonds, 1 cup (250 grams) of sugar and 4 egg whites. Flavour with vanilla or any other flavouring. Pipe on to the baking tin and bake in the oven. Finish off as above.

TULIP. TULIPE—There are a great many different kinds of tulip but only one, the 'wild tulip', a plant growing in the South of France, is edible. It is the root that is eaten, and it may be prepared like Jerusalem artichoke, or sweet potato.

TUN. FÛT—A cask large enough to hold several hogsheads.

TUNNY (TUNA FISH). THON—Fish found in warm and temperate seas. The tunny is a large, strong, spindle-shaped fish.

It lives in the warm parts of the Atlantic and the Mediterranean, and is scarcely ever found beyond the Bay of Biscay. Many species of tunny, all related to the mackerel family, are found in both the Atlantic and Pacific coasts of the United States.

The white tunny or *germon* is found as high as the coast of Brittany. This is similar to the albacore of the Pacific.

The *thonine* which is called the *thouna* at Nice and the *thounina* at Sète is found only in the Mediterranean. It never grows to more than 3 feet in length. It is fished in the region of Nice from May to October. Its flesh is firm, oily and savoury and has some resemblance to veal. Tunny is eaten fresh, salted, smoked or canned in oil.

Tunny (tuna) à la provençale. THON À LA PROVENÇALE—Stud a round cut of tunny (tuna) with anchovy fillets. Marinate it in oil, lemon juice, salt and pepper for an hour.

Just colour the fish on both sides in oil in a sauté pan. Add a chopped onion lightly cooked in butter (or oil), 2 very large tomatoes peeled, seeded and crushed, a small clove of garlic, also crushed, and a bouquet garni. Pour over ¾ cup (1½ decilitres) of white wine.

Finish cooking in the oven, basting often.

Drain the fish and set on a round dish. Cover with the concentrated cooking liquor to which a little *Espagnole sauce* and some capers have been added. Instead of thickening the sauce with Espagnole, a spoonful of

Kneaded butter may be used (see BUTTER, *Compound butters*).

TURBAN—Word much used in French cookery to describe the way some foodstuffs are arranged on a dish in a circle.

The same word is used to describe certain preparations, mostly forcemeat, which are cooked in border moulds. Thus, 'turbans' of fish, crustaceans, various kinds of poultry, game, etc., can be made.

TURBOT—Large European flat fish, one of the most delicate of its kind. Its nearest American relative is the halibut.

The turbot has a lozenge-shaped body. Its skin seems to lack scales completely: they are so minute that they need not be removed.

The turbot has its eyes on the left side of its body, the side which is generally yellowish-grey or brown, dotted with little black and white marks. The other side is white. On the grey or brown side the little conical tubercles which give the turbot its name of *turbot piquant* are to be found.

Turbot double is a species which has coloured skin on both sides. The flesh of this species is mediocre.

The normal size of the turbot is from 16 to 32 inches long. Its flesh is white, firm, flaky and savoury.

The brill, sometimes called *turbot lisse* in French, belongs to the same family.

Small-sized turbots, known as chicken turbot in English, are *turbotins* in French. They are cooked in the same way as ordinary turbot.

Turbot à l'américaine—Proceed as for *Brill à l'américaine**.

Turbot à l'amiral—Proceed as for *Brill à l'amiral**.

Turbot à la Bercy—Proceed as for *Brill à la Bercy**.

Boiled turbot with various sauces. TURBOT BOUILLI—Large turbots, whole, or cut into chunks or *darnes* (like salmon) are cooked in this way.

This fish is cooked in a *court-bouillon** composed of salted milk and water, with slices of lemon, allowing to each quart (litre) of water: ½ cup (1 decilitre) of milk, 2½ teaspoons (15 grams) of salt and one slice of lemon with the skin removed.

To prevent damage during cooking, the head of the turbot can be tied.

The turbot is put into the *turbotière* (a fish kettle specially shaped to cook turbot), using the grid so that it can more easily be removed when cooked. Pour over enough cold *court-bouillon* to cover the fish.

Start boiling gently. As soon as the liquid begins to boil, remove the *turbotière* to a corner of the stove and allow it to poach, allowing 6 minutes to every pound (12 minutes per kilo).

Accompaniment to boiled turbot—The fish, carefully drained and wiped, is set on a large dish covered with a table napkin or placed on the grid of a dish specially designed for boiled fish, and garnished with fresh parsley in bunches.

It is served with boiled potatoes (served in a separate dish) and one or other of the sauces suitable for boiled fish.

Turbot à la bonne femme—Proceed as for *Brill à la bonne femme**.

Braised turbot with various garnishes and sauces. TURBOT BRAISÉ—Turbot left whole, cut in pieces or filleted, is braised in white or red wine, in any of the ways given for *Braised brill* (see BRILL).

Turbot à la cancalaise—Turbot left whole, cut in pieces or filleted, cooked in white wine. Drain the fish, set it on a serving dish; garnish with oysters poached, drained and de-bearded, and shelled crayfish. Coat with *Normande sauce* (see SAUCE) to which the strained oyster liquor has been added.

Cold turbot. TURBOT FROID—Whole turbot or turbot cut in chunks or *darnes* may be served cold.

It is accompanied by one or other of the cold sauces suitable for cold fish, such as *Mayonnaise*, *Tartare*, *Rémoulade*, *Verte*, *Gribiche*, etc. (see SAUCE).

It is served as it is, set on a table napkin and garnished with fresh parsley, or it is surrounded on the serving dish with one or other of the garnishes recommended for cold fish.

Creamed turbot au gratin. TURBOT À LA CRÈME AU GRATIN—Prepared with sliced left-over turbot like *Creamed cod au gratin* (see COD).

Turbot Dugléré (*Mac Fisheries*)

Turbot Dugléré—Proceed as for *Bass Dugléré**.

Fillets of turbot. FILETS DE TURBOT—Turbot is filleted raw, and medium-sized fish should be chosen.

All the methods of preparation given for fillets of brill or sole are applicable to fillet of turbot.

Fried turbot. TURBOT FRIT—In general only very small turbots, fillets or *darnes* are fried. See BRILL, *Fried brill*.

However, Brillat-Savarin, who in his *Twelfth Meditation* devoted a long study to frying, assures his readers that it is possible to fry very large turbots.

He even says that his master cook, La Planche, did this perfectly, and at the conclusion of the *Théorie de la Friture* he compliments him: 'You have tried my "hell", and you have been the first to have the glory of offering to an astonished universe an immense fried turbot. This day there was great jubilation among the elect.'

Turbot fried in batter. FRITOT DE TURBOT—Cut filleted turbot into 'matchsticks'. Put these pieces of fish to soak for 30 minutes in oil, lemon juice, chopped parsley, salt and pepper.

Just before serving, dip the matchsticks one by one into a light batter and fry them in smoking hot deep fat or oil.

Drain, wipe and season with fine dry salt. Served heaped on napkin-covered dish. Garnish with fried parsley and lemon. Serve with *Tomato sauce* (see SAUCE).

Turbot au gratin—Prepared whole in the case of small fish, or cut in pieces if it is large. Proceed as for *Sole au gratin**.

Grilled turbot. TURBOT GRILLÉ—Chicken turbot or *turbotins* are mostly prepared in this way. Large turbots can also be grilled, cut into thickish *darnes* or filleted.

Grilled turbot is accompanied either by *Maître d'hôtel*

butter or by one of the sauces usually served with grilled fish. See BUTTER, *Compound butters* and SAUCE.

Proceed to cook the turbot in the same way as *Grilled brill* (see BRILL).

Turbot kedgeree. CADGERY DE TURBOT—Cut 1 pound (500 grams) of cooked turbot in small slices. Heat this fish in butter. Set in a deep dish in layers alternating with 4 cups (500 grams) of *Pilaf rice**, prepared in the usual way but not too much cooked, and bound with 2½ cups (5 decilitres) of rather thin *Béchamel sauce* (see SAUCE) seasoned with curry. Strew diced hard boiled eggs over each layer of turbot. Coat the last layer of rice with the same sauce.

Turbot or chicken turbot en matelote—Cut the turbot into regular pieces. Prepare as *Sole en matelote à la normande**.

Set on a long dish. Garnish with crayfish, fried smelts and croûtons.

Turbot à la pèlerine—Season the turbot with salt and pepper. Put it on a baking tin lined, for a fish of 4 pounds (2 kilos) with ¾ cup (150 grams) of chopped onion cooked till tender in butter without colouring.

Sprinkle the fish with melted butter. Cook gently in the oven, without adding any moisture.

Set on a long dish. Dilute the pan juices with white wine, add thick fresh cream, boil down, add butter, strain and pour over the fish.

Glaze well in the oven. Garnish with fried scallops set in a mound at each end of the dish.

Turbot à la Saint-Malo—This method is suitable for small fish.

Make shallow cuts on both sides, season with salt and pepper, brush with oil and grill gently.

Put on a serving dish. Surround with boiled potatoes cut into thick round slices and fried in butter. Garnish at each end with fresh parsley. Serve *Saint-Malo sauce* separately (see SAUCE).

Scalloped turbot. COQUILLES DE TURBOT—Prepared with left-over turbot like *Brill in scallop shells**.

Turbot à la vénitienne—Proceed as for *Fillets of sole à la vénitienne* (see SOLE).

Turbot Victoria—Proceed as for *Brill à la Victoria.*

Turbot in white wine. TURBOT AU VIN BLANC—Prepared with the turbot left whole, in chunks or in fillets, like *Brill in white wine.*

TURBOTIÈRE—Square-shaped fish kettle, provided with a removable grid, called *turbotière* because it is chiefly used for cooking turbot and other flat fish.

TUREEN. SOUPIÈRE—Broad, deep dish in which soup is served.

It was not until the eighteenth century that the tureen made its appearance on the French table. Before that soup had been poured out of the kitchen *marmite* directly into covered bowls which were carried, filled, to the guests. In the reign of Louis XV the goldsmith Thomas Germain (see SILVERWARE) made magnificent tureens. The most beautiful were made at Sèvres, Strasbourg, Moustiers, Rouen, etc. In the nineteenth century and twentieth century the tureen continued to make part of the dinner service and to follow the evolution of fashion and style.

TURKEY. DINDE, DINDON, DINDONNEAU—There are two main varieties of turkey: the wild turkey, native of North America, and the farmyard turkey, which is bred in poultry runs. The origin of this bird is uncertain. Some authorities believe that it comes from Bermuda in the West Indies, others that its original habitat was North America.

It seems most likely that the first home of the turkey was that immense tract of land which stretches from the extreme north-western boundary of the United States to the isthmus of Panama, that is to say, the periphery of the Gulf of Mexico.

In Canada and other parts of North America, now so thickly populated, wild turkeys were once very plentiful but the inroads of civilization and agriculture have driven them little by little towards the centre of the continent, which to this day is more sparsely settled.

Brillat-Savarin, who devoted a long paragraph of his *Sixth Meditation* to turkeys and turkey-lovers, refuses to give any credence to the theory that this bird comes from the Old World. 'The turkey', he says, 'is certainly one of the finest gifts made by the New World to the Old.

'Those who always like to know best have said that the turkey was known to the Romans, that it was served at Charlemagne's wedding feast, and that it is thus erroneous to attribute to the Jesuits the credit for this savoury import.

'Only two things can be said in reply to this paradox: (1) The name of the bird (in France *Dinde* or *D'Inde*, meaning from India), since in the past America was known as the West Indies; (2) The face of the turkey which is clearly that of a foreigner (this last argument of the master's seems weak indeed). No wise man could be mistaken about it'.

And Brillat-Savarin declares peremptorily that 'the turkey appeared in Europe towards the end of the seventeenth century; that it was imported by the Jesuits who reared these birds in large numbers especially on a farm which they owned in the region of Bourges; that it is from there that they spread little by little all over France; which is why in popular speech in many parts of the country, people used to, and still do, refer to a turkey as a "Jesuit". America is the only place in which wild turkeys have been found in a state of nature (there are none in Africa); and on the farms of North America, where turkeys are very common, they are bred either from wild eggs hatched by a tame hen or from young poults caught in the woods and tamed, with the result that the flocks are closer to nature and retain more of their natural plumage'.

After having put forward all this evidence of whose authenticity he is convinced, Brillat-Savarin speaks of the influence of the turkey on the economy of the U.S.A., and tells a delightful story of how in Hartford, Connecticut, he had 'the satisfaction of killing a wild turkey' and how he prepared it with his own hands. 'During the whole of our journey back from the hunt', he says, 'I was reflecting on the manner in which I would cook my turkey, and was somewhat troubled for fear that I should not find everything I wanted in Hartford, because I wanted to acquire great merit by the display of my rich prize'.

And Brillat-Savarin says that after having—still with his own hands—prepared partridge wings *en papillote* and cooked grey squirrels in a Madeira *court-bouillon*, he roasted the famous turkey. 'This turkey', he says, 'was delightful to look at, titillating to smell and delicious to taste'.

In French the word *dindon* (turkey-cock) is scarcely ever used in the language of cookery. On menus the bird is almost always called *dindonneau* (young turkey) or sometimes, with reference to a hen bird, *dinde* (turkey hen).

But it must be understood that *dinde* implies a young and consequently tender hen-bird of about 5–8 pounds.

All recipes for *chicken* are suitable for hen turkeys

and young turkey-cocks. Nevertheless, here are a few special recipes for turkey.

Turkey à l'anglaise. DINDONNEAU À L'ANGLAISE—Truss the turkey with the legs pressed tightly against the breast. Poach in a poultry stock. See CHICKEN, *Boiled chicken à l'anglaise.*

Ballottine of turkey à la toulousaine. BALLOTTINE DE DINDONNEAU À LA TOULOUSAINE—Bone a young turkey; stuff it with *Quenelle forcemeat II* (see FORCEMEAT) mixed with a *salpicon** of lambs' sweetbreads, mushrooms and truffles. Roll the turkey into a long tight bundle (*ballottine*). Wrap in a fine cloth. Poach in a very little concentrated poultry stock.

Drain the ballottine. Put it on a serving dish, either directly on the dish or raised on a slice of fried bread. Surround with a *Toulouse garnish* (see GARNISHES). Coat with *Suprême sauce* (see SAUCE) with the concentrated cooking stock added to it.

Ballottine of turkey can be served brown instead of white by cooking it in braising stock as indicated for *Braised chicken* (see CHICKEN). Cooked in this way the *ballottine* can be served with various garnishes such as *Chipolata, Financière, Godard, Turtle*, etc., or with braised vegetables or macaroni or other *pasta* prepared *à l'italienne, à la milanaise* or *à la napolitaine*, or with *risotto*.

Ballottine of turkey to be served cold is prepared in the same way. It is poached, like galantine of chicken, in a jelly stock. After cooling under a weight, it is served, coated with its own jelly (which must first be clarified), or presented in a glass bowl completely covered in jelly.

Braised turkey (with various garnishes). DINDONNEAU BRAISÉ—Cook a turkey in braising stock. When it is ready, drain and untruss it. Put it on a serving dish surrounded with the garnish indicated in the selected recipe. Skim all fat off the braising stock. Boil down and strain the stock. Pour it over the turkey. Braised turkey-hens or cocks can be garnished with different vegetables, some of which should be cooked with the bird, others separately. Among the garnishes most suitable for braised turkey (which can be served as a main course or as a prelude to it) are the following: *Alsacienne*; braised sauerkraut; smoked belly of pork; Strasbourg sausages; *Bourguignonne* (the bird being braised in red wine with mushrooms and glazed onions); belly of pork lardoons; braised celery; mushrooms; chipolatas; *Fermière*; *Financière*; *Languedocienne*; *Napolitaine*; *Milanaise*; *Piémontaise*; *Strasbourgeoise*. See GARNISHES.

Braised stuffed turkey. DINDONNEAU FARCI BRAISÉ—Stuff the turkey with fine stuffing or some other mixture, and proceed as for *Stuffed chicken.* See CHICKEN.

Stuffed turkey is served with various garnishes. All those indicated for chicken may be used.

Casserole or cocotte of turkey. DINDONNEAU EN CASSEROLE, EN COCOTTE—Proceed as for *Casserole* or *Cocotte of chicken.* See CHICKEN.

Turkeys cooked *en casserole* or *en cocotte* can be served with various garnishes such as artichokes, egg-plant (aubergine), mushrooms, very small marrows (zucchini, courgettes), small onions, potatoes, truffles, etc.

Turkey à la chipolata. DINDONNEAU À LA CHIPOLATA—Truss a turkey with the legs tightly pressed against the breast. Bard it. Pot-roast in butter.

Serve it either straight on a serving dish or raised on a platform of sandwich bread fried in butter (when the turkey is raised thus, it can be entirely surrounded by the garnish).

Surround with a garnish of chipolatas, arranged in little clumps with spaces between (see GARNISHES). Pour on the cooking stock diluted with Madeira and thickened brown veal stock or chicken stock boiled down and strained.

Cold turkey. DINDONNEAU FROID—All recipes for cold chicken are suitable for turkey.

Daube of turkey à la bourgeoise. DINDONNEAU EN DAUBE À LA BOURGEOISE—For this dish a tender turkey-hen (5-7 pounds) must be used and not a young turkey cock. Braise the bird in a brown stock as indicated for *Braised chicken* (see CHICKEN). When it is three parts cooked, drain the turkey. Strain the braising stock. Put the bird back in the braising pan. Surround with a *bourgeoise* garnish made of carrots cut into pear shapes (or small new carrots), three parts cooked as for glazed carrots, small glazed onions and pieces of belly of pork, blanched and fried. Pour over the whole the strained braising stock Cover pan and finish cooking in a moderate oven.

Fricassée of turkey. FRICASSÉE DE DINDONNEAU—Using a young and tender turkey, proceed as for *Fricassée of chicken.**

Galantine of hen-turkey en bellevue. DINDE EN GALANTINE EN BELLEVUE—Proceed with a young hen-turkey (5-7 pounds) as indicated for *Galantine of chicken* (see CHICKEN). Cook the turkey in a jelly stock containing a great many gelatinous ingredients (calves' feet, knuckle of veal, poultry carcases, fresh pork skin).

Drain the galantine. Unwrap it. Cool under a weight. Mask the galantine with *White chaud-froid sauce*, flavoured with Madeira and made with some of the poultry stock, the remainder of this being used to make a poultry jelly. See JELLY and SAUCE.

Decorate the galantine with truffles, pickled tongue and the white of hard boiled egg. Highlight with jelly.

Serve on a long dish, decorated with jelly motifs.

This galantine can also be served on a plinth.

Turkey giblets. ABATIS DE DINDONNEAU—Proceed as for giblets of chicken and other poultry. See GIBLETS.

Grilled turkey. DINDONNEAU GRILLÉ—Only very small turkeys are prepared in this way. Proceed as for *Grilled chicken.* See CHICKEN.

Turkey hash. HACHIS DE DINDONNEAU—Proceed, using turkey scraps as for *Poultry hash.* See HASH.

Braised turkey legs with various garnishes. CUISSES DE DINDONNEAU BRAISÉES—The legs of large turkeys, whose wings or breasts have been used in some other way, are prepared thus:

Bone the legs. Fill with a stuffing of some kind. Roll them into little long, tight bundles (*ballottines*). Braise in the usual way in white or brown stock. Glaze in the oven. Arrange on a serving dish. Garnish according to the recipe selected. Mask with their cooking sauce.

Legs of turkey prepared in this way are often called turkey hams.

Turkey liver. FOIE DE DINDONNEAU—All recipes for chicken liver are suitable for turkey liver. They can be served skewered with pilaf or risotto, or sautéed with various garnishes, etc. Like chicken livers, turkey livers can be used as an ingredient of various stuffings.

They are also served colloped (sliced) and sautéed, as a garnish with eggs cooked in different ways, especially omelettes and scrambled eggs.

Hot turkey pâté. PÂTÉ CHAUD DE DINDONNEAU—Using boned turkey, proceed as for *Hot chicken pâté.* See PÂTÉ.

Prepared in the same way (in a pâté crust) turkey pâté can also be served cold. When it is cold, a few tablespoons of concentrated poultry jelly are poured into the pâté through the hole made to allow steam to escape during cooking.

Turkey pinions. AILERONS DE DINDONNEAU—These are usually stuffed and braised, and served with various garnishes. See PINIONS.

Poupeton of turkey Brillat-Savarin. POUPETON DE DINDONNEAU BRILLAT-SAVARIN—Bone a small turkey as for a galantine. Stuff with a mixture of fine veal stuffing and *à gratin stuffing* (see FORCEMEAT) enriched with lambs' sweetbreads braised in white stock, diced *foie gras* and coarsely diced truffles.

Roll the turkey into a long tight bundle. Wrap it in pig's caul, then in butter muslin. Tie it securely.

Put this *poupeton* in a buttered *daube* pan lined with raw ham, onion rings and carrots. Cover and cook gently for 15 minutes. Pour over it a glass of Madeira. Boil down. Moisten with poultry stock and finish cooking in the oven, covered. Strain and boil down the cooking stock and serve as sauce with the turkey.

Turkey *poupeton* can also be served cold. After cooking, it is left to cool under a weight and served masked with poultry jelly.

Ragoût of turkey. RAGOÛT DE DINDONNEAU—Using turkey cut into pieces, proceed as indicated for *Goose ragoût*. Various garnishes can be served with turkey ragoût. Among the most suitable are the following: *Bourgeoise*, new carrots, celeriac, mushrooms, chipolata, artichoke hearts, chestnuts, potatoes. See GARNISHES.

Roast turkey. DINDONNEAU RÔTI—Truss a small turkey and bard the breast with pork fat. Roast on the spit, allowing 20 minutes per pound or in the oven for 25 minutes per pound.

Before the turkey is fully cooked, remove the barding and brown the breast evenly.

Serve with the diluted cooking stock and with watercress.

Roast turkey à l'anglaise (*John Cowderoy*)

Roast turkey à l'anglaise. DINDONNEAU RÔTI À L'ANGLAISE—Stuff the turkey with a sage and onion stuffing prepared as follows: Bake the onions in their skins in the oven. Peel and chop them. Toss in butter. Season with a pinch of chopped sage. Mix with an equal quantity of breadcrumbs, dipped in milk and squeezed, and half their quantity of chopped veal fat.

Roast the turkey in the usual way. Put it on a serving dish surrounded with slices of bacon or grilled sausages. Serve the cooking gravy and *Bread sauce* separately. See SAUCES.

Turkey with chestnut stuffing. DINDONNEAU FARCI AUX MARRONS—Stuff a medium-sized turkey (5 pounds) with best sausage meat, allowing 1¼ to 1½ pounds (600 to 800 grams), according to the size of the bird, mixed with chestnuts two-thirds cooked in clear chicken or veal stock flavoured with celery.

So as to be able to stuff the bird very full, take away the breast bone. Truss the turkey and bard it. Roast on the spit or in the oven, basting frequently during cooking. Serve with its own gravy.

Stuffed turkey-hen grand-duc. DINDE ÉTOUFFÉE GRAND-DUC—'Slit open a hen-turkey (about 6 pounds) along the back and stuff with the following mixture:

'1 pound (500 grams) of chicken rubbed through a fine sieve; 2 cups (½ litre) of double cream; ½ pound (250 grams) of *foie gras*, poached in port wine; rubbed through a sieve. Mix all these ingredients thoroughly and season.

'Add to this mixture 12 truffles, peeled and cooked for 10 minutes in a little liqueur brandy, 24 chicken hearts soaked in water, with all veins removed, steeped in white Malaga wine, drained, dried in a cloth, stuffed with a purée of York ham and poached for 15 minutes in *Truffle essence*. See ESSENCE.

'Fold the stuffed turkey carefully into shape. Wrap in slices of raw ham or bacon. Encase it in a large layer of lining pastry, taking care to keep the shape of the bird as far as possible. Bake in the oven for 2½ hours.

'During cooking, which must be slow, cover the turkey with greaseproof paper folded in four, so that it will cook all through without browning too soon.

'To serve, present the turkey as it comes out of the oven, and serve with it a sauce-boat full of *Demi-glace sauce* (see SAUCE) flavoured with truffle essence.' (Recipe of M. Valmy-Joyeuse, who created this dish in 1906 while he was in charge of the kitchens of the Marquise of Mazenda.)

Truffled turkey. DINDONNEAU TRUFFÉ—Discriminating gourmets believe that to achieve the best results, a truffled bird should be stuffed with truffles four or five days before cooking. After the truffles have fulfilled their function in flavouring the bird, they are removed and discarded and the bird is stuffed afresh with more truffles mixed with pork fat or raw *foie gras*, and then cooked.

We merely mentioned in passing this somewhat complicated method. The following method of preparing truffled turkey (or any other poultry or winged game) is far more practical:

Prepare a *Poultry forcemeat for truffled poultry*. See FORCEMEAT.

Truffling. Draw the turkey, leaving the skin of the neck very long so as to be able to close the opening in the bird securely when trussing. (This can be done by your poultry dealer.)

Under the skin of the turkey, that is to say between the flesh and the skin, insert a dozen large slices of truffle, seasoned and sprinkled with a few drops of brandy. Stuff and truss the turkey and wrap it in a sheet of buttered greaseproof paper. Leave to stand in a cool place for 24 hours at least.

Cooking. Bard the turkey. Wrap it in buttered paper. Roast on the spit in front of a hot fire, allowing 30 minutes per pound, or roast in the oven in a roasting pan, uncovered, for 25 to 30 minutes per pound.

Unwrap and untruss the turkey. Brown it. Put it on a serving dish and serve with its own diluted gravy, enriched, if desired, with *Périgueux sauce*. See SAUCE.

The truffled pork fat stuffing can be made without *foie gras*, but this ingredient greatly improves the flavour.

TURNIP. NAVET—A pot vegetable of European origin with a fleshy and sweetish root. It was cultivated in India before the Aryan invasion.

Young tender turnips are usually easy to digest but large turnips are somewhat indigestible. Turnips have the property of absorbing large quantities of fat (like haricot beans), and for this reason they are traditionally served with fatty meat (mutton, duck, etc.).

Turnips, which are sold in French markets all the year round, are mainly used, like carrots, parsnips, leeks and onions, as pot vegetables. In France, the best turnips for this purpose come from Meaux.

Spring turnips are used in *navarins*, and especially as a garnish for duckling.

Turnips are also used in the preparation of thick and cream soups. They are less commonly eaten as a vegetable on their own.

There are many varieties of turnips which can be put in two main classes, the long-rooted and the flat-rooted. The latter is superior to the first for flavour and sweetness.

Boiled turnips. NAVETS À L'ANGLAISE—Proceed as for *Boiled carrots*. See CARROT.

Turnips in cream. NAVETS À LA CRÈME—Only very tender spring turnips can be prepared in this way. Trim the turnips to look like olives and proceed as for *Carrots à la crème*.*

Glazed turnips (garnish). NAVETS GLACÉS—Proceed as for *Glazed carrots*. See CARROT.

Turnips to be further cooked in the sauce of the main dish can be prepared in this way: Trim the turnips to look like olives (or if they are small, leave them whole). Sauté in butter in a frying-pan. Season with salt and sprinkle with castor (fine) sugar. Sauté for a few seconds over a very high flame to brown them slightly. Finish cooking with the main dish (duck, shoulder of mutton, etc.).

Turnips au gratin or Mornay. NAVETS AU GRATIN DITS MORNAY—Cut the turnips into rather thick round slices. Parboil these slices. Cool under running water. Drain. Cook slowly in butter. When they are ready, put them in an ovenware dish lined with *Mornay sauce* (see SAUCE). Cover with *Mornay sauce*. Sprinkle with grated cheese. Pour on melted butter. Brown slowly.

Turnip mould. PAIN DE NAVETS—Proceed, using purée of turnips, as indicated for *Carrot timbale*.*

Turnips with chopped parsley. NAVETS AUX FINES HERBES—Trim the turnips to look like olives or cut into round slices. Parboil them in salt water until they are fairly tender. Cool under running water and drain.

Sauté the turnips in butter in a frying pan. Season with salt and a large pinch of castor (fine) sugar. Cook slowly, tossing frequently.

At the last moment, sprinkle with chopped parsley.

Turnip purée. PURÉE DE NAVETS—Proceed, using turnips, as indicated in the recipe for *Cardoon purée*.*

Purée of turnip soup—See SOUPS AND BROTHS.

Turnip soufflé. SOUFFLÉ AUX NAVETS—Proceed, using purée of turnips, as indicated for *Carrot soufflé*.*

Stuffed turnips. NAVETS FARCIS—Choose round turnips of equal size. Peel neatly, cut round the base of the stalks and scoop out. Parboil the scooped-out turnips until they are fairly tender.

Make a purée of the scooped-out pulp. Add to it half its weight of mashed potatoes. Mix well, season and add butter.

Stuff the turnips with this mixture, smoothing it into the shape of a dome.

Put the turnips in a buttered baking dish. Pour on melted butter. Finish cooking in the oven, basting frequently.

Stuffed turnips (garnish). NAVETS FARCIS—Neatly peel some large, tender turnips. Press a corer into each one (starting at the base of the stalks). Do not drive the corer through to the other side.

Parboil the turnips until they are fairly tender. Cool them under running water. Drain and remove the cores. Force the cores through a sieve. Add an equal quantity of dry *Duxelles*.*

Fill the turnips with this stuffing. Smooth the surface into a dome.

Put the turnips in a buttered baking dish. Pour on melted butter. Bake in the oven, basting frequently.

As soon as the turnips are cooked, sprinkle with breadcrumbs and brown quickly.

Stuffed turnips à la duxelles. NAVETS FARCIS À LA DUXELLES—Proceed as indicated for *Stuffed turnips*, filling the scooped-out turnips with a *Duxelles** mixture to which the pulp of the turnips has been added after having been stewed and rubbed through a sieve.

Put the turnips in a buttered baking dish. Moisten with a few tablespoons of clear soup or clear veal stock. Sprinkle with breadcrumbs. Pour on melted butter. Bake in a slow oven.

Stuffed turnips à la piémontaise. NAVETS FARCIS À LA PIÉMONTAISE—Proceed as indicated for *Stuffed turnips*, filling the turnips with *Risotto* (see RICE) mixed with the finely diced pulp stewed in butter. Sprinkle with grated Parmesan. Pour on melted butter. Brown in a slow oven.

Turnips in sugar. NAVETS AU SUCRE—Peel and quarter the turnips. Trim to look like olives (parboil them if they are old). Sauté in butter in a frying pan, seasoning with salt and a little sugar. When they are browned, put them in a stew-pan. Moisten with veal stock, cover and stew until all the moisture has evaporated.

Serve in a vegetable dish, or use as a garnish.

TURNOVER. CHAUSSON—In pastry making this name applies particularly to a preparation made with a round sheet of flaky pastry, filled with some composition, folded over, and baked in the oven.

Turnovers are made large or small, and are filled with all kinds of fillings.

Although these confections are included primarily in the domain of sweet pastries, considered as puddings or sweets, the name is extended to cover small preparations served as an *hors-d'oeuvre* or as a small entrée. These turnovers are made with a forcemeat filling or with a *salpicon** of various fishes; there are *foie gras* and truffle turnovers, turnovers filled with purée, or with a *salpicon* of various meats, of fowl, game, etc.

Apple turnover. CHAUSSON AUX POMMES—The chief type of this little pastry is apple turnover which is prepared in the following way:

Fill the centre of a round sheet of *Flaky pastry* (see DOUGH) with a few tablespoons of apples prepared as for a charlotte (sliced, cooked in a sauté pan with butter and sugar, and flavoured with vanilla, cinnamon, or or other flavouring) and completely cold. See CHARLOTTE, *Apple charlotte*.

Fold over the pastry to make it into a turnover.

Join the edges. Set on a buttered baking tin. Mark the top with a few incisions, *gild** with an egg and cook in a 450°F. oven for 15 minutes.

Note. Turnovers stuffed with various fruits can be made in the same way (whole or sliced, according to their size): apricots, pineapples, cherries, peaches, pears, plums etc. These fruits can either be put on the pastry uncooked, or cooked in syrup. When using raw fruits it is best to soak them for a time in sugar and in a liqueur before putting them on to the pastry.

Sweet turnovers can also be made with a preparation of fruit soaked in sugar and liqueurs and combined either with *French pastry cream* (see CREAMS) or with thick fresh cream, or finally with apricot jam.

Sweet turnovers of this kind are usually served warm, but they can also be served cold.

Turnovers à la Cussy. CHAUSSONS À LA CUSSY—These turnovers and the following are served as hors-d'oeuvre or as a small entrée.

Fill some round sheets of *Flaky pastry* (see DOUGH) with a *forcemeat** of creamed whiting (or other white fish) to which anchovy fillets, cut into small strips, and chopped truffles are added. Fold the pastry over into turnovers. Set them on a buttered baking-tin, gild and bake in a 450°F. oven until golden brown.

Turnovers à la lyonnaise. CHAUSSONS À LA LYONNAISE—Fill the middle of little circular sheets of *Flaky pastry* (see DOUGH) with a good spoonful of creamed pike or other white fish finished with *Crayfish butter* (see BUTTER, *Compound butters*) mixed with a preparation of crayfish tails and truffles, flavoured with a little cognac.

Fold over the pastry in the form of a turnover; seal the edges; put them on a buttered baking sheet, gild them with egg, and cook in a hot oven (450°F.) until golden.

Turnovers à la Nantua. CHAUSSONS À LA NANTUA—These are prepared in the same way as *Turnovers à la Lyonnaise*, with a ragoût of *Crayfish tails à la Nantua** in place of the pike forcemeat.

Turnovers à la périgourdine. CHAUSSONS À LA PÉRIGOURDINE—Fill the centres of round sheets of *Flaky pastry* (see DOUGH) with a preparation of *foie gras* and truffles seasoned with salt and pepper and sprinkled with cognac. Fold over the pastry into the form of turnovers. Put them on a buttered baking sheet, and cook them in a hot oven (450°F.); serve very hot.

Turnovers à la reine. CHAUSSONS À LA REINE—Prepared in the same way as *Turnovers à la périgourdine*, but replacing the preparation of *foie gras* and truffles with a purée of creamed chicken, mixed with truffles and mushrooms cut up fine.

Note. The rissoles for which recipes will be found under HORS-D'OEUVRE, *Hot hors-d'oeuvre* are, in fact, turnovers when they are prepared with round circles of pastry and folded over, but in principle this type of turnover is deep fried instead of being cooked in the oven.

TURNSPIT. TOURNEBROCHE—Kitchen utensil which is disappearing more and more, banished by the improvements of modern kitchen equipment.

Old-fashioned turnspits were of various kinds. Some worked mechanically by clockwork, others by animal power—that is to say by a dog shut in a round cage who turned the spit. Others were made to move by a *galopin*, a young apprentice *hasteur*, who, without respite, and burning his face in front of the immense brazier, turned the handle of the spit.

Later spits operated by heat rising from the fire, turning a winged wheel, were installed in the great eating establishments, and still exist in great numbers today.

Monumental power-driven spits, on which a whole side of beef or twenty chickens at a time could be roasted can still be found in some of these establishments.

Nowadays meat and poultry are roasted before the fire in apparatus which functions by gas or electricity.

TURRON (Confectionery). TOURON—*Turron*, which originated in Spain, is a kind of almond paste, flavoured in various ways, often with pistachio nuts, hazel nuts or candied fruits. It is made in many different forms, and there are many kinds both in France and Spain which have very little resemblance to each other. But all *turrons* are made either with almonds or hazel-nuts, however much they may differ in their flavour and decoration.

In France the name *touron* is used for a *petit four* made in the following way:

Ingredients. ½ pound (250 grams) blanched almonds, 3 cups (400 grams) powdered sugar, 4 egg whites, 3½ ounces (100 grams) pounded pistachio nuts, ½ cup (100 grams) *Royal icing* (see ICING), icing or confectioner's sugar, orange peel.

Method. Pound the almonds with 2 egg whites. Add to these almonds half the powdered sugar and knead together on marble. Sprinkle with sugar and roll out ½ inch thick.

Prepare separately the following: chop finely some blanched pistachios with the rest of the sugar mixed with orange peel. Put in a bowl with *Royal icing* and the rest of the egg whites and mix well with a wooden spoon.

Spread this mixture in a uniform layer on the rolled-out sheet of almond paste. Cut out with a round cutter, and with another cutter of lesser diameter cut out the middle of the round pieces turning them into rings. Set these rings on a buttered and floured baking-tin and dry them out in a very low oven.

TURTLE. TORTUE—This is a general term for reptiles with bodies encased in a bony carapace.

There are land turtles (see TERRAPIN) and water turtles. The flesh of both kinds can be eaten, but it is the water turtle that is made into the famous turtle soup.

'Turtle soup is a soup that the English hold in high esteem, and this is fully justified, because, in the opinion of connoisseurs, it does combine the qualities of succulence and nourishment for which it is universally reputed. It is the aristocratic soup *par excellence*, often served at the great diplomatic dinners and ceremonial repasts.

'Turtles are imported from South America, Africa and Australia. The best and the most highly priced on the market come from the West Indies.' (A. Suzanne, *La Cuisine Anglaise*.)

Turtle flesh that has been dried in the sun is also imported from these countries; with this flesh it is doubtless possible to make turtle soup, but the result is not nearly so good. Various other dishes may also be made with turtle, connoisseurs of turtle cookery particularly prizing the flippers.

Turtle flippers. NAGEOIRES DE TORTUE—Cook the flippers, until two-thirds done, in the soup for the same length of time as the rest of the animal, then prepare in different ways. They can be braised in Madeira or white wine, or cooked in one of the following ways:

Turtle flippers à l'américaine. NAGEOIRES DE TORTUE À L'AMÉRICAINE—Braise in white wine. Cover with highly seasoned *Américaine sauce*. See SAUCE.

Simmer for a few minutes.

Turtle flippers à la financière. NAGEOIRES DE TORTUE À LA FINANCIÈRE—Braise in Madeira. Set on a long dish. Surround with a *Financière* garnish (see GARNISHES). Boil down the braising liquor and pour over the flippers.

Turtle flippers à l'indienne. NAGEOIRES DE TORTUE À L'INDIENNE—Braise in white wine. Cover with *Curry sauce* (see SAUCE). Simmer for a few moments. Serve *Rice à l'indienne** separately.

Turtle soup—See SOUPS AND BROTHS.

TURTLE HERBS. HERBES À TORTUE—A mixture of aromatic herbs used to season soups or sauces called *à la tortue*. These herbs, which are sold commercially ready-prepared, are basil, thyme, bay and marjoram.

TURTLE-DOVE. TOURTERELLE—One of the pigeon family found in all Europe, Asia and Africa. The flesh of the turtle-dove is edible. All the methods of preparing pigeon are applicable. See PIGEON.

UDDER. Tetine—Calf's and cow's udder can be braised in the same way as *Noix de veau.*

Before being cooked in a braising base it should be soaked in cold water, blanched, cooled in cold water and flattened under pressure.

It may also be studded with small pieces of bacon fat.

Braised calf's udder should be accompanied by one or other of the garnishes given for *Noix de veau* (see VEAL).

Udder can be eaten fresh, salted or smoked.

UGLI. Aeglé—Common tree of East Indies which generally grows to a great height. Its numerous cylindrical branches are armed with long twin thorns between the leaves.

Its fruit is globular, about the size of an orange, with a thick hard skin. This fruit is commonly called *bilva* or *mahura* by the Indians and is much prized, in spite of its rather strong smell and insipid taste. The English who live in the West Indies eat this fruit baked in the cinders and sprinkled with sugar. It is exported to a certain extent to England and also in the form of jam. It is extremely nourishing although slightly laxative.

The skin of the *ugli* provides scent which is highly valued.

UKHA (Russian cookery)—This is Russian for a fish soup and there is an enormous variety of them. The stock for these can be prepared from any sea or river fish: small perch, bass, ling, pike-perch, pike, tench, cod, eel, salmon, trout and carp, to say nothing of the traditionally famous sturgeon and sterlet.

Boil 1 sliced onion, 1 parsnip, a sprig of parsley, bay leaf and 6 peppercorns in 3½ pints of water for ½ hour. Cool the stock, then add fish, in large portions, if it is meant to be served separately, whole, if it is to be used for stock only. Season with salt and simmer slowly for 25-30 minutes, then remove the main portions; heads, tails and bones from filleted fish can be left to simmer another 15-20 minutes. Strain before use.

For a really good, clear *ukha*, you need an assortment of fish to give it taste, strength, sweetness and a certain interesting viscosity. Perch and bass can be recommended for their flavour and gelatinous qualities, ling and allied fish for sweetness and delicacy.

The best *ukha*, of course, is made of the freshest fish and the more fish you use, the richer the soup, as in the case of meat soups. Small perch used for stock only need to be washed and gutted; the scales need not be scraped off, as this adds to the texture. Perch for stock could be boiled until it disintegrates completely, then strained.

To give *ukha* a perfect translucency, Russian cooks clarify it with caviar. This is how it is done: pound 2 ounces of caviar—either pressed or soft—in a mortar, add 3 or 4 tablespoons of cold water very slowly, a little at a time, and mix well. Dilute with a good cupful of very hot, strained fish stock. Pour half this mixture into the hot soup, stirring all the time, and bring to the boil. Add the second half of the caviar 'clarifier', bring to the boil once again, simmer on the lowest heat for a few minutes, remove from heat and leave to stand for 15 minutes for the caviar to settle. Strain, re-heat and serve either with a nice portion of boiled fish, or with fish *Coulibiac.**

The following are the most famous of traditional *ukhas*: Sterlet ukha with ling roes, Burbot ukha with pike quenelles, Salmon and champagne soup, Sturgeon and pearl barley, Eel and peas, Whitebait and sauerkraut, Carp and sorrel soup.

ULVA. Ulve—Seaweed eaten in certain countries, notably Japan, but which is without any food value.

UMBRA, MUD-MINNOW. Umbre—European fish found in fresh water but not commonly marketed.

UMBRINE OR UMBRA. Ombrine, ombre de mer—Mediterranean fish which is sometimes sold for bass. It resembles the perch and its weight reaches 30 to 32 pounds. The flesh is very delicate and was greatly prized by the Romans. It is prepared like bass.

UNCORKING. Déboucher—The uncorking of a wine bottle must be done without shaking the bottle. Wine-waiters generally use a twist-drill for this purpose, but, unless one has the knack of operating this tool, it is wiser to use a corkscrew.

UNFERMENTED WINE. Moût—Grape juice which has not yet been fermented. The term is more loosely applied to all fruit juices or cereal decoctions intended for fermentation.

It is used also of certain vegetable juices from which alcoholic drinks are made.

UNTRUSSING. Débrider—To untie the string used to truss poultry or winged game.

URANOSCOPUS. Uranoscope—Species of fish found in warm and temperate seas. The only type of uranoscopus found on the coasts of France, very rare in the Atlantic Ocean but common in the Mediterranean, is the *uranoscoperrat* or white hogfish. Its flesh, mediocre in quality, is used in making *bouillabaisse.*

UVAL—French word meaning 'pertaining to grapes'. More particularly the word is used in the phrase *cure uvale*, grape cure, that is a health treatment consisting of raw grapes and fresh grape juice. At the season when grapes are ripe, counters where fresh grapes and grape juice are sold may be seen in certain places, such as the big railway stations in Paris and the grape producing centres. They are called *Stations uvales*.

(*Robert Carrier*)

Veal blanquette

(*Recipes on page 985*)

VACHERIN—Sweet (dessert) made either with meringue 'crowns' mounted one on top of the other on a sweet pastry base, forming a kind of bowl which is decorated with meringue piped through a forcing (pastry) bag and dried out in a very low oven, or with circles of almond paste similarly mounted on top of each other. These *timbales* are filled either with *Chantilly cream* (see CREAMS), ice cream flavoured with vanilla or with some other flavouring, or with a *bombe* mixture.

Vacherin with raspberries

Vacherin with almond paste crown. VACHERIN AVEC COURONNE EN PÂTÉ D'AMANDES—Make almond paste in the following manner:

Almond paste. Pound finely in a mortar 1 pound (475 grams) of sweet almonds including a few bitter almonds (25 grams). Moisten while pounding with the juice of half a lemon. Put the almonds in a copper pan with 3½ cups (500 grams) of icing (confectioner's) sugar and the white of an egg. Mix well.

Dry out over the heat, stirring with the spatula. Cook the almonds, stirring all the time, until the paste no longer sticks to the finger when pressed.

Remove the pan from the fire, spread out the paste on the marble, turn with the spatula so that it cools equally and add to it $\frac{1}{6}$ ounce (5 grams) of gum tragacanth dissolved in water.

To make the vacherin. Roll out some of the paste into a round 8 inches in diameter and $\frac{1}{8}$ inch thick.

With the same paste make a circle 6 inches wide and 2 inches high. Dry the round and the circle at the open oven.

Place the round on paper sprinkled with sugar. Fix the circle on top of this round with rather stiff royal icing, and put into the oven to colour. Cool completely and place on a serving plate. At the last moment fill with very firm *Chantilly cream* (see CREAMS), flavoured with vanilla or other flavouring.

Vacherin with crown of meringue. VACHERIN AVEC COURONNE DE MERINGUE—With a forcing (pastry) bag make circles of ordinary *Meringue** on buttered and floured baking-tins, the diameter of the rings varying according to the size of the sweet to be prepared. Sprinkle with fine sugar and cook in the oven at a low heat until the meringue is well dried.

Put these circles on a baking-tin, one on top of the other. Coat them with meringue. Using a pipe, decorate this 'box', sprinkle it with sugar and dry it again in the oven.

Fix the box, with sugar cooked to the 'crack' stage (260°F.—see SUGAR), to a base of *Chou pastry I* (see DOUGH) and at the last moment, when the vacherin is quite cold, fill with stiffly beaten, vanilla-flavoured cream, which should be rounded into a dome.

VAISSELLE—French collective term (literally 'vessel') for all the plates and dishes used for the table, the kitchen and the house. *Vaisselle plate* is plate, i.e. dishes, etc., of silver (cf. Spanish *plata*, silver). See SILVERWARE, PORCELAIN, FAIENCE.

VALENCIA. VALENCE—Describes Spanish oranges and in Paris, by extension, is used to describe all oranges.

VALENCIENNES—A method of cooking applied in particular to chicken, which includes a rice garnish.

VALESNIKI—A preparation made with cream cheese in the style of kromeskies. See HORS-D'OEUVRE, *Hot hors-d'oeuvre.*

VALOIS (A LA)—Name for various dishes and pastries. Jules Gouffé described a Béarnaise sauce finished off with meat glaze as Valois sauce.

VANILLA. VANILLE—Pod of a climbing plant, a native of Mexico and cultivated in various tropical regions. The pods are gathered before they are completely ripe, plunged into boiling water, then, before they are quite dry, shut in tins, where their aroma develops. The best quality pods, very smooth in flavour, are covered with a frost of vanilline crystals. Three kinds of vanilla are sold commercially:

(1) Fine vanilla, the pods 8 to 12 inches long, the surface black, smooth and frosted.

(2) Woody vanilla, the pods 5 to 8 inches long, reddish-brown, the surface dry and dull and not much frosted.

Branch of vanilla with flowers and pods

(3) *Vanillons*, 4 to 5 inches long, the pods thicker, flat and soft, almost always opened and rarely frosted, the scent stronger and a little bitter.

Yet another sort of vanilla exists which comes from the Indies, yellowish in colour and almost scentless.

The Mexican vanilla is the most highly esteemed; after it come those of Guiana, of Guadaloupe and of Réunion.

Vanilla is sometimes falsified, either by emptying the pods and filling them with a neutral paste or by brushing ordinary vanilla with Peruvian balsam to frost them artificially with benzoic acid crystals.

Vanilla is much used as an aromatic flavouring, either in its original form, in powder form, or as an extract.

VANILLA SUGAR—Sugar flavoured with vanilla.

VANILLINE—Synthetic product, whose flavour and scent are less fine than those of the natural vanilla.

VANNER—French culinary term for stirring a sauce with a spoon to make it smooth and keep a skin from forming.

VARENIKI—See HORS-D'OEUVRE, *Hot hors-d'oeuvre*.

VARIETY MEATS—See OFFAL.

VASQUE—French word for a shallow bowl, generally round in shape, made of all sorts of materials, crystal, moulded glass, china, silver, used for serving all kinds of cold foods, *chaud-froids*, *mousses**, *foie gras en gelée*, etc.

Fresh fruit, cooked fruit, liquid custards and other cold sweets are also served in *vasques*.

VATEL—A celebrated *Maître d'hôtel*, born in 1635 of Swiss parentage, who died in 1671.

'A legend three centuries old presents Vatel to us as the great master-cook of the Louis XIV era. Let us speak solely and briefly of Vatel, and ask ourselves whether the echo of Vatel's culinary genius would have come down to us, without the witty gossip of Madame de Sévigné.

'All we can say up to the present is that in the *État de la Maison du Roi et des Maisons des Princes du sang* we have found no reference to Vatel, and in the formularies which appeared after his death, there is nothing to show that this man, who, we have been given to understand, was the model for all cooks, had any influence at all on the progress of the culinary art in his times.

'No, we have no authentic proof that Vatel was a cook. Nothing has come down to us from him, and yet in all periods almost all the great cooks have handed on their professional work in writing.

'The only authentic document, the only one on which the name of Vatel appears, is the letter addressed on April 24th, 1671, by Madame de Sévigné to Madame de Grignan. She says, "But what I did learn on coming in here, something that I cannot put out of my mind, which affects me so that I no longer know what I am telling you: is that Vatel, the great Vatel, *maître d'hôtel* to M. Fouquet and of late *maître d'hôtel* to M. le Prince, has stabbed himself".

'Thus, in this funeral oration, Madame de Sévigné, well instructed by Moreuil (the owner of the house) as to the standing of Vatel, tells us, in so many words, that he was a *maître d'hôtel*, and in those days, as now, there was a certain distinction between the chief of service at the table and the great master of the kitchen and the cooking.

'And even so, while publishing that very precise letter of Madame de Sévigné, the conscientious author of *L'Histoire de la table*, Louis Nicolardot, commits the error of describing Vatel as a cook.

'In the series of medallions placed at the head of his works, where Carême has inscribed the names of culinary celebrities and gastronomic notabilities of his own and earlier times, we find that of Vatel (spelt Watel), alongside those of Gourville, Grimod de la Reynière, Brillat-Savarin, Berchoux, etc. Then again, it is certain that if Vatel had been a cook, Carême would not have failed to comment on his end as he did for his master, Laguipière, cook to Murat, who died at Vilna during the great retreat from Russia.

'No, Vatel was not a cook; no more than Brillat-Savarin, the Baron Brisse or Fulbert-Dumonteil, who incidentally glorified themselves with "their" recipes, compiled and written by cooks, admirers of their brilliant chronicles.

'While conceding that someone may provide one day authentic proof that Vatel did in fact practise in the kitchen, his sensational suicide none the less shows that he did not have the character of a cook, because he did not know how to make the best of a bad job, could not rise above difficult circumstances.

'If we master cooks, whose coat sleeves could be decorated with four or five chevrons each showing ten years' service, were to cast back our minds, we would all be able to tell of incidents in which disasters were quickly overcome, circumstances which would have demanded hara-kiri if Vatel's example had been followed. But recourse to the bacon-slicer (for want of a sword) would have resolved nothing, and it is in circumstances such as these that the strength of character of the man in charge is revealed and the iron will, the highest possible sense of responsibility and the experience which enables him to make prompt and energetic decisions, are called upon.

'Such a one does not lose his head and think of suicide. An authoritative call to the good will of his team, a few brief clear orders roared into the tumult of clattering copper pots, and the trouble is over: the service goes on. . . .

'But even if Vatel was only a *maître d'hôtel*, we must all the same admit that he was part of the structure. We will conclude like the gentle epicurean poet Berchoux:

"Oh, you who by profession preside at meals
Spare him some regrets, but do not imitate him."
(Philéas Gilbert.)

VATRUSHKI (Russian cookery)—Small open tarts made with *brioche dough* filled with cream cheese and other compositions.

Vatrushki with cream cheese (Russian cooking). VATRUSHKI AU FROMAGE BLANC—Make and roll out some ordinary unsweetened *Brioche dough* (see DOUGH). Cut with a round, fluted-edged pastry-cutter into pieces 4 inches in diameter. Fill with cream cheese.

Crimp up the edges of the dough, put on a baking tray, brush over with egg and bake in a slow oven for 15 to 18 minutes.

Vatrushki can also be made with best *Lining paste* (see DOUGH) or with *Coulibiac dough* (see COULIBIAC).

Vatrushki with onion. VATRUSHKI À L'OIGNON—Prepare as *Vatrushki with cream cheese*, replacing the cheese with onion purée blended with a thick *Velouté sauce*. See SAUCE.

VEAL. VEAU—Flesh of calf, i.e. young of the cow. The best meat comes from animals aged from two and a half to three months, fed exclusively on milk, with some eggs towards the end; it must be white with a slight greenish tinge (reddish colouration shows that the animal has been given solid food); it is not greasy to the touch like pork; its fat is white and satiny and smells of milk. Veal killed too young is more gelatinous and of less nutritional value.

Veal, like beef, is divided into three categories so far as market value is concerned. Since veal butchering differs in France, England and the U.S.A., the joints or cuts designated are the nearest approximations rather than equivalents.

(1) *Cul* or *Quasi* (English Chump end of loin; U.S.A. Heel or round). *Noix* (English Topside; U.S.A. Rump). *Rouelle* (English Fillet; U.S.A. Round roast). *Longe* (English and U.S.A. Loin) with or without kidney. *Carré* (English Best end of neck; U.S.A. Rib roast).

(2) *Épaule* (Shoulder). *Basses-côtes* (English End chops; U.S.A. Shoulder chops). *Poitrine* (Breast). *Ventre* (English Belly; U.S.A. Flank).

Amourettes of veal. AMOURETTES DE VEAU—In French cookery the spinal marrow of veal is known as *amourettes*.

The substance of this marrow has a great resemblance to calf's brains, and all the methods of preparing the latter are applicable to the amourettes.

It may, like the brains, be prepared as a dish by itself; more often, however, it is used as an ingredient of a garnish. See OFFAL OR VARIETY MEATS.

Veal blanquette—Cut 1½ pounds (750 grams) of veal taken from the shoulder, the breast, or end chops (shoulder chops) into uniform square pieces.

Put into a shallow saucepan with enough white stock or light broth (or plain water) to cover the pieces of meat. Add salt and bring to the boil, removing all scum.

Add a carrot, an onion stuck with a clove, a leek and a *bouquet garni* composed of parsley, thyme, bay leaf and celery.

Cook very slowly for an hour and a half.

Thicken three-quarters of the cooking liquor with 3 tablespoons (50 grams) each of butter and flour *roux*. Mix this sauce well, or *Velouté* (see SAUCE), and add to it a handful of mushroom trimmings (from the mushrooms to be used in the blanquette). Cook for 15 minutes, stirring from time to time.

Remove the pieces of veal from their liquid; trim them, that is to say remove little bones which have become loose; put the meat in a sauté pan with a dozen little onions previously cooked in a flour and water *court-bouillon** and a dozen peeled mushrooms.

Strain the sauce through a muslin bag, thicken with 3 egg yolks and ¾ cup (1½ decilitres) of cream and pour over the veal.

Season with a little grated nutmeg and a squeeze of lemon juice. Keep warm on a corner of the stove, the saucepan covered, taking care that it does not boil. Serve in a dish with croûtons of bread fried in butter.

Veal blanquette, various garnishes. BLANQUETTE DE VEAU—Prepare the blanquette as in the preceding recipe. After the first cooking, and after the pieces of veal have been drained, put them back in the sauté pan with the prescribed vegetables. Pour over the strained sauce and finish cooking in the usual way.

Veal blanquette may be prepared with the following: celeriac in quarters, half-cooked in butter, or halved celery hearts; cucumbers cut into chunks and blanched for 3 minutes in boiling salted water; braised lettuce, braised lettuce hearts cut in two; *matignon**; carrots, turnips, celery or leeks, sliced and stewed in butter.

Veal blanquette à l'ancienne. BLANQUETTE DE VEAU À L'ANCIENNE—Like *Blanquette of lamb à l'ancienne*. See LAMB.

Breast of veal. POITRINE DE VEAU—This cut is usually boned, stuffed and braised. It may also be used to make *ragoûts*.

This is the forcemeat which is normally used to stuff it:

Add to 2 pounds (1 kilo) of *Fine pork forcemeat* (see FORCEMEAT), ¾ cup (150 grams) of chopped onion cooked till tender in butter and 1 tablespoon of chopped parsley, and bind with a whole egg. Season with salt, pepper and spices and mix well.

The boned breast may also be stuffed with such forcemeats as quenelle forcemeat, fine pork forcemeat mixed with chopped spinach lightly cooked in butter, sausage meat mixed with dry *Duxelles*,* etc.

The cooking time for a stuffed breast of veal weighing 10 pounds (5 kilos) is 3½ to 4 hours. For the method of braising see CULINARY METHODS.

Breast of veal à l'allemande. POITRINE DE VEAU À L'ALLEMANDE—Poach in light stock a breast of veal stuffed as above. Serve surrounded by vegetables, carrots, leeks, etc., that have been cooked with it, and serve hot *Horseradish sauce* (see SAUCE) separately.

Breast of veal à l'alsacienne. POITRINE DE VEAU À L'ALSACIENNE—The breast is braised until it is half cooked, then finished off in the braising pan with blanched sauerkraut.

Breast of veal à l'anglaise. POITRINE DE VEAU À L'ANGLAISE—The breast having been stuffed with the forcemeat described below, poach it gently in a light stock or salted water. Serve with boiled bacon.

Stuffing for breast of veal. Add to chopped beef or veal kidney some chopped veal udder or crow and breadcrumbs soaked in milk and pressed, all in thirds. Bind this forcemeat with 2 eggs to every 2 pounds (1 kilo) and season.

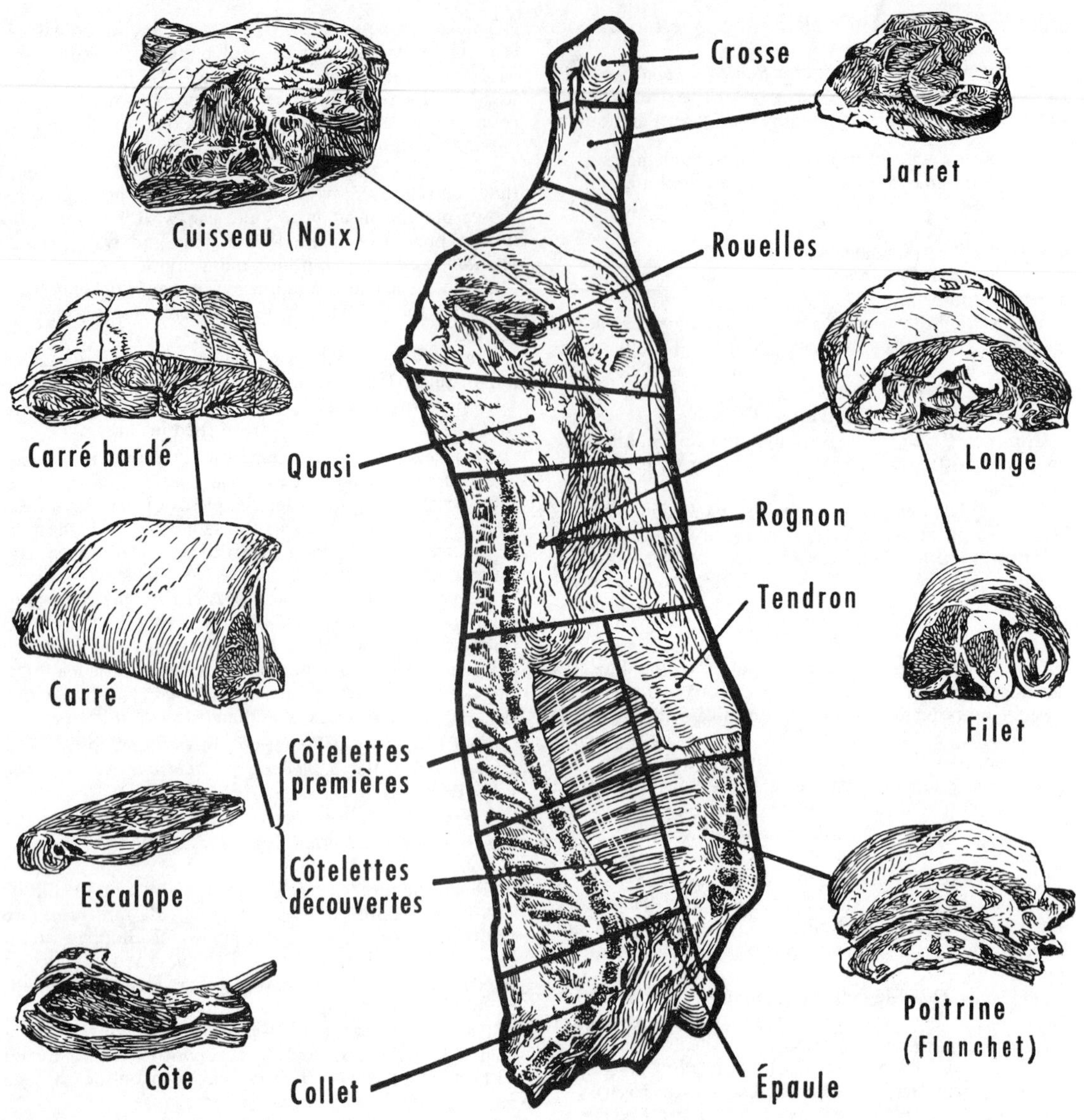

French cuts of veal

Brochettes of veal. BROCHETTES DE VEAU—Cut some fillet (U.S.A. round) of veal into little square pieces about 3 inches thick. Spit them on skewers alternately with blanched pieces of bacon. Season the meat on the skewers, dip in melted butter, cover them with breadcrumbs, sprinkle with more melted butter and cook on the grill.

Carré de veau—See *Rib of veal*, below.

Veal chops. CÔTES DE VEAU—These cuts, taken from the best end of loin (U.S.A. rib) must not be too thin.

Veal chops are generally sautéed in butter, and cooked in this way are served *au naturel*, that is to say, sprinkled with their cooking juices, diluted, boiled down and buttered; they may be garnished in various ways, but should always be sprinkled with their own cooking juices.

Veal chops may also be grilled. In this case they are served with *Maître d'hôtel butter* (see BUTTER, *Compound butters*) or any other sauce usually served with grilled meat. See SAUCE.

Veal chops à l'ancienne. CÔTES DE VEAU À L'ANCIENNE—Cook 6 chops in butter without browning. Set on a round dish. Surround with a garnish composed of cocks' combs and kidneys, lambs' sweetbreads, truffles and mushrooms, heated in Madeira and bound with *Chicken velouté sauce* (see SAUCE) diluted with cream.

As sauce for the chops, dilute the pan juices with Madeira, add equal quantities of concentrated and thickened brown veal stock and fresh cream; simmer down; add butter and strain.

Veal chops with basil. CÔTES DE VEAU AU BASILIC—Season six chops with salt and pepper; sauté in butter. Drain and set on a serving dish. Sprinkle with a sauce made by diluting the pan juices with white wine and adding a few tablespoons of veal stock, $\frac{1}{2}$ teaspoon of chopped basil, and butter.

Veal chops Bellevue (cold). CÔTES DE VEAU BELLEVUE—Braise 6 chops, cut rather thick, and let them cool in the cooking liquor.

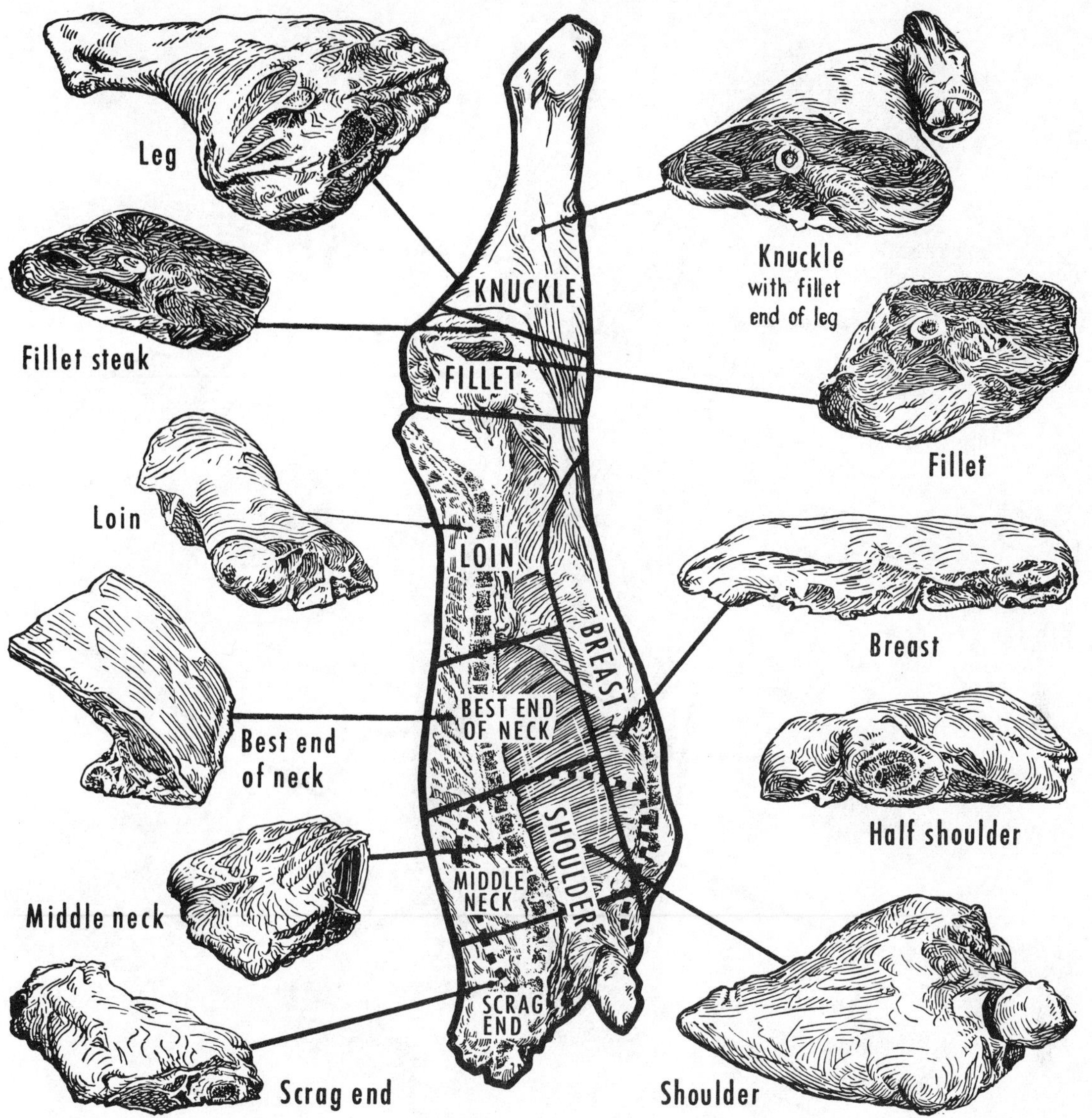

English cuts of veal

Put into an hors-d'oeuvre dish or a deep oval dish, lined with jelly and decorated with mixed vegetables (carrots and turnips in little balls, peas, diced French beans, etc.). The chops must be put in the dish covered with their cooking liquor. Fill the dish with half melted jelly. Chill well on ice.

Turn out the chops on to a long dish. Garnish with chopped jelly.

Veal chops à la bonne femme. Côtes de veau à la bonne femme—Cook lightly in an earthenware casserole, browning them on both sides, 6 veal chops cut rather thick and seasoned with salt and pepper. Add for each chop, 6 small lardoons of lean bacon, blanched and fried lightly in butter, 6 small fried onions and 12 little new potatoes (or an equal quantity of old potatoes cut to look like olives), one-third cooked in butter. Cook gently in the oven. At the last moment add 6 tablespoons of thickened brown gravy. Serve in the casserole in which they were cooked.

Veal chop Bouchère. Côte de veau Bouchère—French culinary name for a chop taken from the collar end of the neck and not trimmed. This cut is generally grilled, but it can also be sautéed in butter.

It is served as it is, accompanied by vegetables to taste.

Veal chops bourguignonne. Côtes de veau bourguignonne—Sauté 6 chops in butter. When half cooked add for each chop 6 small glazed onions, 4 small mushrooms and 6 lardoons of lean, blanched bacon. Cook all together. Set the chops on a serving dish. Dilute the pan juices with red wine, thicken with a tablespoon of *Kneaded butter* (see BUTTER, *Compound butters*), add a teaspoon of meat jelly, cook down, add butter and pour over the chops.

Braised veal chops. Côtes de veau braisées—Cut the chops rather thick; season with salt and pepper. Put it into a buttered sauté dish lined with strips of bacon rind, and chopped onions and carrots. Let these cook gently in the oven, covered, for 10 minutes.

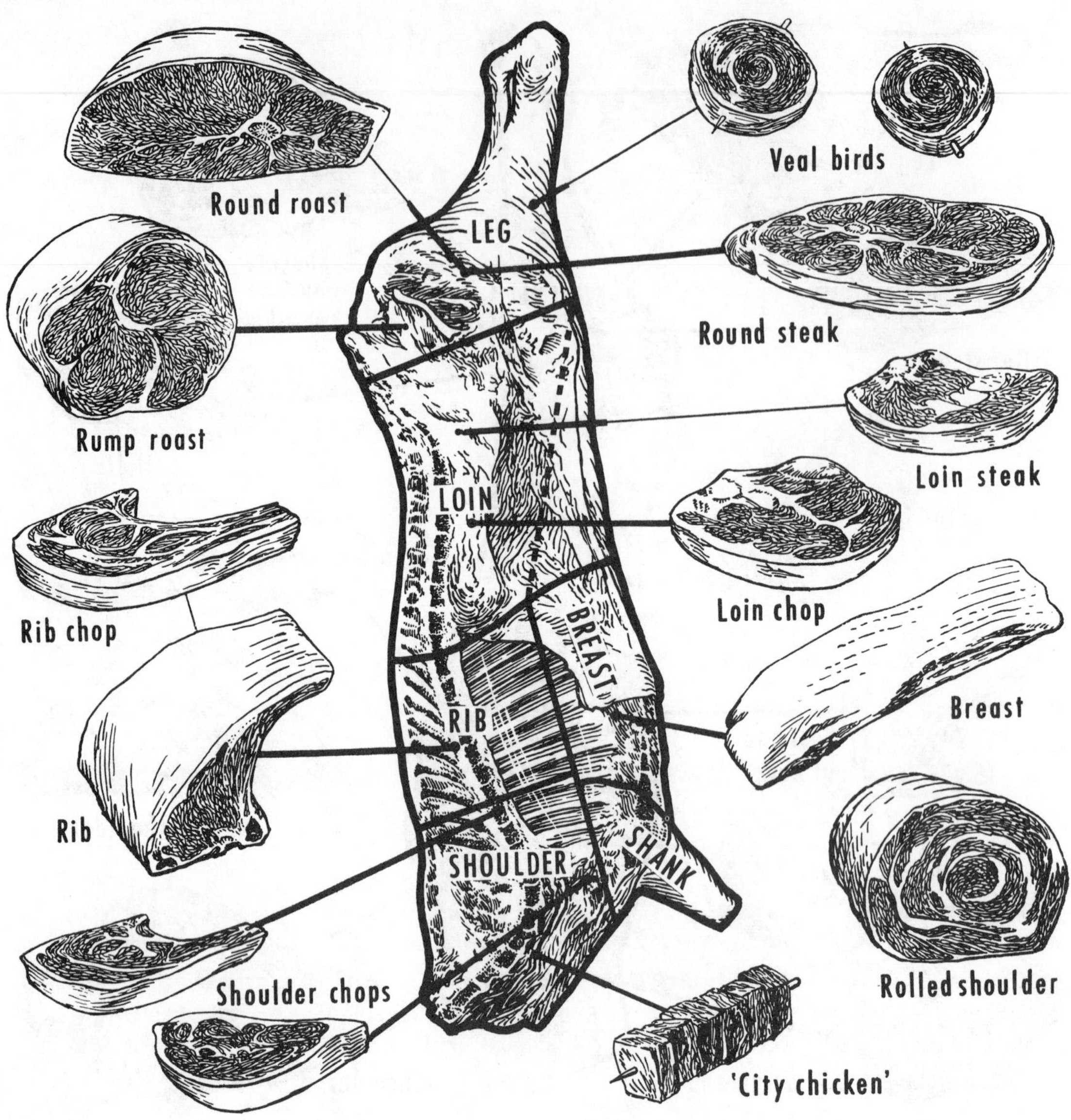

American cuts of veal

Pour in for each chop $\frac{1}{4}$ cup ($\frac{1}{2}$ decilitre) of white wine; boil down. Pour in clear brown stock to halfway up the meat. Add a small *bouquet garni*. Bring to the boil on top of the stove then cook in the oven, covered, for 45 minutes to an hour, according to size.

Drain the chops, set them on a round dish and coat with a sauce made by straining the braising liquor, removing all grease and boiling down.

Note. Braised veal chops can be accompanied by various garnishes. All those indicated elsewhere for sautéed veal chops are applicable.

Veal chops en casserole. CÔTES DE VEAU EN CASSEROLE—Season the chops with salt and pepper. Cook gently in butter in an earthenware casserole. At the last moment sprinkle with thickened veal gravy. Serve in the same casserole.

Veal chops en casserole with various garnishes. CÔTES DE VEAU EN CASSEROLE—When the chops are almost cooked, remove from the casserole. Place in the latter the garnish being used, put back the chop on top and finish cooking all together.

The garnishes most often used for this dish are the following: aubergines (egg-plant) cut in small rounds or squares, sautéed in butter or oil; glazed carrots (either small new carrots or large carrots cut into oval pieces); celeriac cut in oval pieces and simmered in butter; cèpes or other edible fungi, usually cultivated mushrooms, sautéed in butter; cucumbers cut into large olive-shaped pieces, cooked in butter; artichoke bottoms in quarters; French (string) beans cooked in water and tossed in butter; glazed turnips (also cut into olive-shaped pieces); salsify, cooked in a flour and water *court-bouillon** and sautéed in butter; Jerusalem artichokes cooked in butter.

The following may also be used to garnish veal chops cooked *en casserole*, but should be added only when the meat is completely cooked: braised endive; Brussels sprouts, lightly fried in butter; little cauliflower flowerets sautéed in butter; braised chicory; leaf spinach chopped with butter or cream; new broad beans with butter; stewed gombos (okra or ladies' fingers) with tomato; hop shoots in butter; flageolet beans in butter; French (string) beans in butter or cream; braised lettuce; braised chestnuts; noodles in butter; purée of sorrel; peas in butter or *à la française*; quartered tomatoes, stewed in butter.

Veal chops chasseur. CÔTES DE VEAU CHASSEUR—Prepared like *Mutton chops chasseur*.*

Veal chops chaud-froid. CÔTES DE VEAU EN CHAUD-FROID —*In white sauce*. Cook 6 chops in butter without letting them colour. Allow them to cool. Coat with *Chaud-froid sauce* (see SAUCE), to which the pan juices diluted with Madeira or any other wine have been added.

Decorate the top of each chop with truffles, pickled tongue, lean ham, tarragon leaves, etc. Glaze with jelly. Chill well. Set on a round dish and garnish with chopped jelly.

In brown sauce. Braise the chops, browning them. Allow them to cool in the braising liquor. Drain them and coat with *Brown chaud-froid sauce* to which the braising liquor has been added. Decorate and glaze with jelly.

Note. Veal chops *en chaud-froid* may be accompanied by vegetable salad bound with mayonnaise, halves of hard boiled eggs or lettuce hearts.

Veal chops en cocotte. CÔTES DE VEAU EN COCOTTE—Alternative name for *Veal chops en casserole*. *Veal chops à la bonne femme* are also sometimes known by the same name.

Veal chops en cocotte with various garnishes. CÔTES DE VEAU EN COCOTTE—Can be accompanied by any of the garnishes given for *Veal chops en casserole with various garnishes*.

Veal chops à la crème. CÔTES DE VEAU À LA CRÈME—Sauté the chops in butter. Drain and set on a round dish. Coat with the cooking juices diluted with white wine (or Madeira) and fresh cream, cooked down and strained.

It is also permissible to add a tablespoon of *Velouté sauce* (see SAUCE) to the cream to thicken the sauce.

Veal chops à l'indienne. CÔTES DE VEAU À L'INDIENNE—Sauté 4 chops in butter. When browned on both sides, put them into the pan with 2 tablespoons of chopped onion. Season with a teaspoon of curry. Cook gently, covered. Set the chops on a round dish and coat with sauce made in the following way. Dilute the cooking juices with ¼ cup (½ decilitre) of dry white wine. Add 4 tablespoons of thick fresh cream; boil down to a good consistency. Add a squeeze of lemon juice.

Serve *Rice à l'indienne** separately.

Veal chops Cussy. CÔTES DE VEAU CUSSY—Cut a pocket in the veal chops taken from the middle of the best end of the neck (U.S.A. rib) and cut rather thick. Fill with a *salpicon** composed of mushrooms, carrots and lean ham, bound with *Béchamel sauce* (see SAUCE) and well seasoned.

Coat with egg and breadcrumbs. Cook in clarified butter, browning on both sides.

Prepare a creamy *Risotto* (see RICE), bind with cheese and add a *salpicon** of truffles.

Set the chop on a round dish. Garnish with the truffle risotto. Pour around a few tablespoons of tomato-flavoured brown gravy and sprinkle the chop with 2 tablespoons of *Noisette butter*. See BUTTER, *Compound butters*.

Veal chops à la custine. CÔTES DE VEAU À LA CUSTINE—'Braise the veal chops, coat each one with a good tablespoon of *Duxelles*.*

'Dip in the sauce, then in breadcrumbs, then in beaten eggs and in breadcrumbs a second time. Fry until golden in butter and serve with a light tomato sauce.' (Carême's recipe.)

Veal chops à la dreux (old style). CÔTES DE VEAU À LA DREUX—'Stud 12 veal chops (cut rather thick and lightly flattened) with pickled tongue and truffles. Tie the chops with string.

'Line a shallow casserole with the trimmings from the chops, 2 carrots, 2 onions and a *bouquet garni*, cover with thin bards of bacon fat and place the chops on top. Pour over some consommé and a wineglass of Madeira and cook for a good three-quarters of an hour.

'Drain on a *plafond* (an old-fashioned copper baking tin) with a cover on top to keep them under pressure until they are cold.

'Strain the pan juices and remove all grease. Boil down to a light glaze.

'When the chops are cold, trim them carefully so that the tongue and truffles can be seen distinctly; put them in a sauté dish with their glaze and allow to simmer for a quarter of an hour before serving. Set on a dish; garnish the middle with a *Ragoût à la financière** and use the glaze as sauce.' (Plumerey's recipe.)

Veal chops à la dreux (modern style). CÔTES DE VEAU À LA DREUX—Stud the chops, cut rather thick, with pickled tongue and truffles.

Cook gently in butter. When cooked, trim the flat surfaces slightly so that the tongue and truffles show more clearly.

Set on a round dish. Surround with a *Financière garnish* (see GARNISHES). For sauce use the pan juices diluted with Madeira and mixed with thickened brown veal stock.

Veal chops à la duxelles. CÔTES DE VEAU À LA DUXELLES —Sauté the chops in butter. When almost cooked put into the pan 4 good tablespoons of dry *Duxelles*.* Cook all together over a gentle heat for a few moments. Set the chops on a round dish. Sprinkle with the pan juices to which some white wine and tomato-flavoured *Demi-glace sauce* have been added. Sprinkle with chopped parsley.

Veal chops à la fermière. CÔTES DE VEAU À LA FERMIÈRE —Cooked in a cocotte like *Veal chops à la paysanne*, but without potatoes.

Veal chops aux fines herbes. CÔTES DE VEAUX AUX FINES HERBES—Sauté 4 chops in butter. Drain and arrange on a round dish. Dilute the pan juices with ¼ cup (½ decilitre) of white wine to which a teaspoon of chopped shallot has been added. Add some *Demi-glace sauce* (see SAUCE). Allow to boil for a few moments, then add a tablespoon of chopped parsley, chervil and tarragon.

Pour the sauce over the chops.

Veal chops à la gelée (Carême's recipe). CÔTES DE VEAU À LA GELÉE—'Trim the veal chops and stud them with ham and bacon fat or pickled tongue. Put them in a pot lined with bards of bacon fat and put more bards of bacon fat on top. Over these place the trimmings of the chops, 2 carrots, 2 onions, 2 cloves and a good bouquet of thyme, bay leaf and basil; add salt, a glass of white wine, a spoonful of brandy and 2 tablespoons of consommé (for 10 chops). Cover with buttered paper and place the pot on the fire.

'When it has come right to the boil, set the fire above and below the pot (or put it to cook over a gentle heat) in such a way that the chops boil only lightly for 2 hours. This cooking time is for thick chops weighing about ½ pound (250 grams) each.

'After this drain them. When they are almost cold, press them between two *plafonds* (baking tins), putting a weight on top.

'When they are quite cold trim them perfectly; glaze them with their braising liquor cooked down and strained and set them on a dish garnished with chopped jelly. Decorate the top of each chop lightly with jelly. Surround with a pretty border of jelly croûtons.'

Grilled veal chops. CÔTES DE VEAU GRILLÉES—Season the chops with salt and pepper, sprinkle with melted butter or oil and cook under a moderate grill.

Set on a round dish, put a paper frill on the bone and garnish with watercress.

Note. Grilled veal chops are generally served as they are, but can be accompanied by a *Compound butter* (see BUTTER) or some kind of garnish, the most usual being potatoes.

Veal chops à la hongroise. CÔTES DE VEAU À LA HONGROISE—Season the chops with salt and paprika; sauté them in butter. When they are well browned on both sides put into the pan a good tablespoon of chopped onion, cooked till tender in butter and seasoned with paprika. Cook gently, covered.

Drain the chops; set them on a round dish. Coat with a sauce made by diluting the pan juices with white wine then adding cream, cooking down and adding butter.

Veal chops à la languedocienne. CÔTES DE VEAU À LA LANGUEDOCIENNE—Sauté 4 chops in goose fat. When they are browned on both sides put into the pan a tablespoon of chopped onion and 2 tablespoons of raw ham cut in small dice. Cook gently all together. At the last moment add 12 green olives stoned and blanched and a little chopped garlic. Set the chops on a round dish and surround with potatoes cut to look like olives and fried. Pour the sauce and the olives over the chops.

Veal chops à la lyonnaise. CÔTES DE VEAU À LA LYONNAISE—Sauté 4 chops in butter. When almost done, put into the pan 4 tablespoons of chopped onions gently cooked in butter. Finish cooking together. Set the chops on a round dish. Add 2 tablespoons of vinegar, 1 tablespoon of chopped parsley and a little meat glaze to the onions, and pour over the chops.

Veal chops Maintenon. CÔTES DE VEAU MAINTENON—Prepared like *Mutton chop Maintenon.**

Veal chops à la maraîchère. CÔTES DE VEAU À LA MARAÎCHÈRE—Sauté in butter. Garnish with chunks of salsify, cooked in a flour and water *court-bouillon** and fried in butter, Brussels sprouts sautéed in butter and potatoes cut to look like olives and cooked in butter.

For sauce use the pan juices diluted with white wine and with veal gravy added.

Veal chops à la maréchale. CÔTES DE VEAU À LA MARÉCHALE—Flatten the chops lightly; season with salt and pepper and coat with egg and breadcrumbs. Cook in clarified butter.

Garnish with asparagus tips in butter and slices of truffles (placed on top of the chops); pour veal gravy around and sprinkle with *Noisette butter*. See BUTTER, *Compound butters.*

Veal chops à la milanaise. CÔTES DE VEAU À LA MILANAISE—Flatten the veal chops and season with salt and pepper then coat with egg and breadcrumbs mixed with grated Parmesan. Cook in clarified butter. Set on a round dish. Surround with *Macaroni à la milanaise.** Put on top of each chop a slice of peeled lemon and sprinkle with *Noisette butter*. See BUTTER, *Compound butters.*

Note. This is how *Veal chops à la milanaise* are prepared in Paris restaurants. In Italy they are generally served without the macaroni, simply with sautéed potatoes.

Minced veal chops Grimod de la Reyniere. CÔTES DE VEAU HACHÉE GRIMOD DE LA REYNIÈRE—Chop the veal chops finely, adding to each chop one-third of its weight of breadcrumbs soaked in milk and pressed, and a teaspoon of chopped truffles. Season with salt, pepper and a little grated nutmeg.

Put this forcemeat back on to the bone of the chop and re-form it to its original shape. Coat with egg and breadcrumbs and cook in clarified butter. Set on a round dish. Garnish with buttered asparagus tips and surround with concentrated veal gravy. Sprinkle with *Noisette butter*. See BUTTER, *Compound butters.*

Minced veal chops with various vegetables. CÔTES DE VEAU HACHÉES AVEC LÉGUMES—Chop the meat of the chops finely as for the *Chops Grimod de la Reynière*, but without adding truffles.

Re-form the chop. Sauté in clarified butter.

Garnish with vegetables.

Surround with thickened brown veal gravy. Sprinkle with *Noisette butter*. See BUTTER, *Compound butters.*

Veal chops à la Morland. CÔTES DE VEAU À LA MORLAND—'After having prepared 12 veal chops (cutlets) as though to be cooked in the ordinary way, dip them in four beaten eggs and coat them with finely chopped truffles. Sauté them in clarified butter. Set them on a serving dish with a mushroom purée in the middle. Use *Demi-glace sauce*.' See SAUCE. (Carême's recipe.)

Veal chops with mushrooms. CÔTES DE VEAU AUX CHAMPIGNONS—Season 6 chops with salt and pepper. Brown both sides in butter in a sauté pan.

When half cooked put with each chop in the pan 6 peeled mushroom heads (using raw mushrooms).

Set the chops on a round dish. Garnish with the mushrooms.

Sprinkle over the cooking juices diluted with Madeira and *Demi-glace sauce*. See SAUCE.

Veal chops with mushrooms à la crème. CÔTES DE VEAU AUX CHAMPIGNONS À LA CRÈME—As above. After having set the chops on a dish, dilute the cooking juices with Madeira and fresh cream and cook down. Coat the chops and mushrooms with this sauce.

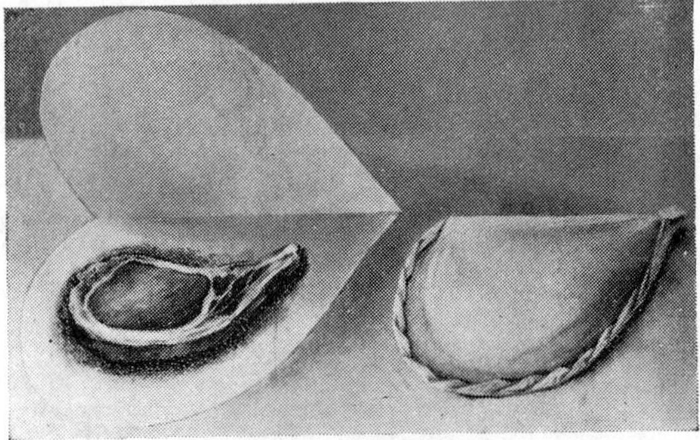

Veal chops en papillote

Veal chops en papillote. CÔTES DE VEAU EN PAPILLOTE—Sauté the chops in butter. Set on a sheet of oiled paper cut in the shape of a heart, placing chop on one half of the heart on top of a slice of cooked ham covered with a tablespoon of rather thick *Duxelles sauce* (see SAUCE). Put another tablespoon of the *Duxelles sauce* on top of the chop and cover with another slice of ham.

Close the *papillote*, folding over the edges like a hem.

Put on a dish and put in the oven long enough to puff up the paper and colour it a little.

Veal chops Parmentier. CÔTES DE VEAU PARMENTIER—Season 4 chops with salt and pepper. Fry in butter on both sides.

When they are half cooked, put in the pan $1\frac{1}{2}$ cups (200 grams) of potatoes cut in pieces $\frac{3}{4}$-inch square. Finish cooking together.

Set the chops on a round dish, surrounded with the potatoes. Pour over the pan juices diluted with 2 tablespoons of veal stock. Sprinkle with chopped parsley.

Veal chops à la paysanne. CÔTES DE VEAU À LA PAYSANNE —Cook 4 chops in butter. When they are almost ready, put into the pan ½ cup (½ decilitre) of vegetable *fondue à la fermière** with the addition of 6 tablespoons of small lean lardoons fried in butter and 1½ cups of potatoes cut in small dice and cooked in butter. Finish cooking altogether. At the end of cooking sprinkle over ½ cup of veal gravy.

Note. Veal chops *à la paysanne* can be cooked and served in an earthenware casserole, as can all dishes cooked *à la paysanne.*

Veal chops à la piémontaise. CÔTES DE VEAU À LA PIÉMONTAISE—Season the chops with salt and pepper; coat with egg and breadcrumbs mixed with grated cheese. Sauté in clarified butter. Garnish with *Risotto à la piémontaise* (see RICE). Pour round *Demi-glace sauce* (see SAUCE) flavoured with tomato.

Veal chops Pojarski. CÔTES DE VEAU POJARSKI—Chop finely the meat of the chops and mix with a quarter of its weight of butter and an equal quantity of breadcrumbs soaked in milk and pressed. Season this forcemeat with salt, pepper and a little grated nutmeg. Put it back on the bone and reconstitute the chops in their original shape. Flour each chop. Cook in clarified butter. Set on a round dish; garnish with the chosen vegetable, and put a slice of peeled lemon on top of each chop. Sprinkle with *Noisette butter.* See BUTTER, *Compound butters.*

Veal chops en portefeuille (grilled). CÔTES DE VEAU EN PORTEFEUILLE—Cut open the lean meat of a veal chop cut rather thick. Season inside and out with salt and pepper, and fill this pocket with some kind of forcemeat. Wrap the chop in a piece of pig's caul (or pork fat), previously soaked in cold water. Cook on the grill at a gentle heat.

Serve with a garnish of vegetables. Pour round some veal gravy with butter added.

Veal chops en portefeuille (sautéed). CÔTES DE VEAU EN PORTEFEUILLE—Prepare the chops as above. Cook in butter in a sauté pan. Set on a round dish. Garnish with the prescribed vegetable. For sauce use the pan juices diluted with white wine and with thickened veal gravy added.

Veal chops à la portugaise. CÔTES DE VEAU À LA PORTUGAISE—Sauté the chops in oil. Set on a round dish. Add to the pan juices for each chop 2 good tablepoons of *Tomato fondue.** Add ½ cup (1 decilitre) of white wine, season with a little garlic, boil down, add 2 teaspoons of chopped parsley and pour over the chops.

Veal chops à la provençale. CÔTES DE VEAU À LA PROVENÇALE—Sauté the chops in a mixture of butter and oil. Set on a round dish; garnish with tomatoes stuffed with *duxelles** covered with grated cheese and browned. Dilute the pan juices with white wine, add some *Tomato sauce* (see SAUCE), and a little garlic for seasoning. Pour over the chops. Sprinkle with chopped parsley.

Sautéed veal chops with various garnishes. CÔTES DE VEAU SAUTÉES—Sauté the chops in butter, set on a round dish and garnish with the prescribed vegetable.

Dilute the pan juices with white wine, add some brown veal gravy and pour over the chops.

Thus prepared, the chops may be garnished with the following vegetables: quartered artichokes or artichoke bottoms; asparagus tips in butter; aubergines (egg-plants) in round or large dice, sautéed in butter or oil; carrots, *à la crème*, glazed or Vichy; celery, braised or simmered in butter; cèpes or other edible fungi sautéed in butter or oil; braised chicory (U.S.A. endive); Brussels sprouts, sautéed in butter; cauliflower, sautéed in butter; zucchini (Italian marrows or courgettes), in rounds or dice, sautéed in butter or oil; braised endive (U.S.A. chicory); leaf spinach stewed in butter, or chopped or sieved in butter, cream or gravy; hop shoots in butter or cream; kidney beans in butter or *à la bretonne*; sweet corn in butter or cream; braised sorrel; peas in butter or *à la française*; potatoes, prepared in various ways; pilaf rice or risotto; salsify in cream, in gravy, or sautéed in butter; halved tomatoes sautéed in butter, grilled, or cooked slowly in butter or oil (*fondue*).

Veal chops with truffles. CÔTES DE VEAU AUX TRUFFES—Season the chops with salt and pepper. Sauté in butter. When almost cooked, put into the pan for each chop 6 rather thick slices of truffles. Set the chops on a round dish and cover with the truffles. Sprinkle with the cooking juices diluted with Madeira and with *Demi-glace sauce* flavoured with truffle essence added.

Veal chops vert-pré. CÔTES DE VEAU VERT-PRÉ—Grill the chops and garnish as for *Entrecôte au vert-pré.* See BEEF, *Entrecôte.*

Veal chops Vichy. CÔTES DE VEAU VICHY—Sauté the chops in butter. When cooked, put into the pan for each chop 5 tablespoons of carrots prepared *à la Vichy* (see CARROT). Sprinkle with the diluted pan juices.

Veal chops à la viennoise. CÔTES DE VEAU À LA VIENNOISE—Prepared like *Escalopes of veal à la viennoise,* below.

Veal chops Zingara. CÔTES DE VEAU ZINGARA—Season with salt and paprika. Sauté in butter. Set the chops on a round dish and put on top a slice of ham sautéed in butter Coat with *Zingara sauce.* See SAUCE.

Escalopes of veal. ESCALOPES DE VEAU—Escalopes of veal are usually cut from the fillet (U.S.A. round) or the best end of the neck (U.S.A. rib) of veal. They can also be taken from the topside or silverside (U.S.A. rump).

These pieces, which average about 3 ounces (100 grams), should be oval, round or heart-shaped. They are lightly flattened and sautéed in butter.

All the recipes given for veal chops are applicable to escalopes. All those given below for escalopes can equally well be used for veal chops.

In the same way, all the recipes given for tournedos (see BEEF) and for *Noisettes* of mutton (see MUTTON), can be applied to veal chops and escalopes.

Escalopes of veal à l'anglaise. ESCALOPES DE VEAU À L'ANGLAISE—Flatten the escalopes lightly; coat them with egg and breadcrumbs. Cook in clarified butter. Set them in a 'crown' on a serving dish and sprinkle with *Noisette butter.* See BUTTER, *Compound butters.*

Escalopes of veal à l'anversoise. ESCALOPES DE VEAU À L'ANVERSOISE—Sauté the escalopes in butter. Set them on croûtons of bread fried in butter. Garnish with *Hop shoots in cream** and small potatoes fried in butter. For sauce use the cooking juices diluted with white wine and with thick brown gravy added.

Escalopes of veal with French (string) beans or other green vegetable. ESCALOPES DE VEAU AUX HARICOTS VERTS —The escalopes can be coated in egg and breadcrumbs or left plain. Sauté them in butter. Set on a round dish. Garnish with French (string) beans in butter and surround with veal gravy. Sprinkle the escalopes with the cooking butter.

Note. Escalopes prepared in this way can be garnished with fresh flageolet beans, new broad beans, asparagus tips, peas, etc., cooked in salted water, drained and mixed with butter.

Escalopes of veal Brancas. ESCALOPES DE VEAU BRANCAS—Cover the escalopes, seasoned with salt and pepper, with a thin layer of *mirepoix** of vegetables cooked till very tender in butter. Coat in egg and breadcrumbs and sauté in clarified butter.

Set on a base of *Annette potatoes* (see POTATOES). Put on top of each escalope a *chiffonnade of lettuce* (see LETTUCE) bound in a rather thick cream sauce.

Pour round the escalopes a few tablespoons of *Demi-glace sauce* (see SAUCE) with Madeira and butter.

Escalopes of veal Casimir. ESCALOPES DE VEAU CASIMIR—Season escalopes taken from the fillet (round) with salt and paprika and sauté them in butter.

Set each on an artichoke bottom cooked gently in butter; put on top a *julienne* of carrot, cut short and thick, stewed in butter with a *julienne* of truffles, cut to the same size, added when the carrots are cooked.

Coat with the cooking juices diluted with cream and seasoned with paprika.

Escalopes of veal with courgettes or aubergines. ESCALOPES DE VEAU AUX COURGETTES, AUX AUBERGINES—Season with salt and pepper 4 escalopes taken from the best end of the neck (U.S.A. rib), trimmed and flattened. Sauté them in butter.

Fry separately in oil 2 courgettes (Italian marrows or zucchini) peeled and cut in round slices, or aubergines (egg-plant) prepared in the same way.

Set the escalopes on a round dish, garnish with the courgettes or aubergines and sprinkle with the cooking juices from the escalopes, diluted with a little white wine and some good, concentrated meat juice which may be seasoned with a little grated garlic. Sprinkle with chopped parsley.

Escalopes of veal à la jardinière. ESCALOPES DE VEAU À LA JARDINIÈRE—The escalopes can be coated in egg and breadcrumbs or left plain. Sauté the escalopes in butter. Set them on a round dish. Garnish with a *jardinière* (see GARNISH) of vegetables bound with butter or cream. Surround with veal gravy and sprinkle with the cooking butter.

Escalopes of veal with rosemary (Italian cookery). ESCALOPES DE VEAU AU ROMARIN—Cut from a piece of boned loin of veal 6 slices about 1 inch thick. Season with salt and pepper and flour them.

Put the slices of loin of veal to cook in a sauté pan with 3 tablespoons (40-50 grams) of very hot butter.

When they are cooked and a good colour on both sides, pour in a glass of white wine; add a small sprig of rosemary, as fresh as possible. Seal the pan hermetically and cook slowly without boiling for 18 to 20 minutes.

Set these slices of loin of veal on a dish and sprinkle them with their juice.

Escalopes of veal à la viennoise. ESCALOPES DE VEAU À LA VIENNOISE—Flatten the escalopes well, season and coat them with egg and breadcrumbs. Cook them in butter. Arrange on a round dish on a layer of *Anchovy butter* (see BUTTER, *Compound butters*). On top of the escalopes put slices of peeled lemon, and on top of each slice of lemon a stoned olive surrounded by a fillet of anchovy.

Set round the escalopes in little heaps the white and yolk of hard boiled eggs, chopped separately, capers and chopped parsley.

Feuilleton of veal 'l'Échelle'. FEUILLETON DE VEAU 'L'ÉCHELLE'—Seal quickly in very hot butter a boned and seasoned fillet (U.S.A. round roast) of veal. Allow to cool. Cut it at regular intervals longways so as to make 'leaves' attached only at the base.

Fill the intervals with a mixture of dry *Duxelles*,* chopped lean ham, truffles cut in dice and an equal quantity of a fine *mirepoix** of vegetables, bound with beaten egg.

Re-form the fillet, cover it with *mirepoix** and wrap it in pig's caul or paper-thin salt pork previously soaked in cold water. Cook covered in the oven in butter.

Set the fillet on a long dish. Garnish with braised lettuce and potatoes fried in butter. For sauce use the cooking juices diluted with Madeira and brown veal gravy.

Feuilleton of cold veal in jelly—See FEUILLETON.

Fillet of veal. FILET DE VEAU—Loin of veal, boned or unboned, a part which in reality includes not only the fillet (U.S.A. sirloin) in the proper sense, but also the part which corresponds to what would be called the eye of the sirloin (U.S.A. tenderloin) in beef. When this piece is served whole it ought to be called loin. It is, in this case, the equivalent of the sirloin of beef.

The true fillet of veal is a very delicate cut and can be prepared alone. From it may also be cut *escalopes*, *noisettes* or *médaillons*, the two last being treated in the same way as the escalopes.

Fillet of veal, cut in square pieces, may also be used to make *sautées à la minute*; they may be skewered to make brochettes, or, lightly flattened, may be grilled.

Veal forcemeat or godiveau—See FORCEMEAT.

Fricadelles of veal. FRICADELLES DE VEAU—Prepared with raw or cooked veal as for *Fricadelles of beef*. See BEEF.

Veal fricandeau. FRICANDEAU—Nowadays this name is given mainly to a dish made of loin of veal (*noix de veau*) larded, braised or roasted (see *Noix de veau* in this section).

Fricassée of veal. FRICASSÉE DE VEAU—Prepared with veal cut into pieces of regular shape and size like *Fricassée of chicken*. See FRICASSÉE.

Grenadins of veal. GRENADINS DE VEAU—Name which describes pieces cut from the topside of veal, like escalopes but smaller and thicker.

They are studded with bacon fat and braised like rump (topside) of veal.

All the garnishes given for rump (topside) of veal, are applicable to *grenadins*.

Knuckle of veal à l'italienne or Osso-bucco. JARRET DE VEAU À L'ITALIENNE—Rounds of knuckle of veal braised in a stock which generally includes tomato purée.

Method. Saw $1\frac{1}{2}$ pounds (750 grams) of knuckle of veal into 8 rounds 2 inches thick, season with salt and pepper, sprinkle with flour and brown nicely in 2-3 tablespoons of lard.

Add 4 tablespoons of chopped onion, cook until pale golden, add 1 cup (2 decilitres) of white wine, cook down, add 4 large tomatoes, peeled, seeded and pressed, and pour in 1 cup (2 decilitres) of white stock or broth. Add a grated clove of garlic and a *bouquet garni** and cook, covered, in the oven for an hour and a half.

Set the pieces of knuckle on a dish and coat them with the concentrated cooking liquor.

Sprinkle over a little lemon juice and some chopped parsley.

Knuckle of veal à la provençale. JARRET DE VEAU À LA PROVENÇALE—Saw the knuckle into chunks of the same thickness. Season with salt and pepper. Cook lightly in oil. Add (for one whole knuckle) $\frac{3}{4}$ cup (150 grams) of finely chopped onion. When the onion is partly cooked, add 4 large tomatoes peeled, seeded and pressed. Season with garlic, pour in $\frac{3}{4}$ cup ($1\frac{1}{2}$ decilitres) of white wine and a few tablespoons of brown veal gravy. Add a *bouquet garni**. Cook, covered, for an hour and a half.

Veal loaf. PAIN DE VEAU—Prepared with *Fine panada forcemeat I*, using veal. See FORCEMEAT.

Loin of veal. LONGE DE VEAU—This cut is the equivalent of the sirloin in beef, and is the part of the carcase which extends from the point of the haunch to the first ribs.

Loin of veal, which is served as a meat entrée, can be braised, cooked covered in the oven, or roasted. When it is roasted it is usually boned first, leaving a strip of skin long enough to wrap round the fillet. The kidney is usually included in this joint, part of the fat surrounding it having been removed.

The loin thus prepared (boned, rolled and with the kidney inside) is sometimes called a *Rognonnade de veau*. It can also be braised.

Braised or baked covered in the oven, the loin of veal can be accompanied by any of the garnishes prescribed for *Noix de veau* (topside or U.S.A. rump of veal).

Matelote of veal. MATELOTE DE VEAU—This is simply *Veal sauté*, the cooking juices diluted with red wine, small onions and mushrooms added and the sauce thickened with *Kneaded butter*. See BUTTER, *Compound butters*.

Médaillons of veal. MÉDAILLONS DE VEAU—Small pieces usually cut from the fillet (U.S.A. sirloin) of veal. These small cuts, which should be round in shape as their name indicates, are prepared like *Escalopes of veal*.

Neck of veal, best end of neck—See *Rib (carré)*.

Noisettes of veal. NOISETTES DE VEAU—Small pieces, round in shape, usually cut from the fillet. Prepared like escalopes.

Noisettes à la Benevent. NOISETTES À LA BENEVENT—'The *noisette* of veal,' says Plumerey, 'is that fat part, oblong in shape, found in the shoulder of veal to the left of the blade bone. In the middle is found an extremely delicate piece of meat about the size of a walnut.

'Procure 16 of these *noisettes*, which should be soaked in water on a corner of the stove for 2 hours and then blanched. Cool in cold water and when nearly cold drain and wipe on a cloth and put them under pressure.

'These noisettes should then be cooked in a braising stock with a *mirepoix** and Madeira.

'They are served garnished with a *macédoine* of vegetables, a purée of sorrel or braised chicory.' (Plumerey's recipe.)

Noix (rump or topside), sous-noix (round or silverside) and fricandeau of veal. NOIX, SOUS-NOIX, FRICANDEAU DE VEAU—The *noix* of veal is the topside (rump), the fleshy upper part of the leg, cut lengthwise.

Below this piece is found another fleshy part, the silverside (the round), which is called in French the *sous-noix* or *noix pâtissière*, also cut lengthwise.

The *noix* is always studded with fine bacon fat, but only the parts next to the bone of the chump end. This part is mostly used for braising. It may also be pot-roasted or roasted. This latter method, however, is seldom used.

The *sous-noix*, or silverside, is also studded with bacon fat and cooked in the same way as the *noix*.

Under the heading CULINARY METHODS all the necessary instructions for braising the *noix* and *sous-noix* of veal will be found.

It is from the *noix* that the piece called the *fricandeau* is cut. This is a slice cut along the grain of the meat and should not be more than $1\frac{1}{2}$ inches thick.

The *fricandeau* is studded with fine bacon fat and usually braised, like the *noix* and *sous-noix*.

Garnishes applicable to the noix (rump or topside), soux-nois (round or silverside) and fricandeau of veal. Bouquetière, *bourgeoise*, endive, mushrooms, *Clamart*, braised chicory, spinach, *jardinière*, various vegetables braised, celery, lettuce, *macédoine*, *milanaise*, sorrel, *piémontaise*, risotto. See GARNISH.

Noix, sous-noix and fricandeau, cold. NOIX, SOUS-NOIX, FRICANDEAU FROIDS—These pieces may be served cold. After having been braised and allowed to cool in the strained braising liquor, they are coated with the same liquor, jellied, and garnished with chopped jelly.

They may be accompanied by any of the garnishes used to garnish cold meat and poultry.

Veal offal or variety meats. ABATS DE VEAU—Veal offal or variety meat is delicate in flavour and lends itself to a considerable number of treatments. See OFFAL OR VARIETY MEATS.

Paupiettes of veal. PAUPIETTES DE VEAU—The paupiettes are made with escalopes of veal cut from the topside or silverside (U.S.A. rump or round), flattened well and rolled up, after having been spread with some forcemeat, usually *Quenelle forcemeat* (see FORCEMEAT) mixed with *duxelles** or chopped truffles.

These paupiettes are very slowly braised, served with some kind of garnish and coated with their braising liquor. All the garnishes given for veal chops or escalopes are applicable to paupiettes.

Paupiettes of veal braised à blanc. PAUPIETTES DE VEAU BRAISÉES À BLANC—Proceed, using paupiettes, in the same way as for *Calf's sweetbreads braised in white stock*. See OFFAL OR VARIETY MEATS.

Paupiettes of veal braised à brun. PAUPIETTES DE VEAU BRAISÉES À BRUN—Spread the paupiettes with *Pork forcemeat* (see FORCEMEAT) mixed with dry *Duxelles** and chopped parsley and bound with egg. Roll them up, bard with bacon and tie them. Put them into a sauté pan, buttered and lined with strips of pork skin (or bacon rinds), and chopped onions and carrots, lightly cooked in butter. Put a *bouquet garni** in the middle. Season with salt and pepper. Cover and allow to cook gently on the stove for 10 minutes, then pour in 1 cup (2 decilitres) of white wine (or Madeira, if more suitable to the accompaniment) for every 10 paupiettes. Boil down this liquid to nothing. Pour in, to three-quarters of the depth of the paupiettes, thickened veal gravy. Cook, covered, in the oven, basting often, for 45 minutes to 1 hour.

Drain the paupiettes, untie them and remove the bards. Glaze them. Set on a serving-dish and coat with the braising liquor, reduced (boiled down) and strained.

Note. Paupiettes braised *à brun* are usually accompanied by vegetables mixed with butter or braised. In some cases these accompaniments can be cooked with the veal, as in *Paupiettes of veal à la bourgeoise*, *à la bourguignonne*, *à la chipolata*, etc.

When the paupiettes are accompanied by buttered vegetables or purée of vegetables, fresh or dried, the vegetables are often served separately.

Paupiettes of veal à la grecque—See PAUPIETTES.

Hot fillet of veal pâté—See PÂTÉS.

Quasi and rouelle of veal (English chump end of loin, U.S.A. heel of round). QUASI ET ROUELLE DE VEAU—The quasi is a piece taken from the leg. It is cooked in a covered pan in butter, or braised.

All the garnishes given for the *noix* (English topside, U.S.A. rump), the *fricandeau*, the *carré* (English best end of neck, U.S.A. rib) and the loin are applicable.

Ragoûts of veal. RAGOÛTS DE VEAU—Made with shoulder, breast and scrag (U.S.A. neck). These, whether boned or not, are cut into pieces 2 inches square. Veal *ragoûts* are made in the same way as those of mutton. (See illustration on next page.)

Rib (carré) of veal. CARRÉ DE VEAU—Best end of neck (U.S.A. rib) is scarcely ever cooked in one piece. This

Veal ragoût

joint is nevertheless excellent, baked, roasted or braised, and provides an enjoyable meat course.

To prepare the whole *carré* proceed as follows: Cut down the top of the joint; remove the spinal bone (this makes the joint much easier to carve). Season and wrap in thin bards of bacon fat.

Roast in the oven, allowing 30 minutes to the pound at 325°F.; pot-roast it or braise it in the usual way.

Set the *carré* (the bacon fat and string removed) on the serving dish. Garnish with watercress and serve with its cooking juices, diluted if the meat has been roasted. If it has been braised or cooked covered surround it with the prescribed garnish.

Note. Any of the garnishes indicated elsewhere for loin or *noix* of veal are applicable to the *carré*, whether roasted, pot-roasted or braised. According to their nature the garnishes are set around the meat or served separately.

Cold rib of veal. CARRÉ DE VEAU FROID—Roast the rib of veal in the usual way, trim it, coat with jelly, set on a serving dish and garnish with cress.

Cold rib of veal may be prepared as described in any of the recipes given elsewhere for loin or *noix* of veal.

Saddle of veal. SELLE DE VEAU—This cut consists of the entire back of the animal.

Saddle of veal is braised, pot-roasted or roasted. It is accompanied by any of the garnishes normally served with meat, notably those given for *Noix* (*topside or rump*) *of veal*.

Veal sautés. SAUTÉS DE VEAU—Usually made from the same cuts as *ragoûts*. After the meat has been lightly fried, the juices in the pan are diluted with white wine, and stock or sauce of some kind, varying according to the recipe, is added.

Cut the veal into pieces of regular size and shape. Season it and cook it lightly in butter, oil or fat, according to the nature of the preparation.

Drain off the fat; dilute the remaining juices with white wine and add veal gravy or *Demi-glace sauce*.

Cook covered for an hour or an hour and a half.

Drain the pieces of meat. Trim them and put into another saucepan; add the prescribed garnish, pour over the strained sauce from which all grease has been removed, and simmer all together for 15 to 20 minutes over a low heat.

Serve in a deep dish or in a border of pilaf rice or risotto.

Note. When thick veal gravy or *Demi-glace sauce* is not available, the veal may be moistened with stock (or water) and thickened with *Kneaded butter* (see BUTTER, *Compound butters*). It may also be treated in the way suggested for *ragoûts*, that is to say it may be sprinkled with flour then moistened with the prescribed liquid.

Veal sauté with aubergines (egg-plant). SAUTÉ DE VEAU AUX AUBERGINES—Like *Lamb sauté with aubergines* (*egg-plant*),* made with shoulder chops or end chops of veal, boned and cut into square pieces.

Veal sauté with cèpes, morels or St George's agarics. SAUTÉ DE VEAU AVEC CÈPES, MORILLES, MOUSSERONS—Proceed as for *Lamb sauté with cèpes*.*

Veal sauté chasseur. SAUTÉ DE VEAU CHASSEUR—Cook 1½ pounds of veal lightly in a mixture of butter and oil. Dilute with a little dry white wine, add 4 chopped shallots and stir in veal stock and *Tomato sauce* (see SAUCE). Add a *bouquet garni*.* Cook for an hour and a half.

Veal sauté Clamart. SAUTÉ DE VEAU CLAMART—Prepare the veal sauté as in the first recipe. When the pieces of veal are almost cooked, drain them and put back in the sauté pan. Cover them with peas cooked *à la française*, but not completely cooked. Pour over the cooking liquor from the sauté, strained and with all grease removed. Finish cooking, covered, in the oven.

Veal sauté à la crème. SAUTÉ DE VEAU À LA CRÈME—Prepared like *Lamb sauté à la crème*,* using veal, boned and cut into small squares.

Veal sauté aux fines herbes. SAUTÉ DE VEAU AUX FINES HERBES—Prepared like *Lamb sauté aux fines herbes*.*

Veal sauté à la hongroise. SAUTÉ DE VEAU À LA HONGROISE—Cook 1½ pounds (750 grams) of veal lightly in butter. When it is half cooked, add 2 tablespoons of chopped onion and sprinkle with paprika. Dilute the pan juices with white wine, then stir in 4 cups (8 decilitres) of light *Velouté sauce* (see SAUCE) and add a *bouquet garni*.* Cook for 1½ hours.

Drain the pieces, trim and put into another sauté pan.

How to turn out a rice border for a sauté of veal

Pour over the sauce, strained and diluted with a few tablespoons of cream. Allow to simmer for 15 minutes. Serve in a deep dish.

Veal sauté à l'indienne. SAUTÉ DE VEAU L'INDIENNE—Cook the veal lightly in butter. When it is half cooked add 2 tablespoons of chopped onion. Cook together for 5 minutes.

Drain off the fat; sprinkle with a teaspoon of curry powder and a tablespoon of flour. Cook till golden; stir in 4 cups (8 decilitres) of white stock; add a good *bouquet garni*. Cook for 1½ hours.

Set in a deep dish and serve *Rice à l'indienne** separately.

Veal sauté à l'italienne. SAUTÉ DE VEAU À L'ITALIENNE—Prepared like *Lamb sauté à l'italienne.**

Veal sauté Marengo. SAUTÉ DE VEAU MARENGO—Cook 1½ pounds (750 grams) of veal lightly in oil. When it is half cooked add 2 tablespoons of chopped onion and a crushed clove of garlic.

Dilute the pan juices with white wine. Stir in 3 cups (6 decilitres) of thickened veal stock and 1 cup (2 decilitres) of *Tomato sauce* (see SAUCE). Add a *bouquet garni.** Cook for 1½ hours.

Drain the pieces, trim them and put them back in a sauté pan with 12 small glacé onions and 12 mushrooms sautéed in oil. Pour over them the sauce, strained and with all grease removed, and simmer for 15 minutes.

Set in a deep dish, sprinkle with crushed parsley and garnish with heart-shaped croûtons fried in butter or oil.

Note. Although a preparation *à la Marengo*, a style chiefly applied to chicken (see CHICKEN, *Chicken sauté à la Marengo*) normally includes truffles, crayfish and fried egg yolks, this veal sauté is garnished only with onions and mushrooms.

Veal sauté à la minute. SAUTÉ DE VEAU À LA MINUTE—Cut boned shoulder chops or end chops of veal into small squares. Season them with salt and pepper and sauté quickly in smoking hot butter. Finish cooking in the oven.

Arrange in a deep dish and pour over a sauce made by diluting the pan juices with ¾ cup (1½ decilitres) of white wine, boiling down, adding a tablespoon of dissolved meat glaze, 3 tablespoons of butter and the juice of half a lemon and stirring well. Sprinkle with chopped parsley.

Veal sauté with mushrooms. SAUTÉ DE VEAU AUX CHAMPIGNONS—Fry lightly in butter 1½ pounds (750 grams) of veal, cut as for a *ragoût* and seasoned with salt and pepper.

Drain off all fat, dilute the pan juices with white wine and add 4 cups (8 decilitres) of stock or thickened veal gravy or a light *Demi-glace sauce*. See SAUCE.

Add a *bouquet garni**; cook very slowly for 1½ hours.

Drain the pieces of meat, trim and put them into another sauté pan with ½ pound (250 grams) of mushrooms previously sautéed in butter (whole if they are small, sliced if they are large).

Pour over the strained sauce from which all grease has been removed. Boil down, if necessary. Allow to simmer all together for 15 minutes.

Veal sauté Parmentier. SAUTÉ DE VEAU PARMENTIER—Prepared like *Chicken sauté Parmentier.**

Veal sauté à la portugaise. SAUTÉ DE VEAU À LA PORTUGAISE—Cook the veal lightly in oil with a tablespoon of chopped onion and a crushed clove of garlic.

Dilute the pan juices with white wine. Stir in 1 cup (2 decilitres) of concentrated and thickened veal gravy and 2 cups (4 decilitres) of *Tomato sauce* (see SAUCE). Season, add a *bouquet garni** and cook for 1½ hours.

Drain the pieces, trim them, put into another sauté pan with 6 or 8 large tomatoes, peeled, seeded, pressed and cooked lightly in oil, add a tablespoon of chopped parsley, pour over the sauce, strained and boiled down, and simmer together for 15 minutes.

Veal sauté à la printanière. SAUTÉ DE VEAU À LA PRINTANIÈRE—Proceed as for *Veal sauté with mushrooms*. Garnish with 4-5 small new carrots (150 grams), 2 small new turnips (100 grams) cut to look like olives, 12 small glazed onions and 1 cup (2 decilitres) of fresh peas.

Small new potatoes may also be added to the garnish.

Veal sauté with red wine I, or Matelote of veal. SAUTÉ DE VEAU AU VIN ROUGE, MATELOTE DE VEAU—Cook 1½ pounds (750 grams) of veal lightly in butter with a large onion cut into quarters.

Pour in 3 cups (6 decilitres) of red wine and 1 cup (2 decilitres) of white stock. Add a crushed clove of garlic and a *bouquet garni**. Cook for 1½ hours.

Drain the pieces, trim and put into another sauté pan with 12 small glazed onions and ¼ pound (125 grams) of mushrooms sautéed in butter.

Pour over the cooking liquor boiled down by one-third, thickened with 2 tablespoons of *Kneaded butter* (see BUTTER, *Compound butters*) and strained. Simmer, covered, for 15 minutes.

Veal sauté with red wine II. SAUTÉ DE VEAU AU VIN ROUGE—Brown the pieces of veal, then sprinkle them with a good tablespoon of flour. Cook till the flour colours lightly; stir in red wine and white stock and finish off in the same way as for *Ragoûts à brun*. See RAGOÛT, *Method of cooking brown ragoûts*.

Shoulder of veal. ÉPAULE DE VEAU—This cut, which is quite large, is generally boned before being cooked.

Once boned, the meat of the shoulder must be well-beaten inside and seasoned with salt and pepper, then rolled and tied. Thus prepared, it can be pot-roasted, roasted or braised. Braised shoulder is prepared in the same way as braised topside (*noix de veau* or U.S.A. rump) and is served with the same garnishes.

The shoulder can also be stuffed with some kind of forcemeat. Boned, it is also used to make *ragoûts, fricassées, blanquettes* and *sautés*.

It is also used to make different kinds of forcemeat.

Shoulder of veal à la boulangère. ÉPAULE DE VEAU À LA BOULANGÈRE—Proceed with a shoulder of veal, boned and rolled, as for *Shoulder of mutton à la boulangère*. See MUTTON.

Shoulder of veal à la bourgeoise. ÉPAULE DE VEAU À LA BOURGEOISE—Rolled, stuffing optional. Braise the shoulder in the usual way (see CULINARY METHODS, *Braising white meat*). Serve with a *Bourgeoise garnish*. See GARNISHES.

Stuffed shoulder of veal. ÉPAULE DE VEAU FARCIE—Bone a medium-sized shoulder of veal and beat the inside surface well. Season with salt, pepper and a pinch of spice. Spread with a thick layer of fine forcemeat or sausage meat mixed with chopped herbs and well seasoned. Roll up the shoulder and tie it to keep in a good shape. Braise in the usual way.

Drain the shoulder and remove the strings. Glaze it and set on a serving dish. Pour over a little of the braising liquor boiled down and strained, and serve either as it is or accompanied by some kind of garnish.

Shoulder of veal stuffed à l'anglaise. ÉPAULE DE VEAU FARCIE À L'ANGLAISE—Stuff the shoulder, boned as above, with a forcemeat made as follows: one-third calf's or ox (beef) kidney, one-third udder or veal fat (both these ingredients finely chopped), one-third breadcrumbs soaked in milk and pressed, and 2 eggs, to each 2 pounds (kilo) of forcemeat, all well seasoned and mixed.

Roll and tie the shoulder. Braise in the usual way or roast, if preferred.

Serve accompanied by boiled bacon and sprinkled with some of the concentrated braising liquor or, if the shoulder is roasted, with its own gravy.

Tendrons (English middle-cut breast, U.S.A. riblets) of veal. TENDRONS DE VEAU—These pieces are cut from the extremities of the ribs, from the point at which the chops are generally cut, to the sternum.

To qualify for the name *tendron* these pieces must include the full width of the breast. Cut across, they are not tendrons. Cut in square pieces they are used to make ragoûts and sautés.

Tendrons are generally braised with very little liquid and can be accompanied by one of the garnishes given either for the *noix* of veal or *fricandeau*, or for the rib or loin. Instead of being braised they may be cooked in butter without moisture in a covered pan.

Tendrons à la bourgeoise. TENDRONS DE VEAU À LA BOURGEOISE—Braise 4 tendrons. When half-cooked add 12 small glazed onions, 12 carrots cut to look like olives and glazed and 2 ounces (50 grams) of streaky (lean) bacon cut in dice, blanched and fried. Finish cooking together. Glaze the meat, set on a serving dish with the garnish and sprinkle with the cooking juices.

Tendrons chasseur. TENDRONS DE VEAU CHASSEUR—Bake the tendrons covered with butter. In the same casserole cook lightly 5 ounces (150 grams) of chopped mushrooms. Dilute the cooking juices with ½ cup (1 decilitre) of white wine, add ½ cup (1 decilitre) of *Demi-glace sauce* and ¼ cup (½ decilitre) of *Tomato sauce*. See SAUCE.

Boil for a few moments, pour over the tendrons and sprinkle with chopped parsley, chervil and tarragon.

Tendrons à la jardinière. TENDRONS DE VEAU À LA JARDINIÈRE—Braise the tendrons or pot-roast them covered with butter. Set them on a serving dish with a *jardinière garnish* (see GARNISHES); sprinkle with their cooking juices.

Tendrons with mushrooms. TENDRONS DE VEAU AUX CHAMPIGNONS—As above. Garnish with 5 ounces (150 grams) of peeled mushrooms.

Tendrons with noodles or risotto. TENDRONS DE VEAU AUX NOUILLES, AU RISOTTO—Braised or pot-roasted tendrons accompanied by noodles or risotto. Sprinkle with their cooking juices.

Tendrons à la provençale. TENDRONS DE VEAU À LA PROVENÇALE—Prepare in the same way as *Knuckle of veal à la provençale*.

Tendrons with risotto. TENDRONS DE VEAU AU RISOTTO—Braise the tendrons with as little liquid as possible. Set them on a round dish and garnish with risotto to which diced mushrooms and truffles has been added.

Tendrons with spinach or sorrel. TENDRONS DE VEAU AUX ÉPINARDS, À L'OSEILLE—Braise the tendrons in the usual way. Serve them sprinkled with their cooking juices accompanied by spinach in butter or sorrel, braised separately.

VEGETABLE. LÉGUME—In current speech a vegetable is any kitchen-garden plant used for food.

We eat vegetables in their natural state. We also eat animals which feed only on vegetables and vegetation. In the last analysis, therefore, it might be said that plants are our only food.

This shows the considerable importance of vegetables in our diet. Furthermore, the infinite variety of dishes available to us is due to the plants, vegetables, and condiments which provide such a rich range of flavours, for they have been fundamental to the art of cooking since that remote time in antiquity when one of our ancestors first hit upon the idea of cooking a piece of meat and a few roots in the same pot.

All the essentials of a balanced diet are present in vegetables: protein, fats, carbohydrates, mineral salts and vitamins. Though the amount of each of these elements varies in different vegetables, in no other type of food are they more readily assimilable.

A vast number of plants, edible in their wild state, have been greatly improved by cultivation and selective breeding. We have today a great many vegetables unknown to our ancestors.

In some vegetables one part is edible, in others, another. Roots, bulbs or tubers are eaten in the case of potatoes, sweet potatoes, yams, root chervil, various kinds of Jerusalem artichoke, carrots, various kinds of turnips, black radishes, radishes, kohlrabi, celeriac, beetroot, black and white salsify, Chinese artichoke, onions, sorrel, etc. We eat the young shoots of asparagus, hops, bramble, etc., and the stems of leeks, edible thistle, celery, beet and rhubarb, etc. We eat the leaves of spinach, orach, tetragonia, purslane, sorrel, all kinds of cabbage, lettuce, chicory, endive, watercress, dandelion, corn-salad, etc. In the case of cauliflowers and artichokes, etc., we eat the flowers.

Tomatoes, cucumbers, small and large marrows (squashes), melons, ladies' fingers (okra), sweet peppers and pumpkins are all fruits. We also eat ripe seeds, such as cereals and pulses, and other seeds before they are fully ripe, such as green peas, sugar-peas and beans, green corn, etc. If we add fungi and truffles to this list, it will be obvious that strict vegetarians need not want for a varied diet.

Most vegetables lose some of their water in cooking (this is true even of boiled vegetables) and, in consequence, suffer a loss of weight. This loss is much more substantial in the case of green vegetables than roots or tubers. Cereals and pulses generally increase in weight in cooking. This is especially true of dried vegetables. Dried vegetables are often soaked in water before cooking. It is always advisable to cook them in the water in which they have been soaking.

Modern methods of conserving and freezing vegetables make them richer in nutritive values than all but the very fresh vegetables, and although they can never replace garden-fresh vegetables, the frozen and canned vegetables provide great variety to the table. See PRESERVATION OF FOOD.

Vegetable fumet. FUMET DE LÉGUMES—This fumet is made by boiling down almost to nothing the stock of different vegetables, such as carrots, onions, leeks and celery.

Vegetable julienne à la bretonne. JULIENNE DE LÉGUMES À LA BRETONNE—Shred finely the white part of 2 leeks (100 grams), 4 stalks (100 grams) of white celery and 1 small onion (50 grams). Stew them slowly in 3 tablespoons (50 grams) of butter. Season. When the vegetables are three-parts cooked, add 4 tablespoons (50 grams) of shredded raw mushrooms.

According to the main dish with which it is to be served, blend either with meat or vegetable *Velouté sauce* (see SAUCE) and a few tablespoons of cream or serve plain.

Vegetable loaves. PAIN DE LÉGUMES—These loaves are usually made, using braised vegetables, mixed with eggs beaten as for an omelette, poured into a buttered plain mould and poached in a *bain-marie** (pan of hot water).

By following the recipe given for *Endive loaf* (see

ENDIVE), various other vegetable loaves can be made: artichoke, aubergine (egg-plant), carrot, cauliflower, spinach, lettuce, turnip, etc.

This type of loaf, made in large moulds, is served as a small entrée. They usually have a sauce, generally a cream sauce, poured over them.

Small vegetable loaves are used as a garnish for meat and broiled, braised or poached poultry. They can also be used for garnishing fish dishes or poached or soft-boiled eggs.

Vegetable pickles (achards) (commercial product)—A mixture of different vegetables and fruit spiced with vinegar and mustard. Achards can be bought ready-made but here is a recipe to prepare it in the home. Divide into quarters, rounds or pieces, according to the nature of each article, the following vegetables: asparagus tips, very small maize (corn), new carrots, white and red radishes, celeriac, turnips and artichoke hearts. Add small bouquets of cauliflower, whole almonds still green and hardly formed (if available—otherwise a few blanched almonds), small green walnuts, cumquats, very small apricots, green apples in quarters, green and red pimentos, mushrooms and gherkins.

Blanch all these ingredients for one minute in boiling salt water, drain them and marinate them for 24 hours in vinegar.

Drain all the vegetables and fruit, mix them together and put them in a jar. Cover with the following marinade: To make 4 quarts (litres) in all, boil 3 quarts (litres) of strong vinegar, remove from fire and add ¼ cup (30 grams) of coriander, ¾ cup (100 grams) of powdered ginger, 7 tablespoons (50 grams) of peppercorns, 4 tablespoons (50 grams) of mustard grains, 4 teaspoons (10 grams) of red pepper, 4 teaspoons (10 grams) of saffron and 2 tablespoons (30 grams) of salt.

Cover the marinade and let it stand for 10 minutes. Strain through a cloth and filter. Add 1 quart (litre) of oil and mix well. Put the vegetables and fruit in jars and cover with the marinade. Seal firmly and expose to the sun for 8 to 10 days.

Vegetable stalks and stumps. MOELLES VÉGÉTALES—The French word *moelle* derives from *molle* (soft) and is applied in cookery to certain tender vegetable stalks and the tender parts of vegetable stumps.

VEGETABLE PEAR—See CHAYOTE.

VELOUTÉ—In cookery this name is used more than anything else as the title for a white sauce made with white veal or chicken stock, a basic sauce which is used as a base for a number of other sauces, notably *Allemande*.

The word is used to describe certain thickened soups. See SOUPS AND BROTHS.

There are meat and fish *veloutés*. The first is obtained by adding white stock (veal or poultry) to white *roux** (a blend of butter and flour). The second are made with fish stock or fish *fumet*.*

When, towards the end of the cooking, egg yolks are added for thickening, the *velouté* becomes *Allemande sauce*. This sauce is used very frequently.

Velouté is the basis for most white sauces. Recipes for these are to be found in alphabetical order under SAUCE.

VENISON. VENAISON—This word is used for the meat of any kind of deer. In French, and formerly in English, it described the meat of any kind of game animal or wild beast killed for food, and *basse venaison* is the meat of hare or wild rabbit.

For other recipes for venison, see ROEBUCK.

Haunch of venison (English cookery). HANCHE DE VENAISON—After having rubbed the quarter of venison with a mixture of flour and pepper, hang it in a cool, well-aired place and leave it for 3 or 4 days.

To cook. Trim and cover completely with a flour and water paste. Wrap in strong paper, tie with string.

Roast on the spit, basting often, allowing 3 to 4 hours for a haunch of deer.

Ten minutes before removing from the spit take off the flour and water paste, pour melted butter over the meat and sprinkle it with salt and flour.

Brown over hot fire.

Note. The custom in England is to serve the haunch of venison with boiled French (string) beans and red-currant jelly.

VENUS—Type of mollusc usually called the cockle, found in all seas.

All types of these are edible. They are eaten raw, like oysters, or cooked like mussels.

VERJUICE. VERJUS—Acid juice extracted from large unripened grapes. This is used like vinegar.

Some writers say that in former times the word *verjus* meant *sauce verte* which was sold in the streets of Paris.

VERMICELLI—A *pasta** whose descriptive name suggests its wormlike form. It is used for soups, puddings and soufflés.

VERMOUTH—Word deriving from the German *vermut* which means absinthe. A white wine flavoured with various bitter ingredients such as absinthe, anise, cinnamon, coriander, bitter orange peel, cloves, quassia, quinine, elderberries, etc.

VERT-PRÉ—Method of preparing certain grilled meats. These grills are garnished with straw potatoes and water-cress and are generally served with *Maître d'hôtel butter* (see BUTTER, *Compound butters*), containing plenty of chopped parsley.

Certain foodstuffs (such as poultry or fish) coated with *Green mayonnaise* (see SAUCE) are also called *vert-pré*.

VERVAIN, VERBENA. VERVEINE—Plant cultivated in gardens. The dried leaves of verbena, which are highly scented, are used to make infusions.

VESPETRO—Old liqueur, now hardly ever made in France, which formerly had a high reputation.

It was made in the district round Metz and its fame, which was very great in the eighteenth century, came chiefly from the fact that Louis XV drank a great deal of it to restore his failing strength.

This liqueur was flavoured with the seeds of angelica, coriander, anise and fennel.

VETCH. GESSE—A name used for several different pulses; some of them are used as food. The cultivated vetch, originally from the Caucasus, then cultivated in Spain, was imported into France about the middle of the seventeenth century. Its seeds are eaten green, like peas.

Chick-vetch is used in the same way as chick-peas.

The tuber-vetch has a starchy root which is roasted in hot ash and which tastes something like chestnuts.

VICHY (Carrots à la)—Carrots are thought to be good for afflictions of the liver and are much used at Vichy whose waters are particularly favourable for hepatic conditions. For the preparation of *Carrots à la Vichy*, see CARROTS.

VICTORIA—In the culinary repertoire there are a great number of dishes dedicated to Queen Victoria. Some of the best known are: *Sole* (*or other fish*) *Victoria*, *Poularde Victoria*, *Salade Victoria* and *Bombe Victoria*.

VICTORIA CAKE—Made like plum cake using 2 pounds (1 kilo) of butter, 3 cups (750 grams) of sugar, ½ pound (250 grams) of ground almonds mixed with 2 eggs, 22 eggs (put in one by one), 11¼ cups (1 kilo 500 grams) of flour mixed with 3 teaspoons (10 grams) of baking powder, 1 pound (500 grams) of crystallized cherries, 13 ounces (400 grams) of chopped peel, ½ cup (1 decilitre) of rum, the grated rind of 2 lemons, 2 teaspoons (5 grams) of cinnamon and 2 teaspoons (5 grams) of powdered cloves.

VIDELLE—Small gadget used in confectionery to remove the stones from some fruits. Also known by this name is a utensil used in pastry-making which is really only a wheel pastry-cutter.

VIENNESE PASTRY. KNUSPER—Make a short pastry from 2¾ cups (350 grams) of sieved flour, 1 cup (225 grams) of butter, ¾ cup (175 grams) of sugar, a teaspoon of cinnamon and, if necessary, a little milk. Let the dough stand for 15 minutes. Roll it out. Put it in a buttered baking tin. Brush the surface with egg and sprinkle with chopped almonds and crystallized sugar. Bake in a medium oven (375°F.). When the cake is a good colour, take it out of the oven. While it is still hot cut it into rectangles. It can be eaten fresh or may be kept for several days in a tin.

VIERGE—Butter mixed with salt, pepper and lemon juice, all beaten will in a bowl until it becomes frothy. This whipped butter is served with asparagus and other boiled vegetables.

VIN DE MARCHÉ OR POT DE VIN—Formerly this was the wine given as a present to someone who had acted as an intermediary in a business transaction. This wine was later replaced by a present of any kind or even by a sum of money.

VIN DES NOCES (MARRIAGE WINE)—This wine was a gift offered to the priest who performed a marriage ceremony. 'In certain dioceses', says M. Chernel (*Dictionnaire historique des institutions, moeurs et coutumes de France*) 'the priest, in blessing the nuptial bed, mixed together red and white wine to symbolize the union of the bride and bridegroom.

'In the diocese of Amiens, the priest began by blessing the bread and wine; he then dipped three *rôties* (rusks) in the wine, one for himself, one for the bridal pair and the third for the friends and relations present at the ceremony. After taking his own, he gave the bridal pair theirs and finished with that of the other guests; then he blessed the bed.'

VINAGE, FORTIFICATION—Addition of alcohol to a must or a wine.

VINAIGRETTE—Mixture of oil and vinegar seasoned with salt and pepper and sometimes with the addition of chopped herbs. See SAUCE, *Cold sauces*.

VINAIGRIER—Small barrel, of wood or earthenware, in which vinegar is made.

VINCENT—Cold sauce prepared with various herbs, blanched, pounded and sieved, and hard boiled eggs. See SAUCE, *Cold sauces*.

VINE. VIGNE—Plant growing wild in Europe and Asia Minor, whose discovery is, in all religions, attributed to divine intervention. It is mentioned in Genesis and in the most ancient Egyptian and Greek documents. In antiquity

Pruning the vine in the Médoc
(*French Government Tourist Office*)

the Greek vine growers of Scio were particularly renowned; among the Romans the wines of Campania, Falernia, Massicus, etc. held first place.

It was first the Greeks and then the Romans who brought the cultivation of the vine to Provence and Gaul. In France itself the vine is cultivated in the region south of a line passing through Mézières, Beauvais, Paris and the lower Loire, and the regions particularly devoted to vine-cultivation are the Aude, the Gard and the Hérault.

The yield of the vine depends on the variety; in general it is considered that 286 pounds (130 kilos) of grapes give 26,418 gallons (a hectolitre) of wine and 35 to 48 pounds (16 to 22 kilos) of marc.

The legend of the vine (*from the Talmud*):
Noah planted the vine.
'What are you doing there?' the devil asked him.
'I am planting a vine.'
'What is the use of that?'

Spraying vines in the Gironde
(*French Government Tourist Office*

'Its fruit, freshly picked or dried, is sweet and good: the pressed juice gladdens the heart of man.'

'Let us work together,' said the devil.

'I should like that,' said Noah.

The vine planted, the devil went in search of a lamb, a lion, a monkey and a pig. He cut their throats and poured their blood on the ground.

That is why when man eats the fruit of the vine he is as gentle as a lamb; when he drinks wine he believes himself a lion; if by chance he drinks too much he grimaces like a monkey and when he is often drunk he is nothing more than a vile pig.

Principal varieties—Among the principal varieties are the following:

RED VARIETIES OF BORDEAUX

Cabernet Franc. The important vineyards for Médoc:

Bunch. Medium, cylindro-conic, pointed, upward-angled.

Fruit. Medium, round, with thick hard skin, covered with bloom, black-violet, crisp.

Juice. Thick, viscous, sweet-tasting, free.

Malbec or Cot. Vines of the Coasts, often mixed with the preceding:

Bunch. Long, large, not very tightly packed.

Fruit. Oval, soft, thin-skinned, black-violet.

Bloom. Pronounced.

Juice. Sweet, pleasant, without positive flavour.

WHITE VARIETIES OF BORDEAUX

Sauvignon. Important vineyards of Sauternes and Château-Yquem, usually mixed with white Sémillon:

Bunch. Small, thick, closely pressed together.

Fruit. Oblong, small, amber-coloured, black-spotted, small-pipped, short stalks.

Juice. Sweet, pleasant.

Sémillon.

Bunch. Large, cylindro-conic.

Fruit. Globular, pale yellow.

RED VARIETIES OF BURGUNDY

Pinot noir. Important vineyard for Burgundy:

Bunch. Small, strongly attached.

Fruit. Small, elliptical by being crammed together, thick-skinned, black, firm, rich in colour, rather velvety.

Juice. Plentiful, sweet, without much flavour.

Gamay. Burgundy-Beaujolais:

Bunch. Close-packed, medium-sized, cylindrical.

Fruit. Long, medium-sized, elliptical, black.

Pineau blanc

WHITE VARIETIES OF BURGUNDY

Pinot, or Pine, or Chardonnay. Important vineyards for Burgundy and Champagne:

Bunch. Small, short, compact.

Fruit. Small, round, light green, golden on side next to the sun, firm flesh.

Flavour. Simple, rather heightened.

Clairette

PRINCIPAL VARIETIES OF THE SOUTH OF FRANCE, RED AND WHITE

Piquepoul. Wines of the south of France:

Bunch. Medium, markedly wing-shaped.

Fruit. Small, oblong, juicy, black or grey.

Grenache. Wines of the Roussillon:

Bunch. Large, woody.

Fruit. Oblong, coloured, very sweet.

Clairette blanche. Picardan and table grapes:

Bunch. Medium-sized, rather long, wing-shaped.

Fruit. Elongated, rather tight, transparent, white.

Marsanne. White Ermitage:

Bunch. Large, grooved.

Fruit. Small, globular, golden yellow.

Syrah. Red Ermitage, *Côte Rôtie*:

Bunch. Large, conical.

Fruit. Medium-sized, elliptical, firm, black, velvety.

Malvoisie. Liqueur wines:

Bunch. Voluminous, wing-shaped.

Fruit. Ovoid, golden on side facing the sun, juicy, very sweet and full tasting.

White muscat. Frontignan:

Bunch. Medium-sized, elongated, quite regular.

Fruit. Medium-sized, round, amber-yellow, firm fleshed, musky, very sweet.

Folle blanche. Brandy:

Bunch. Medium-sized, close packed, rather wing-shaped.

Fruit. Medium-sized, spherical, greenish-white or yellow according to the sun.

Poulsard. Jura wines:

Bunch. Rather loose, markedly wing-shaped.

Fruit. Elliptical, reddish-brown.

Chasselas doré.

Bunch. Medium-sized, conical, wing-shaped.

Fruit. Medium-sized, spherical, fine, thin skin, pale green at first then greenish-white with touches of reddish-gold on the side next to the sun.

Flesh. Crisp, pleasantly sweet, heightened flavour.

Among other varieties there may be mentioned:

Le Corbeau, La Mondeuse. Wines of the Savoy, Isère and Montmélian.

Le Quillaut. Wine of the Jurançon.
Le Tressot à bon vin. Wine of the Rycey.
La Verdesse. Wines of the Grésivaudan.
La Boussase. Wines of the Drôme.
La Précoce de Malingre. Wines of the Paris district.
Le Blanc Brun. Wine of the Arbois.
Le Corbel. Wine of the Ermitage.
Le Grec-Rouge. Wines of the Haute-Loire.
Le Chemin blanc. Wines of Anjou.
Le Burger blanc. Wines of Alsace.
L'Aramon. Wines of the Gard.
L'Altesse verte. Wines of the Loire.
Le Mourvèdre. Wines of Provence.

Vine leaves. FEUILLES DE VIGNE—Tender vine leaves have various uses in cookery.

Certain types of game, especially quail and partridge, are wrapped in vine leaves, as well as being barded with pork fat.

Dolmas à la turque are made by wrapping balls made from a mixture of rice and meat in vine leaves (see DOLMAS).

Tender vine leaves are also used for making fritters.

Very tender vine leaves, finely shredded, are used to flavour green salads.

They are also used in the presentation of fruit in bowls and baskets.

VINEGAR. VINAIGRE—Produce of the acetic fermentation of wine under the action of a fungus, the *mycoderma aceti*, making its first appearance in the form of a light veil, which penetrates the liquid more and more, forming a thick, folded, sticky skin, which is called the *mère de vinaigre*. This micro-organism is developed between 15° and 30°C. (59° and 86°F.).

A good vinegar must be clear and transparent, colourless if it is made from white wine, pinkish if it comes from red wine, but always lighter coloured than the latter; it must have a frankly acid taste, and an aroma recalling that of the wine from which it comes.

Vinegar is made of any kind of alcoholic liquid (alcoholized water, beer, cider, perry, milk, etc.); alcohol vinegar is colourless if it has not been tinted with caramel; it is without taste or smell. Cider vinegar is yellowish, always less acid than wine vinegar; beer vinegar is yellow, slightly bitter; its flavour recalls that of bitter beer; glucose vinegar always has a taste of fermented flour; wood vinegar has an acid taste; vinegar made from *piquettes* or from marc has a characteristic smell.

It is an everyday condiment, serving to conserve some substances in marinades or pickles; it has no disadvantages, so long as acid condiments are not forbidden in the diet. For table use, vinegar is often flavoured with tarragon, onion, shallot, herbs, etc.

The use of vinegar as seasoning for foodstuffs has a high place in the story of human diet. This use is proved, first in Biblical times, by the book of Ruth (II, 14): 'And Boaz said unto her, "At mealtime come thou hither and eat of the bread, and dip thy morsel in the vinegar",' and later in Greek and Roman antiquity, by the words *oxybaphon* and *acetabulum* (vinegar vessel), the names for certain bowls that were placed, filled with vinegar, on the dining table, for guests to dip their bread in.

In the thirteenth century among the street vendors who had the right to cry their wares in Paris, some rolled a barrel in the street, announcing to the *hôteliers* and housewives: 'Vinaigres bons et biaux! vinaigre de moutarde i ail!' ('Good and beautiful vinegars! Mustard and garlic vinegar!').

'In 1657, an edict of Charles IX accorded the bourgeois of Paris the privilege of selling vinegar made from the wine of their vineyards, in small quantities and *à pot*, and it was chiefly this that the young boys sold as they wheeled their barrows from one district to another, with their caps, their aprons lifted and draped on their hips, their half-litre mugs or *chopines* in their hands, crying at every door, '*marchand de vinaigre! du bon vinaigre!*'.

Aromatic vinegar. VINAIGRE AROMATIQUE—A mixture of 4 ounces (125 grams) of vulnerary alcohol with 29 ounces (875 grams) of vinegar.

Raspberry vinegar. VINAIGRE FRAMBOISE—Pour into a stoneware jar 2 quarts (litres) of vinegar and as many raspberries as it can contain; leave for 8 days. Strain without pressure through a horsehair strainer.

Rose vinegar. VINAIGRE ROSAT—Add 3 ounces (100 grams) of red rose petals to a quart (litre) of vinegar and leave to macerate for 10 days.

VIOLET. VIOLETTE—The sweet violet is one of the species of *fleurs pectorales*. Their petals are candied in sugar.

Candied violets are used in pastry-making, confectionery, the making of ices and iced mousses and in the preparation of salads.

VIRGOULEUSE—Name of a winter pear, so called because it comes from the commune of Virgoulée, near Limoges.

VISNISKI (Russian cookery)—A kind of rissole made with *Coulibiac** paste, filled with fish forcemeat seasoned with fennel, and fried.

Fish visniski. VISNISKI AU POISSON—Make some *Coulibiac** dough. Roll out and cut with a round pastry-cutter into pieces about 2 inches in diameter.

Garnish with chopped cooked fish to which chopped fennel has been added. Season and blend with a thick meatless *Velouté* (see SAUCE). The portions of the garnish should be the size of a walnut.

Cover with a round of *Coulibiac* dough of the same size as the first one.

Put the *visniski* on a baking-tray. Let them rise in a warm place for 25 minutes. At the last moment fry in very hot oil. Drain and serve on a napkin.

VITAMINS. VITAMINES—Substances indispensable to nutrition, whose absence can cause serious disorders.

Vitamin A. Derived mainly from carotene, a yellow pigment that is found extensively in vegetable foodstuffs. The vitamin also exists in some animal foods. Its absence gives rise to eye troubles and, in young subjects, a stoppage of growth.

Vitamin B. This was first discovered in the husks of rice. It is nowadays seen as a compound, composed mainly of three factors:

Vitamin B_1. Nitrogen base, related to the alkaloids, destroyed by high temperatures and alkalis. It is an anti-neurotic factor and plays its part in the equilibrium of the nervous system.

Vitamin B_2. Riboflavin, a yellow substance found in milk and in liver. It resists all but very high degrees of heat and alkalis. It has an effect on growth, and its absence causes skin troubles similar to pellagra.

Vitamin B_3. Resists heat, but is destroyed by alkalis; it is a factor in the utilization of foodstuffs by the body.

These three elements are usually found together, but in proportions which vary from one foodstuff to another.

Absence of vitamin B from the diet gives rise to neurotic complaints and to beri-beri. There is a tendency to attribute certain digestive complaints, like constipation, diarrhoea, vomiting, loss of appetite, etc., to a slight deficiency of vitamin B.

Vitamin C. An acid, ascorbic acid, nowadays prepared chemically. Its absence causes scurvy.

Vitamin D. A sterol activated by ultra-violet rays, and today prepared industrially. It is chiefly found in cod liver oil and fish oils. It has been found also in animal fats and in small quantities in milk, cream and cheeses. Shortage of vitamin D would cause rickets.

Vitamin E. It appears to have an effect on growth and its absence may cause sterility. It is found in the oil of cereal germs and in liver.

In practice the discovery of vitamins teaches us what has in fact been known for a long time—the necessity of introducing into our diet a certain amount of raw foods, in the form of *hors-d'oeuvre*, salad and fruits.

Foodstuffs classed in order of richness in vitamins (according to Mlle. Randoin):

Vitamin A. Butter, cod liver oil, liver, egg yolk, beef fat, tomatoes, cream, powdered milk, fatty cheese, spinach, carrots, cabbage, lemon, orange, fish oil, herring, brains, heart, kidney, fat meat, mushrooms, cauliflower, lettuce, cereals, wheat husks, wholemeal bread, fresh peas, beetroot, artichokes, lentils, almonds, nuts, bananas, gourds, white beans.

Vitamin B. Yeast, cereal germs, lentils, egg yolks, brain, liver, cabbage, carrots, spinach, cauliflower, onions, kidneys, fresh or dried peas, apples, pears, beetroot, artichokes, potatoes, wholemeal bread, beans, dried milk, milk whey, malt extract, lemon, orange, tomato, almonds, walnuts, sweet chestnuts, mushrooms, gourd, plums, grapes, bananas, lettuce, lean meat.

Vitamin C. Lemon, orange, cabbage, tomatoes, oysters, onions, lettuce, dandelion, swede turnip, fresh peas, spinach, cauliflower, grapes, banana, beetroot, carrots, French beans, rhubarb, turnips, apples, plums, meat juices, milk, whey.

Vitamin D (anti-richitic). Cod liver oil, fish oil, animal fats, milk, cream.

Vitamin E. Wheat germ oil.

VITELOTTE, KIDNEY POTATO—A type of potato which remains firm when cooked.

VIVEURS—Culinary title given to various preparations characterized by strong seasoning with cayenne or paprika, such as *Potage* or *Consommé des viveurs*.

VOL-AU-VENT—'This entrée', said Carême, 'is pretty and good, without a doubt; it is almost always eaten with pleasure for its extreme delicacy and lightness, but to cook it perfectly demands the utmost care. This is the essential part of the operation, so that the flakiness of the pastry is not lost in dampness'.

To make the pastry. Take half a lump of *Flaky pastry* (see DOUGH) and divide it into two pieces.

Roll out each piece to a thickness of about ¼ inch.

Cut the first piece in a round 6 inches in diameter and place it on a baking sheet which has been brushed with water.

Cut the second piece into a round of the same thickness and remove a round from the middle so as to leave a circle with an interior diameter of 4½ inches and an exterior diameter of 6 inches. Brush the first piece of pastry with water and place the pastry circle on top. Press lightly to fix and leave for 10 minutes.

Brush the top with beaten egg. Lightly cut a circle on the central part which, after cooking, will form the 'lid'. Pink the edges at regular intervals.

Cook in a hot oven for 20 to 25 minutes, according to the size of the vol-au-vent.

After cooking detach the 'lid'.

The vol-au-vent case may, after cooking, be filled with various kinds of mixtures bound with brown and white sauce. Among the most usual garnishes for this purpose are: *Financière*; *Marinière*; purée of chicken, or purée of crustacea; *Toulouse*; various *salpicons**, etc.

VOLAILLE—See CHICKEN.

VOLIÈRE (EN)—Style of serving game birds, much used formerly but now abandoned.

This rather ostentatious presentation was done by placing on the cooked bird, each in its proper position, the head, the tail and the outspread wings. All these were fixed with little wooden pegs.

Peacocks were served in this way in the Middle Ages adorned with their plumage, and holding in their beaks, which were gilded, a little piece of burning tow.

Service *en volière*, applied chiefly to pheasants and woodcock, was in vogue up to the end of the nineteenth century. Quite often, during the same period, game was served under the title of *chasse royale*, a great number of game birds all adorned with their plumage being set on a great silver dish, the largest on croûtons of fried bread and the smallest arranged as a border round the sides.

This type of arrangement has derived from one grander still which was in use until the seventeenth century, consisting of a variety of meats and game arranged in pyramids. Today roasts of game or any other meat are presented in a less ostentatious way. They are simply put on the serving dish or on a croûton of fried bread spread with forcemeat, and garnished with watercress.

VOLNAY—A highly esteemed Burgundy wine which comes from Volnay in the Côte d'Or. See BURGUNDY.

VOSNE—Red wine from the Côte d'Or. See BURGUNDY.

VOUGEOT—One of the greatest Burgundies, from Vougeot, a community of the Côte d'Or, not far from Beaune.

VOUVRAY—Highly reputed white wine from the district of Vouvray, near Tours. This wine, which is highly flavoured and a little musky, is naturally mildly sparkling, but is often treated like Champagne to make it more so.

VOYAGE (Gâteau) (German cookery)—Sweet pastry which keeps for a long time. It is a sort of apricot biscuit with an individual flavour due to the substitution of breadcrumbs for the flour which is generally used to make biscuits.

Ingredients. 1¾ cups (230 grams) fine sugar, 7 whole eggs, 4½ cups (250 grams) breadcrumbs, ½ cup (1 decilitre) apricot jam, 2 teaspoons (10 grams) vanilla sugar.

Method. Cream the sugar and egg yolks together in a basin. Make very fine breadcrumbs by rubbing stale bread in a cloth to turn it into crumbs and putting these through a very fine metal sieve.

Beat the whites of eggs stiffly and fold them lightly into the sugar and yolks mixture, which must become very light, frothy and whitish. Finally, mix in the breadcrumbs and sugar. Fill a forcing-bag fitted with a plain nozzle about ½ inch wide with the mixture.

Make round shapes with this on buttered and floured baking sheets. Cook in a low oven and take them out as soon as they are cooked. Allow to cool in a cake rack.

When these biscuits are quite cold, spread the first with apricot jam flavoured with kirsch. Cover with a second biscuit and spread this with jam also. Superimpose 5 or 6 biscuits in this way and sprinkle the top one with icing sugar mixed with powdered cinnamon.

Wrap at once in silver paper. Keep in a cool place.

WADERS. Chevaliers—Birds of passage (sandpipers, redlegs, gambets, etc.) some of which have delicate meat. They are prepared like *woodcock** and *snipe**.

WAFFLE. Gaufre—The French waffle is a very light type of sweet pastry which, instead of being baked in the oven, like most other types of pastry, is cooked between the two buttered and heated plates of a waffle iron. The plates of the waffle iron, which are fixed to the ends of two long iron stems hinged together, are decorated with embossed patterns, usually squares, though sometimes the waffle-plates are decorated with religious emblems.

Waffles, which have a very long history, are often mentioned in the poems of the end of the twelfth century. At this period waffles were made and sold in the streets. On great religious feast days, the waffle-sellers would set up their stalls at the doors of the churches, and there, in the public view, would bake their waffles, which were eaten piping hot. The best quality waffles were called *métiers*.

Filled waffles I. Gaufres fourrées—*Ingredients.* $3\frac{3}{4}$ cups (500 grams) sieved flour, 1 cup (250 grams) butter, $\frac{1}{4}$ cup (60 grams) fine sugar, 3 eggs, $1\frac{1}{2}$ teaspoons (10 grams) of bicarbonate of soda, half a vanilla pod or 1 teaspoon vanilla extract.

Method. Make a ring of the flour on the table, add the butter, the sugar, the eggs, the bicarbonate and the vanilla. Mix everything together without working the dough too hard.

Mardi-Gras waffles (seventeenth century)

Let this dough stand for 2 hours. Roll it out with a rolling-pin to a thickness of $\frac{3}{4}$ inch and cut it into round or oval shapes with a fluted pastry-cutter.

Moulds for fritters made of waffle batter (*Larousse*)

While the dough is being rolled out, the waffle iron should be heated on both sides.

Butter the waffle iron and put a piece of dough between the plates, close the iron and cook on top of a very hot wood-fired oven or on a gas cooker.

Turn the waffle iron once during the cooking.

Take out the waffles, and, while they are still hot, slice them across. Put the waffles under a weight. Allow them to cool, then spread them with the cream for which a recipe is given below. Sandwich the two halves together and keep them in a tin in a dry place until they are required.

Note. Waffle sandwiches will keep for 2 or 3 days. It is possible, therefore, to cook the waffles in advance and put in the filling as required.

Cream filling for the waffles. Take 1 cup (250 grams) of butter, $1\frac{3}{4}$ cups (250 grams) of icing sugar and 7 ounces (200 grams) of *praline*.*

Warm a basin and place the butter, sugar and praline in it. Work the mixture with a whisk.

When the mixture is blended to a smooth paste, use it as a filling for the waffles.

Filled waffles II. GAUFRES FOURRÉES—*Ingredients.* 3¾ cups (500 grams) of flour, ½ cup (125 grams) of butter, ⅛ cup (30 grams) of fine sugar, 2 packages (15 grams) dry or compressed yeast, 1½ teaspoons (10 grams) of salt, 4 eggs, 1-1¼ cups (2-3 decilitres) of milk.

Mix together as for all other batters.

This waffle dough should be made the night before it is eaten and left to rise in an earthenware dish covered with a cloth. It should be kept in a cool place. Next morning the dough should be shaped into little balls the size of half an egg and put on a floured metal baking sheet. Allow to rise to double their size and proceed with the cooking as in the previous recipe.

Open the irons as soon as the waffles are cooked. Put the waffles under a weight and fill them with cream.

Liége waffles. GAUFRES LIÉGEOISES—Arrange 3¾ cups (500 grams) of sieved flour in a circle on the table. Place in the centre of this circle a package of dry or compressed yeast, enough to cover a sixpence. Mix the yeast with a little warm water, and then mix in a quarter of the flour. Leave this mixture to rise.

Now add a pinch of salt, ½ cup (125 grams) fine sugar, 7 tablespoons (200 grams) of butter, a pinch of ground cinnamon and 4 eggs. Mix. Work the dough with the palm of the hand. Divide it into pieces, each the size of an egg. Roll these pieces into the shape of sausages. Put them on a floured slab and let them stand for half an hour.

Heat a waffle iron. Butter it. Put a sausage of dough between the plates. Cook on both sides over a moderate heat.

Northern waffles or Dutch wafers. GAUFRES DU NORD, GAUFRETTES HOLLANDAISES—*Ingredients.* 1 cup (250 grams) flour, ½ cup (125 grams) sugar, 6 tablespoons (180 grams) butter, 1 white of egg, a small pinch of salt, vanilla or cinnamon or orange or lemon peel according to taste.

Method. Arrange the flour in a circle on the table. Place the sugar, the salt and the desired flavouring in the centre. Moisten and dissolve the sugar in the white of egg, add the butter and mix all these ingredients. Shape the dough into a ball. Cook the waffles in the usual way.

Plain waffles (old recipe). GAUFRES ORDINAIRES—Take 14 ounces of flour and 6 ounces of fresh cream, 1 pound of fine sugar and 4 grains of orange flower water. Beat the flour with half the cream. When it is quite smooth, add the sugar. Next, add the rest of the cream and orange flower water, so that the mixture is as thin as milk. Now, heat the waffle-iron and grease it with a brush dipped in fresh butter melted in an earthenware pan. One and a half spoonfuls of the mixture are placed between the waffle-plates to make each waffle. A little pressure is exerted on the plates to make the waffles thinner.

The waffle iron is set on lighted coals in an oven, and when the waffle is baked on one side, the iron is turned over. To discover whether the waffle is ready, open up the iron a little. If the waffle is a good colour, remove it by sliding a knife under it, and prising it free. While it is still hot, put it in whatever mould will give it the desired shape. Put the waffles, one by one, in the hot cupboard to keep them crisp.

Plain waffles (modern recipe). GAUFRES ORDINAIRES—*Ingredients.* ½ pound (250 grams) butter, ½ pound (250 grams) lump sugar, 16 egg yolks, 7 ounces (200 grams) *praline,** ½ cup (1 decilitre) of water.

Method. Put the sugar and water in a basin. Cook to ball degree, i.e. until a drop of the mixture forms a ball when plunged into cold water (see SUGAR). While the sugar is cooking, skim it until the surface is clear. When it is ready, strain it through a fine strainer.

Put the egg yolks in a basin and pour the sugar on to them in a thin trickle. Mix with a beater, working the mixture until it is quite cold. Next add the butter, softened in advance to the consistency of a paste, then, still whisking, add the *praline.*

Drop a spoonful of this mixture on the waffle iron, which should be heated and buttered in advance. Cook on both sides.

Vanilla waffles. GAUFRES À LA VANILLE—*Ingredients.* 3¾ cups (500 grams) sieved flour, ½ pound (250 grams) butter, 4 whole eggs, 4 tablespoons (65 grams) of sugar, pod of vanilla or 1 teaspoon vanilla extract, 1½ teaspoons (10 grams) bicarbonate of soda.

For the butter cream. ½ pound (250 grams) of butter, 1¾ cups (250 grams) icing sugar, 5 yolks of egg, 1 pod of vanilla or teaspoon vanilla extract.

Method. Arrange the flour in a ring on the table, place in the middle the sugar, butter, eggs, the inside of the vanilla pod (or the extract) and the bicarbonate of soda.

Mix all these ingredients quickly to avoid lumps. Roll the dough into a ball and let it stand for 2 hours.

To make the waffles. Roll out the dough with a rolling-pin to a thickness of ⅛ inch and cut it into oval shapes with a fluted pastry cutter. Place these shapes on a floured slab. Heat the waffle iron and butter the plates lightly. Place the pastry in the middle and close the waffle iron, pressing the plates together. Put it to cook on top of a gas or coal-fired cooker.

Turn over the waffle iron to ensure that the waffle is cooked on both sides. Make sure that the waffle is cooked by opening up the waffle iron.

As soon as the waffle is ready, remove it, slice it across, and put it under a weight to keep it in shape.

Butter cream. Put the ½ pound (250 grams) of butter in a bowl. Work it to the consistency of a paste, add the icing sugar, then the yolks of egg. Mix these ingredients thoroughly. Spread the halves of the waffle (on the inside) with this cream.

Fifteenth century waffle-irons

WAFFLE-IRON. GAUFRIER—Special mould used in the preparation of waffles. It is made of two cast-iron plates which fit together and are embossed with matching designs.

WAGTAIL. HOCHEQUEUE—This little European bird is cooked in the same way as the lark.

WALEWSKA (A LA)—A method of preparing fish, particularly fillets of sole. Fish cooked in this way is poached in fish *fumet,** set on a fireproof dish, garnished with slices of spiny lobster and truffles and coated with *Mornay sauce* with spiny lobster butter. See SAUCE and BUTTER, *Compound butters.*

WALNUT. NOIX—The fruit of the walnut tree, which grows in Europe.

Walnuts and walnut oil have been known from the earliest times. The Greeks knew it four centuries before Christ, and towards the end of the fourth century, the Romans extended its cultivation all over Europe.

Before they are quite ripe walnuts are known as green walnuts. The fleshy casing of the walnut is called the shuck. An excellent liqueur (*brou*) is made from walnut shucks.

When it is fresh, the walnut is very pleasant to eat and easily digestible. The dried walnut, used a great deal in cookery and confectionery, is more difficult to digest, because of its high fat content.

Walnut Ketchup (English condiment)—Put in a tub, with 2 or 3 pounds of rock salt, about 4 pounds (2 kilos) of green walnut shells, mix well and leave for 6 days, crushing the shells from time to time with a pestle. Leave the tub tilted to one side after each operation so that the juice which runs from the fruit can be poured off every day, until only the pulp remains. Put this juice to boil and skim it. As soon as it is skimmed add to this juice ¾ cup (100 grams) of ginger, ¾ cup (100 grams) of powdered spice, ½ cup (60 grams) of cayenne pepper and an equal quantity of cloves. Simmer for half an hour. Put into small bottles the juice and ingredients. Seal hermetically and keep in a very dry place. Leave for several months before using.

WATERCRESS. CRESSON—See also CRESS. Watercress is used raw, to garnish grilled and roast meats, or in salads. Cooked, it provides excellent dishes.

Watercress cooked with butter. CRESSON ÉTUVÉ AU BEURRE—Blanch the cress quickly in salt water, drain it, dry it, and simmer it in butter in the same way as spinach.

Watercress cooked with cream. CRESSON ÉTUVÉ À LA CRÈME—Cook in the same way as above. At the last moment, add a few tablespoons of fresh boiling cream.

Watercress cooked au jus. CRESSON ÉTUVÉ AU JUS—The same as above; finish with the addition of some juice from the roast.

Watercress garnish. GARNITURE DE CRESSON—Trim, wash and drain the cress. Arrange it in bunches beside grilled or roast meat.

Watercress purée. PURÉE DE CRESSON—Simmer some watercress in butter and pass it through a sieve. Add a third of its volume of potato purée. Finish with fresh butter or boiled cream, according to the recipe.

Watercress salad. SALADE DE CRESSON—Trim, wash, drain and dry the watercress. Season in the usual way with oil, vinegar (or lemon juice), salt and pepper.

This salad must only be dressed at the last moment.

Watercress sandwiches. SANDWICHS AU CRESSON—Cover some buttered slices of bread with watercress which has been properly dried, or with a *chiffonnade* of watercress.

Sandwiches can also be made with watercress which has been finely chopped and mixed with a rather thick mayonnaise.

Cream of watercress soup — See SOUPS AND BROTHS.

WATERFISCH—Dutch word used in France for 'freshwater fish'.

The name of *waterfisch* or *patervisch* is used in cookery for a kind of sauce served with freshwater fish, particularly perch.

Waterfisch sauce (cold). SAUCE WATERFISCH—Prepared with the *court-bouillon** of the fish being used with gelatine added, strained and mixed with a *julienne* of vegetables as above but cooked in a *court-bouillon* (or fish *fumet**); add sweet pimentos, gherkins and capers.

Note. This sauce—or, rather, jelly—is used to coat the fish, after it has been cooked in *court-bouillon*, cooled in the same liquid, skinned and wiped dry. It is then decorated with anchovy fillets cut into thin strips. *Rémoulade sauce* (see SAUCE) is served with this dish.

Waterfisch sauce (hot). SAUCE WATERFISCH—Cook gently in butter till soft 2 ounces (50 grams) of carrots, 1 ounce (25 grams) of the white part of leeks, 1 ounce (25 grams) of celery and 1 ounce (25 grams) of parsley roots, all cut in a fine *julienne* (thin strips). When these vegetables are cooked, add a cup (2 decilitres) of *court-bouillon** or fish *fumet**. Reduce the liquid to nothing, then add 4 decilitres of *White wine sauce*. See SAUCE.

WATERMELON. PASTÈQUE—Fruit of a *cucurbitaceae* family plant. There are many varieties, with white, yellow, and red coloured flesh. They can be pleasantly musky or rather insipid. Water melons, unlike ordinary melons, have no central cavity. They are eaten raw or made into jam.

Water parsnip

WATER PARSNIP. BERLE—Aquatic plant the leaves of which have some similarity to those of celery. It is also called *Water parsley*, *Creeping watercress* and *Water smallage*.

The leaves of the water parsnip are eaten in salads.

Only the leaves of this plant should be eaten, as its roots are poisonous.

WATERZOOTJE (Flemish cookery). WATERZOÏ—A fish dish having some analogy with the *cotriade** of the Breton fishermen, but which is solid food rather than a soup.

Method. In Holland and Belgium this preparation is equivalent to bouillabaisse but, not unnaturally, the tomato, garlic and saffron are missing. Moreover it is cooked not with oil, like the celebrated Provençale soup, but with butter.

Line a buttered sauté pan with 1 cup (200 grams) of the white part of celery, chopped, and put on top 4 pounds (2 kilos) of freshwater fish (eel, carp, pike, tench, etc.) cut in chunks of equal size.

Season with salt and pepper, add a *bouquet garni** composed of parsley, thyme, bay leaf and 2 or 3 leaves of sage. Cover with water (or fish *fumet**). Dot over the top 7 tablespoons (100 grams) of butter divided into small pieces.

Begin cooking over a hot fire, then cover the sauté pan and cook very slowly, so that the cooking of the fish and the reduction of the liquid are done at the same time.

Add stock to give the desired consistency and a little biscotte (melba toast) reduced to powder. Remove the *bouquet garni*. Serve with slices of buttered bread.

Chicken waterzootje or waterzoï (*Robert Carrier*)

Chicken waterzootje. WATERZOÏ DE VOLAILLE—Although *Waterzootje* is the name for a fish dish, it is sometimes prepared with jointed chicken (either roasting chicken or fat hen) cooked in a white stock flavoured with onions, leeks, *bouquet garni*, celery, thyme, bay leaf and cloves. Bring to the boil, then add a little white wine. Season with salt and pepper, and continue simmering very slowly for 1½ hours. Cut into pieces, remove *bouquet garni* and serve in the stock, garnished with chopped parsley.

WAXWING. JASEUR—A European bird of the sparrow family. It is edible and is cooked in the same way as lark.

WEEVER. VIVE—Type of European fish found on the sandy coasts. The *greater weaver*, whose firm white flesh is highly esteemed, has an elongated body, pinkish or yellowish in colour with dark bands; it has stiff spines along the dorsal fin, whose pricks are poisonous, even after the fish is dead. All the methods of cooking whiting are applicable to the weever.

Weever en matelote vierge (Carême's recipe). VIVE EN MATELOTE VIERGE—'Take 6 nice weevers, clean them in the usual way, then cut each into three chunks, not using the head; put these pieces into a buttered saucepan with a *bouquet garni*,* chopped onions, 2 cloves of garlic, 2 cloves, salt and grated nutmeg; pour in a bottle of white Burgundy; start cooking over a strong heat, then skim and moderate the heat so that the fish just simmers.

'As soon as it becomes firm to the touch drain it on to a dish and put it immediately into another saucepan; strain the liquor; use its fat, which will serve to keep the fish hot, then make a little white *roux* to thicken the liquid; add the trimmings of 4 punnets of mushrooms which have been peeled and cooked.

'When the sauce has had all grease removed, reduce it, thicken it with 3 egg yolks, strain it through a cloth and keep it hot in a *bain-marie*.

'The pieces of weever should have been kept hot without boiling; arrange them in a pyramid, holding them in place with heart-shaped croûtons of bread fried in butter; pour over the sauce to which the mushrooms will have have been added at the last moment, together with a piece of the finest butter as big as an egg.'

WEIGHTS AND MEASURES. POIDS ET MESURES—In this book we have quoted several old French recipes in which the quantities of the ingredients are given in old units. Often we have indicated the metric equivalents, but here is all the data in a comparative table.

Measures of weight—Livre (pound): this old unit of measure of weight has had varied values, but it is generally accepted to be the equivalent of 489·5 grams.

Marc: equalled half a pound, i.e. 244·75 grams.
Quarteron: quarter of a pound, i.e. about 122 grams.
Once: one-sixteenth part of a pound, i.e. 30·59 grams.
Gros: one-eighth part of an ounce, i.e. 3·825 grams.
Grain: about one-eighteenth of a gram, i.e. 0·053 grams.

Measures of capacity—*Muid* represented 2 *feuillettes* or 4 *quartauts*, i.e. 268·23 litres.

Pinte: equalled 0·93 litre (in Paris).
Quartaut: 72 French pints, i.e. about 67 litres.
Setier: 8 Paris pints, i.e. 7·45 litres.
Chopine: used to be half a French pint.

Some of the old measures of capacity have remained in use, particularly for Champagne wines, the value differing slightly from the old values, the metric equivalents being expressed in round figures. A bottle may at times have the same capacity as the old pint, i.e. 0·93 litre, but the present-day bottle generally equals 0·80 litre.

Muid = 260 litres.
Trentain = 300 litres.
Poinçon = 200 litres.
Caque = 100 litres.
Queue de Reims = 396 litres.
Queue de Champagne = 366 litres.
Sapinée = 30 pints (28 litres).
Velte = 1 setier = 7·45 litres.
Quartaut = 50 litres.
Feuillette = 114 litres.
Pièce = 200 litres.

Old linear measures—The *foot* equalled 0·3248 metre, it was divided into 12 inches of 0·027 metre. The inch equalled 12 lines of 0·225 centimetre.

Note. A complete table of English, American and French weights and measures will be found in the beginning of this book.

WELL. PUITS—Word used for the space left empty in the middle of a circle of flour, in which are placed the different ingredients necessary to make pastry or other mixtures; the central part of food arranged in the form of a crown, 'turban' or circle, where various garnishes are placed; the hollow made in the middle of a cake or pudding; the metal sleeve or chimney in the middle of certain moulds and cake tins.

WELS. SILURE—A large freshwater fish with smooth soft skin and barbelled mouth.

The European *wels*, which is scarcely found at all in France except in the River Doubs, and which is also called the *glanis*, grows up to over 6 feet long and weighs 50 pounds or more.

The dwarf wels, or freshwater catfish, originating in America whence it has been imported and used to stock French rivers, grows to 14 to 24 inches long. Its flesh is very delicate. The pectoral and dorsal fins have spikes, whose prick is disagreeable but not dangerous.

This catfish is prepared like the freshwater burbot.

WELSH RABBIT OR RAREBIT—An English toasted cheese preparation, made as follows:

Put into a saucepan with a little English beer, ½ pound (250 grams) of Gloucester cheese cut in small squares. Add a little English mustard. Cook this mixture on the fire stirring all the time until the cheese has melted. Pour this composition over slices of English bread, toasted and buttered. Brown well under the grill.

WHALE. BALEINE—In the Middle Ages whale meat, under the name of *crapois* or Lenten bacon, was sold on meatless days and formed the staple diet of the poor. The flesh of this cetacean is most indigestible and remains tough even after 24 hours' cooking.

There are several kinds of whales, which differ in name, appearance and size. From the gastronomical point of view, only whale calves are of any interest. The flesh of these is of a reddish colour and somewhat similar to beef in appearance, but it is a long way away from it in taste. Whale meat was not greatly esteemed by our grandfathers, but they did set some store by the tongue of the animal, usually salted, and Ambroise Paré says that 'it is tender and delicious'. They also much appreciated whale fat which they ate 'during Lent, with peas'.

As whale meat can be kept for quite a long time without going bad, sailors used to store it, to cook as required. It can be prepared like tunny (tuna fish).

There are not many recipes for whale meat. Some authors of culinary books, basing their arguments on the fact that whalemeat is eaten by the Eskimos and the Japanese, and on Lacépède's assertion that 'whale meat when salted can be regarded as a delicate dish', have had no hesitation in concocting half a dozen recipes for the preparation of this giant cetacean. It has been proved that whale meat is in fact highly nitrogenous and consequently very restorative.

Dr Félix Brémont tells how he had an occasion to eat whale meat in 1892 in a restaurant near the Halles: 'I will not say anything bad about whale meat, but neither can I find it in me to say anything good about it. Boil a piece of lean beef in water which has been used to wash a not-too-fresh mackerel, and you will have a dish similar to that which was served to me under the name of *Escalope of whale à la Valois*'.

We do not protest against the lack of enthusiasm on the part of Dr Félix Brémont, nor do we entirely agree with him. Is it not certain, is it not an inescapable fact that all animals living on land, swimming in water or flying in air must, sooner or later, play their part in the culinary repertoire of the world?

WHEAT. BLÉ, FROMENT—Cereal crop known and cultivated from the earliest times. Wheat appears to have originated in Chaldea. From there it found its way all over the East and to Italy. The Gauls, according to Herodotus, discovered it as a result of their overseas expeditions. In Caesar's time, it was cultivated in Gaul only on a very limited scale. In the sixteenth century the poor had only barley or rye bread to eat. Wheaten bread was reserved exclusively for the rich man's table.

Wheat grain, which is a fruit in the botanical sense of the word, consists of three parts: shell (or pericarp), nut (or caryopsis) and seed (or embryo).

The shell represents 14·36% of the grain.

The nut, consisting of *gluten*, is filled with starch cells.

According to strain and race, it contains on the average from 9% to 11% of gluten and from 56% to 75% of starch. It represents 84·21% of the grain.

The embryo (1·43% of the grain) is rich in nitrogenous matter and fats. It also contains ferment and odoriferous substances.

In addition to starch and gluten, wheat grain also contains soluble sugar, dextrines and mineral salts (ash).

There is a considerable number of varieties, which can be classified in two groups: hard grain, richer in gluten, and soft grain richer in starch.

The main uses of grain are in the making and manufacture of cereals, flours, pasta products and bread.

WHEATEAR. TRAQUET—Passerine, classed as game; it is quite well thought of and is cooked like lark.

WHIPPED CREAM. CRÈME FOUETTÉE—Cream whipped with a whisk or beaten. See CREAM.

WHISK. FOUET—Utensil to beat eggs, cream, white sauces, *béarnaise*, *hollandaise*, *mayonnaise*, etc. For cooking, whisks made of metal are used. For baking and confectionery whisks made of box-wood or wicker are also used. Modern rotary hand and electric beaters are often used to replace the whisk, but many professionals find these inferior to the whisk.

WHISKY or WHISKEY—A grain spirit from Scotland or Ireland distilled from barley, rye and other cereals, malted and fermented.

WHITEBAIT. BLANCHAILLE—The 'fry' or young of the common herring (*Clupes harengus*) and sprat (*Clupes* *sprattus*), which abound in the Thames and along the coasts of the North Sea. It is also found in vast numbers in the mouth of the Garonne.

These little fishes are mostly fried in deep fat.

All the recipes given for *nonats** (the 'fry' of a small Mediterranean goby) are applicable to whitebait.

WHITE BEET. Poirée—A variety of *chard.**

WHITE-TAIL. Cul-blanc—Several migrant birds are known by this name, especially the wheatear, mightily prized in France as game. This bird is cooked in the same way as lark.

Whiting

WHITING. Merlan—The European whiting is a gadoid fish with a long, somewhat compact body. It has soft, rounded scales. It is greyish or olive green along the back, with copper or pale yellow shading. Its flanks are white, speckled with yellow, and its belly silvery. It is between 10 and 16 inches long. Whiting is caught mainly in the English Channel and the Baltic. Its flesh is fine in texture, flaky and easy to digest.

Another species of whiting, the pollack, is similar in appearance but is yellowish in colour and darker. Its flesh, though of good quality, is less delicate than that of the whiting proper.

The American whiting is also known as silver hake and is fished off the New England coast. The average whiting is 12-14 inches long but larger specimens are not uncommon.

Whiting à l'anglaise. Merlan à l'anglaise—Slit the fish along the back. Remove backbone. Season. Flour. Dip in egg and breadcrumbs and fry in butter, browning well on both sides.

Serve on a dish covered with slightly softened *Maître d'hôtel butter.* See BUTTER, *Compound butters.*

Note. Grilled whiting, served with melted butter and boiled potatoes, is also called *Whiting à l'anglaise.*

Whiting à la Bercy. Merlan à la Bercy—Make a shallow incision along the back. Put the whiting in a buttered fireproof dish. Sprinkle with a teaspoon of chopped shallot.

Season. Moisten with $\frac{1}{2}$ cup (1 decilitre) of white wine. Dot with 2 teaspoons (20 grams) of butter cut into tiny fragments. Bring to the boil on the stove, then bake in the oven, basting frequently.

When the fish is cooked, glaze in a very hot oven.

At the last minute, squeeze a few drops of lemon juice over the fish, and sprinkle with chopped parsley.

Boiled whiting with melted butter or other sauce. Merlan bouilli avec beurre fondu—Boil the whiting in salt water. Drain it. Serve it on a napkin or wire tray. Garnish with potatoes and fresh parsley. Serve with melted butter or any other sauce suitable for boiled fish.

Whiting à la bonne femme. Merlan à la bonne femme—Proceed as for *Brill à la bonne femme.**

Whiting à la cancalaise. Merlan à la cancalaise—Using whiting, proceed as for *Brill à la cancalaise.**

How to Fillet Whiting (*Larousse*)

Make an incision just below the head

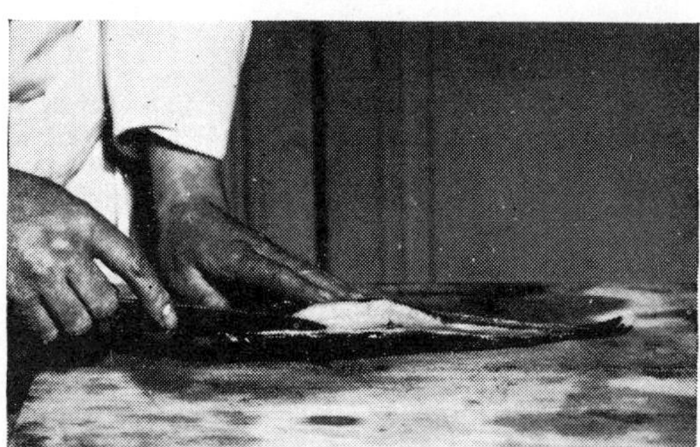

Cut along the length of the backbone

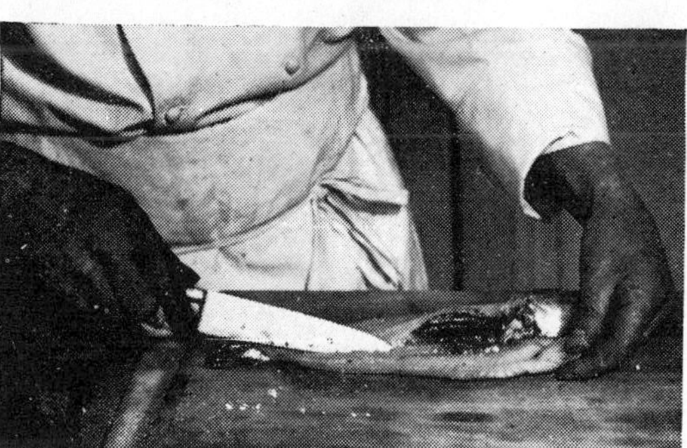

Cut the fillet away completely from the bone and remove

The two fillets cleaned and ready for cooking

Whiting Colbert. MERLAN COLBERT—Slit the whiting along the back and remove backbone. Season with salt and pepper. Sprinkle with flour. Dip in egg and breadcrumbs. Deep fry.

Serve on a long dish. Put into the slit in the fish a tablespoon of *Maître d'hôtel butter*. See BUTTER, *Compound butters*.

Whiting à la dieppoise. MERLAN À LA DIEPPOISE—Proceed as indicated for *Brill à la dieppoise.**

Whiting à l'espagnole. MERLAN À L'ESPAGNOLE—Dip in egg and breadcrumbs as indicated for *Whiting à l'anglaise*. Fry in oil until well browned on both sides. Serve on a bed of *Tomato fondue,** seasoned with a little crushed garlic.

Decorate each end of the dish with a clump of onion rings fried in oil.

Fillets of whiting. FILETS DE MERLAN—Fillets of whiting can be prepared in all ways suitable for whole whiting.

All recipes given for fillets of sea-perch, brill, sole, etc., are also suitable for fillets of whiting.

Whiting forcemeat. FARCE DE MERLAN—Made of whiting, *panade**, cream and eggs, in the same way as *Pike forcemeat*. See FORCEMEATS AND STUFFINGS.

Fried whiting. MERLAN FRIT—Slit the whiting. Dip in milk and flour. Fry at the last moment. Drain and season with very dry table salt.

Serve on a napkin with fried parsley and halved lemon.

Whiting au gratin. MERLAN AU GRATIN—Proceed as indicated for *Sole au gratin.**

Grilled whiting. MERLAN GRILLÉ—Make a shallow incision in the whiting. Season. Dredge with flour. Brush with melted butter or oil and grill under a gentle heat.

Serve on a long dish. Garnish with parsley and slices of lemon. Serve with melted butter, *Maître d'hôtel butter*, or any other sauce especially suitable for grilled fish. See BUTTER, *Compound butters* and SAUCE.

Whiting loaf—See LOAVES, *Fish loaves*.

Whiting en lorgnette (fried). MERLAN FRIT EN LORGNETTE—Fillet a large whiting, starting at the tail and working towards the head. Shave off the flesh very close to the bone. Remove the bone, cutting it off at the base of the head. Season the whiting. Dip in egg and breadcrumbs. Roll the fillets. Skewer them to keep them in shape.

Deep fry in boiling fat at the last minute. Serve on a napkin. Garnish with fried parsley and lemon.

Whiting en lorgnette (poached). MERLAN POCHÉ EN LORGNETTE—Split the whiting open as indicated above and remove the bone. Season the fillets. Spread them with a layer (not too thick) of fish forcemeat and roll them up.

Put the whiting in a buttered baking dish, moistened with very concentrated fish *fumet.** Cook in the oven, basting frequently.

Drain the fish. Put it on a serving-dish, with garnish and sauce as indicated.

Whiting with Italian marrows (zucchini) or aubergines (egg-plant)—MERLAN AUX COURGETTES, AUBERGINES—Season the whiting. Dredge the flour over it. Fry in butter.

Serve on a long dish. Garnish with little Italian marrows (zucchini) or aubergines (egg-plant), diced and sautéed in oil.

Squeeze a little lemon juice over the whiting. Sprinkle with chopped parsley. Pour on 2 tablespoons of browned butter.

Whiting à la meunière. MERLAN À LA MEUNIÈRE—Proceed as indicated for *Bass à la meunière.**

Whiting mousse. MOUSSE DE MERLAN—Using raw whiting, proceed as indicated for *Fish mousse** mixture.

Fill a plain, round, deep dish three-quarters full of this mixture. Cook in a *bain-marie** (pan of hot water).

Turn out on a round dish. Serve garnish and sauce as indicated in the recipe selected.

Whiting with mushrooms. MERLAN AUX CHAMPIGNONS—Proceed as for *Brill with mushrooms.**

Whiting Orly. MERLAN ORLY—Fillet a large raw whiting. Dip the fillets in a light batter. See BATTER.

At the last moment, deep-fry in boiling fat. Drain on a linen cloth. Sprinkle with table salt. Serve on a napkin. Garnish with fried parsley. Serve *Tomato sauce* (see SAUCE) separately.

Whiting with oysters. MERLAN AUX HUÎTRES—Prepare the whiting as indicated for *Brill with oysters.** Garnish with poached oysters, drained and trimmed.

Whiting sur le plat. MERLAN SUR LE PLAT—Make a shallow incision along the back of the whiting. Season. Put it in a buttered fireproof dish. Pour on 2-3 tablespoons of white wine and a few drops of lemon juice. Bring to the boil on the stove and finish cooking in the oven, basting frequently. Serve in the cooking dish.

Whiting Richelieu. MERLAN RICHELIEU—Proceed as for *Whiting à l'anglaise*. Cover with *Maître d'hôtel butter* (see BUTTER, *Compound butters*) and arrange 4 strips of truffle on top.

Whiting paupiettes. MERLAN EN PAUPIETTES—Fillet the whiting. Spread the inside with a thin layer of fish forcemeat. Roll the fillets tightly and poach in concentrated fish stock. Proceed according to the recipe selected.

Note. Paupiettes of whiting can be prepared *à la Bercy*; *à la dieppoise*; *aux fines herbes*; *au gratin*; *à la Nantua*; *à la normande*; in white wine. All garnishes and sauces indicated for sole are suitable for this dish.

Whiting with shrimps. MERLAN AUX CREVETTES—Proceed as for *Brill with shrimps.**

Whiting in wine. MERLAN AU VIN BLANC—Proceed as indicated for *Brill in white wine*.

WHOLEMEAL (WHOLE-WHEAT). BIS—Term applied to loaves of home-made bread which contains a certain proportion of bran, or made of a mixture of wheat and rye flour. The crust of wholemeal bread is of a brown colour. See BREAD.

WHORTLEBERRY OR HUCKLEBERRY. AIRELLE—The French name *airelle* is often used to define different berries; bilberry (U.S.A. huckleberry), whortleberry, etc. The real whortleberry (or red whortleberry) properly speaking, is a small reddish berry, acid in taste, which is used mostly in compotes in germanic countries (*preiselbeere* in German). It is used as a sweet-sour accompaniment to red meats and game. Its properties resemble those of cranberries and bilberries.

Whortleberry or huckleberry accompaniment to cold meats. AIRELLES—Separate berries from the stem. Measure 2 quarts (litres) of berries and wash them, drain and put in a basin. Add 1 cup (2 decilitres) of red wine, a pinch of powdered cinnamon, 5 cloves and 1 pound (500 grams) of fine sugar. Bring to the boil, skim, cook for 30 minutes.

Drain the whortleberries, boil down the juice until it reaches the consistency of a thick syrup. Put the berries back into the syrup and mix well. Let cool and put in jars. Seal firmly and keep in a cool place.

Serve, like gherkins, with boiled beef and with cold meats.

Whortleberry or huckleberry compote. COMPOTE D'AIRELLES—Prepare a syrup of 1 pound (500 grams) of sugar, ¾ cup (2 decilitres) of water, the peel of ½ lemon and a piece of cinnamon bark. Pick over 2 pounds (1 kilo) of whortleberries, remove stalks and put into the syrup. Boil fast.

Remove the berries with a perforated spoon as soon as they are cooked and put into a glass dish.

Boil down the syrup and pour over the fruit. Chill before serving.

Whortlberry or huckleberry jam. CONFITURE D'AIRELLES —For 4 pounds (2 kilos) of seeded whortleberries allow 3 pounds (1½ kilos) of sugar. Melt the sugar with a pint (½ litre) of water in a copper or stainless steel pan.

Put the berries into the pan. Cook, stirring frequently with a wooden spoon to prevent the fruit sticking to the bottom.

Cook and finish off as described in the general rules for making jam. See JAMS AND JELLIES.

Decant into jars and seal.

Whortleberry or huckleberry jelly. GELÉE D'AIRELLES—*Ingredients.* 4 pounds (2 kilos) seeded whortleberries, 2 pounds (1 kilo) seeded red currants and 6 pounds (3 kilos) of sugar.

Method of preparation. Press the whortleberries and the red currants to extract all juice. Put this juice into a pan with the sugar. Mix.

Put on the fire. At the first sign of boiling, skim carefully. Leave to cook for 5 minutes. Check if the jelly is ready.

Leave to stand until lukewarm. Decant into jars and seal.

Whortleberry or huckleberry kissel (Russian cookery). KISSEL D'AIRELLES—Pound 2 pounds (1 kilo) of whortleberries in a mortar, adding to them about 2¾ quarts (2½ litres) of water. Take this mixture out of the mortar and press through a napkin to extract all juice.

Put 6 tablespoons of cornflour (or potato starch) into a pan, pour the juice over it and stir.

Add 1 cup (200 grams) of castor (very fine) sugar. Put on the fire to boil, stirring all the time. As soon as the mixture thickens and becomes transparent, transfer it into a silver dish or a porcelain bowl. Serve hot. Hand very thick cream separately.

WIDERKOMM. VIDRECOME—Large glass used in Germany in the Middle Ages for ceremonial feasts.

WILD ARUM, LORDS AND LADIES. GOUET, PIED-DE-VEAU—This plant has a tuberous stem very rich in starch, which can be extracted and used in cooking. When it is fresh, it contains a bitter, corrosive substance, which can be eliminated by washing or drying.

WILD BOAR. SANGLIER—Wild mammal, very near to the domestic pig (*bête noire*, in French hunting terms). Its flesh, which has a pronounced 'wild' taste, does not make good eating except in the young animals. The flesh of the adult animals is tough and only becomes palatable if left to marinate for a long time.

Up to the age of six months the wild boar in French is called a *marcassin*; from six months to a year, a *bête rousse*; between one year and two, a *bête de compagnie*; after two years, a *ragot*; at three years a wild boar *à son tiers an*; at four years he is a *quartenier*; older, a *porc entier*, and finally, when he is advanced in age, he is given the name of *solitaire* or *ermite*: he can attain the age of thirty.

Only the *marcassins* and the *bêtes rousses* are used in their entirety in the kitchen. Every part of these creatures, leg, saddle, loin, shoulder and back is excellent. In an old boar only the head is eatable, and even then it is necessary to add to it a great number of other ingredients, such as fine pork forcemeat, chicken meat, fresh pork tongue, fat bacon, truffles and pistachios.

Note. Before being cooked, in any way whatever, the meat of the *marcassin* or *bête rousse* should be left for a time in a strong marinade.

Chine of marcassin (young wild boar) à la chipolata. ÉCHINE DE MARCASSIN À LA CHIPOLATA—The chine is the whole or part of the backbone and adhering flesh. After having marinated the chine for several hours, drain and dry it and braise it in a well seasoned braising stock in the usual way. See CULINARY METHODS, *Braising*.

When it is three-quarters cooked, drain the chine. Put it back in the saucepan with a *Chipolata garnish* (see GARNISHES). Pour over the strained juices from the braising; finish cooking, simmering very slowly.

Civet or marcassin (young wild boar). CIVET DE MARCASSIN—Made like *Civet of hare*. See HARE.

Cutlets (U.S.A. chops) of marcassin (young wild boar). CÔTELETTES DE MARCASSIN—Prepared like *Cutlets* (*chops*) *of roebuck* or of *Pork*. See ROEBUCK and PORK.

Wild boar ham. JAMBON DE SANGLIER—This is cured and cooked in exactly the same way as pork ham (see HAM). It can be eaten cooked or raw. It is garnished with a vegetable purée, usually chestnut.

Wild boar ham, sweet-sour. JAMBON DE SANGLIER À L'AIGRE-DOUCE—Braise the ham, in the same way as pork ham. See HAM.

When it is cooked drain it, put on a long dish, pour over a few tablespoons of the strained braising juices, sprinkle with sugar and glaze in the oven.

Finish off the braising juices like a *Romaine sauce* (see SAUCE). Add to this sauce 12 prunes (soaked in water and stoned) and 24 cherries pickled in vinegar. At the last moment, add a little chocolate dissolved in water.

Serve the ham with this sauce, accompanied by some kind of garnish.

This way of preparing wild boar is popular in the north of Europe.

Wild boar ham, sweet-sour, à l'italienne. JAMBON DE SANGLIER, À L'AIGRE-DOUCE, À L'ITALIENNE—Made in every way like the preceding recipe but adding to the sauce some pine kernels, citron peel and chopped candied orange.

Boar's head. HURE DE SANGLIER—The cooking of boar's head, which is a very large dish, involves many different ingredients. The actual boar's head is the most insignificant part of this preparation, because apart from the tongue and a few pieces of lean flesh which are taken off the skull, this cold dish, which, it must be repeated, is very generous in size, uses only the cutaneous parts covering the animal's head.

Ingredients. For a head of about 10 pounds (5 kilos) when cooked: 9 pounds (4 kilos 500 grams) *Fine pork forcemeat* (see FORCEMEAT); 2 pounds (1 kilo) chicken meat (boned, trimmed); 1½ pounds (750 grams) cooked lean ham; 4 fresh pork tongues (heated, skinned and pickled in brine); 1 pound (500 grams) scarlet tongue; 1 pound (500 grams) fat bacon; ¾ pound (400 grams) peeled truffles; 5 ounces (150 grams) blanched pistachios.

Method. Singe and scrape the head carefully, then bone it completely, taking care not to tear the skin. Cut off the ears (which must be cooked separately), take out the tongue and take off the small fleshy pieces from next to the skin.

Trim these pieces of lean flesh and cut them into large regular dice and put them, the tongue and the skin of the head to macerate for 10 hours with carrots, chopped onions, thyme, bay leaf, salt, pepper and spices.

Prepare a *salpicon* by cutting into dice the wild boar's

tongue, the pork tongues, previously cooked, the scarlet tongue, the ham, the chicken and the bacon into dice 1 inch square. Add the truffles cut into large dice, the pistachio nuts and the pieces of lean meat taken from the head of the boar. Marinate for 2 hours with brandy, salt, pepper and spices.

Add to this *salpicon* the fine pork forcemeat and 4 whole eggs. Mix all well together.

Boar's head, after Carême

Spread the skin from the boar's head (the outside downwards) on a cloth that has been soaked in cold water and wrung out. In the middle of this skin put the above mixture. Fold the skin over the mixture, and wrap it completely in the cloth, re-shaping it in its original form, that is to say, making it narrower at the snout. Tie up firmly.

Put the head to cook in a jelly stock, prepared in the usual way (see JELLY), using the bones and trimmings of the boar's head as well as the carcase and trimmings of the chicken.

Cook gently for 4½ hours. One hour before it is ready, put in the ears.

Drain the head and the ears. Leave to stand for 30 minutes, then untie it. Wash the cloth and wring it out well to remove the moisture, then roll the boar's head in the cloth again, securing it firmly with a string, and taking care to keep the shape. (Begin tying the head at the snout end.)

Leave to cool for at least 12 hours.

Untie the boar's head, wipe it carefully. Skewer the two ears, coated with a layer of brown *Chaud-froid sauce* (see SAUCE) or dissolved meat jelly, in their places. Coat the whole of the boar's head (placed on a grid or rack) with the same sauce or with meat jelly, and put back the tusks in their place. Using hard boiled egg white and truffles, make the eyes (the pork butchers use eyes made of enamel).

Decorate with *Montpellier butter* (see BUTTER, *Compound butters*) or with cut-out egg white, truffles and blanched pistachios. Set on a long dish. Glaze with jelly. Chill before serving.

Note. Instead of being set on the platter the boar's head may be put on a slice of buttered bread or a foundation of shaped rice, and truffles may be skewered to the head, although complicated serving arrangements are not recommended.

In home cooking, and even in *grande cuisine*, the boar's head is most often covered, when quite cold, with a thick layer of golden breadcrumbs. In this case the ears are cut up in a *salpicon* before being cooked, and added to the other ingredients. When thus served, the head is a sort of galantine or roll of boar's head.

Loin of marcassin (young wild boar). CARRÉ DE MARCASSIN—Cooked whole like the *Loin of roebuck* (see ROEBUCK) but more often divided into cutlets (chops) which are prepared like those of roebuck or pork.

Noisettes of marcassin (young wild boar). NOISETTES DE MARCASSIN—Like *Noisettes of roebuck*. See ROEBUCK.

Scalloped marcassin (young wild boar). ESCALOPES DE MARCASSIN—All the recipes given for *Scalloped roebuck* or *Noisettes of roebuck* are applicable to young wild boar. See ROEBUCK.

WILD CHICORY. BARBE DE CAPUCIN—A variety of wild chicory blanched by being grown in a dark place. It has a slight bitterness which is not unpleasant.

Wild chicory is greatly valued as a salad, because it is always tender.

It can be prepared like chicory. It can also be cut into short little chunks and pickled in vinegar like gherkins.

WILD THYME. SERPOLET—Labiate-flowered plant, scented and aromatic, used as condiment and for infusions.

WILLIAM—Variety of eating pear that is very juicy and sweet-flavoured. It ripens in September.

Old Médoc vines
(French Government Tourist Office)

WINE. VIN—According to the legal definition, wine is 'the product of the alcoholic fermentation of fresh or dried grapes or the juice of fresh grapes'. Unfortunately a large number of practices that are to some degree tolerated have the effect of making this definition less strict.

The making of wine, which varies in any case a little from region to region, seems to have been done differently in ancient times.

The Greeks dried the grapes in the sun on wicker trays which were brought in each evening to prevent the dew falling on them; they tried to make wine that was strong and heavy, and the Romans, too, liked their wines to be very concentrated; they exposed them to the heat in amphorae. This wine was always mixed with water at mealtimes.

The making of Burgundy wine about 1470, as represented on an old tapestry

Vinification. At the present day, broadly speaking, wine-making in France follows the processes used by many preceding generations, although inventions such as wine presses, pasteurization equipment and corking machines, as well as agricultural equipment and transportation facilities, have changed the picture. The following operations go into the making of wine:

Vendange or harvest. The date at which the grapes are picked naturally varies according to the region, the temperature and local custom; where there is a *ban de vendange* the gathering must not be done before a given date.

In general the grape harvest takes place when the density of the must, taken from a number of bunches, is found to be stationary so that the grape has nothing more to gain from remaining on the plant; as far as possible a spell of fine dry weather is chosen.

Égrappage or removal from the stalks. According to the region and the growth the fruit may next be partly removed from the stalks. This is more usual in making white wine than red, and is also done when the must is acid or the grapes are over-ripe.

An old wine press

Foulage or crushing. Transported into large vats, the grapes are in some remote regions still crushed by feet; mechanical presses are mainly used nowadays.

Cuvaison or fermentation. Once the grape harvest has been crushed (only the making of red wine is being considered at the moment) it is put into huge vats, which are made of wood (for fine wines), stone, brick, or tinned or japanned iron. The success of the fermentation depends to a great extent on the surrounding temperature, so that in cold districts the vats must be thick and the cellars must be heated, whereas in Algeria and Tunisia, thin-walled vats, which are good heat conductors and are cooled by being wrapped in wet cloths, are used.

Fermentation. Fermentation is due to the action of fungi of the species *saccharomyces*, very small in size (the average diameter is 5 to 6 thousandths of a millimetre) which are always to be found on the surface of the skins and which persist in the soil, where they can resist the most intense cold (at —4°C. they become torpid and inactive, but recover their vitality with the first warmth); these yeasts are of different types, among them *saccharomyces apiculatus*, *pastorianus* and *ellipsoidus*, the most active of all, which appears later on the bunches, at the time when the fruit is ripe. Cultivated on barley must, they provide a sort of barley wine which would have been the cervisia of the Gauls. It may be said that each growth has its individual fermenting agent, which has a considerable part to play in fermenting substances that later on will give birth to the bouquet.

By submitting a sterilized must to fermentation with leavens coming from Médoc, Burgundy or Champagne, it is possible to obtain wines which resemble those from which the leaven originated, without ever quite equalling their quality.

For fermentation to take place in the best conditions, the temperature of the cellars should not drop below 18°C. (64°F.) or it will become excessive, to the detriment of the quality of the wine, which thereby loses a large part of its volatile products. The best temperature for fine wines is 25°C. (77°F.).

Generally this fermentation takes place spontaneously, due to the leavening agent in the fruit. Sometimes selected leavens are used either, in the case of a hot country, to obtain a better yield of alcohol by using leavens adapted to higher temperatures, or if the grape harvest has been soaked by rain, when it is advisable to introduce immediately into the vat a fully active yeast which will prevent the development of harmful ferments. It is always advisable in the latter case to use a yeast from the same district as the harvest or from its immediate neighbourhood; from this a ferment is prepared which is in full activity at the time it is put into the vat.

The ferment breaks down the glucose (grape sugar), and from the beginning of fermentation the carbonic gas which is freed raises the solid parts of the grapes, *le chapeau*, at the level of which fermentation is most active. If it is allowed to float, the process is unevenly distributed, the marc evaporates less and acid ferments develop on the surface on contact with the air. These difficulties are prevented by sprinkling and pressing back the 'hat', a risky task, carrying with it some danger of asphyxia. Wine-growers sometimes prefer fermentation to be carried out *à chapeau soumergé*, keeping it down in the must with the aid of wicker racks.

Fermentation, at first quite violent, later becomes calmer. This is generally the moment chosen for the *décuvage*, when the wine is drawn off from the vats. The length of time the wine stays in the vats is variable; a short period gives finer, more delicately flavoured wines, richer in alcohol, less acid and paler in colour; a prolonged period in the vats gives wines that are more robust, stronger and darker in colour. This period lasts from 10 to 15 days in the Médoc, 4 to 8 days in Burgundy and even less in Algeria.

Décuvage. This has the effect of separating the fermented wine from the marc; a tap placed at the base of the vat allows this first wine to be drawn off. This is called the *vin de goutte* or *pied de cuve*, the bottom of the vat.

Pressurage (*pressing*). The solid residue known as marc (if no wine of second growth is to be made) is then put under the press and submitted to moderate pressure; this *vin de presse* is always richer in tannin than the *vin de goutte*, with which it is mixed. The marc is then pressed again, more strongly, giving a more astringent, acid wine, less rich in alcohol. Finally the marc is pressed once more; the wine from this third pressing always has a distinct taste of the husks.

On the average the wine harvest gives 63% *vin de goutte*, 25% wine of the first pressing and 10% wines of the second and third pressings.

Vinification (*white wine*). White wine can be made of white or red grapes, with the exception of a few vines whose juice is coloured. These varieties are called *teinturiers*. The grapes are taken as quickly as possible to the press, without previous crushing and the juice alone is set to ferment. The next step is generally a *débourbage*, arresting the onset of fermentation by strong sulphurization (10 to 15 grams of sulphuric acid or 5 to 7·5 grams per hectolitre) and the must, thus inactivated, is left to rest; it is then strongly aired by being drawn off, in order to eliminate the sulphuric acid, and fermentation begins again more slowly. It is sometimes activated by the addition of selected yeasts, and, as clarification is always slowed down by lack of tannin, this is generally added in the proportion of 4 to 5 grams per hectolitre.

Subsequent operations. The wine is drawn off from the vats into barrels, where fermentation continues, and care is taken to replace any liquid which evaporates, so that the barrels are always full.

Soutirages or drawings off. Drawing-off has the effect of decanting wines from lees; the first *soutirage* takes place two to four weeks after the *décuvage*, the drawing-off from the vats; the second is in January in the South of France and in March and April in colder parts of France.

The part played by the yeasts, though they have by now become much less active, is not yet finished. It is after fermentation that they develop the taste-producing elements, provided that air is excluded; this is why ullage is carried out in the first place and the barrels afterwards placed 'side bung' or *bonde sur le côté*.

Wine presses

Filtering and clarifying. Before being released for consumption the wine is filtered and clarified to give it greater limpidity; different substances are used for this, which, by coagulating on contact with tannin, form a sort of screen which entraps and deposits the particles in suspension.

For this purpose fresh blood is sometimes used, but infrequently, and only for very commonplace wines. As a rule gelatine or dried albumen is used for *vins ordinaires* (10 to 15 grams per hectolitre), very fresh egg whites for fine wines (2 or 3 per hectolitre), and isinglass for white wines (10 to 15 grams per hectolitre).

The technique of *collage*, which is often practised as part of the treatment given to wine after it has arrived in the cellar, is described below.

Other operations are sometimes carried out, such as pasteurization (heating to 55°C. (131°F.) and 60°C. (140°F.), with air excluded, the presence of air giving wine a 'cooked' taste at 35°C. (95°F.)), to assure that the wine will keep. This is chiefly done after blending to amalgamate the mixture. The pasteurization which is sometimes carried out to remedy maladies of the wine will be considered later.

Fortification, where French wines are concerned, is a matter of adding alcohol to wines which are too deficient in it to keep well, thereby raising the content by one or two degrees at the most. This addition of alcohol is legally forbidden for wines destined to be consumed in France and is strictly limited to wines for export.

Other practices have more relation to chemistry than genuine wine-making. If the must is not sweet enough, a special legal decree allows sugar to be added; tartaric acid is added if the must is not acid enough, chalk if it is too acid.

The sugar is inverted by boiling it with must to which a little tartaric acid has been added. To obtain a reduction on the tax this must be carried out in the presence of a government official.

Plâtrage or plastering. This was formerly done, chiefly in the Mediterranean region, to augment the acidity and add brilliance to the colour. The practice has fallen into disuse in France.

Phosphotage (addition of phosphate of lime). This has much the same effect as *plâtrage*, but does not improve the colour.

Tanisage or treatment with tannin. This corrects lack of astringency. Alcohol tannin is used for this purpose.

Salage. Also a very ancient practice, known to the Ancient Greeks, who added sea water to their wines. Usually salt is added (up to 1 gram per litre is permitted) to augment the extract and perhaps to cloak some adulteration such as fortification or watering-down.

Shellisage or addition of glycerine. This makes the wine smooth, gives it body, improves its keeping qualities and, above all, increases the proportion of extract. This addition of glycerine is forbidden by law, and can easily be detected by the expert.

The use of sulphur, in the form of sulphuric acid, obtained by burning sulphurated wicks or by adding alkaline bisulphates is recommended by all oenologists as a preventative against the maladies of the wine. Part of the sulphuric acid is eliminated by the *soutirage* or drawing off.

These chemical processes, which remove wine somewhat from its legal definition, present many disadvantages, especially when several of them are done simultaneously, and they may be dangerous to the consumer.

Among the processes which are plainly fraudulent there may be cited the use of saccharine, of dulcine, of antiseptics and of mineral, vegetable and organic colouring matter.

Ageing of wine. This takes place naturally by the wine being left to rest, in cask, side bung, for one, two or more years, according to the nature of the wine, but can be induced artificially by agitation, by heating, by refrigeration, and by the use of electrical impulses, though these can never replace the effect of natural ageing.

Fine wines are subsequently put into bottles, which has the effect of slowing down the processes resulting from oxydization and etherification; these develop the bouquet, and allow the wine to acquire what is called 'bottle age'.

Wines of second and third pressing. Obtained by adding sugared water to the marc (50 kilograms per hectolitre) and fermenting this anew. These wines always have less extract, cream of tartar and tannin, but they still provide a healthy drink which is worth about two-thirds as much as natural wine.

Piquettes. Made from the fermentation of marcs to which unsweetened water has been added. Very poor in alcohol and extract, they are normally used for home consumption and for blending with wines of second and third pressings.

Wine from dried fruit. Raisins are generally used after having been cooked in warm water; the resulting wines, always white, are characterized by the presence of 0·7% to 1% of levogyrous sugar of which there is no trace in natural wine; they are mostly used for blending.

Sparkling wines. Natural sparkling wines contain a certain amount of unfermented sugar at the time of bottling, thus continuing to ferment after corking, which keeps the carbonic acid gas in solution.

Sparkling Champagne wines have the addition of a 'liqueur' (a solution of sugar candy in some wine, with alcohol added in amounts varying according to the quality). The deposit which forms in the bottle is brought up against the cork by setting the bottle upside down, and expelled after it has coagulated. To obtain a fine sparkling wine a pressure of 4 to 5 atmospheres is required, demanding 10 to 13 degrees on the must-measure. Analyses and calculations make it possible to determine from this the quantity of sugar to be added for the acidity of the wine.

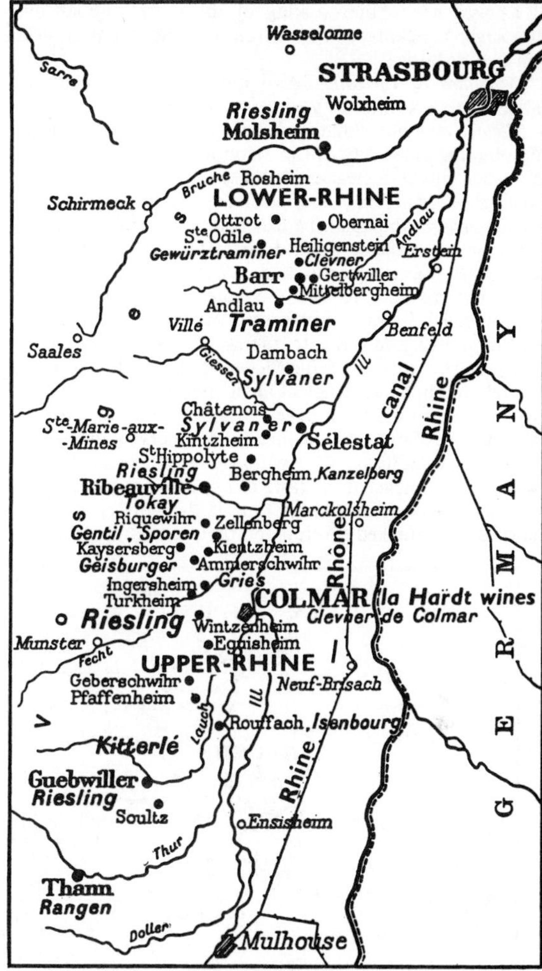

The Vineyards of Alsace

Artificial sparkling wines are made by the introduction of carbonic acid gas in the same way as for artificial Seltzer water, but a fine, creamy, lasting sparkle is never obtained in this way.

Luxury wines: liqueur wines. Wines which are sweeter or richer in alcohol than those in current consumption. The following varieties are distinguished:

Vins doux mutés or *Mistelles*, obtained by adding alcohol to partly fermented must immediately after its extraction (Muscat, Banyuls, Grenache).

Vins doux semi-mutés, obtained by the addition of alcohol to partly fermented must so as to obtain about 15°.

Vins doux passerillés, obtained from musts with a strong sugar content and from raisins dried on the plant, in the sun or in the ovens. The must should be such as to give a wine of 13° to 15° alcoholic content without the addition of alcohol. Part of the sugar should remain, not decomposed.

Wines muted by the addition of alcohol immediately after fermentation while still containing much sugar (Port).

Dry wines fortified after fermentation, like sherry.

Wines with a dry wine base blended to give them smoothness (Madeira, Marsala).

Cooked wines, the cooking of the must augmenting the sugar concentration and transforming it partly into caramel (Malaga).

Maladies of the wine. A liquid which is essentially alive, wine is subject to various maladies.

Fleurs de vin. Small whitish efflorescences which develop on wines deficient in alcohol on contact with the air when ullage is neglected; these are due to a fungus, *mycoderma vini*. The *fleurs du vin* are often the first stage of *acescence*, which can be checked at the outset by the addition of chalk or neutral tartrate of potassium (3·7 grams per gram of acetic acid). When it is marked, the only thing to do is to turn the wine into vinegar.

Amertume, literally 'bitterness', manifests itself chiefly in Burgundies and is due to a ferment which decomposes the glycerine in wines which have been kept too long in barrels and in wines deficient in alcohol. It can be treated, when taken in the early stages, by adding tannin, tartaric acid and alcohol. A simple means of dispersing *amertume* is to mix the affected wine with a younger wine. A wine which has contracted the taste of *amertune* in bottles can re-establish itself in a short time if the bottles are well corked, and stacked carefully on their sides in a properly arranged cellar. On the other hand it is possible to decant the bottles into a perfectly clean, well-fumigated cask, add younger wine and clarify.

Acescence. When casks have not been ullaged regularly, the wine is quickly attacked by *acescence*. This is a very common malady due to an acetic ferment which gives birth to vinegar. This ferment develops best in barrels which have a *vidange*, that is to say a gap between the upper part and the wine inside, and can attack good quality wines, though it principally attacks weak wines whenever they are exposed to heat.

Development of the ferment is prevented by drawing-off the wine and by keeping the barrels full all the time, side bung, so that as little air as possible is allowed to penetrate.

A wine is *piqué*, or pricked, when it is attacked by an acetic ferment. It is very difficult to save a pricked wine. Several methods are advocated. Neutral tartrate of potassium lessens a little the vinegary taste, but the wine so treated must be used immediately.

Pasteurization. The surest way to achieve an appreciable result is to pasteurize the spoiled wine. Heated by means of a pasteurizer, the wine is freed from all the ferment-producing germs which spoil its keeping qualities. There are numerous types of pasteurizers operated by steam, hot air or gas.

The wine to be pasteurized must be clarified and drawn off and have perfect limpidity. To save time the wine can be filtered, then heated to a maximum temperature of 60° to 72°C. (140° to 161°F.). The pasteurized wine should be put into perfectly clean and strongly fumigated barrels which should then be set in a very clean place. This operation, done with care, always has satisfactory results.

Pasteurization can be done in bottles. These are placed upright in a double-bottomed heater which is filled up to the necks of the bottles, of which one, used for testing, is filled with water and provided with a thermometer to show the rise in temperature and the correct moment to remove from the heat.

It must not be thought that pasteurization will restore to its normal state a wine that is badly soured; but it nevertheless has the effect of killing off the existing acetic ferments so that the liquid can be used. Pasteurized wines can remain on ullage, i.e. with an air-filled gap in the barrel, for quite a long time without being affected.

Pasteurization has the effect of ageing the wine. Some people claim that the process benefits the wine, but opinions are divided. Certainly wines that have slight natural alcoholic content or deteriorate quickly can be helped by pasteurization.

Goût d'évent. Wine put into barrels which have not been properly cleaned, are very old or badly corked, loses part of its bouquet and takes on a particular taste which is called *goût d'évent*.

To get rid of this taste the wine is drawn off into a clean well fumigated barrel. If the taste is too strong, the wine should be mixed with another, which has a higher alcohol content. It must then be clarified and drawn off immediately the wine is clear and the *goût d'évent* has gone.

Vins tournés. Wine usually 'turns' as a result of a poor quality grape harvest. It is a common mistake to confuse 'turned' wine with wine that is *piqué* or soured. In cask,

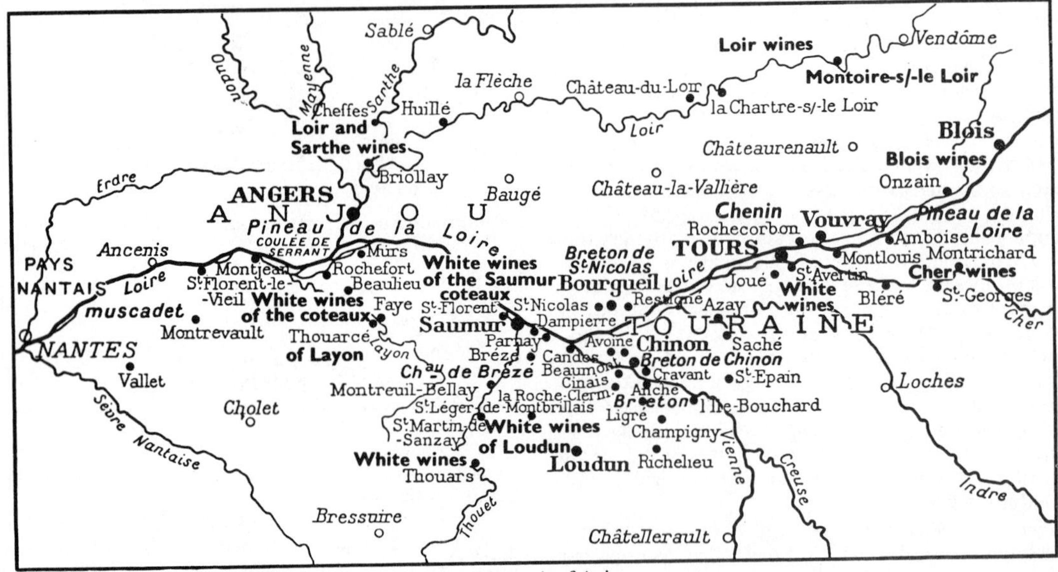

The Vineyards of Anjou

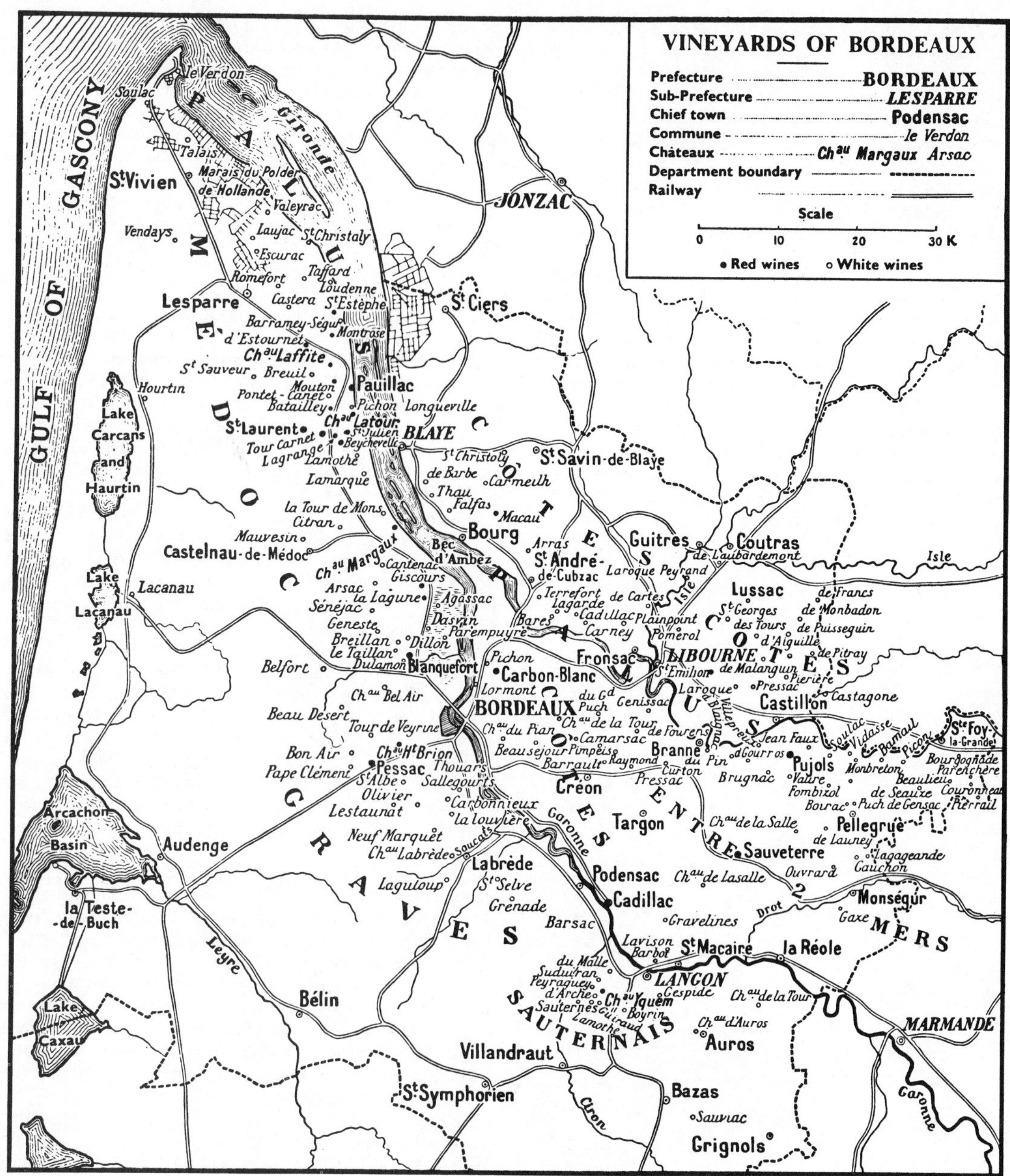

The Vineyards of Bordeaux

wine begins to turn from the bottom, whereas souring always begins on the surface.

A wine that turns completely may be recognized by its dull colour, it is clouded like muddy water and has a smell of rotting organic matter; it has no characteristic of wine.

There are several remedies for turned wine, of which the best and most used is as follows: as soon as it is seen that the wine has turned, citric acid should be added to it, without exceeding the authorized proportion (50 grams per hectolitre). The bright red colour will return in a few days, then, to restore the spoiled wine completely, it should be mixed with another wine of good quality and the mixture clarified. Pasteurization is also indicated in these circumstances; the wine should be heated to a temperature of 60-70°C. (140-158°F.).

Wines which become ropey (*gras*), *stained* (*taché*) *or yellow* (*jaune*). It is said that a wine has become ropey or *gras* when it is oily and viscid. This malady is particularly rampant among the white wines of the centre of France, but it also attacks weak red wines.

One remedy alone: to use alcohol tannin in a proper dosage (8 grams per hectolitre). Shake the wine from time to time for two or three days to mix well, then clarify thoroughly.

If white wine becomes *taché*, that is to say slightly reddened, a combination of sulphuric and animal black can be used to lighten the colour again.

White wines which become yellow are also treated in the same way, but there is also a simpler method, within the reach of all and invariably successful, which is to clarify the yellowed wine according to the instructions given below under the heading *Clarifying wine* (*collage*), then to filter and draw off a fortnight later.

Wines which taste stagnant or mildewed. It often happens that the utensils used in making wine have been badly cleaned or incompletely dried. Water has been left in the casks and has become stagnant. It is therefore understandable that the wine may acquire the same taste.

Wine generally passes unharmed from the press to the vat but if it is put into mildewed casks, the bad taste is quickly communicated. To get rid of this, the wine is drawn off into a clean cask and a litre of pure olive oil is added, the barrel being vigorously shaken. A few days later, when the oil has risen to the surface, the wine is drawn off. Alternatively the oil floating on the top may be expelled by introducing a certain amount of wine through a tube. This takes the place of the oil, which is expelled through the bung-hole.

When a bottled wine contracts a corked taste (*goût de bouchon*), it can be treated in the same way, but it is only rarely that this happens on a scale important enough for this to be done. In general the corked taste is found in one or two bottles only and it is better to sacrifice them.

Casse. Under the name *casse* are known three sorts of malady. *Casse brune*, which may be observed on red and white wines, is due to oxydization and insolubility of the colouring matter under the influence of an oxide. It is seen in wines whose fermentation has been slowed down by too high a temperature or made with grapes attacked by *pourriture grise* (grey rot). Exposed to the air the wine becomes cloudy, forms a considerable deposit and develops a taste first insipid then bitter. At the outset, *casse brune* can be treated with tannin (4 to 10 grams per hectolitre), followed by drawing off into a well fumigated cask or adding bisulphate. It is then clarified and pasteurized.

It can happen that wine develops *casse* simply as a result of a considerable change of temperature, or a long journey. If it is a robust wine it will in these circumstances right itself after a few days.

Casse bleu or *casse ferrique* which attacks white and red wines is due to an excess of iron salts in the wine (the grapes having been tainted with ferruginous earth or contact with iron instruments or receptacles). The iron salts combine with tannin to form ferrous tannates which, by oxydization, are transformed into insoluble ferric tannates. The treatment is to add citric acid (20 to 40 grams per hectolitre), to clarify with egg whites and draw off into a fumigated cask.

Pousse and *tourne* are troubles caused by the presence of an anaerobic bacillus which attacks the tartaric acid and which develops in weak wines; on contact with the air the surface of wine becomes iridescent, it is seen to be discoloured, it loses its clarity and acidity and forms a brownish deposit.

It liberates, at the expense of bitartrate of potassium, lactic acid, propionic acid and carbonic acid gas, which tend to dilate the cask and blow off the bottom. The taste, at first insipid, becomes bitter and nauseating. If the malady is taken at the outset it can be checked by an addition to the wine of tartaric acid (20 to 30 grams per hectolitre), following 30 to 40 hours later by treatment with tannin (10 grams per hectolitre) and sulphur (5 to 8 grams of bisulphate per hectolitre), then clarification with gelatine.

The causes of these troubles are dirty cellars, insufficient care of vessels and utensils used in the wine-making and imperfect cleaning of casks, failure to use only sound grapes or too high a temperature in the cellars.

Wines unsuitable for consumption. According to the decree of February 1st, 1930, wine is considered unfit for consumption if it is suffering from any malady, with or without *acescence*, which gives it an abnormal appearance and taste, and when it has either a deficiency of tartaric acid, or of bitartrates of potassium, or at least two of the following characteristics:

(1) Volatile acids in excess of 1 gram 50 per litre expressed as sulphuric acid;

(2) Total acidity expressed as bitartrate of potassium less than 1 gram 25 per litre;

(3) Ammonia content higher than 20 milligrams per litre.

Care of the finished wine.

The cellar. The first requirement of a cellar is not that it should be extremely cold but that its temperature should be as constant as possible.

In a large town, where there is heavy traffic, it is important to see that the cellar is not shaken when heavy vehicles pass; repeated shocks of this kind can cause lees to rise, which, mixed with the wine, can turn it sour.

A wine cellar must be kept scrupulously clean; no rubbish should be left in it, no vegetables with a strong odour (carrots, cabbage, onions, turnips), no cheese, no barnyard animals and no liquids such as petrol, mineral oils, etc.; all these very easily communicate their aroma *sui generis* to the wine, as has often been observed.

The Vineyards of Burgundy

The wooden stands on which the casks are set must be firmly fixed, 8 to 12 inches above the ground on cross-bars made of wood or stone. In this way the air circulates freely under the barrels and will prevent the hoops becoming damp.

Care should be taken to fix the casks with wedges so that one can be removed without others being shaken, since this might cause the lees to rise.

Clarifying wine (*collage*). It is necessary to clarify (*coller*) wine which is going to be bottled.

The purpose of the *collage* is to give the wine its limpidity; it precipitates to the bottom of the barrel the solids which the liquid holds in suspension, matter which can give rise to the maladies detailed elsewhere.

A barrel of red wine containing 225 litres is clarified with 4 egg whites well beaten in a litre of wine. For white wine a tablet of special gelatine dissolved in ½ litre of hot water for each hectolitre of wine.

The bung having been extracted, 4 or 5 litres of wine are removed with a rubber tube, a special suction pump or a siphon. Failing any of these tools, the barrel can be pierced with a gimlet for the necessary amount of wine to be withdrawn. The clarifying agent is poured in through the bunghole, then with the aid of a round stick split into four at the end the liquid is vigorously whisked to mix in the *colle*. The wine which was drawn off is now poured back, and more wine is added, if needed. The barrel is banged again and again to make the sediment fall and get rid of bubbles, and the bung is replaced. The wine is then rested for 20 days.

Age of wine for bottling. Wines are bottled at different 'ages' according to type.

Bordeaux and Burgundies of the finest growths, rich in tannin and alcohol and full coloured, need to be kept for 3 to 4 years. Chablis and wines other than the *grands crus* can be bottled at the end of 18 months or 2 years. Generally speaking bottling should be done before the wine has lost its bouquet, finesse, its liquorous quality and its colour.

Red wines should have a slightly yellowish tinge; none should taste acid or 'new'.

A wine bottled in these conditions will acquire bouquet and finesse.

The bottles: Cleaning. The bottles are of the same capacity to within a few centilitres, but their shape differs from one wine district to another. It is therefore best to put each wine into bottles which come from its district of origin.

The bottles are washed in hot water in which some soda has been dissolved (20 kilograms to 100 litres). When they are half filled with this solution a quantity of small shot is poured in and the bottles are shaken vigorously to scour the glass thoroughly.

If the bottom of the bottle is very much encrusted, a long-handled brush is used to clean it. It is then rinsed in cold water and turned upside down on a perforated shelf (*planche à égoutter*), on a draining-board of galvanized iron, or on a metal contrivance with spikes. Often today they are dried by hot air.

Bottling, corking, sealing, capping. Bottling should preferably be done in spring or autumn. Cool, dry weather should be chosen, a day when the wind blows from the north or the east. Stormy weather should be avoided.

It is not necessary to draw off the clarified wine before bottling it but it must be verified that it is absolutely clear. This is easily done by filling a glass with wine from the barrel and holding it up to the light.

The next requirement is a tap of rust-proof metal or wood. With a brace and a bit a hole is worked in the base of the barrel, exactly in the middle, and about the same size as the tap, care being taken not to come on a joint. The tap is carefully fixed so that it will not leak. A clean wooden bucket is placed below (or a perfectly clean deep dish) so that none of the wine is lost. One or two bottles are drawn to 'clear', then the others are filled until the barrel is exhausted.

The choice of corks is very important. They must be of fine, soft, supple cork, giving to pressure from the fingers and without blemishes. Before using they should be put into a receptacle and boiling water poured over them. This operation is intended not only to make them more supple, but also to ensure that the cork is freed of any impurities it may contain. They are then drained for an hour in a strainer, and finally soaked for 10 to 15 minutes in good quality alcohol, either brandy or an old marc which has lost its aroma.

It is preferable not to re-use old corks, or to use them only for *vins ordinaires* which are going to be drunk immediately.

The bottles are corked immediately either quite full or with a small space left at the top, so that if strong pressure is exerted on the cork, it will not burst the neck of the bottle.

In private cellars the implement used to knock the cork down into the bottle is simply a kind of bat; the cork is put in and hit with the *batte* until it is well down in the neck.

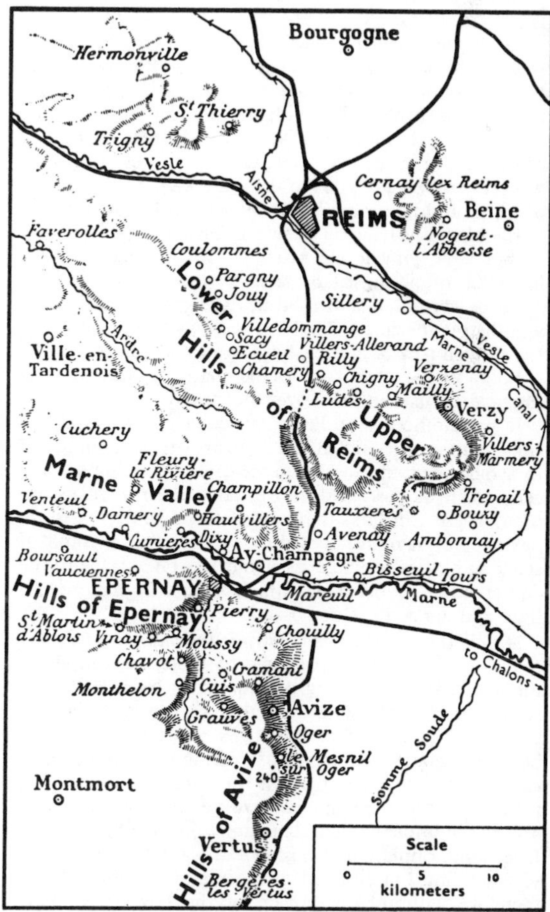

The Vineyards of Champagne

In industrial premises, large restaurants, etc., apparatus is used which allows many bottles to be corked in a very short time without fear of breakage. This work is easily done, and the cork goes down into the wine, so that there is no empty space at the top. The wine can thus only benefit, though naturally the cork must still be of good quality and prepared with the same care.

To seal the corks, Spanish wax is dissolved in boiling water. (This wax is sold in paint shops and by grocers in France.) When the wax is soft, the neck of the bottle is held in the left hand and the base in the right hand and the end of the cork and a very small part of the neck of the bottle are dipped into it. The bottle is gently turned with the right hand for a moment so as to coat the cork and bottle neck well, then the bottle is set upright.

It is essential to add a little fat to the wax so as to make it less breakable and, at the same time, more adhesive.

The purpose of the wax is to preserve the cork and to prevent it from being nibbled by insects, which are always numerous in cellars.

Sealing with wax is now generally replaced by sealing with metal caps, which cover the cork either partly or completely. These are made in many types and sizes.

When a machine is not available, the work is done in the following way: a strong string is attached to a large nail firmly fixed in a wall or door. The string is held in one hand and the bottle with the cap in place is held in the other. The string is wound round the cap just below the ridge which ends the neck, and thus attached is pulled to and fro keeping the string taut, so that the cap is pressed tight.

Placing the bottles. Generally the bottles are set in two rows in this way: at the back a row of bottles with their bottoms against the wall and their necks in front. Then the space in front is filled with another row with bottoms facing forwards with the necks fitting between two necks of the bottles in the back row. On top of these two rows of bottles others are piled in the same way. A tiny bubble of air should be visible in the middle of the body of the bottle when it is lying on its side and will indicate whether or not it is lying level. Attention to this may prevent breaking, often caused by lack of stability.

To be certain that the bottles are exactly horizontal and the pile perfectly steady, it is as well to set laths on top of each row of bottles, both front and back.

For a stack of bottles to be perfectly steady, it is essential to use uniform-sized bottles.

In private houses, in Paris particularly, where space is sometimes very restricted and there are frequent removals, to avoid the trouble and expense of constructing a wine-cellar such as described above, portable iron racks are used. These can hold the equivalent of half a barrel, a barrel or even more, according to size. This method of stacking bottles is much easier but less favourable to the conservation of the wine, which should be exposed to light and air as little as possible.

Appellations controlées (*controlled names*) *of wines and brandies*—The general principle of repressing frauds in the matter of the naming of wine dates from 1905. But it was not until May 6th, 1919, that a law was introduced to control this naming. Even this was still incomplete because it made the mistake of making the name depend entirely on the place in which the wine was made. The result was that sometimes unscrupulous producers were able to sell under a celebrated name some mediocre wines from commonplace plants grown in places unsuitable for vine-growing but situated in the region designated and therefore without any breach of the law, since these wines certainly came from the region indicated.

The vine-growing associations thus demanded the institution of a control for the district names, and this was instituted by the decree of July 30th, 1935. It is still impossible to forbid a vine-grower to give a wine a name of origin that is justified solely by the place in which the grapes were harvested, but from that date onwards consumers could know that only the *Appellations controlées* indicate choice wines and guaranteed quality and finesse.

This control is vested in a state committee of forty members nominated by the French Minister of Agriculture. It includes vine-growers, presidents of vine-growing associations and some high officials of various ministries.

The decisions of this committee are transformed by the Ministry of Agriculture into decrees having the force of law and which determine:

(1) The nature of the soil where the vines must grow which produce the particular wine.

(2) The type of vine and its size.

(3) The processes used to make the wine and *eau-de-vie*, proved traditional processes.

(4) The minimum degree of alcohol.

(5) The maximum production per hectare (2·471 acres) of vines planted, so as to prohibit cultivation detrimental to quality.

Control is carried out in the district of production by agents of the committee who visit the vine-growers and check that the traditional rules are being kept. Later when the wine is in cask it is guaranteed by the State document which accompanies it.

This is the equivalent for fine wines of the *acquit jaune d'or* which already existed for the great brandies called after their place of origin, and which had rendered such service in preventing usurpation of such names.

When the wine in question is sold in bottles it can be recognized by the words APPELLATION CONTROLÉE overprinted on the label.

Appellations controlées can be divided into three categories: (1) Regional names; (2) Sub-regional names; (3) Names of *communes*.

The smaller the territories, the more severe the regulations to which their production is subject. The commune names apply to the most restricted spaces, sometimes part of a commune and sometimes a whole commune, sometimes several communes grouped together but using the name of one. For example the name *Châteauneuf-du-Pape* is used for wines harvested in well defined conditions in certain parts of the territory of Châteauneuf-du-Pape, Bédarrides, Courthezon, Sorgues and Orange.

In Burgundy a singular situation is encountered which is the result of regional *Appellations de climats*. The vineyards of the Côte de Nuits are called *climats*, because of their varying climatic conditions. These are sometimes very restricted in space and are generally the property of several wine-growers all of whose wines are sold under the name of the *climat d'origin* or district of origin of the wine. They produce certain wines that are peculiar to a very small region.

The name of the *climat* or region thus becomes more restricted and higher up the scale than the name of the *commune* which may embrace a varying number of *climats*. For example, the *Grands-Echézeaux* is a celebrated *climat* of the *commune* of Flagey-Echézeaux; it is a name of the place of origin because the land which bears the name belongs to several proprietors who by established custom make use of this name.

A name which gives the place of origin is collectively owned, but the *Château* names apply to private property, such as the châteaux of the Gironde, like *Château d'Yquem*, *Château-Lafite*, *Château-Haut-Brion*. It may be noted that these last also have a regional name: *Château-d'Yquem* for example is a Sauternes, *Château-Margaux* is a Médoc.

To serve wine. SERVICE DES VINS—This is how wine should be served at table according to Grimod de la Reynière (*Almanach des Gourmands*):

'Wines of Orléans, Auxerre, Joigny, Coulanges, Vermanton and other vintages of Basse-Bourgogne, and the common wines of Bordeaux, are generally adopted for the everyday use of the demi-gourmand, or for hosts of a demi-fortune.

'Often, after the soup, a wise gourmet offers a glass of dry Madeira or Teneriffe; *vin ordinaire* occupies the table until the second service; then with the roast it is customary to serve the Beaune, the Pommard, the Clos-Vougeot, the Chambertin or, according to the taste of the guests, the second quality Bordeaux, Saint-Emilion, Château-Margaux, or Graves. The passage of these wines is rapid.

'As soon as the third service has succeeded the roast, with the *entremets*, the vegetables, the elegant pastries, the Bordeaux-Lafite, the delicious Romanée, the Hermitage, the Côte Rôtie, or, if the guests prefer, the white wine of Bordeaux, the Sauternes, the Saint-Péray, etc. should be served. But dessert soon follows the third service; then all the delicious wines of Spain or Greece make their appearance, the old port, the sweet Malvoisie, the Royal-Jurançon, the Malaga and the Muscat, the Rota and the wine of Cyprus. Tokay wine is poured into very small glasses. Finally, to crown the feast, champagne froths into crystal, and gaiety, which has already spread itself among the guests, is manifested in cheerful talk and well-pointed jokes.

'This is, more or less, the order of service of wines. Doubtless the personal taste of each host causes variations to be made from time to time. But the order indicated is generally observed.'

The wines at a dinner should be served as follows:

White wines and sparkling wines. Serve cold. Champagne has everything to gain from being served *frappé*, that is to say in a silver-plated bucket filled with ice. It is not customary when the cork is removed from a champagne bottle to send it shooting through the air. It was different in our fathers' day, when, doubtless in homage to Dom Pérignon who, at the beginning of the eighteenth century invented *champagnisation*, it was the fashion to make the corks explode out of the bottles of the famous nectar of the country of Champagne.

Red Bordeaux wines. Bring the bottles from the cellar 48 hours before the meal; stand in a corner of the room away from direct heat or draughts; serve at about 64°F.

Red Burgundy wines. Bring from the cellar several hours before the meal and set in a rather warm room or in a corner of the dining-room. Burgundies should be served at room temperature (about 59°F.–60°F.).

When wines are old, or have a sediment, it is important to serve them with great care so that they are not muddied. It is usual in this case to lay the bottle, as soon as it is brought from the cellar, in a basket, which, keeping it in a horizontal position, makes pouring possible with the minimum of disturbance. It is preferable to decant

TABLE SHOWING THE SERVING OF WINES

WITH SOUP	WITH HORS-D'OEUVRE AND FISH	AT THE FIRST MAIN COURSE	WITH THE ROAST	WITH THE SWEET COURSE	WITH DESSERT
		Red Bordeaux	*Red Burgundies*		
Madeira	Barsac	Château-Beychevelle	Chambertin	Ermitage Blanc	Alicante (Red)
Marsala	Chablis	Château-Cos-d'Estournel	Clos-Vougeot	Montrachet	Cyprus wine
Port	Château-Carbonnieux	Château-Lafite Château-Latour	Corton	Muscat de Frontignan	Lacrima-Christi
Sherry	Graves	Château-Margaux	Ermitage Rouge	Rhine wines	Malaga
	Château d'Yquem				
Zucco	Meursault	Château-Haut-Brion (Graves)	Musigny		Malvoisie
	Montrachet	Château-Mouton-Rothschild	Côte de Nuits	WITH CHEESE	Muscatel
	Pouilly	Saint-Émilion	Pommard	Red Bordeaux or Burgundy	Port
	Sauternes	Saint-Estèphe	Richebourg	Iced Champagne	Syracuse
	Moselle and Rhine wines	Saint-Julien	Romanée		Ténédos (Turkish)
		Château-Pichon-Longueville	Volnay		Sherry
		Château-Pontet-Canet	Iced Champagne		Iced Champagne

TABLE RELATING WINES TO FOOD

	Red Bordeaux	White Bordeaux	Red Burgundies	White Burgundies	Beaujolais Mâconnais	Côtes du Rhône	Loire	Alsace	Champagne
Oysters		Graves.		Meursault. Petit-Chablis.				Sylvaner.	Natural.
Hors-d'Oeuvre		Château d'Yquem. Entre-deux-mers. Sainte-Croix-du-Mont.		Montrachet. Chablis.	Chardonnay-Mâcon.	White Mâcon.	Vouvray. Pouilly-sur-Loire.	Zwicker. Sylvaner.	
Fish and Crustaceans		Sauternes. Montbazillac.		Meursault. Pouilly.	Solutré-Chaintré.			Traminer. Riesling.	Extra dry.
Entrées, Poultry, White Meat.	Light Graves. Château-Lafite. Château-Latour. Château-Margaux.		Chambelle-Musigny.				Chinon. Château-du-Breuil.		Sec (dry.).
Roasts, Game, Red Meat.	Saint-Émilion. Pomerol.		Gevrey-Chambertin. Morey-Saint-Denis. Clos-Vougeot. Nuits-Saint-Georges. Beaune. Pommard.		Moulin-à-vent.	Château-neuf-du-Pape. Côte-rôtie. Ermitage.	Saint-Nicolas-de-Bourgeuil.		
Cheese: *unfermented.*	Château-Margaux.								Doux (sweet).
fermented.	Pomerol. Saint-Émilion.		Nuits-Saint-Georges.			Côte-rôtie. Château-neuf-du-Pape.			
Foies Gras			Nuits-Saint-Georges.	Grand Montrachet.			Chinon. Muscadet.		
Sweet Course, Dessert		Grand-Sauternes. Château-d'Yquem. Barsac.				Arbois.	Chalonnes. Saumur. Vouvray. Quart-de-Chaume.	Gewurz-traminer.	Demi-sec.
Temperature	Room temperature.	*Frappé* (iced) (Between 0° and 5°C., 32°-48°F.).	Room temperature.	Cold.	Cellar temperature.	Cold.	Very cold.	Very cold.	Usually frappé

TABLES OF WINES ACCORDING TO YEARS

Key. x = Poor to mediocre, xx = average to fair, xxx = good to very good, xxxx = excellent.

	Red Bordeaux	White Bordeaux	Red Burgundies	White Burgundies	Beaujolais Mâconnais	Côtes du Rhône	Loire	Alsace	Champagne
1917	xx	xxx	xx	x	x	xxx	x	xx	xxx
1918	x	xx	x	x	xx	xx	xx	x	xx
1919	xx	xx	xxx	xx	xxxx	xx	x	xx	xxx
1920	xxxx	x	xx	xx	xx	xxxx	x	xx	xxxx
1921	xxx	xxxx	xxx	xxx	xxxx	xxx	xxxx	xxxx	xxxx
1922	xx	xxx	x	xx	xx	xx	x	xx	x
1923	xxx	xx	xxxx	xxxx	xxxx	xxx	xx	xx	xxx
1924	xxxx	xxx	xx	xx	xx	xxx	xxx	xx	xx
1925	x	xx	x	xx	x	xx	x	xx	xx
1926	xxx	xx	xxxx	xxx	xxxx	xxx	xxx	xxxx	xxxx
1927	xx	x	x	xxx	x	xx	x	x	x
1928	xxxx	xxx	xxx	xxxx	xxxx	xxx	xxx	xxxx	xxxx
1929	xxxx	xxxx	xxxx	xxxx	x	xxxx	xxx	xxxx	xxxx
1930	x	x	x	x	x	xx	x	x	x
1931	x	x	x	x	x	x	x	x	x
1932	x	x	xxx	x	x	x	xx	xxx	xx
1933	xxx	xx	xxx	xxx	xxxx	xxx	xxxx	x	xxxx
1934	xxx	xxxx	xx	xxx	xxx	xxxx	xxx	xxxx	xxxx
1935	x	x	x	xxx	x	xx	x	xxxx	x
1936	x	x	x	x	x	xx	x	x	x
1937	xxxx	xxxx	xx	xx	xxx	xxxx	xxx	xxx	xxx
1938	xx	xx	xxx	xx	xx	xx	xx	x	xx
1939	xx	xx	x	xx	x	xxxx	xx	x	x
1940	xx	xx	x	x	xxx	x	xx	xxx	xx
1941	x	x	xx	x	x	x	xx	xxx	xxx
1942	xx	xxx	xx	xx	xxx	xxxx	xxx	xx	xx
1943	xxx	xxxx	xxx	xxx	xx	xxx	xxx	xxxx	xxxx
1944	x	x	x	x	xxx	x	xx	xx	xx
1945	xxxx	xxxx	xxxx	xxx	xxxx	xxxx	xxxx	xxxx	xxx
1946	xx	xx	xx	xxx	xxx	xxx	xxx	xxx	xxx
1947	xxxx	xxxx	xxxx	xxxx	xxx	xxxx	xxxx	xxxx	xxxx
1948	xxx	xxx	xxx	xxx	xxx	xxx	xx	xxx	xx
1949	xxx	xxx	xxx	xxxx	xxx	xxx	xxx	xxx	xxx
1950	xxx	x	xx	xx	xx	xxx	xxx	xxx	xx
1951	x	x	x	x	x	x	xx	x	x
1952	xxx	xxx	xxx	xxx	xxx	xxx	xxx	xxx	xxx
1953	xxxx	xxxx	xxxx	xx	xxxx	xx	xxxx	xxx	xxx
1954	xx	xx	xx	xx	xx	xx	xx	xxx	xx
1955	xxxx	xxxx	xxxx	xxx	xxx	xxx	xxx	xxx	xxx
1956	xx	xx	x	x	x	xxx	xx	xx	x
1957	xxx	xxxx	xxx	xxx	xxx	xxx	xxx	xxx	xxx
1958	xxx	xx	x	xx	xx	xx	xxx	xx	xx
1959	xxx	xxx	xxxx	xxxx	x and xxxx	x	xxxx	xxxx	xxxx
1960	—	—	x	xx	xx	xxx	xx	—	—

the wine, this too being carried out with the greatest possible care.

Wine: health and dietetic value. If it is a truism that wine is bad for some sick persons, it does not follow that it should be forbidden to everybody, particularly not to the healthy.

Taken in moderate quantities, i.e. 50 to 75 centilitres (1 to 1½ pints) a day, 1 litre (quart) for heavy workers, as part of a normal diet, it is a good light stimulant and tonic and an aid to digestion.

Wine is not simply a dilution of alcohol; it contains volatile substances, organic acids, and nitrogenous matter and has real alimentary value. A 75-centilitre (1½-pint) bottle has the same calorific value as a litre (quart) of milk, a pound (500 grams) of bread or 2 pounds (a kilogram) of potatoes.

These findings, confirmed by modern science, are not a modern discovery. The Salernian school formulated them in the twelfth century in one of its sentences, of which the following is a translation:

'As for wine, on the choice, this is our doctrine:
Drink little of it, but let it be good;
Wine serves as a medicine,
Bad wine is a poison.
No adulterated wines, they are bad for the stomach.
A wine that is fresh, natural, sparkling, smooth
Ought to delight taste, scent and sight.'

A story about wine. A bishop who was travelling in Italy charged his secretary to go ahead and mark the inn where he had found the best wine. This he would indicate by inscribing on the door of the inn the word *est*, third person singular of the verb *to be*, signifying in Latin *it is, it exists, there is some*! Passing through Montefiascone where he found some excellent wine, the secretary could only express his enthusiasm by repeating the agreed word three times: 'Est, est, est'. The bishop stayed so long at the inn to confirm his forerunner's good impression that he died there.

Ever since then Montefiascone wine has been named Est-est-est.

HOME-MADE WINES—See BEVERAGES.

WINKLE OR PERIWINKLE. BIGORNEAU—A name applied to many small gastropod molluscs, of the genus *Littorina*. The genus occurs on all coasts from the Arctic and Antarctic to the equator.

In various regions of France this mollusc, with a brown coloured spiral shell with a corneous operculum, is called by different names. Thus in Brittany it is called *vignot* or *vignette*, in Normandy *brelin* and in Aunis *escargot de mer* or *guignette*.

At Croisic and in the Auray region winkle farms have been set up, where winkles are cultivated.

Generally speaking winkles are eaten raw, but they can be cooked like cockles. To eat it, the mollusc is extracted from its shell with a pin.

WINTERTHUR (A LA)—Culinary title for a spiny lobster prepared exactly as *Spiny lobster Cardinal** but stuffed with peeled shrimps as well as a *salpicon** of spiny lobster.

WITLOOF—A Belgian endive blanched in cellars. See ENDIVE, CHICORY.

WOODCOCK. BÉCASSE—The woodcock, which is considered, by people who know what is good, the best winged game, is a migratory bird.

It comes to France about the end of September and stays the whole winter—its mating season. Then, towards the end of February, it flies back to its land of origin.

There are three varieties of woodcock; the large (which is the size of a medium-sized partridge), the medium and the small.

Woodcock

People who like eating woodcock insist that it should be cooked undrawn. Only the gizzard has to be removed.

The woodcock, they say, being insectivorous and baccivorous (insect-eating and berry-eating), should not be drawn any more than thrushes, blackbirds, rails or the garden-warbler, for its full flavour to be appreciated.

But some authors, Fonssagrives, for instance, and some public health specialists hold the view that woodcock is difficult to digest, indeed, harmful to health, especially when it is prepared as a *salmis*.*

This opinion is erroneous, the gourmets assure us, particularly where sound woodcock is concerned, that is birds which are not excessively high.

Allowing winged or ground game to get too high is quite wrong gastronomically and is often done out of sheer snobbery. Meat which has reached the state of decomposition (and some alleged woodcock fanciers would not look at this bird unless it has reached the state of complete decomposition) is certainly difficult to digest and often even toxic.

Some decry the use of *rôtie*, which is usually prepared by spreading pieces of bread fried golden in the dripping with the bird's trail (i.e. the intestines) chopped up finely, blended with a little grated bacon fat or *foie gras*, strengthened with a dash of brandy, seasoned with salt and pepper and flavoured with spices.

The gourmets, however, continue to consider woodcock, as well as the trail, which is normally served with it, one of the most succulent morsels.

Here are the opinions of several gastronomes on this subject:

Pierre Belon wrote:

'The woodcock has plenty of rich fat. It sharpens one's discernment of the wines; those who are well off, knowing this, eat it to appreciate the wine.'

Brillat-Savarin wrote in his *Physiologie du goût*:

'The woodcock is a very distinguished bird but few people know its charms. The woodcock is in its full glory when roasted before the eyes of the hunter, especially the hunter who shot it; the roasting is done and the trail is prepared as desired and the mouth waters in the anticipation of delight.'

If Brillat-Savarin eulogizes roast woodcock, Godard

d'Aucour sings the praises of a different preparation:

'When a woodcock is reduced to a purée
Prepared by skilful art,
This dish, so rare, and not less precious,
Should only be served at the banquets of gods.'

We, for our part, prefer less complicated dishes. And for the true gastronome and woodcock fancier, nothing can rival a roast woodcock cooked to a turn, or woodcock in brandy (*à la fine champagne*).

Woodcock à l'armagnac. Bécasse a l'armagnac—Proceed, using Armagnac, as described in the recipe for *Woodcock in brandy* (*à la fine champagne*).

Woodcock in brandy (à la fine champagne). Bécasse à la fine champagne—Cook the woodcock from 10 to 12 minutes. Cut it into joints (pieces) and put them into a buttered silver casserole or into a low-sided terrine, arranging them in a pyramid. Cover the casserole. Keep hot on a hot-plate *without allowing to boil.*

Dilute the juices in which the woodcock was cooked with a small glass of previously burnt fine champagne brandy. Add the chopped intestines, blended with the blood left from pressing the carcase and the trimmings, one tablespoon of concentrated game stock boiled down to the consistency of a *fumet** and a dash of lemon juice. Season with a pinch of cayenne pepper. Pour this sauce over the woodcock and reheat without allowing it to boil.

Woodcock au calvados. Bécasse au calvados—Proceed, using calvados, as described in the recipe for *Woodcock in brandy* (*à la fine champagne*).

Woodcock in casserole or cocotte. Bécasse en casserole, en cocotte—Truss the woodcock as for an entrée, cover with a thin rasher of bacon or salt pork, put into a casserole or a *cocotte*,* in which some butter has been heated; season and cook in the oven from 15 to 18 minutes, basting frequently. Drain the woodcock and remove trussing string. Put in the casserole a dash of brandy and a few tablespoons of concentrated game stock boiled down to a consistency of a *fumet*, or, if not available use unthickened brown gravy.

As usual with roast woodcock, serve the trail at the same time. This can either be put underneath the bird in the *cocotte* or served separately. For the preparation of trail, see recipe for *Roast woodcock* below.

Woodcock au chambertin. Bécasse au chambertin—A kind of salmi, which can be garnished with truffles and mushrooms.

Truss a woodcock as for entrée and cook in the oven from 8 to 10 minutes.

Divide it into joints. Remove the intestines and keep two-thirds to prepare the *rôtie* and the rest for thickening the sauce.

Put the pieces of woodcock into a buttered silver serving dish, cover with sliced truffles and mushrooms, the latter lightly tossed in butter. Keep hot without allowing to boil.

Chop up the carcase and all the trimmings. Put them into a chambertin wine sauce prepared in the followin manner:

Brown in butter a *mirepoix** consisting of half a carrot and half an onion cut into dice and a scant ounce (25 grams) of raw lean ham, a sprig of thyme and a piece of bay leaf. Moisten with $1\frac{1}{2}$ cups (3 decilitres) of chambertin wine. Boil down completely. Moisten with $1\frac{1}{4}$ cups ($2\frac{1}{2}$ decilitres) of *Demi-glace** (see SAUCE) based on a game *fumet*.* Simmer for 20 minutes. Add to this sauce the chopped carcase and the trimmings of the woodcock and a small glass of previously burnt brandy. Rub through a fine sieve. Put back on the fire, bind, using one-third of the intestines, rubbed through a fine sieve as a liaison. Add a tablespoon of butter and pour over the pieces of woodcock. Heat on a hot-plate without allowing it to boil.

Serve with the *rôtie* made with the rest of the intestines.

Chaud-froid of woodcock. Bécasse en chaud-froid—Cook the woodcock in the oven, leaving it slightly underdone. Joint (divide in pieces), and remove the skin. Coat them with brown *Chaud-froid sauce* based on concentrated game stock (see SAUCE). Decorate each piece with slices of truffles, white of hard boiled eggs, salt beef tongue, or cooked ham, and glaze with jelly. Allow to cool thoroughly. See CHAUD-FROID.

Arrange these pieces of woodcock either in a cut-glass dish on a foundation of well-set jelly, or on a buttered croûton. Garnish with chopped jelly.

Woodcock à la crème. Bécasse à la crème—Prepare the woodcock as described in the preceding recipe. After removing the trussing string, put the bird back in the casserole, sprinkle with a dash of brandy and add a few tablespoons of thick fresh cream. Simmer in the oven for a few moments.

Woodcock en daube à l'ancienne. Bécasse en daube à l'ancienne—Dress the woodcock removing the backbone. Season the inside with *spiced salt* (see SALT). Stuff with a large piece of raw *foie gras*, studded with pieces of truffle, seasoned with spiced salt and sprinkled with brandy.

Enclose the *foie gras* well in the bird. Truss the woodcock as for an entrée and bard with a lean rasher (thin sheet) of bacon.

Put the woodcock into an earthenware casserole in which 2 tablespoons of butter have been heated. Baste with this butter and cook in the oven for 10 minutes.

Add 8 mushroom caps and 8 thick slices of truffles and finish cooking together, with a lid on, for 6 minutes. Drain the woodcock and garnish. Dilute the juices left in the casserole with half a glass of red wine (Bordeaux or Burgundy), reduce, add 1 cup (2 decilitres) of game *fumet*,* or, if this is not available, use *Demi-glace sauce* (see SAUCE) with the chopped carcase of the bird added to it to strengthen it, and strained. Boil for a few moments add finely chopped intestines, blended with 2 tablespoons of brandy and 1 good tablespoon of butter. Strain this sauce.

Remove trussing string and put the woodcock and the garnish into the casserole. Pour the sauce over it, heat for a few moments without allowing it to boil.

Woodcock en daube (cold) I. Bécasse en daube—Prepare and cook the woodcock as described in the above recipe but do not add mushrooms to the garnish.

When the woodcock is cooked, drain it, remove trussing string and barding bacon and put it with some truffles into an oval-shaped earthenware *cocotte*. Cover with the sauce prepared as described in the above recipe, adding some meat jelly, strained and with all the fat carefully skimmed off. Chill.

Woodcock en daube (cold) II. Bécasse en daube—Bone the woodcock completely without tearing the skin. Spread the bird on a piece of muslin, soaked in water, wrung out and stretched out on the table.

Season with spiced salt (see SALT) and sprinkle with a few drops of brandy. Cover the middle with a layer of finely pounded pork forcemeat mixed with one-third of its weight of *à gratin forcemeat* for game (see FORCEMEATS AND STUFFINGS), and the bird's intestines, rubbed through a sieve. On this forcemeat, put a piece of *foie gras* of about $2\frac{1}{2}$ ounces (75 grams) pressing it a little into the mixture. The *foie gras* should be studded with large pieces of uncooked truffles, seasoned with spiced salt, well pressed in and sprinkled with a dash of brandy. Cover the *foie gras* with a layer of forcemeat, enclose the whole in the woodcock and wrap the bird in the piece of muslin.

Tie the *ballottine* with string at both ends and in the middle, tightening it to give the *ballottine* its correct shape.

Put this ballottine to cook for 40 minutes in a concentrated game stock, to which the carcase and the trimmings of the bird have been added.

Drain the ballottine, unwrap it. Rinse the piece of muslin in hot water, wring it out and wrap the ballottine in it once again. Put the ballottine into a *terrine*. Strain the liquor left over in the pan, skim off fat, allow it to cool thoroughly and cover the ballottine with it.

Take the ballottine out of the jelly and unwrap it. Put it in a glass dish on a foundation of well set jelly, clarified in the usual manner (see JELLY) with the liquor left over from cooking the woodcock. Cover the ballottine completely with the half set jelly and chill on ice before serving.

Note. Ballottine of woodcock, as well as ballottine of other game, instead of being arranged in a dish and covered with jelly (which is, be it said, the most practical as well as the most elegant method of arrangement), can be served on a round dish, placed direct on the dish or on a buttered croûton of bread, and garnished with chopped jelly.

It can also be lightly coated with a brown chaud-froid sauce based on a game *fumet**; decorate with pieces of truffles, white of hard boiled eggs and salt beef tongue, and glaze with jelly.

Woodcock à la Diane (cold). BÉCASSE À LA DIANE—The recipe which follows comes from Leopold Mourier:

'Roast the woodcock but remove from heat while still markedly underdone, and cut it into fillets.

'Pound the carcase and the intestines with a piece of *foie gras* the size of a walnut, a piece of butter the size of a hazelnut, some nutmeg and brandy.

'Rub through a sieve and season well.

'Arrange this forcemeat on large pieces of truffles, uncooked and steeped in fine champagne brandy.

'Reshape the woodcock, sandwiching the fillets together with slices of truffles covered with forcemeat. Cover the whole with very concentrated game jelly. Chill thoroughly before serving.'

Woodcock au fumet. BÉCASSE AU FUMET—Prepare like *Woodcock in brandy* (*à la fine champagne*). When it is cooked, but quite underdone, joint it (divide into pieces), put in a silver casserole and finish off on a hot-plate, pouring over it the blood pressed out of the carcase, thickened a little with finely chopped intestines and a dash of previously burnt fine champagne brandy.

Serve the rest of the trail (intestines) on a piece of fried bread.

Woodcock à l'orange. BÉCASSE À L'ORANGE—Cook the woodcock on a spit or in the oven. Arrange it on a croûton spread with the trail. See *Roast woodcock*.

Dilute the pan juices (or the dripping-pan juices) with ½ cup (1 decilitre) of dry white wine, add a few tablespoons of concentrated game stock boiled down to the consistency of a *fumet*.* Simmer for 5 minutes. Add the juice of 1 orange, strain through a fine strainer or muslin bag, add finely shredded rind of 1 orange, blanched and well drained, and blend in a teaspoon of butter. Pour this sauce over the woodcock. Garnish the dish with sections or slices of oranges.

Woodcock with oysters à l'ancienne. BÉCASSE AUX HUÎTRES À L'ANCIENNE—Although a woodcock cannot be considered as abstinence fare, it is often served as such during Lent.

Stuff the woodcock with 8 oysters *à la crème*, i.e. poached in their own liquid, drained, de-bearded and dried, then put into very thick *Velouté sauce* (see SAUCE) based on concentrated fish stock and the liquor left over from the oysters.

Truss the woodcock. Cook in the oven, until light golden.

Spread with finely chopped intestines blended with 2 pounded anchovy fillets, seasoned with salt, pepper, grated nutmeg and lemon juices on a croûton fried in oil and brown the top. Arrange the woodcock on the croûton.

Dilute the juices left over from cooking the woodcock with a dash of brandy, blend in 2 tablespoons of butter and pour over the bird. Surround the woodcock with 4 oysters, dipped in egg and breadcrumbs and fried, and lemon cut in quarters.

Woodcock pâté

Hot woodcock pâté à la périgourdine I. PÂTÉ CHAUD DE BÉCASSE À LA PÉRIGOURDINE—Cut off the breast fillets of 2 woodcocks. Using the boned flesh of the rest of these two birds and adding to it the flesh of another whole woodcock and a quantity of fat bacon equal to half the total weight of the woodcocks' flesh, prepare a very finely pounded forcemeat, season it with salt, pepper and spices and sprinkle with a small glass of brandy.

Coat the bottom and the walls of a pâté dish, lined with short pastry (the pâté baking mould should be the hinged kind, either round or oval in shape).

On the forcemeat put 2 fillets, slightly flattened with a steak-beater. On these place 4 small slices of *foie gras* and 8 thick slices of truffles. Cover with another layer of forcemeat to be followed by the other two fillets, and slices of *foie gras* and truffles. Finish off with another layer of forcemeat. Cover with a lid of pastry cut and rolled out to the size and shape of the diameter of the mould. Seal the edges and crimp with a pastry crimper. Make a small hole or a chimney in the middle of the pâté to allow steam to escape. Decorate with pieces of rolled-out pastry cut in fancy shapes. Brush with yolk of egg. Put on a baking tray and cook in a slow oven for about an hour.

Unhinge the mould, take out the pâté and arrange it on a dish. Through the hole in the top pour in a few tablespoons of *Demi-glace sauce* (see SAUCE), based on a concentrated game stock boiled down to the consistency of a *fumet* and essence of truffles.

Hot woodcock pâté à la périgourdine II. PÂTÉ CHAUD DE BÉCASSE À LA PÉRIGOURDINE—Bone two woodcocks completely. Lay them out on the table and spread each with a forcemeat as described in the above recipe, with *foie gras* and truffles. Roll the woodcocks into ballottines and wrap each in a piece of muslin. Poach for 12 minutes in Madeira-flavoured braising stock, made from the carcases and trimmings of the birds. Drain and allow to cool. When quite cold, unwrap the ballottines.

Meanwhile, prepare a finely pounded forcemeat, composed of two-thirds *à gratin game forcemeat* and one-third *veal forcemeat*. See FORCEMEAT.

Line an oval-shaped hot pâté mould with short pie pastry, then coat the bottom and the wall of the mould with the above forcemeat. Put the ballottines on this forcemeat, laying them side by side. Cover the ballottines with 10 slices of *foie gras* heated in butter and 20 slivers of truffles. Cover with the rest of the forcemeat, put on a lid of rolled out pastry and finish off as described above.

Cook in a slow oven from 40 to 45 minutes. At the last moment pour into the pâté, through the opening in the top, several tablespoons of *Périgueux sauce*. See SAUCE.

Cold woodcock pâté. PÂTÉ FROID DE BÉCASSE—This can be prepared in the same way as *Hot woodcock pâté II.*

Allow the pâté to cool without taking it out of the mould. When it is quite cold, pour into it a few tablespoons of liquid aspic jelly, flavoured with Madeira, port or sherry. Leave to get cold for 12 hours.

Take the pâté out of the mould and serve it on a napkin-covered dish.

Woodcock à la périgourdine. BÉCASSE À LA PÉRIGOURDINE—Stuff the woodcock with a forcemeat of the bird's chopped intestines, *foie gras* and truffles, chopped or cut into dice, seasoned with salt, pepper and spices and strengthened with a dash of Armagnac. Truss the woodcock as for an entrée. Heat 2 tablespoons of butter in an earthenware casserole and put the woodcock in. Season and brown on all sides. Add 6 small peeled truffles. Sprinkle with a small glass of Armagnac. Cook in the oven, uncovered, from 15 to 18 minutes. Remove trussing string. Baste with 4 tablespoons of concentrated game stock boiled down to a consistency of a *fumet.** Serve in the same casserole.

This dish is a variation of *Woodcock à la Souvarov*.

Woodcock pie with truffles. TOURTE DE BÉCASSE AUX TRUFFES—Fill the middle of a round rolled-out piece of *flaky pastry* (see DOUGH), circled with a flaky pastry band, with a layer of *à gratin game forcemeat* (see FORCEMEAT). On this forcemeat put the pieces of two woodcocks jointed (cut into serving pieces) and briskly fried in sizzling butter, just to brown them lightly. Cover with slices of truffles. Season with salt and pepper and scatter over a few small dabs of butter.

Cover with puff paste and seal the edges. Make a hole in the middle of this pastry lid to allow steam to escape. Decorate the top with rolled-out pieces of flaky pastry cut in fancy shapes and brush with yolk of egg. Bake in a hot oven. Remove from the oven, pour into the pie a few tablespoons of concentrated game stock. Serve on a napkin.

Purée of woodcock. PURÉE DE BÉCASSE—Let us first of all say that the woodcock is really too noble a bird to be treated in this manner and we do not hesitate to qualify as barbarians people, even though they may be gastronomes, or fancy themselves as such, who say and write that this dish is the 'height of culinary art'.

Cook a woodcock in the oven for 10 minutes, allow to cool and bone completely. Pound the flesh in a mortar, together with the intestines. Rub this purée through a fine sieve. Put it to heat in a *bain-marie,** in a casserole or in a silver timbale. Add to it a few tablespoons of very concentrated game *fumet,** made from the carcase and the trimmings of the woodcock and doubled with rich *Demi-glace* (see SAUCE). Add 2 tablespoons of fine champagne brandy and stir.

You can add to this purée diced truffles, cooked in Madeira, or a few tablespoons of truffle purée. The woodcock purée can be served by itself, pyramided on a platter and garnished with puff pastry rosettes or heart-shaped croûtons fried in butter. It can also be used as a garnish for various dishes: soft boiled or poached eggs on woodcock purée, and especially for plover eggs.

And, finally, it is used for filling *barquettes* and other tartlets, patties, vol-au-vent cases, and other dishes of similar nature which are served as small entrées, or *entrées volantes*.

Woodcock à la Riche. BÉCASSE À LA RICHE—This dish was the speciality of the old Café Riche. It was very famous for the excellence of its cuisine and disappeared in 1917.

This woodcock is prepared as *Woodcock in brandy* (*à la fine champagne*)*. It is arranged on a croûton of fried bread, spread with *à gratin game forcemeat* (see FORCEMEAT) and the gravy which is poured over the woodcock is thickened with purée of *foie gras* and butter. The bird is jointed (divided into pieces) only at the very last moment.

Roast woodcock. BÉCASSE RÔTIE—Truss the woodcock, drawing the head round and running the beak through the legs. Bard it and tie with string. Cook on a spit on a very lively fire, from 18 to 20 minutes, or in the oven from 15 to 18 minutes.

Arrange the woodcock on a canapé of bread fried in butter, or fried golden in the dripping pan, or in the roasting pan.

Roast woodcock must always be served with its *rôtie*, i.e. croûton of fried bread spread with the intestines of the bird taken out after cooking. It is prepared in the following manner.

Chop up finely the woodcock's intestines (the gizzard having been removed) with an equal quantity of *foie gras* or fresh grated bacon fat, season with salt and pepper and add a pinch of grated nutmeg and a dash of brandy. Spread this mixture on pieces of bread, either fried or cooked in the dripping pan. Sprinkle with freshly ground pepper straight from the pepper mill. Put in a very hot oven for a few moments.

The *rôties*, i.e. pieces of fried bread with the trail on them, can be garnished with peeled grapes. Instead of cognac, the mixture can be flavoured with Armagnac or Calvados.

Finally, we must add that it is customary for making croûtons for serving the trail of woodcock or other winged game, to use crustless bread, or what is called in France 'English bread'. These croûtons can also be made from home-made bread. The trail is best served on this, in our opinion.

Salmis of woodcock. SALMIS DE BÉCASSE—Roast a woodcock for a short time to keep it underdone and cut into joints (pieces). Skin these joints and trim them.

Put them into a buttered sauté pan. Place over them 12 small mushrooms tossed in butter, or sliced large mushrooms, and 8 to 10 slices of truffles, cut not too thin. Sprinkle with a tablespoon of previously burnt brandy. Keep hot, with a lid on, but do not allow to boil.

Chop or pound finely the carcase of the woodcock (the carcase can be chopped together with the intestines, or the trail can be kept for spreading on garnish croûtons).

Add these ingredients to 1 cup (2 decilitres) of dry white wine, boiled down in a pan with 2 small chopped shallots.

Some authors of culinary works maintain that a salmis of woodcock can be prepared without wine of any kind. That is not our view. The salmis is a sauce which should be moistened with white wine, and sometimes with red wine.

Generally speaking, in modern practice, the salmis are moistened with dry white wine. In the old days, they were mainly moistened with red wine.

Moisten with $1\frac{1}{4}$ cups ($2\frac{1}{2}$ decilitres) of thickened brown veal stock, to which $\frac{3}{4}$ cup ($1\frac{1}{2}$ decilitres) of game *fumet** (concentrated game stock) has been added. Boil for 10 minutes. Strain through a sieve pressing with a vegetable presser to extract all the juices from the carcase. Put the strained sauce into a sauté pan, add to it one or two tablespoons of veal stock and cook down to the right consistency. Season the sauce to taste, add a tablespoon of previously burnt brandy, and strain through a fine strainer. Pour this sauce over the pieces of woodcock and heat *without allowing to boil.*

Put the pieces of woodcock into a timbale, pour the sauce over them and garnish with heart-shaped croûtons fried in butter.

The salmis of woodcock can be served on a crôuton, square or rectangular, cooked in butter, and either spread with the trail of the bird or not, as desired. When it is served with heart-shaped croûtons—and this garnish, although not compulsory, is to be recommended—these croûtons can be spread with *à gratin forcemeat*. See FORCEMEAT.

All the recipes for the preparation of various salmis will be found under the entry entitled SALMIS.

Woodcock sauté à la Brillat-Savarin. BÉCASSE SAUTÉE BRILLAT-SAVARIN—Prepare the woodcock as described in the recipe for *Woodcock in champagne*, replacing champagne by Madeira.

Arrange the pieces of woodcock in a pie pastry flan, baked blind. Garnish with a ragoût of cocks' combs and kidneys, sautéed lamb sweetbreads, truffles and mushrooms, bound with greatly reduced *Demi-glace* (see SAUCE) based on a game *fumet.** Pour over the whole the gravy left over from cooking the woodcock.

Woodcock sauté in champagne. BÉCASSE SAUTÉE AU CHAMPAGNE—Cut the woodcock into pieces, uncooked. Use the carcase and the trimmings to prepare a *fumet** and add rich *Demi-glace* (see SAUCE) to it.

Put the pieces of woodcock in a sauté pan just big enough to hold them and brown briskly in butter. Cover the pan with a lid and leave to simmer for 8 minutes. Drain the pieces of woodcock, arrange in a timbale or in a shallow dish and keep hot.

Dilute the pan juices with a glass of dry champagne, add the strained concentrated woodcock *fumet** and boil for a few moments. Thicken this sauce with the chopped intestines, season with a small pinch of cayenne and add a teaspoon of butter and a dash of lemon juice. Strain the sauce and pour it over the woodcock, piping hot.

Woodcock sauté with truffles. BÉCASSE SAUTÉE AUX TRUFFES—Prepare the woodcock as described in the recipe for *Woodcock sauté in champagne*. Rub the woodcock's intestines through a fine sieve, mix with *à gratin forcemeat* (see FORCEMEAT) spread on a croûton fried in butter and brown the top. Arrange the woodcock on this croûton.

In the butter left over from the cooking quickly toss a dozen good thick slices of truffles, season with salt and pepper, moisten with $\frac{1}{2}$ cup (1 decilitre) of Madeira; cook down, add 5 tablespoons of game *fumet** and pour over the woodcock.

Woodcock soufflé. SOUFFLÉ DE BÉCASSE—Bone an uncooked woodcock and prepare a *soufflé** mixture adding a little *foie gras* and the bird's intestines rubbed through a sieve to its flesh.

Fill a buttered soufflé dish three-quarters full with this mixture and poach in the oven, in a *bain-marie** (pan of hot water), from 25 to 35 minutes, according to the size of the dish.

Serve separately *Madeira sauce* based on game essence. See SAUCE.

Woodcock soufflé can also be prepared using cooked flesh, pounded in a mortar and rubbed through a sieve. Add to it either *Demi-glace* or *Velouté sauce* made with concentrated game stock (see SAUCE). Bind with a liaison of 2 yolks of egg and fold in stiffly beaten whites.

This soufflé is cooked like an ordinary soufflé.

Woodcock à la Souvarov. BÉCASSE À LA SOUVAROV—Prepared like *Partridge à la Souvarov.**

Suprême of woodcock

Suprême of woodcock. Prepared like chicken suprêmes. See CHICKEN, *Suprêmes of chicken.*

Timbale of woodcock (hot). TIMBALE DE BÉCASSE—Line a pie-dish with pie pastry and line this with thin rashers of fat bacon. Coat the bottom and the walls of the pie dish with *à gratin game forcemeat* (see FORCEMEAT) mixed with diced truffles.

Bone two woodcocks, stuff with a piece of *foie gras* studded with pieces of truffle, roll into ballottines, brown briskly in butter and put into the pie dish.

Cover the woodcocks and fill in the spaces between and around them with fine forcemeat, mixed with a purée of *foie gras* and the intestines, rubbed through a sieve, well seasoned and flavoured with a dash of brandy. Over this forcemeat, put a layer of *à gratin* game forcemeat, piling it slightly into a dome shape. Cover with thin rashers of fat bacon, then with a rolled out piece of pastry cut to the diameter of the pie dish (sealing the edges to form a ridge above the pie dish). Decorate with pieces of rolled out pastry cut in fancy shapes. Make a hole in the centre to allow steam to escape. Brush with beaten egg and cook in a hot oven for $1\frac{1}{4}$ hours.

Leave to rest for a few moments before taking out of the pie dish. Arrange on a round dish covered with a folded napkin. Pour into the timbale a few tablespoons of *Demi-glace* (see SAUCE) based on concentrated game stock.

Usually hot timbales, whatever their nature, are lined with very ordinary pie pastry, its main quality being its strength as it acts as a receptacle in these circumstances.

To make this dish more delicate, the pie dish can be lined with short pastry which will make it edible. It is usually much appreciated by gastronomes, especially when it is impregnated with juice of woodcock.

Timbale of woodcock (cold). TIMBALE DE BÉCASSE—This is prepared in a pie dish, lined with *Fine lining paste* (see DOUGH) and cooked as described in the recipe for *Hot timbale of woodcock*.

When the pie is cooked, leave to get cold. Pour into it, to fill all the empty spaces, some liquid aspic jelly based on concentrated game stock, flavoured with Madeira or some other wine. Allow to get quite cold before taking out of the pie dish. Serve on a napkin-covered dish.

Truffled woodcock (in casserole). BÉCASSE TRUFFÉE—Prepare the woodcock as described in the recipe below for *Truffled roast woodcock*. Cook it in an earthenware casserole as described in the recipe for *Casserole of woodcock*. At the end of cooking, sprinkle with a dash of brandy and a few tablespoons of game *fumet*.*

Truffled roast woodcock. BÉCASSE TRUFFÉE RÔTIE—Stuff the woodcock (with the backbone removed) with lard mixed with truffles, prepared as described in the recipe for *Forcemeat for truffled poultry* (see FORCEMEATS AND STUFFINGS) with truffles, cut in uniform pieces, tossed for a few moments in the heated lard and seasoned with *spiced salt*. See SALT.

Slip a dozen thin slices of truffle under the skin of the woodcock, raising it gently. Truss and bard the woodcock.

Wrap it in a piece of buttered greaseproof paper and cook it on a spit from 20 to 25 minutes, or in the oven from 18 to 20 minutes.

Arrange the woodcock on a canapé of fried bread, which may be spread with the trail of the bird, as described in the recipe for *Roast woodcock*. Serve it with its own juices or with *Périgueux sauce*. See SAUCE.

Truffled woodcock should be prepared, that is stuffed with truffles and forcemeat, at least two days before it is cooked.

WOODEN PLINTH. MANDRIN—Formerly, these plinths were covered with such substances as modelling fat, butter, decorative sugar motifs, etc., for the presentation of cold dishes displayed on plinths. This method of presentation has now been almost completely abandoned and is merely of historical interest.

In former times, these wooden plinths were much used. Carême, in his writings, often speaks of them for, at that time, dishes were almost always presented on plinths or supports of one kind or another, all more or less elaborately decorated.

Nowadays it is usual to serve cold food either simply laid out on a dish, or, completely covered with jelly in a glass bowl.

WOOD GROUSE. COQ DE BRUYÈRE—A bird belonging to the *Gallinae* order. The wood grouse is the largest type of feathered game which is to be found in Europe. In its size and weight it resembles the turkey.

This bird, which has very delicate flesh, is found in considerable abundance in the countries of northern Europe, in Russia, Poland, Hungary, and in the Black Forest region of Germany.

It is rarer in France, but is still found in the Ardennes, in the Vosges, the Alpes, and the Pyrenees. In these districts the *great grouse* or *grand coq de bruyère*, a magnificent bird, is treated from the culinary point of view in the same way as pheasant.

In north European countries, before preparing this bird it is left to soak for a while, two to three days, in a bath of cream. For its preparation, see PHEASANT.

WOODPECKER. PIC—Edible scansorial bird which is prepared like blackbird or thrush.

WOOD PIGEON. PALOMBE—A species of ring dove or wild pigeon, which is prepared like ordinary pigeon. This bird is called *palombe* or *ramier* in French.

WORMSEED (U.S.A. MEXICAN TEA)—A kind of tea produced by the ambroissier shrub with a sweet-smelling flower. Restorative and stomachic properties are attributed to the infusion of this plant.

WORMWOOD. GÉNÉPI—A name applied to several species of plants, among which are the Alpine yarrow, used in the preparation of medicinal herb-teas, and the musk milfoil, which is believed to aid digestion. The musk milfoil is the main ingredient of a liqueur (*liqueur d'Ira* or *Irabitter*) made in Switzerland and Italy from a number of different Alpine herbs. Originally, the liqueur distilled at the *Grande Chartreuse* bore this name.

WRAP. EMBALLER—To envelope a joint of meat, etc. first in a slice of pork fat or pig's caul, then in a cloth or, in the case of certain puddings and other similar preparations, in a buttered and floured cloth.

XIMENIA. Ximénie—Type of small plant found in hot countries, of which there are a number of species, among them the Ximenia of Gabon which is widespread in Africa. The fruits, known as mountain plums or wild limes, are edible.

YAK. Yack—Long-haired humped grunting wild or domesticated ox of Tibet.

The flesh of the yak is edible; the milk is abundant, rich in butter and casein. It is more like goat's milk than cow's milk.

YAM. Igname—A climbing plant. Its very large root is edible and is prepared in the same way as the sweet potato. A starch product is also extracted from yams, and is much used in cookery and confectionery. It is called Guiana arrowroot.

YEAST. Levure—A microscopic organism of the fungus group, which grows in an environment of sugar, producing by-products all with characteristic smells. There is an infinite number of types. See BEEF, CIDER, BREAD, WINE.

YOGHOURT, YAGOURT. Yaourt—A curdled milk product from the Balkans made with lactic ferments which have a much greater acidifying power than the natural fermenting agents.

The use of yoghourt is not so recent as might be thought, at least in France. History recounts that King François I, suffering from an intestinal complaint which had resisted the whole pharmacopoeia of the day, heard that a Jewish doctor from Constantinople had been responsible for some marvellous cures in similar cases, with milk curds prepared in a certain way, and was able to bring this practitioner to Paris. The doctor arrived on foot with a flock of sheep and cured his royal client, but refused to divulge the secret of his concoction.

The method used in Bulgaria for making yoghourt consists of first of all reducing the partially skimmed milk by one-third over a slow heat. The milk is then divided up into bowls, and when it has cooled to about 30°C. (86°F.) some leaven from a previous fermentation is introduced. It is called *Maya* and it is slipped under the skin which has formed on the surface of the milk without breaking it. The bowls are left for 24 hours at a temperature of about 25°C. (77°F.), then kept for 24 hours in a cool place before being used.

In Europe, since these oriental curds have come into fashion, they have been factory-produced, evaporated whole-cream milk being treated with a pure culture of selected lactic ferments.

YORK HAM. Jambon de York—York ham, which is prepared in the town of the same name in England, has the reputation of being the best in Europe.

Yorkshire pigs are remarkable for their early maturity, but their fat is a little soft, and their meat is accompanied by a large proportion of fat.

YORKSHIRE PUDDING—Yorkshire pudding, which is a sort of thick pancake rather than a pudding in the ordinary sense, is, in England, the obligatory accompaniment to roast beef.

It is made as follows:

Mix together without lumps 3¾ cups (500 grams) of flour with 4 eggs and 4½ cups (1¼ litres) of milk. Season with salt, pepper and grated nutmeg.

Pour this mixture into a deep pan in which has been heated some of the fat from the roast. Bake in the oven.

If the piece of beef is being spit-roasted, place the Yorkshire pudding underneath it when taking it from the oven, so that the pudding is impregnated with the juice dripping from the beef.

Cut the Yorkshire pudding into squares or lozenges and set it on the edges of the dish on which the beef is served, or serve it separately.

YULE LOG—See CAKES, *Christmas Yule log.*

ZABAGLIONE. Sabayon—A sort of cream mousse of Italian origin which is used to coat hot puddings but which can also be served alone in cups.

The word *sabayon* in French is a corruption of the Italian word *zabaglione*, and for this word the dictionary gives the following definition: Composed of the yolks of fresh eggs, sugar, wine and some flavourings, cooked while beating to make it thicken.

Method of preparation. Beat together in a basin until the mixture forms a 'ribbon' 1 cup (250 grams) of sugar and 6 yolks of eggs.

Flavour with a tablespoon of vanilla sugar, or, according to taste, with orange, lemon or tangerine peel, or vanilla extract.

Add 1¼ cups (2½ decilitres) of white wine, sweet or dry. Cook this mixture over the heat in a *bain-marie*, or in a double saucepan, over a very low heat, whisking it vigorously until it becomes frothy and stiff.

Note. Zabaglione is served as a sweet in cups or glasses.

It is also used as an accompaniment to certain hot sweets, mostly puddings. In this case zabaglione is poured over the pudding, or served separately.

Zabaglione à la créole. Sabayon à la créole—Make a zabaglione with white wine, flavouring it with orange peel. As soon as it becomes frothy, cool it by plunging the *bain-marie* (double boiler) into a basin of cold water, without ceasing to whisk.

Add 4 tablespoons of rum and a cup (¼ litre) of stiffly whipped cream. Mix rapidly and serve in a glass bowl set in crushed ice. Serve immediately.

ZAKUSKI—*Hors-d'oeuvre* course in Russia. These *hors-d'oeuvre* sometimes used to be served in a room apart from the dining-room, but it is more usual to serve them actually on the dining table, to be eaten immediately after drinking a glass of vodka.

Zabaglione (*Robert Carrier*)

In a certain corps of the Imperial Guard it was the tradition when entertaining young officers to provoke them to drink so many toasts with the zakuski that they could go no further and had to be carried to the beds which had usually been prepared for them in advance.

ZAMPINO—See PORK, *Stuffed pig's leg.*

ZARA (Maraschino). MARASQUIN DE ZARA—A renowned liqueur made at Zara, a Dalmatian village situated on the Adriatic, which was ceded to Italy by the treaty of Rapallo. This liqueur is much used in pastry-making and confectionery to flavour sweets and ices.

ZEBU—A bovine mammal, widely domesticated in Africa and Asia. Its flesh can be eaten and is prepared like beef.

ZEELAND (Oysters). HUÎTRES DE ZÉLANDE—This province of the Low Countries is made up almost entirely of islands, and is situated at the mouths of the rivers Scheldt and Maas. Zeeland oysters are famous. For various preparations see OYSTER.

ZÉPHIR, ZEPHYR—Name used by some chefs to designate light and frothy preparations.

It is often, quite wrongly, applied to mousses and mousselines of foie gras, fish and chicken.

ZESTE—French for 'peel', the exterior, coloured, flavoured part of the skin of lemon, orange, tangerine, citron, etc.

ZESTER—French culinary term meaning to peel an orange or lemon. This operation is made easier by using a special instrument called a *zesteur.*

ZIBET. ZIBETH—A variety of chives from tropical Asia. Used to season sauces, *ragoûts* and salads.

ZINGARA—Garnish which accompanies small cuts of meat and poultry. It is made up of finely chopped or shredded lean ham, tongue, mushrooms and truffles, bound with *Demi-glace sauce* (see SAUCE) flavoured with tomato and tarragon essence.

ZISTE—French word for the white pith found in oranges and lemons just underneath the coloured peel. This substance has a rather bitter taste.

ZUCCHINI—Italian marrows. In U.S.A. these slender green vegetables are called Italian squash or zucchini. In England they are known as baby marrows or courgettes. For recipes see ITALIAN MARROWS.

ZWIEBACK—A sort of *biscotte* or rusk which is found in all French bakeries.

Marée

French Index

A

B

C

D

E

F

G

H

I

J

K

L

M

N

O

P

S

T

U

V

X Y

Z

Bibliography

GUILLAUME TIREL called TAILLEVENT—Le Viandier c. 1370.

UN BOURGEOIS PARISIEN—Le Ménagier de Paris, 1393.

LA VARENNE—Le Cuisinier François, 1651.
—La Cuisine méthodique, 1662.

MASSIALOT—Le Cuisinier royal en bourgeois, 1691.

VINCENT LA CHAPELLE—La Cuisine moderne, 1735.

MENON—Nouveau Traité de la cuisine, 1739.
—La Cuisine bourgeoise, 1746.
—La Science du Maître d'hôtel cuisinier, 1749.
—Les Soupers de la Cour, 1755.

MARIN—Les Dons de Comus, 1739.

GRIMOD DE LA REYNIÈRE—Almanachs gourmands, 1803 to 1810.
—Le Manuel des Amphitryons, 1808.

VIARD—Le Cuisinier impérial, 1806.

APPERT—L'Art de conserver, 1810, re-named Le Conservateur in 1831.

BEAUVILLIERS—L'Art du Cuisinier, 1814.

CARÊME—Le Pâtissier royal, 1815.
—Le Pâtissier pittoresque, 1815.
—Le Maître d'hôtel français, 1822.
—Le Cuisinier Parisien, 1828.
—L'Art de la Cuisine française au XIXe siècle, 1835, 3 vol. (vols. 4 and 5 were written by Plumerey).

CATHERINE—Manuel de cuisine bourgeoise, 1823.

BOREL—Nouveau Dictionnaire de cuisine, office et pâtisserie, 1825.

BRILLAT-SAVARIN—Le Physiologie du goût, 1826.

DURAND—Le Cuisinier Durand de Nîmes, 1830.

AULAGNIER—Dictionnaire des aliments, 1830.

COMTE DE COURCHAMPS—Néo-Physiologie du goût, 1839.

PLUMEREY—Vols. 4 and 5. L'Art de la Cuisine française au XIXe siècle.

BERNARDI—Le Glacier royal, 1844.
—L'Écuyer tranchant, 1845.

ETIENNE—Traité de l'office, 2 vol. 1845.

DUBOIS and BERNARD—La Cuisine classique, 1856.

RECULET—Le Cuisine praticien, 1859.

PETIT—La Gastronomie en Russie, 1860.

URBAIN DUBOIS—La Cuisine classique, 2nd edition, 1864.
—La Cuisine de tous les pays, 1868.
—La Cuisine artistique, 1872.
—Le Grand Livre des Pâtissiers Confiseurs, 1883.
—L'École des Cuisinières, 1887.
—Nouvelle Cuisine bourgeoise, 1888.
—La Cuisine d'aujourd'hui, 1889.
—La Pâtisserie d'aujourd'hui, 1894.

LACAM—Le Nouveau Pâtissier glacier, 1865.
—Mémorial historique de la pâtisserie, 1888.

GOUFFÉ—Le Livre de Cuisine, 1867.
—Le Livre des Conserves, 1869.
—Le Livre de la Pâtisserie, 1873.
—Le Livre des Soupes et Potages, 1875.

BARON BRISSE—Les 366 menus, 1868.
—La Salle à manger, 1869.
—Cuisine de Carême, 1872.

A. DUMAS—Grand Dictionnaire de Cuisine, 1873.

BERTHE—Traité de l'office, 1876.

MONSELET—Lettres gourmandes suivies de recettes, 1877.

FLORIAN-PHARAON—Cuisine de chasse et de pêche, 1882.

PAPUT-LEBEAU—Le Gastrophile, 1883.

MIQUE GRANDCHAMP—Le Cuisinier à la bonne franquette, 1883.

MORARD—Les Secrets de la cuisine dévoilés, 1886.

GARLIN—La Cuisine moderne, 1887.
—La Pâtisserie moderne, 1888.
—Cuisine ancienne, 1893.

LACAM and CHARABOT—Le Glacier classique et artistique, 1893.

PHILÉAS GILBERT—La Cuisine de tous les mois, 1893.
—La Cuisine, 1925.

A. COLOMBIÉ—Traité de cuisine bourgeoise, 1893.
—Eléments culinaires, 1894.

CH. CHEMIN—L'Art de la Cuisine, 1891.

J. FAVRE—Dictionnaire universel de cuisine, 1883–1890.

CH. DRIESSENS—L'Alphabet de la ménagère, 1894.

GRANDI—130 recettes d'oeufs, 1893.

REBOUL—La Cuisine provençale, 1895.

SCHEIBENBOGEN—Cuisine austro-hongroise, 1896.

A. HÉLIE—La Cuisine maigre, 1897.

L. DUCHARDON—La Cuisine, 1894.

L. TENDRET—La Cuisine au pays de Brillat-Savarin, 1892.

P. SALLES and P. MONTAGNÉ—La Grande Cuisine illustrée, 1900.

ESCOFFIER, PHILÉAS GILBERT and FETU—Le Guide culinaire, 1903.

Mme VATEL—Table, Cuisine, Office, 1903.

A. SUZANNE—La Cuisine anglaise, 1904.

HEYRAUD—La Cuisine à Nice, 1907.

L. AURICOSTE DE LAZARQUE—Cuisine Messine, 1898.

MAILLE—Cuisine comtoise, 1907.

P. MONTAGNÉ and P. GILBERT—La cuisine militaire en garnison et en campagne, 1908.

L. PIGOT—Memorandum du pâtissier entremettier, 1908.
—La Chasse gourmande, 1909.

E. DUVAL—Traité de confiserie moderne, 1908.

E. DARENNE and DUVAL—Traite de pâtisserie moderne, 1909.

ESCOFFIER, P. GILBERT and E. FETU—Le Livre des menus, 1910.

P. MONTAGNÉ and Dr. REGNAULT—La Cuisine diététique, 1910.

DUMONT-LESPINE—La Pâtisserie fine, 1912.
—La Cuisine électrique, 1935.

P. MONTAGNÉ—La Cuisine fine, 1913.
—La Bonne Chère pas chère, 1919.
—Le Festin Occitan, 1929.
—Les Délices de la table, 1931.

PAMPILLE—Les Bons Plats de France.

A. JACQUET—L'Alimentation pratique et économique.

JEAN LAHOR—L'Alimentation à bon marché, 1908.

CL. GAY—Cuisine anglo-américaine, 1913.

L. MONOD—La Cuisine florentine, 1914.

E. RICHARDIN—La Cuisine française aux XIXe et XXe siècles, 1914.

ALI-BAB—Gastronomie pratique, 1919.

ESCOFFIER—L'Aide-Mémoire culinaire, 1919.

A. NIGNON—L'Heptaméron des Gourmets, 1920.
—Éloge de la Cuisine française, 1926.

B. GUEGAN—La Fleur de la Cuisine française, 1920.

J. WERNERT—Hors-d'oeuvre et savories, 1926.

L. ISNARD—La Gastronomie africaine, 1920.

TANTE MARIE—Veritable Cuisine des familles, 1921.

Mme MOLL WEISS—La Cuisine rationnelle, 1925.

Dr. DE POMAINE—Cuisine juive, 1925.

AUSTIN DE CROZE—Les Plats régionaux, 1926.

J. BANNEAU—Le Répertoire de la Pâtisserie, 1925.

P. BOUILLARD—La Gourmandise à bon marché, 1926.
—La Cuisine au coin du feu, 1928.

Mme EBRARD SAINT-ANGE—Le Livre de cuisine, 1927.

P. REBOUX—Plats nouveaux, 1927.
—Plats du jour, 1930.

E. VERDIER—Dissertations gastronomiques, 1928.

ESCOFFIER—Le Riz. La Morue, 1928.

P. MONTAGNÉ and P. SALLES—Le Grand Livre de la Cuisine, 1929.

FOUCOU—Recettes de cuisine provençale, 1929.

M. BOUZY—Poissons, Coquillages, Crustacés, 1929.

E. GREVIN—Nouveau Traité de la Cuisine, 1929.

G. DERYS—L'Art d'être gourmand, 1929.
—Les Plats au vin, recettes d'amateurs, 1937.

LA MAZILLE—La Bonne Cuisine du Périgord, 1929.

PELLAPRAT—Cuisine familiale.
—Guide des Hors-d'oeuvre.
—La Pâtisserie pratique.
—L'Art culinaire moderne.

F. MICHEL—La Conserve de ménage, 1932.

ESCOFFIER—Ma Cuisine, 1934.

BENOIT-PERRAT—Comus en Bresse, 1935.

P. MONTAGNÉ and Dr. GOTTSCHALK—Mon menu, 1936.

R. BRUNET and PELLAPRAT—La Cuisine au vin, 1936.

Additional Reading List

compiled by Elizabeth David

PIERRE HUGUENIN—Les Meilleures Recettes de ma Pauvre Mère, et Quelques Autres Encore. Publication du Comité de la Foire Gastronomique de Dijon. Dijon, Librarie Venot, 1936.

DR. ÉDOUARD DE POMIANE—365 Menus, 365 Recettes. Précédées d'une Étude sur le Régime Alimentaire de Chacun. Éditions Albin Michel, Paris, 22 rue Huyghens, 1938.

COMITÉ BOULONNAIS DE PROPAGANDE POUR LA CONSOMMATION DES PRODUITS DE LA MER—Les Meilleures Recettes Culinaires pour Poissons et Crustacés, 1938.

LES FRÈRES DROUILLET—Gastronomie Nivernaise. Crépin-Leblond, Moulins, 1939.

VILMORIN-ANDRIEUX—Dictionnaire Vilmorin des Plantes Potagères. Vilmorin-Andrieux, 4 Quai de la Mégisserie, Paris, 1948.

DR ALFRED GOTTSCHALK—Histoire de l'Alimentation et de la Gastronomie depuis la Préhistoire jusqu'a nos Jours. 2 vols. Éditions Hippocrate, Le François, 91 boulevard Saint-Germain, Paris, 1948.

LÉON ISNARD—Cuisine Française et Africaine. Éditions Albin Michel, 22 rue Huyghens, Paris, 1949.

CHARLES GAY—Vieux Pots, Saulces et Rosts Memorables. Essai Historique et Meilleures Recettes de la Cuisine Française. Arrault et Cie, Tours, 1950.

GEORGES CHAUDIEU & ACHILLE BONNEVILLE, PRÉSIDENT ET VICE-PRÉSIDENT DE L'ÉCOLE PROFESSIONELLE DE LA BOUCHERIE DE PARIS—Bouchers de Paris. 2 vols. D.E.J. Peyronnet et Cie, 33 rue Vivienne, Paris 2.

P. E. LALOUE—Le Guide de la Charcuterie. Aide-Mémoire de Charcuterie pratique. Guide de la Charcuterie, 191 rue de l'Ermitage, Montreuil-sous-Bois (Seine), 1954. (First published 1950.)

RECETTES ET PAYSAGES—(1) Sud-Ouest et Pyrénées, (2) Sud-Est, Méditerranée, (3) Ile de France, Val de Loire, (4) L'Est de la France, Champagne, Alsace, Lorraine, Bourgogne, Franche-Comté, Bresse, (5) Nord, Bretagne, Normandie, Pays de l'ouest. Publications Françaises, 13 rue de Grenelle, Paris. 1950–1952. (Under the title *Recettes des Provinces de France* the chapters on regional cooking, the recipes and the colour photographs from the above series were collected into one volume edited by CURNONSKY and published by Productions de Paris, in 1959.)

JEAN-NOËL ESCUDIER—La Véritable Cuisine Provençale et Niçoise. Éditions Gallia-Toulon, 1953.

CURNONSKY (Editor)—Cuisine et Vins de France. Librarie Larousse, 13–21 rue Montparnasse and 114 boulevard Raspail, Paris, 1953.

ROBERT-J. COURTINE—Le Plus Doux des Péchés. Éditions Touristiques et Littéraires, Bourg, 1954.

HENRIETTE BABET-CHARTON—La Charcuterie à la Campagne. La Maison Rustique, 26 rue Jacob, Paris. 6th edition, 1954.

ROGER LALLEMAND—La Cuisine de Chez Nois: (1) Le Bourbonnais. (2) Le Nivernais-Morvan. Imprimerie R. Gentil, Gannat (Allier). 1954, 1955.

H. P. PELLAPRAT—Le Poisson dans la Cuisine Française. Flammarion, 26 rue Racine, Paris, 1954.

NOUVEAU LAROUSSE MÉNAGER. Librairie Larousse, 13–21 rue Montparnasse and 114 boulevard Raspail, Paris 6, 1955.

COLLECTION CUISINE ET VINS DE FRANCE—Les sauces, Recettes et Conseils Pratiques. Compagnie Parisienne d'Éditions techniques et commerciales, 94 faubourg St Honoré, Paris, 1957.

L'ART CULINAIRE FRANÇAIS. Les Recettes de Cuisine—Pâtisserie—Conserves—des Maîtres contemporains les plus réputés. Ali-Bab, E. Darenne, E. Duval, A. Escoffier, Ph. Gilbert, A. Guérot, P. Montagné, H-P. Pellaprat, Urbain Dubois, etc. Cuisine Régionale, Cuisine Étrangère. Flammarion, 26 rue Racine, Paris, 1957.

FRANCIS AMUNATÉGUI—L'Art des Mets ou Traité des Plaisirs de la Table. Librairie Arthème Fayard, 18 rue du Saint-Gothard, Paris 14, 1959.

GRINGOIRE, Th. & SAULNIER, L.—Le Répertoire de la Cuisine. Dupont et Malget. Guérins, Successeur, 40 rue Coquillière, Paris. 18th edition, 1961.